HANDBOOK OF
COMMON STOCKS

2018 SUMMER

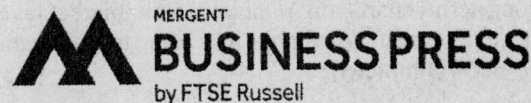

MERGENT
BUSINESS PRESS
by FTSE Russell

INTRODUCTION

Mergent's Handbook of Common Stocks provides quick and easy access to basic financial and business information on more than 900 stocks that are included in the Russell 1000, S&P 500, S&P 400 and Mergent's Dividend Achievers. The Tab Section provides one-line information on New York Stock Exchange companies.

The price charts, statistics, and analyses are presented in a format that provides the investor with the necessary perspective for acting on investment advice or suggestions. It also affords investors the opportunity to make investment decisions on their own.

Statistics and analyses are revised quarterly. Every effort is made to secure the most current operating results and dividend information available. In the case of year-end results, preliminary results are shown and analyzed as they are received. Full statistical presentations of annual report information are shown in the following edition. The schedule below describes the publication dates and company reporting periods usually covered in each edition.

The Winter Edition (published in January) covers quarterly reports and preliminary annual reports through September 30.

The Spring Edition (published in April) covers quarterly reports and preliminary annual reports through December 31.

The Summer Edition (published in July) covers quarterly reports and preliminary annual reports through March 31.

The Fall Edition (published in October) covers quarterly reports and preliminary annual reports through June 30.

Note: For various reasons, some companies may not report in time to meet our publication deadlines. Company reports received close to press time are shown in the Addenda. The remainder of late reports are published and analyzed in the next edition of the Handbook.

The special section on these opening pages contains a number of features, including a guide on how to use this book, a classification of companies by their major line of business based on their NAIC code, outstanding stock price movements by company, plus long-term charts on popular stock market averages. The Addenda provide the latest developments available just prior to publication but after the company reports have been completed.

TABLE OF CONTENTS

Page

HOW TO USE THIS BOOK... 4a

HOW TO USE THIS BOOK

The presentation of historical data and analytical comments provides the answers to four basic questions for each company:

1. What does the company do?
(See G.)
2. How has it done in the past?
(See B, J.)
3. How is it doing now?
(See C, D, H.)
4. How will it fare in the future?
(See I.)

A. CAPSULE STOCK INFORMATION shows where the stock is traded and its symbol, a recent price and price/earnings ratio, plus the yield afforded by the indicated dividend based on a recent price. The indicated dividend is the current annualized dividend based on the most recent price. Some companies are designated as Dividend Achievers. Dividend Achievers have, by *Mergent's* criteria, increased their cash dividend payments for at least ten consecutive years, adjusting for splits. The number of years of consecutive increases is given for each Dividend Achiever.

B. LONG-TERM PRICE CHART illustrates the pattern of monthly stock price movements, fully adjusted for stock dividends and splits. The chart points out the degree of volatility in the price movement of the company's stock and what its long-term trend has been. It also shows how it has performed long-term relative to an initial investment in the S&P 500 Index equal to the price of the company's stock at the beginning of the period shown in the price chart. It indicates areas of price support and resistance, plus other technical points to be considered by the investor. The bars at the base of the long-term price chart indicate the monthly trading volume. Monthly trading volume offers the individual an opportunity to recognize at what periods stock accumulation occurs and what percent of a company's outstanding shares are traded.

PRICE SCORES – Above each company's price/volume chart are its **Mergent's Price Scores**. These are basic measures of the stock's performance. Each stock is measured against the New York Stock Exchange Composite Index.

A score of 100 indicates that the stock did as well as the New York Stock Exchange Composite Index during the time period. A score of less than 100 means that the stock did not do as well; a score of more than 100 means that the stock outperformed the NYSE Composite Index. All stock prices are adjusted for splits and stock dividends. The time periods measured for each company conclude with the date of the recent price shown in the top line of each company's profile.

The **7 YEAR PRICE SCORE** mirrors the common stock's price growth over the previous seven years. The higher the price score, the better the relative performance. It is based on the ratio of the latest 12-month average price to the current seven-year average. This ratio is then indexed against the same ratio for the market as a whole (the New York Stock Exchange Composite Index), which is taken as 100.

The **12 MONTH PRICE SCORE** is a similar measurement but for a shorter period of time. It is based on the ratio of the latest two-month average price to the current 12-month average. As was done for the Long-Term Price Score, this ratio is also indexed to the same ratio for the market as a whole.

C. INTERIM EARNINGS (Per Share) – Figures are reported after the effect of extraordinary items, discontinued operations and cumulative effects of accounting changes. Each figure is for the quarterly period indicated. These figures are essentially as reported by the company, although all figures are adjusted for all stock dividends and splits.

ILLUSTRATIVE INC.

Exchange **A**	Symbol	Price	52Wk Range	Yield	P/E
NYS	100	$57.94 (06/30/2018)	58.67-49.64	3.28	26.70

*7 Year Price Score 99.96   *NYSE Composite Index=100   *12 Month Price Score 96.60

Interim Earnings (Per Share)

Qtr.	Mar	Jun	Sep	Dec
2014	(0.21)	0.37	0.83	0.32
2015	0.74	0.54 **C**	0.53	0.43
2016	0.81	0.10	0.75	0.53
2017	0.50	0.19	0.95	...

Interim Dividends (Per Share)

Amt	Decl	Ex	Rec	Pay
0.463Q	05/09/2017	05/24/2017	05/26/2017	06/15/2017
0.463Q	07/11/2017	08/11/2017	08/15/2017	09/15/2017
0.475Q	10/10/2017	11/14/2017	11/15/2017	12/15/2017 **D**
0.475Q	01/09/2018	02/20/2018	02/21/2018	03/15/2018

Indicated Div: $1.90 (Div. Reinv. Plan)

Valuation Analysis   **Institutional Holding**

Forecast EPS	$3.51	No of Institutions
	(06/30/2018)	1093
Market Cap	$23.9 Billion	Shares
Book Value	$4.9 Billion	442,522,080
Price/Book **E**	4.87	% Held **F**
Price/Sales	1.06	83.49

Business Summary: Containers & Packaging (MIC: 8.1.3 SIC: 2621 NAIC: 322121) **G**

Illustrative Inc. is a paper and packaging company with markets and manufacturing operations in North America, Europe, Latin America, Russia, Asia, Africa and the Middle East. Co.'s businesses are separated into three segments: Industrial Packaging, which manufactures containerboard in the U.S. and its products include linerboard, medium, whitetop, recycled linerboard, recycled medium and saturating kraft; Printing Papers, produces printing and writing papers and its products include uncoated papers and pulp; and Consumer Packaging, produces solid bleached sulfate board and its brands include Paper products.

Recent Developments: For the quarter ended March 31, 2018, income from continuing operations increased 27.8% to US$395.0 million from US$309.0 million in the year-earlier quarter. Net income increased 27.8% to US$395.0 million from US$309.0 million in the year-earlier quarter. Revenues were US$5.91 billion, up 12.3% from US$5.27 billion the year before. Direct operating expenses rose 11.1% to US$4.02 billion from US$3.62 billion in the comparable period the year before. Indirect operating expenses increased 8.3% to US$1.23 billion from US$1.14 billion in the equivalent prior-year period. **H**

Prospects: Our evaluation of Illustrative Incorporated as of Jan. 14, 2018 is the result of our systematic analysis on three basic characteristics: earnings strength, relative valuation, and recent stock price movement. The company has enjoyed a very positive trend in earnings per share over the past 5 quarters and while recent estimates for the company have been mixed, 00 has posted better than expected results. Based on operating earnings yield, the company is undervalued when compared to all of the companies in our coverage universe. Share price changes over the past year indicates that 00 will perform poorly over the near term. **I**

Financial Data

(US$ in Millions)	9 Mos	6 Mos	3 Mos	12/31/2016	12/31/2015	12/31/2014	12/31/2013	12/31/2012
Earnings Per Share	2.17	1.97	1.88	2.18	2.23	1.29	3.11	1.80
Cash Flow Per Share	3.55	6.13	6.04	6.01	6.18	7.19	6.83	6.80
Tang Book Value Per Share	3.62	2.75	2.84	2.38	1.31	3.19	9.44	4.52
Dividends Per Share	1.850	1.827	1.805	1.783	1.640	1.450	1.250	1.087
Dividend Payout % **J**	85.25	92.77	96.01	81.77	73.54	112.40	40.19	60.42
Income Statement								
Total Revenue	17,196	11,283	5,511	21,079	22,365	23,617	29,080	27,833
EBITDA	2,146	1,150	710	2,676	3,034	2,787	2,884	3,095
Depn & Amortn	997	656	324	1,200	1,213	1,308	1,423	1,399
Income Before Taxes	718	215	244	956	1,266	872	849	1,024
Income Taxes	147	(6)	83	247	466	123	(523)	331
Net Income	684	289	209	904	938	555	1,395	794
Average Shares	417	416	416	415	420	432	448	440
Balance Sheet								
Current Assets	7,211	7,237	6,721	6,969	6,477	7,959	9,025	8,905
Total Assets	33,813	33,877	33,301	33,345	30,587	28,684	31,528	32,153
Current Liabilities	4,869	5,002	4,267	4,072	3,924	4,909	5,127	4,998
Long-Term Obligations	11,373	10,392	10,823	11,075	8,900	8,631	8,827	9,696
Total Liabilities	28,899	29,332	28,726	29,004	26,703	23,569	23,423	25,849
Stockholders' Equity	4,914	4,545	4,575	4,341	3,884	5,115	8,105	6,304
Shares Outstanding	412	412	412	411	420	420	436	439
Statistical Record								
Return on Assets %	2.72	2.51	2.42	2.82	3.17	1.84	4.38	2.68
Return on Equity %	19.77	19.12	17.69	21.92	20.85	8.40	19.36	12.25
EBITDA Margin %	12.48	10.19	12.88	12.70	13.57	11.80	9.92	11.12
Net Margin %	3.98	2.56	3.79	4.29	4.19	2.35	4.80	2.85
Asset Turnover	0.68	0.67	0.67	0.66	0.75	0.78	0.91	0.94
Current Ratio	1.48	1.45	1.58	1.71	1.65	1.62	1.76	1.78
Debt to Equity	2.31	2.29	2.37	2.55	2.29	1.69	1.09	1.54
Price Range	58.17-43.60	57.99-41.76	57.99-39.60	54.28-32.58	57.59-36.80	55.25-44.25	49.48-39.28	39.28-27.42
P/E Ratio	26.81-20.09	29.44-21.20	30.85-21.06	24.90-14.94	25.83-16.50	42.83-34.30	15.91-12.63	21.82-15.23
Average Yield %	3.51	3.63	3.80	4.09	3.41	3.00	2.77	3.29

Address: Poplar Avenue,	**Web Site:** www.interncom	**Auditors:** Deloitte & Touche LLP
Memphis, TN 38197	**Officers:** Mark - Chairman, President, Chief	**Investor Contact:** 91-419-171
Telephone: 419-7000 **K**	Executive Officer, Chief Operating Officer Tommy	**Transfer Agents:** Computershare Trust
	- Senior Vice President	Company, N.A., Canton, MA

HOW TO USE THIS BOOK

D. INTERIM DIVIDENDS (Per Share) – The cash dividends are the actual dollar amounts declared by the company. No adjustments have been made for stock dividends and splits. **Ex-Dividend Date**: a stockholder must purchase the stock prior to this date in order to be entitled to the dividend. The **Record Date** indicates the date on which the shareholder had to have been a holder of record in order to qualify for the dividend. The **Payable Date** indicates the date the company paid or intends to pay the dividend. The cash amount shown in the first column is followed by a letter (example "Q" for quarterly) to indicate the frequency of the dividend. A notation of "Dividend payment suspended" indicates that dividend payments have been suspended within the most recent ten years.
Indicated Dividend This is the annualized amount (fully adjusted for splits) of the latest regular cash dividend. Companies with Dividend Reinvestment Plans are indicated here.

E. VALUATION ANALYSIS is a tool for evaluating a company's stock. Included are: Forecast Earnings Per Share (EPS), Market Capitalization, Book Value, Price/Book and Price/Sales.

F. INSTITUTIONAL HOLDINGS – indicates the number of investment companies, insurance companies, mutual funds, bank trust and college endowment funds holding the stock and the total number of shares held as last reported.

G. BUSINESS SUMMARY explains what a company does in terms of the products or services it sells, its markets, and the position the company occupies in its industry. For a quick reference, included are the Company's Standard Industrial Classification (SIC), North American Industry Classification (NAIC) and Mergent's Industry Classification (MIC).

H. RECENT DEVELOPMENTS – This section captures what has happened in the most recent quarter for which results are available. It provides recently released sales, earnings and expense figures.

I. PROSPECTS – This section focuses on what is anticipated for the immediate future, as well as the outlook for the next few years, based on analysis by Mergent.

J. FINANCIAL DATA (fully adjusted for stock dividends and splits) is provided for at least the past seven fiscal years preceded by the most recent three-, six- and nine-month results if available.
Fiscal Years are the annual financial reporting periods as determined by each company. Annual prices and dividends are displayed based on the Company's fiscal year.

Per Share Data:
The Earnings Per Share figure is based on a trailing 12-month period. Earnings per share, and all per share figures, are adjusted for subsequent stock dividends and splits.
Cash Flow Per Share represents the annualized cash flow from operating activities (or for quarters, TTM cash flow from operating activities) divided by the average shares outstanding.
Tangible Book Value Per Share is calculated as stockholders equity (the value of common shares, paid-in capital and retained earnings) minus preferred stock and intangibles such as goodwill, patents and excess acquisition costs, divided by shares outstanding. It demonstrates the underlying cash value of each common share if the company were to be liquidated as of that date.

Dividends Per Share is the total of cash payments made per share to shareholders for the trailing 12-month period.

HOW TO USE THIS BOOK

Dividend Payout % is the proportion of earnings available for common stock that is paid to common shareholders in the form of cash dividends. It is significant because it indicates what percentage of earnings is being reinvested in the business for internal growth.

EDITOR'S NOTE: TTM net income is net income for the last 365 days (normally four reported quarters) ended on the quarterly balance sheet date. Where that last 365 days does not exactly equate to the last four reported quarters the net income for any included partial quarter is adjusted on a pro-rata basis.

INCOME STATEMENT, BALANCE SHEET AND STATISTICAL RECORD

Includes pertinent earnings and balance sheet information essential to analyzing a corporation's performance. The comparisons provide the necessary historical perspective to intelligently review the various operating and financial trends. Generic definitions follow.

Income Statement:

Total Revenues consists of all revenues from operations.

EBITDA represents earnings before, interest, taxes, depreciation and amortization, and special items.

Depreciation and Amortization includes all non-cash charges such as depletion and amortization as well as depreciation.

Income Before Taxes is the remaining income *after* deducting all costs, expenses, property charges, interest etc. but *before* deducting income taxes.

Income Taxes includes the amount charged against earnings to provide for current and deferred income taxes.

Net Income consists of all revenues less all expenses (operating and non-operating), and is presented before preference and common dividends.

Average Shares Outstanding is the weighted average number of shares including common equivalent shares outstanding during the year, as reported by the corporation and fully adjusted for all stock dividends and splits. The use of *average shares* minimizes the distortion in *earnings per share* which could result from issuance of a large amount of stock or the company's purchase of a large amount of its own stock during the year.

Balance Sheet:

Current Assets includes the short-term assets expected to be realized or consumed within one year. Normally includes cash and cash equivalents, short term investments, receivables, prepayments and inventories.

Total Assets represents all of the assets of the company, including tangible and intangible, and current and non-current.

Current Liabilities are all of the obligations of the company normally expected to be paid within one year. Includes bank overdrafts, short-term debt, payables and accruals.

Long-Term Obligations are the total long-term debts (due beyond one year) reported by the company, including bonds, capital lease obligations, notes, mortgages, debentures, etc.

Total Liabilities represents all liabilities of the company, whether current or non-current.

Stockholders' Equity is the sum of all capital stock accounts – paid in capital (including additional premium), retained earnings, and all other capital balances.

Shares Outstanding is the number of shares outstanding as of the date of the company's quarterly/annual report, exclusive of treasury stock and adjusted for subsequent stock dividends and splits.

Statistical Record:

Return on Assets % represents the ratio of annualized net income (or for Mos, TTM net income) to average total assets. This ratio

HOW TO USE THIS BOOK

represents how effectively assets are being used to produce a profit.

Return on Equity % is the ratio of annualized net income (or for Mos, TTM net income) to average stockholders' equity, expressed as a percentage. This ratio illustrates how effectively the investment of the stockholders is being utilized to earn a profit.

EBITDA Margin % represents earnings before interest, taxes, depreciation and amortization as a percentage of total revenue.

Net Margin % is net income expressed as a percentage of total revenues.

Asset Turnover is annualized total revenue (or for Mos, TTM total revenue) divided by average total assets. A measure of efficiency for the use of assets.

Current Ratio represents current assets divided by current liabilities. The higher the figure the better the company is able to meet its current liabilities out of its current assets. A key measure of liquidity for industrial companies.

Debt to Equity is the ratio of long-term obligations to stockholders' equity.

Price Ranges are based on each Company's fiscal year. Where actual stock sales did not take place, a range of lowest bid and highest asked prices is shown.

Price/Earnings Ratio is shown as a range. The figures are calculated by dividing the stock's highest price for the year and its lowest price by the year's earnings per share. Growth stocks tend to command higher P/Es than cyclical stocks.

Average Yield % is the ratio of annual dividends to the real average of the prices over the fiscal year.

EDITOR'S NOTE: In order to preserve the historical relationships between prices, earnings and dividends, figures are not restated to reflect subsequent events. Figures are presented in U.S. dollars unless otherwise indicated.

K. ADDITIONAL INFORMATION on each stock includes the officers of the company, investor relations contact, address, telephone number, web site and transfer agents.

OTHER DEFINITIONS

Factors Pertaining Especially to Real Estate Investment Trusts

Property Income is income from property rental and other associated activities.

Non-Property Income includes interest income and other income not from property activities.

Factors Pertaining Especially to Utilities

PPE Turnover represents annualized total revenue (or for Mos, TTM total revenue) divided by average net property, plant and equipment.

Factors Pertaining Especially to Banks

Interest Income is all interest income, including income from loans and leases, securities and deposits.

Interest Expense is all interest expense, including from loans and leases, securities and deposits.

Net Interest Income is interest income less interest expense. This figure is presented before provision for losses.

Provision for Losses represents the amount charged against earnings to increase the provision made for losses on loans and leases.

Non-Interest Income is any income that is not interest-related. Such income could include trading revenue and gains on the sale of assets.

Non-Interest Expense is all expenses that are not interest-related, including employment costs, office costs, marketing costs, etc.

Net Loans & Leases includes all loans and leases net of provisions for losses. May include commercial, agricultural, real estate, consumer and foreign loans.

Total Deposits are all time and demand deposits entrusted to a bank.

Net Interest Margin % is net interest income before provisions expressed as a

HOW TO USE THIS BOOK

percentage of total interest income. A key measure of bank profitability.

Efficiency Ratio % is non-interest expense expressed as a percentage of total revenue.

, *Loans to Deposits* are net loans and leases divided by total deposits. A key measure of bank liquidity.

Factors Pertaining Especially to Insurance Companies

Premium Income is the amount of insurance premiums received from policyholders. This is the primary revenue source for insurance companies.

Benefits and Claims represents the payments made to policyholders under the terms of insurance contracts.

Loss Ratio % is benefits and claims expressed as a percentage of premium income. A key ratio of insurance company profitability.

ABBREVIATIONS AND SYMBOLS

A...Annual
ASE................Ō.....American Stock Exchange
()...Deficit
(Div. Reinv. Plan)..Dividend Reinvest Plan offered
E..Extra
M...Monthly
N/A.......................Ō.....Not Applicable
N.M............................Not Meaningful
NMS................ National Market Systems
NYS..............New York Stock Exchange
Q...Quarterly
S......................................Semi-Annual
Sp............Ō................Special Dividend
U.....................Ō.....Frequency Unknown

FORDS TOP 50 COMPANIES BY REVENUES

Company Name	Ticker Symbol	Net Income	Norm P/E /5yr avg	Ann FY Sales(mil)
WALMART	WMT	$9,862	1.19	$500,343
ROYAL DUTCH A	RDSA	$12,977	1.54	$311,870
TOYOTA MOTOR	TM	$16,377	0.82	$246,830
BP PLC	BP	$3,389	1.51	$244,582
EXXON MOBIL	XOM	$19,710	1.19	$244,363
BERKSHIRE HATHAW	BRKB	$44,940	1.13	$242,137
APPLE	AAPL	$48,351	1.17	$229,234
UNITEDHEALTH GRP	UNH	$10,558	1.13	$201,159
DAIMLER AG	DDAIF	$12,617	0.75	$199,915
MCKESSON CORP	MCK	$5,070	0.67	$198,533
CVS HEALTH	CVS	$6,622	0.6	$184,765
AMAZON.COM	AMZN	$3,033	2.81	$177,866
AT&T INC	T	$29,450	0.83	$160,546
FORD MOTOR	F	$7,602	0.74	$156,776
AMERISOURCEBERGN	ABC	$364	0.76	$153,144
TOTAL SA	TOT	$8,631	1.48	$149,341
GENERAL MOTORS	GM	-$3,864	0.74	$145,588
CHEVRON	CVX	$9,195	1.61	$141,722
CARDINAL HEALTH	CAH	$1,288	0.65	$129,976
COSTCO WHOLESALE	COST	$2,679	1.03	$129,025
VERIZON COMMUNIC	VZ	$30,101	0.85	$126,034
HONDA MOTOR	HMC	$5,515	0.8	$125,209
KROGER	KR	$1,907	0.68	$122,662
GEN ELECTRIC	GE	-$5,787	0.56	$122,092
WALGREENS BOOTS	WBA	$4,078	0.51	$118,214
J P MORGAN CHASE	JPM	$24,441	1.33	$113,899
FANNIE MAE	FNMA	$2,463	0.44	$112,394
ALPHABET	GOOGL	$12,662	0.97	$110,855
NISSAN MOTOR	NSANY	$5,934	0.86	$104,824
PHILLIPS 66	PSX	$5,106	2.03	$104,622
HOME DEPOT	HD	$8,630	1.05	$100,904
BANK OF AMERICA	BAC	$18,232	1.23	$100,264
EXPRESS SCRIPTS	ESRX	$4,517	0.75	$100,065
SIEMENS AG	SIEGY	$6,084	1.13	$98,885
WELLS FARGO & CO	WFC	$22,183	0.98	$97,741
VALERO ENERGY	VLO	$4,065	1.86	$93,980
BOEING	BA	$8,197	1.59	$93,392
ANTHEM	ANTM	$3,843	1.28	$90,039
MICROSOFT	MSFT	$21,204	1.43	$89,950
DEUTSCHE TELEKOM	DTEGY	$4,149	1.16	$89,843
PETROBRAS	PBR	-$91	1.91	$89,507
CITIGROUP	C	-$6,798	1.11	$87,966
COMCAST	CMCSA	$22,714	0.72	$84,526
HITACHI	HTHIY	$2,068	1	$81,947
IBM	IBM	$5,753	0.96	$79,139
BASF SE	BASFY	$4,283	1.04	$78,745
DELL TECHNOL	DVMT	-$3,728	N/A	$78,660
JOHNSON JOHNSON	JNJ	$1,300	0.99	$76,450

SHORT-TERM PRICE SCORES: COMPANY RANKINGS

25 Highest	SHORT TERM PRICE SCORE	LONG TERM PRICE SCORE	52 WEEK HIGH	52 WEEK LOW	RECENT PRICE
Whiting Petroleum Corp	166.0	17.3	55.46	16.00	52.72
Tenet Healthcare Corp.	165.7	51.3	38.35	12.65	33.57
Genesis Healthcare Inc	163.3	23.0	2.86	0.69	2.29
HollyFrontier Corp	152.3	93.8	81.65	26.19	68.43
Delek US Holdings Inc (New)	148.4	107.6	59.81	20.88	50.17
Twitter Inc	144.2	<fill>	46.76	15.75	43.67
Square Inc	140.7	<fill>	67.59	22.83	61.64
Zendesk Inc	139.9	<fill>	59.43	25.48	54.49
PBF Energy Inc	137.1	<fill>	50.57	19.95	41.93
GrubHub Inc	137.0	<fill>	119.86	43.13	104.91
Boston Beer Co Inc (The)	135.9	84.2	302.55	130.50	299.70
Macy's Inc	132.7	50.1	40.21	17.53	37.43
Oasis Petroleum Inc.	131.9	31.8	13.78	6.95	12.97
Deckers Outdoor Corp.	131.6	96.6	121.94	61.60	112.89
Continental Resources Inc.	131.5	88.5	68.83	30.03	64.76
WPX Energy Inc	131.4	<fill>	19.17	9.27	18.03
American Eagle Outfitters, Inc.	131.1	85.4	25.26	10.62	23.25
Plantronics, Inc.	130.2	95.7	77.69	41.36	76.25
Valero Energy Corp	129.2	136.3	124.44	64.55	110.83
GoDaddy Inc	128.6	<fill>	74.74	41.19	70.60
Grainger (W.W.) Inc.	127.9	84.2	319.62	156.25	308.40
Chipotle Mexican Grill Inc	127.9	60.8	469.94	251.33	431.37
Marathon Oil Corp.	127.6	51.4	21.90	10.77	20.86
Wex Inc	127.1	119.0	192.54	101.80	190.48
Globus Medical Inc	126.9	<fill>	57.41	28.28	50.46
25 Lowest					
TC PipeLines, LP	58.5	73.2	59.30	23.16	25.95
Colony Capital Inc (New)	60.3	<fill>	14.70	5.48	6.24
Macquarie Infrastructure Corp	66.6	79.1	78.97	36.56	42.20
Alexander & Baldwin Inc (REIT)	68.4	<fill>	46.87	20.91	23.50
Diebold Nixdorf Inc	71.4	48.5	28.00	11.50	11.95
Newell Brands Inc	71.9	84.2	53.90	23.12	25.79
Arconic Inc	72.7	79.2	30.84	16.87	17.01
Acuity Brands Inc	73.9	90.7	206.68	110.22	115.87
General Electric Co	74.3	62.0	27.45	12.75	13.61
Penney (J.C.) Co.,Inc. (Holding Co.)	74.6	22.1	5.56	2.30	2.34
Buckeye Partners LP	75.4	61.9	65.90	34.86	35.15
Owens & Minor, Inc.	75.5	54.7	32.51	14.94	16.71
ProAssurance Corp	75.7	87.1	63.00	35.35	35.45
Pitney Bowes Inc	75.7	53.3	15.96	8.45	8.57
Edgewell Personal Care Co	75.9	65.4	76.33	41.40	50.46
Avon Products, Inc.	76.0	18.3	3.80	1.48	1.62
Community Health Systems, Inc.	76.1	19.1	9.96	3.32	3.32
NACCO Industries Inc	76.3	72.1	88.85	31.90	33.75
World Fuel Services Corp.	76.5	56.2	39.81	20.18	20.41
Philip Morris International Inc	77.0	91.6	121.62	76.85	80.74
Tupperware Brands Corp	77.1	68.5	70.36	40.20	41.24
Cooper Tire & Rubber Co.	78.0	89.9	40.35	24.00	26.30
L Brands, Inc	78.0	59.3	62.95	31.68	36.88
RPC, Inc.	78.4	103.9	26.73	13.65	14.57
Belden Inc	78.5	97.6	87.00	54.50	61.12

Ranking by Total Revenues

Based on most recent fiscal year-end figures.

Rank	Company Name	Revenues ($Mill)	Rank	Company Name	Revenues ($Mill)
1.	Walmart Inc	500,343.0	26.	Dell Technologies Inc	78,660.0
2.	Exxon Mobil Corp	244,363.0	27.	Philip Morris International	78,098.0
3.	Berkshire Hathaway Inc	242,137.0	28.	Johnson & Johnson	76,450.0
4.	McKesson Corp	208,357.0	29.	Marathon Petroleum Corp.	75,369.0
5.	UnitedHealth Group Inc	201,159.0	30.	Target Corp	71,879.0
6.	CVS Health Corporation	184,765.0	31.	Lowe's Companies Inc	68,619.0
7.	AT&T Inc	160,546.0	32.	United Parcel Service Inc	65,872.0
8.	Ford Motor Co.	156,776.0	33.	FedEx Corp	65,450.0
9.	AmerisourceBergen Corp.	153,143.8	34.	Procter & Gamble C.	65,058.0
10.	General Motors Co	145,588.0	35.	DowDuPont Inc	62,484.0
11.	Chevron Corporation	141,722.0	36.	MetLife Inc	62,308.0
12.	Cardinal Health, Inc.	129,976.0	37.	Archer Daniels Midland Co.	60,828.0
13.	Verizon Communications	126,034.0	38.	Aetna Inc	60,535.0
14.	Kroger Co	122,662.0	39.	United Technologies Corp	59,837.0
15.	General Electric Co	122,092.0	40.	Prudential Financial Inc	59,689.0
16.	JPMorgan Chase & Co	113,899.0	41.	Sysco Corp	55,371.1
17.	Phillips 66	104,622.0	42.	Disney (Walt) Co.	55,137.0
18.	Home Depot Inc	100,904.0	43.	Humana Inc.	53,767.0
19.	Bank of America Corp	100,264.0	44.	Pfizer Inc	52,546.0
20.	Wells Fargo & Co.	97,741.0	45.	HP Inc	52,056.0
21.	Valero Energy Corp	93,980.0	46.	Lockheed Martin Corp	51,048.0
22.	Boeing Co.	93,392.0	47.	American Intl. Group Inc	49,520.0
23.	Anthem Inc	90,039.4	48.	Centene Corp	48,382.0
24.	Citigroup Inc	87,966.0	49.	Bunge Ltd.	45,794.0
25.	Intl. Bus. Machines Corp	79,139.0	50.	Caterpillar Inc.	45,462.0

Ranking by Net Income

Based on most recent fiscal year-end figures.

Rank	Company Name	Net Income ($Mill)	Rank	Company Name	Net Income ($Mill)
1.	Berkshire Hathaway Inc	44,940.0	26.	Intl. Bus. Machines Corp	5,753.0
2.	Verizon Communications	30,101.0	27.	Norfolk Southern Corp.	5,404.0
3.	AT&T Inc	29,450.0	28.	NextEra Energy Inc	5,378.0
4.	JPMorgan Chase & Co	24,441.0	29.	PNC Financial Services Grp	5,338.0
5.	Wells Fargo & Co.	22,183.0	30.	AbbVie Inc	5,309.0
6.	Pfizer Inc	21,308.0	31.	McDonald's Corp	5,192.3
7.	Exxon Mobil Corp	19,710.0	32.	Phillips 66	5,106.0
8.	Bank of America Corp	18,232.0	33.	BlackRock Inc	4,970.0
9.	Procter & Gamble Co.	15,326.0	34.	United Parcel Service Inc	4,910.0
10.	Union Pacific Corp	10,712.0	35.	3M Co	4,858.0
11.	UnitedHealth Group Inc	10,558.0	36.	AFLAC Inc	4,604.0
12.	Altria Group Inc	10,222.0	37.	FedEx Corp	4,572.0
13.	Walmart Inc	9,862.0	38.	United Technologies Corp	4,552.0
14.	Chevron Corporation	9,195.0	39.	NIKE Inc	4,240.0
15.	Disney (Walt) Co.	8,980.0	40.	Bank of New York Mellon	4,090.0
16.	Home Depot Inc	8,630.0	41.	Valero Energy Corp	4,065.0
17.	Boeing Co.	8,197.0	42.	MetLife Inc	4,010.0
18.	Prudential Financial Inc	7,863.0	43.	Mastercard Inc	3,915.0
19.	Ford Motor Co.	7,602.0	44.	Chubb Ltd	3,861.0
20.	Sprint Corp	7,389.0	45.	Anthem Inc	3,842.8
21.	Visa Inc	6,699.0	46.	Oracle Corp	3,825.0
22.	CVS Health Corporation	6,622.0	47.	Exelon Corp	3,770.0
23.	US Bancorp	6,218.0	48.	Delta Air Lines Inc	3,577.0
24.	Morgan Stanley	6,111.0	49.	Southwest Airlines Co	3,488.0
25.	Philip Morris International	6,035.0	50.	Lowe's Companies Inc	3,447.0

Ranking by Total Assets

Based on most recent fiscal year-end figures.

Rank	Company Name	Assets ($Mill)	Rank	Company Name	Assets ($Mill)
1.	JPMorgan Chase & Co	2,533,600.0	26.	BlackRock Inc	220,217.0
2.	Bank of America Corp	2,281,234.0	27.	General Motors Co	212,482.0
3.	Wells Fargo & Co.	1,951,757.0	28.	SunTrust Banks Inc	205,962.0
4.	Citigroup Inc	1,842,465.0	29.	Walmart Inc	204,522.0
5.	Morgan Stanley	851,733.0	30.	DowDuPont Inc	192,164.0
6.	Prudential Financial Inc	831,921.0	31.	American Express Co.	181,159.0
7.	MetLife Inc	719,892.0	32.	Pfizer Inc	171,797.0
8.	Berkshire Hathaway Inc	702,095.0	33.	Ally Financial Inc	167,148.0
9.	American Intl. Group Inc	498,301.0	34.	Chubb Ltd	167,022.0
10.	US Bancorp	462,040.0	35.	Johnson & Johnson	157,303.0
11.	AT&T Inc	444,097.0	36.	Citizens Financial Group Inc	152,336.0
12.	PNC Financial Services Grp	380,768.0	37.	Ameriprise Financial Inc	147,470.0
13.	General Electric Co	377,945.0	38.	UnitedHealth Group Inc	139,058.0
14.	Bank of New York Mellon	371,758.0	39.	Duke Energy Corp	137,914.0
15.	Capital One Financial Corp	365,693.0	40.	KeyCorp	137,698.0
16.	Exxon Mobil Corp	348,691.0	41.	Oracle Corp	137,264.0
17.	Lincoln National Corp.	281,763.0	42.	AFLAC Inc	137,217.0
18.	Ford Motor Co.	257,808.0	43.	Intl. Bus. Machines Corp	125,356.0
19.	Verizon Communications	257,143.0	44.	Regions Financial Corp	124,294.0
20.	Chevron Corporation	253,806.0	45.	Dell Technologies Inc	122,281.0
21.	Schwab (Charles) Corp	243,274.0	46.	Procter & Gamble Co	120,406.0
22.	State Street Corp.	238,425.0	47.	M & T Bank Corp	118,593.5
23.	Hartford Financial Svcs. Grp	225,260.0	48.	Allergan PLC	118,341.9
24.	Voya Financial Inc	222,532.0	49.	Exelon Corp	116,700.0
25.	BB&T Corp.	221,642.0	50.	Allstate Corp	112,422.0

Ranking by Market Capitalization

Based on most recent fiscal year-end figures and closing prices at 6/29/2018

Rank	Company Name	Market Cap ($Mill)	Rank	Company Name	Market Cap ($Mill)
1.	JPMorgan Chase & Co	354,777.8	26.	McDonald's Corp	123,029.4
2.	Exxon Mobil Corp	350,265.1	27.	General Electric Co	118,207.5
3.	Johnson & Johnson	325,452.1	28.	3M Co	116,791.1
4.	Bank of America Corp	285,828.4	29.	Medtronic PLC	115,719.8
5.	Wells Fargo & Co.	270,152.1	30.	Accenture plc	110,262.9
6.	Walmart Inc	252,739.8	31.	Altria Group Inc	107,483.5
7.	Chevron Corporation	241,602.3	32.	Honeywell International	106,973.0
8.	Visa Inc	236,577.4	33.	Abbott Laboratories	106,926.9
9.	UnitedHealth Group Inc	235,767.1	34.	Union Pacific Corp	104,771.6
10.	Home Depot Inc	225,056.4	35.	NIKE Inc	102,205.0
11.	Pfizer Inc	212,222.4	36.	Salesforce.Com Inc	100,104.0
12.	Verizon Communications	207,875.7	37.	United Technologies Corp	100,031.4
13.	Mastercard Inc	202,454.0	38.	Schlumberger Ltd	92,845.5
14.	AT&T Inc	197,187.5	39.	Lilly (Eli) & Co	92,619.8
15.	Procter & Gamble Co.	196,289.6	40.	Bristol-Myers Squibb Co.	90,455.4
16.	Boeing Co.	195,461.7	41.	Lockheed Martin Corp	84,354.0
17.	Citigroup Inc	194,442.9	42.	American Express Co.	84,315.5
18.	Coca-Cola Co	186,635.8	43.	Morgan Stanley	83,910.3
19.	Oracle Corp	175,409.7	44.	Thermo Fisher Scientific	83,337.3
20.	Merck & Co Inc	163,301.4	45.	US Bancorp	82,155.8
21.	Disney (Walt) Co.	156,221.7	46.	ConocoPhillips	81,460.0
22.	DowDuPont Inc	152,986.3	47.	Caterpillar Inc.	81,117.8
23.	AbbVie Inc	147,024.4	48.	BlackRock Inc	79,931.1
24.	Intl. Bus. Machines Corp	128,240.2	49.	NextEra Energy Inc	78,744.0
25.	Philip Morris International	125,508.2	50.	Lowe's Companies Inc	77,999.8

Ranking by Current Yield
Based on closing prices at 6/29/2018

Rank	Company Name	Yield %	Rank	Company Name	Yield %
1.	Buckeye Partners LP	14.37	26.	Iron Mountain Inc	6.71
2.	NGL Energy Partners LP	12.48	27.	Apple Hospitality REIT Inc	6.71
3.	Energy Transfer Partners LP	11.87	28.	EPR Properties	6.67
4.	Annaly Capital Management	11.66	29.	Tupperware Brands Corp	6.60
5.	CenturyLink Inc	11.59	30.	Kimco Realty Corp	6.59
6.	New Residential Investment	11.44	31.	L Brands, Inc	6.51
7.	Chimera Investment Corp	10.94	32.	Brixmor Property Group Inc	6.31
8.	Global Partners LP	10.85	33.	AT&T Inc	6.23
9.	MFA Financial, Inc.	10.55	34.	Owens & Minor, Inc.	6.22
10.	GameStop Corp	10.43	35.	Enterprise Products Partners	6.22
11.	TC PipeLines, LP	10.02	36.	NY Community Bancorp	6.16
12.	Macquarie Infrastructure	9.48	37.	W.P. Carey Inc	6.15
13.	AmeriGas Partners LP	9.00	38.	Tanger Factory Outlet Center	5.96
14.	Spirit Realty Capital Inc	8.97	39.	PPL Corp	5.74
15.	Starwood Property Trust Inc.	8.84	40.	HCP Inc	5.73
16.	Pitney Bowes Inc	8.75	41.	Philip Morris International	5.65
17.	Omega Healthcare Investors	8.52	42.	Welltower Inc	5.55
18.	Vector Group Ltd	8.39	43.	Ventas Inc	5.55
19.	OUTFRONT Media Inc	7.40	44.	Mercury General Corp.	5.49
20.	VEREIT Inc	7.39	45.	National Health Investors	5.43
21.	Targa Resources Corp	7.36	46.	Magellan Midstream Partner	5.43
22.	Medical Properties Trust	7.12	47.	Ford Motor Co.	5.42
23.	CoreCivic Inc	7.12	48.	Macerich Co (The)	5.21
24.	Energy Transfer Equity LP	7.07	49.	Retail Properties of America	5.18
25.	Colony Capital Inc	7.05	50.	Southern Company	5.18

Ranking by Return on Equity
Based on most recent fiscal year-end figures.

Rank	Company Name	Return on Equity %	Rank	Company Name	Return on Equity %
1.	Burlington Stores Inc	2,048.74	26.	Mettler-Toledo Intl, Inc.	76.56
2.	Boeing Co.	1,398.81	27.	Rite Aid Corp	72.82
3.	Energizer Holdings Inc	731.40	28.	Altria Group Inc	72.63
4.	Kimberly-Clark Corp.	705.26	29.	Southwestern Energy Co	72.24
5.	United Parcel Service Inc	698.93	30.	Mastercard Inc	70.39
6.	Lennox International Inc	697.15	31.	BWX Technologies inc	67.91
7.	Pitney Bowes Inc	615.63	32.	First Data Corp	67.02
8.	Lockheed Martin Corp	483.57	33.	Crown Holdings Inc	66.80
9.	Welbilt Inc	400.60	34.	Sherwin-Williams Co	63.63
10.	Block (H & R), Inc.	368.45	35.	Kellogg Co	61.74
11.	Tempur Sealy Intl, Inc.	311.20	36.	Allison Transmission Hldgs	56.97
12.	Home Depot Inc	299.07	37.	United Rentals Inc	56.63
13.	S&P Global Inc	219.84	38.	Campbell Soup Co	56.26
14.	Sealed Air Corp	213.88	39.	Lowe's Companies Inc	56.17
15.	Taubman Centers Inc	171.13	40.	Berry Global Group Inc	55.44
16.	Clorox Co (The)	167.10	41.	Booz Allen Hamilton Hldg	54.09
17.	Chemours Co	155.42	42.	Brown-Forman Corp	53.39
18.	Laredo Petroleum, Inc	116.04	43.	TJX Companies, Inc.	53.13
19.	Wyndham Destinations	109.42	44.	Zoetis Inc	53.05
20.	AbbVie Inc	109.09	45.	Science Applications Intl	52.71
21.	Hilton Grand Vacations	95.47	46.	FactSet Research Systems	47.96
22.	Hershey Company	92.05	47.	Union Pacific Corp	47.83
23.	Verizon Communications	91.74	48.	Aptiv PLC	47.54
24.	Ciena Corp	86.95	49.	Simon Property Group, Inc.	46.80
25.	MSCI Inc	84.60	50.	Nordstrom, Inc.	46.55

Ranking by High P/E Ratio

Based on closing prices at 6/29/2018

Rank	Company Name	P/E Ratio	Rank	Company Name	P/E Ratio
1.	Twitter Inc	4,367.00	26.	Zayo Group Holdings Inc	114.00
2.	Vishay Intertechnology	2,320.00	27.	Keysight Technologies Inc	113.52
3.	Tennant Co.	1,580.00	28.	Targa Resources Corp	109.98
4.	Brinks Co	996.88	29.	Digital Realty Trust Inc	109.39
5.	Waters Corp.	569.38	30.	HanesBrands Inc	104.86
6.	Jefferies Financial Group	454.80	31.	Merck & Co Inc	104.66
7.	Newmont Mining Corp	419.00	32.	Sun Communities Inc	104.13
8.	McKesson Corp	416.88	33.	United States Cellular Corp	102.89
9.	Boston Scientific Corp.	408.75	34.	American Campus Comm.	97.45
10.	Grace (WR) & Co	407.28	35.	Bristol-Myers Squibb Co.	97.09
11.	GameStop Corp	364.25	36.	Cabot Oil & Gas Corp.	95.20
12.	New York Times Co.	323.75	37.	Cooper Companies, Inc.	90.56
13.	Worldpay Inc	314.54	38.	USG Corp	89.83
14.	Adtalem Global Education	282.94	39.	Healthcare Tr. Of America	86.97
15.	Johnson & Johnson	258.17	40.	DowDuPont Inc	86.74
16.	Abbott Laboratories	234.58	41.	Alleghany Corp.	85.94
17.	Salesforce.Com Inc	213.13	42.	Agilent Technologies	85.89
18.	Diamond Offshore Drilling	208.60	43.	MSA Safety Inc	85.26
19.	Sempra Energy	193.52	44.	GoDaddy Inc	85.06
20.	Macerich Co	189.43	45.	Red Hat Inc	85.04
21.	Devon Energy Corp.	183.17	46.	Catalent Inc	83.78
22.	Bunge Ltd.	170.02	47.	GrubHub Inc	83.26
23.	Vornado Realty Trust	144.94	48.	Quaker Chemical Corp.	79.83
24.	Coca-Cola Co	129.00	49.	Veeva Systems Inc	79.24
25.	Crown Castle Intl. Corp	119.80	50.	Lilly (Eli) & Co	79.01

Ranking by Low P/E Ratio

Based on closing prices at 6/29/2018

Rank	Company Name	P/E Ratio	Rank	Company Name	P/E Ratio
1.	Genworth Financial, Inc.	2.94	26.	Duke Realty Corp	6.35
2.	Sprint Corp	2.94	27.	Torchmark Corp	6.46
3.	Southwestern Energy Co	3.71	28.	Pitney Bowes Inc	6.49
4.	New Residential Investment	3.87	29.	AT&T Inc	6.50
5.	Laredo Petroleum, Inc	4.04	30.	Ciena Corp	6.58
6.	CNX Resources Corp	4.26	31.	Verizon Communications	6.59
7.	KBR Inc	4.75	32.	CenterPoint Energy, Inc	6.81
8.	Alexander & Baldwin Inc	4.84	33.	White Mountains Insur. Grp	6.85
9.	Ryder System, Inc.	4.86	34.	NACCO Industries Inc	6.93
10.	Reinsurance Grp of America	4.94	35.	Lincoln National Corp.	6.95
11.	Annaly Capital Management	4.97	36.	Assured Guaranty Ltd	6.98
12.	Chesapeake Energy Corp.	4.99	37.	BankUnited Inc.	7.07
13.	Prudential Financial Inc	5.22	38.	Macy's Inc	7.12
14.	Santander Consumer USA	5.35	39.	AFLAC Inc	7.23
15.	GATX Corp	5.59	40.	TC PipeLines, LP	7.54
16.	Ford Motor Co.	5.74	41.	Macquarie Infrastructure	7.56
17.	Newell Brands Inc	5.82	42.	Trinity Industries, Inc.	7.65
18.	Spectrum Brands Holdings	5.92	43.	Federated Investors Inc	7.80
19.	Air Lease Corp	5.95	44.	WestRock Co	7.82
20.	Wyndham Destinations Inc	5.97	45.	Block (H & R), Inc.	7.83
21.	Prestige Brands Holdings	6.05	46.	Norfolk Southern Corp.	7.91
22.	Global Partners LP	6.09	47.	Alaska Air Group, Inc.	7.96
23.	Chimera Investment Corp	6.11	48.	Tribune Media Co	7.99
24.	Group 1 Automotive, Inc.	6.18	49.	Unum Group	8.04
25.	Penske Automotive Group	6.31	50.	Realogy Holdings Corp	8.11

CLASSIFICATION BY INDUSTRY

Accommodation and Food Services
Accommodation
Choice Hotels International, Inc.
Extended Stay America Inc
Hilton Grand Vacations
Host Hotels & Resorts Inc.
Hyatt Hotels Corp.
Park Place Entertainment Corp.
Wyndham Worldwide Corp.

Food Services and Drinking Places
Brinker International, Inc.
Chipotle Mexican Grill Inc
*Darden Restaurants, Inc.
*McDonald's Corporation
Ruby Tuesday, Inc.
*Yum! Brands, Inc.

Administrative & Support and Waste Management & Remediation Services
Administrative and Support Services
*Equifax Inc.
*ManpowerGroup
Mid Atlantic Medical Services
Robert Half International, Inc.
*Rollins, Inc.

Waste Management and Remediation Services
Clean Harbors, Inc.
Republic Services, Inc.
*Waste Management, Inc.

Arts, Entertainment, and Recreation
*Carnival Corp.
*Disney (Walt) Company (The)
GTECH Holdings Corp.
Las Vegas Sands Corp.
Live Nation Entertainment, Inc.
MGM Resorts International
Royal Caribbean Cruises Ltd.
Six Flags Entertainment Corp
Vail Resorts Inc
Vista Outdoor Inc

Construction
ABM Industries Incorporated
*Boston Properties, Inc.
CalAtlantic Group Inc
Chicago Bridge & Iron Co., N.V.
Dycom Industries, Inc.
Eagle Materials Inc.
EMCOR Group, Inc.
Fortune Brands Home & Security, Inc.
*Granite Construction Inc.
Horton (D.R.) Inc.
Jacobs Engineering Group Inc.
KB Home
KBR Inc.
Lennar Corporation
Martin Marietta Materials, Inc.
*MDU Resources Group, Inc.

NVR Inc.
Owens Corning
Pulte Homes, Inc.
Quanta Services, Inc.
Toll Brothers, Inc.
TRI Pointe Group Inc.a

Educational Services
DeVry Education Group Inc.
Graham Holdings Co.

Electric Power Generation
Calpine Corp.
Covanta Holding Corp.
NRG Energy, Inc.
Ormat Technologies Inc

Finance and Insurance
Commercial Banking
Ally Financial Inc
Associated Banc-Corp
*BancorpSouth, Inc.
*Bank of America Corporation
*Bank of Hawaii Corporation
*Bank of New York Mellon Corp.
BankUnited Inc.
*BB&T Corporation
*Comerica, Inc.
*Community Bank System, Inc.
Cullen/Frost Bankers, Inc.
First Data Corp.
*First Horizon National Corporation
First Republic Bank (San Francisco, CA)
HRG Group
*Hudson United Bancorp
*J.P. Morgan Chase & Co.
*KeyCorp
*M&T Bank Corporation
*North Fork Bancorporation, Inc.
*PNC Financial Services Group
Prosperity Bancshares Inc.
*Regions Financial Corp.
*State Street Corporation
*SunTrust Banks, Inc.
Synchrony Financial
*Synovus Financial Corporation
*TCF Financial Corp.
TransUnion
*U.S. Bancorp
*Valley National Bancorp
*Wells Fargo & Company
*Wilmington Trust Corporation ·

Direct Health and Medical Insurance Carriers
*AFLAC Incorporated
Cigna Corp.
Humana Inc.
Pacificare Health Systems, Inc.

Reinsurance Group of America
UnitedHealth Group Inc.
Universal American Corp.
*UnumProvident Corporation
WellCare Health Plans Inc.

Direct Life Insurance Carriers

American Equity Investment Life Holding Co.
Assurant Inc.
*Genworth Financial Inc. (Holding Co)
*Lincoln National Corporation
Primerica Inc.
Principal Financial Group, Inc.
*Protective Life Corporation
Prudential Financial, Inc.
*Torchmark Corporation
Voya Financial Inc.

Direct Property and Casualty Insurance Carriers
Allied World Assurance Company Holdings AG
Allmerica Financial Corporation
*Allstate Corporation (The)
*American Financial Group, Inc.
American International Group
Aspen Insurance Holdings Ltd
Berkley (W.R.) Corporation
Berkshire Hathaway Inc.
CNA Financial Corporation
Everest Re Group Ltd
Hanover Insurance Group Inc.
*Kemper Corp.
Leucadia National Corporation
Loews Corporation
Markel Corporation
Mercury General Corporation
ProAssurance Corp.
Progressive Corporation (The)
RenaissanceRe Holdings Ltd
*RLI Corp.
*The St Paul Travelers Companies Inc.
White Mountains Insurance Group, Ltd
XL Capital Ltd

Direct Title Insurance Carriers
Alleghany Corporation
*CoreLogic Inc.
Fidelity National Financial Inc.
First American Financial Corp

Insurance Agencies and Brokerages
Aetna, Inc.
Anthem Inc.
Brown & Brown, Inc.
Centene Corp
Gallagher (Arthur J.) & Company
*Hartford Financial Services Group
Metlife, Inc.
Molina Healthcare Inc.

Mortgage and Nonmortgage Loan Brokers
Community Bancorp, Inc.
Nondepository Credit Intermediation
*American Express Company

Ameriprise Financial Inc.
*Capital One Financial Corp.
Discover Financial Services
Invesco Ltd
Lazard Ltd
*Morgan Stanley

Real Estate Investment Trusts
Alexandria Real Estate Equities, Inc.
American Campus Communities Inc.
American Homes 4 Rent
American Tower Corp
AMB Property Corporation
*Annaly Capital Management Inc.
Apartment Investment & Management Co
Apple Hospitality REIT Inc.
AvalonBay Communities, Inc.
*Brandywine Realty Trust
*Brixmor Property Group Inc
Camden Property Trust
Care Capital Properties Inc.
*Chimera Investment Corp.
Columbia Property Trust Inc
Corporate Office Properties Trust
*Crown Castle International Corp.
CubeSmart
*DCT Industrial Trust Inc.
*DDR Corp
Digital Realty Trust Inc.
Douglas Emmett Inc.
*Duke Realty Corporation
*Education Realty Trust Inc.
Empire State Realty Trust Inc
*Equity Commonwealth
Equity Lifestyle Properties Inc
*Equity Residential Prop. Trust
*EPR Properties
*Essex Property Trust, Inc.
Extra Space Storage Inc
*Federal Realty Investment Trust
General Growth Properties Inc.
*HCP, Inc.
*Healthcare Realty Trust, Inc.
Healthcare Trust of America Inc
*Highwoods Properties, Inc.
*Kilroy Realty Corp.
*Kimco Realty Corp.
LaSalle Hotel Properties
*Liberty Property Trust
*Macerich Company (The)
*Mack-Cali Realty Corporation
Medical Properties Trust Inc.
MFA Financial, Inc.
*Mid-America Apartment Communities Inc
National Health Investors, Inc.
*National Retail Properties Inc.
*Omega Healthcare Investors, Inc.
OUTFRONT Media Inc
Paramount Group Inc
Piedmont Office Realty Trust Inc
*ProLogis
Public Storage, Inc.
Realty Income Corp.

*Regency Centers Corporation
Retail Properties of America, Inc
*Shurgard Storage Centers, Inc.
*Simon Property Group, Inc.
SL Green Realty Corp.
Spirit Reality Capital
Starwood Hotels & Resorts
Sun Communities, Inc.
*Tanger Factory Outlet Centers, Inc.
*Taubman Centers, Inc.
*UDR Inc.
*Universal Health Realty Inc. Trust
*Urban Edge Properties
*Urstadt Biddle Properties Inc.
*Ventas, Inc.
*Vornado Realty Trust
Washington Prime Group
*Weingarten Realty Investors
*Welltower Inc.

Reinsurance Carriers
*Marsh & McLennan Cos. Inc.
*Old Republic International Corp.

Savings Institutions
*Sovereign Bancorp, Inc.
*Webster Financial Corp.

*Securities, Commodity Contracts, and Other
Financial Investments and Related Activities*
Affiliated Managers Group Inc.
Assured Guaranty Ltd
Broadridge Financial Solutions Inc.
*Citigroup Inc.
CME Group Inc.
Eaton Vance Corporation
Federated Investors, Inc.
*Franklin Resources, Inc.
Goldman Sachs Group, Inc.
IntercontinentalExchange Inc.
Janus Capital Group, Inc.
Legg Mason, Inc.
Raymond James Financial, Inc.
*Waddell & Reed Financial, Inc.
Westwood Holdings Group, Inc.

Other Financial Vehicles
BlackRock, Inc.

Health Care and Social Assistance
Brookdale Senior Living Inc.
Community Health Systems, Inc.
DaVita Inc.
Genesis Healthcare Inc.
HCA Holdings Inc.
Health Management Associates
HealthSouth Corp
Kindred Healthcare, Inc.
Laboratory Corp. of America
Mednax, Inc.
*Tenet Healthcare Corporation
Universal Health Services, Inc.

Information
*Cable Networks, Program Distribution and
Internet Service Providers*
Time Warner Inc.

*Information Services and Data Processing
Services*
Alliance Data Systems Corp.
Arista Networks Inc
Black Knight Financial Services Inc.
Concord EFS, Inc.
DST Systems, Inc.
Dun & Bradstreet Corp. (The)
Fair Isaac Corporation
FactSet Research Systems Inc.
FleetCor Technologies Inc.
GoDaddy Inc.
Green Dot Corp
*Hewlett Packard Enterprise Co
Lender Processing Services Inc.
MasterCard Inc.
Nielsen Holdings PLC
NCR Corporation
Square Inc
*Thomson Reuters Corp
Total System Services, Inc.
Vantiv Inc.
VeriFone Systems
Visa Inc.
Western Union Co.

Motion Picture and Sound Recording Industries
Cinemark Holdings Inc
DreamWorks Animation SKG Inc.
News Corp.
Regal Entertainment Group

Publishing Industries
3D Systems Corp.
Guidewire Software Inc
Meredith Corporation
Monster Worldwide Inc.
MSCI Inc.
*New York Times Company
Oracle Corp.
*Reader's Digest Association, Inc.
ServiceNow Inc
Solera Holdings Inc.
Time Inc.
Tyler Technologies, Inc.
Veeva Systems
Veritiv Corp
VMWARE, Inc.
Wiley (John) & Sons Inc.

Radio and Television Broadcasting
Cable One Inc
Dolby Laboratories Inc.
Pandora Media Inc
Tegna Inc
Westwood One, Inc.

Telecommunications
*AT&T Inc

*CenturyLink, Inc.
*Citizens Communications Co.
 Fidelity National Information Services Inc.
 Keysight Technology
 Level 3 Communications, Inc.
 Neustar Inc.
 Qwest Communications International
 Sprint Nextel Corporation
 Sprint Corp
*Telephone and Data Systems, Inc.
 United States Cellular Corp.
*Verizon Communications Inc.
 Zayo Group Holdings Inc

Manufacturing
Beverage and Tobacco Product Manufacturing
*Altria Group, Inc.
 Boston Beer Co., Inc.
*Brown-Forman Corporation
*Coca-Cola Company (The)
 Constellation Brands, Inc.
 Dr Pepper Snapple Group Inc
 Molson Coors Brewing Company
*PepsiCo Inc.
*Philip Morris International Inc.
*Reynolds American Inc.
*Vector Group Inc.

Chemical Manufacturing
*3M Company
*Air Products & Chemicals, Inc.
*Albemarle Corporation
 Alberto-Culver Company
*Avon Products, Inc.
*Cabot Corporation
 Celanese Corp.
 CF Industries Holdings Inc.
 Charles River Laboratories Int.
 Chemours Co
 Chemtura Corp.
*Church & Dwight Company, Inc.
*Clorox Company (The)
*Colgate-Palmolive Company
 Compass Minerals International Inc.
*Dow Chemical Company
*du Pont (E.I.) de Nemours & Co.
*Eastman Chemical Company
*Ecolab, Inc.
*Fuller (H.B.) Company
 Grace (W.R.) Co.
 Huntsman Corp.
 IMC Global, Inc.
*International Flavors & Fragrances
 Monsanto Co.
*Olin Corporation
 Platform Specialty Products Corp
*PPG Industries, Inc.
*Praxair, Inc.
*Procter & Gamble Company
 Rockwood Holdings Inc.
*Rohm & Haas Company
*RPM International Inc.
 Scotts Company (The)
*Sherwin-Williams Company

 Stepan Co.
 Westlake Chemical Corp.
 Univar Inc.
 Versum Materials
*Valspar Corporation (The)

Computer and Electronic Product Manufacturing
 Advanced Micro Devices, Inc.
 Agilent Technologies, Inc.
*Allegheny Technologies Inc.
*Ametek, Inc.
 Ciena Corp.
*Corning Incorporated
*Emerson Electric Co.
 Esterline Technologies Corp
 Fitbit Inc
 Global Payments Inc.
 Harman International Industries
 Juniper Networks Inc.
*Harris Corporation
*HP Inc
 Knowles Corp
*International Business Machines
 Jabil Circuit, Inc.
 L-3 Communications Holdings
 Mettler-Toledo International Inc.
 Micron Technology, Inc.
*Motorola Solutions Inc.
 Plantronics, Inc.
*Raytheon Company
*Rockwell Collins, Inc.
 Teradyne, Inc.
 Teradata Corp.
 Thermo Fisher Scientific Inc.
 TE Connectivity Ltd
 Vishay Intertechnology, Inc.
 Waters Corporation

Electrical Equipment, Appliance, and Component Manufacturing
 Acuity Brands Inc.
 Amphenol Corp.
 Anixter International Inc.
 Belden Inc.
*Eaton Corporation
 Edgewell Personal Care Co.
 Energizer Holdings Inc
 Enersys
*General Electric Company
*Hubbell, Inc.
 Manitowoc Foodservice Inc
 Regal Beloit Corp.
*Rockwell Automation
*Smith (A.O.) Corporation
 Spectrum Brands Holdings Inc
*Whirlpool Corporation

Fabricated Metal Product Manufacturing
*Badger Meter, Inc.
*Ball Corporation
*Crane Co.
 Crown Holdings, Inc.
 Danaher Corporation

Greif Inc.
Orbital ATK Inc
*Parker-Hannifin Corp.
Shaw Group Inc. (The)
*Snap-On Incorporated
*Stanley Works
*Timken Company (The)
Valmont Industries, Inc.

Food Manufacturing
*Archer Daniels Midland Co.
Bunge Ltd
*Campbell Soup Company
*ConAgra Brands, Inc.
Corn Products International Inc.
Dean Foods Company
*Flowers Foods, Inc.
*General Mills, Inc.
*Hershey Foods Corporation
Hillshire Brands Co
*Hormel Foods Corporation
*Kellogg Company
Lamb Weston
*McCormick & Company, Inc.
Mead Johnson Nutrition Co.
Pinnacle Foods Inc.
Post Holdings Inc
Ralcorp Holdings Inc.
*Sensient Technologies Corp.
*Smucker (J.M.) Company
Tootsie Roll Industries, Inc.
TreeHouse Foods Inc
*Tyson Foods, Inc.
Whitewave Foods Co.

Furniture and Related Product Manufacturing
HNI Corporation
Leggett & Platt, Incorporated
*Masco Corporation
Tempur Sealy International Inc.
Steelcase Inc.

Machinery Manufacturing
AGCO Corporation
*Brunswick Corporation
BWX Technologies Inc.
*Caterpillar Inc.
Colfax Corp
*Cummins Inc.
*Curtiss-Wright Corp.
*Deere & Company
*Diebold Nixdorf Inc.
*Donaldson Company, Inc.
*Dover Corporation
Flowserve Corporation
FMC Corporation
Gardner Denver, Inc.
*Graco Inc.
*IDEX Corporation
Ingersoll-Rand Plc
ITT Inc
*Kennametal Inc.
Lindsay Corp
Lennox International Inc.
Pentair Ltd

Roper Technologies Inc.
Terex Corporation
*Tennant Company
*Toro Co. (The)
Varian Medical Systems, Inc.
Watsco Inc.
*Xerox Corporation
Xylem Inc.
*York International Corporation

Medical Equipment and Supplies Manufacturing
Advanced Medical Optics Inc.
Alere Inc.
*Bard (C.R.), Inc.
*Baxter International Inc.
*Becton, Dickinson and Company
Bio-Rad Laboratories, Inc.
Boston Scientific Corporation
CareFusion Corp
Cooper Companies, Inc.
Covidien Plc
Globus Medical
Halyard Health Inc
Hill-Rom Holdings, Inc.
*Medtronic PLC
Mine Safety Appliances Company
ResMed Inc.
Steris plc
Stryker Corporation
*Teleflex Inc.
Zimmer Biomet Holdings, Inc.

Nonmetallic Mineral Product Manufacturing
Brink's Company (The)
Minerals Technologies Inc.
Oil-Dri Corp. of America
Owens-Illinois, Inc.
USG Corporation

Paper and Wood Product Manufacturing
*Avery Dennison Corporation
*Bemis Company, Inc.
*Boise Cascade Corporation
Domtar Corp.
Graphic Packaging Holding Co.
*International Paper Company
*Kimberly-Clark Corporation
*Louisiana-Pacific Corporation
Packaging Corp. of America
*Rayonier Inc.
*Sonoco Products Company
Tenneco Inc.

Petroleum and Coal Products Manufacturing
*Chevron Corp.
*ConocoPhillips
*Exxon Mobil Corporation
*Hess Corp.
HollyFrontier Corp
*Marathon Petroleum Corp
Murphy Oil Corporation
NGL Energy
PBF Energy, Inc.
Phillips 66
Tesoro Corporation

Valero Energy Corporation
Western Refining Inc.

Pharmaceutical Preparation Manufacturing
*Abbott Laboratories
AbbVie Inc.
*Allergan, Inc.
AmerisourceBergen Corporation
Ashland Global
*Bristol-Myers Squibb Company
Catalent Inc
Edwards Lifesciences Corp.
Genentech, Inc.
*Johnson & Johnson
*Lilly (Eli) & Company
*Merck & Co., Inc.
*Pfizer Inc.
Prestige Brands Holdings Inc.
Zoetis Inc.

Plastics and Rubber Products Manufacturing
AptarGroup Inc.
Armstrong World Industry Inc.
Berry Plastics Group Inc.
*Carlisle Companies Incorporated
Hexcel Corp
*Illinois Tool Works, Incorporated
*Myers Industries, Inc.
*Newell Brands Inc.
PolyOne Corp.d
Sealed Air Corporation
Tupperware Brands Corporation
*West Pharmaceutical Services

Primary Metal Manufacturing
*AK Steel Holding Corporation
*Arconic Inc.
Carpenter Technology Corp.
Commercial Metals Co.
*Nucor Corporation
*United States Steel Corporation
*Worthington Industries, Inc.

Printing and Related Support Activities
Deluxe Corporation

Textiles, Apparel, and Leather Manufacturing
Coach, Inc.
Kate Spade & Co.
Michael Kors Holdings Ltd
Mohawk Industries, Inc.
*NIKE, Inc.
PVH Corp.
Ralph Lauren Corp
Under Armour Inc.
*VF Corporation

Transportation Equipment Manufacturing
Allison Transmission Holdings Inc
Autoliv, Inc.
*Boeing Company (The)
*BorgWarner Inc.
Dana Corp
Delphi Automotive Plc
*Ford Motor Company
General Dynamics Corporation

General Motors Co.
*Harley-Davidson, Inc.
*Honeywell International Inc.
Huntington Ingalls Industries Inc
Lear Corp.
*Lockheed Martin Corporation
*Meritor Inc.
*Modine Manufacturing Company
Navistar International Inc.
*Oshkosh Corp.
*Polaris Industries Inc.
Sequa Corporation
Spirit AeroSystems Holdings Inc.
Teledyne Technologies
*Textron Inc.
Thor Industries, Inc.
Transdigm Group Inc.
Trinity Industries, Inc.
*United Technologies Corp.
Visteon Corp.
WABCO Holdings Inc.
Wabtec Corp.

Other Manufacturing
*Brady Corporation
Coty, Inc.
*Estee Lauder Companies, Inc.
Fortive
Macquaire Infrastructure

Mining
Activities Support for Mining
*Baker Hughes Inc.
Diamond Offshore Drilling, Inc.
Dril-Quip, Inc.
Ensco plc
Frank's International N.V.
EOG Resources, Inc.
Halliburton Company
Helmerich & Payne, Inc.
*Marathon Oil Corporation
Noble Corp
Now Inc.
Oceaneering International, Inc.
Oil States International, Inc.
Pride International, Inc.
Rowan Companies Plc
RPC, Inc.
Schlumberger Ltd.
Superior Energy Services, Inc.
Transocean Ltd

Mining (except Oil and Gas)
*Arch Coal, Inc.
CONSOL Energy Inc.
Freeport-McMoRan Inc.
*Massey Energy Co.
Mosaic Co. (The)
Newmont Mining Corporation
*Southern Copper Corp.
Tahoe Resources Inc.
*Vulcan Materials Company

Oil and Gas Extraction
AmeriGas Partners LP

*Anadarko Petroleum Corp.
*Apache Corporation
 Cabot Oil & Gas Corp.
 Chesapeake Energy Corp.
 Cimarex Energy Co.
 Concho Resources Inc
 Continental Resources Inc.
 Delek US Holdings
 Denbury Resources, Inc.
 Devon Energy Corporation
*Kerr-McGee Corporation
 Kosmos Energy Ltd
 Laredo Petroleum, Inc.
 Nabors Industries Ltd.
 Newfield Exploration Co.
 Noble Corp.
 Noble Energy, Inc.
*Occidental Petroleum Corp.
 Pioneer Natural Resources Co.
 QEP Resources Inc
 Range Resources Corp.
 St. Mary Land & Exploration Co.
 Southwestern Energy Company
 Ultra Petroleum Corp
 Whiting Petroleum Corp.
 WPX Energy, Inc.

Other Services
 Aramark
 Clear Channel Outdoor Holdings
 CoreCivic Inc.
 CSRA Inc
 Genpact Ltd
 Hillenbrand Inc.
 Leidos Holdings Inc.
 Northwestern Corp
 Palo Alto Networks, Inc
 Red Hat Inc.
*Regis Corporation
 Reliance Steel & Aluminum Co.
 Salesforce.Com Inc.
 Science Applications International Corp
 Service Corporation International
 ServiceMaster Global Holdings, Inc
 StoneMor Partners LP
 Tableau Software Inc
 Twitter Inc
*Universal Corporation
 Valassis Communications, Inc.
 Workday Inc.
 Wex Inc.
 WestRock Co
 Yelp Inc.

Professional, Scientific, and Technical Services
 Accenture Ltd
 AECOM Technology Corp.
 Agere Systems Inc.
*Block (H & R), Inc.
 Booz Allen Hamilton Holding Corp.
 Convergys Corporation

 Covance Inc.
 Fluor Corporation
 FTI Consulting Inc.
 Gartner Group, Inc.
*Interpublic Group of Companies
 Korn/Ferry International
 Moody's Corporation
*Omnicom Group, Inc.
*PerkinElmer, Inc.
 Quest Diagnostics, Incorporated
 Quintiles IMS Holdings Inc.
*S&P Global Inc
 Synnex Corp.

Real Estate and Rental and Leasing
Real Estate
 Alexander & Baldwin Inc.
 CBRE Group Inc.
 Colony Northstar
 Howard Hughes Corp
 Jones Lang LaSalle Inc.
 Realogy Holdings Corp
 Store Capital
*W.P. Carey & Co. LLC

Rental and Leasing Services
 Air Lease Corp
 United Rentals, Inc.

Retail Trade
Building Material and Garden Equipment and Supplies Dealers
*Home Depot (The), Inc.
*Lowe's Companies, Inc.
 Wesco International, Inc.

Clothing and Clothing Accessories Stores
 American Eagle Outfitters, Inc.
 Burlington Stores Inc.
 Carter's Inc
 Chico's FAS, Inc.
 Deckers Outdoor Corp..
*Foot Locker, Inc.
 Gap, Inc. (The)
 Nordstrom, Inc.
 Payless ShoeSource Inc.
*Tiffany & Co.
 TJX Companies, Inc. (The)

Furniture and Consumer Electronics
 Aaron's, Inc.
 Best Buy Co., Inc.
 GameStop Corp.
*RadioShack Corporation
 Williams-Sonoma, Inc.

General Merchandise Stores
 Big Lots, Inc.
 Dillard's, Inc.
 Dollar General Corp.
 Kohl's Corporation
 Macys Inc.
 Penney (J.C.) Company, Inc.
*Target Corporation
*Wal-Mart Stores, Inc.

Grocery Stores
  Kroger Company (The)
*Ruddick Corporation
  Safeway Inc.

Health and Personal Care Stores
*CVS Health Corp
*Rite Aid Corporation
*Walgreen Co.

Motor Vehicle and Parts Dealers
  Advance Auto Parts, Inc.
  Asbury Automotive Group, Inc.
  AutoNation, Inc.
  AutoZone, Inc.
  Carmax Inc.
  Group 1 Automotive, Inc.
  KAR Auction Services Inc.
  Lithia Motors, Inc
  Penske Automotive Group Inc.
  Sonic Automotive, Inc.

Sporting Goods, Hobby, Book, and Music Stores and other
  Barnes & Noble, Inc.
  Cabelas Inc.
  CST Brands Inc.
  Dick's Sporting Goods, Inc.
  Murphy USA Inc.
  Sally Beauty Holdings Inc.
  Signet Jewelers Ltd.
*Sotheby's Holdings, Inc.

Transportation and Warehousing
  AirTran Holdings, Inc.
  Alaska Air Group, Inc.
*Atmos Energy Corporation
*Buckeye Partners, L.P.
  Delta Air Lines, Inc.
*Energy Transfer Equity L P
*Enterprise Products Partners L.P.
*FedEx Corporation
*GATX Corporation
  Genesee & Wyoming Inc.
  Genesis Energy L.P.
  Global Partners LP
  Iron Mountain Incorporated
  Kansas City Southern
  Kinder Morgan Inc.
  Kirby Corp.
  Magellan Midstream Partners LP
*Norfolk Southern Corporation
*OGE Energy Corp.
*Oneok Inc.
  Plains All American Pipeline, L.P.
*Ryder System, Inc.
  Southwest Airlines Co.
  Targa Resources Corp
  TC PipeLines, LP
*Union Pacific Corp.
  United Parcel Service, Inc.
  Western Gas Resources, Inc.
  Williams Companies, Inc. (The)
  XPO Logistics, Inc.

Utilities
Utilities - Electric
  AES Corporation (The)
*Alliant Energy Corporation
*Ameren Corporation
*American Electric Power Co.
*Avista Corp.
*Black Hills Corporation
*CenterPoint Energy, Inc.
*Cleco Corp.
*CMS Energy Corporation
*Consolidated Edison, Inc.
*Dominion Resources, Inc.
*DTE Energy Co.
*Duke Energy Corporation
*Edison International
*Entergy Corporation
*Eversource Energy
*Exelon Corporation
*FirstEnergy Corporation
*Great Plains Energy Incorporated
*Hawaiian Electric Industries, Inc.
*Idacorp, Inc.
*NextEra Energy Inc.
  New Jersey Resources Corp.
*NiSource, Inc.
*PG&E Corporation
*Pinnacle West Capital Corp.
*PNM Resources, Inc.
*PPL Corporation
*Puget Energy, Inc.
  RRI Energy, Inc.
*SCANA Corporation
*Southern Company (The)
*WEC Energy Group Inc.
*Westar Energy, Inc.
*Xcel Energy, Inc.

Utilities - Natural Gas
*Chesapeake Utilities Corp.
  Antero Resources Corp

*Energen Corporation
*Equitable Resources, Inc.
*National Fuel Gas Company
  Northwest Natural Gas Co.
  One Gas, Inc.
  Oneok Partners LP
  Rice Energy Inc.
*Sempra Energy
  South Jersey Industries, Inc
*Southwest Gas Corporation.
*Spire Inc.
*UGI Corporation
*Vectren Corporation
*WGL Holdings, Inc.

Utilities - Water
*American States Water Co.
  American Water Works Co., Inc.
*Aqua America, Inc.
*California Water Service Group
  SJW Group

Wholesale Trade

Wholesale Trade, Durable Goods
Arrow Electronics, Inc.
*Avnet, Inc.
Ceridian Corporation
*Genuine Parts Company
Grainger (W.W.), Inc.
Hughes Supply, Inc.
MSC Industrial Direct Co., Inc.
National-Oilwell, Inc.
*Owens & Minor, Inc.
*Pitney Bowes Inc.
*Weyerhaeuser Company
World Fuel Services Corp.

Wholesale Trade, Nondurable Goods
Cardinal Health, Inc.
*Crompton Corporation
*Dominos Pizza Inc.
Herbalife Ltd.
*McKesson Corporation
Nu Skin Enterprises, Inc.
Performance Food Group Inc.
*Supervalu Inc.
*Sysco Corporation
US Foods Holding Corp

* Designates companies offering dividend reinvestment plans.

DOW JONES INDUSTRIAL AVERAGE
PRICES - EARNINGS - DIVIDENDS

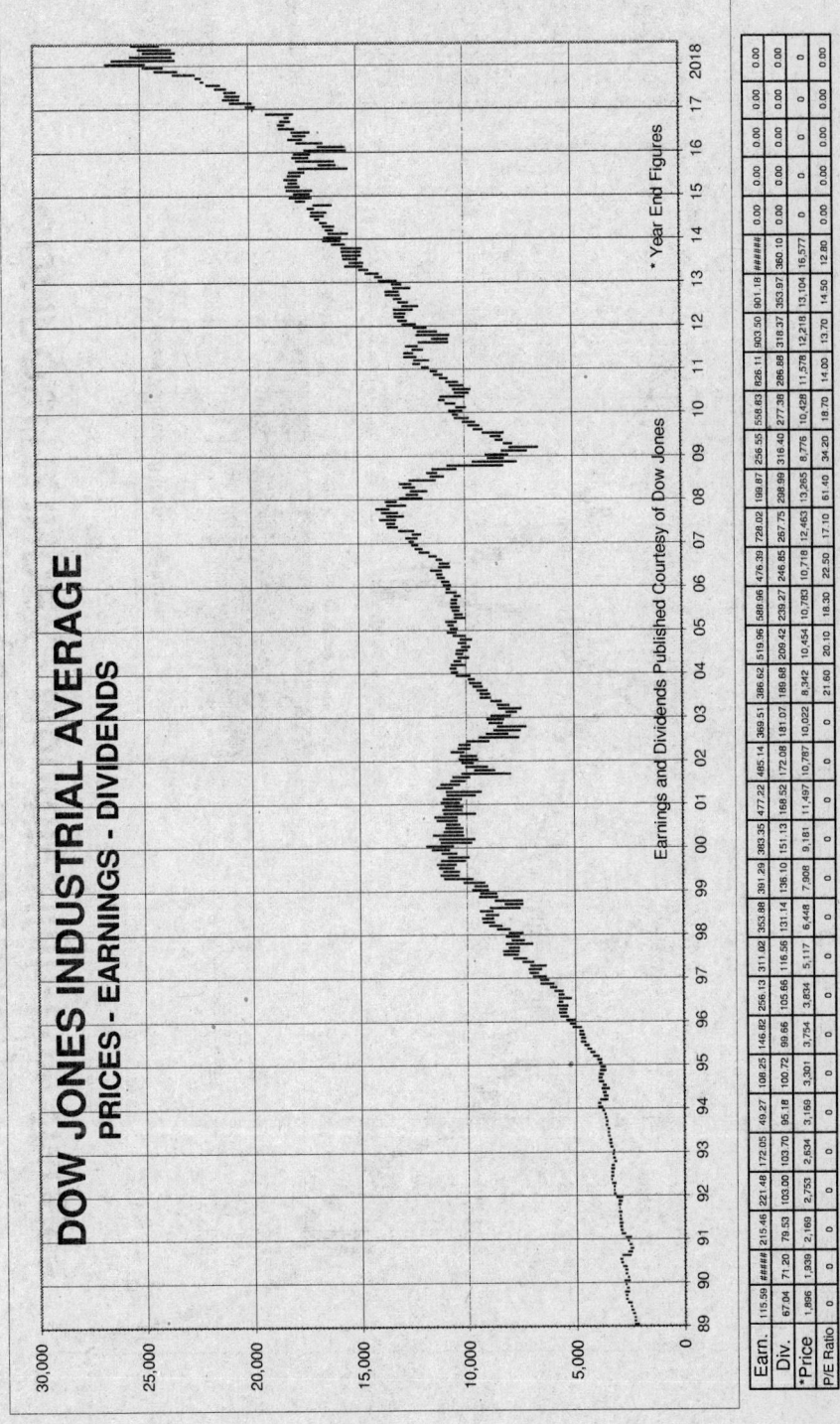

Earnings and Dividends Published Courtesy of Dow Jones

* Year End Figures

Year	Earn.	Div.	*Price	P/E Ratio
89	115.59	67.04	1,896	0
90	#####	71.20	1,939	0
91	215.46	79.53	2,169	0
92	221.48	103.00	2,753	0
93	172.05	103.70	2,634	0
94	49.27	95.18	3,169	0
95	108.25	100.72	3,301	0
96	146.82	99.66	3,754	0
97	256.13	105.66	3,834	0
98	311.02	116.56	5,117	0
99	353.88	131.14	6,448	0
00	391.29	136.10	7,908	0
01	383.35	151.13	9,181	0
02	477.22	168.52	11,497	21.60
03	485.14	172.08	10,787	0
04	369.51	181.07	10,022	21.60
05	386.62	189.68	8,342	20.10
06	519.96	209.27	10,454	18.30
07	589.96	239.27	10,783	20.10
08	476.39	246.85	10,718	22.50
09	728.02	267.75	12,463	17.10
10	199.87	298.99	13,265	34.20
11	256.55	316.40	8,776	61.40
12	558.63	277.38	10,428	18.70
13	826.11	286.88	11,578	14.00
14	903.50	318.37	12,218	13.70
15	901.18	353.97	13,104	14.50
16	#####	360.10	16,577	12.80
17	0.00	0.00	0	0.00
2018	0.00	0.00	0	0.00

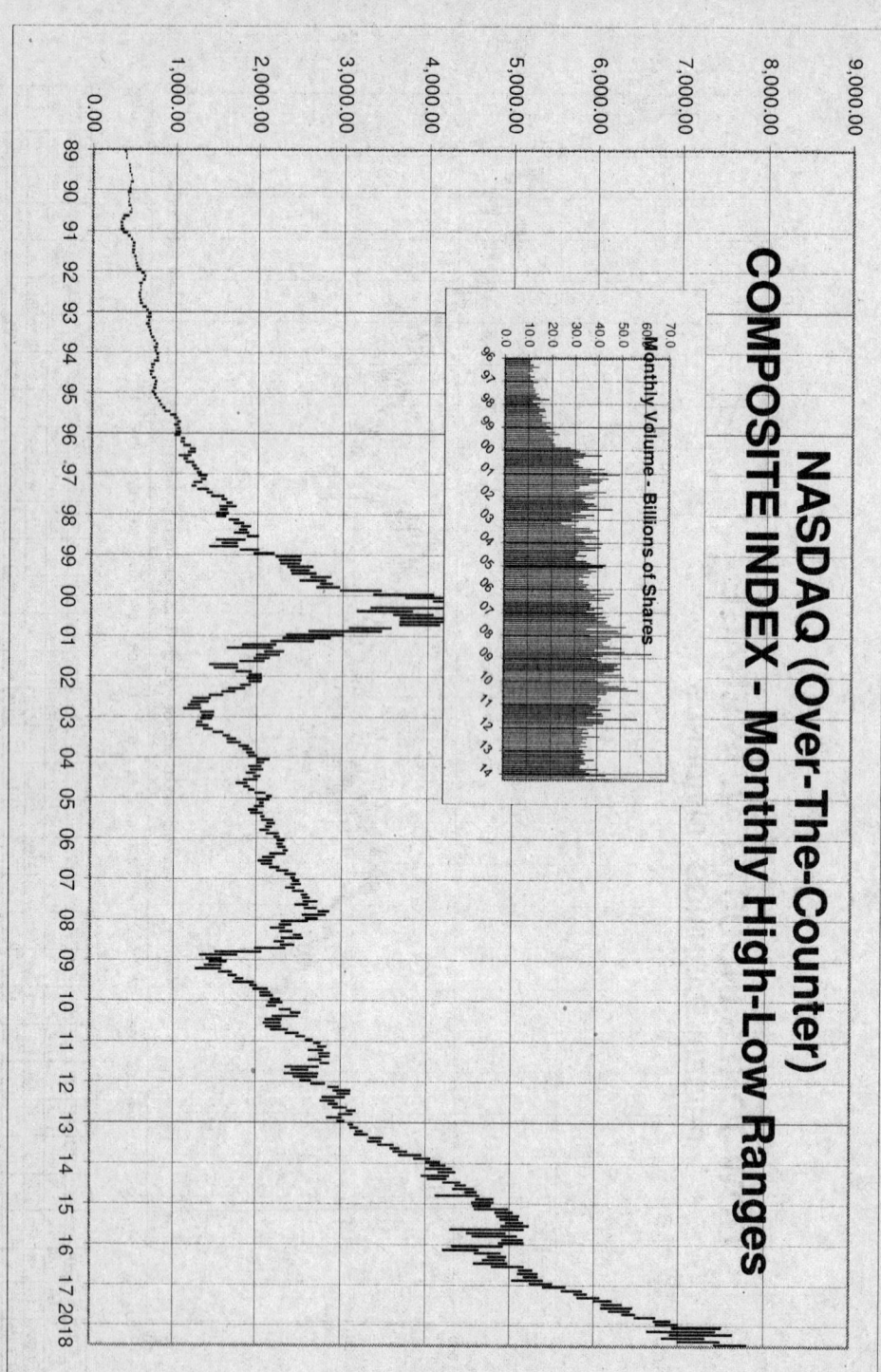

NASDAQ (Over-The-Counter)
COMPOSITE INDEX - Monthly High-Low Ranges

Monthly Volume - Billions of Shares

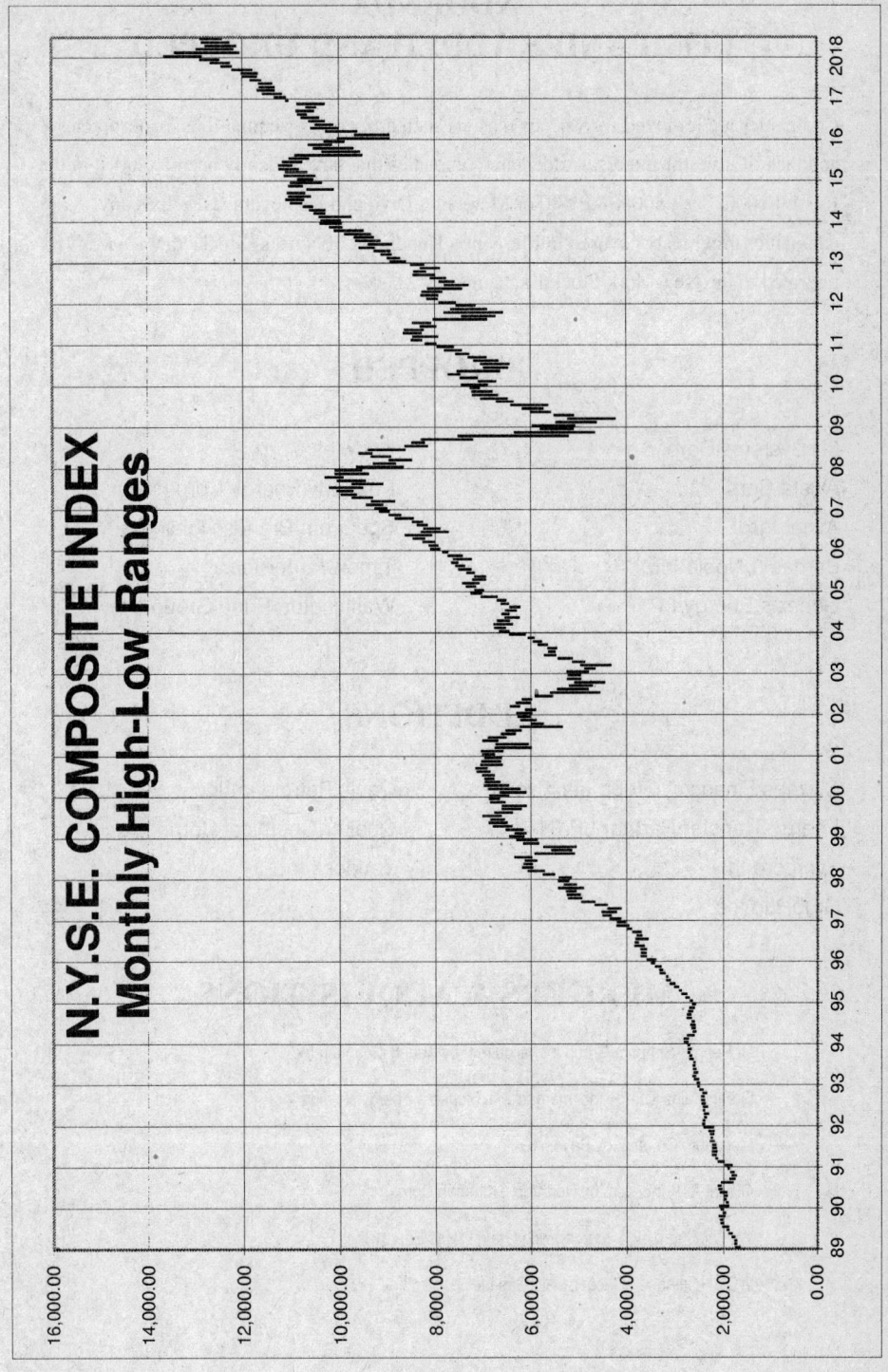

N.Y.S.E. COMPOSITE INDEX
Monthly High-Low Ranges

ADDENDA
COMPANIES ADDED AND DROPPED

Companies are removed for various reasons such as mergers, acquisitions, bankruptcies and lack of investor interest. Added are companies that have recently been included in the Russell 1000, S&P 500, S&P 400 or Mergent's Dividend Achievers, as well as any companies previously covered in Mergent's Handbook of Nasdaq Stocks that have migrated to the New York Stock Exchange.

DROPPED

3D Systems Corp.

Avista Corp.

Avnet Inc.

Barnes & Noble Inc.

Genesis Energy LP

Knowles Corp.

Peabody Energy Corp (New)

Spectrum Brands Holdings

Time Warner Inc.

Washington Prine Group (New)

ADDITIONS

Citizens Financial Group Inc. (New)

Energy Transfer Partner LP (New)

Evercore Inc.

GrubHub Inc.

Oasis Petroleum Inc.

Quaker Chemical Corp.

Zendesk Inc.

MERGERS & ACQUISITIONS

Dr Pepper Snapple Group Inc. acquired. by Keurig Mountain Inc.

Great Plains Energy Inc. merged with Monarch Energy Holding Inc.

Monsanto Co. acq. by Bayer AG

Orbital ATK Inc. acq. by Northrop Grumman Corp.

Westar Energy Inc. merged with Great Plains Energy Inc.

WGL Holdings Inc. acq. by AltaGas Ltd

ADDENDA
RECENT DIVIDEND INCREASES

Company	Increased	Amount	Date	Company	Increased	Amount	Date
AbbVie Inc	0.96	Q	4/12/2018	HNI Corp	0.30	Q	5/17/2018
Alexandria Real Estate Equities Inc	0.93	Q	6/28/2018	IDEX Corporation	0.43	Q	5/14/2018
Alliant Energy Corp	0.34	Q	4/27/2018	International Business Machines	1.57	Q	5/9/2018
American Campus Communities Inc	0.46	Q	5/11/2018	Invesco Ltd	0.30	Q	5/10/2018
American Eagle Outfitters, Inc.	0.14	Q	4/12/2018	Johnson & Johnson	0.90	Q	5/25/2018
American Financial Group Inc	1.50	Q	5/14/2018	Jones Lang LaSalle Inc	0.41	Q	5/17/2018
American Tower Corp (New)	0.77	Q	6/18/2018	KeyCorp	0.12	Q	5/25/2018
American Water Works Co, Inc.	0.46	Q	5/10/2018	Kilroy Realty Corp	0.46	Q	6/28/2018
Ameriprise Financial Inc	0.90	Q	5/4/2018	Kinder Morgan Inc.	0.20	Q	4/27/2018
Amphenol Corp.	0.23	Q	6/15/2018	Legg Mason, Inc.	0.34	Q	6/11/2018
Ashland Global Holdings Inc	0.25	Q	5/31/2018	Leggett & Platt, Inc.	0.38	Q	6/14/2018
Autoliv Inc	0.62	Q	5/22/2018	Lennox International Inc	0.64	Q	6/28/2018
Avery Dennison Corp	0.52	Q	6/5/2018	Lithia Motors Inc	0.29	Q	5/10/2018
Bank of Hawaii Corp	0.60	Q	5/30/2018	M & T Bank Corp	0.80	Q	5/31/2018
Baxter International Inc	0.19	Q	5/31/2018	Magellan Midstream Partners LP	0.94	Q	5/7/2018
BB&T Corp.	0.38	Q	5/10/2018	ManpowerGroup Inc	1.01	Q	5/31/2018
Berkley (WR) Corp	0.50	Q	6/8/2018	MetLife Inc	0.42	Q	5/4/2018
Block (H & R), Inc.	0.25	Q	6/21/2018	MSA Safety Inc	0.38	Q	5/18/2018
Cabot Corp.	0.33	Q	5/24/2018	National Fuel Gas Co. (NJ)	0.43	Q	6/28/2018
Cardinal Health, Inc.	0.48	Q	6/29/2018	Nielsen Holdings PLC	0.35	Q	6/5/2018
Carnival Corp	0.50	Q	5/24/2018	Noble Energy Inc	0.11	Q	5/4/2018
Celanese Corp (DE)	0.54	Q	4/27/2018	Northrop Grumman Corp	1.20	Q	6/1/2018
Chesapeake Utilities Corp.	0.37	Q	6/14/2018	ONEOK Inc	0.80	Q	4/27/2018
Chubb Ltd	0.73	Q	6/21/2018	Packaging Corp of America	0.79	Q	6/14/2018
Cimarex Energy Co	0.16	Q	5/14/2018	Parker Hannifin Corp	0.76	Q	5/9/2018
Clorox Co (The)	0.96	Q	4/24/2018	Penske Automotive Group Inc	0.35	Q	5/18/2018
Colgate-Palmolive Co.	0.42	Q	4/19/2018	Philip Morris International Inc	1.14	Q	6/21/2018
Comerica, Inc.	0.34	Q	6/14/2018	Phillips 66	0.80	Q	5/18/2018
Constellation Brands Inc	0.74	Q	5/9/2018	Portland General Electric Co.	0.36	Q	6/22/2018
Convergys Corp	0.11	Q	6/21/2018	Procter & Gamble Company (The)	0.72	Q	4/19/2018
Cullen/Frost Bankers, Inc.	0.67	Q	5/30/2018	Quest Diagnostics, Inc.	0.50	Q	4/3/2018
Deere & Co.	0.69	Q	6/28/2018	Ralph Lauren Corp	0.63	Q	6/28/2018
Delek US Holdings Inc (New)	0.25	Q	5/18/2018	Raymond James Financial, Inc.	0.30	Q	6/29/2018
Devon Energy Corp.	0.08	Q	6/14/2018	Rayonier Inc.	0.27	Q	6/14/2018
Dollar General Corp	0.29	Q	4/9/2018	Raytheon Co.	0.87	Q	4/10/2018
Donaldson Co. Inc.	0.19	Q	6/8/2018	Realty Income Corp	0.22	Q	6/29/2018
Enterprise Products Partners L.P.	0.43	Q	4/27/2018	Regal Beloit Corp	0.28	Q	6/28/2018
EOG Resources, Inc.	0.19	Q	4/13/2018	RLI Corp	0.22	Q	5/30/2018
Evercore Inc	0.50	Q	5/24/2018	Rockwell Automation, Inc.	0.92	Q	5/11/2018
Extended Stay America Inc	0.22	Q	5/10/2018	Signet Jewelers Ltd	0.37	Q	5/3/2018
Extra Space Storage Inc	0.86	Q	6/14/2018	Sonoco Products Co.	0.41	Q	5/10/2018
Exxon Mobil Corp	0.82	Q	5/11/2018	Southern Company (The)	0.60	Q	5/18/2018
FactSet Research Systems Inc.	0.64	Q	5/30/2018	Southwest Airlines Co	0.16	Q	6/5/2018
Federated Investors Inc (PA)	0.27	Q	5/7/2018	Southwest Gas Holdings Inc	0.52	Q	5/14/2018
FedEx Corp	0.65	Q	6/22/2018	Spirit AeroSystems Holdings Inc	0.12	Q	6/15/2018
First Republic Bank (San Francisco,	0.18	Q	4/25/2018	Tanger Factory Outlet Centers, Inc.	0.35	Q	4/27/2018
Flowers Foods, Inc.	0.18	Q	6/6/2018	TE Connectivity Ltd	0.44	Q	5/24/2018
Foot Locker, Inc.	0.35	Q	4/19/2018	The Gap Inc	0.24	Q	4/10/2018
Fuller (HB) Company	0.16	Q	4/25/2018	Tiffany & Co.	0.55	Q	6/19/2018
General Dynamics Corp	0.93	Q	4/12/2018	Timken Co. (The)	0.28	Q	5/17/2018
Grainger (W.W.) Inc.	1.36	Q	5/11/2018	TJX Companies, Inc.	0.39	Q	5/16/2018
Hewlett Packard Enterprise Co	0.11	Q	6/12/2018	Toll Brothers Inc.	0.11	Q	4/12/2018
Tootsie Roll Industries Inc	0.09	Q	6/15/2018	Versum Materials Inc	0.06	Q	5/14/2018
Torchmark Corp	0.16	Q	4/2/2018	Vishay Intertechnology, Inc.	0.09	Q	6/12/2018
Travelers Companies Inc (The)	0.77	Q	6/7/2018	W.P. Carey Inc	1.02	Q	6/28/2018
UDR Inc	0.32	Q	4/6/2018	Watsco Inc.	1.45	Q	4/13/2018
UGI Corp.	0.26	Q	6/14/2018	Webster Financial Corp	0.33	Q	5/4/2018
UnitedHealth Group Inc	0.90	Q	6/15/2018	Whirlpool Corp	1.15	Q	5/17/2018
Universal Health Realty Income	0.67	Q	6/22/2018	Williams Sonoma Inc	0.43	Q	4/26/2018

ADDENDA

RECENT DIVIDEND DECREASES

Company	Decreased	Amount	Date
CNA Financial Corp	0.30	Q	5/11/2018
Franklin Resources, Inc.	0.23	Q	6/28/2018
LaSalle Hotel Properties	0.23	Q	6/28/2018
Lazard Ltd	0.44	Q	5/4/2018
Macquarie Infrastructure Corp	1.00	Q	5/11/2018
TC PipeLines, LP	0.65	Q	5/8/2018

RECENT AND PENDING NAME CHANGES

OLD NAME	NEW NAME
Colony NorthStar Inc.	Colony Capital Inc.
Halyard Health Inc.	Avanos Medical Inc.
Herbalife Life	Herbalife Nutrition Ltd
HRG Group Inc.	Spectrum Brands Holdings Inc.
Leucadia National Corp.	Jeffries Financial Group Inc.
Wyndham Worldwide Corp.	Wyndham Destinations Inc.

RECENT DIVIDEND STOCK CHANGES

Name	Splits	Ex	Record	Payable
HEICO Corp	25%	6/28/2018	6/21/2018	6/27/2018
Herbalife Nutrition Ltd	2-for-1	5/15/2018	5/7/2018	5/14/2018

The 2018 Dividend Achievers

Companies listed below qualified for the 2018 Summer Edition of Mergent's Dividend Achievers
Also shown are total numbers of consecutive years of dividend growth.

Company Name	Years of Growth	Company Name	Years of Growth
3M Co	58	Dominion Energy	13
Aaron's, Inc.	13	Donaldson Co. Inc.	21
Abbott Laboratories	43	Dover Corp	61
ABM Industries, Inc.	52	Duke Energy Corp	12
AFLAC Inc.	34	Eaton Vance Corp	35
Air Products & Chemicals, Inc.	34	Ecolab, Inc.	24
Albemarle Corp.	22	Edison International	12
Alliant Energy Corp.	13	Emerson Electric Co.	60
Altria Group Inc	51	Enbridge Energy Partners LP	10
American Equity Investment Life Holding Co	13	Energy Transfer Equity LP	10
American Financial Group Inc	11	Energy Transfer Partner LP	15
American States Water Co.	63	Enterprise Products Partners L.P.	18
AmeriGas Partners, L.P.	12	Equity Lifestyle Properties Inc	12
Ameriprise Financial Inc	11	Erie Indemnity Co.	21
AmerisourceBergen Corp.	12	Essex Property Trust, Inc.	22
Amtrust Financial	10	Evercore Inc.	10
Analog Devices, Inc.	13	Eversource Energy	17
AptarGroup Inc.	23	Exxon Mobil Corp.	34
Aqua America Inc	25	FactSet Research Systems Inc.	17
Archer Daniels Midland Co.	42	Federal Realty Investment Trust (MD)	49
Assurant Inc	12	FedEx Corp	13
AT&T Inc	32	Flowers Foods, Inc.	13
Atlantic Tele-Network, Inc.	17	Franklin Resources, Inc.	27
Atmos Energy Corp.	29	Fuller (H.B.) Company	49
Atrion Corp.	13	General Dynamics Corp.	25
Automatic Data Processing Inc.	41	General Mills, Inc.	13
Badger Meter, Inc.	24	Genuine Parts Co.	60
Becton, Dickinson and Co.	44	Gorman-Rupp Co. (The)	44
Bemis Co Inc	33	Graco Inc.	17
Berkley (W. R.) Corp.	15	Grainger (W.W.) Inc.	45
Best Buy Inc	13	Hanover Insurance Group Inc	11
Black Hills Corporation	45	Harris Corp.	15
Brady Corp.	32	Hasbro, Inc.	13
Brown & Brown, Inc.	23	Helmerich & Payne, Inc.	40
Brown-Forman Corp.	32	Holly Energy Partners LP	12
Buckeye Partners, L.P.	21	Hormel Foods Corp.	50
California Water Service Group (DE)	49	Illinois Tool Works, Inc.	54
Cardinal Health, Inc.	20	International Business Machines Corp.	21
Carlisle Companies Inc.	40	International Flavors & Fragrances Inc.	14
Caterpillar Inc.	23	ITT Corporation	14
CenterPoint Energy, Inc	11	Johnson & Johnson	52
Chesapeake Utilities Corp.	13	Kellogg Co	12
Chevron Corporation	29	Kimberly-Clark Corp.	42
Church & Dwight Co., Inc.	20	Kroger Co	10
Clorox Co.	40	Leggett & Platt, Inc.	45
Coca-Cola Co (The)	54	Lindsay Corp	14
Colgate-Palmolive Co.	54	Lockheed Martin Corp.	14
Community Bank System, Inc.	25	Lowe's Companies Inc	55
Compass Minerals International Inc	12	Magellan Midstream Partners LP	15
Consolidated Edison, Inc.	42	McCormick & Co., Inc.	30
CSX Corp.	12	McDonald's Corp	40
Cullen/Frost Bankers, Inc.	23	MDU Resources Group Inc.	26
Cummins, Inc.	11	Mercury General Corp.	30
CVS Health Corporation	13	Meredith Corp.	23
Digital Realty Trust, Inc.	12		

The 2018 Dividend Achievers (continued)

Companies listed below qualified for the 2018 Summer Edition of Mergent's Dividend Achievers
Also shown are total numbers of consecutive years of dividend growth.

Company Name	Years of Growth	Company Name	Years of Growth
MSA Safety Inc	46	South Jersey Industries, Inc.	17
MSC Industrial Direct Co., Inc.	13	Southern Company (The)	15
Nacco Industries	10	Southwest Gas Holdings	10
National Fuel Gas Co. (NJ)	45	Spire Inc.	13
National Health Investors, Inc.	14	Stanley Black & Decker, Inc.	49
National Healthcare Corp.	11	Stepan Co.	49
National Retail Properties Inc	27	Stryker Corp.	24
New Jersey Resources Corp	21	Sunoco Logistics Partners L.P.	14
Newmarket Corp	10	Sysco Corp.	40
NextEra Energy Inc	21	Tanger Factory Outlet Centers, Inc.	23
NIKE, Inc	15	Target Corp	45
Northrop Grumman Corp	13	TC PipeLines, LP	17
Northwest Natural Gas Co.	61	Telephone & Data Systems, Inc.	42
Northwestern Corp.	11	Tennant Co.	44
NU Skin Enterprises, Inc.	15	Texas Instruments Inc.	13
Nucor Corp.	44	The Gap, Inc.	12
Occidental Petroleum Corp	14	Tiffany & Co.	14
OGE Energy	10	TJX Companies, Inc.	20
Oil-Dri Corp. of America	14	Tompkins Financial Corp	20
Old Republic International Corp.	35	Tootsie Roll Industries Inc	53
Omega Healthcare Investors, Inc.	14	Torchmark Corp.	11
Oneok Inc.	14	Toro Co. (The)	13
Owens & Minor, Inc.	19	TransMontaigne Partners L.P.	11
Polaris Industries Inc.	21	Travelers Companies Inc (The)	11
Portland General Electric	10	UGI Corp.	29
PPG Industries, Inc.	45	Union Pacific	10
PPL Corp	17	United Bankshares, Inc.	35
Praxair, Inc.	24	United Technologies Corp.	23
Procter & Gamble Co.	63	Universal Corp.	46
Prosperity Bancshares Inc.	17	Universal Health Realty Income Trust	29
Quaker Chemical Corp	10	Urstadt Biddle Properties Inc	18
Raytheon Co.	12	Vector Group Ltd	18
Realty Income Corp.	22	Vectren Corp	41
Regal Beloit Corp	12	Verizon Communications Inc	12
Republic Services, Inc.	13	VF Corp.	44
RLI Corp.	40	W.P. Carey Inc	18
Robert Half International Inc.	12	Walgreens Boots Alliance Inc	41
Rollins, Inc.	14	Walmart Inc.	41
Roper Industries, Inc	24	Waste Management, Inc. (DE)	13
RPM International Inc (DE)	43	WEC Energy Group Inc	13
Ryder System, Inc.	12	Welltower Inc	13
SCANA Corp	16	West Pharmaceutical Services, Inc.	24
Sensient Technologies Corp.	11	Westlake Chemical Corp	12
Sherwin-Williams Co.	37	Westwood Holdings Group, Inc.	14
SJW Corp.	49	Wiley (John) & Sons Inc.	23
Smith (A.O.) Corp	24	Williams Sonoma Inc	10
Smucker (J.M.) Co.	19	Yum! Brands, Inc.	12
Sonoco Products Co.	33		

AARON'S INC

Exchange	Symbol	Price	52Wk Range	Yield	P/E	Div Acheiver
NYS	AAN	$43.45 (6/29/2018)	48.89-34.44	0.28	10.73	14 Years

*7 Year Price Score 110.23 *NYSE Composite Index=100 *12 Month Price Score 97.91

Interim Earnings (Per Share)

Qtr.	Mar	Jun	Sep	Dec
2015	0.68	0.56	0.33	0.30
2016	0.68	0.53	0.40	0.30
2017	0.74	0.51	0.35	2.46
2018	0.73	...	...	...

Interim Dividends (Per Share)

Amt	Decl	Ex	Rec	Pay
0.028Q	08/15/2017	09/14/2017	09/15/2017	10/02/2017
0.03Q	11/08/2017	12/12/2017	12/13/2017	01/02/2018
0.03Q	03/06/2018	03/22/2018	03/23/2018	04/02/2018
0.03Q	05/14/2018	06/18/2018	06/19/2018	07/06/2018

Indicated Div: $0.12

Valuation Analysis | **Institutional Holding**

Forecast EPS	$3.35	No of Institutions	
	(06/12/2018)	375	
Market Cap	$3.0 Billion	Shares	
Book Value	$1.8 Billion	91,347,080	
Price/Book	1.74	% Held	
Price/Sales	0.87	N/A	

Business Summary: Retail - Furniture & Home Furnishings (MIC: 2.1.6 SIC: 5712 NAIC: 442110)

Aaron's is an omnichannel provider of lease-purchase solutions. Co. is engaged in the sales and lease ownership and specialty retailing of furniture, consumer electronics, home appliances and accessories through its more than 1,860 Company-operated and franchised stores in 47 states and Canada as well as its e-commerce platform, Aarons.com. Co.'s stores carry brands such as Samsung®, Frigidaire®, Hewlett-Packard®, LG®, Whirlpool®, Simmons®, Philips®, Ashley® and Magnavox®. As of Dec. 31, 2017 , Co. had 1,726 Aaron's stores, comprised of 1,175 Company-operated stores in 35 states and Canada, and 551 independently-owned franchised stores in 40 states and Canada.

Recent Developments: For the quarter ended Mar 31 2018, net income decreased 2.0% to US$52.2 million from US$53.3 million in the year-earlier quarter. Revenues were US$954.8 million, up 13.1% from US$844.6 million the year before. Operating income was US$70.1 million versus US$86.5 million in the prior-year quarter, a decrease of 19.0%. Direct operating expenses declined 20.4% to US$53.7 million from US$67.5 million in the comparable period the year before. Indirect operating expenses increased 20.3% from US$690.6 million in the equivalent prior-year period.

Prospects: Our evaluation of Aaron's Inc as of Jan. 21, 2018 is the result of our systematic analysis on three basic characteristics: earnings strength, relative valuation, and recent stock price movement. The company has generated a negative trend in earnings per share over the past 5 quarters and while recent estimates for the company have been mixed, AAN has posted results that fell short of analysts expectations. Based on operating earnings yield, the company is undervalued when compared to all of the companies in our coverage universe. Share price changes over the past year indicates that AAN will perform very well over the near term.

Financial Data

(US$ in Thousands)	3 Mos	12/31/2017	12/31/2016	12/31/2015	12/31/2014	12/31/2013	12/31/2012	12/31/2011
Earnings Per Share	4.05	4.06	1.91	1.86	1.08	1.58	2.25	1.43
Cash Flow Per Share	3.59	2.25	6.42	2.30	(0.68)	4.07	0.79	...
Tang Book Value Per Share	12.81	12.42	9.90	7.59	5.45	12.30	11.83	9.93
Dividends Per Share	0.115	0.113	0.102	0.094	0.086	0.072	0.062	0.054
Dividend Payout %	2.84	2.77	5.37	5.05	7.96	4.56	2.76	3.78
Income Statement								
Total Revenue	954,809	3,383,708	3,207,716	3,179,756	2,725,239	2,234,631	2,222,588	2,024,049
EBITDA	510,884	313,080	292,713	286,274	191,698	240,875	332,806	233,286
Depn & Amortn	440,008	54,800	53,600	52,000	53,700	53,300	53,100	45,200
Income Before Taxes	66,752	239,577	218,422	213,120	121,704	184,960	276,855	183,377
Income Taxes	14,506	(52,959)	79,139	77,411	43,471	64,294	103,812	69,610
Net Income	52,246	292,536	139,283	135,709	78,233	120,666	173,043	113,767
Average Shares	72,018	72,121	73,013	73,043	72,723	76,390	76,826	...
Balance Sheet								
Current Assets	1,505,175	1,626,078	1,630,070	1,617,652	1,409,286	1,353,167	1,342,110	1,283,122
Total Assets	2,719,009	2,692,264	2,615,736	2,658,875	2,456,844	1,827,176	1,812,929	1,735,149
Current Liabilities	604,298	372,870	360,193	374,326	358,690	317,551	271,554	317,844
Long-Term Obligations	358,519	368,798	497,829	610,450	606,082	142,704	141,528	153,789
Total Liabilities	962,817	964,260	1,134,138	1,292,257	1,233,323	687,213	676,803	758,595
Stockholders' Equity	1,756,192	1,728,004	1,481,598	1,366,618	1,223,521	1,139,963	1,136,126	976,554
Shares Outstanding	70,173	70,019	71,448	72,600	72,488	72,956	75,720	75,640
Statistical Record								
Return on Assets %	10.91	11.02	5.27	5.31	3.65	6.63	9.73	7.03
Return on Equity %	17.90	18.23	9.75	10.48	6.62	10.60	16.34	11.63
EBITDA Margin %	53.51	9.25	9.13	9.00	7.03	10.78	14.97	11.53
Net Margin %	5.47	8.65	4.34	4.27	2.87	5.40	7.79	5.62
Asset Turnover	1.31	1.27	1.21	1.24	1.27	1.23	1.25	1.25
Current Ratio	2.49	4.36	4.53	4.32	3.93	4.26	4.94	4.04
Debt to Equity	0.20	0.21	0.34	0.45	0.50	0.13	0.12	0.16
Price Range	48.89-29.25	47.54-26.92	33.97-20.33	40.46-21.74	35.90-23.27	30.60-26.68	31.16-24.83	29.16-19.19
P/E Ratio	12.07-7.22	11.71-6.63	17.79-10.64	21.75-11.69	33.24-21.55	19.37-16.89	13.85-11.04	20.39-13.42
Average Yield %	0.29	0.31	0.41	0.29	0.30	0.25	0.22	0.21

Address: 400 Galleria Parkway S.E., Suite 300, Atlanta, GA 30339-3182
Telephone: 678-402-3000

Web Site: www.aarons.com
Officers: Ray M. Robinson - Chairman R. Charles Loudermilk - Chairman Emeritus, Chairman, Chief Executive Officer

Auditors: Ernst & Young LLP
Investor Contact: 678-402-3116
Transfer Agents: Computershare Investor Services, Canton, MA

ABBVIE INC

Exchange	Symbol	Price	52Wk Range	Yield	P/E
NYS	ABBV	$92.65 (6/29/2018)	123.21-69.85	4.14	23.34

*7 Year Price Score N/A *NYSE Composite Index=100 ***12 Month Price Score 103.68**

TRADING VOLUME (thousand shares)

Interim Earnings (Per Share)

Qtr.	Mar	Jun	Sep	Dec
2015	0.63	0.83	0.74	0.92
2016	0.83	0.98	0.97	0.85
2017	1.06	1.19	1.01	0.03
2018	1.74	...	...	...

Interim Dividends (Per Share)

Amt	Decl	Ex	Rec	Pay
0.64Q	09/08/2017	10/12/2017	10/13/2017	11/15/2017
0.71Q	10/27/2017	01/11/2018	01/12/2018	02/15/2018
0.96Q	02/15/2018	04/12/2018	04/13/2018	05/15/2018
0.96Q	06/14/2018	07/12/2018	07/13/2018	08/15/2018

Indicated Div: $3.84 (Div. Reinv. Plan)

Valuation Analysis **Institutional Holding**

Forecast EPS	$7.77	No of Institutions	
	(06/14/2018)	2374	
Market Cap	$147.0 Billion	Shares	
Book Value	$3.6 Billion		1,270,572,800
Price/Book	41.38	% Held	
Price/Sales	4.96		67.34

Business Summary: Pharmaceuticals (MIC: 4.1.1 SIC: 2834 NAIC: 325412)

AbbVie is a research-based biopharmaceutical company. Co.'s portfolio of products includes a line of therapies that addresses serious diseases such as: HUMIRA (adalimumab) to treat autoimmune diseases; oncology products such as IMBRUVICA (ibrutinib) and Venclexta (venetoclax); virology products such as VIEKIRA PAK for the treatment of hepatitis C and Norvir (ritonavir) for the treatment of human immunodeficiency virus-1 infection; metabolic and hormone products that target conditions such as testosterone deficiency; endocrinology products such as Lupron (leuprolide acetate) for the palliative treatment of advanced prostate cancer, treatment of endometriosis and central precocious puberty.

Recent Developments: For the quarter ended Mar 31 2018, net income increased 62.7% to US$2.78 billion from US$1.71 billion in the year-earlier quarter. Revenues were US$7.93 billion, up 21.4% from US$6.54 billion the year before. Operating income was US$2.90 billion versus US$2.41 billion in the prior-year quarter, an increase of 20.6%. Direct operating expenses rose 19.2% to US$1.93 billion from US$1.62 billion in the comparable period the year before. Indirect operating expenses increased 23.4% to US$3.10 billion from US$2.52 billion in the equivalent prior-year period.

Prospects: Our evaluation of AbbVie Inc. as of Jan. 21, 2018 is the result of our systematic analysis on three basic characteristics: earnings strength, relative valuation, and recent stock price movement. The company has enjoyed a very positive trend in earnings per share over the past 5 quarters and while recent estimates for the company have been mixed, ABBV has posted better than expected results. Based on operating earnings yield, the company is undervalued when compared to all of the companies in our coverage universe. Share price changes over the past year indicates that ABBV will perform very well over the near term.

Financial Data
(US$ in Thousands)

	3 Mos	12/31/2017	12/31/2016	12/31/2015	12/31/2014	12/31/2013	12/31/2012	12/31/2011
Earnings Per Share	3.97	3.30	3.63	3.13	1.10	2.56	3.35	...
Cash Flow Per Share	6.60	6.24	4.33	4.64	2.23	3.94	4.01	...
Dividends Per Share	2.630	2.560	2.280	2.020	1.660	1.600	...	...
Dividend Payout %	66.25	77.58	62.81	64.54	150.91	62.50	...	...
Income Statement								
Total Revenue	7,934,000	28,216,000	25,638,000	22,859,000	19,960,000	18,790,000	18,380,000	17,443,951
EBITDA	3,493,000	10,232,000	10,038,000	8,167,000	3,546,000	6,507,000	6,959,000	4,940,721
Depn & Amortn	445,000	1,501,000	1,189,000	836,000	786,000	897,000	1,150,000	1,272,194
Income Before Taxes	2,797,000	7,727,000	7,884,000	6,645,000	2,369,000	5,332,000	5,725,000	3,668,527
Income Taxes	14,000	2,418,000	1,931,000	1,501,000	595,000	1,204,000	450,000	235,399
Net Income	2,783,000	5,309,000	5,953,000	5,144,000	1,774,000	4,128,000	5,275,000	3,433,128
Average Shares	1,596,000	1,603,000	1,631,000	1,637,000	1,610,000	1,604,000	1,577,000	...
Balance Sheet								
Current Assets	20,444,000	21,223,000	16,187,000	16,314,000	16,088,000	17,848,000	15,354,000	7,354,155
Total Assets	69,342,000	70,786,000	66,099,000	53,050,000	27,547,000	29,198,000	27,008,000	19,657,166
Current Liabilities	17,058,000	16,641,000	9,781,000	10,894,000	11,400,000	6,879,000	6,776,000	5,896,678
Long-Term Obligations	30,906,000	30,953,000	36,440,000	29,240,000	10,565,000	14,292,000	14,630,000	...
Total Liabilities	65,789,000	65,689,000	61,463,000	49,105,000	25,805,000	24,706,000	23,645,000	7,433,453
Stockholders' Equity	3,553,000	5,097,000	4,636,000	3,945,000	1,742,000	4,492,000	3,363,000	12,223,713
Shares Outstanding	1,586,769	1,592,131	1,592,512	1,609,892	1,591,389	1,587,360	1,577,334	...
Statistical Record								
Return on Assets %	9.45	7.76	9.97	12.76	6.25	14.69	22.55	16.83
Return on Equity %	149.25	109.09	138.37	180.90	56.91	105.11	67.50	24.59
EBITDA Margin %	44.03	36.26	39.15	35.73	17.77	34.63	37.86	28.32
Net Margin %	35.08	18.82	23.22	22.50	8.89	21.97	28.70	19.68
Asset Turnover	0.44	0.41	0.43	0.57	0.70	0.67	0.79	0.86
Current Ratio	1.20	1.28	1.65	1.50	1.41	2.59	2.27	1.25
Debt to Equity	8.70	6.07	7.86	7.41	6.06	3.18	4.35	...
Price Range	123.21-63.45	98.21-60.00	67.39-51.18	71.23-48.27	69.71-46.46	54.32-33.71	...	...
P/E Ratio	31.04-15.98	29.76-18.18	18.56-14.10	22.76-15.42	63.37-42.24	21.22-13.17	...	...
Average Yield %	3.04	3.41	3.76	3.25	2.99	3.66	...	...

Address: 1 North Waukegan Road, North Chicago, IL 60064-6400 **Telephone:** 847-932-7900	**Web Site:** www.abbvie.com **Officers:** Richard A. Gonzalez - Chairman, Chief Executive Officer William J. Chase - Executive Vice President, Chief Financial Officer	**Auditors:** Ernst & Young LLP **Investor Contact:** 847-932-7900 **Transfer Agents:** Computershare Trust Company, N.A., Canton, MA

ABBOTT LABORATORIES

Exchange	Symbol	Price	52Wk Range	Yield	P/E	Div Acheiver
NYS	ABT	$60.99 (6/29/2018)	63.62-47.94	1.84	234.58	44 Years

*7 Year Price Score 112.12 *NYSE Composite Index=100 *12 Month Price Score 106.52

Interim Earnings (Per Share)

Qtr.	Mar	Jun	Sep	Dec
2015	1.51	0.52	0.38	0.51
2016	0.21	0.41	(0.22)	0.54
2017	0.24	0.16	0.34	(0.47)
2018	0.23	...	...	...

Interim Dividends (Per Share)

Amt	Decl	Ex	Rec	Pay
0.265Q	09/14/2017	10/12/2017	10/13/2017	11/15/2017
0.28Q	12/15/2017	01/11/2018	01/12/2018	02/15/2018
0.28Q	02/16/2018	04/12/2018	04/13/2018	05/15/2018
0.28Q	06/08/2018	07/12/2018	07/13/2018	08/15/2018

Indicated Div: $1.12 (Div. Reinv. Plan)

Valuation Analysis | **Institutional Holding**

Forecast EPS	$2.86	No of Institutions
	(06/14/2018)	2480
Market Cap	$106.9 Billion	Shares
Book Value	$31.4 Billion	1,552,900,480
Price/Book	3.41	% Held
Price/Sales	3.76	63.62

Business Summary: Medical Instruments & Equipment (MIC: 4.3.1 SIC: 2834 NAIC: 325412)

Abbott Laboratories is engaged in the discovery, development, manufacture, and sale of a line of health care products. Co. has four reportable segments: Established Pharmaceutical Products, which sells a line of branded generic pharmaceutical products internationally; Nutritional Products, which sells adult and pediatric nutritional products; Diagnostic Products, which sells diagnostic systems and tests for blood banks, hospitals, commercial laboratories and alternate-care testing sites; and Vascular Products, which sells coronary, endovascular, structural heart, vessel closure and other medical device products. Non-reportable segments include the Diabetes Care and Medical Optics segments.

Recent Developments: For the quarter ended Mar 31 2018, income from continuing operations increased 6.0% to US$409.0 million from US$386.0 million in the year-earlier quarter. Net income decreased 0.2% to US$418.0 million from US$419.0 million in the year-earlier quarter. Revenues were US$7.39 billion, up 16.7% from US$6.34 billion the year before. Operating income was US$608.0 million versus a loss of US$242.0 million in the prior-year quarter. Direct operating expenses rose 0.2% to US$3.07 billion from US$3.06 billion in the comparable period the year before. Indirect operating expenses increased 5.7% to US$3.72 billion from US$3.52 billion in the equivalent prior-year period.

Prospects: Our evaluation of Abbott Laboratories as of Jan. 21, 2018 is the result of our systematic analysis on three basic characteristics: earnings strength, relative valuation, and recent stock price movement. The company has produced a positive trend in earnings per share over the past 5 quarters and while recent estimates for the company have remained steady, ABT has posted better than expected results. Based on operating earnings yield, the company is about fairly valued when compared to all of the companies in our coverage universe. Share price changes over the past year indicates that ABT will perform very well over the near term.

Financial Data

(US$ in Thousands)	3 Mos	12/31/2017	12/31/2016	12/31/2015	12/31/2014	12/31/2013	12/31/2012	12/31/2011
Earnings Per Share	0.26	0.27	0.94	2.92	1.49	1.62	3.72	3.01
Cash Flow Per Share	3.48	3.20	2.16	1.98	2.42	2.13	5.90	5.76
Tang Book Value Per Share	N.M.	N.M.	5.65	4.08	3.49	6.24	1.50	N.M.
Dividends Per Share	1.075	1.060	1.040	0.960	0.880	0.560	2.010	1.880
Dividend Payout %	413.46	392.59	110.64	32.88	59.06	34.57	54.03	62.46
Income Statement								
Total Revenue	7,390,000	27,390,000	20,853,000	20,405,000	20,247,000	21,848,000	39,873,910	38,851,259
EBITDA	1,514,000	6,032,000	3,098,000	4,713,000	4,139,000	4,330,000	9,674,326	8,855,110
Depn & Amortn	884,000	3,021,000	1,353,000	1,472,000	1,548,000	1,719,000	2,898,534	3,211,523
Income Before Taxes	431,000	2,231,000	1,413,000	3,183,000	2,518,000	2,521,000	6,262,614	5,198,642
Income Taxes	22,000	1,878,000	350,000	577,000	797,000	138,000	299,694	470,193
Net Income	418,000	477,000	1,400,000	4,423,000	2,284,000	2,576,000	5,962,920	4,728,449
Average Shares	1,765,278	1,749,000	1,483,000	1,506,000	1,527,000	1,574,000	1,591,838	1,567,389
Balance Sheet								
Current Assets	14,964,000	20,147,000	26,776,000	14,155,000	15,261,000	49,247,000	31,322,583	23,768,774
Total Assets	70,908,000	76,250,000	52,666,000	41,247,000	41,275,000	42,953,000	67,234,944	60,276,893
Current Liabilities	9,010,000	8,912,000	6,660,000	9,186,000	10,532,000	9,507,000	13,280,176	15,480,228
Long-Term Obligations	21,154,000	27,210,000	20,681,000	5,871,000	3,408,000	3,388,000	18,085,302	12,039,822
Total Liabilities	39,509,000	45,353,000	32,128,000	20,036,000	19,749,000	17,782,000	40,513,983	35,837,060
Stockholders' Equity	31,399,000	30,897,000	20,538,000	21,211,000	21,526,000	25,171,000	26,720,961	24,439,833
Shares Outstanding	1,753,187	1,743,602	1,472,869	1,472,665	1,508,035	1,548,098	1,576,667	1,570,378
Statistical Record								
Return on Assets %	0.67	0.74	2.97	10.72	5.42	4.68	9.33	7.90
Return on Equity %	1.52	1.85	6.69	20.70	9.78	9.93	23.25	20.19
EBITDA Margin %	20.49	22.02	14.86	23.10	20.44	19.82	24.26	22.79
Net Margin %	5.66	1.74	6.71	21.68	11.28	11.79	14.95	12.17
Asset Turnover	0.40	0.42	0.44	0.49	0.48	0.40	0.62	0.65
Current Ratio	1.66	2.26	4.02	1.54	1.45	2.02	2.36	1.54
Debt to Equity	0.67	0.88	1.01	0.28	0.16	0.13	0.68	0.49
Price Range	63.62-42.67	57.47-39.05	45.29-36.34	51.20-39.06	46.37-35.85	38.71-31.34	34.51-25.91	26.95-21.61
P/E Ratio	244.69-164.12	212.85-144.63	48.18-38.66	17.53-13.38	31.12-24.06	23.90-19.35	9.28-6.96	8.95-7.18
Average Yield %	2.04	2.18	2.57	2.07	2.15	1.57	6.66	7.70

Address: 100 Abbott Park Road, Abbott Park, IL 60064-6400 **Telephone:** 224-667-6100	**Web Site:** www.abbott.com **Officers:** Miles D. White - Chairman, Chief Executive Officer Hubert L. Allen - Executive Vice President, Secretary, General Counsel	**Auditors:** Ernst & Young LLP **Investor Contact:** 847-937-7300 **Transfer Agents:** Computershare Trust Company, NA, Providence, RI

ABM INDUSTRIES, INC.

Exchange	Symbol	Price	52Wk Range	Yield	P/E	Div Acheiver
NYS	ABM	$29.18 (6/29/2018)	44.79-28.46	2.40	21.78	53 Years

*7 Year Price Score 102.62 *NYSE Composite Index=100   *12 Month Price Score 77.93

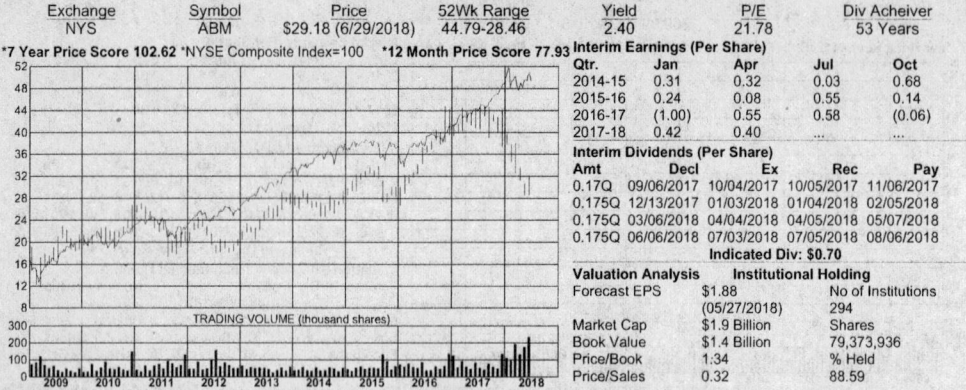

Interim Earnings (Per Share)

Qtr.	Jan	Apr	Jul	Oct
2014-15	0.31	0.32	0.03	0.68
2015-16	0.24	0.08	0.55	0.14
2016-17	(1.00)	0.55	0.58	(0.06)
2017-18	0.42	0.40	...	...

Interim Dividends (Per Share)

Amt	Decl	Ex	Rec	Pay
0.17Q	09/06/2017	10/04/2017	10/05/2017	11/06/2017
0.175Q	12/13/2017	01/03/2018	01/04/2018	02/05/2018
0.175Q	03/06/2018	04/04/2018	04/05/2018	05/07/2018
0.175Q	06/06/2018	07/03/2018	07/05/2018	08/06/2018

Indicated Div: $0.70

Valuation Analysis

		Institutional Holding	
Forecast EPS	$1.88	No of Institutions	
	(05/27/2018)	294	
Market Cap	$1.9 Billion	Shares	
Book Value	$1.4 Billion	79,373,936	
Price/Book	1.34	% Held	
Price/Sales	0.32	88.59	

Business Summary: Sanitation Services (MIC: 7.5.3 SIC: 7349 NAIC: 561720)

ABM Industries is a provider of integrated facility solutions. Co.'s segments are: Janitorial, which provides a range of cleaning services; Facility Services, which provides onsite mechanical engineering and technical services and solutions for facilities and infrastructure systems; Parking, which provides parking and transportation services; Building and Energy Solutions, which provides energy solutions, electrical, heating, ventilation and air conditioning, lighting, and other maintenance and repair services; and Other, which provides facility solutions to airlines and airports related to access control, aircraft cabin cleaning, certain shuttle bus operations, and passenger assistance.

Recent Developments: For the quarter ended Apr 30 2018, income from continuing operations decreased 19.6% to US$25.4 million from US$31.6 million in the year-earlier quarter. Net income decreased 15.0% to US$26.6 million from US$31.3 million in the year-earlier quarter. Revenues were US$1.58 billion, up 20.6% from US$1.31 billion the year before. Operating income was US$45.3 million versus US$51.0 million in the prior-year quarter, a decrease of 11.2%. Indirect operating expenses increased 21.9% to US$1.54 billion from US$1.26 billion in the equivalent prior-year period.

Prospects: Our evaluation of ABM Industries Inc. as of Jan. 21, 2018 is the result of our systematic analysis on three basic characteristics: earnings strength, relative valuation, and recent stock price movement. The company has generated a negative trend in earnings per share over the past 5 quarters and while recent estimates for the company have been raised by analysts, ABM has posted results that fell short of analysts expectations. Based on operating earnings yield, the company is undervalued when compared to all of the companies in our coverage universe. Share price changes over the past year indicates that ABM will perform in line with the market over the near term.

Financial Data

(US$ in Thousands)	6 Mos	3 Mos	10/31/2017	10/31/2016	10/31/2015	10/31/2014	10/31/2013	10/31/2012
Earnings Per Share	1.34	1.49	0.07	1.01	1.33	1.32	1.30	1.14
Cash Flow Per Share	1.38	0.76	0.10	1.48	2.56	2.15	2.47	2.78
Tang Book Value Per Share	N.M.	N.M.	N.M.	N.M.	0.51	N.M.	N.M.	N.M.
Dividends Per Share	0.690	0.685	0.680	0.660	0.640	0.620	0.600	0.580
Dividend Payout %	51.49	45.97	971.43	65.35	48.12	46.97	46.15	50.88
Income Statement								
Total Revenue	3,169,200	1,588,300	5,453,600	5,144,700	4,897,800	5,032,800	4,809,281	4,300,265
EBITDA	97,600	35,800	172,000	112,300	130,600	185,900	179,378	147,117
Depn & Amortn	32,900	16,200	70,100	57,600	57,000	57,300	60,353	50,864
Income Before Taxes	36,600	5,300	82,700	44,300	63,400	117,900	106,133	86,254
Income Taxes	15,100	(22,200)	8,800	(10,400)	18,300	48,800	39,552	29,931
Net Income	54,400	27,800	3,800	57,200	76,300	75,600	72,900	62,582
Average Shares	66,200	66,300	58,300	56,900	57,400	57,100	56,067	54,914
Balance Sheet								
Current Assets	1,215,700	1,218,100	1,235,500	993,700	947,200	927,200	864,632	767,427
Total Assets	3,749,900	3,797,000	3,812,600	2,281,200	2,149,800	2,192,900	2,119,236	1,869,251
Current Liabilities	704,200	699,600	757,800	599,200	568,200	526,400	508,524	473,910
Long-Term Obligations	1,090,300	1,173,400	1,161,300	268,300	158,000	319,800	314,870	215,000
Total Liabilities	2,313,300	2,380,200	2,436,900	1,307,200	1,142,300	1,224,100	1,201,729	1,018,853
Stockholders' Equity	1,436,600	1,416,800	1,375,700	974,000	1,007,500	968,800	917,507	850,398
Shares Outstanding	65,729	65,686	65,502	55,599	56,105	55,691	55,477	54,393
Statistical Record								
Return on Assets %	2.72	2.85	0.12	2.57	3.51	3.51	3.66	3.33
Return on Equity %	7.05	7.61	0.32	5.76	7.72	8.02	8.25	7.58
EBITDA Margin %	3.08	2.25	3.15	2.18	2.67	3.69	3.73	3.42
Net Margin %	1.72	1.75	0.07	1.11	1.56	1.50	1.52	1.46
Asset Turnover	1.95	1.84	1.79	2.32	2.26	2.33	2.41	2.29
Current Ratio	1.73	1.74	1.63	1.66	1.67	1.76	1.70	1.62
Debt to Equity	0.76	0.83	0.84	0.28	0.16	0.33	0.34	0.25
Price Range	44.79-31.13	44.79-37.36	44.79-38.22	40.42-26.58	33.80-26.70	29.43-24.57	28.99-18.27	24.50-17.95
P/E Ratio	33.43-23.23	30.06-25.07	639.86-546.00	40.02-26.32	25.41-20.08	22.30-18.61	22.30-14.05	21.49-15.75
Average Yield %	1.73	1.64	1.62	1.97	2.10	2.29	2.59	2.78

Address: One Liberty Plaza, 7th Floor, New York, NY 10006 **Telephone:** 212-297-0200	**Web Site:** www.abm.com **Officers:** Scott B. Salmirs - President, Chief Executive Officer, Executive Vice President Andrea R. Newborn - Executive Vice President, Corporate Secretary, General Counsel	**Auditors:** KPMG LLP **Investor Contact:** 212-297-0200 **Transfer Agents:** Computershare, Providence, RI

4

ACCENTURE PLC

Exchange	Symbol	Price	52Wk Range	Yield	P/E
NYS	ACN	$163.59 (6/29/2018)	164.74-122.94	1.63	26.22

*7 Year Price Score 124.18 *NYSE Composite Index=100 ***12 Month Price Score 105.65**

Interim Earnings (Per Share)

Qtr.	Nov	Feb	May	Aug
2014-15	1.29	1.08	1.24	1.15
2015-16	1.28	2.08	1.41	1.68
2016-17	1.58	1.33	1.05	1.48
2017-18	1.79	1.37	1.60	...

Interim Dividends (Per Share)

Amt	Decl	Ex	Rec	Pay
1.21S	09/29/2016	10/19/2016	10/21/2016	11/15/2016
1.21S	03/23/2017	04/11/2017	04/13/2017	05/15/2017
1.33S	09/28/2017	10/18/2017	10/19/2017	11/15/2017
1.33S	03/22/2018	04/11/2018	04/12/2018	05/15/2018

Indicated Div: $2.66

Valuation Analysis | **Institutional Holding**

Forecast EPS	N/A	No of Institutions	1583
Market Cap	$105.0 Billion	Shares	550,355,264
Book Value	$9.8 Billion	% Held	72.38
Price/Book	10.71		
Price/Sales	2.58		

Business Summary: Business Services (MIC: 7.5.2 SIC: 7389 NAIC: 561499)

Accenture is a services company. Co.'s operating groups are: Communications, Media and Technology, which serves communications, media, high tech, software and platform companies; Financial Services, which serves the banking, capital markets and insurance industries; Health and Public Service, which serves healthcare payers and providers, government departments and agencies, public service organizations, educational institutions and non-profit organizations; Products, which serves a set of interconnected consumer-relevant industries such as consumer goods and retail; and Resources, which serves the chemicals, energy, forest products, metals and mining, utilities and related industries.

Recent Developments: For the quarter ended May 31 2018, net income increased 50.1% to US$1.06 billion from US$704.8 million in the year-earlier quarter. Revenues were US$10.84 billion, up 15.8% from US$9.36 billion the year before. Operating income was US$1.62 billion versus US$865.4 million in the prior-year quarter, an increase of 87.2%. Direct operating expenses rose 16.6% to US$7.52 billion from US$6.45 billion in the comparable period the year before. Indirect operating expenses decreased 16.9% to US$1.70 billion from US$2.04 billion in the equivalent prior-year period.

Prospects: Our evaluation of Accenture PLC as of July 19, 2015 is the result of our systematic analysis on three basic characteristics: earnings strength, relative valuation, and recent stock price movement. The company has managed to produce a neutral trend in earnings per share over the past 5 quarters and while recent estimates for the company have been raised by analysts, ACN has posted better than expected results. Based on operating earnings yield, the company is about fairly valued when compared to all of the companies in our coverage universe. Share price changes over the past year indicates that ACN will perform in line with the market over the near term.

Financial Data

(US$ in Thousands)	9 Mos	6 Mos	3 Mos	08/31/2017	08/31/2016	08/31/2015	08/31/2014	08/31/2013
Earnings Per Share	6.24	5.69	5.65	5.44	6.45	4.76	4.52	4.93
Cash Flow Per Share	9.17	9.17	7.95	8.02	7.30	6.53	5.50	5.12
Tang Book Value Per Share	7.05	6.90	6.33	6.21	6.14	4.93	5.08	4.71
Dividends Per Share	2.66	2.54	2.54	2.420	2.200	2.040	1.860	1.620
Dividend Payout %	42.63	44.64	44.96	44.49	34.11	42.86	41.15	32.86
Income Statement								
Total Revenue	30,961,179	20,122,325	10,054,493	36,765,478	34,797,661	32,914,424	31,874,678	30,394,285
EBITDA	5,023,969	3,179,870	1,720,028	4,956,454	6,318,398	5,037,040	4,611,862	4,645,433
Depn & Amortn	691,686	453,297	232,633	362,817	729,052	645,923	326,910	324,997
Income Before Taxes	4,351,479	2,738,921	1,494,124	4,616,032	5,603,572	4,410,530	4,297,701	4,339,294
Income Taxes	1,185,256	630,839	305,582	981,100	1,253,969	1,136,741	1,121,743	784,775
Net Income	3,030,383	1,987,363	1,123,660	3,445,149	4,111,892	3,053,581	2,941,498	3,281,878
Average Shares	654,600	656,118	656,671	660,463	667,770	678,757	692,389	712,763
Balance Sheet								
Current Assets	12,336,872	12,284,948	12,303,841	12,097,289	11,976,222	11,579,394	11,904,442	11,844,178
Total Assets	23,250,793	23,132,979	22,974,153	22,689,890	20,609,004	18,266,058	17,930,452	16,867,049
Current Liabilities	9,553,596	9,367,912	9,863,026	9,824,279	8,878,924	8,532,199	8,158,079	8,160,990
Long-Term Obligations	25,958	25,923	22,226	22,163	24,457	25,587	26,403	25,600
Total Liabilities	13,453,468	13,450,292	13,872,023	13,740,413	13,053,742	12,132,333	12,198,417	11,906,863
Stockholders' Equity	9,797,325	9,682,687	9,102,130	8,949,477	7,555,262	6,133,725	5,732,035	4,960,186
Shares Outstanding	641,553	637,479	635,318	636,088	642,590	650,036	656,556	666,355
Statistical Record								
Return on Assets %	17.86	16.61	16.42	15.91	21.10	16.87	16.91	19.57
Return on Equity %	44.12	40.68	43.15	41.75	59.91	51.47	55.02	72.08
EBITDA Margin %	16.23	15.80	17.11	13.48	18.16	15.30	14.47	15.28
Net Margin %	9.79	9.88	11.18	9.37	11.82	9.28	9.23	10.80
Asset Turnover	1.83	1.81	1.74	1.70	1.79	1.82	1.83	1.81
Current Ratio	1.29	1.31	1.25	1.23	1.35	1.36	1.46	1.45
Debt to Equity	N.M.	N.M.	N.M.	N.M.	N.M.	N.M.	N.M.	0.01
Price Range	164.74-122.08	164.74-114.86	148.04-113.21	130.76-109.80	119.65-92.29	105.20-75.85	85.40-70.28	83.09-61.06
P/E Ratio	26.40-19.56	28.95-20.19	26.20-20.04	24.04-20.18	18.55-14.31	22.10-15.93	18.89-15.55	16.85-12.39
Average Yield %	1.85	1.81	1.94	2.00	2.03	2.26	2.35	2.22

Address: 1 Grand Canal Square, Grand Canal Harbour, Dublin, 2
Telephone: 164-620-00

Web Site: www.accenture.com
Officers: Pierre Nanterme - Chairman, Chief Executive Officer Johan G. (Jo) Deblaere - Chief Operating Officer, Region Officer

Auditors: KPMG LLP
Investor Contact: 353-140-78203
Transfer Agents: Computershare, Canton, MA

ACUITY BRANDS INC (HOLDING COMPANY)

Exchange	Symbol	Price	52Wk Range	Yield	P/E
NYS	AYI	$115.87 (6/29/2018)	206.68-110.22	0.45	14.54

*7 Year Price Score 90.66 *NYSE Composite Index=100 *12 Month Price Score 73.92

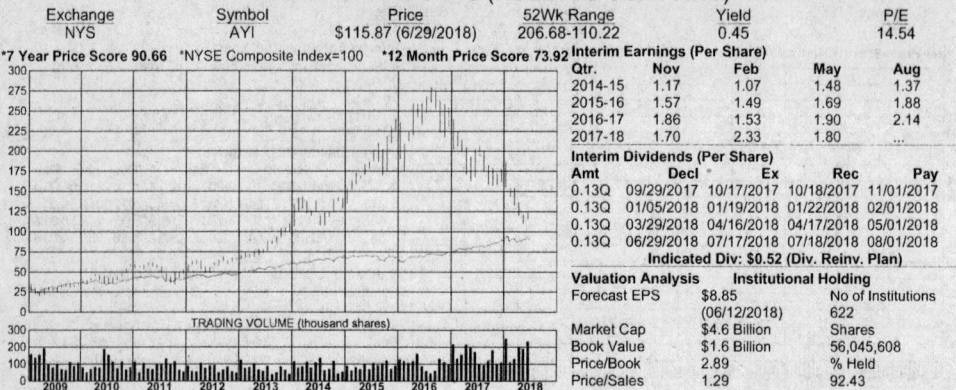

Interim Earnings (Per Share)

Qtr.	Nov	Feb	May	Aug
2014-15	1.17	1.07	1.48	1.37
2015-16	1.57	1.49	1.69	1.88
2016-17	1.86	1.53	1.90	2.14
2017-18	1.70	2.33	1.80	...

Interim Dividends (Per Share)

Amt	Decl	Ex	Rec	Pay
0.13Q	09/29/2017	10/17/2017	10/18/2017	11/01/2017
0.13Q	01/05/2018	01/19/2018	01/22/2018	02/01/2018
0.13Q	03/29/2018	04/16/2018	04/17/2018	05/01/2018
0.13Q	06/29/2018	07/17/2018	07/18/2018	08/01/2018

Indicated Div: $0.52 (Div. Reinv. Plan)

Valuation Analysis

		Institutional Holding	
Forecast EPS	$8.85	No of Institutions	
	(06/12/2018)	622	
Market Cap	$4.6 Billion	Shares	
Book Value	$1.6 Billion	56,045,608	
Price/Book	2.89	% Held	
Price/Sales	1.29	92.43	

Business Summary: Electrical Equipment (MIC: 7.3.1 SIC: 3648 NAIC: 335129)

Acuity Brands is a provider of lighting and building management solutions and services for commercial, institutional, industrial, infrastructure, and residential applications throughout North America and select international markets. Co.'s lighting and building management solutions include devices such as luminaires, lighting controls, power supplies, prismatic skylights, and drivers, as well as integrated systems designed to optimize energy efficiency and comfort for various indoor and outdoor applications. Co.'s solutions portfolio also includes software and services to provide a host of other economic benefits resulting from data analytics that enables the Internet of Things.

Recent Developments: For the quarter ended May 31 2018, net income decreased 11.2% to US$73.0 million from US$82.2 million in the year-earlier quarter. Revenues were US$944.0 million, up 5.9% from US$891.6 million the year before. Operating income was US$105.9 million versus US$131.5 million in the prior-year quarter, a decrease of 19.5%. Direct operating expenses rose 8.2% to US$554.6 million from US$512.7 million in the comparable period the year before. Indirect operating expenses increased 14.6% to US$283.5 million from US$247.4 million in the equivalent prior-year period.

Prospects: Our evaluation of Acuity Brands Inc. as of Jan. 21, 2018 is the result of our systematic analysis on three basic characteristics: earnings strength, relative valuation, and recent stock price movement. The company has produced a positive trend in earnings per share over the past 5 quarters and while recent estimates for the company have been raised by analysts, AYI has posted results that fell short of analysts expectations. Based on operating earnings yield, the company is undervalued when compared to all of the companies in our coverage universe. Share price changes over the past year indicates that AYI will perform in line with the market over the near term.

Financial Data

(US$ in Thousands)	9 Mos	6 Mos	3 Mos	08/31/2017	08/31/2016	08/31/2015	08/31/2014	08/31/2013
Earnings Per Share	7.97	8.07	7.27	7.43	6.63	5.09	4.05	2.95
Cash Flow Per Share	10.83	10.21	9.96	7.34	7.93	6.70	5.45	3.14
Tang Book Value Per Share	3.13	6.78	9.29	7.54	7.54	13.16	8.40	4.18
Dividends Per Share	0.520	0.520	0.520	0.520	0.520	0.520	0.520	0.520
Dividend Payout %	6.52	6.44	7.15	7.00	7.84	10.22	12.84	17.63
Income Statement								
Total Revenue	2,618,900	1,674,900	842,800	3,505,100	3,291,300	2,706,700	2,393,500	2,089,100
EBITDA	371,800	244,000	138,000	571,700	517,700	409,500	329,600	253,300
Depn & Amortn	58,500	38,300	19,000	46,600	40,900	34,400	31,800	29,000
Income Before Taxes	288,800	189,600	110,900	492,600	444,600	343,600	265,700	193,100
Income Taxes	47,400	21,200	39,400	170,900	153,800	121,500	89,900	65,700
Net Income	241,400	168,400	71,500	321,700	290,800	222,100	175,800	127,400
Average Shares	40,500	41,500	42,100	43,300	43,800	43,400	43,000	42,500
Balance Sheet								
Current Assets	1,105,800	1,093,400	1,323,800	1,245,600	1,322,900	1,436,500	1,186,700	913,500
Total Assets	2,882,400	2,750,500	2,961,400	2,899,600	2,948,000	2,429,600	2,168,100	1,903,800
Current Liabilities	672,100	509,600	594,900	600,900	672,500	520,900	470,500	386,200
Long-Term Obligations	356,400	356,500	356,500	356,500	355,000	352,400	353,600	353,600
Total Liabilities	1,282,000	1,114,700	1,235,300	1,234,000	1,288,200	1,069,600	1,004,600	910,300
Stockholders' Equity	1,600,400	1,635,800	1,726,100	1,665,600	1,659,800	1,360,000	1,163,500	993,500
Shares Outstanding	39,968	40,757	41,944	41,871	43,736	43,305	42,862	42,486
Statistical Record								
Return on Assets %	11.83	11.87	10.52	11.00	10.79	9.66	8.63	7.00
Return on Equity %	21.17	19.83	18.03	19.35	19.21	17.60	16.30	13.94
EBITDA Margin %	14.20	14.57	16.37	16.31	15.73	15.13	13.77	12.12
Net Margin %	9.22	10.05	8.48	9.18	8.84	8.21	7.34	6.10
Asset Turnover	1.27	1.23	1.18	1.20	1.22	1.18	1.18	1.15
Current Ratio	1.65	2.15	2.23	2.07	1.97	2.76	2.52	2.37
Debt to Equity	0.22	0.22	0.21	0.21	0.21	0.26	0.30	0.36
Price Range	206.68-110.22	214.01-142.58	254.26-156.39	275.12-162.78	279.15-169.87	211.15-117.71	143.65-84.43	88.34-59.86
P/E Ratio	25.93-13.83	26.52-17.67	34.97-21.51	37.03-21.91	42.10-25.62	41.48-23.13	35.47-20.85	29.95-20.29
Average Yield %	0.32	0.29	0.27	0.25	0.23	0.32	0.44	0.72

Address: 1170 Peachtree Street, N.E., Suite 2300, Atlanta, GA 30309-7676
Telephone: 404-853-1400
Fax: 404-853-1300

Web Site: www.acuitybrands.com
Officers: Vernon J. Nagel - Chairman, President, Chief Executive Officer Richard K. Reece - Executive Vice President, Chief Financial Officer

Auditors: Ernst & Young LLP
Investor Contact: 404-853-1400
Transfer Agents: Computershare Shareowner Services, Pittsburgh, PA

ADTALEM GLOBAL EDUCATION INC

Exchange	Symbol	Price	52Wk Range	Yield	P/E
NYS	ATGE	$48.10 (6/29/2018)	49.90-31.35	N/A	282.94

*7 Year Price Score 99.05 *NYSE Composite Index=100 *12 Month Price Score 111.67

Interim Earnings (Per Share)

Qtr.	Sep	Dec	Mar	Jun
2014-15	0.31	0.65	0.72	0.46
2015-16	0.08	(0.79)	0.81	(0.16)
2016-17	0.39	0.23	0.62	0.67
2017-18	0.20	(1.33)	0.63	...

Interim Dividends (Per Share)

Dividend Payment Suspended

Valuation Analysis — **Institutional Holding**

Valuation Analysis		Institutional Holding	
Forecast EPS	$2.76	No of Institutions	
	(06/11/2018)	373	
Market Cap	$2.9 Billion	Shares	
Book Value	$1.6 Billion	73,654,320	
Price/Book	1.86	% Held	
Price/Sales	1.87	94.03	

TRADING VOLUME (thousand shares)

Business Summary: Educational Services (MIC: 2.2.2 SIC: 8221 NAIC: 611310)

Adtalem Global Education is a provider of educational services. Co.'s institutions and companies provide a range of programs in healthcare, technology, business, accounting, finance and law. Co. conducts its operations through four segments. The Medical and Healthcare segment includes the operations of its Chamberlain University, and Medical and Veterinary Schools. The Professional Education segment includes the operations of Becker Professional Education. The Technology and Business segment includes the operations of Adtalem Education of Brazil. The U.S. Traditional Postsecondary segment includes the operations of its DeVry University and Carrington College.

Recent Developments: For the quarter ended Mar 31 2018, income from continuing operations increased 22.6% to US$44.5 million from US$36.3 million in the year-earlier quarter. Net income decreased 1.8% to US$39.3 million from US$40.0 million in the year-earlier quarter. Revenues were US$342.2 million, up 2.9% from US$332.7 million the year before. Operating income was US$53.8 million versus US$44.0 million in the prior-year quarter, an increase of 22.3%. Direct operating expenses declined 1.4% to US$179.7 million from US$182.2 million in the comparable period the year before. Indirect operating expenses increased 2.0% to US$108.7 million from US$106.5 million in the equivalent prior-year period.

Prospects: Our evaluation of Adtalem Global Education Inc. as of Jan. 21, 2018 is the result of our systematic analysis on three basic characteristics: earnings strength, relative valuation, and recent stock price movement. The company has generated a negative trend in earnings per share over the past 5 quarters and while recent estimates for the company have remained steady, ATGE has posted results that fell short of analysts expectations. Based on operating earnings yield, the company is undervalued when compared to all of the companies in our coverage universe. Share price changes over the past year indicates that ATGE will perform well over the near term.

Financial Data

(US$ in Thousands)	9 Mos	6 Mos	3 Mos	06/30/2017	06/30/2016	06/30/2015	06/30/2014	06/30/2013
Earnings Per Share	0.17	0.16	1.72	1.91	(0.05)	2.14	2.07	1.65
Cash Flow Per Share	3.96	3.96	3.51	3.59	3.61	3.15	4.14	4.07
Tang Book Value Per Share	5.09	4.64	6.20	6.48	10.41	11.14	11.29	9.63
Dividends Per Share	...	...	0.180	0.180	0.360	0.360	0.340	0.340
Dividend Payout %	...	...	10.47	9.42	...	16.82	16.43	20.61
Income Statement								
Total Revenue	1,004,715	662,522	421,025	1,809,800	1,843,537	1,909,943	1,923,371	1,964,375
EBITDA	181,124	111,302	34,081	210,801	67,257	241,918	264,007	250,039
Depn & Amortn	46,208	30,176	19,645	72,188	79,400	85,008	82,739	83,111
Income Before Taxes	132,481	80,212	14,638	134,394	(17,298)	153,660	179,367	164,969
Income Taxes	120,888	113,232	1,678	10,420	(14,542)	18,537	27,699	39,227
Net Income	(29,037)	(68,371)	12,785	122,283	(3,166)	139,899	134,032	106,786
Average Shares	61,965	62,023	63,432	64,019	64,371	65,277	64,853	64,611
Balance Sheet								
Current Assets	539,340	469,809	541,626	471,207	518,105	601,057	577,091	442,164
Total Assets	2,287,305	2,210,722	2,383,596	2,314,035	2,096,996	2,074,193	1,997,636	1,857,018
Current Liabilities	378,626	296,819	450,518	377,327	361,836	321,909	316,812	316,217
Long-Term Obligations	120,000	165,000	135,000	125,000	...	...	...	...
Total Liabilities	729,018	690,763	725,557	644,996	514,909	489,383	464,243	459,862
Stockholders' Equity	1,558,287	1,519,959	1,658,039	1,669,039	1,582,087	1,584,810	1,533,393	1,397,156
Shares Outstanding	60,369	60,295	61,194	62,371	62,549	63,623	63,624	62,946
Statistical Record								
Return on Assets %	0.60	0.64	4.67	5.54	N.M.	6.87	6.95	5.78
Return on Equity %	0.86	0.92	6.74	7.52	N.M.	8.97	9.15	7.76
EBITDA Margin %	18.03	16.80	8.09	11.65	3.65	12.67	13.73	12.73
Net Margin %	N.M.	N.M.	3.04	6.76	N.M.	7.32	6.97	5.44
Asset Turnover	0.67	0.74	0.76	0.82	0.88	0.94	1.00	1.06
Current Ratio	1.42	1.58	1.20	1.25	1.43	1.87	1.82	1.40
Debt to Equity	0.08	0.11	0.08	0.07	...	...	...	...
Price Range	49.75-31.35	45.85-31.35	40.65-22.23	40.65-17.84	32.02-15.84	49.18-29.98	45.99-28.32	34.03-18.35
P/E Ratio	292.65-184.41	286.56-195.94	23.63-12.92	21.28-9.34	...	22.98-14.01	22.22-13.68	20.62-11.12
Average Yield %	...	...	0.55	0.60	1.58	0.89	0.93	1.29

Address: 500 West Monroe, Chicago, IL 60661 Telephone: 630-515-7700	Web Site: www.adtalem.com Officers: Lisa W. Wardell - President, Chief Executive Officer Patrick J. Unzicker - Senior Vice President, Vice President, Chief Financial Officer, Chief Accounting Officer, Treasurer, Controller	Auditors: PricewaterhouseCoopers LLP Investor Contact: 630-353-3800 Transfer Agents: Computershare Investor Services, L.L.C.

7

ADVANCE AUTO PARTS INC

Exchange	Symbol	Price	52Wk Range	Yield	P/E
NYS	AAP	$135.70 (6/29/2018)	139.50-79.38	0.18	19.96

*7 Year Price Score 73.57   *NYSE Composite Index=100   *12 Month Price Score 117.05

TRADING VOLUME (thousand shares)

Interim Earnings (Per Share)

Qtr.	Apr	Jul	Oct	Jan
2015-16	2.00	2.03	1.63	0.74
2016	2.14	1.68	1.53	0.84
2017	1.46	1.17	1.30	2.49
2018	1.84	...	...	...

Interim Dividends (Per Share)

Amt	Decl	Ex	Rec	Pay
0.06Q	08/10/2017	09/21/2017	09/22/2017	10/06/2017
0.06Q	11/07/2017	12/21/2017	12/22/2017	01/05/2018
0.06Q	02/06/2018	03/22/2018	03/23/2018	04/06/2018
0.06Q	05/15/2018	06/21/2018	06/22/2018	07/06/2018

Indicated Div: $0.24

Valuation Analysis / Institutional Holding

Forecast EPS	$6.78 (06/14/2018)	No of Institutions	664
Market Cap	$10.0 Billion	Shares	93,424,872
Book Value	$3.5 Billion	% Held	92.92
Price/Book	2.83		
Price/Sales	1.07		

Business Summary: Retail - Automotive (MIC: 2.1.4 SIC: 5531 NAIC: 441310)

Advance Auto Parts is an automotive aftermarket parts provider in North America, serving both professional installers and do-it-yourself customers as well as independently-owned operators. Co.'s stores and branches provide a selection of brand name, original equipment manufacturer and private label automotive replacement parts, accessories, batteries, and maintenance items for domestic and imported cars, vans, sport utility vehicles and light and heavy duty trucks. As of Dec 30 2017, Co. operated 5,054 total stores and 129 branches primarily under the trade names Advance Auto Parts, Autopart International, Carquest and Worldpac.

Recent Developments: For the quarter ended Apr 21 2018, net income increased 26.6% to US$136.7 million from US$108.0 million in the year-earlier quarter. Revenues were US$2.87 billion, down 0.6% from US$2.89 billion the year before. Operating income was US$198.2 million versus US$179.8 million in the prior-year quarter, an increase of 10.3%. Direct operating expenses declined 1.1% to US$1.60 billion from US$1.62 billion in the comparable period the year before. Indirect operating expenses decreased 1.5% to US$1.07 billion from US$1.09 billion in the equivalent prior-year period.

Prospects: Our evaluation of Advance Auto Parts Inc. as of Jan. 21, 2018 is the result of our systematic analysis on three basic characteristics: earnings strength, relative valuation, and recent stock price movement. The company has produced a positive trend in earnings per share over the past 5 quarters and while recent estimates for the company have been raised by analysts, AAP has posted better than expected results. Based on operating earnings yield, the company is undervalued when compared to all of the companies in our coverage universe. Share price changes over the past year indicates that AAP will perform very poorly over the near term.

Financial Data
(US$ in Thousands)

	3 Mos	12/30/2017	12/31/2016	01/02/2016	01/03/2015	12/28/2013	12/29/2012	12/31/2011
Earnings Per Share	6.80	6.42	6.20	6.40	6.71	5.32	5.22	5.11
Cash Flow Per Share	9.73	8.16	6.83	9.45	9.56	7.50	9.40	10.99
Tang Book Value Per Share	26.61	24.66	17.42	10.69	3.55	17.39	15.06	10.17
Dividends Per Share	0.240	0.240	0.240	0.240	0.240	0.240	0.240	0.240
Dividend Payout %	3.53	3.74	3.87	3.75	3.58	4.51	4.60	4.70
Income Statement								
Total Revenue	2,873,848	9,373,784	9,567,679	9,737,018	9,843,861	6,493,814	6,205,003	6,170,462
EBITDA	270,391	785,960	1,014,726	1,042,024	1,089,842	862,837	843,824	838,404
Depn & Amortn	71,692	206,900	215,981	223,728	235,040	199,821	185,909	174,219
Income Before Taxes	181,017	520,259	738,835	752,888	781,394	626,398	624,074	633,236
Income Taxes	44,290	44,754	279,213	279,490	287,569	234,640	236,404	238,554
Net Income	136,727	475,505	459,622	473,398	493,825	391,758	387,670	394,682
Average Shares	74,205	74,110	73,856	73,733	73,414	73,414	74,062	77,071
Balance Sheet								
Current Assets	5,617,516	5,426,892	5,172,764	4,940,746	4,741,040	3,989,384	3,184,200	2,293,820
Total Assets	8,614,953	8,482,301	8,315,033	8,134,565	7,962,358	5,564,774	4,613,814	3,655,754
Current Liabilities	3,480,139	3,480,097	3,676,046	3,797,477	3,743,066	2,764,785	2,559,638	2,187,875
Long-Term Obligations	1,044,755	1,044,327	1,042,949	1,213,161	1,636,311	1,052,668	604,461	415,136
Total Liabilities	5,068,332	5,067,105	5,398,841	5,673,917	5,959,446	4,048,569	3,403,120	2,807,840
Stockholders' Equity	3,546,621	3,415,196	2,916,192	2,460,648	2,002,912	1,516,205	1,210,694	847,914
Shares Outstanding	74,031	73,936	73,749	73,314	73,074	72,840	73,383	72,799
Statistical Record								
Return on Assets %	5.92	5.68	5.60	5.90	7.18	7.72	9.40	11.29
Return on Equity %	15.35	15.06	17.14	21.27	27.61	28.81	37.77	41.94
EBITDA Margin %	9.41	8.38	10.61	10.70	11.07	13.29	13.60	13.59
Net Margin %	4.76	5.07	4.80	4.86	5.02	6.03	6.25	6.40
Asset Turnover	1.10	1.12	1.17	1.21	1.43	1.28	1.50	1.77
Current Ratio	1.61	1.56	1.41	1.30	1.27	1.44	1.24	1.05
Debt to Equity	0.29	0.31	0.36	0.49	0.82	0.69	0.50	0.49
Price Range	151.47-79.38	174.79-79.38	176.78-136.19	200.38-143.00	161.22-109.63	110.28-71.76	92.37-65.59	72.16-50.04
P/E Ratio	22.28-11.67	27.23-12.36	28.51-21.97	31.31-22.34	24.03-16.34	20.73-13.49	17.70-12.57	14.12-9.79
Average Yield %	0.22	0.20	0.15	0.15	0.18	0.28	0.32	0.38

Address: 5008 Airport Road, Roanoke, VA 24012	Web Site: www.AdvanceAutoParts.com	Auditors: Deloitte & Touche LLP
Telephone: 540-362-4911	Officers: Thomas R. Greco - Chief Executive Officer Robert B. Cushing - Executive Vice President	Investor Contact: 540-561-6444 Transfer Agents: BNY Mellon Shareowner Services, Pittsburgh, PA

AECOM

Exchange	Symbol	Price	52Wk Range	Yield	P/E
NYS	ACM	$33.03 (6/29/2018)	39.62-30.47	N/A	29.23

*7 Year Price Score 95.57   *NYSE Composite Index=100   *12 Month Price Score 94.80

Interim Earnings (Per Share)

Qtr.	Dec	Mar	Jun	Sep
2014-15	(0.73)	0.00	(0.11)	0.01
2015-16	(0.13)	0.27	0.43	0.05
2016-17	0.30	0.65	0.64	0.55
2017-18	0.69	(0.75)	...	

Interim Dividends (Per Share)

No Dividends Paid

Valuation Analysis — **Institutional Holding**

Forecast EPS	$2.70	No of Institutions
	(06/14/2018)	446
Market Cap	$5.3 Billion	Shares
Book Value	$4.0 Billion	156,360,832
Price/Book	1.31	% Held
Price/Sales	0.28	60.98

Business Summary: Construction Services (MIC: 7.5.4 SIC: 8711 NAIC: 541330)

AECOM is a firm positioned to design, build, finance and operate infrastructure assets for governments, businesses and organizations. Co.'s business segments are: Design and Consulting Services, which include of planning, consulting, architectural and engineering design services to commercial and government clients; Construction Services including construction, program and construction management services; Management Services, which include program and facilities management and maintenance, training, logistics, and systems integration and information technology services; and AECOM Capital, which invests in and develops real estate, public-private partnership and infrastructure projects.

Recent Developments: For the quarter ended Mar 31 2018, net loss amounted to US$107.8 million versus net income of US$115.8 million in the year-earlier quarter. Revenues were US$790.9 million, down 82.1% from US$4.43 billion the year before. Operating loss was US$44.1 million versus an income of US$140.9 million in the prior-year quarter. Direct operating expenses rose 9.2% to US$4.65 billion from US$4.26 billion in the comparable period the year before. Indirect operating expenses increased 573.3% to US$185.4 million from US$27.5 million in the equivalent prior-year period.

Prospects: Our evaluation of AECOM as of Jan. 21, 2018 is the result of our systematic analysis on three basic characteristics: earnings strength, relative valuation, and recent stock price movement. The company has managed to produce a neutral trend in earnings per share over the past 5 quarters and while recent estimates for the company have remained steady, ACM has posted better than expected results. Based on operating earnings yield, the company is undervalued when compared to all of the companies in our coverage universe. Share price changes over the past year indicates that ACM will perform poorly over the near term.

Financial Data

(US$ in Thousands)	6 Mos	3 Mos	09/30/2017	09/30/2016	09/30/2015	09/30/2014	09/30/2013	09/30/2012
Earnings Per Share	1.13	2.53	2.13	0.62	(1.04)	2.33	2.35	(0.52)
Cash Flow Per Share	5.24	4.25	4.47	5.25	5.11	3.71	4.06	3.86
Tang Book Value Per Share	N.M.	N.M.	N.M.	N.M.	N.M.	1.64	1.32	2.78
Income Statement								
Total Revenue	9,701,742	4,910,832	18,203,402	17,410,825	17,989,880	8,356,783	8,153,495	8,218,180
EBITDA	192,632	166,600	676,010	451,385	233,182	366,806	426,892	91,029
Depn & Amortn	133,483	62,835	157,100	171,700	191,300	69,100	70,700	77,100
Income Before Taxes	(97,593)	47,600	287,600	21,523	(257,745)	256,864	311,455	(31,167)
Income Taxes	(71,493)	(47,093)	7,706	(37,917)	(80,237)	82,024	92,578	74,416
Net Income	(8,419)	111,314	339,390	96,109	(154,845)	229,854	239,243	(58,567)
Average Shares	159,495	161,847	159,135	156,073	149,605	98,657	101,942	111,875
Balance Sheet								
Current Assets	6,923,960	6,842,040	6,682,222	6,000,771	6,246,085	3,434,113	3,131,602	3,147,293
Total Assets	14,617,332	14,622,951	14,396,956	13,726,745	14,014,298	6,123,377	5,665,623	5,664,568
Current Liabilities	5,641,841	5,676,057	5,578,379	5,304,756	4,836,052	2,455,769	2,053,549	2,078,402
Long-Term Obligations	3,814,976	3,738,900	3,702,109	3,758,966	4,446,527	939,565	1,089,060	907,141
Total Liabilities	10,576,580	10,518,582	10,400,830	10,359,824	10,606,550	3,936,860	3,644,180	3,495,104
Stockholders' Equity	4,040,752	4,104,369	3,996,126	3,366,921	3,407,748	2,186,517	2,021,443	2,169,464
Shares Outstanding	160,237	159,132	157,529	153,901	151,263	96,715	96,016	107,041
Statistical Record								
Return on Assets %	1.28	2.87	2.41	0.69	N.M.	3.90	4.22	N.M.
Return on Equity %	4.78	10.79	9.22	2.83	N.M.	10.92	11.42	N.M.
EBITDA Margin %	1.99	3.39	3.71	2.59	1.30	4.39	5.24	1.11
Net Margin %	N.M.	2.27	1.86	0.55	N.M.	2.75	2.93	N.M.
Asset Turnover	1.35	1.33	1.29	1.25	1.79	1.42	1.44	1.43
Current Ratio	1.23	1.21	1.20	1.13	1.29	1.40	1.52	1.51
Debt to Equity	0.94	0.91	0.93	1.12	1.30	0.43	0.54	0.42
Price Range	39.62-30.47	39.13-30.47	40.13-26.92	36.17-23.15	35.36-24.92	38.13-27.47	35.20-18.87	24.06-14.91
P/E Ratio	35.06-26.96	15.47-12.04	18.84-12.64	58.34-37.34	...	16.36-11.79	14.98-8.03	...

Address: 1999 Avenue of the Stars, Suite 2600, Los Angeles, CA 90067 **Telephone:** 213-593-8000	**Web Site:** www.aecom.com **Officers:** Michael S. Burke - Chairman, President, Chief Executive Officer Daniel R. Tishman - Vice-Chairman	**Auditors:** Ernst & Young LLP **Investor Contact:** 212-973-2982 **Transfer Agents:** Computershare Investor Services, LLC, Canton, MA

AES CORP.

Exchange	Symbol	Price	52Wk Range	Yield	P/E
NYS	AES	$13.41 (6/29/2018)	13.51-10.06	3.88	N/A

*7 Year Price Score 74.82 *NYSE Composite Index=100 *12 Month Price Score 110.14

TRADING VOLUME (thousand shares)

Interim Earnings (Per Share)

Qtr.	Mar	Jun	Sep	Dec
2015	0.20	0.10	0.26	(0.12)
2016	0.19	(0.73)	0.26	(1.43)
2017	(0.04)	0.08	0.23	(2.03)
2018	1.03	...	...	...

Interim Dividends (Per Share)

Amt	Decl	Ex	Rec	Pay
0.12Q	10/13/2017	10/31/2017	11/01/2017	11/15/2017
0.13Q	12/11/2017	01/31/2018	02/01/2018	02/15/2018
0.13Q	04/13/2018	04/30/2018	05/01/2018	05/15/2018
0.13Q	07/16/2018	08/02/2018	08/03/2018	08/17/2018

Indicated Div: $0.52

Valuation Analysis

		Institutional Holding	
Forecast EPS	$1.21	No of Institutions	
	(06/14/2018)	759	
Market Cap	$8.9 Billion	Shares	
Book Value	$4.0 Billion	787,844,608	
Price/Book	2.19	% Held	
Price/Sales	0.91	75.99	

Business Summary: Electric Utilities (MIC: 3.1.1 SIC: 4911 NAIC: 221121)

AES is a holding company. Through its subsidiaries and affiliates, Co. operates a portfolio of electricity generation and distribution businesses. Co. has two lines of business: generation, where Co. owns and/or operates power plants to generate and sell power to customers, such as utilities, industrial users, and other intermediaries; and utilities, where Co. owns and/or operates utilities to generate or purchase, distribute, transmit and sell electricity to end-user customers in the residential, commercial, industrial and governmental sectors within a defined service area. In certain circumstances, Co.'s utilities also generate and sell electricity on the wholesale market.

Recent Developments: For the quarter ended Mar 31 2018, income from continuing operations increased 702.1% to US$778.0 million from US$97.0 million in the year-earlier quarter. Net income increased 692.9% to US$777.0 million from US$98.0 million in the year-earlier quarter. Revenues were US$2.74 billion, up 6.2% from US$2.58 billion the year before. Direct operating expenses rose 3.0% to US$2.08 billion from US$2.02 billion in the comparable period the year before. Indirect operating expenses increased 3.7% to US$56.0 million from US$54.0 million in the equivalent prior-year period.

Prospects: Our evaluation of AES Corp. as of Jan. 21, 2018 is the result of our systematic analysis on three basic characteristics: earnings strength, relative valuation, and recent stock price movement. The company has generated a negative trend in earnings per share over the past 5 quarters and while recent estimates for the company have been mixed, AES has posted results that fell short of analysts expectations. Based on operating earnings yield, the company is undervalued when compared to all of the companies in our coverage universe. Share price changes over the past year indicates that AES will perform very poorly over the near term.

Financial Data

(US$ in Millions)	3 Mos	12/31/2017	12/31/2016	12/31/2015	12/31/2014	12/31/2013	12/31/2012	12/31/2011
Earnings Per Share	(0.69)	(1.76)	(1.71)	0.44	1.06	0.15	(1.21)	0.07
Cash Flow Per Share	3.48	3.77	4.36	3.11	2.49	3.65	3.83	3.71
Tang Book Value Per Share	3.97	2.84	3.13	3.47	3.71	3.44	2.98	2.25
Dividends Per Share	0.490	0.480	0.440	0.400	0.200	0.160	0.040	...
Dividend Payout %	...	...	...	90.91	18.87	106.67	...	...
Income Statement								
Total Revenue	2,740	10,530	13,586	14,963	17,146	15,891	18,141	17,274
EBITDA	1,457	2,702	2,209	3,138	3,886	3,448	2,788	4,536
Depn & Amortn	254	1,005	1,105	1,104	1,204	1,193	1,251	1,154
Income Before Taxes	998	771	137	1,122	1,576	1,048	314	2,179
Income Taxes	231	990	(188)	465	419	343	708	636
Net Income	684	(1,161)	(1,130)	306	769	114	(912)	58
Average Shares	663	660	662	689	724	748	755	783
Balance Sheet								
Current Assets	5,438	6,398	6,411	6,866	7,826	7,739	8,465	9,228
Total Assets	32,573	33,112	36,119	36,850	38,966	40,411	41,830	45,333
Current Liabilities	4,876	6,028	5,272	6,950	6,997	7,653	8,319	8,446
Long-Term Obligations	17,661	17,801	19,160	18,278	18,725	18,869	18,519	20,116
Total Liabilities	28,529	29,810	32,543	33,163	34,616	36,003	37,183	39,309
Stockholders' Equity	4,044	3,302	3,576	3,687	4,350	4,408	4,647	6,024
Shares Outstanding	661	660	659	666	703	722	744	765
Statistical Record								
Return on Assets %	N.M.	N.M.	N.M.	0.81	1.94	0.28	N.M.	0.14
Return on Equity %	N.M.	N.M.	N.M.	7.61	17.56	2.52	N.M.	0.92
EBITDA Margin %	53.18	25.66	16.26	20.97	22.66	21.70	15.37	26.26
Net Margin %	24.96	N.M.	N.M.	2.05	4.49	0.72	N.M.	0.34
Asset Turnover	0.28	0.30	0.37	0.39	0.43	0.39	0.42	0.40
Current Ratio	1.12	1.06	1.22	0.99	1.12	1.01	1.02	1.09
Debt to Equity	4.37	5.39	5.36	4.96	4.30	4.28	3.99	3.34
Price Range	11.95-10.06	11.95-10.23	13.26-8.54	13.94-8.83	15.57-12.79	15.31-10.70	13.80-9.72	13.38-9.44
P/E Ratio	...	...	...	31.68-20.07	14.69-12.07	102.07-71.33	...	191.14-134.86
Average Yield %	4.42	4.28	3.87	3.33	1.40	1.25	0.34	...

Address: 4300 Wilson Boulevard, Arlington, VA 22203	**Web Site:** www.aes.com	**Auditors:** Ernst & Young LLP
Telephone: 703-522-1315	**Officers:** Andres R. Gluski - President, Chief Executive Officer, Executive Vice President, Chief Operating Officer Thomas M. O'Flynn - Executive Vice President, Chief Financial Officer	**Investor Contact:** 703-682-6451
Fax: 703-528-4510		**Transfer Agents:** Computershare Investor Services, Canton, MA

AETNA INC

Exchange	Symbol	Price	52Wk Range	Yield	P/E
NYS	AET	$183.50 (6/29/2018)	193.74-151.44	1.09	17.39

*7 Year Price Score 146.10 *NYSE Composite Index=100 ***12 Month Price Score 102.88**

TRADING VOLUME (thousand shares)

Interim Earnings (Per Share)

Qtr.	Mar	Jun	Sep	Dec
2015	2.20	2.08	1.59	0.91
2016	2.06	2.23	1.70	0.39
2017	(1.11)	3.60	2.52	0.76
2018	3.67	...	...	...

Interim Dividends (Per Share)

Amt	Decl	Ex	Rec	Pay
0.50Q	09/29/2017	10/11/2017	10/12/2017	10/27/2017
0.50Q	12/03/2017	01/10/2018	01/11/2018	01/26/2018
0.50Q	02/23/2018	04/11/2018	04/12/2018	04/27/2018
0.50Q	05/18/2018	07/24/2018	07/25/2018	08/01/2018

Indicated Div: $2.00

Valuation Analysis

Forecast EPS	$10.92
	(06/14/2018)
Market Cap	$60.0 Billion
Book Value	$16.4 Billion
Price/Book	3.66
Price/Sales	0.99

Institutional Holding

No of Institutions	1419
Shares	367,741,952
% Held	89.26

Business Summary: Life & Health (MIC: 5.2.2 SIC: 6324 NAIC: 524114)

Aetna is a health care benefits company. Co. conducts its operations in three business segments: Health Care, which provides medical, pharmacy benefit management services, dental, behavioral health and vision plans provided on both an insured basis and an employer-funded basis and businesses products and services that complement its medical products; Group Insurance, which primarily includes group life insurance and group disability products and long-term care products; and Large Case Pensions, which manages a variety of retirement products (including pension and annuity products) primarily for tax-qualified pension plans.

Recent Developments: For the quarter ended Mar 31 2018, net income amounted to US$1.22 billion versus a net loss of US$379.0 million in the year-earlier quarter. Revenues were US$15.34 billion, up 1.1% from US$15.17 billion the year before. Net premiums earned were US$13.07 billion versus US$13.76 billion in the prior-year quarter, a decrease of 5.0%. Net investment income fell 24.2% to US$197.0 million from US$260.0 million a year ago.

Prospects: Our evaluation of Aetna Inc. as of Jan. 21, 2018 is the result of our systematic analysis on three basic characteristics: earnings strength, relative valuation, and recent stock price movement. The company has generated a negative trend in earnings per share over the past 5 quarters and while recent estimates for the company have been mixed, AET has posted better than expected results. Based on operating earnings yield, the company is undervalued when compared to all of the companies in our coverage universe. Share price changes over the past year indicates that AET will perform well over the near term.

Financial Data
(US$ in Thousands)

	3 Mos	12/31/2017	12/31/2016	12/31/2015	12/31/2014	12/31/2013	12/31/2012	12/31/2011
Earnings Per Share	10.55	5.68	6.41	6.78	5.68	5.33	4.81	5.22
Cash Flow Per Share	6.04	(1.39)	10.56	11.07	9.49	6.41	5.34	6.73
Tang Book Value Per Share	14.28	11.72	16.50	10.84	5.49	4.70	10.30	8.46
Dividends Per Share	2.000	1.750	1.000	1.000	0.900	0.800	0.700	0.450
Dividend Payout %	18.96	30.81	15.60	14.75	15.85	15.01	14.55	8.62
Income Statement								
Premium Income	13,070,000	53,894,000	56,298,000	53,788,800	51,748,500	41,836,600	31,715,400	28,965,000
Total Revenue	15,335,000	60,535,000	63,155,000	60,336,500	58,003,200	47,294,600	36,595,900	33,779,800
Benefits & Claims	10,574,000	1,875,000	2,101,000	2,120,600	2,165,000	2,350,400	2,949,500	1,876,500
Income Before Taxes	1,465,000	2,992,000	3,991,000	4,235,600	3,499,900	2,940,500	2,545,400	3,077,800
Income Taxes	246,000	1,087,000	1,735,000	1,841,000	1,454,700	1,028,600	887,500	1,092,100
Net Income	1,209,000	1,904,000	2,271,000	2,390,200	2,040,800	1,913,600	1,657,900	1,985,700
Average Shares	329,600	335,400	354,300	352,600	359,100	359,200	345,000	380,200
Balance Sheet								
Total Assets	59,197,000	55,151,000	69,146,000	53,424,100	53,402,100	49,871,800	41,494,500	38,593,100
Total Liabilities	42,799,000	39,571,000	51,265,000	37,309,800	38,919,500	35,846,300	31,088,700	28,472,900
Stockholders' Equity	16,398,000	15,580,000	17,881,000	16,114,300	14,482,600	14,025,500	10,405,800	10,120,200
Shares Outstanding	327,100	326,800	351,700	349,500	349,800	362,200	327,600	349,700
Statistical Record								
Return on Assets %	6.05	3.06	3.70	4.47	3.95	4.19	4.13	5.20
Return on Equity %	22.79	11.38	13.32	15.62	14.32	15.67	16.11	19.85
Loss Ratio %	80.90	3.48	3.73	3.94	4.18	5.62	9.30	6.48
Net Margin %	7.88	3.15	3.60	3.96	3.52	4.05	4.53	5.88
Price Range	193.74-127.28	182.73-116.71	134.90-94.31	132.60-87.60	90.84-65.15	68.93-44.38	50.23-35.30	45.90-30.51
P/E Ratio	18.36-12.06	32.17-20.55	21.05-14.71	19.56-12.92	15.99-11.47	12.93-8.33	10.44-7.34	8.79-5.84
Average Yield %	1.23	1.18	0.87	0.92	1.15	1.35	1.65	1.15

Address: 151 Farmington Avenue, Hartford, CT 06156 **Telephone:** 860-273-0123	**Web Site:** www.aetna.com **Officers:** Mark T. Bertolini - Chairman, President, Chief Executive Officer Karen S. Lynch - President	**Auditors:** KPMG LLP **Investor Contact:** 860-273-2402 **Transfer Agents:** Computershare Trust Company, N.A, Providence, RI

AFFILIATED MANAGERS GROUP INC.

Exchange	Symbol	Price	52Wk Range	Yield	P/E
NYS	AMG	$148.67 (6/29/2018)	215.76-148.67	0.81	11.73

*7 Year Price Score 90.67   *NYSE Composite Index=100   *12 Month Price Score 86.45

TRADING VOLUME (thousand shares)

Interim Earnings (Per Share)

Qtr.	Mar	Jun	Sep	Dec
2015	2.28	2.31	1.98	2.71
2016	1.92	1.97	2.00	2.69
2017	2.13	2.22	2.22	5.46
2018	2.77	...	...	...

Interim Dividends (Per Share)

Amt	Decl	Ex	Rec	Pay
0.20Q	07/31/2017	08/08/2017	08/10/2017	08/24/2017
0.20Q	10/30/2017	11/08/2017	11/09/2017	11/22/2017
0.30Q	01/29/2018	02/07/2018	02/08/2018	02/23/2018
0.30Q	04/30/2018	05/09/2018	05/10/2018	05/24/2018

Indicated Div: $1.20

Valuation Analysis

		Institutional Holding	
Forecast EPS	$16.05	No of Institutions	
	(06/14/2018)	762	
Market Cap	$8.1 Billion	Shares	
Book Value	$3.7 Billion	65,785,940	
Price/Book	2.20	% Held	
Price/Sales	3.40	98.12	

Business Summary: Wealth Management (MIC: 5.5.2 SIC: 6282 NAIC: 523920)

Affiliated Managers Group is a global asset management company with equity investments in boutique investment management firms (Affiliates). Co.'s Affiliates provide investment management services globally to institutional, retail and high net worth clients. In addition, Co. provides centralized assistance to its Affiliates in strategic matters, marketing, distribution, product development and operations. Co. operates in three business segments representing its three principal distribution channels: Institutional, Mutual Fund and High Net Worth.

Recent Developments: For the quarter ended Mar 31 2018, net income increased 15.7% to US$224.0 million from US$193.6 million in the year-earlier quarter. Revenues were US$612.4 million, up 12.5% from US$544.3 million the year before. Indirect operating expenses increased 11.2% to US$435.4 million from US$391.7 million in the equivalent prior-year period.

Prospects: Our evaluation of Affiliated Managers Group Inc. as of Jan. 21, 2018 is the result of our systematic analysis on three basic characteristics: earnings strength, relative valuation, and recent stock price movement. The company has produced a positive trend in earnings per share over the past 5 quarters and while recent estimates for the company have been raised by analysts, AMG has posted better than expected results. Based on operating earnings yield, the company is undervalued when compared to all of the companies in our coverage universe. Share price changes over the past year indicates that AMG will perform very well over the near term.

Financial Data
(US$ in Thousands)

	3 Mos	12/31/2017	12/31/2016	12/31/2015	12/31/2014	12/31/2013	12/31/2012	12/31/2011
Earnings Per Share	12.67	12.03	8.57	9.28	8.01	6.55	3.28	3.11
Cash Flow Per Share	22.95	20.90	18.91	22.19	25.31	18.02	12.21	13.68
Dividends Per Share	0.900	0.800	...	...	...	...	...	...
Dividend Payout %	7.10	6.65	...	...	...	...	...	...
Income Statement								
Total Revenue	612,400	2,305,000	2,194,600	2,484,500	2,510,900	2,188,800	1,805,500	1,704,800
EBITDA	236,000	972,400	873,600	992,600	977,600	817,100	644,700	578,800
Depn & Amortn	23,200	106,700	134,500	142,300	139,100	142,200	222,300	97,700
Income Before Taxes	191,200	764,900	645,800	801,700	731,800	555,900	365,500	380,000
Income Taxes	63,500	58,400	235,600	256,900	227,900	194,100	83,800	93,100
Net Income	153,000	689,500	472,800	516,000	452,100	360,500	174,000	164,900
Average Shares	57,000	58,600	57,000	57,200	58,400	56,700	53,000	53,000
Balance Sheet								
Current Assets	866,400	1,116,100	1,084,000	1,304,200	1,316,300	1,210,200	912,300	876,400
Total Assets	8,584,200	8,702,100	8,749,100	7,784,800	7,698,100	6,318,800	6,187,100	5,218,900
Current Liabilities	2,223,700	807,200	729,300	729,400	808,300	514,700	375,800	417,600
Long-Term Obligations	305,100	1,550,300	1,808,000	1,589,600	1,591,800	865,000	1,630,600	1,198,200
Total Liabilities	4,907,200	4,879,900	5,129,500	4,947,700	5,071,100	4,184,600	4,102,900	3,352,900
Stockholders' Equity	3,677,000	3,822,200	3,619,600	2,837,100	2,627,000.	2,134,200	2,084,200	1,866,000
Shares Outstanding	54,300	58,500	58,500	55,800	54,600	53,900	53,900	53,900
Statistical Record								
Return on Assets %	8.38	7.90	5.70	6.67	6.45	5.77	3.04	3.14
Return on Equity %	19.83	18.53	14.61	18.89	18.99	17.09	8.79	9.00
EBITDA Margin %	38.54	42.19	39.81	39.95	38.93	37.33	35.71	33.95
Net Margin %	24.98	29.91	21.54	20.77	18.01	16.47	9.64	9.67
Asset Turnover	0.28	0.26	0.26	0.32	0.36	0.35	0.32	0.32
Current Ratio	0.39	1.38	1.49	1.79	1.63	2.35	2.43	2.10
Debt to Equity	0.08	0.41	0.50	0.56	0.61	0.41	0.78	0.64
Price Range	215.76-149.51	206.51-141.34	179.01-117.80	228.02-144.01	216.88-179.30	216.88-130.15	132.30-96.00	112.20-72.88
P/E Ratio	17.03-11.80	17.17-11.75	20.89-13.75	24.57-15.52	27.08-22.38	33.11-19.87	40.34-29.27	36.08-23.43
Average Yield %	0.50	0.46	...	...	...	...	...	...

Address: 777 South Flagler Drive, West Palm Beach, FL 33401	Web Site: www.amg.com	Auditors: PricewaterhouseCoopers LLP
Telephone: 800-345-1100	Officers: Sean M. Healey - Chairman, Chief Executive Officer Nathaniel Dalton - President, Chief Operating Officer, Chief Executive Officer	Investor Contact: 617-747-3300 Transfer Agents: American Stock Transfer & Trust Company, New York, NY

AFLAC INC

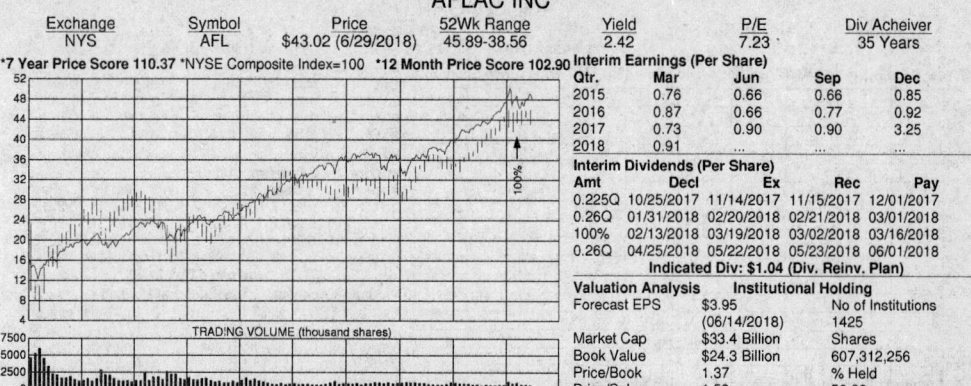

Exchange	Symbol	Price	52Wk Range	Yield	P/E	Div Acheiver
NYS	AFL	$43.02 (6/29/2018)	45.89-38.56	2.42	7.23	35 Years

*7 Year Price Score 110.37 *NYSE Composite Index=100 *12 Month Price Score 102.90

Interim Earnings (Per Share)

Qtr.	Mar	Jun	Sep	Dec
2015	0.76	0.66	0.66	0.85
2016	0.87	0.66	0.77	0.92
2017	0.73	0.90	0.90	3.25
2018	0.91	...	...	...

Interim Dividends (Per Share)

Amt	Decl	Ex	Rec	Pay
0.225Q	10/25/2017	11/14/2017	11/15/2017	12/01/2017
0.26Q	01/31/2018	02/20/2018	02/21/2018	03/01/2018
100%	02/13/2018	03/19/2018	03/02/2018	03/16/2018
0.26Q	04/25/2018	05/22/2018	05/23/2018	06/01/2018

Indicated Div: $1.04 (Div. Reinv. Plan)

Valuation Analysis

		Institutional Holding	
Forecast EPS	$3.95	No of Institutions	
	(06/14/2018)	1425	
Market Cap	$33.4 Billion	Shares	
Book Value	$24.3 Billion	607,312,256	
Price/Book	1.37	% Held	
Price/Sales	1.53	56.32	

Business Summary: Life & Health (MIC: 5.2.2 SIC: 6311 NAIC: 524113)

Aflac Incorporated is a holding company. Co. sells supplemental health and life insurance, which is marketed and administered via its subsidiary, American Family Life Assurance Company of Columbus (Aflac). Aflac operates in the U.S. (Aflac U.S.), which designs the U.S. insurance products to provide supplemental coverage for people having medical or insurance coverage; and as a branch in Japan (Aflac Japan), which provides insurance products to help consumers pay for medical and nonmedical costs that are not reimbursed under Japan's national health insurance system. Aflac U.S. also provides group products via Continental American Insurance Company (CAIC), branded as Aflac Group Insurance.

Recent Developments:
For the quarter ended Mar 31 2018, net income increased 21.1% to US$717.0 million from US$592.0 million in the year-earlier quarter. Revenues were US$5.46 billion, up 2.9% from US$5.31 billion the year before. Net premiums earned were US$4.75 billion versus US$4.64 billion in the prior-year quarter, an increase of 2.3%. Net investment income rose 5.4% to US$837.0 million from US$794.0 million a year ago.

Prospects:
Our evaluation of AFLAC Inc. as of Jan. 21, 2018 is the result of our systematic analysis on three basic characteristics: earnings strength, relative valuation, and recent stock price movement. The company has managed to produce a neutral trend in earnings per share over the past 5 quarters. However, while recent estimates for the company have been mixed, AFL has posted better than expected results. Based on operating earnings yield, the company is undervalued when compared to all of the companies in our coverage universe. Share price changes over the past year indicates that AFL will perform well over the near term.

Financial Data
(US$ in Thousands)	3 Mos	12/31/2017	12/31/2016	12/31/2015	12/31/2014	12/31/2013	12/31/2012	12/31/2011
Earnings Per Share	5.95	5.77	3.21	2.92	3.25	3.38	3.06	2.09
Cash Flow Per Share	7.20	7.74	7.26	7.87	7.26	11.35	15.97	11.62
Tang Book Value Per Share	31.31	31.50	25.24	20.86	20.73	15.91	17.08	14.48
Dividends Per Share	0.915	0.870	0.830	0.790	0.750	0.710	0.670	0.615
Dividend Payout %	15.38	15.08	25.86	27.01	23.08	21.01	21.93	29.43
Income Statement								
Premium Income	4,745,000	18,531,000	19,225,000	17,570,000	19,072,000	20,135,000	22,148,000	20,362,000
Total Revenue	5,464,000	21,667,000	22,559,000	20,872,000	22,728,000	23,939,000	25,364,000	22,171,000
Benefits & Claims	3,042,000	12,181,000	12,919,000	11,746,000	12,937,000	13,813,000	15,330,000	13,749,000
Income Before Taxes	982,000	4,018,000	4,067,000	3,862,000	4,491,000	4,816,000	4,302,000	2,992,000
Income Taxes	265,000	(586,000)	1,408,000	1,329,000	1,540,000	1,658,000	1,436,000	1,028,000
Net Income	717,000	4,604,000	2,659,000	2,533,000	2,951,000	3,158,000	2,866,000	1,964,000
Average Shares	783,852	797,860	827,842	866,344	908,000	934,816	938,574	938,740
Balance Sheet								
Total Assets	147,356,000	137,217,000	129,819,000	118,296,000	119,767,000	121,307,000	131,094,000	117,102,000
Total Liabilities	123,069,000	112,619,000	109,337,000	100,588,000	101,420,000	106,687,000	115,116,000	103,596,000
Stockholders' Equity	24,287,000	24,598,000	20,482,000	17,708,000	18,347,000	14,620,000	15,978,000	13,506,000
Shares Outstanding	775,757	780,910	811,620	848,760	884,890	918,826	935,572	932,620
Statistical Record								
Return on Assets %	3.37	3.45	2.14	2.13	2.45	2.50	2.30	1.80
Return on Equity %	21.19	20.43	13.89	14.05	17.90	20.64	19.39	15.99
Loss Ratio %	64.11	65.73	67.20	66.85	67.83	68.60	69.22	67.52
Net Margin %	13.12	21.25	11.79	12.14	12.98	13.19	11.30	8.86
Price Range	45.84-36.09	44.63-33.57	37.14-27.77	32.99-27.61	33.40-27.90	33.74-24.32	27.35-19.23	29.64-15.73
P/E Ratio	7.71-6.07	7.73-5.82	11.57-8.65	11.30-9.46	10.28-8.58	9.98-7.20	8.94-6.28	14.18-7.53
Average Yield %	2.22	2.23	2.45	2.56	2.44	2.45	2.89	2.62

Address: 1932 Wynnton Road, Columbus, GA 31999 **Telephone:** 706-323-3431 **Fax:** 706-596-3488	**Web Site:** www.aflac.com **Officers:** Daniel P. Amos - Chairman, President, Chief Executive Officer Frederick John Crawford - Executive Vice President, Chief Financial Officer	**Auditors:** KPMG LLP **Investor Contact:** 706-596-3264 **Transfer Agents:** Aflac Incorporated Shareholder Services, Columbus, GA

AGCO CORP.

Exchange	Symbol	Price	52Wk Range	Yield	P/E
NYS	AGCO	$60.72 (6/29/2018)	75.48-59.23	0.99	22.08

*7 Year Price Score 103.43 *NYSE Composite Index=100   *12 Month Price Score 91.09

Interim Earnings (Per Share)

Qtr.	Mar	Jun	Sep	Dec
2015	0.34	1.22	0.77	0.73
2016	0.09	0.61	0.50	0.76
2017	(0.13)	1.14	0.76	0.55
2018	0.30	...	...	...

Interim Dividends (Per Share)

Amt	Decl	Ex	Rec	Pay
0.14Q	07/12/2017	08/11/2017	08/15/2017	09/15/2017
0.14Q	10/26/2017	11/14/2017	11/15/2017	12/15/2017
0.15Q	01/25/2018	02/14/2018	02/15/2018	03/15/2018
0.15Q	04/26/2018	05/14/2018	05/15/2018	06/15/2018

Indicated Div: $0.60

Valuation Analysis

		Institutional Holding	
Forecast EPS	$3.80 (06/13/2018)	No of Institutions	571
Market Cap	$4.8 Billion	Shares	85,637,128
Book Value	$3.1 Billion	% Held	82.26
Price/Book	1.58		
Price/Sales	0.56		

TRADING VOLUME (thousand shares)

Business Summary: Industrial Machinery & Equipment (MIC: 7.2.1 SIC: 3523 NAIC: 333111)

AGCO is a manufacturer and distributor of agricultural equipment and related replacement parts. Co. sells a range of agricultural equipment, including tractors, combines, hay tools, sprayers, forage equipment, seeding and tillage equipment, implements, and grain storage and protein production systems. Co. distributes its products through a combination of over 3,000 independent dealers and distributors as well as Co. utilizes associates and licensees to provide a distribution channel for its products. In addition, Co. provides retail financing through its finance joint ventures with Cooperatieve Centrale Raiffeisen-Boerenleenbank B.A.

Recent Developments: For the quarter ended Mar 31 2018, net income amounted to US$25.0 million versus a net loss of US$8.2 million in the year-earlier quarter. Revenues were US$2.01 billion, up 23.3% from US$1.63 billion the year before. Operating income was US$50.5 million versus US$15.7 million in the prior-year quarter, an increase of 221.7%. Direct operating expenses rose 21.8% to US$1.58 billion from US$1.30 billion in the comparable period the year before. Indirect operating expenses increased 20.0% to US$377.5 million from US$314.6 million in the equivalent prior-year period.

Prospects: Our evaluation of AGCO Corp. as of Jan. 21, 2018 is the result of our systematic analysis on three basic characteristics: earnings strength, relative valuation, and recent stock price movement. The company has produced a positive trend in earnings per share over the past 5 quarters. However, while recent estimates for the company have been mixed, AGCO has posted better than expected results. Based on operating earnings yield, the company is undervalued when compared to all of the companies in our coverage universe. Share price changes over the past year indicates that AGCO will perform well over the near term.

Financial Data
(US$ in Thousands)

	3 Mos	12/31/2017	12/31/2016	12/31/2015	12/31/2014	12/31/2013	12/31/2012	12/31/2011
Earnings Per Share	2.75	2.32	1.96	3.06	4.36	6.01	5.30	5.95
Cash Flow Per Share	5.88	7.27	4.53	6.03	4.69	8.19	6.84	7.59
Tang Book Value Per Share	10.68	10.55	9.97	14.51	19.09	23.27	17.20	11.67
Dividends Per Share	0.570	0.560	0.520	0.480	0.440	0.400	...	...
Dividend Payout %	20.73	24.14	26.53	15.69	10.09	6.66	...	...
Income Statement								
Total Revenue	2,007,500	8,306,500	7,410,500	7,467,300	9,723,700	10,786,900	9,962,200	8,773,200
EBITDA	114,100	608,700	531,600	584,900	877,800	1,120,000	888,300	764,700
Depn & Amortn	75,100	279,800	274,600	260,100	280,400	259,400	229,900	173,500
Income Before Taxes	28,700	283,800	204,900	279,400	539,000	802,600	600,800	561,000
Income Taxes	11,400	133,600	92,200	72,500	187,700	258,500	137,900	24,600
Net Income	24,300	186,400	160,100	266,400	410,400	597,200	522,100	583,300
Average Shares	80,500	80,200	81,700	87,100	94,200	99,400	98,600	98,100
Balance Sheet								
Current Assets	4,061,300	3,627,700	3,165,700	2,898,300	3,527,900	4,517,100	3,954,700	3,662,800
Total Assets	8,448,900	7,971,700	7,168,400	6,501,300	7,395,900	8,438,800	7,721,800	7,257,200
Current Liabilities	2,715,500	2,650,600	2,144,900	2,185,400	2,216,900	2,812,000	2,464,800	2,205,500
Long-Term Obligations	1,989,000	1,618,100	1,610,000	928,800	997,600	938,500	1,035,600	1,409,700
Total Liabilities	5,396,000	4,942,100	4,392,300	3,663,000	3,947,400	4,428,600	4,257,100	4,262,000
Stockholders' Equity	3,052,900	3,029,600	2,776,100	2,838,300	3,448,500	4,010,200	3,464,700	2,995,200
Shares Outstanding	79,525	79,553	79,465	83,814	89,146	97,362	96,815	97,194
Statistical Record								
Return on Assets %	2.79	2.46	2.34	3.83	5.18	7.39	6.95	9.19
Return on Equity %	7.53	6.42	5.69	8.47	11.00	15.98	16.12	20.63
EBITDA Margin %	5.68	7.33	7.17	7.83	9.03	10.38	8.92	8.72
Net Margin %	1.21	2.24	2.16	3.57	4.22	5.54	5.24	6.65
Asset Turnover	1.10	1.10	1.08	1.07	1.23	1.33	1.33	1.38
Current Ratio	1.50	1.37	1.48	1.33	1.59	1.61	1.60	1.66
Debt to Equity	0.65	0.53	0.58	0.33	0.29	0.23	0.30	0.47
Price Range	75.48-58.03	75.48-58.03	60.66-44.02	57.87-42.72	59.19-42.08	64.42-48.02	53.73-38.56	58.13-32.39
P/E Ratio	27.45-21.10	32.53-25.01	30.95-22.46	18.91-13.96	13.58-9.65	10.72-7.99	10.14-7.28	9.77-5.44
Average Yield %	0.83	0.84	1.03	0.98	0.87	0.72	...	...

Address: 4205 River Green Parkway, Duluth, GA 30096 Telephone: 770-813-9200	Web Site: www.agcocorp.com Officers: Martin H. Richenhagen - Chairman, President, Chief Executive Officer Andrew H. Beck - Senior Vice President, Chief Financial Officer, Principal Accounting Officer	Auditors: KPMG LLP Investor Contact: 770-232-8229 Transfer Agents: Computershare Trust Company, N.A., Canton, MA

AGILENT TECHNOLOGIES, INC.

Exchange	Symbol	Price	52Wk Range	Yield	P/E
NYS	A	$61.84 (6/29/2018)	74.82-58.57	0.96	85.89

*7 Year Price Score 127.57 *NYSE Composite Index=100 *12 Month Price Score 96.53

Interim Earnings (Per Share)

Qtr.	Jan	Apr	Jul	Oct
2014-15	0.21	0.25	0.31	0.43
2015-16	0.37	0.28	0.38	0.38
2016-17	0.52	0.50	0.54	0.54
2017-18	(0.99)	0.63	...	...

Interim Dividends (Per Share)

Amt	Decl	Ex	Rec	Pay
0.132Q	09/20/2017	10/02/2017	10/03/2017	10/25/2017
0.149Q	11/15/2017	12/29/2017	01/02/2018	01/24/2018
0.149Q	03/21/2018	04/02/2018	04/03/2018	04/25/2018
0.149Q	05/16/2018	07/02/2018	07/03/2018	07/25/2018

Indicated Div: $0.60

Valuation Analysis | **Institutional Holding**

Forecast EPS	$2.67 (06/13/2018)	No of Institutions	1000
Market Cap	$19.9 Billion	Shares	352,006,016
Book Value	$4.6 Billion	% Held	78.76
Price/Book	4.32		
Price/Sales	4.22		

Business Summary: Medical Instruments & Equipment (MIC: 4.3.1 SIC: 3826 NAIC: 334516)

Agilent Technologies engages in life sciences, diagnostics and applied chemical markets, providing application focused solutions including instruments, software, services and consumables. Co.'s life sciences and applied markets business provides solutions including instruments and software to identify, quantify and analyze the physical and biological properties of substances and products, and interrogate samples at the molecular level. The diagnostics and genomics business includes genomics, nucleic acid contract manufacturing and the pathology, companion diagnostics and reagent partnership businesses. The CrossLab business spans the entire lab with its consumables and services portfolio.

Recent Developments: For the quarter ended Apr 30 2018, net income increased 25.0% to US$205.0 million from US$164.0 million in the year-earlier quarter. Revenues were US$1.21 billion, up 9.4% from US$1.10 billion the year before. Operating income was US$215.0 million versus US$201.0 million in the prior-year quarter, an increase of 7.0%. Direct operating expenses rose 10.2% to US$562.0 million from US$510.0 million in the comparable period the year before. Indirect operating expenses increased 9.7% to US$429.0 million from US$391.0 million in the equivalent prior-year period.

Prospects: Our evaluation of Agilent Technologies Inc. as of Jan. 21, 2018 is the result of our systematic analysis on three basic characteristics: earnings strength, relative valuation, and recent stock price movement. The company has managed to produce a neutral trend in earnings per share over the past 5 quarters and while recent estimates for the company have remained steady, A has posted better than expected results. Based on operating earnings yield, the company is about fairly valued when compared to all of the companies in our coverage universe. Share price changes over the past year indicates that A will perform well over the near term.

Financial Data

(US$ in Millions)	6 Mos	3 Mos	10/31/2017	10/31/2016	10/31/2015	10/31/2014	10/31/2013	10/31/2012
Earnings Per Share	0.72	0.59	2.10	1.40	1.20	1.49	2.10	3.27
Cash Flow Per Share	3.21	3.06	2.76	2.43	1.47	2.14	3.38	3.52
Tang Book Value Per Share	5.22	5.41	5.79	4.07	4.09	5.17	3.98	3.09
Dividends Per Share	0.562	0.545	0.528	0.460	0.400	0.528	0.460	0.300
Dividend Payout %	78.06	92.37	25.14	32.86	33.33	35.44	21.90	9.17
Income Statement								
Total Revenue	2,417	1,211	4,472	4,202	4,038	6,981	6,782	6,858
EBITDA	581	295	954	700	637	944	1,140	1,306
Depn & Amortn	101	51	94	95	98	194	181	171
Income Before Taxes	460	233	803	544	480	646	859	1,043
Income Taxes	575	553	119	82	42	142	135	(110)
Net Income	(115)	(320)	684	462	401	504	724	1,153
Average Shares	326	323	326	329	335	338	345	353
Balance Sheet								
Current Assets	4,525	4,397	4,169	3,635	3,686	5,500	4,983	4,629
Total Assets	8,784	8,698	8,426	7,802	7,479	10,831	10,686	10,536
Current Liabilities	1,365	1,361	1,263	945	976	1,702	1,602	1,893
Long-Term Obligations	1,800	1,800	1,801	1,912	1,655	2,762	2,699	2,112
Total Liabilities	4,171	4,176	3,595	3,559	3,312	5,533	5,400	5,354
Stockholders' Equity	4,613	4,522	4,831	4,243	4,167	5,298	5,286	5,182
Shares Outstanding	322	286	322	323	331	334	332	346
Statistical Record								
Return on Assets %	2.82	2.37	8.43	6.03	4.38	4.68	6.82	11.74
Return on Equity %	5.28	4.44	15.08	10.96	8.47	9.52	13.83	24.23
EBITDA Margin %	24.04	24.36	21.33	16.66	15.78	13.52	16.81	19.04
Net Margin %	N.M.	N.M.	15.30	10.99	9.93	7.22	10.68	16.81
Asset Turnover	0.56	0.56	0.55	0.55	0.44	0.65	0.64	0.70
Current Ratio	3.32	3.23	3.30	3.85	3.78	3.23	3.11	2.45
Debt to Equity	0.39	0.40	0.37	0.45	0.40	0.52	0.51	0.41
Price Range	74.82-55.77	74.82-48.90	68.03-43.21	48.44-34.80	43.55-33.37	43.57-35.79	37.89-25.56	32.79-23.55
P/E Ratio	103.92-77.46	126.81-82.88	32.40-20.58	34.60-24.86	36.29-27.81	29.24-24.02	18.04-12.17	10.03-7.20
Average Yield %	0.86	0.89	0.95	1.08	1.01	1.31	1.46	1.06

Address: 5301 Stevens Creek Blvd., Santa Clara, CA 95051 Telephone: 408-345-8886	Web Site: www.investor.agilent.com Officers: Michael R. (Mike) McMullen - President, Chief Executive Officer, Senior Vice President, Division Officer Didier Hirsch - Senior Vice President, Chief Financial Officer, Chief Accounting Officer	Auditors: PricewaterhouseCoopers LLP Investor Contact: 408-345-8948 Transfer Agents: ComputerShare Investor Services, Chicago, IL

15

AIR LEASE CORP

Exchange	Symbol	Price	52Wk Range	Yield	P/E
NYS	AL	$41.97 (6/29/2018)	50.34-37.36	0.95	5.95

*7 Year Price Score 108.86 *NYSE Composite Index=100 *12 Month Price Score 98.83

TRADING VOLUME (thousand shares)

Interim Earnings (Per Share)

Qtr.	Mar	Jun	Sep	Dec
2015	0.19	0.70	0.71	0.74
2016	0.85	0.84	0.86	0.89
2017	0.78	0.92	0.90	4.23
2018	1.00	...	...	...

Interim Dividends (Per Share)

Amt	Decl	Ex	Rec	Pay
0.075Q	08/03/2017	09/12/2017	09/13/2017	10/06/2017
0.10Q	11/09/2017	12/13/2017	12/14/2017	01/04/2018
0.10Q	02/22/2018	03/19/2018	03/20/2018	04/06/2018
0.10Q	05/10/2018	06/04/2018	06/05/2018	07/10/2018

Indicated Div: $0.40

Valuation Analysis — **Institutional Holding**

Forecast EPS	$4.59	No of Institutions
	(06/13/2018)	373
Market Cap	$4.4 Billion	Shares
Book Value	$4.2 Billion	97,780,256
Price/Book	1.03	% Held
Price/Sales	2.84	86.20

Business Summary: Miscellaneous Transportation Services (MIC: 7.4.5 SIC: 7359 NAIC: 532411)

Air Lease is an aircraft leasing company. Co. is principally engaged in purchasing new commercial jet transport aircraft directly from aircraft manufacturers, such as The Boeing Company and Airbus S.A.S., and leasing those aircraft to airlines. In addition to its leasing activities, Co. sells aircraft from its operating lease portfolio to third parties, including other leasing companies, financial services companies and airlines. Co. also provides fleet management services to investors and owners of aircraft portfolios. As of Dec 31 2017, Co. owned 244 aircraft, comprised of 188 narrowbody jet aircraft and 56 widebody jet aircraft.

Recent Developments: For the quarter ended Mar 31 2018, net income increased 30.3% to US$110.7 million from US$84.9 million in the year-earlier quarter. Revenues were US$381.2 million, up 5.8% from US$360.2 million the year before. Indirect operating expenses increased 6.0% to US$239.9 million from US$226.3 million in the equivalent prior-year period.

Prospects: Our evaluation of Air Lease Corp as of Jan. 21, 2018 is the result of our systematic analysis on three basic characteristics: earnings strength, relative valuation, and recent stock price movement. The company has managed to produce a neutral trend in earnings per share over the past 5 quarters. However, while recent estimates for the company have been mixed, AL has posted better than expected results. Based on operating earnings yield, the company is undervalued when compared to all of the companies in our coverage universe. Share price changes over the past year indicates that AL will perform well over the near term.

Financial Data

(US$ in Thousands)	3 Mos	12/31/2017	12/31/2016	12/31/2015	12/31/2014	12/31/2013	12/31/2012	12/31/2011
Earnings Per Share	7.05	6.82	3.44	2.34	2.38	1.80	1.28	0.59
Cash Flow Per Share	10.47	10.27	9.90	8.19	7.53	6.44	4.85	2.98
Tang Book Value Per Share	40.65	39.83	32.89	29.44	27.07	24.78	23.04	21.61
Dividends Per Share	0.350	0.325	0.225	0.170	0.130	0.105	...	...
Dividend Payout %	4.96	4.77	6.54	7.26	5.46	5.83	...	...
Income Statement								
Total Revenue	381,209	1,516,380	1,419,055	1,222,840	1,050,493	858,675	655,746	336,741
EBITDA	369,460	1,405,253	1,319,121	1,056,857	952,023	765,849	567,605	252,840
Depn & Amortn	151,176	508,352	452,682	397,760	336,657	280,037	216,219	112,307
Income Before Taxes	141,319	609,530	580,238	392,953	394,776	293,442	203,973	82,841
Income Taxes	30,668	(146,622)	205,313	139,562	138,778	103,031	72,054	29,609
Net Income	110,651	756,152	374,925	253,391	255,998	190,411	131,919	53,232
Average Shares	112,230	111,657	110,798	110,628	110,192	108,963	107,656	90,416
Balance Sheet								
Current Assets	271,624	1,871,058	1,581,478	1,244,238	1,434,891	1,432,504	901,114	783,511
Total Assets	15,944,846	15,614,164	13,975,616	12,355,098	10,774,784	9,332,604	7,353,624	5,164,593
Current Liabilities	281,122	1,165,322	1,113,110	1,069,313	889,124	701,070	502,392	338,802
Long-Term Obligations	9,887,499	9,698,785	8,713,874	7,712,421	6,714,362	5,853,317	4,384,732	2,602,799
Total Liabilities	11,718,223	11,486,722	10,593,429	9,335,186	8,002,722	6,809,170	5,021,003	2,988,310
Stockholders' Equity	4,226,623	4,127,442	3,382,187	3,019,912	2,772,062	2,523,434	2,332,621	2,176,283
Shares Outstanding	103,979	103,621	102,844	102,582	102,392	101,822	101,247	100,714
Statistical Record								
Return on Assets %	5.14	5.11	2.84	2.19	2.55	2.28	2.10	1.43
Return on Equity %	20.35	20.14	11.68	8.75	9.67	7.84	5.84	3.13
EBITDA Margin %	96.92	92.67	92.96	86.43	90.63	89.19	86.56	75.08
Net Margin %	29.03	49.87	26.42	20.72	24.37	22.17	20.12	15.81
Asset Turnover	0.10	0.10	0.11	0.11	0.10	0.10	0.10	0.09
Current Ratio	0.97	1.61	1.42	1.16	1.61	2.04	1.79	2.31
Debt to Equity	2.34	2.35	2.58	2.55	2.42	2.32	1.88	1.20
Price Range	50.34-34.91	48.31-34.64	37.02-22.73	40.21-29.83	42.44-30.27	33.29-21.50	25.58-18.62	29.70-17.83
P/E Ratio	7.14-4.95	7.08-5.08	10.76-6.61	17.18-12.75	17.83-12.72	18.49-11.94	19.98-14.55	50.34-30.22
Average Yield %	0.84	0.84	0.72	0.75	0.48	0.36	0.38	...

Address: 2000 Avenue of the Stars, Suite 1000N, Los Angeles, CA 90067
Telephone: 310-553-0555

Web Site: www.airleasecorp.com
Officers: Steven F. Udvar-Házy - Chairman, Chief Executive Officer John L. Plueger - President, Chief Operating Officer, Chief Executive Officer

Auditors: KPMG LLP
Investor Contact: 310-553-0555
Transfer Agents: American Stock Transfer & Trust Company, LLC, Seattle, WA

AIR PRODUCTS & CHEMICALS INC

Exchange	Symbol	Price	52Wk Range	Yield	P/E	Div Acheiver
NYS	APD	$155.73 (6/29/2018)	174.00-142.13	2.83	30.06	35 Years

*7 Year Price Score 109.09 *NYSE Composite Index=100 *12 Month Price Score 101.77

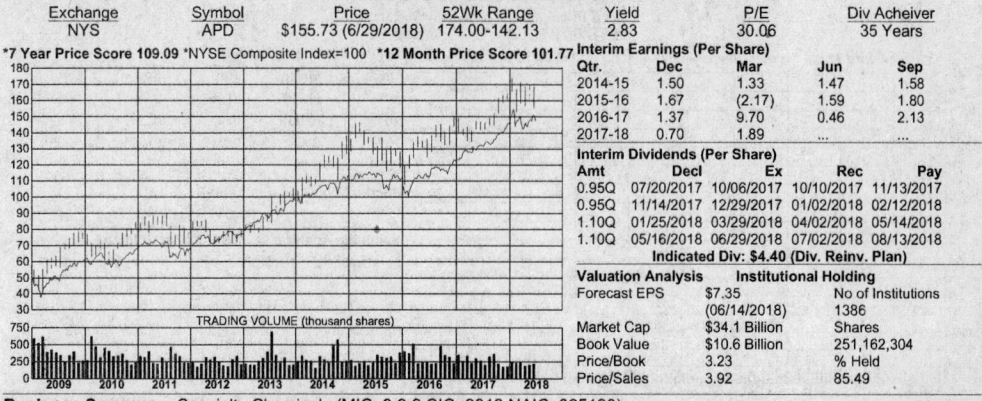

Interim Earnings (Per Share)

Qtr.	Dec	Mar	Jun	Sep
2014-15	1.50	1.33	1.47	1.58
2015-16	1.67	(2.17)	1.59	1.80
2016-17	1.37	9.70	0.46	2.13
2017-18	0.70	1.89	...	...

Interim Dividends (Per Share)

Amt	Decl	Ex	Rec	Pay
0.95Q	07/20/2017	10/06/2017	10/10/2017	11/13/2017
0.95Q	11/14/2017	12/29/2017	01/02/2018	02/12/2018
1.10Q	01/25/2018	03/29/2018	04/02/2018	05/14/2018
1.10Q	05/16/2018	06/29/2018	07/02/2018	08/13/2018

Indicated Div: $4.40 (Div. Reinv. Plan)

Valuation Analysis | **Institutional Holding**

Forecast EPS	$7.35	No of Institutions	
	(06/14/2018)	1386	
Market Cap	$34.1 Billion	Shares	
Book Value	$10.6 Billion	251,162,304	
Price/Book	3.23	% Held	
Price/Sales	3.92	85.49	

Business Summary: Specialty Chemicals (MIC: 8.3.2 SIC: 2813 NAIC: 325120)

Air Products and Chemicals serves energy, electronics, chemicals, metals, and manufacturing customers with solutions that include gases, equipment, and services. Co.'s Industrial Gases business produces atmospheric gases (oxygen, nitrogen, argon, and rare gases); process gases (hydrogen, helium, carbon dioxide, carbon monoxide, syngas, and specialty gases); and equipment for the production or processing of gases, such as air separation units and non-cryogenic generators. Co.'s industrial gases equipment business designs and manufactures equipment for air separation, hydrocarbon recovery and purification, natural gas liquefaction, and liquid helium and liquid hydrogen transport and storage.

Recent Developments: For the quarter ended Mar 31 2018, income from continuing operations increased 36.6% to US$423.6 million from US$310.1 million in the year-earlier quarter. Net income decreased 80.2% to US$423.6 million from US$2.14 billion in the year-earlier quarter. Revenues were US$2.16 billion, up 8.9% from US$1.98 billion the year before. Operating income was US$455.4 million versus US$395.6 million in the prior-year quarter, an increase of 15.1%. Direct operating expenses rose 7.3% to US$1.51 billion from US$1.40 billion in the comparable period the year before. Indirect operating expenses increased 7.2% to US$193.8 million from US$180.7 million in the equivalent prior-year period.

Prospects: Our evaluation of Air Products & Chemicals Inc. as of Jan. 21, 2018 is the result of our systematic analysis on three basic characteristics: earnings strength, relative valuation, and recent stock price movement. The company has produced a positive trend in earnings per share over the past 5 quarters and while recent estimates for the company have been raised by analysts, APD has posted better than expected results. Based on operating earnings yield, the company is about fairly valued when compared to all of the companies in our coverage universe. Share price changes over the past year indicates that APD will perform in line with the market over the near term.

Financial Data

(US$ in Thousands)	6 Mos	3 Mos	09/30/2017	09/30/2016	09/30/2015	09/30/2014	09/30/2013	09/30/2012
Earnings Per Share	5.18	12.99	13.65	2.89	5.88	4.61	4.68	5.44
Cash Flow Per Share	12.68	11.53	11.62	12.48	11.34	10.28	7.41	8.33
Tang Book Value Per Share	42.53	41.09	41.20	25.04	26.05	25.82	22.12	19.38
Dividends Per Share	3.950	3.800	3.620	3.390	3.200	3.020	2.770	2.500
Dividend Payout %	76.25	29.25	26.52	117.30	54.42	65.51	59.19	45.96
Income Statement								
Total Revenue	4,372,300	2,216,600	8,187,600	9,524,400	9,894,900	10,439,000	10,180,400	9,611,700
EBITDA	1,404,900	698,400	2,298,300	2,985,900	2,560,400	2,233,600	2,182,700	2,094,200
Depn & Amortn	467,900	227,900	843,200	893,000	900,400	914,800	864,700	817,200
Income Before Taxes	876,800	440,700	1,336,000	1,983,600	1,561,100	1,203,100	1,182,600	1,158,700
Income Taxes	348,000	291,800	260,900	586,500	415,900	366,000	307,900	287,300
Net Income	571,000	154,600	3,000,400	631,100	1,277,900	991,700	994,200	1,167,300
Average Shares	220,800	220,400	218,000	218,300	217,300	215,200	212,300	214,700
Balance Sheet								
Current Assets	5,396,300	5,355,500	5,876,700	4,317,300	2,910,800	3,294,800	3,439,100	3,415,800
Total Assets	18,511,100	18,208,800	18,467,200	18,055,300	17,438,100	17,779,100	17,850,100	16,941,800
Current Liabilities	1,752,300	1,831,600	2,489,000	3,283,300	3,648,100	2,963,000	3,227,600	2,689,900
Long-Term Obligations	3,442,400	3,414,900	3,402,400	4,918,100	3,949,100	4,824,500	5,056,300	4,584,200
Total Liabilities	7,930,300	7,993,500	8,381,000	10,975,700	10,189,100	10,413,300	10,808,000	10,464,600
Stockholders' Equity	10,580,800	10,215,300	10,086,200	7,079,600	7,249,000	7,365,800	7,042,100	6,477,200
Shares Outstanding	219,193	218,939	218,346	217,350	215,359	213,538	211,179	212,475
Statistical Record								
Return on Assets %	6.28	16.71	16.43	3.55	7.26	5.57	5.72	7.45
Return on Equity %	11.47	32.86	34.96	8.78	17.49	13.77	14.71	18.97
EBITDA Margin %	32.13	31.51	28.07	31.35	25.88	21.40	21.44	21.79
Net Margin %	13.06	6.97	36.65	6.63	12.91	9.50	9.77	12.14
Asset Turnover	0.48	0.50	0.45	0.54	0.56	0.59	0.59	0.61
Current Ratio	3.08	2.92	2.36	1.31	0.80	1.11	1.07	1.27
Debt to Equity	0.33	0.33	0.34	0.69	0.54	0.65	0.72	0.71
Price Range	174.00-134.30	164.62-134.30	151.53-132.26	145.52-107.53	146.19-110.04	126.03-94.84	101.71-71.27	85.68-68.29
P/E Ratio	33.59-25.93	12.67-10.34	11.10-9.69	50.35-37.21	24.86-18.71	27.34-20.57	21.73-15.23	15.75-12.55
Average Yield %	2.58	2.58	2.54	2.68	2.43	2.74	3.30	3.20

Address: 7201 Hamilton Boulevard, Allentown, PA 18195-1501
Telephone: 610-481-4911
Fax: 610-481-5900

Web Site: www.airproducts.com
Officers: Seifollah (Seifi) Ghasemi - Chairman, President, Chief Executive Officer M. Scott Crocco - Chief Financial Officer, Executive Vice President, Senior Vice President, Vice President, Controller, Principal Accounting Officer

Auditors: KPMG LLP
Investor Contact: 610-481-7461
Transfer Agents: Broadridge Corporate Issuer Solutions, Inc., Brentwood, NY

AK STEEL HOLDING CORP.

Exchange	Symbol	Price	52Wk Range	Yield	P/E
NYS	AKS	$4.34 (6/29/2018)	6.78-4.14	N/A	N/A

*7 Year Price Score 72.80 *NYSE Composite Index=100 *12 Month Price Score 87.18

Interim Earnings (Per Share)

Qtr.	Mar	Jun	Sep	Dec
2015	(1.72)	(0.36)	0.04	(0.81)
2016	(0.08)	0.08	0.21	(0.29)
2017	0.19	0.19	(0.02)	(0.35)
2018	0.09	...	...	...

Interim Dividends (Per Share)

No Dividends Paid

Valuation Analysis — **Institutional Holding**

Forecast EPS	$0.76 (06/13/2018)	No of Institutions	420
Market Cap	$1.4 Billion	Shares	
Book Value	N/A	248,137,760	
Price/Book	N/A	% Held	
Price/Sales	0.22	71.70	

TRADING VOLUME (thousand shares)

Business Summary: Non-Precious Metals (MIC: 8.2.2 SIC: 3312 NAIC: 331111)

AK Steel Holding is a producer of flat-rolled carbon, stainless and electrical steels and tubular products through its subsidiary, AK Steel Corporation. Co.'s operations produce flat-rolled carbon to automotive manufacturers, stainless steels to manufacturers and their suppliers in the automotive industry and to manufacturers of food handling, chemical processing, pollution control, medical as well as health equipment, and electrical steels to manufacturers of power transmission and distribution transformers; in sheet and strip form, and carbon and stainless steel that Co. finishes into welded steel tubing. Co. also produces metallurgical coal through its AK Coal Resources, Inc. subsidiary.

Recent Developments: For the quarter ended Mar 31 2018, net income decreased 55.5% to US$44.8 million from US$100.6 million in the year-earlier quarter. Revenues were US$1.66 billion, up 8.2% from US$1.53 billion the year before. Operating income was US$63.6 million versus US$129.7 million in the prior-year quarter, a decrease of 51.0%. Direct operating expenses rose 14.6% to US$1.46 billion from US$1.28 billion in the comparable period the year before. Indirect operating expenses increased 3.8% to US$131.6 million from US$126.8 million in the equivalent prior-year period.

Prospects: Our evaluation of AK Steel Holding Corp. as of Jan. 21, 2018 is the result of our systematic analysis on three basic characteristics: earnings strength, relative valuation, and recent stock price movement. The company has suffered a very negative trend in earnings per share over the past 5 quarters and while recent estimates for the company have been mixed, AKS has posted results that fell short of analysts expectations. Based on operating earnings yield, the company is about fairly valued when compared to all of the companies in our coverage universe. Share price changes over the past year indicates that AKS will perform very poorly over the near term.

Financial Data (US$ in Thousands)	3 Mos	12/31/2017	12/31/2016	12/31/2015	12/31/2014	12/31/2013	12/31/2012	12/31/2011
Earnings Per Share	(0.09)	0.02	(0.03)	(2.86)	(0.65)	(0.34)	(9.06)	(1.41)
Cash Flow Per Share	0.72	0.63	1.32	1.13	(2.18)	(0.81)	(2.39)	(1.64)
Tang Book Value Per Share	...	...	...	...	...	...	...	3.19
Dividends Per Share	...	...	...	...	...	...	0.100	0.200
Income Statement								
Total Revenue	1,658,900	6,080,500	5,882,500	6,692,900	6,505,700	5,570,400	5,933,700	6,468,000
EBITDA	142,400	428,900	441,900	6,200	320,200	324,500	70,100	(21,600)
Depn & Amortn	64,900	226,000	216,600	216,000	201,900	190,100	192,000	185,000
Income Before Taxes	39,900	50,600	61,400	(382,800)	(26,400)	7,000	(208,600)	(254,100)
Income Taxes	(4,900)	(17,000)	3,200	63,400	7,700	(10,400)	790,000	(94,000)
Net Income	28,700	6,200	(7,800)	(509,000)	(96,900)	(46,800)	(1,027,300)	(155,600)
Average Shares	316,000	319,700	230,000	177,200	148,100	135,800	113,000	109,800
Balance Sheet								
Current Assets	2,094,700	1,833,900	1,823,700	1,806,200	2,025,700	1,273,200	1,442,700	1,274,400
Total Assets	4,457,700	4,296,100	4,036,000	4,084,400	4,858,500	3,605,700	3,903,100	4,449,900
Current Liabilities	1,002,400	1,001,000	865,300	1,042,600	1,125,200	831,400	812,400	1,137,100
Long-Term Obligations	2,103,300	2,110,100	1,816,600	2,354,100	2,452,500	1,506,200	1,411,200	650,000
Total Liabilities	4,476,800	4,512,100	4,308,200	5,062,000	5,351,000	3,826,700	4,408,400	4,061,400
Stockholders' Equity	(19,100)	(216,000)	(272,200)	(977,600)	(492,500)	(221,000)	(505,300)	388,500
Shares Outstanding	315,279	314,884	314,160	177,893	177,215	136,380	135,944	110,284
Statistical Record								
Return on Assets %	N.M.	0.15	N.M.	N.M.	N.M.	N.M.	N.M.	N.M.
EBITDA Margin %	8.58	7.05	7.51	0.09	4.92	5.83	1.18	N.M.
Net Margin %	1.73	0.10	N.M.	N.M.	N.M.	N.M.	N.M.	N.M.
Asset Turnover	1.45	1.46	1.44	1.50	1.54	1.48	1.42	1.50
Current Ratio	2.09	1.83	2.11	1.73	1.80	1.53	1.78	1.12
Debt to Equity	...	...	...	...	...	...	...	1.67
Price Range	7.65-4.14	11.11-4.14	10.95-1.83	5.97-2.04	11.19-5.20	8.20-2.82	10.04-3.57	17.61-5.77
P/E Ratio	...	555.50-207.00	...	...	...	...	...	...
Average Yield %	...	...	...	...	...	...	1.60	1.62

Address: 9227 Centre Pointe Drive, West Chester, OH 45069
Telephone: 513-425-5000
Fax: 513-425-5220

Web Site: www.aksteel.com
Officers: Kirk W. Reich - President, Vice President, Chief Operating Officer, Division Officer Roger K. Newport - Chief Executive Officer, Executive Vice President, Senior Vice President, Vice President, Vice President, Chief Financial Officer

Auditors: Ernst & Young LLP
Investor Contact: 513-425-5270
Transfer Agents: Computershare Investor Services, LLC, Canton, MA

ALASKA AIR GROUP, INC.

Exchange	Symbol	Price	52Wk Range	Yield	P/E
NYS	ALK	$60.39 (6/29/2018)	94.63-57.75	2.12	7.96

*7 Year Price Score 108.77 *NYSE Composite Index=100 *12 Month Price Score 87.28

Interim Earnings (Per Share)

Qtr.	Mar	Jun	Sep	Dec
2015	1.12	1.79	2.14	1.51
2016	1.46	2.10	2.07	0.91
2017	0.79	2.38	2.14	3.04
2018	0.03	...	...	...

Interim Dividends (Per Share)

Amt	Decl	Ex	Rec	Pay
0.30Q	08/04/2017	08/18/2017	08/22/2017	09/07/2017
0.30Q	11/03/2017	11/20/2017	11/21/2017	12/07/2017
0.32Q	01/25/2018	02/16/2018	02/20/2018	03/08/2018
0.32Q	05/04/2018	05/21/2018	05/22/2018	06/07/2018

Indicated Div: $1.28

Valuation Analysis   Institutional Holding

Forecast EPS	$4.73	No of Institutions
	(06/13/2018)	727
Market Cap	$7.4 Billion	Shares
Book Value	$3.4 Billion	120,926,968
Price/Book	2.17	% Held
Price/Sales	0.93	84.97

Business Summary: Airlines/Air Freight (MIC: 7.4.4 SIC: 4512 NAIC: 481111)

Alaska Air Group is a holding company. Co.'s Alaska Airlines, Inc. (Alaska) and Virgin America Inc. subsidiaries operate fleets of passenger jets (mainline operations). Alaska also contracts with Co.'s Horizon Air Industries, Inc (Horizon) subsidiary, SkyWest Airlines, Inc. and Peninsula Airways, Inc. for regional capacity. Horizon operates a fleet of turboprop aircraft and sells its capacity to Alaska under a capacity purchase arrangement. Co.'s mainline operations provide passenger service from the western U.S. throughout the contiguous U.S., Alaska, Hawaii, Canada, Mexico, Costa Rica and Cuba; and regional operations carry passengers mainly in Washington, Oregon, Idaho and California.

Recent Developments: For the quarter ended Mar 31 2018, net income decreased 95.7% to US$4.0 million from US$93.0 million in the year-earlier quarter. Revenues were US$1.83 billion, up 5.3% from US$1.74 billion the year before. Operating income was US$29.0 million versus US$157.0 million in the prior-year quarter, a decrease of 81.5%. Direct operating expenses rose 16.5% to US$884.0 million from US$759.0 million in the comparable period the year before. Indirect operating expenses increased 11.5% to US$919.0 million from US$824.0 million in the equivalent prior-year period.

Prospects: Our evaluation of Alaska Air Group Inc. as of Jan. 21, 2018 is the result of our systematic analysis on three basic characteristics: earnings strength, relative valuation, and recent stock price movement. The company has generated a negative trend in earnings per share over the past 5 quarters. However, while recent estimates for the company have been mixed, ALK has posted results that fell short of analysts expectations. Based on operating earnings yield, the company is undervalued when compared to all of the companies in our coverage universe. Share price changes over the past year indicates that ALK will perform in line with the market over the near term.

Financial Data
(US$ in Thousands)

	3 Mos	12/31/2017	12/31/2016	12/31/2015	12/31/2014	12/31/2013	12/31/2012	12/31/2011
Earnings Per Share	7.59	8.35	6.54	6.56	4.42	3.58	2.20	1.67
Cash Flow Per Share	11.58	12.90	11.19	12.34	7.60	7.01	5.31	4.85
Tang Book Value Per Share	11.06	13.37	6.92	19.26	16.18	14.76	10.10	8.27
Dividends Per Share	1.220	1.200	1.100	0.800	0.500	0.200	...	...
Dividend Payout %	16.07	14.37	16.82	12.20	11.31	5.59	...	...
Income Statement								
Total Revenue	1,832,000	7,933,000	5,931,000	5,598,000	5,368,000	5,156,000	4,657,000	4,317,800
EBITDA	111,000	1,631,000	1,711,000	1,619,000	1,276,000	1,103,000	805,000	693,500
Depn & Amortn	94,000	372,000	363,000	320,000	294,000	270,000	264,000	246,900
Income Before Taxes	6,000	1,207,000	1,345,000	1,312,000	975,000	816,000	514,000	393,700
Income Taxes	2,000	173,000	531,000	464,000	370,000	308,000	198,000	149,200
Net Income	4,000	1,034,000	814,000	848,000	605,000	508,000	316,000	244,500
Average Shares	123,630	123,854	124,389	129,372	136,801	141,878	143,568	146,840
Balance Sheet								
Current Assets	2,114,000	2,146,000	2,050,000	1,663,000	1,756,000	1,762,000	1,737,000	1,595,500
Total Assets	10,848,000	10,740,000	9,962,000	6,533,000	6,181,000	5,838,000	5,505,000	5,195,000
Current Liabilities	2,992,000	2,700,000	2,535,000	1,806,000	1,671,000	1,580,000	1,501,000	1,509,600
Long-Term Obligations	2,062,000	2,262,000	2,645,000	571,000	686,000	754,000	871,000	1,099,000
Total Liabilities	7,409,000	7,019,000	7,031,000	4,122,000	4,054,000	3,809,000	4,084,000	4,021,800
Stockholders' Equity	3,439,000	3,721,000	2,931,000	2,411,000	2,127,000	2,029,000	1,421,000	1,173,200
Shares Outstanding	123,350	123,060	123,328	125,175	131,481	137,491	140,753	141,899
Statistical Record								
Return on Assets %	8.88	9.99	9.84	13.34	10.07	8.96	5.89	4.79
Return on Equity %	29.10	31.09	30.39	37.37	29.11	29.45	24.30	21.46
EBITDA Margin %	6.06	20.56	28.85	28.92	23.77	21.39	17.29	16.06
Net Margin %	0.22	13.03	13.72	15.15	11.27	9.85	6.79	5.66
Asset Turnover	0.76	0.77	0.72	0.88	0.89	0.91	0.87	0.85
Current Ratio	0.71	0.79	0.81	0.92	1.05	1.12	1.16	1.06
Debt to Equity	0.60	0.61	0.90	0.24	0.32	0.37	0.61	0.94
Price Range	94.63-61.49	100.24-61.68	91.56-55.66	86.33-58.77	59.77-36.59	39.09-21.55	22.46-16.10	19.13-12.83
P/E Ratio	12.47-8.10	12.00-7.39	14.00-8.51	13.16-8.96	13.52-8.28	10.92-6.02	10.21-7.32	11.45-7.68
Average Yield %	1.59	1.43	1.53	1.12	1.06	1.06	...	...

Address: 19300 International Boulevard, Seattle, WA 98188
Telephone: 206-392-5040

Web Site: www.alaskaair.com
Officers: Bradley D. Tilden - Chairman, Chief Executive Officer Brandon S. Pedersen - Executive Vice President, Vice President, Chief Financial Officer, Controller

Auditors: KPMG LLP
Investor Contact: 206-392-5260
Transfer Agents: Computershare Trust Company N.A., Providence, RI

ALBEMARLE CORP.

Exchange	Symbol	Price	52Wk Range	Yield	P/E	Div Acheiver
NYS	ALB	$94.33 (6/29/2018)	144.58-88.96	1.42	77.32	23 Years

*7 Year Price Score 127.36 *NYSE Composite Index=100 ***12 Month Price Score 82.75**

TRADING VOLUME (thousand shares)

Interim Earnings (Per Share)

Qtr.	Mar	Jun	Sep	Dec
2015	0.40	0.46	0.58	1.56
2016	2.02	(2.78)	1.13	5.31
2017	0.45	0.92	1.06	(1.94)
2018	1.18	...	...	...

Interim Dividends (Per Share)

Amt	Decl	Ex	Rec	Pay
0.32Q	07/10/2017	09/14/2017	09/15/2017	10/02/2017
0.32Q	11/06/2017	12/14/2017	12/15/2017	01/02/2018
0.335Q	02/23/2018	03/14/2018	03/15/2018	04/02/2018
0.335Q	05/08/2018	06/14/2018	06/15/2018	07/02/2018

Indicated Div: $1.34 (Div. Reinv. Plan)

Valuation Analysis | **Institutional Holding**

Forecast EPS	$5.26	No of Institutions
	(06/11/2018)	814
Market Cap	$10.4 Billion	Shares
Book Value	$3.8 Billion	116,753,976
Price/Book	2.75	% Held
Price/Sales	3.29	68.76

Business Summary: Specialty Chemicals (MIC: 8.3.2 SIC: 2821 NAIC: 325211)

Albemarle is a developer, manufacturer and marketer of chemicals across a range of end markets including, among others, the petroleum refining, consumer electronics, energy storage, construction, automotive, lubricants, and pharmaceuticals. Co.'s segments include: Lithium and Advanced Materials, which consisted of Lithium and Performance Catalyst Solutions; Bromine Specialties, which includes products used in fire safety solutions and other specialty chemicals applications; and Refining Solutions, which consisted of two main product lines: Clean Fuels Technologies composed of hydroprocessing catalysts, and Heavy Oil Upgrading composed of fluidized catalytic cracking catalysts and additives.

Recent Developments: For the quarter ended Mar 31 2018, net income increased 121.7% to US$138.9 million from US$62.7 million in the year-earlier quarter. Revenues were US$821.6 million, up 13.8% from US$722.1 million the year before. Operating income was US$182.6 million versus US$121.7 million in the prior-year quarter, an increase of 50.1%. Direct operating expenses rose 10.6% to US$516.7 million from US$467.1 million in the comparable period the year before. Indirect operating expenses decreased 8.2% to US$122.4 million from US$133.3 million in the equivalent prior-year period.

Prospects: Our evaluation of Albemarle Corp. as of Jan. 21, 2018 is the result of our systematic analysis on three basic characteristics: earnings strength, relative valuation, and recent stock price movement. The company has enjoyed a very positive trend in earnings per share over the past 5 quarters and while recent estimates for the company have been mixed, ALB has posted better than expected results. Based on operating earnings yield, the company is about fairly valued when compared to all of the companies in our coverage universe. Share price changes over the past year indicates that ALB will perform very well over the near term.

Financial Data

(US$ in Thousands)	3 Mos	12/31/2017	12/31/2016	12/31/2015	12/31/2014	12/31/2013	12/31/2012	12/31/2011
Earnings Per Share	1.22	0.49	5.68	3.00	1.69	4.90	3.47	4.77
Cash Flow Per Share	3.10	2.74	6.51	3.24	6.26	5.16	5.47	5.38
Tang Book Value Per Share	15.59	14.86	16.89	N.M.	13.74	15.68	16.45	13.37
Dividends Per Share	1.295	1.280	1.220	1.160	1.100	0.960	0.800	0.670
Dividend Payout %	106.15	261.22	21.48	38.67	65.09	19.59	23.05	14.05
Income Statement								
Total Revenue	821,629	3,071,976	2,677,203	3,651,335	2,445,548	2,616,416	2,745,420	2,869,005
EBITDA	202,477	731,648	759,245	671,609	352,437	675,286	495,693	671,797
Depn & Amortn	50,330	169,500	178,800	180,700	97,900	99,300	88,300	83,600
Income Before Taxes	138,609	446,798	515,264	358,187	213,179	544,427	374,593	550,623
Income Taxes	20,361	431,817	96,263	29,122	18,484	136,322	82,533	130,014
Net Income	131,760	54,850	643,675	334,906	133,316	413,171	311,536	436,280
Average Shares	111,867	112,380	113,239	111,556	79,102	84,322	89,884	91,522
Balance Sheet								
Current Assets	2,158,725	2,477,563	3,306,618	1,831,003	3,348,850	1,482,915	1,407,313	1,355,620
Total Assets	7,556,340	7,750,772	8,161,207	9,615,014	5,223,103	3,584,797	3,437,291	3,203,824
Current Liabilities	868,860	1,200,925	1,140,103	1,616,685	1,139,886	436,363	385,009	401,178
Long-Term Obligations	1,436,852	1,415,360	2,121,718	3,174,674	2,223,035	1,054,310	686,588	749,257
Total Liabilities	3,756,030	4,076,223	4,366,145	6,360,622	3,863,638	1,957,436	1,603,693	1,612,547
Stockholders' Equity	3,800,310	3,674,549	3,795,062	3,254,392	1,359,465	1,627,361	1,833,598	1,591,277
Shares Outstanding	110,756	110,546	112,523	112,219	78,030	80,052	88,899	88,841
Statistical Record								
Return on Assets %	1.81	0.69	7.22	4.51	3.03	11.77	9.36	13.91
Return on Equity %	3.64	1.47	18.21	14.52	8.93	23.88	18.14	29.01
EBITDA Margin %	24.64	23.82	28.36	18.39	14.41	25.81	18.06	23.42
Net Margin %	16.04	1.79	24.04	9.17	5.45	15.79	11.35	15.21
Asset Turnover	0.43	0.39	0.30	0.49	0.56	0.75	0.82	0.91
Current Ratio	2.48	2.06	2.90	1.13	2.94	3.40	3.66	3.38
Debt to Equity	0.38	0.39	0.56	0.98	1.64	0.65	0.37	0.47
Price Range	144.58-89.56	144.58-88.05	91.80-47.71	64.38-41.78	72.62-53.16	69.55-57.75	67.70-51.56	71.11-39.00
P/E Ratio	118.51-73.41	295.06-179.69	16.16-8.40	21.46-13.93	42.97-31.46	14.19-11.79	19.51-14.86	14.91-8.18
Average Yield %	1.09	1.11	1.65	2.16	1.71	1.50	1.34	1.17

Address: 4350 Congress Street, Suite 700, Charlotte, NC 28209 Telephone: 980-299-5700	Web Site: www.albemarle.com Officers: Luther C. Kissam - Chairman, President, President (frmr), Chief Executive Officer, Principal Financial Officer, Principal Executive Officer Scott A. Tozier - Executive Vice President, Chief Financial Officer, Senior Vice President, Chief Risk Officer, Principal Accounting Officer, Chief Accounting Officer	Auditors: PricewaterhouseCoopers LLP Investor Contact: 225-388-8011 Transfer Agents: Wells Fargo Bank, N.A. Shareowner Services, St. Paul, MN

ALCOA CORPORATION

Exchange	Symbol	Price	52Wk Range	Yield	P/E
NYS	AA	$46.88 (6/29/2018)	60.23-32.65	N/A	62.51

*7 Year Price Score N/A   *NYSE Composite Index=100   ***12 Month Price Score 103.64**

TRADING VOLUME (thousand shares)

Interim Earnings (Per Share)

Qtr.	Mar	Jun	Sep	Dec
2016	(1.15)	(0.29)	(0.04)	(0.76)
2017	1.21	0.40	0.60	(1.05)
2018	0.80	...	...	...

Interim Dividends (Per Share)

No Dividends Paid

Valuation Analysis | Institutional Holding

Forecast EPS	$4.14	No of Institutions
	(06/14/2018)	536
Market Cap	$8.7 Billion	Shares
Book Value	$5.4 Billion	166,810,704
Price/Book	1.63	% Held
Price/Sales	0.72	N/A

Business Summary: Metal Products (MIC: 8.2.3 SIC: 3353 NAIC: 331315)

Alcoa is a vertically integrated aluminum company which comprised of bauxite mining, alumina refining, aluminum production (smelting, casting, and rolling), and energy generation. As of Dec 31 2017, Co. had more than 40 operating locations (through direct and indirect ownership) in 10 countries around the world, primarily in Australia, Brazil, Canada, Europe, and the United States.

Recent Developments: For the quarter ended Mar 31 2018, net income decreased 11.0% to US$274.0 million from US$308.0 million in the year-earlier quarter. Revenues were US$3.09 billion, up 16.4% from US$2.66 billion the year before. Direct operating expenses rose 17.7% to US$2.38 billion from US$2.02 billion in the comparable period the year before. Indirect operating expenses increased 38.8% to US$297.0 million from US$214.0 million in the equivalent prior-year period.

Prospects: Our evaluation of Alcoa Corporation as of Jan. 21, 2018 is the result of our systematic analysis on three basic characteristics: earnings strength, relative valuation, and recent stock price movement. The company has suffered a very negative trend in earnings per share over the past 5 quarters and while recent estimates for the company have been raised by analysts, AA has posted results that fell short of analysts expectations. Based on operating earnings yield, the company is undervalued when compared to all of the companies in our coverage universe. Share price changes over the past year indicates that AA will perform in line with the market over the near term.

Financial Data
(US$ in Thousands)

	3 Mos	12/31/2017	12/31/2016	12/31/2015	12/31/2014	12/31/2013
Earnings Per Share	0.75	1.16	(2.19)	...	...	...
Cash Flow Per Share	6.48	6.65	(1.69)	...	...	...
Tang Book Value Per Share	28.79	24.42	30.91	...	...	...
Income Statement						
Total Revenue	3,090,000	11,652,000	9,318,000	11,199,000	13,147,000	12,573,000
EBITDA	632,000	2,015,000	799,000	713,000	1,200,000	(1,416,000)
Depn & Amortn	194,000	752,000	718,000	780,000	954,000	1,026,000
Income Before Taxes	412,000	1,159,000	(162,000)	(337,000)	(63,000)	(2,747,000)
Income Taxes	138,000	600,000	184,000	402,000	284,000	123,000
Net Income	150,000	217,000	(400,000)	(863,000)	(256,000)	(2,909,000)
Average Shares	188,000	187,000	183,000	...	...	...
Balance Sheet						
Current Assets	4,149,000	4,238,000	3,181,000	2,566,000	2,917,000	...
Total Assets	17,096,000	17,447,000	16,741,000	16,413,000	18,680,000	...
Current Liabilities	2,976,000	3,252,000	2,821,000	2,404,000	2,735,000	...
Long-Term Obligations	1,445,000	1,388,000	1,424,000	207,000	313,000	...
Total Liabilities	11,728,000	12,924,000	11,087,000	6,971,000	8,081,000	...
Stockholders' Equity	5,368,000	4,523,000	5,654,000	9,442,000	10,599,000	...
Shares Outstanding	186,455	185,200	182,930	...	...	...
Statistical Record						
Return on Assets %	0.83	1.27	N.M.	N.M.	...	...
Return on Equity %	2.53	4.26	N.M.	N.M.	...	...
EBITDA Margin %	20.45	17.29	8.57	6.37	9.13	N.M.
Net Margin %	4.85	1.86	N.M.	N.M.	N.M.	N.M.
Asset Turnover	0.71	0.68	0.56	0.64	...	...
Current Ratio	1.39	1.30	1.13	1.07	1.07	...
Debt to Equity	0.27	0.31	0.25	0.02	0.03	...
Price Range	56.99-29.69	54.14-28.83	32.05-22.91	...	...	...
P/E Ratio	75.99-39.59	46.67-24.85	...	...	...	...

Address: 201 Isabella Street, Suite 500, Pittsburgh, PA 15212-5858
Telephone: 412-315-2900

Web Site: www.alcoa.com
Officers: Roy C. Harvey - President, Chief Executive Officer William F. Oplinger - Executive Vice President, Chief Financial Officer

Auditors: PricewaterhouseCoopers LLP
Transfer Agents: Computershare Trust Company, N.A.

21

ALEXANDER & BALDWIN INC (REIT)

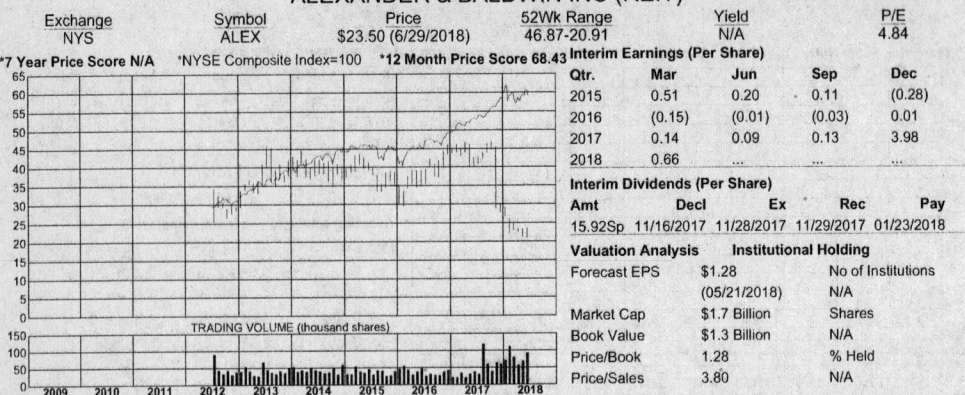

Exchange	Symbol	Price	52Wk Range	Yield	P/E
NYS	ALEX	$23.50 (6/29/2018)	46.87-20.91	N/A	4.84

*7 Year Price Score N/A *NYSE Composite Index=100 *12 Month Price Score 68.43

Interim Earnings (Per Share)

Qtr.	Mar	Jun	Sep	Dec
2015	0.51	0.20	0.11	(0.28)
2016	(0.15)	(0.01)	(0.03)	0.01
2017	0.14	0.09	0.13	3.98
2018	0.66	...	...	...

Interim Dividends (Per Share)

Amt	Decl	Ex	Rec	Pay
15.92Sp	11/16/2017	11/28/2017	11/29/2017	01/23/2018

Valuation Analysis **Institutional Holding**

Forecast EPS	$1.28	No of Institutions
	(05/21/2018)	N/A
Market Cap	$1.7 Billion	Shares
Book Value	$1.3 Billion	N/A
Price/Book	1.28	% Held
Price/Sales	3.80	N/A

Business Summary: REITs (MIC: 5.3.1 SIC: 6798 NAIC: 525930)

Alexander & Baldwin is a Hawaii real estate company. Co. operates in three segments: Commercial Real Estate, which owns, operates and manages retail, industrial and office properties in Hawaii and on the Mainland, and leases urban land in Hawaii to third-party lessees; Land Operations, which engages in planning, zoning, financing, constructing, purchasing, managing, selling, and investing in real property, renewable energy and diversified agribusiness activities; and Materials and Construction, which includes asphalt paving as prime contractor and subcontractor, imports and sells liquid asphalt, and manufactures and sells precast concrete products.

Recent Developments: For the quarter ended Mar 31 2018, net income increased 577.1% to US$47.4 million from US$7.0 million in the year-earlier quarter. Revenues were US$113.3 million, up 21.6% from US$93.2 million the year before. Revenues from property income rose 44.3% to US$64.5 million from US$44.7 million in the corresponding quarter a year earlier.

Prospects: Our evaluation of Alexander & Baldwin Inc. (REIT) as of Jan. 21, 2018 is the result of our systematic analysis on three basic characteristics: earnings strength, relative valuation, and recent stock price movement. The company has suffered a very negative trend in earnings per share over the past 5 quarters and while recent estimates for the company have been raised by analysts, ALEX has posted better than expected results. Based on operating earnings yield, the company is overvalued when compared to all of the companies in our coverage universe. Share price changes over the past year indicates that ALEX will perform in line with the market over the near term.

Financial Data

(US$ in Thousands)	3 Mos	12/31/2017	12/31/2016	12/31/2015	12/31/2014	12/31/2013	12/31/2012	12/31/2011
Earnings Per Share	4.86	4.34	(0.18)	0.54	1.25	0.82	0.48	0.56
Cash Flow Per Share	0.27	(0.03)	2.26	2.63	0.80	(0.86)	0.26	0.25
Tang Book Value Per Share	15.80	10.25	21.71	22.06	21.26	20.42	21.31	...
Dividends Per Share	15.920	15.920	0.250	...	...	...	...	...
Dividend Payout %	327.57	366.82	...	...	...	...	...	...
Income Statement								
Total Revenue	113,300	425,500	387,500	570,500	560,000	365,200	296,700	268,700
EBITDA	13,700	56,400	165,200	117,000	106,700	81,700	66,400	67,200
Depn & Amortn	10,200	32,300	106,100	43,800	55,000	41,700	35,100	34,800
Income Before Taxes	(4,800)	600	35,300	47,600	28,800	23,600	16,500	15,600
Income Taxes	(2,700)	(218,200)	2,600	16,500	(1,400)	8,500	(1,200)	6,800
Net Income	47,300	228,300	(10,200)	29,600	61,400	36,900	20,500	23,500
Average Shares	72,200	53,000	49,400	49,300	49,300	45,100	42,900	42,100
Balance Sheet								
Current Assets	178,500	274,800	138,300	152,500	175,900	171,400	63,400	68,800
Total Assets	2,310,700	2,231,200	2,156,300	2,243,500	2,329,900	2,285,200	1,437,300	1,386,600
Current Liabilities	123,300	926,800	165,100	184,700	183,000	218,200	69,600	90,000
Long-Term Obligations	795,800	585,200	472,700	497,800	631,500	605,500	220,000	327,200
Total Liabilities	990,100	1,576,800	936,200	1,008,300	1,126,000	1,119,300	522,900	660,800
Stockholders' Equity	1,320,600	654,400	1,220,100	1,235,200	1,203,900	1,165,900	914,400	725,800
Shares Outstanding	72,000	49,300	49,000	48,900	48,800	48,600	42,900	...
Statistical Record								
Return on Assets %	12.05	10.41	N.M.	1.29	2.66	1.98	...	1.72
Return on Equity %	21.28	24.36	N.M.	2.43	5.18	3.55	...	3.32
EBITDA Margin %	12.09	13.25	42.63	20.51	19.05	22.37	22.38	25.01
Net Margin %	41.75	53.65	N.M.	5.19	10.96	10.10	6.91	8.75
Asset Turnover	0.20	0.19	0.18	0.25	0.24	0.20	...	0.20
Current Ratio	1.45	0.30	0.84	0.83	0.96	0.79	0.91	0.76
Debt to Equity	0.60	0.89	0.39	0.40	0.52	0.52	0.24	0.45
Price Range	46.87-21.99	46.87-27.62	46.09-29.30	43.52-33.34	44.56-34.74	45.92-29.21	34.25-25.30	...
P/E Ratio	9.64-4.52	10.80-6.36	...	80.59-61.74	35.65-27.79	56.00-35.62	71.35-52.71	...
Average Yield %	42.28	37.60	0.66	...	...	...	...	...

Address: 822 Bishop Street, Honolulu, HI 96813	Web Site: www.alexanderbaldwin.com	Auditors: DELOITTE & TOUCHE LLP
Telephone: 808-525-6611	Officers: Stanley M. Kuriyama - Chairman, President, Chief Executive Officer Christopher J. Benjamin - President, Chief Executive Officer, Chief Operating Officer	Transfer Agents: Computershare Shareowner Services LLC

ALEXANDRIA REAL ESTATE EQUITIES INC

Exchange	Symbol	Price	52Wk Range	Yield	P/E
NYS	ARE	$126.17 (6/29/2018)	134.03-114.58	2.95	48.53

*7 Year Price Score 111.52 *NYSE Composite Index=100 *12 Month Price Score 100.71

TRADING VOLUME (thousand shares)

Interim Earnings (Per Share)

Qtr.	Mar	Jun	Sep	Dec
2015	0.25	0.44	0.46	0.49
2016	(0.05)	(1.72)	0.07	(0.30)
2017	0.29	0.35	0.55	0.38
2018	1.32	...	...	...

Interim Dividends (Per Share)

Amt	Decl	Ex	Rec	Pay
0.86Q	09/06/2017	09/28/2017	09/29/2017	10/16/2017
0.90Q	12/04/2017	12/28/2017	12/29/2017	01/15/2018
0.90Q	03/05/2018	03/28/2018	03/29/2018	04/16/2018
0.93Q	06/04/2018	06/28/2018	06/29/2018	07/16/2018

Indicated Div: $3.72

Valuation Analysis

		Institutional Holding	
Forecast EPS	$2.92	No of Institutions	
	(06/13/2018)	568	
Market Cap	$12.7 Billion	Shares	
Book Value	$6.2 Billion	125,757,480	
Price/Book	2.05	% Held	
Price/Sales	10.79	98.01	

Business Summary: REITs (MIC: 5.3.1 SIC: 6798 NAIC: 525930)

Alexandria Real Estate Equities is an urban office Real Estate Investment Trust focused on collaborative life science and technology campuses in AAA innovation cluster locations. Co. is engaged in the business of providing space for lease in the life science and technology industries. Co. has market presence in key locations, including Greater Boston, San Francisco, New York City, San Diego, Seattle, Maryland, and Research Triangle Park. As of Dec 31 2017, Co. had 213 properties in North America containing of operating properties and development and redevelopment of new Class A properties (under construction or pre-construction), of which 49.0% were single-tenant properties.

Recent Developments: For the quarter ended Mar 31 2018, net income increased 197.6% to US$141.5 million from US$47.6 million in the year-earlier quarter. Revenues were US$320.1 million, up 18.2% from US$270.9 million the year before. Revenues from property income rose 18.3% to US$317.7 million from US$268.5 million in the corresponding quarter a year earlier.

Prospects: Our evaluation of Alexandria Real Estate Equities Inc. as of Jan. 21, 2018 is the result of our systematic analysis on three basic characteristics: earnings strength, relative valuation, and recent stock price movement. The company has enjoyed a very positive trend in earnings per share over the past 5 quarters. Because the company lacks sufficient analyst estimate data, we place greater weight on the historical EPS trend as the measure of earnings strength. Based on operating earnings yield, the company is overvalued when compared to all of the companies in our coverage universe. Share price changes over the past year indicates that ARE will perform well over the near term.

Financial Data

(US$ in Thousands)	3 Mos	12/31/2017	12/31/2016	12/31/2015	12/31/2014	12/31/2013	12/31/2012	12/31/2011
Earnings Per Share	2.60	1.58	(1.99)	1.63	1.01	1.60	1.09	1.73
Cash Flow Per Share	4.72	4.92	5.14	4.79	4.70	4.60	4.90	4.18
Tang Book Value Per Share	60.78	58.88	53.37	49.73	48.43	49.69	48.41	48.65
Dividends Per Share	3.520	3.450	3.230	3.050	2.880	2.610	2.090	1.860
Dividend Payout %	135.38	218.35	...	187.12	285.15	163.13	191.74	107.51
Income Statement								
Total Revenue	320,139	1,128,097	921,706	843,474	726,877	631,151	586,073	573,443
EBITDA	87,526	713,677	376,287	516,121	410,164	400,404	369,778	361,455
Depn & Amortn	(4,202)	406,365	319,039	265,802	232,277	197,927	199,148	161,813
Income Before Taxes	54,813	178,667	(49,705)	144,506	98,588	134,525	101,446	136,235
Net Income	135,630	169,093	(65,901)	144,217	101,574	136,217	102,126	131,418
Average Shares	100,125	92,063	76,103	71,528	71,169	68,038	62,160	59,077
Balance Sheet								
Current Assets	270,240	287,448	151,110	164,455	123,443	95,323	189,367	109,351
Total Assets	12,821,196	12,103,953	10,354,888	8,911,120	8,136,036	7,529,764	7,150,116	6,574,129
Current Liabilities	877,051	855,977	808,585	651,361	547,899	489,762	465,109	361,972
Long-Term Obligations	5,210,798	4,764,807	4,164,025	3,965,795	3,678,579	3,061,061	3,181,949	2,779,264
Total Liabilities	6,626,599	6,154,287	5,459,092	4,936,033	4,307,597	3,612,975	3,708,265	3,199,828
Stockholders' Equity	6,194,597	5,949,666	4,895,796	3,975,087	3,828,439	3,916,789	3,441,851	3,374,301
Shares Outstanding	100,696	99,783	87,665	72,548	71,463	71,172	63,244	61,560
Statistical Record								
Return on Assets %	2.22	1.51	N.M.	1.69	1.30	1.86	1.48	2.11
Return on Equity %	4.72	3.12	N.M.	3.70	2.62	3.70	2.99	4.17
EBITDA Margin %	27.34	63.26	40.83	61.19	56.43	63.44	63.09	63.03
Net Margin %	42.37	14.99	N.M.	17.10	13.97	21.58	17.43	22.92
Asset Turnover	0.10	0.10	0.10	0.10	0.09	0.09	0.09	0.09
Current Ratio	0.31	0.34	0.19	0.25	0.23	0.19	0.41	0.30
Debt to Equity	0.84	0.80	0.85	1.00	0.96	0.78	0.92	0.82
Price Range	134.03-110.52	134.03-108.18	114.52-71.65	102.42-83.40	90.19-63.62	78.09-61.02	76.65-64.75	84.93-57.19
P/E Ratio	51.55-42.51	84.83-68.47	...	62.83-51.17	89.30-62.99	48.81-38.14	70.32-59.40	49.09-33.06
Average Yield %	2.90	2.90	3.28	3.30	3.75	3.83	2.92	2.53

Address: 385 East Colorado Boulevard, Suite 299, Pasadena, CA 91101 **Telephone:** 626-578-0777	**Web Site:** www.are.com **Officers:** Joel S. Marcus - Chairman, President, Chief Executive Officer Dean A. Shigenaga - Co-President, Executive Vice President, Chief Financial Officer, Treasurer	**Auditors:** Ernst & Young LLP **Investor Contact:** 626-396-4828 **Transfer Agents:** American Stock Transfer & Trust Company, LLC, Brooklyn, NY

ALLEGHANY CORP.

Exchange	Symbol	Price	52Wk Range	Yield	P/E
NYS	Y	$574.97 (6/29/2018)	633.80-523.19	N/A	85.94

*7 Year Price Score 103.19 *NYSE Composite Index=100 *12 Month Price Score 97.95

TRADING VOLUME (thousand shares)

Interim Earnings (Per Share)

Qtr.	Mar	Jun	Sep	Dec
2015	7.82	11.40	6.07	9.83
2016	9.96	4.99	10.09	4.51
2017	9.67	6.60	(20.90)	9.95
2018	11.04			

Interim Dividends (Per Share)

No Dividends Paid

Valuation Analysis — **Institutional Holding**

Forecast EPS	$36.35	No of Institutions
	(06/14/2018)	473
Market Cap	$8.8 Billion	Shares
Book Value	$8.4 Billion	16,075,826
Price/Book	1.05	% Held
Price/Sales	1.36	79.84

Business Summary: General Insurance (MIC: 5.2.1 SIC: 6331 NAIC: 524126)

Alleghany is an insurance holding company. Through its Alleghany Insurance Holdings LLC subsidiary, Co. is engaged in the property and casualty insurance business. Co. sources, executes, manages and monitors certain private capital investments through its subsidiary, Alleghany Capital Corporation (Alleghany Capital). Alleghany Capital's investments include: Stranded Oil Resources Corporation; Bourn & Koch, Inc.; R.C. Tway Company, LLC; IPS-Integrated Project Services, LLC; and Jazwares, LLC. Co. has two segments: reinsurance, which consists of property and casualty reinsurance operations; and insurance, which consists of property and casualty insurance operations.

Recent Developments: For the quarter ended Mar 31 2018, net income increased 14.6% to US$171.2 million from US$149.4 million in the year-earlier quarter. Revenues were US$1.58 billion, up 3.4% from US$1.53 billion the year before. Net premiums earned were unchanged at US$1.21 billion versus the prior-year quarter. Net investment income rose 7.4% to US$124.1 million from US$115.5 million a year ago.

Prospects: Our evaluation of Alleghany Corp. as of Jan. 21, 2018 is the result of our systematic analysis on three basic characteristics: earnings strength, relative valuation, and recent stock price movement. The company has generated a negative trend in earnings per share over the past 5 quarters. Because the company lacks sufficient analyst estimate data, we place greater weight on the historical EPS trend as the measure of earnings strength. Based on operating earnings yield, the company is undervalued when compared to all of the companies in our coverage universe. Share price changes over the past year indicates that Y will perform poorly over the near term.

Financial Data
(US$ in Thousands)

	3 Mos	12/31/2017	12/31/2016	12/31/2015	12/31/2014	12/31/2013	12/31/2012	12/31/2011
Earnings Per Share	6.69	5.85	29.59	35.13	41.40	37.44	45.48	16.20
Cash Flow Per Share	31.39	28.92	51.23	20.54	22.72	34.78	32.02	10.63
Tang Book Value Per Share	492.16	501.62	472.17	463.26	450.23	399.42	366.57	325.87
Dividends Per Share	10.000	...	...	...	...	...	...	...
Dividend Payout %	149.48	...	...	...	...	...	...	...
Income Statement								
Premium Income	1,207,856	4,954,990	4,975,777	4,230,286	4,410,647	4,239,216	3,733,005	747,639
Total Revenue	1,584,954	6,424,655	6,131,019	4,999,478	5,231,809	4,971,654	4,753,212	981,837
Benefits & Claims	670,578	3,620,197	2,917,166	2,339,790	2,494,565	2,479,353	2,630,170	429,986
Income Before Taxes	208,604	36,690	647,805	757,368	931,909	855,236	719,276	190,837
Income Taxes	37,422	(63,802)	187,141	195,173	251,777	225,882	17,032	47,586
Net Income	171,575	90,133	456,921	560,315	679,239	628,421	702,244	143,251
Average Shares	15,418	15,410	15,442	15,879	16,405	16,786	15,441	8,811
Balance Sheet								
Total Assets	25,097,256	25,384,317	23,756,591	22,846,333	23,489,436	23,361,088	22,807,967	6,478,089
Total Liabilities	16,723,856	16,870,254	15,816,646	15,291,626	16,016,008	16,437,331	16,404,180	3,552,412
Stockholders' Equity	8,373,400	8,514,063	7,939,945	7,554,707	7,473,428	6,923,757	6,403,787	2,925,677
Shares Outstanding	15,362	15,390	15,410	15,544	16,054	16,766	16,890	8,551
Statistical Record								
Return on Assets %	0.46	0.37	1.96	2.42	2.90	2.72	4.78	2.22
Return on Equity %	1.36	1.10	5.88	7.46	9.44	9.43	15.01	4.91
Loss Ratio %	55.52	73.06	58.63	55.31	56.56	58.49	70.46	57.51
Net Margin %	10.83	1.40	7.45	11.21	12.98	12.64	14.77	14.59
Price Range	633.80-523.19	656.22-523.19	616.13-450.94	515.25-440.61	482.00-363.60	417.39-335.42	355.46-284.25	338.90-277.26
P/E Ratio	94.74-78.20	112.17-89.43	20.82-15.24	14.67-12.54	11.64-8.78	11.15-8.96	7.82-6.25	20.92-17.11
Average Yield %	1.70	...	...	...	...	...	...	...

Address: 1411 Broadway, 34th Floor, New York, NY 10018 **Telephone:** 212-752-1356	**Web Site:** www.alleghany.com **Officers:** John J. Burns - Chairman Weston M. Hicks - President, Chief Executive Officer	**Auditors:** Ernst &Young LLP **Transfer Agents:** Computershare Trust Company, N.A., Providence, RI

ALLEGHENY TECHNOLOGIES, INC

Exchange	Symbol	Price	52Wk Range	Yield	P/E
NYS	ATI	$25.12 (6/29/2018)	29.77-16.93	N/A	N/A

*7 Year Price Score 68.35   *NYSE Composite Index®=100   *12 Month Price Score 111.21

Interim Earnings (Per Share)

Qtr.	Mar	Jun	Sep	Dec
2015	0.09	(0.15)	(1.35)	(2.12)
2016	(0.94)	(0.18)	(4.95)	0.10
2017	0.16	0.09	(1.12)	0.04
2018	0.42	...	...	...

Interim Dividends (Per Share)

Dividend Payment Suspended

Valuation Analysis   Institutional Holding

Forecast EPS	$1.39	No of Institutions
	(06/13/2018)	497
Market Cap	$3.2 Billion	Shares
Book Value	$1.8 Billion	160,856,736
Price/Book	1.71	% Held
Price/Sales	0.87	77.28

Business Summary: Non-Precious Metals (MIC: 8.2.2 SIC: 3317 NAIC: 331210)

Allegheny Technologies is a manufacturer of specialty materials and complex components. Co.'s business segments are High Performance Materials and Components, which produces, converts and distributes materials, including titanium and titanium-based alloys, nickel- and cobalt-based alloys and superalloys, zirconium and related alloys; and Flat Rolled Products, which produces, converts and distributes stainless steel, nickel-based alloys, specialty alloys, and titanium and titanium-based alloys, in a variety of product forms including plate, sheet, engineered strip, and Precision Rolled Strip® products.

Recent Developments: For the quarter ended Mar 31 2018, net income increased 186.7% to US$60.5 million from US$21.1 million in the year-earlier quarter. Revenues were US$979.0 million, up 13.1% from US$865.9 million the year before. Operating income was US$81.5 million versus US$66.9 million in the prior-year quarter, an increase of 21.8%. Direct operating expenses rose 12.0% to US$830.4 million from US$741.1 million in the comparable period the year before. Indirect operating expenses increased 15.9% to US$67.1 million from US$57.9 million in the equivalent prior-year period.

Prospects: Our evaluation of Allegheny Technologies Inc. as of Jan. 21, 2018 is the result of our systematic analysis on three basic characteristics: earnings strength, relative valuation, and recent stock price movement. The company has suffered a very negative trend in earnings per share over the past 5 quarters and while recent estimates for the company have been raised by analysts, ATI has posted results that fell short of analysts expectations. Based on operating earnings yield, the company is overvalued when compared to all of the companies in our coverage universe. Share price changes over the past year indicates that ATI will perform well over the near term.

Financial Data
(US$ in Thousands)

	3 Mos	12/31/2017	12/31/2016	12/31/2015	12/31/2014	12/31/2013	12/31/2012	12/31/2011
Earnings Per Share	(0.57)	(0.83)	(5.97)	(3.53)	(0.03)	1.44	1.43	1.97
Cash Flow Per Share	0.68	0.20	(0.41)	1.22	0.52	3.45	4.02	2.90
Tang Book Value Per Share	10.44	9.60	6.55	13.11	16.72	20.06	16.20	16.34
Dividends Per Share	...	...	0.240	0.620	0.720	0.720	0.720	0.720
Dividend Payout %	...	...	...	...	...	50.00	50.35	36.55
Income Statement								
Total Revenue	979,000	3,525,100	3,134,600	3,719,600	4,223,400	4,043,500	5,031,500	5,183,000
EBITDA	130,800	182,500	(439,700)	(177,900)	286,800	91,000	509,600	606,100
Depn & Amortn	39,800	135,200	170,300	189,900	176,600	180,600	194,000	174,400
Income Before Taxes	65,500	(86,500)	(734,000)	(478,000)	1,500	(154,800)	244,000	339,400
Income Taxes	5,000	(6,800)	(106,900)	(112,100)	(8,700)	(63,600)	76,200	116,300
Net Income	58,000	(91,900)	(640,900)	(377,900)	(2,600)	154,000	158,400	214,300
Average Shares	145,500	110,100	107,300	107,300	107,100	106,800	116,600	113,900
Balance Sheet								
Current Assets	2,051,800	1,915,700	1,766,500	1,867,600	2,482,100	2,950,800	2,510,600	2,569,500
Total Assets	5,350,000	5,185,400	5,170,000	5,751,700	6,582,600	6,898,500	6,247,800	6,046,900
Current Liabilities	759,200	712,600	708,700	686,500	959,900	1,211,000	871,500	861,800
Long-Term Obligations	1,535,300	1,530,600	1,771,900	1,491,800	1,509,100	1,527,400	1,463,000	1,482,000
Total Liabilities	3,503,900	3,446,000	3,814,800	3,668,900	3,984,200	4,004,300	3,768,200	3,571,600
Stockholders' Equity	1,846,100	1,739,400	1,355,200	2,082,800	2,598,400	2,894,200	2,479,600	2,475,300
Shares Outstanding	125,647	125,857	108,925	109,174	108,710	107,983	107,398	106,354
Statistical Record								
Return on Assets %	N.M.	N.M.	N.M.	N.M.	N.M.	2.34	2.57	4.07
Return on Equity %	N.M.	N.M.	N.M.	N.M.	N.M.	5.73	6.38	9.49
EBITDA Margin %	13.36	5.18	N.M.	N.M.	6.79	2.25	10.13	11.69
Net Margin %	5.92	N.M.	N.M.	N.M.	N.M.	3.81	3.15	4.13
Asset Turnover	0.69	0.68	0.57	0.60	0.63	0.62	0.82	0.98
Current Ratio	2.70	2.69	2.49	2.72	2.59	2.44	2.88	2.98
Debt to Equity	0.83	0.88	1.31	0.72	0.58	0.53	0.59	0.60
Price Range	29.77-14.89	25.84-14.89	18.94-7.62	37.45-10.46	46.23-29.86	35.64-26.00	51.62-25.61	72.74-32.78
P/E Ratio	...	...	...	...	...	24.75-18.06	36.10-17.91	36.92-16.64
Average Yield %	...	...	1.61	2.52	1.92	2.39	2.06	1.28

Address: 1000 Six PPG Place, Pittsburgh, PA 15222-5479 **Telephone:** 412-394-2800	**Web Site:** www.atimetals.com **Officers:** Richard J. (Rich) Harshman - Chairman, President, Chief Executive Officer L. Patrick Hassey - Chairman, Outgoing Chief Executive Officer	**Auditors:** Ernst & Young LLP **Investor Contact:** 412-394-3004 **Transfer Agents:** Computershare

ALLERGAN PLC

Exchange	Symbol	Price	52Wk Range	Yield	P/E
NYS	AGN PRA	$166.72 (6/29/2018)	256.15-143.80	N/A	N/A

*7 Year Price Score 80.46 *NYSE Composite Index=100 *12 Month Price Score 84.12

TRADING VOLUME (thousand shares)

Interim Earnings (Per Share)

Qtr.	Mar	Jun	Sep	Dec
2015	(1.85)	(0.80)	13.29	(2.20)
2016	0.47	(1.44)	38.58	0.74
2017	(7.86)	(2.37)	(12.07)	9.09
2018	(0.99)	...	...	...

Interim Dividends (Per Share)

Amt	Decl	Ex	Rec	Pay
13.75Q	04/19/2017	08/11/2017	08/15/2017	09/01/2017
13.75Q	04/19/2017	05/11/2017	05/15/2017	06/01/2017
13.75Q	10/31/2017	11/14/2017	11/15/2017	12/01/2017
13.75Q	10/31/2017	02/14/2018	02/15/2018	03/01/2018

Valuation Analysis | Institutional Holding

Forecast EPS	N/A	No of Institutions
		1288
Market Cap	$56.5 Billion	Shares
Book Value	$72.3 Billion	302,968,544
Price/Book	0.78	% Held
Price/Sales	3.52	N/A

Business Summary: Pharmaceuticals (MIC: 4.1.1 SIC: 2834 NAIC: 325412)

Allergan is a specialty pharmaceutical company engaged in the development, manufacturing, marketing, and distribution of brand name pharmaceutical products, medical aesthetics, biosimilar and over-the-counter pharmaceutical products. Co. has three operating segments: U.S. Specialized Therapeutics, which provides branded products within the U.S., including medical aesthetics, medical dermatology, eye care, neurosciences and urology therapeutic products; U.S. General Medicine, which includes Central Nervous System, gastrointestinal women's health, and anti-infectives products within the U.S.; and International, which provides a range of branded and aesthetics products outside of the U.S.

Recent Developments: For the quarter ended Mar 31 2018, loss from continuing operations was US$283.9 million compared with a loss of US$2.56 billion in the year-earlier quarter. Net loss amounted to US$283.9 million versus a net loss of US$2.56 billion in the year-earlier quarter. Revenues were US$3.67 billion, up 2.8% from US$3.57 billion the year before. Operating loss was US$654.0 million versus a loss of US$906.0 million in the prior-year quarter. Direct operating expenses rose 16.1% to US$522.8 million from US$450.4 million in the comparable period the year before. Indirect operating expenses decreased 5.6% to US$3.80 billion from US$4.03 billion in the equivalent prior-year period.

Prospects: Our evaluation of Allergan PLC as of Aug. 2, 2015 is the result of our systematic analysis on three basic characteristics: earnings strength, relative valuation, and recent stock price movement. The company has managed to produce a neutral trend in earnings per share over the past 5 quarters. However, while recent estimates for the company have been lowered by analysts, AGN has posted better than expected results. Based on operating earnings yield, the company is about fairly valued when compared to all of the companies in our coverage universe. Share price changes over the past year indicates that AGN will perform in line with the market over the near term.

Financial Data
(US$ in Thousands)

	3 Mos	12/31/2017	12/31/2016	12/31/2015	12/31/2014	12/31/2013	12/31/2012	12/31/2011
Earnings Per Share	(6.34)	(13.19)	38.18	10.01	(7.42)	(5.27)	0.76	2.06
Cash Flow Per Share	19.75	17.60	3.69	12.32	10.21	8.53	5.28	5.08
Tang Book Value Per Share	N.M.	N.M.	N.M.	N.M.	N.M.	N.M.	N.M.	1.90
Dividends Per Share	2.820	2.800	55.000	41.097	0.200	0.200	0.200	0.200
DividendPayout %	...	144.05	410.56	...	...	...	...	...
Income Statement								
Total Revenue	3,672,100	15,940,700	14,570,600	15,071,000	13,062,300	8,677,600	5,914,900	4,584,400
EBITDA	1,027,200	(9,187,000)	(1,452,600)	(3,119,700)	(1,078,300)	(207,400)	455,500	633,800
Depn & Amortn	1,760,000	171,500	153,700	128,600	230,900	202,000	97,500	93,600
Income Before Taxes	(966,100)	(10,386,400)	(2,832,000)	(4,430,200)	(1,712,100)	(644,400)	243,800	460,500
Income Taxes	(682,200)	(6,670,400)	(1,897,000)	(1,561,900)	(81,900)	112,700	146,800	196,900
Net Income	(286,100)	(4,125,500)	14,973,400	3,915,200	(1,630,500)	(750,400)	97,300	260,900
Average Shares	334,600	333,800	384,900	367,800	219,700	142,300	128,400	126,500
Balance Sheet								
Current Assets	6,393,300	11,376,700	17,857,900	8,615,400	6,881,700	4,434,700	3,879,700	2,569,700
Total Assets	112,021,300	118,341,900	128,986,300	135,840,700	52,529,100	22,725,900	14,103,500	6,698,300
Current Liabilities	5,816,000	9,848,100	7,874,700	8,328,300	5,018,600	3,294,900	2,710,600	1,839,500
Long-Term Obligations	25,936,400	25,843,500	29,970,800	40,293,400	14,846,300	8,517,400	6,257,100	665,300
Total Liabilities	39,693,400	44,520,800	52,793,600	59,249,300	24,198,000	13,193,800	10,269,700	3,134,700
Stockholders' Equity	72,327,900	73,821,100	76,192,700	76,591,400	28,331,100	9,532,100	3,833,800	3,563,600
Shares Outstanding	339,000	330,200	334,900	394,500	247,600	174,200	127,700	127,200
Statistical Record								
Return on Assets %	N.M.	N.M.	11.28	4.16	N.M.	N.M.	0.93	4.17
Return on Equity %	N.M.	N.M.	19.55	7.46	N.M.	N.M.	2.62	7.62
EBITDA Margin %	27.97	N.M.	N.M.	N.M.	N.M.	N.M.	7.70	13.83
Net Margin %	N.M.	N.M.	102.76	25.98	N.M.	N.M.	1.64	5.69
Asset Turnover	0.13	0.13	0.11	0.16	0.35	0.47	0.57	0.73
Current Ratio	1.10	1.16	2.27	1.03	1.37	1.35	1.43	1.40
Debt to Equity	0.36	0.35	0.39	0.53	0.52	0.89	1.63	0.19
Price Range	256.15-144.02	256.15-163.58	312.50-188.47	339.50-252.10	270.61-167.93	168.00-83.10	90.85-55.89	72.10-50.59
P/E Ratio	...	...	8.18-4.94	33.92-25.18	...	...	119.54-73.54	35.00-24.56
Average Yield %	1.34	1.27	21.96	13.89	0.09	0.16	0.24	0.33

Address: Clonshaugh Business and Technology Park, Coolock, Dublin, 07054 Telephone: 862-261-7000	Web Site: www.allergan.com Officers: Brenton L. Saunders - Chairman, President, Chief Executive Officer Maria Teresa Hilado - Executive Vice President, Chief Financial Officer, Chief Financial Officer	Auditors: PricewaterhouseCoopers LLP Investor Contact: 862-261-7488 Transfer Agents: American Stock Transfer and Trust Company, New York, NY

ALLIANCE DATA SYSTEMS CORP.

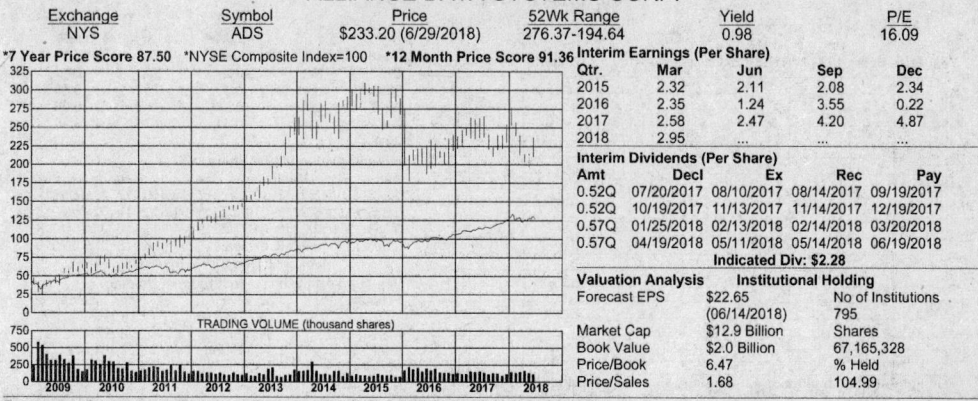

Exchange	Symbol	Price	52Wk Range	Yield	P/E
NYS	ADS	$233.20 (6/29/2018)	276.37-194.64	0.98	16.09

*7 Year Price Score 87.50   *NYSE Composite Index=100   *12 Month Price Score 91.36

Interim Earnings (Per Share)

Qtr.	Mar	Jun	Sep	Dec
2015	2.32	2.11	2.08	2.34
2016	2.35	1.24	3.55	0.22
2017	2.58	2.47	4.20	4.87
2018	2.95	...	...	...

Interim Dividends (Per Share)

Amt	Decl	Ex	Rec	Pay
0.52Q	07/20/2017	08/10/2017	08/14/2017	09/19/2017
0.52Q	10/19/2017	11/13/2017	11/14/2017	12/19/2017
0.57Q	01/25/2018	02/13/2018	02/14/2018	03/20/2018
0.57Q	04/19/2018	05/11/2018	05/14/2018	06/19/2018

Indicated Div: $2.28

Valuation Analysis

		Institutional Holding	
Forecast EPS	$22.65 (06/14/2018)	No of Institutions	795
Market Cap	$12.9 Billion	Shares	67,165,328
Book Value	$2.0 Billion	% Held	104.99
Price/Book	6.47		
Price/Sales	1.68		

TRADING VOLUME (thousand shares)

Business Summary: Business Services (MIC: 7.5.2 SIC: 7389 NAIC: 561499)

Alliance Data Systems is a provider of data-driven marketing and loyalty solutions. Co. provides a portfolio of outsourced marketing solutions, including customer loyalty programs, database marketing services, end-to-end marketing services, analytics and creative services, direct marketing services and private label and co-brand retail credit card programs. Co. focuses on facilitating and managing interactions between its clients and their customers through all consumer marketing channels, including in-store, online, email, social media, mobile, direct mail and telephone. Co.'s products and services are reported under three segments: LoyaltyOne®, Epsilon and Card Services.

Recent Developments: For the quarter ended Mar 31 2018, net income increased 12.0% to US$163.9 million from US$146.4 million in the year-earlier quarter. Revenues were US$1.88 billion, unchanged from the year before. Operating income was US$377.8 million versus US$352.4 million in the prior-year quarter, an increase of 7.2%. Direct operating expenses declined 2.7% to US$1.01 billion from US$1.04 billion in the comparable period the year before. Indirect operating expenses increased 1.7% to US$492.5 million from US$484.5 million in the equivalent prior-year period.

Prospects: Our evaluation of Alliance Data Systems Corp. as of Jan. 21, 2018 is the result of our systematic analysis on three basic characteristics: earnings strength, relative valuation, and recent stock price movement. The company has produced a positive trend in earnings per share over the past 5 quarters. However, while recent estimates for the company have been mixed, ADS has posted better than expected results. Based on operating earnings yield, the company is undervalued when compared to all of the companies in our coverage universe. Share price changes over the past year indicates that ADS will perform poorly over the near term.

Financial Data

(US$ in Thousands)	3 Mos	12/31/2017	12/31/2016	12/31/2015	12/31/2014	12/31/2013	12/31/2012	12/31/2011
Earnings Per Share	14.49	14.10	7.34	8.85	7.87	7.42	6.58	5.45
Cash Flow Per Share	50.04	46.85	35.54	27.57	23.84	20.40	22.62	19.95
Dividends Per Share	2.130	2.080	0.520	...	...	...	...	...
Dividend Payout %	14.70	14.75	7.08	...	...	...	...	...
Income Statement								
Total Revenue	1,884,200	7,719,400	7,138,100	6,439,746	5,302,940	4,319,063	3,641,390	3,173,287
EBITDA	510,900	2,061,200	1,708,200	1,698,049	1,368,994	1,284,440	1,114,038	940,206
Depn & Amortn	133,100	415,700	442,700	436,189	270,527	185,528	139,674	127,526
Income Before Taxes	218,600	1,081,100	837,000	931,676	837,941	793,412	682,904	514,095
Income Taxes	54,700	292,400	319,400	326,248	321,801	297,242	260,648	198,809
Net Income	163,900	788,700	515,800	596,541	506,293	496,170	422,256	315,286
Average Shares	55,700	55,900	58,900	62,301	62,445	66,866	64,143	57,804
Balance Sheet								
Current Assets	23,470,500	24,705,600	19,589,300	16,250,417	13,814,776	10,400,842	9,132,143	6,606,967
Total Assets	29,392,900	30,684,800	25,514,100	22,421,830	20,263,977	13,244,257	12,000,139	8,980,249
Current Liabilities	10,985,500	10,146,700	9,229,500	6,405,559	6,305,483	4,512,498	5,032,777	3,855,171
Long-Term Obligations	5,973,100	13,415,700	10,103,300	10,136,018	8,134,248	2,435,792	2,051,570	2,163,640
Total Liabilities	27,391,500	28,829,500	23,855,900	20,411,800	17,867,597	12,388,496	11,471,652	8,804,283
Stockholders' Equity	2,001,400	1,855,300	1,658,200	2,010,030	2,396,380	855,761	528,487	175,966
Shares Outstanding	55,500	55,400	57,400	60,877	63,812	51,550	49,603	49,830
Statistical Record								
Return on Assets %	2.98	2.81	2.15	2.80	3.02	3.93	4.01	3.65
Return on Equity %	47.91	44.90	28.05	27.08	31.14	71.69	119.55	316.77
EBITDA Margin %	27.11	26.70	23.93	26.37	25.82	29.74	30.59	29.63
Net Margin %	8.70	10.22	7.23	9.26	9.55	11.49	11.60	9.94
Asset Turnover	0.29	0.27	0.30	0.30	0.32	0.34	0.35	0.37
Current Ratio	2.14	2.43	2.12	2.54	2.19	2.30	1.81	1.71
Debt to Equity	2.98	7.23	6.09	5.04	3.39	2.85	3.88	12.30
Price Range	276.37-210.43	264.57-210.43	276.57-177.12	309.91-247.05	294.27-233.67	262.93-144.76	148.02-100.94	105.74-70.68
P/E Ratio	19.07-14.52	18.76-14.92	37.68-24.13	35.02-27.92	37.39-29.69	35.44-19.51	22.50-15.34	19.40-12.97
Average Yield %	0.89	0.88	0.24	...	...	...	...	...

Address: 7500 Dallas Parkway, Suite 700, Plano, TX 75024 **Telephone:** 214-494-3000	**Web Site:** www.alliancedata.com **Officers:** Robert A. Minicucci - Chairman Edward J. Heffernan - President, Chief Executive Officer	**Auditors:** DELOITTE & TOUCHE LLP **Investor Contact:** 212-850-5721 **Transfer Agents:** ComputerShare Investor Services, Providence, RI

ALLIANT ENERGY CORP

Exchange	Symbol	Price	52Wk Range	Yield	P/E	Div Acheiver
NYS	LNT	$42.32 (6/29/2018)	45.18-37.14	3.17	20.54	14 Years

*7 Year Price Score 108.71 *NYSE Composite Index=100 *12 Month Price Score 97.78

Interim Earnings (Per Share)

Qtr.	Mar	Jun	Sep	Dec
2015	0.44	0.30	0.80	0.15
2016	0.42	0.37	0.57	0.28
2017	0.44	0.41	0.73	0.40
2018	0.52	...	...	...

Interim Dividends (Per Share)

Amt	Decl	Ex	Rec	Pay
0.315Q	10/15/2017	10/30/2017	10/31/2017	11/15/2017
0.335Q	01/15/2018	01/30/2018	01/31/2018	02/15/2018
0.335Q	04/16/2018	04/27/2018	04/30/2018	05/15/2018
0.335Q	07/16/2018	07/30/2018	07/31/2018	08/15/2018

Indicated Div: $1.34 (Div. Reinv. Plan)

Valuation Analysis   **Institutional Holding**

Forecast EPS	$2.12	No of Institutions
	(06/03/2018)	678
Market Cap	$9.8 Billion	Shares
Book Value	$4.2 Billion	201,854,672
Price/Book	2.32	% Held
Price/Sales	2.84	57.82

Business Summary: Electric Utilities (MIC: 3.1.1 SIC: 4931 NAIC: 221122)

Alliant Energy is a public utility holding company. Through its subsidiaries, Co. principally generates and distributes electricity and distributes and transports natural gas to retail customers in select markets in Iowa and Wisconsin, and sells electricity to wholesale customers in Wisconsin. At Dec 31 2017, Co. supplied electric and natural gas service to approximately 960,000 electric and approximately 410,000 natural gas customers in the Midwest. Co.'s non-utility operations consist of its non-regulated generation, transportation, and other non-regulated investments including an interest in American Transmission Company LLC, a transmission-only utility operating in the Midwest.

Recent Developments: For the quarter ended Mar 31 2018, income from continuing operations increased 21.6% to US$123.5 million from US$101.6 million in the year-earlier quarter. Net income increased 19.9% to US$123.5 million from US$103.0 million in the year-earlier quarter. Revenues were US$916.3 million, up 7.3% from US$853.9 million the year before. Operating income was US$165.7 million versus US$147.2 million in the prior-year quarter, an increase of 12.6%. Direct operating expenses rose 5.2% to US$603.2 million from US$573.3 million in the comparable period the year before. Indirect operating expenses increased 10.5% to US$147.4 million from US$133.4 million in the equivalent prior-year period.

Prospects: Our evaluation of Alliant Energy Corp. as of Jan. 21, 2018 is the result of our systematic analysis on three basic characteristics: earnings strength, relative valuation, and recent stock price movement. The company has managed to produce a neutral trend in earnings per share over the past 5 quarters. However, while recent estimates for the company have been mixed, LNT has posted results that fell short of analysts expectations. Based on operating earnings yield, the company is undervalued when compared to all of the companies in our coverage universe. Share price changes over the past year indicates that LNT will perform very well over the near term.

Financial Data

(US$ in Thousands)	3 Mos	12/31/2017	12/31/2016	12/31/2015	12/31/2014	12/31/2013	12/31/2012	12/31/2011
Earnings Per Share	2.06	1.99	1.64	1.68	1.73	1.62	1.45	1.37
Cash Flow Per Share	3.19	4.28	3.77	3.87	4.02	3.30	3.79	3.18
Tang Book Value Per Share	18.28	18.08	16.96	16.41	15.50	14.79	14.39	13.84
Dividends Per Share	1.281	1.260	1.175	1.100	1.020	0.940	0.900	0.850
Dividend Payout %	62.16	63.32	71.65	65.48	58.96	58.20	62.28	62.04
Income Statement								
Total Revenue	916,300	3,382,200	3,320,000	3,253,600	3,350,300	3,276,800	3,094,500	3,665,300
EBITDA	298,600	1,186,600	1,006,300	1,027,600	1,020,700	975,800	929,500	870,500
Depn & Amortn	120,400	483,500	406,800	413,700	442,300	411,100	387,900	380,100
Income Before Taxes	119,000	488,000	403,800	427,500	399,600	392,300	388,900	336,400
Income Taxes	16,800	66,700	59,400	70,400	44,300	53,900	89,400	55,100
Net Income	123,500	467,500	381,700	388,400	393,300	376,200	335,700	321,900
Average Shares	231,400	229,700	227,100	225,400	221,600	221,600	221,536	221,356
Balance Sheet								
Current Assets	725,900	905,100	877,100	826,800	1,043,100	1,011,200	994,300	866,500
Total Assets	14,241,800	14,187,800*	13,373,800	12,495,200	12,085,900	11,112,400	10,785,500	9,687,900
Current Liabilities	2,073,500	2,149,000	1,162,000	1,359,300	1,214,700	1,433,300	1,020,000	855,000
Long-Term Obligations	4,056,800	4,010,600	4,315,600	3,522,200	3,606,700	2,977,800	3,136,600	2,703,100
Total Liabilities	10,010,300	10,005,600	9,511,800	8,771,100	8,647,200	7,831,000	7,590,600	6,614,900
Stockholders' Equity	4,231,500	4,182,200	3,862,000	3,724,100	3,438,700	3,281,400	3,194,900	3,073,000
Shares Outstanding	231,481	231,348	227,673	226,918	221,871	221,887	221,974	222,037
Statistical Record								
Return on Assets %	3.52	3.39	2.94	3.16	3.39	3.44	3.27	3.39
Return on Equity %	12.01	11.62	10.04	10.84	11.71	11.62	10.68	10.68
EBITDA Margin %	32.59	35.08	30.31	31.58	30.47	29.78	30.04	23.75
Net Margin %	13.48	13.82	11.50	11.94	11.74	11.48	10.85	8.78
Asset Turnover	0.25	0.25	0.26	0.26	0.29	0.30	0.30	0.39
Current Ratio	0.35	0.42	0.75	0.61	0.86	0.71	0.97	1.01
Debt to Equity	0.96	0.96	1.12	0.95	1.05	0.91	0.98	0.88
Price Range	45.18-37.14	45.18-36.86	40.87-30.79	35.16-27.27	34.66-25.25	26.97-21.95	23.75-21.05	22.16-17.15
P/E Ratio	21.93-18.03	22.70-18.52	24.92-18.77	20.93-16.24	20.03-14.59	16.65-13.55	16.38-14.52	16.18-12.52
Average Yield %	3.10	3.07	3.20	3.60	3.54	3.75	4.07	4.28

Address: 4902 N. Biltmore Lane, Madison, WI 53718 **Telephone:** 608-458-3311 **Fax:** 608-458-4824	**Web Site:** www.alliantenergy.com **Officers:** Patricia L. Kampling - Chairman, President, Chief Executive Officer, Chief Operating Officer Robert J. Durian - Chief Financial Officer, Vice President, Treasurer, Chief Accounting Officer, Controller	**Auditors:** Deloitte & Touche LLP **Investor Contact:** 608-458-3956 **Transfer Agents:** Wells Fargo Shareowner Services, Mendota Heights, MN

ALLISON TRANSMISSION HOLDINGS INC

Exchange	Symbol	Price	52Wk Range	Yield	P/E
NYS	ALSN	$40.49 (6/29/2018)	45.33-33.20	1.48	10.33

*7 Year Price Score N/A   *NYSE Composite Index=100   *12 Month Price Score 102.61

Interim Earnings (Per Share)

Qtr.	Mar	Jun	Sep	Dec
2015	0.38	0.30	0.27	0.08
2016	0.28	0.36	0.27	0.36
2017	0.52	0.63	0.75	1.46
2018	1.08	...	...	...

Interim Dividends (Per Share)

Amt	Decl	Ex	Rec	Pay
0.15Q	08/10/2017	08/17/2017	08/21/2017	08/31/2017
0.15Q	11/08/2017	11/17/2017	11/20/2017	11/30/2017
0.15Q	02/08/2018	02/16/2018	02/20/2018	02/28/2018
0.15Q	05/10/2018	05/18/2018	05/21/2018	05/31/2018

Indicated Div: $0.60

Valuation Analysis

Institutional Holding	
Forecast EPS	$3.90 (06/12/2018)
Market Cap	$5.7 Billion
Book Value	$706.0 Million
Price/Book	8.03
Price/Sales	2.34

No of Institutions	404
Shares	232,870,368
% Held	78.83

Business Summary: Auto Parts (MIC: 1.8.2 SIC: 3714 NAIC: 336350)

Allison Transmission Holdings is a manufacturer of fully-automatic transmissions for medium- and heavy-duty commercial vehicles and medium- and heavy-tactical U.S. defense vehicles. Co.'s transmissions are used in a variety of applications, including on-highway trucks (distribution, refuse, construction, fire and emergency), buses (primarily school, transit and hybrid-transit), motorhomes, off-highway vehicles and equipment (primarily energy, mining and construction) and defense vehicles (wheeled and tracked). Co. also sells branded replacement parts, support equipment and other products necessary to service the installed base of vehicles utilizing Co.'s transmissions.

Recent Developments: For the quarter ended Mar 31 2018, net income increased 81.9% to US$151.0 million from US$83.0 million in the year-earlier quarter. Revenues were US$663.0 million, up 32.9% from US$499.0 million the year before. Operating income was US$222.0 million versus US$149.0 million in the prior-year quarter, an increase of 49.0%. Direct operating expenses rose 29.4% to US$321.0 million from US$248.0 million in the comparable period the year before. Indirect operating expenses increased 17.6% to US$120.0 million from US$102.0 million in the equivalent prior-year period.

Prospects: Our evaluation of Allison Transmission Holding as of Jan. 21, 2018 is the result of our systematic analysis on three basic characteristics: earnings strength, relative valuation, and recent stock price movement. The company has managed to produce a neutral trend in earnings per share over the past 5 quarters. However, while recent estimates for the company have been mixed, ALSN has posted better than expected results. Based on operating earnings yield, the company is undervalued when compared to all of the companies in our coverage universe. Share price changes over the past year indicates that ALSN will perform in line with the market over the near term.

Financial Data
(US$ in Thousands)

	3 Mos	12/31/2017	12/31/2016	12/31/2015	12/31/2014	12/31/2013	12/31/2012	12/31/2011
Earnings Per Share	3.92	3.36	1.27	1.03	1.25	0.88	2.76	0.56
Cash Flow Per Share	5.04	4.42	3.51	3.30	3.10	2.46	2.73	2.59
Dividends Per Share	0.600	0.600	0.600	0.600	0.510	0.420	0.180	...
Dividend Payout %	15.31	17.86	47.24	58.25	40.80	47.73	6.52	...
Income Statement								
Total Revenue	663,000	2,262,000	1,840,200	1,985,800	2,127,400	1,926,800	2,141,800	2,162,800
EBITDA	265,000	800,000	618,100	588,700	699,100	603,000	619,900	623,600
Depn & Amortn	44,000	170,000	175,900	185,400	192,600	204,000	252,500	255,700
Income Before Taxes	191,000	527,000	341,300	288,800	368,100	266,100	216,200	150,600
Income Taxes	40,000	23,000	126,400	106,500	139,500	100,700	(298,000)	47,600
Net Income	151,000	504,000	214,900	182,300	228,600	165,400	514,200	103,000
Average Shares	140,000	150,000	168,800	177,200	182,300	187,900	186,200	183,275
Balance Sheet								
Current Assets	716,000	632,000	547,600	616,800	758,000	606,900	490,300	702,700
Total Assets	4,260,000	4,205,000	4,218,600	4,408,400	4,804,200	4,812,600	4,866,000	5,192,600
Current Liabilities	436,000	417,000	342,200	304,600	345,900	387,200	377,800	449,900
Long-Term Obligations	2,532,000	2,534,000	2,146,800	2,352,700	2,502,600	2,660,400	2,801,300	3,345,000
Total Liabilities	3,554,000	3,516,000	3,138,300	3,219,800	3,406,400	3,373,800	3,509,100	4,370,900
Stockholders' Equity	706,000	689,000	1,080,300	1,188,600	1,397,800	1,438,800	1,356,900	821,700
Shares Outstanding	139,990	139,990	163,795	171,157	179,488	183,376	184,084	181,375
Statistical Record								
Return on Assets %	13.56	11.97	4.97	3.96	4.75	3.42	10.20	1.96
Return on Equity %	79.28	56.97	18.89	14.10	16.12	11.83	47.08	13.18
EBITDA Margin %	39.97	35.37	33.59	29.65	32.86	31.30	28.94	28.83
Net Margin %	22.78	22.28	11.68	9.18	10.75	8.58	24.01	4.76
Asset Turnover	0.57	0.54	0.43	0.43	0.44	0.40	0.42	0.41
Current Ratio	1.64	1.52	1.60	2.02	2.19	1.57	1.30	1.56
Debt to Equity	3.59	3.68	1.99	1.98	1.79	1.85	2.06	4.07
Price Range	45.33-33.20	44.08-32.81	35.02-21.58	33.90-24.64	34.38-26.46	28.04-20.42	25.02-16.21	...
P/E Ratio	11.56-8.47	13.12-9.76	27.57-16.99	32.91-23.92	27.50-21.17	31.86-23.20	9.07-5.87	...
Average Yield %	1.54	1.60	2.15	2.02	1.68	1.76	0.91	...

Address: One Allison Way, Indianapolis, IN 46222 Telephone: 317-242-5000	Web Site: www.allisontransmission.com Officers: Lawrence E. (Larry) Dewey - Chairman, President, Chief Executive Officer David S. Graziosi - President, Chief Executive Officer, Executive Vice President, Chief Financial Officer, Treasurer, Assistant Secretary	Auditors: PricewaterhouseCoopers LLP Investor Contact: 317-242-5000 Transfer Agents: American Stock Transfer & Trust Company, LLC, Brooklyn, NY

ALLSTATE CORP

Exchange	Symbol	Price	52Wk Range	Yield	P/E
NYS	ALL	$91.27 (6/29/2018)	104.91-86.45	2.02	9.92

*7 Year Price Score 125.43 *NYSE Composite Index=100 *12 Month Price Score 97.77

Interim Earnings (Per Share)

Qtr.	Mar	Jun	Sep	Dec
2015	1.53	0.79	1.54	1.18
2016	0.57	0.64	1.31	2.16
2017	1.79	1.49	1.74	3.34
2018	2.63	...	...	...

Interim Dividends (Per Share)

Amt	Decl	Ex	Rec	Pay
0.37Q	07/11/2017	08/29/2017	08/31/2017	10/02/2017
0.37Q	11/16/2017	11/29/2017	11/30/2017	01/02/2018
0.46Q	02/07/2018	03/02/2018	03/05/2018	04/02/2018
0.46Q	05/11/2018	05/30/2018	05/31/2018	07/02/2018

Indicated Div: $1.84 (Div. Reinv. Plan)

Valuation Analysis — **Institutional Holding**

Forecast EPS	$9.15
	(06/14/2018)
Market Cap	$32.1 Billion
Book Value	$23.3 Billion
Price/Book	1.38
Price/Sales	0.83

No of Institutions	1411
Shares	375,254,368
% Held	68.27

TRADING VOLUME (thousand shares)

Business Summary: General Insurance (MIC: 5.2.1 SIC: 6331 NAIC: 524126)

Allstate is a holding company. Through its subsidiaries, Co. provides property-liability insurance and the life insurance, retirement and investment products. Co. has four segments: Allstate Protection, which sells private passenger auto, homeowners, and other property-liability insurance products; Allstate Financial, which sells life insurance and voluntary accident and health insurance products; Discontinued Lines and Coverages, which includes results from property-liability insurance coverage that Co. no longer write and results for certain commercial and other businesses in run-off; and Corporate and Other, which includes holding company activities and certain non-insurance operations.

Recent Developments: For the quarter ended Mar 31 2018, net income increased 40.3% to US$975.0 million from US$695.0 million in the year-earlier quarter. Revenues were US$9.77 billion, up 1.3% from US$9.64 billion the year before. Net premiums earned were US$8.90 billion versus US$8.55 billion in the prior-year quarter, an increase of 4.1%. Net investment income rose 5.1% to US$786.0 million from US$748.0 million a year ago.

Prospects: Our evaluation of Allstate Corp. as of Jan. 21, 2018 is the result of our systematic analysis on three basic characteristics: earnings strength, relative valuation, and recent stock price movement. The company has generated a negative trend in earnings per share over the past 5 quarters. However, while recent estimates for the company have been mixed, ALL has posted better than expected results. Based on operating earnings yield, the company is undervalued when compared to all of the companies in our coverage universe. Share price changes over the past year indicates that ALL will perform very well over the near term.

Financial Data
(US$ in Millions)

	3 Mos	12/31/2017	12/31/2016	12/31/2015	12/31/2014	12/31/2013	12/31/2012	12/31/2011
Earnings Per Share	9.20	8.36	4.67	5.05	6.27	4.81	4.68	1.51
Cash Flow Per Share	11.53	11.92	10.68	9.02	7.50	9.13	6.22	3.70
Tang Book Value Per Share	53.37	52.46	48.11	44.78	46.27	43.33	40.38	34.79
Dividends Per Share	1.570	1.480	1.320	1.200	1.120	1.000	0.880	0.840
Dividend Payout %	17.07	17.70	28.27	23.76	17.86	20.79	18.80	55.63
Income Statement								
Premium Income	8,902	34,678	33,582	32,467	31,086	29,970	28,978	28,180
Total Revenue	9,770	38,524	36,534	35,653	35,239	34,507	33,315	32,654
Benefits & Claims	504	23,852	24,078	22,837	21,193	19,828	20,302	21,922
Income Before Taxes	1,224	3,991	2,754	3,282	4,236	3,396	3,306	960
Income Taxes	249	802	877	1,111	1,386	1,116	1,000	172
Net Income	975	3,189	1,877	2,171	2,850	2,280	2,306	788
Average Shares	359	367	377	406	438	470	493	523
Balance Sheet								
Total Assets	113,289	112,422	108,610	104,656	108,533	123,520	126,947	125,563
Total Liabilities	90,012	89,871	88,037	84,631	86,229	102,040	106,367	106,889
Stockholders' Equity	23,277	22,551	20,573	20,025	22,304	21,480	20,580	18,674
Shares Outstanding	352	355	366	381	418	449	479	501
Statistical Record								
Return on Assets %	3.10	2.89	1.76	2.04	2.46	1.82	1.82	0.61
Return on Equity %	15.61	14.79	9.22	10.26	13.02	10.84	11.72	4.18
Loss Ratio %	5.66	68.78	71.70	70.34	68.18	66.16	70.06	77.79
Net Margin %	9.98	8.28	5.14	6.09	8.09	6.61	6.92	2.41
Price Range	104.91-79.73	104.91-73.09	74.58-57.70	72.58-56.99	71.00-49.55	54.71-40.17	42.62-27.56	34.31-22.68
P/E Ratio	11.40-8.67	12.55-8.74	15.97-12.36	14.37-11.29	11.32-7.90	11.37-8.35	9.11-5.89	22.72-15.02
Average Yield %	1.69	1.68	1.96	1.82	1.89	2.02	2.47	2.91

Address: 2775 Sanders Road, Northbrook, IL 60062 **Telephone:** 847-402-5000	**Web Site:** www.allstate.com **Officers:** Thomas J. Wilson - Chairman, President, Chief Executive Officer Steven E. Shebik - Vice-Chairman, Executive Vice President, Chief Financial Officer	**Auditors:** DELOITTE & TOUCHE LLP **Investor Contact:** 800-416-8803 **Transfer Agents:** Wells Fargo Bank, N.A. Shareowner Services, St. Paul, MN

ALLY FINANCIAL INC

Exchange	Symbol	Price	52Wk Range	Yield	P/E
NYS	ALLY	$26.27 (6/29/2018)	30.83-20.79	1.98	12.16

*7 Year Price Score N/A   ***NYSE Composite Index=100**   ***12 Month Price Score 99.60**

TRADING VOLUME (thousand shares)

Interim Earnings (Per Share)

Qtr.	Mar	Jun	Sep	Dec
2015	1.06	(2.22)	0.47	(1.98)
2016	0.49	0.71	0.43	0.52
2017	0.46	0.55	0.63	0.41
2018	0.57	...	...	...

Interim Dividends (Per Share)

Amt	Decl	Ex	Rec	Pay
0.12Q	07/19/2017	07/28/2017	08/01/2017	08/15/2017
0.12Q	10/11/2017	10/31/2017	11/01/2017	11/15/2017
0.13Q	01/11/2018	01/31/2018	02/01/2018	02/15/2018
0.13Q	04/12/2018	04/30/2018	05/01/2018	05/15/2018

Indicated Div: $0.52

Valuation Analysis   **Institutional Holding**

Forecast EPS	$3.05	No of Institutions
	(06/14/2018)	499
Market Cap	$11.4 Billion	Shares
Book Value	$13.1 Billion	470,254,592
Price/Book	0.87	% Held
Price/Sales	1.15	N/A

Business Summary: Credit & Lending (MIC: 5.4.1 SIC: 6141 NAIC: 522291)

Ally Financial is a financial holding company. Co.'s Dealer Financial Services includes its Automotive Finance and Insurance segments, providing a range of financial services and insurance products to automotive dealerships and their retail customers. Co.'s banking subsidiary, Ally Bank, acquires deposits directly from customers through direct banking via the internet, telephone, mobile, and mail channels. Ally Bank's products include checking, savings, and certificates of deposit, Popmoney person-to-person transfer services, eCheck remote deposit capture and mobile banking. At Dec 31 2017, Co. had total assets of $167.15 billion.

Recent Developments: For the quarter ended Mar 31 2018, income from continuing operations increased 18.3% to US$252.0 million from US$213.0 million in the year-earlier quarter. Net income increased 16.8% to US$250.0 million from US$214.0 million in the year-earlier quarter. Net interest income decreased 3.4% to US$1.32 billion from US$1.37 billion in the year-earlier quarter. Provision for loan losses was US$261.0 million versus US$271.0 million in the prior-year quarter, a decrease of 3.7%. Non-interest income fell 10.6% to US$354.0 million from US$396.0 million, while non-interest expense declined 6.9% to US$1.09 billion.

Prospects: Our evaluation of Ally Financial Inc as of Jan. 21, 2018 is the result of our systematic analysis on three basic characteristics: earnings strength, relative valuation, and recent stock price movement. The company has enjoyed a very positive trend in earnings per share over the past 5 quarters and while recent estimates for the company have been mixed, ALLY has posted better than expected results. Based on operating earnings yield, the company is undervalued when compared to all of the companies in our coverage universe. Share price changes over the past year indicates that ALLY will perform well over the near term.

Financial Data
(US$ in Millions)

	3 Mos	12/31/2017	12/31/2016	12/31/2015	12/31/2014	12/31/2013	12/31/2012	12/31/2011
Earnings Per Share	2.16	2.04	2.15	(2.66)	1.83	(1.64)	0.95	(2.23)
Cash Flow Per Share	9.17	8.99	9.47	10.55	7.07	5.95	12.20	13.31
Tang Book Value Per Share	29.68	30.33	28.00	26.44	29.46	27.00	29.03	22.77
Dividends Per Share	0.450	0.400	0.160	...	...	...	...	...
Dividend Payout %	20.83	19.61	7.44	...	...	...	...	...
Income Statement								
Total Revenue	2,470	9,866	9,835	9,539	9,667	9,577	10,497	13,332
Income Before Taxes	328	1,507	1,581	1,393	1,246	357	(755)	67
Income Taxes	76	581	470	496	321	(59)	(1,284)	179
Net Income	250	929	1,067	1,289	1,150	361	1,196	(157)
Average Shares	438	455	482	482	481	420	412	412
Balance Sheet								
Total Assets	170,021	167,148	163,728	158,581	151,828	151,167	182,347	184,059
Total Liabilities	156,939	153,654	150,411	145,142	136,429	136,959	162,449	164,688
Stockholders' Equity	13,082	13,494	13,317	13,439	15,399	14,208	19,898	19,371
Shares Outstanding	432	437	467	481	480	479	412	412
Statistical Record								
Return on Assets %	0.58	0.56	0.66	0.83	0.76	0.22	0.65	N.M.
Return on Equity %	7.30	6.93	7.95	8.94	7.77	2.12	6.07	N.M.
Net Margin %	10.12	9.42	10.85	13.51	11.90	3.77	11.39	N.M.
Asset Turnover	0.06	0.06	0.06	0.06	0.06	0.06	0.06	0.07
Price Range	30.83-18.22	29.41-18.22	20.40-14.90	23.88-18.33	27.90-20.12	...	...	...
P/E Ratio	14.27-8.44	14.42-8.93	9.49-6.93	...	15.25-10.99	...	...	...
Average Yield %	1.86	1.78	0.88	...	...	...	...	...

Address: Ally Detroit Center, 500 Woodward Avenue, Floor 10, Detroit, MI 48226 **Telephone:** 866-710-4623	**Web Site:** www.ally.com **Officers:** Franklin W. Hobbs - Chairman Jeffrey J. Brown - Chief Executive Officer, Senior Executive Vice President, Division Officer	**Auditors:** Deloitte & Touche LLP **Investor Contact:** 866-710-4623 **Transfer Agents:** Computershare Limited

ALTRIA GROUP INC

Exchange	Symbol	Price	52Wk Range	Yield	P/E	Div Acheiver
NYS	MO	$56.79 (6/29/2018)	74.61-54.52	4.93	10.16	52 Years

*7 Year Price Score 105.55 *NYSE Composite Index=100 *12 Month Price Score 86.61

TRADING VOLUME (thousand shares)

Interim Earnings (Per Share)

Qtr.	Mar	Jun	Sep	Dec
2015	0.52	0.74	0.78	0.64
2016	0.62	0.84	0.56	5.26
2017	0.72	1.03	0.97	2.59
2018	1.00	...	...	...

Interim Dividends (Per Share)

Amt	Decl	Ex	Rec	Pay
0.66Q	08/24/2017	09/14/2017	09/15/2017	10/10/2017
0.66Q	12/06/2017	12/20/2017	12/21/2017	01/10/2018
0.70Q	03/01/2018	03/14/2018	03/15/2018	04/10/2018
0.70Q	05/17/2018	06/14/2018	06/15/2018	07/10/2018

Indicated Div: $2.80 (Div. Reinv. Plan)

Valuation Analysis — **Institutional Holding**

Forecast EPS	$4.00	No of Institutions
	(06/14/2018)	2329
Market Cap	$107.6 Billion	Shares
Book Value	$15.4 Billion	1,588,569,856
Price/Book	6.99	% Held
Price/Sales	4.20	56.90

Business Summary: Tobacco Products (MIC: 1.3.1 SIC: 2111 NAIC: 312221)

Altria Group is a holding company. Co.'s subsidiaries include: Philip Morris USA Inc., which is engaged in the manufacture and sale of cigarettes; John Middleton Co., which is engaged in the manufacture and sale of machine-made cigars and pipe tobacco; and UST LLC, which through its subsidiaries, including U.S. Smokeless Tobacco Company LLC and Ste. Michelle Wine Estates Ltd., is engaged in the manufacture and sale of smokeless tobacco products and wine. Co.'s other operating companies included Nu Mark LLC, a subsidiary that is engaged in the manufacture and sale of tobacco products, and Philip Morris Capital Corporation, a subsidiary that maintains a portfolio of finance assets.

Recent Developments: For the quarter ended Mar 31 2018, net income increased 35.2% to US$1.90 billion from US$1.40 billion in the year-earlier quarter. Revenues were US$6.11 billion, up 0.4% from US$6.08 billion the year before. Operating income was US$2.32 billion versus US$2.24 billion in the prior-year quarter, an increase of 3.4%. Direct operating expenses declined 4.1% to US$3.17 billion from US$3.31 billion in the comparable period the year before. Indirect operating expenses increased 15.5% to US$620.0 million from US$537.0 million in the equivalent prior-year period.

Prospects: Our evaluation of Altria Group Inc. as of Jan. 21, 2018 is the result of our systematic analysis on three basic characteristics: earnings strength, relative valuation, and recent stock price movement. The company has managed to produce a neutral trend in earnings per share over the past 5 quarters and while recent estimates for the company have been mixed, MO has posted better than expected results. Based on operating earnings yield, the company is undervalued when compared to all of the companies in our coverage universe. Share price changes over the past year indicates that MO will perform in line with the market over the near term.

Financial Data

(US$ in Thousands)	3 Mos	12/31/2017	12/31/2016	12/31/2015	12/31/2014	12/31/2013	12/31/2012	12/31/2011
Earnings Per Share	5.59	5.31	7.28	2.67	2.56	2.26	2.06	1.64
Cash Flow Per Share	2.67	2.56	1.94	2.96	2.36	2.19	1.92	1.75
Dividends Per Share	2.630	2.540	2.350	2.170	2.000	1.840	1.700	1.580
Dividend Payout %	47.05	47.83	32.28	81.27	78.13	81.42	82.52	96.34
Income Statement								
Total Revenue	6,108,000	25,576,000	25,744,000	25,434,000	24,522,000	24,466,000	24,618,000	23,800,000
EBITDA	2,343,000	10,189,000	21,987,000	8,342,000	7,764,000	7,212,000	6,604,000	6,321,000
Depn & Amortn	53,000	188,000	183,000	204,000	188,000	212,000	225,000	253,000
Income Before Taxes	2,124,000	9,296,000	21,057,000	7,321,000	6,768,000	5,951,000	5,253,000	4,852,000
Income Taxes	571,000	(399,000)	7,608,000	2,835,000	2,704,000	2,407,000	2,294,000	2,189,000
Net Income	1,894,000	10,222,000	14,239,000	5,241,000	5,070,000	4,535,000	4,180,000	3,390,000
Average Shares	1,899,000	1,921,000	1,952,000	1,961,000	1,978,000	1,999,000	2,024,000	2,064,000
Balance Sheet								
Current Assets	4,824,000	4,344,000	7,260,000	6,086,000	6,878,000	6,590,000	6,315,000	7,131,000
Total Assets	43,899,000	43,202,000	45,932,000	32,535,000	34,475,000	34,859,000	35,329,000	36,962,000
Current Liabilities	7,475,000	6,792,000	7,375,000	7,078,000	7,673,000	7,058,000	8,251,000	7,643,000
Long-Term Obligations	13,033,000	13,030,000	13,881,000	12,915,000	13,693,000	13,992,000	12,419,000	13,089,000
Total Liabilities	28,505,000	27,825,000	33,162,000	29,655,000	31,461,000	30,740,000	32,161,000	33,282,000
Stockholders' Equity	15,394,000	15,377,000	12,770,000	2,880,000	3,014,000	4,119,000	3,168,000	3,680,000
Shares Outstanding	1,893,825	1,901,259	1,943,272	1,960,059	1,971,474	1,993,479	2,009,740	2,044,419
Statistical Record								
Return on Assets %	23.79	22.94	36.19	15.64	14.62	12.92	11.53	9.12
Return on Equity %	77.49	72.63	181.47	177.84	142.16	124.47	121.75	76.42
EBITDA Margin %	38.36	39.84	85.41	32.80	31.66	29.48	26.83	26.56
Net Margin %	31.01	39.97	55.31	20.61	20.68	18.54	16.98	14.24
Asset Turnover	0.57	0.57	0.65	0.76	0.71	0.70	0.68	0.64
Current Ratio	0.65	0.64	0.98	0.86	0.90	0.93	0.77	0.93
Debt to Equity	0.85	0.85	1.09	4.48	4.54	3.40	3.92	3.56
Price Range	77.71-59.27	77.71-61.22	69.87-57.20	61.53-47.54	51.27-34.00	38.57-31.44	36.16-28.14	30.31-23.51
P/E Ratio	13.90-10.60	14.63-11.53	9.60-7.86	23.04-17.81	20.03-13.28	17.07-13.91	17.55-13.66	18.48-14.34
Average Yield %	3.85	3.64	3.68	4.03	4.75	5.19	5.26	5.96

Address: 6601 West Broad Street, Richmond, VA 23230 Telephone: 804-274-2200	Web Site: www.altria.com Officers: Howard A. Willard - Chairman, Chief Executive Officer, Executive Vice President, Chief Operating Officer, Chief Financial Officer William F. Gifford - Vice-Chairman, Executive Vice President, Chief Financial Officer	Auditors: PricewaterhouseCoopers LLP Investor Contact: 804-484-8222 Transfer Agents: Computershare Trust Company, N.A., Providence, RI

AMEREN CORP

Exchange	Symbol	Price	52Wk Range	Yield	P/E
NYS	AEE	$60.85 (6/29/2018)	64.54-52.59	3.01	26.00

*7 Year Price Score 109.26 *NYSE Composite Index=100   *12 Month Price Score 98.62

Interim Earnings (Per Share)

Qtr.	Mar	Jun	Sep	Dec
2015	0.45	0.61	1.41	0.12
2016	0.43	0.61	1.52	0.12
2017	0.42	0.79	1.18	(0.25)
2018	0.62	...	...	...

Interim Dividends (Per Share)

Amt	Decl	Ex	Rec	Pay
0.44Q	08/11/2017	09/12/2017	09/13/2017	09/29/2017
0.458Q	10/13/2017	12/12/2017	12/13/2017	12/29/2017
0.458Q	02/09/2018	03/13/2018	03/14/2018	03/29/2018
0.458Q	05/04/2018	06/12/2018	06/13/2018	06/29/2018

Indicated Div: $1.83 (Div. Reinv. Plan)

Valuation Analysis / Institutional Holding

Forecast EPS	$3.05	No of Institutions
	(06/14/2018)	773
Market Cap	$14.8 Billion	Shares
Book Value	$7.2 Billion	210,391,664
Price/Book	2.05	% Held
Price/Sales	2.37	62.59

Business Summary: Electric Utilities (MIC: 3.1.1 SIC: 4931 NAIC: 221111)

Ameren is a public utility holding company. Through its subsidiary, Union Electric Company, doing business as Ameren Missouri, Co. operates a rate-regulated electric generation, transmission, and distribution business and a rate-regulated natural gas distribution business in Missouri. Through its subsidiary, Ameren Illinois Company, doing business as Ameren Illinois, Co. operates rate-regulated electric transmission, electric distribution, and natural gas distribution businesses in Illinois. As of Dec 31 2017, Ameren Missouri and Ameren Illinois supplied electric service to 1.2 million customers each, and natural gas service to 100,000 customers and 800,000 customers, respectively.

Recent Developments: For the quarter ended Mar 31 2018, net income increased 47.1% to US$153.0 million from US$104.0 million in the year-earlier quarter. Revenues were US$1.59 billion, up 4.6% from US$1.52 billion the year before. Operating income was US$273.0 million versus US$242.0 million in the prior-year quarter, an increase of 12.8%. Direct operating expenses rose 2.5% to US$1.08 billion from US$1.05 billion in the comparable period the year before. Indirect operating expenses increased 5.9% to US$234.0 million from US$221.0 million in the equivalent prior-year period.

Prospects: Our evaluation of Ameren Corp. as of Jan. 21, 2018 is the result of our systematic analysis on three basic characteristics: earnings strength, relative valuation, and recent stock price movement. The company has managed to produce a neutral trend in earnings per share over the past 5 quarters and while recent estimates for the company have been mixed, AEE has posted results that fell short of analysts expectations. Based on operating earnings yield, the company is undervalued when compared to all of the companies in our coverage universe. Share price changes over the past year indicates that AEE will perform very well over the near term.

Financial Data

(US$ in Thousands)	3 Mos	12/31/2017	12/31/2016	12/31/2015	12/31/2014	12/31/2013	12/31/2012	12/31/2011
Earnings Per Share	2.34	2.14	2.68	2.59	2.40	1.18	(4.01)	2.15
Cash Flow Per Share	8.36	8.67	8.73	8.31	6.39	6.98	6.95	7.78
Tang Book Value Per Share	27.99	27.92	27.58	26.94	25.98	25.19	25.51	30.92
Dividends Per Share	1.795	1.778	1.715	1.655	1.610	1.600	1.600	1.555
Dividend Payout %	76.71	83.06	63.99	63.90	67.08	135.59	...	72.33
Income Statement								
Total Revenue	1,585,000	6,177,000	6,076,000	6,098,000	6,053,000	5,838,000	6,828,000	7,531,000
EBITDA	555,000	2,436,000	2,328,000	2,158,000	2,087,000	1,958,000	(397,000)	2,084,000
Depn & Amortn	259,000	974,000	945,000	896,000	813,000	761,000	842,000	829,000
Income Before Taxes	195,000	1,105,000	1,041,000	948,000	970,000	829,000	(1,654,000)	836,000
Income Taxes	42,000	576,000	382,000	363,000	377,000	311,000	(680,000)	310,000
Net Income	151,000	523,000	653,000	630,000	586,000	289,000	(974,000)	519,000
Average Shares	242,900	244,200	243,400	243,600	244,400	244,500	242,600	241,500
Balance Sheet								
Current Assets	1,567,000	1,612,000	1,593,000	1,917,000	2,046,000	1,972,000	2,369,000	2,295,000
Total Assets	26,079,000	25,945,000	24,699,000	23,640,000	22,676,000	21,042,000	21,835,000	23,645,000
Current Liabilities	3,345,000	2,940,000	2,674,000	2,093,000	2,249,000	2,461,000	1,698,000	1,785,000
Long-Term Obligations	6,766,000	7,094,000	6,595,000	6,880,000	6,120,000	5,504,000	6,626,000	6,677,000
Total Liabilities	18,849,000	18,761,000	17,596,000	16,694,000	15,963,000	14,498,000	15,219,000	15,726,000
Stockholders' Equity	7,230,000	7,184,000	7,103,000	6,946,000	6,713,000	6,544,000	6,616,000	7,919,000
Shares Outstanding	243,600	242,600	242,600	242,600	242,600	242,600	242,600	242,600
Statistical Record								
Return on Assets %	2.25	2.07	2.69	2.72	2.68	1.35	N.M.	2.20
Return on Equity %	8.00	7.32	9.27	9.22	8.84	4.39	N.M.	6.63
EBITDA Margin %	35.02	39.44	38.31	35.39	34.48	33.54	N.M.	27.67
Net Margin %	9.53	8.47	10.75	10.33	9.68	4.95	N.M.	6.89
Asset Turnover	0.25	0.24	0.25	0.26	0.28	0.27	0.30	0.32
Current Ratio	0.47	0.55	0.60	0.92	0.91	0.80	1.40	1.29
Debt to Equity	0.94	0.99	0.93	0.99	0.91	0.84	1.00	0.84
Price Range	64.54-52.59	64.54-51.69	53.77-42.13	46.54-37.51	47.92-35.40	37.03-30.72	34.71-28.55	33.81-25.97
P/E Ratio	27.58-22.47	30.16-24.15	20.06-15.72	17.97-14.48	19.97-14.75	31.38-26.03	...	15.73-12.08
Average Yield %	3.12	3.11	3.50	3.96	4.02	4.62	4.96	5.28

Address: 1901 Chouteau Avenue, St. Louis, MO 63103 Telephone: 314-621-3222	Web Site: www.ameren.com Officers: Warner L. Baxter - Chairman, President, Chief Executive Officer Martin J. Lyons - Executive Vice President, Chief Financial Officer	Auditors: PricewaterhouseCoopers LLP Transfer Agents: Ameren Services Company, St. Louis, MO

AMERICAN CAMPUS COMMUNITIES INC

Exchange	Symbol	Price	52Wk Range	Yield	P/E
NYS	ACC	$42.88 (6/29/2018)	49.00-34.80	4.29	97.45

*7 Year Price Score 79.73 *NYSE Composite Index=100 *12 Month Price Score 95.54

Interim Earnings (Per Share)

Qtr.	Mar	Jun	Sep	Dec
2015	0.62	0.14	0.01	0.25
2016	0.36	0.14	0.07	0.19
2017	0.25	(0.02)	(0.01)	0.29
2018	0.18	...	...	...

Interim Dividends (Per Share)

Amt	Decl	Ex	Rec	Pay
0.44Q	08/02/2017	08/10/2017	08/14/2017	08/25/2017
0.44Q	11/01/2017	11/10/2017	11/13/2017	11/27/2017
0.44Q	01/23/2018	02/01/2018	02/02/2018	02/16/2018
0.46Q	05/02/2018	05/11/2018	05/14/2018	05/25/2018

Indicated Div: $1.84

Valuation Analysis

		Institutional Holding	
Forecast EPS	$0.67 (06/14/2018)	No of Institutions	468
Market Cap	$5.9 Billion	Shares	166,840,832
Book Value	$3.5 Billion	% Held	100.00
Price/Book	1.69		
Price/Sales	7.11		

TRADING VOLUME (thousand shares)

Business Summary: REITs (MIC: 5.3.1 SIC: 6798 NAIC: 525930)

American Campus Communities is a real estate investment trust. Through American Campus Communities Operating Partnership L.P., Co. owns, manages and develops student housing properties. Co. focuses on the acquisition, design, financing, development, construction management, leasing and management of student housing properties. Co. has four reportable segments: Wholly-Owned Properties, On-Campus Participating Properties, Development Services and Property Management Services. As of Dec 31 2017, Co.'s property portfolio contained 169 properties, with 132 owned off-campus student housing properties, 32 American Campus Equity properties, and five on-campus participating properties.

Recent Developments: For the quarter ended Mar 31 2018, net income decreased 23.8% to US$26.3 million from US$34.4 million in the year-earlier quarter. Revenues were US$220.4 million, up 14.2% from US$192.9 million the year before. Revenues from property income rose 14.3% to US$216.0 million from US$189.0 million in the corresponding quarter a year earlier.

Prospects: Our evaluation of American Campus Communities Inc. as of Jan. 21, 2018 is the result of our systematic analysis on three basic characteristics: earnings strength, relative valuation, and recent stock price movement. The company has produced a positive trend in earnings per share over the past 5 quarters and while recent estimates for the company have been mixed, ACC has posted results that fell short of analysts expectations. Based on operating earnings yield, the company is overvalued when compared to all of the companies in our coverage universe. Share price changes over the past year indicates that ACC will perform well over the near term.

Financial Data

(US$ in Thousands)	3 Mos	12/31/2017	12/31/2016	12/31/2015	12/31/2014	12/31/2013	12/31/2012	12/31/2011
Earnings Per Share	0.44	0.50	0.75	1.02	0.58	0.98	0.65	0.80
Cash Flow Per Share	2.65	2.37	2.38	2.33	2.47	2.35	2.39	1.89
Tang Book Value Per Share	25.30	25.56	26.05	24.66	24.35	25.05	25.30	18.90
Dividends Per Share	1.760	1.740	1.660	1.580	1.500	1.418	1.350	1.350
Dividend Payout %	400.00	348.00	221.33	154.90	258.62	144.64	207.69	168.75
Income Statement								
Total Revenue	220,409	796,447	786,361	753,381	733,915	657,462	491,290	390,317
EBITDA	50,492	141,787	175,879	206,371	151,286	137,179	118,644	98,873
Depn & Amortn	86	4,500	900	3,700	2,400	13,700	6,800	4,100
Income Before Taxes	26,531	71,110	101,773	119,303	62,692	48,456	57,027	43,143
Income Taxes	281	989	1,150	1,242	1,308	1,020	725	433
Net Income	25,927	69,038	99,061	115,991	62,839	104,644	56,636	56,629
Average Shares	137,499	136,002	130,018	114,032	105,711	105,382	85,309	69,807
Balance Sheet								
Current Assets	93,713	73,942	55,385	68,809	67,144	83,440	72,366	50,679
Total Assets	7,006,952	6,897,370	5,865,913	6,025,947	5,834,748	5,598,040	5,118,962	3,008,582
Current Liabilities	52,932	53,741	76,614	71,988	70,629	65,088	56,046	36,884
Long-Term Obligations	3,134,210	3,024,519	2,125,297	2,967,980	2,972,719	2,744,387	2,221,105	1,447,530
Total Liabilities	3,550,449	3,412,385	2,420,928	3,255,751	3,225,194	2,973,139	2,470,581	1,633,366
Stockholders' Equity	3,456,503	3,484,985	3,444,985	2,770,196	2,609,554	2,624,901	2,648,381	1,375,216
Shares Outstanding	136,600	136,362	132,225	112,350	107,175	104,782	104,665	72,759
Statistical Record								
Return on Assets %	0.94	1.08	1.66	1.96	1.10	1.95	1.39	1.99
Return on Equity %	1.75	1.99	3.18	4.31	2.40	3.97	2.81	4.37
EBITDA Margin %	22.91	17.80	22.37	27.39	20.61	20.86	24.15	25.33
Net Margin %	11.76	8.67	12.60	15.40	8.56	15.92	11.53	14.51
Asset Turnover	0.13	0.12	0.13	0.13	0.13	0.12	0.12	0.14
Current Ratio	1.77	1.38	0.72	0.96	0.95	1.28	1.29	1.37
Debt to Equity	0.91	0.87	0.62	1.07	1.14	1.05	0.84	1.05
Price Range	49.63-34.80	51.43-40.23	54.55-39.33	44.84-32.26	41.88-32.21	47.88-31.80	47.69-40.86	42.39-30.78
P/E Ratio	112.80-79.09	102.86-80.46	72.73-52.44	43.96-31.63	72.21-55.53	48.86-32.45	73.37-62.86	52.99-38.48
Average Yield %	4.01	3.73	3.50	3.98	3.95	3.55	3.04	3.79

Address: 12700 Hill Country Blvd., Suite T-200, Austin, TX 78738
Telephone: 512-732-1000

Web Site: www.americancampus.com
Officers: Edward Lowenthal - Chairman James C. Hopke - President, Chief Operating Officer, Executive Vice President, Executive Vice President, Executive Vice President (frmr)

Auditors: Ernst & Young LLP
Investor Contact: 512-732-1041
Transfer Agents: Wells Fargo Bank N.A., Mendota Heights, MN

AMERICAN EAGLE OUTFITTERS, INC.

Exchange	Symbol	Price	52Wk Range	Yield	P/E
NYS	AEO	$23.25 (6/29/2018)	25.26-10.62	2.37	19.06

*7 Year Price Score 85.43   *NYSE Composite Index=100   *12 Month Price Score 131.13

Interim Earnings (Per Share)

Qtr.	Apr	Jul	Oct	Jan
2015-16	0.15	0.17	0.38	0.42
2016-17	0.22	0.23	0.41	0.30
2017-18	0.14	0.12	0.36	0.52
2018-19	0.22	...	...	...

Interim Dividends (Per Share)

Amt	Decl	Ex	Rec	Pay
0.125Q	09/07/2017	10/05/2017	10/06/2017	10/20/2017
0.125Q	12/05/2017	12/14/2017	12/15/2017	12/29/2017
0.138Q	03/07/2018	04/12/2018	04/13/2018	04/27/2018
0.138Q	06/06/2018	07/12/2018	07/13/2018	07/27/2018

Indicated Div: $0.55

Valuation Analysis

		Institutional Holding	
Forecast EPS	$1.51 (06/19/2018)	No of Institutions	560
Market Cap	$4.1 Billion	Shares	214,575,472
Book Value	$1.2 Billion	% Held	73.96
Price/Book	3.39		
Price/Sales	1.06		

Business Summary: Retail - Apparel and Accessories (MIC: 2.1.5 SIC: 5651 NAIC: 448140)

American Eagle Outfitters is a multi-brand retailer. Co. operates over 1,000 retail stores and online at www.ae.com and www.aerie.com. Co. provides a range of assortment of apparel and accessories for men and women under the American Eagle Outfitters brand, and intimates, apparel and personal care products for women under the Aerie brand. Co. operates stores in the U.S., Canada, Mexico, Hong Kong, China and the U.K. Co. also has license agreements with third-parties to operate American Eagle Outfitters and Aerie stores throughout Asia, Europe, Latin America and the Middle East. As of Feb. 3, 2018, Co. operated 933 American Eagle Outfitters stores and 109 Aerie stand-alone stores.

Recent Developments: For the quarter ended May 5 2018, net income increased 58.2% to US$39.9 million from US$25.2 million in the year-earlier quarter. Revenues were US$823.0 million, up 8.0% from US$761.8 million the year before. Operating income was US$50.7 million versus US$36.9 million in the prior-year quarter, an increase of 37.2%. Direct operating expenses rose 7.1% to US$518.5 million from US$484.0 million in the comparable period the year before. Indirect operating expenses increased 5.3% to US$253.7 million from US$240.9 million in the equivalent prior-year period.

Prospects: Our evaluation of American Eagle Outfitters Inc. as of Jan. 21, 2018 is the result of our systematic analysis on three basic characteristics: earnings strength, relative valuation, and recent stock price movement. The company has enjoyed a very positive trend in earnings per share over the past 5 quarters and while recent estimates for the company have been mixed, AEO has posted results that fell short of analysts expectations. Based on operating earnings yield, the company is undervalued when compared to all of the companies in our coverage universe. Share price changes over the past year indicates that AEO will perform poorly over the near term.

Financial Data

(US$ in Thousands)	3 Mos	02/03/2018	01/28/2017	01/30/2016	01/31/2015	02/01/2014	02/02/2013	01/28/2012
Earnings Per Share	1.22	1.13	1.16	1.11	0.42	0.43	1.16	0.77
Cash Flow Per Share	2.33	2.20	2.02	1.76	1.75	1.20	2.51	1.23
Tang Book Value Per Share	6.51	6.68	6.27	5.45	5.55	5.71	6.08	7.04
Dividends Per Share	0.512	0.500	0.500	0.500	0.500	0.375	2.050	0.440
Dividend Payout %	42.01	44.25	43.10	45.05	119.05	87.21	176.72	57.14
Income Statement								
Total Revenue	822,961	3,795,549	3,609,865	3,521,848	3,282,867	3,305,802	3,475,802	3,159,818
EBITDA	93,680	446,142	487,906	462,487	292,031	258,838	524,794	374,944
Depn & Amortn	42,472	158,969	152,644	140,616	132,529	116,761	122,756	137,934
Income Before Taxes	51,208	287,173	335,262	321,871	159,502	142,077	402,038	237,010
Income Taxes	11,279	83,010	122,813	108,580	70,715	59,094	137,940	85,305
Net Income	39,929	204,163	212,449	218,138	80,322	82,983	232,108	151,705
Average Shares	178,273	180,156	183,835	196,237	195,135	194,475	200,665	196,314
Balance Sheet								
Current Assets	874,596	968,530	901,229	723,375	890,513	923,560	1,141,800	1,287,488
Total Assets	1,730,914	1,816,313	1,782,660	1,612,246	1,696,908	1,694,164	1,756,053	1,950,802
Current Liabilities	434,804	485,221	493,783	463,682	459,093	415,478	435,902	405,401
Total Liabilities	523,533	569,522	578,091	560,870	557,162	527,986	534,866	533,951
Stockholders' Equity	1,207,381	1,246,791	1,204,569	1,051,376	1,139,746	1,166,178	1,221,187	1,416,851
Shares Outstanding	176,217	177,316	181,886	180,135	194,516	193,149	192,604	193,848
Statistical Record								
Return on Assets %	13.01	11.25	12.55	13.22	4.75	4.82	12.32	7.94
Return on Equity %	18.82	16.52	18.89	19.97	6.99	6.97	17.31	10.99
EBITDA Margin %	11.38	11.75	13.52	13.13	8.90	7.83	15.10	11.87
Net Margin %	4.85	5.38	5.89	6.19	2.45	2.51	6.68	4.80
Asset Turnover	2.29	2.09	2.13	2.13	1.94	1.92	1.85	1.65
Current Ratio	2.01	2.00	1.83	1.56	1.94	2.22	2.62	3.18
Price Range	21.77-10.62	19.37-10.62	19.37-13.12	18.35-13.24	14.85-10.28	22.55-12.77	23.80-13.58	16.18-10.17
P/E Ratio	17.84-8.70	17.14-9.40	16.70-11.31	16.53-11.93	35.36-24.48	52.44-29.70	20.52-11.71	21.01-13.21
Average Yield %	3.34	3.58	3.05	3.08	3.93	2.18	10.55	3.21

Address: 77 Hot Metal Street, Pittsburgh, PA 15203-2329 **Telephone:** 412-432-3300	**Web Site:** www.ae.com **Officers:** Jay L. Schottenstein - Executive Chairman, Chairman, Chief Executive Officer, Interim Chief Executive Officer Michael R. Rempell - Executive Vice President, Chief Operating Officer	**Auditors:** Ernst & Young LLP **Investor Contact:** 412-432-3300 **Transfer Agents:** Computershare Trust Company, N.A., Providence, RI

AMERICAN ELECTRIC POWER COMPANY, INC.

Exchange	Symbol	Price	52Wk Range	Yield	P/E
NYS	AEP	$69.25 (6/29/2018)	77.63-62.93	3.58	19.29

*7 Year Price Score 102.76 *NYSE Composite Index=100 *12 Month Price Score 94.02

Interim Earnings (Per Share)

Qtr.	Mar	Jun	Sep	Dec
2015	1.29	0.88	1.06	0.95
2016	1.02	1.02	(1.56)	0.76
2017	1.20	0.76	1.10	0.81
2018	0.92	...	...	...

Interim Dividends (Per Share)

Amt	Decl	Ex	Rec	Pay
0.59Q	07/25/2017	08/08/2017	08/10/2017	09/08/2017
0.62Q	10/24/2017	11/09/2017	11/10/2017	12/08/2017
0.62Q	01/23/2018	02/08/2018	02/09/2018	03/09/2018
0.62Q	04/23/2018	05/09/2018	05/10/2018	06/08/2018

Indicated Div: $2.48 (Div. Reinv. Plan)

Valuation Analysis / **Institutional Holding**

Forecast EPS	$3.90	No of Institutions
	(06/14/2018)	1364
Market Cap	$34.1 Billion	Shares
Book Value	$18.5 Billion	432,109,056
Price/Book	1.84	% Held
Price/Sales	2.19	63.99

Business Summary: Electric Utilities (MIC: 3.1.1 SIC: 4911 NAIC: 221122)

American Electric Power Company is a public utility holding company. The public utility subsidiaries of Co. provide electric service, consisting of generation, transmission and distribution, on an integrated basis to their retail customers. The service areas of Co.'s public utility subsidiaries cover portions of the states of Arkansas, Indiana, Kentucky, Louisiana, Michigan, Ohio, Oklahoma, Tennessee, Texas, Virginia and West Virginia. Transmission networks are interconnected with distribution facilities in the territories served.

Recent Developments: For the quarter ended Mar 31 2018, net income decreased 23.1% to US$456.7 million from US$594.2 million in the year-earlier quarter. Revenues were US$4.05 billion, up 2.9% from US$3.93 billion the year before. Operating income was US$706.0 million versus US$1.09 billion in the prior-year quarter, a decrease of 35.0%. Direct operating expenses rose 7.9% to US$2.52 billion from US$2.33 billion in the comparable period the year before. Indirect operating expenses increased 60.2% to US$825.3 million from US$515.2 million in the equivalent prior-year period.

Prospects: Our evaluation of American Electric Power Company Inc. as of Jan. 21, 2018 is the result of our systematic analysis on three basic characteristics: earnings strength, relative valuation, and recent stock price movement. The company has produced a positive trend in earnings per share over the past 5 quarters and while recent estimates for the company have been mixed, AEP has posted results that fell short of analysts expectations. Based on operating earnings yield, the company is undervalued when compared to all of the companies in our coverage universe. Share price changes over the past year indicates that AEP will perform very well over the near term.

Financial Data
(US$ in Thousands)

	3 Mos	12/31/2017	12/31/2016	12/31/2015	12/31/2014	12/31/2013	12/31/2012	12/31/2011
Earnings Per Share	3.59	3.88	1.24	4.17	3.34	3.04	2.60	4.02
Cash Flow Per Share	8.67	8.68	9.18	9.68	9.44	8.44	7.83	7.86
Tang Book Value Per Share	37.46	37.09	35.27	36.33	34.18	32.79	31.19	30.18
Dividends Per Share	2.420	2.390	2.270	2.150	2.030	1.950	1.880	1.850
Dividend Payout %	67.41	61.60	183.06	51.56	60.78	64.14	72.31	46.02
Income Statement								
Total Revenue	4,048,300	15,424,900	16,380,100	16,453,200	17,020,000	15,357,000	14,945,000	15,116,000
EBITDA	799,500	5,837,500	3,443,700	5,651,500	5,448,000	4,890,000	4,728,000	5,092,000
Depn & Amortn	27,400	2,126,300	2,090,900	2,154,700	2,073,000	1,874,000	1,918,000	1,792,000
Income Before Taxes	540,200	2,816,200	475,600	2,622,900	2,490,000	2,110,000	1,822,000	2,367,000
Income Taxes	102,000	969,700	(73,700)	919,600	942,000	684,000	604,000	818,000
Net Income	454,400	1,912,600	610,900	2,047,100	1,634,000	1,480,000	1,259,000	1,946,000
Average Shares	493,127	492,611	491,662	490,574	488,899	487,040	485,084	482,460
Balance Sheet								
Current Assets	4,135,000	4,253,100	6,033,900	4,072,400	4,478,000	4,310,000	4,589,000	4,182,000
Total Assets	65,609,500	64,729,100	63,467,700	61,683,100	59,633,000	56,414,000	54,367,000	52,223,000
Current Liabilities	9,471,400	8,271,300	9,498,000	7,108,500	7,967,000	6,112,000	6,823,000	6,611,000
Long-Term Obligations	18,844,900	19,419,600	17,378,400	17,740,900	16,181,000	16,828,000	15,586,000	15,083,000
Total Liabilities	47,109,200	46,430,200	46,070,700	43,791,400	42,813,000	40,329,000	39,130,000	37,559,000
Stockholders' Equity	18,500,300	18,298,900	17,397,000	17,891,700	16,820,000	16,085,000	15,237,000	14,664,000
Shares Outstanding	492,512	492,005	491,711	491,052	489,402	487,777	485,668	483,422
Statistical Record								
Return on Assets %	2.79	2.98	0.97	3.37	2.82	2.67	2.36	3.79
Return on Equity %	9.81	10.72	3.45	11.79	9.93	9.45	8.40	13.73
EBITDA Margin %	19.75	37.84	21.02	34:35	32.01	31.84	31.64	33.69
Net Margin %	11.22	12.40	3.73	12.44	9.60	9.64	8.42	12.87
Asset Turnover	0.24	0.24	0.26	0.27	0.29	0.28	0.28	0.29
Current Ratio	0.44	0.51	0.64	0.57	0.56	0.71	0.67	0.63
Debt to Equity	1.02	1.06	1.00	0.99	0.96	1.05	1.02	1.03
Price Range	77.63-63.38	77.63-62.12	71.27-57.64	64.57-52.54	62.91-46.08	51.43-41.92	45.27-37.22	41.65-33.60
P/E Ratio	21.62-17.65	20.01-16.01	57.48-46.48	15.48-12.60	18.84-13.80	16.92-13.79	17.41-14.32	10.36-8.36
Average Yield %	3.42	3.41	3.54	3.79	3.84	4.24	4.59	4.96

Address: 1 Riverside Plaza, Columbus, OH 43215-2373 **Telephone:** 614-716-1000 **Fax:** 614-223-1823	**Web Site:** www.aep.com **Officers:** Nicholas K. Akins - Chairman, President, Chief Executive Officer Brian X. Tierney - Executive Vice President, Chief Financial Officer	**Auditors:** PricewaterhouseCoopers LLP **Investor Contact:** 614-716-2819 **Transfer Agents:** Computershare Trust Company, N.A., Providence, RI

AMERICAN EQUITY INVESTMENT LIFE HOLDING CO

Exchange	Symbol	Price	52Wk Range	Yield	P/E	Div Acheiver
NYS	AEL	$36.00 (6/29/2018)	36.95-25.75	0.72	12.50	14 Years

*7 Year Price Score 118.88 *NYSE Composite Index=100 *12 Month Price Score 109.72

Interim Earnings (Per Share)

Qtr.	Mar	Jun	Sep	Dec
2015	0.07	1.05	1.19	0.39
2016	(0.55)	0.18	(0.09)	1.42
2017	0.60	0.30	0.63	0.40
2018	1.55	...	...	...

Interim Dividends (Per Share)

Amt	Decl	Ex	Rec	Pay
0.20A	11/21/2014	11/26/2014	12/01/2014	12/15/2014
0.22A	11/19/2015	11/25/2015	11/30/2015	12/14/2015
0.24A	11/17/2016	12/01/2016	12/05/2016	12/20/2016
0.26A	11/16/2017	11/28/2017	11/29/2017	12/12/2017

Indicated Div: $0.26

Valuation Analysis / Institutional Holding

Valuation Analysis		Institutional Holding	
Forecast EPS	$3.43	No of Institutions	383
	(06/12/2018)		
Market Cap	$3.2 Billion	Shares	104,451,536
Book Value	$2.5 Billion	% Held	
Price/Book	1.27		105.63
Price/Sales	1.05		

Business Summary: Life & Health (MIC: 5.2.2 SIC: 6311 NAIC: 524113)

American Equity Investment Life Holding is a holding company. Co. is engaged in the development and sale of fixed index and fixed rate annuity products. Co. issues fixed annuity and life insurance products through its wholly-owned life insurance subsidiaries, American Equity Investment Life Insurance Company, American Equity Investment Life Insurance Company of New York, and Eagle Life Insurance Company. Co.'s life insurance products include ordinary and term, universal life and other interest-sensitive life insurance products. Co. was licensed to sell its products in 50 states and the District of Columbia at Dec 31 2017.

Recent Developments: For the quarter ended Mar 31 2018, net income increased 161.3% to US$141.0 million from US$53.9 million in the year-earlier quarter. Revenues were US$118.9 million, down 87.2% from US$927.3 million the year before. Net premiums earned were US$59.8 million versus US$53.0 million in the prior-year quarter, an increase of 12.8%. Net investment income rose 5.2% to US$510.8 million from US$485.6 million a year ago.

Prospects: Our evaluation of American Equity Investment Life Holding Co as of Jan. 21, 2018 is the result of our systematic analysis on three basic characteristics: earnings strength, relative valuation, and recent stock price movement. The company has managed to produce a neutral trend in earnings per share over the past 5 quarters and while recent estimates for the company have been mixed, AEL has posted better than expected results. Based on operating earnings yield, the company is undervalued when compared to all of the companies in our coverage universe. Share price changes over the past year indicates that AEL will perform in line with the market over the near term.

Financial Data
(US$ in Thousands)

	3 Mos	12/31/2017	12/31/2016	12/31/2015	12/31/2014	12/31/2013	12/31/2012	12/31/2011
Earnings Per Share	2.88	1.93	0.97	2.72	1.58	3.38	0.89	1.37
Cash Flow Per Share	10.90	21.60	16.63	6.40	9.51	13.16	12.77	4.67
Tang Book Value Per Share	28.30	31.91	26.04	23.90	28.13	19.63	27.86	24.36
Dividends Per Share	0.260	0.260	0.240	0.220	0.200	0.180	0.150	0.120
Dividend Payout %	9.03	13.47	24.74	8.09	12.66	5.33	16.85	8.76
Income Statement								
Total Revenue	118,872	3,891,652	2,220,282	1,518,937	2,168,973	2,610,692	1,588,558	1,139,775
Income Before Taxes	177,611	316,271	130,247	337,314	196,064	389,332	85,989	132,914
Income Taxes	36,649	141,626	47,004	117,484	70,041	136,049	28,191	46,666
Net Income	140,962	174,645	83,243	219,830	126,023	253,283	57,798	86,248
Average Shares	91,139	90,311	85,605	80,961	79,893	75,040	65,675	63,619
Balance Sheet								
Total Assets	61,301,324	62,030,736	56,053,472	49,041,163	43,989,734	39,621,499	35,133,478	30,874,719
Total Liabilities	58,754,334	59,180,579	53,761,877	47,096,628	41,849,858	38,236,812	33,413,241	29,466,040
Stockholders' Equity	2,546,990	2,850,157	2,291,595	1,944,535	2,139,876	1,384,687	1,720,237	1,408,679
Shares Outstanding	89,983	89,331	88,001	81,354	76,062	70,535	61,750	57,836
Statistical Record								
Return on Assets %	0.44	0.30	0.16	0.47	0.30	0.68	0.17	0.30
Return on Equity %	10.50	6.79	3.92	10.76	7.15	16.31	3.68	7.35
Net Margin %	118.58	4.49	3.75	14.47	5.81	9.70	3.64	7.57
Asset Turnover	0.05	0.07	0.04	0.03	0.05	0.07	0.05	0.04
Price Range	35.50-22.52	32.22-22.34	24.03-12.81	29.67-22.76	29.46-20.43	26.38-12.21	12.95-10.05	13.85-8.17
P/E Ratio	12.33-7.82	16.69-11.58	24.77-13.21	10.91-8.37	18.65-12.93	7.80-3.61	14.55-11.29	10.11-5.96
Average Yield %	0.91	0.97	1.41	0.83	0.83	1.01	1.30	1.03

Address: 6000 Westown Parkway, West Des Moines, IA 50266 Telephone: 515-221-0002	Web Site: www.american-equity.com Officers: David J. Noble - Chairman John M. Matovina - Vice-Chairman, President, Chief Executive Officer, Chief Financial Officer, Treasurer	Auditors: KPMG LLP Investor Contact: 515-221-0002 Transfer Agents: Computershare Trust Company, N.A., Providence, RI

AMERICAN EXPRESS CO.

Exchange	Symbol	Price	52Wk Range	Yield	P/E
NYS	AXP	$98.00 (6/29/2018)	102.70-83.74	1.43	28.00

*7 Year Price Score 102.39   *NYSE Composite Index=100   *12 Month Price Score 104.29

Interim Earnings (Per Share)

Qtr.	Mar	Jun	Sep	Dec
2015	1.48	1.42	1.24	0.90
2016	1.45	2.10	1.20	0.89
2017	1.34	1.47	1.50	(1.33)
2018	1.86	...	...	...

Interim Dividends (Per Share)

Amt	Decl	Ex	Rec	Pay
0.35Q	09/26/2017	10/05/2017	10/06/2017	11/10/2017
0.35Q	11/28/2017	01/04/2018	01/05/2018	02/09/2018
0.35Q	03/12/2018	04/05/2018	04/06/2018	05/10/2018
0.35Q	05/08/2018	07/05/2018	07/06/2018	08/10/2018

Indicated Div: $1.40

Valuation Analysis		Institutional Holding	
Forecast EPS	$7.25	No of Institutions	2044
	(06/13/2018)		
Market Cap	$84.3 Billion	Shares	890,347,072
Book Value	$19.6 Billion	% Held	74.56
Price/Book	4.30		
Price/Sales	2.24		

Business Summary: Credit & Lending (MIC: 5.4.1 SIC: 6153 NAIC: 522210)

American Express, together with its subsidiaries, Co. is a global services company that provides charge and credit card products and travel-related services to consumers and businesses around the world. Co.'s range of products and services includes: charge card, credit card and other payment and financing products; network services; merchant acquisition and processing, servicing and settlement, and point-of-sale marketing and information products and services for merchants; other fee services, including fraud prevention services and the design and operation of customer loyalty programs; expense management products and services; travel-related services; and stored value/prepaid products.

Recent Developments: For the quarter ended Mar 31 2018, net income increased 30.6% to US$1.63 billion from US$1.25 billion in the year-earlier quarter. Net interest income increased 22.6% to US$1.84 billion from US$1.50 billion in the year-earlier quarter. Provision for loan losses was US$775.0 million versus US$573.0 million in the prior-year quarter, an increase of 35.3%. Non-interest income rose 9.3% to US$7.88 billion from US$7.21 billion, while non-interest expense advanced 9.0% to US$6.86 billion.

Prospects: Our evaluation of American Express Co. as of Jan. 21, 2018 is the result of our systematic analysis on three basic characteristics: earnings strength, relative valuation, and recent stock price movement. The company has produced a positive trend in earnings per share over the past 5 quarters and while recent estimates for the company have been raised by analysts, AXP has posted better than expected results. Based on operating earnings yield, the company is undervalued when compared to all of the companies in our coverage universe. Share price changes over the past year indicates that AXP will perform well over the near term.

Financial Data (US$ in Thousands)	3 Mos	12/31/2017	12/31/2016	12/31/2015	12/31/2014	12/31/2013	12/31/2012	12/31/2011
Earnings Per Share	3.50	2.97	5.65	5.05	5.56	4.88	3.89	4.12
Cash Flow Per Share	16.81	15.33	8.79	10.98	10.52	7.90	6.22	8.89
Tang Book Value Per Share	22.81	16.67	18.48	17.68	16.42	14.55	13.31	12.43
Dividends Per Share	1.340	1.310	1.190	1.100	0.980	0.860	0.780	0.720
Dividend Payout %	38.29	44.11	21.06	21.78	17.63	17.62	20.05	17.48
Income Statement								
Total Revenue	10,339,000	35,583,000	33,823,000	34,441,000	35,999,000	34,932,000	33,808,000	32,282,000
Income Before Taxes	2,082,000	7,414,000	8,096,000	7,938,000	8,991,000	7,888,000	6,451,000	6,956,000
Income Taxes	448,000	4,678,000	2,688,000	2,775,000	3,106,000	2,529,000	1,969,000	2,057,000
Net Income	1,634,000	2,736,000	5,408,000	5,163,000	5,885,000	5,359,000	4,482,000	4,935,000
Average Shares	861,000	886,000	935,000	1,003,000	1,051,000	1,089,000	1,141,000	1,184,000
Balance Sheet								
Total Assets	179,956,000	181,159,000	158,893,000	161,184,000	159,103,000	153,375,000	153,140,000	153,337,000
Total Liabilities	160,343,000	162,932,000	138,392,000	140,511,000	138,430,000	133,879,000	134,254,000	134,543,000
Stockholders' Equity	19,613,000	18,227,000	20,501,000	20,673,000	20,673,000	19,496,000	18,886,000	18,794,000
Shares Outstanding	860,000	859,000	904,000	969,000	1,023,000	1,064,000	1,105,000	1,164,000
Statistical Record								
Return on Assets %	1.84	1.61	3.37	3.22	3.77	3.50	2.92	3.29
Return on Equity %	15.45	14.13	26.20	24.97	29.30	27.92	23.72	28.18
Net Margin %	15.80	7.69	15.99	14.99	16.35	15.34	13.26	15.29
Asset Turnover	0.22	0.21	0.21	0.22	0.23	0.23	0.22	0.21
Price Range	101.64-75.55	99.70-75.32	75.32-51.11	93.04-67.87	95.84-80.24	90.73-57.48	61.05-48.24	53.59-42.36
P/E Ratio	29.04-21.59	33.57-25.36	13.33-9.05	18.42-13.44	17.24-14.43	18.59-11.78	15.69-12.40	13.01-10.28
Average Yield %	1.50	1.55	1.86	1.41	1.09	1.18	1.39	1.52

Address: 200 Vesey Street, New York, NY 10285
Telephone: 212-640-2000
Fax: 212-640-0404

Web Site: www.americanexpress.com
Officers: Stephen J. Squeri - Chairman, Chief Executive Officer, Vice-Chairman, Division Officer Richard Petrino - Executive Vice President, Corporate Controller, Principal Accounting Officer

Auditors: PricewaterhouseCoopers LLP
Transfer Agents: Computershare Shareowner Services LLC, Canton, MA

AMERICAN FINANCIAL GROUP INC

Exchange	Symbol	Price	52Wk Range	Yield	P/E	Div Acheiver
NYS	AFG	$107.33 (6/29/2018)	120.49-95.54	1.30	20.72	12 Years

*7 Year Price Score 131.86 *NYSE Composite Index=100 *12 Month Price Score 101.01

Interim Earnings (Per Share)

Qtr.	Mar	Jun	Sep	Dec
2015	0.21	1.57	0.71	1.45
2016	1.14	0.62	1.23	4.35
2017	1.72	1.61	0.13	1.84
2018	1.60	...	...	...

Interim Dividends (Per Share)

Amt	Decl	Ex	Rec	Pay
0.35Q	01/02/2018	01/11/2018	01/15/2018	01/25/2018
0.35Q	04/02/2018	04/12/2018	04/13/2018	04/25/2018
1.50Sp	05/02/2018	05/14/2018	05/15/2018	05/25/2018
0.35Q	07/02/2018	07/12/2018	07/13/2018	07/25/2018

Indicated Div: $1.40 (Div. Reinv. Plan)

Valuation Analysis — **Institutional Holding**

Forecast EPS	$8.55 (06/14/2018)	No of Institutions	533
Market Cap	$9.5 Billion	Shares	73,997,808
Book Value	$5.2 Billion	% Held	53.28
Price/Book	1.84		
Price/Sales	1.38		

Business Summary: General Insurance (MIC: 5.2.1 SIC: 6331 NAIC: 524126)

American Financial Group is a holding company. Co.'s segments include Property and Casualty Insurance, which includes Property and Transportation (inland and ocean marine, agricultural-related, and commercial automobile), Specialty Casualty (executive and professional liability, umbrella and excess liability, excess and surplus, general liability, targeted programs, and workers' compensation), and Specialty Financial (fidelity and surety, and lease and loan services); Annuity, which sells fixed and fixed-indexed annuities in the retail, financial institutions and education markets; and other, which includes commercial real estate operations.

Recent Developments: For the quarter ended Mar 31 2018, net income decreased 9.0% to US$141.0 million from US$155.0 million in the year-earlier quarter. Revenues were US$1.62 billion, up 2.7% from US$1.58 billion the year before. Net premiums earned were US$1.11 billion versus US$1.03 billion in the prior-year quarter, an increase of 8.3%.

Prospects: Our evaluation of American Financial Group Inc. as of Jan. 21, 2018 is the result of our systematic analysis on three basic characteristics: earnings strength, relative valuation, and recent stock price movement. The company has generated a negative trend in earnings per share over the past 5 quarters. However, while recent estimates for the company have been mixed, AFG has posted better than expected results. Based on operating earnings yield, the company is undervalued when compared to all of the companies in our coverage universe. Share price changes over the past year indicates that AFG will perform well over the near term.

Financial Data
(US$ in Thousands)

	3 Mos	12/31/2017	12/31/2016	12/31/2015	12/31/2014	12/31/2013	12/31/2012	12/31/2011
Earnings Per Share	5.18	5.28	7.33	3.94	4.97	5.16	5.09	3.33
Cash Flow Per Share	25.63	20.55	13.20	15.49	13.73	8.51	8.65	6.58
Tang Book Value Per Share	56.07	58.12	54.27	50.22	53.34	49.31	49.37	44.55
Dividends Per Share	4.825	4.787	2.152	2.030	1.910	1.805	0.970	0.662
Dividend Payout %	93.15	90.67	29.37	51.52	38.43	34.98	19.06	19.89
Income Statement								
Premium Income	1,113,000	4,601,000	4,352,000	4,328,000	3,986,000	3,318,000	3,165,000	3,189,000
Total Revenue	1,619,000	6,865,000	6,498,000	6,145,000	5,713,000	5,092,000	5,062,000	4,750,000
Benefits & Claims	834,000	3,873,000	3,595,000	3,558,000	3,306,000	2,731,000	2,779,000	2,623,000
Income Before Taxes	174,000	724,000	787,000	565,000	626,000	689,000	537,000	560,000
Income Taxes	33,000	247,000	119,000	195,000	220,000	236,000	135,000	240,000
Net Income	145,000	475,000	649,000	352,000	452,000	471,000	488,000	343,000
Average Shares	90,400	89,800	88,500	89,400	91,000	91,200	95,900	102,900
Balance Sheet								
Total Assets	60,656,000	60,658,000	55,072,000	49,859,000	47,535,000	42,087,000	39,171,000	36,042,000
Total Liabilities	55,473,000	55,328,000	50,156,000	45,267,000	42,656,000	37,488,000	34,593,000	31,497,000
Stockholders' Equity	5,183,000	5,330,000	4,916,000	4,592,000	4,879,000	4,599,000	4,578,000	4,545,000
Shares Outstanding	88,881	88,275	86,924	87,474	87,708	89,513	88,979	97,846
Statistical Record								
Return on Assets %	0.79	0.82	1.23	0.72	1.01	1.16	1.29	1.00
Return on Equity %	9.00	9.27	13.61	7.43	9.54	10.26	10.67	7.61
Loss Ratio %	74.93	84.18	82.61	82.21	82.94	82.31	87.80	82.25
Net Margin %	8.96	6.92	9.99	5.73	7.91	9.25	9.64	7.22
Price Range	120.49-93.29	109.06-85.86	88.12-65.14	75.17-58.04	62.36-52.93	58.16-39.52	40.25-36.58	37.30-30.09
P/E Ratio	23.26-18.01	20.66-16.26	12.02-8.89	19.08-14.73	12.55-10.65	11.27-7.66	7.91-7.19	11.20-9.04
Average Yield %	4.64	4.83	2.93	3.03	3.28	3.60	2.54	1.94

Address: 301 East Fourth Street, Cincinnati, OH 45202 **Telephone:** 513-579-2121	**Web Site:** www.afginc.com **Officers:** Carl H. Lindner - Co-President, Co-Chief Executive Officer S. Craig Lindner - Co-President, Co-Chief Executive Officer	**Auditors:** Ernst & Young LLP **Investor Contact:** 513-579-6739 **Transfer Agents:** American Stock Transfer & Trust Company, New York, NY

AMERICAN HOMES 4 RENT

Exchange	Symbol	Price	52Wk Range	Yield	P/E
NYS	AMH	$22.18 (6/29/2018)	23.17-18.73	0.90	N/A

*7 Year Price Score N/A   *NYSE Composite Index=100   *12 Month Price Score 96.88

Interim Earnings (Per Share)

Qtr.	Mar	Jun	Sep	Dec
2015	(0.08)	(0.08)	(0.14)	(0.10)
2016	(0.02)	(0.04)	(0.09)	0.01
2017	(0.01)	0.00	0.01	0.00
2018	0.02	...	...	...

Interim Dividends (Per Share)

Amt	Decl	Ex	Rec	Pay
0.05Q	08/03/2017	09/14/2017	09/15/2017	09/29/2017
0.05Q	11/02/2017	12/29/2017	01/02/2018	01/05/2018
0.05Q	02/22/2018	03/14/2018	03/15/2018	04/02/2018
0.05Q	05/03/2018	06/14/2018	06/15/2018	07/02/2018
		Indicated Div: $0.20		

Valuation Analysis

Forecast EPS	$0.16	Institutional Holding	
	(06/11/2018)	No of Institutions	N/A
Market Cap	$6.3 Billion	Shares	
Book Value	$5.1 Billion	N/A	
Price/Book	1.24	% Held	
Price/Sales	6.42	N/A	

TRADING VOLUME (thousand shares)

Business Summary: REITs (MIC: 5.3.1 SIC: 6798 NAIC: 525930)

American Homes 4 Rent is a real estate investment trust which engaged in acquiring, renovating, leasing and operating single-family homes as rental properties. As of Dec 31 2017, Co. owned 51,239 single-family properties in 22 states, including 310 properties held for sale.

Recent Developments: For the quarter ended Mar 31 2018, net income increased 82.5% to US$21.5 million from US$11.8 million in the year-earlier quarter. Revenues were US$258.0 million, up 10.4% from US$233.8 million the year before. Revenues from property income rose 10.6% to US$256.7 million from US$232.1 million in the corresponding quarter a year earlier.

Prospects: Our evaluation of American Homes 4 Rent as of Jan. 21, 2018 is the result of our systematic analysis on three basic characteristics: earnings strength, relative valuation, and recent stock price movement. The company has managed to produce a neutral trend in earnings per share over the past 5 quarters and while recent estimates for the company have remained steady, AMH has posted better than expected results. Based on operating earnings yield, the company is overvalued when compared to all of the companies in our coverage universe. Share price changes over the past year indicates that AMH will perform well over the near term.

Financial Data (US$ in Thousands)	3 Mos	12/31/2017	12/31/2016	12/31/2015	12/31/2014	12/31/2013	12/31/2012	12/31/2011
Earnings Per Share	0.03	(0.01)	(0.14)	(0.40)	(0.34)	(0.36)	(1.42)	(0.01)
Cash Flow Per Share	1.36	1.46	1.19	0.96	0.82	0.13	(0.90)	(0.01)
Tang Book Value Per Share	17.56	17.54	16.73	15.10	15.74	15.17	23.40	0.09
Dividends Per Share	0.200	0.200	0.200	0.200	0.200	0.050	...	...
Income Statement								
Total Revenue	258,004	960,399	878,889	630,576	398,874	139,032	4,540	65
EBITDA	128,941	470,859	401,447	265,196	152,305	51,283	(8,125)	(21)
Depn & Amortn	78,115	281,747	260,154	223,731	165,516	70,987	2,111	21
Income Before Taxes	21,525	76,492	10,446	(47,948)	(33,092)	(20,074)	(10,236)	(42)
Net Income	20,411	80,999	6,695	(62,301)	(48,057)	(32,311)	(10,236)	(42)
Average Shares	286,727	264,254	234,010	210,600	196,348	123,592	7,225	3,301
Balance Sheet								
Current Assets	388,270	182,823	250,241	168,968	185,985	175,419	397,198	...
Total Assets	8,958,033	8,608,768	8,107,210	6,807,786	6,227,351	4,224,144	921,458	3,523
Current Liabilities	264,268	595,080	568,751	291,591	486,723	573,485	16,294	49
Long-Term Obligations	2,824,857	2,137,864	2,600,839	2,580,962	1,571,034	...	...	...
Total Liabilities	3,841,924	3,459,139	3,914,274	3,548,441	2,777,250	1,289,200	16,784	49
Stockholders' Equity	5,116,109	5,149,629	4,192,936	3,259,345	3,450,101	2,934,944	904,674	3,474
Shares Outstanding	285,004	286,749	243,375	207,870	211,473	185,504	38,664	38,664
Statistical Record								
Return on Assets %	1.02	0.97	0.09	N.M.	N.M.	N.M.	N.M.	...
Return on Equity %	1.85	1.73	0.18	N.M.	N.M.	N.M.	N.M.	...
EBITDA Margin %	49.98	49.03	45.68	42.06	38.18	36.89	N.M.	N.M.
Net Margin %	7.91	8.43	0.76	N.M.	N.M.	N.M.	N.M.	N.M.
Asset Turnover	0.11	0.11	0.12	0.10	0.08	0.05	0.01	...
Current Ratio	1.47	0.31	0.44	0.58	0.38	0.31	24.38	...
Debt to Equity	0.55	0.42	0.62	0.79	0.46	...	...	...
Price Range	23.76-18.73	23.77-20.34	22.84-13.21	17.48-15.30	18.51-15.87	16.90-15.22	...	...
Average Yield %	0.92	0.90	1.07	1.21	1.16	0.31	...	...

Address: 30601 Agoura Road, Suite 200, Agoura Hills, CA 91301
Telephone: 805-413-5300

Web Site: www.americanhomes4rent.com
Officers: David P. Singelyn - Chief Executive Officer, Interim Chief Financial Officer John Corrigan - Chief Operating Officer

Auditors: Ernst & Young LLP
Transfer Agents: American Stock Transfer & Trust Company, LLC

40

AMERICAN INTERNATIONAL GROUP INC

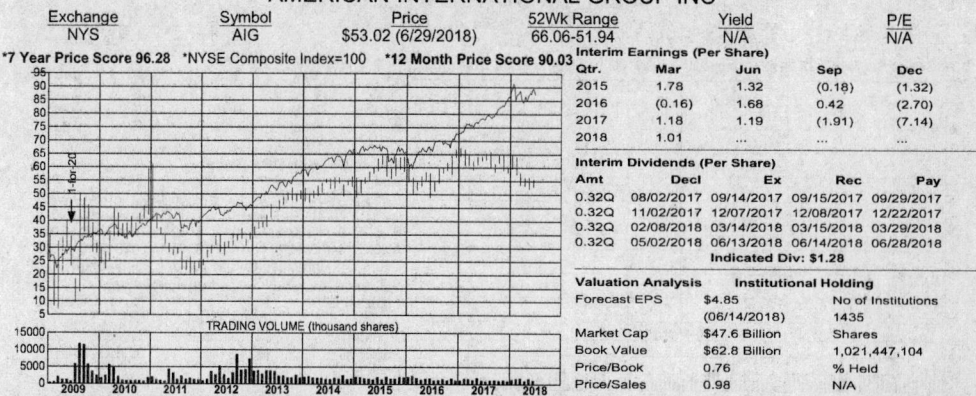

Exchange	Symbol	Price	52Wk Range	Yield	P/E
NYS	AIG	$53.02 (6/29/2018)	66.06-51.94	N/A	N/A

*7 Year Price Score 96.28 *NYSE Composite Index=100 *12 Month Price Score 90.03

Interim Earnings (Per Share)

Qtr.	Mar	Jun	Sep	Dec
2015	1.78	1.32	(0.18)	(1.32)
2016	(0.16)	1.68	0.42	(2.70)
2017	1.18	1.19	(1.91)	(7.14)
2018	1.01	...	...	...

Interim Dividends (Per Share)

Amt	Decl	Ex	Rec	Pay
0.32Q	08/02/2017	09/14/2017	09/15/2017	09/29/2017
0.32Q	11/02/2017	12/07/2017	12/08/2017	12/22/2017
0.32Q	02/08/2018	03/14/2018	03/15/2018	03/29/2018
0.32Q	05/02/2018	06/13/2018	06/14/2018	06/28/2018

Indicated Div: $1.28

Valuation Analysis — **Institutional Holding**

Forecast EPS	$4.85	No of Institutions
	(06/14/2018)	1435
Market Cap	$47.6 Billion	Shares
Book Value	$62.8 Billion	1,021,447,104
Price/Book	0.76	% Held
Price/Sales	0.98	N/A

TRADING VOLUME (thousand shares)

Business Summary: General Insurance (MIC: 5.2.1 SIC: 6331 NAIC: 524126)

American International Group is a holding company. Co.'s business operations consist of Commercial Insurance, Consumer Insurance, Other Operations, and a Legacy Portfolio. Commercial Insurance consists of Liability and Financial Lines and Property and Special Risks. Consumer Insurance consists of Group Retirement, Individual Retirement, Life Insurance and Personal Insurance. Other Operations include Institutional Markets, which consists of stable value wrap products, structured settlement and terminal funding annuities, corporate- and bank-owned life insurance and guaranteed investment contracts. Co.'s Legacy Portfolio includes its Legacy Property and Casualty Run-Off Insurance Lines.

Recent Developments: For the quarter ended Mar 31 2018, income from continuing operations decreased 21.6% to US$950.0 million from US$1.21 billion in the year-earlier quarter. Net income decreased 21.6% to US$949.0 million from US$1.21 billion in the year-earlier quarter. Revenues were US$11.71 billion, down 7.3% from US$12.63 billion the year before. Net premiums earned were US$7.28 billion versus US$7.78 billion in the prior-year quarter, a decrease of 6.5%. Net investment income fell 14.6% to US$2.81 billion from US$3.29 billion a year ago.

Prospects: Our evaluation of American International Group Inc. as of Jan. 21, 2018 is the result of our systematic analysis on three basic characteristics: earnings strength, relative valuation, and recent stock price movement. The company has managed to produce a neutral trend in earnings per share over the past 5 quarters. However, while recent estimates for the company have been mixed, AIG has posted results that fell short of analysts expectations. Based on operating earnings yield, the company is about fairly valued when compared to all of the companies in our coverage universe. Share price changes over the past year indicates that AIG will perform poorly over the near term.

Financial Data

(US$ in Thousands)	3 Mos	12/31/2017	12/31/2016	12/31/2015	12/31/2014	12/31/2013	12/31/2012	12/31/2011
Earnings Per Share	(6.85)	(6.54)	(0.78)	1.65	5.20	6.13	2.04	9.44
Cash Flow Per Share	0.92	(9.23)	2.18	2.21	3.51	3.98	2.17	0.02
Tang Book Value Per Share	69.95	72.49	76.66	75.10	77.69	68.62	66.38	55.33
Dividends Per Share	1.280	1.280	1.280	0.810	0.500	0.200	...	...
Dividend Payout %	...	...	...	49.09	9.62	3.26	...	...
Income Statement								
Premium Income	7,275,000	31,374,000	34,393,000	36,655,000	37,254,000	37,350,000	38,011,000	38,990,000
Total Revenue	11,712,000	49,520,000	52,367,000	58,327,000	64,406,000	68,678,000	65,656,000	64,237,000
Benefits & Claims	5,667,000	29,972,000	32,437,000	31,345,000	28,281,000	29,503,000	31,977,000	33,449,000
Income Before Taxes	1,227,000	1,466,000	(74,000)	3,281,000	10,501,000	9,368,000	9,322,000	(1,065,000)
Income Taxes	277,000	7,526,000	185,000	1,059,000	2,927,000	360,000	1,570,000	(18,036,000)
Net Income	938,000	(6,084,000)	(849,000)	2,196,000	7,529,000	9,085,000	3,438,000	17,798,000
Average Shares	925,266	930,561	1,091,085	1,334,464	1,447,553	1,481,206	1,687,226	1,799,458
Balance Sheet								
Total Assets	499,143,000	498,301,000	498,264,000	496,943,000	515,581,000	541,329,000	548,633,000	555,773,000
Total Liabilities	436,351,000	433,130,000	421,964,000	407,285,000	408,683,000	440,859,000	450,631,000	450,822,000
Stockholders' Equity	62,792,000	65,171,000	76,300,000	89,658,000	106,898,000	100,470,000	98,002,000	104,951,000
Shares Outstanding	897,681	899,044	995,335	1,193,916	1,375,926	1,464,063	1,476,321	1,896,821
Statistical Record								
Return on Assets %	N.M.	N.M.	N.M.	0.43	1.42	1.67	0.62	2.87
Return on Equity %	N.M.	N.M.	N.M.	2.23	7.26	9.15	3.38	18.71
Loss Ratio %	77.90	95.53	94.31	85.51	75.91	78.99	84.13	85.79
Net Margin %	8.01	(12.29)	(1.62)	3.76	11.69	13.23	5.24	27.71
Price Range	66.06-53.41	67.20-58.11	66.70-48.79	64.54-48.87	56.51-46.88	52.30-34.84	37.21-23.54	61.18-20.10
P/E Ratio	...	...	...	39.12-29.62	10.87-9.02	8.53-5.68	18.24-11.54	6.48-2.13
Average Yield %	2.09	2.05	2.23	1.38	0.95	0.45	...	...

Address: 175 Water Street, New York, NY 10038 Telephone: 212-770-7000	Web Site: www.aig.com Officers: Douglas M. Steenland - Chairman Brian Duperreault - President, Chief Executive Officer	Auditors: PricewaterhouseCoopers LLP Transfer Agents: Wells Fargo Bank, N.A. Shareowner Services, St. Paul, MN

AMERICAN STATES WATER CO

Exchange	Symbol	Price	52Wk Range	Yield	P/E	Div Acheiver
NYS	AWR	$57.16 (6/29/2018)	59.45-46.73	1.78	31.23	64 Years

*7 Year Price Score 122.92 *NYSE Composite Index=100 *12 Month Price Score 103.57

Interim Earnings (Per Share)

Qtr.	Mar	Jun	Sep	Dec
2015	0.32	0.41	0.56	0.31
2016	0.28	0.45	0.59	0.30
2017	0.34	0.62	0.57	0.35
2018	0.29	...	...	...

Interim Dividends (Per Share)

Amt	Decl	Ex	Rec	Pay
0.255Q	08/01/2017	08/11/2017	08/15/2017	09/01/2017
0.255Q	10/31/2017	11/14/2017	11/15/2017	12/01/2017
0.255Q	01/31/2018	02/14/2018	02/15/2018	03/01/2018
0.255Q	04/30/2018	05/14/2018	05/15/2018	06/01/2018

Indicated Div: $1.02 (Div. Reinv. Plan)

Valuation Analysis

		Institutional Holding	
Forecast EPS	$1.75	No of Institutions	
	(06/03/2018)	346	
Market Cap	$2.1 Billion	Shares	
Book Value	$531.5 Million	32,599,404	
Price/Book	3.95	% Held	
Price/Sales	4.81	58.65	

Business Summary: Water Utilities (MIC: 3.2.1 SIC: 4941 NAIC: 221310)

American States Water is a holding company. Co. is the parent company of Golden State Water Company (GSWC) and American States Utility Services, Inc. (ASUS) and its subsidiaries. Co. has three reportable segments: water, electric and contracted services. Within the segments, Co. has two principal business units, water and electric service utility operations, conducted through GSWC, and contracted services conducted through ASUS and its subsidiaries. GSWC is a public utility company engaged principally in the purchase, production, distribution and sale of water in 10 counties in the State of California. At Dec 31 2017, GSWC served 258,949 water customers and 24,274 electric customers.

Recent Developments: For the quarter ended Mar 31 2018, net income decreased 15.1% to US$10.8 million from US$12.7 million in the year-earlier quarter. Revenues were US$94.7 million, down 4.1% from US$98.8 million the year before. Operating income was US$18.7 million versus US$24.6 million in the prior-year quarter, a decrease of 23.9%. Direct operating expenses rose 4.5% to US$46.1 million from US$44.1 million in the comparable period the year before. Indirect operating expenses decreased 0.6% to US$30.0 million from US$30.1 million in the equivalent prior-year period.

Prospects: Our evaluation of American States Water Co. as of Jan. 21, 2018 is the result of our systematic analysis on three basic characteristics: earnings strength, relative valuation, and recent stock price movement. The company has managed to produce a neutral trend in earnings per share over the past 5 quarters and while recent estimates for the company have been mixed, AWR has posted results that fell short of analysts expectations. Based on operating earnings yield, the company is about fairly valued when compared to all of the companies in our coverage universe. Share price changes over the past year indicates that AWR will perform well over the near term.

Financial Data

(US$ in Thousands)	3 Mos	12/31/2017	12/31/2016	12/31/2015	12/31/2014	12/31/2013	12/31/2012	12/31/2011
Earnings Per Share	1.83	1.88	1.62	1.60	1.57	1.61	1.41	1.22
Cash Flow Per Share	4.15	3.95	2.65	2.54	4.22	3.51	2.66	2.14
Tang Book Value Per Share	14.44	14.42	13.49	12.73	13.21	12.69	11.79	10.85
Dividends Per Share	1.007	0.994	0.914	0.874	0.831	0.760	0.635	0.550
Dividend Payout %	55.03	52.87	56.42	54.63	52.93	47.20	45.04	45.27
Income Statement								
Total Revenue	94,728	440,603	436,087	458,641	465,791	472,077	466,908	419,274
EBITDA	28,459	168,406	154,822	161,519	161,547	161,144	154,759	133,257
Depn & Amortn	9,726	39,273	39,109	42,674	41,751	40,967	43,234	38,349
Income Before Taxes	13,346	108,341	94,478	98,215	99,106	98,469	90,093	72,086
Income Taxes	2,564	38,974	34,735	37,731	38,048	35,783	35,945	30,076
Net Income	10,782	69,367	59,743	60,484	61,058	62,686	54,148	45,859
Average Shares	36,874	36,844	36,750	37,614	38,880	38,869	38,262	37,674
Balance Sheet								
Current Assets	145,676	155,463	166,875	132,697	209,451	191,617	184,033	165,601
Total Assets	1,423,664	1,416,734	1,470,493	1,348,600	1,378,298	1,310,183	1,280,943	1,238,362
Current Liabilities	196,491	156,662	177,944	123,507	99,290	100,906	93,697	104,370
Long-Term Obligations	281,053	324,941	325,252	325,541	325,798	326,079	332,463	340,395
Total Liabilities	892,140	886,789	976,196	882,655	871,497	817,779	826,364	829,696
Stockholders' Equity	531,524	529,945	494,297	465,945	506,801	492,404	454,579	408,666
Shares Outstanding	36,733	36,680	36,571	36,501	38,286	38,720	38,474	37,577
Statistical Record								
Return on Assets %	4.65	4.81	4.23	4.44	4.54	4.84	4.29	3.77
Return on Equity %	13.10	13.55	12.41	12.44	12.22	13.24	12.51	11.67
EBITDA Margin %	30.04	38.22	35.50	35.22	34.68	34.14	33.15	31.78
Net Margin %	11.38	15.74	13.70	13.19	13.11	13.28	11.60	10.94
Asset Turnover	0.30	0.31	0.31	0.34	0.35	0.36	0.37	0.35
Current Ratio	0.74	0.99	0.94	1.07	2.11	1.90	1.96	1.59
Debt to Equity	0.53	0.61	0.66	0.70	0.64	0.66	0.73	0.83
Price Range	59.45-43.29	57.91-41.22	47.18-37.62	43.57-36.00	38.71-27.15	32.86-23.99	23.99-17.15	18.16-15.64
P/E Ratio	32.49-23.66	30.80-21.93	29.12-23.22	27.23-22.50	24.66-17.29	20.41-14.90	17.01-12.16	14.89-12.82
Average Yield %	1.97	2.05	2.21	2.21	2.64	2.76	3.16	3.20

Address: 630 E. Foothill Boulevard, San Dimas, CA 91773-1212 **Telephone:** 909-394-3600	**Web Site:** www.aswater.com **Officers:** Lloyd E. Ross - Chairman Robert J. Sprowls - President, Chief Executive Officer	**Auditors:** PricewaterhouseCoopers LLP **Investor Contact:** 909-394-3600 **Transfer Agents:** Computershare Shareowner Services, Jersey City, NJ

AMERICAN TOWER CORP

Exchange	Symbol	Price	52Wk Range	Yield	P/E
NYS	AMT	$144.17 (6/29/2018)	152.72-130.93	2.14	54.82

*7 Year Price Score 118.78 *NYSE Composite Index=100 *12 Month Price Score 97.77

Interim Earnings (Per Share)

Qtr.	Mar	Jun	Sep	Dec
2015	0.45	0.30	0.18	0.49
2016	0.58	0.37	0.55	0.47
2017	0.67	0.80	0.69	0.51
2018	0.63	...	...	...

Interim Dividends (Per Share)

Amt	Decl	Ex	Rec	Pay
0.66Q	09/12/2017	09/28/2017	09/29/2017	10/17/2017
0.70Q	12/07/2017	12/27/2017	12/28/2017	01/16/2018
0.75Q	03/08/2018	04/10/2018	04/11/2018	04/27/2018
0.77Q	05/24/2018	06/18/2018	06/19/2018	07/13/2018

Indicated Div: $3.08

Valuation Analysis / Institutional Holding

Forecast EPS	$3.10 (06/14/2018)	No of Institutions 1462
Market Cap	$63.7 Billion	Shares 502,134,688
Book Value	$6.3 Billion	% Held
Price/Book	10.05	N/A
Price/Sales	9.38	

Business Summary: REITs (MIC: 5.3.1 SIC: 6798 NAIC: 525930)

American Tower is a holding company. Through its subsidiaries, Co. is a real estate investment trusts and independent owner, operator and developer of multitenant communications real estate. Co.'s property operations lease space on communications sites to wireless service providers, radio and television broadcast companies, wireless data providers, government agencies and municipalities and tenants in a number of other industries. Co.'s services operations provides tower-related services, including site acquisition, zoning and permitting and structural analysis services, which support its site leasing business, including through the addition of new tenants and equipment on its sites.

Recent Developments: For the quarter ended Mar 31 2018, net income decreased 8.8% to US$280.3 million from US$307.4 million in the year-earlier quarter. Revenues were US$1.74 billion, up 7.8% from US$1.62 billion the year before.

Prospects: Our evaluation of American Tower Corp. as of Jan. 21, 2018 is the result of our systematic analysis on three basic characteristics: earnings strength, relative valuation, and recent stock price movement. The company has managed to produce a neutral trend in earnings per share over the past 5 quarters. However, while recent estimates for the company have been mixed, AMT has posted results that fell short of analysts expectations. Based on operating earnings yield, the company is overvalued when compared to all of the companies in our coverage universe. Share price changes over the past year indicates that AMT will perform very well over the near term.

Financial Data
(US$ in Thousands)

	3 Mos	12/31/2017	12/31/2016	12/31/2015	12/31/2014	12/31/2013	12/31/2012	12/31/2011
Earnings Per Share	2.63	2.67	1.98	1.41	2.00	1.38	1.60	0.99
Cash Flow Per Share	6.97	6.83	6.34	5.21	5.39	4.05	3.57	2.95
Dividends Per Share	2.620	2.620	2.170	1.810	1.400	1.100	0.900	0.350
Dividend Payout %	99.62	98.13	109.60	128.37	70.00	79.71	56.25	35.35
Income Statement								
Total Revenue	1,741,800	6,663,900	5,785,668	4,771,516	4,100,048	3,361,407	2,875,960	2,443,532
EBITDA	877,000	2,795,000	2,565,307	2,059,623	1,973,189	1,451,704	1,492,921	1,150,557
Depn & Amortn	446,300	835,500	758,900	661,400	551,800	483,600	411,900	353,400
Income Before Taxes	249,200	1,256,100	1,125,860	829,962	865,704	541,749	701,294	506,895
Income Taxes	(31,100)	30,700	155,501	157,955	62,505	59,541	107,304	125,080
Net Income	285,200	1,238,900	956,425	685,074	824,910	551,333	637,283	396,462
Average Shares	438,520	431,688	429,283	423,015	400,086	399,146	399,287	400,195
Balance Sheet								
Current Assets	2,797,400	2,038,100	1,689,870	996,468	947,968	952,656	829,528	842,771
Total Assets	34,372,700	33,214,300	30,879,150	26,904,272	21,331,545	20,272,571	14,089,129	12,232,430
Current Liabilities	4,544,700	2,512,100	1,631,269	1,200,029	1,929,692	924,758	632,178	779,591
Long-Term Obligations	18,568,800	19,430,300	18,294,659	17,068,807	13,711,084	14,408,146	8,693,345	7,134,492
Total Liabilities	28,038,500	26,972,800	24,115,255	20,252,593	17,377,985	16,738,406	10,516,028	8,945,210
Stockholders' Equity	6,334,200	6,241,500	6,763,895	6,651,679	3,953,560	3,534,165	3,573,101	3,287,220
Shares Outstanding	441,596	428,820	427,102	423,885	396,698	394,864	395,091	393,642
Statistical Record								
Return on Assets %	3.64	3.87	3.30	2.84	3.97	3.21	4.83	3.51
Return on Equity %	18.32	19.05	14.22	12.92	22.03	15.51	18.53	11.68
EBITDA Margin %	50.35	41.94	44.34	43.16	48.13	43.19	51.91	47.09
Net Margin %	16.37	18.59	16.53	14.36	20.12	16.40	22.16	16.22
Asset Turnover	0.20	0.21	0.20	0.20	0.20	0.20	0.22	0.22
Current Ratio	0.62	0.81	1.04	0.83	0.49	1.03	1.31	1.08
Debt to Equity	2.93	3.11	2.70	2.57	3.47	4.08	2.43	2.17
Price Range	152.72-120.64	152.72-103.01	117.84-83.66	104.06-87.01	105.01-78.83	84.64-68.36	77.27-58.81	60.70-46.35
P/E Ratio	58.07-45.87	57.20-38.58	59.52-42.25	73.80-61.71	52.51-39.41	61.33-49.54	48.29-36.76	61.31-46.82
Average Yield %	1.90	2.01	2.05	1.89	1.55	1.44	1.32	0.68

Address: 116 Huntington Avenue, Boston, MA 02116 Telephone: 617-375-7500	Web Site: www.americantower.com Officers: James D. (Jim) Taiclet - Chairman, President, Chief Executive Officer Thomas A. (Tom) Bartlett - Executive Vice President, Chief Financial Officer, Treasurer	Auditors: DELOITTE & TOUCHE LLP Investor Contact: 617-375-7500 Transfer Agents: Computershare

AMERICAN WATER WORKS CO, INC.

Exchange	Symbol	Price	52Wk Range	Yield	P/E
NYS	AWK	$85.38 (6/29/2018)	92.25-76.06	2.13	34.99

*7 Year Price Score 120.94 *NYSE Composite Index=100 *12 Month Price Score 97.94

Interim Earnings (Per Share)

Qtr.	Mar	Jun	Sep	Dec
2015	0.44	0.68	0.96	0.55
2016	0.46	0.77	0.83	0.57
2017	0.52	0.73	1.13	(0.01)
2018	0.59	...	...	...

Interim Dividends (Per Share)

Amt	Decl	Ex	Rec	Pay
0.415Q	07/28/2017	08/07/2017	08/09/2017	09/01/2017
0.415Q	10/31/2017	11/09/2017	11/10/2017	12/01/2017
0.415Q	12/08/2017	02/06/2018	02/07/2018	03/01/2018
0.455Q	04/20/2018	05/10/2018	05/11/2018	06/01/2018

Indicated Div: $1.82

Valuation Analysis / Institutional Holding

Forecast EPS	$3.29 (06/14/2018)	No of Institutions	891
Market Cap	$15.2 Billion	Shares	188,897,072
Book Value	$5.5 Billion	% Held	80.07
Price/Book	2.79		
Price/Sales	4.52		

Business Summary: Water Utilities (MIC: 3.2.1 SIC: 4941 NAIC: 221310)

American Water Works Company is a holding company. Through its subsidiaries, Co. is a water and wastewater utility company. Co.'s Regulated Businesses provide water and wastewater services as public utilities. Co.'s Market-Based Businesses consists of four segments including Military Services Group, which operates and maintains water and wastewater systems for military bases; Contract Operations Group, which operates and maintains water and wastewater facilities for municipalities, the food and beverage industry; Homeowner Services Group, which provides warranty-type services for homeowners; and Keystone, which provides services for natural gas exploration and production companies.

Recent Developments: For the quarter ended Mar 31 2018, net income increased 14.0% to US$106.0 million from US$93.0 million in the year-earlier quarter. Revenues were US$761.0 million, up 0.7% from US$756.0 million the year before. Operating income was US$217.0 million versus US$230.0 million in the prior-year quarter, a decrease of 5.7%. Direct operating expenses rose 3.9% to US$347.0 million from US$334.0 million in the comparable period the year before. Indirect operating expenses increased 2.6% to US$197.0 million from US$192.0 million in the equivalent prior-year period.

Prospects: Our evaluation of American Water Works Co. Inc. as of Jan. 21, 2018 is the result of our systematic analysis on three basic characteristics: earnings strength, relative valuation, and recent stock price movement. The company has produced a positive trend in earnings per share over the past 5 quarters. However, while recent estimates for the company have been mixed, AWK has posted results that were in line with analysts expectations. Based on operating earnings yield, the company is about fairly valued when compared to all of the companies in our coverage universe. Share price changes over the past year indicates that AWK will perform very well over the near term.

Financial Data

(US$ in Thousands)	3 Mos	12/31/2017	12/31/2016	12/31/2015	12/31/2014	12/31/2013	12/31/2012	12/31/2011
Earnings Per Share	2.44	2.38	2.62	2.64	2.35	2.06	2.01	1.75
Cash Flow Per Share	7.81	8.14	7.15	6.59	6.13	5.04	5.40	4.61
Tang Book Value Per Share	22.87	22.45	21.75	21.02	20.66	19.73	18.28	17.31
Dividends Per Share	1.660	1.620	1.465	1.330	1.210	0.840	1.210	0.900
Dividend Payout %	68.03	68.07	55.92	50.38	51.49	40.78	60.20	51.43
Income Statement								
Total Revenue	761,000	3,357,000	3,302,000	3,159,000	3,011,328	2,901,858	2,876,889	2,666,236
EBITDA	386,000	1,714,000	1,530,000	1,495,000	1,349,306	1,232,271	1,233,328	1,066,028
Depn & Amortn	162,000	460,000	435,000	405,000	356,952	337,653	314,639	268,987
Income Before Taxes	140,000	912,000	770,000	782,000	709,814	605,470	631,258	503,680
Income Taxes	34,000	486,000	302,000	306,000	279,973	236,206	257,008	198,751
Net Income	106,000	426,000	468,000	476,000	423,108	369,264	358,070	309,613
Average Shares	179,000	179,000	179,000	180,000	179,806	179,056	177,671	176,531
Balance Sheet								
Current Assets	729,000	720,000	784,000	657,000	661,369	550,390	499,447	1,397,659
Total Assets	19,728,000	19,482,000	18,482,000	17,241,000	16,130,956	15,069,533	14,718,976	14,776,391
Current Liabilities	2,539,000	2,325,000	2,392,000	1,533,000	1,240,998	1,235,533	994,832	1,489,105
Long-Term Obligations	6,396,000	6,490,000	5,749,000	5,862,000	5,432,744	5,212,881	5,190,509	5,339,947
Total Liabilities	14,277,000	14,097,000	13,264,000	12,192,000	11,215,365	10,341,729	10,273,988	10,536,007
Stockholders' Equity	5,451,000	5,385,000	5,218,000	5,049,000	4,915,591	4,727,804	4,444,988	4,240,384
Shares Outstanding	178,040	178,444	178,096	178,282	179,462	178,379	176,988	175,664
Statistical Record								
Return on Assets %	2.29	2.24	2.61	2.85	2.71	2.48	2.42	2.15
Return on Equity %	8.18	8.04	9.09	9.55	8.78	8.05	8.22	7.40
EBITDA Margin %	50.72	51.06	46.34	47.33	44.81	42.46	42.87	39.98
Net Margin %	13.93	12.69	14.17	15.07	14.05	12.73	12.45	11.61
Asset Turnover	0.18	0.18	0.18	0.19	0.19	0.19	0.19	0.18
Current Ratio	0.29	0.31	0.33	0.43	0.53	0.45	0.50	0.94
Debt to Equity	1.17	1.21	1.10	1.16	1.11	1.10	1.17	1.26
Price Range	92.25-75.25	92.25-70.57	84.76-59.44	60.61-48.63	55.86-41.16	43.50-37.13	38.35-31.38	32.55-25.23
P/E Ratio	37.81-30.84	38.76-29.65	32.35-22.69	22.96-18.42	23.77-17.51	21.12-18.02	19.08-15.61	18.60-14.42
Average Yield %	2.02	2.01	2.02	2.45	2.53	2.05	3.43	3.12

Address: 1025 Laurel Oak Road, Voorhees, NJ 08043 Telephone: 856-346-8200	Web Site: www.amwater.com Officers: George MacKenzie - Chairman Susan N. Story - President, Chief Executive Officer, Senior Vice President, Chief Financial Officer	Auditors: PricewaterhouseCoopers LLP Investor Contact: 856-566-4005 Transfer Agents: American Stock Transfer & Trust Company, Brooklyn, NY

AMERIGAS PARTNERS LP

Exchange	Symbol	Price	52Wk Range	Yield	P/E	Div Acheiver
NYS	APU	$42.22 (6/29/2018)	48.22-39.80	9.00	28.53	13 Years

*7 Year Price Score 79.87   *NYSE Composite Index=100   *12 Month Price Score 94.51

Interim Earnings (Per Share)

Qtr.	Dec	Mar	Jun	Sep
2014-15	(0.49)	2.17	(0.37)	(0.62)
2015-16	0.77	1.74	(0.46)	(1.03)
2016-17	0.87	1.14	(0.62)	(0.31)
2017-18	0.97	1.44	...	...

Interim Dividends (Per Share)

Amt	Decl	Ex	Rec	Pay
0.95Q	07/24/2017	08/08/2017	08/10/2017	08/18/2017
0.95Q	10/26/2017	11/09/2017	11/10/2017	11/17/2017
0.95Q	01/24/2018	02/08/2018	02/09/2018	02/20/2018
0.95Q	04/23/2018	05/09/2018	05/10/2018	05/18/2018

Indicated Div: $3.80

Valuation Analysis

		Institutional Holding	
Forecast EPS	$2.05	No of Institutions	
	(06/12/2018)	342	
Market Cap	$3.9 Billion	Shares	
Book Value	N/A	27,371,484	
Price/Book	N/A	% Held	
Price/Sales	1.43	29.71	

Business Summary: Gas Utilities (MIC: 3.3.1 SIC: 5989 NAIC: 454312)

AmeriGas Partners is a holding company and it conducts its business principally through its subsidiary, AmeriGas Propane, L.P. Co. is a retail propane distributor. As of Sep 30 2017, Co. served about 1,900,000 residential, commercial, industrial, agricultural, wholesale and motor fuel customers in all 50 states from about 1,900 propane distribution locations. AmeriGas Propane, Inc. is Co.'s general partner and is engaged in managing Co.'s operations. In addition to distributing propane, Co. sells, installs and services propane appliances. As part of its overall transportation and distribution infrastructure, Co. operates as an interstate carrier throughout the continental U.S.

Recent Developments: For the quarter ended Mar 31 2018, net income increased 41.6% to US$194.2 million from US$137.1 million in the year-earlier quarter. Revenues were US$1.04 billion, up 20.5% from US$863.7 million the year before. Operating income was US$235.8 million versus US$199.9 million in the prior-year quarter, an increase of 18.0%. Direct operating expenses rose 34.0% to US$514.9 million from US$384.4 million in the comparable period the year before. Indirect operating expenses increased 3.6% to US$289.6 million from US$279.4 million in the equivalent prior-year period.

Prospects: Our evaluation of AmeriGas Partners, L.P. as of Jan. 21, 2018 is the result of our systematic analysis on three basic characteristics: earnings strength, relative valuation, and recent stock price movement. The company has generated a negative trend in earnings per share over the past 5 quarters and while recent estimates for the company have been raised by analysts, APU has posted better than expected results. Based on operating earnings yield, the company is about fairly valued when compared to all of the companies in our coverage universe. Share price changes over the past year indicates that APU will perform poorly over the near term.

Financial Data

(US$ in Thousands)	6 Mos	3 Mos	09/30/2017	09/30/2016	09/30/2015	09/30/2014	09/30/2013	09/30/2012
Earnings Per Share	1.48	1.18	1.25	1.77	1.91	2.82	2.14	(0.11)
Cash Flow Per Share	4.14	3.50	3.84	4.54	5.64	5.17	3.83	4.22
Dividends Per Share	3.800	3.790	3.780	3.720	3.600	3.440	3.280	3.103
Dividend Payout %	256.76	321.19	302.40	210.17	188.48	121.99	153.27	...
Income Statement								
Total Revenue	1,827,628	787,296	2,453,495	2,311,817	2,885,322	3,712,935	3,166,543	2,921,616
EBITDA	458,037	186,642	475,870	520,520	532,913	616,653	551,500	291,468
Depn & Amortn	73,395	37,817	147,741	146,805	152,204	154,020	159,306	134,225
Income Before Taxes	303,070	108,248	167,903	209,620	217,867	297,052	226,762	14,602
Income Taxes	3,034	2,378	2,034	(1,573)	2,898	2,611	1,671	1,931
Net Income	296,245	104,421	162,059	206,984	211,211	289,893	221,222	11,025
Average Shares	93,074	93,080	93,050	93,023	92,977	92,946	92,910	81,433
Balance Sheet								
Current Assets	551,489	581,241	413,774	344,448	366,361	505,908	500,692	523,368
Total Assets	4,140,970	4,192,104	4,059,261	4,057,770	4,141,712	4,364,058	4,409,846	4,517,331
Current Liabilities	569,066	719,174	581,532	588,455	546,294	617,514	616,974	670,845
Long-Term Obligations	2,563,942	2,563,441	2,563,832	2,325,334	2,273,817	2,280,145	2,288,097	2,297,363
Total Liabilities	3,297,746	3,440,306	3,311,362	3,073,549	2,977,496	3,041,544	3,024,743	3,088,223
Shares Outstanding	92,976	92,963	92,958	92,923	92,889	92,867	92,824	92,801
Statistical Record								
Return on Assets %	5.53	4.16	3.99	5.03	4.97	6.61	4.96	0.35
EBITDA Margin %	25.06	23.71	19.40	22.52	18.47	16.61	17.42	9.98
Net Margin %	16.21	13.26	6.61	8.95	7.32	7.81	6.99	0.38
Asset Turnover	0.65	0.61	0.60	0.56	0.68	0.85	0.71	0.92
Current Ratio	0.97	0.81	0.71	0.59	0.67	0.82	0.81	0.78
Price Range	48.22-39.96	49.87-42.09	49.87-42.09	49.89-32.21	52.55-39.73	48.30-41.18	50.00-37.76	46.21-37.19
P/E Ratio	32.58-27.00	42.26-35.67	39.90-33.67	28.19-18.20	27.51-20.80	17.13-14.60	23.36-17.64	...
Average Yield %	8.52	8.36	8.30	8.76	7.65	7.76	7.52	7.36

Address: 460 North Gulph Road, King of Prussia, PA 19406
Telephone: 610-337-7000

Web Site: www.amerigas.com
Officers: John L. Walsh - Executive Chairman, Vice-Chairman, Holding/Parent Company Officer
Jerry E. Sheridan - President, Chief Executive Officer, Vice President, Chief Operating Officer

Auditors: Ernst & Young LLP
Investor Contact: 610-337-7000ext.10
Transfer Agents: ComputerShare Investor Services, Providence, RI

AMERIPRISE FINANCIAL INC

Exchange	Symbol	Price	52Wk Range	Yield	P/E	Div Acheiver
NYS	AMP	$139.88 (6/29/2018)	182.04-127.29	2.57	12.89	12 Years

*7 Year Price Score 119.74 *NYSE Composite Index=100   *12 Month Price Score 91.72

TRADING VOLUME (thousand shares)

Interim Earnings (Per Share)

Qtr.	Mar	Jun	Sep	Dec
2015	2.08	2.23	2.17	2.00
2016	2.09	1.97	1.30	2.44
2017	2.52	2.50	3.24	1.20
2018	3.91	...	...	...

Interim Dividends (Per Share)

Amt	Decl	Ex	Rec	Pay
0.83Q	07/25/2017	08/03/2017	08/07/2017	08/18/2017
0.83Q	10/24/2017	11/03/2017	11/06/2017	11/17/2017
0.83Q	01/24/2018	02/15/2018	02/16/2018	02/28/2018
0.90Q	04/23/2018	05/04/2018	05/07/2018	05/18/2018

Indicated Div: $3.60 (Div. Reinv. Plan)

Valuation Analysis   **Institutional Holding**

Forecast EPS	$14.53	No of Institutions
	(06/12/2018)	1142
Market Cap	$20.3 Billion	Shares
Book Value	$5.8 Billion	166,329,344
Price/Book	3.47	% Held
Price/Sales	1.65	73.34

Business Summary: Wealth Management (MIC: 5.5.2 SIC: 6282 NAIC: 523930)

Ameriprise Financial is a holding company. Co. provides a range of products and services to individual and institutional clients. Co.'s segments include Advice & Wealth Management, which provides financial planning and advice, as well as brokerage services, primarily to retail clients through Co.'s advisors; Asset Management, which provides investment management and advice and investment products to institutional clients; Annuities, which provides variable and fixed annuity products; Protection, which provides a range of products to address the protection and risk management needs of Co.'s retail clients including life, DI and property casualty insurance; and Corporate & Other.

Recent Developments: For the quarter ended Mar 31 2018, net income increased 47.4% to US$594.0 million from US$403.0 million in the year-earlier quarter. Revenues were US$3.17 billion, up 8.3% from US$2.93 billion the year before. Direct operating expenses rose 0.5% to US$1.63 billion from US$1.62 billion in the comparable period the year before. Indirect operating expenses increased 1.6% to US$840.0 million from US$827.0 million in the equivalent prior-year period.

Prospects: Our evaluation of Ameriprise Financial Inc. as of Jan. 21, 2018 is the result of our systematic analysis on three basic characteristics: earnings strength, relative valuation, and recent stock price movement. The company has managed to produce a neutral trend in earnings per share over the past 5 quarters. However, while recent estimates for the company have been mixed, AMP has posted better than expected results. Based on operating earnings yield, the company is undervalued when compared to all of the companies in our coverage universe. Share price changes over the past year indicates that AMP will perform very well over the near term.

Financial Data
(US$ in Millions)

	3 Mos	12/31/2017	12/31/2016	12/31/2015	12/31/2014	12/31/2013	12/31/2012	12/31/2011
Earnings Per Share	10.85	9.44	7.81	8.48	8.30	6.44	4.62	4.37
Cash Flow Per Share	9.95	11.04	11.82	14.16	12.52	6.71	6.86	9.02
Tang Book Value Per Share	40.27	40.90	40.66	42.20	44.37	42.64	44.58	46.21
Dividends Per Share	3.320	3.240	2.920	2.590	2.260	2.010	1.430	0.870
Dividend Payout %	30.60	34.32	37.39	30.54	27.23	31.21	30.95	19.91
Income Statement								
Total Revenue	3,168	12,027	11,696	12,170	12,268	11,199	10,217	10,192
EBITDA	803	2,562	1,982	2,679	3,019	2,395	1,666	1,845
Depn & Amortn	56	141	149	150	144	144	152	143
Income Before Taxes	696	2,214	1,592	2,142	2,547	1,970	1,238	1,385
Income Taxes	102	734	278	455	545	492	335	355
Net Income	594	1,480	1,314	1,562	1,619	1,334	1,029	1,076
Average Shares	152	156	168	184	195	207	222	246
Balance Sheet								
Current Assets	2,201	8,405	7,796	8,133	8,055	7,661	7,265	8,869
Total Assets	144,762	147,470	139,821	145,342	148,810	144,576	134,729	133,986
Current Liabilities	12,050	12,463	11,963	10,440	9,387	8,991	8,351	11,419
Long-Term Obligations	5,055	5,099	5,236	10,246	9,929	8,456	7,384	7,571
Total Liabilities	138,922	141,472	133,529	138,125	140,686	136,384	125,637	123,731
Stockholders' Equity	5,840	5,998	6,292	7,217	8,124	8,192	9,092	10,255
Shares Outstanding	145	146	154	171	183	192	203	221
Statistical Record								
Return on Assets %	1.17	1.03	0.92	1.06	1.10	0.96	0.76	0.81
Return on Equity %	27.70	24.08	19.40	20.36	19.85	15.44	10.61	10.26
EBITDA Margin %	25.35	21.30	16.95	22.01	24.61	21.39	16.31	18.10
Net Margin %	18.75	12.31	11.23	12.83	13.20	11.91	10.07	10.56
Asset Turnover	0.09	0.08	0.08	0.08	0.08	0.08	0.08	0.08
Current Ratio	0.18	0.67	0.65	0.78	0.86	0.85	0.87	0.78
Debt to Equity	0.87	0.85	0.83	1.42	1.22	1.03	0.81	0.74
Price Range	182.04-120.79	171.70-111.55	118.90-76.27	137.81-103.08	136.76-101.47	115.05-62.63	63.52-45.46	64.73-37.34
P/E Ratio	16.78-11.13	18.19-11.82	15.22-9.77	16.25-12.16	16.48-12.23	17.86-9.73	13.75-9.84	14.81-8.54
Average Yield %	2.25	2.35	3.00	2.12	1.92	2.38	2.61	1.63

Address: 1099 Ameriprise Financial Center, Minneapolis, MN 55474
Telephone: 612-671-3131

Web Site: www.ameriprise.com
Officers: James M. Cracchiolo - Chairman, Chief Executive Officer Walter Stanley Berman - Executive Vice President, Chief Financial Officer

Auditors: PricewaterhouseCoopers LLP
Investor Contact: 612-671-2080
Transfer Agents: Computershare Trust Company, N.A, Providence, RI

AMERISOURCEBERGEN CORP.

Exchange	Symbol	Price	52Wk Range	Yield	P/E	Div Acheiver
NYS	ABC	$85.27 (6/29/2018)	105.48-73.23	1.78	22.09	13 Years

*7 Year Price Score 97.55 *NYSE Composite Index=100 *12 Month Price Score 98.51

Interim Earnings (Per Share)
Qtr.	Dec	Mar	Jun	Sep
2014-15	(0.91)	(2.33)	0.89	1.65
2015-16	1.46	2.68	1.56	0.63
2016-17	1.11	1.86	0.23	(1.56)
2017-18	3.90	1.29	...	...

Interim Dividends (Per Share)
Amt	Decl	Ex	Rec	Pay
0.365Q	08/10/2017	08/17/2017	08/21/2017	09/05/2017
0.38Q	11/09/2017	11/17/2017	11/20/2017	12/04/2017
0.38Q	02/07/2018	02/16/2018	02/20/2018	03/05/2018
0.38Q	05/10/2018	05/18/2018	05/21/2018	06/04/2018

Indicated Div: $1.52

Valuation Analysis   Institutional Holding
Forecast EPS	$6.47	No of Institutions
	(06/14/2018)	1063
Market Cap	$18.7 Billion	Shares
Book Value	$3.2 Billion	199,875,552
Price/Book	5.88	% Held
Price/Sales	0.12	73.27

Business Summary: Pharmaceuticals (MIC: 4.1.1 SIC: 5122 NAIC: 424210)

AmerisourceBergen is a pharmaceutical sourcing and distribution services company. Co.'s operations are comprised of the Pharmaceutical Distribution segment and Other. The Pharmaceutical Distribution segment includes: Co.'s AmerisourceBergen Drug Corporation subsidiary, which distributes brand-name and generic pharmaceuticals, over-the-counter healthcare products, home healthcare supplies and equipment, outsourced compounded sterile preparations, and related services to a variety of healthcare providers; and Co.'s AmerisourceBergen Specialty Group Inc. subsidiary, which provides pharmaceutical distribution and additional services to physicians who focus on a variety of disease states.

Recent Developments: For the quarter ended Mar 31 2018, net income decreased 31.4% to US$282.2 million from US$411.5 million in the year-earlier quarter. Revenues were US$41.03 billion, up 10.5% from US$37.15 billion the year before. Operating income was US$481.4 million versus US$625.0 million in the prior-year quarter, a decrease of 23.0%. Direct operating expenses rose 10.8% to US$39.78 billion from US$35.89 billion in the comparable period the year before. Indirect operating expenses increased 22.6% to US$774.3 million from US$631.4 million in the equivalent prior-year period.

Prospects: Our evaluation of AmerisourceBergen Corp. as of Jan. 21, 2018 is the result of our systematic analysis on three basic characteristics: earnings strength, relative valuation, and recent stock price movement. The company has generated a negative trend in earnings per share over the past 5 quarters and while recent estimates for the company have been raised by analysts, ABC has posted better than expected results. Based on operating earnings yield, the company is undervalued when compared to all of the companies in our coverage universe. Share price changes over the past year indicates that ABC will perform poorly over the near term.

Financial Data
(US$ in Thousands)	6 Mos	3 Mos	09/30/2017	09/30/2016	09/30/2015	09/30/2014	09/30/2013	09/30/2012
Earnings Per Share	3.86	4.43	1.64	6.32	(0.62)	1.17	1.84	2.80
Cash Flow Per Share	4.83	8.91	6.89	14.94	18.00	6.44	3.41	5.15
Dividends Per Share	1.490	1.475	1.460	1.360	1.160	0.940	0.840	0.520
Dividend Payout %	38.60	33.30	89.02	21.52	...	80.34	45.65	18.57
Income Statement								
Total Revenue	81,500,190	40,466,332	153,143,826	146,849,686	135,961,803	119,569,127	87,959,167	79,489,596
EBITDA	1,084,414	506,607	1,325,492	1,763,360	561,085	912,379	1,037,045	1,377,084
Depn & Amortn	237,234	111,724	262,420	232,538	187,935	162,089	138,690	118,529
Income Before Taxes	762,679	359,019	917,887	1,390,910	274,149	673,428	824,458	1,163,131
Income Taxes	(423,662)	(502,834)	553,403	(37,019)	409,036	389,398	331,023	454,945
Net Income	1,149,308	861,853	364,484	1,427,929	(134,887)	276,484	433,707	718,986
Average Shares	222,303	220,822	221,602	225,959	217,786	235,405	235,345	256,903
Balance Sheet								
Current Assets	26,397,211	25,296,432	24,303,299	22,851,847	20,334,488	16,800,205	14,393,651	10,987,151
Total Assets	38,395,732	36,361,510	35,316,470	33,656,200	27,736,157	21,532,183	18,918,638	15,444,126
Current Liabilities	28,094,404	26,740,291	26,818,165	25,281,308	22,700,765	17,250,160	14,870,635	11,214,482
Long-Term Obligations	4,640,021	4,617,259	3,781,963	3,870,244	3,493,048	1,995,632	1,396,606	1,446,770
Total Liabilities	35,208,182	33,486,928	33,252,009	31,526,796	27,102,637	19,575,284	16,598,893	12,987,414
Stockholders' Equity	3,187,550	2,874,582	2,064,461	2,129,404	633,520	1,956,899	2,319,745	2,456,712
Shares Outstanding	219,743	218,500	217,993	220,050	206,891	221,908	229,994	235,394
Statistical Record								
Return on Assets %	2.35	2.79	1.06	4.64	N.M.	1.37	2.52	4.71
Return on Equity %	29.91	39.23	17.38	103.08	N.M.	12.93	18.16	26.94
EBITDA Margin %	1.33	1.25	0.87	1.20	0.41	0.76	1.18	1.73
Net Margin %	1.41	2.13	0.24	0.97	N.M.	0.23	0.49	0.90
Asset Turnover	4.38	4.42	4.44	4.77	5.52	5.91	5.12	5.21
Current Ratio	0.94	0.95	0.91	0.90	0.90	0.97	0.97	0.98
Debt to Equity	1.46	1.61	1.83	1.82	5.51	1.02	0.60	0.59
Price Range	105.48-73.23	96.38-73.23	96.38-69.03	105.02-73.66	115.48-75.02	78.33-61.10	62.23-38.99	42.08-35.57
P/E Ratio	27.33-18.97	21.76-16.53	58.77-42.09	16.62-11.66	...	66.95-52.22	33.82-21.19	15.03-12.70
Average Yield %	1.69	1.71	1.72	1.54	1.15	1.34	1.67	1.37

Address: 1300 Morris Drive, Chesterbrook, PA 19087-5594 Telephone: 610-727-7000 Fax: 610-647-0141	Web Site: www.amerisourcebergen.com Officers: Steven H. Collis - Chairman, President, Chief Executive Officer John G. Chou - Executive Vice President, Senior Vice President, Chief Legal Officer, Chief Business Officer, General Counsel, Secretary	Auditors: Ernst & Young LLP Investor Contact: 610-727-7199 Transfer Agents: ComputerShare, College Station, TX

AMETEK INC

Exchange	Symbol	Price	52Wk Range	Yield	P/E
NYS	AME	$72.16 (6/29/2018)	78.79-60.57	0.78	23.13

*7 Year Price Score 116.07 *NYSE Composite Index=100 *12 Month Price Score 102.60

TRADING VOLUME (thousand shares)

Interim Earnings (Per Share)

Qtr.	Mar	Jun	Sep	Dec
2015	0.59	0.64	0.65	0.58
2016	0.57	0.59	0.56	0.47
2017	0.60	0.65	0.66	1.03
2018	0.78	...	...	...

Interim Dividends (Per Share)

Amt	Decl	Ex	Rec	Pay
0.09Q	08/04/2017	09/14/2017	09/15/2017	09/29/2017
0.09Q	11/10/2017	12/05/2017	12/06/2017	12/20/2017
0.14Q	02/01/2018	03/15/2018	03/16/2018	03/29/2018
0.14Q	05/09/2018	06/14/2018	06/15/2018	06/29/2018

Indicated Div: $0.56 (Div. Reinv. Plan)

Valuation Analysis | Institutional Holding

Forecast EPS	$3.15
	(06/14/2018)
Market Cap	$16.7 Billion
Book Value	$4.2 Billion
Price/Book	3.97
Price/Sales	3.74

No of Institutions	798
Shares	237,435,952
% Held	84.69

Business Summary: Electrical Equipment (MIC: 7.3.1 SIC: 3629 NAIC: 335999)

AMETEK is a manufacturer of electronic instruments and electromechanical devices with operations in North America, Europe, Asia and South America. Co.'s products are marketed and sold through two operating groups: the Electronic Instruments Group, which is engaged in the design and manufacture of instruments for the process, power and industrial, and aerospace markets; and the Electromechanical Group, which supplies precision motion control solutions, thermal management systems, specialty metals and electrical interconnects. Co.'s end markets include aerospace and defense, medical, automation, mass transit, petrochemical and other industrial markets.

Recent Developments: For the quarter ended Mar 31 2018, net income increased 30.5% from US$138.9 million in the year-earlier quarter. Revenues were US$1.17 billion, up 16.4% from US$1.01 billion the year before. Operating income was US$258.2 million versus US$217.4 million in the prior-year quarter, an increase of 18.7%. Direct operating expenses rose 16.4% to US$776.8 million from US$667.4 million in the comparable period the year before. Indirect operating expenses increased 12.1% to US$137.7 million from US$122.8 million in the equivalent prior-year period.

Prospects: Our evaluation of Ametek Inc. as of Jan. 21, 2018 is the result of our systematic analysis on three basic characteristics: earnings strength, relative valuation, and recent stock price movement. The company has enjoyed a very positive trend in earnings per share over the past 5 quarters and while recent estimates for the company have been mixed, AME has posted better than expected results. Based on operating earnings yield, the company is about fairly valued when compared to all of the companies in our coverage universe. Share price changes over the past year indicates that AME will perform well over the near term.

Financial Data
(US$ in Thousands)

	3 Mos	12/31/2017	12/31/2016	12/31/2015	12/31/2014	12/31/2013	12/31/2012	12/31/2011
Earnings Per Share	3.12	2.94	2.19	2.45	2.37	2.10	1.88	1.58
Cash Flow Per Share	3.76	3.62	3.25	2.80	2.96	2.71	2.53	2.12
Dividends Per Share	0.410	0.360	0.360	0.360	0.330	0.240	0.220	0.160
Dividend Payout %	13.14	12.24	16.44	14.69	13.92	11.43	11.70	10.13
Income Statement								
Total Revenue	1,172,647	4,300,170	3,840,087	3,974,295	4,021,964	3,594,136	3,334,213	2,989,914
EBITDA	306,344	1,077,985	967,123	966,882	948,484	855,605	791,624	675,244
Depn & Amortn	48,834	183,227	179,716	68,707	63,724	57,238	53,677	48,873
Income Before Taxes	235,824	796,729	693,103	806,380	804,832	724,795	662,475	556,642
Income Taxes	54,484	115,259	180,945	215,521	220,372	207,796	203,343	172,178
Net Income	181,340	681,470	512,158	590,859	584,460	516,999	459,132	384,464
Average Shares	232,965	231,845	233,730	241,586	247,102	246,065	243,986	243,162
Balance Sheet								
Current Assets	1,960,205	1,934,655	1,928,190	1,619,613	1,578,604	1,369,129	1,164,743	1,059,119
Total Assets	8,058,361	7,796,064	7,100,674	6,664,530	6,420,963	5,877,902	5,190,056	4,319,490
Current Liabilities	1,159,923	1,138,663	924,441	1,025,172	936,144	874,545	879,969	628,875
Long-Term Obligations	1,897,633	1,866,166	2,062,644	1,556,045	1,427,825	1,141,750	1,133,121	1,123,416
Total Liabilities	3,853,964	3,768,431	3,844,161	3,409,904	3,181,402	2,741,781	2,654,905	2,266,685
Stockholders' Equity	4,204,397	4,027,633	3,256,513	3,254,626	3,239,561	3,136,121	2,535,151	2,052,805
Shares Outstanding	231,579	231,193	229,378	235,515	241,335	245,006	243,395	240,557
Statistical Record								
Return on Assets %	9.43	9.15	7.42	9.03	9.50	9.34	9.63	9.45
Return on Equity %	19.03	18.71	15.69	18.20	18.33	18.23	19.96	20.09
EBITDA Margin %	26.12	25.07	25.18	24.33	23.58	23.81	23.74	22.58
Net Margin %	15.46	15.85	13.34	14.87	14.53	14.38	13.77	12.86
Asset Turnover	0.58	0.58	0.56	0.61	0.65	0.65	0.70	0.73
Current Ratio	1.69	1.70	2.09	1.58	1.69	1.57	1.32	1.68
Debt to Equity	0.45	0.46	0.63	0.48	0.44	0.36	0.45	0.55
Price Range	78.79-53.20	72.87-49.18	53.59-43.88	57.50-47.90	54.20-46.12	52.67-37.57	38.02-28.17	31.18-20.95
P/E Ratio	25.25-17.05	24.79-16.73	24.47-20.04	23.47-19.55	22.87-19.46	25.08-17.89	20.22-14.98	19.73-13.26
Average Yield %	0.61	0.59	0.75	0.67	0.64	0.54	0.65	0.59

Address: 1100 Cassatt Road, Berwyn, PA 19312-1177 **Telephone:** 610-647-2121 **Fax:** 610-647-0211	**Web Site:** www.ametek.com **Officers:** David A. Zapico - Chairman, Chief Executive Officer, Executive Vice President, Chief Operating Officer, Division Officer William J. Burke - Executive Vice President, Chief Financial Officer, Senior Vice President, Comptroller, Treasurer	**Auditors:** Ernst & Young LLP **Transfer Agents:** American Stock Transfer & Trust Co., New York, NY

AMPHENOL CORP.

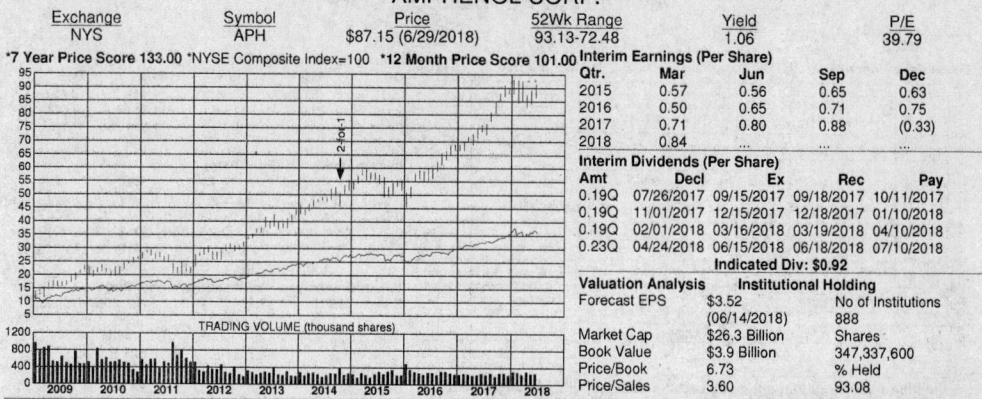

Exchange	Symbol	Price	52Wk Range	Yield	P/E
NYS	APH	$87.15 (6/29/2018)	93.13-72.48	1.06	39.79

*7 Year Price Score 133.00 *NYSE Composite Index=100 *12 Month Price Score 101.00

Interim Earnings (Per Share)

Qtr.	Mar	Jun	Sep	Dec
2015	0.57	0.56	0.65	0.63
2016	0.50	0.65	0.71	0.75
2017	0.71	0.80	0.88	(0.33)
2018	0.84	...	...	...

Interim Dividends (Per Share)

Amt	Decl	Ex	Rec	Pay
0.19Q	07/26/2017	09/15/2017	09/18/2017	10/11/2017
0.19Q	11/01/2017	12/15/2017	12/18/2017	01/10/2018
0.19Q	02/01/2018	03/16/2018	03/19/2018	04/10/2018
0.23Q	04/24/2018	06/15/2018	06/18/2018	07/10/2018

Indicated Div: $0.92

Valuation Analysis | **Institutional Holding**

Forecast EPS	$3.52	No of Institutions
(06/14/2018)		888
Market Cap	$26.3 Billion	Shares
Book Value	$3.9 Billion	347,337,600
Price/Book	6.73	% Held
Price/Sales	3.60	93.08

Business Summary: Electrical Equipment (MIC: 7.3.1 SIC: 3678 NAIC: 334417)

Amphenol is engaged in designing, manufacturing and marketing electrical, electronic and fiber optic connectors, interconnect systems, antennas, sensors and sensor-based products and coaxial and high-speed specialty cable. Co. has two reportable business segments: Interconnect Products and Assemblies, which designs, manufacturers and markets a range of connector and connector systems, antennas and sensors used in a range of applications; and Cable Products and Solutions, which primarily designs, manufacturers and markets cable, other products and components for use primarily in the broadband communications and information technology markets as well as certain applications in other markets.

Recent Developments: For the quarter ended Mar 31 2018, net income increased 18.0% to US$268.3 million from US$227.3 million in the year-earlier quarter. Revenues were US$1.87 billion, up 19.7% from US$1.56 billion the year before. Operating income was US$376.9 million versus US$314.1 million in the prior-quarter, an increase of 20.0%. Direct operating expenses rose 20.7% to US$1.26 billion from US$1.04 billion in the comparable period the year before. Indirect operating expenses increased 14.0% to US$230.0 million from US$201.8 million in the equivalent prior-year period.

Prospects: Our evaluation of Amphenol Corp. as of Jan. 21, 2018 is the result of our systematic analysis on three basic characteristics: earnings strength, relative valuation, and recent stock price movement. The company has managed to produce a neutral trend in earnings per share over the past 5 quarters and while recent estimates for the company have been mixed, APH has posted better than expected results. Based on operating earnings yield, the company is about fairly valued when compared to all of the companies in our coverage universe. Share price changes over the past year indicates that APH will perform well over the near term.

Financial Data

(US$ in Thousands)	3 Mos	12/31/2017	12/31/2016	12/31/2015	12/31/2014	12/31/2013	12/31/2012	12/31/2011
Earnings Per Share	2.19	2.06	2.61	2.41	2.21	1.96	1.70	1.52
Cash Flow Per Share	3.41	3.74	3.49	3.33	2.81	2.42	2.08	1.67
Tang Book Value Per Share	N.M.	N.M.	N.M.	1.77	0.94	9.04	1.56	1.30
Dividends Per Share	0.730	0.700	0.580	0.530	0.450	0.305	0.210	0.030
Dividend Payout %	33.33	33.98	22.22	21.99	20.36	15.56	12.39	1.97
Income Statement								
Total Revenue	1,866,900	7,011,300	6,286,400	5,568,700	5,345,500	4,614,669	4,292,065	3,939,786
EBITDA	439,700	1,651,300	1,419,200	1,274,300	1,200,800	1,031,708	948,721	868,975
Depn & Amortn	60,500	226,800	217,000	171,600	168,100	136,482	121,779	119,439
Income Before Taxes	354,700	1,352,400	1,141,100	1,052,800	972,500	846,645	778,841	716,752
Income Taxes	86,400	691,700	308,500	280,500	257,300	207,896	219,333	187,910
Net Income	265,600	650,500	822,900	763,500	709,100	635,672	555,317	524,191
Average Shares	316,000	316,500	315,200	316,500	320,430	324,548	327,894	343,651
Balance Sheet								
Current Assets	3,937,100	4,656,000	3,591,200	3,850,000	3,504,100	3,157,567	2,706,915	2,181,237
Total Assets	9,403,700	10,003,900	8,498,700	7,458,400	7,027,000	6,168,028	5,215,463	4,445,225
Current Liabilities	2,184,700	1,579,400	1,635,200	1,008,400	1,045,600	1,609,878	888,514	642,415
Long-Term Obligations	2,489,400	3,541,500	2,635,500	2,813,200	2,672,300	1,431,437	1,606,204	1,376,831
Total Liabilities	5,489,800	6,014,100	4,823,800	4,219,900	4,119,600	3,308,519	2,785,504	2,273,456
Stockholders' Equity	3,913,900	3,989,800	3,674,900	3,238,500	2,907,400	2,859,509	2,429,959	2,171,769
Shares Outstanding	302,100	305,700	308,300	308,000	309,884	316,412	319,715	326,244
Statistical Record								
Return on Assets %	7.63	7.03	10.29	10.54	10.75	11.17	11.47	12.39
Return on Equity %	18.15	16.97	23.74	24.85	24.59	24.04	24.07	23.34
EBITDA Margin %	23.55	23.55	22.58	22.88	22.46	22.36	22.10	22.06
Net Margin %	14.23	9.28	13.09	13.71	13.27	13.78	12.94	13.31
Asset Turnover	0.81	0.76	0.79	0.77	0.81	0.81	0.89	0.93
Current Ratio	1.80	2.95	2.20	3.82	3.35	1.96	3.05	3.40
Debt to Equity	0.64	0.89	0.72	0.87	0.92	0.50	0.66	0.63
Price Range	93.13-68.65	91.04-66.60	68.83-45.42	60.20-49.06	55.45-42.34	44.59-32.35	32.51-22.91	29.30-19.90
P/E Ratio	42.53-31.35	44.19-32.33	26.37-17.40	24.98-20.36	25.09-19.16	22.75-16.51	19.12-13.48	19.28-13.09
Average Yield %	0.89	0.91	0.98	0.96	0.93	0.79	0.73	0.12

Address: 358 Hall Avenue, Wallingford, CT 06492 **Telephone:** 203-265-8900 **Fax:** 203-265-8746	**Web Site:** www.amphenol.com **Officers:** Martin H. Loeffler - Chairman, Executive Chairman Richard Adam Norwitt - President, Chief Executive Officer	**Auditors:** DELOITTE & TOUCHE LLP **Transfer Agents:** Computershare Trust Company, N.A., Providence, RI

ANADARKO PETROLEUM CORP

Exchange	Symbol	Price	52Wk Range	Yield	P/E
NYS	APC	$73.25 (6/29/2018)	74.33-40.52	1.37	N/A

*7 Year Price Score 61.38 *NYSE Composite Index=100 *12 Month Price Score 125.35

Interim Earnings (Per Share)

Qtr.	Mar	Jun	Sep	Dec
2015	(6.45)	0.12	(4.41)	(2.45)
2016	(2.03)	(1.36)	(1.61)	(0.90)
2017	(0.58)	(0.76)	(1.27)	1.76
2018	0.22	...	...	...

Interim Dividends (Per Share)

Amt	Decl	Ex	Rec	Pay
0.05Q	08/02/2017	09/12/2017	09/13/2017	09/27/2017
0.05Q	11/15/2017	12/12/2017	12/13/2017	12/27/2017
0.25Q	02/07/2018	03/13/2018	03/14/2018	03/28/2018
0.25Q	05/15/2018	06/12/2018	06/13/2018	06/27/2018

Indicated Div: $1.00 (Div. Reinv. Plan)

Valuation Analysis

Valuation Analysis	**Institutional Holding**	
Forecast EPS	$2.85	No of Institutions
	(06/14/2018)	1320
Market Cap	$36.9 Billion	Shares
Book Value	$8.7 Billion	621,566,080
Price/Book	4.22	% Held
Price/Sales	3.30	84.90

TRADING VOLUME (thousand shares)

Business Summary: Production & Extraction (MIC: 9.1.1 SIC: 1311 NAIC: 211111)

Anadarko Petroleum is an independent exploration and development, production, and marketing of oil, natural gas, and natural gas liquids (NGLs), and in the marketing of liquefied natural gas. In addition, Co. engages in the gathering, processing, treating, and transporting of oil, natural gas, and NGLs. Co. also participates in the hard-minerals business through royalty arrangements. As of Dec 31 2017, Co.'s proved reserves consisted of 1.4 billion barrels of oil equivalent.

Recent Developments: For the quarter ended Mar 31 2018, net income amounted to US$174.0 million versus a net loss of US$275.0 million in the year-earlier quarter. Revenues were US$3.05 billion, down 19.2% from US$3.77 billion the year before. Operating income was US$551.0 million versus a loss of US$100.0 million in the prior-year quarter. Direct operating expenses declined 54.8% to US$877.0 million from US$1.94 billion in the comparable period the year before. Indirect operating expenses decreased 16.1% to US$1.62 billion from US$1.93 billion in the equivalent prior-year period.

Prospects: Our evaluation of Anadarko Petroleum Corp. as of Jan. 21, 2018 is the result of our systematic analysis on three basic characteristics: earnings strength, relative valuation, and recent stock price movement. The company has managed to produce a neutral trend in earnings per share over the past 5 quarters. Because the company lacks sufficient analyst estimate data, we place greater weight on the historical EPS trend as the measure of earnings strength. Based on operating earnings yield, the company is overvalued when compared to all of the companies in our coverage universe. Share price changes over the past year indicates that APC will perform very poorly over the near term.

Financial Data

(US$ in Thousands)	3 Mos	12/31/2017	12/31/2016	12/31/2015	12/31/2014	12/31/2013	12/31/2012	12/31/2011
Earnings Per Share	(0.05)	(0.85)	(5.90)	(13.18)	(3.47)	1.58	4.74	(5.32)
Cash Flow Per Share	8.33	7.32	5.73	(3.69)	16.73	17.71	16.63	5.03
Tang Book Value Per Share	6.13	9.48	11.44	12.76	25.97	32.15	29.87	24.63
Dividends Per Share	0.400	0.200	0.200	1.080	0.990	0.540	0.360	0.360
Dividend Payout %	...	...	...	...	...	34.18	7.59	...
Income Statement								
Total Revenue	3,045,000	11,908,000	7,869,000	8,698,000	18,470,000	14,581,000	13,411,000	13,967,000
EBITDA	1,518,000	3,523,000	1,362,000	(4,261,000)	5,376,000	6,719,000	8,271,000	1,245,000
Depn & Amortn	990,000	4,279,000	4,301,000	4,603,000	4,550,000	3,927,000	3,964,000	3,830,000
Income Before Taxes	300,000	(1,688,000)	(3,829,000)	(9,689,000)	54,000	2,106,000	3,565,000	(3,424,000)
Income Taxes	126,000	(1,477,000)	(1,021,000)	(2,877,000)	1,617,000	1,165,000	1,120,000	(856,000)
Net Income	121,000	(456,000)	(3,071,000)	(6,692,000)	(1,750,000)	801,000	2,391,000	(2,649,000)
Average Shares	519,000	548,000	522,000	508,000	506,000	505,000	502,000	498,000
Balance Sheet								
Current Assets	5,530,000	6,762,000	5,266,000	3,982,000	11,221,000	7,108,000	6,795,000	6,931,000
Total Assets	41,076,000	42,086,000	45,564,000	46,414,000	61,689,000	55,781,000	52,589,000	51,779,000
Current Liabilities	4,734,000	3,906,000	3,328,000	4,181,000	10,234,000	5,703,000	3,994,000	4,899,000
Long-Term Obligations	15,643,000	15,547,000	15,281,000	15,718,000	15,092,000	13,065,000	13,269,000	15,060,000
Total Liabilities	32,335,000	31,390,000	33,352,000	33,595,000	41,964,000	33,924,000	31,960,000	33,674,000
Stockholders' Equity	8,741,000	10,696,000	12,212,000	12,819,000	19,725,000	21,857,000	20,629,000	18,105,000
Shares Outstanding	503,900	530,800	551,200	508,300	506,600	503,700	500,500	498,400
Statistical Record								
Return on Assets %	N.M.	N.M.	N.M.	N.M.	N.M.	1.48	4.57	N.M.
Return on Equity %	N.M.	N.M.	N.M.	N.M.	N.M.	3.77	12.31	N.M.
EBITDA Margin %	49.85	29.59	17.31	N.M.	29.11	46.08	61.67	8.91
Net Margin %	3.97	N.M.	N.M.	N.M.	N.M.	5.49	17.83	N.M.
Asset Turnover	0.26	0.27	0.17	0.16	0.31	0.27	0.26	0.27
Current Ratio	1.17	1.73	1.58	0.95	1.10	1.25	1.70	1.41
Debt to Equity	1.79	1.45	1.25	1.23	0.77	0.60	0.64	0.83
Price Range	62.90-40.52	71.74-40.52	72.69-30.54	94.54-45.67	112.69-72.01	97.76-74.31	88.05-57.12	84.71-60.53
P/E Ratio	...	...	...	...	...	61.87-47.03	18.58-12.05	...
Average Yield %	0.78	0.38	0.38	1.44	1.04	0.62	0.49	0.47

Address: 1201 Lake Robbins Drive, The Woodlands, TX 77380-1046 Telephone: 832-636-1000	Web Site: www.anadarko.com Officers: R. A. Walker - Chairman, President, Chief Executive Officer, Chief Operating Officer Robert G. Gwin - Executive Vice President, Senior Vice President, Chief Financial Officer	Auditors: KPMG LLP Investor Contact: 855-820-6605 Transfer Agents: BNYMellon Shareowner Services, Jersey City, NJ

ANDEAVOR

Exchange	Symbol	Price	52Wk Range	Yield	P/E
NYS	ANDV	$131.18 (6/29/2018)	149.68-89.62	1.80	11.91

*7 Year Price Score 128.67 *NYSE Composite Index=100 *12 Month Price Score 124.86

Interim Earnings (Per Share)

Qtr.	Mar	Jun	Sep	Dec
2015	1.15	4.59	6.13	0.54
2016	0.57	3.47	1.42	0.67
2017	0.42	0.31	3.54	6.04
2018	1.12	....	....	....

Interim Dividends (Per Share)

Amt	Decl	Ex	Rec	Pay
0.59Q	08/07/2017	08/29/2017	08/31/2017	09/15/2017
0.59Q	11/08/2017	11/29/2017	11/30/2017	12/15/2017
0.59Q	02/14/2018	02/27/2018	02/28/2018	03/15/2018
0.59Q	05/07/2018	05/30/2018	05/31/2018	06/15/2018

Indicated Div: $2.36

Valuation Analysis — **Institutional Holding**

Forecast EPS	$8.87	No of Institutions	884
	(06/14/2018)		
Market Cap	$19.8 Billion	Shares	154,669,312
Book Value	$9.6 Billion	% Held	78.82
Price/Book	2.06		
Price/Sales	0.51		

Business Summary: Refining & Marketing (MIC: 9.1.2 SIC: 2911 NAIC: 324110)

Andeavor is a petroleum refining, logistics and marketing company. Co.'s business is organized into three segments: refining, which refines crude oil and other feedstocks into transportation fuels, such as gasoline and gasoline blendstocks, jet fuel and diesel fuel, as well as other products; logistics, which is comprised of Tesoro Logistics LP's assets and operations, including certain crude oil and natural gas gathering assets, natural gas and natural gas liquids processing assets, and crude oil and refined products terminalling, transportation and storage assets acquired from Co. and third parties; and marketing, which sells transportation fuels through branded and unbranded channels.

Recent Developments: For the quarter ended Mar 31 2018, income from continuing operations increased 163.2% to US$229.0 million from US$87.0 million in the year-earlier quarter. Net income increased 172.4% to US$237.0 million from US$87.0 million in the year-earlier quarter. Revenues were US$10.30 billion, up 55.2% from US$6.64 billion the year before. Operating income was US$370.0 million versus US$195.0 million in the prior-year quarter, an increase of 89.7%. Direct operating expenses rose 58.7% to US$8.61 billion from US$5.43 billion in the comparable period the year before. Indirect operating expenses increased 29.9% to US$1.32 billion from US$1.02 billion in the equivalent prior-year period.

Prospects: Our evaluation of Andeavor as of Jan. 21, 2018 is the result of our systematic analysis on three basic characteristics: earnings strength, relative valuation, and recent stock price movement. The company has enjoyed a very positive trend in earnings per share over the past 5 quarters. However, while recent estimates for the company have been mixed, ANDV has posted results that fell short of analysts expectations. Based on operating earnings yield, the company is undervalued when compared to all of the companies in our coverage universe. Share price changes over the past year indicates that ANDV will perform well over the near term.

Financial Data

(US$ in Thousands)	3 Mos	12/31/2017	12/31/2016	12/31/2015	12/31/2014	12/31/2013	12/31/2012	12/31/2011
Earnings Per Share	11.01	10.81	6.12	12.36	6.44	3.00	5.25	3.81
Cash Flow Per Share	11.64	11.63	10.97	17.30	10.61	6.36	11.34	4.87
Tang Book Value Per Share	30.79	32.20	34.20	31.94	24.30	30.33	28.96	24.33
Dividends Per Share	2.320	2.280	2.100	1.850	1.100	0.900	0.270	...
Dividend Payout %	21.07	21.09	34.31	14.97	17.08	30.00	5.14	...
Income Statement								
Total Revenue	10,300,000	34,975,000	24,582,000	28,711,000	40,633,000	37,601,000	32,974,000	30,303,000
EBITDA	662,000	2,187,000	2,075,000	3,331,000	2,052,000	1,140,000	1,671,000	1,342,000
Depn & Amortn	282,000	656,000	537,000	491,000	363,000	322,000	295,000	262,000
Income Before Taxes	278,000	1,092,000	1,264,000	2,623,000	1,454,000	669,000	1,212,000	905,000
Income Taxes	59,000	(560,000)	427,000	936,000	547,000	246,000	442,000	342,000
Net Income	172,000	1,528,000	734,000	1,540,000	843,000	412,000	743,000	546,000
Average Shares	153,800	141,300	119,900	124,600	130,800	137,300	141,500	143,300
Balance Sheet								
Current Assets	6,409,000	6,883,000	7,414,000	4,307,000	5,074,000	5,326,000	4,636,000	4,151,000
Total Assets	28,841,000	28,573,000	20,398,000	16,332,000	16,584,000	13,389,000	10,702,000	9,892,000
Current Liabilities	4,546,000	5,001,000	3,554,000	2,530,000	3,466,000	3,408,000	2,881,000	3,249,000
Long-Term Obligations	8,386,000	7,668,000	6,468,000	4,067,000	4,254,000	2,823,000	1,587,000	1,283,000
Total Liabilities	19,209,000	18,758,000	14,933,000	11,119,000	12,130,000	9,087,000	6,451,000	6,224,000
Stockholders' Equity	9,632,000	9,815,000	5,465,000	5,213,000	4,454,000	4,302,000	4,251,000	3,668,000
Shares Outstanding	151,110	153,285	116,899	119,393	124,960	131,804	138,162	139,964
Statistical Record								
Return on Assets %	6.75	6.24	3.99	9.36	5.63	3.42	7.20	5.86
Return on Equity %	21.83	20.00	13.71	31.86	19.26	9.63	18.71	15.87
EBITDA Margin %	6.43	6.25	8.44	11.60	5.05	3.03	5.07	4.43
Net Margin %	1.67	4.37	2.99	5.36	2.07	1.10	2.25	1.80
Asset Turnover	1.58	1.43	1.33	1.74	2.71	3.12	3.19	3.25
Current Ratio	1.41	1.38	2.09	1.70	1.46	1.56	1.61	1.28
Debt to Equity	0.87	0.78	1.18	0.78	0.96	0.66	0.37	0.35
Price Range	121.13-75.49	115.36-75.49	107.10-68.64	118.24-66.67	78.55-47.47	64.90-40.22	44.73-21.55	29.18-17.98
P/E Ratio	11.00-6.86	10.67-6.98	17.50-11.22	9.57-5.39	12.20-7.37	21.63-13.41	8.52-4.10	7.66-4.72
Average Yield %	2.35	2.44	2.57	1.97	1.84	1.72	0.86	...

Address: 19100 Ridgewood Pkwy., San Antonio, TX 78259-1828	Web Site: www.tsocorp.com	Auditors: Ernst & Young LLP
Telephone: 210-626-6000	Officers: Gregory J. Goff - Chairman, President, Chief Executive Officer Steven M. Sterin - Executive Vice President, Chief Financial Officer	Transfer Agents: American Stock Transfer & Trust Company, New York, NY

ANIXTER INTERNATIONAL INC

Exchange	Symbol	Price	52Wk Range	Yield	P/E
NYS	AXE	$63.30 (6/29/2018)	88.00-56.75	N/A	19.54

*7 Year Price Score 82.06 ***NYSE Composite Index=100** ***12 Month Price Score 83.90**

TRADING VOLUME (thousand shares)

Interim Earnings (Per Share)

Qtr.	Mar	Jun	Sep	Dec
2015	0.57	2.14	0.97	0.13
2016	0.68	0.61	1.21	1.09
2017	0.91	1.18	1.11	0.01
2018	0.94	...	...	...

Interim Dividends (Per Share)

Dividend Payment Suspended

Valuation Analysis		Institutional Holding	
Forecast EPS	$5.81	No of Institutions	
	(06/03/2018)	335	
Market Cap	$2.1 Billion	Shares	
Book Value	$1.5 Billion	41,543,864	
Price/Book	1.43	% Held	
Price/Sales	0.27	77.41	

Business Summary: Electrical Equipment (MIC: 7.3.1 SIC: 5063 NAIC: 423610)

Anixter International is engaged in the distribution of network and security solutions, electrical and electronic solutions, and utility power solutions through Anixter Inc. and its subsidiaries. The Network and Security Solutions segment supplies products and customized supply chain solutions. The Electrical and Electronic Solutions segment supplies wire and cable, control, lighting and electrical bulk products and customized supply chain solutions. The Utility Power Solutions segment supplies electrical transmission and distribution products, power plant maintenance, repair and operations supplies and smart-grid products, and arranges materials management and procurement outsourcing.

Recent Developments: For the quarter ended Mar 31, 2018, net income increased 3.9% to US$32.1 million from US$30.9 million in the year-earlier quarter. Revenues were US$1.96 billion, up 3.6% from US$1.90 billion the year before. Operating income was US$61.6 million versus US$68.9 million in the prior-year quarter, a decrease of 10.6%. Direct operating expenses rose 4.2% to US$1.58 billion from US$1.52 billion in the comparable period the year before. Indirect operating expenses increased 4.0% to US$323.2 million from US$310.8 million in the equivalent prior-year period.

Prospects: Our evaluation of Anixter International Inc. as of Jan. 21, 2018 is the result of our systematic analysis on three basic characteristics: earnings strength, relative valuation, and recent stock price movement. The company has generated a negative trend in earnings per share over the past 5 quarters and while recent estimates for the company have been raised by analysts, AXE has posted results that fell short of analysts expectations. Based on operating earnings yield, the company is undervalued when compared to all of the companies in our coverage universe. Share price changes over the past year indicates that AXE will perform poorly over the near term.

Financial Data
(US$ in Thousands)

	3 Mos	12/29/2017	12/30/2016	01/01/2016	01/02/2015	01/03/2014	12/28/2012	12/31/2011
Earnings Per Share	3.24	3.21	3.59	3.81	5.84	6.04	3.69	5.36
Cash Flow Per Share	1.81	5.49	8.37	2.78	3.17	10.03	4.30	4.22
Tang Book Value Per Share	10.37	8.98	3.36	N.M.	16.62	20.86	19.30	19.55
Dividends Per Share	...	...	...	...	...	5.000	4.500	...
Dividend Payout %	...	...	...	...	...	82.78	121.95	...
Income Statement								
Total Revenue	1,964,200	7,927,400	7,622,800	6,190,500	6,445,500	6,226,500	6,253,100	6,146,900
EBITDA	81,000	376,600	341,700	294,300	378,600	373,500	301,400	387,100
Depn & Amortn	17,100	64,300	65,500	47,600	35,700	30,100	32,500	33,500
Income Before Taxes	45,700	237,600	197,500	182,900	294,800	296,000	209,200	303,500
Income Taxes	13,600	128,600	76,400	86,000	100,000	95,600	84,600	102,800
Net Income	32,100	109,000	120,500	127,600	194,800	200,500	124,800	188,200
Average Shares	34,100	34,000	33,600	33,400	33,300	33,200	33,800	35,100
Balance Sheet								
Current Assets	2,868,500	2,833,800	2,688,500	2,727,800	2,589,800	2,275,700	2,450,100	2,402,900
Total Assets	4,277,300	4,252,200	4,093,600	4,142,000	3,586,500	2,860,800	3,089,600	3,034,000
Current Liabilities	1,298,900	1,350,800	1,263,900	1,156,200	1,030,500	902,400	967,300	1,026,900
Long-Term Obligations	1,286,100	1,247,900	1,378,800	1,642,900	1,207,700	836,000	982,200	806,800
Total Liabilities	2,785,400	2,793,200	2,801,400	2,962,600	2,453,500	1,833,400	2,119,700	2,032,800
Stockholders' Equity	1,491,900	1,459,000	1,292,200	1,179,400	1,133,000	1,027,400	969,900	1,001,200
Shares Outstanding	33,803	33,657	33,437	33,278	33,141	32,853	32,537	33,228
Statistical Record								
Return on Assets %	2.65	2.62	2.93	3.31	6.06	6.63	4.10	6.31
Return on Equity %	7.78	7.95	9.78	11.07	18.08	19.75	12.73	18.71
EBITDA Margin %	4.12	4.75	4.48	4.75	5.87	6.00	4.82	6.30
Net Margin %	1.63	1.37	1.58	2.06	3.02	3.22	2.00	3.06
Asset Turnover	1.92	1.90	1.86	1.61	2.00	2.06	2.05	2.06
Current Ratio	2.21	2.10	2.13	2.36	2.51	2.52	2.53	2.34
Debt to Equity	0.86	0.86	1.07	1.39	1.07	0.81	1.01	0.81
Price Range	88.00-63.15	88.00-63.15	83.65-38.29	88.18-56.66	107.51-76.57	92.36-62.64	73.37-49.76	75.58-45.10
P/E Ratio	27.16-19.49	27.41-19.67	23.30-10.67	23.14-14.87	18.41-13.11	15.29-10.37	19.88-13.49	14.10-8.41
Average Yield %	...	...	...	...	...	6.40	7.30	...

Address: 2301 Patriot Blvd., Glenview, IL 60026	Web Site: www.anixter.com	Auditors: Ernst & Young LLP
Telephone: 224-521-8000	Officers: Samuel Zell - Chairman William A. (Bill) Galvin - Division Officer, President, Chief Operating Officer, Chief Executive Officer	Investor Contact: 224-521-8895
		Transfer Agents: Wells Fargo Shareowner Services, Mendota Heights, MN

ANNALY CAPITAL MANAGEMENT INC

Exchange	Symbol	Price	52Wk Range	Yield	P/E
NYS	NLY	$10.29 (6/29/2018)	12.54-10.03	11.66	4.97

*7 Year Price Score 73.24   *NYSE Composite Index=100   *12 Month Price Score 91.58

Interim Earnings (Per Share)

Qtr.	Mar	Jun	Sep	Dec
2015	(0.52)	0.93	(0.68)	0.69
2016	(0.96)	(0.32)	0.70	1.89
2017	0.41	(0.01)	0.31	0.65
2018	1.12	...	...	...

Interim Dividends (Per Share)

Amt	Decl	Ex	Rec	Pay
0.30Q	09/14/2017	09/28/2017	09/29/2017	10/31/2017
0.30Q	12/14/2017	12/28/2017	12/29/2017	01/31/2018
0.30Q	03/15/2018	03/28/2018	03/29/2018	04/30/2018
0.30Q	06/14/2018	06/28/2018	06/29/2018	07/31/2018

Indicated Div: $1.20 (Div. Reinv. Plan)

Valuation Analysis

		Institutional Holding	
Forecast EPS	$1.17	No of Institutions	
	(06/07/2018)	890	
Market Cap	$11.9 Billion	Shares	
Book Value	$13.9 Billion	865,305,920	
Price/Book	0.86	% Held	
Price/Sales	3.08	51.34	

Business Summary: REITs (MIC: 5.3.1 SIC: 6798 NAIC: 525930)

Annaly Capital Management is a real estate finance company. Co. owns a portfolio of real estate related investments, such as collateralized mortgage obligations, Agency debentures, and mortgage servicing rights. Co.'s investment groups are comprised of agency, which invests in agency mortgage-backed securities and related derivatives; residential credit, which invests in non-agency mortgage-backed assets within securitized products and residential mortgage loan markets; commercial real estate, which invests in commercial mortgage loans, securities, and other commercial real estate investments; and middle market lending, which provides customized debt financing to middle-market businesses.

Recent Developments: For the quarter ended Mar 31 2018, net income increased 201.5% to US$1.33 billion from US$440.4 million in the year-earlier quarter. Revenues were US$1.76 billion, up 153.5% from US$693.6 million the year before.

Prospects: Our evaluation of Annaly Capital Management Inc. as of Jan. 21, 2018 is the result of our systematic analysis on three basic characteristics: earnings strength, relative valuation, and recent stock price movement. The company has generated a negative trend in earnings per share over the past 5 quarters and while recent estimates for the company have remained steady, NLY has posted better than expected results. Based on operating earnings yield, the company is undervalued when compared to all of the companies in our coverage universe. Share price changes over the past year indicates that NLY will perform very well over the near term.

Financial Data
(US$ in Thousands)

	3 Mos	12/31/2017	12/31/2016	12/31/2015	12/31/2014	12/31/2013	12/31/2012	12/31/2011
Earnings Per Share	2.07	1.37	1.39	0.42	(0.96)	3.74	1.71	0.37
Cash Flow Per Share	6.97	6.50	7.05	(3.34)	6.47	(13.61)	7.83	2.77
Tang Book Value Per Share	10.45	10.75	10.41	11.62	13.00	12.03	15.78	16.04
Dividends Per Share	1.993	2.485	3.169	3.169	3.169	3.469	4.019	4.409
Dividend Payout %	96.28	181.40	227.97	754.46	...	92.75	235.01	1,191.55
Income Statement								
Interest Income	879,487	2,493,126	2,210,951	2,170,697	2,632,647	2,918,562	3,259,145	3,579,618
Interest Expense	367,421	1,008,354	657,752	471,596	512,659	624,714	667,172	480,326
Net Interest Income	512,066	1,484,772	1,553,199	1,699,101	2,119,988	2,293,848	2,591,973	3,099,292
Non-Interest Income	878,712	315,350	128,348	(1,035,068)	(2,747,604)	1,676,144	(584,602)	(2,459,576)
Non-Interest Expense	62,510	224,124	250,356	200,240	209,338	232,081	235,559	237,344
Income Before Taxes	1,328,268	1,575,998	1,431,191	463,793	(836,954)	3,737,911	1,771,812	402,372
Income Taxes	564	6,982	(1,595)	(1,954)	5,325	8,213	35,912	59,051
Net Income	1,327,800	1,569,604	1,433,756	466,556	(842,083)	3,729,698	1,735,900	344,461
Average Shares	1,160,103	1,066,351	970,102	947,276	947,539	995,557	1,005,755	874,518
Balance Sheet								
Net Loans & Leases	1,535,685	1,438,322	456,714	278,600	...	...	...	...
Total Assets	100,382,233	101,760,050	87,905,046	75,190,893	88,355,367	81,922,460	133,452,295	109,630,002
Total Liabilities	86,444,969	86,894,577	75,336,866	63,294,919	75,026,876	69,517,405	117,527,851	93,837,088
Stockholders' Equity	13,937,264	14,865,473	12,568,180	11,895,974	13,328,491	12,405,055	15,924,444	15,792,914
Shares Outstanding	1,159,657	1,159,585	1,018,913	935,929	947,643	947,432	947,213	970,161
Statistical Record								
Return on Assets %	2.66	1.66	1.75	0.57	N.M.	3.46	1.42	0.36
Return on Equity %	18.49	11.44	11.69	3.70	N.M.	26.33	10.92	2.68
Net Interest Margin %	58.22	59.55	70.25	78.27	80.53	78.60	79.53	86.58
Efficiency Ratio %	3.56	7.98	10.70	17.63	...	5.05	8.81	21.19
Price Range	12.66-10.03	12.66-10.08	11.25-8.69	11.04-9.06	11.92-9.97	16.13-9.74	17.75-14.01	18.72-15.48
P/E Ratio	6.12-4.85	9.24-7.36	8.09-6.25	26.29-21.57	...	4.31-2.60	10.38-8.19	50.59-41.84
Average Yield %	17.11	21.35	30.57	31.33	28.13	26.57	24.68	25.29

Address: 1211 Avenue of the Americas, New York, NY 10036
Telephone: 212-696-0100
Fax: 212-696-9809

Web Site: www.annaly.com
Officers: Wellington J. Denahan-Norris - Chairman, Vice-Chairman, Chief Executive Officer, Co-Chief Executive Officer, Chief Operating Officer Kevin G. Keyes - President, Chief Executive Officer, Chief Strategy Officer, Managing Director

Auditors: Ernst & Young LLP
Investor Contact: 888-826-6259
Transfer Agents: Computershare Shareowner Services LLC, Jersey City, NJ

ANTHEM INC

Exchange	Symbol	Price	52Wk Range	Yield	P/E
NYS	ANTM	$238.03 (6/29/2018)	258.19-181.44	1.26	15.26

*7 Year Price Score 141.40 *NYSE Composite Index=100 *12 Month Price Score 104.78

Interim Earnings (Per Share)

Qtr.	Mar	Jun	Sep	Dec
2015	3.09	3.13	2.43	0.72
2016	2.63	2.91	2.30	1.37
2017	3.73	3.16	2.80	4.65
2018	4.99	...	...	...

Interim Dividends (Per Share)

Amt	Decl	Ex	Rec	Pay
0.70Q	07/26/2017	09/07/2017	09/08/2017	09/25/2017
0.70Q	10/24/2017	12/04/2017	12/05/2017	12/21/2017
0.75Q	01/30/2018	03/08/2018	03/09/2018	03/23/2018
0.75Q	04/24/2018	06/07/2018	06/08/2018	06/25/2018

Indicated Div: $3.00

Valuation Analysis — **Institutional Holding**

Forecast EPS	$15.40 (06/14/2018)	No of Institutions 1085
Market Cap	$60.8 Billion	Shares 254,938,256
Book Value	$27.0 Billion	% Held
Price/Book	2.25	72.39
Price/Sales	0.68	

Business Summary: Life & Health (MIC: 5.2.2 SIC: 6324 NAIC: 524114)

Anthem is an insurance holding company. Co. provides network-based managed care plans to large and small employer, individual, Medicaid and Medicare markets. Co.'s managed care plans include preferred provider organizations, health maintenance organizations, point-of-service plans, indemnity plans and other hybrid plans, and hospital only and limited benefit products. In addition, Co. provides managed care services to self-funded customers, including claims processing. Co. also provides other insurance products and services such as dental, vision, life and disability insurance benefits, as well as services to the federal government in connection with the Federal Employee Program.

Recent Developments: For the quarter ended Mar 31 2018, net income increased 30.0% to US$1.31 billion from US$1.01 billion in the year-earlier quarter. Revenues were US$22.54 billion, up 0.1% from US$22.53 billion the year before. Net premiums earned were US$20.90 billion versus US$20.95 billion in the prior-year quarter, a decrease of 0.2%. Net investment income rose 10.6% to US$229.2 million from US$207.2 million a year ago.

Prospects: Our evaluation of Anthem Inc. as of Jan. 21, 2018 is the result of our systematic analysis on three basic characteristics: earnings strength, relative valuation, and recent stock price movement. The company has generated a negative trend in earnings per share over the past 5 quarters and while recent estimates for the company have been raised by analysts, ANTM has posted better than expected results. Based on operating earnings yield, the company is undervalued when compared to all of the companies in our coverage universe. Share price changes over the past year indicates that ANTM will perform well over the near term.

Financial Data
(US$ in Thousands)

	3 Mos	12/31/2017	12/31/2016	12/31/2015	12/31/2014	12/31/2013	12/31/2012	12/31/2011
Earnings Per Share	15.60	14.35	9.21	9.38	8.99	8.20	8.18	7.25
Cash Flow Per Share	14.51	16.00	12.16	15.65	12.21	10.23	8.51	9.37
Tang Book Value Per Share	N.M.	N.M.	N.M.	N.M.	N.M.	N.M.	N.M.	4.41
Dividends Per Share	2.800	2.700	2.600	2.500	1.750	1.500	1.150	1.000
Dividend Payout %	17.95	18.82	28.23	26.65	19.47	18.29	14.06	13.79
Income Statement								
Total Revenue	22,537,500	90,039,400	84,863,000	79,156,500	73,874,100	71,023,500	61,711,700	60,710,700
Income Before Taxes	1,780,300	3,963,800	4,555,400	4,631,000	4,368,100	3,840,200	3,865,500	3,957,900
Income Taxes	467,800	121,000	2,085,600	2,071,000	1,808,000	1,205,900	1,210,000	1,311,200
Net Income	1,312,500	3,842,800	2,469,800	2,560,000	2,569,700	2,489,700	2,655,500	2,646,700
Average Shares	262,800	267,800	268,100	272,900	285,900	303,800	324,800	365,100
Balance Sheet								
Total Assets	73,300,400	70,540,000	65,083,100	61,717,800	62,065,000	59,574,500	58,955,400	52,018,800
Total Liabilities	46,288,000	44,037,100	39,982,700	38,673,700	37,813,700	34,809,300	35,152,700	28,730,600
Stockholders' Equity	27,012,400	26,502,900	25,100,400	23,044,100	24,251,300	24,765,200	23,802,700	23,288,200
Shares Outstanding	255,544	256,084	263,747	261,238	268,109	293,273	304,715	339,372
Statistical Record								
Return on Assets %	5.83	5.67	3.88	4.14	4.23	4.20	4.77	5.18
Return on Equity %	15.61	14.89	10.23	10.83	10.49	10.25	11.25	11.24
Net Margin %	5.82	4.27	2.91	3.23	3.48	3.51	4.30	4.36
Price Range	258.19-164.75	234.96-142.79	147.66-117.22	171.04-123.26	129.16-84.25	93.92-58.93	73.80-52.93	81.78-56.86
P/E Ratio	16.55-10.56	16.37-9.95	16.03-12.73	18.23-13.14	14.37-9.37	11.45-7.19	9.02-6.47	11.28-7.84
Average Yield %	1.37	1.45	1.95	1.70	1.62	1.91	1.82	1.46

Address: 120 Monument Circle, Indianapolis, IN 46204-4903 **Telephone:** 800-331-1476	**Web Site:** www.anthemic.com **Officers:** Joseph R. Swedish - Chairman, President, Chief Executive Officer Gail Koziara Boudreaux - President, Chief Executive Officer	**Auditors:** Ernst & Young LLP **Investor Contact:** 212-476-1473 **Transfer Agents:** EquiServe Trust Company, N.A., Providence, RI

ANTERO RESOURCES CORP

Exchange	Symbol	Price	52Wk Range	Yield	P/E
NYS	AR	$21.35 (6/29/2018)	22.16-17.02	N/A	18.89

*7 Year Price Score N/A   *NYSE Composite Index=100   *12 Month Price Score 98.12

Interim Earnings (Per Share)

Qtr.	Mar	Jun	Sep	Dec
2015	1.49	(0.52)	1.93	0.56
2016	(0.02)	(2.12)	0.77	(1.62)
2017	0.85	(0.02)	(0.43)	1.53
2018	0.05	...	...	...

Interim Dividends (Per Share)

No Dividends Paid

Valuation Analysis	Institutional Holding
Forecast EPS $1.37	No of Institutions
(06/14/2018)	376
Market Cap $6.8 Billion	Shares
Book Value $8.2 Billion	519,912,352
Price/Book 0.83	% Held
Price/Sales 1.94	101.26

TRADING VOLUME (thousand shares)

Business Summary: Production & Extraction (MIC: 9.1.1 SIC: 1311 NAIC: 211111)

Antero Resources is an independent oil and natural gas company engaged in the exploration, development and acquisition of natural gas, natural gas liquids (NGLs), and oil properties located in the Appalachian Basin. Co. operates in the following industry segments: the exploration, development and production of natural gas, NGLs, and oil; gathering and compression; water handling and treatment; and marketing of excess firm transportation capacity. As of Dec 31 2017, Co.'s estimated proved reserves were 17.30 trillion cubic feet equivalent, consisting of 11.10 trillion cubic feet of natural gas, 528 million barrels (MMBbl) of ethane, 461.0 MMBbl of C3+ NGLs and 38.0 MMBbl of oil.

Recent Developments: For the year ended Dec 31 2017, net income amounted to US$785.1 million versus a net loss of US$749.4 million in the prior year. Revenues were US$3.66 billion, up 109.5% from US$1.74 billion the year before. Operating income was US$740.1 million versus a loss of US$975.8 million in the prior year. Direct operating expenses rose 9.8% to US$1.65 billion from US$1.50 billion in the comparable period the year before. Indirect operating expenses increased 4.0% to US$1.27 billion from US$1.22 billion in the equivalent prior-year period.

Prospects: Our evaluation of Antero Resources Corp as of Jan. 21, 2018 is the result of our systematic analysis on three basic characteristics: earnings strength, relative valuation, and recent stock price movement. The company has generated a negative trend in earnings per share over the past 5 quarters and while recent estimates for the company have been raised by analysts, AR has posted results that fell short of analysts expectations. Based on operating earnings yield, the company is overvalued when compared to all of the companies in our coverage universe. Share price changes over the past year indicates that AR will perform very poorly over the near term.

Financial Data
(US$ in Thousands)

	3 Mos	12/31/2017	12/31/2016	12/31/2015	12/31/2014	12/31/2013	12/31/2012	12/31/2011
Earnings Per Share	1.13	1.94	(2.88)	3.43	2.57	(0.07)	(1.10)	1.51
Cash Flow Per Share	6.81	6.36	4.20	3.67	3.81	2.06	1.27	1.02
Tang Book Value Per Share	25.85	25.76	19.89	21.42	16.73	13.73	...	...
Income Statement								
Total Revenue	1,028,101	3,655,574	1,744,525	3,954,858	2,720,632	1,313,134	735,718	691,353
EBITDA	375,428	748,593	(983,857)	1,797,986	1,758,515	533,581	636,238	712,816
Depn & Amortn	228,934	10,000	8,900	7,700	479,167	234,941	192,223	181,833
Income Before Taxes	82,068	469,892	(1,246,309)	1,555,886	1,119,297	162,023	346,505	456,485
Income Taxes	9,120	(295,051)	(496,376)	575,890	445,672	186,210	121,229	185,297
Net Income	14,833	615,070	(848,816)	941,364	673,587	(18,930)	(285,069)	392,678
Average Shares	316,911	316,283	294,945	274,143	262,068	260,100	260,100	260,100
Balance Sheet								
Current Assets	800,034	833,087	402,587	1,248,236	1,252,160	333,564	274,606	333,642
Total Assets	15,422,849	15,261,490	14,255,550	14,155,224	11,573,495	6,613,581	3,618,793	3,788,800
Current Liabilities	789,853	762,096	817,388	707,270	1,155,105	622,229	376,296	255,058
Long-Term Obligations	4,876,706	4,800,090	4,703,973	4,708,513	4,362,550	2,078,999	1,444,058	1,317,330
Total Liabilities	7,241,704	7,112,309	7,992,925	8,220,832	7,189,702	3,014,921	1,945,056	1,829,994
Stockholders' Equity	8,181,145	8,149,181	6,262,625	5,934,392	4,383,793	3,598,660	1,673,737	1,958,806
Shares Outstanding	316,524	316,379	314,877	277,035	262,071	262,049	...	...
Statistical Record								
Return on Assets %	2.39	4.17	N.M.	7.32	7.41	N.M.	N.M.	...
Return on Equity %	4.57	8.54	N.M.	18.25	16.88	N.M.	N.M.	...
EBITDA Margin %	36.52	20.48	N.M.	45.46	64.64	40.63	86.48	103.10
Net Margin %	1.44	16.83	N.M.	23.80	24.76	N.M.	N.M.	56.80
Asset Turnover	0.23	0.25	0.12	0.31	0.30	0.26	0.20	...
Current Ratio	1.01	1.09	0.49	1.76	1.08	0.54	0.73	1.31
Debt to Equity	0.60	0.59	0.75	0.79	1.00	0.58	0.86	0.67
Price Range	23.44-17.02	26.16-17.65	30.10-19.77	45.65-19.12	67.41-38.60	63.44-52.01	...	...
P/E Ratio	20.74-15.06	13.48-9.10	...	13.31-5.57	26.23-15.02	...	...	...

Address: 1615 Wynkoop Street, Denver, CO 80202 Telephone: 303-357-7310	Web Site: www.anteroresources.com Officers: Paul M. Rady - Chairman, Chief Executive Officer Glen C. Warren - President, Chief Financial Officer, Secretary	Auditors: KPMG LLP Transfer Agents: American Stock Transfer & Trust Company, LLC

APACHE CORP

Exchange	Symbol	Price	52Wk Range	Yield	P/E
NYS	APA	$46.75 (6/29/2018)	50.22-34.15	2.14	14.47

*7 Year Price Score 49.08 *NYSE Composite Index=100 *12 Month Price Score 98.35

Interim Earnings (Per Share)

Qtr.	Mar	Jun	Sep	Dec
2015	(12.34)	(14.83)	(14.95)	(19.08)
2016	(1.29)	(0.65)	(1.60)	(0.49)
2017	0.56	1.50	0.16	1.19
2018	0.38	...	...	...

Interim Dividends (Per Share)

Amt	Decl	Ex	Rec	Pay
0.25Q	09/13/2017	10/20/2017	10/23/2017	11/22/2017
0.25Q	12/14/2017	01/19/2018	01/22/2018	02/22/2018
0.25Q	02/12/2018	04/20/2018	04/23/2018	05/22/2018
0.25Q	05/24/2018	07/20/2018	07/23/2018	08/22/2018

Indicated Div: $1.00 (Div. Reinv. Plan)

Valuation Analysis

		Institutional Holding	
Forecast EPS	$1.78	No of Institutions	
	(06/14/2018)	1209	
Market Cap	$17.9 Billion	Shares	
Book Value	$7.5 Billion		469,264,416
Price/Book	2.38	% Held	
Price/Sales	2.84		85.01

TRADING VOLUME (thousand shares)

Business Summary: Production & Extraction (MIC: 9.1.1 SIC: 1311 NAIC: 211111)
Apache is an independent energy company that explores for, develops, and produces natural gas, crude oil, and natural gas liquids. As of Dec 31 2017, Co. had exploration and production interests in three geographic areas: the U.S., Egypt, and offshore the U.K. in the North Sea. Co. also has exploration interests in Suriname. As of Dec 31 2017, Co. had total estimated proved reserves of 1.2 billion barrels of oil equivalent, which consisted of 583 million barrels of crude oil, 204 million barrels of natural gas liquids, and 2.3 trillion cubic feet of natural gas.

Recent Developments: For the quarter ended Mar 31 2018, net income decreased 22.8% to US$206.0 million from US$267.0 million in the year-earlier quarter. Revenues were US$1.74 billion, down 7.2% from US$1.88 billion the year before. Direct operating expenses rose 9.4% to US$430.0 million from US$393.0 million in the comparable period the year before. Indirect operating expenses decreased 2.4% to US$924.0 million from US$947.0 million in the equivalent prior-year period.

Prospects: Our evaluation of Apache Corp. as of Jan. 21, 2018 is the result of our systematic analysis on three basic characteristics: earnings strength, relative valuation, and recent stock price movement. The company has managed to produce a neutral trend in earnings per share over the past 5 quarters and while recent estimates for the company have been raised by analysts, APA has posted better than expected results. Based on operating earnings yield, the company is overvalued when compared to all of the companies in our coverage universe. Share price changes over the past year indicates that APA will perform very poorly over the near term.

Financial Data
(US$ in Thousands)

	3 Mos	12/31/2017	12/31/2016	12/31/2015	12/31/2014	12/31/2013	12/31/2012	12/31/2011
Earnings Per Share	3.23	3.41	(3.71)	(61.20)	(14.06)	5.50	4.92	11.47
Cash Flow Per Share	6.77	6.37	6.39	7.89	22.03	24.90	21.80	25.92
Tang Book Value Per Share	19.63	19.47	16.44	6.79	68.66	80.92	73.58	69.38
Dividends Per Share	1.000	1.000	1.000	1.000	0.950	0.770	0.660	0.600
Dividend Payout %	30.96	29.33	...	...	...	14.00	13.41	5.23
Income Statement								
Total Revenue	1,742,000	6,423,000	5,354,000	6,366,000	13,851,000	16,054,000	17,078,000	16,888,000
EBITDA	1,040,000	3,594,000	1,352,000	1,406,000	7,382,000	11,106,000	12,151,000	12,455,000
Depn & Amortn	553,000	2,280,000	2,618,000	29,372,000	10,158,000	6,700,000	7,109,000	4,204,000
Income Before Taxes	388,000	918,000	(1,682,000)	(28,226,000)	(2,906,000)	4,216,000	4,877,000	8,093,000
Income Taxes	182,000	(585,000)	(442,000)	(5,469,000)	1,637,000	1,928,000	2,876,000	3,509,000
Net Income	145,000	1,304,000	(1,405,000)	(23,119,000)	(5,403,000)	2,232,000	2,001,000	4,584,000
Average Shares	384,000	383,000	379,000	378,000	384,000	406,000	391,000	400,000
Balance Sheet								
Current Assets	3,253,000	3,725,000	3,241,000	3,752,000	6,415,000	6,366,000	4,962,000	4,803,000
Total Assets	21,791,000	21,922,000	22,519,000	18,842,000	55,952,000	61,637,000	60,737,000	52,051,000
Current Liabilities	2,342,000	2,564,000	1,843,000	1,841,000	3,664,000	4,700,000	5,536,000	4,963,000
Long-Term Obligations	7,936,000	7,934,000	8,544,000	8,777,000	11,245,000	9,672,000	11,355,000	6,785,000
Total Liabilities	14,289,000	14,506,000	16,281,000	16,276,000	30,015,000	28,241,000	29,406,000	23,058,000
Stockholders' Equity	7,502,000	7,416,000	6,238,000	2,566,000	25,937,000	33,396,000	31,331,000	28,993,000
Shares Outstanding	382,146	380,954	379,439	378,034	376,504	395,772	391,640	384,117
Statistical Record								
Return on Assets %	5.57	5.87	N.M.	N.M.	N.M.	3.65	3.54	9.60
Return on Equity %	17.80	19.10	N.M.	N.M.	N.M.	6.90	6.62	17.18
EBITDA Margin %	59.70	55.96	25.25	22.09	53.30	69.18	71.15	73.75
Net Margin %	8.32	20.30	N.M.	N.M.	N.M.	13.90	11.72	27.14
Asset Turnover	0.28	0.29	0.26	0.17	0.24	0.26	0.30	0.35
Current Ratio	1.39	1.45	1.76	2.04	1.75	1.35	0.90	0.97
Debt to Equity	1.06	1.07	1.37	3.42	0.43	0.29	0.36	0.23
Price Range	53.99-34.15	63.78-38.37	67.35-34.38	71.40-36.20	103.48-55.20	94.42-68.84	111.57-75.07	133.37-76.50
P/E Ratio	16.72-10.57	18.70-11.25	...	...	...	17.17-12.52	22.68-15.26	11.63-6.67
Average Yield %	2.27	2.09	1.87	1.84	1.11	0.93	0.74	0.54

Address: One Post Oak Central, 2000 Post Oak Boulevard, Suite 100, Houston, TX 77056-4400
Telephone: 713-296-6000

Web Site: www.apachecorp.com
Officers: John J. Christmann - President, Chief Executive Officer, Vice President, Region Officer Rebecca A. Hoyt - Senior Vice President, Vice President, Chief Accounting Officer, Controller

Auditors: Ernst & Young LLP
Investor Contact: 281-302-2286
Transfer Agents: Wells Fargo Bank, N.A., South St. Paul, MN

APARTMENT INVESTMENT & MANAGEMENT CO

Exchange	Symbol	Price	52Wk Range	Yield	P/E
NYS	AIV	$42.30 (6/29/2018)	46.45-38.00	3.59	17.63

*7 Year Price Score 97.77 *NYSE Composite Index=100 *12 Month Price Score 94.74

Interim Earnings (Per Share)

Qtr.	Mar	Jun	Sep	Dec
2015	0.58	0.39	0.12	0.43
2016	0.15	1.41	0.07	1.03
2017	0.07	0.10	0.11	1.67
2018	0.52	...	...	...

Interim Dividends (Per Share)

Amt	Decl	Ex	Rec	Pay
0.36Q	07/26/2017	08/16/2017	08/18/2017	08/31/2017
0.36Q	10/25/2017	11/16/2017	11/17/2017	11/30/2017
0.38Q	01/31/2018	02/15/2018	02/16/2018	02/28/2018
0.38Q	05/02/2018	05/17/2018	05/18/2018	05/31/2018

Indicated Div: $1.52

Valuation Analysis | **Institutional Holding**

Forecast EPS	$0.70	No of Institutions
	(06/13/2018)	504
Market Cap	$6.7 Billion	Shares
Book Value	$1.7 Billion	208,136,976
Price/Book	3.98	% Held
Price/Sales	6.61	99.78

Business Summary: REITs (MIC: 5.3.1 SIC: 6798 NAIC: 525930)

Apartment Investment and Management is a self-administered and self-managed real estate investment trust. Co. is focused on the ownership, management, redevelopment and limited development of apartment communities. Co., through its wholly-owned subsidiaries, AIMCO-GP, Inc. and AIMCO-LP Trust, owns a majority of the ownership interests in AIMCO Properties, L.P. (the Aimco Operating Partnership). Co. conducts all of its business through the Aimco Operating Partnership. As of Dec 31 2017, Co.'s real estate portfolio consisted of 182 apartment communities with 43,802 apartment homes. Co.'s reportable segments are conventional and affordable real estate operations.

Recent Developments: For the quarter ended Mar 31 2018, income from continuing operations increased 158.5% to US$45.4 million from US$17.5 million in the year-earlier quarter. Net income increased 457.8% to US$95.7 million from US$17.2 million in the year-earlier quarter. Revenues were US$247.7 million, up 0.5% from US$246.5 million the year before.

Prospects: Our evaluation of Apartment Investment & Management Co. as of Jan. 21, 2018 is the result of our systematic analysis on three basic characteristics: earnings strength, relative valuation, and recent stock price movement. The company has enjoyed a very positive trend in earnings per share over the past 5 quarters. Because the company lacks sufficient analyst estimate data, we place greater weight on the historical EPS trend as the measure of earnings strength. Based on operating earnings yield, the company is overvalued when compared to all of the companies in our coverage universe. Share price changes over the past year indicates that AIV will perform well over the near term.

Financial Data
(US$ in Thousands)

	3 Mos	12/31/2017	12/31/2016	12/31/2015	12/31/2014	12/31/2013	12/31/2012	12/31/2011
Earnings Per Share	2.40	1.96	2.67	1.52	2.06	1.40	0.61	(0.86)
Cash Flow Per Share	2.60	2.52	2.41	2.32	2.21	2.24	2.35	2.17
Tang Book Value Per Share	9.82	9.79	10.64	9.36	7.11	6.16	5.82	2.08
Dividends Per Share	1.460	1.440	1.320	1.180	1.040	0.960	0.760	0.480
Dividend Payout %	60.83	73.47	49.44	77.63	50.49	68.57	124.59	...
Income Statement								
Total Revenue	247,720	1,005,437	995,854	981,310	984,363	974,053	1,033,197	1,079,584
EBITDA	146,149	573,527	590,993	568,089	547,943	549,525	576,113	554,385
Depn & Amortn	92,548	371,850	338,126	311,487	286,422	296,825	350,692	385,191
Income Before Taxes	7,978	15,394	64,275	63,866	47,428	31,711	(11,427)	(131,545)
Income Taxes	(37,388)	(32,126)	(25,208)	(27,524)	(20,047)	(1,959)	(929)	(7,166)
Net Income	83,792	315,774	430,410	248,710	309,249	207,290	132,456	(57,087)
Average Shares	156,740	156,796	156,391	155,570	146,002	145,532	134,479	119,312
Balance Sheet								
Current Assets	139,031	142,541	131,150	137,745	120,416	185,933	368,189	430,784
Total Assets	6,255,290	6,079,040	6,232,818	6,144,194	6,097,028	6,079,413	6,401,380	6,871,862
Current Liabilities	...	...	36,677	36,123	41,919	43,161	30,747	66,091
Long-Term Obligations	4,254,845	4,088,911	3,884,632	3,873,160	4,135,139	4,388,185	4,688,447	5,172,320
Total Liabilities	4,585,100	4,415,896	4,438,915	4,521,803	4,869,293	5,111,956	5,485,955	5,963,533
Stockholders' Equity	1,670,190	1,663,144	1,793,903	1,622,391	1,227,735	967,457	915,425	908,329
Shares Outstanding	157,326	157,189	156,888	156,326	146,403	145,917	145,563	120,916
Statistical Record								
Return on Assets %	6.20	5.13	6.94	4.06	5.08	3.32	1.99	N.M.
Return on Equity %	22.98	18.27	25.13	17.45	28.18	22.02	14.49	N.M.
EBITDA Margin %	59.00	57.04	59.35	57.89	55.66	56.42	55.76	51.35
Net Margin %	33.83	31.41	43.22	25.34	31.42	21.28	12.82	N.M.
Asset Turnover	0.16	0.16	0.16	0.16	0.16	0.16	0.16	0.15
Current Ratio	...	...	3.58	3.81	2.87	4.31	11.97	6.52
Debt to Equity	2.55	2.46	2.17	2.39	3.37	4.54	5.12	5.69
Price Range	46.45-38.00	46.53-42.42	47.59-35.45	41.19-34.85	38.32-25.72	33.20-25.00	28.27-22.40	27.97-20.29
P/E Ratio	19.35-15.83	23.74-21.64	17.82-13.28	27.10-22.93	18.60-12.49	23.71-17.86	46.34-36.72	...
Average Yield %	3.37	3.24	3.14	3.07	3.22	3.22	2.92	1.94

Address: 4582 South Ulster Street, Suite 1100, Denver, CO 80237
Telephone: 303-757-8101
Fax: 303-759-3226

Web Site: www.aimco.com
Officers: Terry Considine - Chairman, Chief Executive Officer Paul L. Beldin - Executive Vice President, Chief Financial Officer, Senior Vice President, Chief Accounting Officer

Auditors: Ernst & Young LLP
Investor Contact: 303-691-4350
Transfer Agents: Computershare Trust Company, N.A., Providence, RI

APPLE HOSPITALITY REIT INC

Exchange	Symbol	Price	52Wk Range	Yield	P/E
NYS	APLE	$17.88 (6/29/2018)	20.12-16.85	6.71	21.29

*7 Year Price Score N/A   *NYSE Composite Index=100   *12 Month Price Score 98.52

TRADING VOLUME (thousand shares)

Interim Earnings (Per Share)

Qtr.	Mar	Jun	Sep	Dec
2015	0.24	0.24	0.27	(0.09)
2016	0.20	0.31	0.07	0.19
2017	0.15	0.39	0.28	(0.01)
2018	0.18	...	...	...

Interim Dividends (Per Share)

Amt	Decl	Ex	Rec	Pay
0.10M	03/19/2018	04/02/2018	04/03/2018	04/16/2018
0.10M	04/19/2018	05/01/2018	05/02/2018	05/15/2018
0.10M	05/21/2018	06/01/2018	06/04/2018	06/18/2018
0.10M	06/20/2018	06/29/2018	07/02/2018	07/16/2018

Indicated Div: $1.20

Valuation Analysis   Institutional Holding

Forecast EPS	$0.93 (06/13/2018)	No of Institutions 273
Market Cap	$4.1 Billion	Shares 152,187,008
Book Value	$3.6 Billion	% Held
Price/Book	1.16	N/A
Price/Sales	3.31	

Business Summary: REITs (MIC: 5.3.1 SIC: 6798 NAIC: 525930)

Apple Hospitality REIT is a real estate investment trust (REIT) that invests in real estate, primarily in the lodging sector, in the U.S. As of Dec 31 2017, Co. owned 239 hotels with an aggregate of 30,322 rooms located in urban, suburban and developing markets throughout 33 states. All of Co.'s hotels operate under Marriott or Hilton brands. The hotels are operated and managed under separate management agreements with 23 hotel management companies, none of which are affiliated with Co. Co. has wholly-owned taxable REIT subsidiaries, which lease all of Co.'s hotels from wholly-owned qualified REIT subsidiaries.

Recent Developments: For the quarter ended Mar 31 2018, net income increased 22.7% to US$42.2 million from US$34.4 million in the year-earlier quarter. Revenues were US$298.4 million, up 1.9% from US$292.9 million the year before. Revenues from property income rose 2.0% to US$274.8 million from US$269.4 million in the corresponding quarter a year earlier.

Prospects: Our evaluation of Apple Hospitality REIT Inc as of Jan. 21, 2018 is the result of our systematic analysis on three basic characteristics: earnings strength, relative valuation, and recent stock price movement. The company has managed to produce a neutral trend in earnings per share over the past 5 quarters. However, while recent estimates for the company have been lowered by analysts, APLE has posted results that fell short of analysts expectations. Based on operating earnings yield, the company is undervalued when compared to all of the companies in our coverage universe. Share price changes over the past year indicates that APLE will perform in line with the market over the near term.

Financial Data

(US$ in Thousands)	3 Mos	12/31/2017	12/31/2016	12/31/2015	12/31/2014	12/31/2013	12/31/2012	12/31/2011
Earnings Per Share	0.84	0.82	0.76	0.65	0.04	1.26	0.82	0.76
Cash Flow Per Share	1.74	1.72	1.73	1.56	1.47	1.51	1.35	1.27
Tang Book Value Per Share	15.44	15.53	15.78	15.18	16.13	14.35	14.74	...
Dividends Per Share	1.100	1.100	1.200	0.800	...	...	...	...
Dividend Payout %	130.95	134.15	157.89	123.08	...	...	...	...
Income Statement								
Total Revenue	298,389	1,238,622	1,041,025	898,314	803,896	387,991	365,586	320,500
EBITDA	99,104	407,181	333,272	278,767	145,437	146,611	129,343	105,408
Depn & Amortn	44,840	176,499	148,163	127,449	113,112	54,827	52,748	49,815
Income Before Taxes	42,345	183,339	145,083	118,186	8,802	83,338	69,850	51,222
Income Taxes	163	847	431	898	1,969	1,422	1,166	1,068
Net Income	42,182	182,492	144,652	117,288	6,833	115,222	75,476	69,988
Average Shares	230,515	223,526	190,856	180,261	171,488	91,308	91,111	91,198
Balance Sheet								
Current Assets	...	29,791	29,425	22,651	32,526	27,518	18,949	...
Total Assets	4,973,371	4,902,338	4,979,883	3,722,775	3,779,749	1,491,281	1,526,017	...
Current Liabilities	89,439	109,057	124,856	77,614	55,555	16,919	13,101	...
Long-Term Obligations	1,327,458	1,222,196	1,337,963	998,103	709,570	162,551	166,783	...
Total Liabilities	1,416,897	1,331,253	1,462,819	1,075,717	765,125	179,470	179,884	...
Stockholders' Equity	3,556,474	3,571,085	3,517,064	2,647,058	3,014,624	1,311,811	1,346,133	...
Shares Outstanding	230,339	229,961	222,938	174,368	186,910	91,392	91,309	91,442
Statistical Record								
Return on Assets %	3.83	3.69	3.32	3.13	0.26	7.64	...	...
Return on Equity %	5.40	5.15	4.68	4.14	0.32	8.67	...	...
EBITDA Margin %	33.21	32.87	32.01	31.03	18.09	37.79	35.38	32.89
Net Margin %	14.14	14.73	13.90	13.06	0.85	29.70	20.65	21.84
Asset Turnover	0.25	0.25	0.24	0.24	0.31	0.26	...	...
Current Ratio	...	0.27	0.24	0.29	0.59	1.63	1.45	...
Debt to Equity	0.37	0.34	0.38	0.38	0.24	0.12	0.12	...
Price Range	20.12-16.85	20.64-17.59	20.59-17.26	20.68-16.38	...	...	...	...
P/E Ratio	23.95-20.06	25.17-21.45	27.09-22.71	31.82-25.20	...	...	...	...
Average Yield %	5.87	5.77	6.32	4.23	...	...	...	...

Address: 814 East Main Street, Richmond, VA 23219 **Telephone:** 804-344-8121	**Web Site:** www.applehospitalityreit.com **Officers:** Glade M. Knight - Executive Chairman, Chief Executive Officer Justin G. Knight - President, Chief Executive Officer	**Auditors:** Ernst & Young LLP

APTARGROUP INC.

Exchange	Symbol	Price	52Wk Range	Yield	P/E	Div Acheiver
NYS	ATR	$93.38 (6/29/2018)	96.13-80.93	1.37	26.45	24 Years

*7 Year Price Score 105.66 *NYSE Composite Index=100 *12 Month Price Score 104.53

Interim Earnings (Per Share)

Qtr.	Mar	Jun	Sep	Dec
2015	0.70	0.90	0.83	0.68
2016	0.67	0.91	0.82	0.77
2017	0.81	1.01	0.83	0.77
2018	0.92	...	...	...

Interim Dividends (Per Share)

Amt	Decl	Ex	Rec	Pay
0.32Q	07/13/2017	07/24/2017	07/26/2017	08/16/2017
0.32Q	10/19/2017	10/31/2017	11/01/2017	11/22/2017
0.32Q	01/18/2018	01/30/2018	01/31/2018	02/21/2018
0.32Q	04/25/2018	05/08/2018	05/09/2018	05/30/2018

Indicated Div: $1.28

Valuation Analysis

Forecast EPS	$3.79 (06/14/2018)	Institutional Holding
Market Cap	$5.8 Billion	No of Institutions 489
Book Value	$1.4 Billion	Shares 81,085,096
Price/Book	4.15	% Held 84.18
Price/Sales	2.27	

Business Summary: Plastics (MIC: 8.4.2 SIC: 3089 NAIC: 326199)

AptarGroup is a provider of a range of packaging, dispensing and sealing solutions, primarily for the beauty, personal care, home care, prescription drug, consumer health care, injectables, food and beverage markets. While Co. provides a range of dispensing and sealing solutions, its primary products are: dispensing pumps, which dispense a spray or lotion from non-pressurized containers; closures, which are plastic caps which allow a product to be dispensed without removing the cap; aerosol valves, which dispense product from pressurized containers; and elastomeric primary packaging components, which include stoppers for infusion, antibiotic, lyophilization and diagnostic vials.

Recent Developments: For the quarter ended Mar 31 2018, net income increased 14.4% to US$59.3 million from US$51.8 million in the year-earlier quarter. Revenues were US$703.4 million, up 17.0% from US$601.3 million the year before. Operating income was US$88.0 million versus US$78.0 million in the prior-year quarter, an increase of 12.7%. Direct operating expenses rose 18.5% to US$455.8 million from US$384.7 million in the comparable period the year before. Indirect operating expenses increased 15.1% to US$159.6 million from US$138.6 million in the equivalent prior-year period.

Prospects: Our evaluation of AptarGroup Inc. as of Jan. 21, 2018 is the result of our systematic analysis on three basic characteristics: earnings strength, relative valuation, and recent stock price movement. The company has managed to produce a neutral trend in earnings per share over the past 5 quarters and while recent estimates for the company have remained steady, ATR has posted better than expected results. Based on operating earnings yield, the company is about fairly valued when compared to all of the companies in our coverage universe. Share price changes over the past year indicates that ATR will perform well over the near term.

Financial Data
(US$ in Thousands)

	3 Mos	12/31/2017	12/31/2016	12/31/2015	12/31/2014	12/31/2013	12/31/2012	12/31/2011
Earnings Per Share	3.53	3.41	3.17	3.09	2.85	2.52	2.38	2.65
Cash Flow Per Share	5.39	5.20	5.20	5.19	4.84	4.32	4.71	3.92
Tang Book Value Per Share	13.76	12.49	10.81	12.89	11.85	16.38	14.81	15.96
Dividends Per Share	1.280	1.280	1.220	1.140	1.090	1.000	0.880	0.800
Dividend Payout %	36.26	37.54	38.49	36.89	38.25	39.68	36.97	30.19
Income Statement								
Total Revenue	703,350	2,469,283	2,330,934	2,317,149	2,597,809	2,520,013	2,331,036	2,337,183
EBITDA	128,264	472,936	458,767	458,955	451,343	427,470	391,629	418,585
Depn & Amortn	41,175	142,755	145,485	134,647	146,893	144,923	133,845	132,048
Income Before Taxes	81,282	295,054	280,688	295,289	288,218	265,266	241,830	274,959
Income Taxes	21,929	74,796	74,893	95,276	94,677	92,457	78,953	91,312
Net Income	59,300	220,030	205,590	199,348	191,658	171,994	162,612	183,683
Average Shares	64,414	64,596	64,849	64,492	67,292	68,208	68,395	69,274
Balance Sheet								
Current Assets	1,793,123	1,670,073	1,270,170	1,294,994	1,213,938	1,198,411	1,038,933	1,143,950
Total Assets	3,283,694	3,137,823	2,606,785	2,438,726	2,437,190	2,497,762	2,324,412	2,159,295
Current Liabilities	566,753	527,748	542,955	411,900	604,738	542,821	455,323	518,849
Long-Term Obligations	1,199,975	1,191,146	772,737	762,524	588,892	354,814	352,860	254,910
Total Liabilities	1,879,227	1,826,085	1,432,835	1,289,315	1,333,783	1,018,005	944,522	869,519
Stockholders' Equity	1,404,467	1,311,738	1,173,950	1,149,411	1,103,407	1,479,757	1,379,890	1,289,776
Shares Outstanding	62,400	61,860	62,146	62,516	61,931	65,384	65,928	65,900
Statistical Record								
Return on Assets %	7.84	7.66	8.13	8.18	7.77	7.13	7.23	8.76
Return on Equity %	17.20	17.70	17.65	17.70	14.84	12.03	12.15	14.30
EBITDA Margin %	18.24	19.15	19.68	19.81	17.37	16.96	16.80	17.91
Net Margin %	8.43	8.91	8.82	8.60	7.38	6.83	6.98	7.86
Asset Turnover	0.89	0.86	0.92	0.95	1.05	1.05	1.04	1.12
Current Ratio	3.16	3.16	2.34	3.14	2.01	2.21	2.28	2.20
Debt to Equity	0.85	0.91	0.66	0.66	0.53	0.24	0.26	0.20
Price Range	91.83-75.80	90.09-71.64	80.46-66.70	75.72-61.38	68.38-56.18	67.81-47.72	55.26-45.80	54.34-42.79
P/E Ratio	26.01-21.47	26.42-21.01	25.38-21.04	24.50-19.86	23.99-19.71	26.91-18.94	23.22-19.24	20.51-16.15
Average Yield %	1.49	1.55	1.61	1.71	1.69	1.72	1.71	1.61

Address: 265 Exchange Drive, Suite 100, Crystal Lake, IL 60014
Telephone: 815-477-0424
Fax: 815-477-0481

Web Site: www.aptar.com
Officers: George L. Fotiades - Chairman Stephan B. Tanda - President, Chief Executive Officer

Auditors: PricewaterhouseCoopers LLP
Investor Contact: 815-477-0424
Transfer Agents: Wells Fargo Shareowner Services, South St. Paul, MN

APTIV PLC

Exchange	Symbol	Price	52Wk Range	Yield	P/E
NYS	APTV	$91.63 (6/29/2018)	102.93-72.64	0.96	18.44

*7 Year Price Score N/A   *NYSE Composite Index=100   *12 Month Price Score 108.20

TRADING VOLUME (thousand shares)

Interim Earnings (Per Share)

Qtr.	Mar	Jun	Sep	Dec
2015	0.72	2.23	1.42	0.70
2016	1.53	0.94	1.07	1.03
2017	1.24	1.38	1.48	0.96
2018	1.15	...	...	...

Interim Dividends (Per Share)

Amt	Decl	Ex	Rec	Pay
0.29Q	07/27/2017	08/07/2017	08/09/2017	08/23/2017
0.29Q	10/26/2017	11/07/2017	11/08/2017	11/22/2017
0.22Q	12/07/2017	02/02/2018	02/05/2018	02/14/2018
0.22Q	04/26/2018	05/08/2018	05/09/2018	05/23/2018

Indicated Div: $0.88

Valuation Analysis

		Institutional Holding	
Forecast EPS	N/A	No of Institutions	824
Market Cap	$24.3 Billion	Shares	
Book Value	$3.5 Billion	277,087,264	
Price/Book	7.00	% Held	
Price/Sales	1.98	90.19	

Business Summary: Auto Parts (MIC: 1.8.2 SIC: 3714 NAIC: 336399)

Aptiv is a vehicle components manufacturer and provides electrical and electronic, powertrain, and safety technology solutions to the global automotive and commercial vehicle markets. Co. has three segments: Electrical / Electronic Architecture, which provides electrical and electronic architectures such as connectors, electrical centers and distribution systems; Powertrain Systems, which provides products for engine management systems and products; and Electronics and Safety, which provides a range of electronic and safety equipment and software in the areas of controls, security, infotainment, communications and safety systems.

Recent Developments: For the quarter ended Mar 31 2018, income from continuing operations increased 38.0% to US$316.0 million from US$229.0 million in the year-earlier quarter. Net income decreased 10.2% to US$316.0 million from US$352.0 million in the year-earlier quarter. Revenues were US$3.63 billion, up 15.5% from US$3.14 billion the year before. Operating income was US$374.0 million versus US$293.0 million in the prior-year quarter, an increase of 27.6%. Direct operating expenses rose 15.8% to US$2.95 billion from US$2.54 billion in the comparable period the year before. Indirect operating expenses increased 1.0% to US$309.0 million from US$306.0 million in the equivalent prior-year period.

Prospects: Our evaluation of Delphi Automotive PLC as of July 26, 2015 is the result of our systematic analysis on three basic characteristics: earnings strength, relative valuation, and recent stock price movement. The company has managed to produce a neutral trend in earnings per share over the past 5 quarters. However, while recent estimates for the company have been lowered by analysts, DLPH has posted better than expected results. Based on operating earnings yield, the company is undervalued when compared to all of the companies in our coverage universe. Share price changes over the past year indicates that DLPH will perform very well over the near term.

Financial Data

(US$ in Millions)	3 Mos	12/31/2017	12/31/2016	12/31/2015	12/31/2014	12/31/2013	12/31/2012	12/31/2011
Earnings Per Share	4.97	5.06	4.59	5.06	4.48	3.89	3.33	2.72
Cash Flow Per Share	5.02	5.49	7.09	5.97	7.11	5.63	4.56	3.27
Tang Book Value Per Share	1.07	0.51	N.M.	N.M.	3.80	5.52	3.39	3.33
Dividends Per Share	1.310	1.380	1.160	1.000	1.000	...	...	...
Dividend Payout %	26.36	27.27	25.27	19.76	22.32	...	...	...
Income Statement								
Total Revenue	3,630	12,884	16,661	15,165	17,023	16,463	15,519	16,041
EBITDA	556	1,817	2,150	2,077	2,316	2,088	1,866	1,994
Depn & Amortn	157	429	570	447	486	436	402	396
Income Before Taxes	370	1,255	1,425	1,508	1,705	1,523	1,345	1,506
Income Taxes	59	223	242	263	282	256	212	305
Net Income	307	1,355	1,257	1,450	1,351	1,212	1,077	1,145
Average Shares	266	268	273	286	301	311	323	421
Balance Sheet								
Current Assets	5,926	5,641	5,419	5,121	5,224	5,752	5,227	5,501
Total Assets	12,560	12,169	12,292	11,973	10,746	11,047	10,176	9,128
Current Liabilities	3,708	3,540	4,148	3,927	3,889	3,894	3,659	3,712
Long-Term Obligations	4,163	4,132	3,959	3,956	2,417	2,351	2,324	1,996
Total Liabilities	9,093	8,870	9,891	9,723	8,236	8,136	7,831	7,440
Stockholders' Equity	3,467	3,299	2,401	2,250	2,510	2,911	2,345	1,688
Shares Outstanding	264	265	269	278	291	306	315	328
Statistical Record								
Return on Assets %	10.59	11.08	10.33	12.76	12.40	11.42	11.13	11.33
Return on Equity %	43.90	47.54	53.91	60.92	49.84	46.12	53.26	31.25
EBITDA Margin %	15.32	14.10	12.90	13.70	13.61	12.68	12.02	12.43
Net Margin %	8.46	10.52	7.54	9.56	7.94	7.36	6.94	7.14
Asset Turnover	0.98	1.05	1.37	1.34	1.56	1.55	1.60	1.59
Current Ratio	1.60	1.59	1.31	1.30	1.34	1.48	1.43	1.48
Debt to Equity	1.20	1.25	1.65	1.76	0.96	0.81	0.99	1.18
Price Range	96.02-61.77	88.77-56.57	71.81-47.75	74.68-55.77	62.10-48.83	50.36-31.51	32.04-18.54	18.54-16.44
P/E Ratio	19.32-12.43	17.54-11.18	15.64-10.40	14.76-11.02	13.86-10.90	12.95-8.10	9.62-5.57	6.81-6.04
Average Yield %	1.62	1.87	2.03	1.49	1.77	...	...	...

Address: C, Ardilaun Court, 112-114	Web Site: www.delphi.com	Auditors: Ernst & Young LLP
St. Stephen's Green, Dublin, 2	Officers: Rajiv L. Gupta - Chairman Kevin P. Clark - President, Chief Executive Officer, Executive Vice President, Senior Vice President, Chief Operating Officer, Chief Financial Officer	Investor Contact: 248-813-2494
Telephone: 125-970-13		Transfer Agents: Computershare Trust Company, N.A., Providence

AQUA AMERICA INC

Exchange	Symbol	Price	52Wk Range	Yield	P/E	Div Acheiver
NYS	WTR	$35.18 (6/29/2018)	39.33-32.44	2.33	25.87	26 Years

*7 Year Price Score 105.14 *NYSE Composite Index=100 *12 Month Price Score 97.29

Interim Earnings (Per Share)

Qtr.	Mar	Jun	Sep	Dec
2015	0.27	0.32	0.38	0.16
2016	0.29	0.33	0.41	0.28
2017	0.28	0.34	0.43	0.30
2018	0.29	...	...	...

Interim Dividends (Per Share)

Amt	Decl	Ex	Rec	Pay
0.205Q	08/01/2017	08/14/2017	08/16/2017	09/01/2017
0.205Q	10/26/2017	11/16/2017	11/17/2017	12/01/2017
0.205Q	02/05/2018	02/15/2018	02/16/2018	03/01/2018
0.205Q	04/25/2018	05/17/2018	05/18/2018	06/01/2018

Indicated Div: $0.82 (Div. Reinv. Plan)

Valuation Analysis

Forecast EPS	$1.40	
	(06/14/2018)	
Market Cap	$6.3 Billion	
Book Value	$2.0 Billion	
Price/Book	3.17	
Price/Sales	7.67	

Institutional Holding

No of Institutions	655
Shares	121,634,992
% Held	58.11

Business Summary: Water Utilities (MIC: 3.2.1 SIC: 4941 NAIC: 221310)

Aqua America is the holding company for regulated utilities providing water or wastewater services in Pennsylvania, Ohio, Texas, Illinois, North Carolina, New Jersey, Indiana, and Virginia. As of Dec 31 2017, Co.'s Aqua Pennsylvania, Inc. subsidiary service territory is located in the suburban areas north and west of the City of Philadelphia and in 27 other counties in Pennsylvania. Co.'s Aqua Resources, Inc. subsidiary provides water and wastewater service through operating and maintenance contracts with municipal authorities and other parties. Co.'s Aqua Infrastructure, LLC subsidiary provides non-utility raw water supply services for firms in the natural gas drilling industry.

Recent Developments: For the quarter ended Mar 31 2018, net income increased 3.6% to US$50.8 million from US$49.1 million in the year-earlier quarter. Revenues were US$194.3 million, up 3.5% from US$187.8 million the year before. Operating income was US$69.3 million versus US$71.1 million in the prior-year quarter, a decrease of 2.5%. Direct operating expenses rose 8.9% to US$73.9 million from US$67.9 million in the comparable period the year before. Indirect operating expenses increased 4.7% to US$51.1 million from US$48.8 million in the equivalent prior-year period.

Prospects: Our evaluation of Aqua America Inc. as of Jan. 21, 2018 is the result of our systematic analysis on three basic characteristics: earnings strength, relative valuation, and recent stock price movement. The company has enjoyed a very positive trend in earnings per share over the past 5 quarters and while recent estimates for the company have remained steady, WTR has posted results that fell short of analysts expectations. Based on operating earnings yield, the company is about fairly valued when compared to all of the companies in our coverage universe. Share price changes over the past year indicates that WTR will perform very well over the near term.

Financial Data

(US$ in Thousands)	3 Mos	12/31/2017	12/31/2016	12/31/2015	12/31/2014	12/31/2013	12/31/2012	12/31/2011
Earnings Per Share	1.36	1.35	1.32	1.14	1.31	1.25	1.12	0.82
Cash Flow Per Share	2.18	2.15	2.23	2.10	2.06	2.09	2.11	2.12
Tang Book Value Per Share	10.85	10.78	10.19	9.58	9.19	8.52	7.75	7.06
Dividends Per Share	0.805	0.792	0.739	0.686	0.634	0.622	0.536	0.504
Dividend Payout %	59.22	58.67	55.95	60.18	48.40	49.76	47.86	61.17
Income Statement								
Total Revenue	194,347	809,525	819,875	814,204	779,903	768,643	757,760	711,956
EBITDA	107,764	480,964	465,765	453,755	442,543	426,922	438,516	405,597
Depn & Amortn	35,967	136,302	130,987	125,290	123,054	119,258	111,767	111,942
Income Before Taxes	48,326	256,321	254,184	251,929	243,092	230,348	248,992	215,853
Income Taxes	(2,131)	16,914	20,978	14,962	25,219	22,690	66,881	71,091
Net Income	50,839	239,738	234,182	201,790	233,239	221,300	196,563	143,069
Average Shares	178,238	178,175	177,846	177,517	177,763	176,814	174,917	173,361
Balance Sheet								
Current Assets	124,142	131,246	128,650	128,370	152,522	171,669	260,894	320,453
Total Assets	6,403,708	6,332,463	6,158,991	5,741,038	5,406,752	5,051,817	4,858,517	4,348,420
Current Liabilities	259,135	284,488	301,536	193,199	225,335	266,910	274,164	425,673
Long-Term Obligations	2,063,066	2,007,753	1,737,605	1,743,612	1,560,655	1,468,583	1,543,954	1,395,457
Total Liabilities	4,431,549	4,374,842	4,308,923	4,015,108	3,751,409	3,516,982	3,472,813	3,097,107
Stockholders' Equity	1,972,159	1,957,621	1,850,068	1,725,930	1,655,343	1,534,835	1,385,704	1,251,313
Shares Outstanding	177,897	177,713	177,394	176,544	176,753	176,750	175,209	173,518
Statistical Record								
Return on Assets %	3.82	3.84	3.93	3.62	4.46	4.47	4.26	3.40
Return on Equity %	12.58	12.59	13.06	11.94	14.62	15.15	14.87	11.80
EBITDA Margin %	55.45	59.41	56.81	55.73	56.74	55.54	57.87	56.97
Net Margin %	26.16	29.61	28.56	24.78	29.91	28.79	25.94	20.10
Asset Turnover	0.13	0.13	0.14	0.15	0.15	0.16	0.16	0.17
Current Ratio	0.48	0.46	0.43	0.66	0.68	0.64	0.95	0.75
Debt to Equity	1.05	1.03	0.94	1.01	0.94	0.96	1.11	1.12
Price Range	39.33-31.30	39.33-29.54	35.66-28.67	30.51-24.49	28.05-22.59	27.99-20.34	21.48-16.94	18.92-15.42
P/E Ratio	28.92-23.01	29.13-21.88	27.02-21.72	26.76-21.48	21.41-17.24	22.39-16.27	19.18-15.13	23.07-18.81
Average Yield %	2.34	2.37	2.35	2.56	2.55	2.54	2.80	2.85

Address: 762 W. Lancaster Avenue, Bryn Mawr, PA 19010-3489 **Telephone:** 610-527-8000	**Web Site:** www.aquaamerica.com **Officers:** Christopher H. (Chris) Franklin - Chairman, Chief Executive Officer, President, Executive Vice President, Senior Vice President, Chief Executive Officer, Region Officer, Executive Vice President, Division Officer, Senior Vice President, Region Officer, Division Officer Daniel J. Schuller - Division Officer, Deputy Chief Financial Officer, Executive Vice President	**Auditors:** PricewaterhouseCoopers LLP **Investor Contact:** 610-645-1191 **Transfer Agents:** Computershare Trust Company, N.A., Providence, RI

ARAMARK

Exchange	Symbol	Price	52Wk Range	Yield	P/E
NYS	ARMK	$37.10 (6/29/2018)	45.99-36.61	1.13	18.74

*7 Year Price Score N/A   *NYSE Composite Index=100   *12 Month Price Score 92.34

Interim Earnings (Per Share)

Qtr.	Dec	Mar	Jun	Sep
2014-15	0.35	0.24	0.14	0.23
2015-16	0.38	0.27	0.18	0.34
2016-17	0.50	0.28	0.26	0.45
2017-18	1.16	0.11		

Interim Dividends (Per Share)

Amt	Decl	Ex	Rec	Pay
0.103Q	08/02/2017	08/14/2017	08/16/2017	09/05/2017
0.105Q	11/14/2017	11/24/2017	11/27/2017	12/07/2017
0.105Q	01/31/2018	02/13/2018	02/14/2018	03/01/2018
0.105Q	05/02/2018	05/16/2018	05/17/2018	05/31/2018

Indicated Div: $0.42

Valuation Analysis

		Institutional Holding	
Forecast EPS	$2.25 (05/27/2018)	No of Institutions	418
Market Cap	$9.1 Billion	Shares	258,793,552
Book Value	$2.8 Billion	% Held	72.38
Price/Book	3.27		
Price/Sales	0.60		

TRADING VOLUME (thousand shares)

Business Summary: Hotels, Restaurants & Travel (MIC: 2.2.1 SIC: 5812 NAIC: 722110)

Aramark is a provider of food, facilities and uniform services to education, healthcare, business and industry, and sports, leisure and corrections clients. Co.'s business segments are: Food and Support Services (FSS) North America and FSS International, manage interrelated services-including food, hospitality and facility services-for school districts, colleges and universities, healthcare facilities, businesses, sports, entertainment and recreational venues, conference and convention centers, national and state parks and correctional institutions; and Uniform and Career Apparel, which provides uniforms and other garments and work clothes and ancillary items such as mats and shop towels.

Recent Developments: For the quarter ended Mar 30 2018, net income decreased 60.5% to US$27.7 million from US$70.2 million in the year-earlier quarter. Revenues were US$3.94 billion, up 8.8% from US$3.62 billion the year before. Operating income was US$136.5 million versus US$191.4 million in the prior-year quarter, a decrease of 28.7%. Direct operating expenses rose 10.4% to US$3.56 billion from US$3.23 billion in the comparable period the year before. Indirect operating expenses increased 18.3% to US$241.3 million from US$204.0 million in the equivalent prior-year period.

Prospects: Our evaluation of Aramark as of Jan. 21, 2018 is the result of our systematic analysis on three basic characteristics: earnings strength, relative valuation, and recent stock price movement. The company has generated a negative trend in earnings per share over the past 5 quarters and while recent estimates for the company have been raised by analysts, ARMK has posted results that fell short of analysts expectations. Based on operating earnings yield, the company is about fairly valued when compared to all of the companies in our coverage universe. Share price changes over the past year indicates that ARMK will perform well over the near term.

Financial Data
(US$ in Thousands)

	6 Mos	3 Mos	09/29/2017	09/30/2016	10/02/2015	10/03/2014	09/27/2013	09/28/2012
Earnings Per Share	1.98	2.15	1.49	1.16	0.96	0.63	0.33	0.49
Cash Flow Per Share	2.64	3.13	4.32	3.34	2.88	1.73	3.46	3.41
Dividends Per Share	0.416	0.414	0.412	0.380	0.345	0.225	...	...
Dividend Payout %	21.01	19.26	27.65	32.76	35.94	35.71	...	...
Income Statement								
Total Revenue	7,904,429	3,965,118	14,604,412	14,415,829	14,329,135	14,832,913	13,945,657	13,505,426
EBITDA	642,244	352,886	1,038,595	975,609	849,925	799,681	748,924	815,174
Depn & Amortn	286,713	133,849	237,900	234,800	226,600	239,900	239,100	236,600
Income Before Taxes	185,079	142,738	520,642	430,931	341,996	229,677	90,629	124,968
Income Taxes	(135,077)	(149,702)	146,455	142,699	105,020	80,218	19,233	18,066
Net Income	319,853	292,284	373,923	287,806	235,946	148,956	69,356	103,551
Average Shares	252,485	252,244	251,557	248,763	246,616	237,451	209,370	209,707
Balance Sheet								
Current Assets	2,976,287	2,812,287	2,653,139	2,492,571	2,379,123	2,464,976	2,287,165	2,185,501
Total Assets	13,732,757	12,526,822	11,006,229	10,582,072	10,224,050	10,455,693	10,267,106	10,487,354
Current Liabilities	2,298,058	2,012,567	2,368,095	2,184,745	2,180,988	2,378,873	2,389,253	2,163,674
Long-Term Obligations	7,749,518	6,976,508	5,190,331	5,223,514	5,212,290	5,355,789	5,758,229	5,971,305
Total Liabilities	10,937,134	9,804,428	8,547,168	8,421,066	8,340,691	8,737,657	9,363,399	9,554,337
Stockholders' Equity	2,795,623	2,722,394	2,459,061	2,161,006	1,883,359	1,718,036	903,707	933,017
Shares Outstanding	246,120	245,752	245,593	244,713	239,917	233,910	201,798	202,573
Statistical Record								
Return on Assets %	4.11	4.72	3.47	2.77	2.29	1.41	0.67	...
Return on Equity %	19.79	21.81	16.23	14.27	13.14	11.18	7.57	...
EBITDA Margin %	8.13	8.90	7.11	6.77	5.93	5.39	5.37	6.04
Net Margin %	4.05	7.37	2.56	2.00	1.65	1.00	0.50	0.77
Asset Turnover	1.25	1.29	1.36	1.39	1.39	1.41	1.35	...
Current Ratio	1.30	1.40	1.12	1.14	1.09	1.04	0.96	1.01
Debt to Equity	2.77	2.56	2.11	2.42	2.77	3.12	6.37	6.40
Price Range	45.99-36.11	43.75-33.08	41.48-33.08	38.21-29.57	33.49-25.35	29.89-22.70	...	...
P/E Ratio	23.23-18.24	20.35-15.39	27.84-22.20	32.94-25.49	34.89-26.41	47.44-36.03	...	...
Average Yield %	1.02	1.06	1.10	1.14	1.12	0.84	...	...

Address: Aramark Tower, 1101 Market Street, Philadelphia, PA 19107
Telephone: 215-238-3000

Web Site: www.aramark.com
Officers: Eric J. Foss - Chairman, President, Chief Executive Officer Stephen P. Bramlage - Executive Vice President, Chief Financial Officer

Auditors: KPMG LLP
Transfer Agents: Computershare Trust Company, N.A.

ARCHER DANIELS MIDLAND CO.

Exchange	Symbol	Price	52Wk Range	Yield	P/E	Div Acheiver
NYS	ADM	$45.83 (6/29/2018)	46.53-38.96	2.92	15.80	43 Years

*7 Year Price Score 86.75 *NYSE Composite Index=100 *12 Month Price Score 104.14

Interim Earnings (Per Share)

Qtr.	Mar	Jun	Sep	Dec
2015	0.77	0.62	0.41	1.18
2016	0.39	0.48	0.58	0.72
2017	0.59	0.48	0.34	1.38
2018	0.70	...	...	...

Interim Dividends (Per Share)

Amt	Decl	Ex	Rec	Pay
0.32Q	08/03/2017	08/15/2017	08/17/2017	09/07/2017
0.32Q	11/02/2017	11/15/2017	11/16/2017	12/07/2017
0.335Q	02/06/2018	02/16/2018	02/20/2018	03/13/2018
0.335Q	05/03/2018	05/16/2018	05/17/2018	06/07/2018

Indicated Div: $1.34 (Div. Reinv. Plan)

Valuation Analysis / Institutional Holding

Forecast EPS	$3.12
(06/12/2018)	
Market Cap	$25.6 Billion
Book Value	$18.7 Billion
Price/Book	1.37
Price/Sales	0.42

No of Institutions 1166
Shares 591,208,448
% Held 69.52

Business Summary: Food (MIC: 1.2.1 SIC: 2041 NAIC: 311211)

Archer Daniels Midland is principally engaged in procuring, transporting, storing, processing, and merchandising agricultural commodities and products. Co. has four segments: Agricultural Services, which buy, store, clean, and transport agricultural commodities and resells these commodities primarily as food and feed ingredients and as raw materials; Corn Processing, which is engaged in corn wet milling and dry milling activities; Oilseeds Processing, which is engaged in the origination, merchandising, crushing, and further processing of oilseeds; and Wild Flavors and Specialty Ingredients, which engages in the manufacturing, sales, and distribution of specialty products.

Recent Developments: For the quarter ended Mar 31 2018, net income increased 16.5% to US$396.0 million from US$340.0 million in the year-earlier quarter. Revenues were US$15.53 billion, up 3.6% from US$14.99 billion the year before. Direct operating expenses rose 3.7% to US$14.64 billion from US$14.12 billion in the comparable period the year before. Indirect operating expenses increased 0.6% to US$529.0 million from US$526.0 million in the equivalent prior-year period.

Prospects: Our evaluation of Archer Daniels Midland Co. as of Jan. 21, 2018 is the result of our systematic analysis on three basic characteristics: earnings strength, relative valuation, and recent stock price movement. The company has generated a negative trend in earnings per share over the past 5 quarters. However, while recent estimates for the company have been mixed, ADM has posted results that fell short of analysts expectations. Based on operating earnings yield, the company is undervalued when compared to all of the companies in our coverage universe. Share price changes over the past year indicates that ADM will perform poorly over the near term.

Financial Data

(US$ in Thousands)	3 Mos	12/31/2017	12/31/2016	12/31/2015	12/31/2014	12/31/2013	12/31/2012	06/30/2012
Earnings Per Share	2.90	2.79	2.16	2.98	3.43	2.02	1.05	1.84
Cash Flow Per Share	(3.15)	3.89	2.50	4.01	7.60	7.91	7.45	4.34
Tang Book Value Per Share	26.41	25.84	23.51	23.88	25.58	29.43	27.87	26.35
Dividends Per Share	1.295	1.280	1.200	1.120	0.960	0.760	0.700	0.685
Dividend Payout %	44.66	45.88	55.56	37.58	27.99	37.62	33.33	37.23
Income Statement								
Total Revenue	15,526,000	60,828,000	62,346,000	67,702,000	81,201,000	89,804,000	46,729,000	89,038,000
EBITDA	610,000	2,179,000	2,518,000	2,930,000	3,853,000	2,751,000	1,331,000	2,470,000
Depn & Amortn	235,000	802,000	787,000	799,000	850,000	827,000	435,000	848,000
Income Before Taxes	317,000	1,153,000	1,530,000	1,894,000	2,758,000	1,613,000	742,000	1,293,000
Income Taxes	68,000	7,000	534,000	438,000	877,000	670,000	303,000	523,000
Net Income	393,000	1,595,000	1,279,000	1,849,000	2,248,000	1,342,000	692,000	1,223,000
Average Shares	565,000	572,000	591,000	621,000	656,000	663,000	661,000	666,000
Balance Sheet								
Current Assets	20,906,000	19,925,000	21,045,000	21,829,000	26,028,000	28,530,000	29,762,000	26,954,000
Total Assets	41,100,000	39,963,000	39,769,000	40,157,000	44,027,000	43,752,000	45,136,000	41,553,000
Current Liabilities	13,285,000	12,570,000	13,173,000	13,505,000	15,602,000	15,658,000	16,993,000	14,626,000
Long-Term Obligations	6,657,000	6,623,000	6,504,000	5,779,000	5,558,000	5,347,000	6,456,000	6,535,000
Total Liabilities	22,368,000	21,650,000	22,596,000	22,258,000	24,452,000	23,596,000	26,216,000	23,584,000
Stockholders' Equity	18,732,000	18,313,000	17,173,000	17,899,000	19,575,000	20,156,000	18,920,000	17,969,000
Shares Outstanding	559,000	557,000	573,000	595,000	637,000	659,000	659,000	659,000
Statistical Record								
Return on Assets %	4.09	4.00	3.19	4.39	5.12	3.02	3.14	2.91
Return on Equity %	9.20	8.99	7.27	9.87	11.32	6.87	7.28	6.63
EBITDA Margin %	3.93	3.58	4.04	4.33	4.75	3.06	2.85	2.77
Net Margin %	2.53	2.62	2.05	2.73	2.77	1.49	1.48	1.37
Asset Turnover	1.52	1.53	1.56	1.61	1.85	2.02	2.12	2.12
Current Ratio	1.57	1.59	1.60	1.62	1.67	1.82	1.75	1.84
Debt to Equity	0.36	0.36	0.38	0.32	0.28	0.27	0.34	0.36
Price Range	46.04-38.96	46.97-38.96	47.72-30.51	53.17-34.18	53.71-38.23	43.79-27.39	29.10-24.48	33.50-24.16
P/E Ratio	15.88-13.43	16.84-13.96	22.09-14.12	17.84-11.47	15.66-11.15	21.68-13.56	27.71-23.31	18.21-13.13
Average Yield %	3.08	2.99	2.96	2.44	2.08	2.15	1.30	2.31

Address: 77 West Wacker Drive, Suite 4600, Chicago, IL 60601	**Web Site:** www.adm.com	**Auditors:** Ernst & Young LLP
Telephone: 312-634-8100	**Officers:** Juan R. Luciano - Chairman, President, Chief Executive Officer, Executive Vice President, Chief Operating Officer Ray G. Young - Executive Vice President, Senior Vice President, Chief Financial Officer	**Investor Contact:** 217-424-5656 **Transfer Agents:** Hickory Point Bank & Trust, fsb, Decatur, IL

ARCONIC INC

Exchange	Symbol	Price	52Wk Range	Yield	P/E
NYS	ARNC	$17.01 (6/29/2018)	30.84-16.87	1.41	N/A

*7 Year Price Score 79.16 *NYSE Composite Index=100 *12 Month Price Score 72.75

Interim Earnings (Per Share)

Qtr.	Mar	Jun	Sep	Dec
2015	0.42	0.30	0.06	(1.71)
2016	0.00	0.27	0.33	(2.91)
2017	0.65	0.43	0.22	(1.59)
2018	0.29	...	...	...

Interim Dividends (Per Share)

Amt	Decl	Ex	Rec	Pay
0.06Q	09/19/2017	11/02/2017	11/03/2017	11/25/2017
0.06Q	01/19/2018	02/01/2018	02/02/2018	02/25/2018
0.06Q	02/15/2018	05/03/2018	05/04/2018	05/25/2018
0.06Q	05/17/2018	08/02/2018	08/03/2018	08/25/2018

Indicated Div: $0.24

Valuation Analysis   Institutional Holding

Forecast EPS	$1.25	No of Institutions
	(06/14/2018)	963
Market Cap	$8.2 Billion	Shares
Book Value	$5.3 Billion	542,074,368
Price/Book	1.56	% Held
Price/Sales	0.62	72.19

TRADING VOLUME (thousand shares)

Business Summary: Non-Precious Metals (MIC: 8.2.2 SIC: 3334 NAIC: 331312)

Arconic is engaged in lightweight metals engineering and manufacturing. Co.'s operations consist of three reportable segments: Global Rolled Products, which produces a range of aluminum sheet and plate products for the aerospace, automotive, commercial transportation, brazing and industrial markets; Engineered Products and Solutions, which develops and manufactures products for the aerospace (commercial and defense), commercial transportation, and power generation end markets; as well as Transportation and Construction Solutions, which produces products that are used mostly in the nonresidential building and construction and commercial transportation end markets.

Recent Developments: For the quarter ended Mar 31 2018, net income decreased 55.6% to US$143.0 million from US$322.0 million in the year-earlier quarter. Revenues were US$3.45 billion, up 7.9% from US$3.19 billion the year before. Operating income was US$333.0 million versus US$283.0 million in the prior-year quarter, an increase of 17.7%. Direct operating expenses rose 12.6% to US$2.77 billion from US$2.46 billion in the comparable period the year before. Indirect operating expenses decreased 23.7% to US$344.0 million from US$451.0 million in the equivalent prior-year period.

Prospects: Our evaluation of Arconic Inc. as of Jan. 21, 2018 is the result of our systematic analysis on three basic characteristics: earnings strength, relative valuation, and recent stock price movement. The company has enjoyed a very positive trend in earnings per share over the past 5 quarters and while recent estimates for the company have been mixed, ARNC has posted results that fell short of analysts expectations. Based on operating earnings yield, the company is about fairly valued when compared to all of the companies in our coverage universe. Share price changes over the past year indicates that ARNC will perform poorly over the near term.

Financial Data
(US$ in Thousands)

	3 Mos	12/31/2017	12/31/2016	12/31/2015	12/31/2014	12/31/2013	12/31/2012	12/31/2011
Earnings Per Share	(0.65)	(0.28)	(2.31)	(0.93)	0.63	(6.42)	0.54	1.65
Cash Flow Per Share	1.17	1.55	1.98	3.77	4.32	4.42	4.20	6.20
Tang Book Value Per Share	N.M.	N.M.	N.M.	12.43	15.45	18.83	21.27	22.67
Dividends Per Share	0.240	0.240	0.090	...	...	0.360	0.360	0.360
Dividend Payout %	...	...	...	...	...	...	66.67	21.82
Income Statement								
Total Revenue	3,445,000	12,960,000	12,394,000	22,534,000	23,906,000	23,032,000	23,700,000	24,951,000
EBITDA	455,000	1,498,000	2,022,000	2,099,000	2,415,000	114,000	2,273,000	3,033,000
Depn & Amortn	142,000	551,000	1,132,000	1,280,000	1,372,000	1,422,000	1,462,000	1,481,000
Income Before Taxes	199,000	470,000	407,000	337,000	589,000	(1,748,000)	352,000	1,048,000
Income Taxes	56,000	544,000	1,476,000	445,000	320,000	428,000	162,000	255,000
Net Income	143,000	(74,000)	(941,000)	(322,000)	268,000	(2,285,000)	191,000	611,000
Average Shares	503,000	451,000	438,000	419,666	393,333	356,666	358,666	387,000
Balance Sheet								
Current Assets	5,895,000	6,378,000	5,892,000	7,953,000	8,269,000	6,969,000	7,700,000	7,713,000
Total Assets	18,219,000	18,718,000	20,038,000	36,528,000	37,399,000	35,742,000	40,179,000	40,120,000
Current Liabilities	2,802,000	2,824,000	2,749,000	5,211,000	5,541,000	6,105,000	5,942,000	6,013,000
Long-Term Obligations	6,309,000	6,806,000	8,044,000	9,044,000	8,769,000	7,607,000	8,311,000	8,640,000
Total Liabilities	12,951,000	13,808,000	14,923,000	24,482,000	25,093,000	25,149,000	26,980,000	26,276,000
Stockholders' Equity	5,268,000	4,910,000	5,115,000	12,046,000	12,306,000	10,593,000	13,199,000	13,844,000
Shares Outstanding	482,832	481,416	438,519	436,720	405,554	357,003	355,737	354,804
Statistical Record								
Return on Assets %	N.M.	N.M.	N.M.	N.M.	0.73	N.M.	0.47	1.54
Return on Equity %	N.M.	N.M.	N.M.	N.M.	2.34	N.M.	1.41	4.45
EBITDA Margin %	13.21	11.56	16.31	9.31	10.10	0.49	9.59	12.16
Net Margin %	4.15	N.M.	N.M.	N.M.	1.12	N.M.	0.81	2.45
Asset Turnover	0.69	0.67	0.44	0.61	0.65	0.61	0.59	0.63
Current Ratio	2.10	2.26	2.14	1.53	1.49	1.14	1.30	1.28
Debt to Equity	1.20	1.39	1.57	0.75	0.71	0.72	0.63	0.62
Price Range	30.84-21.84	30.55-19.19	25.49-15.19	38.47-17.62	39.66-22.76	24.09-17.35	24.25-18.07	40.86-19.20
P/E Ratio	...	...	...	...	62.95-36.13	...	44.90-33.47	24.76-11.64
Average Yield %	0.93	0.94	0.43	...	...	1.86	1.75	1.14

Address: 390 Park Avenue, New York, NY 10022-4608	Web Site: www.arconic.com	Auditors: PricewaterhouseCoopers LLP
Telephone: 212-836-2732	Officers: John C. Plant - Chairman Charles P. (Chip) Blankenship - Chief Executive Officer	Investor Contact: 212-836-2674 Transfer Agents: Computershares

ARISTA NETWORKS INC

Exchange	Symbol	Price	52Wk Range	Yield	P/E
NYS	ANET	$257.49 (6/29/2018)	307.96-143.46	N/A	42.49

*7 Year Price Score N/A   *NYSE Composite Index=100   *12 Month Price Score 115.25

TRADING VOLUME (thousand shares)

Interim Earnings (Per Share)

Qtr.	Mar	Jun	Sep	Dec
2015	0.34	0.33	0.39	0.60
2016	0.48	0.53	0.69	0.79
2017	1.07	1.30	1.68	1.29
2018	1.79	...	...	...

Interim Dividends (Per Share)

No Dividends Paid

Valuation Analysis

		Institutional Holding	
Forecast EPS	$7.11	No of Institutions	
	(06/14/2018)	544	
Market Cap	$19.1 Billion	Shares	
Book Value	$1.8 Billion	42,213,004	
Price/Book	10.37	% Held	
Price/Sales	10.73	N/A	

Business Summary: Computer Hardware & Equipment (MIC: 6.2.1 SIC: 5045 NAIC: 423430)

Arista Networks is a supplier of cloud networking solutions that use software to address the needs of large-scale Internet companies, cloud service providers and data centers. Co.'s cloud networking solutions consist of its Extensible Operating System (EOS), a set of network applications and its Ethernet switching and routing platforms. EOS supports cloud and virtualization solutions, including VMware NSX, Microsoft System Center, OpenStack and other cloud management frameworks. Co. also co-authored the VXLAN protocol specification with VMware. Co.'s EOS+ is a software platform for network programmability and automation, provides an advanced level of programmability.

Recent Developments: For the quarter ended Mar 31 2018, net income increased 74.2% to US$144.5 million from US$83.0 million in the year-earlier quarter. Revenues were US$472.5 million, up 40.8% from US$335.5 million the year before. Operating income was US$138.7 million versus US$73.4 million in the prior-year quarter, an increase of 89.0%. Direct operating expenses rose 39.8% to US$169.6 million from US$121.3 million in the comparable period the year before. Indirect operating expenses increased 16.6% to US$164.2 million from US$140.8 million in the equivalent prior-year period.

Prospects: Our evaluation of Arista Networks Inc as of Jan. 21, 2018 is the result of our systematic analysis on three basic characteristics: earnings strength, relative valuation, and recent stock price movement. The company has produced a positive trend in earnings per share over the past 5 quarters and while recent estimates for the company have been mixed, ANET has posted better than expected results. Based on operating earnings yield, the company is overvalued when compared to all of the companies in our coverage universe. Share price changes over the past year indicates that ANET will perform very well over the near term.

Financial Data

(US$ in Thousands)	3 Mos	12/31/2017	12/31/2016	12/31/2015	12/31/2014	12/31/2013	12/31/2012	12/31/2011
Earnings Per Share	6.06	5.35	2.50	1.67	1.29	0.72	0.39	0.65
Cash Flow Per Share	8.98	8.74	1.91	3.04	2.36	1.27	1.06	0.59
Tang Book Value Per Share	24.82	22.55	15.64	11.57	8.48	2.25	0.43	...
Income Statement								
Total Revenue	472,489	1,646,186	1,129,167	837,591	584,106	361,224	193,408	139,848
EBITDA	148,851	497,740	264,761	162,561	135,513	71,148	41,697	45,500
Depn & Amortn	5,270	20,200	19,400	13,400	10,000	5,000	1,800	1,100
Income Before Taxes	142,894	474,760	242,225	146,009	121,508	58,275	32,975	37,626
Income Taxes	(1,644)	51,559	58,036	24,907	34,658	15,815	11,626	3,591
Net Income	144,538	423,201	184,189	121,102	86,850	42,460	21,349	34,035
Average Shares	80,721	78,977	73,222	71,411	54,590	30,051	24,901	21,345
Balance Sheet								
Current Assets	2,379,174	2,266,429	1,526,126	974,328	679,479	285,523	177,172	...
Total Assets	2,580,034	2,460,860	1,729,007	1,159,890	811,023	364,520	220,168	...
Current Liabilities	457,779	529,905	459,553	235,011	144,373	209,344	46,364	...
Long-Term Obligations	37,138	37,673	39,593	41,210	42,547	43,152	122,926	...
Total Liabilities	734,995	798,946	621,187	371,738	255,365	286,788	201,258	...
Stockholders' Equity	1,845,039	1,661,914	1,107,820	788,152	555,658	77,732	18,910	...
Shares Outstanding	74,338	73,706	70,811	68,132	65,528	31,927	30,305	29,788
Statistical Record								
Return on Assets %	21.45	20.20	12.72	12.29	14.78	14.52	...	...
Return on Equity %	31.55	30.56	19.38	18.02	27.42	87.87	...	...
EBITDA Margin %	31.50	30.24	23.45	19.41	23.20	19.70	21.56	32.54
Net Margin %	30.59	25.71	16.31	14.46	14.87	11.75	11.04	24.34
Asset Turnover	0.79	0.79	0.78	0.85	0.99	1.24	...	...
Current Ratio	5.20	4.28	3.32	4.15	4.71	1.36	3.82	...
Debt to Equity	0.02	0.02	0.04	0.05	0.08	0.56	6.50	...
Price Range	307.96-131.36	243.55-88.23	98.00-53.00	87.68-56.71	93.31-55.00	...	...	...
P/E Ratio	50.82-21.68	45.52-16.49	39.20-21.20	52.50-33.96	72.33-42.64	...	...	...

Address: 5453 Great America Parkway, Santa Clara, CA 95054 **Telephone:** 408-547-5500	**Web Site:** www.arista.com **Officers:** Andy Bechtolsheim - Chairman, Chief Development Officer, Interim Chief Financial Officer, Principal Financial Officer Andreas Bechtolsheim - Executive Officer	**Auditors:** Ernst & Young LLP **Transfer Agents:** Computershare Trust Company, N.A., Canton, MA

ARMSTRONG WORLD INDUSTRIES INC

Exchange	Symbol	Price	52Wk Range	Yield	P/E
NYS	AWI	$63.20 (6/29/2018)	64.90-44.05	N/A	22.41

*7 Year Price Score 100.01 *NYSE Composite Index=100 *12 Month Price Score 108.22

Interim Earnings (Per Share)

Qtr.	Mar	Jun	Sep	Dec
2015	0.83	0.53	0.57	(0.24)
2016	(0.18)	0.30	1.26	0.49
2017	0.56	0.77	0.92	0.62
2018	0.51	...	...	...

Interim Dividends (Per Share)

Dividend Payment Suspended

Valuation Analysis **Institutional Holding**

Forecast EPS	$3.71	No of Institutions
	(06/11/2018)	301
Market Cap	$3.3 Billion	Shares
Book Value	$403.8 Million	65,136,240
Price/Book	8.17	% Held
Price/Sales	4.10	81.62

Business Summary: Construction Materials (MIC: 8.5.1 SIC: 5039 NAIC: 327993)

Armstrong World Industries designs, manufactures and sells ceiling systems (primarily mineral fiber, fiberglass wool and metal) for use in the construction and renovation of residential, commercial and institutional buildings. Co. has three segments: Americas (including Canada); Europe, Middle East and Africa (including Russia); and Pacific Rim. Each of Co.'s segments produce suspended fiber and metal ceilings for use in commercial and institutional settings in addition to sourcing complimentary ceiling products. Each segment also includes Co.'s Worthington Armstrong Venture joint venture, which manufactures suspension system (grid) products that are invoiced by both Co. and WAVE.

Recent Developments: For the quarter ended Mar 31 2018, income from continuing operations increased 16.1% to US$41.2 million from US$35.5 million in the year-earlier quarter. Net income decreased 8.6% to US$27.8 million from US$30.4 million in the year-earlier quarter. Revenues were US$227.3 million, up 3.4% from US$219.8 million the year before. Operating income was US$49.6 million versus US$57.3 million in the prior-year quarter, a decrease of 13.4%. Direct operating expenses rose 10.6% to US$156.5 million from US$141.5 million in the comparable period the year before. Indirect operating expenses increased 1.0% to US$21.2 million from US$21.0 million in the equivalent prior-year period.

Prospects: Our evaluation of Armstrong World Industries Inc. as of Jan. 21, 2018 is the result of our systematic analysis on three basic characteristics: earnings strength, relative valuation, and recent stock price movement. The company has produced a positive trend in earnings per share over the past 5 quarters. However, while recent estimates for the company have been mixed, AWI has posted results that fell short of analysts expectations. Based on operating earnings yield, the company is undervalued when compared to all of the companies in our coverage universe. Share price changes over the past year indicates that AWI will perform very well over the near term.

Financial Data

(US$ in Thousands)	3 Mos	12/31/2017	12/31/2016	12/31/2015	12/31/2014	12/31/2013	12/31/2012	12/31/2011
Earnings Per Share	2.82	2.86	1.87	1.68	1.14	1.60	2.19	1.90
Cash Flow Per Share	3.51	3.20	0.89	3.67	3.80	3.70	3.72	3.64
Tang Book Value Per Share	N.M.	N.M.	N.M.	5.04	2.68	2.76	3.25	10.01
Dividends Per Share	...	...	...	...	...	...	8.550	...
Dividend Payout %	...	...	...	...	...	...	390.41	...
Income Statement								
Total Revenue	227,300	893,600	1,234,500	2,420,000	2,515,300	2,719,900	2,618,900	2,859,500
EBITDA	45,900	277,900	207,600	219,200	293,000	287,100	327,900	297,700
Depn & Amortn	3,600	89,200	89,200	118,300	129,400	109,000	112,700	113,800
Income Before Taxes	33,100	155,100	71,200	57,800	120,100	112,500	164,600	138,200
Income Taxes	8,200	1,500	50,400	71,300	83,200	71,400	76,100	80,700
Net Income	27,800	154,800	104,700	94,200	63,800	94,100	131,300	112,400
Average Shares	53,800	53,900	55,700	55,900	55,400	58,400	59,500	58,800
Balance Sheet								
Current Assets	599,100	648,900	406,200	880,800	811,500	884,000	1,019,900	1,209,300
Total Assets	1,825,100	1,873,500	1,758,000	2,691,900	2,606,200	2,916,600	2,854,300	2,994,700
Current Liabilities	245,100	269,900	224,100	436,300	388,100	410,900	384,700	386,100
Long-Term Obligations	810,100	817,700	848,600	950,900	1,003,000	1,042,600	1,038,000	822,900
Total Liabilities	1,421,300	1,454,200	1,491,600	1,923,100	1,957,100	2,243,400	2,135,200	1,864,500
Stockholders' Equity	403,800	419,300	266,400	768,800	649,100	673,200	719,100	1,130,200
Shares Outstanding	52,198	52,772	54,428	55,359	55,126	54,406	58,934	58,424
Statistical Record								
Return on Assets %	8.50	8.53	4.69	3.56	2.31	3.26	4.48	3.80
Return on Equity %	45.10	45.15	20.17	13.29	9.65	13.52	14.16	10.12
EBITDA Margin %	20.19	31.10	16.82	9.06	11.65	10.56	12.52	10.41
Net Margin %	12.23	17.32	8.48	3.89	2.54	3.46	5.01	3.93
Asset Turnover	0.45	0.49	0.55	0.91	0.91	0.94	0.89	0.97
Current Ratio	2.44	2.40	1.81	2.02	2.09	2.15	2.65	3.13
Debt to Equity	2.01	1.95	3.19	1.24	1.55	1.55	1.44	0.73
Price Range	64.15-41.35	60.55-38.80	45.51-31.45	51.99-38.75	53.19-39.27	49.93-40.06	50.38-33.50	41.61-28.43
P/E Ratio	22.75-14.66	21.17-13.57	24.34-16.82	30.95-23.06	46.65-34.44	31.20-25.04	23.00-15.29	21.90-14.96
Average Yield %	...	...	...	...	...	...	20.81	...

Address: 2500 Columbia Avenue, Lancaster, PA 17603
Telephone: 717-397-0611

Web Site: www.armstrong.com
Officers: Victor D. (Vic) Grizzle - President, Chief Executive Officer, Executive Vice President, Division Officer Brian L. MacNeal - Senior Vice President, Chief Financial Officer

Auditors: KPMG LLP
Investor Contact: 717-396-6354
Transfer Agents: American Stock Transfer & Trust Company, New York, NY

ARROW ELECTRONICS, INC.

Exchange	Symbol	Price	52Wk Range	Yield	P/E
NYS	ARW	$75.28 (6/29/2018)	86.94-72.79	N/A	15.75

*7 Year Price Score 113.86 *NYSE Composite Index=100 *12 Month Price Score 95.24

Interim Earnings (Per Share)

Qtr.	Mar	Jun	Sep	Dec
2015	1.09	1.28	1.15	1.68
2016	1.14	1.45	1.28	1.81
2017	1.26	1.11	1.50	0.61
2018	1.56	...	...	...

Interim Dividends (Per Share)

No Dividends Paid

Valuation Analysis · **Institutional Holding**

Forecast EPS	$8.80	No of Institutions	
	(06/14/2018)	581	
Market Cap	$6.6 Billion	Shares	
Book Value	$5.1 Billion	112,439,984	
Price/Book	1.29	% Held	
Price/Sales	0.24	83.57	

Business Summary: Electrical Equipment (MIC: 7.3.1 SIC: 3679 NAIC: 334419)

Arrow Electronics is a provider of products, services, and solutions to industrial and commercial users of electronic components and enterprise computing solutions. Co. has two business segments: the global components business, which markets and distributes electronic components to original equipment manufacturers and contract manufacturers, and provides a range of capabilities throughout the life cycle of technology products and services; and the global enterprise computing solutions business, which provides computing solutions and services, including datacenter, cloud, security, and analytics solutions to value-added resellers.

Recent Developments: For the quarter ended Mar 31 2018, net income increased 20.2% to US$139.9 million from US$116.3 million in the year-earlier quarter. Revenues were US$6.88 billion, up 19.9% from US$5.74 billion the year before. Operating income was US$236.0 million versus US$193.0 million in the prior-year quarter, an increase of 22.3%. Direct operating expenses rose 20.7% to US$6.01 billion from US$4.98 billion in the comparable period the year before. Indirect operating expenses increased 11.4% to US$632.9 million from US$568.2 million in the equivalent prior-year period.

Prospects: Our evaluation of Arrow Electronics Inc. as of Jan. 21, 2018 is the result of our systematic analysis on three basic characteristics: earnings strength, relative valuation, and recent stock price movement. The company has enjoyed a very positive trend in earnings per share over the past 5 quarters and while recent estimates for the company have remained steady, ARW has posted better than expected results. Based on operating earnings yield, the company is undervalued when compared to all of the companies in our coverage universe. Share price changes over the past year indicates that ARW will perform poorly over the near term.

Financial Data

(US$ in Thousands)	3 Mos	12/31/2017	12/31/2016	12/31/2015	12/31/2014	12/31/2013	12/31/2012	12/31/2011
Earnings Per Share	4.78	4.48	5.68	5.20	4.98	3.85	4.56	5.17
Cash Flow Per Share	0.80	1.40	3.90	6.92	6.82	4.39	6.16	1.06
Tang Book Value Per Share	23.37	25.03	18.94	15.22	18.24	17.16	17.52	16.12
Income Statement								
Total Revenue	6,875,613	26,812,508	23,825,261	23,282,020	22,768,674	21,357,285	20,405,128	21,390,264
EBITDA	245,306	1,047,395	1,057,559	1,023,575	989,978	857,287	954,019	1,051,743
Depn & Amortn	12,994	192,721	199,020	203,028	197,978	168,064	149,896	142,707
Income Before Taxes	187,133	690,864	707,824	685,146	676,015	574,790	702,247	803,065
Income Taxes	46,590	287,126	190,674	191,697	184,943	182,343	203,642	210,485
Net Income	139,094	401,962	522,750	497,726	498,045	399,420	506,332	598,810
Average Shares	89,035	89,766	92,033	95,686	99,947	103,699	111,077	115,932
Balance Sheet								
Current Assets	11,767,213	12,417,759	10,316,721	9,186,471	9,032,607	8,585,770	7,715,301	7,024,591
Total Assets	16,124,805	16,462,809	14,206,366	13,021,930	12,442,856	12,060,883	10,785,687	9,829,079
Current Liabilities	6,955,094	7,956,569	6,689,222	6,056,152	5,838,021	5,301,946	4,910,211	3,958,927
Long-Term Obligations	3,533,050	2,933,045	2,696,334	2,380,575	2,075,453	2,226,132	1,587,478	1,927,823
Total Liabilities	11,025,197	11,511,270	9,792,928	8,879,487	8,288,886	7,880,651	6,802,465	6,160,267
Stockholders' Equity	5,099,608	4,951,539	4,413,438	4,142,443	4,153,970	4,180,232	3,983,222	3,668,812
Shares Outstanding	87,620	87,691	88,913	90,923	95,895	99,936	106,001	111,814
Statistical Record								
Return on Assets %	2.89	2.62	3.83	3.91	4.07	3.50	4.90	6.16
Return on Equity %	8.89	8.58	12.19	12.00	11.95	9.79	13.20	17.31
EBITDA Margin %	3.57	3.91	4.44	4.40	4.35	4.01	4.68	4.92
Net Margin %	2.02	1.50	2.19	2.14	2.19	1.87	2.48	2.80
Asset Turnover	1.89	1.75	1.75	1.83	1.86	1.87	1.97	2.20
Current Ratio	1.69	1.56	1.54	1.52	1.55	1.62	1.57	1.77
Debt to Equity	0.69	0.59	0.61	0.57	0.50	0.53	0.40	0.53
Price Range	86.94-69.97	83.96-69.97	72.44-46.66	64.67-50.79	62.71-46.42	54.25-36.47	42.63-31.02	46.53-25.98
P/E Ratio	18.19-14.64	18.74-15.62	12.75-8.21	12.44-9.77	12.59-9.32	14.09-9.47	9.35-6.80	9.00-5.03

| Address: 9201 East Dry Creek Road, Centennial, CO 80112 | Web Site: www.arrow.com | Auditors: Ernst & Young LLP |
| Telephone: 303-824-4000 | Officers: Michael J. Long - Chairman, President, Chief Executive Officer, Chief Operating Officer Christopher D. (Chris) Stansbury - Senior Vice President, Chief Financial Officer, Vice President, Principal Accounting Officer | Investor Contact: 303-824-4000 Transfer Agents: Wells Fargo Shareowner Services, South St. Paul, MN |

ASBURY AUTOMOTIVE GROUP INC

Exchange	Symbol	Price	52Wk Range	Yield	P/E
NYS	ABG	$68.55 (6/29/2018)	75.85-50.15	N/A	9.86

*7 Year Price Score 95.98   *NYSE Composite Index=100   *12 Month Price Score 109.41

Interim Earnings (Per Share)

Qtr.	Mar	Jun	Sep	Dec
2015	1.30	1.52	1.96	1.65
2016	1.27	1.65	1.47	3.03
2017	1.61	1.52	1.48	2.02
2018	1.93	...	...	...

Interim Dividends (Per Share)

No Dividends Paid

Valuation Analysis		Institutional Holding	
Forecast EPS	$7.65	No of Institutions	
	(06/13/2018)	273	
Market Cap	$1.4 Billion	Shares	
Book Value	$424.3 Million	27,474,050	
Price/Book	3.33	% Held	
Price/Sales	0.22	93.66	

TRADING VOLUME (thousand shares)

Business Summary: Retail - Automotive (MIC: 2.1.4 SIC: 5599 NAIC: 441229)

Asbury Automotive Group is an automotive retailer with store operations conducted by its subsidiaries. As of Dec 31 2017, Co. owned and operated 94 new vehicle franchises, representing 29 brands of automobiles at 80 dealership locations, and 24 collision centers. Co.'s stores provide a range of automotive products and services, including new and used vehicles; parts and service, including vehicle repair and maintenance services, replacement parts, and collision repair services; and finance and insurance products, including arranging vehicle financing through third parties and aftermarket products, such as extended service contracts.

Recent Developments: For the quarter ended Mar 31 2018, net income increased 17.9% to US$40.1 million from US$34.0 million in the year-earlier quarter. Revenues were US$1.61 billion, up 3.7% from US$1.55 billion the year before. Operating income was US$73.2 million versus US$72.3 million in the prior-year quarter, an increase of 1.2%. Direct operating expenses rose 4.0% to US$1.34 billion from US$1.29 billion in the comparable period the year before. Indirect operating expenses increased 2.3% to US$192.2 million from US$187.8 million in the equivalent prior-year period.

Prospects: Our evaluation of Asbury Automotive Group Inc. as of Jan. 21, 2018 is the result of our systematic analysis on three basic characteristics: earnings strength, relative valuation, and recent stock price movement. The company has managed to produce a neutral trend in earnings per share over the past 5 quarters and while recent estimates for the company have been raised by analysts, ABG has posted results that fell short of analysts expectations. Based on operating earnings yield, the company is undervalued when compared to all of the companies in our coverage universe. Share price changes over the past year indicates that ABG will perform very poorly over the near term.

Financial Data

(US$ in Thousands)	3 Mos	12/31/2017	12/31/2016	12/31/2015	12/31/2014	12/31/2013	12/31/2012	12/31/2011
Earnings Per Share	6.95	6.62	7.40	6.41	3.71	3.51	2.61	2.08
Cash Flow Per Share	9.89	12.80	6.31	5.91	2.82	1.65	(0.66)	(5.69)
Tang Book Value Per Share	9.10	8.83	4.85	5.47	10.25	12.92	10.84	8.76
Income Statement								
Total Revenue	1,609,200	6,456,500	6,527,800	6,588,300	5,867,700	5,334,900	4,640,300	4,276,700
EBITDA	79,000	319,800	374,000	366,000	262,700	243,600	208,100	155,000
Depn & Amortn	5,800	32,100	30,700	29,500	26,400	24,300	22,600	22,700
Income Before Taxes	53,400	209,100	267,800	273,400	183,000	165,300	133,300	77,600
Income Taxes	13,300	70,000	100,600	104,000	71,000	64,200	50,000	29,600
Net Income	40,100	139,100	167,200	169,200	111,600	109,100	82,200	67,900
Average Shares	20,800	21,000	22,600	26,400	30,100	31,100	31,500	32,600
Balance Sheet								
Current Assets	1,326,600	1,302,100	1,332,400	1,343,000	1,276,700	1,108,600	986,400	792,500
Total Assets	2,429,400	2,356,700	2,336,100	2,305,900	2,192,000	1,888,600	1,661,400	1,419,400
Current Liabilities	1,101,100	1,058,200	1,104,900	1,007,800	1,041,100	834,200	779,800	636,300
Long-Term Obligations	859,100	862,600	912,700	940,400	678,700	543,300	461,400	439,100
Total Liabilities	2,005,100	1,962,500	2,056,400	1,991,400	1,747,100	1,398,000	1,258,600	1,092,800
Stockholders' Equity	424,300	394,200	279,700	314,500	444,900	490,600	402,800	326,600
Shares Outstanding	20,632	20,813	21,253	24,810	28,523	30,765	31,316	31,320
Statistical Record								
Return on Assets %	6.01	5.93	7.18	7.52	5.47	6.15	5.32	4.67
Return on Equity %	40.19	41.28	56.12	44.56	23.86	24.42	22.48	22.13
EBITDA Margin %	4.91	4.95	5.73	5.56	4.48	4.57	4.48	3.62
Net Margin %	2.49	2.15	2.56	2.57	1.90	2.05	1.77	1.59
Asset Turnover	2.70	2.75	2.80	2.93	2.88	3.01	3.00	2.94
Current Ratio	1.20	1.23	1.21	1.33	1.23	1.33	1.26	1.25
Debt to Equity	2.02	2.19	3.26	2.99	1.53	1.11	1.15	1.34
Price Range	75.85-50.15	69.45-50.15	67.44-45.07	95.54-66.76	77.56-45.42	55.61-32.03	32.03-21.50	21.66-15.04
P/E Ratio	10.91-7.22	10.49-7.58	9.11-6.09	14.90-10.41	20.91-12.24	15.84-9.13	12.27-8.24	10.41-7.23

Address: 2905 Premiere Parkway N.W., Suite 300, Duluth, GA 30097	**Web Site:** www.asburyauto.com	**Auditors:** Ernst & Young LLP
Telephone: 770-418-8200	**Officers:** Craig T. Monaghan - Vice-Chairman, President, Chief Executive Officer David W. Hult - President, Chief Executive Officer, Executive Vice President, Chief Operating Officer	**Investor Contact:** 770-418-8210 **Transfer Agents:** Computershare Trust Company, N.A.

ASHLAND GLOBAL HOLDINGS INC

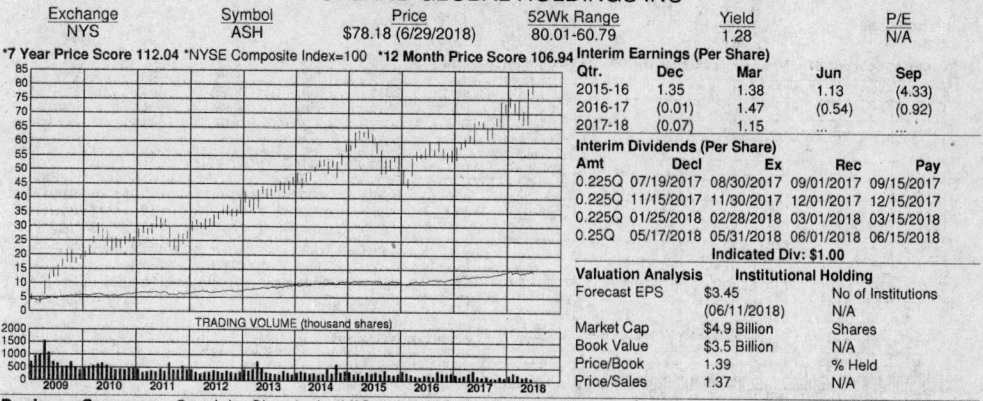

Exchange	Symbol	Price	52Wk Range	Yield	P/E
NYS	ASH	$78.18 (6/29/2018)	80.01-60.79	1.28	N/A

*7 Year Price Score 112.04 *NYSE Composite Index=100 *12 Month Price Score 106.94

Interim Earnings (Per Share)

Qtr.	Dec	Mar	Jun	Sep
2015-16	1.35	1.38	1.13	(4.33)
2016-17	(0.01)	1.47	(0.54)	(0.92)
2017-18	(0.07)	1.15	...	...

Interim Dividends (Per Share)

Amt	Decl	Ex	Rec	Pay
0.225Q	07/19/2017	08/30/2017	09/01/2017	09/15/2017
0.225Q	11/15/2017	11/30/2017	12/01/2017	12/15/2017
0.225Q	01/25/2018	02/28/2018	03/01/2018	03/15/2018
0.25Q	05/17/2018	05/31/2018	06/01/2018	06/15/2018

Indicated Div: $1.00

Valuation Analysis		Institutional Holding	
Forecast EPS	$3.45	No of Institutions	
	(06/11/2018)	N/A	
Market Cap	$4.9 Billion	Shares	
Book Value	$3.5 Billion	N/A	
Price/Book	1.39	% Held	
Price/Sales	1.37	N/A	

Business Summary: Specialty Chemicals (MIC: 8.3.2 SIC: 5169 NAIC: 325199)

Ashland Global Holdings is engaged in providing specialty chemical solutions to customers in a range of consumer and industrial markets. Co. has three segments: Specialty Ingredients, which include various end use markets, such as the oral care, hair care, skin care, home care, pharmaceutical, nutrition, adhesives, coatings, construction, energy, and performance specialties; Composites, which manufactures and sells a range of unsaturated polyester and vinyl ester resins, gelcoats and additives for the reinforced plastics industry; and Intermediates and Solvents, which produces related derivatives used as chemical intermediates and as specialty process solvents in a range of applications.

Recent Developments: For the quarter ended Mar 31 2018, income from continuing operations increased 127.6% to US$66.0 million from US$29.0 million in the year-earlier quarter. Net income decreased 30.5% to US$73.0 million from US$105.0 million in the year-earlier quarter. Revenues were US$974.0 million, up 20.8% from US$806.0 million the year before. Operating income was US$95.0 million versus US$53.0 million in the prior-year quarter, an increase of 79.2%. Direct operating expenses rose 20.9% to US$699.0 million from US$578.0 million in the comparable period the year before. Indirect operating expenses increased 2.9% to US$180.0 million from US$175.0 million in the equivalent prior-year period.

Prospects: Our evaluation of Ashland Global Holdings Inc. as of Jan. 21, 2018 is the result of our systematic analysis on three basic characteristics: earnings strength, relative valuation, and recent stock price movement. The company has generated a negative trend in earnings per share over the past 5 quarters and while recent estimates for the company have remained steady, ASH has posted better than expected results. Based on operating earnings yield, the company is about fairly valued when compared to all of the companies in our coverage universe. Share price changes over the past year indicates that ASH will perform well over the near term.

Financial Data
(US$ in Millions)

	6 Mos	3 Mos	09/30/2017	09/30/2016	09/30/2015	09/30/2014
Earnings Per Share	(0.38)	(0.06)	0.01	(0.46)	4.48	3.00
Cash Flow Per Share	3.06	3.53	4.11	11.13	1.31	7.53
Dividends Per Share	0.900	1.065	1.230	1.560	1.460	1.360
Dividend Payout %	...	...	12,300.00	...	32.59	45.33
Income Statement						
Total Revenue	1,816	842	3,260	4,948	5,387	6,121
EBITDA	137	40	342	552	569	343
Depn & Amortn	4	2	219	260	263	304
Income Before Taxes	68	5	(105)	108	146	(118)
Income Taxes	15	14	7	133	(22)	(188)
Net Income	69	(4)	1	(29)	309	233
Average Shares	64	62	62	64	69	78
Balance Sheet						
Current Assets	1,713	1,964	1,903	2,866	3,093	3,561
Total Assets	8,441	8,655	8,618	9,697	10,054	10,951
Current Liabilities	712	1,003	968	1,216	1,442	1,687
Long-Term Obligations	2,579	2,584	2,584	3,055	3,348	2,942
Total Liabilities	4,930	5,256	5,212	6,350	7,017	7,368
Stockholders' Equity	3,511	3,399	3,406	3,347	3,037	3,583
Shares Outstanding	62	62	62	62	67	...
Statistical Record						
Return on Assets %	N.M.	N.M.	0.01	N.M.	2.94	2.02
Return on Equity %	N.M.	N.M.	0.03	N.M.	9.34	5.73
EBITDA Margin %	7.54	4.75	10.49	11.16	10.56	5.60
Net Margin %	3.80	N.M.	0.03	N.M.	5.74	3.81
Asset Turnover	0.40	0.44	0.36	0.50	0.51	0.53
Current Ratio	2.41	1.96	1.97	2.36	2.14	2.11
Debt to Equity	0.73	0.76	0.76	0.91	1.10	0.82
Price Range	75.71-59.48	73.98-53.39	67.45-52.62	60.33-43.67	64.35-47.16	53.51-41.63
P/E Ratio	...	...	N.M.	...	14.36-10.53	17.84-13.88
Average Yield %	1.34	1.67	2.05	2.92	2.53	2.81

Address: 50 E. RiverCenter Boulevard, Covington, KY 41011 **Telephone:** 859-815-3333	**Web Site:** www.ashland.com **Officers:** William A. Wulfsohn - Chairman, Chief Executive Officer J. Kevin Willis - Senior Vice President, Chief Financial Officer	**Auditors:** Ernst & Young LLP **Transfer Agents:** Wells Fargo Shareowner Services, Mendota Heights, MN

ASPEN INSURANCE HOLDINGS LTD

Exchange	Symbol	Price	52Wk Range	Yield	P/E
NYS	AHL	$40.70 (6/29/2018)	51.75-35.05	2.36	N/A

*7 Year Price Score 83.61 *NYSE Composite Index=100 *12 Month Price Score 98.97

Interim Earnings (Per Share)

Qtr.	Mar	Jun	Sep	Dec
2015	1.87	0.62	0.30	1.74
2016	1.68	0.89	1.40	(1.36)
2017	1.36	1.07	(4.48)	(3.23)
2018	0.38			

Interim Dividends (Per Share)

Amt	Decl	Ex	Rec	Pay
0.24Q	07/26/2017	08/10/2017	08/14/2017	08/29/2017
0.24Q	10/25/2017	11/09/2017	11/10/2017	11/28/2017
0.24Q	02/07/2018	02/22/2018	02/23/2018	03/13/2018
0.24Q	05/02/2018	05/17/2018	05/18/2018	06/05/2018

Indicated Div: $0.96

Valuation Analysis **Institutional Holding**

Forecast EPS	N/A	No of Institutions: 346
Market Cap	$2.4 Billion	Shares
Book Value	$2.9 Billion	72,499,288
Price/Book	0.85	% Held
Price/Sales	0.92	86.12

Business Summary: General Insurance (MIC: 5.2.1 SIC: 6331 NAIC: 524126)

Aspen Insurance Holdings is a holding company. Co. underwrites specialty insurance and reinsurance through its subsidiaries in Bermuda, the U.S. and the U.K. Co. has two segments: reinsurance, which consists of property catastrophe reinsurance, other property reinsurance (risk excess, pro rata and facultative), casualty reinsurance (U.S. treaty, international treaty and global facultative) and specialty reinsurance (credit and surety, agriculture insurance and reinsurance, marine, aviation, terrorism, engineering and other specialty lines), and insurance, which consists of property and casualty insurance, marine, aviation and energy insurance and financial and professional lines insurance.

Recent Developments: For the quarter ended Mar 31 2018, net income decreased 68.1% to US$30.8 million from US$96.5 million in the year-earlier quarter. Revenues were US$683.5 million, down 0.0% from US$683.6 million the year before. Net premiums earned were US$533.5 million versus US$581.1 million in the prior-year quarter, a decrease of 8.2%. Net investment income fell 0.8% to US$47.3 million from US$47.7 million a year ago.

Prospects: Our evaluation of Aspen Insurance Holdings Ltd. as of July 19, 2015 is the result of our systematic analysis on three basic characteristics: earnings strength, relative valuation, and recent stock price movement. The company has managed to produce a neutral trend in earnings per share over the past 5 quarters. However, while recent estimates for the company have been lowered by analysts, AHL has posted better than expected results. Based on operating earnings yield, the company is undervalued when compared to all of the companies in our coverage universe. Share price changes over the past year indicates that AHL will perform in line with the market over the near term.

Financial Data
(US$ in Thousands)

	3 Mos	12/31/2017	12/31/2016	12/31/2015	12/31/2014	12/31/2013	12/31/2012	12/31/2011
Earnings Per Share	(6.26)	(5.22)	2.61	4.54	4.82	4.14	3.38	(1.82)
Cash Flow Per Share	(2.52)	(1.87)	7.47	9.37	9.41	8.47	6.96	4.86
Tang Book Value Per Share	47.42	48.73	59.68	55.82	54.83	50.06	49.03	44.61
Dividends Per Share	...	...	...	...	...	...	...	0.600
Income Statement								
Premium Income	533,500	2,306,600	2,637,300	2,473,300	2,405,300	2,171,800	2,083,500	1,888,500
Total Revenue	683,500	2,653,400	2,938,500	2,753,400	2,646,400	2,423,300	2,329,400	2,077,700
Benefits & Claims	310,200	...	...	...	...	...	...	...
Income Before Taxes	34,400	(281,800)	209,500	337,500	367,900	342,700	295,400	(143,000)
Income Taxes	3,600	(15,400)	6,100	14,400	12,100	13,400	15,000	(37,200)
Net Income	30,600	(267,700)	203,300	322,300	355,000	329,800	280,600	(105,800)
Average Shares	60,513	59,753	61,860	62,687	65,872	69,417	73,689	70,665
Balance Sheet								
Total Assets	13,207,900	12,906,400	12,090,100	11,048,800	10,716,300	10,230,500	10,310,600	9,476,500
Total Liabilities	10,351,800	9,980,600	8,443,200	7,630,200	7,297,500	6,930,600	6,822,400	6,304,900
Stockholders' Equity	2,856,100	2,925,800	3,646,900	3,418,600	3,418,800	3,299,900	3,488,200	3,171,600
Shares Outstanding	59,652	59,474	59,774	60,918	62,017	65,546	70,753	70,655
Statistical Record								
Return on Assets %	N.M.	N.M.	1.75	2.96	3.39	3.21	2.83	N.M.
Return on Equity %	N.M.	N.M.	5.74	9.43	10.57	9.72	8.40	N.M.
Loss Ratio %	58.14	...	...	...	...	...	...	...
Net Margin %	4.48	(10.09)	6.92	11.71	13.41	13.61	12.05	(5.09)
Price Range	53.80-35.05	57.70-36.45	55.50-41.07	51.19-42.32	46.94-36.63	41.31-32.08	33.58-26.17	30.74-22.16
P/E Ratio	...	...	21.26-15.74	11.28-9.32	9.74-7.60	9.98-7.75	9.93-7.74	...
Average Yield %	...	...	...	...	...	...	...	2.26

Address: 141 Front Street, Hamilton, HM 19 **Telephone:** 441-295-8201	**Web Site:** www.aspen.bm **Officers:** Glyn Jones - Chairman Christopher O'Kane - Chief Executive Officer	**Auditors:** KPMG LLP **Investor Contact:** 646-502-1076 **Transfer Agents:** Computershare Investor Services, Jersey City, NJ

ASSOCIATED BANC-CORP

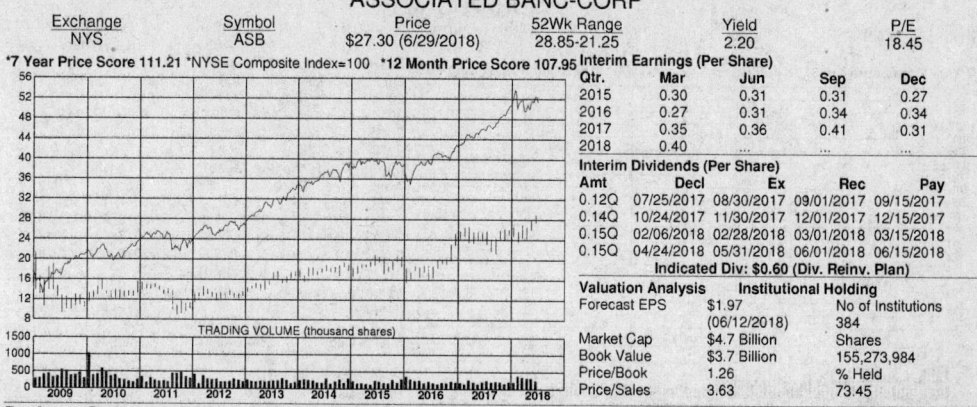

Exchange	Symbol	Price	52Wk Range	Yield	P/E
NYS	ASB	$27.30 (6/29/2018)	28.85-21.25	2.20	18.45

*7 Year Price Score 111.21 *NYSE Composite Index=100 *12 Month Price Score 107.95

Interim Earnings (Per Share)

Qtr.	Mar	Jun	Sep	Dec
2015	0.30	0.31	0.31	0.27
2016	0.27	0.31	0.34	0.34
2017	0.35	0.36	0.41	0.31
2018	0.40	...	...	...

Interim Dividends (Per Share)

Amt	Decl	Ex	Rec	Pay
0.12Q	07/25/2017	08/30/2017	09/01/2017	09/15/2017
0.14Q	10/24/2017	11/30/2017	12/01/2017	12/15/2017
0.15Q	02/06/2018	02/28/2018	03/01/2018	03/15/2018
0.15Q	04/24/2018	05/31/2018	06/01/2018	06/15/2018

Indicated Div: $0.60 (Div. Reinv. Plan)

Valuation Analysis — **Institutional Holding**

Forecast EPS	$1.97	No of Institutions
	(06/12/2018)	384
Market Cap	$4.7 Billion	Shares
Book Value	$3.7 Billion	155,273,984
Price/Book	1.26	% Held
Price/Sales	3.63	73.45

Business Summary: Banking (MIC: 5.1.1 SIC: 6022 NAIC: 522110)

Associated Banc is a bank holding company. Through banking and various nonbanking subsidiaries, Co. provides banking and nonbanking products and services. Co. has three segments: Corporate and Commercial Specialty, which provides lending solutions such as commercial loans, deposit and cash management solutions; Community, Consumer, and Business, which includes lending solutions such as residential mortgages, deposit and transactional solutions; and Risk Management and Shared Services, which includes corporate risk management, credit administration, treasury, finance, operations and technology functions. At Dec 31 2017, Co. had total assets of $30.48 billion and deposits of $22.79 billion.

Recent Developments: For the quarter ended Mar 31 2018, net income increased 23.4% to US$69.5 million from US$56.3 million in the year-earlier quarter. Net interest income increased 16.4% to US$209.9 million from US$180.3 million in the year-earlier quarter. Provision for loan losses was nil versus US$9.0 million in the prior-year quarter, a decrease of 100.0%. Non-interest income rose 13.2% to US$90.4 million from US$79.8 million, while non-interest expense advanced 22.6% to US$213.0 million.

Prospects: Our evaluation of Associated Banc-Corp. as of Jan. 21, 2018 is the result of our systematic analysis on three basic characteristics: earnings strength, relative valuation, and recent stock price movement. The company has managed to produce a neutral trend in earnings per share over the past 5 quarters and while recent estimates for the company have been mixed, ASB has posted better than expected results. Based on operating earnings yield, the company is undervalued when compared to all of the companies in our coverage universe. Share price changes over the past year indicates that ASB will perform in line with the market over the near term.

Financial Data

(US$ in Thousands)	3 Mos	12/31/2017	12/31/2016	12/31/2015	12/31/2014	12/31/2013	12/31/2012	12/31/2011
Earnings Per Share	1.48	1.42	1.26	1.19	1.16	1.10	1.00	0.66
Cash Flow Per Share	2.03	3.04	4.22	2.02	1.35	2.94	2.03	1.79
Tang Book Value Per Share	13.19	13.26	12.38	11.70	11.51	11.12	11.06	10.34
Dividends Per Share	0.530	0.500	0.450	0.410	0.370	0.330	0.230	0.040
Dividend Payout %	35.81	35.21	35.71	34.45	31.90	30.00	23.00	6.06
Income Statement								
Interest Income	261,532	886,605	791,568	753,662	736,745	708,983	718,284	741,622
Interest Expense	51,661	145,385	84,295	77,384	55,778	63,440	92,292	128,791
Net Interest Income	209,871	741,220	707,273	676,278	680,967	645,543	625,992	612,831
Provision for Losses	...	26,000	70,000	37,500	16,000	10,000	3,000	52,000
Non-Interest Income	90,380	332,680	352,883	328,409	290,319	313,099	313,290	282,469
Non-Interest Expense	212,966	709,133	702,560	697,399	679,241	680,749	681,823	659,873
Income Before Taxes	87,285	338,767	287,596	269,788	276,045	267,893	254,459	183,427
Income Taxes	17,829	109,503	87,322	81,487	85,536	79,201	75,486	43,728
Net Income	69,456	229,264	200,274	188,301	190,509	188,692	178,973	139,699
Average Shares	166,432	153,647	149,961	150,603	158,254	165,802	172,357	173,372
Balance Sheet								
Net Loans & Leases	22,663,477	20,604,655	19,896,865	18,564,994	17,482,479	15,692,684	15,375,023	13,902,115
Total Assets	33,366,505	30,483,594	29,139,315	27,715,021	26,821,774	24,226,920	23,487,735	21,924,217
Total Deposits	23,825,602	22,785,962	21,888,448	21,007,665	18,763,504	17,267,167	16,939,865	15,090,655
Total Liabilities	29,653,806	27,246,151	26,048,003	24,777,775	24,021,523	21,335,630	20,551,336	19,058,423
Stockholders' Equity	3,712,699	3,237,443	3,091,312	2,937,246	2,800,251	2,891,290	2,936,399	2,865,794
Shares Outstanding	170,794	152,843	152,120	151,239	151,541	164,138	170,239	174,591
Statistical Record								
Return on Assets %	0.78	0.77	0.70	0.69	0.75	0.79	0.79	0.64
Return on Equity %	7.07	7.25	6.63	6.56	6.69	6.48	6.15	4.64
Net Interest Margin %	80.25	83.60	89.35	89.73	92.43	91.05	87.15	82.63
Efficiency Ratio %	60.52	58.16	61.39	64.45	66.13	66.60	66.10	64.43
Loans to Deposits	0.95	0.90	0.91	0.88	0.93	0.91	0.91	0.92
Price Range	26.90-21.25	26.50-21.25	25.15-15.48	20.84-16.62	19.36-15.58	17.60-13.12	14.63-11.43	15.36-8.95
P/E Ratio	18.18-14.36	18.66-14.96	19.96-12.29	17.51-13.97	16.69-13.43	16.00-11.93	14.63-11.43	23.27-13.56
Average Yield %	2.16	2.04	2.36	2.16	2.08	2.11	1.77	0.31

Address: 433 Main Street, Green Bay, WI 54301	**Web Site:** www.associatedbank.com	**Auditors:** KPMG LLP
Telephone: 920-491-7500	**Officers:** William R. Hutchinson - Chairman Tammy C. Stadler - Executive Vice President, Corporate Controller, Principal Accounting Officer	**Investor Contact:** 920-491-7059
		Transfer Agents: Wells Fargo Shareowner Services, Saint Paul, MN

ASSURANT INC

Exchange	Symbol	Price	52Wk Range	Yield	P/E	Div Acheiver
NYS	AIZ	$103.49 (6/29/2018)	106.27-85.16	2.16	11.85	13 Years

*7 Year Price Score 114.31 *NYSE Composite Index=100 *12 Month Price Score 98.58

TRADING VOLUME (thousand shares)

Interim Earnings (Per Share)

Qtr.	Mar	Jun	Sep	Dec
2015	0.71	0.47	(0.10)	0.96
2016	3.34	2.70	2.37	0.67
2017	2.53	2.16	(1.05)	5.66
2018	1.96	...	...	...

Interim Dividends (Per Share)

Amt	Decl	Ex	Rec	Pay
0.56Q	11/10/2017	11/24/2017	11/27/2017	12/18/2017
0.56Q	01/19/2018	02/23/2018	02/26/2018	03/19/2018
0.56Q	05/11/2018	05/25/2018	05/29/2018	06/19/2018
0.56Q	07/12/2018	08/24/2018	08/27/2018	09/18/2018

Indicated Div: $2.24

Valuation Analysis

		Institutional Holding	
Forecast EPS	$7.49 (06/13/2018)	No of Institutions	592
Market Cap	$5.4 Billion	Shares	66,260,060
Book Value	$4.5 Billion	% Held	79.72
Price/Book	1.21		
Price/Sales	0.84		

Business Summary: Life & Health (MIC: 5.2.2 SIC: 6321 NAIC: 524114)

Assurant is a holding company. Co. is a provider risk management solutions in the housing and lifestyle markets, protecting where consumers live and the goods they buy. Through its operating subsidiaries, Co. provides mobile device protection products and services; extended service contracts and related services for consumer electronics and appliances; vehicle protection services; pre-funded funeral insurance; credit insurance; lender-placed homeowners insurance; manufactured housing and flood insurance; renters insurance and related products; and field services, valuation services and other property risk management services.

Recent Developments: For the quarter ended Mar 31 2018, net income decreased 26.3% to US$106.0 million from US$143.8 million in the year-earlier quarter. Revenues were US$1.64 billion, up 5.6% from US$1.55 billion the year before. Net premiums earned were US$1.12 billion versus US$1.05 billion in the prior-year quarter, an increase of 7.1%. Net investment income rose 8.0% to US$130.2 million from US$120.6 million a year ago.

Prospects: Our evaluation of Assurant Inc. as of Jan. 21, 2018 is the result of our systematic analysis on three basic characteristics: earnings strength, relative valuation, and recent stock price movement. The company has generated a negative trend in earnings per share over the past 5 quarters and while recent estimates for the company have been mixed, AIZ has posted better than expected results. Based on operating earnings yield, the company is undervalued when compared to all of the companies in our coverage universe. Share price changes over the past year indicates that AIZ will perform well over the near term.

Financial Data
(US$ in Thousands)

	3 Mos	12/31/2017	12/31/2016	12/31/2015	12/31/2014	12/31/2013	12/31/2012	12/31/2011
Earnings Per Share	8.73	9.39	9.13	2.05	6.44	6.30	5.67	5.58
Cash Flow Per Share	8.10	9.65	2.19	3.73	5.46	13.41	8.04	8.85
Tang Book Value Per Share	62.12	58.46	54.11	51.83	57.12	51.43	54.43	46.13
Dividends Per Share	2.180	2.150	2.030	1.370	1.060	0.960	0.810	0.700
Dividend Payout %	24.97	22.90	22.23	66.83	16.46	15.24	14.29	12.54
Income Statement								
Total Revenue	1,638,600	6,415,000	7,531,780	10,325,494	10,381,653	9,047,657	8,508,270	8,272,804
Income Before Taxes	136,500	444,500	848,588	201,181	744,137	789,699	757,751	714,955
Income Taxes	30,500	(75,100)	283,238	59,626	273,230	300,792	274,046	169,116
Net Income	106,000	519,600	565,350	141,555	470,907	488,907	483,705	545,839
Average Shares	54,189	55,311	61,934	69,017	73,152	77,654	85,307	97,795
Balance Sheet								
Total Assets	32,427,900	31,843,000	29,709,128	30,043,128	31,562,466	29,714,689	28,946,607	27,115,445
Total Liabilities	27,938,100	27,572,400	25,611,028	25,519,161	26,381,159	24,881,210	23,761,241	22,088,509
Stockholders' Equity	4,489,800	4,270,600	4,098,100	4,523,967	5,181,307	4,833,479	5,185,366	5,026,936
Shares Outstanding	52,570	52,417	55,941	65,850	69,299	71,828	78,664	88,524
Statistical Record								
Return on Assets %	1.55	1.69	1.89	0.46	1.54	1.67	1.72	2.04
Return on Equity %	11.14	12.42	13.08	2.92	9.40	9.76	9.45	11.13
Net Margin %	6.47	8.10	7.51	1.37	4.54	5.40	5.69	6.60
Asset Turnover	0.21	0.21	0.25	0.34	0.34	0.31	0.30	0.31
Price Range	106.27-85.16	106.27-87.74	93.74-66.23	86.81-59.86	69.52-60.81	66.37-34.70	43.35-32.57	41.71-31.23
P/E Ratio	12.17-9.75	11.32-9.34	10.27-7.25	42.35-29.20	10.80-9.44	10.53-5.51	7.65-5.74	7.47-5.60
Average Yield %	2.24	2.18	2.42	1.92	1.60	1.88	2.18	1.88

Address: 28 Liberty Street, 41st Floor, New York, NY 10005 **Telephone:** 212-859-7000	**Web Site:** www.assurant.com **Officers:** Alan B. Colberg - President, Chief Executive Officer, Executive Vice President Richard S. Dziadzio - Executive Vice President, Chief Financial Officer, Treasurer	**Auditors:** PricewaterhouseCoopers LLP **Investor Contact:** 212-859-7197 **Transfer Agents:** Computershare, Providence, RI

ASSURED GUARANTY LTD

Exchange	Symbol	Price	52Wk Range	Yield	P/E
NYS	AGO	$35.73 (6/29/2018)	45.38-33.01	1.79	6.98

*7 Year Price Score 120.27 *NYSE Composite Index=100   *12 Month Price Score 94.68

Interim Earnings (Per Share)

Qtr.	Mar	Jun	Sep	Dec
2015	1.28	1.96	0.88	2.95
2016	0.43	1.09	3.60	1.50
2017	2.49	1.24	1.72	0.48
2018	1.68	...	...	...

Interim Dividends (Per Share)

Amt	Decl	Ex	Rec	Pay
0.142Q	08/02/2017	08/14/2017	08/16/2017	08/30/2017
0.142Q	11/01/2017	11/14/2017	11/15/2017	11/29/2017
0.16Q	02/21/2018	03/06/2018	03/07/2018	03/21/2018
0.16Q	05/02/2018	05/15/2018	05/16/2018	05/30/2018

Indicated Div: $0.64

Valuation Analysis   **Institutional Holding**

Forecast EPS	N/A	No of Institutions 420
Market Cap	$4.1 Billion	Shares
Book Value	$6.8 Billion	141,516,480
Price/Book	0.60	% Held
Price/Sales	2.70	91.20

TRADING VOLUME (thousand shares)

Business Summary: General Insurance (MIC: 5.2.1 SIC: 6351 NAIC: 524298)

Assured Guaranty is a Bermuda-based holding company that provides, through its operating subsidiaries, credit protection products and international public finance including infrastructure and structured finance markets. Co. markets its financial guaranty insurance directly to issuers and underwriters of public finance and structured finance securities as well as to investors in such obligations. Co. guarantees obligations issued principally in the U.S. and the U.K, and also guarantees obligations issued in other countries and regions. Co.'s financial guaranty direct and assumed businesses provide credit protection on public finance, infrastructure and structured finance obligations.

Recent Developments: For the year ended Dec 31 2017, net income decreased 17.1% to US$730.0 million from US$881.0 million in the prior year. Revenues were US$1.74 billion, up 3.7% from US$1.68 billion the year before. Net premiums earned were US$690.0 million versus US$864.0 million in the prior year, a decrease of 20.1%. Net investment income rose 2.5% to US$418.0 million from US$408.0 million a year ago.

Prospects: Our evaluation of Assured Guaranty Ltd. as of Sep. 17, 2017 is the result of our systematic analysis on three basic characteristics: earnings strength, relative valuation, and recent stock price movement. The company has suffered a very negative trend in earnings per share over the past 5 quarters and while recent estimates for the company have been mixed, AGO has posted better than expected results. Based on operating earnings yield, the company is undervalued when compared to all of the companies in our coverage universe. Share price changes over the past year indicates that AGO will perform very well over the near term.

Financial Data
(US$ in Thousands)

	3 Mos	12/31/2017	12/31/2016	12/31/2015	12/31/2014	12/31/2013	12/31/2012	12/31/2011
Earnings Per Share	5.12	5.96	6.56	7.08	6.26	4.30	0.57	4.18
Cash Flow Per Share	3.11	3.59	(1.06)	(0.35)	3.34	1.31	(0.87)	3.68
Tang Book Value Per Share	59.66	58.95	50.82	43.96	36.37	28.08	25.74	25.89
Dividends Per Share	0.588	0.570	0.520	0.480	0.440	0.400	0.360	0.180
Dividend Payout %	11.47	9.56	7.93	6.78	7.03	9.30	63.16	4.31
Income Statement								
Total Revenue	293,000	1,739,000	1,677,000	2,207,000	1,994,000	1,608,000	973,000	1,819,313
Income Before Taxes	217,000	991,000	1,017,000	1,431,000	1,531,000	1,142,000	132,000	1,034,462
Income Taxes	20,000	261,000	136,000	375,000	443,000	334,000	22,000	258,842
Net Income	197,000	730,000	881,000	1,056,000	1,088,000	808,000	110,000	775,620
Average Shares	116,600	122,300	134,100	149,000	173,600	187,600	190,700	185,500
Balance Sheet								
Total Assets	14,019,000	14,433,000	14,151,000	14,544,000	14,925,000	16,287,000	17,242,000	18,091,531
Total Liabilities	7,235,000	7,594,000	7,647,000	8,481,000	9,167,000	11,172,000	12,248,000	13,373,095
Stockholders' Equity	6,784,000	6,839,000	6,504,000	6,063,000	5,758,000	5,115,000	4,994,000	4,718,436
Shares Outstanding	113,709	116,020	127,988	137,928	158,306	182,177	194,003	182,235
Statistical Record								
Return on Assets %	4.25	5.11	6.12	7.17	6.97	4.82	0.62	4.02
Return on Equity %	9.09	10.94	13.98	17.87	20.01	15.99	2.26	18.21
Net Margin %	67.24	41.98	52.53	47.85	54.56	50.25	11.31	42.63
Asset Turnover	0.10	0.12	0.12	0.15	0.13	0.10	0.05	0.09
Price Range	45.38-33.01	45.38-33.65	38.86-22.04	29.52-23.62	26.65-20.73	24.65-14.23	18.98-11.26	19.75-9.19
P/E Ratio	8.86-6.45	7.61-5.65	5.92-3.36	4.17-3.34	4.26-3.31	5.73-3.31	33.30-19.75	4.72-2.20
Average Yield %	1.53	1.44	1.87	1.82	1.84	1.93	2.53	1.27

Address: 30 Woodbourne Avenue, Hamilton, HM 08
Telephone: 441-279-5700
Fax: 441-279-5701

Web Site: www.assuredguaranty.com
Officers: Robin Monro-Davies - Chairman Dominic J. Frederico - President, Chief Executive Officer

Auditors: PricewaterhouseCoopers LLP
Investor Contact: 441-279-5700
Transfer Agents: Mellon Investor Services LLC

AT&T INC

Exchange	Symbol	Price	52Wk Range	Yield	P/E	Div Acheiver
NYS	T	$32.11 (6/29/2018)	39.51-31.40	6.23	6.50	33 Years

*7 Year Price Score 81.73   *NYSE Composite Index=100   *12 Month Price Score 89.16

Interim Earnings (Per Share)

Qtr.	Mar	Jun	Sep	Dec
2015	0.61	0.58	0.50	0.66
2016	0.61	0.55	0.54	0.40
2017	0.56	0.63	0.49	3.07
2018	0.75	...	...	...

Interim Dividends (Per Share)

Amt	Decl	Ex	Rec	Pay
0.49Q	09/29/2017	10/06/2017	10/10/2017	11/01/2017
0.50Q	12/15/2017	01/09/2018	01/10/2018	02/01/2018
0.50Q	03/30/2018	04/09/2018	04/10/2018	05/01/2018
0.50Q	06/29/2018	07/09/2018	07/10/2018	08/01/2018

Indicated Div: $2.00 (Div. Reinv. Plan)

Valuation Analysis | **Institutional Holding**

Forecast EPS	$3.42	No of Institutions
	(06/14/2018)	2967
Market Cap	$197.4 Billion	Shares
Book Value	$145.9 Billion	4,235,675,648
Price/Book	1.35	% Held
Price/Sales	1.24	N/A

TRADING VOLUME (thousand shares)

Business Summary: Services (MIC: 6.1.2 SIC: 4813 NAIC: 517110)

AT&T is a holding company. Co.'s subsidiaries and affiliates operate in the communications and digital entertainment services industry, providing services and equipment that deliver voice, video and broadband services domestically and internationally. The services and products that Co. offer vary by market, and include: wireless communications, data/broadband and internet services, digital video services, local and long-distance telephone services, telecommunications equipment, managed networking, and wholesale services. Co. also owns and operates regional TV sports networks and a network dedicated to game-related programming as well as internet interactive game playing.

Recent Developments: For the quarter ended Mar 31 2018, net income increased 33.2% to US$4.76 billion from US$3.57 billion in the year-earlier quarter. Revenues were US$38.04 billion, down 3.4% from US$39.37 billion the year before. Operating income was US$6.20 billion versus US$6.36 billion in the prior-year quarter, a decrease of 2.4%. Direct operating expenses declined 0.9% to US$17.95 billion from US$18.11 billion in the comparable period the year before. Indirect operating expenses decreased 6.8% to US$13.89 billion from US$14.90 billion in the equivalent prior-year period.

Prospects: Our evaluation of AT&T Inc. as of Jan. 21, 2018 is the result of our systematic analysis on three basic characteristics: earnings strength, relative valuation, and recent stock price movement. The company has managed to produce a neutral trend in earnings per share over the past 5 quarters and while recent estimates for the company have been mixed, T has posted results that fell short of analysts expectations. Based on operating earnings yield, the company is undervalued when compared to all of the companies in our coverage universe. Share price changes over the past year indicates that T will perform in line with the market over the near term.

Financial Data
(US$ in Thousands)

	3 Mos	12/31/2017	12/31/2016	12/31/2015	12/31/2014	12/31/2013	12/31/2012	12/31/2011
Earnings Per Share	4.94	4.76	2.10	2.37	1.19	3.39	1.25	0.66
Cash Flow Per Share	6.31	6.35	6.36	6.38	6.02	6.48	6.73	5.84
Dividends Per Share	1.970	1.960	1.920	1.880	1.840	1.800	1.760	1.720
Dividend Payout %	39.88	41.18	91.43	79.32	154.62	53.10	140.80	260.61
Income Statement								
Total Revenue	38,038,000	160,546,000	163,786,000	146,801,000	132,447,000	128,752,000	127,434,000	126,723,000
EBITDA	13,897,000	41,328,000	45,285,000	44,022,000	31,171,000	48,797,000	30,064,000	25,835,000
Depn & Amortn	5,994,000	19,761,000	20,661,000	19,289,000	17,773,000	17,722,000	16,933,000	16,368,000
Income Before Taxes	6,132,000	15,267,000	19,714,000	20,613,000	9,785,000	27,135,000	9,687,000	5,932,000
Income Taxes	1,382,000	(14,708,000)	6,479,000	7,005,000	3,442,000	9,224,000	2,900,000	2,532,000
Net Income	4,662,000	29,450,000	12,976,000	13,345,000	6,224,000	18,249,000	7,264,000	3,944,000
Average Shares	6,179,999	6,182,999	6,188,999	5,645,999	5,220,999	5,384,999	5,820,999	5,949,999
Balance Sheet								
Current Assets	78,505,000	79,146,000	38,369,000	35,992,000	32,028,000	23,196,000	22,706,000	23,027,000
Total Assets	446,343,000	444,097,000	403,821,000	402,672,000	292,829,000	277,787,000	272,315,000	270,344,000
Current Liabilities	70,580,000	81,389,000	50,576,000	47,816,000	37,282,000	34,995,000	31,787,000	30,794,000
Long-Term Obligations	133,724,000	125,972,000	113,681,000	118,515,000	76,011,000	69,290,000	66,358,000	61,300,000
Total Liabilities	300,423,000	303,236,000	280,686,000	280,001,000	206,459,000	186,799,000	179,953,000	164,810,000
Stockholders' Equity	145,920,000	140,861,000	123,135,000	122,671,000	86,370,000	90,988,000	92,362,000	105,534,000
Shares Outstanding	6,147,540	6,139,424	6,138,993	6,144,939	5,186,912	5,226,315	5,581,394	5,926,511
Statistical Record								
Return on Assets %	7.14	6.95	3.21	3.84	2.18	6.63	2.67	1.46
Return on Equity %	22.72	22.31	10.53	12.77	7.02	19.91	7.32	3.63
EBITDA Margin %	36.53	25.74	27.65	29.99	23.53	37.90	23.59	20.39
Net Margin %	12.26	18.34	7.92	9.09	4.70	14.17	5.70	3.11
Asset Turnover	0.37	0.38	0.41	0.42	0.46	0.47	0.47	0.47
Current Ratio	1.11	0.97	0.76	0.75	0.86	0.66	0.71	0.75
Debt to Equity	0.92	0.89	0.92	0.97	0.88	0.76	0.72	0.58
Price Range	41.69-32.86	43.02-32.86	43.47-33.51	36.18-31.80	36.74-31.86	39.00-33.11	38.34-29.16	31.86-27.33
P/E Ratio	8.44-6.65	9.04-6.90	20.70-15.96	15.27-13.42	30.87-26.77	11.50-9.77	30.67-23.33	48.27-41.41
Average Yield %	5.26	5.08	4.89	5.56	5.32	5.08	5.20	5.86

Address: 208 S. Akard St., Dallas, TX 75202	Web Site: www.att.com	Auditors: Ernst & Young LLP
Telephone: 210-821-4105	Officers: Randall L. Stephenson - Chairman, President, Chief Executive Officer, Senior Executive Vice President, Chief Financial Officer, Chief Operating Officer John Joseph Stephens - Senior Executive Vice President, Chief Financial Officer	Investor Contact: 210-351-2058 Transfer Agents: Computershare Trust Company, N.A, Providence, RI

ATMOS ENERGY CORP.

Exchange	Symbol	Price	52Wk Range	Yield	P/E	Div Acheiver
NYS	ATO	$90.14 (6/29/2018)	92.29-78.03	2.15	16.42	30 Years

*7 Year Price Score 121.19 *NYSE Composite Index=100 *12 Month Price Score 100.98

Interim Earnings (Per Share)

Qtr.	Dec	Mar	Jun	Sep
2014-15	0.96	1.35	0.55	0.23
2015-16	1.00	1.38	0.69	0.32
2016-17	1.19	1.55	0.67	0.33
2017-18	2.89	1.60	...	...

Interim Dividends (Per Share)

Amt	Decl	Ex	Rec	Pay
0.45Q	08/02/2017	08/17/2017	08/21/2017	09/05/2017
0.485Q	11/08/2017	11/24/2017	11/27/2017	12/11/2017
0.485Q	02/06/2018	02/23/2018	02/26/2018	03/12/2018
0.485Q	05/02/2018	05/18/2018	05/21/2018	06/04/2018

Indicated Div: $1.94 (Div. Reinv. Plan)

Valuation Analysis — **Institutional Holding**

Forecast EPS	$3.96	No of Institutions
	(06/14/2018)	604
Market Cap	$10.0 Billion	Shares
Book Value	$4.7 Billion	104,294,088
Price/Book	2.12	% Held
Price/Sales	3.23	71.55

Business Summary: Gas Utilities (MIC: 3.3.1 SIC: 4924 NAIC: 221210)

Atmos Energy is engaged in the regulated natural gas distribution and pipeline and storage businesses. Co. operates in the following segments: distribution, which is primarily comprised of its regulated natural gas distribution and related sales operations in eight states and storage assets located in Kentucky and Tennessee; and pipeline and storage, which is comprised primarily of the pipeline and storage operations of its Atmos Pipeline-Texas division and its natural gas transmission operations in Louisiana. As of Sep 30 2017, Co. delivered natural gas to over 3.0 million residential, commercial, public authority and industrial customers in eight states located primarily in the South.

Recent Developments: For the quarter ended Mar 31 2018, income from continuing operations increased 10.5% to US$179.0 million from US$162.0 million in the year-earlier quarter. Net income increased 8.7% to US$179.0 million from US$164.7 million in the year-earlier quarter. Revenues were US$1.22 billion, up 23.4% from US$988.2 million the year before. Operating income was US$269.0 million versus US$285.2 million in the prior-year quarter, a decrease of 5.7%. Direct operating expenses rose 46.7% to US$627.0 million from US$427.5 million in the comparable period the year before. Indirect operating expenses increased 17.4% to US$323.5 million from US$275.5 million in the equivalent prior-year period.

Prospects: Our evaluation of Atmos Energy Corp. as of Jan. 21, 2018 is the result of our systematic analysis on three basic characteristics: earnings strength, relative valuation, and recent stock price movement. The company has managed to produce a neutral trend in earnings per share over the past 5 quarters. However, while recent estimates for the company have been lowered by analysts, ATO has posted results that fell short of analysts expectations. Based on operating earnings yield, the company is undervalued when compared to all of the companies in our coverage universe. Share price changes over the past year indicates that ATO will perform very well over the near term.

Financial Data

(US$ in Thousands)	6 Mos	3 Mos	09/30/2017	09/30/2016	09/30/2015	09/30/2014	09/30/2013	09/30/2012
Earnings Per Share	5.49	5.44	3.73	3.38	3.09	2.96	2.64	2.37
Cash Flow Per Share	9.55	8.51	8.17	7.66	8.21	7.58	6.77	6.49
Tang Book Value Per Share	35.94	34.55	29.86	26.17	24.16	23.35	20.29	17.93
Dividends Per Share	1.870	1.835	1.800	1.680	1.560	1.480	1.400	1.380
Dividend Payout %	34.06	33.73	48.26	49.70	50.49	50.00	53.03	58.23
Income Statement								
Total Revenue	2,108,601	889,192	2,759,735	3,349,949	4,142,136	4,940,916	3,886,257	3,438,483
EBITDA	686,016	327,900	1,043,909	959,521	903,011	861,070	739,289	678,173
Depn & Amortn	177,755	88,374	319,633	293,096	276,005	254,956	237,607	246,577
Income Before Taxes	449,448	208,017	604,094	550,477	510,765	476,819	373,297	290,422
Income Taxes	(43,676)	(106,115)	221,383	200,373	195,690	187,002	142,599	98,226
Net Income	493,124	314,132	396,421	350,104	315,075	289,817	243,194	216,717
Average Shares	111,706	108,564	106,100	103,524	101,892	97,608	91,711	91,172
Balance Sheet								
Current Assets	622,736	778,910	539,646	681,686	630,985	775,840	683,266	827,962
Total Assets	11,356,322	11,264,720	10,749,596	10,010,889	9,092,945	8,594,704	7,940,401	7,495,675
Current Liabilities	1,349,127	959,410	1,013,443	1,788,281	1,154,823	910,650	978,486	1,275,954
Long-Term Obligations	2,617,892	3,067,469	3,067,045	2,188,779	2,455,388	2,455,986	2,455,671	1,956,305
Total Liabilities	6,634,976	6,701,100	6,850,930	6,547,830	5,898,148	5,508,472	5,359,992	5,136,432
Stockholders' Equity	4,721,346	4,563,620	3,898,666	3,463,059	3,194,797	3,086,232	2,580,409	2,359,243
Shares Outstanding	111,060	110,962	106,104	103,930	101,478	100,388	90,640	90,239
Statistical Record								
Return on Assets %	5.52	5.36	3.82	3.66	3.56	3.51	3.15	2.92
Return on Equity %	14.02	14.17	10.77	10.49	10.03	10.23	9.85	9.37
EBITDA Margin %	32.53	36.88	37.83	28.64	21.80	17.43	19.02	19.72
Net Margin %	23.39	35.33	14.36	10.45	7.61	5.87	6.26	6.30
Asset Turnover	0.29	0.26	0.27	0.35	0.47	0.60	0.50	0.46
Current Ratio	0.46	0.81	0.53	0.38	0.55	0.85	0.70	0.65
Debt to Equity	0.55	0.67	0.79	0.63	0.77	0.80	0.95	0.83
Price Range	92.29-78.03	92.29-73.21	88.69-68.96	81.32-57.82	58.81-47.35	53.40-41.08	45.19-33.20	36.94-30.60
P/E Ratio	16.81-14.21	16.97-13.46	23.78-18.49	24.06-17.11	19.03-15.32	18.04-13.88	17.12-12.58	15.59-12.91
Average Yield %	2.22	2.20	2.27	2.39	2.89	3.11	3.52	4.11

Address: Three Lincoln Centre, Suite 1800, 5430 LBJ Freeway, Dallas, TX 75240
Telephone: 972-934-9227
Fax: 972-855-3075

Web Site: www.atmosenergy.com
Officers: Kim R. Cocklin - Executive Chairman, President, Chief Executive Officer Michael E. Haefner - President, Chief Executive Officer, Chief Operating Officer, Executive Vice President, Senior Vice President

Auditors: Ernst & Young LLP
Investor Contact: 972-855-3729
Transfer Agents: American Stock Transfer & Trust Company, New York, NY

AUTOLIV INC

Exchange	Symbol	Price	52Wk Range	Yield	P/E
NYS	ALV	$103.17 (6/29/2018)	115.08-75.95	2.40	22.04

*7 Year Price Score 109.45 *NYSE Composite Index=100 *12 Month Price Score 110.12

Interim Earnings (Per Share)

Qtr.	Mar	Jun	Sep	Dec
2015	0.40	1.55	1.12	2.10
2016	1.51	1.68	1.56	1.68
2017	1.62	1.47	1.04	0.72
2018	1.45			

Interim Dividends (Per Share)

Amt	Decl	Ex	Rec	Pay
0.60Q	12/12/2017	02/21/2018	02/22/2018	03/08/2018
0.62Q	02/14/2018	05/22/2018	05/23/2018	06/07/2018
0.62Q	05/08/2018	08/21/2018	08/22/2018	09/06/2018
0.00Q	05/24/2018	07/02/2018	06/12/2018	06/29/2018

Indicated Div: $2.48

Valuation Analysis

		Institutional Holding	
Forecast EPS	$7.95 (06/14/2018)	No of Institutions	434
Market Cap	$9.0 Billion	Shares	47,616,216
Book Value	$4.2 Billion	% Held	31.61
Price/Book	2.14		
Price/Sales	0.85		

Business Summary: Auto Parts (MIC: 1.8.2 SIC: 3714 NAIC: 336399)

Autoliv is a holding company. Through its subsidiaries, Co. is a supplier of automotive safety systems with a range of product offerings, including passive safety systems and active safety systems that are sold within its two operating segments: Passive Safety and Electronics. Passive safety products include modules and components for passenger and driver-side airbags, side-impact airbag protection systems, seatbelts, steering wheels, inflator technologies, whiplash protection systems and child seats, and components for such systems as well as passive safety electronic products such as restraint electronics and crash sensors. Active safety products include camera-based vision systems.

Recent Developments: For the quarter ended Mar 31 2018, net income decreased 13.9% to US$122.4 million from US$142.1 million in the year-earlier quarter. Revenues were US$2.81 billion, up 7.8% from US$2.61 billion the year before. Operating income was US$225.4 million versus US$217.6 million in the prior-year quarter, an increase of 3.6%. Direct operating expenses rose 8.1% to US$2.23 billion from US$2.07 billion in the comparable period the year before. Indirect operating expenses increased 8.9% to US$353.8 million from US$324.9 million in the equivalent prior-year period.

Prospects: Our evaluation of Autoliv Inc. as of Jan. 21, 2018 is the result of our systematic analysis on three basic characteristics: earnings strength, relative valuation, and recent stock price movement. The company has generated a negative trend in earnings per share over the past 5 quarters and while recent estimates for the company have been mixed, ALV has posted better than expected results. Based on operating earnings yield, the company is undervalued when compared to all of the companies in our coverage universe. Share price changes over the past year indicates that ALV will perform poorly over the near term.

Financial Data (US$ in Thousands)	3 Mos	12/31/2017	12/31/2016	12/31/2015	12/31/2014	12/31/2013	12/31/2012	12/31/2011
Earnings Per Share	4.68	4.87	6.42	5.17	5.06	5.07	5.08	6.65
Cash Flow Per Share	9.22	10.70	9.82	8.51	7.74	8.77	7.34	8.50
Tang Book Value Per Share	27.02	25.08	18.07	18.86	19.90	24.30	21.48	18.11
Dividends Per Share	2.400	2.380	2.300	2.220	2.120	2.000	1.890	1.730
Dividend Payout %	51.28	48.87	35.83	42.94	41.90	39.45	37.20	26.02
Income Statement								
Total Revenue	2,812,800	10,382,600	10,073,600	9,169,600	9,240,500	8,803,400	8,266,700	8,232,400
EBITDA	229,700	1,015,200	1,242,100	1,052,400	1,024,100	1,041,700	972,000	1,146,900
Depn & Amortn	8,100	425,900	383,000	319,000	305,400	286,000	273,200	268,300
Income Before Taxes	209,600	535,500	801,200	671,000	660,100	726,700	660,500	821,500
Income Taxes	74,500	203,500	242,200	218,200	198,000	244,100	183,000	201,300
Net Income	126,700	427,100	567,100	456,800	467,800	485,800	483,100	623,400
Average Shares	87,300	87,700	88,400	88,400	92,400	95,900	95,100	93,700
Balance Sheet								
Current Assets	4,341,900	4,204,700	4,140,900	4,038,300	4,136,200	3,700,400	3,289,200	3,000,300
Total Assets	8,878,100	8,549,900	8,234,400	7,525,500	7,442,900	6,983,000	6,570,300	6,117,300
Current Liabilities	2,809,500	2,654,600	2,597,600	2,226,400	2,138,600	2,428,500	1,849,800	2,085,900
Long-Term Obligations	1,325,200	1,321,700	1,323,600	1,499,400	1,521,200	279,100	562,900	363,500
Total Liabilities	4,671,900	4,514,800	4,557,200	4,069,900	4,015,800	3,001,700	2,811,700	2,783,900
Stockholders' Equity	4,206,200	4,035,100	3,677,200	3,455,600	3,427,100	3,981,300	3,758,600	3,333,400
Shares Outstanding	87,094	86,972	88,230	88,107	88,726	94,396	95,500	89,293
Statistical Record								
Return on Assets %	4.71	5.09	7.18	6.10	6.49	7.17	7.59	10.58
Return on Equity %	10.17	11.08	15.86	13.27	12.63	12.55	13.59	19.91
EBITDA Margin %	8.17	9.78	12.33	11.48	11.08	11.83	11.76	13.93
Net Margin %	4.50	4.11	5.63	4.98	5.06	5.52	5.84	7.57
Asset Turnover	1.22	1.24	1.27	1.23	1.28	1.30	1.30	1.40
Current Ratio	1.55	1.58	1.59	1.81	1.93	1.52	1.78	1.44
Debt to Equity	0.32	0.33	0.36	0.43	0.44	0.07	0.15	0.11
Price Range	109.65-69.35	93.37-69.35	90.60-67.92	94.23-69.57	77.82-62.15	68.01-46.20	49.74-37.38	60.17-33.24
P/E Ratio	23.43-14.82	19.17-14.24	14.11-10.58	18.23-13.46	15.38-12.28	13.41-9.11	9.79-7.36	9.05-5.00
Average Yield %	2.75	2.93	2.91	2.69	2.97	3.51	4.31	3.66

Address: Klarabergsviadukten 70, Section B7,, Box 70381, SE-107 24, Stockholm, SE-107 24 Telephone: 858-720-600	Web Site: www.autoliv.com Officers: Hasse Johansson - Chairman Mats Backman - Chief Financial Officer, Division Officer	Auditors: Ernst & Young AB Investor Contact: 248-223-8107 Transfer Agents: Computershare Trust Company, N.A., Providence, RI

AUTONATION, INC.

Exchange	Symbol	Price	52Wk Range	Yield	P/E
NYS	AN	$48.58 (6/29/2018)	62.00-38.72	N/A	10.84

*7 Year Price Score 80.97 *NYSE Composite Index=100 *12 Month Price Score 96.87

Interim Earnings (Per Share)

Qtr.	Mar	Jun	Sep	Dec
2015	0.97	1.00	1.04	0.88
2016	0.89	1.08	1.05	1.13
2017	0.97	0.86	1.00	1.61
2018	1.01	...	...	...

Interim Dividends (Per Share)

No Dividends Paid

Valuation Analysis · **Institutional Holding**

Forecast EPS	$4.80	No of Institutions	
	(06/14/2018)	481	
Market Cap	$4.4 Billion	Shares	
Book Value	$2.5 Billion	84,580,720	
Price/Book	1.79	% Held	
Price/Sales	0.20	51.31	

TRADING VOLUME (thousand shares)

Business Summary: Retail - Automotive (MIC: 2.1.4 SIC: 5511 NAIC: 441110)

AutoNation, through its subsidiaries, is an automotive retailer. Co. provides a range of automotive products and services, including new vehicles, used vehicles, parts and service, which includes automotive repair and maintenance services as well as wholesale parts and collision businesses, and automotive finance and insurance products, which include vehicle service and other protection products, as well as the arranging of financing for vehicle purchases through third-party finance sources. As of Dec 31 2017, Co. owned and operated 360 new vehicle franchises from 253 stores located in the U.S. As of Dec 31 2017, Co. had three reportable segments: Domestic, Import, and Premium Luxury.

Recent Developments: For the quarter ended Mar 31 2018, income from continuing operations decreased 5.0% to US$93.3 million from US$98.2 million in the year-earlier quarter. Net income decreased 4.5% to US$93.7 million from US$98.1 million in the year-earlier quarter. Revenues were US$5.26 billion, up 2.3% from US$5.14 billion the year before. Operating income was US$185.8 million versus US$206.7 million in the prior-year quarter, a decrease of 10.1%. Direct operating expenses rose 2.3% to US$4.42 billion from US$4.32 billion in the comparable period the year before. Indirect operating expenses increased 7.1% to US$656.5 million from US$613.1 million in the equivalent prior-year period.

Prospects: Our evaluation of AutoNation Inc. as of Jan. 21, 2018 is the result of our systematic analysis on three basic characteristics: earnings strength, relative valuation, and recent stock price movement. The company has managed to produce a neutral trend in earnings per share over the past 5 quarters. However, while recent estimates for the company have been mixed, AN has posted better than expected results. Based on operating earnings yield, the company is undervalued when compared to all of the companies in our coverage universe. Share price changes over the past year indicates that AN will perform very poorly over the near term.

Financial Data
(US$ in Thousands)

	3 Mos	12/31/2017	12/31/2016	12/31/2015	12/31/2014	12/31/2013	12/31/2012	12/31/2011
Earnings Per Share	4.48	4.43	4.15	3.89	3.52	3.04	2.52	1.91
Cash Flow Per Share	6.01	5.52	4.99	4.50	4.14	3.99	2.55	2.60
Tang Book Value Per Share	4.06	2.92	1.99	4.65	3.55	3.86	1.32	3.72
Income Statement								
Total Revenue	5,259,900	21,534,600	21,609,000	20,862,000	19,108,800	17,517,600	15,668,800	13,832,300
EBITDA	188,300	1,016,900	1,042,000	1,003,900	934,700	846,900	741,800	657,300
Depn & Amortn	1,700	164,200	148,800	132,100	112,600	101,000	92,900	88,000
Income Before Taxes	126,200	636,500	702,300	722,700	682,300	604,400	516,800	461,300
Income Taxes	32,900	201,500	270,600	279,000	262,500	228,600	199,500	177,100
Net Income	93,700	434,600	430,500	442,600	418,700	374,900	316,400	281,400
Average Shares	92,700	98,200	103,800	113,900	118,900	123,300	125,800	147,300
Balance Sheet								
Current Assets	4,646,900	4,797,500	4,714,800	4,711,400	3,999,200	3,830,000	3,361,100	2,676,200
Total Assets	10,220,300	10,271,500	10,060,000	9,558,300	8,399,700	7,914,100	7,203,000	6,198,800
Current Liabilities	5,433,600	5,635,700	5,829,200	5,169,100	3,882,000	3,751,800	3,201,700	2,462,600
Long-Term Obligations	1,958,700	1,959,200	1,611,100	1,753,700	2,103,400	1,809,800	2,066,300	1,634,400
Total Liabilities	7,748,400	7,902,200	7,749,700	7,209,000	6,327,600	5,852,400	5,514,500	4,304,200
Stockholders' Equity	2,471,900	2,369,300	2,310,300	2,349,300	2,072,100	2,061,700	1,688,500	1,894,600
Shares Outstanding	91,329	91,559	100,652	110,804	113,313	120,915	120,856	135,784
Statistical Record								
Return on Assets %	4.24	4.28	4.38	4.93	5.13	4.96	4.71	4.62
Return on Equity %	17.54	18.57	18.43	20.02	20.26	19.99	17.61	14.16
EBITDA Margin %	3.58	4.72	4.82	4.81	4.89	4.83	4.73	4.75
Net Margin %	1.78	2.02	1.99	2.12	2.19	2.14	2.02	2.03
Asset Turnover	2.13	2.12	2.20	2.32	2.34	2.32	2.33	2.27
Current Ratio	0.86	0.85	0.81	0.91	1.03	1.02	1.05	1.09
Debt to Equity	0.79	0.83	0.70	0.75	1.02	0.88	1.22	0.86
Price Range	62.00-38.72	56.25-38.72	59.66-40.26	66.20-56.12	61.23-46.84	54.10-39.59	48.45-32.54	40.93-27.53
P/E Ratio	13.84-8.64	12.70-8.74	14.38-9.70	17.02-14.43	17.39-13.31	17.80-13.02	19.23-12.91	21.43-14.41

Address: 200 S.W. 1st Avenue, Fort Lauderdale, FL 33301 **Telephone:** 954-769-6000	**Web Site:** www.autonation.com **Officers:** Michael J. (Mike) Jackson - Chairman, Chief Executive Officer, President Cheryl S. Miller - Executive Vice President, Chief Financial Officer	**Auditors:** KPMG LLP **Investor Contact:** 954-769-7342 **Transfer Agents:** Computershare Trust Company, N.A.

AUTOZONE, INC.

Exchange	Symbol	Price	52Wk Range	Yield	P/E
NYS	AZO	$670.93 (6/29/2018)	796.95-493.15	N/A	13.69

*7 Year Price Score 90.93 *NYSE Composite Index=100 *12 Month Price Score 101.81

TRADING VOLUME (thousand shares)

Interim Earnings (Per Share)

Qtr.	Nov	Feb	Apr	Aug
2014-15	7.27	6.51	9.57	12.70
2015-16	8.29	7.43	10.77	14.24
2016-17	9.36	8.08	11.44	15.21
2017-18	10.00	10.38	13.42	...

Interim Dividends (Per Share)

No Dividends Paid

Valuation Analysis		Institutional Holding	
Forecast EPS	$49.86	No of Institutions	
	(06/13/2018)	875	
Market Cap	$17.9 Billion	Shares	
Book Value	N/A	30,144,868	
Price/Book	N/A	% Held	
Price/Sales	1.60	71.72	

Business Summary: Retail - Automotive (MIC: 2.1.4 SIC: 5531 NAIC: 441310)

AutoZone is a retailer and a distributor of automotive replacement parts and accessories. At Aug 26 2017, Co. operated 5,465 stores in the U.S., including Puerto Rico; 524 stores in Mexico; 14 stores in Brazil; and 26 Interamerican Motor Corporation branches. Each AutoZone store carries a product line for cars, sport utility vehicles, vans and light trucks, including new and remanufactured automotive hard parts, maintenance items, accessories and non-automotive products. Co. also has commercial programs in AutoZone stores in Mexico and Brazil. Co. also sells the AALLDATA brand automotive diagnostic and repair software through www.alldata.com and www.alldatadiy.com.

Recent Developments: For the quarter ended May 5 2018, net income increased 10.6% to US$366.7 million from US$331.7 million in the year-earlier quarter. Revenues were US$2.66 billion, up 1.6% from US$2.62 billion the year before. Operating income was US$545.8 million versus US$529.6 million in the prior-year quarter, an increase of 3.1%. Direct operating expenses was unchanged at US$1.24 billion versus the comparable period the year before. Indirect operating expenses increased 3.3% to US$877.2 million from US$848.8 million in the equivalent prior-year period.

Prospects: Our evaluation of AutoZone Inc. as of Jan. 21, 2018 is the result of our systematic analysis on three basic characteristics: earnings strength, relative valuation, and recent stock price movement. The company has managed to produce a neutral trend in earnings per share over the past 5 quarters and while recent estimates for the company have been raised by analysts, AZO has posted better than expected results. Based on operating earnings yield, the company is undervalued when compared to all of the companies in our coverage universe. Share price changes over the past year indicates that AZO will perform very poorly over the near term.

Financial Data
(US$ in Thousands)

	9 Mos	6 Mos	3 Mos	08/26/2017	08/27/2016	08/29/2015	08/30/2014	08/31/2013
Earnings Per Share	49.01	47.03	44.73	44.07	40.70	36.03	31.57	27.79
Cash Flow Per Share	67.51	64.30	62.56	55.40	52.92	48.46	40.43	38.73
Income Statement								
Total Revenue	7,662,309	5,002,156	2,589,131	10,888,676	10,635,676	10,187,340	9,475,313	9,147,530
EBITDA	1,225,475	677,779	470,753	2,411,489	2,365,772	2,229,200	2,088,346	2,008,588
Depn & Amortn	5,858	3,927	1,999	331,420	305,377	276,149	258,123	235,490
Income Before Taxes	1,099,431	595,623	429,865	1,925,489	1,912,714	1,802,612	1,662,714	1,587,683
Income Taxes	162,177	25,090	148,862	644,620	671,707	642,371	592,970	571,203
Net Income	937,254	570,533	281,003	1,280,869	1,241,007	1,160,241	1,069,744	1,016,480
Average Shares	27,329	27,882	28,096	29,065	30,488	32,206	33,882	36,581
Balance Sheet								
Current Assets	4,671,277	4,826,307	4,717,192	4,611,255	4,239,573	3,970,294	3,580,612	3,278,013
Total Assets	9,301,769	9,403,719	9,397,084	9,259,781	8,599,787	8,102,349	7,517,858	6,892,089
Current Liabilities	4,918,336	4,947,228	5,067,640	4,766,301	4,690,320	4,712,873	4,541,094	4,169,150
Long-Term Obligations	4,954,697	5,043,541	4,982,984	5,081,238	4,924,119	4,624,876	4,162,890	4,013,267
Total Liabilities	10,663,372	10,734,266	10,922,183	10,688,158	10,387,325	9,803,739	9,139,715	8,579,408
Stockholders' Equity	(1,361,603)	(1,330,547)	(1,525,099)	(1,428,377)	(1,787,538)	(1,701,390)	(1,621,857)	(1,687,319)
Shares Outstanding	26,662	27,251	27,262	27,833	29,118	30,659	32,304	34,293
Statistical Record								
Return on Assets %	14.96	·14.60	14.15	14.38	14.90	14.90	14.89	15.20
EBITDA Margin %	15.99	13.55	18.18	22.15	22.24	21.88	22.04	21.96
Net Margin %	12.23	11.41	10.85	11.76	11.67	11.39	11.29	11.11
Asset Turnover	1.22	1.22	1.21	1.22	1.28	1.31	1.32	1.37
Current Ratio	0.95	0.98	0.93	0.97	0.90	0.84	0.79	0.79
Price Range	796.95-493.15	796.95-493.15	809.87-493.15	809.87-493.15	815.98-695.46	750.13-501.78	543.84-411.89	448.58-344.99
P/E Ratio	16.26-10.06	16.95-10.49	18.11-11.03	18.38-11.19	20.05-17.09	20.82-13.93	17.23-13.05	16.14-12.41

Address: 123 South Front Street, Memphis, TN 38103 Telephone: 901-495-6500	Web Site: www.autozone.com Officers: William C. (Bill) Rhodes - Chairman, President, Chief Executive Officer William T. Giles - Executive Vice President, Chief Financial Officer	Auditors: Ernst & Young LLP Investor Contact: 901-495-6500 Transfer Agents: ComputerShare Investor Services, Providence, RI

AVALONBAY COMMUNITIES, INC.

Exchange	Symbol	Price	52Wk Range	Yield	P/E
NYS	AVB	$171.89 (6/29/2018)	194.28-153.90	3.42	30.32

*7 Year Price Score 90.14 *NYSE Composite Index=100 *12 Month Price Score 93.96

Interim Earnings (Per Share)

Qtr.	Mar	Jun	Sep	Dec
2015	1.56	1.29	1.53	1.12
2016	1.73	1.44	2.59	1.76
2017	1.72	1.20	1.72	1.72
2018	1.03	...	...	...

Interim Dividends (Per Share)

Amt	Decl	Ex	Rec	Pay
1.42Q	09/14/2017	09/28/2017	09/29/2017	10/16/2017
1.42Q	11/09/2017	12/28/2017	12/29/2017	01/16/2018
1.47Q	01/31/2018	03/28/2018	03/29/2018	04/16/2018
1.47Q	05/23/2018	06/28/2018	06/29/2018	07/16/2018

Indicated Div: $5.88 (Div. Reinv. Plan)

Valuation Analysis

Forecast EPS	$4.31	
	(06/14/2018)	
Market Cap	$23.8 Billion	
Book Value	$10.3 Billion	
Price/Book	2.30	
Price/Sales	10.81	

Institutional Holding

No of Institutions	742
Shares	161,952,512
% Held	96.22

Business Summary: REITs (MIC: 5.3.1 SIC: 6798 NAIC: 525930)

AvalonBay Communities is a real estate investment trust. Co. focuses on the development, redevelopment, acquisition, ownership and operation of multifamily communities primarily in New England, the New York/New Jersey metro area, the Mid-Atlantic, the Pacific Northwest, and Northern and Southern California. At Jan 31 2018, Co. owned or held a direct or indirect ownership interest in 267 operating apartment communities containing 77,614 apartment homes in 12 states and the District of Columbia; 21 communities under development; and rights to develop an additional 29 communities. Co. operates its apartment communities under three core brands Avalon, AVA and Eaves by Avalon.

Recent Developments: For the quarter ended Mar 31 2018, net income decreased 39.9% to US$141.6 million from US$235.8 million in the year-earlier quarter. Revenues were US$560.8 million, up 7.4% from US$522.3 million the year before.

Prospects: Our evaluation of AvalonBay Communities Inc. as of Jan. 21, 2018 is the result of our systematic analysis on three basic characteristics: earnings strength, relative valuation, and recent stock price movement. The company has enjoyed a very positive trend in earnings per share over the past 5 quarters. Because the company lacks sufficient analyst estimate data, we place greater weight on the historical EPS trend as the measure of earnings strength. Based on operating earnings yield, the company is about fairly valued when compared to all of the companies in our coverage universe. Share price changes over the past year indicates that AVB will perform well over the near term.

Financial Data

(US$ in Thousands)	3 Mos	12/31/2017	12/31/2016	12/31/2015	12/31/2014	12/31/2013	12/31/2012	12/31/2011
Earnings Per Share	5.67	6.35	7.52	5.51	5.21	2.78	4.32	4.87
Cash Flow Per Share	9.28	9.13	8.33	7.91	6.79	5.71	5.54	4.78
Tang Book Value Per Share	74.78	75.22	74.07	71.83	68.51	66.42	59.76	46.18
Dividends Per Share	5.730	5.680	5.400	5.000	4.640	4.280	3.880	3.570
Dividend Payout %	101.06	89.45	71.81	90.74	89.06	153.96	89.81	73.31
Income Statement								
Total Revenue	560,792	2,158,628	2,045,255	1,856,028	1,685,061	1,462,921	1,038,660	968,711
EBITDA	360,477	1,589,868	1,687,995	1,327,114	1,143,050	815,098	640,856	579,266
Depn & Amortn	165,514	584,150	531,434	477,923	442,682	573,715	260,094	250,269
Income Before Taxes	139,850	806,057	969,051	673,576	519,750	68,981	243,842	160,818
Income Taxes		305	141	1,861	9,368	...	...	...
Net Income	141,643	876,921	1,034,002	742,038	683,567	353,164	423,869	441,622
Average Shares	138,153	138,066	137,461	134,593	131,237	127,265	98,025	90,777
Balance Sheet								
Current Assets	271,407	234,592	362,048	535,405	634,702	406,694	2,808,399	713,926
Total Assets	18,646,447	18,414,821	17,867,271	16,931,305	16,176,723	15,328,143	11,160,078	8,482,390
Current Liabilities	405,246	297,683	280,727	264,474	244,027	227,314	182,648	156,473
Long-Term Obligations	7,599,455	7,329,470	7,030,880	6,456,948	6,525,852	6,145,391	3,851,033	3,632,296
Total Liabilities	8,311,323	8,026,775	7,695,855	7,090,779	7,130,318	6,732,011	4,322,863	4,087,649
Stockholders' Equity	10,335,124	10,388,046	10,171,416	9,840,526	9,046,405	8,596,132	6,837,215	4,394,741
Shares Outstanding	138,208	138,094	137,330	137,002	132,050	129,416	114,403	95,175
Statistical Record								
Return on Assets %	4.27	4.83	5.93	4.48	4.34	2.67	4.30	5.42
Return on Equity %	7.60	8.53	10.31	7.86	7.75	4.58	7.53	11.46
EBITDA Margin %	64.28	73.65	82.53	71.50	67.83	55.72	61.70	59.80
Net Margin %	25.26	40.62	50.56	39.98	40.57	24.14	40.81	45.59
Asset Turnover	0.12	0.12	0.12	0.11	0.11	0.11	0.11	0.12
Current Ratio	0.67	0.79	1.29	2.02	2.60	1.79	15.38	4.56
Debt to Equity	0.74	0.71	0.69	0.66	0.72	0.71	0.56	0.83
Price Range	199.10-153.90	199.10-169.61	191.00-159.75	185.54-159.08	169.20-117.53	141.46-116.86	151.00-124.26	139.51-109.16
P/E Ratio	35.11-27.14	31.35-26.71	25.40-21.24	33.67-28.87	32.48-22.56	50.88-42.04	34.95-28.76	28.65-22.41
Average Yield %	3.16	3.07	3.06	2.91	3.26	3.30	2.81	2.88

Address: Ballston Tower, 671 N. Glebe Road, Suite 800, Arlington, VA 22203 **Telephone:** 703-329-6300 **Fax:** 703-329-9130	**Web Site:** www.avalonbay.com **Officers:** Timothy J. Naughton - Chairman, President, Chief Executive Officer Leo S. Horey - Executive Vice President, Chief Administrative Officer	**Auditors:** Ernst & Young LLP **Investor Contact:** 703-317-4681 **Transfer Agents:** Computershare, Pittsburgh, PA

AVANGRID INC

Exchange	Symbol	Price	52Wk Range	Yield	P/E
NYS	AGR	$52.93 (6/29/2018)	54.26-43.37	3.33	42.34

*7 Year Price Score N/A   *NYSE Composite Index=100   *12 Month Price Score 103.89

Interim Earnings (Per Share)

Qtr.	Mar	Jun	Sep	Dec
2015	0.42	0.04	0.20	0.35
2016	0.69	0.33	0.35	0.68
2017	0.77	0.39	0.32	(0.25)
2018	0.79			

Interim Dividends (Per Share)

Amt	Decl	Ex	Rec	Pay
0.432Q	12/01/2017	12/08/2017	12/11/2017	01/02/2018
0.432Q	02/15/2018	03/08/2018	03/09/2018	04/02/2018
0.432Q	04/25/2018	06/07/2018	06/08/2018	07/02/2018
0.44Q	07/11/2018	09/06/2018	09/07/2018	10/01/2018

Indicated Div: $1.76

Valuation Analysis   **Institutional Holding**

Forecast EPS	$2.39 (06/14/2018)	No of Institutions 290
Market Cap	$16.4 Billion	Shares
Book Value	$15.2 Billion	46,726,092
Price/Book	1.08	% Held
Price/Sales	2.70	N/A

Business Summary: Electric Utilities (MIC: 3.1.1 SIC: 4911 NAIC: 221122)

AVANGRID is an energy services holding company. Through its subsidiaries, Co. is engaged in the regulated energy distribution and renewable energy generation. Co. has two segments: Networks, which include electric transmission and distribution and natural gas distribution, transportation and sales; and Renewables, which has activities relating to renewable energy, mainly wind energy generation and trading related with such activities. As of Dec 31 2017, Networks delivered electricity to about 2.2 million electric utility customers and natural gas to about 1 million natural gas public utility customers. Renewables operated 58 wind farms in 21 states across the United States.

Recent Developments: For the quarter ended Mar 31 2018, net income decreased 0.4% to US$238.0 million from US$239.0 million in the year-earlier quarter. Revenues were US$1.87 billion, up 6.1% from US$1.76 billion the year before. Operating income was US$403.0 million versus US$427.0 million in the prior-year quarter, a decrease of 5.6%. Direct operating expenses rose 11.8% to US$1.10 billion from US$987.0 million in the comparable period the year before. Indirect operating expenses increased 4.4% to US$359.0 million from US$344.0 million in the equivalent prior-year period.

Prospects: Our evaluation of Avangrid Inc as of Jan. 21, 2018 is the result of our systematic analysis on three basic characteristics: earnings strength, relative valuation, and recent stock price movement. The company has generated a negative trend in earnings per share over the past 5 quarters and while recent estimates for the company have been raised by analysts, AGR has posted better than expected results. Based on operating earnings yield, the company is undervalued when compared to all of the companies in our coverage universe. Share price changes over the past year indicates that AGR will perform very well over the near term.

Financial Data

(US$ in Thousands)	3 Mos	12/31/2017	12/31/2016	12/31/2015	12/31/2014	12/31/2013	12/31/2012
Earnings Per Share	1.25	1.23	2.04	1.05	1.70	(0.30)	1.00
Cash Flow Per Share	6.20	5.70	5.03	5.35	5.48	4.84	2.98
Tang Book Value Per Share	37.91	37.61	37.05	36.85	43.25	41.38	...
Dividends Per Share	1.728	1.728	1.728	...	...	...	...
Dividend Payout %	138.24	140.49	84.71	...	...	...	...
Income Statement							
Total Revenue	1,865,000	5,963,000	6,018,000	4,367,000	4,594,000	4,313,000	4,055,000
EBITDA	403,000	1,205,000	2,056,000	1,209,000	1,512,000	752,000	849,000
Depn & Amortn	21,000	802,000	779,000	641,000	563,000	545,000	484,000
Income Before Taxes	308,000	123,000	1,009,000	301,000	706,000	(38,000)	49,000
Income Taxes	72,000	(259,000)	379,000	34,000	282,000	26,000	(121,000)
Net Income	244,000	381,000	630,000	267,000	424,000	(65,000)	243,000
Average Shares	309,793	309,661	309,817	254,605	243,000	243,000	243,000
Balance Sheet							
Current Assets	1,981,000	2,260,000	2,252,000	2,474,000	2,299,000	2,012,000	...
Total Assets	31,483,000	31,671,000	31,309,000	30,743,000	24,252,000	23,209,000	...
Current Liabilities	2,716,000	3,114,000	2,712,000	2,035,000	1,773,000	1,630,000	...
Long-Term Obligations	5,160,000	5,196,000	4,510,000	4,530,000	2,516,000	2,696,000	...
Total Liabilities	16,312,000	16,594,000	16,200,000	15,690,000	11,812,000	11,194,000	...
Stockholders' Equity	15,171,000	15,077,000	15,109,000	15,053,000	12,440,000	12,015,000	...
Shares Outstanding	309,086	309,005	308,993	308,864	243,000	243,000	243,000
Statistical Record							
Return on Assets %	1.23	1.21	2.03	0.97	1.79	...	...
Return on Equity %	2.54	2.52	4.17	1.94	3.47	...	...
EBITDA Margin %	21.61	20.21	34.16	27.68	32.91	17.44	20.94
Net Margin %	13.08	6.39	10.47	6.11	9.23	N.M.	5.99
Asset Turnover	0.19	0.19	0.19	0.16	0.19	...	...
Current Ratio	0.73	0.73	0.83	1.22	1.30	1.23	...
Debt to Equity	0.34	0.34	0.30	0.30	0.20	0.22	...
Price Range	53.07-42.71	53.07-37.80	46.49-35.62	38.40-33.26	...	...	...
P/E Ratio	42.46-34.17	43.15-30.73	22.79-17.46	36.57-31.68	...	...	...
Average Yield %	3.64	3.79	4.26	...	...	...	...

Address: 180 Marsh Hill Road, Orange, CT 06477 **Telephone:** 207-629-1200	**Web Site:** www.avangrid.com **Officers:** Ignacio Sanchez Galan - Chairman James P. Torgerson - Chief Executive Officer	**Auditors:** KPMG LLP **Transfer Agents:** Broadridge Corporate Issuer Solutions, Inc., Philadelphia, PA

AVANOS MEDICAL INC

Exchange	Symbol	Price	52Wk Range	Yield	P/E
NYS	AVNS	$57.25 (6/29/2018)	60.96-38.35	N/A	30.95

*7 Year Price Score N/A *NYSE Composite Index=100 *12 Month Price Score 115.21

Interim Earnings (Per Share)

Qtr.	Mar	Jun	Sep	Dec
2015	0.46	0.17	(10.10)	0.31
2016	0.30	0.14	0.19	0.22
2017	0.27	0.36	0.35	0.71
2018	0.43	...	...	...

Interim Dividends (Per Share)

No Dividends Paid

Valuation Analysis

		Institutional Holding	
Forecast EPS	$0.72	No of Institutions	
	(06/07/2018)	424	
Market Cap	$2.7 Billion	Shares	
Book Value	$1.3 Billion	49,101,688	
Price/Book	2.15	% Held	
Price/Sales	7.23	N/A	

Business Summary: Medical Instruments & Equipment (MIC: 4.3.1 SIC: 3842 NAIC: 339113)

Halyard Health is a medical technology company focused on eliminating pain, speeding recovery and preventing infection for healthcare providers and patients. Co. is organized into two operating segments based on product groupings: Medical Devices, which focused on pain management, respiratory and digestive health to improve patient outcomes and reduce the cost of care that include post-operative pain management solutions, and minimally invasive interventional (or chronic) pain therapies; and Surgical and Infection Prevention, which provides healthcare supplies and solutions that target the prevention of healthcare-associated infections.

Recent Developments: For the quarter ended Mar 31 2018, loss from continuing operations was US$11.3 million compared with a loss of US$14.9 million in the year-earlier quarter. Net income increased 57.8% to US$20.2 million from US$12.8 million in the year-earlier quarter. Revenues were US$156.4 million, up 7.3% from US$145.7 million the year before. Operating loss was US$7.0 million versus a loss of US$17.6 million in the prior-year quarter. Direct operating expenses rose 1.7% to US$65.3 million from US$64.2 million in the comparable period the year before. Indirect operating expenses decreased 1.0% to US$98.1 million from US$99.1 million in the equivalent prior-year period.

Prospects: Our evaluation of Halyard Health Inc. as of Jan. 21, 2018 is the result of our systematic analysis on three basic characteristics: earnings strength, relative valuation, and recent stock price movement. The company has managed to produce a neutral trend in earnings per share over the past 5 quarters and while recent estimates for the company have remained steady, HYH has posted better than expected results. Based on operating earnings yield, the company is about fairly valued when compared to all of the companies in our coverage universe. Share price changes over the past year indicates that HYH will perform well over the near term.

Financial Data

(US$ in Thousands)	3 Mos	12/31/2017	12/31/2016	12/31/2015	12/31/2014	12/31/2013	12/31/2012	12/31/2011
Earnings Per Share	1.85	1.69	0.85	(9.15)	0.58	...	...	...
Cash Flow Per Share	2.85	3.08	4.04	2.09	3.18	...	...	...
Tang Book Value Per Share	7.29	6.43	N.M.	0.59	N.M.	...	...	...
Income Statement								
Total Revenue	156,400	611,600	1,592,300	1,574,400	1,672,100	1,677,500	1,684,000	1,659,900
EBITDA	(3,800)	(24,100)	130,400	(337,700)	147,300	265,200	266,300	249,000
Depn & Amortn	3,200	19,000	43,000	40,000	53,000	39,900	38,300	38,300
Income Before Taxes	(14,800)	(72,200)	55,300	(410,500)	91,200	227,800	229,800	214,600
Income Taxes	(3,500)	(40,100)	15,500	15,800	64,100	73,200	77,200	72,200
Net Income	20,200	79,300	39,800	(426,300)	27,100	154,600	152,600	142,400
Average Shares	46,900	46,800	47,000	46,600	46,538	...	...	...
Balance Sheet								
Current Assets	1,161,100	1,160,700	593,500	676,000	684,900	585,100	593,700	...
Total Assets	2,202,900	2,195,900	2,071,800	2,000,200	2,527,600	2,484,000	2,534,200	...
Current Liabilities	360,600	389,800	324,400	315,200	356,000	310,400	359,100	...
Long-Term Obligations	542,000	541,100	579,000	578,100	632,300	...	...	...
Total Liabilities	951,100	980,500	969,300	944,900	1,036,400	404,900	478,500	...
Stockholders' Equity	1,251,800	1,215,400	1,102,500	1,055,300	1,491,200	2,079,100	2,055,700	...
Shares Outstanding	47,014	46,920	46,681	46,614	46,535	...	...	...
Statistical Record								
Return on Assets %	4.04	3.72	1.95	N.M.	...	6.16	...	...
Return on Equity %	7.28	6.84	3.68	N.M.	...	7.48	...	...
EBITDA Margin %	N.M.	N.M.	8.19	N.M.	8.81	15.81	15.81	15.00
Net Margin %	12.92	12.97	2.50	N.M.	1.62	9.22	9.06	8.58
Asset Turnover	0.17	0.29	0.78	0.70	...	0.67	...	...
Current Ratio	3.22	2.98	1.83	2.14	1.92	1.88	1.65	...
Debt to Equity	0.43	0.45	0.53	0.55	0.42	...	...	...
Price Range	49.89-35.52	48.63-35.52	39.06-23.29	50.41-27.00	45.47-35.82	...	...	...
P/E Ratio	26.97-19.20	28.78-21.02	45.95-27.40	...	78.40-61.76	...	...	...

Address: 5405 Windward Parkway, Suite 100 South, Alpharetta, GA 30004 **Telephone:** 678-425-9273	**Web Site:** www.halyardhealth.com **Officers:** Ronald W. Dollens - Chairman Joseph Fralin Woody - Chief Executive Officer	**Auditors:** Deloitte & Touche LLP **Transfer Agents:** Computershare

AVERY DENNISON CORP

Exchange	Symbol	Price	52Wk Range	Yield	P/E
NYS	AVY	$102.10 (6/29/2018)	122.68-88.37	2.04	31.13

*7 Year Price Score 143.91 *NYSE Composite Index=100 *12 Month Price Score 98.72

Interim Earnings (Per Share)

Qtr.	Mar	Jun	Sep	Dec
2015	0.77	0.68	0.88	0.61
2016	0.98	0.88	0.98	0.69
2017	1.25	1.34	1.20	(0.66)
2018	1.40	...	...	...

Interim Dividends (Per Share)

Amt	Decl	Ex	Rec	Pay
0.45Q	07/27/2017	09/01/2017	09/06/2017	09/20/2017
0.45Q	10/27/2017	12/05/2017	12/06/2017	12/20/2017
0.45Q	01/31/2018	03/06/2018	03/07/2018	03/21/2018
0.52Q	04/26/2018	06/05/2018	06/06/2018	06/20/2018

Indicated Div: $2.08 (Div. Reinv. Plan)

Valuation Analysis | **Institutional Holding**

Forecast EPS	$6.00	No of Institutions
	(06/14/2018)	842
Market Cap	$9.0 Billion	Shares
Book Value	$1.1 Billion	105,947,032
Price/Book	8.25	% Held
Price/Sales	1.32	75.65

Business Summary: Containers & Packaging (MIC: 8.1.3 SIC: 2672 NAIC: 322222)

Avery Dennison operates in three reportable segments: Label and Graphic Materials, which manufactures and sells Fasson®-, JAC®-, and Avery Dennison®-brand pressure-sensitive label and packaging materials, Avery Dennison®- and Mactac®-brand graphics, and Avery Dennison®-brand reflective products; Retail Branding and Information Solutions, which designs, manufactures and sells a range of branding and information solutions; as well as Industrial and Healthcare Materials, which manufactures and sells Fasson®-brand and Avery Dennison®-brand tapes and fasteners, Vancive™-brand medical pressure-sensitive adhesive based materials and products, and performance polymers.

Recent Developments: For the quarter ended Mar 31 2018, net income increased 11.6% to US$125.2 million from US$112.2 million in the year-earlier quarter. Revenues were US$1.78 billion, up 13.0% from US$1.57 billion the year before. Direct operating expenses rose 14.5% to US$1.29 billion from US$1.13 billion in the comparable period the year before. Indirect operating expenses increased 5.8% to US$324.3 million from US$306.5 million in the equivalent prior-year period.

Prospects: Our evaluation of Avery Dennison Corp. as of Jan. 21, 2018 is the result of our systematic analysis on three basic characteristics: earnings strength, relative valuation, and recent stock price movement. The company has enjoyed a very positive trend in earnings per share over the past 5 quarters and while recent estimates for the company have been mixed, AVY has posted better than expected results. Based on operating earnings yield, the company is about fairly valued when compared to all of the companies in our coverage universe. Share price changes over the past year indicates that AVY will perform very well over the near term.

Financial Data
(US$ in Thousands)	3 Mos	12/30/2017	12/31/2016	01/02/2016	01/03/2015	12/28/2013	12/29/2012	12/31/2011
Earnings Per Share	3.28	3.13	3.54	2.95	2.60	2.16	2.08	1.78
Cash Flow Per Share	7.40	7.38	6.59	5.22	3.92	3.26	5.02	4.01
Tang Book Value Per Share	N.M.	N.M.	0.74	2.60	3.07	6.71	6.92	6.94
Dividends Per Share	1.800	1.760	1.600	1.460	1.340	1.140	1.080	1.000
Dividend Payout %	54.88	56.23	45.20	49.49	51.54	52.78	51.92	56.18
Income Statement								
Total Revenue	1,776,400	6,613,800	6,086,500	5,966,900	6,330,300	6,140,000	6,035,600	6,026,300
EBITDA	216,800	779,100	654,500	594,600	563,200	557,700	478,400	471,900
Depn & Amortn	44,500	126,600	117,500	125,200	135,500	135,600	150,100	168,000
Income Before Taxes	159,100	589,500	477,100	408,900	364,400	363,100	255,500	232,900
Income Taxes	33,300	307,700	156,400	134,500	113,300	118,800	86,400	78,500
Net Income	125,200	281,800	320,700	274,300	248,900	215,800	215,400	190,100
Average Shares	89,600	90,100	90,700	92,900	95,700	100,100	103,500	106,800
Balance Sheet								
Current Assets	2,332,300	2,237,900	1,904,800	1,775,400	1,921,300	2,091,800	2,411,700	2,218,800
Total Assets	5,280,500	5,136,900	4,396,400	4,133,700	4,360,200	4,610,600	5,105,300	4,972,700
Current Liabilities	2,081,400	1,971,800	2,004,300	1,459,100	1,597,800	1,554,100	2,074,500	1,647,100
Long-Term Obligations	1,342,700	1,316,300	713,400	963,600	945,300	950,600	702,200	954,200
Total Liabilities	4,190,800	4,090,700	3,470,900	3,168,000	3,293,700	3,118,400	3,524,400	3,314,200
Stockholders' Equity	1,089,700	1,046,200	925,500	965,700	1,066,500	1,492,200	1,580,900	1,658,500
Shares Outstanding	88,015	88,011	88,308	89,967	90,458	96,178	99,915	106,269
Statistical Record								
Return on Assets %	5.87	5.93	7.54	6.48	5.46	4.45	4.29	3.79
Return on Equity %	28.02	28.66	34.01	27.07	19.14	14.08	13.34	11.54
EBITDA Margin %	12.20	11.78	10.75	9.96	8.90	9.08	7.93	7.83
Net Margin %	7.05	4.26	5.27	4.60	3.93	3.51	3.57	3.15
Asset Turnover	1.36	1.39	1.43	1.41	1.39	1.27	1.20	1.20
Current Ratio	1.12	1.13	0.95	1.22	1.20	1.35	1.16	1.35
Debt to Equity	1.23	1.26	0.77	1.00	0.89	0.64	0.44	0.58
Price Range	122.68-79.48	117.10-70.14	78.84-58.16	66.18-51.07	52.67-41.28	50.65-34.92	34.97-26.38	43.11-23.97
P/E Ratio	37.40-24.23	37.41-22.41	22.27-16.43	22.43-17.31	20.26-15.88	23.45-16.17	16.81-12.68	24.22-13.47
Average Yield %	1.80	1.94	2.22	2.49	2.74	2.63	3.54	2.89

Address: 207 Goode Avenue, Glendale, CA 91203
Telephone: 626-304-2000

Web Site: www.averydennison.com
Officers: Mitchell R. Butier - President, Chief Executive Officer, Senior Vice President, Chief Financial Officer, Chief Operating Officer Gregory S. Lovins - Senior Vice President, Chief Financial Officer, Vice President, Interim Chief Financial Officer, Treasurer

Auditors: PricewaterhouseCoopers LLP
Investor Contact: 626-304-2000
Transfer Agents: Broadridge Corporate Issuer Solutions, Inc., Brentwood, NY

AVON PRODUCTS, INC.

Exchange	Symbol	Price	52Wk Range	Yield	P/E
NYS	AVP	$1.62 (6/29/2018)	3.80-1.48	N/A	54.00

*7 Year Price Score 18.26   *NYSE Composite Index=100   *12 Month Price Score 75.95

Interim Earnings (Per Share)

Qtr.	Mar	Jun	Sep	Dec
2015	(0.33)	0.07	(1.58)	(0.76)
2016	(0.38)	0.06	0.07	(0.04)
2017	(0.10)	(0.12)	0.01	0.20
2018	(0.06)	...	...	...

Interim Dividends (Per Share)

Dividend Payment Suspended

Valuation Analysis		Institutional Holding	
Forecast EPS	$0.15	No of Institutions	
	(06/14/2018)	488	
Market Cap	$715.5 Million	Shares	
Book Value	N/A	456,663,488	
Price/Book	N/A	% Held	
Price/Sales	0.12	93.21	

Business Summary: Household & Personal Products (MIC: 1.7.1 SIC: 2844 NAIC: 446120)

Avon Products is a manufacturer and marketer of beauty and related products. Co.'s product categories are Beauty and Fashion and Home. Beauty consists of skincare (which includes personal care), fragrance and color (cosmetics). Fashion and Home consists of fashion jewelry, watches, apparel, footwear, accessories, gift and decorative products, housewares, entertainment and leisure products, children's products and nutritional products. Co.'s business is conducted primarily in one channel, direct selling. Co.'s reportable segments are based on geographic operations in four regions: Europe, Middle East and Africa; South Latin America; North Latin America; and Asia Pacific.

Recent Developments: For the quarter ended Mar 31 2018, net loss amounted to US$21.1 million versus a net loss of US$36.5 million in the year-earlier quarter. Revenues were US$1.39 billion, up 4.5% from US$1.33 billion the year before. Operating income was US$44.9 million versus US$29.8 million in the prior-year quarter, an increase of 50.7%. Direct operating expenses rose 12.1% to US$579.7 million from US$517.1 million in the comparable period the year before. Indirect operating expenses decreased 2.2% to US$768.9 million from US$786.2 million in the equivalent prior-year period.

Prospects: Our evaluation of Avon Products Inc. as of Jan. 21, 2018 is the result of our systematic analysis on three basic characteristics: earnings strength, relative valuation, and recent stock price movement. The company has enjoyed a very positive trend in earnings per share over the past 5 quarters. Because the company lacks sufficient analyst estimate data, we place greater weight on the historical EPS trend as the measure of earnings strength. Based on operating earnings yield, the company is overvalued when compared to all of the companies in our coverage universe. Share price changes over the past year indicates that AVP will perform very poorly over the near term.

Financial Data

(US$ in Thousands)	3 Mos	12/31/2017	12/31/2016	12/31/2015	12/31/2014	12/31/2013	12/31/2012	12/31/2011
Earnings Per Share	0.03	...	(0.29)	(2.60)	(0.88)	(0.13)	(0.10)	1.18
Cash Flow Per Share	0.58	0.62	0.29	0.21	0.83	1.25	1.28	1.52
Tang Book Value Per Share	...	...	...	...	N.M.	1.55	1.13	1.90
Dividends Per Share	...	...	...	0.240	0.240	0.240	0.750	0.920
Dividend Payout %	...	...	...	...	...	...	...	77.97
Income Statement								
Total Revenue	1,393,500	5,715,600	5,717,700	6,160,500	8,851,400	9,955,000	10,717,100	11,291,600
EBITDA	70,300	331,000	235,300	224,700	401,800	422,100	470,200	993,000
Depn & Amortn	27,900	84,300	83,300	94,000	141,300	164,800	162,400	174,000
Income Before Taxes	10,400	120,700	31,200	22,700	164,200	162,600	218,600	742,600
Income Taxes	31,500	100,700	124,600	819,200	549,100	163,600	256,800	216,200
Net Income	(20,300)	22,000	(107,600)	(1,148,900)	(388,600)	(56,400)	(42,500)	513,600
Average Shares	440,900	439,700	437,000	435,200	434,500	433,400	431,900	432,100
Balance Sheet								
Current Assets	2,149,500	2,233,300	1,992,300	2,341,100	2,964,500	3,479,100	3,928,900	4,098,800
Total Assets	3,640,400	3,697,900	3,418,900	3,879,500	5,496,800	6,492,300	7,382,500	7,735,000
Current Liabilities	1,750,800	1,559,600	1,485,700	2,195,100	2,047,200	2,240,500	2,704,600	2,891,000
Long-Term Obligations	1,629,600	1,872,200	1,875,800	2,159,600	2,463,900	2,532,700	2,623,900	2,459,100
Total Liabilities	3,922,900	3,955,100	3,822,200	4,949,800	5,207,000	5,382,200	6,165,400	6,164,600
Stockholders' Equity	(282,500)	(257,200)	(403,300)	(1,070,300)	289,800	1,110,100	1,217,100	1,570,400
Shares Outstanding	441,680	440,300	437,600	435,500	434,700	433,900	432,200	430,800
Statistical Record								
Return on Assets %	1.08	0.62	N.M.	N.M.	N.M.	N.M.	N.M.	6.58
Return on Equity %	...	...	...	...	N.M.	N.M.	N.M.	31.83
EBITDA Margin %	5.04	5.79	4.12	3.65	4.54	4.24	4.39	8.79
Net Margin %	N.M.	0.38	N.M.	N.M.	N.M.	N.M.	N.M.	4.55
Asset Turnover	1.63	1.61	1.56	1.31	1.48	1.43	1.41	1.45
Current Ratio	1.23	1.43	1.34	1.07	1.45	1.55	1.45	1.42
Debt to Equity	...	...	...	...	8.50	2.28	2.16	1.57
Price Range	4.85-1.87	5.93-1.87	6.89-2.38	9.39-2.50	17.22-9.11	24.20-14.36	23.52-13.80	30.91-16.09
P/E Ratio	161.67-62.33	N.M.	...	...	...	...	...	26.19-13.64
Average Yield %	...	...	...	3.93	1.78	1.19	4.42	3.70

Address: Building 6, Chiswick Park, London, W4 5HR Telephone: 160-423-2425	Web Site: www.avon.com Officers: Jan Zijderveld - Chief Executive Officer Jonathan Charles Myers - Chief Operating Officer, Executive Vice President	Auditors: PricewaterhouseCoopers LLP Investor Contact: 212-282-5320 Transfer Agents: Computershare Investor Services, Canton, MA

BADGER METER INC

Exchange	Symbol	Price	52Wk Range	Yield	P/E	Div Acheiver
NYS	BMI	$44.70 (6/29/2018)	51.60-39.30	1.16	39.21	25 Years

*7 Year Price Score 125.39 *NYSE Composite Index=100   **12 Month Price Score 95.66

Interim Earnings (Per Share)

Qtr.	Mar	Jun	Sep	Dec
2015	0.14	0.28	0.29	0.19
2016	0.28	0.33	0.30	0.21
2017	0.30	0.36	0.27	0.25
2018	0.26	...	...	...

Interim Dividends (Per Share)

Amt	Decl	Ex	Rec	Pay
0.13Q	08/11/2017	08/29/2017	08/31/2017	09/15/2017
0.13Q	11/10/2017	11/29/2017	11/30/2017	12/15/2017
0.13Q	02/09/2018	02/27/2018	02/28/2018	03/15/2018
0.13Q	04/27/2018	05/30/2018	05/31/2018	06/15/2018

Indicated Div: $0.52 (Div. Reinv. Plan)

Valuation Analysis / **Institutional Holding**

Forecast EPS	$1.42 (06/13/2018)	No of Institutions	256
Market Cap	$1.3 Billion	Shares	30,409,316
Book Value	$280.7 Million	% Held	69.84
Price/Book	4.64		
Price/Sales	3.21		

Business Summary: Electronic Instruments & Related Products (MIC: 6.2.3 SIC: 3824 NAIC: 334514)

Badger Meter is a manufacturer and marketer of products incorporating flow measurement, control and communication solutions. Co.'s product lines fall into two categories: sales of water meters and related technologies to municipal water utilities (municipal water), which includes mechanical and ultrasonic (electronic) water meters and related technologies and services used by municipal water utilities; and sales of meters to various industries for water and other fluids (flow instrumentation), which includes meters and valves sold worldwide to measure and control materials flowing through a pipe or pipeline including water, air, steam, oil, and other liquids and gases.

Recent Developments: For the year ended Dec 31 2017, net income increased 7.0% to US$34.6 million from US$32.3 million in the prior year. Revenues were US$402.4 million, up 2.2% from US$393.8 million the year before. Operating income was US$55.6 million versus US$50.8 million in the prior year, an increase of 9.6%. Direct operating expenses rose 1.4% to US$246.7 million from US$243.2 million in the comparable period the year before. Indirect operating expenses increased 0.3% to US$100.1 million from US$99.8 million in the equivalent prior-year period.

Prospects: Our evaluation of Badger Meter Inc. as of Jan. 21, 2018 is the result of our systematic analysis on three basic characteristics: earnings strength, relative valuation, and recent stock price movement. The company has generated a negative trend in earnings per share over the past 5 quarters. However, while recent estimates for the company have been mixed, BMI has posted results that fell short of analysts expectations. Based on operating earnings yield, the company is overvalued when compared to all of the companies in our coverage universe. Share price changes over the past year indicates that BMI will perform in line with the market over the near term.

Financial Data

(US$ in Thousands)	3 Mos	12/31/2017	12/31/2016	12/31/2015	12/31/2014	12/31/2013	12/31/2012	12/31/2011
Earnings Per Share	1.14	1.19	1.11	0.90	1.03	0.85	0.97	0.64
Cash Flow Per Share	1.52	1.72	1.94	1.25	1.25	1.21	1.21	1.05
Tang Book Value Per Share	5.35	5.18	5.32	4.37	3.63	3.28	2.69	4.50
Dividends Per Share	0.505	0.490	0.430	0.390	0.370	0.350	0.330	0.300
Dividend Payout %	44.30	41.18	38.74	43.33	35.92	41.18	33.85	47.24
Income Statement								
Total Revenue	105,041	402,440	393,761	377,698	364,768	334,122	319,660	262,915
EBITDA	16,705	67,678	61,480	52,362	54,938	47,619	52,056	34,678
Depn & Amortn	6,712	12,056	10,715	9,993	8,891	8,512	7,587	7,144
Income Before Taxes	9,703	54,833	49,844	41,152	44,912	38,009	43,471	27,349
Income Taxes	2,157	20,262	17,549	15,214	15,234	13,392	15,439	8,188
Net Income	7,546	34,571	32,295	25,938	29,678	24,617	28,032	19,161
Average Shares	29,150	29,111	29,050	28,894	28,756	28,880	28,798	30,098
Balance Sheet								
Current Assets	166,760	158,623	151,012	149,328	141,105	127,163	121,374	101,195
Total Assets	395,266	391,727	349,699	355,480	341,158	316,058	290,453	218,910
Current Liabilities	88,550	93,109	75,838	104,544	107,075	98,041	94,080	22,413
Total Liabilities	114,544	114,275	93,490	123,205	126,827	119,495	119,206	39,629
Stockholders' Equity	280,722	277,452	256,209	232,275	214,331	196,563	171,247	179,281
Shares Outstanding	29,113	29,118	29,118	29,049	28,922	28,823	28,628	30,245
Statistical Record								
Return on Assets %	8.91	9.33	9.13	7.45	9.03	8.12	10.98	8.81
Return on Equity %	12.32	12.96	13.19	11.62	14.45	13.39	15.95	11.02
EBITDA Margin %	15.90	16.82	15.61	13.86	15.06	14.25	16.28	13.19
Net Margin %	7.18	8.59	8.20	6.87	8.14	7.37	8.77	7.29
Asset Turnover	1.08	1.09	1.11	1.08	1.11	1.10	1.25	1.21
Current Ratio	1.88	1.70	1.99	1.43	1.32	1.30	1.29	4.52
Price Range	51.60-35.35	51.60-34.60	38.55-26.61	32.79-27.66	30.02-23.79	27.68-21.27	24.14-14.84	22.59-13.53
P/E Ratio	45.26-31.01	43.36-29.08	34.73-23.97	36.43-30.73	29.15-23.10	32.56-25.02	24.88-15.30	35.30-21.14
Average Yield %	1.14	1.18	1.26	1.30	1.41	1.43	1.78	1.68

Address: 4545 W. Brown Deer Road, Milwaukee, WI 53223 Telephone: 414-355-0400	Web Site: www.badgermeter.com Officers: Richard A. Meeusen - Chairman, President, Chief Executive Officer Richard E. Johnson - Senior Vice President, Chief Financial Officer, Treasurer	Auditors: Ernst & Young LLP Investor Contact: 414-371-5702 Transfer Agents: American Stock Transfer & Trust Company, LLC, New York, NY

BALL CORP

Exchange	Symbol	Price	52Wk Range	Yield	P/E
NYS	BLL	$35.55 (6/29/2018)	42.93-35.25	1.13	29.38

*7 Year Price Score 105.15 *NYSE Composite Index=100 *12 Month Price Score 92.60

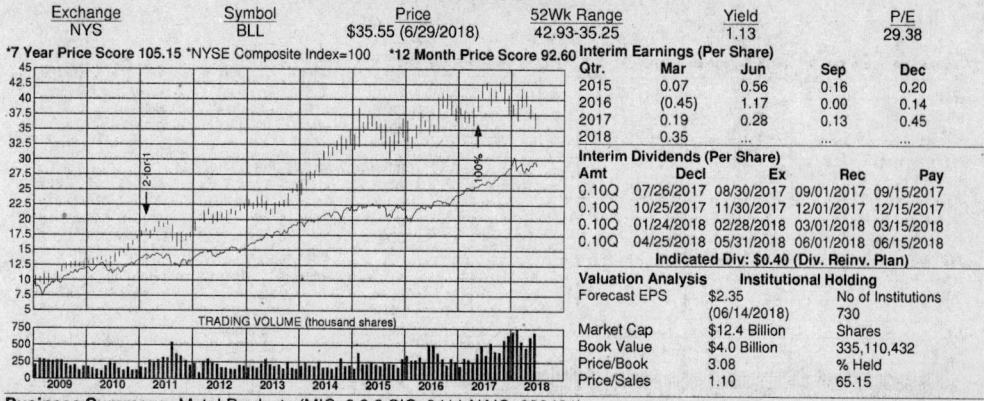

Interim Earnings (Per Share)

Qtr.	Mar	Jun	Sep	Dec
2015	0.07	0.56	0.16	0.20
2016	(0.45)	1.17	0.00	0.14
2017	0.19	0.28	0.13	0.45
2018	0.35	...	...	...

Interim Dividends (Per Share)

Amt	Decl	Ex	Rec	Pay
0.10Q	07/26/2017	08/30/2017	09/01/2017	09/15/2017
0.10Q	10/25/2017	11/30/2017	12/01/2017	12/15/2017
0.10Q	01/24/2018	02/28/2018	03/01/2018	03/15/2018
0.10Q	04/25/2018	05/31/2018	06/01/2018	06/15/2018

Indicated Div: $0.40 (Div. Reinv. Plan)

Valuation Analysis   **Institutional Holding**

Forecast EPS	$2.35	No of Institutions
	(06/14/2018)	730
Market Cap	$12.4 Billion	Shares
Book Value	$4.0 Billion	335,110,432
Price/Book	3.08	% Held
Price/Sales	1.10	65.15

TRADING VOLUME (thousand shares)

Business Summary: Metal Products (MIC: 8.2.3 SIC: 3411 NAIC: 332431)

Ball is a supplier of metal packaging to the beverage, food, personal care and household products industries. Co.'s segments include: beverage packaging, North and Central America; beverage packaging, South America; beverage packaging, Europe, all of which is engaged in manufacturing and sells of metal beverage containers; food and aerosol packaging, which manufacture and sell steel food, aerosol, paint and general line containers, as well as extruded aluminum aerosol containers and aluminum slugs; and aerospace, which manufacture and sell aerospace and other related products and the provision of services used in the defense, civil space and commercial space industries.

Recent Developments: For the quarter ended Mar 31 2018, net income increased 78.6% to US$125.0 million from US$70.0 million in the year-earlier quarter. Revenues were US$2.79 billion, up 12.6% from US$2.47 billion the year before. Operating income was US$226.0 million versus US$152.0 million in the prior-year quarter, an increase of 48.7%. Direct operating expenses rose 13.3% to US$2.24 billion from US$1.98 billion in the comparable period the year before. Indirect operating expenses decreased 6.9% to US$322.0 million from US$346.0 million in the equivalent prior-year period.

Prospects: Our evaluation of Ball Corp. as of Jan. 21, 2018 is the result of our systematic analysis on three basic characteristics: earnings strength, relative valuation, and recent stock price movement. The company has produced a positive trend in earnings per share over the past 5 quarters and while recent estimates for the company have remained steady, BLL has posted results that fell short of analysts expectations. Based on operating earnings yield, the company is undervalued when compared to all of the companies in our coverage universe. Share price changes over the past year indicates that BLL will perform in line with the market over the near term.

Financial Data

(US$ in Thousands)	3 Mos	12/31/2017	12/31/2016	12/31/2015	12/31/2014	12/31/2013	12/31/2012	12/31/2011
Earnings Per Share	1.21	1.05	0.81	1.00	1.65	1.37	1.27	1.31
Cash Flow Per Share	5.15	4.22	0.61	3.67	3.66	2.87	2.75	2.87
Dividends Per Share	0.400	0.365	0.260	0.260	0.260	0.260	0.200	0.140
Dividend Payout %	33.06	34.76	31.90	26.13	15.76	19.05	15.69	10.65
Income Statement								
Total Revenue	2,785,000	10,983,000	9,061,000	7,997,000	8,570,000	8,468,100	8,735,700	8,630,900
EBITDA	351,000	1,311,000	812,000	852,500	1,078,100	1,056,700	1,038,800	1,116,500
Depn & Amortn	125,000	509,000	349,000	247,300	239,500	261,300	248,300	279,600
Income Before Taxes	152,000	514,000	125,000	345,500	645,600	583,600	595,600	659,800
Income Taxes	34,000	165,000	(126,000)	47,000	149,900	149,600	165,000	201,300
Net Income	125,000	374,000	263,000	280,900	470,000	406,800	403,500	444,000
Average Shares	357,552	356,985	322,884	281,968	284,860	298,446	316,168	337,180
Balance Sheet								
Current Assets	4,160,000	3,758,000	3,653,000	2,184,000	2,313,500	2,465,700	2,339,400	2,321,900
Total Assets	17,731,000	17,169,000	16,173,000	9,777,000	7,571,000	7,819,800	7,507,100	7,284,600
Current Liabilities	3,905,000	4,107,000	2,969,000	2,141,600	2,006,800	1,927,400	1,685,800	1,856,100
Long-Term Obligations	7,131,000	6,518,000	7,310,000	5,054,200	2,993,800	3,182,500	3,085,300	2,696,700
Total Liabilities	13,698,000	13,228,000	12,738,000	8,525,700	6,537,900	6,619,900	6,392,500	6,065,500
Stockholders' Equity	4,033,000	3,941,000	3,435,000	1,251,300	1,033,100	1,199,900	1,114,600	1,219,100
Shares Outstanding	349,141	349,881	349,730	284,578	273,932	284,236	299,458	320,631
Statistical Record								
Return on Assets %	2.51	2.24	2.02	3.24	6.11	5.31	5.44	6.25
Return on Equity %	11.27	10.14	11.19	24.59	42.10	35.15	34.49	32.44
EBITDA Margin %	12.60	11.94	8.96	10.66	12.58	12.48	11.89	12.94
Net Margin %	4.49	3.41	2.90	3.51	5.48	4.80	4.62	5.14
Asset Turnover	0.66	0.66	0.70	0.92	1.11	1.10	1.18	1.21
Current Ratio	1.07	0.92	1.23	1.02	1.15	1.28	1.39	1.25
Debt to Equity	1.77	1.65	2.13	4.04	2.90	2.65	2.77	2.21
Price Range	42.93-35.77	42.93-35.77	41.01-31.95	38.58-30.25	35.08-24.14	25.90-20.77	22.73-18.13	20.18-15.11
P/E Ratio	35.48-29.56	40.89-34.06	50.63-39.44	38.58-30.25	21.26-14.63	18.90-15.16	17.90-14.27	15.40-11.53
Average Yield %	1.00	0.92	0.71	0.75	0.86	1.13	0.96	0.78

Address: 10 Longs Peak Drive, P.O. Box 5000, Broomfield, CO 80021-2510
Telephone: 303-469-3131

Web Site: www.ball.com
Officers: John A. Hayes - Chairman, President, Chief Executive Officer Charles E. Baker - Vice President, General Counsel, Corporate Secretary, Assistant Secretary

Auditors: PricewaterhouseCoopers LLP
Investor Contact: 303-460-3537
Transfer Agents: Computershare, Providence, RI

BANCORPSOUTH BANK (TUPELO, MS)

Exchange	Symbol	Price	52Wk Range	Yield	P/E
NYS	BXS	$32.95 (6/29/2018)	35.20-27.55	1.70	18.31

*7 Year Price Score 116.38 *NYSE Composite Index=100 *12 Month Price Score 104.51

TRADING VOLUME (thousand shares)

Interim Earnings (Per Share)

Qtr.	Mar	Jun	Sep	Dec
2015	0.33	0.41	0.36	0.23
2016	0.24	0.37	0.40	0.41
2017	0.41	0.41	0.43	0.42
2018	0.54	...	...	...

Interim Dividends (Per Share)

Amt	Decl	Ex	Rec	Pay
0.14Q	10/25/2017	12/14/2017	12/15/2017	01/02/2018
0.14Q	01/24/2018	03/14/2018	03/15/2018	04/02/2018
0.14Q	04/25/2018	06/14/2018	06/15/2018	07/02/2018

Indicated Div: $0.56 (Div. Reinv. Plan)

Valuation Analysis

		Institutional Holding	
Forecast EPS	$2.28	No of Institutions	
	(06/11/2018)	287	
Market Cap	$3.3 Billion	Shares	
Book Value	$2.1 Billion	82,365,440	
Price/Book	1.59	% Held	
Price/Sales	4.01	75.95	

Business Summary: Banking (MIC: 5.1.1 SIC: 6022 NAIC: 522110)

BancorpSouth is a financial holding company. Through its subsidiary, BancorpSouth Bank, Co. provides financial services to individuals and small-to-medium size businesses. Co. has three segments: Community Banking, which provides deposit products, commercial loans and consumer loans; Insurance Agencies, which serves as agents in the sale of commercial lines of insurance and lines of property and casualty, life, health and employee benefits products and services; and General Corporate and Other, which includes mortgage banking, trust services, credit card activities, investment services and others. At Dec 31 2017, Co. had total assets of $15.30 billion and total deposits of $11.92 billion.

Recent Developments: For the quarter ended Mar 31 2018, net income increased 40.4% to US$53.5 million from US$38.1 million in the year-earlier quarter. Net interest income increased 20.5% to US$138.1 million from US$114.6 million in the year-earlier quarter. Provision for loan losses was unchanged at US$1.0 million versus the prior-year quarter. Non-interest income rose 11.4% to US$78.9 million from US$70.9 million, while non-interest expense advanced 16.2% to US$147.7 million.

Prospects: Our evaluation of BancorpSouth Bank as of Jan. 21, 2018 is the result of our systematic analysis on three basic characteristics: earnings strength, relative valuation, and recent stock price movement. The company has managed to produce a neutral trend in earnings per share over the past 5 quarters. However, while recent estimates for the company have been mixed, BXS has posted better than expected results. Based on operating earnings yield, the company is undervalued when compared to all of the companies in our coverage universe. Share price changes over the past year indicates that BXS will perform poorly over the near term.

Financial Data

(US$ in Thousands)	3 Mos	12/31/2017	12/31/2016	12/31/2015	12/31/2014	12/31/2013	12/31/2012	12/31/2011
Earnings Per Share	1.80	1.67	1.41	1.33	1.21	0.99	0.90	0.45
Cash Flow Per Share	1.84	1.98	1.52	1.39	1.48	2.14	1.42	3.07
Tang Book Value Per Share	14.44	15.44	14.95	14.27	13.40	12.60	12.43	11.88
Dividends Per Share	0.280	0.140	0.450	0.350	0.250	0.120	0.040	0.140
Dividend Payout %	15.56	8.38	31.91	26.32	20.66	12.12	4.44	31.11
Income Statement								
Interest Income	152,195	512,991	483,179	464,378	450,257	449,507	486,424	537,853
Interest Expense	14,117	38,955	29,727	28,696	33,595	50,558	71,833	102,940
Net Interest Income	138,078	474,036	453,452	435,682	416,662	398,949	414,591	434,913
Provision for Losses	1,000	3,000	4,000	(13,000)	...	7,500	28,000	130,081
Non-Interest Income	78,934	268,033	279,030	277,968	269,146	275,066	280,149	270,845
Non-Interest Expense	147,701	507,446	532,038	539,911	518,406	534,849	549,193	533,633
Income Before Taxes	68,311	231,623	196,444	186,739	167,402	131,666	117,547	42,044
Income Taxes	14,820	78,590	63,716	59,248	50,652	37,551	33,252	4,475
Net Income	53,491	153,033	132,728	127,491	116,750	94,115	84,295	37,569
Average Shares	98,942	91,755	94,455	96,124	96,302	95,332	93,864	83,509
Balance Sheet								
Net Loans & Leases	12,319,394	11,074,811	10,855,182	10,404,227	9,711,508	8,874,372	8,601,661	8,758,651
Total Assets	17,185,772	15,298,518	14,724,388	13,798,662	13,326,369	13,029,733	13,397,198	12,995,851
Total Deposits	13,894,301	11,915,596	11,688,141	11,331,161	10,972,339	10,773,836	11,088,146	10,955,189
Total Liabilities	15,125,285	13,585,033	13,000,505	12,143,218	11,720,310	11,516,603	11,948,146	11,732,939
Stockholders' Equity	2,060,487	1,713,485	1,723,883	1,655,444	1,606,059	1,513,130	1,449,052	1,262,912
Shares Outstanding	99,636	90,312	93,696	94,162	96,254	95,231	94,437	83,483
Statistical Record								
Return on Assets %	1.05	1.02	0.93	0.94	0.89	0.71	0.64	0.28
Return on Equity %	8.95	8.90	7.83	7.82	7.49	6.35	6.20	3.02
Net Interest Margin %	90.72	92.41	93.85	93.82	92.54	88.75	85.23	80.86
Efficiency Ratio %	63.90	64.97	69.80	72.73	72.06	73.82	71.64	65.99
Loans to Deposits	0.89	0.93	0.93	0.92	0.89	0.82	0.78	0.80
Price Range	35.20-27.55	34.20-27.55	31.60-18.96	26.93-19.76	25.90-19.62	25.45-14.28	15.57-10.89	16.67-8.34
P/E Ratio	19.56-15.31	20.48-16.50	22.41-13.45	20.25-14.86	21.40-16.21	25.71-14.42	17.30-12.10	37.04-18.53
Average Yield %	0.90	0.46	1.91	1.45	1.09	0.65	0.29	1.12

Address: One Mississippi Plaza, 201 South Spring Street, Tupelo, MS 38804 Telephone: 662-680-2000	Web Site: www.bancorpsouth.com Officers: James D. Rollins - Chairman, Chief Executive Officer Chris A. Bagley - President, Chief Operating Officer, Interim Chief Financial Officer, Treasurer	Auditors: KPMG LLP Investor Contact: 662-680-2000 Transfer Agents: Computershare, Canton, MA

BANK OF AMERICA CORP

Exchange	Symbol	Price	52Wk Range	Yield	P/E
NYS	BAC	$28.19 (6/29/2018)	32.84-22.89	1.70	15.93

*7 Year Price Score 139.53 *NYSE Composite Index=100 *12 Month Price Score 103.85

Interim Earnings (Per Share)

Qtr.	Mar	Jun	Sep	Dec
2015	0.27	0.45	0.37	0.22
2016	0.21	0.36	0.41	0.40
2017	0.41	0.46	0.48	0.21
2018	0.62	...	...	...

Interim Dividends (Per Share)

Amt	Decl	Ex	Rec	Pay
0.12Q	07/26/2017	08/30/2017	09/01/2017	09/29/2017
0.12Q	10/25/2017	11/30/2017	12/01/2017	12/29/2017
0.12Q	01/31/2018	03/01/2018	03/02/2018	03/30/2018
0.12Q	04/25/2018	05/31/2018	06/01/2018	06/29/2018

Indicated Div: $0.48 (Div. Reinv. Plan)

Valuation Analysis

Forecast EPS	$2.48 (06/14/2018)
Market Cap	$286.9 Billion
Book Value	$266.2 Billion
Price/Book	1.08
Price/Sales	2.80

Institutional Holding

No of Institutions	2804
Shares	8,293,237,760
% Held	57.12

Business Summary: Banking (MIC: 5.1.1 SIC: 6021 NAIC: 522110)

Bank of America is a bank and financial holding company. Through its banking and various nonbanking subsidiaries throughout the U.S. and in international markets, Co. serves individual consumers, small- and middle-market businesses, institutional investors, corporations and governments with a range of banking, investing, asset management and other financial and risk management products and services. Co. provides its services and products through four segments: Consumer Banking, Global Wealth & Investment Management, Global Banking and Global Markets. As of Dec 31 2017, Co. had total assets of $2.28 trillion and total deposits of $1.31 trillion.

Recent Developments: For the quarter ended Mar 31 2018, net income increased 29.6% to US$6.92 billion from US$5.34 billion in the year-earlier quarter. Net interest income increased 5.0% to US$11.61 billion from US$11.06 billion in the year-earlier quarter. Provision for loan losses was US$834.0 million versus US$835.0 million in the prior-year quarter, a decrease of 0.1%. Non-interest income rose 2.9% to US$11.52 billion from US$11.19 billion, while non-interest expense declined 1.4% to US$13.90 billion.

Prospects: Our evaluation of Bank of America Corp. as of Jan. 21, 2018 is the result of our systematic analysis on three basic characteristics: earnings strength, relative valuation, and recent stock price movement. The company has enjoyed a very positive trend in earnings per share over the past 5 quarters and while recent estimates for the company have been raised by analysts, BAC has posted better than expected results. Based on operating earnings yield, the company is undervalued when compared to all of the companies in our coverage universe. Share price changes over the past year indicates that BAC will perform in line with the market over the near term.

Financial Data

(US$ in Millions)	3 Mos	12/31/2017	12/31/2016	12/31/2015	12/31/2014	12/31/2013	12/31/2012	12/31/2011
Earnings Per Share	1.77	1.56	1.50	1.31	0.36	0.90	0.25	0.01
Cash Flow Per Share	6.16	1.02	1.78	2.65	2.54	8.65	(1.29)	6.36
Tang Book Value Per Share	16.96	16.87	16.61	15.16	13.91	13.11	12.59	11.98
Dividends Per Share	0.435	0.390	0.250	0.200	0.120	0.040	0.040	0.040
Dividend Payout %	24.58	25.00	16.67	15.27	33.33	4.44	16.00	400.00
Income Statement								
Interest Income	15,599	57,579	51,057	49,800	50,886	55,020	57,400	66,236
Interest Expense	3,991	12,912	9,961	10,549	10,934	12,755	16,744	21,620
Net Interest Income	11,608	44,667	41,096	39,251	39,952	42,265	40,656	44,616
Provision for Losses	834	3,396	3,597	3,161	2,275	3,556	8,169	13,410
Non-Interest Income	11,517	42,685	42,605	43,256	44,295	46,677	42,678	48,838
Non-Interest Expense	13,897	54,743	54,951	57,192	75,117	69,214	72,093	80,274
Income Before Taxes	8,394	29,213	25,153	22,154	6,855	16,172	3,072	(230)
Income Taxes	1,476	10,981	7,247	6,266	2,022	4,741	(1,116)	(1,676)
Net Income	6,918	18,232	17,906	15,888	4,833	11,431	4,188	1,446
Average Shares	10,472	10,779	11,036	11,215	10,584	11,492	10,841	10,254
Balance Sheet								
Net Loans & Leases	933,045	937,786	904,512	898,220	879,808	922,167	903,053	906,179
Total Assets	2,328,478	2,281,234	2,187,702	2,144,316	2,104,534	2,102,273	2,209,974	2,129,046
Total Deposits	1,328,664	1,309,545	1,260,934	1,197,259	1,118,936	1,119,271	1,105,261	1,033,041
Total Liabilities	2,062,254	2,014,088	1,920,862	1,888,111	1,861,063	1,869,588	1,973,018	1,898,945
Stockholders' Equity	266,224	267,146	266,840	256,205	243,471	232,685	236,956	230,101
Shares Outstanding	10,175	10,287	10,052	10,380	10,516	10,591	10,779	10,536
Statistical Record								
Return on Assets %	0.89	0.82	0.82	0.75	0.23	0.53	0.19	0.07
Return on Equity %	7.60	6.83	6.83	6.36	2.03	4.87	1.79	0.63
Net Interest Margin %	74.42	77.58	80.49	78.82	78.51	76.82	70.83	67.36
Efficiency Ratio %	51.25	54.60	58.67	61.46	78.92	68.06	72.04	69.76
Loans to Deposits	0.70	0.72	0.72	0.75	0.79	0.82	0.82	0.88
Price Range	32.84-22.23	29.88-22.05	23.16-11.16	18.45-15.15	18.13-14.51	15.88-11.03	11.61-5.80	15.25-4.99
P/E Ratio	18.55-12.56	19.15-14.13	15.44-7.44	14.08-11.56	50.36-40.31	17.64-12.26	46.44-23.20	N.M.
Average Yield %	1.64	1.58	1.62	1.21	0.73	0.30	0.47	0.40

Address: Bank of America Corporate Center, 100 N. Tryon Street, Charlotte, NC 28255
Telephone: 704-386-5681

Web Site: www.bankofamerica.com
Officers: Brian T. Moynihan - Chairman, President, Chief Executive Officer, Division Officer Terrence P. (Terry) Laughlin - Vice-Chairman, Division Officer, Chief Risk Officer, Executive Officer

Auditors: PricewaterhouseCoopers LLP
Investor Contact: 800-521-3984
Transfer Agents: Computershare Trust Company, N.A., Providence, RI

BANK OF HAWAII CORP

Exchange	Symbol	Price	52Wk Range	Yield	P/E
NYS	BOH	$83.42 (6/29/2018)	88.62-75.00	2.88	18.87

*7 Year Price Score 107.96 *NYSE Composite Index=100 *12 Month Price Score 101.12

Interim Earnings (Per Share)

Qtr.	Mar	Jun	Sep	Dec
2015	0.97	0.95	0.79	0.99
2016	1.16	1.03	1.02	1.02
2017	1.20	1.05	1.08	1.01
2018	1.28	...	...	...

Interim Dividends (Per Share)

Amt	Decl	Ex	Rec	Pay
0.52Q	07/24/2017	08/29/2017	08/31/2017	09/15/2017
0.52Q	10/20/2017	11/29/2017	11/30/2017	12/14/2017
0.52Q	01/19/2018	02/27/2018	02/28/2018	03/14/2018
0.60Q	04/19/2018	05/30/2018	05/31/2018	06/14/2018

Indicated Div: $2.40 (Div. Reinv. Plan)

Valuation Analysis   Institutional Holding

Forecast EPS	$5.30 (06/13/2018)	No of Institutions	421
Market Cap	$3.5 Billion	Shares	46,452,488
Book Value	$1.2 Billion	% Held	
Price/Book	2.84		64.19
Price/Sales	5.12		

Business Summary: Banking (MIC: 5.1.1 SIC: 6022 NAIC: 522110)

Bank of Hawaii is a bank holding company. Through its subsidiary, Bank of Hawaii, Co. provides financial products and services to customers in Hawaii, Guam, and other Pacific Islands. Co. has four segments: Retail Banking, which provides loan and lease, deposit, and retail insurance products; Commercial Banking, which provides corporate banking, commercial real estate loans, commercial lease financing, and deposit products; Investment Services, which includes trust services and investment management; and Treasury and Other, which consists of corporate asset and liability management activities. As of Dec 31 2017, Co. had total assets of $17.09 billion and total deposits of $14.88 billion.

Recent Developments: For the quarter ended Mar 31 2018, net income increased 5.6% to US$54.0 million from US$51.2 million in the year-earlier quarter. Net interest income increased 8.3% to US$119.0 million from US$109.9 million in the year-earlier quarter. Provision for loan losses was US$4.1 million versus US$4.4 million in the prior-year quarter, a decrease of 6.3%. Non-interest income fell 21.2% to US$44.0 million from US$55.9 million, while non-interest expense advanced 6.6% to US$94.4 million.

Prospects: Our evaluation of Bank of Hawaii Corp. as of Jan. 21, 2018 is the result of our systematic analysis on three basic characteristics: earnings strength, relative valuation, and recent stock price movement. The company has managed to produce a neutral trend in earnings per share over the past 5 quarters. However, while recent estimates for the company have been mixed, BOH has posted better than expected results. Based on operating earnings yield, the company is undervalued when compared to all of the companies in our coverage universe. Share price changes over the past year indicates that BOH will perform in line with the market over the near term.

Financial Data
(US$ in Thousands)

	3 Mos	12/31/2017	12/31/2016	12/31/2015	12/31/2014	12/31/2013	12/31/2012	12/31/2011
Earnings Per Share	4.42	4.33	4.23	3.70	3.69	3.38	3.67	3.39
Cash Flow Per Share	4.96	4.14	5.30	5.41	4.77	5.45	4.92	4.88
Tang Book Value Per Share	28.01	27.73	25.95	24.53	22.84	21.41	21.56	20.61
Dividends Per Share	2.060	2.040	1.890	1.800	1.800	1.800	1.800	1.800
Dividend Payout %	46.61	47.11	44.68	48.65	48.78	53.25	49.05	53.10
Income Statement								
Interest Income	132,146	503,794	457,900	432,110	417,633	398,505	420,489	439,693
Interest Expense	13,190	46,556	40,321	38,023	37,977	39,598	43,218	49,485
Net Interest Income	118,956	457,238	417,579	394,087	379,656	358,907	377,271	390,208
Provision for Losses	4,125	16,900	4,750	1,000	(4,864)	...	979	12,690
Non-Interest Income	44,035	185,417	197,343	186,219	180,017	186,223	200,286	197,655
Non-Interest Expense	94,384	357,691	350,578	348,104	326,899	330,963	334,288	348,193
Income Before Taxes	64,482	268,064	259,594	231,202	237,638	214,161	242,290	226,980
Income Taxes	10,442	83,392	78,133	70,498	74,596	63,659	76,214	66,937
Net Income	54,040	184,672	181,461	160,704	163,042	150,502	166,076	160,043
Average Shares	42,358	42,607	42,879	43,454	44,125	44,572	45,249	47,224
Balance Sheet								
Net Loans & Leases	9,832,238	9,708,832	8,908,011	7,780,913	6,794,037	5,986,368	5,747,038	5,418,655
Total Assets	17,136,030	17,089,052	16,492,367	15,455,016	14,787,208	14,084,280	13,728,372	13,846,391
Total Deposits	14,957,133	14,883,968	14,320,240	13,251,103	12,633,089	11,914,656	11,529,482	10,592,623
Total Liabilities	15,894,837	15,857,184	15,330,830	14,338,756	13,732,122	13,072,304	12,706,707	12,843,724
Stockholders' Equity	1,241,193	1,231,868	1,161,537	1,116,260	1,055,086	1,011,976	1,021,665	1,002,667
Shares Outstanding	42,314	42,401	42,635	43,282	43,724	44,490	44,754	45,947
Statistical Record								
Return on Assets %	1.11	1.10	1.13	1.06	1.13	1.08	1.20	1.19
Return on Equity %	15.41	15.43	15.89	14.80	15.78	14.80	16.36	15.89
Net Interest Margin %	90.02	90.76	91.19	91.20	90.91	90.06	89.72	88.75
Efficiency Ratio %	53.57	51.90	53.50	56.30	54.70	56.60	53.85	54.63
Loans to Deposits	0.66	0.65	0.62	0.59	0.54	0.50	0.50	0.51
Price Range	88.62-75.00	90.36-75.00	89.31-55.26	69.22-54.53	61.52-53.53	59.67-44.05	49.60-42.04	49.11-35.03
P/E Ratio	20.05-16.97	20.87-17.32	21.11-13.06	18.71-14.74	16.67-14.51	17.65-13.03	13.51-11.46	14.49-10.33
Average Yield %	2.50	2.47	2.67	2.85	3.12	3.44	3.90	4.07

Address: 130 Merchant Street, Honolulu, HI 96813 **Telephone:** 888-643-3888	**Web Site:** www.boh.com **Officers:** Peter S. Ho - Chairman, President, Chief Executive Officer, Chief Banking Officer Wayne Y. Hamano - Vice-Chairman, Chief Commercial Officer	**Auditors:** Ernst & Young LLP **Investor Contact:** 808-694-8430 **Transfer Agents:** Computershare Investor Services, LLC, Canton, MA

BANK OF NEW YORK MELLON CORP

Exchange	Symbol	Price	52Wk Range	Yield	P/E
NYS	BK	$53.93 (6/29/2018)	58.42-50.15	1.78	13.48

*7 Year Price Score 117.47 *NYSE Composite Index=100 *12 Month Price Score 102.09

Interim Earnings (Per Share)

Qtr.	Mar	Jun	Sep	Dec
2015	0.67	0.73	0.74	0.58
2016	0.73	0.75	0.90	0.77
2017	0.83	0.88	0.94	1.08
2018	1.10	...	...	...

Interim Dividends (Per Share)

Amt	Decl	Ex	Rec	Pay
0.24Q	07/20/2017	07/28/2017	08/01/2017	08/11/2017
0.24Q	10/19/2017	10/30/2017	10/31/2017	11/09/2017
0.24Q	01/18/2018	01/29/2018	01/30/2018	02/09/2018
0.24Q	04/19/2018	04/30/2018	05/01/2018	05/11/2018

Indicated Div: $0.96 (Div. Reinv. Plan)

Valuation Analysis

		Institutional Holding	
Forecast EPS	$4.24	No of Institutions	
	(06/14/2018)	1470	
Market Cap	$54.5 Billion	Shares	
Book Value	$41.7 Billion	964,501,376	
Price/Book	1.31	% Held	
Price/Sales	3.16	77.60	

Business Summary: Banking (MIC: 5.1.1 SIC: 6022 NAIC: 522110)

Bank of New York Mellon is global investments company. Co. divides its businesses into two principal segments, Investment Management and Investment Services. Co. also has an Other segment which includes the leasing portfolio, corporate treasury activities, derivatives and other trading, corporate and bank-owned life insurance and renewable energy investments, and business exits. Co.'s two principal banking subsidiaries are: The Bank of New York Mellon, which houses Co.'s Investment Services businesses and BNY Mellon, National Association which houses Co.'s Wealth Management business. As of Dec 31 2017, Co. had total assets of $371.76 billion and deposits of $244.32 billion.

Recent Developments: For the quarter ended Mar 31 2018, net income increased 24.0% to US$1.16 billion from US$937.0 million in the year-earlier quarter. Net interest income increased 16.0% to US$919.0 million from US$792.0 million in the year-earlier quarter. Credit for loan losses was unchanged at US$5.0 million versus the prior-year quarter. Non-interest income rose 6.8% to US$3.26 billion from US$3.05 billion, while non-interest expense advanced 3.7% to US$2.74 billion.

Prospects: Our evaluation of Bank of New York Mellon Corp. as of Jan. 21, 2018 is the result of our systematic analysis on three basic characteristics: earnings strength, relative valuation, and recent stock price movement. The company has managed to produce a neutral trend in earnings per share over the past 5 quarters and while recent estimates for the company have been raised by analysts, BK has posted results that were in line with analysts expectations. Based on operating earnings yield, the company is undervalued when compared to all of the companies in our coverage universe. Share price changes over the past year indicates that BK will perform in line with the market over the near term.

Financial Data
(US$ in Thousands)

	3 Mos	12/31/2017	12/31/2016	12/31/2015	12/31/2014	12/31/2013	12/31/2012	12/31/2011
Earnings Per Share	4.00	3.72	3.15	2.71	2.15	1.74	2.03	2.03
Cash Flow Per Share	4.94	4.49	5.84	3.74	3.97	(0.56)	1.38	1.81
Tang Book Value Per Share	15.54	15.03	12.32	11.67	11.22	10.67	9.77	7.75
Dividends Per Share	0.910	0.860	0.720	0.680	0.660	0.580	0.520	0.480
Dividend Payout %	22.75	23.12	22.86	25.09	30.70	33.33	25.62	23.65
Income Statement								
Total Revenue	4,640,000	16,617,000	15,674,000	15,494,000	16,046,000	15,326,000	15,249,000	15,334,000
Income Before Taxes	1,444,000	4,610,000	4,725,000	4,235,000	3,563,000	3,712,000	3,302,000	3,617,000
Income Taxes	282,000	496,000	1,177,000	1,013,000	912,000	1,520,000	779,000	1,048,000
Net Income	1,171,000	4,090,000	3,547,000	3,158,000	2,567,000	2,111,000	2,445,000	2,516,000
Average Shares	1,021,731	1,040,290	1,072,013	1,112,511	1,137,480	1,154,441	1,178,430	1,223,026
Balance Sheet								
Total Assets	373,597,000	371,758,000	333,469,000	393,780,000	385,303,000	374,310,000	358,990,000	325,266,000
Total Liabilities	331,869,000	330,507,000	294,658,000	355,743,000	347,862,000	336,789,000	322,559,000	291,849,000
Stockholders' Equity	41,728,000	41,251,000	38,811,000	38,037,000	37,441,000	37,521,000	36,431,000	33,417,000
Shares Outstanding	1,010,676	1,013,442	1,047,488	1,085,342	1,118,227	1,142,249	1,163,490	1,209,674
Statistical Record								
Return on Assets %	1.22	1.16	0.97	0.81	0.68	0.58	0.71	0.88
Return on Equity %	10.73	10.22	9.21	8.37	6.85	5.71	6.98	7.65
Net Margin %	25.24	24.61	22.63	20.38	16.00	13.77	16.03	16.41
Asset Turnover	0.05	0.05	0.04	0.04	0.04	0.04	0.04	0.05
Price Range	58.42-46.20	54.97-43.87	49.17-32.74	45.26-35.66	41.53-30.91	34.94-25.70	26.20-19.51	32.37-17.71
P/E Ratio	14.61-11.55	14.78-11.79	15.61-10.39	16.70-13.16	19.32-14.38	20.08-14.77	12.91-9.61	15.95-8.72
Average Yield %	1.74	1.72	1.79	1.65	1.81	1.94	2.30	1.92

Address: 225 Liberty Street, New York, NY 10286
Telephone: 212-495-1784

Web Site: www.bnymellon.com
Officers: Charles W. Scharf - Chairman, Chief Executive Officer Thomas P. (Todd) Gibbons - Vice-Chairman, Division Officer, Chief Financial Officer, Senior Executive Vice President

Auditors: KPMG LLP
Investor Contact: 412-234-4633
Transfer Agents: Computershare Shareowner Services LLC, Jersey City, NJ

BANKUNITED INC.

Exchange	Symbol	Price	52Wk Range	Yield	P/E
NYS	BKU	$40.85 (6/29/2018)	44.24-30.50	2.06	7.07

*7 Year Price Score 98.03 *NYSE Composite Index=100 *12 Month Price Score 109.06

Interim Earnings (Per Share)

Qtr.	Mar	Jun	Sep	Dec
2015	0.44	0.43	0.95	0.52
2016	0.51	0.52	0.47	0.59
2017	0.57	0.60	0.62	3.79
2018	0.77	...	...	...

Interim Dividends (Per Share)

Amt	Decl	Ex	Rec	Pay
0.21Q	09/25/2017	10/13/2017	10/16/2017	10/31/2017
0.21Q	12/27/2017	01/11/2018	01/12/2018	01/31/2018
0.21Q	03/23/2018	04/11/2018	04/12/2018	04/30/2018
0.21Q	06/25/2018	07/13/2018	07/16/2018	07/31/2018

Indicated Div: $0.84

Valuation Analysis

		Institutional Holding	
Forecast EPS	$3.27 (06/14/2018)	No of Institutions	338
Market Cap	$4.3 Billion	Shares	129,716,504
Book Value	$3.0 Billion	% Held	93.04
Price/Book	1.43		
Price/Sales	3.08		

TRADING VOLUME (thousand shares)

Business Summary: Banking (MIC: 5.1.1 SIC: 6035 NAIC: 522120)

BankUnited is a bank holding company. Through its subsidiary, BankUnited, National Association, Co. provides banking services to individual and corporate customers. Co.'s lending products include small business loans, commercial real estate loans, equipment loans and leases, term loans, formula-based loans, municipal and non-profit loans and leases, commercial and mortgage warehouse lines of credit, letters of credit and consumer loans. Co.'s deposit products including checking accounts, money market deposit accounts, savings accounts and certificates of deposit. As of Dec 31 2017, Co. had total assets of $30.35 billion and total deposits of $21.88 billion.

Recent Developments: For the quarter ended Mar 31 2018, net income increased 36.8% to US$85.2 million from US$62.3 million in the year-earlier quarter. Net interest income increased 7.5% to US$247.8 million from US$230.6 million in the year-earlier quarter. Provision for loan losses was US$3.1 million versus US$12.1 million in the prior-year quarter, a decrease of 74.0%. Non-interest income fell 0.6% to US$28.0 million from US$28.1 million, while non-interest expense advanced 3.4% to US$161.8 million.

Prospects: Our evaluation of BankUnited Inc as of Jan. 21, 2018 is the result of our systematic analysis on three basic characteristics: earnings strength, relative valuation, and recent stock price movement. The company has managed to produce a neutral trend in earnings per share over the past 5 quarters and while recent estimates for the company have been raised by analysts, BKU has posted better than expected results. Based on operating earnings yield, the company is undervalued when compared to all of the companies in our coverage universe. Share price changes over the past year indicates that BKU will perform poorly over the near term.

Financial Data
(US$ in Thousands)

	3 Mos	12/31/2017	12/31/2016	12/31/2015	12/31/2014	12/31/2013	12/31/2012	12/31/2011
Earnings Per Share	5.78	5.58	2.09	2.35	1.95	2.01	2.05	0.62
Cash Flow Per Share	4.00	3.02	2.98	2.13	(0.50)	(0.68)	(3.74)	(2.60)
Tang Book Value Per Share	27.83	27.59	22.47	20.90	19.52	18.41	18.28	15.01
Dividends Per Share	0.840	0.840	0.840	0.630	1.050	0.630	0.720	0.560
Dividend Payout %	14.53	15.05	40.19	26.81	53.85	31.34	35.12	90.32
Income Statement								
Total Revenue	355,762	1,362,365	1,165,634	983,040	867,909	769,927	810,103	801,314
Income Before Taxes	110,831	404,461	335,444	296,893	293,250	318,002	344,865	192,744
Income Taxes	25,596	(209,812)	109,703	45,233	89,035	109,066	133,605	129,576
Net Income	85,235	614,273	225,741	251,660	204,215	208,936	211,260	63,168
Average Shares	105,933	105,857	103,656	102,972	100,595	99,751	93,828	95,605
Balance Sheet								
Total Assets	30,432,536	30,346,986	27,880,151	23,883,467	19,210,529	15,046,649	12,375,953	11,322,038
Total Liabilities	27,399,864	27,320,924	25,461,722	21,639,569	17,157,995	13,117,951	10,569,273	9,786,758
Stockholders' Equity	3,032,672	3,026,062	2,418,429	2,243,898	2,052,534	1,928,698	1,806,680	1,535,280
Shares Outstanding	106,160	106,848	104,166	103,626	101,656	101,013	95,006	97,700
Statistical Record								
Return on Assets %	2.18	2.11	0.87	1.17	1.19	1.52	1.78	0.57
Return on Equity %	22.90	22.56	9.66	11.71	10.26	11.19	12.61	4.53
Net Margin %	23.96	45.09	19.37	25.60	23.53	27.14	26.08	7.88
Asset Turnover	0.05	0.05	0.04	0.05	0.05	0.06	0.07	0.07
Price Range	43.34-30.50	40.90-30.50	38.22-28.13	39.34-26.74	35.38-27.66	33.22-24.44	26.15-22.04	29.72-19.39
P/E Ratio	7.50-5.28	7.33-5.47	18.29-13.46	16.74-11.38	18.14-14.18	16.53-12.16	12.76-10.75	47.94-31.27
Average Yield %	2.31	2.36	2.57	1.82	3.30	2.23	3.00	2.23

Address: 14817 Oak Lane, Miami Lakes, FL 33016 **Telephone:** 305-569-2000	**Web Site:** www.bankunited.com **Officers:** John Adam Kanas - Chairman, President, Chief Executive Officer Rajinder P. Singh - President, Chief Executive Officer, Chief Operating Officer
Auditors: KPMG LLP **Investor Contact:** 305-569-2000 **Transfer Agents:** Registrar and Transfer Company	

BAXTER INTERNATIONAL INC

Exchange	Symbol	Price	52Wk Range	Yield	P/E
NYS	BAX	$73.84 (6/29/2018)	75.41-59.50	1.03	48.90

*7 Year Price Score 125.09 *NYSE Composite Index=100 ***12 Month Price Score 108.27**

Interim Earnings (Per Share)

Qtr.	Mar	Jun	Sep	Dec
2015	0.78	0.60	0.00	0.37
2016	6.12	2.19	0.24	0.46
2017	0.49	0.48	0.45	(0.13)
2018	0.71	...	...	...

Interim Dividends (Per Share)

Amt	Decl	Ex	Rec	Pay
0.16Q	07/18/2017	08/30/2017	09/01/2017	10/02/2017
0.16Q	11/14/2017	11/30/2017	12/01/2017	01/02/2018
0.16Q	02/20/2018	03/01/2018	03/02/2018	04/02/2018
0.19Q	05/08/2018	05/31/2018	06/01/2018	07/02/2018

Indicated Div: $0.76 (Div. Reinv. Plan)

Valuation Analysis

		Institutional Holding	
Forecast EPS	$2.90	No of Institutions	1550
	(06/13/2018)		
Market Cap	$39.6 Billion	Shares	599,643,200
Book Value	$9.1 Billion	% Held	77.03
Price/Book	4.35		
Price/Sales	3.68		

Business Summary: Medical Instruments & Equipment (MIC: 4.3.1 SIC: 3841 NAIC: 339112)

Baxter International provides a broad portfolio of essential healthcare products across its portfolio, including acute and chronic dialysis therapies; sterile intravenous (IV) solutions; infusion systems and devices; parenteral nutrition therapies; inhaled anesthetics; generic injectable pharmaceuticals; and surgical hemostat and sealant products. These products are used by hospitals, kidney dialysis centers, nursing homes, rehabilitation centers, doctors' offices and by patients at home under physician supervision. As of Dec 31 2017, Co. manufactured products in about 20 countries and sells them in about 100 countries.

Recent Developments: For the quarter ended Mar 31 2018, income from continuing operations increased 42.5% to US$389.0 million from US$273.0 million in the year-earlier quarter. Net income increased 43.0% to US$389.0 million from US$272.0 million in the year-earlier quarter. Revenues were US$2.68 billion, up 8.2% from US$2.48 billion the year before. Operating income was US$432.0 million versus US$353.0 million in the prior-year quarter, an increase of 22.4%. Direct operating expenses rose 9.2% to US$1.56 billion from US$1.43 billion in the comparable period the year before. Indirect operating expenses decreased 1.3% to US$682.0 million from US$691.0 million in the equivalent prior-year period.

Prospects: Our evaluation of Baxter International Inc. as of Jan. 21, 2018 is the result of our systematic analysis on three basic characteristics: earnings strength, relative valuation, and recent stock price movement. The company has generated a negative trend in earnings per share over the past 5 quarters and while recent estimates for the company have been mixed, BAX has posted better than expected results. Based on operating earnings yield, the company is about fairly valued when compared to all of the companies in our coverage universe. Share price changes over the past year indicates that BAX will perform well over the near term.

Financial Data
(US$ in Millions)

	3 Mos	12/31/2017	12/31/2016	12/31/2015	12/31/2014	12/31/2013	12/31/2012	12/31/2011
Earnings Per Share	1.51	1.29	9.01	1.76	4.56	3.66	4.18	3.88
Cash Flow Per Share	3.89	3.38	3.02	3.02	5.93	5.89	5.62	4.95
Tang Book Value Per Share	8.36	8.59	8.50	8.78	4.00	3.62	6.63	6.14
Dividends Per Share	0.640	0.610	0.505	1.270	2.050	1.920	1.570	1.265
Dividend Payout %	42.38	47.29	5.60	72.16	44.96	52.46	37.56	32.60
Income Statement								
Total Revenue	2,677	10,561	10,163	9,968	16,671	15,259	14,190	13,893
EBITDA	642	2,033	5,820	1,313	3,589	3,445	3,661	3,537
Depn & Amortn	192	761	800	759	1,005	823	712	670
Income Before Taxes	438	1,217	4,954	428	2,439	2,494	2,862	2,813
Income Taxes	49	493	(12)	35	493	537	563	553
Net Income	389	717	4,965	968	2,497	2,012	2,326	2,224
Average Shares	551	555	551	549	547	549	556	573
Balance Sheet								
Current Assets	6,956	7,263	6,574	11,796	10,351	10,004	9,260	8,650
Total Assets	16,890	17,111	15,546	20,975	25,917	25,869	20,390	19,073
Current Liabilities	2,642	2,821	2,744	5,750	6,042	5,906	4,759	4,857
Long-Term Obligations	3,550	3,509	2,779	3,935	7,606	8,126	5,580	4,749
Total Liabilities	7,791	7,987	7,256	12,129	17,797	17,406	13,452	12,488
Stockholders' Equity	9,099	9,124	8,290	8,846	8,120	8,463	6,938	6,585
Shares Outstanding	536	541	539	547	542	543	546	560
Statistical Record								
Return on Assets %	5.12	4.39	27.12	4.13	9.64	8.70	11.76	12.17
Return on Equity %	9.38	8.23	57.79	11.41	30.12	26.13	34.31	33.82
EBITDA Margin %	23.98	19.25	57.27	13.17	21.53	22.58	25.80	25.46
Net Margin %	14.53	6.79	48.85	9.71	14.98	13.19	16.39	16.01
Asset Turnover	0.66	0.65	0.56	0.43	0.64	0.66	0.72	0.76
Current Ratio	2.63	2.57	2.40	2.05	1.71	1.69	1.95	1.78
Debt to Equity	0.39	0.38	0.34	0.44	0.94	0.96	0.80	0.72
Price Range	72.26-51.86	66.05-44.44	49.16-34.76	42.13-32.27	41.83-36.12	40.43-34.71	37.38-26.64	33.90-25.89
P/E Ratio	47.85-34.34	51.20-34.45	5.46-3.86	23.94-18.34	9.17-7.92	11.05-9.48	8.94-6.37	8.74-6.67
Average Yield %	1.02	1.05	1.15	3.39	5.22	5.10	4.98	4.29

Address: One Baxter Parkway, Deerfield, IL 60015 **Telephone:** 224-948-2000 **Fax:** 847-948-2964	**Web Site:** www.baxter.com **Officers:** Jose E. Almeida - Chairman, President, Chief Executive Officer Giuseppe Accogli - Senior Vice President, Corporate Vice-President, Division Officer	**Auditors:** PricewaterhouseCoopers LLP **Transfer Agents:** Computershare Trust Company, N.A., Providence, RI

BB&T CORP.

Exchange	Symbol	Price	52Wk Range	Yield	P/E
NYS	BBT	$50.44 (6/29/2018)	56.03-43.66	2.97	15.66

*7 Year Price Score 108.32 *NYSE Composite Index=100 *12 Month Price Score 104.83

Interim Earnings (Per Share)

Qtr.	Mar	Jun	Sep	Dec
2015	0.67	0.62	0.64	0.64
2016	0.67	0.66	0.73	0.72
2017	0.46	0.77	0.74	0.77
2018	0.94	...	...	...

Interim Dividends (Per Share)

Amt	Decl	Ex	Rec	Pay
0.33Q	10/23/2017	11/09/2017	11/10/2017	12/01/2017
0.33Q	01/23/2018	02/08/2018	02/09/2018	03/01/2018
0.045Q	02/22/2018	03/05/2018	03/06/2018	03/20/2018
0.375Q	04/24/2018	05/10/2018	05/11/2018	06/01/2018

Indicated Div: $1.50 (Div. Reinv. Plan)

Valuation Analysis / **Institutional Holding**

Forecast EPS	$4.01	No of Institutions	
	(06/14/2018)	1367	
Market Cap	$39.3 Billion	Shares	
Book Value	$29.6 Billion	Shares	590,093,632
Price/Book	1.33	% Held	
Price/Sales	3.19		60.61

Business Summary: Banking (MIC: 5.1.1 SIC: 6021 NAIC: 522110)

BB&T is a financial holding company. Through its subsidiary, Branch Banking and Trust Company, Co. provides loans and lease financing, including insurance premium financing, permanent commercial real estate financing, loan servicing for third-party investors, direct consumer finance loans to individuals, credit card lending, automobile financing, factoring and equipment financing. Co. also markets other services, including deposits; discount and brokerage, annuities and mutual funds; and life insurance, property and casualty insurance, health insurance and commercial general liability insurance. At Dec 31 2017, Co. had total assets of $221.64 billion and total deposits of $157.37 billion.

Recent Developments: For the quarter ended Mar 31 2018, net income increased 85.7% to US$791.0 million from US$426.0 million in the year-earlier quarter. Net interest income increased 1.5% to US$1.63 billion from US$1.61 billion in the year-earlier quarter. Provision for loan losses was US$150.0 million versus US$148.0 million in the prior-year quarter, an increase of 1.4%. Non-interest income rose 0.8% to US$1.18 billion from US$1.17 billion, while non-interest expense declined 19.8% to US$1.69 billion.

Prospects: Our evaluation of BB&T Corp. as of Jan. 21, 2018 is the result of our systematic analysis on three basic characteristics: earnings strength, relative valuation, and recent stock price movement. The company has enjoyed a very positive trend in earnings per share over the past 5 quarters and while recent estimates for the company have been raised by analysts, BBT has posted better than expected results. Based on operating earnings yield, the company is undervalued when compared to all of the companies in our coverage universe. Share price changes over the past year indicates that BBT will perform poorly over the near term.

Financial Data

(US$ in Thousands)	3 Mos	12/31/2017	12/31/2016	12/31/2015	12/31/2014	12/31/2013	12/31/2012	12/31/2011
Earnings Per Share	3.22	2.74	2.77	2.56	2.75	2.19	2.70	1.83
Cash Flow Per Share	6.14	5.80	3.31	3.90	4.54	7.59	5.28	6.55
Tang Book Value Per Share	19.42	19.45	18.88	18.70	18.76	16.59	15.63	14.82
Dividends Per Share	1.335	1.260	1.150	1.050	0.950	1.120	0.760	0.640
Dividend Payout %	41.46	45.99	41.52	41.02	34.55	51.14	28.15	34.97
Income Statement								
Interest Income	1,921,000	7,374,000	7,066,000	6,327,000	6,142,000	6,507,000	6,917,000	6,885,000
Interest Expense	288,000	839,000	745,000	735,000	768,000	891,000	1,060,000	1,378,000
Net Interest Income	1,633,000	6,535,000	6,321,000	5,592,000	5,374,000	5,616,000	5,857,000	5,507,000
Provision for Losses	150,000	547,000	572,000	428,000	251,000	592,000	1,057,000	1,190,000
Non-Interest Income	1,180,000	4,782,000	4,472,000	4,019,000	3,784,000	3,937,000	3,820,000	3,113,000
Non-Interest Expense	1,686,000	7,444,000	6,721,000	6,266,000	5,921,000	5,837,000	5,828,000	5,802,000
Income Before Taxes	977,000	3,326,000	3,500,000	2,917,000	2,986,000	3,124,000	2,792,000	1,628,000
Income Taxes	186,000	911,000	1,058,000	794,000	760,000	1,395,000	764,000	296,000
Net Income	788,000	2,394,000	2,426,000	2,084,000	2,151,000	1,679,000	1,979,000	1,289,000
Average Shares	791,005	810,977	814,916	757,765	728,372	714,363	708,877	705,168
Balance Sheet								
Net Loans & Leases	142,708,000	143,310,000	143,549,000	135,526,000	119,833,000	115,407,000	116,346,000	108,949,000
Total Assets	220,729,000	221,642,000	219,276,000	209,947,000	186,814,000	183,010,000	183,872,000	174,579,000
Total Deposits	158,196,000	157,371,000	160,234,000	149,124,000	129,040,000	127,475,000	133,075,000	124,939,000
Total Liabilities	191,117,000	191,994,000	189,395,000	182,641,000	162,476,000	160,251,000	162,714,000	157,161,000
Stockholders' Equity	29,612,000	29,648,000	29,881,000	27,306,000	24,338,000	22,759,000	21,158,000	17,418,000
Shares Outstanding	779,752	782,006	809,475	780,337	720,698	706,620	699,728	697,143
Statistical Record								
Return on Assets %	1.25	1.09	1.13	1.05	1.16	0.92	1.10	0.78
Return on Equity %	9.26	8.04	8.46	8.07	9.13	7.65	10.23	7.62
Net Interest Margin %	85.01	88.62	89.46	88.38	87.50	86.31	84.68	79.99
Efficiency Ratio %	54.37	61.24	58.25	60.56	59.65	55.89	54.28	58.03
Loans to Deposits	0.90	0.91	0.90	0.91	0.93	0.91	0.87	0.87
Price Range	56.03-41.65	50.45-41.65	47.71-30.28	41.60-34.78	40.77-35.20	37.32-29.11	33.99-25.79	29.17-19.17
P/E Ratio	17.40-12.93	18.41-15.20	17.22-10.93	16.25-13.59	14.83-12.80	17.04-13.29	12.59-9.55	15.94-10.48
Average Yield %	2.79	2.73	3.11	2.74	2.50	3.39	2.51	2.56

Address: 200 West Second Street, Winston-Salem, NC 27101
Telephone: 336-733-2000
Fax: 336-671-2399

Web Site: www.bbt.com
Officers: Kelly S. King - Chairman, Chief Executive Officer, Chief Operating Officer Christopher L. Henson - President, Chief Operating Officer

Auditors: PricewaterhouseCoopers LLP
Investor Contact: 336-733-3021
Transfer Agents: Computershare Trust Company, N.A., Providence, RI

BECTON, DICKINSON & CO

Exchange	Symbol	Price	52Wk Range	Yield	P/E	Div Acheiver
NYS	BDX	$239.56 (6/29/2018)	246.28-191.56	1.25	N/A	45 Years

*7 Year Price Score 128.64 *NYSE Composite Index=100 ***12 Month Price Score 104.70**

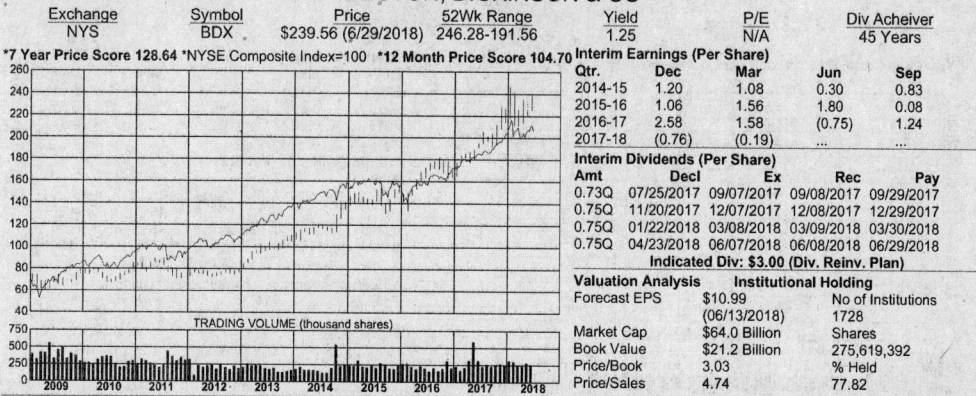

Interim Earnings (Per Share)

Qtr.	Dec	Mar	Jun	Sep
2014-15	1.20	1.08	0.30	0.83
2015-16	1.06	1.56	1.80	0.08
2016-17	2.58	1.58	(0.75)	1.24
2017-18	(0.76)	(0.19)	...	...

Interim Dividends (Per Share)

Amt	Decl	Ex	Rec	Pay
0.73Q	07/25/2017	09/07/2017	09/08/2017	09/29/2017
0.75Q	11/20/2017	12/07/2017	12/08/2017	12/29/2017
0.75Q	01/22/2018	03/08/2018	03/09/2018	03/30/2018
0.75Q	04/23/2018	06/07/2018	06/08/2018	06/29/2018

Indicated Div: $3.00 (Div. Reinv. Plan)

Valuation Analysis / Institutional Holding

Forecast EPS	$10.99	No of Institutions
	(06/13/2018)	1728
Market Cap	$64.0 Billion	Shares
Book Value	$21.2 Billion	275,619,392
Price/Book	3.03	% Held
Price/Sales	4.74	77.82

Business Summary: Medical Instruments & Equipment (MIC: 4.3.1 SIC: 3841 NAIC: 339112)

Becton, Dickinson and Company is a medical technology company engaged in the development, manufacture and sale of a range of medical supplies, devices, laboratory equipment and diagnostic products. Co.'s operations consist of two business segments: BD Medical and BD Life Sciences. BD Medical segment produces an array of medical technologies and devices that are used to help improve healthcare delivery in a range of settings. BD Life Sciences segment provides products for the safe collection and transport of diagnostics specimens, and instruments and reagent systems to detect a range of infectious diseases, healthcare-associated infections and cancers.

Recent Developments:
For the quarter ended Mar 31 2018, net loss amounted to US$12.0 million versus net income of US$344.0 million in the year-earlier quarter. Revenues were US$4.22 billion, up 42.2% from US$2.97 billion the year before. Operating income was US$183.0 million versus US$446.0 million in the prior-year quarter, a decrease of 59.0%. Direct operating expenses rose 70.4% to US$2.62 billion from US$1.54 billion in the comparable period the year before. Indirect operating expenses increased 44.0% to US$1.42 billion from US$987.0 million in the equivalent prior-year period.

Prospects:
Our evaluation of Becton, Dickinson and Co. as of Jan. 21, 2018 is the result of our systematic analysis on three basic characteristics: earnings strength, relative valuation, and recent stock price movement. The company has managed to produce a neutral trend in earnings per share over the past 5 quarters and while recent estimates for the company have been raised by analysts, BDX has posted better than expected results. Based on operating earnings yield, the company is about fairly valued when compared to all of the companies in our coverage universe. Share price changes over the past year indicates that BDX will perform in line with the market over the near term.

Financial Data
(US$ in Thousands)

	6 Mos	3 Mos	09/30/2017	09/30/2016	09/30/2015	09/30/2014	09/30/2013	09/30/2012
Earnings Per Share	(0.46)	1.31	4.60	4.49	3.35	5.99	6.49	5.59
Cash Flow Per Share	9.45	11.11	11.65	12.00	8.54	9.03	8.80	8.22
Tang Book Value Per Share	N.M.	N.M.	N.M.	N.M.	N.M.	14.79	14.07	9.65
Dividends Per Share	2.960	2.940	2.920	2.640	2.400	2.180	1.980	1.800
Dividend Payout %	...	224.43	63.48	58.80	71.64	36.39	30.51	32.20
Income Statement								
Total Revenue	7,302,000	3,080,000	12,093,000	12,483,000	10,282,000	8,446,000	8,054,000	7,708,382
EBITDA	1,257,000	512,000	2,509,000	2,555,000	1,986,000	2,173,000	1,809,000	2,067,671
Depn & Amortn	844,000	291,000	1,088,000	1,114,000	891,000	562,000	546,000	510,938
Income Before Taxes	118,000	107,000	976,000	1,074,000	739,000	1,522,000	1,165,000	1,472,408
Income Taxes	260,000	241,000	(124,000)	97,000	44,000	337,000	236,000	362,880
Net Income	(148,000)	(136,000)	1,100,000	976,000	695,000	1,185,000	1,293,000	1,169,927
Average Shares	267,341	230,038	223,588	217,536	207,509	197,709	199,193	209,181
Balance Sheet								
Current Assets	7,512,000	7,542,000	18,633,000	6,367,000	6,045,000	6,131,000	5,873,000	5,322,071
Total Assets	54,573,000	55,363,000	37,734,000	25,586,000	26,820,000	12,447,000	12,149,000	11,360,909
Current Liabilities	4,426,000	4,895,000	3,342,000	4,400,000	4,386,000	2,235,000	2,130,000	1,978,055
Long-Term Obligations	22,589,000	22,095,000	18,664,000	10,550,000	11,370,000	3,769,000	3,763,000	3,761,112
Total Liabilities	33,420,000	34,115,000	24,783,000	17,953,000	19,656,000	7,396,000	7,106,000	7,225,020
Stockholders' Equity	21,152,000	21,247,000	12,948,000	7,633,000	7,164,000	5,053,000	5,043,000	4,135,889
Shares Outstanding	267,201	266,242	227,942	213,291	210,695	191,892	193,999	196,911
Statistical Record								
Return on Assets %	0.12	1.01	3.47	3.71	3.54	9.64	11.00	10.71
Return on Equity %	0.32	2.80	10.69	13.16	11.38	23.47	28.17	26.03
EBITDA Margin %	17.21	16.62	20.75	20.47	19.32	25.73	22.46	26.82
Net Margin %	N.M.	N.M.	9.10	7.82	6.76	14.03	16.05	15.18
Asset Turnover	0.34	0.31	0.38	0.48	0.52	0.69	0.69	0.71
Current Ratio	1.70	1.54	5.58	1.45	1.38	2.74	2.76	2.69
Debt to Equity	1.07	1.04	1.44	1.38	1.59	0.75	0.75	0.91
Price Range	246.28-177.07	228.21-164.80	205.63-162.80	181.55-132.19	153.86-113.60	120.33-98.33	104.50-74.63	79.91-70.65
P/E Ratio	...	174.21-125.80	44.70-35.39	40.43-29.44	45.93-33.91	20.09-16.42	16.10-11.50	14.30-12.64
Average Yield %	1.44	1.51	1.59	1.67	1.72	1.93	2.18	2.39

Address: 1 Becton Drive, Franklin Lakes, NJ 07417-1880	Web Site: www.bd.com	Auditors: Ernst & Young LLP
Telephone: 201-847-6800	Officers: Vincent A. Forlenza - Chairman, President, Chief Executive Officer, Chief Operating Officer Thomas E. Polen - President, Executive Vice President, Division Officer	Investor Contact: 180-028-46845 Transfer Agents: Computershare Trust Company, N.A., Canton, MA

BELDEN INC

Exchange	Symbol	Price	52Wk Range	Yield	P/E
NYS	BDC	$61.12 (6/29/2018)	87.00-54.50	0.33	74.54

*7 Year Price Score 97.59 *NYSE Composite Index=100 *12 Month Price Score 78.50

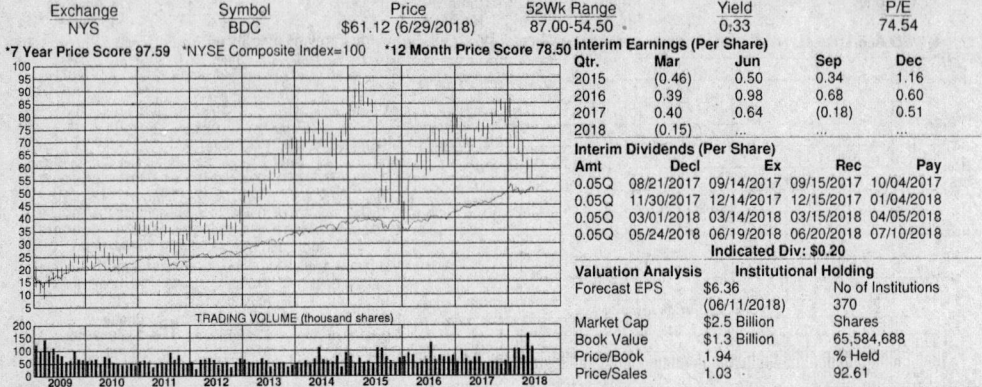

Interim Earnings (Per Share)
Qtr.	Mar	Jun	Sep	Dec
2015	(0.46)	0.50	0.34	1.16
2016	0.39	0.98	0.68	0.60
2017	0.40	0.64	(0.18)	0.51
2018	(0.15)	...	...	...

Interim Dividends (Per Share)
Amt	Decl	Ex	Rec	Pay
0.05Q	08/21/2017	09/14/2017	09/15/2017	10/04/2017
0.05Q	11/30/2017	12/14/2017	12/15/2017	01/04/2018
0.05Q	03/01/2018	03/14/2018	03/15/2018	04/05/2018
0.05Q	05/24/2018	06/19/2018	06/20/2018	07/10/2018

Indicated Div: $0.20

Valuation Analysis
		Institutional Holding	
Forecast EPS	$6.36	No of Institutions	370
	(06/11/2018)		
Market Cap	$2.5 Billion	Shares	
Book Value	$1.3 Billion	65,584,688	
Price/Book	1.94	% Held	
Price/Sales	1.03	92.61	

Business Summary: Electrical Equipment (MIC: 7.3.1 SIC: 3357 NAIC: 335921)

Belden is a signal transmission solutions company. Co. has five segments: Broadcast Solutions, which provides production, distribution, and connectivity systems for television broadcast, cable, satellite, and Internet Protocol television industries; Enterprise Connectivity Solutions, which provides network infrastructure solutions; Industrial Connectivity Solutions, which provides networking components and connectivity products; Industrial IT Solutions, which provides networking systems for markets such as discrete manufacturing, process, including oil and gas, energy and transportation; and Network Security Solutions, which provides software and services that protect against cyberattacks.

Recent Developments: For the quarter ended Apr 1 2018, net income decreased 90.0% to US$2.6 million from US$25.6 million in the year-earlier quarter. Revenues were US$605.6 million, up 9.8% from US$551.4 million the year before. Operating income was US$44.2 million versus US$51.6 million in the prior-year quarter, a decrease of 14.3%. Direct operating expenses rose 14.0% to US$375.0 million from US$329.0 million in the comparable period the year before. Indirect operating expenses increased 9.1% to US$186.4 million from US$170.8 million in the equivalent prior-year period.

Prospects: Our evaluation of Belden Inc. as of Jan. 21, 2018 is the result of our systematic analysis on three basic characteristics: earnings strength, relative valuation, and recent stock price movement. The company has enjoyed a very positive trend in earnings per share over the past 5 quarters and while recent estimates for the company have been mixed, BDC has posted better than expected results. Based on operating earnings yield, the company is undervalued when compared to all of the companies in our coverage universe. Share price changes over the past year indicates that BDC will perform poorly over the near term.

Financial Data
(US$ in Thousands)	3 Mos	12/31/2017	12/31/2016	12/31/2015	12/31/2014	12/31/2013	12/31/2012	12/31/2011
Earnings Per Share	0.82	1.37	2.65	1.54	1.69	2.31	4.23	2.38
Cash Flow Per Share	4.41	6.05	7.46	5.58	4.48	3.75	3.08	3.92
Tang Book Value Per Share	N.M.	N.M.	N.M.	N.M.	N.M.	N.M.	N.M.	4.25
Dividends Per Share	0.200	0.200	0.200	0.200	0.200	0.200	0.200	0.200
Dividend Payout %	24.39	14.60	7.55	12.99	11.83	8.66	4.73	8.40
Income Statement								
Total Revenue	605,565	2,388,643	2,356,672	2,309,222	2,308,265	2,069,193	1,840,739	1,981,953
EBITDA	60,286	331,846	367,096	289,174	261,290	285,131	104,235	224,009
Depn & Amortn	36,318	149,597	145,585	150,391	102,126	94,403	57,892	50,172
Income Before Taxes	6,990	99,348	126,461	38,170	77,591	118,127	(4,662)	126,722
Income Taxes	4,420	6,495	(1,185)	(26,568)	7,114	22,315	(38,194)	24,638
Net Income	2,618	93,210	128,003	66,204	74,449	103,313	194,490	114,345
Average Shares	41,633	42,643	42,557	42,953	43,997	44,737	45,942	48,104
Balance Sheet								
Current Assets	1,183,482	1,372,071	1,478,952	843,164	1,414,150	1,195,498	959,582	925,421
Total Assets	3,766,549	3,840,613	3,806,803	3,315,841	3,262,827	2,751,753	2,584,583	1,788,120
Current Liabilities	589,124	678,928	570,279	549,263	525,359	401,566	452,482	381,566
Long-Term Obligations	1,662,654	1,560,748	1,620,161	1,750,521	1,765,422	1,364,536	1,135,527	550,926
Total Liabilities	2,475,002	2,406,378	2,346,490	2,491,742	2,455,641	1,915,212	1,772,723	1,093,571
Stockholders' Equity	1,291,547	1,434,235	1,460,313	824,099	807,186	836,541	811,860	694,549
Shares Outstanding	41,003	42,019	42,180	41,981	42,464	43,455	44,168	45,825
Statistical Record								
Return on Assets %	1.86	2.44	3.58	2.01	2.48	3.87	8.87	6.56
Return on Equity %	5.09	6.44	11.18	8.12	9.06	12.53	25.75	17.16
EBITDA Margin %	9.96	13.89	15.58	12.52	11.32	13.78	5.66	11.30
Net Margin %	0.43	3.90	5.43	2.87	3.23	4.99	10.57	5.77
Asset Turnover	0.65	0.62	0.66	0.70	0.77	0.78	0.84	1.14
Current Ratio	2.01	2.02	2.59	1.54	2.69	2.98	2.12	2.43
Debt to Equity	1.29	1.09	1.11	2.12	2.19	1.63	1.40	0.79
Price Range	87.00-64.55	86.29-64.68	80.48-37.15	95.14-45.10	80.96-58.56	71.30-44.99	44.99-30.24	40.32-23.93
P/E Ratio	106.10-78.72	62.99-47.21	30.37-14.02	61.78-29.29	47.91-34.65	30.87-19.48	10.64-7.15	16.94-10.05
Average Yield %	0.26	0.26	0.32	0.28	0.28	0.35	0.55	0.59

Address: 1 North Brentwood Boulevard, 15th Floor, St. Louis, MO 63105
Telephone: 314-854-8000
Fax: 314-854-8001

Web Site: www.belden.com
Officers: John S. Stroup - Chairman, President, Chief Executive Officer Ross Rosenberg - Senior Vice President

Auditors: Ernst & Young LLP
Investor Contact: 314-854-8054
Transfer Agents: American Stock Transfer & Trust Company, Brooklyn, NY

BEMIS CO INC

Exchange	Symbol	Price	52Wk Range	Yield	P/E	Div Acheiver
NYS	BMS	$42.21 (6/29/2018)	49.22-40.96	2.94	42.64	34 Years

*7 Year Price Score 86.91   *NYSE Composite Index=100   *12 Month Price Score 93.99

Interim Earnings (Per Share)

Qtr.	Mar	Jun	Sep	Dec
2015	0.55	0.67	0.64	0.58
2016	0.59	0.53	0.72	0.64
2017	0.55	0.30	0.61	(0.44)
2018	0.52	...	...	...

Interim Dividends (Per Share)

Amt	Decl	Ex	Rec	Pay
0.30Q	08/03/2017	08/15/2017	08/17/2017	09/01/2017
0.30Q	11/02/2017	11/14/2017	11/15/2017	12/01/2017
0.31Q	02/08/2018	02/16/2018	02/20/2018	03/01/2018
0.31Q	05/03/2018	05/16/2018	05/17/2018	06/01/2018

Indicated Div: $1.24 (Div. Reinv. Plan)

Valuation Analysis

		Institutional Holding	
Forecast EPS	$2.79 (06/14/2018)	No of Institutions	525
Market Cap	$3.8 Billion	Shares	98,880,840
Book Value	$1.2 Billion	% Held	70.14
Price/Book	3.10		
Price/Sales	0.94		

Business Summary: Containers & Packaging (MIC: 8.1.3 SIC: 2671 NAIC: 322221)

Bemis Co is a manufacturer of packaging products. The majority of Co.'s products are sold to customers in the food industry. The U.S. Packaging segment represents all food, consumer, and industrial products packaging-related manufacturing operations located in the U.S. This segment manufactures multilayer polymer, blown and cast film structures which are then converted to produce packaging for processed and fresh meat, dairy, liquids, and frozen foods. The Global Packaging segment includes all packaging-related manufacturing operations located outside of the U.S. as well as global medical device and pharmaceutical packaging-related manufacturing operations.

Recent Developments: For the quarter ended Mar 31 2018, net income decreased 6.8% to US$47.6 million from US$51.1 million in the year-earlier quarter. Revenues were US$1.03 billion, up 3.2% from US$995.4 million the year before. Operating income was US$80.5 million versus US$88.4 million in the prior-year quarter, a decrease of 8.9%. Direct operating expenses rose 4.1% to US$829.4 million from US$797.1 million in the comparable period the year before. Indirect operating expenses increased 6.9% to US$117.5 million from US$109.9 million in the equivalent prior-year period.

Prospects: Our evaluation of Bemis Co Inc. as of Jan. 21, 2018 is the result of our systematic analysis on three basic characteristics: earnings strength, relative valuation, and recent stock price movement. The company has managed to produce a neutral trend in earnings per share over the past 5 quarters and while recent estimates for the company have been mixed, BMS has posted better than expected results. Based on operating earnings yield, the company is undervalued when compared to all of the companies in our coverage universe. Share price changes over the past year indicates that BMS will perform in line with the market over the near term.

Financial Data

(US$ in Thousands)	3 Mos	12/31/2017	12/31/2016	12/31/2015	12/31/2014	12/31/2013	12/31/2012	12/31/2011
Earnings Per Share	0.99	1.02	2.48	2.44	1.89	2.04	1.66	1.73
Cash Flow Per Share	3.72	4.14	4.63	5.71	2.48	3.63	4.07	4.02
Tang Book Value Per Share	2.67	2.27	0.82	1.14	3.07	4.34	3.93	3.02
Dividends Per Share	1.210	1.200	1.160	1.120	1.080	1.040	1.000	0.960
Dividend Payout %	122.22	117.65	46.77	45.90	57.14	50.98	60.24	55.49
Income Statement								
Total Revenue	1,027,400	4,046,200	4,004,400	4,071,400	4,343,500	5,029,800	5,139,200	5,322,670
EBITDA	124,600	271,300	557,200	559,800	594,500	578,800	555,200	590,232
Depn & Amortn	43,200	152,800	146,100	144,200	170,000	190,300	205,700	221,200
Income Before Taxes	62,500	52,700	350,900	363,900	363,700	320,300	278,600	292,223
Income Taxes	14,900	(41,300)	114,700	122,000	124,600	107,700	104,800	104,900
Net Income	47,600	94,000	236,200	239,300	191,100	212,600	173,800	184,081
Average Shares	91,200	91,900	95,100	97,900	101,200	103,900	103,900	105,072
Balance Sheet								
Current Assets	1,285,200	1,237,100	1,165,500	1,119,000	1,287,800	1,504,500	1,525,000	1,549,011
Total Assets	3,753,800	3,699,900	3,715,700	3,489,800	3,615,100	4,110,200	4,185,700	4,320,444
Current Liabilities	682,700	666,100	576,100	589,100	481,400	601,900	643,000	681,965
Long-Term Obligations	1,544,200	1,542,400	1,527,800	1,353,900	1,315,900	1,421,400	1,417,600	1,554,750
Total Liabilities	2,515,600	2,498,700	2,456,000	2,282,400	2,182,100	2,425,400	2,544,800	2,738,341
Stockholders' Equity	1,238,200	1,201,200	1,259,700	1,207,400	1,433,000	1,684,800	1,640,900	1,582,103
Shares Outstanding	91,000	90,800	92,700	95,100	98,200	101,900	103,200	102,983
Statistical Record								
Return on Assets %	2.40	2.54	6.54	6.74	4.95	5.13	4.08	4.28
Return on Equity %	7.24	7.64	19.10	18.13	12.26	12.79	10.76	10.64
EBITDA Margin %	12.13	6.71	13.91	13.75	13.69	11.51	10.80	11.09
Net Margin %	4.63	2.32	5.90	5.88	4.40	4.23	3.38	3.46
Asset Turnover	1.08	1.09	1.11	1.15	1.12	1.21	1.21	1.24
Current Ratio	1.88	1.86	2.02	1.90	2.68	2.50	2.37	2.27
Debt to Equity	1.25	1.28	1.21	1.12	0.92	0.84	0.86	0.98
Price Range	50.19-40.96	51.65-40.96	54.08-43.25	49.33-39.17	46.08-37.17	42.23-33.46	33.79-29.78	34.25-27.53
P/E Ratio	50.70-41.37	50.64-40.16	21.81-17.44	20.22-16.05	24.38-19.67	20.70-16.40	20.36-17.94	19.80-15.91
Average Yield %	2.65	2.58	2.33	2.48	2.70	2.66	3.17	3.07

Address: 2301 Industrial Drive, Neenah, WI 54956	Web Site: www.bemis.com	Auditors: PricewaterhouseCoopers LLP
Telephone: 920-527-5000	Officers: Timothy M. Manganello - Chairman, William F. Austen - President, Chief Executive Officer, Executive Vice President, Vice President, Chief Operating Officer, Division Officer	Investor Contact: 920-727-4100, Transfer Agents: Wells Fargo Bank, N.A., South St. Paul, MN

BERKLEY (WR) CORP

Exchange	Symbol	Price	52Wk Range	Yield	P/E	Div Acheiver
NYS	WRB	$72.41 (6/29/2018)	78.31-62.54	0.83	15.67	16 Years

*7 Year Price Score 111.45 *NYSE Composite Index=100 *12 Month Price Score 105.56

Interim Earnings (Per Share)

Qtr.	Mar	Jun	Sep	Dec
2015	0.89	0.95	1.18	0.85
2016	0.93	0.85	1.72	1.18
2017	0.96	0.85	1.26	1.21
2018	1.30	...	...	...

Interim Dividends (Per Share)

Amt	Decl	Ex	Rec	Pay
0.14Q	11/13/2017	11/29/2017	11/30/2017	12/14/2017
0.14Q	02/28/2018	03/13/2018	03/14/2018	04/02/2018
0.50Sp	05/31/2018	06/08/2018	06/11/2018	06/18/2018
0.15Q	05/31/2018	06/14/2018	06/15/2018	07/05/2018

Indicated Div: $0.60

Valuation Analysis

		Institutional Holding	
Forecast EPS	$3.65 (06/14/2018)	No of Institutions	564
Market Cap	$8.8 Billion	Shares	123,615,816
Book Value	$5.5 Billion	% Held	63.86
Price/Book	1.61		
Price/Sales	1.14		

TRADING VOLUME (thousand shares)

Business Summary: General Insurance (MIC: 5.2.1 SIC: 6331 NAIC: 524126)

W. R. Berkley is an insurance holding company. Co. operates in two segments of the property casualty insurance business: Insurance, which includes commercial insurance business, including excess and surplus lines and admitted lines, throughout the U.S., as well as insurance business in the U.K., Continental Europe, South America, Canada, Mexico, Scandinavia, Asia and Australia; and Reinsurance, which provides reinsurance business on a facultative and treaty basis in the U.S., U.K., Continental Europe, Australia, the Asia-Pacific region and South Africa. Co. also invests in equity securities, merger arbitrage securities, investment funds, private equity, loans and real estate related assets.

Recent Developments: For the quarter ended Mar 31 2018, net income increased 34.4% to US$167.6 million from US$124.7 million in the year-earlier quarter. Revenues were US$1.89 billion, up 1.1% from US$1.87 billion the year before. Net premiums earned were unchanged at US$1.57 billion versus the prior-year quarter. Net investment income rose 17.2% to US$174.5 million from US$148.9 million a year ago.

Prospects: Our evaluation of Berkley (W. R.) Corp. as of Jan. 21, 2018 is the result of our systematic analysis on three basic characteristics: earnings strength, relative valuation, and recent stock price movement. The company has generated a negative trend in earnings per share over the past 5 quarters. However, while recent estimates for the company have been mixed, WRB has posted better than expected results. Based on operating earnings yield, the company is about fairly valued when compared to all of the companies in our coverage universe. Share price changes over the past year indicates that WRB will perform in line with the market over the near term.

Financial Data
(US$ in Thousands)

	3 Mos	12/31/2017	12/31/2016	12/31/2015	12/31/2014	12/31/2013	12/31/2012	12/31/2011
Earnings Per Share	4.62	4.26	4.68	3.87	4.86	3.55	3.56	2.71
Cash Flow Per Share	4.87	5.69	6.90	7.10	5.75	6.06	4.91	4.80
Tang Book Value Per Share	43.38	43.06	40.45	36.06	35.02	31.96	31.01	28.49
Dividends Per Share	1.560	1.550	1.510	0.470	1.430	0.390	1.350	0.310
Dividend Payout %	33.77	36.38	32.26	12.14	29.42	10.99	37.92	11.44
Income Statement								
Premium Income	1,567,408	6,311,419	6,293,348	6,040,609	5,744,418	5,226,537	4,673,516	4,160,867
Total Revenue	1,891,247	7,684,764	7,654,184	7,206,457	7,128,928	6,408,534	5,823,554	5,155,984
Benefits & Claims	963,219	4,002,348	3,845,800	3,656,270	3,490,567	3,197,024	2,948,479	2,658,365
Income Before Taxes	210,990	772,770	896,438	732,030	952,196	698,888	701,928	518,283
Income Taxes	43,417	219,433	292,953	227,923	302,593	193,587	191,285	123,550
Net Income	166,396	549,094	601,916	503,694	648,884	499,925	510,592	394,803
Average Shares	128,125	129,017	128,552	130,188	133,652	140,742	143,314	145,672
Balance Sheet								
Total Assets	24,587,832	24,299,917	23,364,844	21,730,967	21,716,691	20,551,796	20,155,896	18,487,731
Total Liabilities	19,136,056	18,888,573	18,317,636	17,130,721	17,126,746	16,215,761	15,849,679	14,479,305
Stockholders' Equity	5,451,776	5,411,344	5,047,208	4,600,246	4,589,945	4,336,035	4,306,217	4,008,426
Shares Outstanding	121,543	121,514	121,193	123,307	126,748	132,233	136,017	137,520
Statistical Record								
Return on Assets %	2.46	2.30	2.66	2.32	3.07	2.46	2.64	2.19
Return on Equity %	11.14	10.50	12.44	10.96	14.54	11.57	12.25	10.24
Loss Ratio %	61.45	63.41	61.11	60.53	60.76	61.17	63.09	63.89
Net Margin %	8.80	7.15	7.86	6.99	9.10	7.80	8.77	7.66
Price Range	73.43-62.54	72.98-62.54	66.75-47.95	58.41-48.40	53.96-37.93	45.39-37.74	40.21-33.85	35.68-26.71
P/E Ratio	15.89-13.54	17.13-14.68	14.26-10.25	15.09-12.51	11.10-7.80	12.79-10.63	11.29-9.51	13.17-9.86
Average Yield %	2.27	2.26	2.66	0.89	3.13	0.92	3.60	1.00

Address: 475 Steamboat Road, Greenwich, CT 06830 Telephone: 203-629-3000	Web Site: www.wrberkley.com Officers: William R. Berkley - Executive Chairman, Chairman, Chief Executive Officer W. Robert Berkley - President, Chief Executive Officer, Chief Operating Officer	Auditors: KPMG LLP Investor Contact: 203-629-3040 Transfer Agents: Wells Fargo Bank, N.A., Mendota Heights, MN

BERKSHIRE HATHAWAY INC

Exchange	Symbol	Price	52Wk Range	Yield	P/E
NYS	BRK B	$282040 (6/29/2018)	325915.00-254700.00	N/A	11.67

*7 Year Price Score 117.29 *NYSE Composite Index=100   *12 Month Price Score 99.84

Interim Earnings (Per Share)

Qtr.	Mar	Jun	Sep	Dec
2015	3143.00	2442.00	5737.00	3333.00
2016	3401.00	3042.00	4379.00	3823.00
2017	2469.00	2592.00	2473.00	19793.00
2018	(692.00)	...	...	...

Interim Dividends (Per Share)

No Dividends Paid

Valuation Analysis		Institutional Holding	
Forecast EPS	$13526.35	No of Institutions	2735
	(06/10/2018)		
Market Cap	$464.0 Billion	Shares	
Book Value	$347.4 Billion		1,024,661,440
Price/Book	1.34	% Held	
Price/Sales	1.97		15.99

Business Summary: General Insurance (MIC: 5.2.1 SIC: 6331 NAIC: 524126)

Berkshire Hathaway is a holding company. Co.'s subsidiaries are engaged in several business activities which include: underwriting private passenger automobile insurance; operation of a railroad system in North America; regulated electric and gas utility; manufacturing of products including industrial, consumer and building products; wholesale distribution of groceries and non-food items; provider of services including aviation pilot training, electronic components distribution and retailing businesses, including automotive dealerships; and manufactured housing and related consumer financing, transportation equipment, manufacturing and leasing, and furniture leasing.

Recent Developments: For the quarter ended Mar 31 2018, net loss amounted to US$1.07 billion versus net income of US$4.14 billion in the year-earlier quarter. Revenues were US$58.47 billion, down 9.2% from US$64.37 billion the year before. Net premiums earned were US$13.37 billion versus US$21.75 billion in the prior-year quarter, a decrease of 38.5%.

Prospects: Our evaluation of Berkshire Hathaway Inc. as of Aug. 27, 2017 is the result of our systematic analysis on three basic characteristics: earnings strength, relative valuation, and recent stock price movement. The company has produced a positive trend in earnings per share over the past 5 quarters. However, while recent estimates for the company have been lowered by analysts, BRK.B has posted results that fell short of analysts expectations. Based on operating earnings yield, the company is about fairly valued when compared to all of the companies in our coverage universe. Share price changes over the past year indicates that BRK.B will perform poorly over the near term.

Financial Data
(US$ in Thousands)

	3 Mos	12/31/2017	12/31/2016	12/31/2015	12/31/2014	12/31/2013	12/31/2012	12/31/2011
Earnings Per Share	24,166.00	27,326.00	14,645.00	14,656.00	12,092.00	11,850.00	8,977.00	6,215.00
Cash Flow Per Share	21,293.55	27,833.87	19,738.16	19,164.63	19,477.25	16,855.55	12,652.36	12,410.52
Tang Book Value Per Share	142,129.05	142,578.70	103,406.82	111,777.28	109,230.64	100,294.17	81,027.67	67,625.75
Income Statement								
Premium Income	13,373,000	60,597,000	45,881,000	41,294,000	41,253,000	36,684,000	34,545,000	32,075,000
Total Revenue	58,473,000	242,137,000	223,604,000	210,821,000	194,673,000	182,150,000	162,463,000	143,688,000
Benefits & Claims	10,250,000	54,509,000	36,037,000	31,940,000	31,587,000	26,347,000	25,227,000	25,708,000
Income Before Taxes	(1,924,000)	20,900,000	32,744,000	34,946,000	28,105,000	28,796,000	22,236,000	15,314,000
Income Taxes	(452,000)	(21,515,000)	9,240,000	10,532,000	7,935,000	8,951,000	6,924,000	4,568,000
Net Income	(1,138,000)	44,940,000	24,074,000	24,083,000	19,872,000	19,476,000	14,824,000	10,254,000
Average Shares	1,644	1,644	1,643	1,643	1,643	1,643	1,651	1,649
Balance Sheet								
Total Assets	702,651,000	702,095,000	620,854,000	552,257,000	526,186,000	484,931,000	427,452,000	392,647,000
Total Liabilities	355,250,000	353,799,000	337,853,000	296,707,000	286,016,000	263,041,000	239,805,000	227,797,000
Stockholders' Equity	347,401,000	348,296,000	283,001,000	255,550,000	240,170,000	221,890,000	187,647,000	164,850,000
Shares Outstanding	1,645	1,644	1,644	1,643	1,642	1,643	1,642	1,650
Statistical Record								
Return on Assets %	5.86	6.79	4.09	4.47	3.93	4.27	3.61	2.68
Return on Equity %	12.41	14.24	8.92	9.72	8.60	9.51	8.39	6.37
Loss Ratio %	76.65	89.95	78.54	77.35	76.57	71.82	73.03	80.15
Net Margin %	(1.95)	18.56	10.77	11.42	10.21	10.69	9.12	7.14
Price Range	325915-242510	299360-238100	249711-187001	226680-192200	229300-164075	178275-134060	135936-114500	131300-100000
P/E Ratio	13.49-10.04	10.96-8.71	17.05-12.77	15.47-13.11	18.96-13.57	15.04-11.31	15.14-12.75	21.13-16.09

Address: 3555 Farnam Street, Omaha, NE 68131 **Telephone:** 402-346-1400	**Web Site:** www.berkshirehathaway.com **Officers:** Warren E. Buffett - Chairman, Chief Executive Officer Charles T. Munger - Vice-Chairman	**Auditors:** DELOITTE & TOUCHE LLP **Transfer Agents:** Wells Fargo Bank, N.A., St. Paul, MN

BERRY GLOBAL GROUP INC

Exchange	Symbol	Price	52Wk Range	Yield	P/E
NYS	BERY	$45.94 (6/29/2018)	61.03-45.68	N/A	13.28

'7 Year Price Score N/A *NYSE Composite Index=100 **'12 Month Price Score 86.64**

Interim Earnings (Per Share)

Qtr.	Dec	Mar	Jun	Sep
2014-15	0.11	0.31	(0.11)	0.39
2015-16	0.03	0.47	0.76	0.61
2016-17	0.40	0.54	0.79	0.81
2017-18	1.20	0.66	...	...

Interim Dividends (Per Share)

No Dividends Paid

Valuation Analysis

		Institutional Holding	
Forecast EPS	$3.62	No of Institutions	467
	(06/14/2018)		
Market Cap	$6.0 Billion	Shares	
Book Value	$1.3 Billion		134,946,080
Price/Book	4.64	% Held	
Price/Sales	0.80		99.29

Business Summary: Plastics (MIC: 8.4.2 SIC: 3089 NAIC: 326199)

Berry Global Group is a provider of plastic consumer packaging, nonwoven specialty materials and engineered materials. Co. operates in three operating segments: Health, Hygiene & Specialties, which consists of nonwoven specialty materials used in hygiene, infection prevention, personal care, industrial, construction, and filtration applications; Consumer Packaging, which consists of containers, foodservice items, closures, overcaps, bottles, prescription vials, tubes, and printed films; and Engineered Materials, which consists of pipeline corrosion protection solutions, tapes and adhesives, polyethylene based film products, can liners, and specialty coated and laminated products.

Recent Developments: For the quarter ended Mar 31 2018, net income increased 25.0% to US$90.0 million from US$72.0 million in the year-earlier quarter. Revenues were US$1.97 billion, up 8.9% from US$1.81 billion the year before. Operating income was US$188.0 million versus US$175.0 million in the prior-year quarter, an increase of 7.4%. Direct operating expenses rose 9.8% to US$1.60 billion from US$1.45 billion in the comparable period the year before. Indirect operating expenses increased 2.8% to US$183.0 million from US$178.0 million in the equivalent prior-year period.

Prospects: Our evaluation of Berry Global Group Inc. as of Jan. 21, 2018 is the result of our systematic analysis on three basic characteristics: earnings strength, relative valuation, and recent stock price movement. The company has managed to produce a neutral trend in earnings per share over the past 5 quarters and while recent estimates for the company have been raised by analysts, BERY has posted better than expected results. Based on operating earnings yield, the company is undervalued when compared to all of the companies in our coverage universe. Share price changes over the past year indicates that BERY will perform well over the near term.

Financial Data
(US$ in Millions)

	6 Mos	3 Mos	09/30/2017	10/01/2016	09/26/2015	09/27/2014	09/28/2013	09/29/2012
Earnings Per Share	3.46	3.34	2.56	1.89	0.70	0.51	0.48	0.02
Cash Flow Per Share	7.06	7.52	7.66	6.98	5.36	4.55	4.10	5.76
Income Statement								
Total Revenue	3,743	1,776	7,095	6,489	4,881	4,958	4,647	4,766
EBITDA	598	283	1,239	1,124	663	646	670	687
Depn & Amortn	261	129	521	525	350	358	341	355
Income Before Taxes	209	92	449	308	122	67	85	4
Income Taxes	(44)	(71)	109	72	36	4	28	2
Net Income	253	163	340	236	86	62	57	2
Average Shares	135	136	132	125	123	121	119	86
Balance Sheet								
Current Assets	2,261	1,981	2,004	1,792	1,383	1,432	1,337	1,233
Total Assets	9,107	8,420	8,476	7,653	5,028	5,268	5,135	5,106
Current Liabilities	1,162	1,154	1,134	1,031	705	767	684	646
Long-Term Obligations	5,992	5,502	5,608	5,712	3,648	3,860	3,875	4,431
Total Liabilities	7,804	7,249	7,464	7,435	5,096	5,385	5,334	5,561
Stockholders' Equity	1,303	1,171	1,012	218	(68)	(117)	(199)	(455)
Shares Outstanding	131	131	130	122	119	117	115	83
Statistical Record								
Return on Assets %	5.33	5.67	4.23	3.66	1.68	1.20	1.12	0.04
Return on Equity %	46.95	63.93	55.44	309.58	...	...	...	...
EBITDA Margin %	15.98	15.93	17.46	17.32	13.58	13.03	14.42	14.41
Net Margin %	6.76	9.18	4.79	3.64	1.76	1.25	1.23	0.04
Asset Turnover	0.85	0.93	0.88	1.01	0.95	0.96	0.91	0.93
Current Ratio	1.95	1.72	1.77	1.74	1.96	1.87	1.95	1.91
Debt to Equity	4.60	4.70	5.54	26.20	...	...	...	...
Price Range	61.03-47.52	60.79-47.50	58.77-42.81	45.97-28.42	36.80-23.14	26.21-18.12	24.99-13.48	...
P/E Ratio	17.64-13.73	18.20-14.22	22.96-16.72	24.32-15.04	52.57-33.06	51.39-35.53	52.06-28.08	...

Address: 101 Oakley Street, Evansville, IN 47710

Telephone: 812-424-2904

Web Site: www.berryplastics.com
Officers: Thomas E. (Tom) Salmon - Chairman, President, Chief Operating Officer, Division Officer, Chief Executive Officer Mark W. Miles - Executive Vice President, Chief Financial Officer, Treasurer, Controller

Auditors: Ernst & Young LLP
Investor Contact: 812-.30-6.2964
Transfer Agents: Computershare Trust Company, N.A.

BEST BUY INC

Exchange	Symbol	Price	52Wk Range	Yield	P/E	Div Acheiver
NYS	BBY	$74.58 (6/29/2018)	78.78-52.59	2.41	22.07	14 Years

*7 Year Price Score 145.23 *NYSE Composite Index=100 *12 Month Price Score 110.83

Interim Earnings (Per Share)

Qtr.	Apr	Jul	Oct	Jan
2015-16	0.36	0.46	0.36	1.38
2016-17	0.70	0.61	0.61	1.89
2017-18	0.60	0.67	0.78	1.21
2018-19	0.72	...	...	...

Interim Dividends (Per Share)

Amt	Decl	Ex	Rec	Pay
0.34Q	08/30/2017	09/18/2017	09/19/2017	10/10/2017
0.34Q	11/17/2017	12/06/2017	12/07/2017	12/28/2017
0.45Q	03/01/2018	03/21/2018	03/22/2018	04/12/2018
0.45Q	05/25/2018	06/13/2018	06/14/2018	07/05/2018

Indicated Div: $1.80 (Div. Reinv. Plan)

Valuation Analysis

		Institutional Holding	
Forecast EPS	$5.00	No of Institutions	913
	(06/11/2018)	Shares	
Market Cap	$21.0 Billion		297,079,552
Book Value	$3.4 Billion	% Held	
Price/Book	6.13		70.92
Price/Sales	0.49		

Business Summary: Retail - Appliances and Electronics (MIC: 2.1.7 SIC: 5731 NAIC: 443112)

Best Buy is a provider of technology products, services and solutions. Co. provides these products and services to the customers who visit its stores, engage with Geek Squad agents or use its websites or mobile applications. Co. has two reportable segments: Domestic and International. Co.'s Domestic and International segments have offerings in six categories: Consumer Electronics, Computing and Mobile Phones, Entertainment, Appliances, Services and Other. As of Feb 3 2018, Co. had approximately 1,200 large-format and 300 small-format stores throughout its Domestic and International segments.

Recent Developments: For the quarter ended May 5 2018, net income increased 10.6% to US$208.0 million from US$188.0 million in the year-earlier quarter. Revenues were US$9.11 billion, up 6.8% from US$8.53 billion the year before. Operating income was US$265.0 million versus US$300.0 million in the prior-year quarter, a decrease of 11.7%. Direct operating expenses rose 7.3% to US$6.98 billion from US$6.51 billion in the comparable period the year before. Indirect operating expenses increased 8.0% to US$1.86 billion from US$1.72 billion in the equivalent prior-year period.

Prospects: Our evaluation of Best Buy Inc. as of Jan. 21, 2018 is the result of our systematic analysis on three basic characteristics: earnings strength, relative valuation, and recent stock price movement. The company has managed to produce a neutral trend in earnings per share over the past 5 quarters and while recent estimates for the company have been raised by analysts, BBY has posted results that were in line with analysts expectations. Based on operating earnings yield, the company is undervalued when compared to all of the companies in our coverage universe. Share price changes over the past year indicates that BBY will perform poorly over the near term.

Financial Data
(US$ in Thousands)

	3 Mos	02/03/2018	01/28/2017	01/30/2016	01/31/2015	02/01/2014	02/02/2013	03/03/2012
Earnings Per Share	3.38	3.26	3.81	2.56	3.49	1.53	(1.30)	(3.36)
Cash Flow Per Share	7.44	7.01	8.01	3.83	5.55	3.21	4.66	8.84
Tang Book Value Per Share	10.66	11.26	13.77	12.15	12.84	9.98	6.50	6.01
Dividends Per Share	1.470	1.360	1.570	1.430	0.720	0.680	0.660	0.620
Dividend Payout %	43.49	41.72	41.21	55.86	20.63	44.44	...	...
Income Statement								
Total Revenue	9,109,000	42,151,000	39,403,000	39,528,000	40,339,000	42,410,000	45,085,000	50,705,000
EBITDA	452,000	2,575,000	2,542,000	2,047,000	2,133,000	1,903,000	758,000	2,122,000
Depn & Amortn	176,000	683,000	654,000	657,000	656,000	716,000	832,000	945,000
Income Before Taxes	257,000	1,817,000	1,816,000	1,310,000	1,387,000	1,087,000	(186,000)	1,043,000
Income Taxes	49,000	818,000	609,000	503,000	141,000	398,000	231,000	709,000
Net Income	208,000	1,000,000	1,228,000	897,000	1,233,000	532,000	(441,000)	(1,231,000)
Average Shares	288,300	307,100	322,600	350,700	353,600	347,600	338,600	366,300
Balance Sheet								
Current Assets	8,930,000	9,829,000	10,516,000	9,886,000	11,729,000	10,485,000	12,047,000	10,297,000
Total Assets	12,082,000	13,049,000	13,856,000	13,519,000	15,256,000	14,013,000	16,787,000	16,005,000
Current Liabilities	7,055,000	7,817,000	7,122,000	6,925,000	7,777,000	7,436,000	10,810,000	8,855,000
Long-Term Obligations	792,000	811,000	1,321,000	1,339,000	1,580,000	1,612,000	1,153,000	1,685,000
Total Liabilities	8,662,000	9,437,000	9,147,000	9,141,000	10,261,000	10,027,000	13,726,000	12,260,000
Stockholders' Equity	3,420,000	3,612,000	4,709,000	4,378,000	4,995,000	3,986,000	3,061,000	3,745,000
Shares Outstanding	281,000	282,988	311,108	323,779	351,468	346,751	338,276	341,400
Statistical Record								
Return on Assets %	8.15	7.31	9.00	6.25	8.45	3.46	N.M.	N.M.
Return on Equity %	25.76	23.65	27.10	19.19	27.53	15.14	N.M.	N.M.
EBITDA Margin %	4.96	6.11	6.45	5.18	5.29	4.49	1.68	4.18
Net Margin %	2.28	2.37	3.12	2.27	3.06	1.25	N.M.	N.M.
Asset Turnover	3.41	3.08	2.89	2.75	2.76	2.76	2.99	2.95
Current Ratio	1.27	1.26	1.48	1.43	1.51	1.41	1.11	1.16
Debt to Equity	0.23	0.22	0.28	0.31	0.32	0.40	0.38	0.45
Price Range	78.06-50.42	78.06-42.14	49.31-26.93	41.77-25.87	39.91-22.78	44.33-15.12	27.51-11.29	33.03-22.12
P/E Ratio	23.09-14.92	23.94-12.93	12.94-7.07	16.32-10.11	11.44-6.53	28.97-9.88	...	...
Average Yield %	2.35	2.42	4.36	4.13	2.35	2.20	3.62	2.25

Address: 7601 Penn Avenue South, Richfield, MN 55423
Telephone: 612-291-1000

Web Site: www.bestbuy.com
Officers: Hubert Joly - Chairman, President, Chief Executive Officer Richard M. Schulze - Chairman Emeritus, Chairman

Auditors: Deloitte & Touche LLP
Investor Contact: 612-291-1000
Transfer Agents: Computershare, Providence, RI

BIG LOTS, INC.

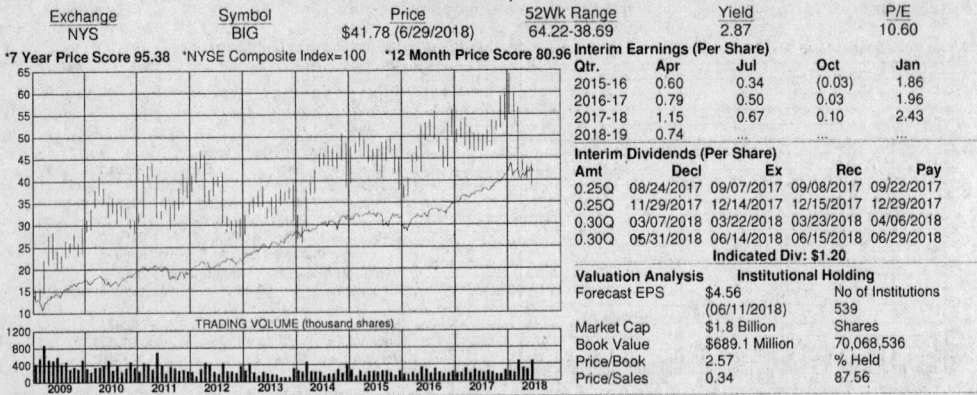

Interim Earnings (Per Share)

Qtr.	Apr	Jul	Oct	Jan
2015-16	0.60	0.34	(0.03)	1.86
2016-17	0.79	0.50	0.03	1.96
2017-18	1.15	0.67	0.10	2.43
2018-19	0.74	...	...	...

Interim Dividends (Per Share)

Amt	Decl	Ex	Rec	Pay
0.25Q	08/24/2017	09/07/2017	09/08/2017	09/22/2017
0.25Q	11/29/2017	12/14/2017	12/15/2017	12/29/2017
0.30Q	03/07/2018	03/22/2018	03/23/2018	04/06/2018
0.30Q	05/31/2018	06/14/2018	06/15/2018	06/29/2018

Indicated Div: $1.20

Valuation Analysis

		Institutional Holding	
Forecast EPS	$4.56 (06/11/2018)	No of Institutions	539
Market Cap	$1.8 Billion	Shares	70,068,536
Book Value	$689.1 Million	% Held	87.56
Price/Book	2.57		
Price/Sales	0.34		

Business Summary: Retail - General Merchandise/Department Stores (MIC: 2.1.1 SIC: 5331 NAIC: 452990)

Big Lots is a retailer. At Feb 3 2018, Co. operated a total of 1,416 stores. Co.'s merchandising categories are Furniture (upholstery, mattress, and case goods departments), Seasonal (lawn and garden, and other holiday departments), Soft Home (home decor, frames, bedding, utility bedding, bath, window, textile, and area rugs departments), Food (beverage and grocery, candy and snacks, and specialty foods departments), Consumables (health and beauty, plastics, chemical, and pet departments), Hard Home (small appliances, table top, stationery, and home maintenance departments), and Electronics, Toys, and Accessories (electronics, jewelry, hosiery, toys, and infant accessories departments).

Recent Developments: For the year ended Feb 3 2018, net income increased 24.2% to US$189.8 million from US$152.8 million in the prior year. Revenues were US$5.27 billion, up 1.4% from US$5.20 billion the year before. Operating income was US$301.4 million versus US$248.0 million in the prior year, an increase of 21.5%. Direct operating expenses rose 0.9% to US$3.13 billion from US$3.10 billion in the comparable period the year before. Indirect operating expenses decreased 0.6% to US$1.84 billion from US$1.85 billion in the equivalent prior-year period.

Prospects: Our evaluation of Big Lots Inc. as of Jan. 21, 2018 is the result of our systematic analysis on three basic characteristics: earnings strength, relative valuation, and recent stock price movement. The company has generated a negative trend in earnings per share over the past 5 quarters and while recent estimates for the company have been raised by analysts, BIG has posted better than expected results. Based on operating earnings yield, the company is undervalued when compared to all of the companies in our coverage universe. Share price changes over the past year indicates that BIG will perform poorly over the near term.

Financial Data

(US$ in Thousands)	3 Mos	02/03/2018	01/28/2017	01/30/2016	01/31/2015	02/01/2014	02/02/2013	01/28/2012
Earnings Per Share	3.94	4.38	3.32	2.80	2.06	2.16	2.93	2.99
Cash Flow Per Share	6.22	5.75	6.90	6.80	5.81	3.46	4.62	4.67
Tang Book Value Per Share	16.28	15.97	14.70	14.67	14.92	15.66	13.00	12.75
Dividends Per Share	1.050	1.000	0.840	0.760	0.510	...	...	...
Dividend Payout %	26.65	22.83	25.30	27.14	24.76			
Income Statement								
Total Revenue	1,267,983	5,270,980	5,200,439	5,190,582	5,177,078	5,301,912	5,400,119	5,202,250
EBITDA	74,374	419,165	369,732	353,233	344,188	304,326	404,805	435,702
Depn & Amortn	28,529	117,100	120,400	122,700	119,700	115,100	106,300	90,280
Income Before Taxes	44,269	295,354	244,241	226,850	221,900	185,887	294,313	341,892
Income Taxes	13,030	105,522	91,458	83,842	85,239	61,118	117,148	134,657
Net Income	31,239	189,832	152,828	142,873	114,276	125,295	177,121	207,064
Average Shares	42,218	43,300	45,974	50,964	55,552	57,958	60,476	69,419
Balance Sheet								
Current Assets	1,052,171	1,021,973	994,379	994,432	1,038,429	1,121,061	1,090,630	1,006,656
Total Assets	1,726,986	1,651,726	1,607,707	1,640,370	1,635,891	1,739,599	1,753,626	1,641,310
Current Liabilities	636,312	589,608	678,595	678,448	587,829	577,447	629,634	584,820
Long-Term Obligations	174,000	199,800	106,400	62,300	62,100	77,000	171,200	65,900
Total Liabilities	1,037,874	982,139	957,077	919,900	846,341	838,172	995,484	818,077
Stockholders' Equity	689,112	669,587	650,630	720,470	789,550	901,427	758,142	823,233
Shares Outstanding	42,338	41,925	44,259	49,101	52,912	57,548	57,269	63,609
Statistical Record								
Return on Assets %	10.19	11.46	9.44	8.75	6.79	7.19	10.27	12.73
Return on Equity %	25.25	28.29	22.35	18.98	13.55	15.14	22.04	23.46
EBITDA Margin %	5.87	7.95	7.11	6.81	6.65	5.74	7.50	8.38
Net Margin %	2.46	3.60	2.94	2.75	2.21	2.36	3.28	3.98
Asset Turnover	3.15	3.18	3.21	3.18	3.08	3.04	3.13	3.20
Current Ratio	1.65	1.73	1.47	1.47	1.77	1.94	1.73	1.72
Debt to Equity	0.25	0.30	0.16	0.09	0.08	0.09	0.23	0.08
Price Range	64.22-41.32	64.22-46.45	56.02-36.19	50.96-35.88	50.80-25.71	38.96-26.79	46.81-26.86	44.04-29.02
P/E Ratio	16.30-10.49	14.66-10.61	16.87-10.90	18.20-12.81	24.66-12.48	18.04-12.40	15.98-9.17	14.73-9.71
Average Yield %	2.06	1.94	1.75	1.94	1.68	1.22	...	...

BIO-RAD LABORATORIES INC

Exchange	Symbol	Price	52Wk Range	Yield	P/E
NYS	BIO	$288.54 (6/29/2018)	303.88-212.27	N/A	11.35

*7 Year Price Score 136.10 *NYSE Composite Index=100 *12 Month Price Score 112.15

Interim Earnings (Per Share)

Qtr.	Mar	Jun	Sep	Dec
2015	0.61	0.97	0.59	1.68
2016	0.42	0.61	0.62	(0.70)
2017	0.41	0.17	0.91	2.58
2018	21.77	...	...	...

Interim Dividends (Per Share)

No Dividends Paid

Valuation Analysis

		Institutional Holding	
Forecast EPS	$6.09	No of Institutions	
	(05/26/2018)	434	
Market Cap	$8.6 Billion	Shares	
Book Value	$4.5 Billion	22,967,450	
Price/Book	1.92	% Held	
Price/Sales	3.89	61.43	

Business Summary: Biotechnology (MIC: 4.1.2 SIC: 3826 NAIC: 334516)

Bio-Rad Laboratories is a manufacturer and distributor of its own life science research and clinical diagnostics products. Co. has two primary segments: Life Science, which is engaged in developing, manufacturing and marketing a range of reagents, apparatus and laboratory instruments used for biological research; and Clinical Diagnostics, which designs, manufactures, sells and supports test systems, informatics systems, test kits and quality controls that serve clinical laboratories in the diagnostics market. Co. sells its products and services to a diverse client base comprised of scientific research, healthcare, education and government customers.

Recent Developments: For the quarter ended Mar 31 2018, net income increased to US$656.8 million from US$12.4 million in the year-earlier quarter. Revenues were US$551.5 million, up 10.3% from US$500.1 million the year before. Operating income was US$43.6 million versus US$26.2 million in the prior-year quarter, an increase of 66.5%. Direct operating expenses rose 8.4% to US$249.3 million from US$230.0 million in the comparable period the year before. Indirect operating expenses increased 6.0% to US$258.6 million from US$243.9 million in the equivalent prior-year period.

Prospects: Our evaluation of Bio-Rad Laboratories Inc. as of Jan. 21, 2018 is the result of our systematic analysis on three basic characteristics: earnings strength, relative valuation, and recent stock price movement. The company has managed to produce a neutral trend in earnings per share over the past 5 quarters and while recent estimates for the company have remained steady, BIO has posted better than expected results. Based on operating earnings yield, the company is overvalued when compared to all of the companies in our coverage universe. Share price changes over the past year indicates that BIO will perform well over the near term.

Financial Data

(US$ in Thousands)	3 Mos	12/31/2017	12/31/2016	12/31/2015	12/31/2014	12/31/2013	12/31/2012	12/31/2011
Earnings Per Share	25.43	4.07	0.95	3.85	3.05	2.69	5.72	6.26
Cash Flow Per Share	6.73	3.50	7.33	6.38	9.46	6.14	9.83	9.27
Tang Book Value Per Share	127.82	75.54	65.86	60.64	49.21	48.75	44.04	36.03
Income Statement								
Total Revenue	551,519	2,160,153	2,068,172	2,019,441	2,175,044	2,132,694	2,069,235	2,073,529
EBITDA	901,671	249,319	191,702	289,239	290,088	307,456	393,043	401,697
Depn & Amortn	34,300	148,700	142,900	131,800	149,900	147,200	130,400	121,000
Income Before Taxes	863,689	97,805	41,560	145,847	131,557	112,385	222,931	235,762
Income Taxes	206,915	(24,444)	13,435	32,754	42,712	34,574	59,084	57,739
Net Income	656,774	122,249	28,125	113,093	88,845	77,790	163,778	178,223
Average Shares	30,171	30,034	29,646	29,409	29,133	28,906	28,642	28,468
Balance Sheet								
Current Assets	1,977,116	1,976,649	1,844,524	1,777,596	1,716,367	1,747,856	1,929,932	1,798,155
Total Assets	6,214,912	4,273,012	3,850,504	3,711,542	3,341,278	3,388,790	3,436,753	3,096,803
Current Liabilities	456,198	502,696	471,322	441,351	446,761	487,472	469,920	459,115
Long-Term Obligations	434,678	434,581	434,186	435,707	435,710	435,615	732,414	731,698
Total Liabilities	1,726,821	1,342,762	1,263,745	1,221,039	1,156,123	1,202,068	1,426,018	1,352,866
Stockholders' Equity	4,488,091	2,930,250	2,586,759	2,490,503	2,185,155	2,186,722	2,010,735	1,743,937
Shares Outstanding	29,804	29,785	29,576	29,359	29,069	28,776	28,481	28,184
Statistical Record								
Return on Assets %	15.08	3.01	0.74	3.21	2.64	2.28	5.00	5.79
Return on Equity %	21.31	4.43	1.10	4.84	4.06	3.71	8.70	10.87
EBITDA Margin %	163.49	11.54	9.27	14.32	13.34	14.42	18.99	19.37
Net Margin %	119.08	5.66	1.36	5.60	4.08	3.65	7.91	8.60
Asset Turnover	0.44	0.53	0.55	0.57	0.65	0.62	0.63	0.67
Current Ratio	4.33	3.93	3.91	4.03	3.84	3.59	4.11	3.92
Debt to Equity	0.10	0.15	0.17	0.17	0.20	0.20	0.36	0.42
Price Range	274.11-199.34	271.30-182.91	183.46-123.93	151.93-113.77	133.73-106.48	126.00-105.05	114.25-92.30	126.34-87.54
P/E Ratio	10.78-7.84	66.66-44.94	193.12-130.45	39.46-29.55	43.85-34.91	46.84-39.05	19.97-16.14	20.18-13.98

Address: 1000 Alfred Nobel Drive, Hercules, CA 94547 Telephone: 510-724-7000	Web Site: www.bio-rad.com Officers: Norman D. Schwartz - Chairman, President, Chief Executive Officer Michael Crowley - Executive Vice President	Auditors: KPMG LLP Investor Contact: 510-741-6104 Transfer Agents: Computershare, Canton, MA

BLACK HILLS CORPORATION

Exchange	Symbol	Price	52Wk Range	Yield	P/E	Div Acheiver
NYS	BKH	$61.21 (6/29/2018)	70.83-50.66	3.10	14.30	46 Years

*7 Year Price Score 97.56 *NYSE Composite Index=100 *12 Month Price Score 94.56

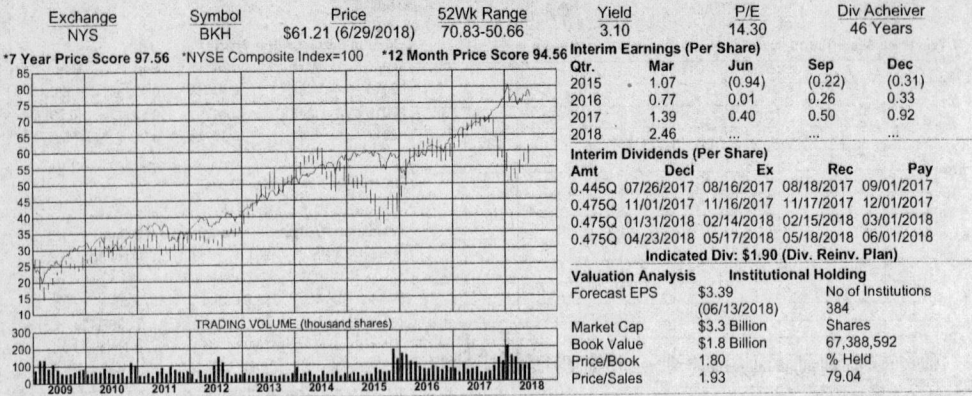

Interim Earnings (Per Share)

Qtr.	Mar	Jun	Sep	Dec
2015	1.07	(0.94)	(0.22)	(0.31)
2016	0.77	0.01	0.26	0.33
2017	1.39	0.40	0.50	0.92
2018	2.46	...	...	...

Interim Dividends (Per Share)

Amt	Decl	Ex	Rec	Pay
0.445Q	07/26/2017	08/16/2017	08/18/2017	09/01/2017
0.475Q	11/01/2017	11/16/2017	11/17/2017	12/01/2017
0.475Q	01/31/2018	02/14/2018	02/15/2018	03/01/2018
0.475Q	04/23/2018	05/17/2018	05/18/2018	06/01/2018

Indicated Div: $1.90 (Div. Reinv. Plan)

Valuation Analysis — **Institutional Holding**

Forecast EPS	$3.39	No of Institutions
(06/13/2018)		384
Market Cap	$3.3 Billion	Shares
Book Value	$1.8 Billion	67,388,592
Price/Book	1.80	% Held
Price/Sales	1.93	79.04

Business Summary: Electric Utilities (MIC: 3.1.1 SIC: 4911 NAIC: 221121)

Black Hills is a holding company. Through its subsidiaries, Co. has the following segments: Electric Utilities, which generates, transmits and distributes electricity in South Dakota, Wyoming, Colorado and Montana; Gas Utilities, which serves natural gas utility customers in Arkansas, Colorado, Iowa, Nebraska, Kansas and Wyoming; Power Generation, which produces electric power from its generating plants and sells the electric capacity and energy primarily to Co.'s utilities; and Mining, which produces and sells the coal to electric generation facilities.

Recent Developments: For the quarter ended Mar 31 2018, income from continuing operations increased 70.1% to US$139.0 million from US$81.7 million in the year-earlier quarter. Net income increased 70.5% to US$136.6 million from US$80.1 million in the year-earlier quarter. Revenues were US$575.4 million, up 5.1% from US$547.5 million the year before. Operating income is US$148.3 million versus US$150.2 million in the prior-year quarter, a decrease of 1.3%. Direct operating expenses rose 8.8% to US$363.7 million from US$334.3 million in the comparable period the year before. Indirect operating expenses increased 0.6% to US$63.4 million from US$63.0 million in the equivalent prior-year period.

Prospects: Our evaluation of Black Hills Corp. as of Jan. 21, 2018 is the result of our systematic analysis on three basic characteristics: earnings strength, relative valuation, and recent stock price movement. The company has generated a negative trend in earnings per share over the past 5 quarters. However, while recent estimates for the company have been mixed, BKH has posted results that fell short of analysts expectations. Based on operating earnings yield, the company is undervalued when compared to all of the companies in our coverage universe. Share price changes over the past year indicates that BKH will perform very well over the near term.

Financial Data

(US$ in Thousands)	3 Mos	12/31/2017	12/31/2016	12/31/2015	12/31/2014	12/31/2013	12/31/2012	12/31/2011
Earnings Per Share	4.28	3.21	1.37	(0.71)	2.89	2.59	1.85	1.24
Cash Flow Per Share	8.46	8.05	6.16	9.45	7.29	7.35	7.21	5.61
Tang Book Value Per Share	9.55	7.51	5.75	21.54	22.82	21.37	19.80	19.40
Dividends Per Share	1.840	1.810	1.680	1.620	1.560	1.520	1.480	1.460
Dividend Payout %	42.99	56.39	122.63	...	53.98	58.69	80.00	117.74
Income Statement								
Total Revenue	575,389	1,680,266	1,572,974	1,304,605	1,393,570	1,275,852	1,173,884	1,272,188
EBITDA	150,070	613,030	419,042	193,413	412,428	434,978	408,195	281,493
Depn & Amortn	1,900	196,507	195,223	161,734	150,210	147,980	160,187	135,591
Income Before Taxes	113,175	281,742	93,106	(49,522)	194,177	177,540	136,895	57,468
Income Taxes	(25,802)	73,367	10,475	(22,160)	65,395	61,608	48,400	18,224
Net Income	133,004	177,034	72,970	(32,111)	128,781	114,962	81,528	49,730
Average Shares	54,122	55,120	53,271	45,288	44,598	44,419	44,073	40,081
Balance Sheet								
Current Assets	492,105	570,782	466,814	822,151	454,036	345,288	405,106	758,921
Total Assets	6,626,989	6,658,902	6,515,444	4,655,501	4,279,806	3,875,178	3,729,471	4,127,083
Current Liabilities	788,564	649,101	527,932	422,029	651,281	378,394	734,889	878,067
Long-Term Obligations	2,858,787	3,109,400	3,211,189	1,866,866	1,267,589	1,396,948	938,877	1,280,409
Total Liabilities	4,808,219	4,949,928	4,900,805	3,189,634	2,903,782	2,567,430	2,496,962	2,917,747
Stockholders' Equity	1,818,770	1,708,974	1,614,639	1,465,867	1,376,024	1,307,748	1,232,509	1,209,336
Shares Outstanding	53,594	53,540	53,382	51,192	44,671	44,499	44,206	43,924
Statistical Record								
Return on Assets %	3.56	2.69	1.30	N.M.	3.16	3.02	2.07	1.27
Return on Equity %	13.37	10.65	4.72	N.M.	9.60	9.05	6.66	4.31
EBITDA Margin %	26.08	36.48	26.64	14.83	29.60	34.09	34.77	22.13
Net Margin %	23.12	10.54	4.64	N.M.	9.24	9.01	6.95	3.91
Asset Turnover	0.26	0.26	0.28	0.29	0.34	0.34	0.30	0.32
Current Ratio	0.62	0.88	0.88	1.95	0.70	0.91	0.55	0.86
Debt to Equity	1.57	1.82	1.99	1.27	0.92	1.07	0.76	1.06
Price Range	71.88-50.66	71.88-57.44	64.08-45.57	53.12-37.29	61.39-47.48	54.82-36.34	36.95-30.67	34.80-26.61
P/E Ratio	16.79-11.84	22.39-17.89	46.77-33.26	...	21.24-16.43	21.17-14.03	19.97-16.58	28.06-21.46
Average Yield %	2.90	2.75	2.87	3.54	2.84	3.21	4.40	4.65

Address: 7001 Mount Rushmore Road, Rapid City, SD 57702	Web Site: www.blackhillscorp.com	Auditors: Deloitte & Touche LLP
Telephone: 605-721-1700	Officers: David R. Emery - Chairman, President, Chief Executive Officer Linden R. Evans - President, Chief Operating Officer, Division Officer	Investor Contact: 605-721-1171 Transfer Agents: Wells Fargo Shareowner Services, St. Paul, MN

BLACKROCK INC

Exchange	Symbol	Price	52Wk Range	Yield	P/E
NYS	BLK	$499.04 (6/29/2018)	593.26-412.19	2.31	15.75

*7 Year Price Score 124.59 *NYSE Composite Index=100 *12 Month Price Score 104.86

Interim Earnings (Per Share)

Qtr.	Mar	Jun	Sep	Dec
2015	4.84	4.84	5.00	5.11
2016	3.92	4.73	5.26	5.12
2017	5.23	5.22	5.78	14.00
2018	6.68	...	...	...

Interim Dividends (Per Share)

Amt	Decl	Ex	Rec	Pay
2.50Q	07/20/2017	08/31/2017	09/05/2017	09/22/2017
2.50Q	11/16/2017	12/01/2017	12/04/2017	12/21/2017
2.88Q	01/11/2018	03/06/2018	03/07/2018	03/22/2018
2.88Q	05/23/2018	06/06/2018	06/07/2018	06/21/2018

Indicated Div: $11.52

Valuation Analysis

		Institutional Holding	
Forecast EPS	$27.73 (06/14/2018)	No of Institutions	1526
Market Cap	$80.0 Billion	Shares	159,469,968
Book Value	$32.0 Billion	% Held	74.23
Price/Book	2.50		
Price/Sales	6.04		

Business Summary: Finance Intermediaries & Services (MIC: 5.5.1 SIC: 6211 NAIC: 523120)

BlackRock is an investment management firm. Co.'s products include single- and multi-asset portfolios investing in equities, fixed income, alternatives and money market instruments. Products are provided directly and via intermediaries in a variety of vehicles, including open-end and closed-end mutual funds, iShares® exchange-traded funds, collective investment funds and other pooled investment vehicles. Co. also provides its BlackRock Solutions® investment and risk management technology platform, Aladdin®, risk analytics, advisory and technology services and solutions to institutional and wealth management investors. As of Dec 31 2017, Co. had $6.29 trillion of assets under management.

Recent Developments: For the quarter ended Mar 31 2018, net income increased 26.0% to US$1.09 billion from US$868.0 million in the year-earlier quarter. Revenues were US$3.58 billion, up 15.9% from US$3.09 billion the year before. Operating income was US$1.38 billion versus US$1.14 billion in the prior-year quarter, an increase of 20.3%. Indirect operating expenses increased 13.3% to US$2.21 billion from US$1.95 billion in the equivalent prior-year period.

Prospects: Our evaluation of BlackRock Inc. as of Jan. 21, 2018 is the result of our systematic analysis on three basic characteristics: earnings strength, relative valuation, and recent stock price movement. The company has enjoyed a very positive trend in earnings per share over the past 5 quarters and while recent estimates for the company have been raised by analysts, BLK has posted better than expected results. Based on operating earnings yield, the company is about fairly valued when compared to all of the companies in our coverage universe. Share price changes over the past year indicates that BLK will perform poorly over the near term.

Financial Data
(US$ in Thousands)

	3 Mos	12/31/2017	12/31/2016	12/31/2015	12/31/2014	12/31/2013	12/31/2012	12/31/2011
Earnings Per Share	31.68	30.23	19.04	19.79	19.25	16.87	13.79	12.37
Cash Flow Per Share	24.05	23.61	13.06	18.05	18.31	21.40	12.77	15.34
Tang Book Value Per Share	8.63	7.60	N.M.	N.M.	N.M.	N.M.	N.M.	N.M.
Dividends Per Share	10.380	10.000	9.160	8.720	7.720	6.720	6.000	5.500
Dividend Payout %	32.77	33.08	48.11	44.06	40.10	39.83	43.51	44.46
Income Statement								
Total Revenue	3,583,000	12,491,000	11,155,000	11,401,000	11,081,000	10,180,000	9,337,000	9,081,000
EBITDA	1,401,000	5,703,000	4,888,000	5,049,000	4,901,000	4,473,000	3,971,000	3,605,000
Depn & Amortn	11,000	221,000	223,000	243,000	274,000	289,000	286,000	294,000
Income Before Taxes	1,359,000	5,277,000	4,460,000	4,602,000	4,395,000	3,973,000	3,470,000	3,135,000
Income Taxes	265,000	270,000	1,290,000	1,250,000	1,131,000	1,022,000	1,030,000	796,000
Net Income	1,089,000	4,970,000	3,172,000	3,345,000	3,294,000	2,932,000	2,458,000	2,337,000
Average Shares	162,918	164,415	166,579	169,038	171,112	173,828	178,017	187,116
Balance Sheet								
Current Assets	8,655,000	9,593,000	8,441,000	8,320,000	7,843,000	6,637,000	6,856,000	5,466,000
Total Assets	216,017,000	220,217,000	220,177,000	225,261,000	239,808,000	219,873,000	200,451,000	179,896,000
Current Liabilities	2,209,000	3,314,000	2,974,000	3,039,000	2,900,000	2,831,000	2,716,000	2,428,000
Long-Term Obligations	5,036,000	5,014,000	4,915,000	4,930,000	4,938,000	4,939,000	5,687,000	4,690,000
Total Liabilities	184,039,000	188,392,000	191,079,000	196,758,000	212,442,000	193,413,000	175,048,000	154,848,000
Stockholders' Equity	31,978,000	31,825,000	29,098,000	28,503,000	27,366,000	26,460,000	25,403,000	25,048,000
Shares Outstanding	160,308	159,977	161,534	163,461	164,786	166,589	168,875	138,463
Statistical Record								
Return on Assets %	2.33	2.26	1.42	1.44	1.43	1.40	1.29	1.30
Return on Equity %	17.00	16.32	10.98	11.97	12.24	11.31	9.72	9.14
EBITDA Margin %	39.10	45.66	43.82	44.29	44.23	43.94	42.53	39.70
Net Margin %	30.39	39.79	28.44	29.34	29.73	28.80	26.33	25.74
Asset Turnover	0.06	0.06	0.05	0.05	0.05	0.05	0.05	0.05
Current Ratio	3.92	2.89	2.84	2.74	2.70	2.34	2.52	2.25
Debt to Equity	0.16	0.16	0.17	0.17	0.18	0.19	0.22	0.19
Price Range	593.26-377.10	518.86-371.64	398.45-289.72	380.33-293.52	364.40-286.39	316.47-206.71	209.29-163.37	207.06-141.77
P/E Ratio	18.73-11.90	17.16-12.29	20.93-15.22	19.22-14.83	18.93-14.88	18.76-12.25	15.18-11.85	16.74-11.46
Average Yield %	2.24	2.36	2.62	2.51	2.42	2.49	3.23	3.07

Address: 55 East 52nd Street, New York, NY 10055 **Telephone:** 212-810-5300	**Web Site:** www.blackrock.com **Officers:** Laurence D. Fink - Chairman, Chief Executive Officer Robert S. (Rob) Kapito - President	**Auditors:** Deloitte & Touche LLP **Transfer Agents:** Computershare, Jersey City, NJ

BLOCK (H & R), INC.

Exchange	Symbol	Price	52Wk Range	Yield	P/E
NYS	HRB	$22.78 (6/29/2018)	31.51-22.50	4.39	7.83

*7 Year Price Score 84.26 *NYSE Composite Index=100 *12 Month Price Score 97.62

Interim Earnings (Per Share)

Qtr.	Jul	Oct	Jan	Apr
2013-14	(0.42)	(0.39)	(0.78)	3.31
2014-15	(0.42)	(0.41)	(0.13)	2.68
2015-16	(0.36)	(0.55)	(0.35)	2.76
2016-17	(0.56)	(0.68)	(0.50)	3.66
2017-18	(0.63)	(0.74)	(1.18)	5.45

Interim Dividends (Per Share)

Amt	Decl	Ex	Rec	Pay
0.24Q	08/21/2017	09/12/2017	09/13/2017	10/02/2017
0.24Q	11/03/2017	12/01/2017	12/04/2017	01/02/2018
0.24Q	02/27/2018	03/12/2018	03/13/2018	04/02/2018
0.25Q	06/12/2018	06/21/2018	06/22/2018	07/02/2018

Indicated Div: $1.00 (Div. Reinv. Plan)

Valuation Analysis

		Institutional Holding	
Forecast EPS	$1.89 (06/07/2018)	No of Institutions	712
Market Cap	$4.8 Billion	Shares	
Book Value	$393.7 Million		272,760,864
Price/Book	12.11	% Held	
Price/Sales	1.51		78.98

Business Summary: Miscellaneous Consumer Services (MIC: 2.2.3 SIC: 7291 NAIC: 541213)

H&R Block and its subsidiaries are engaged in providing assisted and do-it-yourself tax return preparations solutions through multiple channels (including in-person, online and mobile applications, and desktop software) and distribute Co.'s financial products and services to the public in the U.S., Canada, Australia, and their respective territories. In addition to its tax services and products, Co. also provides additional services, including refund transfers, H&R Block Emerald Advance® lines of credit, H&R Block Emerald Prepaid MasterCard®, peace of Mind® Extended Service Plan, Tax Identity Shield®, Refund Advance Loans and, for Co.'s Canadian clients, an Instant Cash Back® refund option.

Recent Developments: For the year ended Apr 30 2018, income from continuing operations increased 48.9% to US$626.9 million from US$420.9 million a year earlier. Net income increased 49.9% to US$613.1 million from US$408.9 million in the prior year. Revenues were US$3.16 billion, up 4.1% from US$3.04 billion the year before. Direct operating expenses rose 5.8% to US$1.74 billion from US$1.64 billion in the comparable period the year before. Indirect operating expenses decreased 1.2% to US$668.2 million from US$676.0 million in the equivalent prior-year period.

Prospects: Our evaluation of Block (H & R) Inc. as of Jan. 21, 2018 is the result of our systematic analysis on three basic characteristics: earnings strength, relative valuation, and recent stock price movement. The company has suffered a very negative trend in earnings per share over the past 5 quarters and while recent estimates for the company have remained steady, HRB has posted better than expected results. Based on operating earnings yield, the company is undervalued when compared to all of the companies in our coverage universe. Share price changes over the past year indicates that HRB will perform well over the near term.

Financial Data

(US$ in Thousands)	04/30/2018	04/30/2017	04/30/2016	04/30/2015	04/30/2014	04/30/2013	04/30/2012	04/30/2011
Earnings Per Share	2.91	1.91	1.49	1.71	1.72	1.58	0.89	1.31
Cash Flow Per Share	4.07	2.58	2.13	2.28	2.96	1.82	1.21	1.66
Tang Book Value Per Share	N.M.	...	N.M.	3.48	2.79	2.00	2.17	0.77
Dividends Per Share	0.960	0.880	0.800	0.800	0.800	0.800	0.700	0.600
Dividend Payout %	32.99	46.07	53.69	46.78	46.51	50.63	78.65	45.80
Income Statement								
Total Revenue	3,159,931	3,036,314	3,038,153	3,078,658	3,024,295	2,905,943	2,893,771	3,774,296
EBITDA	854,643	821,608	730,693	889,351	851,816	770,211	645,370	769,225
Depn & Amortn	103,400	103,200	100,800	101,300	84,700	68,200	69,300	92,200
Income Before Taxes	668,732	629,287	569,479	742,805	767,116	702,011	576,070	677,025
Income Taxes	41,823	208,370	185,926	256,061	267,019	236,853	230,102	257,620
Net Income	613,149	408,945	374,267	473,663	475,157	433,948	265,932	406,110
Average Shares	210,213	214,095	250,818	277,136	276,027	274,359	298,601	309,777
Balance Sheet								
Current Assets	1,891,713	1,346,039	1,222,298	2,951,301	3,114,006	2,462,343	2,500,994	2,477,731
Total Assets	3,140,949	2,694,108	2,857,775	4,515,420	4,693,529	4,537,779	4,649,567	5,207,961
Current Liabilities	843,651	939,280	1,039,605	1,878,289	2,313,116	2,012,205	2,526,428	2,214,675
Long-Term Obligations	1,494,609	1,493,017	1,501,925	505,298	505,837	905,958	409,115	1,049,754
Total Liabilities	2,747,238	2,754,991	2,834,672	2,682,471	3,136,980	3,274,232	3,323,675	3,758,387
Stockholders' Equity	393,711	(60,883)	23,103	1,832,949	1,556,549	1,263,547	1,325,892	1,449,574
Shares Outstanding	209,254	207,171	220,517	275,275	274,228	272,635	292,119	305,366
Statistical Record								
Return on Assets %	21.02	14.73	10.12	10.29	10.29	9.45	5.38	7.78
Return on Equity %	368.45	...	40.22	27.95	33.70	33.52	19.11	28.10
EBITDA Margin %	27.05	27.06	24.05	28.89	28.17	26.50	22.30	20.38
Net Margin %	19.40	13.47	12.32	15.39	15.71	14.93	9.19	10.76
Asset Turnover	1.08	1.09	0.82	0.67	0.66	0.63	0.59	0.72
Current Ratio	2.24	1.43	1.18	1.57	1.35	1.22	0.99	1.12
Debt to Equity	3.80	...	65.01	0.28	0.32	0.72	0.31	0.72
Price Range	31.51-23.86	24.79-19.46	37.40-20.24	35.64-27.64	32.19-26.05	29.42-14.47	17.48-12.73	18.92-10.62
P/E Ratio	10.83-8.20	12.98-10.19	25.10-13.58	20.84-16.16	18.72-15.15	18.62-9.16	19.64-14.30	14.44-8.11
Average Yield %	3.54	3.88	2.47	2.48	2.76	4.11	4.51	4.18

Address: One H&R Block Way, Kansas City, MO 64105 **Telephone:** 816-854-3000	**Web Site:** www.hrblock.com **Officers:** Robert A. Gerard - Chairman Jeffrey J. Jones - President, Chief Executive Officer, Chief Executive Officer - Designate	**Auditors:** DELOITTE & TOUCHE LLP **Transfer Agents:** Wells Fargo Shareowner Services, St. Paul, MN

BOEING CO. (THE)

Exchange	Symbol	Price	52Wk Range	Yield	P/E
NYS	BA	$335.51 (6/29/2018)	371.56-197.75	2.04	21.99

*7 Year Price Score 166.60 *NYSE Composite Index=100 *12 Month Price Score 115.88

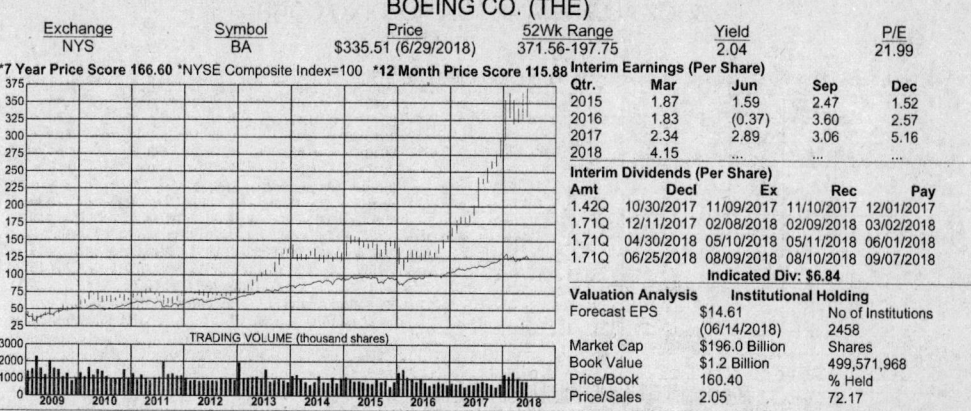

Interim Earnings (Per Share)
Qtr.	Mar	Jun	Sep	Dec
2015	1.87	1.59	2.47	1.52
2016	1.83	(0.37)	3.60	2.57
2017	2.34	2.89	3.06	5.16
2018	4.15	...	...	...

Interim Dividends (Per Share)
Amt	Decl	Ex	Rec	Pay
1.42Q	10/30/2017	11/09/2017	11/10/2017	12/01/2017
1.71Q	12/11/2017	02/08/2018	02/09/2018	03/02/2018
1.71Q	04/30/2018	05/10/2018	05/11/2018	06/01/2018
1.71Q	06/25/2018	08/09/2018	08/10/2018	09/07/2018

Indicated Div: $6.84

Valuation Analysis
Forecast EPS	$14.61
	(06/14/2018)
Market Cap	$196.0 Billion
Book Value	$1.2 Billion
Price/Book	160.40
Price/Sales	2.05

Institutional Holding
No of Institutions	2458
Shares	499,571,968
% Held	72.17

Business Summary: Aerospace (MIC: 7.1.1 SIC: 3721 NAIC: 336411)

Boeing is an aerospace firm. Co. has five segments: Commercial Airplanes; Defense, Space and Security (BDS), which is comprised of the Boeing Military Aircraft (BMA), Network and Space Systems (N&SS) and Global Services and Support (GSS) segments; and Boeing Capital (BCC). Commercial Airplanes segment provides commercial jet aircraft and provides related support services. N&SS provides defense and intelligence systems and intelligence systems. GS&S segment provides support solutions. BCC segment facilitates, arranges, structures and provides selective financing solutions for Co.'s Boeing customers.

Recent Developments: For the quarter ended Mar 31 2018, net income increased 56.9% to US$2.48 billion from US$1.58 billion in the year-earlier quarter. Revenues were US$23.38 billion, up 6.5% from US$21.96 billion the year before. Operating income was US$2.88 billion versus US$2.21 billion in the prior-year quarter, an increase of 30.3%. Direct operating expenses rose 4.2% to US$18.82 billion from US$18.07 billion in the comparable period the year before. Indirect operating expenses were unchanged at US$1.68 billion versus the equivalent prior-year period.

Prospects: Our evaluation of Boeing Co. as of Jan. 21, 2018 is the result of our systematic analysis on three basic characteristics: earnings strength, relative valuation, and recent stock price movement. The company has generated a negative trend in earnings per share over the past 5 quarters and while recent estimates for the company have been mixed, BA has posted better than expected results. Based on operating earnings yield, the company is about fairly valued when compared to all of the companies in our coverage universe. Share price changes over the past year indicates that BA will perform very well over the near term.

Financial Data
(US$ in Millions)	3 Mos	12/31/2017	12/31/2016	12/31/2015	12/31/2014	12/31/2013	12/31/2012	12/31/2011
Earnings Per Share	15.26	13.43	7.61	7.44	7.38	5.96	5.11	5.34
Cash Flow Per Share	24.09	22.12	16.48	13.63	12.17	10.78	9.91	5.39
Tang Book Value Per Share	N.M.	N.M.	N.M.	N.M.	0.96	9.07	N.M.	N.M.
Dividends Per Share	5.970	5.680	4.360	3.640	2.920	1.940	1.760	1.680
Dividend Payout %	39.12	42.29	57.29	48.92	39.57	32.55	34.44	31.46
Income Statement								
Total Revenue	23,382	93,392	94,571	96,114	90,762	86,623	81,698	68,735
EBITDA	-3,368	11,751	6,989	8,513	8,597	7,742	7,353	6,935
Depn & Amortn	501	1,548	1,418	1,357	1,414	1,338	1,248	1,322
Income Before Taxes	2,765	9,843	5,265	6,881	6,850	6,018	5,642	5,115
Income Taxes	362	1,850	673	1,979	1,691	1,646	2,007	1,382
Net Income	2,477	8,197	4,895	5,176	5,446	4,585	3,900	4,018
Average Shares	597	610	642	695	736	767	761	753
Balance Sheet								
Current Assets	86,543	65,161	62,488	68,234	67,785	65,074	57,309	49,810
Total Assets	113,549	92,333	89,997	94,408	99,198	92,663	88,896	79,986
Current Liabilities	75,532	56,269	50,134	50,412	56,717	51,486	44,982	41,274
Long-Term Obligations	10,471	9,782	9,568	8,730	8,141	8,072	8,973	10,018
Total Liabilities	112,327	91,978	89,180	88,073	90,533	77,788	83,029	76,471
Stockholders' Equity	1,222	355	817	6,335	8,665	14,875	5,867	3,515
Shares Outstanding	584	591	617	666	706	747	755	744
Statistical Record								
Return on Assets %	9.08	8.99	5.29	5.35	5.68	5.05	4.61	5.41
Return on Equity %	1,400.61	1,398.81	136.51	69.01	46.27	44.21	82.91	127.94
EBITDA Margin %	14.40	12.58	7.39	8.86	9.47	8.94	9.00	10.09
Net Margin %	10.59	8.78	5.18	5.39	6.00	5.29	4.77	5.85
Asset Turnover	0.94	1.02	1.02	0.99	0.95	0.95	0.96	0.93
Current Ratio	1.15	1.16	1.25	1.35	1.20	1.26	1.27	1.21
Debt to Equity	8.57	27.55	11.71	1.38	0.94	0.54	1.53	2.85
Price Range	364.64-175.62	297.90-156.97	157.81-108.44	158.31-125.49	144.37-118.34	138.36-73.65	77.27-67.24	79.95-57.41
P/E Ratio	23.90-11.51	22.18-11.69	20.74-14.25	21.28-16.87	19.56-16.04	23.21-12.36	15.12-13.16	14.97-10.75
Average Yield %	2.33	2.64	3.27	2.54	2.27	1.88	2.40	2.41

Address: 100 North Riverside Plaza, Chicago, IL 60606-1596 **Telephone:** 312-544-2000	**Web Site:** www.boeing.com **Officers:** Dennis A. Muilenburg - Chairman, Vice-Chairman, President, Chief Executive Officer, Chief Operating Officer, Executive Vice President, Division Officer Gregory D. (Greg) Smith - Executive Vice President, Vice President, Chief Financial Officer, Chief Accounting Officer, Corporate Controller	**Auditors:** DELOITTE & TOUCHE LLP **Investor Contact:** 312-544-2000 **Transfer Agents:** Computershare Trust Company, N.A., Providence, RI

BOOZ ALLEN HAMILTON HOLDING CORP.

Exchange	Symbol	Price	52Wk Range	Yield	P/E
NYS	BAH	$43.73 (6/29/2018)	45.55-32.30	1.74	21.33

*7 Year Price Score 120.62 *NYSE Composite Index=100 *12 Month Price Score 112.01

Interim Earnings (Per Share)

Qtr.	Jun	Sep	Dec	Mar
2013-14	0.48	0.45	0.31	0.30
2014-15	0.47	0.42	0.35	0.28
2015-16	0.43	0.37	0.71	0.43
2016-17	0.45	0.41	0.37	0.44
2017-18	0.53	0.47	0.47	0.58

Interim Dividends (Per Share)

Amt	Decl	Ex	Rec	Pay
0.17Q	08/03/2017	08/10/2017	08/14/2017	08/31/2017
0.17Q	11/06/2017	11/13/2017	11/14/2017	11/30/2017
0.19Q	02/05/2018	02/14/2018	02/14/2018	02/28/2018
0.19Q	05/24/2018	06/13/2018	06/14/2018	06/29/2018

Indicated Div: $0.76

Valuation Analysis / **Institutional Holding**

Forecast EPS	$2.46	No of Institutions
(06/12/2018)		358
Market Cap	$6.3 Billion	Shares
Book Value	$554.6 Million	242,460,400
Price/Book	11.31	% Held
Price/Sales	1.02	92.22

Business Summary: Business Services (MIC: 7.5.2 SIC: 8742 NAIC: 541611)

Booz Allen Hamilton Holding is a holding company. Co. provides management and technology, consulting, and engineering services to the U.S. and international governments, corporations, and non-profit organizations. Co.'s services include: Consulting, which focuses on develop solutions for specific domains, human capital, and operations; Analytics, which include decision analysts' capabilities, and data scientists; Digital Solutions, which include Software Developers and Systems Architects; Engineering, which include engineers that provide prototyping, reverse engineering, and Networks and Information Technology Infrastructure; and Cyber, which focuses on prevention against cyber attacks.

Recent Developments: For the year ended Mar 31 2018, net income increased 20.8% to US$305.1 million from US$252.5 million in the prior year. Revenues were US$6.17 billion, up 6.3% from US$5.80 billion the year before. Operating income was US$520.1 million versus US$484.2 million in the prior year, an increase of 7.4%. Direct operating expenses rose 6.4% to US$4.73 billion from US$4.44 billion in the comparable period the year before. Indirect operating expenses increased 5.3% to US$923.4 million from US$877.0 million in the equivalent prior-year period.

Prospects: Our evaluation of Booz Allen Hamilton Holding as of Jan. 21, 2018 is the result of our systematic analysis on three basic characteristics: earnings strength, relative valuation, and recent stock price movement. The company has managed to produce a neutral trend in earnings per share over the past 5 quarters and while recent estimates for the company have been raised by analysts, BAH has posted better than expected results. Based on operating earnings yield, the company is undervalued when compared to all of the companies in our coverage universe. Share price changes over the past year indicates that BAH will perform in line with the market over the near term.

Financial Data

(US$ in Thousands)	03/31/2018	03/31/2017	03/31/2016	03/31/2015	03/31/2014	03/31/2013	03/31/2012	03/31/2011
Earnings Per Share	2.05	1.67	1.94	1.52	1.54	1.45	1.70	0.66
Cash Flow Per Share	2.53	2.58	1.70	2.13	2.35	3.46	2.76	2.59
Dividends Per Share	0.700	0.620	0.540	1.460	2.400	8.360	0.090	...
Dividend Payout %	34.15	37.13	27.84	96.05	155.84	576.55	5.29	...
Income Statement								
Total Revenue	6,171,853	5,804,284	5,405,738	5,274,770	5,478,693	5,758,059	5,859,218	5,591,296
EBITDA	568,373	520,498	500,377	510,450	516,417	497,895	450,752	311,956
Depn & Amortn	48,100	46,300	50,100	52,700	57,600	59,300	58,800	52,000
Income Before Taxes	438,004	411,900	379,462	385,918	380,787	368,311	343,874	128,064
Income Taxes	132,893	159,410	85,368	153,349	148,599	149,253	103,919	43,370
Net Income	305,111	252,490	294,094	232,569	232,188	219,058	239,955	84,694
Average Shares	147,750	150,274	149,719	150,375	148,681	144,854	140,812	127,448
Balance Sheet								
Current Assets	1,488,719	1,294,480	1,189,771	1,163,208	1,255,977	1,424,352	1,657,663	1,365,649
Total Assets	3,603,366	3,373,105	3,010,171	2,877,493	2,940,818	3,177,528	3,314,791	3,024,023
Current Liabilities	1,036,166	1,101,401	939,913	848,994	917,104	964,646	914,446	866,135
Long-Term Obligations	1,755,479	1,470,174	1,484,448	1,569,272	1,585,231	1,659,611	922,925	964,328
Total Liabilities	3,048,738	2,799,514	2,601,683	2,690,995	2,769,182	2,950,735	2,429,606	2,116,773
Stockholders' Equity	554,628	573,591	408,488	186,498	171,636	226,793	1,185,185	907,250
Shares Outstanding	143,446	148,887	147,992	149,089	149,295	146,206	142,552	140,215
Statistical Record								
Return on Assets %	8.75	7.91	9.96	7.99	7.59	6.75	7.55	2.78
Return on Equity %	54.09	51.42	98.59	129.88	116.55	31.03	22.87	11.96
EBITDA Margin %	9.21	8.97	9.26	9.68	9.43	8.65	7.69	5.58
Net Margin %	4.94	4.35	5.44	4.41	4.24	3.80	4.10	1.51
Asset Turnover	1.77	1.82	1.83	1.81	1.79	1.77	1.84	1.84
Current Ratio	1.44	1.18	1.27	1.37	1.37	1.48	1.81	1.58
Debt to Equity	3.17	2.56	3.63	8.41	9.24	7.32	0.78	1.06
Price Range	40.02-31.90	38.20-27.24	31.13-24.45	30.46-20.82	22.16-12.90	19.06-11.90	19.87-13.52	20.00-18.00
P/E Ratio	19.52-15.56	22.87-16.31	16.05-12.60	20.04-13.70	14.39-8.38	13.14-8.21	11.69-7.95	30.30-27.27
Average Yield %	1.91	1.93	1.94	5.87	13.04	56.23	0.52	...

Address: 8283 Greensboro Drive, McLean, VA 22102 Telephone: 703-902-5000	Web Site: www.boozallen.com Officers: Ralph W. Shrader - Chairman, President, Chief Executive Officer Horacio D. Rozanski - President, Executive Vice President, Chief Operating Officer, Chief Executive Officer	Auditors: Ernst & Young LLP Investor Contact: 703-377-5332 Transfer Agents: Computershare, Jersey City, NJ

BORGWARNER INC

*7 Year Price Score 90.03   *NYSE Composite Index=100   *12 Month Price Score 95.38

Interim Earnings (Per Share)

Qtr.	Mar	Jun	Sep	Dec
2015	0.79	0.65	0.70	0.56
2016	0.75	0.76	0.39	(1.35)
2017	0.89	1.01	0.88	(0.69)
2018	1.07	...	...	...

Interim Dividends (Per Share)

Amt	Decl	Ex	Rec	Pay
0.14Q	07/27/2017	08/30/2017	09/01/2017	09/15/2017
0.17Q	11/09/2017	11/30/2017	12/01/2017	12/15/2017
0.17Q	02/08/2018	02/28/2018	03/01/2018	03/15/2018
0.17Q	04/26/2018	05/31/2018	06/01/2018	06/15/2018

Indicated Div: $0.68

Valuation Analysis   Institutional Holding

Forecast EPS	$4.42	No of Institutions
	(06/14/2018)	842
Market Cap	$9.1 Billion	Shares
Book Value	$3.9 Billion	232,656,192
Price/Book	2.32	% Held
Price/Sales	0.89	89.36

Business Summary: Auto Parts (MIC: 1.8.2 SIC: 3714 NAIC: 336350)

Borg Warner is a supplier of technology solutions for combustion, hybrid and electric vehicles. These products are manufactured and sold primarily to original equipment manufacturers (OEMs) of light vehicles. Co.'s products are also sold to other OEMs of commercial vehicles and off-highway vehicles. Co.'s products fall into two reporting segments: Engine and Drivetrain. The Engine segment's products include turbochargers, timing systems, emissions systems, thermal systems, thermostats, diesel cold start and gasoline ignition technology. The Drivetrain segment's products include friction, mechanical and controls products, torque management, and rotating electrical components.

Recent Developments: For the quarter ended Mar 31 2018, net income increased 18.6% to US$236.8 million from US$199.6 million in the year-earlier quarter. Revenues were US$2.78 billion, up 15.7% from US$2.41 billion the year before. Operating income was US$333.5 million versus US$291.5 million in the prior-year quarter, an increase of 14.4%. Direct operating expenses rose 16.0% to US$2.19 billion from US$1.89 billion in the comparable period the year before. Indirect operating expenses increased 14.9% to US$258.3 million from US$224.8 million in the equivalent prior-year period.

Prospects: Our evaluation of Borg Warner Inc. as of Jan. 21, 2018 is the result of our systematic analysis on three basic characteristics: earnings strength, relative valuation, and recent stock price movement. The company has enjoyed a very positive trend in earnings per share over the past 5 quarters and while recent estimates for the company have been mixed, BWA has posted better than expected results. Based on operating earnings yield, the company is undervalued when compared to all of the companies in our coverage universe. Share price changes over the past year indicates that BWA will perform in line with the market over the near term.

Financial Data

(US$ in Thousands)	3 Mos	12/31/2017	12/31/2016	12/31/2015	12/31/2014	12/31/2013	12/31/2012	12/31/2011
Earnings Per Share	2.27	2.08	0.55	2.70	2.86	2.70	2.09	2.23
Cash Flow Per Share	5.51	5.61	4.82	3.87	3.53	3.14	3.89	3.24
Tang Book Value Per Share	7.31	6.37	4.96	5.71	9.98	9.63	7.33	4.42
Dividends Per Share	0.620	0.590	0.530	0.520	0.510	0.250	...	...
Dividend Payout %	27.31	28.37	96.36	19.26	17.83	9.26	...	...
Income Statement								
Total Revenue	2,784,300	9,799,300	9,071,000	8,023,200	8,305,100	7,436,600	7,183,200	7,114,700
EBITDA	445,300	1,484,900	617,300	1,259,900	1,294,100	1,154,600	1,046,800	1,100,800
Depn & Amortn	109,200	407,800	391,400	320,200	330,400	299,400	293,900	303,300
Income Before Taxes	321,500	1,012,400	147,600	886,800	932,800	825,800	718,200	727,700
Income Taxes	94,900	580,300	30,300	280,400	292,600	218,300	238,600	195,300
Net Income	225,100	439,900	118,500	609,700	655,800	624,300	500,900	550,100
Average Shares	210,766	211,548	215,328	225,648	228,924	231,337	242,754	256,936
Balance Sheet								
Current Assets	3,697,800	3,543,200	2,911,600	3,135,300	2,970,800	2,798,500	2,472,800	2,137,800
Total Assets	10,034,800	9,787,600	8,834,700	8,841,500	7,228,000	6,917,000	6,400,800	5,958,600
Current Liabilities	2,436,600	2,425,200	2,091,800	2,357,300	2,168,200	1,623,900	1,603,100	1,905,400
Long-Term Obligations	2,131,500	2,103,700	2,043,600	2,124,600	716,300	1,021,000	823,800	751,300
Total Liabilities	6,124,100	6,070,800	5,616,400	5,287,800	3,611,800	3,356,400	3,318,200	3,570,700
Stockholders' Equity	3,910,700	3,716,800	3,218,300	3,553,700	3,616,200	3,560,600	3,082,600	2,387,900
Shares Outstanding	210,101	210,812	212,262	219,324	226,430	227,932	231,145	217,028
Statistical Record								
Return on Assets %	4.98	4.72	1.34	7.59	9.27	9.38	8.08	9.56
Return on Equity %	13.01	12.69	3.49	17.01	18.28	18.80	18.26	23.68
EBITDA Margin %	15.99	15.15	6.81	15.70	15.58	15.53	14.57	15.47
Net Margin %	8.08	4.49	1.31	7.60	7.90	8.39	6.97	7.73
Asset Turnover	1.06	1.05	1.02	1.00	1.17	1.12	1.16	1.24
Current Ratio	1.52	1.46	1.39	1.33	1.37	1.72	1.54	1.12
Debt to Equity	0.55	0.57	0.63	0.60	0.20	0.29	0.27	0.31
Price Range	57.91-37.99	55.68-37.99	43.23-27.69	63.01-38.89	67.38-50.24	55.96-35.42	43.52-30.27	40.83-28.07
P/E Ratio	25.51-16.74	26.77-18.26	78.60-50.35	23.34-14.40	23.56-17.57	20.73-13.12	20.83-14.48	18.31-12.59
Average Yield %	1.29	1.30	1.53	1.00	0.86	0.56	...	...

Address: 3850 Hamlin Road, Auburn Hills, MI 48326 **Telephone:** 248-754-9200	**Web Site:** www.borgwarner.com **Officers:** James R. Verrier - President, Chief Executive Officer, Vice President, Chief Operating Officer Ronald T. Hundzinski - Executive Vice President, Chief Financial Officer, Vice President, Treasurer, Controller	**Auditors:** PricewaterhouseCoopers LLP **Investor Contact:** 248-754-0881 **Transfer Agents:** BNY Mellon Shareowner Services, Jersey City, NJ

BOSTON BEER CO INC (THE)

Exchange	Symbol	Price	52Wk Range	Yield	P/E
NYS	SAM	$299.70 (6/29/2018)	302.55-130.50	N/A	35.43

*7 Year Price Score 84.15   *NYSE Composite Index=100   *12 Month Price Score 135.86

Interim Earnings (Per Share)

Qtr.	Mar	Jun	Sep	Dec
2015	1.00	2.18	2.85	1.23
2016	0.53	2.06	2.48	1.74
2017	0.45	2.35	2.78	2.55
2018	0.78	...	...	...

Interim Dividends (Per Share)

No Dividends Paid

Valuation Analysis		Institutional Holding	
Forecast EPS	$7.60	No of Institutions	353
	(06/14/2018)		
Market Cap	$3.5 Billion	Shares	12,231,454
Book Value	$436.9 Million		
Price/Book	8.04	% Held	59.65
Price/Sales	3.94		

Business Summary: Beverages (MIC: 1.2.2 SIC: 2082 NAIC: 312120)

Boston Beer Company is engaged in the business of selling alcohol beverages throughout the U.S. and in selected international markets. Co. consists of two operating segments that each produce and sell alcohol beverages. The first is the Boston Beer Company operating segment comprised of Co.'s Samuel Adams®, Twisted Tea® and Angry Orchard® brands. The second is the A&S Brewing Collaborative operating segment which is comprised of The Traveler Beer Company, Coney Island Brewing Company, Angel City Brewing Company and Concrete Beach Brewing Company. Co. produces malt beverages, hard cider and hard seltzer at Co.-owned breweries and under contract arrangements at other brewery locations.

Recent Developments: For the quarter ended Mar 31 2018, net income increased 63.0% to US$9.3 million from US$5.7 million in the year-earlier quarter. Revenues were US$190.5 million, up 17.8% from US$161.7 million the year before. Operating income was US$9.2 million versus US$4.0 million in the prior-year quarter, an increase of 129.3%. Direct operating expenses rose 10.6% to US$94.4 million from US$85.4 million in the comparable period the year before. Indirect operating expenses increased 20.1% to US$86.9 million from US$72.3 million in the equivalent prior-year period.

Prospects: Our evaluation of Boston Beer Co. Inc. as of Jan. 21, 2018 is the result of our systematic analysis on three basic characteristics: earnings strength, relative valuation, and recent stock price movement. The company has generated a negative trend in earnings per share over the past 5 quarters and while recent estimates for the company have been raised by analysts, SAM has posted better than expected results. Based on operating earnings yield, the company is about fairly valued when compared to all of the companies in our coverage universe. Share price changes over the past year indicates that SAM will perform well over the near term.

Financial Data
(US$ in Thousands)

	3 Mos	12/30/2017	12/31/2016	12/26/2015	12/27/2014	12/28/2013	12/29/2012	12/31/2011
Earnings Per Share	8.46	8.09	6.79	7.25	6.69	5.18	4.39	4.81
Cash Flow Per Share	11.13	11.33	12.10	12.89	10.92	7.85	7.47	5.50
Tang Book Value Per Share	36.97	36.13	35.81	35.87	33.09	23.41	18.93	14.30
Income Statement								
Total Revenue	190,457	862,992	906,446	959,934	903,007	739,053	580,222	513,000
EBITDA	21,773	166,793	186,253	198,354	180,373	138,210	115,686	121,946
Depn & Amortn	12,820	51,200	49,300	43,400	34,800	25,700	20,200	18,500
Income Before Taxes	9,158	116,142	137,121	155,010	145,594	112,541	95,517	103,500
Income Taxes	(152)	17,093	49,772	56,596	54,851	42,149	36,050	37,441
Net Income	9,310	99,049	87,349	98,414	90,743	70,392	59,467	66,059
Average Shares	11,831	12,180	12,796	13,520	13,484	13,504	13,435	13,741
Balance Sheet								
Current Assets	174,903	168,348	201,238	223,603	207,462	164,278	162,342	125,723
Total Assets	579,887	569,624	623,297	645,400	605,161	444,075	359,484	272,488
Current Liabilities	99,923	101,758	101,519	111,160	110,170	104,377	88,894	67,049
Long-Term Obligations	...	...	411	471	528	584	566	...
Total Liabilities	142,961	146,101	176,715	184,179	169,021	141,990	114,393	87,743
Stockholders' Equity	436,926	423,523	446,582	461,221	436,140	302,085	245,091	184,745
Shares Outstanding	11,718	11,621	12,368	12,756	13,069	12,747	12,811	12,822
Statistical Record								
Return on Assets %	17.59	16.65	13.55	15.78	17.34	17.57	18.87	24.48
Return on Equity %	23.53	22.83	18.93	21.99	24.65	25.80	27.75	37.10
EBITDA Margin %	11.43	19.33	20.55	20.66	19.97	18.70	19.94	23.77
Net Margin %	4.89	11.48	9.64	10.25	10.05	9.52	10.25	12.88
Asset Turnover	1.53	1.45	1.41	1.54	1.73	1.84	1.84	1.90
Current Ratio	1.75	1.65	1.98	2.01	1.88	1.57	1.83	1.88
Price Range		200.70-129.90	194.60-129.90	204.25-146.42	323.99-197.05	297.78-203.81	259.25-134.45	139.24-94.52	112.88-72.13
P/E Ratio		23.72-15.35	24.05-16.06	30.08-21.56	44.69-27.18	44.51-30.46	50.05-25.96	31.72-21.53	23.47-15.00

Address: One Design Center Place, Suite 850, Boston, MA 02210
Telephone: 617-368-5000
Fax: 617-368-5500

Web Site: www.bostonbeer.com
Officers: C. James Koch - Chairman David A. Burwick - President, Chief Executive Officer

Auditors: Deloitte & Touche LLP
Investor Contact: 617-368-5060
Transfer Agents: Computershare Shareowner Services LLC, Jersey City, NJ

BOSTON PROPERTIES INC

Exchange	Symbol	Price	52Wk Range	Yield	P/E
NYS	BXP	$125.42 (6/29/2018)	130.96-112.09	2.55	36.46

*7 Year Price Score 83.63   ***NYSE Composite Index=100**   ***12 Month Price Score 98.17**

Interim Earnings (Per Share)

Qtr.	Mar	Jun	Sep	Dec
2015	1.11	0.52	1.20	0.91
2016	1.18	0.63	0.50	0.95
2017	0.63	0.87	0.76	0.67
2018	1.14	...	...	...

Interim Dividends (Per Share)

Amt	Decl	Ex	Rec	Pay
0.75Q	09/15/2017	09/28/2017	09/29/2017	10/31/2017
0.80Q	12/18/2017	12/28/2017	12/29/2017	01/30/2018
0.80Q	03/15/2018	03/28/2018	03/29/2018	04/30/2018
0.80Q	06/14/2018	06/28/2018	06/29/2018	07/31/2018

Indicated Div: $3.20

Valuation Analysis

		Institutional Holding	
Forecast EPS	$2.80 (06/13/2018)	No of Institutions	692
Market Cap	$19.4 Billion	Shares	194,238,128
Book Value	$5.9 Billion	% Held	100.28
Price/Book	3.29		
Price/Sales	7.36		

Business Summary: REITs (MIC: 5.3.1 SIC: 6798 NAIC: 525930)

Boston Properties is a self-administered and self-managed real estate investment trust, with substantial in-house capabilities and resources in acquisitions, development, financing, capital markets, construction management, property management, marketing, leasing, accounting, risk management, tax and legal services. At Dec 31 2017, Co. owned or had interests in 179 commercial real estate properties, including twelve properties under construction/redevelopment. As of Dec 31 2017, Co.'s properties consisted of: 167 office properties, six residential properties (including four under construction), five retail properties and one hotel.

Recent Developments: For the quarter ended Mar 31 2018, income from continuing operations increased 3.9% to US$119.9 million from US$115.4 million in the year-earlier quarter. Net income increased 87.2% to US$216.3 million from US$115.6 million in the year-earlier quarter. Revenues were US$661.2 million, up 4.6% from US$632.2 million the year before. Revenues from property income rose 3.6% to US$640.8 million from US$618.3 million in the corresponding quarter a year earlier.

Prospects: Our evaluation of Boston Properties Inc. as of Jan. 21, 2018 is the result of our systematic analysis on three basic characteristics: earnings strength, relative valuation, and recent stock price movement. The company has enjoyed a very positive trend in earnings per share over the past 5 quarters. Because the company lacks sufficient analyst estimate data, we place greater weight on the historical EPS trend as the measure of earnings strength. Based on operating earnings yield, the company is overvalued when compared to all of the companies in our coverage universe. Share price changes over the past year indicates that BXP will perform well over the near term.

Financial Data
(US$ in Thousands)

	3 Mos	12/31/2017	12/31/2016	12/31/2015	12/31/2014	12/31/2013	12/31/2012	12/31/2011
Earnings Per Share	3.44	2.93	3.26	3.73	2.83	4.86	1.92	1.86
Cash Flow Per Share	5.74	5.89	6.73	5.21	4.54	5.11	4.27	4.16
Tang Book Value Per Share	36.79	36.38	36.32	35.87	35.90	36.56	34.35	33.23
Dividends Per Share	3.100	3.050	2.700	3.850	7.100	4.850	2.300	2.050
Dividend Payout %	90.12	104.10	82.82	103.22	250.88	99.79	119.79	110.22
Income Statement								
Total Revenue	661,151	2,602,076	2,550,820	2,490,821	2,396,998	2,135,539	1,876,267	1,759,526
EBITDA	373,823	1,535,614	1,588,549	1,472,991	1,429,565	1,640,851	1,112,752	1,061,245
Depn & Amortn	165,797	617,547	694,403	639,542	628,573	565,397	454,044	439,184
Income Before Taxes	119,454	543,586	481,297	401,253	345,249	628,574	245,144	227,930
Net Income	178,646	462,439	512,785	583,106	443,611	749,811	289,650	272,679
Average Shares	154,705	154,390	153,977	153,844	153,308	152,521	150,711	146,218
Balance Sheet								
Current Assets	1,417,437	1,459,130	1,311,774	1,650,256	2,988,994	3,133,405	2,152,220	2,836,349
Total Assets	19,583,939	19,372,233	18,851,643	18,379,456	19,886,767	20,162,251	15,462,321	14,782,966
Current Liabilities	590,396	554,186	672,765	792,415	1,289,267	867,235	382,051	316,145
Long-Term Obligations	10,339,313	10,271,611	9,796,133	9,216,513	10,086,984	11,521,508	8,912,369	8,704,138
Total Liabilities	13,704,911	13,558,276	13,065,348	12,670,021	14,189,469	14,369,786	10,254,380	9,861,316
Stockholders' Equity	5,879,028	5,813,957	5,786,295	5,709,435	5,697,298	5,792,465	5,207,941	4,921,650
Shares Outstanding	154,362	154,325	153,790	153,579	153,113	152,983	151,601	148,107
Statistical Record								
Return on Assets %	2.81	2.42	2.75	3.05	2.22	4.21	1.91	1.94
Return on Equity %	9.29	7.97	8.90	10.22	7.72	13.63	5.70	5.83
EBITDA Margin %	56.54	59.01	62.28	59.14	59.64	76.84	59.31	60.31
Net Margin %	27.02	17.77	20.10	23.41	18.51	35.11	15.44	15.50
Asset Turnover	0.14	0.14	0.14	0.13	0.12	0.12	0.12	0.13
Current Ratio	2.40	2.63	1.95	2.08	2.32	3.61	5.63	8.97
Debt to Equity	1.76	1.77	1.69	1.61	1.77	1.99	1.71	1.77
Price Range	136.87-112.09	139.88-117.70	143.61-108.18	144.74-108.65	136.28-100.37	114.59-98.27	116.07-97.49	112.36-84.66
P/E Ratio	39.79-32.58	47.74-40.17	44.05-33.18	38.80-29.13	48.16-35.47	23.58-20.22	60.45-50.78	60.41-45.52
Average Yield %	2.51	2.41	2.12	2.99	6.00	4.58	2.17	2.10

Address: Prudential Center, 800 Boylston Street, Suite 1900, Boston, MA 02199-8103 **Telephone:** 617-236-3300	**Web Site:** www.bostonproperties.com **Officers:** Mortimer B. Zuckerman - Chairman Emeritus, Chairman, Executive Chairman, Chief Executive Officer Douglas T. Linde - President	**Auditors:** PricewaterhouseCoopers LLP **Investor Contact:** 617-236-3322 **Transfer Agents:** Computershare Trust Company, N.A., Providence, RI

BOSTON SCIENTIFIC CORP.

Exchange	Symbol	Price	52Wk Range	Yield	P/E
NYS	BSX	$32.70 (6/29/2018)	34.32-24.79	N/A	408.75

*7 Year Price Score 142.71 *NYSE Composite Index=100 *12 Month Price Score 110.21

TRADING VOLUME (thousand shares)

Interim Earnings (Per Share)

Qtr.	Mar	Jun	Sep	Dec
2015	0.00	0.08	(0.15)	(0.11)
2016	0.15	(0.15)	0.17	0.09
2017	0.21	0.11	0.20	(0.44)
2018	0.21	...	...	...

Interim Dividends (Per Share)

No Dividends Paid

Valuation Analysis		Institutional Holding	
Forecast EPS	$1.39	No of Institutions	
	(06/14/2018)	947	
Market Cap	$45.1 Billion	Shares	
Book Value	$7.0 Billion	1,478,277,760	
Price/Book	6.42	% Held	
Price/Sales	4.87	79.73	

Business Summary: Medical Instruments & Equipment (MIC: 4.3.1 SIC: 3841 NAIC: 339112)

Boston Scientific is a developer, manufacturer and marketer of medical devices. Co.'s products include: drug-eluting coronary stent systems, coronary therapies, and structural heart therapy for Interventional Cardiology; stents, peripheral embolization devices and vena cava filters for Peripheral Interventions; a range of implantable devices that monitor the heart for Cardiac Rhythm Management; steerable radio frequency ablation catheters for Electrophysiology; devices for gastroenterology and interventional bronchoscopy for Endoscopy; devices to treat urological and pelvic conditions for Urology and Public Health; and Precision SpectraTM Spinal Cord Stimulator Systems for Neuromodulation

Recent Developments: For the quarter ended Mar 31 2018, net income increased 2.8% to US$298.0 million from US$290.0 million in the year-earlier quarter. Revenues were US$2.38 billion, up 10.1% from US$2.16 billion the year before. Operating income was US$407.0 million versus US$364.0 million in the prior-year quarter, an increase of 11.8%. Direct operating expenses rose 3.4% to US$672.0 million from US$650.0 million in the comparable period the year before. Indirect operating expenses increased 13.4% to US$1.30 billion from US$1.15 billion in the equivalent prior-year period.

Prospects: Our evaluation of Boston Scientific Corp. as of Jan. 21, 2018 is the result of our systematic analysis on three basic characteristics: earnings strength, relative valuation, and recent stock price movement. The company has produced a positive trend in earnings per share over the past 5 quarters and while recent estimates for the company have been mixed, BSX has posted better than expected results. Based on operating earnings yield, the company is undervalued when compared to all of the companies in our coverage universe. Share price changes over the past year indicates that BSX will perform in line with the market over the near term.

Financial Data
(US$ in Thousands)

	3 Mos	12/31/2017	12/31/2016	12/31/2015	12/31/2014	12/31/2013	12/31/2012	12/31/2011
Earnings Per Share	0.08	0.08	0.25	(0.18)	(0.09)	(0.09)	(2.89)	0.29
Cash Flow Per Share	1.09	1.04	0.71	0.45	0.96	0.81	0.89	0.67
Income Statement								
Total Revenue	2,379,000	9,048,000	8,386,000	7,477,000	7,380,000	7,143,000	7,249,000	7,622,000
EBITDA	451,000	1,436,000	675,000	(97,000)	(11,000)	374,000	(3,563,000)	1,219,000
Depn & Amortn	68,000	279,000	270,000	274,000	287,000	279,000	288,000	296,000
Income Before Taxes	323,000	933,000	177,000	(650,000)	(509,000)	(223,000)	(4,107,000)	642,000
Income Taxes	26,000	828,000	(170,000)	(411,000)	(390,000)	(102,000)	(39,000)	201,000
Net Income	298,000	104,000	347,000	(239,000)	(119,000)	(121,000)	(4,068,000)	441,000
Average Shares	1,396,800	1,392,700	1,377,200	1,341,200	1,324,300	1,341,200	1,406,700	1,519,000
Balance Sheet								
Current Assets	4,080,000	3,822,000	3,239,000	3,471,000	3,606,000	3,011,000	3,022,000	3,105,000
Total Assets	19,202,000	19,042,000	18,096,000	18,133,000	17,042,000	16,571,000	17,154,000	21,290,000
Current Liabilities	4,988,000	5,654,000	3,587,000	2,430,000	2,846,000	1,824,000	1,772,000	1,807,000
Long-Term Obligations	4,803,000	3,815,000	5,420,000	5,674,000	3,859,000	4,237,000	4,252,000	4,257,000
Total Liabilities	12,173,000	12,029,000	11,363,000	11,813,000	10,585,000	10,032,000	10,284,000	9,937,000
Stockholders' Equity	7,030,000	7,012,000	6,733,000	6,320,000	6,457,000	6,539,000	6,870,000	11,353,000
Shares Outstanding	1,379,621	1,373,496	1,362,104	1,346,647	1,327,451	1,322,296	1,355,711	1,449,055
Statistical Record								
Return on Assets %	0.60	0.56	1.91	N.M.	N.M.	N.M.	N.M.	2.03
Return on Equity %	1.59	1.51	5.30	N.M.	N.M.	N.M.	N.M.	3.89
EBITDA Margin %	18.96	15.87	8.05	N.M.	N.M.	5.24	N.M.	15.99
Net Margin %	12.53	1.15	4.14	N.M.	N.M.	N.M.	N.M.	5.79
Asset Turnover	0.50	0.49	0.46	0.43	0.44	0.42	0.38	0.35
Current Ratio	0.82	0.68	0.90	1.43	1.27	1.65	1.71	1.72
Debt to Equity	0.68	0.54	0.80	0.90	0.60	0.65	0.62	0.37
Price Range	29.80-24.42	29.80-21.88	24.48-16.07	18.94-13.22	13.98-11.37	12.38-5.73	6.36-4.97	7.79-5.09
P/E Ratio	372.50-305.25	372.50-273.50	97.92-64.28	...	...	...	...	26.86-17.55

Address: 300 Boston Scientific Way, Marlborough, MA 01752-1234 Telephone: 508-683-4000	Web Site: www.bostonscientific.com Officers: Michael F. Mahoney - Chairman, President, Chief Executive Officer Kevin J. Ballinger - Executive Vice President, Senior Vice President, Division Officer	Auditors: Ernst & Young LLP Investor Contact: 508-650-8023 Transfer Agents: Computershare Shareowner Services, Providence, RI

BRADY CORP

Exchange	Symbol	Price	52Wk Range
NYS	BRC	$38.55 (6/29/2018)	40.65-31.95

Yield	P/E	Div Acheiver
2.15	25.03	33 Years

*7 Year Price Score 97.20   *NYSE Composite Index=100   *12 Month Price Score 103.10

Interim Earnings (Per Share)

Qtr.	Oct	Jan	Apr	Jul
2014-15	0.26	0.23	0.34	(0.77)
2015-16	0.37	0.30	0.42	0.50
2016-17	0.44	0.49	0.43	0.48
2017-18	0.49	0.08	0.49	...

Interim Dividends (Per Share)

Amt	Decl	Ex	Rec	Pay
0.207Q	09/06/2017	10/06/2017	10/10/2017	10/31/2017
0.207Q	11/14/2017	01/09/2018	01/10/2018	01/31/2018
0.207Q	02/21/2018	04/06/2018	04/09/2018	04/30/2018
0.207Q	05/23/2018	07/09/2018	07/10/2018	07/31/2018

Indicated Div: $0.83 (Div. Reinv. Plan)

Valuation Analysis

		Institutional Holding	
Forecast EPS	$1.99	No of Institutions	268
	(06/04/2018)		
Market Cap	$1.9 Billion	Shares	
Book Value	$734.6 Million	51,316,888	
Price/Book	2.53	% Held	
Price/Sales	1.59	76.05	

TRADING VOLUME (thousand shares)

Business Summary: Printing (MIC: 7.5.5 SIC: 3999 NAIC: 339950)

Brady is a manufacturer and supplier of identification solutions and workplace safety products that identify and protect premises, products and people. Co. has two segments: Identification Solutions, which includes industrial and healthcare identification products in several categories, including facility identification and protection, product identification, wire identification, people identification, patient identification, and custom wristbands; and Workplace Safety, which includes workplace safety and compliance products in several categories, including safety and compliance signs, tags, and labels, informational and architectural signage, asset tracking labels, and first aid products.

Recent Developments: For the quarter ended Apr 30 2018, net income increased 15.3% to US$26.0 million from US$22.6 million in the year-earlier quarter. Revenues were US$298.4 million, up 8.2% from US$275.9 million the year before. Operating income was US$37.7 million versus US$31.6 million in the prior-year quarter, an increase of 19.5%. Direct operating expenses rose 8.3% to US$147.3 million from US$136.0 million in the comparable period the year before. Indirect operating expenses increased 4.6% to US$113.4 million from US$108.4 million in the equivalent prior-year period.

Prospects: Our evaluation of Brady Corp. as of Jan. 21, 2018 is the result of our systematic analysis on three basic characteristics: earnings strength, relative valuation, and recent stock price movement. The company has managed to produce a neutral trend in earnings per share over the past 5 quarters and while recent estimates for the company have remained steady, BRC has posted better than expected results. Based on operating earnings yield, the company is undervalued when compared to all of the companies in our coverage universe. Share price changes over the past year indicates that BRC will perform in line with the market over the near term.

Financial Data

(US$ in Thousands)	9 Mos	6 Mos	3 Mos	07/31/2017	07/31/2016	07/31/2015	07/31/2014	07/31/2013
Earnings Per Share	1.54	1.48	1.89	1.84	1.58	0.06	(0.89)	(3.02)
Cash Flow Per Share	2.75	2.58	2.81	2.82	2.74	1.82	1.80	2.80
Tang Book Value Per Share	5.21	4.60	4.42	4.08	2.26	1.67	2.48	1.09
Dividends Per Share	0.828	0.825	0.823	0.820	0.810	0.800	0.780	0.760
Dividend Payout %	53.73	55.74	43.52	44.57	51.27	1,333.33	...	...
Income Statement								
Total Revenue	876,352	577,931	290,151	1,113,316	1,120,625	1,171,731	1,225,034	1,152,109
EBITDA	128,266	84,319	42,191	152,326	140,544	63,506	(12,082)	(33,380)
Depn & Amortn	19,047	12,840	6,564	20,190	23,375	27,355	26,727	48,725
Income Before Taxes	106,766	69,787	34,764	126,632	109,345	24,995	(53,109)	(98,746)
Income Taxes	50,657	39,678	8,928	30,987	29,235	20,093	(4,963)	42,070
Net Income	56,109	30,109	25,836	95,645	80,110	2,987	(45,968)	(154,535)
Average Shares	52,729	52,719	52,383	51,956	50,769	51,383	51,866	51,330
Balance Sheet								
Current Assets	425,050	414,122	423,642	407,814	407,424	408,582	463,842	512,490
Total Assets	1,033,407	1,034,385	1,057,613	1,050,223	1,043,964	1,062,897	1,253,665	1,438,683
Current Liabilities	181,394	171,672	193,785	187,198	166,727	209,247	291,945	323,497
Long-Term Obligations	58,157	70,615	93,810	104,536	211,982	200,774	159,296	201,150
Total Liabilities	298,760	302,412	344,942	350,083	440,366	475,209	520,589	607,886
Stockholders' Equity	734,647	731,973	712,671	700,140	603,598	587,688	733,076	830,797
Shares Outstanding	48,205	51,777	51,559	51,353	50,459	51,319	51,322	52,173
Statistical Record								
Return on Assets %	7.95	7.65	9.39	9.13	7.58	0.26	N.M.	N.M.
Return on Equity %	11.63	11.40	14.91	14.67	13.41	0.45	N.M.	N.M.
EBITDA Margin %	14.64	14.59	14.54	13.68	12.54	5.42	N.M.	N.M.
Net Margin %	6.40	5.21	8.90	8.59	7.15	0.25	N.M.	N.M.
Asset Turnover	1.14	1.12	1.07	1.06	1.06	1.01	0.91	0.76
Current Ratio	2.34	2.41	2.19	2.18	2.44	1.95	1.59	1.58
Debt to Equity	0.08	0.10	0.13	0.15	0.35	0.34	0.22	0.24
Price Range	39.80-31.95	39.80-31.95	39.80-31.95	39.80-31.86	32.64-19.92	28.91-21.19	35.54-24.26	36.33-26.34
P/E Ratio	25.84-20.75	26.89-21.59	21.06-16.90	21.63-17.32	20.66-12.35	481.83-353.17	...	...
Average Yield %	2.24	2.23	2.25	2.27	3.20	3.12	2.69	2.38

Address: 6555 West Good Hope Road, Milwaukee, WI 53223
Telephone: 414-358-6600

Web Site: www.bradycorp.com
Officers: J. Michael Nauman - President, Chief Executive Officer Thomas J. Felmer - Interim President, Interim Chief Executive Officer, Senior Vice President, Chief Financial Officer, Division Officer

Auditors: DELOITTE & TOUCHE LLP
Investor Contact: 414-438-6940
Transfer Agents: Wells Fargo Bank Minnesota, N.A., St. Paul, MN

111

BRANDYWINE REALTY TRUST

Exchange	Symbol	Price	52Wk Range	Yield	P/E
NYS	BDN	$16.88 (6/29/2018)	18.58-15.32	4.27	21.37

*7 Year Price Score 95.52   *NYSE Composite Index=100   *12 Month Price Score 95.42

Interim Earnings (Per Share)

Qtr.	Mar	Jun	Sep	Dec
2015	0.04	0.01	0.10	(0.36)
2016	0.25	(0.02)	0.03	(0.08)
2017	0.11	0.02	0.11	0.41
2018	0.25	...	...	...

Interim Dividends (Per Share)

Amt	Decl	Ex	Rec	Pay
0.16Q	09/12/2017	10/03/2017	10/04/2017	10/18/2017
0.18Q	12/07/2017	01/08/2018	01/09/2018	01/23/2018
0.18Q	02/28/2018	04/03/2018	04/04/2018	04/18/2018
0.18Q	05/23/2018	07/05/2018	07/06/2018	07/20/2018

Indicated Div: $0.72 (Div. Reinv. Plan)

Valuation Analysis

		Institutional Holding	
Forecast EPS	$0.46 (06/13/2018)	No of Institutions	378
Market Cap	$3.0 Billion	Shares	
Book Value	$1.8 Billion		243,859,680
Price/Book	1.63	% Held	
Price/Sales	5.73		96.29

Business Summary: REITs (MIC: 5.3.1 SIC: 6798 NAIC: 525930)

Brandywine Realty Trust is a self-administered and self-managed real estate investment trust that provides leasing, property management, development, redevelopment, acquisition and other tenant-related services for a portfolio of office, residential, retail and mixed-use properties. As of Dec 31 2017, Co. owned 93 properties (the Properties) and economic interests in 13 unconsolidated real estate ventures (the Real Estate Ventures). The Properties and the properties owned by the Real Estate Ventures are located in or near Philadelphia, PA; Metropolitan Washington, D.C.; Southern New Jersey; Richmond, VA; Wilmington, DE and Austin, TX.

Recent Developments: For the quarter ended Mar 31 2018, net income increased 110.2% to US$44.7 million from US$21.3 million in the year-earlier quarter. Revenues were US$136.4 million, up 4.2% from US$130.9 million the year before. Revenues from property income rose 3.4% to US$134.4 million from US$130.0 million in the corresponding quarter a year earlier.

Prospects: Our evaluation of Brandywine Realty Trust as of Jan. 21, 2018 is the result of our systematic analysis on three basic characteristics: earnings strength, relative valuation, and recent stock price movement. The company has enjoyed a very positive trend in earnings per share over the past 5 quarters. Because the company lacks sufficient analyst estimate data, we place greater weight on the historical EPS trend as the measure of earnings strength. Based on operating earnings yield, the company is overvalued when compared to all of the companies in our coverage universe. Share price changes over the past year indicates that BDN will perform well over the near term.

Financial Data
(US$ in Thousands)

	3 Mos	12/31/2017	12/31/2016	12/31/2015	12/31/2014	12/31/2013	12/31/2012	12/31/2011
Earnings Per Share	0.79	0.65	0.19	(0.21)	...	0.23	(0.06)	(0.10)
Cash Flow Per Share	1.01	1.04	0.98	1.10	1.14	1.20	1.09	1.32
Tang Book Value Per Share	10.01	9.90	10.24	10.43	11.39	11.28	11.72	12.52
Dividends Per Share	0.660	0.640	0.620	0.600	0.600	0.600	0.600	0.600
Dividend Payout %	83.54	98.46	326.32	...	...	260.87	...	...
Income Statement								
Total Revenue	136,358	520,493	525,463	602,631	596,982	562,210	559,833	581,805
EBITDA	68,400	397,918	330,475	305,294	344,407	367,574	310,238	337,860
Depn & Amortn	3,275	185,173	191,624	219,936	210,946	205,715	206,148	220,284
Income Before Taxes	45,668	129,537	52,004	(29,929)	6,814	35,318	(32,895)	(17,007)
Income Taxes	138	(628)	...	...	...	...	...	...
Net Income	44,329	120,850	40,191	(30,401)	6,975	42,777	6,595	(4,499)
Average Shares	179,788	176,808	176,010	178,162	166,202	154,414	143,257	135,444
Balance Sheet								
Current Assets	392,843	389,877	355,989	218,912	410,310	406,891	139,213	125,595
Total Assets	4,037,936	3,995,448	4,099,213	4,554,511	4,859,173	4,765,095	4,506,709	4,557,718
Current Liabilities	137,678	182,123	165,056	158,518	184,369	180,912	178,178	193,393
Long-Term Obligations	1,940,032	1,930,828	2,013,112	2,384,717	2,451,308	2,595,381	2,465,330	2,393,995
Total Liabilities	2,188,233	2,166,268	2,232,869	2,620,586	2,718,346	2,864,875	2,754,431	2,701,127
Stockholders' Equity	1,849,703	1,829,180	1,866,344	1,933,925	2,140,827	1,900,220	1,752,278	1,856,591
Shares Outstanding	178,442	178,285	175,140	174,688	179,293	156,731	143,538	142,690
Statistical Record								
Return on Assets %	3.54	2.99	0.93	N.M.	0.14	0.92	0.15	N.M.
Return on Equity %	7.76	6.54	2.11	N.M.	0.35	2.34	0.36	N.M.
EBITDA Margin %	50.16	76.45	62.89	50.66	57.69	65.38	55.42	58.07
Net Margin %	32.51	23.22	7.65	N.M.	1.17	7.61	1.18	N.M.
Asset Turnover	0.13	0.13	0.12	0.13	0.12	0.12	0.12	0.13
Current Ratio	2.85	2.14	2.16	1.38	2.23	2.25	0.78	0.65
Debt to Equity	1.05	1.06	1.08	1.23	1.15	1.37	1.41	1.29
Price Range	18.58-15.32	18.58-15.74	16.87-11.29	17.00-11.72	16.29-13.77	15.94-12.18	12.88-9.40	12.76-7.09
P/E Ratio	23.52-19.39	28.58-24.22	88.79-59.42	...	N.M.	69.30-52.96	...	...
Average Yield %	3.85	3.76	4.15	4.23	4.00	4.36	5.17	5.65

Address: 2929 Walnut Street, Suite 1700, Philadelphia, PA 19104	Web Site: www.brandywinerealty.com	Auditors: PricewaterhouseCoopers LLP
Telephone: 610-325-5600	Officers: Gerard H. Sweeney - President, Chief Executive Officer Thomas E. Wirth - Executive Vice President, Chief Financial Officer, Principal Accounting Officer	Investor Contact: 610-832-7702 Transfer Agents: Computershare, Providence, RI

BRIGHT HORIZONS FAMILY SOLUTIONS, INC

Exchange	Symbol	Price	52Wk Range	Yield	P/E
NYS	BFAM	$102.52 (6/29/2018)	108.09-75.84	N/A	40.68

*7 Year Price Score N/A *NYSE Composite Index=100 *12 Month Price Score 109.50

TRADING VOLUME (thousand shares)

Interim Earnings (Per Share)

Qtr.	Mar	Jun	Sep	Dec
2015	0.35	0.43	0.33	0.39
2016	0.40	0.50	0.37	0.28
2017	0.68	0.54	0.51	0.85
2018	0.62	...	...	...

Interim Dividends (Per Share)

No Dividends Paid

Valuation Analysis | Institutional Holding

Forecast EPS	$3.15	No of Institutions
	(06/13/2018)	N/A
Market Cap	$5.9 Billion	Shares
Book Value	$737.2 Million	N/A
Price/Book	8.00	% Held
Price/Sales	3.31	N/A

Business Summary: Services (MIC: 6.1.2 SIC: 8351 NAIC: 624410)

Bright Horizons Family Solutions is a provider of child care, early education, back-up dependent care and educational advisory services. Co. provides services under contracts with employers. Co.'s service offerings include center-based full service child care and early education, back-up dependent care, and educational advisory services. Co.'s center-based child care services have two models: a profit and loss model; and a cost-plus model. Co. also provides back-up dependent care services through its full-service centers, its back-up centers, as well as through its Back-Up Care Advantage program. Co.'s educational advisory services consist of its EdAssist and College Coach services.

Recent Developments: For the quarter ended Mar 31 2018, net income decreased 9.9% to US$37.3 million from US$41.4 million in the year-earlier quarter. Revenues were US$463.7 million, up 9.8% from US$422.2 million the year before. Operating income was US$55.3 million versus US$51.4 million in the prior-year quarter, an increase of 7.5%. Direct operating expenses rose 10.4% to US$350.1 million from US$317.2 million in the comparable period the year before. Indirect operating expenses increased 8.8% to US$58.3 million from US$53.5 million in the equivalent prior-year period.

Prospects: Our evaluation of Bright Horizons Family Solutions Inc as of Jan. 21, 2018 is the result of our systematic analysis on three basic characteristics: earnings strength, relative valuation, and recent stock price movement. The company has generated a negative trend in earnings per share over the past 5 quarters and while recent estimates for the company have been mixed, BFAM has posted better than expected results. Based on operating earnings yield, the company is about fairly valued when compared to all of the companies in our coverage universe. Share price changes over the past year indicates that BFAM will perform well over the near term.

Financial Data
(US$ in Thousands)

	3 Mos	12/31/2017	12/31/2016	12/31/2015	12/31/2014	12/31/2013	12/31/2012	12/31/2011
Earnings Per Share	2.52	2.59	1.55	1.50	1.07	0.20	(12.62)	(11.32)
Cash Flow Per Share	4.04	4.01	3.59	2.80	2.66	2.55	17.61	22.20
Income Statement								
Total Revenue	463,657	1,740,905	1,569,841	1,458,445	1,352,999	1,218,776	1,070,938	973,701
EBITDA	55,749	300,200	271,363	260,291	224,319	118,127	129,864	115,671
Depn & Amortn	465	94,761	85,242	78,689	77,399	72,775	34,400	28,000
Income Before Taxes	43,781	161,400	143,197	140,156	112,314	4,811	11,752	5,587
Income Taxes	6,483	4,437	48,437	46,229	40,279	(7,533)	3,243	825
Net Income	37,298	156,963	94,760	93,927	72,035	12,623	8,162	4,759
Average Shares	59,448	60,253	60,594	62,360	67,244	64,509	6,058	6,016
Balance Sheet								
Current Assets	196,346	192,461	154,399	152,713	223,158	165,170	136,017	124,205
Total Assets	2,514,480	2,468,644	2,359,017	2,150,541	2,141,076	2,102,670	1,913,632	1,771,164
Current Liabilities	511,723	460,655	387,580	305,343	279,423	255,088	201,893	193,672
Long-Term Obligations	1,043,788	1,046,011	1,054,009	905,661	911,627	756,323	904,607	794,443
Total Liabilities	1,777,303	1,719,584	1,671,150	1,422,933	1,390,117	1,213,533	1,313,418	1,204,770
Stockholders' Equity	737,177	749,060	687,867	727,608	750,959	889,137	600,214	566,394
Shares Outstanding	57,544	58,013	58,910	60,008	61,534	65,302	7,389	7,335
Statistical Record								
Return on Assets %	6.25	6.50	4.19	4.38	3.39	0.63	0.44	0.27
Return on Equity %	20.90	21.85	13.35	12.71	8.78	1.70	1.40	0.84
EBITDA Margin %	12.02	17.24	17.29	17.85	16.58	9.69	12.13	11.88
Net Margin %	8.04	9.02	6.04	6.44	5.32	1.04	0.76	0.49
Asset Turnover	0.73	0.72	0.69	0.68	0.64	0.61	0.58	0.56
Current Ratio	0.38	0.42	0.40	0.50	0.80	0.65	0.67	0.64
Debt to Equity	1.42	1.40	1.53	1.24	1.21	0.85	1.51	1.40
Price Range	104.67-70.04	94.71-68.01	72.30-60.59	68.58-44.22	47.14-35.94	38.15-27.50	...	...
P/E Ratio	41.54-27.79	36.57-26.26	46.65-39.09	45.72-29.48	44.06-33.59	190.75-137.50	...	...

Address: 200 Talcott Avenue South, Watertown, MA 02472	**Web Site:** www.brighthorizons.com	**Auditors:** DELOITTE & TOUCHE LLP
Telephone: 617-673-8000	**Officers:** David H. Lissy - Executive Chairman, Chief Executive Officer Linda A. Mason - Chairman	**Transfer Agents:** Wells Fargo Shareowner Services SM, St. Paul, MN

BRINKER INTERNATIONAL, INC.

Exchange	Symbol	Price	52Wk Range	Yield	P/E
NYS	EAT	$47.60 (6/29/2018)	52.12-29.89	3.19	17.18

*7 Year Price Score 71.00   ***NYSE Composite Index=100**   ***12 Month Price Score 122.16**

Interim Earnings (Per Share)

Qtr.	Sep	Dec	Mar	Jun*
2014-15	0.49	0.64	1.02	0.91
2015-16	0.54	0.80	1.00	1.09
2016-17	0.42	0.69	0.86	1.01
2017-18	0.20	0.54	1.02	...

Interim Dividends (Per Share)

Amt	Decl	Ex	Rec	Pay
0.38Q	08/10/2017	09/07/2017	09/08/2017	09/28/2017
0.38Q	11/16/2017	12/07/2017	12/08/2017	12/28/2017
0.38Q	02/06/2018	03/08/2018	03/09/2018	03/29/2018
0.38Q	04/30/2018	06/07/2018	06/08/2018	06/28/2018

Indicated Div: $1.52

TRADING VOLUME (thousand shares)

Valuation Analysis		Institutional Holding	
Forecast EPS	$3.52	No of Institutions	453
	(06/14/2018)		
Market Cap	$2.1 Billion	Shares	69,087,808
Book Value	N/A	% Held	83.03
Price/Book	N/A		
Price/Sales	0.67		

Business Summary: Hotels, Restaurants & Travel (MIC: 2.2.1 SIC: 5812 NAIC: 722110)

Brinker International owns, develops, operates and franchises the Chili's® Grill & Bar (Chili's) and Maggiano's Little Italy® (Maggiano's) restaurant brands. Co.'s Chili's restaurant menu features American food and Fresh Mex and Fresh Tex offerings, including burgers, ribs and fajitas, as well as margaritas. Co.'s Maggiano's restaurant features lunch and dinner menu in the form of appetizers and entrees with pasta, chicken, seafood, veal, steaks and desserts, including a selection of cocktails and wines. As of June 28 2017, Co.'s system of Co.-owned and franchised restaurants included 1,674 restaurants located in 49 states and Washington, D.C. Co. also has restaurants in other countries.

Recent Developments: For the quarter ended Mar 28 2018, net income increased 10.7% to US$46.9 million from US$42.4 million in the year-earlier quarter. Revenues were US$812.5 million, up 0.2% from US$810.6 million the year before. Operating income was US$72.7 million versus US$72.9 million in the prior-year quarter, a decrease of 0.2%. Direct operating expenses rose 1.1% to US$662.9 million from US$655.9 million in the comparable period the year before. Indirect operating expenses decreased 6.0% to US$76.9 million from US$81.9 million in the equivalent prior-year period.

Prospects: Our evaluation of Brinker International Inc. as of Jan. 21, 2018 is the result of our systematic analysis on three basic characteristics: earnings strength, relative valuation, and recent stock price movement. The company has produced a positive trend in earnings per share over the past 5 quarters and while recent estimates for the company have been raised by analysts, EAT has posted results that fell short of analysts expectations. Based on operating earnings yield, the company is undervalued when compared to all of the companies in our coverage universe. Share price changes over the past year indicates that EAT will perform poorly over the near term.

Financial Data

(US$ in Thousands)	9 Mos	6 Mos	3 Mos	06/28/2017	06/29/2016	06/24/2015	06/25/2014	06/26/2013
Earnings Per Share	2.77	2.61	2.76	2.94	3.42	3.05	2.26	2.20
Cash Flow Per Share	6.76	6.28	6.15	6.20	6.71	5.86	5.45	4.06
Tang Book Value Per Share	...	...	...	...	...	...	N.M.	0.11
Dividends Per Share	1.480	1.440	1.400	1.360	1.280	1.120	0.960	0.800
Dividend Payout %	53.43	55.17	50.72	46.26	37.43	36.72	42.48	36.36
Income Statement								
Total Revenue	2,318,324	1,505,790	739,390	3,150,837	3,257,489	3,002,278	2,905,452	2,846,098
EBITDA	159,410	85,462	29,516	260,043	475,329	458,525	380,460	390,914
Depn & Amortn	1,449	966	483	1,988	156,368	145,242	136,081	131,481
Income Before Taxes	115,207	56,291	15,149	208,508	286,387	284,277	216,288	230,315
Income Taxes	33,048	21,048	5,272	57,685	85,642	87,583	62,249	66,956
Net Income	82,159	35,243	9,877	150,823	200,745	196,694	154,039	163,359
Average Shares	45,973	46,880	48,732	51,250	58,684	64,404	68,152	74,158
Balance Sheet								
Current Assets	144,019	194,474	140,876	154,392	176,774	189,717	210,854	198,591
Total Assets	1,336,879	1,400,545	1,368,625	1,413,700	1,472,716	1,435,873	1,490,604	1,452,603
Current Liabilities	448,997	451,876	414,362	446,428	432,443	418,475	466,110	390,211
Long-Term Obligations	1,361,705	1,365,255	1,353,659	1,319,829	1,113,949	970,825	832,302	780,121
Total Liabilities	1,945,421	1,953,405	1,907,653	1,907,381	1,685,815	1,514,333	1,427,510	1,303,246
Stockholders' Equity	(608,542)	(552,860)	(539,028)	(493,681)	(213,099)	(78,460)	63,094	149,357
Shares Outstanding	43,843	46,339	47,233	48,440	55,420	60,585	64,558	67,444
Statistical Record								
Return on Assets %	9.69	8.85	9.72	10.48	13.58	13.48	10.50	11.34
Return on Equity %	...	...	...	...	...	...	145.41	71.34
EBITDA Margin %	6.88	5.68	3.99	8.25	14.59	15.27	13.09	13.74
Net Margin %	3.54	2.34	1.34	4.79	6.16	6.55	5.30	5.74
Asset Turnover	2.28	2.16	2.22	2.19	2.20	2.06	1.98	1.98
Current Ratio	0.32	0.43	0.34	0.35	0.41	0.45	0.45	0.51
Debt to Equity	...	...	...	...	...	...	13.19	5.22
Price Range	45.46-29.89	50.49-29.89	55.19-29.89	55.19-36.93	59.90-43.42	63.12-44.16	55.00-38.19	41.60-28.71
P/E Ratio	16.41-10.79	19.34-11.45	20.00-10.83	18.77-12.56	17.51-12.70	20.70-14.48	24.34-16.90	18.91-13.05
Average Yield %	4.03	3.72	3.25	2.89	2.60	2.04	2.08	2.32

Address: 6820 LBJ Freeway, Dallas, TX 75240	Web Site: www.brinker.com	Auditors: KPMG LLP
Telephone: 972-980-9917	Officers: Joseph M. (Joe) DePinto - Chairman Wyman T. Roberts - President, Chief Executive Officer	Investor Contact: 972-980-9917 Transfer Agents: Computershare, Canton, MA

BRINKS CO (THE)

Exchange	Symbol	Price	52Wk Range	Yield	P/E
NYS	BCO	$79.75 (6/29/2018)	87.85-66.30	0.75	996.88

*7 Year Price Score 167.26 *NYSE Composite Index=100   *12 Month Price Score 97.88

Interim Earnings (Per Share)

Qtr.	Mar	Jun	Sep	Dec
2015	(0.06)	(0.26)	0.15	(0.07)
2016	(0.06)	0.01	0.48	0.25
2017	0.67	0.28	0.38	(1.01)
2018	0.43	...	...	...

Interim Dividends (Per Share)

Amt	Decl	Ex	Rec	Pay
0.15Q	10/17/2017	11/10/2017	11/13/2017	12/01/2017
0.15Q	01/15/2018	02/07/2018	02/08/2018	03/01/2018
0.15Q	05/03/2018	05/17/2018	05/18/2018	06/01/2018
0.15Q	07/13/2018	07/26/2018	07/27/2018	09/01/2018

Indicated Div: $0.60

Valuation Analysis

		Institutional Holding	
Forecast EPS	$3.75	No of Institutions	
	(06/14/2018)	427	
Market Cap	$4.1 Billion	Shares	
Book Value	$342.1 Million	59,784,448	
Price/Book	11.87	% Held	
Price/Sales	1.18	105.25	

Business Summary: Business Services (MIC: 7.5.2 SIC: 4731 NAIC: 488510)

Brink's is a provider of logistics and security solutions including cash-in-transit, Automated teller machine (ATM) replenishment and maintenance, cash management services, including vault outsourcing, money processing, and intelligent safe services, international transportation of valuables, and payment services. Co.'s primary services include: Cash-in-Transit Services, which include the transportation of: cash between businesses and financial institutions; ATM Services, which provides customers who own and operate ATMs a variety of service options; and Cash Management Services, which include money processing and other cash management services.

Recent Developments: For the quarter ended Mar 31 2018, income from continuing operations decreased 37.5% to US$25.3 million from US$40.5 million in the year-earlier quarter. Net income decreased 37.0% to US$25.5 million from US$40.5 million in the year-earlier quarter. Revenues were US$879.1 million, up 11.5% from US$788.4 million the year before. Operating income was US$64.8 million versus US$70.9 million in the prior-year quarter, a decrease of 8.6%. Direct operating expenses rose 13.6% to US$693.6 million from US$610.3 million in the comparable period the year before. Indirect operating expenses increased 12.6% to US$120.7 million from US$107.2 million in the equivalent prior-year period.

Prospects: Our evaluation of Brink's Co as of Jan. 21, 2018 is the result of our systematic analysis on three basic characteristics: earnings strength, relative valuation, and recent stock price movement. The company has generated a negative trend in earnings per share over the past 5 quarters. However, while recent estimates for the company have been mixed, BCO has posted better than expected results. Based on operating earnings yield, the company is about fairly valued when compared to all of the companies in our coverage universe. Share price changes over the past year indicates that BCO will perform very well over the near term.

Financial Data

(US$ in Thousands)	3 Mos	12/31/2017	12/31/2016	12/31/2015	12/31/2014	12/31/2013	12/31/2012	12/31/2011
Earnings Per Share	0.08	0.32	0.68	(0.24)	(1.71)	1.16	1.83	1.55
Cash Flow Per Share	5.54	4.97	3.34	4.24	2.88	4.14	5.16	5.17
Tang Book Value Per Share	N.M.	N.M.	2.64	2.13	3.67	8.42	4.22	2.41
Dividends Per Share	0.600	0.550	0.400	0.400	0.400	0.400	0.400	0.400
Dividend Payout %	750.00	171.88	58.82	...	...	34.48	21.86	25.81
Income Statement								
Total Revenue	879,100	3,347,000	3,020,600	3,061,400	3,562,300	3,942,200	3,842,100	3,885,500
EBITDA	87,900	239,700	167,500	81,100	(27,400)	345,300	342,000	332,100
Depn & Amortn	38,800	28,900	23,200	24,900	5,500	181,400	174,600	162,400
Income Before Taxes	35,600	181,100	126,500	40,600	(53,300)	141,500	148,500	151,600
Income Taxes	11,400	157,700	78,500	66,500	36,700	52,000	26,900	59,400
Net Income	22,300	16,700	34,500	(11,900)	(83,900)	56,800	88,900	74,500
Average Shares	52,100	51,800	50,600	49,300	49,000	49,000	48,600	48,100
Balance Sheet								
Current Assets	1,507,300	1,488,200	843,700	777,700	907,600	1,102,700	995,500	933,900
Total Assets	3,099,100	3,059,600	1,994,800	1,946,700	2,192,200	2,498,000	2,553,900	2,406,200
Current Liabilities	852,600	834,900	753,800	641,800	728,400	798,600	743,000	702,100
Long-Term Obligations	1,137,700	1,139,600	247,600	358,100	373,300	330,500	335,600	335,300
Total Liabilities	2,757,000	2,742,200	1,657,700	1,628,800	1,758,200	1,804,100	2,052,100	1,998,200
Stockholders' Equity	342,100	317,400	337,100	317,900	434,000	693,900	501,800	408,000
Shares Outstanding	50,900	50,500	50,000	48,900	48,600	48,400	47,800	46,900
Statistical Record								
Return on Assets %	0.16	0.66	1.75	N.M.	N.M.	2.25	3.57	3.19
Return on Equity %	1.16	5.10	10.51	N.M.	N.M.	9.50	19.49	16.12
EBITDA Margin %	10.00	7.16	5.55	2.65	N.M.	8.76	8.90	8.55
Net Margin %	2.54	0.50	1.14	N.M.	N.M.	1.44	2.31	1.92
Asset Turnover	1.31	1.32	1.53	1.48	1.52	1.56	1.54	1.66
Current Ratio	1.77	1.78	1.12	1.21	1.25	1.38	1.34	1.33
Debt to Equity	3.33	3.59	0.73	1.13	0.86	0.48	0.67	0.82
Price Range	87.85-53.10	87.00-41.30	45.10-26.04	33.54-22.41	35.57-20.10	34.44-24.37	29.62-21.05	34.28-21.85
P/E Ratio	N.M.	271.88-129.06	66.32-38.29	...	...	29.69-21.01	16.19-11.50	22.12-14.10
Average Yield %	0.81	0.82	1.19	1.39	1.49	1.41	1.61	1.43

Address: 1801 Bayberry Court,	Web Site: www.brinks.com	Auditors: DELOITTE & TOUCHE LLP
Richmond, VA 23226-8100	Officers: Douglas A. Pertz - President, Chief	Investor Contact: 804-289-9708
Telephone: 804-289-9600	Executive Officer Ronald J. (Ron) Domanico -	Transfer Agents: Computershare,
	Executive Vice President, Chief Financial Officer	Providence, RI

BRISTOL-MYERS SQUIBB CO.

Exchange	Symbol	Price	52Wk Range	Yield	P/E
NYS	BMY	$55.34 (6/29/2018)	68.98-50.53	2.89	97.09

*7 Year Price Score 93.16 *NYSE Composite Index=100 *12 Month Price Score 87.01

Interim Earnings (Per Share)

Qtr.	Mar	Jun	Sep	Dec
2015	0.71	(0.08)	0.42	(0.12)
2016	0.71	0.70	0.72	0.53
2017	0.94	0.56	0.51	(1.41)
2018	0.91	...	...	...

Interim Dividends (Per Share)

Amt	Decl	Ex	Rec	Pay
0.39Q	09/13/2017	10/05/2017	10/06/2017	11/01/2017
0.40Q	12/07/2017	01/04/2018	01/05/2018	02/01/2018
0.40Q	03/01/2018	04/05/2018	04/06/2018	05/01/2018
0.40Q	06/14/2018	07/05/2018	07/06/2018	08/01/2018

Indicated Div: $1.60

Valuation Analysis | **Institutional Holding**

Forecast EPS	$3.40	No of Institutions
	(06/14/2018)	2386
Market Cap	$90.5 Billion	Shares
Book Value	$12.8 Billion	1,451,588,480
Price/Book	7.07	% Held
Price/Sales	4.30	67.12

TRADING VOLUME (thousand shares)

Business Summary: Pharmaceuticals (MIC: 4.1.1 SIC: 2834 NAIC: 325412)

Bristol-Myers Squibb is engaged in the discovery, development, licensing, manufacturing, marketing, distribution and sale of biopharmaceutical products. Co. has products in the following therapeutic classes: oncology; cardiovascular; immunoscience; and virology, including human immunodeficiency virus (HIV) infection. Co.'s products include: Empliciti, a humanized monoclonal antibody for the treatment of multiple myeloma; Yervoy, a monoclonal antibody for the treatment of patients with unresectable or metastatic melanoma; Baraclude, an oral antiviral agent for the treatment of chronic hepatitis B; and Reyataz is a protease inhibitor for the treatment of HIV.

Recent Developments: For the quarter ended Mar 31 2018, net income decreased 2.0% to US$1.50 billion from US$1.53 billion in the year-earlier quarter. Revenues were US$5.19 billion, up 5.4% from US$4.93 billion the year before. Direct operating expenses rose 25.2% to US$1.58 billion from US$1.27 billion in the comparable period the year before. Indirect operating expenses decreased 6.6% to US$2.23 billion from US$2.39 billion in the equivalent prior-year period.

Prospects: Our evaluation of Bristol-Myers Squibb Co. as of Jan. 21, 2018 is the result of our systematic analysis on three basic characteristics: earnings strength, relative valuation, and recent stock price movement. The company has generated a negative trend in earnings per share over the past 5 quarters. However, while recent estimates for the company have been mixed, BMY has posted results that fell short of analysts expectations. Based on operating earnings yield, the company is undervalued when compared to all of the companies in our coverage universe. Share price changes over the past year indicates that BMY will perform well over the near term.

Financial Data
(US$ in Millions)

	3 Mos	12/31/2017	12/31/2016	12/31/2015	12/31/2014	12/31/2013	12/31/2012	12/31/2011
Earnings Per Share	0.57	0.61	2.65	0.93	1.20	1.54	1.16	2.16
Cash Flow Per Share	3.42	3.21	1.70	1.10	1.90	2.16	4.14	2.85
Tang Book Value Per Share	2.95	2.26	4.76	3.57	3.66	3.48	N.M.	4.29
Dividends Per Share	1.570	1.560	1.140	1.490	1.450	1.760	1.360	1.320
Dividend Payout %	275.44	255.74	43.02	160.22	120.83	114.29	117.24	61.11
Income Statement								
Total Revenue	5,193	20,776	19,427	16,560	15,879	16,385	17,621	21,244
EBITDA	1,949	6,009	6,530	2,761	3,127	3,543	2,798	7,202
Depn & Amortn	163	682	448	500	543	453	382	448
Income Before Taxes	1,740	5,131	5,915	2,077	2,381	2,891	2,340	6,700
Income Taxes	284	4,156	1,408	446	352	311	(161)	1,721
Net Income	1,486	1,007	4,457	1,565	2,004	2,563	1,960	3,709
Average Shares	1,640	1,652	1,680	1,679	1,670	1,662	1,688	1,717
Balance Sheet								
Current Assets	14,649	14,854	13,704	10,415	14,608	18,916	9,521	15,318
Total Assets	33,083	33,551	33,707	31,748	33,749	38,592	35,897	32,970
Current Liabilities	9,624	9,563	8,841	8,017	8,461	12,440	8,279	7,780
Long-Term Obligations	5,775	6,975	5,716	6,550	7,242	7,981	6,568	5,376
Total Liabilities	20,290	21,810	17,530	17,482	18,897	23,438	22,274	17,014
Stockholders' Equity	12,793	11,741	16,177	14,266	14,852	15,154	13,623	15,956
Shares Outstanding	1,634	1,625	1,664	1,669	1,661	1,649	1,630	1,690
Statistical Record								
Return on Assets %	2.78	2.99	13.58	4.78	5.54	6.88	5.68	11.58
Return on Equity %	6.76	7.21	29.20	10.75	13.36	-17.81	13.22	23.42
EBITDA Margin %	37.53	28.92	33.61	16.67	19.69	21.62	15.88	33.90
Net Margin %	28.62	4.85	22.94	9.45	12.62	15.64	11.12	17.46
Asset Turnover	0.64	0.62	0.59	0.51	0.44	0.44	0.51	0.66
Current Ratio	1.52	1.55	1.55	1.30	1.73	1.52	1.15	1.97
Debt to Equity	0.45	0.59	0.35	0.46	0.49	0.53	0.48	0.34
Price Range	68.98-51.66	65.35-46.82	76.77-49.23	70.71-57.30	61.30-46.59	53.84-32.59	36.15-30.81	35.29-24.97
P/E Ratio	121.02-90.63	107.13-76.75	28.97-18.58	76.03-61.61	51.08-38.83	34.96-21.16	31.16-26.56	16.34-11.56
Average Yield %	2.62	2.71	1.80	2.31	2.78	4.02	4.08	4.56

Address: 345 Park Avenue, New York, NY 10154	**Web Site:** www.bms.com	**Auditors:** DELOITTE & TOUCHE LLP
Telephone: 212-546-4000	**Officers:** Giovanni Caforio - Chairman, Chief Executive Officer, Executive Vice President, Chief Commercial Officer, Chief Operating Officer, Division Officer Sandra Leung - Executive Vice President, General Counsel, Senior Vice President, Corporate Secretary	**Investor Contact:** 609-252-4611
Fax: 212-546-4020		**Transfer Agents:** Wells Fargo Shareowner Services, Mendota Heights, MN

BRIXMOR PROPERTY GROUP INC

Exchange	Symbol	Price	52Wk Range	Yield	P/E
NYS	BRX	$17.43 (6/29/2018)	20.00-13.98	6.31	18.35

*7 Year Price Score N/A *NYSE Composite Index=100 *12 Month Price Score 91.97

Interim Earnings (Per Share)

Qtr.	Mar	Jun	Sep	Dec
2015	0.10	0.18	0.18	0.19
2016	0.20	0.21	0.19	0.30
2017	0.23	0.25	0.27	0.23
2018	0.20	...	...	...

Interim Dividends (Per Share)

Amt	Decl	Ex	Rec	Pay
0.26Q	07/31/2017	10/04/2017	10/05/2017	10/16/2017
0.275Q	10/30/2017	01/03/2018	01/04/2018	01/16/2018
0.275Q	02/12/2018	04/04/2018	04/05/2018	04/16/2018
0.275Q	04/30/2018	07/05/2018	07/06/2018	07/16/2018

Indicated Div: $1.10 (Div. Reinv. Plan)

Valuation Analysis

		Institutional Holding	
Forecast EPS	$0.82	No of Institutions	
	(06/13/2018)	395	
Market Cap	$5.3 Billion	Shares	
Book Value	$2.9 Billion	339,383,648	
Price/Book	1.84	% Held	
Price/Sales	4.14	100.79	

Business Summary: REITs (MIC: 5.3.1 SIC: 6798 NAIC: 525930)

Brixmor Property Group is an internally-managed real estate investment trust. Brixmor Operating Partnership LP and subsidiaries (Operating Partnership) is the entity through which Co. conducts substantially all of its operations and owns substantially all of its assets. Co. is engaged in the ownership, management, leasing, acquisition, disposition and redevelopment of retail shopping centers through the Operating Partnership. As of Dec 31 2017, Co.'s portfolio was comprised of 486 shopping centers. In addition, Co. has one land parcel currently under development.

Recent Developments: For the quarter ended Mar 31 2018, net income decreased 14.8% to US$61.0 million from US$71.7 million in the year-earlier quarter. Revenues were US$317.2 million, down 2.6% from US$325.8 million the year before. Revenues from property income fell 2.5% to US$243.3 million from US$249.6 million in the corresponding quarter a year earlier.

Prospects: Our evaluation of Brixmor Property Group Inc as of Jan. 21, 2018 is the result of our systematic analysis on three basic characteristics: earnings strength, relative valuation, and recent stock price movement. The company has generated a negative trend in earnings per share over the past 5 quarters and while recent estimates for the company have remained steady, BRX has posted better than expected results. Based on operating earnings yield, the company is undervalued when compared to all of the companies in our coverage universe. Share price changes over the past year indicates that BRX will perform in line with the market over the near term.

Financial Data
(US$ in Thousands)

	3 Mos	12/31/2017	12/31/2016	12/31/2015	12/31/2014	12/31/2013	12/31/2012	12/31/2011
Earnings Per Share	0.95	0.98	0.91	0.65	0.36	(0.50)	...	...
Cash Flow Per Share	1.87	1.81	1.88	1.79	1.97	1.76	...	...
Tang Book Value Per Share	9.45	9.55	9.60	9.59	9.79	10.29	23.04	24.85
Dividends Per Share	1.055	1.040	0.980	0.900	0.727	...	...	...
Dividend Payout %	111.05	106.12	107.69	138.46	201.94	...	...	...
Income Statement								
Total Revenue	317,175	1,283,180	1,275,772	1,265,980	1,236,599	1,174,697	1,125,797	565,619
EBITDA	110,003	538,293	526,064	482,117	402,055	287,090	323,882	443,976
Depn & Amortn	(6,094)	16,566	22,270	40,343	29,264	41,921	91,519	85,142
Income Before Taxes	61,022	295,432	277,665	197,077	110,581	(101,995)	(152,879)	154,761
Net Income	61,022	300,293	275,628	193,720	89,002	(93,534)	(122,567)	115,351
Average Shares	304,278	305,281	305,060	305,017	244,588	188,993	...	...
Balance Sheet								
Current Assets	457,502	490,396	403,872	400,625	410,941	473,399	445,320	480,713
Total Assets	8,987,858	9,153,926	9,319,685	9,498,007	9,702,402	10,171,916	9,603,729	10,032,266
Current Liabilities	504,171	569,340	553,636	603,439	679,102	709,529	632,112	691,154
Long-Term Obligations	5,622,111	5,676,238	5,838,889	5,974,266	6,042,997	5,981,289	6,499,356	6,694,549
Total Liabilities	6,126,282	6,245,578	6,396,801	6,628,224	6,798,692	7,807,981	7,860,767	8,152,213
Stockholders' Equity	2,861,576	2,908,348	2,922,884	2,869,783	2,903,710	2,363,935	1,742,962	1,880,053
Shares Outstanding	302,826	304,620	304,343	299,138	296,552	229,689	75,649	75,649
Statistical Record								
Return on Assets %	3.16	3.25	2.92	2.02	0.90	N.M.	N.M.	...
Return on Equity %	10.02	10.30	9.49	6.71	3.38	N.M.	N.M.	...
EBITDA Margin %	34.68	41.95	41.23	38.08	32.51	24.44	28.77	78.49
Net Margin %	19.24	23.40	21.60	15.30	7.20	N.M.	N.M.	20.39
Asset Turnover	0.14	0.14	0.14	0.13	0.12	0.12	0.11	...
Current Ratio	0.91	0.86	0.73	0.66	0.61	0.67	0.70	0.70
Debt to Equity	1.96	1.95	2.00	2.08	2.08	2.53	3.73	3.56
Price Range	21.84-14.23	25.29-17.47	28.96-21.10	27.39-22.23	25.24-20.13	20.94-19.66	...	...
P/E Ratio	22.99-14.98	25.81-17.83	31.82-23.19	42.14-34.20	70.11-55.92	...	...	...
Average Yield %	5.80	5.21	3.80	3.62	3.23	...	...	...

Address: 450 Lexington Avenue, New York, NY 10017 **Telephone:** 212-869-3000	**Web Site:** www.brixmor.com **Officers:** John G. Schreiber - Chairman James M. Taylor - President, Chief Executive Officer	**Auditors:** Deloitte & Touche LLP **Transfer Agents:** Computershare Trust Company, N.A., Canton, MA

BROADRIDGE FINANCIAL SOLUTIONS INC

Exchange	Symbol	Price	52Wk Range	Yield	P/E	Div Acheiver
NYS	BR	$115.10 (6/29/2018)	119.63-72.28	1.27	33.95	10 Years

*7 Year Price Score 151.76 *NYSE Composite Index=100 *12 Month Price Score 120.50

Interim Earnings (Per Share)

Qtr.	Sep	Dec	Mar	Jun
2014-15	0.26	0.28	0.43	1.35
2015-16	0.28	0.33	0.52	1.40
2016-17	0.28	0.25	0.63	1.55
2017-18	0.42	0.52	0.90	...

Interim Dividends (Per Share)

Amt	Decl	Ex	Rec	Pay
0.365Q	08/09/2017	09/14/2017	09/15/2017	10/03/2017
0.365Q	11/16/2017	12/14/2017	12/15/2017	01/03/2018
0.365Q	02/06/2018	03/14/2018	03/15/2018	04/03/2018
0.365Q	05/03/2018	06/14/2018	06/15/2018	07/03/2018

Indicated Div: $1.46

Valuation Analysis · Institutional Holding

Forecast EPS	$4.21	No of Institutions	
	(06/12/2018)	846	
Market Cap	$13.5 Billion	Shares	
Book Value	$1.2 Billion	143,495,408	
Price/Book	11.62	% Held	
Price/Sales	N/A	82.92	

Business Summary: Finance Intermediaries & Services (MIC: 5.5.1 SIC: 7389 NAIC: 523999)

Broadridge Financial Solutions provides investor communications and technology solutions to banks, broker-dealers, mutual funds and corporate issuers. Co.'s businesses operate in two business segments: Investor Communication Solutions, which involves the processing and distribution of proxy materials to investors in equity securities and mutual funds, as well as the facilitation of related vote processing; and Global Technology and Operations, which provides a suite of computerized real-time transaction processing services that automate the securities transaction lifecycle, from desktop productivity tools, data aggregation, performance reporting, and portfolio management.

Recent Developments: For the quarter ended Mar 31 2018, net income increased 43.7% to US$109.1 million from US$75.9 million in the year-earlier quarter. Revenues were US$1.07 billion, up 6.2% from US$1.01 billion the year before. Operating income was US$130.0 million versus US$109.7 million in the prior-year quarter, an increase of 18.5%. Direct operating expenses rose 3.8% to US$803.1 million from US$773.7 million in the comparable period the year before. Indirect operating expenses increased 10.6% to US$138.8 million from US$125.5 million in the equivalent prior-year period.

Prospects: Our evaluation of Broadridge Financial Solutions Inc. as of Jan. 21, 2018 is the result of our systematic analysis on three basic characteristics: earnings strength, relative valuation, and recent stock price movement. The company has managed to produce a neutral trend in earnings per share over the past 5 quarters. However, while recent estimates for the company have been mixed, BR has posted better than expected results. Based on operating earnings yield, the company is about fairly valued when compared to all of the companies in our coverage universe. Share price changes over the past year indicates that BR will perform well over the near term.

Financial Data

(US$ in Thousands)	9 Mos	6 Mos	3 Mos	06/30/2017	06/30/2016	06/30/2015	06/30/2014	06/30/2013
Earnings Per Share	3.39	3.12	2.85	2.70	2.53	2.32	2.12	1.69
Cash Flow Per Share	...	5.69	4.38	4.37	3.69	3.60	3.24	2.22
Dividends Per Share	1.425	1.390	1.355	1.320	1.200	1.080	0.840	0.720
Dividend Payout %	42.04	44.55	47.54	48.89	47.43	46.55	39.62	42.60
Income Statement								
Total Revenue	3,009,500	1,937,600	924,800	4,142,600	2,897,000	2,694,200	2,558,000	2,430,800
EBITDA	426,500	259,500	114,200	662,100	570,300	530,300	475,500	392,400
Depn & Amortn	94,900	62,100	30,500	126,100	70,500	63,300	58,100	57,000
Income Before Taxes	303,000	177,800	74,300	493,300	474,000	444,400	395,500	323,200
Income Taxes	81,900	65,800	24,400	161,400	161,400	151,800	132,500	111,100
Net Income	221,100	112,000	49,900	326,800	307,500	287,100	263,000	212,100
Average Shares	120,900	120,300	119,800	120,800	121,600	124,000	124,100	125,400
Balance Sheet								
Current Assets	1,203,000	1,051,200	1,034,300	989,600	1,289,100	861,400	880,600	807,000
Total Assets	3,484,700	3,249,900	3,224,500	3,149,800	2,879,800	2,368,100	2,192,100	2,018,200
Current Liabilities	767,300	586,000	609,400	744,900	693,000	508,900	484,400	469,500
Long-Term Obligations	1,203,100	1,222,700	1,292,400	1,102,100	897,600	689,400	524,100	524,500
Total Liabilities	2,323,000	2,175,900	2,186,600	2,146,000	1,834,300	1,440,300	1,230,400	1,202,200
Stockholders' Equity	1,161,800	1,074,000	1,037,900	1,003,800	1,045,500	927,800	961,700	816,000
Shares Outstanding	117,300	116,600	116,500	116,500	118,300	118,200	119,500	119,000
Statistical Record								
Return on Assets %	...	12.06	11.12	10.84	11.69	12.59	12.49	10.59
Return on Equity %	...	36.41	32.84	31.89	31.08	30.39	29.59	25.45
EBITDA Margin %	14.17	13.39	12.35	15.98	19.69	19.68	18.59	16.14
Net Margin %	7.35	5.78	5.40	7.89	10.61	10.66	10.28	8.73
Asset Turnover	...	1.38	1.35	1.37	1.10	1.18	1.22	1.21
Current Ratio	1.57	1.79	1.70	1.33	1.86	1.69	1.82	1.72
Debt to Equity	1.04	1.14	1.25	1.10	0.86	0.74	0.54	0.64
Price Range	109.69-66.66	91.61-65.74	81.56-60.56	77.65-60.56	65.36-49.64	55.53-39.11	42.13-26.93	27.97-20.41
P/E Ratio	32.36-19.66	29.36-21.07	28.62-21.25	28.76-22.43	25.83-19.62	23.94-16.86	19.87-12.70	16.55-12.08
Average Yield %	1.70	1.83	1.92	1.93	2.12	2.29	2.24	3.04

Address: 5 Dakota Drive, Lake Success, NY 11042 **Telephone:** 516-472-5400	**Web Site:** www.broadridge.com **Officers:** Leslie A. Brun - Chairman Timothy C. Gokey - President, Chief Operating Officer, Senior Vice President, Chief Development Officer	**Auditors:** Deloitte & Touche LLP **Investor Contact:** 516-472-5400 **Transfer Agents:** Broadridge Corporate Issuer Solutions, Inc.

BROOKDALE SENIOR LIVING INC

Exchange	Symbol	Price	52Wk Range	Yield	P/E
NYS	BKD	$9.09 (6/29/2018)	14.73-6.47	N/A	N/A

*7 Year Price Score 35.92   *NYSE Composite Index=100   *12 Month Price Score 82.79

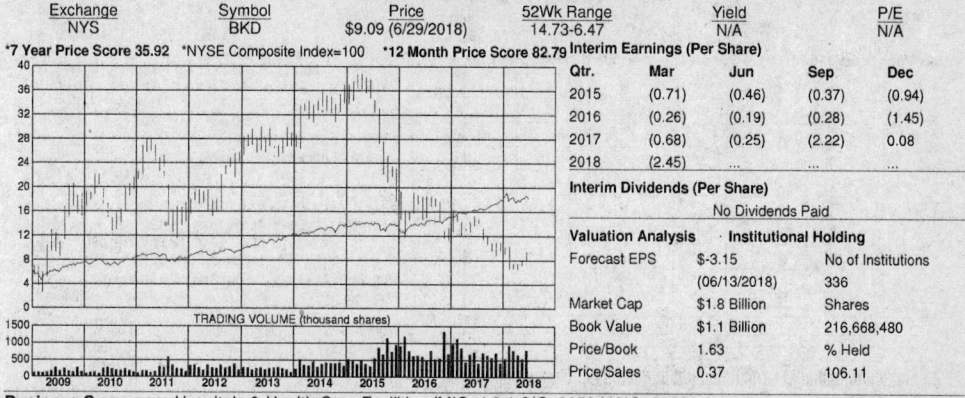

Interim Earnings (Per Share)

Qtr.	Mar	Jun	Sep	Dec
2015	(0.71)	(0.46)	(0.37)	(0.94)
2016	(0.26)	(0.19)	(0.28)	(1.45)
2017	(0.68)	(0.25)	(2.22)	0.08
2018	(2.45)	...	...	...

Interim Dividends (Per Share)

No Dividends Paid

Valuation Analysis   Institutional Holding

Forecast EPS	$-3.15	No of Institutions
	(06/13/2018)	336
Market Cap	$1.8 Billion	Shares
Book Value	$1.1 Billion	216,668,480
Price/Book	1.63	% Held
Price/Sales	0.37	106.11

Business Summary: Hospitals & Health Care Facilities (MIC: 4.2.1 SIC: 8052 NAIC: 623311)

Brookdale Senior Living is a holding company. Through its subsidiaries, Co. operates independent living, assisted living and dementia-care communities and continuing care retirement centers (CCRCs). Through its ancillary services programs, Co. also provide a range of outpatient therapy, home health and hospice services to residents of many of its communities and to seniors living outside of its communities. As of Dec 31 2017, Co. operated 129 retirement center communities (24,476 units), 822 assisted living communities (56,718 units) and 72 CCRCs (19,388 units).

Recent Developments: For the quarter ended Mar 31 2018, net loss amounted to US$457.2 million versus a net loss of US$126.4 million in the year-earlier quarter. Revenues were US$1.19 billion, down 2.4% from US$1.22 billion the year before. Operating loss was US$413.8 million versus an income of US$48.1 million in the prior-year quarter. Direct operating expenses declined 6.3% to US$632.3 million from US$674.5 million in the comparable period the year before. Indirect operating expenses increased 96.1% to US$968.7 million from US$494.1 million in the equivalent prior-year period.

Prospects: Our evaluation of Brookdale Senior Living Inc. as of Jan. 21, 2018 is the result of our systematic analysis on three basic characteristics: earnings strength, relative valuation, and recent stock price movement. The company has produced a positive trend in earnings per share over the past 5 quarters. Because the company lacks sufficient analyst estimate data, we place greater weight on the historical EPS trend as the measure of earnings strength. Based on operating earnings yield, the company is overvalued when compared to all of the companies in our coverage universe. Share price changes over the past year indicates that BKD will perform poorly over the near term.

Financial Data

(US$ in Thousands)	3 Mos	12/31/2017	12/31/2016	12/31/2015	12/31/2014	12/31/2013	12/31/2012	12/31/2011
Earnings Per Share	(4.84)	(3.07)	(2.18)	(2.48)	(1.01)	(0.03)	(0.54)	(0.56)
Cash Flow Per Share	1.81	1.97	1.96	1.59	1.64	2.96	2.38	2.22
Tang Book Value Per Share	4.46	5.00	6.79	8.52	10.64	5.89	5.79	6.19
Income Statement								
Total Revenue	1,187,234	4,747,116	4,976,980	4,960,608	3,831,706	2,891,966	2,770,085	2,457,918
EBITDA	(257,978)	227,637	495,966	558,601	445,043	396,848	331,158	318,473
Depn & Amortn	109,871	479,400	514,200	721,000	529,100	264,100	248,500	247,100
Income Before Taxes	(437,406)	(573,294)	(400,918)	(549,560)	(330,902)	(3,312)	(60,113)	(67,267)
Income Taxes	15,585	(16,515)	5,378	(92,209)	(181,305)	1,756	2,044	2,340
Net Income	(457,188)	(571,419)	(404,397)	(457,477)	(148,990)	(3,584)	(65,645)	(68,175)
Average Shares	186,880	186,155	185,653	184,333	148,185	123,671	121,991	121,161
Balance Sheet								
Current Assets	892,071	901,872	619,504	497,943	614,789	294,862	309,038	280,875
Total Assets	7,187,428	7,675,449	9,217,687	10,048,564	10,521,363	4,737,757	4,665,978	4,466,061
Current Liabilities	1,064,305	1,095,776	731,142	840,148	877,762	870,844	1,121,503	620,950
Long-Term Obligations	4,530,389	4,539,790	5,829,912	6,196,809	5,993,691	2,434,624	2,169,826	2,415,971
Total Liabilities	6,107,384	6,144,721	7,139,705	7,589,676	7,639,639	3,716,820	3,663,261	3,425,853
Stockholders' Equity	1,080,044	1,530,728	2,077,982	2,458,888	2,881,724	1,020,937	1,002,717	1,040,208
Shares Outstanding	193,797	191,275	190,045	188,338	187,037	127,726	126,689	125,354
Statistical Record								
EBITDA Margin %	N.M.	4.80	9.97	11.26	11.61	13.72	11.95	12.96
Asset Turnover	0.61	0.56	0.52	0.48	0.50	0.62	0.61	0.55
Current Ratio	0.84	0.82	0.85	0.59	0.70	0.34	0.28	0.45
Debt to Equity	4.19	2.97	2.81	2.52	2.08	2.38	2.16	2.32
Price Range	15.24-6.53	16.27-8.81	19.30-11.27	38.74-17.69	36.86-26.37	29.97-24.96	25.72-15.19	28.05-11.54

Address: 111 Westwood Place, Suite 400, Brentwood, TN 37027 **Telephone:** 615-221-2250	**Web Site:** www.brookdale.com **Officers:** William B. Doniger - Vice-Chairman William B. Doniger - Vice-Chairman	**Auditors:** Ernst & Young LLP **Investor Contact:** 615-564-8104 **Transfer Agents:** American Stock Transfer & Trust Company, New York, NY

BROWN & BROWN INC

Exchange	Symbol	Price	52Wk Range	Yield	P/E	Div Acheiver
NYS	BRO	$27.73 (6/29/2018)	28.59-21.36	1.08	18.74	24 Years

*7 Year Price Score 118.72 *NYSE Composite Index=100 *12 Month Price Score 108.63

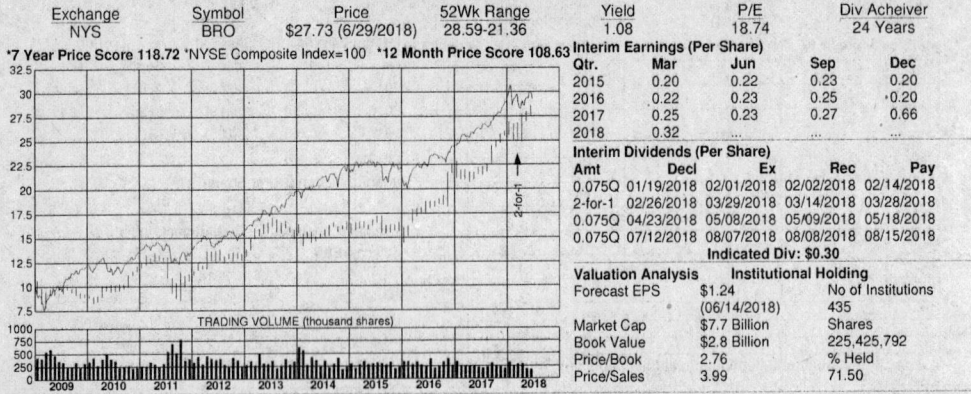

Interim Earnings (Per Share)

Qtr.	Mar	Jun	Sep	Dec
2015	0.20	0.22	0.23	0.20
2016	0.22	0.23	0.25	·0.20
2017	0.25	0.23	0.27	0.66
2018	0.32	...	...	...

Interim Dividends (Per Share)

Amt	Decl	Ex	Rec	Pay
0.075Q	01/19/2018	02/01/2018	02/02/2018	02/14/2018
2-for-1	02/26/2018	03/29/2018	03/14/2018	03/28/2018
0.075Q	04/23/2018	05/08/2018	05/09/2018	05/18/2018
0.075Q	07/12/2018	08/07/2018	08/08/2018	08/15/2018

Indicated Div: $0.30

Valuation Analysis

		Institutional Holding	
Forecast EPS	$1.24 (06/14/2018)	No of Institutions	435
Market Cap	$7.7 Billion	Shares	225,425,792
Book Value	$2.8 Billion	% Held	71.50
Price/Book	2.76		
Price/Sales	3.99		

Business Summary: Brokers & Intermediaries (MIC: 5.2.3 SIC: 6411 NAIC: 524210)

Brown & Brown is an insurance agency, wholesale brokerage, insurance programs and service organization. Co. markets and sells insurance products and services, primarily in the property, casualty and employee benefits areas. Co. has four segments: Retail, which provides a range of insurance products and services; National Programs, which provides programs, that can be grouped into five categories: Professional Programs, Arrowhead Insurance Programs, Commercial Programs, Public Entity-Related Programs, and the National Flood Program; Wholesale Brokerage, which markets and sells excess and surplus commercial and personal lines insurance; and Services, which provides insurance-related services.

Recent Developments: For the quarter ended Mar 31 2018, net income increased 29.6% to US$90.8 million from US$70.1 million in the year-earlier quarter. Revenues were US$501.5 million, up 7.8% from US$465.1 million the year before.

Prospects: Our evaluation of Brown & Brown Inc. as of Jan. 21, 2018 is the result of our systematic analysis on three basic characteristics: earnings strength, relative valuation, and recent stock price movement. The company has produced a positive trend in earnings per share over the past 5 quarters and while recent estimates for the company have been raised by analysts, BRO has posted better than expected results. Based on operating earnings yield, the company is about fairly valued when compared to all of the companies in our coverage universe. Share price changes over the past year indicates that BRO will perform in line with the market over the near term.

Financial Data

(US$ in Thousands)	3 Mos	12/31/2017	12/31/2016	12/31/2015	12/31/2014	12/31/2013	12/31/2012	12/31/2011
Earnings Per Share	1.48	1.41	0.91	0.85	0.70	0.74	0.63	0.56
Cash Flow Per Share	1.60	1.62	1.37	1.49	1.37	1.38	0.79	0.86
Dividends Per Share	0.285	0.278	0.251	0.226	0.205	0.185	0.172	0.163
Dividend Payout %	19.32	19.75	27.61	26.62	29.08	25.00	27.38	28.76
Income Statement								
Total Revenue	501,461	1,881,347	1,766,629	1,660,509	1,575,796	1,363,279	1,200,032	1,013,542
EBITDA	154,613	510,738	483,980	462,707	389,052	391,534	336,281	297,045
Depn & Amortn	26,501	22,700	21,000	20,900	20,895	17,485	15,373	12,392
Income Before Taxes	118,441	449,722	423,499	402,559	339,749	357,609	304,811	270,521
Income Taxes	27,613	50,092	166,008	159,241	132,853	140,497	120,766	106,526
Net Income	90,828	399,630	257,491	243,318	206,896	217,112	184,045	163,995
Average Shares	275,714	277,586	275,608	280,224	285,782	285,248	284,020	280,528
Balance Sheet								
Current Assets	2,074,602	2,242,156	1,760,737	1,537,389	1,570,108	928,036	759,512	708,127
Total Assets	5,615,083	5,747,550	5,287,343	5,012,739	4,956,458	3,649,508	3,128,058	2,607,011
Current Liabilities	1,634,632	1,987,474	1,445,157	1,328,547	1,269,153	906,877	567,781	481,620
Long-Term Obligations	851,548	856,141	1,018,372	1,079,878	1,152,846	380,000	450,000	250,033
Total Liabilities	2,844,490	3,164,851	2,927,132	2,862,963	2,842,713	1,642,367	1,320,725	963,048
Stockholders' Equity	2,770,593	2,582,699	2,360,211	2,149,776	2,113,745	2,007,141	1,807,333	1,643,963
Shares Outstanding	276,074	276,210	280,208	277,970	286,972	290,838	287,756	286,704
Statistical Record								
Return on Assets %	7.78	7.24	4.99	4.88	4.81	6.41	6.40	6.55
Return on Equity %	16.21	16.17	11.39	11.41	10.04	11.38	10.64	10.41
EBITDA Margin %	30.83	27.15	27.40	27.87	24.69	28.72	28.02	29.31
Net Margin %	18.11	21.24	14.58	14.65	13.13	15.93	15.34	16.18
Asset Turnover	0.35	0.34	0.34	0.33	0.37	0.40	0.42	0.40
Current Ratio	1.27	1.13	1.22	1.16	1.24	1.02	1.34	1.47
Debt to Equity	0.31	0.33	0.43	0.50	0.55	0.19	0.25	0.15
Price Range	26.89-20.66	25.97-20.66	22.56-14.44	17.23-15.37	16.63-14.14	17.06-12.73	13.82-11.15	13.46-8.50
P/E Ratio	18.17-13.96	18.41-14.65	24.79-15.86	20.28-18.08	23.76-20.20	23.05-17.20	21.94-17.69	24.03-15.18
Average Yield %	1.20	1.22	1.38	1.39	1.32	1.18	1.36	1.41

Address: 220 South Ridgewood Avenue, Daytona Beach, FL 32114 **Telephone:** 386-252-9601	**Web Site:** www.bbinsurance.com **Officers:** J. Hyatt Brown - Chairman J. Powell Brown - President, Chief Executive Officer	**Auditors:** DELOITTE & TOUCHE LLP **Investor Contact:** 386-252-9601 **Transfer Agents:** American Stock Transfer & Trust Co., Brooklyn, NY

BROWN-FORMAN CORP

Exchange	Symbol	Price	52Wk Range	Yield	P/E	Div Acheiver
NYS	BF B	$49.01 (6/29/2018)	59.22-37.82	1.29	33.11	33 Years

*7 Year Price Score 113.78 *NYSE Composite Index=100 *12 Month Price Score 109.04

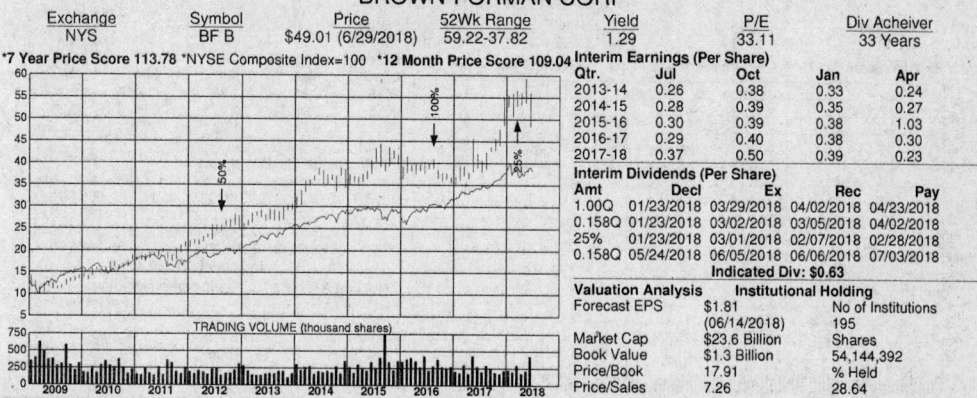

Interim Earnings (Per Share)

Qtr.	Jul	Oct	Jan	Apr
2013-14	0.26	0.38	0.33	0.24
2014-15	0.28	0.39	0.35	0.27
2015-16	0.30	0.39	0.38	1.03
2016-17	0.29	0.40	0.38	0.30
2017-18	0.37	0.50	0.39	0.23

Interim Dividends (Per Share)

Amt	Decl	Ex	Rec	Pay
1.00Q	01/23/2018	03/29/2018	04/02/2018	04/23/2018
0.158Q	01/23/2018	03/02/2018	03/05/2018	04/02/2018
25%	01/23/2018	03/01/2018	02/07/2018	02/28/2018
0.158Q	05/24/2018	06/05/2018	06/06/2018	07/03/2018

Indicated Div: $0.63

Valuation Analysis / Institutional Holding

Forecast EPS	$1.81	No of Institutions
	(06/14/2018)	195
Market Cap	$23.6 Billion	Shares
Book Value	$1.3 Billion	54,144,392
Price/Book	17.91	% Held
Price/Sales	7.26	28.64

Business Summary: Beverages (MIC: 1.2.2 SIC: 2084 NAIC: 312130)

Brown-Forman primarily manufactures, bottles, imports, exports, markets, and sells a range of alcoholic beverage brands. Co.'s principal brands include, among other, Jack Daniel's Tennessee Whiskey; Jack Daniel's Tennessee Honey; Jack Daniel's RTDs; Gentleman Jack Rare Tennessee Whiskey; Jack Daniel's Tennessee Fire; Jack Daniel's Single Barrel Collection; Jack Daniel's Winter Jack; Jack Daniel's Sinatra Select; Jack Daniel's No. 27 Gold Tennessee Whiskey; Jack Daniel's Tennessee Rye; Korbel California Champagnes; Korbel California Brandy; Woodford Reserve Kentucky Bourbon; Woodford Reserve Double Oaked; Woodford Reserve Kentucky Rye Whiskey; Finlandia Vodkas; and Slane Irish Whiskey.

Recent Developments: For the year ended Apr 30 2018, net income increased 7.2% to US$717.0 million from US$669.0 million in the prior year. Revenues were US$3.25 billion, up 8.5% from US$2.99 billion the year before. Operating income was US$1.04 billion versus US$989.0 million in the prior year, an increase of 5.1%. Direct operating expenses rose 7.5% to US$1.05 billion from US$973.0 million in the comparable period the year before. Indirect operating expenses increased 12.7% to US$1.16 billion from US$1.03 billion in the equivalent prior-year period.

Prospects: Our evaluation of Brown-Forman Corp. as of Jan. 21, 2018 is the result of our systematic analysis on three basic characteristics: earnings strength, relative valuation, and recent stock price movement. The company has produced a positive trend in earnings per share over the past 5 quarters and while recent estimates for the company have been raised by analysts, BF.B has posted better than expected results. Based on operating earnings yield, the company is about fairly valued when compared to all of the companies in our coverage universe. Share price changes over the past year indicates that BF.B will perform very well over the near term.

Financial Data

(US$ in Thousands)	04/30/2018	04/30/2017	04/30/2016	04/30/2015	04/30/2014	04/30/2013	04/30/2012	04/30/2011
Earnings Per Share	1.48	1.37	2.09	1.28	1.22	1.10	0.95	1.04
Cash Flow Per Share	1.32	1.32	1.03	1.15	1.22	1.01	0.96	0.97
Tang Book Value Per Share	N.M.	N.M.	0.76	1.32	1.38	0.64	1.47	1.41
Dividends Per Share	1.608	0.564	0.524	0.484	0.436	1.991	0.357	0.597
Dividend Payout %	108.65	41.23	25.10	37.69	35.62	180.97	37.64	57.44
Income Statement								
Total Revenue	3,248,000	2,994,000	3,089,000	3,134,000	2,991,000	2,849,000	2,723,000	2,586,000
EBITDA	1,103,000	1,047,000	1,589,000	1,078,000	1,021,000	949,000	837,000	911,000
Depn & Amortn	64,000	58,000	56,000	51,000	50,000	51,000	49,000	56,000
Income Before Taxes	977,000	933,000	1,489,000	1,002,000	947,000	865,000	760,000	829,000
Income Taxes	260,000	264,000	422,000	318,000	288,000	274,000	247,000	257,000
Net Income	717,000	669,000	1,067,000	684,000	659,000	591,000	513,000	572,000
Average Shares	484,248	488,076	510,700	532,707	537,705	537,465	540,375	549,423
Balance Sheet								
Current Assets	2,555,000	2,351,000	2,233,000	2,254,000	2,177,000	1,821,000	1,749,000	1,976,000
Total Assets	4,976,000	4,625,000	4,183,000	4,193,000	4,103,000	3,626,000	3,477,000	3,712,000
Current Liabilities	821,000	970,000	791,000	958,000	561,000	473,000	404,000	707,000
Long-Term Obligations	2,341,000	1,689,000	1,230,000	748,000	997,000	997,000	503,000	504,000
Total Liabilities	3,660,000	3,255,000	2,621,000	2,288,000	2,071,000	1,998,000	1,408,000	1,652,000
Stockholders' Equity	1,316,000	1,370,000	1,562,000	1,905,000	2,032,000	1,628,000	2,069,000	2,060,000
Shares Outstanding	481,001	480,107	494,355	521,750	533,637	534,267	532,777	543,712
Statistical Record								
Return on Assets %	14.94	15.19	25.41	16.49	17.05	16.64	14.23	16.12
Return on Equity %	53.39	45.63	61.38	34.75	36.01	31.97	24.78	28.93
EBITDA Margin %	33.96	34.97	51.44	34.40	34.14	33.31	30.74	35.23
Net Margin %	22.08	22.34	34.54	21.83	22.03	20.74	18.84	22.12
Asset Turnover	0.68	0.68	0.74	0.76	0.77	0.80	0.76	0.73
Current Ratio	3.11	2.42	2.82	2.35	3.88	3.85	4.33	2.79
Debt to Equity	1.78	1.23	0.79	0.39	0.49	0.61	0.24	0.24
Price Range	56.52-37.82	40.85-35.17	44.32-36.09	38.82-33.44	36.19-26.60	28.74-22.40	23.09-16.60	19.47-14.52
P/E Ratio	38.19-25.55	29.82-25.67	21.21-17.27	30.33-26.13	29.67-21.80	26.13-20.36	24.30-17.47	18.72-13.96
Average Yield %	3.43	1.50	1.31	1.33	1.45	7.73	1.76	3.51

Address: 850 Dixie Highway, Louisville, KY 40210
Telephone: 502-585-1100
Fax: 502-774-7876

Web Site: www.brown-forman.com
Officers: Paul C. Varga - Chairman, Chief Executive Officer Geo. Garvin Brown - Chairman, Executive Vice President

Auditors: PricewaterhouseCoopers LLP
Transfer Agents: Computershare, Providence, RI

BRUNSWICK CORP.

Exchange	Symbol	Price	52Wk Range	Yield	P/E
NYS	BC	$64.48 (6/29/2018)	68.77-48.63	1.18	37.27

*7 Year Price Score 108.70 *NYSE Composite Index=100 *12 Month Price Score 108.75

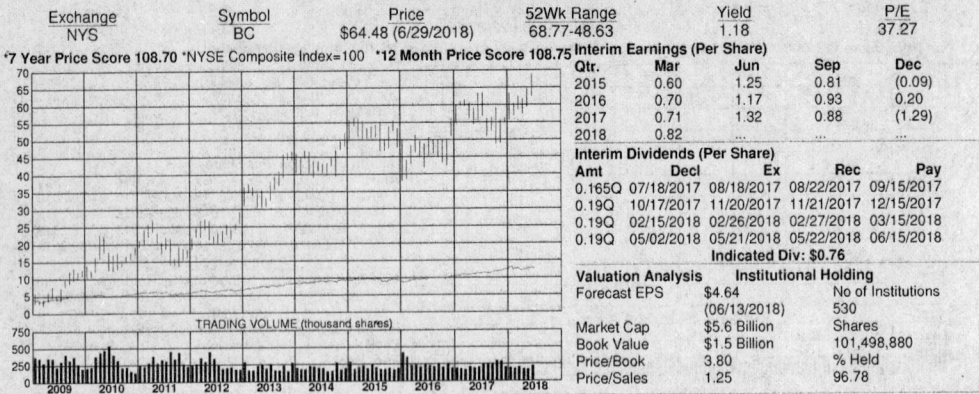

Interim Earnings (Per Share)

Qtr.	Mar	Jun	Sep	Dec
2015	0.60	1.25	0.81	(0.09)
2016	0.70	1.17	0.93	0.20
2017	0.71	1.32	0.88	(1.29)
2018	0.82	...	...	...

Interim Dividends (Per Share)

Amt	Decl	Ex	Rec	Pay
0.165Q	07/18/2017	08/18/2017	08/22/2017	09/15/2017
0.19Q	10/17/2017	11/20/2017	11/21/2017	12/15/2017
0.19Q	02/15/2018	02/26/2018	02/27/2018	03/15/2018
0.19Q	05/02/2018	05/21/2018	05/22/2018	06/15/2018

Indicated Div: $0.76

Valuation Analysis   **Institutional Holding**

Forecast EPS	$4.64	No of Institutions
	(06/13/2018)	530
Market Cap	$5.6 Billion	Shares
Book Value	$1.5 Billion	101,498,880
Price/Book	3.80	% Held
Price/Sales	1.25	96.78

Business Summary: Leisure Equipment (MIC: 1.6.1 SIC: 3511 NAIC: 333611)

Brunswick is a designer, manufacturer and marketer of recreation products. Co. operates in three reportable segments: marine engine, which manufactures and markets a range of outboard, sterndrive and inboard engine and propulsion systems; boat, which designs, manufactures and markets fiberglass pleasure boats, yachts and sport yachts, sport cruisers and sport boats, fishing boats, pontoon boats, utility boats, deck boats, inflatable boats, and aluminum boats; and fitness, which designs, manufactures and markets a line of cardiovascular fitness equipment and strength-training equipment under the Life Fitness, Hammer Strength, Cybex, Indoor Cycling Group and SCIFIT brands.

Recent Developments: For the quarter ended Mar 31 2018, income from continuing operations increased 8.5% to US$80.5 million from US$74.2 million in the year-earlier quarter. Net income increased 12.3% to US$72.9 million from US$64.9 million in the year-earlier quarter. Revenues were US$1.16 billion, up 6.8% from US$1.08 billion the year before. Operating income was US$115.4 million versus US$103.4 million in the prior-year quarter, an increase of 11.6%. Direct operating expenses rose 7.6% to US$847.6 million from US$787.8 million in the comparable period the year before. Indirect operating expenses increased 0.8% to US$192.4 million from US$190.9 million in the equivalent prior-year period.

Prospects: Our evaluation of Brunswick Corp. as of Jan. 21, 2018 is the result of our systematic analysis on three basic characteristics: earnings strength, relative valuation, and recent stock price movement. The company has managed to produce a neutral trend in earnings per share over the past 5 quarters and while recent estimates for the company have been mixed, BC has posted results that fell short of analysts' expectations. Based on operating earnings yield, the company is undervalued when compared to all of the companies in our coverage universe. Share price changes over the past year indicates that BC will perform poorly over the near term.

Financial Data

(US$ in Thousands)	3 Mos	12/31/2017	12/31/2016	12/31/2015	12/31/2014	12/31/2013	12/31/2012	12/31/2011
Earnings Per Share	1.73	1.62	3.00	2.56	2.58	8.20	0.54	0.78
Cash Flow Per Share	4.77	4.48	4.61	3.48	2.53	1.87	1.78	1.00
Tang Book Value Per Share	10.42	10.43	9.65	10.21	8.94	7.70	N.M.	N.M.
Dividends Per Share	0.710	0.685	0.615	0.525	0.450	0.100	0.050	0.050
Dividend Payout %	41.04	42.28	20.50	20.51	17.44	1.22	9.26	6.41
Income Statement								
Total Revenue	1,155,400	4,510,000	4,488,500	4,105,700	3,838,700	3,887,500	3,717,600	3,748,000
EBITDA	143,300	450,800	508,200	423,000	393,000	358,700	335,900	269,100
Depn & Amortn	27,800	89,800	97,100	85,900	78,300	84,800	85,900	97,200
Income Before Taxes	109,300	337,200	385,400	311,500	286,100	231,500	184,800	94,000
Income Taxes	29,800	156,000	115,300	87,800	93,000	(545,600)	33,600	17,400
Net Income	72,900	146,400	276,000	241,400	245,700	769,200	50,000	71,900
Average Shares	88,800	90,100	92,000	94,300	95,100	93,800	92,400	92,200
Balance Sheet								
Current Assets	1,862,700	1,846,700	1,688,500	1,984,900	1,967,800	1,508,600	1,360,100	1,356,100
Total Assets	3,404,600	3,358,200	3,284,700	3,152,500	3,134,400	2,915,800	2,424,200	2,494,000
Current Liabilities	1,076,400	1,035,100	964,900	908,100	900,100	883,100	937,200	908,100
Long-Term Obligations	428,900	431,800	436,500	442,500	450,200	453,400	563,600	690,400
Total Liabilities	1,923,800	1,875,300	1,844,600	1,871,200	1,962,900	1,877,400	2,346,500	2,463,100
Stockholders' Equity	1,480,800	1,482,900	1,440,100	1,281,300	1,171,500	1,038,400	77,700	30,900
Shares Outstanding	87,277	87,537	89,317	90,813	92,694	92,409	89,631	89,104
Statistical Record								
Return on Assets %	4.62	4.41	8.55	7.68	8.12	28.81	2.03	2.78
Return on Equity %	10.45	10.02	20.23	19.68	22.24	137.84	91.83	141.95
EBITDA Margin %	12.40	10.00	11.32	10.30	10.24	9.23	9.04	7.18
Net Margin %	6.31	3.25	6.15	5.88	6.40	19.79	1.34	1.92
Asset Turnover	1.35	1.36	1.39	1.31	1.27	1.46	1.51	1.45
Current Ratio	1.73	1.78	1.75	2.19	2.19	1.71	1.45	1.49
Debt to Equity	0.29	0.29	0.30	0.35	0.38	0.44	7.25	22.34
Price Range	63.42-48.63	63.42-48.63	56.03-37.98	56.39-46.50	51.94-38.95	46.48-29.09	29.09-18.49	27.01-13.50
P/E Ratio	36.66-28.11	39.15-30.02	18.68-12.66	22.03-18.16	20.13-15.10	5.67-3.55	53.87-34.24	34.63-17.31
Average Yield %	1.25	1.20	1.31	1.01	1.03	0.27	0.21	0.26

Address: 26125 N. Riverwoods Blvd., Suite 500, Mettawa, IL 60045-3420 **Telephone:** 847-735-4700	**Web Site:** www.brunswick.com **Officers:** Mark D. Schwabero - Chairman, President, Chief Executive Officer, Chief Operating Officer, Vice President, Division Officer Christopher E. Clawson - Vice President, Division Officer	**Auditors:** DELOITTE & TOUCHE LLP **Investor Contact:** 847-735-4612 **Transfer Agents:** ComputerShare Investor Services, Providence, RI

BUCKEYE PARTNERS LP

Exchange	Symbol	Price	52Wk Range	Yield	P/E	Div Acheiver
NYS	BPL	$35.15 (6/29/2018)	65.90-34.86	14.37	11.05	22 Years

*7 Year Price Score 61.92   *NYSE Composite Index=100   *12 Month Price Score 75.44

TRADING VOLUME (thousand shares)

Interim Earnings (Per Share)

Qtr.	Mar	Jun	Sep	Dec
2015	0.87	0.71	0.78	1.04
2016	1.01	1.07	1.19	0.75
2017	0.88	0.80	0.81	0.83
2018	0.74	...	...	...

Interim Dividends (Per Share)

Amt	Decl	Ex	Rec	Pay
1.263Q	08/04/2017	08/10/2017	08/14/2017	08/21/2017
1.263Q	11/03/2017	11/09/2017	11/13/2017	11/20/2017
1.263Q	02/09/2018	02/16/2018	02/20/2018	02/27/2018
1.263Q	05/04/2018	05/11/2018	05/14/2018	05/21/2018

Indicated Div: $5.05

Valuation Analysis / Institutional Holding

Forecast EPS	$3.15	No of Institutions	
	(06/12/2018)	520	
Market Cap	$5.4 Billion	Shares	119,845,232
Book Value	N/A	% Held	73.86
Price/Book	N/A		
Price/Sales	1.39		

Business Summary: Equipment & Services (MIC: 9.1.3 SIC: 4613 NAIC: 486910)

Buckeye Partners is a holding company. Through its subsidiaries, Co. owns and operates integrated assets providing midstream logistic solutions, including transportation, storage, processing and marketing of liquid petroleum products. Co. has three segments: Domestic Pipelines & Terminals, which provide pipeline transportation services; Global Marine Terminals, which provide marine accessible bulk storage and blending services, rail and truck rack loading/unloading, along with petroleum processing services in the East Coast and Gulf Coast regions of the U.S. and in the Caribbean; and Merchant Services, which distribute refined petroleum products in the continental U.S. and in the Caribbean.

Recent Developments:
For the quarter ended Mar 31 2018, net income decreased 7.3% to US$117.1 million from US$126.3 million in the year-earlier quarter. Revenues were US$1.18 billion, up 22.1% from US$969.3 million the year before. Operating income was US$169.5 million versus US$172.6 million in the prior-year quarter, a decrease of 1.8%. Direct operating expenses rose 32.5% to US$940.2 million from US$709.5 million in the comparable period the year before. Indirect operating expenses decreased 15.9% to US$73.4 million from US$87.2 million in the equivalent prior-year period.

Prospects:
Our evaluation of Buckeye Partners, L.P. as of Jan. 21, 2018 is the result of our systematic analysis on three basic characteristics: earnings strength, relative valuation, and recent stock price movement. The company has managed to produce a neutral trend in earnings per share over the past 5 quarters. However, while recent estimates for the company have been lowered by analysts, BPL has posted results that fell short of analysts expectations. Based on operating earnings yield, the company is undervalued when compared to all of the companies in our coverage universe. Share price changes over the past year indicates that BPL will perform very poorly over the near term.

Financial Data
(US$ in Thousands)

	3 Mos	12/31/2017	12/31/2016	12/31/2015	12/31/2014	12/31/2013	12/31/2012	12/31/2011
Earnings Per Share	3.18	3.32	4.03	3.40	2.28	1.49	2.32	1.20
Cash Flow Per Share	6.26	6.23	5.41	5.54	5.03	3.60	4.53	4.47
Dividends Per Share	5.037	5.013	4.825	4.625	4.425	4.225	4.150	4.025
Dividend Payout %	158.41	150.98	119.73	136.03	194.08	283.56	178.88	335.42
Income Statement								
Total Revenue	1,183,105	3,648,145	3,248,376	3,453,434	6,620,247	5,054,101	4,357,242	4,759,610
EBITDA	173,098	886,915	920,121	762,914	643,319	601,036	458,956	329,291
Depn & Amortn	3,900	202,800	186,600	158,700	148,400	122,700	120,200	105,500
Income Before Taxes	110,093	458,532	538,599	432,884	323,684	347,416	223,776	104,230
Income Taxes	490	872	1,460	874	451	1,060	(675)	...
Net Income	112,373	478,802	535,608	437,223	272,954	160,273	226,417	108,501
Average Shares	149,532	143,144	132,927	128,617	119,899	107,677	97,635	90,772
Balance Sheet								
Current Assets	519,996	656,598	1,318,897	551,550	632,299	901,086	634,322	626,036
Total Assets	10,215,511	10,304,659	9,421,103	8,369,281	8,086,088	7,005,563	5,981,009	5,570,376
Current Liabilities	446,188	685,360	399,548	504,309	621,955	685,043	594,366	554,979
Long-Term Obligations	4,587,949	4,658,321	4,217,695	3,732,824	3,388,986	3,092,711	2,735,244	2,393,574
Total Liabilities	5,405,763	5,713,722	5,009,380	4,633,892	4,383,460	3,939,898	3,608,696	3,267,207
Shares Outstanding	153,155	146,677	140,263	129,523	127,043	115,063	98,345	93,273
Statistical Record								
Return on Assets %	4.66	4.85	6.00	5.31	3.62	2.47	3.91	2.37
EBITDA Margin %	14.63	24.31	28.33	22.09	9.72	11.89	10.53	6.92
Net Margin %	9.50	13.12	16.49	12.66	4.12	3.17	5.20	2.28
Asset Turnover	0.38	0.37	0.36	0.42	0.88	0.78	0.75	1.04
Current Ratio	1.17	0.96	3.30	1.09	1.02	1.32	1.07	1.13
Price Range	69.64-37.39	72.62-44.59	74.40-50.35	82.04-54.00	83.91-66.87	73.13-45.41	64.17-44.65	68.52-57.61
P/E Ratio	21.90-11.76	21.87-13.43	18.46-12.49	24.13-15.88	36.80-29.33	49.08-30.48	27.66-19.25	57.10-48.01
Average Yield %	8.96	8.92	7.18	6.42	5.76	6.59	7.84	6.30

Address: One Greenway Plaza, Suite 600, Houston, TX 77046
Telephone: 832-615-8600

Web Site: www.buckeye.com
Officers: Gary L. Bohnsack - Associate/Affiliate Company Officer Clark C. Smith - President, Chief Executive Officer, Chief Operating Officer, Associate/Affiliate Company Officer

Auditors: DELOITTE & TOUCHE LLP
Investor Contact: 800-422-2825
Transfer Agents: First Chicago Trust Company a Division of Equiserv, Jersey City, NJ

BUNGE LTD.

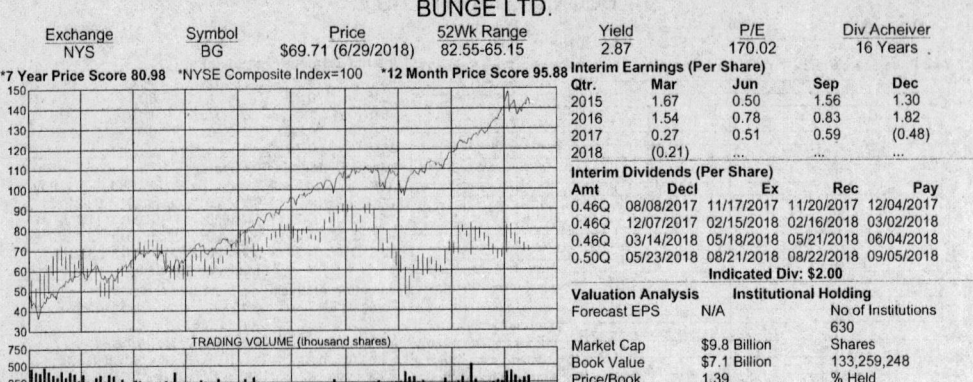

Exchange	Symbol	Price	52Wk Range	Yield	P/E	Div Acheiver
NYS	BG	$69.71 (6/29/2018)	82.55-65.15	2.87	170.02	16 Years

*7 Year Price Score 80.98 *NYSE Composite Index=100 *12 Month Price Score 95.88

Interim Earnings (Per Share)

Qtr.	Mar	Jun	Sep	Dec
2015	1.67	0.50	1.56	1.30
2016	1.54	0.78	0.83	1.82
2017	0.27	0.51	0.59	(0.48)
2018	(0.21)	...	...	...

Interim Dividends (Per Share)

Amt	Decl	Ex	Rec	Pay
0.46Q	08/08/2017	11/17/2017	11/20/2017	12/04/2017
0.46Q	12/07/2017	02/15/2018	02/16/2018	03/02/2018
0.46Q	03/14/2018	05/18/2018	05/21/2018	06/04/2018
0.50Q	05/23/2018	08/21/2018	08/22/2018	09/05/2018

Indicated Div: $2.00

Valuation Analysis

Forecast EPS	N/A	

Institutional Holding

No of Institutions: 630

Market Cap	$9.8 Billion	Shares
Book Value	$7.1 Billion	133,259,248
Price/Book	1.39	% Held
Price/Sales	0.22	73.88

TRADING VOLUME (thousand shares)

Business Summary: Food (MIC: 1.2.1 SIC: 2079 NAIC: 311225)

Bunge is a holding company. Through its subsidiaries, Co. is an agribusiness and food company operating in the farm field to consumer foods. Co.'s segments include: Agribusiness, which purchases, stores, transports, processes and sells agricultural commodities and commodity products; Food and Ingredients, which include edible oil and milling products; Sugar and Bioenergy, in which Co. is a producer of sugar and ethanol in Brazil, and a trader and merchandiser of sugar; and Fertilizer, in which Co. produces, blends and distributes a range of nitrogen, phosphate and potassium fertilizers, including phosphate-based liquid and solid nitrogen fertilizers, through its operations in Argentina.

Recent Developments: For the quarter ended Mar 31 2018, loss from continuing operations was US$17.0 million compared with income of US$54.0 million in the year-earlier quarter. Net loss amounted to US$19.0 million versus net income of US$48.0 million in the year-earlier quarter. Revenues were US$10.64 billion, down 4.3% from US$11.12 billion the year before. Direct operating expenses declined 3.8% to US$10.26 billion from US$10.66 billion in the comparable period the year before. Indirect operating expenses decreased 9.0% to US$344.0 million from US$378.0 million in the equivalent prior-year period.

Prospects: Our evaluation of Bunge Ltd. as of July 19, 2015 is the result of our systematic analysis on three basic characteristics: earnings strength, relative valuation, and recent stock price movement. The company has produced a positive trend in earnings per share over the past 5 quarters. However, while recent estimates for the company have been lowered by analysts, BG has posted better than expected results. Based on operating earnings yield, the company is undervalued when compared to all of the companies in our coverage universe. Share price changes over the past year indicates that BG will perform well over the near term.

Financial Data
(US$ in Millions)

	3 Mos	12/31/2017	12/31/2016	12/31/2015	12/31/2014	12/31/2013	12/31/2012	12/31/2011
Earnings Per Share	0.41	0.89	5.01	5.07	3.17	1.55	0.19	6.07
Cash Flow Per Share	(3.47)	7.17	13.58	4.25	9.57	15.12	(3.12)	17.83
Tang Book Value Per Share	33.88	39.96	41.18	35.14	49.08	57.17	65.09	68.93
Dividends Per Share	1.800	1.760	1.600	1.440	1.280	1.140	1.040	0.960
Dividend Payout %	439.02	197.75	31.94	28.40	40.38	73.55	547.37	15.82
Income Statement								
Total Revenue	10,641	45,794	42,679	43,455	57,161	61,347	60,991	58,743
EBITDA	206	1,035	1,696	1,784	1,570	1,825	1,117	1,637
Depn & Amortn	142	580	517	518	576	524	504	497
Income Before Taxes	2	230	996	1,051	734	1,014	372	940
Income Taxes	19	56	220	296	249	904	(6)	44
Net Income	(21)	160	745	791	515	306	64	942
Average Shares	140	141	148	152	147	148	147	155
Balance Sheet								
Current Assets	13,376	10,403	11,092	10,916	13,081	17,772	17,264	13,128
Total Assets	23,084	18,871	19,188	17,922	21,432	26,781	27,280	23,275
Current Liabilities	8,550	6,215	7,684	7,340	8,704	12,535	11,561	6,947
Long-Term Obligations	5,446	4,160	3,069	2,934	2,855	3,179	3,532	3,348
Total Liabilities	16,019	11,723	12,044	11,481	12,986	16,924	16,418	11,568
Stockholders' Equity	7,065	7,148	7,144	6,441	8,446	9,857	10,862	11,707
Shares Outstanding	140	140	139	142	145	147	146	143
Statistical Record								
Return on Assets %	0.42	0.84	4.00	4.02	2.14	1.13	0.25	3.82
Return on Equity %	1.27	2.24	10.94	10.63	5.63	2.95	0.57	7.87
EBITDA Margin %	1.94	2.26	3.97	4.11	2.75	2.97	1.83	2.79
Net Margin %	N.M.	0.35	1.75	1.82	0.90	0.50	0.10	1.60
Asset Turnover	2.07	2.41	2.29	2.21	2.37	2.27	2.41	2.38
Current Ratio	1.56	1.67	1.44	1.49	1.50	1.42	1.49	1.89
Debt to Equity	0.77	0.58	0.43	0.46	0.34	0.32	0.33	0.29
Price Range	83.22-65.15	83.22-65.15	73.61-47.79	92.85-61.81	92.91-73.51	83.11-66.40	73.82-57.22	75.44-55.51
P/E Ratio	202.98-158.90	93.51-73.20	14.69-9.54	18.31-12.19	29.31-23.19	53.62-42.84	388.53-301.16	12.43-9.14
Average Yield %	2.44	2.39	2.59	1.79	1.58	1.51	1.59	1.45

Address: 50 Main Street, White Plains, NY 10606
Telephone: 914-684-2800

Web Site: www.bunge.com
Officers: Thomas M. Boehlert - Executive Vice President, Chief Financial Officer Deborah Borg - Executive Vice President, Chief Human Resources Officer

Auditors: Deloitte & Touche LLP
Investor Contact: 914-684-2800
Transfer Agents: Computershare Investor Services LLC

BURLINGTON STORES INC

Exchange	Symbol	Price	52Wk Range	Yield	P/E
NYS	BURL	$150.53 (6/29/2018)	156.43-80.27	N/A	25.30

*7 Year Price Score N/A   *NYSE Composite Index=100   *12 Month Price Score 126.84

TRADING VOLUME (thousand shares)

Interim Earnings (Per Share)

Qtr.	Apr	Jul	Oct	Jan
2015-16	0.34	0.14	0.20	1.30
2016-17	0.52	0.28	0.45	1.76
2017-18	0.73	0.66	0.65	3.44
2018-19	1.20	...	...	...

Interim Dividends (Per Share)

No Dividends Paid

Valuation Analysis

		Institutional Holding	
Forecast EPS	$6.02	No of Institutions	
	(06/10/2018)	457	
Market Cap	$10.2 Billion	Shares	
Book Value	$111.3 Million	78,568,592	
Price/Book	91.47	% Held	
Price/Sales	1.62	97.33	

Business Summary: Retail - Apparel and Accessories (MIC: 2.1.5 SIC: 5311 NAIC: 452111)

Burlington Stores is a holding company. Through its indirect subsidiary, Burlington Coat Factory Warehouse Corporation, operated 629 retail stores, inclusive of an internet store, selling apparel, footwear and accessories for men, women and children. A majority of those stores provide a home furnishing and linens department and a juvenile furniture department. As of Feb 3 2018, Co. operated stores under the names Burlington Stores, Cohoes Fashions, Super Baby Depot, MJM Designer Shoes and one online store. Co.'s trademarks include Burlington Stores, BCF, Burlington, Burlington Coat Factory, Cohoes, Luxury Linens, MJM Designer Shoes, and Baby Depot.

Recent Developments: For the quarter ended May 5 2018, net income increased 57.7% to US$82.6 million from US$52.4 million in the year-earlier quarter. Revenues were US$1.52 billion, up 12.8% from US$1.35 billion the year before. Direct operating expenses rose 12.1% to US$892.7 million from US$796.4 million in the comparable period the year before. Indirect operating expenses increased 10.7% to US$532.0 million from US$480.5 million in the equivalent prior-year period.

Prospects: Our evaluation of Burlington Stores Inc as of Jan. 21, 2018 is the result of our systematic analysis on three basic characteristics: earnings strength, relative valuation, and recent stock price movement. The company has managed to produce a neutral trend in earnings per share over the past 5 quarters and while recent estimates for the company have been raised by analysts, BURL has posted better than expected results. Based on operating earnings yield, the company is about fairly valued when compared to all of the companies in our coverage universe. Share price changes over the past year indicates that BURL will perform poorly over the near term.

Financial Data
(US$ in Thousands)

	3 Mos	02/03/2018	01/28/2017	01/30/2016	01/31/2015	02/01/2014	02/02/2013	01/28/2012
Earnings Per Share	5.95	5.48	3.01	1.99	0.87	(0.39)	(2.92)	(3.12)
Cash Flow Per Share	9.54	8.75	8.57	4.43	4.09	0.79	9.68	5.55
Income Statement								
Total Revenue	1,524,708	6,110,043	5,590,950	5,129,843	4,849,634	4,461,987	4,165,504	3,887,531
EBITDA	114,721	669,257	551,073	448,175	336,981	307,697	290,892	253,801
Depn & Amortn	201	181,500	161,700	150,300	148,200	147,600	147,800	135,100
Income Before Taxes	99,999	428,980	333,212	238,876	105,036	32,358	29,165	(10,420)
Income Taxes	17,411	44,128	117,339	88,394	39,081	16,208	3,864	(4,148)
Net Income	82,588	384,852	215,873	150,482	65,955	16,150	25,301	(6,272)
Average Shares	68,970	70,288	71,721	75,443	75,865	370,040	45,982	45,146
Balance Sheet								
Current Assets	1,100,901	1,100,433	928,324	932,982	987,483	1,016,520	879,654	877,988
Total Assets	2,825,446	2,812,829	2,574,483	2,580,147	2,624,569	2,621,092	2,478,082	2,501,143
Current Liabilities	1,091,649	1,119,631	996,834	886,588	933,117	903,816	740,055	505,287
Long-Term Obligations	1,122,552	1,113,808	1,128,843	1,303,497	1,249,276	1,369,159	1,335,532	1,605,464
Total Liabilities	2,714,175	2,726,055	2,624,295	2,679,169	2,690,520	2,771,560	2,558,351	2,612,088
Stockholders' Equity	111,271	86,774	(49,812)	(99,022)	(65,951)	(150,468)	(80,269)	(110,945)
Shares Outstanding	67,612	67,871	70,180	72,071	75,254	73,686	51,835	51,046
Statistical Record								
Return on Assets %	15.42	14.06	8.40	5.80	2.52	0.64	1.00	...
Return on Equity %	1,179.80	2,048.74	...	...	...	...	...	...
EBITDA Margin %	7.52	10.95	9.86	8.74	6.95	6.90	6.98	6.53
Net Margin %	5.42	6.30	3.86	2.93	1.36	0.36	0.61	N.M.
Asset Turnover	2.33	2.23	2.18	1.98	1.85	1.75	1.65	...
Current Ratio	1.01	0.98	0.93	1.05	1.06	1.12	1.19	1.74
Debt to Equity	10.09	12.84	...	...	...	...	...	...
Price Range	139.36-80.27	127.61-80.27	89.68-49.71	61.02-40.70	51.60-24.26	32.50-24.86	...	...
P/E Ratio	23.42-13.49	23.29-14.65	29.79-16.51	30.66-20.45	59.31-27.89	...	...	...

Address: 2006 Route 130 North, Burlington, NJ 08016 **Telephone:** 609-387-7800	**Web Site:** www.burlingtonstores.com **Officers:** Thomas A. (Tom) Kingsbury - Chairman, President, Chief Executive Officer Joyce Manning Magrini - Executive Vice President	**Auditors:** Deloitte & Touche LLP **Transfer Agents:** American Stock Transfer & Trust Company, LLC, Brooklyn, NY

BWX TECHNOLOGIES INC

Exchange	Symbol	Price	52Wk Range	Yield	P/E
		$62.32 (6/29/2018)	70.94-48.60	1.03	39.69

*7 Year Price Score 159.61 *NYSE Composite Index=100 *12 Month Price Score 107.18

TRADING VOLUME (thousand shares)

Interim Earnings (Per Share)

Qtr.	Mar	Jun	Sep	Dec
2015	0.42	(0.16)	0.96	(0.01)
2016	0.46	0.55	0.39	0.36
2017	0.55	0.61	0.46	(0.16)
2018	0.66			

Interim Dividends (Per Share)

Amt	Decl	Ex	Rec	Pay
0.11Q	08/04/2017	08/17/2017	08/21/2017	09/08/2017
0.11Q	11/03/2017	11/17/2017	11/20/2017	12/13/2017
0.16Q	02/22/2018	03/09/2018	03/12/2018	03/29/2018
0.16Q	05/04/2018	05/17/2018	05/18/2018	06/06/2018

Indicated Div: $0.64

Valuation Analysis / Institutional Holding

Forecast EPS	$2.55	No of Institutions	
	(06/11/2018)	409	
Market Cap	$6.2 Billion	Shares	
Book Value	$345.1 Million	111,866,296	
Price/Book	18.00	% Held	
Price/Sales	3.62	102.62	

Business Summary: Industrial Machinery & Equipment (MIC: 7.2.1 SIC: 3511 NAIC: 333611)

BWX Technologies is a manufacturer of nuclear components and a service provider. Co. operates in three reportable segments: Nuclear Operations, which designs and manufactures naval nuclear reactors for the U.S. Department of Energy/National Nuclear Security Administration's Naval Nuclear Propulsion Program; Technical Services, which provides various services to the U.S. Government, including uranium processing, environmental site restoration services and management and operating services for various U.S. Government-owned facilities; and Nuclear Energy, which supplies commercial nuclear steam generators and components to nuclear utility customers.

Recent Developments: For the quarter ended Mar 31 2018, net income increased 19.0% to US$66.4 million from US$55.8 million in the year-earlier quarter. Revenues were US$457.5 million, up 6.8% from US$428.2 million the year before. Operating income was US$79.9 million versus US$76.3 million in the prior-year quarter, an increase of 4.7%. Direct operating expenses rose 8.0% to US$327.4 million from US$303.2 million in the comparable period the year before. Indirect operating expenses increased 3.0% to US$50.2 million from US$48.7 million in the equivalent prior-year period.

Prospects: Our evaluation of BWX Technologies Inc. as of Jan. 21, 2018 is the result of our systematic analysis on three basic characteristics: earnings strength, relative valuation, and recent stock price movement. The company has generated a negative trend in earnings per share over the past 5 quarters. However, while recent estimates for the company have been mixed, BWXT has posted results that fell short of analysts expectations. Based on operating earnings yield, the company is about fairly valued when compared to all of the companies in our coverage universe. Share price changes over the past year indicates that BWXT will perform very well over the near term.

Financial Data
(US$ in Thousands)

	3 Mos	12/31/2017	12/31/2016	12/31/2015	12/31/2014	12/31/2013	12/31/2012	12/31/2011
Earnings Per Share	1.57	1.47	1.76	1.22	0.27	3.07	1.91	1.43
Cash Flow Per Share	2.60	2.24	2.33	3.09	0.69	1.23	1.56	1.48
Tang Book Value Per Share	0.21	N.M.	N.M.	0.37	4.77	7.26	6.12	4.65
Dividends Per Share	0.490	0.420	0.360	0.320	0.400	0.340	0.080	...
Dividend Payout %	31.21	28.57	20.45	26.23	148.15	11.07	4.19	...
Income Statement								
Total Revenue	457,463	1,687,738	1,550,573	1,415,529	2,923,019	3,269,208	3,291,359	2,952,040
EBITDA	94,709	342,942	297,341	242,819	63,161	512,987	314,353	221,281
Depn & Amortn	14,061	47,300	48,400	55,300	92,900	62,200	59,400	61,800
Income Before Taxes	77,866	282,168	241,199	207,669	(36,290)	449,115	252,709	156,280
Income Taxes	18,603	147,415	73,656	80,416	(15,991)	184,583	101,861	72,982
Net Income	66,441	147,844	183,057	131,465	29,388	346,078	227,695	169,654
Average Shares	100,512	100,369	103,840	107,583	108,761	112,685	119,021	118,404
Balance Sheet								
Current Assets	702,850	873,090	693,571	647,294	1,473,802	1,437,424	1,521,086	1,487,076
Total Assets	1,539,539	1,712,339	1,579,815	1,382,139	2,856,936	2,609,153	2,840,355	2,789,111
Current Liabilities	327,055	528,126	439,876	353,780	819,636	927,228	1,079,288	1,154,807
Long-Term Obligations	471,367	481,059	497,724	285,000	285,000	225	430	633
Total Liabilities	1,194,398	1,426,945	1,429,797	1,116,423	1,858,232	1,444,466	1,853,920	1,963,317
Stockholders' Equity	345,141	285,394	150,018	265,716	998,704	1,164,687	986,435	825,794
Shares Outstanding	99,665	99,417	99,290	105,297	106,688	110,468	115,235	118,107
Statistical Record								
Return on Assets %	10.04	8.98	12.33	6.20	1.08	12.70	8.07	6.41
Return on Equity %	57.55	67.91	87.82	20.79	2.72	32.18	25.06	22.05
EBITDA Margin %	20.70	20.32	19.18	17.15	2.16	15.69	9.55	7.50
Net Margin %	14.52	8.76	11.81	9.29	1.01	10.59	6.92	5.75
Asset Turnover	1.09	1.03	1.04	0.67	1.07	1.20	1.17	1.12
Current Ratio	2.15	1.65	1.58	1.83	1.80	1.55	1.41	1.29
Debt to Equity	1.37	1.69	3.32	1.07	0.29	N.M.	N.M.	N.M.
Price Range	67.37-46.34	62.45-39.22	40.52-27.09	32.23-19.33	25.39-19.81	24.70-18.11	19.84-16.47	25.45-13.27
P/E Ratio	42.91-29.52	42.48-26.68	23.02-15.39	26.42-15.84	94.05-73.38	8.05-5.90	10.38-8.62	17.80-9.28
Average Yield %	0.87	0.82	1.02	1.28	1.77	1.59	0.44	...

Address: 800 Main Street, 4th Floor, Lynchburg, VA 24504 **Telephone:** 980-365-4300	**Web Site:** www.bwxt.com **Officers:** Rex D. Geveden - Chief Operating Officer, President, Chief Executive Officer David S. Black - Vice President, Chief Accounting Officer, Senior Vice President, Chief Financial Officer, Treasurer	**Auditors:** DELOITTE & TOUCHE LLP **Investor Contact:** 704-625-4944 **Transfer Agents:** Computershare Trust Company, N.A., Canton, MA

CABLE ONE INC

Exchange	Symbol	Price	52Wk Range	Yield	P/E
NYS	CABO	$733.29 (6/29/2018)	762.27-619.00	0.95	17.46

*7 Year Price Score N/A   *NYSE Composite Index=100   *12 Month Price Score 94.63

TRADING VOLUME (thousand shares)

Interim Earnings (Per Share)

Qtr.	Mar	Jun	Sep	Dec
2015	3.78	3.67	3.30	4.44
2016	4.65	4.62	3.63	4.23
2017	5.80	4.97	5.48	24.48
2018	7.08	...	...	...

Interim Dividends (Per Share)

Amt	Decl	Ex	Rec	Pay
1.75Q	08/02/2017	08/11/2017	08/15/2017	09/01/2017
1.75Q	11/07/2017	11/20/2017	11/21/2017	12/08/2017
1.75Q	02/06/2018	02/16/2018	02/20/2018	03/09/2018
1.75Q	05/08/2018	05/21/2018	05/22/2018	06/08/2018

Indicated Div: $7.00

Valuation Analysis   **Institutional Holding**

Forecast EPS	$30.48	No of Institutions
	(06/14/2018)	293
Market Cap	$4.2 Billion	Shares
Book Value	$699.9 Million	5,023,816
Price/Book	6.01	% Held
Price/Sales	4.13	N/A

Business Summary: Business Services (MIC: 7.5.2 SIC: 4841 NAIC: 515210)

Cable One is a provider of data, video and voice services in 21 Western, Midwestern and Southern states. Co. provides these broadband services to residential and business customers in more than 750 communities. The markets Co. serves are primarily non-metropolitan, secondary markets, with majority of its customers located in seven states: Arizona, Idaho, Illinois, Mississippi, Missouri, Oklahoma and Texas. Co.'s product lines include residential data services, residential video services, residential voice services, business services, and advertising. As of Dec 31 2017, Co. provided service to 797,537 residential and business customers.

Recent Developments: For the quarter ended Mar 31 2018, net income increased 26.6% to US$40.7 million from US$32.1 million in the year-earlier quarter. Revenues were US$265.8 million, up 28.1% from US$207.4 million the year before. Operating income was US$64.7 million versus US$58.6 million in the prior-year quarter, an increase of 10.4%. Direct operating expenses rose 37.1% to US$94.7 million from US$69.1 million in the comparable period the year before. Indirect operating expenses increased 33.3% to US$106.4 million from US$79.8 million in the equivalent prior-year period.

Prospects: Our evaluation of Cable ONE Inc. as of Jan. 21, 2018 is the result of our systematic analysis on three basic characteristics: earnings strength, relative valuation, and recent stock price movement. The company has produced a positive trend in earnings per share over the past 5 quarters and while recent estimates for the company have remained steady, CABO has posted better than expected results. Based on operating earnings yield, the company is about fairly valued when compared to all of the companies in our coverage universe. Share price changes over the past year indicates that CABO will perform in line with the market over the near term.

Financial Data

(US$ in Thousands)	3 Mos	12/31/2017	12/31/2016	12/31/2015	12/31/2014	12/31/2013	12/31/2012
Earnings Per Share	42.01	40.72	17.14	15.19	147,309.00	104,511.00	93,911.00
Cash Flow Per Share	59.78	57.13	43.73	42.10	...	...	...
Dividends Per Share	6.750	6.500	6.000	1.500	...	...	...
Dividend Payout %	16.07	15.96	35.01	9.87	...	...	...
Income Statement							
Total Revenue	265,761	960,029	819,625	807,266	814,812	825,707	804,992
EBITDA	112,248	410,265	335,528	302,110	372,009	289,811	276,711
Depn & Amortn	46,970	173,600	142,200	140,600	134,000	125,500	126,500
Income Before Taxes	50,555	189,801	163,107	145,420	238,009	164,311	150,211
Income Taxes	9,902	(44,227)	64,168	56,387	90,700	59,800	56,300
Net Income	40,653	234,028	98,939	89,033	147,309	104,511	93,911
Average Shares	5,742	5,747	5,770	5,860	...	...	...
Balance Sheet							
Current Assets	247,226	242,384	185,937	166,353	50,121	46,768	...
Total Assets	2,213,786	2,218,329	1,397,271	1,408,595	1,262,040	1,248,344	...
Current Liabilities	132,097	170,604	111,143	126,832	95,623	105,142	...
Long-Term Obligations	1,157,273	1,160,682	530,886	545,301	...	...	...
Total Liabilities	1,513,876	1,546,913	942,760	973,249	408,752	413,085	...
Stockholders' Equity	699,910	671,416	454,511	435,346	853,288	835,259	...
Shares Outstanding	5,732	5,731	5,708	5,833	...	...	...
Statistical Record							
Return on Assets %	13.28	12.95	7.03	...	11.74	...	...
Return on Equity %	40.90	41.57	22.18	...	17.45	...	...
EBITDA Margin %	42.24	42.73	40.94	37.42	45.66	35.10	34.37
Net Margin %	15.30	24.38	12.07	11.03	18.08	12.66	11.67
Asset Turnover	0.56	0.53	0.58	...	0.65	...	...
Current Ratio	1.87	1.42	1.67	1.31	0.52	0.44	...
Debt to Equity	1.65	1.73	1.17	1.25	...	...	...
Price Range	762.27-624.47	762.27-570.00	623.87-396.52	490.48-376.91	...	...	...
P/E Ratio	18.14-14.86	18.72-14.00	36.40-23.13	32.29-24.81	...	...	...
Average Yield %	0.95	0.94	1.18	0.35	...	...	...

Address: 210 E. Earll Drive, Phoenix, AZ 85012	Web Site: www.cableone.net	Auditors: PricewaterhouseCoopers LLP
Telephone: 602-364-6000	Officers: Julia M. Laulis - Chairman, President, Chief Executive Officer, Chief Operating Officer Michael E. Bowker - Senior Vice President, Chief Sales Officer, Chief Marketing Officer, Chief Operating Officer	Transfer Agents: Computershare Trust Company, N.A.

CABOT CORP.

Exchange	Symbol	Price	52Wk Range	Yield	P/E
NYS	CBT	$61.77 (6/29/2018)	68.48-51.21	2.14	N/A

*7 Year Price Score 102.73 *NYSE Composite Index=100 *12 Month Price Score 101.62

Interim Earnings (Per Share)

Qtr.	Dec	Mar	Jun	Sep
2014-15	0.69	0.41	(7.04)	0.61
2015-16	(0.11)	0.76	0.88	0.83
2016-17	0.85	1.18	0.71	1.06
2017-18	(1.98)	(2.80)	...	...

Interim Dividends (Per Share)

Amt	Decl	Ex	Rec	Pay
0.315Q	11/10/2017	11/22/2017	11/24/2017	12/08/2017
0.315Q	01/12/2018	02/22/2018	02/23/2018	03/09/2018
0.33Q	05/09/2018	05/24/2018	05/25/2018	06/08/2018
0.33Q	07/13/2018	08/30/2018	08/31/2018	09/14/2018

Indicated Div: $1.32

Valuation Analysis | **Institutional Holding**

Forecast EPS	$4.10	No of Institutions	
	(06/07/2018)	441	
Market Cap	$3.8 Billion	Shares	
Book Value	$1.2 Billion	67,827,776	
Price/Book	3.14	% Held	
Price/Sales	1.29	86.79	

Business Summary: Specialty Chemicals (MIC: 8.3.2 SIC: 2895 NAIC: 325182)

Cabot is a chemicals and performance materials. Co.'s business segments are: Reinforcement Materials, which include rubber blacks products are used in tires and industrial products; Performance Chemicals, which designs, manufactures and sells materials that deliver performance in a customer applications across the automotive, construction and infrastructure; Purification Solutions, which include activated carbon products are used for the purification of water, air, food and beverages, pharmaceuticals and other liquids and gases; and Specialty Fluids, which produces and markets cesium formate as a drilling and completion fluid for use primarily in high pressure oil and gas well construction.

Recent Developments: For the quarter ended Mar 31 2018, net loss amounted to US$163.0 million versus net income of US$80.0 million in the year-earlier quarter. Revenues were US$818.0 million, up 20.6% from US$678.0 million the year before. Operating loss was US$158.0 million versus an income of US$90.0 million in the prior-year quarter. Direct operating expenses rose 23.4% to US$628.0 million from US$509.0 million in the comparable period the year before. Indirect operating expenses increased 340.5% to US$348.0 million from US$79.0 million in the equivalent prior-year period.

Prospects: Our evaluation of Cabot Corp. as of Jan. 21, 2018 is the result of our systematic analysis on three basic characteristics: earnings strength, relative valuation, and recent stock price movement. The company has managed to produce a neutral trend in earnings per share over the past 5 quarters and while recent estimates for the company have been raised by analysts, CBT has posted results that fell short of analysts expectations. Based on operating earnings yield, the company is undervalued when compared to all of the companies in our coverage universe. Share price changes over the past year indicates that CBT will perform poorly over the near term.

Financial Data

(US$ in Thousands)	6 Mos	3 Mos	09/30/2017	09/30/2016	09/30/2015	09/30/2014	09/30/2013	09/30/2012
Earnings Per Share	(3.01)	0.97	3.80	2.36	(5.27)	3.03	2.36	5.99
Cash Flow Per Share	5.99	4.57	5.46	6.26	7.87	4.89	6.57	6.53
Tang Book Value Per Share	16.44	16.18	19.21	15.79	14.84	16.45	17.77	15.83
Dividends Per Share	1.260	1.245	1.230	1.040	0.880	0.840	0.800	0.760
Dividend Payout %	...	128.35	32.37	44.07	...	27.72	33.90	12.69
Income Statement								
Total Revenue	1,538,000	720,000	2,717,000	2,411,000	2,871,000	3,647,000	3,463,000	3,300,000
EBITDA	21,000	141,000	479,000	397,000	(159,000)	544,000	438,000	440,000
Depn & Amortn	79,000	39,000	147,000	154,000	169,000	184,000	176,000	153,000
Income Before Taxes	(79,000)	92,000	288,000	194,000	(377,000)	308,000	205,000	245,000
Income Taxes	198,000	205,000	29,000	34,000	(45,000)	92,000	58,000	55,000
Net Income	(295,000)	(122,000)	241,000	149,000	(334,000)	199,000	153,000	388,000
Average Shares	61,800	61,900	62,700	62,900	63,400	65,100	64,500	64,200
Balance Sheet								
Current Assets	1,387,000	1,281,000	1,262,000	1,089,000	1,048,000	1,364,000	1,495,000	1,443,000
Total Assets	3,117,000	3,189,000	3,314,000	3,044,000	3,075,000	4,084,000	4,233,000	4,399,000
Current Liabilities	833,000	788,000	742,000	398,000	441,000	630,000	844,000	919,000
Long-Term Obligations	631,000	631,000	661,000	918,000	970,000	1,004,000	1,020,000	1,172,000
Total Liabilities	1,901,000	1,841,000	1,834,000	1,770,000	1,841,000	2,142,000	2,282,000	2,586,000
Stockholders' Equity	1,216,000	1,348,000	1,480,000	1,274,000	1,234,000	1,942,000	1,951,000	1,813,000
Shares Outstanding	61,818	61,796	61,884	62,210	62,458	64,382	63,970	63,347
Statistical Record								
Return on Assets %	N.M.	2.12	7.58	4.86	N.M.	4.79	3.54	10.26
Return on Equity %	N.M.	5.13	17.50	11.85	N.M.	10.22	8.13	23.45
EBITDA Margin %	1.37	19.58	17.63	16.47	N.M.	14.92	12.65	13.33
Net Margin %	N.M.	N.M.	8.87	6.18	N.M.	5.46	4.42	11.76
Asset Turnover	0.96	0.92	0.85	0.79	0.80	0.88	0.80	0.87
Current Ratio	1.67	1.63	1.70	2.74	2.38	2.17	1.77	1.57
Debt to Equity	0.52	0.47	0.45	0.72	0.79	0.52	0.52	0.65
Price Range	68.48-50.75	64.26-50.75	60.90-48.21	53.41-31.56	50.77-30.90	60.30-42.48	43.93-32.41	44.66-23.27
P/E Ratio	...	66.25-52.32	16.03-12.69	22.63-13.37	...	19.90-14.02	18.61-13.73	7.46-3.88
Average Yield %	2.18	2.21	2.27	2.33	2.11	1.58	2.09	2.07

Address: Two Seaport Lane, Suite 1300, Boston, MA 02210-2019	**Auditors:** DELOITTE & TOUCHE LLP
Telephone: 617-345-0100	**Investor Contact:** 617-342-6090
Web Site: www.cabotcorp.com	**Transfer Agents:** Computershare Trust Company, N.A., Providence, RI
Officers: Sean D. Keohane - President, Chief Executive Officer, Executive Vice President, Division Officer Erica McLaughlin - Senior Vice President, Chief Financial Officer	

CABOT OIL & GAS CORP.

Exchange	Symbol	Price	52Wk Range	Yield	P/E
NYS	COG	$23.80 (6/29/2018)	29.44-21.95	1.01	95.20

*7 Year Price Score 77.71 ***NYSE Composite Index=100** ***12 Month Price Score 89.79**

Interim Earnings (Per Share)

Qtr.	Mar	Jun	Sep	Dec
2015	0.10	(0.07)	(0.04)	(0.27)
2016	(0.12)	(0.14)	(0.02)	(0.64)
2017	0.23	0.05	0.04	(0.09)
2018	0.25	...	...	...

Interim Dividends (Per Share)

Amt	Decl	Ex	Rec	Pay
0.05Q	07/27/2017	08/08/2017	08/10/2017	08/24/2017
0.05Q	10/25/2017	11/07/2017	11/08/2017	11/17/2017
0.06Q	01/03/2018	01/23/2018	01/24/2018	02/07/2018
0.06Q	05/02/2018	05/15/2018	05/16/2018	05/30/2018

Indicated Div: $0.24

Valuation Analysis

		Institutional Holding	
Forecast EPS	$1.11	No of Institutions	
	(06/14/2018)	798	
Market Cap	$10.8 Billion	Shares	
Book Value	$2.4 Billion	501,925,792	
Price/Book	4.48	% Held	
Price/Sales	6.27	90.57	

Business Summary: Production & Extraction (MIC: 9.1.1 SIC: 1311 NAIC: 211111)

Cabot Oil & Gas is an independent oil and gas company engaged in the development, exploitation and exploration of oil and gas properties. Co. also transports, stores, gathers and purchases natural gas for resale. Co.'s exploration, development and production operations are primarily concentrated in two unconventional plays: the Marcellus Shale in northeast Pennsylvania and the Eagle Ford Shale in south Texas. Co. also has operations in various other conventional and unconventional plays throughout the continental U.S. As of Dec 31 2017, Co. had proved natural gas reserves of 9.353 trillion cubic feet and proved crude oil and natural gas liquids reserves of 62.3 million barrels.

Recent Developments: For the quarter ended Mar 31 2018, net income increased 10.9% to US$117.2 million from US$105.7 million in the year-earlier quarter. Revenues were US$473.2 million, down 8.6% from US$517.8 million the year before. Operating income was US$177.0 million versus US$190.1 million in the prior-year quarter, a decrease of 6.9%. Direct operating expenses declined 9.9% to US$137.1 million from US$152.2 million in the comparable period the year before. Indirect operating expenses decreased 9.4% to US$159.0 million from US$175.6 million in the equivalent prior-year period.

Prospects: Our evaluation of Cabot Oil & Gas Corp. as of Jan. 21, 2018 is the result of our systematic analysis on three basic characteristics: earnings strength, relative valuation, and recent stock price movement. The company has suffered a very negative trend in earnings per share over the past 5 quarters. However, while recent estimates for the company have been mixed, COG has posted results that fell short of analysts expectations. Based on operating earnings yield, the company is overvalued when compared to all of the companies in our coverage universe. Share price changes over the past year indicates that COG will perform in line with the market over the near term.

Financial Data

(US$ in Thousands)	3 Mos	12/31/2017	12/31/2016	12/31/2015	12/31/2014	12/31/2013	12/31/2012	12/31/2011
Earnings Per Share	0.25	0.22	(0.91)	(0.28)	0.25	0.66	0.31	0.29
Cash Flow Per Share	1.96	1.94	0.86	1.79	2.97	2.44	1.55	1.20
Tang Book Value Per Share	5.31	5.48	5.52	4.85	5.19	5.29	5.07	5.04
Dividends Per Share	0.210	0.170	0.080	0.080	0.080	0.060	0.040	0.030
Dividend Payout %	84.00	77.27	...	...	32.00	9.09	12.90	10.34
Income Statement								
Total Revenue	473,227	1,764,219	1,155,677	1,357,150	2,173,011	1,746,278	1,204,546	979,864
EBITDA	178,125	527,772	26,425	529,888	740,620	1,205,225	762,803	654,372
Depn & Amortn	1,195	573,591	595,211	626,665	637,514	654,745	456,670	347,522
Income Before Taxes	156,872	(127,949)	(657,122)	(193,688)	29,321	485,538	237,840	235,187
Income Taxes	39,641	(328,828)	(242,475)	(73,382)	(72,067)	205,765	106,110	112,779
Net Income	117,231	100,393	(417,124)	(113,891)	104,468	279,773	131,730	122,408
Average Shares	461,549	465,551	456,847	413,696	417,601	422,375	421,986	421,522
Balance Sheet								
Current Assets	1,236,118	764,957	715,881	144,786	413,447	378,899	270,310	345,800
Total Assets	4,538,401	4,727,344	5,122,569	5,261,899	5,437,716	4,981,080	4,616,313	4,331,493
Current Liabilities	510,491	630,050	257,812	235,552	499,018	407,905	444,139	343,344
Long-Term Obligations	1,218,231	1,217,891	1,520,530	2,005,000	1,752,000	1,147,000	1,012,000	950,000
Total Liabilities	2,131,885	2,203,439	2,554,902	3,252,711	3,294,983	2,776,478	2,484,866	2,226,725
Stockholders' Equity	2,406,516	2,523,905	2,567,667	2,009,188	2,142,733	2,204,602	2,131,447	2,104,768
Shares Outstanding	452,817	460,611	465,150	413,875	413,022	416,396	420,050	417,230
Statistical Record								
Return on Assets %	2.29	2.04	N.M.	N.M.	2.01	5.83	2.94	2.94
Return on Equity %	4.38	3.94	N.M.	N.M.	4.81	12.90	6.20	6.16
EBITDA Margin %	37.64	29.92	2.29	39.04	34.08	69.02	63.33	66.78
Net Margin %	24.77	5.69	N.M.	N.M.	4.81	16.02	10.94	12.49
Asset Turnover	0.35	0.36	0.22	0.25	0.42	0.36	0.27	0.24
Current Ratio	2.42	1.21	2.78	0.61	0.83	0.93	0.61	1.01
Debt to Equity	0.51	0.48	0.59	1.00	0.82	0.52	0.47	0.45
Price Range	29.44-21.50	29.44-20.77	26.50-15.48	35.40-15.03	41.61-28.48	39.93-23.77	25.54-14.77	22.15-9.36
P/E Ratio	117.76-86.00	133.82-94.41	...	...	166.44-113.92	60.50-36.01	82.37-47.65	76.37-32.27
Average Yield %	0.82	0.69	0.35	0.30	0.23	0.18	0.20	0.20

Address: Three Memorial City Plaza, 840 Gessner Road, Suite 1400, Houston, TX 77024 **Telephone:** 281-589-4600 **Fax:** 281-589-4653	**Web Site:** www.cabotog.com **Officers:** Dan O. Dinges - Chairman, President, Chief Executive Officer Scott C. Schroeder - Executive Vice President, Chief Financial Officer	**Auditors:** PricewaterhouseCoopers LLP **Investor Contact:** 281-589-4993 **Transfer Agents:** Wells Fargo Bank N.A., Mendota Heights, MN

CALIFORNIA WATER SERVICE GROUP (DE)

Exchange	Symbol	Price	52Wk Range	Yield	P/E	Div Acheiver
NYS	CWT	$38.95 (6/29/2018)	45.60-35.40	1.93	29.29	50 Years

*7 Year Price Score 123.26 *NYSE Composite Index=100 *12 Month Price Score 97.96

Interim Earnings (Per Share)

Qtr.	Mar	Jun	Sep	Dec
2015	0.03	0.21	0.52	0.18
2016	(0.02)	0.24	0.48	0.31
2017	0.02	0.39	0.70	0.29
2018	(0.05)	...	...	...

Interim Dividends (Per Share)

Amt	Decl	Ex	Rec	Pay
0.18Q	07/26/2017	08/03/2017	08/07/2017	08/18/2017
0.18Q	10/25/2017	11/03/2017	11/06/2017	11/17/2017
0.188Q	01/31/2018	02/09/2018	02/12/2018	02/23/2018
0.188Q	04/25/2018	05/04/2018	05/07/2018	05/18/2018

Indicated Div: $0.75 (Div. Reinv. Plan)

Valuation Analysis

		Institutional Holding	
Forecast EPS	$1.40 (06/2018)	No of Institutions	329
Market Cap	$1.9 Billion	Shares	42,029,424
Book Value	$681.3 Million	% Held	
Price/Book	2.75		63.99
Price/Sales	2.77		

Business Summary: Water Utilities (MIC: 3.2.1 SIC: 4941 NAIC: 221310)

California Water Service Group is a holding company. Through its subsidiaries, Co. produces, purchases, stores, treats, tests, distributes and sells water for domestic, industrial, public and irrigation uses, and for fire protection. Co. also provides non-regulated water-related services under agreements with municipalities and other private companies. The non-regulated services include water system operation, billing and meter reading, the lease of communication antenna sites, lab services, and promotion of other non- regulated services. As of Dec 31 2017, Co. provided service to approximately 484,900 customers in approximately 100 California communities through 20 separate districts.

Recent Developments: For the quarter ended Mar 31 2018, net loss amounted to US$2.5 million versus net income of US$1.1 million in the year-earlier quarter. Revenues were US$132.2 million, up 8.4% from US$122.0 million the year before. Operating income was US$8.1 million versus US$10.6 million in the prior-year quarter, a decrease of 23.7%. Direct operating expenses rose 9.9% to US$70.7 million from US$64.3 million in the comparable period the year before. Indirect operating expenses increased 13.4% to US$53.5 million from US$47.2 million in the equivalent prior-year period.

Prospects: Our evaluation of California Water Service Group as of Jan. 21, 2018 is the result of our systematic analysis on three basic characteristics: earnings strength, relative valuation, and recent stock price movement. The company has generated a negative trend in earnings per share over the past 5 quarters and while recent estimates for the company have remained steady, CWT has posted better than expected results. Based on operating earnings yield, the company is about fairly valued when compared to all of the companies in our coverage universe. Share price changes over the past year indicates that CWT will perform well over the near term.

Financial Data
(US$ in Thousands)

	3 Mos	12/31/2017	12/31/2016	12/31/2015	12/31/2014	12/31/2013	12/31/2012	12/31/2011
Earnings Per Share	1.33	1.40	1.01	0.94	1.19	1.02	1.17	0.90
Cash Flow Per Share	3.37	3.08	3.32	3.02	2.68	2.68	3.14	2.66
Tang Book Value Per Share	14.12	14.39	13.69	13.36	13.05	12.49	11.24	10.69
Dividends Per Share	0.728	0.720	0.690	0.670	0.650	0.640	0.630	0.615
Dividend Payout %	54.70	51.43	68.32	71.28	54.62	62.75	53.85	68.33
Income Statement								
Total Revenue	132,247	666,890	609,370	588,368	597,499	584,103	559,966	501,814
EBITDA	27,136	209,481	170,036	160,783	174,346	156,421	154,252	143,439
Depn & Amortn	21,207	79,512	66,074	64,007	64,119	61,331	57,973	53,063
Income Before Taxes	(2,774)	96,109	73,479	69,545	83,465	66,301	68,184	60,737
Income Taxes	(229)	28,928	24,804	24,528	26,727	19,047	19,356	23,025
Net Income	(2,545)	67,181	48,675	45,017	56,738	47,254	48,828	37,712
Average Shares	48,030	48,009	47,956	47,880	47,829	46,417	41,892	41,772
Balance Sheet								
Current Assets	165,785	227,873	142,069	127,578	154,124	139,490	146,564	113,888
Total Assets	2,716,507	2,740,375	2,411,745	2,246,095	2,187,351	1,959,855	1,995,924	1,854,587
Current Liabilities	464,317	490,959	250,230	148,455	217,706	166,584	243,067	151,875
Long-Term Obligations	515,670	515,793	531,745	512,287	419,233	426,142	434,467	481,632
Total Liabilities	2,035,196	2,046,913	1,752,274	1,603,940	1,560,725	1,361,099	1,522,212	1,404,758
Stockholders' Equity	681,311	693,462	659,471	642,155	626,626	598,756	473,712	449,829
Shares Outstanding	48,074	48,012	47,964	47,875	47,806	47,740	41,908	41,817
Statistical Record								
Return on Assets %	2.46	2.61	2.08	2.03	2.74	2.39	2.53	2.13
Return on Equity %	9.53	9.93	7.46	7.10	9.26	8.81	10.55	8.52
EBITDA Margin %	20.52	31.41	27.90	27.33	29.18	26.78	27.55	28.58
Net Margin %	N.M.	10.07	7.99	7.65	9.50	8.09	8.72	7.52
Asset Turnover	0.26	0.26	0.26	0.27	0.29	0.30	0.29	0.28
Current Ratio	0.36	0.46	0.57	0.86	0.71	0.84	0.60	0.75
Debt to Equity	0.76	0.74	0.81	0.80	0.67	0.71	0.92	1.07
Price Range	45.60-33.25	45.60-32.50	36.80-22.96	25.96-19.68	26.09-20.44	23.23-18.35	19.21-17.22	19.21-16.89
P/E Ratio	34.29-25.00	32.57-23.21	36.44-22.73	27.62-20.94	21.92-17.18	22.77-17.99	16.42-14.72	21.34-18.77
Average Yield %	1.86	1.90	2.31	2.87	2.78	3.12	3.46	3.37

Address: 1720 North First Street, San Jose, CA 95112 Telephone: 408-367-8200	Web Site: www.calwatergroup.com Officers: Peter C. Nelson - Chairman, President, Chief Executive Officer Martin A. Kropelnicki - President, Chief Executive Officer, Vice President, Chief Financial Officer, Chief Operating Officer	Auditors: Deloitte & Touche LLP Investor Contact: 408-367-8200 Transfer Agents: American Stock Transfer & Trust Company, Brooklyn, NY

CALLON PETROLEUM CO. (DE)

Exchange	Symbol	Price	52Wk Range	Yield	P/E
NYS	CPE	$10.74 (6/29/2018)	14.26-9.54	N/A	17.61

*7 Year Price Score 109.85 *NYSE Composite Index=100 *12 Month Price Score 101.88

Interim Earnings (Per Share)

Qtr.	Mar	Jun	Sep	Dec
2015	(0.21)	(0.11)	(1.72)	(1.67)
2016	(0.51)	(0.61)	0.14	0.07
2017	0.22	0.16	0.08	0.10
2018	0.27	...	...	...

Interim Dividends (Per Share)

No Dividends Paid

Valuation Analysis

		Institutional Holding	
Forecast EPS	$0.91	No of Institutions	
	(06/14/2018)	392	
Market Cap	$2.2 Billion	Shares	
Book Value	$1.9 Billion	287,295,776	
Price/Book	1.13	% Held	
Price/Sales	5.26	71.26	

TRADING VOLUME (thousand shares)

Business Summary: Production & Extraction (MIC: 9.1.1 SIC: 1311 NAIC: 211111)

Callon Petroleum is engaged in the exploration, development, acquisition and production of oil and natural gas properties in the Permian Basin in West Texas. As of Dec 31 2017, Co.'s estimated net proved reserves totaled 137.0 million barrels of oil equivalents and included 107.1 million barrels of oil and 179.4 billion cubic feet of natural gas.

Recent Developments: For the quarter ended Mar 31 2018, net income increased 18.3% to US$55.8 million from US$47.1 million in the year-earlier quarter. Revenues were US$127.4 million, up 56.6% from US$81.4 million the year before. Operating income was US$61.0 million versus US$32.2 million in the prior-year quarter, an increase of 89.1%. Direct operating expenses rose 14.1% to US$21.5 million from US$18.8 million in the comparable period the year before. Indirect operating expenses increased 48.5% to US$45.0 million from US$30.3 million in the equivalent prior-year period.

Prospects: Our evaluation of Callon Petroleum Co. as of Jan. 21, 2018 is the result of our systematic analysis on three basic characteristics: earnings strength, relative valuation, and recent stock price movement. The company has generated a negative trend in earnings per share over the past 5 quarters. However, while recent estimates for the company have been mixed, CPE has posted results that fell short of analysts expectations. Based on operating earnings yield, the company is about fairly valued when compared to all of the companies in our coverage universe. Share price changes over the past year indicates that CPE will perform very poorly over the near term.

Financial Data
(US$ in Thousands)

	3 Mos	12/31/2017	12/31/2016	12/31/2015	12/31/2014	12/31/2013	12/31/2012	12/31/2011
Earnings Per Share	0.61	0.56	(0.78)	(3.77)	0.65	(0.01)	0.07	2.70
Cash Flow Per Share	1.33	1.14	0.94	1.32	2.10	1.35	1.29	2.09
Tang Book Value Per Share	9.46	9.20	8.62	4.53	7.85	6.92	5.18	5.05
Income Statement								
Total Revenue	127,440	366,474	200,851	137,512	151,862	102,569	110,733	127,644
EBITDA	57,169	124,756	(79,163)	(179,689)	71,508	14,235	14,612	48,676
Depn & Amortn	453	900	793	865	836	750	760	645
Income Before Taxes	56,256	121,697	(91,827)	(201,665)	60,900	7,391	4,744	36,314
Income Taxes	495	1,273	(14)	38,474	23,134	3,104	2,223	(67,036)
Net Income	55,761	120,424	(91,813)	(240,139)	37,766	4,304	2,747	104,149
Average Shares	202,588	202,102	126,258	65,708	45,961	40,133	40,337	38,582
Balance Sheet								
Current Assets	147,172	144,860	725,126	62,252	60,457	29,564	19,923	63,076
Total Assets	2,835,519	2,693,296	2,267,587	788,594	876,770	423,953	378,173	367,460
Current Liabilities	238,535	205,773	131,550	87,877	98,812	62,793	38,477	27,317
Long-Term Obligations	670,374	620,196	390,219	328,565	335,000	75,748	120,668	125,345
Total Liabilities	924,375	837,330	534,185	425,836	443,035	144,859	172,202	168,505
Stockholders' Equity	1,911,144	1,855,966	1,733,402	362,758	433,735	279,094	205,971	198,955
Shares Outstanding	201,947	201,836	201,041	80,087	55,225	40,345	39,800	39,398
Statistical Record								
Return on Assets %	4.99	4.85	N.M.	N.M.	5.81	1.07	0.73	35.56
Return on Equity %	6.99	6.71	N.M.	N.M.	10.60	1.77	1.35	96.99
EBITDA Margin %	44.86	34.04	N.M.	N.M.	47.09	13.88	13.20	38.13
Net Margin %	43.75	32.86	N.M.	N.M.	24.87	4.20	2.48	81.59
Asset Turnover	0.16	0.15	0.13	0.17	0.23	0.26	0.30	0.44
Current Ratio	0.62	0.70	5.51	0.71	0.61	0.47	0.52	2.31
Debt to Equity	0.35	0.33	0.23	0.91	0.77	0.27	0.59	0.63
Price Range	13.61-9.54	16.07-9.54	17.64-5.23	10.01-4.78	11.94-4.14	7.59-3.27	7.65-3.88	9.23-3.27
P/E Ratio	22.31-15.64	28.70-17.04	...	...	18.37-6.37	...	109.29-55.43	3.42-1.21

Address: 200 North Canal Street, Natchez, MS 39120 **Telephone:** 601-442-1601	**Web Site:** www.callon.com **Officers:** Joseph C. Gatto - President, Chief Executive Officer, Chief Financial Officer, Senior Vice President, Treasurer James P. (Jim) Ulm - Chief Financial Officer, Senior Vice President	**Auditors:** Grant Thornton LLP **Investor Contact:** 601-442-1601 **Transfer Agents:** American Stock Transfer & Trust Company, New York, NY

CAMDEN PROPERTY TRUST

Exchange	Symbol	Price	52Wk Range	Yield	P/E
NYS	CPT	$91.13 (6/29/2018)	95.70-78.55	3.38	42.39

*7 Year Price Score 95.24   *NYSE Composite Index=100   *12 Month Price Score 98.62

TRADING VOLUME (thousand shares)

Interim Earnings (Per Share)

Qtr.	Mar	Jun	Sep	Dec
2015	1.27	0.40	0.41	0.67
2016	0.46	4.92	3.21	0.45
2017	0.39	0.43	0.38	0.93
2018	0.41			

Interim Dividends (Per Share)

Amt	Decl	Ex	Rec	Pay
0.75Q	09/08/2017	09/28/2017	09/29/2017	10/17/2017
0.75Q	12/01/2017	12/14/2017	12/15/2017	01/17/2018
0.77Q	02/01/2018	03/28/2018	03/30/2018	04/17/2018
0.77Q	06/15/2018	06/28/2018	06/29/2018	07/17/2018

Indicated Div: $3.08

Valuation Analysis

		Institutional Holding	
Forecast EPS	$1.80 (06/14/2018)	No of Institutions	511
Market Cap	$9.4 Billion	Shares	
Book Value	$3.4 Billion		108,241,784
Price/Book	2.76	% Held	
Price/Sales	10.00		96.64

Business Summary: REITs (MIC: 5.3.1 SIC: 6798 NAIC: 525930)

Camden Property Trust is a real estate investment trust. Co. is primarily engaged in the ownership, management, development, redevelopment, acquisition, and construction of multifamily apartment communities. Co.'s properties typically consist of mid-rise buildings or two and three story buildings in a landscaped setting and provide residents with a variety of amenities common to multifamily rental properties. As of Dec 31 2017, Co. owned interests in, operated, or was developing 162 multifamily properties comprised of 55,143 apartment homes across the U.S. Co. also own land holdings which it may develop into multifamily communities.

Recent Developments: For the quarter ended Mar 31 2018, net income increased 12.6% to US$40.5 million from US$36.0 million in the year-earlier quarter. Revenues were US$232.5 million, up 2.9% from US$225.9 million the year before. Revenues from property income rose 5.1% to US$230.7 million from US$219.5 million in the corresponding quarter a year earlier.

Prospects: Our evaluation of Camden Property Trust as of Jan. 21, 2018 is the result of our systematic analysis on three basic characteristics: earnings strength, relative valuation, and recent stock price movement. The company has produced a positive trend in earnings per share over the past 5 quarters. Because the company lacks sufficient analyst estimate data, we place greater weight on the historical EPS trend as the measure of earnings strength. Based on operating earnings yield, the company is overvalued when compared to all of the companies in our coverage universe. Share price changes over the past year indicates that CPT will perform very well over the near term.

Financial Data
(US$ in Thousands)

	3 Mos	12/31/2017	12/31/2016	12/31/2015	12/31/2014	12/31/2013	12/31/2012	12/31/2011
Earnings Per Share	2.15	2.13	9.05	2.76	3.27	3.78	3.30	0.66
Cash Flow Per Share	4.72	4.75	4.93	4.75	4.75	4.64	3.86	3.37
Tang Book Value Per Share	32.96	33.14	30.82	28.87	28.85	27.85	26.64	21.97
Dividends Per Share	3.020	3.000	7.250	2.800	2.640	2.520	2.240	1.960
Dividend Payout %	140.47	140.85	80.11	101.45	80.73	66.67	67.88	296.97
Income Statement								
Total Revenue	232,476	928,691	891,024	900,260	858,589	810,048	744,315	677,263
EBITDA	128,889	545,986	793,167	608,360	628,446	453,904	468,132	329,751
Depn & Amortn	70,224	263,974	250,146	257,082	238,989	223,198	213,480	187,668
Income Before Taxes	39,084	195,262	449,876	253,966	296,194	132,577	150,370	29,669
Income Taxes	388	1,224	1,617	1,872	1,903	1,826	1,208	2,220
Net Income	39,395	196,422	819,823	249,315	292,089	336,364	285,465	49,379
Average Shares	96,046	92,515	89,903	89,490	88,468	88,494	85,556	73,701
Balance Sheet								
Current Assets	139,834	401,843	369,854	41,688	185,793	52,117	66,285	91,270
Total Assets	6,128,375	6,173,748	6,028,152	6,037,612	6,056,907	5,632,141	5,385,172	4,622,075
Current Liabilities	227,850	252,639	256,015	242,851	256,767	205,742	180,317	154,994
Long-Term Obligations	2,204,940	2,204,598	2,480,588	2,724,687	2,743,539	2,530,766	2,510,468	2,432,112
Total Liabilities	2,744,997	2,768,385	3,013,279	3,221,055	3,241,305	2,940,605	2,822,073	2,765,433
Stockholders' Equity	3,383,378	3,405,363	3,014,873	2,816,557	2,815,602	2,691,536	2,563,099	1,856,642
Shares Outstanding	102,640	102,769	97,818	97,571	97,604	96,660	96,201	84,517
Statistical Record								
Return on Assets %	3.33	3.22	13.55	4.12	5.00	6.11	5.69	1.06
Return on Equity %	6.30	6.12	28.04	8.85	10.61	12.80	12.88	2.71
EBITDA Margin %	55.44	58.79	89.02	67.58	73.20	56.03	62.89	48.69
Net Margin %	16.95	21.15	92.01	27.69	34.02	41.52	38.35	7.29
Asset Turnover	0.16	0.15	0.15	0.15	0.15	0.15	0.15	0.15
Current Ratio	0.61	1.59	1.44	0.17	0.72	0.25	0.37	0.59
Debt to Equity	0.65	0.65	0.82	0.97	0.97	0.94	0.98	1.31
Price Range	95.70-78.55	95.70-79.06	90.67-70.55	81.28-69.45	77.87-56.88	75.46-56.79	71.59-59.61	69.32-53.09
P/E Ratio	44.51-36.53	44.93-37.12	10.02-7.80	29.45-25.16	23.81-17.39	19.96-15.02	21.69-18.06	105.03-80.44
Average Yield %	3.45	3.44	8.87	3.68	3.77	3.76	3.39	3.27

Address: 11 Greenway Plaza, Suite 2400, Houston, TX 77046 **Telephone:** 713-354-2500	**Web Site:** www.camdenliving.com **Officers:** Richard J. Campo - Chairman, Chief Executive Officer D. Keith Oden - President	**Auditors:** Deloitte & Touche LLP **Investor Contact:** 713-354-2549 **Transfer Agents:** American Stock Transfer and Trust Company, New York, NY

CAMPBELL SOUP CO

Exchange	Symbol	Price	52Wk Range	Yield	P/E
NYS	CPB	$40.54 (6/29/2018)	54.19-33.19	3.45	25.50

*7 Year Price Score 80.07 *NYSE Composite Index=100 *12 Month Price Score 81.74

Interim Earnings (Per Share)

Qtr.	Oct	Jan	Apr	Jul
2014-15	0.74	0.66	0.58	0.23
2015-16	0.62	0.85	0.59	(0.26)
2016-17	0.94	0.33	0.58	1.04
2017-18	0.91	0.95	(1.31)	...

Interim Dividends (Per Share)

Amt	Decl	Ex	Rec	Pay
0.35Q	09/27/2017	10/12/2017	10/13/2017	10/30/2017
0.35Q	11/16/2017	01/09/2018	01/10/2018	01/29/2018
0.35Q	03/21/2018	04/10/2018	04/11/2018	04/30/2018
0.35Q	06/27/2018	07/12/2018	07/13/2018	07/30/2018

Indicated Div: $1.40 (Div. Reinv. Plan)

Valuation Analysis   **Institutional Holding**

Forecast EPS	$2.86	No of Institutions
	(06/14/2018)	880
Market Cap	$12.2 Billion	Shares
Book Value	$1.4 Billion	198,768,992
Price/Book	8.69	% Held
Price/Sales	1.50	41.37

TRADING VOLUME (thousand shares)

Business Summary: Food (MIC: 1.2.1 SIC: 2032 NAIC: 311422)

Campbell Soup is a manufacturer and marketer of food and beverage products. Co. manages its businesses in three segments: Americas Simple Meals and Beverages, which includes the retail and food service businesses in the U.S., Canada and Latin America; Global Biscuits and Snacks, which includes Pepperidge Farm cookies, crackers, bakery and frozen products in U.S. retail, Arnott's biscuits in Australia and Asia Pacific, and Kelsen cookies globally; and Campbell Fresh, which includes Bolthouse Farms fresh carrots, carrot ingredients, refrigerated beverages and refrigerated salad dressings, Garden Fresh Gourmet salsa, hummus, dips and tortilla chips, and the U.S. refrigerated soup business.

Recent Developments:
For the quarter ended Apr 29 2018, net loss amounted to US$393.0 million versus net income of US$176.0 million in the year-earlier quarter. Revenues were US$2.13 billion, up 14.7% from US$1.85 billion the year before. Operating loss was US$475.0 million versus an income of US$298.0 million in the prior-year quarter. Direct operating expenses rose 26.9% to US$1.51 billion from US$1.19 billion in the comparable period the year before. Indirect operating expenses increased 197.8% to US$1.09 billion from US$367.0 million in the equivalent prior-year period.

Prospects:
Our evaluation of Campbell Soup Co. as of Jan. 21, 2018 is the result of our systematic analysis on three basic characteristics: earnings strength, relative valuation, and recent stock price movement. The company has generated a negative trend in earnings per share over the past 5 quarters and while recent estimates for the company have been raised by analysts, CPB has posted results that fell short of analysts expectations. Based on operating earnings yield, the company is undervalued when compared to all of the companies in our coverage universe. Share price changes over the past year indicates that CPB will perform poorly over the near term.

Financial Data
(US$ in Thousands)	9 Mos	6 Mos	3 Mos	07/30/2017	07/31/2016	08/02/2015	08/03/2014	07/28/2013
Earnings Per Share	1.59	3.48	2.86	2.89	1.81	2.21	2.59	1.44
Cash Flow Per Share	4.33	4.27	4.18	4.24	4.75	3.80	2.82	3.25
Dividends Per Share	1.400	1.400	1.400	1.400	1.248	1.248	1.248	1.160
Dividend Payout %	88.05	40.23	48.95	48.44	68.95	56.47	48.19	80.56
Income Statement								
Total Revenue	6,466,000	4,341,000	2,161,000	7,890,000	7,961,000	8,082,000	8,268,000	8,052,000
EBITDA	217,000	816,000	494,000	1,699,000	1,248,000	1,381,000	1,479,000	1,473,000
Depn & Amortn	37,000	161,000	82,000	299,000	288,000	286,000	287,000	393,000
Income Before Taxes	76,000	593,000	382,000	1,293,000	849,000	990,000	1,073,000	955,000
Income Taxes	(91,000)	33,000	107,000	406,000	286,000	299,000	347,000	275,000
Net Income	167,000	560,000	275,000	887,000	563,000	691,000	818,000	458,000
Average Shares	301,000	301,000	302,000	307,000	311,000	313,000	316,000	317,000
Balance Sheet								
Current Assets	2,329,000	1,928,000	1,996,000	1,900,000	1,908,000	2,092,000	2,100,000	2,221,000
Total Assets	14,566,000	8,336,000	7,746,000	7,726,000	7,837,000	8,089,000	8,113,000	8,323,000
Current Liabilities	3,403,000	3,012,000	2,583,000	2,395,000	2,555,000	2,806,000	2,989,000	3,282,000
Long-Term Obligations	8,080,000	2,247,000	2,269,000	2,499,000	2,314,000	2,552,000	2,244,000	2,544,000
Total Liabilities	13,162,000	6,394,000	6,065,000	6,089,000	6,312,000	6,709,000	6,498,000	7,106,000
Stockholders' Equity	1,404,000	1,942,000	1,681,000	1,637,000	1,525,000	1,380,000	1,615,000	1,217,000
Shares Outstanding	301,000	301,000	323,000	301,000	308,000	310,000	313,000	312,000
Statistical Record								
Return on Assets %	4.41	13.25	11.02	11.43	7.09	8.55	9.79	6.18
Return on Equity %	33.62	61.78	53.21	56.26	38.87	46.27	56.83	43.43
EBITDA Margin %	3.36	18.80	22.86	21.53	15.68	17.09	17.89	18.29
Net Margin %	2.58	12.90	12.73	11.24	7.07	8.55	9.89	5.69
Asset Turnover	0.74	0.99	0.99	1.02	1.00	1.00	0.99	1.09
Current Ratio	0.68	0.64	0.77	0.79	0.75	0.75	0.70	0.68
Debt to Equity	5.75	1.16	1.35	1.53	1.52	1.85	1.39	2.09
Price Range	58.96-40.36	63.84-45.13	63.84-45.13	63.84-50.96	67.55-46.15	49.31-41.60	47.89-38.60	48.14-32.47
P/E Ratio	37.08-25.38	18.34-12.97	22.32-15.78	22.09-17.63	37.32-25.50	22.31-18.82	18.49-14.90	33.43-22.55
Average Yield %	2.87	2.65	2.53	2.44	2.20	2.75	2.87	2.93

Address: 1 Campbell Place, Camden, NJ 08103-1799
Telephone: 856-342-4800
Fax: 856-342-3878

Web Site: www.campbellsoupcompany.com
Officers: Les C. Vinney - Chairman Keith R. McLoughlin - Interim President, Interim Chief Executive Officer

Auditors: PricewaterhouseCoopers LLP
Investor Contact: 180-084-02865
Transfer Agents: Computershare Trust Company, N.A., Providence, RI

CAPITAL ONE FINANCIAL CORP

Exchange	Symbol	Price	52Wk Range	Yield	P/E
NYS	COF	$91.90 (6/29/2018)	105.71-78.21	1.74	20.15

*7 Year Price Score 102.65 *NYSE Composite Index=100 *12 Month Price Score 100.54

TRADING VOLUME (thousand shares)

Interim Earnings (Per Share)

Qtr.	Mar	Jun	Sep	Dec
2015	2.00	1.50	1.98	1.59
2016	1.84	1.69	1.90	1.47
2017	1.54	1.94	2.14	(2.14)
2018	2.62	...	...	...

Interim Dividends (Per Share)

Amt	Decl	Ex	Rec	Pay
0.40Q	07/27/2017	08/03/2017	08/07/2017	08/17/2017
0.40Q	11/02/2017	11/10/2017	11/13/2017	11/24/2017
0.40Q	02/01/2018	02/09/2018	02/12/2018	02/23/2018
0.40Q	05/03/2018	05/11/2018	05/14/2018	05/24/2018

Indicated Div: $1.60

Valuation Analysis

		Institutional Holding	
Forecast EPS	$10.17 (06/19/2018)	No of Institutions	1278
Market Cap	$44.7 Billion	Shares	523,640,256
Book Value	$49.2 Billion	% Held	86.75
Price/Book	0.91		
Price/Sales	1.45		

Business Summary: Banking (MIC: 5.1.1 SIC: 6021 NAIC: 522110)

Capital One Financial is a financial services holding company with banking and non-banking subsidiaries. As of Dec 31 2017, Co.'s subsidiaries included: Capital One Bank (USA), NA, which provides credit and debit card products, other lending products and deposit products; and Capital One, NA, which provides banking products and financial services to consumers, small businesses and commercial clients. Co.'s principal operations are organized into three segments based on the products and services provided or the type of customer served: Credit Card, Consumer Banking and Commercial Banking. As of Dec 31 2017, Co. had total assets of $365.69 billion and total deposits of $243.70 billion.

Recent Developments: For the quarter ended Mar 31 2018, income from continuing operations increased 68.9% to US$1.34 billion from US$795.0 million in the year-earlier quarter. Net income increased 66.2% to US$1.35 billion from US$810.0 million in the year-earlier quarter. Net interest income increased 4.5% to US$5.72 billion from US$5.47 billion in the year-earlier quarter. Provision for loan losses was US$1.67 billion versus US$1.99 billion in the prior-year quarter, a decrease of 16.0%. Non-interest income rose 12.3% to US$1.19 billion from US$1.06 billion, while non-interest expense advanced 4.0% to US$3.57 billion.

Prospects: Our evaluation of Capital One Financial Corp. as of Jan. 21, 2018 is the result of our systematic analysis on three basic characteristics: earnings strength, relative valuation, and recent stock price movement. The company has enjoyed a very positive trend in earnings per share over the past 5 quarters and while recent estimates for the company have been raised by analysts, COF has posted results that fell short of analysts expectations. Based on operating earnings yield, the company is undervalued when compared to all of the companies in our coverage universe. Share price changes over the past year indicates that COF will perform poorly over the near term.

Financial Data

(US$ in Thousands)	3 Mos	12/31/2017	12/31/2016	12/31/2015	12/31/2014	12/31/2013	12/31/2012	12/31/2011
Earnings Per Share	4.56	3.49	6.89	7.07	7.59	6.96	6.16	6.80
Cash Flow Per Share	25.93	29.29	23.42	18.69	16.52	17.22	16.11	16.35
Tang Book Value Per Share	71.35	70.43	68.71	62.22	56.15	48.48	45.68	34.95
Dividends Per Share	1.600	1.600	1.600	1.500	1.200	0.950	0.200	0.200
Dividend Payout %	35.09	45.85	23.22	21.22	15.81	13.65	3.25	2.94
Income Statement								
Interest Income	6,637,000	25,222,000	22,891,000	20,459,000	19,397,000	19,898,000	18,964,000	14,987,000
Interest Expense	919,000	2,762,000	2,018,000	1,625,000	1,579,000	1,792,000	2,375,000	2,246,000
Net Interest Income	5,718,000	22,460,000	20,873,000	18,834,000	17,818,000	18,106,000	16,589,000	12,741,000
Provision for Losses	1,674,000	7,551,000	6,459,000	4,536,000	3,541,000	3,453,000	4,415,000	2,360,000
Non-Interest Income	1,191,000	4,777,000	4,628,000	4,579,000	4,472,000	4,278,000	4,807,000	3,538,000
Non-Interest Expense	3,573,000	14,194,000	13,558,000	12,996,000	12,180,000	12,514,000	11,946,000	9,332,000
Income Before Taxes	1,662,000	5,492,000	5,484,000	5,881,000	6,569,000	6,417,000	5,035,000	4,587,000
Income Taxes	319,000	3,375,000	1,714,000	1,869,000	2,146,000	2,025,000	1,301,000	1,334,000
Net Income	1,346,000	1,982,000	3,751,000	4,050,000	4,428,000	4,159,000	3,517,000	3,147,000
Average Shares	490,800	484,200	509,800	548,000	571,900	587,600	566,000	459,000
Balance Sheet								
Net Loans & Leases	242,187,000	247,942,000	240,126,000	225,625,000	204,559,000	193,102,000	200,934,000	131,843,000
Total Assets	362,857,000	365,693,000	357,033,000	334,048,000	308,854,000	297,048,000	312,918,000	206,019,000
Total Deposits	250,847,000	243,702,000	236,768,000	217,721,000	205,548,000	204,523,000	212,485,000	128,226,000
Total Liabilities	313,654,000	316,963,000	309,519,000	286,764,000	263,801,000	255,304,000	272,419,000	176,353,000
Stockholders' Equity	49,203,000	48,730,000	47,514,000	47,284,000	45,053,000	41,744,000	40,499,000	29,666,000
Shares Outstanding	485,879	485,525	480,218	527,259	553,391	572,675	582,207	459,947
Statistical Record								
Return on Assets %	0.71	0.55	1.08	1.26	1.46	1.36	1.35	1.56
Return on Equity %	5.18	4.12	7.89	8.77	10.20	10.11	10.00	11.20
Net Interest Margin %	86.15	89.05	91.18	92.06	91.86	90.99	87.48	85.01
Efficiency Ratio %	45.64	47.31	49.27	51.91	51.03	51.76	50.25	50.38
Loans to Deposits	0.97	1.02	1.01	1.04	1.00	0.94	0.95	1.03
Price Range	105.71-76.92	100.50-76.92	90.62-58.15	91.71-71.55	84.95-68.66	76.61-50.80	61.40-43.75	56.21-37.63
P/E Ratio	23.18-16.87	28.80-22.04	13.15-8.44	12.97-10.12	11.19-9.05	11.01-7.30	9.97-7.10	8.27-5.53
Average Yield %	1.81	1.86	2.24	1.88	1.53	1.53	0.37	0.42

Address: 1680 Capital One Drive, McLean, VA 22102 **Telephone:** 703-720-1000	**Web Site:** www.capitalone.com **Officers:** Richard D. Fairbank - Chairman, President, Chief Executive Officer Timothy P. Golden - Senior Vice President, Controller, Principal Accounting Officer	**Auditors:** Ernst & Young LLP **Investor Contact:** 703-720-2455 **Transfer Agents:** ComputerShare Investor Services, Providence, RI	

CARDINAL HEALTH, INC.

Exchange	Symbol	Price	52Wk Range	Yield	P/E	Div Acheiver
NYS	CAH	$48.83 (6/29/2018)	78.69-48.83	3.90	9.11	21 Years

*7 Year Price Score 80.50 *NYSE Composite Index=100 *12 Month Price Score 83.54

Interim Earnings (Per Share)

Qtr.	Sep	Dec	Mar	Jun
2014-15	0.78	0.86	1.09	0.88
2015-16	1.15	0.98	1.17	1.02
2016-17	0.96	1.02	1.20	0.86
2017-18	0.36	3.33	0.81	...

Interim Dividends (Per Share)

Amt	Decl	Ex	Rec	Pay
0.462Q	08/09/2017	09/29/2017	10/02/2017	10/15/2017
0.462Q	11/08/2017	12/29/2017	01/02/2018	01/15/2018
0.462Q	02/07/2018	03/29/2018	04/02/2018	04/15/2018
0.476Q	05/09/2018	06/29/2018	07/02/2018	07/15/2018

Indicated Div: $1.91

Valuation Analysis **Institutional Holding**

Forecast EPS	$4.92	No of Institutions
	(06/14/2018)	1064
Market Cap	$15.2 Billion	Shares
Book Value	$7.5 Billion	351,168,448
Price/Book	2.01	% Held
Price/Sales	0.11	82.57

Business Summary: Pharmaceuticals (MIC: 4.1.1 SIC: 5122 NAIC: 424210)

Cardinal Health is a healthcare services and products company. Co.'s segments are: Pharmaceutical and Medical. The Pharmaceutical segment distributes branded and generic pharmaceutical, specialty pharmaceutical, over-the-counter healthcare and consumer products; operates nuclear pharmacies and radiopharmaceutical manufacturing facilities; provides pharmacy management services to hospitals as well as medication therapy management and patient outcomes services. The Medical segment manufactures, sources and distributes Cardinal Health branded medical, surgical and laboratory products, which are sold in the U.S., Canada, Europe, Asia and other markets.

Recent Developments: For the quarter ended Mar 31 2018, net income decreased 33.2% to US$255.0 million from US$382.0 million in the year-earlier quarter. Revenues were US$33.63 billion, up 5.7% from US$31.82 billion the year before. Operating income was US$546.0 million versus US$605.0 million in the prior-year quarter, a decrease of 9.8%. Direct operating expenses rose 5.4% to US$31.72 billion from US$30.09 billion in the comparable period the year before. Indirect operating expenses increased 21.7% to US$1.37 billion from US$1.12 billion in the equivalent prior-year period.

Prospects: Our evaluation of Cardinal Health Inc. as of Jan. 21, 2018 is the result of our systematic analysis on three basic characteristics: earnings strength, relative valuation, and recent stock price movement. The company has generated a negative trend in earnings per share over the past 5 quarters and while recent estimates for the company have been raised by analysts, CAH has posted better than expected results. Based on operating earnings yield, the company is undervalued when compared to all of the companies in our coverage universe. Share price changes over the past year indicates that CAH will perform very poorly over the near term.

Financial Data

(US$ in Thousands)	9 Mos	6 Mos	3 Mos	06/30/2017	06/30/2016	06/30/2015	06/30/2014	06/30/2013
Earnings Per Share	5.36	5.75	3.44	4.03	4.32	3.62	3.38	0.97
Cash Flow Per Share	9.39	6.30	7.16	3.74	9.06	7.65	7.40	5.06
Tang Book Value Per Share	N.M.	N.M.	N.M.	N.M.	N.M.	0.73	1.58	1.18
Dividends Per Share	1.850	1.836	1.823	1.809	1.610	1.415	1.250	1.090
Dividend Payout %	34.51	31.93	52.98	44.89	37.27	39.07	36.98	112.37
Income Statement								
Total Revenue	101,460,000	67,827,000	32,641,000	129,976,000	121,546,000	102,531,000	91,084,000	101,093,000
EBITDA	1,989,000	1,183,000	488,000	2,439,000	2,731,000	2,362,000	2,196,000	1,270,000
Depn & Amortn	779,000	520,000	229,000	314,000	277,000	254,000	265,000	259,000
Income Before Taxes	959,000	495,000	178,000	1,924,000	2,276,000	1,967,000	1,798,000	888,000
Income Taxes	(466,000)	(675,000)	61,000	630,000	845,000	755,000	635,000	553,000
Net Income	1,422,000	1,168,000	115,000	1,288,000	1,427,000	1,215,000	1,166,000	334,000
Average Shares	315,000	316,000	318,000	320,000	330,000	335,000	345,000	344,000
Balance Sheet								
Current Assets	23,513,000	25,188,000	23,725,000	28,345,000	21,956,000	21,752,000	17,939,000	17,770,000
Total Assets	41,031,000	42,905,000	41,940,000	40,112,000	34,122,000	30,142,000	26,033,000	25,819,000
Current Liabilities	21,427,000	23,125,000	22,407,000	21,221,000	19,701,000	17,243,000	15,115,000	14,590,000
Long-Term Obligations	9,027,000	9,057,000	9,068,000	9,068,000	4,952,000	5,211,000	3,171,000	3,686,000
Total Liabilities	33,494,000	35,306,000	35,262,000	33,304,000	27,568,000	23,886,000	19,632,000	19,844,000
Stockholders' Equity	7,537,000	7,599,000	6,678,000	6,808,000	6,554,000	6,256,000	6,401,000	5,975,000
Shares Outstanding	311,000	315,000	315,000	316,000	322,000	328,000	337,000	339,000
Statistical Record								
Return on Assets %	4.51	4.68	2.87	3.47	4.43	4.33	4.50	1.33
Return on Equity %	23.93	26.19	16.59	19.28	22.22	19.20	18.84	5.47
EBITDA Margin %	1.96	1.74	1.50	1.88	2.25	2.30	2.41	1.26
Net Margin %	1.40	1.72	0.35	0.99	1.17	1.19	1.28	0.33
Asset Turnover	3.57	3.40	3.42	3.50	3.77	3.65	3.51	4.04
Current Ratio	1.10	1.09	1.06	1.34	1.11	1.26	1.19	1.22
Debt to Equity	1.20	1.19	1.36	1.33	0.76	0.83	0.50	0.62
Price Range	82.71-55.00	83.80-55.00	83.80-64.36	84.92-65.17	90.85-73.69	91.50-68.56	73.54-47.02	48.76-37.75
P/E Ratio	15.43-10.26	14.57-9.57	24.36-18.71	21.07-16.17	21.03-17.06	25.28-18.94	21.76-13.91	50.27-38.92
Average Yield %	2.67	2.56	2.45	2.35	1.95	1.74	2.01	2.54

Address: 7000 Cardinal Place, Dublin, OH 43017	**Web Site:** www.cardinalhealth.com	**Auditors:** Ernst & Young LLP
Telephone: 614-757-5000	**Officers:** George S. Barrett - Executive Chairman, Chairman, Chief Executive Officer Michael C. Kaufmann - Chief Executive Officer, Chief Financial Officer, Division Officer	**Investor Contact:** 614-757-7115 **Transfer Agents:** Computershare Trust Company, N.A., Canton, MA

CARLISLE COMPANIES INC.

Exchange	Symbol	Price	52Wk Range	Yield	P/E	Div Acheiver
NYS	CSL	$108.31 (6/29/2018)	118.75-92.40	1.37	11.15	41 Years

*7 Year Price Score 103.32 *NYSE Composite Index=100 *12 Month Price Score 100.82

Interim Earnings (Per Share)

Qtr.	Mar	Jun	Sep	Dec
2015	0.59	1.43	1.56	1.24
2016	1.05	1.75	(0.15)	1.16
2017	0.94	1.58	1.37	1.82
2018	4.94	...	...	...

Interim Dividends (Per Share)

Amt	Decl	Ex	Rec	Pay
0.37Q	08/07/2017	08/16/2017	08/18/2017	09/01/2017
0.37Q	11/06/2017	11/16/2017	11/17/2017	12/01/2017
0.37Q	02/06/2018	02/16/2018	02/20/2018	03/01/2018
0.37Q	05/01/2018	05/14/2018	05/15/2018	06/01/2018

Indicated Div: $1.48 (Div. Reinv. Plan)

Valuation Analysis | **Institutional Holding**

Forecast EPS	$5.79	No of Institutions
	(06/14/2018)	506
Market Cap	$6.6 Billion	Shares
Book Value	$2.7 Billion	64,545,224
Price/Book	2.42	% Held
Price/Sales	1.56	87.44

Business Summary: Rubber Products (MIC: 8.4.1 SIC: 3069 NAIC: 326299)

Carlisle Companies is a holding company. Through its subsidiaries, Co. is a manufacturing company that designs, manufactures, and markets a range of products that are marketed as a component to original equipment manufacturers, distributors, as well as directly to end-users. Co.'s products include: rubber, thermoplastic polyolefin, and polyvinyl chloride membrane roofing systems; wire, cable, connectors, contacts, and cable assemblies for the transfer of power and data; industrial liquid and powder finishing equipment and integrated system solutions; brakes and friction material; and commercial and institutional foodservice permanentware, table coverings, cookware, and catering equipment.

Recent Developments: For the quarter ended Mar 31 2018, income from continuing operations was unchanged at US$57.9 million compared with the year-earlier quarter. Net income increased 401.0% to US$309.6 million from US$61.8 million in the year-earlier quarter. Revenues were US$984.7 million, up 27.2% from US$774.0 million the year before. Operating income was US$94.7 million versus US$89.5 million in the prior-year quarter, an increase of 5.8%. Direct operating expenses rose 34.2% to US$735.3 million from US$547.9 million in the comparable period the year before. Indirect operating expenses increased 13.3% to US$154.7 million from US$136.6 million in the equivalent prior-year period.

Prospects: Our evaluation of Carlisle Companies Inc. as of Jan. 21, 2018 is the result of our systematic analysis on three basic characteristics: earnings strength, relative valuation, and recent stock price movement. The company has managed to produce a neutral trend in earnings per share over the past 5 quarters. However, while recent estimates for the company have been mixed, CSL has posted better than expected results. Based on operating earnings yield, the company is about fairly valued when compared to all of the companies in our coverage universe. Share price changes over the past year indicates that CSL will perform poorly over the near term.

Financial Data

(US$ in Thousands)	3 Mos	12/31/2017	12/31/2016	12/31/2015	12/31/2014	12/31/2013	12/31/2012	12/31/2011
Earnings Per Share	9.71	5.71	3.82	4.82	3.82	3.22	4.22	2.86
Cash Flow Per Share	7.46	7.27	8.25	8.16	4.61	6.53	7.75	3.11
Tang Book Value Per Share	3.61	N.M.	7.99	5.08	9.72	8.60	3.36	2.85
Dividends Per Share	1.460	1.440	1.300	1.100	0.940	0.840	0.760	0.700
Dividend Payout %	15.04	25.22	34.03	22.82	24.61	26.09	18.01	24.48
Income Statement								
Total Revenue	984,700	4,089,900	3,675,400	3,543,200	3,204,000	2,943,000	3,629,400	3,224,500
EBITDA	143,800	586,600	516,200	575,400	473,000	442,200	498,900	343,200
Depn & Amortn	51,000	84,900	75,100	73,500	64,700	75,400	74,600	68,100
Income Before Taxes	78,300	468,200	410,500	467,900	376,100	333,000	398,800	253,900
Income Taxes	20,400	102,900	159,700	148,300	124,400	97,800	131,500	72,000
Net Income	309,600	365,500	250,100	319,700	251,300	209,700	270,200	180,300
Average Shares	62,164	63,551	64,883	65,804	65,304	64,806	63,610	62,495
Balance Sheet								
Current Assets	2,218,100	1,644,600	1,355,200	1,319,500	1,611,500	1,535,000	1,205,300	1,214,100
Total Assets	5,503,800	5,299,800	3,965,800	3,954,100	3,758,700	3,493,000	3,457,300	3,137,900
Current Liabilities	706,200	658,600	513,500	605,900	392,200	376,400	470,600	613,500
Long-Term Obligations	1,586,400	1,586,200	596,400	598,700	749,800	751,000	752,500	604,300
Total Liabilities	2,783,000	2,771,500	1,498,900	1,606,700	1,553,700	1,506,900	1,669,200	1,637,800
Stockholders' Equity	2,720,800	2,528,300	2,466,900	2,347,400	2,205,000	1,986,100	1,788,100	1,500,100
Shares Outstanding	60,759	61,839	64,257	64,051	64,691	63,658	63,127	61,664
Statistical Record								
Return on Assets %	12.81	7.89	6.30	8.29	6.93	6.03	8.17	6.36
Return on Equity %	23.41	14.63	10.36	14.05	.11.99	11.11	16.39	12.69
EBITDA Margin %	14.60	14.34	14.04	16.24	14.76	15.03	13.75	10.64
Net Margin %	31.44	8.94	6.80	9.02	7.84	7.13	7.44	5.59
Asset Turnover	0.88	0.88	0.93	0.92	0.88	0.85	1.10	1.14
Current Ratio	3.14	2.50	2.64	2.18	4.11	4.08	2.56	1.98
Debt to Equity	0.58	0.63	0.24	0.26	0.34	0.38	0.42	0.40
Price Range	118.75-92.40	115.91-92.40	115.96-77.82	104.60-84.11	91.54-71.67	79.62-58.76	59.36-45.56	50.55-30.52
P/E Ratio	12.23-9.52	20.30-16.18	30.36-20.37	21.70-17.45	23.96-18.76	24.73-18.25	14.07-10.80	17.67-10.67
Average Yield %	1.40	1.39	1.29	1.16	1.14	1.24	1.45	1.65

Address: 16430 North Scottsdale Road, Suite 400, Scottsdale, AZ 85254 **Telephone:** 480-781-5000	**Web Site:** www.carlisle.com **Officers:** D. Christian Koch - President, Chief Operating Officer, Region Officer, Chief Executive Officer Robert M. Roche - Chief Financial Officer, Vice President
	Auditors: DELOITTE & TOUCHE LLP **Investor Contact:** 800-897-9071 **Transfer Agents:** Computershare Investor Services, LLC, Chicago, IL

CARMAX INC.

Exchange	Symbol	Price	52Wk Range	Yield	P/E
NYS	KMX	$72.87 (6/29/2018)	80.19-58.77	N/A	19.23

*7 Year Price Score 106.98 *NYSE Composite Index=100 *12 Month Price Score 102.71

TRADING VOLUME (thousand shares)

Interim Earnings (Per Share)

Qtr.	May	Aug	Nov	Feb
2015-16	0.86	0.82	0.63	0.71
2016-17	0.90	0.84	0.72	0.81
2017-18	1.13	0.98	0.81	0.67
2018-19	1.33	...	...	...

Interim Dividends (Per Share)

No Dividends Paid

Valuation Analysis

		Institutional Holding	
Forecast EPS	$4.58	No of Institutions	
	(06/13/2018)	737	
Market Cap	$12.9 Billion	Shares	
Book Value	$3.4 Billion	218,292,224	
Price/Book	3.81	% Held	
Price/Sales	0.74	95.29	

Business Summary: Retail - Automotive (MIC: 2.1.4 SIC: 5521 NAIC: 441120)

CarMax is a holding company. Through its subsidiaries, Co. is engaged as a retailer of used vehicles. Co. operates in two segments: CarMax Sales Operations, which sells used vehicles, purchases used vehicles from customers and other sources, sells related products and services, and arranges financing options for customers; and CarMax Auto Finance, which consists of finance operation that provides vehicle financing to customer buying vehicles from Co. Co.'s products and services include retail merchandising, wholesale auctions, extended protection plans, reconditioning and service, and customer credit. As of Feb 28 2017, Co. operated 173 used car stores in 86 U.S. television markets.

Recent Developments: For the quarter ended May 31 2018, net income increased 12.7% to US$238.7 million from US$211.7 million in the year-earlier quarter. Revenues were US$4.79 billion, up 5.5% from US$4.54 billion the year before. Direct operating expenses rose 6.1% to US$4.13 billion from US$3.89 billion in the comparable period the year before. Indirect operating expenses increased 9.9% to US$341.7 million from US$310.9 million in the equivalent prior-year period.

Prospects: Our evaluation of Carmax Inc. as of Jan. 21, 2018 is the result of our systematic analysis on three basic characteristics: earnings strength, relative valuation, and recent stock price movement. The company has managed to produce a neutral trend in earnings per share over the past 5 quarters and while recent estimates for the company have been mixed, KMX has posted better than expected results. Based on operating earnings yield, the company is undervalued when compared to all of the companies in our coverage universe. Share price changes over the past year indicates that KMX will perform in line with the market over the near term.

Financial Data

(US$ in Thousands)	3 Mos	02/28/2018	02/28/2017	02/29/2016	02/28/2015	02/28/2014	02/28/2013	02/29/2012
Earnings Per Share	3.79	3.60	3.26	3.03	2.73	2.16	1.87	1.79
Cash Flow Per Share	(0.23)	(0.44)	(2.46)	(0.73)	(4.49)	(2.74)	(3.41)	(0.27)
Tang Book Value Per Share	19.15	18.45	16.66	14.92	15.11	14.96	13.36	11.77
Income Statement								
Total Revenue	4,792,592	17,120,209	15,875,118	15,149,675	14,268,716	12,574,299	10,962,818	10,003,599
EBITDA	267,486	1,292,953	1,203,521	1,173,302	1,099,504	918,556	816,008	775,824
Depn & Amortn	45,343	158,600	140,700	127,000	105,700	90,400	82,300	75,200
Income Before Taxes	319,684	1,063,608	1,006,405	1,009,944	969,331	797,322	701,351	666,910
Income Taxes	81,028	399,496	379,435	386,516	371,973	304,736	267,067	253,115
Net Income	238,656	664,112	626,970	623,428	597,358	492,586	434,284	413,795
Average Shares	179,421	184,470	192,215	205,540	218,691	227,584	231,823	230,721
Balance Sheet								
Current Assets	2,957,494	3,061,444	2,873,630	2,471,781	2,599,038	2,643,224	2,310,131	1,853,448
Total Assets	17,756,167	17,486,272	16,279,356	14,481,576	13,198,201	11,707,157	9,888,602	8,331,543
Current Liabilities	1,288,202	1,174,058	1,105,787	1,005,193	997,173	875,497	684,173	646,313
Long-Term Obligations	12,861,152	12,752,812	11,826,438	10,342,323	8,818,750	7,340,431	6,009,627	4,863,318
Total Liabilities	14,372,406	14,169,423	13,170,776	11,576,790	10,041,416	8,390,160	6,869,435	5,658,431
Stockholders' Equity	3,383,761	3,316,849	3,108,580	2,904,786	3,156,785	3,316,997	3,019,167	2,673,112
Shares Outstanding	176,719	179,747	186,548	194,712	208,869	221,685	225,906	227,118
Statistical Record								
Return on Assets %	4.04	3.93	4.08	4.49	4.80	4.56	4.77	5.44
Return on Equity %	21.15	20.67	20.85	20.51	18.45	15.55	15.26	16.62
EBITDA Margin %	5.58	7.55	7.58	7.74	7.71	7.31	7.44	7.76
Net Margin %	4.98	3.88	3.95	4.12	4.19	3.92	3.96	4.14
Asset Turnover	1.01	1.01	1.03	1.09	1.15	1.16	1.20	1.32
Current Ratio	2.30	2.61	2.60	2.46	2.61	3.02	3.38	2.87
Debt to Equity	3.80	3.84	3.80	3.56	2.79	2.21	1.99	1.82
Price Range	76.81-58.77	76.81-55.37	68.60-45.70	74.73-42.15	68.30-42.88	53.05-38.38	40.10-25.22	35.38-23.41
P/E Ratio	20.27-15.51	21.34-15.38	21.04-14.02	24.66-13.91	25.02-15.71	24.56-17.77	21.44-13.49	19.77-13.08

Address: 12800 Tuckahoe Creek Parkway, Richmond, VA 23238 Telephone: 804-747-0422	Web Site: www.carmax.com Officers: William D. (Bill) Nash - President, Executive Vice President, Senior Vice President, Vice President, Chief Executive Officer Thomas W. Reedy - Executive Vice President, Senior Vice President, Chief Financial Officer	Auditors: KPMG LLP Investor Contact: 804-935-4591 Transfer Agents: American Stock Transfer & Trust Company, LLC, Brooklyn, NY

CARNIVAL CORP

Exchange	Symbol	Price	52Wk Range	Yield	P/E
NYS	CCL	$57.31 (6/29/2018)	71.94-57.16	3.49	14.69

*7 Year Price Score 116.93 *NYSE Composite Index=100 *12 Month Price Score 93.38

Interim Earnings (Per Share)

Qtr.	Feb	May	Aug	Nov
2014-15	0.06	0.29	1.56	0.35
2015-16	0.18	0.80	1.93	0.84
2016-17	0.48	0.52	1.83	0.75
2017-18	0.54	0.78	...	...

Interim Dividends (Per Share)

Amt	Decl	Ex	Rec	Pay
0.40Q	07/18/2017	08/23/2017	08/25/2017	09/15/2017
0.45Q	10/19/2017	11/22/2017	11/24/2017	12/15/2017
0.45Q	01/18/2018	02/22/2018	02/23/2018	03/16/2018
0.50Q	04/11/2018	05/24/2018	05/25/2018	06/15/2018

Indicated Div: $2.00 (Div. Reinv. Plan)

Valuation Analysis

		Institutional Holding	
Forecast EPS	$4.23	No of Institutions	
	(06/14/2018)	1171	
Market Cap	$40.7 Billion	Shares	
Book Value	$23.9 Billion		496,961,248
Price/Book	1.70	% Held	
Price/Sales	2.22		59.52

Business Summary: Hotels, Restaurants & Travel (MIC: 2.2.1 SIC: 4489 NAIC: 483212)

Carnival is a leisure travel company. Co. operates ships within global, regional and national cruise brands that sell tailored cruise products and services. Co.'s North America segment includes Carnival Cruise Lines, Princess Cruises, Holland America Line, and Seabourn. Co.'s Europe, Australia & Asia segment includes Costa Cruises, AIDA Cruises, P&O Cruises (U.K.), and P&O Cruises (Australia), and Cunard. Co. also has a Cruise Support segment that represents its port destinations and private islands. In additon, Co. has a Tour and Other segment, which includes Holland America Princess Alaska Tours, a tour company in Alaska and the Canadian Yukon.

Recent Developments: For the quarter ended May 31 2018, net income increased 48.0% to US$561.0 million from US$379.0 million in the year-earlier quarter. Revenues were US$4.36 billion, up 10.4% from US$3.95 billion the year before. Operating income was US$559.0 million versus US$500.0 million in the prior-year quarter, an increase of 11.8%. Direct operating expenses rose 10.1% to US$2.68 billion from US$2.44 billion in the comparable period the year before. Indirect operating expenses increased 10.7% to US$1.12 billion from US$1.01 billion in the equivalent prior-year period.

Prospects: Our evaluation of Carnival Corp. as of Jan. 21, 2018 is the result of our systematic analysis on three basic characteristics: earnings strength, relative valuation, and recent stock price movement. The company has managed to produce a neutral trend in earnings per share over the past 5 quarters. However, while recent estimates for the company have been lowered by analysts, CCL has posted better than expected results. Based on operating earnings yield, the company is undervalued when compared to all of the companies in our coverage universe. Share price changes over the past year indicates that CCL will perform well over the near term.

Financial Data

(US$ in Thousands)	6 Mos	3 Mos	11/30/2017	11/30/2016	11/30/2015	11/30/2014	11/30/2013	11/30/2012
Earnings Per Share	3.90	3.64	3.59	3.72	2.26	1.59	1.39	1.67
Cash Flow Per Share	7.79	7.61	7.37	6.87	5.85	4.42	3.66	3.84
Tang Book Value Per Share	27.85	28.17	27.92	25.36	25.29	25.60	25.84	25.05
Dividends Per Share	1.800	1.700	1.600	1.350	1.100	1.000	1.500	1.000
Dividend Payout %	46.15	46.70	44.57	36.29	48.67	62.89	107.91	59.88
Income Statement								
Total Revenue	8,589,000	4,232,000	17,510,000	16,389,000	15,714,000	15,884,000	15,456,000	15,382,000
EBITDA	2,047,000	923,000	4,701,000	4,783,000	3,634,000	3,160,000	2,968,000	3,155,000
Depn & Amortn	1,000,000	488,000	1,846,000	1,738,000	1,626,000	1,635,000	1,588,000	1,527,000
Income Before Taxes	955,000	390,000	2,666,000	2,828,000	1,799,000	1,245,000	1,072,000	1,302,000
Income Taxes	3,000	...	60,000	49,000	42,000	9,000	(6,000)	4,000
Net Income	951,000	391,000	2,606,000	2,779,000	1,757,000	1,236,000	1,078,000	1,298,000
Average Shares	715,000	719,000	725,000	747,000	779,000	778,000	777,000	779,000
Balance Sheet								
Current Assets	2,278,000	1,667,000	1,596,000	1,689,000	2,451,000	1,503,000	1,937,000	1,821,000
Total Assets	42,184,000	41,441,000	40,778,000	38,936,000	39,237,000	39,532,000	40,104,000	39,161,000
Current Liabilities	9,308,000	8,851,000	8,800,000	7,072,000	6,956,000	6,921,000	6,720,000	7,340,000
Long-Term Obligations	8,172,000	7,445,000	6,993,000	8,357,000	7,413,000	7,363,000	8,092,000	7,168,000
Total Liabilities	18,251,000	17,060,000	16,562,000	16,339,000	15,466,000	15,244,000	15,548,000	15,232,000
Stockholders' Equity	23,933,000	24,382,000	24,216,000	22,597,000	23,771,000	24,288,000	24,556,000	23,929,000
Shares Outstanding	711,000	716,000	718,000	726,000	772,000	777,000	776,000	776,000
Statistical Record								
Return on Assets %	6.84	6.60	6.54	7.09	4.46	3.10	2.72	3.33
Return on Equity %	12.06	11.25	11.13	11.95	7.31	5.06	4.45	5.42
EBITDA Margin %	23.83	21.81	26.85	29.18	23.13	19.89	19.20	20.51
Net Margin %	11.07	9.24	14.88	16.96	11.18	7.78	6.97	8.44
Asset Turnover	0.44	0.45	0.44	0.42	0.40	0.40	0.39	0.39
Current Ratio	0.24	0.19	0.18	0.24	0.35	0.22	0.29	0.25
Debt to Equity	0.34	0.31	0.29	0.37	0.31	0.30	0.33	0.30
Price Range	71.94-62.28	71.94-55.53	69.48-49.88	55.14-41.92	54.08-42.39	44.16-33.88	39.32-31.60	39.16-29.48
P/E Ratio	18.45-15.97	19.76-15.26	19.35-13.89	14.82-11.27	23.93-18.76	27.77-21.31	28.29-22.73	23.45-17.65
Average Yield %	2.71	2.62	2.60	2.79	2.29	2.59	4.22	2.97

Address: 3655 N.W. 87th Avenue, Miami, FL 33178-2428 Telephone: 305-599-2600	Web Site: www.carnivalcorporation.com Officers: Micky Meir Arison - Chairman, Chief Executive Officer, Associate/Affiliate Company Officer Arnold W. Donald - President, Chief Executive Officer, Associate/Affiliate Company Officer	Auditors: PricewaterhouseCoopers LLP Investor Contact: 305-406-5539 Transfer Agents: ComputerShare Investor Services, Providence, RI

CARPENTER TECHNOLOGY CORP.

Exchange	Symbol	Price	52Wk Range	Yield	P/E
NYS	CRS	$52.57 (6/29/2018)	60.43-36.96	1.37	14.68

*7 Year Price Score 83.61   ***NYSE Composite Index=100**   ***12 Month Price Score 114.93**

Interim Earnings (Per Share)

Qtr.	Sep	Dec	Mar	Jun
2014-15	0.25	0.45	(0.03)	0.43
2015-16	0.18	0.23	(0.51)	0.31
2016-17	(0.13)	0.15	0.44	0.54
2017-18	0.49	1.92	0.63	...

Interim Dividends (Per Share)

Amt	Decl	Ex	Rec	Pay
0.18Q	08/09/2017	08/18/2017	08/22/2017	09/07/2017
0.18Q	10/10/2017	10/23/2017	10/24/2017	12/07/2017
0.18Q	01/24/2018	02/05/2018	02/06/2018	03/01/2018
0.18Q	04/18/2018	04/30/2018	05/01/2018	06/07/2018

Indicated Div: $0.72

Valuation Analysis

		Institutional Holding	
Forecast EPS	$2.37	No of Institutions	
	(06/12/2018)	373	
Market Cap	$2.5 Billion	Shares	
Book Value	$1.4 Billion	54,208,596	
Price/Book	1.80	% Held	
Price/Sales	1.20	89.43	

Business Summary: Non-Precious Metals (MIC: 8.2.2 SIC: 3312 NAIC: 331111)

Carpenter Technology is engaged in the manufacturing, fabrication and distribution of metals. Co. produces and distributes premium specialty alloys, including titanium alloys, powder metals, stainless steels, alloy steels, and tool steels as well as drilling tools. Co.'s superalloy and titanium powder technologies support a range of products and manufacturing techniques. Co.'s segments are Specialty Alloys Operations, which consists of alloy and stainless steel manufacturing operations; and Performance Engineered Products, which includes the Dynamet titanium business, the Carpenter Powder Products business, the Amega West business and the Latrobe and Mexico distribution businesses.

Recent Developments: For the quarter ended Dec 31 2017, net income increased to US$92.1 million from US$7.0 million in the year-earlier quarter. Revenues were US$487.8 million, up 14.1% from US$427.4 million the year before. Operating income was US$40.8 million versus US$15.4 million in the prior-year quarter, an increase of 164.9%. Direct operating expenses rose 10.2% to US$402.1 million from US$364.9 million in the comparable period the year before. Indirect operating expenses decreased 4.7% to US$44.9 million from US$47.1 million in the equivalent prior-year period.

Prospects: Our evaluation of Carpenter Technology Corp. as of Jan. 21, 2018 is the result of our systematic analysis on three basic characteristics: earnings strength, relative valuation, and recent stock price movement. The company has produced a positive trend in earnings per share over the past 5 quarters and while recent estimates for the company have been raised by analysts, CRS has posted better than expected results. Based on operating earnings yield, the company is about fairly valued when compared to all of the companies in our coverage universe. Share price changes over the past year indicates that CRS will perform very well over the near term.

Financial Data

(US$ in Thousands)	9 Mos	6 Mos	3 Mos	06/30/2017	06/30/2016	06/30/2015	06/30/2014	06/30/2013
Earnings Per Share	3.58	3.39	1.62	0.99	0.23	1.11	2.47	2.73
Cash Flow Per Share	3.91	3.65	2.51	2.75	5.33	5.37	4.50	4.07
Tang Book Value Per Share	22.11	21.58	19.32	18.61	17.10	19.81	21.94	18.01
Dividends Per Share	0.720	0.720	0.720	0.720	0.720	0.720	0.720	0.720
Dividend Payout %	20.11	21.24	44.44	72.73	313.04	64.86	29.15	26.37
Income Statement								
Total Revenue	1,539,700	967,500	479,800	1,797,600	1,813,400	2,226,700	2,173,000	2,271,700
EBITDA	215,800	141,400	71,100	205,500	155,200	223,800	305,900	321,300
Depn & Amortn	87,200	58,000	28,700	105,800	106,500	107,200	93,300	85,100
Income Before Taxes	106,600	68,900	35,200	70,200	20,900	89,000	195,800	215,500
Income Taxes	(39,100)	(46,600)	11,800	23,200	10,200	30,400	63,600	70,300
Net Income	145,700	115,500	23,400	47,000	11,300	58,700	132,800	146,100
Average Shares	47,700	47,600	47,300	47,100	48,200	52,700	53,600	53,400
Balance Sheet								
Current Assets	1,191,300	1,159,500	1,111,700	1,093,600	1,010,700	1,070,400	1,194,500	1,281,500
Total Assets	2,991,900	2,944,100	2,892,500	2,878,100	2,794,300	2,905,900	3,057,500	2,882,900
Current Liabilities	401,100	387,800	381,600	396,000	298,800	322,100	430,600	421,200
Long-Term Obligations	546,300	548,300	549,800	550,000	611,300	607,100	604,300	604,200
Total Liabilities	1,620,800	1,607,300	1,661,500	1,679,500	1,689,400	1,580,000	1,553,200	1,579,800
Stockholders' Equity	1,371,100	1,336,800	1,231,000	1,198,600	1,104,900	1,325,900	1,504,300	1,303,100
Shares Outstanding	46,928	46,894	46,803	46,753	46,600	50,318	53,137	52,773
Statistical Record								
Return on Assets %	5.89	5.65	2.68	1.66	0.40	1.97	4.47	5.30
Return on Equity %	13.52	13.11	6.51	4.08	0.93	4.15	9.46	12.14
EBITDA Margin %	14.02	14.61	14.82	11.43	8.56	10.05	14.08	14.14
Net Margin %	9.46	11.94	4.88	2.61	0.62	2.64	6.11	6.43
Asset Turnover	0.70	0.68	0.66	0.63	0.63	0.75	0.73	0.82
Current Ratio	2.97	2.99	2.91	2.76	3.38	3.32	2.77	3.04
Debt to Equity	0.40	0.41	0.45	0.46	0.55	0.46	0.40	0.46
Price Range	54.09-34.66	52.84-34.66	48.03-31.25	43.63-31.25	40.56-25.16	64.32-35.69	66.64-45.59	55.70-43.77
P/E Ratio	15.11-9.68	15.59-10.22	29.65-19.29	44.07-31.57	176.35-109.39	57.95-32.15	26.98-18.46	20.40-16.03
Average Yield %	1.63	1.74	1.88	1.91	2.17	1.55	1.21	1.47

Address: 1735 Market Street, 15th Floor, Philadelphia, PA 19103	**Web Site:** www.cartech.com	**Auditors:** PricewaterhouseCoopers LLP
Telephone: 610-208-2000	**Officers:** Gregory A. Pratt - Interim Executive Chairman, Chairman, Interim President, Interim Chief Executive Officer Tony R. Thene - President, Chief Executive Officer, Senior Vice President, Chief Financial Officer	**Investor Contact:** 610-208-3476 **Transfer Agents:** American Stock Transfer & Trust Company

CARS.COM INC

7 Year Price Score N/A **NYSE Composite Index=100** **12 Month Price Score 99.56**

TRADING VOLUME (thousand shares)

Interim Earnings (Per Share)

Qtr.	Mar	Jun	Sep	Dec
2016	0.47	0.59	0.72	(0.41)
2017	0.38	0.35	0.29	2.12
2018	0.01	...	...	...

Interim Dividends (Per Share)

No Dividends Paid

Valuation Analysis / Institutional Holding

Valuation Analysis		Institutional Holding	
Forecast EPS	$0.94	No of Institutions	
	(06/18/2018)		298
Market Cap	$2.0 Billion	Shares	
Book Value	$1.7 Billion		82,327,552
Price/Book	1.22	% Held	
Price/Sales	3.22		N/A

Business Summary: IT Services (MIC: 6.3.1 SIC: 7374 NAIC: 518210)

Cars.com is a digital automotive marketplace that creates connections between customers (car dealerships and automotive original equipment manufacturers) and consumers (individuals researching cars or looking to purchase a car). Co. provides a range of digital solutions targeting buyers and sellers of automobiles and automobile services. Co.'s main product, digital automotive marketplace, connects buyers and sellers on Cars.com™. Co. also operates Auto.com™, DealerRater.com®, NewCars.com® and PickupTrucks.com™, which are specialized websites directed toward different consumer segments. Co. also has DealerInspire.com® and LaunchDigitalMarketing.com® as part of its portfolio.

Recent Developments: For the quarter ended Mar 31 2018, net income decreased 96.5% to US$929,000 from US$26.9 million in the year-earlier quarter. Revenues were US$160.0 million, up 4.4% from US$153.2 million the year before. Operating income was US$7.2 million versus US$27.2 million in the prior-year quarter, a decrease of 73.6%. Direct operating expenses rose 20.0% to US$19.1 million from US$15.9 million in the comparable period the year before. Indirect operating expenses increased 21.4% to US$133.7 million from US$110.1 million in the equivalent prior-year period.

Prospects: Our evaluation of Cars.com Inc. as of Jan. 21, 2018 is the result of our systematic analysis on three basic characteristics: earnings strength, relative valuation, and recent stock price movement. The company has suffered a very negative trend in earnings per share over the past 5 quarters and while recent estimates for the company have been mixed, CARS has posted results that fell short of analysts expectations. Based on operating earnings yield, the company is undervalued when compared to all of the companies in our coverage universe. Share price changes over the past year indicates that CARS will perform very poorly over the near term.

Financial Data (US$ in Thousands)	3 Mos	12/31/2017	12/31/2016	12/31/2015	12/31/2014
Earnings Per Share	2.77	3.13	1.37	...	...
Cash Flow Per Share	2.35	2.59	2.77	...	...
Income Statement					
Total Revenue	159,957	626,262	633,106	596,510	145,939
EBITDA	25,105	145,333	251,787	230,496	34,382
Depn & Amortn	17,955	10,800	74,829	72,658	18,164
Income Before Taxes	1,193	122,162	176,958	157,838	16,218
Income Taxes	264	(102,281)	588	...	...
Net Income	929	224,443	176,370	157,838	16,218
Average Shares	72,122	71,727	71,598	...	...
Balance Sheet					
Current Assets	148,009	142,639	119,541	98,517	...
Total Assets	2,664,086	2,511,039	2,547,266	2,473,667	...
Current Liabilities	109,104	90,149	71,984	88,370	...
Long-Term Obligations	681,846	557,194	...	...	...
Total Liabilities	985,729	831,911	129,981	169,148	...
Stockholders' Equity	1,678,357	1,679,128	2,417,285	2,304,519	...
Shares Outstanding	71,864	71,627	...	...	...
Statistical Record					
Return on Assets %	7.66	8.87	7.01	...	...
Return on Equity %	9.74	10.96	7.45	...	...
EBITDA Margin %	15.69	23.21	39.77	38.64	23.56
Net Margin %	0.58	35.84	27.86	26.46	11.11
Asset Turnover	0.24	0.25	0.25	...	...
Current Ratio	1.36	1.58	1.66	1.11	...
Debt to Equity	0.41	0.33	...	...	...
Price Range	31.97-22.00	29.98-22.00	...	...	...
P/E Ratio	11.54-7.94	9.58-7.03	...	...	...

Address: 300 S. Riverside Plaza, Suite 1000, Chicago, IL 60606 **Telephone:** 312-601-5000	**Web Site:** www.cars.com **Officers:** Scott E. Forbes - Chairman Thomas Alex Vetter - President, Chief Executive Officer	**Auditors:** Ernst & Young LLP **Transfer Agents:** Wells Fargo Shareowner Services, Mendota Heights, MN

CARTER'S INC

Exchange	Symbol	Price	52Wk Range	Yield	P/E
NYS	CRI	$108.39 (6/29/2018)	122.77-84.28	1.66	17.51

*7 Year Price Score 106.59 *NYSE Composite Index=100 *12 Month Price Score 102.87

Interim Earnings (Per Share)

Qtr.	Mar	Jun	Sep	Dec
2015	0.94	0.68	1.51	1.38
2016	1.04	0.71	1.60	1.74
2017	0.95	0.78	1.71	2.81
2018	0.89	...	...	...

Interim Dividends (Per Share)

Amt	Decl	Ex	Rec	Pay
0.37Q	08/17/2017	08/25/2017	08/29/2017	09/08/2017
0.37Q	11/08/2017	11/17/2017	11/20/2017	12/01/2017
0.45Q	02/22/2018	03/09/2018	03/12/2018	03/23/2018
0.45Q	05/17/2018	05/25/2018	05/29/2018	06/15/2018

Indicated Div: $1.80

Valuation Analysis

Valuation Analysis	Institutional Holding	
Forecast EPS	$6.46	No of Institutions
	(06/12/2018)	550
Market Cap	$5.1 Billion	Shares
Book Value	$854.8 Million	60,699,304
Price/Book	5.97	% Held
Price/Sales	1.49	87.62

Business Summary: Apparel, Footwear & Accessories (MIC: 1.4.2 SIC: 5641 NAIC: 315291)

Carter's is a marketer of apparel for babies and young children. Under its Carter's brand, Co. designs, sources, and markets a range of products, mainly for sizes newborn to eight. Under its OshKosh B'gosh (OshKosh) brand, Co. designs, sources, and markets a range of young children's apparel, mainly for children in sizes newborn to 12. Co. provides several product categories, including baby, sleepwear, playclothes, and related accessories. As of Dec 30 2017, Co. operated 466 Carter's and 131 OshKosh stores in the U.S. Products are also sold through 179 co-branded retail stores in Canada and 41 retail stores in Mexico, in addition to its international wholesale, licensing and online channels.

Recent Developments: For the quarter ended Mar 31 2018, net income decreased 8.9% to US$42.5 million from US$46.6 million in the year-earlier quarter. Revenues were US$755.8 million, up 3.1% from US$732.8 million the year before. Operating income was US$60.3 million versus US$78.5 million in the prior-year quarter, a decrease of 23.1%. Direct operating expenses rose 1.5% to US$423.3 million from US$417.1 million in the comparable period the year before. Indirect operating expenses increased 14.7% to US$272.2 million from US$237.2 million in the equivalent prior-year period.

Prospects: Our evaluation of Carter Holdings Inc. as of Jan. 21, 2018 is the result of our systematic analysis on three basic characteristics: earnings strength, relative valuation, and recent stock price movement. The company has enjoyed a very positive trend in earnings per share over the past 5 quarters and while recent estimates for the company have been mixed, CRI has posted better than expected results. Based on operating earnings yield, the company is undervalued when compared to all of the companies in our coverage universe. Share price changes over the past year indicates that CRI will perform in line with the market over the near term.

Financial Data

(US$ in Thousands)	3 Mos	12/30/2017	12/31/2016	01/02/2016	01/03/2015	12/28/2013	12/29/2012	12/31/2011
Earnings Per Share	6.19	6.24	5.08	4.50	3.62	2.75	2.69	1.94
Cash Flow Per Share	6.62	6.94	7.42	5.96	5.28	3.69	4.80	1.41
Tang Book Value Per Share	4.50	4.52	6.19	7.52	5.45	3.38	8.28	5.30
Dividends Per Share	1.560	1.480	1.320	0.880	0.760	0.480	...	...
Dividend Payout %	25.20	23.72	25.98	19.56	20.99	17.45	...	...
Income Statement								
Total Revenue	755,786	3,400,410	3,199,184	3,013,879	2,893,868	2,638,711	2,381,734	2,109,734
EBITDA	83,180	505,147	495,970	463,136	405,093	330,521	301,631	220,536
Depn & Amortn	22,489	84,416	73,419	68,417	74,937	68,288	39,500	32,500
Income Before Taxes	52,872	391,032	396,070	368,188	302,906	249,465	255,391	180,888
Income Taxes	10,403	88,268	137,964	130,366	108,236	89,058	94,241	66,872
Net Income	42,469	302,764	258,106	237,822	194,670	160,407	161,150	114,016
Average Shares	47,391	48,146	50,375	52,334	53,093	57,522	59,069	58,214
Balance Sheet								
Current Assets	935,083	1,017,669	1,057,086	1,131,465	1,041,458	970,381	957,703	782,147
Total Assets	1,975,206	2,067,999	1,946,597	2,009,113	1,893,096	1,812,484	1,630,109	1,402,709
Current Liabilities	225,936	328,624	277,609	262,718	247,971	269,139	244,235	152,753
Long-Term Obligations	617,541	617,306	580,376	584,431	586,000	586,000	186,000	236,000
Total Liabilities	1,120,392	1,210,906	1,158,473	1,134,062	1,106,412	1,111,753	644,630	597,000
Stockholders' Equity	854,814	857,093	788,124	875,051	786,684	700,731	985,479	805,709
Shares Outstanding	47,113	47,178	48,948	51,764	52,712	54,541	59,126	58,595
Statistical Record								
Return on Assets %	15.47	15.12	13.09	12.22	10.34	9.34	10.66	8.60
Return on Equity %	36.71	36.91	31.12	28.70	25.75	19.08	18.04	15.39
EBITDA Margin %	11.01	14.86	15.50	15.37	14.00	12.53	12.66	10.45
Net Margin %	5.62	8.90	8.07	7.89	6.73	6.08	6.77	5.40
Asset Turnover	1.77	1.70	1.62	1.55	1.54	1.54	1.57	1.59
Current Ratio	4.14	3.10	3.81	4.31	4.20	3.61	3.92	5.12
Debt to Equity	0.72	0.72	0.74	0.67	0.74	0.84	0.19	0.29
Price Range	122.77-80.35	117.59-78.32	111.47-84.16	108.98-80.98	87.31-64.84	77.33-55.55	57.44-39.49	40.62-27.04
P/E Ratio	19.83-12.98	18.84-12.55	21.94-16.57	24.22-18.00	24.12-17.91	28.12-20.20	21.35-14.68	20.94-13.94
Average Yield %	1.57	1.61	1.36	0.94	1.00	0.71	...	...

Address: Phipps Tower, 3438 Peachtree Road N.E., Suite 1800, Atlanta, GA 30326	Web Site: www.carters.com	Auditors: PricewaterhouseCoopers LLP
Telephone: 678-791-1000	Officers: Michael Dennis Casey - Chairman, President, Chief Executive Officer Brian J. Lynch - President, Executive Vice President	Investor Contact: 404-745-2889 Transfer Agents: American Stock Transfer & Trust Company, LLC, Brooklyn, NY

CATALENT INC

Exchange	Symbol	Price	52Wk Range	Yield	P/E
NYS	CTLT	$41.89 (6/29/2018)	47.39-33.75	N/A	83.78

*7 Year Price Score N/A   ***NYSE Composite Index=100**   ***12 Month Price Score 98.61**

TRADING VOLUME (thousand shares)

Interim Earnings (Per Share)

Qtr.	Sep	Dec	Mar	Jun
2014-15	(0.18)	0.37	0.25	1.26
2015-16	0.07	0.24	0.08	0.50
2016-17	0.04	0.14	0.21	0.49
2017-18	0.03	(0.16)	0.14	...

Interim Dividends (Per Share)

No Dividends Paid

Valuation Analysis   Institutional Holding

Forecast EPS	$1.67	No of Institutions
	(06/14/2018)	338
Market Cap	$5.6 Billion	Shares
Book Value	$1.1 Billion	157,379,104
Price/Book	5.23	% Held
Price/Sales	2.33	N/A

Business Summary: Pharmaceuticals (MIC: 4.1.1 SIC: 2834 NAIC: 325412)

Catalent is a holding company. Co. is a provider of delivery technologies and development solutions for drugs, biologics and consumer and animal health products. Co.'s segments include: Softgel Technologies, which provides formulation, development and manufacturing services for soft capsules; Drug Delivery Solutions, which provides various formulation delivery technologies, and related solutions including: development and manufacturing of a range of oral dose forms including fast-dissolve tablets and controlled release products; and Clinical Supply Services, which provides manufacturing, packaging, storage and inventory management for drugs and biologics in clinical trials.

Recent Developments: For the quarter ended Mar 31 2018, net income decreased 26.9% to US$19.0 million from US$26.0 million in the year-earlier quarter. Revenues were US$627.9 million, up 17.9% from US$532.6 million the year before. Operating income was US$73.1 million versus US$64.6 million in the prior-year quarter, an increase of 13.2%. Direct operating expenses rose 19.4% to US$436.2 million from US$365.2 million in the comparable period the year before. Indirect operating expenses increased 15.4% to US$118.6 million from US$102.8 million in the equivalent prior-year period.

Prospects: Our evaluation of Catalent Inc as of Jan. 21, 2018 is the result of our systematic analysis on three basic characteristics: earnings strength, relative valuation, and recent stock price movement. The company has managed to produce a neutral trend in earnings per share over the past 5 quarters and while recent estimates for the company have remained steady, CTLT has posted better than expected results. Based on operating earnings yield, the company is about fairly valued when compared to all of the companies in our coverage universe. Share price changes over the past year indicates that CTLT will perform very well over the near term.

Financial Data

(US$ in Thousands)	9 Mos	6 Mos	3 Mos	06/30/2017	06/30/2016	06/30/2015	06/30/2014	06/30/2013
Earnings Per Share	0.50	0.57	0.87	0.87	0.89	1.75	0.21	(0.62)
Cash Flow Per Share	2.79	2.85	2.66	2.40	1.24	1.44	2.38	1.84
Income Statement								
Total Revenue	1,778,100	1,150,200	543,900	2,075,400	1,848,100	1,830,800	1,827,700	1,800,300
EBITDA	240,000	142,200	27,500	327,900	327,600	311,800	331,000	350,500
Depn & Amortn	96,000	60,800	1,300	102,200	94,200	94,300	100,500	171,200
Income Before Taxes	62,600	29,900	1,900	135,600	144,900	112,500	67,400	(23,900)
Income Taxes	61,700	48,000	(1,900)	25,800	33,700	(97,700)	49,500	24,100
Net Income	900	(18,100)	3,800	109,800	111,500	212,200	16,200	(46,700)
Average Shares	135,109	132,983	127,784	126,737	125,870	121,348	76,123	74,970
Balance Sheet								
Current Assets	1,214,400	1,075,500	1,330,100	1,059,800	790,200	737,500	687,500	677,900
Total Assets	4,554,100	4,387,100	3,784,800	3,454,300	3,091,100	3,145,400	3,090,200	3,056,800
Current Liabilities	557,500	484,000	457,100	469,000	391,200	399,000	453,000	410,300
Long-Term Obligations	2,706,500	2,672,500	2,082,900	2,055,100	1,832,800	1,864,100	2,685,400	2,656,600
Total Liabilities	3,485,700	3,381,600	2,746,000	2,730,800	2,455,200	2,511,400	3,461,400	3,467,500
Stockholders' Equity	1,068,400	1,005,500	1,038,800	723,500	635,900	634,000	(371,200)	(410,700)
Shares Outstanding	133,369	133,318	132,841	125,049	124,712	124,319	74,821	74,796
Statistical Record								
Return on Assets %	1.60	1.85	3.15	3.36	3.57	6.81	0.53	N.M.
Return on Equity %	7.33	8.75	13.19	16.15	17.51	161.49	...	...
EBITDA Margin %	13.50	12.36	5.06	15.80	17.73	17.03	18.11	19.47
Net Margin %	0.05	N.M.	0.70	5.29	6.03	11.59	0.89	N.M.
Asset Turnover	0.61	0.61	0.63	0.63	0.59	0.59	0.59	0.58
Current Ratio	2.18	2.22	2.91	2.26	2.02	1.85	1.52	1.65
Debt to Equity	2.53	2.66	2.01	2.84	2.88	2.94	...	...
Price Range	47.39-27.66	43.02-25.88	41.67-21.85	38.02-21.85	34.21-20.86	31.96-19.85	...	...
P/E Ratio	94.78-55.32	75.47-45.40	47.90-25.11	43.70-25.11	38.44-23.44	18.26-11.34	...	...

Address: 14 Schoolhouse Road, Somerset, NJ 08873 **Telephone:** 732-537-6200	**Web Site:** www.catalent.com **Officers:** John R. Chiminski - Chairman, President, Chief Executive Officer Wetteny Joseph - Chief Financial Officer, Senior Vice President, Division Officer	**Auditors:** Ernst & Young LLP **Transfer Agents:** Computershare Trust Company, N.A.

CATERPILLAR INC.

Exchange	Symbol	Price	52Wk Range	Yield	P/E	Div Acheiver
NYS	CAT	$135.67 (6/29/2018)	170.89-106.51	2.54	36.87	24 Years

*7 Year Price Score 117.03 *NYSE Composite Index=100 *12 Month Price Score 104.76

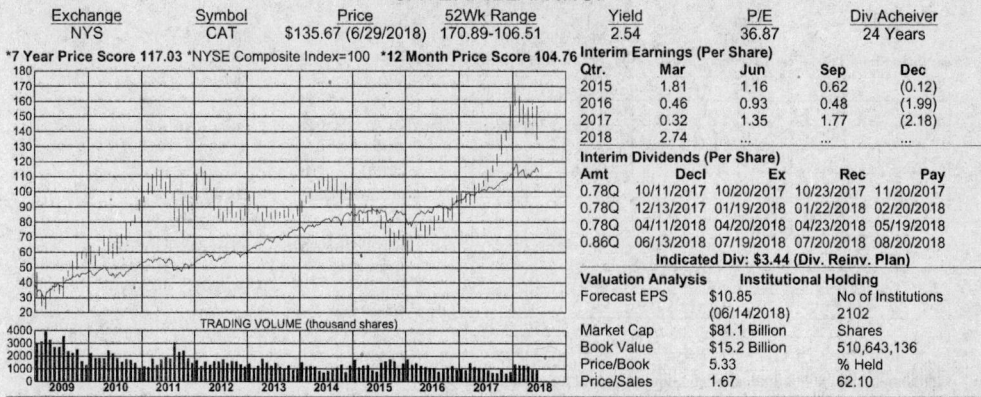

Interim Earnings (Per Share)

Qtr.	Mar	Jun	Sep	Dec
2015	1.81	1.16	0.62	(0.12)
2016	0.46	0.93	0.48	(1.99)
2017	0.32	1.35	1.77	(2.18)
2018	2.74	...	...	...

Interim Dividends (Per Share)

Amt	Decl	Ex	Rec	Pay
0.78Q	10/11/2017	10/20/2017	10/23/2017	11/20/2017
0.78Q	12/13/2017	01/19/2018	01/22/2018	02/20/2018
0.78Q	04/11/2018	04/20/2018	04/23/2018	05/19/2018
0.86Q	06/13/2018	07/19/2018	07/20/2018	08/20/2018

Indicated Div: $3.44 (Div. Reinv. Plan)

Valuation Analysis — **Institutional Holding**

Forecast EPS	$10.85	No of Institutions
	(06/14/2018)	2102
Market Cap	$81.1 Billion	Shares
Book Value	$15.2 Billion	510,643,136
Price/Book	5.33	% Held
Price/Sales	1.67	62.10

Business Summary: Construction Services (MIC: 7.5.4 SIC: 3531 NAIC: 333120)

Caterpillar manufactures construction and mining equipment, diesel and natural gas engines, industrial gas turbines and diesel-electric locomotives. Co. has five segments: Construction Industries, which provides machinery for infrastructure, forestry and building construction applications; Resource Industries, which provides machinery for mining, quarry, waste, and material handling applications; Energy and Transportation, which provides reciprocating engines, turbines, diesel-electric locomotives and related parts; Financial Products Segment, which provides financing for Co.'s products; and All Other operating segments, which provides business strategy and product management.

Recent Developments: For the quarter ended Mar 31 2018, net income increased 759.3% to US$1.67 billion from US$194.0 million in the year-earlier quarter. Revenues were US$12.86 billion, up 30.9% from US$9.82 billion the year before. Operating income was US$2.11 billion versus US$380.0 million in the prior-year quarter, an increase of 454.7%. Direct operating expenses rose 26.0% to US$8.57 billion from US$6.80 billion in the comparable period the year before. Indirect operating expenses decreased 17.3% to US$2.19 billion from US$2.64 billion in the equivalent prior-year period.

Prospects: Our evaluation of Caterpillar Inc. as of Jan. 21, 2018 is the result of our systematic analysis on three basic characteristics: earnings strength, relative valuation, and recent stock price movement. The company has enjoyed a very positive trend in earnings per share over the past 5 quarters and while recent estimates for the company have been mixed, CAT has posted better than expected results. Based on operating earnings yield, the company is about fairly valued when compared to all of the companies in our coverage universe. Share price changes over the past year indicates that CAT will perform well over the near term.

Financial Data

(US$ in Thousands)	3 Mos	12/31/2017	12/31/2016	12/31/2015	12/31/2014	12/31/2013	12/31/2012	12/31/2011
Earnings Per Share	3.68	1.26	(0.11)	3.50	5.88	5.75	8.48	7.40
Cash Flow Per Share	8.52	9.64	9.57	11.23	13.05	15.80	8.01	10.87
Tang Book Value Per Share	11.15	9.01	8.13	9.23	11.51	16.08	10.04	2.22
Dividends Per Share	3.110	3.100	3.080	2.940	2.600	2.240	1.960	1.800
Dividend Payout %	84.51	246.03	...	84.00	44.22	29.91	29.25	24.32
Income Statement								
Total Revenue	12,859,000	45,462,000	38,537,000	47,011,000	55,184,000	55,656,000	65,875,000	60,138,000
EBITDA	3,082,000	7,814,000	3,947,000	6,654,000	8,986,000	9,030,000	11,921,000	10,158,000
Depn & Amortn	681,000	2,555,000	2,707,000	2,705,000	2,795,000	2,710,000	2,421,000	2,211,000
Income Before Taxes	2,134,000	4,082,000	139,000	2,855,000	5,083,000	5,128,000	8,236,000	6,725,000
Income Taxes	472,000	3,339,000	192,000	742,000	1,380,000	1,319,000	2,528,000	1,720,000
Net Income	1,665,000	754,000	(67,000)	2,102,000	3,695,000	3,789,000	5,681,000	4,928,000
Average Shares	608,000	599,300	584,300	601,300	628,900	658,600	669,600	666,100
Balance Sheet								
Current Assets	37,357,000	36,244,000	31,967,000	34,418,000	38,867,000	38,335,000	42,524,000	38,128,000
Total Assets	78,014,000	76,962,000	74,704,000	78,497,000	84,681,000	84,896,000	89,356,000	81,446,000
Current Liabilities	27,402,000	26,931,000	26,132,000	26,303,000	27,877,000	27,297,000	29,755,000	28,561,000
Long-Term Obligations	23,165,000	23,847,000	22,818,000	25,247,000	27,784,000	26,719,000	27,752,000	24,944,000
Total Liabilities	62,808,000	63,265,000	61,567,000	63,688,000	67,935,000	64,085,000	71,824,000	68,563,000
Stockholders' Equity	15,206,000	13,697,000	13,137,000	14,809,000	16,746,000	20,811,000	17,532,000	12,883,000
Shares Outstanding	597,904	597,625	586,486	582,321	606,166	637,822	655,048	647,533
Statistical Record								
Return on Assets %	2.86	0.99	N.M.	2.58	4.36	4.35	6.63	6.78
Return on Equity %	15.47	5.62	N.M.	13.32	19.68	19.76	37.25	41.57
EBITDA Margin %	23.97	17.19	10.24	14.15	16.28	16.22	18.10	16.89
Net Margin %	12.95	1.66	N.M.	4.47	6.70	6.81	8.62	8.19
Asset Turnover	0.62	0.60	0.50	0.58	0.65	0.64	0.77	0.83
Current Ratio	1.36	1.35	1.22	1.31	1.39	1.40	1.43	1.33
Debt to Equity	1.52	1.74	1.74	1.70	1.66	1.28	1.58	1.94
Price Range	170.89-92.27	158.42-91.39	97.33-57.91	91.88-63.79	111.40-86.17	99.49-80.43	116.20-79.64	115.41-70.55
P/E Ratio	46.44-25.07	125.73-72.53	...	26.25-18.23	18.95-14.65	17.30-13.99	13.70-9.39	15.60-9.53
Average Yield %	2.43	2.75	3.92	3.73	2.58	1.98	2.64	1.86

Address: 510 Lake Cook Road, Suite 100, Deerfield, IL 60015 Telephone: 224-551-4000	Web Site: www.caterpillar.com Officers: David L. Calhoun - Chairman Donald James (Jim) Umpleby - Group President, Chief Executive Officer	Auditors: PricewaterhouseCoopers LLP Investor Contact: 309-675-4549 Transfer Agents: ComputerShare, College Station, TX

CBRE GROUP INC

Exchange	Symbol	Price	52Wk Range	Yield	P/E
NYS	CBRE	$47.74 (6/29/2018)	49.05-34.91	N/A	22.84

*7 Year Price Score 117.54 *NYSE Composite Index=100 *12 Month Price Score 109.36

TRADING VOLUME (thousand shares)

Interim Earnings (Per Share)

Qtr.	Mar	Jun	Sep	Dec
2015	0.28	0.37	0.44	0.54
2016	0.24	0.36	0.31	0.78
2017	0.38	0.58	0.58	0.49
2018	0.44	...	...	...

Interim Dividends (Per Share)

No Dividends Paid

Valuation Analysis

Valuation Analysis		Institutional Holding	
Forecast EPS	$3.12	No of Institutions	
	(06/12/2018)	800	
Market Cap	$16.2 Billion	Shares	
Book Value	$4.4 Billion	399,532,448	
Price/Book	3.72	% Held	
Price/Sales	1.02	N/A	

Business Summary: Property, Real Estate & Development (MIC: 5.3.2 SIC: 6531 NAIC: 531210)

CBRE Group is a holding company. Through its subsidiaries, Co. is a commercial real estate services and investment firm. Co. has five segments: The Americas, which consists of operations located in the U.S., Canada and Latin America; Europe, Middle East and Africa, which mainly consists of operations in Europe; Asia Pacific, which includes operations in Asia, Australia and New Zealand; Global Investment Management business, which consists of investment management operations in North America, Europe and Asia Pacific; and Development Services business, which consists of real estate development and investment activities primarily in the U.S.

Recent Developments: For the quarter ended Mar 31 2018, net income increased 8.1% to US$150.1 million from US$138.9 million in the year-earlier quarter. Revenues were US$4.67 billion, up 15.4% from US$4.05 billion the year before.

Prospects: Our evaluation of CBRE Group Inc. as of Jan. 21, 2018 is the result of our systematic analysis on three basic characteristics: earnings strength, relative valuation, and recent stock price movement. The company has generated a negative trend in earnings per share over the past 5 quarters and while recent estimates for the company have been mixed, CBG has posted better than expected results. Based on operating earnings yield, the company is undervalued when compared to all of the companies in our coverage universe. Share price changes over the past year indicates that CBG will perform well over the near term.

Financial Data
(US$ in Thousands)

	3 Mos	12/31/2017	12/31/2016	12/31/2015	12/31/2014	12/31/2013	12/31/2012	12/31/2011
Earnings Per Share	2.09	2.03	1.69	1.63	1.45	0.95	0.97	0.74
Cash Flow Per Share	2.37	2.10	1.34	1.96	2.00	2.27	0.90	1.13
Income Statement								
Total Revenue	4,673,952	14,209,608	13,071,589	10,855,810	9,049,918	7,184,794	6,514,099	5,905,411
EBITDA	211,080	1,246,847	971,375	966,650	904,150	671,456	672,374	519,768
Depn & Amortn	29,733	166,000	151,200	137,200	122,800	98,100	76,200	54,200
Income Before Taxes	156,110	953,886	683,375	716,881	675,548	444,563	428,749	324,762
Income Taxes	46,164	466,147	296,662	320,853	263,759	187,187	185,322	189,103
Net Income	150,288	691,479	571,973	547,132	484,503	316,538	315,555	239,162
Average Shares	342,589	340,783	338,424	336,414	334,171	331,762	327,044	323,723
Balance Sheet								
Current Assets	5,754,300	5,452,527	5,122,450	5,305,223	3,524,504	2,879,812	4,084,550	3,550,047
Total Assets	11,907,442	11,483,830	10,779,587	11,017,943	7,647,105	6,998,414	7,809,542	7,219,143
Current Liabilities	4,869,655	4,606,645	4,525,429	4,994,157	2,875,634	2,605,740	2,972,293	2,680,648
Long-Term Obligations	1,758,188	1,999,603	2,548,126	2,645,111	1,852,416	1,866,890	2,543,707	2,611,187
Total Liabilities	7,549,811	7,464,400	7,765,100	8,305,291	5,387,275	5,102,629	6,270,331	6,067,662
Stockholders' Equity	4,357,631	4,019,430	3,014,487	2,712,652	2,259,830	1,895,785	1,539,211	1,151,481
Shares Outstanding	339,737	339,459	337,279	334,230	332,991	331,927	330,082	327,972
Statistical Record								
Return on Assets %	6.52	6.21	5.23	5.86	6.62	4.28	4.19	3.88
Return on Equity %	18.82	19.66	19.92	22.01	23.32	18.43	23.39	23.22
EBITDA Margin %	4.52	8.77	7.43	8.90	9.99	9.35	10.32	8.80
Net Margin %	3.22	4.87	4.38	5.04	5.35	4.41	4.84	4.05
Asset Turnover	1.46	1.28	1.20	1.16	1.24	0.97	0.86	0.96
Current Ratio	1.18	1.18	1.13	1.06	1.23	1.11	1.37	1.32
Debt to Equity	0.40	0.50	0.85	0.98	0.82	0.98	1.65	2.27
Price Range	47.88-32.48	44.20-30.04	34.58-23.32	38.92-30.93	35.06-25.47	26.31-19.90	20.86-15.10	29.70-12.78
P/E Ratio	22.91-15.54	21.77-14.80	20.46-13.80	23.88-18.98	24.18-17.57	27.69-20.95	21.51-15.57	40.14-17.27

Address: 400 South Hope Street, 25th Floor, Los Angeles, CA 90071
Telephone: 213-613-3333

Web Site: www.cbre.com
Officers: Robert E. Sulentic - President, Chief Executive Officer James R. Groch - Chief Financial Officer, Director, Executive Vice President, Chief Investment Officer, Global Chief Investment Officer, Division Officer

Auditors: KPMG LLP
Investor Contact: 213-613-3732
Transfer Agents: Broadridge Corporate Issuer Solutions, Inc., Edgewood, NY

CBS CORP

Exchange	Symbol	Price	52Wk Range	Yield	P/E
NYS	CBS	$56.22 (6/29/2018)	67.56-48.74	1.28	19.87

*7 Year Price Score 91.48   ***NYSE Composite Index=100**   ***12 Month Price Score 91.35**

Interim Earnings (Per Share)

Qtr.	Mar	Jun	Sep	Dec
2015	0.78	0.67	0.88	0.56
2016	1.02	0.93	1.07	(0.21)
2017	(0.61)	0.14	1.46	(0.09)
2018	1.32	...	...	...

Interim Dividends (Per Share)

Amt	Decl	Ex	Rec	Pay
0.18Q	07/26/2017	09/07/2017	09/08/2017	10/01/2017
0.18Q	11/21/2017	12/08/2017	12/11/2017	01/01/2018
0.18Q	02/01/2018	03/08/2018	03/09/2018	04/01/2018
0.18Q	05/25/2018	06/07/2018	06/08/2018	07/01/2018

Indicated Div: $0.72

Valuation Analysis   **Institutional Holding**

Forecast EPS	$5.25	No of Institutions
	(06/14/2018)	1063
Market Cap	$21.4 Billion	Shares
Book Value	$2.0 Billion	374,241,280
Price/Book	10.80	% Held
Price/Sales	1.52	N/A

Business Summary: Radio & Television (MIC: 2.3.1 SIC: 4833 NAIC: 515120)

CBS is a mass media company. Co.'s segments include: Entertainment, which is composed of the CBS® Television Network, CBS Television Studios®, CBS Studios International™, CBS Television Distribution™, CBS Interactive™, CBS Films®, CBS All Access®, and CBSN®; Cable Networks, which is composed of Showtime Networks, CBS Sports Network®, and Smithsonian Networks™, which operates Smithsonian Channel™; Publishing, which is composed of Simon & Schuster, which publishes and distributes books under imprints such as Simon & Schuster®, Pocket Books®, Scribner®, Gallery Books®, Touchstone® and Atria Books®; and Local Media, which is composed of CBS Television Stations and CBS Local Digital Media™.

Recent Developments: For the quarter ended Mar 31 2018, income from continuing operations increased 12.6% to US$511.0 million from US$454.0 million in the year-earlier quarter. Net income amounted to US$511.0 million versus a net loss of US$252.0 million in the year-earlier quarter. Revenues were US$3.76 billion, up 12.5% from US$3.34 billion the year before. Operating income was US$772.0 million versus US$726.0 million in the prior-year quarter, an increase of 6.3%. Direct operating expenses rose 15.7% to US$2.40 billion from US$2.07 billion in the comparable period the year before. Indirect operating expenses increased 8.5% to US$589.0 million from US$543.0 million in the equivalent prior-year period.

Prospects: Our evaluation of CBS Corp. as of Jan. 21, 2018 is the result of our systematic analysis on three basic characteristics: earnings strength, relative valuation, and recent stock price movement. The company has managed to produce a neutral trend in earnings per share over the past 5 quarters. However, while recent estimates for the company have been mixed, CBS has posted better than expected results. Based on operating earnings yield, the company is undervalued when compared to all of the companies in our coverage universe. Share price changes over the past year indicates that CBS will perform in line with the market over the near term.

Financial Data
(US$ in Thousands)

	3 Mos	12/31/2017	12/31/2016	12/31/2015	12/31/2014	12/31/2013	12/31/2012	12/31/2011
Earnings Per Share	2.83	0.88	2.81	2.89	5.27	3.01	2.39	1.92
Cash Flow Per Share	2.32	2.21	3.78	2.88	2.32	3.08	2.82	2.63
Dividends Per Share	0.720	0.720	0.660	0.600	0.540	0.480	0.440	0.350
Dividend Payout %	25.44	81.82	23.49	20.76	10.25	15.95	18.41	18.23
Income Statement								
Total Revenue	3,761,000	13,692,000	13,166,000	13,886,000	13,806,000	15,284,000	14,089,000	14,245,000
EBITDA	817,000	2,575,000	2,814,000	2,631,000	2,763,000	3,622,000	3,326,000	2,938,000
Depn & Amortn	56,000	203,000	205,000	240,000	249,000	357,000	369,000	426,000
Income Before Taxes	660,000	1,979,000	2,230,000	2,023,000	2,164,000	2,897,000	2,561,000	2,083,000
Income Taxes	135,000	633,000	628,000	587,000	762,000	978,000	892,000	755,000
Net Income	511,000	357,000	1,261,000	1,413,000	2,959,000	1,879,000	1,574,000	1,305,000
Average Shares	386,000	407,000	448,000	489,000	561,000	624,000	659,000	681,000
Balance Sheet								
Current Assets	6,191,000	6,273,000	6,063,000	5,747,000	5,589,000	5,370,000	5,720,000	5,543,000
Total Assets	20,591,000	20,843,000	24,238,000	23,765,000	24,072,000	26,387,000	26,466,000	26,197,000
Current Liabilities	4,069,000	3,972,000	3,708,000	3,560,000	4,033,000	4,207,000	3,941,000	3,933,000
Long-Term Obligations	9,470,000	9,464,000	8,902,000	8,226,000	6,510,000	5,940,000	5,904,000	5,958,000
Total Liabilities	18,608,000	18,865,000	20,549,000	18,202,000	17,102,000	16,421,000	16,253,000	16,289,000
Stockholders' Equity	1,983,000	1,978,000	3,689,000	5,563,000	6,970,000	9,966,000	10,213,000	9,908,000
Shares Outstanding	381,000	383,000	412,000	463,000	507,000	596,000	630,000	651,000
Statistical Record								
Return on Assets %	5.14	1.58	5.24	5.91	11.73	7.11	5.96	4.99
Return on Equity %	46.01	12.60	27.18	22.55	34.94	18.62	15.60	13.23
EBITDA Margin %	21.72	18.81	21.37	18.95	20.01	23.70	23.61	20.62
Net Margin %	13.59	2.61	9.58	10.18	21.43	12.29	11.17	9.16
Asset Turnover	0.65	0.61	0.55	0.58	0.55	0.58	0.53	0.54
Current Ratio	1.52	1.58	1.64	1.61	1.39	1.28	1.45	1.41
Debt to Equity	4.78	4.78	2.41	1.48	0.93	0.60	0.58	0.60
Price Range	69.51-49.27	69.51-54.46	64.85-42.65	63.35-38.67	67.55-48.91	63.74-37.52	38.05-27.27	29.54-18.95
P/E Ratio	24.56-17.41	78.99-61.89	23.08-15.18	21.92-13.38	12.82-9.28	21.18-12.47	15.92-11.41	15.39-9.87
Average Yield %	1.20	1.15	1.23	1.12	0.92	0.95	1.33	1.43

Address: 51 W. 52nd Street, New York, NY 10019
Telephone: 212-975-4321

Web Site: www.cbscorporation.com
Officers: Leslie Moonves - Chairman, President, Chief Executive Officer Sumner M. Redstone - Chairman Emeritus, Executive Chairman

Auditors: PricewaterhouseCoopers LLP
Investor Contact: 187-722-70787
Transfer Agents: Wells Fargo Shareowner Services, St. Paul, MN

CELANESE CORP (DE)

Exchange	Symbol	Price	52Wk Range	Yield	P/E
NYS	CE	$111.06 (6/29/2018)	117.97-93.36	1.94	14.89

*7 Year Price Score 130.25 *NYSE Composite Index=100 *12 Month Price Score 105.78

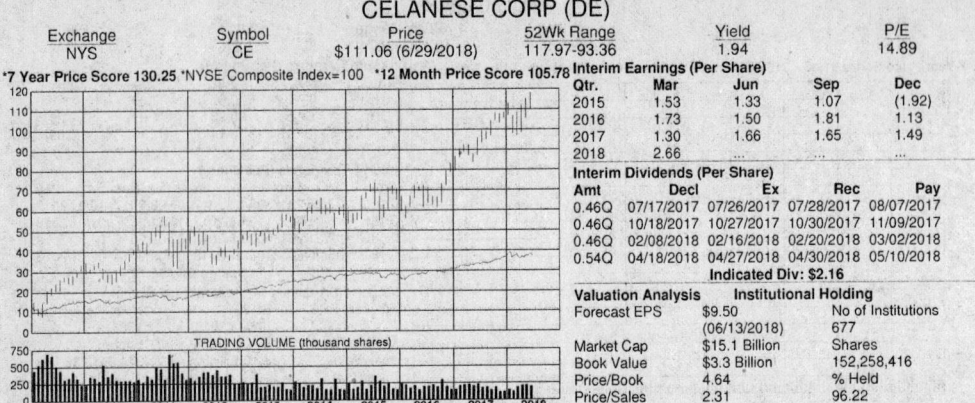

Interim Earnings (Per Share)

Qtr.	Mar	Jun	Sep	Dec
2015	1.53	1.33	1.07	(1.92)
2016	1.73	1.50	1.81	1.13
2017	1.30	1.66	1.65	1.49
2018	2.66	...	...	...

Interim Dividends (Per Share)

Amt	Decl	Ex	Rec	Pay
0.46Q	07/17/2017	07/26/2017	07/28/2017	08/07/2017
0.46Q	10/18/2017	10/27/2017	10/30/2017	11/09/2017
0.46Q	02/08/2018	02/16/2018	02/20/2018	03/02/2018
0.54Q	04/18/2018	04/27/2018	04/30/2018	05/10/2018

Indicated Div: $2.16

Valuation Analysis

		Institutional Holding	
Forecast EPS	$9.50	No of Institutions	
	(06/13/2018)	677	
Market Cap	$15.1 Billion	Shares	
Book Value	$3.3 Billion	152,258,416	
Price/Book	4.64	% Held	
Price/Sales	2.31	96.22	

Business Summary: Specialty Chemicals (MIC: 8.3.2 SIC: 5169 NAIC: 424690)

Celanese is a technology and specialty materials company. Co.'s segments include: Advanced Engineered Materials, which includes its engineered materials business that uses polymer technology to produce a portfolio of specialty polymers used automotive, medical and electronics products, as well as other consumer and industrial applications; Consumer Specialties, which includes Co.'s cellulose derivatives and food ingredients businesses; Industrial Specialties, which includes Co.'s emulsion polymers and ethylene vinyl acetate polymers businesses; and Acetyl Intermediates, which includes its intermediate chemistry business, which produces and supplies acetyl products.

Recent Developments: For the quarter ended Mar 31 2018, income from continuing operations increased 99.5% to US$367.0 million from US$184.0 million in the year-earlier quarter. Net income increased 98.4% to US$365.0 million from US$184.0 million in the year-earlier quarter. Revenues were US$1.85 billion, up 25.8% from US$1.47 billion the year before. Operating income was US$343.0 million versus US$170.0 million in the prior-year quarter, an increase of 101.8%. Direct operating expenses rose 19.2% to US$1.34 billion from US$1.12 billion in the comparable period the year before. Indirect operating expenses decreased 4.4% to US$172.0 million from US$180.0 million in the equivalent prior-year period.

Prospects: Our evaluation of Celanese Corp. as of Jan. 21, 2018 is the result of our systematic analysis on three basic characteristics: earnings strength, relative valuation, and recent stock price movement. The company has enjoyed a very positive trend in earnings per share over the past 5 quarters and while recent estimates for the company have been raised by analysts, CE has posted better than expected results. Based on operating earnings yield, the company is undervalued when compared to all of the companies in our coverage universe. Share price changes over the past year indicates that CE will perform well over the near term.

Financial Data

(US$ in Thousands)	3 Mos	12/31/2017	12/31/2016	12/31/2015	12/31/2014	12/31/2013	12/31/2012	12/31/2011
Earnings Per Share	7.46	6.09	6.18	2.00	4.00	6.91	3.79	3.82
Cash Flow Per Share	5.55	5.82	6.14	5.71	6.21	4.80	4.55	4.08
Tang Book Value Per Share	13.32	11.66	11.36	10.55	12.67	11.21	4.94	2.45
Dividends Per Share	1.840	1.740	1.380	1.150	0.930	0.525	0.270	0.220
Dividend Payout %	24.66	28.57	22.33	57.50	23.25	7.60	7.12	5.76
Income Statement								
Total Revenue	1,851,000	6,140,000	5,389,000	5,674,000	6,802,000	6,510,000	6,418,000	6,763,000
EBITDA	385,000	1,317,000	1,283,000	782,000	1,133,000	1,912,000	910,000	1,075,000
Depn & Amortn	6,000	305,000	290,000	357,000	292,000	312,000	312,000	294,000
Income Before Taxes	348,000	892,000	875,000	307,000	695,000	1,429,000	415,000	563,000
Income Taxes	65,000	213,000	122,000	201,000	314,000	508,000	48,000	149,000
Net Income	363,000	843,000	900,000	304,000	624,000	1,101,000	605,000	607,000
Average Shares	136,383	138,317	145,668	152,287	156,166	159,334	159,796	158,947
Balance Sheet								
Current Assets	3,006,000	2,792,000	2,472,000	2,787,000	2,698,000	3,182,000	2,839,000	2,703,000
Total Assets	9,780,000	9,538,000	8,357,000	8,586,000	8,818,000	9,018,000	9,000,000	8,518,000
Current Liabilities	1,602,000	1,559,000	1,077,000	1,550,000	1,338,000	1,545,000	1,355,000	1,385,000
Long-Term Obligations	3,343,000	3,315,000	2,890,000	2,468,000	2,608,000	2,887,000	2,930,000	2,873,000
Total Liabilities	6,527,000	6,651,000	5,769,000	6,208,000	6,000,000	6,319,000	7,270,000	7,177,000
Stockholders' Equity	3,253,000	2,887,000	2,588,000	2,378,000	2,818,000	2,699,000	1,730,000	1,341,000
Shares Outstanding	135,855	135,769	140,660	146,782	152,902	156,939	159,642	156,463
Statistical Record								
Return on Assets %	11.32	9.42	10.59	3.49	7.00	12.22	6.89	7.23
Return on Equity %	34.89	30.79	36.15	11.70	22.62	49.72	39.29	53.55
EBITDA Margin %	20.80	21.45	23.81	13.78	16.66	29.37	14.18	15.90
Net Margin %	19.61	13.73	16.70	5.36	9.17	16.91	9.43	8.98
Asset Turnover	0.72	0.69	0.63	0.65	0.76	0.72	0.73	0.81
Current Ratio	1.88	1.79	2.30	1.80	2.02	2.06	2.10	1.95
Debt to Equity	1.03	1.15	1.12	1.04	0.93	1.07	1.69	2.14
Price Range	112.96-83.79	108.50-79.51	83.30-55.81	73.72-53.41	66.05-48.83	58.25-41.97	52.22-33.28	57.66-31.49
P/E Ratio	15.14-11.23	17.82-13.06	13.48-9.03	36.86-26.70	16.51-12.21	8.43-6.07	13.78-8.78	15.09-8.24
Average Yield %	1.85	1.83	2.03	1.81	1.59	1.06	0.64	0.49

Address: 222 West Las Colinas Blvd.,	Web Site: www.celanese.com	Auditors: KPMG LLP
Suite 900N, Irving, TX 75039-5421	Officers: Mark C. Rohr - Chairman, Chief Executive	Investor Contact: 972-443-4965
Telephone: 972-443-4000	Officer Scott McDougald Sutton - Chief Operating	Transfer Agents: ComputerShare
	Officer, Executive Vice President, Division Officer	Investor Services, Providence, RI

CENTENE CORP

Exchange	Symbol	Price	52Wk Range	Yield	P/E
NYS	CNC	$123.21 (6/29/2018)	125.75-79.42	N/A	21.10

*7 Year Price Score 159.09 *NYSE Composite Index=100 *12 Month Price Score 115.44

Interim Earnings (Per Share)

Qtr.	Mar	Jun	Sep	Dec
2015	0.51	0.72	0.76	0.89
2016	(0.14)	0.97	0.83	1.56
2017	0.79	1.47	1.16	1.30
2018	1.91	...	...	...

Interim Dividends (Per Share)

No Dividends Paid

Valuation Analysis

	Institutional Holding	
Forecast EPS	$7.06	No of Institutions
	(06/14/2018)	858
Market Cap	$21.8 Billion	Shares
Book Value	$7.5 Billion	185,843,008
Price/Book	2.90	% Held
Price/Sales	0.44	100.11

Business Summary: Hospitals & Health Care Facilities (MIC: 4.2.1 SIC: 6324 NAIC: 524114)

Centene is a healthcare enterprise that provides a portfolio of services to government sponsored healthcare programs. Co. operates in two segments: Managed Care, which provides health plan coverage to individuals through government subsidized programs, including Medicaid, the State Children's Health Insurance Program, Long Term Care, Foster Care, dual-eligible individuals, the Supplemental Security Income Program, also known as the Aged, Blind or Disabled Program, Medicare, and Health Insurance Marketplace; and Specialty Services, which consists of Co.'s specialty companies providing a range of healthcare services and products.

Recent Developments: For the quarter ended Mar 31 2018, net income increased 156.1% to US$338.0 million from US$132.0 million in the year-earlier quarter. Revenues were US$13.19 billion, up 12.5% from US$11.72 billion the year before.

Prospects: Our evaluation of Centene Corp. as of Jan. 21, 2018 is the result of our systematic analysis on three basic characteristics: earnings strength, relative valuation, and recent stock price movement. The company has generated a negative trend in earnings per share over the past 5 quarters and while recent estimates for the company have been mixed, CNC has posted better than expected results. Based on operating earnings yield, the company is undervalued when compared to all of the companies in our coverage universe. Share price changes over the past year indicates that CNC will perform very well over the near term.

Financial Data
(US$ in Thousands)

	3 Mos	12/31/2017	12/31/2016	12/31/2015	12/31/2014	12/31/2013	12/31/2012	12/31/2011
Earnings Per Share	5.84	4.69	3.43	2.88	2.25	1.47	0.01	1.06
Cash Flow Per Share	12.00	8.64	11.57	5.52	10.51	3.53	2.70	2.61
Tang Book Value Per Share	3.90	4.05	N.M.	9.64	7.35	7.56	6.46	6.16
Income Statement								
Total Revenue	13,194,000	48,382,000	40,607,000	22,760,000	16,560,000	10,863,329	8,667,612	5,340,582
EBITDA	620,000	1,706,000	1,622,000	818,000	557,000	348,108	58,948	237,454
Depn & Amortn	39,000	317,000	248,000	78,000	65,000	52,234	50,112	42,249
Income Before Taxes	513,000	1,134,000	1,157,000	697,000	457,000	268,917	(11,624)	174,885
Income Taxes	175,000	326,000	599,000	339,000	196,000	107,080	(329)	66,522
Net Income	340,000	828,000	562,000	355,000	271,000	165,099	1,859	111,218
Average Shares	177,690	176,702	163,975	123,066	120,360	112,494	107,428	104,948
Balance Sheet								
Current Assets	10,976,000	8,703,000	8,365,000	3,605,000	3,034,000	1,800,173	1,373,602	940,010
Total Assets	25,170,000	21,855,000	20,197,000	7,339,000	5,838,000	3,529,300	2,741,682	2,190,336
Current Liabilities	10,890,000	9,332,000	8,623,000	3,629,000	2,900,000	1,559,121	1,197,090	837,613
Long-Term Obligations	5,172,000	4,695,000	4,651,000	1,216,000	888,000	665,697	535,481	348,344
Total Liabilities	17,667,000	15,005,000	14,302,000	5,182,000	4,094,000	2,295,259	1,788,626	1,254,702
Stockholders' Equity	7,503,000	6,850,000	5,895,000	2,157,000	1,744,000	1,234,041	953,056	935,634
Shares Outstanding	176,795	173,437	171,919	120,342	118,433	110,638	104,658	101,729
Statistical Record								
Return on Assets %	4.42	3.94	4.07	5.39	5.79	5.27	0.08	5.38
Return on Equity %	15.16	12.99	13.92	18.20	18.20	15.10	0.20	12.86
EBITDA Margin %	4.70	3.53	3.99	3.59	3.36	3.20	0.68	4.45
Net Margin %	2.58	1.71	1.38	1.56	1.64	1.52	0.02	2.08
Asset Turnover	2.14	2.30	2.94	3.45	3.54	3.46	3.51	2.58
Current Ratio	1.01	0.93	0.97	0.99	1.05	1.15	1.15	1.12
Debt to Equity	0.69	0.69	0.79	0.56	0.51	0.54	0.56	0.37
Price Range	111.59-69.77	103.02-58.31	75.39-50.68	81.48-51.92	53.58-27.83	33.19-20.45	25.40-13.42	20.27-12.67
P/E Ratio	19.11-11.95	21.97-12.43	21.98-14.78	28.29-18.03	23.81-12.37	22.58-13.91	N.M.	19.12-11.95

Address: 7700 Forsyth Boulevard, St. Louis, MO 63105 **Telephone:** 314-725-4477 **Fax:** 314-725-5180	**Web Site:** www.centene.com **Officers:** Michael F. Neidorff - Chairman, Chief Executive Officer, President Jeffrey A. Schwaneke - Executive Vice President, Chief Financial Officer, Treasurer, Senior Vice President, Vice President, Chief Accounting Officer, Corporate Controller	**Auditors:** KPMG LLP **Transfer Agents:** Broadridge Corporate Issuer Solutions, Inc., Philadelphia, PA

CENTERPOINT ENERGY, INC

Exchange	Symbol	Price	52Wk Range	Yield	P/E	Div Acheiver
NYS	CNP	$27.71 (6/29/2018)	30.45-24.92	4.01	6.81	12 Years

*7 Year Price Score 97.74   *NYSE Composite Index=100   *12 Month Price Score 92.97

Interim Earnings (Per Share)

Qtr.	Mar	Jun	Sep	Dec
2015	0.30	0.18	(0.91)	(1.18)
2016	0.36	(0.01)	0.41	0.24
2017	0.44	0.31	0.39	2.99
2018	0.38	...	...	...

Interim Dividends (Per Share)

Amt	Decl	Ex	Rec	Pay
0.268Q	07/27/2017	08/14/2017	08/16/2017	09/08/2017
0.268Q	10/25/2017	11/15/2017	11/16/2017	12/08/2017
0.278Q	12/13/2017	02/14/2018	02/15/2018	03/08/2018
0.278Q	04/26/2018	05/16/2018	05/17/2018	06/14/2018

Indicated Div: $1.11 (Div. Reinv. Plan)

Valuation Analysis   **Institutional Holding**

Forecast EPS	$1.60	No of Institutions
	(06/12/2018)	824
Market Cap	$12.0 Billion	Shares
Book Value	$4.9 Billion	419,674,432
Price/Book	2.46	% Held
Price/Sales	1.19	75.19

Business Summary: Electric Utilities (MIC: 3.1.1 SIC: 4911 NAIC: 221111)

CenterPoint Energy is a public utility holding company whose subsidiaries include: CenterPoint Energy Houston Electric, LLC, which engages in the electric transmission and distribution business in the Texas Gulf Coast area; CenterPoint Energy Resources Corp. (CERC Corp.), which owns and operates natural gas distribution systems; and CenterPoint Energy Services, Inc., which obtains and provides variable and fixed-price physical natural gas supplies and services mainly to commercial and industrial customers and electric and natural gas utilities. CERC Corp. also owns interests in Enable Midstream Partners, LP, which owns, operates and develops natural gas and crude oil infrastructure assets.

Recent Developments: For the quarter ended Mar 31 2018, net income decreased 14.1% to US$165.0 million from US$192.0 million in the year-earlier quarter. Revenues were US$3.16 billion, up 15.4% from US$2.74 billion the year before. Operating income was US$251.0 million versus US$291.0 million in the prior-year quarter, a decrease of 13.7%. Direct operating expenses rose 16.8% to US$2.48 billion from US$2.12 billion in the comparable period the year before. Indirect operating expenses increased 32.0% to US$425.0 million from US$322.0 million in the equivalent prior-year period.

Prospects: Our evaluation of Centerpoint Energy Inc. as of Jan. 21, 2018 is the result of our systematic analysis on three basic characteristics: earnings strength, relative valuation, and recent stock price movement. The company has generated a negative trend in earnings per share over the past 5 quarters and while recent estimates for the company have been mixed, CNP has posted results that fell short of analysts expectations. Based on operating earnings yield, the company is undervalued when compared to all of the companies in our coverage universe. Share price changes over the past year indicates that CNP will perform well over the near term.

Financial Data

(US$ in Thousands)	3 Mos	12/31/2017	12/31/2016	12/31/2015	12/31/2014	12/31/2013	12/31/2012	12/31/2011
Earnings Per Share	4.07	4.13	1.00	(1.61)	1.42	0.72	0.97	3.17
Cash Flow Per Share	3.68	3.30	4.46	4.34	3.25	3.76	4.34	4.44
Tang Book Value Per Share	9.25	8.86	6.03	6.10	8.62	8.13	6.62	5.93
Dividends Per Share	1.080	1.070	1.030	0.990	0.950	0.830	0.810	0.790
Dividend Payout %	26.54	25.91	103.00	...	66.90	115.28	83.51	24.92
Income Statement								
Total Revenue	3,155,000	9,614,000	7,528,000	7,386,000	9,226,000	8,106,000	7,452,000	8,450,000
EBITDA	243,000	2,224,000	2,033,000	1,930,000	2,061,000	1,608,000	1,857,000	2,256,000
Depn & Amortn	6,000	1,036,000	1,126,000	970,000	1,013,000	531,000	562,000	529,000
Income Before Taxes	143,000	798,000	478,000	503,000	577,000	593,000	726,000	1,144,000
Income Taxes	47,000	(729,000)	254,000	(438,000)	274,000	470,000	340,000	404,000
Net Income	165,000	1,792,000	432,000	(692,000)	611,000	311,000	417,000	1,357,000
Average Shares	431,000	434,000	431,000	430,000	432,000	430,930	429,794	428,724
Balance Sheet								
Current Assets	3,049,000	3,395,000	2,923,000	2,689,000	3,268,000	2,658,000	2,874,000	2,337,000
Total Assets	22,410,000	22,736,000	21,829,000	21,334,000	23,200,000	21,870,000	22,871,000	21,703,000
Current Liabilities	2,616,000	3,069,000	3,080,000	2,467,000	3,475,000	3,019,000	3,575,000	2,593,000
Long-Term Obligations	8,176,000	8,195,000	7,532,000	7,901,000	8,009,000	7,817,000	8,357,000	8,641,000
Total Liabilities	17,553,000	18,048,000	18,369,000	17,873,000	18,652,000	17,541,000	18,570,000	17,481,000
Stockholders' Equity	4,857,000	4,688,000	3,460,000	3,461,000	4,548,000	4,329,000	4,301,000	4,222,000
Shares Outstanding	431,471	431,044	430,682	430,000	430,000	429,000	428,000	426,000
Statistical Record								
Return on Assets %	7.96	8.04	2.00	N.M.	2.71	1.39	1.87	6.49
Return on Equity %	42.05	43.99	12.45	N.M.	13.77	7.21	9.76	36.58
EBITDA Margin %	7.70	23.13	27.01	26.13	22.34	19.84	24.92	26.70
Net Margin %	5.23	18.64	5.74	N.M.	6.62	3.84	5.60	16.06
Asset Turnover	0.45	0.43	0.35	0.33	0.41	0.36	0.33	0.40
Current Ratio	1.17	1.11	0.95	1.09	0.94	0.88	0.80	0.90
Debt to Equity	1.68	1.75	2.18	2.28	1.76	1.81	1.94	2.05
Price Range	30.45-25.85	30.45-24.59	24.84-16.90	23.63-16.14	25.54-21.54	25.16-19.25	21.75-18.23	21.29-15.20
P/E Ratio	7.48-6.35	7.37-5.95	24.84-16.90	...	17.99-15.17	34.94-26.74	22.42-18.79	6.72-4.79
Average Yield %	3.81	3.80	4.70	5.05	3.95	3.58	4.04	4.27

Address: 1111 Louisiana, Houston, TX 77002	Web Site: www.centerpointenergy.com	Auditors: DELOITTE & TOUCHE LLP
Telephone: 713-207-1111	Officers: Milton Carroll - Executive Chairman Scott M. Prochazka - President, Chief Executive Officer, Executive Vice President, Chief Operating Officer	Investor Contact: 713-207-6500 Transfer Agents: CenterPoint Energy Investor Services

CENTURYLINK INC

Exchange	Symbol	Price	52Wk Range	Yield	P/E
NYS	CTL	$18.64 (6/29/2018)	23.97-13.62	11.59	9.23

*7 Year Price Score 47.25   *NYSE Composite Index=100   *12 Month Price Score 99.24

Interim Earnings (Per Share)

Qtr.	Mar	Jun	Sep	Dec
2015	0.34	0.26	0.37	0.61
2016	0.44	0.36	0.28	0.08
2017	0.30	0.03	0.17	1.71
2018	0.11	...	...	...

Interim Dividends (Per Share)

Amt	Decl	Ex	Rec	Pay
0.54Q	08/22/2017	08/31/2017	09/05/2017	09/15/2017
0.54Q	11/14/2017	11/24/2017	11/27/2017	12/11/2017
0.54Q	02/21/2018	03/02/2018	03/05/2018	03/16/2018
0.54Q	05/23/2018	06/01/2018	06/04/2018	06/15/2018

Indicated Div: $2.16 (Div. Reinv. Plan)

Valuation Analysis

		Institutional Holding	
Forecast EPS	$1.00	No of Institutions	
	(06/13/2018)	1071	
Market Cap	$20.1 Billion	Shares	926,906,688
Book Value	$23.4 Billion	% Held	
Price/Book	0.86	% Held	70.23
Price/Sales	1.04		

Business Summary: Services (MIC: 6.1.2 SIC: 4813 NAIC: 517110)

CenturyLink is a holding company. Through its subsidiaries, Co. is a communications company. Co.'s communications services include local and long-distance voice, broadband, Multi-Protocol Label Switching, private line (including special access), Ethernet, colocation, hosting (including cloud hosting and managed hosting), data integration, video, network, public access, Voice over Internet Protocol, information technology and other ancillary services. Co. has two segments: Business, which provides products and services to enterprise, wholesale and governmental customers, including other communication providers; and Consumer, which provides products and services to residential consumers.

Recent Developments:
For the quarter ended Mar 31 2018, net income decreased 29.4% to US$115.0 million from US$163.0 million in the year-earlier quarter. Revenues were US$5.95 billion, up 41.2% from US$4.21 billion the year before. Operating income was US$750.0 million versus US$631.0 million in the prior-year quarter, an increase of 18.9%. Direct operating expenses rose 48.5% to US$2.80 billion from US$1.89 billion in the comparable period the year before. Indirect operating expenses increased 41.5% to US$2.39 billion from US$1.69 billion in the equivalent prior-year period.

Prospects:
Our evaluation of CenturyLink, Inc. as of Jan. 21, 2018 is the result of our systematic analysis on three basic characteristics: earnings strength, relative valuation, and recent stock price movement. The company has managed to produce a neutral trend in earnings per share over the past 5 quarters. However, while recent estimates for the company have been mixed, CTL has posted results that fell short of analysts expectations. Based on operating earnings yield, the company is undervalued when compared to all of the companies in our coverage universe. Share price changes over the past year indicates that CTL will perform poorly over the near term.

Financial Data

(US$ in Thousands)	3 Mos	12/31/2017	12/31/2016	12/31/2015	12/31/2014	12/31/2013	12/31/2012	12/31/2011
Earnings Per Share	2.02	2.21	1.16	1.58	1.36	(0.40)	1.25	1.07
Cash Flow Per Share	4.21	6.18	8.52	9.29	9.13	9.25	9.75	7.89
Dividends Per Share	2.160	2.160	2.160	2.160	2.160	2.160	2.900	2.900
Dividend Payout %	106.93	97.74	186.21	136.71	158.82	...	232.00	271.03
Income Statement								
Total Revenue	5,945,000	17,656,000	17,470,000	17,900,000	18,031,000	18,095,000	18,376,000	15,351,000
EBITDA	2,054,000	4,731,000	5,029,000	5,464,000	5,379,000	4,474,000	5,667,000	4,621,000
Depn & Amortn	1,283,000	2,710,000	2,691,000	2,836,000	2,958,000	2,952,000	3,098,000	2,601,000
Income Before Taxes	236,000	540,000	1,020,000	1,316,000	1,110,000	224,000	1,250,000	948,000
Income Taxes	121,000	(849,000)	394,000	438,000	338,000	463,000	473,000	375,000
Net Income	115,000	1,389,000	626,000	878,000	772,000	(239,000)	777,000	573,000
Average Shares	1,069,183	628,693	540,679	555,093	569,739	600,892	622,285	534,121
Balance Sheet								
Current Assets	4,183,000	4,194,000	5,162,000	2,650,000	3,576,000	3,907,000	3,613,000	3,523,000
Total Assets	74,793,000	75,611,000	47,017,000	47,604,000	50,147,000	51,787,000	54,020,000	56,139,000
Current Liabilities	4,767,000	4,857,000	5,349,000	4,604,000	3,918,000	4,409,000	4,595,000	4,019,000
Long-Term Obligations	36,940,000	37,283,000	18,185,000	18,722,000	20,121,000	20,181,000	19,400,000	21,356,000
Total Liabilities	51,350,000	52,120,000	33,618,000	33,544,000	35,124,000	34,596,000	34,731,000	35,312,000
Stockholders' Equity	23,443,000	23,491,000	13,399,000	14,060,000	15,023,000	17,191,000	19,289,000	20,827,000
Shares Outstanding	1,078,632	1,069,169	546,545	543,800	568,517	583,637	625,658	618,514
Statistical Record								
Return on Assets %	2.21	2.27	1.32	1.80	1.51	N.M.	1.41	1.47
Return on Equity %	7.30	7.53	4.55	6.04	4.79	N.M.	3.86	3.76
EBITDA Margin %	34.55	26.80	28.79	30.53	29.83	24.73	30.84	30.10
Net Margin %	1.93	7.87	3.58	4.91	4.28	N.M.	4.23	3.73
Asset Turnover	0.32	0.29	0.37	0.37	0.35	0.34	0.33	0.39
Current Ratio	0.88	0.86	0.97	0.58	0.91	0.89	0.79	0.88
Debt to Equity	1.58	1.59	1.36	1.33	1.34	1.17	1.01	1.03
Price Range	27.31-13.62	27.31-13.62	32.80-22.24	40.52-24.38	41.81-28.09	41.76-30.30	42.95-36.59	46.73-31.82
P/E Ratio	13.52-6.74	12.36-6.16	28.28-19.17	25.65-15.43	30.74-20.65	...	34.36-29.27	43.67-29.74
Average Yield %	10.72	9.72	7.73	6.87	5.92	4.59	7.37	7.49

Address: 100 CenturyLink Drive, Monroe, LA 71203	Web Site: www.centurylink.com	Auditors: KPMG LLP
Telephone: 318-388-9000	Officers: Jeffrey K. Storey - President, Chief Executive Officer, Chief Operating Officer Stacey W. Goff - Executive Vice President, Chief Administrative Officer, Secretary, General Counsel	Investor Contact: 800-833-1188
Fax: 318-789-8656		Transfer Agents: Computershare Trust Company, Providence, RI

CF INDUSTRIES HOLDINGS INC

Exchange	Symbol	Price	52Wk Range	Yield	P/E
NYS	CF	$44.40 (6/29/2018)	45.95-27.58	2.70	23.37

7 Year Price Score 74.65 *NYSE Composite Index=100 *12 Month Price Score 109.46

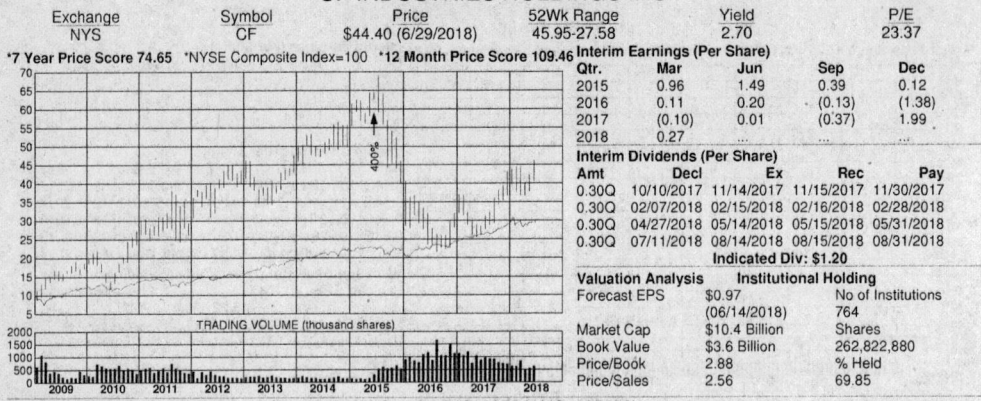

Interim Earnings (Per Share)

Qtr.	Mar	Jun	Sep	Dec
2015	0.96	1.49	0.39	0.12
2016	0.11	0.20	(0.13)	(1.38)
2017	(0.10)	0.01	(0.37)	1.99
2018	0.27	...	...	...

Interim Dividends (Per Share)

Amt	Decl	Ex	Rec	Pay
0.30Q	10/10/2017	11/14/2017	11/15/2017	11/30/2017
0.30Q	02/07/2018	02/15/2018	02/16/2018	02/28/2018
0.30Q	04/27/2018	05/14/2018	05/15/2018	05/31/2018
0.30Q	07/11/2018	08/14/2018	08/15/2018	08/31/2018

Indicated Div: $1.20

Valuation Analysis

Forecast EPS	$0.97 (06/14/2018)	Institutional Holding	
		No of Institutions	764
Market Cap	$10.4 Billion	Shares	
Book Value	$3.6 Billion		262,822,880
Price/Book	2.88	% Held	
Price/Sales	2.56		69.85

Business Summary: Agricultural Chemicals (MIC: 8.3.3 SIC: 2879 NAIC: 325320)

CF Industries Holdings is a manufacturer and distributor of nitrogen fertilizer and other nitrogen products. Co.'s reportable segments include: ammonia, which produces anhydrous ammonia (ammonia), its nitrogen fertilizer product that contains 82.0% nitrogen; granular urea, which produces granular urea that contains 46.0% nitrogen; urea ammonium nitrate (UAN), which produces UAN, a liquid fertilizer product with a nitrogen content that ranges from 28.0% to 32.0%; ammonium nitrate (AN), which produces AN, a nitrogen-based product with a nitrogen content between 29.0% and 35.0%; and Other; which includes diesel exhaust fluid, urea liquor, nitric acid, as well as compound fertilizer products.

Recent Developments: For the quarter ended Mar 31 2018, net income amounted to US$88.0 million versus a net loss of US$9.0 million in the year-earlier quarter. Revenues were US$957.0 million, down 7.7% from US$1.04 billion the year before. Operating income was US$161.0 million versus US$58.0 million in the prior-year quarter, an increase of 177.6%. Direct operating expenses declined 17.5% to US$767.0 million from US$930.0 million in the comparable period the year before. Indirect operating expenses decreased 40.8% to US$29.0 million from US$49.0 million in the equivalent prior-year period.

Prospects: Our evaluation of CF Industries Holdings Inc. as of Jan. 21, 2018 is the result of our systematic analysis on three basic characteristics: earnings strength, relative valuation, and recent stock price movement. The company has managed to produce a neutral trend in earnings per share over the past 5 quarters. Because the company lacks sufficient analyst estimate data, we place greater weight on the historical EPS trend as the measure of earnings strength. Based on operating earnings yield, the company is overvalued when compared to all of the companies in our coverage universe. Share price changes over the past year indicates that CF will perform well over the near term.

Financial Data

(US$ in Thousands)	3 Mos	12/31/2017	12/31/2016	12/31/2015	12/31/2014	12/31/2013	12/31/2012	12/31/2011
Earnings Per Share	1.90	1.53	(1.19)	2.96	5.42	4.95	5.72	4.40
Cash Flow Per Share	6.66	6.99	2.64	5.12	5.50	4.98	7.42	5.99
Tang Book Value Per Share	5.20	5.18	4.30	7.06	8.76	10.51	12.04	7.43
Dividends Per Share	1.200	1.200	1.200	1.200	1.000	0.440	0.320	0.200
Dividend Payout %	63.16	78.43	...	40.54	18.46	8.89	5.60	4.55
Income Statement								
Total Revenue	957,000	4,130,000	3,685,000	4,308,300	4,743,200	5,474,700	6,104,000	6,097,900
EBITDA	340,000	271,000	190,000	1,289,600	2,375,400	2,726,100	3,333,300	3,157,100
Depn & Amortn	185,000	102,000	89,000	65,400	53,900	410,600	419,800	416,200
Income Before Taxes	98,000	(134,000)	(94,000)	1,092,600	2,144,200	2,168,000	2,782,500	2,595,400
Income Taxes	17,000	(575,000)	(81,000)	395,800	773,000	686,500	964,200	926,500
Net Income	63,000	358,000	(277,000)	699,900	1,390,300	1,464,600	1,848,700	1,539,200
Average Shares	234,800	233,900	233,100	236,100	256,500	296,000	323,500	350,000
Balance Sheet								
Current Assets	1,660,000	1,465,000	2,655,000	1,127,100	2,614,500	2,630,100	2,807,600	1,798,600
Total Assets	13,522,000	13,463,000	15,131,000	12,738,900	11,338,200	10,678,100	10,166,900	8,974,500
Current Liabilities	626,000	580,000	686,000	1,215,200	979,700	828,300	950,200	1,031,200
Long-Term Obligations	4,693,000	4,692,000	5,778,000	5,592,700	4,592,500	3,098,100	1,600,000	1,617,800
Total Liabilities	9,928,000	9,884,000	11,783,000	8,703,700	7,128,500	5,602,000	4,264,700	4,427,500
Stockholders' Equity	3,594,000	3,579,000	3,348,000	4,035,200	4,209,700	5,076,100	5,902,200	4,547,000
Shares Outstanding	233,358	233,287	233,114	233,081	241,673	279,240	314,753	327,102
Statistical Record								
Return on Assets %	3.09	2.50	N.M.	5.81	12.63	14.05	19.26	17.36
Return on Equity %	12.92	10.34	N.M.	16.98	29.94	26.68	35.29	35.81
EBITDA Margin %	35.53	6.56	5.16	29.93	50.08	49.79	54.61	51.77
Net Margin %	6.58	8.67	N.M.	16.25	29.31	26.75	30.29	25.24
Asset Turnover	0.28	0.29	0.26	0.36	0.43	0.53	0.64	0.69
Current Ratio	2.65	2.53	3.87	0.93	2.67	3.18	2.95	1.74
Debt to Equity	1.31	1.31	1.73	1.39	1.09	0.61	0.27	0.36
Price Range	44.56-25.51	43.07-25.51	40.81-21.43	68.92-40.07	56.55-44.98	47.41-34.06	44.90-30.76	37.96-24.20
P/E Ratio	23.45-13.43	28.15-16.67	...	23.28-13.54	10.43-8.30	9.58-6.88	7.85-5.38	8.63-5.50
Average Yield %	3.51	3.73	4.22	2.13	1.99	1.09	0.83	0.68

Address: 4 Parkway North, Suite 400, Deerfield, IL 60015	Web Site: www.cfindustries.com	Auditors: KPMG LLP
Telephone: 847-405-2400	Officers: Stephen A. Furbacher - Chairman W. Anthony Will - President, Chief Executive Officer, Senior Vice President, Vice President	Investor Contact: 847-405-2550 Transfer Agents: Computershare, Providence, RI

CHARLES RIVER LABORATORIES INTERNATIONAL INC.

Exchange	Symbol	Price	52Wk Range	Yield	P/E
NYS	CRL	$112.26 (6/29/2018)	118.09-96.72	N/A	42.20

*7 Year Price Score 131.79 *NYSE Composite Index=100 *12 Month Price Score 100.73

Interim Earnings (Per Share)

Qtr.	Mar	Jun	Sep	Dec
2015	0.66	1.02	0.79	0.66
2016	0.78	0.73	0.79	0.93
2017	0.97	1.12	1.08	(0.62)
2018	1.08	...	...	...

Interim Dividends (Per Share)

No Dividends Paid

Valuation Analysis	Institutional Holding	
Forecast EPS	$5.85	No of Institutions
	(06/14/2018)	497
Market Cap	$5.4 Billion	Shares
Book Value	$1.1 Billion	63,118,760
Price/Book	4.72	% Held
Price/Sales	2.82	96.80

Business Summary: Biotechnology (MIC: 4.1.2 SIC: 8731 NAIC: 541710)

Charles River Laboratories International is a contract research organization engaged in laboratory animal medicine and science to develop a portfolio of discovery and safety assessment services. Co. has three segments: Research Models and Services, which is engaged in supplying research models to the drug development industry; Discovery and Safety Assessment, which provides discovery and safety assessment services that include in vivo and in vitro studies, supporting laboratory services, and non-clinical consulting and program management to support product development; and Manufacturing Support, which includes its Microbial Solutions, Avian Vaccine Services and Biologics Testing Solutions.

Recent Developments: For the quarter ended Mar 31 2018, income from continuing operations increased 13.4% to US$53.3 million from US$47.0 million in the year-earlier quarter. Net income increased 13.4% to US$53.2 million from US$47.0 million in the year-earlier quarter. Revenues were US$494.0 million, up 10.8% from US$445.8 million the year before. Operating income was US$67.8 million versus US$69.7 million in the prior-year quarter, a decrease of 2.7%. Direct operating expenses rose 13.9% to US$312.5 million from US$274.4 million in the comparable period the year before. Indirect operating expenses increased 11.8% to US$113.6 million from US$101.6 million in the equivalent prior-year period.

Prospects: Our evaluation of Charles River Laboratories International Inc. as of Jan. 21, 2018 is the result of our systematic analysis on three basic characteristics: earnings strength, relative valuation, and recent stock price movement. The company has generated a negative trend in earnings per share over the past 5 quarters and while recent estimates for the company have been mixed, CRL has posted better than expected results. Based on operating earnings yield, the company is undervalued when compared to all of the companies in our coverage universe. Share price changes over the past year indicates that CRL will perform very well over the near term.

Financial Data

(US$ in Thousands)	3 Mos	12/30/2017	12/31/2016	12/26/2015	12/27/2014	12/28/2013	12/29/2012	12/31/2011
Earnings Per Share	2.66	2.54	3.23	3.13	2.66	2.12	2.01	2.14
Cash Flow Per Share	7.20	6.72	6.29	6.22	5.42	4.39	4.35	4.00
Tang Book Value Per Share	N.M.	N.M.	N.M.	0.29	3.64	6.85	6.37	4.80
Income Statement								
Total Revenue	493,970	1,857,601	1,681,432	1,363,302	1,297,662	1,165,528	1,129,530	1,142,647
EBITDA	84,217	457,212	376,015	304,386	284,848	255,202	243,774	259,126
Depn & Amortn	10,268	131,170	126,699	94,929	96,457	96,636	81,275	85,231
Income Before Taxes	63,040	296,955	222,921	195,428	177,595	138,327	129,746	132,662
Income Taxes	9,772	171,369	66,835	43,391	47,671	32,911	27,628	17,140
Net Income	52,631	123,355	154,765	149,313	126,698	102,828	97,295	109,566
Average Shares	48,828	48,564	47,958	47,634	47,558	48,489	48,406	51,318
Balance Sheet								
Current Assets	843,348	826,625	656,832	559,234	606,898	552,550	485,252	425,843
Total Assets	3,001,003	2,929,922	2,711,800	2,068,497	1,885,192	1,644,621	1,586,344	1,558,320
Current Liabilities	407,098	463,504	429,593	311,761	296,170	247,034	342,247	216,797
Long-Term Obligations	1,129,581	1,114,105	1,207,696	845,997	745,958	642,352	527,136	703,187
Total Liabilities	1,861,177	1,884,842	1,875,032	1,335,430	1,212,989	1,003,637	985,539	1,032,737
Stockholders' Equity	1,139,826	1,045,080	836,768	733,067	672,203	640,984	600,805	525,583
Shares Outstanding	47,905	47,402	47,363	46,698	47,327	47,553	48,220	48,875
Statistical Record								
Return on Assets %	4.54	4.38	6.37	7.57	7.20	6.38	6.20	6.55
Return on Equity %	12.82	13.15	19.40	21.31	19.35	16.61	17.32	17.77
EBITDA Margin %	17.05	24.61	22.36	22.33	21.95	21.90	21.58	22.68
Net Margin %	10.65	6.64	9.20	10.95	9.76	8.82	8.61	9.59
Asset Turnover	0.67	0.66	0.69	0.69	0.74	0.72	0.72	0.68
Current Ratio	2.07	1.78	1.53	1.79	2.05	2.24	1.42	1.96
Debt to Equity	0.99	1.07	1.44	1.15	1.11	1.00	0.88	1.34
Price Range	118.09-87.09	118.09-76.53	88.44-67.10	84.20-61.59	65.59-50.74	53.33-37.47	41.24-27.39	42.47-25.95
P/E Ratio	44.39-32.74	46.49-30.13	27.38-20.77	26.90-19.68	24.66-19.08	25.16-17.67	20.52-13.63	19.85-12.13

Address: 251 Ballardvale Street, Wilmington, MA 01887	**Web Site:** www.criver.com	**Auditors:** PricewaterhouseCoopers LLP
Telephone: 781-222-6000	**Officers:** James C. Foster - Chairman, President, Chief Executive Officer Davide A. Molho - President, Chief Operating Officer, Corporate Executive Vice-President, Division Officer	**Investor Contact:** 781-222-6000
		Transfer Agents: ComputerShare Investor Services, Providence, RI

CHEMOURS CO (THE)

Exchange	Symbol	Price	52Wk Range	Yield	P/E
NYS	CC	$44.36 (6/29/2018)	57.23-37.92	0.90	9.46

*7 Year Price Score N/A   *NYSE Composite Index=100   *12 Month Price Score 97.81

Interim Earnings (Per Share)

Qtr.	Mar	Jun	Sep	Dec
2015	0.24	(0.10)	(0.16)	(0.48)
2016	0.28	(0.10)	1.11	(1.26)
2017	0.79	0.84	1.08	1.19
2018	1.58	...	...	...

Interim Dividends (Per Share)

Amt	Decl	Ex	Rec	Pay
0.03Q	08/02/2017	08/15/2017	08/17/2017	09/15/2017
0.03Q	11/07/2017	11/17/2017	11/20/2017	12/15/2017
0.17Q	11/30/2017	02/14/2018	02/15/2018	03/15/2018
0.17Q	05/01/2018	05/16/2018	05/17/2018	06/15/2018

Indicated Div: $0.40

Valuation Analysis

Forecast EPS	$5.85 (06/13/2018)
Market Cap	$7.9 Billion
Book Value	$997.0 Million
Price/Book	7.94
Price/Sales	1.22

Institutional Holding

No of Institutions	651
Shares	160,939,184
% Held	N/A

TRADING VOLUME (thousand shares)

Business Summary: Specialty Chemicals (MIC: 8.3.2 SIC: 2899 NAIC: 325998)

Chemours is a provider of performance chemicals. Co. has three reportable segments: Titanium Technologies, Fluoroproducts and Chemical Solutions. Co.'s Titanium Technologies segment is a producer of titanium dioxide, a white pigment used to deliver whiteness, brightness, opacity and protection in a variety of applications. Co.'s Fluoroproducts segment is a provider of fluoroproducts, such as refrigerants and industrial fluoropolymer resins. Co.'s Chemical Solutions segment is a provider of industrial chemicals used in gold production, oil and gas, water treatment and other industries.

Recent Developments: For the quarter ended Mar 31 2018, net income increased 96.7% to US$297.0 million from US$151.0 million in the year-earlier quarter. Revenues were US$1.73 billion, up 20.4% from US$1.44 billion the year before. Direct operating expenses rose 10.4% to US$1.19 billion from US$1.08 billion in the comparable period the year before. Indirect operating expenses decreased 4.4% to US$173.0 million from US$181.0 million in the equivalent prior-year period.

Prospects: Our evaluation of The Chemours Company as of Jan. 21, 2018 is the result of our systematic analysis on three basic characteristics: earnings strength, relative valuation, and recent stock price movement. The company has produced a positive trend in earnings per share over the past 5 quarters and while recent estimates for the company have been mixed, CC has posted better than expected results. Based on operating earnings yield, the company is undervalued when compared to all of the companies in our coverage universe. Share price changes over the past year indicates that CC will perform very well over the near term.

Financial Data

(US$ in Millions)	3 Mos	12/31/2017	12/31/2016	12/31/2015	12/31/2014	12/31/2013	12/31/2012
Earnings Per Share	4.69	3.91	0.04	(0.50)	2.21	2.34	...
Cash Flow Per Share	4.36	3.46	3.26	1.01	...	...	...
Tang Book Value Per Share	4.66	3.79	N.M.	N.M.	...	...	...
Dividends Per Share	0.260	0.120	0.120	0.580	...	...	...
Dividend Payout %	5.54	3.07	300.00	...	...	...	...
Income Statement							
Total Revenue	1,730	6,183	5,400	5,717	6,432	6,859	7,365
EBITDA	493	1,363	454	186	784	809	1,720
Depn & Amortn	72	269	281	264	254	255	260
Income Before Taxes	369	879	(40)	(210)	530	554	1,460
Income Taxes	84	165	(18)	(98)	149	152	427
Net Income	297	746	7	(90)	400	423	1,057
Average Shares	188	190	183	181	181	181	...
Balance Sheet							
Current Assets	3,584	3,493	2,553	2,301	1,962	1,980	...
Total Assets	7,484	7,293	6,060	6,298	5,978	5,621	...
Current Liabilities	1,622	1,648	1,771	1,466	1,407	1,471	...
Long-Term Obligations	4,141	4,097	3,529	3,915	...	...	...
Total Liabilities	6,487	6,433	5,960	6,172	2,309	2,407	...
Stockholders' Equity	997	860	100	126	3,669	3,214	...
Shares Outstanding	178	182	182	181	181	181	...
Statistical Record							
Return on Assets %	12.97	11.17	0.11	...	6.90	...	...
Return on Equity %	132.30	155.42	6.18	...	11.62	...	...
EBITDA Margin %	28.50	22.04	8.41	3.25	12.19	11.79	23.35
Net Margin %	17.17	12.07	0.13	N.M.	6.22	6.17	14.35
Asset Turnover	0.94	0.93	0.87	...	1.11	...	...
Current Ratio	2.21	2.12	1.44	1.57	1.39	1.35	...
Debt to Equity	4.15	4.76	35.29	31.07	...	...	...
Price Range	57.23-35.09	57.23-21.22	26.96-3.12	20.85-4.72	...	...	...
P/E Ratio	12.20-7.48	14.64-5.43	674.00-78.00	...	...	...	...
Average Yield %	0.55	0.28	1.04	6.49	...	...	...

Address: 1007 Market Street, Wilmington, DE 19899 **Telephone:** 302-773-1000	**Web Site:** www.chemours.com **Officers:** Richard H. Brown - Chairman Mark P. Vergnano - President, Chief Executive Officer, Holding/Parent Company Officer	**Auditors:** PricewaterhouseCoopers LLP **Transfer Agents:** Computershare Trust Company, N.A.

CHESAPEAKE ENERGY CORP.

Exchange	Symbol	Price	52Wk Range	Yield	P/E
NYS	CHK	$5.24 (6/29/2018)	5.24-2.63	N/A	4.99

*7 Year Price Score 21.34 *NYSE Composite Index=100 *12 Month Price Score 109.61

Interim Earnings (Per Share)

Qtr.	Mar	Jun	Sep	Dec
2015	(5.72)	(6.27)	(7.08)	(3.36)
2016	(1.44)	(2.48)	(1.54)	(0.98)
2017	0.08	0.47	(0.05)	0.34
2018	0.29	...	...	...

Interim Dividends (Per Share)

Dividend Payment Suspended

Valuation Analysis		Institutional Holding	
Forecast EPS	$0.81	No of Institutions	
	(06/14/2018)	797	
Market Cap	$4.8 Billion	Shares	
Book Value	N/A	633,651,584	
Price/Book	N/A	% Held	
Price/Sales	0.52	82.43	

Business Summary: Production & Extraction (MIC: 9.1.1 SIC: 1311 NAIC: 211111)

Chesapeake Energy is an oil and natural gas exploration and production company engaged in the acquisition, exploration and development of properties for the production of oil, natural gas and natural gas liquids (NGL) from underground reservoirs. Co. also owns oil and natural gas marketing and natural gas gathering and compression businesses. Co.'s operations are located onshore in the U.S. Co. has two geographic operating divisions: Southern Division, and Northern Division. As of Dec 31 2017, Co. had estimated total proved reserves of 260.0 million barrels of oil, 8.60 trillion cubic feet of natural gas, and 219.0 million barrels of NGL.

Recent Developments: For the quarter ended Mar 31 2018, net income increased 108.5% to US$294.0 million from US$141.0 million in the year-earlier quarter. Revenues were US$2.49 billion, down 9.6% from US$2.75 billion the year before. Operating income was US$278.0 million versus US$241.0 million in the prior-year quarter, an increase of 15.4%. Direct operating expenses rose 4.3% to US$534.0 million from US$512.0 million in the comparable period the year before. Indirect operating expenses decreased 16.1% to US$1.68 billion from US$2.00 billion in the equivalent prior-year period.

Prospects: Our evaluation of Chesapeake Energy Corp. as of Jan. 21, 2018 is the result of our systematic analysis on three basic characteristics: earnings strength, relative valuation, and recent stock price movement. The company has suffered a very negative trend in earnings per share over the past 5 quarters and while recent estimates for the company have been raised by analysts, CHK has posted better than expected results. Based on operating earnings yield, the company is undervalued when compared to all of the companies in our coverage universe. Share price changes over the past year indicates that CHK will perform very poorly over the near term.

Financial Data

(US$ in Thousands)	3 Mos	12/31/2017	12/31/2016	12/31/2015	12/31/2014	12/31/2013	12/31/2012	12/31/2011
Earnings Per Share	1.05	0.90	(6.45)	(22.43)	1.87	0.73	(1.46)	2.32
Cash Flow Per Share	1.44	0.82	(0.27)	1.86	7.03	7.07	4.40	9.27
Tang Book Value Per Share	...	...	...	...	20.87	19.47	18.83	20.57
Dividends Per Share	...	...	...	0.175	0.350	0.350	0.350	0.250
Dividend Payout %	...	...	...	...	18.72	47.95	...	10.78
Income Statement								
Total Revenue	2,489,000	9,496,000	7,872,000	12,764,000	20,951,000	17,506,000	12,316,000	11,635,000
EBITDA	703,000	2,376,000	(3,186,000)	(16,552,000)	6,204,000	4,572,000	1,914,000	4,847,000
Depn & Amortn	286,000	995,000	1,107,000	2,229,000	2,915,000	2,903,000	2,811,000	1,923,000
Income Before Taxes	294,000	955,000	(4,589,000)	(19,098,000)	3,200,000	1,442,000	(974,000)	2,880,000
Income Taxes	...	2,000	(190,000)	(4,463,000)	1,144,000	548,000	(380,000)	1,123,000
Net Income	293,000	949,000	(4,401,000)	(14,685,000)	1,917,000	724,000	(769,000)	1,742,000
Average Shares	1,053,000	906,000	764,000	662,000	772,000	653,000	643,000	752,000
Balance Sheet								
Current Assets	1,224,000	1,525,000	2,142,000	2,480,000	7,468,000	3,656,000	2,948,000	3,177,000
Total Assets	12,086,000	12,425,000	13,028,000	17,357,000	40,751,000	41,782,000	41,611,000	41,835,000
Current Liabilities	2,354,000	2,356,000	3,648,000	3,685,000	5,863,000	5,515,000	6,266,000	7,082,000
Long-Term Obligations	9,325,000	9,921,000	9,938,000	10,383,000	11,184,000	12,917,000	12,356,000	10,824,000
Total Liabilities	12,306,000	12,921,000	14,488,000	15,219,000	23,848,000	25,787,000	26,042,000	25,211,000
Stockholders' Equity	(220,000)	(496,000)	(1,460,000)	2,138,000	16,903,000	15,995,000	15,569,000	16,624,000
Shares Outstanding	908,377	906,492	895,058	663,357	663,329	664,190	664,319	659,335
Statistical Record								
Return on Assets %	9.27	7.46	N.M.	N.M.	4.65	1.74	N.M.	4.41
Return on Equity %	...	...	N.M.	N.M.	11.65	4.59	N.M.	10.93
EBITDA Margin %	28.24	25.02	N.M.	N.M.	29.61	26.12	15.54	41.66
Net Margin %	11.77	9.99	N.M.	N.M.	9.15	4.14	N.M.	14.97
Asset Turnover	0.78	0.75	0.52	0.44	0.51	0.42	0.29	0.29
Current Ratio	0.52	0.65	0.59	0.67	1.27	0.66	0.47	0.45
Debt to Equity	...	...	...	4.86	0.66	0.81	0.79	0.65
Price Range	6.32-2.63	7.18-3.51	8.05-1.59	21.26-3.72	29.50-16.71	27.13-15.62	24.07-12.75	33.50-20.75
P/E Ratio	6.02-2.50	7.98-3.90	...	...	15.78-8.94	37.17-21.39	...	14.44-8.95
Average Yield %	...	...	...	1.51	1.42	1.63	1.90	0.90

Address: 6100 North Western Avenue, Oklahoma City, OK 73118	Web Site: www.chk.com	Auditors: PricewaterhouseCoopers LLP
Telephone: 405-848-8000	Officers: R. Brad Martin - Chairman Archie W. Dunham - Chairman Emeritus	Investor Contact: 405-935-4763 Transfer Agents: Computershare Trust Company, N.A., Canton, MA

CHESAPEAKE UTILITIES CORP.

Exchange	Symbol	Price	52Wk Range	Yield	P/E	Div Acheiver
NYS	CPK	$79.95 (6/29/2018)	85.55-66.65	1.85	19.89	14 Years

*7 Year Price Score 124.13 *NYSE Composite Index=100   *12 Month Price Score 99.82

Interim Earnings (Per Share)

Qtr.	Mar	Jun	Sep	Dec
2015	1.44	0.41	0.33	0.56
2016	1.33	0.52	0.29	0.72
2017	1.17	0.37	0.42	1.59
2018	1.64			

Interim Dividends (Per Share)

Amt	Decl	Ex	Rec	Pay
0.325Q	08/02/2017	09/14/2017	09/15/2017	10/05/2017
0.325Q	11/08/2017	12/14/2017	12/15/2017	01/05/2018
0.325Q	02/27/2018	03/14/2018	03/15/2018	04/05/2018
0.37Q	05/09/2018	06/14/2018	06/15/2018	07/05/2018

Indicated Div: $1.48 (Div. Reinv. Plan)

Valuation Analysis | **Institutional Holding**

Forecast EPS	$3.50	No of Institutions
	(06/11/2018)	237
Market Cap	$1.3 Billion	Shares
Book Value	$505.2 Million	11,884,029
Price/Book	2.59	% Held
Price/Sales	1.95	54.31

Business Summary: Gas Utilities (MIC: 3.3.1 SIC: 4923 NAIC: 221210)

Chesapeake Utilities is a energy company engaged, through its operating divisions and subsidiaries, in various energy and other businesses. Co. operates within two reportable segments: Regulated Energy and Unregulated Energy. Co.'s regulated energy businesses consist of: regulated natural gas distribution operations; regulated natural gas transmission operations; and regulated electric distribution operations. Co.'s unregulated energy segment provides propane distribution, propane and crude oil wholesale marketing operation, natural gas marketing operation, and Co.'s natural gas supply, gathering and processing operation.

Recent Developments: For the quarter ended Mar 31 2018, net income increased 40.3% to US$26.9 million from US$19.1 million in the year-earlier quarter. Revenues were US$239.4 million, up 29.3% from US$185.2 million the year before. Operating income was US$40.4 million versus US$35.1 million in the prior-year quarter, an increase of 15.1%. Direct operating expenses rose 34.8% to US$184.4 million from US$136.7 million in the comparable period the year before. Indirect operating expenses increased 9.4% to US$14.6 million from US$13.3 million in the equivalent prior-year period.

Prospects: Our evaluation of Chesapeake Utilities Corp. as of Jan. 21, 2018 is the result of our systematic analysis on three basic characteristics: earnings strength, relative valuation, and recent stock price movement. The company has enjoyed a very positive trend in earnings per share over the past 5 quarters. However, while recent estimates for the company have been lowered by analysts, CPK has posted better than expected results. Based on operating earnings yield, the company is about fairly valued when compared to all of the companies in our coverage universe. Share price changes over the past year indicates that CPK will perform very well over the near term.

Financial Data

(US$ in Thousands)	3 Mos	12/31/2017	12/31/2016	12/31/2015	12/31/2014	12/31/2013	12/31/2012	12/31/2011
Earnings Per Share	4.02	3.55	2.86	2.72	2.47	2.26	1.99	1.91
Cash Flow Per Share	7.14	6.74	6.62	6.97	5.45	5.05	4.57	4.96
Tang Book Value Per Share	29.25	28.11	26.32	22.35	20.08	18.78	17.35	16.28
Dividends Per Share	1.300	1.280	1.202	1.133	1.067	1.013	0.960	0.910
Dividend Payout %	32.34	36.06	42.05	41.64	43.18	44.84	48.16	47.56
Income Statement								
Total Revenue	239,356	617,583	498,860	459,244	498,834	444,306	392,502	418,027
EBITDA	42,750	93,200	90,989	85,029	76,096	69,229	62,453	59,727
Depn & Amortn	2,276	8,122	7,334	6,978	6,577	6,123	5,547	5,116
Income Before Taxes	36,810	72,433	73,016	68,045	60,037	54,872	48,159	45,611
Income Taxes	9,955	14,309	28,341	26,905	23,945	22,085	19,296	17,989
Net Income	26,855	58,124	44,675	41,140	36,092	32,787	28,863	27,622
Average Shares	16,402	16,383	15,613	15,143	14,604	14,543	14,507	14,476
Balance Sheet								
Current Assets	137,834	178,587	141,151	112,538	122,373	126,409	100,597	127,760
Total Assets	1,427,450	1,417,434	1,229,219	1,068,586	904,469	837,522	733,746	709,066
Current Liabilities	374,323	413,000	334,051	279,593	194,235	221,942	162,166	157,499
Long-Term Obligations	222,014	197,395	136,954	149,340	158,486	117,592	101,907	110,285
Total Liabilities	922,209	931,140	783,133	710,448	604,147	558,749	477,148	468,286
Stockholders' Equity	505,241	486,294	446,086	358,138	300,322	278,773	256,598	240,780
Shares Outstanding	16,363	16,344	16,303	15,270	14,588	14,457	14,396	14,350
Statistical Record								
Return on Assets %	4.94	4.39	3.88	4.17	4.14	4.17	3.99	4.00
Return on Equity %	13.63	12.47	11.08	12.50	12.46	12.25	11.57	11.83
EBITDA Margin %	17.86	15.09	18.24	18.51	15.25	15.58	15.91	14.29
Net Margin %	11.22	9.41	8.96	8.96	7.24	7.38	7.35	6.61
Asset Turnover	0.50	0.47	0.43	0.47	0.57	0.57	0.54	0.61
Current Ratio	0.37	0.43	0.42	0.40	0.63	0.57	0.62	0.81
Debt to Equity	0.44	0.41	0.31	0.42	0.53	0.42	0.40	0.46
Price Range	85.55-66.65	85.55-63.40	70.00-53.54	60.31-45.54	52.60-37.78	40.48-30.27	32.45-26.83	29.55-25.21
P/E Ratio	21.28-16.58	24.10-17.86	24.48-18.72	22.17-16.74	21.30-15.30	17.91-13.39	16.31-13.48	15.47-13.20
Average Yield %	1.71	1.71	1.93	2.21	2.44	2.88	3.25	3.37

Address: 909 Silver Lake Boulevard, Dover, DE 19904
Telephone: 302-734-6799

Web Site: www.chpk.com
Officers: John R. Schimkaitis - Vice-Chairman, Chief Executive Officer Michael P. McMasters - President, Executive Vice President, Chief Operating Officer

Auditors: Baker Tilly Virchow Krause, L
Investor Contact: 888-742-5275
Transfer Agents: Computershare Trust Company, N.A., Providence, RI

CHEVRON CORPORATION

Exchange	Symbol	Price	52Wk Range	Yield	P/E	Div Acheiver
NYS	CVX	$126.43 (6/29/2018)	133.60-103.04	3.54	23.68	30 Years

*7 Year Price Score 86.56   *NYSE Composite Index=100   *12 Month Price Score 104.98

Interim Earnings (Per Share)

Qtr.	Mar	Jun	Sep	Dec
2015	1.37	0.30	1.09	(0.31)
2016	(0.39)	(0.78)	0.68	0.22
2017	1.41	0.77	1.03	1.64
2018	1.90	...	...	...

Interim Dividends (Per Share)

Amt	Decl	Ex	Rec	Pay
1.08Q	07/26/2017	08/16/2017	08/18/2017	09/11/2017
1.08Q	10/25/2017	11/16/2017	11/17/2017	12/11/2017
1.12Q	01/31/2018	02/15/2018	02/16/2018	03/12/2018
1.12Q	04/25/2018	05/17/2018	05/18/2018	06/11/2018

Indicated Div: $4.48 (Div. Reinv. Plan)

Valuation Analysis   Institutional Holding

Forecast EPS	$8.25	No of Institutions
	(06/14/2018)	3013
Market Cap	$241.6 Billion	Shares
Book Value	$150.4 Billion	1,593,537,536
Price/Book	1.61	% Held
Price/Sales	1.65	59.08

Business Summary: Refining & Marketing (MIC: 9.1.2 SIC: 2911 NAIC: 324110)

Chevron is engaged in energy and chemicals operations. Upstream operations consist of, among others, exploring for, developing and producing crude oil and natural gas; transporting, storage and marketing of natural gas; and a gas-to-liquids plant. Downstream operations consist of, among others, refining crude oil into petroleum products; marketing of crude oil and refined products; and manufacturing and marketing of commodity petrochemicals, plastics for industrial uses and fuel and lubricant additives. At Dec 31 2017, Co. had net proved reserves of 6.54 billion barrels of crude oil, condensate, natural gas liquids and synthetic oil, and 30.74 trillion cubic feet of natural gas.

Recent Developments: For the quarter ended Mar 31 2018, net income increased 35.6% to US$3.66 billion from US$2.70 billion in the year-earlier quarter. Revenues were US$37.76 billion, up 13.0% from US$33.42 billion the year before. Direct operating expenses rose 17.4% to US$25.93 billion from US$22.09 billion in the comparable period the year before. Indirect operating expenses decreased 17.6% to US$6.76 billion from US$8.20 billion in the equivalent prior-year period.

Prospects: Our evaluation of Chevron Corporation as of Jan. 21, 2018 is the result of our systematic analysis on three basic characteristics: earnings strength, relative valuation, and recent stock price movement. The company has generated a negative trend in earnings per share over the past 5 quarters and while recent estimates for the company have been raised by analysts, CVX has posted results that fell short of analysts expectations. Based on operating earnings yield, the company is about fairly valued when compared to all of the companies in our coverage universe. Share price changes over the past year indicates that CVX will perform poorly over the near term.

Financial Data

(US$ in Millions)	3 Mos	12/31/2017	12/31/2016	12/31/2015	12/31/2014	12/31/2013	12/31/2012	12/31/2011
Earnings Per Share	5.34	4.85	(0.27)	2.45	10.14	11.09	13.32	13.44
Cash Flow Per Share	11.43	10.90	6.84	10.42	16.72	18.27	19.85	20.69
Tang Book Value Per Share	76.31	75.39	74.53	78.67	80.03	75.50	67.75	58.92
Dividends Per Share	4.360	4.320	4.290	4.280	4.210	3.900	3.510	3.090
Dividend Payout %	81.65	89.07	...	174.69	41.52	35.17	26.35	22.99
Income Statement								
Total Revenue	37,764	141,722	114,472	138,477	211,970	228,848	241,909	253,706
EBITDA	9,521	28,877	17,498	25,879	47,995	50,091	59,745	60,545
Depn & Amortn	4,289	19,349	19,457	21,037	16,793	14,186	13,413	12,911
Income Before Taxes	5,073	9,221	(2,160)	4,842	31,202	35,905	46,332	47,634
Income Taxes	1,414	(48)	(1,729)	132	11,892	14,308	19,996	20,626
Net Income	3,638	9,195	(497)	4,587	19,241	21,423	26,179	26,895
Average Shares	1,913	1,898	1,873	1,875	1,898	1,932	1,965	2,001
Balance Sheet								
Current Assets	31,726	28,560	29,619	35,347	42,232	50,250	55,720	53,234
Total Assets	256,442	253,806	260,078	266,103	266,026	253,753	232,982	209,474
Current Liabilities	30,630	27,737	31,785	26,464	31,926	33,018	34,212	33,600
Long-Term Obligations	31,144	33,571	35,286	33,664	24,028	20,057	12,065	9,812
Total Liabilities	106,086	105,682	114,522	113,387	110,998	104,640	96,458	88,092
Stockholders' Equity	150,356	148,124	145,556	152,716	155,028	149,113	136,524	121,382
Shares Outstanding	1,910	1,904	1,891	1,882	1,879	1,913	1,946	1,981
Statistical Record								
Return on Assets %	3.94	3.58	N.M.	1.72	7.40	8.80	11.80	13.64
Return on Equity %	6.84	6.26	N.M.	2.98	12.65	15.00	20.25	23.75
EBITDA Margin %	25.21	20.38	15.29	18.69	22.64	21.89	24.70	23.86
Net Margin %	9.63	6.49	N.M.	3.31	9.08	9.36	10.82	10.60
Asset Turnover	0.57	0.55	0.43	0.52	0.82	0.94	1.09	1.29
Current Ratio	1.04	1.03	0.93	1.34	1.32	1.52	1.63	1.58
Debt to Equity	0.21	0.23	0.24	0.22	0.15	0.13	0.09	0.08
Price Range	133.60-103.04	125.98-103.04	118.77-78.98	112.78-70.02	134.85-100.86	127.76-108.14	117.96-96.41	109.66-89.88
P/E Ratio	25.02-19.30	25.98-21.25	...	46.03-28.58	13.30-9.95	11.52-9.75	8.86-7.24	8.16-6.69
Average Yield %	3.85	3.88	4.30	4.44	3.49	3.25	3.26	3.07

Address: 6001 Bollinger Canyon Road, San Ramon, CA 94583-2324	Web Site: www.chevron.com	Auditors: PricewaterhouseCoopers LLP
Telephone: 925-842-1000	**Officers:** Christine L. Cavallo - Assistant Secretary, Managing Counsel Michael K. Wirth - Chairman, Vice-Chairman, Chief Executive Officer, Executive Vice President, Executive Vice President (frmr)	**Investor Contact:** 925-842-5690
Fax: 925-894-6017		**Transfer Agents:** Computershare, Providence, RI

CHIMERA INVESTMENT CORP

Exchange	Symbol	Price	52Wk Range	Yield	P/E
NYS	CIM	$18.28 (6/29/2018)	19.72-16.24	10.94	6.11

*7 Year Price Score 93.69 *NYSE Composite Index=100 *12 Month Price Score 99.04

Interim Earnings (Per Share)

Qtr.	Mar	Jun	Sep	Dec
2015	0.33	0.57	(0.24)	0.60
2016	0.44	0.39	0.92	1.16
2017	0.84	0.56	0.69	0.52
2018	1.22	...	...	...

Interim Dividends (Per Share)

Amt	Decl	Ex	Rec	Pay
0.50Q	08/01/2017	09/27/2017	09/28/2017	10/27/2017
0.50Q	11/01/2017	12/28/2017	12/29/2017	01/30/2018
0.50Q	02/13/2018	03/28/2018	03/29/2018	04/30/2018
0.50Q	05/02/2018	06/28/2018	06/29/2018	07/31/2018

Indicated Div: $2.00 (Div. Reinv. Plan)

Valuation Analysis

		Institutional Holding	
Forecast EPS	$2.32	No of Institutions	
	(05/28/2018)	.388	
Market Cap	$3.4 Billion	Shares	
Book Value	$3.7 Billion	198,630,384	
Price/Book	0.93	% Held	
Price/Sales	2.68	67.24	

Business Summary: REITs (MIC: 5.3.1 SIC: 6798 NAIC: 525930)

Chimera Investment is a real estate investment trust engaged in investing in mortgage assets. Co.'s investment portfolio includes: Residential Mortgage-Backed Securities, which invests in mortgage pass-through certificates issued or guaranteed; Agency commercial mortgage-backed securities, which each Government National Mortgage Association Construction Loan Certificates is backed by a single multifamily property or health care facilities; residential mortgage loans, which invests in residential mortgage loans primarily through direct and secondary market purchases; and other Asset-Backed Securities, which invests in securities issued in various collaterized debt obligations offerings.

Recent Developments: For the quarter ended Mar 31 2018, net income increased 46.8% to US$239.0 million from US$162.8 million in the year-earlier quarter. Revenues were US$414.6 million, up 35.7% from US$305.6 million the year before.

Prospects: Our evaluation of Chimera Investment Corp. as of Jan. 21, 2018 is the result of our systematic analysis on three basic characteristics: earnings strength, relative valuation, and recent stock price movement. The company has suffered a very negative trend in earnings per share over the past 5 quarters and while recent estimates for the company have remained steady, CIM has posted better than expected results. Based on operating earnings yield, the company is undervalued when compared to all of the companies in our coverage universe. Share price changes over the past year indicates that CIM will perform well over the near term.

Financial Data
(US$ in Thousands)

	3 Mos	12/31/2017	12/31/2016	12/31/2015	12/31/2014	12/31/2013	12/31/2012	12/31/2011
Earnings Per Share	2.99	2.61	2.92	1.25	2.85	1.75	1.60	0.65
Cash Flow Per Share	3.33	2.60	2.94	1.99	0.89	1.48	1.63	2.18
Tang Book Value Per Share	19.63	19.35	16.64	15.70	17.55	16.21	17.24	14.83
Dividends Per Share	2.000	2.000	2.440	1.440	1.800	2.800	1.900	2.550
Dividend Payout %	66.89	76.63	83.56	115.20	63.16	160.00	118.75	392.31
Income Statement								
Total Revenue	414,614	1,168,349	992,902	603,111	768,360	498,786	513,493	337,320
EBITDA	241,596	513,018	557,001	271,308	528,190	299,773	276,037	89,781
Depn & Amortn	2,555	(11,758)	4,975	20,958	(61,017)	(62,915)	(51,731)	(48,154)
Income Before Taxes	239,041	524,776	552,026	250,350	589,207	362,688	327,768	137,935
Income Taxes	34	108	83	1,000.00	2	2	1,000.00	606
Net Income	239,007	524,668	551,943	250,349	589,205	362,686	327,767	137,329
Average Shares	188,176	188,287	188,024	199,650	205,508	205,514	205,499	205,434
Balance Sheet								
Current Assets	199,421	164,358	257,411	180,309	235,719	110,623	660,483	255,624
Total Assets	21,330,728	21,222,070	16,684,908	15,344,646	19,155,005	6,936,081	7,742,489	7,747,135
Current Liabilities	8,143,864	7,975,145	6,267,110	8,127,509	10,425,034	1,957,862	1,622,897	2,789,220
Long-Term Obligations	9,516,121	9,594,437	7,275,221	4,249,911	5,095,278	...	...	...
Total Liabilities	17,659,985	17,587,093	13,561,375	12,398,458	15,547,315	3,604,571	4,200,010	4,699,516
Stockholders' Equity	3,670,743	3,634,977	3,123,533	2,946,188	3,607,690	3,331,510	3,542,479	3,047,619
Shares Outstanding	186,969	187,809	187,739	187,711	205,546	205,525	205,519	205,493
Statistical Record								
Return on Assets %	2.88	2.77	3.44	1.45	4.52	4.94	4.22	1.74
Return on Equity %	16.73	15.53	18.14	7.64	16.98	10.55	9.92	4.08
EBITDA Margin %	58.27	43.91	56.10	44.98	68.74	60.10	53.76	26.62
Net Margin %	57.65	44.91	55.59	41.51	76.68	72.71	63.83	40.71
Asset Turnover	0.06	0.06	0.06	0.03	0.06	0.07	0.07	0.04
Current Ratio	0.02	0.02	0.04	0.02	0.02	0.06	0.41	0.09
Debt to Equity	2.59	2.64	2.33	1.44	1.41	...	...	...
Price Range	20.83-16.24	20.83-17.09	17.64-11.39	16.45-12.86	16.95-14.95	16.60-13.05	15.60-10.65	21.55-12.55
P/E Ratio	6.97-5.43	7.98-6.55	6.04-3.90	13.16-10.29	5.95-5.25	9.49-7.46	9.75-6.66	33.15-19.31
Average Yield %	10.75	10.60	16.17	9.79	11.36	18.40	14.05	14.75

Address: 520 Madison Avenue, 32nd Floor, New York, NY 10022
Telephone: 212-626-2300

Web Site: www.chimerareit.com
Officers: Matthew Lambiase - President, Chief Executive Officer Choudhary Yarlagadda - Chief Operating Officer

Auditors: Ernst & Young LLP
Investor Contact: 866-315-9930
Transfer Agents: Computershare Shareowner Services LLC, Jersey City, NJ

CHIPOTLE MEXICAN GRILL INC

Exchange	Symbol	Price	52Wk Range	Yield	P/E
NYS	CMG	$431.37 (6/29/2018)	469.94-251.33	N/A	64.48

*7 Year Price Score 60.80 *NYSE Composite Index=100 *12 Month Price Score 127.86

Interim Earnings (Per Share)

Qtr.	Mar	Jun	Sep	Dec
2015	3.88	4.45	4.59	2.18
2016	(0.88)	0.87	0.27	0.54
2017	1.60	2.32	0.69	1.55
2018	2.13	...	...	...

Interim Dividends (Per Share)

No Dividends Paid

Valuation Analysis / Institutional Holding

Valuation Analysis		Institutional Holding	
Forecast EPS	$8.63	No of Institutions	
	(06/14/2018)	730	
Market Cap	$12.0 Billion	Shares	
Book Value	$1.4 Billion	28,703,132	
Price/Book	8.80	% Held	
Price/Sales	2.63	89.02	

TRADING VOLUME (thousand shares)

Business Summary: Hotels, Restaurants & Travel (MIC: 2.2.1 SIC: 5812 NAIC: 722110)

Chipotle Mexican Grill together with its subsidiaries operates Chipotle Mexican Grill restaurants, which serve a focused menu of burritos, tacos, burrito bowls (a burrito without the tortilla) and salads. As of Dec 31 2017, Co. operated 2,363 Chipotle restaurants throughout the U.S., as well as 37 international Chipotle restaurants, and Co. also had 8 restaurants in operation in other non-Chipotle concepts. Co. also makes a variety of extras such as guacamole, salsas and tortilla chips seasoned with lime juice and salt. In addition to sodas, fruit and tea drinks and organic milk, most of Co.'s restaurants also provides a selection of beer and margaritas.

Recent Developments: For the quarter ended Mar 31 2018, net income increased 28.9% to US$59.4 million from US$46.1 million in the year-earlier quarter. Revenues were US$1.15 billion, up 7.4% from US$1.07 billion the year before. Operating income was US$92.8 million versus US$73.2 million in the prior-year quarter, an increase of 26.8%. Direct operating expenses rose 5.1% to US$924.1 million from US$879.2 million in the comparable period the year before. Indirect operating expenses increased 12.9% to US$131.5 million from US$116.4 million in the equivalent prior-year period.

Prospects: Our evaluation of Chipotle Mexican Grill Inc. as of Jan. 21, 2018 is the result of our systematic analysis on three basic characteristics: earnings strength, relative valuation, and recent stock price movement. The company has suffered a very negative trend in earnings per share over the past 5 quarters. However, while recent estimates for the company have been mixed, CMG has posted results that fell short of analysts expectations. Based on operating earnings yield, the company is overvalued when compared to all of the companies in our coverage universe. Share price changes over the past year indicates that CMG will perform very poorly over the near term.

Financial Data
(US$ in Thousands)

	3 Mos	12/31/2017	12/31/2016	12/31/2015	12/31/2014	12/31/2013	12/31/2012	12/31/2011
Earnings Per Share	6.69	6.17	0.77	15.10	14.13	10.47	8.75	6.76
Cash Flow Per Share	18.55	16.39	11.90	21.98	21.98	17.08	13.29	13.17
Tang Book Value Per Share	48.23	47.90	47.91	68.86	64.15	48.86	39.37	32.71
Income Statement								
Total Revenue	1,148,397	4,476,412	3,904,384	4,501,223	4,108,269	3,214,591	2,731,224	2,269,548
EBITDA	139,723	439,091	185,107	900,235	824,777	630,525	541,815	425,500
Depn & Amortn	46,915	163,348	146,368	130,368	110,474	96,054	84,130	74,938
Income Before Taxes	94,202	275,743	38,739	769,867	714,303	534,471	457,685	349,705
Income Taxes	34,756	99,490	15,801	294,265	268,929	207,033	179,685	134,760
Net Income	59,446	176,253	22,938	475,602	445,374	327,438	278,000	214,945
Average Shares	27,950	28,561	29,770	31,494	31,512	31,281	31,783	31,775
Balance Sheet								
Current Assets	630,439	629,535	522,374	814,647	878,479	666,307	546,607	501,192
Total Assets	2,097,444	2,045,692	2,026,103	2,725,066	2,546,285	2,009,280	1,668,667	1,425,308
Current Liabilities	367,320	323,893	281,793	279,942	245,710	199,228	186,852	157,453
Long-Term Obligations	...	...	...	...	...	...	3,386	3,529
Total Liabilities	733,399	681,247	623,610	597,092	533,916	470,992	422,741	381,082
Stockholders' Equity	1,364,045	1,364,445	1,402,493	2,127,974	2,012,369	1,538,288	1,245,926	1,044,226
Shares Outstanding	27,826	28,026	28,814	30,584	31,027	31,033	31,093	31,252
Statistical Record								
Return on Assets %	9.12	8.66	0.96	18.04	19.55	17.81	17.92	16.88
Return on Equity %	13.68	12.74	1.30	22.97	25.09	23.52	24.21	23.17
EBITDA Margin %	12.17	9.81	4.74	20.00	20.08	19.61	19.84	18.75
Net Margin %	5.18	3.94	0.59	10.57	10.84	10.19	10.18	9.47
Asset Turnover	2.19	2.20	1.64	1.71	1.80	1.75	1.76	1.78
Current Ratio	1.72	1.94	1.85	2.91	3.58	3.34	2.93	3.18
Price Range	496.14-251.33	496.14-268.70	533.69-359.92	757.77-479.85	692.69-476.28	546.97-280.94	440.40-236.24	343.52-212.66
P/E Ratio	74.16-37.57	80.41-43.55	693.10-467.43	50.18-31.78	49.02-33.71	52.24-26.83	50.33-27.00	50.82-31.46

Address: 1401 Wynkoop Street, Suite 500, Denver, CO 80202 Telephone: 303-595-4000	Web Site: www.chipotle.com Officers: M. Steven (Steve) Ells - Chairman, Chief Executive Officer, Co-Chief Executive Officer, Executive Chairman Brian R. Niccol - Chief Executive Officer	Auditors: Ernst & Young LLP Investor Contact: 303-595-4000 Transfer Agents: Wells Fargo Shareowner Services, Mendota Heights, MN

CHOICE HOTELS INTERNATIONAL, INC.

Exchange	Symbol	Price	52Wk Range	Yield	P/E
NYS	CHH	$75.60 (6/29/2018)	84.60-60.05	1.14	38.77

*7 Year Price Score 118.25 *NYSE Composite Index=100 *12 Month Price Score 106.86

Interim Earnings (Per Share)

Qtr.	Mar	Jun	Sep	Dec
2015	0.37	0.62	0.72	0.51
2016	0.35	0.68	0.84	0.56
2017	0.51	0.79	0.84	(0.12)
2018	0.44	...	...	...

Interim Dividends (Per Share)

Amt	Decl	Ex	Rec	Pay
0.215Q	09/18/2017	09/29/2017	10/02/2017	10/17/2017
0.215Q	12/18/2017	12/29/2017	01/02/2018	01/17/2018
0.215Q	02/26/2018	03/29/2018	04/02/2018	04/17/2018
0.215Q	04/20/2018	06/29/2018	07/02/2018	07/17/2018

Indicated Div: $0.86

Valuation Analysis

		Institutional Holding	
Forecast EPS	$3.71	No of Institutions	
	(06/04/2018)	285	
Market Cap	$4.3 Billion	Shares	
Book Value	N/A	34,035,940	
Price/Book	N/A	% Held	
Price/Sales	4.20	N/A	

TRADING VOLUME (thousand shares)

Business Summary: Hotels, Restaurants & Travel (MIC: 2.2.1 SIC: 7011 NAIC: 721110)

Choice Hotels International is a hotel franchisor with 6,514 hotels (516,122 rooms) in 50 states, the District of Columbia and over 40 countries and territories outside the U.S. Co. franchises lodging properties under the following brand names: Comfort Inn®, Comfort Suites®, Quality®, Clarion®, Sleep Inn®, Econo Lodge®, Rodeway Inn®, MainStay Suites®, Suburban Extended Stay Hotel®, Cambria® hotels & suites, and Ascend Hotel Collection®. Co.'s brand names include Comfort Inn, Comfort Suites, Quality, Clarion, Ascend Hotel Collection, Sleep Inn, Econo Lodge, Rodeway Inn, MainStay Suites, Suburban Extended Stay Hotel and Cambria hotels & suites.

Recent Developments: For the quarter ended Mar 31 2018, net income increased 3.4% to US$25.1 million from US$24.3 million in the year-earlier quarter. Revenues were US$209.4 million, up 10.9% from US$188.9 million the year before. Operating income was US$46.2 million versus US$45.4 million in the prior-year quarter, an increase of 1.9%. Indirect operating expenses increased 13.7% to US$163.1 million from US$143.5 million in the equivalent prior-year period.

Prospects: Our evaluation of Choice Hotels International Inc. as of Jan. 21, 2018 is the result of our systematic analysis on three basic characteristics: earnings strength, relative valuation, and recent stock price movement. The company has generated a negative trend in earnings per share over the past 5 quarters and while recent estimates for the company have been mixed, CHH has posted better than expected results. Based on operating earnings yield, the company is about fairly valued when compared to all of the companies in our coverage universe. Share price changes over the past year indicates that CHH will perform well over the near term.

Financial Data
(US$ in Thousands)

	3 Mos	12/31/2017	12/31/2016	12/31/2015	12/31/2014	12/31/2013	12/31/2012	12/31/2011
Earnings Per Share	1.95	2.02	2.46	2.22	2.10	1.91	2.07	1.85
Cash Flow Per Share	4.21	4.59	2.71	2.81	3.19	2.62	2.79	2.29
Dividends Per Share	0.860	0.860	0.830	0.790	0.750	0.740	11.150	0.740
Dividend Payout %	44.10	42.57	33.74	35.59	35.71	38.74	538.65	40.00
Income Statement								
Total Revenue	209,394	1,007,356	924,641	859,878	757,970	724,307	691,509	638,793
EBITDA	56,407	272,862	245,999	230,439	217,241	199,374	197,005	172,021
Depn & Amortn	10,278	5,200	5,600	4,300	3,100	3,100	2,400	2,600
Income Before Taxes	36,429	228,543	199,488	184,886	174,416	156,284	168,956	157,788
Income Taxes	5,375	109,104	60,609	55,956	52,285	44,317	48,481	47,661
Net Income	25,086	114,893	139,371	128,029	123,160	112,601	120,687	110,396
Average Shares	57,111	56,526	56,155	57,273	58,256	58,335	57,653	58,934
Balance Sheet								
Current Assets	231,845	402,933	344,873	310,953	351,414	258,646	233,470	194,796
Total Assets	1,052,017	927,607	852,468	717,010	647,270	539,899	510,772	447,689
Current Liabilities	269,270	294,497	263,668	208,016	200,098	174,338	176,137	184,565
Long-Term Obligations	795,745	725,292	839,409	812,945	782,082	783,471	847,150	252,032
Total Liabilities	1,311,934	1,139,709	1,163,817	1,112,909	1,076,071	1,004,144	1,059,676	473,250
Stockholders' Equity	(259,917)	(212,102)	(311,349)	(395,899)	(428,801)	(464,245)	(548,904)	(25,561)
Shares Outstanding	56,660	56,679	56,299	56,336	57,337	58,638	58,171	58,277
Statistical Record								
Return on Assets %	11.37	12.91	17.71	18.77	20.75	21.43	25.11	25.69
EBITDA Margin %	26.94	27.09	26.60	26.80	28.66	27.53	28.49	26.93
Net Margin %	11.98	11.41	15.07	14.89	16.25	15.55	17.45	17.28
Asset Turnover	1.04	1.13	1.18	1.26	1.28	1.38	1.44	1.49
Current Ratio	0.86	1.37	1.31	1.49	1.76	1.48	1.33	1.06
Price Range	84.60-60.05	78.70-53.50	56.70-41.85	64.85-46.62	57.34-43.71	49.71-33.62	44.21-30.80	41.25-26.54
P/E Ratio	43.38-30.79	38.96-26.49	23.05-17.01	29.21-21.00	27.30-20.81	26.03-17.60	21.36-14.88	22.30-14.35
Average Yield %	1.23	1.33	1.71	1.43	1.52	1.79	31.06	2.11

Address: 1 Choice Hotels Circle, Suite 400, Rockville, MD 20850
Telephone: 301-592-5000

Web Site: www.choicehotels.com
Officers: Stewart Bainum - Chairman Patrick S. Pacious - President, Chief Operating Officer, Executive Vice President

Auditors: Ernst & Young LLP
Investor Contact: 301-592-5026
Transfer Agents: Computershare, Providence, RI

CHUBB LTD

Exchange	Symbol	Price	52Wk Range	Yield	P/E
NYS	CB	$127.02 (6/29/2018)	156.15-124.57	2.30	15.55

*7 Year Price Score 107.68 *NYSE Composite Index=100 *12 Month Price Score 90.57

TRADING VOLUME (thousand shares)

Interim Earnings (Per Share)

Qtr.	Mar	Jun	Sep	Dec
2015	2.05	2.86	1.62	2.09
2016	0.97	1.54	2.88	3.43
2017	2.31	2.77	(0.15)	3.25
2018	2.30	...	...	...

Interim Dividends (Per Share)

Amt	Decl	Ex	Rec	Pay
0.71Q	08/10/2017	09/28/2017	09/29/2017	10/20/2017
0.71Q	11/16/2017	12/28/2017	12/29/2017	01/19/2018
0.71Q	02/22/2018	03/28/2018	03/29/2018	04/20/2018
0.73Q	05/17/2018	06/21/2018	06/22/2018	07/13/2018

Indicated Div: $2.92 (Div. Reinv. Plan)

Valuation Analysis | **Institutional Holding**

Forecast EPS	N/A	No of Institutions 1409
Market Cap	$59.2 Billion	Shares
Book Value	$51.3 Billion	494,591,040
Price/Book	1.15	% Held
Price/Sales	1.82	N/A

Business Summary: General Insurance (MIC: 5.2.1 SIC: 6331 NAIC: 524130)

Chubb is a holding company. Through its subsidiaries, Co. is an insurance and reinsurance organization. Co. provides commercial insurance products and service offerings such as risk management programs. Co. provides insurance products ranging from Directors & Officers and professional liability to several specialty-casualty and umbrella and excess casualty lines. Co. also provides personal lines insurance coverage including homeowners, umbrella liability and recreational marine products. Co.'s segments are: North America Commercial P&C Insurance, North America Personal P&C Insurance, North America Agricultural Insurance, Overseas General Insurance, Global Reinsurance, and Life Insurance.

Recent Developments: For the quarter ended Mar 31 2018, net income decreased 1.0% to US$1.08 billion from US$1.09 billion in the year-earlier quarter. Revenues were US$7.83 billion, up 4.3% from US$7.51 billion the year before. Net premiums earned were US$7.03 billion versus US$6.77 billion in the prior-year quarter, an increase of 3.8%. Net investment income rose 8.2% to US$806.0 million from US$745.0 million a year ago.

Prospects: Our evaluation of Chubb Ltd. as of Sep. 17, 2017 is the result of our systematic analysis on three basic characteristics: earnings strength, relative valuation, and recent stock price movement. The company has generated a negative trend in earnings per share over the past 5 quarters and while recent estimates for the company have been mixed, CB has posted better than expected results. Based on operating earnings yield, the company is undervalued when compared to all of the companies in our coverage universe. Share price changes over the past year indicates that CB will perform well over the near term.

Financial Data
(US$ in Thousands)

	3 Mos	12/31/2017	12/31/2016	12/31/2015	12/31/2014	12/31/2013	12/31/2012	12/31/2011
Earnings Per Share	8.17	8.19	8.87	8.62	8.42	10.92	7.89	4.65
Cash Flow Per Share	8.68	9.64	11.41	11.87	13.40	11.80	11.72	10.26
Tang Book Value Per Share	62.61	62.78	56.18	72.26	72.61	68.93	66.28	58.43
Dividends Per Share	2.840	2.820	2.740	2.660	2.700	2.020	2.060	1.380
Dividend Payout %	34.76	34.43	30.89	30.86	32.07	18.50	26.11	29.68
Income Statement								
Premium Income	7,027,000	29,034,000	28,749,000	17,213,000	17,426,000	16,613,000	15,677,000	15,387,000
Total Revenue	7,831,000	32,243,000	31,469,000	18,987,000	19,171,000	19,261,000	17,936,000	16,834,000
Benefits & Claims	4,253,000	19,130,000	16,640,000	10,027,000	10,166,000	9,863,000	10,174,000	9,921,000
Income Before Taxes	1,158,000	3,304,000	4,686,000	3,183,000	3,256,000	4,119,000	2,896,000	2,053,000
Income Taxes	135,000	(139,000)	815,000	462,000	634,000	480,000	270,000	506,000
Net Income	1,082,000	3,861,000	4,135,000	2,834,000	2,853,000	3,758,000	2,706,000	1,585,000
Average Shares	469,473	471,196	465,949	328,835	338,986	344,147	342,746	340,780
Balance Sheet								
Total Assets	168,781,000	167,022,000	159,786,000	102,366,000	98,248,000	94,510,000	92,545,000	87,505,000
Total Liabilities	117,494,000	115,850,000	111,511,000	73,231,000	68,661,000	65,685,000	65,014,000	62,989,000
Stockholders' Equity	51,287,000	51,172,000	48,275,000	29,135,000	29,587,000	28,825,000	27,531,000	24,516,000
Shares Outstanding	465,831	463,833	465,968	324,563	328,659	339,793	340,321	336,927
Statistical Record								
Return on Assets %	2.34	2.36	3.15	2.83	2.96	4.02	3.00	1.86
Return on Equity %	7.66	7.76	10.65	9.65	9.77	13.34	10.37	6.68
Loss Ratio %	60.52	65.89	57.88	58.25	58.34	59.37	64.90	64.48
Net Margin %	13.82	11.97	13.14	14.93	14.88	19.51	15.09	9.42
Price Range	156.15-134.57	155.19-128.48	133.32-108.00	119.47-99.72	117.58-92.19	103.53-79.80	81.70-68.98	73.33-58.98
P/E Ratio	19.11-16.47	18.95-15.69	15.03-12.18	13.86-11.57	13.96-10.95	9.48-7.31	10.35-8.74	15.77-12.68
Average Yield %	1.95	1.98	2.22	2.43	2.60	2.21	2.76	2.12

Address: Baerengasse 32, Zurich, CH-8001	Web Site: www.acegroup.com	Auditors: PricewaterhouseCoopers LLP
Telephone: 434-567-600	Officers: Evan G. Greenberg - Chairman, Vice-Chairman, President, Chief Executive Officer, Chief Operating Officer John W. Keogh - Executive Vice Chairman, Vice-Chairman, Chief Operating Officer	

CHURCH & DWIGHT CO INC

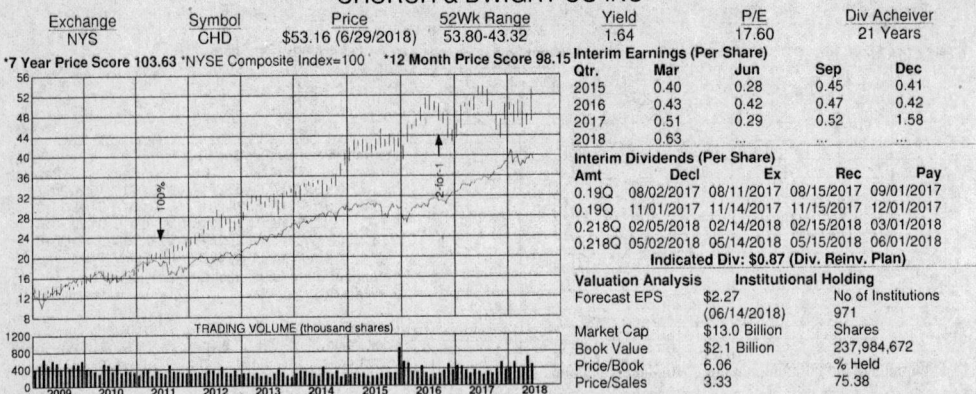

Exchange	Symbol	Price	52Wk Range	Yield	P/E	Div Acheiver
NYS	CHD	$53.16 (6/29/2018)	53.80-43.32	1.64	17.60	21 Years

*7 Year Price Score 103.63 *NYSE Composite Index=100 *12 Month Price Score 98.15

Interim Earnings (Per Share)

Qtr.	Mar	Jun	Sep	Dec
2015	0.40	0.28	0.45	0.41
2016	0.43	0.42	0.47	0.42
2017	0.51	0.29	0.52	1.58
2018	0.63	...	...	...

Interim Dividends (Per Share)

Amt	Decl	Ex	Rec	Pay
0.19Q	08/02/2017	08/11/2017	08/15/2017	09/01/2017
0.19Q	11/01/2017	11/14/2017	11/15/2017	12/01/2017
0.218Q	02/05/2018	02/14/2018	02/15/2018	03/01/2018
0.218Q	05/02/2018	05/14/2018	05/15/2018	06/01/2018

Indicated Div: $0.87 (Div. Reinv. Plan)

Valuation Analysis / **Institutional Holding**

Forecast EPS	$2.27	No of Institutions
	(06/14/2018)	971
Market Cap	$13.0 Billion	Shares
Book Value	$2.1 Billion	237,984,672
Price/Book	6.06	% Held
Price/Sales	3.33	75.38

TRADING VOLUME (thousand shares)

Business Summary: Household & Personal Products (MIC: 1.7.1 SIC: 2841 NAIC: 325611)

Church & Dwight develops, manufactures and markets a range of household, personal care and specialty products. Co. sells its products under a variety of brands via a distribution platform that includes supermarkets, mass merchandisers, wholesale clubs, drugstores, convenience stores, home stores, dollar, pet and other specialty stores and websites. Co. has three segments: Consumer Domestic, which sells household and personal care products; Consumer International, which sells personal care products, some of which use the same brands as its domestic lines, in international markets; and Specialty Products Division, which has an animal productivity business with products for animal agriculture.

Recent Developments: For the quarter ended Mar 31 2018, net income increased 20.0% to US$157.8 million from US$131.5 million in the year-earlier quarter. Revenues were US$1.01 billion, up 14.7% from US$877.2 million the year before. Operating income was US$220.3 million versus US$196.1 million in the prior-year quarter, an increase of 12.3%. Direct operating expenses rose 16.0% to US$554.5 million from US$477.9 million in the comparable period the year before. Indirect operating expenses increased 13.8% to US$231.2 million from US$203.2 million in the equivalent prior-year period.

Prospects: Our evaluation of Church & Dwight Co. Inc. as of Jan. 21, 2018 is the result of our systematic analysis on three basic characteristics: earnings strength, relative valuation, and recent stock price movement. The company has managed to produce a neutral trend in earnings per share over the past 5 quarters and while recent estimates for the company have been mixed, CHD has posted better than expected results. Based on operating earnings yield, the company is about fairly valued when compared to all of the companies in our coverage universe. Share price changes over the past year indicates that CHD will perform in line with the market over the near term.

Financial Data

(US$ in Thousands)	3 Mos	12/31/2017	12/31/2016	12/31/2015	12/31/2014	12/31/2013	12/31/2012	12/31/2011
Earnings Per Share	3.02	2.90	1.75	1.53	1.50	1.40	1.23	1.06
Cash Flow Per Share	2.88	2.72	2.54	2.31	2.00	1.80	1.86	1.53
Tang Book Value Per Share	N.M.	N.M.	N.M.	N.M.	N.M.	N.M.	N.M.	0.94
Dividends Per Share	0.787	0.760	0.710	0.670	0.620	0.560	0.480	0.340
Dividend Payout %	26.08	26.21	40.57	43.65	41.20	40.14	39.18	32.08
Income Statement								
Total Revenue	1,006,000	3,776,200	3,493,100	3,394,800	3,297,600	3,194,300	2,921,900	2,749,300
EBITDA	254,400	795,400	784,100	730,000	697,800	682,400	603,600	543,100
Depn & Amortn	35,700	60,900	59,700	58,300	57,100	59,700	56,000	49,800
Income Before Taxes	198,600	681,900	696,700	641,200	613,300	595,000	533,600	484,600
Income Taxes	42,900	(50,700)	246,900	225,000	211,000	203,400	192,700	185,000
Net Income	157,800	743,400	459,000	410,400	413,900	394,400	349,800	309,600
Average Shares	250,000	256,100	262,100	267,200	275,000	282,400	285,400	291,600
Balance Sheet								
Current Assets	891,400	1,000,200	756,800	906,000	1,032,500	1,115,800	933,800	755,200
Total Assets	5,942,900	6,014,800	4,354,100	4,256,900	4,381,300	4,259,700	4,098,100	3,117,600
Current Liabilities	1,230,700	935,000	1,001,900	872,700	905,300	651,200	725,600	383,600
Long-Term Obligations	1,802,100	2,103,400	693,400	692,800	698,600	649,500	649,400	249,700
Total Liabilities	3,799,600	3,796,800	2,376,200	2,233,700	2,279,400	1,959,400	2,037,200	1,077,000
Stockholders' Equity	2,143,300	2,218,000	1,977,900	2,023,200	2,101,900	2,299,900	2,060,900	2,040,600
Shares Outstanding	244,489	247,629	253,962	259,908	266,703	277,929	277,562	284,574
Statistical Record								
Return on Assets %	14.76	14.34	10.63	9.50	9.58	9.44	9.67	10.21
Return on Equity %	37.74	35.43	22.88	19.90	18.81	18.09	17.01	15.83
EBITDA Margin %	25.29	21.06	22.45	21.50	21.16	21.36	20.66	19.75
Net Margin %	15.69	19.69	13.14	12.09	12.55	12.35	11.97	11.26
Asset Turnover	0.75	0.73	0.81	0.79	0.76	0.76	0.81	0.91
Current Ratio	0.72	1.07	0.76	1.04	1.14	1.71	1.29	1.97
Debt to Equity	0.84	0.95	0.35	0.34	0.33	0.28	0.32	0.12
Price Range	53.80-43.32	53.80-43.32	51.67-39.12	45.28-38.78	40.27-31.03	33.45-26.79	29.38-22.40	23.17-17.14
P/E Ratio	17.81-14.34	18.55-14.94	29.53-22.35	29.60-25.35	26.84-20.69	23.90-19.13	23.89-18.21	21.86-16.17
Average Yield %	1.59	1.55	1.52	1.58	1.79	1.81	1.85	1.67

Address: 500 Charles Ewing Boulevard, Ewing, NJ 08628 Telephone: 609-806-1200 Fax: 609-497-7269	Web Site: www.churchdwight.com Officers: James R. (Jim) Craigie - Chairman, Chief Executive Officer Matthew Thomas Farrell - President, Chief Executive Officer, Executive Vice President, Chief Financial Officer, Chief Operating Officer	Auditors: DELOITTE & TOUCHE LLP Investor Contact: 609-497-7111 Transfer Agents: Computershare Inc., Canton, MA

CIENA CORP

Exchange	Symbol	Price	52Wk Range	Yield	P/E
NYS	CIEN	$26.51 (6/29/2018)	27.49-19.57	N/A	6.58

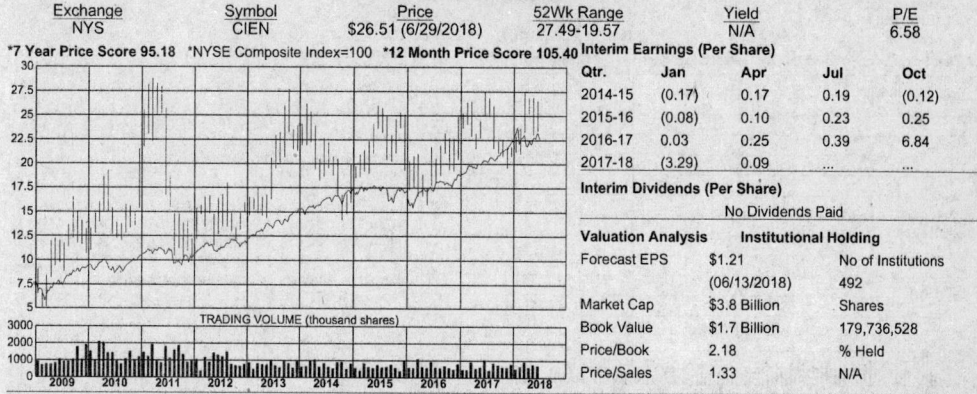

*7 Year Price Score 95.18 *NYSE Composite Index=100 *12 Month Price Score 105.40

Interim Earnings (Per Share)

Qtr.	Jan	Apr	Jul	Oct
2014-15	(0.17)	0.17	0.19	(0.12)
2015-16	(0.08)	0.10	0.23	0.25
2016-17	0.03	0.25	0.39	6.84
2017-18	(3.29)	0.09	...	...

Interim Dividends (Per Share)

No Dividends Paid

Valuation Analysis / **Institutional Holding**

Forecast EPS	$1.21	No of Institutions
	(06/13/2018)	492
Market Cap	$3.8 Billion	Shares
Book Value	$1.7 Billion	179,736,528
Price/Book	2.18	% Held
Price/Sales	1.33	N/A

Business Summary: IT Services (MIC: 6.3.1 SIC: 7373 NAIC: 541512)

Ciena provides equipment, software and services that support the transport, switching, aggregation, service delivery and management of voice, video and data traffic on communications networks. Co.'s Converged Packet Optical, Packet Networking, and Optical Transport products are used by communications service providers, cable and multiservice operators, Web-scale providers, submarine network operators, governments, enterprises, research and education institutions, and other network operators. To complement its solutions, Co. provides a range of transformation and automation services that help customers to design, optimize, integrate, deploy, manage and maintain their networks.

Recent Developments: For the quarter ended Apr 30 2018, net income decreased 63.6% to US$13.9 million from US$38.0 million in the year-earlier quarter. Revenues were US$730.0 million, up 3.2% from US$707.0 million the year before. Operating income was US$32.1 million versus US$57.8 million in the prior-year quarter, a decrease of 44.5%. Direct operating expenses rose 12.3% to US$436.7 million from US$388.8 million in the comparable period the year before. Indirect operating expenses increased 0.3% to US$261.2 million from US$260.4 million in the equivalent prior-year period.

Prospects: Our evaluation of CIENA Corp. as of Jan. 21, 2018 is the result of our systematic analysis on three basic characteristics: earnings strength, relative valuation, and recent stock price movement. The company has generated a negative trend in earnings per share over the past 5 quarters. However, while recent estimates for the company have been lowered by analysts, CIEN has posted results that fell short of analysts expectations. Based on operating earnings yield, the company is undervalued when compared to all of the companies in our coverage universe. Share price changes over the past year indicates that CIEN will perform poorly over the near term.

Financial Data

(US$ in Thousands)	6 Mos	3 Mos	10/31/2017	10/31/2016	10/31/2015	10/31/2014	10/31/2013	10/31/2012
Earnings Per Share	4.03	4.19	7.53	0.51	0.10	(0.38)	(0.83)	(1.45)
Cash Flow Per Share	1.82	2.06	1.65	2.09	2.21	0.85	0.44	1.08
Tang Book Value Per Share	9.66	9.65	12.36	2.52	1.19	...	...	...
Income Statement								
Total Revenue	1,376,113	646,135	2,801,687	2,600,573	2,445,669	2,288,289	2,082,546	1,833,923
EBITDA	58,004	21,962	322,061	269,682	202,050	125,295	89,203	45,951
Depn & Amortn	11,824	5,912	112,913	130,990	125,966	103,751	119,608	125,797
Income Before Taxes	24,908	4,577	156,126	86,718	23,764	(26,673)	(80,191)	(134,699)
Income Taxes	484,415	477,940	(1,105,827)	14,134	12,097	13,964	5,240	9,322
Net Income	(459,507)	(473,363)	1,261,953	72,584	11,667	(40,637)	(85,431)	(144,021)
Average Shares	147,973	143,922	169,919	150,704	120,101	105,783	102,350	99,341
Balance Sheet								
Current Assets	1,985,422	1,923,422	2,006,311	2,013,192	1,864,210	1,693,190	1,395,802	1,415,690
Total Assets	3,506,554	3,469,384	3,951,711	2,882,442	2,695,051	2,072,632	1,802,770	1,881,143
Current Liabilities	989,755	933,376	1,037,743	891,862	667,034	781,136	615,055	684,970
Long-Term Obligations	585,538	584,601	657,095	1,050,289	1,285,433	1,279,380	1,212,019	1,225,806
Total Liabilities	1,762,435	1,713,244	1,815,369	2,116,101	2,074,175	2,142,247	1,885,447	1,970,115
Stockholders' Equity	1,744,119	1,756,140	2,136,342	766,341	620,876	(69,615)	(82,677)	(88,972)
Shares Outstanding	143,427	144,180	143,043	139,767	135,612	106,979	103,705	100,601
Statistical Record								
Return on Assets %	24.21	24.80	36.93	2.60	0.49	N.M.	N.M.	N.M.
Return on Equity %	58.72	61.43	86.95	10.44	4.23	...	...	...
EBITDA Margin %	4.22	3.40	11.50	10.37	8.26	5.48	4.28	2.51
Net Margin %	N.M.	N.M.	45.04	2.79	0.48	N.M.	N.M.	N.M.
Asset Turnover	0.91	0.89	0.82	0.93	1.03	1.18	1.13	0.95
Current Ratio	2.01	2.06	1.93	2.26	2.79	2.17	2.27	2.07
Debt to Equity	0.34	0.33	0.31	1.37	2.07	...	...	...
Price Range	27.50-19.57	27.50-19.57	27.50-19.21	25.30-15.73	26.03-14.81	26.20-14.16	27.67-12.42	17.98-10.38
P/E Ratio	6.82-4.86	6.56-4.67	3.65-2.55	49.61-30.84	260.30-148.10	...	...	...

Address: 7035 Ridge Road, Hanover, MD 21076
Telephone: 410-694-5700
Fax: 410-694-5750

Web Site: www.ciena.com
Officers: Patrick H. Nettles - Executive Chairman
Gary B. Smith - President, Chief Executive Officer

Auditors: PricewaterhouseCoopers LLP
Transfer Agents: Computershare Trust Company, N.A., Providence, RI

CIGNA CORP

Exchange	Symbol	Price	52Wk Range	Yield	P/E
NYS	CI	$169.95 (6/29/2018)	226.22-164.00	0.02	16.69

*7 Year Price Score 138.39 *NYSE Composite Index=100 *12 Month Price Score 92.17

Interim Earnings (Per Share)

Qtr.	Mar	Jun	Sep	Dec
2015	2.04	2.26	2.10	1.64
2016	2.00	1.97	1.76	1.47
2017	2.30	3.15	2.21	1.10
2018	3.72	...	...	...

Interim Dividends (Per Share)

Amt	Decl	Ex	Rec	Pay
0.04A	02/25/2015	03/10/2015	03/12/2015	04/10/2015
0.04A	02/24/2016	03/09/2016	03/11/2016	04/11/2016
0.04A	02/22/2017	03/08/2017	03/10/2017	04/10/2017
0.04A	02/28/2018	03/09/2018	03/12/2018	04/10/2018

Indicated Div: $0.04 (Div. Reinv. Plan)

Valuation Analysis

		Institutional Holding	
Forecast EPS	$13.20 (06/14/2018)	No of Institutions	1248
Market Cap	$41.3 Billion	Shares	261,625,808
Book Value	$14.2 Billion	% Held	82.69
Price/Book	2.91		
Price/Sales	0.97		

Business Summary: Life & Health (MIC: 5.2.2 SIC: 6324 NAIC: 524114)

Cigna is a holding company. Co. is a health services organization. Through its subsidiaries, Co. provides medical, dental, disability, life and accident insurance and related products and services, the majority of which are provide through employers and other groups such as governmental and non-governmental organizations, unions and associations. Co. also provides commercial health and dental insurance, Medicare and Medicaid products and health, life and accident insurance coverages to individuals in the U.S. and selected international markets. Co.'s segments include: Global Health Care; Global Supplemental Benefits; Group Disability and Life; and Other Operations.

Recent Developments: For the quarter ended Mar 31 2018, net income increased 54.6% to US$917.0 million from US$593.0 million in the year-earlier quarter. Revenues were US$11.38 billion, up 8.6% from US$10.47 billion the year before. Net premiums earned were US$9.00 billion versus US$8.15 billion in the prior-year quarter, an increase of 10.4%. Net investment income rose 8.6% to US$329.0 million from US$303.0 million a year ago.

Prospects: Our evaluation of Cigna Corp. as of Jan. 21, 2018 is the result of our systematic analysis on three basic characteristics: earnings strength, relative valuation, and recent stock price movement. The company has generated a negative trend in earnings per share over the past 5 quarters and while recent estimates for the company have been raised by analysts, CI has posted better than expected results. Based on operating earnings yield, the company is undervalued when compared to all of the companies in our coverage universe. Share price changes over the past year indicates that CI will perform well over the near term.

Financial Data

(US$ in Millions)	3 Mos	12/31/2017	12/31/2016	12/31/2015	12/31/2014	12/31/2013	12/31/2012	12/31/2011
Earnings Per Share	10.18	8.77	7.19	8.04	7.83	5.18	5.61	4.84
Cash Flow Per Share	18.71	16.29	15.72	10.61	7.56	2.57	8.23	5.51
Tang Book Value Per Share	32.99	31.03	30.14	23.45	18.46	16.47	13.18	18.14
Dividends Per Share	0.040	0.040	0.040	0.040	0.040	0.040	0.040	0.040
Dividend Payout %	0.39	0.46	0.56	0.50	0.51	0.77	0.71	0.83
Income Statement								
Premium Income	8,999	32,307	30,626	29,642	27,214	28,976	26,187	19,089
Total Revenue	11,380	41,616	39,668	37,876	34,914	32,380	29,119	21,998
Benefits & Claims	1,455	25,406	24,486	23,290	21,334	20,865	17,859	12,724
Income Before Taxes	1,218	3,606	2,979	3,327	3,304	2,176	2,477	1,968
Income Taxes	301	1,374	1,136	1,250	1,210	698	853	640
Net Income	915	2,237	1,867	2,094	2,102	1,476	1,623	1,327
Average Shares	245	255	259	260	268	284	289	274
Balance Sheet								
Total Assets	63,141	61,753	59,360	57,088	55,896	54,336	53,734	51,047
Total Liabilities	48,946	48,018	45,637	45,053	45,122	43,769	43,965	42,703
Stockholders' Equity	14,195	13,735	13,723	12,035	10,774	10,567	9,769	8,344
Shares Outstanding	243	243	256	256	259	275	285	285
Statistical Record								
Return on Assets %	4.11	3.69	3.20	3.71	3.81	2.73	3.09	2.74
Return on Equity %	17.97	16.29	14.46	18.36	19.70	14.52	17.87	17.71
Loss Ratio %	16.17	78.64	79.95	78.57	78.39	72.01	68.20	66.66
Net Margin %	8.04	5.38	4.71	5.53	6.02	4.56	5.57	6.03
Price Range	226.22-146.49	211.73-135.72	146.55-116.03	169.77-101.06	105.20-75.64	88.18-53.46	54.49-39.66	52.62-36.66
P/E Ratio	22.22-14.39	24.14-15.48	20.38-16.14	21.12-12.57	13.44-9.66	17.02-10.32	9.71-7.07	10.87-7.57
Average Yield %	0.02	0.02	0.03	0.03	0.04	0.06	0.09	0.09

Address: 900 Cottage Grove Road, Bloomfield, CT 06002
Telephone: 860-226-6000
Fax: 860-226-6741

Web Site: www.cigna.com
Officers: Isaiah Harris - Chairman David M. Cordani - President, Chief Executive Officer

Auditors: PricewaterhouseCoopers LLP
Investor Contact: 215-761-1414
Transfer Agents: Computershare Shareowner Services, Providence, RI

CIMAREX ENERGY CO

Exchange	Symbol	Price	52Wk Range	Yield	P/E
NYS	XEC	$101.74 (6/29/2018)	128.66-83.67	0.63	17.63

*7 Year Price Score 85.43   *NYSE Composite Index=100   *12 Month Price Score 88.96

Interim Earnings (Per Share)

Qtr.	Mar	Jun	Sep	Dec
2015	(4.84)	(6.47)	(8.21)	(6.78)
2016	(2.00)	(2.91)	(0.14)	0.42
2017	1.38	1.02	0.96	1.83
2018	1.96	...	...	...

Interim Dividends (Per Share)

Amt	Decl	Ex	Rec	Pay
0.08Q	09/01/2017	11/14/2017	11/15/2017	12/01/2017
0.08Q	12/08/2017	02/14/2018	02/15/2018	03/01/2018
0.16Q	02/23/2018	05/14/2018	05/15/2018	06/01/2018
0.16Q	05/11/2018	08/14/2018	08/15/2018	08/31/2018

Indicated Div: $0.64

Valuation Analysis   Institutional Holding

Forecast EPS	$7.32	No of Institutions
	(06/14/2018)	736
Market Cap	$9.7 Billion	Shares
Book Value	$2.8 Billion	113,993,520
Price/Book	3.53	% Held
Price/Sales	4.76	90.07

Business Summary: Production & Extraction (MIC: 9.1.1 SIC: 1311 NAIC: 211111)

Cimarex Energy is an independent oil and gas exploration and production company. Co.'s operations are mainly located in Oklahoma, Texas and New Mexico. Co.'s operations are focused in two main areas: the Permian Basin and the Mid-Continent region. Co.'s Permian Basin region encompasses west Texas and southeast New Mexico. Co.'s Mid-Continent region consists of Oklahoma and the Texas Panhandle. As of Dec 31 2017, Co.'s proved oil and gas reserves totaled 3.35 trillion cubic feet of natural gas equivalent, consisted of 1.61 trillion cubic feet of gas, and 137.2 million barrels of oil and 153.9 million barrels of natural gas liquids.

Recent Developments: For the quarter ended Mar 31 2018, net income increased 42.3% to US$186.3 million from US$131.0 million in the year-earlier quarter. Revenues were US$567.1 million, up 26.8% from US$447.2 million the year before. Operating income was US$250.7 million versus US$221.5 million in the prior-year quarter, an increase of 13.2%. Direct operating expenses rose 0.3% to US$126.3 million from US$125.9 million in the comparable period the year before. Indirect operating expenses increased 90.5% to US$190.2 million from US$99.8 million in the equivalent prior-year period.

Prospects: Our evaluation of Cimarex Energy Co as of Jan. 21, 2018 is the result of our systematic analysis on three basic characteristics: earnings strength, relative valuation, and recent stock price movement. The company has suffered a very negative trend in earnings per share over the past 5 quarters and while recent estimates for the company have been raised by analysts, XEC has posted better than expected results. Based on operating earnings yield, the company is about fairly valued when compared to all of the companies in our coverage universe. Share price changes over the past year indicates that XEC will perform very poorly over the near term.

Financial Data

(US$ in Thousands)	3 Mos	12/31/2017	12/31/2016	12/31/2015	12/31/2014	12/31/2013	12/31/2012	12/31/2011
Earnings Per Share	5.77	5.19	(4.62)	(25.92)	5.78	6.47	4.07	6.15
Cash Flow Per Share	13.13	11.73	6.40	7.44	18.90	15.53	14.03	15.06
Tang Book Value Per Share	22.33	20.41	18.29	22.96	44.30	39.03	32.96	28.44
Dividends Per Share	0.320	0.320	0.400	0.640	0.620	0.540	0.460	0.380
Dividend Payout %	5.55	6.17	...	...	10.73	8.35	11.30	6.18
Income Statement								
Total Revenue	567,134	1,918,249	1,257,345	1,452,619	2,424,176	1,998,051	1,623,938	1,757,889
EBITDA	388,099	1,179,900	(130,304)	(2,948,304)	1,648,862	1,533,030	1,088,609	1,238,496
Depn & Amortn	132,859	446,031	465,936	778,923	806,021	615,874	513,916	390,461
Income Before Taxes	243,267	681,996	(658,264)	(3,782,384)	805,901	893,700	560,550	841,481
Income Taxes	56,949	187,667	(227,215)	(1,373,436)	298,697	329,011	206,727	311,549
Net Income	186,318	494,329	(431,049)	(2,408,948)	507,204	564,689	353,823	529,932
Average Shares	93,737	93,509	93,379	92,992	85,810	85,409	85,034	86,232
Balance Sheet								
Current Assets	977,990	935,635	969,304	1,077,930	931,804	469,139	470,137	457,895
Total Assets	5,260,364	5,042,639	4,681,693	5,243,286	8,725,293	7,253,135	6,305,152	5,428,577
Current Liabilities	658,298	679,574	522,302	410,067	776,327	683,167	645,862	616,339
Long-Term Obligations	1,487,330	1,486,920	1,487,939	1,485,620	1,500,000	924,000	750,000	405,000
Total Liabilities	2,508,771	2,474,361	2,321,629	2,445,608	4,224,661	3,230,927	2,830,416	2,297,964
Stockholders' Equity	2,751,593	2,568,278	2,360,064	2,797,678	4,500,632	4,022,208	3,474,736	3,130,613
Shares Outstanding	95,433	95,437	95,123	94,820	87,592	87,152	86,595	85,774
Statistical Record								
Return on Assets %	11.39	10.17	N.M.	N.M.	6.35	8.33	6.01	10.83
Return on Equity %	22.15	20.06	N.M.	N.M.	11.90	15.06	10.68	18.46
EBITDA Margin %	68.43	61.51	N.M.	N.M.	68.02	76.73	67.04	70.45
Net Margin %	32.85	25.77	N.M.	N.M.	20.92	28.26	21.79	30.15
Asset Turnover	0.42	0.39	0.25	0.21	0.30	0.29	0.28	0.36
Current Ratio	1.49	1.38	1.86	2.63	1.20	0.69	0.73	0.74
Debt to Equity	0.54	0.58	0.63	0.53	0.33	0.23	0.22	0.13
Price Range	128.66-91.33	142.47-91.33	143.25-75.60	129.44-85.27	148.77-92.73	110.43-57.73	86.41-46.96	117.56-53.37
P/E Ratio	22.30-15.83	27.45-17.60	...	...	25.74-16.04	17.07-8.92	21.23-11.54	19.12-8.68
Average Yield %	0.30	0.28	0.35	0.58	0.51	0.67	0.74	0.45

Address: 1700 Lincoln Street, Suite 3700, Denver, CO 80203 Telephone: 303-295-3995	Web Site: www.cimarex.com Officers: Thomas E. Jorden - Chairman, Executive Vice President, President, Chief Executive Officer Krista L. Johnson - Division Officer	Auditors: KPMG LLP Investor Contact: 303-295-3995 Transfer Agents: Continental Stock Transfer & Trust Company, New York, NY

CINEMARK HOLDINGS INC

Exchange	Symbol	Price	52Wk Range	Yield	P/E
NYS	CNK	$35.08 (6/29/2018)	43.31-32.29	3.65	16.63

*7 Year Price Score 91.00   *NYSE Composite Index=100   *12 Month Price Score 96.25

Interim Earnings (Per Share)

Qtr.	Mar	Jun	Sep	Dec
2015	0.37	0.61	0.40	0.50
2016	0.50	0.46	0.56	0.66
2017	0.68	0.44	0.33	0.81
2018	0.53	...	...	...

Interim Dividends (Per Share)

Amt	Decl	Ex	Rec	Pay
0.29Q	08/10/2017	08/29/2017	08/31/2017	09/13/2017
0.29Q	11/17/2017	11/30/2017	12/01/2017	12/15/2017
0.32Q	02/23/2018	03/07/2018	03/08/2018	03/22/2018
0.32Q	05/25/2018	06/07/2018	06/08/2018	06/22/2018

Indicated Div: $1.28

Valuation Analysis   Institutional Holding

Forecast EPS	$2.21	No of Institutions
	(06/14/2018)	432
Market Cap	$4.1 Billion	Shares
Book Value	$1.5 Billion	135,103,520
Price/Book	2.81	% Held
Price/Sales	1.37	86.88

Business Summary: Entertainment (MIC: 2.3.2 SIC: 7832 NAIC: 512131)

Cinemark Holdings is a holding company. Through its subsidiaries, Co. is engaged in the motion picture exhibition industry, with theatres in the U. S., Brazil, Argentina, Chile, Colombia, Peru, Ecuador, Honduras, El Salvador, Nicaragua, Costa Rica, Panama, Guatemala, Bolivia, Curacao and Paraguay. At Dec 31 2017, Co. managed its business under two segments: U.S. markets and international markets. As of the same date, Co. operated 533 theatres and 5,959 screens in the U.S. and Latin America. Co. develops and expands new platforms and markets adaptive concepts for its theatre circuit, such as XD, Luxury Lounger recliner seats, Cinemark Reserve, motion seats, CineArts and other concepts.

Recent Developments: For the quarter ended Mar 31 2018, net income decreased 22.5% to US$62.2 million from US$80.2 million in the year-earlier quarter. Revenues were US$780.0 million, up 0.0% from US$779.6 million the year before. Operating income was US$102.2 million versus US$131.2 million in the prior-year quarter, a decrease of 22.1%. Direct operating expenses rose 2.1% to US$391.2 million from US$383.3 million in the comparable period the year before. Indirect operating expenses increased 8.1% to US$286.6 million from US$265.1 million in the equivalent prior-year period.

Prospects: Our evaluation of Cinemark Holdings Inc. as of Jan. 21, 2018 is the result of our systematic analysis on three basic characteristics: earnings strength, relative valuation, and recent stock price movement. The company has generated a negative trend in earnings per share over the past 5 quarters. However, while recent estimates for the company have been mixed, CNK has posted results that fell short of analysts expectations. Based on operating earnings yield, the company is undervalued when compared to all of the companies in our coverage universe. Share price changes over the past year indicates that CNK will perform in line with the market over the near term.

Financial Data

(US$ in Thousands)	3 Mos	12/31/2017	12/31/2016	12/31/2015	12/31/2014	12/31/2013	12/31/2012	12/31/2011
Earnings Per Share	2.11	2.26	2.19	1.87	1.66	1.28	1.47	1.14
Cash Flow Per Share	3.98	4.57	3.90	3.96	3.97	2.72	3.48	3.47
Dividends Per Share	1.190	1.160	1.080	1.000	1.000	0.920	0.840	0.840
Dividend Payout %	56.40	51.33	49.32	53.48	60.24	71.88	57.14	73.68
Income Statement								
Total Revenue	779,971	2,991,547	2,918,765	2,852,609	2,626,990	2,682,894	2,473,531	2,279,613
EBITDA	169,775	644,154	637,692	610,472	548,557	522,345	544,395	465,124
Depn & Amortn	61,281	235,093	207,091	186,898	173,138	160,071	143,394	150,149
Income Before Taxes	78,638	309,392	328,684	319,541	267,320	241,182	283,709	199,981
Income Taxes	25,097	79,358	103,819	128,939	96,064	113,316	125,398	73,050
Net Income	62,021	264,180	255,091	216,869	192,610	148,470	168,949	130,557
Average Shares	116,143	116,059	115,783	115,399	114,966	114,396	113,824	113,224
Balance Sheet								
Current Assets	591,740	657,570	676,317	715,151	741,010	729,599	845,161	627,118
Total Assets	4,413,471	4,470,893	4,306,633	4,126,497	4,151,980	4,144,163	3,863,226	3,522,408
Current Liabilities	387,349	468,913	443,225	439,793	414,407	395,712	338,204	305,027
Long-Term Obligations	2,021,098	2,031,522	2,016,722	1,981,882	2,016,552	2,025,453	1,893,571	1,691,633
Total Liabilities	2,953,529	3,077,098	3,044,815	3,026,789	3,039,180	3,050,741	2,779,161	2,509,531
Stockholders' Equity	1,459,942	1,393,795	1,261,818	1,099,708	1,112,800	1,093,422	1,084,065	1,012,877
Shares Outstanding	116,778	116,475	116,210	115,924	115,700	115,382	114,949	114,201
Statistical Record								
Return on Assets %	5.60	6.02	6.03	5.24	4.64	3.71	4.56	3.76
Return on Equity %	17.72	19.90	21.54	19.60	17.46	13.64	16.07	12.83
EBITDA Margin %	21.77	21.53	21.85	21.40	20.88	19.47	22.01	20.40
Net Margin %	7.95	8.83	8.74	7.60	7.33	5.53	6.83	5.73
Asset Turnover	0.68	0.68	0.69	0.69	0.63	0.67	0.67	0.66
Current Ratio	1.53	1.40	1.53	1.63	1.79	1.84	2.50	2.06
Debt to Equity	1.38	1.46	1.60	1.80	1.81	1.85	1.75	1.67
Price Range	44.46-32.29	44.58-32.29	42.23-27.15	45.52-31.56	36.37-27.73	34.17-25.98	27.20-18.04	21.75-16.82
P/E Ratio	21.07-15.30	19.73-14.29	19.28-12.40	24.34-16.88	21.91-16.70	26.70-20.30	18.50-12.27	19.08-14.75
Average Yield %	3.15	2.99	2.99	2.62	3.07	3.06	3.66	4.31

Address: 3900 Dallas Parkway, Suite 500, Plano, TX 75093 **Telephone:** 972-665-1000	**Web Site:** www.cinemark.com **Officers:** Lee Roy Mitchell - Chairman Mark Zoradi - Chief Executive Officer	**Auditors:** Deloitte & Touche LLP **Investor Contact:** 972-665-1500 **Transfer Agents:** Wells Fargo Shareholder Services

CITIGROUP INC

Exchange	Symbol	Price	52Wk Range	Yield	P/E
NYS	C	$66.92 (6/29/2018)	80.08-65.46	N/A	N/A

*7 Year Price Score 116.06 *NYSE Composite Index=100 *12 Month Price Score 94.12

Interim Earnings (Per Share)

Qtr.	Mar	Jun	Sep	Dec
2015	1.51	1.51	1.35	1.02
2016	1.10	1.24	1.24	1.14
2017	1.35	1.28	1.42	(7.03)
2018	1.68	...	...	...

Interim Dividends (Per Share)

Amt	Decl	Ex	Rec	Pay
0.32Q	07/19/2017	08/03/2017	08/07/2017	08/25/2017
0.32Q	10/18/2017	11/03/2017	11/06/2017	11/22/2017
0.32Q	01/18/2018	02/02/2018	02/05/2018	02/23/2018
0.32Q	04/25/2018	05/04/2018	05/07/2018	05/25/2018

Indicated Div: $1.28

Valuation Analysis — **Institutional Holding**

Forecast EPS	$6.56	No of Institutions	
	(06/19/2018)	2352	
Market Cap	$170.6 Billion	Shares	
Book Value	$201.9 Billion	2,696,652,032	
Price/Book	0.85	% Held	
Price/Sales	1.89	N/A	

Business Summary: Banking (MIC: 5.1.1 SIC: 6021 NAIC: 522110)

Citigroup is a financial services holding company, providing consumers, corporations, governments and institutions with a range of financial products and services. Co.'s activities are conducted through the: Global Consumer Banking, which provides traditional banking services to retail customers through retail banking, including commercial banking, and Citi-branded cards and Citi retail services; and Institutional Clients Group, which provides a range of wholesale banking products and services, including, among others, fixed income and equity sales and trading, and foreign exchange. As of Dec 31 2017, Co. had total assets of $1.84 trillion and total deposits of $960.00 billion.

Recent Developments: For the quarter ended Mar 31 2018, income from continuing operations increased 12.9% to US$4.65 billion from US$4.12 billion in the year-earlier quarter. Net income increased 13.2% to US$4.64 billion from US$4.10 billion in the year-earlier quarter. Net interest income increased 2.0% to US$11.17 billion from US$10.96 billion in the year-earlier quarter. Provision for loan losses was US$1.83 billion versus US$1.63 billion in the prior-year quarter, an increase of 12.2%. Non-interest income rose 3.9% to US$7.70 billion from US$7.41 billion, while non-interest expense advanced 1.8% to US$10.95 billion.

Prospects: Our evaluation of Citigroup Inc. as of Jan. 21, 2018 is the result of our systematic analysis on three basic characteristics: earnings strength, relative valuation, and recent stock price movement. The company has enjoyed a very positive trend in earnings per share over the past 5 quarters and while recent estimates for the company have been raised by analysts, C has posted better than expected results. Based on operating earnings yield, the company is undervalued when compared to all of the companies in our coverage universe. Share price changes over the past year indicates that C will perform well over the near term.

Financial Data

(US$ in Thousands)	3 Mos	12/31/2017	12/31/2016	12/31/2015	12/31/2014	12/31/2013	12/31/2012	12/31/2011
Earnings Per Share	(2.65)	(2.98)	4.72	5.40	2.20	4.35	2.44	3.63
Cash Flow Per Share	0.54	(3.18)	18.62	13.23	14.99	18.91	4.86	15.38
Tang Book Value Per Share	60.81	59.96	64.03	60.03	56.24	54.41	50.57	48.88
Dividends Per Share	1.120	0.960	0.420	0.160	0.040	0.040	0.040	0.030
Dividend Payout %	...	...	8.90	2.96	1.82	0.92	1.64	0.83
Income Statement								
Interest Income	16,332,000	61,204,000	57,615,000	58,551,000	61,683,000	62,970,000	68,138,000	72,681,000
Interest Expense	5,160,000	16,517,000	12,511,000	11,921,000	13,690,000	16,177,000	20,535,000	24,234,000
Net Interest Income	11,172,000	44,687,000	45,104,000	46,630,000	47,993,000	46,793,000	47,603,000	48,447,000
Provision for Losses	1,831,000	7,503,000	6,749,000	7,108,000	6,828,000	7,604,000	10,848,000	11,773,000
Non-Interest Income	7,700,000	26,762,000	24,771,000	29,724,000	28,889,000	29,573,000	22,570,000	29,906,000
Non-Interest Expense	10,951,000	41,185,000	41,649,000	44,420,000	55,690,000	49,265,000	51,389,000	51,956,000
Income Before Taxes	6,090,000	22,761,000	21,477,000	24,826,000	14,364,000	19,497,000	7,936,000	14,624,000
Income Taxes	1,441,000	29,388,000	6,444,000	7,440,000	6,864,000	5,867,000	27,000	3,521,000
Net Income	4,620,000	(6,798,000)	14,912,000	17,242,000	7,313,000	13,673,000	7,541,000	11,067,000
Average Shares	2,563,000	2,698,500	2,888,300	3,007,700	3,037,000	3,041,600	3,015,500	2,998,800
Balance Sheet								
Net Loans & Leases	660,584,000	654,679,000	612,309,000	604,991,000	628,641,000	645,824,000	630,009,000	617,127,000
Total Assets	1,922,104,000	1,842,465,000	1,792,077,000	1,731,210,000	1,842,530,000	1,880,382,000	1,864,660,000	1,873,878,000
Total Deposits	1,001,219,000	959,822,000	929,406,000	907,887,000	899,332,000	968,273,000	930,560,000	865,936,000
Total Liabilities	1,720,189,000	1,641,725,000	1,566,957,000	1,509,353,000	1,631,996,000	1,676,043,000	1,675,611,000	1,696,072,000
Stockholders' Equity	201,915,000	200,740,000	225,120,000	221,857,000	210,534,000	204,339,000	189,049,000	177,806,000
Shares Outstanding	2,549,934	2,569,909	2,772,392	2,953,279	3,023,918	3,029,243	3,028,884	2,923,878
Statistical Record								
Return on Assets %	N.M.	N.M.	0.84	0.96	0.39	0.73	0.40	0.58
Return on Equity %	N.M.	N.M.	6.65	7.98	3.53	6.95	4.10	6.49
Net Interest Margin %	68.41	73.01	78.29	79.64	77.81	74.31	69.86	66.66
Efficiency Ratio %	45.57	46.82	50.55	50.32	61.49	53.23	56.65	50.65
Loans to Deposits	0.66	0.68	0.66	0.67	0.70	0.67	0.68	0.71
Price Range	80.08-57.72	77.10-55.68	61.09-34.98	60.34-46.95	56.37-45.68	53.29-39.56	40.17-24.82	51.30-23.11
P/E Ratio	...	...	12.94-7.41	11.17-8.69	25.62-20.76	12.25-9.09	16.46-10.17	14.13-6.37
Average Yield %	1.61	1.46	0.91	0.39	0.30	0.08	0.12	0.08

Address: 388 Greenwich Street, New York, NY 10013 **Telephone:** 212-559-1000	**Web Site:** www.citigroup.com **Officers:** Michael E. O'Neill - Chairman Michael S. Helfer - Vice-Chairman, General Counsel, Corporate Secretary	**Auditors:** KPMG LLP **Investor Contact:** 212-559-2718 **Transfer Agents:** Computershare Trust Company, N.A., Providence, RI

CITIZENS FINANCIAL GROUP INC

Exchange	Symbol	Price	52Wk Range	Yield	P/E
NYS	CFG	$38.90 (6/29/2018)	47.87-32.08	2.26	11.37

*7 Year Price Score N/A   ***NYSE Composite Index=100**   ***12 Month Price Score 100.83**

Interim Earnings (Per Share)

Qtr.	Mar	Jun	Sep	Dec
2015	0.38	0.35	0.40	0.42
2016	0.41	0.46	0.56	0.55
2017	0.61	0.63	0.68	1.33
2018	0.78	...	...	...

Interim Dividends (Per Share)

Amt	Decl	Ex	Rec	Pay
0.18Q	07/19/2017	07/31/2017	08/02/2017	08/16/2017
0.18Q	10/18/2017	10/31/2017	11/01/2017	11/15/2017
0.22Q	01/18/2018	01/31/2018	02/01/2018	02/15/2018
0.22Q	04/18/2018	05/01/2018	05/02/2018	05/16/2018

Indicated Div: $0.88

Valuation Analysis

		Institutional Holding	
Forecast EPS	$3.45 (06/19/2018)	No of Institutions	740
Market Cap	$19.0 Billion	Shares	532,256,224
Book Value	$20.1 Billion	% Held	N/A
Price/Book	0.95		
Price/Sales	2.87		

Business Summary: Banking (MIC: 5.1.1 SIC: 6036 NAIC: 522120)

Citizens Financial Group is a bank holding company. Co.'s principal business activity is banking, conducted through its subsidiaries Citizens Bank, N.A. and Citizens Bank of Pennsylvania. Co. provides a set of banking products and services through its two operating segments, Consumer Banking and Commercial Banking. As of Dec 31 2017, Co. conducted its operations through approximately 1,150 branches operating in an 11-state footprint across the New England, Mid-Atlantic and Midwest regions and through its online, telephone and mobile banking platforms. As of Dec 31 2017, Co. had total assets of $152.34 billion and total deposits of $115.9 billion.

Recent Developments: For the quarter ended Mar 31 2018, net income increased 21.3% to US$388.0 million from US$320.0 million in the year-earlier quarter. Net interest income increased 8.6% to US$1.09 billion from US$1.01 billion in the year-earlier quarter. Provision for loan losses was US$78.0 million versus US$96.0 million in the prior-year quarter, a decrease of 18.8%. Non-interest income fell 2.1% to US$371.0 million from US$379.0 million, while non-interest expense advanced 3.4% to US$883.0 million.

Prospects: Our evaluation of Citizens Financial Group Inc as of Jan. 21, 2018 is the result of our systematic analysis on three basic characteristics: earnings strength, relative valuation, and recent stock price movement. The company has produced a positive trend in earnings per share over the past 5 quarters. Because the company lacks sufficient analyst estimate data, we place greater weight on the historical EPS trend as the measure of earnings strength. Based on operating earnings yield, the company is undervalued when compared to all of the companies in our coverage universe. Share price changes over the past year indicates that CFG will perform poorly over the near term.

Financial Data

(US$ in Thousands)	3 Mos	12/31/2017	12/31/2016	12/31/2015	12/31/2014	12/31/2013	12/31/2012	12/31/2011
Earnings Per Share	3.42	3.25	1.97	1.55	1.55	(6.12)	1.15	0.90
Cash Flow Per Share	3.56	3.75	2.85	2.29	2.50	4.73	3.05	4.43
Tang Book Value Per Share	26.51	26.76	24.66	23.73	22.70	22.00	22.89	...
Dividends Per Share	0.720	0.640	0.460	0.400	0.100	2.120	0.270	...
Dividend Payout %	21.05	19.69	23.35	25.81	6.45	...	23.48	...
Income Statement								
Interest Income	1,328,000	4,920,000	4,266,000	3,854,000	3,664,000	3,501,000	3,846,000	4,204
Interest Expense	237,000	747,000	508,000	452,000	363,000	443,000	619,000	884
Net Interest Income	1,091,000	4,173,000	3,758,000	3,402,000	3,301,000	3,058,000	3,227,000	3,320
Provision for Losses	78,000	321,000	369,000	302,000	319,000	479,000	413,000	882
Non-Interest Income	371,000	1,534,000	1,497,000	1,422,000	1,678,000	1,632,000	1,667,000	1,711
Non-Interest Expense	883,000	3,474,000	3,352,000	3,259,000	3,392,000	7,679,000	3,457,000	3,371 .
Income Before Taxes	501,000	1,912,000	1,534,000	1,263,000	1,268,000	(3,468,000)	1,024,000	778
Income Taxes	113,000	260,000	489,000	423,000	403,000	(42,000)	381,000	272
Net Income	388,000	1,652,000	1,045,000	840,000	865,000	(3,426,000)	643,000	506
Average Shares	489,266	503,685	523,930	538,220	557,724	559,998	559,998	559
Balance Sheet								
Net Loans & Leases	110,979,000	110,099,000	107,058,000	98,191,000	92,496,000	85,892,000	86,639,000	...
Total Assets	153,453,000	152,336,000	149,520,000	138,208,000	132,857,000	122,154,000	127,053,000	...
Total Deposits	115,730,000	115,089,000	109,804,000	102,539,000	95,707,000	86,903,000	95,148,000	...
Total Liabilities	133,394,000	132,066,000	129,773,000	118,562,000	113,589,000	102,958,000	102,924,000	...
Stockholders' Equity	20,059,000	20,270,000	19,747,000	19,646,000	19,268,000	19,196,000	24,129,000	...
Shares Outstanding	487,551	490,812	511,954	527,774	545,884	559,998	559,998	...
Statistical Record								
Return on Assets %	1.13	1.09	0.72	0.62	0.68	N.M.	...	...
Return on Equity %	8.62	8.26	5.29	4.32	4.50	N.M.	...	...
Net Interest Margin %	82.15	84.82	88.09	88.27	90.09	87.35	83.91	78.97
Efficiency Ratio %	51.97	53.83	58.16	61.77	63.50	149.60	62.71	56.99
Loans to Deposits	0.96	0.96	0.97	0.96	0.97	0.99	0.91	...
Price Range	47.87-32.08	42.63-32.08	36.46-18.14	28.32-22.63	25.51-21.80	...	...	...
P/E Ratio	14.00-9.38	13.12-9.87	18.51-9.21	18.27-14.60	16.46-14.06	...	...	...
Average Yield %	1.87	1.75	1.90	1.57	0.42	...	...	...

Address: One Citizens Plaza, Providence, RI 02903 **Telephone:** 401-456-7000 **Fax:** 401-455-5927	**Web Site:** www.citizensbank.com **Officers:** Bruce Van Saun - Chairman, Chief Executive Officer Mary Ellen Baker - Executive Vice President, Division Officer	**Auditors:** DELOITTE & TOUCHE LLP **Transfer Agents:** Common Stock is Computershare Trust Company, N.A.

CLEAN HARBORS INC

Exchange	Symbol	Price	52Wk Range	Yield	P/E
NYS	CLH	$55.55 (6/29/2018)	58.05-45.45	N/A	29.08

*7 Year Price Score 78.77   *NYSE Composite Index=100   *12 Month Price Score 97.00

TRADING VOLUME (thousand shares)

Interim Earnings (Per Share)

Qtr.	Mar	Jun	Sep	Dec
2015	(0.12)	0.18	0.69	0.02
2016	(0.36)	0.07	(0.18)	(0.22)
2017	(0.37)	0.45	0.21	1.47
2018	(0.22)	...	...	...

Interim Dividends (Per Share)

No Dividends Paid

Valuation Analysis	Institutional Holding	
Forecast EPS	$0.84	No of Institutions
	(06/12/2018)	372
Market Cap	$3.1 Billion	Shares
Book Value	$1.1 Billion	66,954,300
Price/Book	2.73	% Held
Price/Sales	1.04	95.00

Business Summary: Sanitation Services (MIC: 7.5.3 SIC: 4953 NAIC: 562112)

Clean Harbors is a provider of environmental, energy and industrial services throughout North America. Co. has six operating segments: Technical Services, which provides a range of hazardous material management services; Industrial and Field Services, which provides industrial and specialty services; Safety-Kleen, which provides a range of environmental services such as parts cleaning, containerized waste services, used oil collection, and other complementary products and services; Oil, Gas and Lodging Services, which provides fluid handling, surface rentals, seismic support services, directional boring services, as well as lodges and remote workforce accommodation facilities.

Recent Developments: For the quarter ended Mar 31 2018, net loss amounted to US$12.6 million versus a net loss of US$21.4 million in the year-earlier quarter. Revenues were US$749.8 million, up 8.8% from US$688.9 million the year before. Operating income was US$11.0 million versus US$5.4 million in the prior-year quarter, an increase of 102.3%. Direct operating expenses rose 10.0% to US$546.4 million from US$496.6 million in the comparable period the year before. Indirect operating expenses increased 2.9% to US$192.4 million from US$186.9 million in the equivalent prior-year period.

Prospects: Our evaluation of Clean Harbors Inc. as of Jan. 21, 2018 is the result of our systematic analysis on three basic characteristics: earnings strength, relative valuation, and recent stock price movement. The company has enjoyed a very positive trend in earnings per share over the past 5 quarters and while recent estimates for the company have been mixed, CLH has posted results that fell short of analysts expectations. Based on operating earnings yield, the company is overvalued when compared to all of the companies in our coverage universe. Share price changes over the past year indicates that CLH will perform poorly over the near term.

Financial Data

(US$ in Thousands)	3 Mos	12/31/2017	12/31/2016	12/31/2015	12/31/2014	12/31/2013	12/31/2012	12/31/2011
Earnings Per Share	1.91	1.76	(0.69)	0.76	(0.47)	1.57	2.40	2.39
Cash Flow Per Share	4.97	5.01	4.50	6.80	4.93	6.86	6.00	3.39
Tang Book Value Per Share	3.35	4.26	2.10	2.37	4.76	5.52	4.40	12.01
Income Statement								
Total Revenue	749,778	2,944,978	2,755,226	3,275,137	3,401,636	3,509,656	2,187,908	1,984,136
EBITDA	77,208	395,897	339,241	420,199	355,590	434,761	338,456	348,302
Depn & Amortn	66,516	251,400	247,000	234,000	239,400	212,500	163,439	124,235
Income Before Taxes	(9,578)	58,689	8,716	109,646	38,522	143,885	127,730	184,678
Income Taxes	3,053	(42,050)	48,589	65,544	66,850	48,319	(1,944)	57,426
Net Income	(12,631)	100,739	(39,873)	44,102	(28,328)	95,566	129,674	127,252
Average Shares	56,457	57,200	57,532	58,434	60,311	60,728	54,079	53,324
Balance Sheet								
Current Assets	1,079,822	1,154,056	1,092,871	921,196	1,126,433	1,171,179	1,086,793	891,868
Total Assets	3,684,816	3,706,570	3,681,920	3,431,428	3,704,278	3,953,678	3,825,806	2,085,803
Current Liabilities	524,684	503,817	504,668	517,120	572,471	639,545	569,052	381,742
Long-Term Obligations	1,625,259	1,625,537	1,633,272	1,382,543	1,395,000	1,401,435	1,402,879	530,578
Total Liabilities	2,539,290	2,518,368	2,597,679	2,335,146	2,441,407	2,478,039	2,393,734	1,184,816
Stockholders' Equity	1,145,526	1,188,202	1,084,241	1,096,282	1,262,871	1,475,639	1,432,072	900,987
Shares Outstanding	56,244	56,501	57,297	57,593	58,903	60,672	60,385	53,182
Statistical Record								
Return on Assets %	2.99	2.73	N.M.	1.24	N.M.	2.46	4.38	6.90
Return on Equity %	9.91	8.87	N.M.	3.74	N.M.	6.57	11.09	15.13
EBITDA Margin %	10.30	13.44	12.31	12.83	10.45	12.39	15.47	17.55
Net Margin %	N.M.	3.42	N.M.	1.35	N.M.	2.72	5.93	6.41
Asset Turnover	0.82	0.80	0.77	0.92	0.89	0.90	0.74	1.08
Current Ratio	2.06	2.29	2.17	1.78	1.97	1.83	1.91	2.34
Debt to Equity	1.42	1.37	1.51	1.26	1.10	0.95	0.98	0.59
Price Range	61.33-48.06	61.33-49.98	57.78-39.35	58.87-40.22	64.51-44.98	62.53-50.30	70.30-47.16	64.17-40.58
P/E Ratio	32.11-25.16	34.85-28.40	...	77.46-52.92	...	39.83-32.04	29.29-19.65	26.85-16.98

Address: 42 Longwater Drive, Norwell, MA 02061-9149 Telephone: 781-792-5000	Web Site: www.cleanharbors.com Officers: Alan S. McKim - Chairman, President, Chief Executive Officer Michael Louis Battles - Executive Vice President, Chief Financial Officer, Chief Accounting Officer, Corporate Controller, Senior Vice President	Auditors: DELOITTE & TOUCHE LLP Investor Contact: 617-542-5300 Transfer Agents: American Stock Transfer & Trust Company, New York, NY

CLOROX CO (THE)

Exchange	Symbol	Price	52Wk Range	Yield	P/E	Div Acheiver
NYS	CLX	$135.25 (6/29/2018)	149.69-114.80	2.84	22.10	41 Years

*7 Year Price Score 103.18 *NYSE Composite Index=100 *12 Month Price Score 93.01

Interim Earnings (Per Share)

Qtr.	Sep	Dec	Mar	Jun
2014-15	0.68	0.95	1.30	1.44
2015-16	1.33	1.13	1.23	1.25
2016-17	1.36	1.14	1.31	1.52
2017-18	1.46	1.77	1.37	...

Interim Dividends (Per Share)

Amt	Decl	Ex	Rec	Pay
0.84Q	09/12/2017	10/24/2017	10/25/2017	11/13/2017
0.84Q	11/14/2017	01/23/2018	01/24/2018	02/09/2018
0.96Q	02/13/2018	04/24/2018	04/25/2018	05/11/2018
0.96Q	05/21/2018	07/31/2018	08/01/2018	08/17/2018

Indicated Div: $3.84 (Div. Reinv. Plan)

Valuation Analysis

		Institutional Holding	
Forecast EPS	$6.17	No of Institutions	
	(06/14/2018)	1289	
Market Cap	$17.5 Billion	Shares	
Book Value	$837.0 Million	127,535,672	
Price/Book	20.92	% Held	
Price/Sales	2.88	71.52	

Business Summary: Household & Personal Products (MIC: 1.7.1 SIC: 2842 NAIC: 325612)

Clorox is a manufacturer and marketer of consumer products. Co. sells its products via mass retail and grocery outlets, warehouse, clubs, and e-commerce channels, among others. Co. markets consumer brand names, including its namesake bleach and cleaning products, Pine-Sol® cleaners, Liquid-Plumr® clog removers, Poett® home care products, Fresh Step® cat litter, Glad® bags, wraps and container products, Kingsford® and Match Light® charcoal, RenewLife® digestive health products, Hidden Valley® dressings and sauces, Brita® water-filtration products, and Burt's Bees® personal care products. Co. also markets to services channels, including infection control products for the healthcare industry.

Recent Developments: For the quarter ended Mar 31 2018, income from continuing operations increased 5.2% to US$181.0 million from US$172.0 million in the year-earlier quarter. Net income increased 5.2% to US$181.0 million from US$172.0 million in the year-earlier quarter. Revenues were US$1.52 billion, up 2.7% from US$1.48 billion the year before. Direct operating expenses rose 5.0% to US$868.0 million from US$827.0 million in the comparable period the year before. Indirect operating expenses increased 1.0% to US$407.0 million from US$403.0 million in the equivalent prior-year period.

Prospects: Our evaluation of Clorox Co. as of Jan. 21, 2018 is the result of our systematic analysis on three basic characteristics: earnings strength, relative valuation, and recent stock price movement. The company has generated a negative trend in earnings per share over the past 5 quarters and while recent estimates for the company have been raised by analysts, CLX has posted better than expected results. Based on operating earnings yield, the company is about fairly valued when compared to all of the companies in our coverage universe. Share price changes over the past year indicates that CLX will perform well over the near term.

Financial Data

(US$ in Thousands)	9 Mos	6 Mos	3 Mos	06/30/2017	06/30/2016	06/30/2015	06/30/2014	06/30/2013
Earnings Per Share	6.12	6.06	5.43	5.33	4.92	4.37	4.23	4.30
Cash Flow Per Share	7.40	7.11	7.41	6.73	5.99	6.71	5.92	5.91
Dividends Per Share	3.320	3.280	3.240	3.200	3.080	2.960	2.840	2.560
Dividend Payout %	54.25	54.13	59.67	60.04	62.60	67.73	67.14	59.53
Income Statement								
Total Revenue	4,433,000	2,916,000	1,500,000	5,973,000	5,761,000	5,655,000	5,591,000	5,623,000
EBITDA	930,000	628,000	340,000	1,261,000	1,216,000	1,154,000	1,116,000	1,124,000
Depn & Amortn	121,000	81,000	40,000	163,000	165,000	165,000	169,000	171,000
Income Before Taxes	748,000	506,000	279,000	1,014,000	968,000	893,000	847,000	834,000
Income Taxes	142,000	81,000	87,000	330,000	335,000	315,000	299,000	279,000
Net Income	606,000	425,000	192,000	701,000	648,000	580,000	558,000	572,000
Average Shares	131,900	131,655	131,509	131,566	131,717	132,776	131,742	132,969
Balance Sheet								
Current Assets	2,373,000	1,680,000	1,520,000	1,514,000	1,485,000	1,429,000	1,395,000	1,420,000
Total Assets	5,444,000	4,758,000	4,600,000	4,573,000	4,518,000	4,164,000	4,258,000	4,311,000
Current Liabilities	2,013,000	1,380,000	1,376,000	1,809,000	1,558,000	1,405,000	1,638,000	1,134,000
Long-Term Obligations	1,789,000	1,788,000	1,787,000	1,391,000	1,797,000	1,796,000	1,595,000	2,170,000
Total Liabilities	4,607,000	3,998,000	4,008,000	4,031,000	4,221,000	4,046,000	4,104,000	4,165,000
Stockholders' Equity	837,000	760,000	592,000	542,000	297,000	118,000	154,000	146,000
Shares Outstanding	129,489	129,348	128,923	129,014	129,355	128,614	128,796	130,366
Statistical Record								
Return on Assets %	16.02	17.11	15.75	15.42	14.89	13.77	13.02	13.20
Return on Equity %	130.06	154.95	162.09	167.10	311.44	426.47	372.00	10,400.00
EBITDA Margin %	20.98	21.54	22.67	21.11	21.11	20.41	19.96	19.99
Net Margin %	13.67	14.57	12.80	11.74	11.25	10.26	9.98	10.17
Asset Turnover	1.21	1.30	1.33	1.31	1.32	1.34	1.30	1.30
Current Ratio	1.18	1.22	1.10	0.84	0.95	1.02	0.85	1.25
Debt to Equity	2.14	2.35	3.02	2.57	6.05	15.22	10.36	14.86
Price Range	149.69-124.22	149.69-118.72	141.15-112.25	141.15-112.25	138.39-104.02	111.93-86.39	95.83-81.49	89.53-70.10
P/E Ratio	24.46-20.30	24.70-19.59	25.99-20.67	26.48-21.06	28.13-21.14	25.61-19.77	22.65-19.26	20.82-16.30
Average Yield %	2.46	2.45	2.51	2.49	2.50	2.91	3.23	3.27

Address: 1221 Broadway, Oakland, CA 94612-1888	Web Site: www.thecloroxcompany.com	Auditors: Ernst & Young LLP
Telephone: 510-271-7000	Officers: Benno O. Dorer - Chairman, Chief Executive Officer, Executive Vice President, Senior Vice President, Division Officer Kevin Jacobsen - Senior Vice President, Chief Financial Officer	Transfer Agents: Computershare, Providence, RI

CMS ENERGY CORP

Exchange	Symbol	Price	52Wk Range	Yield	P/E	Div Acheiver
NYS	CMS	$47.28 (6/29/2018)	50.55-41.77	3.02	26.41	10 Years

*7 Year Price Score 110.59 *NYSE Composite Index=100 *12 Month Price Score 96.61

Interim Earnings (Per Share)

Qtr.	Mar	Jun	Sep	Dec
2015	0.73	0.25	0.53	0.38
2016	0.59	0.45	0.67	0.28
2017	0.71	0.33	0.61	(0.01)
2018	0.86	...	...	...

Interim Dividends (Per Share)

Amt	Decl	Ex	Rec	Pay
0.333Q	07/20/2017	08/02/2017	08/04/2017	08/31/2017
0.333Q	10/19/2017	11/02/2017	11/03/2017	11/30/2017
0.357Q	02/05/2018	02/15/2018	02/16/2018	02/28/2018
0.357Q	04/19/2018	05/03/2018	05/04/2018	05/31/2018

Indicated Div: $1.43

Valuation Analysis — **Institutional Holding**

Forecast EPS	$2.33
	(06/14/2018)
Market Cap	$13.4 Billion
Book Value	$4.6 Billion
Price/Book	2.91
Price/Sales	1.99

No of Institutions 750
Shares 320,788,224
% Held 91.20

Business Summary: Electric Utilities (MIC: 3.1.1 SIC: 4931 NAIC: 221119)

CMS Energy is a holding company. Co. has several subsidiaries, including Consumers Energy Company (Consumers), an electric and gas utility, and CMS Enterprises Company (CMS Enterprises), primarily a domestic independent power producer. Consumers serves individuals and businesses operating in the alternative energy, automotive, chemical, metal, and food products industries, as well as a group of other industries. CMS Enterprises, through its subsidiaries and equity investments, is engaged primarily in independent power production and owns power generation facilities fueled mostly by natural gas and renewable sources. Co. has three segments: electric utility, gas utility, and enterprises.

Recent Developments: For the quarter ended Mar 31 2018, net income increased 21.1% to US$241.0 million from US$199.0 million in the year-earlier quarter. Revenues were US$1.95 billion, up 6.8% from US$1.83 billion the year before. Operating income was US$363.0 million versus US$388.0 million in the prior-year quarter, a decrease of 6.4%. Direct operating expenses rose 11.5% to US$1.22 billion from US$1.10 billion in the comparable period the year before. Indirect operating expenses increased 6.7% to US$366.0 million from US$343.0 million in the equivalent prior-year period.

Prospects: Our evaluation of CMS Energy Corp. as of Jan. 21, 2018 is the result of our systematic analysis on three basic characteristics: earnings strength, relative valuation, and recent stock price movement. The company has managed to produce a neutral trend in earnings per share over the past 5 quarters and while recent estimates for the company have remained steady, CMS has posted better than expected results. Based on operating earnings yield, the company is undervalued when compared to all of the companies in our coverage universe. Share price changes over the past year indicates that CMS will perform very well over the near term.

Financial Data

(US$ in Millions)	3 Mos	12/31/2017	12/31/2016	12/31/2015	12/31/2014	12/31/2013	12/31/2012	12/31/2011
Earnings Per Share	1.79	1.64	1.98	1.89	1.74	1.66	1.42	1.58
Cash Flow Per Share	6.28	6.09	5.85	5.95	5.35	5.37	4.75	4.66
Tang Book Value Per Share	16.27	15.77	15.23	14.21	13.34	12.98	12.10	11.92
Dividends Per Share	1.355	1.330	1.240	1.160	1.080	1.020	0.960	0.840
Dividend Payout %	75.70	81.10	62.63	61.38	62.07	61.45	67.61	53.16
Income Statement								
Total Revenue	1,953	6,583	6,399	6,456	7,179	6,566	6,253	6,503
EBITDA	666	2,178	2,053	1,916	1,801	1,766	1,587	1,549
Depn & Amortn	279	881	811	750	685	628	598	546
Income Before Taxes	278	871	813	782	714	743	605	597
Income Taxes	40	424	273	271	250	302	245	191
Net Income	241	460	551	523	477	452	382	415
Average Shares	282	280	278	276	274	271	268	263
Balance Sheet								
Current Assets	2,207	2,475	2,280	2,320	2,597	2,526	2,422	2,565
Total Assets	22,868	23,050	21,622	20,340	19,185	17,416	17,131	16,452
Current Liabilities	2,482	2,784	2,655	2,302	2,014	1,945	1,797	2,338
Long-Term Obligations	9,082	9,214	8,750	8,559	8,139	7,239	6,863	6,207
Total Liabilities	18,272	18,609	17,369	16,402	15,515	13,962	13,937	13,424
Stockholders' Equity	4,596	4,441	4,253	3,938	3,670	3,454	3,194	3,028
Shares Outstanding	282	281	279	277	275	266	264	254
Statistical Record								
Return on Assets %	2.26	2.06	2.62	2.65	2.61	2.62	2.27	2.59
Return on Equity %	11.20	10.58	13.42	13.75	13.39	13.60	12.25	14.26
EBITDA Margin %	34.10	33.09	32.08	29.68	25.09	26.90	25.38	23.82
Net Margin %	12.34	6.99	8.61	8.10	6.64	6.88	6.11	6.38
Asset Turnover	0.30	0.29	0.30	0.33	0.39	0.38	0.37	0.41
Current Ratio	0.89	0.89	0.86	1.01	1.29	1.30	1.35	1.10
Debt to Equity	1.98	2.07	2.06	2.17	2.22	2.10	2.15	2.05
Price Range	50.55-41.77	50.55-41.51	46.17-35.61	38.20-31.39	36.42-26.12	29.94-24.38	24.81-21.33	22.35-17.16
P/E Ratio	28.24-23.34	30.82-25.31	23.32-17.98	20.21-16.61	20.93-15.01	18.04-14.69	17.47-15.02	14.15-10.86
Average Yield %	2.92	2.87	2.99	3.35	3.60	3.77	4.16	4.26

Address: One Energy Plaza, Jackson, MI 49201	Web Site: www.cmsenergy.com	Auditors: PricewaterhouseCoopers LLP
Telephone: 517-788-0550	Officers: John G. Russell - Chairman, President, Chief Executive Officer Patricia K. Poppe - President, Chief Executive Officer, Division Officer	Investor Contact: 517-788-1868 Transfer Agents: Investor Services Department, Jackson, MI

CNA FINANCIAL CORP

Exchange	Symbol	Price	52Wk Range	Yield	P/E
NYS	CNA	$45.68 (6/29/2018)	55.08-45.21	2.63	13.36

*7 Year Price Score 109.90 *NYSE Composite Index=100 *12 Month Price Score 92.77

Interim Earnings (Per Share)

Qtr.	Mar	Jun	Sep	Dec
2015	0.86	0.51	0.66	(0.26)
2016	0.25	0.77	1.26	0.89
2017	0.96	1.00	0.53	0.82
2018	1.07	...	...	...

Interim Dividends (Per Share)

Amt	Decl	Ex	Rec	Pay
0.30Q	10/30/2017	11/10/2017	11/13/2017	11/29/2017
2.00Sp	02/12/2018	02/23/2018	02/26/2018	03/14/2018
0.30Q	02/12/2018	02/23/2018	02/26/2018	03/14/2018
0.30Q	04/30/2018	05/11/2018	05/14/2018	05/30/2018

Indicated Div: $1.20

Valuation Analysis

		Institutional Holding	
Forecast EPS	$4.17 (06/13/2018)	No of Institutions	300
Market Cap	$12.4 Billion	Shares	275,904,320
Book Value	$11.4 Billion		
Price/Book	1.09	% Held	99.33
Price/Sales	1.27		

Business Summary: General Insurance (MIC: 5.2.1 SIC: 6331 NAIC: 524126)

CNA Financial is an insurance holding company. Co.'s insurance products include commercial property and casualty coverages, including surety. Co.'s services include risk management, information services, warranty and claims administration. Co.'s products and services are marketed through independent agents, brokers and managing general underwriters to a range of customers, including businesses, insurance companies, and other groups. Co.'s core business, commercial property and casualty insurance operations are reported in three segments: Specialty, Commercial and International. Co.'s non-core businesses are managed in two segments: Life & Group Non-Core and Corporate & Other Non-Core.

Recent Developments: For the quarter ended Mar 31 2018, net income increased 11.9% to US$291.0 million from US$260.0 million in the year-earlier quarter. Revenues were US$2.54 billion, up 8.8% from US$2.33 billion the year before. Net premiums earned were US$1.79 billion versus US$1.65 billion in the prior-year quarter, an increase of 8.5%. Net investment income fell 10.1% to US$490.0 million from US$545.0 million a year ago.

Prospects: Our evaluation of CNA Financial Corp. as of Jan. 21, 2018 is the result of our systematic analysis on three basic characteristics: earnings strength, relative valuation, and recent stock price movement. The company has suffered a very negative trend in earnings per share over the past 5 quarters. However, while recent estimates for the company have been mixed, CNA has posted better than expected results. Based on operating earnings yield, the company is undervalued when compared to all of the companies in our coverage universe. Share price changes over the past year indicates that CNA will perform well over the near term.

Financial Data
(US$ in Thousands)

	3 Mos	12/31/2017	12/31/2016	12/31/2015	12/31/2014	12/31/2013	12/31/2012	12/31/2011
Earnings Per Share	3.42	3.30	3.17	1.77	2.55	3.47	2.33	2.28
Cash Flow Per Share	4.38	4.63	5.22	5.13	5.34	4.46	4.63	6.32
Tang Book Value Per Share	41.55	44.60	43.71	42.94	46.83	46.33	45.14	42.40
Dividends Per Share	3.150	3.100	3.000	3.000	2.000	0.800	0.600	0.400
Dividend Payout %	92.11	93.94	94.64	169.49	78.43	23.05	25.75	17.54
Income Statement								
Premium Income	1,785,000	6,988,000	6,924,000	6,921,000	7,212,000	7,271,000	6,882,000	6,603,000
Total Revenue	2,535,000	9,542,000	9,366,000	9,101,000	9,692,000	10,113,000	9,547,000	8,947,000
Benefits & Claims	...	5,310,000	5,283,000	5,384,000	5,591,000	5,947,000	5,896,000	5,489,000
Income Before Taxes	346,000	1,310,000	1,137,000	549,000	1,207,000	1,313,000	872,000	877,000
Income Taxes	55,000	411,000	278,000	70,000	319,000	376,000	244,000	246,000
Net Income	291,000	899,000	859,000	479,000	691,000	937,000	628,000	614,000
Average Shares	272,400	272,100	271,100	270,700	270,600	270,200	269,800	269,600
Balance Sheet								
Total Assets	57,649,000	56,567,000	55,233,000	55,047,000	55,566,000	57,194,000	58,522,000	55,179,000
Total Liabilities	46,224,000	44,323,000	43,264,000	43,291,000	42,772,000	44,543,000	46,208,000	43,622,000
Stockholders' Equity	11,425,000	12,244,000	11,969,000	11,756,000	12,794,000	12,651,000	12,314,000	11,557,000
Shares Outstanding	271,371	271,205	270,495	270,274	269,980	269,717	269,399	269,274
Statistical Record								
Return on Assets %	1.65	1.61	1.55	0.87	1.23	1.62	1.10	1.11
Return on Equity %	8.05	7.43	7.22	3.90	5.43	7.51	5.25	5.46
Loss Ratio %	...	75.99	76.30	77.79	77.52	81.79	85.67	83.13
Net Margin %	11.48	9.42	9.17	5.26	7.13	9.27	6.58	6.86
Price Range	55.08-43.30	54.98-40.21	42.07-28.21	43.40-34.24	43.08-36.29	42.89-28.01	30.67-25.91	31.04-21.58
P/E Ratio	16.11-12.66	16.66-12.18	13.27-8.90	24.52-19.34	16.89-14.23	12.36-8.07	13.16-11.12	13.61-9.46
Average Yield %	6.28	6.49	8.96	7.82	5.01	2.27	2.14	1.48

Address: 333 S. Wabash, Chicago, IL 60604
Telephone: 312-822-5000
Fax: 312-822-6419

Web Site: www.cna.com
Officers: Dino E. Robusto - Chairman, Chief Executive Officer James Anderson - Senior Vice President, Executive Vice President, Chief Financial Officer

Auditors: Deloitte & Touche LLP
Investor Contact: 312-822-4278
Transfer Agents: Wells Fargo Bank, N.A., St. Paul, MN

CNX RESOURCES CORP

Exchange	Symbol	Price	52Wk Range	Yield	P/E
NYS	CNX	$17.78 (6/29/2018)	17.90-11.70	N/A	4.26

*7 Year Price Score 51.72   *NYSE Composite Index=100   *12 Month Price Score 112.09

Interim Earnings (Per Share)

Qtr.	Mar	Jun	Sep	Dec
2015	0.34	(2.64)	0.52	0.13
2016	(0.43)	(2.05)	0.11	(1.34)
2017	(0.17)	0.73	(0.11)	1.20
2018	2.35			

Interim Dividends (Per Share)

Dividend Payment Suspended

Valuation Analysis   Institutional Holding

Forecast EPS	$0.70	No of Institutions
	(06/12/2018)	486
Market Cap	$3.9 Billion	Shares
Book Value	$4.3 Billion	248,171,456
Price/Book	0.89	% Held
Price/Sales	3.10	98.17

Business Summary: Production & Extraction (MIC: 9.1.1 SIC: 1311 NAIC: 211111)

CNX Resources is an energy company operated through two primary divisions, Exploration and Production (E&P) and Pennsylvania (PA) Mining Operations. The E&P division is focused on Appalachian area natural gas and liquids activities, including production, gathering, processing and acquisition of natural gas properties in the Appalachian Basin. The PA Mining Operations division is focused on the extraction and preparation of coal, also in the Appalachian Basin. As of Dec 31 2017, Co. had total proved developed and undeveloped reserves of 7.58 trillion cubic feet equivalent.

Recent Developments: For the quarter ended Mar 31 2018, income from continuing operations was US$545.5 million compared with a loss of US$91.0 million in the year-earlier quarter. Net income amounted to US$545.5 million versus a net loss of US$39.0 million in the year-earlier quarter. Revenues were US$495.7 million, up 54.9% from US$319.9 million the year before. Direct operating expenses rose 11.3% to US$149.4 million from US$134.2 million in the comparable period the year before. Indirect operating expenses decreased 38.4% to US$174.4 million from US$283.3 million in the equivalent prior-year period.

Prospects: Our evaluation of CNX Resources Corp. as of Jan. 21, 2018 is the result of our systematic analysis on three basic characteristics: earnings strength, relative valuation, and recent stock price movement. The company has generated a negative trend in earnings per share over the past 5 quarters. However, while recent estimates for the company have been mixed, CNX has posted results that fell short of analysts expectations. Based on operating earnings yield, the company is overvalued when compared to all of the companies in our coverage universe. Share price changes over the past year indicates that CNX will perform poorly over the near term.

Financial Data
(US$ in Thousands)

	3 Mos	12/31/2017	12/31/2016	12/31/2015	12/31/2014	12/31/2013	12/31/2012	12/31/2011
Earnings Per Share	4.17	1.65	(3.70)	(1.64)	0.70	2.87	1.70	2.76
Cash Flow Per Share	3.17	2.83	2.04	2.21	4.07	2.88	3.19	6.74
Tang Book Value Per Share	15.65	17.43	16.55	20.53	23.14	21.85	17.33	15.90
Dividends Per Share	...	...	0.010	0.145	0.250	0.375	0.625	0.425
Dividend Payout %	...	...	...	...	35.71	13.07	36.76	15.40
Income Statement								
Total Revenue	495,729	1,455,131	2,026,375	3,114,401	3,726,804	3,299,685	5,430,307	6,117,242
EBITDA	799,713	692,060	264,024	349,970	977,879	726,395	1,344,772	1,662,302
Depn & Amortn	1,922	412,036	598,503	649,601	571,191	461,122	627,438	626,005
Income Before Taxes	759,240	118,581	(525,955)	(498,900)	183,124	46,075	497,274	787,953
Income Taxes	213,694	(176,458)	10,010	(134,425)	14,347	(33,189)	109,201	155,456
Net Income	527,563	380,747	(848,102)	(374,885)	163,090	660,442	388,470	632,497
Average Shares	224,182	230,951	229,387	229,186	231,580	230,077	229,141	229,003
Balance Sheet								
Current Assets	406,944	852,504	626,139	804,763	1,166,350	1,445,592	1,539,094	1,897,977
Total Assets	8,122,229	6,931,913	9,183,981	10,929,902	11,759,530	11,393,667	12,670,909	12,525,700
Current Liabilities	437,671	441,679	940,014	1,680,937	1,147,961	1,119,971	1,387,099	1,388,397
Long-Term Obligations	2,229,776	2,207,373	2,762,069	2,748,205	3,275,878	3,163,559	3,174,586	3,177,423
Total Liabilities	3,777,988	3,032,014	5,385,586	6,227,875	6,430,072	6,387,378	8,717,117	8,914,815
Stockholders' Equity	4,344,241	3,899,899	3,798,395	4,702,027	5,329,458	5,006,289	3,953,792	3,610,885
Shares Outstanding	218,639	223,743	229,443	229,054	230,265	229,145	228,094	227,056
Statistical Record								
Return on Assets %	10.90	4.73	N.M.	N.M.	1.41	5.49	3.08	5.14
Return on Equity %	23.11	9.89	N.M.	N.M.	3.16	14.74	10.24	19.30
EBITDA Margin %	161.32	47.56	13.03	11.24	26.24	22.01	24.76	27.17
Net Margin %	106.42	26.17	N.M.	N.M.	4.38	20.02	7.15	10.34
Asset Turnover	0.15	0.18	0.20	0.27	0.32	0.27	0.43	0.50
Current Ratio	0.93	1.93	0.67	0.48	1.02	1.29	1.11	1.37
Debt to Equity	0.51	0.57	0.73	0.58	0.61	0.63	0.80	0.88
Price Range	17.90-11.35	16.30-11.35	18.39-4.16	28.64-5.42	39.58-26.80	32.05-22.11	32.84-22.35	46.28-26.44
P/E Ratio	4.29-2.72	9.88-6.88	...	...	56.54-38.28	11.17-7.70	19.32-13.15	16.77-9.58
Average Yield %	...	...	0.08	0.85	0.75	1.35	2.29	1.10

Address: CNX Center, 1000 CONSOL Energy Drive, Suite 400, Canonsburg, PA 15317-6506
Telephone: 724-485-4000

Web Site: www.cnx.com
Officers: William N. Thorndike - Chairman Nicholas J. DeIuliis - President, Chief Executive Officer, Executive Vice President, Chief Operating Officer

Auditors: Ernst & Young LLP
Investor Contact: 724-485-3157
Transfer Agents: ComputerShare, College Station, TX

COCA-COLA CO (THE)

Exchange	Symbol	Price	52Wk Range	Yield	P/E	Div Acheiver
NYS	KO	$43.86 (6/29/2018)	48.53-41.55	3.56	129.00	55 Years

*7 Year Price Score 88.61   *NYSE Composite Index=100   *12 Month Price Score 94.39

TRADING VOLUME (thousand shares)

Interim Earnings (Per Share)

Qtr.	Mar	Jun	Sep	Dec
2015	0.35	0.71	0.33	0.28
2016	0.34	0.79	0.24	0.12
2017	0.27	0.32	0.33	(0.63)
2018	0.32	...	...	...

Interim Dividends (Per Share)

Amt	Decl	Ex	Rec	Pay
0.37Q	07/20/2017	09/14/2017	09/15/2017	10/02/2017
0.37Q	10/19/2017	11/30/2017	12/01/2017	12/15/2017
0.39Q	02/15/2018	03/14/2018	03/15/2018	04/02/2018
0.39Q	04/26/2018	06/14/2018	06/15/2018	07/02/2018

Indicated Div: $1.56 (Div. Reinv. Plan)

Valuation Analysis   Institutional Holding

Forecast EPS	$2.08	No of Institutions
	(06/14/2018)	2674
Market Cap	$186.8 Billion	Shares
Book Value	$19.6 Billion	3,336,877,824
Price/Book	9.53	% Held
Price/Sales	5.51	60.01

Business Summary: Beverages (MIC: 1.2.2 SIC: 2086 NAIC: 312111)

Coca-Cola is a beverage company. Co. owns or licenses and markets nonalcoholic beverage brands including sparkling beverages and a variety of still beverages such as waters, flavored waters and enhanced waters, juices and juice drinks, ready-to-drink teas and coffees, sports drinks, dairy, and energy drinks. Co.'s nonalcoholic sparkling beverage brands include Coca-Cola and Sprite. Co. markets, manufactures and sells beverage concentrates and syrups, including fountain syrups; and finished sparkling and still beverages. Co.'s operating structure consists of the following operating segments: Europe, Middle East and Africa; Latin America; North America; Asia Pacific; and Bottling Investments.

Recent Developments: For the quarter ended Mar 30 2018, income from continuing operations increased 12.1% to US$1.33 billion from US$1.18 billion in the year-earlier quarter. Net income increased 18.2% to US$1.40 billion from US$1.18 billion in the year-earlier quarter. Revenues were US$7.63 billion, down 16.4% from US$9.12 billion the year before. Operating income was US$1.81 billion versus US$1.96 billion in the prior-year quarter, a decrease of 7.7%. Direct operating expenses declined 22.1% to US$2.74 billion from US$3.51 billion in the comparable period the year before. Indirect operating expenses decreased 15.5% to US$3.08 billion from US$3.64 billion in the equivalent prior-year period.

Prospects: Our evaluation of Coca-Cola Co as of Jan. 21, 2018 is the result of our systematic analysis on three basic characteristics: earnings strength, relative valuation, and recent stock price movement. The company has enjoyed a very positive trend in earnings per share over the past 5 quarters and while recent estimates for the company have been mixed, KO has posted better than expected results. Based on operating earnings yield, the company is about fairly valued when compared to all of the companies in our coverage universe. Share price changes over the past year indicates that KO will perform in line with the market over the near term.

Financial Data

(US$ in Thousands)	3 Mos	12/31/2017	12/31/2016	12/31/2015	12/31/2014	12/31/2013	12/31/2012	12/31/2011
Earnings Per Share	0.34	0.29	1.49	1.67	1.60	1.90	1.97	1.85
Cash Flow Per Share	1.60	1.64	2.03	2.42	2.42	2.38	2.36	2.07
Tang Book Value Per Share	0.61	0.10	0.45	0.33	0.90	1.26	1.22	0.88
Dividends Per Share	1.500	1.480	1.400	1.320	1.220	1.120	1.020	0.940
Dividend Payout %	441.18	510.34	93.96	79.04	76.25	58.95	51.78	50.95
Income Statement								
Total Revenue	7,626,000	35,410,000	41,863,000	44,294,000	45,998,000	46,854,000	48,017,000	46,542,000
EBITDA	2,026,000	7,021,000	8,989,000	11,112,000	10,181,000	12,547,000	12,639,000	12,355,000
Depn & Amortn	270,000	1,186,000	1,597,000	1,753,000	1,736,000	1,743,000	1,723,000	1,672,000
Income Before Taxes	1,691,000	5,671,000	7,301,000	9,116,000	8,556,000	10,875,000	10,990,000	10,749,000
Income Taxes	506,000	5,560,000	1,586,000	2,239,000	2,201,000	2,851,000	2,723,000	2,805,000
Net Income	1,368,000	1,248,000	6,527,000	7,351,000	7,098,000	8,584,000	9,019,000	8,572,000
Average Shares	4,305,999	4,323,999	4,366,999	4,404,999	4,449,999	4,508,999	4,583,999	4,645,999
Balance Sheet								
Current Assets	38,042,000	36,545,000	34,010,000	33,395,000	32,986,000	31,304,000	30,328,000	25,497,000
Total Assets	93,282,000	87,896,000	87,270,000	90,093,000	92,023,000	90,055,000	86,174,000	79,974,000
Current Liabilities	31,480,000	27,194,000	26,532,000	26,930,000	32,374,000	27,811,000	27,821,000	24,283,000
Long-Term Obligations	29,792,000	31,182,000	29,684,000	28,407,000	19,063,000	19,154,000	14,736,000	13,656,000
Total Liabilities	73,672,000	70,824,000	64,208,000	64,539,000	61,703,000	56,882,000	53,384,000	48,339,000
Stockholders' Equity	19,610,000	17,072,000	23,062,000	25,554,000	30,320,000	33,173,000	32,790,000	31,635,000
Shares Outstanding	4,259,000	4,259,000	4,288,000	4,323,999	4,365,999	4,401,999	4,468,999	4,525,999
Statistical Record								
Return on Assets %	1.55	1.42	7.34	8.07	7.80	9.74	10.83	11.21
Return on Equity %	6.75	6.22	26.78	26.31	22.36	26.03	27.92	27.37
EBITDA Margin %	26.57	19.83	21.47	25.09	22.13	26.78	26.32	26.55
Net Margin %	17.94	3.52	15.59	16.60	15.43	18.32	18.78	18.42
Asset Turnover	0.37	0.40	0.47	0.49	0.51	0.53	0.58	0.61
Current Ratio	1.21	1.34	1.28	1.24	1.02	1.13	1.09	1.05
Debt to Equity	1.52	1.83	1.29	1.11	0.63	0.58	0.45	0.43
Price Range	48.53-42.33	47.43-40.44	46.89-40.17	43.84-37.99	44.83-37.10	43.09-36.25	40.56-33.49	35.62-30.80
P/E Ratio	142.74-124.50	163.55-139.45	31.47-26.96	26.25-22.75	28.02-23.19	22.68-19.08	20.59-17.00	19.25-16.65
Average Yield %	3.32	3.34	3.22	3.20	2.99	2.82	2.75	2.82

Address: One Coca-Cola Plaza, Atlanta, GA 30313
Telephone: 404-676-2121
Fax: 404-676-6792

Web Site: www.coca-colacompany.com
Officers: Ahmet Muhtar Kent - Chairman, President, Chief Executive Officer James Quincey - President, Chief Executive Officer, Chief Operating Officer, Region Officer

Auditors: Ernst & Young LLP
Investor Contact: 404-676-7563
Transfer Agents: Computershare Trust Company, N.A., Providence, RI

COLGATE-PALMOLIVE CO.

Exchange	Symbol	Price	52Wk Range	Yield	P/E	Div Acheiver
NYS	CL	$64.81 (6/29/2018)	77.50-61.65	2.59	27.46	55 Years

*7 Year Price Score 89.87   *NYSE Composite Index=100   *12 Month Price Score 88.83

Interim Earnings (Per Share)

Qtr.	Mar	Jun	Sep	Dec
2015	0.59	0.63	0.80	(0.50)
2016	0.59	0.67	0.78	0.68
2017	0.64	0.59	0.68	0.37
2018	0.72	...	...	...

Interim Dividends (Per Share)

Amt	Decl	Ex	Rec	Pay
0.40Q	09/26/2017	10/20/2017	10/23/2017	11/15/2017
0.40Q	01/11/2018	01/22/2018	01/23/2018	02/15/2018
0.42Q	03/07/2018	04/19/2018	04/20/2018	05/15/2018
0.42Q	06/18/2018	07/17/2018	07/18/2018	08/15/2018

Indicated Div: $1.68 (Div. Reinv. Plan)

Valuation Analysis   **Institutional Holding**

Forecast EPS	$3.10	No of Institutions
	(06/14/2018)	2028
Market Cap	$56.5 Billion	Shares
Book Value	N/A	763,083,776
Price/Book	N/A	% Held
Price/Sales	3.60	69.22

TRADING VOLUME (thousand shares)

Business Summary: Household & Personal Products (MIC: 1.7.1 SIC: 2844 NAIC: 325611)

Colgate-Palmolive is engaged primarily in the manufacture and market a range of consumer products. Co. has two product segments. Oral, Personal and Home Care products include toothpaste, toothbrushes and mouthwash, bar and liquid hand soaps, shower gels, shampoos, conditioners, deodorants and antiperspirants, laundry and dishwashing detergents, fabric conditioners, household cleaners, bleaches and other similar items. These products are sold to retail trade customers and wholesale distributors. Pet Nutrition products include pet nutrition products manufactured and marketed by Hill's Pet Nutrition. The principal customers for Pet Nutrition products are pet supply retailers and veterinarians.

Recent Developments: For the quarter ended Mar 31 2018, net income increased 11.0% to US$678.0 million from US$611.0 million in the year-earlier quarter. Revenues were US$4.00 billion, up 6.4% from US$3.76 billion the year before. Operating income was US$983.0 million versus US$912.0 million in the prior-year quarter, an increase of 7.8%. Direct operating expenses rose 6.8% to US$1.59 billion from US$1.49 billion in the comparable period the year before. Indirect operating expenses increased 5.0% to US$1.43 billion from US$1.36 billion in the equivalent prior-year period.

Prospects: Our evaluation of Colgate-Palmolive Co. as of Jan. 21, 2018 is the result of our systematic analysis on three basic characteristics: earnings strength, relative valuation, and recent stock price movement. The company has managed to produce a neutral trend in earnings per share over the past 5 quarters and while recent estimates for the company have been mixed, CL has posted results that fell short of analysts expectations. Based on operating earnings yield, the company is about fairly valued when compared to all of the companies in our coverage universe. Share price changes over the past year indicates that CL will perform in line with the market over the near term.

Financial Data

(US$ in Thousands)	3 Mos	12/31/2017	12/31/2016	12/31/2015	12/31/2014	12/31/2013	12/31/2012	12/31/2011
Earnings Per Share	2.36	2.28	2.72	1.52	2.36	2.38	2.58	2.47
Cash Flow Per Share	3.40	3.46	3.51	3.27	3.60	3.44	3.35	2.97
Dividends Per Share	1.600	1.590	1.550	1.500	1.420	1.330	1.220	1.135
Dividend Payout %	67.80	69.74	56.99	98.68	60.17	55.88	47.38	45.95
Income Statement								
Total Revenue	4,002,000	15,454,000	15,195,000	16,034,000	17,277,000	17,420,000	17,085,000	16,734,000
EBITDA	1,088,000	3,613,000	3,860,000	2,814,000	3,582,000	3,583,000	3,913,000	3,863,000
Depn & Amortn	129,000	35,000	33,000	33,000	32,000	32,000	31,000	28,000
Income Before Taxes	924,000	3,476,000	3,728,000	2,755,000	3,526,000	3,560,000	3,867,000	3,783,000
Income Taxes	246,000	1,313,000	1,152,000	1,215,000	1,194,000	1,155,000	1,243,000	1,235,000
Net Income	634,000	2,024,000	2,441,000	1,384,000	2,180,000	2,241,000	2,472,000	2,431,000
Average Shares	879,900	887,800	898,400	909,700	924,300	939,900	960,200	984,000
Balance Sheet								
Current Assets	4,292,000	4,639,000	4,338,000	4,384,000	4,863,000	4,822,000	4,556,000	4,402,000
Total Assets	13,144,000	12,676,000	12,123,000	11,958,000	13,459,000	13,876,000	13,394,000	12,724,000
Current Liabilities	3,980,000	3,408,000	3,305,000	3,534,000	3,946,000	4,470,000	3,736,000	3,716,000
Long-Term Obligations	6,550,000	6,566,000	6,520,000	6,269,000	5,644,000	4,749,000	4,926,000	4,430,000
Total Liabilities	13,393,000	12,736,000	12,366,000	12,257,000	12,314,000	11,571,000	11,205,000	10,349,000
Stockholders' Equity	(249,000)	(60,000)	(243,000)	(299,000)	1,145,000	2,305,000	2,189,000	2,375,000
Shares Outstanding	872,320	874,701	883,108	892,738	906,712	919,946	935,728	960,036
Statistical Record								
Return on Assets %	16.32	16.32	20.22	10.89	15.95	16.44	18.88	20.35
Return on Equity %	...	...	...	327.19	126.38	99.73	108.03	96.28
EBITDA Margin %	27.19	23.38	25.40	17.55	20.73	20.57	22.90	23.08
Net Margin %	15.84	13.10	16.06	8.63	12.62	12.86	14.47	14.53
Asset Turnover	1.23	1.25	1.26	1.26	1.26	1.28	1.30	1.40
Current Ratio	1.08	1.36	1.31	1.24	1.23	1.08	1.22	1.18
Debt to Equity	...	...	...	...	4.93	2.06	2.25	1.87
Price Range	77.50-68.19	77.23-64.53	75.27-62.45	71.46-60.37	71.00-60.17	66.26-52.27	55.31-44.13	46.98-37.97
P/E Ratio	32.84-28.89	33.87-28.30	27.67-22.96	47.01-39.72	30.08-25.50	27.84-21.96	21.44-17.10	19.02-15.37
Average Yield %	2.20	2.20	2.21	2.23	2.15	2.23	2.42	2.66

Address: 300 Park Avenue, New York, NY 10022
Telephone: 212-310-2000
Fax: 212-310-3284

Web Site: www.colgatepalmolive.com
Officers: Ian M. Cook - Chairman, President, Chief Executive Officer Franck J. Moison - Vice-Chairman, Division Officer

Auditors: PricewaterhouseCoopers LLP
Investor Contact: 212-310-2575
Transfer Agents: Computershare, Providence, RI

COLFAX CORP

Exchange	Symbol	Price	52Wk Range	Yield	P/E
NYS	CFX	$30.65 (6/29/2018)	43.16-29.84	N/A	27.61

*7 Year Price Score 72.34 *NYSE Composite Index=100 *12 Month Price Score 83.76

Interim Earnings (Per Share)

Qtr.	Mar	Jun	Sep	Dec
2015	0.42	0.42	0.15	0.35
2016	0.18	0.32	0.23	0.31
2017	0.31	0.43	0.37	0.11
2018	0.20	...	...	...

Interim Dividends (Per Share)

No Dividends Paid

Valuation Analysis **Institutional Holding**

Forecast EPS	$2.15	No of Institutions
	(06/13/2018)	286
Market Cap	$3.8 Billion	Shares
Book Value	$3.6 Billion	96,729,984
Price/Book	1.05	% Held
Price/Sales	1.06	104.82

Business Summary: Industrial Machinery & Equipment (MIC: 7.2.1 SIC: 3561 NAIC: 333911)

Colfax provides gas- and fluid-handling and fabrication technology products and services to commercial and governmental customers. Co.'s gas- and fluid-handling segment is a supplier of a range of products, including centrifugal and axial fans, rotary heat exchangers, gas compressors, centrifugal and positive displacement pumps, which serves customers in the power generation, oil, gas and petrochemical, mining, marine (including defense) and general industrial and other end markets. Co.'s fabrication technology segment formulates, develops, manufactures and supplies consumable products and equipment for use in the cutting and joining of steels, aluminum and other metals and metal alloys.

Recent Developments: For the quarter ended Mar 30 2018, income from continuing operations decreased 17.0% to US$31.9 million from US$38.4 million in the year-earlier quarter. Net income decreased 30.0% to US$29.0 million from US$41.5 million in the year-earlier quarter. Revenues were US$880.9 million, up 20.1% from US$733.6 million the year before. Operating income was US$62.2 million versus US$60.2 million in the prior-year quarter, an increase of 3.2%. Direct operating expenses rose 23.6% to US$610.3 million from US$493.8 million in the comparable period the year before. Indirect operating expenses increased 16.1% to US$208.4 million from US$179.6 million in the equivalent prior-year period.

Prospects: Our evaluation of Colfax Corp. as of Jan. 21, 2018 is the result of our systematic analysis on three basic characteristics: earnings strength, relative valuation, and recent stock price movement. The company has generated a negative trend in earnings per share over the past 5 quarters and while recent estimates for the company have been raised by analysts, CFX has posted better than expected results. Based on company earnings yield, the company is about fairly valued when compared to all of the companies in our coverage universe. Share price changes over the past year indicates that CFX will perform poorly over the near term.

Financial Data
(US$ in Thousands)

	3 Mos	12/31/2017	12/31/2016	12/31/2015	12/31/2014	12/31/2013	12/31/2012	12/31/2011
Earnings Per Share	1.11	1.22	1.04	1.34	3.02	1.56	(0.92)	0.10
Cash Flow Per Share	1.42	1.78	2.00	2.45	3.18	3.65	1.80	1.31
Income Statement								
Total Revenue	880,925	3,300,184	3,647,047	3,967,053	4,624,476	4,207,209	3,913,856	693,392
EBITDA	84,440	81,451	317,215	375,345	504,053	484,492	211,709	39,006
Depn & Amortn	36,987	52,300	79,200	90,700	94,500	78,100	71,700	13,100
Income Before Taxes	37,865	(11,986)	207,999	236,902	358,248	302,795	48,439	19,987
Income Taxes	5,986	42,554	62,808	49,724	(62,025)	93,652	90,703	15,432
Net Income	24,535	151,090	128,111	167,739	392,098	178,628	(64,402)	4,555
Average Shares	124,080	123,229	123,198	124,869	122,666	100,366	91,069	44,268
Balance Sheet								
Current Assets	2,163,227	2,069,832	1,785,597	1,759,765	2,099,463	2,138,346	2,130,782	351,208
Total Assets	6,879,214	6,709,697	6,385,459	6,732,919	7,245,098	6,582,853	6,129,727	1,088,543
Current Liabilities	1,095,478	1,097,380	1,106,674	1,116,344	1,285,535	1,375,090	1,175,458	240,042
Long-Term Obligations	1,122,077	1,055,305	1,286,738	1,411,755	1,529,389	1,457,642	1,693,512	101,518
Total Liabilities	3,274,657	3,209,282	3,488,588	3,662,944	4,098,272	4,068,964	4,217,375	899,268
Stockholders' Equity	3,604,557	3,500,415	2,896,871	3,069,975	3,146,826	2,513,889	1,912,352	189,275
Shares Outstanding	123,477	123,245	122,780	123,486	123,730	101,921	94,067	43,697
Statistical Record								
Return on Assets %	2.06	2.31	1.95	2.40	5.67	2.81	N.M.	0.43
Return on Equity %	4.14	4.72	4.28	5.40	13.85	8.07	N.M.	2.25
EBITDA Margin %	9.59	2.47	8.70	9.46	10.90	11.52	5.41	5.63
Net Margin %	2.79	4.58	3.51	4.23	8.48	4.25	N.M.	0.66
Asset Turnover	0.54	0.50	0.55	0.57	0.67	0.66	1.08	0.66
Current Ratio	1.97	1.89	1.61	1.58	1.63	1.56	1.81	1.46
Debt to Equity	0.31	0.30	0.44	0.46	0.49	0.58	0.89	0.54
Price Range	43.16-30.92	43.16-34.88	39.75-19.29	53.47-22.00	74.92-47.20	63.69-40.35	40.35-24.80	31.80-18.17
P/E Ratio	38.88-27.86	35.38-28.59	38.22-18.55	39.90-16.42	24.81-15.63	40.83-25.87	...	318.00-181.70

Address: 420 National Business Parkway, 5th Floor, Annapolis Junction, MD 20701
Telephone: 301-323-9000

Web Site: www.colfaxcorp.com
Officers: Mitchell P. Rales - Chairman Shyam Kambeyanda - Senior Vice President, Division Officer

Auditors: Ernst & Young LLP
Investor Contact: 301-323-9090
Transfer Agents: Registrar and Transfer Company, Cranford, NJ

COLONY CAPITAL INC

Exchange	Symbol	Price	52Wk Range	Yield	P/E
NYS	CLNY	$6.24 (6/29/2018)	14.70-5.48	7.05	N/A

*7 Year Price Score N/A   *NYSE Composite Index=100   *12 Month Price Score 60.33

Interim Earnings (Per Share)

Qtr.	Mar	Jun	Sep	Dec
2015	0.11	0.19	0.21	0.09
2016	0.09	0.06	0.13	(0.07)
2017	(0.01)	0.07	0.00	(0.69)
2018	(0.14)	...	...	...

Interim Dividends (Per Share)

Amt	Decl	Ex	Rec	Pay
0.27Q	08/03/2017	09/28/2017	09/30/2017	10/16/2017
0.27Q	11/02/2017	12/28/2017	12/29/2017	01/15/2018
0.11Q	02/26/2018	03/28/2018	03/29/2018	04/16/2018
0.11Q	05/08/2018	06/28/2018	06/29/2018	07/16/2018

Indicated Div: $0.44

Valuation Analysis

Forecast EPS	$-0.45 (06/10/2018)
Market Cap	$3.1 Billion
Book Value	$8.0 Billion
Price/Book	0.39
Price/Sales	1.10

Institutional Holding

No of Institutions	473
Shares	439,004,512
% Held	N/A

TRADING VOLUME (thousand shares)
2009 2010 2011 2012 2013 2014 2015 2016 2017 2018

Business Summary: REITs (MIC: 5.3.1 SIC: 6531 NAIC: 531390)

NorthStar Asset Management Group is an asset management firm. Co.'s primary business lines are as follows: NorthStar Listed Companies, and Retail Companies, which provides asset management and other services on a fee basis by managing the day-to-day activities of the NorthStar Listed Companies, and Retail Companies; Broker-dealer, which raises capital in the retail market through NorthStar Securities and earned dealer manager fees for selling equity in the Retail Companies; Direct Investments, which invest in strategic partnerships and joint ventures with third-parties. As of Dec 31 2017, Co. had $43.00 billion of assets under management.

Recent Developments: For the quarter ended Mar 31 2018, loss from continuing operations was US$26.4 million compared with income of US$39.6 million in the year-earlier quarter. Net loss amounted to US$26.3 million versus net income of US$52.2 million in the year-earlier quarter. Revenues were US$666.7 million, up 9.8% from US$607.2 million the year before. Revenues from property income rose 30.0% to US$554.7 million from US$426.9 million in the corresponding quarter a year earlier.

Prospects: Our evaluation of Colony Northstar Inc. as of Jan. 21, 2018 is the result of our systematic analysis on three basic characteristics: earnings strength, relative valuation, and recent stock price movement. The company has generated a negative trend in earnings per share over the past 5 quarters. However, while recent estimates for the company have been mixed, CLNS has posted results that fell short of analysts expectations. Based on operating earnings yield, the company is overvalued when compared to all of the companies in our coverage universe. Share price changes over the past year indicates that CLNS will perform very well over the near term.

Financial Data
(US$ in Thousands)

	3 Mos	12/31/2017	12/31/2016	12/31/2015	12/31/2014	12/31/2013	12/31/2012	12/31/2011
Earnings Per Share	(0.76)	(0.64)	0.21	0.60	0.10	(0.01)	(0.09)	(0.14)
Cash Flow Per Share	1.18	1.03	0.92	0.84	0.25	(0.03)	(0.11)	(0.12)
Tang Book Value Per Share	9.69	9.69	N.M.	0.92	1.03	...	...	...
Dividends Per Share	0.920	2.213	0.400	0.400	0.100	...	...	...
Dividend Payout %	...	...	190.48	66.67	100.00	...	...	...
Income Statement								
Total Revenue	666,664	2,796,734	398,542	435,821	259,142	89,938	50,761	13,055
EBITDA	66,098	851,555	164,833	201,022	22,661	(1,921)	(17,257)	(25,620)
Depn & Amortn	157,587	453,300	75,121	59,253	900	74	65	62
Income Before Taxes	(91,489)	(176,567)	63,798	140,991	21,761	(1,995)	(17,322)	(25,682)
Income Taxes	(32,808)	(98,399)	11,022	21,869	1,622	...	...	...
Net Income	(41,327)	(197,891)	42,281	119,794	19,100	(1,995)	(17,322)	(25,682)
Average Shares	530,680	532,600	185,111	193,119	194,408	187,815	187,815	183,442
Balance Sheet								
Current Assets	1,154,817	1,422,426	241,011	220,077	198,950	30,724	19,851	...
Total Assets	23,564,492	24,785,650	850,627	374,821	266,987	31,709	20,257	...
Current Liabilities	689,138	470,095	91,165	197,148	65,239	3,283	2,343	...
Long-Term Obligations	10,495,429	10,827,810	468,425	...	...	...	...	...
Total Liabilities	15,563,519	16,377,725	666,515	199,756	65,239	3,341	2,382	...
Stockholders' Equity	8,000,973	8,407,925	184,112	175,065	201,748	28,368	17,875	...
Shares Outstanding	501,379	543,335	193,639	189,898	196,686	...	...	...
Statistical Record								
Return on Assets %	N.M.	N.M.	6.88	37.33	12.79	N.M.	...	...
Return on Equity %	N.M.	N.M.	23.48	63.58	16.60	N.M.	...	...
EBITDA Margin %	9.91	30.45	41.36	46.12	8.74	N.M.	N.M.	N.M.
Net Margin %	N.M.	N.M.	10.61	27.49	7.37	N.M.	N.M.	N.M.
Asset Turnover	0.12	0.22	0.65	1.36	1.74	3.46	...	...
Current Ratio	1.68	3.03	2.64	1.12	3.05	9.36	8.47	...
Debt to Equity	1.31	1.29	2.54	...	...	...	...	...
Price Range	14.70-5.50	14.70-11.41	...	...	...	...	...	...
Average Yield %	7.70	16.60	...	...	...	...	...	...

Address: 515 South Flower Street, 44th Floor, Los Angeles, CA 90071
Telephone: 310-282-8820

Web Site: www.clns.com
Officers: David T. Hamamoto - Chairman, Chief Executive Officer, Holding/Parent Company Officer Albert Tylis - President, Holding/Parent Company Officer

Auditors: Ernst & Young LLP
Transfer Agents: American Stock Transfer & Trust Company, LLC, Brookly, NY

COLUMBIA PROPERTY TRUST INC

Exchange	Symbol	Price	52Wk Range	Yield	P/E
NYS	CXP	$22.71 (6/29/2018)	23.16-19.61	3.52	26.72

*7 Year Price Score N/A   ***NYSE Composite Index=100**   ***12 Month Price Score 100.87**

Interim Earnings (Per Share)

Qtr.	Mar	Jun	Sep	Dec
2015	0.04	0.07	0.16	0.08
2016	0.05	0.11	0.30	0.22
2017	0.61	0.01	0.84	(0.01)
2018	0.01	...	...	...

Interim Dividends (Per Share)

Amt	Decl	Ex	Rec	Pay
0.20Q	08/07/2017	08/30/2017	09/01/2017	09/15/2017
0.20Q	11/13/2017	11/30/2017	12/01/2017	01/04/2018
0.20Q	02/08/2018	02/28/2018	03/01/2018	03/15/2018
0.20Q	05/15/2018	05/31/2018	06/01/2018	06/15/2018

Indicated Div: $0.80

Valuation Analysis   **Institutional Holding**

Forecast EPS	$0.10 (06/13/2018)	No of Institutions 295
Market Cap	$2.7 Billion	Shares 103,527,912
Book Value	$2.8 Billion	% Held
Price/Book	0.95	20.92
Price/Sales	9.60	

Business Summary: REITs (MIC: 5.3.1 SIC: 6798 NAIC: 525930)

Columbia Property Trust is a real estate investment trust that owns and operates commercial real estate properties. Co. conducts its business primarily through Columbia Property Trust Operating Partnership, L.P., which acquires, develops, owns, leases, and operates real properties directly, through wholly owned subsidiaries, or through joint ventures. Co. typically invests in office properties. As of Dec 31 2017, Co. owned 19 operating properties, of which 14 were wholly owned and five were owned through unconsolidated joint ventures. These properties are located primarily in New York, San Francisco, Washington, D.C., and Atlanta.

Recent Developments: For the quarter ended Mar 31 2018, income from continuing operations decreased 4.5% to US$1.5 million from US$1.6 million in the year-earlier quarter. Net income decreased 98.0% to US$1.5 million from US$74.7 million in the year-earlier quarter. Revenues were US$73.7 million, down 10.3% from US$82.2 million the year before.

Prospects: Our evaluation of Columbia Property Trust Inc as of Jan. 21, 2018 is the result of our systematic analysis on three basic characteristics: earnings strength, relative valuation, and recent stock price movement. The company has managed to produce a neutral trend in earnings per share over the past 5 quarters. Because the company lacks sufficient analyst estimate data, we place greater weight on the historical EPS trend as the measure of earnings strength. Based on operating earnings yield, the company is overvalued when compared to all of the companies in our coverage universe. Share price changes over the past year indicates that CXP will perform well over the near term.

Financial Data
(US$ in Thousands)

	3 Mos	12/31/2017	12/31/2016	12/31/2015	12/31/2014	12/31/2013	12/31/2012	12/31/2011
Earnings Per Share	0.85	1.45	0.68	0.36	0.74	0.12	0.36	0.40
Cash Flow Per Share	0.60	0.51	1.56	1.79	1.90	1.63	1.84	2.06
Tang Book Value Per Share	23.62	20.78	20.04	20.40	21.03	21.14	22.33	23.64
Dividends Per Share	0.800	0.800	1.200	1.200	1.200	0.300	1.880	2.000
Dividend Payout %	94.12	55.17	176.47	333.33	162.16	250.00	522.22	500.00
Income Statement								
Total Revenue	73,710	289,000	473,543	566,065	540,797	526,578	576,691	576,389
EBITDA	42,616	129,040	188,826	231,811	206,241	214,067	227,930	231,471
Depn & Amortn	28,790	80,394	108,543	131,490	117,766	119,835	120,307	119,772
Income Before Taxes	(266)	(2,341)	19,962	22,279	20,039	26,320	41,103	47,789
Income Taxes	7	(213)	445	378	662	500	586	(276)
Net Income	1,498	176,041	84,281	44,619	92,635	15,720	48,039	56,642
Average Shares	119,350	121,159	123,228	124,847	124,918	134,085	136,672	135,680
Balance Sheet								
Current Assets	23,503	103,930	288,059	153,377	273,224	220,861	187,756	170,017
Total Assets	4,638,800	4,511,539	4,299,793	4,678,118	4,738,878	4,592,482	5,730,949	5,776,567
Current Liabilities	105,772	148,963	167,755	136,113	106,276	99,678	104,778	75,678
Long-Term Obligations	1,646,676	1,784,941	1,534,438	1,845,830	1,800,066	1,609,179	2,236,296	2,115,486
Total Liabilities	1,796,341	1,979,603	1,797,025	2,063,924	2,005,400	1,804,659	2,467,443	2,316,765
Stockholders' Equity	2,842,459	2,531,936	2,502,768	2,614,194	2,733,478	2,787,823	3,263,506	3,459,802
Shares Outstanding	118,601	119,789	122,184	124,363	124,973	124,830	136,900	136,549
Statistical Record								
Return on Assets %	2.33	4.00	1.87	0.95	1.99	0.30	0.83	...
Return on Equity %	3.81	6.99	3.29	1.67	3.36	0.52	1.43	...
EBITDA Margin %	57.82	44.65	39.88	40.95	38.14	40.65	39.52	40.16
Net Margin %	2.03	60.91	17.80	7.88	17.13	2.99	8.33	9.83
Asset Turnover	0.06	0.07	0.11	0.12	0.12	0.10	0.10	...
Current Ratio	0.22	0.70	1.72	1.13	2.57	2.22	1.79	2.25
Debt to Equity	0.58	0.70	0.61	0.71	0.66	0.58	0.69	0.61
Price Range	23.16-19.61	23.43-20.62	24.63-19.81	27.67-21.16	29.13-23.12	25.07-22.16	...	...
P/E Ratio	27.25-23.07	16.16-14.22	36.22-29.13	76.86-58.78	39.36-31.24	208.92-184.67	...	...
Average Yield %	3.67	3.63	5.46	4.81	4.67	1.29	...	...

Address: 1170 Peachtree Street NE, Suite 600, Atlanta, GA 30309 **Telephone:** 404-465-2200	**Web Site:** www.columbiapropertytrust.com **Officers:** John L. Dixon - Chairman E. Nelson Mills - President, Chief Executive Officer	**Auditors:** Deloitte & Touche LLP **Transfer Agents:** DST Systems Inc

COMERICA, INC.

*7 Year Price Score 140.29 ***NYSE Composite Index=100** ***12 Month Price Score 110.21**

Interim Earnings (Per Share)

Qtr.	Mar	Jun	Sep	Dec
2015	0.73	0.73	0.74	0.64
2016	0.34	0.58	0.84	0.92
2017	1.11	1.13	1.26	0.64
2018	1.59	...	...	...

Interim Dividends (Per Share)

Amt	Decl	Ex	Rec	Pay
0.30Q	07/25/2017	09/14/2017	09/15/2017	10/01/2017
0.30Q	11/07/2017	12/14/2017	12/15/2017	01/01/2018
0.30Q	01/23/2018	03/14/2018	03/15/2018	04/01/2018
0.34Q	04/24/2018	06/14/2018	06/15/2018	07/01/2018

Indicated Div: $1.36 (Div. Reinv. Plan)

Valuation Analysis **Institutional Holding**

Forecast EPS	$6.78	No of Institutions
	(06/14/2018)	829
Market Cap	$15.7 Billion	Shares
Book Value	$8.0 Billion	178,442,720
Price/Book	1.96	% Held
Price/Sales	4.67	79.00

TRADING VOLUME (thousand shares)

Business Summary: Banking (MIC: 5.1.1 SIC: 6021 NAIC: 522110)

Comerica is a financial holding company. Co.'s principal activity is lending to and accepting deposits from businesses and individuals. Co.'s business segments are: Business Bank, which provides products and services to middle market businesses, multinational corporations and governmental entities; Retail Bank, which includes small business banking and personal financial services; and Wealth Management, which provides products and services consisting of fiduciary services, private banking, retirement services, investment management and advisory services, investment banking and brokerage services. As of Dec 31 2017, Co. had total assets of $71.57 billion and deposits of $57.90 billion.

Recent Developments: For the quarter ended Mar 31 2018, net income increased 39.1% to US$281.0 million from US$202.0 million in the year-earlier quarter. Net interest income increased 16.8% to US$549.0 million from US$470.0 million in the year-earlier quarter. Provision for loan losses was US$12.0 million versus US$16.0 million in the prior-year quarter, a decrease of 25.0%. Non-interest income fell 10.0% to US$244.0 million from US$271.0 million, while non-interest expense declined 2.4% to US$446.0 million.

Prospects: Our evaluation of Comerica Inc. as of Jan. 21, 2018 is the result of our systematic analysis on three basic characteristics: earnings strength, relative valuation, and recent stock price movement. The company has managed to produce a neutral trend in earnings per share over the past 5 quarters and while recent estimates for the company have been raised by analysts, CMA has posted better than expected results. Based on operating earnings yield, the company is undervalued when compared to all of the companies in our coverage universe. Share price changes over the past year indicates that CMA will perform poorly over the near term.

Financial Data

(US$ in Thousands)	3 Mos	12/31/2017	12/31/2016	12/31/2015	12/31/2014	12/31/2013	12/31/2012	12/31/2011
Earnings Per Share	4.62	4.14	2.68	2.84	3.16	2.85	2.67	2.09
Cash Flow Per Share	6.13	6.34	2.86	4.90	3.57	4.57	3.94	4.88
Tang Book Value Per Share	46.38	46.07	44.47	43.03	41.35	39.24	36.87	34.80
Dividends Per Share	1.160	1.090	0.890	0.830	0.790	0.680	0.550	0.400
Dividend Payout %	25.11	26.33	33.21	29.23	25.00	23.86	20.60	19.14
Income Statement								
Interest Income	590,000	2,182,000	1,909,000	1,784,000	1,750,000	1,784,000	1,863,000	1,809,000
Interest Expense	41,000	121,000	112,000	95,000	95,000	112,000	135,000	156,000
Net Interest Income	549,000	2,061,000	1,797,000	1,689,000	1,655,000	1,672,000	1,728,000	1,653,000
Provision for Losses	12,000	74,000	248,000	147,000	27,000	46,000	79,000	153,000
Non-Interest Income	244,000	1,107,000	1,051,000	1,050,000	868,000	826,000	818,000	792,000
Non-Interest Expense	446,000	1,860,000	1,930,000	1,842,000	1,658,000	1,722,000	1,757,000	1,762,000
Income Before Taxes	335,000	1,234,000	670,000	750,000	870,000	730,000	710,000	530,000
Income Taxes	54,000	491,000	193,000	229,000	277,000	189,000	189,000	137,000
Net Income	281,000	743,000	477,000	521,000	593,000	541,000	521,000	393,000
Average Shares	175,000	178,000	177,000	181,000	185,000	187,000	192,000	186,000
Balance Sheet								
Net Loans & Leases	48,542,000	48,461,000	48,358,000	48,450,000	47,999,000	44,872,000	45,428,000	41,953,000
Total Assets	72,335,000	71,567,000	72,978,000	71,877,000	69,190,000	65,227,000	65,359,000	61,008,000
Total Deposits	57,635,000	57,903,000	58,985,000	59,853,000	57,486,000	53,292,000	52,202,000	47,755,000
Total Liabilities	64,335,000	63,604,000	65,182,000	64,317,000	61,788,000	58,074,000	58,417,000	54,140,000
Stockholders' Equity	8,000,000	7,963,000	7,796,000	7,560,000	7,402,000	7,153,000	6,942,000	6,868,000
Shares Outstanding	172,474	172,858	175,313	175,707	179,018	182,304	188,275	197,333
Statistical Record								
Return on Assets %	1.13	1.03	0.66	0.74	0.88	0.83	0.82	0.69
Return on Equity %	10.32	9.43	6.20	6.96	8.15	7.68	7.52	6.21
Net Interest Margin %	93.05	94.45	94.13	94.67	94.57	93.72	92.75	91.38
Efficiency Ratio %	53.48	56.55	65.20	65.00	63.33	65.98	65.54	67.74
Loans to Deposits	0.84	0.84	0.82	0.81	0.83	0.84	0.87	0.88
Price Range	102.21-64.46	87.74-64.46	70.03-31.02	52.65-40.41	52.37-43.06	47.63-30.34	33.57-26.72	43.36-21.98
P/E Ratio	22.12-13.95	21.19-15.57	26.13-11.57	18.54-14.23	16.57-13.63	16.71-10.65	12.57-10.01	20.75-10.52
Average Yield %	1.46	1.49	1.95	1.82	1.63	1.73	1.81	1.25

Address: Comerica Bank Tower, 1717 Main Street, MC 6404, Dallas, TX 75201 **Telephone:** 214-462-6831	**Web Site:** www.comerica.com **Officers:** Ralph W. Babb - Chairman, President, Chief Executive Officer Curtis C. Farmer - Vice-Chairman, President, Executive Vice President	**Auditors:** Ernst & Young LLP **Investor Contact:** 214-462-6831 **Transfer Agents:** Wells Fargo Shareowner Services, St. Paul, MN

COMMERCIAL METALS CO.

Exchange	Symbol	Price	52Wk Range	Yield	P/E
NYS	CMC	$21.11 (6/29/2018)	26.13-17.08	2.27	43.98

*7 Year Price Score 101.15 *NYSE Composite Index=100 *12 Month Price Score 105.85

Interim Earnings (Per Share)

Qtr.	Nov	Feb	May	Aug
2014-15	0.30	0.46	0.49	(0.05)
2015-16	0.21	0.09	0.17	0.00
2016-17	0.05	0.26	0.34	(0.26)
2017-18	0.31	0.09	0.34	...

Interim Dividends (Per Share)

Amt	Decl	Ex	Rec	Pay
0.12Q	10/24/2017	11/07/2017	11/08/2017	11/22/2017
0.12Q	01/02/2018	01/12/2018	01/16/2018	01/31/2018
0.12Q	03/21/2018	04/03/2018	04/04/2018	04/19/2018
0.12Q	06/20/2018	07/03/2018	07/05/2018	07/19/2018
		Indicated Div: $0.48		

Valuation Analysis — **Institutional Holding**

Forecast EPS	$1.49	No of Institutions
	(06/14/2018)	389
Market Cap	$2.5 Billion	Shares
Book Value	$1.5 Billion	132,345,152
Price/Book	1.70	% Held
Price/Sales	0.55	83.44

Business Summary: Non-Precious Metals (MIC: 8.2.2 SIC: 3312 NAIC: 331111)

Commercial Metals manufactures, recycles and markets steel and metal products, related materials and services. Co. has five segments: Americas Recycling , which processes scrap metals; Americas Mills, which, via its mills, produces rebar, angles, flats, rounds, channels, fence post sections and other shapes; Americas Fabrication, which bends, welds, cuts and fabricates steel, and sells or rents products for the installation of concrete; International Mill, which comprises its mill, recycling and fabrication operations in Poland; and International Marketing and Distribution, which sells, distributes and processes steel products, ferrous and nonferrous metals and other industrial products.

Recent Developments: For the quarter ended May 31 2018, income from continuing operations increased 34.1% to US$42.3 million from US$31.6 million in the year-earlier quarter. Net income increased 1.8% to US$40.0 million from US$39.3 million in the year-earlier quarter. Revenues were US$1.20 billion, up 15.3% from US$1.04 billion the year before. Direct operating expenses rose 15.6% to US$1.04 billion from US$896.3 million in the comparable period the year before. Indirect operating expenses increased 6.7% to US$112.9 million from US$105.9 million in the equivalent prior-year period.

Prospects: Our evaluation of Commercial Metals Co. as of Jan. 21, 2018 is the result of our systematic analysis on three basic characteristics: earnings strength, relative valuation, and recent stock price movement. The company has produced a positive trend in earnings per share over the past 5 quarters and while recent estimates for the company have been raised by analysts, CMC has posted better than expected results. Based on operating earnings yield, the company is about fairly valued when compared to all of the companies in our coverage universe. Share price changes over the past year indicates that CMC will perform very poorly over the near term.

Financial Data

(US$ in Thousands)	9 Mos	6 Mos	3 Mos	08/31/2017	08/31/2016	08/31/2015	08/31/2014	08/31/2013
Earnings Per Share	0.48	0.48	0.65	0.39	0.47	1.20	0.97	0.66
Cash Flow Per Share	2.11	1.81	1.21	1.51	5.08	2.69	1.17	1.27
Tang Book Value Per Share	11.87	11.87	11.75	11.54	11.35	10.83	10.81	10.26
Dividends Per Share	0.480	0.480	0.480	0.480	0.480	0.480	0.480	0.480
Dividend Payout %	100.00	100.00	73.85	123.08	102.13	40.00	49.48	72.73
Income Statement								
Total Revenue	3,335,285	2,130,801	1,238,519	4,569,675	4,610,526	5,988,605	7,039,959	6,889,575
EBITDA	232,188	131,913	89,032	202,465	266,764	447,470	350,959	326,622
Depn & Amortn	99,443	66,316	32,193	113,414	119,343	125,182	128,407	124,078
Income Before Taxes	107,442	51,805	50,314	45,004	85,190	244,528	144,811	132,936
Income Taxes	23,465	10,153	11,778	12,454	12,647	83,206	42,724	57,979
Net Income	86,946	46,980	36,810	46,332	54,762	141,634	115,551	77,315
Average Shares	118,254	118,269	117,857	117,364	116,623	117,949	118,607	117,552
Balance Sheet								
Current Assets	1,994,956	1,648,038	1,600,497	1,713,900	2,048,125	2,307,101	2,553,791	2,366,195
Total Assets	3,245,493	2,910,480	2,898,576	2,975,131	3,130,869	3,372,302	3,688,520	3,494,801
Current Liabilities	511,936	530,325	500,123	608,438	821,118	617,348	891,153	781,109
Long-Term Obligations	1,139,103	799,834	803,785	805,580	757,948	1,277,882	1,281,042	1,278,814
Total Liabilities	1,792,717	1,459,193	1,463,776	1,574,374	1,763,597	2,053,101	2,340,040	2,224,802
Stockholders' Equity	1,452,716	1,451,287	1,434,800	1,400,757	1,367,272	1,319,201	1,348,480	1,269,999
Shares Outstanding	117,014	116,825	116,630	115,793	114,635	115,635	117,829	117,010
Statistical Record								
Return on Assets %	1.76	1.88	2.61	1.52	1.68	4.01	3.22	2.23
Return on Equity %	4.00	4.03	5.56	3.35	4.07	10.62	8.83	6.14
EBITDA Margin %	6.96	6.19	7.19	4.43	5.79	7.47	4.99	4.74
Net Margin %	2.61	2.20	2.97	1.01	1.19	2.37	1.64	1.12
Asset Turnover	1.37	1.54	1.60	1.50	1.41	1.70	1.96	1.99
Current Ratio	3.90	3.11	3.20	2.82	2.49	3.74	2.87	3.03
Debt to Equity	0.78	0.55	0.56	0.58	0.55	0.97	0.95	1.01
Price Range	26.13-17.08	25.97-17.08	24.34-17.08	24.34-14.77	18.30-12.91	18.54-12.99	20.58-14.91	17.41-12.74
P/E Ratio	54.44-35.58	54.10-35.58	37.45-26.28	62.41-37.87	38.94-27.47	15.45-10.83	21.22-15.37	26.38-19.30
Average Yield %	2.30	2.41	2.45	2.51	3.07	3.02	2.61	3.21

Address: 6565 North MacArthur Blvd., Irving, TX 75039	**Web Site:** www.cmc.com	**Auditors:** Deloitte & Touche LLP
Telephone: 214-689-4300	**Officers:** Barbara R. Smith - Chairman, President, Chief Executive Officer, Chief Operating Officer, Chief Financial Officer, Senior Vice President Tracy L. Porter - Executive Vice President, Senior Vice President, Division Officer, Chief Operating Officer	**Investor Contact:** 214-689-4300
Fax: 214-689-5886		**Transfer Agents:** StockTrans®, a Broadridge Company

COMMUNITY BANK SYSTEM INC

Exchange	Symbol	Price	52Wk Range	Yield	P/E	Div Acheiver
NYS	CBU	$59.07 (6/29/2018)	61.98-49.11	2.30	18.23	26 Years

*7 Year Price Score 113.48 *NYSE Composite Index=100 *12 Month Price Score 107.00

TRADING VOLUME (thousand shares)

Interim Earnings (Per Share)

Qtr.	Mar	Jun	Sep	Dec
2015	0.54	0.58	0.60	0.47
2016	0.55	0.58	0.61	0.58
2017	0.57	0.35	0.68	1.43
2018	0.78	...	...	...

Interim Dividends (Per Share)

Amt	Decl	Ex	Rec	Pay
0.34Q	08/16/2017	09/14/2017	09/15/2017	10/10/2017
0.34Q	11/16/2017	12/14/2017	12/15/2017	01/10/2018
0.34Q	02/21/2018	03/14/2018	03/15/2018	04/10/2018
0.34Q	05/17/2018	06/14/2018	06/15/2018	07/10/2018

Indicated Div: $1.36 (Div. Reinv. Plan)

Valuation Analysis / Institutional Holding

Valuation Analysis		Institutional Holding	
Forecast EPS	$3.12	No of Institutions	
	(06/07/2018)	265	
Market Cap	$3.0 Billion	Shares	
Book Value	$1.6 Billion		43,505,128
Price/Book	1.84	% Held	
Price/Sales	5.33		71.89

Business Summary: Banking (MIC: 5.1.1 SIC: 6021 NAIC: 522110)

Community Bank System is a financial holding company. Through its Community Bank, N.A. subsidiary, Co. operates as a community bank provides a range of banking and financial services to retail, commercial, and municipal customers in New York, Pennsylvania, Vermont and Western Massachusetts. Through its Benefit Plans Administrative Services, Inc. subsidiary, Co. provides employee benefit services in the U.S. and Puerto Rico. Through other subsidiaries, Co. provides wealth management, retirement planning, higher educational planning, fiduciary, risk management, and personal financial planning services. At Dec 31 2017, Co. had total assets of $10.75 billion and total deposit of $8.44 billion.

Recent Developments: For the quarter ended Mar 31 2018, net income increased 52.7% to US$40.1 million from US$26.3 million in the year-earlier quarter. Net interest income increased 25.8% to US$84.6 million from US$67.3 million in the year-earlier quarter. Provision for loan losses was US$3.7 million versus US$1.8 million in the prior-year quarter, an increase of 101.3%. Non-interest income rose 29.7% to US$57.5 million from US$44.3 million, while non-interest expense advanced 17.3% to US$86.3 million.

Prospects: Our evaluation of Community Bank System Inc. as of Jan. 21, 2018 is the result of our systematic analysis on three basic characteristics: earnings strength, relative valuation, and recent stock price movement. The company has managed to produce a neutral trend in earnings per share over the past 5 quarters and while recent estimates for the company have been mixed, CBU has posted better than expected results. Based on operating earnings yield, the company is undervalued when compared to all of the companies in our coverage universe. Share price changes over the past year indicates that CBU will perform poorly over the near term.

Financial Data

(US$ in Thousands)	3 Mos	12/31/2017	12/31/2016	12/31/2015	12/31/2014	12/31/2013	12/31/2012	12/31/2011
Earnings Per Share	3.24	3.03	2.32	2.19	2.22	1.94	1.93	2.01
Cash Flow Per Share	4.08	3.88	2.97	2.84	3.04	2.58	2.76	2.73
Tang Book Value Per Share	15.94	15.98	16.14	15.00	14.75	12.00	13.01	11.19
Dividends Per Share	1.340	1.320	1.260	1.220	1.160	1.100	1.060	1.000
Dividend Payout %	41.36	43.56	54.31	55.71	52.25	56.70	54.92	49.75
Income Statement								
Interest Income	88,404	329,455	285,187	259,622	256,220	264,159	281,400	270,969
Interest Expense	3,780	13,780	11,291	11,202	11,792	26,065	50,976	61,556
Net Interest Income	84,624	315,675	273,896	248,420	244,428	238,094	230,424	209,413
Provision for Losses	3,679	10,984	8,076	6,447	7,178	7,992	9,108	4,736
Non-Interest Income	57,491	202,423	155,625	123,299	119,020	102,180	99,246	89,222
Non-Interest Expense	86,331	347,149	266,848	233,055	226,580	221,255	211,757	190,372
Income Before Taxes	52,105	159,965	154,597	132,217	129,690	111,027	108,805	103,527
Income Taxes	11,999	9,248	50,785	40,987	38,337	32,198	31,737	30,385
Net Income	40,106	150,717	103,812	91,230	91,353	78,829	77,068	73,142
Average Shares	51,497	49,470	44,485	41,401	41,029	40,504	39,671	36,182
Balance Sheet								
Net Loans & Leases	6,179,555	6,209,635	4,903,745	4,756,906	4,191,907	4,065,492	3,822,688	3,429,344
Total Assets	10,966,555	10,746,198	8,666,437	8,552,669	7,489,440	7,095,864	7,496,800	6,488,275
Total Deposits	8,771,092	8,444,420	7,075,954	6,873,474	5,935,264	5,896,044	5,628,039	4,795,245
Total Liabilities	9,335,089	9,110,883	7,468,337	7,412,022	6,501,536	6,220,052	6,594,022	5,713,692
Stockholders' Equity	1,631,466	1,635,315	1,198,100	1,140,647	987,904	875,812	902,778	774,583
Shares Outstanding	50,883	50,696	44,437	43,774	40,747	40,431	39,625	36,986
Statistical Record								
Return on Assets %	1.66	1.55	1.20	1.14	1.25	1.08	1.10	1.23
Return on Equity %	11.24	10.64	8.85	8.57	9.80	8.86	9.16	10.59
Net Interest Margin %	95.72	95.82	96.04	95.69	95.40	90.13	81.88	77.28
Efficiency Ratio %	59.17	65.27	60.54	60.86	60.38	60.40	55.63	52.85
Loans to Deposits	0.70	0.74	0.69	0.69	0.71	0.69	0.68	0.72
Price Range	58.03-49.11	62.32-49.11	62.24-34.47	43.13-33.60	39.91-32.84	40.27-27.36	29.38-25.55	28.34-21.81
P/E Ratio	17.91-15.16	20.57-16.21	26.83-14.86	19.69-15.34	17.98-14.79	20.76-14.10	15.22-13.24	14.10-10.85
Average Yield %	2.46	2.38	2.87	2.87	3.27	3.18	3.42	4.03

Address: 5790 Widewaters Parkway, DeWitt, NY 13214-1883 Telephone: 315-445-2282	Web Site: www.communitybankna.com Officers: Sally A. Steele - Chairman Mark E. Tryniski - President, Chief Executive Officer	Auditors: PricewaterhouseCoopers LLP Investor Contact: 315-445-3121 Transfer Agents: American Stock Transfer & Trust Company LLC, Brooklyn, NY

COMMUNITY HEALTH SYSTEMS, INC.

Exchange	Symbol	Price	52Wk Range	Yield	P/E
NYS	CYH	$3.32 (6/29/2018)	9.96-3.32	N/A	N/A

*7 Year Price Score 19.10   *NYSE Composite Index=100   *12 Month Price Score 76.10

Interim Earnings (Per Share)

Qtr.	Mar	Jun	Sep	Dec
2015	0.68	0.95	0.44	(0.71)
2016	0.10	(12.91)	(0.71)	(1.99)
2017	(1.79)	(1.22)	(0.98)	(18.01)
2018	(0.22)	...	...	...

Interim Dividends (Per Share)

Dividend Payment Suspended

Valuation Analysis | Institutional Holding

Forecast EPS	$-1.25	No of Institutions
	(06/13/2018)	349
Market Cap	$386.1 Million	Shares
Book Value	N/A	145,235,344
Price/Book	N/A	% Held
Price/Sales	0.03	96.07

TRADING VOLUME (thousand shares)

Business Summary: Hospitals & Health Care Facilities (MIC: 4.2.1 SIC: 8062 NAIC: 622110)

Community Health Systems is an operator of general acute care hospitals and outpatient facilities. Services provided via Co.'s hospitals and affiliated businesses include general acute care, emergency room, general and specialty surgery, critical care, internal medicine, obstetrics, diagnostic, psychiatric and rehabilitation services. Co. also provides additional outpatient services at urgent care centers, occupational medicine clinics, imaging centers, cancer centers, ambulatory surgery centers and home health and hospice agencies. At Dec 31 2017, Co. owned or leased 125 hospitals, comprised of 123 general acute care hospitals and two stand-alone rehabilitation or psychiatric hospitals.

Recent Developments: For the quarter ended Mar 31 2018, loss from continuing operations was US$6.0 million compared with a loss of US$176.0 million in the year-earlier quarter. Net loss amounted to US$6.0 million versus a net loss of US$177.0 million in the year-earlier quarter. Revenues were US$3.69 billion, down 17.8% from US$4.49 billion the year before. Operating income was US$212.0 million versus US$71.0 million in the prior-year quarter, an increase of 198.6%. Indirect operating expenses decreased 21.2% to US$3.48 billion from US$4.42 billion in the equivalent prior-year period.

Prospects: Our evaluation of Community Health Systems Inc. as of Jan. 21, 2018 is the result of our systematic analysis on three basic characteristics: earnings strength, relative valuation, and recent stock price movement. The company has suffered a very negative trend in earnings per share over the past 5 quarters. Because the company lacks sufficient analyst estimate data, we place greater weight on the historical EPS trend as the measure of earnings strength. Based on operating earnings yield, the company is overvalued when compared to all of the companies in our coverage universe. Share price changes over the past year indicates that CYH will perform very poorly over the near term.

Financial Data
(US$ in Thousands)

	3 Mos	12/31/2017	12/31/2016	12/31/2015	12/31/2014	12/31/2013	12/31/2012	12/31/2011
Earnings Per Share	(20.43)	(22.00)	(15.54)	1.37	0.82	1.51	2.96	2.23
Cash Flow Per Share	5.67	6.92	10.24	8.05	14.47	11.75	14.31	14.03
Dividends Per Share	...	...	...	...	...	...	0.250	...
Dividend Payout %	...	...	...	...	...	...	8.45	...
Income Statement								
Total Revenue	3,689,000	15,353,000	18,438,000	19,437,000	18,639,000	12,997,693	13,028,985	13,626,168
EBITDA	389,000	(1,057,000)	304,000	2,495,000	1,341,000	1,661,043	1,810,229	1,726,131
Depn & Amortn	181,000	861,000	1,100,000	1,174,000	75,000	782,675	725,558	657,665
Income Before Taxes	(20,000)	(2,849,000)	(1,758,000)	348,000	294,000	263,221	461,738	424,056
Income Taxes	(7,000)	(449,000)	(104,000)	116,000	82,000	88,594	157,502	137,653
Net Income	(25,000)	(2,459,000)	(1,721,000)	158,000	92,000	141,203	265,640	201,948
Average Shares	112,291	111,769	110,730	115,272	112,549	93,815	89,806	90,666
Balance Sheet								
Current Assets	3,993,000	4,068,000	4,666,000	5,166,000	5,566,000	3,747,963	3,419,142	2,846,089
Total Assets	17,311,000	17,450,000	21,944,000	26,861,000	27,421,000	17,117,295	16,606,335	15,208,840
Current Liabilities	2,263,000	2,356,000	2,887,000	3,072,000	3,589,000	2,457,483	2,143,220	1,911,139
Long-Term Obligations	13,855,000	13,880,000	14,789,000	16,822,000	16,681,000	9,286,495	9,451,394	8,782,798
Total Liabilities	18,086,000	18,217,000	20,329,000	22,842,000	23,418,000	14,049,468	13,875,128	12,811,744
Stockholders' Equity	(775,000)	(767,000)	1,615,000	4,019,000	4,003,000	3,067,827	2,731,207	2,397,096
Shares Outstanding	116,301	114,651	113,876	112,757	116,725	95,011	91,950	90,571
Statistical Record								
Return on Assets %	N.M.	N.M.	N.M.	0.58	0.41	0.84	1.67	1.35
Return on Equity %	N.M.	N.M.	N.M.	3.94	2.60	4.87	10.33	8.81
EBITDA Margin %	10.54	N.M.	1.65	12.84	7.19	12.78	13.89	12.67
Net Margin %	N.M.	N.M.	N.M.	0.81	0.49	1.09	2.04	1.48
Asset Turnover	0.75	0.78	0.75	0.72	0.84	0.77	0.82	0.91
Current Ratio	1.76	1.73	1.62	1.68	1.55	1.53	1.60	1.49
Debt to Equity	...	...	9.16	4.19	4.17	3.03	3.46	3.66
Price Range	10.32-3.96	10.32-3.99	21.84-4.66	52.71-20.73	47.29-28.99	42.13-25.30	26.06-13.74	34.65-12.59
P/E Ratio	...	...	...	38.48-15.13	57.67-35.35	27.90-16.76	8.80-4.64	15.54-5.64
Average Yield %	...	...	...	...	...	...	1.21	...

Address: 4000 Meridian Boulevard, Franklin, TN 37067 **Telephone:** 615-465-7000	**Web Site:** www.chs.net **Officers:** Wayne T. Smith - Chairman, President, Chief Executive Officer Tim L. Hingtgen - President, Executive Vice President, Chief Operating Officer

Auditors: Deloitte & Touche LLP
Investor Contact: 615-465-7000
Transfer Agents: Registrar and Transfer Company, Cranford, NJ

COMPASS MINERALS INTERNATIONAL INC

Exchange	Symbol	Price	52Wk Range	Yield	P/E	Div Acheiver
NYS	CMP	$65.75 (6/29/2018)	75.65-58.85	4.38	66.41	13 Years

*7 Year Price Score 69.74   ***NYSE Composite Index=100**   ***12 Month Price Score 99.35**

Interim Earnings (Per Share)

Qtr.	Mar	Jun	Sep	Dec
2015	1.79	0.39	0.80	1.72
2016	1.46	0.18	0.27	2.87
2017	0.63	(0.19)	0.94	(0.13)
2018	0.37	...	...	...

Interim Dividends (Per Share)

Amt	Decl	Ex	Rec	Pay
0.72Q	08/04/2017	08/30/2017	09/01/2017	09/15/2017
0.72Q	11/09/2017	11/30/2017	12/01/2017	12/15/2017
0.72Q	02/13/2018	02/28/2018	03/01/2018	03/15/2018
0.72Q	05/09/2018	05/31/2018	06/01/2018	06/15/2018

Indicated Div: $2.88

Valuation Analysis   **Institutional Holding**

Forecast EPS	$2.98	No of Institutions
	(06/14/2018)	473
Market Cap	$2.2 Billion	Shares
Book Value	$669.1 Million	50,008,768
Price/Book	3.33	% Held
Price/Sales	1.57	91.00

Business Summary: Mining (MIC: 8.2.4 SIC: 1499 NAIC: 212399)

Compass Minerals International is a holding company. Through its wholly owned subsidiaries, Co. is a provider of minerals, including salt, plant nutrition minerals, and chemicals. Co. has three reportable segments: Salt, which products include rock salt, mechanically evaporated salt, solar evaporated salt, brine magnesium chloride and flake magnesium chloride; Plant Nutrition North America, which includes sulfate of potash specialty fertilizer and micronutrients; and Plant Nutrition South America, which manufactures, distributes and markets an array of specialty plant nutrients and supplements developed and formulated from primary and secondary nutrients, micronutrients and biostimulants.

Recent Developments: For the quarter ended Mar 31 2018, net income decreased 41.4% to US$12.6 million from US$21.5 million in the year-earlier quarter. Revenues were US$437.9 million, up 12.9% from US$387.8 million the year before. Operating income was US$26.6 million versus US$41.4 million in the prior-year quarter, a decrease of 35.7%. Direct operating expenses rose 21.7% to US$372.5 million from US$306.2 million in the comparable period the year before. Indirect operating expenses decreased 3.5% from US$40.2 million to US$38.8 million from US$40.2 million in the equivalent prior-year period.

Prospects: Our evaluation of Compass Minerals International Inc. as of Jan. 21, 2018 is the result of our systematic analysis on three basic characteristics: earnings strength, relative valuation, and recent stock price movement. The company has enjoyed a very positive trend in earnings per share over the past 5 quarters. However, while recent estimates for the company have been lowered by analysts, CMP has posted results that fell short of analysts expectations. Based on operating earnings yield, the company is about fairly valued when compared to all of the companies in our coverage universe. Share price changes over the past year indicates that CMP will perform very poorly over the near term.

Financial Data

(US$ in Thousands)	3 Mos	12/31/2017	12/31/2016	12/31/2015	12/31/2014	12/31/2013	12/31/2012	12/31/2011
Earnings Per Share	0.99	1.25	4.79	4.69	6.44	3.88	2.65	4.45
Cash Flow Per Share	5.81	4.34	4.94	4.09	7.24	7.13	4.57	7.67
Tang Book Value Per Share	3.79	4.32	4.36	14.73	14.25	14.39	12.89	11.78
Dividends Per Share	2.880	2.880	2.780	2.640	2.400	2.180	1.980	1.800
Dividend Payout %	290.91	230.40	58.04	56.29	37.27	56.19	74.72	40.45
Income Statement								
Total Revenue	437,900	1,364,400	1,138,000	1,098,700	1,282,500	1,129,600	941,900	1,105,700
EBITDA	31,400	279,200	325,100	315,500	391,100	266,200	195,300	284,500
Depn & Amortn	600	124,400	92,300	79,500	79,200	74,200	65,800	66,200
Income Before Taxes	17,100	101,900	198,700	214,500	291,800	174,100	111,300	197,300
Income Taxes	4,400	60,000	34,600	55,300	73,900	43,300	22,400	48,300
Net Income	12,600	42,700	162,700	159,200	217,900	130,800	88,900	149,000
Average Shares	33,836	33,820	33,780	33,692	33,581	33,420	33,135	32,934
Balance Sheet								
Current Assets	596,500	737,500	715,000	512,300	702,700	577,400	506,900	515,800
Total Assets	2,412,800	2,571,000	2,466,500	1,628,900	1,637,200	1,404,800	1,300,600	1,205,500
Current Liabilities	251,100	268,000	372,000	170,800	237,700	257,600	199,300	326,800
Long-Term Obligations	1,218,200	1,330,400	1,194,800	722,100	622,500	474,700	478,400	326,700
Total Liabilities	1,743,700	1,876,400	1,749,400	989,200	983,600	850,600	797,100	758,900
Stockholders' Equity	669,100	694,600	717,100	639,700	653,600	554,200	503,500	446,600
Shares Outstanding	33,849	33,827	33,789	33,701	33,609	33,476	33,272	33,023
Statistical Record								
Return on Assets %	1.43	1.70	7.92	9.75	14.33	9.67	7.08	12.85
Return on Equity %	4.83	6.05	23.92	24.62	36.08	24.73	18.66	37.51
EBITDA Margin %	7.17	20.46	28.57	28.72	30.50	23.57	20.73	25.73
Net Margin %	2.88	3.13	14.30	14.49	16.99	11.58	9.44	13.48
Asset Turnover	0.60	0.54	0.55	0.67	0.84	0.84	0.75	0.95
Current Ratio	2.38	2.75	1.92	3.00	2.96	2.24	2.54	1.58
Debt to Equity	1.82	1.92	1.67	1.13	0.95	0.86	0.95	0.73
Price Range	75.65-58.85	83.60-60.10	81.85-66.62	95.60-72.12	97.20-77.09	91.64-71.09	78.85-68.38	97.61-64.80
P/E Ratio	76.41-59.44	66.88-48.08	17.09-13.91	20.38-15.38	15.09-11.97	23.62-18.32	29.75-25.80	21.93-14.56
Average Yield %	4.30	4.16	3.76	3.08	2.76	2.78	2.68	2.17

Address: 9900 West 109th Street, Suite 100, Overland Park, KS 66210
Telephone: 913-344-9200

Web Site: www.compassminerals.com
Officers: Francis Joseph (Fran) Malecha - President, Chief Executive Officer James D. Standen - Interim Chief Financial Officer, Chief Financial Officer, Principal Financial Officer, Principal Accounting Officer, Treasurer, Vice President

Auditors: Ernst & Young LLP
Investor Contact: 913-344-9200
Transfer Agents: Computershare Trust Company, N.A., Providence, RI

CONAGRA BRANDS INC

Exchange	Symbol	Price	52Wk Range	Yield	P/E
NYS	CAG	$35.73 (6/29/2018)	38.94-32.43	2.38	16.62

*7 Year Price Score 99.31   *NYSE Composite Index=100   *12 Month Price Score 101.87

Interim Earnings (Per Share)
Qtr.	Aug	Nov	Feb	May
2014-15	1.12	0.02	(2.23)	0.49
2015-16	(2.65)	0.35	0.46	0.27
2016-17	0.42	0.28	0.41	0.35
2017-18	0.36	0.54	0.90	...

Interim Dividends (Per Share)
Amt	Decl	Ex	Rec	Pay
0.212Q	07/20/2017	07/27/2017	07/31/2017	08/31/2017
0.212Q	09/21/2017	10/30/2017	10/31/2017	11/30/2017
0.212Q	12/12/2017	01/29/2018	01/30/2018	03/01/2018
0.212Q	04/20/2018	04/27/2018	04/30/2018	05/31/2018

Indicated Div: $0.85 (Div. Reinv. Plan)

Valuation Analysis
		Institutional Holding	
Forecast EPS	$2.25	No of Institutions	1045
	(06/14/2018)		
Market Cap	$14.1 Billion	Shares	400,899,680
Book Value	$3.7 Billion	% Held	65.82
Price/Book	3.78		
Price/Sales	1.79		

TRADING VOLUME (thousand shares)

Business Summary: Food (MIC: 1.2.1 SIC: 2038 NAIC: 311412)

Conagra Brands is a packaged goods food company. Co.'s segments are: Grocery & Snacks, which includes branded, shelf stable food products sold in various retail channels; Refrigerated & Frozen, which includes branded, temperature controlled food products sold in various retail channels; International, which includes branded food products sold in retail and foodservice channels outside of the U.S.; Foodservice, which includes branded and customized food products for sale to restaurants and other foodservice establishments; and Commercial Foods, which included commercially branded and private label food and ingredients, which were sold to commercial and industrial customers, among others.

Recent Developments: For the quarter ended Feb 25 2018, income from continuing operations increased 94.5% to US$349.2 million from US$179.5 million in the year-earlier quarter. Net income increased 101.8% to US$363.7 million from US$180.2 million in the year-earlier quarter. Revenues were US$1.99 billion, up 0.7% from US$1.98 billion the year before. Direct operating expenses rose 2.6% to US$1.40 billion from US$1.36 billion in the comparable period the year before. Indirect operating expenses decreased 6.4% to US$370.0 million from US$395.4 million in the equivalent prior-year period.

Prospects: Our evaluation of Conagra Brands Inc. as of Jan. 21, 2018 is the result of our systematic analysis on three basic characteristics: earnings strength, relative valuation, and recent stock price movement. The company has managed to produce a neutral trend in earnings per share over the past 5 quarters and while recent estimates for the company have been raised by analysts, CAG has posted better than expected results. Based on operating earnings yield, the company is undervalued when compared to all of the companies in our coverage universe. Share price changes over the past year indicates that CAG will perform poorly over the near term.

Financial Data
(US$ in Thousands)	9 Mos	6 Mos	3 Mos	05/28/2017	05/29/2016	05/31/2015	05/25/2014	05/26/2013
Earnings Per Share	2.15	1.66	1.40	1.46	(1.56)	(0.60)	0.70	1.85
Cash Flow Per Share	2.93	2.59	2.37	2.73	2.79	3.42	3.69	3.45
Dividends Per Share	0.838	0.825	0.863	0.900	1.000	1.000	1.000	0.990
Dividend Payout %	38.95	49.70	61.61	61.64	...	...	142.86	53.51
Income Statement								
Total Revenue	5,972,100	3,977,600	1,804,200	7,826,900	11,642,900	15,832,400	17,702,600	15,491,400
EBITDA	1,093,000	760,000	344,700	958,600	4,551,400	(55,100)	1,066,800	1,480,600
Depn & Amortn	193,400	129,000	64,700	33,600	3,670,000	108,500	111,400	56,200
Income Before Taxes	785,400	556,600	243,600	729,500	583,600	(495,500)	576,400	1,148,800
Income Taxes	138,100	229,500	120,000	254,700	225,400	234,000	298,200	400,200
Net Income	738,800	376,000	152,500	639,300	(677,000)	(252,600)	303,100	773,900
Average Shares	402,500	410,400	419,200	436,000	438,500	426,100	427,500	417,600
Balance Sheet								
Current Assets	2,058,100	2,056,300	2,125,000	2,013,200	3,576,700	3,667,700	4,230,800	4,379,800
Total Assets	10,463,200	10,400,100	10,225,600	10,096,300	13,390,600	17,542,200	19,366,400	20,405,300
Current Liabilities	1,990,700	1,850,300	2,053,600	1,720,500	2,532,400	3,310,200	2,642,400	3,401,300
Long-Term Obligations	3,232,900	3,261,800	2,767,000	2,769,200	4,917,800	6,888,900	8,767,600	8,886,900
Total Liabilities	6,742,700	6,702,400	6,431,800	6,105,500	9,677,000	13,016,200	14,107,900	15,140,900
Stockholders' Equity	3,720,500	3,697,700	3,793,800	3,990,800	3,713,600	4,526,000	5,258,500	5,264,400
Shares Outstanding	393,519	400,660	408,498	416,519	438,064	428,204	421,915	419,465
Statistical Record								
Return on Assets %	8.49	6.48	5.25	5.46	N.M.	N.M.	1.53	4.87
Return on Equity %	22.42	17.36	16.12	16.64	N.M.	N.M.	5.78	15.99
EBITDA Margin %	18.30	19.11	19.11	12.25	39.09	N.M.	6.03	9.56
Net Margin %	12.37	9.45	8.45	8.17	N.M.	N.M.	1.71	5.00
Asset Turnover	0.75	0.72	0.67	0.67	0.75	0.84	0.89	0.98
Current Ratio	1.03	1.11	1.03	1.17	1.41	1.11	1.60	1.29
Debt to Equity	0.87	0.88	0.73	0.69	1.32	1.52	1.67	1.69
Price Range	41.50-32.43	41.50-32.43	41.50-33.07	41.50-33.23	36.13-29.12	30.27-22.36	28.97-21.99	28.14-18.53
P/E Ratio	19.30-15.08	25.00-19.54	29.64-23.62	28.42-22.76	...	...	41.39-31.42	15.21-10.01
Average Yield %	2.28	2.22	2.30	2.38	3.04	...	3.74	4.29

Address: 222 Merchandise Mart Plaza, Suite 1300, Chicago, IL 60654 **Telephone:** 312-549-5000	**Web Site:** www.conagrafoods.com **Officers:** Richard H. Lenny - Chairman Sean M. Connolly - President, Chief Executive Officer	**Auditors:** KPMG LLP **Investor Contact:** 402-240-4154 **Transfer Agents:** Wells Fargo Shareowner Services, St. Paul, MN

CUBESMART

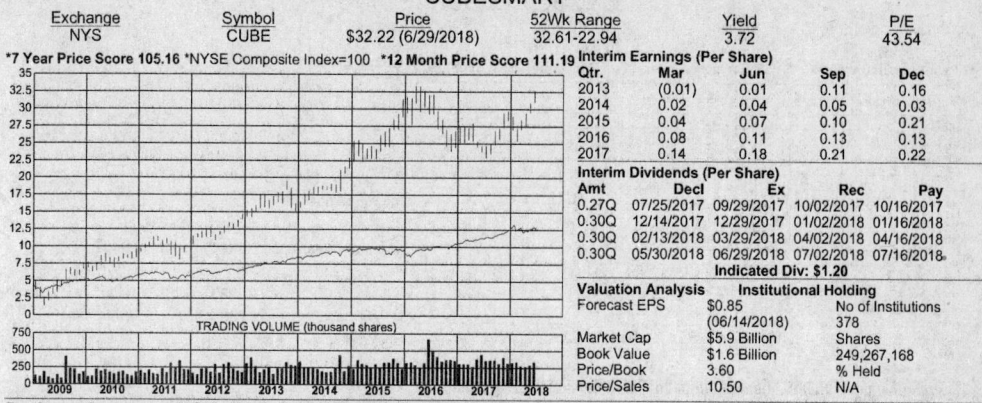

Exchange	Symbol	Price	52Wk Range	Yield	P/E
NYS	CUBE	$32.22 (6/29/2018)	32.61-22.94	3.72	43.54

*7 Year Price Score 105.16 ***NYSE Composite Index=100** ***12 Month Price Score 111.19**

Interim Earnings (Per Share)

Qtr.	Mar	Jun	Sep	Dec
2013	(0.01)	0.01	0.11	0.16
2014	0.02	0.04	0.05	0.03
2015	0.04	0.07	0.10	0.21
2016	0.08	0.11	0.13	0.13
2017	0.14	0.18	0.21	0.22

Interim Dividends (Per Share)

Amt	Decl	Ex	Rec	Pay
0.27Q	07/25/2017	09/29/2017	10/02/2017	10/16/2017
0.30Q	12/14/2017	12/29/2017	01/02/2018	01/16/2018
0.30Q	02/13/2018	03/29/2018	04/02/2018	04/16/2018
0.30Q	05/30/2018	06/29/2018	07/02/2018	07/16/2018

Indicated Div: $1.20

Valuation Analysis

Forecast EPS	$0.85 (06/14/2018)
Market Cap	$5.9 Billion
Book Value	$1.6 Billion
Price/Book	3.60
Price/Sales	10.50

Institutional Holding

No of Institutions	378
Shares	249,267,168
% Held	N/A

TRADING VOLUME (thousand shares)

Business Summary: REITs (MIC: 5.3.1 SIC: 6798 NAIC: 525930)

CubeSmart is a real estate company focused primarily on the ownership, operation, management, acquisition, and development of self-storage properties. At Dec 31 2017, Co. owned 484 self-storage properties in 23 states and in the District of Columbia, and managed 452 stores for third parties in 26 states, bringing the total number of stores it owned and/or managed to 936. Co.'s customers rent storage cubes typically on a month-to-month basis. Additionally, some of Co.'s stores provide outside storage areas for vehicles and boats. Co.'s stores are designed to accommodate both residential and commercial customers, with features such as aisles and load-bearing capabilities for truck access.

Recent Developments: For the year ended Dec 31 2017, net income increased 53.4% to US$135.6 million from US$88.4 million in the prior year. Revenues were US$558.9 million, up 9.6% from US$510.0 million the year before.

Prospects: Our evaluation of CubeSmart as of Jan. 21, 2018 is the result of our systematic analysis on three basic characteristics: earnings strength, relative valuation, and recent stock price movement. The company has produced a positive trend in earnings per share over the past 5 quarters and while recent estimates for the company have remained steady, CUBE has posted better than expected results. Based on operating earnings yield, the company is about fairly valued when compared to all of the companies in our coverage universe. Share price changes over the past year indicates that CUBE will perform well over the near term.

Financial Data

(US$ in Thousands)	12/31/2017	12/31/2016	12/31/2015	12/31/2014	12/31/2013	12/31/2012	12/31/2011	12/31/2010
Earnings Per Share	0.74	0.45	0.42	0.14	0.26	(0.03)	(0.02)	(0.08)
Cash Flow Per Share	1.63	1.47	1.28	1.11	1.06	0.95	0.82	0.76
Tang Book Value Per Share	8.93	9.15	9.33	8.69	7.77	7.51	7.83	7.35
Dividends Per Share	1.110	0.900	0.690	0.550	0.460	0.430	0.280	0.100
Dividend Payout %	150.00	200.00	164.29	392.86	176.92	...	...	...
Income Statement								
Total Revenue	558,943	510,039	444,521	376,963	318,395	283,076	237,605	216,826
EBITDA	344,906	308,456	279,340	210,616	171,944	155,016	123,492	104,635
Depn & Amortn	148,319	164,442	154,113	129,003	117,488	118,573	81,869	70,850
Income Before Taxes	136,997	91,038	79,167	32,621	11,560	(7,551)	(4,771)	(9,851)
Net Income	134,288	87,905	77,712	26,379	41,448	1,817	(398)	(7,393)
Average Shares	181,448	179,533	170,191	150,863	137,742	124,548	102,976	93,998
Balance Sheet								
Current Assets	37,594	20,843	96,458	14,413	15,355	10,565	20,360	16,141
Total Assets	3,545,336	3,475,028	3,114,834	2,786,339	2,358,624	2,150,319	1,875,979	1,478,819
Current Liabilities	199,127	143,415	124,122	97,736	77,930	77,571	62,916	43,936
Long-Term Obligations	1,634,990	1,595,743	1,262,212	1,173,851	1,138,818	1,023,759	758,441	615,457
Total Liabilities	1,916,202	1,819,646	1,471,507	1,338,313	1,266,348	1,160,528	920,066	754,603
Stockholders' Equity	1,629,134	1,655,382	1,643,327	1,448,026	1,092,276	989,791	955,913	724,216
Shares Outstanding	182,215	180,083	174,667	163,956	139,328	131,794	122,058	98,596
Statistical Record								
Return on Assets %	3.83	2.66	2.63	1.03	1.84	0.09	N.M.	N.M.
Return on Equity %	8.18	5.32	5.03	2.08	3.98	0.19	N.M.	N.M.
EBITDA Margin %	61.71	60.48	62.84	55.87	54.00	54.76	51.97	48.26
Net Margin %	24.03	17.23	17.48	7.00	13.02	0.64	N.M.	N.M.
Asset Turnover	0.16	0.15	0.15	0.15	0.14	0.14	0.14	0.14
Current Ratio	0.19	0.15	0.78	0.15	0.20	0.14	0.32	0.37
Debt to Equity	1.00	0.96	0.77	0.81	1.04	1.03	0.79	0.85
Price Range	29.65-22.94	33.30-23.88	31.42-22.07	22.92-15.63	19.48-14.24	14.67-10.30	11.39-8.04	9.56-6.31
P/E Ratio	40.07-31.00	74.00-53.07	74.81-52.55	163.71-111.64	74.92-54.77	...	...	...
Average Yield %	4.26	3.10	2.71	2.96	2.80	3.50	2.79	1.25

Address: 5 Old Lancaster Road, Malvern, PA 19355	Web Site: www.cubesmart.com	Auditors: KPMG LLP
Telephone: 610-535-5000	Officers: William M. Diefenderfer - Chairman Christopher P. Marr - President, Chief Executive Officer, Chief Operating Officer, Chief Investment Officer, Treasurer	Investor Contact: 610-293-5700 Transfer Agents: American Stock Transfer & Trust Co., LLC, Brooklyn, NY

CONCHO RESOURCES INC

Exchange	Symbol	Price	52Wk Range	Yield	P/E
NYS	CXO	$138.35 (6/29/2018)	161.66-108.05	N/A	18.18

*7 Year Price Score 99.45 *NYSE Composite Index=100 *12 Month Price Score 99.32

TRADING VOLUME (thousand shares)

Interim Earnings (Per Share)

Qtr.	Mar	Jun	Sep	Dec
2015	0.06	(1.02)	1.49	(0.02)
2016	(7.95)	(2.04)	(0.38)	(0.67)
2017	4.37	1.02	(0.77)	1.78
2018	5.58	...	...	...

Interim Dividends (Per Share)

No Dividends Paid

Valuation Analysis   Institutional Holding

Forecast EPS	$4.09	No of Institutions
	(06/14/2018)	684
Market Cap	$20.6 Billion	Shares
Book Value	$9.7 Billion	166,490,976
Price/Book	2.12	% Held
Price/Sales	7.06	95.04

Business Summary: Production & Extraction (MIC: 9.1.1 SIC: 1311 NAIC: 211111)

Concho Resources is an independent oil and natural gas company engaged in the acquisition, development, exploration and production of oil and natural gas properties. Co.'s four core operating areas include: Northern Delaware Basin, which comprised the Avalon Shale, Bone Spring and Wolfcamp; Southern Delaware Basin, where it mainly targets the Bone Spring and Wolfcamp formations; Midland Basin, where it mainly targets the Spraberry and Wolfcamp zones; and New Mexico Shelf, where it mainly targets the Yeso, San Andres and Grayburg formations. At Dec 31 2017, Co.'s total estimated proved reserves of 840.0 million barrels of oil equivalents consisted of about 60.0% oil and 40.0% natural gas.

Recent Developments: For the quarter ended Mar 31 2018, net income increased 28.5% to US$835.0 million from US$650.0 million in the year-earlier quarter. Revenues were US$947.0 million, up 54.7% from US$612.0 million the year before. Operating income was US$1.02 billion versus US$1.06 billion in the prior-year quarter, a decrease of 3.7%. Direct operating expenses rose 48.1% to US$200.0 million from US$135.0 million in the comparable period the year before. Indirect operating income amounted to US$275.0 million compared with an income of US$584.0 million in the equivalent prior-year period.

Prospects: Our evaluation of Concho Resources Inc. as of Jan. 21, 2018 is the result of our systematic analysis on three basic characteristics: earnings strength, relative valuation, and recent stock price movement. The company has suffered a very negative trend in earnings per share over the past 5 quarters and while recent estimates for the company have been raised by analysts, CXO has posted better than expected results. Based on operating earnings yield, the company is overvalued when compared to all of the companies in our coverage universe. Share price changes over the past year indicates that CXO will perform very poorly over the near term.

Financial Data
(US$ in Thousands)

	3 Mos	12/31/2017	12/31/2016	12/31/2015	12/31/2014	12/31/2013	12/31/2012	12/31/2011
Earnings Per Share	7.61	6.41	(10.85)	0.54	4.88	2.39	4.15	5.28
Cash Flow Per Share	12.01	11.51	10.25	7.48	15.38	13.13	11.96	11.69
Tang Book Value Per Share	65.18	59.77	52.02	53.56	46.49	35.49	32.86	28.42
Income Statement								
Total Revenue	947,000	2,586,000	1,634,988	1,803,573	2,660,147	2,319,919	1,819,814	1,739,967
EBITDA	1,125,000	1,048,000	(2,114,418)	330,955	2,052,361	1,348,348	1,417,104	1,293,188
Depn & Amortn	6,000	21,000	20,600	18,300	979,740	772,608	575,128	428,377
Income Before Taxes	1,089,000	881,000	(2,338,536)	97,271	855,960	357,159	659,271	746,451
Income Taxes	254,000	(75,000)	(876,090)	31,371	317,785	118,237	251,041	285,848
Net Income	835,000	956,000	(1,462,446)	65,900	538,175	251,003	431,689	548,137
Average Shares	148,462	147,956	134,755	120,373	109,132	103,913	103,972	103,653
Balance Sheet								
Current Assets	719,000	592,000	546,494	1,314,550	1,188,396	520,875	458,882	411,023
Total Assets	14,381,000	13,732,000	12,119,326	12,641,876	11,799,963	9,591,164	8,589,437	6,849,576
Current Liabilities	1,109,000	1,165,000	753,186	596,420	1,427,193	756,868	740,086	701,477
Long-Term Obligations	2,370,000	2,691,000	2,740,580	3,332,188	3,517,320	3,630,421	3,101,103	2,080,141
Total Liabilities	4,643,000	4,817,000	4,496,633	5,699,325	6,519,175	5,833,215	5,123,241	3,868,837
Stockholders' Equity	9,738,000	8,915,000	7,622,693	6,942,551	5,280,788	3,757,949	3,466,196	2,980,739
Shares Outstanding	149,070	148,726	146,058	129,137	113,004	105,095	104,581	103,700
Statistical Record								
Return on Assets %	8.24	7.40	N.M.	0.54	5.03	2.76	5.58	8.97
Return on Equity %	12.49	11.56	N.M.	1.08	11.91	6.95	13.36	20.44
EBITDA Margin %	118.80	40.53	N.M.	18.35	77.15	58.12	77.87	74.32
Net Margin %	88.17	36.97	N.M.	3.65	20.23	10.82	23.72	31.50
Asset Turnover	0.21	0.20	0.13	0.15	0.25	0.26	0.24	0.28
Current Ratio	0.65	0.51	0.73	2.20	0.83	0.69	0.62	0.59
Debt to Equity	0.24	0.30	0.36	0.48	0.67	0.97	0.89	0.70
Price Range	161.66-108.05	153.92-108.05	143.25-72.52	128.31-86.67	148.00-83.01	120.72-80.14	113.43-77.80	109.79-67.25
P/E Ratio	21.24-14.20	24.01-16.86	...	237.61-160.50	30.33-17.01	50.51-33.53	27.33-18.75	20.79-12.74

Address: One Concho Center, 600 West Illinois Avenue, Midland, TX 79701	Web Site: www.concho.com	Auditors: Grant Thornton LLP
Telephone: 432-683-7443	Officers: Timothy A. Leach - Chairman, President, Chief Executive Officer Jack F. Harper - President,	Investor Contact: 432-685-2533
Fax: 432-683-7441	Chief Financial Officer, Executive Vice President, Treasurer, Senior Vice President, Chief of Staff	Transfer Agents: American Stock Transfer & Trust Company, New York, NY

CONDUENT INC

Exchange	Symbol	Price	52Wk Range	Yield	P/E
NYS	CNDT	$18.17 (6/29/2018)	20.85-15.05	N/A	29.31

*7 Year Price Score N/A   *NYSE Composite Index=100   *12 Month Price Score 110.12

Interim Earnings (Per Share)

Qtr.	Mar	Jun	Sep	Dec
2016	(0.12)	(0.05)	0.01	(4.69)
2017	(0.04)	(0.03)	(0.09)	1.00
2018	(0.26)	...	...	...

Interim Dividends (Per Share)

No Dividends Paid

Valuation Analysis   Institutional Holding

Forecast EPS	$1.02	No of Institutions
	(06/14/2018)	361
Market Cap	$3.8 Billion	Shares
Book Value	$3.7 Billion	196,935,040
Price/Book	1.05	% Held
Price/Sales	0.65	N/A

TRADING VOLUME (thousand shares)

Business Summary: Business Services (MIC: 7.5.2 SIC: 7389 NAIC: 813910)

Conduent is a holding company. Through its subsidiaries, Co. is a provider of business process services in transaction-intensive processing, analytics and automation. Co.'s reportable segments are: Commercial Industries, which delivers end-to-end business-to-business and business-to-customer services including customer care, human resource management, finance and accounting, workforce learning services and legal business services; Healthcare, which provides services and solutions and subject matter personnel to providers, payers, pharmaceutical and life science companies and government agencies; and Public Sector, which provides government-centric business process services.

Recent Developments: For the quarter ended Mar 31 2018, loss from continuing operations was US$50.0 million compared with a loss of US$10.0 million in the year-earlier quarter. Net loss amounted to US$50.0 million versus a net loss of US$6.0 million in the year-earlier quarter. Revenues were US$1.42 billion, down 8.6% from US$1.55 billion the year before. Direct operating expenses declined 9.7% to US$1.17 billion from US$1.29 billion in the comparable period the year before. Indirect operating expenses increased 8.9% to US$306.0 million from US$281.0 million in the equivalent prior-year period.

Prospects: Our evaluation of Conduent Inc. as of Jan. 21, 2018 is the result of our systematic analysis on three basic characteristics: earnings strength, relative valuation, and recent stock price movement. The company has suffered a very negative trend in earnings per share over the past 5 quarters and while recent estimates for the company have remained steady, CNDT has posted better than expected results. Based on operating earnings yield, the company is undervalued when compared to all of the companies in our coverage universe. Share price changes over the past year indicates that CNDT will perform poorly over the near term.

Financial Data
(US$ in Millions)

	3 Mos	12/31/2017	12/31/2016	12/31/2015	12/31/2014	12/31/2013
Earnings Per Share	0.62	0.83	(4.85)	...	...	...
Cash Flow Per Share	1.80	1.48	0.53	...	...	...
Income Statement						
Total Revenue	1,420	6,022	6,408	6,662	6,938	6,879
EBITDA	(19)	489	(777)	(129)	523	709
Depn & Amortn	2	368	410	376	395	385
Income Before Taxes	(54)	(16)	(1,227)	(574)	10	207
Income Taxes	(4)	(193)	(244)	(238)	(24)	72
Net Income	(50)	181	(983)	(414)	(81)	182
Average Shares	205	206	202	...	...	...
Balance Sheet						
Current Assets	2,620	2,710	1,917	1,874	3,252	...
Total Assets	7,511	7,548	7,709	9,058	10,954	...
Current Liabilities	1,374	1,368	1,402	2,741	4,139	...
Long-Term Obligations	1,972	1,979	1,913	37	43	...
Total Liabilities	3,859	3,877	4,279	3,896	5,543	...
Stockholders' Equity	3,652	3,671	3,430	5,162	5,411	...
Shares Outstanding	210	210	202	...	...	...
Statistical Record						
Return on Assets %	1.80	2.37	N.M.	N.M.	...	...
Return on Equity %	3.86	5.10	N.M.	N.M.	...	...
EBITDA Margin %	N.M.	8.12	N.M.	N.M.	7.54	10.31
Net Margin %	N.M.	3.01	N.M.	N.M.	N.M.	2.65
Asset Turnover	0.77	0.79	0.76	0.67	...	...
Current Ratio	1.91	1.98	1.37	0.68	0.79	...
Debt to Equity	0.54	0.54	0.56	0.01	0.01	...
Price Range	20.01-15.05	17.70-13.31	...	...	...	...
P/E Ratio	32.27-24.27	21.33-16.04	...	...	...	...

Address: 100 Campus Drive, Suite 200, Florham Park, NJ 07932 **Telephone:** 844-663-2638	**Web Site:** www.conduent.com **Officers:** Ashok Vemuri - Chief Executive Officer Douglas H. Marshall - Secretary	**Auditors:** PricewaterhouseCoopers LLP **Transfer Agents:** Computershare Trust Company, N.A.

CONOCOPHILLIPS

Exchange	Symbol	Price	52Wk Range	Yield	P/E
NYS	COP	$69.62 (6/29/2018)	70.66-42.50	1.64	N/A

*7 Year Price Score 77.21 *NYSE Composite Index=100 *12 Month Price Score 122.19

Interim Earnings (Per Share)

Qtr.	Mar	Jun	Sep	Dec
2015	0.22	(0.15)	(0.87)	(2.78)
2016	(1.18)	(0.86)	(0.84)	(0.03)
2017	0.47	(2.78)	0.34	1.28
2018	0.75	...	...	...

Interim Dividends (Per Share)

Amt	Decl	Ex	Rec	Pay
0.265Q	10/06/2017	10/13/2017	10/16/2017	12/01/2017
0.285Q	02/01/2018	02/09/2018	02/12/2018	03/01/2018
0.285Q	05/04/2018	05/11/2018	05/14/2018	06/01/2018
0.285Q	07/11/2018	07/20/2018	07/23/2018	09/04/2018

Indicated Div: $1.14 (Div. Reinv. Plan)

Valuation Analysis | **Institutional Holding**

Forecast EPS	$4.16	No of Institutions
	(06/14/2018)	2176
Market Cap	$81.5 Billion	Shares
Book Value	$30.5 Billion	1,085,715,584
Price/Book	2.67	% Held
Price/Sales	2.41	63.21

Business Summary: Production & Extraction (MIC: 9.1.1 SIC: 1311 NAIC: 211111)

ConocoPhillips explores for, produces, transports and markets crude oil, bitumen, natural gas, liquefied natural gas and natural gas liquids. Co. has six segments: Alaska, which operates in Alaska; Lower 48, which operates in the U.S. Lower 48 states and the Gulf of Mexico; Canada, which operates in western Canada and northeastern Alberta; Europe and North Africa, which has activities in Norway, the U.K. and Libya; Asia Pacific and Middle East, which has activities in China, Indonesia, Malaysia, Australia, Qatar, Timor-Leste and Brunei; and Other International, which has activities in Colombia and Chile. At Dec 31 2017, Co.'s proved reserves totaled 5.04 billion barrels of oil equivalent.

Recent Developments: For the quarter ended Mar 31 2018, net income increased 50.3% to US$900.0 million from US$599.0 million in the year-earlier quarter. Revenues were US$8.96 billion, up 15.3% from US$7.77 billion the year before. Direct operating expenses rose 9.0% to US$4.89 billion from US$4.48 billion in the comparable period the year before. Indirect operating expenses decreased 34.7% to US$2.30 billion from US$3.52 billion in the equivalent prior-year period.

Prospects: Our evaluation of ConocoPhillips as of Jan. 21, 2018 is the result of our systematic analysis on three basic characteristics: earnings strength, relative valuation, and recent stock price movement. The company has generated a negative trend in earnings per share over the past 5 quarters and while recent estimates for the company have been raised by analysts, COP has posted better than expected results. Based on operating earnings yield, the company is overvalued when compared to all of the companies in our coverage universe. Share price changes over the past year indicates that COP will perform very poorly over the near term.

Financial Data

(US$ in Thousands)	3 Mos	12/31/2017	12/31/2016	12/31/2015	12/31/2014	12/31/2013	12/31/2012	12/31/2011
Earnings Per Share	(0.41)	(0.70)	(2.91)	(3.58)	5.51	7.38	6.72	8.97
Cash Flow Per Share	6.51	5.80	3.53	6.10	13.53	13.07	11.16	14.29
Tang Book Value Per Share	26.11	26.00	28.27	32.17	42.16	42.49	39.33	47.56
Dividends Per Share	1.080	1.060	1.000	2.940	2.840	2.700	2.640	2.640
Dividend Payout %	...	...	...	...	51.54	36.59	39.29	29.43
Income Statement								
Total Revenue	8,961,000	32,584,000	24,360,000	30,935,000	55,517,000	58,248,000	62,004,000	251,226,000
EBITDA	3,372,000	5,328,000	4,777,000	2,794,000	18,367,000	22,492,000	22,712,000	31,907,000
Depn & Amortn	1,412,000	6,845,000	9,062,000	9,113,000	8,329,000	7,434,000	6,580,000	7,934,000
Income Before Taxes	1,776,000	(2,615,000)	(5,530,000)	(7,239,000)	9,390,000	14,446,000	15,423,000	23,001,000
Income Taxes	876,000	(1,822,000)	(1,971,000)	(2,868,000)	3,583,000	6,409,000	7,942,000	10,499,000
Net Income	888,000	(855,000)	(3,615,000)	(4,428,000)	6,869,000	9,156,000	8,428,000	12,436,000
Average Shares	1,186,454	1,221,038	1,245,440	1,241,919	1,245,863	1,239,803	1,253,093	1,387,100
Balance Sheet								
Current Assets	13,187,000	16,512,000	8,609,000	8,789,000	15,068,000	19,023,000	23,989,000	30,218,000
Total Assets	70,727,000	73,362,000	89,772,000	97,484,000	116,539,000	118,057,000	117,144,000	153,230,000
Current Liabilities	7,109,000	9,397,000	6,909,000	9,256,000	11,537,000	15,129,000	17,443,000	28,068,000
Long-Term Obligations	16,709,000	17,128,000	26,186,000	23,453,000	22,383,000	21,073,000	20,770,000	21,610,000
Total Liabilities	40,181,000	42,755,000	54,798,000	57,722,000	64,628,000	65,967,000	69,157,000	88,006,000
Stockholders' Equity	30,546,000	30,607,000	34,974,000	39,762,000	51,911,000	52,090,000	47,987,000	65,224,000
Shares Outstanding	1,170,066	1,177,107	1,237,269	1,235,995	1,231,352	1,225,939	1,220,017	1,285,669
Statistical Record								
Return on Assets %	N.M.	N.M.	N.M.	N.M.	5.86	7.79	6.22	8.04
Return on Equity %	N.M.	N.M.	N.M.	N.M.	13.21	18.30	14.85	18.59
EBITDA Margin %	37.63	16.35	19.61	9.03	33.08	38.61	36.63	12.70
Net Margin %	9.91	N.M.	N.M.	N.M.	12.37	15.72	13.59	4.95
Asset Turnover	0.43	0.40	0.26	0.29	0.47	0.50	0.46	1.62
Current Ratio	1.85	1.76	1.25	0.95	1.31	1.26	1.38	1.08
Debt to Equity	0.55	0.56	0.75	0.59	0.43	0.40	0.43	0.33
Price Range	60.67-42.50	56.23-42.50	52.64-31.88	69.88-42.19	86.76-61.69	74.34-56.81	59.63-50.82	61.91-46.49
P/E Ratio	...	...	...	...	15.75-11.20	10.07-7.70	8.87-7.56	6.90-5.18
Average Yield %	2.17	2.22	2.35	5.05	3.83	4.18	4.71	4.84

Address: 600 North Dairy Ashford, Houston, TX 77079
Telephone: 281-293-1000
Fax: 281-661-7636

Web Site: www.conocophillips.com
Officers: Ryan M. Lance - Chairman, Chief Executive Officer, Division Officer Don E. Wallette - Executive Vice President, Chief Financial Officer, Executive Vice President (frmr)

Auditors: El Sayed El Ayouty & Co.
Investor Contact: 212-207-1996
Transfer Agents: Computershare, Canton, MA

CONSOLIDATED EDISON INC

Exchange	Symbol	Price	52Wk Range	Yield	P/E	Div Acheiver
NYS	ED	$77.98 (6/29/2018)	89.66-71.39	3.67	15.44	43 Years

*7 Year Price Score 98.66 *NYSE Composite Index=100 *12 Month Price Score 92.59

Interim Earnings (Per Share)

Qtr.	Mar	Jun	Sep	Dec
2015	1.26	0.74	1.45	0.59
2016	1.05	0.77	1.62	0.66
2017	1.27	0.57	1.48	1.63
2018	1.37	...	...	...

Interim Dividends (Per Share)

Amt	Decl	Ex	Rec	Pay
0.69Q	07/20/2017	08/14/2017	08/16/2017	09/15/2017
0.69Q	10/19/2017	11/14/2017	11/15/2017	12/15/2017
0.715Q	01/18/2018	02/13/2018	02/14/2018	03/15/2018
0.715Q	04/19/2018	05/15/2018	05/16/2018	06/15/2018

Indicated Div: $2.86 (Div. Reinv. Plan)

Valuation Analysis

Forecast EPS	$4.27	No of Institutions
	(06/14/2018)	1200
Market Cap	$24.3 Billion	Shares
Book Value	$15.7 Billion	222,765,888
Price/Book	1.55	% Held
Price/Sales	1.99	46.85

Institutional Holding

Business Summary: Electric Utilities (MIC: 3.1.1 SIC: 4931 NAIC: 221121)

Consolidated Edison is a holding company. Co. owns Consolidated Edison Company of New York, Inc., which at Dec 31 2017, provided electricity, gas and steam to about 3.4 million customers in New York City and Westchester County, 1.1 million customers in Manhattan, the Bronx, Queens and Westchester County, and 1,600 customers in Manhattan, respectively. Co. also owns Orange and Rockland Utilities, Inc., which delivers electricity and natural gas to customers in southeastern New York and northern New Jersey; The Clean Energy Businesses, which develop, own and operate renewable and energy infrastructure projects; and Consolidated Edison Transmission, LLC, which invests in transmission projects.

Recent Developments: For the quarter ended Mar 31 2018, net income increased 10.3% to US$428.0 million from US$388.0 million in the year-earlier quarter. Revenues were US$3.36 billion, up 4.2% from US$3.23 billion the year before. Operating income was US$755.0 million versus US$812.0 million in the prior-year quarter, a decrease of 7.0%. Direct operating expenses rose 9.4% to US$1.69 billion from US$1.55 billion in the comparable period the year before. Indirect operating expenses increased 5.4% to US$918.0 million from US$871.0 million in the equivalent prior-year period.

Prospects: Our evaluation of Consolidated Edison Inc. as of Jan. 21, 2018 is the result of our systematic analysis on three basic characteristics: earnings strength, relative valuation, and recent stock price movement. The company has managed to produce a neutral trend in earnings per share over the past 5 quarters and while recent estimates for the company have remained steady, ED has posted results that fell short of analysts expectations. Based on operating earnings yield, the company is undervalued when compared to all of the companies in our coverage universe. Share price changes over the past year indicates that ED will perform very well over the near term.

Financial Data

(US$ in Thousands)	3 Mos	12/31/2017	12/31/2016	12/31/2015	12/31/2014	12/31/2013	12/31/2012	12/31/2011
Earnings Per Share	5.05	4.94	4.12	4.05	3.71	3.61	3.86	3.57
Cash Flow Per Share	9.86	10.96	11.48	11.18	9.67	8.71	8.85	10.72
Tang Book Value Per Share	48.54	47.93	45.07	43.08	41.46	40.33	39.05	38.30
Dividends Per Share	2.785	2.760	2.680	2.600	2.520	2.460	2.420	2.400
Dividend Payout %	55.15	55.87	65.05	64.20	67.92	68.14	62.69	67.23
Income Statement								
Total Revenue	3,364,000	12,033,000	12,075,000	12,554,000	12,919,000	12,354,000	12,188,000	12,938,000
EBITDA	712,000	3,943,000	3,645,000	3,529,000	3,424,000	3,291,000	3,342,000	3,189,000
Depn & Amortn	(28,000)	1,217,000	1,006,000	1,078,000	1,173,000	1,034,000	997,000	933,000
Income Before Taxes	545,000	1,997,000	1,943,000	1,798,000	1,660,000	1,538,000	1,741,000	1,662,000
Income Taxes	117,000	472,000	698,000	605,000	568,000	476,000	600,000	600,000
Net Income	428,000	1,525,000	1,245,000	1,193,000	1,092,000	1,062,000	1,141,000	1,062,000
Average Shares	311,600	308,800	301,900	294,400	294,000	294,400	294,500	294,400
Balance Sheet								
Current Assets	3,773,000	3,537,000	3,406,000	3,836,000	3,854,000	3,891,000	3,451,000	3,638,000
Total Assets	48,900,000	48,111,000	48,255,000	45,642,000	44,308,000	40,647,000	41,209,000	39,214,000
Current Liabilities	5,651,000	4,902,000	3,843,000	4,720,000	3,781,000	4,730,000	3,945,000	2,987,000
Long-Term Obligations	14,730,000	14,731,000	14,735,000	12,006,000	11,631,000	10,490,000	10,064,000	10,145,000
Total Liabilities	33,246,000	32,693,000	33,957,000	32,590,000	31,732,000	28,402,000	29,340,000	27,565,000
Stockholders' Equity	15,654,000	15,418,000	14,298,000	13,052,000	12,576,000	12,245,000	11,869,000	11,649,000
Shares Outstanding	311,000	310,000	305,000	293,000	292,876	292,872	292,871	292,888
Statistical Record								
Return on Assets %	3.22	3.17	2.64	2.65	2.57	2.59	2.83	2.82
Return on Equity %	10.38	10.26	9.08	9.31	8.80	8.81	9.68	9.27
EBITDA Margin %	21.17	32.77	30.19	28.11	26.50	26.64	27.42	24.65
Net Margin %	12.72	12.67	10.31	9.50	8.45	8.60	9.36	8.21
Asset Turnover	0.25	0.25	0.26	0.28	0.30	0.30	0.30	0.34
Current Ratio	0.67	0.72	0.89	0.81	1.02	0.82	0.87	1.22
Debt to Equity	0.94	0.96	1.03	0.92	0.92	0.86	0.85	0.87
Price Range	89.66-74.35	89.66-72.64	81.67-64.27	71.40-57.21	68.50-52.46	63.66-54.33	64.94-54.10	62.59-48.85
P/E Ratio	17.75-14.72	18.15-14.70	19.82-15.60	17.63-14.13	18.46-14.14	17.63-15.05	16.82-14.02	17.53-13.68
Average Yield %	3.40	3.40	3.62	4.11	4.39	4.25	4.07	4.46

Address: 4 Irving Place, New York, NY 10003	**Web Site:** www.conedison.com	**Auditors:** PricewaterhouseCoopers LLP
Telephone: 212-460-4600	**Officers:** John McAvoy - Chairman, President, Chief Executive Officer Elizabeth D. Moore - Senior Vice President, General Counsel	**Investor Contact:** 212-460-6611
		Transfer Agents: Computershare, Pittsburgh, PA

CONSTELLATION BRANDS INC

Exchange	Symbol	Price	52Wk Range	Yield	P/E
NYS	STZ	$218.87 (6/29/2018)	234.22-191.73	1.35	16.44

*7 Year Price Score 160.65 *NYSE Composite Index=100 *12 Month Price Score 103.02

Interim Earnings (Per Share)

Qtr.	May	Aug	Nov	Feb
2015-16	1.18	1.49	1.33	1.19
2016-17	1.55	1.75	1.98	2.25
2017-18	2.00	2.48	2.44	4.62
2018-19	3.77	...	...	...

Interim Dividends (Per Share)

Amt	Decl	Ex	Rec	Pay
0.52Q	10/04/2017	11/06/2017	11/07/2017	11/21/2017
0.52Q	01/04/2018	02/08/2018	02/09/2018	02/23/2018
0.74Q	03/28/2018	05/09/2018	05/10/2018	05/24/2018
0.74Q	06/28/2018	08/09/2018	08/10/2018	08/24/2018

Indicated Div: $2.96

TRADING VOLUME (thousand shares)

Valuation Analysis

		Institutional Holding	
Forecast EPS	$9.60 (06/14/2018)	No of Institutions	1218
Market Cap	$41.8 Billion	Shares	181,184,208
Book Value	$10.6 Billion	% Held	76.09
Price/Book	3.96		
Price/Sales	5.44		

Business Summary: Beverages (MIC: 1.2.2 SIC: 2084 NAIC: 312130)

Constellation Brands is an international beverage alcohol company. Co. produces and markets beer, wine and spirits with operations in the U.S., Mexico, New Zealand, Italy and Canada. Co. has two business divisions: Beer, which import, market and sells in the U.S. Mexican Beer brands in the import category and sells Ballast Point brand in the craft beer category; and Wine and Spirits, which sells a number of wine brands across all categories, such as table wine, sparkling wine and dessert wine, across popular, premium and luxury categories, complemented by certain premium spirits brands.

Recent Developments: For the quarter ended May 31 2018, net income increased 86.1% to US$746.3 million from US$401.0 million in the year-earlier quarter. Revenues were US$2.05 billion, up 6.1% from US$1.93 billion the year before. Operating income was US$625.4 million versus US$561.1 million in the prior-year quarter, an increase of 11.5%. Direct operating expenses rose 6.2% to US$998.5 million from US$940.2 million in the comparable period the year before. Indirect operating expenses decreased 0.9% to US$423.2 million from US$427.2 million in the equivalent prior-year period.

Prospects: Our evaluation of Constellation Brands Inc. as of Jan. 21, 2018 is the result of our systematic analysis on three basic characteristics: earnings strength, relative valuation, and recent stock price movement. The company has generated a negative trend in earnings per share over the past 5 quarters and while recent estimates for the company have been raised by analysts, STZ has posted better than expected results. Based on operating earnings yield, the company is about fairly valued when compared to all of the companies in our coverage universe. Share price changes over the past year indicates that STZ will perform very well over the near term.

Financial Data

(US$ in Thousands)	3 Mos	02/28/2018	02/28/2017	02/29/2016	02/28/2015	02/28/2014	02/28/2013	02/29/2012
Earnings Per Share	13.31	11.55	7.52	5.18	4.17	9.83	2.04	2.13
Cash Flow Per Share	10.73	9.92	8.51	7.17	5.61	4.39	3.05	3.83
Dividends Per Share	2.300	2.080	1.600	1.240	...	...	...	...
Dividend Payout %	17.28	18.01	21.28	23.94	...	...	...	...
Income Statement								
Total Revenue	2,047,100	7,585,000	7,331,500	6,548,400	6,028,000	4,867,700	2,796,100	2,654,300
EBITDA	714,100	2,574,000	2,693,300	1,985,000	1,697,800	2,593,000	625,800	584,900
Depn & Amortn	88,700	386,500	293,900	221,000	202,000	155,300	115,400	98,400
Income Before Taxes	537,600	1,855,500	2,066,100	1,450,100	1,158,100	2,114,500	283,300	305,500
Income Taxes	155,700	11,900	554,200	440,600	343,400	259,200	128,600	89,000
Net Income	743,800	2,318,900	1,535,100	1,054,900	839,300	1,943,100	387,800	445,000
Average Shares	197,060	200,745	204,099	203,821	201,224	197,570	190,307	208,655
Balance Sheet								
Current Assets	3,604,800	3,474,000	3,230,000	2,977,600	2,910,800	2,747,200	2,471,200	2,034,300
Total Assets	23,096,700	20,538,700	18,602,400	16,965,000	15,144,500	14,302,100	7,638,100	7,109,900
Current Liabilities	1,990,500	1,944,700	2,697,600	2,272,300	1,130,700	2,025,700	677,900	1,199,600
Long-Term Obligations	9,416,400	9,417,600	7,720,700	6,816,200	7,137,500	6,373,300	3,277,800	2,421,400
Total Liabilities	12,540,300	12,492,600	11,711,200	10,405,400	9,373,800	9,320,800	4,777,800	4,433,900
Stockholders' Equity	10,556,400	8,046,100	6,891,200	6,559,600	5,770,700	4,981,300	2,860,300	2,676,000
Shares Outstanding	191,153	191,306	194,598	199,458	194,541	191,470	184,776	214,601
Statistical Record								
Return on Assets %	12.65	11.85	8.63	6.55	5.70	17.71	5.26	6.22
Return on Equity %	29.64	31.05	22.83	17.06	15.61	49.56	14.01	16.98
EBITDA Margin %	34.88	33.94	36.74	30.31	28.17	53.27	22.38	22.04
Net Margin %	36.33	30.57	20.94	16.11	13.92	39.92	13.87	16.77
Asset Turnover	0.37	0.39	0.41	0.41	0.41	0.44	0.38	0.37
Current Ratio	1.81	1.79	1.20	1.31	2.57	1.36	3.65	1.70
Debt to Equity	0.89	1.17	1.12	1.04	1.24	1.28	1.15	0.90
Price Range	234.22-179.14	228.57-155.79	171.24-138.71	154.36-110.91	115.78-77.97	82.07-43.25	44.71-18.69	22.97-16.63
P/E Ratio	17.60-13.46	19.79-13.49	22.77-18.45	29.80-21.41	27.76-18.70	8.35-4.40	21.92-9.16	10.78-7.81
Average Yield %	1.09	1.06	1.01	0.97	...	...	...	...

Address: 207 High Point Drive, Building 100, Victor, NY 14564 Telephone: 585-678-7100	Web Site: www.cbrands.com Officers: Richard Sands - Chairman William A. Newlands - President, Executive Vice President, Chief Operating Officer, Division Officer	Auditors: KPMG LLP Investor Contact: 585-678-7483 Transfer Agents: Computershare Shareowner Services, College Station, TX

CONTINENTAL RESOURCES INC.

Exchange	Symbol	Price	52Wk Range	Yield	P/E
NYS	CLR	$64.76 (6/29/2018)	68.83-30.03	N/A	23.64

*7 Year Price Score 88.50 *NYSE Composite Index=100 *12 Month Price Score 131.54

Interim Earnings (Per Share)

Qtr.	Mar	Jun	Sep	Dec
2015	(0.36)	0.00	(0.22)	(0.38)
2016	(0.54)	(0.32)	(0.30)	0.07
2017	0.00	(0.17)	0.03	2.25
2018	0.63	...	...	...

Interim Dividends (Per Share)

No Dividends Paid

Valuation Analysis   **Institutional Holding**

Forecast EPS	$3.15	No of Institutions
	(06/14/2018)	563
Market Cap	$24.4 Billion	Shares
Book Value	$5.4 Billion	96,821,376
Price/Book	4.54	% Held
Price/Sales	6.81	24.79

Business Summary: Production & Extraction (MIC: 9.1.1 SIC: 1311 NAIC: 211111)

Continental Resources is an independent crude oil and natural gas company with properties in the North, South and East regions of the U.S. The North region consists of properties north of Kansas and west of the Mississippi River and includes North Dakota Bakken, Montana Bakken, and the Red River units. The South region includes all properties south of Nebraska and west of the Mississippi River including various plays in the South Central Oklahoma Oil Province and Sooner Trend Anadarko Canadian Kingfisher areas of Oklahoma. As of Dec 31 2017, Co.'s estimated proved reserves were 1,331 million barrels of crude oil equivalent.

Recent Developments: For the quarter ended Mar 31 2018, net income increased to US$233.9 million from US$469,000 in the year-earlier quarter. Revenues were US$1.14 billion, up 66.5% from US$685.4 million the year before. Operating income was US$380.7 million versus US$77.2 million in the prior-year quarter, an increase of 393.0%. Direct operating expenses rose 94.5% to US$227.4 million from US$116.9 million in the comparable period the year before. Indirect operating expenses increased 8.5% to US$532.9 million from US$491.3 million in the equivalent prior-year period.

Prospects: Our evaluation of Continental Resources Inc. as of Jan. 21, 2018 is the result of our systematic analysis on three basic characteristics: earnings strength, relative valuation, and recent stock price movement. The company has generated a negative trend in earnings per share over the past 5 quarters and while recent estimates for the company have been raised by analysts, CLR has posted better than expected results. Based on operating earnings yield, the company is overvalued when compared to all of the companies in our coverage universe. Share price changes over the past year indicates that CLR will perform very poorly over the near term.

Financial Data
(US$ in Thousands)

	3 Mos	12/31/2017	12/31/2016	12/31/2015	12/31/2014	12/31/2013	12/31/2012	12/31/2011
Earnings Per Share	2.74	2.11	(1.08)	(0.96)	2.64	2.06	2.04	1.21
Cash Flow Per Share	6.72	5.60	3.03	5.03	9.10	6.96	4.49	3.01
Tang Book Value Per Share	14.26	13.68	11.49	12.52	13.35	10.65	8.52	6.38
Income Statement								
Total Revenue	1,141,028	3,120,828	1,980,273	2,680,167	4,801,618	3,455,150	2,572,520	1,649,789
EBITDA	836,935	2,121,400	1,397,675	1,524,448	3,214,277	2,413,761	1,990,602	1,156,011
Depn & Amortn	455,559	1,670,838	1,709,567	1,746,454	1,368,311	965,437	694,698	391,844
Income Before Taxes	305,482	156,067	(632,454)	(535,085)	1,562,038	1,213,049	1,155,196	687,445
Income Taxes	71,536	(633,380)	(232,775)	(181,417)	584,697	448,830	415,811	258,373
Net Income	233,946	789,447	(399,679)	(353,668)	977,341	764,219	739,385	429,072
Average Shares	374,181	373,768	370,380	369,540	370,758	369,698	363,692	356,460
Balance Sheet								
Current Assets	1,291,055	1,251,725	913,233	822,339	1,389,601	1,147,266	946,783	936,373
Total Assets	14,377,517	14,199,651	13,811,776	14,919,808	15,145,070	11,941,182	9,140,009	5,646,086
Current Liabilities	1,391,277	1,330,242	932,393	923,028	1,952,013	1,473,156	1,125,865	1,111,801
Long-Term Obligations	6,163,775	6,351,405	6,577,697	7,115,644	5,995,837	4,713,821	3,537,771	1,254,301
Total Liabilities	9,016,296	9,068,448	9,509,780	10,250,908	10,177,226	7,988,064	5,976,310	3,337,960
Stockholders' Equity	5,361,221	5,131,203	4,301,996	4,668,900	4,967,844	3,953,118	3,163,699	2,308,126
Shares Outstanding	376,057	375,219	374,492	372,959	372,005	371,317	371,209	361,743
Statistical Record								
Return on Assets %	7.25	5.64	N.M.	N.M.	7.22	7.25	9.97	9.29
Return on Equity %	21.16	16.74	N.M.	N.M.	21.91	21.48	26.95	24.40
EBITDA Margin %	73.35	67.98	70.58	56.88	66.94	69.86	77.38	70.07
Net Margin %	20.50	25.30	N.M.	N.M.	20.35	22.12	28.74	26.01
Asset Turnover	0.25	0.22	0.14	0.18	0.35	0.33	0.35	0.36
Current Ratio	0.93	0.94	0.98	0.89	0.71	0.78	0.84	0.84
Debt to Equity	1.15	1.24	1.53	1.52	1.21	1.19	1.12	0.54
Price Range	58.95-30.03	53.41-30.03	58.01-16.04	52.63-20.00	80.64-30.95	60.50-36.53	47.47-31.29	36.06-22.72
P/E Ratio	21.51-10.96	25.31-14.23	...	...	30.55-11.72	29.37-17.74	23.27-15.34	29.80-18.77

Address: 20 N. Broadway, Oklahoma City, OK 73102 **Telephone:** 405-234-9000	**Web Site:** www.clr.com **Officers:** Harold G. Hamm - Chairman, Chief Executive Officer Jeffrey B. Hume - Vice-Chairman, President, Chief Operating Officer	**Auditors:** Grant Thornton LLP **Investor Contact:** 405-234-9127 **Transfer Agents:** American Stock Transfer & Trust Company, New York

CONVERGYS CORP

Exchange	Symbol	Price	52Wk Range	Yield	P/E
NYS	CVG	$24.44 (6/29/2018)	26.65-21.47	1.80	21.25

*7 Year Price Score 92.85 *NYSE Composite Index=100 *12 Month Price Score 99.44

Interim Earnings (Per Share)

Qtr.	Mar	Jun	Sep	Dec
2015	0.37	0.28	0.56	0.40
2016	0.43	0.32	0.46	0.19
2017	0.38	0.40	0.35	0.10
2018	0.30	...	...	...

Interim Dividends (Per Share)

Amt	Decl	Ex	Rec	Pay
0.10Q	08/08/2017	09/21/2017	09/22/2017	10/06/2017
0.10Q	11/07/2017	12/21/2017	12/22/2017	01/05/2018
0.10Q	02/21/2018	03/22/2018	03/23/2018	04/06/2018
0.11Q	05/08/2018	06/21/2018	06/22/2018	07/06/2018

Indicated Div: $0.44

Valuation Analysis — **Institutional Holding**

Forecast EPS	$1.69 (05/30/2018)	No of Institutions 412
Market Cap	$2.2 Billion	Shares
Book Value	$1.4 Billion	120,969,376
Price/Book	1.63	% Held
Price/Sales	0.82	84.39

Business Summary: IT Services (MIC: 6.3.1 SIC: 7373 NAIC: 541512)

Convergys is a provider of integrated agent, analytics and technology solutions. Co.'s contact center technology solutions include: multichannel interaction solutions; cross-channel integration framework; real-time decisioning engine; robotic process automation; intelligent notifications; campaign management; personalized care; personalized selling; agent productivity; and retention. Co.'s team delivers data-driven insights to enhance customer experience through analytics and consulting, and software solutions, including integrated customer experience analytics and Voice of Customer SaaS software for measuring customer satisfaction. As of Dec 31 2017, Co. operated 140 contact centers.

Recent Developments: For the quarter ended Mar 31 2018, net income decreased 21.4% to US$29.8 million from US$37.9 million in the year-earlier quarter. Revenues were US$674.2 million, down 7.3% from US$727.6 million the year before. Operating income was US$34.5 million versus US$48.8 million in the prior-year quarter, a decrease of 29.3%. Direct operating expenses declined 7.2% to US$417.7 million from US$450.2 million in the comparable period the year before. Indirect operating expenses decreased 2.9% to US$222.0 million from US$228.6 million in the equivalent prior-year period.

Prospects: Our evaluation of Convergys Corp. as of Jan. 21, 2018 is the result of our systematic analysis on three basic characteristics: earnings strength, relative valuation, and recent stock price movement. The company has managed to produce a neutral trend in earnings per share over the past 5 quarters. However, while recent estimates for the company have been mixed, CVG has posted results that fell short of analysts expectations. Based on operating earnings yield, the company is undervalued when compared to all of the companies in our coverage universe. Share price changes over the past year indicates that CVG will perform well over the near term.

Financial Data

(US$ in Thousands)	3 Mos	12/31/2017	12/31/2016	12/31/2015	12/31/2014	12/31/2013	12/31/2012	12/31/2011
Earnings Per Share	1.15	1.22	1.40	1.61	1.13	0.56	0.86	2.72
Cash Flow Per Share	2.65	2.82	3.18	2.54	2.59	2.03	1.00	1.64
Tang Book Value Per Share	1.63	1.66	0.97	1.32	0.21	6.74	7.32	4.88
Dividends Per Share	0.400	0.390	0.350	0.310	0.270	0.240	0.150	...
Dividend Payout %	34.78	31.97	25.00	19.25	23.89	42.86	17.44	...
Income Statement								
Total Revenue	674,200	2,792,100	2,913,600	2,950,600	2,855,500	2,046,100	2,005,000	2,262,000
EBITDA	57,800	303,200	326,200	336,700	291,500	228,000	125,300	265,000
Depn & Amortn	23,800	105,100	122,200	141,500	142,900	85,500	82,400	86,900
Income Before Taxes	29,500	179,800	185,900	177,000	129,300	131,000	29,300	162,000
Income Taxes	(300)	58,400	52,900	8,600	12,800	72,500	1,100	118,900
Net Income	29,800	121,400	143,000	169,000	120,000	60,900	100,600	334,800
Average Shares	98,200	99,900	102,500	104,700	106,200	109,200	117,100	122,900
Balance Sheet								
Current Assets	856,500	857,700	784,800	823,400	890,900	1,060,400	1,100,600	951,100
Total Assets	2,386,300	2,414,700	2,371,800	2,358,100	2,516,500	1,956,700	2,037,900	2,325,900
Current Liabilities	359,500	323,000	347,600	338,400	368,500	292,600	286,500	382,200
Long-Term Obligations	230,000	267,700	297,000	337,400	368,400	60,200	59,900	121,000
Total Liabilities	1,011,900	1,037,000	1,055,900	1,081,900	1,289,300	667,100	666,000	914,400
Stockholders' Equity	1,374,400	1,377,700	1,315,900	1,276,200	1,227,200	1,289,600	1,371,900	1,411,500
Shares Outstanding	91,499	91,800	94,700	96,800	99,400	100,800	105,900	115,400
Statistical Record								
Return on Assets %	4.73	5.07	6.03	6.93	5.37	3.05	4.60	15.04
Return on Equity %	8.36	9.01	11.00	13.50	9.54	4.58	7.21	25.80
EBITDA Margin %	8.57	10.86	11.20	11.41	10.21	11.14	6.25	11.72
Net Margin %	4.42	4.35	4.91	5.73	4.20	2.98	5.02	14.80
Asset Turnover	1.14	1.17	1.23	1.21	1.28	1.02	0.92	1.02
Current Ratio	2.38	2.66	2.26	2.43	2.42	3.62	3.84	2.49
Debt to Equity	0.17	0.19	0.23	0.26	0.30	0.05	0.04	0.09
Price Range	26.65-20.69	26.65-20.33	30.78-22.83	26.47-19.16	22.60-17.45	21.22-15.88	16.83-12.19	14.72-8.61
P/E Ratio	23.17-17.99	21.84-16.66	21.99-16.31	16.44-11.90	20.00-15.44	37.89-28.36	19.57-14.17	5.41-3.17
Average Yield %	1.69	1.63	1.30	1.31	1.32	1.32	1.03	...

Address: 201 East Fourth Street, Cincinnati, OH 45202 Telephone: 513-723-7000	Web Site: www.convergys.com Officers: Andrea J. Ayers - President, Chief Executive Officer, Division Officer Andre S. Valentine - Senior Vice President, Controller, Chief Financial Officer	Auditors: Ernst & Young LLP Investor Contact: 513-723-7000 Transfer Agents: ComputerShare Investment Services, LLC, Canto

COOPER COMPANIES, INC. (THE)

Exchange	Symbol	Price	52Wk Range	Yield	P/E
NYS	COO	$235.45 (6/29/2018)	254.90-217.88	0.03	90.56

*7 Year Price Score 126.35 *NYSE Composite Index=100 *12 Month Price Score 96.61

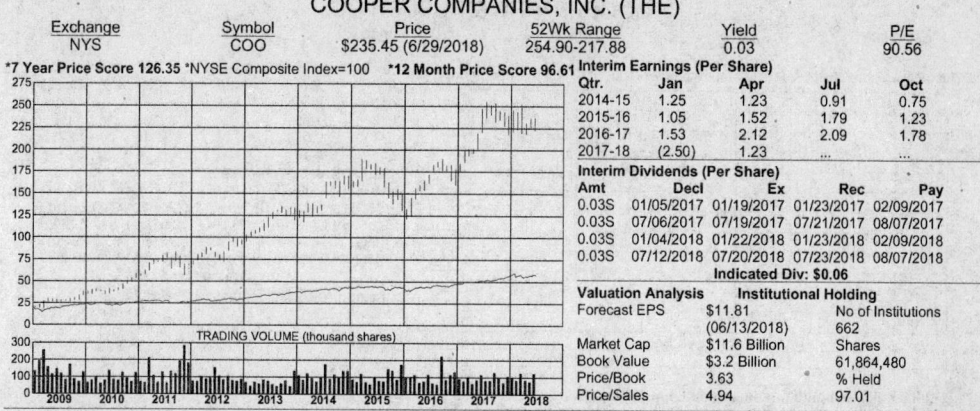

Interim Earnings (Per Share)

Qtr.	Jan	Apr	Jul	Oct
2014-15	1.25	1.23	0.91	0.75
2015-16	1.05	1.52	1.79	1.23
2016-17	1.53	2.12	2.09	1.78
2017-18	(2.50)	1.23	...	...

Interim Dividends (Per Share)

Amt	Decl	Ex	Rec	Pay
0.03S	01/05/2017	01/19/2017	01/23/2017	02/09/2017
0.03S	07/06/2017	07/19/2017	07/21/2017	08/07/2017
0.03S	01/04/2018	01/22/2018	01/23/2018	02/09/2018
0.03S	07/12/2018	07/20/2018	07/23/2018	08/07/2018

Indicated Div: $0.06

Valuation Analysis

		Institutional Holding	
Forecast EPS	$11.81	No of Institutions	
	(06/13/2018)	662	
Market Cap	$11.6 Billion	Shares	
Book Value	$3.2 Billion	61,864,480	
Price/Book	3.63	% Held	
Price/Sales	4.94	97.01	

Business Summary: Medical Instruments & Equipment (MIC: 4.3.1 SIC: 3851 NAIC: 339115)

Cooper Companies is a global medical device company. Co. operates through two business units, CooperVision, Inc. (CooperVision) and CooperSurgical, Inc. (CooperSurgical). CooperVision is a global manufacturer providing products for contact lens wearers. CooperVision develops, manufactures and markets a broad range of single-use, two-week and monthly contact lenses, featuring advanced materials and optics. CooperSurgical's business competes in the general health care market with a focus on advancing the health of families through a diversified portfolio of products and services focusing on women's health, including medical devices, fertility, genomics, diagnostics, and contraception.

Recent Developments: For the quarter ended Apr 30 2018, net income decreased 41.9% to US$60.9 million from US$104.9 million in the year-earlier quarter. Revenues were US$631.3 million, up 20.8% from US$522.4 million the year before. Operating income was US$74.7 million versus US$117.1 million in the prior-year quarter, a decrease of 36.2%. Direct operating expenses rose 27.1% to US$226.8 million from US$178.5 million in the comparable period the year before. Indirect operating expenses increased 45.4% to US$329.8 million from US$226.8 million in the equivalent prior-year period.

Prospects: Our evaluation of Cooper Companies Inc. as of Jan. 21, 2018 is the result of our systematic analysis on three basic characteristics: earnings strength, relative valuation, and recent stock price movement. The company has managed to produce a neutral trend in earnings per share over the past 5 quarters and while recent estimates for the company have been raised by analysts, COO has posted better than expected results. Based on operating earnings yield, the company is about fairly valued when compared to all of the companies in our coverage universe. Share price changes over the past year indicates that COO will perform in line with the market over the near term.

Financial Data

(US$ in Thousands)	6 Mos	3 Mos	10/31/2017	10/31/2016	10/31/2015	10/31/2014	10/31/2013	10/31/2012
Earnings Per Share	2.60	3.49	7.52	5.59	4.14	5.51	5.96	5.05
Cash Flow Per Share	11.21	10.46	12.14	10.47	8.07	9.46	8.56	6.56
Tang Book Value Per Share	N.M.	N.M.	6.48	1.93	1.23	N.M.	17.05	12.55
Dividends Per Share	0.060	0.060	0.060	0.060	0.060	0.060	0.060	0.060
Dividend Payout %	2.31	1.72	0.80	1.07	1.45	1.09	1.01	1.19
Income Statement								
Total Revenue	1,221,300	590,000	2,139,000	1,966,814	1,797,060	1,717,776	1,587,725	1,445,136
EBITDA	238,600	129,200	495,800	382,613	380,147	442,700	446,788	398,437
Depn & Amortn	72,700	36,000	68,400	60,790	146,559	138,201	125,349	111,214
Income Before Taxes	128,800	74,800	394,000	295,633	215,485	296,534	312,271	275,452
Income Taxes	190,400	197,300	21,100	20,699	10,341	24,705	15,365	26,808
Net Income	(61,600)	(122,500)	372,900	273,917	203,523	269,856	296,151	248,339
Average Shares	49,600	48,900	49,600	49,026	49,179	48,960	49,685	49,152
Balance Sheet								
Current Assets	1,272,400	1,175,500	953,200	934,458	841,818	791,617	747,241	657,860
Total Assets	6,414,400	6,268,600	4,858,700	4,475,918	4,460,610	4,458,340	3,137,261	2,941,384
Current Liabilities	460,400	415,700	396,100	536,455	569,172	442,182	321,253	262,552
Long-Term Obligations	2,442,400	2,372,900	1,149,300	1,107,384	1,105,764	1,280,833	301,670	348,422
Total Liabilities	3,226,500	3,112,300	1,683,000	1,776,051	1,793,101	1,888,462	732,726	748,633
Stockholders' Equity	3,187,900	3,156,300	3,175,700	2,699,867	2,667,509	2,569,878	2,404,535	2,192,751
Shares Outstanding	49,100	49,000	48,800	48,785	48,268	48,143	47,995	48,440
Statistical Record								
Return on Assets %	2.34	3.20	7.99	6.11	4.56	7.11	9.74	8.90
Return on Equity %	4.26	5.84	12.69	10.18	7.77	10.85	12.88	11.99
EBITDA Margin %	19.54	21.90	23.18	19.45	21.15	25.77	28.14	27.57
Net Margin %	N.M.	N.M.	17.43	13.93	11.33	15.71	18.65	17.18
Asset Turnover	0.42	0.41	0.46	0.44	0.40	0.45	0.52	0.52
Current Ratio	2.76	2.83	2.41	1.74	1.48	1.79	2.33	2.51
Debt to Equity	0.77	0.75	0.36	0.41	0.41	0.50	0.13	0.16
Price Range	254.90-201.05	254.90-184.61	254.90-159.50	189.90-121.01	189.09-137.62	164.29-117.30	134.97-89.40	100.67-56.64
P/E Ratio	98.04-77.33	73.04-52.90	33.90-21.21	33.97-21.65	45.67-33.24	29.82-21.29	22.65-15.00	19.93-11.22
Average Yield %	0.03	0.03	0.03	0.04	0.04	0.04	0.05	0.08

Address: 6140 Stoneridge Mall Road, Suite 590, Pleasanton, CA 94588 **Telephone:** 925-460-3600 **Fax:** 925-460-3648	**Web Site:** www.coopercos.com **Officers:** Albert G. (Al) White - President, Chief Executive Officer, Chief Financial Officer, Executive Vice President, Chief Strategy Officer, Vice President, Treasurer Daniel G. McBride - Executive Vice President, Vice President, Chief Operating Officer, General Counsel, Chief Risk Officer	**Auditors:** KPMG LLP **Investor Contact:** 925-460-3663 **Transfer Agents:** American Stock Transfer & Trust Company, New York, NY

COOPER TIRE & RUBBER CO.

Exchange	Symbol	Price	52Wk Range	Yield	P/E
NYS	CTB	$26.30 (6/29/2018)	40.35-24.00	1.60	18.65

*7 Year Price Score 89.86 *NYSE Composite Index=100 *12 Month Price Score 77.96

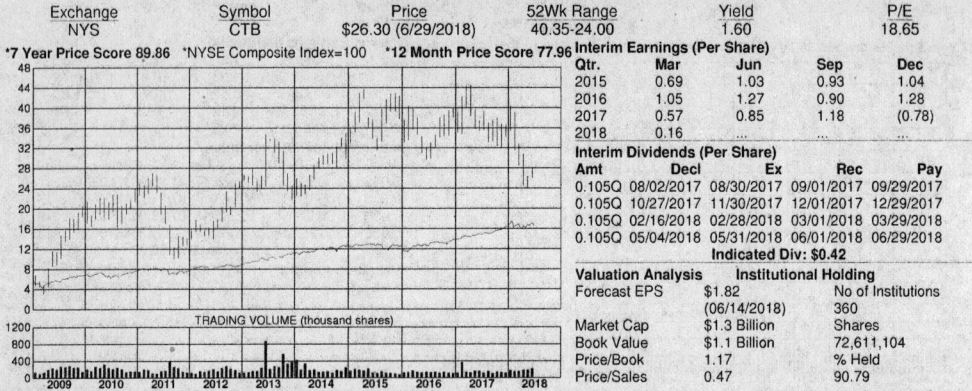

Interim Earnings (Per Share)

Qtr.	Mar	Jun	Sep	Dec
2015	0.69	1.03	0.93	1.04
2016	1.05	1.27	0.90	1.28
2017	0.57	0.85	1.18	(0.78)
2018	0.16	...	...	...

Interim Dividends (Per Share)

Amt	Decl	Ex	Rec	Pay
0.105Q	08/02/2017	08/30/2017	09/01/2017	09/29/2017
0.105Q	10/27/2017	11/30/2017	12/01/2017	12/29/2017
0.105Q	02/16/2018	02/28/2018	03/01/2018	03/29/2018
0.105Q	05/04/2018	05/31/2018	06/01/2018	06/29/2018

Indicated Div: $0.42

Valuation Analysis — Institutional Holding

Forecast EPS	$1.82	No of Institutions	
	(06/14/2018)	360	
Market Cap	$1.3 Billion	Shares	
Book Value	$1.1 Billion	72,611,104	
Price/Book	1.17	% Held	
Price/Sales	0.47	90.79	

TRADING VOLUME (thousand shares)

Business Summary: Auto Parts (MIC: 1.8.2 SIC: 3011 NAIC: 326211)

Cooper Tire & Rubber is a manufacturer and marketer of replacement tires. In its Americas Tire Operations segment, Co. manufactures and markets passenger car and light truck tires, primarily for sale in the U.S. replacement market, and also supplies passenger car tires to the U.S., Mexican, Central American and South American markets. In its International Tire Operations segment, Co.'s U.K. entity manufactures and markets passenger car, light truck, motorcycle and racing tires and tire retread material for the domestic and global markets, and its Serbian entity manufactures light vehicle tires primarily for the European markets and for export.

Recent Developments: For the quarter ended Mar 31 2018, net income decreased 69.4% to US$9.0 million from US$29.4 million in the year-earlier quarter. Revenues were US$601.5 million, down 6.5% from US$643.0 million the year before. Operating income was US$26.5 million versus US$58.0 million in the prior-year quarter, a decrease of 54.4%. Direct operating expenses declined 1.4% to US$517.0 million from US$524.4 million in the comparable period the year before. Indirect operating expenses decreased 4.2% to US$58.0 million from US$60.6 million in the equivalent prior-year period.

Prospects: Our evaluation of Cooper Tire & Rubber Co. as of Jan. 21, 2018 is the result of our systematic analysis on three basic characteristics: earnings strength, relative valuation, and recent stock price movement. The company has managed to produce a neutral trend in earnings per share over the past 5 quarters and while recent estimates for the company have been mixed, CTB has posted better than expected results. Based on operating earnings yield, the company is undervalued when compared to all of the companies in our coverage universe. Share price changes over the past year indicates that CTB will perform very poorly over the near term.

Financial Data
(US$ in Thousands)

	3 Mos	12/31/2017	12/31/2016	12/31/2015	12/31/2014	12/31/2013	12/31/2012	12/31/2011
Earnings Per Share	1.41	1.81	4.51	3.69	3.42	1.73	3.49	4.02
Cash Flow Per Share	3.02	3.39	5.67	5.27	5.20	4.30	7.24	2.02
Tang Book Value Per Share	18.94	18.44	16.65	14.81	11.82	12.81	9.32	8.69
Dividends Per Share	0.420	0.420	0.420	0.420	0.420	0.420	0.420	0.420
Dividend Payout %	29.79	23.20	9.31	11.38	12.28	24.28	12.03	10.45
Income Statement								
Total Revenue	601,496	2,854,656	2,924,869	2,972,901	3,424,809	3,439,233	4,200,836	3,927,158
EBITDA	27,020	450,843	562,634	523,215	550,230	427,101	570,191	288,703
Depn & Amortn	9,210	182,232	173,315	167,578	175,073	187,034	174,755	121,556
Income Before Taxes	12,434	243,925	367,093	334,028	348,519	212,971	368,450	134,146
Income Taxes	3,451	147,180	115,799	118,224	111,697	79,406	116,024	(135,457)
Net Income	8,285	95,400	248,381	212,766	213,578	111,013	220,371	253,503
Average Shares	51,179	52,673	55,090	57,623	62,401	64,282	63,224	63,012
Balance Sheet								
Current Assets	1,453,739	1,388,317	1,420,518	1,334,630	1,427,552	1,454,790	1,449,695	1,263,980
Total Assets	2,678,982	2,607,735	2,619,395	2,436,176	2,489,931	2,738,147	2,801,160	2,501,005
Current Liabilities	560,514	505,353	500,814	433,003	511,365	564,583	655,141	651,017
Long-Term Obligations	295,221	295,987	297,094	296,412	298,931	320,959	336,142	329,496
Total Liabilities	1,538,259	1,480,639	1,543,381	1,456,928	1,646,139	1,747,281	2,043,536	1,923,204
Stockholders' Equity	1,140,723	1,127,096	1,076,014	979,248	843,792	990,866	757,624	577,801
Shares Outstanding	50,605	50,941	52,999	55,832	58,151	63,386	63,158	62,298
Statistical Record								
Return on Assets %	2.76	3.65	9.80	8.64	8.17	4.01	8.29	10.55
Return on Equity %	6.53	8.66	24.10	23.34	23.28	12.70	32.91	48.82
EBITDA Margin %	4.49	15.79	19.24	17.60	16.07	12.42	13.57	7.35
Net Margin %	1.38	3.34	8.49	7.16	6.24	3.23	5.25	6.46
Asset Turnover	1.06	1.09	1.15	1.21	1.31	1.24	1.58	1.63
Current Ratio	2.59	2.75	2.84	3.08	2.79	2.58	2.21	1.94
Debt to Equity	0.26	0.26	0.28	0.30	0.35	0.32	0.44	0.57
Price Range	44.45-28.35	44.45-32.00	40.30-29.53	43.69-31.46	34.98-22.27	34.66-21.62	25.36-13.85	26.98-10.02
P/E Ratio	31.52-20.11	24.56-17.68	8.94-6.55	11.84-8.53	10.23-6.51	20.03-12.50	7.27-3.97	6.71-2.49
Average Yield %	1.16	1.13	1.19	1.10	1.49	1.53	2.29	2.26

Address: 701 Lima Avenue, Findlay, OH 45840	**Web Site:** www.coopertire.com	**Auditors:** Ernst & Young LLP
Telephone: 419-423-1321	**Officers:** Bradley E. Hughes - President, Chief Executive Officer, Chief Operating Officer, Senior Vice President, Chief Financial Officer, Vice President, Treasurer Ginger M. Jones - Chief Financial Officer, Senior Vice President, Vice President	**Investor Contact:** 419-424-4165
Fax: 419-424-4305		**Transfer Agents:** Computershare Inc., Canton, MA

CORECIVIC INC

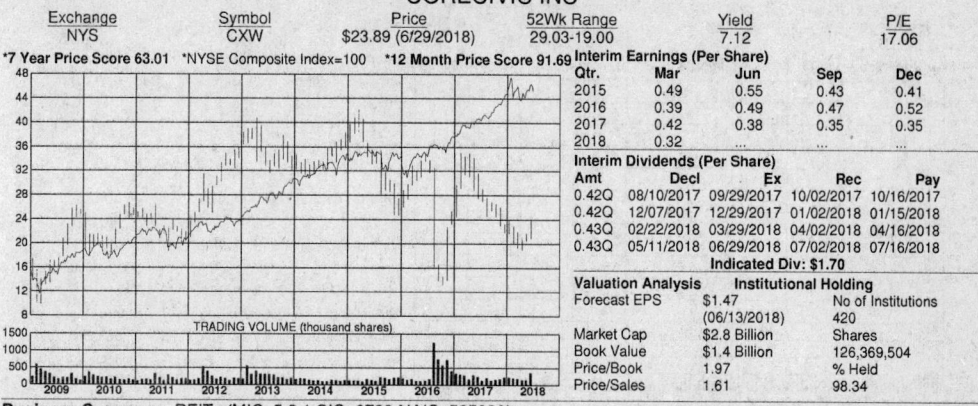

Exchange	Symbol	Price	52Wk Range	Yield	P/E
NYS	CXW	$23.89 (6/29/2018)	29.03-19.00	7.12	17.06

*7 Year Price Score 63.01 *NYSE Composite Index=100 *12 Month Price Score 91.69

Interim Earnings (Per Share)

Qtr.	Mar	Jun	Sep	Dec
2015	0.49	0.55	0.43	0.41
2016	0.39	0.49	0.47	0.52
2017	0.42	0.38	0.35	0.35
2018	0.32	...	...	...

Interim Dividends (Per Share)

Amt	Decl	Ex	Rec	Pay
0.42Q	08/10/2017	09/29/2017	10/02/2017	10/16/2017
0.42Q	12/07/2017	12/29/2017	01/02/2018	01/15/2018
0.43Q	02/22/2018	03/29/2018	04/02/2018	04/16/2018
0.43Q	05/11/2018	06/29/2018	07/02/2018	07/16/2018

Indicated Div: $1.70

Valuation Analysis **Institutional Holding**

Forecast EPS	$1.47	No of Institutions
	(06/13/2018)	420
Market Cap	$2.8 Billion	Shares
Book Value	$1.4 Billion	126,369,504
Price/Book	1.97	% Held
Price/Sales	1.61	98.34

TRADING VOLUME (thousand shares)

Business Summary: REITs (MIC: 5.3.1 SIC: 6798 NAIC: 525930)

CoreCivic is a real estate investment trust. Co. is the owner of partnership correctional, detention, and residential reentry facilities and prison operators. As of Dec 31 2017, Co. owned and managed 70 correctional, detention, and residential reentry facilities, and managed an additional seven correctional and detention facilities owned by Co.'s government partners, with a total design capacity of approximately 78,000 beds in 19 states. In addition, Co.'s facilities provide a variety of rehabilitation and educational programs, such as basic education, and faith-based services. Co. also makes available to offenders' certain health care, food services, and work and recreational programs.

Recent Developments: For the quarter ended Mar 31 2018, net income decreased 24.5% to US$37.8 million from US$50.0 million in the year-earlier quarter. Revenues were US$440.9 million, down 1.1% from US$445.7 million the year before.

Prospects: Our evaluation of CoreCivic Inc. as of Jan. 21, 2018 is the result of our systematic analysis on three basic characteristics: earnings strength, relative valuation, and recent stock price movement. The company has generated a negative trend in earnings per share over the past 5 quarters and while recent estimates for the company have remained steady, CXW has posted better than expected results. Based on operating earnings yield, the company is undervalued when compared to all of the companies in our coverage universe. Share price changes over the past year indicates that CXW will perform in line with the market over the near term.

Financial Data
(US$ in Thousands)

	3 Mos	12/31/2017	12/31/2016	12/31/2015	12/31/2014	12/31/2013	12/31/2012	12/31/2011
Earnings Per Share	1.40	1.50	1.87	1.88	1.66	2.70	1.56	1.54
Cash Flow Per Share	3.03	2.89	3.19	3.42	3.65	3.37	2.84	3.35
Tang Book Value Per Share	11.72	11.57	11.74	11.82	12.34	12.60	15.08	14.02
Dividends Per Share	1.690	1.680	2.040	2.160	2.040	8.600	0.600	...
Dividend Payout %	120.71	112.00	109.09	114.89	122.89	318.52	38.46	...
Income Statement								
Total Revenue	440,916	1,765,498	1,849,785	1,793,087	1,646,867	1,694,297	1,759,885	1,735,613
EBITDA	59,639	406,186	461,727	431,311	355,500	327,523	417,172	440,851
Depn & Amortn	891	145,700	165,800	151,400	114,000	112,800	114,100	109,100
Income Before Taxes	39,712	191,951	228,172	230,215	201,965	169,597	244,709	258,811
Income Taxes	1,935	13,911	8,253	8,361	6,943	(134,995)	87,586	96,301
Net Income	37,777	178,040	219,919	221,854	195,022	300,835	156,761	162,510
Average Shares	118,359	118,465	117,791	117,785	117,312	111,250	100,623	105,535
Balance Sheet								
Current Assets	288,600	327,490	298,824	342,058	365,985	352,734	350,742	359,429
Total Assets	3,264,450	3,272,398	3,271,604	3,356,018	3,127,191	3,007,425	2,974,742	3,019,631
Current Liabilities	285,844	290,838	272,193	324,595	318,988	254,406	166,458	198,362
Long-Term Obligations	1,455,265	1,452,717	1,435,169	1,447,077	1,200,000	1,205,000	1,111,545	1,245,014
Total Liabilities	1,830,240	1,820,790	1,812,641	1,893,270	1,645,691	1,504,918	1,453,122	1,611,609
Stockholders' Equity	1,434,210	1,451,608	1,458,963	1,462,748	1,481,500	1,502,507	1,521,620	1,408,022
Shares Outstanding	118,544	118,204	117,554	117,232	116,764	115,923	100,105	99,528
Statistical Record								
Return on Assets %	5.10	5.44	6.62	6.84	6.36	10.06	5.22	5.41
Return on Equity %	11.44	12.23	15.01	15.07	13.07	19.90	10.67	11.29
EBITDA Margin %	13.53	23.01	24.96	24.05	21.59	19.33	23.70	25.40
Net Margin %	8.57	10.08	11.89	12.37	11.84	17.76	8.91	9.36
Asset Turnover	0.54	0.54	0.56	0.55	0.54	0.57	0.59	0.58
Current Ratio	1.01	1.13	1.10	1.05	1.15	1.39	2.11	1.81
Debt to Equity	1.01	1.00	0.98	0.99	0.81	0.80	0.73	0.88
Price Range	34.94-19.27	35.03-21.77	35.02-13.18	42.10-24.62	38.33-31.13	40.78-31.60	35.87-20.96	26.35-18.64
P/E Ratio	24.96-13.76	23.35-14.51	18.73-7.05	22.39-13.10	23.09-18.75	15.10-11.70	22.99-13.44	17.11-12.10
Average Yield %	6.52	5.98	7.77	6.40	6.00	24.14	2.03	...

Address: 10 Burton Hills Blvd., Nashville, TN 37215
Telephone: 615-263-3000

Web Site: www.cca.com
Officers: John D. Ferguson - Chairman, Vice-Chairman, President, Chief Executive Officer
Kim M. White - Executive Vice President

Auditors: Ernst & Young LLP
Investor Contact: 615-263-3005
Transfer Agents: American Stock Transfer and Trust Company LLC, New York, NY

CORELOGIC INC.

Exchange	Symbol	Price	52Wk Range	Yield	P/E
NYS	CLGX	$51.90 (6/29/2018)	55.48-42.44	N/A	26.75

*7 Year Price Score 116.77 *NYSE Composite Index=100 *12 Month Price Score 109.88

TRADING VOLUME (thousand shares)

Interim Earnings (Per Share)

Qtr.	Mar	Jun	Sep	Dec
2015	0.32	0.36	0.31	0.41
2016	0.31	0.45	0.39	0.04
2017	0.18	0.48	0.36	0.76
2018	0.34	...	...	...

Interim Dividends (Per Share)

No Dividends Paid

Valuation Analysis   **Institutional Holding**

Forecast EPS	$2.71	No of Institutions
	(06/04/2018)	339
Market Cap	$4.2 Billion	Shares
Book Value	$1.0 Billion	87,663,792
Price/Book	4.20	% Held
Price/Sales	2.28	N/A

Business Summary: Business Services (MIC: 7.5.2 SIC: 7374 NAIC: 519190)

CoreLogic is a property information, analytics and data-enabled services provider operating in North America, Western Europe and Asia Pacific. Co. has two segments: Property Intelligence, which owns or licenses real property, mortgage and consumer information, including loan information, property sales and characteristic information, and property risk and replacement cost; and Risk Management and Work Flow segment, which owns or licenses real property information, mortgage information and consumer information, including loan information, property sales and characteristic information, natural hazard data, parcel maps, employment verification, criminal records and eviction records.

Recent Developments: For the quarter ended Mar 31 2018, income from continuing operations increased 123.2% to US$28.4 million from US$12.7 million in the year-earlier quarter. Net income increased 83.2% to US$28.3 million from US$15.4 million in the year-earlier quarter. Revenues were US$444.9 million, up 1.1% from US$439.9 million the year before. Operating income was US$44.4 million versus US$32.6 million in the prior-year quarter, an increase of 36.4%. Direct operating expenses declined 5.0% to US$239.4 million from US$252.0 million in the comparable period the year before. Indirect operating expenses increased 3.7% to US$161.1 million from US$155.3 million in the equivalent prior-year period.

Prospects: Our evaluation of CoreLogic Inc. as of Jan. 21, 2018 is the result of our systematic analysis on three basic characteristics: earnings strength, relative valuation, and recent stock price movement. The company has enjoyed a very positive trend in earnings per share over the past 5 quarters and while recent estimates for the company have been mixed, CLGX has posted better than expected results. Based on operating earnings yield, the company is about fairly valued when compared to all of the companies in our coverage universe. Share price changes over the past year indicates that CLGX will perform well over the near term.

Financial Data

(US$ in Thousands)	3 Mos	12/31/2017	12/31/2016	12/31/2015	12/31/2014	12/31/2013	12/31/2012	12/31/2011
Earnings Per Share	1.94	1.78	1.19	1.41	0.79	1.11	1.09	(0.68)
Cash Flow Per Share	4.78	4.59	4.71	3.69	3.54	3.72	3.52	1.47
Income Statement								
Total Revenue	444,900	1,851,117	1,952,557	1,528,110	1,405,040	1,330,630	1,567,633	1,338,547
EBITDA	67,756	314,616	303,957	308,216	241,940	246,708	297,044	212,390
Depn & Amortn	23,176	83,900	82,200	73,700	68,300	61,800	77,300	63,700
Income Before Taxes	27,418	168,892	163,974	173,226	106,658	137,259	167,276	90,400
Income Taxes	(711)	18,172	54,524	57,394	29,770	34,473	80,396	67,175
Net Income	28,287	152,162	106,550	127,844	73,200	107,728	112,293	(74,609)
Average Shares	82,820	85,234	89,122	90,564	92,429	97,109	104,050	109,712
Balance Sheet								
Current Assets	420,999	430,268	391,887	542,266	500,625	641,614	589,924	655,979
Total Assets	4,067,179	4,077,413	3,907,534	3,701,050	3,516,362	3,003,355	3,029,827	3,110,071
Current Liabilities	607,465	613,366	668,421	614,476	550,590	538,027	517,091	527,252
Long-Term Obligations	1,660,241	1,683,524	1,496,889	1,315,511	1,319,211	811,776	792,324	846,027
Total Liabilities	3,059,170	3,069,537	2,904,550	2,651,560	2,502,195	1,958,982	1,860,526	1,867,550
Stockholders' Equity	1,008,009	1,007,876	1,002,984	1,049,490	1,014,167	1,044,373	1,169,301	1,242,521
Shares Outstanding	81,636	80,885	84,368	88,228	89,343	91,254	97,698	106,544
Statistical Record								
Return on Assets %	4.13	3.81	2.79	3.54	2.25	3.57	3.65	N.M.
Return on Equity %	16.31	15.13	10.35	12.39	7.11	9.73	9.29	N.M.
EBITDA Margin %	15.23	17.00	15.57	20.17	17.22	18.54	18.95	15.87
Net Margin %	6.36	8.22	5.46	8.37	5.21	8.10	7.16	N.M.
Asset Turnover	0.46	0.46	0.51	0.42	0.43	0.44	0.51	0.42
Current Ratio	0.69	0.70	0.59	0.88	0.91	1.19	1.14	1.24
Debt to Equity	1.65	1.67	1.49	1.25	1.30	0.78	0.68	0.68
Price Range	49.10-39.90	49.10-35.01	42.56-32.19	42.18-30.75	35.86-26.00	35.93-21.88	28.00-12.55	20.91-7.80
P/E Ratio	25.31-20.57	27.58-19.67	35.76-27.05	29.91-21.81	45.39-32.91	32.37-19.71	25.69-11.51	...

Address: 40 Pacifica, Irvine, CA 92618-7471 **Telephone:** 949-214-1000	**Web Site:** www.corelogic.com **Officers:** Paul F. Folino - Chairman Frank D. Martell - President, Interim President, Chief Executive Officer, Interim Chief Executive Officer, Chief Operating Officer, Chief Financial Officer, Principal Financial Officer	**Auditors:** PricewaterhouseCoopers LLP **Investor Contact:** 703-610-5410 **Transfer Agents:** Wells Fargo Shareowner Services, South Saint Paul, MN

CORNING INC

Exchange	Symbol	Price	52Wk Range	Yield	P/E
NYS	GLW	$27.51 (6/29/2018)	34.85-26.35	2.62	N/A

*7 Year Price Score 119.78 *NYSE Composite Index=100 *12 Month Price Score 91.53

Interim Earnings (Per Share)

Qtr.	Mar	Jun	Sep	Dec
2015	0.29	0.36	0.15	0.18
2016	(0.36)	1.87	0.26	1.42
2017	0.07	0.42	0.39	(1.55)
2018	(0.72)	...	...	...

Interim Dividends (Per Share)

Amt	Decl	Ex	Rec	Pay
0.155Q	07/19/2017	08/29/2017	08/31/2017	09/29/2017
0.155Q	10/04/2017	11/15/2017	11/16/2017	12/15/2017
0.18Q	02/07/2018	02/27/2018	02/28/2018	03/29/2018
0.18Q	04/26/2018	05/30/2018	05/31/2018	06/29/2018

Indicated Div: $0.72

Valuation Analysis — **Institutional Holding**

Forecast EPS	$1.71	No of Institutions
	(06/13/2018)	1562
Market Cap	$22.9 Billion	Shares
Book Value	$14.4 Billion	818,106,048
Price/Book	1.59	% Held
Price/Sales	2.23	63.70

Business Summary: Electrical Equipment (MIC: 7.3.1 SIC: 3211 NAIC: 327211)

Corning is a provider of high-performance glass. Co. operates in five reportable segments: Display Technologies, which manufactures glass substrates for matrix liquid crystal displays; Optical Communications, which is engaged in delivering optical solutions; Environmental Technologies, which manufactures ceramic substrates and filter products for emissions control in mobile and stationary applications; Specialty Materials, which manufactures products that provide material formulations for glass, glass ceramics and fluoride crystals; and Life Sciences segment, which include consumables (plastic vessels, specialty surfaces and media), as well as general labware and equipment.

Recent Developments: For the quarter ended Mar 31 2018, net loss amounted to US$589.0 million versus net income of US$86.0 million in the year-earlier quarter. Revenues were US$2.50 billion, up 5.3% from US$2.38 billion the year before. Operating income was US$194.0 million versus US$413.0 million in the prior-year quarter, a decrease of 53.0%. Direct operating expenses rose 8.5% to US$1.55 billion from US$1.42 billion in the comparable period the year before. Indirect operating expenses increased 41.4% to US$761.0 million from US$538.0 million in the equivalent prior-year period.

Prospects: Our evaluation of Corning Inc. as of Jan. 21, 2018 is the result of our systematic analysis on three basic characteristics: earnings strength, relative valuation, and recent stock price movement. The company has generated a negative trend in earnings per share over the past 5 quarters. However, while recent estimates for the company have been lowered by analysts, GLW has posted better than expected results. Based on operating earnings yield, the company is undervalued when compared to all of the companies in our coverage universe. Share price changes over the past year indicates that GLW will perform in line with the market over the near term.

Financial Data
(US$ in Thousands)

	3 Mos	12/31/2017	12/31/2016	12/31/2015	12/31/2014	12/31/2013	12/31/2012	12/31/2011
Earnings Per Share	(1.46)	(0.66)	3.23	1.00	1.73	1.34	1.15	1.77
Cash Flow Per Share	2.52	2.24	2.46	2.30	3.61	1.92	2.14	2.04
Tang Book Value Per Share	11.50	12.63	14.28	12.75	13.84	14.02	13.60	13.30
Dividends Per Share	0.645	0.620	0.540	0.480	0.400	0.390	0.315	0.225
Dividend Payout %	...	...	16.72	48.00	23.12	29.10	27.39	12.71
Income Statement								
Total Revenue	2,500,000	10,116,000	9,390,000	9,111,000	9,715,000	7,819,000	8,012,000	7,890,000
EBITDA	(142,000)	2,564,000	4,730,000	2,490,000	4,599,000	3,040,000	2,396,000	2,766,000
Depn & Amortn	323,000	1,158,000	1,195,000	1,184,000	1,200,000	1,002,000	997,000	957,000
Income Before Taxes	(504,000)	1,296,000	3,408,000	1,187,000	3,302,000	1,926,000	1,302,000	1,739,000
Income Taxes	124,000	2,154,000	(3,000)	147,000	1,096,000	512,000	389,000	408,000
Net Income	(589,000)	(497,000)	3,695,000	1,339,000	2,472,000	1,961,000	1,728,000	2,805,000
Average Shares	848,000	1,021,000	1,144,000	1,343,000	1,427,000	1,462,000	1,506,000	1,583,000
Balance Sheet								
Current Assets	7,663,000	8,827,000	9,048,000	8,269,000	10,238,000	8,891,000	9,695,000	8,677,000
Total Assets	26,834,000	27,494,000	27,899,000	28,547,000	30,063,000	28,478,000	29,375,000	27,848,000
Current Liabilities	2,995,000	3,209,000	2,751,000	2,814,000	2,324,000	1,746,000	1,956,000	2,097,000
Long-Term Obligations	4,808,000	4,749,000	3,646,000	3,910,000	3,227,000	3,272,000	3,382,000	2,364,000
Total Liabilities	12,421,000	11,796,000	10,006,000	9,759,000	8,484,000	7,316,000	7,889,000	6,770,000
Stockholders' Equity	14,413,000	15,698,000	17,893,000	18,788,000	21,579,000	21,162,000	21,486,000	21,078,000
Shares Outstanding	832,000	858,000	926,000	1,130,000	1,274,000	1,399,000	1,470,000	1,515,000
Statistical Record								
Return on Assets %	N.M.	N.M.	13.06	4.57	8.45	6.78	6.02	10.45
Return on Equity %	N.M.	N.M.	20.09	6.63	11.57	9.20	8.10	13.87
EBITDA Margin %	N.M.	25.35	50.37	27.33	47.34	38.88	29.91	35.06
Net Margin %	N.M.	N.M.	39.35	14.70	25.45	25.08	21.57	35.55
Asset Turnover	0.37	0.37	0.33	0.31	0.33	0.27	0.28	0.29
Current Ratio	2.56	2.75	3.29	2.94	4.41	5.09	4.96	4.14
Debt to Equity	0.33	0.30	0.20	0.21	0.15	0.15	0.16	0.11
Price Range	34.85-26.32	32.64-24.19	24.94-16.69	25.00-15.97	23.32-17.05	17.82-11.79	14.62-10.88	23.37-11.88
P/E Ratio	...	...	7.72-5.17	25.00-15.97	13.48-9.86	13.30-8.80	12.71-9.46	13.20-6.71
Average Yield %	2.14	2.13	2.55	2.36	1.97	2.67	2.45	1.29

Address: One Riverfront Plaza, Corning, NY 14831	**Web Site:** www.corning.com	**Auditors:** PricewaterhouseCoopers LLP
Telephone: 607-974-9000	**Officers:** Wendell P. Weeks - Chairman, President, Chief Executive Officer Lawrence D. McRae - Vice-Chairman, Corporate Development Officer, Executive Vice President, Senior Vice President	**Investor Contact:** 888-267-6464
		Transfer Agents: ComputerShare Investor Services, Chicago, IL

CORPORATE OFFICE PROPERTIES TRUST

Exchange	Symbol	Price	52Wk Range	Yield	P/E
NYS	OFC	$28.99 (6/29/2018)	35.45-24.96	3.79	51.77

*7 Year Price Score 89.21   *NYSE Composite Index=100   *12 Month Price Score 92.38

Interim Earnings (Per Share)

Qtr.	Mar	Jun	Sep	Dec
2015	0.10	0.13	0.91	0.59
2016	0.03	(0.54)	0.25	0.23
2017	0.18	0.08	0.21	0.10
2018	0.17	...	...	...

Interim Dividends (Per Share)

Amt	Decl	Ex	Rec	Pay
0.275Q	08/11/2017	09/28/2017	09/30/2017	10/16/2017
0.275Q	11/09/2017	12/28/2017	12/29/2017	01/16/2018
0.275Q	02/22/2018	03/28/2018	03/30/2018	04/16/2018
0.275Q	05/10/2018	06/28/2018	06/29/2018	07/16/2018

Indicated Div: $1.10

Valuation Analysis   **Institutional Holding**

Forecast EPS	$0.74	No of Institutions
	(06/14/2018)	398
Market Cap	$3.0 Billion	Shares
Book Value	$1.4 Billion	129,903,168
Price/Book	2.09	% Held
Price/Sales	4.71	108.37

TRADING VOLUME (thousand shares)

Business Summary: REITs (MIC: 5.3.1 SIC: 6798 NAIC: 525930)

Corporate Office Properties Trust is a real estate investment trust. Through Corporate Office Properties, L.P. and subsidiaries, Co. is engaged in owning, managing, leasing, developing and acquiring office and data center properties. The majority of Co.'s portfolio is in locations that support U.S. Government agencies and their contractors, most of whom are engaged in national security, defense and information technology related activities. As of Dec 31 2017, Co.'s properties included the following: 159 operating office properties; 10 office properties under, or contractually committed for, construction or redevelopment; 1,000 acres of land that Co. controlled; and a wholesale data center.

Recent Developments: For the quarter ended Mar 31 2018, net income decreased 17.4% to US$18.8 million from US$22.7 million in the year-earlier quarter. Revenues were US$155.5 million, up 11.2% from US$139.8 million the year before. Revenues from property income rose 1.2% to US$128.3 million from US$126.8 million in the corresponding quarter a year earlier.

Prospects: Our evaluation of Corporate Office Properties Trust as of Jan. 21, 2018 is the result of our systematic analysis on three basic characteristics: earnings strength, relative valuation, and recent stock price movement. The company has produced a positive trend in earnings per share over the past 5 quarters. Because the company lacks sufficient analyst estimate data, we place greater weight on the historical EPS trend as the measure of earnings strength. Based on operating earnings yield, the company is about fairly valued when compared to all of the companies in our coverage universe. Share price changes over the past year indicates that OFC will perform very well over the near term.

Financial Data

(US$ in Thousands)	3 Mos	12/31/2017	12/31/2016	12/31/2015	12/31/2014	12/31/2013	12/31/2012	12/31/2011
Earnings Per Share	0.56	0.57	(0.03)	1.74	0.25	0.83	(0.03)	(1.94)
Cash Flow Per Share	1.94	2.33	2.45	2.17	2.20	1.87	2.60	2.19
Tang Book Value Per Share	13.29	13.10	12.92	13.19	12.96	12.78	11.81	14.53
Dividends Per Share	1.100	1.100	1.100	1.100	1.100	1.100	1.100	1.650
Dividend Payout %	196.43	192.98	...	63.22	440.00	132.53	...	...
Income Statement								
Total Revenue	155,476	612,820	574,328	625,466	586,473	523,360	528,007	556,841
EBITDA	70,748	269,552	184,019	345,394	258,146	228,094	208,502	100,078
Depn & Amortn	34,857	134,228	132,719	140,025	136,086	113,214	113,480	127,444
Income Before Taxes	18,466	64,659	(26,419)	120,812	34,590	36,704	7,570	(123,044)
Income Taxes	55	1,098	244	199	310	1,978	381	(10,679)
Net Income	17,150	70,091	11,439	178,300	40,255	93,707	20,977	(117,675)
Average Shares	101,143	99,155	94,502	97,667	88,263	85,224	73,454	69,382
Balance Sheet								
Current Assets	92,189	56,133	262,844	100,454	48,703	95,283	51,398	69,917
Total Assets	3,596,238	3,578,484	3,780,885	3,909,312	3,670,257	3,629,952	3,653,759	3,867,524
Current Liabilities	151,436	162,706	169,815	159,081	183,908	159,357	154,252	161,011
Long-Term Obligations	1,866,664	1,844,186	1,904,001	2,077,752	1,920,057	1,927,703	2,019,168	2,426,303
Total Liabilities	2,179,887	2,192,447	2,257,826	2,364,787	2,218,834	2,204,368	2,288,335	2,732,099
Stockholders' Equity	1,416,351	1,386,037	1,523,059	1,544,525	1,451,423	1,425,584	1,365,424	1,135,425
Shares Outstanding	102,150	101,292	98,498	94,531	93,255	87,394	80,952	72,011
Statistical Record								
Return on Assets %	1.80	1.90	0.30	4.70	1.10	2.57	0.56	N.M.
Return on Equity %	4.46	4.82	0.74	11.90	2.80	6.71	1.67	N.M.
EBITDA Margin %	45.50	43.99	32.04	55.22	44.02	43.58	39.49	17.97
Net Margin %	11.03	11.44	1.99	28.51	6.86	17.90	3.97	N.M.
Asset Turnover	0.17	0.17	0.15	0.17	0.16	0.14	0.14	0.14
Current Ratio	0.61	0.34	1.55	0.63	0.26	0.60	0.33	0.43
Debt to Equity	1.32	1.33	1.25	1.35	1.32	1.35	1.48	2.14
Price Range	35.79-24.96	35.79-29.01	31.34-20.04	30.75-20.34	29.29-23.69	29.75-21.79	26.12-20.96	36.74-19.37
P/E Ratio	63.91-44.57	62.79-50.89	...	17.67-11.69	117.16-94.76	35.84-26.25		
Average Yield %	3.51	3.35	4.10	4.36	4.06	4.31	4.69	5.56

Address: 6711 Columbia Gateway Drive, Suite 300, Columbia, MD 21046 Telephone: 443-285-5400	Web Site: www.copt.com Officers: Jay H. Shidler - Chairman Clay W. Hamlin - Vice-Chairman	Auditors: PricewaterhouseCoopers LLP Investor Contact: 443-285-5400 Transfer Agents: Wells Fargo Shareowner Services, St. Paul, MN

COTY, INC.

Exchange	Symbol	Price	52Wk Range	Yield	P/E
NYS	COTY	$14.10 (6/29/2018)	21.53-13.11	3.55	N/A

*7 Year Price Score N/A   ***NYSE Composite Index=100**   ***12 Month Price Score 82.11**

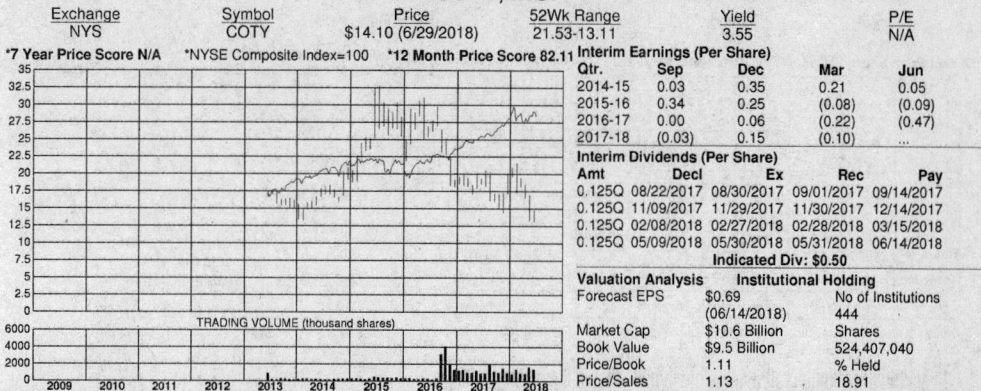

Interim Earnings (Per Share)

Qtr.	Sep	Dec	Mar	Jun
2014-15	0.03	0.35	0.21	0.05
2015-16	0.34	0.25	(0.08)	(0.09)
2016-17	0.00	0.06	(0.22)	(0.47)
2017-18	(0.03)	0.15	(0.10)	...

Interim Dividends (Per Share)

Amt	Decl	Ex	Rec	Pay
0.125Q	08/22/2017	08/30/2017	09/01/2017	09/14/2017
0.125Q	11/09/2017	11/29/2017	11/30/2017	12/14/2017
0.125Q	02/08/2018	02/27/2018	02/28/2018	03/15/2018
0.125Q	05/09/2018	05/30/2018	05/31/2018	06/14/2018

Indicated Div: $0.50

Valuation Analysis   **Institutional Holding**

Forecast EPS	$0.69	No of Institutions
	(06/14/2018)	444
Market Cap	$10.6 Billion	Shares
Book Value	$9.5 Billion	524,407,040
Price/Book	1.11	% Held
Price/Sales	1.13	18.91

TRADING VOLUME (thousand shares)

Business Summary: Household & Personal Products (MIC: 1.7.1 SIC: 2844 NAIC: 325620)

Coty is a beauty company. Co. is organized into three divisions, which is also its operating and reportable segments: Consumer Beauty, which primarily focuses on color cosmetics, retail hair coloring and styling products, body care and mass fragrances primarily in the mass retail channel, e-commerce and social selling direct-to-consumer platform; Luxury, which primarily focuses on fragrances, skincare and cosmetics across various regions and channels, including travel retail; and Professional Beauty, which primarily focuses on servicing salon owners and salon personnel in both hair and nail care, covering salon segments and salon client needs.

Recent Developments: For the quarter ended Mar 31 2018, net loss amounted to US$60.1 million versus a net loss of US$159.4 million in the year-earlier quarter. Revenues were US$2.22 billion, up 9.4% from US$2.03 billion the year before. Operating income was US$19.9 million versus a loss of US$192.5 million in the prior-year quarter. Direct operating expenses declined 0.5% to US$812.4 million from US$816.1 million in the comparable period the year before. Indirect operating expenses decreased 1.3% to US$1.39 billion from US$1.41 billion in the equivalent prior-year period.

Prospects: Our evaluation of Coty, Inc. as of Jan. 21, 2018 is the result of our systematic analysis on three basic characteristics: earnings strength, relative valuation, and recent stock price movement. The company has generated a negative trend in earnings per share over the past 5 quarters and while recent estimates for the company have been raised by analysts, COTY has posted better than expected results. Based on operating earnings yield, the company is overvalued when compared to all of the companies in our coverage universe. Share price changes over the past year indicates that COTY will perform very poorly over the near term.

Financial Data

(US$ in Thousands)	9 Mos	6 Mos	3 Mos	06/30/2017	06/30/2016	06/30/2015	06/30/2014	06/30/2013
Earnings Per Share	(0.45)	(0.57)	(0.66)	(0.66)	0.44	0.64	(0.26)	0.42
Cash Flow Per Share	0.32	0.54	1.02	1.18	1.45	1.49	1.41	1.22
Dividends Per Share	0.500	0.500	0.500	0.650	0.250	0.200	0.200	0.150
Dividend Payout %	...	...	...	...	56.82	31.25	...	35.71
Income Statement								
Total Revenue	7,098,600	4,875,900	2,238,300	7,650,300	4,349,100	4,395,200	4,551,600	4,649,100
EBITDA	761,700	552,400	192,700	(159,400)	373,100	462,500	189,400	564,600
Depn & Amortn	543,500	350,500	168,700	280,000	152,400	156,200	165,000	169,400
Income Before Taxes	13,600	69,300	(41,400)	(658,000)	138,800	233,300	(44,100)	318,700
Income Taxes	(28,800)	(33,200)	(25,300)	(259,500)	(40,400)	(26,100)	20,100	116,800
Net Income	12,500	89,500	(19,700)	(422,200)	156,900	232,500	(97,400)	168,000
Average Shares	750,100	752,700	748,600	642,800	354,200	362,900	381,700	396,400
Balance Sheet								
Current Assets	3,910,600	3,879,200	4,249,500	3,581,500	1,938,400	1,856,400	2,784,800	2,416,900
Total Assets	23,765,000	23,445,600	23,573,100	22,548,200	7,100,200	6,018,900	6,592,500	6,470,000
Current Liabilities	3,941,800	4,155,800	3,948,500	3,803,600	1,855,200	1,526,200	1,597,300	1,463,200
Long-Term Obligations	7,628,600	7,145,800	7,541,900	6,928,300	4,001,000	2,605,900	3,260,100	2,590,100
Total Liabilities	14,265,700	14,016,500	14,120,800	13,233,500	6,740,000	5,049,100	5,748,700	4,976,000
Stockholders' Equity	9,499,300	9,429,100	9,452,300	9,314,700	360,200	969,800	843,800	1,494,000
Shares Outstanding	750,500	749,800	749,400	747,900	337,100	360,800	353,900	383,800
Statistical Record								
Return on Assets %	N.M.	N.M.	N.M.	N.M.	2.39	3.69	N.M.	2.66
Return on Equity %	N.M.	N.M.	N.M.	N.M.	23.53	25.64	N.M.	13.31
EBITDA Margin %	10.73	11.33	8.61	N.M.	8.58	10.52	4.16	12.14
Net Margin %	0.18	1.84	N.M.	N.M.	3.61	5.29	N.M.	3.61
Asset Turnover	0.40	0.40	0.57	0.52	0.66	0.70	0.70	0.73
Current Ratio	0.99	0.93	1.08	0.94	1.04	1.22	1.74	1.65
Debt to Equity	0.80	0.76	0.80	0.74	11.11	2.69	3.86	1.73
Price Range	21.53-14.36	20.54-14.36	25.10-16.00	29.75-17.05	32.68-21.79	32.45-15.94	17.85-13.25	17.52-16.61
P/E Ratio	...	...	...	...	74.27-49.52	50.70-24.91	...	41.71-39.55
Average Yield %	2.73	2.76	2.62	3.07	0.91	0.96	1.26	0.88

Address: 350 Fifth Avenue, New York, NY 10118
Telephone: 212-389-7300

Web Site: www.coty.com
Officers: Lambertus J.H. (Bart) Becht - Chairman, Interim Chief Executive Officer Camillo Pane - Chief Executive Officer, Executive Vice President

Auditors: Deloitte & Touche LLP
Investor Contact: 212-389-7300

CRANE CO.

Exchange	Symbol	Price	52Wk Range	Yield	P/E
NYS	CR	$80.13 (6/29/2018)	99.94-72.19	1.75	27.44

*7 Year Price Score 111.95 *NYSE Composite Index=100 *12 Month Price Score 97.36

TRADING VOLUME (thousand shares)

Interim Earnings (Per Share)

Qtr.	Mar	Jun	Sep	Dec
2015	0.87	0.95	0.97	1.11
2016	0.93	1.15	1.07	(1.09)
2017	1.05	1.14	1.13	(0.48)
2018	1.13	...	...	...

Interim Dividends (Per Share)

Amt	Decl	Ex	Rec	Pay
0.33Q	07/24/2017	08/29/2017	08/31/2017	09/08/2017
0.33Q	10/23/2017	11/29/2017	11/30/2017	12/08/2017
0.35Q	01/29/2018	02/27/2018	02/28/2018	03/09/2018
0.35Q	04/23/2018	05/30/2018	05/31/2018	06/08/2018

Indicated Div: $1.40

Valuation Analysis / Institutional Holding

Forecast EPS	$5.60 (06/13/2018)	No of Institutions	476
Market Cap	$4.8 Billion	Shares	53,046,496
Book Value	$1.4 Billion	% Held	70.02
Price/Book	3.32		
Price/Sales	1.65		

Business Summary: Industrial Machinery & Equipment (MIC: 7.2.1 SIC: 3499 NAIC: 332999)

Crane is a manufacturer of industrial products. Co. has four segments: Fluid Handling, which provides fluid handling equipment; Payment and Merchandising Technologies, which provides technology payment acceptance products and vending equipment and related solutions; Aerospace and Electronics, which provides products such as custom designed, engineered products used in landing systems, sensing and utility systems, fluid management, seat actuation, power and microelectronic applications, and microwave systems; and Engineered Materials, which manufactures fiberglass-reinforced plastic panels and coils for use in the manufacturing of recreational vehicles, truck bodies, truck trailers.

Recent Developments: For the quarter ended Mar 31 2018, net income increased 8.5% to US$68.7 million from US$63.3 million in the year-earlier quarter. Revenues were US$799.1 million, up 18.7% from US$673.4 million the year before. Operating income was US$94.3 million versus US$93.3 million in the prior-year quarter, an increase of 1.1%. Direct operating expenses rose 21.4% to US$521.2 million from US$429.5 million in the comparable period the year before. Indirect operating expenses increased 21.9% to US$183.6 million from US$150.6 million in the equivalent prior-year period.

Prospects: Our evaluation of Crane Co. as of Jan. 21, 2018 is the result of our systematic analysis on three basic characteristics: earnings strength, relative valuation, and recent stock price movement. The company has managed to produce a neutral trend in earnings per share over the past 5 quarters and while recent estimates for the company have been mixed, CR has posted better than expected results. Based on operating earnings yield, the company is undervalued when compared to all of the companies in our coverage universe. Share price changes over the past year indicates that CR will perform in line with the market over the near term.

Financial Data
(US$ in Thousands)

	3 Mos	12/31/2017	12/31/2016	12/31/2015	12/31/2014	12/31/2013	12/31/2012	12/31/2011
Earnings Per Share	2.92	2.84	2.07	3.89	3.23	3.73	3.72	0.44
Cash Flow Per Share	6.50	5.35	5.42	3.95	4.50	4.14	4.08	2.58
Dividends Per Share	1.340	1.320	1.320	1.320	1.260	1.160	1.080	0.980
Dividend Payout %	45.89	46.48	63.77	33.93	39.01	31.10	29.03	222.73
Income Statement								
Total Revenue	799,100	2,786,000	2,748,000	2,740,500	2,924,997	2,595,281	2,579,068	2,545,867
EBITDA	126,100	442,100	238,900	411,300	360,365	389,309	349,957	84,974
Depn & Amortn	27,900	41,000	40,200	39,100	41,700	38,700	40,400	39,900
Income Before Taxes	84,400	367,500	164,100	336,500	281,156	326,016	284,605	20,454
Income Taxes	15,700	195,000	40,300	106,500	87,587	105,065	88,416	(6,062)
Net Income	68,700	171,800	122,800	228,900	192,672	219,502	216,993	26,315
Average Shares	61,000	60,400	59,300	58,800	59,603	58,839	58,293	59,204
Balance Sheet								
Current Assets	1,636,900	1,518,500	1,315,700	1,203,500	1,195,184	1,149,092	1,180,521	1,032,232
Total Assets	4,490,500	3,593,500	3,428,000	3,341,600	3,450,785	3,559,607	2,889,878	2,843,531
Current Liabilities	912,000	837,500	520,800	572,800	640,025	668,902	511,888	533,095
Long-Term Obligations	1,138,500	494,100	745,300	749,300	749,213	749,170	399,092	398,914
Total Liabilities	3,045,700	2,248,300	2,294,200	2,202,200	2,391,033	2,355,288	1,971,495	2,029,978
Stockholders' Equity	1,444,800	1,345,200	1,133,800	1,139,400	1,059,752	1,204,319	918,383	813,553
Shares Outstanding	59,827	59,411	58,964	58,109	58,121	58,185	57,106	57,614
Statistical Record								
Return on Assets %	4.47	4.89	3.62	6.74	5.50	6.81	7.55	0.95
Return on Equity %	13.31	13.86	10.77	20.82	17.02	20.68	24.99	2.93
EBITDA Margin %	15.78	15.87	8.69	15.01	12.32	15.00	13.57	3.34
Net Margin %	8.60	6.17	4.47	8.35	6.59	8.46	8.41	1.03
Asset Turnover	0.73	0.79	0.81	0.81	0.83	0.80	0.90	0.92
Current Ratio	1.79	1.81	2.53	2.10	1.87	1.72	2.31	1.94
Debt to Equity	0.79	0.37	0.66	0.66	0.71	0.62	0.43	0.49
Price Range	99.94-72.19	90.46-71.55	77.36-43.14	69.78-45.27	76.33-53.63	67.25-46.28	51.07-35.53	51.06-34.03
P/E Ratio	34.23-24.72	31.85-25.19	37.37-20.84	17.94-11.64	23.63-16.60	18.03-12.41	13.73-9.55	116.05-77.34
Average Yield %	1.61	1.69	2.23	2.33	1.87	1.99	2.54	2.18

Address: 100 First Stamford Place, Stamford, CT 06902 Telephone: 203-363-7300	Web Site: www.craneco.com Officers: R. S. Evans - Chairman Max H. Mitchell - President, Chief Executive Officer, Executive Vice President, Chief Operating Officer	Auditors: DELOITTE & TOUCHE LLP Investor Contact: 203-363-7352 Transfer Agents: First Chicago Trust Company of New York, Jersey City, NJ

CROWN CASTLE INTERNATIONAL CORP

Exchange	Symbol	Price	52Wk Range	Yield	P/E
NYS	CCI	$107.82 (6/29/2018)	114.03-96.64	3.90	119.80

*7 Year Price Score 107.03 *NYSE Composite Index=100 *12 Month Price Score 96.93

Interim Earnings (Per Share)

Qtr.	Mar	Jun	Sep	Dec
2015	0.34	3.42	0.28	0.38
2016	0.11	0.22	0.26	0.36
2017	0.33	0.31	0.21	0.17
2018	0.21	...	...	...

Interim Dividends (Per Share)

Amt	Decl	Ex	Rec	Pay
0.95Q	08/03/2017	09/14/2017	09/15/2017	09/29/2017
1.05Q	10/18/2017	12/14/2017	12/15/2017	12/29/2017
1.05Q	02/21/2018	03/15/2018	03/16/2018	03/30/2018
1.05Q	05/17/2018	06/14/2018	06/15/2018	06/29/2018

Indicated Div: $4.20

Valuation Analysis

	Institutional Holding
Forecast EPS $1.23 (06/14/2018)	No of Institutions 1051
Market Cap $44.7 Billion	Shares 458,585,504
Book Value $12.8 Billion	
Price/Book 3.49	% Held 95.95
Price/Sales 9.65	

Business Summary: REITs (MIC: 5.3.1 SIC: 6798 NAIC: 525930)

Crown Castle International owns, operates and leases shared wireless infrastructure, including: towers and other structures, such as rooftops and fiber supporting small cell networks. Co.'s core business is providing access, including space or capacity, to its shared wireless infrastructure via long-term contracts in various forms, including license, sublease and lease agreements. As part of its effort to provide wireless infrastructure solutions, Co. also provides certain network services relating to its wireless infrastructure, consisting of site development services relating to existing or new tenant equipment installations on its wireless infrastructure and installation services.

Recent Developments: For the quarter ended Mar 31 2018, net income decreased 4.2% to US$114.0 million from US$119.0 million in the year-earlier quarter. Revenues were US$1.30 billion, up 27.9% from US$1.02 billion the year before. Revenues from property income rose 34.5% to US$1.15 billion from US$857.0 million in the corresponding quarter a year earlier.

Prospects: Our evaluation of Crown Castle International Corp. as of Jan. 21, 2018 is the result of our systematic analysis on three basic characteristics: earnings strength, relative valuation, and recent stock price movement. The company has managed to produce a neutral trend in earnings per share over the past 5 quarters and while recent estimates for the company have been raised by analysts, CCI has posted results that fell short of analysts expectations. Based on operating earnings yield, the company is overvalued when compared to all of the companies in our coverage universe. Share price changes over the past year indicates that CCI will perform well over the near term.

Financial Data
(US$ in Thousands)

	3 Mos	12/31/2017	12/31/2016	12/31/2015	12/31/2014	12/31/2013	12/31/2012	12/31/2011
Earnings Per Share	0.90	1.01	0.95	4.42	1.04	0.26	0.64	0.52
Cash Flow Per Share	5.01	5.35	5.22	5.39	5.01	4.15	2.66	2.27
Dividends Per Share	4.000	3.900	3.605	3.345	0.820	...	...	...
Dividend Payout %	444.44	386.14	379.47	75.68	78.85	...	...	...
Income Statement								
Total Revenue	1,299,000	4,355,605	3,921,225	3,663,851	3,689,884	3,022,384	2,432,680	2,032,729
EBITDA	279,000	1,957,414	1,720,790	1,773,951	1,718,209	1,442,904	1,136,215	1,074,528
Depn & Amortn	2,000	914,900	832,700	774,900	757,400	562,100	438,900	387,800
Income Before Taxes	118,000	470,593	373,854	473,829	388,134	292,529	100,827	179,807
Income Taxes	4,000	26,043	16,881	(51,457)	(10,640)	198,628	(100,061)	8,347
Net Income	114,000	444,550	356,973	1,520,992	390,513	90,111	188,584	171,077
Average Shares	410,000	383,221	340,879	334,062	333,265	299,293	291,270	285,947
Balance Sheet								
Current Assets	1,074,000	1,133,780	1,324,761	981,245	931,502	892,683	1,581,324	599,152
Total Assets	32,250,000	32,229,570	22,675,092	22,036,245	21,143,276	20,594,908	16,088,709	10,545,096
Current Liabilities	1,187,000	1,292,082	961,355	855,369	898,935	756,387	1,237,858	402,106
Long-Term Obligations	15,616,000	16,044,369	12,069,393	12,143,019	11,807,526	11,490,914	10,923,186	6,853,182
Total Liabilities	19,418,000	19,890,488	15,117,977	14,947,024	14,427,051	13,668,191	13,149,963	7,853,819
Stockholders' Equity	12,832,000	12,339,082	7,557,115	7,089,221	6,716,225	6,926,717	2,938,746	2,691,277
Shares Outstanding	415,000	406,280	360,536	333,771	333,856	334,070	293,164	284,449
Statistical Record								
Return on Assets %	1.57	1.62	1.59	7.04	1.87	0.49	1.41	1.63
Return on Equity %	4.35	4.47	4.86	22.03	5.72	1.83	6.68	6.27
EBITDA Margin %	21.48	44.94	43.88	48.42	46.57	47.74	46.71	52.86
Net Margin %	8.78	10.21	9.10	41.51	10.58	2.98	7.75	8.42
Asset Turnover	0.17	0.16	0.17	0.17	0.18	0.16	0.18	0.19
Current Ratio	0.90	0.88	1.38	1.15	1.04	1.18	1.28	1.49
Debt to Equity	1.22	1.30	1.60	1.71	1.76	1.66	3.72	2.55
Price Range	114.03-93.69	114.03-84.36	102.56-78.22	88.71-76.58	84.75-68.96	79.77-66.66	72.16-44.92	46.17-37.37
P/E Ratio	126.70-104.10	112.90-83.52	107.96-82.34	20.07-17.33	81.49-66.31	306.81-256.38	112.75-70.19	88.79-71.87
Average Yield %	3.84	3.92	4.01	4.00	1.07	...	...	...

Address: 1220 Augusta Drive, Suite 600, Houston, TX 77057-2261 **Telephone:** 713-570-3000	**Web Site:** www.crowncastle.com **Officers:** J. Landis Martin - Chairman Jay A. Brown - President, Chief Executive Officer, Chief Financial Officer, Senior Vice President, Treasurer	**Auditors:** PricewaterhouseCoopers LLP **Investor Contact:** 713-570-3050 **Transfer Agents:** Mellon Investor Services LLC, Jersey City, NJ

CROWN HOLDINGS INC

Exchange	Symbol	Price	52Wk Range	Yield	P/E
NYS	CCK	$44.76 (6/29/2018)	61.17-43.34	N/A	19.55

*7 Year Price Score 94.26   *NYSE Composite Index=100   *12 Month Price Score 81.48

Interim Earnings (Per Share)

Qtr.	Mar	Jun	Sep	Dec
2015	0.32	1.02	1.01	0.47
2016	0.57	1.21	1.31	0.47
2017	0.77	0.94	1.32	(0.64)
2018	0.67	...	...	...

Interim Dividends (Per Share)

No Dividends Paid

Valuation Analysis   Institutional Holding

Forecast EPS	$5.45	No of Institutions
(06/14/2018)		579
Market Cap	$6.0 Billion	Shares
Book Value	$765.0 Million	152,245,568
Price/Book	7.86	% Held
Price/Sales	0.67	82.09

TRADING VOLUME (thousand shares)

Business Summary: Metal Products (MIC: 8.2.3 SIC: 3411 NAIC: 332431)

Crown Holdings is engaged in the design, manufacture and sale of packaging products for consumer goods. Co.'s primary products include steel and aluminum cans for food, beverage, household and other consumer products, glass bottles for beverage products and metal vacuum closures and caps. These products are sold through Co.'s sales organization to the soft drink, food, citrus, brewing, household products, personal care and various other industries. Co.'s business is organized geographically within three divisions: Americas, which include Americas Beverage segment and North America Food segment; European, which includes European Beverage segment and European Food segment; and Asia-Pacific.

Recent Developments: For the quarter ended Mar 31 2018, net income decreased 15.0% to US$113.0 million from US$133.0 million in the year-earlier quarter. Revenues were US$2.20 billion, up 15.6% from US$1.90 billion the year before. Operating income was US$221.0 million versus US$225.0 million in the prior-year quarter, a decrease of 1.8%. Direct operating expenses rose 17.8% to US$1.87 billion from US$1.59 billion in the comparable period the year before. Indirect operating expenses increased 19.8% to US$103.0 million from US$86.0 million in the equivalent prior-year period.

Prospects: Our evaluation of Crown Holdings Inc. as of Jan. 21, 2018 is the result of our systematic analysis on three basic characteristics: earnings strength, relative valuation, and recent stock price movement. The company has produced a positive trend in earnings per share over the past 5 quarters and while recent estimates for the company have remained steady, CCK has posted results that fell short of analysts expectations. Based on operating earnings yield, the company is undervalued when compared to all of the companies in our coverage universe. Share price changes over the past year indicates that CCK will perform in line with the market over the near term.

Financial Data

(US$ in Thousands)	3 Mos	12/31/2017	12/31/2016	12/31/2015	12/31/2014	12/31/2013	12/31/2012	12/31/2011
Earnings Per Share	2.29	2.38	3.56	2.82	2.79	2.30	3.75	1.83
Cash Flow Per Share	2.46	5.62	6.70	6.93	6.65	6.34	4.22	2.50
Income Statement								
Total Revenue	2,197,000	8,698,000	8,284,000	8,762,000	9,097,000	8,656,000	8,470,000	8,644,000
EBITDA	285,000	1,313,000	1,247,000	1,135,000	952,000	941,000	1,035,000	948,000
Depn & Amortn	65,000	247,000	247,000	237,000	190,000	134,000	180,000	140,000
Income Before Taxes	152,000	829,000	769,000	639,000	516,000	576,000	636,000	587,000
Income Taxes	39,000	401,000	186,000	178,000	41,000	148,000	(17,000)	194,000
Net Income	90,000	323,000	496,000	393,000	387,000	324,000	557,000	282,000
Average Shares	133,800	135,610	139,310	139,140	138,500	140,700	148,400	154,300
Balance Sheet								
Current Assets	5,261,000	3,074,000	2,841,000	3,049,000	3,624,000	3,180,000	2,750,000	2,603,000
Total Assets	13,079,000	10,663,000	9,599,000	10,020,000	9,708,000	8,030,000	7,490,000	6,868,000
Current Liabilities	2,861,000	3,250,000	2,896,000	2,908,000	2,926,000	2,920,000	2,518,000	2,285,000
Long-Term Obligations	7,778,000	5,217,000	4,717,000	5,255,000	5,007,000	3,469,000	3,289,000	3,337,000
Total Liabilities	12,314,000	10,062,000	9,233,000	9,876,000	9,589,000	8,026,000	7,652,000	7,341,000
Stockholders' Equity	765,000	601,000	366,000	144,000	119,000	4,000	(162,000)	(473,000)
Shares Outstanding	134,307	134,275	139,840	139,441	139,000	138,207	143,136	148,449
Statistical Record								
Return on Assets %	2.67	3.19	5.04	3.98	4.36	4.18	7.74	4.10
Return on Equity %	46.79	66.80	193.98	298.86	629.27	...	...	...
EBITDA Margin %	12.97	15.10	15.05	12.95	10.46	10.87	12.22	10.97
Net Margin %	4.10	3.71	5.99	4.49	4.25	3.74	6.58	3.26
Asset Turnover	0.78	0.86	0.84	0.89	1.03	1.12	1.18	1.26
Current Ratio	1.84	0.95	0.98	1.05	1.24	1.09	1.09	1.14
Debt to Equity	10.17	8.68	12.89	36.49	42.08	867.25	...	...
Price Range	61.17-48.30	61.17-52.48	57.09-44.21	56.63-44.31	52.31-40.12	45.22-36.81	38.79-32.69	41.19-29.30
P/E Ratio	26.71-21.09	25.70-22.05	16.04-12.42	20.08-15.71	18.75-14.38	19.66-16.00	10.34-8.72	22.51-16.01

Address: One Crown Way, Philadelphia, PA 19154-4599 **Telephone:** 215-698-5100	**Web Site:** www.crowncork.com **Officers:** John W. Conway - Chairman, President, Chief Executive Officer, Chief Operating Officer Timothy J. Donahue - President, Chief Executive Officer, Executive Vice President, Chief Financial Officer, Chief Operating Officer	**Auditors:** PricewaterhouseCoopers LLP **Investor Contact:** 215-698-5341 **Transfer Agents:** Wells Fargo Shareowner Services, St. Paul, MN

CULLEN/FROST BANKERS, INC.

Exchange	Symbol	Price	52Wk Range	Yield	P/E	Div Acheiver
NYS	CFR	$108.24 (6/29/2018)	120.77-81.59	2.48	18.53	24 Years

*7 Year Price Score 112.43 *NYSE Composite Index=100 *12 Month Price Score 112.59

Interim Earnings (Per Share)

Qtr.	Mar	Jun	Sep	Dec
2015	1.10	1.11	1.17	0.89
2016	1.07	1.11	1.24	1.28
2017	1.28	1.29	1.41	1.53
2018	1.61	...	...	...

Interim Dividends (Per Share)

Amt	Decl	Ex	Rec	Pay
0.57Q	07/27/2017	08/29/2017	08/31/2017	09/15/2017
0.57Q	10/26/2017	11/29/2017	11/30/2017	12/15/2017
0.57Q	01/24/2018	02/27/2018	02/28/2018	03/15/2018
0.67Q	04/25/2018	05/30/2018	05/31/2018	06/15/2018

Indicated Div: $2.68

Valuation Analysis / **Institutional Holding**

Forecast EPS	$6.74 (06/13/2018)	No of Institutions 501
Market Cap	$6.9 Billion	Shares 66,619,248
Book Value	$3.2 Billion	% Held 76.26
Price/Book	2.13	
Price/Sales	5.44	

Business Summary: Banking (MIC: 5.1.1 SIC: 6021 NAIC: 522110)

Cullen/Frost Bankers is a financial holding company and a bank holding company. Through its subsidiaries, Co. provides commercial and consumer banking services, and trust and investment management, insurance, brokerage, mutual funds, leasing, treasury management, capital markets advisory and item processing services throughout various Texas markets. Co. has two segments: Banking, which includes commercial and consumer banking services, and its Frost Insurance Agency; and Frost Wealth Advisors, which includes fee-based services within private trust, retirement services, and financial management services. At Dec 31 2017, Co. had total assets of $31.75 billion and deposits of $26.87 billion.

Recent Developments: For the quarter ended Mar 31 2018, net income increased 25.4% to US$106.5 million from US$84.9 million in the year-earlier quarter. Net interest income increased 10.2% to US$229.7 million from US$208.5 million in the year-earlier quarter. Provision for loan losses was US$6.9 million versus US$8.0 million in the prior-year quarter, a decrease of 12.7%. Non-interest income rose 9.3% to US$91.4 million from US$83.7 million, while non-interest expense advanced 4.6% to US$196.6 million.

Prospects: Our evaluation of Cullen/Frost Bankers Inc. as of Jan. 21, 2018 is the result of our systematic analysis on three basic characteristics: earnings strength, relative valuation, and recent stock price movement. The company has managed to produce a neutral trend in earnings per share over the past 5 quarters and while recent estimates for the company have been raised by analysts, CFR has posted better than expected results. Based on operating earnings yield, the company is undervalued when compared to all of the companies in our coverage universe. Share price changes over the past year indicates that CFR will perform in line with the market over the near term.

Financial Data

(US$ in Thousands)

	3 Mos	12/31/2017	12/31/2016	12/31/2015	12/31/2014	12/31/2013	12/31/2012	12/31/2011
Earnings Per Share	5.84	5.51	4.70	4.28	4.29	3.80	3.86	3.54
Cash Flow Per Share	9.73	8.45	7.00	6.27	4.62	2.88	4.88	4.49
Tang Book Value Per Share	38.24	39.28	34.60	33.60	32.32	30.16	30.48	28.48
Dividends Per Share	2.280	2.250	2.150	2.100	2.030	1.980	1.900	1.830
Dividend Payout %	39.04	40.83	45.74	49.07	47.32	52.11	49.22	51.69
Income Statement								
Interest Income	243,326	892,947	788,412	749,496	701,471	642,500	631,612	623,017
Interest Expense	13,578	26,525	12,076	12,864	14,537	21,945	26,751	41,241
Net Interest Income	229,748	866,422	776,336	736,632	686,934	620,555	604,861	581,776
Provision for Losses	6,945	35,460	51,673	51,845	16,314	20,582	10,080	27,445
Non-Interest Income	91,445	336,470	349,708	328,730	320,144	302,818	288,787	290,002
Non-Interest Expense	196,611	759,069	732,960	693,718	654,740	611,910	575,093	558,098
Income Before Taxes	117,637	408,363	341,411	319,799	336,024	290,881	308,475	286,235
Income Taxes	11,157	44,214	37,150	40,471	58,047	53,015	70,523	68,700
Net Income	106,480	364,149	304,261	279,328	277,977	237,866	237,952	217,535
Average Shares	64,662	64,662	62,968	63,473	62,973	61,116	61,643	61,277
Balance Sheet								
Net Loans & Leases	13,214,144	12,990,301	11,822,347	11,350,672	10,887,993	9,423,262	9,119,395	7,884,982
Total Assets	31,459,232	31,747,880	30,196,319	28,567,118	28,277,775	24,312,939	23,124,069	20,317,245
Total Deposits	26,677,778	26,872,389	25,811,575	24,343,595	24,135,930	20,688,786	19,497,366	16,756,748
Total Liabilities	28,215,802	28,450,017	27,193,791	25,676,775	25,426,372	21,798,778	20,706,587	18,033,708
Stockholders' Equity	3,243,430	3,297,863	3,002,528	2,890,343	2,851,403	2,514,161	2,417,482	2,283,537
Shares Outstanding	63,793	63,475	63,474	61,982	63,149	60,566	61,479	61,263
Statistical Record								
Return on Assets %	1.24	1.18	1.03	0.98	1.06	1.00	1.09	1.15
Return on Equity %	12.17	11.56	10.30	9.73	10.36	9.65	10.10	10.01
Net Interest Margin %	94.42	97.03	98.47	98.28	97.93	96.58	95.76	93.38
Efficiency Ratio %	58.73	61.74	64.40	64.34	64.09	64.73	62.48	61.13
Loans to Deposits	0.50	0.48	0.46	0.47	0.45	0.46	0.47	0.47
Price Range	110.67-81.59	101.40-81.59	88.77-42.55	80.10-59.40	81.67-68.06	75.58-54.27	60.67-53.66	62.57-44.29
P/E Ratio	18.95-13.97	18.40-14.81	18.89-9.05	18.71-13.88	19.04-15.86	19.89-14.28	15.72-13.90	17.68-12.51
Average Yield %	2.38	2.44	3.27	3.05	2.66	2.98	3.36	3.36

Address: 100 W. Houston Street, San Antonio, TX 78205
Telephone: 210-220-4011
Fax: 210-220-5578

Web Site: www.frostbank.com
Officers: Phillip D. Green - Chairman, President, Chief Executive Officer, Group Executive Vice President, Chief Financial Officer Paul H. Bracher - President

Auditors: Ernst & Young LLP
Investor Contact: 210-220-5632
Transfer Agents: American Stock Transfer & Trust Company, LLC, Brooklyn, NY

CUMMINS, INC.

Exchange	Symbol	Price	52Wk Range	Yield	P/E	Div Acheiver
NYS	CMI	$133.00 (6/29/2018)	192.50-132.32	3.43	23.88	12 Years

*7 Year Price Score 103.03 *NYSE Composite Index=100 *12 Month Price Score 86.23

TRADING VOLUME (thousand shares)

Interim Earnings (Per Share)

Qtr.	Mar	Jun	Sep	Dec
2015	2.14	2.62	2.14	0.94
2016	1.87	2.40	1.72	2.24
2017	2.36	2.53	2.71	(1.63)
2018	1.96	...	...	...

Interim Dividends (Per Share)

Amt	Decl	Ex	Rec	Pay
1.08Q	10/10/2017	11/16/2017	11/17/2017	12/01/2017
1.08Q	02/13/2018	02/22/2018	02/23/2018	03/08/2018
1.08Q	05/08/2018	05/17/2018	05/18/2018	06/01/2018
1.14Q	07/10/2018	08/21/2018	08/22/2018	09/04/2018

Indicated Div: $4.56 (Div. Reinv. Plan)

Valuation Analysis

		Institutional Holding	
Forecast EPS	$13.23 (06/13/2018)	No of Institutions	1375
Market Cap	$21.9 Billion	Shares	166,837,232
Book Value	$7.4 Billion	% Held	73.27
Price/Book	2.96		
Price/Sales	1.02		

Business Summary: Auto Parts (MIC: 1.8.2 SIC: 3519 NAIC: 333618)

Cummins is a diesel engine manufacturer. Co.'s reportable operating segments consist of: Engine, which manufactures and markets diesel and natural gas powered engines; Distribution, which engages in wholesaling engines, generator sets and service parts, as well as performing service and repair activities on its products; Components, which sells filtration products, aftertreatment systems, turbochargers and fuel systems; and Power Systems, which designs, manufactures and sells engines for industrial applications (including mining, oil and gas and marine), standby and prime power generator sets, alternators and other power components.

Recent Developments: For the quarter ended Apr 1 2018, net income decreased 19.8% to US$325.0 million from US$405.0 million in the year-earlier quarter. Revenues were US$5.57 billion, up 21.4% from US$4.59 billion the year before. Operating income was US$530.0 million versus US$540.0 million in the prior-year quarter, a decrease of 1.9%. Direct operating expenses rose 26.3% to US$4.37 billion from US$3.46 billion in the comparable period the year before. Indirect operating expenses increased 13.9% to US$670.0 million from US$588.0 million in the equivalent prior-year period.

Prospects: Our evaluation of Cummins Inc. as of Jan. 21, 2018 is the result of our systematic analysis on three basic characteristics: earnings strength, relative valuation, and recent stock price movement. The company has managed to produce a neutral trend in earnings per share over the past 5 quarters and while recent estimates for the company have been raised by analysts, CMI has posted better than expected results. Based on operating earnings yield, the company is undervalued when compared to all of the companies in our coverage universe. Share price changes over the past year indicates that CMI will perform in line with the market over the near term.

Financial Data
(US$ in Thousands)

	3 Mos	12/31/2017	12/31/2016	12/31/2015	12/31/2014	12/31/2013	12/31/2012	12/31/2011
Earnings Per Share	5.57	5.97	8.23	7.84	9.02	7.91	8.67	9.55
Cash Flow Per Share	10.80	13.67	11.42	11.56	12.41	11.17	8.07	10.74
Tang Book Value Per Share	32.46	31.41	36.05	37.65	38.02	35.84	30.50	25.66
Dividends Per Share	4.265	4.210	4.000	3.510	2.810	2.250	1.800	1.325
Dividend Payout %	76.57	70.52	48.60	44.77	31.15	28.45	20.76	13.87
Income Statement								
Total Revenue	5,570,000	20,428,000	17,509,000	19,110,000	19,221,000	17,301,000	17,334,000	18,048,000
EBITDA	545,000	2,895,000	2,410,000	2,485,000	2,826,000	2,451,000	2,565,000	2,945,000
Depn & Amortn	5,000	467,000	434,000	419,000	351,000	318,000	287,000	264,000
Income Before Taxes	523,000	2,365,000	1,930,000	2,025,000	2,434,000	2,119,000	2,271,000	2,671,000
Income Taxes	198,000	1,371,000	474,000	555,000	698,000	531,000	533,000	725,000
Net Income	325,000	999,000	1,394,000	1,399,000	1,651,000	1,483,000	1,645,000	1,848,000
Average Shares	165,700	167,270	169,336	178,406	183,079	187,417	189,668	193,597
Balance Sheet								
Current Assets	9,201,000	8,928,000	7,707,000	7,947,000	9,055,000	8,639,000	7,167,000	7,091,000
Total Assets	18,392,000	18,075,000	15,011,000	15,134,000	15,776,000	14,728,000	12,548,000	11,668,000
Current Liabilities	5,832,000	5,677,000	4,325,000	3,803,000	4,021,000	3,368,000	3,136,000	3,657,000
Long-Term Obligations	1,571,000	1,588,000	1,568,000	1,576,000	1,589,000	1,672,000	698,000	658,000
Total Liabilities	10,998,000	10,816,000	8,136,000	7,728,000	8,027,000	7,218,000	5,945,000	6,176,000
Stockholders' Equity	7,394,000	7,259,000	6,875,000	7,406,000	7,749,000	7,510,000	6,603,000	5,492,000
Shares Outstanding	164,772	165,700	168,200	175,200	182,200	186,700	189,800	192,000
Statistical Record								
Return on Assets %	5.45	6.04	9.22	9.05	10.82	10.87	13.55	16.75
Return on Equity %	12.75	14.14	19.47	18.46	21.64	21.02	27.13	36.37
EBITDA Margin %	9.78	14.17	13.76	13.00	14.70	14.17	14.80	16.32
Net Margin %	5.83	4.89	7.96	7.32	8.59	8.57	9.49	10.24
Asset Turnover	1.26	1.23	1.16	1.24	1.26	1.27	1.43	1.64
Current Ratio	1.58	1.57	1.78	2.09	2.25	2.57	2.29	1.94
Debt to Equity	0.21	0.22	0.23	0.21	0.21	0.22	0.11	0.12
Price Range	192.50-144.34	180.35-137.42	146.46-83.52	147.85-85.21	160.55-123.70	140.97-103.66	128.00-83.53	120.18-79.91
P/E Ratio	34.56-25.91	30.21-23.02	17.80-10.15	18.86-10.87	17.80-13.71	17.82-13.10	14.76-9.63	12.58-8.37
Average Yield %	2.59	2.65	3.44	2.80	1.95	1.85	1.75	1.32

Address: 500 Jackson Street, P.O. Box 3005, Columbus, IN 47202-3005
Telephone: 812-377-5000
Fax: 812-377-4937

Web Site: www.cummins.com
Officers: Norman Thomas Linebarger - Chairman, President, Chief Executive Officer, Executive Vice President, Vice President, Chief Financial Officer, Chief Operating Officer, Division Officer Richard Joseph (Rich) Freeland - President, Vice President, Chief Operating Officer, Division Officer

Auditors: PricewaterhouseCoopers LLP
Investor Contact: 812-377-3121
Transfer Agents: Wells Fargo Shareowner Services

CURTISS-WRIGHT CORP.

Exchange	Symbol	Price	52Wk Range	Yield	P/E
NYS	CW	$119.02 (6/29/2018)	142.06-91.78	0.50	23.57

*7 Year Price Score 140.62 *NYSE Composite Index=100 *12 Month Price Score 105.15

Interim Earnings (Per Share)

Qtr.	Mar	Jun	Sep	Dec
2015	0.33	0.53	0.71	1.48
2016	0.73	0.88	1.02	1.52
2017	0.73	1.13	1.43	1.51
2018	0.98	...	...	...

Interim Dividends (Per Share)

Amt	Decl	Ex	Rec	Pay
0.15Q	09/13/2017	10/05/2017	10/06/2017	10/20/2017
0.15Q	11/16/2017	11/28/2017	11/29/2017	12/08/2017
0.15Q	02/07/2018	03/28/2018	03/29/2018	04/12/2018
0.15Q	05/16/2018	06/20/2018	06/21/2018	07/05/2018

Indicated Div: $0.60

Valuation Analysis

		Institutional Holding	
Forecast EPS	$5.61	No of Institutions	
	(06/14/2018)	400	
Market Cap	$5.3 Billion	Shares	
Book Value	$1.6 Billion	46,858,192	
Price/Book	3.33	% Held	
Price/Sales	2.29	82.00	

Business Summary: Industrial Machinery & Equipment (MIC: 7.2.1 SIC: 3599 NAIC: 333999)

Curtiss-Wright is a multinational manufacturing and service company that designs, manufactures, and overhauls precision components and provides engineered products and services to the aerospace, defense, power generation, and general industrial markets. Co. operates through three segments: Commercial/Industrial, which provide industrial vehicle products such as electronic throttle control devices and transmission shifters; Defense, which provide Commercial Off-the-Shelf embedded computing board level modules, integrated subsystems, flight test equipment, instrumentation and control systems; and Power, which provide a range of hardware, pumps, valves, and fastening systems.

Recent Developments: For the quarter ended Mar 31 2018, net income increased 34.1% to US$43.6 million from US$32.5 million in the year-earlier quarter. Revenues were US$547.5 million, up 4.6% from US$523.6 million the year before. Operating income was US$64.5 million versus US$47.7 million in the prior-year quarter, an increase of 35.2%. Direct operating expenses rose 2.7% to US$366.3 million from US$356.7 million in the comparable period the year before. Indirect operating expenses decreased 2.1% to US$116.7 million from US$119.2 million in the equivalent prior-year period.

Prospects: Our evaluation of Curtiss-Wright Corp. as of Jan. 21, 2018 is the result of our systematic analysis on three basic characteristics: earnings strength, relative valuation, and recent stock price movement. The company has managed to produce a neutral trend in earnings per share over the past 5 quarters and while recent estimates for the company have been mixed, CW has posted better than expected results. Based on operating earnings yield, the company is about fairly valued when compared to all of the companies in our coverage universe. Share price changes over the past year indicates that CW will perform in line with the market over the near term.

Financial Data

(US$ in Thousands)	3 Mos	12/31/2017	12/31/2016	12/31/2015	12/31/2014	12/31/2013	12/31/2012	12/31/2011
Earnings Per Share	5.05	4.80	4.15	3.05	2.31	2.88	2.40	2.77
Cash Flow Per Share	7.75	8.80	9.51	3.48	6.91	5.06	3.25	4.36
Tang Book Value Per Share	3.54	2.31	1.55	N.M.	2.73	N.M.	N.M.	4.48
Dividends Per Share	0.580	0.560	0.520	0.520	0.520	0.390	0.350	0.320
Dividend Payout %	11.49	11.67	12.53	17.05	22.51	13.54	14.58	11.55
Income Statement								
Total Revenue	547,522	2,271,026	2,108,931	2,205,683	2,243,126	2,510,771	2,097,716	2,054,130
EBITDA	93,782	402,690	371,809	375,932	349,338	306,573	224,491	265,323
Depn & Amortn	24,601	61,600	62,600	64,700	66,600	71,600	62,800	59,500
Income Before Taxes	60,977	299,619	267,961	275,194	246,944	197,953	135,362	184,989
Income Taxes	17,334	84,728	78,579	82,946	76,995	59,972	43,073	54,566
Net Income	43,643	214,891	187,329	145,461	113,338	137,981	113,844	130,423
Average Shares	44,678	44,761	45,045	47,616	49,075	47,912	47,412	47,013
Balance Sheet								
Current Assets	1,352,777	1,401,860	1,414,811	1,316,620	1,571,075	1,337,283	1,175,761	1,167,134
Total Assets	3,179,059	3,236,321	3,037,781	3,029,378	3,399,511	3,458,274	3,114,588	2,652,837
Current Liabilities	541,285	590,997	675,262	525,187	571,993	534,593	639,748	505,384
Long-Term Obligations	813,576	813,989	815,630	953,083	953,279	958,604	751,990	583,928
Total Liabilities	1,600,084	1,708,521	1,746,590	1,773,955	1,921,078	1,905,569	1,801,996	1,423,798
Stockholders' Equity	1,578,975	1,527,800	1,291,191	1,255,423	1,478,433	1,552,705	1,312,592	1,229,039
Shares Outstanding	44,235	44,123	44,181	44,621	47,904	47,638	46,449	46,484
Statistical Record								
Return on Assets %	7.29	6.85	6.16	4.53	3.31	4.20	3.94	5.33
Return on Equity %	15.57	15.25	14.67	10.64	7.48	9.63	8.93	10.92
EBITDA Margin %	17.13	17.73	17.63	17.04	15.57	12.21	10.70	12.92
Net Margin %	7.97	9.46	8.88	6.59	5.05	5.50	5.43	6.35
Asset Turnover	0.74	0.72	0.69	0.69	0.65	0.76	0.73	0.84
Current Ratio	2.50	2.37	2.10	2.51	2.75	2.50	1.84	2.31
Debt to Equity	0.52	0.53	0.63	0.76	0.64	0.62	0.57	0.48
Price Range	139.88-83.41	124.20-83.41	107.06-63.70	77.08-61.97	73.16-58.77	62.23-31.05	40.82-28.90	38.26-26.16
P/E Ratio	27.70-16.52	25.88-17.38	25.80-15.35	25.27-20.32	31.67-25.44	21.61-10.78	17.01-12.04	13.81-9.44
Average Yield %	0.53	0.56	0.62	0.75	0.78	0.95	1.06	0.98

Address: 13925 Ballantyne Corporate Place, Suite 400, Charlotte, NC 28277 **Telephone:** 704-869-4600	**Web Site:** www.curtisswright.com **Officers:** David C. Adams - Chairman, Chief Executive Officer, President, Vice President, Co-Chief Operating Officer, Chief Operating Officer Thomas P. Quinly - Vice President, Chief Operating Officer	**Auditors:** DELOITTE & TOUCHE LLP **Investor Contact:** 973-541-3700 **Transfer Agents:** Broadridge Corporate Issuer Solutions, Inc., Brentwood, NY

CVS HEALTH CORPORATION

Exchange	Symbol	Price	52Wk Range	Yield	P/E	Div Acheiver
NYS	CVS	$64.35 (6/29/2018)	83.63-60.60	3.11	9.88	14 Years

*7 Year Price Score 80.44   ***NYSE Composite Index=100**   ***12 Month Price Score 89.92**

Interim Earnings (Per Share)

Qtr.	Mar	Jun	Sep	Dec
2015	1.07	1.12	1.11	1.34
2016	1.04	0.86	1.43	1.58
2017	0.92	1.07	1.26	3.20
2018	0.98	...	...	...

Interim Dividends (Per Share)

Amt	Decl	Ex	Rec	Pay
0.50Q	09/19/2017	10/23/2017	10/24/2017	11/03/2017
0.50Q	12/29/2017	01/23/2018	01/24/2018	02/02/2018
0.50Q	03/14/2018	04/20/2018	04/23/2018	05/03/2018
0.50Q	07/11/2018	07/24/2018	07/25/2018	08/01/2018

Indicated Div: $2.00 (Div. Reinv. Plan)

Valuation Analysis   **Institutional Holding**

Forecast EPS	$7.00	No of Institutions
	(06/14/2018)	2261
Market Cap	$65.4 Billion	Shares
Book Value	$38.7 Billion	1,066,842,688
Price/Book	1.69	% Held
Price/Sales	0.35	75.58

Business Summary: Retail - Food & Beverage, Drug & Tobacco (MIC: 2.1.2 SIC: 5912 NAIC: 446110)

CVS Health is a pharmacy health care provider. Co. has three reportable segments: Pharmacy Services, which provides pharmacy benefit management services, and through its SilverScript Insurance Company subsidiary, is a provider of drug benefits to eligible beneficiaries under the federal government's Medicare Part D program; Retail/LTC, which sells prescription drugs and a range of over-the-counter and personal care products, beauty and cosmetic products, and general merchandise (front store products); and Corporate, which provides management and administrative services to support the overall operations of Co.

Recent Developments: For the quarter ended Mar 31 2018, income from continuing operations increased 3.7% to US$998.0 million from US$962.0 million in the year-earlier quarter. Net income increased 4.7% to US$998.0 million from US$953.0 million in the year-earlier quarter. Revenues were US$45.69 billion, up 2.6% from US$44.51 billion the year before. Operating income was US$1.95 billion versus US$1.79 billion in the prior-year quarter, an increase of 8.5%. Direct operating expenses rose 2.3% to US$38.83 billion from US$37.94 billion in the comparable period the year before. Indirect operating expenses increased 2.8% to US$4.91 billion from US$4.78 billion in the equivalent prior-year period.

Prospects: Our evaluation of CVS Health Corp. as of Jan. 21, 2018 is the result of our systematic analysis on three basic characteristics: earnings strength, relative valuation, and recent stock price movement. The company has produced a positive trend in earnings per share over the past 5 quarters. However, while recent estimates for the company have been mixed, CVS has posted better than expected results. Based on operating earnings yield, the company is undervalued when compared to all of the companies in our coverage universe. Share price changes over the past year indicates that CVS will perform very poorly over the near term.

Financial Data

(US$ in Thousands)	3 Mos	12/31/2017	12/31/2016	12/31/2015	12/31/2014	12/31/2013	12/31/2012	12/31/2011
Earnings Per Share	6.51	6.44	4.90	4.63	3.96	3.74	3.03	2.57
Cash Flow Per Share	6.72	7.85	9.36	7.52	7.01	4.75	5.23	4.38
Tang Book Value Per Share	N.M.	N.M.	N.M.	N.M.	0.04	1.58	1.26	1.33
Dividends Per Share	2.000	2.000	1.700	1.400	1.100	0.900	0.650	0.500
Dividend Payout %	30.72	31.06	34.69	30.24	27.78	24.06	21.45	19.46
Income Statement								
Total Revenue	45,693,000	184,765,000	177,526,000	153,290,000	139,367,000	126,761,000	123,133,000	107,100,000
EBITDA	2,587,000	11,009,000	11,395,000	10,954,000	9,678,000	9,437,000	8,180,000	7,898,000
Depn & Amortn	644,000	1,700,000	1,700,000	1,500,000	1,400,000	1,400,000	1,300,000	1,568,000
Income Before Taxes	1,470,000	8,268,000	8,637,000	8,616,000	7,678,000	7,528,000	6,323,000	5,746,000
Income Taxes	472,000	1,637,000	3,317,000	3,386,000	3,033,000	2,928,000	2,441,000	2,258,000
Net Income	998,000	6,622,000	5,317,000	5,237,000	4,644,000	4,592,000	3,877,000	3,461,000
Average Shares	1,019,000	1,024,000	1,079,000	1,126,000	1,169,000	1,226,000	1,280,000	1,347,000
Balance Sheet								
Current Assets	71,798,000	31,229,000	31,042,000	30,378,000	25,983,000	25,325,000	19,852,000	18,594,000
Total Assets	135,139,000	95,131,000	94,462,000	93,657,000	74,252,000	71,526,000	65,912,000	64,543,000
Current Liabilities	30,248,000	30,648,000	26,250,000	23,169,000	19,027,000	15,425,000	13,790,000	11,956,000
Long-Term Obligations	61,552,000	22,181,000	25,615,000	26,267,000	11,695,000	12,841,000	9,133,000	9,208,000
Total Liabilities	96,466,000	57,440,000	57,632,000	56,461,000	36,294,000	33,588,000	28,208,000	26,492,000
Stockholders' Equity	38,673,000	37,691,000	36,830,000	37,196,000	37,958,000	37,938,000	37,704,000	38,051,000
Shares Outstanding	1,016,000	1,014,000	1,061,000	1,101,000	1,140,000	1,180,000	1,231,000	1,298,000
Statistical Record								
Return on Assets %	5.85	6.99	5.64	6.24	6.37	6.68	5.93	5.46
Return on Equity %	18.39	17.77	14.33	13.94	12.24	12.14	10.21	9.14
EBITDA Margin %	5.66	5.96	6.42	7.15	6.94	7.44	6.64	7.37
Net Margin %	2.18	3.58	3.00	3.42	3.33	3.62	3.15	3.23
Asset Turnover	1.63	1.95	1.88	1.83	1.91	1.84	1.88	1.69
Current Ratio	2.37	1.02	1.18	1.31	1.37	1.64	1.44	1.56
Debt to Equity	1.59	0.59	0.70	0.71	0.31	0.34	0.24	0.24
Price Range	83.63-60.60	83.92-66.80	106.10-73.53	113.45-91.56	98.25-65.44	71.58-48.35	49.24-41.46	41.16-32.06
P/E Ratio	12.85-9.31	13.03-10.37	21.65-15.01	24.50-19.78	24.81-16.53	19.14-12.93	16.25-13.68	16.02-12.47
Average Yield %	2.64	2.58	1.83	1.38	1.40	1.54	1.43	1.39

Address: One CVS Drive, Woonsocket, RI 02895	**Web Site:** www.cvshealth.com	**Auditors:** Ernst & Young LLP
Telephone: 401-765-1500	**Officers:** David W. Dorman - Chairman Larry J. Merlo - President, Chief Executive Officer	**Investor Contact:** 800-201-0938
Fax: 401-762-2137		**Transfer Agents:** Computershare, Providence, RI

DAVITA INC

Exchange	Symbol	Price	52Wk Range	Yield	P/E
NYS	DVA	$69.44 (6/29/2018)	80.03-53.89	N/A	33.07

*7 Year Price Score 83.48 *NYSE Composite Index=100 *12 Month Price Score 102.58

Interim Earnings (Per Share)

Qtr.	Mar	Jun	Sep	Dec
2015	(0.52)	0.78	1.00	(0.02)
2016	0.47	0.26	2.76	0.81
2017	2.29	0.65	(1.14)	1.61
2018	0.98	...	...	...

Interim Dividends (Per Share)

No Dividends Paid

Valuation Analysis   Institutional Holding

Forecast EPS	$4.09	No of Institutions
	(06/13/2018)	729
Market Cap	$12.4 Billion	Shares
Book Value	$4.6 Billion	182,001,632
Price/Book	2.71	% Held
Price/Sales	1.24	81.15

Business Summary: Diagnostic & Health Related Services (MIC: 4.2.2 SIC: 8092 NAIC: 621492)

DaVita operates two divisions, DaVita Kidney Care (Kidney Care) and DaVita Medical Group (DMG). Kidney Care is comprised of Co.'s U.S. dialysis and related lab services, its ancillary services and strategic initiatives, for patients suffering from chronic kidney failure. Co.'s DMG division is a patient- and physician-focused integrated healthcare delivery and management company. As of Dec 31 2017, Co. provided dialysis and administrative services in the U.S. through a network of 2,510 outpatient dialysis centers in 46 states and the District of Columbia. Co. also provides acute inpatient dialysis services in approximately 900 hospitals and related laboratory services throughout the U.S.

Recent Developments: For the quarter ended Mar 31 2018, income from continuing operations decreased 53.2% to US$231.0 million from US$493.9 million in the year-earlier quarter. Net income decreased 55.0% to US$225.2 million from US$500.3 million in the year-earlier quarter. Revenues were US$2.85 billion, up 8.3% from US$2.63 billion the year before. Operating income was US$410.7 million versus US$875.9 million in the prior-year quarter, a decrease of 53.1%. Direct operating expenses rose 9.9% to US$2.04 billion from US$1.85 billion in the comparable period the year before. Indirect operating expenses amounted to US$403.2 million compared with an income of US$96.7 million in the equivalent prior-year period.

Prospects: Our evaluation of Davita Inc. as of Jan. 21, 2018 is the result of our systematic analysis on three basic characteristics: earnings strength, relative valuation, and recent stock price movement. The company has managed to produce a neutral trend in earnings per share over the past 5 quarters and while recent estimates for the company have been mixed, DVA has posted results that fell short of analysts expectations. Based on operating earnings yield, the company is undervalued when compared to all of the companies in our coverage universe. Share price changes over the past year indicates that DVA will perform very poorly over the near term.

Financial Data

(US$ in Thousands)	3 Mos	12/31/2017	12/31/2016	12/31/2015	12/31/2014	12/31/2013	12/31/2012	12/31/2011
Earnings Per Share	2.10	3.47	4.29	1.25	3.33	2.95	2.73	2.48
Cash Flow Per Share	7.85	10.11	9.71	7.35	6.87	8.45	5.72	6.23
Income Statement								
Total Revenue	2,849,444	10,876,634	14,745,105	13,781,837	12,795,106	11,764,050	8,186,280	6,731,806
EBITDA	557,912	2,383,189	2,435,967	1,588,675	2,125,042	1,893,470	1,573,291	1,397,979
Depn & Amortn	142,799	544,129	545,734	475,484	428,309	373,107	299,810	249,060
Income Before Taxes	301,597	1,408,426	1,475,851	704,811	1,286,439	1,090,420	984,927	907,829
Income Taxes	70,737	323,859	455,813	295,726	446,343	381,013	359,845	325,292
Net Income	178,686	663,618	879,874	269,732	723,114	633,446	536,017	478,001
Average Shares	181,834	191,348	204,904	216,251	216,927	214,763	195,942	193,064
Balance Sheet								
Current Assets	8,673,555	8,744,358	3,980,228	4,503,280	3,876,797	3,472,278	2,878,794	2,281,608
Total Assets	18,942,372	18,948,193	18,741,257	18,514,875	17,942,715	17,098,877	16,018,596	8,892,172
Current Liabilities	2,947,523	3,041,177	2,696,445	2,399,138	2,088,652	2,462,049	2,018,174	1,153,116
Long-Term Obligations	9,279,885	9,158,018	8,947,327	9,001,308	8,383,280	8,141,231	8,326,534	4,417,624
Total Liabilities	14,361,692	14,258,164	14,093,210	13,644,095	12,772,202	12,666,398	12,255,459	6,751,097
Stockholders' Equity	4,580,680	4,690,029	4,648,047	4,870,780	5,170,513	4,432,479	3,763,137	2,141,075
Shares Outstanding	178,463	182,462	194,554	209,754	215,640	213,163	210,997	187,282
Statistical Record								
Return on Assets %	2.06	3.52	4.71	1.48	4.13	3.83	4.29	5.62
Return on Equity %	8.12	14.21	18.44	5.37	15.06	15.46	18.11	23.21
EBITDA Margin %	19.58	21.91	16.52	11.53	16.61	16.10	19.22	20.77
Net Margin %	6.27	6.10	5.97	1.96	5.65	5.38	6.55	7.10
Asset Turnover	0.52	0.58	0.79	0.76	0.73	0.71	0.66	0.79
Current Ratio	2.94	2.88	1.48	1.88	1.86	1.41	1.43	1.98
Debt to Equity	2.03	1.95	1.92	1.85	1.62	1.84	2.21	2.06
Price Range	80.03-53.89	72.36-53.89	78.44-55.16	84.23-67.79	78.07-62.74	65.59-53.76	57.49-38.56	44.68-30.32
P/E Ratio	38.11-25.66	20.85-15.53	18.28-12.86	67.38-54.23	23.44-18.84	22.24-18.22	21.06-14.13	18.02-12.23

Address: 2000 16th Street, Denver, CO 80202	Web Site: www.davita.com	Auditors: KPMG LLP
Telephone: 303-405-2100	Officers: Kent J. Thiry - Chairman, Co-Chairman, Chief Executive Officer Robert J. Margolis - Co-Chairman	Investor Contact: 310-536-2585 / Transfer Agents: Computershare

DANAHER CORP

Exchange	Symbol	Price	52Wk Range	Yield	P/E
NYS	DHR	$98.68 (6/29/2018)	103.80-79.29	0.65	27.34

*7 Year Price Score 118.60 *NYSE Composite Index=100 *12 Month Price Score 106.37

TRADING VOLUME (thousand shares)

Interim Earnings (Per Share)

Qtr.	Mar	Jun	Sep	Dec
2015	0.79	0.97	2.01	0.99
2016	1.09	0.94	0.56	1.06
2017	0.72	0.79	0.81	1.21
2018	0.80	...	...	...

Interim Dividends (Per Share)

Amt	Decl	Ex	Rec	Pay
0.14Q	09/12/2017	09/28/2017	09/29/2017	10/27/2017
0.14Q	12/05/2017	12/28/2017	12/29/2017	01/26/2018
0.16Q	02/20/2018	03/28/2018	03/29/2018	04/27/2018
0.16Q	05/08/2018	06/28/2018	06/29/2018	07/27/2018

Indicated Div: $0.64

Valuation Analysis

		Institutional Holding	
Forecast EPS	$4.45 (06/14/2018)	No of Institutions	1651
Market Cap	$68.9 Billion	Shares	628,558,720
Book Value	$27.2 Billion	% Held	76.22
Price/Book	2.54		
Price/Sales	3.66		

Business Summary: Medical Instruments & Equipment (MIC: 4.3.1 SIC: 3823 NAIC: 334513)

Danaher designs, manufactures and markets professional, medical, industrial and commercial products and services, Co.'s business consists of four segments: Life Sciences, which provides research tools to study the basic building blocks of life; Diagnostics, which provides analytical instruments, reagents, consumables, software and services that hospitals, physicians' offices, and reference laboratories ; Dental, which provides products that are used to diagnose, treat and prevent disease and ailments of the teeth, gums and supporting bone; and Environmental & Applied Solutions, which its water quality business provides instrumentation, services and disinfection systems.

Recent Developments: For the quarter ended Mar 30 2018, income from continuing operations increased 17.1% to US$566.6 million from US$483.8 million in the year-earlier quarter. Net income increased 12.0% to US$566.6 million from US$506.1 million in the year-earlier quarter. Revenues were US$4.70 billion, up 11.6% from US$4.21 billion the year before. Operating income was US$743.0 million versus US$617.0 million in the prior-year quarter, an increase of 20.4%. Direct operating expenses rose 9.6% to US$2.05 billion from US$1.87 billion in the comparable period the year before. Indirect operating expenses increased 10.7% to US$1.90 billion from US$1.72 billion in the equivalent prior-year period.

Prospects: Our evaluation of Danaher Corp. as of Jan. 21, 2018 is the result of our systematic analysis on three basic characteristics: earnings strength, relative valuation, and recent stock price movement. The company has enjoyed a very positive trend in earnings per share over the past 5 quarters and while recent estimates for the company have remained steady, DHR has posted better than expected results. Based on operating earnings yield, the company is about fairly valued when compared to all of the companies in our coverage universe. Share price changes over the past year indicates that DHR will perform in line with the market over the near term.

Financial Data

(US$ in Thousands)	3 Mos	12/31/2017	12/31/2016	12/31/2015	12/31/2014	12/31/2013	12/31/2012	12/31/2011
Earnings Per Share	3.61	3.53	3.65	4.74	3.63	3.80	3.36	3.11
Cash Flow Per Share	5.36	5.00	5.08	5.45	5.35	5.15	4.91	3.88
Tang Book Value Per Share	N.M.	N.M.	N.M.	N.M.	N.M.	0.14	N.M.	N.M.
Dividends Per Share	0.580	0.560	0.570	0.540	0.400	0.100	0.100	0.090
Dividend Payout %	16.07	15.86	15.62	11.39	11.02	2.63	2.98	2.89
Income Statement								
Total Revenue	4,695,400	18,329,700	16,882,400	20,563,100	19,913,800	19,118,000	18,260,400	16,090,540
EBITDA	1,071,600	3,671,800	3,340,500	4,055,000	4,140,400	4,236,100	3,593,000	2,868,219
Depn & Amortn	320,800	577,800	545,000	573,500	552,600	529,900	497,800	350,660
Income Before Taxes	713,100	2,938,800	2,611,300	3,324,000	3,481,800	3,566,000	2,940,900	2,381,069
Income Taxes	146,500	469,000	457,900	725,300	883,400	871,000	711,500	512,562
Net Income	566,600	2,492,100	2,553,700	3,357,400	2,598,400	2,695,000	2,392,200	2,172,264
Average Shares	709,500	706,100	699,800	708,500	716,100	711,000	713,100	701,191
Balance Sheet								
Current Assets	7,075,100	6,850,000	6,665,100	7,836,700	9,431,300	9,113,700	7,587,800	6,272,357
Total Assets	47,145,200	46,648,600	45,295,300	48,222,200	36,991,700	34,672,200	32,941,000	29,949,447
Current Liabilities	4,442,900	4,792,300	6,874,000	6,170,400	5,396,400	4,527,400	4,206,100	4,172,028
Long-Term Obligations	10,410,700	10,327,400	9,674,200	12,025,200	3,401,500	3,436,700	5,287,600	5,206,800
Total Liabilities	19,955,300	20,290,400	22,292,500	24,531,900	13,613,600	12,286,900	13,924,500	13,044,713
Stockholders' Equity	27,189,900	26,358,200	23,002,800	23,690,300	23,378,100	22,385,300	19,016,500	16,904,783
Shares Outstanding	698,500	696,600	692,200	686,800	704,300	698,100	687,500	687,730
Statistical Record								
Return on Assets %	5.53	5.42	5.45	7.88	7.25	7.97	7.59	8.33
Return on Equity %	10.01	10.10	10.91	14.27	11.36	13.02	13.28	14.19
EBITDA Margin %	22.82	20.03	19.79	19.72	20.79	22.16	19.68	17.83
Net Margin %	12.07	13.60	15.13	16.33	13.05	14.10	13.10	13.50
Asset Turnover	0.41	0.40	0.36	0.48	0.56	0.57	0.58	0.62
Current Ratio	1.59	1.43	0.97	1.27	1.75	2.01	1.80	1.50
Debt to Equity	0.38	0.39	0.42	0.51	0.15	0.15	0.28	0.31
Price Range	103.80-79.29	94.62-78.78	81.84-63.35	73.78-62.06	65.98-54.34	58.51-42.37	43.07-36.63	42.27-30.63
P/E Ratio	28.75-21.96	26.80-22.32	22.42-17.36	15.57-13.09	18.18-14.97	15.40-11.15	12.82-10.90	13.59-9.85
Average Yield %	0.65	0.65	0.76	0.81	0.68	0.20	0.25	0.24

Address: 2200 Pennsylvania Avenue, N.W., Suite 800W, Washington, DC 20037-1701 **Telephone:** 202-828-0850 **Fax:** 202-828-0860	**Web Site:** www.danaher.com **Officers:** Steven M. Rales - Chairman Thomas Patrick (Tom) Joyce - President, Chief Executive Officer, Executive Vice President	**Auditors:** Ernst & Young LLP **Investor Contact:** 202-828-0850 **Transfer Agents:** Computershare, Providence, RI

DARDEN RESTAURANTS, INC.

Exchange	Symbol	Price	52Wk Range	Yield	P/E
NYS	DRI	$107.06 (6/29/2018)	108.87-77.05	2.80	24.84

*7 Year Price Score 121.92 *NYSE Composite Index=100 *12 Month Price Score 104.48

Interim Earnings (Per Share)

Qtr.	Aug	Nov	Feb	May
2014-15	3.81	(0.26)	1.05	0.83
2015-16	0.67	0.33	0.82	1.08
2016-17	0.87	0.64	1.32	0.98
2017-18	0.93	0.67	1.73	...

Interim Dividends (Per Share)

Amt	Decl	Ex	Rec	Pay
0.63Q	09/21/2017	10/06/2017	10/10/2017	11/01/2017
0.63Q	12/14/2017	01/09/2018	01/10/2018	02/01/2018
0.63Q	03/22/2018	04/09/2018	04/10/2018	05/01/2018
0.75Q	06/20/2018	07/09/2018	07/10/2018	08/01/2018

Indicated Div: $3.00 (Div. Reinv. Plan)

Valuation Analysis

		Institutional Holding	
Forecast EPS	$5.51	No of Institutions	
	(06/14/2018)	921	
Market Cap	$13.3 Billion	Shares	
Book Value	$2.1 Billion	144,230,432	
Price/Book	6.24	% Held	
Price/Sales	1.68	83.70	

Business Summary: Hotels, Restaurants & Travel (MIC: 2.2.1 SIC: 5812 NAIC: 722110)

Darden Restaurants is a restaurant company. Co. has four reportable segments: Olive Garden; LongHorn Steakhouse; Fine Dining (which includes The Capital Grille and Eddie V's); and Other Business (which includes Cheddar's Scratch Kitchen, Yard House, Seasons 52, Bahama Breeze, consumer-packaged goods and franchise activities). As of May 28 2017, Co. owned and operated 1,695 restaurants through subsidiaries in the U.S. and Canada. As of May 28 2017, Co. also had 78 restaurants operated by independent third parties pursuant to area development and franchise agreements.

Recent Developments: For the quarter ended Feb 25 2018, income from continuing operations increased 31.4% to US$218.5 million from US$166.3 million in the year-earlier quarter. Net income increased 31.5% to US$217.8 million from US$165.6 million in the year-earlier quarter. Revenues were US$2.13 billion, up 13.3% from US$1.88 billion the year before. Operating income was US$233.4 million versus US$229.5 million in the prior-year quarter, an increase of 1.7%. Direct operating expenses rose 14.4% to US$1.65 billion from US$1.44 billion in the comparable period the year before. Indirect operating expenses increased 18.6% to US$247.9 million from US$209.0 million in the equivalent prior-year period.

Prospects: Our evaluation of Darden Restaurants Inc. as of Jan. 21, 2018 is the result of our systematic analysis on three basic characteristics: earnings strength, relative valuation, and recent stock price movement. The company has produced a positive trend in earnings per share over the past 5 quarters and while recent estimates for the company have been raised by analysts, DRI has posted better than expected results. Based on operating earnings yield, the company is undervalued when compared to all of the companies in our coverage universe. Share price changes over the past year indicates that DRI will perform well over the near term.

Financial Data

(US$ in Thousands)	9 Mos	6 Mos	3 Mos	05/28/2017	05/29/2016	05/31/2015	05/25/2014	05/26/2013
Earnings Per Share	4.31	3.90	3.87	3.80	2.90	5.47	2.15	3.13
Cash Flow Per Share	7.82	7.59	7.38	7.41	6.46	6.74	4.25	7.38
Tang Book Value Per Share	N.M.	N.M.	N.M.	N.M.	4.00	7.00	5.37	3.74
Dividends Per Share	2.450	2.380	2.310	2.240	2.100	2.200	2.200	2.000
Dividend Payout %	56.84	61.03	59.69	58.95	72.41	40.22	102.33	63.90
Income Statement								
Total Revenue	5,946,000	3,817,600	1,936,100	7,170,200	6,933,500	6,764,000	6,285,600	8,551,900
EBITDA	538,000	304,300	174,600	951,400	916,000	695,500	627,100	1,056,100
Depn & Amortn	1,200	900	100	273,900	293,800	327,900	318,200	407,800
Income Before Taxes	388,900	272,900	159,500	637,300	449,700	175,300	174,600	522,400
Income Taxes	(39,500)	63,000	38,200	154,800	90,000	(21,100)	(8,600)	109,800
Net Income	421,500	203,700	119,000	479,100	375,000	709,500	286,200	411,900
Average Shares	125,700	125,500	127,300	126,000	129,300	129,700	133,200	131,600
Balance Sheet								
Current Assets	569,600	485,200	483,000	799,800	820,300	1,056,400	1,976,400	764,900
Total Assets	5,454,700	5,317,600	5,223,500	5,504,200	4,582,600	5,994,700	7,100,700	6,936,900
Current Liabilities	1,467,500	1,418,000	1,258,300	1,289,200	1,187,100	1,196,700	1,618,500	1,416,400
Long-Term Obligations	926,400	935,600	936,600	936,600	440,000	1,452,300	2,533,400	2,548,700
Total Liabilities	3,329,800	3,341,500	3,164,800	3,402,500	2,630,600	3,661,200	4,943,800	4,877,400
Stockholders' Equity	2,124,900	1,976,100	2,058,700	2,101,700	1,952,000	2,333,500	2,156,900	2,059,500
Shares Outstanding	123,789	123,533	123,673	125,400	126,200	126,700	132,300	130,300
Statistical Record								
Return on Assets %	10.76	10.08	10.17	9.53	7.11	10.66	4.09	6.41
Return on Equity %	26.61	25.75	25.28	23.70	17.55	31.09	13.61	21.17
EBITDA Margin %	9.05	7.97	9.02	13.27	13.21	10.28	9.98	12.35
Net Margin %	7.09	5.34	6.15	6.68	5.41	10.49	4.55	4.82
Asset Turnover	1.56	1.56	1.54	1.43	1.31	1.02	0.90	1.33
Current Ratio	0.39	0.34	0.38	0.62	0.69	0.88	1.22	0.54
Debt to Equity	0.44	0.47	0.45	0.45	0.23	0.62	1.17	1.24
Price Range	99.31-74.16	92.69-71.55	92.69-60.63	88.40-59.68	67.78-53.93	62.44-39.18	48.94-40.99	51.23-39.79
P/E Ratio	23.04-17.21	23.77-18.35	23.95-15.67	23.26-15.71	23.37-18.60	11.41-7.16	22.76-19.07	16.37-12.71
Average Yield %	2.84	2.92	2.99	3.15	3.39		4.89	4.43

Address: 1000 Darden Center Drive, Orlando, FL 32837 **Telephone:** 407-245-4000	**Web Site:** www.darden.com **Officers:** Charles M. (Chuck) Sonsteby - Chairman Eugene I. (Gene) Lee - President, President (frmr), Chief Executive Officer, Interim Chief Executive Officer, Division Officer	**Auditors:** KPMG LLP **Investor Contact:** 800-832-7336 **Transfer Agents:** Wells Fargo Shareowner Services, Mendota Heights, MN

DANA INC

Exchange	Symbol	Price	52Wk Range	Yield	P/E
NYS	DAN	$20.19 (6/29/2018)	34.88-20.19	1.98	21.95

7 Year Price Score 116.28 *NYSE Composite Index=100* **12 Month Price Score 82.11**

Interim Earnings (Per Share)

Qtr.	Mar	Jun	Sep	Dec
2015	0.38	0.36	0.75	(0.49)
2016	0.30	0.36	0.39	3.31
2017	0.51	0.47	0.46	(0.74)
2018	0.73	...	...	...

Interim Dividends (Per Share)

Amt	Decl	Ex	Rec	Pay
0.06Q	07/26/2017	08/09/2017	08/11/2017	09/01/2017
0.06Q	10/25/2017	11/09/2017	11/10/2017	12/01/2017
0.10Q	02/16/2018	03/01/2018	03/02/2018	03/23/2018
0.10Q	04/26/2018	05/10/2018	05/11/2018	06/01/2018

Indicated Div: $0.40

Valuation Analysis

	Institutional Holding	
Forecast EPS	$3.00	No of Institutions
	(06/14/2018)	423
Market Cap	$2.9 Billion	Shares
Book Value	$1.1 Billion	168,898,640
Price/Book	2.66	% Held
Price/Sales	0.38	N/A

Business Summary: Auto Parts (MIC: 1.8.2 SIC: 3714 NAIC: 336399)

Dana is a holding company. Through its subsidiaries, Co is a provider of driveline, sealing and thermal-management products its customer base. Co. has four segments: Light Vehicle Driveline Technologies, which include front axles, rear axles, drive shafts, differentials, torque couplings and modular assemblies; Commercial Vehicle Driveline Technologies, which include steer axles, drive axles, drive shafts, and tire inflation systems; Off-Highway Driveline Technologies, which include front axles, rear axles, driveshafts, transmissions, torque converters, tire inflation systems, and electronic controls; and Power Technologies, which include gaskets, cover modules and heat shields.

Recent Developments: For the quarter ended Mar 31 2018, net income increased 38.8% to US$111.0 million from US$80.0 million in the year-earlier quarter. Revenues were US$2.14 billion, up 25.7% from US$1.70 billion the year before. Direct operating expenses rose 27.4% to US$1.83 billion from US$1.44 billion in the comparable period the year before. Indirect operating expenses increased 7.3% to US$133.0 million from US$124.0 million in the equivalent prior-year period.

Prospects: Our evaluation of Dana Inc. as of Jan. 21, 2018 is the result of our systematic analysis on three basic characteristics: earnings strength, relative valuation, and recent stock price movement. The company has generated a negative trend in earnings per share over the past 5 quarters and while recent estimates for the company have been mixed, DAN has posted better than expected results. Based on operating earnings yield, the company is undervalued when compared to all of the companies in our coverage universe. Share price changes over the past year indicates that DAN will perform very well over the near term.

Financial Data

(US$ in Thousands)	3 Mos	12/31/2017	12/31/2016	12/31/2015	12/31/2014	12/31/2013	12/31/2012	12/31/2011
Earnings Per Share	0.92	0.71	4.36	0.99	1.84	(0.09)	1.40	1.02
Cash Flow Per Share	3.54	3.82	2.62	2.55	3.23	3.94	2.28	2.52
Tang Book Value Per Share	5.51	4.91	6.66	3.64	4.94	4.16	4.48	3.29
Dividends Per Share	0.280	0.240	0.240	0.230	0.200	0.200	0.200	...
Dividend Payout %	30.43	33.80	5.50	23.23	10.87	...	14.29	...
Income Statement								
Total Revenue	2,138,000	7,209,000	5,826,000	6,060,000	6,617,000	6,769,000	7,224,000	7,592,000
EBITDA	242,000	704,000	497,000	566,000	576,000	704,000	701,000	655,000
Depn & Amortn	68,000	233,000	182,000	174,000	213,000	262,000	277,000	307,000
Income Before Taxes	153,000	380,000	215,000	292,000	260,000	368,000	364,000	296,000
Income Taxes	48,000	283,000	(424,000)	82,000	(70,000)	119,000	51,000	85,000
Net Income	108,000	111,000	640,000	159,000	319,000	244,000	300,000	219,000
Average Shares	147,500	146,900	146,800	160,000	173,500	146,400	214,700	215,300
Balance Sheet								
Current Assets	3,164,000	2,882,000	2,284,000	2,474,000	2,954,000	3,165,000	2,953,000	3,049,000
Total Assets	5,945,000	5,644,000	4,860,000	4,326,000	4,930,000	5,129,000	5,144,000	5,305,000
Current Liabilities	1,861,000	1,702,000	1,253,000	1,091,000	1,261,000	1,268,000	1,310,000	1,493,000
Long-Term Obligations	1,755,000	1,759,000	1,595,000	1,553,000	1,613,000	1,567,000	803,000	831,000
Total Liabilities	4,841,000	4,631,000	3,703,000	3,598,000	3,850,000	3,820,000	3,301,000	3,568,000
Stockholders' Equity	1,104,000	1,013,000	1,157,000	728,000	1,080,000	1,309,000	1,843,000	1,737,000
Shares Outstanding	145,465	144,984	143,938	150,068	166,070	145,338	148,264	147,319
Statistical Record								
Return on Assets %	2.56	2.11	13.90	3.44	6.34	4.75	5.73	4.21
Return on Equity %	13.20	10.23	67.72	17.59	26.71	15.48	16.71	12.80
EBITDA Margin %	11.32	9.77	8.53	9.34	8.70	10.40	9.70	8.63
Net Margin %	5.05	1.54	10.99	2.62	4.82	3.60	4.15	2.88
Asset Turnover	1.36	1.37	1.26	1.31	1.32	1.32	1.38	1.46
Current Ratio	1.70	1.69	1.82	2.27	2.34	2.50	2.25	2.04
Debt to Equity	1.59	1.74	1.38	2.13	1.49	1.20	0.44	0.48
Price Range	34.88-17.57	33.04-17.57	19.74-10.09	23.20-13.11	24.60-17.21	23.32-15.52	16.55-11.31	18.99-9.95
P/E Ratio	37.91-19.10	46.54-24.75	4.53-2.31	23.43-13.24	13.37-9.35	...	11.82-8.08	18.62-9.75
Average Yield %	1.07	1.01	1.74	1.20	0.93	1.05	1.43	...

Address: 3939 Technology Drive, Maumee, OH 43537
Telephone: 419-887-3000
Fax: 419-887-5200

Web Site: www.dana.com
Officers: James K. Kamsickas - President, Chief Executive Officer Jonathan M. Collins - Executive Vice President, Senior Vice President, Chief Financial Officer

Auditors: PricewaterhouseCoopers LLP
Investor Contact: 800-537-8823
Transfer Agents: Wells Fargo Shareowner Services

DCT INDUSTRIAL TRUST INC

Exchange	Symbol	Price	52Wk Range	Yield	P/E
NYS	DCT	$66.73 (6/29/2018)	67.07-52.27	2.16	45.39

*7 Year Price Score 129.16 *NYSE Composite Index=100 *12 Month Price Score 109.61

Interim Earnings (Per Share)

Qtr.	Mar	Jun	Sep	Dec
2015	0.32	0.20	0.09	0.43
2016	0.41	0.24	0.17	0.22
2017	0.16	0.45	0.28	0.22
2018	0.52	...	...	...

Interim Dividends (Per Share)

Amt	Decl	Ex	Rec	Pay
0.31Q	08/03/2017	10/05/2017	10/06/2017	10/18/2017
0.36Q	11/02/2017	12/21/2017	12/22/2017	01/04/2018
0.36Q	02/01/2018	03/28/2018	03/30/2018	04/11/2018
0.36Q	04/29/2018	06/28/2018	06/29/2018	07/11/2018

Indicated Div: $1.44 (Div. Reinv. Plan)

Valuation Analysis — **Institutional Holding**

Forecast EPS	$0.78
	(06/13/2018)
Market Cap	$6.3 Billion
Book Value	$2.0 Billion
Price/Book	3.16
Price/Sales	14.65

No of Institutions	388
Shares	122,703,120
% Held	100.98

Business Summary: REITs (MIC: 5.3.1 SIC: 6798 NAIC: 525930)

DCT Industrial Trust is an industrial real estate company engaged in the ownership, acquisition, development, leasing and management of bulk-distribution and light-industrial properties located in the U.S. As of Dec 31 2017, Co. owned interests in approximately 74.8 million square feet of properties leased to approximately 850 customers, including: 398 consolidated operating properties; six consolidated properties which are shell-construction complete and in lease-up; one consolidated properties under redevelopment; three consolidated value-add acquisitions; and 21 unconsolidated properties. In addition, Co. has 19 projects under construction and several projects in pre-development.

Recent Developments: For the quarter ended Mar 31 2018, net income increased 222.6% to US$50.9 million from US$15.8 million in the year-earlier quarter. Revenues were US$109.8 million, up 3.7% from US$105.9 million the year before. Revenues from property income rose 3.8% to US$109.4 million from US$105.4 million in the corresponding quarter a year earlier.

Prospects: Our evaluation of DCT Industrial Trust Inc. as of Jan. 21, 2018 is the result of our systematic analysis on three basic characteristics: earnings strength, relative valuation, and recent stock price movement. The company has managed to produce a neutral trend in earnings per share over the past 5 quarters. However, while recent estimates for the company have been mixed, DCT has posted better than expected results. Based on operating earnings yield, the company is overvalued when compared to all of the companies in our coverage universe. Share price changes over the past year indicates that DCT will perform well over the near term.

Financial Data
(US$ in Thousands)

	3 Mos	12/31/2017	12/31/2016	12/31/2015	12/31/2014	12/31/2013	12/31/2012	12/31/2011
Earnings Per Share	1.47	1.11	1.03	1.05	0.58	0.20	(0.24)	(0.44)
Cash Flow Per Share	2.57	2.64	2.46	2.27	2.04	2.05	1.87	1.76
Tang Book Value Per Share	21.13	20.83	20.35	19.84	19.88	19.28	18.97	19.65
Dividends Per Share	1.340	1.290	1.180	1.130	0.280	1.120	...	1.120
Dividend Payout %	91.16	116.22	114.56	107.62	48.28	560.00	...	...
Income Statement								
Total Revenue	109,807	424,468	392,776	354,697	336,526	289,005	260,779	253,449
EBITDA	107,194	338,653	319,327	306,533	250,734	188,584	171,674	159,340
Depn & Amortn	41,232	168,245	161,334	156,010	148,992	137,120	126,687	128,989
Income Before Taxes	49,946	104,349	94,509	96,428	40,069	(11,656)	(23,996)	(33,900)
Income Taxes	81	2,267	591	736	...	...	...	...
Net Income	48,823	103,494	93,060	94,048	49,164	15,870	(15,086)	(25,250)
Average Shares	93,837	92,688	89,982	88,514	83,572	74,692	63,707	60,647
Balance Sheet								
Current Assets	80,984	25,290	17,632	49,599	23,410	44,847	22,772	12,834
Total Assets	4,055,841	4,010,672	3,808,142	3,632,355	3,451,534	3,265,963	3,057,199	2,793,298
Current Liabilities	167,376	185,166	155,603	165,389	140,055	115,615	103,025	87,706
Long-Term Obligations	1,750,926	1,722,354	1,628,928	1,556,472	1,409,045	1,452,367	1,452,314	1,252,783
Total Liabilities	2,068,382	2,059,111	1,946,093	1,880,371	1,701,702	1,722,157	1,728,135	1,585,329
Stockholders' Equity	1,987,459	1,951,561	1,862,049	1,751,984	1,749,832	1,543,806	1,329,064	1,207,969
Shares Outstanding	94,075	93,707	91,516	88,313	88,012	80,066	70,077	61,485
Statistical Record								
Return on Assets %	3.49	2.65	2.49	2.66	1.46	0.50	N.M.	N.M.
Return on Equity %	7.14	5.43	5.14	5.37	2.99	1.10	N.M.	N.M.
EBITDA Margin %	97.62	79.78	81.30	86.42	74.51	65.25	65.83	62.87
Net Margin %	44.46	24.38	23.69	26.52	14.61	5.49	N.M.	N.M.
Asset Turnover	0.11	0.11	0.11	0.10	0.10	0.09	0.09	0.09
Current Ratio	0.48	0.14	0.11	0.30	0.17	0.39	0.22	0.15
Debt to Equity	0.88	0.88	0.87	0.89	0.81	0.94	1.09	1.04
Price Range	61.42-48.12	61.42-44.18	50.43-33.90	38.60-31.31	36.47-27.64	33.32-25.96	27.44-20.28	23.32-16.08
P/E Ratio	41.78-32.73	55.33-39.80	48.96-33.00	36.76-29.82	62.88-47.66	166.60-129.80	...	...
Average Yield %	2.39	2.40	2.71	3.24	0.88	3.81	...	5.51

Address: 555 17th Street, Suite 3700, Denver, CO 80202 **Telephone:** 303-597-2400	**Web Site:** www.dctindustrial.com **Officers:** Thomas F. August - Chairman Philip L. Hawkins - President, Chief Executive Officer, President (frmr)	**Auditors:** Ernst & Young LLP **Investor Contact:** 303-597-1550 **Transfer Agents:** BNY Mellon Shareowner Services, Jersey City, NJ

DDR CORP

Exchange	Symbol	Price	52Wk Range	Yield	P/E
NYS	DDR PRH	$14.78 (6/29/2018)	17.81-11.01	N/A	N/A

*7 Year Price Score 45.36   *NYSE Composite Index=100   *12 Month Price Score 92.52

Interim Earnings (Per Share)

Qtr.	Mar	Jun	Sep	Dec
2015	(1.38)	0.06	0.30	0.48
2016	0.22	0.20	(0.36)	0.16
2017	(0.32)	0.12	(0.04)	(1.24)
2018	(0.34)	...	...	...

Interim Dividends (Per Share)

Amt	Decl	Ex	Rec	Pay
0.461Q	06/11/2013	06/27/2013	07/01/2013	07/15/2013
0.461Q	09/12/2013	09/27/2013	10/01/2013	10/15/2013
0.461Q	12/10/2013	12/27/2013	12/31/2013	01/15/2014
0.461Q	03/11/2014	03/28/2014	04/01/2014	04/15/2014

Valuation Analysis   **Institutional Holding**

Forecast EPS	$-0.28	No of Institutions
	(06/21/2018)	424
Market Cap	$2.7 Billion	Shares
Book Value	$2.8 Billion	422,023,232
Price/Book	0.98	% Held
Price/Sales	3.04	N/A

Business Summary: REITs (MIC: 5.3.1 SIC: 6798 NAIC: 525930)

DDR is a self-administered and self-managed real estate investment trust (REIT), engaged in the business of acquiring, owning, developing, redeveloping, expanding, leasing, financing and managing shopping centers. As of Dec 31 2017, Co.'s portfolio consisted of 273 shopping centers (including 137 shopping centers owned through joint ventures). These properties consist of 261 shopping centers owned in the United States and 12 in Puerto Rico. At Dec 31 2017, Co. owned and managed approximately 92 million total square feet of gross leasable area through all its properties (wholly-owned and joint venture). Co. also owns more than 250 acres of undeveloped land.

Recent Developments: For the quarter ended Mar 31 2018, loss from continuing operations was US$63.9 million compared with a loss of US$92.2 million in the year-earlier quarter. Net loss amounted to US$53.9 million versus a net loss of US$54.0 million in the year-earlier quarter. Revenues were US$215.1 million, down 10.5% from US$240.4 million the year before. Revenues from property income fell 11.6% to US$200.0 million from US$226.4 million in the corresponding quarter a year earlier.

Prospects: Our evaluation of DDR Corp. as of Jan. 21, 2018 is the result of our systematic analysis on three basic characteristics: earnings strength, relative valuation, and recent stock price movement. The company has suffered a very negative trend in earnings per share over the past 5 quarters. Because the company lacks sufficient analyst estimate data, we place greater weight on the historical EPS trend as the measure of earnings strength. Based on operating earnings yield, the company is overvalued when compared to all of the companies in our coverage universe. Share price changes over the past year indicates that DDR will perform poorly over the near term.

Financial Data

(US$ in Thousands)	3 Mos	12/31/2017	12/31/2016	12/31/2015	12/31/2014	12/31/2013	12/31/2012	12/31/2011
Earnings Per Share	(1.50)	(1.48)	0.20	(0.54)	0.50	(0.28)	(0.42)	(0.56)
Cash Flow Per Share	2.04	2.23	2.53	2.41	2.35	2.29	2.08	2.02
Tang Book Value Per Share	11.25	11.87	14.48	15.34	16.85	17.25	17.87	18.99
Dividends Per Share	...	1.520	1.520	...	...	1.080	0.960	0.440
Dividend Payout %	...	...	760.00	...	...	...	...	...
Income Statement								
Total Revenue	215,068	921,588	1,005,805	1,028,071	985,675	888,788	800,375	771,018
EBITDA	(23,910)	113,244	546,096	380,784	664,370	541,388	421,954	409,683
Depn & Amortn	10,103	353,676	391,666	396,730	431,204	338,277	265,195	245,069
Income Before Taxes	(72,712)	(400,715)	(26,105)	(228,460)	11,973	(2,219)	(48,866)	(55,272)
Income Taxes	(18)	12,418	1,781	6,286	1,855	2,713	1,160	1,044
Net Income	(54,153)	(241,685)	60,012	(72,168)	117,282	(10,175)	(25,822)	(15,854)
Average Shares	184,560	183,681	182,780	180,473	179,061	163,213	145,863	135,736
Balance Sheet								
Current Assets	251,503	281,677	210,095	204,143	221,218	327,991	249,778	283,557
Total Assets	6,910,446	7,170,073	8,197,518	9,097,088	9,541,895	9,693,073	8,055,837	7,469,425
Current Liabilities	396,603	423,323	457,538	494,082	509,660	470,520	370,234	286,949
Long-Term Obligations	3,741,520	3,849,312	4,493,968	5,139,537	5,234,707	5,294,673	4,319,143	4,104,584
Total Liabilities	4,143,029	4,279,141	4,960,003	5,641,903	5,771,647	5,788,412	4,713,699	4,423,741
Stockholders' Equity	2,767,417	2,890,932	3,237,515	3,455,185	3,770,248	3,904,661	3,342,138	3,045,684
Shares Outstanding	184,379	183,949	182,675	182,173	179,877	179,174	157,130	138,140
Statistical Record								
Return on Assets %	N.M.	N.M.	0.69	N.M.	1.22	N.M.	N.M.	N.M.
Return on Equity %	N.M.	N.M.	1.79	N.M.	3.06	N.M.	N.M.	N.M.
EBITDA Margin %	N.M.	12.29	54.29	37.04	67.40	60.91	52.72	53.14
Net Margin %	N.M.	N.M.	5.97	N.M.	11.90	N.M.	N.M.	N.M.
Asset Turnover	0.12	0.12	0.12	0.11	0.10	0.10	0.10	0.10
Current Ratio	0.63	0.67	0.46	0.41	0.43	0.70	0.67	0.99
Debt to Equity	1.35	1.33	1.39	1.49	1.39	1.36	1.29	1.35
Price Range	21.21-11.29	25.54-12.23	32.87-24.37	33.61-24.35	30.87-24.86	32.04-24.68	26.18-20.27	24.99-16.79
P/E Ratio	...	...	164.34-121.83	...	61.74-49.72	...	...	...
Average Yield %	...	8.69	5.38	...	...	3.89	3.96	2.05

Address: 3300 Enterprise Parkway, Beachwood, OH 44122	**Web Site:** www.ddr.com	**Auditors:** PricewaterhouseCoopers LLP
Telephone: 216-755-5500	**Officers:** David R. Lukes - President, Chief Executive Officer Michael A. Makinen - Executive Vice President, Chief Operating Officer	**Transfer Agents:** Computershare, Providence, RI
Fax: 216-755-1500		

DEAN FOODS CO.

Exchange	Symbol	Price	52Wk Range	Yield	P/E
NYS	DF	$10.51 (6/29/2018)	17.14-8.16	3.43	N/A

*7 Year Price Score 55.92 *NYSE Composite Index=100 *12 Month Price Score 89.19

Interim Earnings (Per Share)

Qtr.	Mar	Jun	Sep	Dec
2015	(0.78)	0.28	0.22	0.20
2016	0.43	0.36	0.16	0.36
2017	(0.11)	0.19	0.02	0.57
2018	0.00			

Interim Dividends (Per Share)

Amt	Decl	Ex	Rec	Pay
0.09Q	08/09/2017	08/17/2017	08/21/2017	08/30/2017
0.09Q	11/08/2017	11/17/2017	11/20/2017	12/05/2017
0.09Q	03/07/2018	03/16/2018	03/19/2018	03/28/2018
0.09Q	05/09/2018	05/18/2018	05/21/2018	05/31/2018

Indicated Div: $0.36

Valuation Analysis — **Institutional Holding**

Forecast EPS	$0.66	No of Institutions
	(06/11/2018)	416
Market Cap	$959.9 Million	Shares
Book Value	$650.4 Million	111,336,576
Price/Book	1.48	% Held
Price/Sales	0.12	N/A

Business Summary: Food (MIC: 1.2.1 SIC: 2024 NAIC: 311520)

Dean Foods is a food and beverage company and a processor and direct-to-store distributor of fluid milk and other dairy and dairy case products. Co. manufactures, markets and distributes a branded and private label dairy and dairy case products, including fluid milk, ice cream, cultured dairy products, creamers, ice cream mix and other dairy products to retailers, educational institutions and governmental entities. Co.'s portfolio includes DairyPurewhite, TruMoo®, Alta Dena ®, Berkeley Farms ®, Country Fresh ®, Dean's ®, Friendly's ®, Garelick Farms ®, LAND O LAKES ®, Mayfield ® and more. Co. also makes and distributes ice cream, cultured products, juices, teas and bottled water.

Recent Developments: For the quarter ended Mar 31 2018, net loss amounted to US$265,000 versus a net loss of US$9.8 million in the year-earlier quarter. Revenues were US$1.98 billion, down 0.8% from US$2.00 billion the year before. Operating income was US$15.3 million versus US$4.1 million in the prior-year quarter, an increase of 278.8%. Direct operating expenses was unchanged at US$1.53 billion versus the comparable period the year before. Indirect operating expenses decreased 5.5% to US$433.2 million from US$458.2 million in the equivalent prior-year period.

Prospects: Our evaluation of Dean Foods Co. as of Jan. 21, 2018 is the result of our systematic analysis on three basic characteristics: earnings strength, relative valuation, and recent stock price movement. The company has enjoyed a very positive trend in earnings per share over the past 5 quarters and while recent estimates for the company have been mixed, DF has posted results that fell short of analysts expectations. Based on operating earnings yield, the company is undervalued when compared to all of the companies in our coverage universe. Share price changes over the past year indicates that DF will perform very poorly over the near term.

Financial Data
(US$ in Thousands)

	3 Mos	12/31/2017	12/31/2016	12/31/2015	12/31/2014	12/31/2013	12/31/2012	12/31/2011
Earnings Per Share	...	0.67	1.31	(0.09)	(0.22)	8.58	1.70	(17.18)
Cash Flow Per Share	1.71	1.59	2.82	4.37	1.63	(3.38)	4.76	4.90
Tang Book Value Per Share	5.29	5.36	5.04	5.02	5.74	6.62	N.M.	...
Dividends Per Share	0.360	0.360	0.360	0.280	0.280	...	...	...
Dividend Payout %	...	53.73	27.48	...	...	...	...	...
Income Statement								
Total Revenue	1,980,507	7,795,025	7,710,226	8,121,661	9,503,196	9,016,321	11,462,277	13,055,493
EBITDA	19,953	252,014	442,098	224,856	168,125	649,061	675,077	(1,789,108)
Depn & Amortn	5,078	165,810	172,652	171,353	159,389	165,469	246,583	10,539
Income Before Taxes	842	21,243	202,651	(13,310)	(52,283)	283,034	263,922	(2,052,598)
Income Taxes	1,107	(26,179)	82,034	(5,229)	(32,096)	(42,325)	146,509	(456,811)
Net Income	(265)	61,588	119,929	(8,508)	(20,296)	813,178	158,622	(1,575,621)
Average Shares	91,192	91,273	91,510	93,298	93,916	94,796	93,065	91,694
Balance Sheet								
Current Assets	1,002,123	1,019,879	1,058,630	1,077,563	1,180,060	1,150,698	2,202,778	1,716,322
Total Assets	2,444,714	2,503,829	2,606,227	2,528,015	2,769,636	2,802,045	5,687,091	5,754,363
Current Liabilities	626,310	672,195	847,787	761,895	794,451	781,087	1,340,993	1,495,542
Long-Term Obligations	906,063	912,074	745,245	840,932	916,481	896,564	3,077,258	3,563,389
Total Liabilities	1,794,354	1,847,882	1,995,671	1,982,511	2,142,318	2,087,730	5,329,904	5,857,761
Stockholders' Equity	650,360	655,947	610,556	545,504	627,318	714,315	357,187	(103,398)
Shares Outstanding	91,332	91,123	90,586	91,428	94,080	94,831	92,781	91,872
Statistical Record								
Return on Assets %	2.86	2.41	4.66	N.M.	N.M.	19.16	2.77	N.M.
Return on Equity %	11.42	9.73	20.69	N.M.	N.M.	151.78	124.66	N.M.
EBITDA Margin %	1.01	3.23	5.73	2.77	1.77	7.20	5.89	N.M.
Net Margin %	N.M.	0.79	1.56	N.M.	N.M.	9.02	1.38	N.M.
Asset Turnover	3.13	3.05	3.00	3.07	3.41	2.12	2.00	1.90
Current Ratio	1.60	1.52	1.25	1.41	1.49	1.47	1.64	1.15
Debt to Equity	1.39	1.39	1.22	1.54	1.46	1.26	8.62	...
Price Range	20.05-8.29	21.91-9.09	22.00-15.88	19.56-15.41	19.40-12.70	22.70-14.35	17.48-9.82	12.91-7.41
P/E Ratio		32.70-13.57	16.79-12.12	...	...	2.65-1.67	10.28-5.78	...
Average Yield %	2.75	2.33	1.97	1.61	1.76	...	...	...

Address: 2711 North Haskell Avenue, Suite 3400, Dallas, TX 75204
Telephone: 214-303-3400

Web Site: www.deanfoods.com
Officers: Tom C. Davis - Chairman Ralph P. Scozzafava - Executive Vice President, Chief Operating Officer, Chief Commercial Officer, Chief Executive Officer

Auditors: DELOITTE & TOUCHE LLP
Investor Contact: 214-303-3400
Transfer Agents: Computershare Shareowner Services LLC, Providence, RI

DECKERS OUTDOOR CORP.

Exchange	Symbol	Price	52Wk Range	Yield	P/E
NYS	DECK	$112.89 (6/29/2018)	121.94-61.60	N/A	31.53

*7 Year Price Score 96.58   *NYSE Composite Index=100   *12 Month Price Score 131.57

Interim Earnings (Per Share)

Qtr.	Mar	Jun	Sep	Dec
2013	0.03	(0.85)	0.95	4.04
Qtr.	Jun	Sep	Dec	Mar
2014-15	(1.07)	1.17	4.50	0.07
2015-16	(1.43)	1.11	4.78	(0.70)
2016-17	(1.84)	1.21	1.27	(0.48)
2017-18	(1.32)	1.54	2.69	0.67

Interim Dividends (Per Share)

No Dividends Paid

Valuation Analysis   Institutional Holding

Forecast EPS	$6.35	No of Institutions
	(06/04/2018)	450
Market Cap	$3.4 Billion	Shares
Book Value	$940.8 Million	40,577,876
Price/Book	3.65	% Held
Price/Sales	1.81	95.56

TRADING VOLUME (thousand shares)

Business Summary: Apparel, Footwear & Accessories (MIC: 1.4.2 SIC: 3021 NAIC: 316211)

Deckers Outdoor is engaged in designing, marketing and distributing footwear, apparel and accessories. Co. markets its products primarily under five brands. The UGG® brand is comprised of a line of footwear for women, men and children. Teva® is an outdoor active lifestyle brand, and the product line includes sandals, shoes, and boots. Sanuk® is a surf lifestyle footwear brand, and it includes Co.'s SIDEWALK SURFERS shoe, Yoga Mat and Beer Cozy sandal collections. Co.' other brands include: Hoka One One®, a line of running footwear; and Koolaburra® by UGG, a line of casual footwear using sheepskin and other plush materials. At Mar 31 2017, Co. had a total of 160 retail stores worldwide.

Recent Developments: For the year ended Mar 31 2018, net income increased to US$114.4 million from US$5.7 million in the prior year. Revenues were US$1.90 billion, up 6.3% from US$1.79 billion the year before. Operating income was US$222.6 million versus a loss of US$1.9 million in the prior year. Direct operating expenses rose 1.8% to US$971.7 million from US$954.9 million in the comparable period the year before. Indirect operating expenses decreased 15.3% to US$709.1 million from US$837.2 million in the equivalent prior-year period.

Prospects: Our evaluation of Deckers Outdoor Corp. as of Jan. 21, 2018 is the result of our systematic analysis on three basic characteristics: earnings strength, relative valuation, and recent stock price movement. The company has generated a negative trend in earnings per share over the past 5 quarters and while recent estimates for the company have been raised by analysts, DECK has posted better than expected results. Based on operating earnings yield, the company is undervalued when compared to all of the companies in our coverage universe. Share price changes over the past year indicates that DECK will perform poorly over the near term.

Financial Data

(US$ in Thousands)	03/31/2018	03/31/2017	03/31/2016	03/31/2015	03/31/2014	12/31/2013	12/31/2012	12/31/2011
Earnings Per Share	3.58	0.18	3.70	4.66	(0.08)	4.18	3.45	5.07
Cash Flow Per Share	10.31	6.21	3.85	4.93	5.61	7.60	4.43	0.78
Tang Book Value Per Share	28.54	27.36	23.63	21.67	19.34	19.24	14.95	16.06
Income Statement								
Total Revenue	1,903,339	1,790,147	1,875,197	1,817,057	294,716	1,556,618	1,414,398	1,377,283
EBITDA	270,796	52,183	212,303	274,445	10,278	250,015	221,108	314,308
Depn & Amortn	48,572	52,628	50,024	49,293	10,569	41,439	33,367	28,977
Income Before Taxes	220,696	(6,986)	156,885	221,139	(742)	205,557	184,118	285,262
Income Taxes	106,302	(12,696)	34,620	59,359	1,943	59,868	55,104	83,404
Net Income	114,394	5,710	122,265	161,780	(2,685)	145,689	128,866	199,052
Average Shares	31,996	32,355	33,039	34,733	34,621	34,829	37,334	39,265
Balance Sheet								
Current Assets	910,690	820,821	785,765	686,593	623,862	829,304	691,586	817,902
Total Assets	1,264,379	1,191,780	1,278,068	1,169,933	1,064,204	1,259,729	1,068,064	1,146,196
Current Liabilities	189,166	159,051	238,498	167,542	122,215	320,518	267,017	232,079
Long-Term Obligations	31,504	32,082	32,631	33,154	...	...	...	...
Total Liabilities	323,600	237,525	310,597	232,921	175,355	371,610	329,263	310,260
Stockholders' Equity	940,779	954,255	967,471	937,012	888,849	888,119	738,801	835,936
Shares Outstanding	30,447	31,987	32,020	33,292	34,624	34,618	34,400	38,692
Statistical Record								
Return on Assets %	9.31	0.46	9.96	14.48	N.M.	12.52	11.61	20.36
Return on Equity %	12.07	0.59	12.80	17.72	N.M.	17.91	16.32	26.74
EBITDA Margin %	14.23	2.92	11.32	15.10	3.49	16.06	15.63	22.82
Net Margin %	6.01	0.32	6.52	8.90	N.M.	9.36	9.11	14.45
Asset Turnover	1.55	1.45	1.53	1.63	1.03	1.34	1.27	1.41
Current Ratio	4.81	5.16	3.29	4.10	5.10	2.59	2.59	3.52
Debt to Equity	0.03	0.03	0.03	0.04	...	...	...	...
Price Range	98.29-55.78	88.57-44.99	76.58-42.27	99.38-66.05	88.56-72.86	86.09-36.12	90.21-28.63	117.66-72.38
P/E Ratio	27.46-15.58	380.94-249.94	20.70-11.42	21.33-14.17	...	20.60-8.64	26.15-8.30	23.21-14.28

Address: 250 Coromar Drive, Goleta, CA 93117	**Web Site:** www.deckers.com	**Auditors:** KPMG LLP
Telephone: 805-967-7611	**Officers:** John M. Gibbons - Chairman David Powers - Chief Executive Officer, Division Officer	**Investor Contact:** 203-.68-2.8200
		Transfer Agents: Mellon Investor Services LLC, South Hackensack, NJ

DEERE & CO.

Exchange	Symbol	Price	52Wk Range	Yield	P/E
NYS	DE	$139.80 (6/29/2018)	171.49-115.44	1.97	25.19

*7 Year Price Score 121.63 *NYSE Composite Index=100 ***12 Month Price Score 101.94**

TRADING VOLUME (thousand shares)

Interim Earnings (Per Share)

Qtr.	Jan	Apr	Jul	Oct
2014-15	1.12	2.03	1.53	1.10
2015-16	0.80	1.56	1.55	0.90
2016-17	0.61	2.49	1.97	1.57
2017-18	(1.66)	3.67	...	...

Interim Dividends (Per Share)

Amt	Decl	Ex	Rec	Pay
0.60Q	08/30/2017	09/28/2017	09/29/2017	11/01/2017
0.60Q	12/06/2017	12/28/2017	12/29/2017	02/01/2018
0.60Q	02/28/2018	03/28/2018	03/29/2018	05/01/2018
0.69Q	05/30/2018	06/28/2018	06/29/2018	08/01/2018

Indicated Div: $2.76 (Div. Reinv. Plan)

Valuation Analysis | Institutional Holding

Forecast EPS	$9.58
	(06/13/2018)
Market Cap	$45.3 Billion
Book Value	$10.4 Billion
Price/Book	4.35
Price/Sales	1.35

No of Institutions	1660
Shares	272,754,848
% Held	54.77

Business Summary: Industrial Machinery & Equipment (MIC: 7.2.1 SIC: 3523 NAIC: 332212)

Deere & Co. and its subsidiaries (collectively, John Deere) operates in three business segments: Agriculture and Turf, which manufactures and distributes agriculture and turf equipment and related service parts including tractors, loaders, harvesting equipment, scrapers, as well as tillage, seeding and application equipment; Construction and Forestry, which manufactures and distributes a range of machines and service parts used in construction, earthmoving, material handling and timber harvesting; and Financial Services, which primarily finances sales and leases by John Deere dealers of new and used agriculture and turf equipment and construction and forestry equipment.

Recent Developments: For the quarter ended Apr 29 2018, net income increased 49.7% to US$1.21 billion from US$808.3 million in the year-earlier quarter. Revenues were US$10.72 billion, up 29.4% from US$8.29 billion the year before. Direct operating expenses rose 35.1% to US$7.33 billion from US$5.43 billion in the comparable period the year before. Indirect operating expenses increased 18.5% to US$2.00 billion from US$1.69 billion in the equivalent prior-year period.

Prospects: Our evaluation of Deere & Co. as of Jan. 21, 2018 is the result of our systematic analysis on three basic characteristics: earnings strength, relative valuation, and recent stock price movement. The company has produced a positive trend in earnings per share over the past 5 quarters and while recent estimates for the company have been raised by analysts, DE has posted better than expected results. Based on operating earnings yield, the company is about fairly valued compared to all of the companies in our coverage universe. Share price changes over the past year indicates that DE will perform in line with the market over the near term.

Financial Data
(US$ in Thousands)

	6 Mos	3 Mos	10/29/2017	10/31/2016	10/31/2015	10/31/2014	10/31/2013	10/31/2012
Earnings Per Share	5.55	4.37	6.68	4.81	5.77	8.63	9.09	7.63
Cash Flow Per Share	3.56	5.10	6.92	11.91	11.21	9.71	8.45	2.93
Tang Book Value Per Share	17.05	13.84	25.81	17.79	18.80	23.74	25.00	15.00
Dividends Per Share	2.400	2.400	2.400	2.400	2.400	2.220	1.990	1.790
Dividend Payout %	43.24	54.92	35.93	49.90	41.59	25.72	21.89	23.46
Income Statement								
Total Revenue	17,633,500	6,913,500	29,737,700	26,644,000	28,862,800	36,066,900	37,795,400	36,157,100
EBITDA	3,442,400	1,267,400	4,779,300	3,688,700	4,152,100	6,157,400	6,861,700	6,072,200
Depn & Amortn	950,800	463,200	726,000	701,000	692,000	696,000	637,000	555,000
Income Before Taxes	1,901,600	517,900	3,153,800	2,224,000	2,780,100	4,797,400	5,483,400	4,734,400
Income Taxes	1,234,700	1,057,500	971,100	700,100	840,100	1,626,500	1,945,900	1,659,400
Net Income	673,200	(535,100)	2,159,100	1,523,900	1,940,000	3,161,700	3,537,300	3,064,700
Average Shares	329,200	322,800	323,300	316,600	336,000	366,100	389,200	401,500
Balance Sheet								
Current Assets	19,513,200	16,746,000	18,851,400	12,176,600	12,492,000	14,019,600	15,316,900	16,942,400
Total Assets	69,873,000	66,577,500	65,786,300	57,981,400	57,947,600	61,336,400	59,521,300	56,265,800
Current Liabilities	25,231,000	22,779,500	22,692,600	19,236,100	20,408,600	21,232,500	21,979,000	19,092,000
Long-Term Obligations	26,278,600	26,421,800	25,891,000	23,760,000	23,833,000	24,381,000	21,578,000	22,453,000
Total Liabilities	59,462,700	57,324,900	56,229,000	51,461,400	51,204,200	52,273,800	49,255,500	49,423,700
Stockholders' Equity	10,410,300	9,252,600	9,557,300	6,520,000	6,743,400	9,062,600	10,265,800	6,842,100
Shares Outstanding	324,284	323,787	321,841	314,767	316,687	345,504	373,802	387,805
Statistical Record								
Return on Assets %	2.83	2.31	3.51	2.62	3.25	5.23	6.11	5.85
Return on Equity %	20.17	17.66	27.01	22.92	24.55	32.72	41.35	44.81
EBITDA Margin %	19.52	18.33	16.07	13.84	14.39	17.07	18.15	16.79
Net Margin %	3.82	N.M.	7.26	5.72	6.72	8.77	9.36	8.48
Asset Turnover	0.52	0.51	0.48	0.46	0.48	0.60	0.65	0.69
Current Ratio	0.77	0.74	0.83	0.63	0.61	0.66	0.70	0.89
Debt to Equity	2.52	2.86	2.71	3.64	3.53	2.69	2.10	3.28
Price Range	171.49-110.79	171.49-107.05	133.25-88.06	88.30-71.78	97.33-72.89	94.53-80.01	95.05-80.90	88.40-70.59
P/E Ratio	30.90-19.96	39.24-24.50	19.95-13.18	18.36-14.92	16.87-12.63	10.95-9.27	10.46-8.90	11.59-9.25
Average Yield %	1.74	1.90	2.10	2.98	2.73	2.54	2.31	2.24

Address: One John Deere Place, Moline, IL 61265 **Telephone:** 309-765-8000 **Fax:** 309-765-9929	**Web Site:** www.johndeere.com **Officers:** Samuel R. Allen - Chairman, President, Chief Executive Officer, Chief Operating Officer, Division Officer Rajesh Kalathur - Senior Vice President, Chief Financial Officer	**Auditors:** DELOITTE & TOUCHE LLP **Investor Contact:** 309-765-4491 **Transfer Agents:** ComputerShare, College Station, TX

DELEK US HOLDINGS INC

Exchange	Symbol	Price	52Wk Range	Yield	P/E
NYS	DK	$50.17 (6/29/2018)	59.81-20.88	1.99	16.08

*7 Year Price Score 107.55 *NYSE Composite Index=100 *12 Month Price Score 148.42

Interim Earnings (Per Share)

Qtr.	Mar	Jun	Sep	Dec
2015	(0.28)	0.79	0.29	(0.52)
2016	(0.47)	(0.11)	(2.61)	0.70
2017	0.18	(0.61)	1.29	2.87
2018	(0.43)	...	...	...

Interim Dividends (Per Share)

Amt	Decl	Ex	Rec	Pay
0.15Q	08/02/2017	08/21/2017	08/23/2017	09/13/2017
0.15Q	11/09/2017	11/21/2017	11/22/2017	12/15/2017
0.20Q	02/26/2018	03/09/2018	03/12/2018	03/26/2018
0.25Q	05/07/2018	05/18/2018	05/21/2018	06/04/2018

Indicated Div: $1.00

Valuation Analysis — **Institutional Holding**

Forecast EPS	$4.40	No of Institutions
	(06/14/2018)	N/A
Market Cap	$4.2 Billion	Shares
Book Value	$1.6 Billion	N/A
Price/Book	2.60	% Held
Price/Sales	0.50	N/A

TRADING VOLUME (thousand shares)

Business Summary: Refining & Marketing (MIC: 9.1.2 SIC: 2911 NAIC: 324110)

Delek US Holdings is an energy business focused on petroleum refining and the transportation, storage and wholesale distribution of crude oil, intermediate and refined products. Co. has two segments: refining, which operates independent refineries in Tyler, TX and El Dorado, AR; and logistics, which gathers, transports and stores crude oil and markets, distributes, transports and stores refined products in select regions of the southeastern U.S. and west Texas for both Co.'s refining segment and third parties. Co.'s refining segment also includes biodiesel facilities that are involved in the production of biodiesel fuels and related activities, located in Crossett, AR and Cleburne, TX.

Recent Developments: For the quarter ended Mar 31 2018, loss from continuing operations was US$11.8 million compared with income of US$15.3 million in the year-earlier quarter. Net loss amounted to US$20.0 million versus net income of US$15.3 million in the year-earlier quarter. Revenues were US$2.35 billion, up 99.1% from US$1.18 billion the year before. Operating income was US$38.8 million versus US$29.8 million in the prior-year quarter, an increase of 30.2%. Direct operating expenses rose 97.2% to US$2.04 billion from US$1.04 billion in the comparable period the year before. Indirect operating expenses increased 132.7% to US$271.6 million from US$116.7 million in the equivalent prior-year period.

Prospects: Our evaluation of Delek US Holdings Inc. as of Jan. 21, 2018 is the result of our systematic analysis on three basic characteristics: earnings strength, relative valuation, and recent stock price movement. The company has suffered a very negative trend in earnings per share over the past 5 quarters and while recent estimates for the company have been raised by analysts, DK has posted better than expected results. Based on operating earnings yield, the company is overvalued when compared to all of the companies in our coverage universe. Share price changes over the past year indicates that DK will perform very poorly over the near term.

Financial Data

(US$ in Thousands)	3 Mos	12/31/2017	12/31/2016	12/31/2015	12/31/2014	12/31/2013	12/31/2012	12/31/2011
Earnings Per Share	3.12	4.00	(2.49)	0.32	3.35	1.96	4.57	2.78
Cash Flow Per Share	2.23	4.64	4.32	2.96	5.39	1.73	7.86	2.30
Tang Book Value Per Share	8.23	9.07	15.38	16.92	15.92	14.33	13.58	9.76
Dividends Per Share	0.500	0.300	0.600	0.600	1.000	0.950	0.600	0.330
Dividend Payout %	16.03	7.50	...	187.50	29.85	48.47	13.13	11.87
Income Statement								
Total Revenue	2,353,200	7,267,100	4,197,900	5,762,000	8,324,300	8,706,800	8,726,700	7,198,200
EBITDA	47,900	526,000	(179,800)	215,000	477,600	329,500	551,400	369,800
Depn & Amortn	44,900	149,500	115,100	132,700	110,200	85,500	78,300	70,800
Income Before Taxes	(28,800)	286,700	(347,800)	25,100	327,600	206,600	427,600	247,800
Income Taxes	(17,000)	(29,200)	(171,500)	(16,600)	101,600	70,900	151,600	84,700
Net Income	(34,900)	288,800	(153,700)	19,400	198,600	117,700	272,800	158,300
Average Shares	82,252	72,303	61,921	61,320	59,355	60,047	59,644	57,026
Balance Sheet								
Current Assets	2,856,500	2,611,800	1,402,200	988,800	1,247,400	1,410,500	1,359,700	1,050,600
Total Assets	6,084,700	5,935,200	2,985,100	3,324,900	2,891,400	2,834,400	2,623,700	2,230,600
Current Liabilities	2,138,900	2,671,700	940,500	759,700	857,200	1,080,800	999,100	994,700
Long-Term Obligations	1,770,800	875,400	748,500	880,500	533,300	376,600	310,000	358,400
Total Liabilities	4,466,500	4,284,600	1,993,200	2,171,600	1,889,700	1,899,400	1,724,400	1,577,200
Stockholders' Equity	1,618,200	1,650,600	991,900	1,153,300	1,001,700	935,000	899,300	653,400
Shares Outstanding	83,973	80,770	61,954	62,137	57,271	59,229	59,619	58,036
Statistical Record								
Return on Assets %	5.37	6.48	N.M.	0.62	6.94	4.31	11.21	9.38
Return on Equity %	18.55	21.86	N.M.	1.80	20.51	12.83	35.04	28.87
EBITDA Margin %	2.04	7.24	N.M.	3.73	5.74	3.78	6.32	5.14
Net Margin %	N.M.	3.97	N.M.	0.34	2.39	1.35	3.13	2.20
Asset Turnover	1.87	1.63	1.33	1.85	2.91	3.19	3.59	4.27
Current Ratio	1.34	0.98	1.49	1.30	1.46	1.31	1.36	1.06
Debt to Equity	1.09	0.53	0.75	0.76	0.53	0.40	0.34	0.55
Price Range	40.70-20.88	35.08-20.88	24.89-11.88	40.86-22.45	35.77-25.87	40.50-20.17	27.39-11.13	17.25-6.89
P/E Ratio	13.04-6.69	8.77-5.22	...	127.69-70.16	10.68-7.72	20.66-10.29	5.99-2.44	6.21-2.48
Average Yield %	1.74	1.17	3.67	1.84	3.25	3.08	3.07	2.57

Address: 7102 Commerce Way, Brentwood, TN 37027 Telephone: 615-771-6701	Web Site: www.Delekus.com Officers: Ezra Uzi Yemin - Chairman, President, Chief Executive Officer Kevin L. Kremke - Executive Vice President, Chief Financial Officer	Auditors: Ernst & Young LLP Investor Contact: 615-435-1366 Transfer Agents: American Stock Transfer & Trust Company, Brooklyn, NY

DELL TECHNOLOGIES INC

Exchange	Symbol	Price	52Wk Range	Yield	P/E
NYS	DVMT	$84.58 (6/29/2018)	89.57-60.36	N/A	N/A

*7 Year Price Score N/A   *NYSE Composite Index=100   *12 Month Price Score 106.47

Interim Earnings (Per Share)

Qtr.	Apr	Jul	Oct	Jan
2015-16	(1.24)	(0.65)	(0.44)	(0.38)
2016-17	0.14	1.41	(4.51)	(2.66)
2017-18	(2.57)	(1.97)	(2.05)	(0.51)
2018-19	2.33	...	...	...

Interim Dividends (Per Share)

No Dividends Paid

Valuation Analysis   Institutional Holding

Forecast EPS	$6.13	No of Institutions
	(06/14/2018)	769
Market Cap	$65.0 Billion	Shares
Book Value	$11.3 Billion	190,148,800
Price/Book	5.73	% Held
Price/Sales	0.79	N/A

Business Summary: Computer Hardware & Equipment (MIC: 6.2.1 SIC: 3571 NAIC: 334111)

Dell Technologies is a holding company. Through its subsidiaries, Co. is engaged in providing information technology solutions. Co. is organized into three business units: Client Solutions Group, which has offerings that include hardware, such as desktop personal computers, notebooks and tablets, and peripherals, such as monitors, printers, and projectors, as well as third-party software, and peripherals; Infrastructure Solutions Group, which enables the digital transformation of Co.'s enterprise customers through Co.'s cloud and big data solutions, which are built upon a data center infrastructure; and VMware, which provides virtualization and cloud infrastructure solutions.

Recent Developments: For the quarter ended May 4 2018, loss from continuing operations was US$538.0 million compared with a loss of US$1.20 billion in the year-earlier quarter. Net loss amounted to US$538.0 million versus a net loss of US$1.20 billion in the year-earlier quarter. Revenues were US$21.36 billion, up 18.6% from US$18.00 billion the year before. Operating loss was US$153.0 million versus a loss of US$1.27 billion in the prior-year quarter. Direct operating expenses rose 14.3% to US$15.48 billion from US$13.54 billion in the comparable period the year before. Indirect operating expenses increased 5.3% to US$6.03 billion from US$5.73 billion in the equivalent prior-year period.

Prospects: Our evaluation of Dell Technologies Inc. as of Jan. 21, 2018 is the result of our systematic analysis on three basic characteristics: earnings strength, relative valuation, and recent stock price movement. The company has enjoyed a very positive trend in earnings per share over the past 5 quarters. Because the company lacks sufficient analyst estimate data, we place greater weight on the historical EPS trend as the measure of earnings strength. Based on operating earnings yield, the company is undervalued when compared to all of the companies in our coverage universe. Share price changes over the past year indicates that DVMT will perform well over the near term.

Financial Data
(US$ in Thousands)

	3 Mos	02/02/2018	02/03/2017	01/29/2016	01/30/2015
Earnings Per Share	...	(7.08)	(4.22)	(2.72)	(3.02)
Cash Flow Per Share	10.08	8.87	3.18	5.35	6.31
Income Statement					
Total Revenue	21,356,000	78,660,000	61,642,000	50,911,000	54,142,000
EBITDA	(87,000)	1,312,000	(1,656,000)	714,000	885,000
Depn & Amortn	36,000	7,000,000	3,700,000	2,000,000	2,100,000
Income Before Taxes	(623,000)	(5,688,000)	(5,356,000)	(1,286,000)	(1,215,000)
Income Taxes	(85,000)	(1,833,000)	(1,619,000)	(118,000)	(107,000)
Net Income	(636,000)	(3,728,000)	(1,672,000)	(1,104,000)	(1,221,000)
Average Shares	199,000	567,000	478,000	405,000	404,000
Balance Sheet					
Current Assets	41,231,000	38,957,000	30,773,000	23,573,000	...
Total Assets	123,217,000	122,281,000	118,206,000	45,122,000	...
Current Liabilities	44,114,000	45,892,000	38,135,000	25,310,000	...
Long-Term Obligations	44,770,000	43,998,000	43,061,000	10,650,000	...
Total Liabilities	111,888,000	112,571,000	104,732,000	43,550,000	...
Stockholders' Equity	11,329,000	9,710,000	13,474,000	1,572,000	...
Shares Outstanding	768,000	769,000	778,000	405,000	...
Statistical Record					
EBITDA Margin %	N.M.	1.67	N.M.	1.40	1.63
Asset Turnover	0.69	0.66	0.74	...	...
Current Ratio	0.93	0.85	0.81	0.93	...
Debt to Equity	3.95	4.53	3.20	6.77	...
Price Range	89.11-60.36	89.11-60.36	64.35-42.75	...	...

Address: One Dell Way, Round Rock, TX 78682
Telephone: 800-289-3355

Web Site: www.delltechnologies.com
Officers: Michael S. Dell - Chairman, Chief Executive Officer Marius Haas - President, Chief Commercial Officer

Auditors: PricewaterhouseCoopers LLP
Investor Contact: 800-289-3355

DELTA AIR LINES INC (DE)

Exchange	Symbol	Price	52Wk Range	Yield	P/E
NYS	DAL	$49.54 (6/29/2018)	60.13-45.21	2.83	10.54

*7 Year Price Score 124.30 *NYSE Composite Index=100 *12 Month Price Score 99.95

Interim Earnings (Per Share)

Qtr.	Mar	Jun	Sep	Dec
2015	0.90	1.83	1.65	1.26
2016	1.21	2.03	1.70	0.87
2017	0.82	1.68	1.64	0.82
2018	0.77	1.47	...	...

Interim Dividends (Per Share)

Amt	Decl	Ex	Rec	Pay
0.305Q	11/03/2017	11/16/2017	11/17/2017	12/08/2017
0.305Q	02/09/2018	02/22/2018	02/23/2018	03/16/2018
0.305Q	04/27/2018	05/10/2018	05/11/2018	06/01/2018
0.35Q	07/12/2018	07/25/2018	07/26/2018	08/16/2018

Indicated Div: $1.40

Valuation Analysis **Institutional Holding**

Forecast EPS	$5.57	No of Institutions
	(06/14/2018)	1315
Market Cap	$34.2 Billion	Shares
Book Value	$12.9 Billion	759,510,016
Price/Book	2.66	% Held
Price/Sales	0.80	0.01

Business Summary: Airlines/Air Freight (MIC: 7.4.4 SIC: 4512 NAIC: 481111)

Delta Air Lines provides scheduled air transportation for passengers and cargo in the U.S. and around the world. Co.'s route network is centered around a system of hub and international gateway airports that it operates in Amsterdam, Atlanta, Boston, Detroit, London-Heathrow, Los Angeles, Minneapolis-St. Paul, New York-LaGuardia, New York-JFK, Paris-Charles de Gaulle, Salt Lake City, Seattle and Tokyo-Narita. Each of these operations includes flights that gather and distribute traffic from markets in the geographic region surrounding the hub or gateway to domestic and international cities and to other hubs or gateways. Co.'s network is supported by a fleet of aircraft varied in size.

Recent Developments: For the quarter ended June 30 2018, net income decreased 13.6% to US$1.03 billion from US$1.19 billion in the year-earlier quarter. Revenues were US$11.78 billion, up 9.6% from US$10.75 billion the year before. Operating income was US$1.68 billion versus US$1.98 billion in the prior-year quarter, a decrease of 15.2%. Direct operating expenses rose 19.4% to US$5.00 billion from US$4.19 billion in the comparable period the year before. Indirect operating expenses increased 11.4% to US$5.10 billion from US$4.58 billion in the equivalent prior-year period.

Prospects: Our evaluation of Delta Air Lines Inc. as of Jan. 21, 2018 is the result of our systematic analysis on three basic characteristics: earnings strength, relative valuation, and recent stock price movement. The company has managed to produce a neutral trend in earnings per share over the past 5 quarters and while recent estimates for the company have been raised by analysts, DAL has posted better than expected results. Based on operating earnings yield, the company is undervalued when compared to all of the companies in our coverage universe. Share price changes over the past year indicates that DAL will perform poorly over the near term.

Financial Data

(US$ in Thousands)	6 Mos	3 Mos	12/31/2017	12/31/2016	12/31/2015	12/31/2014	12/31/2013	12/31/2012
Earnings Per Share	4.70	4.91	4.95	5.79	5.63	0.78	12.29	1.19
Cash Flow Per Share	11.10	10.36	7.15	9.57	9.95	5.92	5.31	2.92
Dividends Per Share	1.220	1.117	1.015	0.675	0.450	0.300	0.120	...
Dividend Payout %	25.96	22.76	20.51	11.66	7.99	38.46	0.98	...
Income Statement								
Total Revenue	21,743,000	9,968,000	41,244,000	39,639,000	40,704,000	40,362,000	37,773,000	36,670,000
EBITDA	3,481,000	1,430,000	8,297,000	8,924,000	9,438,000	3,422,000	4,779,000	3,430,000
Depn & Amortn	1,200,000	610,000	2,200,000	1,900,000	1,800,000	1,700,000	1,400,000	1,400,000
Income Before Taxes	2,090,000	718,000	5,701,000	6,636,000	7,157,000	1,072,000	2,527,000	1,025,000
Income Taxes	518,000	171,000	2,124,000	2,263,000	2,631,000	413,000	(8,013,000)	16,000
Net Income	1,572,000	547,000	3,577,000	4,373,000	4,526,000	659,000	10,540,000	1,009,000
Average Shares	697,000	706,000	723,000	755,000	804,000	845,000	858,000	850,000
Balance Sheet								
Current Assets	7,641,000	7,724,000	7,844,000	7,451,000	9,056,000	12,465,000	9,651,000	8,272,000
Total Assets	55,796,000	54,078,000	53,292,000	51,261,000	53,134,000	54,121,000	52,252,000	44,550,000
Current Liabilities	19,269,000	20,012,000	18,573,000	15,239,000	17,526,000	16,879,000	14,152,000	13,270,000
Long-Term Obligations	8,562,000	6,360,000	6,592,000	6,201,000	6,766,000	8,561,000	9,795,000	11,082,000
Total Liabilities	42,940,000	41,521,000	39,382,000	38,974,000	42,284,000	45,308,000	40,609,000	46,681,000
Stockholders' Equity	12,856,000	12,557,000	13,910,000	12,287,000	10,850,000	8,813,000	11,643,000	(2,131,000)
Shares Outstanding	691,331	702,478	707,197	730,737	778,783	825,258	851,443	851,402
Statistical Record								
Return on Assets %	6.17	6.67	6.84	8.35	8.44	1.24	21.78	2.29
Return on Equity %	25.23	27.61	27.31	37.70	46.04	6.44	221.61	...
EBITDA Margin %	16.01	14.35	20.12	22.51	23.19	8.48	12.65	9.35
Net Margin %	7.23	5.49	8.67	11.03	11.12	1.63	27.90	2.75
Asset Turnover	0.80	0.80	0.79	0.76	0.76	0.76	0.78	0.83
Current Ratio	0.40	0.39	0.42	0.49	0.52	0.74	0.68	0.62
Debt to Equity	0.67	0.51	0.47	0.50	0.62	0.97	0.84	...
Price Range	60.13-45.21	60.13-44.03	56.43-44.03	51.78-33.36	52.26-40.00	49.23-27.47	29.34-11.87	12.10-8.01
P/E Ratio	12.79-9.62	12.25-8.97	11.40-8.89	8.94-5.76	9.28-7.10	63.12-35.22	2.39-0.97	10.17-6.73
Average Yield %	2.32	2.17	2.03	1.56	0.98	0.80	0.60	...

Address: Post Office Box 20706, Atlanta, GA 30320-6001 **Telephone:** 404-715-2600	**Web Site:** www.delta.com **Officers:** Glen W. Hauenstein - President, Executive Vice President, Chief Revenue Officer, Executive Vice President (frmr) Edward H. Bastian - Chief Executive Officer, President, Executive Vice President, Chief Financial Officer, Senior Vice President, Vice President, Controller, Division Officer	**Auditors:** Ernst & Young LLP **Investor Contact:** 404-715-2170 **Transfer Agents:** Wells Fargo Shareowner Services, St. Paul, MN

DELUXE CORP

Exchange	Symbol	Price	52Wk Range	Yield	P/E
NYS	DLX	$66.21 (6/29/2018)	77.69-66.19	1.81	13.62

*7 Year Price Score 109.39 *NYSE Composite Index=100   ***12 Month Price Score 94.41**

Interim Earnings (Per Share)

Qtr.	Mar	Jun	Sep	Dec
2015	0.91	1.11	1.13	1.20
2016	1.18	1.18	1.19	1.10
2017	1.16	1.22	0.59	1.74
2018	1.31	...	...	...

Interim Dividends (Per Share)

Amt	Decl	Ex	Rec	Pay
0.30Q	07/27/2017	08/17/2017	08/21/2017	09/05/2017
0.30Q	10/26/2017	11/17/2017	11/20/2017	12/04/2017
0.30Q	01/25/2018	02/16/2018	02/20/2018	03/05/2018
0.30Q	05/02/2018	05/18/2018	05/21/2018	06/04/2018

Indicated Div: $1.20

Valuation Analysis   **Institutional Holding**

Forecast EPS	$5.70	No of Institutions
	(06/13/2018)	505
Market Cap	$3.2 Billion	Shares
Book Value	$1.1 Billion	55,900,828
Price/Book	3.01	% Held
Price/Sales	1.61	83.33

Business Summary: Printing (MIC: 7.5.5 SIC: 2761 NAIC: 323116)

Deluxe is engaged in providing payment solutions. Co.'s product and service offerings are comprised of: Checks, which is a provider of checks in the U.S.; Marketing solutions and other services, which utilize digital printing and web-to-print solutions to provide promotional solutions such as postcards, brochures, retail packaging supplies, and apparel; Forms, which is a provider of printed forms to small businesses, including deposit tickets, billing forms, work orders, job proposals; and Accessories and other products, which provide small business owners with the customized documents necessary to manage their business.

Recent Developments: For the quarter ended Mar 31 2018, net income increased 11.0% to US$63.3 million from US$57.1 million in the year-earlier quarter. Revenues were US$491.9 million, up 0.9% from US$487.8 million the year before. Operating income was US$87.7 million versus US$85.0 million in the prior-year quarter, an increase of 3.2%. Direct operating expenses rose 5.3% to US$188.8 million from US$179.3 million in the comparable period the year before. Indirect operating expenses decreased 3.6% to US$215.4 million from US$223.5 million in the equivalent prior-year period.

Prospects: Our evaluation of Deluxe Corp. as of Jan. 21, 2018 is the result of our systematic analysis on three basic characteristics: earnings strength, relative valuation, and recent stock price movement. The company has managed to produce a neutral trend in earnings per share over the past 5 quarters and while recent estimates for the company have remained steady, DLX has posted better than expected results. Based on operating earnings yield, the company is undervalued when compared to all of the companies in our coverage universe. Share price changes over the past year indicates that DLX will perform in line with the market over the near term.

Financial Data

(US$ in Thousands)	3 Mos	12/31/2017	12/31/2016	12/31/2015	12/31/2014	12/31/2013	12/31/2012	12/31/2011
Earnings Per Share	4.86	4.72	4.65	4.36	3.96	3.65	3.32	2.80
Cash Flow Per Share	7.22	7.03	6.56	6.23	5.63	5.17	4.79	4.61
Dividends Per Share	1.200	1.200	1.200	1.200	1.150	1.000	1.000	1.000
Dividend Payout %	24.69	25.42	25.81	27.52	29.04	27.40	30.12	35.71
Income Statement								
Total Revenue	491,914	1,965,556	1,849,062	1,772,817	1,674,082	1,584,824	1,514,917	1,417,596
EBITDA	125,546	563,622	531,356	485,646	448,627	430,484	408,982	389,020
Depn & Amortn	36,549	229,436	168,668	137,400	114,917	111,124	111,382	125,139
Income Before Taxes	83,418	312,827	340,386	327,947	297,181	281,059	250,753	216,084
Income Taxes	20,082	82,672	111,004	109,318	97,387	94,407	80,261	71,489
Net Income	63,336	230,155	229,382	218,629	199,794	186,652	170,492	144,595
Average Shares	48,017	48,448	48,975	49,825	50,262	51,010	51,076	51,415
Balance Sheet								
Current Assets	399,938	392,966	398,230	325,988	318,890	319,313	219,743	192,575
Total Assets	2,273,816	2,208,827	2,184,338	1,844,402	1,688,391	1,569,529	1,412,440	1,388,809
Current Liabilities	375,633	425,770	415,684	751,043	467,248	490,071	220,110	300,367
Long-Term Obligations	741,702	665,260	722,806	196,222	393,401	385,115	652,581	656,131
Total Liabilities	1,222,146	1,193,814	1,303,368	1,099,333	1,040,894	1,019,072	979,505	1,086,120
Stockholders' Equity	1,051,670	1,015,013	880,970	745,069	647,497	550,457	432,935	302,689
Shares Outstanding	47,841	47,953	48,546	49,019	49,742	50,344	50,614	50,826
Statistical Record								
Return on Assets %	10.66	10.48	11.36	12.38	12.27	12.52	12.14	10.72
Return on Equity %	24.07	24.28	28.14	31.40	33.36	37.96	46.23	54.68
EBITDA Margin %	25.52	28.67	28.74	27.39	26.80	27.16	27.00	27.44
Net Margin %	12.88	11.71	12.41	12.33	11.93	11.78	11.25	10.20
Asset Turnover	0.89	0.89	0.92	1.00	1.03	1.06	1.08	1.05
Current Ratio	1.06	0.92	0.96	0.43	0.68	0.65	1.00	0.64
Debt to Equity	0.71	0.66	0.82	0.26	0.61	0.70	1.51	2.17
Price Range	77.69-63.73	76.84-67.03	73.04-51.00	69.57-53.36	63.54-45.52	52.19-32.24	32.24-21.51	28.12-18.05
P/E Ratio	15.99-13.79	16.28-14.20	15.71-10.97	15.96-12.24	16.05-11.49	14.30-8.83	9.71-6.48	10.04-6.45
Average Yield %	1.68	1.69	1.89	1.93	2.08	2.44	3.76	4.21

Address: 3680 Victoria St. N.,
Shoreview, MN 55126-2966
Telephone: 651-483-7111
Fax: 651-483-7337

Web Site: www.deluxe.com
Officers: Lee J. Schram - Chief Executive Officer
Keith A. Bush - Senior Vice President, Chief Financial Officer

Auditors: PricewaterhouseCoopers LLP
Investor Contact: 651-787-1068
Transfer Agents: Wells Fargo Bank
Minnesota, N.A., St. Paul, MN

DEVON ENERGY CORP.

Exchange	Symbol	Price	52Wk Range	Yield	P/E
NYS	DVN	$43.96 (6/29/2018)	44.81-29.54	0.73	183.17

*7 Year Price Score 56.08 *NYSE Composite Index=100 *12 Month Price Score 109.60

TRADING VOLUME (thousand shares)

Interim Earnings (Per Share)

Qtr.	Mar	Jun	Sep	Dec
2015	(8.88)	(6.94)	(8.64)	(11.10)
2016	(6.44)	(3.04)	1.89	0.70
2017	1.07	0.80	0.43	(0.61)
2018	(0.38)			

Interim Dividends (Per Share)

Amt	Decl	Ex	Rec	Pay
0.06Q	09/13/2017	12/14/2017	12/15/2017	12/29/2017
0.06Q	11/29/2017	03/14/2018	03/15/2018	03/29/2018
0.08Q	03/07/2018	06/14/2018	06/15/2018	06/29/2018
0.08Q	06/06/2018	09/13/2018	09/14/2018	09/28/2018

Indicated Div: $0.32

Valuation Analysis

		Institutional Holding	
Forecast EPS	$1.62 (06/14/2018)	No of Institutions	1263
Market Cap	$23.1 Billion	Shares	542,921,856
Book Value	$8.9 Billion	% Held	77.05
Price/Book	2.59		
Price/Sales	1.63		

Business Summary: Production & Extraction (MIC: 9.1.1 SIC: 1311 NAIC: 211111)

Devon Energy is an independent energy company engaged primarily in the exploration, development and production of oil, natural gas and natural gas liquids. Co.'s operations are concentrated in various North American onshore areas in the U.S. and Canada. Co.'s operating areas consist of Barnett Shale, Delaware Basin, Eagle Ford, Heavy Oil, Rockies Oil, and the STACK development, located in Oklahoma's Canadian, Kingfisher and Blaine counties. Co. also owns natural gas pipelines, plants and treatment facilities through its ownership in EnLink Midstream Partners, L.P. As of Dec 31 2017, Co. had 2.15 billion barrels of oil equivalent proved reserves.

Recent Developments: For the quarter ended Mar 31 2018, net income amounted to US$153.0 million versus net income of US$317.0 million in the year-earlier quarter. Revenues were US$3.81 billion, up 7.3% from US$3.55 billion the year before. Direct operating expenses rose 22.1% to US$2.21 billion from US$1.81 billion in the comparable period the year before. Indirect operating expenses increased 25.8% to US$1.78 billion from US$1.41 billion in the equivalent prior-year period.

Prospects: Our evaluation of Devon Energy Corp. as of Jan. 21, 2018 is the result of our systematic analysis on three basic characteristics: earnings strength, relative valuation, and recent stock price movement. The company has generated a negative trend in earnings per share over the past 5 quarters and while recent estimates for the company have been raised by analysts, DVN has posted better than expected results. Based on operating earnings yield, the company is about fairly valued when compared to all of the companies in our coverage universe. Share price changes over the past year indicates that DVN will perform very poorly over the near term.

Financial Data
(US$ in Thousands)

	3 Mos	12/31/2017	12/31/2016	12/31/2015	12/31/2014	12/31/2013	12/31/2012	12/31/2011
Earnings Per Share	0.24	1.70	(6.52)	(35.55)	3.91	(0.06)	(0.52)	11.25
Cash Flow Per Share	5.54	5.59	3.43	13.23	14.77	13.52	12.36	15.11
Tang Book Value Per Share	12.41	13.09	3.75	4.83	37.25	36.06	37.44	38.19
Dividends Per Share	0.240	0.240	0.420	0.960	0.940	0.860	0.800	0.670
Dividend Payout %	100.00	14.12	...	...	24.04	...	...	5.96
Income Statement								
Total Revenue	3,810,000	13,949,000	12,197,000	13,145,000	19,566,000	10,397,000	9,502,000	11,454,000
EBITDA	356,000	2,970,000	(987,000)	(17,622,000)	7,904,000	3,346,000	2,864,000	6,869,000
Depn & Amortn	537,000	2,074,000	1,986,000	3,129,000	3,319,000	2,780,000	2,811,000	2,248,000
Income Before Taxes	(181,000)	896,000	(3,877,000)	(21,268,000)	4,059,000	149,000	(317,000)	4,290,000
Income Taxes	(28,000)	(182,000)	(173,000)	(6,065,000)	2,368,000	169,000	(132,000)	2,156,000
Net Income	(197,000)	898,000	(3,302,000)	(14,454,000)	1,607,000	(20,000)	(206,000)	4,704,000
Average Shares	520,000	523,000	507,000	407,000	407,000	402,000	400,000	414,000
Balance Sheet								
Current Assets	3,635,000	4,791,000	3,772,000	4,026,000	6,498,000	8,005,000	8,971,000	9,305,000
Total Assets	29,316,000	30,241,000	25,913,000	29,532,000	50,637,000	42,877,000	43,326,000	41,117,000
Current Liabilities	3,482,000	3,315,000	2,616,000	3,295,000	5,935,000	6,655,000	6,003,000	6,738,000
Long-Term Obligations	9,628,000	10,291,000	10,154,000	12,137,000	9,830,000	7,956,000	8,455,000	5,969,000
Total Liabilities	20,411,000	20,987,000	19,986,000	22,483,000	29,098,000	22,378,000	22,048,000	19,687,000
Stockholders' Equity	8,905,000	9,254,000	5,927,000	7,049,000	21,539,000	20,499,000	21,278,000	21,430,000
Shares Outstanding	525,600	525,000	523,000	418,000	409,000	406,000	406,000	403,700
Statistical Record								
Return on Assets %	0.49	3.20	N.M.	N.M.	3.44	N.M.	N.M.	12.71
Return on Equity %	1.77	11.83	N.M.	N.M.	7.65	N.M.	N.M.	23.13
EBITDA Margin %	9.34	21.29	N.M.	N.M.	40.40	32.18	30.14	59.97
Net Margin %	N.M.	6.44	N.M.	N.M.	8.21	N.M.	N.M.	41.07
Asset Turnover	0.51	0.50	0.44	0.33	0.42	0.24	0.22	0.31
Current Ratio	1.04	1.45	1.44	1.22	1.09	1.20	1.49	1.38
Debt to Equity	1.08	1.11	1.71	1.72	0.46	0.39	0.40	0.28
Price Range	44.81-29.54	49.01-29.54	48.33-18.65	69.03-28.67	79.50-52.66	65.52-51.44	75.81-51.15	93.10-53.34
P/E Ratio	186.71-123.08	28.83-17.38	...	...	20.33-13.47	...	...	8.28-4.74
Average Yield %	0.67	0.64	1.17	1.81	1.39	1.49	1.33	0.88

Address: 333 West Sheridan Avenue, Oklahoma City, OK 73102-5015 **Telephone:** 405-235-3611	**Web Site:** www.devonenergy.com **Officers:** John Richels - Chairman, Vice-Chairman, President, Chief Executive Officer David A. Hager - President, Chief Executive Officer, Executive Vice President, Chief Operating Officer	**Auditors:** KPMG LLP **Investor Contact:** 405-552-4505 **Transfer Agents:** Computershare Trust Company, N.A., Providence, RI

DIAMOND OFFSHORE DRILLING, INC.

Exchange	Symbol	Price	52Wk Range	Yield	P/E
NYS	DO	$20.86 (6/29/2018)	21.22-10.22	N/A	208.60

*7 Year Price Score 32.29   *NYSE Composite Index=100   *12 Month Price Score 119.14

Interim Earnings (Per Share)

Qtr.	Mar	Jun	Sep	Dec
2015	(1.86)	0.66	0.99	(1.79)
2016	0.64	(4.30)	0.10	0.84
2017	0.17	0.12	0.08	(0.24)
2018	0.14	...	...	...

Interim Dividends (Per Share)

Dividend Payment Suspended

Valuation Analysis

		Institutional Holding	
Forecast EPS	$-0.54	No of Institutions	
	(06/14/2018)	452	
Market Cap	$2.9 Billion	Shares	
Book Value	$3.8 Billion	171,716,448	
Price/Book	0.76	% Held	
Price/Sales	2.04	99.71	

Business Summary: Equipment & Services (MIC: 9.1.3 SIC: 1381 NAIC: 213111)

Diamond Offshore Drilling engaged in offshore drilling, providing contract drilling services to the energy industry around the globe with a fleet of 17 offshore drilling rigs. As of Dec 31 2017, Co.'s fleet consists of consisting of four drillships and seven ultra-deepwater, four deepwater and two mid-water semisubmersible rigs. Co.'s fleet enables Co. to offer services in the floater market on a worldwide basis.

Recent Developments: For the quarter ended Mar 31 2018, net income decreased 17.9% to US$19.3 million from US$23.5 million in the year-earlier quarter. Revenues were US$295.5 million, down 21.0% from US$374.2 million the year before. Operating income was US$512,000 versus US$50.9 million in the prior-year quarter, a decrease of 99.0%. Direct operating expenses declined 10.2% to US$192.2 million from US$214.0 million in the comparable period the year before. Indirect operating expenses decreased 6.0% to US$102.8 million from US$109.4 million in the equivalent prior-year period.

Prospects: Our evaluation of Diamond Offshore Drilling Inc. as of Jan. 21, 2018 is the result of our systematic analysis on three basic characteristics: earnings strength, relative valuation, and recent stock price movement. The company has suffered a very negative trend in earnings per share over the past 5 quarters. However, while recent estimates for the company have been lowered by analysts, DO has posted better than expected results. Based on operating earnings yield, the company is about fairly valued when compared to all of the companies in our coverage universe. Share price changes over the past year indicates that DO will perform very poorly over the near term.

Financial Data

(US$ in Thousands)	3 Mos	12/31/2017	12/31/2016	12/31/2015	12/31/2014	12/31/2013	12/31/2012	12/31/2011
Earnings Per Share	0.10	0.13	(2.72)	(2.00)	2.81	3.95	5.18	6.92
Cash Flow Per Share	3.49	3.60	4.70	5.37	7.22	7.67	9.41	10.21
Tang Book Value Per Share	27.52	27.50	27.34	29.99	32.46	33.35	32.92	31.17
Dividends Per Share	...	...	...	0.500	3.500	3.500	3.500	3.500
Dividend Payout %	...	...	...	...	124.56	88.61	67.57	50.58
Income Statement								
Total Revenue	295,510	1,485,746	1,600,342	2,419,393	2,814,671	2,920,421	2,986,508	3,322,419
EBITDA	83,364	438,310	2,627	202,426	1,032,926	1,186,474	1,352,300	1,644,352
Depn & Amortn	81,825	348,695	381,760	493,162	456,483	388,092	392,913	398,612
Income Before Taxes	(25,142)	(21,440)	(468,299)	(381,348)	515,191	774,240	918,081	1,179,271
Income Taxes	(44,463)	(39,786)	(95,796)	(107,063)	128,180	225,554	197,604	216,729
Net Income	19,321	18,346	(372,503)	(274,285)	387,011	548,686	720,477	962,542
Average Shares	137,495	137,265	137,168	137,157	137,523	139,064	139,048	139,038
Balance Sheet								
Current Assets	879,969	886,653	505,807	669,595	899,059	2,718,110	2,132,943	1,992,683
Total Assets	6,193,083	6,250,570	6,371,877	7,164,889	8,021,289	8,391,434	7,235,286	6,964,157
Current Liabilities	195,026	223,288	340,499	625,723	856,646	745,582	485,546	427,291
Long-Term Obligations	1,972,634	1,972,225	1,980,884	1,994,773	1,994,526	2,244,189	1,496,066	1,495,823
Total Liabilities	2,413,451	2,476,309	2,621,743	3,052,119	3,569,726	3,754,176	2,658,892	2,631,094
Stockholders' Equity	3,779,632	3,774,261	3,750,134	4,112,770	4,451,563	4,637,258	4,576,394	4,333,063
Shares Outstanding	137,342	137,227	137,169	137,158	137,147	139,035	139,031	139,027
Statistical Record								
Return on Assets %	0.23	0.29	N.M.	N.M.	4.72	7.02	10.12	14.06
Return on Equity %	0.37	0.49	N.M.	N.M.	8.52	11.91	16.13	23.49
EBITDA Margin %	28.21	29.50	0.16	8.37	36.70	40.63	45.28	49.49
Net Margin %	6.54	1.23	N.M.	N.M.	13.75	18.79	24.12	28.97
Asset Turnover	0.23	0.24	0.24	0.32	0.34	0.37	0.42	0.49
Current Ratio	4.51	3.97	1.49	1.07	1.05	3.65	4.39	4.66
Debt to Equity	0.52	0.52	0.53	0.49	0.45	0.48	0.33	0.35
Price Range	20.13-10.22	19.49-10.22	26.11-14.80	37.23-16.81	56.92-29.37	76.48-55.39	72.43-55.61	80.14-52.90
P/E Ratio	201.30-102.20	149.92-78.62	...	...	20.26-10.45	19.36-14.02	13.98-10.74	11.58-7.64
Average Yield %	...	...	...	1.91	7.82	5.24	5.37	5.18

Address: 15415 Katy Freeway, Houston, TX 77094
Telephone: 281-492-5300
Fax: 281-492-5316

Web Site: www.diamondoffshore.com
Officers: James S. Tisch - Chairman Marc Gerard Rex Edwards - President, Chief Executive Officer

Auditors: Deloitte & Touche LLP
Investor Contact: 281-492-5393
Transfer Agents: Computershare, Providence, R.I.

DICK'S SPORTING GOODS, INC

Exchange	Symbol	Price	52Wk Range	Yield	P/E
NYS	DKS	$35.25 (6/29/2018)	40.49-24.39	2.55	11.48

*7 Year Price Score 55.75   *NYSE Composite Index=100   *12 Month Price Score 109.92

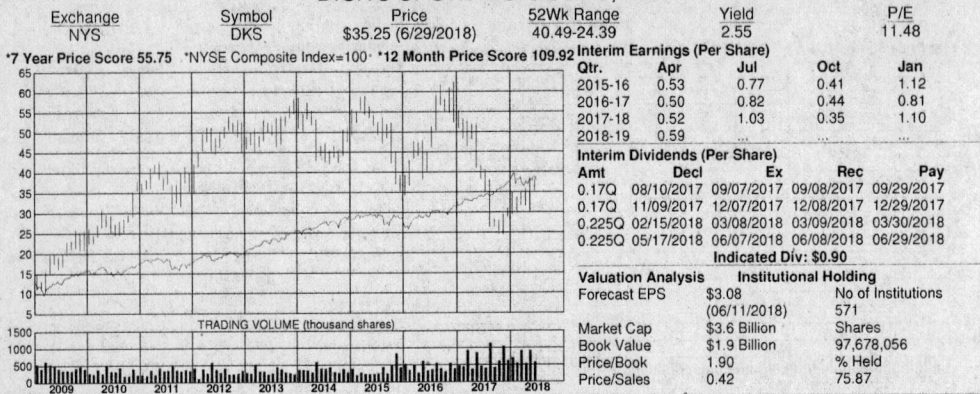

Interim Earnings (Per Share)

Qtr.	Apr	Jul	Oct	Jan
2015-16	0.53	0.77	0.41	1.12
2016-17	0.50	0.82	0.44	0.81
2017-18	0.52	1.03	0.35	1.10
2018-19	0.59	...	...	...

Interim Dividends (Per Share)

Amt	Decl	Ex	Rec	Pay
0.17Q	08/10/2017	09/07/2017	09/08/2017	09/29/2017
0.17Q	11/09/2017	12/07/2017	12/08/2017	12/29/2017
0.225Q	02/15/2018	03/08/2018	03/09/2018	03/30/2018
0.225Q	05/17/2018	06/07/2018	06/08/2018	06/29/2018

Indicated Div: $0.90

Valuation Analysis

		Institutional Holding	
Forecast EPS	$3.08	No of Institutions	
	(06/11/2018)	571	
Market Cap	$3.6 Billion	Shares	
Book Value	$1.9 Billion	97,678,056	
Price/Book	1.90	% Held	
Price/Sales	0.42	75.87	

Business Summary: Retail - Specialty (MIC: 2.1.3 SIC: 5941 NAIC: 451110)

Dick's Sporting Goods is an omni-channel sporting goods retailer offering sports equipment, apparel, footwear and accessories through a blend of dedicated associates, in-store services and specialty shop-in-shops. Co. also owns and operates Golf Galaxy, Field & Stream, and Dick's Team Sports HQ, an all-in-one youth sports digital platform offering free league management services, mobile apps for scheduling, communications and live scorekeeping, custom uniforms and FanWear. Co.'s Dick's Sporting Goods stores unites several sports specialty stores under one roof. Through eCommerce, Co. continues to develop its online content and capabilities to enhance the online experience.

Recent Developments: For the quarter ended May 5 2018, net income increased 3.2% to US$60.1 million from US$58.2 million in the year-earlier quarter. Revenues were US$1.91 billion, up 4.6% from US$1.83 billion the year before. Operating income was US$87.3 million versus US$90.1 million in the prior-year quarter, a decrease of 3.0%. Direct operating expenses rose 5.1% to US$1.35 billion from US$1.28 billion in the comparable period the year before. Indirect operating expenses increased 4.7% to US$473.0 million from US$451.8 million in the equivalent prior-year period.

Prospects: Our evaluation of Dick's Sporting Goods Inc. as of Jan. 21, 2018 is the result of our systematic analysis on three basic characteristics: earnings strength, relative valuation, and recent stock price movement. The company has generated a negative trend in earnings per share over the past 5 quarters and while recent estimates for the company have been raised by analysts, DKS has posted better than expected results. Based on operating earnings yield, the company is undervalued when compared to all of the companies in our coverage universe. Share price changes over the past year indicates that DKS will perform very poorly over the near term.

Financial Data
(US$ in Thousands)

	3 Mos	02/03/2018	01/28/2017	01/30/2016	01/31/2015	02/01/2014	02/02/2013	01/28/2012
Earnings Per Share	3.07	3.01	2.56	2.83	2.84	2.69	2.31	2.10
Cash Flow Per Share	6.81	6.86	6.85	5.60	5.10	3.30	3.55	3.42
Tang Book Value Per Share	14.76	15.09	13.99	13.24	12.88	11.52	10.47	11.39
Dividends Per Share	0.735	0.680	0.605	0.550	0.500	0.500	2.500	0.500
Dividend Payout %	23.94	22.59	23.63	19.43	17.61	18.59	108.23	23.81
Income Statement								
Total Revenue	1,909,719	8,590,472	7,921,981	7,270,965	6,814,479	6,213,173	5,836,119	5,211,802
EBITDA	142,879	730,684	670,878	715,387	720,829	702,836	621,159	558,994
Depn & Amortn	56,433	221,300	206,600	180,500	161,600	153,800	125,300	113,100
Income Before Taxes	83,790	501,337	458,422	530,875	556,014	546,107	489,825	432,026
Income Taxes	23,705	177,892	171,026	200,484	211,816	208,509	199,116	168,120
Net Income	60,085	323,445	287,396	330,391	344,198	337,598	290,709	263,906
Average Shares	102,153	107,586	112,216	116,794	121,238	125,628	125,995	125,768
Balance Sheet								
Current Assets	2,163,566	2,006,085	1,995,678	1,812,690	1,850,384	1,620,071	1,595,889	1,868,393
Total Assets	4,319,414	4,203,939	4,058,296	3,559,336	3,436,198	3,071,487	2,887,807	2,996,452
Current Liabilities	1,312,555	1,425,014	1,397,415	1,191,675	1,118,833	1,002,587	1,000,768	940,146
Long-Term Obligations	338,869	60,084	4,679	5,324	5,913	6,476	7,762	151,596
Total Liabilities	2,421,204	2,262,438	2,128,807	1,770,149	1,603,973	1,379,308	1,300,483	1,363,707
Stockholders' Equity	1,898,210	1,941,501	1,929,489	1,789,187	1,832,225	1,692,179	1,587,324	1,632,745
Shares Outstanding	102,514	103,028	110,330	111,751	118,106	120,966	123,005	121,333
Statistical Record								
Return on Assets %	7.52	7.70	7.57	9.47	10.61	11.36	9.72	9.46
Return on Equity %	16.86	16.44	15.50	18.30	19.59	20.64	17.76	17.66
EBITDA Margin %	7.48	8.51	8.47	9.84	10.58	11.31	10.64	10.73
Net Margin %	3.15	3.77	3.63	4.54	5.05	5.43	4.98	5.06
Asset Turnover	2.01	2.05	2.09	2.08	2.10	2.09	1.95	1.87
Current Ratio	1.65	1.41	1.43	1.52	1.65	1.62	1.59	1.99
Debt to Equity	0.18	0.03	N.M.	N.M.	N.M.	N.M.	N.M.	0.09
Price Range	51.68-24.39	53.17-24.39	62.25-36.57	58.98-34.24	57.26-41.90	58.58-45.11	53.93-40.80	42.58-29.86
P/E Ratio	16.83-7.94	17.66-8.10	24.32-14.29	20.84-12.10	20.16-14.75	21.78-16.77	23.35-17.66	20.28-14.22
Average Yield %	2.25	1.83	1.20	1.12	1.03	0.97	5.12	1.33

Address: 345 Court Street, Coraopolis, PA 15108
Telephone: 724-273-3400

Web Site: www.DICKS.com
Officers: Edward W. Stack - Chairman, Chief Executive Officer William J. Colombo - Vice-Chairman, Chief Marketing Officer

Auditors: DELOITTE & TOUCHE LLP
Transfer Agents: American Stock Transfer & Trust Company, New York, NY

DIEBOLD NIXDORF INC

Exchange	Symbol	Price	52Wk Range	Yield	P/E
NYS	DBD	$11.95 (6/29/2018)	28.00-11.50	3.35	N/A

*7 Year Price Score 48.47 *NYSE Composite Index=100 *12 Month Price Score 71.38

Interim Earnings (Per Share)

Qtr.	Mar	Jun	Sep	Dec
2015	(0.04)	0.34	0.33	0.49
2016	2.56	(0.32)	(1.44)	(1.14)
2017	(0.78)	(0.41)	(0.47)	(1.43)
2018	(0.94)	...	...	...

Interim Dividends (Per Share)

Amt	Decl	Ex	Rec	Pay
0.10Q	04/26/2017	05/17/2017	05/19/2017	06/09/2017
0.10Q	07/13/2017	08/23/2017	08/25/2017	09/15/2017
0.10Q	10/18/2017	11/16/2017	11/17/2017	12/08/2017
0.10Q	02/01/2018	02/23/2018	02/26/2018	03/16/2018

Indicated Div: $0.40 (Div. Reinv. Plan)

Valuation Analysis — **Institutional Holding**

Forecast EPS	$1.03	No of Institutions
	(06/11/2018)	388
Market Cap	$907.7 Million	Shares
Book Value	$426.9 Million	116,411,464
Price/Book	2.13	% Held
Price/Sales	0.20	101.15

Business Summary: Computer Hardware & Equipment (MIC: 6.2.1 SIC: 3578 NAIC: 333313)

Diebold Nixdorf provides connected commerce services, software and technology. Co.'s financial self-service products are primarily automated teller machines and other equipment primarily used in the banking industry which include both hardware and the software required for the equipment to operate as intended. Co. also provides provides global product sales, service, installation, project management for longer-term contracts and monitoring of original equipment manufacturer electronic security products to financial, government, retail and commercial customers. Co. also designs, manufactures and/or procures and installs physical security and facility products.

Recent Developments: For the quarter ended Mar 31 2018, net loss amounted to US$63.3 million versus a net loss of US$52.2 million in the year-earlier quarter. Revenues were US$1.06 billion, down 3.5% from US$1.10 billion the year before. Operating loss was US$21.0 million versus a loss of US$48.6 million in the prior-year quarter. Direct operating expenses declined 4.3% to US$823.3 million from US$860.3 million in the comparable period the year before. Indirect operating expenses decreased 10.0% to US$261.9 million from US$291.1 million in the equivalent prior-year period.

Prospects: Our evaluation of Diebold Nixdorf Inc. as of Jan. 21, 2018 is the result of our systematic analysis on three basic characteristics: earnings strength, relative valuation, and recent stock price movement. The company has managed to produce a neutral trend in earnings per share over the past 5 quarters. However, while recent estimates for the company have been mixed, DBD has posted better than expected results. Based on operating earnings yield, the company is undervalued when compared to all of the companies in our coverage universe. Share price changes over the past year indicates that DBD will perform poorly over the near term.

Financial Data

(US$ in Thousands)	3 Mos	12/31/2017	12/31/2016	12/31/2015	12/31/2014	12/31/2013	12/31/2012	12/31/2011
Earnings Per Share	(3.25)	(3.09)	(0.48)	1.12	1.76	(2.85)	1.23	2.24
Cash Flow Per Share	(0.51)	0.49	0.41	0.57	2.90	1.95	2.14	3.35
Tang Book Value Per Share	N.M.	N.M.	N.M.	3.86	5.56	6.51	8.49	9.18
Dividends Per Share	0.400	0.400	0.963	1.150	1.150	1.150	1.140	1.120
Dividend Payout %	...	...	...	102.68	65.34	...	92.68	50.00
Income Statement								
Total Revenue	1,064,200	4,609,300	3,316,300	2,419,300	3,051,053	2,857,491	2,991,693	2,835,848
EBITDA	45,700	14,200	(75,100)	119,000	250,211	(40,422)	199,203	249,397
Depn & Amortn	67,100	92,900	61,800	40,700	48,202	50,151	51,447	50,549
Income Before Taxes	(43,900)	(175,700)	(238,300)	45,800	170,589	(119,807)	117,426	164,392
Income Taxes	19,400	29,800	(67,600)	(13,700)	53,570	56,715	29,905	12,815
Net Income	(70,900)	(233,100)	(33,000)	73,700	114,417	(181,605)	78,454	144,815
Average Shares	75,800	75,500	69,100	65,600	65,154	63,659	63,914	64,792
Balance Sheet								
Current Assets	2,413,500	2,508,400	2,619,600	1,643,600	1,655,530	1,555,350	1,814,857	1,732,355
Total Assets	5,178,400	5,250,200	5,270,300	2,249,300	2,342,136	2,183,491	2,592,987	2,517,443
Current Liabilities	1,847,200	1,799,400	1,824,500	955,800	1,027,723	893,736	838,855	824,217
Long-Term Obligations	1,712,500	1,787,100	1,691,400	613,100	479,794	480,242	617,534	606,154
Total Liabilities	4,751,500	4,780,200	4,678,900	1,836,900	1,810,532	1,586,727	1,783,024	1,690,457
Stockholders' Equity	426,900	470,000	591,400	412,400	531,604	596,764	809,963	826,986
Shares Outstanding	75,955	75,558	75,144	65,001	64,632	64,068	63,240	62,513
Statistical Record								
Return on Assets %	N.M.	N.M.	N.M.	3.21	5.06	N.M.	3.06	5.75
Return on Equity %	N.M.	N.M.	N.M.	15.61	20.28	N.M.	9.56	16.20
EBITDA Margin %	4.29	0.31	N.M.	4.92	8.20	N.M.	6.66	8.79
Net Margin %	N.M.	N.M.	N.M.	3.05	3.75	N.M.	2.62	5.11
Asset Turnover	0.88	0.88	0.88	1.05	1.35	1.20	1.17	1.13
Current Ratio	1.31	1.39	1.44	1.72	1.61	1.74	2.16	2.10
Debt to Equity	4.01	3.80	2.86	1.49	0.90	0.80	0.76	0.73
Price Range	30.70-14.30	31.60-16.15	30.09-21.20	37.83-29.36	40.61-32.35	35.10-27.61	40.68-28.26	36.94-24.76
P/E Ratio	...	...	...	33.78-26.21	23.07-18.38	...	33.07-22.98	16.49-11.05
Average Yield %	1.88	1.66	3.77	3.40	3.12	3.73	3.30	3.58

Address: 5995 Mayfair Road, P.O. Box 3077, North Canton, OH 44720-8077 **Telephone:** 330-490-4000	**Web Site:** www.diebold.com **Officers:** Gary G. Greenfield - Chairman Gerrard Schmid - President, Chief Executive Officer	**Auditors:** KPMG LLP **Investor Contact:** 330-490-6319 **Transfer Agents:** Wells Fargo Shareowner Services

DIGITAL REALTY TRUST INC

Exchange	Symbol	Price	52Wk Range	Yield	P/E	Div Acheiver
NYS	DLR	$111.58 (6/29/2018)	126.04-97.95	3.62	109.39	13 Years

*7 Year Price Score 114.55 *NYSE Composite Index=100   *12 Month Price Score 95.51

Interim Earnings (Per Share)

Qtr.	Mar	Jun	Sep	Dec
2015	0.75	0.86	0.28	(0.32)
2016	0.27	0.19	1.25	0.48
2017	0.41	0.36	(0.02)	0.26
2018	0.42	...	...	...

Interim Dividends (Per Share)

Amt	Decl	Ex	Rec	Pay
0.93Q	08/07/2017	09/14/2017	09/15/2017	09/29/2017
0.93Q	11/03/2017	12/14/2017	12/15/2017	01/12/2018
1.01Q	03/01/2018	03/14/2018	03/15/2018	03/30/2018
1.01Q	05/08/2018	06/14/2018	06/15/2018	06/29/2018

Indicated Div: $4.04

Valuation Analysis

		Institutional Holding	
Forecast EPS	$1.10 (06/13/2018)	No of Institutions	876
Market Cap	$23.0 Billion	Shares	245,447,712
Book Value	$10.3 Billion	% Held	108.74
Price/Book	2.24		
Price/Sales	8.66		

TRADING VOLUME (thousand shares)

Business Summary: REITs (MIC: 5.3.1 SIC: 6798 NAIC: 525930)

Digital Realty Trust is engaged in the business of owning, acquiring, developing and managing data centers. Co. provides data center, colocation and interconnection solutions for domestic and international tenants ranging from financial services, cloud and information technology services, to manufacturing, energy, healthcare, and consumer products. As of Dec. 31 2017, Co.'s portfolio consisted of 205 data centers, including seven held-for-sale data centers and 18 data centers held as investments in unconsolidated joint ventures, of which 152 are located throughout the U.S., 38 are located in Europe, seven are located in Asia, five are located in Australia and three are located in Canada.

Recent Developments: For the quarter ended Mar 31 2018, net income increased 30.2% to US$110.1 million from US$84.6 million in the year-earlier quarter. Revenues were US$744.4 million, up 35.2% from US$550.6 million the year before. Revenues from property income rose 35.1% to US$743.5 million from US$550.5 million in the corresponding quarter a year earlier.

Prospects: Our evaluation of Digital Realty Trust Inc. as of Jan. 21, 2018 is the result of our systematic analysis on three basic characteristics: earnings strength, relative valuation, and recent stock price movement. The company has managed to produce a neutral trend in earnings per share over the past 5 quarters. However, while recent estimates for the company have been mixed, DLR has posted results that fell short of analysts expectations. Based on operating earnings yield, the company is overvalued when compared to all of the companies in our coverage universe. Share price changes over the past year indicates that DLR will perform very well over the near term.

Financial Data

(US$ in Thousands)	3 Mos	12/31/2017	12/31/2016	12/31/2015	12/31/2014	12/31/2013	12/31/2012	12/31/2011
Earnings Per Share	1.02	0.99	2.20	1.56	0.99	2.12	1.48	1.32
Cash Flow Per Share	5.06	5.88	6.07	5.78	4.92	5.13	4.68	4.07
Tang Book Value Per Share	26.39	28.05	20.94	19.67	20.87	22.70	23.14	18.42
Dividends Per Share	3.800	3.720	3.520	3.400	3.320	3.120	2.920	2.720
Dividend Payout %	372.55	375.76	160.00	217.95	335.35	147.17	197.30	206.06
Income Statement								
Total Revenue	744,368	2,457,928	2,142,213	1,763,336	1,616,438	1,482,259	1,279,067	1,062,710
EBITDA	308,188	1,373,224	1,387,107	1,074,431	941,142	988,010	759,770	630,622
Depn & Amortn	125,102	879,585	720,930	578,064	557,356	486,805	393,995	327,400
Income Before Taxes	106,059	238,652	425,133	292,551	195,364	311,945	210,559	157,132
Income Taxes	3,374	7,901	10,385	6,451	5,238	1,292	2,647	(42)
Net Income	106,627	248,259	426,187	296,689	200,183	314,488	210,334	156,265
Average Shares	206,507	174,895	150,679	138,865	133,637	128,127	116,006	99,169
Balance Sheet								
Current Assets	339,028	289,528	225,974	252,460	188,807	278,333	268,617	186,376
Total Assets	21,581,917	21,404,345	12,192,585	11,451,267	9,526,784	9,685,745	8,819,214	6,098,566
Current Liabilities	1,012,490	1,179,979	969,072	735,268	720,942	765,196	739,861	390,588
Long-Term Obligations	9,147,712	8,648,618	5,838,607	5,934,241	4,673,127	4,961,892	4,278,565	2,940,210
Total Liabilities	11,328,066	11,001,362	7,096,570	6,951,135	5,648,528	6,075,229	5,350,909	3,575,649
Stockholders' Equity	10,253,851	10,402,983	5,096,015	4,500,132	3,878,256	3,610,516	3,468,305	2,522,917
Shares Outstanding	205,874	205,470	159,019	146,384	135,626	128,455	125,140	106,039
Statistical Record								
Return on Assets %	1.60	1.48	3.60	2.83	2.08	3.40	2.81	2.73
Return on Equity %	3.55	3.20	8.86	7.08	5.35	8.89	7.00	6.97
EBITDA Margin %	41.40	55.87	64.75	60.93	58.22	66.66	59.40	59.34
Net Margin %	14.32	10.10	19.89	16.83	12.38	21.22	16.44	14.70
Asset Turnover	0.16	0.15	0.18	0.17	0.17	0.16	0.17	0.19
Current Ratio	0.33	0.25	0.23	0.34	0.26	0.36	0.36	0.48
Debt to Equity	0.89	0.83	1.15	1.32	1.20	1.37	1.23	1.17
Price Range	126.04-97.95	126.04-99.36	112.10-72.50	77.01-61.52	70.27-49.12	73.77-44.53	80.31-59.28	67.14-50.63
P/E Ratio	123.57-96.03	127.31-100.36	50.95-32.95	49.37-39.44	70.98-49.62	34.80-21.00	54.26-40.05	50.86-38.36
Average Yield %	3.35	3.28	3.43	5.01	5.56	5.21	4.12	4.61

| Address: Four Embarcadero Center, Suite 3200, San Francisco, CA 94111
Telephone: 415-738-6500
Fax: 415-738-6501 | Web Site: www.digitalrealty.com
Officers: Laurence A. Chapman - Chairman A. William Stein - Interim Chief Executive Officer, Chief Executive Officer, Chief Financial Officer, Chief Investment Officer | Auditors: KPMG LLP
Investor Contact: 415-738-6500
Transfer Agents: American Stock Transfer & Trust Company, New York, NY |

DILLARD'S INC.

Exchange	Symbol	Price	52Wk Range	Yield	P/E
NYS	DDS	$94.50 (6/29/2018)	97.51-50.48	0.42	11.55

*7 Year Price Score 69.81 ***NYSE Composite Index=100** ***12 Month Price Score 119.53**

Interim Earnings (Per Share)

Qtr.	Apr	Jul	Oct	Jan
2015-16	2.66	0.75	1.19	2.26
2016-17	2.17	0.35	0.67	1.69
2017-18	2.12	(0.58)	0.50	5.37
2018-19	2.89	...	...	...

Interim Dividends (Per Share)

Amt	Decl	Ex	Rec	Pay
0.10Q	08/17/2017	09/28/2017	09/29/2017	10/30/2017
0.10Q	11/17/2017	12/28/2017	12/29/2017	02/05/2018
0.10Q	03/01/2018	03/28/2018	03/30/2018	05/07/2018
0.10Q	05/19/2018	06/28/2018	06/29/2018	08/06/2018

Indicated Div: $0.40

Valuation Analysis

		Institutional Holding	
Forecast EPS	$6.08 (06/10/2018)	No of Institutions	346
Market Cap	$2.6 Billion	Shares	34,981,812
Book Value	$1.7 Billion	% Held	70.48
Price/Book	1.55		
Price/Sales	0.40		

Business Summary: Retail - General Merchandise/Department Stores (MIC: 2.1.1 SIC: 5311 NAIC: 452111)

Dillard's is a fashion apparel, cosmetics and home furnishing retailer. As of Feb 3 2018 , Co. operated 292 Dillard's stores, including 24 clearance centers, and an Internet store offering a wide selection of merchandise including fashion apparel for women, men and children, accessories, cosmetics, home furnishings and other consumer goods. Co. also operates a contracting construction company, CDI Contractors, LLC, a portion of whose business includes constructing and remodeling stores for Co. As of Feb 3 2018, Co. operated retail department stores in 29 states, primarily in the southwest, southeast and midwest regions of the U. S.

Recent Developments: For the quarter ended May 5 2018, net income increased 21.5% to US$80.5 million from US$66.3 million in the year-earlier quarter. Revenues were US$1.49 billion, up 2.6% from US$1.45 billion the year before. Direct operating expenses rose 3.8% to US$903.0 million from US$870.0 million in the comparable period the year before. Indirect operating expenses increased 0.9% to US$484.4 million from US$480.3 million in the equivalent prior-year period.

Prospects: Our evaluation of Dillard's Inc. as of Jan. 21, 2018 is the result of our systematic analysis on three basic characteristics: earnings strength, relative valuation, and recent stock price movement. The company has managed to produce a neutral trend in earnings per share over the past 5 quarters and while recent estimates for the company have been mixed, DDS has posted better than expected results. Based on operating earnings yield, the company is undervalued when compared to all of the companies in our coverage universe. Share price changes over the past year indicates that DDS will perform very poorly over the near term.

Financial Data

(US$ in Thousands)	3 Mos	02/03/2018	01/28/2017	01/30/2016	01/31/2015	02/01/2014	02/02/2013	01/28/2012
Earnings Per Share	8.18	7.51	4.93	6.91	7.79	7.10	6.87	8.52
Cash Flow Per Share	9.06	9.15	15.11	11.57	14.39	11.04	10.69	9.39
Tang Book Value Per Share	60.94	60.77	53.41	49.98	49.02	45.33	41.24	41.50
Dividends Per Share	0.370	0.340	0.280	0.260	0.240	0.220	5.200	0.190
Dividend Payout %	4.52	4.53	5.68	3.76	3.08	3.10	75.69	2.23
Income Statement								
Total Revenue	1,490,725	6,422,676	6,418,009	6,754,545	6,780,129	6,691,777	6,751,595	6,399,765
EBITDA	173,731	507,269	564,734	719,707	823,074	815,729	809,346	726,728
Depn & Amortn	56,471	232,000	244,000	250,000	251,000	255,000	260,000	258,000
Income Before Taxes	103,238	212,689	257,675	408,784	510,768	496,224	479,750	396,669
Income Taxes	22,690	(7,800)	88,500	140,770	179,480	173,400	145,060	(62,518)
Net Income	80,548	221,324	169,220	269,370	331,853	323,671	335,962	463,909
Average Shares	27,849	29,487	34,308	39,005	42,603	45,586	48,911	54,448
Balance Sheet								
Current Assets	2,045,383	1,729,851	1,837,921	1,668,883	1,888,442	1,660,156	1,491,980	1,591,729
Total Assets	3,781,463	3,673,169	3,888,136	3,865,625	4,170,071	4,050,739	4,048,744	4,306,137
Current Liabilities	1,278,289	1,039,701	976,517	751,216	885,323	778,311	767,116	870,364
Long-Term Obligations	568,051	568,309	730,094	822,054	820,704	821,544	822,309	823,938
Total Liabilities	2,099,377	1,965,014	2,170,719	2,070,320	2,150,801	2,058,542	2,078,569	2,254,118
Stockholders' Equity	1,682,086	1,708,155	1,717,417	1,795,305	2,019,270	1,992,197	1,970,175	2,052,019
Shares Outstanding	27,601	28,106	32,157	35,920	41,192	43,948	47,769	49,441
Statistical Record								
Return on Assets %	5.97	5.76	4.38	6.72	8.10	8.01	7.91	10.72
Return on Equity %	13.97	12.71	9.66	14.16	16.59	16.38	16.44	22.48
EBITDA Margin %	11.65	7.90	8.80	10.66	12.14	12.19	11.99	11.36
Net Margin %	5.40	3.45	2.64	3.99	4.89	4.84	4.98	7.25
Asset Turnover	1.64	1.67	1.66	1.69	1.65	1.66	1.59	1.48
Current Ratio	1.60	1.66	1.88	2.22	2.13	2.13	1.94	1.83
Debt to Equity	0.34	0.33	0.43	0.46	0.41	0.41	0.42	0.40
Price Range	87.97-46.93	78.87-46.93	87.74-54.65	142.22-61.24	125.81-83.60	97.21-75.77	89.05-43.89	60.28-38.56
P/E Ratio	10.75-5.74	10.50-6.25	17.80-11.09	20.58-8.86	16.15-10.73	13.69-10.67	12.96-6.39	7.08-4.53
Average Yield %	0.59	0.60	0.42	0.26	0.22	0.26	7.26	0.40

Address: 1600 Cantrell Road, Little Rock, AR 72201
Telephone: 501-376-5200

Web Site: www.dillards.com
Officers: William T. Dillard - Chairman, Chief Executive Officer Alex Dillard - President

Auditors: KPMG LLP
Investor Contact: 501-376-5965
Transfer Agents: Registrar and Transfer Company, Cranford, NJ

DISCOVER FINANCIAL SERVICES

Exchange	Symbol	Price	52Wk Range	Yield	P/E
NYS	DFS	$70.41 (6/29/2018)	81.31-57.66	1.99	12.12

*7 Year Price Score 106.42 *NYSE Composite Index=100 *12 Month Price Score 103.67

TRADING VOLUME (thousand shares)

Interim Earnings (Per Share)

Qtr.	Mar	Jun	Sep	Dec
2015	1.28	1.33	1.38	1.15
2016	1.35	1.47	1.56	1.41
2017	1.43	1.40	1.59	1.00
2018	1.82	...	...	...

Interim Dividends (Per Share)

Amt	Decl	Ex	Rec	Pay
0.35Q	07/25/2017	08/22/2017	08/24/2017	09/07/2017
0.35Q	10/19/2017	11/21/2017	11/22/2017	12/07/2017
0.35Q	01/18/2018	02/21/2018	02/22/2018	03/08/2018
0.35Q	04/20/2018	05/23/2018	05/24/2018	06/07/2018

Indicated Div: $1.40

Valuation Analysis / Institutional Holding

Forecast EPS	$7.77 (06/14/2018)	No of Institutions	1168
Market Cap	$24.7 Billion	Shares	391,496,768
Book Value	$10.9 Billion		
Price/Book	2.28	% Held	71.16
Price/Sales	2.09		

Business Summary: Credit & Lending (MIC: 5.4.1 SIC: 6141 NAIC: 522210)

Discover Financial Services is a bank holding and financial holding company. Co. operates two segments: Direct Banking, which includes Discover-branded credit cards issued to individuals on the Discover Network and other consumer products and services, including private student loans, personal loans, home equity loans, and other consumer lending and deposit products; and Payment Services, which includes PULSE electronic funds transfer network, Diners Club International global payments network, and its Network Partners business that provides payment transaction processing and settlement services. As of Dec 31 2017, Co. had total assets of $100.09 billion and total deposits of $58.76 billion.

Recent Developments: For the quarter ended Mar 31 2018, net income increased 18.1% to US$666.0 million from US$564.0 million in the year-earlier quarter. Net interest income increased 11.0% to US$2.10 billion from US$1.89 billion in the year-earlier quarter. Provision for loan losses was US$751.0 million versus US$586.0 million in the prior-year quarter, an increase of 28.2%. Non-interest income rose 6.3% to US$475.0 million from US$447.0 million, while non-interest expense advanced 9.4% to US$968.0 million.

Prospects: Our evaluation of Discover Financial Services as of Jan. 21, 2018 is the result of our systematic analysis on three basic characteristics: earnings strength, relative valuation, and recent stock price movement. The company has produced a positive trend in earnings per share over the past 5 quarters and while recent estimates for the company have been mixed, DFS has posted better than expected results. Based on operating earnings yield, the company is undervalued when compared to all of the companies in our coverage universe. Share price changes over the past year indicates that DFS will perform poorly over the near term.

Financial Data
(US$ in Thousands)

	3 Mos	12/31/2017	12/31/2016	12/31/2015	12/31/2014	12/31/2013	11/30/2012	11/30/2011
Earnings Per Share	5.81	5.42	5.77	5.13	4.90	4.96	4.46	4.06
Cash Flow Per Share	15.30	13.93	10.90	8.82	8.28	7.24	5.84	6.66
Tang Book Value Per Share	28.15	27.69	26.60	24.41	22.58	20.71	17.56	14.75
Dividends Per Share	1.350	1.300	1.160	1.080	0.920	0.600	0.400	0.200
Dividend Payout %	23.24	23.99	20.10	21.05	18.78	12.10	8.97	4.93
Income Statement								
Total Revenue	3,044,000	11,545,000	10,497,000	10,002,000	9,611,000	9,370,000	8,984,000	8,550,313
Income Before Taxes	856,000	3,537,000	3,656,000	3,612,000	3,694,000	3,944,000	3,753,000	3,511,244
Income Taxes	190,000	1,438,000	1,263,000	1,315,000	1,371,000	1,474,000	1,408,000	1,284,536
Net Income	666,000	2,099,000	2,393,000	2,297,000	2,323,000	2,470,000	2,345,000	2,226,708
Average Shares	355,000	374,000	406,000	437,498	463,412	486,861	520,000	542,626
Balance Sheet								
Total Assets	101,967,000	100,087,000	92,308,000	86,936,000	83,126,000	79,340,000	75,283,000	68,783,937
Total Liabilities	91,096,000	89,195,000	80,985,000	75,661,000	71,992,000	68,531,000	65,505,000	60,541,726
Stockholders' Equity	10,871,000	10,892,000	11,323,000	11,275,000	11,134,000	10,809,000	9,778,000	8,242,211
Shares Outstanding	351,416	357,920	388,766	421,678	449,188	472,244	497,871	528,830
Statistical Record								
Return on Assets %	2.24	2.18	2.66	2.70	2.86	3.19	3.25	3.44
Return on Equity %	19.89	18.90	21.12	20.50	21.17	24.00	25.96	30.30
Net Margin %	21.88	18.18	22.80	22.97	24.17	26.36	26.10	26.04
Asset Turnover	0.12	0.12	0.12	0.12	0.12	0.12	0.12	0.13
Price Range	81.31-57.66	77.50-57.66	73.18-43.25	65.49-50.60	66.38-52.21	55.95-37.80	41.61-23.07	27.52-18.02
P/E Ratio	13.99-9.92	14.30-10.64	12.68-7.50	12.77-9.86	13.55-10.66	11.28-7.62	9.33-5.17	6.78-4.44
Average Yield %	2.01	1.99	2.07	1.89	1.52	1.28	1.19	0.87

Address: 2500 Lake Cook Road, Riverwoods, IL 60015 **Telephone:** 224-405-0900	**Web Site:** www.discover.com **Officers:** David W. Nelms - Chairman, Chief Executive Officer Roger C. Hochschild - President, Chief Operating Officer	**Auditors:** Deloitte & Touche LLP **Investor Contact:** 224-405-4555 **Transfer Agents:** Computershare, Jersey City, NJ

DISNEY (WALT) CO. (THE)

Exchange	Symbol	Price	52Wk Range	Yield	P/E
NYS	DIS	$104.81 (6/29/2018)	112.47-96.93	1.60	13.96

*7 Year Price Score 101.54 *NYSE Composite Index=100 *12 Month Price Score 98.04

Interim Earnings (Per Share)

Qtr.	Dec	Mar	Jun	Sep
2014-15	1.27	1.23	1.45	0.95
2015-16	1.73	1.30	1.59	1.10
2016-17	1.55	1.50	1.51	1.14
2017-18	2.91	1.95	...	...

Interim Dividends (Per Share)

Amt	Decl	Ex	Rec	Pay
0.78S	11/30/2016	12/08/2016	12/12/2016	01/11/2017
0.78S	06/28/2017	07/06/2017	07/10/2017	07/27/2017
0.84S	11/29/2017	12/08/2017	12/11/2017	01/11/2018
0.84S	06/26/2018	07/06/2018	07/09/2018	07/26/2018

Indicated Div: $1.68

Valuation Analysis — **Institutional Holding**

Forecast EPS	$7.07	No of Institutions
	(06/14/2018)	2805
Market Cap	$157.2 Billion	Shares
Book Value	$45.2 Billion	1,256,874,752
Price/Book	3.48	% Held
Price/Sales	2.76	59.06

Business Summary: Entertainment (MIC: 2.3.2 SIC: 4841 NAIC: 515210)

Walt Disney is an entertainment company. Co.'s segments are: Media Networks, which includes cable and broadcast television networks; television production and distribution operations, domestic television stations and radio networks and stations; Parks and Resorts, which owns and operates the Disneyland Resort, and the Disney Cruise Line, among others; Studio Entertainment, which produces and acquires live-action and animated motion pictures, direct-to-video content, musical recordings and live stage plays; and Consumer Products and Interactive Media, which licenses Co.'s trade names, characters and visual and literary properties to manufacturers, game developers, publishers and retailers.

Recent Developments: For the quarter ended Mar 31 2018, net income increased 22.7% to US$3.12 billion from US$2.54 billion in the year-earlier quarter. Revenues were US$14.55 billion, up 9.1% from US$13.34 billion the year before. Direct operating expenses rose 8.1% to US$7.53 billion from US$6.97 billion in the comparable period the year before. Indirect operating expenses increased 14.3% to US$2.99 billion from US$2.62 billion in the equivalent prior-year period.

Prospects: Our evaluation of Disney (Walt) Co. as of Jan. 21, 2018 is the result of our systematic analysis on three basic characteristics: earnings strength, relative valuation, and recent stock price movement. The company has managed to produce a neutral trend in earnings per share over the past 5 quarters and while recent estimates for the company have been raised by analysts, DIS has posted results that fell short of analysts expectations. Based on operating earnings yield, the company is undervalued when compared to all of the companies in our coverage universe. Share price changes over the past year indicates that DIS will perform in line with the market over the near term.

Financial Data

(US$ in Thousands)	6 Mos	3 Mos	09/30/2017	10/01/2016	10/03/2015	09/27/2014	09/28/2013	09/29/2012
Earnings Per Share	7.51	7.06	5.69	5.73	4.90	4.26	3.38	3.13
Cash Flow Per Share	9.59	8.81	7.89	8.13	6.34	5.64	5.29	4.45
Tang Book Value Per Share	4.56	3.29	1.93	5.32	5.95	5.65	5.96	5.41
Dividends Per Share	1.620	1.620	1.560	1.420	1.810	0.860	0.750	0.600
Dividend Payout %	21.57	22.95	27.42	24.78	36.94	20.19	22.19	19.17
Income Statement								
Total Revenue	29,899,000	15,351,000	55,137,000	55,632,000	52,465,000	48,813,000	45,041,000	42,278,000
EBITDA	9,260,000	4,573,000	16,635,000	16,729,000	15,525,000	13,657,000	11,140,000	10,989,000
Depn & Amortn	1,364,000	742,000	2,782,000	2,527,000	2,354,000	2,288,000	2,192,000	1,987,000
Income Before Taxes	7,624,000	3,702,000	13,468,000	13,942,000	13,054,000	11,392,000	8,713,000	8,633,000
Income Taxes	85,000	(728,000)	4,422,000	5,078,000	5,016,000	4,242,000	2,984,000	3,087,000
Net Income	7,360,000	4,423,000	8,980,000	9,391,000	8,382,000	7,501,000	6,136,000	5,682,000
Average Shares	1,510,000	1,521,000	1,578,000	1,639,000	1,709,000	1,759,000	1,813,000	1,818,000
Balance Sheet								
Current Assets	16,808,000	17,274,000	15,889,000	16,966,000	16,758,000	15,176,000	14,109,000	13,709,000
Total Assets	97,943,000	97,734,000	95,789,000	92,033,000	88,182,000	84,186,000	81,241,000	74,898,000
Current Liabilities	19,728,000	19,875,000	19,595,000	16,842,000	16,334,000	13,292,000	11,704,000	12,813,000
Long-Term Obligations	18,766,000	20,082,000	19,119,000	16,483,000	12,773,000	12,676,000	13,050,000	10,981,000
Total Liabilities	52,792,000	54,445,000	54,474,000	48,768,000	43,657,000	39,228,000	35,812,000	35,139,000
Stockholders' Equity	45,151,000	43,289,000	41,315,000	43,265,000	44,525,000	44,958,000	45,429,000	39,759,000
Shares Outstanding	1,500,000	1,500,000	1,500,000	1,600,000	1,600,000	1,707,000	1,800,000	1,780,000
Statistical Record								
Return on Assets %	12.09	11.54	9.59	10.45	9.57	9.09	7.88	7.75
Return on Equity %	25.80	25.26	21.29	21.45	18.43	16.64	14.45	14.77
EBITDA Margin %	30.97	29.79	30.17	30.07	29.59	27.98	24.73	25.99
Net Margin %	24.62	28.81	16.29	16.88	15.98	15.37	13.62	13.44
Asset Turnover	0.60	0.59	0.59	0.62	0.60	0.59	0.58	0.58
Current Ratio	0.85	0.87	0.81	1.01	1.03	1.14	1.21	1.07
Debt to Equity	0.42	0.46	0.46	0.38	0.29	0.28	0.29	0.28
Price Range	115.84-96.93	115.84-96.93	115.84-90.83	120.07-88.85	121.69-81.74	90.94-63.59	67.67-47.06	52.92-29.00
P/E Ratio	15.42-12.91	16.41-13.73	20.36-15.96	20.95-15.51	24.83-16.68	21.35-14.93	20.02-13.92	16.91-9.27
Average Yield %	1.54	1.52	1.49	1.41	1.77	1.09	1.29	1.41

Address: 500 South Buena Vista Street, Burbank, CA 91521
Telephone: 818-560-1000

Web Site: www.disney.com
Officers: Robert A. (Bob) Iger - Chairman, President, Chief Executive Officer Alan N. Braverman - Senior Executive Vice President, General Counsel, Secretary

Auditors: PricewaterhouseCoopers LLP
Investor Contact: 818-553-7200
Transfer Agents: Broadridge Corporate Issuer Solutions, Brentwood, NY

DOLBY LABORATORIES INC

Exchange	Symbol	Price	52Wk Range	Yield	P/E
NYS	DLB	$61.69 (6/29/2018)	70.19-48.25	1.04	76.16

*7 Year Price Score 114.13 *NYSE Composite Index=100 *12 Month Price Score 102.80

Interim Earnings (Per Share)

Qtr.	Dec	Mar	Jun	Sep
2014-15	0.40	0.56	0.34	0.46
2015-16	0.30	0.66	0.62	0.22
2016-17	0.51	0.49	0.73	0.22
2017-18	(0.80)	0.66	...	...

Interim Dividends (Per Share)

Amt	Decl	Ex	Rec	Pay
0.14Q	07/24/2017	08/03/2017	08/07/2017	08/15/2017
0.16Q	10/25/2017	11/03/2017	11/06/2017	11/15/2017
0.16Q	01/24/2018	02/02/2018	02/05/2018	02/14/2018
0.16Q	04/24/2018	05/04/2018	05/07/2018	05/16/2018

Indicated Div: $0.64

Valuation Analysis

		Institutional Holding	
Forecast EPS	$0.89	No of Institutions	
	(06/13/2018)	420	
Market Cap	$6.4 Billion	Shares	
Book Value	$2.1 Billion	65,117,792	
Price/Book	2.99	% Held	
Price/Sales	5.65	46.24	

Business Summary: Manufacturing (MIC: 6.1.1 SIC: 3663 NAIC: 334220)

Dolby Laboratories designs and manufactures audio and imaging products for the cinema, television, broadcast, and entertainment industries. Co. has various licensing models: a two-tier model, an integrated licensing model, a patent licensing model, and collaboration arrangements. Co.'s Cinema Imaging Products include digital cinema server used on digital cinema projectors. Co.'s Dolby Cinema Audio Products include cinema processors, amplifiers, and loudspeakers. Co.'s Dolby Conference Phone is a hardware component of the Dolby Voice conferencing solution. Co.'s other products include broadcast hardware and software used to encode, transmit, and decode multiple channels of audio.

Recent Developments: For the quarter ended Mar 30 2018, net income increased 39.5% to US$70.8 million from US$50.7 million in the year-earlier quarter. Revenues were US$301.4 million, up 12.7% from US$267.5 million the year before. Operating income was US$86.3 million versus US$63.3 million in the prior-year quarter, an increase of 36.4%. Direct operating expenses rose 14.8% to US$31.0 million from US$27.0 million in the comparable period the year before. Indirect operating expenses increased 3.9% to US$184.1 million from US$177.2 million in the equivalent prior-year period.

Prospects: Our evaluation of Dolby Laboratories Inc. as of Jan. 21, 2018 is the result of our systematic analysis on three basic characteristics: earnings strength, relative valuation, and recent stock price movement. The company has managed to produce a neutral trend in earnings per share over the past 5 quarters. However, while recent estimates for the company have been lowered by analysts, DLB has posted results that fell short of analysts expectations. Based on operating earnings yield, the company is about fairly valued when compared to all of the companies in our coverage universe. Share price changes over the past year indicates that DLB will perform well over the near term.

Financial Data
(US$ in Thousands)

	6 Mos	3 Mos	09/29/2017	09/30/2016	09/25/2015	09/26/2014	09/27/2013	09/28/2012
Earnings Per Share	0.81	0.64	1.95	1.81	1.75	1.99	1.84	2.46
Cash Flow Per Share	3.02	3.12	3.66	3.49	3.03	3.55	2.70	3.66
Tang Book Value Per Share	15.75	14.94	16.01	14.25	13.58	13.38	11.40	13.41
Dividends Per Share	0.600	0.580	0.560	0.480	0.400	...	4.000	...
Dividend Payout %	74.07	90.63	28.72	26.52	22.86	...	217.39	...
Income Statement								
Total Revenue	589,152	287,797	1,081,454	1,025,738	970,638	960,176	909,674	926,264
EBITDA	168,180	81,830	300,594	282,345	289,621	310,672	284,773	393,376
Depn & Amortn	1,472	742	53,400	52,000	48,200	38,100	37,400	30,600
Income Before Taxes	174,317	84,834	256,644	235,904	245,782	276,099	250,646	368,991
Income Taxes	185,030	166,312	54,217	49,502	62,542	67,379	60,344	103,857
Net Income	(10,991)	(81,622)	201,802	185,860	181,390	206,103	189,271	264,302
Average Shares	107,001	102,552	103,286	102,424	103,862	103,632	102,788	107,541
Balance Sheet								
Current Assets	1,154,665	1,035,511	1,011,434	759,730	918,330	1,005,851	812,722	970,286
Total Assets	2,606,639	2,514,709	2,533,554	2,310,106	2,133,293	1,984,012	1,737,945	1,960,798
Current Liabilities	213,149	223,182	245,773	213,083	209,681	189,370	172,815	156,840
Total Liabilities	459,210	465,002	396,812	339,850	326,225	273,995	256,835	240,529
Stockholders' Equity	2,147,429	2,049,707	2,136,742	1,970,256	1,807,068	1,710,017	1,481,110	1,720,269
Shares Outstanding	104,097	103,274	102,155	101,422	101,034	102,268	101,739	103,095
Statistical Record								
Return on Assets %	3.48	2.76	8.36	8.23	8.84	11.11	10.26	13.78
Return on Equity %	4.15	3.30	9.85	9.68	10.34	12.95	11.86	15.66
EBITDA Margin %	28.55	28.43	27.80	27.53	29.84	32.36	31.30	42.47
Net Margin %	N.M.	N.M.	18.66	18.12	18.69	21.47	20.81	28.53
Asset Turnover	0.46	0.46	0.45	0.45	0.47	0.52	0.49	0.48
Current Ratio	5.42	4.64	4.12	3.57	4.38	5.31	4.70	6.19
Price Range	70.19-48.25	63.25-45.19	59.07-45.19	54.54-30.50	45.99-30.91	46.93-34.39	35.60-28.98	45.11-26.28
P/E Ratio	86.65-59.57	98.83-70.61	30.29-23.17	30.13-16.85	26.28-17.66	23.58-17.28	19.35-15.75	18.34-10.68
Average Yield %	1.05	1.09	1.11	1.15	1.02	...	12.23	...

Address: 1275 Market Street, San Francisco, CA 94103-1410 **Telephone:** 415-558-0200	**Web Site:** www.dolby.com **Officers:** Peter Gotcher - Chairman Kevin J. Yeaman - President, Chief Executive Officer	**Auditors:** KPMG LLP **Transfer Agents:** Computershare Trust Company, N.A., Providence, RI

DOLLAR GENERAL CORP

Exchange	Symbol	Price	52Wk Range	Yield	P/E
NYS	DG	$98.60 (6/29/2018)	105.34-69.04	1.18	16.49

*7 Year Price Score 108.58 *NYSE Composite Index=100 *12 Month Price Score 105.25

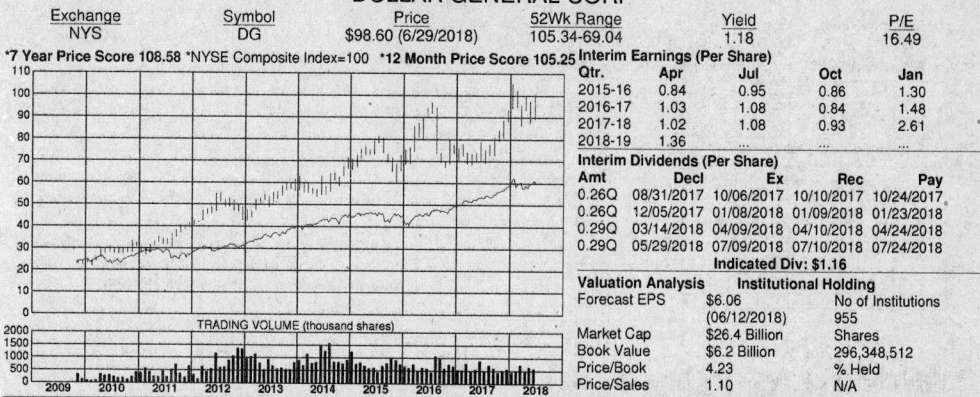

Interim Earnings (Per Share)

Qtr.	Apr	Jul	Oct	Jan
2015-16	0.84	0.95	0.86	1.30
2016-17	1.03	1.08	0.84	1.48
2017-18	1.02	1.08	0.93	2.61
2018-19	1.36	...	...	...

Interim Dividends (Per Share)

Amt	Decl	Ex	Rec	Pay
0.26Q	08/31/2017	10/06/2017	10/10/2017	10/24/2017
0.26Q	12/05/2017	01/08/2018	01/09/2018	01/23/2018
0.29Q	03/14/2018	04/09/2018	04/10/2018	04/24/2018
0.29Q	05/29/2018	07/09/2018	07/10/2018	07/24/2018

Indicated Div: $1.16

Valuation Analysis

		Institutional Holding	
Forecast EPS	$6.06	No of Institutions	955
	(06/12/2018)		
Market Cap	$26.4 Billion	Shares	296,348,512
Book Value	$6.2 Billion	% Held	
Price/Book	4.23	N/A	
Price/Sales	1.10		

Business Summary: Retail - General Merchandise/Department Stores (MIC: 2.1.1 SIC: 5331 NAIC: 452990)

Dollar General is a discount retailer providing a range of merchandise. At Mar 2 2018, Co. operated 14,609 stores located in 44 states, primarily in the southern, southwestern, midwestern and eastern U.S. Co.'s consumables category includes paper and cleaning products, packaged food, perishables, snacks, health and beauty; seasonal products include decorations, toys, batteries, small electronics, automotive and home office supplies; home products include kitchen supplies, cookware, frames, craft supplies and kitchen, and bed and bath soft goods; and apparel category includes casual everyday apparel, as well as socks, underwear, disposable diapers, shoes and accessories.

Recent Developments: For the quarter ended May 4 2018, net income increased 30.5% to US$364.9 million from US$279.5 million in the year-earlier quarter. Revenues were US$6.11 billion, up 9.0% from US$5.61 billion the year before. Operating income was US$490.2 million versus US$473.8 million in the prior-year quarter, an increase of 3.5%. Direct operating expenses rose 8.7% to US$4.25 billion from US$3.91 billion in the comparable period the year before. Indirect operating expenses increased 12.0% to US$1.37 billion from US$1.23 billion in the equivalent prior-year period.

Prospects: Our evaluation of Dollar General Inc. as of Jan. 21, 2018 is the result of our systematic analysis on three basic characteristics: earnings strength, relative valuation, and recent stock price movement. The company has managed to produce a neutral trend in earnings per share over the past 5 quarters and while recent estimates for the company have been raised by analysts, DG has posted results that fell short of analysts expectations. Based on operating earnings yield, the company is undervalued when compared to all of the companies in our coverage universe. Share price changes over the past year indicates that DG will perform poorly over the near term.

Financial Data
(US$ in Thousands)

	3 Mos	02/02/2018	02/03/2017	01/29/2016	01/30/2015	01/31/2014	02/01/2013	02/03/2012
Earnings Per Share	5.98	5.63	4.43	3.95	3.49	3.17	2.85	2.22
Cash Flow Per Share	6.86	6.63	5.61	4.69	4.33	3.77	3.41	3.03
Tang Book Value Per Share	2.61	2.18	N.M.	N.M.	0.56	N.M.	N.M.	N.M.
Dividends Per Share	1.070	1.040	1.000	0.880	...	...	...	...
Dividend Payout %	17.89	18.47	22.57	22.28	...	...	...	...
Income Statement								
Total Revenue	6,114,463	23,470,967	21,986,598	20,368,562	18,909,588	17,504,167	16,022,128	14,807,188
EBITDA	599,519	2,407,616	2,441,749	2,290,568	2,104,993	2,032,614	1,902,520	1,673,889
Depn & Amortn	109,335	403,300	378,300	350,600	335,900	315,300	277,200	243,700
Income Before Taxes	465,411	1,907,280	1,965,628	1,853,024	1,680,861	1,628,330	1,497,394	1,225,289
Income Taxes	100,559	368,320	714,495	687,944	615,516	603,214	544,732	458,604
Net Income	364,852	1,538,960	1,251,133	1,165,080	1,065,345	1,025,116	952,662	766,685
Average Shares	269,135	273,362	282,261	295,211	305,681	323,854	334,469	345,117
Balance Sheet								
Current Assets	4,166,036	4,247,852	3,677,771	3,432,410	3,532,609	3,205,607	2,677,113	2,275,074
Total Assets	12,493,230	12,516,911	11,672,204	11,257,885	11,224,104	10,867,524	10,367,682	9,688,520
Current Liabilities	2,525,332	2,964,878	2,622,805	1,995,596	1,987,740	1,811,971	1,738,547	1,509,902
Long-Term Obligations	2,862,497	2,604,613	2,710,576	2,969,175	2,639,427	2,742,788	2,771,336	2,617,891
Total Liabilities	6,256,912	6,391,137	6,266,004	5,880,009	5,514,066	5,465,331	5,382,352	5,013,938
Stockholders' Equity	6,236,318	6,125,774	5,406,294	5,377,876	5,710,038	5,402,193	4,985,330	4,674,582
Shares Outstanding	267,557	268,733	275,212	286,694	303,447	317,058	327,069	338,089
Statistical Record								
Return on Assets %	13.37	12.76	10.74	10.39	9.67	9.68	9.53	7.84
Return on Equity %	27.61	26.76	22.83	21.07	19.23	19.79	19.78	17.26
EBITDA Margin %	9.80	10.26	11.11	11.25	11.13	11.61	11.87	11.30
Net Margin %	5.97	6.56	5.69	5.72	5.63	5.86	5.95	5.18
Asset Turnover	1.97	1.95	1.89	1.82	1.72	1.65	1.60	1.51
Current Ratio	1.65	1.43	1.40	1.72	1.78	1.77	1.54	1.51
Debt to Equity	0.46	0.43	0.50	0.55	0.46	0.51	0.56	0.56
Price Range	105.34-69.04	105.34-68.35	96.71-66.97	81.18-60.02	71.29-53.50	62.87-43.80	55.06-41.64	42.70-26.85
P/E Ratio	17.62-11.55	18.71-12.14	21.83-15.12	20.55-15.19	20.43-15.33	19.83-13.82	19.32-14.61	19.23-12.09
Average Yield %	1.26	1.32	1.25	1.21	...	...	...	...

Address: 100 Mission Ridge, Goodlettsville, TN 37072
Telephone: 615-855-4000
Fax: 615-855-5527

Web Site: www.dollargeneral.com
Officers: Michael M. Calbert - Chairman, Chairman (frmr) Todd J. Vasos - Chief Executive Officer, Executive Vice President, Chief Merchandising Officer, Chief Operating Officer, Division Officer

Auditors: Ernst & Young LLP
Investor Contact: 615-855-4000
Transfer Agents: Wells Fargo Bank, N.A., St. Paul, MN

DOMINION ENERGY INC

Exchange	Symbol	Price	52Wk Range	Yield	P/E	Div Acheiver
NYS	D	$68.18 (6/29/2018)	84.91-61.75	4.90	15.22	14 Years

*7 Year Price Score 90.40   *NYSE Composite Index=100   *12 Month Price Score 85.76

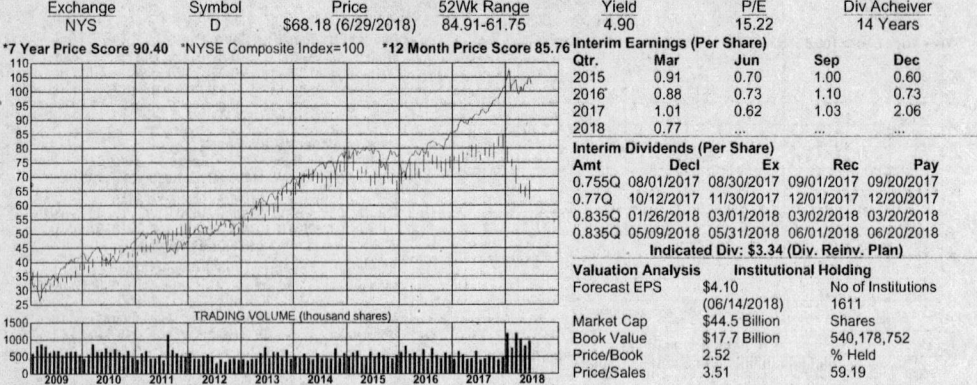

Interim Earnings (Per Share)

Qtr.	Mar	Jun	Sep	Dec
2015	0.91	0.70	1.00	0.60
2016	0.88	0.73	1.10	0.73
2017	1.01	0.62	1.03	2.06
2018	0.77	...	...	...

Interim Dividends (Per Share)

Amt	Decl	Ex	Rec	Pay
0.755Q	08/01/2017	08/30/2017	09/01/2017	09/20/2017
0.77Q	10/12/2017	11/30/2017	12/01/2017	12/20/2017
0.835Q	01/26/2018	03/01/2018	03/02/2018	03/20/2018
0.835Q	05/09/2018	05/31/2018	06/01/2018	06/20/2018

Indicated Div: $3.34 (Div. Reinv. Plan)

Valuation Analysis   Institutional Holding

Forecast EPS	$4.10	No of Institutions
	(06/14/2018)	1611
Market Cap	$44.5 Billion	Shares
Book Value	$17.7 Billion	540,178,752
Price/Book	2.52	% Held
Price/Sales	3.51	59.19

Business Summary: Electric Utilities (MIC: 3.1.1 SIC: 4911 NAIC: 221121)

Dominion Energy is a producer and transporter of energy. Co.'s subsidiary, Dominion Gas Holdings, LLC conducts business activities through a regulated interstate natural gas transmission pipeline and underground storage system in the Northeast, mid-Atlantic and Midwest states, regulated gas transportation and distribution operations in Ohio, and gas gathering and processing activities primarily in West Virginia, Ohio and Pennsylvania. Co.'s nonregulated operations include merchant generation, energy marketing and price risk management activities, and retail energy marketing operations. As of Dec 31 2017, Co. served over 6.0 million utility and retail energy customers in 14 states.

Recent Developments: For the quarter ended Mar 31 2018, net income decreased 22.0% to US$526.0 million from US$674.0 million in the year-earlier quarter. Revenues were US$3.47 billion, up 2.4% from US$3.38 billion the year before. Operating income was US$875.0 million versus US$1.08 billion in the prior-year quarter, a decrease of 18.9%. Direct operating expenses rose 15.0% to US$1.89 billion from US$1.65 billion in the comparable period the year before. Indirect operating expenses increased 5.9% to US$697.0 million from US$658.0 million in the equivalent prior-year period.

Prospects: Our evaluation of Dominion Energy Inc. as of Jan. 21, 2018 is the result of our systematic analysis on three basic characteristics: earnings strength, relative valuation, and recent stock price movement. The company has managed to produce a neutral trend in earnings per share over the past 5 quarters and while recent estimates for the company have been mixed, D has posted better than expected results. Based on operating earnings yield, the company is undervalued when compared to all of the companies in our coverage universe. Share price changes over the past year indicates that D will perform very well over the near term.

Financial Data

(US$ in Thousands)	3 Mos	12/31/2017	12/31/2016	12/31/2015	12/31/2014	12/31/2013	12/31/2012	12/31/2011
Earnings Per Share	4.48	4.72	3.44	3.20	2.24	2.93	0.53	2.45
Cash Flow Per Share	6.80	7.15	6.68	7.55	5.90	5.93	7.20	5.21
Tang Book Value Per Share	17.28	15.58	12.08	14.77	13.57	14.20	12.43	13.90
Dividends Per Share	3.115	3.035	2.800	2.590	2.400	2.250	2.110	1.970
Dividend Payout %	69.53	64.30	81.40	80.94	107.14	76.79	398.11	80.41
Income Statement								
Total Revenue	3,466,000	12,586,000	11,737,000	11,683,000	12,436,000	13,120,000	13,093,000	14,379,000
EBITDA	1,547,000	6,497,000	5,726,000	5,401,000	4,531,000	4,971,000	2,822,000	4,328,000
Depn & Amortn	572,000	2,202,000	1,849,000	1,669,000	1,560,000	1,390,000	1,443,000	1,288,000
Income Before Taxes	661,000	3,090,000	2,867,000	2,828,000	1,778,000	2,704,000	497,000	2,171,000
Income Taxes	135,000	(30,000)	655,000	905,000	452,000	892,000	146,000	745,000
Net Income	503,000	2,999,000	2,123,000	1,899,000	1,310,000	1,697,000	302,000	1,408,000
Average Shares	650,500	636,000	617,100	593,700	584,500	579,500	573,900	574,600
Balance Sheet								
Current Assets	4,281,000	4,334,000	4,248,000	4,191,000	5,615,000	5,940,000	5,140,000	5,430,000
Total Assets	77,354,000	76,585,000	71,610,000	58,797,000	54,327,000	50,096,000	46,838,000	45,614,000
Current Liabilities	9,339,000	9,636,000	8,115,000	8,120,000	7,198,000	6,994,000	7,763,000	6,962,000
Long-Term Obligations	31,120,000	30,948,000	30,231,000	23,616,000	21,805,000	19,330,000	16,851,000	17,394,000
Total Liabilities	59,665,000	59,443,000	57,005,000	46,133,000	42,772,000	38,197,000	36,013,000	33,911,000
Stockholders' Equity	17,689,000	17,142,000	14,605,000	12,664,000	11,555,000	11,899,000	10,825,000	11,703,000
Shares Outstanding	653,000	645,000	628,000	596,000	585,000	581,000	576,000	570,000
Statistical Record								
Return on Assets %	3.82	4.05	3.25	3.36	2.51	3.50	0.65	3.18
Return on Equity %	17.60	18.89	15.53	15.68	11.17	14.94	2.67	11.75
EBITDA Margin %	44.63	51.62	48.79	46.23	36.43	37.89	21.55	30.10
Net Margin %	14.51	23.83	18.09	16.25	10.53	12.93	2.31	9.79
Asset Turnover	0.17	0.17	0.18	0.21	0.24	0.27	0.28	0.33
Current Ratio	0.46	0.45	0.52	0.52	0.78	0.85	0.66	0.78
Debt to Equity	1.76	1.81	2.07	1.86	1.89	1.62	1.56	1.49
Price Range	84.91-67.30	84.91-71.68	78.92-67.47	79.27-64.89	80.23-63.51	67.80-51.80	54.97-49.19	53.53-42.26
P/E Ratio	18.95-15.02	17.99-15.19	22.94-19.61	24.77-20.28	35.82-28.35	23.14-17.68	103.72-92.81	21.85-17.25
Average Yield %	4.00	3.88	3.82	3.65	3.43	3.79	4.05	4.14

Address: 120 Tredegar Street, Richmond, VA 23219	Web Site: www.dom.com	Auditors: DELOITTE & TOUCHE LLP
Telephone: 804-819-2000	Officers: Thomas F. Farrell - Chairman, President, Chief Executive Officer Mark F. McGettrick - Executive Vice President, Chief Financial Officer	Investor Contact: 804-819-2205
Fax: 804-775-5819		Transfer Agents: Dominion Resources Services, Inc. Richmond, VA

DOMINOS PIZZA INC.

Exchange	Symbol	Price	52Wk Range	Yield	P/E
NYS	DPZ	$282.17 (6/29/2018)	292.39-168.71	0.78	42.95

*7 Year Price Score 161.41 *NYSE Composite Index=100 *12 Month Price Score 121.42

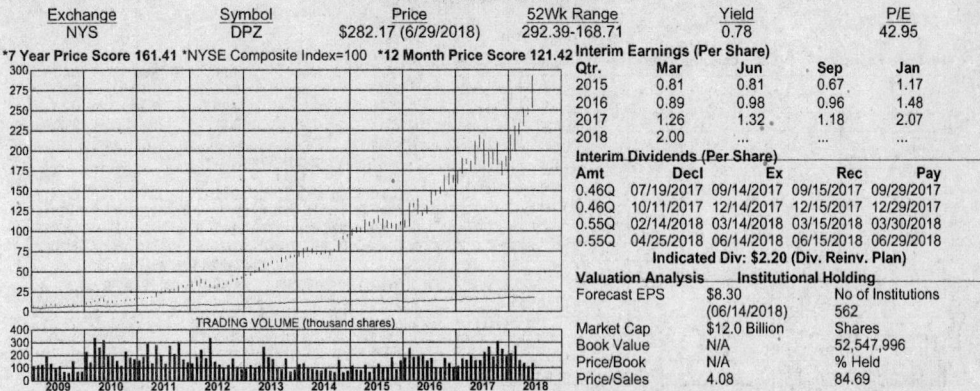

Interim Earnings (Per Share)

Qtr.	Mar	Jun	Sep	Jan
2015	0.81	0.81	0.67	1.17
2016	0.89	0.98	0.96	1.48
2017	1.26	1.32	1.18	2.07
2018	2.00	...	...	...

Interim Dividends (Per Share)

Amt	Decl	Ex	Rec	Pay
0.46Q	07/19/2017	09/14/2017	09/15/2017	09/29/2017
0.46Q	10/11/2017	12/14/2017	12/15/2017	12/29/2017
0.55Q	02/14/2018	03/14/2018	03/15/2018	03/30/2018
0.55Q	04/25/2018	06/14/2018	06/15/2018	06/29/2018

Indicated Div: $2.20 (Div. Reinv. Plan)

Valuation Analysis — **Institutional Holding**

Forecast EPS	$8.30
	(06/14/2018)
Market Cap	$12.0 Billion
Book Value	N/A
Price/Book	N/A
Price/Sales	4.08

No of Institutions	562
Shares	52,547,996
% Held	84.69

Business Summary: Hotels, Restaurants & Travel (MIC: 2.2.1 SIC: 5812 NAIC: 722211)

Domino's Pizza is involved in the: retail sales of food through Co.-owned Domino's Pizza stores; sales of food, equipment and supplies to Co.-owned and franchised Domino's Pizza stores; and receipt of royalties and fees from domestic and international Domino's Pizza franchisees. Co.'s menu features pizza products with varying sizes and crust types. Co.'s typical store also provides oven-baked sandwiches, pasta, boneless chicken and wings, bread side items, desserts and Coca-Cola® soft drink products. International markets vary toppings by country and culture, such as squid topping in Japan, and feature regional specialty items, such as a banana and cinnamon dessert pizza in Brazil.

Recent Developments: For the quarter ended Mar 25 2018, net income increased 42.2% to US$88.8 million from US$62.5 million in the year-earlier quarter. Revenues were US$785.4 million, up 25.8% from US$624.2 million the year before. Operating income was US$133.5 million versus US$116.0 million in the prior-year quarter, an increase of 15.0%. Direct operating expenses rose 12.8% to US$485.5 million from US$430.4 million in the comparable period the year before. Indirect operating expenses increased 113.9% to US$166.4 million from US$77.8 million in the equivalent prior-year period.

Prospects: Our evaluation of Dominos Pizza Inc. as of Jan. 21, 2018 is the result of our systematic analysis on three basic characteristics: earnings strength, relative valuation, and recent stock price movement. The company has produced a positive trend in earnings per share over the past 5 quarters. However, while recent estimates for the company have been mixed, DPZ has posted better than expected results. Based on operating earnings yield, the company is about fairly valued when compared to all of the companies in our coverage universe. Share price changes over the past year indicates that DPZ will perform poorly over the near term.

Financial Data
(US$ in Thousands)

	3 Mos	12/31/2017	01/01/2017	01/03/2016	12/28/2014	12/29/2013	12/30/2012	01/01/2012
Earnings Per Share	6.57	5.83	4.30	3.47	2.86	2.48	1.91	1.71
Cash Flow Per Share	7.87	7.38	5.92	5.33	3.51	3.51	3.13	2.61
Dividends Per Share	1.930	1.840	1.520	1.240	1.000	0.800	3.000	...
Dividend Payout %	29.38	31.56	35.35	35.73	34.97	32.26	157.07	...
Income Statement								
Total Revenue	785,371	2,787,979	2,472,628	2,216,528	1,993,833	1,802,223	1,678,439	1,652,193
EBITDA	134,653	576,577	498,600	450,266	386,895	345,688	320,098	289,377
Depn & Amortn	1,177	55,345	44,558	44,827	41,534	31,877	37,767	30,232
Income Before Taxes	103,670	400,153	344,658	306,215	258,623	225,099	181,187	167,806
Income Taxes	14,843	122,248	129,980	113,426	96,036	82,114	68,795	62,445
Net Income	88,827	277,905	214,678	192,789	162,587	142,985	112,392	105,361
Average Shares	44,377	47,677	49,923	55,532	56,931	57,720	58,997	61,653
Balance Sheet								
Current Assets	536,423	579,780	495,873	602,637	428,361	351,540	306,267	326,843
Total Assets	798,300	836,753	716,295	799,845	619,280	525,255	478,197	480,543
Current Liabilities	384,766	398,285	403,698	375,983	265,608	254,611	229,498	197,175
Long-Term Obligations	3,117,193	3,121,490	2,148,990	2,181,460	1,523,546	1,512,299	1,536,443	1,450,369
Total Liabilities	3,569,164	3,572,137	2,599,438	2,600,096	1,838,745	1,815,457	1,813,720	1,690,282
Stockholders' Equity	(2,770,864)	(2,735,384)	(1,883,143)	(1,800,251)	(1,219,465)	(1,290,202)	(1,335,523)	(1,209,739)
Shares Outstanding	42,625	42,898	48,100	49,838	55,553	55,768	56,313	57,741
Statistical Record								
Return on Assets %	39.50	35.79	28.40	26.73	28.49	28.58	23.51	22.45
EBITDA Margin %	17.15	20.68	20.16	20.31	19.40	19.18	19.07	17.51
Net Margin %	11.31	9.97	8.68	8.70	8.15	7.93	6.70	6.38
Asset Turnover	3.83	3.59	3.27	3.07	3.49	3.60	3.51	3.52
Current Ratio	1.39	1.46	1.23	1.60	1.61	1.38	1.33	1.66
Price Range	231.59-168.71	218.88-158.36	172.26-104.16	119.43-94.17	95.93-67.17	70.68-43.55	43.46-28.75	34.91-16.17
P/E Ratio	35.25-25.68	37.54-27.16	40.06-24.22	34.42-27.14	33.54-23.49	28.50-17.56	22.75-15.05	20.42-9.46
Average Yield %	0.98	0.97	1.09	1.16	1.29	1.36	8.44	

Address: 30 Frank Lloyd Wright Drive, Ann Arbor, MI 48105	**Web Site:** www.dominos.com	**Auditors:** PricewaterhouseCoopers LLP
Telephone: 734-930-3030	**Officers:** David A. Brandon - Chairman, Chief Executive Officer Jeffrey D. Lawrence - Executive Vice President, Chief Financial Officer	**Investor Contact:** 734-930-3008
		Transfer Agents: ComputerShare Investor Services, Providence, RI

DOMTAR CORP

*7 Year Price Score 96.15 *NYSE Composite Index=100 *12 Month Price Score 106.82

Interim Earnings (Per Share)

Qtr.	Mar	Jun	Sep	Dec
2015	0.56	0.60	0.17	0.90
2016	0.06	0.29	0.94	0.75
2017	0.32	0.61	1.11	(6.15)
2018	0.86	...	...	...

Interim Dividends (Per Share)

Amt	Decl	Ex	Rec	Pay
0.415Q	08/02/2017	09/29/2017	10/02/2017	10/16/2017
0.415Q	11/01/2017	12/29/2017	01/02/2018	01/15/2018
0.435Q	02/08/2018	03/29/2018	04/02/2018	04/16/2018
0.435Q	05/09/2018	07/02/2018	07/03/2018	07/16/2018

Indicated Div: $1.74

Valuation Analysis

		Institutional Holding	
Forecast EPS	$3.81	No of Institutions	
	(06/13/2018)	N/A	
Market Cap	$3.9 Billion	Shares	
Book Value	$2.5 Billion	N/A	
Price/Book	1.57	% Held	
Price/Sales	0.75	N/A	

Business Summary: Paper & Forest Products (MIC: 8.1.2 SIC: 2621 NAIC: 322121)

Domtar is engaged in designing, manufacturing, marketing and distributing a range of fiber-based products including communication papers, specialty and packaging papers and absorbent hygiene products. Co. is also a marketer and producer of a broad line of incontinence care products as well as infant diapers. Co. operates the following business segments: Pulp and Paper, which consists of the design, manufacturing, marketing and distribution of communication, specialty and packaging papers, as well as softwood, fluff and hardwood market pulp; and Personal Care, which consists of the design, manufacturing, marketing and distribution of absorbent hygiene products.

Recent Developments: For the quarter ended Mar 31 2018, net income increased 170.0% to US$54.0 million from US$20.0 million in the year-earlier quarter. Revenues were US$1.35 billion, up 3.3% from US$1.30 billion the year before. Operating income was US$77.0 million versus US$38.0 million in the prior-year quarter, an increase of 102.6%. Direct operating expenses was unchanged at US$1.08 billion versus the comparable period the year before. Indirect operating expenses decreased 0.5% to US$184.0 million from US$185.0 million in the equivalent prior-year period.

Prospects: Our evaluation of Domtar Corp. as of Jan. 21, 2018 is the result of our systematic analysis on three basic characteristics: earnings strength, relative valuation, and recent stock price movement. The company has managed to produce a neutral trend in earnings per share over the past 5 quarters and while recent estimates for the company have been raised by analysts, UFS has posted better than expected results. Based on operating earnings yield, the company is undervalued when compared to all of the companies in our coverage universe. Share price changes over the past year indicates that UFS will perform in line with the market over the near term.

Financial Data
(US$ in Thousands)

	3 Mos	12/31/2017	12/31/2016	12/31/2015	12/31/2014	12/31/2013	12/31/2012	12/31/2011
Earnings Per Share	(3.57)	(4.11)	2.04	2.24	6.64	1.36	2.38	4.54
Cash Flow Per Share	7.15	7.16	7.41	7.16	9.78	6.17	7.63	11.07
Tang Book Value Per Share	29.54	29.51	24.25	24.06	25.96	30.94	33.07	35.44
Dividends Per Share	1.680	1.660	1.645	1.600	1.400	1.050	0.850	0.650
Dividend Payout %	...	...	80.64	71.43	21.08	77.21	35.71	14.32
Income Statement								
Total Revenue	1,345,000	5,157,000	5,098,000	5,264,000	5,563,000	5,391,000	5,482,000	5,612,000
EBITDA	160,000	(15,000)	552,000	628,000	727,000	527,000	752,000	968,000
Depn & Amortn	79,000	302,000	329,000	340,000	363,000	366,000	385,000	376,000
Income Before Taxes	65,000	(383,000)	157,000	156,000	261,000	72,000	236,000	505,000
Income Taxes	11,000	(125,000)	29,000	14,000	(170,000)	(20,000)	58,000	133,000
Net Income	54,000	(258,000)	128,000	142,000	431,000	91,000	172,000	365,000
Average Shares	62,900	62,700	62,700	63,400	64,900	66,800	72,200	80,400
Balance Sheet								
Current Assets	1,665,000	1,657,000	1,568,000	1,554,000	1,670,000	2,077,000	2,015,000	1,934,000
Total Assets	5,151,000	5,212,000	5,680,000	5,663,000	6,185,000	6,278,000	6,123,000	5,869,000
Current Liabilities	713,000	741,000	753,000	788,000	926,000	709,000	758,000	716,000
Long-Term Obligations	1,103,000	1,129,000	1,218,000	1,219,000	1,181,000	1,510,000	1,128,000	837,000
Total Liabilities	2,658,000	2,729,000	3,004,000	3,011,000	3,295,000	3,496,000	3,246,000	2,897,000
Stockholders' Equity	2,493,000	2,483,000	2,676,000	2,652,000	2,890,000	2,782,000	2,877,000	2,972,000
Shares Outstanding	62,831	62,695	62,588	62,849	64,010	64,837	69,692	73,500
Statistical Record								
Return on Assets %	N.M.	N.M.	2.25	2.40	6.92	1.47	2.86	6.14
Return on Equity %	N.M.	N.M.	4.79	5.12	15.20	3.22	5.87	11.82
EBITDA Margin %	11.90	N.M.	10.83	11.93	13.07	9.78	13.72	17.25
Net Margin %	4.01	N.M.	2.51	2.70	7.75	1.69	3.14	6.50
Asset Turnover	0.96	0.95	0.90	0.89	0.89	0.87	0.91	0.94
Current Ratio	2.34	2.24	2.08	1.97	1.80	2.93	2.66	2.70
Debt to Equity	0.44	0.45	0.46	0.46	0.41	0.54	0.39	0.28
Price Range	64.64-47.33	63.91-47.33	54.86-42.41	59.49-44.24	63.73-37.66	51.34-34.01	49.87-35.13	50.51-33.08
P/E Ratio	...	...	26.89-20.79	26.56-19.75	9.60-5.67	37.75-25.00	20.95-14.76	11.13-7.29
Average Yield %	3.07	3.13	3.37	3.04	2.88	2.64	2.07	1.55

Address: 234 Kingsley Park Drive, Fort Mill, SC 29715
Telephone: 803-802-7500

Web Site: www.domtar.com
Officers: Harold H. MacKay - Chairman John D. Williams - President, Chief Executive Officer

Auditors: PricewaterhouseCoopers LLP
Investor Contact: 514-848-5555
Transfer Agents: ComputerShare Investor Services, Providence, RI

DONALDSON CO. INC.

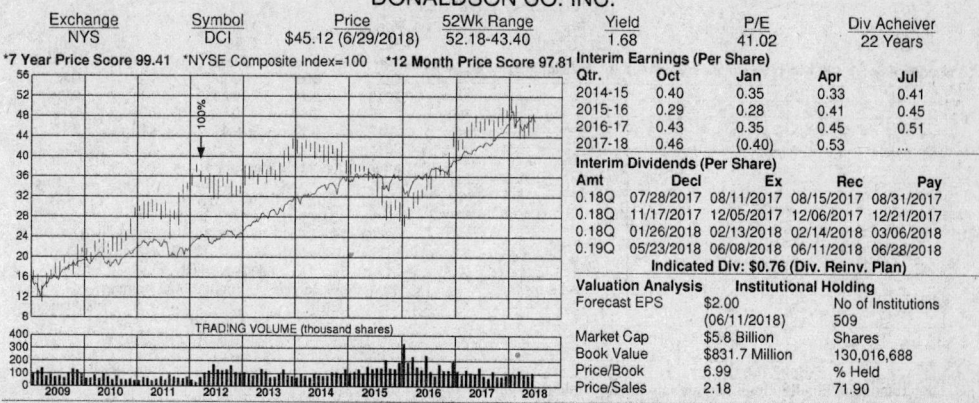

Exchange	Symbol	Price	52Wk Range	Yield	P/E	Div Acheiver
NYS	DCI	$45.12 (6/29/2018)	52.18-43.40	1.68	41.02	22 Years

*7 Year Price Score 99.41 *NYSE Composite Index=100 *12 Month Price Score 97.81

Interim Earnings (Per Share)

Qtr.	Oct	Jan	Apr	Jul
2014-15	0.40	0.35	0.33	0.41
2015-16	0.29	0.28	0.41	0.45
2016-17	0.43	0.35	0.45	0.51
2017-18	0.46	(0.40)	0.53	...

Interim Dividends (Per Share)

Amt	Decl	Ex	Rec	Pay
0.18Q	07/28/2017	08/11/2017	08/15/2017	08/31/2017
0.18Q	11/17/2017	12/05/2017	12/06/2017	12/21/2017
0.18Q	01/26/2018	02/13/2018	02/14/2018	03/06/2018
0.19Q	05/23/2018	06/08/2018	06/11/2018	06/28/2018

Indicated Div: $0.76 (Div. Reinv. Plan)

Valuation Analysis | **Institutional Holding**

Forecast EPS	$2.00 (06/11/2018)	No of Institutions	509
Market Cap	$5.8 Billion	Shares	130,016,688
Book Value	$831.7 Million	% Held	71.90
Price/Book	6.99		
Price/Sales	2.18		

Business Summary: Industrial Machinery & Equipment (MIC: 7.2.1 SIC: 3564 NAIC: 333411)

Donaldson Company is a manufacturer of filtration systems and replacement parts. Co. has two reporting segments: Engine Products, with products including replacement filters for both air and liquid filtration applications, air filtration systems, liquid filtration systems for fuel, lube and hydraulic applications, and exhaust and emissions systems; and Industrial Products, with products including dust, fume and mist collectors, compressed air purification systems, air filtration systems for gas turbines, polytetrafluoroethylene membrane-based products and air and gas filtration systems for applications including hard disk drives and semi-conductor manufacturing.

Recent Developments: For the quarter ended Apr 30 2018, net income increased 16.3% to US$69.9 million from US$60.1 million in the year-earlier quarter. Revenues were US$700.0 million, up 15.1% from US$608.2 million the year before. Operating income was US$100.9 million versus US$88.5 million in the prior-year quarter, an increase of 14.0%. Direct operating expenses rose 16.1% to US$460.4 million from US$396.7 million in the comparable period the year before. Indirect operating expenses increased 12.8% to US$138.7 million from US$123.0 million in the equivalent prior-year period.

Prospects: Our evaluation of Donaldson Co. Inc. as of Jan. 21, 2018 is the result of our systematic analysis on three basic characteristics: earnings strength, relative valuation, and recent stock price movement. The company has enjoyed a very positive trend in earnings per share over the past 5 quarters and while recent estimates for the company have been raised by analysts, DCI has posted better than expected results. Based on operating earnings yield, the company is about fairly valued when compared to all of the companies in our coverage universe. Share price changes over the past year indicates that DCI will perform in line with the market over the near term.

Financial Data

(US$ in Thousands)

	9 Mos	6 Mos	3 Mos	07/31/2017	07/31/2016	07/31/2015	07/31/2014	07/31/2013
Earnings Per Share	1.10	1.02	1.77	1.74	1.42	1.49	1.76	1.64
Cash Flow Per Share	1.88	1.96	2.10	2.34	2.13	1.55	2.18	2.13
Tang Book Value Per Share	4.30	4.17	4.61	4.37	3.76	3.81	5.70	6.01
Dividends Per Share	0.715	0.710	0.705	0.700	0.685	0.665	0.575	0.410
Dividend Payout %	65.00	69.61	39.83	40.23	48.24	44.63	32.67	25.00
Income Statement								
Total Revenue	2,009,500	1,309,500	644,800	2,371,900	2,220,300	2,371,213	2,473,466	2,436,948
EBITDA	333,200	174,200	91,300	410,300	346,900	370,660	432,903	417,891
Depn & Amortn	57,400	2,800	1,400	68,800	68,800	66,900	62,000	58,800
Income Before Taxes	260,100	161,100	84,700	322,000	257,400	288,603	360,703	348,181
Income Taxes	182,200	153,100	23,800	89,200	66,600	80,492	100,479	100,804
Net Income	77,900	8,000	60,900	232,800	190,800	208,111	260,224	247,377
Average Shares	131,900	130,600	132,700	134,100	134,800	139,381	147,641	150,455
Balance Sheet								
Current Assets	1,249,200	1,279,900	1,204,300	1,151,000	1,009,700	1,030,716	1,225,277	1,055,662
Total Assets	2,095,000	2,131,300	2,032,400	1,979,700	1,788,600	1,809,534	1,942,411	1,743,556
Current Liabilities	397,700	435,000	415,100	484,100	543,800	560,647	609,580	476,435
Long-Term Obligations	687,500	667,700	631,700	537,300	351,800	389,218	243,726	102,774
Total Liabilities	1,263,300	1,309,000	1,156,100	1,129,600	1,021,200	1,034,765	939,928	658,369
Stockholders' Equity	831,700	822,300	876,300	850,100	767,400	774,769	1,002,483	1,085,187
Shares Outstanding	128,912	129,858	129,849	130,605	132,892	134,598	140,405	146,152
Statistical Record								
Return on Assets %	7.35	6.90	12.32	12.36	10.58	11.09	14.12	14.24
Return on Equity %	17.93	17.05	28.45	28.79	24.68	23.42	24.93	24.80
EBITDA Margin %	16.58	13.30	14.16	17.30	15.62	15.63	17.50	17.15
Net Margin %	3.88	0.61	9.44	9.81	8.59	8.78	10.52	10.15
Asset Turnover	1.34	1.31	1.29	1.26	1.23	1.26	1.34	1.40
Current Ratio	3.14	2.94	2.90	2.38	1.86	1.84	2.01	2.22
Debt to Equity	0.83	0.81	0.72	0.63	0.46	0.50	0.24	0.09
Price Range	52.18-43.40	52.18-41.58	48.17-36.02	47.96-35.64	36.88-26.17	42.91-31.93	43.58-35.15	39.26-32.02
P/E Ratio	47.44-39.45	51.16-40.76	27.21-20.35	27.56-20.48	25.97-18.43	28.80-21.43	24.76-19.97	23.94-19.52
Average Yield %	1.52	1.53	1.58	1.66	2.20	1.75	1.41	1.15

Address: 1400 West 94th Street, Minneapolis, MN 55431 **Telephone:** 952-887-3131	**Web Site:** www.donaldson.com **Officers:** Tod E. Carpenter - President, Chief Executive Officer, Chief Operating Officer, Division Officer Scott J. Robinson - Chief Financial Officer, Vice President	**Auditors:** PricewaterhouseCoopers LLP **Investor Contact:** 952-887-3753 **Transfer Agents:** Wells Fargo Shareowner Services, St. Paul, MN

DOUGLAS EMMETT INC

Exchange	Symbol	Price	52Wk Range	Yield	P/E
NYS	DEI	$40.18 (6/29/2018)	41.39-34.93	2.49	63.78

*7 Year Price Score 106.12 *NYSE Composite Index=100   ***12 Month Price Score 98.81**

Interim Earnings (Per Share)

Qtr.	Mar	Jun	Sep	Dec
2015	0.12	0.09	0.08	0.09
2016	0.10	0.12	0.21	0.13
2017	0.12	0.13	0.15	0.17
2018	0.17	...	...	...

Interim Dividends (Per Share)

Amt	Decl	Ex	Rec	Pay
0.23Q	09/07/2017	09/28/2017	09/29/2017	10/13/2017
0.25Q	12/07/2017	12/28/2017	12/29/2017	01/15/2018
0.25Q	03/01/2018	03/28/2018	03/29/2018	04/17/2018
0.25Q	05/31/2018	06/28/2018	06/29/2018	07/13/2018

Indicated Div: $1.00

Valuation Analysis / Institutional Holding

Forecast EPS	$0.73 (06/10/2018)	No of Institutions	360
Market Cap	$6.8 Billion	Shares	213,182,208
Book Value	$2.5 Billion	% Held	99.45
Price/Book	2.78		
Price/Sales	8.23		

TRADING VOLUME (thousand shares)

Business Summary: REITs (MIC: 5.3.1 SIC: 6798 NAIC: 525930)

Douglas Emmett is a real estate investment trust. Through its interest in Douglas Emmett Properties, LP and its subsidiaries, its consolidated joint ventures (JVs), and its investments in its unconsolidated institutional real estate funds, Co. owns or partially owns, acquires, develops and manages real estate, consisting primarily of office and multifamily properties. At Dec 31 2017, Co. owned a portfolio of 63 office properties (including ancillary retail space), which included 10 office properties owned by its consolidated JVs, 10 multifamily properties containing 3,380 apartment units, and the fee interests in two parcels of land subject to ground leases.

Recent Developments: For the quarter ended Mar 31 2018, net income increased 49.8% to US$32.6 million from US$21.8 million in the year-earlier quarter. Revenues were US$212.2 million, up 9.1% from US$194.5 million the year before.

Prospects: Our evaluation of Douglas Emmett Inc. as of Jan. 21, 2018 is the result of our systematic analysis on three basic characteristics: earnings strength, relative valuation, and recent stock price movement. The company has enjoyed a very positive trend in earnings per share over the past 5 quarters. However, while recent estimates for the company have been mixed, DEI has posted results that were in line with analysts expectations. Based on operating earnings yield, the company is overvalued when compared to all of the companies in our coverage universe. Share price changes over the past year indicates that DEI will perform well over the near term.

Financial Data
(US$ in Thousands)

	3 Mos	12/31/2017	12/31/2016	12/31/2015	12/31/2014	12/31/2013	12/31/2012	12/31/2011
Earnings Per Share	0.63	0.58	0.55	0.39	0.30	0.31	0.16	0.01
Cash Flow Per Share	2.43	2.50	2.27	1.86	1.71	1.71	1.50	1.65
Tang Book Value Per Share	14.44	14.34	12.63	13.07	13.38	13.78	13.97	14.17
Dividends Per Share	0.960	0.940	0.890	0.850	0.810	0.740	0.630	0.490
Dividend Payout %	153.60	162.07	160.65	220.21	270.00	238.71	393.75	4,900.00
Income Statement								
Total Revenue	212,247	812,052	742,551	635,774	599,539	591,536	578,999	575,337
EBITDA	69,334	514,554	461,201	394,153	376,447	368,540	363,307	362,143
Depn & Amortn	3,803	270,856	241,102	197,639	198,799	188,253	186,559	208,563
Income Before Taxes	32,631	98,522	73,951	61,061	49,141	49,739	30,055	5,125
Net Income	28,206	94,443	85,397	58,384	44,621	45,311	22,942	1,451
Average Shares	169,625	161,230	153,190	150,604	176,221	174,802	173,120	159,966
Balance Sheet								
Current Assets	305,413	294,881	215,036	190,262	102,071	121,375	441,788	471,484
Total Assets	8,323,900	8,292,641	7,613,705	6,066,161	5,954,596	5,847,789	6,103,807	6,231,602
Current Liabilities	229,300	272,395	223,267	157,027	168,196	176,297	171,914	193,074
Long-Term Obligations	4,098,900	4,117,390	4,369,537	3,611,276	3,435,290	3,241,140	3,441,140	3,624,156
Total Liabilities	5,865,048	5,855,117	5,692,562	4,139,950	4,011,138	3,877,392	4,124,151	4,366,496
Stockholders' Equity	2,458,852	2,437,524	1,921,143	1,926,211	1,943,458	1,970,397	1,979,656	1,865,106
Shares Outstanding	169,900	169,564	151,530	146,919	144,869	142,605	141,245	131,070
Statistical Record								
Return on Assets %	1.30	1.19	1.25	0.97	0.76	0.76	0.37	0.02
Return on Equity %	4.79	4.33	4.43	3.02	2.28	2.29	1.19	0.08
EBITDA Margin %	32.67	63.36	62.11	62.00	62.79	62.30	62.75	62.94
Net Margin %	13.29	11.63	11.50	9.18	7.44	7.66	3.96	0.25
Asset Turnover	0.10	0.10	0.11	0.11	0.10	0.10	0.09	0.09
Current Ratio	1.33	1.08	0.96	1.21	0.61	0.69	2.57	2.44
Debt to Equity	1.67	1.69	2.27	1.87	1.77	1.64	1.74	1.94
Price Range	41.39-34.93	41.39-36.46	38.70-24.95	31.79-26.85	29.38-23.29	28.18-22.27	24.48-18.46	21.05-15.54
P/E Ratio	65.70-55.44	71.36-62.86	70.36-45.36	81.51-68.85	97.93-77.63	90.90-71.84	153.00-115.38	N.M.
Average Yield %	2.48	2.42	2.65	2.89	2.96	3.02	2.78	2.63

Address: 808 Wilshire Boulevard, Suite 200, Santa Monica, CA 90401 Telephone: 310-255-7700	Web Site: www.douglasemmett.com Officers: Dan A. Emmett - Chairman Jordan L. Kaplan - President, Chief Executive Officer	Auditors: Ernst & Young LLP Investor Contact: 310-255-7751 Transfer Agents: Computershare Investor Services

DOVER CORP

Exchange	Symbol	Price	52Wk Range	Yield	P/E	Div Acheiver
NYS	DOV	$73.20 (6/29/2018)	86.41-64.75	2.57	14.94	62 Years

*7 Year Price Score 108.32 *NYSE Composite Index=100 *12 Month Price Score 98.52

Interim Earnings (Per Share)

Qtr.	Mar	Jun	Sep	Dec
2015	1.28	2.07	1.19	0.91
2016	0.64	0.76	0.83	1.03
2017	1.09	1.04	1.14	1.88
2018	0.84	...	...	...

Interim Dividends (Per Share)

Amt	Decl	Ex	Rec	Pay
0.47Q	11/03/2017	11/29/2017	11/30/2017	12/15/2017
0.47Q	02/09/2018	02/27/2018	02/28/2018	03/15/2018
0.00Q	04/18/2018	05/09/2018	04/30/2018	05/09/2018
0.47Q	05/04/2018	05/30/2018	05/31/2018	06/15/2018

Indicated Div: $1.88 (Div. Reinv. Plan)

Valuation Analysis **Institutional Holding**

Forecast EPS	$4.80	No of Institutions
	(06/14/2018)	1003
Market Cap	$11.3 Billion	Shares
Book Value	$4.4 Billion	169,981,904
Price/Book	2.55	% Held
Price/Sales	1.43	77.70

Business Summary: Industrial Machinery & Equipment (MIC: 7.2.1 SIC: 3559 NAIC: 333220)

Dover is a global manufacturer delivering equipment and components, specialty systems, consumable supplies, software and digital solutions and support services through four operating segments: Energy, which provides solutions and services for production and processing of fuels worldwide; Engineered Systems, which designs, manufactures and services critical equipment and components; Fluids, which is focused on the handling of critical fluids across the retail fueling, chemical, hygienic, oil and gas and industrial end markets; and Refrigeration & Food Equipment, which provides equipment and systems serving the commercial refrigeration and food service industries.

Recent Developments: For the quarter ended Mar 31 2018, net income decreased 23.7% to US$131.4 million from US$172.2 million in the year-earlier quarter. Revenues were US$1.92 billion, up 6.0% from US$1.81 billion the year before. Operating income was US$194.8 million versus US$174.9 million in the prior-year quarter, an increase of 11.4%. Direct operating expenses rose 5.2% to US$1.21 billion from US$1.15 billion in the comparable period the year before. Indirect operating expenses increased 5.7% to US$514.1 million from US$486.3 million in the equivalent prior-year period.

Prospects: Our evaluation of Dover Corp. as of Jan. 21, 2018 is the result of our systematic analysis on three basic characteristics: earnings strength, relative valuation, and recent stock price movement. The company has enjoyed a very positive trend in earnings per share over the past 5 quarters and while recent estimates for the company have been mixed, DOV has posted better than expected results. Based on operating earnings yield, the company is about fairly valued when compared to all of the companies in our coverage universe. Share price changes over the past year indicates that DOV will perform in line with the market over the near term.

Financial Data
(US$ in Thousands)

	3 Mos	12/31/2017	12/31/2016	12/31/2015	12/31/2014	12/31/2013	12/31/2012	12/31/2011
Earnings Per Share	4.90	5.15	3.25	5.46	4.59	5.78	4.41	4.74
Cash Flow Per Share	5.04	5.28	5.54	6.02	5.70	6.88	6.93	5.69
Dividends Per Share	1.850	1.820	1.720	1.640	1.550	1.450	1.330	1.180
Dividend Payout %	37.76	35.34	52.92	30.04	33.77	25.09	30.16	24.89
Income Statement								
Total Revenue	1,921,579	7,830,436	6,794,342	6,956,311	7,752,728	8,729,813	8,104,339	7,950,140
EBITDA	243,639	1,301,834	994,469	1,095,383	1,373,465	1,593,512	1,460,528	1,386,757
Depn & Amortn	49,133	191,285	175,495	167,516	152,079	235,358	201,816	175,997
Income Before Taxes	160,757	973,843	689,332	800,610	1,094,207	1,237,412	1,137,571	1,095,164
Income Taxes	29,322	162,178	180,440	204,729	316,067	271,607	304,452	248,799
Net Income	131,435	811,665	508,892	869,829	775,235	1,003,129	811,070	895,243
Average Shares	157,090	157,744	156,636	159,172	168,842	173,547	183,993	188,887
Balance Sheet								
Current Assets	2,951,999	3,207,120	2,589,191	2,420,779	2,896,822	3,240,162	3,027,844	3,397,130
Total Assets	10,543,040	10,657,653	10,115,991	8,619,763	9,090,385	10,838,172	10,443,943	9,501,450
Current Liabilities	2,080,588	2,298,193	1,940,318	1,367,182	2,039,354	1,615,580	1,986,628	1,202,981
Long-Term Obligations	3,032,003	2,986,702	3,206,637	2,617,342	2,253,041	2,599,201	2,189,350	2,186,230
Total Liabilities	6,097,418	6,274,473	6,316,245	4,975,188	5,389,660	5,460,776	5,524,713	4,570,895
Stockholders' Equity	4,445,622	4,383,180	3,799,746	3,644,575	3,700,725	5,377,396	4,919,230	4,930,555
Shares Outstanding	154,677	154,823	155,428	155,003	163,011	169,906	174,717	183,591
Statistical Record								
Return on Assets %	7.42	7.81	5.42	9.82	7.78	9.43	8.11	9.91
Return on Equity %	18.36	19.84	13.63	23.68	17.08	19.48	16.42	18.93
EBITDA Margin %	12.68	16.63	14.64	15.75	17.72	18.25	18.02	17.44
Net Margin %	6.84	10.37	7.49	12.50	10.00	11.49	10.01	11.26
Asset Turnover	0.76	0.75	0.72	0.79	0.78	0.82	0.81	0.88
Current Ratio	1.42	1.40	1.33	1.77	1.42	2.01	1.52	2.82
Debt to Equity	0.68	0.68	0.84	0.72	0.61	0.48	0.45	0.44
Price Range	86.41-62.20	81.88-61.62	62.26-42.50	62.77-45.19	73.51-54.69	64.64-44.00	44.60-34.11	46.76-29.89
P/E Ratio	17.63-12.69	15.90-11.97	19.16-13.08	11.50-8.28	16.02-11.92	11.18-7.61	10.11-7.73	9.87-6.31
Average Yield %	2.52	2.64	3.16	3.01	2.35	2.68	3.34	2.95

Address: 3005 Highland Parkway, Downers Grove, IL 60515
Telephone: 630-541-1540

Web Site: www.dovercorporation.com
Officers: Michael F. Johnston - Chairman Richard Joseph Tobin - President, Chief Executive Officer

Auditors: PricewaterhouseCoopers LLP
Investor Contact: 212-922-1640
Transfer Agents: ComputerShare Investor Services, Providence, RI

DOWDUPONT INC

Exchange	Symbol	Price	52Wk Range	Yield	P/E
NYS	DWDP	$65.92 (6/29/2018)	77.02-62.04	2.31	86.74

*7 Year Price Score N/A   ***NYSE Composite Index=100**   ***12 Month Price Score N/A**

Interim Earnings (Per Share)

Qtr.	Mar	Jun	Sep	Dec
2018	0.47	...	...	...

Interim Dividends (Per Share)

Amt	Decl	Ex	Rec	Pay
0.38Q	11/02/2017	11/14/2017	11/15/2017	12/15/2017
0.38Q	02/15/2018	02/27/2018	02/28/2018	03/15/2018
0.38Q	04/25/2018	05/30/2018	05/31/2018	06/15/2018
0.38Q	06/25/2018	08/30/2018	08/31/2018	09/14/2018

Indicated Div: $1.52

Valuation Analysis   **Institutional Holding**

Forecast EPS	$4.20	No of Institutions	
	(06/14/2018)	1966	
Market Cap	$153.0 Billion	Shares	
Book Value	$101.3 Billion	1,645,553,792	
Price/Book	1.51	% Held	
Price/Sales	2.16	N/A	

TRADING VOLUME (thousand shares)

2009 2010 2011 2012 2013 2014 2015 2016 2017 2018

Business Summary: Plastics (MIC: 8.4.2 SIC: 2821 NAIC: 325211)

DowDuPont is a holding company comprised of The Dow Chemical Company and E.I. du Pont de Nemours & Company. Co. is comprised of three divisions: Agriculture; Materials Science and Specialty Products. The Agriculture division offers a portfolio of products and technologies, and a pipeline of germplasm, traits and crop protection. The Materials Science division offers solutions within the packaging, infrastructure and consumer care markets. The Science and Specialty Products division assists customers with solving problems in the electronics and imaging, industrial biosciences, nutrition & health, safety & construction, sustainable solutions, transportation and advanced polymers industries.

Recent Developments: For the year ended Dec 31 2017, income from continuing operations decreased 62.1% to US$1.67 billion from US$4.40 billion a year earlier. Net income decreased 63.9% to US$1.59 billion from US$4.40 billion in the prior year. Revenues were US$62.48 billion, up 29.7% from US$48.16 billion the year before. Direct operating expenses rose 33.9% to US$50.41 billion from US$37.64 billion in the comparable period the year before. Indirect operating expenses increased 61.4% to US$11.53 billion from US$7.14 billion in the equivalent prior-year period.

Prospects: Our evaluation of DowDuPont Inc. as of Jan. 21, 2018 is the result of our systematic analysis on three basic characteristics: earnings strength, relative valuation, and recent stock price movement. The company has generated a negative trend in earnings per share over the past 5 quarters. Because the company lacks sufficient analyst estimate data, we place greater weight on the historical EPS trend as the measure of earnings strength. Based on operating earnings yield, the company is about fairly valued when compared to all of the companies in our coverage universe. Share price changes over the past year indicates that DWDP will perform in line with the market over the near term.

Financial Data

(US$ in Millions)	3 Mos	12/31/2017	12/31/2016	12/31/2015
Earnings Per Share	0.76	0.91	3.52	6.15
Cash Flow Per Share	2.62	5.50	5.04	6.73
Tang Book Value Per Share	3.36	3.24	3.87	...
Dividends Per Share	0.760	0.380	1.840	1.720
Dividend Payout %	100.00	41.76	52.27	27.97
Income Statement				
Total Revenue	21,510	62,484	48,158	48,778
EBITDA	2,338	5,132	7,396	12,458
Depn & Amortn	703	3,768	2,674	2,327
Income Before Taxes	1,285	429	3,971	9,256
Income Taxes	389	(476)	9	2,147
Net Income	1,104	1,460	4,318	7,685
Average Shares	2,335	1,598	1,123	1,241
Balance Sheet				
Current Assets	49,733	49,893	23,659	...
Total Assets	192,441	192,164	79,511	...
Current Liabilities	26,617	26,128	12,604	...
Long-Term Obligations	29,343	30,056	20,456	...
Total Liabilities	91,181	91,834	53,524	...
Stockholders' Equity	101,260	100,330	25,987	...
Shares Outstanding	2,321	2,328	1,211	...
Statistical Record				
Return on Assets %	1.23	1.07	5.84	...
Return on Equity %	2.61	2.31	16.77	...
EBITDA Margin %	10.87	8.21	15.36	25.54
Net Margin %	5.13	2.34	8.97	15.76
Asset Turnover	0.52	0.46	0.65	...
Current Ratio	1.87	1.91	1.88	...
Debt to Equity	0.29	0.30	0.79	...
Price Range	77.02-62.41	73.32-64.68	...	...
P/E Ratio	101.34-82.12	80.57-71.08	...	...
Average Yield %	1.07	0.54	...	...

Address: c/o The Dow Chemical Company, 2030 Dow Center, Midland, MI 48674
Telephone: 989-636-1000

Web Site: www.dow-dupont.com
Officers: Andrew N. Liveris - Executive Chairman
Edward D. Breen - Chief Executive Officer

Auditors: DELOITTE & TOUCHE LLP
Investor Contact: 180-042-28193

DRIL-QUIP INC

Exchange	Symbol	Price	52Wk Range	Yield	P/E
NYS	DRQ	$51.40 (6/29/2018)	56.35-36.20	N/A	N/A

*7 Year Price Score 52.15 *NYSE Composite Index=100 *12 Month Price Score 102.14

Interim Earnings (Per Share)

Qtr.	Mar	Jun	Sep	Dec
2015	1.38	1.01	1.32	1.28
2016	0.97	0.96	0.51	0.03
2017	0.00	0.00	(0.78)	(1.91)
2018	(0.20)	...	...	...

Interim Dividends (Per Share)

No Dividends Paid

Valuation Analysis   **Institutional Holding**

Forecast EPS	$-0.32	No of Institutions	
	(06/14/2018)	346	
Market Cap	$2.0 Billion	Shares	
Book Value	$1.3 Billion	55,548,724	
Price/Book	1.50	% Held	
Price/Sales	4.50	99.79	

TRADING VOLUME (thousand shares)

Business Summary: Equipment & Services (MIC: 9.1.3 SIC: 3533 NAIC: 333132)

Dril-Quip designs, manufactures, sells and services offshore drilling and production equipment. Co.'s primary products consist of subsea and surface wellheads, subsea and surface production trees, subsea control systems and manifolds, mudline hanger systems, specialty connectors and associated pipe, drilling and production riser systems, liner hangers, wellhead connectors and diverters. Co. also provides technical advisory assistance on an as-requested basis during installation of its products, as well as rework and reconditioning services for customer-owned Co.'s products. Co.'s customers may rent or purchase running tools from Co. for use in the installation and retrieval of its products.

Recent Developments: For the quarter ended Mar 31 2018, net loss amounted to US$7.4 million versus net income of US$94,000 in the year-earlier quarter. Revenues were US$99.2 million, down 16.8% from US$119.2 million the year before. Operating loss was US$6.3 million versus a loss of US$870,000 in the prior-year quarter. Direct operating expenses declined 17.8% to US$67.8 million from US$82.4 million in the comparable period the year before. Indirect operating expenses were unchanged at US$37.7 million versus the equivalent prior-year period.

Prospects: Our evaluation of Dril-Quip Inc. as of Jan. 21, 2018 is the result of our systematic analysis on three basic characteristics: earnings strength, relative valuation, and recent stock price movement. The company has enjoyed a very positive trend in earnings per share over the past 5 quarters. However, while recent estimates for the company have been mixed, DRQ has posted better than expected results. Based on operating earnings yield, the company is overvalued when compared to all of the companies in our coverage universe. Share price changes over the past year indicates that DRQ will perform very poorly over the near term.

Financial Data

(US$ in Thousands)	3 Mos	12/31/2017	12/31/2016	12/31/2015	12/31/2014	12/31/2013	12/31/2012	12/31/2011
Earnings Per Share	(2.89)	(2.69)	2.47	4.98	5.19	4.16	2.94	2.36
Cash Flow Per Share	2.86	2.88	6.55	4.96	3.74	3.99	(0.20)	2.54
Tang Book Value Per Share	31.97	31.69	34.19	34.90	31.98	30.54	26.35	23.03
Income Statement								
Total Revenue	99,173	455,469	538,731	844,310	930,957	872,372	733,031	601,342
EBITDA	1,964	(30,536)	144,459	279,335	309,948	252,845	187,916	152,652
Depn & Amortn	8,241	38,600	31,600	30,500	31,200	29,300	26,224	23,013
Income Before Taxes	(4,482)	(65,644)	115,868	249,771	279,380	224,097	162,122	130,004
Income Taxes	2,901	34,995	22,647	57,763	70,668	54,270	42,913	34,737
Net Income	(7,383)	(100,639)	93,221	192,008	208,712	169,827	119,209	95,267
Average Shares	37,729	37,457	37,667	38,531	40,190	40,865	40,523	40,322
Balance Sheet								
Current Assets	1,002,131	1,008,549	1,056,711	1,124,298	1,127,140	1,078,813	924,388	799,302
Total Assets	1,397,862	1,399,805	1,461,404	1,428,250	1,449,251	1,394,612	1,231,447	1,085,858
Current Liabilities	87,238	99,911	101,480	100,815	198,642	142,790	155,089	151,000
Total Liabilities	92,753	105,344	104,980	103,792	204,059	152,594	165,015	160,614
Stockholders' Equity	1,305,109	1,294,461	1,356,424	1,324,458	1,245,192	1,242,018	1,066,432	925,244
Shares Outstanding	38,136	38,132	37,797	37,951	38,932	40,673	40,475	40,175
Statistical Record								
Return on Assets %	N.M.	N.M.	6.43	13.35	14.68	12.93	10.26	9.37
Return on Equity %	N.M.	N.M.	6.94	14.94	16.78	14.71	11.94	10.87
EBITDA Margin %	1.98	N.M.	26.81	33.08	33.29	28.98	25.64	25.39
Net Margin %	N.M.	N.M.	17.30	22.74	22.42	19.47	16.26	15.84
Asset Turnover	0.31	0.32	0.37	0.59	0.65	0.66	0.63	0.59
Current Ratio	11.49	10.09	10.41	11.15	5.67	7.56	5.96	5.29
Price Range	56.35-36.20	67.10-36.20	65.65-47.50	80.20-55.11	115.81-70.00	119.38-73.05	76.61-58.72	81.36-49.38
P/E Ratio	...	...	26.58-19.23	16.10-11.07	22.31-13.49	28.70-17.56	26.06-19.97	34.47-20.92

Address: 6401 N. Eldridge Parkway, Houston, TX 77041	**Web Site:** www.dril-quip.com	**Auditors:** PricewaterhouseCoopers LLP
Telephone: 713-939-7711	**Officers:** John V. Lovoi - Chairman Blake T. DeBerry - President, Chief Executive Officer, Senior Vice President	**Investor Contact:** 713-939-7711
Fax: 713-939-8063		**Transfer Agents:** Computershare, Jersey City, NJ

DTE ENERGY CO

Exchange	Symbol	Price	52Wk Range	Yield	P/E
NYS	DTE	$103.63 (6/29/2018)	115.99-94.70	3.41	16.99

*7 Year Price Score 107.44 *NYSE Composite Index=100 *12 Month Price Score 93.59

Interim Earnings (Per Share)

Qtr.	Mar	Jun	Sep	Dec
2015	1.53	0.61	1.47	0.44
2016	1.37	0.84	1.88	0.73
2017	2.23	0.99	1.51	1.60
2018	2.00	...	...	...

Interim Dividends (Per Share)

Amt	Decl	Ex	Rec	Pay
0.882Q	11/03/2017	12/15/2017	12/18/2017	01/15/2018
0.882Q	02/02/2018	03/16/2018	03/19/2018	04/15/2018
0.882Q	05/03/2018	06/15/2018	06/18/2018	07/15/2018
0.882Q	06/21/2018	09/14/2018	09/17/2018	10/15/2018

Indicated Div: $3.53

Valuation Analysis   **Institutional Holding**

Forecast EPS	$5.78	No of Institutions	
	(06/13/2018)	873	
Market Cap	$18.8 Billion	Shares	
Book Value	$9.9 Billion	157,820,288	
Price/Book	1.90	% Held	
Price/Sales	1.43	63.93	

Business Summary: Electric Utilities (MIC: 3.1.1 SIC: 4911 NAIC: 221111)

DTE Energy is a holding company. Co. is engaged in the generation, purchase, distribution and sale of electricity in southeastern Michigan through its DTE Electric Company subsidiary, as well as in the purchase, storage, transportation, distribution and sale of natural gas throughout Michigan and the sale of storage and transportation capacity through its DTE Gas Company subsidiary. Co.'s non-utility operations are: natural gas pipelines, gathering and storage businesses; power and industrial projects; and energy marketing and trading operations. As of Dec 31 2017, DTE Electric and DTE Gas Company served approximately 2.2 million and 1.3 million, respectively, customers throughout Michigan.

Recent Developments: For the quarter ended Mar 31 2018, net income decreased 10.9% to US$351.0 million from US$394.0 million in the year-earlier quarter. Revenues were US$3.75 billion, up 16.0% from US$3.24 billion the year before. Operating income was US$504.0 million versus US$585.0 million in the prior-year quarter, a decrease of 13.8%. Direct operating expenses rose 24.7% to US$2.86 billion from US$2.29 billion in the comparable period the year before. Indirect operating expenses increased 8.7% to US$389.0 million from US$358.0 million in the equivalent prior-year period.

Prospects: Our evaluation of DTE Energy Co. as of Jan. 21, 2018 is the result of our systematic analysis on three basic characteristics: earnings strength, relative valuation, and recent stock price movement. The company has generated a negative trend in earnings per share over the past 5 quarters and while recent estimates for the company have been mixed, DTE has posted results that fell short of analysts expectations. Based on operating earnings yield, the company is undervalued when compared to all of the companies in our coverage universe. Share price changes over the past year indicates that DTE will perform very well over the near term.

Financial Data

(US$ in Thousands)	3 Mos	12/31/2017	12/31/2016	12/31/2015	12/31/2014	12/31/2013	12/31/2012	12/31/2011
Earnings Per Share	6.10	6.32	4.83	4.05	5.10	3.76	3.55	4.18
Cash Flow Per Share	12.04	11.83	11.61	10.68	10.39	12.31	12.88	11.88
Tang Book Value Per Share	37.07	35.41	32.79	37.14	35.07	32.64	30.29	29.05
Dividends Per Share	3.415	3.357	3.055	2.840	2.690	2.585	2.415	2.322
Dividend Payout %	55.98	53.13	63.25	70.12	52.75	68.75	68.03	55.56
Income Statement								
Total Revenue	3,753,000	12,607,000	10,630,000	10,337,000	12,301,000	9,661,000	8,791,000	8,897,000
EBITDA	566,000	1,912,000	1,646,000	1,485,000	1,771,000	1,420,000	1,465,000	1,536,000
Depn & Amortn	15,000	101,000	89,000	98,000	77,000	71,000	75,000	65,000
Income Before Taxes	419,000	1,287,000	1,105,000	950,000	1,275,000	922,000	960,000	987,000
Income Taxes	68,000	175,000	271,000	230,000	364,000	254,000	286,000	267,000
Net Income	361,000	1,134,000	868,000	727,000	905,000	661,000	610,000	711,000
Average Shares	180,000	179,000	179,000	179,000	177,000	175,000	172,000	170,000
Balance Sheet								
Current Assets	2,957,000	3,081,000	2,762,000	2,575,000	3,087,000	2,806,000	2,915,000	3,196,000
Total Assets	33,841,000	33,767,000	32,041,000	28,737,000	27,974,000	25,935,000	26,339,000	26,009,000
Current Liabilities	2,541,000	2,812,000	2,437,000	2,528,000	2,577,000	3,189,000	2,768,000	2,628,000
Long-Term Obligations	12,185,000	12,185,000	11,269,000	8,835,000	8,343,000	7,214,000	7,014,000	7,187,000
Total Liabilities	23,953,000	24,255,000	23,030,000	19,965,000	19,647,000	18,014,000	18,966,000	19,000,000
Stockholders' Equity	9,888,000	9,512,000	9,011,000	8,772,000	8,327,000	7,921,000	7,373,000	7,009,000
Shares Outstanding	181,483	179,386	179,432	179,470	176,991	177,087	172,351	169,247
Statistical Record								
Return on Assets %	3.32	3.45	2.85	2.56	3.36	2.53	2.32	2.79
Return on Equity %	11.48	12.24	9.74	8.50	11.14	8.64	8.46	10.36
EBITDA Margin %	15.08	15.17	15.48	14.37	14.40	14.70	16.66	17.26
Net Margin %	9.62	9.00	8.17	7.03	7.36	6.84	6.94	7.99
Asset Turnover	0.40	0.38	0.35	0.36	0.46	0.37	0.33	0.35
Current Ratio	1.16	1.10	1.13	1.02	1.20	0.88	1.05	1.22
Debt to Equity	1.23	1.28	1.25	1.01	1.00	0.91	0.95	1.03
Price Range	115.99-98.49	115.99-97.10	100.10-78.38	91.54-73.78	90.18-65.10	72.90-60.05	62.10-52.96	55.05-44.03
P/E Ratio	19.01-16.15	18.35-15.36	20.72-16.23	22.60-18.22	17.68-12.76	19.39-15.97	17.49-14.92	13.17-10.53
Average Yield %	3.18	3.15	3.34	3.52	3.55	3.84	4.18	4.69

Address: One Energy Plaza, Detroit, MI 48226-1279	**Web Site:** www.dteenergy.com	**Auditors:** PricewaterhouseCoopers LLP
Telephone: 313-235-4000	**Officers:** Gerard M Anderson - Chairman, Chief Executive Officer, President Jeffrey A. Jewell - Vice President, Controller, Chief Accounting Officer	**Transfer Agents:** Wells Fargo Bank, N.A.

DUKE ENERGY CORP

Exchange	Symbol	Price	52Wk Range	Yield	P/E	Div Acheiver
NYS	DUK	$79.08 (6/29/2018)	91.09-72.12	4.69	18.74	13 Years

*7 Year Price Score 89.45 *NYSE Composite Index=100 ***12 Month Price Score 92.12**

Interim Earnings (Per Share)

Qtr.	Mar	Jun	Sep	Dec
2015	1.22	0.78	1.35	0.69
2016	1.01	0.74	1.70	(0.33)
2017	1.02	0.98	1.36	1.00
2018	0.88	...	...	...

Interim Dividends (Per Share)

Amt	Decl	Ex	Rec	Pay
0.89Q	10/26/2017	11/16/2017	11/17/2017	12/18/2017
0.89Q	01/05/2018	02/15/2018	02/16/2018	03/16/2018
0.89Q	05/03/2018	05/17/2018	05/18/2018	06/18/2018
0.927Q	07/06/2018	08/16/2018	08/17/2018	09/17/2018

Indicated Div: $3.71 (Div. Reinv. Plan)

Valuation Analysis | **Institutional Holding**

Forecast EPS	$4.73 (06/14/2018)	No of Institutions	1829
Market Cap	$55.4 Billion	Shares	549,281,472
Book Value	$41.8 Billion	% Held	N/A
Price/Book	1.33		
Price/Sales	2.31		

Business Summary: Electric Utilities (MIC: 3.1.1 SIC: 4931 NAIC: 221122)

Duke Energy is an energy company. Through its subsidiaries, Co. conducts its operations in three reportable operating segments: Electric Utilities and Infrastructure, which provides retail electric service through the generation, transmission, distribution and sale of electricity; Gas Utilities and Infrastructure, which conducts natural gas operations primarily through the regulated public utilities of Piedmont and Duke Energy Ohio; and Commercial Renewables, which primarily acquires, builds, develops and operates wind and solar renewable generation throughout the continental U.S. The portfolio includes nonregulated renewable energy and energy storage businesses.

Recent Developments: For the year ended Dec 31 2017, income from continuing operations increased 19.1% to US$3.07 billion from US$2.58 billion a year earlier. Net income increased 41.2% to US$3.06 billion from US$2.17 billion in the prior year. Revenues were US$23.57 billion, up 3.6% from US$22.74 billion the year before. Operating income was US$5.78 billion versus US$5.34 billion in the prior year, an increase of 8.2%. Direct operating expenses declined 1.6% to US$12.77 billion from US$12.98 billion in the comparable period the year before. Indirect operating expenses increased 13.3% to US$5.01 billion from US$4.43 billion in the equivalent prior-year period.

Prospects: Our evaluation of Duke Energy Corp. Holding Co as of Jan. 21, 2018 is the result of our systematic analysis on three basic characteristics: earnings strength, relative valuation, and recent stock price movement. The company has managed to produce a neutral trend in earnings per share over the past 5 quarters. However, while recent estimates for the company have been mixed, DUK has posted better than expected results. Based on operating earnings yield, the company is undervalued when compared to all of the companies in our coverage universe. Share price changes over the past year indicates that DUK will perform very well over the near term.

Financial Data

(US$ in Thousands)	3 Mos	12/31/2017	12/31/2016	12/31/2015	12/31/2014	12/31/2013	12/31/2012	12/31/2011
Earnings Per Share	4.22	4.36	3.11	4.05	2.66	3.76	3.07	3.84
Cash Flow Per Share	9.61	9.48	9.81	9.62	9.32	9.04	9.11	8.27
Tang Book Value Per Share	31.95	31.92	30.87	33.99	34.73	35.40	34.40	41.68
Dividends Per Share	3.525	3.490	3.360	3.240	3.150	3.090	3.030	2.970
Dividend Payout %	83.53	80.05	108.04	80.00	118.42	82.18	49.84	77.34
Income Statement								
Total Revenue	6,135,000	23,565,000	22,743,000	23,459,000	23,925,000	24,598,000	19,624,000	14,529,000
EBITDA	2,431,000	10,166,000	9,524,000	9,256,000	9,076,000	8,547,000	6,147,000	5,137,000
Depn & Amortn	1,089,000	4,046,000	3,880,000	3,613,000	3,507,000	3,229,000	2,652,000	2,026,000
Income Before Taxes	827,000	4,147,000	3,749,000	4,068,000	4,004,000	3,798,000	2,303,000	2,305,000
Income Taxes	181,000	1,196,000	1,156,000	1,326,000	1,669,000	1,261,000	705,000	752,000
Net Income	620,000	3,059,000	2,152,000	2,816,000	1,883,000	2,665,000	1,768,000	1,706,000
Average Shares	701,000	700,000	691,000	694,000	707,000	706,000	575,000	444,333
Balance Sheet								
Current Assets	8,279,000	8,453,000	8,039,000	8,322,000	11,575,000	10,516,000	10,122,000	6,880,000
Total Assets	138,541,000	137,914,000	132,761,000	121,156,000	120,709,000	114,779,000	113,856,000	62,526,000
Current Liabilities	12,998,000	12,482,000	11,551,000	11,400,000	11,233,000	8,644,000	10,029,000	5,528,000
Long-Term Obligations	49,030,000	49,035,000	45,576,000	37,495,000	37,213,000	38,152,000	36,351,000	18,679,000
Total Liabilities	96,749,000	96,175,000	91,728,000	81,429,000	79,834,000	73,449,000	72,900,000	39,754,000
Stockholders' Equity	41,792,000	41,739,000	41,033,000	39,727,000	40,875,000	41,330,000	40,956,000	22,772,000
Shares Outstanding	701,000	700,000	700,000	688,000	707,000	706,000	704,000	445,333
Statistical Record								
Return on Assets %	2.17	2.26	1.69	2.33	1.60	2.33	2.00	2.81
Return on Equity %	7.14	7.39	5.31	6.99	4.58	6.48	5.53	7.53
EBITDA Margin %	39.63	43.14	41.88	39.46	37.94	34.75	31.32	35.36
Net Margin %	10.11	12.98	9.46	12.00	7.87	10.83	9.01	11.74
Asset Turnover	0.18	0.17	0.18	0.19	0.20	0.22	0.22	0.24
Current Ratio	0.64	0.68	0.70	0.73	1.03	1.22	1.01	1.24
Debt to Equity	1.17	1.17	1.11	0.94	0.91	0.92	0.89	0.82
Price Range	91.09-74.32	91.09-76.50	87.23-71.04	89.36-65.83	86.83-67.13	75.20-63.80	69.84-59.87	66.18-51.75
P/E Ratio	21.59-17.61	20.89-17.55	28.05-22.84	22.06-16.25	32.64-25.24	20.00-16.97	22.75-19.50	17.23-13.48
Average Yield %	4.22	4.15	4.27	4.33	4.27	4.46	2.36	5.22

Address: 550 South Tryon Street, Charlotte, NC 28202-1803
Telephone: 704-382-3853

Web Site: www.duke-energy.com
Officers: Lynn J. Good - Chairman, President, Chief Executive Officer, Vice-Chairman, Group Executive, Chief Financial Officer Melissa H. Anderson - Executive Vice President, Chief Human Resources Officer, Senior Vice President

Auditors: Deloitte & Touche LLP
Investor Contact: 704-382-4070
Transfer Agents: Duke Energy, Charlotte, NC

DUKE REALTY CORP

Exchange	Symbol	Price	52Wk Range	Yield	P/E
NYS	DRE	$29.03 (6/29/2018)	30.14-24.52	2.76	6.35

*7 Year Price Score 111.68 *NYSE Composite Index=100 *12 Month Price Score 101.29

Interim Earnings (Per Share)

Qtr.	Mar	Jun	Sep	Dec
2015	0.19	1.30	0.22	0.07
2016	0.12	0.31	0.32	0.13
2017	0.20	3.38	0.46	0.53
2018	0.20	...	...	...

Interim Dividends (Per Share)

Amt	Decl	Ex	Rec	Pay
0.20Q	10/25/2017	11/15/2017	11/16/2017	11/30/2017
0.85Sp	11/21/2017	11/30/2017	12/01/2017	12/12/2017
0.20Q	01/31/2018	02/14/2018	02/15/2018	02/28/2018
0.20Q	04/25/2018	05/15/2018	05/16/2018	05/31/2018

Indicated Div: $0.80 (Div. Reinv. Plan)

Valuation Analysis — **Institutional Holding**

Forecast EPS	$0.54 (06/13/2018)	No of Institutions 614
Market Cap	$10.4 Billion	Shares 406,936,096
Book Value	$4.5 Billion	% Held N/A
Price/Book	2.29	
Price/Sales	12.42	

Business Summary: REITs (MIC: 5.3.1 SIC: 6798 NAIC: 525930)

Duke Realty is a self-administered and self-managed real estate investment trust and is the sole general partner of Duke Realty Limited Partnership. As of Dec 31 2017, Co. owned or jointly controlled 509 industrial, medical office and other properties; and owned, including through ownership interests in unconsolidated joint ventures 1,900 acres of land and controlled an additional 1,600 acres through purchase options. Co. had two operating segments at Dec 31 2017, the first consisting of the ownership and rental of industrial real estate investments. The second segment consists of various real estate services such as property management, asset management, maintenance and leasing.

Recent Developments: For the quarter ended Mar 31 2018, income from continuing operations increased 12.4% to US$73.5 million from US$65.4 million in the year-earlier quarter. Net income increased 4.1% to US$73.6 million from US$70.8 million in the year-earlier quarter. Revenues were US$234.6 million, up 29.5% from US$181.1 million the year before. Revenues from property income rose 12.7% to US$193.5 million from US$171.7 million in the corresponding quarter a year earlier.

Prospects: Our evaluation of Duke Realty Corp. as of Jan. 21, 2018 is the result of our systematic analysis on three basic characteristics: earnings strength, relative valuation, and recent stock price movement. The company has generated a negative trend in earnings per share over the past 5 quarters. Because the company lacks sufficient analyst estimate data, we place greater weight on the historical EPS trend as the measure of earnings strength. Based on operating earnings yield, the company is overvalued when compared to all of the companies in our coverage universe. Share price changes over the past year indicates that DRE will perform well over the near term.

Financial Data

(US$ in Thousands)	3 Mos	12/31/2017	12/31/2016	12/31/2015	12/31/2014	12/31/2013	12/31/2012	12/31/2011
Earnings Per Share	4.57	4.56	0.88	1.77	0.60	0.47	(0.48)	0.11
Cash Flow Per Share	1.27	1.26	1.28	1.10	1.32	1.35	1.11	1.34
Tang Book Value Per Share	12.70	12.72	9.77	9.22	8.31	7.86	7.04	7.59
Dividends Per Share	1.630	1.620	0.730	0.890	0.680	0.680	0.680	0.680
Dividend Payout %	35.67	35.53	82.95	50.28	113.33	144.68	...	618.18
Income Statement								
Total Revenue	234,557	780,934	902,244	949,432	1,164,704	1,081,790	1,109,440	1,274,274
EBITDA	170,050	541,813	658,239	611,171	639,454	517,941	414,918	480,821
Depn & Amortn	78,947	242,606	255,419	253,683	290,279	288,583	262,825	267,222
Income Before Taxes	75,566	226,925	265,279	188,581	130,808	2,350	(92,563)	(8,796)
Income Taxes	10,329	(357)	(589)	(3,928)	(844)	(5,080)	(103)	(194)
Net Income	72,963	1,634,431	312,143	615,310	243,588	190,592	(73,977)	95,565
Average Shares	360,400	362,011	357,076	352,197	340,446	326,712	267,900	259,598
Balance Sheet								
Current Assets	296,758	193,474	159,375	174,619	211,786	182,908	216,229	382,211
Total Assets	7,427,674	7,388,196	6,772,002	6,917,113	7,754,839	7,752,614	7,560,101	7,004,437
Current Liabilities	197,676	178,939	254,002	263,318	323,687	308,945	319,071	282,480
Long-Term Obligations	2,496,456	2,422,891	2,908,477	3,341,739	4,453,403	4,254,376	4,446,170	3,809,589
Total Liabilities	2,894,169	2,855,352	3,306,184	3,735,181	4,894,514	4,739,371	4,968,687	4,289,751
Stockholders' Equity	4,533,505	4,532,844	3,465,818	3,181,932	2,860,325	3,013,243	2,591,414	2,714,686
Shares Outstanding	357,025	356,361	354,756	345,285	344,112	326,399	279,423	252,927
Statistical Record								
Return on Assets %	22.76	23.08	4.55	8.39	3.14	2.49	N.M.	1.30
Return on Equity %	40.93	40.87	9.37	20.37	8.29	6.80	N.M.	3.38
EBITDA Margin %	72.50	69.38	72.96	64.37	54.90	47.88	37.40	37.73
Net Margin %	31.11	209.29	34.60	64.81	20.91	17.62	N.M.	7.50
Asset Turnover	0.12	0.11	0.13	0.13	0.15	0.14	0.15	0.17
Current Ratio	1.50	1.08	0.63	0.66	0.65	0.59	0.68	1.35
Debt to Equity	0.55	0.53	0.84	1.05	1.56	1.41	1.72	1.40
Price Range	30.14-24.52	30.14-24.04	28.79-18.76	22.58-17.61	20.63-14.53	18.71-13.87	15.77-12.02	15.51-9.70
P/E Ratio	6.60-5.37	6.61-5.27	32.72-21.32	12.76-9.95	34.38-24.22	39.81-29.51	...	141.00-88.18
Average Yield %	5.87	5.83	3.00	4.40	3.86	4.24	4.82	5.31

Address: 600 East 96th Street, Suite 100, Indianapolis, IN 46240 **Telephone:** 317-808-6000	**Web Site:** www.dukerealty.com **Officers:** James B. (Jim) Connor - Senior Executive Vice President, Chief Operating Officer, Region Officer, Chairman, President, Chief Executive Officer Peter D. Harrington - Executive Vice President	**Auditors:** KPMG LLP **Investor Contact:** 317-808-6060 **Transfer Agents:** American Stock Transfer & Trust Company, New York, NY

DUN & BRADSTREET CORP (DE)

Exchange	Symbol	Price	52Wk Range	Yield	P/E	Div Acheiver
NYS	DNB	$122.65 (6/29/2018)	133.42-105.35	1.70	24.14	10 Years

*7 Year Price Score 90.81   *NYSE Composite Index=100   *12 Month Price Score 103.75

Interim Earnings (Per Share)

Qtr.	Mar	Jun	Sep	Dec
2015	1.13	(0.22)	1.62	2.11
2016	0.82	0.51	(0.80)	2.12
2017	0.42	1.22	1.45	0.70
2018	1.71	...	...	...

Interim Dividends (Per Share)

Amt	Decl	Ex	Rec	Pay
0.502Q	08/02/2017	08/21/2017	08/23/2017	09/08/2017
0.502Q	10/19/2017	11/21/2017	11/22/2017	12/08/2017
0.522Q	02/12/2018	02/21/2018	02/22/2018	03/09/2018
0.522Q	05/09/2018	05/22/2018	05/23/2018	06/08/2018

Indicated Div: $2.09

Valuation Analysis

		Institutional Holding	
Forecast EPS	$8.49	No of Institutions	
	(06/13/2018)	530	
Market Cap	$4.5 Billion	Shares	
Book Value	N/A	44,653,024	
Price/Book	N/A	% Held	
Price/Sales	2.55	70.85	

TRADING VOLUME (thousand shares)

Business Summary: Business Services (MIC: 7.5.2 SIC: 7323 NAIC: 561450)

Dun & Bradstreet is a provider of commercial data, analytics and insight on businesses. Customers use Co.'s Risk Management Solutions™ to mitigate credit, compliance and supplier risk, increase cash flow and drive profitability, and Co.'s Sales & Marketing Solutions™ to use data to grow sales and improve marketing effectiveness and also for data management capabilities. Co. manages and reports its business through two segments: Americas, which consists of its operations in the U.S., Canada, and its Latin America Worldwide Network; and Non-Americas, which consists of its operations in the U.K., Greater China, India, and its European and Asia Pacific Worldwide Networks.

Recent Developments: For the quarter ended Mar 31 2018, income from continuing operations increased 292.0% to US$63.9 million from US$16.3 million in the year-earlier quarter. Net income increased 312.3% to US$63.9 million from US$15.5 million in the year-earlier quarter. Revenues were US$418.2 million, up 9.6% from US$381.5 million the year before. Operating income was US$94.7 million versus US$41.3 million in the prior-year quarter, an increase of 129.3%. Direct operating expenses declined 1.7% to US$139.2 million from US$141.6 million in the comparable period the year before. Indirect operating expenses decreased 7.2% to US$184.3 million from US$198.6 million in the equivalent prior-year period.

Prospects: Our evaluation of Dun & Bradstreet Corp. as of Jan. 21, 2018 is the result of our systematic analysis on three basic characteristics: earnings strength, relative valuation, and recent stock price movement. The company has enjoyed a very positive trend in earnings per share over the past 5 quarters and while recent estimates for the company have remained steady, DNB has posted better than expected results. Based on operating earnings yield, the company is undervalued when compared to all of the companies in our coverage universe. Share price changes over the past year indicates that DNB will perform in line with the market over the near term.

Financial Data

(US$ in Thousands)	3 Mos	12/31/2017	12/31/2016	12/31/2015	12/31/2014	12/31/2013	12/31/2012	12/31/2011
Earnings Per Share	5.08	3.79	2.65	4.64	7.99	6.54	6.43	5.28
Cash Flow Per Share	7.68	7.76	8.82	9.51	8.64	8.52	7.83	6.40
Dividends Per Share	2.030	2.010	1.930	1.850	1.760	1.600	1.520	1.440
Dividend Payout %	39.96	53.03	72.83	39.87	22.03	24.46	23.64	27.27
Income Statement								
Total Revenue	418,200	1,742,500	1,703,700	1,637,100	1,681,800	1,655,200	1,663,000	1,758,500
EBITDA	104,400	393,000	264,200	335,600	398,500	443,500	428,200	415,900
Depn & Amortn	10,200	12,200	9,300	6,200	8,300	8,100	11,200	12,300
Income Before Taxes	80,900	322,700	203,600	280,000	348,600	396,000	378,300	368,100
Income Taxes	15,900	179,700	99,900	74,200	52,600	135,500	83,100	109,200
Net Income	63,900	140,900	97,400	168,800	294,400	258,500	295,500	260,300
Average Shares	37,300	37,200	36,800	36,400	36,900	39,500	46,000	49,300
Balance Sheet								
Current Assets	463,700	1,093,700	944,400	959,600	935,900	822,400	747,400	726,900
Total Assets	1,943,300	2,480,900	2,209,200	2,273,600	1,986,200	1,890,300	1,991,800	1,977,100
Current Liabilities	899,000	1,052,400	1,010,000	959,200	1,158,900	852,300	876,700	953,500
Long-Term Obligations	1,293,900	1,645,600	1,594,500	1,804,100	1,352,200	1,516,000	1,290,700	963,900
Total Liabilities	2,793,200	3,308,200	3,211,200	3,390,400	3,189,500	2,938,700	3,009,200	2,721,000
Stockholders' Equity	(849,900)	(827,300)	(1,002,000)	(1,116,800)	(1,203,300)	(1,048,400)	(1,017,400)	(743,900)
Shares Outstanding	37,000	36,900	36,800	36,100	35,900	37,800	41,300	47,700
Statistical Record								
Return on Assets %	8.97	6.01	4.33	7.93	15.19	13.32	14.85	13.41
EBITDA Margin %	24.96	22.55	15.51	20.50	23.69	26.79	25.75	23.65
Net Margin %	15.28	8.09	5.72	10.31	17.51	15.62	17.77	14.80
Asset Turnover	0.84	0.74	0.76	0.77	0.87	0.85	0.84	0.91
Current Ratio	0.52	1.04	0.94	1.00	0.81	0.96	0.85	0.76
Price Range	130.23-102.24	125.41-100.75	140.73-87.91	135.92-100.97	127.37-94.87	123.42-78.17	86.50-63.34	86.45-59.25
P/E Ratio	25.64-20.13	33.09-26.58	53.11-33.17	29.29-21.76	15.94-11.87	18.87-11.95	13.45-9.85	16.37-11.22
Average Yield %	1.77	1.79	1.64	1.55	1.58	1.64	1.95	1.94

Address: 103 JFK Parkway, Short Hills, NJ 07078	**Web Site:** www.dnb.com	**Auditors:** PricewaterhouseCoopers LLP
Telephone: 973-921-5500	**Officers:** Thomas J. Manning - Chairman, Interim Chief Executive Officer Christie A. Hill - Senior Vice President, Chief Legal Officer, General Counsel, Corporate Secretary	**Investor Contact:** 973-921-5914 **Transfer Agents:** Computershare Shareowner Services LLC, Providence, RI

DYCOM INDUSTRIES, INC.

Exchange	Symbol	Price	52Wk Range	Yield	P/E
NYS	DY	$94.51 (6/29/2018)	122.80-76.07	N/A	N/A

*7 Year Price Score 154.10 *NYSE Composite Index=100* ***12 Month Price Score 98.89**

TRADING VOLUME (thousand shares)

Interim Earnings (Per Share)

Qtr.	Oct	Jan	Apr	Jul
2016-17	1.59	0.74	1.22	1.38
2017-18	0.90	...	...	0.00
Qtr.	Apr	Jan	Apr	Jan
2018-19	0.53	...	...	...

Interim Dividends (Per Share)

No Dividends Paid

Valuation Analysis

		Institutional Holding	
Forecast EPS	$4.68	No of Institutions	
	(06/14/2018)	449	
Market Cap	$2.9 Billion	Shares	
Book Value	$747.0 Million	42,580,232	
Price/Book	3.95	% Held	
Price/Sales	N/A	81.55	

Business Summary: Construction Services (MIC: 7.5.4 SIC: 1623 NAIC: 237130)

Dycom Industries is a provider of specialty contracting services throughout the U.S. and in Canada. Co. provides program management, engineering, construction, maintenance, and installation services for telecommunications providers, underground facility locating services for various utilities, including telecommunications providers, and other construction and maintenance services for electric and gas utilities. Co. provides the labor, tools and equipment to design, engineer, locate, maintain, expand, install and upgrade the telecommunications infrastructure. Also, Co. provides underground facility locating services to a variety of utility companies, including telecommunication providers.

Recent Developments: For the quarter ended Oct 28 2017, net income decreased 43.6% to US$28.8 million from US$51.1 million in the year-earlier quarter. Revenues were US$756.2 million, down 5.4% from US$799.2 million the year before. Direct operating expenses declined 2.3% to US$600.8 million from US$615.0 million in the comparable period the year before. Indirect operating expenses increased 13.2% to US$107.2 million from US$94.8 million in the equivalent prior-year period.

Prospects: Our evaluation of Dycom Industries Inc. as of Jan. 21, 2018 is the result of our systematic analysis on three basic characteristics: earnings strength, relative valuation, and recent stock price movement. The company has generated a negative trend in earnings per share over the past 5 quarters and while recent estimates for the company have been mixed, DY has posted better than expected results. Based on operating earnings yield, the company is about fairly valued when compared to all of the companies in our coverage universe. Share price changes over the past year indicates that DY will perform poorly over the near term.

Financial Data

(US$ in Thousands)	3 Mos	01/27/2018	07/29/2017	07/30/2016	07/25/2015	07/26/2014	07/27/2013	07/28/2012
Earnings Per Share	0.53	2.15	4.92	3.89	2.41	1.15	1.04	1.14
Cash Flow Per Share	...	10.37	8.20	7.96	4.18	2.50	3.24	1.94
Tang Book Value Per Share	7.79	7.43	5.35	1.57	3.43	2.93	1.06	5.01
Income Statement								
Total Revenue	731,375	1,411,348	3,066,880	2,672,542	2,022,312	1,811,593	1,608,612	1,201,119
EBITDA	77,134	139,071	410,914	346,561	241,940	167,663	146,289	137,465
Depn & Amortn	43,259	72,961	123,125	105,514	79,331	74,517	64,756	56,187
Income Before Taxes	23,709	46,550	250,425	206,327	135,584	66,319	58,199	64,561
Income Taxes	6,478	(22,285)	93,208	77,587	51,260	26,341	23,011	25,183
Net Income	17,231	68,835	157,217	128,740	84,324	39,978	35,188	39,378
Average Shares	32,407	32,054	31,984	33,115	35,026	34,816	33,782	34,481
Balance Sheet								
Current Assets	936,082	904,786	938,518	851,234	696,632	605,736	541,134	376,947
Total Assets	1,883,010	1,840,956	1,899,307	1,719,716	1,358,864	1,212,354	1,154,208	772,193
Current Liabilities	275,860	259,612	318,538	322,627	226,710	196,532	199,815	114,563
Long-Term Obligations	731,736	733,843	738,265	706,202	521,841	446,863	444,169	187,500
Total Liabilities	1,136,028	1,115,960	1,227,724	1,162,429	851,664	727,420	725,847	379,262
Stockholders' Equity	746,982	724,996	671,583	557,287	507,200	484,934	428,361	392,931
Shares Outstanding	31,193	31,185	31,087	31,420	33,381	33,990	33,264	33,587
Statistical Record								
Return on Assets %	...	7.38	8.71	8.23	6.58	3.39	3.66	5.28
Return on Equity %	...	19.77	25.66	23.80	17.05	8.78	8.59	10.60
EBITDA Margin %	10.55	9.85	13.40	12.97	11.96	9.26	9.09	11.44
Net Margin %	2.36	4.88	5.13	4.82	4.17	2.21	2.19	3.28
Asset Turnover	...	1.51	1.70	1.71	1.58	1.54	1.67	1.61
Current Ratio	3.39	3.49	2.95	2.64	3.07	3.08	2.71	3.29
Debt to Equity	0.98	1.01	1.10	1.27	1.03	0.92	1.04	0.48
Price Range	122.80-76.07	120.60-76.07	108.99-71.34	95.94-48.61	69.62-25.67	33.52-24.77	26.77-13.09	23.79-12.59
P/E Ratio	231.70-143.53	56.09-35.38	22.15-14.50	24.66-12.50	28.89-10.65	29.15-21.54	25.74-12.59	20.87-11.04

Address: 11780 US Highway 1, Suite 600, Palm Beach Gardens, FL 33408 **Telephone:** 561-627-7171 **Fax:** 561-627-7709	**Web Site:** www.dycomind.com **Officers:** Steven E. Nielsen - Chairman, President, Chief Executive Officer Timothy R. Estes - Executive Vice President, Chief Operating Officer	**Auditors:** PricewaterhouseCoopers LLP **Investor Contact:** 561-627-7171 **Transfer Agents:** American Stock Transfer & Trust Company, New York, NY

Exchange	Symbol	Price	52Wk Range	Yield	P/E
NYS	EXP	$104.97 (6/29/2018)	120.30-87.24	0.38	19.88

*7 Year Price Score 114.20 *NYSE Composite Index=100 *12 Month Price Score 100.66

Interim Earnings (Per Share)

Qtr.	Jun	Sep	Dec	Mar
2013-14	0.60	0.80	0.63	0.46
2014-15	0.75	1.00	1.03	0.93
2015-16	0.75	0.59	0.92	0.79
2016-17	0.93	1.25	1.17	0.75
2017-18	1.13	1.31	2.08	0.76

Interim Dividends (Per Share)

Amt	Decl	Ex	Rec	Pay
0.10Q	08/07/2017	10/05/2017	10/06/2017	11/07/2017
0.10Q	11/01/2017	12/21/2017	12/22/2017	01/26/2018
0.10Q	02/01/2018	04/11/2018	04/12/2018	05/11/2018
0.10Q	05/24/2018	06/21/2018	06/22/2018	07/20/2018

Indicated Div: $0.40

Valuation Analysis

		Institutional Holding	
Forecast EPS	$6.41	No of Institutions	
	(06/12/2018)	486	
Market Cap	$5.1 Billion	Shares	
Book Value	$1.4 Billion	55,672,504	
Price/Book	3.58	% Held	
Price/Sales	3.66	96.61	

Business Summary: Construction Materials (MIC: 8.5.1 SIC: 3241 NAIC: 327310)

Eagle Materials is a holding company. Co. operates in five business segments: Cement, Gypsum Wallboard, Recycled Paperboard, Oil and Gas Proppants and Concrete and Aggregates. These operations are conducted in the U.S. and include the mining of limestone and the manufacture, production, distribution and sale of portland cement and slag, the grinding of slag, the mining of gypsum and the manufacture and sale of gypsum wallboard, the manufacture and sale of recycled paperboard to the gypsum wallboard industry and other paperboard converters, the sale of readymix concrete and the mining and sale of aggregates and sand used in hydraulic fracturing.

Recent Developments: For the year ended Mar 31 2018, net income increased 29.5% to US$256.6 million from US$198.2 million in the prior year. Revenues were US$1.39 billion, up 14.5% from US$1.21 billion the year before. Direct operating expenses rose 16.5% to US$1.05 billion from US$899.2 million in the comparable period the year before. Indirect operating expenses amounted to US$39.2 million compared with an income of US$5.1 million in the equivalent prior-year period.

Prospects: Our evaluation of Eagle Materials Inc. as of Jan. 21, 2018 is the result of our systematic analysis on three basic characteristics: earnings strength, relative valuation, and recent stock price movement. The company has produced a positive trend in earnings per share over the past 5 quarters and while recent estimates for the company have been mixed, EXP has posted results that fell short of analysts expectations. Based on operating earnings yield, the company is about fairly valued when compared to all of the companies in our coverage universe. Share price changes over the past year indicates that EXP will perform poorly over the near term.

Financial Data

(US$ in Thousands)	03/31/2018	03/31/2017	03/31/2016	03/31/2015	03/31/2014	03/31/2013	03/31/2012	03/31/2011
Earnings Per Share	5.28	4.10	3.05	3.71	2.49	1.22	0.42	0.34
Cash Flow Per Share	7.01	6.92	5.36	4.72	3.48	2.67	1.37	1.00
Tang Book Value Per Share	24.41	19.98	18.03	15.91	13.40	10.78	7.10	6.93
Dividends Per Share	0.400	0.400	0.400	0.400	0.400	0.400	0.300	0.400
Dividend Payout %	7.58	9.76	13.11	10.78	16.06	32.79	71.43	117.65
Income Statement								
Total Revenue	1,386,520	1,211,220	1,143,492	1,066,368	898,396	642,562	495,023	462,180
EBITDA	365,781	360,764	280,952	289,403	229,575	122,512	58,905	73,916
Depn & Amortn	109,600	86,000	84,200	69,700	67,300	55,100	48,900	48,200
Income Before Taxes	228,543	252,133	180,169	207,960	143,993	51,589	(6,616)	9,196
Income Taxes	15,330	96,300	66,660	66,074	57,561	26,352	3,180	1,913
Net Income	256,632	198,219	152,592	186,853	124,243	57,744	18,732	14,849
Average Shares	48,645	48,361	50,070	50,372	49,939	47,340	44,515	44,251
Balance Sheet								
Current Assets	458,735	400,624	380,003	366,635	306,960	261,271	191,841	174,626
Total Assets	2,368,003	2,247,124	1,883,635	1,882,591	1,511,529	1,476,233	985,145	982,810
Current Liabilities	179,329	229,519	120,589	184,576	108,820	100,229	77,043	70,350
Long-Term Obligations	620,922	605,253	499,714	455,714	371,759	489,259	262,259	287,000
Total Liabilities	950,313	1,043,674	843,104	871,998	680,030	780,063	512,634	523,246
Stockholders' Equity	1,417,690	1,203,450	1,040,531	1,010,593	831,499	696,170	472,511	459,564
Shares Outstanding	48,282	48,453	48,526	50,245	50,053	49,503	45,269	44,447
Statistical Record								
Return on Assets %	11.12	9.60	8.08	11.01	8.32	4.69	1.90	1.49
Return on Equity %	19.58	17.67	14.84	20.29	16.27	9.88	4.01	3.28
EBITDA Margin %	26.38	29.79	24.57	27.14	25.55	19.07	11.90	15.99
Net Margin %	18.51	16.37	13.34	17.52	13.83	8.99	3.78	3.21
Asset Turnover	0.60	0.59	0.61	0.63	0.60	0.52	0.50	0.46
Current Ratio	2.56	1.75	3.15	1.99	2.82	2.61	2.49	2.48
Debt to Equity	0.44	0.50	0.48	0.45	0.45	0.70	0.56	0.62
Price Range	120.30-87.24	108.70-68.78	87.68-46.85	104.73-69.80	90.88-61.72	71.57-29.84	35.81-15.68	32.79-21.79
P/E Ratio	22.78-16.52	26.51-16.78	28.75-15.36	28.23-18.81	36.50-24.79	58.66-24.46	85.26-37.33	96.44-64.09
Average Yield %	0.39	0.46	0.56	0.46	0.54	0.83	1.18	1.47

Address: 3811 Turtle Creek Blvd.,
Suite 1100, Dallas, TX 75219
Telephone: 214-432-2000
Fax: 214-432-2100

Web Site: www.eaglematerials.com
Officers: Richard R. Stewart - Chairman,
Vice-Chairman Michael R. Nicolais - Vice-Chairman

Auditors: Ernst & Young LLP
Investor Contact: 214-432-2000
Transfer Agents: Computershare, Inc.,
Providence , RI

EASTMAN CHEMICAL CO

Exchange	Symbol	Price	52Wk Range	Yield	P/E
NYS	EMN	$99.96 (6/29/2018)	110.84-82.77	2.24	10.42

*7 Year Price Score 105.79 *NYSE Composite Index=100 *12 Month Price Score 108.46

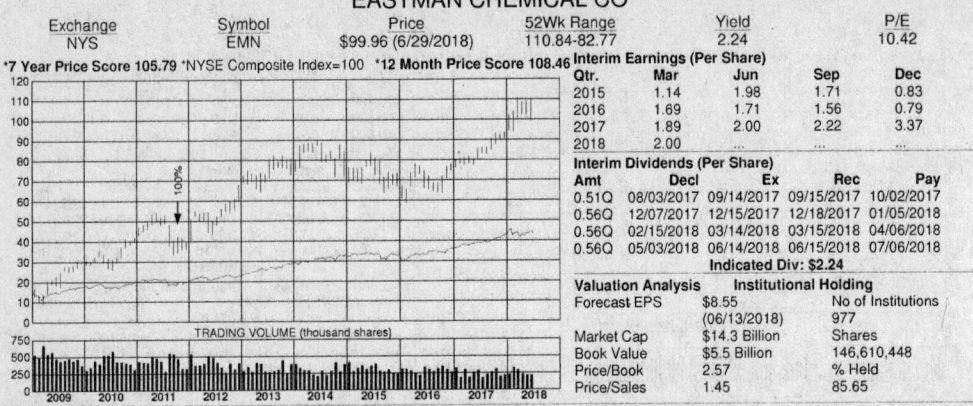

Interim Earnings (Per Share)
Qtr.	Mar	Jun	Sep	Dec
2015	1.14	1.98	1.71	0.83
2016	1.69	1.71	1.56	0.79
2017	1.89	2.00	2.22	3.37
2018	2.00	...	...	...

Interim Dividends (Per Share)
Amt	Decl	Ex	Rec	Pay
0.51Q	08/03/2017	09/14/2017	09/15/2017	10/02/2017
0.56Q	12/07/2017	12/15/2017	12/18/2017	01/05/2018
0.56Q	02/15/2018	03/14/2018	03/15/2018	04/06/2018
0.56Q	05/03/2018	06/14/2018	06/15/2018	07/06/2018

Indicated Div: $2.24

Valuation Analysis
		Institutional Holding	
Forecast EPS	$8.55	No of Institutions	
	(06/13/2018)	977	
Market Cap	$14.3 Billion	Shares	
Book Value	$5.5 Billion	146,610,448	
Price/Book	2.57	% Held	
Price/Sales	1.45	85.65	

Business Summary: Plastics (MIC: 8.4.2 SIC: 2821 NAIC: 325211)

Eastman Chemical is a chemical company that produces a range of materials, specialty additives, chemicals, and fibers. Co.'s segments are: Additives & Functional Products, which manufactures chemicals for products in the coatings and tires industries; Adhesives & Plasticizers, which manufactures coatings and inks additives, adhesives resins, tire additives and others; Advanced Materials, which manufactures specialty plastics, interlayers, and performance films; Chemical Intermediates, which manufactures intermediates, plasticizers, and functional amines; and Fibers, which manufactures acetate tow, acetate yarn, and acetyl chemical products.

Recent Developments: For the quarter ended Mar 31 2018, net income increased 3.9% to US$290.0 million from US$279.0 million in the year-earlier quarter. Revenues were US$2.61 billion, up 13.2% from US$2.30 billion the year before. Direct operating expenses rose 19.3% to US$2.03 billion from US$1.70 billion in the comparable period the year before. Indirect operating expenses increased 4.8% to US$218.0 million from US$208.0 million in the equivalent prior-year period.

Prospects: Our evaluation of Eastman Chemical Co. as of Jan. 21, 2018 is the result of our systematic analysis on three basic characteristics: earnings strength, relative valuation, and recent stock price movement. The company has generated a negative trend in earnings per share over the past 5 quarters and while recent estimates for the company have been raised by analysts, EMN has posted better than expected results. Based on operating earnings yield, the company is undervalued when compared to all of the companies in our coverage universe. Share price changes over the past year indicates that EMN will perform in line with the market over the near term.

Financial Data
(US$ in Thousands)

	3 Mos	12/31/2017	12/31/2016	12/31/2015	12/31/2014	12/31/2013	12/31/2012	12/31/2011
Earnings Per Share	9.59	9.47	5.75	5.66	4.97	7.44	2.93	4.86
Cash Flow Per Share	10.99	11.44	9.38	10.85	9.42	8.42	7.73	4.47
Tang Book Value Per Share	N.M.	N.M.	N.M.	N.M.	N.M.	N.M.	N.M.	10.69
Dividends Per Share	2.140	2.090	1.890	1.660	1.450	1.250	1.080	0.990
Dividend Payout %	22.31	22.07	32.87	29.33	29.18	16.80	36.86	20.37
Income Statement								
Total Revenue	2,607,000	9,549,000	9,008,000	9,648,000	9,527,000	9,350,000	8,102,000	7,178,000
EBITDA	561,000	1,950,000	1,716,000	1,794,000	1,532,000	2,204,000	1,101,000	1,301,000
Depn & Amortn	152,000	420,000	412,000	402,000	355,000	345,000	309,000	261,000
Income Before Taxes	350,000	1,289,000	1,049,000	1,129,000	990,000	1,679,000	649,000	964,000
Income Taxes	60,000	(99,000)	190,000	275,000	235,000	507,000	206,000	307,000
Net Income	290,000	1,384,000	854,000	848,000	751,000	1,165,000	437,000	696,000
Average Shares	144,800	146,100	148,400	149,800	151,100	156,500	149,100	143,100
Balance Sheet								
Current Assets	3,483,000	3,143,000	2,866,000	2,878,000	3,173,000	2,840,000	2,594,000	2,302,000
Total Assets	16,366,000	15,999,000	15,457,000	15,611,000	16,072,000	11,845,000	11,619,000	6,184,000
Current Liabilities	2,029,000	1,982,000	1,795,000	2,056,000	2,022,000	1,470,000	1,364,000	1,114,000
Long-Term Obligations	6,311,000	6,147,000	6,311,000	6,608,000	7,248,000	4,254,000	4,779,000	1,445,000
Total Liabilities	10,821,000	10,596,000	10,925,000	11,670,000	12,562,000	8,049,000	8,676,000	4,314,000
Stockholders' Equity	5,545,000	5,403,000	4,532,000	3,941,000	3,510,000	3,796,000	2,943,000	1,870,000
Shares Outstanding	142,635	142,915	146,438	147,761	148,596	152,416	153,894	136,915
Statistical Record								
Return on Assets %	8.69	8.80	5.48	5.35	5.38	9.93	4.90	11.44
Return on Equity %	27.38	27.86	20.10	22.76	20.56	34.57	18.11	39.81
EBITDA Margin %	21.52	20.42	19.05	18.59	16.08	23.57	13.59	18.12
Net Margin %	11.12	14.49	9.48	8.79	7.88	12.46	5.39	9.70
Asset Turnover	0.61	0.61	0.58	0.61	0.68	0.80	0.91	1.18
Current Ratio	1.72	1.59	1.60	1.40	1.57	1.93	1.90	2.07
Debt to Equity	1.14	1.14	1.39	1.68	2.06	1.12	1.62	0.77
Price Range	110.84-77.25	93.42-75.92	78.21-58.43	83.75-63.30	90.20-71.49	82.60-64.06	68.05-40.09	54.08-33.31
P/E Ratio	11.56-8.06	9.86-8.02	13.60-10.16	14.80-11.18	18.15-14.38	11.10-8.61	23.23-13.68	11.13-6.85
Average Yield %	2.40	2.49	2.72	2.27	1.75	1.69	2.03	2.23

Address: 200 South Wilcox Drive, Kingsport, TN 37662	**Web Site:** www.eastman.com	**Auditors:** PricewaterhouseCoopers LLP
Telephone: 423-229-2000	**Officers:** Mark J. Costa - Chairman, President, Chief Executive Officer, Executive Vice President, Chief Marketing Officer Mark J. Costa - Chairman, President, Chief Executive Officer, Executive Vice President, Chief Marketing Officer	**Investor Contact:** 212-835-1620 **Transfer Agents:** American Stock Transfer & Trust Company, New York, NY

EATON CORP PLC

Exchange	Symbol	Price	52Wk Range	Yield	P/E
NYS	ETN	$74.74 (6/29/2018)	87.86-70.44	3.53	10.93

*7 Year Price Score 99.18 *NYSE Composite Index=100 *12 Month Price Score 97.19

Interim Earnings (Per Share)

Qtr.	Mar	Jun	Sep	Dec
2015	0.99	1.14	0.96	1.14
2016	0.88	1.07	1.15	1.12
2017	0.96	1.15	3.14	1.45
2018	1.10	...	...	...

Interim Dividends (Per Share)

Amt	Decl	Ex	Rec	Pay
0.60Q	10/24/2017	11/02/2017	11/03/2017	11/17/2017
0.66Q	02/28/2018	03/09/2018	03/12/2018	03/23/2018
0.66Q	04/24/2018	05/03/2018	05/04/2018	05/18/2018
0.66Q	07/24/2018	08/02/2018	08/03/2018	08/17/2018

Indicated Div: $2.64

Valuation Analysis

		Institutional Holding	
Forecast EPS	N/A	No of Institutions	1216
Market Cap	$32.7 Billion	Shares	
Book Value	$17.3 Billion		390,955,264
Price/Book	1.89	% Held	
Price/Sales	1.57		69.40

Business Summary: Electrical Equipment (MIC: 7.3.1 SIC: 3599 NAIC: 336399)

Eaton is a power management company providing energy-efficient solutions. Co.'s segments are: Electrical Products, which includes electrical components, industrial components, residential products, and single phase power quality; Electrical Systems and Services, which includes power distribution and assemblies, three phase power quality, and hazardous duty electrical equipment; Hydraulics, which provides power products, fluid conveyance products, filtration systems solutions, industrial drum and disc brakes, and golf grips; Aerospace, which supplies aerospace fuel, hydraulics and pneumatic systems; and Vehicle, which provides drivetrain and powertrain systems and critical components.

Recent Developments: For the quarter ended Mar 31 2018, net income increased 12.2% to US$487.0 million from US$434.0 million in the year-earlier quarter. Revenues were US$5.25 billion, up 8.3% from US$4.85 billion the year before. Direct operating expenses rose 8.0% to US$3.57 billion from US$3.31 billion in the comparable period the year before. Indirect operating expenses increased 2.6% to US$1.05 billion from US$1.02 billion in the equivalent prior-year period.

Prospects: Our evaluation of Eaton Corp PLC as of Sep. 17, 2017 is the result of our systematic analysis on three basic characteristics: earnings strength, relative valuation, and recent stock price movement. The company has enjoyed a very positive trend in earnings per share over the past 5 quarters and while recent estimates for the company have remained steady, ETN has posted results that fell short of analysts expectations. Based on operating earnings yield, the company is undervalued when compared to all of the companies in our coverage universe. Share price changes over the past year indicates that ETN will perform in line with the market over the near term.

Financial Data
(US$ in Millions)

	3 Mos	12/31/2017	12/31/2016	12/31/2015	12/31/2014	12/31/2013	12/31/2012	12/31/2011
Earnings Per Share	6.84	6.68	4.21	4.23	3.76	3.90	3.46	3.93
Cash Flow Per Share	5.79	6.00	5.59	5.09	3.96	4.83	4.77	3.69
Dividends Per Share	2.460	2.400	2.280	2.200	1.960	1.680	1.520	1.360
Dividend Payout %	35.96	35.93	54.16	52.01	52.13	43.08	43.93	34.61
Income Statement								
Total Revenue	5,251	20,404	19,747	20,855	22,552	22,046	16,311	16,049
EBITDA	865	4,090	2,846	2,856	2,502	2,671	2,057	2,227
Depn & Amortn	230	476	486	479	514	516	598	556
Income Before Taxes	565	3,368	2,127	2,145	1,761	1,884	1,251	1,553
Income Taxes	78	382	202	164	(42)	11	31	201
Net Income	488	2,985	1,922	1,979	1,793	1,861	1,217	1,350
Average Shares	441	447	456	467	476	476	350	342
Balance Sheet								
Current Assets	8,129	8,337	6,941	6,616	8,100	8,731	7,844	5,826
Total Assets	32,668	32,623	30,419	31,031	33,529	35,491	35,848	17,873
Current Liabilities	5,396	5,075	5,485	4,625	5,355	4,914	5,431	3,637
Long-Term Obligations	6,845	7,167	6,711	7,781	8,024	8,969	9,762	3,366
Total Liabilities	15,405	15,370	15,522	15,845	17,743	18,700	20,762	10,404
Stockholders' Equity	17,263	17,253	14,897	15,186	15,786	16,791	15,086	7,469
Shares Outstanding	437	439	449	458	467	475	470	334
Statistical Record								
Return on Assets %	9.61	9.47	6.24	6.13	5.20	5.22	4.52	7.69
Return on Equity %	18.76	18.57	12.74	12.78	11.01	11.68	10.76	18.21
EBITDA Margin %	16.47	20.05	14.41	13.69	11.09	12.12	12.61	13.88
Net Margin %	9.29	14.63	9.73	9.49	7.95	8.44	7.46	8.41
Asset Turnover	0.66	0.65	0.64	0.65	0.65	0.62	0.61	0.91
Current Ratio	1.51	1.64	1.27	1.43	1.51	1.78	1.44	1.60
Debt to Equity	0.40	0.42	0.45	0.51	0.51	0.53	0.65	0.45
Price Range	87.86-70.44	81.51-66.88	69.86-47.27	73.50-49.74	79.44-58.27	76.75-54.18	54.66-37.04	56.22-34.16
P/E Ratio	12.85-10.30	12.20-10.01	16.59-11.23	17.38-11.76	21.13-15.50	19.68-13.89	15.80-10.71	14.31-8.69
Average Yield %	3.16	3.19	3.69	3.50	2.75	2.57	3.25	2.85

Address: Eaton House, 30 Pembroke Road, Dublin 4, 44114-2584
Telephone: 353-163-72900

Web Site: www.eaton.com
Officers: Craig Arnold - Chairman, Chief Executive Officer Richard H. Fearon - Vice-Chairman, Chief Financial Officer, Chief Planning Officer

Auditors: Ernst & Young LLP
Investor Contact: 216-523-4205
Transfer Agents: Computershare Shareowner Services, Jersey City, NJ

EATON VANCE CORP

Exchange	Symbol	Price	52Wk Range	Yield	P/E	Div Acheiver
NYS	EV	$52.19 (6/29/2018)	60.87-45.44	2.38	19.47	36 Years

*7 Year Price Score 111.92 *NYSE Composite Index=100 *12 Month Price Score 102.20

Interim Earnings (Per Share)

Qtr.	Jan	Apr	Jul	Oct
2014-15	0.21	0.58	0.57	0.53
2015-16	0.50	0.48	0.55	0.57
2016-17	0.53	0.62	0.58	0.69
2017-18	0.63	0.78	...	...

Interim Dividends (Per Share)

Amt	Decl	Ex	Rec	Pay
0.31Q	10/12/2017	10/30/2017	10/31/2017	11/15/2017
0.31Q	01/10/2018	01/30/2018	01/31/2018	02/15/2018
0.31Q	04/11/2018	04/27/2018	04/30/2018	05/15/2018
0.31Q	07/10/2018	07/30/2018	07/31/2018	08/15/2018

Indicated Div: $1.24

Valuation Analysis

		Institutional Holding	
Forecast EPS	$3.21	No of Institutions	
	(06/05/2018)	538	
Market Cap	$6.2 Billion	Shares	
Book Value	$1.1 Billion	111,350,928	
Price/Book	5.72	% Held	
Price/Sales	3.82	79.78	

Business Summary: Wealth Management (MIC: 5.5.2 SIC: 6282 NAIC: 523930)

Eaton Vance, through its subsidiaries, manages active equity, income and alternative strategies across a range of investment styles and asset classes, including U.S. and global equities, floating-rate bank loans, municipal bonds, global income, high-yield and investment grade bonds. Through its subsidiary, Parametric Portfolio Associates LLC, Co. provides portfolio implementation and overlay services, including tax-managed and non-tax-managed custom core equity strategies, centralized portfolio management of multi-manager portfolios and customized exposure management services. As of Oct 31 2017, Co. had $422.3 billion in assets under management.

Recent Developments: For the quarter ended Apr 30 2018, net income increased 24.2% to US$96.4 million from US$77.6 million in the year-earlier quarter. Revenues were US$414.3 million, up 10.6% from US$374.6 million the year before. Operating income was US$132.7 million versus US$117.9 million in the prior-year quarter, an increase of 12.5%. Direct operating expenses rose 7.9% to US$34.5 million from US$32.0 million in the comparable period the year before. Indirect operating expenses increased 9.9% to US$247.0 million from US$224.7 million in the equivalent prior-year period.

Prospects: Our evaluation of Eaton Vance Corp. as of Jan. 21, 2018 is the result of our systematic analysis on three basic characteristics: earnings strength, relative valuation, and recent stock price movement. The company has produced a positive trend in earnings per share over the past 5 quarters and while recent estimates for the company have been raised by analysts, EV has posted results that fell short of analysts expectations. Based on operating earnings yield, the company is about fairly valued when compared to all of the companies in our coverage universe. Share price changes over the past year indicates that EV will perform in line with the market over the near term.

Financial Data

(US$ in Thousands)	6 Mos	3 Mos	10/31/2017	10/31/2016	10/31/2015	10/31/2014	10/31/2013	10/31/2012
Earnings Per Share	2.68	2.52	2.42	2.12	1.92	2.44	1.53	1.72
Cash Flow Per Share	0.52	0.38	0.59	3.09	1.94	0.85	1.00	1.59
Tang Book Value Per Share	6.25	6.24	5.58	3.59	2.82	3.05	3.01	3.42
Dividends Per Share	1.210	1.180	1.150	1.075	1.015	0.910	1.820	0.770
Dividend Payout %	45.15	46.83	47.52	50.71	52.86	37.30	118.95	44.77
Income Statement								
Total Revenue	835,673	421,412	1,529,010	1,342,860	1,403,563	1,450,294	1,357,503	1,209,036
EBITDA	282,504	144,392	483,264	432,158	416,908	546,788	425,313	473,015
Depn & Amortn	8,705	4,277	9,100	10,900	11,400	10,900	13,000	16,900
Income Before Taxes	261,451	134,114	469,169	408,052	369,384	491,149	359,453	403,738
Income Taxes	82,661	48,617	173,666	153,630	143,214	186,710	143,896	142,385
Net Income	174,657	78,056	282,131	241,307	230,299	304,316	193,841	203,465
Average Shares	123,779	123,941	116,418	113,982	118,155	121,595	122,444	115,126
Balance Sheet								
Current Assets	719,260	747,247	811,008	610,346	816,015	580,522	668,767	632,423
Total Assets	2,498,208	2,397,009	2,330,901	1,732,576	2,116,471	1,860,086	2,407,249	1,979,491
Current Liabilities	241,497	197,098	320,079	269,937	277,047	275,719	255,222	227,985
Long-Term Obligations	708,947	655,586	631,441	573,967	970,850	725,637	1,100,415	946,605
Total Liabilities	1,405,734	1,297,756	1,319,505	1,028,787	1,496,240	1,204,910	1,737,465	1,367,419
Stockholders' Equity	1,092,474	1,099,253	1,011,396	703,789	620,231	655,176	669,784	612,072
Shares Outstanding	119,642	120,513	118,520	113,987	115,885	118,261	121,631	116,291
Statistical Record								
Return on Assets %	13.89	14.41	13.89	12.50	11.58	14.26	8.84	10.65
Return on Equity %	34.48	32.51	32.90	36.35	36.11	45.94	30.24	37.84
EBITDA Margin %	33.81	34.26	31.61	32.18	29.70	37.70	31.33	39.12
Net Margin %	20.90	18.52	18.45	17.97	16.41	20.98	14.28	16.83
Asset Turnover	0.70	0.77	0.75	0.70	0.71	0.68	0.62	0.63
Current Ratio	2.98	3.79	2.53	2.26	2.95	2.11	2.62	2.77
Debt to Equity	0.65	0.60	0.62	0.82	1.57	1.11	1.64	1.55
Price Range	60.87-42.96	60.87-41.80	51.90-34.60	40.18-27.18	44.00-33.06	43.63-34.29	44.18-28.14	29.70-21.78
P/E Ratio	22.71-16.03	24.15-16.59	21.45-14.30	18.95-12.82	22.92-17.22	17.88-14.05	28.88-18.39	17.27-12.66
Average Yield %	2.34	2.41	2.54	3.09	2.56	2.38	4.80	2.92

Address: Two International Place, Boston, MA 02110
Telephone: 617-482-8260
Fax: 617-482-2396

Web Site: www.eatonvance.com
Officers: Thomas E. Faust - Chairman, President, Chief Executive Officer Jeffrey P. Beale - Vice President, Chief Administrative Officer

Auditors: Deloitte & Touche LLP
Investor Contact: 617-482-8260
Transfer Agents: ComputerShare Investor Services, Providence, RI

ECOLAB INC

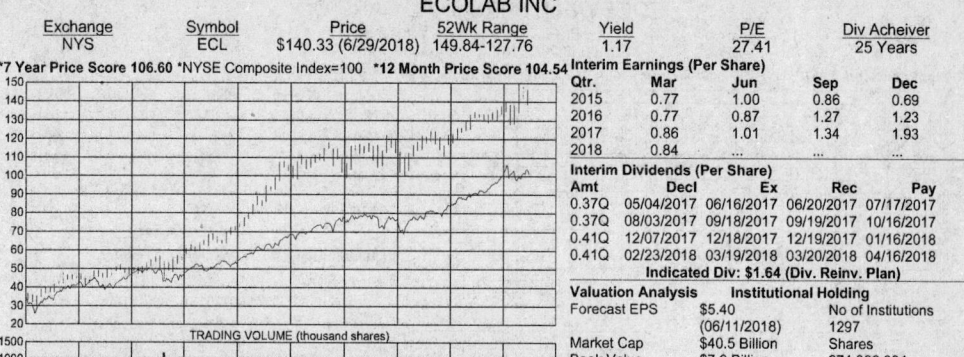

Exchange	Symbol	Price	52Wk Range	Yield	P/E	Div Acheiver
NYS	ECL	$140.33 (6/29/2018)	149.84-127.76	1.17	27.41	25 Years

*7 Year Price Score 106.60 *NYSE Composite Index=100 *12 Month Price Score 104.54

Interim Earnings (Per Share)

Qtr.	Mar	Jun	Sep	Dec
2015	0.77	1.00	0.86	0.69
2016	0.77	0.87	1.27	1.23
2017	0.86	1.01	1.34	1.93
2018	0.84	...	...	...

Interim Dividends (Per Share)

Amt	Decl	Ex	Rec	Pay
0.37Q	05/04/2017	06/16/2017	06/20/2017	07/17/2017
0.37Q	08/03/2017	09/18/2017	09/19/2017	10/16/2017
0.41Q	12/07/2017	12/18/2017	12/19/2017	01/16/2018
0.41Q	02/23/2018	03/19/2018	03/20/2018	04/16/2018

Indicated Div: $1.64 (Div. Reinv. Plan)

Valuation Analysis / **Institutional Holding**

Forecast EPS	$5.40	No of Institutions
	(06/11/2018)	1297
Market Cap	$40.5 Billion	Shares
Book Value	$7.6 Billion	274,336,384
Price/Book	5.33	% Held
Price/Sales	2.86	94.94

Business Summary: Specialty Chemicals (MIC: 8.3.2 SIC: 2842 NAIC: 325612)

Ecolab is a provider of water, hygiene and energy technologies and services that protect people and resources. Co.'s products and technologies are used in water treatment, pollution control, energy conservation, oil production and refining, steelmaking, and other industrial processes. Co. has four segments: Global Industrial, which consists of the Water, Food and Beverage, Paper and Textile Care operating segments; Global Institutional, which consists of the consists of the Institutional, Specialty and Healthcare operating segments; Global Energy, which consists of the Energy operating segment; as well as Other, which consists of the Pest Elimination and Equipment Care operating segments.

Recent Developments: For the quarter ended Mar 31 2018, net income decreased 3.5% to US$248.2 million from US$257.3 million in the year-earlier quarter. Revenues were US$3.47 billion, up 9.8% from US$3.16 billion the year before. Operating income was US$354.3 million versus US$357.2 million in the prior-year quarter, a decrease of 0.8%. Direct operating expenses rose 12.4% to US$2.08 billion from US$1.85 billion in the comparable period the year before. Indirect operating expenses increased 8.5% to US$1.03 billion from US$953.4 million in the equivalent prior-year period.

Prospects: Our evaluation of Ecolab Inc. as of Jan. 21, 2018 is the result of our systematic analysis on three basic characteristics: earnings strength, relative valuation, and recent stock price movement. The company has enjoyed a very positive trend in earnings per share over the past 5 quarters and while recent estimates for the company have remained steady, ECL has posted better than expected results. Based on operating earnings yield, the company is about fairly valued when compared to all of the companies in our coverage universe. Share price changes over the past year indicates that ECL will perform in line with the market over the near term.

Financial Data

(US$ in Thousands)	3 Mos	12/31/2017	12/31/2016	12/31/2015	12/31/2014	12/31/2013	12/31/2012	12/31/2011
Earnings Per Share	5.12	5.13	4.14	3.32	3.93	3.16	2.35	1.91
Cash Flow Per Share	7.46	7.22	6.61	6.75	6.05	5.20	4.10	2.89
Dividends Per Share	1.560	1.520	1.420	1.340	1.155	0.965	0.830	0.725
Dividend Payout %	30.47	29.63	34.30	40.36	29.39	30.54	35.32	37.96
Income Statement								
Total Revenue	3,470,900	13,838,300	13,152,800	13,545,100	14,280,500	13,253,400	11,838,700	6,798,500
EBITDA	604,800	2,605,800	2,476,000	2,121,300	2,513,000	2,074,600	1,757,300	1,084,800
Depn & Amortn	231,100	586,000	561,000	560,000	558,000	514,000	468,000	331,000
Income Before Taxes	317,300	1,764,800	1,650,400	1,317,700	1,698,400	1,298,300	1,012,600	679,600
Income Taxes	69,100	242,400	403,300	300,500	476,200	324,700	311,300	216,300
Net Income	247,300	1,508,400	1,229,600	1,002,100	1,202,800	967,800	703,600	462,500
Average Shares	292,700	294,000	296,700	301,400	305,900	305,900	298,900	242,100
Balance Sheet								
Current Assets	4,596,800	4,596,400	4,279,400	4,447,500	4,871,100	4,698,400	4,892,000	5,396,000
Total Assets	20,184,300	19,962,400	18,330,200	18,641,700	19,466,700	19,636,500	17,572,300	18,240,800
Current Liabilities	3,982,800	3,431,800	3,019,400	4,764,400	4,386,600	3,488,700	3,052,700	3,166,300
Long-Term Obligations	6,397,700	6,758,300	6,145,700	4,260,200	4,864,000	6,043,500	5,736,100	6,613,200
Total Liabilities	12,583,300	12,343,900	11,429,100	11,731,800	12,150,200	12,292,200	11,495,300	12,574,100
Stockholders' Equity	7,601,000	7,618,500	6,901,100	6,909,900	7,315,900	7,344,300	6,077,000	5,666,700
Shares Outstanding	288,500	289,322	291,825	295,967	299,852	301,135	294,722	291,974
Statistical Record								
Return on Assets %	7.62	7.88	6.63	5.26	6.15	5.20	3.92	4.00
Return on Equity %	20.85	20.78	17.76	14.09	16.41	14.42	11.95	11.87
EBITDA Margin %	17.42	18.83	18.82	15.66	17.60	15.65	14.84	15.96
Net Margin %	7.12	10.90	9.35	7.40	8.42	7.30	5.94	6.80
Asset Turnover	0.72	0.72	0.71	0.71	0.73	0.71	0.66	0.59
Current Ratio	1.15	1.34	1.42	0.93	1.11	1.35	1.60	1.70
Debt to Equity	0.84	0.89	0.89	0.62	0.66	0.82	0.94	1.17
Price Range	140.34-124.47	137.42-117.86	124.05-100.14	122.10-98.93	118.07-98.03	107.99-71.90	72.72-58.02	57.81-44.53
P/E Ratio	27.41-24.31	26.79-22.97	29.96-24.19	36.78-29.80	30.04-24.94	34.17-22.75	30.94-24.69	30.27-23.31
Average Yield %	1.18	1.18	1.23	1.18	1.06	1.08	1.27	1.40

Address: 1 Ecolab Place, St. Paul, MN 55102	**Web Site:** www.ecolab.com	**Auditors:** PricewaterhouseCoopers LLP
Telephone: 800-232-6522	**Officers:** Douglas M. Baker - Chairman, President, Chief Executive Officer, Chief Operating Officer Timothy Beastrom - Assistant Secretary	**Investor Contact:** 651-293-2545 **Transfer Agents:** Elavon Financial Services DAC

245

EDGEWELL PERSONAL CARE CO

Exchange	Symbol	Price	52Wk Range	Yield	P/E
NYS	EPC	$50.46 (6/29/2018)	76.33-41.40	N/A	N/A

*7 Year Price Score 65.37 *NYSE Composite Index=100 *12 Month Price Score 75.90

Interim Earnings (Per Share)

Qtr.	Dec	Mar	Jun	Sep
2014-15	1.69	(1.41)	(1.17)	(3.54)
2015-16	0.39	1.10	0.61	0.88
2016-17	0.58	1.14	0.95	(2.57)
2017-18	0.12	1.20	...	...

Interim Dividends (Per Share)

No Dividends Paid

Valuation Analysis | **Institutional Holding**

Forecast EPS	$3.43	No of Institutions	
	(06/14/2018)	514	
Market Cap	$2.7 Billion	Shares	
Book Value	$1.7 Billion	68,311,576	
Price/Book	1.57	% Held	
Price/Sales	N/A	79.04	

TRADING VOLUME (thousand shares)

Business Summary: Household & Personal Products (MIC: 1.7.1 SIC: 2844 NAIC: 325620)

Edgewell Personal Care is a manufacturer and marketer of personal care products in the wet shave, sun and skin care, feminine care and infant care categories. Co. manages its business in four segments: Wet Shave, which manufactures and distributes Schick and Wilkinson Sword razor systems, composed of razor handles and refillable blades, and disposable shave products for men and women; Sun and Skin Care, in which Co. sells its products under the Banana Boat, Hawaiian Tropic, Bulldog® and Wet Ones brand names; Feminine Care, in which Co. markets products under the Playtex, Stayfree, Carefree and o.b. brands; and All Other, which includes infant care, pet care and miscellaneous other products.

Recent Developments: For the quarter ended Mar 31 2018, net income decreased 0.9% to US$65.1 million from US$65.7 million in the year-earlier quarter. Revenues were US$608.1 million, down 0.5% from US$611.0 million the year before. Direct operating expenses rose 1.5% to US$306.0 million from US$301.4 million in the comparable period the year before. Indirect operating expenses decreased 1.7% to US$216.3 million from US$220.1 million in the equivalent prior-year period.

Prospects: Our evaluation of Edgewell Personal Care Co. as of Jan. 21, 2018 is the result of our systematic analysis on three basic characteristics: earnings strength, relative valuation, and recent stock price movement. The company has generated a negative trend in earnings per share over the past 5 quarters and while recent estimates for the company have been raised by analysts, EPC has posted results that fell short of analysts expectations. Based on operating earnings yield, the company is undervalued when compared to all of the companies in our coverage universe. Share price changes over the past year indicates that EPC will perform in line with the market over the near term.

Financial Data
(US$ in Thousands)

	6 Mos	3 Mos	09/30/2017	09/30/2016	09/30/2015	09/30/2014	09/30/2013	09/30/2012
Earnings Per Share	(0.30)	(0.36)	0.10	2.99	(4.44)	5.69	6.47	6.22
Cash Flow Per Share	...	6.03	5.17	2.97	2.40	9.23	12.08	9.71
Income Statement								
Total Revenue	1,076,400	468,300	2,298,400	2,362,000	2,421,200	4,447,700	4,466,000	4,567,200
EBITDA	204,100	75,700	90,400	365,300	(285,200)	716,400	863,100	829,400
Depn & Amortn	49,200	24,800	74,100	73,600	73,700	120,300	164,700	136,700
Income Before Taxes	118,900	33,100	(52,900)	219,900	(458,700)	473,500	567,900	565,400
Income Taxes	47,100	26,400	(58,600)	41,200	(162,600)	117,400	160,900	156,500
Net Income	71,800	6,700	5,700	178,700	(275,300)	356,100	407,000	408,900
Average Shares	54,100	55,600	57,500	59,700	62,000	62,600	62,900	65,700
Balance Sheet								
Current Assets	1,004,400	1,180,600	1,186,200	1,452,000	1,636,600	2,729,600	2,568,400	2,522,600
Total Assets	4,079,200	4,172,500	4,188,800	4,771,500	4,991,700	6,928,700	6,717,400	6,731,200
Current Liabilities	551,900	445,400	524,400	868,200	666,800	1,573,700	1,153,400	1,307,500
Long-Term Obligations	1,404,100	1,678,700	1,525,400	1,544,200	1,704,000	1,768,900	1,998,800	2,138,600
Total Liabilities	2,348,000	2,516,700	2,447,100	2,942,500	3,127,600	4,406,400	4,263,800	4,661,700
Stockholders' Equity	1,731,200	1,655,800	1,741,700	1,829,000	1,864,100	2,522,300	2,453,600	2,069,500
Shares Outstanding	53,997	54,151	56,017	57,914	60,176	61,824	62,324	61,522
Statistical Record								
Return on Assets %	...	N.M.	0.13	3.65	N.M.	5.22	6.05	6.09
Return on Equity %	...	N.M.	0.32	9.65	N.M.	14.31	18.00	19.55
EBITDA Margin %	18.96	16.16	3.93	15.47	N.M.	16.11	19.33	18.16
Net Margin %	6.67	1.43	0.25	7.57	N.M.	8.01	9.11	8.95
Asset Turnover	...	0.53	0.51	0.48	0.41	0.65	0.66	0.68
Current Ratio	1.82	2.65	2.26	1.67	2.45	1.73	2.23	1.93
Debt to Equity	0.81	1.01	0.88	0.84	0.91	0.70	0.81	1.03
Price Range	77.31-46.10	81.71-56.64	81.75-69.72	87.48-69.84	107.28-78.40	92.73-67.59	80.20-52.29	59.13-47.72
P/E Ratio	...	817.50-697.20		29.26-23.36	...	16.30-11.88	12.40-8.08	9.51-7.67

Address: 1350 Timberlake Manor Parkway, Chesterfield, MO 63017 **Telephone:** 314-594-1900	**Web Site:** www.edgewell.com **Officers:** David P. Hatfield - Chairman, President, Chief Executive Officer John N. Hill - Vice President	**Auditors:** PricewaterhouseCoopers LLP **Investor Contact:** 314-982-2013 **Transfer Agents:** Continental Stock Transfer & Trust Company, New York, NY

EDISON INTERNATIONAL

Exchange	Symbol	Price	52Wk Range	Yield	P/E	Div Acheiver
NYS	EIX	$63.27 (6/29/2018)	82.64-58.07	3.82	49.05	13 Years

*7 Year Price Score 96.43 *NYSE Composite Index=100 *12 Month Price Score 87.41

Interim Earnings (Per Share)

Qtr.	Mar	Jun	Sep	Dec
2015	0.91	1.15	1.28	(0.24)
2016	0.82	0.84	1.27	1.03
2017	1.10	0.85	1.43	(1.66)
2018	0.67	...	...	...

Interim Dividends (Per Share)

Amt	Decl	Ex	Rec	Pay
0.542Q	08/24/2017	09/28/2017	09/29/2017	10/31/2017
0.605Q	12/07/2017	12/28/2017	12/29/2017	01/31/2018
0.605Q	02/22/2018	03/28/2018	03/29/2018	04/30/2018
0.605Q	06/21/2018	06/29/2018	07/02/2018	07/31/2018

Indicated Div: $2.42 (Div. Reinv. Plan)

Valuation Analysis | **Institutional Holding**

Forecast EPS	$4.10	No of Institutions
	(06/14/2018)	938
Market Cap	$20.6 Billion	Shares
Book Value	$11.7 Billion	317,205,760
Price/Book	1.76	% Held
Price/Sales	1.66	78.25

Business Summary: Electric Utilities (MIC: 3.1.1 SIC: 4911 NAIC: 221111)

Edison International is a holding company. Through its principal subsidiary, Southern California Edison Company (SCE), Co. is primarily engaged in the business of supplying and delivering electricity. Co. is also the parent company of Edison Energy Group, a company that engaged in businesses focused on providing energy services and distributing solar to commercial and industrial customers. SCE supplies electricity to its customers through transmission and distribution networks. Its transmission facilities include sub-transmission facilities and are located primarily in California as well as in Nevada and Arizona.

Recent Developments: For the quarter ended Mar 31 2018, income from continuing operations decreased 38.3% to US$242.0 million from US$392.0 million in the year-earlier quarter. Net income decreased 38.3% to US$242.0 million from US$392.0 million in the year-earlier quarter. Revenues were US$2.56 billion, up 4.1% from US$2.46 billion the year before. Operating income was US$330.0 million versus US$471.0 million in the prior-year quarter, a decrease of 29.9%. Direct operating expenses rose 15.3% to US$1.60 billion from US$1.39 billion in the comparable period the year before. Indirect operating expenses increased 4.8% to US$633.0 million from US$604.0 million in the equivalent prior-year period.

Prospects: Our evaluation of Edison International as of Jan. 21, 2018 is the result of our systematic analysis on three basic characteristics: earnings strength, relative valuation, and recent stock price movement. The company has generated a negative trend in earnings per share over the past 5 quarters. However, while recent estimates for the company have been lowered by analysts, EIX has posted better than expected results. Based on operating earnings yield, the company is undervalued when compared to all of the companies in our coverage universe. Share price changes over the past year indicates that EIX will perform very well over the near term.

Financial Data

(US$ in Thousands)	3 Mos	12/31/2017	12/31/2016	12/31/2015	12/31/2014	12/31/2013	12/31/2012	12/31/2011
Earnings Per Share	1.29	1.72	3.97	3.10	4.89	2.78	(0.56)	(0.11)
Cash Flow Per Share	10.94	11.00	9.96	13.83	9.96	9.83	10.20	11.98
Tang Book Value Per Share	35.90	35.82	36.82	34.89	33.64	30.50	28.95	30.86
Dividends Per Share	2.295	2.232	1.982	1.732	1.482	1.367	1.313	1.285
Dividend Payout %	177.91	129.80	49.94	55.89	30.32	49.19	...	...
Income Statement								
Total Revenue	2,564,000	12,320,000	11,869,000	11,524,000	13,413,000	12,581,000	11,862,000	12,760,000
EBITDA	856,000	3,191,000	3,688,000	3,539,000	4,349,000	3,377,000	4,005,000	2,310,000
Depn & Amortn	479,000	1,610,000	1,520,000	1,420,000	1,815,000	1,622,000	1,634,000	1,889,000
Income Before Taxes	211,000	949,000	1,590,000	1,568,000	1,979,000	1,221,000	1,860,000	(350,000)
Income Taxes	(31,000)	281,000	177,000	486,000	443,000	242,000	267,000	(288,000)
Net Income	218,000	565,000	1,311,000	1,020,000	1,612,000	915,000	(183,000)	(37,000)
Average Shares	327,000	328,000	330,000	329,000	329,000	329,000	330,000	326,000
Balance Sheet								
Current Assets	2,992,000	3,729,000	2,123,000	2,654,000	4,019,000	3,312,000	2,672,000	4,484,000
Total Assets	51,943,000	52,580,000	51,319,000	50,310,000	50,186,000	46,646,000	44,394,000	48,039,000
Current Liabilities	4,647,000	7,068,000	5,912,000	4,927,000	5,479,000	4,881,000	3,744,000	4,348,000
Long-Term Obligations	13,367,000	11,642,000	10,175,000	10,964,000	10,234,000	9,825,000	9,231,000	13,689,000
Total Liabilities	40,247,000	40,909,000	39,323,000	38,942,000	39,226,000	36,708,000	34,962,000	37,984,000
Stockholders' Equity	11,696,000	11,671,000	11,996,000	11,368,000	10,960,000	9,938,000	9,432,000	10,055,000
Shares Outstanding	325,811	325,811	325,811	325,811	325,811	325,811	325,811	325,811
Statistical Record								
Return on Assets %	0.81	1.09	2.57	2.03	3.33	2.01	N.M.	N.M.
Return on Equity %	3.55	4.77	11.19	9.14	15.43	9.45	N.M.	N.M.
EBITDA Margin %	33.39	25.90	31.07	30.71	32.42	26.84	33.76	18.10
Net Margin %	8.50	4.59	11.05	8.85	12.02	7.27	N.M.	N.M.
Asset Turnover	0.24	0.24	0.23	0.23	0.28	0.28	0.26	0.27
Current Ratio	0.64	0.53	0.36	0.54	0.73	0.68	0.71	1.03
Debt to Equity	1.14	1.00	0.85	0.96	0.93	0.99	0.98	1.36
Price Range	82.64-58.07	82.64-63.24	78.55-58.28	69.05-55.58	68.27-45.07	53.98-44.36	47.96-39.98	41.52-33.29
P/E Ratio	64.06-45.02	48.05-36.77	19.79-14.68	22.27-17.93	13.96-9.22	19.42-15.96	...	...
Average Yield %	3.08	2.87	2.81	2.82	2.63	2.85	2.96	3.37

Address: 2244 Walnut Grove Avenue, P.O. Box 976, Rosemead, CA 91770
Telephone: 626-302-2222

Web Site: www.edisoninvestor.com
Officers: William P. Sullivan - Chairman Pedro J. Pizarro - President, Chief Executive Officer

Auditors: PricewaterhouseCoopers LLP
Transfer Agents: Wells Fargo Shareowner Services, St. Paul, MN

EDUCATION REALTY TRUST INC

Exchange	Symbol	Price	52Wk Range	Yield	P/E
NYS	EDR	$41.50 (6/29/2018)	41.58-30.30	3.76	45.11

*7 Year Price Score 83.72 'NYSE Composite Index=100 *12 Month Price Score 103.83

Interim Earnings (Per Share)

Qtr.	Mar	Jun	Sep	Dec
2015	0.14	0.06	(0.10)	0.29
2016	0.26	0.26	(0.05)	0.20
2017	0.21	0.07	(0.01)	0.33
2018	0.53	...		

Interim Dividends (Per Share)

Amt	Decl	Ex	Rec	Pay
0.39Q	07/13/2017	07/27/2017	07/31/2017	08/15/2017
0.39Q	10/12/2017	10/30/2017	10/31/2017	11/15/2017
0.39Q	01/11/2018	01/30/2018	01/31/2018	02/15/2018
0.39Q	04/12/2018	04/27/2018	04/30/2018	05/15/2018

Indicated Div: $1.56 (Div. Reinv. Plan)

Valuation Analysis

		Institutional Holding	
Forecast EPS	$0.82 (06/13/2018)	No of Institutions	341
Market Cap	$3.1 Billion	Shares	
Book Value	$1.9 Billion		116,188,624
Price/Book	1.69	% Held	
Price/Sales	9.36		102.33

TRADING VOLUME (thousand shares)

Business Summary: REITs (MIC: 5.3.1 SIC: 6798 NAIC: 525930)

Education Realty Trust is a real estate investment trust. Co. is engaged in developing, acquiring, owning and managing collegiate housing communities located near university campuses. Co. selectively develops collegiate housing communities for its own account and also provides third-party management services as well as third-party development consulting services on collegiate housing development projects for universities and other third parties. As of Dec 31 2017, Co. owned 70 collegiate housing communities located in 24 states containing 36,420 beds in 13,701 apartment units on or near 41 university campuses.

Recent Developments: For the quarter ended Mar 31 2018, net income increased 151.4% to US$40.6 million from US$16.1 million in the year-earlier quarter. Revenues were US$90.7 million, up 5.7% from US$85.8 million the year before. Revenues from property income rose 8.6% to US$87.7 million from US$80.8 million in the corresponding quarter a year earlier.

Prospects: Our evaluation of Education Realty Trust Inc. as of Jan. 21, 2018 is the result of our systematic analysis on three basic characteristics: earnings strength, relative valuation, and recent stock price movement. The company has produced a positive trend in earnings per share over the past 5 quarters and while recent estimates for the company have remained steady, EDR has posted better than expected results. Based on operating earnings yield, the company is overvalued when compared to all of the companies in our coverage universe. Share price changes over the past year indicates that EDR will perform well over the near term.

Financial Data

(US$ in Thousands)	3 Mos	12/31/2017	12/31/2016	12/31/2015	12/31/2014	12/31/2013	12/31/2012	12/31/2011
Earnings Per Share	0.92	0.60	0.65	0.40	1.09	0.12	0.24	(0.45)
Cash Flow Per Share	1.79	2.04	1.91	2.01	2.08	2.03	1.13	1.63
Tang Book Value Per Share	24.49	24.29	24.54	21.68	20.53	18.87	19.99	18.23
Dividends Per Share	1.550	1.540	1.500	1.460	1.380	1.260	1.020	0.720
Dividend Payout %	168.48	256.67	230.77	365.00	126.61	1,050.00	425.00	...
Income Statement								
Total Revenue	90,728	331,066	288,968	255,162	225,793	184,376	144,951	125,447
EBITDA	24,778	64,539	40,155	46,152	38,916	24,930	18,595	7,348
Depn & Amortn	363	1,600	1,700	1,500	900	600	2,438	450
Income Before Taxes	19,344	46,195	21,760	18,327	15,394	5,493	835	(12,413)
Income Taxes	66	584	684	347	261	203	(884)	(95)
Net Income	40,958	47,440	44,924	19,911	47,055	4,323	8,421	(11,014)
Average Shares	76,385	74,465	69,600	49,991	43,277	38,489	34,105	25,161
Balance Sheet								
Current Assets	27,393	35,276	46,679	48,787	32,993	40,355	30,621	84,090
Total Assets	3,063,991	3,015,164	2,506,185	2,001,831	1,811,637	1,610,565	1,324,687	977,809
Current Liabilities	1,154,889	182,907	148,599	104,694	94,170	91,144	75,087	46,175
Long-Term Obligations	(2,911)	933,449	517,196	638,707	711,137	779,581	477,846	358,504
Total Liabilities	1,207,562	1,170,428	706,166	765,132	822,848	884,841	566,965	415,942
Stockholders' Equity	1,856,429	1,844,736	1,800,019	1,236,699	988,789	725,724	757,722	561,867
Shares Outstanding	75,808	75,779	73,075	56,879	47,999	38,246	37,687	30,600
Statistical Record								
Return on Assets %	2.50	1.72	1.99	1.04	2.75	0.29	0.73	N.M.
Return on Equity %	3.96	2.60	2.95	1.79	5.49	0.58	1.27	N.M.
EBITDA Margin %	27.31	19.49	13.90	18.09	17.24	13.52	12.83	5.86
Net Margin %	45.14	14.33	15.55	7.80	20.84	2.34	5.81	N.M.
Asset Turnover	0.12	0.12	0.13	0.13	0.13	0.13	0.13	0.15
Current Ratio	0.02	0.19	0.31	0.47	0.35	0.44	0.41	1.82
Debt to Equity	...	0.51	0.29	0.52	0.72	1.07	0.63	0.64
Price Range	41.35-30.30	42.61-34.57	48.47-35.63	39.59-28.08	37.38-25.95	35.13-25.20	35.37-29.49	30.69-21.78
P/E Ratio	44.95-32.93	71.02-57.62	74.57-54.82	98.98-70.20	34.29-23.81	292.75-210.00	147.38-122.88	...
Average Yield %	4.25	3.99	3.57	4.29	4.40	4.22	3.15	2.81

Address: 999 South Shady Grove Road, Suite 600, Memphis, TN 38120 Telephone: 901-259-2500	Web Site: www.edrtrust.com Officers: Randall L. (Randy) Churchey - Chairman, President, Chief Executive Officer Thomas Trubiana - President, Executive Vice President, Senior Vice President, Chief Investment Officer	Auditors: Deloitte & Touche LLP Investor Contact: 901-259-2500 Transfer Agents: American Stock Transfer & Trust Co. LLC, New York, NY

EDWARDS LIFESCIENCES CORP

Exchange	Symbol	Price	52Wk Range	Yield	P/E
NYS	EW	$145.57 (6/29/2018)	153.90-101.38	N/A	55.99

*7 Year Price Score 142.12 *NYSE Composite Index=100 *12 Month Price Score 113.33

Interim Earnings (Per Share)

Qtr.	Mar	Jun	Sep	Dec
2015	0.56	0.51	0.54	0.64
2016	0.66	0.58	0.65	0.72
2017	1.06	0.86	0.79	(0.01)
2018	0.96	...	...	...

Interim Dividends (Per Share)

Amt	Decl	Ex	Rec	Pay
100%	11/19/2015	12/14/2015	11/30/2015	12/11/2015

Valuation Analysis

		Institutional Holding	
Forecast EPS	$4.62 (06/14/2018)	No of Institutions	1073
Market Cap	$30.7 Billion	Shares	202,219,072
Book Value	$3.2 Billion	% Held	83.07
Price/Book	9.45		
Price/Sales	8.90		

Business Summary: Medical Instruments & Equipment (MIC: 4.3.1 SIC: 3842 NAIC: 339113)

Edwards Lifesciences is engaged in patient-focused technology for structural heart disease and critical care monitoring. Co.'s products and technologies are categorized into three areas: Transcatheter Heart Valve Therapy, which provides transcatheter heart valve replacement technologies designed for the nonsurgical replacement of heart valves; Surgical Heart Valve Therapy, which provides surgical tissue heart valve products, surgical heart valve repair therapies and cardiac cannula devices; and Critical Care, which provides hemodynamic monitoring systems used to measure a patient's heart function and fluid status in surgical and intensive care settings.

Recent Developments: For the quarter ended Mar 31 2018, net income decreased 10.3% to US$206.6 million from US$230.2 million in the year-earlier quarter. Revenues were US$894.8 million, up 1.3% from US$883.5 million the year before. Operating income was US$252.5 million versus US$298.3 million in the prior-year quarter, a decrease of 15.4%. Direct operating expenses rose 8.3% to US$233.6 million from US$215.6 million in the comparable period the year before. Indirect operating expenses increased 10.6% to US$408.7 million from US$369.6 million in the equivalent prior-year period.

Prospects: Our evaluation of Edwards Lifesciences Corp. as of Jan. 21, 2018 is the result of our systematic analysis on three basic characteristics: earnings strength, relative valuation, and recent stock price movement. The company has generated a negative trend in earnings per share over the past 5 quarters and while recent estimates for the company have been raised by analysts, EW has posted results that fell short of analysts expectations. Based on operating earnings yield, the company is about fairly valued when compared to all of the companies in our coverage universe. Share price changes over the past year indicates that EW will perform in line with the market over the near term.

Financial Data

(US$ in Thousands)	3 Mos	12/31/2017	12/31/2016	12/31/2015	12/31/2014	12/31/2013	12/31/2012	12/31/2011
Earnings Per Share	2.60	2.70	2.61	2.25	3.74	1.72	1.24	0.99
Cash Flow Per Share	4.87	4.74	3.30	2.55	4.80	2.12	1.62	1.37
Tang Book Value Per Share	7.69	6.49	8.45	7.75	8.31	5.11	4.50	4.04
Income Statement								
Total Revenue	894,800	3,435,300	2,963,700	2,493,700	2,322,900	2,045,500	1,899,600	1,678,600
EBITDA	281,800	1,111,900	809,900	690,400	1,212,300	574,000	435,400	321,900
Depn & Amortn	19,100	74,100	63,600	58,700	57,500	53,100	44,000	44,000
Income Before Taxes	263,500	1,034,900	737,900	622,400	1,144,000	515,700	391,800	278,200
Income Taxes	56,900	451,300	168,400	127,500	332,900	123,600	97,900	46,900
Net Income	206,600	583,600	569,500	494,900	811,100	391,700	293,200	236,700
Average Shares	215,100	215,900	217,800	220,300	217,000	227,600	236,600	238,800
Balance Sheet								
Current Assets	2,716,900	2,532,100	2,240,000	2,047,900	2,294,600	1,725,800	1,291,900	1,168,500
Total Assets	5,825,100	5,695,800	4,510,000	4,059,300	3,524,300	2,724,700	2,221,500	1,980,500
Current Liabilities	1,314,500	1,402,900	532,500	476,200	434,400	345,600	347,400	335,200
Long-Term Obligations	456,000	438,400	822,300	599,900	598,100	593,100	189,300	150,400
Total Liabilities	2,579,400	2,739,600	1,891,000	1,556,200	1,332,900	1,165,500	742,200	642,600
Stockholders' Equity	3,245,700	2,956,200	2,619,000	2,503,100	2,191,400	1,559,200	1,479,300	1,337,900
Shares Outstanding	210,700	209,700	211,600	215,400	215,600	218,600	228,600	228,200
Statistical Record								
Return on Assets %	10.56	11.44	13.26	13.05	25.96	15.84	13.92	12.63
Return on Equity %	18.70	20.94	22.18	21.08	43.25	25.78	20.76	17.89
EBITDA Margin %	31.49	32.37	27.33	27.69	52.19	28.06	22.92	19.18
Net Margin %	23.09	16.99	19.22	19.85	34.92	19.15	15.43	14.10
Asset Turnover	0.65	0.67	0.69	0.66	0.74	0.83	0.90	0.90
Current Ratio	2.07	1.80	4.21	4.30	5.28	4.99	3.72	3.49
Debt to Equity	0.14	0.15	0.31	0.24	0.27	0.38	0.13	0.11
Price Range	142.34-93.09	120.15-89.49	121.36-74.52	82.56-61.93	66.74-32.09	47.28-30.72	54.88-34.22	45.68-31.25
P/E Ratio	54.75-35.80	44.50-33.14	46.50-28.55	36.69-27.52	17.84-8.58	27.49-17.86	44.25-27.59	46.14-31.57

Address: One Edwards Way, Irvine, CA 92614 **Telephone:** 949-250-2500	**Web Site:** www.edwards.com **Officers:** Michael A. Mussallem - Chairman, Chief Executive Officer Donald E. Bobo - Corporate Vice-President	**Auditors:** PricewaterhouseCoopers LLP **Transfer Agents:** ComputerShare Investor Services, Providence, RI

EMCOR GROUP, INC.

Exchange	Symbol	Price	52Wk Range	Yield	P/E
NYS	EME	$76.18 (6/29/2018)	84.14-62.45	0.42	19.63

*7 Year Price Score 127.83 *NYSE Composite Index=100 *12 Month Price Score 100.96

Interim Earnings (Per Share)

Qtr.	Mar	Jun	Sep	Dec
2015	0.52	0.74	0.66	0.81
2016	0.56	0.90	0.84	0.67
2017	0.87	0.95	1.09	0.90
2018	0.94	...	...	...

Interim Dividends (Per Share)

Amt	Decl	Ex	Rec	Pay
0.08Q	10/03/2017	10/16/2017	10/17/2017	10/30/2017
0.08Q	01/05/2018	01/12/2018	01/16/2018	01/30/2018
0.08Q	04/04/2018	04/13/2018	04/16/2018	04/30/2018
0.08Q	07/09/2018	07/19/2018	07/20/2018	07/31/2018

Indicated Div: $0.32

Valuation Analysis | **Institutional Holding**

Forecast EPS	$4.50 (06/13/2018)	No of Institutions	500
Market Cap	$4.5 Billion	Shares	75,418,416
Book Value	$1.7 Billion	% Held	96.84
Price/Book	2.63		
Price/Sales	0.58		

Business Summary: Construction Services (MIC: 7.5.4 SIC: 1731 NAIC: 238210)

EMCOR Group is an electrical and mechanical construction and facilities services firm. In addition, Co. provides a number of building services and industrial services. Co.'s services are provided through its operating subsidiaries and joint venture entities. Co. focuses on providing construction services relating to electrical and mechanical systems and in providing various services relating to the operation, maintenance and management of facilities, including refineries and petrochemical plants. Co. also provides its construction services indirectly by acting as a subcontractor to contractors, systems suppliers, property managers and other subcontractors.

Recent Developments: For the quarter ended Mar 31 2018, income from continuing operations increased 4.8% to US$55.7 million from US$53.1 million in the year-earlier quarter. Net income increased 5.3% to US$55.4 million from US$52.6 million in the year-earlier quarter. Revenues were US$1.90 billion, up 0.5% from US$1.89 billion the year before. Operating income was US$78.7 million versus US$82.8 million in the prior-year quarter, a decrease of 4.9%. Direct operating expenses was unchanged at US$1.63 billion versus the comparable period the year before. Indirect operating expenses increased 3.7% to US$190.4 million from US$183.6 million in the equivalent prior-year period.

Prospects: Our evaluation of EMCOR Group Inc. as of Jan. 21, 2018 is the result of our systematic analysis on three basic characteristics: earnings strength, relative valuation, and recent stock price movement. The company has generated a negative trend in earnings per share over the past 5 quarters and while recent estimates for the company have been mixed, EME has posted better than expected results. Based on operating earnings yield, the company is undervalued when compared to all of the companies in our coverage universe. Share price changes over the past year indicates that EME will perform in line with the market over the near term.

Financial Data
(US$ in Thousands)

	3 Mos	12/31/2017	12/31/2016	12/31/2015	12/31/2014	12/31/2013	12/31/2012	12/31/2011
Earnings Per Share	3.88	3.82	2.97	2.72	2.52	1.82	2.16	1.91
Cash Flow Per Share	5.32	6.18	4.34	4.25	3.72	2.24	2.76	2.24
Tang Book Value Per Share	4.13	3.63	1.17	2.63	1.27	1.34	6.51	4.48
Dividends Per Share	0.320	0.320	0.320	0.320	0.320	0.180	0.510	0.050
Dividend Payout %	8.25	8.38	10.77	11.76	12.70	9.89	23.61	2.62
Income Statement								
Total Revenue	1,900,388	7,686,999	7,551,524	6,718,726	6,424,965	6,417,158	6,346,679	5,613,459
EBITDA	89,409	419,048	388,266	361,277	364,344	277,620	310,929	264,543
Depn & Amortn	10,668	88,494	79,808	74,195	74,466	67,328	60,962	53,750
Income Before Taxes	76,289	318,749	296,494	278,823	281,645	202,651	244,248	201,352
Income Taxes	20,633	90,699	111,199	106,256	103,528	75,297	95,362	76,764
Net Income	55,374	227,196	181,935	172,286	168,664	123,792	146,584	130,826
Average Shares	59,064	59,618	61,206	63,307	67,062	68,076	67,738	68,375
Balance Sheet								
Current Assets	2,169,777	2,284,509	2,210,847	2,067,419	1,886,603	1,930,105	2,044,453	1,936,653
Total Assets	3,841,999	3,965,904	3,894,170	3,546,470	3,388,967	3,465,915	3,107,070	3,014,076
Current Liabilities	1,512,297	1,650,952	1,511,774	1,413,728	1,283,417	1,298,743	1,294,519	1,330,913
Long-Term Obligations	291,478	294,786	408,296	300,065	316,399	335,331	154,112	153,335
Total Liabilities	2,151,183	2,292,637	2,357,081	2,069,759	1,972,954	1,999,650	1,760,990	1,779,342
Stockholders' Equity	1,690,816	1,673,267	1,537,089	1,476,711	1,416,013	1,466,265	1,346,080	1,234,734
Shares Outstanding	58,450	58,798	59,946	61,067	62,981	66,896	66,964	66,444
Statistical Record								
Return on Assets %	6.01	5.78	4.88	4.97	4.92	3.77	4.78	4.53
Return on Equity %	14.26	14.15	12.04	11.91	11.70	8.80	11.33	10.96
EBITDA Margin %	4.70	5.45	5.14	5.38	5.67	4.33	4.90	4.71
Net Margin %	2.91	2.96	2.41	2.56	2.63	1.93	2.31	2.33
Asset Turnover	2.01	1.96	2.02	1.94	1.87	1.95	2.07	1.95
Current Ratio	1.43	1.38	1.46	1.46	1.47	1.49	1.58	1.46
Debt to Equity	0.17	0.18	0.27	0.20	0.22	0.23	0.11	0.12
Price Range	84.14-60.39	83.64-60.39	73.04-42.47	51.68-39.96	47.79-39.07	43.78-34.61	34.70-25.76	32.65-18.58
P/E Ratio	21.69-15.56	21.90-15.81	24.59-14.30	19.00-14.69	18.96-15.50	24.05-19.02	16.06-11.93	17.09-9.73
Average Yield %	0.45	0.47	0.60	0.69	0.73	0.46	1.76	0.18

Address: 301 Merritt Seven, Norwalk, CT 06851-1092	Web Site: www.emcorgroup.com	Auditors: Ernst & Young LLP
Telephone: 203-849-7800	Officers: Anthony J. Guzzi - President, Chief Executive Officer Mark A. Pompa - Executive Vice President, Chief Financial Officer	Investor Contact: 203-849-7938 Transfer Agents: Computershare Shareowner Services, Pittsburgh, PA

EMERSON ELECTRIC CO.

Exchange	Symbol	Price	52Wk Range	Yield	P/E	Div Acheiver
NYS	EMR	$69.14 (6/29/2018)	74.08-58.00	2.81	24.78	61 Years

*7 Year Price Score 93.48   *NYSE Composite Index=100   *12 Month Price Score 105.28

Interim Earnings (Per Share)

Qtr.	Dec	Mar	Jun	Sep
2014-15	0.75	1.42	0.84	0.98
2015-16	0.53	0.57	0.74	0.68
2016-17	0.48	0.45	0.64	0.78
2017-18	0.61	0.76	...	...

Interim Dividends (Per Share)

Amt	Decl	Ex	Rec	Pay
0.48Q	08/01/2017	08/09/2017	08/11/2017	09/11/2017
0.485Q	11/07/2017	11/16/2017	11/17/2017	12/11/2017
0.485Q	02/06/2018	02/15/2018	02/16/2018	03/09/2018
0.485Q	05/01/2018	05/10/2018	05/11/2018	06/11/2018

Indicated Div: $1.94 (Div. Reinv. Plan)

Valuation Analysis

Forecast EPS	$3.18	Institutional Holding	
	(06/14/2018)	No of Institutions	
		2000	
Market Cap	$43.7 Billion	Shares	
Book Value	$8.5 Billion	576,797,312	
Price/Book	5.14	% Held	
Price/Sales	2.64	65.60	

Business Summary: Electrical Equipment (MIC: 7.3.1 SIC: 3679 NAIC: 334419)

Emerson Electric is organized into five business segments: process management, which provides measurement, control and diagnostic capabilities for automated industrial processes producing items such as fuels, chemicals, foods, medicines and power; industrial automation, which brings integrated manufacturing solutions to various industries; climate technologies, which provides heating, air conditioning and refrigeration technology; commercial and residential solutions, which provides tools for professionals and homeowners, residential storage systems and appliance solutions.

Recent Developments: For the quarter ended Mar 31 2018, income from continuing operations increased 27.3% to US$489.0 million from US$384.0 million in the year-earlier quarter. Net income increased 63.0% to US$489.0 million from US$300.0 million in the year-earlier quarter. Revenues were US$4.25 billion, up 18.9% from US$3.57 billion the year before. Direct operating expenses rose 20.1% to US$2.42 billion from US$2.02 billion in the comparable period the year before. Indirect operating expenses increased 18.9% to US$1.03 billion from US$868.0 million in the equivalent prior-year period.

Prospects: Our evaluation of Emerson Electric Co. as of Jan. 21, 2018 is the result of our systematic analysis on three basic characteristics: earnings strength, relative valuation, and recent stock price movement. The company has managed to produce a neutral trend in earnings per share over the past 5 quarters and while recent estimates for the company have been raised by analysts, EMR has posted better than expected results. Based on operating earnings yield, the company is about fairly valued when compared to all of the companies in our coverage universe. Share price changes over the past year indicates that EMR will perform poorly over the near term.

Financial Data
(US$ in Thousands)

	6 Mos	3 Mos	09/30/2017	09/30/2016	09/30/2015	09/30/2014	09/30/2013	09/30/2012
Earnings Per Share	2.79	2.48	2.35	2.52	3.99	3.03	2.76	2.67
Cash Flow Per Share	3.87	3.32	2.98	4.46	3.76	5.27	5.08	4.17
Tang Book Value Per Share	0.74	0.97	2.36	4.29	N.M.	1.79	1.99	0.60
Dividends Per Share	1.930	1.925	1.920	1.900	1.880	1.720	1.640	1.600
Dividend Payout %	69.18	77.62	81.70	75.40	47.12	56.77	59.42	59.93
Income Statement								
Total Revenue	8,064,000	3,816,000	15,264,000	14,522,000	22,304,000	24,537,000	24,669,000	24,412,000
EBITDA	1,506,000	672,000	3,050,000	2,979,000	5,053,000	4,285,000	4,155,000	4,085,000
Depn & Amortn	271,000	131,000	550,000	475,000	721,000	743,000	741,000	746,000
Income Before Taxes	1,161,000	503,000	2,335,000	2,316,000	4,161,000	3,348,000	3,196,000	3,115,000
Income Taxes	278,000	109,000	660,000	697,000	1,428,000	1,164,000	1,130,000	1,091,000
Net Income	874,000	392,000	1,518,000	1,635,000	2,710,000	2,147,000	2,004,000	1,968,000
Average Shares	636,000	640,500	643,400	646,800	676,500	704,100	722,900	734,600
Balance Sheet								
Current Assets	7,725,000	8,152,000	8,252,000	9,960,000	10,049,000	10,867,000	10,999,000	10,126,000
Total Assets	19,785,000	19,858,000	19,589,000	21,743,000	22,088,000	24,177,000	24,711,000	23,818,000
Current Liabilities	5,945,000	6,192,000	5,045,000	8,008,000	7,800,000	8,454,000	7,625,000	7,133,000
Long-Term Obligations	3,357,000	3,375,000	3,794,000	4,062,000	4,289,000	3,559,000	4,055,000	3,787,000
Total Liabilities	11,293,000	11,509,000	10,871,000	14,175,000	14,007,000	14,058,000	14,126,000	13,523,000
Stockholders' Equity	8,492,000	8,349,000	8,718,000	7,568,000	8,081,000	10,119,000	10,585,000	10,295,000
Shares Outstanding	631,535	634,221	641,691	642,796	654,608	696,605	706,660	724,113
Statistical Record								
Return on Assets %	9.66	8.58	7.35	7.44	11.72	8.78	8.26	8.23
Return on Equity %	21.71	19.94	18.64	20.84	29.78	20.74	19.20	18.97
EBITDA Margin %	18.68	17.61	19.98	20.51	22.66	17.46	16.84	16.73
Net Margin %	10.84	10.27	9.94	11.26	12.15	8.75	8.12	8.06
Asset Turnover	0.89	0.85	0.74	0.66	0.96	1.00	1.02	1.02
Current Ratio	1.30	1.32	1.64	1.24	1.29	1.29	1.44	1.42
Debt to Equity	0.40	0.40	0.44	0.54	0.53	0.35	0.38	0.37
Price Range	74.05-57.44	69.98-56.14	64.15-49.41	56.34-42.29	65.77-43.04	70.26-61.79	66.50-47.32	53.37-40.69
P/E Ratio	26.54-20.59	28.22-22.64	27.30-21.03	22.36-16.78	16.48-10.79	23.19-20.39	24.09-17.14	19.99-15.24
Average Yield %	3.02	3.15	3.30	3.75	3.29	2.60	2.93	3.27

Address: 8000 W. Florissant Avenue, St. Louis, MO 63136 Telephone: 314-553-2000	Web Site: www.emerson.com Officers: David N. Farr - Chairman, President, Chief Executive Officer Edward L. Monser - President, Chief Operating Officer	Auditors: KPMG LLP Investor Contact: 314-553-2197 Transfer Agents: Computershare, Inc., Providence, RI

EMPIRE STATE REALTY TRUST INC

Exchange	Symbol	Price	52Wk Range	Yield	P/E
NYS	ESRT	$17.10 (6/29/2018)	21.07-16.00	2.46	45.00

*7 Year Price Score N/A *NYSE Composite Index=100 *12 Month Price Score 87.91

Interim Earnings (Per Share)

Qtr.	Mar	Jun	Sep	Dec
2015	0.03	0.10	0.10	0.07
2016	.0.06	0.09	0.12	0.11
2017	0.06	0.10	0.12	0.10
2018	0.06	...	...	...

Interim Dividends (Per Share)

Amt	Decl	Ex	Rec	Pay
0.105Q	08/09/2017	09/14/2017	09/15/2017	09/29/2017
0.105Q	11/24/2017	12/14/2017	12/15/2017	12/29/2017
0.105Q	03/02/2018	03/14/2018	03/15/2018	03/30/2018
0.105Q	05/18/2018	06/14/2018	06/15/2018	06/29/2018

Indicated Div: $0.42

Valuation Analysis

		Institutional Holding	
Forecast EPS	$0.21	No of Institutions	
	(06/11/2018)	246	
Market Cap	$2.8 Billion	Shares	
Book Value	$1.2 Billion	155,945,456	
Price/Book	2.40	% Held	
Price/Sales	3.93	87.61	

TRADING VOLUME (thousand shares)

Business Summary: REITs (MIC: 5.3.1 SIC: 6798 NAIC: 525930)

Empire State Realty Trust is a real estate investment trust that owns, manages, operates, acquires and repositions office and retail properties in Manhattan and the greater New York metropolitan area. As of Dec 31 2017, Co. owned 14 office properties encompassing approximately 9.4 million rentable square feet of office space. Empire State Realty OP, L.P. conducts substantially all of Co.'s business. Co. has two segments: real estate, which includes all activities related to the ownership, management, operation, acquisition, repositioning and disposition of its real estate assets; and observatory, which operates the 86th and 102nd floor observatories at the Empire State Building.

Recent Developments: For the quarter ended Mar 31 2018, net income decreased 5.7% to US$18.1 million from US$19.1 million in the year-earlier quarter. Revenues were US$168.5 million, up 2.1% from US$165.0 million the year before. Revenues from property income rose 5.3% to US$140.1 million from US$133.1 million in the corresponding quarter a year earlier.

Prospects: Our evaluation of Empire State Realty Trust Inc as of Jan. 21, 2018 is the result of our systematic analysis on three basic characteristics: earnings strength, relative valuation, and recent stock price movement. The company has produced a positive trend in earnings per share over the past 5 quarters and while recent estimates for the company have remained steady, ESRT has posted results that fell short of analysts expectations. Based on operating earnings yield, the company is overvalued when compared to all of the companies in our coverage universe. Share price changes over the past year indicates that ESRT will perform well over the near term.

Financial Data
(US$ in Thousands)

	3 Mos	12/31/2017	12/31/2016	12/31/2015	12/31/2014	12/31/2013	10/06/2013	12/31/2012
Earnings Per Share	0.38	0.39	0.38	0.29	0.27	0.79	...	...
Cash Flow Per Share	1.23	1.21	1.63	1.78	1.41	(5.86)	...	...
Tang Book Value Per Share	1.92	4.19	4.25	0.28	N.M.	N.M.	...	...
Dividends Per Share	0.420	0.420	0.400	0.340	0.340	0.080	...	...
Dividend Payout %	110.53	107.69	105.26	117.24	125.93	10.06	...	...
Income Statement								
Total Revenue	168,496	712,468	678,000	657,634	635,326	127,583	206,072	260,294
EBITDA	37,172	312,889	290,886	259,688	230,826	256,525	49,028	123,991
Depn & Amortn	1,783	119,490	106,343	108,319	89,505	49,947	50,475	35,302
Income Before Taxes	17,798	124,926	113,396	83,877	74,865	193,431	(52,107)	34,295
Income Taxes	(260)	6,673	6,146	3,949	4,655	...	...	...
Net Income	10,002	63,583	52,392	34,666	27,143	75,245	(37,232)	48,643
Average Shares	296,827	298,049	277,568	266,621	254,506	95,611	...	...
Balance Sheet								
Current Assets	752,170	530,197	615,885	112,565	106,005	116,364	...	83,767
Total Assets	4,141,813	3,931,347	3,890,953	3,300,650	3,296,495	2,476,061	...	1,052,553
Current Liabilities	150,278	157,935	181,247	159,989	137,011	113,314	...	59,533
Long-Term Obligations	1,918,280	1,688,721	1,612,331	1,632,416	1,611,652	1,208,112	...	996,489
Total Liabilities	2,960,280	2,755,061	2,728,813	2,767,917	2,819,853	2,090,903	...	1,063,412
Stockholders' Equity	1,173,529	1,168,282	1,154,136	524,729	468,638	385,158	...	(10,859)
Shares Outstanding	164,369	161,477	155,840	120,023	107,191	95,606	...	...
Statistical Record								
Return on Assets %	1.58	1.63	1.45	1.05	0.94	...	...	4.72
Return on Equity %	5.44	5.48	6.22	6.98	6.36	...	...	...
EBITDA Margin %	22.06	43.92	42.90	39.49	36.33	201.07	23.79	47.63
Net Margin %	5.94	8.92	7.73	5.27	4.27	58.98	N.M.	18.69
Asset Turnover	0.18	0.18	0.19	0.20	0.22	...	...	0.25
Current Ratio	5.01	3.36	3.40	0.70	0.77	1.03	...	1.41
Debt to Equity	1.63	1.45	1.40	3.11	3.44	3.14	...	...
Price Range	21.63-16.31	21.92-19.76	22.17-14.67	18.96-15.94	17.88-14.19	15.55-13.27	13.20-13.10	...
P/E Ratio	56.92-42.92	56.21-50.67	58.34-38.61	65.38-54.97	66.22-52.56	19.68-16.80	...	...
Average Yield %	2.10	2.03	2.11	1.91	2.14	0.56	...	...

Address: 111 West 33rd Street, 12th Floor, New York, NY 10120	Web Site: www.empirestaterealtytrust.com	Auditors: Ernst & Young LLP
Telephone: 212-687-8700	Officers: Anthony E. Malkin - Chairman, President, Chief Executive Officer John B. Kessler - President, Chief Operating Officer	Transfer Agents: American Stock Transfer & Trust Company, LLC

ENCOMPASS HEALTH CORP

Exchange	Symbol	Price	52Wk Range	Yield	P/E
NYS	EHC	$67.72 (6/29/2018)	69.24-42.49	1.48	24.01

*7 Year Price Score 116.55 *NYSE Composite Index=100 *12 Month Price Score 123.52

Interim Earnings (Per Share)

Qtr.	Mar	Jun	Sep	Dec
2015	0.44	0.45	0.52	0.50
2016	0.61	0.65	0.64	0.69
2017	0.70	0.70	0.67	0.61
2018	0.84	...	...	...

Interim Dividends (Per Share)

Amt	Decl	Ex	Rec	Pay
0.25Q	07/20/2017	09/29/2017	10/02/2017	10/16/2017
0.25Q	10/20/2017	12/29/2017	01/02/2018	01/16/2018
0.25Q	02/23/2018	03/29/2018	04/02/2018	04/16/2018
0.25Q	05/04/2018	06/29/2018	07/02/2018	07/16/2018

Indicated Div: $1.00

Valuation Analysis / **Institutional Holding**

Forecast EPS	$3.38	No of Institutions
	(06/13/2018)	498
Market Cap	$6.7 Billion	Shares
Book Value	$1.2 Billion	125,123,568
Price/Book	5.59	% Held
Price/Sales	1.67	N/A

Business Summary: Hospitals & Health Care Facilities (MIC: 4.2.1 SIC: 8093 NAIC: 623110)

Encompass Health is a provider of post-acute healthcare services, providing both facility-based and home-based post-acute services in 36 states and Puerto Rico through its network of inpatient rehabilitation hospitals, home health agencies, and hospice agencies. Co. manages its operations using two operating segments: inpatient rehabilitation and home health and hospice. As of Dec 31 2017, Co. operated hospitals in 31 states and Puerto Rico. Co. also managed four inpatient rehabilitation units. As of Dec 31 2017, Co.'s Encompass Home Health and Hospice business operated home health and hospice agencies in 28 states, with concentrations in the Southeast, Oklahoma, and Texas.

Recent Developments: For the quarter ended Mar 31 2018, income from continuing operations increased 24.8% to US$105.7 million from US$84.7 million in the year-earlier quarter. Net income increased 24.6% to US$105.2 million from US$84.4 million in the year-earlier quarter. Revenues were US$1.05 billion, up 9.3% from US$957.1 million the year before. Direct operating expenses rose 10.5% to US$141.2 million from US$127.8 million in the comparable period the year before. Indirect operating expenses increased 10.3% to US$735.7 million from US$666.7 million in the equivalent prior-year period.

Prospects: Our evaluation of Encompass Health Corp. as of Jan. 21, 2018 is the result of our systematic analysis on three basic characteristics: earnings strength, relative valuation, and recent stock price movement. The company has managed to produce a neutral trend in earnings per share over the past 5 quarters and while recent estimates for the company have been raised by analysts, EHC has posted better than expected results. Based on operating earnings yield, the company is undervalued when compared to all of the companies in our coverage universe. Share price changes over the past year indicates that EHC will perform in line with the market over the near term.

Financial Data
(US$ in Thousands)

	3 Mos	12/31/2017	12/31/2016	12/31/2015	12/31/2014	12/31/2013	12/31/2012	12/31/2011
Earnings Per Share	2.82	2.69	2.59	1.91	2.29	2.58	1.69	1.96
Cash Flow Per Share	7.08	7.01	6.78	5.42	5.13	5.34	4.34	3.67
Tang Book Value Per Share	N.M.	N.M.	N.M.	N.M.	N.M.	N.M.	1.29	0.26
Dividends Per Share	0.990	0.980	0.940	0.880	0.780	0.360	...	...
Dividend Payout %	35.11	36.43	36.29	46.07	34.06	13.95	...	...
Income Statement								
Total Revenue	1,046,000	3,919,000	3,646,000	3,115,700	2,374,300	2,247,200	2,134,900	2,026,900
EBITDA	214,900	754,600	746,600	620,800	565,300	552,300	480,400	413,900
Depn & Amortn	45,900	111,800	102,300	91,000	79,900	67,900	59,000	63,600
Income Before Taxes	133,400	488,400	472,200	386,900	376,200	384,000	327,300	230,900
Income Taxes	30,000	160,600	163,900	141,900	110,700	12,700	108,600	37,100
Net Income	83,800	256,300	247,600	183,100	222,000	323,600	185,000	208,700
Average Shares	99,400	99,300	99,500	101,000	100,700	102,100	108,100	109,200
Balance Sheet								
Current Assets	708,500	702,200	654,500	598,700	686,600	580,400	636,800	391,000
Total Assets	4,939,600	4,893,700	4,681,900	4,606,100	3,408,800	2,534,400	2,423,800	2,271,200
Current Liabilities	572,000	517,500	475,600	426,400	364,300	311,600	300,900	313,200
Long-Term Obligations	2,544,400	2,545,400	2,979,300	3,134,700	2,110,800	1,505,200	1,239,900	1,235,800
Total Liabilities	3,742,600	3,712,000	3,946,000	3,994,700	2,842,400	2,096,600	1,790,000	1,766,800
Stockholders' Equity	1,197,000	1,181,700	735,900	611,400	566,400	437,800	633,800	504,400
Shares Outstanding	98,800	98,305	88,929	90,130	87,788	87,993	95,685	95,246
Statistical Record								
Return on Assets %	5.67	5.35	5.32	4.57	7.47	13.05	7.86	8.99
Return on Equity %	27.65	26.73	36.65	31.09	44.21	60.40	32.42	51.75
EBITDA Margin %	20.54	19.25	20.48	19.92	23.81	24.58	22.50	20.42
Net Margin %	8.01	6.54	6.79	5.88	9.35	14.40	8.67	10.30
Asset Turnover	0.83	0.82	0.78	0.78	0.80	0.91	0.91	0.87
Current Ratio	1.24	1.36	1.38	1.40	1.88	1.86	2.12	1.25
Debt to Equity	2.13	2.15	4.05	5.13	3.73	3.44	1.96	2.45
Price Range	58.57-42.37	50.10-38.61	43.05-30.91	47.93-33.04	41.74-30.05	36.48-21.11	24.63-16.82	28.16-14.25
P/E Ratio	20.77-15.02	18.62-14.35	16.62-11.93	25.09-17.30	18.23-13.12	14.14-8.18	14.57-9.95	14.37-7.27
Average Yield %	2.06	2.18	2.42	2.11	2.15	1.20	...	...

Address: 9001 Liberty Parkway, Birmingham, AL 35243	**Web Site:** www.healthsouth.com	**Auditors:** PricewaterhouseCoopers LLP
Telephone: 205-967-7116	**Officers:** Leo I. (Lee) Higdon - Chairman Jon F. Hanson - Chairman	**Investor Contact:** 205-968-6400
		Transfer Agents: Computershare Investor Services, Canton, MA

ENERGEN CORP.

Exchange	Symbol	Price	52Wk Range	Yield	P/E
NYS	EGN	$72.82 (6/29/2018)	72.82-47.35	N/A	18.11

*7 Year Price Score 80.16   *NYSE Composite Index=100   *12 Month Price Score 116.71

Interim Earnings (Per Share)

Qtr.	Mar	Jun	Sep	Dec
2015	(0.21)	(1.52)	(2.89)	(7.71)
2016	(2.34)	0.38	0.55	(0.56)
2017	0.34	0.30	(0.19)	2.69
2018	1.22			

Interim Dividends (Per Share)

Dividend Payment Suspended

Valuation Analysis

	Institutional Holding	
Forecast EPS	$3.39	No of Institutions
	(06/14/2018)	515
Market Cap	$7.1 Billion	Shares
Book Value	$3.6 Billion	111,131,944
Price/Book	1.99	% Held
Price/Sales	6.58	82.79

TRADING VOLUME (thousand shares)

Business Summary: Production & Extraction (MIC: 9.1.1 SIC: 1311 NAIC: 211111)

Energen is an oil and natural gas exploration and production company engaged in the exploration, development and production of oil, natural gas liquids and natural gas. Co.'s operations are primarily located within the Midland Basin, the Delaware Basin and the Central Basin Platform areas of the Permian Basin in west Texas and New Mexico. In addition, Co. explores for and develops new reservoirs, primarily in areas in which it has an operating presence. As of Dec 31 2017, Co. had 444.0 million barrels of oil equivalents proved reserves, which consisted of 577.49 billion cubic feet of natural gas, 90.78 million barrels of natural gas liquids, and 257.01 million barrels of oil.

Recent Developments: For the quarter ended Mar 31 2018, net income increased 256.0% to US$118.9 million from US$33.4 million in the year-earlier quarter. Revenues were US$356.2 million, up 47.8% from US$240.9 million the year before. Operating income was US$165.1 million versus US$61.3 million in the prior-year quarter, an increase of 169.3%. Direct operating expenses rose 39.0% to US$75.2 million from US$54.1 million in the comparable period the year before. Indirect operating expenses decreased 7.7% to US$115.9 million from US$125.5 million in the equivalent prior-year period.

Prospects: Our evaluation of Energen Corp. as of Jan. 21, 2018 is the result of our systematic analysis on three basic characteristics: earnings strength, relative valuation, and recent stock price movement. The company has generated a negative trend in earnings per share over the past 5 quarters and while recent estimates for the company have been raised by analysts, EGN has posted better than expected results. Based on operating earnings yield, the company is overvalued when compared to all of the companies in our coverage universe. Share price changes over the past year indicates that EGN will perform poorly over the near term.

Financial Data

(US$ in Thousands)	3 Mos	12/31/2017	12/31/2016	12/31/2015	12/31/2014	12/31/2013	12/31/2012	12/31/2011
Earnings Per Share	4.02	3.14	(1.77)	(12.43)	7.75	2.82	3.51	3.59
Cash Flow Per Share	7.91	5.86	3.09	9.39	9.68	12.82	10.17	10.57
Tang Book Value Per Share	36.52	35.40	32.17	36.78	46.84	39.36	37.14	33.79
Dividends Per Share	...	...	...	0.080	0.470	0.580	0.560	0.540
Dividend Payout %	...	...	...	...	6.06	20.57	15.95	15.04
Income Statement								
Total Revenue	356,171	961,045	532,889	878,554	1,679,213	1,738,650	1,617,169	1,483,479
EBITDA	289,553	629,129	237,709	(843,839)	726,706	895,474	882,535	734,144
Depn & Amortn	124,210	483,376	447,961	593,789	548,564	527,845	419,598	283,997
Income Before Taxes	155,095	107,387	(247,151)	(1,480,736)	140,371	298,429	397,381	405,325
Income Taxes	36,180	(199,441)	(79,638)	(535,005)	40,728	105,282	143,819	145,701
Net Income	118,915	306,828	(167,513)	(945,731)	568,032	204,554	253,562	259,624
Average Shares	97,818	97,707	94,475	76,078	73,274	72,470	72,316	72,332
Balance Sheet								
Current Assets	192,655	191,393	505,911	246,340	919,360	427,231	425,120	444,168
Total Assets	5,205,764	5,033,895	4,579,823	4,613,693	6,138,258	6,622,212	6,175,890	5,237,416
Current Liabilities	363,898	322,244	338,204	287,521	560,323	1,109,893	1,159,782	543,879
Long-Term Obligations	755,964	782,861	527,443	776,087	1,038,563	1,343,464	1,103,528	1,153,700
Total Liabilities	1,650,917	1,595,438	1,459,221	1,717,833	2,723,654	3,764,193	3,499,200	2,805,253
Stockholders' Equity	3,554,847	3,438,457	3,120,602	2,895,860	3,414,604	2,858,019	2,676,690	2,432,163
Shares Outstanding	97,327	97,135	97,013	78,743	72,895	72,606	72,069	71,970
Statistical Record								
Return on Assets %	8.00	6.38	N.M.	N.M.	8.90	3.20	4.43	5.41
Return on Equity %	11.70	9.36	N.M.	N.M.	18.11	7.39	9.90	11.32
EBITDA Margin %	81.30	65.46	44.61	N.M.	43.28	51.50	54.57	49.49
Net Margin %	33.39	31.93	N.M.	N.M.	33.83	11.77	15.68	17.50
Asset Turnover	0.22	0.20	0.12	0.16	0.26	0.27	0.28	0.31
Current Ratio	0.53	0.59	1.50	0.86	1.64	0.38	0.37	0.82
Debt to Equity	0.21	0.23	0.17	0.27	0.30	0.47	0.41	0.47
Price Range	62.86-46.77	59.37-46.77	62.07-22.90	75.46-40.45	90.10-55.49	85.31-44.87	55.50-40.85	65.01-38.80
P/E Ratio	15.64-11.63	18.91-14.89	...	...	11.63-7.16	30.25-15.91	15.81-11.64	18.11-10.81
Average Yield %	...	...	...	0.13	0.62	0.97	1.15	1.00

Address: 605 Richard Arrington, Birmingham, AL 35203-2707 **Telephone:** 205-326-2700	**Web Site:** www.energen.com **Officers:** James T. McManus - Chairman, President, Chief Executive Officer, Chief Operating Officer Charles W. Porter - Vice President, Chief Financial Officer, Treasurer	**Auditors:** PricewaterhouseCoopers LLP **Investor Contact:** 205-326-8421 **Transfer Agents:** Computershare Shareowner Services LLC, Providence, RI

ENERGIZER HOLDINGS INC

Exchange	Symbol	Price	52Wk Range	Yield	P/E
NYS	ENR	$62.96 (6/29/2018)	62.96-41.14	1.84	30.56

*7 Year Price Score N/A   *NYSE Composite Index=100   *12 Month Price Score 114.68

Interim Earnings (Per Share)

Qtr.	Dec	Mar	Jun	Sep
2014-15	0.99	(1.11)	(0.32)	0.38
2015-16	1.05	0.26	0.39	0.34
2016-17	1.52	0.75	0.40	0.55
2017-18	0.98	0.13	...	...

Interim Dividends (Per Share)

Amt	Decl	Ex	Rec	Pay
0.275Q	07/31/2017	08/17/2017	08/21/2017	09/12/2017
0.29Q	11/13/2017	11/29/2017	11/30/2017	12/14/2017
0.29Q	01/29/2018	02/16/2018	02/20/2018	03/13/2018
0.29Q	04/30/2018	05/18/2018	05/21/2018	06/13/2018

Indicated Div: $1.16

Valuation Analysis / Institutional Holding

Forecast EPS	$3.36 (06/11/2018)	No of Institutions	437
Market Cap	$3.8 Billion	Shares	68,500,400
Book Value	$44.7 Million	% Held	N/A
Price/Book	84.07		
Price/Sales	2.11		

TRADING VOLUME (thousand shares)

Business Summary: Household & Personal Products (MIC: 1.7.1 SIC: 3692 NAIC: 335912)

Energizer Holdings is a manufacturer, marketer and distributor of household batteries, specialty batteries and lighting products under the Energizer® and Eveready® brand names, and a designer and marketer of automotive fragrance and appearance products marketed under the Refresh Your Car!®, California Scents®, Driven®, Bahama & Co.®, LEXOL®, and Eagle One® brands. Co. provides batteries using lithium, alkaline, carbon zinc, nickel metal hydride, zinc air and silver oxide. Co. also distributes, markets, and licenses lighting products including headlights, lanterns, children's lights and area lights. Co. markets its flashlights under the Hard Case®, Dolphin®, and WeatherReady® sub-brands.

Recent Developments: For the quarter ended Mar 31 2018, net income decreased 83.4% to US$7.8 million from US$46.9 million in the year-earlier quarter. Revenues were US$374.4 million, up 4.3% from US$359.0 million the year before. Direct operating expenses rose 7.7% to US$205.9 million from US$191.1 million in the comparable period the year before. Indirect operating expenses increased 33.7% to US$133.3 million from US$99.7 million in the equivalent prior-year period.

Prospects: Our evaluation of Energizer Holdings Co. as of Jan. 21, 2018 is the result of our systematic analysis on three basic characteristics: earnings strength, relative valuation, and recent stock price movement. The company has generated a negative trend in earnings per share over the past 5 quarters and while recent estimates for the company have been raised by analysts, ENR has posted better than expected results. Based on operating earnings yield, the company is undervalued when compared to all of the companies in our coverage universe. Share price changes over the past year indicates that ENR will perform very poorly over the near term.

Financial Data

(US$ in Thousands)	6 Mos	3 Mos	09/30/2017	09/30/2016	09/30/2015	09/30/2014	09/30/2013	09/30/2012
Earnings Per Share	2.06	2.68	3.22	2.04	(0.06)	...	...	...
Cash Flow Per Share	3.91	4.09	3.20	3.12	2.60	...	...	...
Dividends Per Share	1.130	1.115	1.100	1.000	0.250	...	...	...
Dividend Payout %	54.85	41.60	34.16	49.02	...	...	...	...
Income Statement								
Total Revenue	947,700	573,300	1,755,700	1,634,200	1,631,600	1,840,400	2,012,200	2,087,700
EBITDA	172,300	135,200	371,300	250,700	114,300	308,200	284,900	381,800
Depn & Amortn	5,600	2,800	44,900	30,700	37,100	40,300	54,800	55,300
Income Before Taxes	136,800	119,000	273,300	165,700	(700)	215,200	162,000	257,600
Income Taxes	68,600	58,600	71,800	38,000	3,300	57,900	47,100	70,600
Net Income	68,200	60,400	201,500	127,700	(4,000)	157,300	114,900	187,000
Average Shares	61,100	61,500	62,600	62,500	62,200	...	...	...
Balance Sheet								
Current Assets	1,047,800	1,039,000	1,020,200	889,500	1,126,500	747,100	753,000	...
Total Assets	1,772,400	1,764,100	1,823,600	1,731,500	1,629,600	1,194,700	1,238,800	...
Current Liabilities	552,300	546,900	582,000	533,100	467,800	380,400	395,100	...
Long-Term Obligations	977,300	977,900	978,500	981,700	995,000	...	...	...
Total Liabilities	1,727,700	1,730,400	1,738,500	1,761,500	1,689,700	470,200	501,100	...
Stockholders' Equity	44,700	33,700	85,100	(30,000)	(60,100)	724,500	737,700	...
Shares Outstanding	59,686	59,685	60,708	61,672	62,195	...	...	...
Statistical Record								
Return on Assets %	7.27	9.65	11.34	7.58	N.M.	...	...	...
Return on Equity %	228.16	652.16	731.40	...	N.M.	...	...	...
EBITDA Margin %	18.18	23.58	21.15	15.34	7.01	16.75	14.16	18.29
Net Margin %	7.20	10.54	11.48	7.81	N.M.	8.55	5.71	8.96
Asset Turnover	1.02	1.03	0.99	0.97	1.16	...	...	...
Current Ratio	1.90	1.90	1.75	1.67	2.41	1.96	1.91	...
Debt to Equity	21.86	29.02	11.50	...	...	...	...	...
Price Range	59.82-41.14	59.82-41.14	59.82-41.14	52.35-30.23	42.31-33.00	...	...	...
P/E Ratio	29.04-19.97	22.32-15.35	18.58-12.78	25.66-14.82	...	...	...	...
Average Yield %	2.27	2.25	2.23	2.35	0.64	...	...	...

Address: 533 Maryville University Drive, St. Louis, MO 63141 **Telephone:** 314-985-2000	**Web Site:** www.energizerholdings.com **Officers:** J. Patrick Mulcahy - Chairman Alan R. Hoskins - President, Chief Executive Officer	**Auditors:** PricewaterhouseCoopers LLP **Transfer Agents:** Continental Stock Transfer and Trust Company

ENERGY TRANSFER EQUITY LP

Exchange	Symbol	Price	52Wk Range	Yield	P/E	Div Acheiver
NYS	ETE	$17.25 (6/29/2018)	19.18-14.17	7.07	18.55	11 Years

*7 Year Price Score 76.88   *NYSE Composite Index=100   *12 Month Price Score 99.57

TRADING VOLUME (thousand shares)

Interim Earnings (Per Share)

Qtr.	Mar	Jun	Sep	Dec
2015	0.26	0.28	0.28	0.30
2016	0.30	0.23	0.19	0.21
2017	0.21	0.18	0.22	0.22
2018	0.31	...	...	...

Interim Dividends (Per Share)

Amt	Decl	Ex	Rec	Pay
0.285Q	07/27/2017	08/03/2017	08/07/2017	08/21/2017
0.295Q	10/26/2017	11/06/2017	11/07/2017	11/20/2017
0.305Q	01/29/2018	02/07/2018	02/08/2018	02/20/2018
0.305Q	04/26/2018	05/04/2018	05/07/2018	05/21/2018

Indicated Div: $1.22 (Div. Reinv. Plan)

Valuation Analysis / Institutional Holding

Forecast EPS	$1.74 (06/14/2018)	No of Institutions	536
Market Cap	$18.6 Billion	Shares	
Book Value	N/A	Shares	551,533,248
Price/Book	N/A	% Held	
Price/Sales	0.43		46.58

Business Summary: Equipment & Services (MIC: 9.1.3 SIC: 4922 NAIC: 486210)

Energy Transfer Equity is a holding company. Co.'s segments are: Investment in Energy Transfer Partners, L.P., which includes intrastate transportation and storage operations, interstate transportation and storage operations, midstream operations, liquids transportation and services operations, investment in Sunoco Logistics Partners L.P., and retail marketing operations; Investment in Sunoco LP, which includes wholesale and retail operations; and Investment in Lake Charles liquefied natural gas (LNG), which provides terminal services for shippers by receiving LNG at the facility for storage and delivering such LNG to shippers, either in liquid state or gaseous state after regasification.

Recent Developments: For the quarter ended Mar 31 2018, income from continuing operations increased 120.0% to US$726.0 million from US$330.0 million in the year-earlier quarter. Net income increased 53.3% to US$489.0 million from US$319.0 million in the year-earlier quarter. Revenues were US$11.88 billion, up 23.0% from US$9.66 billion the year before. Operating income was US$1.10 billion versus US$757.0 million in the prior-year quarter, an increase of 45.3%. Direct operating expenses rose 23.1% to US$9.25 billion from US$7.51 billion in the comparable period the year before. Indirect operating expenses increased 10.3% to US$1.54 billion from US$1.39 billion in the equivalent prior-year period.

Prospects: Our evaluation of Energy Transfer Equity L.P. as of Jan. 21, 2018 is the result of our systematic analysis on three basic characteristics: earnings strength, relative valuation, and recent stock price movement. The company has managed to produce a neutral trend in earnings per share over the past 5 quarters. However, while recent estimates for the company have been mixed, ETE has posted results that fell short of analysts expectations. Based on operating earnings yield, the company is undervalued when compared to all of the companies in our coverage universe. Share price changes over the past year indicates that ETE will perform poorly over the near term.

Financial Data

(US$ in Thousands)	3 Mos	12/31/2017	12/31/2016	12/31/2015	12/31/2014	12/31/2013	12/31/2012	12/31/2011
Earnings Per Share	0.93	0.83	0.92	1.11	0.57	0.17	0.28	0.34
Cash Flow Per Share	5.26	4.11	3.26	2.89	2.92	2.16	1.01	1.54
Dividends Per Share	1.170	1.150	1.140	1.020	0.750	0.652	0.625	0.588
Dividend Payout %	125.81	138.55	123.91	91.89	130.43	372.50	221.24	170.29
Income Statement								
Total Revenue	11,882,000	40,523,000	37,504,000	42,126,000	55,691,000	48,335,000	16,964,000	8,240,703
EBITDA	1,107,000	4,692,000	3,475,000	4,136,000	3,677,000	2,488,000	3,044,000	1,724,322
Depn & Amortn	4,000	2,204,000	2,089,000	1,776,000	1,223,000	1,128,000	801,000	556,569
Income Before Taxes	637,000	566,000	(446,000)	717,000	1,085,000	139,000	1,225,000	427,942
Income Taxes	(10,000)	(1,833,000)	(217,000)	(100,000)	357,000	93,000	54,000	16,883
Net Income	363,000	954,000	995,000	1,189,000	633,000	196,000	304,000	309,811
Average Shares	1,154,700	1,150,800	1,078,600	1,064,400	1,090,800	1,121,800	1,066,888	891,873
Balance Sheet								
Current Assets	6,593,000	10,683,000	6,985,000	5,410,000	6,153,000	6,536,000	5,597,000	1,455,444
Total Assets	82,909,000	86,246,000	79,011,000	71,189,000	64,469,000	50,330,000	48,904,000	20,896,793
Current Liabilities	7,261,000	7,897,000	7,277,000	4,910,000	6,782,000	6,500,000	5,845,000	1,841,313
Long-Term Obligations	41,779,000	43,671,000	42,858,000	36,837,000	29,653,000	22,562,000	21,440,000	10,946,864
Total Liabilities	84,089,000	87,442,000	80,705,000	72,121,000	63,805,000	49,252,000	46,791,000	20,843,309
Shares Outstanding	1,079,145	1,079,145	1,046,947	1,046,923	1,080,613	1,122,926	1,119,822	891,890
Statistical Record								
Return on Assets %	1.32	1.15	1.32	1.75	1.10	0.40	0.87	1.62
EBITDA Margin %	9.32	11.58	9.27	9.82	6.60	5.15	17.94	20.92
Net Margin %	3.06	2.35	2.65	2.82	1.14	0.41	1.79	3.76
Asset Turnover	0.53	0.49	0.50	0.62	0.97	0.97	0.48	0.43
Current Ratio	0.91	1.35	0.96	1.10	0.91	1.01	0.96	0.79
Price Range	19.73-14.20	19.86-15.15	19.59-4.05	35.24-11.09	32.24-19.62	20.62-11.37	11.95-8.60	11.56-8.02
P/E Ratio	21.22-15.27	23.93-18.25	21.29-4.40	31.75-9.99	56.56-34.43	121.31-66.88	42.67-30.71	33.99-23.58
Average Yield %	6.78	6.47	8.51	3.71	2.85	4.23	5.89	5.87

Address: 8111 Westchester Drive, Suite 600, Dallas, TX 75225 Telephone: 214-981-0700	Web Site: www.energytransfer.com Officers: Kelcy L. Warren - Chairman John W. McReynolds - President, Chief Financial Officer	Auditors: Grant Thornton LLP Investor Contact: 214-981-0700 Transfer Agents: American Stock Transfer & Trust, Brooklyn, NY

ENERGY TRANSFER PARTNERS LP

Exchange	Symbol	Price	52Wk Range	Yield	P/E	Div Acheiver
NYS	ETP	$19.04 (6/29/2018)	21.35-15.71	11.87	17.00	15 Years

*7 Year Price Score 52.33 *NYSE Composite Index=100 ***12 Month Price Score 100.34**

Interim Earnings (Per Share)

Qtr.	Mar	Jun	Sep	Dec
2015	(0.10)	0.83	(0.07)	(0.24)
2016	0.18	0.34	0.16	0.30
2017	1.42	(0.04)	0.33	0.59
2018	0.24	...	...	...

Interim Dividends (Per Share)

Amt	Decl	Ex	Rec	Pay
0.55Q	07/27/2017	08/03/2017	08/07/2017	08/14/2017
0.565Q	10/26/2017	11/06/2017	11/07/2017	11/14/2017
0.565Q	01/27/2018	02/07/2018	02/08/2018	02/14/2018
0.565Q	04/26/2018	05/04/2018	05/07/2018	05/15/2018

Indicated Div: $2.26

Valuation Analysis / **Institutional Holding**

Valuation Analysis		Institutional Holding	
Forecast EPS	$1.06	No of Institutions	
	(06/14/2018)	72	
Market Cap	$22.2 Billion	Shares	
Book Value	N/A	13,669,721	
Price/Book	N/A	% Held	
Price/Sales	0.73	44.72	

Business Summary: Equipment & Services (MIC: 9.1.3 SIC: 4612 NAIC: 486110)

Energy Transfer Partners, through its subsidiaries, conduct activities such as natural gas operations; and interstate natural gas transportation and storage; and crude oil, natural gas liquid and refined product. Co.'s segment includes: Intrastate Transportation and Storage, which owns and operates a natural gas open-access interstate pipeline network; Midstream, which consists of natural gas gathering, compression, treating, processing, storage, and transportation; NGL and Refined Products Transportation and Services, which transport, store and execute acquisition and marketing activities utilizing a network of pipelines, storage and blending facilities.

Recent Developments: For the quarter ended Mar 31 2018, net income increased 47.7% to US$879.0 million from US$595.0 million in the year-earlier quarter. Revenues were US$8.28 billion, up 123.7% from US$3.70 billion the year before. Operating income was US$973.0 million versus US$635.0 million in the prior-year quarter, an increase of 53.2%. Direct operating expenses rose 126.4% to US$6.59 billion from US$2.91 billion in the comparable period the year before. Indirect operating expenses increased 361.3% to US$715.0 million from US$155.0 million in the equivalent prior-year period.

Prospects: Our evaluation of Sunoco Logistics Partners L.P. as of Apr. 23, 2017 is the result of our systematic analysis on three basic characteristics: earnings strength, relative valuation, and recent stock price movement. The company has produced a positive trend in earnings per share over the past 5 quarters. However, while recent estimates for the company have been mixed, SXL has posted better than expected results. Based on operating earnings yield, the company is overvalued when compared to all of the companies in our coverage universe. Share price changes over the past year indicates that SXL will perform very poorly over the near term.

Financial Data

(US$ in Thousands)	3 Mos	12/31/2017	12/31/2016	12/31/2015	12/31/2014	12/31/2013	12/31/2012	10/04/2012
Earnings Per Share	1.12	0.93	0.98	0.42	0.51	1.63	0.55	1.57
Cash Flow Per Share	5.28	4.34	2.91	2.38	2.66	3.61	1.35	2.61
Dividends Per Share	2.215	2.170	1.978	1.715	1.426	1.174	0.917	0.865
Dividend Payout %	197.77	233.33	201.84	408.33	279.66	72.23	166.82	55.12
Income Statement								
Total Revenue	8,280,000	29,054,000	9,151,000	10,486,000	18,088,000	16,639,000	3,194,000	9,950,000
EBITDA	1,860,000	4,548,000	1,330,000	921,000	676,000	824,000	221,000	556,000
Depn & Amortn	603,000	2,334,000	437,000	369,000	284,000	243,000	57,000	78,000
Income Before Taxes	911,000	849,000	736,000	418,000	325,000	504,000	150,000	413,000
Income Taxes	(40,000)	(1,496,000)	27,000	21,000	25,000	30,000	8,000	24,000
Net Income	715,000	2,081,000	705,000	393,000	291,000	463,000	139,000	381,000
Average Shares	1,167,800	1,037,800	305,400	251,700	214,100	208,600	208,200	207,800
Balance Sheet								
Current Assets	5,748,000	6,528,000	2,906,000	1,848,000	2,349,000	3,073,000	2,390,000	...
Total Assets	77,495,000	77,965,000	18,849,000	15,489,000	13,644,000	11,897,000	10,361,000	...
Current Liabilities	6,223,000	6,994,000	2,138,000	1,663,000	2,311,000	2,736,000	2,131,000	...
Long-Term Obligations	33,109,000	32,687,000	7,313,000	5,591,000	4,260,000	2,503,000	1,732,000	...
Total Liabilities	49,496,000	49,696,000	9,889,000	7,682,000	6,966,000	5,693,000	4,289,000	...
Stockholders' Equity	...	...	300,000	286,000	...	...	...	...
Shares Outstanding	1,164,000	1,164,112	331,798	278,266	226,072	207,699	207,546	...
Statistical Record								
Return on Assets %	5.07	4.30	4.10	2.70	2.28	4.16	1.75	...
Return on Equity %	...	...	239.96	...	...	...	...	...
EBITDA Margin %	22.46	15.65	14.53	8.78	3.74	4.95	6.92	5.59
Net Margin %	8.64	7.16	7.70	3.75	1.61	2.78	4.35	3.83
Asset Turnover	0.62	0.60	0.53	0.72	1.42	1.50	0.40	...
Current Ratio	0.92	0.93	1.36	1.11	1.02	1.12	1.12	...
Debt to Equity	...	...	24.38	19.55	...	...	...	...
Price Range	24.49-15.71	26.71-15.71	31.47-16.49	46.00-22.07	51.13-36.60	37.74-24.86	25.95-22.53	25.02-14.41
P/E Ratio	21.87-14.03	28.72-16.89	32.11-16.83	109.52-52.55	100.25-71.76	23.15-15.25	47.18-40.96	15.94-9.18
Average Yield %	11.41	10.35	7.55	4.75	3.19	3.67	3.71	4.54

Address: 8111 Westchester Drive, Suite 600, Dallas, TX 75225
Telephone: 214-981-0700

Web Site: www.energytransfer.com
Officers: Marshall S. (Mackie) McCrea - Chairman, Chief Operating Officer, Chief Commercial Officer Kurt A. Lauterbach - Senior Vice President

Auditors: Grant Thornton LLP
Transfer Agents: American Stock Transfer & Trust Compan, New York, NY

ENERSYS

Exchange	Symbol	Price	52Wk Range	Yield	P/E
NYS	ENS	$74.64 (6/29/2018)	81.92-61.45	0.94	26.95

*7 Year Price Score 99.86   *NYSE Composite Index=100   *12 Month Price Score 107.10

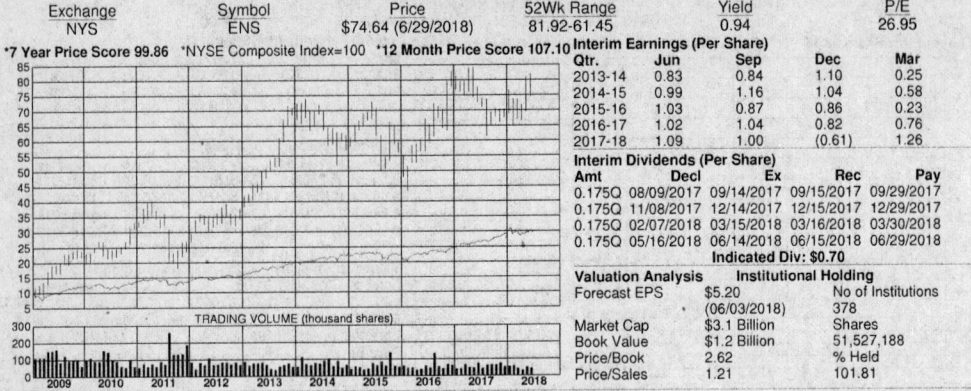

Interim Earnings (Per Share)

Qtr.	Jun	Sep	Dec	Mar
2013-14	0.83	0.84	1.10	0.25
2014-15	0.99	1.16	1.04	0.58
2015-16	1.03	0.87	0.86	0.23
2016-17	1.02	1.04	0.82	0.76
2017-18	1.09	1.00	(0.61)	1.26

Interim Dividends (Per Share)

Amt	Decl	Ex	Rec	Pay
0.175Q	08/09/2017	09/14/2017	09/15/2017	09/29/2017
0.175Q	11/08/2017	12/14/2017	12/15/2017	12/29/2017
0.175Q	02/07/2018	03/15/2018	03/16/2018	03/30/2018
0.175Q	05/16/2018	06/14/2018	06/15/2018	06/29/2018

Indicated Div: $0.70

Valuation Analysis   **Institutional Holding**

Forecast EPS	$5.20	No of Institutions
	(06/03/2018)	378
Market Cap	$3.1 Billion	Shares
Book Value	$1.2 Billion	51,527,188
Price/Book	2.62	% Held
Price/Sales	1.21	101.81

Business Summary: Electrical Equipment (MIC: 7.3.1 SIC: 5063 NAIC: 423610)

EnerSys is a manufacturer, marketer and distributor of industrial batteries. Co. also manufactures, markets and distributes products such as battery chargers, power equipment, battery accessories, and outdoor cabinet enclosures. Additionally, Co. provides related aftermarket and customer-support services for its products. Co. has two primary product lines: reserve power, which are used for backup power for the ongoing operation of applications in telecommunications systems, uninterruptible power systems, applications for computer and computer-controlled systems, and other power applications; and motive power products, which are used to provide power for electric industrial forklifts.

Recent Developments: For the year ended Mar 31 2018, net income decreased 24.3% to US$119.8 million from US$158.2 million in the prior year. Revenues were US$2.58 billion, up 9.1% from US$2.37 billion the year before. Operating income was US$269.4 million versus US$235.9 million in the prior year, an increase of 14.2%. Direct operating expenses rose 12.1% to US$1.92 billion from US$1.72 billion in the comparable period the year before. Indirect operating expenses decreased 6.6% to US$387.6 million from US$414.8 million in the equivalent prior-year period.

Prospects: Our evaluation of Enersys as of Jan. 21, 2018 is the result of our systematic analysis on three basic characteristics: earnings strength, relative valuation, and recent stock price movement. The company has generated a negative trend in earnings per share over the past 5 quarters and while recent estimates for the company have remained steady, ENS has posted better than expected results. Based on operating earnings yield, the company is undervalued when compared to all of the companies in our coverage universe. Share price changes over the past year indicates that ENS will perform very poorly over the near term.

Financial Data

(US$ in Thousands)	03/31/2018	03/31/2017	03/31/2016	03/31/2015	03/31/2014	03/31/2013	03/31/2012	03/31/2011
Earnings Per Share	2.77	3.64	2.99	3.77	3.02	3.42	2.93	2.27
Cash Flow Per Share	4.95	5.67	6.93	4.26	4.08	5.09	4.18	1.55
Tang Book Value Per Share	16.60	14.29	11.58	11.63	14.01	15.05	12.09	10.63
Dividends Per Share	0.700	0.700	0.700	0.700	0.500	...	...	...
Dividend Payout %	25.27	19.23	23.41	18.57	16.56	...	...	...
Income Statement								
Total Revenue	2,581,891	2,367,149	2,316,249	2,505,512	2,474,433	2,277,559	2,283,369	1,964,462
EBITDA	309,201	280,280	251,966	318,244	230,545	296,828	256,275	217,381
Depn & Amortn	45,874	45,388	47,686	49,261	49,693	47,876	48,532	43,517
Income Before Taxes	238,326	212,695	181,937	249,339	163,747	230,233	191,259	151,826
Income Taxes	118,493	54,472	50,113	67,814	16,980	65,275	47,292	38,018
Net Income	119,594	160,214	136,150	181,188	150,328	166,508	144,003	113,426
Average Shares	43,119	44,012	45,474	48,052	49,788	48,635	49,216	50,044
Balance Sheet								
Current Assets	1,539,587	1,418,915	1,296,239	1,233,418	1,300,700	1,152,962	1,071,673	997,948
Total Assets	2,486,925	2,293,029	2,214,488	2,163,047	2,321,858	1,987,867	1,919,279	1,828,387
Current Liabilities	491,530	467,431	451,171	433,371	581,403	467,559	460,301	463,572
Long-Term Obligations	579,590	587,705	606,398	495,973	288,132	155,476	237,110	249,378
Total Liabilities	1,291,250	1,189,573	1,201,357	1,122,817	1,065,843	818,466	887,084	854,056
Stockholders' Equity	1,195,675	1,103,456	1,013,131	1,040,230	1,256,015	1,169,401	1,032,195	974,331
Shares Outstanding	41,915	43,447	43,189	44,068	46,942	47,840	47,800	50,034
Statistical Record								
Return on Assets %	5.00	7.11	6.20	8.08	6.98	8.52	7.66	6.52
Return on Equity %	10.40	15.14	13.22	15.78	12.40	15.13	14.31	12.93
EBITDA Margin %	11.98	11.84	10.88	12.70	9.32	13.03	11.22	11.07
Net Margin %	4.63	6.77	5.88	7.23	6.08	7.31	6.31	5.77
Asset Turnover	1.08	1.05	1.06	1.12	1.15	1.17	1.22	1.13
Current Ratio	3.13	3.04	2.87	2.85	2.24	2.47	2.33	2.15
Debt to Equity	0.48	0.53	0.60	0.48	0.23	0.13	0.23	0.26
Price Range	83.96-61.45	82.71-52.44	72.75-43.39	71.81-51.83	73.87-42.78	45.58-30.16	40.01-17.91	39.75-21.08
P/E Ratio	30.31-22.18	22.72-14.41	24.33-14.51	19.05-13.75	24.46-14.17	13.33-8.82	13.66-6.11	17.51-9.29
Average Yield %	0.98	1.01	1.17	1.11	0.84	...	...	...

Address: 2366 Bernville Road, Reading, PA 19605
Telephone: 610-208-1991

Web Site: www.enersys.com
Officers: David M. Shaffer - President, Chief Executive Officer Todd M. Sechrist - Executive Vice President, Chief Operating Officer, Region Officer

Auditors: Ernst & Young LLP
Investor Contact: 610-236-4040
Transfer Agents: Computershare

ENSCO PLC

Exchange	Symbol	Price	52Wk Range	Yield	P/E
NYS	ESV	$7.26 (6/29/2018)	7.43-4.16	0.55	N/A

*7 Year Price Score 13.94 *NYSE Composite Index=100 *12 Month Price Score 114.77

Interim Earnings (Per Share)

Qtr.	Mar	Jun	Sep	Dec
2015	1.38	1.11	1.34	(10.61)
2016	0.74	2.04	0.28	0.06
2017	(0.09)	(0.15)	(0.08)	(0.59)
2018	(0.32)	...	...	...

Interim Dividends (Per Share)

Amt	Decl	Ex	Rec	Pay
0.01Q	08/29/2017	09/08/2017	09/11/2017	09/22/2017
0.01Q	11/07/2017	12/01/2017	12/04/2017	12/15/2017
0.01Q	02/20/2018	03/02/2018	03/05/2018	03/16/2018
0.01Q	05/22/2018	06/01/2018	06/04/2018	06/15/2018

Indicated Div: $0.04

Valuation Analysis

		Institutional Holding	
Forecast EPS	N/A	No of Institutions	560
Market Cap	$3.2 Billion	Shares	494,966,464
Book Value	$8.6 Billion	% Held	
Price/Book	0.37	N/A	
Price/Sales	1.77		

Business Summary: Equipment & Services (MIC: 9.1.3 SIC: 1381 NAIC: 213111)

Ensco is an offshore contract drilling company engaged in providing offshore contract drilling services to the international oil and gas industry. As of Dec 31 2017, Co. owned and operated an offshore drilling rig fleet of 62 rigs. Co.'s rig fleet includes 12 drillships, 11 semisubmersible rigs, four moored semisubmersible rigs and 38 jackup rigs, including rigs under construction. Co.'s business consists of three operating segments: floaters, which includes its drillships and semisubmersible rigs; jackups; and other, which consists of management services on rigs owned by third-parties. Co.'s two reportable segments, floaters and jackups, provide one service, contract drilling.

Recent Developments: For the quarter ended Mar 31 2018, loss from continuing operations was US$140.4 million compared with a loss of US$24.0 million in the year-earlier quarter. Net loss amounted to US$140.5 million versus a net loss of US$24.6 million in the year-earlier quarter. Revenues were US$417.0 million, down 11.5% from US$471.1 million the year before. Operating loss was US$51.3 million versus an income of US$57.8 million in the prior-year quarter. Direct operating expenses rose 16.9% to US$325.2 million from US$278.1 million in the comparable period the year before. Indirect operating expenses increased 5.8% to US$143.1 million from US$135.2 million in the equivalent prior-year period.

Prospects: Our evaluation of Ensco PLC as of Jan. 21, 2018 is the result of our systematic analysis on three basic characteristics: earnings strength, relative valuation, and recent stock price movement. The company has suffered a very negative trend in earnings per share over the past 5 quarters. However, while recent estimates for the company have been mixed, ESV has posted better than expected results. Based on operating earnings yield, the company is undervalued when compared to all of the companies in our coverage universe. Share price changes over the past year indicates that ESV will perform well over the near term.

Financial Data
(US$ in Thousands)

	3 Mos	12/31/2017	12/31/2016	12/31/2015	12/31/2014	12/31/2013	12/31/2012	12/31/2011
Earnings Per Share	(1.14)	(0.91)	3.13	(6.88)	(16.88)	6.07	5.04	3.08
Cash Flow Per Share	0.45	0.78	3.85	7.31	8.89	8.58	9.56	3.81
Tang Book Value Per Share	19.63	19.99	27.23	27.65	33.68	40.39	36.26	32.01
Dividends Per Share	0.040	0.040	0.040	0.600	3.000	2.250	1.500	1.400
Dividend Payout %	...	...	1.28	...	...	37.07	29.76	45.45
Income Statement								
Total Revenue	417,000	1,843,000	2,776,400	4,063,400	4,564,500	4,919,800	4,300,700	2,842,700
EBITDA	39,000	447,200	1,657,800	(692,300)	(1,862,500)	2,412,600	2,126,000	1,234,200
Depn & Amortn	98,400	444,800	445,300	572,500	537,900	611,900	558,600	418,900
Income Before Taxes	(122,000)	(196,000)	997,500	(1,471,200)	(2,548,800)	1,658,500	1,466,600	736,600
Income Taxes	18,400	109,200	108,500	(13,900)	140,500	225,600	244,400	131,000
Net Income	(140,100)	(303,700)	890,200	(1,594,800)	(3,902,600)	1,418,200	1,169,700	600,400
Average Shares	433,600	332,500	279,100	232,200	231,600	231,100	229,700	192,600
Balance Sheet								
Current Assets	1,578,700	1,612,000	3,279,300	2,285,100	2,934,800	1,535,200	1,723,900	1,644,700
Total Assets	14,533,700	14,625,900	14,374,500	13,637,000	16,059,900	19,472,900	18,565,300	17,871,200
Current Liabilities	573,300	758,500	854,400	775,500	1,104,600	1,047,300	989,700	1,323,400
Long-Term Obligations	4,987,300	4,750,700	4,942,600	5,895,100	5,885,600	4,718,900	4,798,400	4,877,600
Total Liabilities	5,940,100	5,893,800	6,123,900	7,124,100	7,844,900	6,681,300	6,718,900	6,991,900
Stockholders' Equity	8,593,600	8,732,100	8,250,600	6,512,900	8,215,000	12,791,600	11,846,400	10,879,300
Shares Outstanding	437,150	435,950	303,050	235,350	234,250	233,550	232,450	230,950
Statistical Record								
Return on Assets %	N.M.	N.M.	6.34	N.M.	N.M.	7.46	6.40	4.82
Return on Equity %	N.M.	N.M.	12.03	N.M.	N.M.	11.51	10.27	7.13
EBITDA Margin %	9.35	24.26	59.71	N.M.	N.M.	49.04	49.43	43.42
Net Margin %	N.M.	N.M.	32.06	N.M.	N.M.	28.83	27.20	21.12
Asset Turnover	0.13	0.13	0.20	0.27	0.26	0.26	0.24	0.23
Current Ratio	2.75	2.13	3.84	2.95	2.66	1.47	1.74	1.24
Debt to Equity	0.58	0.54	0.60	0.91	0.72	0.37	0.41	0.45
Price Range	9.35-4.16	11.81-4.16	15.89-6.64	31.93-13.53	57.33-26.41	65.45-51.73	60.33-42.21	59.57-39.51
P/E Ratio	...	...	5.08-2.12	...	...	10.78-8.52	11.97-8.38	19.34-12.83
Average Yield %	0.69	0.58	0.42	2.86	6.34	3.83	2.80	2.72

Address: 6 Chesterfield Gardens, London, W1J5BQ	Web Site: www.enscoplc.com	Auditors: KPMG LLP
Telephone: 207-659-4660	Officers: Carl G. Trowell - President, Chief Executive Officer Patrick Carey Lowe - Executive Vice President, Chief Operating Officer, Senior Vice President	Investor Contact: 713-430-4607 Transfer Agents: Computershare Trust Company, N.A.

ENTERGY CORP

Exchange	Symbol	Price	52Wk Range	Yield	P/E
NYS	ETR	$80.79 (6/29/2018)	87.42-72.02	4.41	31.68

*7 Year Price Score 88.04 *NYSE Composite Index=100 *12 Month Price Score 98.36

Interim Earnings (Per Share)

Qtr.	Mar	Jun	Sep	Dec
2015	1.65	0.83	(4.04)	0.55
2016	1.28	3.16	2.16	(9.86)
2017	0.46	2.27	2.21	(2.66)
2018	0.73	...	...	...

Interim Dividends (Per Share)

Amt	Decl	Ex	Rec	Pay
0.87Q	07/28/2017	08/08/2017	08/10/2017	09/01/2017
0.89Q	10/27/2017	11/08/2017	11/09/2017	12/01/2017
0.89Q	01/26/2018	02/07/2018	02/08/2018	03/01/2018
0.89Q	04/11/2018	05/09/2018	05/10/2018	06/01/2018

Indicated Div: $3.56

Valuation Analysis

		Institutional Holding	
Forecast EPS	$6.35	No of Institutions	896
	(06/14/2018)		
Market Cap	$14.6 Billion	Shares	186,650,624
Book Value	$8.2 Billion	% Held	84.14
Price/Book	1.79		
Price/Sales	1.30		

Business Summary: Electric Utilities (MIC: 3.1.1 SIC: 4911 NAIC: 221122)

Entergy is engaged in electric power production and retail electric distribution operations. Co. operates through two business segments: Utility, which generates, transmits, distributes and sells electric power to retail and wholesale customers in Arkansas, Louisiana, Mississippi, and Texas, as well as provides natural gas utility services to customers in and around Baton Rouge, LA, and New Orleans, LA; and Entergy Wholesale Commodities, which includes theownership, operation, and decommissioning of nuclear power plants located in the northern U.S. and the sale of the electric power produced by its operating plants.

Recent Developments: For the quarter ended Mar 31 2018, net income increased 58.3% to US$136.2 million from US$86.1 million in the year-earlier quarter. Revenues were US$2.72 billion, up 5.2% from US$2.59 billion the year before. Direct operating expenses declined 7.9% to US$1.83 billion from US$1.99 billion in the comparable period the year before. Indirect operating expenses increased 32.7% to US$555.2 million from US$418.3 million in the equivalent prior-year period.

Prospects: Our evaluation of Entergy Corp. as of Jan. 21, 2018 is the result of our systematic analysis on three basic characteristics: earnings strength, relative valuation, and recent stock price movement. The company has enjoyed a very positive trend in earnings per share over the past 5 quarters. However, while recent estimates for the company have been mixed, ETR has posted better than expected results. Based on operating earnings yield, the company is undervalued when compared to all of the companies in our coverage universe. Share price changes over the past year indicates that ETR will perform very well over the near term.

Financial Data

(US$ in Thousands)	3 Mos	12/31/2017	12/31/2016	12/31/2015	12/31/2014	12/31/2013	12/31/2012	12/31/2011
Earnings Per Share	2.55	2.28	(3.26)	(0.99)	5.22	3.99	4.76	7.55
Cash Flow Per Share	14.67	14.60	16.72	18.37	21.67	17.90	16.54	17.63
Tang Book Value Per Share	43.12	43.28	44.15	51.56	54.91	53.07	50.65	49.73
Dividends Per Share	3.520	3.500	3.420	3.340	3.320	3.320	3.320	3.320
Dividend Payout %	138.04	153.51	...	...	63.60	83.21	69.75	43.97
Income Statement								
Total Revenue	2,723,881	11,074,481	10,845,645	11,513,251	12,494,921	11,390,947	10,302,079	11,229,073
EBITDA	857,832	3,420,647	1,262,772	1,773,982	4,157,567	3,373,366	3,112,375	3,783,583
Depn & Amortn	525,181	2,078,578	2,123,291	2,117,236	2,127,892	2,012,076	1,771,649	1,745,455
Income Before Taxes	179,863	967,923	(1,381,762)	(799,661)	1,549,854	956,553	899,218	1,653,635
Income Taxes	43,663	542,570	(817,259)	(642,927)	589,597	225,981	30,855	286,263
Net Income	132,761	425,353	(564,503)	(156,734)	960,257	730,572	868,363	1,367,372
Average Shares	181,431	180,535	178,885	179,176	180,296	178,570	177,737	178,370
Balance Sheet								
Current Assets	3,655,734	3,285,331	3,684,268	4,067,412	4,389,633	3,929,691	3,683,126	3,622,703
Total Assets	47,281,525	46,707,149	45,904,434	44,647,681	46,527,854	43,406,446	43,202,502	40,701,699
Current Liabilities	5,232,672	5,036,207	3,200,096	3,089,958	3,848,891	4,060,572	4,106,321	4,950,699
Long-Term Obligations	15,613,260	14,337,274	14,492,237	13,138,557	12,529,819	12,171,367	11,954,859	10,082,134
Total Liabilities	39,108,783	38,516,831	37,619,440	35,072,705	36,215,369	33,469,220	33,724,902	31,459,918
Stockholders' Equity	8,172,742	8,190,318	8,284,994	9,574,976	10,312,485	9,937,226	9,477,600	9,241,781
Shares Outstanding	180,799	180,517	179,129	178,389	179,240	178,370	177,807	176,355
Statistical Record								
Return on Assets %	1.01	0.92	N.M.	N.M.	2.14	1.69	2.06	3.44
Return on Equity %	5.70	5.16	N.M.	N.M.	9.48	7.53	9.25	15.15
EBITDA Margin %	31.49	30.89	11.64	15.41	33.27	29.61	30.21	33.69
Net Margin %	4.87	3.84	N.M.	N.M.	7.69	6.41	8.43	12.18
Asset Turnover	0.24	0.24	0.24	0.25	0.28	0.26	0.24	0.28
Current Ratio	0.70	0.65	1.15	1.32	1.14	0.97	0.90	0.73
Debt to Equity	1.91	1.75	1.75	1.37	1.22	1.22	1.26	1.09
Price Range	87.42-72.02	87.42-70.44	82.03-66.56	89.90-61.53	91.16-60.52	72.35-60.85	73.06-62.04	74.18-59.57
P/E Ratio	34.28-28.24	38.34-30.89	...	...	17.46-11.59	18.13-15.25	15.35-13.03	9.83-7.89
Average Yield %	4.46	4.49	4.55	4.58	4.47	5.06	4.91	4.86

Address: 639 Loyola Avenue, New Orleans, LA 70113	**Web Site:** www.entergy.com	**Auditors:** Deloitte & Touche LLP	
Telephone: 504-576-4000	**Officers:** Leo P. Denault - Chairman, Chief Executive Officer, Executive Vice President, Chief Financial Officer Andrew S. Marsh - Executive Vice President, Chief Financial Officer	**Investor Contact:** 504-576-4879 **Transfer Agents:** Wells Fargo Shareowner Services, St. Paul, MN	

ENTERPRISE PRODUCTS PARTNERS L.P.

Exchange	Symbol	Price	52Wk Range	Yield	P/E	Div Acheiver
NYS	EPD	$27.67 (6/29/2018)	29.52-23.89	6.22	20.50	19 Years

*7 Year Price Score 74.60 *NYSE Composite Index=100 *12 Month Price Score 104.77

Interim Earnings (Per Share)

Qtr.	Mar	Jun	Sep	Dec
2015	0.32	0.28	0.32	0.34
2016	0.32	0.27	0.30	0.31
2017	0.36	0.30	0.28	0.36
2018	0.41	...	...	...

Interim Dividends (Per Share)

Amt	Decl	Ex	Rec	Pay
0.422Q	10/12/2017	10/30/2017	10/31/2017	11/07/2017
0.425Q	01/12/2018	01/30/2018	01/31/2018	02/07/2018
0.427Q	04/10/2018	04/27/2018	04/30/2018	05/08/2018
0.43Q	07/09/2018	07/30/2018	07/31/2018	08/08/2018

Indicated Div: $1.72 (Div. Reinv. Plan)

Valuation Analysis — **Institutional Holding**

Forecast EPS	$1.62	No of Institutions
	(06/14/2018)	1289
Market Cap	$60.1 Billion	Shares
Book Value	N/A	881,920,256
Price/Book	N/A	% Held
Price/Sales	1.92	32.35

Business Summary: Equipment & Services (MIC: 9.1.3 SIC: 4922 NAIC: 486210)

Enterprise Products Partners provides midstream energy services to producers and consumers of natural gas, natural gas liquids (NGLs), crude oil, petrochemicals and refined products. Co.'s midstream energy operations include: natural gas gathering, treating, processing, transportation and storage; NGL transportation, fractionation, storage, and export and import terminals (including liquefied petroleum gases, and ethane); crude oil gathering, transportation, storage and terminals; petrochemical and refined products transportation, storage and terminals, and related services; and a marine transportation business that operates on the U.S. inland and Intracoastal Waterway systems.

Recent Developments: For the quarter ended Mar 31 2018, net income increased 18.2% to US$911.5 million from US$771.0 million in the year-earlier quarter. Revenues were US$9.30 billion, up 27.0% from US$7.32 billion the year before. Operating income was US$1.14 billion versus US$1.03 billion in the prior-year quarter, an increase of 10.4%. Direct operating expenses rose 29.8% to US$8.22 billion from US$6.33 billion in the comparable period the year before. Indirect operating income amounted to US$62.7 million compared with an income of US$44.4 million in the equivalent prior-year period.

Prospects: Our evaluation of Enterprise Products Partners L.P. as of Jan. 21, 2018 is the result of our systematic analysis on three basic characteristics: earnings strength, relative valuation, and recent stock price movement. The company has managed to produce a neutral trend in earnings per share over the past 5 quarters. However, while recent estimates for the company have been mixed, EPD has posted results that fell short of analysts expectations. Based on operating earnings yield, the company is undervalued when compared to all of the companies in our coverage universe. Share price changes over the past year indicates that EPD will perform very poorly over the near term.

Financial Data

(US$ in Thousands)	3 Mos	12/31/2017	12/31/2016	12/31/2015	12/31/2014	12/31/2013	12/31/2012	12/31/2011
Earnings Per Share	1.35	1.30	1.20	1.26	1.47	1.41	1.36	1.19
Cash Flow Per Share	2.32	2.18	1.95	2.04	2.25	2.16	1.67	2.02
Dividends Per Share	1.683	1.668	1.590	1.510	1.430	1.350	1.266	1.202
Dividend Payout %	124.63	128.27	132.50	119.84	97.28	95.74	93.45	101.05
Income Statement								
Total Revenue	9,298,500	29,241,500	23,022,300	27,027,900	47,951,200	47,727,000	42,583,100	44,313,000
EBITDA	1,384,800	4,736,000	4,412,700	4,305,700	4,630,900	4,311,300	4,018,000	3,588,700
Depn & Amortn	331,800	1,296,100	1,215,700	1,161,600	1,114,100	1,012,400	900,500	776,600
Income Before Taxes	800,900	2,455,300	2,214,400	2,182,300	2,597,100	2,497,300	2,346,500	2,069,100
Income Taxes	5,100	25,700	23,400	(2,500)	23,100	57,500	(17,200)	27,200
Net Income	900,700	2,799,300	2,513,100	2,521,200	2,787,400	2,596,900	2,419,900	2,046,900
Average Shares	2,177,200	2,154,300	2,089,100	1,998,600	1,895,200	1,842,600	1,786,400	1,719,800
Balance Sheet								
Current Assets	6,791,000	6,506,400	6,528,200	4,313,000	5,490,700	7,023,400	5,843,100	6,068,700
Total Assets	55,482,300	54,418,100	52,194,000	48,952,000	47,100,700	40,138,700	35,934,400	34,125,100
Current Liabilities	8,839,600	9,295,100	8,250,500	7,166,600	7,873,700	8,238,700	7,755,700	7,432,400
Long-Term Obligations	23,016,400	21,713,700	21,120,900	20,826,700	19,157,400	16,226,500	14,655,200	14,029,400
Total Liabilities	32,729,000	31,870,900	30,147,000	28,656,900	29,037,500	24,923,900	22,746,700	22,011,700
Shares Outstanding	2,171,413	2,161,090	2,117,588	2,012,553	1,937,324	1,871,370	1,806,667	1,772,281
Statistical Record								
Return on Assets %	5.49	5.25	4.96	5.25	6.39	6.83	6.89	6.25
EBITDA Margin %	14.89	16.20	19.17	15.93	9.66	9.03	9.44	8.10
Net Margin %	9.69	9.57	10.92	9.33	5.81	5.44	5.68	4.62
Asset Turnover	0.58	0.55	0.45	0.56	1.10	1.25	1.21	1.35
Current Ratio	0.77	0.70	0.79	0.60	0.70	0.85	0.75	0.82
Price Range	29.40-23.89	29.86-23.89	29.93-19.79	36.83-21.86	41.11-31.84	33.15-25.04	27.44-23.11	23.20-18.75
P/E Ratio	21.78-17.70	22.97-18.38	24.94-16.49	29.23-17.35	27.97-21.66	23.51-17.76	20.18-17.00	19.50-15.76
Average Yield %	6.38	6.25	6.12	5.04	3.91	4.50	4.94	5.64

Address: 1100 Louisiana Street, 10th Floor, Houston, TX 77002 **Telephone:** 713-381-6500	**Web Site:** www.enterpriseproducts.com **Officers:** Randa Duncan Williams - Chairman Richard H. Bachmann - Vice-Chairman	**Auditors:** DELOITTE & TOUCHE LLP **Investor Contact:** 866-230-0745 **Transfer Agents:** Wells Fargo Shareowner Services, South St. Paul, MN

ENVISION HEALTHCARE CORP

Exchange	Symbol	Price	52Wk Range	Yield	P/E
NYS	EVHC	$44.01 (6/29/2018)	62.94-24.79	N/A	38.61

*7 Year Price Score N/A   *NYSE Composite Index=100   *12 Month Price Score 99.98

Interim Earnings (Per Share)

Qtr.	Mar	Jun	Sep	Dec
2016	0.53	0.80	0.69	(2.50)
2017	(3.84)	0.45	0.23	1.17
2018	(0.71)	...	...	...

Interim Dividends (Per Share)

No Dividends Paid

Valuation Analysis | **Institutional Holding**

Forecast EPS	$3.62	No of Institutions
(06/12/2018)		N/A
Market Cap	$5.3 Billion	Shares
Book Value	$6.5 Billion	N/A
Price/Book	0.83	% Held
Price/Sales	0.66	N/A

TRADING VOLUME (thousand shares)

Business Summary: Hospitals & Health Care Facilities (MIC: 4.2.1 SIC: 8011 NAIC: 621399)

Envision Healthcare is a provider of healthcare services. Co. has three reportable segments: physician services, which include Co.'s hospital-based and non-hospital-based physician services businesses; medical transportation, which include Co.'s community-based medical transportation services, including emergency (911), non-emergency, managed transportation, air ambulance and disaster response services; and ambulatory services, which include Co.'s ambulatory surgery business, which acquires, develops, owns and operates ambulatory surgery centers and surgical hospitals in partnership with physicians and health systems.

Recent Developments: For the quarter ended Mar 31 2018, income from continuing operations increased 1.1% to US$88.1 million from US$87.1 million in the year-earlier quarter. Net loss amounted to US$35.2 million versus a net loss of US$391.1 million in the year-earlier quarter. Revenues were US$2.08 billion, up 10.6% from US$1.88 billion the year before. Operating income was US$157.4 million versus US$155.9 million in the prior-year quarter, an increase of 1.0%. Indirect operating expenses increased 11.4% to US$1.92 billion from US$1.72 billion in the equivalent prior-year period.

Prospects: Our evaluation of Envision Healthcare Corp. as of Jan. 21, 2018 is the result of our systematic analysis on three basic characteristics: earnings strength, relative valuation, and recent stock price movement. The company has generated a negative trend in earnings per share over the past 5 quarters. However, while recent estimates for the company have been mixed, EVHC has posted results that fell short of analysts expectations. Based on operating earnings yield, the company is undervalued when compared to all of the companies in our coverage universe. Share price changes over the past year indicates that EVHC will perform very poorly over the near term.

Financial Data
(US$ in Thousands)

	3 Mos	12/31/2017	12/31/2016	12/31/2015	12/31/2014	12/31/2013
Earnings Per Share	1.14	(1.93)	(0.47)	3.16	0.66	0.04
Cash Flow Per Share	6.11	6.73	7.10	11.19	1.51	0.36
Income Statement						
Total Revenue	2,077,000	7,819,300	3,696,000	2,566,900	4,397,644	3,728,312
EBITDA	155,700	242,400	371,100	626,700	474,109	354,675
Depn & Amortn	4,300	64,400	47,800	25,400	155,629	158,588
Income Before Taxes	87,800	(53,100)	180,900	479,800	209,110	10,178
Income Taxes	5,500	(496,800)	(900)	113,800	89,498	(994)
Net Income	(86,400)	(228,000)	(18,600)	163,000	125,508	5,995
Average Shares	122,354	120,943	59,002	51,612	189,921	156,962
Balance Sheet						
Current Assets	2,534,000	4,744,300	2,411,300	537,700	1,363,239	...
Total Assets	14,384,500	16,572,600	16,708,900	6,499,300	4,703,753	...
Current Liabilities	1,118,300	1,395,100	1,154,300	385,900	576,868	...
Long-Term Obligations	4,608,500	6,263,300	5,791,600	2,358,000	2,025,877	...
Total Liabilities	7,933,000	10,045,500	9,977,800	4,205,900	2,943,176	...
Stockholders' Equity	6,451,500	6,527,100	6,731,100	2,293,400	1,760,577	...
Shares Outstanding	121,105	121,021	117,478	54,294	183,679	...
Statistical Record						
Return on Assets %	0.84	N.M.	N.M.	2.91	...	...
Return on Equity %	2.05	N.M.	N.M.	8.04	...	...
EBITDA Margin %	7.50	3.10	10.04	24.41	10.78	9.51
Net Margin %	N.M.	N.M.	N.M.	6.35	2.85	0.16
Asset Turnover	0.52	0.47	0.32	0.46	...	...
Current Ratio	2.27	3.40	2.09	1.39	2.36	...
Debt to Equity	0.71	0.96	0.86	1.03	1.15	...
Price Range	63.36-24.79	72.48-24.79	71.75-63.29	...	...	...
P/E Ratio	55.58-21.75	...	...	...	...	...

Address: 1A Burton Hills Boulevard, Nashville, TN 37215	Web Site: www.evhc.net	Auditors: DELOITTE & TOUCHE LLP
Telephone: 615-665-1283	Officers: Christopher A. Holden - President, Chief Executive Officer Karey L. Witty - Chief Operating Officer, Executive Vice President	Transfer Agents: American Stock Transfer & Trust, Brooklyn, NY

EOG RESOURCES, INC.

Exchange	Symbol	Price	52Wk Range	Yield	P/E
NYS	EOG	$124.43 (6/29/2018)	127.45-83.15	0.59	22.58

*7 Year Price Score 103.21 *NYSE Composite Index=100 *12 Month Price Score 113.50

Interim Earnings (Per Share)

Qtr.	Mar	Jun	Sep	Dec
2015	(0.31)	0.01	(7.47)	(0.52)
2016	(0.86)	(0.53)	(0.35)	(0.24)
2017	0.05	0.04	0.17	4.20
2018	1.10	...	...	...

Interim Dividends (Per Share)

Amt	Decl	Ex	Rec	Pay
0.168Q	09/19/2017	10/16/2017	10/17/2017	10/31/2017
0.168Q	12/13/2017	01/16/2018	01/17/2018	01/31/2018
0.185Q	02/27/2018	04/13/2018	04/16/2018	04/30/2018
0.185Q	04/25/2018	07/16/2018	07/17/2018	07/31/2018

Indicated Div: $0.74

Valuation Analysis

		Institutional Holding	
Forecast EPS	$5.25	No of Institutions	1453
	(06/14/2018)		
Market Cap	$72.0 Billion	Shares	576,967,104
Book Value	$16.8 Billion	% Held	97.96
Price/Book	4.28		
Price/Sales	5.87		

TRADING VOLUME (thousand shares)

Business Summary: Production & Extraction (MIC: 9.1.1 SIC: 1311 NAIC: 211111)

EOG Resources, together with its subsidiaries, explores for, develops, produces and markets crude oil and natural gas primarily in producing basins in the U.S., The Republic of Trinidad and Tobago, the U.K., The People's Republic of China, Canada and, from time to time, select other international areas. As of Dec 31 2017, Co.'s total estimated net proved reserves were 2,527 million barrels of oil equivalent, of which 1,313.0 million barrels (MMBbl) were crude oil and condensate reserves, 503.0 MMBbl were natural gas liquids reserves and 4,263.00 billion cubic feet, or 711.0 million barrels of oil equivalent, were natural gas reserves.

Recent Developments: For the quarter ended Mar 31 2018, net income increased to US$638.6 million from US$28.5 million in the year-earlier quarter. Revenues were US$3.68 billion, up 41.0% from US$2.61 billion the year before. Operating income was US$874.6 million versus US$107.7 million in the prior-year quarter, an increase of 711.7%. Direct operating expenses rose 22.4% to US$578.4 million from US$472.6 million in the comparable period the year before. Indirect operating expenses increased 9.8% to US$2.23 billion from US$2.03 billion in the equivalent prior-year period.

Prospects: Our evaluation of EOG Resources Inc. as of Jan. 21, 2018 is the result of our systematic analysis on three basic characteristics: earnings strength, relative valuation, and recent stock price movement. The company has generated a negative trend in earnings per share over the past 5 quarters and while recent estimates for the company have been raised by analysts, EOG has posted better than expected results. Based on operating earnings yield, the company is overvalued when compared to all of the companies in our coverage universe. Share price changes over the past year indicates that EOG will perform very poorly over the near term.

Financial Data
(US$ in Thousands)

	3 Mos	12/31/2017	12/31/2016	12/31/2015	12/31/2014	12/31/2013	12/31/2012	12/31/2011
Earnings Per Share	5.51	4.46	(1.98)	(8.29)	5.32	4.02	1.05	2.05
Cash Flow Per Share	8.54	7.42	4.25	6.59	15.92	13.56	9.76	8.71
Tang Book Value Per Share	29.10	28.15	24.24	23.54	32.30	28.23	24.45	23.49
Dividends Per Share	0.670	0.670	0.670	0.670	0.511	0.366	0.335	0.318
Dividend Payout %	12.16	15.02	...	...	9.61	9.11	31.75	15.49
Income Statement								
Total Revenue	3,681,162	11,208,320	7,650,632	8,757,428	18,035,340	14,487,118	11,682,636	10,126,115
EBITDA	1,623,906	4,344,941	2,277,593	(3,370,519)	9,193,814	7,273,322	4,663,995	4,636,543
Depn & Amortn	748,591	3,409,387	3,553,417	3,313,644	3,997,041	3,600,976	3,169,703	2,516,381
Income Before Taxes	813,359	661,182	(1,557,505)	(6,921,556)	4,995,315	3,436,886	1,280,740	1,909,799
Income Taxes	174,770	(1,921,397)	(460,819)	(2,397,041)	2,079,828	1,239,777	710,461	818,676
Net Income	638,589	2,582,579	(1,096,686)	(4,524,515)	2,915,487	2,197,109	570,279	1,091,123
Average Shares	579,726	578,693	553,384	545,697	548,539	546,228	541,524	532,536
Balance Sheet								
Current Assets	3,585,097	3,279,108	3,554,603	2,592,244	5,416,021	4,072,015	3,589,884	3,253,938
Total Assets	30,740,517	29,833,078	29,459,433	26,975,244	34,762,687	30,574,238	27,336,578	24,838,797
Current Liabilities	2,836,758	2,725,542	2,027,291	1,819,287	3,384,308	2,861,716	2,924,058	2,522,319
Long-Term Obligations	6,071,604	6,030,836	6,979,779	6,653,685	5,903,354	5,906,642	5,905,602	5,009,166
Total Liabilities	13,899,878	13,549,805	15,477,852	14,032,209	17,050,105	15,155,779	14,051,814	12,197,893
Stockholders' Equity	16,840,639	16,283,273	13,981,581	12,943,035	17,712,582	15,418,459	13,284,764	12,640,904
Shares Outstanding	578,812	578,476	576,700	549,858	548,294	546,171	543,264	538,038
Statistical Record								
Return on Assets %	10.65	8.71	N.M.	N.M.	8.92	7.59	2.18	4.70
Return on Equity %	20.75	17.07	N.M.	N.M.	17.60	15.31	4.39	9.54
EBITDA Margin %	44.11	38.77	29.77	N.M.	50.98	50.21	39.92	45.79
Net Margin %	17.35	23.04	N.M.	N.M.	16.17	15.17	4.88	10.78
Asset Turnover	0.41	0.38	0.27	0.28	0.55	0.50	0.45	0.44
Current Ratio	1.26	1.20	1.75	1.42	1.60	1.42	1.23	1.29
Debt to Equity	0.36	0.37	0.50	0.51	0.33	0.38	0.44	0.40
Price Range	118.47-83.15	109.41-83.15	108.01-60.24	99.74-68.36	117.98-80.87	92.58-56.72	62.19-41.98	59.84-34.20
P/E Ratio	21.50-15.09	24.53-18.64	...	...	22.18-15.20	23.03-14.11	59.22-39.98	29.19-16.69
Average Yield %	0.69	0.70	0.80	0.79	0.52	0.50	0.62	0.64

Address: 1111 Bagby, Sky Lobby 2, Houston, TX 77002
Telephone: 713-651-7000

Web Site: www.eogresources.com
Officers: William R. Thomas - Chairman, Chief Executive Officer, President, Senior Executive Vice President Gary L. Thomas - President, Senior Executive Vice President, Chief Operating Officer

Auditors: Deloitte & Touche LLP
Investor Contact: 713-651-7000
Transfer Agents: Computershare Trust Company, N.A., Providence, RI

EPR PROPERTIES

Exchange	Symbol	Price	52Wk Range	Yield	P/E
NYS	EPR	$64.79 (6/29/2018)	73.81-53.04	6.67	22.73

*7 Year Price Score 89.98 ***NYSE Composite Index=100** ***12 Month Price Score 94.23**

Interim Earnings (Per Share)

Qtr.	Mar	Jun	Sep	Dec
2015	0.64	0.75	0.76	0.78
2016	0.77	0.77	0.81	0.82
2017	0.75	1.02	0.77	0.74
2018	0.32	...	...	...

Interim Dividends (Per Share)

Amt	Decl	Ex	Rec	Pay
0.36M	03/19/2018	03/28/2018	03/29/2018	04/16/2018
0.36M	04/17/2018	04/27/2018	04/30/2018	05/15/2018
0.36M	05/17/2018	05/30/2018	05/31/2018	06/15/2018
0.36M	06/18/2018	06/28/2018	06/29/2018	07/16/2018

Indicated Div: $4.32 (Div. Reinv. Plan)

Valuation Analysis **Institutional Holding**

Forecast EPS	$3.33	No of Institutions
	(06/14/2018)	497
Market Cap	$4.8 Billion	Shares
Book Value	$2.9 Billion	89,093,912
Price/Book	1.67	% Held
Price/Sales	8.00	N/A

Business Summary: REITs (MIC: 5.3.1 SIC: 6798 NAIC: 525930)

EPR Properties is a real estate investment trust. Co.'s operating segments are: Entertainment, which consists of investments in megaplex theatres, entertainment retail centers, family entertainment centers and other retail parcels; Education, which consists of investments in public charter schools, early education centers and K-12 private schools; Recreation, which consists of investments in ski areas, waterparks, golf entertainment complexes and other recreation; and Other, which consists of land under ground lease, property under development and land held for development related to the Adelaar casino and resort project in Sullivan County, NY.

Recent Developments: For the quarter ended Mar 31 2018, net income decreased 45.2% to US$29.5 million from US$53.9 million in the year-earlier quarter. Revenues were US$155.0 million, up 20.0% from US$129.1 million the year before. Revenues from property income rose 20.0% to US$132.9 million from US$110.8 million in the corresponding quarter a year earlier.

Prospects: Our evaluation of EPR Properties as of Jan. 14, 2018 is the result of our systematic analysis on three basic characteristics: earnings strength, relative valuation, and recent stock price movement. The company has generated a negative trend in earnings per share over the past 5 quarters. Because the company lacks sufficient analyst estimate data, we place greater weight on the historical EPS trend as the measure of earnings strength. Based on operating earnings yield, the company is undervalued when compared to all of the companies in our coverage universe. Share price changes over the past year indicates that EPR will perform very well over the near term.

Financial Data

(US$ in Thousands)	3 Mos	12/31/2017	12/31/2016	12/31/2015	12/31/2014	12/31/2013	12/31/2012	12/31/2011
Earnings Per Share	2.85	3.29	3.17	2.93	2.86	3.24	1.98	1.80
Cash Flow Per Share	5.74	5.49	4.82	4.79	4.61	4.87	4.42	4.20
Tang Book Value Per Share	38.69	39.10	34.11	33.95	33.57	32.54	31.13	31.36
Dividends Per Share	4.140	4.080	3.840	3.630	3.420	3.160	3.000	2.800
Dividend Payout %	145.26	124.01	121.14	123.89	119.58	97.52	151.52	155.56
Income Statement								
Total Revenue	154,968	575,991	493,242	421,017	385,051	343,064	321,786	301,659
EBITDA	102,325	527,519	425,960	359,661	322,977	291,819	256,797	216,395
Depn & Amortn	37,481	129,100	103,900	85,900	63,000	50,700	47,300	45,000
Income Before Taxes	30,507	265,295	224,916	193,846	178,707	160,063	132,841	99,716
Income Taxes	1,020	2,399	553	482	4,228	(14,176)	...	...
Net Income	29,538	262,968	224,982	194,532	179,633	180,226	121,556	115,228
Average Shares	74,180	71,254	63,474	58,328	54,444	48,214	47,049	46,901
Balance Sheet								
Current Assets	128,904	152,679	128,018	73,962	63,690	60,210	73,393	68,942
Total Assets	6,238,866	6,191,493	4,865,022	4,217,270	3,702,048	3,272,276	2,946,730	2,733,995
Current Liabilities	231,835	235,341	193,496	161,482	130,036	108,926	118,000	81,597
Long-Term Obligations	3,131,437	3,028,827	2,485,625	1,981,920	1,645,523	1,475,336	1,368,832	1,154,295
Total Liabilities	3,363,272	3,264,168	2,679,121	2,143,402	1,775,936	1,584,639	1,487,209	1,263,946
Stockholders' Equity	2,875,594	2,927,325	2,185,901	2,073,868	1,926,112	1,687,637	1,459,521	1,470,049
Shares Outstanding	74,318	74,125	63,647	60,823	57,125	51,655	46,887	46,726
Statistical Record								
Return on Assets %	4.23	4.76	4.94	4.91	5.15	5.80	4.27	4.07
Return on Equity %	9.33	10.29	10.53	9.73	9.94	11.45	8.28	7.50
EBITDA Margin %	66.03	91.58	86.36	85.43	83.88	85.06	79.80	71.73
Net Margin %	19.06	45.65	45.61	46.21	46.65	52.53	37.78	38.20
Asset Turnover	0.11	0.10	0.11	0.11	0.11	0.11	0.11	0.11
Current Ratio	0.56	0.65	0.66	0.46	0.49	0.55	0.62	0.84
Debt to Equity	1.09	1.03	1.14	0.96	0.85	0.87	0.94	0.79
Price Range	76.65-53.18	77.56-63.11	84.46-54.09	65.58-49.57	60.80-48.60	60.70-45.93	48.11-40.40	49.88-35.91
P/E Ratio	26.89-18.66	23.57-19.18	26.64-17.06	22.38-16.92	21.26-16.99	18.73-14.18	24.30-20.40	27.71-19.95
Average Yield %	6.13	5.72	5.43	6.33	6.32	6.23	6.72	6.28

Address: 909 Walnut Street, Suite 200, Kansas City, MO 64106
Telephone: 816-472-1700
Fax: 816-472-5794

Web Site: www.eprkc.com
Officers: Robert J. Druten - Chairman Gregory K. Silvers - President, Chief Executive Officer, Executive Vice President, Vice President, Chief Operating Officer, Chief Development Officer, Secretary, General Counsel

Auditors: KPMG LLP
Transfer Agents: Computershare Trust Company, N. A., Providence, RI

EQT CORP

Exchange	Symbol	Price	52Wk Range	Yield	P/E
NYS	EQT	$55.18 (6/29/2018)	67.02-45.73	0.22	50.16

*7 Year Price Score 65.28 *NYSE Composite Index=100 *12 Month Price Score 91.13

Interim Earnings (Per Share)

Qtr.	Mar	Jun	Sep	Dec
2015	1.14	0.04	0.27	(0.88)
2016	0.04	(1.55)	(0.05)	(1.13)
2017	0.95	0.24	0.13	6.72
2018	(5.99)	...	...	...

Interim Dividends (Per Share)

Amt	Decl	Ex	Rec	Pay
0.03Q	10/11/2017	11/09/2017	11/10/2017	12/01/2017
0.03Q	01/17/2018	02/13/2018	02/14/2018	03/01/2018
0.03Q	04/18/2018	05/10/2018	05/11/2018	06/01/2018
0.03Q	07/11/2018	08/09/2018	08/10/2018	09/01/2018

Indicated Div: $0.12

Valuation Analysis

		Institutional Holding	
Forecast EPS	$2.36 (06/14/2018)	No of Institutions	852
Market Cap	$14.6 Billion	Shares	263,097,136
Book Value	$11.7 Billion	% Held	N/A
Price/Book	1.25		
Price/Sales	3.74		

Business Summary: Production & Extraction (MIC: 9.1.1 SIC: 1311 NAIC: 211111)

EQT conducts its business through five business segments: EQT Production, EQM Gathering, EQM Transmission, RMP Gathering and RMP Water. EQT Production is a natural gas producer in the United States. EQM Gathering and EQM Transmission provide gathering, transmission and storage services. RMP Gathering provides natural gas gathering services to Co. RMP Water provides water services that support well completion activities and collects and recycles or disposes of flowback and produced water for Co. in Washington and Greene Counties, PA and Belmont County, OH. As of Dec 31 2017, Co. had total proved reserves of 21.4 trillion cubic feet of proved natural gas, NGL and crude oil reserves.

Recent Developments: For the quarter ended Mar 31 2018, net loss amounted to US$1.44 billion versus net income of US$250.7 million in the year-earlier quarter. Revenues were US$1.43 billion, up 60.3% from US$894.2 million the year before. Operating loss was US$1.72 billion versus an income of US$391.0 million in the prior-year quarter. Direct operating expenses rose 40.7% to US$276.0 million from US$196.2 million in the comparable period the year before. Indirect operating expenses increased 838.5% to US$2.88 billion from US$307.0 million in the equivalent prior-year period.

Prospects: Our evaluation of EQT Corp. as of Jan. 21, 2018 is the result of our systematic analysis on three basic characteristics: earnings strength, relative valuation, and recent stock price movement. The company has suffered a very negative trend in earnings per share over the past 5 quarters. However, while recent estimates for the company have been lowered by analysts, EQT has posted better than expected results. Based on operating earnings yield, the company is overvalued when compared to all of the companies in our coverage universe. Share price changes over the past year indicates that EQT will perform poorly over the near term.

Financial Data

(US$ in Thousands)	3 Mos	12/31/2017	12/31/2016	12/31/2015	12/31/2014	12/31/2013	12/31/2012	12/31/2011
Earnings Per Share	1.10	8.04	(2.71)	0.56	2.54	2.57	1.22	3.19
Cash Flow Per Share	7.65	8.74	6.36	7.99	9.33	7.97	5.47	6.13
Tang Book Value Per Share	33.97	40.04	33.91	33.29	30.23	26.74	24.01	24.04
Dividends Per Share	0.120	0.120	0.120	0.120	0.120	0.120	0.880	0.880
Dividend Payout %	10.91	1.49	...	21.43	4.72	4.67	72.13	27.59
Income Statement								
Total Revenue	1,433,583	3,378,015	1,608,348	2,339,762	2,469,710	1,862,011	1,641,608	1,639,934
EBITDA	(1,690,331)	956,235	681,313	1,392,308	1,539,546	1,340,416	985,611	1,234,754
Depn & Amortn	23,600	10,940	927,920	819,216	679,298	676,570	499,118	339,297
Income Before Taxes	(1,783,944)	742,523	(394,527)	426,561	723,711	521,158	301,707	759,129
Income Taxes	(338,965)	(1,115,619)	(263,464)	104,675	214,092	175,186	105,296	279,360
Net Income	(1,585,994)	1,508,529	(452,983)	85,171	386,965	390,572	183,395	479,769
Average Shares	264,877	187,727	166,978	152,939	152,513	151,787	150,506	150,209
Balance Sheet								
Current Assets	1,191,581	1,163,055	1,828,219	2,251,019	1,904,323	1,255,425	852,845	1,690,134
Total Assets	27,632,346	29,522,604	15,472,922	13,976,172	12,064,900	9,792,053	8,849,862	8,772,719
Current Liabilities	1,108,676	1,232,237	804,640	795,819	833,479	523,410	570,465	804,910
Long-Term Obligations	7,456,826	7,323,555	3,289,459	2,793,343	2,822,889	2,490,354	2,502,969	2,527,627
Total Liabilities	15,916,024	16,202,986	9,612,641	8,898,381	7,482,085	5,757,265	5,246,042	5,178,889
Stockholders' Equity	11,716,322	13,319,618	5,860,281	5,077,791	4,582,815	4,034,788	3,603,820	3,593,830
Shares Outstanding	265,000	264,320	172,827	152,554	151,596	150,884	150,109	149,477
Statistical Record								
Return on Assets %	N.M.	6.71	N.M.	0.65	3.54	4.19	2.08	6.05
Return on Equity %	N.M.	15.73	N.M.	1.76	8.98	10.23	5.08	14.38
EBITDA Margin %	N.M.	28.31	42.36	59.51	62.34	71.99	60.04	75.29
Net Margin %	N.M.	44.66	N.M.	3.64	15.67	20.98	11.17	29.26
Asset Turnover	0.18	0.15	0.11	0.18	0.23	0.24	0.19	0.21
Current Ratio	1.07	0.94	2.27	2.83	2.28	2.40	1.50	2.10
Debt to Equity	0.64	0.55	0.56	0.55	0.62	0.62	0.69	0.70
Price Range	67.02-45.73	67.02-50.83	79.33-49.53	91.95-47.75	109.84-75.38	92.56-57.19	62.74-44.00	68.35-44.44
P/E Ratio	60.93-41.57	8.34-6.32	...	164.20-85.27	43.24-29.68	36.02-22.25	51.43-36.07	21.43-13.92
Average Yield %	0.21	0.20	0.18	0.16	0.12	0.15	1.64	1.64

Address: 625 Liberty Avenue, Suite 1700, Pittsburgh, PA 15222
Telephone: 412-553-5700

Web Site: www.eqt.com
Officers: David L. Porges - Chairman, President, Chief Executive Officer, Associate/Affiliate Company Officer, Interim President, Interim Chief Executive Officer Robert Joseph McNally - Senior Vice President, Chief Financial Officer

Auditors: Ernst & Young LLP
Investor Contact: 412-553-7833
Transfer Agents: Computershare, College Station, TX

EQUIFAX INC

Exchange	Symbol	Price	52Wk Range	Yield	P/E
NYS	EFX	$125.11 (6/29/2018)	146.26-92.98	1.25	28.96

*7 Year Price Score 112.88 *NYSE Composite Index=100 *12 Month Price Score 95.98

Interim Earnings (Per Share)
Qtr.	Mar	Jun	Sep	Dec
2015	0.73	0.92	0.98	0.93
2016	0.85	1.08	1.09	1.02
2017	1.26	1.36	0.79	1.42
2018	0.75	...	...	...

Interim Dividends (Per Share)
Amt	Decl	Ex	Rec	Pay
0.39Q	08/04/2017	08/23/2017	08/25/2017	09/15/2017
0.39Q	11/09/2017	11/22/2017	11/24/2017	12/15/2017
0.39Q	03/01/2018	03/09/2018	03/12/2018	03/30/2018
0.39Q	05/03/2018	05/24/2018	05/25/2018	06/15/2018

Indicated Div: $1.56

Valuation Analysis
Forecast EPS	$5.93
	(06/14/2018)
Market Cap	$15.1 Billion
Book Value	$3.3 Billion
Price/Book	4.60
Price/Sales	4.43

Institutional Holding
No of Institutions	754
Shares	155,944,608
% Held	87.07

Business Summary: Business Services (MIC: 7.5.2 SIC: 7323 NAIC: 561450)

Equifax Inc. is a provider of information solutions and human resources business process outsourcing services for businesses, governments and consumers. Co.'s products and services are based on databases of consumer and business information. Co. uses statistical techniques and software tools to analyze all available data, creating insights, decision-making solutions and processing services for its clients. Co. also provides information, technology and services to support debt collections and recovery management. Additionally, Co. provides payroll-related and human resource management business process outsourcing services in the U.S.

Recent Developments: For the quarter ended Mar 31 2018, net income decreased 39.6% to US$93.8 million from US$155.4 million in the year-earlier quarter. Revenues were US$865.7 million, up 4.0% from US$832.2 million the year before. Operating income was US$144.2 million versus US$218.6 million in the prior-year quarter, a decrease of 34.0%. Direct operating expenses rose 14.0% to US$342.8 million from US$300.8 million in the comparable period the year before. Indirect operating expenses increased 21.1% to US$378.7 million from US$312.8 million in the equivalent prior-year period.

Prospects: Our evaluation of Equifax Inc. as of Jan. 21, 2018 is the result of our systematic analysis on three basic characteristics: earnings strength, relative valuation, and recent stock price movement. The company has managed to produce a neutral trend in earnings per share over the past 5 quarters and while recent estimates for the company have been mixed, EFX has posted better than expected results. Based on operating earnings yield, the company is undervalued when compared to all of the companies in our coverage universe. Share price changes over the past year indicates that EFX will perform poorly over the near term.

Financial Data
(US$ in Thousands)

	3 Mos	12/31/2017	12/31/2016	12/31/2015	12/31/2014	12/31/2013	12/31/2012	12/31/2011
Earnings Per Share	4.32	4.83	4.04	3.55	2.97	2.84	2.22	1.88
Cash Flow Per Share	6.92	6.79	6.65	6.25	5.08	4.67	4.13	3.35
Dividends Per Share	1.560	1.560	1.320	1.160	1.000	0.880	0.720	0.640
Dividend Payout %	36.11	32.30	32.67	32.68	33.67	30.99	32.43	34.04
Income Statement								
Total Revenue	865,700	3,362,200	3,144,900	2,663,600	2,436,400	2,303,900	2,160,500	1,959,800
EBITDA	226,100	1,130,300	1,089,000	900,400	847,000	790,900	659,000	628,200
Depn & Amortn	79,000	290,900	268,700	200,000	204,200	190,300	163,400	164,900
Income Before Taxes	123,200	746,600	728,200	636,600	574,200	530,400	440,200	408,200
Income Taxes	29,400	148,600	233,100	201,800	200,200	188,900	159,400	168,000
Net Income	90,900	587,300	488,800	429,100	367,400	351,800	272,100	232,900
Average Shares	121,300	121,500	121,100	120,900	123,500	123,700	122,500	123,700
Balance Sheet								
Current Assets	917,400	998,400	672,900	561,600	605,100	648,400	529,700	452,300
Total Assets	7,196,100	7,233,400	6,664,000	4,509,000	4,674,200	4,539,900	4,511,100	3,508,600
Current Liabilities	1,538,900	1,673,500	1,259,600	603,800	823,100	662,500	646,500	362,800
Long-Term Obligations	1,739,600	1,739,000	2,086,800	1,145,900	1,145,700	1,145,500	1,447,400	966,000
Total Liabilities	3,921,400	4,059,000	4,001,300	2,198,100	2,474,100	2,239,200	2,577,900	1,806,200
Stockholders' Equity	3,274,700	3,174,400	2,662,700	2,310,900	2,200,100	2,300,700	1,933,200	1,702,400
Shares Outstanding	120,300	120,100	119,900	118,700	119,400	121,900	120,400	119,600
Statistical Record								
Return on Assets %	7.51	8.45	8.73	9.35	7.97	7.77	6.77	6.71
Return on Equity %	17.03	20.12	19.60	19.02	16.33	16.62	14.93	13.73
EBITDA Margin %	26.12	33.62	34.63	33.80	34.76	34.33	30.50	32.05
Net Margin %	10.50	17.47	15.54	16.11	15.08	15.27	12.59	11.88
Asset Turnover	0.49	0.48	0.56	0.58	0.53	0.51	0.54	0.56
Current Ratio	0.60	0.60	0.53	0.93	0.74	0.98	0.82	1.25
Debt to Equity	0.53	0.55	0.78	0.50	0.52	0.50	0.75	0.57
Price Range	146.26-92.98	146.26-92.98	136.43-93.22	113.61-80.00	82.15-65.04	69.35-53.13	54.93-38.42	39.81-28.79
P/E Ratio	33.86-21.52	30.28-19.25	33.77-23.07	32.00-22.54	27.66-21.90	24.42-18.71	24.74-17.31	21.18-15.31
Average Yield %	1.24	1.23	1.10	1.18	1.36	1.45	1.56	1.82

Address: 1550 Peachtree Street, N.W., Atlanta, GA 30309	**Web Site:** www.equifax.com	**Auditors:** Ernst & Young LLP
Telephone: 404-885-8000	**Officers:** Mark W. Begor - Chief Executive Officer John W. Gamblé - Chief Financial Officer, Corporate Vice-President	**Investor Contact:** 404-885-8804 **Transfer Agents:** American Stock Transfer & Trust Company, Brookly, NY

EQUITY COMMONWEALTH

Exchange	Symbol	Price	52Wk Range	Yield	P/E
NYS	EQC	$31.50 (6/29/2018)	32.32-28.10	N/A	21.28

*7 Year Price Score 96.94 ***NYSE Composite Index=100** ***12 Month Price Score 100.63**

Interim Earnings (Per Share)

Qtr.	Mar	Jun	Sep	Dec
2015	0.05	0.04	0.18	0.29
2016	0.31	0.56	0.67	0.08
2017	0.17	(0.06)	0.25	(0.19)
2018	1.48	...	...	...

Interim Dividends (Per Share)

Dividend Payment Suspended

Valuation Analysis **Institutional Holding**

Forecast EPS	$0.08	No of Institutions	
	(06/05/2018)	367	
Market Cap	$3.8 Billion	Shares	
Book Value	$3.4 Billion	155,136,768	
Price/Book	1.13	% Held	
Price/Sales	12.77	N/A	

Business Summary: REITs (MIC: 5.3.1 SIC: 6798 NAIC: 525930)

Equity Commonwealth is an internally managed and self-advised real estate investment trust engaged in the ownership and operation primarily of office buildings. At Dec 31 2017, Co.'s portfolio included 16 properties (26 buildings).

Recent Developments: For the quarter ended Mar 31 2018, net income increased 687.8% to US$187.7 million from US$23.8 million in the year-earlier quarter. Revenues were US$58.6 million, down 41.1% from US$99.6 million the year before. Revenues from property income fell 45.7% to US$43.5 million from US$80.2 million in the corresponding quarter a year earlier.

Prospects: Our evaluation of Equity Commonwealth as of Jan. 21, 2018 is the result of our systematic analysis on three basic characteristics: earnings strength, relative valuation, and recent stock price movement. The company has managed to produce a neutral trend in earnings per share over the past 5 quarters. Because the company lacks sufficient analyst estimate data, we place greater weight on the historical EPS trend as the measure of earnings strength. Based on operating earnings yield, the company is overvalued when compared to all of the companies in our coverage universe. Share price changes over the past year indicates that EQC will perform in line with the market over the near term.

Financial Data

(US$ in Thousands)	3 Mos	12/31/2017	12/31/2016	12/31/2015	12/31/2014	12/31/2013	12/31/2012	12/31/2011
Earnings Per Share	1.48	0.17	1.62	0.56	(0.19)	(1.97)	(1.81)	0.81
Cash Flow Per Share	0.83	0.81	1.30	1.41	1.60	2.09	3.30	3.40
Tang Book Value Per Share	27.01	25.60	25.33	23.62	22.64	23.06	29.49	33.32
Dividends Per Share	...	...	...	...	0.250	1.000	1.750	2.000
Dividend Payout %	...	...	...	...	...	...	...	246.91
Income Statement								
Total Revenue	58,588	340,571	500,680	714,891	861,857	885,536	1,013,092	911,948
EBITDA	209,709	129,138	410,332	349,436	119,101	336,587	476,565	400,352
Depn & Amortn	14,705	73,169	102,695	145,888	166,076	178,353	188,123	166,444
Income Before Taxes	190,669	30,166	233,639	102,221	(188,644)	(13,548)	85,626	40,602
Income Taxes	3,007	500	745	2,364	3,191	2,634	3,207	1,347
Net Income	187,599	29,656	232,894	99,857	24,012	(177,060)	(95,421)	109,984
Average Shares	127,097	125,129	126,768	129,437	125,163	112,378	83,750	84,726
Balance Sheet								
Current Assets	3,148,455	2,730,954	2,253,237	2,009,650	644,874	468,319	372,239	418,224
Total Assets	4,137,306	4,236,945	4,526,075	5,244,372	5,761,639	6,646,434	8,189,634	7,447,026
Current Liabilities	55,644	73,955	103,555	133,925	176,248	187,216	231,002	193,346
Long-Term Obligations	678,527	848,578	1,141,667	1,710,324	2,207,665	3,005,410	4,349,821	3,577,331
Total Liabilities	737,016	937,579	1,265,628	1,875,885	2,442,056	3,282,848	5,084,206	3,878,509
Stockholders' Equity	3,400,290	3,299,366	3,260,447	3,368,487	3,319,583	3,363,586	3,105,428	3,568,517
Shares Outstanding	121,457	124,217	123,994	126,349	129,607	118,386	83,804	83,721
Statistical Record								
Return on Assets %	4.47	0.68	4.75	1.81	0.39	N.M.	N.M.	1.57
Return on Equity %	5.79	0.90	7.01	2.99	0.72	N.M.	N.M.	3.28
EBITDA Margin %	357.94	37.92	81.95	48.88	13.82	38.01	47.04	43.90
Net Margin %	320.20	8.71	46.52	13.97	2.79	N.M.	N.M.	12.06
Asset Turnover	0.07	0.08	0.10	0.13	0.14	0.12	0.13	0.13
Current Ratio	56.58	36.93	21.76	15.01	3.66	2.50	1.61	2.16
Debt to Equity	0.20	0.26	0.35	0.51	0.67	0.89	1.40	1.00
Price Range	32.51-28.10	32.51-29.80	31.77-25.41	29.67-25.21	28.06-22.40	26.26-15.71	20.61-13.58	28.71-15.95
P/E Ratio	21.97-18.99	191.24-175.29	19.61-15.69	52.98-45.02	...	...	...	35.44-19.69
Average Yield %	...	...	...	...	0.96	4.53	10.25	8.77

Address: Two North Riverside Plaza, Suite 2100, Chicago, IL 60606 **Telephone:** 312-646-2800 **Fax:** 617-332-2261	**Web Site:** www.eqcre.com **Officers:** Samuel Zell - Chairman David A. Helfand - President, Chief Executive Officer, Interim Chief Financial Officer	**Auditors:** Ernst & Young LLP **Investor Contact:** 617-796-8222 **Transfer Agents:** Wells Fargo Bank, National Association, Mendota Heights, MN

EQUITY LIFESTYLE PROPERTIES INC

Exchange	Symbol	Price	52Wk Range	Yield	P/E	Div Acheiver
NYS	ELS	$91.90 (6/29/2018)	92.58-81.55	2.39	41.77	13 Years

*7 Year Price Score 126.71 *NYSE Composite Index=100 *12 Month Price Score 101.55

Interim Earnings (Per Share)

Qtr.	Mar	Jun	Sep	Dec
2015	0.32	0.38	0.43	0.41
2016	0.60	0.42	0.48	0.43
2017	0.65	0.45	0.56	0.51
2018	0.68	...	...	...

Interim Dividends (Per Share)

Amt	Decl	Ex	Rec	Pay
0.487Q	07/25/2017	09/28/2017	09/29/2017	10/13/2017
0.487Q	11/02/2017	12/28/2017	12/29/2017	01/12/2018
0.55Q	02/27/2018	03/28/2018	03/30/2018	04/13/2018
0.55Q	05/01/2018	06/28/2018	06/29/2018	07/13/2018
		Indicated Div: $2.20		

Valuation Analysis — **Institutional Holding**

Forecast EPS	$2.37	No of Institutions
	(06/14/2018)	364
Market Cap	$8.2 Billion	Shares
Book Value	$1.0 Billion	97,268,000
Price/Book	7.89	% Held
Price/Sales	8.69	88.28

Business Summary: REITs (MIC: 5.3.1 SIC: 6798 NAIC: 525930)

Equity Lifestyle Properties is an owner and operator of lifestyle-oriented properties (Properties) consisting of manufactured home communities and recreational vehicle (RV) resorts and campgrounds. Co. owns the land and provides its customers the opportunity to place factory built homes, cottages, cabins or RVs either permanently or on a long-term or short-term basis. Co.'s customers may lease individual developed areas (Sites) or enter right-to-use contracts which provide them access to specific Properties for limited stays. Co. was a real estate networks with a portfolio, as of Dec 31 2017, of 406 properties consisting of 151,323 sites located throughout the U.S. and Canada.

Recent Developments: For the quarter ended Mar 31 2018, net income increased 1.7% to US$64.2 million from US$63.1 million in the year-earlier quarter. Revenues were US$246.0 million, up 5.9% from US$232.4 million the year before. Revenues from property income rose 5.9% to US$241.7 million from US$228.2 million in the corresponding quarter a year earlier.

Prospects: Our evaluation of Equity Lifestyle Properties Inc. as of Jan. 21, 2018 is the result of our systematic analysis on three basic characteristics: earnings strength, relative valuation, and recent stock price movement. The company has enjoyed a very positive trend in earnings per share over the past 5 quarters. Because the company lacks sufficient analyst estimate data, we place greater weight on the historical EPS trend as the measure of earnings strength. Based on operating earnings yield, the company is overvalued when compared to all of the companies in our coverage universe. Share price changes over the past year indicates that ELS will perform very well over the near term.

Financial Data

(US$ in Thousands)	3 Mos	12/31/2017	12/31/2016	12/31/2015	12/31/2014	12/31/2013	12/31/2012	12/31/2011
Earnings Per Share	2.20	2.17	1.92	1.54	1.41	1.28	0.66	0.32
Cash Flow Per Share	4.39	4.42	4.16	4.20	3.43	3.08	2.86	2.47
Tang Book Value Per Share	11.64	11.65	10.20	9.36	9.25	9.09	8.69	11.28
Dividends Per Share	2.013	1.950	1.700	1.500	1.300	1.000	0.875	0.750
Dividend Payout %	91.48	89.86	88.54	97.40	92.20	78.13	132.58	234.38
Income Statement								
Total Revenue	246,025	925,312	870,435	821,654	776,809	728,375	709,877	580,073
EBITDA	121,917	429,902	405,078	366,852	358,057	304,235	302,661	226,687
Depn & Amortn	33,232	122,720	118,521	114,698	111,872	110,505	105,578	86,463
Income Before Taxes	62,982	206,612	184,527	146,423	133,890	75,208	72,559	40,556
Net Income	60,222	197,589	173,263	139,371	128,005	116,199	69,391	36,598
Average Shares	94,577	93,425	92,569	91,907	91,511	91,196	90,862	80,660
Balance Sheet								
Current Assets	108,804	112,005	122,235	146,586	139,440	126,668	115,929	158,489
Total Assets	3,690,083	3,610,032	3,478,987	3,420,061	3,446,339	3,391,639	3,398,226	3,496,101
Current Liabilities	350,055	309,973	305,861	281,657	255,066	236,066	204,058	212,138
Long-Term Obligations	2,238,889	2,200,017	2,091,279	2,145,713	2,212,246	2,192,368	2,269,866	2,284,683
Total Liabilities	2,656,920	2,578,078	2,470,444	2,494,993	2,534,346	2,498,306	2,538,978	2,569,774
Stockholders' Equity	1,033,163	1,031,954	1,008,543	925,068	911,993	893,333	859,248	926,327
Shares Outstanding	88,738	88,585	85,529	84,253	83,879	83,313	83,193	82,156
Statistical Record								
Return on Assets %	5.55	5.57	5.01	4.06	3.74	3.42	2.01	1.32
Return on Equity %	19.18	19.37	17.87	15.17	14.18	13.26	7.75	6.35
EBITDA Margin %	49.55	46.46	46.54	44.65	46.09	41.77	42.64	39.08
Net Margin %	24.48	21.35	19.91	16.96	16.48	15.95	9.78	6.31
Asset Turnover	0.26	0.26	0.25	0.24	0.23	0.21	0.21	0.21
Current Ratio	0.31	0.36	0.40	0.52	0.55	0.54	0.57	0.75
Debt to Equity	2.17	2.13	2.07	2.32	2.43	2.45	2.64	2.47
Price Range	91.71-77.06	91.71-71.35	83.16-63.80	66.81-51.55	52.42-36.13	42.77-33.48	36.49-31.91	36.05-27.29
P/E Ratio	41.69-35.03	42.26-32.88	43.31-33.23	43.38-33.47	37.18-25.62	33.41-26.16	55.30-48.35	112.66-85.27
Average Yield %	2.34	2.33	2.33	2.32	2.64	2.98	2.67	2.44

Address: Two North Riverside Plaza, Suite 800, Chicago, IL 60606 **Telephone:** 312-279-1400	**Web Site:** www.equitylifestyleproperties.com **Officers:** Samuel Zell - Chairman, Chief Executive Officer, Co-Chairman Howard Walker - Co-Vice Chairman, Vice-Chairman	**Auditors:** Ernst & Young LLP **Investor Contact:** 180-024-75279 **Transfer Agents:** American Stock Transfer and Trust Company, LLC, New York, NY

EQUITY RESIDENTIAL

Exchange	Symbol	Price	52Wk Range	Yield	P/E
NYS	EQR	$63.69 (6/29/2018)	70.37-55.26	3.39	35.19

*7 Year Price Score 80.59   ***NYSE Composite Index=100**   ***12 Month Price Score 96.71**

Interim Earnings (Per Share)

Qtr.	Mar	Jun	Sep	Dec
2015	0.49	0.78	0.53	0.56
2016	9.76	0.59	0.56	0.76
2017	0.39	0.53	0.37	0.34
2018	0.57	...	...	...

Interim Dividends (Per Share)

Amt	Decl	Ex	Rec	Pay
0.504Q	09/15/2017	09/22/2017	09/25/2017	10/13/2017
0.504Q	12/19/2017	12/29/2017	01/02/2018	01/12/2018
0.54Q	03/15/2018	03/23/2018	03/26/2018	04/13/2018
0.54Q	06/14/2018	06/22/2018	06/25/2018	07/13/2018

Indicated Div: $2.16

Valuation Analysis

		Institutional Holding	
Forecast EPS	$1.48	No of Institutions	
	(06/04/2018)	812	
Market Cap	$23.5 Billion	Shares	
Book Value	$10.3 Billion	449,374,464	
Price/Book	2.28	% Held	
Price/Sales	9.38	97.83	

Business Summary: REITs (MIC: 5.3.1 SIC: 6798 NAIC: 525930)

Equity Residential is a real estate investment trust focused on the acquisition, development and management of apartment properties. Co. is the general partner of, and as of Dec. 31, 2017 owned an approximate 96.4% ownership interest in ERP Operating Limited Partnership (ERPOP). All of Co.'s property ownership, development and related business operations are conducted through ERPOP and those entities/subsidiaries owned or controlled by ERPOP. As of Dec 31 2017, Co., directly or indirectly through investments in title holding entities, owned all or a portion of 305 properties located in 10 states and the District of Columbia.

Recent Developments: For the quarter ended Mar 31 2018, net income increased 47.1% to US$220.5 million from US$149.9 million in the year-earlier quarter. Revenues were US$633.0 million, up 4.8% from US$604.1 million the year before.

Prospects: Our evaluation of Equity Residential Properties Trust as of Jan. 21, 2018 is the result of our systematic analysis on three basic characteristics: earnings strength, relative valuation, and recent stock price movement. The company has produced a positive trend in earnings per share over the past 5 quarters. However, while recent estimates for the company have been mixed, EQR has posted better than expected results. Based on operating earnings yield, the company is overvalued when compared to all of the companies in our coverage universe. Share price changes over the past year indicates that EQR will perform well over the near term.

Financial Data

(US$ in Thousands)	3 Mos	12/31/2017	12/31/2016	12/31/2015	12/31/2014	12/31/2013	12/31/2012	12/31/2011
Earnings Per Share	1.81	1.63	11.68	2.36	1.73	5.16	2.70	2.95
Cash Flow Per Share	3.63	3.45	3.04	3.73	3.67	2.45	3.45	2.71
Tang Book Value Per Share	27.84	27.73	27.86	28.60	28.44	29.01	22.27	18.38
Dividends Per Share	2.051	2.015	13.015	2.210	2.000	1.850	1.780	1.580
Dividend Payout %	113.33	123.62	111.43	93.64	115.61	35.85	65.93	53.56
Income Statement								
Total Revenue	633,016	2,471,406	2,425,800	2,744,965	2,614,748	2,387,702	2,123,715	1,989,463
EBITDA	400,834	1,586,034	1,551,367	1,771,773	1,671,163	1,496,672	1,325,589	1,222,391
Depn & Amortn	207,406	743,749	705,649	765,895	758,861	1,013,353	684,992	663,616
Income Before Taxes	79,525	456,005	416,612	558,380	448,485	(121,076)	312,108	80,509
Income Taxes	213	478	1,613	917	1,394	1,169	539	728
Net Income	211,809	603,454	4,292,163	870,120	631,308	1,830,613	841,719	893,585
Average Shares	383,018	382,678	381,992	380,620	377,735	354,305	319,766	312,065
Balance Sheet								
Current Assets	94,711	100,762	219,088	155,115	160,468	199,737	872,161	546,850
Total Assets	20,383,870	20,570,599	20,704,148	23,157,328	22,950,614	22,834,545	17,201,000	16,659,303
Current Liabilities	743,094	430,638	463,348	559,305	507,329	512,203	441,759	367,692
Long-Term Obligations	8,425,159	8,957,291	8,987,258	10,968,498	10,844,861	10,766,254	8,529,244	9,721,061
Total Liabilities	10,094,698	10,328,135	10,475,070	12,686,960	12,582,158	12,327,344	9,911,187	10,990,288
Stockholders' Equity	10,289,172	10,242,464	10,229,078	10,470,368	10,368,456	10,507,201	7,289,813	5,669,015
Shares Outstanding	368,211	368,018	365,870	364,755	362,855	360,479	325,054	297,508
Statistical Record								
Return on Assets %	3.28	2.92	19.52	3.77	2.76	9.14	4.96	5.44
Return on Equity %	6.53	5.90	41.36	8.35	6.05	20.57	12.96	16.61
EBITDA Margin %	63.32	64.18	63.95	64.55	63.91	62.68	62.42	61.44
Net Margin %	33.46	24.42	176.94	31.70	24.14	76.67	39.63	44.92
Asset Turnover	0.12	0.12	0.11	0.12	0.11	0.12	0.13	0.12
Current Ratio	0.13	0.23	0.47	0.28	0.32	0.39	1.97	1.49
Debt to Equity	0.82	0.87	0.88	1.05	1.05	1.02	1.17	1.71
Price Range	70.37-55.26	70.37-50.90	81.59-58.81	81.97-68.95	74.55-51.87	60.75-50.45	65.47-54.06	63.68-49.66
P/E Ratio	38.88-30.53	43.17-36.75	6.99-5.04	34.73-29.22	43.09-29.98	11.77-9.78	24.25-20.02	21.59-16.83
Average Yield %	3.17	3.08	19.16	2.90	3.19	3.34	3.00	2.79

Address: Two North Riverside Plaza, Chicago, IL 60606 **Telephone:** 312-474-1300	**Web Site:** www.equityapartments.com **Officers:** Samuel Zell - Chairman David J. Neithercut - President, Chief Executive Officer	**Auditors:** Ernst & Young LLP **Investor Contact:** 888-879-6356 **Transfer Agents:** Computershare Trust Company, N.A, Providence, RI

ESSEX PROPERTY TRUST INC

Exchange	Symbol	Price	52Wk Range	Yield	P/E	Div Acheiver
NYS	ESS	$239.07 (6/29/2018)	269.39-217.81	3.11	45.62	23 Years

*7 Year Price Score 101.18 *NYSE Composite Index=100 *12 Month Price Score 95.27

Interim Earnings (Per Share)

Qtr.	Mar	Jun	Sep	Dec
2015	0.92	0.70	0.65	1.22
2016	1.19	1.10	1.00	2.98
2017	2.72	1.08	1.21	1.57
2018	1.38	...	...	...

Interim Dividends (Per Share)

Amt	Decl	Ex	Rec	Pay
1.75Q	09/19/2017	09/28/2017	09/29/2017	10/16/2017
1.75Q	12/13/2017	12/28/2017	12/29/2017	01/16/2018
1.86Q	02/21/2018	03/28/2018	03/29/2018	04/16/2018
1.86Q	05/21/2018	06/28/2018	06/29/2018	07/13/2018

Indicated Div: $7.44 (Div. Reinv. Plan)

Valuation Analysis

Forecast EPS	$4.88 (06/14/2018)
Market Cap	$15.8 Billion
Book Value	N/A
Price/Book	N/A
Price/Sales	11.48

Institutional Holding

No of Institutions	621
Shares	79,170,912
% Held	67.64

TRADING VOLUME (thousand shares)

Business Summary: REITs (MIC: 5.3.1 SIC: 6798 NAIC: 525930)

Essex Property Trust is a self-administered and self-managed real estate investment trust. Co. owns all of its interest in its real estate and other investments directly or indirectly through Essex Portfolio, L.P. Co. is engaged primarily in the ownership, operation, management, acquisition, development and redevelopment of primarily apartment communities. As of Dec 31 2017, Co. owned or had ownership interests in 247 apartment communities (aggregating 60,239 apartment homes), one operating commercial buildings, and seven active development projects. The communities are located in Southern California, Northern California and the Seattle metropolitan areas.

Recent Developments: For the quarter ended Mar 31 2018, net income decreased 48.5% to US$96.6 million from US$187.6 million in the year-earlier quarter. Revenues were US$347.3 million, up 3.5% from US$335.4 million the year before. Revenues from property income rose 3.5% to US$344.9 million from US$333.2 million in the corresponding quarter a year earlier.

Prospects: Our evaluation of Essex Property Trust Inc. as of Jan. 21, 2018 is the result of our systematic analysis on three basic characteristics: earnings strength, relative valuation, and recent stock price movement. The company has enjoyed a very positive trend in earnings per share over the past 5 quarters. Because the company lacks sufficient analyst estimate data, we place greater weight on the historical EPS trend as the measure of earnings strength. Based on operating earnings yield, the company is overvalued when compared to all of the companies in our coverage universe. Share price changes over the past year indicates that ESS will perform very well over the near term.

Financial Data
(US$ in Thousands)

	3 Mos	12/31/2017	12/31/2016	12/31/2015	12/31/2014	12/31/2013	12/31/2012	12/31/2011
Earnings Per Share	5.24	6.57	6.27	3.49	2.06	4.04	3.41	1.24
Cash Flow Per Share	12.28	11.64	10.85	9.52	8.72	8.19	7.61	6.66
Tang Book Value Per Share	...	95.03	94.50	94.28	93.42	48.51	46.52	40.37
Dividends Per Share	7.110	7.000	6.400	5.760	5.110	4.840	4.400	4.160
Dividend Payout %	135.69	106.54	102.07	165.04	248.06	119.80	129.03	335.48
Income Statement								
Total Revenue	347,255	1,363,899	1,294,001	1,194,407	969,305	613,703	543,425	475,558
EBITDA	105,726	1,017,702	998,708	833,735	583,880	383,426	356,549	288,820
Depn & Amortn	(4,821)	447,814	412,237	421,673	336,595	193,518	170,686	152,542
Income Before Taxes	63,865	371,598	394,122	226,378	94,545	96,941	99,452	61,723
Income Taxes	...	...	4,410	...	...	...	...	...
Net Income	90,918	433,059	414,979	232,120	122,150	156,283	125,284	47,070
Average Shares	66,082	65,898	65,587	65,061	56,696	37,335	35,124	32,628
Balance Sheet								
Current Assets	407,348	352,056	350,461	279,825	237,583	212,105	201,002	176,107
Total Assets	12,642,667	12,495,706	12,217,408	12,005,091	11,562,874	5,186,839	4,847,223	4,036,964
Current Liabilities	356,902	300,691	284,305	272,634	261,248	125,857	115,302	94,440
Long-Term Obligations	5,718,970	5,689,126	5,563,260	5,315,464	5,109,817	3,033,524	2,818,683	2,360,858
Total Liabilities	6,217,463	6,218,300	6,025,230	5,767,358	5,540,202	3,297,871	3,078,070	2,595,088
Stockholders' Equity	...	6,277,406	6,192,178	6,237,733	6,022,672	1,888,968	1,769,153	1,441,876
Shares Outstanding	66,044	66,054	65,527	65,379	63,682	37,421	36,442	33,888
Statistical Record								
Return on Assets %	2.75	3.50	3.42	1.97	1.46	3.12	2.81	1.21
Return on Equity %	...	6.95	6.66	3.79	3.09	8.54	7.78	3.63
EBITDA Margin %	30.45	74.62	77.18	69.80	60.24	62.48	65.61	60.73
Net Margin %	26.18	31.75	32.07	19.43	12.60	25.47	23.05	9.90
Asset Turnover	0.11	0.11	0.11	0.10	0.12	0.12	0.12	0.12
Current Ratio	1.14	1.17	1.23	1.03	0.91	1.69	1.74	1.86
Debt to Equity	...	0.91	0.90	0.85	0.85	1.61	1.59	1.64
Price Range	269.39-217.81	269.39-221.72	240.04-192.26	244.29-206.60	212.86-143.51	170.47-141.49	160.33-136.94	146.45-110.77
P/E Ratio	51.41-41.57	41.00-33.75	38.28-30.66	70.00-59.20	103.33-69.67	42.20-35.02	47.02-40.16	118.10-89.33
Average Yield %	2.86	2.82	2.89	2.57	2.82	3.13	2.96	3.20

Address: 1100 Park Place Suite 200, San Mateo, CA 94403	**Web Site:** www.essex.com
Telephone: 650-655-7800	**Officers:** George M. Marcus - Chairman Michael J. Schall - President, Chief Executive Officer, Senior Executive Vice President, Chief Operating Officer

Auditors: KPMG LLP
Investor Contact: 650-494-3700
Transfer Agents: Computershare, LLC

ESTERLINE TECHNOLOGIES CORP

Exchange	Symbol	Price	52Wk Range	Yield	P/E
NYS	ESL	$73.80 (6/29/2018)	100.10-68.45	N/A	40.55

*7 Year Price Score 79.10 ***NYSE Composite Index=100** ***12 Month Price Score 90.25**

Interim Earnings (Per Share)

Qtr.	Jan	May	Jul	Sep
2014-15	(0.26)	0.63	0.92	0.62
2015-16	0.17	0.50	0.99	1.76
2016-17	0.54	1.17	1.01	1.18
2017-18	(1.17)	0.80	...	...

Interim Dividends (Per Share)

No Dividends Paid

Valuation Analysis   **Institutional Holding**

Forecast EPS	$3.66	No of Institutions
	(06/13/2018)	340
Market Cap	$2.2 Billion	Shares
Book Value	$1.8 Billion	36,439,936
Price/Book	1.21	% Held
Price/Sales	1.07	97.30

Business Summary: Electronic Instruments & Related Products (MIC: 6.2.3 SIC: 3823 NAIC: 334513)

Esterline Technologies is a manufacturing company principally serving aerospace and defense customers. Co. designs, manufactures and markets engineered products and systems for application within the industries it serves. Co. focuses in three key technology segments: Avionics and Controls, which includes avionics systems, control and communication systems, and interface technologies capabilities; Sensors and Systems, which includes power systems, connection technologies and advanced sensors capabilities; and Advanced Materials, which includes engineered materials and defense technologies capabilities.

Recent Developments: For the quarter ended Mar 30 2018, income from continuing operations decreased 30.4% to US$24.0 million from US$34.4 million in the year-earlier quarter. Net income decreased 30.6% to US$23.9 million from US$34.4 million in the year-earlier quarter. Revenues were US$517.6 million, up 1.7% from US$509.1 million the year before. Operating income was US$33.9 million versus US$55.4 million in the prior-year quarter, a decrease of 38.8%. Direct operating expenses rose 6.6% to US$353.9 million from US$331.9 million in the comparable period the year before. Indirect operating expenses increased 6.6% to US$129.8 million from US$121.8 million in the equivalent prior-year period.

Prospects: Our evaluation of Esterline Technologies Corp. as of Jan. 21, 2018 is the result of our systematic analysis on three basic characteristics: earnings strength, relative valuation, and recent stock price movement. The company has generated a negative trend in earnings per share over the past 5 quarters and while recent estimates for the company have been raised by analysts, ESL has posted results that fell short of analysts expectations. Based on operating earnings yield, the company is undervalued when compared to all of the companies in our coverage universe. Share price changes over the past year indicates that ESL will perform in line with the market over the near term.

Financial Data
(US$ in Thousands)

	6 Mos	3 Mos	09/29/2017	09/30/2016	10/02/2015	10/31/2014	10/25/2013	10/26/2012
Earnings Per Share	1.82	2.19	3.91	3.42	1.91	3.16	5.19	3.60
Cash Flow Per Share	6.48	7.03	6.52	5.68	5.10	6.69	8.07	6.33
Tang Book Value Per Share	13.28	12.53	14.14	6.21	1.47	10.82	5.21	N.M.
Income Statement								
Total Revenue	999,674	482,045	2,002,195	1,992,631	1,774,449	2,051,169	1,969,754	1,992,318
EBITDA	114,860	52,849	253,011	219,659	190,534	299,489	292,377	241,706
Depn & Amortn	54,303	26,216	58,200	49,500	45,000	56,200	55,400	52,400
Income Before Taxes	45,533	19,327	165,130	140,435	116,022	210,834	197,849	143,533
Income Taxes	55,868	53,789	38,928	22,535	18,956	44,274	30,085	29,958
Net Income	(11,104)	(34,981)	117,387	101,685	59,612	102,418	164,734	112,535
Average Shares	29,726	29,903	30,003	29,764	31,215	32,448	31,738	31,282
Balance Sheet								
Current Assets	1,320,867	1,274,567	1,280,457	1,175,788	1,128,814	1,169,504	1,091,715	1,035,693
Total Assets	3,139,527	3,115,056	3,130,323	3,032,031	3,007,030	3,193,467	3,262,112	3,227,117
Current Liabilities	402,062	371,954	393,430	398,498	410,809	408,129	408,092	396,346
Long-Term Obligations	766,082	782,287	759,424	853,796	867,786	609,720	667,859	838,060
Total Liabilities	1,346,572	1,334,327	1,293,716	1,431,474	1,469,563	1,305,650	1,388,507	1,616,636
Stockholders' Equity	1,792,955	1,780,729	1,836,607	1,600,557	1,537,467	1,887,817	1,873,605	1,610,481
Shares Outstanding	29,427	29,721	29,981	29,428	29,546	31,854	31,441	30,869
Statistical Record								
Return on Assets %	1.81	2.19	3.82	3.38	2.09	3.12	5.09	3.42
Return on Equity %	3.20	3.95	6.85	6.50	3.78	5.36	9.48	7.11
EBITDA Margin %	11.49	10.96	12.64	11.02	10.74	14.60	14.84	12.13
Net Margin %	N.M.	N.M.	5.86	5.10	3.36	4.99	8.36	5.65
Asset Turnover	0.67	0.67	0.65	0.66	0.62	0.63	0.61	0.60
Current Ratio	3.29	3.43	3.25	2.95	2.75	2.87	2.68	2.61
Debt to Equity	0.43	0.44	0.41	0.53	0.56	0.32	0.36	0.52
Price Range	101.60-68.45	101.60-69.35	101.60-69.90	95.78-51.76	120.06-71.14	121.48-78.27	84.80-55.42	75.20-48.71
P/E Ratio	55.82-37.61	46.39-31.67	25.98-17.88	28.01-15.13	62.86-37.25	38.44-24.77	16.34-10.68	20.89-13.53

Address: 500 108th Avenue N.E.,	Web Site: www.esterline.com	Auditors: Ernst & Young LLP
Bellevue, WA 98004	Officers: Curtis C. Reusser - Chairman, President,	Investor Contact: 425-453-9400
Telephone: 425-453-9400	Chief Executive Officer Stephen M. Nolan - Executive	Transfer Agents: Mellon Investor
	Vice President, Chief Financial Officer	Services LLC, Ridgefield , NJ

EVERCORE INC

Exchange	Symbol	Price	52Wk Range	Yield	P/E	Div Acheiver
NYS	EVR	$105.45 (6/29/2018)	112.05-70.35	1.90	33.80	10 Years

*7 Year Price Score 136.07 *NYSE Composite Index=100 *12 Month Price Score 119.06

Interim Earnings (Per Share)

Qtr.	Mar	Jun	Sep	Dec
2015	0.10	0.26	0.16	0.46
2016	0.12	0.55	0.79	0.98
2017	1.76	0.41	1.04	(0.43)
2018	2.10	...	...	...

Interim Dividends (Per Share)

Amt	Decl	Ex	Rec	Pay
0.34Q	07/26/2017	08/23/2017	08/25/2017	09/08/2017
0.40Q	10/23/2017	11/22/2017	11/24/2017	12/08/2017
0.40Q	01/29/2018	02/22/2018	02/23/2018	03/09/2018
0.50Q	04/24/2018	05/24/2018	05/25/2018	06/08/2018

Indicated Div: $2.00

Valuation Analysis — **Institutional Holding**

Forecast EPS	$7.42	No of Institutions
	(06/13/2018)	452
Market Cap	$4.3 Billion	Shares
Book Value	$549.9 Million	48,010,536
Price/Book	7.85	% Held
Price/Sales	2.43	N/A

Business Summary: Finance Intermediaries & Services (MIC: 5.5.1 SIC: 6282 NAIC: 523110)

Evercore is an investment banking advisory firm. Co. operates through two business segments: Investment Banking, which provides advice to clients on mergers, acquisitions, divestitures and other corporate transactions, underwrites securities offerings and raises funds for financial sponsors; and Investment Management, which focuses on Institutional Asset Management, through which Co. manages financial assets for institutional investors and provides fiduciary services to corporate employee benefit plans, and Wealth Management, through which Co. provides wealth management services, and Private Equity business, which holds investments in entities that manage private equity funds.

Recent Developments: For the quarter ended Mar 31 2018, net income increased 15.9% to US$109.7 million from US$94.6 million in the year-earlier quarter. Revenues were US$463.6 million, up 19.7% from US$387.2 million the year before. Operating income was US$112.5 million versus US$111.3 million in the prior-year quarter, an increase of 1.1%. Indirect operating expenses increased 27.2% to US$351.0 million from US$275.9 million in the equivalent prior-year period.

Prospects: Our evaluation of Evercore Inc. as of Jan. 21, 2018 is the result of our systematic analysis on three basic characteristics: earnings strength, relative valuation, and recent stock price movement. The company has generated a negative trend in earnings per share over the past 5 quarters. However, while recent estimates for the company have been mixed, EVR has posted better than expected results. Based on operating earnings yield, the company is undervalued when compared to all of the companies in our coverage universe. Share price changes over the past year indicates that EVR will perform poorly over the near term.

Financial Data
(US$ in Thousands)

	3 Mos	12/31/2017	12/31/2016	12/31/2015	12/31/2014	12/31/2013	12/31/2012	12/31/2011
Earnings Per Share	3.12	2.80	2.43	0.98	2.08	1.38	0.89	0.23
Cash Flow Per Share	13.78	13.03	10.58	9.60	6.03	6.17	5.46	5.68
Tang Book Value Per Share	9.66	9.98	8.60	7.50	7.27	8.67	6.91	6.76
Dividends Per Share	1.480	1.420	1.270	1.150	1.030	0.910	0.820	0.740
Dividend Payout %	47.44	50.71	52.26	117.35	49.52	65.94	92.13	321.74
Income Statement								
Total Revenue	463,563	1,704,349	1,440,052	1,223,273	915,858	765,428	642,373	524,264
EBITDA	119,261	443,837	274,334	139,139	179,203	136,718	71,497	39,243
Depn & Amortn	6,712	15,026	13,160	10,469	8,256	6,543	5,962	3,431
Income Before Taxes	112,549	428,811	261,174	128,670	170,947	130,175	65,535	35,812
Income Taxes	4,938	258,442	119,303	77,030	68,756	63,689	30,908	22,724
Net Income	95,543	125,454	107,528	42,863	86,874	53,262	28,889	6,952
Average Shares	45,463	44,826	44,193	43,699	41,843	38,481	32,548	29,397
Balance Sheet								
Current Assets	808,967	1,000,205	925,633	749,464	682,956	537,859	526,747	485,860
Total Assets	1,417,653	1,584,886	1,662,346	1,479,171	1,446,556	1,180,783	1,145,218	1,043,592
Current Liabilities	324,307	464,052	463,421	408,049	385,080	284,159	320,906	302,897
Long-Term Obligations	168,510	175,146	184,647	141,800	127,776	103,226	101,375	99,664
Total Liabilities	867,793	1,040,922	1,135,048	974,619	895,275	678,202	716,712	635,928
Stockholders' Equity	549,860	543,964	527,298	504,552	551,281	502,581	428,506	407,664
Shares Outstanding	40,951	39,102	39,190	39,623	36,255	33,069	29,577	27,941
Statistical Record								
Return on Assets %	9.84	7.73	6.83	2.93	6.61	4.58	2.63	0.72
Return on Equity %	25.28	23.42	20.78	8.12	16.49	11.44	6.89	1.96
EBITDA Margin %	25.73	26.04	19.05	11.37	19.57	17.86	11.13	7.49
Net Margin %	20.61	7.36	7.47	3.50	9.49	6.96	4.50	1.33
Asset Turnover	1.25	1.05	0.91	0.84	0.70	0.66	0.59	0.54
Current Ratio	2.49	2.16	2.00	1.84	1.77	1.89	1.64	1.60
Debt to Equity	0.31	0.32	0.35	0.28	0.23	0.21	0.24	0.24
Price Range	101.80-67.80	92.20-67.80	71.55-40.61	59.15-46.88	63.14-45.29	60.53-30.19	30.19-20.83	37.01-20.93
P/E Ratio	32.63-21.73	32.93-24.21	29.44-16.71	60.36-47.84	30.36-21.77	43.86-21.88	33.92-23.40	160.91-91.00
Average Yield %	1.82	1.84	2.43	2.18	1.93	2.06	3.12	2.45

Address: 55 East 52nd Street, 38th floor, New York, NY 10055	**Web Site:** www.evercore.com	**Auditors:** Deloitte & Touche LLP
Telephone: 212-857-3100	**Officers:** John S. Weinberg - Executive Chairman	**Investor Contact:** 212-857-3100
Fax: 212-857-3101	Roger C. Altman - Senior Chairman, Co-Chairman, Co-Chief Executive Officer	**Transfer Agents:** Computershare, College Station, TX

EVEREST RE GROUP LTD

Exchange	Symbol	Price	52Wk Range	Yield	P/E
NYS	RE	$230.48 (6/29/2018)	271.12-210.36	2.26	25.05

*7 Year Price Score 114.80 *NYSE Composite Index=100 *12 Month Price Score 95.41

Interim Earnings (Per Share)

Qtr.	Mar	Jun	Sep	Dec
2015	7.19	4.68	2.00	8.18
2016	4.00	3.67	7.06	8.98
2017	7.07	5.95	(15.73)	13.87
2018	5.11	...	...	...

Interim Dividends (Per Share)

Amt	Decl	Ex	Rec	Pay
1.25Q	08/23/2017	09/01/2017	09/06/2017	09/20/2017
1.30Q	11/09/2017	11/28/2017	11/29/2017	12/13/2017
1.30Q	02/21/2018	03/06/2018	03/07/2018	03/21/2018
1.30Q	05/16/2018	05/29/2018	05/30/2018	06/13/2018

Indicated Div: $5.20

Valuation Analysis

		Institutional Holding	
Forecast EPS	N/A	No of Institutions	648
Market Cap	$9.4 Billion	Shares	47,505,172
Book Value	$8.3 Billion	% Held	79.97
Price/Book	1.13		
Price/Sales	1.38		

Business Summary: General Insurance (MIC: 5.2.1 SIC: 6331 NAIC: 524126)

Everest Re Group is a holding company. Through its subsidiaries, Co.'s principal business is underwriting of reinsurance and insurance in the U.S., Bermuda and international markets. Co. operates following segments: U.S. Reinsurance, which writes property and casualty reinsurance and specialty lines of business, including Marine, Aviation, Surety and Accident and Health business; International, which writes foreign property and casualty reinsurance; Bermuda, which provides reinsurance and insurance to worldwide property and casualty markets and and reinsurance to the U.K and European markets; and Insurance, which writes property and casualty insurance within the U.S. and Canada.

Recent Developments: For the quarter ended Mar 31 2018, net income decreased 27.9% to US$210.3 million from US$291.6 million in the year-earlier quarter. Revenues were US$1.75 billion, up 17.5% from US$1.48 billion the year before. Net premiums earned were US$1.62 billion versus US$1.31 billion in the prior-year quarter, an increase of 23.4%. Net investment income rose 13.1% to US$138.3 million from US$122.3 million a year ago.

Prospects: Our evaluation of Everest Re Group Ltd. as of Sep. 17, 2017 is the result of our systematic analysis on three basic characteristics: earnings strength, relative valuation, and recent stock price movement. The company has suffered a very negative trend in earnings per share over the past 5 quarters. However, while recent estimates for the company have been mixed, RE has posted better than expected results. Based on operating earnings yield, the company is undervalued when compared to all of the companies in our coverage universe. Share price changes over the past year indicates that RE will perform very well over the near term.

Financial Data

(US$ in Thousands)	3 Mos	12/31/2017	12/31/2016	12/31/2015	12/31/2014	12/31/2013	12/31/2012	12/31/2011
Earnings Per Share	9.20	11.36	23.68	22.10	25.91	25.44	15.79	(1.49)
Cash Flow Per Share	24.13	28.64	33.13	30.14	28.95	22.59	12.76	12.26
Tang Book Value Per Share	203.62	204.95	197.45	178.21	166.75	146.57	130.96	112.99
Dividends Per Share	5.100	5.050	4.700	4.000	3.200	2.190	1.920	1.920
Dividend Payout %	55.43	44.45	19.85	18.10	12.35	8.61	12.16	...
Income Statement								
Premium Income	1,619,427	5,937,840	5,320,466	5,481,459	5,169,135	4,753,543	4,164,628	4,101,347
Total Revenue	1,745,157	6,608,071	5,794,346	5,837,889	5,790,589	5,640,836	4,922,810	4,693,961
Benefits & Claims	1,057,177	4,522,581	3,139,629	3,101,915	2,906,534	2,800,251	2,745,265	3,726,204
Income Before Taxes	217,643	405,184	1,099,844	1,208,509	1,446,115	1,554,966	939,526	(233,947)
Income Taxes	7,325	(63,784)	103,500	134,021	187,652	289,706	110,572	(153,461)
Net Income	210,318	468,968	996,344	977,869	1,199,156	1,259,382	828,954	(80,486)
Average Shares	40,689	40,843	41,628	43,877	45,802	49,056	52,067	53,916
Balance Sheet								
Total Assets	23,513,196	23,591,792	21,321,504	21,426,175	20,817,824	19,808,036	19,777,907	18,893,555
Total Liabilities	15,169,016	15,222,560	13,246,108	13,817,590	13,366,704	12,839,760	13,044,440	12,822,180
Stockholders' Equity	8,344,180	8,369,232	8,075,396	7,608,585	7,451,120	6,968,276	6,733,467	6,071,375
Shares Outstanding	40,978	40,835	40,898	42,694	44,685	47,543	51,417	53,736
Statistical Record								
Return on Assets %	1.70	2.09	4.65	4.63	5.90	6.36	4.28	N.M.
Return on Equity %	4.64	5.70	12.67	12.99	16.63	18.38	12.91	N.M.
Loss Ratio %	65.28	76.17	59.01	56.59	56.23	58.91	65.92	90.85
Net Margin %	12.05	7.10	17.20	16.75	20.71	22.33	16.84	(1.71)
Price Range	271.12-210.36	271.12-210.36	218.38-169.21	191.54-166.99	176.27-137.48	159.13-109.95	114.60-83.35	93.76-73.50
P/E Ratio	29.47-22.87	23.87-18.52	9.22-7.15	8.67-7.56	6.80-5.31	6.26-4.32	7.26-5.28	...
Average Yield %	2.12	2.12	2.47	2.22	2.01	1.63	1.91	2.28

Address: Seon Place - 4th Floor, 141 Front Street, P.O. Box HM 845, Hamilton, HM 19
Telephone: 441-295-0006
Fax: 441-295-4828

Web Site: www.everestregroup.com
Officers: Joseph V. Taranto - Chairman, Chief Executive Officer Dominic James Addesso - President, Chief Executive Officer, Executive Vice President, Chief Financial Officer

Auditors: PricewaterhouseCoopers LLP
Investor Contact: 908-604-3169
Transfer Agents: Computershare Trust Company, N.A., Providence, RI

EVERSOURCE ENERGY

Exchange	Symbol	Price	52Wk Range	Yield	P/E	Div Acheiver
NYS	ES	$58.61 (6/29/2018)	65.81-52.87	3.45	18.67	18 Years

*7 Year Price Score 100.62 *NYSE Composite Index=100 *12 Month Price Score 92.79

Interim Earnings (Per Share)

Qtr.	Mar	Jun	Sep	Dec
2015	0.80	0.65	0.74	0.57
2016	0.77	0.64	0.83	0.72
2017	0.82	0.72	0.82	0.75
2018	0.85	...	...	...

Interim Dividends (Per Share)

Amt	Decl	Ex	Rec	Pay
0.475Q	09/06/2017	09/18/2017	09/19/2017	09/29/2017
0.475Q	12/05/2017	12/15/2017	12/18/2017	12/29/2017
0.505Q	02/07/2018	03/05/2018	03/06/2018	03/30/2018
0.505Q	05/02/2018	05/23/2018	05/24/2018	06/29/2018

Indicated Div: $2.02 (Div. Reinv. Plan)

Valuation Analysis / Institutional Holding

Forecast EPS	$3.25	No of Institutions
	(06/14/2018)	129
Market Cap	$19.6 Billion	Shares
Book Value	$11.2 Billion	24,690,404
Price/Book	1.75	% Held
Price/Sales	2.47	65.19

Business Summary: Electric Utilities (MIC: 3.1.1 SIC: 4911 NAIC: 221122)

Eversource Energy is a public utility holding company, which engaged primarily in the energy delivery business through its utility subsidiaries. As of Dec 31 2017, Connecticut Light and Power Company furnished retail franchise electric service to 1.2 million customers in 149 cities and towns in Connecticut; NSTAR Electric Company served 1.4 million customers in Boston and 139 cities and towns in eastern and western Massachusetts, including Cape Cod, Martha's Vineyard and the greater Springfield metropolitan area; and Public Service Company of New Hampshire served 515,000 retail customers in 211 cities and towns in New Hampshire.

Recent Developments: For the quarter ended Mar 31 2018, net income increased 3.9% to US$271.4 million from US$261.3 million in the year-earlier quarter. Revenues were US$2.29 billion, up 8.7% from US$2.11 billion the year before. Operating income was US$442.5 million versus US$501.0 million in the prior-year quarter, a decrease of 11.7%. Direct operating expenses rose 17.2% to US$1.28 billion from US$1.09 billion in the comparable period the year before. Indirect operating expenses increased 10.5% to US$566.1 million from US$512.2 million in the equivalent prior-year period.

Prospects: Our evaluation of Eversource Energy as of Jan. 21, 2018 is the result of our systematic analysis on three basic characteristics: earnings strength, relative valuation, and recent stock price movement. The company has managed to produce a neutral trend in earnings per share over the past 5 quarters. However, while recent estimates for the company have been mixed, ES has posted results that fell short of analysts expectations. Based on operating earnings yield, the company is undervalued when compared to all of the companies in our coverage universe. Share price changes over the past year indicates that ES will perform well over the near term.

Financial Data
(US$ in Thousands)

	3 Mos	12/31/2017	12/31/2016	12/31/2015	12/31/2014	12/31/2013	12/31/2012	12/31/2011
Earnings Per Share	3.14	3.11	2.96	2.76	2.58	2.49	1.89	2.22
Cash Flow Per Share	5.50	6.32	6.83	4.49	5.17	5.28	4.18	5.47
Tang Book Value Per Share	20.24	21.01	22.70	21.54	20.37	19.32	18.21	21.03
Dividends Per Share	1.930	1.900	1.780	1.670	1.570	1.470	1.323	1.100
Dividend Payout %	61.46	61.09	60.14	60.51	60.85	59.04	69.99	49.55
Income Statement								
Total Revenue	2,287,962	7,751,952	7,639,129	7,954,827	7,741,856	7,301,204	6,273,787	4,465,657
EBITDA	707,981	2,769,964	2,621,245	2,464,247	2,272,125	2,170,106	1,656,958	1,124,083
Depn & Amortn	249,460	773,802	715,466	665,856	614,657	610,777	519,010	302,192
Income Before Taxes	340,892	1,574,407	1,504,818	1,425,971	1,295,362	1,220,630	808,003	571,466
Income Taxes	83,766	578,892	554,997	539,967	468,297	426,941	274,926	170,953
Net Income	269,546	987,996	942,302	878,485	819,546	786,007	525,945	394,693
Average Shares	317,992	318,031	318,454	318,432	317,417	316,211	277,993	177,804
Balance Sheet								
Current Assets	2,771,436	2,487,099	2,477,672	2,618,786	2,692,465	2,087,049	2,227,295	1,357,472
Total Assets	37,039,983	36,220,386	32,053,173	30,580,309	29,777,975	27,795,537	28,302,824	15,647,066
Current Liabilities	4,096,018	3,589,045	3,638,605	2,989,790	3,134,381	3,275,651	3,643,690	1,947,682
Long-Term Obligations	12,015,992	11,775,889	8,829,354	8,805,574	8,606,017	7,776,833	7,200,156	4,614,913
Total Liabilities	25,856,269	25,134,144	21,341,439	20,228,094	19,801,160	18,184,009	19,065,774	11,634,396
Stockholders' Equity	11,183,714	11,086,242	10,711,734	10,352,215	9,976,815	9,611,528	9,237,050	4,012,670
Shares Outstanding	333,878	316,885	316,885	317,191	316,983	315,273	314,053	177,158
Statistical Record								
Return on Assets %	2.88	2.89	3.00	2.91	2.85	2.80	2.39	2.62
Return on Equity %	9.08	9.07	8.92	8.64	8.37	8.34	7.92	9.94
EBITDA Margin %	30.94	35.73	34.31	30.98	29.35	29.72	26.41	25.17
Net Margin %	11.78	12.75	12.34	11.04	10.59	10.77	8.38	8.84
Asset Turnover	0.23	0.23	0.24	0.26	0.27	0.26	0.28	0.30
Current Ratio	0.68	0.69	0.68	0.88	0.86	0.64	0.61	0.70
Debt to Equity	1.07	1.06	0.82	0.85	0.86	0.81	0.78	1.15
Price Range	65.81-56.11	65.81-54.25	60.25-50.58	56.40-45.41	56.15-41.52	45.33-38.67	40.57-33.53	36.31-30.46
P/E Ratio	20.96-17.87	21.16-17.44	20.35-17.09	20.43-16.45	21.76-16.09	18.20-15.53	21.47-17.74	16.36-13.72
Average Yield %	3.15	3.13	3.22	3.34	3.41	3.49	3.53	3.23

Address: 300 Cadwell Drive, Springfield, MA 01104	**Web Site:** www.eversource.com	**Auditors:** Deloitte & Touche LLP
Telephone: 800-286-5000	**Officers:** James J. (Jim) Judge - Chairman, President, Chief Executive Officer, Executive Vice President, Chief Financial Officer Werner J. Schweiger - Executive Vice President, Chief Operating Officer	**Investor Contact:** 860-728-4650 **Transfer Agents:** ComputerShare Investor Services, Providence, RI

EXELON CORP

Exchange	Symbol	Price	52Wk Range	Yield	P/E
NYS	EXC	$42.60 (6/29/2018)	42.60-35.52	3.24	12.17

*7 Year Price Score 89.22 ***NYSE Composite Index=100** ***12 Month Price Score 103.34**

Interim Earnings (Per Share)

Qtr.	Mar	Jun	Sep	Dec
2015	0.80	0.74	0.69	0.32
2016	0.19	0.29	0.53	0.22
2017	1.07	0.09	0.85	1.96
2018	0.60	...	...	...

Interim Dividends (Per Share)

Amt	Decl	Ex	Rec	Pay
0.328Q	07/25/2017	08/11/2017	08/15/2017	09/08/2017
0.328Q	09/25/2017	11/14/2017	11/15/2017	12/08/2017
0.345Q	01/30/2018	02/14/2018	02/15/2018	03/09/2018
0.345Q	05/01/2018	05/14/2018	05/15/2018	06/08/2018

Indicated Div: $1.38

Valuation Analysis

		Institutional Holding	
Forecast EPS	$3.10	No of Institutions	
	(06/14/2018)	1341	
Market Cap	$41.1 Billion	Shares	
Book Value	$30.2 Billion	897,315,712	
Price/Book	1.36	% Held	
Price/Sales	1.19	72.43	

TRADING VOLUME (thousand shares)

Business Summary: Electric Utilities (MIC: 3.1.1 SIC: 4931 NAIC: 221122)

Exelon is a utility services holding company engaged through its principal subsidiaries in the energy generation and energy distribution and transmission businesses. Co. has 12 reportable segments consisting of Exelon Generation Company, LLC's six reportable segments (Mid-Atlantic, Midwest, New England, New York, Electric Reliability Council of Texas and Other Power Regions in Generation), Commonwealth Edison Company; PECO Energy Company, and Baltimore Gas and Electric Company and Pepco Holdings, Inc.'s three utility reportable segments (Potomac Electric Power Company, Delmarva Power & Light Company and Atlantic City Electric Company).

Recent Developments: For the quarter ended Mar 31 2018, net income decreased 34.5% to US$636.0 million from US$971.0 million in the year-earlier quarter. Revenues were US$9.69 billion, up 10.8% from US$8.75 billion the year before. Operating income was US$1.10 billion versus US$1.31 billion in the prior-year quarter, a decrease of 15.8%. Direct operating expenses rose 12.2% to US$7.11 billion from US$6.34 billion in the comparable period the year before. Indirect operating expenses increased 34.4% to US$1.48 billion from US$1.10 billion in the equivalent prior-year period.

Prospects: Our evaluation of Exelon Corp. as of Jan. 21, 2018 is the result of our systematic analysis on three basic characteristics: earnings strength, relative valuation, and recent stock price movement. The company has produced a positive trend in earnings per share over the past 5 quarters and while recent estimates for the company have been mixed, EXC has posted results that fell short of analysts expectations. Based on operating earnings yield, the company is undervalued when compared to all of the companies in our coverage universe. Share price changes over the past year indicates that EXC will perform well over the near term.

Financial Data

(US$ in Thousands)	3 Mos	12/31/2017	12/31/2016	12/31/2015	12/31/2014	12/31/2013	12/31/2012	12/31/2011
Earnings Per Share	3.50	3.97	1.22	2.54	1.88	2.00	1.42	3.75
Cash Flow Per Share	8.05	7.90	9.11	8.56	5.18	7.41	7.49	7.32
Tang Book Value Per Share	24.40	24.06	20.74	25.34	23.41	23.68	22.33	17.86
Dividends Per Share	1.327	1.310	1.264	1.240	1.240	1.455	2.100	2.100
Dividend Payout %	37.93	33.00	103.61	48.82	65.96	72.75	147.89	56.00
Income Statement								
Total Revenue	9,693,000	33,531,000	31,360,000	29,447,000	27,429,000	24,888,000	23,489,000	18,924,000
EBITDA	1,074,000	10,424,000	9,861,000	9,222,000	8,007,000	8,055,000	7,556,000	8,408,000
Depn & Amortn	1,000	5,111,000	6,349,000	4,860,000	4,476,000	3,960,000	4,754,000	3,782,000
Income Before Taxes	702,000	3,756,000	1,989,000	3,330,000	2,506,000	2,763,000	1,889,000	3,953,000
Income Taxes	59,000	(125,000)	761,000	1,073,000	666,000	1,044,000	627,000	1,457,000
Net Income	585,000	3,770,000	1,134,000	2,269,000	1,623,000	1,719,000	1,160,000	2,495,000
Average Shares	968,000	949,000	927,000	893,000	864,000	860,000	819,000	665,000
Balance Sheet								
Current Assets	11,533,000	11,834,000	12,412,000	15,334,000	12,097,000	10,137,000	10,133,000	5,489,000
Total Assets	117,018,000	116,700,000	114,904,000	95,384,000	86,814,000	79,924,000	78,554,000	55,092,000
Current Liabilities	10,153,000	10,796,000	13,457,000	9,118,000	8,762,000	7,728,000	7,784,000	4,989,000
Long-Term Obligations	33,294,000	32,565,000	32,216,000	24,286,000	20,010,000	18,271,000	18,854,000	12,189,000
Total Liabilities	86,787,000	86,843,000	89,067,000	69,398,000	64,013,000	56,999,000	56,843,000	40,620,000
Stockholders' Equity	30,231,000	29,857,000	25,837,000	25,986,000	22,801,000	22,925,000	21,711,000	14,472,000
Shares Outstanding	965,381	963,335	924,035	919,924	859,833	857,290	854,781	663,368
Statistical Record								
Return on Assets %	2.87	3.26	1.08	2.49	1.95	2.17	1.73	4.65
Return on Equity %	11.84	13.54	4.36	9.30	7.10	7.70	6.39	17.75
EBITDA Margin %	11.08	31.09	31.44	31.32	29.19	32.36	32.17	44.43
Net Margin %	6.04	11.24	3.62	7.71	5.92	6.91	4.94	13.18
Asset Turnover	0.29	0.29	0.30	0.32	0.33	0.31	0.35	0.35
Current Ratio	1.14	1.10	0.92	1.68	1.38	1.31	1.30	1.10
Debt to Equity	1.10	1.09	1.25	0.93	0.88	0.80	0.87	0.84
Price Range	42.39-33.50	42.39-33.50	37.50-26.78	37.99-25.46	38.63-26.62	37.78-26.90	42.07-28.57	45.34-39.77
P/E Ratio	12.11-9.57	10.68-8.44	30.74-21.95	14.96-10.02	20.55-14.16	18.89-13.45	29.63-20.12	12.09-10.61
Average Yield %	3.51	3.51	3.76	3.87	3.70	4.69	5.72	4.95

Address: 10 South Dearborn Street, P.O. Box 805379, Chicago, IL 60680-5379 **Telephone:** 800-483-3220	**Web Site:** www.exeloncorp.com **Officers:** Mayo A. Shattuck - Chairman, Executive Chairman Christopher M. (Chris) Crane - President, Chief Executive Officer, Chief Operating Officer	**Auditors:** PricewaterhouseCoopers LLP **Investor Contact:** 312-394-2345 **Transfer Agents:** Wells Fargo

EXTENDED STAY AMERICA INC

Exchange	Symbol	Price	52Wk Range	Yield	P/E
NMS	STAY	$21.61 (6/29/2018)	22.52-16.46	4.07	56.87

*7 Year Price Score N/A *NYSE Composite Index=100 *12 Month Price Score 105.55

Interim Earnings (Per Share)

Qtr.	Mar	Jun	Sep	Dec
2015	0.11	0.28	0.18	(0.02)
2016	0.08	0.30	0.23	(0.26)
2017	0.12	0.27	0.28	(0.25)
2018	0.08	...	...	...

Interim Dividends (Per Share)

Amt	Decl	Ex	Rec	Pay
0.21Q	08/01/2017	08/11/2017	08/15/2017	08/29/2017
0.21Q	11/07/2017	11/20/2017	11/21/2017	12/05/2017
0.21Q	02/27/2018	03/12/2018	03/13/2018	03/27/2018
0.22Q	04/26/2018	05/10/2018	05/11/2018	05/25/2018

Indicated Div: $0.88

Valuation Analysis

		Institutional Holding	
Forecast EPS	$1.14 (06/13/2018)	No of Institutions	319
Market Cap	$4.1 Billion	Shares	208,681,216
Book Value	$758.2 Million	% Held	
Price/Book	5.43		97.10
Price/Sales	3.19		

Business Summary: Hotels, Restaurants & Travel (MIC: 2.2.1 SIC: 7011 NAIC: 721110)

Extended Stay America is an owner/operator of Co.-branded hotels in North America. Co.'s business operates in the extended stay segment of the lodging industry. As of Dec 31 2017, Co. owned and operated 624 hotels comprising about 68,600 rooms located in 44 states across the U.S. Co. operates all of its hotels under the Extended Stay America brand, which serves the mid-price extended stay segment. Co.'s hotels feature fully-furnished rooms with in-room kitchens, complimentary grab-and-go breakfast, free WiFi, flat screen TVs and on-site guest laundry. Co.'s guests include business travelers, leisure travelers, professionals, persons relocating and anyone else in need of temporary housing.

Recent Developments: For the quarter ended Mar 31 2018, net income increased 93.6% to US$31.1 million from US$16.1 million in the year-earlier quarter. Revenues were US$297.8 million, up 2.3% from US$291.0 million the year before. Operating income was US$68.7 million versus US$52.9 million in the prior-year quarter, an increase of 29.8%. Direct operating expenses rose 0.7% to US$142.6 million from US$141.7 million in the comparable period the year before. Indirect operating expenses decreased 10.4% to US$86.4 million from US$96.4 million in the equivalent prior-year period.

Prospects: Our evaluation of Extended Stay America Inc as of Jan. 21, 2018 is the result of our systematic analysis on three basic characteristics: earnings strength, relative valuation, and recent stock price movement. The company has generated a negative trend in earnings per share over the past 5 quarters and while recent estimates for the company have been mixed, STAY has posted results that fell short of analysts expectations. Based on operating earnings yield, the company is undervalued when compared to all of the companies in our coverage universe. Share price changes over the past year indicates that STAY will perform poorly over the near term.

Financial Data

(US$ in Thousands)	3 Mos	12/31/2017	12/31/2016	12/31/2015	12/31/2014	12/31/2013	12/31/2012	12/31/2011
Earnings Per Share	0.38	0.41	0.35	0.55	0.19	0.49	...	...
Cash Flow Per Share	2.36	2.30	2.08	2.10	1.82	1.78	...	...
Tang Book Value Per Share	3.57	3.67	3.65	3.89	3.43	3.20	...	...
Dividends Per Share	0.840	0.820	0.740	0.910	0.530	...	...	...
Dividend Payout %	221.05	200.00	211.43	165.45	278.95	...	...	...
Income Statement								
Total Revenue	297,767	1,282,725	1,270,593	1,284,753	1,213,475	1,132,818	1,011,462	942,728
EBITDA	125,138	590,690	583,549	701,237	532,182	480,178	414,210	386,047
Depn & Amortn	56,606	229,216	221,309	203,897	187,207	168,053	129,938	120,438
Income Before Taxes	36,892	231,702	197,703	359,558	195,611	77,666	26,923	53,685
Income Taxes	5,797	59,514	34,351	76,536	45,057	(4,990)	4,642	7,050
Net Income	14,852	78,847	69,932	113,040	39,596	86,231	20,732	45,573
Average Shares	192,566	193,670	200,736	204,567	204,508	176,268	...	...
Balance Sheet								
Current Assets	270,582	172,552	126,609	475,819	221,258	129,362	183,744	350,272
Total Assets	3,991,214	4,076,005	4,180,304	4,528,900	4,481,120	4,449,687	4,491,734	4,357,304
Current Liabilities	208,241	188,257	193,303	243,969	172,440	175,122	124,362	119,253
Long-Term Obligations	2,474,168	2,534,768	2,585,274	2,762,388	2,891,369	2,926,045	3,605,708	2,680,219
Total Liabilities	3,232,987	3,295,422	3,385,472	3,649,227	3,691,602	3,705,111	3,742,076	2,807,859
Stockholders' Equity	758,227	780,583	794,832	879,673	789,518	744,576	...	...
Shares Outstanding	190,631	192,099	195,406	204,593	204,517	204,788	...	...
Statistical Record								
Return on Assets %	1.74	1.91	1.60	2.51	0.89	1.93	0.47	...
Return on Equity %	9.10	10.01	8.33	13.54	5.16	...	...	...
EBITDA Margin %	42.03	46.05	45.93	54.58	43.86	42.39	40.95	40.95
Net Margin %	4.99	6.15	5.50	8.80	3.26	7.61	2.05	4.83
Asset Turnover	0.32	0.31	0.29	0.29	0.27	0.25	0.23	...
Current Ratio	1.30	0.92	0.65	1.95	1.28	0.74	1.48	2.94
Debt to Equity	3.26	3.25	3.25	3.14	3.66	3.93	...	...
Price Range	21.05-15.76	20.87-15.50	16.93-10.95	21.30-15.75	26.57-17.63	26.26-23.41	...	...
P/E Ratio	55.39-41.47	50.90-37.80	48.37-31.29	38.73-28.64	139.84-92.79	53.59-47.78	...	...
Average Yield %	4.44	4.52	5.06	4.82	2.33	...	...	...

Address: 11525 N. Community House Road, Suite 100, Charlotte, NC 28277
Telephone: 980-345-1600

Web Site: www.esa.com
Officers: Douglas G. Geoga - Chairman Jonathan S. Halkyard - Chief Financial Officer, Chief Operating Officer, Interim Chief Financial Officer, President, Chief Executive Officer

Auditors: Deloitte & Touche LLP
Transfer Agents: American Stock Transfer & Trust Company, LLC

EXTRA SPACE STORAGE INC

Exchange	Symbol	Price	52Wk Range	Yield	P/E
NYS	EXR	$99.81 (6/29/2018)	100.96-74.13	3.45	26.13

*7 Year Price Score 115.08 *NYSE Composite Index=100 *12 Month Price Score 111.82

Interim Earnings (Per Share)

Qtr.	Mar	Jun	Sep	Dec
2015	0.46	0.47	0.58	0.05
2016	0.66	0.66	0.93	0.67
2017	0.64	0.69	0.74	1.69
2018	0.70	...	...	...

Interim Dividends (Per Share)

Amt	Decl	Ex	Rec	Pay
0.78Q	08/25/2017	09/14/2017	09/15/2017	09/29/2017
0.78Q	11/10/2017	12/14/2017	12/15/2017	12/29/2017
0.78Q	02/15/2018	03/14/2018	03/15/2018	03/29/2018
0.86Q	05/24/2018	06/14/2018	06/15/2018	06/29/2018

Indicated Div: $3.44

Valuation Analysis

		Institutional Holding	
Forecast EPS	$2.87 (06/14/2018)	No of Institutions	594
Market Cap	$12.6 Billion	Shares	167,761,824
Book Value	$2.3 Billion	% Held	95.74
Price/Book	5.37		
Price/Sales	11.16		

Business Summary: REITs (MIC: 5.3.1 SIC: 6798 NAIC: 525930)

Extra Space Storage is a real estate investment trust. Substantially all of Co.'s business is conducted through Extra Space Storage LP. Co. operate in three segments: rental operations, which include rental operations of stores in which Co. has an ownership interest; tenant reinsurance, which include the reinsurance of risks relating to the loss of goods stored by tenants in Co.'s stores; and property management, acquisition and development, which include managing, acquiring, developing and selling stores. At Dec 31 2017, Co. had direct and indirect equity interests in 1,061 storage facilities, and Co. managed 422 stores for third parties.

Recent Developments: For the quarter ended Mar 31 2018, net income increased 6.3% to US$95.4 million from US$89.7 million in the year-earlier quarter. Revenues were US$285.5 million, up 8.5% from US$263.0 million the year before. Revenues from property income rose 7.1% to US$247.9 million from US$231.5 million in the corresponding quarter a year earlier.

Prospects: Our evaluation of Extra Space Storage Inc. as of Jan. 21, 2018 is the result of our systematic analysis on three basic characteristics: earnings strength, relative valuation, and recent stock price movement. The company has managed to produce a neutral trend in earnings per share over the past 5 quarters. However, while recent estimates for the company have been mixed, EXR has posted better than expected results. Based on operating earnings yield, the company is about fairly valued when compared to all of the companies in our coverage universe. Share price changes over the past year indicates that EXR will perform well over the near term.

Financial Data

(US$ in Thousands)	3 Mos	12/31/2017	12/31/2016	12/31/2015	12/31/2014	12/31/2013	12/31/2012	12/31/2011
Earnings Per Share	3.82	3.76	2.91	1.56	1.53	1.53	1.14	0.54
Cash Flow Per Share	5.21	4.74	4.30	3.07	2.92	2.44	2.10	1.57
Tang Book Value Per Share	18.59	18.66	17.83	16.81	14.87	15.14	13.44	10.71
Dividends Per Share	3.120	3.120	2.930	2.240	1.810	1.450	0.850	0.560
Dividend Payout %	81.68	82.98	100.69	143.59	118.30	94.77	74.56	103.70
Income Statement								
Total Revenue	285,485	1,105,009	991,875	782,270	647,155	520,613	409,396	329,830
EBITDA	189,891	840,297	633,209	419,908	375,990	310,253	236,757	180,834
Depn & Amortn	55,979	185,903	174,906	123,751	109,531	104,963	79,516	65,358
Income Before Taxes	93,175	502,516	330,842	205,476	188,903	137,855	91,613	52,291
Income Taxes	1,342	3,625	15,847	11,148	7,570	9,984	5,413	1,155
Net Income	88,256	479,013	366,127	189,474	178,355	172,076	117,309	50,449
Average Shares	132,682	134,155	125,948	126,918	121,435	113,105	106,523	96,683
Balance Sheet								
Current Assets	54,064	88,891	74,353	244,197	126,293	187,741	78,720	85,031
Total Assets	7,470,624	7,455,137	7,091,446	6,071,407	4,402,107	3,977,140	3,223,477	2,516,250
Current Liabilities	226,406	190,087	468,083	120,916	204,193	61,272	137,299	260,079
Long-Term Obligations	4,396,888	4,460,217	3,941,223	3,499,621	2,232,597	1,948,723	1,496,425	1,154,484
Total Liabilities	5,126,870	5,104,386	4,846,554	3,982,330	2,664,682	2,218,670	1,731,670	1,497,303
Stockholders' Equity	2,343,754	2,350,751	2,244,892	2,089,077	1,737,425	1,758,470	1,491,807	1,018,947
Shares Outstanding	126,068	126,007	125,881	124,119	116,360	115,755	110,737	94,783
Statistical Record								
Return on Assets %	6.69	6.59	5.55	3.62	4.26	4.78	4.08	2.12
Return on Equity %	21.18	20.85	16.85	9.90	10.20	10.59	9.32	5.31
EBITDA Margin %	66.52	76.04	63.84	53.68	58.10	59.59	57.83	54.83
Net Margin %	30.91	43.35	36.91	24.22	27.56	33.05	28.65	15.30
Asset Turnover	0.16	0.15	0.15	0.15	0.15	0.14	0.14	0.14
Current Ratio	0.24	0.47	0.16	2.02	0.62	3.06	0.57	0.33
Debt to Equity	1.88	1.90	1.76	1.68	1.29	1.11	1.00	1.13
Price Range	88.19-71.79	87.86-71.64	94.38-68.78	90.22-58.64	60.12-41.79	48.65-36.39	36.39-24.00	24.48-17.40
P/E Ratio	23.09-18.79	23.37-19.05	32.43-23.64	57.83-37.59	39.29-27.31	31.80-23.78	31.92-21.05	45.33-32.22
Average Yield %	3.87	3.97	3.50	3.10	3.48	3.44	2.76	2.70

Address: 2795 East Cottonwood Parkway, Suite 300, Salt Lake City, UT 84121
Telephone: 801-365-4600

Web Site: www.extraspace.com
Officers: Kenneth M. Woolley - Executive Chairman, Chairman, Chief Executive Officer Spencer F. Kirk - Chairman, President, Chief Executive Officer

Auditors: Ernst & Young LLP
Investor Contact: 801-365-4600
Transfer Agents: American Stock Transfer & Trust Company

EXXON MOBIL CORP

Exchange	Symbol	Price	52Wk Range	Yield	P/E	Div Acheiver
NYS	XOM	$82.73 (6/29/2018)	89.07-72.81	3.96	17.34	35 Years

*7 Year Price Score 75.21 *NYSE Composite Index=100 *12 Month Price Score 98.58

Interim Earnings (Per Share)

Qtr.	Mar	Jun	Sep	Dec
2015	1.17	1.00	1.01	0.67
2016	0.43	0.41	0.63	0.41
2017	0.95	0.78	0.93	1.97
2018	1.09	...	...	...

Interim Dividends (Per Share)

Amt	Decl	Ex	Rec	Pay
0.77Q	07/26/2017	08/10/2017	08/14/2017	09/11/2017
0.77Q	10/25/2017	11/10/2017	11/13/2017	12/11/2017
0.77Q	01/31/2018	02/09/2018	02/12/2018	03/09/2018
0.82Q	04/25/2018	05/11/2018	05/14/2018	06/11/2018

Indicated Div: $3.28 (Div. Reinv. Plan)

Valuation Analysis		Institutional Holding	
Forecast EPS	$4.92 (06/14/2018)	No of Institutions	3332
Market Cap	$431.4 Billion	Shares	2,964,337,408
Book Value	$188.2 Billion	% Held	45.00
Price/Book	2.29		
Price/Sales	1.73		

Business Summary: Production & Extraction (MIC: 9.1.1 SIC: 1311 NAIC: 211111)

Exxon Mobil is engaged in the exploration for, and production of, crude oil and natural gas, manufacture of petroleum products and transportation and sale of crude oil, natural gas and petroleum products. Co. is a manufacturer and marketer of commodity petrochemicals, including olefins, aromatics, polyethylene and polypropylene plastics and a variety of specialty products. As of Dec 31 2017, Co. had total proved reserves of 21.22 billion barrels of oil-equivalent, which consisted of 8.92 billion barrels of crude oil, 1.62 billion barrels of natural gas liquids, 1,012.0 million barrels of bitumen, 473.0 million barrels of synthetic oil, and 55.15 trillion cubic ft. of natural gas.

Recent Developments: For the year ended Dec 31 2017, net income increased 137.0% to US$19.85 billion from US$8.38 billion in the prior year. Revenues were US$244.36 billion, up 17.4% from US$208.11 billion the year before. Direct operating expenses rose 19.3% to US$162.35 billion from US$136.10 billion in the comparable period the year before. Indirect operating expenses decreased 1.3% to US$62.74 billion from US$63.59 billion in the equivalent prior-year period.

Prospects: Our evaluation of Exxon Mobil Corp. as of Jan. 21, 2018 is the result of our systematic analysis on three basic characteristics: earnings strength, relative valuation, and recent stock price movement. The company has managed to produce a neutral trend in earnings per share over the past 5 quarters and while recent estimates for the company have been raised by analysts, XOM has posted better than expected results. Based on operating earnings yield, the company is about fairly valued when compared to all of the companies in our coverage universe. Share price changes over the past year indicates that XOM will perform poorly over the near term.

Financial Data

(US$ in Thousands)	3 Mos	12/31/2017	12/31/2016	12/31/2015	12/31/2014	12/31/2013	12/31/2012	12/31/2011
Earnings Per Share	4.77	4.63	1.88	3.85	7.60	7.37	9.70	8.42
Cash Flow Per Share	7.12	7.06	5.27	7.23	10.54	10.16	12.10	11.36
Tang Book Value Per Share	36.09	44.28	40.34	41.10	41.51	40.14	36.84	32.61
Dividends Per Share	3.080	3.060	2.980	2.880	2.700	2.460	2.180	1.850
Dividend Payout %	64.57	66.09	158.51	74.81	35.53	33.38	22.47	21.97
Income Statement								
Total Revenue	68,211,000	244,363,000	226,094,000	268,882,000	411,939,000	438,255,000	482,295,000	486,429,000
EBITDA	11,914,000	39,168,000	30,730,000	40,325,000	69,213,000	74,902,000	94,941,000	89,087,000
Depn & Amortn	4,470,000	19,893,000	22,308,000	18,048,000	17,297,000	17,182,000	15,888,000	15,583,000
Income Before Taxes	7,240,000	18,674,000	7,969,000	21,966,000	51,630,000	57,711,000	78,726,000	73,257,000
Income Taxes	2,457,000	(1,174,000)	(406,000)	5,415,000	18,015,000	24,263,000	31,045,000	31,051,000
Net Income	4,650,000	19,710,000	7,840,000	16,150,000	32,520,000	32,580,000	44,880,000	41,060,000
Average Shares	4,270,000	4,256,000	4,177,000	4,196,000	4,282,000	4,418,999	4,627,999	4,874,999
Balance Sheet								
Current Assets	48,315,000	47,134,000	41,416,000	42,623,000	52,910,000	59,308,000	64,460,000	72,963,000
Total Assets	348,826,000	348,691,000	330,314,000	336,758,000	349,493,000	346,808,000	333,795,000	331,052,000
Current Liabilities	60,306,000	57,771,000	47,638,000	53,976,000	64,633,000	71,724,000	64,139,000	77,505,000
Long-Term Obligations	20,781,000	24,406,000	28,932,000	19,925,000	11,653,000	6,891,000	7,928,000	9,322,000
Total Liabilities	160,631,000	161,003,000	162,989,000	165,947,000	175,094,000	172,805,000	167,932,000	176,656,000
Stockholders' Equity	188,195,000	187,688,000	167,325,000	170,811,000	174,399,000	174,003,000	165,863,000	154,396,000
Shares Outstanding	5,214,999	4,239,000	4,148,000	4,156,000	4,201,000	4,334,999	4,501,999	4,733,999
Statistical Record								
Return on Assets %	5.87	5.81	2.34	4.71	9.34	9.57	13.46	12.96
Return on Equity %	11.14	11.10	4.62	9.36	18.67	19.17	27.95	27.26
EBITDA Margin %	17.47	16.03	13.59	15.00	16.80	17.09	19.69	18.31
Net Margin %	6.82	8.07	3.47	6.01	7.89	7.43	9.31	8.44
Asset Turnover	0.72	0.72	0.68	0.78	1.18	1.29	1.45	1.54
Current Ratio	0.80	0.82	0.87	0.79	0.82	0.83	1.01	0.94
Debt to Equity	0.11	0.13	0.17	0.12	0.07	0.04	0.05	0.06
Price Range	89.07-72.81	90.89-76.10	95.12-73.18	93.37-68.71	104.38-86.41	101.51-85.16	93.48-77.60	87.98-68.03
P/E Ratio	18.67-15.26	19.63-16.44	50.60-38.93	24.25-17.85	13.73-11.37	13.77-11.55	9.64-8.00	10.45-8.08
Average Yield %	3.80	3.74	3.46	3.48	2.78	2.72	2.52	2.32

Address: 5959 Las Colinas Boulevard, Irving, TX 75039-2298	Web Site: www.exxonmobil.com	Auditors: PricewaterhouseCoopers LLP
Telephone: 972-940-6000	Officers: Rex W. Tillerson - Chairman, President, Chief Executive Officer Darren W. Woods - President, Chairman, Senior Vice President, President, Vice President, Chief Executive Officer, Division Officer, Senior Vice President, Vice President, Division Officer	Investor Contact: 180-025-21800
Fax: 972-444-1505		Transfer Agents: ComputerShare, College Station, TX

FNB CORP

Exchange	Symbol	Price	52Wk Range	Yield	P/E
NYS	FNB	$13.42 (6/29/2018)	14.76-12.12	3.58	17.43

*7 Year Price Score 87.34   ***NYSE Composite Index=100**   ***12 Month Price Score 97.52**

Interim Earnings (Per Share)

Qtr.	Mar	Jun	Sep	Dec
2015	0.22	0.22	0.22	0.21
2016	0.12	0.19	0.24	0.23
2017	0.09	0.22	0.23	0.06
2018	0.26	...	...	...

Interim Dividends (Per Share)

Amt	Decl	Ex	Rec	Pay
0.12Q	08/16/2017	08/30/2017	09/01/2017	09/15/2017
0.12Q	10/18/2017	11/30/2017	12/01/2017	12/15/2017
0.12Q	02/21/2018	03/02/2018	03/05/2018	03/15/2018
0.12Q	05/16/2018	05/31/2018	06/01/2018	06/15/2018

Indicated Div: $0.48

Valuation Analysis

		Institutional Holding	
Forecast EPS	$1.12	No of Institutions	
	(06/11/2018)	437	
Market Cap	$4.3 Billion	Shares	
Book Value	$4.4 Billion	298,535,744	
Price/Book	0.98	% Held	
Price/Sales	3.28	81.15	

Business Summary: Banking (MIC: 5.1.1 SIC: 6021 NAIC: 522110)

FNB is a financial holding company. Through its subsidiaries, Co. provides commercial banking, consumer banking, insurance and wealth management solutions. Co.'s commercial banking solutions include corporate banking, small business banking, investment real estate financing, business credit, capital markets and lease financing. Co.'s consumer banking products and services include deposit products, mortgage lending, consumer lending, mobile and online banking services. Co.'s wealth management services include asset management, private banking and insurance. As of Dec 31 2017, Co. had total assets of $31.42 billion and total deposits of $22.40 billion.

Recent Developments: For the quarter ended Mar 31 2018, net income increased 277.6% to US$86.8 million from US$23.0 million in the year-earlier quarter. Net interest income increased 30.9% to US$226.1 million from US$172.8 million in the year-earlier quarter. Provision for loan losses was US$14.5 million versus US$10.9 million in the prior-year quarter, an increase of 33.6%. Non-interest income rose 22.5% to US$67.5 million from US$55.1 million, while non-interest expense declined 8.8% to US$171.1 million.

Prospects: Our evaluation of F.N.B. Corp. as of Jan. 21, 2018 is the result of our systematic analysis on three basic characteristics: earnings strength, relative valuation, and recent stock price movement. The company has generated a negative trend in earnings per share over the past 5 quarters and while recent estimates for the company have been mixed, FNB has posted results that fell short of analysts expectations. Based on operating earnings yield, the company is undervalued when compared to all of the companies in our coverage universe. Share price changes over the past year indicates that FNB will perform poorly over the near term.

Financial Data

(US$ in Thousands)	3 Mos	12/31/2017	12/31/2016	12/31/2015	12/31/2014	12/31/2013	12/31/2012	12/31/2011
Earnings Per Share	0.77	0.63	0.78	0.86	0.80	0.80	0.79	0.70
Cash Flow Per Share	1.45	0.92	1.42	1.28	2.67	2.64	3.90	2.33
Tang Book Value Per Share	6.14	6.06	6.47	6.33	5.95	5.38	4.92	4.80
Dividends Per Share	0.480	0.480	0.480	0.480	0.480	0.480	0.480	0.480
Dividend Payout %	62.34	76.19	61.54	55.81	60.00	60.00	60.76	68.57
Income Statement								
Interest Income	272,927	980,326	678,963	546,795	508,983	440,386	431,906	391,125
Interest Expense	46,822	133,892	67,451	48,573	42,686	44,344	59,055	74,617
Net Interest Income	226,105	846,434	611,512	498,222	466,297	396,042	372,851	316,508
Provision for Losses	14,495	61,073	55,752	40,441	38,648	31,090	31,302	33,641
Non-Interest Income	67,503	252,449	201,761	162,410	158,274	135,778	131,463	119,918
Non-Interest Expense	171,083	681,541	511,133	390,549	379,253	338,170	318,829	283,734
Income Before Taxes	108,030	356,269	246,388	229,642	206,670	162,560	154,183	119,051
Income Taxes	21,268	157,065	75,497	69,993	62,620	44,756	43,773	32,004
Net Income	86,762	199,204	170,891	159,649	144,050	117,804	110,410	87,047
Average Shares	325,766	303,857	207,768	176,338	169,078	147,809	140,640	125,012
Balance Sheet								
Net Loans & Leases	21,121,132	20,916,277	14,738,884	12,048,428	11,121,112	9,395,310	8,033,345	6,756,005
Total Assets	31,652,353	31,417,635	21,844,817	17,557,662	16,127,090	13,563,405	12,023,976	9,786,483
Total Deposits	22,497,089	22,399,725	16,065,647	12,623,463	11,382,208	10,198,232	9,082,174	7,289,768
Total Liabilities	27,218,900	27,008,441	19,273,200	15,461,480	14,105,634	11,789,022	10,621,907	8,576,284
Stockholders' Equity	4,433,453	4,409,194	2,571,617	2,096,182	2,021,456	1,774,383	1,402,069	1,210,199
Shares Outstanding	323,686	323,465	211,059	175,441	173,992	158,967	139,929	127,220
Statistical Record								
Return on Assets %	0.85	0.75	0.87	0.95	0.97	0.92	1.01	0.93
Return on Equity %	5.98	5.71	7.30	7.75	7.59	7.42	8.43	7.65
Net Interest Margin %	82.84	86.34	90.07	91.12	91.61	89.93	86.33	80.92
Efficiency Ratio %	50.25	55.29	58.04	55.07	56.84	58.69	56.59	55.52
Loans to Deposits	0.94	0.93	0.92	0.95	0.98	0.92	0.88	0.93
Price Range	14.87-12.12	16.30-12.12	16.40-11.18	14.64-11.89	13.65-11.49	13.29-10.62	12.44-9.95	11.46-8.19
P/E Ratio	19.31-15.74	25.87-19.24	21.03-14.33	17.02-13.83	17.06-14.36	16.61-13.27	15.75-12.59	16.37-11.70
Average Yield %	3.47	3.40	3.69	3.69	3.60	3.84	3.99	4.77

Address: One North Shore Center, 12 Federal Street, Pittsburgh, PA 15212
Telephone: 800-555-5455

Web Site: www.fnb-online.com
Officers: Vincent J. Delie - Chairman, President, Chief Executive Officer, Division Officer Vincent J. Calabrese - Chief Financial Officer, Corporate Controller, Principal Accounting Officer

Auditors: Ernst & Young LLP
Investor Contact: 724-983-3429
Transfer Agents: ComputerShare, College Station, TX

FACTSET RESEARCH SYSTEMS INC.

Exchange	Symbol	Price	52Wk Range	Yield	P/E	Div Acheiver
NYS	FDS	$198.10 (6/29/2018)	215.79-155.53	1.29	31.59	18 Years

*7 Year Price Score 111.39 *NYSE Composite Index=100 *12 Month Price Score 104.87

Interim Earnings (Per Share)

Qtr.	Nov	Feb	May	Aug
2014-15	1.32	1.46	1.45	1.48
2015-16	1.43	1.63	1.62	3.51
2016-17	1.66	1.68	1.66	1.51
2017-18	1.77	1.33	...	...

Interim Dividends (Per Share)

Amt	Decl	Ex	Rec	Pay
0.56Q	08/11/2017	08/29/2017	08/31/2017	09/19/2017
0.56Q	11/08/2017	11/29/2017	11/30/2017	12/19/2017
0.56Q	02/07/2018	02/27/2018	02/28/2018	03/20/2018
0.64Q	05/07/2018	05/30/2018	05/31/2018	06/19/2018

Indicated Div: $2.56

Valuation Analysis / Institutional Holding

Valuation Analysis		Institutional Holding	
Forecast EPS	$8.53	No of Institutions	580
	(05/30/2018)		
Market Cap	$7.7 Billion	Shares	48,730,104
Book Value	$612.1 Million	% Held	92.45
Price/Book	12.60		
Price/Sales	5.92		

Business Summary: Business Services (MIC: 7.5.2 SIC: 7371 NAIC: 541511)

FactSet Research Systems provides financial information and analytical applications for the global investment community. Co. provides information to financial investment personnel through its analytics, service, content, and technology. Co. supports the workflow of both buy-side and sell-side clients. From streaming real-time data to historical information, including quotes, estimates, news and commentary, Co. provides content through desktop, wireless and off-platform solutions. Co.'s application provides tools and resources including company and industry analyses, screening tools, portfolio analysis, risk profiles, alpha-testing, portfolio optimization and research management solutions.

Recent Developments: For the quarter ended Nov 30 2017, net income increased 5.7% to US$70.4 million from US$66.6 million in the year-earlier quarter. Revenues were US$329.1 million, up 14.3% from US$288.1 million the year before. Operating income was US$89.1 million versus US$90.3 million in the prior-year quarter, a decrease of 1.4%. Direct operating expenses rose 26.9% to US$161.5 million from US$127.3 million in the comparable period the year before. Indirect operating expenses increased 11.4% to US$78.5 million from US$70.5 million in the equivalent prior-year period.

Prospects: Our evaluation of FactSet Research Systems Inc. as of Jan. 21, 2018 is the result of our systematic analysis on three basic characteristics: earnings strength, relative valuation, and recent stock price movement. The company has enjoyed a very positive trend in earnings per share over the past 5 quarters and while recent estimates for the company have been raised by analysts, FDS has posted better than expected results. Based on operating earnings yield, the company is about fairly valued when compared to all of the companies in our coverage universe. Share price changes over the past year indicates that FDS will perform poorly over the near term.

Financial Data
(US$ in Thousands)

	6 Mos	3 Mos	08/31/2017	08/31/2016	08/31/2015	08/31/2014	08/31/2013	08/31/2012
Earnings Per Share	6.27	6.62	6.51	8.19	5.71	4.92	4.45	4.12
Cash Flow Per Share	8.88	8.46	8.13	8.08	7.37	6.25	6.15	5.17
Tang Book Value Per Share	N.M.	N.M.	N.M.	N.M.	4.44	4.39	6.02	5.94
Dividends Per Share	2.240	2.180	2.120	1.880	1.660	1.480	1.320	1.160
Dividend Payout %	35.73	32.93	32.57	22.95	29.07	30.08	29.66	28.16
Income Statement								
Total Revenue	664,372	329,141	1,221,179	1,127,092	1,006,768	920,335	858,112	805,793
EBITDA	212,955	100,465	378,912	485,429	356,854	329,364	299,310	300,805
Depn & Amortn	28,372	14,286	28,000	23,300	23,100	25,900	28,400	26,100
Income Before Taxes	178,392	86,179	344,312	460,993	333,754	303,464	270,910	274,705
Income Taxes	54,876	15,800	86,053	122,178	92,703	91,921	72,273	85,896
Net Income	123,516	70,379	258,259	338,815	241,051	211,543	198,637	188,809
Average Shares	39,846	39,680	39,642	41,365	42,235	42,970	44,624	45,810
Balance Sheet								
Current Assets	472,067	427,012	409,376	369,276	304,174	249,775	318,034	299,125
Total Assets	1,472,492	1,430,602	1,413,315	1,019,161	736,671	663,212	690,197	694,143
Current Liabilities	186,493	161,600	201,139	158,210	139,780	127,291	118,253	113,176
Long-Term Obligations	574,702	574,666	575,000	300,000	35,000	...	...	...
Total Liabilities	860,402	812,385	853,624	501,780	205,087	152,130	148,418	141,879
Stockholders' Equity	612,090	618,217	559,691	517,381	531,584	511,082	541,779	552,264
Shares Outstanding	38,927	39,110	39,023	40,038	41,316	41,792	43,324	44,279
Statistical Record								
Return on Assets %	19.61	21.16	21.23	38.49	34.44	31.26	28.70	27.86
Return on Equity %	44.96	47.01	47.96	64.42	46.24	40.18	36.31	35.28
EBITDA Margin %	32.05	30.52	31.03	43.07	35.45	35.79	34.88	37.33
Net Margin %	18.59	21.38	21.15	30.06	23.94	22.99	23.15	23.43
Asset Turnover	1.03	1.02	1.00	1.28	1.44	1.36	1.24	1.19
Current Ratio	2.53	2.64	2.04	2.33	2.18	1.96	2.69	2.64
Debt to Equity	0.94	0.93	1.03	0.58	0.07	...	...	...
Price Range	208.69-155.53	199.88-155.53	183.17-151.67	178.81-136.40	173.20-116.34	127.86-101.94	111.60-87.45	108.52-82.24
P/E Ratio	33.28-24.81	30.19-23.49	28.14-23.30	21.83-16.65	30.33-20.37	25.99-20.72	25.08-19.65	26.34-19.96
Average Yield %	1.26	1.28	1.28	1.18	1.18	1.11	1.33	1.23

Address: 601 Merritt 7, Norwalk, CT 06851
Telephone: 203-810-1000
Fax: 203-810-1001

Web Site: www.factset.com
Officers: Philip A. Hadley - Chairman, Chief Executive Officer Gene D. Fernandez - Chief Technology Officer, Chief Products Officer

Auditors: Ernst & Young LLP
Transfer Agents: Computershare Shareowner Services

FAIR ISAAC CORP

Exchange	Symbol	Price	52Wk Range	Yield	P/E
NYS	FICO	$193.32 (6/29/2018)	202.12-131.75	N/A	49.32

*7 Year Price Score 152.22 *NYSE Composite Index=100 *12 Month Price Score 115.34

Interim Earnings (Per Share)

Qtr.	Dec	Mar	Jun	Sep
2014-15	0.43	0.58	0.62	1.02
2015-16	0.59	0.72	1.08	1.00
2016-17	1.16	0.78	0.78	1.25
2017-18	0.86	1.03	...	...

Interim Dividends (Per Share)

Dividend Payment Suspended

Valuation Analysis — **Institutional Holding**

Forecast EPS	$6.42	No of Institutions
	(06/20/2018)	421
Market Cap	$5.8 Billion	Shares
Book Value	$370.7 Million	37,600,948
Price/Book	15.56	% Held
Price/Sales	5.90	89.00

Business Summary: Internet & Software (MIC: 6.3.2 SIC: 7372 NAIC: 511210)

Fair Isaac provides a range of analytical solutions, credit scoring and credit account management products and services to banks, and credit reporting agencies. Co.'s segments are: Applications, which includes pre-configured decision management applications designed for a specific type of business problem or process; Scores, which includes Co.'s business-to-business scoring solutions and services, Co.'s myFICO® solutions for consumers, and associated services; and Decision Management Software, which is composed of analytic and decision management software tools that clients can use to create their own custom decision management applications, and its FICO® Decision Management Suite.

Recent Developments: For the quarter ended Mar 31 2018, net income increased 28.7% to US$32.3 million from US$25.1 million in the year-earlier quarter. Revenues were US$257.9 million, up 12.9% from US$228.4 million the year before. Operating income was US$48.1 million versus US$40.0 million in the prior-year quarter, an increase of 20.1%. Direct operating expenses rose 8.9% to US$78.5 million from US$72.1 million in the comparable period the year before. Indirect operating expenses increased 13.0% to US$131.3 million from US$116.2 million in the equivalent prior-year period.

Prospects: Our evaluation of Fair, Isaac & Co. Inc. as of Jan. 21, 2018 is the result of our systematic analysis on three basic characteristics: earnings strength, relative valuation, and recent stock price movement. The company has enjoyed a very positive trend in earnings per share over the past 5 quarters and while recent estimates for the company have remained steady, FICO has posted results that fell short of analysts expectations. Based on operating earnings yield, the company is overvalued when compared to all of the companies in our coverage universe. Share price changes over the past year indicates that FICO will perform well over the near term.

Financial Data
(US$ in Thousands)

	6 Mos	3 Mos	09/30/2017	09/30/2016	09/30/2015	09/30/2014	09/30/2013	09/30/2012
Earnings Per Share	3.92	3.67	3.98	3.39	2.65	2.72	2.48	2.64
Cash Flow Per Share	6.81	7.36	7.31	5.93	4.23	5.17	3.85	3.71
Dividends Per Share	...	0.020	0.040	0.080	0.080	0.080	0.080	0.080
Dividend Payout %	...	0.54	1.01	2.36	3.02	2.94	3.23	3.03
Income Statement								
Total Revenue	493,179	235,321	932,169	881,356	838,781	788,985	743,444	676,423
EBITDA	91,807	42,205	189,823	185,184	152,061	173,598	175,746	189,204
Depn & Amortn	3,472	1,788	12,709	13,982	13,673	11,917	13,535	21,544
Income Before Taxes	74,759	33,957	151,324	144,569	109,238	133,131	131,984	136,243
Income Taxes	15,185	6,658	23,068	35,121	22,736	38,252	41,889	44,239
Net Income	59,574	27,299	128,256	109,448	86,502	94,879	90,095	92,004
Average Shares	31,300	31,561	32,245	32,308	32,609	34,864	36,292	36,063
Balance Sheet								
Current Assets	333,219	299,136	310,931	267,638	286,602	288,527	249,188	259,325
Total Assets	1,290,895	1,240,845	1,255,620	1,221,052	1,230,163	1,192,298	1,161,547	1,158,611
Current Liabilities	368,546	353,280	326,655	246,077	243,875	341,404	165,880	209,605
Long-Term Obligations	512,868	462,834	462,801	494,000	516,000	376,000	447,000	455,000
Total Liabilities	920,192	855,203	829,083	774,224	793,165	737,684	630,870	684,205
Stockholders' Equity	370,703	385,642	426,537	446,828	436,998	454,614	530,677	474,406
Shares Outstanding	29,835	30,246	30,243	30,935	31,290	32,047	34,786	34,839
Statistical Record								
Return on Assets %	9.84	9.55	10.36	8.91	7.14	8.06	7.77	8.02
Return on Equity %	31.30	29.14	29.37	24.70	19.40	19.26	17.93	19.52
EBITDA Margin %	18.62	17.94	20.36	21.01	18.13	22.00	23.64	27.97
Net Margin %	12.08	11.60	13.76	12.42	10.31	12.03	12.12	13.60
Asset Turnover	0.77	0.77	0.75	0.72	0.69	0.67	0.64	0.59
Current Ratio	0.90	0.85	0.95	1.09	1.18	0.85	1.50	1.24
Debt to Equity	1.38	1.20	1.09	1.11	1.18	0.83	0.84	0.96
Price Range	178.09-125.93	158.13-120.17	145.54-111.42	132.87-81.01	97.25-53.89	64.88-51.00	55.29-40.62	45.95-20.26
P/E Ratio	45.43-32.13	43.09-32.74	36.57-27.99	39.19-23.90	36.70-20.34	23.85-18.75	22.29-16.38	17.41-7.67
Average Yield %	...	0.01	0.03	0.08	0.10	0.14	0.17	0.20

Address: 181 Metro Drive, Suite 700, San Jose, CA 95110-1346 **Telephone:** 408-535-1500	**Web Site:** www.fico.com **Officers:** Braden R. Kelly - Chairman William J. Lansing - Chief Executive Officer	**Auditors:** DELOITTE & TOUCHE LLP **Investor Contact:** 800-213-5542 **Transfer Agents:** Computershare, College Station, TX

FEDERAL REALTY INVESTMENT TRUST (MD)

Exchange	Symbol	Price	52Wk Range	Yield	P/E	Div Acheiver
NYS	FRT	$126.55 (6/29/2018)	135.03-108.11	3.16	31.64	50 Years

*7 Year Price Score 81.33 *NYSE Composite Index=100 *12 Month Price Score 95.77

Interim Earnings (Per Share)

Qtr.	Mar	Jun	Sep	Dec
2015	0.67	0.63	0.75	0.98
2016	1.10	0.78	0.82	0.80
2017	0.78	1.05	1.47	0.67
2018	0.81	...	...	...

Interim Dividends (Per Share)

Amt	Decl	Ex	Rec	Pay
1.00Q	07/31/2017	09/21/2017	09/22/2017	10/16/2017
1.00Q	11/01/2017	12/29/2017	01/02/2018	01/16/2018
1.00Q	02/13/2018	03/13/2018	03/14/2018	04/16/2018
1.00Q	05/02/2018	06/21/2018	06/22/2018	07/16/2018

Indicated Div: $4.00 (Div. Reinv. Plan)

Valuation Analysis

		Institutional Holding	
Forecast EPS	$3.16	No of Institutions	567
	(06/13/2018)		
Market Cap	$9.3 Billion	Shares	89,819,560
Book Value	$2.3 Billion	% Held	94.47
Price/Book	4.12		
Price/Sales	10.58		

TRADING VOLUME (thousand shares)

Business Summary: REITs (MIC: 5.3.1 SIC: 6798 NAIC: 525930)

Federal Realty Investment Trust is an equity real estate investment trust that focuses on the ownership, management, and redevelopment of retail and mixed-use properties. Co.'s properties are located primarily in communities in selected metropolitan markets in the Northeast and Mid-Atlantic regions of the U.S., as well as in California and South Florida. As of Dec 31 2017, Co. owned or had a majority interest in community and neighborhood shopping centers and mixed-use properties which were operated as 104 predominantly retail real estate projects.

Recent Developments: For the quarter ended Mar 31 2018, income from continuing operations increased 3.0% to US$59.6 million from US$57.9 million in the year-earlier quarter. Net income increased 8.4% to US$62.9 million from US$58.1 million in the year-earlier quarter. Revenues were US$225.4 million, up 8.7% from US$207.4 million the year before. Revenues from property income rose 7.9% to US$220.6 million from US$204.4 million in the corresponding quarter a year earlier.

Prospects: Our evaluation of Federal Realty Investment Trust as of Jan. 14, 2018 is the result of our systematic analysis on three basic characteristics: earnings strength, relative valuation, and recent stock price movement. The company has managed to produce a neutral trend in earnings per share over the past 5 quarters. Because the company lacks sufficient analyst estimate data, we place greater weight on the historical EPS trend as the measure of earnings strength. Based on operating earnings yield, the company is overvalued when compared to all of the companies in our coverage universe. Share price changes over the past year indicates that FRT will perform well over the near term.

Financial Data
(US$ in Thousands)

	3 Mos	12/31/2017	12/31/2016	12/31/2015	12/31/2014	12/31/2013	12/31/2012	12/31/2011
Earnings Per Share	4.00	3.97	3.50	3.03	2.41	2.46	2.35	2.28
Cash Flow Per Share	6.34	6.37	5.90	5.23	5.14	4.81	4.63	3.92
Tang Book Value Per Share	28.57	28.82	27.32	23.80	23.24	21.56	19.70	18.98
Dividends Per Share	3.980	3.960	3.840	3.620	3.300	3.020	2.840	2.720
Dividend Payout %	99.50	99.75	109.71	119.47	136.93	122.76	120.85	119.30
Income Statement								
Total Revenue	225,405	857,348	801,591	744,012	686,090	637,413	608,018	553,059
EBITDA	144,255	536,065	514,580	455,878	431,306	401,956	397,301	354,561
Depn & Amortn	58,110	216,050	193,585	174,796	170,814	161,099	142,039	126,568
Income Before Taxes	60,140	220,365	226,375	188,678	166,645	136,313	142,615	129,746
Net Income	61,247	289,914	249,910	210,219	164,535	162,681	151,925	143,917
Average Shares	72,968	72,233	71,049	68,981	67,492	65,483	64,056	62,603
Balance Sheet								
Current Assets	207,555	255,494	170,021	173,066	192,230	228,920	166,497	199,925
Total Assets	6,293,625	6,275,755	5,423,279	4,911,709	4,546,870	4,219,294	3,898,565	3,659,908
Current Liabilities	274,100	288,930	289,481	228,309	220,420	221,427	181,571	160,948
Long-Term Obligations	3,335,414	3,284,766	2,798,452	2,642,366	2,409,677	2,321,862	2,208,602	2,110,410
Total Liabilities	4,041,998	4,009,049	3,446,546	3,247,960	2,942,469	2,771,134	2,611,753	2,443,816
Stockholders' Equity	2,251,627	2,266,706	1,976,733	1,663,749	1,604,401	1,448,160	1,286,812	1,216,092
Shares Outstanding	73,216	73,090	71,995	69,493	68,605	66,701	64,815	63,544
Statistical Record								
Return on Assets %	4.94	4.96	4.82	4.45	3.75	4.01	4.01	4.22
Return on Equity %	13.94	13.66	13.69	12.86	10.78	11.90	12.11	12.17
EBITDA Margin %	64.00	62.53	64.19	61.27	62.86	63.06	65.34	64.11
Net Margin %	27.17	33.82	31.18	28.25	23.98	25.52	24.99	26.02
Asset Turnover	0.15	0.15	0.15	0.16	0.16	0.16	0.16	0.16
Current Ratio	0.76	0.88	0.59	0.76	0.87	1.03	0.92	1.24
Debt to Equity	1.48	1.45	1.42	1.59	1.50	1.60	1.72	1.74
Price Range	137.48-108.11	145.29-120.52	170.35-136.98	150.27-124.96	137.18-100.90	117.96-96.21	110.03-89.23	92.45-75.31
P/E Ratio	34.37-27.03	36.60-30.36	48.67-39.14	49.59-41.24	56.92-41.87	47.95-39.11	46.82-37.97	40.55-33.03
Average Yield %	3.15	3.02	2.52	2.60	2.75	2.85	2.80	3.22

Address: 1626 East Jefferson Street, Rockville, MD 20852 **Telephone:** 301-998-8100	**Web Site:** www.federalrealty.com **Officers:** Donald C. Wood - President, Chief Executive Officer, Principal Financial Officer Daniel Guglielmone - Executive Vice President, Chief Financial Officer, Treasurer	**Auditors:** Grant Thornton LLP **Investor Contact:** 800-658-8980 **Transfer Agents:** American Stock Transfer & Trust Company, New York, NY

FEDERATED INVESTORS INC (PA)

Exchange	Symbol	Price	52Wk Range	Yield	P/E
NYS	FII	$23.32 (6/29/2018)	36.53-22.96	4.63	7.80

*7 Year Price Score 89.58 *NYSE Composite Index=100 *12 Month Price Score 79.34

Interim Earnings (Per Share)

Qtr.	Mar	Jun	Sep	Dec
2015	0.35	0.40	0.42	0.45
2016	0.44	0.51	0.54	0.55
2017	0.49	0.53	0.56	1.30
2018	0.60	...	...	...

Interim Dividends (Per Share)

Amt	Decl	Ex	Rec	Pay
0.25Q	07/27/2017	08/04/2017	08/08/2017	08/15/2017
0.25Q	10/26/2017	11/07/2017	11/08/2017	11/15/2017
0.25Q	01/25/2018	02/07/2018	02/08/2018	02/15/2018
0.27Q	04/26/2018	05/07/2018	05/08/2018	05/15/2018

Indicated Div: $1.08

Valuation Analysis — **Institutional Holding**

Forecast EPS	$2.38	No of Institutions
	(06/14/2018)	488
Market Cap	$2.4 Billion	Shares
Book Value	$799.6 Million	119,744,008
Price/Book	2.96	% Held
Price/Sales	2.16	83.85

Business Summary: Wealth Management (MIC: 5.5.2 SIC: 6282 NAIC: 523930)

Federated Investors, together with its subsidiaries, is a provider of investment management products and related financial services. Co. sponsors, markets and provides investment-related services to various investment products, including mutual funds and Separate Accounts (which include separately managed accounts, institutional accounts, sub-advised funds and other managed products) in both domestic and international markets. Co. markets these funds to banks, broker/dealers and other financial intermediaries who use them to meet the needs of their customers, including retail investors, corporations and retirement plans. As of Dec 31 2017, Co. had $397.6 billion in assets under management.

Recent Developments: For the quarter ended Mar 31 2018, net income increased 17.6% to US$60.0 million from US$51.0 million in the year-earlier quarter. Revenues were US$263.9 million, down 3.5% from US$273.5 million the year before. Operating income was US$79.7 million versus US$77.8 million in the prior-year quarter, an increase of 2.4%. Indirect operating expenses decreased 5.9% to US$184.2 million from US$195.7 million in the equivalent prior-year period.

Prospects: Our evaluation of Federated Investors Inc. as of Jan. 21, 2018 is the result of our systematic analysis on three basic characteristics: earnings strength, relative valuation, and recent stock price movement. The company has managed to produce a neutral trend in earnings per share over the past 5 quarters and while recent estimates for the company have been mixed, FII has posted better than expected results. Based on operating earnings yield, the company is undervalued when compared to all of the companies in our coverage universe. Share price changes over the past year indicates that FII will perform very well over the near term.

Financial Data
(US$ in Thousands)	3 Mos	12/31/2017	12/31/2016	12/31/2015	12/31/2014	12/31/2013	12/31/2012	12/31/2011
Earnings Per Share	2.99	2.87	2.03	1.62	1.42	1.55	1.79	1.45
Cash Flow Per Share	2.94	2.78	2.54	2.32	1.91	2.59	3.14	1.13
Tang Book Value Per Share	0.62	0.24	N.M.	N.M.	N.M.	N.M.	N.M.	N.M.
Dividends Per Share	1.000	1.000	2.000	1.000	1.000	0.980	2.470	0.960
Dividend Payout %	33.44	34.84	98.52	61.73	70.42	63.23	137.99	66.21
Income Statement								
Total Revenue	263,852	1,102,924	1,143,371	926,609	859,250	878,365	945,706	895,114
EBITDA	81,085	367,874	354,807	288,405	258,963	280,579	331,052	271,718
Depn & Amortn	839	11,100	9,700	9,200	10,000	9,100	8,100	8,300
Income Before Taxes	78,916	352,002	340,934	274,906	239,352	259,015	308,511	246,371
Income Taxes	18,910	57,101	119,420	102,920	89,530	92,660	110,883	91,288
Net Income	60,331	291,341	208,919	169,807	149,236	162,177	188,088	150,906
Average Shares	97,189	97,412	99,117	100,477	100,723	100,669	100,313	100,632
Balance Sheet								
Current Assets	441,013	437,274	359,760	395,828	342,055	339,318	300,062	366,511
Total Assets	1,235,327	1,231,410	1,155,107	1,187,203	1,140,519	1,135,797	1,090,061	1,150,856
Current Liabilities	99,635	128,849	162,538	159,208	149,321	214,205	181,134	187,356
Long-Term Obligations	165,000	170,000	165,750	191,250	216,750	198,333	276,250	318,750
Total Liabilities	435,707	470,195	560,281	539,387	531,025	569,678	594,629	608,897
Stockholders' Equity	799,620	761,215	594,826	647,816	609,494	566,119	495,432	541,959
Shares Outstanding	101,445	101,109	101,998	104,103	104,927	104,798	104,450	103,752
Statistical Record								
Return on Assets %	25.50	24.42	17.79	14.59	13.11	14.57	16.74	13.10
Return on Equity %	42.77	42.97	33.53	27.01	25.39	30.55	36.16	29.20
EBITDA Margin %	30.73	33.35	31.03	31.12	30.14	31.94	35.01	30.36
Net Margin %	22.87	26.42	18.27	18.33	17.37	18.46	19.89	16.86
Asset Turnover	0.92	0.92	0.97	0.80	0.75	0.79	0.84	0.78
Current Ratio	4.43	3.39	2.21	2.49	2.29	1.58	1.66	1.96
Debt to Equity	0.21	0.22	0.28	0.30	0.36	0.35	0.56	0.59
Price Range	36.53-25.48	36.53-25.26	32.93-23.29	35.34-28.29	33.86-25.73	30.52-20.23	23.45-15.83	28.00-14.38
P/E Ratio	12.22-8.52	12.73-8.80	16.22-11.47	21.81-17.46	23.85-18.12	19.69-13.05	13.10-8.84	19.31-9.92
Average Yield %	3.31	3.51	6.89	3.08	3.39	3.74	12.01	4.35

Address: Federated Investors Tower, Pittsburgh, PA 15222-3779 **Telephone:** 412-288-1900	**Web Site:** www.federatedinvestors.com **Officers:** John F. Donahue - Chairman Paul A. Uhlman - Vice President	**Auditors:** Ernst & Young LLP **Transfer Agents:** ComputerShare Investor Services, Providence, RI

FEDEX CORP

Exchange	Symbol	Price	52Wk Range
NYS	FDX	$227.06 (6/29/2018)	274.32-203.55

Yield	P/E	Div Acheiver
1.15	13.86	14 Years

*7 Year Price Score 126.29 *NYSE Composite Index=100 *12 Month Price Score 103.62

Interim Earnings (Per Share)

Qtr.	Aug	Nov	Feb	May
2014-15	2.10	2.14	2.01	(2.60)
2015-16	2.42	2.44	1.84	(0.20)
2016-17	2.65	2.59	2.07	3.76
2017-18	2.19	2.84	7.59	...

Interim Dividends (Per Share)

Amt	Decl	Ex	Rec	Pay
0.50Q	08/18/2017	09/08/2017	09/11/2017	10/02/2017
0.50Q	11/17/2017	12/08/2017	12/11/2017	01/02/2018
0.50Q	02/16/2018	03/09/2018	03/12/2018	04/02/2018
0.65Q	06/11/2018	06/22/2018	06/25/2018	07/09/2018

Indicated Div: $2.60 (Div. Reinv. Plan)

Valuation Analysis

		Institutional Holding	
Forecast EPS	$17.36	No of Institutions	
	(06/13/2018)	1869	
Market Cap	$60.7 Billion	Shares	
Book Value	$18.9 Billion	239,404,880	
Price/Book	3.21	% Held	
Price/Sales	0.95	72.37	

TRADING VOLUME (thousand shares)

Business Summary: Airlines/Air Freight (MIC: 7.4.4 SIC: 4513 NAIC: 492110)

FedEx provides transportation, e-commerce and business services through companies under the FedEx brand. These companies are included in the following segments: Federal Express Corporation, an express transportation company; TNT Express B.V., an international express transportation, small-package ground delivery and freight transportation company; FedEx Ground Package System, Inc., a provider of small-package ground delivery services; FedEx Freight, Inc., a provider of less-than-truckload freight services; and FedEx Corporate Services, Inc., which provides sales, marketing, information technology, communications, customer services, technical support, billing and collections services.

Recent Developments: For the quarter ended Feb 28 2018, net income increased 269.0% to US$2.07 billion from US$562.0 million in the year-earlier quarter. Revenues were US$16.53 billion, up 10.2% from US$15.00 billion the year before. Operating income was US$1.00 billion versus US$1.03 billion in the prior-year quarter, a decrease of 2.3%. Direct operating expenses rose 11.2% to US$7.14 billion from US$6.42 billion in the comparable period the year before. Indirect operating expenses increased 11.0% to US$8.39 billion from US$7.56 billion in the equivalent prior-year period.

Prospects: Our evaluation of FedEx Corp. as of Jan. 21, 2018 is the result of our systematic analysis on three basic characteristics: earnings strength, relative valuation, and recent stock price movement. The company has managed to produce a neutral trend in earnings per share over the past 5 quarters and while recent estimates for the company have been raised by analysts, FDX has posted better than expected results. Based on operating earnings yield, the company is undervalued when compared to all of the companies in our coverage universe. Share price changes over the past year indicates that FDX will perform poorly over the near term.

Financial Data

(US$ in Thousands)	9 Mos	6 Mos	3 Mos	05/31/2017	05/31/2016	05/31/2015	05/31/2014	05/31/2013
Earnings Per Share	16.38	10.86	10.61	11.07	6.51	3.65	6.75	4.91
Cash Flow Per Share	12.86	14.15	16.97	18.53	20.62	18.96	13.89	14.88
Tang Book Value Per Share	42.77	36.32	34.44	33.25	26.50	39.60	39.27	46.05
Dividends Per Share	1.900	1.800	1.700	1.600	1.000	0.800	0.600	0.560
Dividend Payout %	11.60	16.57	16.02	14.45	15.36	21.92	8.89	11.41
Income Statement								
Total Revenue	48,136,000	31,610,000	15,297,000	60,319,000	50,365,000	47,453,000	45,567,000	44,287,000
EBITDA	5,651,000	3,866,000	1,847,000	7,958,000	5,655,000	4,448,000	6,031,000	4,816,000
Depn & Amortn	2,293,000	1,507,000	751,000	2,900,000	2,600,000	2,600,000	2,600,000	2,300,000
Income Before Taxes	2,995,000	2,121,000	982,000	4,579,000	2,740,000	1,627,000	3,289,000	2,455,000
Income Taxes	(450,000)	750,000	386,000	1,582,000	920,000	577,000	1,192,000	894,000
Net Income	3,445,000	1,371,000	596,000	2,997,000	1,820,000	1,050,000	2,097,000	1,561,000
Average Shares	273,000	272,000	272,000	270,000	279,000	287,000	310,000	317,000
Balance Sheet								
Current Assets	13,575,000	12,881,000	12,722,000	12,628,000	11,989,000	10,941,000	9,683,000	11,274,000
Total Assets	51,851,000	50,281,000	49,350,000	48,552,000	46,064,000	37,069,000	33,070,000	33,567,000
Current Liabilities	9,503,000	8,227,000	7,790,000	7,918,000	8,008,000	5,957,000	5,312,000	5,750,000
Long-Term Obligations	16,017,000	15,180,000	15,137,000	14,909,000	13,838,000	7,249,000	4,736,000	2,739,000
Total Liabilities	32,957,000	33,226,000	32,732,000	32,479,000	32,280,000	22,076,000	17,793,000	16,169,000
Stockholders' Equity	18,894,000	17,055,000	16,618,000	16,073,000	13,784,000	14,993,000	15,277,000	17,398,000
Shares Outstanding	267,215	267,889	268,147	268,257	265,524	282,430	318,000	318,000
Statistical Record								
Return on Assets %	9.05	6.11	6.06	6.34	4.37	2.99	6.29	4.92
Return on Equity %	26.20	18.70	18.71	20.08	12.61	6.94	12.84	9.72
EBITDA Margin %	11.74	12.23	12.07	13.19	11.23	9.37	13.24	10.87
Net Margin %	7.16	4.34	3.90	4.97	3.61	2.21	4.60	3.52
Asset Turnover	1.29	1.29	1.28	1.28	1.21	1.35	1.37	1.40
Current Ratio	1.43	1.57	1.63	1.59	1.50	1.84	1.82	1.96
Debt to Equity	0.85	0.89	0.91	0.93	1.00	0.48	0.31	0.16
Price Range	274.32-183.56	231.46-183.56	219.06-158.89	201.02-146.13	184.98-123.18	182.03-139.21	144.53-95.71	109.07-84.34
P/E Ratio	16.75-11.21	21.31-16.90	20.65-14.98	18.16-13.20	28.41-18.92	49.87-38.14	21.41-14.18	22.21-17.18
Average Yield %	0.87	0.88	0.88	0.89	0.89	0.64	0.49	0.60

Address: 942 South Shady Grove Road, Memphis, TN 38120 Telephone: 901-818-7500	Web Site: www.fedex.com Officers: Frederick W. Smith - Chairman, President, Chief Executive Officer David J. Bronczek - President, Chief Operating Officer	Auditors: Ernst & Young LLP Investor Contact: 901-818-7200 Transfer Agents: ComputerShare Investor Services, Providence, RI

FIDELITY NATIONAL FINANCIAL INC

Exchange	Symbol	Price	52Wk Range	Yield	P/E
NYS	FNF	$37.62 (6/29/2018)	41.85-31.82	3.19	15.17

*7 Year Price Score N/A   *NYSE Composite Index=100   *12 Month Price Score 99.74

Interim Earnings (Per Share)

Qtr.	Mar	Jun	Sep	Dec
2015	0.30	0.56	0.53	0.51
2016	0.26	0.67	0.58	0.83
2017	0.25	0.63	0.62	0.88
2018	0.35	...	...	...

Interim Dividends (Per Share)

Amt	Decl	Ex	Rec	Pay
0.27Q	10/25/2017	12/14/2017	12/15/2017	12/29/2017
0.30Q	01/30/2018	03/15/2018	03/16/2018	03/30/2018
0.30Q	05/02/2018	06/14/2018	06/15/2018	06/29/2018
0.30Q	07/17/2018	09/13/2018	09/14/2018	09/28/2018

Indicated Div: $1.20

Valuation Analysis

Forecast EPS	$2.78 (06/13/2018)
Market Cap	$10.3 Billion
Book Value	$4.5 Billion
Price/Book	2.32
Price/Sales	1.36

Institutional Holding

No of Institutions	633
Shares	283,608,256
% Held	101.20

TRADING VOLUME (thousand shares)

Business Summary: General Insurance (MIC: 5.2.1 SIC: 6361 NAIC: 524127)

Fidelity National Financial is a title insurance holding company. Co. has organized its business into two groups, FNF Group and FNF Ventures (FNFV). Through its FNF Group, Co. provides title insurance, escrow and other title related services, including trust activities, trustee's sales guarantees, recordings and reconveyances and home warranty products and technology and transaction services to the real estate and mortgage industries. Through its FNFV group, Co. owns majority and minority equity investment stakes in a number of entities, including American Blue Ribbon Holdings, LLC, Ceridian HCM, Inc. and Digital Insurance, Inc.

Recent Developments: For the quarter ended Mar 31 2018, income from continuing operations increased 63.3% to US$98.0 million from US$60.0 million in the year-earlier quarter. Net income increased 21.0% to US$98.0 million from US$81.0 million in the year-earlier quarter. Revenues were US$1.69 billion, up 3.0% from US$1.64 billion the year before. Net premiums earned were US$1.04 billion versus US$1.05 billion in the prior-year quarter, a decrease of 1.1%.

Prospects: Our evaluation of Fidelity National Financial Inc. as of Jan. 21, 2018 is the result of our systematic analysis on three basic characteristics: earnings strength, relative valuation, and recent stock price movement. The company has managed to produce a neutral trend in earnings per share over the past 5 quarters and while recent estimates for the company have been raised by analysts, FNF has posted better than expected results. Based on operating earnings yield, the company is about fairly valued when compared to all of the companies in our coverage universe. Share price changes over the past year indicates that FNF will perform very well over the near term.

Financial Data
(US$ in Thousands)

	3 Mos	12/31/2017	12/31/2016	12/31/2015	12/31/2014	12/31/2013	12/31/2012	12/31/2011
Earnings Per Share	2.48	2.38	2.34	1.89	0.75	1.71	2.68	1.66
Cash Flow Per Share	2.75	2.72	4.26	3.31	4.11	2.10	2.80	0.57
Tang Book Value Per Share	4.05	3.95	N.M.	N.M.	N.M.	10.18	7.48	9.16
Dividends Per Share	1.070	1.020	0.880	0.800	0.370	0.660	0.580	...
Dividend Payout %	43.15	42.86	37.61	42.33	49.33	38.60	21.64	...
Income Statement								
Premium Income	1,036,000	4,893,000	4,723,000	4,286,000	3,671,000	4,152,000	3,836,500	3,261,100
Total Revenue	1,693,000	7,663,000	9,554,000	9,132,000	8,024,000	8,565,000	7,201,700	4,839,600
Benefits & Claims	47,000	238,000	157,000	246,000	228,000	291,000	279,300	222,300
Income Before Taxes	127,000	864,000	1,072,000	867,000	392,000	651,000	843,400	414,800
Income Taxes	31,000	235,000	372,000	290,000	312,000	205,000	246,700	134,400
Net Income	97,000	771,000	650,000	527,000	583,000	402,000	606,500	369,500
Average Shares	280,000	278,000	280,000	286,000	142,000	235,000	226,000	222,700
Balance Sheet								
Total Assets	9,018,000	9,151,000	14,463,000	13,931,000	13,868,000	10,524,000	9,902,600	7,862,100
Total Liabilities	4,560,000	4,704,000	8,467,000	8,177,000	7,874,000	5,456,000	5,634,600	4,229,400
Stockholders' Equity	4,458,000	4,447,000	5,996,000	5,754,000	5,994,000	5,068,000	4,268,000	3,632,700
Shares Outstanding	274,576	274,431	338,622	347,999	371,777	250,340	228,545	220,677
Statistical Record								
Return on Assets %	6.86	6.53	4.57	3.79	4.78	3.94	6.81	4.69
Return on Equity %	15.25	14.77	11.03	8.97	10.54	8.61	15.31	10.47
Loss Ratio %	4.54	4.86	3.32	5.74	6.21	7.01	7.28	6.82
Net Margin %	5.73	10.06	6.80	5.77	7.27	4.69	8.42	7.63
Price Range	41.85-27.45	40.63-24.17	27.60-21.25	28.73-23.34	25.87-18.83	...	...	...
P/E Ratio	16.88-11.07	17.07-10.16	11.80-9.08	15.20-12.35	34.50-25.10	...	...	...
Average Yield %	3.04	3.19	3.55	3.04	1.76	...	...	...

Address: 601 Riverside Avenue, Jacksonville, FL 32204
Telephone: 904-854-8100

Web Site: www.fnf.com
Officers: Michael J. Nolan - President, Co-Chief Operating Officer Raymond R. (Randy) Quirk - President, Chief Executive Officer

Auditors: Ernst & Young LLP
Investor Contact: 904-854-8120
Transfer Agents: Continental Stock Transfer & Trust Company, New York, NY

FIDELITY NATIONAL INFORMATION SERVICES INC

Exchange	Symbol	Price	52Wk Range	Yield	P/E
NYS	FIS	$106.03 (6/29/2018)	107.72-85.40	1.21	26.12

7 Year Price Score 128.86 *NYSE Composite Index=100 *12 Month Price Score 106.68

Interim Earnings (Per Share)

Qtr.	Mar	Jun	Sep	Dec
2015	0.39	0.84	0.62	0.34
2016	0.17	0.37	0.56	0.62
2017	0.41	0.40	0.18	2.94
2018	0.54	...	...	...

Interim Dividends (Per Share)

Amt	Decl	Ex	Rec	Pay
0.29Q	07/20/2017	09/14/2017	09/15/2017	09/29/2017
0.29Q	10/26/2017	12/14/2017	12/15/2017	12/29/2017
0.32Q	02/01/2018	03/15/2018	03/16/2018	03/30/2018
0.32Q	04/24/2018	06/14/2018	06/15/2018	06/29/2018

Indicated Div: $1.28

Valuation Analysis / Institutional Holding

Forecast EPS	$5.24 (06/13/2018)	No of Institutions 983
Market Cap	$35.0 Billion	Shares 346,709,824
Book Value	$10.5 Billion	% Held
Price/Book	3.33	N/A
Price/Sales	3.92	

Business Summary: Business Services (MIC: 7.5.2 SIC: 7389 NAIC: 561499)

Fidelity National Information Services is a provider of financial services technology. Co.'s segments are: Integrated Financial Solutions, which serves the regional and community bank and savings institution market for transaction and account processing, payment solutions, channel solutions, lending and wealth management solutions, digital channels, risk and compliance solutions, and services; Global Financial Solutions, which provides an array of capital markets and asset management and insurance solutions, as well as banking and payments solutions and consulting and transformation services; and Corporate and Other, which includes global commercial services and retail check processing.

Recent Developments: For the quarter ended Mar 31 2018, net income increased 40.7% to US$190.0 million from US$135.0 million in the year-earlier quarter. Revenues were US$2.07 billion, down 3.8% from US$2.15 billion the year before. Operating income was US$294.0 million versus US$246.0 million in the prior-year quarter, an increase of 19.5%. Direct operating expenses declined 5.2% to US$1.41 billion from US$1.49 billion in the comparable period the year before. Indirect operating expenses decreased 12.9% to US$358.0 million from US$411.0 million in the equivalent prior-year period.

Prospects: Our evaluation of Fidelity National Information Services Inc. as of Jan. 21, 2018 is the result of our systematic analysis on three basic characteristics: earnings strength, relative valuation, and recent stock price movement. The company has enjoyed a very positive trend in earnings per share over the past 5 quarters and while recent estimates for the company have been mixed, FIS has posted better than expected results. Based on operating earnings yield, the company is undervalued when compared to all of the companies in our coverage universe. Share price changes over the past year indicates that FIS will perform well over the near term.

Financial Data
(US$ in Thousands)

	3 Mos	12/31/2017	12/31/2016	12/31/2015	12/31/2014	12/31/2013	12/31/2012	12/31/2011
Earnings Per Share	4.06	3.93	1.72	2.19	2.35	1.68	1.55	1.53
Cash Flow Per Share	4.97	5.28	5.89	3.99	4.09	3.66	3.58	3.90
Dividends Per Share	1.190	1.160	1.040	1.040	0.960	0.880	0.800	0.200
Dividend Payout %	29.31	29.52	60.47	47.49	40.85	52.38	51.61	13.07
Income Statement								
Total Revenue	2,066,000	9,123,000	9,241,000	6,595,200	6,413,800	6,070,700	5,807,600	5,745,700
EBITDA	464,000	1,553,000	1,474,000	1,359,400	1,341,000	1,132,200	1,171,700	1,113,800
Depn & Amortn	167,000	180,000	185,000	139,100	130,100	119,000	117,800	110,700
Income Before Taxes	225,000	1,036,000	906,000	1,036,900	1,053,400	825,000	831,200	744,300
Income Taxes	34,000	(319,000)	317,000	378,800	335,100	309,220	270,900	239,000
Net Income	182,000	1,319,000	568,000	631,500	679,100	493,100	461,200	469,600
Average Shares	334,000	336,000	330,000	288,700	288,700	294,200	297,500	307,000
Balance Sheet								
Current Assets	3,735,000	3,606,000	4,282,000	3,511,400	2,473,100	2,351,900	1,844,200	1,682,700
Total Assets	24,405,000	24,517,000	26,031,000	26,268,800	14,520,500	13,960,100	13,549,700	13,848,300
Current Liabilities	3,816,000	3,923,000	3,151,000	2,363,900	1,598,900	1,672,700	1,256,800	1,354,900
Long-Term Obligations	8,040,000	7,718,000	10,146,000	11,497,800	5,054,600	4,339,800	4,231,600	4,550,600
Total Liabilities	13,910,000	13,682,000	16,290,000	16,947,800	7,963,800	7,379,600	6,908,800	7,345,300
Stockholders' Equity	10,495,000	10,835,000	9,741,000	9,321,000	6,556,700	6,580,500	6,640,900	6,503,000
Shares Outstanding	330,000	333,000	328,000	324,500	284,900	290,600	294,100	292,900
Statistical Record								
Return on Assets %	5.51	5.22	2.17	3.10	4.77	3.58	3.36	3.35
Return on Equity %	13.38	12.82	5.94	7.95	10.34	7.46	7.00	7.28
EBITDA Margin %	22.46	17.02	15.95	20.61	20.91	18.65	20.18	19.38
Net Margin %	8.81	14.46	6.15	9.58	10.59	8.12	7.94	8.17
Asset Turnover	0.36	0.36	0.35	0.32	0.45	0.44	0.42	0.41
Current Ratio	0.98	0.92	1.36	1.49	1.55	1.41	1.47	1.24
Debt to Equity	0.77	0.71	1.04	1.23	0.77	0.66	0.64	0.70
Price Range	102.88-79.13	96.62-76.98	80.84-56.04	73.50-58.52	64.04-48.87	53.68-34.81	36.97-26.43	33.54-22.55
P/E Ratio	25.34-19.49	24.59-19.59	47.00-32.58	33.56-26.72	27.25-20.80	31.95-20.72	23.85-17.05	21.92-14.74
Average Yield %	1.30	1.33	1.46	1.59	1.73	2.01	2.48	0.69

Address: 601 Riverside Avenue, Jacksonville, FL 32204 Telephone: 904-438-6000	Web Site: www.fisglobal.com Officers: Gary A. Norcross - Chairman, President, Corporate Executive Vice President, Chief Operating Officer, Chief Executive Officer Marc M. Mayo - Executive Vice President, Chief Legal Officer, Corporate Secretary	Auditors: KPMG LLP Investor Contact: 904-438-6000 Transfer Agents: Computershare Investor Services, LLC, Chicago, IL

FIRST AMERICAN FINANCIAL CORP

Exchange	Symbol	Price	52Wk Range	Yield	P/E
NYS	FAF	$51.72 (6/29/2018)	62.09-44.11	2.94	N/A

*7 Year Price Score 132.22 *NYSE Composite Index=100 *12 Month Price Score 96.49

Interim Earnings (Per Share)

Qtr.	Mar	Jun	Sep	Dec
2015	0.34	0.85	0.69	0.74
2016	0.47	0.92	0.96	0.73
2017	0.52	1.09	0.19	1.96
2018	0.67	...	...	...

Interim Dividends (Per Share)

Amt	Decl	Ex	Rec	Pay
0.38Q	08/16/2017	09/07/2017	09/08/2017	09/15/2017
0.38Q	11/08/2017	12/07/2017	12/08/2017	12/15/2017
0.38Q	01/24/2018	03/07/2018	03/08/2018	03/15/2018
0.38Q	05/08/2018	06/07/2018	06/08/2018	06/15/2018

Indicated Div: $1.52

Valuation Analysis   **Institutional Holding**

Forecast EPS	$4.43	No of Institutions
	(06/13/2018)	471
Market Cap	$5.8 Billion	Shares
Book Value	$3.5 Billion	108,285,120
Price/Book	1.66	% Held
Price/Sales	N/A	93.40

Business Summary: General Insurance (MIC: 5.2.1 SIC: 6361 NAIC: 524127)

First American Financial is a holding company. Through its subsidiaries, Co. is engaged in the business of providing financial services through its two segments. The title insurance and services segment provides title insurance, closing and/or escrow services and similar or related services domestically and internationally in connection with residential and commercial real estate transactions. It maintains, manages and provides access to title plant records and images and, in addition, provides banking, trust, document custodial and investment advisory services. The specialty insurance segment issues property and casualty insurance policies and sells home warranty products.

Recent Developments: For the quarter ended Mar 31 2018, net income increased 31.2% to US$76.2 million from US$58.1 million in the year-earlier quarter. Revenues were US$1.30 billion, down 1.5% from US$1.32 billion the year before. Net premiums earned were US$1.07 billion versus US$1.10 billion in the prior-year quarter, a decrease of 2.7%. Net investment income rose 12.7% to US$37.1 million from US$32.9 million a year ago.

Prospects: Our evaluation of First American Financial Corp. as of Jan. 21, 2018 is the result of our systematic analysis on three basic characteristics: earnings strength, relative valuation, and recent stock price movement. The company has produced a positive trend in earnings per share over the past 5 quarters and while recent estimates for the company have been mixed, FAF has posted better than expected results. Based on operating earnings yield, the company is undervalued when compared to all of the companies in our coverage universe. Share price changes over the past year indicates that FAF will perform well over the near term.

Financial Data
(US$ in Thousands)

	3 Mos	12/31/2017	12/31/2016	12/31/2015	12/31/2014	12/31/2013	12/31/2012	12/31/2011
Earnings Per Share	3.91	3.76	3.09	2.62	2.15	1.71	2.77	0.73
Cash Flow Per Share	...	5.66	4.42	5.08	3.37	3.54	4.03	1.27
Tang Book Value Per Share	20.09	20.44	17.39	16.00	14.48	14.74	13.48	10.91
Dividends Per Share	1.480	1.440	1.200	1.000	0.840	0.480	0.360	0.240
Dividend Payout %	37.85	38.30	38.83	38.17	39.07	28.07	13.00	32.88
Income Statement								
Total Revenue	1,297,388	5,772,363	5,575,846	5,175,456	4,677,949	4,956,077	4,541,821	3,820,574
Income Before Taxes	93,065	445,331	477,581	432,765	350,560	310,708	467,406	130,293
Income Taxes	16,893	23,468	134,105	143,895	116,345	123,644	165,678	51,714
Net Income	76,227	423,049	342,993	288,086	233,534	186,367	301,041	78,276
Average Shares	113,035	112,435	111,156	109,826	108,688	109,102	108,542	106,914
Balance Sheet								
Total Assets	9,546,789	9,573,222	8,831,777	8,254,351	7,666,100	6,520,600	6,050,847	5,370,337
Total Liabilities	6,076,254	6,093,267	5,823,598	5,495,849	5,093,183	4,067,551	3,702,782	3,341,737
Stockholders' Equity	3,470,535	3,479,955	3,008,179	2,758,502	2,572,917	2,453,049	2,348,065	2,028,600
Shares Outstanding	111,545	110,925	109,944	109,098	107,541	105,900	107,239	105,410
Statistical Record								
Return on Assets %	...	4.60	4.00	3.62	3.29	2.96	5.26	1.40
Return on Equity %	...	13.04	11.86	10.81	9.29	7.76	13.72	3.91
Net Margin %	5.88	7.33	6.15	5.57	4.99	3.76	6.63	2.05
Asset Turnover	...	0.63	0.65	0.65	0.66	0.79	0.79	0.68
Price Range	62.09-38.01	57.02-36.83	43.35-32.44	42.36-32.65	34.30-24.92	28.26-20.53	24.69-12.75	17.06-10.51
P/E Ratio	15.88-9.72	15.16-9.80	14.03-10.50	16.17-12.46	15.95-11.59	16.53-12.01	8.91-4.60	23.37-14.40
Average Yield %	2.93	3.16	3.14	2.70	2.99	1.97	1.94	1.65

Address: 1 First American Way, Santa Ana, CA 92707-5913
Telephone: 714-250-3000
Fax: 714-250-3151

Web Site: www.firstam.com
Officers: Parker S. Kennedy - Executive Chairman, Chairman Dennis J. Gilmore - Chief Executive Officer

Auditors: PricewaterhouseCoopers LLP
Investor Contact: 714-250-5214
Transfer Agents: Wells Fargo Shareowner Services

FIRST DATA CORP

Exchange	Symbol	Price	52Wk Range	Yield	P/E
NYS	FDC	$20.93 (6/29/2018)	21.95-14.99	N/A	12.84

*7 Year Price Score N/A ***NYSE Composite Index=100** ***12 Month Price Score 109.92**

TRADING VOLUME (thousand shares)

Interim Earnings (Per Share)

Qtr.	Mar	Jun	Sep	Dec
2015	(112,000)	(26000.00)	(126000.00)	(1.60)
2016	(0.06)	0.17	0.14	0.21
2017	0.04	0.20	0.31	1.01
2018	0.11	...	...	...

Interim Dividends (Per Share)

No Dividends Paid

Valuation Analysis   Institutional Holding

Forecast EPS	$1.45	No of Institutions
	(06/14/2018)	527
Market Cap	$19.4 Billion	Shares
Book Value	$3.4 Billion	546,505,920
Price/Book	5.78	% Held
Price/Sales	1.69	N/A

Business Summary: IT Services (MIC: 6.3.1 SIC: 7389 NAIC: 561499)

First Data engages in commerce-enabling technology and solutions, for merchants, financial institutions, and card issuers. Co. segments are: Global Business Solutions, which provides retail point-of-sale (POS) merchant acquiring and eCommerce services as well as next-generation offerings, and cloud-based Clover POS operating system; Global Financial Solutions, which provides credit and retail private-label card processing, as well as licensed financial software systems, and lending solutions; and Network & Security Solutions, which provides electronic funds transfer network solutions, debit card processing solutions, stored value network solutions, and security and fraud solutions.

Recent Developments: For the quarter ended Mar 31 2018, net income increased 69.6% to US$134.0 million from US$79.0 million in the year-earlier quarter. Revenues were US$2.28 billion, down 18.5% from US$2.80 billion the year before. Operating income was US$348.0 million versus US$326.0 million in the prior-year quarter, an increase of 6.7%. Direct operating expenses declined 0.3% to US$779.0 million from US$781.0 million in the comparable period the year before. Indirect operating expenses decreased 31.8% to US$1.16 billion from US$1.69 billion in the equivalent prior-year period.

Prospects: Our evaluation of First Data Corp as of Jan. 21, 2018 is the result of our systematic analysis on three basic characteristics: earnings strength, relative valuation, and recent stock price movement. The company has enjoyed a very positive trend in earnings per share over the past 5 quarters. However, while recent estimates for the company have been mixed, FDC has posted results that fell short of analysts expectations. Based on operating earnings yield, the company is undervalued when compared to all of the companies in our coverage universe. Share price changes over the past year indicates that FDC will perform poorly over the near term.

Financial Data

(US$ in Thousands)	3 Mos	12/31/2017	12/31/2016	12/31/2015	12/31/2014	12/31/2013	12/31/2012	12/31/2011
Earnings Per Share	1.63	1.56	0.46	(7.70)	(458,000)	(952,000)	(736,000)	(516,000)
Cash Flow Per Share	2.34	2.23	2.33	4.13	...	...	...	...
Income Statement								
Total Revenue	2,282,000	12,052,000	11,584,000	11,451,000	11,151,800	10,808,900	10,680,300	10,713,600
EBITDA	616,000	1,971,000	1,849,000	421,000	2,503,700	2,287,600	2,310,400	2,409,800
Depn & Amortn	271,000	321,000	300,000	290,000	1,163,300	1,211,900	1,330,900	1,344,200
Income Before Taxes	112,000	713,000	481,000	(1,406,000)	(402,000)	(793,900)	(909,500)	(759,600)
Income Taxes	27,000	(729,000)	81,000	101,000	82,100	86,500	(224,000)	(270,100)
Net Income	101,000	1,465,000	420,000	(1,481,000)	(457,800)	(869,100)	(700,900)	(516,100)
Average Shares	946,000	940,000	921,001	192,263	1	1	1	1
Balance Sheet								
Current Assets	20,490,000	23,372,000	17,417,000	10,786,000	9,954,400	10,076,100	11,883,400	13,315,500
Total Assets	45,415,000	48,269,000	40,292,000	34,362,000	34,269,300	35,239,800	37,899,000	40,276,300
Current Liabilities	20,229,000	23,293,000	16,717,000	10,645,000	9,530,600	9,618,000	11,344,900	12,820,200
Long-Term Obligations	17,908,000	17,927,000	18,131,000	18,737,000	20,711,400	22,556,800	22,528,900	22,521,700
Total Liabilities	42,050,000	45,117,000	39,072,000	33,694,000	34,721,200	36,729,400	38,497,500	40,179,700
Stockholders' Equity	3,365,000	3,152,000	1,220,000	668,000	(451,900)	(1,489,600)	(598,500)	96,600
Shares Outstanding	929,000	925,000	911,959	899,203	1,000.00	1,000.00	1,000.00	1,000.00
Statistical Record								
Return on Assets %	3.80	3.31	1.12	N.M.	N.M.	N.M.	N.M.	N.M.
Return on Equity %	64.72	67.02	44.37	N.M.	...	...	...	N.M.
EBITDA Margin %	26.99	16.35	15.96	3.68	22.45	21.16	21.63	22.49
Net Margin %	4.43	12.16	3.63	N.M.	N.M.	N.M.	N.M.	N.M.
Asset Turnover	0.29	0.27	0.31	0.33	0.32	0.30	0.27	0.28
Current Ratio	1.01	1.00	1.04	1.01	1.04	1.05	1.05	1.04
Debt to Equity	5.32	5.69	14.86	28.05	...	...	...	233.14
Price Range	19.08-14.81	19.08-14.81	16.02-8.67	17.80-15.36	...	...	...	...
P/E Ratio	11.71-9.09	12.23-9.49	34.83-18.85	...	...	...	...	...

Address: 225 Liberty Street, 29th Floor, New York, NY 10281 Telephone: 800-735-3362	Web Site: www.firstdata.com Officers: Frank J. Bisignano - Chairman, Chief Executive Officer Joseph J. Plumeri - Vice-Chairman	Auditors: Ernst & Young LLP Investor Contact: 800-735-3362 Transfer Agents: Wells Fargo Bank Minnesota, South St. Paul, MN

FIRST HORIZON NATIONAL CORP

Exchange	Symbol	Price	52Wk Range	Yield	P/E
NYS	FHN	$17.84 (6/29/2018)	20.61-16.05	2.69	26.24

*7 Year Price Score 113.30 *NYSE Composite Index=100 *12 Month Price Score 98.11

Interim Earnings (Per Share)

Qtr.	Mar	Jun	Sep	Dec
2015	(0.33)	0.22	0.25	0.20
2016	0.20	0.24	0.27	0.23
2017	0.23	0.38	0.28	(0.25)
2018	0.27	...	...	...

Interim Dividends (Per Share)

Amt	Decl	Ex	Rec	Pay
0.09Q	07/25/2017	09/07/2017	09/08/2017	10/02/2017
0.09Q	10/24/2017	11/02/2017	11/03/2017	01/02/2018
0.12Q	01/23/2018	03/08/2018	03/09/2018	04/02/2018
0.12Q	04/24/2018	06/07/2018	06/08/2018	07/02/2018

Indicated Div: $0.48

Valuation Analysis   **Institutional Holding**

Forecast EPS	$1.48	No of Institutions
	(06/13/2018)	504
Market Cap	$5.8 Billion	Shares
Book Value	$4.3 Billion	319,461,760
Price/Book	1.36	% Held
Price/Sales	3.55	74.42

Business Summary: Banking (MIC: 5.1.1 SIC: 6021 NAIC: 522110)

First Horizon National is a bank holding company. Co. provides financial services primarily through its subsidiary, First Tennessee Bank National Association. Co. business segments are: regional banking, which provides financial products and services; fixed income, which consists of fixed income securities sales, trading, and strategies for institutional clients; corporate, which consists of unallocated corporate expenses, expense on subordinated debt issuances, and unallocated interest income; and non-strategic, which consists of the wind-down national consumer lending activities. As of Dec 31 2017, Co. had total assets of $41.42 billion and total deposits of $30.62 billion.

Recent Developments: For the quarter ended Mar 31 2018, net income increased 62.7% to US$95.0 million from US$58.4 million in the year-earlier quarter. Net interest income increased 58.8% to US$301.2 million from US$189.7 million in the year-earlier quarter. Credit for loan losses was unchanged at US$1.0 million versus the prior-year quarter. Non-interest income rose 16.3% to US$136.0 million from US$116.9 million, while non-interest expense advanced 41.0% to US$313.3 million.

Prospects: Our evaluation of First Horizon National Corp. as of Jan. 21, 2018 is the result of our systematic analysis on three basic characteristics: earnings strength, relative valuation, and recent stock price movement. The company has managed to produce a neutral trend in earnings per share over the past 5 quarters. However, while recent estimates for the company have been mixed, FHN has posted better than expected results. Based on operating earnings yield, the company is undervalued when compared to all of the companies in our coverage universe. Share price changes over the past year indicates that FHN will perform in line with the market over the near term.

Financial Data
(US$ in Thousands)

	3 Mos	12/31/2017	12/31/2016	12/31/2015	12/31/2014	12/31/2013	12/31/2012	12/31/2011
Earnings Per Share	0.68	0.65	0.94	0.34	0.91	0.10	(0.11)	0.50
Cash Flow Per Share	(0.46)	(0.07)	0.78	1.57	3.00	1.81	1.49	0.17
Tang Book Value Per Share	7.97	8.01	9.00	8.51	8.63	7.92	7.98	8.10
Dividends Per Share	0.390	0.360	0.280	0.240	0.200	0.200	0.040	0.040
Dividend Payout %	57.35	55.38	29.79	70.59	21.98	200.00	...	8.00
Income Statement								
Interest Income	363,355	989,930	817,909	736,405	709,249	732,053	798,953	832,437
Interest Expense	62,182	147,616	88,825	82,685	81,531	94,679	110,286	131,605
Net Interest Income	301,173	842,314	729,084	653,720	627,718	637,374	688,667	700,832
Provision for Losses	(1,000)	...	11,000	9,000	27,000	55,000	78,000	44,000
Non-Interest Income	136,017	490,219	552,441	517,325	550,044	584,577	671,329	786,011
Non-Interest Expense	313,265	1,023,661	925,204	1,053,791	841,211	1,158,601	1,383,701	1,292,995
Income Before Taxes	124,925	308,872	345,321	108,254	309,551	8,350	(101,705)	149,848
Income Taxes	29,931	131,892	106,810	10,941	78,501	(32,169)	(85,262)	15,836
Net Income	92,174	165,515	227,046	85,879	219,523	29,602	(27,759)	131,196
Average Shares	330,344	244,453	235,292	236,266	236,735	239,794	248,349	262,861
Balance Sheet								
Net Loans & Leases	27,833,011	28,168,751	19,498,700	17,602,602	16,139,003	15,505,417	16,833,556	16,426,673
Total Assets	40,463,195	41,423,388	28,555,231	26,195,136	25,672,887	23,789,833	25,520,140	24,789,384
Total Deposits	30,818,951	30,620,362	22,672,363	19,967,478	18,068,939	16,734,956	16,629,709	16,213,009
Total Liabilities	36,186,098	37,138,331	26,145,578	23,850,981	23,377,350	21,584,513	23,306,099	22,399,912
Stockholders' Equity	4,277,097	4,285,057	2,409,653	2,344,155	2,295,537	2,205,320	2,214,041	2,389,472
Shares Outstanding	327,193	326,736	233,623	238,586	234,219	236,369	243,597	257,468
Statistical Record								
Return on Assets %	0.58	0.47	0.83	0.33	0.89	0.12	N.M.	0.53
Return on Equity %	6.01	4.94	9.53	3.70	9.75	1.34	N.M.	5.50
Net Interest Margin %	82.89	85.09	89.14	88.77	88.50	87.07	86.20	84.19
Efficiency Ratio %	62.73	69.16	67.52	84.05	66.80	88.00	94.11	79.89
Loans to Deposits	0.90	0.92	0.86	0.88	0.89	0.93	1.01	1.01
Price Range	20.61-16.05	20.76-16.05	20.61-11.62	16.20-12.31	13.91-11.18	12.55-9.72	10.89-7.55	12.53-5.63
P/E Ratio	30.31-23.60	31.94-24.69	21.93-12.36	47.65-36.21	15.29-12.29	125.50-97.20	...	25.06-11.26
Average Yield %	2.10	1.94	1.90	1.65	1.66	1.80	0.44	0.43

Address: 165 Madison Avenue, Memphis, TN 38103	**Web Site:** www.firsthorizon.com	**Auditors:** KPMG LLP
Telephone: 901-523-4444	**Officers:** D. Bryan Jordan - Chairman, President, Chief Executive Officer Michael E. Kisber - President	**Investor Contact:** 800-410-4577
		Transfer Agents: Wells Fargo

FIRST INDUSTRIAL REALTY TRUST INC

Exchange	Symbol	Price	52Wk Range	Yield	P/E
NYS	FR	$33.34 (6/29/2018)	33.67-27.75	2.61	18.52

*7 Year Price Score 120.87 *NYSE Composite Index=100 *12 Month Price Score 104.74

Interim Earnings (Per Share)

Qtr.	Mar	Jun	Sep	Dec
2015	0.02	0.13	0.13	0.40
2016	0.14	0.43	0.27	0.20
2017	0.19	0.32	0.36	0.82
2018	0.30	...	...	...

Interim Dividends (Per Share)

Amt	Decl	Ex	Rec	Pay
0.21Q	08/02/2017	09/28/2017	09/29/2017	10/16/2017
0.21Q	11/07/2017	12/28/2017	12/29/2017	01/16/2018
0.218Q	02/21/2018	03/28/2018	03/29/2018	04/16/2018
0.218Q	05/10/2018	06/28/2018	06/29/2018	07/16/2018

Indicated Div: $0.87

Valuation Analysis   **Institutional Holding**

Forecast EPS	$0.81	No of Institutions
	(06/13/2018)	391
Market Cap	$4.0 Billion	Shares
Book Value	$1.4 Billion	156,617,696
Price/Book	2.78	% Held
Price/Sales	10.08	101.48

Business Summary: REITs (MIC: 5.3.1 SIC: 6798 NAIC: 525930)

First Industrial Realty Trust is a real estate investment trust that owns, manages, acquires, sells, develops, and redevelops industrial real estate. As of Dec 31 2017, Co.'s in-service portfolio consisted of 164 bulk warehouse properties, 92 regional warehouse properties, 183 light industrial properties and 45 R&D/flex properties and located in 21 states. Co.'s in-service portfolio includes properties that have reached stabilized occupancy, developed and redeveloped properties and acquired properties that are occupied at acquisition or one year from the acquisition date. Co.'s operations are conducted via First Industrial, L.P., of which Co. is the sole general partner.

Recent Developments: For the quarter ended Mar 31 2018, net income increased 59.5% to US$37.5 million from US$23.5 million in the year-earlier quarter. Revenues were US$99.8 million, up 2.5% from US$97.4 million the year before. Revenues from property income rose 0.3% to US$75.2 million from US$74.9 million in the corresponding quarter a year earlier.

Prospects: Our evaluation of First Industrial Realty Trust Inc. as of Jan. 21, 2018 is the result of our systematic analysis on three basic characteristics: earnings strength, relative valuation, and recent stock price movement. The company has produced a positive trend in earnings per share over the past 5 quarters. Because the company lacks sufficient analyst estimate data, we place greater weight on the historical EPS trend as the measure of earnings strength. Based on operating earnings yield, the company is about fairly valued when compared to all of the companies in our coverage universe. Share price changes over the past year indicates that FR will perform well over the near term.

Financial Data
(US$ in Thousands)

	3 Mos	12/31/2017	12/31/2016	12/31/2015	12/31/2014	12/31/2013	12/31/2012	12/31/2011
Earnings Per Share	1.80	1.69	1.05	0.67	0.42	0.24	(0.24)	(0.34)
Cash Flow Per Share	1.58	1.62	1.50	1.47	1.25	1.18	1.49	1.09
Tang Book Value Per Share	11.72	11.66	10.35	9.37	9.18	9.98	10.84	11.39
Dividends Per Share	0.848	0.840	0.760	0.510	0.410	0.340	...	...
Dividend Payout %	47.08	49.70	72.38	76.12	97.62	141.67	...	...
Income Statement								
Total Revenue	99,771	396,402	378,020	365,762	344,599	328,226	327,273	317,835
EBITDA	81,630	363,933	284,936	240,244	186,627	173,292	167,149	163,368
Depn & Amortn	30,434	94,078	95,514	92,955	93,457	94,271	100,074	95,931
Income Before Taxes	37,550	209,494	126,773	76,767	20,004	4,592	(17,017)	(32,731)
Income Taxes	86	1,193	1,089	117	238	(213)	5,522	450
Net Income	36,292	201,456	121,232	73,802	49,110	40,307	(1,318)	(7,445)
Average Shares	120,211	118,787	115,370	110,781	110,325	106,995	91,468	80,616
Balance Sheet								
Current Assets	144,517	51,355	26,218	32,604	18,685	13,282	9,534	13,215
Total Assets	3,044,595	2,941,062	2,793,263	2,718,051	2,581,995	2,597,510	2,608,842	2,666,657
Current Liabilities	144,516	157,833	151,146	148,664	128,596	115,859	111,901	97,322
Long-Term Obligations	1,401,881	1,296,997	1,347,092	1,442,411	1,349,846	1,296,806	1,335,766	1,479,483
Total Liabilities	1,600,137	1,513,262	1,551,822	1,644,951	1,533,045	1,470,660	1,505,463	1,639,981
Stockholders' Equity	1,444,458	1,427,800	1,241,441	1,073,100	1,048,950	1,126,850	1,103,379	1,026,676
Shares Outstanding	120,557	119,883	117,107	111,027	110,600	109,980	98,767	86,807
Statistical Record								
Return on Assets %	7.35	7.03	4.39	2.78	1.90	1.55	N.M.	N.M.
Return on Equity %	16.01	15.09	10.45	6.96	4.51	3.61	N.M.	N.M.
EBITDA Margin %	81.82	91.81	75.38	65.68	54.16	52.80	51.07	51.40
Net Margin %	36.38	50.82	32.07	20.18	14.25	12.28	N.M.	N.M.
Asset Turnover	0.14	0.14	0.14	0.14	0.13	0.13	0.12	0.12
Current Ratio	1.00	0.33	0.17	0.22	0.15	0.11	0.09	0.14
Debt to Equity	0.97	0.91	1.09	1.34	1.29	1.15	1.21	1.44
Price Range	32.82-26.63	32.82-25.35	29.61-19.32	23.08-18.69	21.16-16.42	18.81-14.08	14.10-10.30	12.67-7.54
P/E Ratio	18.23-14.79	19.42-15.00	28.20-18.40	34.45-27.90	50.38-39.10	78.38-58.67	...	...
Average Yield %	2.83	2.87	3.01	2.44	2.21	2.05	...	...

Address: 311 S. Wacker Drive, Suite 3900, Chicago, IL 60606 **Telephone:** 312-344-4300 **Fax:** 312-922-6320	**Web Site:** www.firstindustrial.com **Officers:** Bruce W. Duncan - Chairman, President, Chief Executive Officer Peter E. Baccile - President, Chief Executive Officer	**Auditors:** PricewaterhouseCoopers LLP **Investor Contact:** 312-344-4320 **Transfer Agents:** Barack Ferrazzano Kirschbaum & Nagelberg LLP

FIRST REPUBLIC BANK (SAN FRANCISCO, CA)

Exchange	Symbol	Price	52Wk Range	Yield	P/E
NYS	FRC	$96.79 (6/29/2018)	105.17-84.96	0.74	21.85

*7 Year Price Score 129.79 *NYSE Composite Index=100 *12 Month Price Score 101.70

Interim Earnings (Per Share)

Qtr.	Mar	Jun	Sep	Dec
2015	0.71	0.80	0.82	0.84
2016	0.88	0.97	1.00	1.03
2017	1.01	1.06	1.14	1.10
2018	1.13	...	...	...

Interim Dividends (Per Share)

Amt	Decl	Ex	Rec	Pay
0.17Q	10/13/2017	10/25/2017	10/26/2017	11/09/2017
0.17Q	01/16/2018	01/24/2018	01/25/2018	02/08/2018
0.18Q	04/13/2018	04/25/2018	04/26/2018	05/10/2018
0.18Q	07/13/2018	07/25/2018	07/26/2018	08/09/2018

Indicated Div: $0.72

Valuation Analysis — **Institutional Holding**

Forecast EPS	$4.77	No of Institutions
	(06/14/2018)	634
Market Cap	$15.7 Billion	Shares
Book Value	$7.8 Billion	205,180,960
Price/Book	2.00	% Held
Price/Sales	5.09	N/A

Business Summary: Banking (MIC: 5.1.1 SIC: 6029 NAIC: 522110)

First Republic Bank is a commercial bank and trust company. Co. focuses on providing personalized, relationship-based services, including private banking, private business banking, real estate lending and wealth management services, including trust and custody services. Co. conducts its business through two reportable business segments: Commercial Banking and Wealth Management. Co. provides its services in the following areas: San Francisco, Palo Alto, Los Angeles, Santa Barbara, Newport Beach, San Diego, Portland, OR; Boston, New York City, Greenwich and Palm Beach, FL. As of Dec 31 2017, Co. had total assets of $87.78 billion and total deposits of $68.92 billion.

Recent Developments: For the quarter ended Mar 31 2018, net income increased 12.6% to US$199.1 million from US$176.8 million in the year-earlier quarter. Net interest income increased 17.6% to US$587.8 million from US$499.7 million in the year-earlier quarter. Provision for loan losses was US$13.0 million versus US$9.1 million in the prior-year quarter, an increase of 43.0%. Non-interest income rose 31.2% to US$133.1 million from US$101.5 million, while non-interest expense advanced 21.9% to US$461.6 million.

Prospects: Our evaluation of First Republic Bank as of Jan. 21, 2018 is the result of our systematic analysis on three basic characteristics: earnings strength, relative valuation, and recent stock price movement. The company has managed to produce a neutral trend in earnings per share over the past 5 quarters. However, while recent estimates for the company have been lowered by analysts, FRC has posted better than expected results. Based on operating earnings yield, the company is undervalued when compared to all of the companies in our coverage universe. Share price changes over the past year indicates that FRC will perform in line with the market over the near term.

Financial Data

(US$ in Thousands)	3 Mos	12/31/2017	12/31/2016	12/31/2015	12/31/2014	12/31/2013	12/31/2012	12/31/2011
Earnings Per Share	4.43	4.31	3.93	3.18	3.07	3.10	2.76	2.65
Cash Flow Per Share	6.32	6.42	5.72	...	3.64	4.28	3.37	0.50
Tang Book Value Per Share	41.07	40.03	34.94	29.80	26.21	22.61	19.93	18.10
Dividends Per Share	0.680	0.670	0.630	0.590	0.540	0.360	0.300	...
Dividend Payout %	15.35	15.55	16.03	18.55	17.59	11.61	10.87	...
Income Statement								
Total Revenue	821,576	2,912,079	2,375,685	1,989,145	1,801,364	1,600,368	1,455,940	1,300,887
Income Before Taxes	246,279	912,202	827,596	690,668	669,883	663,559	601,347	554,732
Income Taxes	47,196	154,542	154,168	168,523	182,877	201,489	197,337	198,039
Net Income	199,083	757,660	673,428	522,145	487,006	462,070	402,472	352,088
Average Shares	164,839	162,340	154,095	145,510	140,497	135,949	134,189	132,724
Balance Sheet								
Total Assets	90,223,508	87,780,507	73,277,772	58,981,285	48,353,330	42,112,763	34,387,677	27,791,801
Total Liabilities	82,386,970	79,962,206	66,369,120	53,275,602	43,574,863	37,952,716	30,989,133	25,274,039
Stockholders' Equity	7,836,538	7,818,301	6,908,652	5,705,683	4,778,467	4,160,047	3,398,544	2,517,762
Shares Outstanding	161,862	161,695	154,292	146,109	138,268	132,768	131,273	129,371
Statistical Record								
Return on Assets %	0.94	0.94	1.02	0.97	1.08	1.21	1.29	1.40
Return on Equity %	10.45	10.29	10.65	9.96	10.90	12.23	13.57	15.12
Net Margin %	24.23	26.02	28.35	26.25	27.04	28.87	27.64	27.07
Asset Turnover	0.04	0.04	0.04	0.04	0.04	0.04	0.05	0.05
Price Range	105.17-84.96	105.17-86.62	92.14-56.59	69.28-47.62	55.62-45.77	52.72-32.78	34.95-29.53	34.60-22.48
P/E Ratio	23.74-19.18	24.40-20.10	23.45-14.40	21.79-14.97	18.12-14.91	17.01-10.57	12.66-10.70	13.06-8.48
Average Yield %	0.71	0.70	0.87	0.97	1.06	0.85	0.92	...

Address: 111 Pine Street, 2nd Floor, San Francisco, CA 94111
Telephone: 415-392-1400

Web Site: www.firstrepublic.com
Officers: James H. Herbert - Chairman, Chief Executive Officer Katherine August-deWilde - Vice-Chairman, President, Chief Operating Officer

Auditors: KPMG LLP
Investor Contact: 415-392-1400
Transfer Agents: Common and Preferred Stock – Computershare Shareowner Services, LLC

FIRSTENERGY CORP

Exchange	Symbol	Price	52Wk Range	Yield	P/E
NYS	FE	$35.91 (6/29/2018)	36.47-29.06	4.01	N/A

*7 Year Price Score 71.92 ***NYSE Composite Index=100** ***12 Month Price Score 103.75**

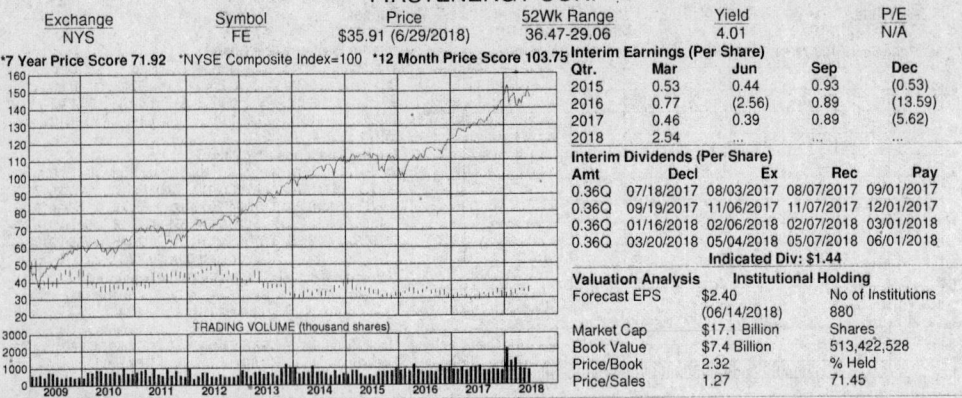

Interim Earnings (Per Share)

Qtr.	Mar	Jun	Sep	Dec
2015	0.53	0.44	0.93	(0.53)
2016	0.77	(2.56)	0.89	(13.59)
2017	0.46	0.39	0.89	(5.62)
2018	2.54			

Interim Dividends (Per Share)

Amt	Decl	Ex	Rec	Pay
0.36Q	07/18/2017	08/03/2017	08/07/2017	09/01/2017
0.36Q	09/19/2017	11/06/2017	11/07/2017	12/01/2017
0.36Q	01/16/2018	02/06/2018	02/07/2018	03/01/2018
0.36Q	03/20/2018	05/04/2018	05/07/2018	06/01/2018

Indicated Div: $1.44

Valuation Analysis

		Institutional Holding	
Forecast EPS	$2.40	No of Institutions	880
	(06/14/2018)		
Market Cap	$17.1 Billion	Shares	513,422,528
Book Value	$7.4 Billion	% Held	71.45
Price/Book	2.32		
Price/Sales	1.27		

Business Summary: Electric Utilities (MIC: 3.1.1 SIC: 4911 NAIC: 221121)

FirstEnergy is a public utility holding company. Through its utility operating subsidiaries, Ohio Edison Company, The Cleveland Electric Illuminating Company, The Toledo Edison Company, Pennsylvania Power Company, Jersey Central Power & Light Company, Metropolitan Edison Company, Pennsylvania Electric Company, Monongahela Power Company, The Potomac Edison Company, West Penn Power Company, American Transmission Systems, Inc. and also Trans-Allegheny Interstate Line Company (the Utilities), Co. is engaged in providing electric service. The Utilities' combined service areas encompass approximately 65,000 square miles in Ohio, Pennsylvania, West Virginia, Maryland, New Jersey and New York.

Recent Developments: For the quarter ended Mar 31 2018, income from continuing operations decreased 31.1% to US$177.0 million from US$257.0 million in the year-earlier quarter. Net income increased 567.8% to US$1.37 billion from US$205.0 million in the year-earlier quarter. Revenues were US$2.98 billion, up 4.2% from US$2.86 billion the year before. Operating income was US$597.0 million versus US$628.0 million in the prior-year quarter, a decrease of 4.9%. Direct operating expenses rose 1.7% to US$1.01 billion from US$995.0 million in the comparable period the year before. Indirect operating expenses increased 11.0% to US$1.37 billion from US$1.23 billion in the equivalent prior-year period.

Prospects: Our evaluation of FirstEnergy Corp. as of Jan. 21, 2018 is the result of our systematic analysis on three basic characteristics: earnings strength, relative valuation, and recent stock price movement. The company has enjoyed a very positive trend in earnings per share over the past 5 quarters and while recent estimates for the company have been mixed, FE has posted better than expected results. Based on operating earnings yield, the company is undervalued when compared to all of the companies in our coverage universe. Share price changes over the past year indicates that FE will perform well over the near term.

Financial Data

(US$ in Thousands)	3 Mos	12/31/2017	12/31/2016	12/31/2015	12/31/2014	12/31/2013	12/31/2012	12/31/2011
Earnings Per Share	(1.80)	(3.88)	(14.49)	1.37	0.71	0.94	1.84	2.21
Cash Flow Per Share	4.50	8.58	7.89	8.17	6.46	6.37	5.54	7.68
Tang Book Value Per Share	3.34	N.M.	1.41	14.17	14.25	14.99	15.87	16.35
Dividends Per Share	1.440	1.440	1.440	1.440	1.440	2.200	2.200	2.200
Dividend Payout %	...	...	...	105.11	202.82	234.04	119.57	99.55
Income Statement								
Total Revenue	2,976,000	14,017,000	14,562,000	15,026,000	15,049,000	14,917,000	15,303,000	16,258,000
EBITDA	958,000	1,408,000	(6,865,000)	3,190,000	2,346,000	2,713,000	3,377,000	3,502,000
Depn & Amortn	294,000	1,138,000	1,313,000	1,282,000	-1,220,000	1,202,000	1,124,000	1,121,000
Income Before Taxes	429,000	(829,000)	(9,232,000)	893,000	171,000	570,000	1,324,000	1,443,000
Income Taxes	252,000	895,000	(3,055,000)	315,000	(42,000)	195,000	553,000	574,000
Net Income	1,369,000	(1,724,000)	(6,177,000)	578,000	299,000	392,000	770,000	885,000
Average Shares	478,000	444,000	426,000	424,000	421,000	419,000	419,000	401,000
Balance Sheet								
Current Assets	2,310,000	3,108,000	2,950,000	3,040,000	3,876,000	3,887,000	3,768,000	3,355,000
Total Assets	38,795,000	42,257,000	43,148,000	52,187,000	52,166,000	50,424,000	50,406,000	47,326,000
Current Liabilities	5,065,000	4,077,000	7,126,000	5,602,000	5,561,000	7,637,000	7,605,000	4,855,000
Long-Term Obligations	16,740,000	21,115,000	18,192,000	19,192,000	19,176,000	15,831,000	15,179,000	15,716,000
Total Liabilities	31,420,000	38,332,000	36,907,000	39,766,000	39,746,000	37,732,000	37,322,000	34,046,000
Stockholders' Equity	7,375,000	3,925,000	6,241,000	12,421,000	12,420,000	12,692,000	13,084,000	13,280,000
Shares Outstanding	476,909	445,334	442,344	423,560	421,102	418,628	418,216	418,216
Statistical Record								
Return on Assets %	N.M.	N.M.	N.M.	1.11	0.58	0.78	1.57	2.16
Return on Equity %	N.M.	N.M.	N.M.	4.65	2.38	3.04	5.83	8.11
EBITDA Margin %	32.19	10.04	N.M.	21.23	15.59	18.19	22.07	21.54
Net Margin %	46.00	N.M.	N.M.	3.85	1.99	2.63	5.03	5.44
Asset Turnover	0.33	0.33	0.30	0.29	0.29	0.30	0.31	0.40
Current Ratio	0.46	0.76	0.41	0.54	0.70	0.51	0.50	0.69
Debt to Equity	2.27	5.38	2.91	1.55	1.54	1.25	1.16	1.18
Price Range	35.05-28.16	35.05-28.16	36.60-30.06	41.37-29.12	40.77-30.22	46.60-31.60	50.87-40.72	46.02-36.25
P/E Ratio	...	...	...	30.20-21.26	57.42-42.56	49.57-33.62	27.65-22.13	20.82-16.40
Average Yield %	4.58	4.63	4.32	4.22	4.26	5.67	4.88	5.24

Address: 76 South Main Street, Akron, OH 44308
Telephone: 800-736-3402

Web Site: www.firstenergycorp.com
Officers: Donald T. Misheff - Chairman Charles E. Jones - President, Chief Executive Officer, Division Officer

Auditors: PricewaterhouseCoopers LLP
Investor Contact: 330-384-3859
Transfer Agents: American Stock Transfer & Trust Company, LLC, New York, NY

FLEETCOR TECHNOLOGIES INC

Exchange	Symbol	Price	52Wk Range	Yield	P/E
NYS	FLT	$210.65 (6/29/2018)	221.72-138.74	N/A	24.81

*7 Year Price Score 123.45 *NYSE Composite Index=100 *12 Month Price Score 112.50

Interim Earnings (Per Share)

Qtr.	Mar	Jun	Sep	Dec
2015	1.00	1.05	1.24	0.56
2016	1.17	1.21	1.36	1.00
2017	1.31	1.39	2.18	3.04
2018	1.88	...	...	...

Interim Dividends (Per Share)

No Dividends Paid

Valuation Analysis		Institutional Holding	
Forecast EPS	$10.43	No of Institutions	
	(06/12/2018)	545	
Market Cap	$18.9 Billion	Shares	
Book Value	$3.9 Billion	92,820,816	
Price/Book	4.86	% Held	
Price/Sales	8.16	86.96	

TRADING VOLUME (thousand shares)

Business Summary: Business Services (MIC: 7.5.2 SIC: 7389 NAIC: 561499)

FleetCor Technologies is engaged in workforce payment products. Co. primarily go to market with its fuel card payments product solutions, corporate payments products, toll products, lodging cards and gift cards. Co.'s primary products are primarily sold to businesses, retailers, major oil companies and marketers and government entities. Co.'s payment programs enable its customers to manage and control their commercial payments, card programs, and employee spending and provide card-accepting merchants. Co. also provides a suite of fleet related and workforce payment solution products, including mobile telematics services, fleet maintenance management and employee benefit.

Recent Developments: For the quarter ended Mar 31 2018, net income increased 41.4% to US$174.9 million from US$123.7 million in the year-earlier quarter. Revenues were US$585.5 million, up 12.5% from US$520.4 million the year before. Operating income was US$260.1 million versus US$195.1 million in the prior-year quarter, an increase of 33.3%. Indirect operating expenses were unchanged at US$325.4 million versus the equivalent prior-year period.

Prospects: Our evaluation of FleetCor Technologies Inc. as of Jan. 21, 2018 is the result of our systematic analysis on three basic characteristics: earnings strength, relative valuation, and recent stock price movement. The company has enjoyed a very positive trend in earnings per share over the past 5 quarters and while recent estimates for the company have been raised by analysts, FLT has posted better than expected results. Based on operating earnings yield, the company is about fairly valued when compared to all of the companies in our coverage universe. Share price changes over the past year indicates that FLT will perform poorly over the near term.

Financial Data
(US$ in Thousands)

	3 Mos	12/31/2017	12/31/2016	12/31/2015	12/31/2014	12/31/2013	12/31/2012	12/31/2011
Earnings Per Share	8.49	7.91	4.75	3.85	4.24	3.36	2.52	1.76
Cash Flow Per Share	9.16	7.42	7.60	8.20	7.21	4.59	1.62	3.47
Income Statement								
Total Revenue	585,500	2,249,538	1,831,546	1,702,865	1,199,390	895,171	707,534	519,591
EBITDA	333,225	1,312,349	949,306	855,251	657,634	486,243	370,283	255,344
Depn & Amortn	72,841	258,449	198,135	190,240	107,249	66,213	46,476	31,090
Income Before Taxes	229,319	946,754	679,275	593,672	521,529	403,569	310,790	210,877
Income Taxes	54,382	153,390	190,534	173,573	144,236	119,068	94,591	63,542
Net Income	174,937	740,200	452,385	362,431	368,707	284,501	216,199	147,335
Average Shares	93,250	93,594	95,213	94,139	86,982	84,655	85,736	83,654
Balance Sheet								
Current Assets	3,907,065	3,549,701	2,527,693	1,945,172	2,137,350	1,353,512	1,195,354	1,122,925
Total Assets	11,692,465	11,318,359	9,626,732	7,891,868	8,674,506	3,932,235	2,721,870	2,324,492
Current Liabilities	4,307,676	4,095,502	3,296,318	2,248,021	2,896,618	1,908,898	1,142,222	1,121,747
Long-Term Obligations	2,867,532	2,902,104	2,521,727	2,061,415	2,168,953	474,939	485,217	278,429
Total Liabilities	7,804,413	7,641,837	6,542,694	5,061,821	5,921,369	2,688,342	1,808,048	1,513,056
Stockholders' Equity	3,888,052	3,676,522	3,084,038	2,830,047	2,753,137	1,243,893	913,822	811,436
Shares Outstanding	89,637	89,803	91,836	92,376	91,662	82,471	81,037	81,860
Statistical Record								
Return on Assets %	7.29	7.07	5.15	4.38	5.85	8.55	8.55	7.74
Return on Equity %	21.89	21.90	15.26	12.98	18.45	26.37	24.99	20.50
EBITDA Margin %	56.91	58.34	51.83	50.22	54.83	54.32	52.33	49.14
Net Margin %	29.88	32.90	24.70	21.28	30.74	31.78	30.56	28.36
Asset Turnover	0.21	0.21	0.21	0.21	0.19	0.27	0.28	0.27
Current Ratio	0.91	0.87	0.77	0.87	0.74	0.71	1.05	1.00
Debt to Equity	0.74	0.79	0.82	0.73	0.79	0.38	0.53	0.34
Price Range	212.50-131.26	193.38-131.26	175.53-113.39	163.86-137.02	156.05-101.69	122.70-53.65	53.65-30.55	37.51-25.25
P/E Ratio	25.03-15.46	24.45-16.59	36.95-23.87	42.56-35.59	36.80-23.98	36.52-15.97	21.29-12.12	21.31-14.35

Address: 5445 Triangle Parkway, Peachtree Corners, GA 30092 Telephone: 770-449-0479	Web Site: www.fleetcor.com Officers: Ronald F. Clarke - Chairman, Chief Executive Officer Eric R. Dey - Chief Financial Officer	Auditors: Ernst & Young LLP Investor Contact: 770-449-0479 Transfer Agents: American Stock Transfer & Trust Company, LLC, Brooklyn, NY

FLOOR & DECOR HOLDINGS INC

Exchange	Symbol	Price	52Wk Range	Yield	P/E
NYS	FND	$49.33 (6/29/2018)	57.50-32.95	N/A	41.45

*7 Year Price Score N/A *NYSE Composite Index=100 *12 Month Price Score 114.07

Interim Earnings (Per Share)

Qtr.	Mar	Jun	Sep	Dec
2016	0.08	0.06	0.16	0.19
2017	0.13	0.20	0.22	0.47
2018	0.30	...	...	...

Interim Dividends (Per Share)

No Dividends Paid

Valuation Analysis / Institutional Holding

Forecast EPS	$1.00	No of Institutions
	(06/12/2018)	197
Market Cap	$4.7 Billion	Shares
Book Value	$487.6 Million	94,835,944
Price/Book	9.72	% Held
Price/Sales	3.20	N/A

Business Summary: Construction Materials (MIC: 8.5.1 SIC: 5211 NAIC: 423310)

Floor & Decor is a holding company. Through its subsidiaries, Co. is a highly differentiated, rapidly growing specialty retailer of hard surface flooring and related accessories. Co. offers a broad in-stock assortment of tile, wood, laminate, and natural stone flooring along with decorative and installation accessories at everyday low prices. Co.'s stores appeal to a variety of customers, including professional installers and commercial businesses, Do it Yourself customers and customers who buy the products for professional installation. Co. also sells products through its Website, FloorandDecor.com. As of Dec. 28, 2017, Co. operates 83 warehouse-format stores across 31 states.

Recent Developments: For the quarter ended Mar 29 2018, net income increased 186.4% to US$31.9 million from US$11.1 million in the year-earlier quarter. Revenues were US$402.9 million, up 31.1% from US$307.3 million the year before. Operating income was US$36.5 million versus US$22.7 million in the prior-year quarter, an increase of 61.0%. Direct operating expenses rose 30.7% to US$237.6 million from US$181.8 million in the comparable period the year before. Indirect operating expenses increased 25.4% to US$128.9 million from US$102.8 million in the equivalent prior-year period.

Prospects: Our evaluation of Floor & Decor Holdings Inc. as of Jan. 21, 2018 is the result of our systematic analysis on three basic characteristics: earnings strength, relative valuation, and recent stock price movement. The company has suffered a very negative trend in earnings per share over the past 5 quarters and while recent estimates for the company have been raised by analysts, FND has posted better than expected results. Based on operating earnings yield, the company is overvalued when compared to all of the companies in our coverage universe. Share price changes over the past year indicates that FND will perform very poorly over the near term.

Financial Data
(US$ in Thousands)

	3 Mos	12/28/2017	12/29/2016	12/31/2015	12/25/2014
Earnings Per Share	1.19	1.03	0.49	0.31	0.18
Cash Flow Per Share	0.98	1.21	1.08	0.24	0.52
Tang Book Value Per Share	1.57	1.11	N.M.	N.M.	...
Income Statement					
Total Revenue	402,948	1,384,767	1,050,759	784,012	584,588
EBITDA	35,461	148,584	79,828	70,923	58,440
Depn & Amortn	(1,045)	36,255	12,512	18,531	24,759
Income Before Taxes	34,722	98,552	54,513	43,006	24,732
Income Taxes	2,851	(4,236)	11,474	16,199	9,634
Net Income	31,871	102,788	43,039	26,807	15,098
Average Shares	104,665	99,660	88,430	86,280	85,651
Balance Sheet					
Current Assets	486,418	503,212	336,215	305,190	...
Total Assets	1,075,882	1,067,992	831,166	748,888	...
Current Liabilities	331,083	359,300	243,714	196,574	...
Long-Term Obligations	169,805	185,562	387,243	176,323	...
Total Liabilities	588,285	625,132	696,883	436,523	...
Stockholders' Equity	487,597	442,860	134,283	312,365	...
Shares Outstanding	96,094	95,509	83,518	83,373	83,333
Statistical Record					
Return on Assets %	12.71	10.88	5.46	...	...
Return on Equity %	38.99	35.82	19.32	...	...
EBITDA Margin %	8.80	10.73	7.60	9.05	10.00
Net Margin %	7.91	7.42	4.10	3.42	2.58
Asset Turnover	1.52	1.47	1.33	...	...
Current Ratio	1.47	1.40	1.38	1.55	...
Debt to Equity	0.35	0.42	2.88	0.56	...
Price Range	52.12-32.05	49.59-32.05	...	...	...
P/E Ratio	43.80-26.93	48.15-31.12	...	...	...

Address: 2233 Lake Park Drive, Smyrna, GA 30080
Telephone: 404-471-1634

Web Site: www.FloorandDecor.com
Officers: Norman H. Axelrod - Chairman George Vincent West - Vice-Chairman

Auditors: Ernst & Young LLP
Transfer Agents: American Stock Transfer & Trust Company, LLC

FLOWERS FOODS, INC.

Exchange	Symbol	Price	52Wk Range	Yield	P/E	Div Acheiver
NYS	FLO	$20.83 (6/29/2018)	22.71-17.00	3.46	31.56	14 Years

*7 Year Price Score 83.62   *NYSE Composite Index=100   ***12 Month Price Score 104.70**

Interim Earnings (Per Share)

Qtr.	Apr	Jul	Oct	Jan
2015-16	0.29	0.24	0.21	0.15

Qtr.	Apr	Jul	Oct	Dec
2016	0.28	0.24	0.19	0.06
2017	0.29	0.21	(0.16)	0.37
2018	0.24	...	...	...

Interim Dividends (Per Share)

Amt	Decl	Ex	Rec	Pay
0.17Q	08/18/2017	08/30/2017	09/01/2017	09/15/2017
0.17Q	11/17/2017	11/30/2017	12/01/2017	12/15/2017
0.17Q	02/16/2018	03/01/2018	03/02/2018	03/16/2018
0.18Q	05/24/2018	06/06/2018	06/07/2018	06/21/2018

Indicated Div: $0.72 (Div. Reinv. Plan)

Valuation Analysis   **Institutional Holding**

Forecast EPS	$1.07	No of Institutions
	(06/14/2018)	462
Market Cap	$4.4 Billion	Shares
Book Value	$1.3 Billion	165,937,952
Price/Book	3.40	% Held
Price/Sales	1.11	94.84

Business Summary: Food (MIC: 1.2.1 SIC: 2053 NAIC: 311813)

Flowers Foods is a producer and marketer of bakery products. Co. operates two business segments: a direct-store-delivery (DSD) and a warehouse delivery (warehouse). The DSD segment produces breads, buns, rolls, tortillas and snack cakes to retail and foodservice customers. The Warehouse segment produces snack cakes and frozen breads and rolls. Co.'s fresh and frozen products are delivered to customers' warehouse nationwide through contract carriers. Co.'s Warehouse Segment markets a line of breads and rolls under the Alpine Valley bread brand primarily for retail and foodservice customers. This segment's snack cakes are sold under the Mrs. Freshley's, Broad Street Bakery, and store brands.

Recent Developments: For the quarter ended Apr 21 2018, net income decreased 15.2% to US$51.2 million from US$60.4 million in the year-earlier quarter. Revenues were US$1.21 billion, up 1.6% from US$1.19 billion the year before. Operating income was US$76.6 million versus US$98.2 million in the prior-year quarter, a decrease of 22.0%. Direct operating expenses rose 2.8% to US$625.1 million from US$608.1 million in the comparable period the year before. Indirect operating expenses increased 4.8% to US$504.7 million from US$481.4 million in the equivalent prior-year period.

Prospects: Our evaluation of Flowers Foods Inc. as of Jan. 21, 2018 is the result of our systematic analysis on three basic characteristics: earnings strength, relative valuation, and recent stock price movement. The company has enjoyed a very positive trend in earnings per share over the past 5 quarters. However, while recent estimates for the company have been mixed, FLO has posted better than expected results. Based on operating earnings yield, the company is about fairly valued when compared to all of the companies in our coverage universe. Share price changes over the past year indicates that FLO will perform in line with the market over the near term.

Financial Data
(US$ in Thousands)

	3 Mos	12/30/2017	12/31/2016	01/02/2016	01/03/2015	12/28/2013	12/29/2012	12/31/2011
Earnings Per Share	0.66	0.71	0.78	0.89	0.82	1.09	0.65	0.60
Cash Flow Per Share	1.51	0.71	1.66	1.54	1.47	1.30	1.06	0.66
Tang Book Value Per Share	0.44	0.21	N.M.	N.M.	0.93	0.66	0.97	1.95
Dividends Per Share	0.680	0.670	0.625	0.568	0.485	0.444	0.420	0.389
Dividend Payout %	103.03	94.37	80.13	63.76	59.15	40.75	64.29	64.81
Income Statement								
Total Revenue	1,206,453	3,920,733	3,926,885	3,778,505	3,748,973	3,751,005	3,046,491	2,773,356
EBITDA	116,871	282,357	380,257	414,679	392,595	441,933	311,911	276,526
Depn & Amortn	44,189	119,445	116,367	116,800	117,200	106,700	93,400	87,500
Income Before Taxes	69,781	149,293	249,537	293,031	268,054	322,373	208,772	191,966
Income Taxes	18,534	(827)	85,761	103,840	92,315	91,479	72,651	68,538
Net Income	51,247	150,120	163,776	189,191	175,739	230,894	136,121	123,428
Average Shares	211,311	210,435	210,354	213,356	213,092	211,927	207,673	205,321
Balance Sheet								
Current Assets	533,220	507,191	476,842	537,515	460,563	487,405	464,451	378,570
Total Assets	2,670,257	2,659,724	2,761,068	2,885,168	2,408,974	2,504,014	1,995,849	1,553,998
Current Liabilities	373,804	393,951	340,624	403,738	315,553	327,782	354,958	268,419
Long-Term Obligations	818,141	820,141	946,667	933,932	728,940	892,478	535,016	283,406
Total Liabilities	1,378,726	1,409,047	1,550,988	1,642,086	1,285,930	1,427,825	1,137,229	795,030
Stockholders' Equity	1,291,531	1,250,677	1,210,080	1,243,082	1,123,044	1,076,189	858,620	758,968
Shares Outstanding	210,813	210,526	208,422	212,266	209,347	208,562	207,409	203,971
Statistical Record								
Return on Assets %	5.21	2.77	5.82	7.17	7.04	10.29	7.69	8.60
Return on Equity %	11.11	6.10	13.39	16.04	15.72	23.93	16.88	15.92
EBITDA Margin %	9.69	7.20	9.68	10.97	10.47	11.78	10.24	9.97
Net Margin %	4.25	3.83	4.17	5.01	4.69	6.16	4.47	4.45
Asset Turnover	1.46	0.72	1.39	1.43	1.50	1.67	1.72	1.93
Current Ratio	1.43	1.29	1.40	1.33	1.46	1.49	1.31	1.41
Debt to Equity	0.63	0.66	0.78	0.75	0.65	0.83	0.62	0.37
Price Range	22.69-17.00	20.84-17.00	21.85-14.60	27.09-18.85	22.19-17.67	25.39-15.51	16.09-12.30	15.31-10.81
P/E Ratio	34.38-25.76	29.35-23.94	28.01-18.72	30.44-21.18	27.06-21.55	23.29-14.23	24.75-18.92	25.52-18.02
Average Yield %	3.55	3.54	3.54	2.51	2.43	2.08	3.01	2.99

Address: 1919 Flowers Circle,	**Web Site:** www.flowersfoods.com	**Auditors:** PricewaterhouseCoopers LLP
Thomasville, GA 31757	**Officers:** Allen L. Shiver - President, Chief Executive	**Investor Contact:** 229-227-2348
Telephone: 229-226-9110	Officer R. Steve Kinsey - Executive Vice President,	**Transfer Agents:** Computershare,
	Chief Financial Officer, Chief Administrative Officer	Providence, RI

FLOWSERVE CORP

Exchange	Symbol	Price	52Wk Range	Yield	P/E
NYS	FLS	$40.40 (6/29/2018)	47.88-37.58	1.88	N/A

*7 Year Price Score 68.65 ***NYSE Composite Index=100** ***12 Month Price Score 98.94**

Interim Earnings (Per Share)

Qtr.	Mar	Jun	Sep	Dec
2015	0.20	0.56	0.70	0.54
2016	0.29	0.48	(0.16)	0.50
2017	0.11	0.32	0.36	(0.81)
2018	0.12	...	...	...

Interim Dividends (Per Share)

Amt	Decl	Ex	Rec	Pay
0.19Q	09/05/2017	09/21/2017	09/22/2017	10/06/2017
0.19Q	12/21/2017	01/04/2018	01/05/2018	01/19/2018
0.19Q	02/28/2018	03/28/2018	03/29/2018	04/13/2018
0.19Q	05/24/2018	06/21/2018	06/22/2018	07/06/2018
		Indicated Div: $0.76		

Valuation Analysis — **Institutional Holding**

Forecast EPS	$1.60	No of Institutions
(06/14/2018)		615
Market Cap	$5.3 Billion	Shares
Book Value	$1.7 Billion	158,437,456
Price/Book	3.13	% Held
Price/Sales	1.42	85.00

TRADING VOLUME (thousand shares)

Business Summary: Industrial Machinery & Equipment (MIC: 7.2.1 SIC: 3561 NAIC: 333911)

Flowserve manufactures and provides aftermarket service flow control systems. Co. develops and manufactures flow control equipment integral to the movement, control and protection of the flow of materials in its customers' processes. Co.'s segments include: Engineered Product Division for long lead time, custom and other engineered pumps and pump systems, mechanical seals, auxiliary systems and replacement parts and related services; Industrial Product Division for engineered and pre-configured industrial pumps and pump systems and related products and services; and Flow Control Division for engineered and industrial valves, control valves, actuators and controls and related services.

Recent Developments: For the quarter ended Mar 31 2018, net income decreased 14.7% to US$16.5 million from US$19.3 million in the year-earlier quarter. Revenues were US$920.0 million, up 6.2% from US$866.3 million the year before. Operating income was US$45.4 million versus US$50.7 million in the prior-year quarter, a decrease of 10.3%. Direct operating expenses rose 8.6% to US$648.5 million from US$597.3 million in the comparable period the year before. Indirect operating expenses increased 3.5% to US$226.0 million from US$218.3 million in the equivalent prior-year period.

Prospects: Our evaluation of Flowserve Corp. as of Jan. 21, 2018 is the result of our systematic analysis on three basic characteristics: earnings strength, relative valuation, and recent stock price movement. The company has produced a positive trend in earnings per share over the past 5 quarters and while recent estimates for the company have been mixed, FLS has posted better than expected results. Based on operating earnings yield, the company is about fairly valued when compared to all of the companies in our coverage universe. Share price changes over the past year indicates that FLS will perform poorly over the near term.

Financial Data
(US$ in Thousands)

	3 Mos	12/31/2017	12/31/2016	12/31/2015	12/31/2014	12/31/2013	12/31/2012	12/31/2011
Earnings Per Share	(0.01)	0.02	1.11	2.00	3.76	3.41	2.84	2.55
Cash Flow Per Share	1.43	2.38	1.74	3.13	4.17	3.44	3.29	1.31
Tang Book Value Per Share	1.88	1.74	1.76	1.66	5.34	4.39	4.75	6.56
Dividends Per Share	0.760	0.570	0.760	0.720	0.640	0.560	0.480	0.427
Dividend Payout %	...	2,850.00	68.47	36.00	17.02	16.42	16.92	16.75
Income Statement								
Total Revenue	919,954	3,660,831	3,991,462	4,561,030	4,877,885	4,954,619	4,751,339	4,510,201
EBITDA	64,015	408,154	369,430	575,041	873,024	797,681	725,751	693,897
Depn & Amortn	28,913	101,438	99,897	99,501	93,307	90,695	88,572	90,653
Income Before Taxes	21,862	250,415	212,200	412,335	721,075	654,004	594,613	568,644
Income Taxes	8,571	258,679	75,286	148,922	208,305	204,701	160,766	158,524
Net Income	15,143	2,652	145,060	267,669	518,824	485,530	448,339	428,582
Average Shares	131,095	131,358	130,975	133,811	137,843	142,429	157,968	168,306
Balance Sheet								
Current Assets	2,411,313	2,558,745	2,331,361	2,631,792	2,794,163	2,847,382	2,740,216	2,628,354
Total Assets	4,770,316	4,910,474	4,742,762	5,103,850	4,968,020	5,036,733	4,810,958	4,622,614
Current Liabilities	1,052,961	1,242,908	1,178,141	1,359,962	1,471,875	1,558,099	1,590,625	1,470,321
Long-Term Obligations	1,501,423	1,499,658	1,485,258	1,570,836	1,101,791	1,127,619	869,116	451,593
Total Liabilities	3,085,089	3,255,887	3,094,528	3,437,373	3,036,458	3,166,354	2,920,739	2,352,801
Stockholders' Equity	1,685,227	1,654,587	1,648,234	1,666,477	1,931,562	1,870,379	1,890,219	2,269,813
Shares Outstanding	130,520	130,322	129,813	129,090	134,349	137,163	144,405	161,718
Statistical Record								
Return on Assets %	N.M.	0.05	2.94	5.32	10.37	9.86	9.48	9.44
Return on Equity %	N.M.	0.16	8.73	14.88	27.29	25.82	21.50	19.60
EBITDA Margin %	6.96	11.15	9.26	12.61	17.90	16.10	15.27	15.39
Net Margin %	1.65	0.07	3.63	5.87	10.64	9.80	9.44	9.50
Asset Turnover	0.78	0.76	0.81	0.91	0.98	1.01	1.00	0.99
Current Ratio	2.29	2.06	1.98	1.94	1.90	1.83	1.72	1.79
Debt to Equity	0.89	0.91	0.90	0.94	0.57	0.60	0.46	0.20
Price Range	51.14-37.58	51.85-37.58	52.32-35.40	62.86-39.85	81.55-54.80	78.83-48.93	48.93-33.39	45.00-23.33
P/E Ratio	...	N.M.	47.14-31.89	31.43-19.93	21.69-14.57	23.12-14.35	17.23-11.76	17.65-9.15
Average Yield %	1.73	1.26	1.67	1.42	0.88	0.96	1.19	1.19

Address: 5215 N. O'Connor Blvd.,	Web Site: www.flowserve.com	Auditors: PricewaterhouseCoopers LLP
Suite 2300, Irving, TX 75039	Officers: Roger L. Fix - Chairman Robert Scott Rowe	Transfer Agents: Wells Fargo Bank,
Telephone: 972-443-6500	- President, Chief Executive Officer	N.A., Mendota Heights, MN
Fax: 972-443-6800		

FLUOR CORP.

Exchange	Symbol	Price	52Wk Range	Yield	P/E
NYS	FLR	$48.78 (6/29/2018)	61.48-37.23	N/A	60.98

*7 Year Price Score N/A *NYSE Composite Index=100 *12 Month Price Score N/A

Interim Earnings (Per Share)

Qtr.	Mar	Jun	Sep	Dec
2015	0.96	1.00	1.17	(0.32)
2016	0.74	0.72	0.03	0.50
2017	0.43	(0.17)	0.67	0.43
2018	(0.13)	...	...	...

Interim Dividends (Per Share)

Amt	Decl	Ex	Rec	Pay
0.21Q	08/02/2017	08/31/2017	09/05/2017	10/03/2017
0.21Q	11/01/2017	12/04/2017	12/05/2017	01/03/2018
0.21Q	01/31/2018	02/28/2018	03/01/2018	04/03/2018
0.21Q	05/02/2018	05/31/2018	06/01/2018	07/03/2018

Indicated Div: $0.84

Valuation Analysis   **Institutional Holding**

Forecast EPS	$2.17	No of Institutions
	(06/13/2018)	789
Market Cap	N/A	Shares
Book Value	$3.0 Billion	142,010,832
Price/Book	N/A	% Held
Price/Sales	N/A	77.17

Business Summary: Construction Services (MIC: 7.5.4 SIC: 1629 NAIC: 237990)

Fluor is a holding company. Through its subsidiaries, Co. provides engineering, procurement, construction, fabrication and modularization, commissioning and maintenance as well as project management services. Co. serves a set of industries including oil and gas, chemicals and petrochemicals, mining and metals, transportation, power, life sciences and manufacturing. Co. is also a service provider to the U.S. federal government and governments abroad; and it performs operations, maintenance and asset integrity activities for industrial clients. Co. has four segments: Energy, Chemicals & Mining; Industrial, Infrastructure & Power; Maintenance, Modification & Asset Integrity; and Government.

Recent Developments: For the quarter ended Mar 31 2018, net loss amounted to US$12.1 million versus net income of US$77.4 million in the year-earlier quarter. Revenues were US$4.82 billion, down 0.3% from US$4.84 billion the year before. Direct operating expenses rose 1.7% to US$4.77 billion from US$4.69 billion in the comparable period the year before. Indirect operating expenses increased 18.2% to US$66.9 million from US$56.6 million in the equivalent prior-year period.

Prospects: Our evaluation of Fluor Corp. as of Jan. 21, 2018 is the result of our systematic analysis on three basic characteristics: earnings strength, relative valuation, and recent stock price movement. The company has produced a positive trend in earnings per share over the past 5 quarters and while recent estimates for the company have been mixed, FLR has posted better than expected results. Based on operating earnings yield, the company is overvalued when compared to all of the companies in our coverage universe. Share price changes over the past year indicates that FLR will perform very poorly over the near term.

Financial Data

(US$ in Thousands)	3 Mos	12/31/2017	12/31/2016	12/31/2015	12/31/2014	12/31/2013	12/31/2012	12/31/2011
Earnings Per Share	0.80	1.36	2.00	2.81	3.20	4.06	2.71	3.40
Cash Flow Per Share	1.40	4.31	5.06	5.86	4.08	4.85	3.75	5.16
Tang Book Value Per Share	17.18	19.85	18.62	20.76	20.17	22.59	19.96	19.53
Dividends Per Share	0.840	0.840	0.840	0.840	0.840	0.640	0.640	0.500
Dividend Payout %	105.00	61.76	42.00	29.89	26.25	15.76	23.62	14.71
Income Statement								
Total Revenue	4,823,770	19,520,970	19,036,525	18,114,048	21,531,577	27,351,573	27,577,135	23,381,399
EBITDA	71,095	651,572	825,156	944,371	1,408,916	1,397,141	946,368	1,187,395
Depn & Amortn	70,571	225,269	225,913	189,738	192,594	207,098	212,381	201,939
Income Before Taxes	(9,055)	386,441	546,600	726,552	1,204,909	1,177,599	733,505	1,001,816
Income Taxes	3,006	121,972	219,151	245,888	352,815	354,573	162,438	303,729
Net Income	(17,590)	191,377	281,401	412,512	510,909	667,711	456,330	593,728
Average Shares	140,099	140,893	140,912	146,722	159,616	164,354	168,491	174,564
Balance Sheet								
Current Assets	5,694,762	5,601,257	5,610,270	5,278,287	5,758,047	6,003,683	6,094,137	5,880,623
Total Assets	9,425,226	9,327,692	9,216,417	7,631,506	8,194,429	8,323,850	8,276,043	8,270,276
Current Liabilities	4,078,306	3,574,170	3,816,029	2,935,352	3,330,853	3,407,160	3,887,114	3,840,111
Long-Term Obligations	1,607,653	1,591,598	1,517,949	992,664	991,685	496,604	520,205	513,500
Total Liabilities	6,428,915	5,985,382	6,091,226	4,634,159	5,083,558	4,566,863	4,934,748	4,874,751
Stockholders' Equity	2,996,311	3,342,310	3,125,191	2,997,347	3,110,871	3,756,987	3,341,295	3,395,525
Shares Outstanding	140,597	139,918	139,258	139,018	148,633	161,287	162,359	168,979
Statistical Record								
Return on Assets %	1.22	2.06	3.33	5.21	6.19	8.04	5.50	7.48
Return on Equity %	3.64	5.92	9.17	13.51	14.88	18.81	13.51	17.23
EBITDA Margin %	1.47	3.34	4.33	5.21	6.54	5.11	3.43	5.08
Net Margin %	N.M.	0.98	1.48	2.28	2.37	2.44	1.65	2.54
Asset Turnover	2.10	2.11	2.25	2.29	2.61	3.30	3.32	2.94
Current Ratio	1.40	1.57	1.47	1.80	1.73	1.76	1.57	1.53
Debt to Equity	0.54	0.48	0.49	0.33	0.32	0.13	0.16	0.15

Address: 6700 Las Colinas Boulevard, Irving, TX 75039
Telephone: 469-398-7000

Web Site: www.fluor.com
Officers: David T. Seaton - Chairman, Chief Executive Officer, Chief Operating Officer, Division Officer Bruce A. Stanski - Executive Vice President, Chief Financial Officer, Division Officer

Auditors: Ernst & Young LLP
Investor Contact: 469-398-7189
Transfer Agents: Computershare, Pittsburgh, PA

FMC CORP.

Exchange	Symbol	Price	52Wk Range	Yield	P/E
NYS	FMC	$89.21 (6/29/2018)	98.17-73.05	0.74	12.97

*7 Year Price Score 115.07 *NYSE Composite Index=100 *12 Month Price Score 100.28

Interim Earnings (Per Share)

Qtr.	Mar	Jun	Sep	Dec
2015	(0.35)	5.52	(0.02)	(1.52)
2016	0.36	0.49	0.59	0.12
2017	(0.93)	0.56	0.41	3.95
2018	1.96	...	...	...

Interim Dividends (Per Share)

Amt	Decl	Ex	Rec	Pay
0.165Q	07/21/2017	09/28/2017	09/29/2017	10/19/2017
0.165Q	12/12/2017	12/28/2017	12/29/2017	01/18/2018
0.165Q	02/16/2018	03/28/2018	03/29/2018	04/19/2018
0.165Q	04/24/2018	06/28/2018	06/29/2018	07/19/2018

Indicated Div: $0.66

Valuation Analysis

Forecast EPS	$6.10
	(06/13/2018)
Market Cap	$12.0 Billion
Book Value	$3.0 Billion
Price/Book	4.02
Price/Sales	3.44

Institutional Holding

No of Institutions	778
Shares	137,575,536
% Held	87.63

Business Summary: Agricultural Chemicals (MIC: 8.3.3 SIC: 2812 NAIC: 325181)

FMC is chemical company serving agricultural, consumer and industrial markets globally. Co. operates in three business segments: FMC Agricultural Solutions, FMC Health and Nutrition and FMC Lithium. Co.'s FMC Agricultural Solutions segment develops, markets and sells three classes of crop protection chemicals, including insecticides, herbicides and fungicides. The FMC Health and Nutrition segment focuses on nutritional ingredients, health excipients, and functional health ingredients. Co.'s FMC Lithium segment manufactures lithium for use in a range of lithium products, which are used primarily in energy storage, specialty polymers and chemical synthesis application.

Recent Developments: For the quarter ended Mar 31 2018, income from continuing operations increased 484.7% to US$263.1 million from US$45.0 million in the year-earlier quarter. Net income amounted to US$269.6 million versus a net loss of US$123.8 million in the year-earlier quarter. Revenues were US$1.21 billion, up 103.1% from US$596.0 million the year before. Direct operating expenses rose 72.7% to US$656.0 million from US$379.8 million in the comparable period the year before. Indirect operating expenses increased 25.1% to US$188.6 million from US$150.8 million in the equivalent prior-year period.

Prospects: Our evaluation of FMC Corp. as of Jan. 21, 2018 is the result of our systematic analysis on three basic characteristics: earnings strength, relative valuation, and recent stock price movement. The company has enjoyed a very positive trend in earnings per share over the past 5 quarters and while recent estimates for the company have been mixed, FMC has posted better than expected results. Based on operating earnings yield, the company is about fairly valued when compared to all of the companies in our coverage universe. Share price changes over the past year indicates that FMC will perform very well over the near term.

Financial Data

(US$ in Thousands)	3 Mos	12/31/2017	12/31/2016	12/31/2015	12/31/2014	12/31/2013	12/31/2012	12/31/2011
Earnings Per Share	6.88	3.99	1.56	3.66	2.29	2.16	3.00	2.55
Cash Flow Per Share	2.17	2.50	3.71	(2.68)	2.80	2.43	2.61	2.68
Tang Book Value Per Share	N.M.	N.M.	2.63	1.62	6.73	6.21	7.05	5.92
Dividends Per Share	0.660	0.660	0.660	0.660	0.600	0.540	0.405	0.300
Dividend Payout %	9.59	16.54	42.31	18.03	26.20	25.00	13.50	11.76
Income Statement								
Total Revenue	1,210,700	2,878,600	3,282,400	3,276,500	4,037,700	3,874,800	3,748,300	3,377,900
EBITDA	404,700	325,500	507,900	23,900	649,300	753,600	757,300	688,400
Depn & Amortn	39,100	65,700	86,400	74,100	103,900	94,600	99,100	101,100
Income Before Taxes	331,700	180,700	338,800	(130,300)	485,900	616,800	612,900	547,900
Income Taxes	68,700	264,100	93,900	47,400	73,500	148,600	146,700	136,500
Net Income	267,200	535,800	209,100	489,000	307,500	293,900	416,200	365,900
Average Shares	136,157	134,255	134,538	133,696	134,282	136,137	138,813	143,308
Balance Sheet								
Current Assets	4,335,600	3,652,700	2,849,200	2,971,900	2,934,400	2,945,000	2,181,800	1,869,400
Total Assets	10,149,100	9,206,300	6,139,300	6,325,900	5,340,500	5,235,200	4,373,900	3,743,500
Current Liabilities	2,686,000	2,209,400	1,438,200	1,453,300	1,910,400	1,986,700	1,135,400	919,900
Long-Term Obligations	2,993,200	2,993,400	1,798,800	2,036,300	1,153,400	1,154,100	908,800	779,100
Total Liabilities	7,162,500	6,524,500	4,181,600	4,460,200	3,810,000	3,715,400	2,893,600	2,502,900
Stockholders' Equity	2,986,600	2,681,800	1,957,700	1,865,700	1,530,500	1,519,800	1,480,300	1,240,600
Shares Outstanding	134,514	134,330	133,690	133,655	133,317	132,885	137,670	139,674
Statistical Record								
Return on Assets %	11.46	6.98	3.35	8.38	5.82	6.12	10.23	10.36
Return on Equity %	38.13	23.10	10.91	28.80	20.16	19.59	30.51	30.85
EBITDA Margin %	33.43	11.31	15.47	0.73	16.08	19.45	20.20	20.38
Net Margin %	22.07	18.61	6.37	14.92	7.62	7.58	11.10	10.83
Asset Turnover	0.43	0.38	0.53	0.56	0.76	0.81	0.92	0.96
Current Ratio	1.61	1.65	1.98	2.04	1.54	1.48	1.92	2.03
Debt to Equity	1.00	1.12	0.92	1.09	0.75	0.76	0.61	0.63
Price Range	98.17-69.59	95.54-57.03	59.00-33.53	64.59-32.93	83.10-51.60	75.46-55.45	58.59-43.48	46.43-32.91
P/E Ratio	14.27-10.11	23.94-14.29	37.82-21.49	17.65-9.00	36.29-22.53	34.94-25.67	19.53-14.49	18.21-12.91
Average Yield %	0.79	0.85	1.44	1.31	0.88	0.83	0.77	0.75

Address: 2929 Walnut Street, Philadelphia, PA 19104 **Telephone:** 215-299-6000 **Fax:** 215-299-5998	**Web Site:** www.fmc.com **Officers:** Pierre R. Brondeau - Chairman, President, Chief Executive Officer Mark A. Douglas - Division Officer, President, Chief Operating Officer	**Auditors:** KPMG LLP **Investor Contact:** 215-299-6119 **Transfer Agents:** Wells Fargo Bank, N.A., Mendota Heights, MN

FOOT LOCKER, INC.

Exchange	Symbol	Price	52Wk Range	Yield	P/E
NYS	FL	$52.65 (6/29/2018)	58.92-29.24	2.62	23.40

*7 Year Price Score 74.05 *NYSE Composite Index=100 *12 Month Price Score 117.03

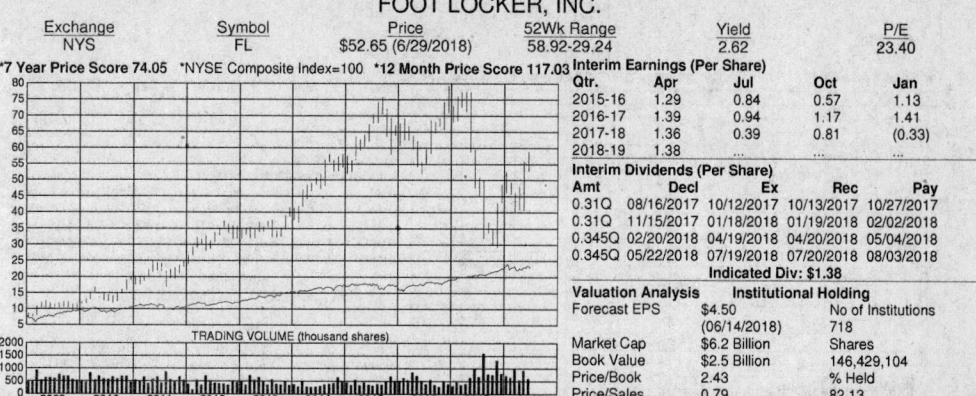

Interim Earnings (Per Share)

Qtr.	Apr	Jul	Oct	Jan
2015-16	1.29	0.84	0.57	1.13
2016-17	1.39	0.94	1.17	1.41
2017-18	1.36	0.39	0.81	(0.33)
2018-19	1.38	...	...	...

Interim Dividends (Per Share)

Amt	Decl	Ex	Rec	Pay
0.31Q	08/16/2017	10/12/2017	10/13/2017	10/27/2017
0.31Q	11/15/2017	01/18/2018	01/19/2018	02/02/2018
0.345Q	02/20/2018	04/19/2018	04/20/2018	05/04/2018
0.345Q	05/22/2018	07/19/2018	07/20/2018	08/03/2018

Indicated Div: $1.38

Valuation Analysis   **Institutional Holding**

Forecast EPS	$4.50	No of Institutions
(06/14/2018)		718
Market Cap	$6.2 Billion	Shares
Book Value	$2.5 Billion	146,429,104
Price/Book	2.43	% Held
Price/Sales	0.79	82.13

Business Summary: Retail - Apparel and Accessories (MIC: 2.1.5 SIC: 5661 NAIC: 448210)

Foot Locker is a retailer of athletically inspired shoes and apparel. Co. operates in two reportable segments: Athletic Stores and Direct-to-Customers. The Athletic Stores segment is an athletic footwear and apparel retailers, with formats that include Foot Locker, Kids Foot Locker, Lady Foot Locker, Champs Sports, Footaction, and Runners Point. The Direct-to-Customers segment includes Footlocker.com, Inc. and other affiliates, including Eastbay, Inc., and Co.'s international ecommerce businesses, which sell to customers through their Internet and mobile sites and catalogs. As of Feb 3 2018, Co. operated 3,310 mall-based stores in the U. S., Canada, Europe, Australia, and New Zealand.

Recent Developments: For the quarter ended May 5 2018, net income decreased 8.3% to US$165.0 million from US$180.0 million in the year-earlier quarter. Revenues were US$2.03 billion, up 1.2% from US$2.00 billion the year before. Operating income was US$224.0 million versus US$268.0 million in the prior-year quarter, a decrease of 16.4%. Direct operating expenses rose 2.9% to US$1.36 billion from US$1.32 billion in the comparable period the year before. Indirect operating expenses increased 7.3% to US$442.0 million from US$412.0 million in the equivalent prior-year period.

Prospects: Our evaluation of Foot Locker Inc. as of Jan. 21, 2018 is the result of our systematic analysis on three basic characteristics: earnings strength, relative valuation, and recent stock price movement. The company has managed to produce a neutral trend in earnings per share over the past 5 quarters and while recent estimates for the company have been raised by analysts, FL has posted better than expected results. Based on operating earnings yield, the company is undervalued when compared to all of the companies in our coverage universe. Share price changes over the past year indicates that FL will perform very poorly over the near term.

Financial Data

(US$ in Thousands)	3 Mos	02/03/2018	01/28/2017	01/30/2016	01/31/2015	02/01/2014	02/02/2013	01/28/2012
Earnings Per Share	2.25	2.22	4.91	3.84	3.56	2.85	2.58	1.80
Cash Flow Per Share	9.01	6.29	6.11	5.37	4.96	3.58	2.71	3.26
Tang Book Value Per Share	19.97	19.30	19.11	17.17	16.26	15.58	14.61	12.61
Dividends Per Share	1.275	1.240	1.100	1.000	0.880	0.800	0.720	0.660
Dividend Payout %	56.67	55.86	22.40	26.04	24.72	28.07	27.91	36.67
Income Statement								
Total Revenue	2,025,000	7,782,000	7,766,000	7,412,000	7,151,000	6,505,000	6,182,000	5,623,000
EBITDA	272,000	749,000	1,164,000	989,000	953,000	801,000	730,000	551,000
Depn & Amortn	45,000	173,000	158,000	148,000	139,000	133,000	118,000	110,000
Income Before Taxes	229,000	578,000	1,004,000	837,000	809,000	663,000	607,000	435,000
Income Taxes	64,000	294,000	340,000	296,000	289,000	234,000	210,000	157,000
Net Income	165,000	284,000	664,000	541,000	520,000	429,000	397,000	278,000
Average Shares	119,100	127,900	135,100	140,800	146,000	150,500	154,000	154,400
Balance Sheet								
Current Assets	2,540,000	2,551,000	2,633,000	2,606,000	2,456,000	2,350,000	2,363,000	2,079,000
Total Assets	3,963,000	3,961,000	3,840,000	3,775,000	3,577,000	3,487,000	3,367,000	3,050,000
Current Liabilities	653,000	616,000	612,000	700,000	696,000	626,000	636,000	548,000
Long-Term Obligations	125,000	125,000	127,000	129,000	132,000	136,000	133,000	135,000
Total Liabilities	1,420,000	1,442,000	1,130,000	1,222,000	1,081,000	991,000	990,000	940,000
Stockholders' Equity	2,543,000	2,519,000	2,710,000	2,553,000	2,496,000	2,496,000	2,377,000	2,110,000
Shares Outstanding	117,261	119,829	131,496	136,977	140,864	145,427	150,070	151,619
Statistical Record								
Return on Assets %	6.86	7.16	17.49	14.76	14.76	12.55	12.17	9.38
Return on Equity %	10.03	10.69	25.30	21.49	20.89	17.66	17.41	13.48
EBITDA Margin %	13.43	9.62	14.99	13.34	13.33	12.31	11.81	9.80
Net Margin %	8.15	3.65	8.55	7.30	7.27	6.59	6.42	4.94
Asset Turnover	1.99	1.96	2.05	2.02	2.03	1.90	1.90	1.90
Current Ratio	3.89	4.14	4.30	3.72	3.53	3.75	3.72	3.79
Debt to Equity	0.05	0.05	0.05	0.05	0.05	0.05	0.06	0.06
Price Range	77.35-29.24	77.35-29.24	79.20-51.79	75.76-52.43	57.98-36.73	41.44-31.79	37.27-26.24	26.67-16.77
P/E Ratio	34.38-13.00	34.84-13.17	16.13-10.55	19.73-13.65	16.29-10.32	14.54-11.15	14.45-10.17	14.82-9.32
Average Yield %	2.84	2.37	1.71	1.54	1.74	2.26	2.21	3.04

Address: 330 West 34th Street, New York, NY 10001 Telephone: 212-720-3700	Web Site: www.footlocker-inc.com Officers: Richard A. Johnson - Chairman, President, Chief Executive Officer, Executive Vice President, Chief Operating Officer, Division Officer Lauren B. Peters - Executive Vice President, Chief Financial Officer	Auditors: KPMG LLP Investor Contact: 212-720-3700 Transfer Agents: Computershare, Providence, R.I.

FORD MOTOR CO. (DE)

Exchange	Symbol	Price	52Wk Range	Yield	P/E
NYS	F	$11.07 (6/29/2018)	13.23-10.24	5.42	5.74

*7 Year Price Score 69.99 *NYSE Composite Index=100 *12 Month Price Score 98.15

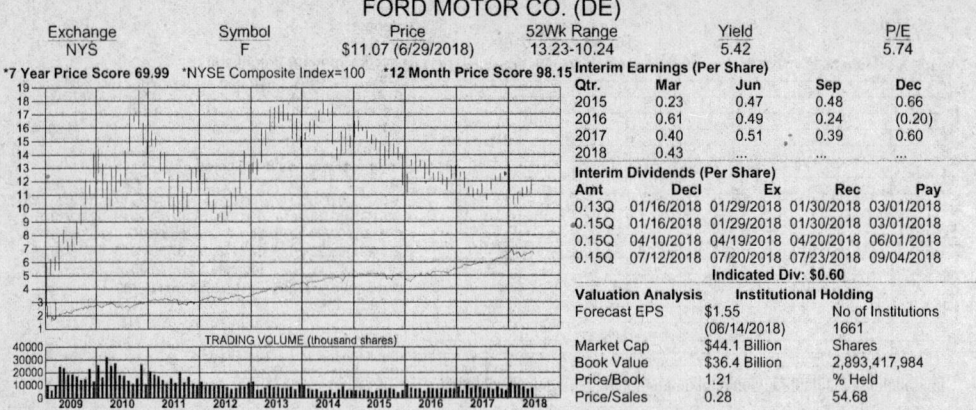

Interim Earnings (Per Share)

Qtr.	Mar	Jun	Sep	Dec
2015	0.23	0.47	0.48	0.66
2016	0.61	0.49	0.24	(0.20)
2017	0.40	0.51	0.39	0.60
2018	0.43	...	...	...

Interim Dividends (Per Share)

Amt	Decl	Ex	Rec	Pay
0.13Q	01/16/2018	01/29/2018	01/30/2018	03/01/2018
0.15Q	01/16/2018	01/29/2018	01/30/2018	03/01/2018
0.15Q	04/10/2018	04/19/2018	04/20/2018	06/01/2018
0.15Q	07/12/2018	07/20/2018	07/23/2018	09/04/2018

Indicated Div: $0.60

Valuation Analysis — **Institutional Holding**

Forecast EPS	$1.55 (06/14/2018)	No of Institutions 1661
Market Cap	$44.1 Billion	Shares
Book Value	$36.4 Billion	2,893,417,984
Price/Book	1.21	% Held
Price/Sales	0.28	54.68

Business Summary: Autos- Manufacturing (MIC: 1.8.1 SIC: 3711 NAIC: 336111)

Ford Motor's business includes designing, manufacturing, marketing, and servicing Ford cars, trucks, and SUVs, as well as Lincoln luxury vehicles. Co. has four operating segments: Automotive, which includes the sale of Ford and Lincoln brand vehicles, service parts, and accessories; Financial Services, which includes its vehicle-related financing and leasing activities at its subsidiary, Ford Motor Credit Company LLC; Ford Smart Mobility LLC, a subsidiary formed to design, build, grow, and invest in emerging mobility services; and Central Treasury Operations, which engages in decision making for investments, risk management activities, and providing financing for the Automotive segment.

Recent Developments: For the quarter ended Mar 31 2018, net income increased 9.1% to US$1.75 billion from US$1.60 billion in the year-earlier quarter. Revenues were US$41.96 billion, up 7.2% from US$39.15 billion the year before. Direct operating expenses rose 9.3% to US$35.75 billion from US$32.70 billion in the comparable period the year before. Indirect operating expenses increased 2.1% to US$5.09 billion from US$4.98 billion in the equivalent prior-year period.

Prospects: Our evaluation of Ford Motor Co. as of Jan. 21, 2018 is the result of our systematic analysis on three basic characteristics: earnings strength, relative valuation, and recent stock price movement. The company has enjoyed a very positive trend in earnings per share over the past 5 quarters. However, while recent estimates for the company have been mixed, F has posted better than expected results. Based on operating earnings yield, the company is undervalued when compared to all of the companies in our coverage universe. Share price changes over the past year indicates that F will perform well over the near term.

Financial Data
(US$ in Millions)

	3 Mos	12/31/2017	12/31/2016	12/31/2015	12/31/2014	12/31/2013	12/31/2012	12/31/2011
Earnings Per Share	1.93	1.90	1.15	1.84	0.80	1.76	1.42	4.94
Cash Flow Per Share	4.35	4.55	4.97	4.07	3.71	2.65	2.36	2.58
Tang Book Value Per Share	9.13	8.78	7.34	7.22	6.27	6.69	4.04	3.81
Dividends Per Share	0.730	0.650	0.850	0.600	0.500	0.400	0.200	0.050
Dividend Payout %	37.82	34.21	73.91	32.61	62.50	22.73	14.08	1.01
Income Statement								
Total Revenue	41,959	156,776	151,800	149,558	144,077	146,917	134,252	136,264
EBITDA	1,837	12,606	10,283	15,681	10,475	13,522	14,343	15,758
Depn & Amortn	...	4,987	4,667	4,332	4,252	4,064	3,655	3,533
Income Before Taxes	1,695	6,947	5,016	8,434	3,067	5,932	7,132	8,181
Income Taxes	174	520	2,189	2,881	1,156	(147)	2,056	(11,541)
Net Income	1,736	7,602	4,596	7,373	3,187	7,155	5,665	20,213
Average Shares	3,998	3,999	4,000	4,003	4,046	4,088	4,016	4,112
Balance Sheet								
Current Assets	123,264	115,902	108,461	43,495	39,016	44,276	43,305	41,667
Total Assets	267,230	257,808	237,951	224,925	208,527	202,026	190,554	178,348
Current Liabilities	99,878	94,600	90,281	78,336	73,963	74,131	73,428	73,038
Long-Term Obligations	105,351	102,666	93,301	89,856	79,999	76,625	66,296	59,177
Total Liabilities	230,830	222,918	208,781	196,283	183,722	175,643	174,607	163,320
Stockholders' Equity	36,400	34,890	29,170	28,642	24,805	26,383	15,947	15,028
Shares Outstanding	3,985	3,974	3,975	3,970	3,956	3,944	3,923	3,923
Statistical Record								
Return on Assets %	3.03	3.07	1.98	3.40	1.55	3.65	3.06	11.78
Return on Equity %	23.13	23.73	15.86	27.59	12.45	33.81	36.48	281.62
EBITDA Margin %	4.38	8.04	6.77	10.48	7.27	9.20	10.68	11.56
Net Margin %	4.14	4.85	3.03	4.93	2.21	4.87	4.22	14.83
Asset Turnover	0.62	0.63	0.65	0.69	0.70	0.75	0.73	0.79
Current Ratio	1.23	1.23	1.20	0.56	0.53	0.60	0.59	0.57
Debt to Equity	2.89	2.94	3.20	3.14	3.23	2.90	4.16	3.94
Price Range	13.23-10.24	13.17-10.56	14.09-11.17	16.57-12.90	17.84-13.54	17.76-12.13	12.96-8.92	18.79-9.37
P/E Ratio	6.85-5.31	6.93-5.56	12.25-9.71	9.01-7.01	22.30-16.92	10.09-6.89	9.13-6.28	3.80-1.90
Average Yield %	6.34	5.51	6.73	4.00	3.15	2.61	1.83	0.38

Address: One American Road, Dearborn, MI 48126 **Telephone:** 313-322-3000	**Web Site:** www.corporate.ford.com **Officers:** William Clay Ford - Executive Chairman, Chairman James Patrick (Jim) Hackett - President, Chief Executive Officer	**Auditors:** PricewaterhouseCoopers LLP **Investor Contact:** 313-845-8540 **Transfer Agents:** Computershare Trust Company, N.A., Providence, RI

FORTIVE CORP

Exchange	Symbol	Price	52Wk Range	Yield	P/E
NYS	FTV	$77.11 (6/29/2018)	81.07-62.18	0.36	24.64

*7 Year Price Score N/A   *NYSE Composite Index=100   *12 Month Price Score 103.97

Interim Earnings (Per Share)

Qtr.	Mar	Jun	Sep	Dec
2016	0.53	0.69	0.65	0.64
2017	0.57	0.68	0.76	0.95
2018	0.74	...	...	...

Interim Dividends (Per Share)

Amt	Decl	Ex	Rec	Pay
0.07Q	08/03/2017	08/23/2017	08/25/2017	09/29/2017
0.07Q	11/02/2017	11/22/2017	11/24/2017	12/29/2017
0.07Q	01/23/2018	02/22/2018	02/23/2018	03/29/2018
0.07Q	04/12/2018	05/24/2018	05/25/2018	06/29/2018

Indicated Div: $0.28

Valuation Analysis

		Institutional Holding	
Forecast EPS	$3.49	No of Institutions	
	(06/13/2018)	934	
Market Cap	$26.9 Billion	Shares	
Book Value	$4.1 Billion	299,950,016	
Price/Book	6.57	% Held	
Price/Sales	3.92	N/A	

Business Summary: Industrial Machinery & Equipment (MIC: 7.2.1 SIC: 3823 NAIC: 334513)

Fortive is a diversified industrial growth company comprising businesses in recognized markets globally. Co. designs, develops, services, manufactures and markets engineered products, software and services. Co. operates through two segments: Professional Instrumentation, which provides essential products, software and services used to create actionable intelligence by measuring and monitoring a range of physical parameters in industrial applications, including electrical current, radio frequency signals, distance, pressure and temperature; and Industrial Technologies, which provides technical equipment, components, software and services for manufacturing, repair and transportation markets.

Recent Developments: For the quarter ended Mar 30 2018, net income increased 30.8% to US$261.2 million from US$199.7 million in the year-earlier quarter. Revenues were US$1.74 billion, up 13.4% from US$1.54 billion the year before. Operating income was US$338.2 million versus US$295.6 million in the prior-year quarter, an increase of 14.4%. Direct operating expenses rose 9.9% to US$869.9 million from US$791.2 million in the comparable period the year before. Indirect operating expenses increased 18.8% to US$532.6 million from US$448.4 million in the equivalent prior-year period.

Prospects: Our evaluation of Fortive Corp. as of Jan. 21, 2018 is the result of our systematic analysis on three basic characteristics: earnings strength, relative valuation, and recent stock price movement. The company has managed to produce a neutral trend in earnings per share over the past 5 quarters and while recent estimates for the company have been mixed, FTV has posted better than expected results. Based on operating earnings yield, the company is about fairly valued when compared to all of the companies in our coverage universe. Share price changes over the past year indicates that FTV will perform well over the near term.

Financial Data

(US$ in Thousands)	3 Mos	12/31/2017	12/31/2016	12/31/2015	12/31/2014	12/31/2013
Earnings Per Share	3.13	2.96	2.51	...	...	...
Cash Flow Per Share	3.44	3.39	3.28	...	...	...
Dividends Per Share	0.280	0.280	0.140	...	...	...
Dividend Payout %	8.95	9.46	5.58	...	...	...
Income Statement						
Total Revenue	1,740,700	6,656,000	6,224,300	6,178,800	6,337,200	5,961,900
EBITDA	397,500	1,479,200	1,337,000	1,357,700	1,357,200	1,221,200
Depn & Amortn	60,000	109,000	91,000	88,000	78,000	78,000
Income Before Taxes	312,900	1,284,200	1,197,000	1,269,700	1,279,200	1,143,200
Income Taxes	51,700	239,700	324,700	405,900	395,800	312,300
Net Income	261,200	1,044,500	872,300	863,800	883,400	830,900
Average Shares	354,400	352,600	347,300	...	...	...
Balance Sheet						
Current Assets	3,079,700	2,936,800	2,488,700	1,594,100	1,683,400	...
Total Assets	10,655,400	10,500,600	8,189,800	7,210,600	7,355,600	...
Current Liabilities	1,461,400	1,602,300	1,466,500	1,323,500	1,285,000	...
Long-Term Obligations	3,996,900	4,056,200	3,358,000	...	...	...
Total Liabilities	6,563,000	6,710,300	5,501,900	2,031,100	2,126,300	...
Stockholders' Equity	4,092,400	3,790,300	2,687,900	5,179,500	5,229,300	...
Shares Outstanding	348,500	347,800	345,900	...	...	...
Statistical Record						
Return on Assets %	11.71	11.18	11.30	11.86	...	...
Return on Equity %	31.69	32.25	22.11	16.60	...	...
EBITDA Margin %	22.84	22.22	21.48	21.97	21.42	20.48
Net Margin %	15.01	15.69	14.01	13.98	13.94	13.94
Asset Turnover	0.73	0.71	0.81	0.85	...	...
Current Ratio	2.11	1.83	1.70	1.20	1.31	...
Debt to Equity	0.98	1.07	1.25	...	...	...
Price Range	80.27-59.62	74.65-53.66	55.97-47.49	...	...	...
P/E Ratio	25.65-19.05	25.22-18.13	22.30-18.92	...	...	...
Average Yield %	0.41	0.43	0.27	...	...	...

Address: 6920 Seaway Blvd., Everett, WA 98203 **Telephone:** 425-446-5000	**Web Site:** www.fortive.com **Officers:** Alan G. Spoon - Chairman James A. Lico - President, Chief Executive Officer	**Auditors:** Ernst & Young LLP **Transfer Agents:** Computershare Trust Company, N.A.

FORTUNE BRANDS HOME & SECURITY, INC.

Exchange	Symbol	Price	52Wk Range	Yield	P/E
NYS	FBHS	$53.69 (6/29/2018)	73.13-53.30	1.49	17.72

*7 Year Price Score N/A   *NYSE Composite Index=100   *12 Month Price Score 87.02

Interim Earnings (Per Share)

Qtr.	Mar	Jun	Sep	Dec
2015	0.25	0.49	0.66	0.54
2016	0.35	0.80	0.78	0.66
2017	0.50	0.88	0.83	0.83
2018	0.49	...	...	...

Interim Dividends (Per Share)

Amt	Decl	Ex	Rec	Pay
0.18Q	09/26/2017	11/22/2017	11/24/2017	12/13/2017
0.20Q	12/08/2017	02/22/2018	02/23/2018	03/14/2018
0.20Q	04/30/2018	05/24/2018	05/25/2018	06/13/2018
0.20Q	07/13/2018	08/30/2018	08/31/2018	09/19/2018
		Indicated Div: $0.80		

Valuation Analysis | **Institutional Holding**

Forecast EPS	$3.63	No of Institutions
	(06/12/2018)	688
Market Cap	$7.8 Billion	Shares
Book Value	$2.4 Billion	155,230,032
Price/Book	3.32	% Held
Price/Sales	1.46	90.29

Business Summary: Household Appliances, Electronics & Goods (MIC: 1.5.1 SIC: 1522 NAIC: 236115)

Fortune Brands Home & Security is a holding company, which provides home and security products. Co. has four business segments: Cabinets, which manufactures custom, semi-custom and stock cabinetry, and vanities; Plumbing, which manufactures or assembles and sells faucets, accessories, kitchen sinks and waste disposals; Doors, which manufactures and sells fiberglass and steel entry door systems and urethane millwork product lines; and Security, which manufactures and sells key-controlled and combination padlocks, bicycle and cable locks, built-in locker locks, door hardware, automotive, trailer and towing locks, electronic access control solutions, and other safety and security devices.

Recent Developments: For the quarter ended Mar 31 2018, income from continuing operations decreased 3.0% to US$75.1 million from US$77.4 million in the year-earlier quarter. Net income decreased 3.2% to US$74.9 million from US$77.4 million in the year-earlier quarter. Revenues were US$1.25 billion, up 5.7% from US$1.19 billion the year before. Operating income was US$119.4 million versus US$111.0 million in the prior-year quarter, an increase of 7.6%. Direct operating expenses rose 5.5% to US$815.0 million from US$772.7 million in the comparable period the year before. Indirect operating expenses increased 5.6% to US$320.2 million from US$303.1 million in the equivalent prior-year period.

Prospects: Our evaluation of Fortune Brands Home & Security Inc. as of Jan. 21, 2018 is the result of our systematic analysis on three basic characteristics: earnings strength, relative valuation, and recent stock price movement. The company has managed to produce a neutral trend in earnings per share over the past 5 quarters and while recent estimates for the company have been mixed, FBHS has posted better than expected results. Based on operating earnings yield, the company is about fairly valued when compared to all of the companies in our coverage universe. Share price changes over the past year indicates that FBHS will perform in line with the market over the near term.

Financial Data

(US$ in Thousands)	3 Mos	12/31/2017	12/31/2016	12/31/2015	12/31/2014	12/31/2013	12/31/2012	12/31/2011
Earnings Per Share	3.03	3.03	2.62	1.93	0.95	1.34	0.71	(0.23)
Cash Flow Per Share	3.78	3.92	4.20	2.58	1.57	1.80	1.76	1.13
Tang Book Value Per Share	N.M.	N.M.	N.M.	N.M.	0.85	2.26	1.93	0.36
Dividends Per Share	0.740	0.720	0.640	0.560	0.480	0.300	...	3.540
Dividend Payout %	24.42	23.76	24.43	29.02	50.53	22.39	...	...
Income Statement								
Total Revenue	1,254,600	5,283,300	4,984,900	4,579,400	4,013,600	4,157,400	3,591,100	3,328,600
EBITDA	156,200	814,500	753,900	606,900	498,300	442,500	264,000	94,300
Depn & Amortn	34,000	130,300	122,700	115,100	96,000	90,400	101,300	111,500
Income Before Taxes	107,500	634,800	582,100	459,900	391,900	344,900	154,000	(43,600)
Income Taxes	32,400	159,500	169,700	153,400	118,300	114,000	34,300	(9,000)
Net Income	75,000	472,600	413,200	315,000	158,100	229,700	118,700	(35,600)
Average Shares	152,100	155,800	157,800	163,000	166,300	171,300	166,100	155,200
Balance Sheet								
Current Assets	1,644,500	1,601,700	1,445,200	1,418,700	1,299,100	1,327,400	1,228,000	953,500
Total Assets	5,552,000	5,511,400	5,128,500	4,878,600	4,052,900	4,178,100	3,873,700	3,637,900
Current Liabilities	1,140,800	906,800	842,800	757,900	699,600	738,700	632,600	597,800
Long-Term Obligations	1,538,000	1,507,600	1,431,100	1,171,600	643,700	350,000	297,500	389,300
Total Liabilities	3,195,200	2,911,900	2,767,000	2,427,700	1,793,400	1,528,700	1,492,600	1,517,100
Stockholders' Equity	2,356,800	2,599,500	2,361,500	2,450,900	2,259,500	2,649,400	2,381,100	2,120,800
Shares Outstanding	145,922	151,906	153,412	159,906	158,140	166,667	163,855	156,008
Statistical Record								
Return on Assets %	8.80	8.88	8.24	7.05	3.84	5.71	3.15	N.M.
Return on Equity %	19.65	19.05	17.13	13.37	6.44	9.13	5.26	N.M.
EBITDA Margin %	12.45	15.42	15.12	13.25	12.42	10.64	7.35	2.83
Net Margin %	5.98	8.95	8.29	6.88	3.94	5.53	3.31	N.M.
Asset Turnover	1.00	0.99	0.99	1.03	0.98	1.03	0.95	0.84
Current Ratio	1.44	1.77	1.71	1.87	1.86	1.80	1.94	1.60
Debt to Equity	0.65	0.58	0.61	0.48	0.28	0.13	0.12	0.18
Price Range	73.13-57.89	69.32-53.89	64.04-45.27	56.47-43.04	47.83-36.77	45.70-29.22	30.33-16.82	17.03-12.20
P/E Ratio	24.14-19.11	22.88-17.79	24.44-17.28	29.26-22.30	50.35-38.71	34.10-21.81	42.72-23.69	...
Average Yield %	1.14	1.14	1.14	1.16	1.14	0.77	...	23.37

Address: 520 Lake Cook Road, Deerfield, IL 60015-5611 **Telephone:** 847-484-4400	**Web Site:** www.fbhs.com **Officers:** Christopher J. Klein - President, Chief Executive Officer Patrick D. Hallinan - Senior Vice President, Chief Financial Officer	**Auditors:** PricewaterhouseCoopers LLP **Transfer Agents:** Wells Fargo Shareowner Services, Mendota Heights, MN

FRANKLIN RESOURCES, INC.

Exchange	Symbol	Price	52Wk Range	Yield	P/E	Div Acheiver
NYS	BEN	$32.05 (6/29/2018)	47.28-31.80	2.87	26.49	28 Years

*7 Year Price Score 73.85   *NYSE Composite Index=100   *12 Month Price Score 81.69

Interim Earnings (Per Share)

Qtr.	Dec	Mar	Jun	Sep
2014-15	0.91	0.98	0.82	0.59
2015-16	0.74	0.61	0.77	0.82
2016-17	0.77	0.74	0.73	0.76
2017-18	(1.06)	0.78	...	...

Interim Dividends (Per Share)

Amt	Decl	Ex	Rec	Pay
0.23Q	12/12/2017	12/22/2017	12/26/2017	01/10/2018
0.23Q	02/14/2018	03/28/2018	03/29/2018	04/12/2018
3.00Sp	02/14/2018	03/28/2018	03/29/2018	04/12/2018
0.23Q	06/12/2018	06/28/2018	06/29/2018	07/13/2018

Indicated Div: $0.92 (Div. Reinv. Plan)

Valuation Analysis

		Institutional Holding	
Forecast EPS	$3.17	No of Institutions	
	(06/14/2018)	902	
Market Cap	$17.4 Billion	Shares	
Book Value	$10.1 Billion	304,399,648	
Price/Book	1.73	% Held	
Price/Sales	2.69	49.77	

Business Summary: Wealth Management (MIC: 5.5.2 SIC: 6282 NAIC: 523930)

Franklin Resources is a holding company that, operates as Franklin Templeton Investments®. Co. is a global investment management organization that provides investment management and related services. Co. provides its investment investment products and services under its Franklin®, Templeton®, Franklin Mutual Series®, Franklin Bissett®, Fiduciary Trust™, Darby®, Balanced Equity Management®, K2® and LibertyShares® brand names. Co.'s products include investment funds and institutional and separately-managed accounts. Co.'s investment funds include U.S.-registered funds, non-U.S.-registered funds, and unregistered funds. At Sep 30 2017, Co.'s total assets under management were $753.20 billion.

Recent Developments: For the quarter ended Mar 31 2018, net income increased 11.0% to US$482.9 million from US$435.0 million in the year-earlier quarter. Revenues were US$1.62 billion, up 1.1% from US$1.60 billion the year before. Operating income was US$555.7 million versus US$555.5 million in the prior-year quarter, an increase of 0.0%. Direct operating expenses declined 2.5% to US$521.5 million from US$534.8 million in the comparable period the year before. Indirect operating expenses increased 5.9% to US$540.6 million from US$510.3 million in the equivalent prior-year period.

Prospects: Our evaluation of Franklin Resources Inc. as of Jan. 21, 2018 is the result of our systematic analysis on three basic characteristics: earnings strength, relative valuation, and recent stock price movement. The company has generated a negative trend in earnings per share over the past 5 quarters and while recent estimates for the company have been raised by analysts, BEN has posted better than expected results. Based on operating earnings yield, the company is undervalued when compared to all of the companies in our coverage universe. Share price changes over the past year indicates that BEN will perform in line with the market over the near term.

Financial Data

(US$ in Thousands)	6 Mos	3 Mos	09/30/2017	09/30/2016	09/30/2015	09/30/2014	09/30/2013	09/30/2012
Earnings Per Share	1.21	1.17	3.01	2.94	3.29	3.79	3.37	2.98
Cash Flow Per Share	2.60	1.83	2.03	2.95	3.66	3.42	3.22	1.66
Tang Book Value Per Share	14.43	17.24	18.73	17.05	15.88	14.86	12.23	11.09
Dividends Per Share	3.860	0.830	0.800	0.720	1.100	0.480	1.390	1.027
Dividend Payout %	319.01	70.94	26.58	24.49	33.43	12.66	41.25	34.41
Income Statement								
Total Revenue	3,233,300	1,615,500	6,392,200	6,618,000	7,948,700	8,491,400	7,985,000	7,101,000
EBITDA	1,250,600	622,500	2,499,300	2,537,500	3,202,000	3,462,400	3,068,900	2,701,700
Depn & Amortn	40,500	19,100	81,500	81,000	81,600	82,600	76,900	67,900
Income Before Taxes	1,238,800	616,400	2,441,200	2,443,100	3,091,600	3,341,500	2,952,600	2,609,600
Income Taxes	1,373,700	1,223,500	759,400	742,100	923,700	997,900	855,900	762,700
Net Income	(140,100)	(583,300)	1,696,700	1,726,700	2,035,300	2,384,300	2,150,200	1,931,400
Average Shares	545,500	550,700	559,100	583,800	614,900	625,200	634,100	643,200
Balance Sheet								
Current Assets	9,625,500	10,068,900	9,751,600	9,277,600	9,306,800	8,644,100	7,474,400	6,996,500
Total Assets	17,690,000	18,074,400	17,534,000	16,098,800	16,335,700	16,357,100	15,390,300	14,751,500
Current Liabilities	3,739,000	2,134,500	1,114,700	997,300	1,117,800	1,220,200	1,731,800	1,709,100
Long-Term Obligations	1,078,800	1,095,500	1,097,600	2,083,400	2,155,300	2,149,000	2,306,000	2,839,100
Total Liabilities	7,631,600	6,316,300	4,914,000	4,163,000	4,494,700	4,773,000	5,317,200	5,550,200
Stockholders' Equity	10,058,400	11,758,100	12,620,000	11,935,800	11,841,000	11,584,100	10,073,100	9,201,300
Shares Outstanding	541,695	552,406	554,865	570,345	603,517	622,893	630,917	636,626
Statistical Record								
Return on Assets %	3.99	3.93	10.09	10.62	12.45	15.02	14.27	13.50
Return on Equity %	6.25	5.68	13.82	14.48	17.38	22.02	22.31	21.73
EBITDA Margin %	38.68	38.53	39.10	38.34	40.28	40.78	38.43	38.05
Net Margin %	N.M.	N.M.	26.54	26.09	25.61	28.08	26.93	27.20
Asset Turnover	0.37	0.38	0.38	0.41	0.49	0.53	0.53	0.50
Current Ratio	2.57	4.72	8.75	9.30	8.33	7.08	4.32	4.09
Debt to Equity	0.11	0.09	0.09	0.17	0.18	0.19	0.23	0.31
Price Range	47.28-34.11	47.28-39.74	47.28-33.18	41.92-30.67	58.84-36.36	58.51-49.52	56.11-41.55	42.67-30.13
P/E Ratio	39.07-28.19	40.41-33.97	15.71-11.02	14.26-10.43	17.88-11.05	15.44-13.07	16.65-12.33	14.32-10.11
Average Yield %	9.05	1.94	1.93	1.97	2.17	0.88	2.94	2.78

Address: One Franklin Parkway, San Mateo, CA 94403	**Web Site:** www.franklinresources.com	**Auditors:** PricewaterhouseCoopers LLP
Telephone: 650-312-2000	**Officers:** Gregory E. Johnson - Chairman, President, Chief Executive Officer Rupert H. Johnson - Vice-Chairman	**Investor Contact:** 650-312-4091
Fax: 650-312-3655		**Transfer Agents:** Computershare, Pittsburgh, PA

FREEPORT-MCMORAN INC

Exchange	Symbol	Price	52Wk Range	Yield	P/E
NYS	FCX	$17.26 (6/29/2018)	19.99-11.89	N/A	11.06

*7 Year Price Score 52.58   *NYSE Composite Index=100   *12 Month Price Score 100.90

TRADING VOLUME (thousand shares)

Interim Earnings (Per Share)

Qtr.	Mar	Jun	Sep	Dec
2015	(2.38)	(1.78)	(3.58)	(3.54)
2016	(3.35)	(0.38)	0.16	0.29
2017	0.16	0.18	0.19	0.72
2018	0.47	...	...	...

Interim Dividends (Per Share)

Dividend Payment Suspended

Valuation Analysis   Institutional Holding

Forecast EPS	$1.98	No of Institutions
	(06/14/2018)	1262
Market Cap	$25.0 Billion	Shares
Book Value	$8.7 Billion	1,234,528,768
Price/Book	2.89	% Held
Price/Sales	1.39	76.92

Business Summary: Non-Precious Metals (MIC: 8.2.2 SIC: 1021 NAIC: 212234)

Freeport-McMoRan is a mining company. Co. operates assets with proven and probable reserves of copper, gold and molybdenum, and Co. is the publicly traded copper producer. Co.'s portfolio of assets includes the Grasberg minerals district in Indonesia (copper and gold deposits), and mining operations in the Americas, including the Morenci minerals district in North America and the Cerro Verde operation in South America.

Recent Developments: For the quarter ended Mar 31 2018, income from continuing operations increased 209.0% to US$828.0 million from US$268.0 million in the year-earlier quarter. Net income increased 167.0% to US$817.0 million from US$306.0 million in the year-earlier quarter. Revenues were US$4.87 billion, up 45.7% from US$3.34 billion the year before. Operating income was US$1.46 billion versus US$597.0 million in the prior-year quarter, an increase of 144.4%. Direct operating expenses rose 26.5% to US$3.26 billion from US$2.58 billion in the comparable period the year before. Indirect operating expenses decreased 10.2% to US$150.0 million from US$167.0 million in the equivalent prior-year period.

Prospects: Our evaluation of Freeport-McMoRan Inc. as of Jan. 21, 2018 is the result of our systematic analysis on three basic characteristics: earnings strength, relative valuation, and recent stock price movement. The company has suffered a very negative trend in earnings per share over the past 5 quarters and while recent estimates for the company have been raised by analysts, FCX has posted better than expected results. Based on operating earnings yield, the company is undervalued when compared to all of the companies in our coverage universe. Share price changes over the past year indicates that FCX will perform very poorly over the near term.

Financial Data

(US$ in Thousands)	3 Mos	12/31/2017	12/31/2016	12/31/2015	12/31/2014	12/31/2013	12/31/2012	12/31/2011
Earnings Per Share	1.56	1.25	(3.16)	(11.31)	(1.26)	2.64	3.19	4.78
Cash Flow Per Share	3.63	3.24	2.82	2.98	5.42	6.13	3.97	6.99
Tang Book Value Per Share	5.97	5.30	3.98	6.03	17.28	17.96	18.13	16.16
Dividends Per Share	...	...	...	0.573	1.250	2.250	1.188	1.500
Dividend Payout %	...	...	...	...	...	85.23	37.23	31.38
Income Statement								
Total Revenue	4,868,000	16,403,000	14,830,000	15,877,000	21,438,000	20,921,000	18,010,000	20,880,000
EBITDA	1,938,000	5,417,000	(107,000)	(9,879,000)	4,069,000	8,228,000	6,852,000	10,056,000
Depn & Amortn	451,000	1,714,000	2,610,000	3,497,000	3,863,000	2,797,000	1,179,000	926,000
Income Before Taxes	1,336,000	2,902,000	(3,472,000)	(14,021,000)	(424,000)	4,913,000	5,487,000	8,818,000
Income Taxes	506,000	883,000	371,000	(1,935,000)	324,000	1,475,000	1,510,000	3,087,000
Net Income	692,000	1,817,000	(4,315,000)	(12,195,000)	(1,268,000)	2,680,000	3,041,000	4,560,000
Average Shares	1,458,000	1,454,000	1,318,000	1,082,000	1,039,000	1,006,000	954,000	955,000
Balance Sheet								
Current Assets	10,106,000	10,779,000	10,435,000	7,462,000	9,045,000	9,972,000	10,297,000	10,047,000
Total Assets	36,637,000	37,302,000	37,317,000	46,577,000	58,795,000	63,473,000	35,440,000	32,070,000
Current Liabilities	4,344,000	5,038,000	4,265,000	4,307,000	5,172,000	4,773,000	3,343,000	2,940,000
Long-Term Obligations	11,123,000	11,703,000	14,795,000	19,779,000	18,492,000	20,394,000	3,525,000	3,533,000
Total Liabilities	27,981,000	29,325,000	31,266,000	38,749,000	40,508,000	42,539,000	17,897,000	16,428,000
Stockholders' Equity	8,656,000	7,977,000	6,051,000	7,828,000	18,287,000	20,934,000	17,543,000	15,642,000
Shares Outstanding	1,449,000	1,448,000	1,445,000	1,246,000	1,039,000	1,038,000	949,000	948,000
Statistical Record								
Return on Assets %	6.23	4.87	N.M.	N.M.	N.M.	5.42	8.98	14.84
Return on Equity %	30.47	25.91	N.M.	N.M.	N.M.	13.93	18.28	32.40
EBITDA Margin %	39.81	33.02	N.M.	N.M.	18.98	39.33	38.05	48.16
Net Margin %	14.22	11.08	N.M.	N.M.	N.M.	12.81	16.89	21.84
Asset Turnover	0.49	0.44	0.35	0.30	0.35	0.42	0.53	0.68
Current Ratio	2.33	2.14	2.45	1.73	1.75	2.09	3.08	3.42
Debt to Equity	1.29	1.47	2.45	2.53	1.01	0.97	0.20	0.23
Price Range	19.99-11.21	19.27-11.21	16.21-3.74	23.66-6.12	39.04-21.03	37.74-26.82	46.50-30.81	60.92-29.87
P/E Ratio	12.81-7.19	15.42-8.97	...	...	...	14.30-10.16	14.58-9.66	12.74-6.25
Average Yield %	...	...	...	3.70	3.80	6.90	3.19	3.16

Address: 333 North Central Avenue, Phoenix, AZ 85004-2189 **Telephone:** 602-366-8100	**Web Site:** www.fcx.com **Officers:** Richard C. Adkerson - Vice-Chairman, President, Chief Executive Officer, President (frmr), Chief Executive Officer (frmr), Chief Financial Officer Kathleen L. Quirk - Executive Vice President, Chief Financial Officer, Treasurer	**Auditors:** Ernst & Young LLP **Investor Contact:** 602-366-8400 **Transfer Agents:** Computershare, Canton, MA

FULLER (HB) COMPANY

Exchange	Symbol	Price	52Wk Range	Yield	P/E	Div Acheiver
NYS	FUL	$53.68 (6/29/2018)	58.64-47.36	1.15	30.50	50 Years

*7 Year Price Score 102.02 *NYSE Composite Index=100 *12 Month Price Score 98.29

Interim Earnings (Per Share)

Qtr.	Feb	May	Aug	Nov
2014-15	0.19	0.49	0.52	0.49
2015-16	0.37	0.65	0.64	0.76
2016-17	0.29	0.50	0.49	(0.15)
2017-18	0.92	...	...	...

Interim Dividends (Per Share)

Amt	Decl	Ex	Rec	Pay
0.15Q	10/05/2017	10/18/2017	10/19/2017	11/02/2017
0.15Q	01/18/2018	01/31/2018	02/01/2018	02/15/2018
0.155Q	04/12/2018	04/25/2018	04/26/2018	05/10/2018
0.155Q	07/12/2018	07/25/2018	07/26/2018	08/09/2018

Indicated Div: $0.62 (Div. Reinv. Plan)

Valuation Analysis — **Institutional Holding**

Forecast EPS	$3.20	No of Institutions
	(06/13/2018)	341
Market Cap	$2.7 Billion	Shares
Book Value	$1.1 Billion	69,190,472
Price/Book	2.42	% Held
Price/Sales	1.08	89.49

Business Summary: Specialty Chemicals (MIC: 8.3.2 SIC: 2891 NAIC: 325520)

H.B. Fuller formulates, manufactures and markets adhesives, sealants and other chemical products. Co.'s Americas Adhesives, Europe, India, Middle East and Africa, and Asia Pacific segments manufacture and supply adhesives products in the assembly, packaging, converting, nonwoven and hygiene, performance wood, flooring, textile, flexible packaging, graphic arts, and envelope markets. Co.'s Construction Products segment provides floor preparation, grouts and mortars for tile setting as well as sealants and related products for heating, ventilation and air conditioning installations. Co.'s Engineering Adhesives segment provides adhesives to markets such as transportation and electronics.

Recent Developments: For the quarter ended Mar 3 2018, net income increased 221.4% to US$47.7 million from US$14.8 million in the year-earlier quarter. Revenues were US$713.1 million, up 41.7% from US$503.3 million the year before. Direct operating expenses rose 44.2% to US$525.4 million from US$364.3 million in the comparable period the year before. Indirect operating expenses increased 33.7% to US$151.0 million from US$112.9 million in the equivalent prior-year period.

Prospects: Our evaluation of Fuller (H.B.) Company as of Jan. 21, 2018 is the result of our systematic analysis on three basic characteristics: earnings strength, relative valuation, and recent stock price movement. The company has managed to produce a neutral trend in earnings per share over the past 5 quarters. However, while recent estimates for the company have been mixed, FUL has posted results that fell short of analysts expectations. Based on operating earnings yield, the company is undervalued when compared to all of the companies in our coverage universe. Share price changes over the past year indicates that FUL will perform well over the near term.

Financial Data

(US$ in Thousands)	3 Mos	12/02/2017	12/03/2016	11/28/2015	11/29/2014	11/30/2013	12/01/2012	12/03/2011
Earnings Per Share	1.76	1.13	2.42	1.69	0.97	1.89	2.48	1.79
Cash Flow Per Share	1.83	2.80	3.84	4.20	0.60	2.67	2.20	2.06
Tang Book Value Per Share	N.M.	N.M.	7.30	6.11	8.71	8.91	5.82	9.38
Dividends Per Share	0.600	0.590	0.550	0.510	0.460	0.385	0.330	0.295
Dividend Payout %	34.09	52.21	22.73	30.18	47.42	20.37	13.31	16.48
Income Statement								
Total Revenue	713,079	2,306,043	2,094,605	2,083,660	2,104,454	2,046,968	1,886,239	1,557,552
EBITDA	77,424	185,788	270,424	237,746	164,236	204,722	162,100	154,763
Depn & Amortn	36,665	87,315	77,685	74,890	65,524	58,795	54,490	31,054
Income Before Taxes	13,214	58,699	167,425	138,345	79,312	127,544	89,548	114,992
Income Taxes	(32,632)	9,086	50,436	55,855	34,348	39,949	30,479	34,951
Net Income	47,682	58,242	124,128	86,680	49,773	96,761	125,622	89,105
Average Shares	51,898	51,619	51,270	51,393	51,255	51,136	50,618	49,866
Balance Sheet								
Current Assets	1,117,481	1,144,992	811,253	801,051	765,136	794,694	799,344	596,590
Total Assets	4,374,053	4,360,646	2,058,254	2,042,252	1,869,006	1,873,028	1,786,320	1,227,709
Current Liabilities	522,827	504,913	391,844	349,525	317,199	360,778	350,119	254,985
Long-Term Obligations	2,328,819	2,398,927	588,145	669,606	547,735	472,315	475,112	179,611
Total Liabilities	3,254,030	3,317,019	1,120,378	1,169,332	978,959	942,963	1,008,047	522,505
Stockholders' Equity	1,120,023	1,043,627	937,876	872,920	890,047	930,065	778,273	705,204
Shares Outstanding	50,533	50,388	50,141	50,074	50,310	50,228	49,903	49,449
Statistical Record								
Return on Assets %	2.79	1.81	5.96	4.44	2.67	5.30	8.36	7.36
Return on Equity %	8.81	5.88	13.49	9.86	5.48	11.36	16.98	13.11
EBITDA Margin %	10.86	8.06	12.91	11.41	7.80	10.00	8.59	9.94
Net Margin %	6.69	2.53	5.93	4.16	2.37	4.73	6.66	5.72
Asset Turnover	0.77	0.72	1.01	1.07	1.13	1.12	1.26	1.29
Current Ratio	2.14	2.27	2.07	2.29	2.41	2.20	2.28	2.34
Debt to Equity	2.08	2.30	0.63	0.77	0.62	0.51	0.61	0.25
Price Range	58.64-47.36	58.64-47.09	48.82-32.71	45.74-32.73	52.74-37.46	51.32-32.55	34.00-21.34	25.19-17.06
P/E Ratio	33.32-26.91	51.89-41.67	20.17-13.52	27.07-19.37	54.37-38.62	27.15-17.22	13.71-8.60	14.07-9.53
Average Yield %	1.14	1.14	1.28	1.25	0.99	0.95	1.11	1.37

Address: 1200 Willow Lake Boulevard, St. Paul, MN 55110-5101	**Web Site:** www.hbfuller.com	**Auditors:** KPMG LLP
Telephone: 651-236-5900	**Officers:** Lee R. Mitau - Chairman R. William Van Sant - Vice-Chairman	**Investor Contact:** 651-236-5062
Fax: 651-236-5161		**Transfer Agents:** Wells Fargo Shareholder Services, St. Paul, MN

GALLAGHER (ARTHUR J.) & CO.

Exchange	Symbol	Price	52Wk Range	Yield	P/E
NYS	AJG	$65.28 (6/29/2018)	72.63-56.76	2.51	17.60

*7 Year Price Score 112.19 *NYSE Composite Index=100 ***12 Month Price Score 102.59**

Interim Earnings (Per Share)

Qtr.	Mar	Jun	Sep	Dec
2015	0.13	0.81	0.75	0.35
2016	0.26	0.84	0.69	0.53
2017	0.31	0.95	0.71	0.57
2018	1.48	...	...	...

Interim Dividends (Per Share)

Amt	Decl	Ex	Rec	Pay
0.39Q	07/26/2017	08/30/2017	09/01/2017	09/15/2017
0.39Q	10/25/2017	11/30/2017	12/01/2017	12/15/2017
0.41Q	01/24/2018	03/01/2018	03/02/2018	03/16/2018
0.41Q	04/25/2018	05/31/2018	06/01/2018	06/15/2018

Indicated Div: $1.64 (Div. Reinv. Plan)

Valuation Analysis		Institutional Holding	
Forecast EPS	$3.50	No of Institutions	
	(06/14/2018)	814	
Market Cap	$11.9 Billion	Shares	
Book Value	$4.5 Billion	185,081,856	
Price/Book	2.63	% Held	
Price/Sales	1.81	90.81	

Business Summary: Brokers & Intermediaries (MIC: 5.2.3 SIC: 6411 NAIC: 524210)

Arthur J. Gallagher & Co. is a holding company. Through its subsidiaries, Co. provides insurance brokerage and consulting services and third-party claims settlement and administration services. Co.'s segments are brokerage, which comprised of retail and wholesale insurance brokerage operations; and risk management, which provides contract claim settlement and administration services for enterprises that choose to self-insure some or all of their property/casualty coverages and for insurance companies that choose to outsource some or all of their property/casualty claims departments. Co. also provides integrated disability management programs, and information services, among others.

Recent Developments: For the quarter ended Mar 31 2018, net income increased 18.2% to US$286.0 million from US$242.0 million in the year-earlier quarter. Revenues were US$1.84 billion, up 11.6% from US$1.65 billion the year before.

Prospects: Our evaluation of Gallagher (Arthur J.) & Co. as of Jan. 21, 2018 is the result of our systematic analysis on three basic characteristics: earnings strength, relative valuation, and recent stock price movement. The company has managed to produce a neutral trend in earnings per share over the past 5 quarters and while recent estimates for the company have been mixed, AJG has posted better than expected results. Based on operating earnings yield, the company is undervalued when compared to all of the companies in our coverage universe. Share price changes over the past year indicates that AJG will perform well over the near term.

Financial Data
(US$ in Thousands)

	3 Mos	12/31/2017	12/31/2016	12/31/2015	12/31/2014	12/31/2013	12/31/2012	12/31/2011
Earnings Per Share	3.71	2.54	2.32	2.06	1.97	2.06	1.59	1.28
Cash Flow Per Share	2.57	4.74	3.49	3.79	2.63	2.71	2.83	2.53
Dividends Per Share	1.580	1.560	1.520	1.480	1.440	1.400	1.360	1.320
Dividend Payout %	42.59	61.42	65.52	71.84	73.10	67.96	85.53	103.13
Income Statement								
Total Revenue	1,837,700	6,159,600	5,594,800	5,392,400	4,626,500	3,179,600	2,520,300	2,134,700
EBITDA	282,800	499,200	460,500	387,400	336,800	327,900	286,700	243,700
Depn & Amortn	40,500	121,100	103,600	93,900	69,400	53,400	41,400	35,900
Income Before Taxes	242,300	378,100	356,900	293,500	267,400	274,500	245,300	207,800
Income Taxes	(43,700)	(121,100)	(88,100)	(95,600)	(36,000)	5,900	50,300	63,700
Net Income	273,700	463,100	414,400	356,800	303,400	268,600	195,000	144,100
Average Shares	185,000	182,100	178,400	173,200	154,300	130,500	122,500	112,500
Balance Sheet								
Current Assets	8,533,300	5,170,600	4,416,100	4,335,800	3,811,200	2,875,600	2,429,500	2,199,400
Total Assets	16,127,500	12,897,400	11,489,600	10,913,800	10,010,000	6,860,500	5,352,300	4,483,500
Current Liabilities	7,742,400	4,912,300	4,611,700	4,191,700	3,642,700	3,284,800	2,362,900	2,073,600
Long-Term Obligations	2,792,100	2,691,900	2,144,600	2,075,000	2,125,000	825,000	725,000	675,000
Total Liabilities	11,612,900	8,792,200	7,893,000	7,275,500	6,780,600	4,775,000	3,693,700	3,239,900
Stockholders' Equity	4,514,600	4,105,200	3,596,600	3,638,300	3,229,400	2,085,500	1,658,600	1,243,600
Shares Outstanding	182,100	181,000	178,300	176,900	164,600	133,600	125,600	114,700
Statistical Record								
Return on Assets %	4.88	3.80	3.69	3.41	3.60	4.40	3.95	3.57
Return on Equity %	16.66	12.03	11.42	10.39	11.42	14.35	13.40	12.26
EBITDA Margin %	15.39	8.10	8.23	7.18	7.28	10.31	11.38	11.42
Net Margin %	14.89	7.52	7.41	6.62	6.56	8.45	7.74	6.75
Asset Turnover	0.47	0.51	0.50	0.52	0.55	0.52	0.51	0.53
Current Ratio	1.10	1.05	0.96	1.03	1.05	0.88	1.03	1.06
Debt to Equity	0.62	0.66	0.60	0.57	0.66	0.40	0.44	0.54
Price Range	72.63-54.73	66.96-52.24	52.12-36.24	49.50-40.08	49.39-43.59	48.11-34.65	37.73-32.76	33.82-24.51
P/E Ratio	19.58-14.75	26.36-20.57	22.47-15.62	24.03-19.46	25.07-22.13	23.35-16.82	23.73-20.60	26.42-19.15
Average Yield %	2.56	2.66	3.27	3.23	3.11	3.26	3.84	4.51

Address: 2850 W. Golf Road, Rolling Meadows, IL 60008-4050	Web Site: www.ajg.com	Auditors: Ernst & Young LLP
Telephone: 630-773-3800	Officers: J. Patrick (Pat) Gallagher - Chairman, President, Chief Executive Officer Douglas K. (Doug) Howell - Corporate Vice-President, Chief Financial Officer	Investor Contact: 630-285-3501 Transfer Agents: Computershare Investor Services, Canton, MA

GAMESTOP CORP

Exchange	Symbol	Price	52Wk Range	Yield	P/E
NYS	GME	$14.57 (6/29/2018)	22.17-12.46	10.43	364.25

*7 Year Price Score 45.90   *NYSE Composite Index=100   *12 Month Price Score 78.57

Interim Earnings (Per Share)

Qtr.	Apr	Jul	Oct	Jan
2015-16	0.68	0.24	0.53	2.33
2016-17	0.63	0.27	0.49	2.01
2017-18	0.58	0.22	0.59	(1.05)
2018-19	0.28	...	...	...

Interim Dividends (Per Share)

Amt	Decl	Ex	Rec	Pay
0.38Q	08/21/2017	09/07/2017	09/08/2017	09/21/2017
0.38Q	11/17/2017	11/30/2017	12/01/2017	12/12/2017
0.38Q	02/21/2018	03/02/2018	03/05/2018	03/20/2018
0.38Q	05/31/2018	06/11/2018	06/12/2018	06/26/2018

Indicated Div: $1.52

Valuation Analysis   **Institutional Holding**

Forecast EPS	$3.08	No of Institutions
	(06/13/2018)	569
Market Cap	$1.5 Billion	Shares
Book Value	$2.2 Billion	135,060,464
Price/Book	0.68	% Held
Price/Sales	0.16	58.25

TRADING VOLUME (thousand shares)

Business Summary: Retail - Appliances and Electronics (MIC: 2.1.7 SIC: 5734 NAIC: 443120)

GameStop is a family of specialty retail brands. Through its video game brand stores and e-commerce sites, Co. is the omnichannel retailer of video game products. Co. also provide mobile and consumer technology products through its AT&T® authorized retailer stores, Cricket WirelessTM reseller pre-paid wireless stores and Simply Mac stores. In addition, Co. is a retailer of collectible pop-culture themed products. Co. has five reportable segments, which are comprised of four geographic Video Game Brands segments: U.S., Canada, Australia and Europe, and a Technology Brands segment. Co.'s Technology Brands segment includes its Spring Mobile and Simply Mac businesses.

Recent Developments: For the quarter ended May 5 2018, net income decreased 52.2% to US$28.2 million from US$59.0 million in the year-earlier quarter. Revenues were US$1.93 billion, down 5.5% from US$2.05 billion the year before. Operating income was US$57.1 million versus US$101.1 million in the prior-year quarter, a decrease of 43.5%. Direct operating expenses declined 5.0% to US$1.28 billion from US$1.34 billion in the comparable period the year before. Indirect operating expenses decreased 0.2% to US$600.2 million from US$601.4 million in the equivalent prior-year period.

Prospects: Our evaluation of GameStop Corp. as of Jan. 21, 2018 is the result of our systematic analysis on three basic characteristics: earnings strength, relative valuation, and recent stock price movement. The company has generated a negative trend in earnings per share over the past 5 quarters. However, while recent estimates for the company have been mixed, GME has posted better than expected results. Based on operating earnings yield, the company is undervalued when compared to all of the companies in our coverage universe. Share price changes over the past year indicates that GME will perform poorly over the near term.

Financial Data

(US$ in Thousands)	3 Mos	02/03/2018	01/28/2017	01/30/2016	01/31/2015	02/01/2014	02/02/2013	01/28/2012
Earnings Per Share	0.04	0.34	3.40	3.78	3.47	2.99	(2.13)	2.41
Cash Flow Per Share	1.57	4.22	5.21	6.21	4.29	6.53	4.92	4.48
Tang Book Value Per Share	3.54	3.73	0.21	2.65	4.08	5.57	6.34	5.95
Dividends Per Share	1.520	1.520	1.480	1.440	1.320	1.100	0.800	...
Dividend Payout %	3,800.00	447.06	43.53	38.10	38.04	36.79	...	...
Income Statement								
Total Revenue	1,934,000	9,224,600	8,607,900	9,363,800	9,296,000	9,039,500	8,886,700	9,550,500
EBITDA	91,500	274,000	709,400	793,100	762,800	726,400	138,500	760,600
Depn & Amortn	34,400	138,400	151,700	144,900	144,500	152,900	180,100	191,700
Income Before Taxes	43,400	80,300	504,700	625,200	608,300	568,800	(44,900)	549,100
Income Taxes	15,200	45,600	151,500	222,400	215,200	214,600	224,900	210,600
Net Income	28,200	34,700	353,200	402,800	393,100	354,200	(269,700)	339,900
Average Shares	102,000	101,500	103,800	106,700	113,200	118,400	126,400	141,000
Balance Sheet								
Current Assets	1,851,600	2,538,700	2,140,700	1,938,800	2,062,500	1,949,600	2,010,900	1,997,300
Total Assets	4,308,400	5,041,600	4,975,900	4,334,900	4,246,300	4,091,400	4,133,600	4,847,400
Current Liabilities	1,214,700	1,915,600	1,761,500	1,794,400	1,639,700	1,726,000	1,715,300	1,633,900
Long-Term Obligations	818,600	817,900	815,000	350,000	350,600	1,600	...	...
Total Liabilities	2,124,900	2,827,100	2,721,800	2,253,900	2,178,600	1,840,000	1,847,300	1,805,300
Stockholders' Equity	2,183,500	2,214,500	2,254,100	2,081,000	2,067,700	2,251,400	2,286,300	3,042,100
Shares Outstanding	101,900	101,300	101,000	103,300	107,700	115,300	118,200	136,800
Statistical Record								
Return on Assets %	0.09	0.68	7.61	9.41	9.46	8.64	N.M.	6.88
Return on Equity %	0.18	1.53	16.34	19.47	18.25	15.65	N.M.	11.48
EBITDA Margin %	4.73	2.97	8.24	8.47	8.21	8.04	1.56	7.96
Net Margin %	1.46	0.38	4.10	4.30	4.23	3.92	N.M.	3.56
Asset Turnover	2.03	1.81	1.85	2.19	2.24	2.20	1.95	1.93
Current Ratio	1.52	1.33	1.22	1.08	1.26	1.13	1.17	1.22
Debt to Equity	0.37	0.37	0.36	0.17	0.17	N.M.	...	...
Price Range	24.95-12.62	26.52-16.00	33.38-20.73	47.44-25.06	46.10-31.92	57.59-23.54	27.83-15.73	28.21-19.50
P/E Ratio	623.75-315.50	78.00-47.06	9.82-6.10	12.55-6.63	13.29-9.20	19.26-7.87	...	11.71-8.09
Average Yield %	8.13	7.22	5.33	3.62	3.36	2.68	3.68	...

Address: 625 Westport Parkway, Grapevine, TX 76051 **Telephone:** 817-424-2000	**Web Site:** www.gamestop.com **Officers:** Daniel A. DeMatteo - Executive Chairman, Interim Chief Executive Officer, Interim Chief Executive Officer Shane S. Kim - Interim Chief Executive Officer	**Auditors:** DELOITTE & TOUCHE LLP **Transfer Agents:** Computershare, Providence, RI

GARTNER INC

Exchange	Symbol	Price	52Wk Range	Yield	P/E
NYS	IT	$132.90 (6/29/2018)	142.14-113.41	N/A	N/A

*7 Year Price Score 127.62 *NYSE Composite Index=100 *12 Month Price Score 103.92

Interim Earnings (Per Share)

Qtr.	Mar	Jun	Sep	Dec
2015	0.32	0.61	0.36	0.77
2016	0.48	0.57	0.36	0.79
2017	0.43	(1.03)	(0.53)	1.23
2018	(0.22)	...	...	...

Interim Dividends (Per Share)

No Dividends Paid

Valuation Analysis		Institutional Holding	
Forecast EPS	$3.74	No of Institutions	593
	(06/12/2018)		
Market Cap	$12.1 Billion	Shares	159,017,968
Book Value	$987.6 Million		
Price/Book	12.27	% Held	88.45
Price/Sales	3.32		

Business Summary: IT Services (MIC: 6.3.1 SIC: 8741 NAIC: 561110)

Gartner is an information technology research and advisory company. Co. works with clients to research, analyze and interpret the business of IT within the context of their individual roles. Co. manages its business through three reportable segments: Research, Consulting and Events. The Research segment consists primarily of subscription-based research products, access to research inquiry, peer networking services, and membership programs. The Consulting segment consists primarily of consulting, measurement engagements, and advisory services. The Events segment consists of various symposia, conferences and exhibitions.

Recent Developments: For the quarter ended Mar 31 2018, net loss amounted to US$19.6 million versus net income of US$36.4 million in the year-earlier quarter. Revenues were US$963.6 million, up 54.1% from US$625.2 million the year before. Operating loss was US$8.7 million versus an income of US$53.5 million in the prior-year quarter. Direct operating expenses rose 50.3% to US$357.2 million from US$237.6 million in the comparable period the year before. Indirect operating expenses increased 84.1% to US$615.1 million from US$334.0 million in the equivalent prior-year period.

Prospects: Our evaluation of Gartner Inc. as of Jan. 21, 2018 is the result of our systematic analysis on three basic characteristics: earnings strength, relative valuation, and recent stock price movement. The company has enjoyed a very positive trend in earnings per share over the past 5 quarters and while recent estimates for the company have remained steady, IT has posted better than expected results. Based on operating earnings yield, the company is overvalued when compared to all of the companies in our coverage universe. Share price changes over the past year indicates that IT will perform in line with the market over the near term.

Financial Data
(US$ in Thousands)

	3 Mos	12/31/2017	12/31/2016	12/31/2015	12/31/2014	12/31/2013	12/31/2012	12/31/2011
Earnings Per Share	(0.55)	0.04	2.31	2.06	2.03	1.93	1.73	1.39
Cash Flow Per Share	3.15	2.88	4.42	4.12	3.88	3.39	2.99	2.66
Income Statement								
Total Revenue	963,565	3,311,494	2,444,540	2,163,056	2,021,441	1,784,213	1,615,808	1,468,588
EBITDA	10,466	237,293	375,544	340,135	324,996	309,722	274,257	244,176
Depn & Amortn	18,278	240,174	61,997	47,142	39,426	34,446	29,802	32,025
Income Before Taxes	(42,871)	(127,817)	288,431	272,211	274,683	266,439	235,596	202,184
Income Taxes	(23,284)	(131,096)	94,849	96,576	90,917	83,638	69,693	65,282
Net Income	(19,587)	3,279	193,582	175,635	183,766	182,801	165,903	136,902
Average Shares	91,005	89,790	83,820	85,056	90,719	94,830	95,842	98,846
Balance Sheet								
Current Assets	2,310,662	2,588,608	1,343,196	1,140,997	1,096,658	1,084,882	927,466	705,785
Total Assets	6,915,028	7,283,173	2,367,335	2,174,686	1,904,351	1,783,582	1,621,277	1,379,872
Current Liabilities	3,185,856	2,822,585	1,460,249	1,323,492	1,215,218	1,159,923	1,070,000	921,137
Long-Term Obligations	2,186,061	2,899,124	664,391	790,000	385,000	136,250	115,000	150,000
Total Liabilities	5,927,457	6,299,708	2,306,457	2,307,086	1,743,180	1,422,266	1,314,604	1,198,088
Stockholders' Equity	987,571	983,465	60,878	(132,400)	161,171	361,316	306,673	181,784
Shares Outstanding	91,210	90,822	82,651	82,338	87,520	91,965	93,361	93,343
Statistical Record								
Return on Assets %	N.M.	0.07	8.50	8.61	9.97	10.74	11.03	10.27
Return on Equity %	N.M.	0.63	...	1,220.92	70.34	54.73	67.74	74.23
EBITDA Margin %	1.09	7.17	15.36	15.72	16.08	17.36	16.97	16.63
Net Margin %	N.M.	0.10	7.92	8.12	9.09	10.25	10.27	9.32
Asset Turnover	0.71	0.69	1.07	1.06	1.10	1.05	1.07	1.10
Current Ratio	0.73	0.92	0.92	0.86	0.90	0.94	0.87	0.77
Debt to Equity	2.21	2.95	10.91	...	2.39	0.38	0.37	0.83
Price Range	142.14-107.99	129.53-90.56	104.93-79.86	93.87-77.92	87.40-62.51	71.22-46.02	51.01-34.67	43.01-32.19
P/E Ratio	...	N.M.	45.42-34.57	45.57-37.83	43.05-30.79	36.90-23.84	29.49-20.04	30.94-23.16

Address: P.O. Box 10212, 56 Top Gallant Road, Stamford, CT 06902-7700	Web Site: www.gartner.com	Auditors: KPMG LLP
Telephone: 203-316-1111	Officers: James C. Smith - Chairman Eugene A. (Gene) Hall - Chief Executive Officer	Investor Contact: 203-316-6537 Transfer Agents: American Stock Transfer & Trust Company, LLC, New York, NY

GATX CORP

Exchange	Symbol	Price	52Wk Range	Yield	P/E
NYS	GATX	$74.23 (6/29/2018)	75.79-56.54	2.37	5.59

*7 Year Price Score 100.58 *NYSE Composite Index=100 *12 Month Price Score 107.49

Interim Earnings (Per Share)

Qtr.	Mar	Jun	Sep	Dec
2015	1.39	1.03	0.91	1.36
2016	1.66	1.49	2.36	0.80
2017	1.44	1.35	1.25	8.71
2018	1.98	...	...	...

Interim Dividends (Per Share)

Amt	Decl	Ex	Rec	Pay
0.42Q	07/28/2017	09/14/2017	09/15/2017	09/30/2017
0.42Q	10/27/2017	12/14/2017	12/15/2017	12/31/2017
0.44Q	01/26/2018	03/02/2018	03/05/2018	03/31/2018
0.44Q	05/01/2018	06/14/2018	06/15/2018	06/30/2018

Indicated Div: $1.76 (Div. Reinv. Plan)

Valuation Analysis **Institutional Holding**

Forecast EPS	$4.70 (06/10/2018)	No of Institutions 365
Market Cap	$2.8 Billion	Shares 56,561,384
Book Value	$1.8 Billion	% Held 91.92
Price/Book	1.52	
Price/Sales	2.05	

Business Summary: Miscellaneous Transportation Services (MIC: 7.4.5 SIC: 4741 NAIC: 488210)

GATX is a railcar lessor, owning fleets in North America, Europe, and Asia. In addition, Co. operates a fleet of U.S.-flagged vessels on the Great Lakes and jointly with Rolls-Royce plc, Co. owns aircraft spare engine lease portfolios. Co. leases tank cars, freight cars, and locomotives in North America, tank cars and freight cars in Europe and freight cars in India and Russia. As of Dec 31 2017, Co. had a wholly owned fleet of approximately 147,005 railcars. As of the same date, Co. also had an ownership interest in an affiliate investment that owned approximately 2,100 railcars, and Co. managed approximately 300 railcars for other third-party owners.

Recent Developments: For the quarter ended Mar 31 2018, net income increased 32.7% to US$76.3 million from US$57.5 million in the year-earlier quarter. Revenues were US$305.3 million, down 3.4% from US$316.1 million the year before. Direct operating expenses rose 3.1% to US$184.1 million from US$178.6 million in the comparable period the year before. Indirect operating expenses increased 2.3% to US$53.5 million from US$52.3 million in the equivalent prior-year period.

Prospects: Our evaluation of GATX Corp. as of Jan. 21, 2018 is the result of our systematic analysis on three basic characteristics: earnings strength, relative valuation, and recent stock price movement. The company has generated a negative trend in earnings per share over the past 5 quarters and while recent estimates for the company have been raised by analysts, GATX has posted results that fell short of analysts expectations. Based on operating earnings yield, the company is undervalued when compared to all of the companies in our coverage universe. Share price changes over the past year indicates that GATX will perform very poorly over the near term.

Financial Data
(US$ in Thousands)

	3 Mos	12/31/2017	12/31/2016	12/31/2015	12/31/2014	12/31/2013	12/31/2012	12/31/2011
Earnings Per Share	13.29	12.75	6.29	4.69	4.48	3.59	2.88	2.35
Cash Flow Per Share	13.77	12.80	15.42	12.40	9.98	8.64	7.89	6.61
Tang Book Value Per Share	46.49	45.05	32.18	28.60	27.78	28.39	24.57	22.22
Dividends Per Share	1.700	1.680	1.600	1.520	1.320	1.240	1.200	1.160
Dividend Payout %	12.79	13.18	25.44	32.41	29.46	34.54	41.67	49.36
Income Statement								
Total Revenue	305,300	1,376,900	1,418,300	1,449,900	1,451,000	1,321,000	1,243,200	1,308,500
EBITDA	204,300	697,600	763,700	728,700	676,600	593,400	559,800	386,700
Depn & Amortn	81,800	322,700	310,200	303,300	287,000	267,800	249,400	238,500
Income Before Taxes	82,600	214,400	305,400	270,300	231,200	159,000	143,800	148,200
Income Taxes	20,600	(243,700)	95,700	110,900	75,700	65,500	26,100	37,400
Net Income	76,300	502,000	257,100	205,300	205,000	169,300	137,300	110,800
Average Shares	38,500	39,400	40,900	43,800	45,800	47,100	47,600	47,200
Balance Sheet								
Current Assets	435,900	512,800	538,600	455,200	576,700	804,900	620,600	713,800
Total Assets	7,468,000	7,422,400	7,105,400	6,894,200	6,937,500	6,549,600	6,055,400	5,857,500
Current Liabilities	145,800	158,600	178,600	178,300	238,000	183,200	451,000	164,200
Long-Term Obligations	4,371,700	4,384,200	4,268,100	4,196,800	4,202,100	3,847,400	3,294,300	3,518,500
Total Liabilities	5,628,300	5,629,700	5,758,200	5,614,000	5,623,500	5,152,600	4,811,200	4,730,200
Stockholders' Equity	1,839,700	1,792,700	1,347,200	1,280,200	1,314,000	1,397,000	1,244,200	1,127,300
Shares Outstanding	37,694	37,895	39,442	41,970	44,198	45,868	46,898	46,653
Statistical Record								
Return on Assets %	7.15	6.91	3.66	2.97	3.04	2.69	2.30	1.96
Return on Equity %	32.30	31.98	19.52	15.83	15.12	12.82	11.55	9.89
EBITDA Margin %	66.92	50.66	53.85	50.26	46.63	44.92	45.03	29.55
Net Margin %	24.99	36.46	18.13	14.16	14.13	12.82	11.04	8.47
Asset Turnover	0.19	0.19	0.20	0.21	0.22	0.21	0.21	0.23
Current Ratio	2.99	3.23	3.02	2.55	2.42	4.39	1.38	4.35
Debt to Equity	2.38	2.45	3.17	3.28	3.20	2.75	2.65	3.12
Price Range	72.37-56.54	65.54-56.54	64.17-35.12	62.95-39.87	69.10-51.00	53.85-43.30	44.90-35.93	44.33-29.70
P/E Ratio	5.45-4.25	5.14-4.43	10.20-5.58	13.42-8.50	15.42-11.38	15.00-12.06	15.59-12.48	18.86-12.64
Average Yield %	2.70	2.77	3.47	2.90	2.12	2.54	2.88	3.14

Address: 222 West Adams Street, Chicago, IL 60606-5314
Telephone: 312-621-6200

Web Site: www.gatx.com
Officers: Brian A. Kenney - Chairman, President, Chief Executive Officer N. Gocke Tezel - Vice President, Senior Vice President, Division Officer

Auditors: Ernst & Young LLP
Investor Contact: 312-621-6262
Transfer Agents: Computershare, Canton, MA

GENERAL DYNAMICS CORP

Exchange	Symbol	Price	52Wk Range	Yield	P/E	Div Acheiver
NYS	GD	$186.41 (6/29/2018)	229.95-185.89	2.00	19.16	26 Years

*7 Year Price Score 130.80 *NYSE Composite Index=100   *12 Month Price Score 94.95

Interim Earnings (Per Share)

Qtr.	Mar	Jun	Sep	Dec
2015	2.14	2.27	2.28	2.40
2016	2.30	2.44	2.21	2.58
2017	2.48	2.45	2.52	2.11
2018	2.65	...	...	...

Interim Dividends (Per Share)

Amt	Decl	Ex	Rec	Pay
0.84Q	08/02/2017	10/05/2017	10/06/2017	11/10/2017
0.84Q	12/06/2017	01/18/2018	01/19/2018	02/09/2018
0.93Q	03/07/2018	04/12/2018	04/13/2018	05/11/2018
0.93Q	06/06/2018	07/05/2018	07/06/2018	08/10/2018

Indicated Div: $3.72

Valuation Analysis

Forecast EPS	$11.05 (06/14/2018)
Market Cap	$55.4 Billion
Book Value	$11.8 Billion
Price/Book	4.70
Price/Sales	1.78

Institutional Holding

No of Institutions	1601
Shares	300,507,776
% Held	85.42

TRADING VOLUME (thousand shares)

Business Summary: Aerospace (MIC: 7.1.1 SIC: 3721 NAIC: 336411)

General Dynamics is an aerospace and defense company. Co. has four business groups: Aerospace, which produces Gulfstream aircraft, provides aircraft services and performs aircraft completions for other original equipment manufacturers; Combat Systems, which provides combat vehicles, weapons systems and munitions; Information Systems and Technology, which provides command, control, communication, computers, intelligence, surveillance and reconnaissance solutions and information technology services; and Marine Systems, which designs, constructs and repairs surface ships and submarines. Co. also does business with non-U.S. governments and corporate and individual buyers of business aircraft.

Recent Developments: For the quarter ended Apr 1 2018, net income increased 4.7% to US$799.0 million from US$763.0 million in the year-earlier quarter. Revenues were US$7.54 billion, up 1.3% from US$7.44 billion the year before. Operating income was US$1.01 billion versus US$1.05 billion in the prior-year quarter, a decrease of 3.6%. Direct operating expenses rose 1.1% to US$5.99 billion from US$5.92 billion in the comparable period the year before. Indirect operating expenses increased 13.8% to US$537.0 million from US$472.0 million in the equivalent prior-year period.

Prospects: Our evaluation of General Dynamics Corp. as of Jan. 21, 2018 is the result of our systematic analysis on three basic characteristics: earnings strength, relative valuation, and recent stock price movement. The company has managed to produce a neutral trend in earnings per share over the past 5 quarters. However, while recent estimates for the company have been mixed, GD has posted better than expected results. Based on operating earnings yield, the company is undervalued when compared to all of the companies in our coverage universe. Share price changes over the past year indicates that GD will perform in line with the market over the near term.

Financial Data

(US$ in Millions)	3 Mos	12/31/2017	12/31/2016	12/31/2015	12/31/2014	12/31/2013	12/31/2012	12/31/2011
Earnings Per Share	9.73	9.56	9.52	9.08	7.42	6.67	(0.94)	6.87
Cash Flow Per Share	9.62	12.97	7.19	7.78	11.12	8.86	7.58	8.89
Tang Book Value Per Share	N.M.	N.M.	N.M.	N.M.	N.M.	3.70	N.M.	N.M.
Dividends Per Share	3.360	3.280	2.970	2.690	2.420	2.190	2.040	1.830
Dividend Payout %	34.53	34.31	31.20	29.63	32.61	25.19	...	26.64
Income Statement								
Total Revenue	7,535	30,973	31,353	31,469	30,852	31,218	31,513	32,677
EBITDA	1,096	4,621	4,776	4,667	4,384	4,249	1,317	4,451
Depn & Amortn	109	441	454	482	496	556	620	592
Income Before Taxes	960	4,077	4,231	4,102	3,802	3,607	541	3,718
Income Taxes	161	1,165	1,169	1,137	1,129	1,121	873	1,166
Net Income	799	2,912	2,955	2,965	2,533	2,357	(332)	2,526
Average Shares	301	304	310	326	341	353	353	367
Balance Sheet								
Current Assets	20,464	18,328	15,447	14,571	17,407	17,886	15,744	15,368
Total Assets	37,219	35,046	32,872	31,997	35,355	35,448	34,309	34,883
Current Liabilities	15,242	13,099	12,846	12,445	13,751	12,194	11,620	11,145
Long-Term Obligations	3,981	3,980	2,988	2,898	3,410	3,908	3,908	3,907
Total Liabilities	25,445	23,611	21,896	21,259	23,526	20,947	22,919	21,651
Stockholders' Equity	11,774	11,435	10,976	10,738	11,829	14,501	11,390	13,232
Shares Outstanding	297	296	302	312	332	353	353	356
Statistical Record								
Return on Assets %	8.37	8.58	9.09	8.80	7.16	6.76	N.M.	7.49
Return on Equity %	26.37	25.99	27.14	26.28	19.24	18.21	N.M.	19.03
EBITDA Margin %	14.55	14.92	15.23	14.83	14.21	13.61	4.18	13.62
Net Margin %	10.60	9.40	9.42	9.42	8.21	7.55	N.M.	7.73
Asset Turnover	0.88	0.91	0.96	0.93	0.87	0.90	0.91	0.97
Current Ratio	1.34	1.40	1.20	1.17	1.27	1.47	1.35	1.38
Debt to Equity	0.34	0.35	0.27	0.27	0.29	0.27	0.34	0.30
Price Range	229.95-185.85	213.86-175.32	178.67-124.18	153.28-131.27	145.36-94.46	95.55-64.57	74.09-61.96	78.11-55.67
P/E Ratio	23.63-19.10	22.37-18.34	18.77-13.04	16.88-14.46	19.59-12.73	14.33-9.68	...	11.37-8.10
Average Yield %	1.64	1.67	2.03	1.91	2.04	2.11	3.73	2.66

Address: 2941 Fairview Park Drive, Suite 100, Falls Church, VA 22042-4513	Web Site: www.generaldynamics.com	Auditors: KPMG LLP
Telephone: 703-876-3000	Officers: Phebe N. Novakovic - Chairman, President, Chief Executive Officer, Senior Vice President, Chief Operating Officer Jason W. Aiken - Senior Vice President, Vice President, Chief Financial Officer	Investor Contact: 703-876-3583 Transfer Agents: Computershare, Providence, RI

GENERAL ELECTRIC CO

Exchange	Symbol	Price	52Wk Range	Yield	P/E
NYS	GE	$13.61 (6/29/2018)	27.45-12.75	3.53	N/A

*7 Year Price Score 62.03   *NYSE Composite Index=100   *12 Month Price Score 74.32

TRADING VOLUME (thousand shares)

Interim Earnings (Per Share)

Qtr.	Mar	Jun	Sep	Dec
2015	(1.35)	(0.13)	0.25	0.62
2016	(0.01)	0.30	0.22	0.38
2017	0.07	0.13	0.21	(1.13)
2018	(0.14)	...	...	...

Interim Dividends (Per Share)

Amt	Decl	Ex	Rec	Pay
0.24Q	09/07/2017	09/15/2017	09/18/2017	10/25/2017
0.12Q	12/08/2017	12/26/2017	12/27/2017	01/25/2018
0.12Q	02/09/2018	02/23/2018	02/26/2018	04/25/2018
0.12Q	06/08/2018	06/15/2018	06/18/2018	07/25/2018

Indicated Div: $0.48 (Div. Reinv. Plan)

Valuation Analysis   Institutional Holding

Forecast EPS	$0.94	No of Institutions
	(06/13/2018)	3016
Market Cap	$118.2 Billion	Shares
Book Value	$59.5 Billion	6,157,541,376
Price/Book	1.99	% Held
Price/Sales	0.96	49.22

Business Summary: Electrical Equipment (MIC: 7.3.1 SIC: 3699 NAIC: 335999)

General Electric is a digital industrial company. Co.'s segments include: Power, which serves power generation, industrial, government and other customers worldwide with products and services related to energy production and water reuse; GE Renewable Energy, which makes renewable power sources; Oil & Gas, which serves all segments of the oil and gas industry, from drilling, completion, production and oil field operations, to transportation via liquefied natural gas and pipelines; Aviation, which designs and produces commercial and military aircraft engines, integrated digital components, electric power and mechanical aircraft systems; and Healthcare, which provides healthcare technologies.

Recent Developments: For the quarter ended Mar 31 2018, income from continuing operations increased 746.2% to US$440.0 million from US$52.0 million in the year-earlier quarter. Net loss amounted to US$1.11 billion versus a net loss of US$187.0 million in the year-earlier quarter. Revenues were US$28.66 billion, up 6.6% from US$26.88 billion the year before. Direct operating expenses rose 5.8% to US$22.97 billion from US$21.71 billion in the comparable period the year before. Indirect operating expenses increased 1.2% to US$5.49 billion from US$5.43 billion in the equivalent prior-year period.

Prospects: Our evaluation of General Electric Co as of Jan. 21, 2018 is the result of our systematic analysis on three basic characteristics: earnings strength, relative valuation, and recent stock price movement. The company has generated a negative trend in earnings per share over the past 5 quarters. However, while recent estimates for the company have been lowered by analysts, GE has posted results that fell short of analysts expectations. Based on operating earnings yield, the company is undervalued when compared to all of the companies in our coverage universe. Share price changes over the past year indicates that GE will perform in line with the market over the near term.

Financial Data

(US$ in Millions)	3 Mos	12/31/2017	12/31/2016	12/31/2015	12/31/2014	12/31/2013	12/31/2012	12/31/2011
Earnings Per Share	(0.93)	(0.72)	0.89	(0.61)	1.50	1.27	1.29	1.23
Cash Flow Per Share	1.33	1.20	(0.03)	2.00	2.76	2.80	2.97	3.15
Tang Book Value Per Share	N.M.	N.M.	N.M.	1.71	3.72	3.84	3.61	3.00
Dividends Per Share	0.720	0.840	0.930	0.920	0.890	0.790	0.700	0.610
Dividend Payout %	...	...	104.49	...	59.33	62.20	54.26	49.59
Income Statement								
Total Revenue	28,660	122,092	123,693	117,386	148,589	146,045	147,359	147,300
EBITDA	3,611	7,005	20,887	13,302	28,500	27,978	31,529	36,375
Depn & Amortn	1,913	10,927	6,832	1,653	1,789	1,711	1,615	1,732
Income Before Taxes	413	(8,791)	9,030	8,186	17,229	16,151	17,406	20,098
Income Taxes	(27)	(3,043)	(464)	6,485	1,772	676	2,504	5,732
Net Income	(1,147)	(5,786)	8,831	(6,126)	15,233	13,057	13,641	14,151
Average Shares	8,696	8,687	9,130	10,016	10,123	10,289	10,564	10,620
Balance Sheet								
Current Assets	112,419	128,356	138,872	151,993	179,041	171,249	162,740	165,198
Total Assets	358,109	377,945	365,183	492,692	648,349	656,560	685,328	717,242
Current Liabilities	73,533	79,378	81,998	108,197	208,440	206,572	221,403	253,379
Long-Term Obligations	106,469	108,575	105,080	145,301	200,414	221,665	236,084	243,459
Total Liabilities	298,595	313,683	289,356	394,418	520,190	525,994	562,302	600,804
Stockholders' Equity	59,514	64,263	75,828	98,274	128,159	130,566	123,026	116,438
Shares Outstanding	8,685	8,680	8,742	9,379	10,057	10,060	10,405	10,573
Statistical Record								
Return on Assets %	N.M.	N.M.	2.05	N.M.	2.33	1.95	1.94	1.93
Return on Equity %	N.M.	N.M.	10.12	N.M.	11.78	10.30	11.36	12.02
EBITDA Margin %	12.60	5.74	16.89	11.33	19.18	19.16	21.40	24.69
Net Margin %	N.M.	N.M.	7.14	N.M.	10.25	8.94	9.26	9.61
Asset Turnover	0.35	0.33	0.29	0.21	0.23	0.22	0.21	0.20
Current Ratio	1.53	1.62	1.69	1.40	0.86	0.83	0.74	0.65
Debt to Equity	1.79	1.69	1.39	1.48	1.56	1.70	1.92	2.09
Price Range	30.27-12.89	31.70-17.36	32.93-27.45	31.28-23.27	28.03-23.95	28.03-20.90	23.12-18.15	21.52-14.69
P/E Ratio	...	...	37.00-30.84	...	18.69-15.97	22.07-16.46	17.92-14.07	17.50-11.94
Average Yield %	3.22	3.23	3.06	3.43	3.42	3.29	3.46	3.36

Address: 41 Farnsworth Street, Boston, MA 02210	**Web Site:** www.ge.com	**Auditors:** KPMG LLP
Telephone: 617-443-3000	**Officers:** John Leonard Flannery - Chairman, Chief Executive Officer, Division Officer David Leon Joyce - Vice-Chairman, Division Officer	**Investor Contact:** 203-373-2460
		Transfer Agents: Computershare, Pittsburgh, PA

GENERAL MILLS INC

Exchange	Symbol	Price	52Wk Range	Yield	P/E	Div Acheiver
NYS	GIS	$44.26 (6/29/2018)	60.20-41.21	4.43	12.16	14 Years

*7 Year Price Score 80.66 *NYSE Composite Index=100 *12 Month Price Score 82.87

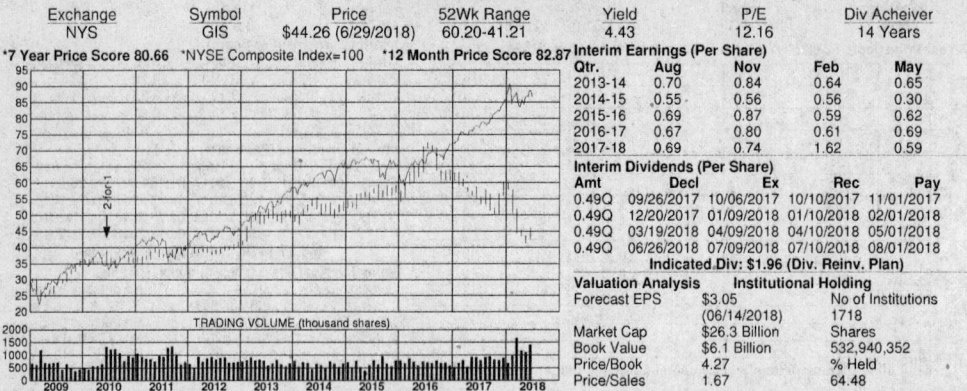

Interim Earnings (Per Share)

Qtr.	Aug	Nov	Feb	May
2013-14	0.70	0.84	0.64	0.65
2014-15	0.55	0.56	0.56	0.30
2015-16	0.69	0.87	0.59	0.62
2016-17	0.67	0.80	0.61	0.69
2017-18	0.69	0.74	1.62	0.59

Interim Dividends (Per Share)

Amt	Decl	Ex	Rec	Pay
0.49Q	09/26/2017	10/06/2017	10/10/2017	11/01/2017
0.49Q	12/20/2017	01/09/2018	01/10/2018	02/01/2018
0.49Q	03/19/2018	04/09/2018	04/10/2018	05/01/2018
0.49Q	06/26/2018	07/09/2018	07/10/2018	08/01/2018

Indicated.Div: $1.96 (Div. Reinv. Plan)

Valuation Analysis   **Institutional Holding**

Forecast EPS	$3.05	No of Institutions
	(06/14/2018)	1718
Market Cap	$26.3 Billion	Shares
Book Value	$6.1 Billion	532,940,352
Price/Book	4.27	% Held
Price/Sales	1.67	64.48

Business Summary: Food (MIC: 1.2.1 SIC: 2043 NAIC: 311230)

General Mills manufactures and markets branded consumer foods sold through retail stores. Co. has four segments: North America Retail, which provides cereals, refrigerated yogurt, soup, meal kits, refrigerated and frozen dough products, dessert and baking mixes, frozen pizza and pizza snacks, grain, fruit and savory snacks, and organic products; Convenience Stores & Foodservice, which provides cereals, snacks, yogurt, frozen meals, frozen dough products, and baking mixes; Europe & Australia, which includes retail and foodservice businesses in the Europe and Australia region; and Asia & Latin America, which includes retail and foodservice businesses in the Asia and South America regions.

Recent Developments: For the year ended May 27 2018, net income increased 27.2% to US$2.16 billion from US$1.70 billion in the prior year. Revenues were US$15.74 billion, up 0.8% from US$15.62 billion the year before. Operating income was US$2.51 billion versus US$2.57 billion in the prior year, a decrease of 2.2%. Direct operating expenses rose 2.6% to US$10.31 billion from US$10.06 billion in the comparable period the year before. Indirect operating expenses decreased 2.6% to US$2.92 billion from US$3.00 billion in the equivalent prior-year period.

Prospects: Our evaluation of General Mills Inc. as of Jan. 21, 2018 is the result of our systematic analysis on three basic characteristics: earnings strength, relative valuation, and recent stock price movement. The company has managed to produce a neutral trend in earnings per share over the past 5 quarters and while recent estimates for the company have been raised by analysts, GIS has posted better than expected results. Based on operating earnings yield, the company is undervalued when compared to all of the companies in our coverage universe. Share price changes over the past year indicates that GIS will perform poorly over the near term.

Financial Data

(US$ in Thousands)	05/27/2018	05/28/2017	05/29/2016	05/31/2015	05/25/2014	05/26/2013	05/27/2012	05/29/2011
Earnings Per Share	3.64	2.77	2.77	1.97	2.83	2.79	2.35	2.70
Cash Flow Per Share	4.94	3.95	4.40	4.15	4.05	4.52	3.72	2.38
Dividends Per Share	1.960	1.920	1.780	1.670	1.550	1.320	1.220	1.120
Dividend Payout %	53.85	69.31	64.26	84.77	54.77	47.31	51.91	41.48
Income Statement								
Total Revenue	15,740,400	15,619,800	16,563,100	17,630,300	17,909,600	17,774,100	16,657,900	14,880,200
EBITDA	3,128,100	3,170,000	3,315,500	2,665,600	3,542,800	3,439,800	3,103,900	3,247,100
Depn & Amortn	618,800	603,600	608,100	588,300	585,400	588,000	541,500	472,600
Income Before Taxes	2,135,600	2,271,300	2,403,600	1,761,900	2,655,000	2,534,900	2,210,500	2,428,200
Income Taxes	57,300	655,200	755,200	586,800	883,300	741,200	709,600	721,100
Net Income	2,131,000	1,657,500	1,697,400	1,221,300	1,824,400	1,855,200	1,567,300	1,798,300
Average Shares	585,700	598,000	611,900	618,800	645,700	665,600	666,700	664,800
Balance Sheet								
Current Assets	4,123,700	4,061,400	3,937,200	3,785,700	4,393,500	4,298,900	3,691,400	3,902,000
Total Assets	30,624,000	21,812,600	21,712,300	21,964,500	23,145,700	22,658,000	21,096,800	18,674,500
Current Liabilities	7,341,900	5,330,800	5,014,700	4,890,100	5,423,500	5,293,900	3,843,200	3,659,200
Long-Term Obligations	12,668,700	7,642,900	7,057,700	7,607,700	6,423,500	5,926,100	6,161,900	5,542,500
Total Liabilities	24,482,900	17,484,700	16,782,100	16,967,800	16,610,900	15,985,800	14,675,100	12,309,000
Stockholders' Equity	6,141,100	4,327,900	4,930,200	4,996,700	6,534,800	6,672,200	6,421,700	6,365,500
Shares Outstanding	593,100	576,900	596,800	598,700	612,300	640,800	648,500	644,800
Statistical Record								
Return on Assets %	8.15	7.64	7.79	5.33	7.99	8.50	7.90	9.92
Return on Equity %	40.82	35.90	34.29	20.84	27.70	28.41	24.58	30.65
EBITDA Margin %	19.87	20.29	20.02	15.12	19.78	19.35	18.63	21.82
Net Margin %	13.54	10.61	10.25	6.93	10.19	10.44	9.41	12.09
Asset Turnover	0.60	0.72	0.76	0.77	0.78	0.81	0.84	0.82
Current Ratio	0.56	0.76	0.79	0.77	0.81	0.81	0.96	1.07
Debt to Equity	2.06	1.77	1.43	1.52	0.98	0.89	0.96	0.87
Price Range	60.20-41.21	72.64-55.91	65.36-54.12	57.14-48.86	54.40-46.36	50.93-37.55	41.05-34.95	39.95-33.57
P/E Ratio	16.54-11.32	26.22-20.18	23.60-19.54	29.01-24.80	19.22-16.56	18.25-13.46	17.47-14.87	14.80-12.43
Average Yield %	3.71	3.03	3.05	3.14	3.09	3.13	3.16	3.07

Address: Number One General Mills Boulevard, Minneapolis, MN 55426
Telephone: 763-764-7600
Fax: 763-764-8330

Web Site: www.generalmills.com
Officers: Jeffrey L. (Jeff) Harmening - Chairman, President, Chief Executive Officer, Chief Operating Officer, Executive Vice President, Region Officer Donal L. Mulligan - Chief Financial Officer, Executive Vice President

Auditors: KPMG LLP
Investor Contact: 180-024-55703
Transfer Agents: Wells Fargo Bank, N.A., St. Paul, MN

GENERAL MOTORS CO

Exchange	Symbol	Price	52Wk Range	Yield	P/E
NYS	GM	$39.40 (6/29/2018)	46.48-34.76	3.86	N/A

*7 Year Price Score 99.25   *NYSE Composite Index=100   *12 Month Price Score 100.88

Interim Earnings (Per Share)

Qtr.	Mar	Jun	Sep	Dec
2015	0.56	0.67	0.84	3.84
2016	1.24	1.81	1.76	1.19
2017	1.70	1.09	(2.03)	(3.45)
2018	0.72	...	...	...

Interim Dividends (Per Share)

Amt	Decl	Ex	Rec	Pay
0.38Q	07/24/2017	09/07/2017	09/08/2017	09/22/2017
0.38Q	10/23/2017	12/07/2017	12/08/2017	12/21/2017
0.38Q	02/05/2018	03/08/2018	03/09/2018	03/23/2018
0.38Q	04/25/2018	06/07/2018	06/08/2018	06/22/2018

Indicated Div: $1.52

Valuation Analysis   **Institutional Holding**

Forecast EPS	$6.42	No of Institutions
	(06/14/2018)	1378
Market Cap	$55.5 Billion	Shares
Book Value	$34.3 Billion	1,178,371,712
Price/Book	1.62	% Held
Price/Sales	0.38	73.63

Business Summary: Autos- Manufacturing (MIC: 1.8.1 SIC: 3711 NAIC: 336111)

General Motors designs, builds and sells cars, trucks, crossovers and automobile parts. Co. also provides automotive financing services through its subsidiary, General Motors Financial Company, Inc. Co.'s automotive operations serves customers through its automotive segments: GM North America, GM Europe, GM International Operations and GM South America. In addition to the products sold to its dealers for consumer retail sales, Co. also sells vehicles directly or through its dealer network to fleet customers, including daily rental car companies, commercial fleet customers, leasing companies and governments. Co. also provides aftersale vehicle services and products via its dealer network.

Recent Developments: For the quarter ended Mar 31 2018, income from continuing operations decreased 58.7% to US$1.11 billion from US$2.69 billion in the year-earlier quarter. Net income decreased 60.3% to US$1.04 billion from US$2.62 billion in the year-earlier quarter. Revenues were US$36.10 billion, down 3.1% from US$37.27 billion the year before. Operating income was US$529.0 million versus US$2.58 billion in the prior-year quarter, a decrease of 79.5%. Direct operating expenses rose 2.7% to US$33.20 billion from US$32.33 billion in the comparable period the year before. Indirect operating expenses increased 0.7% to US$2.37 billion from US$2.36 billion in the equivalent prior-year period.

Prospects: Our evaluation of General Motors Co. as of Jan. 21, 2018 is the result of our systematic analysis on three basic characteristics: earnings strength, relative valuation, and recent stock price movement. The company has generated a negative trend in earnings per share over the past 5 quarters and while recent estimates for the company have been raised by analysts, GM has posted better than expected results. Based on operating earnings yield, the company is undervalued when compared to all of the companies in our coverage universe. Share price changes over the past year indicates that GM will perform well over the near term.

Financial Data

(US$ in Millions)	3 Mos	12/31/2017	12/31/2016	12/31/2015	12/31/2014	12/31/2013	12/31/2012	12/31/2011
Earnings Per Share	(3.67)	(2.60)	6.00	5.91	1.65	2.38	2.92	4.58
Cash Flow Per Share	11.18	11.83	10.71	7.55	6.27	9.07	6.75	5.32
Tang Book Value Per Share	20.23	20.78	25.09	21.96	18.04	20.30	12.49	N.M.
Dividends Per Share	1.520	1.520	1.520	1.380	1.200	...	...	...
Dividend Payout %	...	...	25.33	23.35	72.73	...	...	...
Income Statement								
Total Revenue	36,099	145,588	166,380	152,356	155,929	155,427	152,256	150,276
EBITDA	2,329	21,682	14,312	10,566	7,135	9,997	(22,705)	9,782
Depn & Amortn	1,800	11,666	4,767	5,220	5,403	5,078	7,908	4,108
Income Before Taxes	928	9,731	9,402	5,524	2,152	5,648	(30,257)	5,985
Income Taxes	466	11,533	2,416	(1,897)	228	2,127	(34,831)	(110)
Net Income	1,046	(3,864)	9,427	9,687	3,949	5,346	6,188	9,190
Average Shares	1,430	1,492	1,570	1,640	1,687	1,676	1,675	1,668
Balance Sheet								
Current Assets	71,435	68,744	76,203	78,007	83,670	81,501	69,996	60,247
Total Assets	218,726	212,482	221,690	194,520	177,677	166,344	149,422	144,603
Current Liabilities	82,716	76,890	85,181	71,466	65,701	62,412	53,992	48,932
Long-Term Obligations	69,471	67,254	55,600	43,549	31,853	22,025	10,532	11,650
Total Liabilities	184,428	177,481	177,854	154,649	142,220	123,737	113,178	106,483
Stockholders' Equity	34,298	35,001	43,836	39,871	35,457	42,607	36,244	38,120
Shares Outstanding	1,409	1,402	1,497	1,544	1,610	1,589	1,366	1,564
Statistical Record								
Return on Assets %	N.M.	N.M.	4.52	5.21	2.30	3.39	4.20	6.48
Return on Equity %	N.M.	N.M.	22.46	25.72	10.12	13.56	16.60	24.74
EBITDA Margin %	6.45	14.89	8.60	6.94	4.58	6.43	N.M.	6.51
Net Margin %	2.90	N.M.	5.67	6.36	2.53	3.44	4.06	6.12
Asset Turnover	0.64	0.67	0.80	0.82	0.91	0.98	1.03	1.06
Current Ratio	0.86	0.89	0.89	1.09	1.27	1.31	1.30	1.23
Debt to Equity	2.03	1.92	1.27	1.09	0.90	0.52	0.29	0.31
Price Range	46.48-32.42	46.48-32.42	37.66-26.90	38.87-27.28	40.95-29.69	41.53-26.33	28.83-18.80	38.98-19.05
P/E Ratio	...	...	6.28-4.48	6.58-4.62	24.82-17.99	17.45-11.06	9.87-6.44	8.51-4.16
Average Yield %	3.94	4.04	4.85	4.02	3.47	...	...	...

Address: 300 Renaissance Center, Detroit, MI 48265-3000 **Telephone:** 313-667-1500	**Web Site:** www.gm.com **Officers:** Mary T. Barra - Chairman, Chief Executive Officer, Senior Vice President Daniel (Dan) Ammann - President, Senior Vice President, Chief Financial Officer	**Auditors:** Ernst & Young LLP **Transfer Agents:** Computershare Trust Company, N.A., Providence, RI

GENESEE & WYOMING INC.

Exchange	Symbol	Price	52Wk Range	Yield	P/E
NYS	GWR	$81.32 (6/29/2018)	83.53-65.11	N/A	8.51

*7 Year Price Score 79.01 *NYSE Composite Index=100 *12 Month Price Score 104.41

TRADING VOLUME (thousand shares)

Interim Earnings (Per Share)

Qtr.	Mar	Jun	Sep	Dec
2015	0.42	0.92	1.10	1.47
2016	0.47	0.83	0.98	0.14
2017	0.42	0.74	0.80	6.83
2018	1.19	...	...	...

Interim Dividends (Per Share)

No Dividends Paid

Valuation Analysis		Institutional Holding	
Forecast EPS	$3.85	No of Institutions	
	(06/13/2018)	433	
Market Cap	$5.0 Billion	Shares	
Book Value	$3.7 Billion	69,493,112	
Price/Book	1.37	% Held	
Price/Sales	2.22	90.43	

Business Summary: Rail (MIC: 7.4.3 SIC: 4011 NAIC: 482111)

Genesee & Wyoming owns and operates freight railroads worldwide that are organized in 10 operating regions. Co. has three segments: North American Operations, which includes eight regions that serve 41 U.S. states and four Canadian provinces and includes 115 short line and regional freight railroads with more than 13,000 track-miles; Australian Operations, which provides rail freight services in New South Wales, including in the Hunter Valley coal supply chain, the Northern Territory and South Australia; and U.K./European Operations, which is led by Freightliner Group Limited, a rail maritime intermodal operator and a rail freight company.

Recent Developments: For the quarter ended Mar 31 2018, net income increased 178.6% to US$76.0 million from US$27.3 million in the year-earlier quarter. Revenues were US$574.7 million, up 10.7% from US$519.1 million the year before. Operating income was US$86.9 million versus US$75.9 million in the prior-year quarter, an increase of 14.5%. Direct operating expenses rose 18.4% to US$200.0 million from US$169.0 million in the comparable period the year before. Indirect operating expenses increased 4.9% to US$287.7 million from US$274.2 million in the equivalent prior-year period.

Prospects: Our evaluation of Genesee & Wyoming Inc. as of Jan. 21, 2018 is the result of our systematic analysis on three basic characteristics: earnings strength, relative valuation, and recent stock price movement. The company has generated a negative trend in earnings per share over the past 5 quarters and while recent estimates for the company have been mixed, GWR has posted results that fell short of analysts expectations. Based on operating earnings yield, the company is about fairly valued when compared to all of the companies in our coverage universe. Share price changes over the past year indicates that GWR will perform poorly over the near term.

Financial Data

(US$ in Thousands)	3 Mos	12/31/2017	12/31/2016	12/31/2015	12/31/2014	12/31/2013	12/31/2012	12/31/2011
Earnings Per Share	9.56	8.79	2.42	3.89	4.58	4.79	1.02	2.79
Cash Flow Per Share	8.00	7.78	7.08	8.37	8.89	7.69	3.99	4.35
Tang Book Value Per Share	15.44	13.50	4.77	9.77	21.13	16.87	12.51	13.42
Income Statement								
Total Revenue	574,661	2,208,044	2,001,527	2,000,401	1,639,012	1,569,011	874,916	829,096
EBITDA	150,863	593,628	462,325	526,623	557,830	501,510	209,116	253,098
Depn & Amortn	65,990	192,900	172,300	159,100	135,000	119,200	66,600	59,700
Income Before Taxes	60,135	295,519	215,491	300,931	368,113	318,387	83,396	158,024
Income Taxes	(15,890)	(261,259)	74,395	75,894	107,107	46,296	46,402	38,531
Net Income	75,098	549,051	141,137	225,037	260,755	271,296	52,433	119,484
Average Shares	62,887	62,464	58,256	57,848	56,972	56,679	51,316	42,772
Balance Sheet								
Current Assets	653,120	589,533	485,338	576,560	548,426	548,330	465,252	240,199
Total Assets	8,070,776	8,034,897	7,634,958	6,795,604	5,595,753	5,319,821	5,226,115	2,294,157
Current Liabilities	460,785	467,781	479,110	533,814	464,238	456,508	416,744	261,271
Long-Term Obligations	2,341,563	2,303,442	2,306,915	2,223,306	1,548,051	1,540,346	1,770,566	569,026
Total Liabilities	4,389,936	4,456,363	4,740,376	4,276,143	3,238,894	3,172,026	3,331,654	1,333,523
Stockholders' Equity	3,680,840	3,578,534	2,894,582	2,519,461	2,356,859	2,147,795	1,894,461	960,634
Shares Outstanding	61,930	62,647	62,120	57,738	53,958	53,543	47,088	42,450
Statistical Record								
Return on Assets %	7.58	7.01	1.95	3.63	4.78	5.15	1.39	5.48
Return on Equity %	18.04	16.96	5.20	9.23	11.58	13.42	3.66	13.44
EBITDA Margin %	26.25	26.88	23.10	26.33	34.03	31.96	23.90	30.53
Net Margin %	13.07	24.87	7.05	11.25	15.91	17.29	5.99	14.41
Asset Turnover	0.29	0.28	0.28	0.32	0.30	0.30	0.23	0.38
Current Ratio	1.42	1.26	1.01	1.08	1.18	1.20	1.12	0.92
Debt to Equity	0.64	0.64	0.80	0.88	0.66	0.72	0.93	0.59
Price Range	83.53-62.60	79.48-62.60	80.01-44.55	105.15-50.28	105.51-83.33	101.77-76.08	76.28-48.08	61.98-45.19
P/E Ratio	8.74-6.55	9.04-7.12	33.06-18.41	27.03-12.93	23.04-18.19	21.25-15.88	74.78-47.14	22.22-16.20

Address: 20 West Avenue, Darien, CT 06820
Telephone: 203-202-8900

Web Site: www.gwrr.com
Officers: John C. Hellmann - Chairman, President, Chief Executive Officer Timothy J. Gallagher - Chief Financial Officer

Auditors: PricewaterhouseCoopers LLP
Transfer Agents: Computershare, Providence, RI

GENESIS HEALTHCARE INC

Exchange	Symbol	Price	52Wk Range	Yield	P/E
NYS	GEN	$2.29 (6/29/2018)	2.86-0.69	N/A	N/A

*7 Year Price Score 23.04   *NYSE Composite Index=100   *12 Month Price Score 163.32

Interim Earnings (Per Share)

Qtr.	Mar	Jun	Sep	Dec
2015	(1.50)	(0.22)	(0.32)	(3.07)
2016	(0.48)	(0.26)	(0.23)	0.14
2017	(0.55)	(0.70)	(3.94)	(0.91)
2018	(0.70)	...	...	...

Interim Dividends (Per Share)

No Dividends Paid

Valuation Analysis   Institutional Holding

Forecast EPS	$-1.65	No of Institutions
	(06/12/2018)	28
Market Cap	$365.1 Million	Shares
Book Value	N/A	1,463,447
Price/Book	N/A	% Held
Price/Sales	0.07	36.90

TRADING VOLUME (thousand shares)

Business Summary: Hospitals & Health Care Facilities (MIC: 4.2.1 SIC: 8051 NAIC: 623110)

Genesis Healthcare is a holding company. As of Dec 31 2017, Co. provided inpatient services through its network of 470 nursing and assisted/senior living facilities across 30 states, consisting of 444 skilled nursing facilities and 26 stand-alone assisted/senior living facilities. As of Dec 31 2017, Co. had three operating segments: inpatient services, which includes the operation of nursing facilities and assisted/senior living facilities; rehabilitation therapy services, which includes Co.'s integrated and third-party rehabilitation and respiratory therapy services; and all other services, which provides a range of other specialty medical services, including physician services.

Recent Developments: For the quarter ended Mar 31 2018, loss from continuing operations was US$108.7 million compared with a loss of US$83.6 million in the year-earlier quarter. Net loss amounted to US$108.7 million versus a net loss of US$83.6 million in the year-earlier quarter. Revenues were US$1.30 billion, down 6.3% from US$1.39 billion the year before. Indirect operating expenses decreased 4.7% to US$1.27 billion from US$1.34 billion in the equivalent prior-year period.

Prospects: Our evaluation of Genesis Healthcare Inc. as of Jan. 21, 2018 is the result of our systematic analysis on three basic characteristics: earnings strength, relative valuation, and recent stock price movement. The company has produced a positive trend in earnings per share over the past 5 quarters. Because the company lacks sufficient analyst estimate data, we place greater weight on the historical EPS trend as the measure of earnings strength. Based on operating earnings yield, the company is overvalued when compared to all of the companies in our coverage universe. Share price changes over the past year indicates that GEN will perform very poorly over the near term.

Financial Data
(US$ in Thousands)

	3 Mos	12/31/2017	12/31/2016	12/31/2015	12/31/2014	12/31/2013	12/31/2012	12/31/2011
Earnings Per Share	(6.25)	(6.15)	(0.82)	(4.97)	(0.02)	(0.28)	0.57	(5.47)
Cash Flow Per Share	0.71	1.28	0.76	0.10	0.69	1.28	1.14	2.68
Tang Book Value Per Share	...	...	...	...	0.20	0.11	N.M.	N.M.
Income Statement								
Total Revenue	1,301,072	5,373,740	5,732,430	5,619,224	833,256	842,272	872,623	869,701
EBITDA	58,434	(232,260)	624,445	371,445	51,958	46,485	93,535	(140,125)
Depn & Amortn	51,503	238,200	234,700	218,800	24,300	23,600	24,200	23,300
Income Before Taxes	(108,106)	(969,842)	(138,799)	(355,164)	(3,582)	(11,038)	32,087	(201,705)
Income Taxes	347	(10,427)	(17,435)	172,524	(1,248)	(2,905)	12,438	3,516
Net Income	(68,538)	(578,982)	(64,013)	(426,195)	(907)	(10,484)	21,597	(203,266)
Average Shares	98,252	94,217	152,532	85,755	38,125	37,533	37,589	37,145
Balance Sheet								
Current Assets	952,934	939,907	1,058,987	1,011,493	161,383	142,417	138,825	143,331
Total Assets	4,771,539	4,787,865	5,779,201	6,091,470	650,956	643,416	682,636	695,000
Current Liabilities	859,401	899,194	857,560	798,665	115,292	97,788	104,303	98,378
Long-Term Obligations	4,997,697	5,005,175	5,011,424	5,335,573	398,389	411,495	435,629	471,069
Total Liabilities	5,930,726	5,872,092	6,269,524	6,527,777	555,697	551,184	582,805	617,787
Stockholders' Equity	(1,159,187)	(1,084,227)	(490,323)	(436,307)	95,259	92,232	99,831	77,213
Shares Outstanding	159,446	159,406	154,531	153,554	39,994	39,793	38,543	38,001
Statistical Record								
Return on Assets %	N.M.	N.M.	N.M.	N.M.	N.M.	N.M.	3.13	N.M.
Return on Equity %	...	...	...	...	N.M.	N.M.	24.33	N.M.
EBITDA Margin %	4.49	N.M.	10.89	6.61	6.24	5.52	10.72	N.M.
Net Margin %	N.M.	N.M.	N.M.	N.M.	N.M.	N.M.	2.47	N.M.
Asset Turnover	1.01	1.02	0.96	1.67	1.29	1.27	1.26	1.07
Current Ratio	1.11	1.05	1.23	1.27	1.40	1.46	1.33	1.46
Debt to Equity	...	...	...	...	4.18	4.46	4.36	6.10
Price Range	2.67-0.69	4.69-0.69	4.36-1.38	9.22-3.42	8.91-4.28	7.36-4.20	8.02-5.18	15.56-3.40
P/E Ratio	...	...	...	...	...	...	14.07-9.09	...

Address: 101 East State Street, Kennett Square, PA 19348	**Web Site:** www.genesishcc.com	**Auditors:** KPMG LLP
Telephone: 610-444-6350	**Officers:** George V. Hager - Chief Executive Officer Paul D. Bach - Chief Operating Officer	**Transfer Agents:** Wells Fargo Shareowner Services, South St. Paul, MN

GENPACT LTD

Exchange	Symbol	Price	52Wk Range	Yield	P/E
NYS	G	$28.93 (6/29/2018)	34.76-27.39	1.04	20.37

*7 Year Price Score 114.22 *NYSE Composite Index=100   *12 Month Price Score 97.65

TRADING VOLUME (thousand shares)

Interim Earnings (Per Share)

Qtr.	Mar	Jun	Sep	Dec
2015	0.20	0.28	0.31	0.29
2016	0.27	0.31	0.33	0.37
2017	0.26	0.36	0.38	0.35
2018	0.33	...	...	...

Interim Dividends (Per Share)

Amt	Decl	Ex	Rec	Pay
0.06Q	08/18/2017	09/07/2017	09/08/2017	09/21/2017
0.06Q	11/22/2017	12/07/2017	12/08/2017	12/20/2017
0.075Q	02/12/2018	03/08/2018	03/09/2018	03/21/2018
0.075Q	05/08/2018	06/07/2018	06/08/2018	06/20/2018

Indicated Div: $0.30

Valuation Analysis

		Institutional Holding	
Forecast EPS	N/A	No of Institutions	335
Market Cap	$5.5 Billion	Shares	184,582,816
Book Value	$1.4 Billion	% Held	
Price/Book	4.04		88.09
Price/Sales	1.97		

Business Summary: Business Services (MIC: 7.5.2 SIC: 8742 NAIC: 541618)

Genpact is engaged in business process management and services. Co.'s business focuses on industry verticals in banking and financial services, capital markets, consumer product goods, healthcare, high tech, infrastructure, manufacturing and services, insurance, and life sciences. In addition, Co.'s process knowledge spans a number of service areas, including analytics and research, collections and customer services, consulting and transformation services, core industry operations services, enterprise application services, finance and accounting services, IT infrastructure management services, and supply chain and procurement services.

Recent Developments: For the year ended Dec 31 2017, net income decreased 2.5% to US$260.8 million from US$267.5 million in the prior year. Revenues were US$2.74 billion, up 6.5% from US$2.57 billion the year before. Operating income was US$328.6 million versus US$340.8 million in the prior year, a decrease of 3.6%. Direct operating expenses rose 8.3% to US$1.68 billion from US$1.55 billion in the comparable period the year before. Indirect operating expenses increased 7.3% to US$724.6 million from US$675.3 million in the equivalent prior-year period.

Prospects: Our evaluation of Genpact Ltd. as of Sep. 17, 2017 is the result of our systematic analysis on three basic characteristics: earnings strength, relative valuation, and recent stock price movement. The company has managed to produce a neutral trend in earnings per share over the past 5 quarters and while recent estimates for the company have remained steady, G has posted better than expected results. Based on operating earnings yield, the company is undervalued when compared to all of the companies in our coverage universe. Share price changes over the past year indicates that G will perform well over the near term.

Financial Data
(US$ in Thousands)

	3 Mos	12/31/2017	12/31/2016	12/31/2015	12/31/2014	12/31/2013	12/31/2012	12/31/2011
Earnings Per Share	1.42	1.34	1.28	1.09	0.85	0.97	0.78	0.81
Cash Flow Per Share	1.56	1.85	1.67	1.51	1.23	1.36	1.38	1.20
Tang Book Value Per Share	N.M.	N.M.	0.73	0.79	0.52	1.17	0.44	1.77
Dividends Per Share	0.255	0.240	...	...	...	...	2.240	...
Dividend Payout %	17.96	17.91	...	...	...	...	287.18	...
Income Statement								
Total Revenue	688,912	2,736,929	2,570,756	2,461,044	2,279,438	2,131,997	1,901,971	1,600,436
EBITDA	106,808	438,182	426,536	409,892	356,352	399,175	348,457	323,415
Depn & Amortn	22,699	81,321	73,009	76,186	72,572	70,053	69,351	67,279
Income Before Taxes	76,009	325,126	337,343	312,554	254,385	305,982	262,992	262,059
Income Taxes	12,075	59,742	62,098	61,937	57,419	71,100	78,419	70,656
Net Income	64,695	263,111	269,684	239,817	192,002	229,717	178,216	184,294
Average Shares	196,288	197,049	210,126	219,145	225,168	235,754	229,532	226,354
Balance Sheet								
Current Assets	1,326,500	1,433,895	1,227,037	1,195,069	1,188,508	1,276,144	1,128,767	985,119
Total Assets	3,397,127	3,449,621	2,885,880	2,793,489	2,742,537	2,689,367	2,605,927	2,403,387
Current Liabilities	871,190	838,784	731,355	594,480	622,114	461,693	517,818	661,828
Long-Term Obligations	999,404	1,009,351	700,652	739,536	651,974	656,258	659,412	75,631
Total Liabilities	2,031,130	2,025,577	1,599,232	1,489,133	1,457,401	1,366,628	1,437,516	970,329
Stockholders' Equity	1,365,997	1,424,044	1,286,648	1,304,356	1,285,136	1,322,739	1,168,411	1,433,058
Shares Outstanding	190,613	192,825	198,794	211,472	218,684	231,262	225,480	222,347
Statistical Record								
Return on Assets %	8.70	8.31	9.47	8.66	7.07	8.68	7.10	8.58
Return on Equity %	21.55	19.41	20.76	18.52	14.72	18.44	13.66	12.66
EBITDA Margin %	15.50	16.01	16.59	16.66	15.63	18.72	18.32	20.21
Net Margin %	9.39	9.61	10.49	9.74	8.42	10.77	9.37	11.52
Asset Turnover	0.89	0.86	0.90	0.89	0.84	0.81	0.76	0.74
Current Ratio	1.52	1.71	1.68	2.01	1.91	2.76	2.18	1.49
Debt to Equity	0.73	0.71	0.54	0.57	0.51	0.50	0.56	0.05
Price Range	34.76-23.37	32.66-23.37	28.39-22.70	25.85-18.87	19.30-14.28	21.19-15.46	18.66-14.45	17.83-13.09
P/E Ratio	24.48-16.46	24.37-17.44	22.18-17.73	23.72-17.31	22.71-16.80	21.85-15.94	23.92-18.53	22.01-16.16
Average Yield %	0.88	0.86	...	...	...	...	13.73	...

Address: Canon's Court, 22 Victoria Street, Hamilton, HM12	Web Site: www.genpact.com	Auditors: KPMG
Telephone: 441-295-2244	Officers: N. V. (Tiger) Tyagarajan - President, Chief Executive Officer Edward J. Fitzpatrick - Chief Financial Officer	Investor Contact: 144-129-52244 Transfer Agents: Computershare, Providence, RI

GENUINE PARTS CO.

Exchange	Symbol	Price	52Wk Range	Yield	P/E	Div Acheiver
NYS	GPC	$91.79 (6/29/2018)	107.58-80.48	3.14	N/A	61 Years

*7 Year Price Score 88.57   *NYSE Composite Index=100   *12 Month Price Score 99.36

Interim Earnings (Per Share)

Qtr.	Mar	Jun	Sep	Dec
2015	1.05	1.28	1.24	1.07
2016	1.05	1.28	1.24	1.03
2017	1.08	1.29	1.08	0.74
2018	1.20	...	...	...

Interim Dividends (Per Share)

Amt	Decl	Ex	Rec	Pay
0.675Q	08/21/2017	09/07/2017	09/08/2017	10/02/2017
0.675Q	11/20/2017	12/07/2017	12/08/2017	01/02/2018
0.72Q	02/19/2018	03/08/2018	03/09/2018	04/02/2018
0.72Q	04/23/2018	06/07/2018	06/08/2018	07/02/2018

Indicated Div: $2.88 (Div. Reinv. Plan)

Valuation Analysis

		Institutional Holding	
Forecast EPS	$5.64	No of Institutions	
	(06/14/2018)	997	
Market Cap	$13.5 Billion	Shares	
Book Value	$3.5 Billion	142,692,112	
Price/Book	3.84	% Held	
Price/Sales	N/A	67.70	

TRADING VOLUME (thousand shares)

Business Summary: Auto Parts (MIC: 1.8.2 SIC: 5013 NAIC: 423120)

Genuine Parts is a service organization engaged in the distribution of automotive replacement parts, industrial replacement parts, office products and electrical/electronic materials. Co.'s Automotive Parts Group distributes automotive parts and accessory items. Co.'s Industrial Parts Group distributes industrial replacement parts and related supplies such as bearings and material handling products. Co.'s Office Products Group engages in the wholesale distribution a line of office and other business related products. Co.'s Electrical/Electronic Materials Group distributes materials to electrical and electronic manufacturers, and industrial assembly and specialty wire and cable markets.

Recent Developments: For the quarter ended Mar 31 2018, net income increased 10.2% to US$176.6 million from US$160.2 million in the year-earlier quarter. Revenues were US$4.59 billion, up 17.4% from US$3.91 billion the year before. Direct operating expenses rose 14.6% to US$3.15 billion from US$2.75 billion in the comparable period the year before. Indirect operating expenses increased 30.1% to US$1.19 billion from US$918.6 million in the equivalent prior-year period.

Prospects: Our evaluation of Genuine Parts Co. as of Jan. 21, 2018 is the result of our systematic analysis on three basic characteristics: earnings strength, relative valuation, and recent stock price movement. The company has managed to produce a neutral trend in earnings per share over the past 5 quarters. However, while recent estimates for the company have been mixed, GPC has posted results that fell short of analysts expectations. Based on operating earnings yield, the company is about fairly valued when compared to all of the companies in our coverage universe. Share price changes over the past year indicates that GPC will perform very poorly over the near term.

Financial Data
(US$ in Thousands)

	3 Mos	12/31/2017	12/31/2016	12/31/2015	12/31/2014	12/31/2013	12/31/2012	12/31/2011
Earnings Per Share	...	4.18	4.59	4.63	4.61	4.40	4.14	3.58
Cash Flow Per Share	...	5.54	6.33	7.64	5.15	6.83	5.82	3.99
Tang Book Value Per Share	N.M.	N.M.	10.91	11.89	12.50	13.39	16.15	16.08
Dividends Per Share	2.745	2.700	2.630	2.460	2.300	2.150	1.980	1.800
Dividend Payout %	...	64.59	57.30	53.13	49.89	48.86	47.83	50.28
Income Statement								
Total Revenue	4,586,294	16,308,801	15,339,713	15,280,044	15,341,647	14,077,843	13,013,868	12,458,877
EBITDA	311,791	1,218,445	1,242,911	1,287,018	1,291,140	1,205,232	1,137,797	1,006,778
Depn & Amortn	58,363	167,691	147,487	141,675	148,313	133,957	98,383	88,936
Income Before Taxes	229,319	1,009,268	1,074,340	1,123,681	1,117,739	1,044,304	1,018,932	890,806
Income Taxes	52,743	392,511	387,100	418,009	406,453	359,345	370,891	325,690
Net Income	176,576	616,757	687,240	705,672	711,286	684,959	648,041	565,116
Average Shares	147,322	147,701	149,804	152,496	154,375	155,714	156,420	157,660
Balance Sheet								
Current Assets	7,581,612	7,312,893	5,948,431	5,555,316	5,592,525	5,221,491	4,820,131	4,576,596
Total Assets	12,759,394	12,412,381	8,859,400	8,144,771	8,246,238	7,680,297	6,807,061	5,879,591
Current Liabilities	5,757,472	5,474,025	4,244,150	3,940,654	3,584,115	3,183,044	2,487,638	1,812,073
Long-Term Obligations	2,564,111	2,605,713	589,221	287,642	540,040	527,815	283,748	534,186
Total Liabilities	9,249,315	9,000,229	5,665,672	4,998,204	4,944,990	4,331,223	3,809,174	3,096,356
Stockholders' Equity	3,510,079	3,412,152	3,193,728	3,146,567	3,301,248	3,349,074	2,997,887	2,783,235
Shares Outstanding	146,737	146,652	148,410	150,081	153,113	153,773	154,841	155,651
Statistical Record								
Return on Assets %	...	5.80	8.06	8.61	8.93	9.46	10.19	9.96
Return on Equity %	...	18.67	21.62	21.89	21.39	21.58	22.36	20.27
EBITDA Margin %	6.80	7.47	8.10	8.42	8.42	8.56	8.74	8.08
Net Margin %	3.85	3.78	4.48	4.62	4.64	4.87	4.98	4.54
Asset Turnover	...	1.53	1.80	1.86	1.93	1.94	2.05	2.20
Current Ratio	1.32	1.34	1.40	1.41	1.56	1.64	1.94	2.53
Debt to Equity	0.73	0.76	0.18	0.09	0.16	0.16	0.09	0.19
Price Range	107.58-80.48	100.67-80.48	105.24-77.40	106.57-79.53	108.31-77.75	85.03-63.58	66.38-58.53	61.96-46.73
P/E Ratio	...	24.08-19.25	22.93-16.86	23.02-17.18	23.49-16.87	19.32-14.45	16.03-14.14	17.31-13.05
Average Yield %	3.01	2.96	2.75	2.72	2.59	2.77	3.16	3.34

Address: 2999 Wildwood Parkway, Atlanta, GA 30339
Telephone: 678-934-5000

Web Site: www.genpt.com
Officers: Paul D. Donahue - President, Chief Executive Officer, Executive Vice President, Division Officer Carol B. Yancey - Executive Vice President, Vice President, Chief Financial Officer, Corporate Secretary

Auditors: Ernst & Young LLP
Investor Contact: 770-953-1700
Transfer Agents: Computershare, Providence, RI

GENWORTH FINANCIAL, INC. (HOLDING CO)

Exchange	Symbol	Price	52Wk Range	Yield	P/E
NYS	GNW	$4.50 (6/29/2018)	4.82-2.69	N/A	2.94

*7 Year Price Score 36.80 ***NYSE Composite Index=100** ***12 Month Price Score 109.20**

TRADING VOLUME (thousand shares)

Interim Earnings (Per Share)

Qtr.	Mar	Jun	Sep	Dec
2015	0.31	(0.39)	(0.57)	(0.59)
2016	0.11	0.34	(0.76)	(0.25)
2017	0.31	0.40	0.21	0.70
2018	0.22	...	...	...

Interim Dividends (Per Share)

No Dividends Paid

Valuation Analysis

Valuation Analysis		Institutional Holding	
Forecast EPS	$1.00	No of Institutions	
	(06/04/2018)	496	
Market Cap	$2.3 Billion	Shares	
Book Value	$13.0 Billion	425,563,616	
Price/Book	0.17	% Held	
Price/Sales	0.27	80.64	

Business Summary: Life & Health (MIC: 5.2.2 SIC: 6311 NAIC: 524113)

Genworth Financial is a holding company. Co. operates its business through five operating segments: U.S. Mortgage Insurance, which provides mortgage insurance products predominantly insuring prime-based, individually underwritten residential mortgage loans; Canada Mortgage Insurance, which provides flow mortgage insurance and also provide bulk mortgage insurance in Canada; Australia Mortgage Insurance, which provides flow mortgage insurance and also provide bulk mortgage insurance in Australia; U.S. Life Insurance, which provides long-term care insurance products, and service life insurance; and Runoff, which includes the results of non-strategic products which are no longer actively sold.

Recent Developments: For the quarter ended Mar 31 2018, income from continuing operations decreased 23.6% to US$165.0 million from US$216.0 million in the year-earlier quarter. Net income decreased 23.6% to US$165.0 million from US$216.0 million in the year-earlier quarter. Revenues were US$2.12 billion, down 2.6% from US$2.17 billion the year before. Net premiums earned were unchanged at US$1.14 billion versus the prior-year quarter. Net investment income rose 1.8% to US$804.0 million from US$790.0 million a year ago.

Prospects: Our evaluation of Genworth Financial Inc. as of Jan. 21, 2018 is the result of our systematic analysis on three basic characteristics: earnings strength, relative valuation, and recent stock price movement. The company has managed to produce a neutral trend in earnings per share over the past 5 quarters and while recent estimates for the company have been raised by analysts, GNW has posted results that fell short of analysts expectations. Based on operating earnings yield, the company is undervalued when compared to all of the companies in our coverage universe. Share price changes over the past year indicates that GNW will perform poorly over the near term.

Financial Data
(US$ in Millions)

	3 Mos	12/31/2017	12/31/2016	12/31/2015	12/31/2014	12/31/2013	12/31/2012	12/31/2011
Earnings Per Share	1.53	1.63	(0.56)	(1.24)	(2.51)	1.12	0.65	0.25
Cash Flow Per Share	4.02	5.12	3.71	3.20	4.91	2.83	1.95	6.37
Tang Book Value Per Share	25.31	26.29	24.69	25.03	29.45	26.52	30.34	29.96
Income Statement								
Premium Income	1,140	4,004	4,160	4,579	5,431	5,148	5,038	5,705
Total Revenue	2,115	8,295	8,369	8,548	9,565	9,403	10,023	10,344
Income Before Taxes	228	729	320	(15)	(1,276)	1,050	712	314
Income Taxes	63	(207)	358	(9)	(228)	324	189	53
Net Income	112	817	(277)	(615)	(1,244)	560	323	122
Average Shares	502	501	498	497	496	498	494	493
Balance Sheet								
Total Assets	103,773	105,297	104,658	106,431	111,358	108,045	113,312	114,302
Total Liabilities	90,755	91,879	92,014	93,607	96,435	93,652	96,775	97,761
Stockholders' Equity	13,018	13,418	12,644	12,824	14,923	14,393	16,537	16,541
Shares Outstanding	501	499	498	498	497	495	492	491
Statistical Record								
Return on Assets %	0.74	0.78	N.M.	N.M.	N.M.	0.51	0.28	0.11
Return on Equity %	5.99	6.27	N.M.	N.M.	N.M.	3.62	1.95	0.80
Net Margin %	5.30	9.85	(3.31)	(7.19)	(13.01)	5.96	3.22	1.18
Price Range	4.16-2.72	4.16-3.11	5.22-1.61	9.15-3.47	18.60-7.64	15.63-7.51	9.34-4.12	14.31-4.92
P/E Ratio	2.72-1.78	2.55-1.91	...	...	...	13.96-6.71	14.37-6.34	57.24-19.68

Address: 6620 West Broad Street, Richmond, VA 23230 **Telephone:** 804-281-6000	**Web Site:** www.genworth.com **Officers:** Thomas J. McInerney - President, Chief Executive Officer Kelly L. Groh - Executive Vice President, Chief Financial Officer, Controller, Division Officer	**Auditors:** KPMG LLP **Transfer Agents:** Computershare Shareowner Services LLC, College Station, TX

GGP INC

Exchange	Symbol	Price	52Wk Range	Yield	P/E
NYS	GGP	$20.43 (6/29/2018)	24.07-19.01	4.31	32.43

*7 Year Price Score 76.75 *NYSE Composite Index=100 *12 Month Price Score 93.26

Interim Earnings (Per Share)

Qtr.	Mar	Jun	Sep	Dec
2015	0.66	0.44	0.13	0.20
2016	0.20	0.19	0.70	0.25
2017	0.11	0.13	0.23	0.21
2018	0.06	...	...	...

Interim Dividends (Per Share)

Amt	Decl	Ex	Rec	Pay
0.22Q	08/02/2017	10/12/2017	10/13/2017	10/31/2017
0.22Q	10/31/2017	12/14/2017	12/15/2017	01/05/2018
0.22Q	02/07/2018	04/12/2018	04/13/2018	04/30/2018
0.22Q	05/03/2018	07/12/2018	07/13/2018	07/31/2018

Indicated Div: $0.88 (Div. Reinv. Plan)

Valuation Analysis		Institutional Holding	
Forecast EPS	$0.53	No of Institutions	N/A
	(06/11/2018)		
Market Cap	$19.6 Billion	Shares	N/A
Book Value	$8.7 Billion	% Held	N/A
Price/Book	2.26		
Price/Sales	8.38		

Business Summary: REITs (MIC: 5.3.1 SIC: 6798 NAIC: 525930)

GGP is a self-administered and self-managed real estate investment trust. Co., through its subsidiaries and affiliates, is an owner and operator of retail properties with a property portfolio primarily comprised of Class A retail real estate. As of Dec 31 2017, Co. owned, either entirely or with joint venture partners, 125 retail properties located throughout the U.S. Co. provides management and other services to substantially all of its properties, including properties which Co. owns through joint venture arrangements. Substantially all of Co.'s business is conducted through GGP Operating Partnership, LP, GGP Nimbus, LP, and GGP Limited Partnership.

Recent Developments: For the quarter ended Mar 31 2018, net income decreased 40.3% to US$65.9 million from US$110.4 million in the year-earlier quarter. Revenues were US$574.2 million, up 1.4% from US$566.3 million the year before. Revenues from property income rose 2.7% to US$531.8 million from US$518.0 million in the corresponding quarter a year earlier.

Prospects: Our evaluation of GGP Inc. as of Jan. 21, 2018 is the result of our systematic analysis on three basic characteristics: earnings strength, relative valuation, and recent stock price movement. The company has enjoyed a very positive trend in earnings per share over the past 5 quarters. Because the company lacks sufficient analyst estimate data, we place greater weight on the historical EPS trend as the measure of earnings strength. Based on operating earnings yield, the company is about fairly valued when compared to all of the companies in our coverage universe. Share price changes over the past year indicates that GGP will perform poorly over the near term.

Financial Data

(US$ in Thousands)	3 Mos	12/31/2017	12/31/2016	12/31/2015	12/31/2014	12/31/2013	12/31/2012	12/31/2011
Earnings Per Share	0.63	0.68	1.34	1.43	0.69	0.31	(0.52)	(0.37)
Cash Flow Per Share	1.38	1.44	1.28	1.20	1.07	0.96	0.86	0.53
Tang Book Value Per Share	8.52	8.66	9.13	8.63	7.68	7.77	6.99	7.50
Dividends Per Share	0.880	0.880	1.060	0.710	0.630	0.510	0.420	0.400
Dividend Payout %	139.68	129.41	79.10	49.65	91.30	164.52	...	...
Income Statement								
Total Revenue	574,166	2,327,862	2,346,446	2,403,906	2,535,559	2,527,387	2,511,850	2,742,942
EBITDA	162,571	999,915	1,578,398	1,575,382	1,091,273	1,051,835	350,236	1,734,610
Depn & Amortn	2,378	28,309	41,154	62,106	76,615	84,229	105,871	1,086,639
Income Before Taxes	31,416	491,227	1,026,004	954,855	343,986	238,745	(563,805)	(308,177)
Income Taxes	(280)	(10,896)	901	(38,334)	7,253	345	9,091	9,256
Net Income	64,036	657,334	1,288,367	1,374,561	665,850	302,528	(481,233)	(313,172)
Average Shares	960,293	947,559	952,333	951,062	944,721	934,068	938,049	981,136
Balance Sheet								
Current Assets	968,045	916,243	1,475,449	1,306,451	1,036,239	1,056,170	885,675	791,327
Total Assets	23,258,197	23,349,954	22,732,746	24,073,555	25,335,734	25,762,303	27,282,405	29,518,151
Current Liabilities	1,112,628	1,024,992	972,706	797,770	929,250	963,183	1,170,509	1,882,067
Long-Term Obligations	13,140,068	13,044,044	12,642,004	14,433,745	16,216,555	15,891,340	16,186,358	17,335,706
Total Liabilities	14,599,628	14,554,294	14,096,982	15,803,512	17,729,815	17,659,182	19,660,707	21,034,822
Stockholders' Equity	8,658,569	8,795,660	8,635,764	8,270,043	7,605,919	8,103,121	7,621,698	8,483,329
Shares Outstanding	958,318	956,982	884,097	882,397	884,912	911,194	939,049	935,307
Statistical Record								
Return on Assets %	2.69	2.85	5.49	5.56	2.61	1.14	N.M.	N.M.
Return on Equity %	7.15	7.54	15.20	17.32	8.48	3.85	N.M.	N.M.
EBITDA Margin %	28.31	42.95	67.27	65.53	43.04	41.62	13.94	63.24
Net Margin %	11.15	28.24	54.91	57.18	26.26	11.97	N.M.	N.M.
Asset Turnover	0.10	0.10	0.10	0.10	0.10	0.10	0.09	0.09
Current Ratio	0.87	0.89	1.52	1.64	1.12	1.10	0.76	0.42
Debt to Equity	1.52	1.48	1.46	1.75	2.13	1.96	2.12	2.04
Price Range	24.26-19.01	26.00-19.01	31.97-24.25	31.46-24.37	28.66-19.54	23.33-18.69	20.99-14.36	16.90-11.01
P/E Ratio	38.51-30.17	38.24-27.96	23.86-18.10	22.00-17.04	41.54-28.32	75.26-60.29	...	...
Average Yield %	3.94	3.84	3.81	2.56	2.67	2.50	2.34	2.78

Address: 110 N. Wacker Dr., Chicago, IL 60606	Web Site: www.ggp.com	Auditors: Deloitte & Touche LLP
Telephone: 312-960-5000	Officers: John Bucksbaum - Chairman Shobi Khan - President, Chief Operating Officer	Investor Contact: 312-960-5529
		Transfer Agents: American Stock Transfer & Trust Company, LLC, Brooklyn, NY

GLOBAL PARTNERS LP

Exchange	Symbol	Price	52Wk Range	Yield	P/E
NYS	GLP	$17.05 (6/29/2018)	18.45-15.30	10.85	6.09

*7 Year Price Score 52.67   *NYSE Composite Index=100   *12 Month Price Score 98.08

Interim Earnings (Per Share)

Qtr.	Mar	Jun	Sep	Dec
2015	0.92	0.15	0.16	(0.09)
2016	(0.21)	(0.22)	(3.54)	(1.94)
2017	0.68	0.07	0.44	0.56
2018	1.73	...	...	...

Interim Dividends (Per Share)

Amt	Decl	Ex	Rec	Pay
0.463Q	07/28/2017	08/07/2017	08/09/2017	08/14/2017
0.463Q	10/27/2017	11/08/2017	11/09/2017	11/14/2017
0.463Q	01/29/2018	02/08/2018	02/09/2018	02/14/2018
0.463Q	04/27/2018	05/09/2018	05/10/2018	05/15/2018

Indicated Div: $1.85

Valuation Analysis

Forecast EPS	$1.97 (06/12/2018)
Market Cap	$573.8 Million
Book Value	N/A
Price/Book	N/A
Price/Sales	0.06

Institutional Holding

No of Institutions	83
Shares	16,958,768
% Held	41.85

Business Summary: Equipment & Services (MIC: 9.1.3 SIC: 5171 NAIC: 424710)

Global Partners is a midstream logistics and marketing company that engages in the purchasing, selling, storing and logistics of transporting petroleum and related products. Co.'s segments are: Wholesale, which sells, gathers, stores and transports refined petroleum products, renewable fuels, crude oil and propane; Gasoline Distribution and Station Operations, which sells branded and unbranded gasoline to gasoline station operators and sub-jobbers; and Commercial, which includes sales and deliveries to end user customers in the public sector and to commercial and industrial end users of unbranded gasoline, home heating oil, diesel, kerosene, residual oil, bunker fuel and natural gas.

Recent Developments: For the quarter ended Mar 31 2018, net income increased 160.7% to US$58.7 million from US$22.5 million in the year-earlier quarter. Revenues were US$2.80 billion, up 23.4% from US$2.27 billion the year before. Operating income was US$79.2 million versus US$45.6 million in the prior-year quarter, an increase of 73.6%. Direct operating expenses rose 24.8% to US$2.66 billion from US$2.13 billion in the comparable period the year before. Indirect operating expenses decreased 31.0% to US$65.1 million from US$94.4 million in the equivalent prior-year period.

Prospects: For the Quarter ended Mar. 31, 2017, Co. posted a solid first quarter and continued to position the Partnership for growth. Net income attributable to the Partnership in the first quarter of 2017 was $22.9 million, or $0.68 per diluted limited partner unit, compared with a net loss attributable to the Partnership of $7.0 million, or $0.21 per limited partner unit, in the first quarter of 2016. EBITDA in the first quarter of 2017 was $71.9 million compared with EBITDA of $42.6 million in the comparable period of 2016. Adjusted EBITDA was $60.1 million in the first quarter of 2017 compared with Adjusted EBITDA of $48.7 million in the same period of 2016.

Financial Data
(US$ in Thousands)

	3 Mos	12/31/2017	12/31/2016	12/31/2015	12/31/2014	12/31/2013	12/31/2012	12/31/2011
Earnings Per Share	2.80	1.74	(5.91)	1.11	3.95	1.42	1.71	0.87
Cash Flow Per Share	3.78	10.37	(3.57)	1.94	12.58	9.34	8.78	(0.82)
Dividends Per Share	1.850	1.850	1.850	2.735	2.527	2.340	2.058	2.000
Dividend Payout %	66.07	106.32	...	246.40	63.99	164.79	120.32	229.89
Income Statement								
Total Revenue	2,802,891	8,920,552	8,239,639	10,314,852	17,269,954	19,589,608	17,625,997	14,835,729
EBITDA	81,029	216,184	(49,651)	217,023	233,207	143,309	123,088	75,029
Depn & Amortn	1,822	96,400	102,600	102,300	67,500	57,900	38,500	24,400
Income Before Taxes	57,762	33,554	(238,570)	41,391	117,943	41,872	48,320	19,420
Income Taxes	(913)	(23,563)	53	(1,873)	963	819	1,577	68
Net Income	59,042	58,752	(199,412)	43,563	114,709	42,615	46,743	19,352
Average Shares	33,802	33,634	33,525	32,323	27,502	27,560	26,567	21,474
Balance Sheet								
Current Assets	936,180	878,135	1,075,466	867,035	961,223	1,374,311	1,506,933	1,412,864
Total Assets	2,355,184	2,320,169	2,564,020	2,663,675	2,039,977	2,427,922	2,329,752	1,868,851
Current Liabilities	662,640	668,657	799,225	594,734	707,491	972,572	1,045,195	771,054
Long-Term Obligations	1,108,727	957,774	1,025,850	1,075,564	601,936	909,968	762,754	731,095
Total Liabilities	1,919,788	1,929,216	2,171,365	2,015,886	1,453,035	2,012,685	1,893,291	1,553,562
Shares Outstanding	33,652	33,875	33,773	33,737	30,835	27,491	27,540	21,792
Statistical Record								
Return on Assets %	4.05	2.41	N.M.	1.85	5.13	1.79	2.22	1.09
EBITDA Margin %	2.89	2.42	N.M.	2.10	1.35	0.73	0.70	0.51
Net Margin %	2.11	0.66	N.M.	0.42	0.66	0.22	0.27	0.13
Asset Turnover	4.04	3.65	3.14	4.39	7.73	8.23	8.37	8.38
Current Ratio	1.41	1.31	1.35	1.46	1.36	1.41	1.44	1.83
Price Range	20.20-15.35	21.55-16.05	19.50-12.31	41.82-15.26	45.32-31.68	40.65-25.35	27.81-20.19	29.83-14.86
P/E Ratio	7.21-5.48	12.39-9.22	...	37.68-13.75	11.47-8.02	28.63-17.85	16.26-11.81	34.29-17.08
Average Yield %	10.47	10.09	12.54	8.21	6.37	6.74	8.67	8.53

Address: P.O. Box 9161, 800 South Street, Waltham, MA 02454-9161
Telephone: 781-894-8800

Web Site: www.globalp.com
Officers: Richard Slifka - Chairman Eric S. Slifka - President, Chief Executive Officer, Associate/Affiliate Company Officer

Auditors: Ernst & Young LLP
Investor Contact: 781-894-8800
Transfer Agents: American Stock Transfer and Trust Company, New Yor, NY

GLOBAL PAYMENTS INC

Exchange	Symbol	Price	52Wk Range	Yield	P/E
NYS	GPN	$111.49 (6/29/2018)	118.48-88.31	0.04	34.20

*7 Year Price Score 160.57 *NYSE Composite Index=100 *12 Month Price Score 107.34

Interim Earnings (Per Share)

Qtr.	Aug	Nov	Feb	May
2016-17	0.55	0.32	...	(0.99)
Qtr.	Mar	Jun	Sep	Dec
2017	0.32	0.44	0.71	1.54
2018	0.57	...	...	...

Interim Dividends (Per Share)

Amt	Decl	Ex	Rec	Pay
0.01Q	08/02/2017	09/14/2017	09/15/2017	09/29/2017
0.01Q	11/02/2017	12/14/2017	12/15/2017	12/29/2017
0.01Q	01/31/2018	03/15/2018	03/16/2018	03/30/2018
0.01Q	04/27/2018	06/14/2018	06/15/2018	06/29/2018
		Indicated Div: $0.04		

Valuation Analysis

	Institutional Holding	
Forecast EPS	$5.11	No of Institutions
	(06/14/2018)	705
Market Cap	$17.8 Billion	Shares
Book Value	$4.0 Billion	177,876,896
Price/Book	4.50	% Held
Price/Sales	4.62	83.95

Business Summary: Business Services (MIC: 7.5.2 SIC: 7389 NAIC: 561499)

Global Payments provides payment technology services. Co.'s payment solutions enable its merchant customers to accept card, electronic, check and digital-based payments at the point of sale. Co.'s products include terminal sales and deployment, authorization processing, settlement and funding processing, customer support and help-desk functions, chargeback resolution, industry compliance, Payment Card Industry security, consolidated billing and statements and on-line reporting. Through its wholesale channel, Co. provides payment services to merchants via independent sales organizations. Co.'s credit and debit card transaction processing includes the processing of international card brands.

Recent Developments: For the quarter ended Mar 31 2018, net income increased 84.3% to US$97.6 million from US$53.0 million in the year-earlier quarter. Revenues were US$795.0 million, down 13.6% from US$919.8 million the year before. Operating income was US$156.2 million versus US$105.0 million in the prior-year quarter, an increase of 48.8%. Direct operating expenses declined 44.6% to US$252.4 million from US$455.9 million in the comparable period the year before. Indirect operating expenses increased 7.7% to US$386.4 million from US$358.9 million in the equivalent prior-year period.

Prospects: Our evaluation of Global Payments Inc. as of Jan. 21, 2018 is the result of our systematic analysis on three basic characteristics: earnings strength, relative valuation, and recent stock price movement. The company has managed to produce a neutral trend in earnings per share over the past 5 quarters and while recent estimates for the company have been mixed, GPN has posted better than expected results. Based on operating earnings yield, the company is about fairly valued when compared to all of the companies in our coverage universe. Share price changes over the past year indicates that GPN will perform well over the near term.

Financial Data

(US$ in Thousands)	3 Mos	12/31/2017	12/31/2016	05/31/2016	05/31/2015	05/31/2014	05/31/2013	05/31/2012
Earnings Per Share	3.26	3.01	0.81	2.04	2.06	1.69	1.38	1.19
Cash Flow Per Share	3.16	3.31	5.59	4.41	3.17	1.35	1.55	(1.10)
Tang Book Value Per Share	N.M.	N.M.	N.M.	N.M.	N.M.	N.M.	N.M.	1.00
Dividends Per Share	0.043	0.043	0.020	0.040	0.040	0.040	0.040	0.040
Dividend Payout %	1.33	1.44	2.47	1.96	1.94	2.37	2.90	3.38
Income Statement								
Total Revenue	794,977	3,975,163	2,202,896	2,898,150	2,773,718	2,554,236	2,375,923	2,203,847
EBITDA	254,208	896,746	432,280	538,633	594,084	527,544	468,978	406,445
Depn & Amortn	98,038	337,878	194,329	113,689	137,487	122,045	111,765	99,096
Income Before Taxes	122,259	392,683	173,344	360,912	417,110	377,350	334,284	300,447
Income Taxes	24,673	(101,387)	35,661	70,695	107,995	107,398	95,571	82,881
Net Income	91,399	468,425	124,931	271,666	278,040	245,286	216,125	188,161
Average Shares	160,035	155,528	154,231	133,167	134,922	145,376	156,454	158,862
Balance Sheet								
Current Assets	4,157,878	4,303,579	3,116,006	2,851,313	3,302,295	1,643,444	1,214,492	1,248,739
Total Assets	12,903,297	12,998,069	10,664,350	10,509,952	5,793,548	4,018,650	3,125,056	2,688,143
Current Liabilities	3,908,919	3,815,590	2,851,956	2,430,727	3,015,904	1,211,618	704,114	837,285
Long-Term Obligations	4,176,851	4,559,408	4,260,827	4,379,744	1,680,000	1,376,002	891,134	236,565
Total Liabilities	8,951,691	9,203,542	8,033,559	7,763,476	5,035,572	3,021,423	1,978,971	1,515,959
Stockholders' Equity	3,951,606	3,794,527	2,630,791	2,746,476	757,976	997,227	1,146,085	1,172,184
Shares Outstanding	159,532	159,180	152,185	154,421	130,557	137,691	150,852	157,102
Statistical Record								
Return on Assets %	4.47	3.96	2.59	3.32	5.67	6.87	7.44	6.21
Return on Equity %	15.29	14.58	12.58	15.46	31.68	22.89	18.65	15.92
EBITDA Margin %	31.98	22.56	19.62	18.59	21.42	20.65	19.74	18.44
Net Margin %	11.50	11.78	5.67	9.37	10.02	9.60	9.10	8.54
Asset Turnover	0.34	0.34	0.46	0.35	0.57	0.72	0.82	0.73
Current Ratio	1.06	1.13	1.09	1.17	1.09	1.36	1.72	1.49
Debt to Equity	1.06	1.20	1.62	1.59	2.22	1.38	0.78	0.20
Price Range	118.21-77.50	104.27-70.50	79.23-66.42	77.69-51.09	52.70-33.98	36.50-22.91	25.50-19.94	26.74-19.66
P/E Ratio	36.26-23.77	34.64-23.42	97.81-82.00	38.08-25.04	25.58-16.50	21.60-13.55	18.48-14.45	22.47-16.53
Average Yield %	0.04	0.05	0.03	0.06	0.10	0.13	0.18	0.17

Address: 3550 Lenox Road, Atlanta, GA 30326	Web Site: www.globalpaymentsinc.com	Auditors: DELOITTE & TOUCHE LLP
Telephone: 770-829-8000	Officers: William I. Jacobs - Chairman David E. Mangum - President, Senior Executive Vice President, Chief Financial Officer, Chief Operating Officer	Investor Contact: 770-829-8234
		Transfer Agents: Computershare Trust Company, N.A, Canton, MA

GLOBUS MEDICAL INC

Exchange	Symbol	Price	52Wk Range	Yield	P/E
NYS	GMED	$50.46 (6/29/2018)	57.41-28.28	N/A	42.40

*7 Year Price Score N/A   *NYSE Composite Index=100   *12 Month Price Score 126.86

Interim Earnings (Per Share)

Qtr.	Mar	Jun	Sep	Dec
2015	0.26	0.25	0.28	0.39
2016	0.29	0.27	0.27	0.25
2017	0.30	0.29	0.26	0.25
2018	0.39	...	...	...

Interim Dividends (Per Share)

No Dividends Paid

Valuation Analysis

		Institutional Holding
Forecast EPS	$1.52	No of Institutions
	(06/13/2018)	N/A
Market Cap	$4.9 Billion	Shares
Book Value	$1.0 Billion	N/A
Price/Book	4.77	% Held
Price/Sales	7.49	N/A

TRADING VOLUME (thousand shares)

Business Summary: Medical Instruments & Equipment (MIC: 4.3.1 SIC: 3841 NAIC: 339112)

Globus Medical is a medical device company focused on the design, development and commercialization of musculoskeletal implants. Co. provides a portfolio of products addressing a range of spinal pathologies, anatomies and surgical approaches. All of Co.'s products fall into one of two categories: Innovative Fusion or Disruptive Technologies. Co.'s Innovative Fusion products are used to treat degenerative, deformity, tumor, and trauma conditions. Co.'s pipeline of Disruptive Technology products includes products that allow for minimally invasive surgical techniques, regenerative biologics technologies; and interventional pain management solutions.

Recent Developments: For the quarter ended Mar 31 2018, net income increased 37.7% to US$39.5 million from US$28.7 million in the year-earlier quarter. Revenues were US$174.4 million, up 11.9% from US$155.8 million the year before. Operating income was US$45.6 million versus US$40.3 million in the prior-year quarter, an increase of 13.2%. Direct operating expenses rose 6.7% to US$38.0 million from US$35.6 million in the comparable period the year before. Indirect operating expenses increased 13.7% to US$90.8 million from US$79.9 million in the equivalent prior-year period.

Prospects: Our evaluation of Globus Medical Inc as of Jan. 21, 2018 is the result of our systematic analysis on three basic characteristics: earnings strength, relative valuation, and recent stock price movement. The company has managed to produce a neutral trend in earnings per share over the past 5 quarters and while recent estimates for the company have been mixed, GMED has posted better than expected results. Based on operating earnings yield, the company is about fairly valued when compared to all of the companies in our coverage universe. Share price changes over the past year indicates that GMED will perform poorly over the near term.

Financial Data
(US$ in Thousands)

	3 Mos	12/31/2017	12/31/2016	12/31/2015	12/31/2014	12/31/2013	12/31/2012	12/31/2011
Earnings Per Share	1.19	1.10	1.08	1.17	0.97	0.73	0.80	0.67
Cash Flow Per Share	1.64	1.66	1.79	1.28	0.84	1.01	0.85	1.05
Tang Book Value Per Share	8.47	7.92	6.93	6.19	5.26	4.54	3.96	3.66
Income Statement								
Total Revenue	174,411	635,977	563,994	544,753	474,371	434,459	385,994	331,478
EBITDA	46,571	211,995	196,050	195,327	159,686	120,870	132,293	113,849
Depn & Amortn	785	42,067	38,771	22,522	21,044	18,869	17,640	16,900
Income Before Taxes	48,077	169,928	157,279	172,805	138,642	102,001	114,653	96,949
Income Taxes	8,539	62,580	52,938	60,021	46,157	33,389	40,822	36,165
Net Income	39,538	107,348	104,341	112,784	92,485	68,612	73,831	60,784
Average Shares	100,496	97,887	96,432	96,073	95,457	94,192	92,208	74,823
Balance Sheet								
Current Assets	614,925	620,342	513,766	544,799	470,025	416,808	360,110	258,775
Total Assets	1,127,660	1,078,502	927,637	834,100	703,547	566,304	447,133	329,390
Current Liabilities	82,552	93,073	79,892	82,691	89,412	67,942	39,508	29,271
Total Liabilities	100,792	110,724	95,559	118,776	118,093	93,944	60,631	46,914
Stockholders' Equity	1,026,868	967,778	832,078	715,324	585,454	472,360	386,502	282,476
Shares Outstanding	97,163	96,657	95,929	95,319	94,705	93,442	91,270	72,528
Statistical Record								
Return on Assets %	11.32	10.70	11.81	14.67	14.57	13.54	18.96	20.40
Return on Equity %	12.47	11.93	13.45	17.34	17.49	15.98	22.01	23.81
EBITDA Margin %	26.70	33.33	34.76	35.86	33.66	27.82	34.27	34.35
Net Margin %	22.67	16.88	18.50	20.70	19.50	15.79	19.13	18.34
Asset Turnover	0.63	0.63	0.64	0.71	0.75	0.86	0.99	1.11
Current Ratio	7.45	6.67	6.43	6.59	5.26	6.13	9.11	8.84
Price Range	51.73-28.28	41.64-24.79	27.82-20.65	28.24-20.66	26.95-18.14	20.18-10.49	18.75-10.37	...
P/E Ratio	43.47-23.76	37.85-22.54	25.76-19.12	24.14-17.66	27.78-18.70	27.64-14.37	23.44-12.96	...

Address: 2560 General Armistead Avenue, Audubon, PA 19403 **Telephone:** 610-930-1800 **Fax:** 302-636-5454	**Web Site:** www.globusmedical.com **Officers:** David C. Paul - Chairman, Chief Executive Officer Anthony L. Williams - President, Vice President, Corporate Counsel, Secretary	**Auditors:** Deloitte & Touche LLP **Investor Contact:** 610-930-1800 **Transfer Agents:** Broadridge Corporate Issuer Solutions, Inc., Philadelphia, PA

GODADDY INC

Exchange	Symbol	Price	52Wk Range	Yield	P/E
NYS	GDDY	$70.60 (6/29/2018)	74.74-41.19	N/A	85.06

*7 Year Price Score N/A   ***NYSE Composite Index=100**   ***12 Month Price Score 128.65**

Interim Earnings (Per Share)

Qtr.	Mar	Jun	Sep	Dec
2015	(0.34)	(0.46)	(0.04)	0.01
2016	(0.15)	(0.11)	0.05	(0.02)
2017	0.01	0.10	0.17	0.54
2018	0.02	...	...	...

Interim Dividends (Per Share)

No Dividends Paid

Valuation Analysis   **Institutional Holding**

Forecast EPS	$0.44	No of Institutions
	(06/12/2018)	313
Market Cap	$12.0 Billion	Shares
Book Value	$548.3 Million	161,128,528
Price/Book	21.95	% Held
Price/Sales	5.07	N/A

Business Summary: Internet & Software (MIC: 6.3.2 SIC: 7373 NAIC: 541512)

GoDaddy is a holding company. Co. is a technology provider to small businesses, web design personnel and individuals, delivering cloud-based products and personalized Customer Care. Co. provides website building, hosting and security tools to help customers construct and protect their online presence. Co. provides applications and access to relevant third party products helping them connect to their customers, manage and grow their businesses and get found online. Co. has designed and developed a set of cloud-based technology products enabling its customers to establish a digital presence, connect with their customers and manage their ventures.

Recent Developments: For the quarter ended Mar 31 2018, net income amounted to US$4.2 million versus a net loss of US$3.1 million in the year-earlier quarter. Revenues were US$633.2 million, up 29.3% from US$489.7 million the year before. Operating income was US$26.8 million versus US$5.7 million in the prior-year quarter, an increase of 370.2%. Direct operating expenses rose 21.8% to US$215.3 million from US$176.8 million in the comparable period the year before. Indirect operating expenses increased 27.3% to US$391.1 million from US$307.2 million in the equivalent prior-year period.

Prospects: Our evaluation of GoDaddy Inc as of Jan. 21, 2018 is the result of our systematic analysis on three basic characteristics: earnings strength, relative valuation, and recent stock price movement. The company has suffered a very negative trend in earnings per share over the past 5 quarters and while recent estimates for the company have remained steady, GDDY has posted results that were in line with analysts expectations. Based on operating earnings yield, the company is overvalued when compared to all of the companies in our coverage universe. Share price changes over the past year indicates that GDDY will perform well over the near term.

Financial Data
(US$ in Thousands)

	3 Mos	12/31/2017	12/31/2016	12/31/2015	12/31/2014	12/31/2013	12/31/2012
Earnings Per Share	0.83	0.79	(0.21)	(0.81)	(1.11)	(1.58)	(2.21)
Cash Flow Per Share	3.61	4.37	4.83	4.42	1.40	1.21	0.84
Income Statement							
Total Revenue	633,200	2,231,900	1,847,900	1,607,300	1,387,262	1,130,845	910,903
EBITDA	85,500	278,600	104,700	9,900	(5,558)	(79,874)	(125,033)
Depn & Amortn	57,800	88,800	69,000	61,300	55,574	50,174	75,145
Income Before Taxes	3,900	106,800	(21,500)	(120,600)	(146,129)	(201,026)	(279,270)
Income Taxes	(300)	(18,900)	400	(200)	(2,824)	(1,142)	(218)
Net Income	3,300	136,400	(16,500)	(47,400)	(143,305)	(199,884)	(279,052)
Average Shares	178,787	177,054	79,835	58,676	128,567	126,663	126,098
Balance Sheet							
Current Assets	1,221,300	1,059,500	932,800	693,900	460,882	405,875	...
Total Assets	5,931,000	5,738,300	3,786,900	3,498,800	3,264,805	3,213,130	...
Current Liabilities	1,912,500	1,810,700	1,262,200	1,113,600	972,749	858,529	...
Long-Term Obligations	2,574,200	2,410,800	1,035,700	1,039,800	1,413,939	1,083,934	...
Total Liabilities	5,382,700	5,251,800	3,224,400	3,073,000	2,854,414	2,342,382	...
Stockholders' Equity	548,300	486,500	562,500	425,800	410,391	870,748	...
Shares Outstanding	170,440	167,999	167,112	157,481	129,003	127,559	126,200
Statistical Record							
Return on Assets %	2.83	2.86	N.M.	N.M.	N.M.	...	...
Return on Equity %	24.26	26.01	N.M.	N.M.	N.M.	...	...
EBITDA Margin %	13.50	12.48	5.67	0.62	N.M.	N.M.	N.M.
Net Margin %	0.52	6.11	N.M.	N.M.	N.M.	N.M.	N.M.
Asset Turnover	0.48	0.47	0.51	0.48	0.43	...	...
Current Ratio	0.64	0.59	0.74	0.62	0.47	0.47	...
Debt to Equity	4.69	4.96	1.84	2.44	3.45	1.24	...
Price Range	63.98-36.09	51.06-34.41	36.82-24.25	34.24-23.59	...	...	...
P/E Ratio	77.08-43.48	64.63-43.56	...	...	...	...	...

Address: 14455 N. Hayden Road, Scottsdale, AZ 85260 **Telephone:** 480-505-8800	**Web Site:** www.godaddy.com **Officers:** Charles J. (Chuck) Robel - Chairman Scott W. Wagner - President, Chief Operating Officer, Chief Financial Officer, Chief Executive Officer	**Auditors:** Ernst & Young LLP **Transfer Agents:** American Stock Transfer & Trust Company, LLC, Brooklyn, NY

GORMAN-RUPP COMPANY (THE)

Exchange	Symbol	Price	52Wk Range
NYS	GRC	$35.00 (6/29/2018)	35.86-25.47

Yield	P/E	Div Acheiver
1.43	29.17	45 Years

*7 Year Price Score 89.41 *NYSE Composite Index=100 *12 Month Price Score 108.82

TRADING VOLUME (thousand shares)

Interim Earnings (Per Share)

Qtr.	Mar	Jun	Sep	Dec
2015	0.28	0.25	0.22	0.21
2016	0.24	0.25	0.27	0.19
2017	0.19	0.30	0.22	0.31
2018	0.37	...	...	...

Interim Dividends (Per Share)

Amt	Decl	Ex	Rec	Pay
0.115Q	07/28/2017	08/11/2017	08/15/2017	09/08/2017
0.125Q	10/27/2017	11/14/2017	11/15/2017	12/08/2017
0.125Q	01/26/2018	02/14/2018	02/15/2018	03/09/2018
0.125Q	04/27/2018	05/14/2018	05/15/2018	06/08/2018

Indicated Div: $0.50

Valuation Analysis

Forecast EPS	$1.47 (06/14/2018)
Market Cap	$913.7 Million
Book Value	$332.5 Million
Price/Book	2.75
Price/Sales	2.38

Institutional Holding

No of Institutions	152
Shares	16,723,578
% Held	54.10

Business Summary: Industrial Machinery & Equipment (MIC: 7.2.1 SIC: 3561 NAIC: 333911)

Gorman-Rupp designs, manufactures and globally sells pumps and pump systems for use in water, wastewater, construction, dewatering, industrial, petroleum, original equipment, agriculture, fire protection, heating, ventilating and air conditioning, military and other liquid-handling applications. Co.'s product line consists of pump models ranging in size from 1/4 inch to nearly 15 feet. The types of pumps which Co. produces include self priming centrifugal, standard centrifugal, magnetic drive centrifugal, axial and mixed flow, vertical turbine line shaft, submersible, high pressure booster, rotary gear, diaphragm, bellows and oscillating.

Recent Developments: For the quarter ended Mar 31 2018, net income increased 89.9% to US$9.6 million from US$5.1 million in the year-earlier quarter. Revenues were US$96.6 million, up 4.3% from US$92.6 million the year before. Operating income was US$11.9 million versus US$8.7 million in the prior-year quarter, an increase of 36.9%. Direct operating expenses was unchanged at US$70.4 million versus the comparable period the year before. Indirect operating expenses increased 5.6% to US$14.4 million from US$13.6 million in the equivalent prior-year period.

Prospects: Our evaluation of Gorman-Rupp Co. as of Jan. 21, 2018 is the result of our systematic analysis on three basic characteristics: earnings strength, relative valuation, and recent stock price movement. The company has managed to produce a neutral trend in earnings per share over the past 5 quarters and while recent estimates for the company have been raised by analysts, GRC has posted better than expected results. Based on operating earnings yield, the company is about fairly valued when compared to all of the companies in our coverage universe. Share price changes over the past year indicates that GRC will perform in line with the market over the near term.

Financial Data
(US$ in Thousands)

	3 Mos	12/31/2017	12/31/2016	12/31/2015	12/31/2014	12/31/2013	12/31/2012	12/31/2011
Earnings Per Share	1.20	1.02	0.95	0.96	1.38	1.15	1.07	1.10
Cash Flow Per Share	1.92	1.66	2.04	1.55	1.10	1.92	1.24	0.81
Tang Book Value Per Share	11.29	11.02	9.96	9.43	9.22	8.86	7.71	7.21
Dividends Per Share	0.480	0.470	0.430	0.405	0.370	0.330	0.312	0.283
Dividend Payout %	40.00	46.08	45.26	42.19	26.81	28.70	29.10	25.84
Income Statement								
Total Revenue	96,604	379,389	382,071	406,150	434,925	391,665	375,691	359,490
EBITDA	16,256	52,878	52,011	52,548	68,349	57,865	54,513	54,144
Depn & Amortn	3,600	13,500	15,529	15,282	14,615	13,588	12,066	11,459
Income Before Taxes	12,656	39,378	36,482	37,266	53,734	44,277	42,447	42,685
Income Taxes	3,039	12,823	11,599	12,157	17,593	14,173	14,244	13,881
Net Income	9,617	26,555	24,883	25,109	36,141	30,104	28,203	28,804
Average Shares	26,106	26,100	26,087	26,192	26,256	26,249	26,242	26,234
Balance Sheet								
Current Assets	238,427	227,934	203,900	189,391	200,709	189,289	175,675	155,872
Total Assets	405,116	395,015	382,818	364,201	380,904	355,638	335,183	298,700
Current Liabilities	49,263	45,696	49,352	43,460	64,346	60,760	64,821	50,873
Total Liabilities	72,568	69,520	79,930	77,180	98,937	91,498	100,464	83,936
Stockholders' Equity	332,548	325,495	302,888	287,021	281,967	264,140	234,719	214,764
Shares Outstanding	26,106	26,106	26,093	26,083	26,260	26,253	26,246	26,238
Statistical Record								
Return on Assets %	7.86	6.83	6.64	6.74	9.81	8.72	8.87	9.84
Return on Equity %	9.73	8.45	8.41	8.83	13.24	12.07	12.51	13.89
EBITDA Margin %	16.83	13.94	13.61	12.94	15.72	14.77	14.51	15.06
Net Margin %	9.96	7.00	6.51	6.18	8.31	7.69	7.51	8.01
Asset Turnover	0.97	0.98	1.02	1.09	1.18	1.13	1.18	1.23
Current Ratio	4.84	4.99	4.13	4.36	3.12	3.12	2.71	3.06
Price Range	33.47-24.07	33.47-24.07	33.94-21.26	32.12-22.19	39.18-28.87	34.13-21.44	27.51-20.89	28.39-18.24
P/E Ratio	27.89-20.06	32.81-23.60	35.73-22.38	33.46-23.11	28.39-20.92	29.68-18.64	25.71-19.52	25.81-16.58
Average Yield %	1.65	1.59	1.59	1.47	1.16	1.23	1.35	1.22

Address: 600 South Airport Road, Mansfield, OH 44903	**Web Site:** www.gormanrupp.com	**Auditors:** Ernst & Young LLP
Telephone: 419-755-1011	**Officers:** James C. Gorman - Chairman Jeffrey S. Gorman - President, Chief Executive Officer	**Investor Contact:** 419-755-1397
Fax: 419-755-1233		**Transfer Agents:** Broadridge Corporate Issuer Solutions, Inc., Brentwood, NY

GRACE (WR) & CO

Exchange	Symbol	Price	52Wk Range	Yield	P/E
NYS	GRA	$73.31 (6/29/2018)	76.60-60.27	1.31	407.28

*7 Year Price Score 86.05 ***NYSE Composite Index=100** ***12 Month Price Score 101.21**

TRADING VOLUME (thousand shares)

Interim Earnings (Per Share)

Qtr.	Mar	Jun	Sep	Dec
2015	0.72	0.78	0.19	0.30
2016	(0.04)	0.55	0.56	0.22
2017	0.63	0.64	0.70	(1.80)
2018	0.64	...	...	...

Interim Dividends (Per Share)

Amt	Decl	Ex	Rec	Pay
0.21Q	07/27/2017	08/15/2017	08/17/2017	09/07/2017
0.21Q	10/25/2017	11/14/2017	11/15/2017	12/07/2017
0.24Q	02/08/2018	02/28/2018	03/01/2018	03/22/2018
0.24Q	04/25/2018	05/15/2018	05/16/2018	06/06/2018

Indicated Div: $0.96

Valuation Analysis / Institutional Holding

Forecast EPS	$3.90	No of Institutions
	(06/11/2018)	403
Market Cap	$4.9 Billion	Shares
Book Value	$239.2 Million	64,302,648
Price/Book	20.62	% Held
Price/Sales	2.82	85.33

Business Summary: Specialty Chemicals (MIC: 8.3.2 SIC: 2819 NAIC: 331311)

Grace (W.R.) is engaged in the production and sale of specialty chemicals and specialty materials through two reportable business segments: Grace Catalysts Technologies; and Grace Materials Technologies. Grace Catalysts Technologies produces and sells catalysts and related products and technologies used in refining, petrochemical and other chemical manufacturing applications. Grace Materials Technologies produces and sells specialty materials, including silica-based and silica-alumina-based materials, used in coatings, consumer, industrial, and pharmaceutical applications, as follows: coatings and print media applications, consumer/pharma applications, and chemical Process applications.

Recent Developments: For the quarter ended Mar 31 2018, net income increased 1.2% to US$43.4 million from US$42.9 million in the year-earlier quarter. Revenues were US$431.5 million, up 8.4% from US$398.0 million the year before. Direct operating expenses rose 7.0% to US$262.0 million from US$244.8 million in the comparable period the year before. Indirect operating expenses increased 9.8% to US$101.3 million from US$92.3 million in the equivalent prior-year period.

Prospects: Our evaluation of Grace (W.R.) Co. as of Jan. 21, 2018 is the result of our systematic analysis on three basic characteristics: earnings strength, relative valuation, and recent stock price movement. The company has generated a negative trend in earnings per share over the past 5 quarters and while recent estimates for the company have been mixed, GRA has posted better than expected results. Based on operating earnings yield, the company is undervalued when compared to all of the companies in our coverage universe. Share price changes over the past year indicates that GRA will perform poorly over the near term.

Financial Data

(US$ in Thousands)	3 Mos	12/31/2017	12/31/2016	12/31/2015	12/31/2014	12/31/2013	12/31/2012	12/31/2011
Earnings Per Share	0.18	0.16	1.33	1.99	3.63	3.30	1.23	3.57
Cash Flow Per Share	5.51	4.69	3.81	0.19	(19.55)	6.75	6.04	2.95
Tang Book Value Per Share	N.M.	N.M.	N.M.	N.M.	N.M.	N.M.	0.38	N.M.
Dividends Per Share	0.870	0.840	0.510	...	...	...	...	...
Dividend Payout %	483.33	525.00	38.35	...	...	...	...	...
Income Statement								
Total Revenue	431,500	1,716,500	1,598,600	3,051,500	3,243,000	3,060,700	3,155,500	3,211,900
EBITDA	107,100	360,600	302,400	499,400	552,900	490,100	194,000	520,400
Depn & Amortn	25,000	96,100	85,700	109,300	112,500	108,600	108,200	110,000
Income Before Taxes	62,800	185,000	136,200	289,200	314,600	337,700	39,300	368,300
Income Taxes	24,800	200,500	59,000	164,700	57,000	102,900	(37,300)	114,700
Net Income	43,600	11,200	94,100	144,200	276,300	256,100	94,100	269,400
Average Shares	67,700	68,200	70,500	72,600	76,200	77,700	76,300	75,500
Balance Sheet								
Current Assets	727,600	728,600	654,800	1,184,500	1,690,900	2,294,400	2,440,200	2,149,100
Total Assets	2,945,100	2,907,000	2,911,800	3,676,000	4,095,200	5,396,100	5,090,200	4,496,700
Current Liabilities	465,600	448,200	480,800	707,400	1,182,100	635,600	646,300	635,600
Long-Term Obligations	1,531,700	1,523,800	1,507,600	2,144,300	1,919,000	29,600	35,800	21,600
Total Liabilities	2,705,900	2,650,400	2,543,000	3,468,200	3,729,300	4,835,500	4,781,800	4,337,300
Stockholders' Equity	239,200	256,400	368,800	207,800	365,900	560,600	308,400	159,400
Shares Outstanding	67,295	67,780	68,309	70,533	72,922	77,046	75,565	73,886
Statistical Record								
Return on Assets %	0.41	0.38	2.85	3.71	5.82	4.88	1.96	6.14
Return on Equity %	3.77	3.58	32.55	50.27	59.64	58.94	40.12	643.73
EBITDA Margin %	24.82	21.01	18.92	16.37	17.05	16.01	6.15	16.20
Net Margin %	10.10	0.65	5.89	4.73	8.52	8.37	2.98	8.39
Asset Turnover	0.60	0.59	0.48	0.79	0.68	0.58	0.66	0.73
Current Ratio	1.56	1.63	1.36	1.67	1.43	3.61	3.78	3.38
Debt to Equity	6.40	5.94	4.09	10.32	5.24	0.05	0.12	0.14
Price Range	76.60-60.37	76.60-66.38	79.93-63.12	83.89-68.23	83.47-65.35	79.35-53.96	54.98-37.05	41.78-25.19
P/E Ratio	425.56-335.39	478.75-414.88	60.10-47.46	42.15-34.29	22.99-18.00	24.05-16.35	44.70-30.12	11.70-7.06
Average Yield %	1.24	1.19	0.70	...	...	...	...	...

Address: 7500 Grace Drive, Columbia, MD 21044-4098 Telephone: 410-531-4000	Web Site: www.grace.com Officers: Hudson La Force - President, Senior Vice President, Chief Operating Officer, Chief Financial Officer, Chief Executive Officer Mark A. Shelnitz - Senior Vice President, Vice President, Secretary, General Counsel	Auditors: PricewaterhouseCoopers LLP Investor Contact: 410-531-4167 Transfer Agents: Computershare Shareowner Services LLC, Providence, RI

GRACO INC

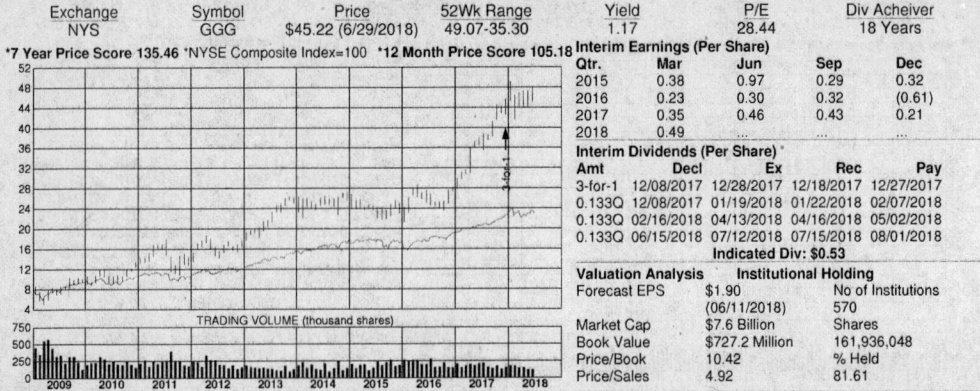

Exchange	Symbol	Price	52Wk Range	Yield	P/E	Div Acheiver
NYS	GGG	$45.22 (6/29/2018)	49.07-35.30	1.17	28.44	18 Years

*7 Year Price Score 135.46 *NYSE Composite Index=100 *12 Month Price Score 105.18

Interim Earnings (Per Share)

Qtr.	Mar	Jun	Sep	Dec
2015	0.38	0.97	0.29	0.32
2016	0.23	0.30	0.32	(0.61)
2017	0.35	0.46	0.43	0.21
2018	0.49	...	...	...

Interim Dividends (Per Share)

Amt	Decl	Ex	Rec	Pay
3-for-1	12/08/2017	12/28/2017	12/18/2017	12/27/2017
0.133Q	12/08/2017	01/19/2018	01/22/2018	02/07/2018
0.133Q	02/16/2018	04/13/2018	04/16/2018	05/02/2018
0.133Q	06/15/2018	07/12/2018	07/15/2018	08/01/2018

Indicated Div: $0.53

Valuation Analysis — **Institutional Holding**

Forecast EPS	$1.90 (06/11/2018)	No of Institutions 570
Market Cap	$7.6 Billion	Shares 161,936,048
Book Value	$727.2 Million	% Held 81.61
Price/Book	10.42	
Price/Sales	4.92	

Business Summary: Industrial Machinery & Equipment (MIC: 7.2.1 SIC: 3561 NAIC: 333911)

Graco, together with its subsidiaries, design, manufacture and market equipment used to move, measure, control, dispense and spray fluid and powder materials. Co. has three segments: Industrial, which includes Co.'s Industrial Products and Applied Fluid Technologies divisions and markets equipment and pre-engineered packages for moving and applying paints, coatings, sealants, adhesives and other fluids; Process, which includes Co.'s Process, Oil and Natural Gas, and Lubrication divisions and markets pumps, valves, meters and accessories to move and dispense fluids; and Contractor, which markets sprayers for architectural coatings for painting, corrosion control, texture and line striping.

Recent Developments: For the quarter ended Mar 30 2018, net income increased 40.8% to US$85.5 million from US$60.7 million in the year-earlier quarter. Revenues were US$406.3 million, up 19.3% from US$340.6 million the year before. Operating income was US$111.7 million versus US$87.4 million in the prior-year quarter, an increase of 27.7%. Direct operating expenses rose 18.9% to US$183.9 million from US$154.7 million in the comparable period the year before. Indirect operating expenses increased 12.5% to US$110.7 million from US$98.4 million in the equivalent prior-year period.

Prospects: Our evaluation of Graco Inc. as of Jan. 21, 2018 is the result of our systematic analysis on three basic characteristics: earnings strength, relative valuation, and recent stock price movement. The company has generated a negative trend in earnings per share over the past 5 quarters and while recent estimates for the company have been mixed, GGG has posted better than expected results. Based on operating earnings yield, the company is about fairly valued when compared to all of the companies in our coverage universe. Share price changes over the past year indicates that GGG will perform very well over the near term.

Financial Data
(US$ in Thousands)

	3 Mos	12/29/2017	12/30/2016	12/25/2015	12/26/2014	12/27/2013	12/28/2012	12/30/2011
Earnings Per Share	1.59	1.45	0.24	1.95	1.22	1.12	0.81	0.77
Cash Flow Per Share	2.05	2.02	1.59	1.10	1.34	1.33	1.05	0.90
Tang Book Value Per Share	1.45	1.53	0.80	0.06	0.70	1.60	0.65	1.17
Dividends Per Share	0.492	0.480	0.440	0.400	0.367	0.333	0.300	0.280
Dividend Payout %	30.97	33.10	185.89	20.48	30.14	29.76	37.19	36.21
Income Statement								
Total Revenue	406,348	1,474,744	1,329,293	1,286,485	1,221,130	1,104,024	1,012,456	895,283
EBITDA	123,312	392,796	143,045	518,056	357,906	330,369	258,799	239,459
Depn & Amortn	12,651	29,500	28,800	25,700	24,100	23,400	22,200	20,600
Income Before Taxes	107,428	347,094	96,655	474,713	315,073	288,822	217,326	209,728
Income Taxes	21,918	94,682	55,981	129,000	89,500	78,000	68,200	67,400
Net Income	85,510	252,412	40,674	345,713	225,573	210,822	149,126	142,328
Average Shares	175,649	174,318	170,880	177,021	185,235	188,370	185,133	184,110
Balance Sheet								
Current Assets	716,234	631,926	503,362	509,017	859,507	792,593	776,996	582,970
Total Assets	1,491,531	1,379,205	1,243,109	1,391,352	1,544,778	1,327,228	1,321,734	874,309
Current Liabilities	280,630	234,426	177,985	194,616	174,480	168,853	151,671	131,282
Long-Term Obligations	285,195	226,035	305,685	392,695	615,000	408,370	556,480	300,000
Total Liabilities	764,352	656,142	669,289	755,801	948,746	692,863	867,620	551,569
Stockholders' Equity	727,179	723,063	573,820	635,551	596,032	634,365	454,114	322,740
Shares Outstanding	167,606	169,318	167,503	167,297	177,595	183,009	182,300	179,242
Statistical Record								
Return on Assets %	19.76	19.36	3.04	23.61	15.75	15.96	13.62	20.32
Return on Equity %	42.84	39.14	6.62	56.30	36.77	38.84	38.50	48.64
EBITDA Margin %	30.35	26.63	10.76	40.27	29.31	29.92	25.56	26.75
Net Margin %	21.04	17.12	3.06	26.87	18.47	19.10	14.73	15.90
Asset Turnover	1.10	1.13	0.99	0.88	0.85	0.84	0.92	1.28
Current Ratio	2.55	2.70	2.83	2.62	4.93	4.69	5.12	4.44
Debt to Equity	0.39	0.31	0.53	0.62	1.03	0.64	1.23	0.93
Price Range	49.07-30.84	45.63-27.70	28.67-21.19	27.14-21.60	27.14-22.00	26.29-16.95	18.67-13.32	17.95-10.82
P/E Ratio	30.86-19.40	31.47-19.10	119.47-88.28	13.92-11.08	22.25-18.04	23.47-15.13	23.05-16.44	23.31-14.06
Average Yield %	1.22	1.31	1.71	1.66	1.46	1.71	1.84	1.96

Address: 88 - 11th Avenue Northeast, Minneapolis, MN 55413 Telephone: 612-623-6000 Fax: 612-623-6777	Web Site: www.graco.com Officers: Lee R. Mitau - Chairman Patrick J. McHale - President, Chief Executive Officer	Auditors: DELOITTE & TOUCHE LLP Transfer Agents: Wells Fargo Bank, N.A., St. Paul, MN

GRAHAM HOLDINGS CO.

Exchange	Symbol	Price	52Wk Range	Yield	P/E
NYS	GHC	$586.10 (6/29/2018)	624.60-542.80	0.91	10.12

*7 Year Price Score 108.03 *NYSE Composite Index=100 *12 Month Price Score 100.32

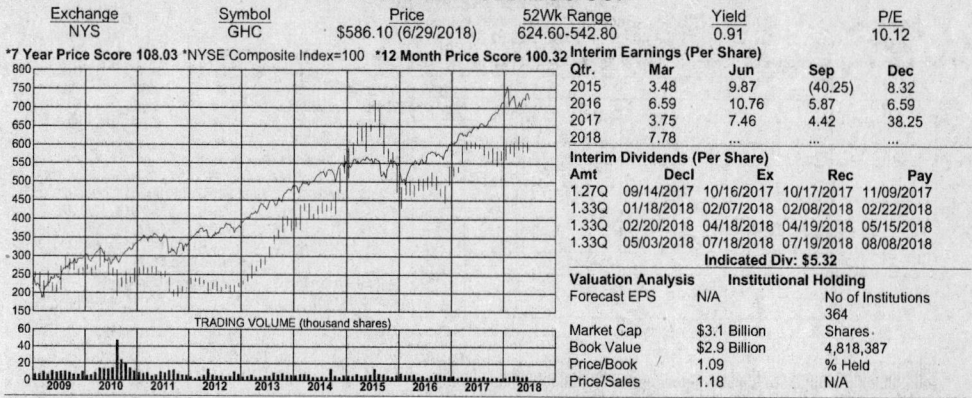

Interim Earnings (Per Share)

Qtr.	Mar	Jun	Sep	Dec
2015	3.48	9.87	(40.25)	8.32
2016	6.59	10.76	5.87	6.59
2017	3.75	7.46	4.42	38.25
2018	7.78	...	...	...

Interim Dividends (Per Share)

Amt	Decl	Ex	Rec	Pay
1.27Q	09/14/2017	10/16/2017	10/17/2017	11/09/2017
1.33Q	01/18/2018	02/07/2018	02/08/2018	02/22/2018
1.33Q	02/20/2018	04/18/2018	04/19/2018	05/15/2018
1.33Q	05/03/2018	07/18/2018	07/19/2018	08/08/2018

Indicated Div: $5.32

Valuation Analysis

Forecast EPS: N/A

Market Cap	$3.1 Billion
Book Value	$2.9 Billion
Price/Book	1.09
Price/Sales	1.18

Institutional Holding

No of Institutions	364
Shares	4,818,387
% Held	N/A

Business Summary: Educational Services (MIC: 2.2.2 SIC: 8299 NAIC: 611699)

Graham Holdings is an education and media company. Co.'s Kaplan, Inc. subsidiary provides a variety of educational services, both domestically and outside the U.S. Co.'s education business includes Kaplan University, which focuses on online education; its test preparation businesses; and businesses in Europe and the Asia Pacific region. Co.'s media operations comprise the ownership and operation of television broadcasting, plus Slate and Foreign Policy magazines. As of Dec 31 2017, Co. owned and operated seven television broadcast stations. Also, as of Dec 31 2017, Co. owned home health and hospice providers, four industrial companies and Social Code LLC, a marketing solutions provider.

Recent Developments: For the quarter ended Mar 31 2018, net income increased 103.8% to US$43.0 million from US$21.1 million in the year-earlier quarter. Revenues were US$659.4 million, up 13.2% from US$582.7 million the year before. Operating income was US$44.2 million versus US$10.3 million in the prior-year quarter, an increase of 331.2%. Direct operating expenses rose 12.1% to US$365.2 million from US$325.7 million in the comparable period the year before. Indirect operating expenses increased 1.3% to US$250.1 million from US$246.8 million in the equivalent prior-year period.

Prospects: Our evaluation of Graham Holdings Co. as of Jan. 21, 2018 is the result of our systematic analysis on three basic characteristics: earnings strength, relative valuation, and recent stock price movement. The company has generated a negative trend in earnings per share over the past 5 quarters. Because the company lacks sufficient analyst estimate data, we place greater weight on the historical EPS trend as the measure of earnings strength. Based on operating earnings yield, the company is undervalued when compared to all of the companies in our coverage universe. Share price changes over the past year indicates that GHC will perform in line with the market over the near term.

Financial Data
(US$ in Thousands)

	3 Mos	12/31/2017	12/31/2016	12/31/2015	12/31/2014	12/31/2013	12/31/2012	12/31/2011
Earnings Per Share	57.91	53.89	29.80	(17.87)	195.03	32.05	17.39	14.70
Cash Flow Per Share	35.89	48.60	46.87	13.06	57.55	45.30	64.66	50.53
Tang Book Value Per Share	232.83	231.68	207.30	231.59	204.94	195.10	93.42	80.74
Dividends Per Share	5.140	5.080	4.840	9.100	10.200	...	19.600	9.400
Dividend Payout %	8.88	9.43	16.24	...	5.23	...	112.71	63.95
Income Statement								
Total Revenue	659,436	2,591,846	2,481,890	2,586,114	3,535,166	3,487,864	4,017,653	4,214,833
EBITDA	85,711	317,030	382,163	7,530	1,483,888	568,612	429,119	524,491
Depn & Amortn	25,026	103,687	91,271	96,978	222,697	246,798	290,044	283,733
Income Before Taxes	53,986	186,038	258,595	(120,193)	1,226,741	288,011	106,524	211,679
Income Taxes	13,600	(119,700)	81,200	20,500	406,100	110,000	71,600.	96,300
Net Income	42,891	302,044	168,590	(100,655)	1,293,843	236,865	132,113	117,150
Average Shares	5,473	5,552	5,589	5,727	6,559	7,333	7,404	7,905
Balance Sheet								
Current Assets	1,521,436	1,735,804	1,871,346	1,860,722	1,690,703	1,702,387	1,453,762	1,245,625
Total Assets	4,760,958	4,937,823	4,432,670	4,352,951	5,752,319	5,811,046	5,105,069	5,016,986
Current Liabilities	1,152,583	878,612	818,961	725,149	1,050,792	934,109	1,126,286	995,556
Long-Term Obligations	91,079	486,561	485,719	399,926	399,545	447,608	453,384	452,229
Total Liabilities	1,876,045	2,022,678	1,979,729	1,862,253	2,601,510	2,500,314	2,507,945	2,403,795
Stockholders' Equity	2,884,913	2,915,145	2,452,941	2,490,698	3,150,809	3,310,732	2,597,124	2,613,191
Shares Outstanding	5,363	5,504	5,576	5,803	5,798	7,387	7,427	7,591
Statistical Record								
Return on Assets %	7.06	6.45	3.83	N.M.	22.38	4.34	2.60	2.32
Return on Equity %	12.07	11.25	6.80	N.M.	40.05	8.02	5.06	4.33
EBITDA Margin %	13.00	12.23	15.40	0.29	41.98	16.30	10.68	12.44
Net Margin %	6.50	11.65	6.79	N.M.	36.60	6.79	3.29	2.78
Asset Turnover	0.58	0.55	0.56	0.51	0.61	0.64	0.79	0.83
Current Ratio	1.32	1.98	2.29	2.57	1.61	1.82	1.29	1.25
Debt to Equity	0.03	0.17	0.20	0.16	0.13	0.14	0.17	0.17
Price Range	610.10-542.80	610.10-514.95	541.95-428.09	718.70-471.59	571.19-370.98	406.93-220.66	241.68-198.03	272.60-189.12
P/E Ratio	10.54-9.37	11.32-9.56	18.19-14.37	...	2.93-1.90	12.70-6.88	13.90-11.39	18.54-12.87
Average Yield %	0.88	0.89	0.99	1.50	2.33	...	8.91	3.95

Address: 1300 North 17th Street, Arlington, VA 22209 Telephone: 703-345-6300	Web Site: www.ghco.com Officers: Donald E. Graham - Chairman, Chief Executive Officer Timothy J. O'Shaughnessy - President, Chief Executive Officer	Auditors: PricewaterhouseCoopers LLP Investor Contact: 703-345-6300 Transfer Agents: ComputerShare Investor Services, Providence, RI

GRAINGER (W.W.) INC.

Exchange	Symbol	Price	52Wk Range	Yield	P/E	Div Acheiver
NYS	GWW	$308.40 (6/29/2018)	319.62-156.25	1.76	27.63	46 Years

*7 Year Price Score 84.21   *NYSE Composite Index=100   *12 Month Price Score 127.87

TRADING VOLUME (thousand shares)

Interim Earnings (Per Share)

Qtr.	Mar	Jun	Sep	Dec
2015	3.07	3.25	2.92	2.34
2016	2.98	2.79	3.05	1.05
2017	2.93	1.67	2.79	2.63
2018	4.07	...	...	...

Interim Dividends (Per Share)

Amt	Decl	Ex	Rec	Pay
1.28Q	07/26/2017	08/10/2017	08/14/2017	09/01/2017
1.28Q	10/25/2017	11/10/2017	11/13/2017	12/01/2017
1.28Q	01/31/2018	02/09/2018	02/12/2018	03/01/2018
1.36Q	04/25/2018	05/11/2018	05/14/2018	06/01/2018

Indicated Div: $5.44

Valuation Analysis / Institutional Holding

Forecast EPS	$14.95	No of Institutions	931
(06/11/2018)			
Market Cap	$17.3 Billion	Shares	55,690,728
Book Value	$1.8 Billion	% Held	69.42
Price/Book	9.76		
Price/Sales	1.62		

Business Summary: Electrical Equipment (MIC: 7.3.1 SIC: 5099 NAIC: 423990)

W.W. Grainger is a distributor of maintenance, repair and operating (MRO) supplies and other related products and services used by businesses and institutions mainly in the U.S. and Canada, and also in Europe, Asia and Latin America. Co.'s U.S. segment provides MRO supplies and other related products and services through sales representatives, catalogs, eCommerce and local branches. Co.'s Canadian segment, through its Acklands – Grainger Inc. subsidiary, distributes tools, fasteners, safety supplies, welding and shop equipment and other items. Co.'s Other businesses include Zoro Tools, Inc. in the U.S. and MonotaRO Co., Ltd. in Japan and other operations in Europe, Asia and Latin America.

Recent Developments: For the quarter ended Mar 31 2018, net income increased 31.7% to US$240.8 million from US$182.9 million in the year-earlier quarter. Revenues were US$2.77 billion, up 8.9% from US$2.54 billion the year before. Operating income was US$334.8 million versus US$292.5 million in the prior-year quarter, an increase of 14.5%. Direct operating expenses rose 10.0% to US$1.67 billion from US$1.52 billion in the comparable period the year before. Indirect operating expenses increased 4.2% to US$756.9 million from US$726.7 million in the equivalent prior-year period.

Prospects: Our evaluation of Grainger (W.W.) Inc. as of Jan. 21, 2018 is the result of our systematic analysis on three basic characteristics: earnings strength, relative valuation, and recent stock price movement. The company has managed to produce a neutral trend in earnings per share over the past 5 quarters and while recent estimates for the company have been mixed, GWW has posted better than expected results. Based on operating earnings yield, the company is undervalued when compared to all of the companies in our coverage universe. Share price changes over the past year indicates that GWW will perform poorly over the near term.

Financial Data

(US$ in Thousands)	3 Mos	12/31/2017	12/31/2016	12/31/2015	12/31/2014	12/31/2013	12/31/2012	12/31/2011
Earnings Per Share	11.16	10.02	9.87	11.58	11.45	11.13	9.52	9.07
Cash Flow Per Share	18.24	18.32	16.55	15.19	14.05	14.20	11.66	10.71
Tang Book Value Per Share	11.62	10.25	11.64	19.68	40.08	39.58	35.70	30.30
Dividends Per Share	5.120	5.060	4.830	4.590	4.170	3.590	3.060	2.520
Dividend Payout %	45.88	50.50	48.94	39.64	36.42	32.26	32.14	27.78
Income Statement								
Total Revenue	2,766,401	10,424,858	10,137,204	9,973,384	9,964,953	9,437,758	8,950,045	8,078,185
EBITDA	406,459	1,220,983	1,281,866	1,456,850	1,550,737	1,478,203	1,290,256	1,207,436
Depn & Amortn	63,931	170,000	166,000	162,000	208,326	180,613	159,049	149,200
Income Before Taxes	318,491	973,095	1,050,251	1,262,445	1,334,386	1,287,599	1,117,789	1,051,213
Income Taxes	66,209	312,881	386,220	465,531	522,090	479,850	418,940	385,115
Net Income	231,545	585,730	605,928	768,996	801,729	797,036	689,881	658,423
Average Shares	56,403	57,983	60,839	65,765	69,205	70,576	71,181	71,176
Balance Sheet								
Current Assets	3,307,162	3,205,989	3,020,229	3,048,642	2,967,549	3,044,285	2,900,640	2,694,900
Total Assets	5,902,811	5,804,254	5,694,307	5,857,755	5,284,252	5,266,328	5,014,598	4,716,062
Current Liabilities	1,504,332	1,506,661	1,628,937	1,788,534	1,261,716	1,195,790	1,080,003	1,387,925
Long-Term Obligations	2,244,406	2,248,036	1,840,946	1,388,414	404,536	445,513	467,048	175,055
Total Liabilities	4,132,213	4,114,122	3,896,372	3,591,121	2,074,380	2,015,890	1,990,686	2,087,277
Stockholders' Equity	1,770,598	1,690,132	1,797,935	2,266,634	3,209,872	3,250,438	3,023,912	2,628,785
Shares Outstanding	56,017	56,328	58,804	62,028	67,432	68,853	69,478	69,962
Statistical Record								
Return on Assets %	11.00	10.19	10.46	13.80	15.20	15.51	14.14	15.28
Return on Equity %	36.04	33.58	29.73	28.08	24.82	25.41	24.34	27.24
EBITDA Margin %	14.69	11.71	12.65	14.61	15.56	15.66	14.42	14.95
Net Margin %	8.37	5.62	5.98	7.71	8.05	8.45	7.71	8.15
Asset Turnover	1.82	1.81	1.75	1.79	1.89	1.84	1.83	1.87
Current Ratio	2.20	2.13	1.85	1.70	2.35	2.55	2.69	1.94
Debt to Equity	1.27	1.33	1.02	0.61	0.13	0.14	0.15	0.07
Price Range	288.75-156.25	258.16-156.25	239.62-182.78	255.22-190.83	269.22-229.29	274.01-202.37	219.90-177.10	192.31-126.11
P/E Ratio	25.87-14.00	25.76-15.59	24.28-18.52	22.04-16.48	23.51-20.03	24.62-18.18	23.10-18.60	21.20-13.90
Average Yield %	2.48	2.50	2.18	2.02	1.67	1.45	1.52	1.67

Address: 100 Grainger Parkway, Lake Forest, IL 60045-5201 **Telephone:** 847-535-1000 **Fax:** 847-535-0878	**Web Site:** www.grainger.com **Officers:** Donald G. Macpherson - Chairman, Chief Executive Officer, Chief Operating Officer John L. Howard - Senior Vice President, General Counsel	**Auditors:** Ernst & Young LLP **Investor Contact:** 847-535-0409 **Transfer Agents:** Computershare Trust Company, N.A., Providence, RI

GRANITE CONSTRUCTION INC

Exchange	Symbol	Price	52Wk Range	Yield	P/E
NYS	GVA	$55.66 (6/29/2018)	67.84-47.37	0.93	27.69

*7 Year Price Score 120.58 *NYSE Composite Index=100 ***12 Month Price Score 96.30**

Interim Earnings (Per Share)

Qtr.	Mar	Jun	Sep	Dec
2015	(0.22)	0.24	0.77	0.72
2016	(0.28)	0.35	0.92	0.42
2017	(0.60)	0.35	1.14	0.81
2018	(0.29)	...	...	...

Interim Dividends (Per Share)

Amt	Decl	Ex	Rec	Pay
0.13Q	09/13/2017	09/28/2017	09/29/2017	10/13/2017
0.13Q	12/07/2017	12/28/2017	12/29/2017	01/12/2018
0.13Q	02/06/2018	03/28/2018	03/30/2018	04/13/2018
0.13Q	06/07/2018	06/28/2018	06/29/2018	07/13/2018

Indicated Div: $0.52 (Div. Reinv. Plan)

Valuation Analysis | **Institutional Holding**

Forecast EPS	$3.18	No of Institutions
	(05/27/2018)	374
Market Cap	$2.2 Billion	Shares
Book Value	$915.4 Million	49,786,784
Price/Book	2.43	% Held
Price/Sales	0.72	90.53

Business Summary: Construction Services (MIC: 7.5.4 SIC: 1629 NAIC: 237990)

Granite Construction is a holding company. Through its subsidiaries, Co. is a heavy civil contractor and a construction materials producer. Co.'s segments are: Construction, which performs construction management and civil construction projects focused on new construction and improvement of streets, roads, highways, bridges, site work and other infrastructure projects; Large Project Construction, which focuses on infrastructure projects such as highways, mass transit facilities, bridges, tunnels, waterway locks and dams, pipelines and airport infrastructure; and Construction Materials, which mines and processes aggregates and operates plants that produce construction materials.

Recent Developments: For the quarter ended Mar 31 2018, net loss amounted to US$9.7 million versus a net loss of US$23.9 million in the year-earlier quarter. Revenues were US$563.4 million, up 20.3% from US$468.4 million the year before. Operating loss was US$12.8 million versus a loss of US$36.4 million in the prior-year quarter. Direct operating expenses rose 14.4% to US$507.1 million from US$443.3 million in the comparable period the year before. Indirect operating expenses increased 12.3% to US$69.1 million from US$61.6 million in the equivalent prior-year period.

Prospects: Our evaluation of Granite Construction Inc. as of Jan. 21, 2018 is the result of our systematic analysis on three basic characteristics: earnings strength, relative valuation, and recent stock price movement. The company has enjoyed a very positive trend in earnings per share over the past 5 quarters. However, while recent estimates for the company have been mixed, GVA has posted better than expected results. Based on operating earnings yield, the company is overvalued when compared to all of the companies in our coverage universe. Share price changes over the past year indicates that GVA will perform poorly over the near term.

Financial Data

(US$ in Thousands)	3 Mos	12/31/2017	12/31/2016	12/31/2015	12/31/2014	12/31/2013	12/31/2012	12/31/2011
Earnings Per Share	2.01	1.71	1.42	1.52	0.64	(0.94)	1.15	1.31
Cash Flow Per Share	2.39	3.67	1.84	1.70	1.10	0.14	2.38	2.42
Tang Book Value Per Share	21.52	22.35	21.00	19.93	18.90	18.71	20.00	20.66
Dividends Per Share	0.520	0.520	0.520	0.520	0.520	0.520	0.520	0.520
Dividend Payout %	25.87	30.41	36.62	34.21	81.25	...	45.22	39.69
Income Statement								
Total Revenue	563,379	2,989,713	2,514,617	2,371,029	2,275,270	2,266,901	2,083,037	2,009,531
EBITDA	2,408	167,214	159,326	173,339	131,883	9,968	138,818	150,724
Depn & Amortn	15,511	63,800	61,000	61,000	64,900	62,700	51,800	56,000
Income Before Taxes	(14,017)	97,356	89,185	100,217	54,696	(65,333)	79,041	87,240
Income Taxes	(4,131)	28,662	30,162	35,179	19,721	(19,263)	21,109	23,348
Net Income	(11,423)	69,098	57,122	60,485	25,346	(36,423)	45,283	51,161
Average Shares	39,908	40,372	40,225	39,868	39,795	38,803	39,076	38,473
Balance Sheet								
Current Assets	1,111,633	1,232,078	1,088,992	985,222	970,178	950,203	1,022,057	909,722
Total Assets	1,759,227	1,871,978	1,733,453	1,627,860	1,620,494	1,617,155	1,729,487	1,547,799
Current Liabilities	578,218	655,274	529,934	466,045	462,826	497,570	531,272	448,468
Long-Term Obligations	176,011	178,453	229,498	245,081	275,621	276,868	271,070	218,413
Total Liabilities	843,791	926,870	847,465	788,623	826,109	835,215	899,534	748,602
Stockholders' Equity	915,436	945,108	885,988	839,237	794,385	781,940	829,953	799,197
Shares Outstanding	40,047	39,871	39,621	39,412	39,186	38,917	38,730	38,682
Statistical Record								
Return on Assets %	4.74	3.83	3.39	3.72	1.57	N.M.	2.76	3.32
Return on Equity %	9.18	7.55	6.60	7.41	3.22	N.M.	5.54	6.56
EBITDA Margin %	0.43	5.59	6.34	7.31	5.80	0.44	6.66	7.50
Net Margin %	N.M.	2.31	2.27	2.55	1.11	N.M.	2.17	2.55
Asset Turnover	1.79	1.66	1.49	1.46	1.41	1.35	1.27	1.30
Current Ratio	1.92	1.88	2.05	2.11	2.10	1.91	1.92	2.03
Debt to Equity	0.19	0.19	0.26	0.29	0.35	0.35	0.33	0.27
Price Range	67.84-45.71	66.66-45.71	61.30-36.25	44.25-29.12	40.29-30.52	37.54-26.83	34.43-21.66	29.26-17.15
P/E Ratio	33.75-22.74	38.98-26.73	43.17-25.53	29.11-19.16	62.95-47.69	...	29.94-18.83	22.34-13.09
Average Yield %	0.92	0.95	1.11	1.46	1.46	1.66	1.89	2.13

Address: 585 West Beach Street, Watsonville, CA 95076 **Telephone:** 831-724-1011	**Web Site:** www.graniteconstruction.com **Officers:** David H. Watts - Chairman James H. Roberts - President, Chief Executive Officer, Executive Vice President, Chief Operating Officer (frmr), Interim Chief Operating Officer, Division Officer	**Auditors:** PricewaterhouseCoopers LLP **Investor Contact:** 831-724-1011 **Transfer Agents:** Computershare, Canton, MA

GRAPHIC PACKAGING HOLDING CO

Exchange	Symbol	Price	52Wk Range	Yield	P/E
NYS	GPK	$14.51 (6/29/2018)	16.68-12.70	2.07	15.27

*7 Year Price Score 109.71 *NYSE Composite Index=100 *12 Month Price Score 97.32

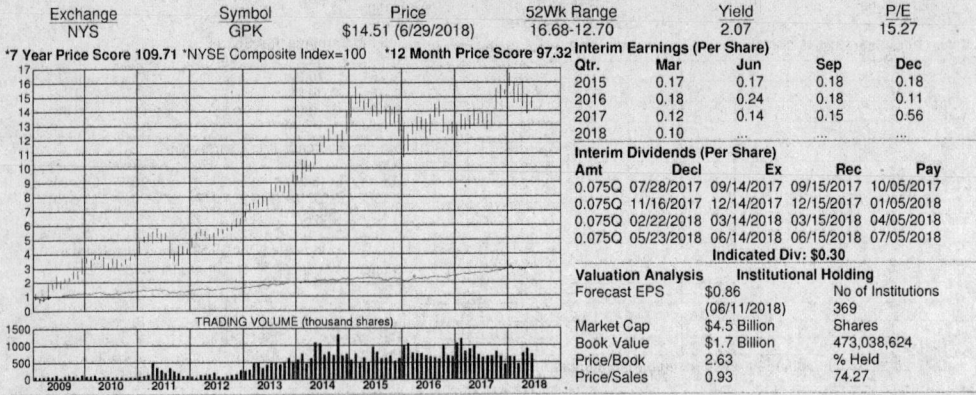

Interim Earnings (Per Share)

Qtr.	Mar	Jun	Sep	Dec
2015	0.17	0.17	0.18	0.18
2016	0.18	0.24	0.18	0.11
2017	0.12	0.14	0.15	0.56
2018	0.10	...	...	...

Interim Dividends (Per Share)

Amt	Decl	Ex	Rec	Pay
0.075Q	07/28/2017	09/14/2017	09/15/2017	10/05/2017
0.075Q	11/16/2017	12/14/2017	12/15/2017	01/05/2018
0.075Q	02/22/2018	03/14/2018	03/15/2018	04/05/2018
0.075Q	05/23/2018	06/14/2018	06/15/2018	07/05/2018

Indicated Div: $0.30

Valuation Analysis — **Institutional Holding**

Forecast EPS	$0.86	No of Institutions	369
	(06/11/2018)		
Market Cap	$4.5 Billion	Shares	473,038,624
Book Value	$1.7 Billion	% Held	74.27
Price/Book	2.63		
Price/Sales	0.93		

Business Summary: Containers & Packaging (MIC: 8.1.3 SIC: 2657 NAIC: 322212)

Graphic Packaging Holding is a provider of paper-based packaging solutions for a range of products to food, beverage and other consumer products companies. Co. is a producer of folding cartons. Co. operates in three geographic areas: Americas, Europe and Asia Pacific. Co. has three segments: Paperboard Mills, which produces primarily coated unbleached kraft and coated recycled board; Americas Paperboard Packaging, which includes paperboard packaging folding cartons sold primarily to Consumer Packaged Goods (CPG) companies in the Americas; and Europe Paperboard Packaging, which includes paperboard packaging folding cartons sold primarily to CPG companies in Europe.

Recent Developments: For the quarter ended Mar 31 2018, net income increased 15.4% to US$42.7 million from US$37.0 million in the year-earlier quarter. Revenues were US$1.48 billion, up 39.0% from US$1.06 billion the year before. Operating income was US$74.0 million versus US$71.6 million in the prior-year quarter, an increase of 3.4%. Direct operating expenses rose 40.9% to US$1.25 billion from US$889.6 million in the comparable period the year before. Indirect operating expenses increased 48.1% to US$148.5 million from US$100.3 million in the equivalent prior-year period.

Prospects: Our evaluation of Graphic Packaging Holding Co. as of Jan. 21, 2018 is the result of our systematic analysis on three basic characteristics: earnings strength, relative valuation, and recent stock price movement. The company has enjoyed a very positive trend in earnings per share over the past 5 quarters. However, while recent estimates for the company have been mixed, GPK has posted results that fell short of analysts expectations. Based on operating earnings yield, the company is about fairly valued when compared to all of the companies in our coverage universe. Share price changes over the past year indicates that GPK will perform in line with the market over the near term.

Financial Data
(US$ in Thousands)

	3 Mos	12/31/2017	12/31/2016	12/31/2015	12/31/2014	12/31/2013	12/31/2012	12/31/2011
Earnings Per Share	0.95	0.96	0.71	0.70	0.27	0.42	0.31	0.73
Cash Flow Per Share	0.96	1.66	1.99	1.79	1.60	1.32	1.19	1.03
Dividends Per Share	0.300	0.300	0.225	0.200	...	...	...	...
Dividend Payout %	31.58	31.25	31.69	28.57	...	...	...	...
Income Statement								
Total Revenue	1,476,000	4,403,700	4,298,100	4,160,200	4,240,500	4,478,100	4,337,100	4,206,300
EBITDA	186,100	611,200	636,000	654,700	435,000	547,000	534,100	419,600
Depn & Amortn	109,800	268,500	240,000	227,600	221,600	232,500	222,700	231,400
Income Before Taxes	47,500	253,000	319,400	359,300	132,700	212,600	200,300	43,300
Income Taxes	5,100	(45,500)	93,200	130,400	45,400	67,400	82,500	(229,800)
Net Income	29,900	300,200	228,000	230,100	89,700	146,600	122,600	276,900
Average Shares	311,300	311,900	321,500	330,700	330,500	349,700	396,200	381,700
Balance Sheet								
Current Assets	1,825,100	1,169,900	1,114,900	1,066,800	1,220,900	1,232,200	1,203,100	1,314,100
Total Assets	7,130,300	4,863,000	4,603,400	4,256,100	4,331,300	4,559,300	4,620,800	4,649,700
Current Liabilities	1,003,300	851,400	779,800	732,200	676,700	711,200	752,900	645,500
Long-Term Obligations	3,043,500	2,213,200	2,088,500	1,838,900	1,942,100	2,176,200	2,253,500	2,335,700
Total Liabilities	5,421,700	3,571,100	3,546,900	3,154,400	3,319,000	3,497,000	3,646,800	3,481,800
Stockholders' Equity	1,708,600	1,291,900	1,056,500	1,101,700	1,012,300	1,062,300	974,000	1,167,900
Shares Outstanding	310,279	309,715	313,533	324,688	327,044	324,746	344,534	389,474
Statistical Record								
Return on Assets %	4.97	6.34	5.13	5.36	2.02	3.19	2.64	6.06
Return on Equity %	21.02	25.57	21.07	21.77	8.65	14.40	11.42	28.92
EBITDA Margin %	12.61	13.88	14.80	15.74	10.26	12.22	12.31	9.98
Net Margin %	2.03	6.82	5.30	5.53	2.12	3.27	2.83	6.58
Asset Turnover	0.82	0.93	0.97	0.97	0.95	0.98	0.93	0.92
Current Ratio	1.82	1.37	1.43	1.46	1.80	1.73	1.60	2.04
Debt to Equity	1.78	1.71	1.98	1.67	1.92	2.05	2.31	2.00
Price Range	16.68-12.70	15.83-12.26	14.60-10.74	15.75-12.24	14.05-9.17	9.60-6.46	6.50-4.49	5.78-3.16
P/E Ratio	17.56-13.37	16.49-12.77	20.56-15.13	22.50-17.49	52.04-33.96	22.86-15.38	20.97-14.48	7.92-4.33
Average Yield %	2.09	2.19	1.73	1.41	...	...	...	...

Address: 1500 Riveredge Parkway, Suite 100, Atlanta, GA 30328	**Web Site:** www.graphicpkg.com	**Auditors:** Ernst & Young LLP
Telephone: 770-240-7200	**Officers:** Philip R. Martens - Chairman Stephen M. Humphrey - Vice-Chairman	**Transfer Agents:** Broadridge Corporate Issuer Solutions, Inc., Ardmore, PA

GREIF INC

Exchange	Symbol	Price	52Wk Range	Yield	P/E
NYS	GEF	$52.89 (6/29/2018)	64.87-49.80	3.18	17.40

*7 Year Price Score 96.17 *NYSE Composite Index=100 *12 Month Price Score 101.35

Interim Earnings (Per Share)
Qtr.	Jan	Apr	Jul	Oct
2014-15	0.52	0.35	0.15	0.21
2015-16	(0.19)	0.53	0.78	0.15
2016-17	0.10	0.61	0.74	0.57
2017-18	0.96	0.77	...	...

Interim Dividends (Per Share)
Amt	Decl	Ex	Rec	Pay
0.42Q	08/29/2017	09/15/2017	09/18/2017	10/01/2017
0.42Q	12/05/2017	12/15/2017	12/18/2017	01/01/2018
0.42Q	02/27/2018	03/16/2018	03/19/2018	04/01/2018
0.42Q	06/05/2018	06/15/2018	06/18/2018	07/01/2018

Indicated Div: $1.68

Valuation Analysis / Institutional Holding
Forecast EPS	$3.55	No of Institutions	
	(06/10/2018)	329	
Market Cap	$2.5 Billion	Shares	
Book Value	$1.1 Billion	29,372,380	
Price/Book	2.33	% Held	
Price/Sales	0.67	47.66	

Business Summary: Containers & Packaging (MIC: 8.1.3 SIC: 2655 NAIC: 322214)

Greif is a producer of industrial packaging products and services. Co. has four segments: Rigid Industrial Packaging and Services, which provides steel, fibre and plastic drums, rigid intermediate bulk containers, closure systems for industrial packaging products, transit protection products, water bottles and reconditioned containers, and services; Paper Packaging and Services, which sells containerboard, corrugated sheets, corrugated containers and other corrugated products; Flexible Products and Services, which produces flexible intermediate bulk containers and related services; and Land Management, which focuses on the harvesting and regeneration of its U.S. timber properties.

Recent Developments: For the quarter ended Apr 30 2018, net income increased 30.1% to US$51.9 million from US$39.9 million in the year-earlier quarter. Revenues were US$968.3 million, up 9.1% from US$887.4 million the year before. Operating income was US$87.7 million versus US$81.5 million in the prior-year quarter, an increase of 7.6%. Direct operating expenses rose 9.6% to US$773.0 million from US$705.5 million in the comparable period the year before. Indirect operating expenses increased 7.2% to US$107.6 million from US$100.4 million in the equivalent prior-year period.

Prospects: Our evaluation of Greif Bros. Corp. as of Jan. 21, 2018 is the result of our systematic analysis on three basic characteristics: earnings strength, relative valuation, and recent stock price movement. The company has produced a positive trend in earnings per share over the past 5 quarters. However, while recent estimates for the company have been mixed, GEF has posted better than expected results. Based on operating earnings yield, the company is undervalued when compared to all of the companies in our coverage universe. Share price changes over the past year indicates that GEF will perform in line with the market over the near term.

Financial Data
(US$ in Thousands)

	6 Mos	3 Mos	10/31/2017	10/31/2016	10/31/2015	10/31/2014	10/31/2013	10/31/2012
Earnings Per Share	3.04	2.88	2.02	1.28	1.23	1.56	2.52	2.17
Cash Flow Per Share	6.13	6.18	6.38	6.28	4.32	5.49	5.27	9.98
Tang Book Value Per Share	4.12	3.83	3.32	1.72	1.59	2.00	2.08	0.55
Dividends Per Share	1.680	1.680	1.680	1.680	1.680	1.680	1.680	1.680
Dividend Payout %	55.26	58.33	83.17	131.25	136.59	107.69	66.67	77.42
Income Statement								
Total Revenue	1,874,000	905,700	3,638,200	3,323,600	3,616,700	4,239,100	4,353,400	4,269,500
EBITDA	207,100	89,500	367,200	324,000	303,000	369,600	459,400	408,400
Depn & Amortn	64,100	31,700	106,800	107,400	113,400	129,800	131,900	131,400
Income Before Taxes	116,700	44,500	200,300	141,200	114,800	158,000	243,700	187,100
Income Taxes	5,500	(15,600)	67,200	66,500	48,400	115,000	97,600	56,800
Net Income	101,600	56,500	118,600	74,900	71,900	91,500	147,300	126,100
Average Shares	25,941	25,800	25,822	25,756	25,674	25,552	25,400	25,200
Balance Sheet								
Current Assets	1,088,600	1,044,000	994,500	920,300	1,008,500	1,154,700	1,094,000	1,064,000
Total Assets	3,346,800	3,328,100	3,232,300	3,153,000	3,315,700	3,667,400	3,882,200	3,856,900
Current Liabilities	667,100	633,400	687,600	659,200	647,000	851,700	801,700	862,000
Long-Term Obligations	1,020,500	1,010,800	937,800	974,600	1,116,200	1,087,400	1,207,200	1,175,300
Total Liabilities	2,260,300	2,240,600	2,189,900	2,173,800	2,300,100	2,525,300	2,599,000	2,656,100
Stockholders' Equity	1,086,500	1,087,500	1,042,400	979,200	1,015,600	1,142,100	1,283,200	1,200,800
Shares Outstanding	47,949	47,924	47,843	47,791	47,813	47,723	47,576	47,403
Statistical Record								
Return on Assets %	5.44	5.20	3.71	2.31	2.06	2.42	3.81	3.12
Return on Equity %	17.30	16.62	11.73	7.49	6.66	7.55	11.86	10.32
EBITDA Margin %	11.05	9.88	10.09	9.75	8.38	8.72	10.55	9.57
Net Margin %	5.42	6.24	3.26	2.25	1.99	2.16	3.38	2.95
Asset Turnover	1.16	1.14	1.14	1.02	1.04	1.12	1.13	1.06
Current Ratio	1.63	1.65	1.45	1.40	1.56	1.36	1.36	1.23
Debt to Equity	0.94	0.93	0.90	1.00	1.10	0.95	0.94	0.98
Price Range	64.87-49.80	64.87-51.20	61.23-45.59	49.59-24.00	48.17-27.84	55.74-42.68	57.43-40.00	56.50-38.90
P/E Ratio	21.34-16.38	22.52-17.78	30.31-22.57	38.74-18.75	39.16-22.63	35.73-27.36	22.79-15.87	26.04-17.93
Average Yield %	2.96	2.94	3.01	4.66	4.35	3.28	3.36	3.63

Address: 425 Winter Road, Delaware, OH 43015	**Web Site:** www.greif.com	**Auditors:** DELOITTE & TOUCHE LLP
Telephone: 740-549-6000	**Officers:** Michael J. Gasser - Chairman Peter G. Watson - President, Chief Executive Officer, Chief Operating Officer, Division Officer	**Investor Contact:** 740-549-6000
		Transfer Agents: The Bank of NEw York Mellon (Luxembourg) S.A., Luxembourg

GROUP 1 AUTOMOTIVE, INC.

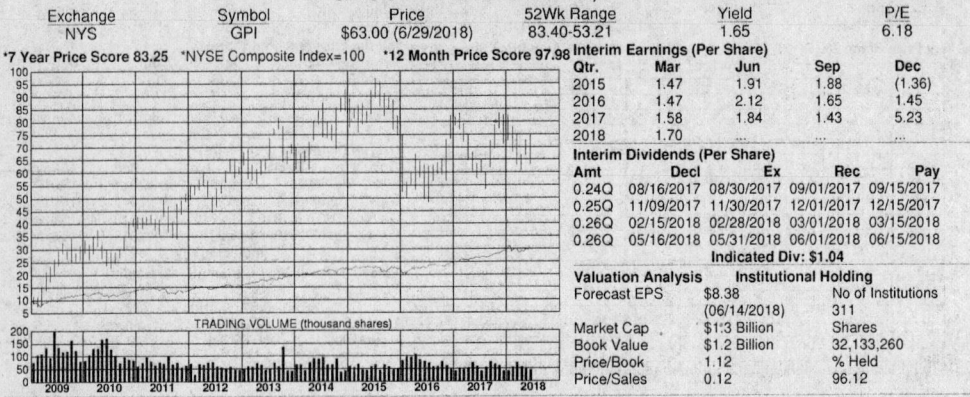

Exchange	Symbol	Price	52Wk Range	Yield	P/E
NYS	GPI	$63.00 (6/29/2018)	83.40-53.21	1.65	6.18

*7 Year Price Score 83.25   *NYSE Composite Index=100   *12 Month Price Score 97.98

Interim Earnings (Per Share)

Qtr.	Mar	Jun	Sep	Dec
2015	1.47	1.91	1.88	(1.36)
2016	1.47	2.12	1.65	1.45
2017	1.58	1.84	1.43	5.23
2018	1.70	...	...	...

Interim Dividends (Per Share)

Amt	Decl	Ex	Rec	Pay
0.24Q	08/16/2017	08/30/2017	09/01/2017	09/15/2017
0.25Q	11/09/2017	11/30/2017	12/01/2017	12/15/2017
0.26Q	02/15/2018	02/28/2018	03/01/2018	03/15/2018
0.26Q	05/16/2018	05/31/2018	06/01/2018	06/15/2018

Indicated Div: $1.04

Valuation Analysis

Forecast EPS	$8.38	
(06/14/2018)		No of Institutions 311
Market Cap	$1.3 Billion	Institutional Holding
Book Value	$1.2 Billion	Shares 32,133,260
Price/Book	1.12	% Held 96.12
Price/Sales	0.12	

Business Summary: Retail - Automotive (MIC: 2.1.4 SIG: 5511 NAIC: 441110)

Group 1 Automotive is an operator in the automotive retail industry. At Dec 31 2017, Co. owned and operated 227 franchises, representing 32 brands of automobiles, at 173 dealership locations and 48 collision centers. Co. owns 151 franchises at 115 dealership locations and 30 collision service centers in the U.S., 55 franchises at 42 dealership locations and 11 collision centers in the U.K. and 21 franchises at 16 dealership locations and seven collision center in Brazil. Via its dealerships, Co. sells new and used cars and light trucks, arranges related vehicle financing; sells service and insurance contracts; provides automotive maintenance and repair services; and sells vehicle parts.

Recent Developments: For the quarter ended Mar 31 2018, net income increased 5.5% to US$35.8 million from US$33.9 million in the year-earlier quarter. Revenues were US$2.86 billion, up 13.5% from US$2.52 billion the year before. Operating income was US$79.1 million versus US$80.1 million in the prior-year quarter, a decrease of 1.3%. Direct operating expenses rose 14.3% to US$2.44 billion from US$2.14 billion in the comparable period the year before. Indirect operating expenses increased 12.3% to US$340.7 million from US$303.4 million in the equivalent prior-year period.

Prospects: Our evaluation of Group 1 Automotive Inc. as of Jan. 21, 2018 is the result of our systematic analysis on three basic characteristics: earnings strength, relative valuation, and recent stock price movement. The company has produced a positive trend in earnings per share over the past 5 quarters and while recent estimates for the company have been raised by analysts, GPI has posted better than expected results. Based on operating earnings yield, the company is undervalued when compared to all of the companies in our coverage universe. Share price changes over the past year indicates that GPI will perform very poorly over the near term.

Financial Data
(US$ in Thousands)

	3 Mos	12/31/2017	12/31/2016	12/31/2015	12/31/2014	12/31/2013	12/31/2012	12/31/2011
Earnings Per Share	10.20	10.08	6.67	3.90	3.60	4.32	4.19	3.47
Cash Flow Per Share	13.60	9.74	18.14	6.09	8.48	2.27	(3.47)	9.00
Tang Book Value Per Share	N.M.	N.M.	N.M.	N.M.	N.M.	1.05	5.03	4.62
Dividends Per Share	0.990	0.970	0.910	0.830	0.700	0.650	0.590	0.480
Dividend Payout %	9.71	9.62	13.64	21.28	19.44	15.05	14.08	13.83
Income Statement								
Total Revenue	2,860,026	11,123,721	10,887,612	10,632,505	9,937,889	8,918,581	7,476,100	6,079,765
EBITDA	79,724	399,772	391,434	325,538	298,007	308,333	261,496	220,603
Depn & Amortn	650	57,900	51,200	47,200	42,300	35,800	31,500	27,100
Income Before Taxes	46,167	219,003	227,371	182,171	164,400	191,895	160,735	132,094
Income Taxes	10,353	5,561	80,306	88,172	71,396	77,903	60,526	49,700
Net Income	35,814	213,442	147,065	93,999	93,004	113,992	100,209	82,394
Average Shares	20,307	20,425	21,170	23,152	24,885	25,314	22,688	22,409
Balance Sheet								
Current Assets	2,413,198	2,329,186	2,150,587	2,202,955	2,035,219	1,967,938	1,566,181	1,175,584
Total Assets	5,058,478	4,871,065	4,461,903	4,414,929	4,141,492	3,819,478	3,023,015	2,476,343
Current Liabilities	2,267,158	2,198,487	2,053,117	2,039,470	1,922,199	1,865,176	1,395,578	1,044,947
Long-Term Obligations	1,376,770	1,318,184	1,212,809	1,203,436	1,008,837	663,689	555,016	482,601
Total Liabilities	3,880,399	3,746,783	3,531,703	3,496,677	3,163,482	2,755,209	2,130,226	1,669,243
Stockholders' Equity	1,178,079	1,124,282	930,200	918,252	978,010	1,064,269	892,789	807,100
Shares Outstanding	20,930	20,898	21,405	23,415	24,339	24,314	22,726	22,707
Statistical Record								
Return on Assets %	4.51	4.57	3.30	2.20	2.34	3.33	3.63	3.52
Return on Equity %	20.06	20.78	15.87	9.91	9.11	11.65	11.76	10.35
EBITDA Margin %	2.79	3.59	3.60	3.06	3.00	·3.46	3.50	3.63
Net Margin %	1.25	1.92	1.35	0.88	0.94	1.28	1.34	1.36
Asset Turnover	2.40	2.38	2.45	2.49	2.50	2.61	2.71	2.60
Current Ratio	1.06	1.06	1.05	1.08	1.06	1.06	1.12	1.13
Debt to Equity	1.17	1.17	1.30	1.31	1.03	0.62	0.62	0.60
Price Range	83.40-53.21	83.40-53.21	82.35-48.20	96.97-74.61	92.94-60.32	81.74-55.45	65.51-44.29	51.80-33.93
P/E Ratio	8.18-5.22	8.27-5.28	12.35-7.23	24.86-19.13	25.82-16.76	18.92-12.84	15.63-10.57	14.93-9.78
Average Yield %	1.44	1.39	1.49	0.97	0.93	0.97	1.06	1.15

Address: 800 Gessner, Suite 500, Houston, TX 77024
Telephone: 713-647-5700
Fax: 713-647-5858

Web Site: www.group1auto.com
Officers: Earl J. Hesterberg - President, Chief Executive Officer John C. Rickel - Senior Vice President, Chief Financial Officer

Auditors: Ernst & Young LLP
Transfer Agents: American Stock Transfer & Trust Company LLC, Brooklyn, NY

GRUBHUB INC

Exchange	Symbol	Price	52Wk Range	Yield	P/E
NYS	GRUB	$104.91 (6/29/2018)	119.86-43.13	N/A	83.26

*7 Year Price Score N/A   *NYSE Composite Index=100   *12 Month Price Score 137.03

Interim Earnings (Per Share)

Qtr.	Mar	Jun	Sep	Dec
2015	0.12	0.11	0.08	0.13
2016	0.12	0.15	0.15	0.16
2017	0.20	0.17	0.15	0.60
2018	0.34	...	...	...

Interim Dividends (Per Share)

No Dividends Paid

Valuation Analysis   Institutional Holding

Forecast EPS	$1.78	No of Institutions
	(06/21/2018)	368
Market Cap	$9.2 Billion	Shares
Book Value	$1.2 Billion	104,487,432
Price/Book	7.91	% Held
Price/Sales	12.06	N/A

TRADING VOLUME (thousand shares)

Business Summary: Internet & Software (MIC: 6.3.2 SIC: 7389 NAIC: 425110)

Grubhub and its wholly-owned subsidiaries provide an online and mobile platform for restaurant pick-up and delivery orders. Diners enter their delivery address or use geo-location within the mobile applications and Co. displays the menus and other relevant information for restaurants in its network. Orders may be placed directly online, via mobile applications or over the phone. In addition, Co. provides delivery services to restaurants on its platform that do not have their own delivery operations. As of Dec 31 2016, Co. connected more than 50,000 local restaurants with diners in more than 1,100 cities across the U.S.

Recent Developments: For the quarter ended Mar 31 2018, net income increased 73.7% to US$30.8 million from US$17.7 million in the year-earlier quarter. Revenues were US$232.6 million, up 49.0% from US$156.1 million the year before. Operating income was US$31.6 million versus US$24.8 million in the prior-year quarter, an increase of 27.4%. Direct operating expenses rose 56.3% to US$113.6 million from US$72.7 million in the comparable period the year before. Indirect operating expenses increased 49.0% to US$87.4 million from US$58.7 million in the equivalent prior-year period.

Prospects: Our evaluation of GrubHub Inc as of Jan. 21, 2018 is the result of our systematic analysis on three basic characteristics: earnings strength, relative valuation, and recent stock price movement. The company has produced a positive trend in earnings per share over the past 5 quarters. However, while recent estimates for the company have been mixed, GRUB has posted better than expected results. Based on operating earnings yield, the company is overvalued when compared to all of the companies in our coverage universe. Share price changes over the past year indicates that GRUB will perform very well over the near term.

Financial Data

(US$ in Thousands)	3 Mos	12/31/2017	12/31/2016	12/31/2015	12/31/2014	12/31/2013	12/31/2012	12/31/2011
Earnings Per Share	1.26	1.12	0.58	0.44	0.30	0.12	0.19	0.36
Cash Flow Per Share	1.98	1.77	1.15	0.53	0.99	1.00	0.94	1.02
Tang Book Value Per Share	0.73	0.14	2.59	2.30	1.99	N.M.	0.22	...
Income Statement								
Total Revenue	232,570	683,067	493,331	361,825	253,873	137,143	82,299	60,611
EBITDA	52,886	141,523	119,024	90,578	68,339	28,366	14,803	14,069
Depn & Amortn	21,334	51,773	35,172	28,649	23,355	13,477	6,071	4,078
Income Before Taxes	30,530	89,648	83,852	61,929	44,984	14,889	8,732	9,991
Income Taxes	(236)	(9,335)	34,295	23,852	20,721	8,142	813	(5,220)
Net Income	30,766	98,983	49,557	38,077	24,263	6,747	7,919	15,211
Average Shares	90,091	88,182	86,135	85,706	81,698	56,645	42,666	42,505
Balance Sheet								
Current Assets	398,286	360,483	396,337	356,274	353,029	122,159	62,005	...
Total Assets	1,578,255	1,543,769	1,197,507	1,060,248	979,702	762,812	206,255	...
Current Liabilities	189,391	174,548	110,490	89,612	111,005	92,591	58,168	...
Long-Term Obligations	143,121	169,645	...	...	...	...	...	...
Total Liabilities	421,035	425,953	225,388	182,652	209,180	187,022	68,367	...
Stockholders' Equity	1,157,220	1,117,816	972,119	877,596	770,522	575,790	137,888	...
Shares Outstanding	87,287	86,790	85,692	84,979	81,905	53,757	31,218	31,319
Statistical Record								
Return on Assets %	7.95	7.22	4.38	3.73	2.78	1.39	...	...
Return on Equity %	10.39	9.47	5.34	4.62	3.60	1.89	...	...
EBITDA Margin %	22.74	20.72	24.13	25.03	26.92	20.68	17.99	23.21
Net Margin %	13.23	14.49	10.05	10.52	9.56	4.92	9.62	25.10
Asset Turnover	0.54	0.50	0.44	0.35	0.29	0.28	...	...
Current Ratio	2.10	2.07	3.59	3.98	3.18	1.32	1.07	...
Debt to Equity	0.12	0.15	...	...	...	...	...	...
Price Range	110.89-32.89	74.09-32.89	43.89-18.34	47.18-22.97	45.21-30.00	...	...	...
P/E Ratio	88.01-26.10	66.15-29.37	75.67-31.62	107.23-52.20	150.70-100.00	...	...	...

Address: 111 W. Washington Street, Suite 2100, Chicago, IL 60602
Telephone: 877-585-7878

Web Site: www.grubhub.com
Officers: Brian P. McAndrews - Chairman Adam J. DeWitt - President, Chief Financial Officer, Treasurer

Auditors: Crowe Horwath LLP
Transfer Agents: American Stock Transfer & Trust Company, LLC., Brooklyn, NY

GUIDEWIRE SOFTWARE INC

Exchange	Symbol	Price	52Wk Range	Yield	P/E
NYS	GWRE	$88.78 (6/29/2018)	95.06-68.25	N/A	N/A

*7 Year Price Score N/A   *NYSE Composite Index=100   *12 Month Price Score 112.38

Interim Earnings (Per Share)

Qtr.	Oct	Jan	Apr	Jul
2014-15	(0.04)	0.06	(0.04)	0.17
2015-16	(0.02)	0.01	(0.01)	0.22
2016-17	(0.11)	0.05	(0.02)	0.36
2017-18	(0.12)	(0.59)	(0.62)	...

Interim Dividends (Per Share)

No Dividends Paid

Valuation Analysis   Institutional Holding

Forecast EPS	$1.09	No of Institutions
	(06/14/2018)	340
Market Cap	$7.1 Billion	Shares
Book Value	$1.3 Billion	94,910,704
Price/Book	5.40	% Held
Price/Sales	12.01	97.47

TRADING VOLUME (thousand shares)

Business Summary: Internet & Software (MIC: 6.3.2 SIC: 7372 NAIC: 511210)

Guidewire Software is a provider of software products and subscription services for the property and casualty industry. Guidewire InsurancePlatform™ consists of applications to support core operations, data management and analytics, and digital engagement. Guidewire InsuranceSuite™ and Guidewire InsuranceNow™ provide transactional systems of record that support the insurance lifecycle. Guidewire InsuranceSuite is a system comprised of three primary applications (ClaimCenter, PolicyCenter and BillingCenter) that can be deployed on-premise or in the cloud. Guidewire InsuranceNow is a cloud-based system that provides policy, billing and claims management functionality to insurers.

Recent Developments: For the quarter ended Apr 30 2018, net loss amounted to US$48.6 million versus a net loss of US$1.8 million in the year-earlier quarter. Revenues were US$140.5 million, up 13.8% from US$123.4 million the year before. Operating loss was US$29.2 million versus a loss of US$4.3 million in the prior-year quarter. Direct operating expenses rose 44.4% to US$74.3 million from US$51.5 million in the comparable period the year before. Indirect operating expenses increased 24.9% to US$95.3 million from US$76.3 million in the equivalent prior-year period.

Prospects: Our evaluation of Guidewire Software Inc as of Jan. 21, 2018 is the result of our systematic analysis on three basic characteristics: earnings strength, relative valuation, and recent stock price movement. The company has managed to produce a neutral trend in earnings per share over the past 5 quarters and while recent estimates for the company have remained steady, GWRE has posted better than expected results. Based on operating earnings yield, the company is overvalued when compared to all of the companies in our coverage universe. Share price changes over the past year indicates that GWRE will perform very well over the near term.

Financial Data
(US$ in Thousands)

	9 Mos	6 Mos	3 Mos	07/31/2017	07/31/2016	07/31/2015	07/31/2014	07/31/2013
Earnings Per Share	(0.97)	(0.37)	0.27	0.28	0.20	0.14	0.21	0.25
Cash Flow Per Share	1.55	1.61	1.58	1.85	1.38	0.91	1.15	0.58
Tang Book Value Per Share	10.89	8.20	10.35	9.07	10.13	9.52	9.21	3.67
Income Statement								
Total Revenue	412,428	271,959	108,171	514,284	424,446	380,537	350,246	300,649
EBITDA	(54,293)	(27,823)	(30,867)	34,023	22,432	20,495	23,896	21,214
Depn & Amortn	7,234	4,161	2,110	6,600	6,500	6,000	5,300	4,500
Income Before Taxes	(56,519)	(28,510)	(31,069)	33,277	20,782	16,740	19,946	17,212
Income Taxes	46,572	25,959	(22,155)	12,053	5,806	6,855	5,225	1,829
Net Income	(103,091)	(54,469)	(8,914)	21,224	14,976	9,885	14,721	15,383
Average Shares	78,777	76,859	75,187	75,328	73,765	72,314	69,112	61,943
Balance Sheet								
Current Assets	1,126,627	638,938	667,634	679,240	707,672	661,644	516,430	210,093
Total Assets	1,832,533	1,283,694	1,150,148	1,078,901	916,178	799,947	757,227	312,270
Current Liabilities	188,694	172,729	135,432	163,616	119,083	104,409	95,386	74,784
Long-Term Obligations	302,184	...	...	...	...	...	...	...
Total Liabilities	512,666	196,205	161,747	185,620	132,243	110,559	106,541	83,841
Stockholders' Equity	1,319,867	1,087,489	988,401	893,281	783,935	689,388	650,686	228,429
Shares Outstanding	80,263	77,281	75,362	75,007	73,039	71,005	69,082	57,909
Statistical Record								
Return on Assets %	N.M.	N.M.	1.96	2.13	1.74	1.27	2.75	5.16
Return on Equity %	N.M.	N.M.	2.26	2.53	2.03	1.48	3.35	7.46
EBITDA Margin %	N.M.	N.M.	N.M.	6.62	5.29	5.39	6.82	7.06
Net Margin %	N.M.	N.M.	N.M.	4.13	3.53	2.60	4.20	5.12
Asset Turnover	0.42	0.52	0.51	0.52	0.49	0.49	0.65	1.01
Current Ratio	5.97	3.70	4.93	4.15	5.94	6.34	5.41	2.81
Debt to Equity	0.23	...	...	...	...	...	...	...
Price Range	91.17-60.50	82.77-52.31	80.06-49.33	72.81-49.33	63.79-43.05	60.08-39.76	57.38-34.85	45.47-24.64
P/E Ratio	...	...	296.52-182.70	260.04-176.18	318.95-215.25	429.14-284.00	273.24-165.95	181.88-98.56

Address: 1001 E. Hillsdale Blvd., Suite 800, Foster City, CA 94404
Telephone: 650-357-9100
Fax: 650-357-9101

Web Site: www.guidewire.com
Officers: Peter P. Gassner - Chairman Marcus S. Ryu - President, Chief Executive Officer

Auditors: KPMG LLP
Investor Contact: 650-357-5282
Transfer Agents: Computershare Shareowner Services LLC, Canton, MA

HALLIBURTON COMPANY

Exchange	Symbol	Price	52Wk Range	Yield	P/E
NYS	HAL	$45.06 (6/29/2018)	56.83-38.66	1.60	N/A

*7 Year Price Score 83.83   *NYSE Composite Index=100   *12 Month Price Score 105.27

Interim Earnings (Per Share)

Qtr.	Mar	Jun	Sep	Dec
2015	(0.76)	0.06	(0.06)	(0.03)
2016	(2.81)	(3.73)	0.01	(0.16)
2017	(0.04)	0.03	0.42	(0.94)
2018	0.05	...	...	...

Interim Dividends (Per Share)

Amt	Decl	Ex	Rec	Pay
0.18Q	11/03/2017	12/06/2017	12/07/2017	12/28/2017
0.18Q	02/19/2018	03/06/2018	03/07/2018	03/28/2018
0.18Q	05/18/2018	06/05/2018	06/06/2018	06/27/2018
0.18Q	07/12/2018	09/04/2018	09/05/2018	09/26/2018

Indicated Div: $0.72

Valuation Analysis

		Institutional Holding	
Forecast EPS	$2.44	No of Institutions	
	(06/14/2018)	1525	
Market Cap	$39.4 Billion	Shares	
Book Value	$8.4 Billion	866,550,912	
Price/Book	4.71	% Held	
Price/Sales	1.79	70.89	

Business Summary: Equipment & Services (MIC: 9.1.3 SIC: 1389 NAIC: 213112)

Halliburton provides services and products to the oil and natural gas industry throughout the lifecycle of the reservoir, from locating hydrocarbons and managing geological data, to drilling and formation evaluation, well construction and completion, and optimizing production. Co. has two segments: Completion and Production, which delivers cementing, stimulation, intervention, pressure control, specialty chemicals, artificial lift and completion services; and Drilling and Evaluation, which provides field and reservoir modeling, drilling, evaluation and precise wellbore placement solutions that enable customers to model, measure, drill and optimize their well construction activities.

Recent Developments: For the quarter ended Mar 31 2018, net income amounted to US$47.0 million versus a net loss of US$32.0 million in the year-earlier quarter. Revenues were US$5.74 billion, up 34.1% from US$4.28 billion the year before. Operating income was US$354.0 million versus US$203.0 million in the prior-year quarter, an increase of 74.4%. Direct operating expenses rose 25.9% to US$5.06 billion from US$4.02 billion in the comparable period the year before. Indirect operating expenses increased 487.3% to US$323.0 million from US$55.0 million in the equivalent prior-year period.

Prospects: Our evaluation of Halliburton Co. as of Jan. 21, 2018 is the result of our systematic analysis on three basic characteristics: earnings strength, relative valuation, and recent stock price movement. The company has enjoyed a very positive trend in earnings per share over the past 5 quarters and while recent estimates for the company have been mixed, HAL has posted better than expected results. Based on operating earnings yield, the company is overvalued when compared to all of the companies in our coverage universe. Share price changes over the past year indicates that HAL will perform very poorly over the near term.

Financial Data

(US$ in Thousands)	3 Mos	12/31/2017	12/31/2016	12/31/2015	12/31/2014	12/31/2013	12/31/2012	12/31/2011
Earnings Per Share	(0.44)	(0.53)	(6.69)	(0.79)	4.11	2.36	2.84	3.08
Cash Flow Per Share	3.47	2.84	(1.97)	3.41	4.79	4.95	3.94	4.01
Tang Book Value Per Share	6.47	6.45	8.08	15.60	16.44	13.44	14.67	12.40
Dividends Per Share	0.720	0.720	0.720	0.720	0.630	0.525	0.360	0.360
Dividend Payout %	...	...	...	...	15.33	22.25	12.68	11.69
Income Statement								
Total Revenue	5,740,000	20,620,000	15,887,000	23,633,000	32,870,000	29,402,000	28,503,000	24,829,000
EBITDA	723,000	2,831,000	(5,483,000)	1,346,000	7,221,000	4,995,000	5,748,000	6,071,000
Depn & Amortn	394,000	1,556,000	1,503,000	1,835,000	2,126,000	1,900,000	1,628,000	1,359,000
Income Before Taxes	189,000	682,000	(7,625,000)	(936,000)	4,712,000	2,764,000	3,822,000	4,449,000
Income Taxes	142,000	1,131,000	(1,858,000)	(274,000)	1,275,000	648,000	1,235,000	1,439,000
Net Income	46,000	(463,000)	(5,763,000)	(671,000)	3,500,000	2,125,000	2,635,000	2,839,000
Average Shares	878,000	870,000	861,000	853,000	852,000	902,000	928,000	922,000
Balance Sheet								
Current Assets	11,035,000	10,777,000	11,677,000	21,609,000	15,068,000	13,704,000	13,086,000	11,577,000
Total Assets	25,191,000	25,085,000	27,000,000	36,942,000	32,240,000	29,223,000	27,410,000	23,677,000
Current Liabilities	4,969,000	4,862,000	4,023,000	5,359,000	5,883,000	5,026,000	4,752,000	4,121,000
Long-Term Obligations	10,428,000	10,430,000	12,214,000	14,687,000	7,840,000	7,816,000	4,820,000	4,820,000
Total Liabilities	16,826,000	16,763,000	17,591,000	21,480,000	15,973,000	15,642,000	11,645,000	10,479,000
Stockholders' Equity	8,365,000	8,322,000	9,409,000	15,462,000	16,267,000	13,581,000	15,765,000	13,198,000
Shares Outstanding	875,000	873,000	866,000	856,000	848,000	849,000	929,000	921,000
Statistical Record								
Return on Assets %	N.M.	N.M.	N.M.	N.M.	11.39	7.50	10.29	13.53
Return on Equity %	N.M.	N.M.	N.M.	N.M.	23.45	14.48	18.15	24.09
EBITDA Margin %	12.60	13.73	N.M.	5.70	21.97	16.99	20.17	24.45
Net Margin %	0.80	N.M.	N.M.	N.M.	10.65	7.23	9.24	11.43
Asset Turnover	0.88	0.79	0.50	0.68	1.07	1.04	1.11	1.18
Current Ratio	2.22	2.22	2.90	4.03	2.56	2.73	2.75	2.81
Debt to Equity	1.25	1.25	1.30	0.95	0.48	0.58	0.31	0.37
Price Range	56.83-38.66	58.21-38.66	55.07-28.48	49.21-33.40	74.02-37.82	56.26-34.69	38.51-26.70	57.27-28.68
P/E Ratio	...	...	...	...	18.01-9.20	23.84-14.70	13.56-9.40	18.59-9.31
Average Yield %	1.59	1.55	1.72	1.75	1.07	1.16	1.09	0.83

Address: 3000 North Sam Houston Parkway East, Houston, TX 77032	Web Site: www.halliburton.com	Auditors: KPMG LLP
Telephone: 281-871-2699	Officers: David J. Lesar - Executive Chairman, Chairman, President, Chief Executive Officer Jeffrey Allen Miller - President, Chief Operating Officer, Executive Vice President, Chief Executive Officer	Investor Contact: 888-669-3920 Transfer Agents: Computershare Shareowner Services, Jersey City, NJ

HANESBRANDS INC

Exchange	Symbol	Price	52Wk Range	Yield	P/E
NYS	HBI	$22.02 (6/29/2018)	25.67-16.51	2.72	104.86

*7 Year Price Score 87.37 *NYSE Composite Index=100 *12 Month Price Score 87.92

TRADING VOLUME (thousand shares)

Interim Earnings (Per Share)

Qtr.	Mar	Jun	Sep	Dec
2015	0.13	0.23	0.40	0.30
2016	0.21	0.34	0.45	0.41
2017	0.18	0.47	0.55	(1.03)
2018	0.22	...	...	...

Interim Dividends (Per Share)

Amt	Decl	Ex	Rec	Pay
0.15Q	07/25/2017	08/11/2017	08/15/2017	09/06/2017
0.15Q	10/24/2017	11/13/2017	11/14/2017	12/05/2017
0.15Q	02/08/2018	02/16/2018	02/20/2018	03/13/2018
0.15Q	04/24/2018	05/14/2018	05/15/2018	06/05/2018

Indicated Div: $0.60

Valuation Analysis

Forecast EPS	$1.76
	(06/03/2018)
Market Cap	$7.9 Billion
Book Value	$705.7 Million
Price/Book	11.24
Price/Sales	1.21

Institutional Holding

No of Institutions	910
Shares	402,597,376
% Held	89.59

Business Summary: Apparel, Footwear & Accessories (MIC: 1.4.2 SIC: 2389 NAIC: 313312)

Hanesbrands is a marketer of basic innerwear and activewear apparel in the U.S., Europe, Australia and Asia/Pacific under several apparel brands. Co. has four segments: Innerwear, which focuses on main apparel products, such as intimate apparel, men's underwear, women's panties, children's underwear, socks and hosiery; Activewear, which sells products such as T-shirts and fleece to both retailers and wholesalers as well as provides uniforms for athletic programs; Direct to Consumer, which includes Co.'s domestic Co.-operated outlet stores and website operations; and International, which includes products in Innerwear and Activewear segments.

Recent Developments: For the quarter ended Mar 31 2018, income from continuing operations increased 8.7% to US$79.4 million from US$73.1 million in the year-earlier quarter. Net income increased 12.5% to US$79.4 million from US$70.6 million in the year-earlier quarter. Revenues were US$1.47 billion, up 6.6% from US$1.38 billion the year before. Operating income was US$146.1 million versus US$126.4 million in the prior-year quarter, an increase of 15.5%. Direct operating expenses rose 6.2% to US$892.6 million from US$840.8 million in the comparable period the year before. Indirect operating expenses increased 4.8% to US$432.9 million from US$413.1 million in the equivalent prior-year period.

Prospects: Our evaluation of Hanesbrands Inc. as of Jan. 21, 2018 is the result of our systematic analysis on three basic characteristics: earnings strength, relative valuation, and recent stock price movement. The company has managed to produce a neutral trend in earnings per share over the past 5 quarters. However, while recent estimates for the company have been mixed, HBI has posted results that were in line with analysts expectations. Based on operating earnings yield, the company is undervalued when compared to all of the companies in our coverage universe. Share price changes over the past year indicates that HBI will perform poorly over the near term.

Financial Data

(US$ in Thousands)	3 Mos	12/30/2017	12/31/2016	01/02/2016	01/03/2015	12/28/2013	12/29/2012	12/31/2011
Earnings Per Share	0.21	0.17	1.40	1.06	1.32	1.08	0.55	0.90
Cash Flow Per Share	1.52	1.79	1.59	0.57	1.66	1.98	1.86	0.57
Tang Book Value Per Share	N.M.	N.M.	N.M.	N.M.	N.M.	0.76	1.13	0.27
Dividends Per Share	0.600	0.600	0.440	0.400	0.300	0.150	...	...
Dividend Payout %	285.71	352.94	31.43	37.74	22.67	13.85	...	...
Income Statement								
Total Revenue	1,471,504	6,471,410	6,028,199	5,731,549	5,324,746	4,627,802	4,525,721	4,637,143
EBITDA	174,565	834,192	827,066	695,811	659,557	588,575	492,836	562,629
Depn & Amortn	34,268	122,487	103,175	103,903	98,202	90,890	93,036	90,725
Income Before Taxes	94,534	537,270	571,199	473,873	464,968	395,801	262,945	315,607
Income Taxes	15,125	473,279	34,272	45,018	60,449	65,307	30,502	48,919
Net Income	79,409	61,894	539,382	428,855	404,519	330,494	164,681	266,688
Average Shares	363,291	369,426	384,566	403,659	306,033	305,469	300,807	297,753
Balance Sheet								
Current Assets	3,399,826	3,386,370	3,298,420	2,917,867	2,765,232	2,243,666	2,027,525	2,330,791
Total Assets	7,327,775	6,894,775	6,907,734	5,619,040	5,221,781	4,090,048	3,631,700	4,034,669
Current Liabilities	1,677,760	1,778,745	1,602,922	1,503,909	1,486,602	999,278	875,668	933,719
Long-Term Obligations	4,185,252	3,702,054	3,507,685	2,254,162	1,613,997	1,467,000	1,317,500	1,807,777
Total Liabilities	6,622,080	6,208,573	5,683,820	4,343,149	3,835,009	2,859,425	2,744,834	3,353,608
Stockholders' Equity	705,695	686,202	1,223,914	1,275,891	1,386,772	1,230,623	886,866	681,061
Shares Outstanding	360,363	360,125	378,687	391,670	300,591	298,366	294,809	292,551
Statistical Record								
Return on Assets %	0.98	0.90	8.64	7.93	8.55	8.58	4.31	6.84
Return on Equity %	8.50	6.50	43.27	32.30	30.41	31.30	21.06	43.00
EBITDA Margin %	11.86	12.89	13.72	12.14	12.39	12.72	10.89	12.13
Net Margin %	5.40	0.96	8.95	7.48	7.60	7.14	3.64	5.75
Asset Turnover	0.91	0.94	0.97	1.06	1.13	1.20	1.18	1.19
Current Ratio	2.03	1.90	2.06	1.94	1.86	2.25	2.32	2.50
Debt to Equity	5.93	5.39	2.87	1.77	1.16	1.19	1.49	2.65
Price Range	25.67-18.38	25.67-18.98	31.18-21.53	34.58-26.54	28.93-16.04	17.74-8.90	9.13-5.55	8.31-5.46
P/E Ratio	122.24-87.52	151.00-111.65	22.27-15.38	32.62-25.03	21.92-12.15	16.42-8.24	16.59-10.09	9.24-6.07
Average Yield %	2.74	2.72	1.66	1.29	1.31	1.12	...	...

Address: 1000 East Hanes Mill Road, Winston-Salem, NC 27105	Web Site: www.Hanes.com	Auditors: PricewaterhouseCoopers LLP
Telephone: 336-519-8080	Officers: Richard A. Noll - Chairman, Executive Chairman, Chief Executive Officer Gerald W. Evans - Chief Executive Officer, Chief Operating Officer, Co-Chief Operating Officer, Division Officer	Investor Contact: 336-519-8080
		Transfer Agents: ComputerShare Investor Services, Providence, RI

HANOVER INSURANCE GROUP INC

Exchange	Symbol	Price	52Wk Range	Yield	P/E	Div Acheiver
NYS	THG	$119.56 (6/29/2018)	123.22-87.90	1.81	24.65	12 Years

*7 Year Price Score 125.59 *NYSE Composite Index=100 *12 Month Price Score 109.95

Interim Earnings (Per Share)

Qtr.	Mar	Jun	Sep	Dec
2015	1.22	2.68	1.74	1.76
2016	1.80	0.05	2.06	(0.30)
2017	1.05	1.83	0.26	1.19
2018	1.57	...	...	...

Interim Dividends (Per Share)

Amt	Decl	Ex	Rec	Pay
0.50Q	08/15/2017	09/14/2017	09/15/2017	09/29/2017
0.54Q	12/05/2017	12/14/2017	12/15/2017	12/29/2017
0.54Q	02/27/2018	03/08/2018	03/09/2018	03/29/2018
0.54Q	05/15/2018	06/07/2018	06/08/2018	06/29/2018

Indicated Div: $2.16

Valuation Analysis **Institutional Holding**

Forecast EPS	$8.50	No of Institutions
	(06/13/2018)	446
Market Cap	$5.1 Billion	Shares
Book Value	$2.9 Billion	52,134,896
Price/Book	*1.74	% Held
Price/Sales	0.97	N/A

TRADING VOLUME (thousand shares)

Business Summary: General Insurance (MIC: 5.2.1 SIC: 6331 NAIC: 524126)

The Hanover Insurance Group is a holding company. Through its subsidiaries, Co. provides property and casualty insurance products and services. Co. has four segments: Commercial Lines, which include commercial multiple peril, commercial automobile, workers' compensation, and other commercial coverages; Personal Lines, which include personal automobile, homeowners, and other personal coverages; Chaucer Holdings Limited, which includes marine and aviation, property, energy, casualty and other coverages; and Other, which provides investment advisory services to affiliates and also manages assets for unaffiliated institutions such as insurance companies, retirement plans and foundations.

Recent Developments: For the quarter ended Mar 31 2018, income from continuing operations increased 50.0% to US$67.8 million from US$45.2 million in the year-earlier quarter. Net income increased 49.8% to US$67.7 million from US$45.2 million in the year-earlier quarter. Revenues were US$1.33 billion, up 5.6% from US$1.26 billion the year before. Net premiums earned were US$1.26 billion versus US$1.18 billion in the prior-year quarter, an increase of 7.0%. Net investment income rose 16.6% to US$82.9 million from US$71.1 million a year ago.

Prospects: Our evaluation of Hanover Insurance Group Inc. as of Jan. 21, 2018 is the result of our systematic analysis on three basic characteristics: earnings strength, relative valuation, and recent stock price movement. The company has suffered a very negative trend in earnings per share over the past 5 quarters. However, while recent estimates for the company have been mixed, THG has posted better than expected results. Based on operating earnings yield, the company is overvalued when compared to all of the companies in our coverage universe. Share price changes over the past year indicates that THG will perform in line with the market over the near term.

Financial Data

(US$ in Thousands)	3 Mos	12/31/2017	12/31/2016	12/31/2015	12/31/2014	12/31/2013	12/31/2012	12/31/2011
Earnings Per Share	4.85	4.33	3.59	7.40	6.28	5.59	1.23	0.81
Cash Flow Per Share	16.04	16.58	17.19	9.99	12.83	8.71	9.11	4.90
Tang Book Value Per Share	64.01	66.00	63.04	61.82	60.58	55.14	54.41	52.11
Dividends Per Share	2.080	2.040	1.880	1.690	1.520	1.360	1.230	1.125
Dividend Payout %	42.89	47.11	52.37	22.84	24.20	24.33	100.00	138.89
Income Statement								
Premium Income	1,263,600	4,833,400	4,628,100	4,704,800	4,710,300	4,450,500	4,239,100	3,598,600
Total Revenue	1,330,900	5,184,400	4,945,800	5,034,000	5,067,600	4,793,700	4,590,700	3,931,600
Benefits & Claims	785,800	3,128,700	2,964,700	2,884,100	2,927,500	2,761,100	2,974,400	2,550,800
Income Before Taxes	80,600	301,500	192,300	439,400	378,000	329,100	28,700	22,300
Income Taxes	12,800	98,500	36,200	108,600	95,700	83,400	(17,400)	(9,600)
Net Income	67,700	186,200	155,100	331,500	282,000	251,000	55,900	37,100
Average Shares	43,100	43,000	43,200	44,800	44,900	44,900	45,300	45,800
Balance Sheet								
Total Assets	15,334,200	15,469,600	14,220,400	13,790,900	13,759,700	13,378,700	13,484,900	12,624,400
Total Liabilities	12,421,100	12,471,900	11,362,900	10,946,500	10,915,700	10,784,200	10,889,500	10,114,600
Stockholders' Equity	2,913,100	2,997,700	2,857,500	2,844,400	2,844,000	2,594,500	2,595,400	2,509,800
Shares Outstanding	42,500	42,500	42,400	43,000	43,900	43,700	44,300	44,600
Statistical Record								
Return on Assets %	1.40	1.25	1.10	2.41	2.08	1.87	0.43	0.35
Return on Equity %	7.16	6.36	5.43	11.66	10.37	9.67	2.18	1.49
Loss Ratio %	62.19	64.73	64.06	61.30	62.15	62.04	70.17	70.88
Net Margin %	5.09	3.59	3.14	6.59	5.56	5.24	1.22	0.94
Price Range	120.84-80.59	108.85-80.59	91.66-74.10	86.58-68.18	73.30-53.14	60.99-38.74	41.39-33.99	48.82-31.22
P/E Ratio	24.92-16.62	25.14-18.61	25.53-20.64	11.70-9.21	11.67-8.46	10.91-6.93	33.65-27.63	60.27-38.54
Average Yield %	2.10	2.19	2.27	2.22	2.44	2.67	3.25	2.83

Address: 440 Lincoln Street, Worcester, MA 01653
Telephone: 508-855-1000
Fax: 508-855-6332

Web Site: www.hanover.com
Officers: Micheal P. Angelini - Chairman Mark Leo Berthiaume - Executive Vice President, Chief Administrative Officer

Auditors: PricewaterhouseCoopers LLP
Investor Contact: 508-855-2063
Transfer Agents: ComputerShare Investor Services, Providence, RI

HARLEY-DAVIDSON INC

Exchange	Symbol	Price	52Wk Range	Yield	P/E
NYS	HOG	$42.08 (6/29/2018)	55.95-40.02	3.52	14.12

'7 Year Price Score 71.10   **'NYSE Composite Index=100**   **'12 Month Price Score 89.23**

Interim Earnings (Per Share)

Qtr.	Mar	Jun	Sep	Dec
2015	1.27	1.44	0.69	0.28
2016	1.36	1.55	0.64	0.28
2017	1.05	1.48	0.40	0.07
2018	1.03			

Interim Dividends (Per Share)

Amt	Decl	Ex	Rec	Pay
0.365Q	08/29/2017	09/11/2017	09/12/2017	09/22/2017
0.365Q	11/28/2017	12/14/2017	12/15/2017	12/29/2017
0.37Q	02/05/2018	02/13/2018	02/14/2018	03/02/2018
0.37Q	05/10/2018	05/30/2018	05/31/2018	06/15/2018

Indicated Div: $1.48 (Div. Reinv. Plan)

Valuation Analysis   **Institutional Holding**

Forecast EPS	$3.24	No of Institutions	
	(06/14/2018)	802	
Market Cap	$7.0 Billion	Shares	
Book Value	$2.0 Billion		199,207,552
Price/Book	3.51	% Held	
Price/Sales	1.23		78.22

Business Summary: Autos- Manufacturing (MIC: 1.8.1 SIC: 3751 NAIC: 336991)

Harley-Davidson is the parent company for the groups of companies doing business as Harley-Davidson Motor Company and Harley-Davidson Financial Services (HDFS). Co. operates in two reportable segments: Motorcycles & Related Products (Motorcycles) and Financial Services. The primary business of the Motorcycles segment is to design, manufacture and sell at wholesale on-road Harley-Davidson motorcycles as well as a line of motorcycle parts, accessories, general merchandise and related services. HDFS is engaged in the business of financing and servicing wholesale inventory receivables and retail consumer loans, primarily for the purchase of Harley-Davidson motorcycles.

Recent Developments: For the quarter ended Apr 1 2018, net income decreased 6.2% to US$174.8 million from US$186.4 million in the year-earlier quarter. Revenues were US$1.54 billion, up 2.7% from US$1.50 billion the year before. Operating income was US$236.4 million versus US$289.2 million in the prior-year quarter, a decrease of 18.2%. Direct operating expenses rose 3.0% to US$968.7 million from US$940.8 million in the comparable period the year before. Indirect operating expenses increased 23.9% to US$337.0 million from US$272.0 million in the equivalent prior-year period.

Prospects: Our evaluation of Harley-Davidson Inc. as of Jan. 21, 2018 is the result of our systematic analysis on three basic characteristics: earnings strength, relative valuation, and recent stock price movement. The company has enjoyed a very positive trend in earnings per share over the past 5 quarters. However, while recent estimates for the company have been mixed, HOG has posted better than expected results. Based on operating earnings yield, the company is undervalued when compared to all of the companies in our coverage universe. Share price changes over the past year indicates that HOG will perform poorly over the near term.

Financial Data

(US$ in Thousands)	3 Mos	12/31/2017	12/31/2016	12/31/2015	12/31/2014	12/31/2013	12/31/2012	12/31/2011
Earnings Per Share	2.98	3.02	3.83	3.69	3.88	3.28	2.72	2.55
Cash Flow Per Share	6.17	5.84	6.52	5.43	5.30	4.39	3.52	3.80
Tang Book Value Per Share	11.65	10.64	10.61	9.67	13.60	13.54	11.18	10.37
Dividends Per Share	1.465	1.460	1.400	1.240	1.100	0.840	0.620	0.475
Dividend Payout %	49.16	48.34	36.55	33.60	28.35	25.61	22.79	18.63
Income Statement								
Total Revenue	1,542,121	5,647,224	5,996,458	5,995,402	6,228,508	5,899,872	5,580,506	5,311,713
EBITDA	259,984	1,207,987	1,359,069	1,463,875	1,466,782	1,326,633	1,176,523	1,018,338
Depn & Amortn	22,144	313,144	305,488	301,595	179,300	167,072	168,978	180,408
Income Before Taxes	230,150	863,839	1,023,911	1,150,163	1,283,320	1,114,305	961,512	792,664
Income Taxes	55,387	342,080	331,747	397,956	438,709	380,312	337,587	244,586
Net Income	174,763	521,759	692,164	752,207	844,611	733,993	623,925	599,114
Average Shares	169,174	172,932	180,535	203,686	217,706	224,071	229,229	234,918
Balance Sheet								
Current Assets	4,220,154	3,884,742	3,853,852	3,983,154	3,948,095	3,988,803	4,050,936	4,542,206
Total Assets	10,277,621	9,972,672	9,890,240	9,991,167	9,528,097	9,405,040	9,170,773	9,674,164
Current Liabilities	3,795,103	3,158,170	2,862,562	2,752,578	2,389,286	2,509,586	1,503,082	2,698,618
Long-Term Obligations	4,108,511	4,587,258	4,666,975	4,845,388	3,761,528	3,416,713	4,370,544	3,843,886
Total Liabilities	8,281,672	8,128,395	7,970,082	8,151,513	6,618,811	6,395,554	6,613,149	7,253,908
Stockholders' Equity	1,995,949	1,844,277	1,920,158	1,839,654	2,909,286	3,009,486	2,557,624	2,420,256
Shares Outstanding	166,436	168,090	175,947	184,733	211,876	219,959	226,100	230,540
Statistical Record								
Return on Assets %	4.96	5.25	6.94	7.71	8.92	7.90	6.60	6.27
Return on Equity %	25.58	27.72	36.72	31.68	28.54	26.37	25.00	25.90
EBITDA Margin %	16.86	21.39	22.66	24.42	23.55	22.49	21.08	19.17
Net Margin %	11.33	9.24	11.54	12.55	13.56	12.44	11.18	11.28
Asset Turnover	0.55	0.57	0.60	0.61	0.66	0.64	0.59	0.56
Current Ratio	1.11	1.23	1.35	1.45	1.65	1.59	2.70	1.68
Debt to Equity	2.06	2.49	2.43	2.63	1.29	1.14	1.71	1.59
Price Range	62.05-41.44	62.94-44.78	62.07-37.49	66.13-45.12	73.94-55.48	69.36-48.69	53.49-39.33	45.91-32.10
P/E Ratio	20.82-13.91	20.84-14.83	16.21-9.79	17.92-12.23	19.06-14.30	21.15-14.84	19.67-14.46	18.00-12.59
Average Yield %	2.92	2.76	2.82	2.20	1.66	1.45	1.35	1.24

Address: 3700 West Juneau Avenue, Milwaukee, WI 53208 **Telephone:** 414-342-4680	**Web Site:** www.harley-davidson.com **Officers:** Michael J. Cave - Chairman Matthew S. Levatich - President, Chief Executive Officer	**Auditors:** Ernst & Young LLP **Transfer Agents:** Computershare, Inc., Providence, RI

HARRIS CORP.

Exchange	Symbol	Price	52Wk Range	Yield	P/E	Div Acheiver
NYS	HRS	$144.54 (6/29/2018)	169.00-109.08	1.58	27.80	16 Years

*7 Year Price Score 145.51 *NYSE Composite Index=100 *12 Month Price Score 104.54

Interim Earnings (Per Share)

Qtr.	Sep	Dec	Mar	Jun
2014-15	1.18	1.32	1.20	(0.58)
2015-16	1.18	(1.23)	1.34	1.28
2016-17	1.27	1.40	0.69	1.07
2017-18	1.32	1.15	1.66	...

Interim Dividends (Per Share)

Amt	Decl	Ex	Rec	Pay
0.57Q	08/25/2017	09/07/2017	09/08/2017	09/22/2017
0.57Q	10/26/2017	11/16/2017	11/17/2017	12/01/2017
0.57Q	02/23/2018	03/07/2018	03/08/2018	03/21/2018
0.57Q	04/27/2018	05/31/2018	06/01/2018	06/15/2018

Indicated Div: $2.28 (Div. Reinv. Plan)

Valuation Analysis

		Institutional Holding	
Forecast EPS	$6.48	No of Institutions	
	(06/14/2018)	1013	
Market Cap	$17.1 Billion	Shares	
Book Value	$3.1 Billion	150,228,864	
Price/Book	5.46	% Held	
Price/Sales	2.83	77.71	

Business Summary: Defense (MIC: 7.1.2 SIC: 3812 NAIC: 334511)

Harris, together with its subsidiaries, provides technology-based solutions. Co. has three segments: Communication Systems, which serves markets in tactical communications and defense products and in public safety networks; Electronic Systems, which provides electronic warfare, avionics, and command, control, communications, computers, intelligence, surveillance and reconnaissance solutions and air traffic management solutions; and Space and Intelligence Systems, which provides intelligence, space protection, geospatial, Earth observation, universe exploration, positioning, navigation and timing, and environmental solutions for national security, defense, civil and commercial customers.

Recent Developments: For the quarter ended Mar 30 2018, income from continuing operations increased 23.8% to US$203.0 million from US$164.0 million in the year-earlier quarter. Net income increased 136.5% to US$201.0 million from US$85.0 million in the year-earlier quarter. Revenues were US$1.57 billion, up 5.3% from US$1.49 billion the year before. Operating income was US$256.0 million versus US$275.0 million in the prior-year quarter, a decrease of 6.9%. Direct operating expenses rose 5.1% to US$1.01 billion from US$958.0 million in the comparable period the year before. Indirect operating expenses increased 19.1% to US$305.0 million from US$256.0 million in the equivalent prior-year period.

Prospects: Our evaluation of Harris Corp. as of Jan. 21, 2018 is the result of our systematic analysis on three basic characteristics: earnings strength, relative valuation, and recent stock price movement. The company has managed to produce a neutral trend in earnings per share over the past 5 quarters and while recent estimates for the company have been raised by analysts, HRS has posted better than expected results. Based on operating earnings yield, the company is about fairly valued when compared to all of the companies in our coverage universe. Share price changes over the past year indicates that HRS will perform very well over the near term.

Financial Data

(US$ in Thousands)	9 Mos	6 Mos	3 Mos	06/30/2017	07/01/2016	07/03/2015	06/27/2014	06/28/2013
Earnings Per Share	5.20	4.23	4.48	4.44	2.59	3.11	4.95	1.01
Cash Flow Per Share	2.62	5.46	5.21	4.65	7.48	7.95	8.03	7.56
Dividends Per Share	2.240	2.200	2.160	2.120	2.000	1.880	1.680	1.480
Dividend Payout %	43.08	52.01	48.21	47.75	77.22	60.45	33.94	146.53
Income Statement								
Total Revenue	4,516,000	2,948,000	1,413,000	5,900,000	7,467,000	5,083,000	5,012,000	5,111,700
EBITDA	979,000	665,000	334,000	1,222,000	992,000	760,000	1,028,300	917,800
Depn & Amortn	181,000	123,000	62,000	147,000	200,000	155,000	142,100	146,400
Income Before Taxes	675,000	460,000	231,000	905,000	611,000	477,000	795,400	664,500
Income Taxes	166,000	154,000	64,000	267,000	266,000	143,000	256,200	202,700
Net Income	501,000	300,000	161,000	553,000	324,000	334,000	534,800	113,000
Average Shares	121,000	120,900	121,200	124,300	125,000	106,800	107,300	111,200
Balance Sheet								
Current Assets	2,414,000	2,132,000	2,127,000	2,073,000	2,608,000	3,524,000	1,991,300	1,948,100
Total Assets	10,070,000	9,856,000	10,099,000	10,090,000	11,996,000	13,129,000	4,931,200	4,858,400
Current Liabilities	2,146,000	1,741,000	1,918,000	1,926,000	1,964,000	2,281,000	1,114,600	1,297,400
Long-Term Obligations	3,391,000	3,391,000	3,395,000	3,396,000	4,120,000	5,053,000	1,575,800	1,577,100
Total Liabilities	6,933,000	6,862,000	7,112,000	7,162,000	8,940,000	9,732,000	3,105,200	3,297,100
Stockholders' Equity	3,137,000	2,994,000	2,987,000	2,928,000	3,056,000	3,397,000	1,826,000	1,561,300
Shares Outstanding	118,552	118,577	119,045	119,628	124,643	123,675	105,509	106,933
Statistical Record								
Return on Assets %	5.97	4.81	5.06	5.02	2.59	3.64	10.96	2.17
Return on Equity %	20.89	16.78	18.34	18.53	10.07	12.58	31.66	6.47
EBITDA Margin %	21.68	22.56	23.64	20.71	13.29	14.95	20.52	17.95
Net Margin %	11.09	10.18	11.39	9.37	4.34	6.57	10.67	2.21
Asset Turnover	0.57	0.56	0.56	0.54	0.60	0.55	1.03	0.98
Current Ratio	1.12	1.22	1.11	1.08	1.33	1.54	1.79	1.50
Debt to Equity	1.08	1.13	1.14	1.16	1.35	1.49	0.86	1.01
Price Range	162.07-107.18	144.50-99.99	131.80-88.98	113.82-81.54	89.48-70.28	82.46-61.52	77.55-49.08	51.97-39.95
P/E Ratio	31.17-20.61	34.16-23.64	29.42-19.86	25.64-18.36	34.55-27.14	26.51-19.78	15.67-9.92	51.46-39.55
Average Yield %	1.72	1.85	1.98	2.10	2.52	2.57	2.54	3.14

Address: 1025 West NASA Boulevard, Melbourne, FL 32919
Telephone: 321-727-9100

Web Site: www.harris.com
Officers: William M. Brown - Chairman, President, Chief Executive Officer Rahul Ghai - Chief Financial Officer, Senior Vice President

Auditors: Ernst & Young LLP
Investor Contact: 321-727-9383
Transfer Agents: Computershare, Canton, MA

HARTFORD FINANCIAL SERVICES GROUP INC.

Exchange	Symbol	Price	52Wk Range	Yield	P/E
NYS	HIG	$51.13 (6/29/2018)	59.11-50.29	1.96	N/A

*7 Year Price Score 117.51 *NYSE Composite Index=100 *12 Month Price Score 95.22

Interim Earnings (Per Share)

Qtr.	Mar	Jun	Sep	Dec
2015	1.08	0.96	0.90	1.02
2016	0.79	0.54	1.12	(0.18)
2017	1.00	(0.11)	0.64	(10.15)
2018	1.64	...	...	...

Interim Dividends (Per Share)

Amt	Decl	Ex	Rec	Pay
0.23Q	07/20/2017	08/30/2017	09/01/2017	10/02/2017
0.25Q	10/23/2017	11/30/2017	12/01/2017	01/02/2018
0.25Q	02/22/2018	03/02/2018	03/05/2018	04/02/2018
0.25Q	05/17/2018	05/31/2018	06/01/2018	07/02/2018

Indicated Div: $1.00

Valuation Analysis | **Institutional Holding**

Forecast EPS	$4.55
	(06/14/2018)
Market Cap	$18.3 Billion
Book Value	$13.1 Billion
Price/Book	1.39
Price/Sales	1.08

No of Institutions	993
Shares	429,488,672
% Held	91.43

TRADING VOLUME (thousand shares)

Business Summary: General Insurance (MIC: 5.2.1 SIC: 6331 NAIC: 524126)

Hartford Financial Services Group is a holding company. Through its subsidiaries, Co. provides property and casualty insurance, group life and disability products, mutual funds and exchange-traded products. Co. has six segments: Commercial Lines, which provides workers' compensation, property, automobile, marine, livestock, liability and umbrella coverages; Personal Lines, which provides automobile, homeowners and personal umbrella coverages; Property & Casualty Other Operations, which includes property and casualty operations; Group Benefits, which provides group life, accident and disability coverage, voluntary benefits and group retiree health; Mutual Funds; and Talcott Resolution.

Recent Developments: For the quarter ended Mar 31 2018, income from continuing operations increased 41.3% to US$428.0 million from US$303.0 million in the year-earlier quarter. Net income increased 57.9% to US$597.0 million from US$378.0 million in the year-earlier quarter. Revenues were US$4.69 billion, up 12.5% from US$4.17 billion the year before. Net premiums earned were US$3.93 billion versus US$3.44 billion in the prior-year quarter, an increase of 14.2%. Net investment income rose 10.0% to US$451.0 million from US$410.0 million a year ago.

Prospects: Our evaluation of Hartford Financial Services Group Inc. as of Jan. 21, 2018 is the result of our systematic analysis on three basic characteristics: earnings strength, relative valuation, and recent stock price movement. The company has suffered a very negative trend in earnings per share over the past 5 quarters. However, while recent estimates for the company have been mixed, HIG has posted better than expected results. Based on operating earnings yield, the company is undervalued when compared to all of the companies in our coverage universe. Share price changes over the past year indicates that HIG will perform well over the near term.

Financial Data
(US$ in Thousands)

	3 Mos	12/31/2017	12/31/2016	12/31/2015	12/31/2014	12/31/2013	12/31/2012	12/31/2011
Earnings Per Share	(7.98)	(8.61)	2.27	3.96	1.73	0.34	(0.18)	1.30
Cash Flow Per Share	7.48	6.01	5.31	6.63	4.27	2.76	6.11	5.11
Tang Book Value Per Share	31.18	32.35	43.69	42.67	42.93	40.61	48.67	48.24
Dividends Per Share	0.960	0.940	0.860	0.780	0.660	0.500	0.400	0.400
Dividend Payout %	...	...	37.89	19.70	38.15	147.06	...	30.77
Income Statement								
Premium Income	3,927,000	14,141,000	13,811,000	13,577,000	13,336,000	13,226,000	13,631,000	14,088,000
Total Revenue	4,691,000	16,974,000	18,300,000	18,377,000	18,614,000	26,236,000	26,412,000	21,859,000
Income Before Taxes	519,000	723,000	804,000	1,978,000	1,699,000	63,000	(527,000)	230,000
Income Taxes	91,000	985,000	(92,000)	305,000	350,000	(247,000)	(494,000)	(346,000)
Net Income	597,000	(3,131,000)	896,000	1,682,000	798,000	176,000	(38,000)	662,000
Average Shares	363,900	363,700	394,800	425,200	460,200	484,400	437,700	478,000
Balance Sheet								
Total Assets	216,666,000	225,260,000	223,432,000	228,348,000	245,013,000	277,884,000	298,513,000	304,064,000
Total Liabilities	203,523,000	211,766,000	206,529,000	210,706,000	226,293,000	258,979,000	276,066,000	281,154,000
Stockholders' Equity	13,143,000	13,494,000	16,903,000	17,642,000	18,720,000	18,905,000	22,447,000	22,910,000
Shares Outstanding	358,077	356,835	373,949	401,821	424,415	453,290	436,305	442,539
Statistical Record								
Return on Assets %	N.M.	N.M.	0.40	0.71	0.31	0.06	N.M.	0.21
Return on Equity %	N.M.	N.M.	5.17	9.25	4.24	0.85	N.M.	3.06
Net Margin %	12.73	(18.45)	4.90	9.15	4.29	0.67	(0.14)	3.03
Price Range	59.11-47.26	57.65-47.05	48.58-37.63	49.53-38.90	42.27-32.18	36.62-22.44	22.88-15.93	30.80-14.92
P/E Ratio	...	...	21.40-16.58	12.51-9.82	24.43-18.60	107.71-66.00	...	23.69-11.48
Average Yield %	1.79	1.81	1.97	1.78	1.81	1.68	2.07	1.73

Address: One Hartford Plaza, Hartford, CT 06155 Telephone: 860-547-5000	Web Site: www.thehartford.com Officers: Christopher J. Swift - Chairman, Chief Executive Officer, Executive Vice President, Chief Financial Officer, Principal Accounting Officer Douglas G. (Doug) Elliot - President, Executive Vice President, Division Officer	Auditors: DELOITTE & TOUCHE LLP Investor Contact: 860-547-8691 Transfer Agents: BNY Mellon Shareowner Services, Jersey City, NY

HAWAIIAN ELECTRIC INDUSTRIES INC

Exchange	Symbol	Price	52Wk Range	Yield	P/E
NYS	HE	$34.30 (6/29/2018)	38.35-31.73	3.62	21.71

*7 Year Price Score 94.95 *NYSE Composite Index=100 *12 Month Price Score 97.11

Interim Earnings (Per Share)

Qtr.	Mar	Jun	Sep	Dec
2015	0.31	0.33	0.47	0.39
2016	0.30	0.41	1.17	0.41
2017	0.31	0.36	0.55	0.30
2018	0.37	...	...	...

Interim Dividends (Per Share)

Amt	Decl	Ex	Rec	Pay
0.31Q	08/01/2017	08/21/2017	08/23/2017	09/12/2017
0.31Q	10/31/2017	11/21/2017	11/22/2017	12/12/2017
0.31Q	02/01/2018	02/21/2018	02/22/2018	03/13/2018
0.31Q	05/09/2018	05/22/2018	05/23/2018	06/12/2018

Indicated Div: $1.24

Valuation Analysis

		Institutional Holding	
Forecast EPS	$1.90	No of Institutions	
	(06/14/2018)	405	
Market Cap	$3.7 Billion	Shares	
Book Value	$2.1 Billion	67,077,068	
Price/Book	1.76	% Held	
Price/Sales	1.43	46.77	

TRADING VOLUME (thousand shares)

Business Summary: Electric Utilities (MIC: 3.1.1 SIC: 4911 NAIC: 221122)

Hawaiian Electric Industries is a holding company. Through its subsidiaries, Co. is engaged in electric utility and banking businesses. Co.'s subsidiary, Hawaiian Electric Company, Inc., and its subsidiaries, Hawaii Electric Light Company, Inc. and Maui Electric Company, Limited, are regulated electric public utilities engaged in the production, purchase, transmission, distribution and sale of electricity. In addition, Co.'s subsidiary, American Savings Bank, F.S.B. is engaged in the origination, purchase and sale of loans, residential mortgage lending, construction and development lending, multifamily residential and commercial real estate lending, consumer lending and commercial lending.

Recent Developments: For the quarter ended Mar 31 2018, net income increased 17.5% to US$40.7 million from US$34.7 million in the year-earlier quarter. Revenues were US$645.9 million, up 9.2% from US$591.6 million the year before. Operating income was US$71.9 million versus US$69.7 million in the prior-year quarter, an increase of 3.1%. Direct operating expenses rose 10.0% to US$574.0 million from US$521.8 million in the comparable period the year before.

Prospects: Our evaluation of Hawaiian Electric Industries Inc. as of Jan. 21, 2018 is the result of our systematic analysis on three basic characteristics: earnings strength, relative valuation, and recent stock price movement. The company has managed to produce a neutral trend in earnings per share over the past 5 quarters and while recent estimates for the company have been mixed, HE has posted results that fell short of analysts expectations. Based on operating earnings yield, the company is undervalued when compared to all of the companies in our coverage universe. Share price changes over the past year indicates that HE will perform well over the near term.

Financial Data

(US$ in Thousands)	3 Mos	12/31/2017	12/31/2016	12/31/2015	12/31/2014	12/31/2013	12/31/2012	12/31/2011
Earnings Per Share	1.58	1.52	2.29	1.50	1.64	1.62	1.42	1.44
Cash Flow Per Share	3.32	3.87	4.57	3.34	2.96	3.31	2.41	2.62
Tang Book Value Per Share	18.78	18.84	18.59	17.49	17.00	16.58	15.79	15.45
Dividends Per Share	1.240	1.240	1.240	1.240	1.240	1.240	1.240	1.240
Dividend Payout %	78.48	81.58	54.15	82.67	75.61	76.54	87.32	86.11
Income Statement								
Total Revenue	645,874	2,555,625	2,380,654	2,602,982	3,239,542	3,238,470	3,374,995	3,242,335
EBITDA	135,186	551,432	640,773	513,447	508,457	481,041	441,592	443,812
Depn & Amortn	61,836	200,658	194,273	183,966	172,762	160,061	150,389	148,152
Income Before Taxes	53,276	276,580	373,841	254,788	261,922	247,747	217,407	216,052
Income Taxes	12,556	109,393	123,695	93,021	91,712	84,341	76,859	75,932
Net Income	40,720	167,187	250,146	161,767	170,210	163,406	140,548	140,120
Average Shares	109,024	108,933	108,309	106,721	102,937	99,623	97,338	95,820
Balance Sheet								
Current Assets	521,279	534,796	527,620	553,922	558,540	659,367	678,507	712,351
Total Assets	12,702,718	13,099,828	12,425,506	11,790,196	11,184,161	10,340,044	10,149,132	9,592,731
Current Liabilities	6,537,519	6,228,093	5,717,433	5,292,882	4,954,148	4,717,006	4,552,246	4,380,070
Long-Term Obligations	1,784,432	1,874,656	1,811,637	1,915,128	1,797,202	1,737,459	1,618,798	1,573,299
Total Liabilities	10,576,648	10,968,149	10,324,460	9,828,263	9,358,440	8,578,681	8,520,974	8,026,489
Stockholders' Equity	2,126,070	2,131,679	2,101,046	1,961,933	1,825,721	1,761,363	1,628,158	1,566,242
Shares Outstanding	108,841	108,787	108,583	107,460	102,565	101,259	97,928	96,038
Statistical Record								
Return on Assets %	1.37	1.31	2.06	1.41	1.58	1.60	1.42	1.50
Return on Equity %	8.20	7.90	12.28	8.54	9.49	9.64	8.78	9.09
EBITDA Margin %	20.93	21.58	26.92	19.73	15.70	14.85	13.08	13.69
Net Margin %	6.30	6.54	10.51	6.21	5.25	5.05	4.16	4.32
Asset Turnover	0.21	0.20	0.20	0.23	0.30	0.32	0.34	0.35
Current Ratio	0.08	0.09	0.09	0.10	0.11	0.14	0.15	0.16
Debt to Equity	0.84	0.88	0.86	0.98	0.98	0.99	0.99	1.00
Price Range	38.35-31.73	38.35-31.83	34.48-27.74	34.83-27.23	34.62-23.22	28.30-23.97	29.24-24.00	26.75-21.06
P/E Ratio	24.27-20.08	25.23-20.94	15.06-12.11	23.22-18.15	21.11-14.16	17.47-14.80	20.59-16.90	18.58-14.62
Average Yield %	3.64	3.65	4.00	4.05	4.77	4.72	4.69	5.04

Address: 1001 Bishop Street, Suite 2900, Honolulu, HI 96813
Telephone: 808-543-5662
Fax: 808-543-7966

Web Site: www.hei.com
Officers: Jeffrey N. Watanabe - Chairman Constance H. Lau - President, Chief Executive Officer

Auditors: DELOITTE & TOUCHE LLP
Investor Contact: 808-543-7384
Transfer Agents: Continental Stock Transfer & Trust Company, New York, NY

HCA HEALTHCARE INC

Exchange	Symbol	Price	52Wk Range	Yield	P/E
NYS	HCA	$102.60 (6/29/2018)	107.79-74.22	1.36	13.88

*7 Year Price Score 119.32 *NYSE Composite Index=100 *12 Month Price Score 112.86

Interim Earnings (Per Share)

Qtr.	Mar	Jun	Sep	Dec
2015	1.36	1.18	1.05	1.39
2016	1.69	1.65	1.59	2.37
2017	1.74	1.75	1.15	1.31
2018	3.18	...	...	...

Interim Dividends (Per Share)

Amt	Decl	Ex	Rec	Pay
2.50Q	10/23/2012	10/31/2012	11/02/2012	11/16/2012
2.00Q	12/06/2012	12/13/2012	12/17/2012	12/21/2012
0.35Q	01/30/2018	02/28/2018	03/01/2018	03/30/2018
0.35Q	05/01/2018	05/31/2018	06/01/2018	06/29/2018

Indicated Div: $1.40

Valuation Analysis | **Institutional Holding**

Forecast EPS	$8.81	No of Institutions
	(06/21/2018)	814
Market Cap	$36.0 Billion	Shares
Book Value	N/A	293,897,344
Price/Book	N/A	% Held
Price/Sales	0.81	N/A

Business Summary: Hospitals & Health Care Facilities (MIC: 4.2.1 SIC: 8062 NAIC: 622110)

HCA Healthcare is a holding company. Through its subsidiaries, partnerships and joint ventures (collectively, its affiliates), Co. owns and operates hospitals and related health care entities. At Dec 31 2017, these affiliates operated 179 hospitals, comprised of 175 general, acute care hospitals, three psychiatric hospitals, and one rehabilitation hospital; as well as operated 120 surgery centers. Co. also operates outpatient health care facilities, such as ambulatory surgery centers, emergency care facilities, urgent care facilities, walk-in clinics, diagnostic and imaging centers, rehabilitation and physical therapy centers, radiation and oncology therapy centers, and physician practices.

Recent Developments: For the quarter ended Mar 31 2018, net income increased 65.0% to US$1.28 billion from US$777.0 million in the year-earlier quarter. Revenues were US$11.42 billion, up 7.5% from US$10.62 billion the year before. Indirect operating expenses increased 3.4% to US$9.88 billion from US$9.56 billion in the equivalent prior-year period.

Prospects: Our evaluation of HCA Healthcare Inc. as of Jan. 21, 2018 is the result of our systematic analysis on three basic characteristics: earnings strength, relative valuation, and recent stock price movement. The company has generated a negative trend in earnings per share over the past 5 quarters. However, while recent estimates for the company have been mixed, HCA has posted results that fell short of analysts expectations. Based on operating earnings yield, the company is undervalued when compared to all of the companies in our coverage universe. Share price changes over the past year indicates that HCA will perform poorly over the near term.

Financial Data
(US$ in Millions)

	3 Mos	12/31/2017	12/31/2016	12/31/2015	12/31/2014	12/31/2013	12/31/2012	12/31/2011
Earnings Per Share	7.39	5.95	7.30	4.99	4.16	3.37	3.49	4.97
Cash Flow Per Share	15.52	14.98	14.70	11.43	10.21	8.27	9.46	8.25
Dividends Per Share	0.350	...	...	...	...	...	6.500	...
Dividend Payout %	4.74	...	...	...	...	...	186.25	...
Income Statement								
Total Revenue	11,423	43,614	41,490	39,678	36,918	34,182	33,013	29,682
EBITDA	1,969	8,137	8,409	7,456	6,979	6,498	6,329	6,801
Depn & Amortn	8	2,111	1,946	1,880	1,798	1,733	1,673	1,461
Income Before Taxes	1,530	4,336	4,756	3,911	3,438	2,917	2,858	3,303
Income Taxes	257	1,638	1,378	1,261	1,108	950	888	719
Net Income	1,144	2,216	2,890	2,129	1,875	1,556	1,605	2,465
Average Shares	359	372	395	426	450	461	459	495
Balance Sheet								
Current Assets	10,391	9,977	9,086	9,232	8,930	8,037	7,763	7,233
Total Assets	37,299	36,593	33,758	32,744	31,199	28,831	28,075	26,898
Current Liabilities	7,478	6,158	5,834	5,516	5,480	5,695	6,172	5,554
Long-Term Obligations	31,594	32,858	31,160	30,255	29,307	27,590	27,495	25,645
Total Liabilities	43,543	43,399	41,060	40,343	39,093	37,101	37,735	35,156
Stockholders' Equity	(6,244)	(6,806)	(7,302)	(7,599)	(7,894)	(8,270)	(9,660)	(8,258)
Shares Outstanding	350	350	370	398	420	439	443	437
Statistical Record								
Return on Assets %	7.60	6.30	8.67	6.66	6.25	5.47	5.82	9.71
EBITDA Margin %	17.24	18.66	20.27	18.79	18.90	19.01	19.17	22.91
Net Margin %	10.01	5.08	6.97	5.37	5.08	4.55	4.86	8.30
Asset Turnover	1.25	1.24	1.24	1.24	1.23	1.20	1.20	1.17
Current Ratio	1.39	1.62	1.56	1.67	1.63	1.41	1.26	1.30
Price Range	103.90-74.22	90.49-74.22	82.02-62.83	94.81-64.47	75.00-47.65	48.54-30.17	33.87-20.80	35.24-17.66
P/E Ratio	14.06-10.04	15.21-12.47	11.24-8.61	19.00-12.92	18.03-11.45	14.40-8.95	9.70-5.96	7.09-3.55
Average Yield %	0.41	...	...	...	...	...	23.25	...

Address: One Park Plaza, Nashville, TN 37203
Telephone: 615-344-9551

Web Site: www.hcahealthcare.com
Officers: R. Milton Johnson - Chairman, President, Chief Executive Officer, Chief Financial Officer
William B. Rutherford - Executive Vice President, Chief Financial Officer

Auditors: Ernst & Young LLP
Investor Contact: 615-344-2688
Transfer Agents: Wells Fargo
Shareowner Services, St. Paul, MN

HCP INC

Exchange	Symbol	Price	52Wk Range	Yield	P/E
NYS	HCP	$25.82 (6/29/2018)	32.55-21.64	5.73	N/A

*7 Year Price Score 59.71 ***NYSE Composite Index=100** ***12 Month Price Score 92.09**

Interim Earnings (Per Share)

Qtr.	Mar	Jun	Sep	Dec
2015	(0.52)	0.36	0.25	(1.29)
2016	0.25	0.64	0.32	0.12
2017	0.97	0.04	(0.02)	(0.13)
2018	0.08	...	...	...

Interim Dividends (Per Share)

Amt	Decl	Ex	Rec	Pay
0.37Q	07/27/2017	08/03/2017	08/07/2017	08/22/2017
0.37Q	10/26/2017	11/03/2017	11/06/2017	11/21/2017
0.37Q	02/01/2018	02/14/2018	02/15/2018	03/02/2018
0.37Q	04/26/2018	05/04/2018	05/07/2018	05/22/2018

Indicated Div: $1.48 (Div. Reinv. Plan)

Valuation Analysis — **Institutional Holding**

Forecast EPS	$0.47	No of Institutions
	(06/11/2018)	903
Market Cap	$12.1 Billion	Shares
Book Value	$5.2 Billion	528,179,392
Price/Book	2.33	% Held
Price/Sales	6.61	N/A

TRADING VOLUME (thousand shares)

Business Summary: REITs (MIC: 5.3.1 SIC: 6798 NAIC: 525930)

HCP is a real estate investment trust, which, together with its consolidated entities, invests primarily in real estate serving the healthcare industry in the U.S. Co. acquires, develops, leases, manages and disposes of healthcare real estate and provides financing to healthcare providers. Co.'s portfolio is comprised of investments in the following healthcare segments: senior housing triple-net (SH NNN), senior housing operating portfolio (SHOP), life science, and medical office. At Dec 31 2017, Co. also had interests in 14 hospitals, 61 care homes in the U.K., one post-acute/skilled nursing facility, interests in 72 senior housing facilities and four life science facilities.

Recent Developments: For the quarter ended Mar 31 2018, net income decreased 90.7% to US$43.2 million from US$464.2 million in the year-earlier quarter. Revenues were US$479.2 million, down 2.6% from US$492.2 million the year before. Revenues from property income fell 0.1% to US$459.6 million from US$460.1 million in the corresponding quarter a year earlier.

Prospects: Our evaluation of HCP Inc. as of Jan. 21, 2018 is the result of our systematic analysis on three basic characteristics: earnings strength, relative valuation, and recent stock price movement. The company has produced a positive trend in earnings per share over the past 5 quarters. Because the company lacks sufficient analyst estimate data, we place greater weight on the historical EPS trend as the measure of earnings strength. Based on operating earnings yield, the company is about fairly valued when compared to all of the companies in our coverage universe. Share price changes over the past year indicates that HCP will perform well over the near term.

Financial Data
(US$ in Thousands)

	3 Mos	12/31/2017	12/31/2016	12/31/2015	12/31/2014	12/31/2013	12/31/2012	12/31/2011
Earnings Per Share	(0.03)	0.88	1.34	(1.21)	2.00	2.13	1.90	1.29
Cash Flow Per Share	1.81	1.81	2.59	2.64	2.72	2.53	2.42	1.82
Tang Book Value Per Share	10.24	10.42	10.74	18.65	22.19	22.28	21.95	20.37
Dividends Per Share	1.480	1.480	2.095	2.260	2.180	2.100	2.000	1.920
Dividend Payout %	...	168.18	156.34	...	109.00	98.59	105.26	148.84
Income Statement								
Total Revenue	479,197	1,848,378	2,129,294	2,544,312	2,266,279	2,099,878	1,900,722	1,725,386
EBITDA	121,688	1,281,669	830,490	(88,546)	1,332,231	1,280,621	1,171,691	919,658
Depn & Amortn	9,255	563,553	(1,197)	(1,295)	(949)	(6,646)	(2,232)	(4,510)
Income Before Taxes	37,331	410,400	367,284	(566,847)	893,438	852,015	756,793	504,831
Income Taxes	(5,336)	(1,333)	4,473	(9,011)	250	5,815	(1,636)	1,249
Net Income	40,232	414,169	627,747	(559,235)	922,233	970,837	832,540	538,891
Average Shares	469,695	468,935	467,403	462,795	458,796	455,702	428,316	400,218
Balance Sheet								
Current Assets	169,436	122,936	182,106	456,045	269,125	365,279	319,671	101,740
Total Assets	14,067,571	14,088,461	15,759,265	21,449,849	21,369,940	20,075,870	19,915,555	17,408,475
Current Liabilities	391,942	454,317	475,505	511,512	517,657	417,237	399,903	399,620
Long-Term Obligations	7,965,591	7,880,466	9,189,495	11,069,003	9,759,773	8,661,627	8,693,820	7,722,619
Total Liabilities	8,861,280	8,787,456	10,211,670	12,106,206	10,634,643	9,352,570	9,364,318	8,374,993
Stockholders' Equity	5,206,291	5,301,005	5,547,595	9,343,643	10,735,297	10,723,300	10,551,237	9,033,482
Shares Outstanding	469,725	469,435	468,081	465,488	459,746	456,960	453,191	408,629
Statistical Record								
Return on Assets %	N.M.	2.78	3.36	N.M.	4.45	4.86	4.45	3.51
Return on Equity %	N.M.	7.64	8.41	N.M.	8.60	9.13	8.48	6.34
EBITDA Margin %	25.39	69.34	39.00	N.M.	58.78	60.99	61.64	53.30
Net Margin %	8.40	22.41	29.48	N.M.	40.69	46.23	43.80	31.23
Asset Turnover	0.13	0.12	0.11	0.12	0.11	0.11	0.10	0.11
Current Ratio	0.43	0.27	0.38	0.89	0.52	0.88	0.80	0.25
Debt to Equity	1.53	1.49	1.66	1.18	0.91	0.81	0.82	0.85
Price Range	33.39-21.64	33.39-25.21	36.72-23.79	43.89-29.81	41.49-32.94	50.32-32.46	42.98-34.48	38.02-26.19
P/E Ratio	...	37.94-28.65	27.40-17.75	...	20.75-16.47	23.63-15.24	22.62-18.15	29.47-20.30
Average Yield %	5.30	4.98	6.62	6.26	5.82	5.14	5.10	5.70

Address: 1920 Main Street, Suite 1200, Irvine, CA 92614	**Web Site:** www.hcpi.com	**Auditors:** Deloitte & Touche LLP
Telephone: 949-407-0700	**Officers:** Brian G. Cartwright - Chairman Thomas M. (Tom) Herzog - Chief Executive Officer, Chief Financial Officer, Chief Financial Officer (frmr), Executive Vice President, President	**Investor Contact:** 562-733-5309
Fax: 562-733-5200		**Transfer Agents:** Wells Fargo Shareowner Services, Saint Paul, MN

HEALTHCARE REALTY TRUST, INC.

Exchange	Symbol	Price	52Wk Range	Yield	P/E
NYS	HR	$29.08 (6/29/2018)	34.65-26.31	4.13	N/A

*7 Year Price Score 92.08   *NYSE Composite Index=100   *12 Month Price Score 89.29

Interim Earnings (Per Share)

Qtr.	Mar	Jun	Sep	Dec
2015	0.05	0.18	0.27	0.19
2016	0.09	0.12	0.10	0.47
2017	0.28	0.22	0.02	(0.32)
2018	0.07	...	...	...

Interim Dividends (Per Share)

Amt	Decl	Ex	Rec	Pay
0.30Q	08/01/2017	08/09/2017	08/11/2017	08/31/2017
0.30Q	10/31/2017	11/15/2017	11/16/2017	11/30/2017
0.30Q	02/13/2018	02/22/2018	02/23/2018	03/06/2018
0.30Q	05/01/2018	05/15/2018	05/16/2018	05/31/2018

Indicated Div: $1.20 (Div. Reinv. Plan)

Valuation Analysis | **Institutional Holding**

Forecast EPS	$0.36	No of Institutions
	(06/11/2018)	344
Market Cap	$3.6 Billion	Shares
Book Value	$1.8 Billion	151,161,168
Price/Book	2.06	% Held
Price/Sales	8.43	97.30

Business Summary: REITs (MIC: 5.3.1 SIC: 6798 NAIC: 525930)

Healthcare Realty Trust is a self-managed and self-administered real estate investment trust that owns, leases, manages, acquires, finances, develops and redevelops income-producing real estate properties associated primarily with the delivery of outpatient healthcare services. Co. had gross investments in 201 real estate properties, construction in progress, land held for development and corporate property at Dec 31 2017. Co. also provided property management services for 160 healthcare-related properties nationwide, as of Dec 31 2017.

Recent Developments: For the quarter ended Mar 31 2018, net income decreased 71.2% to US$9.2 million from US$31.8 million in the year-earlier quarter. Revenues were US$112.1 million, up 7.1% from US$104.6 million the year before. Revenues from property income rose 7.3% to US$110.2 million from US$102.7 million in the corresponding quarter a year earlier.

Prospects: Our evaluation of Healthcare Realty Trust Inc. as of Jan. 21, 2018 is the result of our systematic analysis on three basic characteristics: earnings strength, relative valuation, and recent stock price movement. The company has managed to produce a neutral trend in earnings per share over the past 5 quarters. Because the company lacks sufficient analyst estimate data, we place greater weight on the historical EPS trend as the measure of earnings strength. Based on operating earnings yield, the company is overvalued when compared to all of the companies in our coverage universe. Share price changes over the past year indicates that HR will perform very well over the near term.

Financial Data

(US$ in Thousands)	3 Mos	12/31/2017	12/31/2016	12/31/2015	12/31/2014	12/31/2013	12/31/2012	12/31/2011
Earnings Per Share	(0.01)	.0.18	0.78	0.70	0.33	0.08	0.07	...
Cash Flow Per Share	1.55	1.52	1.39	1.62	1.32	1.33	1.47	1.44
Tang Book Value Per Share	14.09	14.12	13.99	12.02	12.13	12.76	12.60	12.67
Dividends Per Share	1.200	1.200	1.200	1.200	1.200	1.200	1.200	1.200
Dividend Payout %	...	666.67	153.85	171.43	363.64	1,500.00	1,714.29	...
Income Statement								
Total Revenue	112,124	424,499	411,630	388,471	370,855	336,926	316,350	296,649
EBITDA	20,601	221,274	259,590	230,900	205,776	149,623	167,987	151,069
Depn & Amortn	(754)	141,776	116,483	106,530	99,384	88,380	85,122	78,088
Income Before Taxes	9,180	23,096	85,756	58,836	33,979	(12,268)	7,812	(3,057)
Net Income	9,180	23,092	85,571	69,436	31,887	6,946	5,465	(214)
Average Shares	123,347	118,017	109,387	99,880	96,759	90,940	80,127	72,720
Balance Sheet								
Current Assets	39,914	78,515	127,307	76,302	75,019	196,018	225,067	154,719
Total Assets	3,183,420	3,193,585	3,040,647	2,816,726	2,757,510	2,729,662	2,539,972	2,521,022
Current Liabilities	62,318	70,995	78,880	75,522	70,612	74,853	65,809	72,735
Long-Term Obligations	1,306,951	1,283,880	1,264,370	1,431,494	1,403,692	1,348,459	1,293,044	1,393,537
Total Liabilities	1,418,872	1,403,702	1,387,233	1,573,979	1,536,456	1,486,185	1,419,028	1,516,216
Stockholders' Equity	1,764,548	1,789,883	1,653,414	1,242,747	1,221,054	1,243,477	1,120,944	1,004,806
Shares Outstanding	125,198	125,132	116,417	101,517	98,828	95,924	87,514	77,843
Statistical Record								
Return on Assets %	0.01	0.74	2.91	2.49	1.16	0.26	0.22	N.M.
Return on Equity %	0.02	1.34	5.89	5.64	2.59	0.59	0.51	N.M.
EBITDA Margin %	18.37	52.13	63.06	59.44	55.49	44.41	53.10	50.93
Net Margin %	8.19	5.44	20.79	17.87	8.60	2.06	1.73	N.M.
Asset Turnover	0.14	0.14	0.14	0.14	0.14	0.13	0.12	0.12
Current Ratio	0.64	1.11	1.61	1.01	1.06	2.62	3.42	2.13
Debt to Equity	0.74	0.72	0.76	1.15	1.15	1.08	1.15	1.39
Price Range	36.17-26.55	36.17-29.80	36.50-27.74	30.94-22.11	27.81-21.22	30.52-20.98	24.93-18.56	23.63-15.16
P/E Ratio	...	200.94-165.56	46.79-35.56	44.20-31.59	84.27-64.30	381.50-262.25	356.14-265.14	N.M.
Average Yield %	3.75	3.69	3.80	4.62	4.86	4.76	5.30	6.04

Address: 3310 West End Avenue, Suite 700, Nashville, TN 37203 **Telephone:** 615-269-8175	**Web Site:** www.healthcarerealty.com **Officers:** David R. Emery - Executive Chairman, Chairman, Chief Executive Officer Todd J. Meredith - President, Chief Executive Officer, Executive Vice President	**Auditors:** BDO USA, LLP **Transfer Agents:** Wells Fargo Shareowner Services, Mendota Heights, MN

HEALTHCARE TRUST OF AMERICA INC

Exchange	Symbol	Price	52Wk Range	Yield	P/E
NYS	HTA	$26.96 (6/29/2018)	31.78-24.32	4.53	86.97

*7 Year Price Score N/A ***NYSE Composite Index=100** ***12 Month Price Score 89.28**

Interim Earnings (Per Share)

Qtr.	Mar	Jun	Sep	Dec
2015	0.05	0.07	0.05	0.08
2016	0.08	0.09	0.04	0.12
2017	0.09	(0.03)	0.07	0.22
2018	0.05	...	...	...

Interim Dividends (Per Share)

Amt	Decl	Ex	Rec	Pay
0.305Q	07/31/2017	09/29/2017	10/02/2017	10/06/2017
0.305Q	10/24/2017	12/29/2017	01/02/2018	01/09/2018
0.305Q	02/15/2018	04/02/2018	04/03/2018	04/10/2018
0.305Q	04/27/2018	07/03/2018	07/05/2018	07/10/2018

Indicated Div: $1.22

Valuation Analysis — **Institutional Holding**

Forecast EPS	$0.31	No of Institutions
	(06/12/2018)	374
Market Cap	$5.5 Billion	Shares
Book Value	$3.2 Billion	244,738,128
Price/Book	1.71	% Held
Price/Sales	8.31	68.40

TRADING VOLUME (thousand shares)

Business Summary: REITs (MIC: 5.3.1 SIC: 6798 NAIC: 525930)

Healthcare Trust of America is a real estate investment trust and an owners and operators of medical office buildings (MOBs) in the U.S. Co. focuses on owning and operating MOBs that serve healthcare delivery and are located on health system campuses, near university medical centers, or in community core outpatient locations. Co.'s properties include health systems such as Baylor Scott & White Health, Highmark-Allegheny Health Network, Community Health Systems, Greenville Health System and Ascension Health. As of Dec 31 2017, Co.'s portfolio consisted of approximately 24.1 million square feet of gross leasable area.

Recent Developments: For the quarter ended Mar 31 2018, net income decreased 28.5% to US$10.0 million from US$14.0 million in the year-earlier quarter. Revenues were US$175.7 million, up 41.3% from US$124.3 million the year before. Revenues from property income rose 41.6% to US$175.6 million from US$124.0 million in the corresponding quarter a year earlier.

Prospects: Our evaluation of Healthcare Trust Of America as of Jan. 21, 2018 is the result of our systematic analysis on three basic characteristics: earnings strength, relative valuation, and recent stock price movement. The company has produced a positive trend in earnings per share over the past 5 quarters and while recent estimates for the company have remained steady, HTA has posted results that fell short of analysts expectations. Based on operating earnings yield, the company is overvalued when compared to all of the companies in our coverage universe. Share price changes over the past year indicates that HTA will perform very well over the near term.

Financial Data
(US$ in Thousands)

	3 Mos	12/31/2017	12/31/2016	12/31/2015	12/31/2014	12/31/2013	12/31/2012	12/31/2011
Earnings Per Share	0.31	0.34	0.33	0.26	0.37	0.20	(0.22)	0.04
Cash Flow Per Share	1.57	1.70	1.49	1.52	1.41	1.30	1.05	1.00
Tang Book Value Per Share	15.23	15.48	11.58	10.53	11.22	11.29	9.05	11.33
Dividends Per Share	1.210	1.210	1.190	1.170	0.290	...	...	...
Dividend Payout %	390.32	355.88	360.61	450.00	78.38	...	...	...
Income Statement								
Total Revenue	175,661	613,990	460,928	403,822	371,505	319,899	299,644	274,438
EBITDA	104,002	389,330	283,432	244,047	246,753	820,036	100,625	112,877
Depn & Amortn	68,303	239,044	175,285	151,614	140,400	755,000	72,000	65,566
Income Before Taxes	9,446	64,795	47,345	33,557	45,994	23,577	(24,368)	5,593
Net Income	9,802	63,916	45,912	32,931	45,371	24,261	(24,424)	5,541
Average Shares	209,177	185,278	140,259	128,004	121,168	114,969	111,356	112,195
Balance Sheet								
Current Assets	68,938	118,560	25,045	28,962	31,212	36,195	46,896	98,867
Total Assets	6,359,835	6,449,582	3,747,844	3,172,300	3,041,650	2,752,334	2,414,090	2,291,629
Current Liabilities	134,574	167,852	105,034	94,933	101,042	82,893	63,443	47,801
Long-Term Obligations	2,780,291	2,781,031	1,768,905	1,590,696	1,412,461	1,214,241	1,037,359	639,149
Total Liabilities	3,129,716	3,170,800	2,060,570	1,792,876	1,594,511	1,365,128	1,159,824	724,289
Stockholders' Equity	3,230,119	3,278,782	1,687,274	1,379,424	1,447,139	1,387,206	1,254,266	1,567,340
Shares Outstanding	205,179	204,892	141,719	127,026	125,087	118,440	107,326	114,245
Statistical Record								
Return on Assets %	1.19	1.25	1.32	1.06	1.57	0.94	N.M.	0.24
Return on Equity %	2.46	2.57	2.99	2.33	3.20	1.84	N.M.	0.36
EBITDA Margin %	59.21	63.41	61.49	60.43	66.42	256.34	33.58	41.13
Net Margin %	5.58	10.41	9.96	8.15	12.21	7.58	N.M.	2.02
Asset Turnover	0.13	0.12	0.13	0.13	0.13	0.12	0.13	0.12
Current Ratio	0.51	0.71	0.24	0.31	0.31	0.44	0.74	2.07
Debt to Equity	0.86	0.85	1.05	1.15	0.98	0.88	0.83	0.41
Price Range	32.92-24.85	32.92-28.69	34.64-26.30	29.94-22.69	27.40-19.66	26.56-19.46	21.78-18.28	...
P/E Ratio	106.19-80.16	96.82-84.38	104.97-79.70	115.15-87.27	74.05-53.14	132.80-97.30	...	...
Average Yield %	4.07	3.95	3.95	4.50	1.22	...	...	...

Address: 16435 N. Scottsdale Road, Suite 320, Scottsdale, AZ 85254
Telephone: 480-998-3478
Fax: 480-991-0755

Web Site: www.htareit.com
Officers: Scott D. Peters - Chairman, President, Chief Executive Officer Robert A. Milligan - Executive Vice President, Chief Financial Officer, Secretary, Treasurer

Auditors: Deloitte & Touche LLP
Investor Contact: 480-998-3478
Transfer Agents: DST Systems, Inc., Kansas City, MO

HEICO CORP

Exchange	Symbol	Price	52Wk Range	Yield	P/E	Div Acheiver
NYS	HEI	$72.93 (6/29/2018)	76.66-45.98	0.16	44.20	10 Years

*7 Year Price Score 158.21 *NYSE Composite Index=100 *12 Month Price Score 115.67

Interim Earnings (Per Share)

Qtr.	Jan	Apr	Jul	Oct
2014-15	0.21	0.25	0.26	0.29
2015-16	0.24	0.29	0.32	0.33
2016-17	0.30	0.34	0.34	0.39
2017-18	0.48	0.44	...	...

Interim Dividends (Per Share)

Amt	Decl	Ex	Rec	Pay
0.07Q	12/15/2017	01/02/2018	01/03/2018	01/17/2018
25%	12/15/2017	01/18/2018	01/03/2018	01/17/2018
25%	06/11/2018	06/28/2018	06/21/2018	06/27/2018
0.06Q	06/11/2018	07/10/2018	07/11/2018	07/19/2018

Indicated Div: $0.12

Valuation Analysis

		Institutional Holding	
Forecast EPS	$1.84	No of Institutions	
	(06/10/2018)	361	
Market Cap	$9.7 Billion	Shares	
Book Value	$1.3 Billion	34,982,016	
Price/Book	7.59	% Held	
Price/Sales	5.87	35.16	

Business Summary: Aerospace (MIC: 7.1.1 SIC: 3724 NAIC: 336412)

HEICO is a holding company engaged as a manufacturer of Federal Aviation Administration-approved jet engine and aircraft component replacement parts, other than the original equipment manufacturers and their subcontractors. Co. also manufactures a range of electronic equipment for the aviation, defense, space, medical, telecommunications and electronics industries. Co. has two operating segments: Flight Support Group, which uses proprietary technology to design and manufacture jet engine and aircraft component replacement parts for sale; and Electronic Technologies Group, which designs, manufactures and sells various types of electronic, microwave and electro-optical products.

Recent Developments: For the quarter ended Apr 30 2018, net income increased 29.9% to US$66.0 million from US$50.8 million in the year-earlier quarter. Revenues were US$430.6 million, up 16.8% from US$368.7 million the year before. Operating income was US$91.6 million versus US$76.5 million in the prior-year quarter, an increase of 19.6%. Direct operating expenses rose 15.1% to US$262.7 million from US$228.3 million in the comparable period the year before. Indirect operating expenses increased 19.5% to US$76.3 million from US$63.8 million in the equivalent prior-year period.

Prospects: Our evaluation of Heico Corp. as of Jan. 21, 2018 is the result of our systematic analysis on three basic characteristics: earnings strength, relative valuation, and recent stock price movement. The company has managed to produce a neutral trend in earnings per share over the past 5 quarters and while recent estimates for the company have been raised by analysts, HEI has posted better than expected results. Based on projected earnings yield, the company is overvalued when compared to all of the companies in our coverage universe. Share price changes over the past year indicates that HEI will perform very well over the near term.

Financial Data
(US$ in Thousands)

	6 Mos	3 Mos	10/31/2017	10/31/2016	10/31/2015	10/31/2014	10/31/2013	10/31/2012
Earnings Per Share	1.65	1.55	1.37	1.17	1.01	0.92	0.78	0.66
Cash Flow Per Share	2.06	2.00	2.09	1.90	1.33	1.47	1.02	1.07
Dividends Per Share	0.134	0.134	0.122	0.102	0.090	0.301	1.162	0.055
Dividend Payout %	8.12	8.65	8.88	8.73	8.88	32.64	148.36	8.44
Income Statement								
Total Revenue	835,012	404,410	1,524,813	1,376,258	1,188,648	1,132,311	1,008,757	897,347
EBITDA	209,324	98,944	329,650	285,722	247,390	221,113	197,878	175,207
Depn & Amortn	38,089	19,024	21,900	20,400	17,800	17,100	13,400	11,600
Income Before Taxes	161,606	75,195	297,960	257,050	224,964	198,572	180,761	161,175
Income Taxes	23,900	3,500	90,300	80,900	71,400	59,800	56,200	54,500
Net Income	124,770	65,152	185,985	156,192	133,364	121,293	102,396	85,147
Average Shares	136,588	136,390	135,587	133,144	132,443	131,744	130,824	130,124
Balance Sheet								
Current Assets	694,726	662,432	631,892	584,221	503,612	431,293	441,472	367,911
Total Assets	2,627,881	2,570,442	2,512,431	2,039,475	1,736,381	1,489,214	1,533,015	1,192,846
Current Liabilities	230,051	229,056	249,437	214,421	168,387	152,220	161,286	131,514
Long-Term Obligations	683,362	668,527	673,528	457,814	367,241	328,691	376,818	131,194
Total Liabilities	1,352,054	1,331,030	1,351,351	1,076,096	926,524	789,730	926,669	576,173
Stockholders' Equity	1,275,827	1,239,412	1,161,080	963,379	809,863	699,484	606,346	616,673
Shares Outstanding	132,735	132,103	132,003	131,423	130,611	129,972	129,640	129,060
Statistical Record								
Return on Assets %	9.33	9.14	8.17	8.25	8.27	8.03	7.51	7.96
Return on Equity %	19.28	18.76	17.51	17.57	17.67	18.58	16.74	14.82
EBITDA Margin %	25.07	24.47	21.62	20.76	20.81	19.53	19.62	19.52
Net Margin %	14.94	16.11	12.20	11.35	11.22	10.71	10.15	9.49
Asset Turnover	0.69	0.69	0.67	0.73	0.74	0.75	0.74	0.84
Current Ratio	3.02	2.89	2.53	2.72	2.99	2.83	2.74	2.80
Debt to Equity	0.54	0.54	0.58	0.48	0.45	0.47	0.62	0.21
Price Range	73.84-45.32	66.98-38.69	59.07-34.01	38.01-24.76	32.18-24.32	33.03-23.80	28.39-15.54	19.95-14.01
P/E Ratio	44.75-27.47	43.21-24.96	43.11-24.83	32.49-21.16	31.86-24.08	35.91-25.87	36.40-19.93	30.23-21.23
Average Yield %	0.23	0.26	0.26	0.33	0.31	1.08	5.61	0.33

Address: 3000 Taft Street, Hollywood, FL 33021	**Web Site:** www.heico.com	**Auditors:** Deloitte & Touche LLP	
Telephone: 954-987-4000	**Officers:** Laurans A. Mendelson - Chairman, Chief Executive Officer Eric A. Mendelson - Co-President, Division Officer	**Investor Contact:** 954-987-4000	
		Transfer Agents: Computershare Shareowner Services LLC, Providence, RI	

HELMERICH & PAYNE, INC.

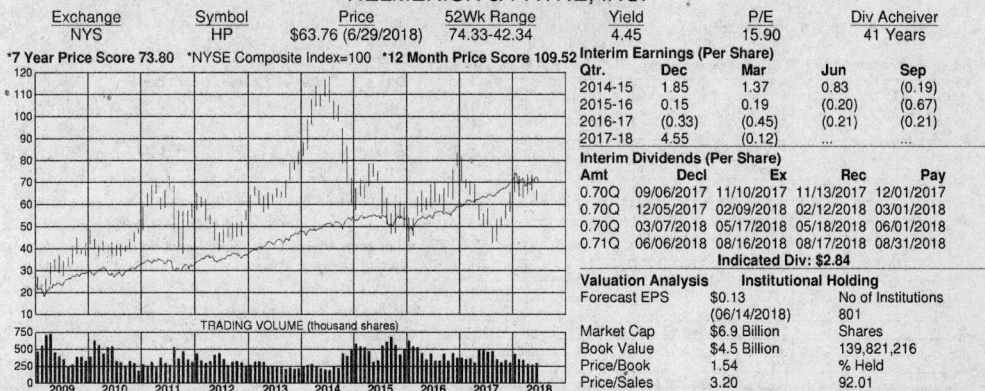

Exchange	Symbol	Price	52Wk Range	Yield	P/E	Div Acheiver
NYS	HP	$63.76 (6/29/2018)	74.33-42.34	4.45	15.90	41 Years

*7 Year Price Score 73.80   ***NYSE Composite Index=100**   ***12 Month Price Score 109.52**

Interim Earnings (Per Share)

Qtr.	Dec	Mar	Jun	Sep
2014-15	1.85	1.37	0.83	(0.19)
2015-16	0.15	0.19	(0.20)	(0.67)
2016-17	(0.33)	(0.45)	(0.21)	(0.21)
2017-18	4.55	(0.12)	...	...

Interim Dividends (Per Share)

Amt	Decl	Ex	Rec	Pay
0.70Q	09/06/2017	11/10/2017	11/13/2017	12/01/2017
0.70Q	12/05/2017	02/09/2018	02/12/2018	03/01/2018
0.70Q	03/07/2018	05/17/2018	05/18/2018	06/01/2018
0.71Q	06/06/2018	08/16/2018	08/17/2018	08/31/2018

Indicated Div: $2.84

Valuation Analysis   **Institutional Holding**

Forecast EPS	$0.13	No of Institutions
(06/14/2018)		801
Market Cap	$6.9 Billion	Shares
Book Value	$4.5 Billion	139,821,216
Price/Book	1.54	% Held
Price/Sales	3.20	92.01

TRADING VOLUME (thousand shares)

Business Summary: Equipment & Services (MIC: 9.1.3 SIC: 1381 NAIC: 213111)

Helmerich & Payne is primarily engaged in contract drilling of oil and gas wells for others. Co.'s contract drilling business is composed of three segments: U.S. Land, which drills primarily in Oklahoma, California, Texas, Wyoming, Colorado, Louisiana, Mississippi, Pennsylvania, Ohio, New Mexico and North Dakota; Offshore, which is conducted in the Gulf of Mexico and Equatorial Guinea; and International Land, which conducts drilling operations in five international locations: Ecuador, Colombia, Argentina, Bahrain and United Arab Emirates. Co. is also engaged in the ownership, development and operation of commercial real estate and the research and development of rotary steerable technology.

Recent Developments: For the quarter ended Mar 31 2018, loss from continuing operations was US$1.6 million compared with a loss of US$48.5 million in the year-earlier quarter. Net loss amounted to US$11.9 million versus a net loss of US$48.8 million in the year-earlier quarter. Revenues were US$577.5 million, up 42.5% from US$405.3 million the year before. Operating loss was US$1.3 million versus a loss of US$65.7 million in the prior-year quarter. Direct operating expenses rose 29.9% to US$385.6 million from US$296.8 million in the comparable period the year before. Indirect operating expenses increased 10.9% to US$193.2 million from US$174.1 million in the equivalent prior-year period.

Prospects: Our evaluation of Helmerich & Payne Inc. as of Jan. 21, 2018 is the result of our systematic analysis on three basic characteristics: earnings strength, relative valuation, and recent stock price movement. The company has produced a positive trend in earnings per share over the past 5 quarters. Because the company lacks sufficient analyst estimate data, we place greater weight on the historical EPS trend as the measure of earnings strength. Based on operating earnings yield, the company is overvalued when compared to all of the companies in our coverage universe. Share price changes over the past year indicates that HP will perform very poorly over the near term.

Financial Data

(US$ in Thousands)	6 Mos	3 Mos	09/30/2017	09/30/2016	09/30/2015	09/30/2014	09/30/2013	09/30/2012
Earnings Per Share	4.01	3.68	(1.20)	(0.54)	3.87	6.46	6.79	5.34
Cash Flow Per Share	3.75	3.30	3.29	6.96	13.17	10.38	9.38	9.34
Tang Book Value Per Share	40.01	40.81	37.40	42.20	45.44	45.19	41.64	36.28
Dividends Per Share	2.800	2.800	2.800	2.763	2.750	2.438	0.870	0.280
Dividend Payout %	69.83	76.09	...	...	71.06	37.73	12.81	5.24
Income Statement								
Total Revenue	1,141,571	564,087	1,804,741	1,624,232	3,165,441	3,719,707	3,387,614	3,151,802
EBITDA	3,207	4,316	414,577	545,667	1,281,841	1,622,934	1,574,396	1,297,402
Depn & Amortn	531	266	585,543	598,587	606,992	523,549	455,623	387,549
Income Before Taxes	(5,554)	1,000.00	(184,598)	(72,667)	665,647	1,096,314	1,114,297	902,580
Income Taxes	(504,563)	(500,641)	(56,735)	(19,677)	243,375	387,548	392,844	328,971
Net Income	488,227	500,106	(128,212)	(56,828)	422,225	708,719	736,639	581,045
Average Shares	108,868	109,095	108,500	107,996	108,570	109,141	107,879	108,377
Balance Sheet								
Current Assets	1,130,983	1,166,346	1,235,267	1,572,686	1,439,007	1,277,366	1,258,211	895,228
Total Assets	6,261,792	6,362,096	6,439,988	6,832,019	7,152,012	6,721,861	6,264,827	5,721,085
Current Liabilities	340,185	355,762	344,385	330,120	351,228	507,526	452,273	381,164
Long-Term Obligations	493,433	493,168	492,902	491,847	492,443	40,000	80,000	195,000
Total Liabilities	1,758,639	1,771,746	2,275,397	2,271,094	2,254,560	1,830,884	1,821,100	1,886,087
Stockholders' Equity	4,503,153	4,590,350	4,164,591	4,560,925	4,897,452	4,890,977	4,443,727	3,834,998
Shares Outstanding	108,876	108,845	108,604	108,077	107,767	108,232	106,716	105,697
Statistical Record								
Return on Assets %	6.94	6.24	N.M.	N.M.	6.09	10.91	12.29	10.81
Return on Equity %	10.03	8.98	N.M.	N.M.	8.63	15.18	17.80	16.31
EBITDA Margin %	0.28	0.77	22.98	33.60	40.49	43.63	46.48	41.16
Net Margin %	42.77	88.66	N.M.	N.M.	13.34	19.05	21.75	18.44
Asset Turnover	0.34	0.31	0.27	0.23	0.46	0.57	0.57	0.59
Current Ratio	3.32	3.28	3.59	4.76	4.10	2.52	2.78	2.35
Debt to Equity	0.11	0.11	0.12	0.11	0.10	0.01	0.02	0.05
Price Range	74.33-42.34	81.11-42.34	83.46-42.34	69.77-42.85	97.87-46.50	118.29-68.95	70.82-45.22	65.13-37.39
P/E Ratio	18.54-10.56	22.04-11.51	...	...	25.29-12.02	18.31-10.67	10.43-6.66	12.20-7.00
Average Yield %	4.84	4.76	4.48	4.75	4.01	2.52	1.44	0.54

Address: 1437 South Boulder Avenue, Tulsa, OK 74119
Telephone: 918-742-5531
Fax: 918-742-0237

Web Site: www.hpinc.com
Officers: Hans Helmerich - Chairman, President, Chief Executive Officer John W. Lindsay - President, Chief Executive Officer, Executive Vice President, Chief Operating Officer

Auditors: Ernst & Young LLP
Investor Contact: 918-588-5207
Transfer Agents: Computershare Investor Services LLC, Providence, RI

HERBALIFE NUTRITION LTD

Exchange	Symbol	Price	52Wk Range	Yield	P/E
NYS	HLF	$53.72 (6/29/2018)	56.48-30.98	N/A	40.09

*7 Year Price Score 112.77 *NYSE Composite Index=100 *12 Month Price Score 126.63

Interim Earnings (Per Share)

Qtr.	Mar	Jun	Sep	Dec
2015	0.46	0.48	0.55	0.49
2016	0.56	(0.14)	0.51	0.57
2017	0.49	0.81	0.33	(0.34)
2018	0.54	...	...	...

Interim Dividends (Per Share)

Dividend Payment Suspended

Valuation Analysis   Institutional Holding

Forecast EPS	N/A	No of Institutions
		343
Market Cap	$8.9 Billion	Shares
Book Value	N/A	89,269,376
Price/Book	N/A	% Held
Price/Sales	1.98	79.98

Business Summary: Household & Personal Products (MIC: 1.7.1 SIC: 5122 NAIC: 424210)

Herbalife Nutrition is a holding company. Through its subsidiaries, Co. is a nutrition company that sells its products to and through a network of independent members. Co. has five product groups: weight management, which provides for meal replacement, protein shakes, drink mixes, weight loss solutions and healthy snacks; targeted nutrition, which provides dietary and nutritional supplements; energy, sports and fitness, which provide products that support a healthy active lifestyle; outer nutrition, which provides for facial skin care, body care, and hair care; and literature, promotional and other, which provide start-up kits, sales tools, and educational materials.

Recent Developments: For the year ended Dec 31 2017, net income decreased 17.7% to US$213.9 million from US$260.0 million in the prior year. Revenues were US$4.43 billion, down 1.4% from US$4.49 billion the year before. Operating income was US$617.1 million versus US$458.1 million in the prior year, an increase of 34.7%. Direct operating expenses declined 0.7% to US$848.6 million from US$854.6 million in the comparable period the year before. Indirect operating expenses decreased 6.7% to US$2.96 billion from US$3.18 billion in the equivalent prior-year period.

Prospects: Our evaluation of Herbalife Ltd. as of Aug. 2, 2015 is the result of our systematic analysis on three basic characteristics: earnings strength, relative valuation, and recent stock price movement. The company has managed to produce a neutral trend in earnings per share over the past 5 quarters. However, while recent estimates for the company have been mixed, HLF has posted better than expected results. Based on operating earnings yield, the company is undervalued when compared to all of the companies in our coverage universe. Share price changes over the past year indicates that HLF will perform poorly over the near term.

Financial Data
(US$ in Thousands)

	3 Mos	12/31/2017	12/31/2016	12/31/2015	12/31/2014	12/31/2013	12/31/2012	12/31/2011
Earnings Per Share	1.34	1.29	1.51	1.99	1.70	2.46	2.02	1.65
Cash Flow Per Share	3.93	3.73	2.21	3.81	2.96	3.77	2.52	2.17
Tang Book Value Per Share	...	...	N.M.	...	...	0.67	0.02	0.62
Dividends Per Share	...	...	...	...	0.150	0.600	0.600	0.365
Dividend Payout %	...	...	...	...	8.82	24.44	29.63	22.12
Income Statement								
Total Revenue	1,176,900	4,427,700	4,488,400	4,469,000	4,958,600	4,825,308	4,072,330	3,454,537
EBITDA	157,000	697,600	538,800	663,800	582,000	816,377	732,347	631,170
Depn & Amortn	25,600	80,100	80,700	82,500	81,500	81,100	70,900	68,900
Income Before Taxes	91,500	471,200	364,700	486,400	421,300	716,717	650,906	559,779
Income Taxes	9,400	257,300	104,700	147,300	112,600	189,192	173,716	147,201
Net Income	82,100	213,900	260,000	339,100	308,700	527,525	477,190	412,578
Average Shares	152,600	165,800	172,200	170,600	181,600	214,890	235,712	249,692
Balance Sheet								
Current Assets	1,951,100	1,860,300	1,462,500	1,566,300	1,393,400	1,643,120	963,848	768,819
Total Assets	2,968,700	2,895,100	2,565,400	2,477,900	2,374,900	2,473,701	1,703,944	1,446,209
Current Liabilities	910,900	906,800	791,500	1,024,400	874,800	922,178	716,891	548,689
Long-Term Obligations	2,109,100	2,165,700	1,438,400	1,392,500	1,711,700	850,019	431,305	202,079
Total Liabilities	3,187,700	3,229,800	2,369,100	2,531,400	2,709,300	1,922,255	1,283,189	886,021
Stockholders' Equity	(219,000)	(334,700)	196,300	(53,500)	(334,400)	551,446	420,755	560,188
Shares Outstanding	166,200	164,600	186,200	185,400	184,400	202,200	213,800	231,600
Statistical Record								
Return on Assets %	6.46	7.83	10.28	13.98	12.73	25.25	30.21	30.81
Return on Equity %	871.07	...	363.15	...	284.46	108.52	97.03	78.78
EBITDA Margin %	13.34	15.76	12.00	14.85	11.74	16.92	17.98	18.27
Net Margin %	6.98	4.83	5.79	7.59	6.23	10.93	11.72	11.94
Asset Turnover	1.38	1.62	1.78	1.84	2.05	2.31	2.58	2.58
Current Ratio	2.14	2.05	1.85	1.53	1.59	1.78	1.34	1.40
Debt to Equity	...	...	7.33	...	...	1.54	1.03	0.36
Price Range	49.99-28.57	39.38-24.59	34.01-21.71	30.39-14.85	40.91-18.58	40.41-16.10	36.34-13.03	31.18-15.94
P/E Ratio	37.31-21.32	30.53-19.07	22.52-14.38	15.27-7.46	24.06-10.93	16.42-6.54	17.99-6.45	18.90-9.66
Average Yield %					0.54	2.25	2.26	1.48

Address: P.O. Box 309GT, Ugland House, South Church Street, KY1-1104 **Telephone:** 213-745-0500	**Web Site:** www.herbalife.com **Officers:** Michael O. Johnson - Chairman, Chief Executive Officer Desmond (Des) Walsh - Executive Vice Chairman, President	**Auditors:** PricewaterhouseCoopers LLP **Transfer Agents:** Mellon Investor Services LLC, South Hackensack, NJ

HERSHEY COMPANY (THE)

Exchange	Symbol	Price	52Wk Range	Yield	P/E
NYS	HSY	$93.06 (6/29/2018)	115.45-89.54	2.82	19.67

*7 Year Price Score 91.60   *NYSE Composite Index=100   *12 Month Price Score 87.97

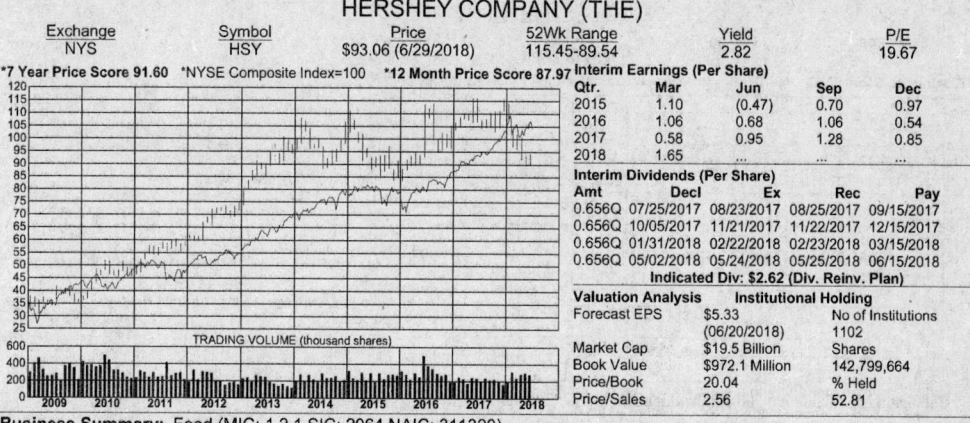

Interim Earnings (Per Share)

Qtr.	Mar	Jun	Sep	Dec
2015	1.10	(0.47)	0.70	0.97
2016	1.06	0.68	1.06	0.54
2017	0.58	0.95	1.28	0.85
2018	1.65	...	...	...

Interim Dividends (Per Share)

Amt	Decl	Ex	Rec	Pay
0.656Q	07/25/2017	08/23/2017	08/25/2017	09/15/2017
0.656Q	10/05/2017	11/21/2017	11/22/2017	12/15/2017
0.656Q	01/31/2018	02/22/2018	02/23/2018	03/15/2018
0.656Q	05/02/2018	05/24/2018	05/25/2018	06/15/2018

Indicated Div: $2.62 (Div. Reinv. Plan)

Valuation Analysis

		Institutional Holding	
Forecast EPS	$5.33	No of Institutions	
	(06/20/2018)	1102	
Market Cap	$19.5 Billion	Shares	
Book Value	$972.1 Million	142,799,664	
Price/Book	20.04	% Held	
Price/Sales	2.56	52.81	

Business Summary: Food (MIC: 1.2.1 SIC: 2064 NAIC: 311320)

Hershey is engaged in the production of chocolate and non-chocolate confectionery. Co. has two reportable segments: North America, which is responsible for Co.'s chocolate and sugar confectionery market position, as well as Co.'s grocery and growing snacks market positions, in the U.S. and Canada; and International and Other, which includes all other countries where Co. manufactures, imports, markets, sells or distributes chocolate and non-chocolate confectionery and other products. Co.'s principal product offerings include chocolate and non-chocolate confectionery products; gum and mint refreshment products; pantry items; and snack items such as spreads, meat snacks, bars and snack bites.

Recent Developments: For the quarter ended Apr 1 2018, net income increased 257.0% to US$350.7 million from US$98.2 million in the year-earlier quarter. Revenues were US$1.97 billion, up 4.9% from US$1.88 billion the year before. Operating income was US$480.5 million versus US$197.2 million in the prior-year quarter, an increase of 143.6%. Direct operating expenses rose 2.8% to US$997.9 million from US$970.3 million in the comparable period the year before. Indirect operating expenses decreased 30.7% to US$493.5 million from US$712.1 million in the equivalent prior-year period.

Prospects: Our evaluation of Hershey Foods Corp. as of Jan. 21, 2018 is the result of our systematic analysis on three basic characteristics: earnings strength, relative valuation, and recent stock price movement. The company has generated a negative trend in earnings per share over the past 5 quarters and while recent estimates for the company have been mixed, HSY has posted better than expected results. Based on operating earnings yield, the company is about fairly valued when compared to all of the companies in our coverage universe. Share price changes over the past year indicates that HSY will perform well over the near term.

Financial Data

(US$ in Thousands)	3 Mos	12/31/2017	12/31/2016	12/31/2015	12/31/2014	12/31/2013	12/31/2012	12/31/2011
Earnings Per Share	4.73	3.66	3.34	2.32	3.77	3.61	2.89	2.74
Cash Flow Per Share	9.11	5.89	4.58	5.54	3.77	5.30	4.85	2.56
Tang Book Value Per Share	N.M.	N.M.	N.M.	N.M.	1.66	3.72	1.05	0.98
Dividends Per Share	2.586	2.548	2.402	2.236	2.040	1.810	1.560	1.380
Dividend Payout %	54.67	69.62	71.92	96.38	54.11	50.14	53.98	50.36
Income Statement								
Total Revenue	1,971,959	7,515,426	7,440,181	7,386,626	7,421,768	7,146,079	6,644,252	6,080,788
EBITDA	552,986	1,420,542	1,421,359	1,252,548	1,601,107	1,540,708	1,321,185	1,270,791
Depn & Amortn	74,416	211,592	231,735	244,928	211,532	201,033	210,037	215,763
Income Before Taxes	449,231	1,110,668	1,099,481	901,847	1,306,043	1,251,319	1,015,579	962,845
Income Taxes	98,512	354,131	379,437	388,896	459,131	430,849	354,648	333,883
Net Income	350,203	782,981	720,044	512,951	846,912	820,470	660,931	628,962
Average Shares	211,955	213,742	215,304	220,651	224,837	227,203	228,337	229,919
Balance Sheet								
Current Assets	2,270,496	2,001,910	1,816,778	1,848,598	2,247,047	2,487,334	2,113,485	2,046,558
Total Assets	7,332,798	5,553,726	5,524,333	5,344,371	5,629,516	5,357,488	4,754,839	4,412,199
Current Liabilities	3,705,507	2,076,543	1,909,443	2,217,912	1,935,647	1,408,022	1,471,110	1,173,775
Long-Term Obligations	2,059,934	2,061,023	2,347,455	1,557,091	1,548,963	1,795,142	1,530,967	1,748,500
Total Liabilities	6,360,670	4,638,388	4,738,477	4,346,374	4,174,454	3,752,654	3,718,090	3,563,177
Stockholders' Equity	972,128	915,338	785,856	997,997	1,455,062	1,604,834	1,036,749	849,022
Shares Outstanding	209,342	210,860	212,259	216,777	221,044	223,894	223,786	225,205
Statistical Record								
Return on Assets %	15.91	14.14	13.21	9.35	15.42	16.23	14.38	14.48
Return on Equity %	111.88	92.05	80.51	41.82	55.36	62.12	69.91	71.83
EBITDA Margin %	28.04	18.90	19.10	16.96	21.57	21.56	19.88	20.90
Net Margin %	17.76	10.42	9.68	6.94	11.41	11.48	9.95	10.34
Asset Turnover	1.20	1.36	1.37	1.35	1.35	1.41	1.45	1.40
Current Ratio	0.61	0.96	0.95	0.83	1.16	1.77	1.44	1.74
Debt to Equity	2.12	2.25	2.99	1.56	1.06	1.12	1.48	2.06
Price Range	115.96-96.06	115.96-102.87	113.89-83.32	110.78-83.58	108.07-88.15	100.90-72.22	74.64-59.49	62.00-46.37
P/E Ratio	24.52-20.31	31.68-28.11	34.10-24.95	47.75-36.03	28.67-23.38	27.95-20.01	25.83-20.58	22.63-16.92
Average Yield %	2.40	2.35	2.48	2.36	2.09	2.02	2.30	2.48

Address: 100 Crystal A. Drive, Hershey, PA 17033	Web Site: www.hersheys.com	Auditors: Ernst & Young LLP
Telephone: 717-534-4200	Officers: Michele G. Buck - President, Chief Executive Vice President	Investor Contact: 800-539-0261
Fax: 717-531-6161		Transfer Agents: Computershare, Providence, RI

HESS CORP

Exchange	Symbol	Price	52Wk Range	Yield	P/E
NYS	HES	$66.89 (6/29/2018)	66.89-38.09	1.49	N/A

*7 Year Price Score 63.67   *NYSE Composite Index=100   *12 Month Price Score 125.95

Interim Earnings (Per Share)

Qtr.	Mar	Jun	Sep	Dec
2015	(1.37)	(1.99)	(0.98)	(6.43)
2016	(1.72)	(1.29)	(1.12)	(15.81)
2017	(1.07)	(1.46)	(2.02)	(8.57)
2018	(0.38)	...	...	...

Interim Dividends (Per Share)

Amt	Decl	Ex	Rec	Pay
0.25Q	09/06/2017	09/15/2017	09/18/2017	09/29/2017
0.25Q	12/06/2017	12/15/2017	12/18/2017	12/29/2017
0.25Q	03/07/2018	03/16/2018	03/19/2018	03/29/2018
0.25Q	06/05/2018	06/15/2018	06/18/2018	06/29/2018

Indicated Div: $1.00

Valuation Analysis

Forecast EPS	$-0.48 (06/14/2018)	**Institutional Holding** No of Institutions 834
Market Cap	$20.6 Billion	Shares 342,431,104
Book Value	$10.6 Billion	% Held N/A
Price/Book	1.94	
Price/Sales	3.73	

Business Summary: Production & Extraction (MIC: 9.1.1 SIC: 1311 NAIC: 211111)

Hess is an exploration and production company engaged in exploration, development, production, transportation, purchase and sale of crude oil, natural gas liquids, and natural gas with production operations located primarily in the U.S., Denmark, the Malaysia/Thailand Joint Development Area and Malaysia. Co. conducts exploration activities primarily offshore Guyana, Suriname, Canada and in the Gulf of Mexico. As of Dec 31 2017, Co. had total proved developed and undeveloped reserves of 1.15 billion barrels of oil equivalent, consisted of 830.0 million barrels of crude oil and condensate and natural gas liquids, as well as 1.94 billion cubic feet of natural gas.

Recent Developments: For the quarter ended Mar 31 2018, net loss amounted to US$65.0 million versus a net loss of US$296.0 million in the year-earlier quarter. Revenues were US$1.39 billion, up 10.8% from US$1.25 billion the year before. Direct operating expenses rose 16.3% to US$685.0 million from US$589.0 million in the comparable period the year before. Indirect operating expenses decreased 28.4% to US$697.0 million from US$974.0 million in the equivalent prior-year period.

Prospects: Our evaluation of Hess Corp. as of Jan. 21, 2018 is the result of our systematic analysis on three basic characteristics: earnings strength, relative valuation, and recent stock price movement. The company has generated a negative trend in earnings per share over the past 5 quarters. Because the company lacks sufficient analyst estimate data, we place greater weight on the historical EPS trend as the measure of earnings strength. Based on operating earnings yield, the company is overvalued when compared to all of the companies in our coverage universe. Share price changes over the past year indicates that HES will perform very poorly over the near term.

Financial Data
(US$ in Thousands)

	3 Mos	12/31/2017	12/31/2016	12/31/2015	12/31/2014	12/31/2013	12/31/2012	12/31/2011
Earnings Per Share	(12.43)	(13.12)	(19.92)	(10.78)	7.53	14.82	5.95	5.01
Cash Flow Per Share	2.60	3.01	2.56	6.99	14.70	14.47	16.68	14.79
Tang Book Value Per Share	33.25	33.93	44.73	66.46	71.18	70.24	55.29	47.68
Dividends Per Share	1.000	1.000	1.000	1.000	1.000	0.700	0.400	0.400
Dividend Payout %	...	...	...	...	13.28	4.72	6.72	7.98
Income Statement								
Total Revenue	1,390,000	5,405,000	4,844,000	6,561,000	11,439,000	24,421,000	38,373,000	37,871,000
EBITDA	528,000	(2,570,000)	(272,000)	38,000	5,983,000	7,669,000	7,106,000	5,250,000
Depn & Amortn	417,000	2,883,000	3,244,000	3,955,000	3,224,000	2,770,000	2,949,000	2,406,000
Income Before Taxes	8,000	(5,778,000)	(3,854,000)	(4,258,000)	2,436,000	4,493,000	3,738,000	2,461,000
Income Taxes	73,000	(1,837,000)	2,222,000	(1,299,000)	744,000	525,000	1,675,000	785,000
Net Income	(106,000)	(4,074,000)	(6,132,000)	(3,056,000)	2,317,000	5,052,000	2,025,000	1,703,000
Average Shares	309,500	314,100	309,900	283,600	307,700	340,900	340,300	339,898
Balance Sheet								
Current Assets	5,014,000	6,157,000	4,276,000	4,404,000	6,687,000	8,599,000	8,387,000	8,339,000
Total Assets	22,072,000	23,112,000	28,621,000	34,195,000	38,578,000	42,754,000	43,441,000	39,136,000
Current Liabilities	1,904,000	2,435,000	2,251,000	2,628,000	4,851,000	6,558,000	8,382,000	8,100,000
Long-Term Obligations	6,372,000	6,397,000	6,694,000	6,544,000	5,919,000	5,420,000	7,324,000	6,005,000
Total Liabilities	11,467,000	12,061,000	14,087,000	14,809,000	16,373,000	18,034,000	22,351,000	20,620,000
Stockholders' Equity	10,605,000	11,051,000	14,534,000	19,386,000	22,205,000	24,720,000	21,090,000	18,516,000
Shares Outstanding	308,055	315,053	316,523	286,045	285,834	325,314	341,527	339,976
Statistical Record								
Return on Assets %	N.M.	N.M.	N.M.	N.M.	5.70	11.72	4.89	4.57
Return on Equity %	N.M.	N.M.	N.M.	N.M.	9.88	22.06	10.20	9.67
EBITDA Margin %	37.99	N.M.	N.M.	0.58	52.30	31.40	18.52	13.86
Net Margin %	N.M.	N.M.	N.M.	N.M.	20.26	20.69	5.28	4.50
Asset Turnover	0.22	0.21	0.15	0.18	0.28	0.57	0.93	1.02
Current Ratio	2.63	2.53	1.90	1.68	1.38	1.31	1.00	1.03
Debt to Equity	0.60	0.58	0.46	0.34	0.27	0.22	0.35	0.32
Price Range	54.72-38.09	62.82-38.09	65.14-34.38	78.09-47.44	101.10-65.45	84.06-52.96	67.00-39.95	87.03-49.46
P/E Ratio	...	...	...	...	13.43-8.69	5.67-3.57	11.26-6.71	17.37-9.87
Average Yield %	2.18	2.14	1.90	1.56	1.15	0.97	0.76	0.57

Address: 1185 Avenue of the Americas, New York, NY 10036 **Telephone:** 212-997-8500	**Web Site:** www.hess.com **Officers:** James H. Quigley - Chairman John B. Hess - Chairman, Chief Executive Officer	**Auditors:** Ernst & Young LLP **Investor Contact:** 212-536-8940 **Transfer Agents:** Computershare, Providence, RI

HEWLETT PACKARD ENTERPRISE CO

Exchange	Symbol	Price	52Wk Range	Yield	P/E
NYS	HPE	$14.61 (6/29/2018)	19.41-13.06	3.08	N/A

*7 Year Price Score N/A *NYSE Composite Index=100 *12 Month Price Score 102.19

Interim Earnings (Per Share)

Qtr.	Jan	Apr	Jul	Oct
2014-15	0.30	0.16	0.13	0.75
2015-16	0.15	0.18	1.32	0.18
2016-17	0.16	(0.37)	0.10	0.32
2017-18	0.89	0.49	...	...

Interim Dividends (Per Share)

Amt	Decl	Ex	Rec	Pay
0.00Q	08/04/2017	09/01/2017	08/21/2017	09/01/2017
0.075Q	11/09/2017	12/12/2017	12/13/2017	01/03/2018
0.075Q	01/18/2018	03/13/2018	03/14/2018	04/04/2018
0.113Q	04/05/2018	06/12/2018	06/13/2018	07/04/2018

Indicated Div: $0.45 (Div. Reinv. Plan)

Valuation Analysis

		Institutional Holding	
Forecast EPS	$1.46	No of Institutions	896
	(06/07/2018)		
Market Cap	$22.3 Billion	Shares	1,364,453,760
Book Value	$23.9 Billion		
Price/Book	0.93	% Held	
Price/Sales	N/A		N/A

Business Summary: IT Services (MIC: 6.3.1 SIC: 7379 NAIC: 541519)

Hewlett Packard Enterprise is a technology company. Co. organizes its business into the following five segments: Enterprise Group, which provides customers with technology infrastructure they need to optimize IT; Software, which allows customers to automate IT operations to accelerate and secure business processes; Enterprise Services, which brings Co.'s solutions together through its consulting and support personnel; Financial Services, which enables IT consumption models, financial architectures and customized investment solutions for customers; and Corporate Investments, which includes Hewlett Packard Labs and certain cloud-related business incubation projects, among others.

Recent Developments: For the quarter ended Apr 30 2018, income from continuing operations was US$850.0 million compared with a loss of US$478.0 million in the year-earlier quarter. Net income amounted to US$778.0 million versus a net loss of US$612.0 million in the year-earlier quarter. Revenues were US$7.47 billion, up 9.7% from US$6.81 billion the year before. Operating income was US$397.0 million versus US$195.0 million in the prior-year quarter, an increase of 103.6%. Direct operating expenses rose 8.3% to US$5.13 billion from US$4.73 billion in the comparable period the year before. Indirect operating expenses increased 3.5% to US$1.95 billion from US$1.88 billion in the equivalent prior-year period.

Prospects: Our evaluation of Hewlett Packard Enterprise Co. as of Jan. 21, 2018 is the result of our systematic analysis on three basic characteristics: earnings strength, relative valuation, and recent stock price movement. The company has generated a negative trend in earnings per share over the past 5 quarters and while recent estimates for the company have remained steady, HPE has posted better than expected results. Based on operating earnings yield, the company is undervalued when compared to all of the companies in our coverage universe. Share price changes over the past year indicates that HPE will perform poorly over the near term.

Financial Data

(US$ in Millions)	6 Mos	3 Mos	10/31/2017	10/31/2016	10/31/2015	10/31/2014	10/31/2013	10/31/2012
Earnings Per Share	1.80	0.94	0.21	1.82	1.34	...	...	...
Cash Flow Per Share	...	1.57	0.54	2.88	2.03	...	...	...
Tang Book Value Per Share	3.59	3.49	3.08	3.71	2.49	...	...	...
Dividends Per Share	0.280	0.270	0.260	0.220	...	...	...	...
Dividend Payout %	15.56	28.72	123.81	12.09	...	...	...	...
Income Statement								
Total Revenue	15,142	7,674	28,871	50,123	52,107	55,123	57,371	61,042
EBITDA	(398)	(512)	3,408	8,471	5,715	6,718	7,692	(8,981)
Depn & Amortn	150	78	2,521	3,755	3,952	4,106	4,428	4,841
Income Before Taxes	(785)	(679)	295	4,155	1,470	2,244	2,871	(14,314)
Income Taxes	(3,105)	(2,139)	(164)	918	(991)	596	820	447
Net Income	2,214	1,436	344	3,161	2,461	1,648	2,051	(14,761)
Average Shares	1,582	1,619	1,674	1,739	1,834	...	...	...
Balance Sheet								
Current Assets	19,792	20,499	21,444	28,917	31,173	22,031	24,379	...
Total Assets	59,876	61,619	61,406	79,679	81,270	65,071	68,775	...
Current Liabilities	19,084	19,343	18,924	22,531	22,151	19,760	20,912	...
Long-Term Obligations	9,970	10,040	10,182	12,608	15,103	485	617	...
Total Liabilities	35,944	37,668	37,940	48,231	47,735	28,295	30,787	...
Stockholders' Equity	23,932	23,951	23,466	31,448	33,535	36,776	37,988	...
Shares Outstanding	1,527	1,567	1,595	1,666	1,742	...	...	...
Statistical Record								
Return on Assets %	...	2.19	0.49	3.92	...	2.46	...	...
Return on Equity %	...	5.46	1.25	9.70	...	4.41	...	...
EBITDA Margin %	N.M.	N.M.	11.80	16.90	10.97	12.19	13.41	N.M.
Net Margin %	14.62	18.71	1.19	6.31	4.72	2.99	3.57	N.M.
Asset Turnover	...	0.42	0.41	0.62	...	0.82	...	...
Current Ratio	1.04	1.06	1.13	1.28	1.41	1.11	1.17	...
Debt to Equity	0.42	0.42	0.43	0.40	0.45	0.01	0.02	...
Price Range	19.41-13.06	16.97-13.06	15.14-12.95	13.81-7.17	10.10-8.75	...	...	...
P/E Ratio	10.78-7.26	18.05-13.89	72.10-61.68	7.59-3.94	7.54-6.53	...	...	...
Average Yield %	1.86	1.90	1.86	2.11	...	...	...	...

Address: 3000 Hanover Street, Palo Alto, CA 94304 **Telephone:** 650-687-5817	**Web Site:** www.hpe.com **Officers:** Patricia F. Russo - Chairman Antonio F. Neri - President, Chief Executive Officer, Executive Vice President, Division Officer	**Auditors:** Ernst & Young LLP **Transfer Agents:** Wells Fargo Shareowner Services

HEXCEL CORP.

Exchange	Symbol	Price	52Wk Range	Yield	P/E
NYS	HXL	$66.38 (6/29/2018)	73.26-51.04	0.75	21.62

*7 Year Price Score 119.16 *NYSE Composite Index=100 *12 Month Price Score 109.97

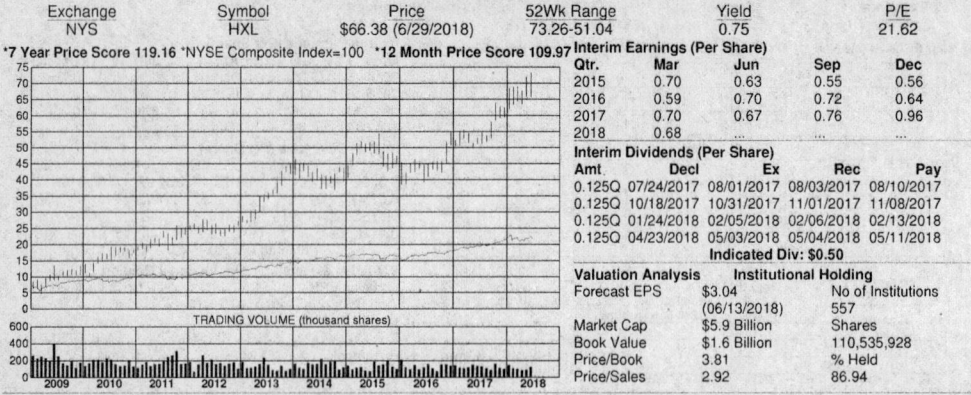

Interim Earnings (Per Share)

Qtr.	Mar	Jun	Sep	Dec
2015	0.70	0.63	0.55	0.56
2016	0.59	0.70	0.72	0.64
2017	0.70	0.67	0.76	0.96
2018	0.68	...	...	...

Interim Dividends (Per Share)

Amt	Decl	Ex	Rec	Pay
0.125Q	07/24/2017	08/01/2017	08/03/2017	08/10/2017
0.125Q	10/18/2017	10/31/2017	11/01/2017	11/08/2017
0.125Q	01/24/2018	02/05/2018	02/06/2018	02/13/2018
0.125Q	04/23/2018	05/03/2018	05/04/2018	05/11/2018

Indicated Div: $0.50

Valuation Analysis | **Institutional Holding**

Forecast EPS	$3.04 (06/13/2018)	No of Institutions 557
Market Cap	$5.9 Billion	Shares
Book Value	$1.6 Billion	110,535,928
Price/Book	3.81	% Held
Price/Sales	2.92	86.94

Business Summary: Plastics (MIC: 8.4.2 SIC: 2821 NAIC: 325211)

Hexcel is a composites company with two reportable segments. The Composite Materials segment manufactures and markets carbon fibers, fabrics and specialty reinforcements, prepregs and other fiber-reinforced matrix materials, structural adhesives, honeycomb, molding compounds, tooling materials, polyurethane systems and laminates that are incorporated into several applications, including military and commercial aircraft, wind turbine blades, recreational products, transport (cars, boats, trains) and other industrial applications. The Engineered Products segment manufactures and markets composite structures and precision machined honeycomb parts primarily for use in the aerospace industry.

Recent Developments: For the quarter ended Mar 31 2018, net income decreased 4.6% to US$61.6 million from US$64.6 million in the year-earlier quarter. Revenues were US$540.1 million, up 12.8% from US$478.8 million the year before. Operating income was US$82.4 million versus US$78.6 million in the prior-year quarter, an increase of 4.8%. Direct operating expenses rose 15.3% to US$397.5 million from US$344.7 million in the comparable period the year before. Indirect operating expenses increased 8.5% to US$60.2 million from US$55.5 million in the equivalent prior-year period.

Prospects: Our evaluation of Hexcel Corp. as of Jan. 21, 2018 is the result of our systematic analysis on three basic characteristics: earnings strength, relative valuation, and recent stock price movement. The company has enjoyed a very positive trend in earnings per share over the past 5 quarters and while recent estimates for the company have been mixed, HXL has posted better than expected results. Based on operating earnings yield, the company is about fairly valued when compared to all of the companies in our coverage universe. Share price changes over the past year indicates that HXL will perform in line with the market over the near term.

Financial Data

(US$ in Thousands)	3 Mos	12/31/2017	12/31/2016	12/31/2015	12/31/2014	12/31/2013	12/31/2012	12/31/2011
Earnings Per Share	3.07	3.09	2.65	2.44	2.12	1.84	1.61	1.35
Cash Flow Per Share	4.86	4.73	4.31	3.14	3.29	2.73	2.31	1.73
Tang Book Value Per Share	15.76	15.03	12.83	11.99	11.41	11.12	9.37	7.54
Dividends Per Share	0.485	0.470	0.430	0.400	...	...	...	...
Dividend Payout %	15.80	15.21	16.23	16.39				
Income Statement								
Total Revenue	540,100	1,973,300	2,004,300	1,861,200	1,855,500	1,678,200	1,578,200	1,392,400
EBITDA	82,700	454,100	453,000	408,800	376,500	329,200	304,900	242,400
Depn & Amortn	300	103,500	93,300	76,400	71,200	59,300	57,200	55,300
Income Before Taxes	74,400	323,200	337,600	318,200	297,300	262,600	237,700	175,500
Income Taxes	14,100	42,500	90,300	83,000	89,300	76,000	74,100	41,600
Net Income	61,600	284,000	249,800	237,200	209,400	187,900	164,300	135,500
Average Shares	91,200	91,900	94,200	97,200	98,700	102,100	102,000	100,700
Balance Sheet								
Current Assets	715,900	656,700	607,000	633,800	681,700	656,400	575,700	524,300
Total Assets	2,884,700	2,780,900	2,400,600	2,187,400	2,036,400	1,836,100	1,603,100	1,376,100
Current Liabilities	270,800	262,100	271,900	292,600	310,600	268,700	235,300	247,500
Long-Term Obligations	835,600	805,600	684,400	576,500	415,000	292,000	240,000	238,300
Total Liabilities	1,322,200	1,285,800	1,155,700	1,007,800	886,500	675,700	609,000	573,900
Stockholders' Equity	1,562,500	1,495,100	1,244,900	1,179,600	1,149,900	1,160,400	994,100	802,200
Shares Outstanding	89,600	89,600	91,400	93,500	95,500	98,900	99,900	98,800
Statistical Record								
Return on Assets %	10.29	10.96	10.86	11.23	10.81	10.93	11.00	10.29
Return on Equity %	19.89	20.73	20.55	20.36	18.13	17.44	18.24	18.54
EBITDA Margin %	15.31	23.01	22.60	21.96	20.29	19.62	19.32	17.41
Net Margin %	11.41	14.39	12.46	12.74	11.29	11.20	10.41	9.73
Asset Turnover	0.75	0.76	0.87	0.88	0.96	0.98	1.06	1.06
Current Ratio	2.64	2.51	2.23	2.17	2.19	2.44	2.45	2.12
Debt to Equity	0.53	0.54	0.55	0.49	0.36	0.25	0.24	0.30
Price Range	69.08-49.76	63.76-49.76	54.97-38.38	54.48-40.38	46.40-36.92	44.69-26.50	27.80-22.53	25.84-17.58
P/E Ratio	22.50-16.21	20.63-16.10	20.74-14.48	22.33-16.55	21.89-17.42	24.29-14.40	17.27-13.99	19.14-13.02
Average Yield %	0.84	0.84	0.86	0.97	0.83	...	...	...

Address: Two Stamford Plaza, 281 Tresser Boulevard, Stamford, CT 06901-3238
Telephone: 203-969-0666

Web Site: www.hexcel.com
Officers: Patrick Winterlich - Executive Vice President, Chief Financial Officer Nick L. Stanage - Chairman, President, Chief Executive Officer, Chief Operating Officer

Auditors: Ernst & Young LLP
Investor Contact: 203-969-0666
Transfer Agents: American Stock Transfer & Trust Company, New York, NY

HIGHWOODS PROPERTIES, INC.

Exchange	Symbol	Price	52Wk Range	Yield	P/E
NYS	HIW	$50.73 (6/29/2018)	52.88-41.50	3.65	28.50

*7 Year Price Score 94.14 *NYSE Composite Index=100 *12 Month Price Score 96.86

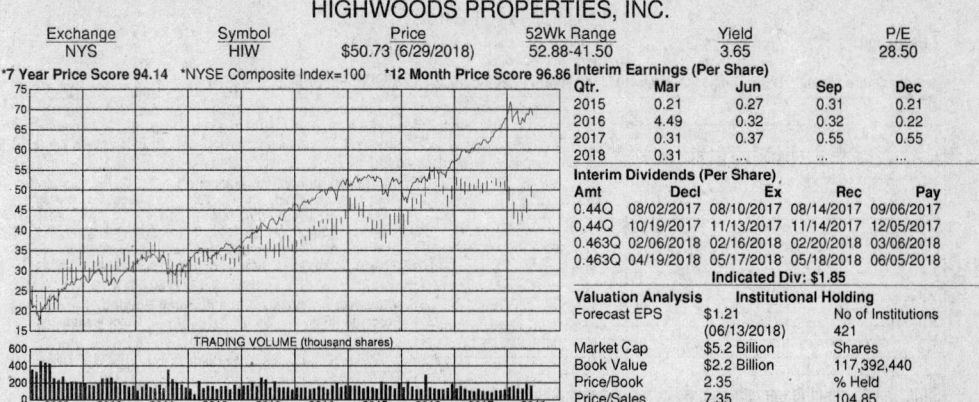

Interim Earnings (Per Share)

Qtr.	Mar	Jun	Sep	Dec
2015	0.21	0.27	0.31	0.21
2016	4.49	0.32	0.32	0.22
2017	0.31	0.37	0.55	0.55
2018	0.31	...	...	...

Interim Dividends (Per Share)

Amt	Decl	Ex	Rec	Pay
0.44Q	08/02/2017	08/10/2017	08/14/2017	09/06/2017
0.44Q	10/19/2017	11/13/2017	11/14/2017	12/05/2017
0.463Q	02/06/2018	02/16/2018	02/20/2018	03/06/2018
0.463Q	04/19/2018	05/17/2018	05/18/2018	06/05/2018

Indicated Div: $1.85

Valuation Analysis

		Institutional Holding	
Forecast EPS	$1.21	No of Institutions	
	(06/13/2018)	421	
Market Cap	$5.2 Billion	Shares	
Book Value	$2.2 Billion	117,392,440	
Price/Book	2.35	% Held	
Price/Sales	7.35	104.85	

Business Summary: REITs (MIC: 5.3.1 SIC: 6798 NAIC: 525930)

Highwoods Properties is an integrated office real estate investment trust that that owns, develops, acquires, leases and manages properties primarily in the business districts of Atlanta, Greensboro, Memphis, Nashville, Orlando, Pittsburgh, Raleigh, Richmond and Tampa. Co.'s primary business is the operation, acquisition and development of office properties. Co. provides a line of real estate services to its customers. Co. provides its customers with services such as build-to-suit construction and space modification, including tenant improvements and expansions. Co. conducts its activities through Highwoods Realty Limited Partnership.

Recent Developments: For the quarter ended Mar 31 2018, net income increased 2.3% to US$34.2 million from US$33.5 million in the year-earlier quarter. Revenues were US$180.4 million, up 6.5% from US$169.4 million the year before.

Prospects: Our evaluation of Highwoods Properties Inc. as of Jan. 21, 2018 is the result of our systematic analysis on three basic characteristics: earnings strength, relative valuation, and recent stock price movement. The company has enjoyed a very positive trend in earnings per share over the past 5 quarters. Because the company lacks sufficient analyst estimate data, we place greater weight on the historical EPS trend as the measure of earnings strength. Based on operating earnings yield, the company is about fairly valued when compared to all of the companies in our coverage universe. Share price changes over the past year indicates that HIW will perform well over the near term.

Financial Data
(US$ in Thousands)

	3 Mos	12/31/2017	12/31/2016	12/31/2015	12/31/2014	12/31/2013	12/31/2012	12/31/2011
Earnings Per Share	1.78	1.78	5.30	1.00	1.19	1.44	1.02	0.54
Cash Flow Per Share	3.50	3.43	3.10	3.06	2.94	3.01	2.54	2.70
Tang Book Value Per Share	21.34	21.22	20.73	16.36	16.09	16.11	14.08	13.12
Dividends Per Share	1.783	1.760	2.500	1.700	1.700	1.700	1.700	1.700
Dividend Payout %	100.14	98.88	47.17	170.00	142.86	118.06	166.67	314.81
Income Statement								
Total Revenue	180,438	702,737	665,634	604,671	608,468	556,810	516,102	482,852
EBITDA	52,048	482,743	415,770	387,910	397,498	336,792	299,864	276,021
Depn & Amortn	388	231,688	224,707	223,384	203,324	190,227	165,420	147,786
Income Before Taxes	33,724	184,259	116,753	80,443	113,761	60,459	45,683	39,623
Net Income	33,072	185,365	524,290	97,078	110,964	125,457	79,595	45,125
Average Shares	106,165	105,594	101,398	97,406	93,800	88,836	79,678	76,189
Balance Sheet								
Current Assets	303,681	312,861	268,832	201,274	214,021	176,797	173,550	173,957
Total Assets	4,695,455	4,623,791	4,561,050	4,493,432	4,004,909	3,807,101	3,350,428	3,180,992
Current Liabilities	206,258	228,215	313,885	248,107	237,633	218,962	172,146	148,821
Long-Term Obligations	2,112,584	2,014,333	1,948,047	2,499,614	2,094,908	1,982,963	1,888,520	1,934,657
Total Liabilities	2,459,419	2,403,973	2,424,695	2,892,125	2,480,698	2,329,801	2,190,288	2,198,779
Stockholders' Equity	2,236,036	2,219,818	2,136,355	1,601,307	1,524,211	1,477,300	1,160,140	982,213
Shares Outstanding	103,421	103,266	101,665	96,091	92,907	89,920	80,311	72,647
Statistical Record								
Return on Assets %	4.03	4.04	11.55	2.28	2.84	3.51	2.43	1.49
Return on Equity %	8.50	8.51	27.98	6.21	7.39	9.51	7.41	4.37
EBITDA Margin %	28.85	68.69	62.46	64.15	65.33	60.49	58.10	57.16
Net Margin %	18.33	26.38	78.77	16.05	18.24	22.53	15.42	9.35
Asset Turnover	0.15	0.15	0.15	0.14	0.16	0.16	0.16	0.16
Current Ratio	1.47	1.37	0.86	0.81	0.90	0.81	1.01	1.17
Debt to Equity	0.94	0.91	0.91	1.56	1.37	1.34	1.63	1.97
Price Range	52.88-41.50	53.19-48.87	55.74-39.01	48.14-36.82	45.13-35.82	41.07-33.00	35.48-29.71	36.92-26.51
P/E Ratio	29.71-23.31	29.88-27.46	10.52-7.36	48.14-36.82	37.92-30.10	28.52-22.92	34.78-29.13	68.37-49.09
Average Yield %	3.58	3.44	5.15	3.96	4.21	4.64	5.17	5.30

Address: 3100 Smoketree Court, Suite 600, Raleigh, NC 27604	Web Site: www.highwoods.com	Auditors: DELOITTE & TOUCHE LLP
Telephone: 919-872-4924	Officers: O. Temple Sloan - Chairman Edward J. Fritsch - President, Chief Executive Officer	Investor Contact: 919-431-1529
Fax: 919-431-1439		Transfer Agents: Wells Fargo Shareholder Services, Mendota Heights, MN

HILL-ROM HOLDINGS, INC.

Exchange	Symbol	Price	52Wk Range	Yield	P/E
NYS	HRC	$87.34 (6/29/2018)	94.34-72.79	0.92	30.54

*7 Year Price Score 134.92 *NYSE Composite Index=100 *12 Month Price Score 107.12

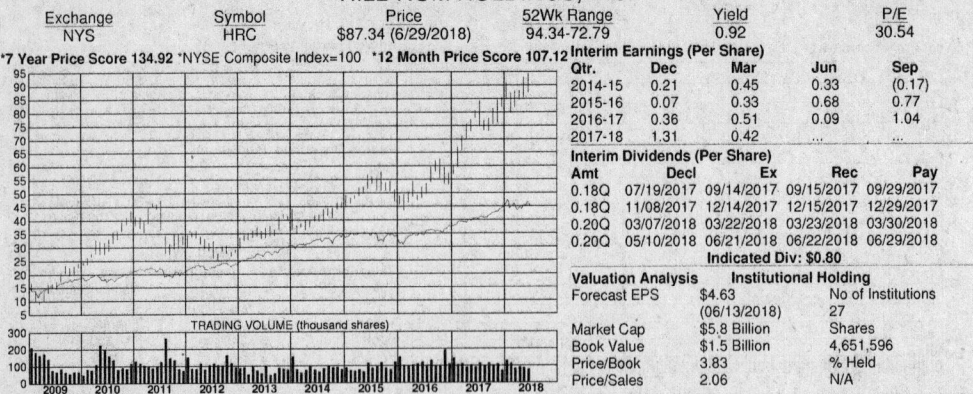

Interim Earnings (Per Share)

Qtr.	Dec	Mar	Jun	Sep
2014-15	0.21	0.45	0.33	(0.17)
2015-16	0.07	0.33	0.68	0.77
2016-17	0.36	0.51	0.09	1.04
2017-18	1.31	0.42	...	...

Interim Dividends (Per Share)

Amt	Decl	Ex	Rec	Pay
0.18Q	07/19/2017	09/14/2017	09/15/2017	09/29/2017
0.18Q	11/08/2017	12/14/2017	12/15/2017	12/29/2017
0.20Q	03/07/2018	03/22/2018	03/23/2018	03/30/2018
0.20Q	05/10/2018	06/21/2018	06/22/2018	06/29/2018

Indicated Div: $0.80

Valuation Analysis

Forecast EPS	$4.63
	(06/13/2018)
Market Cap	$5.8 Billion
Book Value	$1.5 Billion
Price/Book	3.83
Price/Sales	2.06

Institutional Holding

No of Institutions	27
Shares	4,651,596
% Held	N/A

Business Summary: Medical Instruments & Equipment (MIC: 4.3.1 SIC: 3841 NAIC: 339112)

Hill-Rom Holdings is a medical technology company. Co.'s products and services include: Patient Support Systems, which include a variety of specialty frames and surfaces, such as Medical Surgical beds, Intensive Care Unit beds, and Bariatric patient beds, patient mobility solutions, non-invasive therapeutic products and surfaces, and Co.'s communications technologies and software solutions; Front Line Care, which include its patient monitoring and diagnostics products from its Welch Allyn Holdings, Inc. and Mortara Instruments, Inc. and its respiratory health products; and Surgical Solutions, which include surgical tables, lights, and pendants utilized within the operating room setting.

Recent Developments: For the quarter ended Mar 31 2018, net income decreased 16.2% to US$28.5 million from US$34.0 million in the year-earlier quarter. Revenues were US$710.5 million, up 4.7% from US$678.9 million the year before. Operating income was US$46.1 million versus US$63.6 million in the prior-year quarter, a decrease of 27.5%. Direct operating expenses rose 1.6% to US$360.1 million from US$354.5 million in the comparable period the year before. Indirect operating expenses increased 16.7% from US$260.8 million in the equivalent prior-year period.

Prospects: Our evaluation of Hil-Rom Holdings, Inc. as of Jan. 21, 2018 is the result of our systematic analysis on three basic characteristics: earnings strength, relative valuation, and recent stock price movement. The company has generated a negative trend in earnings per share over the past 5 quarters and while recent estimates for the company have been raised by analysts, HRC has posted better than expected results. Based on operating earnings yield, the company is about fairly valued when compared to all of the companies in our coverage universe. Share price changes over the past year indicates that HRC will perform well over the near term.

Financial Data
(US$ in Thousands)

	6 Mos	3 Mos	09/30/2017	09/30/2016	09/30/2015	09/30/2014	09/30/2013	09/30/2012
Earnings Per Share	2.86	2.95	1.99	1.86	0.82	1.04	1.74	1.94
Cash Flow Per Share	4.69	5.06	4.74	4.29	3.73	3.65	4.39	4.20
Tang Book Value Per Share	N.M.	N.M.	N.M.	N.M.	N.M.	2.53	4.50	3.07
Dividends Per Share	0.740	0.720	0.710	0.670	0.632	0.595	0.525	0.487
Dividend Payout %	25.87	24.41	35.68	36.02	77.13	57.21	30.17	25.13
Income Statement								
Total Revenue	1,380,200	669,700	2,743,700	2,655,200	1,988,200	1,686,100	1,716,200	1,634,500
EBITDA	202,100	105,300	482,700	437,700	201,700	231,400	224,700	243,900
Depn & Amortn	102,500	51,400	210,800	209,000	118,200	106,400	71,200	73,900
Income Before Taxes	52,300	30,800	183,000	138,300	65,100	115,200	144,000	163,500
Income Taxes	(64,500)	(57,500)	50,700	15,500	18,300	54,600	39,000	42,700
Net Income	116,800	88,300	133,600	124,100	47,700	60,600	105,000	120,800
Average Shares	67,597	67,432	67,225	66,596	58,536	58,523	60,250	62,120
Balance Sheet								
Current Assets	1,201,000	1,118,300	1,166,200	1,082,100	1,141,000	779,300	688,000	681,800
Total Assets	4,504,700	4,460,500	4,528,700	4,262,400	4,457,600	1,752,100	1,586,800	1,627,600
Current Liabilities	650,500	637,300	658,700	662,300	578,800	442,300	345,400	378,100
Long-Term Obligations	2,025,600	2,036,300	2,120,400	1,938,400	2,175,200	364,900	225,800	237,500
Total Liabilities	2,994,300	3,003,400	3,170,500	3,035,200	3,310,700	945,600	728,100	815,000
Stockholders' Equity	1,510,400	1,457,100	1,358,200	1,227,200	1,146,900	806,500	858,700	812,600
Shares Outstanding	66,230	66,139	65,813	65,705	65,165	57,439	58,523	60,796
Statistical Record								
Return on Assets %	4.28	4.60	3.04	2.84	1.54	3.63	6.53	8.23
Return on Equity %	13.95	14.98	10.33	10.43	4.88	7.28	12.57	15.50
EBITDA Margin %	14.64	15.72	17.59	16.48	10.14	13.72	13.09	14.92
Net Margin %	8.46	13.19	4.87	4.67	2.40	3.59	6.12	7.39
Asset Turnover	0.63	0.65	0.62	0.61	0.64	1.01	1.07	1.11
Current Ratio	1.85	1.75	1.77	1.63	1.97	1.76	1.99	1.80
Debt to Equity	1.34	1.40	1.56	1.58	1.90	0.45	0.26	0.29
Price Range	91.01-69.88	85.36-56.76	84.17-52.92	61.98-43.29	57.79-40.58	44.39-35.13	37.62-26.40	35.96-25.30
P/E Ratio	31.82-24.43	28.94-19.24	42.30-26.59	33.32-23.27	70.48-49.49	42.68-33.78	21.62-15.17	18.54-13.04
Average Yield %	0.93	0.97	1.04	1.31	1.28	1.49	1.59	1.55

Address: 130 East Randolph Street, Suite 1000, Chicago, IL 60601
Telephone: 312-819-7200
Fax: 812-934-8189

Web Site: www.Hill-Rom.com
Officers: William G. (Bill) Dempsey - Executive Chairman John J. Greisch - President, Chief Executive Officer

Auditors: PricewaterhouseCoopers LLP
Investor Contact: 812-931-2199
Transfer Agents: Computershare Trust Company, N.A., Providence, RI

HILTON GRAND VACATIONS INC

Exchange	Symbol	Price	52Wk Range	Yield	P/E
NYS	HGV	$34.70 (6/29/2018)	47.30-34.05	N/A	11.27

*7 Year Price Score N/A ***NYSE Composite Index=100** ***12 Month Price Score 95.76**

TRADING VOLUME (thousand shares)

Interim Earnings (Per Share)

Qtr.	Mar	Jun	Sep	Dec
2016	0.48	0.48	0.35	0.39
2017	0.51	0.51	0.43	1.84
2018	0.30	...	...	...

Interim Dividends (Per Share)

No Dividends Paid

Valuation Analysis		Institutional Holding	
Forecast EPS	$3.04	No of Institutions	
	(06/14/2018)	306	
Market Cap	$3.4 Billion	Shares	
Book Value	$400.0 Million	119,467,112	
Price/Book	8.40	% Held	
Price/Sales	2.00	N/A	

Business Summary: Hotels, Restaurants & Travel (MIC: 2.2.1 SIC: 7011 NAIC: 721110)

Hilton Grand Vacations is a timeshare company engaged in developing, marketing, selling and managing timeshare resorts primarily under the Hilton Grand Vacations brand. Co.'s operations primarily consist of: selling vacation ownership intervals for Co. and third parties; operating its resorts; financing and servicing loans provided to consumers for their timeshare purchases; and managing its points-based Hilton Grand Vacations Club exchange program. As of Dec 31 2017, Co. had 48 timeshare properties, comprised of 8,102 units, located in the U.S. and Europe and feature condominium-style accommodations.

Recent Developments: For the quarter ended Mar 31 2018, net income decreased 40.0% to US$30.0 million from US$50.0 million in the year-earlier quarter. Revenues were US$367.0 million, down 8.0% from US$399.0 million the year before. Direct operating expenses declined 42.4% to US$19.0 million from US$33.0 million in the comparable period the year before. Indirect operating expenses increased 6.4% to US$301.0 million from US$283.0 million in the equivalent prior-year period.

Prospects: Our evaluation of Hilton Grand Vacations Inc. as of Jan. 21, 2018 is the result of our systematic analysis on three basic characteristics: earnings strength, relative valuation, and recent stock price movement. The company has managed to produce a neutral trend in earnings per share over the past 5 quarters. However, while recent estimates for the company have been mixed, HGV has posted results that fell short of analysts expectations. Based on operating earnings yield, the company is undervalued when compared to all of the companies in our coverage universe. Share price changes over the past year indicates that HGV will perform very well over the near term.

Financial Data
(US$ in Millions)

	3 Mos	12/31/2017	12/31/2016	12/31/2015	12/31/2014	12/31/2013
Earnings Per Share	3.08	3.28	1.70	...	...	...
Cash Flow Per Share	2.48	3.60	1.59	...	...	...
Tang Book Value Per Share	3.38	4.50	0.98	...	...	...
Income Statement						
Total Revenue	367	1,711	1,583	1,475	1,317	1,224
EBITDA	47	354	334	331	324	274
Depn & Amortn	1	17	12	10	8	8
Income Before Taxes	39	310	293	292	280	218
Income Taxes	10	(16)	125	118	113	90
Net Income	30	327	168	174	167	128
Average Shares	99	99	99	...	...	...
Balance Sheet						
Current Assets	1,909	1,989	1,812	1,556	1,445	...
Total Assets	2,365	2,384	2,180	1,724	1,621	...
Current Liabilities	388	443	334	304	278	...
Long-Term Obligations	1,023	1,065	1,184	1,136	1,344	...
Total Liabilities	1,965	1,866	2,013	1,830	1,994	...
Stockholders' Equity	400	518	167	(106)	(373)	...
Shares Outstanding	96	99	98	...	...	...
Statistical Record						
Return on Assets %	13.14	14.33	8.58	10.40	...	...
Return on Equity %	98.08	95.47	549.31	...	...	...
EBITDA Margin %	12.81	20.69	21.10	22.44	24.60	22.39
Net Margin %	8.17	19.11	10.61	11.80	12.68	10.46
Asset Turnover	0.72	0.75	0.81	0.88	...	...
Current Ratio	4.92	4.49	5.43	5.12	5.20	...
Debt to Equity	2.56	2.06	7.09	...	...	...
Price Range	47.30-28.66	42.71-24.99	...	...	...	...
P/E Ratio	15.36-9.31	13.02-7.62	...	...	...	...

Address: 6355 MetroWest Boulevard, Suite 180, Orlando, FL 32835 **Telephone:** 407-613-3100	**Web Site:** www.hiltongrandvacations.com **Officers:** Leonard A. Potter - Chairman Mark D. Wang - President, Chief Executive Officer	**Auditors:** Ernst & Young LLP **Transfer Agents:** Wells Fargo Bank

HNI CORP

Exchange	Symbol	Price	52Wk Range	Yield	P/E
NYS	HNI	$37.20 (6/29/2018)	42.86-32.99	3.17	18.88

*7 Year Price Score 78.97   *NYSE Composite Index=100   *12 Month Price Score 98.46

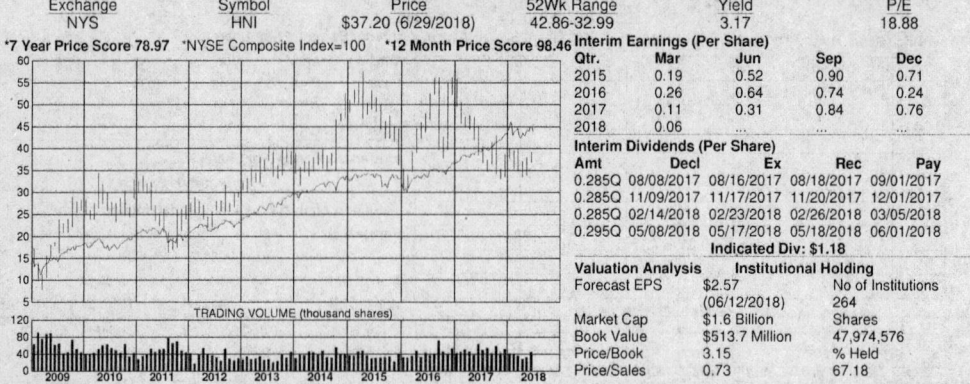

Interim Earnings (Per Share)

Qtr.	Mar	Jun	Sep	Dec
2015	0.19	0.52	0.90	0.71
2016	0.26	0.64	0.74	0.24
2017	0.11	0.31	0.84	0.76
2018	0.06	...	...	...

Interim Dividends (Per Share)

Amt	Decl	Ex	Rec	Pay
0.285Q	08/08/2017	08/16/2017	08/18/2017	09/01/2017
0.285Q	11/09/2017	11/17/2017	11/20/2017	12/01/2017
0.285Q	02/14/2018	02/23/2018	02/26/2018	03/05/2018
0.295Q	05/08/2018	05/17/2018	05/18/2018	06/01/2018

Indicated Div: $1.18

Valuation Analysis   Institutional Holding

Forecast EPS	$2.57	No of Institutions
	(06/12/2018)	264
Market Cap	$1.6 Billion	Shares
Book Value	$513.7 Million	47,974,576
Price/Book	3.15	% Held
Price/Sales	0.73	67.18

Business Summary: Office Equipment & Furniture (MIC: 7.5.1 SIC: 2522 NAIC: 337214)

HNI is a provider of office furniture and hearth products. Co. designs, manufactures and markets a range of office furniture systems and seating across a range of price points. Co.'s office furniture portfolio includes panel-based and freestanding furniture systems and complementary products such as seating, storage, tables and relocatable architectural walls. In addition, Co. manufactures and markets prefabricated fireplaces, hearth stoves and related products. Co.'s line of hearth products includes a range of gas, wood and pellet burning fireplaces, inserts, stoves, facings and accessories. Co.'s products are marketed predominantly in the U.S. and Canada.

Recent Developments: For the quarter ended Mar 31 2018, net income decreased 48.5% to US$2.5 million from US$4.8 million in the year-earlier quarter. Revenues were US$505.1 million, up 5.7% from US$477.7 million the year before. Operating income was US$3.7 million versus US$7.9 million in the prior-year quarter, a decrease of 53.5%. Direct operating expenses rose 8.0% to US$328.2 million from US$303.9 million in the comparable period the year before. Indirect operating expenses increased 4.5% to US$173.2 million from US$165.8 million in the equivalent prior-year period.

Prospects: Our evaluation of HNI Corp. as of Jan. 21, 2018 is the result of our systematic analysis on three basic characteristics: earnings strength, relative valuation, and recent stock price movement. The company has generated a negative trend in earnings per share over the past 5 quarters and while recent estimates for the company have been mixed, HNI has posted better than expected results. Based on operating earnings yield, the company is undervalued when compared to all of the companies in our coverage universe. Share price changes over the past year indicates that HNI will perform very poorly over the near term.

Financial Data

(US$ in Thousands)	3 Mos	12/30/2017	12/31/2016	01/02/2016	01/03/2015	12/28/2013	12/29/2012	12/31/2011
Earnings Per Share	1.97	2.00	1.88	2.32	1.35	1.39	1.07	1.01
Cash Flow Per Share	3.10	3.05	5.04	3.93	3.69	3.66	3.21	3.01
Tang Book Value Per Share	0.62	0.53	4.76	4.51	3.06	3.33	2.94	3.31
Dividends Per Share	1.140	1.130	1.090	1.045	0.990	0.960	0.950	0.920
Dividend Payout %	57.87	56.50	57.98	45.04	73.33	69.06	88.79	91.09
Income Statement								
Total Revenue	505,069	2,175,882	2,203,489	2,304,419	2,222,695	2,059,964	2,004,003	1,833,450
EBITDA	3,643	133,184	190,892	210,176	158,949	142,287	130,987	127,774
Depn & Amortn	(43)	56,494	57,200	46,500	46,100	36,300	43,360	46,287
Income Before Taxes	1,462	70,612	128,911	157,170	104,931	96,707	77,604	70,159
Income Taxes	(999)	(19,286)	43,273	51,764	43,776	33,338	29,278	24,411
Net Income	2,510	89,795	85,577	105,436	61,471	63,683	48,967	45,986
Average Shares	44,134	44,839	45,502	45,440	45,578	45,956	45,819	45,694
Balance Sheet								
Current Assets	460,081	488,880	433,041	438,370	455,559	433,228	404,940	434,040
Total Assets	1,345,139	1,391,550	1,330,234	1,263,925	1,239,334	1,134,705	1,079,631	1,054,258
Current Liabilities	427,855	489,703	463,473	435,900	457,333	411,584	395,885	388,910
Long-Term Obligations	250,000	240,000	180,000	185,000	197,736	150,197	150,372	150,540
Total Liabilities	831,399	877,482	829,631	786,971	824,747	698,377	659,272	635,201
Stockholders' Equity	513,740	514,068	500,603	476,954	414,587	436,328	420,359	419,057
Shares Outstanding	43,529	43,354	44,078	44,158	44,165	44,981	44,950	44,855
Statistical Record								
Return on Assets %	6.55	6.62	6.62	8.45	5.09	5.77	4.60	4.49
Return on Equity %	17.24	17.75	17.56	23.72	14.21	14.91	11.70	11.15
EBITDA Margin %	0.72	6.12	8.66	9.12	7.15	6.91	6.54	6.97
Net Margin %	0.50	4.13	3.88	4.58	2.77	3.09	2.44	2.51
Asset Turnover	1.65	1.60	1.70	1.85	1.84	1.87	1.88	1.79
Current Ratio	1.08	1.00	0.93	1.01	1.00	1.05	1.02	1.12
Debt to Equity	0.49	0.47	0.36	0.39	0.48	0.34	0.36	0.36
Price Range	47.52-32.99	55.91-32.99	56.26-30.91	57.58-36.06	52.53-31.50	40.34-30.02	31.68-21.95	33.75-16.23
P/E Ratio	24.12-16.75	27.95-16.50	29.93-16.44	24.82-15.54	38.91-23.33	29.02-21.60	29.61-20.51	33.42-16.07
Average Yield %	2.92	2.72	2.47	2.17	2.55	2.70	3.59	3.63

Address: 600 East Second Street, Muscatine, IA 52761-0071	Web Site: www.hnicorp.com	Auditors: KPMG LLP
Telephone: 563-272-7400	Officers: Stanley A. (Stan) Askren - Chairman, President, Chief Executive Officer Jeffrey D. Lorenger - President, Executive Vice President, Division Officer, Chief Executive Officer	Investor Contact: 563-272-7400
Fax: 563-272-7114		Transfer Agents: EQ Shareowner Services, St. Paul, MN

HOLLYFRONTIER CORP

Exchange	Symbol	Price	52Wk Range	Yield	P/E
NYS	HFC	$68.43 (6/29/2018)	81.65-26.19	1.93	10.90

*7 Year Price Score 93.82   *NYSE Composite Index=100   *12 Month Price Score 152.32

Interim Earnings (Per Share)

Qtr.	Mar	Jun	Sep	Dec
2015	1.16	1.88	1.04	(0.19)
2016	0.12	(2.33)	0.42	0.30
2017	(0.26)	0.33	1.53	2.92
2018	1.50	...	...	...

Interim Dividends (Per Share)

Amt	Decl	Ex	Rec	Pay
0.33Q	07/31/2017	08/21/2017	08/23/2017	09/20/2017
0.33Q	11/08/2017	11/20/2017	11/21/2017	12/13/2017
0.33Q	02/14/2018	02/27/2018	02/28/2018	03/14/2018
0.33Q	05/09/2018	05/22/2018	05/23/2018	06/14/2018

Indicated Div: $1.32

Valuation Analysis

		Institutional Holding	
Forecast EPS	$5.06	No of Institutions	
	(06/14/2018)	684	
Market Cap	$12.1 Billion	Shares	
Book Value	$5.6 Billion	190,897,024	
Price/Book	2.17	% Held	
Price/Sales	0.79	N/A	

Business Summary: Refining & Marketing (MIC: 9.1.2 SIC: 2911 NAIC: 324110)

HollyFrontier is a petroleum refiner that produces products such as gasoline, diesel fuel, jet fuel, specialty lubricant products, and asphalt. Co. has two reportable segments, Refining and its subsidiary, Holly Energy Partners, L.P. (HEP). Refining segment activities involve the purchase and refining of crude oil and wholesale of refined products, such as gasoline, diesel fuel and jet fuel. The HEP segment includes all of the operations of HEP, which owns and operates logistics and refinery assets consisting of petroleum product and crude oil pipelines, terminals, tankage, loading rack facilities and processing units in the Mid-Continent, Southwest and Rocky Mountain regions of the U.S.

Recent Developments: For the quarter ended Mar 31 2018, net income amounted to US$288.9 million versus a net loss of US$37.8 million in the year-earlier quarter. Revenues were US$4.13 billion, up 34.0% from US$3.08 billion the year before. Operating income was US$395.8 million versus a loss of US$33.5 million in the prior-year quarter. Direct operating expenses rose 22.2% to US$3.24 billion from US$2.65 billion in the comparable period the year before. Indirect operating expenses increased 6.1% to US$489.3 million from US$461.0 million in the equivalent prior-year period.

Prospects: Our evaluation of HollyFrontier Corp. as of Jan. 21, 2018 is the result of our systematic analysis on three basic characteristics: earnings strength, relative valuation, and recent stock price movement. The company has enjoyed a very positive trend in earnings per share over the past 5 quarters and while recent estimates for the company have been raised by analysts, HFC has posted better than expected results. Based on operating earnings yield, the company is undervalued when compared to all of the companies in our coverage universe. Share price changes over the past year indicates that HFC will perform well over the near term.

Financial Data

(US$ in Thousands)	3 Mos	12/31/2017	12/31/2016	12/31/2015	12/31/2014	12/31/2013	12/31/2012	12/31/2011
Earnings Per Share	6.28	4.52	(1.48)	3.90	1.42	3.64	8.38	6.42
Cash Flow Per Share	7.50	5.40	3.41	5.19	3.85	4.34	8.08	8.44
Tang Book Value Per Share	18.89	17.62	14.99	16.21	16.28	18.45	18.25	13.70
Dividends Per Share	1.320	1.320	1.320	1.310	3.260	3.200	3.100	1.337
Dividend Payout %	21.02	29.20	...	33.59	229.58	87.91	36.99	20.83
Income Statement								
Total Revenue	4,128,427	14,251,299	10,535,700	13,237,920	19,764,327	20,160,560	20,090,724	15,439,528
EBITDA	403,256	1,256,714	131,854	1,485,685	770,523	1,437,565	3,067,372	1,841,434
Depn & Amortn	503	286,500	247,900	233,300	261,800	213,600	182,900	125,000
Income Before Taxes	372,620	856,353	(185,747)	1,212,306	469,507	1,161,471	2,785,072	1,639,395
Income Taxes	85,037	(12,379)	19,411	406,060	141,172	391,576	1,027,962	581,991
Net Income	268,091	805,395	(260,453)	740,101	281,292	735,842	1,727,172	1,023,397
Average Shares	177,954	177,196	176,101	188,940	197,428	201,234	206,184	159,294
Balance Sheet								
Current Assets	3,292,913	3,062,828	2,851,009	1,448,065	2,782,998	3,896,444	4,470,265	4,659,124
Total Assets	10,912,074	10,692,154	9,435,661	8,388,299	9,230,640	10,056,739	10,328,997	10,314,621
Current Liabilities	1,465,006	1,422,710	1,083,229	860,615	1,251,403	1,674,490	1,654,444	2,629,061
Long-Term Obligations	2,382,874	2,498,993	2,235,137	1,040,040	1,054,890	997,519	1,336,238	1,214,742
Total Liabilities	5,330,616	5,321,325	4,754,267	3,134,884	3,707,056	4,057,119	4,276,043	5,110,611
Stockholders' Equity	5,581,458	5,370,829	4,681,394	5,253,415	5,523,584	5,999,620	6,052,954	5,204,010
Shares Outstanding	176,778	177,407	177,345	180,234	196,086	198,830	203,551	209,332
Statistical Record								
Return on Assets %	10.94	8.00	N.M.	8.40	2.92	7.22	16.69	14.60
Return on Equity %	21.99	16.02	N.M.	13.73	4.88	12.21	30.60	34.68
EBITDA Margin %	9.77	8.82	1.25	11.22	3.90	7.13	15.27	11.93
Net Margin %	6.49	5.65	N.M.	5.59	1.42	3.65	8.60	6.63
Asset Turnover	1.50	1.42	1.18	1.50	2.05	1.98	1.94	2.20
Current Ratio	2.25	2.15	2.63	1.68	2.22	2.33	2.70	1.77
Debt to Equity	0.43	0.47	0.48	0.20	0.19	0.17	0.22	0.23
Price Range	52.51-23.90	51.63-23.90	41.11-22.31	53.80-30.19	52.63-36.11	58.43-39.73	47.38-25.24	38.20-20.39
P/E Ratio	8.36-3.81	11.42-5.29	...	13.79-7.74	37.06-25.43	16.05-10.91	5.65-3.01	5.95-3.18
Average Yield %	3.61	4.12	4.51	3.01	7.06	6.81	8.65	4.56

Address: 2828 N. Harwood, Suite 1300, Dallas, TX 75201-1507 **Telephone:** 214-871-3555	**Web Site:** www.hollyfrontier.com **Officers:** George J. Damiris - President, Chief Executive Officer, Executive Vice President, Chief Operating Officer, Senior Vice President Richard L. Voliva - Executive Vice President, Senior Vice President, Chief Financial Officer	**Auditors:** Ernst & Young LLP **Investor Contact:** 214-871-3555 **Transfer Agents:** Wells Fargo Shareowner Services, Mendota Heights, MN

HOME DEPOT INC

Exchange	Symbol	Price	52Wk Range	Yield	P/E
NYS	HD	$195.10 (6/29/2018)	207.23-144.58	2.11	25.34

*7 Year Price Score 135.90 *NYSE Composite Index=100 *12 Month Price Score 107.33

Interim Earnings (Per Share)

Qtr.	Apr	Jul	Oct	Jan
2015-16	1.21	1.73	1.35	1.17
2016-17	1.44	1.97	1.60	1.45
2017-18	1.67	2.25	1.84	1.53
2018-19	2.08	...	...	...

Interim Dividends (Per Share)

Amt	Decl	Ex	Rec	Pay
0.89Q	08/17/2017	08/29/2017	08/31/2017	09/14/2017
0.89Q	11/16/2017	11/29/2017	11/30/2017	12/14/2017
1.03Q	02/20/2018	03/07/2018	03/08/2018	03/22/2018
1.03Q	05/17/2018	05/30/2018	05/31/2018	06/14/2018

Indicated Div: $4.12 (Div. Reinv. Plan)

Valuation Analysis / **Institutional Holding**

Forecast EPS	$9.44
	(06/14/2018)
Market Cap	$225.1 Billion
Book Value	$1.7 Billion
Price/Book	133.46
Price/Sales	2.21

No of Institutions	2767
Shares	1,041,881,280
% Held	61.88

TRADING VOLUME (thousand shares)

Business Summary: Retail - Hardware & Home Improvement (MIC: 2.1.8 SIC: 5211 NAIC: 444110)

The Home Depot is a home improvement retailer that sells a range of building materials, home improvement products, lawn and garden products, and decor items and provides a number of services. As of Jan 28 2018, Co. had 2,284 The Home Depot stores located throughout the U.S., including the Commonwealth of Puerto Rico and the territories of the U.S. Virgin Islands and Guam, Canada and Mexico. Co. serves two primary customer groups: Do-It-Yourself customers and professional customers ("Pros"). Co. also serves Do-It-For-Me customers which are customers that are typically home owners who purchase materials and hire Pros to complete the project or installation.

Recent Developments: For the year ended Jan 28 2018, net income increased 8.5% to US$8.63 billion from US$7.96 billion in the prior year. Revenues were US$100.90 billion, up 6.7% from US$94.60 billion the year before. Operating income was US$14.68 billion versus US$13.43 billion in the prior year, an increase of 9.3%. Direct operating expenses rose 6.8% to US$66.55 billion from US$62.28 billion in the comparable period the year before. Indirect operating expenses increased 4.2% to US$19.68 billion from US$18.89 billion in the equivalent prior-year period.

Prospects: Our evaluation of Home Depot Inc. as of Jan. 21, 2018 is the result of our systematic analysis on three basic characteristics: earnings strength, relative valuation, and recent stock price movement. The company has managed to produce a neutral trend in earnings per share over the past 5 quarters and while recent estimates for the company have been raised by analysts, HD has posted better than expected results. Based on operating earnings yield, the company is about fairly valued when compared to all of the companies in our coverage universe. Share price changes over the past year indicates that HD will perform in line with the market over the near term.

Financial Data

(US$ in Thousands)	3 Mos	01/28/2018	01/29/2017	01/31/2016	02/01/2015	02/02/2014	02/03/2013	01/29/2012
Earnings Per Share	7.70	7.29	6.45	5.46	4.71	3.76	3.00	2.47
Cash Flow Per Share	9.94	10.24	7.98	7.36	6.18	5.37	4.58	4.27
Tang Book Value Per Share	N.M.	N.M.	1.86	3.37	6.10	8.14	11.19	10.92
Dividends Per Share	3.700	3.560	2.760	2.360	1.880	1.560	1.160	1.040
Dividend Payout %	48.05	48.83	42.79	43.22	39.92	41.49	38.67	42.11
Income Statement								
Total Revenue	24,947,000	100,904,000	94,595,000	88,519,000	83,176,000	78,812,000	74,754,000	70,395,000
EBITDA	3,913,000	16,743,000	15,400,000	13,637,000	12,255,000	10,923,000	9,450,000	8,343,000
Depn & Amortn	532,000	2,062,000	1,973,000	1,863,000	1,786,000	1,757,000	1,684,000	1,682,000
Income Before Taxes	3,142,000	13,698,000	12,491,000	11,021,000	9,976,000	8,467,000	7,221,000	6,068,000
Income Taxes	738,000	5,068,000	4,534,000	4,012,000	3,631,000	3,082,000	2,686,000	2,185,000
Net Income	2,404,000	8,630,000	7,957,000	7,009,000	6,345,000	5,385,000	4,535,000	3,883,000
Average Shares	1,158,000	1,184,000	1,234,000	1,283,000	1,346,000	1,434,000	1,511,000	1,570,000
Balance Sheet								
Current Assets	21,214,000	18,933,000	17,724,000	16,993,000	15,302,000	15,279,000	15,372,000	14,520,000
Total Assets	46,650,000	44,529,000	42,966,000	42,549,000	39,946,000	40,518,000	41,084,000	40,518,000
Current Liabilities	18,133,000	16,194,000	14,133,000	12,526,000	11,269,000	10,749,000	11,462,000	9,376,000
Long-Term Obligations	24,244,000	24,267,000	22,349,000	20,888,000	16,869,000	14,691,000	9,475,000	10,758,000
Total Liabilities	44,963,000	43,075,000	38,633,000	36,233,000	30,624,000	27,996,000	23,307,000	22,620,000
Stockholders' Equity	1,687,000	1,454,000	4,333,000	6,316,000	9,322,000	12,522,000	17,777,000	17,898,000
Shares Outstanding	1,154,000	1,158,000	1,203,000	1,252,000	1,307,000	1,380,000	1,484,000	1,537,000
Statistical Record								
Return on Assets %	19.70	19.78	18.66	17.04	15.81	13.23	10.94	9.66
Return on Equity %	319.35	299.07	149.85	89.89	58.25	35.64	25.01	21.17
EBITDA Margin %	15.69	16.59	16.28	15.41	14.73	13.86	12.64	11.85
Net Margin %	9.64	8.55	8.41	7.92	7.63	6.83	6.07	5.52
Asset Turnover	2.23	2.31	2.22	2.15	2.07	1.94	1.80	1.75
Current Ratio	1.17	1.17	1.25	1.36	1.36	1.42	1.34	1.55
Debt to Equity	14.37	16.69	5.16	3.31	1.81	1.17	0.53	0.60
Price Range	207.23-144.58	207.23-136.49	138.77-111.85	134.74-104.43	107.62-74.97	82.34-63.92	67.82-44.39	45.41-28.51
P/E Ratio	26.91-18.78	28.43-18.72	21.51-17.34	24.68-19.13	22.85-15.92	21.90-17.00	22.61-14.80	18.38-11.54
Average Yield %	2.19	2.23	2.11	2.00	2.15	2.06	2.08	2.83

Address: 2455 Paces Ferry Road, Atlanta, GA 30339	**Web Site:** www.homedepot.com	**Auditors:** KPMG LLP
Telephone: 770-433-8211	**Officers:** Craig A. Menear - Chairman, President, Chief Executive Officer, Executive Vice President, Region Officer Carol B. Tome - Executive Vice President, Chief Financial Officer	**Investor Contact:** 770-384-4388
Fax: 770-431-2707		**Transfer Agents:** Computershare Trust Company, N.A., Providence, RI

HONEYWELL INTERNATIONAL INC

Exchange	Symbol	Price	52Wk Range	Yield	P/E
NYS	HON	$144.05 (6/29/2018)	164.99-133.29	2.07	62.09

*7 Year Price Score 121.91 ***NYSE Composite Index=100** ***12 Month Price Score 99.08**

Interim Earnings (Per Share)

Qtr.	Mar	Jun	Sep	Dec
2015	1.41	1.51	1.60	1.53
2016	1.53	1.66	1.60	1.34
2017	1.71	1.80	1.75	(3.12)
2018	1.89	...	...	...

Interim Dividends (Per Share)

Amt	Decl	Ex	Rec	Pay
0.665Q	07/28/2017	08/16/2017	08/18/2017	09/08/2017
0.745Q	09/29/2017	11/16/2017	11/17/2017	12/08/2017
0.745Q	02/08/2018	02/22/2018	02/23/2018	03/09/2018
0.745Q	04/23/2018	05/17/2018	05/18/2018	06/08/2018

Indicated Div: $2.98 (Div. Reinv. Plan)

Valuation Analysis	Institutional Holding	
Forecast EPS	$8.03	No of Institutions
	(06/14/2018)	2273
Market Cap	$107.6 Billion	Shares
Book Value	$17.6 Billion	689,559,552
Price/Book	6.11	% Held
Price/Sales	2.60	80.82

Business Summary: Auto Parts (MIC: 1.8.2 SIC: 3714 NAIC: 336312)

Honeywell International is a technology and manufacturing company. Co. has four segments: Aerospace, which supplies products, software and services for aircraft and vehicles; Home and Building Technologies, which provides products, software, solutions and technologies that assist owners of homes stay connected and in control of their comfort, security and energy use; Performance Materials and Technologies, which provides advanced materials, process technologies and automation solutions; and Safety and Productivity Solutions, which provides safety products such as personal protection equipment and footwear, and productivity solutions products and services such as gas detection technology.

Recent Developments: For the quarter ended Mar 31 2018, net income increased 8.9% to US$1.45 billion from US$1.33 billion in the year-earlier quarter. Revenues were US$10.39 billion, up 9.5% from US$9.49 billion the year before. Direct operating expenses rose 10.2% to US$7.19 billion from US$6.53 billion in the comparable period the year before. Indirect operating expenses increased 3.7% to US$1.48 billion from US$1.42 billion in the equivalent prior-year period.

Prospects: Our evaluation of Honeywell International Inc. as of Jan. 21, 2018 is the result of our systematic analysis on three basic characteristics: earnings strength, relative valuation, and recent stock price movement. The company has managed to produce a neutral trend in earnings per share over the past 5 quarters and while recent estimates for the company have been mixed, HON has posted better than expected results. Based on operating earnings yield, the company is undervalued when compared to all of the companies in our coverage universe. Share price changes over the past year indicates that HON will perform well over the near term.

Financial Data

(US$ in Thousands)	3 Mos	12/31/2017	12/31/2016	12/31/2015	12/31/2014	12/31/2013	12/31/2012	12/31/2011
Earnings Per Share	2.32	2.14	6.20	6.04	5.33	4.92	3.69	2.61
Cash Flow Per Share	8.21	7.83	7.17	6.99	6.40	5.51	4.48	3.63
Tang Book Value Per Share	N.M.	N.M.	N.M.	N.M.	3.68	2.65	N.M.	N.M.
Dividends Per Share	2.820	2.740	2.450	2.148	1.867	1.680	1.528	1.370
Dividend Payout %	121.55	128.04	39.52	35.55	35.04	34.15	41.40	52.49
Income Statement								
Total Revenue	10,392,000	40,534,000	39,302,000	38,581,000	40,306,000	39,055,000	37,665,000	36,529,000
EBITDA	2,280,000	7,745,000	7,374,000	7,434,000	6,665,000	6,304,000	4,783,000	3,248,000
Depn & Amortn	288,000	717,000	726,000	672,000	667,000	670,000	660,000	699,000
Income Before Taxes	1,909,000	6,863,000	6,416,000	6,556,000	5,782,000	5,376,000	3,830,000	2,231,000
Income Taxes	458,000	5,204,000	1,601,000	1,739,000	1,489,000	1,450,000	944,000	417,000
Net Income	1,438,000	1,655,000	4,809,000	4,768,000	4,239,000	3,924,000	2,926,000	2,067,000
Average Shares	761,000	772,100	775,300	789,300	795,200	797,300	791,900	791,600
Balance Sheet								
Current Assets	25,587,000	26,002,000	23,058,000	20,053,000	22,191,000	21,164,000	17,598,000	16,134,000
Total Assets	60,948,000	59,387,000	54,146,000	49,316,000	45,451,000	45,435,000	41,853,000	39,808,000
Current Liabilities	18,755,000	18,861,000	16,331,000	18,371,000	14,773,000	14,181,000	13,045,000	12,275,000
Long-Term Obligations	12,738,000	12,573,000	12,182,000	5,554,000	6,046,000	6,801,000	6,395,000	6,881,000
Total Liabilities	43,348,000	42,106,000	34,774,000	30,743,000	27,575,000	27,801,000	28,728,000	29,002,000
Stockholders' Equity	17,600,000	17,281,000	19,372,000	18,573,000	17,876,000	17,634,000	13,125,000	10,806,000
Shares Outstanding	746,929	750,900	760,800	770,400	782,200	783,800	782,800	774,700
Statistical Record								
Return on Assets %	3.05	2.92	9.27	10.06	9.33	8.99	7.15	5.32
Return on Equity %	9.32	9.03	25.28	26.16	23.87	25.51	24.39	19.25
EBITDA Margin %	21.94	19.11	18.76	19.27	16.54	16.14	12.70	8.89
Net Margin %	13.84	4.08	12.24	12.36	10.52	10.05	7.77	5.66
Asset Turnover	0.72	0.71	0.76	0.81	0.89	0.89	0.92	0.94
Current Ratio	1.36	1.38	1.41	1.09	1.50	1.49	1.35	1.31
Debt to Equity	0.72	0.73	0.63	0.30	0.34	0.39	0.49	0.64
Price Range	164.99-122.50	155.96-116.18	119.20-95.69	106.69-91.07	101.40-84.63	90.85-63.11	63.92-52.62	61.65-41.70
P/E Ratio	71.12-52.80	72.88-54.29	19.23-15.43	17.66-15.08	19.02-15.88	18.47-12.83	17.32-14.26	23.62-15.98
Average Yield %	1.98	2.03	2.20	2.11	2.00	2.13	2.60	2.55

Address: 115 Tabor Road, Morris Plains, NJ 07950 Telephone: 973-455-2000 Fax: 973-455-4807	Web Site: www.honeywell.com Officers: Darius Adamczyk - Chairman, President, Chief Executive Officer, Chief Operating Officer, Division Officer Krishna Mikkilineni - Senior Vice President	Auditors: Deloitte & Touche LLP Investor Contact: 973-455-2222 Transfer Agents: American Stock Transfer & Trust Company, LLC, Brookly, NY

HORMEL FOODS CORP.

Exchange	Symbol	Price	52Wk Range	Yield	P/E	Div Acheiver
NYS	HRL	$37.21 (6/29/2018)	37.68-30.15	2.02	21.39	51 Years

*7 Year Price Score 102.54 *NYSE Composite Index=100 *12 Month Price Score 105.31

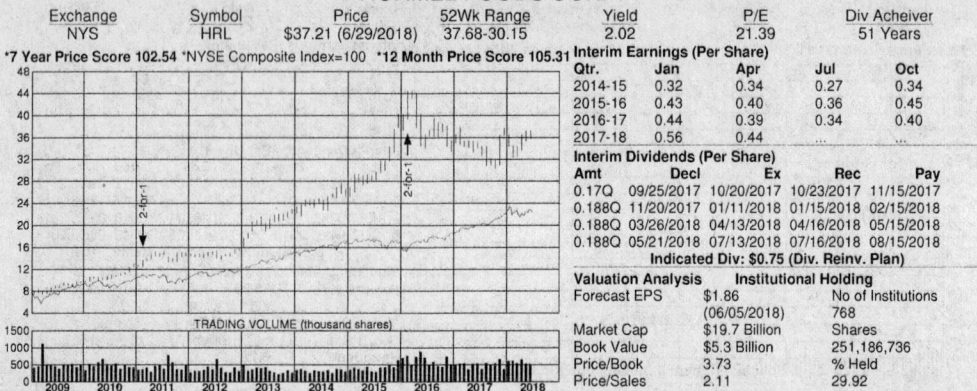

Interim Earnings (Per Share)

Qtr.	Jan	Apr	Jul	Oct
2014-15	0.32	0.34	0.27	0.34
2015-16	0.43	0.40	0.36	0.45
2016-17	0.44	0.39	0.34	0.40
2017-18	0.56	0.44	...	...

Interim Dividends (Per Share)

Amt	Decl	Ex	Rec	Pay
0.17Q	09/25/2017	10/20/2017	10/23/2017	11/15/2017
0.188Q	11/20/2017	01/11/2018	01/15/2018	02/15/2018
0.188Q	03/26/2018	04/13/2018	04/16/2018	05/15/2018
0.188Q	05/21/2018	07/13/2018	07/16/2018	08/15/2018

Indicated Div: $0.75 (Div. Reinv. Plan)

Valuation Analysis   **Institutional Holding**

Forecast EPS	$1.86	No of Institutions
	(06/05/2018)	768
Market Cap	$19.7 Billion	Shares
Book Value	$5.3 Billion	251,186,736
Price/Book	3.73	% Held
Price/Sales	2.11	29.92

Business Summary: Food (MIC: 1.2.1 SIC: 2011 NAIC: 311611)

Hormel Foods is engaged in the production of a variety of meat and food products and the marketing of those products throughout the U.S. and internationally. Co.'s business is reported in five segments: Grocery Products, which processes, markets, and sells shelf-stable food products; Refrigerated Foods, which processes, markets, and sells pork, beef, chicken, and turkey products; Jennie-O Turkey Store, which processes, markets, and sells turkey products; Specialty Foods, which processes, markets, and sells nutritional and private label shelf-stable products; and International and Other, which manufactures, markets, and sells Co.'s products internationally.

Recent Developments: For the quarter ended Apr 29 2018, net income increased 12.6% to US$237.5 million from US$210.9 million in the year-earlier quarter. Revenues were US$2.33 billion, up 6.5% from US$2.19 billion the year before. Operating income was US$306.4 million versus US$316.0 million in the prior-year quarter, a decrease of 3.1%. Direct operating expenses rose 7.9% to US$1.83 billion from US$1.70 billion in the comparable period the year before. Indirect operating expenses increased 11.4% to US$190.3 million from US$170.9 million in the equivalent prior-year period.

Prospects: Our evaluation of Hormel Foods Corp. as of Jan. 21, 2018 is the result of our systematic analysis on three basic characteristics: earnings strength, relative valuation, and recent stock price movement. The company has managed to produce a neutral trend in earnings per share over the past 5 quarters and while recent estimates for the company have been raised by analysts, HRL has posted better than expected results. Based on operating earnings yield, the company is undervalued when compared to all of the companies in our coverage universe. Share price changes over the past year indicates that HRL will perform in line with the market over the near term.

Financial Data

(US$ in Thousands)	6 Mos	3 Mos	10/29/2017	10/30/2016	10/25/2015	10/26/2014	10/27/2013	10/28/2012
Earnings Per Share	1.74	1.69	1.57	1.64	1.27	1.12	0.97	0.93
Cash Flow Per Share	2.25	2.15	1.91	1.85	1.88	1.42	1.21	0.99
Tang Book Value Per Share	2.46	2.21	3.39	3.24	2.78	3.46	3.79	3.93
Dividends Per Share	0.715	0.698	0.680	0.580	0.500	0.400	0.340	0.300
Dividend Payout %	41.09	41.27	43.31	35.37	39.37	35.87	34.87	32.26
Income Statement								
Total Revenue	4,661,861	2,331,293	9,167,519	9,523,224	9,263,863	9,316,256	8,751,654	8,230,670
EBITDA	656,260	322,180	1,380,239	1,425,565	1,185,009	1,053,431	919,805	854,452
Depn & Amortn	80,316	39,123	139,360	140,355	141,576	139,396	134,329	128,469
Income Before Taxes	565,031	281,634	1,239,055	1,278,530	1,033,256	904,567	777,994	719,644
Income Taxes	61,315	1,954	431,542	426,698	369,879	316,126	268,431	253,374
Net Income	540,491	303,107	846,735	890,052	686,088	602,677	526,211	500,050
Average Shares	542,811	543,482	539,116	542,473	541,002	540,432	540,448	537,782
Balance Sheet								
Current Assets	1,850,780	1,948,269	2,026,523	2,029,912	2,063,032	2,132,771	2,047,413	2,320,684
Total Assets	7,829,749	7,858,848	6,975,908	6,370,067	6,139,831	5,455,619	4,915,880	4,563,966
Current Liabilities	1,148,461	1,323,514	1,058,212	1,053,196	1,214,025	954,692	784,009	786,300
Long-Term Obligations	624,763	624,726	250,000	250,000	250,000	250,000	250,000	250,000
Total Liabilities	2,542,544	2,707,517	2,040,001	1,922,061	2,141,633	1,849,941	1,604,840	1,744,511
Stockholders' Equity	5,287,205	5,151,331	4,935,907	4,448,006	3,998,198	3,605,678	3,311,040	2,819,455
Shares Outstanding	530,132	529,988	528,423	528,483	528,411	527,226	527,316	526,088
Statistical Record								
Return on Assets %	13.24	12.86	12.69	14.00	11.87	11.65	11.13	11.39
Return on Equity %	18.88	18.81	18.05	20.73	18.10	17.47	17.21	18.31
EBITDA Margin %	14.08	13.82	15.06	14.97	12.79	11.31	10.51	10.38
Net Margin %	11.59	13.00	9.24	9.35	7.41	6.47	6.01	6.08
Asset Turnover	1.32	1.30	1.37	1.50	1.60	1.80	1.85	1.87
Current Ratio	1.61	1.47	1.92	1.93	1.70	2.23	2.61	2.95
Debt to Equity	0.12	0.12	0.05	0.06	0.06	0.07	0.08	0.09
Price Range	37.68-30.15	37.87-30.15	38.50-30.27	44.47-33.09	34.24-25.07	26.27-21.11	22.06-14.77	15.34-13.74
P/E Ratio	21.66-17.33	22.41-17.84	24.52-19.28	27.12-20.17	26.96-19.74	23.46-18.85	22.74-15.22	16.49-14.77
Average Yield %	2.12	2.05	1.99	1.52	1.75	1.69	1.77	2.07

Address: 1 Hormel Place, Austin, MN 55912-3680
Telephone: 507-437-5611
Fax: 507-437-5489

Web Site: www.hormel.com
Officers: James P. Snee - Chairman, President, Chief Executive Officer, Chief Operating Officer, Vice President, Group Vice President, Division Officer James N. Sheehan - Senior Vice President, Chief Financial Officer, Vice President, Chief Accounting Officer, Controller

Auditors: Ernst & Young LLP
Investor Contact: 507-437-5248
Transfer Agents: Wells Fargo Shareowner Services, Mendota Heights, MN

HORTON (DR) INC

Exchange	Symbol	Price	52Wk Range	Yield	P/E
NYS	DHI	$41.00 (6/29/2018)	52.87-34.36	1.22	13.76

*7 Year Price Score 131.55 *NYSE Composite Index=100 *12 Month Price Score 97.41

Interim Earnings (Per Share)

Qtr.	Dec	Mar	Jun	Sep
2014-15	0.39	0.40	0.60	0.64
2015-16	0.42	0.52	0.66	0.75
2016-17	0.55	0.60	0.76	0.82
2017-18	0.49	0.91	...	...

Interim Dividends (Per Share)

Amt	Decl	Ex	Rec	Pay
0.10Q	07/26/2017	08/07/2017	08/09/2017	08/23/2017
0.125Q	11/09/2017	11/30/2017	12/01/2017	12/15/2017
0.125Q	01/31/2018	02/22/2018	02/23/2018	03/09/2018
0.125Q	04/26/2018	05/10/2018	05/11/2018	05/25/2018

Indicated Div: $0.50

Valuation Analysis **Institutional Holding**

Forecast EPS	$3.70	No of Institutions
	(06/14/2018)	936
Market Cap	$15.5 Billion	Shares
Book Value	$8.2 Billion	388,339,680
Price/Book	1.89	% Held
Price/Sales	1.03	95.02

Business Summary: Builders (MIC: 2.2.5 SIC: 1531 NAIC: 236117)

D.R. Horton a homebuilding company. Co. constructs and sells homes under the D.R. Horton, America's Builder, Emerald Homes, Express Homes, Freedom Homes and Pacific Ridge Homes names. Co.'s business operations consist of homebuilding, financial services and other activities. Co. sells single-family detached homes, as well as attached homes, such as townhomes, duplexes, triplexes and condominiums. Co.'s financial services operations provide mortgage financing and title agency services to homebuyers in its homebuilding markets. In addition, Co. has subsidiaries that engage in conducting insurance-related operations, constructing and owning income-producing rental properties, among others.

Recent Developments: For the quarter ended Mar 31 2018, net income increased 53.1% to US$350.8 million from US$229.2 million in the year-earlier quarter. Revenues were US$3.79 billion, up 16.7% from US$3.25 billion the year before. Direct operating expenses rose 16.1% to US$2.96 billion from US$2.55 billion in the comparable period the year before. Indirect operating expenses increased 12.1% to US$389.4 million from US$347.5 million in the equivalent prior-year period.

Prospects: Our evaluation of Horton (D.R.) Inc. as of Jan. 21, 2018 is the result of our systematic analysis on three basic characteristics: earnings strength, relative valuation, and recent stock price movement. The company has managed to produce a neutral trend in earnings per share over the past 5 quarters and while recent estimates for the company have been raised by analysts, DHI has posted better than expected results. Based on operating earnings yield, the company is undervalued when compared to all of the companies in our coverage universe. Share price changes over the past year indicates that DHI will perform very well over the near term.

Financial Data

(US$ in Thousands)	6 Mos	3 Mos	09/30/2017	09/30/2016	09/30/2015	09/30/2014	09/30/2013	09/30/2012
Earnings Per Share	2.98	2.67	2.74	2.36	2.03	1.50	1.33	2.77
Cash Flow Per Share	1.27	1.05	1.16	1.66	1.91	(1.94)	(3.82)	(0.93)
Tang Book Value Per Share	21.43	20.71	20.45	18.00	15.75	13.77	12.45	11.07
Dividends Per Share	0.450	0.425	0.400	0.320	0.250	0.138	0.188	0.150
Dividend Payout %	15.10	15.92	14.60	13.56	12.32	9.17	14.10	5.42
Income Statement								
Total Revenue	7,127,600	3,332,700	14,091,000	12,157,400	10,824,000	8,024,900	6,259,300	4,354,000
EBITDA	835,800	390,100	1,637,000	1,390,800	1,161,200	840,600	676,700	278,400
Depn & Amortn	2,400	1,200	49,400	50,800	50,300	36,600	22,300	18,800
Income Before Taxes	833,400	388,900	1,602,100	1,353,500	1,123,400	814,200	657,800	242,900
Income Taxes	296,400	202,400	563,700	467,200	372,700	280,700	195,100	(713,400)
Net Income	540,300	189,300	1,038,400	886,300	750,700	533,500	462,700	956,300
Average Shares	383,900	383,800	378,900	375,100	369,800	366,600	364,900	359,000
Balance Sheet								
Current Assets	11,357,600	11,167,200	10,366,900	9,778,200	9,376,200	8,549,300	7,397,900	5,821,500
Total Assets	13,218,100	12,957,300	12,184,600	11,558,900	11,151,000	10,202,500	8,856,400	7,248,200
Current Liabilities	875,500	949,000	911,400	849,200	784,600	747,300	636,400	377,600
Long-Term Obligations	3,233,900	3,258,100	2,871,600	3,271,300	3,811,500	3,682,800	3,509,000	2,493,100
Total Liabilities	5,019,200	5,075,300	4,437,500	4,766,400	5,256,700	5,086,700	4,797,900	3,656,100
Stockholders' Equity	8,198,900	7,882,000	7,747,100	6,792,500	5,894,300	5,115,800	4,058,500	3,592,100
Shares Outstanding	377,409	375,693	374,986	372,923	368,647	364,586	322,943	320,891
Statistical Record								
Return on Assets %	9.09	8.28	8.75	7.78	7.03	5.60	5.75	15.13
Return on Equity %	14.82	13.74	14.28	13.93	13.64	11.63	12.10	30.70
EBITDA Margin %	11.73	11.71	11.62	11.44	10.73	10.47	10.81	6.39
Net Margin %	7.58	5.68	7.37	7.29	6.94	6.65	7.39	21.96
Asset Turnover	1.20	1.18	1.19	1.07	1.01	0.84	0.78	0.69
Current Ratio	12.97	11.77	11.37	11.51	11.95	11.44	11.62	15.42
Debt to Equity	0.39	0.41	0.37	0.48	0.65	0.72	0.86	0.69
Price Range	52.87-32.28	51.45-27.56	39.93-27.28	34.41-23.23	32.21-19.49	25.10-17.69	27.60-17.77	22.37-8.45
P/E Ratio	17.74-10.83	19.27-10.32	14.57-9.96	14.58-9.84	15.87-9.60	16.73-11.79	20.75-13.36	8.08-3.05
Average Yield %	1.11	1.15	1.24	1.05	0.95	0.63	0.86	0.98

Address: 1341 Horton Circle, Arlington, TX 76011 **Telephone:** 817-390-8200	**Web Site:** www.drhorton.com **Officers:** Donald R. Horton - Chairman David V. Auld - President, Chief Executive Officer, Executive Vice President, Chief Operating Officer, Division Officer	**Auditors:** PricewaterhouseCoopers LLP **Investor Contact:** 817-390-8200 **Transfer Agents:** American Stock Transfer & Trust Co., New York, NY

HP INC

Exchange	Symbol	Price	52Wk Range	Yield	P/E
NYS	HPQ	$22.69 (6/29/2018)	24.65-17.19	2.46	8.73

*7 Year Price Score 121.20 *NYSE Composite Index=100 *12 Month Price Score 105.37

Interim Earnings (Per Share)

Qtr.	Jan	Apr	Jul	Oct
2014-15	0.73	0.55	0.47	0.73
2015-16	0.33	0.36	0.45	0.28
2016-17	0.36	0.33	0.41	0.39
2017-18	1.16	0.64		

Interim Dividends (Per Share)

Amt	Decl	Ex	Rec	Pay
0.139Q	11/14/2017	12/12/2017	12/13/2017	01/03/2018
0.139Q	01/29/2018	03/13/2018	03/14/2018	04/04/2018
0.139Q	05/14/2018	06/12/2018	06/13/2018	07/05/2018
0.139Q	06/19/2018	09/11/2018	09/12/2018	10/03/2018

Indicated Div: $0.56 (Div. Reinv. Plan)

Valuation Analysis | **Institutional Holding**

Forecast EPS	$2.00	No of Institutions
	(06/10/2018)	1533
Market Cap	$36.6 Billion	Shares
Book Value	N/A	1,669,759,232
Price/Book	N/A	% Held
Price/Sales	0.66	70.79

Business Summary: Computer Hardware & Equipment (MIC: 6.2.1 SIC: 3571 NAIC: 334111)

HP is a provider of personal computing and other access devices, imaging and printing products, and related technologies, solutions and services. Co. has three business segments: Personal Systems, which provides commercial personal computers (PCs), consumer PCs, workstations, thin clients, commercial tablets and mobility devices, retail point-of-sale systems, displays and other related accessories, software, support, and services for the commercial and consumer markets; Printing, which provides consumer and commercial printer hardware, supplies, media, solutions and services, and scanning devices; and Corporate Investments, which includes HP Labs and certain business incubation projects.

Recent Developments: For the quarter ended Apr 30 2018, net income increased 89.3% to US$1.06 billion from US$559.0 million in the year-earlier quarter. Revenues were US$14.00 billion, up 13.1% from US$12.39 billion the year before. Operating income was US$964.0 million versus US$818.0 million in the prior-year quarter, an increase of 17.8%. Direct operating expenses rose 13.0% to US$11.30 billion from US$10.00 billion in the comparable period the year before. Indirect operating expenses increased 11.1% to US$1.74 billion from US$1.57 billion in the equivalent prior-year period.

Prospects: Our evaluation of HP Inc as of Jan. 21, 2018 is the result of our systematic analysis on three basic characteristics: earnings strength, relative valuation, and recent stock price movement. The company has enjoyed a very positive trend in earnings per share over the past 5 quarters. However, while recent estimates for the company have been mixed, HPQ has posted results that fell short of analysts expectations. Based on operating earnings yield, the company is undervalued when compared to all of the companies in our coverage universe. Share price changes over the past year indicates that HPQ will perform well over the near term.

Financial Data

(US$ in Millions)	6 Mos	3 Mos	10/31/2017	10/31/2016	10/31/2015	10/31/2014	10/31/2013	10/31/2012
Earnings Per Share	2.60	2.29	1.48	1.43	2.48	2.62	2.62	(6.41)
Cash Flow Per Share	2.76	2.37	2.18	1.86	3.58	6.55	6.00	5.34
Dividends Per Share	0.544	0.537	0.531	0.496	0.672	0.610	0.554	0.504
Dividend Payout %	20.92	23.47	35.86	34.69	27.10	23.30	21.16	...
Income Statement								
Total Revenue	28,520	14,517	52,056	48,238	103,355	111,454	112,298	120,357
EBITDA	1,138	980	3,939	3,881	9,090	11,485	11,704	(5,973)
Depn & Amortn	40	20	354	332	4,031	4,300	4,573	5,084
Income Before Taxes	988	905	3,276	3,761	4,732	6,557	6,510	(11,933)
Income Taxes	(2,008)	(1,033)	750	1,095	178	1,544	1,397	717
Net Income	2,996	1,938	2,526	2,496	4,554	5,013	5,113	(12,650)
Average Shares	1,646	1,669	1,702	1,743	1,836	1,912	1,950	1,974
Balance Sheet								
Current Assets	19,433	21,217	22,318	18,468	51,787	50,145	50,364	50,637
Total Assets	32,087	35,245	32,913	29,010	106,882	103,206	105,676	108,768
Current Liabilities	23,127	23,349	22,412	18,808	42,191	43,735	45,521	46,666
Long-Term Obligations	4,494	6,340	6,747	6,758	21,780	16,039	16,608	21,789
Total Liabilities	33,950	37,987	36,321	32,899	79,114	76,475	78,407	86,332
Stockholders' Equity	(1,863)	(2,742)	(3,408)	(3,889)	27,768	26,731	27,269	22,436
Shares Outstanding	1,611	1,641	1,650	1,712	1,803	1,839	1,907	1,962
Statistical Record								
Return on Assets %	14.32	12.15	8.16	3.66	4.34	4.80	4.77	N.M.
Return on Equity %	...	...	...	20.85	16.71	18.57	20.57	N.M.
EBITDA Margin %	3.99	6.75	7.57	8.05	8.79	10.30	10.42	N.M.
Net Margin %	10.50	13.35	4.85	5.17	4.41	4.50	4.55	N.M.
Asset Turnover	1.83	1.70	1.68	0.71	0.98	1.07	1.05	1.01
Current Ratio	0.84	0.91	1.00	0.98	1.23	1.15	1.11	1.09
Debt to Equity	...	...	...	...	0.78	0.60	0.61	0.97
Price Range	24.65-17.19	23.91-14.99	22.12-14.35	15.65-9.02	18.49-11.15	17.32-11.06	12.39-5.32	13.57-6.29
P/E Ratio	9.48-6.61	10.44-6.55	14.95-9.70	10.94-6.31	7.45-4.50	6.61-4.22	4.73-2.03	...
Average Yield %	2.65	2.78	2.94	3.90	4.48	4.20	5.93	4.91

Address: 1501 Page Mill Road, Palo Alto, CA 94304 **Telephone:** 650-857-1501	**Web Site:** www.hp.com **Officers:** Charles V. (Chip) Bergh - Chairman Dion J. Weisler - President, Chief Executive Officer, Division Officer	**Auditors:** Ernst & Young LLP **Investor Contact:** 800-286-5977 **Transfer Agents:** Wells Fargo Shareowner Services, St. Paul, MN

HOST HOTELS & RESORTS INC

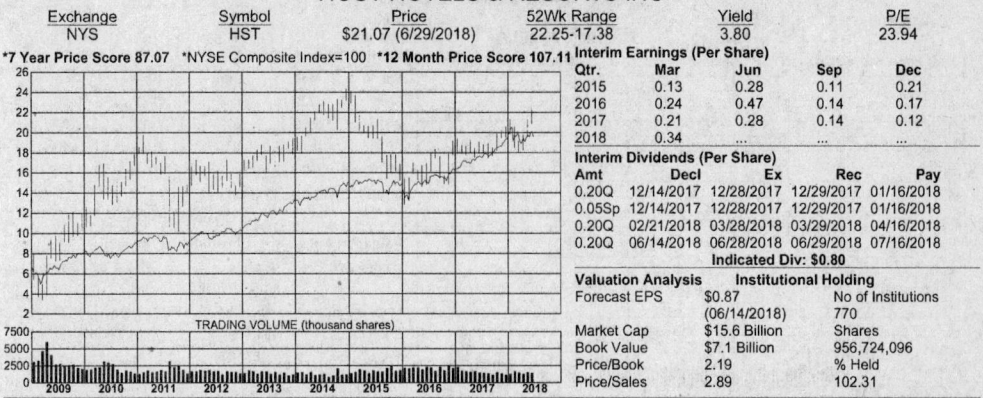

Exchange	Symbol	Price	52Wk Range	Yield	P/E
NYS	HST	$21.07 (6/29/2018)	22.25-17.38	3.80	23.94

*7 Year Price Score 87.07   *NYSE Composite Index=100   *12 Month Price Score 107.11

Interim Earnings (Per Share)

Qtr.	Mar	Jun	Sep	Dec
2015	0.13	0.28	0.11	0.21
2016	0.24	0.47	0.14	0.17
2017	0.21	0.28	0.14	0.12
2018	0.34	...	...	...

Interim Dividends (Per Share)

Amt	Decl	Ex	Rec	Pay
0.20Q	12/14/2017	12/28/2017	12/29/2017	01/16/2018
0.05Sp	12/14/2017	12/28/2017	12/29/2017	01/16/2018
0.20Q	02/21/2018	03/28/2018	03/29/2018	04/16/2018
0.20Q	06/14/2018	06/28/2018	06/29/2018	07/16/2018

Indicated Div: $0.80

Valuation Analysis

		Institutional Holding	
Forecast EPS	$0.87 (06/14/2018)	No of Institutions	770
Market Cap	$15.6 Billion	Shares	956,724,096
Book Value	$7.1 Billion	% Held	102.31
Price/Book	2.19		
Price/Sales	2.89		

TRADING VOLUME (thousand shares)

Business Summary: REITs (MIC: 5.3.1 SIC: 6798 NAIC: 525930)

Host Hotels & Resorts is a real estate investment trust, which owns properties and conducts operations through Host Hotels & Resorts, L.P. As of Feb 21, 2018, Co.'s lodging portfolio consisted of 93 primarily luxury and upper-upscale hotels containing approximately 52,000 rooms, with the majority located in the United States, and with six of the properties located outside of the U.S. in Brazil, Canada and Mexico. In addition, Co. owns non-controlling interests in four domestic and two international joint ventures and a timeshare venture in Hawaii.

Recent Developments: For the quarter ended Mar 31 2018, net income increased 59.0% to US$256.0 million from US$161.0 million in the year-earlier quarter. Revenues were US$1.35 billion, unchanged from the year before.

Prospects: Our evaluation of Host Marriott Corp. as of Jan. 21, 2018 is the result of our systematic analysis on three basic characteristics: earnings strength, relative valuation, and recent stock price movement. The company has generated a negative trend in earnings per share over the past 5 quarters. However, while recent estimates for the company have been mixed, HST has posted results that were in line with analysts expectations. Based on operating earnings yield, the company is about fairly valued when compared to all of the companies in our coverage universe. Share price changes over the past year indicates that HST will perform in line with the market over the near term.

Financial Data

(US$ in Millions)	3 Mos	12/31/2017	12/31/2016	12/31/2015	12/31/2014	12/31/2013	12/31/2012	12/31/2011
Earnings Per Share	0.88	0.76	1.02	0.74	0.96	0.42	0.08	(0.02)
Cash Flow Per Share	1.72	1.67	1.75	1.56	1.52	1.37	1.09	0.95
Tang Book Value Per Share	9.60	9.43	9.48	9.41	9.71	9.58	9.42	9.47
Dividends Per Share	0.850	0.850	0.850	0.800	0.750	0.460	0.300	0.140
Dividend Payout %	96.59	111.84	83.33	108.11	78.13	109.52	375.00	...
Income Statement								
Total Revenue	1,346	5,387	5,430	5,387	5,354	5,166	5,286	4,998
EBITDA	293	1,540	1,672	1,477	1,670	558	395	337
Depn & Amortn	2	758	731	737	725	10	3	3
Income Before Taxes	250	621	790	510	735	248	42	(17)
Income Taxes	4	80	40	9	14	21	31	(1)
Net Income	253	564	762	558	732	317	61	(15)
Average Shares	739	739	743	752	786	747	719	693
Balance Sheet								
Current Assets	469	914	374	254	684	893	453	862
Total Assets	12,064	11,693	11,408	11,784	12,207	12,814	12,994	13,068
Current Liabilities	233	283	278	243	298	214	194	175
Long-Term Obligations	4,266	3,954	3,649	4,017	3,992	4,759	5,411	5,753
Total Liabilities	4,965	4,720	4,414	4,720	4,871	5,586	6,169	6,391
Stockholders' Equity	7,099	6,973	6,994	7,064	7,336	7,228	6,825	6,677
Shares Outstanding	739	739	737	750	755	754	724	705
Statistical Record								
Return on Assets %	5.53	4.88	6.55	4.65	5.85	2.46	0.47	N.M.
Return on Equity %	9.33	8.08	10.81	7.75	10.05	4.51	0.90	N.M.
EBITDA Margin %	21.77	28.59	30.79	27.42	31.19	10.80	7.47	6.74
Net Margin %	18.80	10.47	14.03	10.36	13.67	6.14	1.15	N.M.
Asset Turnover	0.45	0.47	0.47	0.45	0.43	0.40	0.40	0.39
Current Ratio	2.01	3.23	1.35	1.05	2.30	4.17	2.34	4.93
Debt to Equity	0.60	0.57	0.52	0.57	0.54	0.66	0.79	0.86
Price Range	21.30-17.38	20.58-17.38	19.18-12.82	24.14-15.20	24.33-18.00	19.44-15.67	17.25-13.78	19.77-10.17
P/E Ratio	24.20-19.75	27.08-22.87	18.80-12.57	32.62-20.54	25.34-18.75	46.29-37.31	215.63-172.25	...
Average Yield %	4.49	4.57	5.24	4.12	3.49	2.60	1.92	0.90

Address: 6903 Rockledge Drive, Suite 1500, Bethesda, MD 20817	Web Site: www.hosthotels.com	Auditors: KPMG LLP
Telephone: 240-744-1000	Officers: Richard E. Marriott - Chairman James F. Risoleo - President, Chief Executive Officer, Executive Vice President, Chief Investment Officer, Region Officer	Transfer Agents: Computershare Trust Company, N.A., Providence, RI

HOWARD HUGHES CORP

Exchange	Symbol	Price	52Wk Range	Yield	P/E
NYS	HHC	$132.50 (6/29/2018)	139.79-114.47	N/A	34.87

*7 Year Price Score 94.03 *NYSE Composite Index=100 *12 Month Price Score 103.36

Interim Earnings (Per Share)

Qtr.	Mar	Jun	Sep	Dec
2015	(2.68)	0.18	0.76	0.59
2016	2.69	0.16	0.19	1.01
2017	0.13	0.07	0.24	3.46
2018	0.03	...	...	...

Interim Dividends (Per Share)

No Dividends Paid

Valuation Analysis / Institutional Holding

Valuation Analysis		Institutional Holding	
Forecast EPS	$2.03	No of Institutions	
	(06/11/2018)	343	
Market Cap	$5.7 Billion	Shares	
Book Value	$3.1 Billion	42,298,656	
Price/Book	1.85	% Held	
Price/Sales	5.53	81.57	

TRADING VOLUME (thousand shares)

Business Summary: Property, Real Estate & Development (MIC: 5.3.2 SIC: 6552 NAIC: 531312)

Howard Hughes is engaged in the development of master planned communities, in the ownership, management and redevelopment of revenue-generating real estate assets, and in the development of other real estate assets in the form of entitled and unentitled land and residential condominium developments. Co.'s segments are: Master Planned Communities, which includes the development and sale of residential and commercial land, primarily in large-scale long-term projects; Operating Assets, which contains properties, investments and other assets that generate revenue; and Strategic Developments, which focuses on development projects, in which it creates or executes strategic plans for these assets.

Recent Developments: For the quarter ended Mar 31 2018, net income decreased 67.6% to US$1.8 million from US$5.7 million in the year-earlier quarter. Revenues were US$161.7 million, down 30.2% from US$231.8 million the year before.

Prospects: Our evaluation of Howard Hughes Corp as of Jan. 21, 2018 is the result of our systematic analysis on three basic characteristics: earnings strength, relative valuation, and recent stock price movement. The company has suffered a very negative trend in earnings per share over the past 5 quarters and while recent estimates for the company have been mixed, HHC has posted results that fell short of analysts expectations. Based on operating earnings yield, the company is overvalued when compared to all of the companies in our coverage universe. Share price changes over the past year indicates that HHC will perform well over the near term.

Financial Data
(US$ in Thousands)

	3 Mos	12/31/2017	12/31/2016	12/31/2015	12/31/2014	12/31/2013	12/31/2012	12/31/2011
Earnings Per Share	3.80	3.91	4.73	1.60	(0.60)	(1.87)	(3.36)	1.17
Cash Flow Per Share	6.76	7.71	1.49	0.61	(1.48)	3.28	4.00	2.28
Tang Book Value Per Share	69.02	73.56	64.53	59.43	56.10	56.56	58.36	61.26
Income Statement								
Total Revenue	161,679	1,100,120	1,035,005	797,088	634,565	474,610	376,886	275,691
EBITDA	31,828	272,250	410,201	286,603	53,409	(68,211)	(113,357)	125,703
Depn & Amortn	29,289	116,401	81,878	82,275	50,683	29,637	19,455	14,012
Income Before Taxes	(11,994)	95,324	263,958	146,999	16,104	(78,553)	(124,339)	121,567
Income Taxes	558	(45,801)	118,450	24,001	62,960	9,570	6,887	(18,325)
Net Income	1,474	168,404	202,303	126,719	(23,531)	(73,790)	(128,288)	147,180
Average Shares	43,363	43,089	42,729	42,754	39,464	39,449	38,127	38,982
Balance Sheet								
Current Assets	1,049,108	1,064,775	825,933	619,114	721,665	1,383,235	680,397	696,934
Total Assets	6,737,986	6,729,064	6,367,382	5,721,582	5,119,931	4,567,868	3,503,042	3,395,149
Current Liabilities	710,094	682,568	1,105,125	913,731	898,955	808,099	503,733	459,073
Long-Term Obligations	2,895,771	2,857,945	2,690,747	2,443,962	1,993,470	1,514,623	688,312	606,477
Total Liabilities	3,664,548	3,546,078	3,799,644	3,361,465	2,896,168	2,329,284	1,197,804	1,070,564
Stockholders' Equity	3,073,438	3,182,986	2,567,738	2,360,117	2,223,763	2,238,584	2,305,238	2,324,585
Shares Outstanding	42,986	43,270	39,790	39,714	39,638	39,576	39,498	37,945
Statistical Record								
Return on Assets %	2.50	2.57	3.34	2.34	N.M.	N.M.	N.M.	4.59
Return on Equity %	5.78	5.86	8.19	5.53	N.M.	N.M.	N.M.	6.54
EBITDA Margin %	19.69	24.75	39.63	35.96	8.42	N.M.	N.M.	45.60
Net Margin %	0.91	15.31	19.55	15.90	N.M.	N.M.	N.M.	53.39
Asset Turnover	0.16	0.17	0.17	0.15	0.13	0.12	0.11	0.09
Current Ratio	1.48	1.56	0.75	0.68	0.80	1.71	1.35	1.52
Debt to Equity	0.94	0.90	1.05	1.04	0.90	0.68	0.30	0.26
Price Range		139.13-114.47	131.79-105.33	121.71-81.34	159.12-108.49	160.00-118.04	121.13-71.25	75.12-44.27	76.48-37.31
P/E Ratio		36.61-30.12	33.71-26.94	25.73-17.20	99.45-67.81	...	...	...	65.37-31.89

Address: 13355 Noel Road, 22nd Floor, Dallas, TX 75240	**Web Site:** www.howardhughes.com
Telephone: 214-741-7744	**Officers:** William A. (Bill) Ackman - Chairman Grant Herlitz - President, Interim Chief Financial Officer
Fax: 214-741-3021	
	Auditors: Ernst & Young LLP
	Transfer Agents: Computershare, Jersey City, NJ

HUBBELL INC.

Exchange	Symbol	Price	52Wk Range	Yield	P/E	Div Acheiver
NYS	HUBB	$105.74 (6/29/2018)	139.21-102.51	2.91	24.48	10 Years

*7 Year Price Score 94.95 *NYSE Composite Index=100 *12 Month Price Score 88.93

Interim Earnings (Per Share)

Qtr.	Mar	Jun	Sep	Dec
2015	1.07	1.37	1.27	1.06
2016	1.08	1.45	1.56	1.16
2017	1.13	1.43	1.47	0.37
2018	1.05	...	...	...

Interim Dividends (Per Share)

Amt	Decl	Ex	Rec	Pay
0.70Q	07/21/2017	08/29/2017	08/31/2017	09/15/2017
0.77Q	10/20/2017	11/29/2017	11/30/2017	12/15/2017
0.77Q	01/26/2018	02/27/2018	02/28/2018	03/15/2018
0.77Q	04/20/2018	05/30/2018	05/31/2018	06/15/2018

Indicated Div: $3.08

Valuation Analysis | **Institutional Holding**

Forecast EPS	$7.06	No of Institutions	
	(06/11/2018)	466	
Market Cap	$5.8 Billion	Shares	
Book Value	$1.7 Billion	56,346,336	
Price/Book	3.49	% Held	
Price/Sales	1.52	3.29	

Business Summary: Electrical Equipment (MIC: 7.3.1 SIC: 3613 NAIC: 334417)

Hubbell is primarily engaged in the design, manufacture and sale of electrical and electronic products a range of non-residential and residential construction, industrial and utility applications. Co. has two segments: electrical, which comprised of businesses that sell stock and custom products including standard and application wiring device products, rough-in electrical products, connector and grounding products, lighting fixtures and controls, as well as other electrical equipment; and power, which consists of operations that design and manufacture various distribution, transmission, substation and telecommunications products primarily used by the electrical utility industry.

Recent Developments: For the quarter ended Mar 31 2018, net income decreased 6.4% to US$59.8 million from US$63.9 million in the year-earlier quarter. Revenues were US$991.2 million, up 16.3% from US$852.3 million the year before. Operating income was US$99.6 million versus US$107.8 million in the prior-year quarter, a decrease of 7.6%. Direct operating expenses rose 20.1% to US$708.3 million from US$589.7 million in the comparable period the year before. Indirect operating expenses increased 18.4% to US$183.3 million from US$154.8 million in the equivalent prior-year period.

Prospects: Hubbell Inc., through its wholly-owned subsidiary, Hubbell Power Systems, Inc., through its wholly-owned subsidiary, Yellow Merger Sub, Inc., merged with and into Meter Readings Holding Group, LLC in 2018. With this merger, there will be some improvements in earnings forcast. Recently the company has generated a negative trend in earnings per share over the past quarters. However, with this acquisition, there were some improvements in the annual and quarted earnings.

Financial Data
(US$ in Thousands)

	3 Mos	12/31/2017	12/31/2016	12/31/2015	12/31/2014	12/31/2013	12/31/2012	12/31/2011
Earnings Per Share	4.32	4.39	5.24	4.77	5.48	5.47	5.00	4.42
Cash Flow Per Share	5.77	6.92	7.16	5.74	6.66	6.46	5.89	5.61
Tang Book Value Per Share	N.M.	1.55	3.07	7.61	12.47	13.85	10.43	7.96
Dividends Per Share	2.940	2.870	2.590	...	...	1.850	1.680	1.520
Dividend Payout %	68.06	65.38	49.43	...	...	33.82	33.60	34.39
Income Statement								
Total Revenue	991,200	3,668,800	3,505,200	3,390,400	3,359,400	3,183,900	3,044,400	2,871,600
EBITDA	133,100	545,500	527,200	500,800	566,600	549,900	516,700	466,500
Depn & Amortn	40,000	57,500	53,400	51,200	49,900	45,300	44,100	45,800
Income Before Taxes	75,800	443,100	430,400	418,600	485,500	473,800	441,800	389,800
Income Taxes	16,000	193,200	132,600	136,500	158,300	144,000	139,700	119,600
Net Income	58,300	243,100	293,000	277,300	325,300	326,500	299,700	267,900
Average Shares	55,100	55,100	55,700	58,000	59,200	59,600	59,800	60,400
Balance Sheet								
Current Assets	1,720,800	1,604,100	1,551,300	1,387,800	1,629,400	1,632,400	1,456,200	1,353,500
Total Assets	4,975,400	3,720,600	3,525,000	3,208,700	3,322,800	3,187,200	2,947,000	2,846,500
Current Liabilities	898,500	706,100	589,600	603,100	499,200	467,000	447,400	492,100
Long-Term Obligations	1,903,200	987,100	990,500	595,900	597,600	597,200	596,700	596,300
Total Liabilities	3,313,400	2,086,400	1,932,200	1,468,100	1,395,700	1,280,800	1,285,800	1,378,700
Stockholders' Equity	1,662,000	1,634,200	1,592,800	1,740,600	1,927,100	1,906,400	1,661,200	1,467,800
Shares Outstanding	54,800	54,882	55,532	57,836	58,496	59,172	59,236	59,179
Statistical Record								
Return on Assets %	5.63	6.71	8.68	8.49	9.99	10.65	10.32	9.65
Return on Equity %	14.73	15.07	17.53	15.12	16.97	18.30	19.10	18.31
EBITDA Margin %	13.43	14.87	15.04	14.77	16.87	17.27	16.97	16.25
Net Margin %	5.88	6.63	8.36	8.18	9.68	10.25	9.84	9.33
Asset Turnover	0.90	1.01	1.04	1.04	1.03	1.04	1.05	1.03
Current Ratio	1.92	2.27	2.63	2.30	3.26	3.50	3.25	2.75
Debt to Equity	1.15	0.60	0.62	0.34	0.31	0.31	0.36	0.41
Price Range	139.21-109.89	137.50-109.89	118.54-86.29	116.29-82.96	126.41-101.44	110.90-84.63	86.48-67.80	72.70-47.97
P/E Ratio	32.22-25.44	31.32-25.03	22.62-16.47	24.38-17.39	23.07-18.51	20.27-15.47	17.30-13.56	16.45-10.85
Average Yield %	2.42	2.42	2.48	...	...	1.84	2.12	2.44

Address: 40 Waterview Drive, Shelton, CT 06484 **Telephone:** 475-882-4000	**Web Site:** www.hubbell.com **Officers:** David G. Nord - Chairman, President, Chief Executive Officer, Senior Vice President, Chief Financial Officer, Chief Operating Officer William R. Sperry - Senior Vice President, Chief Financial Officer	**Auditors:** PricewaterhouseCoopers LLP **Transfer Agents:** Computershare Inc.

HUDSON PACIFIC PROPERTIES INC

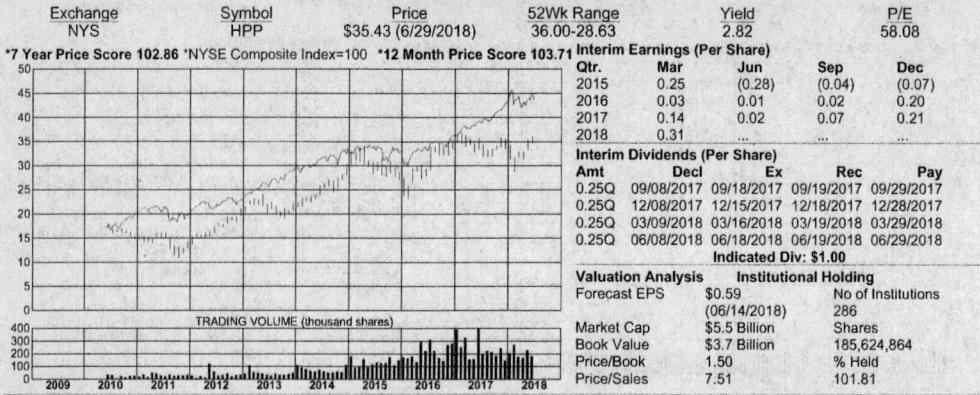

Exchange	Symbol	Price	52Wk Range	Yield	P/E
NYS	HPP	$35.43 (6/29/2018)	36.00-28.63	2.82	58.08

*7 Year Price Score 102.86 *NYSE Composite Index=100 *12 Month Price Score 103.71

Interim Earnings (Per Share)

Qtr.	Mar	Jun	Sep	Dec
2015	0.25	(0.28)	(0.04)	(0.07)
2016	0.03	0.01	0.02	0.20
2017	0.14	0.02	0.07	0.21
2018	0.31	...	...	...

Interim Dividends (Per Share)

Amt	Decl	Ex	Rec	Pay
0.25Q	09/08/2017	09/18/2017	09/19/2017	09/29/2017
0.25Q	12/08/2017	12/15/2017	12/18/2017	12/28/2017
0.25Q	03/09/2018	03/16/2018	03/19/2018	03/29/2018
0.25Q	06/08/2018	06/18/2018	06/19/2018	06/29/2018

Indicated Div: $1.00

Valuation Analysis

Forecast EPS	$0.59 (06/14/2018)
Market Cap	$5.5 Billion
Book Value	$3.7 Billion
Price/Book	1.50
Price/Sales	7.51

Institutional Holding

No of Institutions	286
Shares	185,624,864
% Held	101.81

TRADING VOLUME (thousand shares)

Business Summary: REITs (MIC: 5.3.1 SIC: 6531 NAIC: 531312)

Hudson Pacific Properties is a holding company operating through Hudson Pacific Properties, L.P. Co. is focused on acquiring, repositioning, developing and operating office and media and entertainment properties throughout Northern and Southern California and the Pacific Northwest. Co. has two segments: office properties and media and entertainment properties. As of Dec 31 2017, the office properties segment included 54 properties totaling approximately 13.3 million square feet, while the media and entertainment segment included two properties, the Sunset Gower Studios property and the Sunset Bronson Studios property, totaling approximately 1.2 million square feet located in Hollywood, CA.

Recent Developments: For the quarter ended Mar 31 2018, net income increased 117.6% to US$52.6 million from US$24.2 million in the year-earlier quarter. Revenues were US$174.1 million, up 3.5% from US$168.3 million the year before.

Prospects: Our evaluation of Hudson Pacific Properties Inc as of Jan. 21, 2018 is the result of our systematic analysis on three basic characteristics: earnings strength, relative valuation, and recent stock price movement. The company has enjoyed a very positive trend in earnings per share over the past 5 quarters. However, while recent estimates for the company have been lowered by analysts, HPP has posted better than expected results. Based on operating earnings yield, the company is overvalued when compared to all of the companies in our coverage universe. Share price changes over the past year indicates that HPP will perform well over the near term.

Financial Data

(US$ in Thousands)	3 Mos	12/31/2017	12/31/2016	12/31/2015	12/31/2014	12/31/2013	12/31/2012	12/31/2011
Earnings Per Share	0.61	0.44	0.25	(0.19)	0.15	(0.27)	(0.41)	(0.35)
Cash Flow Per Share	1.70	1.91	2.06	2.03	0.96	0.75	1.03	1.09
Tang Book Value Per Share	23.58	23.39	22.75	18.70	15.50	15.02	14.71	15.99
Dividends Per Share	1.000	1.000	0.800	0.575	0.500	0.500	0.500	0.500
Dividend Payout %	163.93	227.27	320.00	...	333.33	...	...	...
Income Statement								
Total Revenue	174,118	728,139	639,639	520,850	253,415	205,558	166,156	142,189
EBITDA	84,753	469,139	390,843	272,841	125,194	98,660	72,895	63,527
Depn & Amortn	11,696	284,638	271,301	238,380	75,606	72,047	59,136	48,358
Income Before Taxes	52,563	94,561	43,758	(16,082)	23,686	1,415	(5,006)	(2,238)
Net Income	49,240	68,590	27,984	(16,397)	9,955	(14,833)	(17,190)	(10,434)
Average Shares	156,714	153,882	110,369	85,927	66,509	55,182	41,640	29,392
Balance Sheet								
Current Assets	200,361	215,100	202,325	181,040	109,518	77,389	63,833	42,990
Total Assets	6,448,291	6,622,070	6,678,998	6,254,035	2,340,885	2,131,274	1,559,690	1,152,791
Current Liabilities	146,588	279,549	278,061	254,105	137,634	86,625	67,908	51,776
Long-Term Obligations	2,240,688	2,421,380	2,688,010	2,260,716	918,059	931,308	582,085	399,871
Total Liabilities	2,778,449	2,974,122	3,565,538	4,578,024	1,151,534	1,117,353	707,002	515,003
Stockholders' Equity	3,669,842	3,647,948	3,113,460	1,676,011	1,189,351	1,013,921	852,688	637,788
Shares Outstanding	155,626	155,602	136,492	89,153	66,797	57,230	47,496	33,840
Statistical Record								
Return on Assets %	1.47	1.03	0.43	N.M.	0.45	N.M.	N.M.	N.M.
Return on Equity %	2.62	2.03	1.17	N.M.	0.90	N.M.	N.M.	N.M.
EBITDA Margin %	48.68	64.43	61.10	52.38	49.40	48.00	43.87	44.68
Net Margin %	28.28	9.42	4.37	N.M.	3.93	N.M.	N.M.	N.M.
Asset Turnover	0.11	0.11	0.10	0.12	0.11	0.11	0.12	0.13
Current Ratio	1.37	0.77	0.73	0.71	0.80	0.89	0.94	0.83
Debt to Equity	0.61	0.66	0.86	1.35	0.77	0.92	0.68	0.63
Price Range	35.79-28.63	36.65-31.73	35.27-22.97	33.95-27.17	30.34-21.42	23.99-19.03	21.06-13.62	16.07-10.85
P/E Ratio	58.67-46.93	83.30-72.11	141.08-91.88	...	202.27-142.80	...	...	...
Average Yield %	3.01	2.93	2.65	1.90	2.00	2.34	2.93	3.54

Address: 11601 Wilshire Blvd., Ninth Floor, Los Angeles, CA 90025 Telephone: 310-445-5700 Fax: 310-445-5710	Web Site: www.hudsonpacificproperties.com Officers: Victor J. Coleman - Chairman, Chief Executive Officer Mark T. Lammas - Chief Financial Officer, Chief Operating Officer, Treasurer	Auditors: Ernst & Young LLP Investor Contact: 310-829-5400 Transfer Agents: Computershare, Canton, MA

HUMANA INC.

Exchange	Symbol	Price	52Wk Range	Yield	P/E
NYS	HUM	$297.63 (6/29/2018)	306.95-230.77	0.67	23.25

*7 Year Price Score 140.96 ***NYSE Composite Index=100** ***12 Month Price Score 109.43**

TRADING VOLUME (thousand shares)

Interim Earnings (Per Share)

Qtr.	Mar	Jun	Sep	Dec
2015	2.82	2.85	2.09	0.67
2016	1.56	2.06	2.98	(2.66)
2017	7.49	4.46	3.44	1.37
2018	3.53	...	...	...

Interim Dividends (Per Share)

Amt	Decl	Ex	Rec	Pay
0.40Q	08/17/2017	09/28/2017	09/29/2017	10/27/2017
0.40Q	11/02/2017	12/28/2017	12/29/2017	01/26/2018
0.50Q	02/06/2018	03/28/2018	03/30/2018	04/27/2018
0.50Q	04/19/2018	06/28/2018	06/29/2018	07/27/2018

Indicated Div: $2.00

Valuation Analysis | **Institutional Holding**

Forecast EPS	$13.95	No of Institutions
	(06/14/2018)	984
Market Cap	$41.0 Billion	Shares
Book Value	$10.1 Billion	161,741,824
Price/Book	4.06	% Held
Price/Sales	0.75	88.13

Business Summary: Life & Health (MIC: 5.2.2 SIC: 6324 NAIC: 524114)

Humana is a holding company. Through its subsidiaries, Co. is a health and well-being company. Co. manages its business with three segments: Retail, which consists of Medicare and commercial insured medical and specialty health insurance benefits, including dental, vision, and other supplemental health and financial protection products; Group, which consists of employer group commercial fully-insured medical and specialty health insurance benefits, including dental, vision, and other supplemental health and voluntary benefit products; and Healthcare Services, which includes pharmacy solutions, provider services, home based services, clinical programs, and predictive modeling, among others.

Recent Developments: For the quarter ended Mar 31 2018, net income decreased 56.0% to US$491.0 million from US$1.12 billion in the year-earlier quarter. Revenues were US$14.28 billion, up 3.8% from US$13.76 billion the year before. Net premiums earned were US$13.81 billion versus US$13.40 billion in the prior-year quarter, an increase of 3.1%.

Prospects: Our evaluation of Humana Inc. as of Jan. 21, 2018 is the result of our systematic analysis on three basic characteristics: earnings strength, relative valuation, and recent stock price movement. The company has generated a negative trend in earnings per share over the past 5 quarters and while recent estimates for the company have been mixed, HUM has posted better than expected results. Based on operating earnings yield, the company is about fairly valued when compared to all of the companies in our coverage universe. Share price changes over the past year indicates that HUM will perform poorly over the near term.

Financial Data
(US$ in Thousands)

	3 Mos	12/31/2017	12/31/2016	12/31/2015	12/31/2014	12/31/2013	12/31/2012	12/31/2011
Earnings Per Share	12.80	16.81	4.07	8.44	7.36	7.73	7.47	8.46
Cash Flow Per Share	25.61	28.04	12.93	5.81	10.49	10.90	11.88	12.57
Tang Book Value Per Share	45.91	47.65	49.65	47.75	39.67	36.25	32.89	32.46
Dividends Per Share	1.700	1.890	0.870	1.150	1.110	1.070	1.030	0.750
Dividend Payout %	13.28	11.24	21.38	13.63	15.08	13.84	13.79	8.87
Income Statement								
Premium Income	13,811,000	52,380,000	53,021,000	52,409,000	45,959,000	38,829,000	37,009,000	35,106,000
Total Revenue	14,279,000	53,767,000	54,379,000	54,289,000	48,500,000	41,313,000	39,126,000	36,832,000
Benefits & Claims	11,670,000	43,496,000	45,007,000	44,269,000	38,166,000	32,564,000	30,985,000	28,823,000
Income Before Taxes	707,000	4,020,000	1,552,000	2,431,000	2,170,000	1,921,000	1,911,000	2,235,000
Income Taxes	216,000	1,572,000	938,000	1,155,000	1,023,000	690,000	689,000	816,000
Net Income	491,000	2,448,000	614,000	1,276,000	1,147,000	1,231,000	1,222,000	1,419,000
Average Shares	138,830	145,585	150,917	151,142	155,874	159,151	163,457	167,827
Balance Sheet								
Total Assets	33,453,000	27,178,000	25,396,000	24,705,000	23,466,000	20,735,000	19,979,000	17,708,000
Total Liabilities	23,372,000	17,336,000	14,711,000	14,359,000	13,820,000	11,419,000	11,132,000	9,645,000
Stockholders' Equity	10,081,000	9,842,000	10,685,000	10,346,000	9,646,000	9,316,000	8,847,000	8,063,000
Shares Outstanding	137,682	137,678	149,305	148,288	149,604	154,030	158,331	164,004
Statistical Record								
Return on Assets %	5.60	9.31	2.44	5.30	5.19	6.05	6.47	8.39
Return on Equity %	17.96	23.85	5.82	12.77	12.10	13.56	14.41	18.94
Loss Ratio %	84.50	83.04	84.89	84.47	83.04	83.87	83.72	82.10
Net Margin %	3.44	4.55	1.13	2.35	2.36	2.98	3.12	3.85
Price Range	291.23-206.14	260.86-195.24	216.76-153.38	214.92-139.09	149.07-95.59	105.25-66.01	95.50-61.60	89.83-54.74
P/E Ratio	22.75-16.10	15.52-11.61	53.26-37.69	25.46-16.48	20.25-12.99	13.62-8.54	12.78-8.25	10.62-6.47
Average Yield %	0.69	0.82	0.49	0.65	0.91	1.26	1.32	1.01

Address: 500 West Main Street, Louisville, KY 40202 **Telephone:** 502-580-1000	**Web Site:** www.humana.com **Officers:** Kurt J. Hilzinger - Chairman Bruce D. Broussard - President, Chief Executive Officer	**Auditors:** PricewaterhouseCoopers LLP **Investor Contact:** 502-580-3644 **Transfer Agents:** American Stock Transfer & Trust Company, LLC, Brooklyn, NY

HUNTINGTON INGALLS INDUSTRIES, INC.

Exchange	Symbol	Price	52Wk Range	Yield	P/E
NYS	HII	$216.79 (6/29/2018)	270.88-186.16	1.33	19.05

⁴7 Year Price Score 158.02 *NYSE Composite Index=100 **12 Month Price Score 93.97**

TRADING VOLUME (thousand shares)

Interim Earnings (Per Share)

Qtr.	Mar	Jun	Sep	Dec
2015	1.79	3.20	2.29	1.08
2016	2.87	2.80	2.27	4.21
2017	2.56	3.21	3.27	1.42
2018	3.48	...	...	...

Interim Dividends (Per Share)

Amt	Decl	Ex	Rec	Pay
0.60Q	07/25/2017	08/23/2017	08/25/2017	09/08/2017
0.72Q	11/07/2017	11/22/2017	11/24/2017	12/08/2017
0.72Q	02/08/2018	02/22/2018	02/23/2018	03/09/2018
0.72Q	05/01/2018	05/24/2018	05/25/2018	06/08/2018

Indicated Div: $2.88

Valuation Analysis **Institutional Holding**

Forecast EPS	$15.96	No of Institutions
	(06/14/2018)	658
Market Cap	$9.7 Billion	Shares
Book Value	$1.7 Billion	45,317,296
Price/Book	5.63	% Held
Price/Sales	1.27	86.12

Business Summary: Defense (MIC: 7.1.2 SIC: 3731 NAIC: 336611)

Huntington Ingalls Industries is a military shipbuilding company and a provider of professional services to partners in government and industry. Co. has three segments: Ingalls Shipbuilding, which designs and constructs non-nuclear ships for the U.S. Navy and U.S. Coast Guard, including amphibious assault ships, and surface combatants; Newport News Shipbuilding, which is designing and constructing nuclear-powered ships, such as aircraft carriers and submarines, and the refueling and overhaul and the inactivation of such ships; and Technical Solutions, which includes businesses that are focused on life-cycle sustainment services to the U.S. Navy fleet and other maritime customers.

Recent Developments: For the quarter ended Mar 31 2018, net income increased 31.1% to US$156.0 million from US$119.0 million in the year-earlier quarter. Revenues were US$1.87 billion, up 8.7% from US$1.72 billion the year before. Operating income was US$191.0 million versus US$168.0 million in the prior-year quarter, an increase of 13.7%. Direct operating expenses rose 8.3% to US$1.50 billion from US$1.38 billion in the comparable period the year before. Indirect operating expenses increased 6.8% to US$188.0 million from US$176.0 million in the equivalent prior-year period.

Prospects: Our evaluation of Huntington Ingalls Industries Inc. as of Jan. 21, 2018 is the result of our systematic analysis on three basic characteristics: earnings strength, relative valuation, and recent stock price movement. The company has generated a negative trend in earnings per share over the past 5 quarters and while recent estimates for the company have been mixed, HII has posted better than expected results. Based on operating earnings yield, the company is undervalued when compared to all of the companies in our coverage universe. Share price changes over the past year indicates that HII will perform well over the near term.

Financial Data

(US$ in Thousands)	3 Mos	12/31/2017	12/31/2016	12/31/2015	12/31/2014	12/31/2013	12/31/2012	12/31/2011
Earnings Per Share	11.38	10.46	12.14	8.36	6.86	5.18	2.91	(1.93)
Cash Flow Per Share	18.66	17.81	17.52	17.29	14.67	4.75	6.70	10.82
Tang Book Value Per Share	0.04	0.73	N.M.	0.83	N.M.	2.30	N.M.	N.M.
Dividends Per Share	2.640	2.520	2.100	1.700	1.000	0.500	0.100	...
Dividend Payout %	23.20	24.09	17.30	20.33	14.58	9.65	3.44	...
Income Statement								
Total Revenue	1,874,000	7,441,000	7,068,000	7,020,000	6,957,000	6,820,000	6,708,000	6,575,000
EBITDA	261,000	1,071,000	1,044,000	949,000	850,000	738,000	542,000	294,000
Depn & Amortn	51,000	205,000	186,000	180,000	194,000	226,000	184,000	184,000
Income Before Taxes	195,000	772,000	784,000	632,000	507,000	394,000	241,000	6,000
Income Taxes	39,000	293,000	211,000	228,000	169,000	133,000	95,000	100,000
Net Income	156,000	479,000	573,000	404,000	338,000	261,000	146,000	(94,000)
Average Shares	44,800	45,800	47,200	48,300	49,300	50,400	50,100	48,800
Balance Sheet								
Current Assets	2,210,000	2,195,000	2,142,000	2,284,000	2,546,000	2,676,000	2,484,000	2,268,000
Total Assets	6,376,000	6,374,000	6,352,000	6,024,000	6,269,000	6,225,000	6,392,000	6,001,000
Current Liabilities	1,463,000	1,391,000	1,343,000	1,274,000	1,312,000	1,392,000	1,384,000	1,372,000
Long-Term Obligations	1,280,000	1,279,000	1,278,000	1,273,000	1,592,000	1,700,000	1,779,000	1,830,000
Total Liabilities	4,658,000	4,616,000	4,699,000	4,534,000	4,904,000	4,704,000	5,725,000	5,129,000
Stockholders' Equity	1,718,000	1,758,000	1,653,000	1,490,000	1,365,000	1,521,000	667,000	872,000
Shares Outstanding	44,600	45,100	46,200	46,900	48,300	48,700	49,600	48,821
Statistical Record								
Return on Assets %	8.18	7.53	9.23	6.57	5.41	4.14	2.35	N.M.
Return on Equity %	30.75	28.09	36.36	28.30	23.42	23.86	18.92	N.M.
EBITDA Margin %	13.93	14.39	14.77	13.52	12.22	10.82	8.08	4.47
Net Margin %	8.32	6.44	8.11	5.75	4.86	3.83	2.18	N.M.
Asset Turnover	1.20	1.17	1.14	1.14	1.11	1.08	1.08	2.19
Current Ratio	1.51	1.58	1.59	1.79	1.94	1.92	1.79	1.65
Debt to Equity	0.75	0.73	0.77	0.85	1.17	1.12	2.67	2.10
Price Range	270.88-185.22	251.96-185.22	187.96-121.41	143.55-103.98	115.48-87.91	90.01-43.17	44.96-31.80	41.50-22.85
P/E Ratio	23.80-16.28	24.09-17.71	15.48-10.00	17.17-12.44	16.83-12.81	17.38-8.33	15.45-10.93	...
Average Yield %	1.19	1.20	1.36	1.38	1.00	0.82	0.26	...

Address: 4101 Washington Avenue, Newport News, VA 23607
Telephone: 757-380-2000

Web Site: www.huntingtoningalls.com
Officers: Thomas B. Fargo - Chairman C. Michael Petters - President, Chief Executive Officer

Auditors: DELOITTE & TOUCHE LLP
Investor Contact: 757-688-5572
Transfer Agents: Computershare Trust Company, N.A., Providence, RI

HUNTSMAN CORP

Exchange	Symbol	Price	52Wk Range	Yield	P/E
NYS	HUN	$29.20 (6/29/2018)	35.29-25.13	2.23	8.56

*7 Year Price Score 121.35 *NYSE Composite Index=100 *12 Month Price Score 101.52

Interim Earnings (Per Share)

Qtr.	Mar	Jun	Sep	Dec
2015	0.02	0.12	0.22	0.02
2016	0.24	0.36	0.23	0.53
2017	0.31	0.69	0.60	1.01
2018	1.11	...	...	...

Interim Dividends (Per Share)

Amt	Decl	Ex	Rec	Pay
0.125Q	08/21/2017	09/14/2017	09/15/2017	09/29/2017
0.125Q	11/06/2017	12/14/2017	12/15/2017	12/29/2017
0.163Q	02/23/2018	03/14/2018	03/15/2018	03/30/2018
0.163Q	05/15/2018	06/14/2018	06/15/2018	06/29/2018

Indicated Div: $0.65

Valuation Analysis — **Institutional Holding**

Forecast EPS	$3.15
(06/13/2018)	
Market Cap	$7.0 Billion
Book Value	$2.9 Billion
Price/Book	2.41
Price/Sales	0.75

No of Institutions	596
Shares	234,912,800
% Held	74.22

Business Summary: Specialty Chemicals (MIC: 8.3.2 SIC: 2899 NAIC: 325199)

Huntsman is a manufacturer of organic chemical products and of inorganic chemical products. Co. operates in five segments: Polyurethanes, which provides polyurethane chemicals, including methyl diphenyl diisocyanate products, propylene oxide, polyols, propylene glycol and thermoplastic polyurethane; Performance Products, which provides amines, surfactants and maleic anhydride; Advanced Materials, which provides epoxy, acrylic and polyurethane-based polymer products; Textile Effects, which provides textile chemicals, dyes and digital inks; and Pigments and Additives, which provides titanium dioxide, functional additives, color pigments, timber treatment and water treatment chemicals.

Recent Developments: For the quarter ended Mar 31 2018, income from continuing operations increased 138.4% to US$236.0 million from US$99.0 million in the year-earlier quarter. Net income increased 280.4% to US$350.0 million from US$92.0 million in the year-earlier quarter. Revenues were US$2.30 billion, up 18.8% from US$1.93 billion the year before. Operating income was US$296.0 million versus US$162.0 million in the prior-year quarter, an increase of 82.7%. Direct operating expenses rose 13.8% to US$1.76 billion from US$1.54 billion in the comparable period the year before. Indirect operating expenses increased 7.0% to US$244.0 million from US$228.0 million in the equivalent prior-year period.

Prospects: Our evaluation of Huntsman Corp. as of Jan. 21, 2018 is the result of our systematic analysis on three basic characteristics: earnings strength, relative valuation, and recent stock price movement. The company has enjoyed a very positive trend in earnings per share over the past 5 quarters. However, while recent estimates for the company have been mixed, HUN has posted better than expected results. Based on operating earnings yield, the company is undervalued when compared to all of the companies in our coverage universe. Share price changes over the past year indicates that HUN will perform very well over the near term.

Financial Data

(US$ in Thousands)	3 Mos	12/31/2017	12/31/2016	12/31/2015	12/31/2014	12/31/2013	12/31/2012	12/31/2011
Earnings Per Share	3.41	2.61	1.36	0.38	1.31	0.53	1.51	1.02
Cash Flow Per Share	5.35	5.11	4.59	2.37	3.14	2.95	3.25	1.54
Tang Book Value Per Share	11.32	10.09	4.65	5.23	6.41	7.33	6.66	6.18
Dividends Per Share	0.537	0.500	0.500	0.500	0.500	0.500	0.400	0.400
Dividend Payout %	15.76	19.16	36.76	131.58	38.17	94.34	26.49	39.22
Income Statement								
Total Revenue	2,295,000	8,358,000	9,657,000	10,299,000	11,578,000	11,079,000	11,187,000	11,221,000
EBITDA	385,000	1,097,000	1,045,000	752,000	1,016,000	876,000	1,165,000	999,000
Depn & Amortn	82,000	298,000	400,000	377,000	413,000	415,000	399,000	398,000
Income Before Taxes	276,000	634,000	443,000	170,000	398,000	271,000	540,000	352,000
Income Taxes	53,000	64,000	87,000	46,000	51,000	125,000	169,000	109,000
Net Income	274,000	636,000	326,000	93,000	323,000	128,000	363,000	247,000
Average Shares	245,900	243,900	239,600	245,400	246,000	242,400	240,600	241,700
Balance Sheet								
Current Assets	6,385,000	5,979,000	3,555,000	3,834,000	5,039,000	4,159,000	4,119,000	3,946,000
Total Assets	10,703,000	10,244,000	9,189,000	9,820,000	11,002,000	9,188,000	8,884,000	8,657,000
Current Liabilities	3,283,000	3,265,000	1,778,000	1,917,000	2,332,000	2,159,000	2,181,000	1,826,000
Long-Term Obligations	2,298,000	2,258,000	4,136,000	4,626,000	4,939,000	3,639,000	3,418,000	3,734,000
Total Liabilities	7,793,000	7,624,000	7,902,000	8,378,000	9,224,000	7,208,000	7,111,000	6,995,000
Stockholders' Equity	2,910,000	2,620,000	1,287,000	1,442,000	1,778,000	1,980,000	1,773,000	1,662,000
Shares Outstanding	239,831	240,213	236,370	237,080	243,416	240,401	238,273	235,746
Statistical Record								
Return on Assets %	8.26	6.55	3.42	0.89	3.20	1.42	4.13	2.84
Return on Equity %	38.24	32.56	23.83	5.78	17.19	6.82	21.08	14.31
EBITDA Margin %	16.78	13.13	10.82	7.30	8.78	7.91	10.41	8.90
Net Margin %	11.94	7.61	3.38	0.90	2.79	1.16	3.24	2.20
Asset Turnover	0.92	0.86	1.01	0.99	1.15	1.23	1.27	1.29
Current Ratio	1.94	1.83	2.00	2.00	2.16	1.93	1.89	2.16
Debt to Equity	0.79	0.86	3.21	3.21	2.78	1.84	1.93	2.25
Price Range	35.29-23.38	33.42-19.21	20.33-7.91	24.40-9.33	28.88-21.22	24.60-15.90	17.07-9.82	20.95-8.78
P/E Ratio	10.35-6.86	12.80-7.36	14.95-5.82	64.21-24.55	22.05-16.20	46.42-30.00	11.30-6.50	20.54-8.61
Average Yield %	1.88	1.93	3.38	2.71	1.98	2.59	2.84	2.61

Address: 10003 Woodloch Forest Drive, The Woodlands, TX 77380 **Telephone:** 281-719-6000	**Web Site:** www.huntsman.com **Officers:** Peter R. Huntsman - Chairman, President, Chief Executive Officer Sean Douglas - Vice President, Treasurer, Executive Vice President, Chief Financial Officer	**Auditors:** DELOITTE & TOUCHE LLP **Investor Contact:** 801-584-5959 **Transfer Agents:** Computershare, Providence, RI

HYATT HOTELS CORP

Exchange	Symbol	Price	52Wk Range	Yield	P/E
NYS	H	$77.15 (6/29/2018)	84.24-54.62	0.78	15.97

*7 Year Price Score 110.47 *NYSE Composite Index=100 *12 Month Price Score 111.54

Interim Earnings (Per Share)

Qtr.	Mar	Jun	Sep	Dec
2015	0.15	0.27	0.18	0.26
2016	0.25	0.49	0.47	0.31
2017	0.54	0.68	0.14	0.61
2018	3.40	...	...	...

Interim Dividends (Per Share)

Amt	Decl	Ex	Rec	Pay
0.15Q	02/14/2018	03/21/2018	03/22/2018	03/29/2018
0.15Q	05/31/2018	06/18/2018	06/19/2018	06/28/2018

Indicated Div: $0.60

Valuation Analysis / Institutional Holding

Valuation Analysis		Institutional Holding	
Forecast EPS	$1.46	No of Institutions	
	(06/20/2018)	307	
Market Cap	$9.1 Billion	Shares	
Book Value	$4.2 Billion	47,061,720	
Price/Book	2.17	% Held	
Price/Sales	1.98	24.57	

Price chart and TRADING VOLUME (thousand shares) 2009-2018

Business Summary: Hotels, Restaurants & Travel (MIC: 2.2.1 SIC: 7011 NAIC: 721110)

Hyatt Hotels is a hospitality company engaged in the development, ownership, operation, management, franchising, licensing or provision of services to a portfolio of properties, consisting of service hotels, select service hotels, resorts and other properties, including timeshare, fractional and other forms of residential and vacation properties. Co.'s hotels and resorts operate under seven brands: Park Hyatt, Grand Hyatt, Hyatt Regency, Hyatt, Andaz, Hyatt Centric and The Unbound Collection by Hyatt. Co.'s two select service brands are Hyatt Place and Hyatt House, an extended stay brand. As of Dec 31 2017, Co.'s worldwide hotel portfolio consisted of 719 hotels (182,913 rooms).

Recent Developments: For the quarter ended Mar 31 2018, net income increased 647.3% to US$411.0 million from US$55.0 million in the year-earlier quarter. Revenues were US$1.11 billion, down 1.5% from US$1.13 billion the year before. Direct operating expenses declined 3.7% to US$852.0 million from US$885.0 million in the comparable period the year before. Indirect operating expenses decreased 4.3% to US$178.0 million from US$186.0 million in the equivalent prior-year period.

Prospects: Our evaluation of Hyatt Hotels Corp. as of Jan. 21, 2018 is the result of our systematic analysis on three basic characteristics: earnings strength, relative valuation, and recent stock price movement. The company has suffered a very negative trend in earnings per share over the past 5 quarters and while recent estimates for the company have been mixed, H has posted better than expected results. Based on operating earnings yield, the company is overvalued when compared to all of the companies in our coverage universe. Share price changes over the past year indicates that H will perform poorly over the near term.

Financial Data
(US$ in Thousands)

	3 Mos	12/31/2017	12/31/2016	12/31/2015	12/31/2014	12/31/2013	12/31/2012	12/31/2011
Earnings Per Share	4.83	1.98	1.52	0.86	2.23	1.30	0.53	0.67
Cash Flow Per Share	4.42	4.97	3.67	3.77	3.09	2.88	3.02	2.33
Tang Book Value Per Share	31.60	22.71	24.30	24.33	26.44	25.82	26.53	26.38
Dividends Per Share	0.150	...	...	...	...	...	...	...
Dividend Payout %	3.11	...	...	...	...	...	...	...
Income Statement								
Total Revenue	1,109,000	4,685,000	4,429,000	4,328,000	4,415,000	4,184,000	3,949,000	3,698,000
EBITDA	580,000	620,000	574,000	603,000	869,000	673,000	470,000	399,000
Depn & Amortn	(5,000)	335,000	315,000	289,000	324,000	320,000	327,000	288,000
Income Before Taxes	574,000	353,000	221,000	258,000	500,000	322,000	117,000	79,000
Income Taxes	150,000	323,000	85,000	70,000	179,000	116,000	8,000	(28,000)
Net Income	411,000	249,000	204,000	124,000	344,000	207,000	88,000	113,000
Average Shares	120,778	126,346	133,939	143,999	154,350	159,189	165,377	169,240
Balance Sheet								
Current Assets	2,196,000	1,327,000	1,139,000	1,124,000	1,709,000	1,163,000	1,758,000	1,591,000
Total Assets	7,987,000	7,672,000	7,749,000	7,596,000	8,143,000	8,177,000	7,640,000	7,507,000
Current Liabilities	1,051,000	966,000	924,000	1,107,000	730,000	871,000	618,000	568,000
Long-Term Obligations	1,439,000	1,440,000	1,445,000	1,047,000	1,381,000	1,289,000	1,229,000	1,221,000
Total Liabilities	3,799,000	4,137,000	3,846,000	3,605,000	3,516,000	3,408,000	2,819,000	2,689,000
Stockholders' Equity	4,188,000	3,535,000	3,903,000	3,991,000	4,627,000	4,769,000	4,821,000	4,818,000
Shares Outstanding	118,012	118,984	130,815	136,233	149,081	156,111	162,066	165,162
Statistical Record								
Return on Assets %	7.49	3.23	2.65	1.58	4.22	2.62	1.16	1.53
Return on Equity %	14.93	6.70	5.15	2.88	7.32	4.32	1.82	2.27
EBITDA Margin %	52.30	13.23	12.96	13.93	19.68	16.09	11.90	10.79
Net Margin %	37.06	5.31	4.61	2.87	7.79	4.95	2.23	3.06
Asset Turnover	0.59	0.61	0.58	0.55	0.54	0.53	0.52	0.50
Current Ratio	2.09	1.37	1.23	1.02	2.34	1.34	2.84	2.80
Debt to Equity	0.34	0.41	0.37	0.26	0.30	0.27	0.25	0.25
Price Range	81.69-53.29	73.88-50.64	57.69-35.77	61.76-45.86	63.74-45.88	49.85-38.57	44.10-33.74	49.57-29.79
P/E Ratio	16.91-11.03	37.31-25.58	37.95-23.53	71.81-53.33	28.58-20.57	38.35-29.67	83.21-63.66	73.99-44.46
Average Yield %	0.23	...	...	...	...	...	...	...

Address: 150 North Riverside Plaza, Chicago, IL 60606	Web Site: www.hyatt.com	Auditors: Deloitte & Touche LLP
Telephone: 312-750-1234	Officers: Thomas J. Pritzker - Executive Chairman Mark S. Hoplamazian - President, Chief Executive Officer	Investor Contact: 312-750-1234 Transfer Agents: Wells Fargo Shareowner Services, South St. Paul, MN

IDACORP INC

Exchange	Symbol	Price	52Wk Range	Yield	P/E
NYS	IDA	$92.24 (6/29/2018)	98.81-81.05	2.56	21.55

*7 Year Price Score 114.86 *NYSE Composite Index=100 *12 Month Price Score 100.29

Interim Earnings (Per Share)

Qtr.	Mar	Jun	Sep	Dec
2015	0.47	1.31	1.46	0.63
2016	0.51	1.12	1.65	0.66
2017	0.66	0.99	1.80	0.77
2018	0.72	...	...	...

Interim Dividends (Per Share)

Amt	Decl	Ex	Rec	Pay
0.55Q	07/20/2017	08/04/2017	08/08/2017	08/30/2017
0.59Q	10/19/2017	11/03/2017	11/06/2017	11/30/2017
0.59Q	01/18/2018	02/02/2018	02/05/2018	02/28/2018
0.59Q	04/19/2018	05/04/2018	05/07/2018	05/30/2018

Indicated Div: $2.36 (Div. Reinv. Plan)

Valuation Analysis

		Institutional Holding	
Forecast EPS	$4.20	No of Institutions	
	(05/22/2018)	408	
Market Cap	$4.6 Billion	Shares	
Book Value	$2.3 Billion	55,016,924	
Price/Book	2.06	% Held	
Price/Sales	3.43	75.01	

Business Summary: Electric Utilities (MIC: 3.1.1 SIC: 4911 NAIC: 221122)

Idacorp is a holding company. Co.'s principal operating subsidiary, Idaho Power Co. (Idaho Power), is an electric utility engaged in the generation, transmission, distribution, sale, and purchase of electric energy and capacity and is regulated by the state regulatory commissions of Idaho and Oregon and by the Federal Energy Regulatory Commission. Idaho Power's joint venture, Idaho Energy Resources Co., mines and supplies coal to the Jim Bridger generating plant owned in part by Idaho Power. As of Dec 31 2017, Idaho Power provided electric utility service to about 545,000 general business customers in southern Idaho and eastern Oregon, of which over 454,000 were residential customers.

Recent Developments: For the quarter ended Mar 31 2018, net income increased 9.4% to US$36.1 million from US$33.0 million in the year-earlier quarter. Revenues were US$310.1 million, up 2.5% from US$302.5 million the year before. Operating income was US$50.6 million versus US$53.6 million in the prior-year quarter, a decrease of 5.7%. Direct operating expenses rose 4.2% to US$249.1 million from US$238.9 million in the comparable period the year before. Indirect operating expenses increased 4.7% to US$10.5 million from US$10.0 million in the equivalent prior-year period.

Prospects: Our evaluation of Idacorp Inc. as of Jan. 21, 2018 is the result of our systematic analysis on three basic characteristics: earnings strength, relative valuation, and recent stock price movement. The company has managed to produce a neutral trend in earnings per share over the past 5 quarters. However, while recent estimates for the company have been mixed, IDA has posted better than expected results. Based on operating earnings yield, the company is undervalued when compared to all of the companies in our coverage universe. Share price changes over the past year indicates that IDA will perform very well over the near term.

Financial Data
(US$ in Thousands)

	3 Mos	12/31/2017	12/31/2016	12/31/2015	12/31/2014	12/31/2013	12/31/2012	12/31/2011
Earnings Per Share	4.28	4.21	3.94	3.87	3.85	3.64	3.37	3.36
Cash Flow Per Share	8.25	8.70	6.89	7.03	7.27	6.10	4.98	6.27
Tang Book Value Per Share	43.60	44.68	42.55	40.65	38.58	36.53	34.71	32.78
Dividends Per Share	2.280	2.240	2.080	1.920	1.760	1.570	1.370	1.200
Dividend Payout %	53.27	53.21	52.79	49.61	45.71	43.13	40.65	35.71
Income Statement								
Total Revenue	310,107	1,349,486	1,262,020	1,270,289	1,282,524	1,246,214	1,080,662	1,026,756
EBITDA	96,231	492,439	447,342	449,151	410,942	453,348	393,185	305,246
Depn & Amortn	40,068	162,091	143,661	138,110	132,987	129,735	123,941	119,789
Income Before Taxes	34,990	250,474	221,646	229,107	198,154	242,581	195,375	113,931
Income Taxes	2,894	48,660	36,429	45,760	16,772	72,226	26,113	(52,133)
Net Income	36,142	212,419	198,288	194,679	193,480	182,417	168,761	166,693
Average Shares	50,463	50,424	50,373	50,292	50,199	50,126	50,010	49,558
Balance Sheet								
Current Assets	637,904	443,601	440,312	462,036	442,101	476,611	367,253	310,972
Total Assets	6,261,678	6,045,405	6,289,897	6,023,314	5,716,853	5,364,563	5,319,516	4,960,609
Current Liabilities	331,837	200,749	249,715	242,306	241,781	250,372	351,303	368,247
Long-Term Obligations	1,833,576	1,746,123	1,744,614	1,725,410	1,614,438	1,615,258	1,466,632	1,387,550
Total Liabilities	4,004,510	3,794,020	4,135,991	3,965,430	3,763,652	3,513,913	3,560,763	3,302,955
Stockholders' Equity	2,257,168	2,251,385	2,153,906	2,057,884	1,953,201	1,850,650	1,758,753	1,657,654
Shares Outstanding	50,392	50,392	50,396	50,340	50,269	50,232	50,156	49,951
Statistical Record								
Return on Assets %	3.45	3.44	3.21	3.32	3.49	3.41	3.27	3.46
Return on Equity %	9.76	9.64	9.39	9.71	10.17	10.11	9.85	10.45
EBITDA Margin %	31.03	36.49	35.45	35.36	32.04	36.38	36.38	29.73
Net Margin %	11.65	15.74	15.71	15.33	15.09	14.64	15.62	16.23
Asset Turnover	0.22	0.22	0.20	0.22	0.23	0.23	0.21	0.21
Current Ratio	1.92	2.21	1.76	1.91	1.83	1.90	1.05	0.84
Debt to Equity	0.81	0.78	0.81	0.84	0.83	0.87	0.83	0.84
Price Range	98.81-81.05	98.81-77.98	81.87-65.73	70.34-55.77	69.99-50.77	53.88-43.31	44.80-38.28	42.55-34.31
P/E Ratio	23.09-18.94	23.47-18.52	20.78-16.68	18.18-14.41	18.18-13.19	14.80-11.90	13.29-11.36	12.66-10.21
Average Yield %	2.60	2.58	2.77	3.05	3.13	3.22	3.28	3.10

Address: 1221 W. Idaho Street, Boise, ID 83702-5627
Telephone: 208-388-2200

Web Site: www.idacorpinc.com
Officers: Robert A. Tinstman - Chairman Darrel T. Anderson - President, Chief Executive Officer, Executive Vice President, Chief Financial Officer

Auditors: Deloitte & Touche LLP
Investor Contact: 208-388-2664
Transfer Agents: Wells Fargo Shareowner Services, Mendota Heights, MN

IDEX CORPORATION

Exchange	Symbol	Price	52Wk Range	Yield	P/E
NYS	IEX	$136.48 (6/29/2018)	150.37-112.67	1.26	29.41

*7 Year Price Score 138.42 *NYSE Composite Index=100 *12 Month Price Score 104.27

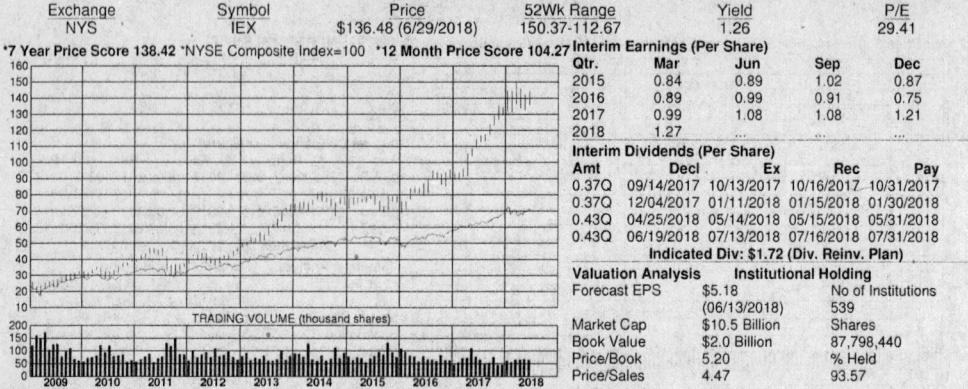

Interim Earnings (Per Share)

Qtr.	Mar	Jun	Sep	Dec
2015	0.84	0.89	1.02	0.87
2016	0.89	0.99	0.91	0.75
2017	0.99	1.08	1.08	1.21
2018	1.27	...	...	...

Interim Dividends (Per Share)

Amt	Decl	Ex	Rec	Pay
0.37Q	09/14/2017	10/13/2017	10/16/2017	10/31/2017
0.37Q	12/04/2017	01/11/2018	01/15/2018	01/30/2018
0.43Q	04/25/2018	05/14/2018	05/15/2018	05/31/2018
0.43Q	06/19/2018	07/13/2018	07/16/2018	07/31/2018

Indicated Div: $1.72 (Div. Reinv. Plan)

Valuation Analysis **Institutional Holding**

Forecast EPS	$5.18	No of Institutions
	(06/13/2018)	539
Market Cap	$10.5 Billion	Shares
Book Value	$2.0 Billion	87,798,440
Price/Book	5.20	% Held
Price/Sales	4.47	93.57

Business Summary: Industrial Machinery & Equipment (MIC: 7.2.1 SIC: 3561 NAIC: 333911)

IDEX is an applied solutions business that sells of pumps, valves, flow meters and other fluidics systems and components and engineered products. Co. has three segments: Fluid and Metering Technologies, which designs, produces and distributes displacement pumps, valves, flow meters, injectors, and other fluid-handling pump modules and systems; Health and Science Technologies, which distribute fluidics, rotary lobe pumps, roll compaction and drying systems used in beverage, food processing, pharmaceutical and cosmetics; and Fire and Safety/Diversified Products, which produces firefighting pumps and controls, rescue tools, lifting bags and other components for the fire and rescue industry.

Recent Developments: For the quarter ended Mar 31 2018, net income increased 30.4% to US$99.0 million from US$75.9 million in the year-earlier quarter. Revenues were US$612.3 million, up 10.6% from US$553.6 million the year before. Operating income was US$136.7 million versus US$115.7 million in the prior-year quarter, an increase of 18.2%. Direct operating expenses rose 10.9% to US$335.7 million from US$302.6 million in the comparable period the year before. Indirect operating expenses increased 3.5% to US$140.0 million from US$135.3 million in the equivalent prior-year period.

Prospects: Our evaluation of IDEX Corp. as of Jan. 21, 2018 is the result of our systematic analysis on three basic characteristics: earnings strength, relative valuation, and recent stock price movement. The company has managed to produce a neutral trend in earnings per share over the past 5 quarters and while recent estimates for the company have been mixed, IEX has posted better than expected results. Based on operating earnings yield, the company is about fairly valued when compared to all of the companies in our coverage universe. Share price changes over the past year indicates that IEX will perform very well over the near term.

Financial Data

(US$ in Thousands)	3 Mos	12/31/2017	12/31/2016	12/31/2015	12/31/2014	12/31/2013	12/31/2012	12/31/2011
Earnings Per Share	4.64	4.36	3.53	3.62	3.45	3.09	0.45	2.32
Cash Flow Per Share	5.49	5.68	5.26	4.67	4.62	4.93	3.93	2.64
Dividends Per Share	1.480	1.450	1.340	1.240	1.070	0.890	0.770	0.660
Dividend Payout %	31.90	33.26	37.96	34.25	31.01	28.80	171.11	28.45
Income Statement								
Total Revenue	612,324	2,287,312	2,113,043	2,020,668	2,147,767	2,024,130	1,954,258	1,838,451
EBITDA	152,335	546,064	463,166	476,407	477,522	439,662	169,939	338,717
Depn & Amortn	11,203	45,902	49,038	42,426	43,187	44,327	41,485	35,504
Income Before Taxes	130,132	455,273	368,512	392,345	392,440	353,129	86,204	273,881
Income Taxes	31,174	118,016	97,403	109,538	113,054	97,914	48,574	80,024
Net Income	98,958	337,257	271,109	282,807	279,386	255,215	37,630	193,857
Average Shares	77,739	77,333	76,758	77,972	80,728	82,489	83,641	83,543
Balance Sheet								
Current Assets	1,069,288	1,004,043	822,721	862,684	1,075,791	990,953	881,865	789,161
Total Assets	3,485,459	3,399,628	3,154,944	2,805,443	2,908,070	2,887,577	2,785,390	2,836,107
Current Liabilities	316,282	360,975	309,158	309,597	411,968	304,609	291,427	258,278
Long-Term Obligations	859,731	858,788	1,014,235	839,707	765,006	772,005	779,241	806,366
Total Liabilities	1,468,574	1,513,086	1,611,050	1,362,152	1,421,619	1,314,588	1,320,392	1,322,972
Stockholders' Equity	2,016,885	1,886,542	1,543,894	1,443,291	1,486,451	1,572,989	1,464,998	1,513,135
Shares Outstanding	76,883	76,693	76,440	76,534	78,765	81,195	82,726	83,233
Statistical Record								
Return on Assets %	10.84	10.29	9.07	9.90	9.64	9.00	1.34	7.43
Return on Equity %	19.70	19.66	18.10	19.31	18.26	16.80	2.52	13.42
EBITDA Margin %	24.88	23.87	21.92	23.58	22.23	21.72	8.70	18.42
Net Margin %	16.16	14.74	12.83	14.00	13.01	12.61	1.93	10.54
Asset Turnover	0.71	0.70	0.71	0.71	0.74	0.71	0.69	0.70
Current Ratio	3.38	2.78	2.66	2.79	2.61	3.25	3.03	3.06
Debt to Equity	0.43	0.46	0.66	0.58	0.51	0.49	0.53	0.53
Price Range	150.37-91.72	135.57-89.34	95.64-68.33	80.00-68.86	81.58-66.43	73.85-46.53	46.53-36.00	47.08-29.80
P/E Ratio	32.41-19.77	31.09-20.49	27.09-19.36	22.10-19.02	23.65-19.26	23.90-15.06	103.40-80.00	20.29-12.84
Average Yield %	1.21	1.31	1.58	1.64	1.43	1.52	1.87	1.67

Address: 1925 West Field Court, Lake Forest, IL 60045 **Telephone:** 847-498-7070	**Web Site:** www.idexcorp.com **Officers:** Andrew K. Silvernail - Chairman, President, Chief Executive Officer William K. Grogan - Senior Vice President, Chief Financial Officer	**Auditors:** DELOITTE & TOUCHE LLP **Investor Contact:** 847-498-7070 **Transfer Agents:** Computershare, Providence, RI

ILLINOIS TOOL WORKS, INC.

Exchange	Symbol	Price	52Wk Range	Yield	P/E	Div Acheiver
NYS	ITW	$138.54 (6/29/2018)	178.88-135.60	2.25	26.49	55 Years

*7 Year Price Score 131.64 ***NYSE Composite Index=100** ***12 Month Price Score 93.21**

Interim Earnings (Per Share)

Qtr.	Mar	Jun	Sep	Dec
2015	1.21	1.30	1.39	1.23
2016	1.29	1.46	1.50	1.45
2017	1.54	1.69	1.85	(0.21)
2018	1.90	...	...	...

Interim Dividends (Per Share)

Amt	Decl	Ex	Rec	Pay
0.78Q	08/04/2017	09/28/2017	09/29/2017	10/10/2017
0.78Q	10/27/2017	12/28/2017	12/29/2017	01/10/2018
0.78Q	02/15/2018	03/28/2018	03/30/2018	04/10/2018
0.78Q	05/04/2018	06/28/2018	06/29/2018	07/11/2018

Indicated Div: $3.12 (Div. Reinv. Plan)

Valuation Analysis / Institutional Holding

Valuation Analysis		Institutional Holding	
Forecast EPS	$7.75	No of Institutions	
	(06/14/2018)	1686	
Market Cap	$46.9 Billion	Shares	
Book Value	$4.2 Billion	364,128,032	
Price/Book	11.29	% Held	
Price/Sales	3.22	64.67	

Business Summary: Industrial Machinery & Equipment (MIC: 7.2.1 SIC: 3569 NAIC: 333999)

Illinois Tool Works manufactures industrial products and equipment. Co. has seven segments: Automotive original equipment manufacturers, which produces components and fasteners; Food Equipment, which produces commercial food equipment; Test & Measurement and Electronics, which produces equipment, consumables, and related software; Welding, which produces arc welding equipment, consumables and accessories; Polymers & Fluids, which produces adhesives, sealants, lubrication and cutting fluids; Construction Products, which produce engineered fastening systems and solutions; and Specialty Products, which produces beverage packaging equipment and consumables, product coding and marking equipment.

Recent Developments: For the quarter ended Mar 31 2018, net income increased 21.6% to US$652.0 million from US$536.0 million in the year-earlier quarter. Revenues were US$3.74 billion, up 7.9% from US$3.47 billion the year before. Operating income was US$903.0 million versus US$807.0 million in the prior-year quarter, an increase of 11.9%. Direct operating expenses rose 8.9% to US$2.18 billion from US$2.00 billion in the comparable period the year before. Indirect operating expenses decreased 0.2% to US$660.0 million from US$661.0 million in the equivalent prior-year period.

Prospects: Our evaluation of Illinois Tool Works Inc. as of Jan. 21, 2018 is the result of our systematic analysis on three basic characteristics: earnings strength, relative valuation, and recent stock price movement. The company has managed to produce a neutral trend in earnings per share over the past 5 quarters and while recent estimates for the company have been mixed, ITW has posted better than expected results. Based on operating earnings yield, the company is about fairly valued when compared to all of the companies in our coverage universe. Share price changes over the past year indicates that ITW will perform well over the near term.

Financial Data

(US$ in Thousands)	3 Mos	12/31/2017	12/31/2016	12/31/2015	12/31/2014	12/31/2013	12/31/2012	12/31/2011
Earnings Per Share	5.23	4.86	5.70	5.13	7.28	3.74	6.06	4.19
Cash Flow Per Share	7.28	6.98	6.47	6.25	4.02	5.67	4.40	3.98
Tang Book Value Per Share	N.M.	N.M.	N.M.	N.M.	0.92	6.55	6.09	5.35
Dividends Per Share	2.990	2.860	2.400	2.070	1.810	1.600	1.480	1.400
Dividend Payout %	57.17	58.85	42.11	40.35	24.86	42.78	24.42	33.41
Income Statement								
Total Revenue	3,744,000	14,314,000	13,599,000	13,405,000	14,484,000	14,135,000	17,924,000	17,786,583
EBITDA	1,030,000	3,947,000	3,516,000	3,372,000	265,135,000	3,099,000	3,485,000	3,334,240
Depn & Amortn	115,000	462,000	470,000	475,000	262,242,000	549,000	611,000	589,669
Income Before Taxes	849,000	3,270,000	2,847,000	2,723,000	2,708,000	2,361,000	3,633,000	2,592,714
Income Taxes	197,000	1,583,000	873,000	820,000	809,000	717,000	1,108,000	575,700
Net Income	652,000	1,687,000	2,035,000	1,899,000	2,946,000	1,679,000	2,870,000	2,071,384
Average Shares	342,800	346,800	357,100	370,100	404,600	449,300	473,200	494,646
Balance Sheet								
Current Assets	6,423,000	7,278,000	6,123,000	6,720,000	8,076,000	9,816,000	7,960,000	6,849,346
Total Assets	16,163,000	16,780,000	15,201,000	15,729,000	17,678,000	19,966,000	19,309,000	17,983,514
Current Liabilities	2,925,000	3,053,000	2,760,000	2,368,000	3,533,000	6,034,000	2,651,000	2,976,727
Long-Term Obligations	6,889,000	7,478,000	7,177,000	6,896,000	5,981,000	2,793,000	4,589,000	3,488,198
Total Liabilities	12,004,000	12,195,000	10,947,000	10,505,000	10,859,000	10,263,000	8,748,000	7,965,723
Stockholders' Equity	4,159,000	4,585,000	4,254,000	5,224,000	6,819,000	9,703,000	10,561,000	10,017,791
Shares Outstanding	338,800	341,500	346,900	363,710	382,900	430,200	455,100	483,608
Statistical Record								
Return on Assets %	11.38	10.55	13.12	11.37	15.65	8.55	15.35	12.10
Return on Equity %	41.68	38.17	42.82	31.54	35.66	16.57	27.82	21.37
EBITDA Margin %	27.51	27.57	25.85	25.15	1,830.54	21.92	19.44	18.75
Net Margin %	17.41	11.79	14.96	14.17	20.34	11.88	16.01	11.65
Asset Turnover	0.92	0.90	0.88	0.80	0.77	0.72	0.96	1.04
Current Ratio	2.20	2.38	2.22	2.84	2.29	1.63	3.00	2.30
Debt to Equity	1.66	1.63	1.69	1.32	0.88	0.29	0.43	0.35
Price Range	178.88-130.17	169.25-121.61	127.93-81.05	99.81-80.09	97.21-76.78	84.08-59.77	62.95-47.79	59.02-40.15
P/E Ratio	34.20-24.89	34.83-25.02	22.44-14.22	19.46-15.61	13.35-10.55	22.48-15.98	10.39-7.89	14.09-9.58
Average Yield %	1.97	2.00	2.21	2.24	2.10	2.27	2.61	2.74

Address: 155 Harlem Avenue, Glenview, IL 60025 Telephone: 847-724-7500	Web Site: www.itw.com Officers: E. Scott Santi - Chairman, Chief Executive Officer, Vice-Chairman, President, Chief Operating Officer Christopher A. O'Herlihy - Vice-Chairman, Executive Vice President	Auditors: DELOITTE & TOUCHE LLP Investor Contact: 847-657-4104 Transfer Agents: Computershare Trust Company, N.A., Providence, RI

INTERCONTINENTAL EXCHANGE INC

Exchange	Symbol	Price	52Wk Range	Yield	P/E
NYS	ICE	$73.55 (6/29/2018)	75.98-64.30	1.31	17.64

*7 Year Price Score 125.90 *NYSE Composite Index=100 *12 Month Price Score 102.31

Interim Earnings (Per Share)

Qtr.	Mar	Jun	Sep	Dec
2015	0.56	0.51	0.55	0.66
2016	0.62	0.60	0.57	0.58
2017	0.84	0.70	0.62	2.06
2018	0.79	...		

Interim Dividends (Per Share)

Amt	Decl	Ex	Rec	Pay
0.24Q	02/07/2018	12/13/2018	12/14/2018	12/31/2018
0.24Q	02/07/2018	03/14/2018	03/15/2018	03/29/2018
0.24Q	02/07/2018	06/13/2018	06/14/2018	06/29/2018
0.24Q	02/07/2018	09/12/2018	09/13/2018	09/28/2018

Indicated Div: $0.96

Valuation Analysis **Institutional Holding**

Forecast EPS	$3.54	No of Institutions
	(06/14/2018)	959
Market Cap	$42.7 Billion	Shares
Book Value	$17.0 Billion	569,110,080
Price/Book	2.52	% Held
Price/Sales	7.19	86.82

Business Summary: Finance Intermediaries & Services (MIC: 5.5.1 SIC: 6231 NAIC: 523210)

IntercontinentalExchange is an operator of regulated exchanges, clearing houses and listings venues, and a provider of data services for commodity and financial markets. Co. operates regulated marketplaces for listing, trading and clearing a range of derivatives and securities contracts across main asset classes, including energy and agricultural commodities, interest rates, equities, equity derivatives, exchange traded funds, credit derivatives, bonds and currencies. Co. provides end-to-end market data services to support the trading, investment, risk management and connectivity needs of customers. Co.'s business is conducted as two segments: Trading and Clearing and Data and Listings.

Recent Developments: For the quarter ended Mar 31 2018, net income decreased 7.2% to US$474.0 million from US$511.0 million in the year-earlier quarter. Revenues were US$1.58 billion, up 7.4% from US$1.47 billion the year before. Operating income was US$650.0 million versus US$582.0 million in the prior-year quarter, an increase of 11.7%. Direct operating expenses rose 16.4% to US$355.0 million from US$305.0 million in the comparable period the year before. Indirect operating expenses decreased 1.5% to US$575.0 million from US$584.0 million in the equivalent prior-year period.

Prospects: Our evaluation of IntercontinentalExchange Inc. as of Jan. 21, 2018 is the result of our systematic analysis on three basic characteristics: earnings strength, relative valuation, and recent stock price movement. The company has managed to produce a neutral trend in earnings per share over the past 5 quarters. However, while recent estimates for the company have been mixed, ICE has posted better than expected results. Based on operating earnings yield, the company is about fairly valued when compared to all of the companies in our coverage universe. Share price changes over the past year indicates that ICE will perform in line with the market over the near term.

Financial Data
(US$ in Thousands)

	3 Mos	12/31/2017	12/31/2016	12/31/2015	12/31/2014	12/31/2013	12/31/2012	12/31/2011
Earnings Per Share	4.17	4.23	2.37	2.28	1.71	0.64	1.50	1.38
Cash Flow Per Share	3.52	3.54	3.60	2.36	2.57	1.88	2.01	1.95
Tang Book Value Per Share	N.M.	N.M.	N.M.	N.M.	N.M.	N.M.	2.50	1.01
Dividends Per Share	0.840	0.800	0.680	0.580	0.520	0.130	...	...
Dividend Payout %	20.14	18.91	28.69	25.46	30.41	20.25	...	...
Income Statement								
Total Revenue	1,580,000	5,834,000	5,958,000	4,682,000	4,221,000	1,795,000	1,362,965	1,327,491
EBITDA	807,000	2,961,000	2,462,000	1,963,000	1,685,000	638,000	888,368	848,824
Depn & Amortn	138,000	257,000	255,000	213,000	182,000	85,000	61,400	56,500
Income Before Taxes	617,000	2,517,000	2,029,000	1,653,000	1,407,000	500,000	789,692	759,239
Income Taxes	143,000	(25,000)	580,000	358,000	402,000	230,000	227,955	237,498
Net Income	464,000	2,514,000	1,422,000	1,274,000	981,000	254,000	551,576	509,673
Average Shares	586,000	594,000	599,000	560,000	575,000	395,000	366,830	369,475
Balance Sheet								
Current Assets	56,634,000	53,562,000	57,133,000	53,313,000	50,245,000	44,259,000	33,750,087	32,605,391
Total Assets	82,062,000	78,264,000	82,003,000	77,987,000	68,279,000	64,818,000	37,214,842	36,147,864
Current Liabilities	57,946,000	54,171,000	58,617,000	54,743,000	50,539,000	44,342,000	32,245,697	31,800,314
Long-Term Obligations	4,269,000	4,267,000	3,871,000	4,717,000	2,247,000	3,923,000	969,500	837,500
Total Liabilities	65,084,000	61,340,000	66,286,000	63,179,000	55,919,000	52,235,000	33,571,465	33,026,339
Stockholders' Equity	16,978,000	16,924,000	15,717,000	14,808,000	12,360,000	12,583,000	3,643,377	3,121,525
Shares Outstanding	581,000	583,000	595,000	595,000	565,000	575,000	362,370	362,125
Statistical Record								
Return on Assets %	3.07	3.14	1.77	1.74	1.47	0.50	1.50	1.62
Return on Equity %	15.13	15.40	9.29	9.38	7.87	3.13	16.26	17.28
EBITDA Margin %	51.08	50.75	41.32	41.93	39.92	35.54	65.18	63.94
Net Margin %	29.37	43.09	23.87	27.21	23.24	14.15	40.47	38.39
Asset Turnover	0.07	0.07	0.07	0.06	0.06	0.04	0.04	0.04
Current Ratio	0.98	0.99	0.97	0.97	0.99	1.00	1.05	1.03
Debt to Equity	0.25	0.25	0.25	0.32	0.18	0.31	0.27	0.27
Price Range	75.83-58.07	72.07-56.22	59.66-45.99	52.83-40.97	45.56-36.69	45.21-24.76	28.47-22.43	26.94-20.78
P/E Ratio	18.18-13.93	17.04-13.29	25.17-19.41	23.17-17.97	26.65-21.46	70.64-38.69	18.98-14.95	19.52-15.06
Average Yield %	1.25	1.26	1.30	1.23	1.28	0.37	...	...

Address: 5660 New Northside Drive, Atlanta, GA 30328 **Telephone:** 770-857-4700 **Fax:** 770-937-0020	**Web Site:** www.theice.com **Officers:** Jeffrey C. Sprecher - Chairman, Chief Executive Officer Charles A. Vice - President, Chief Operating Officer, Vice-Chairman	**Auditors:** Ernst & Young LLP **Investor Contact:** 770-857-4726 **Transfer Agents:** Computershare Trust Company, N.A., Providence, RI

INGERSOLL-RAND PLC

Exchange	Symbol	Price	52Wk Range	Yield	P/E
NYS	IR	$89.73 (6/29/2018)	96.60-80.39	2.36	17.59

*7 Year Price Score 114.62 *NYSE Composite Index=100 *12 Month Price Score 99.85

TRADING VOLUME (thousand shares)

Interim Earnings (Per Share)

Qtr.	Mar	Jun	Sep	Dec
2015	0.19	0.29	1.12	0.88
2016	0.58	2.86	1.44	0.76
2017	0.45	1.38	1.43	1.81
2018	0.48	...	...	...

Interim Dividends (Per Share)

Amt	Decl	Ex	Rec	Pay
0.45Q	10/03/2017	12/07/2017	12/08/2017	12/29/2017
0.45Q	02/07/2018	03/08/2018	03/09/2018	03/30/2018
0.45Q	04/04/2018	06/07/2018	06/08/2018	06/29/2018
0.53Q	06/11/2018	09/06/2018	09/07/2018	09/28/2018

Indicated Div: $2.12

Valuation Analysis   **Institutional Holding**

Forecast EPS	N/A	No of Institutions
		983
Market Cap	$22.3 Billion	Shares
Book Value	$7.1 Billion	231,635,536
Price/Book	3.14	% Held
Price/Sales	1.53	70.07

Business Summary: Industrial Machinery & Equipment (MIC: 7.2.1 SIC: 3585 NAIC: 333415)

Ingersoll-Rand provides products, services and solutions to enhance air in homes and buildings, transport and protect food. Co.'s segments are: Climate. which includes Trane® and American Standard® Heating & Air Conditioning, providing heating, ventilation and air conditioning systems, and commercial and residential building services, parts, support and controls, energy services and building automation as well as transport temperature control solutions; and Industrial, which includes compressed air and gas systems and services, power tools, material handling systems, ARO® fluid management equipment, as well as Club Car® golf, utility and rough terrain vehicles.

Recent Developments: For the quarter ended Mar 31 2018, income from continuing operations increased 4.6% to US$133.5 million from US$127.6 million in the year-earlier quarter. Net income increased 2.5% to US$124.1 million from US$121.1 million in the year-earlier quarter. Revenues were US$3.38 billion, up 12.8% from US$3.00 billion the year before. Operating income was US$243.4 million versus US$215.0 million in the prior-year quarter, an increase of 13.2%. Direct operating expenses rose 13.8% to US$2.42 billion from US$2.13 billion in the comparable period the year before. Indirect operating expenses increased 9.3% to US$720.9 million from US$659.5 million in the equivalent prior-year period.

Prospects: Our evaluation of Ingersoll-Rand Plc. as of Sep. 17, 2017 is the result of our systematic analysis on three basic characteristics: earnings strength, relative valuation, and recent stock price movement. The company has produced a positive trend in earnings per share over the past 5 quarters and while recent estimates for the company have remained steady, IR has posted better than expected results. Based on operating earnings yield, the company is undervalued when compared to all of the companies in our coverage universe. Share price changes over the past year indicates that IR will perform well over the near term.

Financial Data

(US$ in Thousands)	3 Mos	12/31/2017	12/31/2016	12/31/2015	12/31/2014	12/31/2013	12/31/2012	12/31/2011
Earnings Per Share	5.10	5.05	5.65	2.48	3.40	2.07	3.28	1.01
Cash Flow Per Share	5.99	5.98	5.77	3.21	3.60	3.98	3.88	3.65
Dividends Per Share	1.750	1.700	1.360	1.160	1.000	0.630	0.690	0.590
Dividend Payout %	34.31	33.66	24.07	46.77	29.41	30.43	21.04	58.42
Income Statement								
Total Revenue	3,384,500	14,197,600	13,508,900	13,300,700	12,891,400	12,350,500	14,034,900	14,782,000
EBITDA	329,200	1,841,600	1,774,500	1,657,200	1,613,600	1,297,700	1,758,600	1,107,100
Depn & Amortn	93,400	217,300	216,700	209,500	199,900	199,500	238,800	236,200
Income Before Taxes	166,500	1,417,900	1,344,300	1,235,300	1,201,600	832,200	1,282,600	616,800
Income Taxes	33,000	80,200	281,500	540,800	293,700	189,000	227,000	187,200
Net Income	120,400	1,302,600	1,476,200	664,600	931,700	618,800	1,018,600	343,200
Average Shares	253,000	258,100	261,700	267,800	274,300	298,300	310,600	339,300
Balance Sheet								
Current Assets	6,071,500	6,119,100	5,579,300	4,609,400	5,707,900	5,716,700	4,942,700	5,182,600
Total Assets	18,365,100	18,173,300	17,397,400	16,738,800	17,298,500	17,658,100	18,492,900	18,754,200
Current Liabilities	4,320,700	4,828,000	3,590,300	3,648,400	3,666,100	3,408,600	4,161,300	4,124,500
Long-Term Obligations	3,745,500	2,957,000	3,709,400	3,734,800	3,741,700	3,153,500	2,269,300	2,879,300
Total Liabilities	11,284,400	11,033,000	10,753,600	10,922,100	11,311,100	10,589,200	11,345,100	11,826,600
Stockholders' Equity	7,080,700	7,140,300	6,643,800	5,816,700	5,987,400	7,068,900	7,147,800	6,927,600
Shares Outstanding	248,000	249,479	259,006	261,251	262,899	282,700	295,605	297,116
Statistical Record								
Return on Assets %	7.33	7.32	8.63	3.91	5.33	3.42	5.45	1.77
Return on Equity %	19.11	18.90	23.63	11.26	14.27	8.71	14.43	4.60
EBITDA Margin %	9.73	12.97	13.14	12.46	12.52	10.51	12.53	7.49
Net Margin %	3.56	9.17	10.93	5.00	7.23	5.01	7.26	2.32
Asset Turnover	0.82	0.80	0.79	0.78	0.74	0.68	0.75	0.76
Current Ratio	1.41	1.27	1.55	1.26	1.56	1.68	1.19	1.26
Debt to Equity	0.53	0.41	0.56	0.64	0.62	0.45	0.32	0.42
Price Range	96.60-81.22	95.61-74.90	78.75-48.80	70.91-50.61	64.59-53.57	71.42-47.96	48.87-31.86	52.08-26.48
P/E Ratio	18.94-15.93	18.93-14.83	13.94-8.64	28.59-20.41	19.00-15.76	34.50-23.17	14.90-9.71	51.56-26.22
Average Yield %	1.98	1.98	2.11	1.85	1.66	1.08	1.62	1.47

Address: 170/175 Lakeview Dr., Airside Business Park, Swords Telephone: 018-707-400	Web Site: www.ingersollrand.com Officers: Michael W. Lamach - Chairman, Chief Executive Officer, President, Chief Operating Officer Susan K. Carter - Senior Vice President, Chief Financial Officer	Auditors: PricewaterhouseCoopers LLP Transfer Agents: The Bank of New York Mellon, New York, NY

INGREDION INC

Exchange	Symbol	Price	52Wk Range	Yield	P/E
NYS	INGR	$110.70 (6/29/2018)	146.04-109.54	2.17	15.21

*7 Year Price Score 116.22 *NYSE Composite Index=100 *12 Month Price Score 88.97

Interim Earnings (Per Share)

Qtr.	Mar	Jun	Sep	Dec
2015	1.15	1.47	1.48	1.42
2016	1.73	1.58	1.93	1.26
2017	1.68	1.78	2.26	1.34
2018	1.90	...	...	...

Interim Dividends (Per Share)

Amt	Decl	Ex	Rec	Pay
0.60Q	09/15/2017	09/29/2017	10/02/2017	10/25/2017
0.60Q	12/15/2017	12/29/2017	01/02/2018	01/25/2018
0.60Q	03/21/2018	03/29/2018	04/02/2018	04/25/2018
0.60Q	05/16/2018	06/29/2018	07/02/2018	07/25/2018

Indicated Div: $2.40

Valuation Analysis

		Institutional Holding	
Forecast EPS	$7.52 (06/14/2018)	No of Institutions	718
Market Cap	$8.0 Billion	Shares	86,530,064
Book Value	$3.0 Billion	% Held	
Price/Book	2.63	N/A	
Price/Sales	1.37		

TRADING VOLUME (thousand shares)

Business Summary: Food (MIC: 1.2.1 SIC: 2046 NAIC: 311221)

Ingredion is an ingredients solutions provider. Co. supplies a range of customers in various industries, including the food, beverage, paper and corrugating, brewing, pharmaceutical, textile and personal care industries. Co.'s product line includes starches and sweeteners, animal feed products and edible corn oil. Co.'s starch-based products include both food-grade and industrial starches, and biomaterials. Co.'s sweetener products include glucose syrups, high maltose syrups, high fructose corn syrup, caramel color, dextrose, polyols, maltodextrins and glucose and syrup solids. Co. operates four segments: North America, South America, Asia Pacific and Europe, Middle East and Africa.

Recent Developments: For the quarter ended Mar 31 2018, net income increased 12.6% to US$143.0 million from US$127.0 million in the year-earlier quarter. Revenues were US$1.47 billion, up 1.1% from US$1.45 billion the year before. Operating income was US$197.0 million versus US$193.0 million in the prior-year quarter, an increase of 2.1%. Direct operating expenses rose 1.2% to US$1.12 billion from US$1.10 billion in the comparable period the year before. Indirect operating expenses decreased 0.6% to US$157.0 million from US$158.0 million in the equivalent prior-year period.

Prospects: Our evaluation of Ingredion Inc as of Jan. 21, 2018 is the result of our systematic analysis on three basic characteristics: earnings strength, relative valuation, and recent stock price movement. The company has managed to produce a neutral trend in earnings per share over the past 5 quarters and while recent estimates for the company have been mixed, INGR has posted better than expected results. Based on operating earnings yield, the company is undervalued when compared to all of the companies in our coverage universe. Share price changes over the past year indicates that INGR will perform in line with the market over the near term.

Financial Data

(US$ in Thousands)	3 Mos	12/31/2017	12/31/2016	12/31/2015	12/31/2014	12/31/2013	12/31/2012	12/31/2011
Earnings Per Share	7.28	7.06	6.55	5.51	4.74	5.05	5.47	5.32
Cash Flow Per Share	10.90	10.68	10.63	9.58	9.93	8.04	9.54	3.93
Tang Book Value Per Share	24.16	22.15	17.66	15.82	19.76	20.97	20.13	15.75
Dividends Per Share	2.300	2.200	1.900	1.740	1.680	1.560	0.920	0.660
Dividend Payout %	31.59	31.16	29.01	31.58	35.44	30.89	16.82	12.41
Income Statement								
Total Revenue	1,469,000	5,832,000	5,704,000	5,621,000	5,668,000	6,328,000	6,532,000	6,219,000
EBITDA	236,000	1,046,000	1,001,000	848,000	775,000	804,000	874,000	880,000
Depn & Amortn	54,000	209,000	196,000	194,000	195,000	194,000	211,000	211,000
Income Before Taxes	182,000	769,000	742,000	599,000	520,000	547,000	596,000	593,000
Income Taxes	39,000	237,000	246,000	187,000	157,000	144,000	167,000	170,000
Net Income	140,000	519,000	485,000	402,000	355,000	396,000	428,000	416,000
Average Shares	73,600	73,500	74,100	73,000	74,900	78,300	78,200	78,200
Balance Sheet								
Current Assets	2,292,000	2,415,000	2,252,000	1,950,000	2,144,000	2,214,000	2,360,000	2,102,000
Total Assets	5,975,000	6,080,000	5,782,000	5,074,000	5,091,000	5,360,000	5,592,000	5,317,000
Current Liabilities	909,000	957,000	978,000	742,000	721,000	820,000	933,000	926,000
Long-Term Obligations	1,512,000	1,744,000	1,850,000	1,819,000	1,804,000	1,717,000	1,724,000	1,801,000
Total Liabilities	2,935,000	3,189,000	3,217,000	2,930,000	2,914,000	2,956,000	3,155,000	3,213,000
Stockholders' Equity	3,040,000	2,891,000	2,565,000	2,144,000	2,177,000	2,404,000	2,437,000	2,104,000
Shares Outstanding	72,240	71,994	72,414	71,616	71,322	74,311	77,031	75,882
Statistical Record								
Return on Assets %	9.09	8.75	8.91	7.91	6.79	7.23	7.83	8.01
Return on Equity %	19.03	19.02	20.54	18.61	15.50	16.36	18.80	20.39
EBITDA Margin %	16.07	17.94	17.55	15.09	13.67	12.71	13.38	14.15
Net Margin %	9.53	8.90	8.50	7.15	6.26	6.26	6.55	6.69
Asset Turnover	0.99	0.98	1.05	1.11	1.08	1.16	1.19	1.20
Current Ratio	2.52	2.52	2.30	2.63	2.97	2.70	2.53	2.27
Debt to Equity	0.50	0.60	0.72	0.85	0.83	0.71	0.71	0.86
Price Range	146.04-114.09	141.71-114.09	139.64-86.60	99.34-76.49	86.85-58.88	74.01-61.70	66.59-45.59	59.36-37.74
P/E Ratio	20.06-15.67	20.07-16.16	21.32-13.22	18.03-13.88	18.32-12.42	14.66-12.22	12.17-8.33	11.16-7.09
Average Yield %	1.82	1.78	1.60	2.03	2.27	2.31	1.65	1.33

Address: 5 Westbrook Corporate Center, Westchester, IL 60154
Telephone: 708-551-2600
Fax: 708-551-2700

Web Site: www.ingredion.com
Officers: Ilene S. Gordon - Executive Chairman, President, Chief Executive Officer James D. Gray - Chief Financial Officer, Executive Vice President

Auditors: KPMG LLP
Investor Contact: 708-551-2592
Transfer Agents: Computershare, Providence, RI

INTERNATIONAL BUSINESS MACHINES CORP

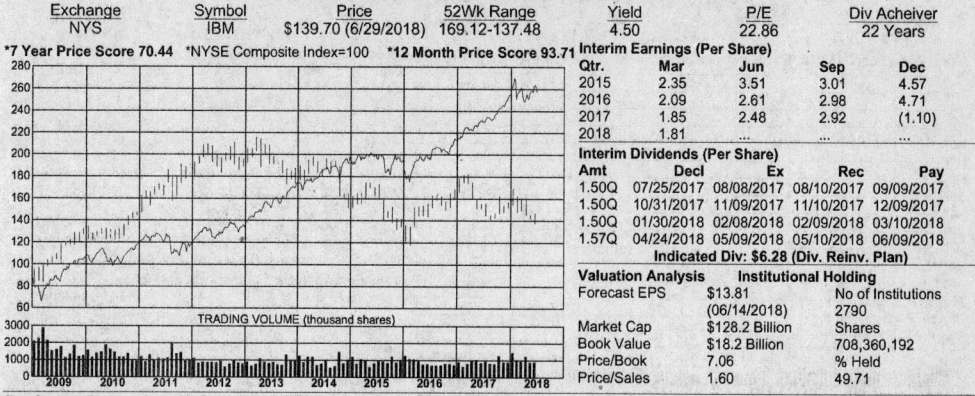

Exchange	Symbol	Price	52Wk Range	Yield	P/E	Div Acheiver
NYS	IBM	$139.70 (6/29/2018)	169.12-137.48	4.50	22.86	22 Years

*7 Year Price Score 70.44   *NYSE Composite Index=100   *12 Month Price Score 93.71

Interim Earnings (Per Share)

Qtr.	Mar	Jun	Sep	Dec
2015	2.35	3.51	3.01	4.57
2016	2.09	2.61	2.98	4.71
2017	1.85	2.48	2.92	(1.10)
2018	1.81	...	...	...

Interim Dividends (Per Share)

Amt	Decl	Ex	Rec	Pay
1.50Q	07/25/2017	08/08/2017	08/10/2017	09/09/2017
1.50Q	10/31/2017	11/09/2017	11/10/2017	12/09/2017
1.50Q	01/30/2018	02/08/2018	02/09/2018	03/10/2018
1.57Q	04/24/2018	05/09/2018	05/10/2018	06/09/2018

Indicated Div: $6.28 (Div. Reinv. Plan)

Valuation Analysis

		Institutional Holding	
Forecast EPS	$13.81	No of Institutions	
	(06/14/2018)	2790	
Market Cap	$128.2 Billion	Shares	
Book Value	$18.2 Billion	708,360,192	
Price/Book	7.06	% Held	
Price/Sales	1.60	49.71	

Business Summary: IT Services (MIC: 6.3.1 SIC: 7379 NAIC: 541519)

International Business Machines consist of five segments: Cognitive Solutions, comprises a portfolio that help clients to identify insights and inform decision-making; Global Business Services, provides clients with consulting, application management services and global process services; Technology Services & Cloud Platforms, provides IT infrastructure services creating business value for clients; Systems, provides clients with infrastructure technologies to help meet the new requirements; and Global Financing, facilitates clients' acquisition of information technology systems, software and services.

Recent Developments: For the quarter ended Mar 31 2018, income from continuing operations decreased 4.4% to US$1.68 billion from US$1.75 billion in the year-earlier quarter. Net income decreased 4.1% to US$1.68 billion from US$1.75 billion in the year-earlier quarter. Revenues were US$19.07 billion, up 5.0% from US$18.16 billion the year before. Direct operating expenses rose 6.0% to US$10.83 billion from US$10.21 billion in the comparable period the year before. Indirect operating expenses increased 7.7% to US$6.53 billion from US$6.07 billion in the equivalent prior-year period.

Prospects: Our evaluation of International Business Machines Corp. as of Jan. 21, 2018 is the result of our systematic analysis on three basic characteristics: earnings strength, relative valuation, and recent stock price movement. The company has managed to produce a neutral trend in earnings per share over the past 5 quarters and while recent estimates for the company have been mixed, IBM has posted better than expected results. Based on operating earnings yield, the company is undervalued when compared to all of the companies in our coverage universe. Share price changes over the past year indicates that IBM will perform poorly over the near term.

Financial Data
(US$ in Thousands)

	3 Mos	12/31/2017	12/31/2016	12/31/2015	12/31/2014	12/31/2013	12/31/2012	12/31/2011
Earnings Per Share	6.11	6.14	12.38	13.42	11.90	14.94	14.37	13.06
Cash Flow Per Share	18.87	17.93	17.70	17.38	16.80	15.85	17.10	16.58
Dividends Per Share	6.000	5.900	5.500	5.000	4.250	3.700	3.300	2.900
Dividend Payout %	98.20	96.09	44.43	37.26	35.71	24.77	22.96	22.21
Income Statement								
Total Revenue	19,072,000	79,139,000	79,919,000	81,741,000	92,793,000	99,751,000	104,507,000	106,916,000
EBITDA	2,344,000	16,412,000	17,233,000	20,196,000	24,872,000	24,530,000	26,928,000	26,093,000
Depn & Amortn	1,114,000	4,541,000	4,381,000	3,855,000	4,492,000	4,678,000	4,676,000	4,815,000
Income Before Taxes	1,136,000	11,400,000	12,330,000	15,945,000	19,986,000	19,524,000	21,902,000	21,003,000
Income Taxes	(540,000)	5,642,000	449,000	2,581,000	4,234,000	3,041,000	5,298,000	5,148,000
Net Income	1,679,000	5,753,000	11,872,000	13,190,000	12,022,000	16,483,000	16,604,000	15,855,000
Average Shares	925,400	937,385	958,714	982,700	1,010,000	1,094,486	1,155,449	1,213,767
Balance Sheet								
Current Assets	49,122,000	49,735,000	43,888,000	42,504,000	49,422,000	51,350,000	49,433,000	50,928,000
Total Assets	125,285,000	125,356,000	117,470,000	110,495,000	117,532,000	126,223,000	119,213,000	116,433,000
Current Liabilities	35,733,000	37,363,000	36,275,000	34,269,000	39,600,000	40,154,000	43,625,000	42,123,000
Long-Term Obligations	40,410,000	39,837,000	34,655,000	33,428,000	35,073,000	32,856,000	24,088,000	22,857,000
Total Liabilities	107,119,000	107,762,000	99,224,000	96,233,000	105,664,000	103,431,000	100,353,000	96,294,000
Stockholders' Equity	18,166,000	17,594,000	18,246,000	14,262,000	11,868,000	22,792,000	18,860,000	20,138,000
Shares Outstanding	917,968	922,179	945,867	965,728	990,523	1,054,390	1,117,367	1,163,182
Statistical Record								
Return on Assets %	4.68	4.74	10.39	11.57	9.86	13.43	14.05	13.79
Return on Equity %	31.14	32.10	72.84	100.96	69.37	79.15	84.92	73.43
EBITDA Margin %	12.29	20.74	21.56	24.71	26.80	24.59	25.77	24.41
Net Margin %	8.80	7.27	14.86	16.14	12.96	16.52	15.89	14.83
Asset Turnover	0.66	0.65	0.70	0.72	0.76	0.81	0.88	0.93
Current Ratio	1.37	1.33	1.21	1.24	1.25	1.28	1.13	1.21
Debt to Equity	2.22	2.26	1.90	2.34	2.96	1.44	1.28	1.14
Price Range	174.52-139.70	181.95-139.70	168.51-117.85	174.40-131.75	197.77-151.41	215.80-172.80	211.00-179.16	194.56-146.76
P/E Ratio	28.56-22.86	29.63-22.75	13.61-9.52	13.00-9.82	16.62-12.72	14.44-11.57	14.68-12.47	14.90-11.24
Average Yield %	3.91	3.74	3.66	3.22	2.33	1.91	1.68	1.70

Address: One New Orchard Road, Armonk, NY 10504	Web Site: www.ibm.com	Auditors: PricewaterhouseCoopers LLP
Telephone: 914-499-1900	Officers: Virginia M. (Ginni) Rometty - Chairman, President, Chief Executive Officer, Senior Vice President Martin J. Schroeter - Senior Vice President, Chief Financial Officer, General Manager, Division Officer	Investor Contact: 914-499-7777
Fax: 914-765-4190		Transfer Agents: Computershare Trust Company, N.A., Providence, RI

INTERNATIONAL FLAVORS & FRAGRANCES INC.

Exchange	Symbol	Price	52Wk Range	Yield	P/E	Div Acheiver
NYS	IFF	$123.96 (6/29/2018)	156.87-122.13	2.23	31.78	15 Years

*7 Year Price Score 112.18 *NYSE Composite Index=100   *12 Month Price Score 89.94

Interim Earnings (Per Share)

Qtr.	Mar	Jun	Sep	Dec
2015	1.57	1.29	1.31	0.98
2016	1.47	1.46	1.12	1.00
2017	1.45	1.38	1.39	(0.50)
2018	1.63	...	...	...

Interim Dividends (Per Share)

Amt	Decl	Ex	Rec	Pay
0.69Q	08/02/2017	09/22/2017	09/25/2017	10/06/2017
0.69Q	12/13/2017	12/28/2017	12/29/2017	01/08/2018
0.69Q	03/06/2018	03/23/2018	03/26/2018	04/06/2018
0.69Q	05/02/2018	06/22/2018	06/25/2018	07/06/2018

Indicated Div: $2.76 (Div. Reinv. Plan)

Valuation Analysis   **Institutional Holding**

Forecast EPS	$6.30 (06/11/2018)	No of Institutions	747
Market Cap	$9.8 Billion	Shares	93,164,312
Book Value	$1.8 Billion	% Held	76.37
Price/Book	5.52		
Price/Sales	2.79		

Business Summary: Specialty Chemicals (MIC: 8.3.2 SIC: 2869 NAIC: 325199)

International Flavors & Fragrances and its subsidiaries is a manufacturer of flavors and fragrances (including cosmetic active ingredients) used to impart flavor or fragrance in a variety of consumer products. Co.'s products are sold principally to manufacturers of perfumes and cosmetics, hair and other personal care products, soaps and detergents, cleaning products, dairy, meat and other processed foods, beverages, snacks and savory foods, sweet and baked goods, and pharmaceutical and oral care products. Co. operates in two business segments, Flavors, which develops different flavors and taste for Co.'s customers; and Fragrances, which has two sources, Fragrance Compounds and Ingredients.

Recent Developments: For the quarter ended Mar 31 2018, net income increased 11.8% to US$129.4 million from US$115.8 million in the year-earlier quarter. Revenues were US$930.9 million, up 12.4% from US$828.3 million the year before. Operating income was US$174.9 million versus US$130.1 million in the prior-year quarter, an increase of 34.4%. Direct operating expenses rose 12.9% to US$525.1 million from US$465.2 million in the comparable period the year before. Indirect operating expenses decreased 0.9% to US$231.0 million from US$233.0 million in the equivalent prior-year period.

Prospects: Our evaluation of International Flavors & Fragrances Inc. as of Jan. 21, 2018 is the result of our systematic analysis on three basic characteristics: earnings strength, relative valuation, and recent stock price movement. The company has managed to produce a neutral trend in earnings per share over the past 5 quarters and while recent estimates for the company have been mixed, IFF has posted better than expected results. Based on operating earnings yield, the company is about fairly valued when compared to all of the companies in our coverage universe. Share price changes over the past year indicates that IFF will perform well over the near term.

Financial Data

(US$ in Thousands)	3 Mos	12/31/2017	12/31/2016	12/31/2015	12/31/2014	12/31/2013	12/31/2012	12/31/2011
Earnings Per Share	3.90	3.72	5.05	5.16	5.06	4.29	3.09	3.26
Cash Flow Per Share	4.53	4.94	6.70	5.39	6.40	5.01	3.98	2.35
Tang Book Value Per Share	2.45	1.42	3.29	4.29	9.49	9.42	6.70	4.89
Dividends Per Share	2.710	2.660	2,400	2,060	1.720	1.460	1.300	1.160
Dividend Payout %	69.49	71.51	47.52	39.92	33.99	34.03	42.07	35.58
Income Statement								
Total Revenue	930,928	3,398,719	3,116,350	3,023,189	3,088,533	2,952,896	2,821,446	2,788,018
EBITDA	184,617	720,502	679,069	659,963	684,482	615,204	561,835	493,512
Depn & Amortn	9,185	118,094	102,363	74,800	89,354	83,227	76,667	75,327
Income Before Taxes	158,837	537,045	523,717	539,101	549,061	485,210	443,415	373,546
Income Taxes	29,421	241,380	118,686	119,854	134,518	131,666	189,281	106,680
Net Income	129,416	295,665	405,031	419,247	414,543	353,544	254,134	266,866
Average Shares	79,393	79,370	79,981	80,891	81,494	81,930	81,833	81,467
Balance Sheet								
Current Assets	1,970,341	1,896,544	1,609,014	1,455,884	1,710,027	1,652,903	1,572,559	1,317,220
Total Assets	4,681,276	4,598,926	4,016,984	3,721,454	3,494,621	3,331,731	3,249,600	2,965,581
Current Liabilities	716,752	768,768	898,297	742,128	518,808	560,366	622,732	564,566
Long-Term Obligations	1,676,211	1,632,186	1,066,855	937,844	934,232	932,665	881,104	778,248
Total Liabilities	2,908,126	2,914,724	2,390,740.	2,131,136	1,976,060	1,868,659	2,000,792	1,861,169
Stockholders' Equity	1,773,150	1,684,202	1,626,244	1,590,318	1,518,561	1,463,072	1,248,808	1,104,412
Shares Outstanding	78,920	78,947	79,213	80,022	80,777	81,384	81,626	80,921
Statistical Record								
Return on Assets %	6.92	6.86	10.44	11.62	12.15	10.74	8.16	9.14
Return on Equity %	18.20	17.86	25.12	26.97	27.81	26.07	21.54	25.37
EBITDA Margin %	19.83	21.20	21.79	21.83	22.16	20.83	19.91	17.70
Net Margin %	13.90	8.70	13.00	13.87	13.42	11.97	9.01	9.57
Asset Turnover	0.78	0.79	0.80	0.84	0.90	0.90	0.91	0.96
Current Ratio	2.75	2.47	1.79	1.96	3.30	2.95	2.53	2.33
Debt to Equity	0.95	0.97	0.66	0.59	0.62	0.64	0.71	0.70
Price Range	156.87-128.98	155.44-115.26	142.97-100.49	122.77-98.15	105.43-83.84	89.89-66.54	67.41-52.88	65.24-51.31
P/E Ratio	40.22-33.07	41.78-30.98	28.31-19.90	23.79-19.02	20.84-16.57	20.95-15.51	21.82-17.11	20.01-15.74
Average Yield %	1.91	1.95	1.93	1.81	1.77	1.85	2.21	1.97

Address: 521 West 57th Street, New York, NY 10019-2960 **Telephone:** 212-765-5500	**Web Site:** www.iff.com **Officers:** Andreas Fibig - Chairman, Chief Executive Officer Francisco Fortanet - Executive Vice President, Senior Vice President	**Auditors:** PricewaterhouseCoopers LLP **Investor Contact:** 212-765-5500 **Transfer Agents:** American Stock Transfer & Trust Company, New York, NY

INTERNATIONAL PAPER CO

Exchange	Symbol	Price	52Wk Range	Yield	P/E
NYS	IP	$52.08 (6/29/2018)	65.08-50.15	3.65	8.18

*7 Year Price Score 100.57 *NYSE Composite Index=100 *12 Month Price Score 95.39

Interim Earnings (Per Share)

Qtr.	Mar	Jun	Sep	Dec
2015	0.74	0.54	0.53	0.43
2016	0.81	0.10	0.75	0.53
2017	0.50	0.19	0.95	3.49
2018	1.74	...	...	...

Interim Dividends (Per Share)

Amt	Decl	Ex	Rec	Pay
0.475Q	10/10/2017	11/14/2017	11/15/2017	12/15/2017
0.475Q	01/09/2018	02/20/2018	02/21/2018	03/15/2018
0.475Q	05/08/2018	05/24/2018	05/25/2018	06/15/2018
0.475Q	07/10/2018	08/14/2018	08/15/2018	09/17/2018

Indicated Div: $1.90 (Div. Reinv. Plan)

Valuation Analysis / **Institutional Holding**

Forecast EPS	$5.07	No of Institutions
	(06/13/2018)	1236
Market Cap	$21.6 Billion	Shares
Book Value	$7.2 Billion	447,229,536
Price/Book	2.98	% Held
Price/Sales	0.99	83.49

Business Summary: Containers & Packaging (MIC: 8.1.3 SIC: 2621 NAIC: 322121)

International Paper is a paper and packaging company with markets and manufacturing operations in North America, Europe, Latin America, Russia, Asia, Africa and the Middle East. Co.'s businesses are separated into three segments: Industrial Packaging, which manufactures containerboard in the U.S. and its products include linerboard, medium, whitetop, recycled linerboard, recycled medium and saturating kraft; Printing Papers, produces printing and writing papers and its products include uncoated papers and pulp; and Consumer Packaging, produces solid bleached sulfate board and its brands include Everest®, Fortress®, and Starcote®.£

Recent Developments: For the quarter ended Mar 31 2018, income from continuing operations increased 88.5% to US$362.0 million from US$192.0 million in the year-earlier quarter. Net income increased 249.3% to US$730.0 million from US$209.0 million in the year-earlier quarter. Revenues were US$5.62 billion, up 9.5% from US$5.13 billion the year before. Direct operating expenses rose 8.5% to US$3.95 billion from US$3.64 billion in the comparable period the year before. Indirect operating expenses increased 6.8% to US$1.18 billion from US$1.10 billion in the equivalent prior-year period.

Prospects: Our evaluation of International Paper Co. as of Jan. 21, 2018 is the result of our systematic analysis on three basic characteristics: earnings strength, relative valuation, and recent stock price movement. The company has enjoyed a very positive trend in earnings per share over the past 5 quarters and while recent estimates for the company have been mixed, IP has posted better than expected results. Based on operating earnings yield, the company is undervalued when compared to all of the companies in our coverage universe. Share price changes over the past year indicates that IP will perform poorly over the near term.

Financial Data

(US$ in Millions)	3 Mos	12/31/2017	12/31/2016	12/31/2015	12/31/2014	12/31/2013	12/31/2012	12/31/2011
Earnings Per Share	6.37	5.13	2.18	2.23	1.29	3.11	1.80	3.07
Cash Flow Per Share	4.32	4.26	6.01	6.18	7.19	6.83	6.80	6.19
Tang Book Value Per Share	9.25	7.53	2.38	1.33	3.19	9.44	4.52	9.78
Dividends Per Share	1.875	1.863	1.783	1.640	1.450	1.250	1.087	0.975
Dividend Payout %	29.43	36.31	81.77	73.54	112.40	40.19	60.42	31.76
Income Statement								
Total Revenue	5,621	21,743	21,079	22,365	23,617	29,080	27,833	26,034
EBITDA	797	2,620	2,676	3,034	2,787	2,884	3,095	3,262
Depn & Amortn	306	1,200	1,200	1,213	1,308	1,423	1,399	1,263
Income Before Taxes	356	848	956	1,266	872	849	1,024	1,458
Income Taxes	89	(1,085)	247	466	123	(523)	331	311
Net Income	729	2,144	904	938	555	1,395	794	1,341
Average Shares	418	417	415	420	432	448	440	437
Balance Sheet								
Current Assets	7,260	8,277	6,969	6,477	7,959	9,025	8,905	10,456
Total Assets	34,030	33,903	33,345	30,587	28,684	31,528	32,153	26,993
Current Liabilities	4,465	5,102	4,072	3,924	4,909	5,127	4,998	4,738
Long-Term Obligations	10,759	10,846	11,075	8,900	8,631	8,827	9,696	9,189
Total Liabilities	26,785	27,381	29,004	26,703	23,569	23,423	25,849	20,373
Stockholders' Equity	7,245	6,522	4,341	3,884	5,115	8,105	6,304	6,620
Shares Outstanding	414	412	411	412	420	436	439	436
Statistical Record								
Return on Assets %	7.91	6.38	2.82	3.17	1.84	4.38	2.68	5.12
Return on Equity %	45.08	39.47	21.92	20.85	8.40	19.36	12.25	19.93
EBITDA Margin %	14.18	12.05	12.70	13.57	11.80	9.92	11.12	12.53
Net Margin %	12.97	9.86	4.29	4.19	2.35	4.80	2.85	5.15
Asset Turnover	0.65	0.65	0.66	0.75	0.78	0.91	0.94	0.99
Current Ratio	1.63	1.62	1.71	1.65	1.62	1.76	1.78	2.21
Debt to Equity	1.49	1.66	2.55	2.29	1.69	1.09	1.54	1.39
Price Range	65.08-49.64	58.67-49.64	54.28-32.58	57.59-36.80	55.25-44.25	49.48-39.28	39.28-27.42	32.40-22.33
P/E Ratio	10.22-7.79	11.44-9.68	24.90-14.94	25.83-16.50	42.83-34.30	15.91-12.63	21.82-15.23	10.55-7.27
Average Yield %	3.35	3.41	4.09	3.41	3.00	2.77	3.29	3.51

Address: 6400 Poplar Avenue, Memphis, TN 38197 **Telephone:** 901-419-7000	**Web Site:** www.internationalpaper.com **Officers:** Mark S. Sutton - Chairman, Chief Executive Officer, Sharon R. Ryan - Senior Vice President, General Counsel	**Auditors:** DELOITTE & TOUCHE LLP **Investor Contact:** 901-419-1731 **Transfer Agents:** Computershare Trust Company, N.A., Canton, MA

INTERPUBLIC GROUP OF COMPANIES INC.

Exchange	Symbol	Price	52Wk Range	Yield	P/E
NYS	IPG	$23.44 (6/29/2018)	25.57-18.45	3.58	17.11

*7 Year Price Score 97.00 *NYSE Composite Index=100 *12 Month Price Score 105.56

Interim Earnings (Per Share)

Qtr.	Mar	Jun	Sep	Dec
2015	0.00	0.29	0.18	0.62
2016	0.01	0.38	0.32	0.78
2017	0.05	0.24	0.37	0.80
2018	(0.04)	...	...	...

Interim Dividends (Per Share)

Amt	Decl	Ex	Rec	Pay
0.18Q	07/26/2017	08/30/2017	09/01/2017	09/15/2017
0.18Q	10/25/2017	11/30/2017	12/01/2017	12/15/2017
0.21Q	02/13/2018	02/28/2018	03/01/2018	03/15/2018
0.21Q	05/24/2018	06/01/2018	06/04/2018	06/18/2018

Indicated Div: $0.84

Valuation Analysis   Institutional Holding

Forecast EPS	$1.71 (06/14/2018)	No of Institutions 719
Market Cap	$9.0 Billion	Shares
Book Value	$2.1 Billion	506,802,720
Price/Book	4.29	% Held
Price/Sales	1.09	88.43

Business Summary: Advertising (MIC: 2.3.4 SIC: 7311 NAIC: 541810)

Interpublic Group of Companies is engaged in providing advertising and marketing services. Co. has two reportale segments: Integrated Agency Networks (IAN) and Constituency Management Group (CMG). Within IAN, Co.'s agencies provide a range of communications and marketing services. Co.'s digital agencies provide digital capabilities and service their own client rosters while also serving as digital partners. In addition, Co.'s domestic integrated agencies provide advertising, marketing communications services and/or marketing services. CMG provides clients with a range of services such as public relations, meeting and event production, and sports and entertainment marketing, among others.

Recent Developments: For the quarter ended Mar 31 2018, net loss amounted to US$16.1 million versus net income of US$21.3 million in the year-earlier quarter. Revenues were US$2.17 billion, up 5.1% from US$2.06 billion the year before. Operating income was US$38.8 million versus US$34.7 million in the prior-year quarter, an increase of 11.8%. Direct operating expenses rose 4.9% to US$2.05 billion from US$1.95 billion in the comparable period the year before. Indirect operating expenses increased 6.4% to US$81.1 million from US$76.2 million in the equivalent prior-year period.

Prospects: Our evaluation of Interpublic Group of Cos. Inc. as of Jan. 21, 2018 is the result of our systematic analysis on three basic characteristics: earnings strength, relative valuation, and recent stock price movement. The company has managed to produce a neutral trend in earnings per share over the past 5 quarters. However, while recent estimates for the company have been mixed, IPG has posted results that fell short of analysts expectations. Based on operating earnings yield, the company is undervalued when compared to all of the companies in our coverage universe. Share price changes over the past year indicates that IPG will perform poorly over the near term.

Financial Data

(US$ in Thousands)	3 Mos	12/31/2017	12/31/2016	12/31/2015	12/31/2014	12/31/2013	12/31/2012	12/31/2011
Earnings Per Share	1.37	1.46	1.49	1.09	1.12	0.61	0.94	0.99
Cash Flow Per Share	1.37	2.26	1.29	1.65	1.60	1.41	0.82	0.59
Dividends Per Share	0.750	0.720	0.600	0.480	0.380	0.300	0.240	0.240
Dividend Payout %	54.74	49.32	40.27	44.04	33.93	49.18	25.53	24.24
Income Statement								
Total Revenue	2,169,100	7,882,400	7,846,600	7,613,800	7,537,100	7,122,300	6,956,200	7,014,600
EBITDA	45,800	1,083,300	1,039,000	956,100	910,500	696,600	903,100	968,100
Depn & Amortn	31,400	135,900	138,300	130,900	132,300	130,600	124,300	130,700
Income Before Taxes	(1,500)	876,000	830,200	762,200	720,700	468,000	674,800	738,400
Income Taxes	12,700	281,900	198,000	282,800	216,500	181,200	213,300	190,200
Net Income	(14,100)	579,000	608,500	454,600	477,100	267,900	446,700	532,300
Average Shares	383,400	397,300	408,000	415,700	425,400	429,600	481,400	540,600
Balance Sheet								
Current Assets	6,963,500	7,464,100	7,438,000	7,693,100	7,810,200	8,084,000	8,738,300	8,286,800
Total Assets	12,240,100	12,695,200	12,485,200	12,585,100	12,747,200	12,905,000	13,493,900	12,876,600
Current Liabilities	7,322,500	7,678,200	7,706,000	7,584,300	7,463,300	8,165,300	7,701,700	8,032,600
Long-Term Obligations	1,288,200	1,285,600	1,280,700	1,610,300	1,623,500	1,129,800	2,060,800	1,210,900
Total Liabilities	10,131,600	10,494,200	10,468,100	10,619,600	10,630,900	10,689,800	11,073,300	10,414,900
Stockholders' Equity	2,108,500	2,201,000	2,017,100	1,965,500	2,116,300	2,215,200	2,420,600	2,461,700
Shares Outstanding	385,519	383,200	391,600	403,200	413,800	424,500	417,500	449,500
Statistical Record								
Return on Assets %	4.54	4.60	4.84	3.59	3.72	2.03	3.38	4.10
Return on Equity %	26.69	27.45	30.47	22.27	22.03	11.56	18.25	21.33
EBITDA Margin %	2.11	13.74	13.24	12.56	12.08	9.78	12.98	13.80
Net Margin %	N.M.	7.35	7.75	5.97	6.33	3.76	6.42	7.59
Asset Turnover	0.69	0.63	0.62	0.60	0.59	0.54	0.53	0.54
Current Ratio	0.95	0.97	0.97	1.01	1.05	0.99	1.13	1.03
Debt to Equity	0.61	0.58	0.63	0.82	0.77	0.51	0.85	0.49
Price Range	25.57-18.45	25.57-18.45	24.60-20.30	23.65-18.27	20.83-16.05	17.70-11.02	11.97-9.45	13.20-6.95
P/E Ratio	18.66-13.47	17.51-12.64	16.51-13.62	21.70-16.76	18.60-14.33	29.02-18.07	12.73-10.05	13.33-7.02
Average Yield %	3.39	3.20	2.63	2.27	2.06	2.01	2.20	2.29

Address: 909 Third Avenue, New York, NY 10022 **Telephone:** 212-704-1200	**Web Site:** www.interpublic.com **Officers:** Michael I. Roth - Chairman, Chief Executive Officer Frank Mergenthaler - Executive Vice President, Chief Financial Officer	**Auditors:** PricewaterhouseCoopers LLP **Transfer Agents:** Computershare Shareowner Services LLC, Jersey City, NJ

INTREXON CORP

*7 Year Price Score N/A *NYSE Composite Index=100 *12 Month Price Score 95.81

Interim Earnings (Per Share)

Qtr.	Mar	Jun	Sep	Dec
2015	0.25	(0.37)	(0.34)	(0.29)
2016	(0.55)	(0.42)	(0.24)	(0.37)
2017	(0.26)	(0.16)	(0.33)	(0.23)
2018	(0.33)	...	...	...

Interim Dividends (Per Share)

No Dividends Paid

Valuation Analysis   Institutional Holding

Forecast EPS	$-1.17	No of Institutions
	(05/29/2018)	N/A
Market Cap	$1.8 Billion	Shares
Book Value	$553.1 Million	N/A
Price/Book	3.26	% Held
Price/Sales	8.14	N/A

Business Summary: Biotechnology (MIC: 4.1.2 SIC: 8731 NAIC: 541710)

Intrexon uses synthetic biology to focus on programming biological systems to alleviate disease, remediate environmental challenges, and provide sustainable food and industrial chemicals. Co.'s technologies include: its UltraVector gene design and fabrication platform and its library of modular DNA components; Cell Systems Informatics; RheoSwitch inducible gene switch; AttSite Recombinases; Protein Engineering; Laser-Enabled Analysis and Processing; ActoBiotics platform; and AdenoVerse technology platform. Co.'s primary domestic operations are in California, Florida, Maryland, and Virginia, and its primary international operations are in Belgium and Hungary.

Recent Developments: For the quarter ended Mar 31 2018, net loss amounted to US$43.2 million versus a net loss of US$32.4 million in the year-earlier quarter. Revenues were US$43.8 million, down 18.4% from US$53.7 million the year before. Operating loss was US$48.5 million versus a loss of US$31.4 million in the prior-year quarter. Direct operating expenses declined 3.1% to US$15.3 million from US$15.8 million in the comparable period the year before. Indirect operating expenses increased 11.1% to US$77.0 million from US$69.3 million in the equivalent prior-year period.

Prospects: Our evaluation of Intrexon Corp as of Jan. 21, 2018 is the result of our systematic analysis on three basic characteristics: earnings strength, relative valuation, and recent stock price movement. The company has suffered a very negative trend in earnings per share over the past 5 quarters. Because the company lacks sufficient analyst estimate data, we place greater weight on the historical EPS trend as the measure of earnings strength. Based on operating earnings yield, the company is overvalued when compared to all of the companies in our coverage universe. Share price changes over the past year indicates that XON will perform very poorly over the near term.

Financial Data
(US$ in Thousands)

	3 Mos	12/31/2017	12/31/2016	12/31/2015	12/31/2014	12/31/2013	12/31/2012	12/31/2011
Earnings Per Share	(1.05)	(0.98)	(1.58)	(0.76)	(0.83)	(1.40)	(18.77)	(18.92)
Cash Flow Per Share	(0.86)	(0.87)	(0.47)	0.32	(0.20)	(1.31)	(11.09)	(15.60)
Tang Book Value Per Share	1.29	1.21	1.50	2.41	2.17	3.20	9.82	8.78
Income Statement								
Total Revenue	43,843	230,981	190,926	173,605	71,930	23,760	13,925	8,171
EBITDA	(46,773)	(122,340)	(172,973)	(70,802)	(74,421)	(35,836)	(76,591)	(82,025)
Depn & Amortn	3,456	11,951	9,387	7,872	6,178	4,325	4,957	3,078
Income Before Taxes	(44,858)	(115,417)	(173,031)	(78,034)	(80,459)	(40,302)	(81,600)	(85,280)
Income Taxes	(4,086)	(2,880)	(3,877)	1,016	(103)	...	...	...
Net Income	(41,988)	(117,018)	(186,612)	(84,493)	(81,822)	(38,980)	(81,874)	(85,280)
Average Shares	127,693	119,998	117,983	111,066	99,170	40,951	5,533	5,240
Balance Sheet								
Current Assets	187,545	154,047	315,181	323,801	174,773	187,556	13,533	22,978
Total Assets	895,666	846,851	949,068	982,046	576,272	469,472	151,646	114,828
Current Liabilities	86,854	80,173	94,605	75,904	47,482	19,829	16,717	17,599
Long-Term Obligations	7,425	7,535	7,562	7,598	8,694	1,663	42	97
Total Liabilities	342,557	313,220	388,831	287,968	191,511	102,750	66,540	34,406
Stockholders' Equity	553,109	533,631	560,237	694,078	384,761	366,722	85,106	80,422
Shares Outstanding	129,239	122,087	118,688	116,658	100,557	97,053	5,661	5,453
Statistical Record								
Asset Turnover	0.24	0.26	0.20	0.22	0.14	0.08	0.10	...
Current Ratio	2.16	1.92	3.33	4.27	3.68	9.46	0.81	1.31
Debt to Equity	0.01	0.01	0.01	0.01	0.02	N.M.	N.M.	N.M.
Price Range	25.67-11.33	26.25-11.33	38.53-21.17	68.05-24.90	35.16-14.61	28.36-16.85	...	...

Address: 20374 Seneca Meadows Parkway, Germantown, MD 20876 Telephone: 301-556-9900	Web Site: www.dna.com Officers: Randal J. Kirk - Chairman, Chief Executive Officer Thomas Bostick - Chief Operating Officer	Auditors: PricewaterhouseCoopers LLP Transfer Agents: American Stock Transfer & Trust Company, LLC

INVESCO LTD

Exchange	Symbol	Price	52Wk Range	Yield	P/E
NYS	IVZ	$26.56 (6/29/2018)	38.40-26.51	4.41	9.35

*7 Year Price Score 86.23 *NYSE Composite Index=100 *12 Month Price Score 81.60

Interim Earnings (Per Share)

Qtr.	Mar	Jun	Sep	Dec
2015	0.60	0.60	0.58	0.48
2016	0.38	0.54	0.58	0.55
2017	0.52	0.58	0.65	0.99
2018	0.62	...	...	...

Interim Dividends (Per Share)

Amt	Decl	Ex	Rec	Pay
0.29Q	07/27/2017	08/15/2017	08/17/2017	09/01/2017
0.29Q	10/25/2017	11/13/2017	11/14/2017	12/04/2017
0.29Q	01/30/2018	02/14/2018	02/15/2018	03/02/2018
0.30Q	04/26/2018	05/10/2018	05/11/2008	06/01/2018

Indicated Div: $1.17

Valuation Analysis   Institutional Holding

Forecast EPS   N/A

No of Institutions 847

Market Cap	$10.9 Billion
Book Value	$8.9 Billion
Price/Book	1.23
Price/Sales	2.05

Shares 408,853,312

% Held N/A

TRADING VOLUME (thousand shares)

Business Summary: Wealth Management (MIC: 5.5.2 SIC: 6282 NAIC: 523930)

Invesco is an investment manager. Co. provides a range of investment capabilities and outcomes, delivered through a set of investment vehicles. Co. sole business is investment management. Co. operates in the retail and institutional markets in North America, Europe, Middle East and Africa, and Asia Pacific. Co.'s asset classes include money market, balanced, equity, fixed income, and alternatives. Co.'s distribution channels consist of: Retail, which is a provider of retail investment solutions to clients in primary markets; and Institutional, which provides investment solutions to institutional investors. As of Dec 31 2017, Co.'s assets under management was US$937.60 billion.

Recent Developments: For the quarter ended Mar 31 2018, net income increased 23.8% to US$265.2 million from US$214.2 million in the year-earlier quarter. Revenues were US$1.36 billion, up 13.7% from US$1.19 billion the year before. Operating income was US$321.1 million versus US$257.9 million in the prior-year quarter, an increase of 24.5%. Indirect operating expenses increased 10.7% to US$1.03 billion from US$934.7 million in the equivalent prior-year period.

Prospects: Our evaluation of Invesco Ltd as of Sep. 17, 2017 is the result of our systematic analysis on three basic characteristics: earnings strength, relative valuation, and recent stock price movement. The company has managed to produce a neutral trend in earnings per share over the past 5 quarters and while recent estimates for the company have remained steady, IVZ has posted better than expected results. Based on operating earnings yield, the company is undervalued when compared to all of the companies in our coverage universe. Share price changes over the past year indicates that IVZ will perform well over the near term.

Financial Data
(US$ in Thousands)

	3 Mos	12/31/2017	12/31/2016	12/31/2015	12/31/2014	12/31/2013	12/31/2012	12/31/2011
Earnings Per Share	2.84	2.75	2.06	2.26	2.27	2.10	1.49	1.57
Cash Flow Per Share	2.44	3.35	0.31	2.46	2.76	1.74	1.81	2.08
Tang Book Value Per Share	1.78	1.34	N.M.	0.85	1.16	0.60	N.M.	N.M.
Dividends Per Share	1.160	1.150	1.110	1.060	0.975	0.848	0.640	0.477
Dividend Payout %	40.85	41.82	53.88	46.90	42.95	40.36	42.95	30.41
Income Statement								
Total Revenue	1,355,800	5,160,300	4,734,400	5,122,900	5,147,100	4,644,600	4,177,000	4,092,200
EBITDA	376,500	1,565,300	1,365,800	1,414,600	1,426,500	1,258,900	847,500	925,600
Depn & Amortn	33,600	99,400	87,300	83,000	76,800	71,300	65,400	117,400
Income Before Taxes	323,900	1,384,500	1,197,300	1,327,000	1,362,300	1,219,700	829,800	877,600
Income Taxes	68,400	268,200	338,300	398,000	390,600	336,900	272,200	286,100
Net Income	253,900	1,127,300	854,200	968,100	988,100	940,300	677,100	729,700
Average Shares	411,800	409,900	415,000	429,300	435,600	448,500	453,800	464,700
Balance Sheet								
Current Assets	22,906,600	22,842,600	17,529,100	16,888,400	12,009,700	10,505,200	3,907,600	3,834,100
Total Assets	31,619,100	31,668,800	25,734,300	25,073,200	20,462,500	19,270,500	17,492,400	19,347,000
Current Liabilities	14,906,100	1,591,800	1,466,700	1,524,400	3,852,600	3,737,500	2,713,000	2,974,400
Long-Term Obligations	6,579,100	6,875,600	6,505,500	7,509,800	6,738,900	5,770,300	5,085,400	6,582,500
Total Liabilities	22,723,800	22,972,700	18,230,500	17,187,900	12,136,500	10,877,900	9,175,600	11,227,900
Stockholders' Equity	8,895,300	8,696,100	7,503,800	7,885,300	8,326,000	8,392,600	8,316,800	8,119,100
Shares Outstanding	410,762	407,100	403,800	417,500	429,900	433,100	441,400	446,000
Statistical Record								
Return on Assets %	4.02	3.93	3.35	4.25	4.97	5.12	3.67	3.67
Return on Equity %	14.12	13.92	11.07	11.94	11.82	11.25	8.22	8.91
EBITDA Margin %	27.77	30.33	28.85	27.61	27.71	27.10	20.29	22.62
Net Margin %	18.73	21.85	18.04	18.90	19.20	20.25	16.21	17.83
Asset Turnover	0.18	0.18	0.19	0.23	0.26	0.25	0.23	0.21
Current Ratio	1.54	14.35	11.95	11.08	3.12	2.81	1.44	1.29
Debt to Equity	0.74	0.79	0.87	0.95	0.81	0.69	0.61	0.81
Price Range	38.40-30.03	37.67-28.92	33.48-23.16	41.85-30.39	41.28-31.77	36.55-25.64	26.84-20.35	27.42-14.85
P/E Ratio	13.52-10.57	13.70-10.52	16.25-11.24	18.52-13.45	18.19-14.00	17.40-12.21	18.01-13.66	17.46-9.46
Average Yield %	3.38	3.43	3.74	2.88	2.61	2.70	2.69	2.18

Address: 1555 Peachtree Street N.E., Suite 1800, Atlanta, GA 30309 **Telephone:** 404-892-0896	**Web Site:** www.invesco.com **Officers:** Ben F. Johnson - Chairman Martin L. Flanagan - President, Chief Executive Officer	**Auditors:** PricewaterhouseCoopers LLP **Investor Contact:** 404-439-4605 **Transfer Agents:** BNY Mellon Shareowner Services, Pittsburg, PA

INVITATION HOMES INC

Exchange	Symbol	Price	52Wk Range	Yield	P/E
NYS	INVH	$23.06 (6/29/2018)	24.10-20.55	1.91	N/A

*7 Year Price Score N/A   ***NYSE Composite Index=100**   ***12 Month Price Score 99.09**

Interim Earnings (Per Share)

Qtr.	Mar	Jun	Sep	Dec
2017	(0.08)	0.02	(0.07)	(0.12)
2018	(0.03)	...	...	...

Interim Dividends (Per Share)

Amt	Decl	Ex	Rec	Pay
0.08Q	08/04/2017	08/11/2017	08/15/2017	08/31/2017
0.08Q	10/13/2017	10/23/2017	10/24/2017	11/07/2017
0.11Q	02/02/2018	02/12/2018	02/13/2018	02/28/2018
0.11Q	05/04/2018	05/14/2018	05/15/2018	05/31/2018

Indicated Div: $0.44

Valuation Analysis | Institutional Holding

Forecast EPS	$-0.03	No of Institutions
	(06/13/2018)	314
Market Cap	$12.0 Billion	Shares
Book Value	$8.5 Billion	548,933,824
Price/Book	1.41	% Held
Price/Sales	9.68	N/A

TRADING VOLUME (thousand shares)

2009 2010 2011 2012 2013 2014 2015 2016 2017 2018

Business Summary: Property, Real Estate & Development (MIC: 5.3.2 SIC: 6519 NAIC: 531190)

Invitation Homes is a owner and operator of single-family homes for lease, providing residents homes in neighborhoods across America. Co. operates one reportable segment related to acquiring, renovating, leasing, and operating single-family homes as rental properties, including single-family homes in planned unit developments. As of Dec 31 2016, Co. owned 48,298 single-family rental homes and had 36,469 homes in its Same Store portfolio.

Recent Developments: For the quarter ended Mar 31 2018, loss from continuing operations was US$23.1 million compared with a loss of US$56.7 million in the year-earlier quarter. Net loss amounted to US$17.6 million versus a net loss of US$42.4 million in the year-earlier quarter. Revenues were US$423.7 million, up 77.5% from US$238.8 million the year before.

Prospects: Our evaluation of Invitation Homes Inc as of Jan. 21, 2018 is the result of our systematic analysis on three basic characteristics: earnings strength, relative valuation, and recent stock price movement. The company has managed to produce a neutral trend in earnings per share over the past 5 quarters. Because the company lacks sufficient analyst estimate data, we place greater weight on the historical EPS trend as the measure of earnings strength. Based on operating earnings yield, the company is overvalued when compared to all of the companies in our coverage universe. Share price changes over the past year indicates that INVH will perform very poorly over the near term.

Financial Data
(US$ in Thousands)

	3 Mos	12/31/2017	12/31/2016	12/31/2015	12/31/2014
Earnings Per Share	(0.20)	(0.26)	(0.32)	...	...
Cash Flow Per Share	0.61	0.77	0.48	...	...
Tang Book Value Per Share	15.78	15.80	6.31	...	...
Dividends Per Share	0.330	0.220	...	...	...
Income Statement					
Total Revenue	423,669	1,054,456	922,587	836,049	658,722
EBITDA	222,810	414,875	452,312	356,321	173,475
Depn & Amortn	153,593	297,627	263,093	245,065	207,289
Income Before Taxes	(23,082)	(139,722)	(96,829)	(162,480)	(269,626)
Net Income	(17,269)	(105,337)	(78,239)	(160,208)	(269,861)
Average Shares	519,660	339,423	519,372	...	...
Balance Sheet					
Current Assets	390,748	416,562	420,211	493,992	561,715
Total Assets	18,696,445	18,683,638	9,732,351	9,796,978	9,199,653
Current Liabilities	349,519	340,102	174,565	163,986	163,142
Long-Term Obligations	9,668,850	9,651,662	7,570,279	7,725,957	6,564,643
Total Liabilities	10,204,509	10,185,553	7,774,928	7,909,947	6,743,052
Stockholders' Equity	8,491,936	8,498,085	1,957,423	1,887,031	2,456,601
Shares Outstanding	520,364	519,173	310,376	...	...
Statistical Record					
EBITDA Margin %	52.59	39.34	49.03	42.62	26.34
Asset Turnover	0.09	0.07	0.09	0.09	...
Current Ratio	1.12	1.22	2.41	3.01	3.44
Debt to Equity	1.14	1.14	3.87	4.09	2.67
Price Range	24.10-20.55	24.10-20.00	...	...	...
Average Yield %	1.48	0.99	...	...	...

Address: 1717 Main Street, Suite 2000, Dallas, TX 75201
Telephone: 972-421-3600

Web Site: www.invitationhomes.com
Officers: Bryce Blair - Executive Chairman Frederick C. (Fred) Tuomi - President, Chief Executive Officer

Auditors: DELOITTE & TOUCHE LLP
Investor Contact: 972-421-3600
Transfer Agents: Computershare Trust Company, N.A.

IQVIA HOLDINGS INC

Exchange	Symbol	Price	52Wk Range	Yield	P/E
NYS	IQV	$99.82 (6/29/2018)	108.56-87.57	N/A	16.98

*7 Year Price Score N/A *NYSE Composite Index=100 *12 Month Price Score 100.90

Interim Earnings (Per Share)

Qtr.	Mar	Jun	Sep	Dec
2015	0.68	0.67	0.89	0.84
2016	0.88	0.71	0.82	(1.65)
2017	0.31	0.34	0.38	4.84
2018	0.32	...	...	...

Interim Dividends (Per Share)

No Dividends Paid

Valuation Analysis   **Institutional Holding**

Forecast EPS	$5.40	No of Institutions
	(06/14/2018)	624
Market Cap	$20.7 Billion	Shares
Book Value	$8.2 Billion	207,741,488
Price/Book	2.53	% Held
Price/Sales	2.08	6.20

Business Summary: Biotechnology (MIC: 4.1.2 SIC: 8731 NAIC: 541710)

IQVIA Holdings is an integrated information and technology-enabled healthcare service provider. Co. has three operating segments: Commercial Solutions, Research & Development Solutions and Integrated Engagement Services. Co.'s principal Commercial Solutions offerings include: national information offerings and sub-national information offerings. Co.'s principal Research & Development Solutions offerings include: project management and clinical monitoring, clinical trial support services, and Q2 Solutions. Co.'s principal Integrated Engagement Services offerings include: health care provider engagement services, patient engagement services, and medical affairs services.

Recent Developments: For the quarter ended Mar 31 2018, net income decreased 28.4% to US$73.0 million from US$102.0 million in the year-earlier quarter. Revenues were US$2.56 billion, up 8.6% from US$2.36 billion the year before. Operating income was US$183.0 million versus US$202.0 million in the prior-year quarter, a decrease of 9.4%. Direct operating expenses rose 8.3% to US$1.65 billion from US$1.53 billion in the comparable period the year before. Indirect operating expenses increased 15.2% to US$728.0 million from US$632.0 million in the equivalent prior-year period.

Prospects: Our evaluation of IQVIA Holdings Inc. as of Jan. 21, 2018 is the result of our systematic analysis on three basic characteristics: earnings strength, relative valuation, and recent stock price movement. The company has produced a positive trend in earnings per share over the past 5 quarters and while recent estimates for the company have been raised by analysts, IQV has posted better than expected results. Based on operating earnings yield, the company is about fairly valued when compared to all of the companies in our coverage universe. Share price changes over the past year indicates that IQV will perform very well over the near term.

Financial Data
(US$ in Thousands)

	3 Mos	12/31/2017	12/31/2016	12/31/2015	12/31/2014	12/31/2013	12/31/2012	12/31/2011
Earnings Per Share	5.88	5.88	0.76	3.08	2.72	1.77	1.51	2.05
Cash Flow Per Share	5.28	4.45	5.75	3.87	3.37	3.20	2.89	1.38
Income Statement								
Total Revenue	2,563,000	9,739,000	6,878,000	5,737,619	5,459,998	5,099,545	4,865,513	4,327,748
EBITDA	182,000	795,000	941,000	781,263	727,069	572,016	506,257	411,821
Depn & Amortn	3,000	125,000	322,000	144,793	127,701	129,329	107,525	122,020
Income Before Taxes	85,000	331,000	479,000	538,995	502,189	323,116	267,428	184,675
Income Taxes	19,000	(987,000)	345,000	158,989	150,056	95,965	93,364	15,105
Net Income	69,000	1,309,000	115,000	387,205	356,383	226,591	177,546	241,772
Average Shares	212,000	222,600	152,000	125,630	131,083	127,862	117,796	117,936
Balance Sheet								
Current Assets	3,724,000	3,450,000	3,337,000	2,411,985	2,146,083	1,945,688	1,509,994	1,365,478
Total Assets	23,235,000	22,742,000	21,208,000	3,926,316	3,305,832	3,066,797	2,499,153	2,322,917
Current Liabilities	3,199,000	2,904,000	2,705,000	1,594,176	1,471,900	1,482,247	1,317,964	1,192,133
Long-Term Obligations	10,342,000	10,122,000	7,108,000	2,419,293	2,292,491	2,035,586	2,366,268	1,951,708
Total Liabilities	15,039,000	14,633,000	12,575,000	4,490,533	4,009,893	3,734,210	3,858,676	3,293,301
Stockholders' Equity	8,196,000	8,109,000	8,633,000	(564,217)	(704,061)	(667,413)	(1,359,523)	(970,384)
Shares Outstanding	207,700	208,100	235,400	119,377	124,129	129,652	115,764	115,966
Statistical Record								
Return on Assets %	5.87	5.96	0.91	10.71	11.18	8.14	7.34	...
Return on Equity %	16.54	15.64	2.84	...	...	...	...	...
EBITDA Margin %	7.10	8.16	13.68	13.62	13.32	11.22	10.41	9.52
Net Margin %	2.69	13.44	1.67	6.75	6.53	4.44	3.65	5.59
Asset Turnover	0.45	0.44	0.55	1.59	1.71	1.83	2.01	...
Current Ratio	1.16	1.19	1.23	1.51	1.46	1.31	1.15	1.15
Debt to Equity	1.26	1.25	0.82	...	...	...	...	...
Price Range	108.56-78.23	108.56-75.35	81.06-55.91	79.10-57.07	60.66-45.80	46.48-41.58	...	...
P/E Ratio	18.46-13.30	18.46-12.81	106.66-73.57	25.68-18.53	22.30-16.84	26.26-23.49	...	...

Address: 4820 Emperor Blvd., Durham, NC 27703

Telephone: 919-998-2000

Web Site: www.quintiles.com

Officers: Ari Bousbib - Chairman, President, Chief Executive Officer Michael R. McDonnell - Executive Vice President, Chief Financial Officer, Chief Financial Officer

Auditors: PricewaterhouseCoopers LLP

Investor Contact: 919-998-2000

Transfer Agents: American Stock Transfer & Trust Company, LLC, Brooklyn, NY

IRON MOUNTAIN INC

Exchange	Symbol	Price	52Wk Range	Yield	P/E
NYS	IRM	$35.01 (6/29/2018)	41.44-30.89	6.71	55.57

*7 Year Price Score 87.44 *NYSE Composite Index=100 *12 Month Price Score 92.25

Interim Earnings (Per Share)

Qtr.	Mar	Jun	Sep	Dec
2015	0.19	0.25	0.11	0.03
2016	0.30	(0.06)	0.03	0.19
2017	0.22	0.30	0.09	0.08
2018	0.16	...	...	...

Interim Dividends (Per Share)

Amt	Decl	Ex	Rec	Pay
0.55Q	07/27/2017	09/14/2017	09/15/2017	10/02/2017
0.588Q	10/24/2017	12/14/2017	12/15/2017	01/02/2018
0.588Q	02/14/2018	03/14/2018	03/15/2018	04/02/2018
0.588Q	05/24/2018	06/14/2018	06/15/2018	07/02/2018

Indicated Div: $2.35

Valuation Analysis / Institutional Holding

Valuation Analysis		Institutional Holding	
Forecast EPS	$1.08	No of Institutions	
	(06/06/2018)	668	
Market Cap	$10.0 Billion	Shares	
Book Value	$2.3 Billion	281,634,816	
Price/Book	4.43	% Held	
Price/Sales	2.53	91.13	

Business Summary: REITs (MIC: 5.3.1 SIC: 4225 NAIC: 493110)

Iron Mountain stores records, primarily physical records and data backup media, and provides information management services that help organizations protect their information, comply with regulations, and enable corporate disaster recovery. Co. provides storage and information management services to commercial, legal, financial, healthcare, insurance, life sciences, energy, businesses services, entertainment and government organizations. Co. operates in the following business segments: North American Records and Information Management Business, North American Data Management Business, Western European Business, Other International Business, and Corporate and Other Business.

Recent Developments: For the quarter ended Mar 31 2018, income from continuing operations decreased 22.5% to US$45.6 million from US$58.8 million in the year-earlier quarter. Net income decreased 22.8% to US$45.2 million from US$58.5 million in the year-earlier quarter. Revenues were US$1.04 billion, up 11.0% from US$938.9 million the year before. Operating income was US$164.6 million versus US$147.8 million in the prior-year quarter, an increase of 11.4%. Direct operating expenses rose 5.2% to US$448.7 million from US$426.7 million in the comparable period the year before. Indirect operating expenses increased 17.8% to US$429.2 million from US$364.4 million in the equivalent prior-year period.

Prospects: Our evaluation of Iron Mountain Inc. as of Jan. 21, 2018 is the result of our systematic analysis on three basic characteristics: earnings strength, relative valuation, and recent stock price movement. The company has produced a positive trend in earnings per share over the past 5 quarters and while recent estimates for the company have remained steady, IRM has posted better than expected results. Based on operating earnings yield, the company is about fairly valued when compared to all of the companies in our coverage universe. Share price changes over the past year indicates that IRM will perform very well over the near term.

Financial Data

(US$ in Thousands)	3 Mos	12/31/2017	12/31/2016	12/31/2015	12/31/2014	12/31/2013	12/31/2012	12/31/2011
Earnings Per Share	0.63	0.69	0.42	0.58	1.66	0.51	0.98	2.02
Cash Flow Per Share	2.42	2.71	2.20	2.57	2.42	2.66	2.49	3.16
Dividends Per Share	2.275	2.237	2.005	1.910	5.371	1.080	5.120	0.938
Dividend Payout %	361.11	324.28	477.38	329.31	323.57	211.76	522.45	46.41
Income Statement								
Total Revenue	1,042,458	3,845,578	3,511,453	3,007,976	3,117,693	3,025,923	3,005,255	3,014,703
EBITDA	312,203	975,963	822,832	727,156	788,647	700,048	821,563	848,794
Depn & Amortn	167,795	406,283	365,526	301,219	304,557	282,856	280,598	290,638
Income Before Taxes	46,782	216,105	146,644	162,066	223,373	163,018	298,366	352,900
Income Taxes	1,168	25,947	44,944	37,713	(97,275)	63,057	114,873	106,488
Net Income	44,684	183,821	104,824	123,241	326,119	97,262	171,708	395,538
Average Shares	285,993	266,845	247,267	212,118	196,749	192,412	174,867	195,938
Balance Sheet								
Current Assets	1,524,873	1,950,315	1,112,107	857,912	917,719	933,607	1,024,092	914,450
Total Assets	11,998,149	10,972,402	9,486,800	6,350,587	6,570,342	6,653,005	6,358,339	6,041,258
Current Liabilities	1,231,062	1,330,173	1,046,557	841,831	856,736	959,101	904,953	849,030
Long-Term Obligations	8,020,873	6,896,971	6,078,206	4,757,610	4,611,436	4,119,139	3,732,116	3,280,268
Total Liabilities	9,738,402	8,674,964	7,550,253	5,841,746	5,713,987	5,605,667	5,208,368	4,795,570
Stockholders' Equity	2,259,747	2,297,438	1,936,547	508,841	856,355	1,047,338	1,149,971	1,245,688
Shares Outstanding	285,923	283,110	263,682	211,340	209,818	191,426	190,005	172,140
Statistical Record								
Return on Assets %	1.57	1.80	1.32	1.91	4.93	1.50	2.76	6.36
Return on Equity %	8.19	8.68	8.55	18.05	34.26	8.85	14.30	24.71
EBITDA Margin %	29.95	25.38	23.43	24.17	25.30	23.14	27.34	28.16
Net Margin %	4.29	4.78	2.99	4.10	10.46	3.21	5.71	13.12
Asset Turnover	0.36	0.38	0.44	0.47	0.47	0.47	0.48	0.48
Current Ratio	1.24	1.47	1.06	1.02	1.07	0.97	1.13	1.08
Debt to Equity	3.55	3.00	3.14	9.35	5.38	3.93	3.25	2.63
Price Range	41.44-30.89	41.44-33.10	41.25-24.56	41.09-26.13	40.27-25.90	39.54-25.30	37.69-27.41	35.40-24.39
P/E Ratio	65.78-49.03	60.06-47.97	98.21-58.48	70.84-45.05	24.26-15.60	77.53-49.61	38.46-27.97	17.52-12.07
Average Yield %	6.24	6.07	5.85	5.76	16.71	3.47	16.15	3.07

Address: One Federal Street, Boston, MA 02110	**Web Site:** www.ironmountain.com	**Auditors:** DELOITTE & TOUCHE LLP
Telephone: 617-535-4766	**Officers:** William L. Meaney - Chief Executive Officer Stuart B. Brown - Executive Vice President, Chief Financial Officer	**Investor Contact:** 617-535-4766
		Transfer Agents: Computershare, Providence, RI

385

ITT INC

Exchange	Symbol	Price	52Wk Range	Yield	P/E
NYS	ITT	$52.27 (6/29/2018)	57.43-39.05	1.03	27.37

*7 Year Price Score 108.62 *NYSE Composite Index=100 *12 Month Price Score 106.38

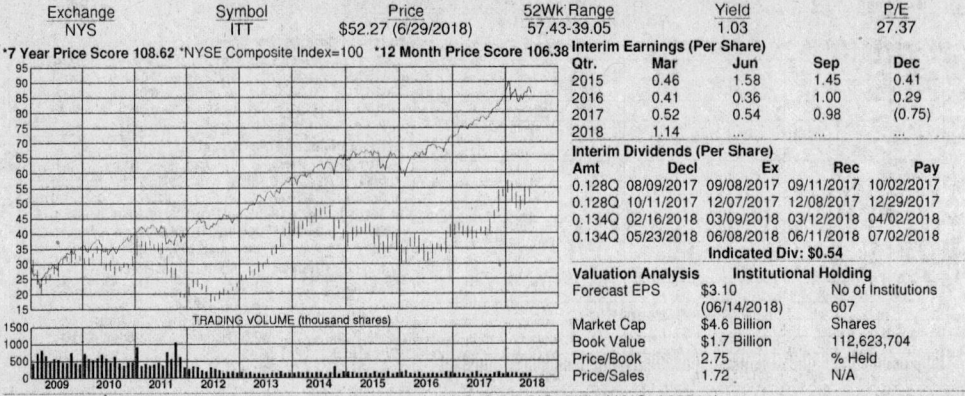

Interim Earnings (Per Share)

Qtr.	Mar	Jun	Sep	Dec
2015	0.46	1.58	1.45	0.41
2016	0.41	0.36	1.00	0.29
2017	0.52	0.54	0.98	(0.75)
2018	1.14			

Interim Dividends (Per Share)

Amt	Decl	Ex	Rec	Pay
0.128Q	08/09/2017	09/08/2017	09/11/2017	10/02/2017
0.128Q	10/11/2017	12/07/2017	12/08/2017	12/29/2017
0.134Q	02/16/2018	03/09/2018	03/12/2018	04/02/2018
0.134Q	05/23/2018	06/08/2018	06/11/2018	07/02/2018

Indicated Div: $0.54

Valuation Analysis

Forecast EPS	$3.10 (06/14/2018)
Market Cap	$4.6 Billion
Book Value	$1.7 Billion
Price/Book	2.75
Price/Sales	1.72

Institutional Holding

No of Institutions	607
Shares	112,623,704
% Held	N/A

Business Summary: Industrial Machinery & Equipment (MIC: 7.2.1 SIC: 3561 NAIC: 333911)

ITT is a manufacturer of components and customized technology solutions for the energy, transportation and industrial markets. Co.'s segments are: Industrial Process, which manufactures engineered fluid process equipment and provides plant and aftermarket services and parts; Motion Technologies, which manufactures brake components and specialized sealing solutions, shock absorbers and damping technologies; Interconnect Solutions, which manufactures and designs a range of engineered harsh environment connector solutions; and Control Technologies, which manufactures equipment, including fuel management, actuation, noise and energy absorption, and environmental control system components.

Recent Developments: For the quarter ended Mar 31 2018, income from continuing operations increased 121.4% to US$101.2 million from US$45.7 million in the year-earlier quarter. Net income increased 122.1% to US$101.3 million from US$45.6 million in the year-earlier quarter. Revenues were US$689.3 million, up 10.1% from US$625.8 million the year before. Operating income was US$110.6 million versus US$57.0 million in the prior-year quarter, an increase of 94.0%. Direct operating expenses rose 10.0% to US$465.1 million from US$422.7 million in the comparable period the year before. Indirect operating expenses decreased 22.2% to US$113.6 million from US$146.1 million in the equivalent prior-year period.

Prospects: Our evaluation of ITT Inc as of Jan. 21, 2018 is the result of our systematic analysis on three basic characteristics: earnings strength, relative valuation, and recent stock price movement. The company has managed to produce a neutral trend in earnings per share over the past 5 quarters. However, while recent estimates for the company have been mixed, ITT has posted better than expected results. Based on operating earnings yield, the company is about fairly valued when compared to all of the companies in our coverage universe. Share price changes over the past year indicates that ITT will perform in line with the market over the near term.

Financial Data

(US$ in Thousands)	3 Mos	12/31/2017	12/31/2016	12/31/2015	12/31/2014	12/31/2013	12/31/2012	12/31/2011
Earnings Per Share	1.91	1.28	2.07	3.88	1.99	5.29	1.33	(1.40)
Cash Flow Per Share	2.99	2.80	2.69	2.56	2.67	2.49	2.65	(3.48)
Tang Book Value Per Share	6.54	5.80	5.13	4.12	5.11	4.61	N.M.	0.89
Dividends Per Share	0.518	0.512	0.372	0.473	0.440	0.400	0.364	1.591
Dividend Payout %	27.12	40.00	17.97	12.20	22.11	7.56	27.37	...
Income Statement								
Total Revenue	689,300	2,585,300	2,405,400	2,485,600	2,654,600	2,496,900	2,227,800	2,119,000
EBITDA	129,500	387,700	331,700	450,500	336,400	245,200	201,000	(189,000)
Depn & Amortn	20,700	78,300	74,100	70,700	72,900	63,400	54,600	57,000
Income Before Taxes	108,800	309,400	258,400	382,300	262,000	180,500	149,100	(318,000)
Income Taxes	7,600	194,600	76,000	70,100	71,300	(309,600)	39,600	260,000
Net Income	101,200	113,500	186,100	351,800	184,500	488,500	125,400	(130,000)
Average Shares	89,000	89,000	89,900	90,700	92,800	92,300	94,100	92,800
Balance Sheet								
Current Assets	1,598,000	1,478,700	1,401,800	1,497,700	1,636,200	1,665,500	1,540,400	1,762,000
Total Assets	3,871,500	3,700,200	3,601,700	3,723,600	3,631,500	3,740,200	3,386,100	3,671,000
Current Liabilities	1,009,100	899,400	866,200	953,100	775,400	832,600	805,300	834,000
Long-Term Obligations	...	...	...	...	...	...	...	4,000
Total Liabilities	2,212,900	2,104,100	2,175,300	2,361,500	2,416,600	2,539,200	2,682,900	2,977,000
Stockholders' Equity	1,658,600	1,596,100	1,426,400	1,362,100	1,214,900	1,201,000	703,200	694,000
Shares Outstanding	87,400	88,200	88,400	89,500	91,000	91,000	92,100	93,500
Statistical Record								
Return on Assets %	4.47	3.11	5.07	9.57	5.01	13.71	3.54	N.M.
Return on Equity %	10.71	7.51	13.31	27.30	15.27	51.31	17.90	N.M.
EBITDA Margin %	18.79	15.00	13.79	18.12	12.67	9.82	9.02	N.M.
Net Margin %	14.68	4.39	7.74	14.15	6.95	19.56	5.63	N.M.
Asset Turnover	0.70	0.71	0.65	0.68	0.72	0.70	0.63	0.26
Current Ratio	1.58	1.64	1.62	1.57	2.11	2.00	1.91	2.11
Debt to Equity	...	...	...	...	...	...	...	0.01
Price Range	57.43-38.01	54.31-38.01	42.73-29.89	43.40-33.05	49.24-37.55	43.50-23.46	24.95-17.14	38.27-18.80
P/E Ratio	30.07-19.90	42.43-29.70	20.64-14.44	11.19-8.52	24.74-18.87	8.22-4.43	18.76-12.89	...
Average Yield %	1.13	1.19	1.05	1.22	1.00	1.25	1.72	5.13

Address: 1133 Westchester Avenue, White Plains, NY 10604 **Telephone:** 914-641-2000	**Web Site:** www.itt.com **Officers:** Denise L. Ramos - President, Chief Executive Officer, Senior Vice President, Chief Financial Officer Lori B. Marino - Corporate Secretary	**Auditors:** Deloitte & Touche LLP **Investor Contact:** 914-641-2030 **Transfer Agents:** Wells Fargo Shareowner Services

JABIL INC

*7 Year Price Score 103.19 *NYSE Composite Index=100 *12 Month Price Score 97.27

Interim Earnings (Per Share)

Qtr.	Nov	Feb	May	Aug
2014-15	0.37	0.27	0.37	0.45
2015-16	0.68	0.41	0.03	0.20
2016-17	0.47	0.11	(0.14)	0.24
2017-18	0.35	0.21	...	...

Interim Dividends (Per Share)

Amt	Decl	Ex	Rec	Pay
0.08Q	07/20/2017	08/11/2017	08/15/2017	09/01/2017
0.08Q	10/19/2017	11/14/2017	11/15/2017	12/01/2017
0.08Q	01/25/2018	02/14/2018	02/15/2018	03/01/2018
0.08Q	04/19/2018	05/14/2018	05/15/2018	06/01/2018

Indicated Div: $0.32

Valuation Analysis

		Institutional Holding	
Forecast EPS	$2.60	No of Institutions	
	(06/14/2018)	566	
Market Cap	$4.8 Billion	Shares	
Book Value	$2.3 Billion	201,547,728	
Price/Book	2.09	% Held	
Price/Sales	0.23	76.01	

Business Summary: Electrical Equipment (MIC: 7.3.1 SIC: 3672 NAIC: 334412)

Jabil provides electronics design, production and product management services to companies in the automotive and transportation, capital equipment, consumer lifestyles and wearable technologies, computing and storage, defense and aerospace, digital home, healthcare, industrial and energy, mobility, networking and telecommunications, packaging, point of sale and printing industries. Co. has two segments: Electronics Manufacturing Services, which is focused around Information Technology, supply chain design and engineering, technologies centered on core electronics; and Diversified Manufacturing Services, which provides engineering solutions and a focus on material sciences and technologies.

Recent Developments: For the quarter ended Feb 28 2018, net income increased 86.5% to US$37.5 million from US$20.1 million in the year-earlier quarter. Revenues were US$5.30 billion, up 19.2% from US$4.45 billion the year before. Operating income was US$129.5 million versus US$83.2 million in the prior-year quarter, an increase of 55.7%. Direct operating expenses rose 20.1% to US$4.90 billion from US$4.08 billion in the comparable period the year before. Indirect operating expenses decreased 4.0% to US$267.6 million from US$278.7 million in the equivalent prior-year period.

Prospects: Our evaluation of Jabil Circuit Inc. as of Jan. 21, 2018 is the result of our systematic analysis on three basic characteristics: earnings strength, relative valuation, and recent stock price movement. The company has suffered a very negative trend in earnings per share over the past 5 quarters and while recent estimates for the company have remained steady, JBL has posted results that fell short of analysts expectations. Based on operating earnings yield, the company is undervalued when compared to all of the companies in our coverage universe. Share price changes over the past year indicates that JBL will perform well over the near term.

Financial Data

(US$ in Thousands)	6 Mos	3 Mos	08/31/2017	08/31/2016	08/31/2015	08/31/2014	08/31/2013	08/31/2012
Earnings Per Share	0.66	0.56	0.69	1.32	1.45	1.19	1.79	1.87
Cash Flow Per Share	6.92	5.94	6.91	4.80	6.40	2.46	5.98	3.07
Tang Book Value Per Share	7.87	7.93	8.22	8.27	8.17	8.32	7.85	9.18
Dividends Per Share	0.320	0.320	0.320	0.320	0.320	0.320	0.320	0.320
Dividend Payout %	48.48	57.14	46.38	24.24	22.07	26.89	17.88	17.11
Income Statement								
Total Revenue	10,886,633	5,585,532	19,063,121	18,353,086	17,899,196	15,762,146	18,336,894	17,151,941
EBITDA	278,788	149,851	1,142,162	1,199,374	1,069,333	681,594	923,379	966,513
Depn & Amortn	19,869	9,979	760,380	696,621	529,149	485,157	418,154	353,525
Income Before Taxes	193,701	107,439	256,233	375,345	422,046	72,123	386,064	508,900
Income Taxes	92,254	43,520	129,066	120,449	127,861	73,711	15,973	112,811
Net Income	101,103	63,795	129,090	254,095	284,019	241,313	371,482	394,687
Average Shares	176,953	180,203	185,838	192,750	196,005	202,497	207,815	211,181
Balance Sheet								
Current Assets	7,036,175	6,922,128	6,626,683	5,848,381	5,866,309	5,359,017	5,820,245	5,639,328
Total Assets	11,488,257	11,519,565	11,095,995	10,322,677	9,603,207	8,479,746	9,153,781	7,803,141
Current Liabilities	6,765,060	7,249,724	6,870,593	5,568,056	5,675,141	4,321,097	4,864,434	3,858,996
Long-Term Obligations	2,181,478	1,693,433	1,632,592	2,074,012	1,346,558	1,669,585	1,690,426	1,658,326
Total Liabilities	9,206,162	9,189,826	8,742,481	7,884,506	7,288,351	6,237,918	6,818,494	5,698,084
Stockholders' Equity	2,282,095	2,329,739	2,353,514	2,438,171	2,314,856	2,241,828	2,335,287	2,105,057
Shares Outstanding	172,063	176,305	177,727	186,998	192,068	194,113	203,164	206,028
Statistical Record								
Return on Assets %	1.13	0.95	1.21	2.54	3.14	2.74	4.38	5.30
Return on Equity %	5.18	4.46	5.39	10.66	12.47	10.54	16.73	19.82
EBITDA Margin %	2.56	2.68	5.99	6.53	5.97	4.32	5.04	5.64
Net Margin %	0.93	1.14	0.68	1.38	1.59	1.53	2.03	2.30
Asset Turnover	1.90	1.77	1.78	1.84	1.98	1.79	2.16	2.30
Current Ratio	1.04	0.95	0.96	1.05	1.03	1.24	1.20	1.46
Debt to Equity	0.96	0.73	0.69	0.85	0.58	0.74	0.72	0.79
Price Range	31.46-24.38	31.46-20.50	31.46-20.41	25.93-16.88	24.83-17.66	24.04-15.67	23.90-16.57	27.13-15.76
P/E Ratio	47.67-36.94	56.18-36.61	45.59-29.58	19.64-12.79	17.12-12.18	20.20-13.17	13.35-9.26	14.51-8.43
Average Yield %	1.12	1.14	1.23	1.55	1.49	1.63	1.63	1.51

Address: 10560 Dr. Martin Luther King, Jr. Street North, St. Petersburg, FL 33716
Telephone: 727-577-9749

Web Site: www.jabil.com
Officers: Timothy L. Main - Chairman, President, Chief Executive Officer Thomas A. Sansone - Vice-Chairman

Auditors: Ernst & Young LLP
Investor Contact: 727-803-3349
Transfer Agents: Computershare, Providence, RI

JACOBS ENGINEERING GROUP, INC.

Exchange	Symbol	Price	52Wk Range	Yield	P/E
NYS	JEC	$63.49 (6/29/2018)	71.05-49.58	0.95	33.77

*7 Year Price Score 97.54   *NYSE Composite Index=100   *12 Month Price Score 102.56

TRADING VOLUME (thousand shares)

Interim Earnings (Per Share)

Qtr.	Dec	Mar	Jun	Sep
2014-15	0.77	0.64	0.73	0.25
2015-16	0.38	0.54	0.57	0.24
2016-17	0.50	0.41	0.74	0.78
2017-18	0.02	0.34	...	...

Interim Dividends (Per Share)

Amt	Decl	Ex	Rec	Pay
0.15Q	07/18/2017	08/02/2017	08/04/2017	09/01/2017
0.15Q	09/27/2017	10/12/2017	10/13/2017	11/10/2017
0.15Q	01/18/2018	02/15/2018	02/16/2018	03/16/2018
0.15Q	05/03/2018	05/17/2018	05/18/2018	06/15/2018

Indicated Div: $0.60

Valuation Analysis

		Institutional Holding	
Forecast EPS	$4.29 (06/14/2018)	No of Institutions	830
Market Cap	$9.0 Billion	Shares	144,625,472
Book Value	$5.9 Billion	% Held	
Price/Book	1.52		89.03
Price/Sales	0.76		

Business Summary: Construction Services (MIC: 7.5.4 SIC: 1629 NAIC: 236210)

Jacobs Engineering Group provides four categories of services: Project Services, which designs and engineers process plants, buildings, infrastructure projects, technology and manufacturing facilities, consumer products manufacturing facilities, power plants and stations, pulp and paper plants, and other facilities; Process, Scientific, and Systems Consulting Services, which provides a range of consulting services; Construction Services, which provides field construction services to private and public sector clients; and Operations and Maintenance Services, which provides management and support services over all aspects of the operations of a facility.

Recent Developments: For the quarter ended Mar 30 2018, net income increased 17.6% to US$51.9 million from US$44.2 million in the year-earlier quarter. Revenues were US$3.94 billion, up 70.9% from US$2.30 billion the year before. Operating income was US$146.3 million versus US$68.2 million in the prior-year quarter, an increase of 114.6%. Direct operating expenses rose 67.9% to US$3.16 billion from US$1.88 billion in the comparable period the year before. Indirect operating expenses increased 78.6% to US$627.1 million from US$351.1 million in the equivalent prior-year period.

Prospects: Our evaluation of Jacobs Engineering Group Inc. as of Jan. 21, 2018 is the result of our systematic analysis on three basic characteristics: earnings strength, relative valuation, and recent stock price movement. The company has managed to produce a neutral trend in earnings per share over the past 5 quarters and while recent estimates for the company have been raised by analysts, JEC has posted better than expected results. Based on operating earnings yield, the company is undervalued when compared to all of the companies in our coverage universe. Share price changes over the past year indicates that JEC will perform poorly over the near term.

Financial Data

(US$ in Thousands)	6 Mos	3 Mos	09/29/2017	09/30/2016	10/02/2015	09/26/2014	09/27/2013	09/28/2012
Earnings Per Share	1.88	1.95	2.42	1.73	2.40	2.48	3.23	2.94
Cash Flow Per Share	3.02	4.16	4.83	5.68	3.81	5.55	3.48	2.36
Tang Book Value Per Share	N.M.	N.M.	9.02	7.02	7.22	7.61	14.98	11.30
Dividends Per Share	0.600	0.600	0.450	...	...	...	...	...
Dividend Payout %	31.91	30.77	18.60	...	...	...	...	...
Income Statement								
Total Revenue	6,685,338	2,750,311	10,022,788	10,964,157	12,114,832	12,695,157	11,818,376	10,893,778
EBITDA	279,970	84,701	519,017	424,106	591,670	689,322	767,933	699,797
Depn & Amortn	95,187	39,527	122,513	129,971	149,292	145,412	98,874	100,824
Income Before Taxes	164,083	41,916	393,217	286,723	430,137	542,166	661,548	593,336
Income Taxes	109,590	39,355	105,842	72,208	101,255	190,054	221,366	202,382
Net Income	50,750	2,163	293,727	210,463	302,971	328,108	423,093	378,954
Average Shares	142,833	125,145	120,147	121,483	126,110	132,371	130,945	128,692
Balance Sheet								
Current Assets	4,457,271	4,546,955	2,996,180	2,864,470	3,282,976	3,892,071	4,039,558	3,612,077
Total Assets	12,601,866	12,691,757	7,380,859	7,360,022	7,785,926	8,453,659	7,274,144	6,839,433
Current Liabilities	2,983,233	3,063,056	1,926,227	1,782,686	1,981,166	2,349,846	1,887,619	1,747,052
Long-Term Obligations	2,511,800	2,587,933	235,000	385,330	584,434	764,075	415,086	528,260
Total Liabilities	6,665,299	6,822,646	2,952,507	3,094,746	3,494,181	3,984,404	3,061,047	3,116,960
Stockholders' Equity	5,936,567	5,869,111	4,428,352	4,265,276	4,291,745	4,469,255	4,213,097	3,722,473
Shares Outstanding	141,714	141,556	120,385	120,950	123,152	131,752	131,639	129,935
Statistical Record								
Return on Assets %	2.38	2.38	4.00	2.79	3.67	4.18	6.01	5.90
Return on Equity %	4.65	4.74	6.78	4.93	6.80	7.58	10.69	10.80
EBITDA Margin %	4.19	3.08	5.18	3.87	4.88	5.43	6.50	6.42
Net Margin %	0.76	0.08	2.93	1.92	2.50	2.58	3.58	3.48
Asset Turnover	1.20	1.03	1.36	1.45	1.47	1.62	1.68	1.70
Current Ratio	1.49	1.48	1.56	1.61	1.66	1.66	2.14	2.07
Debt to Equity	0.42	0.44	0.05	0.09	0.14	0.17	0.10	0.14
Price Range	71.05-49.58	68.51-49.58	62.17-49.25	55.57-35.06	49.68-36.65	66.81-49.52	62.33-38.43	47.61-31.55
P/E Ratio	37.79-26.37	35.13-25.43	25.69-20.35	32.12-20.27	20.70-15.27	26.94-19.97	19.30-11.90	16.19-10.73
Average Yield %	1.03	1.06	0.82	...	...	...	...	...

Address: 1999 Bryan Street, Suite 1200, Dallas, TX 75201 **Telephone:** 214-583-8500	**Web Site:** www.jacobs.com **Officers:** Steven J. Demetriou - Chairman, President, Chief Executive Officer Kevin C. Berryman - Executive Vice President, Chief Financial Officer	**Auditors:** Ernst & Young, LLP **Transfer Agents:** Wells Fargo Shareowner Services, South St. Paul, MN

JBG SMITH PROPERTIES

Exchange	Symbol	Price	52Wk Range	Yield	P/E
NYS	JBGS	$36.47 (6/29/2018)	38.55-31.04	N/A	N/A

*7 Year Price Score N/A *NYSE Composite Index=100 *12 Month Price Score 106.72

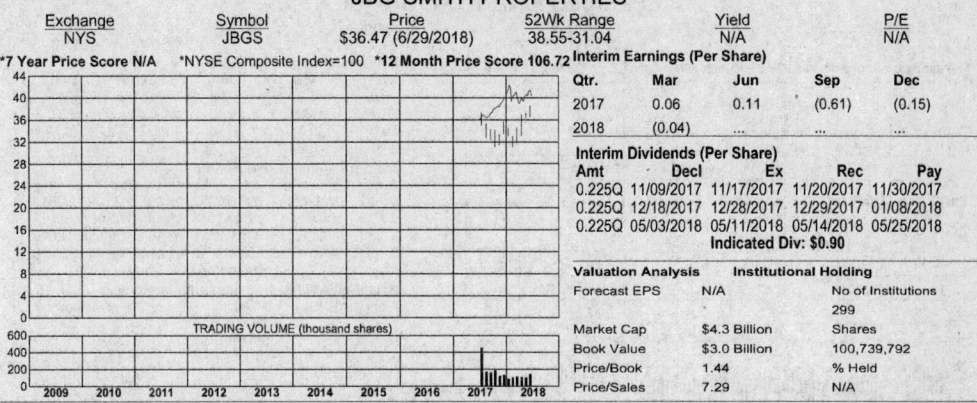

Interim Earnings (Per Share)

Qtr.	Mar	Jun	Sep	Dec
2017	0.06	0.11	(0.61)	(0.15)
2018	(0.04)	...	...	...

Interim Dividends (Per Share)

Amt	Decl	Ex	Rec	Pay
0.225Q	11/09/2017	11/17/2017	11/20/2017	11/30/2017
0.225Q	12/18/2017	12/28/2017	12/29/2017	01/08/2018
0.225Q	05/03/2018	05/11/2018	05/14/2018	05/25/2018

Indicated Div: $0.90

Valuation Analysis / Institutional Holding

Forecast EPS	N/A	No of Institutions 299
Market Cap	$4.3 Billion	Shares
Book Value	$3.0 Billion	100,739,792
Price/Book	1.44	% Held
Price/Sales	7.29	N/A

Business Summary: REITs (MIC: 5.3.1 SIC: 6798 NAIC: 525930)

JBG SMITH Properties operates as a real estate investment trust. Co. owns, operates, and develops mixed use real estate properties. Co. manages residential, office, retail, and mixed-use properties.

Recent Developments: For the quarter ended Mar 31 2018, net loss amounted to US$4.8 million versus net income of US$6.3 million in the year-earlier quarter. Revenues were US$163.0 million, up 40.2% from US$116.3 million the year before. Revenues from property income rose 41.2% to US$161.9 million from US$114.7 million in the corresponding quarter a year earlier.

Prospects: Our evaluation of JBG SMITH Properties as of Jan. 21, 2018 is the result of our systematic analysis on three basic characteristics: earnings strength, relative valuation, and recent stock price movement. The company has produced a positive trend in earnings per share over the past 5 quarters. Because the company lacks sufficient analyst estimate data, we place greater weight on the historical EPS trend as the measure of earnings strength. Based on operating earnings yield, the company is overvalued when compared to all of the companies in our coverage universe. Share price changes over the past year indicates that JBGS will perform very poorly over the near term.

Financial Data
(US$ in Thousands)

	3 Mos	12/31/2017	12/31/2016	12/31/2015	12/31/2014
Earnings Per Share	(0.69)	(0.70)	0.62	0.49	0.81
Cash Flow Per Share	0.59	0.70	1.34	...	...
Tang Book Value Per Share	23.48	25.18	...	...	...
Dividends Per Share	0.450	0.450	...	...	...
Income Statement					
Total Revenue	163,037	543,013	478,519	470,607	472,923
EBITDA	15,194	135,098	246,512	246,785	250,007
Depn & Amortn	2,204	167,741	133,719	144,188	111,388
Income Before Taxes	(5,694)	(88,996)	64,299	54,482	82,820
Income Taxes	(908)	(9,912)	1,083	420	242
Net Income	(4,190)	(71,753)	61,974	49,628	81,299
Average Shares	117,955	105,359	100,571	100,571	100,571
Balance Sheet					
Current Assets	300,841	385,291	65,643	110,883	...
Total Assets	6,061,746	6,071,807	3,660,640	3,575,878	3,357,744
Current Liabilities	130,185	138,607	324,155	137,004	...
Long-Term Obligations	2,133,484	2,187,980	1,165,014	1,302,956	...
Total Liabilities	3,064,772	3,101,199	1,538,951	1,516,902	...
Stockholders' Equity	2,996,974	2,970,608	2,121,689	2,058,976	1,988,347
Shares Outstanding	117,955	117,955	...	...	...
Statistical Record					
Return on Assets %	...	N.M.	1.71	...	...
Return on Equity %	...	N.M.	2.96	...	...
EBITDA Margin %	9.32	24.88	51.52	52.44	52.86
Net Margin %	N.M.	N.M.	12.95	10.55	17.19
Asset Turnover	...	0.11	0.13	...	...
Current Ratio	2.31	2.78	0.20	0.81	...
Debt to Equity	0.71	0.74	0.55	0.63	...
Price Range	37.24-31.04	37.24-31.10	...	...	...
Average Yield %	1.35	1.35	...	...	...

Address: 4445 Willard Avenue, Suite 400, Chevy Chase, MD 20815
Telephone: 240-333-3600

Web Site: www.jbgsmith.com
Officers: Steven Roth - Chairman Robert A. Stewart - Executive Vice-Chairman

Auditors: Deloitte & Touche LLP
Investor Contact: 240-333-3600
Transfer Agents: American Stock Transfer & Trust Company, LLC, Brookly, NY

JEFFERIES FINANCIAL GROUP INC

Exchange	Symbol	Price	52Wk Range	Yield	P/E
NYS	JEF	$22.74 (6/29/2018)	28.01-21.77	1.76	454.80

*7 Year Price Score 83.41 *NYSE Composite Index=100 *12 Month Price Score 91.40

Interim Earnings (Per Share)

Qtr.	Mar	Jun	Sep	Dec
2015	0.99	0.04	(0.47)	0.15
2016	(0.60)	0.15	0.41	0.37
2017	0.75	0.16	0.27	(0.72)
2018	0.34	...	...	...

Interim Dividends (Per Share)

Amt	Decl	Ex	Rec	Pay
0.10Q	07/27/2017	09/15/2017	09/18/2017	09/29/2017
0.10Q	10/26/2017	12/12/2017	12/13/2017	12/27/2017
0.10Q	02/22/2018	03/16/2018	03/19/2018	03/30/2018
0.10Q	05/23/2018	06/15/2018	06/18/2018	06/29/2018

Indicated Div: $0.40

Valuation Analysis

Forecast EPS	$0.84	Institutional Holding	
	(05/21/2018)	No of Institutions	707
Market Cap	$8.1 Billion	Shares	313,496,032
Book Value	$10.4 Billion	Shares	
Price/Book	0.78	% Held	91.50
Price/Sales	0.72		

Business Summary: Agricultural Livestock (MIC: 1.1.2 SIC: 5147 NAIC: 311612)

Jefferies Financial Group is a holding company. Co.'s financial services businesses include Jefferies (investment banking and capital markets), Leucadia Asset Management (asset management), Berkadia (commercial mortgage banking, investment sales and servicing), FXCM Group, LLC (provider of online foreign exchange trading services), HomeFed (a real estate company) and Foursight Capital (vehicle finance). Co. also owns and has investments in an array of other businesses, including beef processing, insurance and consumer products, oil and gas exploration and development, automobile dealerships, fixed wireless broadband services in Italy, manufacturing, and a gold and silver mining project.

Recent Developments: For the quarter ended Mar 31 2018, net income decreased 52.7% to US$139.1 million from US$293.9 million in the year-earlier quarter. Revenues were US$2.68 billion, down 6.5% from US$2.87 billion the year before. Direct operating expenses rose 14.3% to US$1.75 billion from US$1.53 billion in the comparable period the year before. Indirect operating expenses increased 5.6% to US$853.5 million from US$808.2 million in the equivalent prior-year period.

Prospects: Our evaluation of Leucadia National Corp. as of Jan. 21, 2018 is the result of our systematic analysis on three basic characteristics: earnings strength, relative valuation, and recent stock price movement. The company has suffered a very negative trend in earnings per share over the past 5 quarters. Because the company lacks sufficient analyst estimate data, we place greater weight on the historical EPS trend as the measure of earnings strength. Based on operating earnings yield, the company is undervalued when compared to all of the companies in our coverage universe. Share price changes over the past year indicates that LUK will perform poorly over the near term.

Financial Data

(US$ in Thousands)	3 Mos	12/31/2017	12/31/2016	12/31/2015	12/31/2014	12/31/2013	12/31/2012	12/31/2011
Earnings Per Share	0.05	0.45	0.34	0.74	0.54	1.06	3.44	0.10
Cash Flow Per Share	2.35	2.91	1.64	(2.05)	(2.65)	2.07	0.90	0.04
Tang Book Value Per Share	22.21	21.81	21.53	21.72	20.97	20.46	24.18	21.66
Dividends Per Share	0.362	0.325	0.250	0.250	0.250	0.250	0.250	0.250
Dividend Payout %	725.00	72.22	73.53	33.78	46.30	23.58	7.27	250.00
Income Statement								
Total Revenue	2,680,793	11,436,393	10,062,617	10,886,458	11,486,485	10,429,491	9,193,689	1,570,768
EBITDA	101,546	1,360,613	437,324	529,740	499,613	576,930	1,229,214	888,098
Depn & Amortn	3,385	164,039	166,789	172,073	139,744	138,964	170,113	95,233
Income Before Taxes	74,554	1,088,715	161,832	246,255	242,695	353,002	966,520	680,988
Income Taxes	(32,495)	760,967	122,109	109,947	165,971	110,741	376,494	270,253
Net Income	125,697	171,726	130,001	283,650	208,368	372,637	854,466	25,231
Average Shares	373,461	370,701	371,518	372,431	373,333	347,734	248,914	244,573
Balance Sheet								
Current Assets	32,185,849	14,962,068	12,952,561	12,075,445	15,583,132	14,499,058	2,521,266	1,253,479
Total Assets	49,001,494	47,169,108	45,071,307	46,339,812	52,623,908	47,866,781	9,349,118	9,263,189
Current Liabilities	8,718,385	10,126,211	8,343,947	11,187,884	11,389,283	19,336,501	1,280,479	877,132
Long-Term Obligations	9,754,617	7,885,783	7,380,443	7,407,594	8,527,929	8,180,865	918,126	1,875,571
Total Liabilities	38,617,414	36,938,151	34,818,207	35,813,601	42,196,750	37,639,319	2,581,850	3,088,793
Stockholders' Equity	10,384,080	10,230,957	10,253,100	10,526,211	10,427,158	10,227,462	6,767,268	6,174,396
Shares Outstanding	357,215	356,227	359,425	362,617	367,498	364,541	244,582	244,582
Statistical Record								
Return on Assets %	0.03	0.37	0.28	0.57	0.41	1.30	9.16	0.27
Return on Equity %	0.14	1.68	1.25	2.71	2.02	4.39	13.17	0.38
EBITDA Margin %	3.79	11.90	4.35	4.87	4.35	5.53	13.37	56.54
Net Margin %	4.69	1.50	1.29	2.61	1.81	3.57	9.29	1.61
Asset Turnover	0.24	0.25	0.22	0.22	0.23	0.36	0.99	0.17
Current Ratio	3.69	1.48	1.55	1.08	1.37	0.75	1.97	1.43
Debt to Equity	0.94	0.77	0.72	0.70	0.82	0.80	0.14	0.30
Price Range	28.01-21.85	27.20-22.27	24.00-14.45	25.20-16.08	28.65-21.04	32.20-23.79	29.72-19.84	39.02-20.42
P/E Ratio	560.20-437.00	60.44-49.49	70.59-42.50	34.05-21.73	53.06-38.96	30.38-22.44	8.64-5.77	390.20-204.20
Average Yield %	1.43	1.28	1.38	1.14	0.98	0.91	1.06	0.82

Address: 520 Madison Avenue, New York, NY 10022	Web Site: www.leucadia.com	Auditors: DELOITTE & TOUCHE LLP
Telephone: 212-460-1900	Officers: Joseph S. Steinberg - Chairman, President	Investor Contact: 212-460-1900
Fax: 212-598-4869	Brian P. Friedman - President	Transfer Agents: American Stock Transfer & Trust Company, LLC, Brooklyn, NY

JOHNSON & JOHNSON

Exchange	Symbol	Price	52Wk Range	Yield	P/E	Div Acheiver
NYS	JNJ	$121.34 (6/29/2018)	148.14-119.40	2.97	258.17	53 Years

*7 Year Price Score 107.91 *NYSE Composite Index=100   ***12 Month Price Score 91.28**

Interim Earnings (Per Share)

Qtr.	Mar	Jun	Sep	Dec
2015	1.53	1.61	1.20	1.15
2016	1.54	1.43	1.53	1.38
2017	1.61	1.40	1.37	(3.90)
2018	1.60	...	...	...

Interim Dividends (Per Share)

Amt	Decl	Ex	Rec	Pay
0.84Q	07/17/2017	08/25/2017	08/29/2017	09/12/2017
0.84Q	10/19/2017	11/27/2017	11/28/2017	12/12/2017
0.84Q	01/02/2018	02/26/2018	02/27/2018	03/13/2018
0.90Q	04/26/2018	05/25/2018	05/29/2018	06/12/2018

Indicated Div: $3.60 (Div. Reinv. Plan)

Valuation Analysis

		Institutional Holding	
Forecast EPS	$8.12	No of Institutions	
	(06/14/2018)	3506	
Market Cap	$325.5 Billion	Shares	
Book Value	$63.3 Billion	2,320,759,552	
Price/Book	5.15	% Held	
Price/Sales	4.14	66.52	

Business Summary: Pharmaceuticals (MIC: 4.1.1 SIC: 2834 NAIC: 325412)

Johnson & Johnson, is engaged in the research and development, manufacture and sale of a range of products in the health care field. Co. is organized into three business segments: Consumer, which includes a range of products used in the baby care, oral care, beauty, over-the-counter pharmaceutical, women's health and wound care markets. Pharmaceutical, which is focused on five therapeutic areas: immunology, infectious diseases and vaccines, neuroscience, oncology, and cardiovascular and metabolic diseases. Medical Devices, which includes products used in the orthopaedic, surgery, cardiovascular, diabetes care and vision care fields.

Recent Developments: For the quarter ended Apr 1 2018, net income decreased 1.2% to US$4.37 billion from US$4.42 billion in the year-earlier quarter. Revenues were US$20.01 billion, up 12.6% from US$17.77 billion the year before. Direct operating expenses rose 22.3% to US$6.61 billion from US$5.41 billion in the comparable period the year before. Indirect operating expenses increased 16.7% to US$7.91 billion from US$6.78 billion in the equivalent prior-year period.

Prospects: Our evaluation of Johnson & Johnson as of Jan. 21, 2018 is the result of our systematic analysis on three basic characteristics: earnings strength, relative valuation, and recent stock price movement. The company has managed to produce a neutral trend in earnings per share over the past 5 quarters and while recent estimates for the company have remained steady, JNJ has posted better than expected results. Based on operating earnings yield, the company is undervalued when compared to all of the companies in our coverage universe. Share price changes over the past year indicates that JNJ will perform well over the near term.

Financial Data
(US$ in Millions)

	3 Mos	12/31/2017	01/01/2017	01/03/2016	12/28/2014	12/29/2013	12/30/2012	01/01/2012
Earnings Per Share	0.47	0.47	5.93	5.48	5.70	4.81	3.86	3.49
Cash Flow Per Share	8.11	7.84	6.87	6.84	6.58	6.22	5.61	5.24
Tang Book Value Per Share	N.M.	N.M.	7.66	8.62	7.44	8.26	4.91	8.37
Dividends Per Share	3.360	3.320	3.150	2.950	2.760	2.590	2.400	2.250
Dividend Payout %	714.89	706.38	53.12	53.83	48.42	53.85	62.18	64.47
Income Statement								
Total Revenue	20,009	76,450	71,890	70,074	74,331	71,312	67,224	65,030
EBITDA	7,372	22,022	23,861	23,320	24,927	19,942	17,889	15,993
Depn & Amortn	1,746	3,800	3,700	3,700	3,898	4,063	3,646	3,152
Income Before Taxes	5,481	17,673	19,803	19,196	20,563	15,471	13,775	12,361
Income Taxes	1,114	16,373	3,263	3,787	4,240	1,640	3,261	2,689
Net Income	4,367	1,300	16,540	15,409	16,323	13,831	10,853	9,672
Average Shares	2,732	2,746	2,789	2,813	2,864	2,878	2,813	2,776
Balance Sheet								
Current Assets	42,768	43,088	65,032	60,210	59,311	56,407	46,116	54,316
Total Assets	156,625	157,303	141,208	133,411	131,119	132,683	121,347	113,644
Current Liabilities	27,081	30,537	26,287	27,747	25,085	25,675	24,262	22,811
Long-Term Obligations	29,837	30,675	22,442	12,857	15,122	13,328	11,489	12,969
Total Liabilities	93,370	97,143	70,790	62,261	61,367	58,630	56,521	56,564
Stockholders' Equity	63,255	60,160	70,418	71,150	69,752	74,053	64,826	57,080
Shares Outstanding	2,683	2,683	2,707	2,756	2,784	2,821	2,779	2,725
Statistical Record								
Return on Assets %	0.83	0.87	12.08	11.46	12.41	10.92	9.26	8.96
Return on Equity %	1.86	2.00	23.43	21.52	22.76	19.97	17.85	17.07
EBITDA Margin %	36.84	28.81	33.19	33.28	33.54	27.96	26.61	24.59
Net Margin %	21.83	1.70	23.01	21.99	21.96	19.40	16.14	14.87
Asset Turnover	0.52	0.51	0.53	0.52	0.57	0.56	0.57	0.60
Current Ratio	1.58	1.41	2.47	2.17	2.36	2.20	1.90	2.38
Debt to Equity	0.47	0.51	0.32	0.18	0.22	0.18	0.18	0.23
Price Range	148.14-121.37	143.62-111.76	125.40-95.75	106.39-90.73	109.07-86.62	95.63-70.10	72.52-61.78	67.92-57.66
P/E Ratio	315.19-258.23	305.57-237.79	21.15-16.15	19.41-16.56	19.14-15.20	19.88-14.57	18.79-16.01	19.46-16.52
Average Yield %	2.51	2.56	2.77	2.96	2.74	3.02	3.58	3.54

Address: One Johnson & Johnson Plaza, New Brunswick, NJ 08933	**Web Site:** www.jnj.com	**Auditors:** PricewaterhouseCoopers LLP
Telephone: 732-524-0400	**Officers:** Alex Gorsky - Chairman, Chief Executive	**Investor Contact:** 800-950-5089
Fax: 732-214-0332	Officer, Division Officer Dominic J. Caruso - Executive Vice President, Vice President, Chief Financial Officer	**Transfer Agents:** Computershare Trust Company, N.A., Canton, MA

JONES LANG LASALLE INC

Exchange	Symbol	Price	52Wk Range	Yield	P/E
NYS	JLL	$165.99 (6/29/2018)	177.30-116.70	0.49	26.82

*7 Year Price Score 103.17 *NYSE Composite Index=100 ***12 Month Price Score 112.06**

Interim Earnings (Per Share)

Qtr.	Mar	Jun	Sep	Dec
2015	0.92	1.98	2.43	4.31
2016	0.56	1.73	1.05	3.63
2017	0.24	1.71	1.89	1.71
2018	0.88	...	...	...

Interim Dividends (Per Share)

Amt	Decl	Ex	Rec	Pay
0.33S	11/02/2016	11/10/2016	11/15/2016	12/15/2016
0.35S	05/05/2017	05/11/2017	05/15/2017	06/15/2017
0.37S	11/06/2017	11/15/2017	11/16/2017	12/15/2017
0.41S	05/08/2018	05/17/2018	05/18/2018	06/15/2018

Indicated Div: $0.82

Valuation Analysis

Forecast EPS	$10.38	
	(06/14/2018)	
Market Cap	$7.6 Billion	
Book Value	$3.4 Billion	
Price/Book	2.20	
Price/Sales	0.76	

Institutional Holding

No of Institutions	553
Shares	52,630,024
% Held	94.50

TRADING VOLUME (thousand shares)

Business Summary: Property, Real Estate & Development (MIC: 5.3.2 SIC: 6531 NAIC: 531210)

Jones Lang LaSalle is a financial services company that provides real estate services on a local, regional and global basis to owner, occupier, investor and developer clients. Services provided include: agency leasing; capital markets; corporate finance; energy and sustainability services; facility management outsourcing (occupiers); investment management; logistics and supply-chain management; mortgage origination and servicing; project and development management/construction; property management (investors); real estate investment banking/merchant banking; research; consulting and advisory services; tenant representation; valuations; and value recovery and receivership services.

Recent Developments: For the quarter ended Mar 31 2018, net income increased 453.2% to US$42.6 million from US$7.7 million in the year-earlier quarter. Revenues were US$3.56 billion, up 14.0% from US$3.12 billion the year before.

Prospects: Our evaluation of Jones Lang LaSalle Inc. as of Jan. 21, 2018 is the result of our systematic analysis on three basic characteristics: earnings strength, relative valuation, and recent stock price movement. The company has produced a positive trend in earnings per share over the past 5 quarters and while recent estimates for the company have been raised by analysts, JLL has posted better than expected results. Based on operating earnings yield, the company is undervalued when compared to all of the companies in our coverage universe. Share price changes over the past year indicates that JLL will perform well over the near term.

Financial Data
(US$ in Thousands)

	3 Mos	12/31/2017	12/31/2016	12/31/2015	12/31/2014	12/31/2013	12/31/2012	12/31/2011
Earnings Per Share	6.19	5.55	6.98	9.65	8.52	5.98	4.63	3.70
Cash Flow Per Share	16.36	17.42	4.74	8.36	11.16	6.62	7.45	4.90
Tang Book Value Per Share	8.54	5.04	N.M.	7.11	9.82	5.26	1.17	N.M.
Dividends Per Share	0.720	0.720	0.640	0.560	0.480	0.440	0.400	0.300
Dividend Payout %	11.63	12.97	9.17	5.80	5.63	7.36	8.64	8.11
Income Statement								
Total Revenue	3,555,200	7,932,400	6,803,800	5,965,671	5,429,603	4,461,591	3,932,830	3,584,544
EBITDA	98,400	735,200	633,600	664,756	583,869	439,819	355,603	313,805
Depn & Amortn	42,100	198,300	179,700	134,958	118,205	71,000	66,200	62,600
Income Before Taxes	42,500	480,700	408,600	501,671	437,343	334,101	254,230	215,614
Income Taxes	13,500	267,800	108,000	132,805	97,588	92,092	69,244	56,387
Net Income	40,300	254,200	318,200	438,672	386,063	269,865	208,050	164,384
Average Shares	45,905	45,758	45,528	45,414	45,260	45,072	44,799	44,367
Balance Sheet								
Current Assets	4,389,500	3,354,900	3,299,700	2,650,807	2,118,176	1,724,228	1,515,529	1,300,884
Total Assets	9,204,200	8,014,500	7,629,400	6,205,159	5,075,336	4,597,353	4,351,499	3,932,636
Current Liabilities	3,838,300	3,210,000	2,966,300	2,505,193	2,047,011	1,658,424	1,661,971	1,348,617
Long-Term Obligations	1,012,800	675,300	1,178,100	529,999	275,000	430,000	444,000	463,000
Total Liabilities	5,769,400	4,771,300	4,839,700	3,516,396	2,688,539	2,417,684	2,400,316	2,241,507
Stockholders' Equity	3,434,800	3,243,200	2,789,700	2,688,763	2,386,797	2,179,669	1,951,183	1,691,129
Shares Outstanding	45,490	45,373	45,213	45,049	44,828	44,447	44,054	43,470
Statistical Record								
Return on Assets %	3.45	3.25	4.59	7.78	7.98	6.03	5.01	4.51
Return on Equity %	9.00	8.43	11.58	17.29	16.91	13.07	11.39	10.08
EBITDA Margin %	2.77	9.27	9.31	11.14	10.75	9.86	9.04	8.75
Net Margin %	1.13	3.20	4.68	7.35	7.11	6.05	5.29	4.59
Asset Turnover	1.20	1.01	0.98	1.06	1.12	1.00	0.95	0.98
Current Ratio	1.14	1.05	1.11	1.06	1.03	1.04	0.91	0.96
Debt to Equity	0.29	0.21	0.42	0.20	0.12	0.20	0.23	0.27
Price Range	177.30-102.62	153.03-99.21	160.19-88.65	179.35-142.69	153.43-101.95	102.80-82.15	87.08-63.21	107.72-47.04
P/E Ratio	28.64-16.58	27.57-17.88	22.95-12.70	18.59-14.79	18.01-11.97	17.19-13.74	18.81-13.65	29.11-12.71
Average Yield %	0.53	0.59	0.57	0.35	0.38	0.47	0.53	0.37

Address: 200 East Randolph Drive, Chicago, IL 60601 **Telephone:** 312-782-5800 **Fax:** 312-782-4339	**Web Site:** www.jll.com **Officers:** Sheila A. Penrose - Chairman Christian Ulbrich - President, Chief Executive Officer, Region Officer	**Auditors:** KPMG LLP **Investor Contact:** 312-782-5800 **Transfer Agents:** Computershare, Pittsburgh, PA

JPMORGAN CHASE & CO

Exchange	Symbol	Price	52Wk Range	Yield	P/E
NYS	JPM	$104.20 (6/29/2018)	118.77-88.42	2.15	14.80

*7 Year Price Score 132.15 ***NYSE Composite Index=100** ***12 Month Price Score 103.13**

TRADING VOLUME (thousand shares)

Interim Earnings (Per Share)

Qtr.	Mar	Jun	Sep	Dec
2015	1.45	1.54	1.68	1.32
2016	1.35	1.55	1.58	1.71
2017	1.65	1.82	1.76	1.09
2018	2.37	...	...	...

Interim Dividends (Per Share)

Amt	Decl	Ex	Rec	Pay
0.56Q	09/19/2017	10/05/2017	10/06/2017	10/31/2017
0.56Q	12/12/2017	01/04/2018	01/05/2018	01/31/2018
0.56Q	03/20/2018	04/05/2018	04/06/2018	04/30/2018
0.56Q	05/15/2018	07/05/2018	07/06/2018	07/31/2018

Indicated Div: $2.24 (Div. Reinv. Plan)

Valuation Analysis / Institutional Holding

Valuation Analysis		Institutional Holding	
Forecast EPS	$9.04	No of Institutions	
	(06/14/2018)	3289	
Market Cap	$354.8 Billion	Shares	
Book Value	$256.2 Billion	3,203,198,464	
Price/Book	1.38	% Held	
Price/Sales	2.99	71.83	

Business Summary: Banking (MIC: 5.1.1 SIC: 6021 NAIC: 522110)

JPMorgan Chase is a financial holding company. Through its subsidiaries, Co. acts as a financial services firm and banking institution providing investment banking, financial services for consumers and businesses, commercial banking, financial transaction processing and asset management. Co.'s consumer business is the Consumer and Community Banking segment. Co.'s wholesale business segments are Corporate and Investment Bank, Commercial Banking, and Asset and Wealth Management. Under the J.P. Morgan and Chase brands, Co. serves customers in the corporate, institutional and government clients. As of Dec 31 2017, Co. had total assets of $2.53 trillion and total deposits of $1.44 trillion.

Recent Developments:
For the quarter ended Mar 31 2018, net income increased 35.1% to US$8.71 billion from US$6.45 billion in the year-earlier quarter. Net interest income increased 10.3% to US$13.31 billion from US$12.06 billion in the year-earlier quarter. Provision for loan losses was US$1.17 billion versus US$1.32 billion in the prior-year quarter, a decrease of 11.4%. Non-interest income rose 13.4% to US$14.60 billion from US$12.88 billion, while non-interest expense advanced 5.2% to US$16.08 billion.

Prospects:
Our evaluation of J.P. Morgan Chase & Co. as of Jan. 21, 2018 is the result of our systematic analysis on three basic characteristics: earnings strength, relative valuation, and recent stock price movement. The company has managed to produce a neutral trend in earnings per share over the past 5 quarters and while recent estimates for the company have been raised by analysts, JPM has posted better than expected results. Based on operating earnings yield, the company is undervalued when compared to all of the companies in our coverage universe. Share price changes over the past year indicates that JPM will perform in line with the market over the near term.

Financial Data

(US$ in Millions)	3 Mos	12/31/2017	12/31/2016	12/31/2015	12/31/2014	12/31/2013	12/31/2012	12/31/2011
Earnings Per Share	7.04	6.31	6.19	6.00	5.29	4.35	5.20	4.48
Cash Flow Per Share	(5.08)	(0.70)	5.57	19.85	9.72	28.54	6.57	24.60
Tang Book Value Per Share	51.57	51.16	48.83	45.46	41.92	37.46	36.01	31.05
Dividends Per Share	2.120	2.040	1.840	1.680	1.560	1.360	1.150	0.800
Dividend Payout %	30.11	32.33	29.73	28.00	29.49	31.26	22.12	17.86
Income Statement								
Interest Income	17,695	64,372	55,901	50,973	51,531	52,996	56,063	61,293
Interest Expense	4,383	14,275	9,818	7,463	7,897	9,677	11,153	13,604
Net Interest Income	13,312	50,097	46,083	43,510	43,634	43,319	44,910	47,689
Provision for Losses	1,165	5,290	5,361	3,827	3,139	225	3,385	7,574
Non-Interest Income	14,595	49,527	49,585	50,033	50,571	53,287	52,121	49,545
Non-Interest Expense	16,080	58,434	55,771	59,014	61,274	70,467	64,729	62,911
Income Before Taxes	10,662	35,900	34,536	30,702	29,792	25,914	28,917	26,749
Income Taxes	1,950	11,459	9,803	6,260	8,030	7,991	7,633	7,773
Net Income	8,712	24,441	24,733	24,442	21,762	17,923	21,284	18,976
Average Shares	3,480	3,577	3,650	3,733	3,798	3,815	3,823	3,921
Balance Sheet								
Net Loans & Leases	921,049	917,093	880,989	823,744	743,151	722,154	711,860	696,111
Total Assets	2,609,785	2,533,600	2,490,972	2,351,698	2,573,126	2,415,689	2,359,141	2,265,792
Total Deposits	1,486,961	1,443,982	1,375,179	1,279,715	1,363,427	1,287,765	1,193,593	1,127,806
Total Liabilities	2,353,584	2,277,907	2,236,782	2,104,125	2,341,061	2,204,511	2,155,072	2,082,219
Stockholders' Equity	256,201	255,693	254,190	247,573	232,065	211,178	204,069	183,573
Shares Outstanding	3,405	3,426	3,562	3,664	3,715	3,757	3,804	3,773
Statistical Record								
Return on Assets %	1.04	0.97	1.02	0.99	0.87	0.75	0.92	0.87
Return on Equity %	10.43	9.59	9.83	10.19	9.82	8.63	10.95	10.55
Net Interest Margin %	75.23	77.82	82.44	85.36	84.68	81.74	80.11	77.80
Efficiency Ratio %	49.80	51.30	52.87	58.43	60.01	66.30	59.83	56.76
Loans to Deposits	0.62	0.64	0.64	0.64	0.55	0.56	0.60	0.62
Price Range	118.77-82.15	107.83-82.15	87.13-53.07	70.08-54.38	63.15-53.31	58.48-43.97	46.27-31.00	48.00-28.38
P/E Ratio	16.87-11.67	17.09-13.02	14.08-8.57	11.68-9.06	11.94-10.08	13.44-10.11	8.90-5.96	10.71-6.33
Average Yield %	2.16	2.22	2.80	2.63	2.68	2.62	2.93	2.03

Address: 270 Park Avenue, New York, NY 10017	Web Site: www.jpmorganchase.com	Auditors: PricewaterhouseCoopers LLP
Telephone: 212-270-6000	**Officers:** James (Jamie) Dimon - Chairman, President, Chief Executive Officer Gordon A. Smith - Co-President, Co-Chief Operating Officer, Division Officer	**Investor Contact:** 212-270-7325 **Transfer Agents:** Computershare Shareowner Services LLC, Jersey City, NY

JUNIPER NETWORKS INC

Exchange	Symbol	Price	52Wk Range	Yield	P/E
NYS	JNPR	$27.42 (6/29/2018)	29.96-24.05	2.63	44.23

*7 Year Price Score 91.13 *NYSE Composite Index=100 *12 Month Price Score 97.62

Interim Earnings (Per Share)

Qtr.	Mar	Jun	Sep	Dec
2015	0.19	0.40	0.51	0.50
2016	0.23	0.36	0.45	0.49
2017	0.28	0.47	0.43	(0.38)
2018	0.10	...	...	...

Interim Dividends (Per Share)

Amt	Decl	Ex	Rec	Pay
0.10Q	07/25/2017	08/30/2017	09/01/2017	09/22/2017
0.10Q	10/24/2017	11/30/2017	12/01/2017	12/22/2017
0.18Q	01/30/2018	02/28/2018	03/01/2018	03/22/2018
0.18Q	05/02/2018	05/31/2018	06/01/2018	06/22/2018

Indicated Div: $0.72

Valuation Analysis   **Institutional Holding**

Forecast EPS	$1.83 (06/11/2018)	No of Institutions	736
Market Cap	$9.6 Billion	Shares	397,997,408
Book Value	$4.3 Billion	% Held	80.01
Price/Book	2.21		
Price/Sales	1.96		

Business Summary: Peripherals (MIC: 6.2.2 SIC: 3661 NAIC: 334210)

Juniper Networks designs, develops, and sells products and services for networks. Co. sells its products in three geographic regions: Americas; Europe, Middle East, and Africa; and Asia Pacific. Co. sells its network products and service offerings across routing, switching, and security. Co.'s products address network requirements for service providers, cloud providers, national governments, research and public sector organizations and other enterprises. Co.'s portfolio addresses various domains in the network: core; edge; access and aggregation; data centers; and campus and branch. Co.'s product families and service offerings are routing products, switching products, and security products.

Recent Developments: For the quarter ended Mar 31 2018, net income decreased 68.4% to US$34.4 million from US$108.8 million in the year-earlier quarter. Revenues were US$1.08 billion, down 11.3% from US$1.22 billion the year before. Operating income was US$55.5 million versus US$156.3 million in the prior-year quarter, a decrease of 64.5%. Direct operating expenses declined 2.2% to US$464.2 million from US$474.4 million in the comparable period the year before. Indirect operating expenses decreased 4.6% to US$562.9 million from US$590.3 million in the equivalent prior-year period.

Prospects: Our evaluation of Juniper Networks Inc. as of Jan. 21, 2018 is the result of our systematic analysis on three basic characteristics: earnings strength, relative valuation, and recent stock price movement. The company has generated a negative trend in earnings per share over the past 5 quarters. However, while recent estimates for the company have been mixed, JNPR has posted better than expected results. Based on operating earnings yield, the company is undervalued when compared to all of the companies in our coverage universe. Share price changes over the past year indicates that JNPR will perform in line with the market over the near term.

Financial Data

(US$ in Thousands)	3 Mos	12/31/2017	12/31/2016	12/31/2015	12/31/2014	12/31/2013	12/31/2012	12/31/2011
Earnings Per Share	0.62	0.80	1.53	1.59	(0.73)	0.86	0.35	0.79
Cash Flow Per Share	2.77	3.34	2.89	2.28	1.67	1.68	1.23	1.86
Tang Book Value Per Share	3.17	3.99	4.59	4.04	4.48	6.34	5.53	5.77
Dividends Per Share	0.480	0.400	0.400	0.400	0.200	...	...	...
Dividend Payout %	77.42	50.00	26.14	25.16	...	...	...	...
Income Statement								
Total Revenue	1,082,600	5,027,200	4,990,100	4,857,800	4,627,100	4,669,100	4,365,400	4,448,709
EBITDA	108,200	1,062,800	1,074,200	1,055,200	112,500	723,400	492,800	759,082
Depn & Amortn	55,700	202,800	184,500	141,500	141,900	148,200	159,400	147,566
Income Before Taxes	41,400	811,800	827,400	852,200	(86,300)	525,500	291,500	571,716
Income Taxes	7,000	505,600	234,700	218,500	248,000	85,700	105,000	146,704
Net Income	34,400	306,200	592,700	633,700	(334,300)	439,800	186,500	425,136
Average Shares	360,600	384,200	387,800	399,400	457,400	510,300	526,200	541,417
Balance Sheet								
Current Assets	3,920,700	4,184,500	3,971,900	2,912,400	2,971,900	3,703,900	3,600,700	4,439,661
Total Assets	9,078,500	9,833,800	9,656,500	8,619,200	8,403,100	10,326,000	9,832,100	9,983,820
Current Liabilities	1,830,000	1,738,200	1,735,900	1,801,900	1,527,700	1,441,400	1,422,000	1,466,703
Long-Term Obligations	1,787,700	2,136,300	2,133,700	1,648,800	1,349,000	999,300	999,200	999,034
Total Liabilities	4,753,800	5,152,900	4,694,000	4,044,800	3,484,000	3,023,800	2,833,100	2,894,638
Stockholders' Equity	4,324,700	4,680,900	4,962,500	4,574,400	4,919,100	7,302,200	6,999,000	7,089,182
Shares Outstanding	349,000	365,500	381,100	384,000	416,200	495,200	508,400	526,409
Statistical Record								
Return on Assets %	2.48	3.14	6.47	7.45	N.M.	4.36	1.88	4.61
Return on Equity %	4.96	6.35	12.40	13.35	N.M.	6.15	2.64	6.21
EBITDA Margin %	9.99	21.14	21.53	21.72	2.43	15.49	11.29	17.06
Net Margin %	3.18	6.09	11.88	13.05	N.M.	9.42	4.27	9.56
Asset Turnover	0.52	0.52	0.54	0.57	0.49	0.46	0.44	0.48
Current Ratio	2.14	2.41	2.29	1.62	1.95	2.57	2.53	3.03
Debt to Equity	0.41	0.46	0.43	0.36	0.27	0.14	0.14	0.14
Price Range	30.89-24.05	30.89-24.40	28.68-21.24	32.23-21.39	27.95-18.57	22.57-15.69	23.88-14.27	44.46-17.08
P/E Ratio	49.82-38.79	38.61-30.50	18.75-13.88	20.27-13.45	...	26.24-18.24	68.23-40.77	56.28-21.62
Average Yield %	1.73	1.43	1.64	1.52	0.84	...	...	...

Address: 1133 Innovation Way, Sunnyvale, CA 94089
Telephone: 408-745-2000
Fax: 408-745-2100

Web Site: www.juniper.net
Officers: Scott G. Kriens - Chairman, Chief Executive Officer Pradeep S. Sindhu - Chairman, Vice-Chairman, Executive Vice President, Chief Scientific Officer, Chief Technology Officer

Auditors: Ernst & Young LLP
Investor Contact: 408-936-5396
Transfer Agents: Wells Fargo Shareowner Services, Mendota Heights, MN

KANSAS CITY SOUTHERN

Exchange	Symbol	Price	52Wk Range	Yield	P/E
NYS	KSU	$105.96 (6/29/2018)	113.70-101.31	1.36	11.54

*7 Year Price Score 91.41   *NYSE Composite Index=100   *12 Month Price Score 99.77

Interim Earnings (Per Share)

Qtr.	Mar	Jun	Sep	Dec
2015	0.91	1.01	1.20	1.28
2016	0.99	1.11	1.12	1.20
2017	1.38	1.27	1.23	5.28
2018	1.40	...	...	...

Interim Dividends (Per Share)

Amt	Decl	Ex	Rec	Pay
0.36Q	08/15/2017	09/08/2017	09/11/2017	10/04/2017
0.36Q	11/10/2017	12/28/2017	12/29/2017	01/17/2018
0.36Q	01/23/2018	03/09/2018	03/12/2018	04/04/2018
0.36Q	05/18/2018	06/08/2018	06/11/2018	07/05/2018

Indicated Div: $1.44

Valuation Analysis   **Institutional Holding**

Forecast EPS	$6.12	No of Institutions	
	(06/14/2018)	830	
Market Cap	$10.9 Billion	Shares	
Book Value	$4.6 Billion	119,714,760	
Price/Book	2.36	% Held	
Price/Sales	4.16	89.72	

Business Summary: Rail (MIC: 7.4.3 SIC: 4011 NAIC: 482111)

Kansas City Southern is a holding company that has railroad investments in the U.S., Mexico and Panama. Co. is engaged primarily in the freight rail transportation business operating through a single coordinated rail network. As of Dec 31 2017, Co.'s coordinated rail network comprised approximately 6,700 route miles extending from the midwest and southeast portions of the U.S. south into Mexico and connected with all other Class I railroads, providing shippers with an alternative to other railroad routes and giving direct access to Mexico and the southeast and southwest U.S. through alternate interchange hubs.

Recent Developments: For the quarter ended Mar 31 2018, net income decreased 1.4% to US$144.9 million from US$146.9 million in the year-earlier quarter. Revenues were US$638.6 million, up 4.8% from US$609.5 million the year before. Operating income was US$218.7 million versus US$210.7 million in the prior-year quarter, an increase of 3.8%. Direct operating expenses rose 7.8% to US$81.3 million from US$75.4 million in the comparable period the year before. Indirect operating expenses increased 4.7% to US$338.6 million from US$323.4 million in the equivalent prior-year period.

Prospects: Our evaluation of Kansas City Southern Industries Inc. as of Jan. 21, 2018 is the result of our systematic analysis on three basic characteristics: earnings strength, relative valuation, and recent stock price movement. The company has managed to produce a neutral trend in earnings per share over the past 5 quarters. Because the company lacks sufficient analyst estimate data, we place greater weight on the historical EPS trend as the measure of earnings strength. Based on operating earnings yield, the company is undervalued when compared to all of the companies in our coverage universe. Share price changes over the past year indicates that KSU will perform very well over the near term.

Financial Data

(US$ in Thousands)	3 Mos	12/31/2017	12/31/2016	12/31/2015	12/31/2014	12/31/2013	12/31/2012	12/31/2011
Earnings Per Share	9.18	9.16	4.43	4.40	4.55	3.18	3.43	3.00
Cash Flow Per Share	10.13	9.82	8.47	8.29	8.22	7.26	6.12	5.90
Tang Book Value Per Share	44.92	44.09	38.31	36.03	33.96	30.52	28.06	25.10
Dividends Per Share	1.410	1.380	1.320	1.320	1.120	0.860	0.780	...
Dividend Payout %	15.36	15.07	29.80	30.00	24.62	27.04	22.74	...
Income Statement								
Total Revenue	638,600	2,582,900	2,334,200	2,418,800	2,577,100	2,369,300	2,238,600	2,098,300
EBITDA	329,500	1,283,900	1,050,800	1,020,800	1,022,900	836,700	896,300	752,100
Depn & Amortn	83,300	320,900	305,000	284,600	258,100	223,300	198,800	186,200
Income Before Taxes	220,700	862,800	648,100	654,300	692,000	532,800	597,100	436,800
Income Taxes	76,800	(89,600)	182,800	187,300	208,800	198,300	237,000	123,100
Net Income	144,500	962,000	478,100	483,500	502,600	351,400	377,300	330,300
Average Shares	102,976	105,040	107,761	109,915	110,433	110,340	110,080	109,830
Balance Sheet								
Current Assets	565,900	680,100	648,000	537,000	818,300	942,400	522,300	642,500
Total Assets	9,128,100	9,198,700	8,817,500	8,341,000	8,091,000	7,435,400	6,395,900	6,173,000
Current Liabilities	823,800	971,700	744,400	757,600	898,800	730,600	424,800	437,400
Long-Term Obligations	2,230,200	2,235,500	2,271,500	2,045,000	1,841,000	1,856,900	1,547,600	1,602,800
Total Liabilities	4,513,600	4,649,800	4,727,600	4,426,700	4,335,500	4,064,800	3,299,300	3,408,500
Stockholders' Equity	4,614,500	4,548,900	4,089,900	3,914,300	3,755,500	3,370,600	3,096,600	2,764,500
Shares Outstanding	102,600	103,036	106,606	108,461	110,392	110,229	110,131	109,910
Statistical Record								
Return on Assets %	10.66	10.68	5.56	5.88	6.47	5.08	5.99	5.59
Return on Equity %	21.89	22.27	11.91	12.61	14.11	10.87	12.84	12.71
EBITDA Margin %	51.60	49.71	45.02	42.20	39.69	35.31	40.04	35.84
Net Margin %	22.63	37.24	20.48	19.99	19.50	14.83	16.85	15.74
Asset Turnover	0.29	0.29	0.27	0.29	0.33	0.34	0.36	0.36
Current Ratio	0.69	0.70	0.87	0.71	0.91	1.29	1.23	1.47
Debt to Equity	0.48	0.49	0.56	0.52	0.49	0.55	0.50	0.58
Price Range	113.70-85.76	113.44-80.82	99.47-64.35	122.03-70.01	125.88-91.12	125.20-83.48	83.82-62.54	69.17-46.00
P/E Ratio	12.39-9.34	12.38-8.82	22.45-14.53	27.73-15.91	27.67-20.03	39.37-26.25	24.44-18.23	23.06-15.33
Average Yield %	1.37	1.41	1.50	1.35	1.02	0.79	1.06	...

Address: 427 West 12th Street, Kansas City, MO 64105	**Web Site:** www.kcsouthern.com	**Auditors:** KPMG LLP
Telephone: 816-983-1303	**Officers:** Robert J. Druten - Chairman Patrick J. Ottensmeyer - President, Chief Executive Officer, Executive Vice President	**Investor Contact:** 816-983-1551
Fax: 816-556-0297		**Transfer Agents:** Computershare Trust Company, N.A., Providence, RI

KAR AUCTION SERVICES INC.

Exchange	Symbol	Price	52Wk Range	Yield	P/E
NYS	KAR	$54.80 (6/29/2018)	56.64-40.31	2.55	19.71

*7 Year Price Score 123.10 ***NYSE Composite Index=100** ***12 Month Price Score 106.47**

Interim Earnings (Per Share)

Qtr.	Mar	Jun	Sep	Dec
2015	0.38	0.41	0.37	0.35
2016	0.44	0.44	0.39	0.33
2017	0.50	0.41	0.46	1.25
2018	0.66	...	...	...

Interim Dividends (Per Share)

Amt	Decl	Ex	Rec	Pay
0.32Q	08/08/2017	09/19/2017	09/20/2017	10/03/2017
0.35Q	10/31/2017	12/19/2017	12/20/2017	01/05/2018
0.35Q	02/20/2018	03/21/2018	03/22/2018	04/04/2018
0.35Q	05/08/2018	06/20/2018	06/21/2018	07/05/2018

Indicated Div: $1.40

Valuation Analysis   **Institutional Holding**

Forecast EPS	$2.99 (06/14/2018)	No of Institutions N/A
Market Cap	$7.4 Billion	Shares
Book Value	$1.5 Billion	N/A
Price/Book	4.87	% Held
Price/Sales	2.09	N/A

TRADING VOLUME (thousand shares)

Business Summary: Retail - Automotive (MIC: 2.1.4 SIC: 5521 NAIC: 441120)

KAR Auction Services is a provider of used car auction services and salvage auction services in North America and the U.K. Co. operates three business segments: ADESA Inc. Auctions, which encompasses all physical and online wholesale auctions throughout North America (U.S., Canada and Mexico); Insurance Auto Auctions, Inc., which encompasses all salvage auctions throughout North America (U.S. and Canada); and Automotive Finance Corporation, which engaged in the business of providing short-term, inventory-secured financing to independent, used vehicle dealers. As of Dec 31 2017, Co. had a North American network of 75 whole car auction locations and 175 salvage vehicle auction sites.

Recent Developments: For the quarter ended Mar 31 2018, net income increased 30.1% to US$90.0 million from US$69.2 million in the year-earlier quarter. Revenues were US$950.5 million, up 9.7% from US$866.6 million the year before. Operating income was US$157.8 million versus US$143.5 million in the prior-year quarter, an increase of 10.0%. Direct operating expenses rose 6.7% to US$535.0 million from US$501.2 million in the comparable period the year before. Indirect operating expenses increased 16.1% to US$257.7 million from US$221.9 million in the equivalent prior-year period.

Prospects: Our evaluation of KAR Aucton Services Inc. as of Jan. 21, 2018 is the result of our systematic analysis on three basic characteristics: earnings strength, relative valuation, and recent stock price movement. The company has managed to produce a neutral trend in earnings per share over the past 5 quarters. However, while recent estimates for the company have been mixed, KAR has posted better than expected results. Based on corporate earnings yield, the company is undervalued when compared to all of the companies in our coverage universe. Share price changes over the past year indicates that KAR will perform poorly over the near term.

Financial Data
(US$ in Thousands)

	3 Mos	12/31/2017	12/31/2016	12/31/2015	12/31/2014	12/31/2013	12/31/2012	12/31/2011
Earnings Per Share	2.78	2.62	1.60	1.51	1.19	0.48	0.66	0.52
Cash Flow Per Share	4.45	4.32	2.61	3.39	3.08	3.15	2.12	2.25
Dividends Per Share	1.340	1.310	1.190	1.080	1.020	0.820	0.190	...
Dividend Payout %	48.20	50.00	74.38	71.52	85.71	170.83	28.79	...
Income Statement								
Total Revenue	950,500	3,458,000	3,150,100	2,639,600	2,364,500	2,173,300	1,963,400	1,886,300
EBITDA	160,600	664,000	583,700	506,700	419,000	318,200	343,400	304,800
Depn & Amortn	2,700	102,000	89,600	74,800	67,800	64,300	72,400	71,700
Income Before Taxes	116,400	398,000	355,300	340,500	265,000	149,200	151,600	90,000
Income Taxes	26,400	36,000	132,900	125,900	95,700	81,500	59,600	17,800
Net Income	90,000	362,000	222,400	214,600	169,300	67,700	92,000	72,200
Average Shares	135,800	138,000	139,100	142,300	141,800	140,800	139,000	137,800
Balance Sheet								
Current Assets	3,411,100	3,137,400	2,841,200	2,446,100	2,074,900	1,791,500	1,581,400	1,373,200
Total Assets	7,266,200	6,984,300	6,557,600	5,791,800	5,351,500	5,127,200	4,922,300	4,779,100
Current Liabilities	2,627,900	2,389,200	2,335,000	2,226,100	1,590,600	1,434,600	1,286,900	1,196,200
Long-Term Obligations	2,664,300	2,667,700	2,365,100	1,719,300	1,736,600	1,734,700	1,774,600	1,816,900
Total Liabilities	5,746,100	5,499,400	5,160,300	4,405,700	3,804,400	3,645,400	3,478,600	3,435,900
Stockholders' Equity	1,520,100	1,484,900	1,397,300	1,386,100	1,547,100	1,481,800	1,443,700	1,343,200
Shares Outstanding	134,956	134,315	136,639	137,795	141,316	139,027	136,657	136,271
Statistical Record								
Return on Assets %	5.53	5.35	3.59	3.85	3.23	1.35	1.89	1.55
Return on Equity %	25.95	25.12	15.94	14.63	11.18	4.63	6.58	5.58
EBITDA Margin %	16.90	19.20	18.53	19.20	17.72	14.64	17.49	16.16
Net Margin %	9.47	10.47	7.06	8.13	7.16	3.12	4.69	3.83
Asset Turnover	0.51	0.51	0.51	0.47	0.45	0.43	0.40	0.41
Current Ratio	1.30	1.31	1.22	1.10	1.30	1.25	1.23	1.15
Debt to Equity	1.75	1.80	1.69	1.24	1.12	1.17	1.23	1.35
Price Range	56.64-40.31	51.43-40.31	43.88-31.98	39.52-33.77	35.18-26.44	30.15-19.30	20.63-13.49	20.91-11.52
P/E Ratio	20.37-14.50	19.63-15.39	27.43-19.99	26.17-22.36	29.56-22.22	62.81-40.21	31.26-20.44	40.21-22.15
Average Yield %	2.84	2.90	2.99	2.91	3.33	3.34	1.11	...

Address: 13085 Hamilton Crossing Boulevard, Carmel, IN 46032 **Telephone:** 800-923-3725	**Web Site:** www.karauctionservices.com **Officers:** James P. Hallett - Chief Executive Officer Donald S. Gottwald - Chief Operating Officer	**Auditors:** KPMG LLP **Investor Contact:** 317-249-4390

KB HOME

Exchange	Symbol	Price	52Wk Range	Yield	P/E
NYS	KBH	$27.24 (6/29/2018)	38.58-20.71	0.37	24.54

*7 Year Price Score 132.08 *NYSE Composite Index=100 *12 Month Price Score 95.45

Interim Earnings (Per Share)

Qtr.	Feb	May	Aug	Nov
2014-15	0.08	0.10	0.23	0.43
2015-16	0.14	0.17	0.42	0.40
2016-17	0.15	0.33	0.51	0.85
2017-18	(0.82)	0.57	...	...

Interim Dividends (Per Share)

Amt	Decl	Ex	Rec	Pay
0.025Q	10/05/2017	11/01/2017	11/02/2017	11/16/2017
0.025Q	01/25/2018	02/07/2018	02/08/2018	02/22/2018
0.025Q	04/12/2018	05/02/2018	05/03/2018	05/17/2018
0.025Q	07/12/2018	08/01/2018	08/02/2018	08/16/2018

Indicated Div: $0.10

Valuation Analysis

Forecast EPS	$1.74 (06/14/2018)
Market Cap	$2.4 Billion
Book Value	$1.9 Billion
Price/Book	1.25
Price/Sales	0.53

Institutional Holding

No of Institutions	441
Shares	95,315,832
% Held	94.29

Business Summary: Builders (MIC: 2.2.5 SIC: 1531 NAIC: 236115)

KB Home is a builder of attached and detached single-family residential homes, townhomes and condominiums. Co. has five segments, comprised of four homebuilding segments and one financial services segment. Co. organizes its homebuilding operations into four segments: West Coast, Southwest, Central and Southeast. Co.'s financial services segment provides property and casualty insurance and, in certain instances, earthquake, flood and personal property insurance to its homebuyers in the same markets as its homebuilding segments, and provides title services in the majority of its markets located within its Central and Southeast homebuilding segments.

Recent Developments: For the year ended Nov 30 2017, net income increased 71.0% to US$180.6 million from US$105.6 million in the prior year. Revenues were US$4.37 billion, up 21.5% from US$3.59 billion the year before. Direct operating expenses rose 19.9% to US$3.65 billion from US$3.04 billion in the comparable period the year before. Indirect operating expenses increased 9.5% to US$426.4 million from US$389.4 million in the equivalent prior-year period.

Prospects: Our evaluation of KB HOME as of Jan. 21, 2018 is the result of our systematic analysis on three basic characteristics: earnings strength, relative valuation, and recent stock price movement. The company has suffered a very negative trend in earnings per share over the past 5 quarters. However, while recent estimates for the company have been mixed, KBH has posted better than expected results. Based on operating earnings yield, the company is undervalued when compared to all of the companies in our coverage universe. Share price changes over the past year indicates that KBH will perform very well over the near term.

Financial Data
(US$ in Thousands)

	6 Mos	3 Mos	11/30/2017	11/30/2016	11/30/2015	11/30/2014	11/30/2013	11/30/2012
Earnings Per Share	1.11	0.87	1.85	1.12	0.85	9.25	0.46	(0.76)
Cash Flow Per Share	6.38	5.15	5.98	2.20	1.97	(7.07)	(5.37)	0.45
Tang Book Value Per Share	21.83	21.17	20.08	18.23	16.51	15.60	5.69	4.29
Dividends Per Share	0.100	0.100	0.100	0.100	0.100	0.100	0.100	0.138
Dividend Payout %	9.01	11.49	5.41	8.93	11.76	1.08	21.74	...
Income Statement								
Total Revenue	1,973,046	871,623	4,368,529	3,594,646	3,032,030	2,400,949	2,097,130	1,560,115
EBITDA	124,584	47,020	295,037	163,887	149,353	126,229	103,094	(9,964)
Depn & Amortn	3,125	1,552	2,800	3,600	3,400	2,400	1,900	1,600
Income Before Taxes	123,740	46,471	287,170	154,916	124,555	93,522	39,296	(80,850)
Income Taxes	138,300	117,300	109,400	43,700	42,400	(823,400)	(1,600)	(20,100)
Net Income	(13,947)	(71,255)	180,595	105,615	84,643	918,391	39,963	(58,953)
Average Shares	101,159	87,155	98,316	96,278	102,857	99,314	91,559	77,106
Balance Sheet								
Current Assets	4,422,329	4,263,563	4,230,184	4,229,657	4,038,359	3,731,616	2,946,327	2,338,519
Total Assets	5,094,736	4,957,101	5,041,515	5,131,624	5,015,371	4,757,550	3,193,635	2,561,698
Current Liabilities	534,623	477,927	296,635	302,920	262,795	238,508	193,844	165,936
Long-Term Obligations	2,353,848	2,359,570	2,324,845	2,640,149	2,625,536	2,576,525	2,150,498	1,722,815
Total Liabilities	3,180,093	3,104,379	3,115,204	3,408,479	3,324,537	3,161,640	2,657,549	2,184,892
Stockholders' Equity	1,914,643	1,852,722	1,926,311	1,723,145	1,690,834	1,595,910	536,086	376,806
Shares Outstanding	87,688	87,506	95,924	94,504	102,411	102,289	94,246	87,837
Statistical Record								
Return on Assets %	2.40	1.92	3.55	2.08	1.73	23.10	1.39	N.M.
Return on Equity %	6.54	5.30	9.90	6.17	5.15	86.15	8.76	N.M.
EBITDA Margin %	6.31	5.39	6.75	4.56	4.93	5.26	4.92	N.M.
Net Margin %	N.M.	N.M.	4.13	2.94	2.79	38.25	1.91	N.M.
Asset Turnover	0.90	0.90	0.86	0.71	0.62	0.60	0.73	0.61
Current Ratio	8.27	8.92	14.26	13.96	15.37	15.65	15.20	14.09
Debt to Equity	1.23	1.27	1.21	1.53	1.55	1.61	4.01	4.57
Price Range	38.58-20.71	38.58-17.75	31.36-15.07	16.62-9.58	17.32-11.87	20.67-13.78	24.82-14.04	16.90-6.34
P/E Ratio	34.76-18.66	44.34-20.40	16.95-8.15	14.84-8.55	20.38-13.96	2.23-1.49	53.96-30.52	...
Average Yield %	0.37	0.40	0.47	0.71	0.68	0.58	0.54	1.31

Address: 10990 Wilshire Boulevard, Los Angeles, CA 90024	**Web Site:** www.kbhome.com	**Auditors:** Ernst & Young LLP
Telephone: 310-231-4000	**Officers:** Jeffrey T. Mezger - Chairman, President, Chief Executive Officer Matthew W. Mandino - Executive Vice President, Chief Operating Officer	**Investor Contact:** 310-231-4000
Fax: 310-231-4222		**Transfer Agents:** ComputerShare Investor Services, Providence, RI

KBR INC

Exchange	Symbol	Price	52Wk Range	Yield	P/E
NYS	KBR	$17.92 (6/29/2018)	21.59-14.67	1.79	4.75

*7 Year Price Score 63.34 *NYSE Composite Index=100 *12 Month Price Score 99.79

Interim Earnings (Per Share)

Qtr.	Mar	Jun	Sep	Dec
2015	0.30	0.43	0.38	0.29
2016	0.30	0.32	(0.44)	(0.61)
2017	0.26	0.54	0.32	1.94
2018	0.97	...	...	...

Interim Dividends (Per Share)

Amt	Decl	Ex	Rec	Pay
0.08Q	08/10/2017	09/14/2017	09/15/2017	10/13/2017
0.08Q	10/11/2017	12/14/2017	12/15/2017	01/15/2018
0.08Q	02/06/2018	03/14/2018	03/15/2018	04/13/2018
0.08Q	05/17/2018	06/14/2018	06/15/2018	07/13/2018

Indicated Div: $0.32

Valuation Analysis / Institutional Holding

Forecast EPS	$1.40	No of Institutions
	(06/14/2018)	396
Market Cap	$2.5 Billion	Shares
Book Value	$1.5 Billion	179,539,104
Price/Book	1.67	% Held
Price/Sales	0.61	85.86

Business Summary: Construction Services (MIC: 7.5.4 SIC: 1629 NAIC: 237990)

KBR is a provider of differentiated, professional services and technologies across the asset and program life-cycle within the government services and hydrocarbons industries. Co.'s segments include: Government Services, which provides life-cycle support solutions to defense, space, aviation and other programs and missions for government agencies; Technology & Consulting, which provides licensed technologies and consulting services to the hydrocarbons value chain, from wellhead to crude refining and through refining and petrochemicals to specialty chemicals production; and Engineering & Construction, which provides project and program delivery capability globally.

Recent Developments: For the quarter ended Mar 31 2018, net income increased 265.8% to US$139.0 million from US$38.0 million in the year-earlier quarter. Revenues were US$1.04 billion, down 6.1% from US$1.11 billion the year before. Operating income was US$181.0 million versus US$63.0 million in the prior-year quarter, an increase of 187.3%. Direct operating expenses declined 6.5% to US$957.0 million from US$1.02 billion in the comparable period the year before. Indirect operating income amounted to US$100.0 million compared with an expense of US$19.0 million in the equivalent prior-year period.

Prospects: Our evaluation of KBR Inc. as of Jan. 21, 2018 is the result of our systematic analysis on three basic characteristics: earnings strength, relative valuation, and recent stock price movement. The company has enjoyed a very positive trend in earnings per share over the past 5 quarters and while recent estimates for the company have been mixed, KBR has posted better than expected results. Based on operating earnings yield, the company is undervalued when compared to all of the companies in our coverage universe. Share price changes over the past year indicates that KBR will perform poorly over the near term.

Financial Data
(US$ in Thousands)

	3 Mos	12/31/2017	12/31/2016	12/31/2015	12/31/2014	12/31/2013	12/31/2012	12/31/2011
Earnings Per Share	3.77	3.06	(0.43)	1.40	(8.66)	1.54	0.97	3.16
Cash Flow Per Share	1.27	1.37	0.43	0.33	1.16	1.96	0.96	4.33
Tang Book Value Per Share	0.11	0.16	N.M.	4.97	3.98	11.88	11.27	9.66
Dividends Per Share	0.320	0.320	0.320	0.320	0.320	0.320	0.200	0.200
Dividend Payout %	8.49	10.46	...	22.86	...	20.78	20.62	6.33
Income Statement								
Total Revenue	1,038,000	4,171,000	4,268,000	5,096,000	6,366,000	7,283,000	7,921,000	9,261,000
EBITDA	169,000	225,000	(27,000)	198,000	(879,000)	385,000	360,000	661,000
Depn & Amortn	13,000	27,000	31,000	35,000	61,000	54,000	65,000	71,000
Income Before Taxes	150,000	177,000	(58,000)	163,000	(940,000)	326,000	288,000	572,000
Income Taxes	34,000	(193,000)	84,000	86,000	421,000	136,000	86,000	32,000
Net Income	138,000	434,000	(61,000)	203,000	(1,262,000)	229,000	144,000	480,000
Average Shares	140,000	141,000	142,000	144,000	146,000	149,000	149,000	151,000
Balance Sheet								
Current Assets	1,633,000	1,425,000	2,047,000	1,844,000	2,544,000	3,010,000	3,668,000	3,442,000
Total Assets	4,364,000	3,674,000	4,144,000	3,412,000	4,199,000	5,516,000	5,767,000	5,673,000
Current Liabilities	1,320,000	1,071,000	1,559,000	1,412,000	2,024,000	1,828,000	2,277,000	2,284,000
Long-Term Obligations	569,000	498,000	684,000	51,000	63,000	...	84,000	88,000
Total Liabilities	2,852,000	2,445,000	3,387,000	2,347,000	3,257,000	2,899,000	3,225,000	3,178,000
Stockholders' Equity	1,512,000	1,229,000	757,000	1,065,000	942,000	2,617,000	2,542,000	2,495,000
Shares Outstanding	140,624	140,166	142,803	142,058	144,837	148,195	147,584	148,143
Statistical Record								
Return on Assets %	12.85	11.10	N.M.	5.33	N.M.	4.06	2.51	8.66
Return on Equity %	46.22	43.71	N.M.	20.23	N.M.	8.88	5.70	20.25
EBITDA Margin %	16.28	5.39	N.M.	3.89	N.M.	5.29	4.54	7.14
Net Margin %	13.29	10.41	N.M.	3.98	N.M.	3.14	1.82	5.18
Asset Turnover	0.99	1.07	1.13	1.34	1.31	1.29	1.38	1.67
Current Ratio	1.24	1.33	1.31	1.31	1.26	1.65	1.61	1.51
Debt to Equity	0.38	0.41	0.90	0.05	0.07	...	0.03	0.04
Price Range	21.59-13.63	21.09-13.63	17.60-11.76	20.60-14.26	33.62-15.23	36.29-28.01	37.93-22.91	39.12-22.20
P/E Ratio	5.73-3.62	6.89-4.45	...	14.71-10.19	...	23.56-18.19	39.10-23.62	12.38-7.03
Average Yield %	1.88	1.94	2.16	1.82	1.35	1.00	0.68	0.62

Address: 601 Jefferson Street, Suite 3400, Houston, TX 77002	Web Site: www.kbr.com	Auditors: KPMG LLP
	Officers: Stuart J.B. Bradie - President, Chief Executive Officer Eileen G. Akerson - Executive Vice President, General Counsel, Secretary, Division Officer	Investor Contact: 713-753-5082
Telephone: 713-753-3011		Transfer Agents: American Stock Transfer & Trust Company, Brooklyn, NY

KELLOGG CO

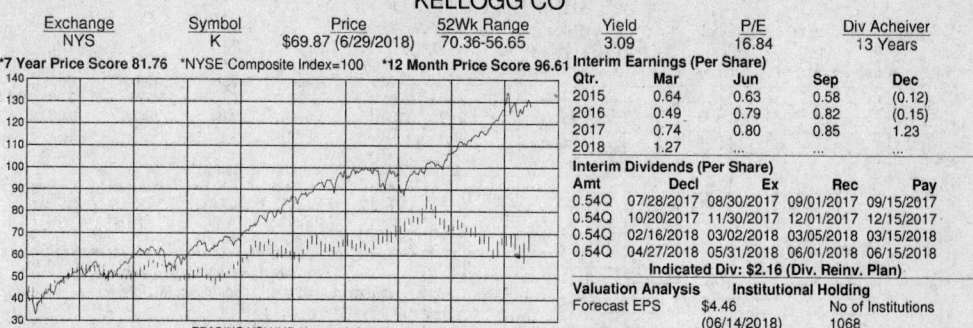

Exchange	Symbol	Price	52Wk Range	Yield	P/E	Div Acheiver
NYS	K	$69.87 (6/29/2018)	70.36-56.65	3.09	16.84	13 Years

*7 Year Price Score 81.76   *NYSE Composite Index=100   *12 Month Price Score 96.61

Interim Earnings (Per Share)

Qtr.	Mar	Jun	Sep	Dec
2015	0.64	0.63	0.58	(0.12)
2016	0.49	0.79	0.82	(0.15)
2017	0.74	0.80	0.85	1.23
2018	1.27	...	...	...

Interim Dividends (Per Share)

Amt	Decl	Ex	Rec	Pay
0.54Q	07/28/2017	08/30/2017	09/01/2017	09/15/2017
0.54Q	10/20/2017	11/30/2017	12/01/2017	12/15/2017
0.54Q	02/16/2018	03/02/2018	03/05/2018	03/15/2018
0.54Q	04/27/2018	05/31/2018	06/01/2018	06/15/2018

Indicated Div: $2.16 (Div. Reinv. Plan)

Valuation Analysis

		Institutional Holding	
Forecast EPS	$4.46	No of Institutions	
	(06/14/2018)	1068	
Market Cap	$24.2 Billion	Shares	
Book Value	$2.5 Billion	460,933,440	
Price/Book	9.55	% Held	
Price/Sales	1.86	69.81	

Business Summary: Food (MIC: 1.2.1 SIC: 2043 NAIC: 311230)

Kellogg manufactures and markets cereal and convenience foods. Co.'s products are cereals and foods such as cookies, crackers, savory snacks, toaster pastries, cereal bars, fruit-flavored snacks, frozen waffles and veggie foods. Co.'s cereal products are marketed under the Kellogg's name and sold to the grocery trade. Co. also markets cookies, crackers, crisps, and other convenience foods, under brands such as Kellogg's, Keebler, Cheez-It, Murray, Austin and Famous Amos. Co. operates the following segments: U.S. Morning Foods; U.S. Snacks; U.S. Specialty; North America Other; Europe; Latin America; and Asia Pacific.

Recent Developments: For the quarter ended Mar 31 2018, net income increased 66.9% to US$444.0 million from US$266.0 million in the year-earlier quarter. Revenues were US$3.40 billion, up 4.7% from US$3.25 billion the year before. Operating income was US$510.0 million versus US$280.0 million in the prior-year quarter, an increase of 82.1%. Direct operating expenses rose 2.9% to US$2.15 billion from US$2.09 billion in the comparable period the year before. Indirect operating expenses decreased 15.7% to US$742.0 million from US$880.0 million in the equivalent prior-year period.

Prospects: Our evaluation of Kellogg Co as of Jan. 21, 2018 is the result of our systematic analysis on three basic characteristics: earnings strength, relative valuation, and recent stock price movement. The company has managed to produce a neutral trend in earnings per share over the past 5 quarters and while recent estimates for the company have been mixed, K has posted better than expected results. Based on operating earnings yield, the company is undervalued when compared to all of the companies in our coverage universe. Share price changes over the past year indicates that K will perform poorly over the near term.

Financial Data

(US$ in Thousands)	3 Mos	12/30/2017	12/31/2016	01/02/2016	01/03/2015	12/28/2013	12/29/2012	12/31/2011
Earnings Per Share	4.15	3.62	1.96	1.72	1.75	4.94	2.67	3.38
Cash Flow Per Share	4.81	4.74	4.66	4.79	4.93	4.99	4.92	4.42
Dividends Per Share	2.140	2.120	2.040	1.980	1.900	1.800	1.740	1.670
Dividend Payout %	51.57	58.56	104.08	115.12	108.57	36.44	65.17	49.41
Income Statement								
Total Revenue	3,401,000	12,923,000	13,014,000	13,525,000	14,580,000	14,792,000	14,197,000	13,198,000
EBITDA	702,000	2,411,000	1,850,000	1,534,000	1,537,000	3,373,000	2,034,000	2,334,000
Depn & Amortn	122,000	481,000	517,000	534,000	503,000	532,000	448,000	369,000
Income Before Taxes	511,000	1,674,000	927,000	773,000	825,000	2,606,000	1,325,000	1,732,000
Income Taxes	67,000	412,000	233,000	159,000	186,000	792,000	363,000	503,000
Net Income	444,000	1,269,000	694,000	614,000	632,000	1,807,000	961,000	1,231,000
Average Shares	348,000	350,000	354,000	356,000	360,000	365,000	360,000	364,000
Balance Sheet								
Current Assets	3,320,000	3,036,000	2,940,000	3,236,000	3,340,000	3,267,000	3,380,000	3,027,000
Total Assets	16,702,000	16,350,000	15,111,000	15,265,000	15,153,000	15,474,000	15,184,000	11,901,000
Current Liabilities	4,515,000	4,479,000	4,474,000	5,739,000	4,364,000	3,835,000	4,523,000	3,313,000
Long-Term Obligations	7,881,000	7,836,000	6,698,000	5,289,000	5,935,000	6,330,000	6,082,000	5,037,000
Total Liabilities	14,164,000	14,138,000	13,201,000	13,137,000	12,364,000	11,929,000	12,765,000	10,141,000
Stockholders' Equity	2,538,000	2,212,000	1,910,000	2,128,000	2,789,000	3,545,000	2,419,000	1,760,000
Shares Outstanding	347,000	345,602	351,069	350,024	356,002	362,801	361,266	357,301
Statistical Record								
Return on Assets %	9.03	8.09	4.58	4.05	4.06	11.82	7.12	10.40
Return on Equity %	63.86	61.74	34.47	25.04	19.63	60.76	46.12	63.01
EBITDA Margin %	20.64	18.66	14.22	11.34	10.54	22.80	14.33	17.68
Net Margin %	13.05	9.82	5.33	4.54	4.33	12.22	6.77	9.33
Asset Turnover	0.81	0.82	0.86	0.89	0.94	0.97	1.05	1.11
Current Ratio	0.74	0.68	0.66	0.56	0.77	0.85	0.75	0.91
Debt to Equity	3.11	3.54	3.51	2.49	2.13	1.79	2.51	2.86
Price Range	73.49-58.87	76.44-58.87	86.98-69.96	73.51-61.31	69.39-56.90	67.46-55.85	56.86-46.51	57.56-48.25
P/E Ratio	17.71-14.19	21.12-16.26	44.38-35.69	42.74-35.65	39.65-32.51	13.66-11.31	21.30-17.42	17.03-14.28
Average Yield %	3.17	3.07	2.67	2.99	2.98	2.89	3.38	3.13

Address: One Kellogg Square, P.O. Box 3599, Battle Creek, MI 49016-3599 Telephone: 269-961-2000	Web Site: www.kelloggcompany.com Officers: Gary H. Pilnick - Vice-Chairman, Corporate Development Officer, Chief Legal Officer, Senior Vice President, General Counsel, Secretary Steven A. (Steve) Cahillane - President, Chief Executive Officer	Auditors: PricewaterhouseCoopers LLP Investor Contact: 269-961-2800 Transfer Agents: Wells Fargo Bank, N.A., St. Paul, MN

KEMPER CORP (DE)

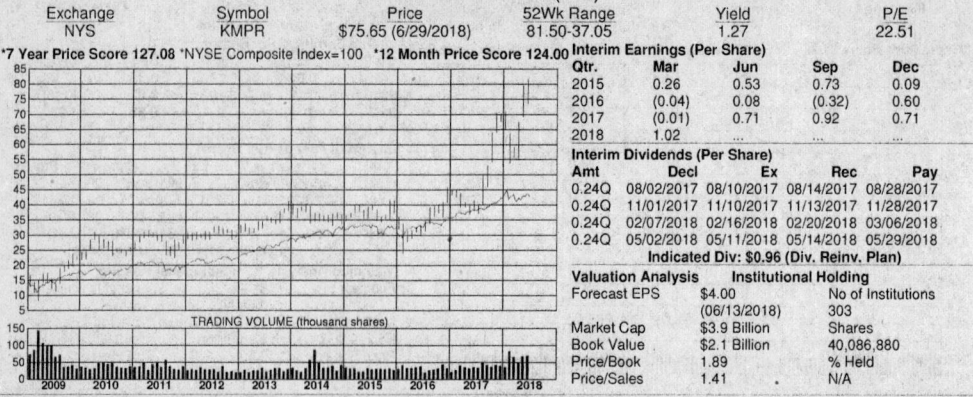

Exchange	Symbol	Price	52Wk Range	Yield	P/E
NYS	KMPR	$75.65 (6/29/2018)	81.50-37.05	1.27	22.51

*7 Year Price Score 127.08 *NYSE Composite Index=100 *12 Month Price Score 124.00

Interim Earnings (Per Share)

Qtr.	Mar	Jun	Sep	Dec
2015	0.26	0.53	0.73	0.09
2016	(0.04)	0.08	(0.32)	0.60
2017	(0.01)	0.71	0.92	0.71
2018	1.02	...	...	...

Interim Dividends (Per Share)

Amt	Decl	Ex	Rec	Pay
0.24Q	08/02/2017	08/10/2017	08/14/2017	08/28/2017
0.24Q	11/01/2017	11/10/2017	11/13/2017	11/28/2017
0.24Q	02/07/2018	02/16/2018	02/20/2018	03/06/2018
0.24Q	05/02/2018	05/11/2018	05/14/2018	05/29/2018

Indicated Div: $0.96 (Div. Reinv. Plan)

Valuation Analysis — **Institutional Holding**

Forecast EPS	$4.00 (06/13/2018)	No of Institutions	303
Market Cap	$3.9 Billion	Shares	40,086,880
Book Value	$2.1 Billion	% Held	N/A
Price/Book	1.89		
Price/Sales	1.41		

Business Summary: General Insurance (MIC: 5.2.1 SIC: 6311 NAIC: 524113)

Kemper is an insurance holding company, with subsidiaries that provide automobile, homeowners, life, health, and other insurance products to individuals and businesses. Co. conducts its operations through two operating segments: Property and Casualty Insurance and Life and Health Insurance. The Property and Casualty Insurance segment's principal products are personal automobile insurance, both preferred and nonstandard, homeowners insurance, other personal insurance and commercial automobile insurance. The Life and Health Insurance segment's principal products are individual life, accident, health and property insurance. Co. conducts its operations solely in the U.S.

Recent Developments: For the quarter ended Mar 31 2018, income from continuing operations was US$53.6 million compared with a loss of US$400,000 in the year-earlier quarter. Net income amounted to US$53.8 million versus a net loss of US$300,000 in the year-earlier quarter. Revenues were US$693.0 million, up 6.4% from US$651.4 million the year before. Net premiums earned were US$609.8 million versus US$563.4 million in the prior-year quarter, an increase of 8.2%. Net investment income fell 2.9% to US$79.2 million from US$81.6 million a year ago.

Prospects: Our evaluation of Kemper Corp. as of Jan. 21, 2018 is the result of our systematic analysis on three basic characteristics: earnings strength, relative valuation, and recent stock price movement. The company has managed to produce a neutral trend in earnings per share over the past 5 quarters. However, while recent estimates for the company have been mixed, KMPR has posted better than expected results. Based on operating earnings yield, the company is overvalued when compared to all of the companies in our coverage universe. Share price changes over the past year indicates that KMPR will perform very well over the near term.

Financial Data
(US$ in Thousands)

	3 Mos	12/31/2017	12/31/2016	12/31/2015	12/31/2014	12/31/2013	12/31/2012	12/31/2011
Earnings Per Share	3.36	2.33	0.33	1.65	2.12	3.80	1.74	1.38
Cash Flow Per Share	5.17	4.69	4.69	4.17	2.49	2.15	1.11	(0.41)
Tang Book Value Per Share	33.78	34.83	32.22	32.52	33.94	31.26	31.65	31.61
Dividends Per Share	0.960	0.960	0.960	0.960	0.960	0.960	0.960	0.960
Dividend Payout %	28.57	41.20	290.91	58.18	45.28	25.26	55.17	69.57
Income Statement								
Premium Income	609,800	2,350,000	2,220,000	2,009,600	1,862,200	2,025,800	2,107,100	2,173,600
Total Revenue	693,000	2,723,400	2,521,900	2,340,800	2,196,600	2,426,500	2,462,300	2,495,000
Income Before Taxes	67,000	161,100	3,500	100,300	160,200	314,400	122,400	82,600
Income Taxes	13,400	41,200	(9,200)	20,100	47,600	99,900	30,600	11,700
Net Income	53,800	120,900	16,800	85,700	114,500	217,700	103,400	83,700
Average Shares	51,868	51,577	51,214	51,683	53,867	56,983	58,999	60,366
Balance Sheet								
Total Assets	8,371,000	8,376,200	8,210,500	8,036,100	7,833,400	7,656,400	8,009,100	8,085,900
Total Liabilities	6,307,200	6,260,600	6,235,300	6,043,700	5,742,700	5,604,900	5,847,400	5,869,800
Stockholders' Equity	2,063,800	2,115,600	1,975,200	1,992,400	2,090,700	2,051,500	2,161,700	2,216,100
Shares Outstanding	51,533	51,462	51,270	51,326	52,418	55,653	58,454	60,248
Statistical Record								
Return on Assets %	2.10	1.46	0.21	1.08	1.48	2.78	1.28	1.02
Return on Equity %	8.65	5.91	0.84	4.20	5.53	10.33	4.71	3.87
Net Margin %	7.76	4.44	0.67	3.66	5.21	8.97	4.20	3.35
Price Range	70.95-36.70	70.45-36.70	45.65-23.80	41.44-34.25	40.88-32.97	41.13-29.50	32.93-27.98	31.42-22.29
P/E Ratio	21.12-10.92	30.24-15.75	138.33-72.12	25.12-20.76	19.28-15.55	10.82-7.76	18.93-16.08	22.77-16.15
Average Yield %	1.83	2.00	2.79	2.56	2.62	2.79	3.18	3.46

Address: One East Wacker Drive, Chicago, IL 60601 **Telephone:** 312-661-4600	**Web Site:** www.kemper.com **Officers:** Robert Joseph Joyce - Chairman Joseph P. Lacher - President, Chief Executive Officer	**Auditors:** DELOITTE & TOUCHE LLP **Investor Contact:** 312-661-4930 **Transfer Agents:** Computershare Trust Company, N.A., Providence, RI

KENNAMETAL INC.

Exchange	Symbol	Price	52Wk Range	Yield	P/E
NYS	KMT	$35.90 (6/29/2018)	51.92-33.40	2.23	18.89

*7 Year Price Score 89.60 ***NYSE Composite Index=100** ***12 Month Price Score 90.06**

TRADING VOLUME (thousand shares)

Interim Earnings (Per Share)

Qtr.	Sep	Dec	Mar	Jun
2014-15	0.49	(4.89)	(0.58)	0.27
2015-16	(0.08)	(2.12)	0.20	(0.83)
2016-17	(0.27)	0.09	0.48	0.31
2017-18	0.48	0.50	0.61	...

Interim Dividends (Per Share)

Amt	Decl	Ex	Rec	Pay
0.20Q	08/02/2017	08/16/2017	08/18/2017	08/31/2017
0.20Q	11/01/2017	11/13/2017	11/14/2017	11/29/2017
0.20Q	01/30/2018	02/12/2018	02/13/2018	02/28/2018
0.20Q	05/02/2018	05/14/2018	05/15/2018	05/30/2018

Indicated Div: $0.80 (Div. Reinv. Plan)

Valuation Analysis

		Institutional Holding	
Forecast EPS	$2.60	No of Institutions	
	(06/13/2018)	438	
Market Cap	$2.9 Billion	Shares	
Book Value	$1.2 Billion	101,757,304	
Price/Book	2.47	% Held	
Price/Sales	1.28	91.85	

Business Summary: Industrial Machinery & Equipment (MIC: 7.2.1 SIC: 3541 NAIC: 333512)

Kennametal engages in the development and application of tungsten carbides, ceramics, materials and solutions used in metal cutting and mission-critical wear applications. Co.'s product offering includes a selection of standard and customized technologies for metalworking applications, such as turning, milling, hole making, tooling systems and services. End users of Co.'s metalworking products include manufacturers engaged in a range of industries including: the manufacturers of transportation vehicles and components, machine tools and light and heavy machinery; airframe and aerospace components; and energy-related components for the oil and gas industry, as well as power generation.

Recent Developments: For the quarter ended Mar 31 2018, net income increased 33.9% to US$53.1 million from US$39.7 million in the year-earlier quarter. Revenues were US$607.9 million, up 15.0% from US$528.6 million the year before. Operating income was US$85.4 million versus US$57.9 million in the prior-year quarter, an increase of 47.4%. Direct operating expenses rose 13.5% to US$388.5 million from US$342.4 million in the comparable period the year before. Indirect operating expenses increased 4.5% to US$134.1 million from US$128.4 million in the equivalent prior-year period.

Prospects: Our evaluation of Kennametal Inc. as of Jan. 21, 2018 is the result of our systematic analysis on three basic characteristics: earnings strength, relative valuation, and recent stock price movement. The company has produced a positive trend in earnings per share over the past 5 quarters and while recent estimates for the company have been mixed, KMT has posted better than expected results. Based on operating earnings yield, the company is undervalued when compared to all of the companies in our coverage universe. Share price changes over the past year indicates that KMT will perform well over the near term.

Financial Data
(US$ in Thousands)

	9 Mos	6 Mos	3 Mos	06/30/2017	06/30/2016	06/30/2015	06/30/2014	06/30/2013
Earnings Per Share	1.90	1.77	1.36	0.61	(2.83)	(4.71)	1.99	2.52
Cash Flow Per Share	3.58	2.61	1.86	2.39	2.74	4.43	3.46	3.58
Tang Book Value Per Share	8.53	7.79	7.03	6.51	5.75	8.09	7.76	10.76
Dividends Per Share	0.800	0.800	0.800	0.800	0.800	0.720	0.720	0.640
Dividend Payout %	42.11	45.20	58.82	131.15	...	...	36.18	25.40
Income Statement								
Total Revenue	1,721,734	1,113,799	542,454	2,058,368	2,098,436	2,647,195	2,837,190	2,589,373
EBITDA	288,981	176,648	82,827	218,373	(53,353)	(224,485)	391,482	407,185
Depn & Amortn	81,022	53,399	26,438	107,656	117,466	131,664	130,222	113,104
Income Before Taxes	186,111	108,870	49,240	81,875	(198,571)	(387,615)	228,809	266,609
Income Taxes	51,204	27,074	9,602	29,895	25,313	(16,654)	66,611	59,693
Net Income	131,651	80,785	39,183	49,138	(225,968)	(373,896)	158,366	203,265
Average Shares	83,109	82,778	82,123	81,169	79,835	79,342	79,667	80,612
Balance Sheet								
Current Assets	1,240,587	1,128,382	1,075,915	1,113,901	1,075,341	1,258,546	1,525,196	1,499,473
Total Assets	2,617,862	2,475,861	2,399,700	2,415,496	2,368,793	2,849,529	3,868,086	3,301,039
Current Liabilities	477,790	407,621	396,967	461,478	427,275	482,744	562,756	467,593
Long-Term Obligations	696,087	695,722	695,357	694,991	699,558	735,885	981,666	703,626
Total Liabilities	1,430,537	1,349,456	1,337,720	1,398,202	1,404,470	1,503,722	1,938,830	1,519,213
Stockholders' Equity	1,187,325	1,126,405	1,061,980	1,017,294	964,323	1,345,807	1,929,256	1,781,826
Shares Outstanding	81,626	81,573	80,967	80,665	79,694	79,375	78,672	77,842
Statistical Record								
Return on Assets %	6.31	6.10	4.67	2.05	N.M.	N.M.	4.42	6.42
Return on Equity %	14.65	14.22	11.00	4.96	N.M.	N.M.	8.53	11.87
EBITDA Margin %	16.78	15.86	15.27	10.61	N.M.	N.M.	13.80	15.73
Net Margin %	7.65	7.25	7.22	2.39	N.M.	N.M.	5.58	7.85
Asset Turnover	0.92	0.93	0.90	0.86	0.80	0.79	0.79	0.82
Current Ratio	2.60	2.77	2.71	2.41	2.52	2.61	2.71	3.21
Debt to Equity	0.59	0.62	0.65	0.68	0.73	0.55	0.51	0.39
Price Range	51.92-33.40	48.97-31.73	42.40-26.96	42.40-20.67	34.12-15.91	46.35-30.99	52.07-38.16	43.34-32.19
P/E Ratio	27.33-17.58	27.67-17.93	31.18-19.82	69.51-33.89	...	...	26.17-19.18	17.20-12.77
Average Yield %	1.93	2.03	2.22	2.40	3.23	1.89	1.58	1.65

Address: 600 Grant Street, Suite 5100, Pittsburgh, PA 15219-2706 **Telephone:** 412-248-8000	**Web Site:** www.kennametal.com **Officers:** Lawrence W. Stranghoener - Chairman (frmr), Chairman Christopher (Chris) Rossi - President, Chief Executive Officer	**Auditors:** PricewaterhouseCoopers LLP **Investor Contact:** 724-539-6559 **Transfer Agents:** Computershare, Jersey City, NJ

KEYCORP

Exchange	Symbol	Price	52Wk Range	Yield	P/E
NYS ●	KEY	$19.54 (6/29/2018)	22.15-16.47	3.48	15.89

'7 Year Price Score 119.61 **'NYSE Composite Index=100** **'12 Month Price Score 101.79**

Interim Earnings (Per Share)

Qtr.	Mar	Jun	Sep	Dec
2015	0.26	0.27	0.25	0.26
2016	0.22	0.23	0.17	0.19
2017	0.27	0.36	0.32	0.17
2018	0.38	...	...	...

Interim Dividends (Per Share)

Amt	Decl	Ex	Rec	Pay
0.105Q	11/16/2017	11/27/2017	11/28/2017	12/15/2017
0.105Q	01/11/2018	02/26/2018	02/27/2018	03/15/2018
0.12Q	05/09/2018	05/25/2018	05/29/2018	06/15/2018
0.17Q	07/11/2018	08/27/2018	08/28/2018	09/14/2018

Indicated Div: $0.68 (Div. Reinv. Plan)

Valuation Analysis / Institutional Holding

Forecast EPS	$1.70 (06/14/2018)	No of Institutions	1050
Market Cap	$20.8 Billion	Shares	1,022,841,664
Book Value	$14.9 Billion	% Held	70.65
Price/Book	1.39		
Price/Sales	2.98		

TRADING VOLUME (thousand shares)

Business Summary: Banking (MIC: 5.1.1 SIC: 6021 NAIC: 522110)

KeyCorp is a bank holding company. Through its subsidiaries, Co. provides a range of retail and commercial banking, commercial leasing, investment management, consumer finance, commercial mortgage servicing and other servicing, and investment banking products and services to individual, corporate and institutional clients through two main segments: Key Community Bank and Key Corporate Bank. Co.'s bank and trust company subsidiary also provide personal and institutional trust custody services, securities lending, personal financial and planning services, and access to mutual funds, among others. At Dec 31 2017, Co. had total assets of $137.70 billion and total deposits of $105.24 billion.

Recent Developments: For the quarter ended Mar 31 2018, income from continuing operations increased 28.0% to US$416.0 million from US$325.0 million in the year-earlier quarter. Net income increased 28.6% to US$418.0 million from US$325.0 million in the year-earlier quarter. Net interest income increased 2.8% to US$944.0 million from US$918.0 million in the year-earlier quarter. Provision for loan losses was US$61.0 million versus US$63.0 million in the prior-year quarter, a decrease of 3.2%. Non-interest income rose 4.2% to US$601.0 million from US$577.0 million, while non-interest expense was unchanged at US$1.01 billion.

Prospects: Our evaluation of KeyCorp as of Jan. 21, 2018 is the result of our systematic analysis on three basic characteristics: earnings strength, relative valuation, and recent stock price movement. The company has generated a negative trend in earnings per share over the past 5 quarters and while recent estimates for the company have been raised by analysts, KEY has posted better than expected results. Based on operating earnings yield, the company is undervalued when compared to all of the companies in our coverage universe. Share price changes over the past year indicates that KEY will perform poorly over the near term.

Financial Data

(US$ in Thousands)

	3 Mos	12/31/2017	12/31/2016	12/31/2015	12/31/2014	12/31/2013	12/31/2012	12/31/2011
Earnings Per Share	1.23	1.13	0.80	1.05	0.99	0.97	0.89	0.87
Cash Flow Per Share	1.90	1.69	1.82	1.35	1.51	1.74	1.44	2.03
Tang Book Value Per Share	10.32	10.33	9.96	11.16	10.57	10.00	9.54	9.11
Dividends Per Share	0.400	0.380	0.330	0.290	0.250	0.215	0.180	0.100
Dividend Payout %	32.52	33.63	41.25	27.62	25.25	22.16	20.22	11.49
Income Statement								
Interest Income	1,137,000	4,390,000	3,319,000	2,622,000	2,554,000	2,620,000	2,705,000	2,889,000
Interest Expense	193,000	613,000	400,000	274,000	261,000	295,000	441,000	622,000
Net Interest Income	944,000	3,777,000	2,919,000	2,348,000	2,293,000	2,325,000	2,264,000	2,267,000
Provision for Losses	61,000	229,000	266,000	166,000	59,000	130,000	229,000	(60,000)
Non-Interest Income	601,000	2,478,000	2,071,000	1,880,000	1,797,000	1,766,000	1,967,000	1,808,000
Non-Interest Expense	1,006,000	4,098,000	3,756,000	2,840,000	2,759,000	2,820,000	2,907,000	2,790,000
Income Before Taxes	478,000	1,928,000	968,000	1,222,000	1,272,000	1,141,000	1,095,000	1,345,000
Income Taxes	62,000	637,000	179,000	303,000	326,000	271,000	239,000	369,000
Net Income	418,000	1,296,000	791,000	916,000	900,000	910,000	858,000	920,000
Average Shares	1,071,786	1,088,593	938,536	844,489	878,199	912,571	943,259	935,801
Balance Sheet								
Net Loans & Leases	88,875,000	86,635,000	86,284,000	59,719,000	57,321,000	54,220,000	52,533,000	49,299,000
Total Assets	137,049,000	137,698,000	136,453,000	95,133,000	93,821,000	92,934,000	89,236,000	88,785,000
Total Deposits	104,751,000	105,235,000	104,087,000	71,046,000	71,998,000	69,262,000	65,993,000	61,956,000
Total Liabilities	122,105,000	122,675,000	121,213,000	84,387,000	83,291,000	82,631,000	78,965,000	78,880,000
Stockholders' Equity	14,944,000	15,023,000	15,240,000	10,746,000	10,530,000	10,303,000	10,271,000	9,905,000
Shares Outstanding	1,064,938	1,069,084	1,079,313	835,751	859,403	890,724	925,768	953,007
Statistical Record								
Return on Assets %	1.02	0.95	0.68	0.97	0.96	1.00	0.96	1.02
Return on Equity %	9.29	8.56	6.07	8.61	8.64	8.85	8.48	8.75
Net Interest Margin %	83.03	86.04	87.95	89.55	89.78	88.74	83.70	78.47
Efficiency Ratio %	57.88	59.67	69.68	63.08	63.41	64.30	62.22	59.40
Loans to Deposits	0.85	0.82	0.83	0.84	0.80	0.78	0.80	0.80
Price Range	22.15-16.47	20.44-16.47	18.54-10.00	15.65-12.16	14.51-12.14	13.46-8.42	9.04-6.89	9.71-5.71
P/E Ratio	18.01-13.39	18.09-14.58	23.17-12.50	14.90-11.58	14.66-12.26	13.88-8.68	10.16-7.74	11.16-6.56
Average Yield %	2.11	2.07	2.60	2.08	1.85	1.94	2.22	1.27

Address: 127 Public Square, Cleveland, OH 44114-1306	**Web Site:** www.key.com	**Auditors:** Ernst & Young LLP
Telephone: 216-689-3000	**Officers:** Beth E. Mooney - Chairman, Vice-Chairman, President, Chief Executive Officer, Chief Operating Officer Christopher M. Gorman - Co-Vice Chairman, Division Officer	**Investor Contact:** 216-689-3000 **Transfer Agents:** Computershare Investor Services LLC, Providence, RI

KEYSIGHT TECHNOLOGIES INC

Exchange	Symbol	Price	52Wk Range	Yield	P/E
NYS	KEYS	$59.03 (6/29/2018)	61.92-38.69	N/A	113.52

*7 Year Price Score N/A   *NYSE Composite Index=100   *12 Month Price Score 121.63

Interim Earnings (Per Share)

Qtr.	Jan	Apr	Jul	Oct
2014-15	0.41	0.56	0.41	1.62
2015-16	0.37	0.51	0.53	0.54
2016-17	0.63	0.27	(0.10)	(0.22)
2017-18	0.50	0.34	...	...

Interim Dividends (Per Share)

No Dividends Paid

Valuation Analysis   **Institutional Holding**

Forecast EPS	$2.99	No of Institutions
	(06/14/2018)	478
Market Cap	$11.0 Billion	Shares
Book Value	$2.5 Billion	182,720,912
Price/Book	4.37	% Held
Price/Sales	3.12	N/A

Business Summary: Industrial Machinery & Equipment (MIC: 7.2.1 SIC: 3823 NAIC: 334513)

Keysight Technologies is a measurement company providing electronic design and test solutions to communications and electronics industries. Co. provides electronic design and test instruments and systems and related software, software design tools, and related services that are used in the design, development, manufacture, installation, deployment and operation of electronics equipment. Related services include start-up assistance, instrument productivity, application services and instrument calibration and repair. Co. also provides customization, consulting and optimization services throughout the customer's product lifecycle.

Recent Developments: For the quarter ended Apr 30 2018, net income increased 30.6% to US$64.0 million from US$49.0 million in the year-earlier quarter. Revenues were US$990.0 million, up 31.5% from US$753.0 million the year before. Operating income was US$100.0 million versus US$42.0 million in the prior-year quarter, an increase of 138.1%. Direct operating expenses rose 31.4% to US$603.0 million from US$459.0 million in the comparable period the year before. Indirect operating expenses increased 13.9% to US$287.0 million from US$252.0 million in the equivalent prior-year period.

Prospects: Our evaluation of Keysight Technologies Inc. as of Jan. 21, 2018 is the result of our systematic analysis on three basic characteristics: earnings strength, relative valuation, and recent stock price movement. The company has enjoyed a very positive trend in earnings per share over the past 5 quarters and while recent estimates for the company have been raised by analysts, KEYS has posted better than expected results. Based on operating earnings yield, the company is undervalued when compared to all of the companies in our coverage universe. Share price changes over the past year indicates that KEYS will perform in line with the market over the near term.

Financial Data

(US$ in Millions)	6 Mos	3 Mos	10/31/2017	10/31/2016	10/31/2015	10/31/2014	10/31/2013	10/31/2012
Earnings Per Share	0.52	0.45	0.56	1.95	3.00	2.35	...	...
Cash Flow Per Share	2.36	2.04	1.74	2.44	2.22	3.37	...	...
Tang Book Value Per Share	N.M.	N.M.	N.M.	3.35	2.10	2.14	...	...
Income Statement								
Total Revenue	1,827	837	3,189	2,918	2,856	2,933	2,888	3,315
EBITDA	255	74	344	495	514	552	566	801
Depn & Amortn	157	78	92	85	81	74	65	55
Income Before Taxes	60	(23)	179	366	388	475	501	746
Income Taxes	(98)	(117)	77	31	(125)	83	44	(95)
Net Income	158	94	102	335	513	392	457	841
Average Shares	190	189	182	172	171	167	...	...
Balance Sheet								
Current Assets	2,189	2,275	2,177	1,854	1,579	1,850	972	993
Total Assets	5,923	6,050	5,933	3,803	3,508	3,050	2,028	2,133
Current Liabilities	953	886	819	644	686	769	560	595
Long-Term Obligations	1,789	2,028	2,038	1,100	1,099	1,099	...	...
Total Liabilities	3,400	3,566	3,623	2,290	2,206	2,281	783	828
Stockholders' Equity	2,523	2,484	2,310	1,513	1,302	769	1,245	1,305
Shares Outstanding	186	187	186	169	169	167	...	...
Statistical Record								
Return on Assets %	1.71	1.75	2.10	9.14	15.65	...	21.97	...
Return on Equity %	4.35	4.21	5.34	23.74	49.54	...	35.84	...
EBITDA Margin %	13.96	8.84	10.79	16.96	18.00	18.82	19.60	24.16
Net Margin %	8.65	11.23	3.20	11.48	17.96	13.37	15.82	25.37
Asset Turnover	0.59	0.67	0.66	0.80	0.87	...	1.39	...
Current Ratio	2.30	2.57	2.66	2.88	2.30	2.41	1.74	1.67
Debt to Equity	0.71	0.82	0.88	0.73	0.84	1.43	...	...
Price Range	54.62-36.34	47.65-35.30	44.67-31.82	33.37-21.18	38.89-29.54	31.50-28.25	...	...
P/E Ratio	105.04-69.88	105.89-78.44	79.77-56.82	17.11-10.86	12.96-9.85	13.40-12.02	...	...

Address: 1400 Fountaingrove Parkway, Santa Rosa, CA 95403 **Telephone:** 800-829-4444	**Web Site:** www.keysight.com **Officers:** Paul N. Clark - Chairman Ronald S. Nersesian - President, Chief Executive Officer	**Auditors:** PricewaterhouseCoopers LLP **Transfer Agents:** Computershare Trust Company, N.A.

KILROY REALTY CORP

Exchange	Symbol	Price	52Wk Range	Yield	P/E
NYS	KRC	$75.64 (6/29/2018)	77.34-63.72	2.41	46.98

*7 Year Price Score 95.95 *NYSE Composite Index=100 *12 Month Price Score 103.41

Interim Earnings (Per Share)

Qtr.	Mar	Jun	Sep	Dec
2015	0.45	0.61	1.09	0.24
2016	1.84	0.31	0.54	0.28
2017	0.26	0.30	0.67	0.28
2018	0.36	...	...	...

Interim Dividends (Per Share)

Amt	Decl	Ex	Rec	Pay
0.425Q	09/13/2017	09/28/2017	09/29/2017	10/18/2017
0.425Q	12/12/2017	12/28/2017	12/29/2017	01/12/2018
0.425Q	02/14/2018	03/28/2018	03/29/2018	04/18/2018
0.455Q	05/23/2018	06/28/2018	06/29/2018	07/18/2018

Indicated Div: $1.82

Valuation Analysis

		Institutional Holding	
Forecast EPS	$1.36	No of Institutions	
	(06/14/2018)	389	
Market Cap	$7.5 Billion	Shares	
Book Value	$3.7 Billion	139,976,224	
Price/Book	2.03	% Held	
Price/Sales	10.35	110.59	

TRADING VOLUME (thousand shares)

Business Summary: REITs (MIC: 5.3.1 SIC: 6798 NAIC: 525930)

Kilroy Realty is a real estate investment trust, which owns, develops, acquires and manages real estate assets, consisting primarily of Class A properties in the coastal regions of Los Angeles, Orange County, San Diego County, the San Francisco Bay Area and greater Seattle. Co. owns its interests in all of its properties through Kilroy Realty, L.P. (the Operating Partnership) and Kilroy Realty Finance Partnership, L.P. and generally conducts substantially all of its operations through the Operating Partnership. As of Dec 31 2017, Co. had a stabilized portfolio of 101 office properties and one residential property.

Recent Developments: For the quarter ended Mar 31 2018, net income increased 9.9% to US$41.0 million from US$37.3 million in the year-earlier quarter. Revenues were US$182.8 million, up 2.0% from US$179.3 million the year before.

Prospects: Our evaluation of Kilroy Realty Corp. as of Jan. 21, 2018 is the result of our systematic analysis on three basic characteristics: earnings strength, relative valuation, and recent stock price movement. The company has enjoyed a very positive trend in earnings per share over the past 5 quarters. Because the company lacks sufficient analyst estimate data, we place greater weight on the historical EPS trend as the measure of earnings strength. Based on operating earnings yield, the company is overvalued when compared to all of the companies in our coverage universe. Share price changes over the past year indicates that KRC will perform well over the near term.

Financial Data

(US$ in Thousands)	3 Mos	12/31/2017	12/31/2016	12/31/2015	12/31/2014	12/31/2013	12/31/2012	12/31/2011
Earnings Per Share	1.61	1.51	2.97	2.42	1.95	0.36	2.56	0.87
Cash Flow Per Share	3.49	3.54	3.73	3.03	2.95	3.11	2.59	2.44
Tang Book Value Per Share	37.30	37.53	35.94	32.28	28.68	27.62	26.66	21.18
Dividends Per Share	1.700	1.650	3.375	1.400	1.400	1.400	1.400	1.400
Dividend Payout %	105.59	109.27	113.64	57.85	71.79	388.89	54.69	160.92
Income Statement								
Total Revenue	182,822	719,001	642,572	581,275	521,725	465,098	404,912	367,131
EBITDA	52,562	431,652	529,837	455,543	280,123	235,372	209,613	199,897
Depn & Amortn	(1,873)	190,500	172,000	159,500	153,800	145,300	125,900	106,000
Income Before Taxes	40,971	180,615	303,798	238,604	59,313	15,837	5,447	5,059
Net Income	36,246	164,612	293,788	234,081	180,219	43,880	270,914	66,015
Average Shares	99,213	98,727	93,023	90,395	84,967	79,108	69,639	56,717
Balance Sheet								
Current Assets	343,987	350,789	497,339	270,943	274,582	233,031	396,317	120,363
Total Assets	6,965,932	6,802,838	6,706,633	5,939,469	5,633,736	5,111,028	4,616,084	3,446,795
Current Liabilities	473,165	293,085	424,697	281,315	258,729	229,957	183,658	104,405
Long-Term Obligations	2,545,295	2,347,063	2,320,123	2,238,508	2,469,413	2,204,938	2,040,935	1,821,286
Total Liabilities	3,279,073	3,102,045	3,163,638	2,768,503	2,967,526	2,649,716	2,426,454	2,079,440
Stockholders' Equity	3,686,859	3,700,793	3,542,995	3,170,966	2,666,210	2,461,312	2,189,630	1,367,355
Shares Outstanding	98,839	98,620	93,219	92,258	86,259	82,153	74,926	58,819
Statistical Record								
Return on Assets %	2.40	2.44	4.63	4.05	3.35	0.90	6.70	2.11
Return on Equity %	4.49	4.54	8.73	8.02	7.03	1.89	15.19	5.22
EBITDA Margin %	28.75	60.03	82.46	78.37	53.69	50.61	51.77	54.45
Net Margin %	19.83	22.89	45.72	40.27	34.54	9.43	66.91	17.98
Asset Turnover	0.10	0.11	0.10	0.10	0.10	0.10	0.10	0.12
Current Ratio	0.73	1.20	1.17	0.96	1.06	1.01	2.16	1.15
Debt to Equity	0.69	0.63	0.65	0.71	0.93	0.90	0.93	1.33
Price Range	77.09-63.72	77.91-67.47	76.88-47.38	78.86-62.83	71.10-50.18	59.58-47.37	49.88-37.92	41.94-29.25
P/E Ratio	47.88-39.58	51.60-44.68	25.89-15.95	32.59-25.96	36.46-25.73	165.50-131.58	19.48-14.81	48.21-33.62
Average Yield %	2.37	2.26	5.16	2.00	2.29	2.69	3.05	3.75

Address: 12200 W. Olympic Boulevard, Suite 200, Los Angeles, CA 90064
Telephone: 310-481-8400

Web Site: www.kilroyrealty.com
Officers: John B. Kilroy - Chairman, President, Chief Executive Officer Justin William Smart - Executive Vice President

Auditors: Deloitte & Touche LLP
Investor Contact: 310-481-8400
Transfer Agents: Computershare Trust Company, N.A., Canton, MA

KIMBERLY-CLARK CORP.

Exchange	Symbol	Price	52Wk Range	Yield	P/E	Div Acheiver
NYS	KMB	$105.34 (6/29/2018)	129.11-98.52	3.80	20.70	43 Years

*7 Year Price Score 88.11 *NYSE Composite Index=100 *12 Month Price Score 89.18

Interim Earnings (Per Share)

Qtr.	Mar	Jun	Sep	Dec
2015	1.27	(0.83)	1.41	0.92
2016	1.50	1.56	1.52	1.41
2017	1.57	1.49	1.60	1.74
2018	0.26	...	...	...

Interim Dividends (Per Share)

Amt	Decl	Ex	Rec	Pay
0.97Q	08/01/2017	09/07/2017	09/08/2017	10/03/2017
0.97Q	11/16/2017	12/07/2017	12/08/2017	01/03/2018
1.00Q	01/23/2018	03/08/2018	03/09/2018	04/03/2018
1.00Q	05/10/2018	06/07/2018	06/08/2018	07/03/2018

Indicated Div: $4.00 (Div. Reinv. Plan)

Valuation Analysis / **Institutional Holding**

Forecast EPS	$6.84	No of Institutions
	(06/14/2018)	1902
Market Cap	$36.8 Billion	Shares
Book Value	$317.0 Million	341,498,784
Price/Book	116.08	% Held
Price/Sales	1.99	64.22

Business Summary: Household & Personal Products (MIC: 1.7.1 SIC: 2679 NAIC: 322299)

Kimberly-Clark is engaged in the manufacturing and marketing of a range of products made from natural or synthetic fibers using technologies in fibers, nonwovens and absorbency. Co. is organized into three operating segments: personal care brands, which provides disposable diapers, training and youth pants, swimpants, baby wipes, feminine and incontinence care products, and other related products; consumer tissue, which provides facial and bathroom tissue, paper towels, napkins and related products; and K-C professional, which provides wipers, tissue, towels, apparel, soaps and sanitizers.

Recent Developments: For the year ended Dec 31 2017, net income increased 4.5% to US$2.32 billion from US$2.22 billion in the prior year. Revenues were US$18.26 billion, up 0.3% from US$18.20 billion the year before. Operating income was US$3.30 billion versus US$3.32 billion in the prior year, a decrease of 0.5%. Direct operating expenses rose 1.3% to US$11.71 billion from US$11.55 billion in the comparable period the year before. Indirect operating expenses decreased 2.4% to US$3.25 billion from US$3.33 billion in the equivalent prior-year period.

Prospects: Our evaluation of Kimberly-Clark Corp. as of Jan. 21, 2018 is the result of our systematic analysis on three basic characteristics: earnings strength, relative valuation, and recent stock price movement. The company has produced a positive trend in earnings per share over the past 5 quarters and while recent estimates for the company have been mixed, KMB has posted better than expected results. Based on operating earnings yield, the company is undervalued when compared to all of the companies in our coverage universe. Share price changes over the past year indicates that KMB will perform well over the near term.

Financial Data

(US$ in Thousands)	3 Mos	12/31/2017	12/31/2016	12/31/2015	12/31/2014	12/31/2013	12/31/2012	12/31/2011
Earnings Per Share	5.09	6.40	5.99	2.77	4.04	5.53	4.42	3.99
Cash Flow Per Share	8.66	8.28	8.97	6.34	7.60	7.92	8.34	5.78
Tang Book Value Per Share	N.M.	N.M.	...	...	N.M.	3.95	5.01	5.54
Dividends Per Share	3.910	3.880	3.680	3.520	3.360	3.240	2.960	2.800
Dividend Payout %	76.82	60.63	61.44	127.08	83.17	58.59	66.97	70.18
Income Statement								
Total Revenue	4,731,000	18,259,000	18,202,000	18,591,000	19,724,000	21,152,000	21,063,000	20,846,000
EBITDA	449,000	4,023,000	4,022,000	2,359,000	3,383,000	3,247,000	2,715,000	2,466,000
Depn & Amortn	211,000	724,000	705,000	746,000	862,000	39,000	29,000	24,000
Income Before Taxes	174,000	2,991,000	3,009,000	1,335,000	2,255,000	2,945,000	2,420,000	2,183,000
Income Taxes	104,000	776,000	922,000	418,000	856,000	929,000	768,000	660,000
Net Income	93,000	2,278,000	2,166,000	1,013,000	1,526,000	2,142,000	1,750,000	1,591,000
Average Shares	352,600	355,900	361,700	366,300	377,400	387,300	396,100	398,600
Balance Sheet								
Current Assets	5,372,000	5,211,000	5,115,000	5,426,000	5,559,000	6,550,000	6,589,000	6,283,000
Total Assets	15,303,000	15,151,000	14,602,000	14,842,000	15,526,000	18,919,000	19,873,000	19,373,000
Current Liabilities	6,674,000	5,858,000	5,846,000	6,349,000	6,226,000	5,848,000	6,091,000	5,397,000
Long-Term Obligations	6,081,000	6,472,000	6,439,000	6,106,000	5,630,000	5,386,000	5,070,000	5,426,000
Total Liabilities	14,986,000	14,461,000	14,646,000	14,952,000	14,725,000	13,991,000	14,339,000	13,577,000
Stockholders' Equity	317,000	690,000	(44,000)	(110,000)	801,000	4,928,000	5,534,000	5,796,000
Shares Outstanding	349,329	351,106	356,568	360,860	365,336	380,799	389,275	395,660
Statistical Record								
Return on Assets %	12.03	15.31	14.67	6.67	8.86	11.04	8.89	8.11
Return on Equity %	798.23	705.26	...	293.20	53.27	40.95	30.81	25.97
EBITDA Margin %	9.49	22.03	22.10	12.69	17.15	15.35	12.89	11.83
Net Margin %	1.97	12.48	11.90	5.45	7.74	10.13	8.31	7.63
Asset Turnover	1.23	1.23	1.23	1.22	1.15	1.09	1.07	1.06
Current Ratio	0.80	0.89	0.87	0.85	0.89	1.12	1.08	1.16
Debt to Equity	19.18	9.38	...	...	7.03	1.09	0.92	0.94
Price Range	133.91-104.74	135.00-109.87	138.13-112.15	129.54-103.35	118.28-98.99	105.15-80.54	84.28-68.18	70.93-59.97
P/E Ratio	26.31-20.58	21.09-17.17	23.06-18.72	46.77-37.31	29.28-24.50	19.02-14.56	19.07-15.42	17.78-15.03
Average Yield %	3.24	3.14	2.91	3.13	3.16	3.45	3.85	4.34

Address: P.O. Box 619100, Dallas, TX 75261-9100	**Web Site:** www.kimberly-clark.com	**Auditors:** DELOITTE & TOUCHE LLP
Telephone: 972-281-1200	**Officers:** Thomas J. Falk - Chairman, Chief Executive Officer, President Michael D. Hsu - President, Chief Operating Officer, Division Officer	**Investor Contact:** .972-281-1440
		Transfer Agents: ComputerShare Investor Services, Providence, RI

KIMCO REALTY CORP

Exchange	Symbol	Price	52Wk Range	Yield	P/E
NYS	KIM	$16.99 (6/29/2018)	21.02-13.24	6.59	16.66

*7 Year Price Score 63.14   *NYSE Composite Index=100   *12 Month Price Score 89.81

Interim Earnings (Per Share)

Qtr.	Mar	Jun	Sep	Dec
2015	0.71	0.27	0.15	0.86
2016	0.31	0.46	(0.13)	0.16
2017	0.15	0.31	0.24	0.17
2018	0.30	...	...	...

Interim Dividends (Per Share)

Amt	Decl	Ex	Rec	Pay
0.27Q	07/26/2017	10/03/2017	10/04/2017	10/16/2017
0.28Q	10/25/2017	12/29/2017	01/02/2018	01/16/2018
0.28Q	01/31/2018	04/02/2018	04/03/2018	04/16/2018
0.28Q	04/24/2018	07/02/2018	07/03/2018	07/16/2018

Indicated Div: $1.12 (Div. Reinv. Plan)

Valuation Analysis

		Institutional Holding	
Forecast EPS	$0.77	No of Institutions	
	(06/13/2018)	679	
Market Cap	$7.2 Billion	Shares	
Book Value	$5.4 Billion	455,666,016	
Price/Book	1.33	% Held	
Price/Sales	5.96	93.66	

Business Summary: REITs (MIC: 5.3.1 SIC: 6798 NAIC: 525930)

Kimco Realty is a real estate investment trust engages in the ownership, management, development and operation of open-air shopping centers. As of Dec 31 2017, Co. had interests in 493 shopping center properties located in 29 states, Puerto Rico and Canada. In addition, as of Dec 31 2017, Co. had 372 other property interests, through Co.'s preferred equity investments and other real estate investments. Co.'s ownership interests in real estate consist of its consolidated portfolio and portfolios where it owns an economic interest, such as properties in Co.'s investment real estate management programs, where Co. partners with institutional investors and also retains management.

Recent Developments: For the quarter ended Mar 31 2018, income from continuing operations increased 13.7% to US$87.0 million from US$76.5 million in the year-earlier quarter. Net income increased 84.1% to US$144.0 million from US$78.2 million in the year-earlier quarter. Revenues were US$304.1 million, up 3.6% from US$293.6 million the year before. Revenues from property income rose 2.0% to US$236.0 million from US$231.3 million in the corresponding quarter a year earlier.

Prospects: Our evaluation of Kimco Realty Corp. as of Jan. 21, 2018 is the result of our systematic analysis on three basic characteristics: earnings strength, relative valuation, and recent stock price movement. The company has enjoyed a very positive trend in earnings per share over the past 5 quarters. Because the company lacks sufficient analyst estimate data, we place greater weight on the historical EPS trend as the measure of earnings strength. Based on operating earnings yield, the company is undervalued when compared to all of the companies in our coverage universe. Share price changes over the past year indicates that KIM will perform well over the near term.

Financial Data

(US$ in Thousands)	3 Mos	12/31/2017	12/31/2016	12/31/2015	12/31/2014	12/31/2013	12/31/2012	12/31/2011
Earnings Per Share	1.02	0.87	0.79	2.00	0.89	0.43	0.42	0.27
Cash Flow Per Share	1.53	1.45	1.41	1.20	1.54	1.40	1.18	1.10
Tang Book Value Per Share	12.77	12.67	12.37	12.21	11.59	11.31	11.69	11.51
Dividends Per Share	1.090	1.090	1.035	0.975	0.915	0.855	0.780	0.730
Dividend Payout %	106.86	125.29	131.01	48.75	102.81	198.84	185.71	270.37
Income Statement								
Total Revenue	304,078	1,200,834	1,170,792	1,166,769	993,897	946,673	922,304	873,694
EBITDA	191,499	696,287	614,416	693,273	577,993	489,434	522,236	540,049
Depn & Amortn	81,382	360,811	355,320	344,527	273,093	257,855	262,742	251,139
Income Before Taxes	60,174	146,329	68,025	168,916	102,107	34,667	34,069	80,441
Income Taxes	52	(880)	72,545	60,230	22,438	34,520	3,939	19,537
Net Income	144,090	426,075	378,850	894,115	424,001	236,281	266,073	169,051
Average Shares	424,521	424,019	419,709	412,851	411,038	408,614	406,689	407,669
Balance Sheet								
Current Assets	414,473	441,535	332,410	372,351	449,943	375,860	339,529	296,229
Total Assets	11,372,502	11,763,726	11,230,600	11,344,171	10,285,728	9,663,630	9,740,807	9,614,516
Current Liabilities	132,209	4,910,734	4,197,519	4,026,569	3,432,819	3,414,833	3,400,526	3,221,217
Long-Term Obligations	5,097,322	882,787	1,139,117	1,614,982	1,428,131	1,035,354	1,003,190	1,130,499
Total Liabilities	5,947,936	6,369,482	5,974,461	6,297,871	5,510,943	5,031,213	4,975,647	4,928,130
Stockholders' Equity	5,424,566	5,394,244	5,256,139	5,046,300	4,774,785	4,632,417	4,765,160	4,686,386
Shares Outstanding	424,899	425,646	425,034	413,430	411,819	409,731	407,782	406,937
Statistical Record								
Return on Assets %	4.36	3.71	3.35	8.27	4.25	2.44	2.74	1.74
Return on Equity %	9.28	8.00	7.33	18.21	9.01	5.03	5.61	3.51
EBITDA Margin %	62.98	57.98	52.48	59.42	58.15	51.70	56.62	61.81
Net Margin %	47.39	35.48	32.36	76.63	42.66	24.96	28.85	19.35
Asset Turnover	0.11	0.10	0.10	0.11	0.10	0.10	0.10	0.09
Current Ratio	3.13	0.09	0.08	0.09	0.13	0.11	0.10	0.09
Debt to Equity	0.94	0.16	0.22	0.32	0.30	0.22	0.21	0.24
Price Range	22.72-14.01	26.07-17.30	32.17-24.71	28.33-22.26	25.91-19.75	25.00-19.25	21.03-16.27	20.30-14.11
P/E Ratio	22.27-13.74	29.97-19.89	40.72-31.28	14.16-11.13	29.11-22.19	58.14-44.77	50.07-38.74	75.19-52.26
Average Yield %	5.93	5.32	3.67	3.85	4.00	3.97	4.08	4.17

Address: 3333 New Hyde Park Road, New Hyde Park, NY 11042-0020 **Telephone:** 516-869-9000	**Web Site:** www.kimcorealty.com **Officers:** Milton Cooper - Executive Chairman Ross Cooper - President, Chief Investment Officer	**Auditors:** PricewaterhouseCoopers LLP **Transfer Agents:** Wells Fargo Shareholder Services, St. Paul, MN

KINDER MORGAN INC.

*7 Year Price Score 48.94 ***NYSE Composite Index=100** ***12 Month Price Score 92.96**

Interim Earnings (Per Share)

Qtr.	Mar	Jun	Sep	Dec
2015	0.20	0.15	0.08	(0.33)
2016	0.12	0.15	(0.10)	0.08
2017	0.18	0.15	0.15	(0.47)
2018	0.22	...	...	...

Interim Dividends (Per Share)

Amt	Decl	Ex	Rec	Pay
0.125Q	07/19/2017	07/27/2017	07/31/2017	08/15/2017
0.125Q	10/18/2017	10/30/2017	10/31/2017	11/15/2017
0.125Q	01/17/2018	01/30/2018	01/31/2018	02/15/2018
0.20Q	04/18/2018	04/27/2018	04/30/2018	05/15/2018

Indicated Div: $0.80 (Div. Reinv. Plan)

Valuation Analysis   Institutional Holding

Forecast EPS	$0.87	No of Institutions
	(06/14/2018)	1329
Market Cap	$38.9 Billion	Shares
Book Value	$34.2 Billion	1,680,227,456
Price/Book	1.14	% Held
Price/Sales	2.84	48.99

Business Summary: Equipment & Services (MIC: 9.1.3 SIC: 4923 NAIC: 221210)

Kinder Morgan is an energy infrastructure company in North America. Co.'s segments are: Natural Gas Pipelines, which include natural gas sales, transportation, storage, gathering, processing and treating, and the terminaling of liquified natural gas; carbon dioxide (CO2), which produces, transports, and markets CO2 to oil fields; Terminals, which includes the ownership and/or operation of liquids and bulk terminal facilities and Jones Act tankers; Products Pipelines, which includes the operation of refined petroleum products, natural gas liquids and crude oil and condensate pipelines; and Kinder Morgan Canada, which includes the ownership and operation of the Trans Mountain pipeline system.

Recent Developments: For the quarter ended Mar 31 2018, net income increased 21.8% to US$542.0 million from US$445.0 million in the year-earlier quarter. Revenues were US$3.42 billion, unchanged from the year before. Operating income was US$949.0 million versus US$977.0 million in the prior-year quarter, a decrease of 2.9%. Direct operating expenses rose 2.8% to US$1.64 billion from US$1.59 billion in the comparable period the year before. Indirect operating expenses decreased 2.6% to US$831.0 million from US$853.0 million in the equivalent prior-year period.

Prospects: Our evaluation of Kinder Morgan, Inc. as of Jan. 21, 2018 is the result of our systematic analysis on three basic characteristics: earnings strength, relative valuation, and recent stock price movement. The company has produced a positive trend in earnings per share over the past 5 quarters and while recent estimates for the company have been raised by analysts, KMI has posted better than expected results. Based on positive earnings yield, the company is about fairly valued when compared to all of the companies in our coverage universe. Share price changes over the past year indicates that KMI will perform very poorly over the near term.

Financial Data

(US$ in Thousands)	3 Mos	12/31/2017	12/31/2016	12/31/2015	12/31/2014	12/31/2013	12/31/2012	12/31/2011
Earnings Per Share	0.05	0.01	0.25	0.10	0.89	1.15	0.35	0.74
Cash Flow Per Share	2.12	2.06	2.14	2.42	3.93	3.92	3.07	3.35
Tang Book Value Per Share	4.08	3.78	4.02	3.49	3.35	N.M.	N.M.	N.M.
Dividends Per Share	0.500	0.500	0.500	1.930	1.700	1.560	1.340	0.740
Dividend Payout %	1,000.00	5,000.00	200.00	1,930.00	191.01	135.65	382.86	100.00
Income Statement								
Total Revenue	3,418,000	13,705,000	13,058,000	14,403,000	16,226,000	14,070,000	9,973,000	8,264,900
EBITDA	985,000	5,437,000	4,917,000	4,468,000	6,345,000	5,891,000	3,913,000	2,571,600
Depn & Amortn	32,000	2,022,000	1,970,000	2,059,000	1,862,000	1,663,000	1,324,000	1,022,200
Income Before Taxes	486,000	1,583,000	1,141,000	358,000	2,685,000	2,553,000	1,190,000	869,100
Income Taxes	164,000	1,938,000	917,000	564,000	648,000	742,000	139,000	362,800
Net Income	524,000	183,000	708,000	253,000	1,026,000	1,193,000	315,000	594,400
Average Shares	2,207,000	2,230,000	2,230,000	2,193,000	1,137,000	1,036,000	908,000	707,600
Balance Sheet								
Current Assets	2,628,000	2,715,000	3,229,000	2,824,000	3,752,000	3,868,000	3,674,000	1,663,300
Total Assets	79,011,000	79,055,000	80,305,000	84,104,000	83,198,000	75,185,000	68,185,000	30,717,000
Current Liabilities	5,429,000	6,181,000	5,924,000	4,065,000	6,362,000	6,075,000	5,209,000	4,529,000
Long-Term Obligations	35,543,000	35,015,000	37,354,000	42,406,000	40,246,000	33,887,000	32,000,000	14,356,400
Total Liabilities	44,821,000	45,419,000	45,874,000	48,985,000	49,122,000	62,092,000	54,320,000	27,396,500
Stockholders' Equity	34,190,000	33,636,000	34,431,000	35,119,000	34,076,000	13,093,000	13,865,000	3,320,500
Shares Outstanding	2,203,966	2,217,110	2,230,103	2,229,224	2,125,147	1,030,677	1,035,668	803,344
Statistical Record								
Return on Assets %	0.34	0.23	0.86	0.30	1.30	1.66	0.64	1.99
Return on Equity %	0.78	0.54	2.03	0.73	4.35	8.85	3.66	17.59
EBITDA Margin %	28.82	39.67	37.66	31.02	39.10	41.87	39.24	31.11
Net Margin %	15.33	1.34	5.42	1.76	6.32	8.48	3.16	7.19
Asset Turnover	0.17	0.17	0.16	0.17	0.20	0.20	0.20	0.28
Current Ratio	0.48	0.44	0.55	0.69	0.59	0.64	0.71	0.37
Debt to Equity	1.04	1.04	1.08	1.21	1.18	2.59	2.31	4.32
Price Range	21.75-14.81	22.94-16.76	23.13-12.01	44.57-14.54	43.01-30.96	41.09-32.58	39.85-30.76	32.17-23.66
P/E Ratio	435.00-296.20	N.M.	92.52-48.04	445.70-145.40	48.33-34.79	35.73-28.33	113.86-87.89	43.47-31.97
Average Yield %	2.68	2.53	2.61	5.52	4.70	4.20	3.87	2.60

Address: 1001 Louisiana Street, Suite 1000, Houston, TX 77002
Telephone: 713-369-9000

Web Site: www.kindermorgan.com
Officers: Richard D. Kinder - Executive Chairman, Chairman, Chief Executive Officer Steven J. Kean - President, Chief Executive Officer, Executive Vice President, Chief Operating Officer

Auditors: PricewaterhouseCoopers LLP
Investor Contact: 713-369-9449
Transfer Agents: Computershare Investor Services, LLC

KIRBY CORP.

Exchange	Symbol	Price	52Wk Range	Yield	P/E
NYS	KEX	$83.60 (6/29/2018)	93.30-60.05	N/A	14.77

*7 Year Price Score 79.60   *NYSE Composite Index=100   *12 Month Price Score 120.02

Interim Earnings (Per Share)

Qtr.	Mar	Jun	Sep	Dec
2015	1.09	1.04	1.04	0.94
2016	0.71	0.72	0.59	0.60
2017	0.51	0.48	0.52	4.12
2018	0.54	...	...	...

Interim Dividends (Per Share)

No Dividends Paid

Valuation Analysis | **Institutional Holding**

Forecast EPS	$3.00	No of Institutions	
(06/03/2018)		389	
Market Cap	$5.0 Billion	Shares	
Book Value	$3.1 Billion	72,625,984	
Price/Book	1.59	% Held	
Price/Sales	2.02	94.09	

Business Summary: Shipping (MIC: 7.4.2 SIC: 4449 NAIC: 483211)

Kirby is a tank barge operator. Co. has two segments: marine transportation, which provides marine transportation services, operating tank barges and towing vessels transporting bulk liquid products throughout the Mississippi River System, coastwise along all three U.S. coasts, and in Alaska and Hawaii; and diesel engine services, which provides services for diesel engines, reduction gears and ancillary products for marine and power generation applications, distributes and services diesel engines, transmissions and pumps, and manufactures oilfield service equipment for land-based oilfield service and oil and gas operator and producer markets.

Recent Developments: For the quarter ended Mar 31 2018, net income increased 18.2% to US$32.7 million from US$27.6 million in the year-earlier quarter. Revenues were US$741.7 million, up 50.8% from US$491.7 million the year before. Operating income was US$50.7 million versus US$46.0 million in the prior-year quarter, an increase of 10.2%. Direct operating expenses rose 60.5% to US$553.3 million from US$344.8 million in the comparable period the year before. Indirect operating expenses increased 36.5% to US$137.7 million from US$100.9 million in the equivalent prior-year period.

Prospects: Our evaluation of Kirby Corp. as of Jan. 21, 2018 is the result of our systematic analysis on three basic characteristics: earnings strength, relative valuation, and recent stock price movement. The company has enjoyed a very positive trend in earnings per share over the past 5 quarters and while recent estimates for the company have been mixed, KEX has posted better than expected results. Based on operating earnings yield, the company is about fairly valued when compared to all of the companies in our coverage universe. Share price changes over the past year indicates that KEX will perform very poorly over the near term.

Financial Data
(US$ in Thousands)

	3 Mos	12/31/2017	12/31/2016	12/31/2015	12/31/2014	12/31/2013	12/31/2012	12/31/2011
Earnings Per Share	5.66	5.62	2.62	4.11	4.93	4.44	3.73	3.33
Cash Flow Per Share	4.83	6.39	7.72	9.53	7.74	10.67	5.86	5.76
Tang Book Value Per Share	33.09	32.55	33.63	31.31	29.24	24.97	19.42	17.20
Income Statement								
Total Revenue	741,688	2,214,418	1,770,673	2,147,532	2,566,318	2,242,195	2,112,658	1,850,417
EBITDA	65,014	330,729	478,166	605,469	672,779	612,260	519,578	447,559
Depn & Amortn	12,703	236,534	233,262	225,470	197,312	176,058	154,943	135,257
Income Before Taxes	42,531	72,723	227,214	361,261	454,006	408,330	340,250	294,400
Income Taxes	9,865	(240,889)	84,942	133,742	169,782	152,379	127,907	109,255
Net Income	32,471	313,187	141,406	226,684	282,006	253,061	209,438	183,026
Average Shares	59,493	55,361	53,512	54,826	56,867	56,552	55,674	54,413
Balance Sheet								
Current Assets	1,056,654	957,082	646,555	640,776	803,154	544,006	596,256	529,329
Total Assets	5,714,500	5,127,427	4,303,499	4,156,266	4,141,909	3,682,517	3,653,128	2,960,411
Current Liabilities	531,158	480,306	358,338	361,917	594,027	345,989	355,020	358,800
Long-Term Obligations	1,423,267	992,403	722,802	778,834	600,000	749,150	1,070,110	763,000
Total Liabilities	2,576,005	2,016,607	1,894,181	1,887,455	1,887,873	1,671,831	1,958,160	1,517,886
Stockholders' Equity	3,138,495	3,110,820	2,409,318	2,268,811	2,254,036	2,010,686	1,694,968	1,442,525
Shares Outstanding	59,672	59,689	53,855	53,720	56,870	56,846	56,585	55,744
Statistical Record								
Return on Assets %	6.38	6.64	3.33	5.46	7.21	6.90	6.32	7.70
Return on Equity %	11.43	11.35	6.03	10.02	13.23	13.66	13.31	14.09
EBITDA Margin %	8.77	14.94	27.00	28.19	26.22	27.31	24.59	24.19
Net Margin %	4.38	14.14	7.99	10.56	10.99	11.29	9.91	9.89
Asset Turnover	0.49	0.47	0.42	0.52	0.66	0.61	0.64	0.78
Current Ratio	1.99	1.99	1.80	1.77	1.35	1.57	1.68	1.48
Debt to Equity	0.45	0.32	0.30	0.34	0.27	0.37	0.63	0.53
Price Range	78.25-60.05	73.10-60.05	72.71-45.77	83.90-50.86	123.25-80.32	99.25-61.89	70.00-45.39	65.99-43.75
P/E Ratio	13.83-10.61	13.01-10.69	27.75-17.47	20.41-12.37	25.00-16.29	22.35-13.94	18.77-12.17	19.82-13.14

Address: 55 Waugh Drive, Suite 1000, Houston, TX 77007 **Telephone:** 713-435-1000 **Fax:** 713-435-1010	**Web Site:** www.kirbycorp.com **Officers:** David W. Grzebinski - President, Chief Executive Officer, Interim Chief Financial Officer, Chief Operating Officer, Chief Financial Officer, Executive Vice President William G. Harvey - Executive Vice President, Chief Financial Officer	**Auditors:** KPMG LLP **Transfer Agents:** Computershare Trust Company, N.A., Providence, RI

KOHL'S CORP.

Exchange	Symbol	Price	52Wk Range	Yield	P/E
NYS	KSS	$72.90 (6/29/2018)	78.32-36.63	3.35	14.05

*7 Year Price Score 84.99 *NYSE Composite Index=100 *12 Month Price Score 124.95

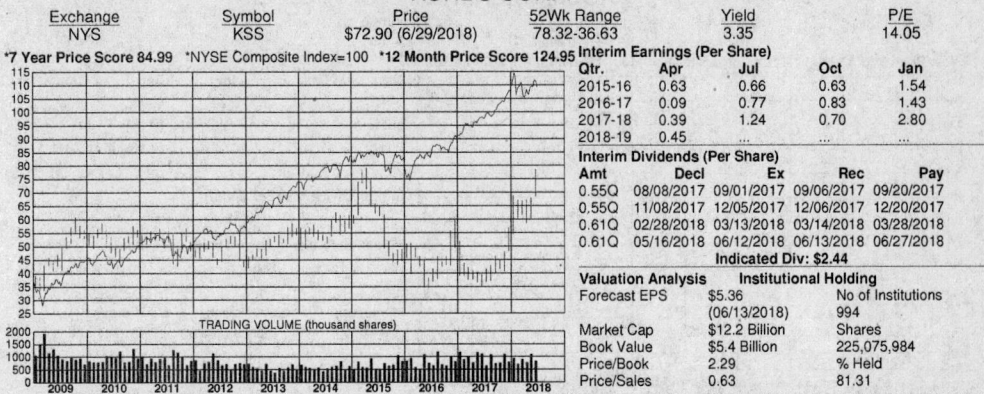

Interim Earnings (Per Share)

Qtr.	Apr	Jul	Oct	Jan
2015-16	0.63	0.66	0.63	1.54
2016-17	0.09	0.77	0.83	1.43
2017-18	0.39	1.24	0.70	2.80
2018-19	0.45	...	...	...

Interim Dividends (Per Share)

Amt	Decl	Ex	Rec	Pay
0.55Q	08/08/2017	09/01/2017	09/06/2017	09/20/2017
0.55Q	11/08/2017	12/05/2017	12/06/2017	12/20/2017
0.61Q	02/28/2018	03/13/2018	03/14/2018	03/28/2018
0.61Q	05/16/2018	06/12/2018	06/13/2018	06/27/2018
		Indicated Div: $2.44		

Valuation Analysis — **Institutional Holding**

Forecast EPS	$5.36	No of Institutions
	(06/13/2018)	994
Market Cap	$12.2 Billion	Shares
Book Value	$5.4 Billion	225,075,984
Price/Book	2.29	% Held
Price/Sales	0.63	81.31

TRADING VOLUME (thousand shares)

Business Summary: Retail - General Merchandise/Department Stores (MIC: 2.1.1 SIC: 5311 NAIC: 452111)

Kohl's sells private label, exclusive and national brand apparel, footwear, accessories, beauty and home products. As of Feb 3 2018, Co. operated 1,158 department stores, a website (www.Kohls.com), 12 FILA outlets, and four Off-Aisle clearance centers. Co.'s website includes merchandise that is available in its stores, as well as merchandise that is available only on-line. Co.'s private brands include Apt. 9, Croft & Barrow, Jumping Beans, SO and Sonoma Goods for Life. Co.'s exclusive brands include Food Network, Jennifer Lopez, Marc Anthony, Rock & Republic and Simply Vera Vera Wang.

Recent Developments: For the quarter ended May 5 2018, net income increased 13.6% to US$75.0 million from US$66.0 million in the year-earlier quarter. Revenues were US$4.21 billion, up 3.5% from US$4.07 billion the year before. Operating income was US$210.0 million versus US$185.0 million in the prior-year quarter, an increase of 13.5%. Direct operating expenses rose 2.8% to US$2.50 billion from US$2.43 billion in the comparable period the year before. Indirect operating expenses increased 3.4% to US$1.50 billion from US$1.45 billion in the equivalent prior-year period.

Prospects: Our evaluation of Kohl's Corp. as of Jan. 21, 2018 is the result of our systematic analysis on three basic characteristics: earnings strength, relative valuation, and recent stock price movement. The company has produced a positive trend in earnings per share over the past 5 quarters and while recent estimates for the company have been raised by analysts, KSS has posted results that fell short of analysts expectations. Based on operating earnings yield, the company is undervalued when compared to all of the companies in our coverage universe. Share price changes over the past year indicates that KSS will perform very poorly over the near term.

Financial Data

(US$ in Thousands)	3 Mos	02/03/2018	01/28/2017	01/30/2016	01/31/2015	02/01/2014	02/02/2013	01/28/2012
Earnings Per Share	5.19	5.12	3.11	3.46	4.24	4.05	4.17	4.30
Cash Flow Per Share	12.32	9.96	12.10	7.66	10.00	8.67	5.30	7.96
Tang Book Value Per Share	31.88	32.30	29.75	29.52	29.81	28.33	27.24	26.35
Dividends Per Share	2.260	2.200	2.000	1.800	1.560	1.400	1.280	1.000
Dividend Payout %	43.55	42.97	64.31	52.02	36.79	34.57	30.70	23.26
Income Statement								
Total Revenue	4,208,000	19,095,000	18,686,000	19,204,000	19,023,000	19,031,000	19,279,000	18,804,000
EBITDA	411,000	2,407,000	2,121,000	2,318,000	2,575,000	2,631,000	2,723,000	2,936,000
Depn & Amortn	243,000	991,000	938,000	934,000	886,000	889,000	833,000	778,000
Income Before Taxes	97,000	1,117,000	875,000	1,057,000	1,349,000	1,404,000	1,561,000	1,859,000
Income Taxes	22,000	258,000	319,000	384,000	482,000	515,000	575,000	692,000
Net Income	75,000	859,000	556,000	673,000	867,000	889,000	986,000	1,167,000
Average Shares	167,000	168,000	179,000	195,000	204,000	220,000	237,000	271,000
Balance Sheet								
Current Assets	4,983,000	5,331,000	5,247,000	5,076,000	5,698,000	5,292,000	4,719,000	4,775,000
Total Assets	12,916,000	13,340,000	13,574,000	13,606,000	14,431,000	14,378,000	13,905,000	14,094,000
Current Liabilities	2,830,000	2,651,000	2,974,000	2,714,000	2,859,000	2,736,000	2,535,000	2,590,000
Long-Term Obligations	3,864,000	4,388,000	4,480,000	4,581,000	4,651,000	4,722,000	4,448,000	4,150,000
Total Liabilities	7,560,000	7,914,000	8,397,000	8,115,000	8,440,000	8,400,000	7,857,000	7,586,000
Stockholders' Equity	5,356,000	5,426,000	5,177,000	5,491,000	5,991,000	5,978,000	6,048,000	6,508,000
Shares Outstanding	168,000	168,000	174,000	186,000	201,000	211,000	222,000	247,000
Statistical Record								
Return on Assets %	6.64	6.28	4.10	4.81	6.04	6.30	6.93	8.46
Return on Equity %	16.77	15.94	10.45	11.75	14.53	14.83	15.45	16.02
EBITDA Margin %	9.77	12.61	11.35	12.07	13.54	13.82	14.12	15.61
Net Margin %	1.78	4.50	2.98	3.50	4.56	4.67	5.11	6.21
Asset Turnover	1.49	1.40	1.38	1.37	1.32	1.35	1.35	1.36
Current Ratio	1.76	2.01	1.76	1.87	1.99	1.93	1.86	1.84
Debt to Equity	0.72	0.81	0.87	0.83	0.78	0.79	0.74	0.64
Price Range	68.83-35.32	68.83-35.32	59.43-34.49	79.07-42.85	62.50-49.09	58.47-45.21	55.11-41.81	57.00-42.60
P/E Ratio	13.26-6.81	13.44-6.90	19.11-11.09	22.85-12.38	14.74-11.58	14.44-11.16	13.22-10.03	13.26-9.91
Average Yield %	4.59	5.06	4.55	3.05	2.78	2.72	2.63	1.95

Address: N56 W17000 Ridgewood Drive, Menomonee Falls, WI 53051
Telephone: 262-703-7000
Fax: 262-703-6373

Web Site: www.kohls.com
Officers: Sona Chawla - President, President-elect, Chief Operating Officer Michelle D. Gass - Chief Executive Officer, Chief Executive Officer-elect, Chief Customer Officer, Chief Merchandising Officer

Auditors: Ernst & Young LLP
Investor Contact: 262-703-1440
Transfer Agents: Wells Fargo Shareowner Services, St. Paul, MN

KOSMOS ENERGY LTD

Exchange	Symbol	Price	52Wk Range	Yield	P/E
NYS	KOS	$8.27 (6/29/2018)	8.53-5.30	N/A	N/A

*7 Year Price Score 63.17 *NYSE Composite Index=100 *12 Month Price Score 107.76

Interim Earnings (Per Share)

Qtr.	Mar	Jun	Sep	Dec
2015	(0.21)	(0.20)	0.15	0.07
2016	(0.15)	(0.28)	(0.15)	(0.15)
2017	(0.07)	(0.02)	(0.16)	(0.31)
2018	(0.13)	...	...	...

Interim Dividends (Per Share)

No Dividends Paid

Valuation Analysis

		Institutional Holding	
Forecast EPS	N/A	No of Institutions	197
Market Cap	$3.3 Billion	Shares	
Book Value	$843.4 Million	521,466,560	
Price/Book	3.88	% Held	
Price/Sales	5.35	84.23	

TRADING VOLUME (thousand shares)

Business Summary: Production & Extraction (MIC: 9.1.1 SIC: 1311 NAIC: 211111)

Kosmos Energy is a holding company. Through its subsidiaries, Co. operates as an oil and gas exploration and production company focused on areas along the Atlantic Margins. Co.'s assets include production and development projects offshore Ghana and Equatorial Guinea, discoveries and exploration potential offshore Mauritania and Senegal, and exploration licenses offshore Cote d'Ivoire, Equatorial Guinea, Morocco, Sao Tome and Principe, and Suriname. As of Dec 31 2017, Co. had total net proved developed and undeveloped reserves of 89,000,000 barrels of oil equivalent, consisting of 82,000,000 barrels of oil, condensate, and natural gas liquids, and 49,000,000,000 cubic feet of natural gas.

Recent Developments: For the year ended Dec 31 2017, net loss amounted to US$222.8 million versus a net loss of US$283.8 million in the prior year. Revenues were US$636.8 million, up 65.3% from US$385.4 million the year before. Direct operating expenses rose 6.3% to US$126.9 million from US$119.4 million in the comparable period the year before. Indirect operating expenses increased 22.7% to US$687.8 million from US$560.6 million in the equivalent prior-year period.

Prospects: Our evaluation of Kosmos Energy Ltd as of Jan. 21, 2018 is the result of our systematic analysis on three basic characteristics: earnings strength, relative valuation, and recent stock price movement. The company has produced a positive trend in earnings per share over the past 5 quarters. Because the company lacks sufficient analyst estimate data, we place greater weight on the historical EPS trend as the measure of earnings strength. Based on operating earnings yield, the company is overvalued when compared to all of the companies in our coverage universe. Share price changes over the past year indicates that KOS will perform poorly over the near term.

Financial Data
(US$ in Thousands)

	3 Mos	12/31/2017	12/31/2016	12/31/2015	12/31/2014	12/31/2013	12/31/2012	12/31/2011
Earnings Per Share	(0.62)	(0.57)	(0.74)	(0.18)	0.72	(0.24)	(0.18)	0.06
Cash Flow Per Share	0.63	0.61	0.13	1.15	1.17	1.39	1.00	1.03
Tang Book Value Per Share	2.13	2.30	2.80	3.44	3.46	2.56	2.65	2.61
Income Statement								
Total Revenue	127,177	636,836	385,355	471,556	882,738	852,428	672,209	676,780
EBITDA	(1,336)	150,892	(118,917)	269,245	812,116	326,465	264,963	321,454
Depn & Amortn	51,600	244,900	131,500	146,600	188,300	213,700	178,600	156,662
Income Before Taxes	(74,574)	(171,603)	(294,564)	85,436	578,268	75,954	34,156	99,043
Income Taxes	(24,348)	44,937	(10,784)	155,272	298,898	166,998	101,184	76,686
Net Income	(50,226)	(222,792)	(283,780)	(69,836)	279,370	(91,044)	(67,028)	22,357
Average Shares	395,600	388,375	385,402	382,610	386,119	376,819	371,847	354,810
Balance Sheet								
Current Assets	448,875	533,602	475,187	734,148	1,010,476	734,961	750,118	1,112,481
Total Assets	3,030,528	3,192,603	3,341,465	3,203,050	2,972,766	2,345,826	2,366,123	2,551,934
Current Liabilities	358,508	428,730	370,025	456,741	448,771	219,324	190,253	339,607
Long-Term Obligations	1,265,196	1,282,797	1,321,874	860,878	794,269	900,000	1,000,000	1,110,000
Total Liabilities	2,187,124	2,295,491	2,260,266	1,877,537	1,633,807	1,353,491	1,337,217	1,531,208
Stockholders' Equity	843,404	897,112	1,081,199	1,325,513	1,338,959	992,335	1,028,906	1,020,726
Shares Outstanding	395,716	389,410	386,757	385,090	386,887	387,574	388,691	390,530
Statistical Record								
Return on Assets %	N.M.	N.M.	N.M.	N.M.	10.51	N.M.	N.M.	1.05
Return on Equity %	N.M.	N.M.	N.M.	N.M.	23.97	N.M.	N.M.	3.23
EBITDA Margin %	N.M.	23.69	N.M.	57.10	92.00	38.30	39.42	47.50
Net Margin %	N.M.	N.M.	N.M.	N.M.	31.65	N.M.	N.M.	3.30
Asset Turnover	0.20	0.19	0.12	0.15	0.33	0.36	0.27	0.32
Current Ratio	1.25	1.24	1.28	1.61	2.25	3.35	3.94	3.28
Debt to Equity	1.50	1.43	1.22	0.65	0.59	0.91	0.97	1.09
Price Range	8.53-5.30	8.53-5.59	7.05-3.50	9.78-4.73	11.23-7.09	13.00-9.75	14.73-9.29	19.24-10.53
P/E Ratio	...	...	...	...	15.60-9.85	...	...	320.67-175.50

Address: Clarendon House, 2 Church Street, Hamilton, HM 11 Telephone: 441-295-5950	Web Site: www.kosmosenergy.com Officers: Andrew G. Inglis - Chairman, Chief Executive Officer Thomas P. Chambers - Senior Vice President, Chief Financial Officer	Auditors: Ernst & Young LLP Investor Contact: 214-445-9669 Transfer Agents: Computershare Trust Company, N.A., United States

KROGER CO (THE)

Exchange	Symbol	Price	52Wk Range	Yield	P/E	Div Acheiver
NYS	KR	$28.45 (6/29/2018)	31.34-19.94	1.97	N/A	11 Years

*7 Year Price Score 81.37   ***NYSE Composite Index=100**   ***12 Month Price Score 102.61**

Interim Earnings (Per Share)

Qtr.	May	Aug	Oct	Jan
2015-16	0.63	0.44	0.43	0.56
2016-17	0.70	0.40	0.41	0.53
2017-18	0.32	0.39	0.44	0.94
2018-19	2.37	...	...	...

Interim Dividends (Per Share)

Amt	Decl	Ex	Rec	Pay
0.125Q	09/14/2017	11/14/2017	11/15/2017	12/01/2017
0.125Q	01/19/2018	02/14/2018	02/15/2018	03/01/2018
0.125Q	03/15/2018	05/14/2018	05/15/2018	06/01/2018
0.14Q	06/28/2018	08/14/2018	08/15/2018	09/01/2018

Indicated Div: $0.56

Valuation Analysis / Institutional Holding

Valuation Analysis		Institutional Holding	
Forecast EPS	$2.11	No of Institutions	
	(06/07/2018)	1138	
Market Cap	$22.6 Billion	Shares	
Book Value	$7.0 Billion	866,210,304	
Price/Book	3.25	% Held	
Price/Sales	N/A	70.16	

TRADING VOLUME (thousand shares)

Business Summary: Retail - Food & Beverage, Drug & Tobacco (MIC: 2.1.2 SIC: 5411 NAIC: 445110)

Kroger operates supermarkets, multi-department stores, jewelry stores, and convenience stores. Co. also manufactures and processes some of the food for sale in its supermarkets. As of Feb 3 2018, Co. operated 2,782 supermarkets under a variety of local banner names in 35 states and the District of Columbia of which 2,268 have pharmacies and 1,489 have fuel centers. In addition to the supermarkets, Co. operated 782 convenience stores, 274 jewelry stores and an online retailer. The convenience stores provide a limited assortment of staple food items and general merchandise and, in most cases, sell fuel. Co. also operated 37 food production plants, primarily bakeries and dairies.

Recent Developments: For the quarter ended May 26 2018, net income increased 579.5% to US$2.02 billion from US$297.0 million in the year-earlier quarter. Revenues were US$37.53 billion, up 3.4% from US$36.29 billion the year before. Operating income was US$1.03 billion versus US$631.0 million in the prior-year quarter, an increase of 63.1%. Direct operating expenses rose 3.8% to US$29.36 billion from US$28.28 billion in the comparable period the year before. Indirect operating expenses decreased 3.2% to US$7.14 billion from US$7.37 billion in the equivalent prior-year period.

Prospects: Our evaluation of Kroger Co. as of Jan. 21, 2018 is the result of our systematic analysis on three basic characteristics: earnings strength, relative valuation, and recent stock price movement. The company has enjoyed a very positive trend in earnings per share over the past 5 quarters and while recent estimates for the company have been raised by analysts, KR has posted better than expected results. Based on operating earnings yield, the company is undervalued when compared to all of the companies in our coverage universe. Share price changes over the past year indicates that KR will perform very poorly over the near term.

Financial Data

(US$ in Thousands)	3 Mos	02/03/2018	01/28/2017	01/30/2016	01/31/2015	02/01/2014	02/02/2013	01/28/2012
Earnings Per Share	...	2.09	2.05	2.06	1.72	1.45	1.39	0.51
Cash Flow Per Share	...	3.75	4.55	5.02	4.26	3.30	2.61	2.26
Tang Book Value Per Share	3.70	3.34	2.72	3.15	2.41	2.51	2.89	2.53
Dividends Per Share	0.500	0.490	0.450	0.395	0.340	0.308	0.248	0.215
Dividend Payout %		23.44	21.95	19.17	19.77	21.21	17.87	42.57
Income Statement								
Total Revenue	37,530,000	122,662,000	115,337,000	109,830,000	108,465,000	98,375,000	96,751,000	90,374,000
EBITDA	3,567,000	4,521,000	5,776,000	5,665,000	5,085,000	4,428,000	4,416,000	2,916,000
Depn & Amortn	741,000	2,436,000	2,340,000	2,089,000	1,948,000	1,703,000	1,652,000	1,638,000
Income Before Taxes	2,634,000	1,484,000	2,914,000	3,094,000	2,649,000	2,282,000	2,302,000	843,000
Income Taxes	616,000	(405,000)	957,000	1,045,000	902,000	751,000	794,000	247,000
Net Income	2,026,000	1,907,000	1,975,000	2,039,000	1,728,000	1,519,000	1,497,000	602,000
Average Shares	846,000	904,000	958,000	980,000	994,000	1,040,000	1,074,000	1,186,000
Balance Sheet								
Current Assets	10,286,000	11,117,000	10,340,000	9,892,000	8,911,000	8,830,000	7,959,000	7,325,000
Total Assets	36,561,000	37,197,000	36,505,000	33,897,000	30,556,000	29,281,000	24,652,000	23,476,000
Current Liabilities	13,476,000	14,197,000	12,860,000	12,971,000	11,403,000	10,705,000	11,057,000	9,105,000
Long-Term Obligations	12,059,000	12,029,000	11,825,000	9,709,000	9,771,000	9,653,000	6,145,000	6,850,000
Total Liabilities	29,591,000	30,266,000	29,807,000	27,077,000	25,144,000	23,897,000	20,445,000	19,495,000
Stockholders' Equity	6,970,000	6,931,000	6,698,000	6,820,000	5,412,000	5,384,000	4,207,000	3,981,000
Shares Outstanding	796,000	870,000	924,000	967,000	974,000	1,016,000	1,028,000	1,122,000
Statistical Record								
Return on Assets %	...	5.09	5.63	6.34	5.79	5.65	6.12	2.57
Return on Equity %	...	27.53	29.30	33.43	32.10	31.76	35.97	13.01
EBITDA Margin %	9.50	3.69	5.01	5.16	4.69	4.50	4.56	3.23
Net Margin %	5.40	1.55	1.71	1.86	1.59	1.54	1.55	0.67
Asset Turnover	...	3.27	3.29	3.42	3.64	3.66	3.96	3.86
Current Ratio	0.76	0.78	0.80	0.76	0.78	0.82	0.72	0.80
Debt to Equity	1.73	1.74	1.77	1.42	1.81	1.79	1.46	1.72
Price Range	31.34-19.94	34.22-19.94	40.65-28.84	42.64-33.66	34.67-17.69	21.71-13.84	13.95-10.56	12.91-10.65
P/E Ratio	...	16.37-9.54	19.83-14.07	20.70-16.34	20.16-10.28	14.97-9.54	10.03-7.59	25.32-20.87
Average Yield %	2.04	1.87	1.30	1.05	1.33	1.68	2.07	1.82

Address: 1014 Vine Street, Cincinnati, OH 45202
Telephone: 513-762-4000
Fax: 513-762-1400

Web Site: www.thekrogerco.com
Officers: W. Rodney McMullen - Chairman, Vice-Chairman, President, Chief Executive Officer, Chief Operating Officer Michael J. Donnelly - Executive Vice President, Executive Vice President (frmr), Senior Vice President, Chief Operating Officer

Auditors: PricewaterhouseCoopers LLP
Investor Contact: 513-762-4366
Transfer Agents: Wells Fargo Shareowner Services, Saint Paul, MN

LABORATORY CORPORATION OF AMERICA HOLDINGS

Exchange	Symbol	Price	52Wk Range	Yield	P/E
NYS	LH	$179.53 (6/29/2018)	189.41-147.99	N/A	14.91

*7 Year Price Score 114.35 *NYSE Composite Index=100 *12 Month Price Score 108.53

Interim Earnings (Per Share)

Qtr.	Mar	Jun	Sep	Dec
2015	0.01	1.64	1.49	1.10
2016	1.55	1.91	1.71	1.77
2017	1.84	1.82	1.74	6.81
2018	1.67	...	...	...

Interim Dividends (Per Share)

No Dividends Paid

Valuation Analysis

	Institutional Holding	
Forecast EPS	$11.55	No of Institutions
	(06/14/2018)	1076
Market Cap	$18.3 Billion	Shares
Book Value	$7.0 Billion	121,629,536
Price/Book	2.62	% Held
Price/Sales	1.69	85.89

TRADING VOLUME (thousand shares)

Business Summary: Diagnostic & Health Related Services (MIC: 4.2.2 SIC: 8071 NAIC: 621511)
Laboratory Corporation of America Holdings is a life sciences company, providing clinical laboratory and end-to-end drug development services. Co. reports its business in two segments: LabCorp Diagnostics (LCD) and Covance Drug Development (CDD). LCD is an independent clinical laboratory business providing testing through an integrated network of primary and specialty laboratories supported by information technology system, logistics, local labs providing response testing and approximately 1,750 patient service centers located throughout the U.S. CDD provides a range of drug research and development and market access services to biopharmaceutical companies and medical device companies.

Recent Developments: For the quarter ended Mar 31 2018, net income decreased 5.9% to US$172.5 million from US$183.3 million in the year-earlier quarter. Revenues were US$2.85 billion, up 18.0% from US$2.41 billion the year before. Operating income was US$305.4 million versus US$318.1 million in the prior-year quarter, a decrease of 4.0%. Direct operating expenses rose 21.6% to US$2.07 billion from US$1.70 billion in the comparable period the year before. Indirect operating expenses increased 20.1% to US$473.6 million from US$394.4 million in the equivalent prior-year period.

Prospects: Our evaluation of Laboratory Corp. of America Holdings as of Jan. 21, 2018 is the result of our systematic analysis on three basic characteristics: earnings strength, relative valuation, and recent stock price movement. The company has enjoyed a very positive trend in earnings per share over the past 5 quarters and while recent estimates for the company have been mixed, LH has posted better than expected results. Based on operating earnings yield, the company is undervalued when compared to all of the companies in our coverage universe. Share price changes over the past year indicates that LH will perform in line with the market over the near term.

Financial Data

(US$ in Thousands)	3 Mos	12/31/2017	12/31/2016	12/31/2015	12/31/2014	12/31/2013	12/31/2012	12/31/2011
Earnings Per Share	12.04	12.21	7.02	4.34	5.91	6.25	5.99	5.11
Cash Flow Per Share	13.55	14.25	11.44	9.94	8.71	9.08	8.77	8.56
Income Statement								
Total Revenue	2,848,300	10,441,400	9,641,800	8,680,100	6,011,600	5,808,300	5,671,400	5,542,300
EBITDA	445,300	1,665,500	1,627,800	1,266,900	1,079,500	1,139,900	1,158,400	1,085,600
Depn & Amortn	142,800	306,800	311,100	269,900	157,600	144,700	141,100	141,500
Income Before Taxes	239,000	1,123,600	1,097,600	722,100	812,400	898,700	922,800	856,600
Income Taxes	69,000	(139,100)	372,300	294,100	314,100	340,200	359,400	333,000
Net Income	173,200	1,268,200	732,100	436,900	511,200	573,800	583,100	519,700
Average Shares	103,400	103,900	104,300	100,600	86,400	91,800	97,400	101,800
Balance Sheet								
Current Assets	2,896,600	2,682,600	2,478,700	2,663,000	1,692,700	1,432,100	1,391,800	1,084,800
Total Assets	16,831,700	16,568,000	14,247,000	14,221,700	7,301,800	6,965,900	6,795,000	6,136,600
Current Liabilities	2,104,000	2,046,100	1,827,600	1,701,500	976,300	735,700	1,028,500	797,400
Long-Term Obligations	6,359,300	6,344,600	5,300,000	5,992,100	2,682,700	2,889,100	2,175,000	2,085,500
Total Liabilities	9,847,700	9,738,000	8,741,200	9,277,300	4,481,300	4,474,600	4,077,600	3,633,100
Stockholders' Equity	6,984,000	6,830,000	5,505,800	4,944,400	2,820,500	2,491,300	2,717,400	2,503,500
Shares Outstanding	102,100	101,900	102,700	101,300	84,600	85,700	93,500	97,800
Statistical Record								
Return on Assets %	7.99	8.23	5.13	4.06	7.17	8.34	8.99	8.43
Return on Equity %	19.77	20.56	13.97	11.25	19.25	22.03	22.28	20.91
EBITDA Margin %	15.63	15.95	16.88	14.60	17.96	19.63	20.43	19.59
Net Margin %	6.08	12.15	7.59	5.03	8.50	9.88	10.28	9.38
Asset Turnover	0.69	0.68	0.68	0.81	0.84	0.84	0.87	0.90
Current Ratio	1.38	1.31	1.36	1.57	1.73	1.95	1.35	1.36
Debt to Equity	0.91	0.93	0.96	1.21	0.95	1.16	0.80	0.83
Price Range	178.11-137.51	163.95-129.07	140.98-100.94	128.18-106.86	109.58-87.86	107.39-86.41	95.25-82.37	100.83-75.99
P/E Ratio	14.79-11.42	13.43-10.57	20.08-14.38	29.53-24.62	18.54-14.87	17.18-13.83	15.90-13.75	19.73-14.87

Address: 358 South Main Street, Burlington, NC 27215 Telephone: 336-229-1127	Web Site: www.labcorp.com Officers: David P. King - Chairman, President, Chief Executive Officer Glenn A. Eisenberg - Executive Vice President, Chief Financial Officer, Principal Accounting Officer, Treasurer	Auditors: PricewaterhouseCoopers LLP Investor Contact: 336-436-5076 Transfer Agents: American Stock Transfer & Trust Company, Brooklyn, NY

L BRANDS, INC

Exchange	Symbol	Price	52Wk Range	Yield	P/E
NYS	LB	$36.88 (6/29/2018)	62.95-31.68	6.51	11.31

*7 Year Price Score 59.34 ***NYSE Composite Index=100** ***12 Month Price Score 77.98**

Interim Earnings (Per Share)

Qtr.	Apr	Jul	Oct	Jan
2015-16	0.84	0.68	0.55	2.14
2016-17	0.52	0.87	0.42	2.17
2017-18	0.33	0.48	0.30	2.31
2018-19	0.17	...	...	...

Interim Dividends (Per Share)

Amt	Decl	Ex	Rec	Pay
0.60Q	08/04/2017	08/17/2017	08/21/2017	09/01/2017
0.60Q	11/10/2017	11/22/2017	11/24/2017	12/08/2017
0.60Q	02/08/2018	02/22/2018	02/23/2018	03/09/2018
0.60Q	05/18/2018	05/31/2018	06/01/2018	06/15/2018

Indicated Div: $2.40 (Div. Reinv. Plan)

Valuation Analysis / Institutional Holding

Valuation Analysis		Institutional Holding	
Forecast EPS	$2.76	No of Institutions	796
	(06/14/2018)		
Market Cap	$10.3 Billion	Shares	252,893,952
Book Value	N/A	% Held	N/A
Price/Book	N/A		
Price/Sales	0.80		

Business Summary: Retail - Apparel and Accessories (MIC: 2.1.5 SIC: 5621 NAIC: 448120)

L Brands is a retailer of women's apparel, personal care, beauty and home fragrance categories. Co. sells its merchandise through company-owned retail stores in the U.S., Canada, the U.K. and Greater China, and through its websites and other channels. Co.'s other international operations are primarily through franchise, license and wholesale partners. Co. operates the following retail brands: Victoria's Secret, PINK, Bath & Body Works, La Senza, and Henri Bendel. Co. has three segments: Victoria's Secret, Bath & Body Works and Victoria's Secret and Bath & Body Works International. As of Feb 3 2018, Co. had a total of 3,075 company-owned retail stores in operation.

Recent Developments: For the quarter ended May 5 2018, net income decreased 48.9% to US$48.0 million from US$94.0 million in the year-earlier quarter. Revenues were US$2.63 billion, up 7.8% from US$2.44 billion the year before. Operating income was US$155.0 million versus US$209.0 million in the prior-year quarter, a decrease of 25.8%. Direct operating expenses rose 9.6% to US$1.68 billion from US$1.53 billion in the comparable period the year before. Indirect operating expenses increased 13.7% to US$789.0 million from US$694.0 million in the equivalent prior-year period.

Prospects: Our evaluation of L Brands, Inc. as of Jan. 21, 2018 is the result of our systematic analysis on three basic characteristics: earnings strength, relative valuation, and recent stock price movement. The company has enjoyed a very positive trend in earnings per share over the past 5 quarters. However, while recent estimates for the company have been mixed, LB has posted better than expected results. Based on operating earnings yield, the company is undervalued when compared to all of the companies in our coverage universe. Share price changes over the past year indicates that LB will perform well over the near term.

Financial Data
(US$ in Thousands)

	3 Mos	02/03/2018	01/28/2017	01/30/2016	01/31/2015	02/01/2014	02/02/2013	01/28/2012
Earnings Per Share	3.26	3.42	3.98	4.22	3.50	3.05	2.54	2.70
Cash Flow Per Share	4.73	4.87	6.60	6.44	6.13	4.32	4.58	4.18
Dividends Per Share	2.400	2.400	4.400	4.000	2.360	1.200	5.000	3.800
Dividend Payout %	73.62	70.18	110.55	94.79	67.43	39.34	196.85	140.74
Income Statement								
Total Revenue	2,626,000	12,632,000	12,574,000	12,154,000	11,454,000	10,773,000	10,459,000	10,364,000
EBITDA	294,000	2,289,000	2,608,000	2,725,000	2,398,000	2,166,000	1,983,000	1,860,000
Depn & Amortn	137,000	571,000	518,000	457,000	438,000	406,000	386,000	387,000
Income Before Taxes	59,000	1,312,000	1,696,000	1,934,000	1,636,000	1,446,000	1,281,000	1,227,000
Income Taxes	11,000	329,000	538,000	681,000	594,000	543,000	528,000	377,000
Net Income	48,000	983,000	1,158,000	1,253,000	1,042,000	903,000	753,000	850,000
Average Shares	282,000	287,000	291,000	297,000	298,000	296,000	297,000	314,000
Balance Sheet								
Current Assets	2,890,000	3,293,000	3,465,000	4,156,000	3,232,000	3,150,000	2,205,000	2,368,000
Total Assets	7,749,000	8,149,000	8,170,000	8,493,000	7,544,000	7,198,000	6,019,000	6,108,000
Current Liabilities	1,858,000	2,031,000	2,014,000	1,875,000	1,679,000	1,826,000	1,538,000	1,526,000
Long-Term Obligations	5,719,000	5,707,000	5,700,000	5,715,000	4,765,000	4,761,000	4,477,000	3,481,000
Total Liabilities	8,720,000	8,902,000	8,899,000	8,752,000	7,526,000	7,568,000	7,034,000	5,971,000
Stockholders' Equity	(971,000)	(753,000)	(729,000)	(259,000)	18,000	(370,000)	(1,015,000)	137,000
Shares Outstanding	278,000	280,000	286,000	290,000	292,000	291,000	289,000	295,000
Statistical Record								
Return on Assets %	11.99	11.85	13.94	15.67	14.18	13.70	12.22	13.57
Return on Equity %	...	...	...	...	...	...	...	105.68
EBITDA Margin %	11.20	18.12	20.74	22.42	20.94	20.11	18.96	17.95
Net Margin %	1.83	7.78	9.21	10.31	9.10	8.38	7.20	8.20
Asset Turnover	1.64	1.52	1.51	1.52	1.56	1.63	1.70	1.65
Current Ratio	1.56	1.62	1.72	2.22	1.92	1.73	1.43	1.55
Debt to Equity	...	...	...	...	264.72	...	...	25.41
Price Range	62.95-34.32	62.95-36.06	96.56-59.01	100.22-77.87	87.05-50.87	65.60-42.85	52.15-40.83	45.22-28.92
P/E Ratio	19.31-10.53	18.41-10.54	24.26-14.83	23.75-18.45	24.87-14.53	21.51-14.05	20.53-16.07	16.75-10.71
Average Yield %	5.22	4.92	5.98	4.41	3.62	2.21	10.58	10.00

Address: Three Limited Parkway, Columbus, OH 43230
Telephone: 614-415-7000

Web Site: www.lb.com
Officers: Leslie H. Wexner - Chairman, Chief Executive Officer Stuart B. Burgdoerfer - Executive Vice President, Chief Financial Officer

Auditors: Ernst & Young LLP
Investor Contact: 614-415-6400
Transfer Agents: American Stock Transfer & Trust Company, Brookly, NY

LAREDO PETROLEUM, INC

Exchange	Symbol	Price	52Wk Range	Yield	P/E
NYS	LPI	$9.62 (6/29/2018)	13.28-7.57	N/A	4.04

*7 Year Price Score N/A   *NYSE Composite Index=100   *12 Month Price Score 87.90

Interim Earnings (Per Share)

Qtr.	Mar	Jun	Sep	Dec
2015	0.00	(1.88)	(4.01)	(4.72)
2016	(0.85)	(0.33)	0.04	(0.07)
2017	0.28	0.25	0.05	1.72
2018	0.36	...	...	...

Interim Dividends (Per Share)

No Dividends Paid

Valuation Analysis

		Institutional Holding	
Forecast EPS	$1.14	No of Institutions	
	(06/14/2018)	246	
Market Cap	$2.3 Billion	Shares	
Book Value	$941.8 Million	345,598,752	
Price/Book	2.43	% Held	
Price/Sales	2.57	N/A	

TRADING VOLUME (thousand shares)

Business Summary: Production & Extraction (MIC: 9.1.1 SIC: 1311 NAIC: 211111)

Laredo Petroleum is an independent energy company focused on the acquisition, exploration and development of oil and natural gas properties, and the transportation of oil and natural gas from such properties. Co. operates through two segments: exploration and production of oil and natural gas properties, which is conducted by Co. through the exploration and development of its acreage in the Permian Basin; and midstream and marketing, which buys, sells, gathers and transports oil, natural gas and water through Co.'s subsidiary, Laredo Midstream Services, LLC. As of Dec 31 2017, Co.'s total estimated proved reserves were 215.9 million barrels of oil equivalent, of which 89.0% were developed.

Recent Developments: For the quarter ended Mar 31 2018, net income increased 26.7% to US$86.5 million from US$68.3 million in the year-earlier quarter. Revenues were US$259.7 million, up 37.4% from US$189.0 million the year before. Operating income was US$93.2 million versus US$51.3 million in the prior-year quarter, an increase of 81.6%. Direct operating expenses rose 23.6% to US$95.1 million from US$76.9 million in the comparable period the year before. Indirect operating expenses increased 17.5% to US$71.4 million from US$60.7 million in the equivalent prior-year period.

Prospects: Our evaluation of Laredo Petroleum, Inc. as of Jan. 21, 2018 is the result of our systematic analysis on three basic characteristics: earnings strength, relative valuation, and recent stock price movement. The company has suffered a very negative trend in earnings per share over the past 5 quarters and while recent estimates for the company have been raised by analysts, LPI has posted results that fell short of analysts expectations. Based on operating earnings yield, the company is undervalued when compared to all of the companies in our coverage universe. Share price changes over the past year indicates that LPI will perform very poorly over the near term.

Financial Data

(US$ in Thousands)	3 Mos	12/31/2017	12/31/2016	12/31/2015	12/31/2014	12/31/2013	12/31/2012	12/31/2011
Earnings Per Share	2.38	2.29	(1.16)	(11.10)	1.85	0.88	0.48	0.98
Cash Flow Per Share	1.96	1.61	1.58	1.59	3.53	2.75	2.96	3.21
Tang Book Value Per Share	3.95	3.16	0.75	0.61	10.88	8.92	6.48	5.96
Income Statement								
Total Revenue	259,696	822,162	597,378	606,640	793,885	665,257	588,080	510,270
EBITDA	100,378	636,761	(171,119)	(2,284,387)	556,030	295,619	183,416	217,800
Depn & Amortn	793	5,900	5,900	6,500	5,100	4,400	3,300	2,400
Income Before Taxes	86,520	542,289	(270,142)	(2,393,680)	430,051	191,055	94,603	164,928
Income Taxes	...	1,800	...	(176,945)	164,286	74,507	32,949	59,374
Net Income	86,520	548,974	(260,739)	(2,209,936)	265,573	118,000	61,654	105,554
Average Shares	239,319	240,122	225,512	199,158	143,554	134,378	128,171	108,099
Balance Sheet								
Current Assets	185,193	235,382	154,777	332,232	365,253	307,609	137,437	122,938
Total Assets	2,087,531	2,023,289	1,782,346	1,813,287	3,932,549	2,623,760	2,338,304	1,627,652
Current Liabilities	239,666	277,419	187,945	216,815	425,025	253,969	262,068	214,361
Long-Term Obligations	847,300	791,855	1,353,909	1,416,226	1,801,295	1,051,538	1,216,760	636,961
Total Liabilities	1,145,701	1,257,710	1,601,773	1,681,840	2,369,348	1,351,504	1,506,581	867,639
Stockholders' Equity	941,830	765,579	180,573	131,447	1,563,201	1,272,256	831,723	760,013
Shares Outstanding	238,320	242,521	241,929	213,808	143,686	142,671	128,298	127,617
Statistical Record								
Return on Assets %	29.04	28.85	N.M.	N.M.	8.10	4.76	3.10	7.83
Return on Equity %	94.95	116.04	N.M.	N.M.	18.73	11.22	7.73	18.03
EBITDA Margin %	38.65	77.45	N.M.	N.M.	70.04	44.44	31.19	42.68
Net Margin %	33.32	66.77	N.M.	N.M.	33.45	17.74	10.48	20.69
Asset Turnover	0.46	0.43	0.33	0.21	0.24	0.27	0.30	0.38
Current Ratio	0.77	0.85	0.82	1.53	0.86	1.21	0.52	0.57
Debt to Equity	0.90	1.03	7.50	10.77	1.15	0.83	1.46	0.84
Price Range	14.83-7.57	15.21-9.49	15.99-4.10	15.80-7.05	30.98-7.39	33.52-15.95	26.80-17.41	22.30-18.10
P/E Ratio	6.23-3.18	6.64-4.14	...	...	16.75-3.99	38.09-18.13	55.83-36.27	22.76-18.47

Address: 15 W. Sixth Street, Suite 900, Tulsa, OK 74119 Telephone: 918-513-4570	Web Site: www.laredopetro.com Officers: Randy A. Foutch - Chairman, Chief Executive Officer Richard C. Buterbaugh - Chief Financial Officer, Executive Vice President, Associate/Affiliate Company Officer	Auditors: Grant Thornton LLP Investor Contact: 918-858-5504 Transfer Agents: American Stock Transfer and Trust Company, Brooklyn, NY

LAS VEGAS SANDS CORP

Exchange	Symbol	Price	52Wk Range	Yield	P/E
NYS	LVS	$76.36 (6/29/2018)	81.27-59.66	3.93	15.97

*7 Year Price Score 98.02 *NYSE Composite Index=100 *12 Month Price Score 110.73

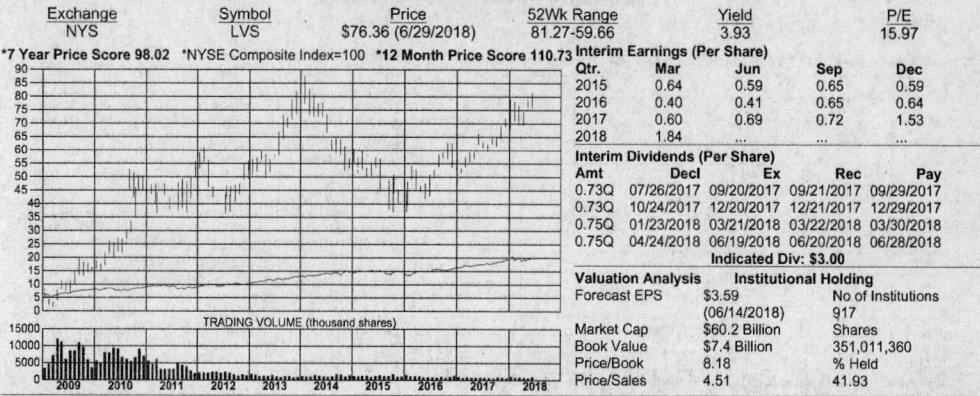

Interim Earnings (Per Share)

Qtr.	Mar	Jun	Sep	Dec
2015	0.64	0.59	0.65	0.59
2016	0.40	0.41	0.65	0.64
2017	0.60	0.69	0.72	1.53
2018	1.84	...	...	...

Interim Dividends (Per Share)

Amt	Decl	Ex	Rec	Pay
0.73Q	07/26/2017	09/20/2017	09/21/2017	09/29/2017
0.73Q	10/24/2017	12/20/2017	12/21/2017	12/29/2017
0.75Q	01/23/2018	03/21/2018	03/22/2018	03/30/2018
0.75Q	04/24/2018	06/19/2018	06/20/2018	06/28/2018

Indicated Div: $3.00

Valuation Analysis — **Institutional Holding**

Forecast EPS	$3.59	No of Institutions	
	(06/14/2018)	917	
Market Cap	$60.2 Billion	Shares	
Book Value	$7.4 Billion	351,011,360	
Price/Book	8.18	% Held	
Price/Sales	4.51	41.93	

Business Summary: Hotels, Restaurants & Travel (MIC: 2.2.1 SIC: 7011 NAIC: 721120)

Las Vegas Sands is a developer of destination properties (integrated resorts) that feature accommodations, gaming, entertainment and retail, convention and exhibition facilities, restaurants and other amenities. Through its 70.1% ownership of Sands China Ltd., Co. owns and operates resort properties, including The Venetian Macao Resort Hotel, Sands Cotai Central, the Four Seasons Hotel Macao, Cotai Strip and the Plaza Casino, and the Sands Macao. In Singapore, Co. owns and operates the Marina Bay Sands, while its properties in the U.S. include The Venetian Resort Hotel Casino and The Palazzo Resort Hotel Casino, the Sands Expo and Convention Center and the Sands Casino Resort Bethlehem.

Recent Developments: For the quarter ended Mar 31 2018, net income increased 179.1% to US$1.62 billion from US$579.0 million in the year-earlier quarter. Revenues were US$3.58 billion, up 16.7% from US$3.07 billion the year before. Operating income was US$1.16 billion versus US$764.0 million in the prior-year quarter, an increase of 51.6%. Direct operating expenses rose 13.1% to US$1.75 billion from US$1.55 billion in the comparable period the year before. Indirect operating expenses decreased 11.3% to US$667.0 million from US$752.0 million in the equivalent prior-year period.

Prospects: Our evaluation of Las Vegas Sands Corp. as of Jan. 21, 2018 is the result of our systematic analysis on three basic characteristics: earnings strength, relative valuation, and recent stock price movement. The company has generated a negative trend in earnings per share over the past 5 quarters and while recent estimates for the company have been raised by analysts, LVS has posted better than expected results. Based on operating earnings yield, the company is about fairly valued when compared to all of the companies in our coverage universe. Share price changes over the past year indicates that LVS will perform in line with the market over the near term.

Financial Data

(US$ in Thousands)	3 Mos	12/31/2017	12/31/2016	12/31/2015	12/31/2014	12/31/2013	12/31/2012	12/31/2011
Earnings Per Share	4.78	3.54	2.10	2.47	3.52	2.79	1.85	1.56
Cash Flow Per Share	6.31	5.74	5.07	4.33	6.00	5.40	3.78	3.66
Tang Book Value Per Share	9.22	8.11	7.64	8.49	8.93	9.24	8.48	10.60
Dividends Per Share	2.940	2.920	2.880	2.600	2.000	1.400	3.750	...
Dividend Payout %	61.51	82.49	137.14	105.26	56.82	50.18	202.70	...
Income Statement								
Total Revenue	3,579,000	12,882,000	11,410,000	11,688,461	14,583,849	13,769,885	11,131,132	9,410,745
EBITDA	1,148,000	4,609,000	3,708,000	3,949,486	5,200,486	4,498,054	3,275,631	3,239,918
Depn & Amortn	19,000	1,246,000	1,189,000	1,077,469	1,119,237	1,099,668	977,743	876,540
Income Before Taxes	1,045,000	3,052,000	2,255,000	2,621,882	3,832,711	3,143,512	2,062,576	2,094,823
Income Taxes	(571,000)	(209,000)	239,000	236,185	244,640	188,836	180,763	211,704
Net Income	1,456,000	2,806,000	1,670,000	1,966,236	2,840,629	2,305,997	1,524,093	1,560,123
Average Shares	790,000	792,000	795,000	797,596	808,019	826,316	824,556	811,816
Balance Sheet								
Current Assets	3,394,000	3,207,000	3,098,000	3,609,250	5,190,499	5,515,539	4,477,514	5,397,152
Total Assets	21,504,000	20,687,000	20,469,000	20,987,421	22,361,691	22,724,264	22,163,652	22,244,123
Current Liabilities	2,874,000	2,948,000	2,806,000	2,464,135	2,712,494	3,129,665	2,622,823	2,498,706
Long-Term Obligations	9,508,000	9,344,000	9,428,000	9,372,645	9,892,913	9,382,752	10,132,265	9,577,131
Total Liabilities	14,141,000	14,194,000	14,292,000	14,170,680	15,148,105	15,058,770	15,101,810	14,393,434
Stockholders' Equity	7,363,000	6,493,000	6,177,000	6,816,741	7,213,586	7,665,494	7,061,842	7,850,689
Shares Outstanding	789,000	789,484	794,960	794,645	798,258	818,702	824,297	733,249
Statistical Record								
Return on Assets %	18.21	13.64	8.03	9.07	12.60	10.27	6.85	7.21
Return on Equity %	56.62	44.29	25.63	28.03	38.18	31.32	20.38	20.78
EBITDA Margin %	32.08	35.78	32.50	33.79	35.66	32.67	29.43	34.43
Net Margin %	40.68	21.78	14.64	16.82	19.48	16.75	13.69	16.58
Asset Turnover	0.64	0.63	0.55	0.54	0.65	0.61	0.50	0.43
Current Ratio	1.18	1.09	1.10	1.46	1.91	1.76	1.71	2.16
Debt to Equity	1.29	1.44	1.53	1.37	1.37	1.22	1.43	1.22
Price Range	79.03-55.56	71.97-51.69	62.84-36.97	60.56-36.98	87.81-52.31	78.87-46.16	61.05-36.41	50.60-36.34
P/E Ratio	16.53-11.62	20.33-14.60	29.92-17.60	24.52-14.97	24.95-14.86	28.27-16.54	33.00-19.68	32.44-23.29
Average Yield %	4.50	4.80	5.69	5.08	2.81	2.35	7.91	...

Address: 3355 Las Vegas Boulevard South, Las Vegas, NV 89109 **Telephone:** 702-414-1000	**Web Site:** www.sands.com **Officers:** Sheldon Gary Adelson - Chairman, Chief Executive Officer, Treasurer George Tanasijevich - Managing Director	**Auditors:** DELOITTE & TOUCHE LLP **Transfer Agents:** American Stock Transfer & Trust Company, New York, NY

LASALLE HOTEL PROPERTIES

Exchange	Symbol	Price	52Wk Range	Yield	P/E
NYS	LHO	$34.23 (6/29/2018)	35.64-24.41	2.63	44.45

*7 Year Price Score 81.31 *NYSE Composite Index=100 *12 Month Price Score 112.13

Interim Earnings (Per Share)

Qtr.	Mar	Jun	Sep	Dec
2015	0.00	0.49	0.39	0.21
2016	0.05	0.49	1.34	0.19
2017	0.67	0.49	0.27	0.11
2018	(0.10)	...	...	...

Interim Dividends (Per Share)

Amt	Decl	Ex	Rec	Pay
0.45Q	09/15/2017	09/28/2017	09/29/2017	10/16/2017
0.45Q	12/15/2017	12/28/2017	12/29/2017	01/16/2018
0.45Q	03/15/2018	03/28/2018	03/29/2018	04/16/2018
0.225Q	06/15/2018	06/28/2018	06/29/2018	07/16/2018

Indicated Div: $0.90

Valuation Analysis

		Institutional Holding	
Forecast EPS	$0.54	No of Institutions	
	(06/12/2018)	362	
Market Cap	$3.8 Billion	Shares	
Book Value	$2.3 Billion	146,802,256	
Price/Book	1.61	% Held	
Price/Sales	3.52	105.52	

Business Summary: REITs (MIC: 5.3.1 SIC: 6798 NAIC: 525930)

LaSalle Hotel Properties is a self-administered and self-managed real estate investment trust. Co. primarily buys, owns, redevelops and leases full-service hotels located in convention, resort and urban business markets. As of Dec 31 2017, Co. owned interests in 41 hotels located in seven states and the District of Columbia. Substantially all of Co.'s assets are held directly or indirectly by, and all of its operations are conducted through, the LaSalle Hotel Operating Partnership, L.P. (Operating Partnership). Co. owned, through a combination of direct and indirect interests, 99.9% of the common units of the Operating Partnership at Dec 31 2017.

Recent Developments: For the quarter ended Mar 31 2018, loss from continuing operations was US$7.0 million compared with income of US$7.2 million in the year-earlier quarter. Net loss amounted to US$7.0 million versus net income of US$81.6 million in the year-earlier quarter. Revenues were US$223.0 million, down 12.3% from US$254.4 million the year before.

Prospects: Our evaluation of LaSalle Hotel Properties as of Jan. 21, 2018 is the result of our systematic analysis on three basic characteristics: earnings strength, relative valuation, and recent stock price movement. The company has managed to produce a neutral trend in earnings per share over the past 5 quarters. Because the company lacks sufficient analyst estimate data, we place greater weight on the historical EPS trend as the measure of earnings strength. Based on operating earnings yield, the company is about fairly valued when compared to all of the companies in our coverage universe. Share price changes over the past year indicates that LHO will perform poorly over the near term.

Financial Data
(US$ in Thousands)

	3 Mos	12/31/2017	12/31/2016	12/31/2015	12/31/2014	12/31/2013	12/31/2012	12/31/2011
Earnings Per Share	0.77	1.54	2.07	1.09	1.88	0.73	0.52	0.16
Cash Flow Per Share	2.41	2.49	3.18	3.00	2.72	2.53	2.52	2.04
Tang Book Value Per Share	21.27	21.84	22.62	21.02	21.64	20.23	19.41	21.07
Dividends Per Share	1.800	1.800	1.800	1.725	1.405	0.960	0.710	0.440
Dividend Payout %	233.77	116.88	86.96	158.26	74.73	131.51	136.54	275.00
Income Statement								
Total Revenue	223,023	1,104,815	1,227,619	1,216,584	1,109,778	977,293	867,075	719,007
EBITDA	45,859	326,068	386,454	377,099	340,212	287,844	254,179	201,699
Depn & Amortn	47,524	177,800	191,791	191,167	162,798	149,282	125,127	112,175
Income Before Taxes	(10,991)	111,470	154,441	134,537	122,598	90,725	80,639	49,868
Income Taxes	(4,027)	1,699	5,784	(1,292)	2,306	470	9,062	7,048
Net Income	(6,962)	195,034	252,781	135,552	212,845	89,935	71,296	43,617
Average Shares	112,163	113,364	113,164	113,096	104,545	97,228	85,897	81,326
Balance Sheet								
Current Assets	273,731	450,845	185,090	71,181	166,039	63,773	80,989	60,954
Total Assets	3,656,589	3,814,941	3,944,079	4,074,817	3,699,949	3,581,038	3,256,570	2,833,275
Current Liabilities	228,002	218,359	263,766	267,540	230,473	216,513	145,420	110,635
Long-Term Obligations	1,078,012	1,120,121	1,118,707	1,429,794	1,021,090	1,255,062	1,252,220	951,397
Total Liabilities	1,309,266	1,341,790	1,386,014	1,700,550	1,258,240	1,477,647	1,403,444	1,067,662
Stockholders' Equity	2,347,323	2,473,151	2,558,065	2,374,267	2,441,709	2,103,391	1,853,126	1,765,613
Shares Outstanding	110,379	113,209	113,088	112,959	112,824	103,963	95,445	83,786
Statistical Record								
Return on Assets %	2.80	5.03	6.29	3.49	5.85	2.63	2.34	1.68
Return on Equity %	4.32	7.75	10.22	5.63	9.37	4.55	3.93	2.72
EBITDA Margin %	20.56	29.51	31.48	31.00	30.66	29.45	29.31	28.05
Net Margin %	N.M.	17.65	20.59	11.14	19.18	9.20	8.22	6.07
Asset Turnover	0.28	0.28	0.31	0.31	0.30	0.29	0.28	0.28
Current Ratio	1.20	2.06	0.70	0.27	0.72	0.29	0.56	0.55
Debt to Equity	0.46	0.45	0.44	0.60	0.42	0.60	0.68	0.54
Price Range	31.60-24.41	31.65-27.60	30.91-20.15	43.47-25.10	41.64-28.89	32.13-23.36	30.12-22.57	29.38-15.72
P/E Ratio	41.04-31.70	20.55-17.92	14.93-9.73	39.88-23.03	22.15-15.37	44.01-32.00	57.92-43.40	183.63-98.25
Average Yield %	6.29	6.17	7.16	4.99	4.05	3.50	2.65	1.80

Address: 7550 Wisconsin Avenue, 10th Floor, Bethesda, MD 20814	**Web Site:** www.lasallehotels.com	**Auditors:** KPMG LLP
Telephone: 301-941-1500	**Officers:** Stuart L. Scott - Acting Chairman Michael D. Barnello - President, Chief Executive Officer	**Investor Contact:** 301-941-1516
Fax: 301-941-1553		**Transfer Agents:** Wells Fargo Bank, N.A., Saint Paul, MN

LAUDER (ESTEE) COS., INC. (THE)

Exchange	Symbol	Price	52Wk Range	Yield	P/E
NYS	EL	$142.69 (6/29/2018)	158.03-93.86	1.07	46.48

*7 Year Price Score 125.97 *NYSE Composite Index=100 ***12 Month Price Score 113.62**

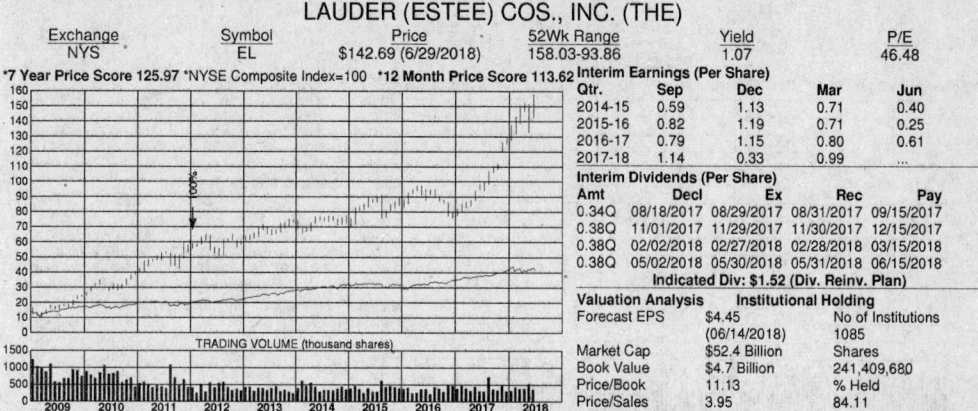

Interim Earnings (Per Share)

Qtr.	Sep	Dec	Mar	Jun
2014-15	0.59	1.13	0.71	0.40
2015-16	0.82	1.19	0.71	0.25
2016-17	0.79	1.15	0.80	0.61
2017-18	1.14	0.33	0.99	...

Interim Dividends (Per Share)

Amt	Decl	Ex	Rec	Pay
0.34Q	08/18/2017	08/29/2017	08/31/2017	09/15/2017
0.38Q	11/01/2017	11/29/2017	11/30/2017	12/15/2017
0.38Q	02/02/2018	02/27/2018	02/28/2018	03/15/2018
0.38Q	05/02/2018	05/29/2018	05/31/2018	06/15/2018

Indicated Div: $1.52 (Div. Reinv. Plan)

Valuation Analysis / **Institutional Holding**

Forecast EPS	$4.45	No of Institutions
	(06/14/2018)	1085
Market Cap	$52.4 Billion	Shares
Book Value	$4.7 Billion	241,409,680
Price/Book	11.13	% Held
Price/Sales	3.95	84.11

Business Summary: Household & Personal Products (MIC: 1.7.1 SIC: 2844 NAIC: 325620)

Estee Lauder Companies is a manufacturer and marketer of skin care, makeup, fragrance and hair care products. Co.'s products are sold under a number of brand names including: Estee Lauder, Clinique, Origins, M.A.C, Bobbi Brown, La Mer, Jo Malone London, Aveda and Too Faced. Co. is also the licensee for fragrances and/or cosmetics sold under various designer brand names, including Tommy Hilfiger, Donna Karan New York, DKNY, Michael Kors and Tom Ford. Additionally, Co. manufactures and sells products under the Prescriptives, RODIN olio lusso and FLIRT! brands. Co. also develops and sells products under a license from Kiton.

Recent Developments: For the quarter ended Mar 31 2018, net income increased 24.7% to US$374.0 million from US$300.0 million in the year-earlier quarter. Revenues were US$3.37 billion, up 18.0% from US$2.86 billion the year before. Operating income was US$497.0 million versus US$427.0 million in the prior-year quarter, an increase of 16.4%. Direct operating expenses rose 15.6% to US$683.0 million from US$591.0 million in the comparable period the year before. Indirect operating expenses increased 19.1% to US$2.19 billion from US$1.84 billion in the equivalent prior-year period.

Prospects: Our evaluation of Lauder (Estee) Cos. Inc. as of Jan. 21, 2018 is the result of our systematic analysis on three basic characteristics: earnings strength, relative valuation, and recent stock price movement. The company has produced a positive trend in earnings per share over the past 5 quarters. However, while recent estimates for the company have been mixed, EL has posted better than expected results. Based on operating earnings yield, the company is about fairly valued when compared to all of the companies in our coverage universe. Share price changes over the past year indicates that EL will perform very well over the near term.

Financial Data

(US$ in Thousands)	9 Mos	6 Mos	3 Mos	06/30/2017	06/30/2016	06/30/2015	06/30/2014	06/30/2013
Earnings Per Share	3.07	2.88	3.70	3.35	2.96	2.82	3.06	2.58
Cash Flow Per Share	6.74	6.58	5.55	4.90	4.82	5.12	3.98	3.16
Tang Book Value Per Share	4.05	3.63	4.05	3.10	5.44	5.79	7.32	5.76
Dividends Per Share	1.440	1.400	1.360	1.320	1.140	0.920	0.780	1.080
Dividend Payout %	46.91	48.61	36.76	39.40	38.51	32.62	25.49	41.86
Income Statement								
Total Revenue	10,388,000	7,018,000	3,274,000	11,824,000	11,262,300	10,780,400	10,968,800	10,181,700
EBITDA	2,117,000	1,504,000	680,000	2,120,000	2,011,500	2,006,300	2,205,700	1,878,900
Depn & Amortn	342,000	226,000	112,000	428,000	401,200	400,000	378,100	329,800
Income Before Taxes	1,719,000	1,239,000	549,000	1,617,000	1,555,200	1,560,600	1,776,800	1,475,200
Income Taxes	790,000	684,000	119,000	361,000	434,400	467,200	567,700	451,400
Net Income	922,000	550,000	427,000	1,249,000	1,114,600	1,088,900	1,204,100	1,019,800
Average Shares	375,700	376,100	375,400	373,000	376,600	385,700	393,100	394,900
Balance Sheet								
Current Assets	6,169,000	5,975,000	5,507,000	4,964,000	4,225,100	4,468,500	4,825,200	4,297,200
Total Assets	12,772,000	12,604,000	12,202,000	11,568,000	9,223,300	8,239,200	7,868,800	7,145,200
Current Liabilities	3,388,000	3,403,000	3,142,000	2,823,000	2,680,500	2,135,600	2,056,700	1,934,600
Long-Term Obligations	3,363,000	3,374,000	3,383,000	3,383,000	1,910,000	1,607,500	1,324,700	1,326,000
Total Liabilities	8,061,000	8,039,000	7,471,000	7,184,000	5,651,400	4,596,000	4,013,900	3,858,300
Stockholders' Equity	4,711,000	4,565,000	4,731,000	4,384,000	3,571,900	3,643,200	3,854,900	3,286,900
Shares Outstanding	367,301	368,073	368,522	368,103	367,759	374,882	382,884	387,994
Statistical Record								
Return on Assets %	9.51	9.04	12.83	12.01	12.73	13.52	16.04	14.85
Return on Equity %	26.07	25.77	32.95	31.40	30.81	29.04	33.72	33.88
EBITDA Margin %	20.38	21.43	20.77	17.93	17.86	18.61	20.11	18.45
Net Margin %	8.88	7.84	13.04	10.56	9.90	10.10	10.98	10.02
Asset Turnover	1.10	1.07	1.14	1.14	1.29	1.34	1.46	1.48
Current Ratio	1.82	1.76	1.75	1.76	1.58	2.09	2.35	2.22
Debt to Equity	0.71	0.74	0.72	0.77	0.53	0.44	0.34	0.40
Price Range	149.72-83.50	129.62-77.33	110.35-75.84	98.19-75.84	97.13-75.73	90.22-70.40	76.77-64.71	71.80-50.56
P/E Ratio	48.77-27.20	45.01-26.85	29.82-20.50	29.31-22.64	32.81-25.58	31.99-24.96	25.09-21.15	27.83-19.60
Average Yield %	1.28	1.41	1.52	1.52	1.30	1.17	1.10	1.73

Address: 767 Fifth Avenue, New York, NY 10153
Telephone: 212-572-4200

Web Site: www.elcompanies.com
Officers: William P. Lauder - Executive Chairman
Leonard A. Lauder - Chairman Emeritus, Chairman

Auditors: KPMG LLP
Investor Contact: 800-308-2334
Transfer Agents: Computershare, Providence, RI

LAZARD LTD

Exchange	Symbol	Price	52Wk Range	Yield	P/E	Div Acheiver
NYS	LAZ	$48.91 (6/29/2018)	59.40-40.66	3.60	21.27	10 Years

*7 Year Price Score 99.09 ***NYSE Composite Index=100** ***12 Month Price Score 103.38**

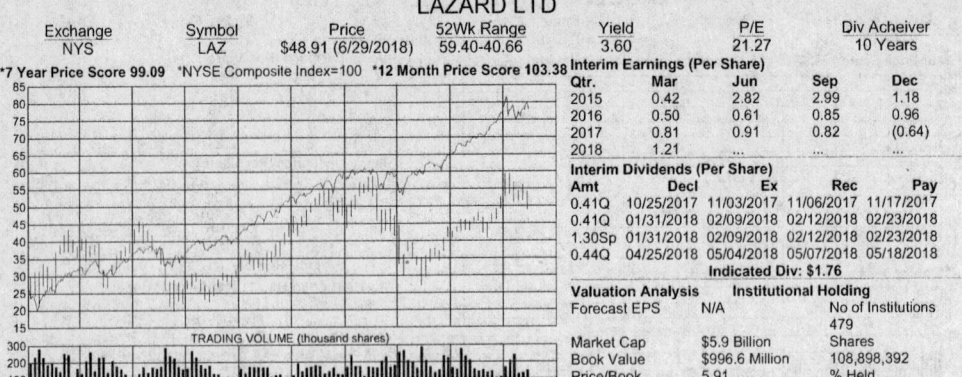

Interim Earnings (Per Share)

Qtr.	Mar	Jun	Sep	Dec
2015	0.42	2.82	2.99	1.18
2016	0.50	0.61	0.85	0.96
2017	0.81	0.91	0.82	(0.64)
2018	1.21	...	...	...

Interim Dividends (Per Share)

Amt	Decl	Ex	Rec	Pay
0.41Q	10/25/2017	11/03/2017	11/06/2017	11/17/2017
0.41Q	01/31/2018	02/09/2018	02/12/2018	02/23/2018
1.30Sp	01/31/2018	02/09/2018	02/12/2018	02/23/2018
0.44Q	04/25/2018	05/04/2018	05/07/2018	05/18/2018

Indicated Div: $1.76

Valuation Analysis

		Institutional Holding	
Forecast EPS	N/A	No of Institutions	479
Market Cap	$5.9 Billion	Shares	108,898,392
Book Value	$996.6 Million	% Held	87.66
Price/Book	5.91		
Price/Sales	2.08		

Business Summary: Finance Intermediaries & Services (MIC: 5.5.1 SIC: 6282 NAIC: 523930)

Lazard is a financial advisory and asset management firm. Co. focuses primarily on two business segments: Financial Advisory, which provides a range of financial advisory services regarding mergers and acquisitions and other strategic matters, restructurings, capital structure, capital raising and various other financial matters; and Asset Management, which provides a range of global investment solutions and investment management services in equity and fixed income strategies, alternative investments and private equity funds to corporations, public funds, sovereign entities, endowments and foundations, labor funds, financial intermediaries and private clients.

Recent Developments: For the quarter ended Mar 31 2018, net income increased 46.4% to US$161.7 million from US$110.4 million in the year-earlier quarter. Revenues were US$768.2 million, up 20.5% from US$637.4 million the year before. Operating income was US$185.8 million versus US$150.2 million in the prior-year quarter, an increase of 23.7%. Direct operating expenses declined 3.2% to US$13.5 million from US$14.0 million in the comparable period the year before. Indirect operating expenses increased 20.2% to US$568.9 million from US$473.3 million in the equivalent prior-year period.

Prospects: Our evaluation of Lazard Ltd. as of Dec. 31, 2017 is the result of our systematic analysis on three basic characteristics: earnings strength, relative valuation, and recent stock price movement. The company has managed to produce a neutral trend in earnings per share over the past 5 quarters. However, while recent estimates for the company have been lowered by analysts, LAZ has posted better than expected results. Based on operating earnings yield, the company is undervalued when compared to all of the companies in our coverage universe. Share price changes over the past year indicates that LAZ will perform very well over the near term.

Financial Data
(US$ in Thousands)

	3 Mos	12/31/2017	12/31/2016	12/31/2015	12/31/2014	12/31/2013	12/31/2012	12/31/2011
Earnings Per Share	2.30	1.91	2.92	7.40	3.20	1.21	0.65	1.36
Cash Flow Per Share	7.36	8.35	4.81	7.08	6.02	4.36	4.11	3.37
Tang Book Value Per Share	5.05	6.79	6.99	7.86	2.94	1.63	1.53	2.79
Dividends Per Share	2.940	2.810	2.690	2.350	1.200	1.000	1.160	0.605
Dividend Payout %	127.83	147.12	92.12	31.76	37.50	82.64	178.46	44.49
Income Statement								
Total Revenue	768,205	2,697,829	2,383,663	2,404,767	2,363,017	2,064,733	1,994,013	1,919,638
EBITDA	287,586	866,458	585,972	21,986	560,316	261,671	163,099	271,994
Depn & Amortn	101,758	41,012	68,511	38,606	40,851	44,864	39,214	36,495
Income Before Taxes	185,828	825,446	517,461	(16,620)	519,465	216,807	123,885	235,499
Income Taxes	24,167	565,599	123,769	(1,009,552)	85,402	51,693	31,100	44,940
Net Income	159,692	253,583	387,698	986,373	427,277	160,212	84,309	174,917
Average Shares	132,142	132,479	132,633	133,244	133,813	133,737	129,325	137,629
Balance Sheet								
Current Assets	2,538,474	3,026,422	2,245,765	2,054,105	1,875,226	1,661,082	1,685,959	1,869,789
Total Assets	4,485,095	4,928,677	4,556,508	4,486,766	3,332,236	3,011,137	2,986,893	3,081,936
Current Liabilities	1,287,457	1,709,667	1,113,149	1,186,512	942,468	803,528	740,989	678,015
Long-Term Obligations	1,190,830	1,190,383	1,195,805	1,007,378	1,060,365	1,064,184	1,094,713	1,096,934
Total Liabilities	3,488,534	3,728,874	3,320,521	3,173,311	2,625,492	2,450,928	2,417,237	2,355,793
Stockholders' Equity	996,561	1,199,803	1,235,987	1,313,455	706,744	560,209	569,656	726,143
Shares Outstanding	120,406	119,018	122,137	125,512	122,315	120,739	115,413	119,517
Statistical Record								
Return on Assets %	6.89	5.35	8.55	25.23	13.47	5.34	2.77	5.38
Return on Equity %	28.44	20.82	30.33	97.65	67.45	28.36	12.98	25.38
EBITDA Margin %	37.44	32.12	24.58	0.91	23.71	12.67	8.18	14.17
Net Margin %	20.79	9.40	16.26	41.02	18.08	7.76	4.23	9.11
Asset Turnover	0.64	0.57	0.53	0.62	0.75	0.69	0.66	0.59
Current Ratio	1.97	1.77	2.02	1.73	1.99	2.07	2.28	2.76
Debt to Equity	1.19	0.99	0.97	0.77	1.50	1.90	1.92	1.51
Price Range	59.40-40.66	52.50-40.61	45.01-27.00	58.78-41.47	54.96-41.37	45.32-29.84	31.49-22.33	45.95-19.65
P/E Ratio	25.83-17.68	27.49-21.26	15.41-9.25	7.94-5.60	17.18-12.93	37.45-24.66	48.45-34.35	33.79-14.45
Average Yield %	6.11	6.24	7.45	4.65	2.44	2.77	4.18	1.78

Address: Clarendon House, 2 Church Street, Hamilton, HM 11
Telephone: 441-295-1422

Web Site: www.lazard.com
Officers: Kenneth M. Jacobs - Chairman, Chief Executive Officer Evan L. Russo - Chief Financial Officer, Associate/Affiliate Company Officer

Auditors: Deloitte & Touche LLP
Investor Contact: 212-632-6637
Transfer Agents: Computershare, Pittsburgh, PA

LEAR CORP.

Exchange	Symbol	Price	52Wk Range	Yield	P/E
NYS	LEA	$185.81 (6/29/2018)	205.34-141.14	1.51	9.58

*7 Year Price Score 144.45 *NYSE Composite Index=100 *12 Month Price Score 109.11

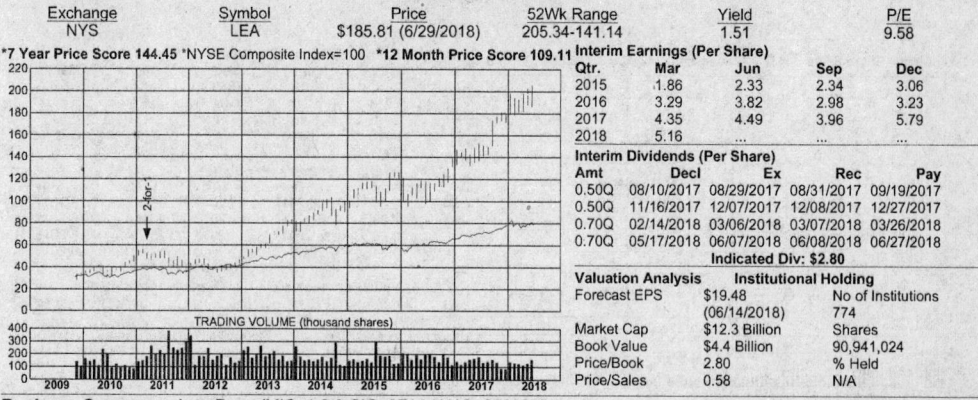

Interim Earnings (Per Share)

Qtr.	Mar	Jun	Sep	Dec
2015	1.86	2.33	2.34	3.06
2016	3.29	3.82	2.98	3.23
2017	4.35	4.49	3.96	5.79
2018	5.16	...	...	...

Interim Dividends (Per Share)

Amt	Decl	Ex	Rec	Pay
0.50Q	08/10/2017	08/29/2017	08/31/2017	09/19/2017
0.50Q	11/16/2017	12/07/2017	12/08/2017	12/27/2017
0.70Q	02/14/2018	03/06/2018	03/07/2018	03/26/2018
0.70Q	05/17/2018	06/07/2018	06/08/2018	06/27/2018

Indicated Div: $2.80

Valuation Analysis

Forecast EPS	$19.48	No of Institutions
	(06/14/2018)	774
Market Cap	$12.3 Billion	Shares
Book Value	$4.4 Billion	90,941,024
Price/Book	2.80	% Held
Price/Sales	0.58	N/A

Institutional Holding

TRADING VOLUME (thousand shares)

Business Summary: Auto Parts (MIC: 1.8.2 SIC: 3714 NAIC: 336360)

Lear is a designer and manufacturer of automotive seating and electrical distribution systems and related components. Co. has two segments: seating, which consists of the design, development, engineering, assembly and delivery of seat systems, and the design, development, engineering and manufacture of seat components, including seat covers and surface materials such as leather and fabric, and seating-related electrical and electronics (including software products); and e-systems, which consists of the design, development, engineering, manufacture, assembly and supply of electrical distribution systems, electronic modules and related components and software for light vehicles globally.

Recent Developments: For the quarter ended Mar 31 2018, net income increased 17.5% to US$374.2 million from US$318.5 million in the year-earlier quarter. Revenues were US$5.73 billion, up 14.7% from US$5.00 billion the year before. Direct operating expenses rose 15.5% to US$5.10 billion from US$4.42 billion in the comparable period the year before. Indirect operating expenses increased 1.6% to US$168.5 million from US$165.8 million in the equivalent prior-year period.

Prospects: Our evaluation of Lear Corp. as of Jan. 21, 2018 is the result of our systematic analysis on three basic characteristics: earnings strength, relative valuation, and recent stock price movement. The company has managed to produce a neutral trend in earnings per share over the past 5 quarters and while recent estimates for the company have been raised by analysts, LEA has posted better than expected results. Based on operating earnings yield, the company is undervalued when compared to all of the companies in our coverage universe. Share price changes over the past year indicates that LEA will perform in line with the market over the near term.

Financial Data

(US$ in Thousands)	3 Mos	12/31/2017	12/31/2016	12/31/2015	12/31/2014	12/31/2013	12/31/2012	12/31/2011
Earnings Per Share	19.40	18.59	13.33	9.59	8.23	4.99	12.85	5.08
Cash Flow Per Share	25.95	26.01	22.32	16.56	11.57	9.64	7.40	7.62
Tang Book Value Per Share	44.22	41.11	27.88	25.16	28.62	28.34	28.57	17.95
Dividends Per Share	2.200	2.000	1.200	1.000	0.800	0.680	0.560	0.500
Dividend Payout %	11.34	10.76	9.00	10.43	9.72	13.63	4.36	9.84
Income Statement								
Total Revenue	5,733,700	20,467,000	18,557,600	18,211,400	17,727,300	16,234,000	14,567,000	14,156,500
EBITDA	588,700	2,040,100	1,799,000	1,466,000	1,165,800	964,000	938,400	901,700
Depn & Amortn	120,200	427,700	378,200	347,800	310,900	285,500	239,600	246,300
Income Before Taxes	447,800	1,526,700	1,338,300	1,031,500	787,400	610,100	648,900	615,700
Income Taxes	77,700	197,500	370,200	285,500	121,400	192,700	(638,000)	68,800
Net Income	353,700	1,313,400	975,100	745,500	672,400	431,400	1,282,800	540,700
Average Shares	67,562	69,277	73,124	77,767	81,728	86,415	99,825	106,344
Balance Sheet								
Current Assets	7,099,700	6,613,000	5,649,300	5,286,600	5,379,600	4,922,500	4,873,500	4,761,500
Total Assets	12,681,200	11,945,900	9,900,600	9,405,800	9,150,200	8,330,900	8,194,100	7,010,900
Current Liabilities	5,296,400	4,854,300	4,182,300	3,839,600	3,957,800	3,579,100	3,216,900	3,063,500
Long-Term Obligations	1,950,000	1,951,500	1,898,000	1,931,700	1,475,000	1,057,100	626,300	695,400
Total Liabilities	8,281,800	7,795,400	6,843,400	6,478,400	6,191,400	5,285,000	4,707,000	4,574,500
Stockholders' Equity	4,399,400	4,150,500	3,057,200	2,927,400	2,958,800	3,045,900	3,487,100	2,436,400
Shares Outstanding	66,371	66,873	69,431	74,464	78,021	80,751	95,942	100,686
Statistical Record								
Return on Assets %	11.69	12.02	10.07	8.04	7.69	5.22	16.83	7.93
Return on Equity %	35.22	36.44	32.50	25.33	22.40	13.21	43.19	22.08
EBITDA Margin %	10.27	9.97	9.69	8.05	6.58	5.94	6.44	6.37
Net Margin %	6.17	6.42	5.25	4.09	3.79	2.66	8.81	3.82
Asset Turnover	1.82	1.87	1.92	1.96	2.03	1.96	1.91	2.08
Current Ratio	1.34	1.36	1.35	1.38	1.36	1.38	1.51	1.55
Debt to Equity	0.44	0.47	0.62	0.66	0.50	0.35	0.18	0.29
Price Range	197.99-132.08	180.89-132.08	138.80-94.98	126.34-93.40	103.28-71.97	83.11-46.84	47.01-34.81	55.96-36.03
P/E Ratio	10.21-6.81	9.73-7.10	10.41-7.13	13.17-9.74	12.55-8.74	16.66-9.39	3.66-2.71	11.02-7.09
Average Yield %	1.34	1.31	1.05	0.90	0.90	1.06	1.35	1.05

Address: 21557 Telegraph Road, Southfield, MI 48033	Web Site: www.lear.com	Auditors: Ernst & Young LLP
Telephone: 248-447-1500	**Officers:** Raymond E. Scott - President, Chief Executive Officer, Division Officer, Executive Vice President, Senior Vice President Jeffrey H. Vanneste - Chief Financial Officer, Senior Vice President	**Investor Contact:** 248-447-1500
Fax: 248-447-5250		**Transfer Agents:** Computershare Trust Company, Canton, MA

LEGG MASON, INC.

Exchange	Symbol	Price	52Wk Range	Yield	P/E
NYS	LM	$34.73 (6/29/2018)	46.14-34.73	3.92	11.54

*7 Year Price Score 84.94   *NYSE Composite Index=100   *12 Month Price Score 93.61

Interim Earnings (Per Share)

Qtr.	Jun	Sep	Dec	Mar
2013-14	0.38	0.70	0.67	0.58
2014-15	0.61	0.04	0.67	0.72
2015-16	0.84	0.58	(1.31)	(0.42)
2016-17	0.31	0.63	0.50	0.75
2017-18	0.52	0.78	1.58	0.15

Interim Dividends (Per Share)

Amt	Decl	Ex	Rec	Pay
0.28Q	07/26/2017	10/04/2017	10/05/2017	10/23/2017
0.28Q	10/31/2017	12/19/2017	12/20/2017	01/15/2018
0.28Q	01/31/2018	03/14/2018	03/15/2018	04/16/2018
0.34Q	04/25/2018	06/11/2018	06/12/2018	07/09/2018

Indicated Div: $1.36

Valuation Analysis

		Institutional Holding	
Forecast EPS	$3.45	No of Institutions	
	(06/20/2018)	587	
Market Cap	$2.9 Billion	Shares	
Book Value	$3.8 Billion	111,694,392	
Price/Book	0.77	% Held	
Price/Sales	0.94	71.80	

Business Summary: Wealth Management (MIC: 5.5.2 SIC: 6282 NAIC: 523930)

Legg Mason is a holding company. Through its subsidiaries, Co. is an asset management company that provides investment management and related services to institutional and individual clients, company-sponsored mutual funds and other pooled investment vehicles. Co.'s investment advisory services include discretionary and non-discretionary management of separate investment accounts in numerous investment styles for institutional and individual investors. Co.'s investment products include proprietary mutual funds ranging from money market and other liquidity products. Co. also provides other domestic and offshore funds. As of Mar 31 2018, Co. had assets under management of $754.13 billion.

Recent Developments: For the year ended Mar 31 2018, net income increased 17.3% to US$336.4 million from US$286.7 million in the prior year. Revenues were US$3.14 billion, up 8.8% from US$2.89 billion the year before. Operating income was US$324.0 million versus US$422.2 million in the prior year, a decrease of 23.3%. Indirect operating expenses increased 14.3% to US$2.82 billion from US$2.46 billion in the equivalent prior-year period.

Prospects: Our evaluation of Legg Mason Inc. as of Jan. 21, 2018 is the result of our systematic analysis on three basic characteristics: earnings strength, relative valuation, and recent stock price movement. The company has generated a negative trend in earnings per share over the past 5 quarters and while recent estimates for the company have been raised by analysts, LM has posted better than expected results. Based on operating earnings yield, the company is undervalued when compared to all of the companies in our coverage universe. Share price changes over the past year indicates that LM will perform in line with the market over the near term.

Financial Data

(US$ in Thousands)	03/31/2018	03/31/2017	03/31/2016	03/31/2015	03/31/2014	03/31/2013	03/31/2012	03/31/2011
Earnings Per Share	3.01	2.18	(0.25)	2.04	2.33	(2.65)	1.54	1.63
Cash Flow Per Share	5.43	5.37	4.22	5.07	3.59	2.28	3.46	2.65
Tang Book Value Per Share	N.M.	N.M.	N.M.	N.M.	2.67	2.96	3.90	3.87
Dividends Per Share	1.120	0.880	0.800	0.640	0.520	0.440	0.320	0.200
Dividend Payout %	37.21	40.37	...	31.37	22.32	...	20.78	12.27
Income Statement								
Total Revenue	3,140,322	2,886,902	2,660,844	2,819,106	2,741,757	2,612,650	2,662,574	2,784,317
EBITDA	417,592	557,449	77,908	473,913	529,030	(367,430)	472,981	550,856
Depn & Amortn	72,986	80,213	60,297	55,086	62,845	87,848	93,795	102,748
Income Before Taxes	233,840	370,878	(25,218)	367,993	419,641	(510,607)	303,083	365,197
Income Taxes	(102,510)	84,175	7,692	125,284	137,805	(150,859)	72,052	119,434
Net Income	285,075	227,256	(25,032)	237,080	284,784	(353,327)	220,817	253,923
Average Shares	91,194	100,799	107,406	113,246	122,383	133,226	143,349	155,484
Balance Sheet								
Current Assets	1,928,382	1,801,747	2,385,128	1,922,035	2,128,383	1,942,862	2,457,794	2,446,556
Total Assets	8,152,534	8,290,415	7,520,446	7,073,977	7,111,349	7,269,660	8,555,747	8,707,756
Current Liabilities	982,042	809,387	841,553	815,046	821,245	702,466	975,782	968,972
Long-Term Obligations	2,221,810	2,221,867	1,740,985	1,058,089	1,038,826	1,302,351	1,407,321	1,479,396
Total Liabilities	4,328,129	4,307,041	3,306,883	2,589,076	2,386,625	2,451,309	2,878,456	2,937,372
Stockholders' Equity	3,824,405	3,983,374	4,213,563	4,484,901	4,724,724	4,818,351	5,677,291	5,770,384
Shares Outstanding	84,606	95,726	107,011	111,469	117,173	125,341	139,874	150,218
Statistical Record								
Return on Assets %	3.47	2.87	N.M.	3.34	3.96	N.M.	2.55	2.93
Return on Equity %	7.30	5.54	N.M.	5.15	5.97	N.M.	3.85	4.37
EBITDA Margin %	13.30	19.31	2.93	16.81	19.30	N.M.	17.76	19.78
Net Margin %	9.08	7.87	N.M.	8.41	10.39	N.M.	8.29	9.12
Asset Turnover	0.38	0.37	0.36	0.40	0.38	0.33	0.31	0.32
Current Ratio	1.96	2.23	2.83	2.36	2.59	2.77	2.52	2.52
Debt to Equity	0.58	0.56	0.41	0.24	0.22	0.27	0.25	0.26
Price Range	46.14-35.65	37.72-27.77	55.58-25.20	58.92-43.36	49.04-29.76	32.15-22.38	37.53-22.95	37.58-25.17
P/E Ratio	15.33-11.84	17.30-12.74	...	28.88-21.25	21.05-12.77	...	24.37-14.90	23.06-15.44
Average Yield %	2.86	2.67	1.83	1.24	1.39	1.68	1.10	0.62

Address: 100 International Drive, Baltimore, MD 21202
Telephone: 410-539-0000

Web Site: www.leggmason.com
Officers: Joseph A. Sullivan - Chairman, President, Chief Executive Officer, Acting Chief Executive Officer, Senior Executive Vice President, Chief Administrative Officer Peter H. Nachtwey - Chief Financial Officer, Senior Executive Vice President

Auditors: PricewaterhouseCoopers LLP
Investor Contact: 410-454-5246
Transfer Agents: American Stock Transfer & Trust Company, New York, NY

LEGGETT & PLATT, INC.

Exchange	Symbol	Price	52Wk Range	Yield	P/E	Div Acheiver
NYS	LEG	$44.64 (6/29/2018)	53.80-40.38	3.41	21.46	46 Years

*7 Year Price Score 97.67 *NYSE Composite Index=100 *12 Month Price Score 91.14

Interim Earnings (Per Share)

Qtr.	Mar	Jun	Sep	Dec
2015	0.50	0.54	0.67	0.57
2016	0.63	0.87	0.67	0.59
2017	0.62	0.64	0.60	0.27
2018	0.57	...	...	...

Interim Dividends (Per Share)

Amt	Decl	Ex	Rec	Pay
0.36Q	08/03/2017	09/14/2017	09/15/2017	10/13/2017
0.36Q	11/07/2017	12/14/2017	12/15/2017	01/12/2018
0.36Q	02/21/2018	03/14/2018	03/15/2018	04/13/2018
0.38Q	05/15/2018	06/14/2018	06/15/2018	07/13/2018

Indicated Div: $1.52

Valuation Analysis

Forecast EPS	$2.65		Institutional Holding	
	(06/10/2018)		No of Institutions	689
Market Cap	$5.9 Billion		Shares	134,378,848
Book Value	$1.2 Billion		% Held	
Price/Book	4.90		% Held	69.21
Price/Sales	1.46			

TRADING VOLUME (thousand shares)

Business Summary: Furniture (MIC: 1.6.2 SIC: 2519 NAIC: 337121)

Leggett & Platt designs and produces engineered components and products. Co. has four segments: Residential Furnishings, which supplies a variety of components used by bedding and upholstered furniture manufacturers in the assembly of their finished products; Commercial Products, which designs, manufactures, and distributes a range of components and products primarily for the office seating market; Industrial Materials, which supplies steel wire; and Specialized Products, which designs, manufactures and sells products including automotive seating components, tubing for the aerospace industry, machinery and equipment, and service van interiors.

Recent Developments: For the quarter ended Mar 31 2018, income from continuing operations decreased 9.5% to US$77.9 million from US$86.1 million in the year-earlier quarter. Net income decreased 9.5% to US$77.9 million from US$86.1 million in the year-earlier quarter. Revenues were US$1.03 billion, up 7.1% from US$960.3 million the year before. Operating income was US$107.4 million versus US$115.9 million in the prior-year quarter, a decrease of 7.3%. Direct operating expenses rose 10.6% to US$811.4 million from US$733.6 million in the comparable period the year before. Indirect operating expenses decreased 0.7% to US$110.0 million from US$110.8 million in the equivalent prior-year period.

Prospects: Our evaluation of Leggett & Platt Inc. as of Jan. 21, 2018 is the result of our systematic analysis on three basic characteristics: earnings strength, relative valuation, and recent stock price movement. The company has produced a positive trend in earnings per share over the past 5 quarters and while recent estimates for the company have been mixed, LEG has posted better than expected results. Based on operating earnings yield, the company is undervalued when compared to all of the companies in our coverage universe. Share price changes over the past year indicates that LEG will perform in line with the market over the near term.

Financial Data

(US$ in Thousands)	3 Mos	12/31/2017	12/31/2016	12/31/2015	12/31/2014	12/31/2013	12/31/2012	12/31/2011
Earnings Per Share	2.08	2.13	2.76	2.28	0.68	1.34	1.70	1.04
Cash Flow Per Share	3.18	3.26	4.00	2.55	2.70	2.87	3.11	2.26
Tang Book Value Per Share	1.20	1.51	1.01	0.64	0.89	1.87	1.67	1.82
Dividends Per Share	1.440	1.420	1.340	1.260	1.220	1.180	1.140	1.100
Dividend Payout %	69.23	66.67	48.55	55.26	179.41	88.06	67.06	105.77
Income Statement								
Total Revenue	1,028,800	3,943,800	3,749,900	3,917,200	3,782,300	3,746,000	3,720,800	3,636,000
EBITDA	140,800	583,900	628,700	590,800	441,100	400,900	457,400	354,700
Depn & Amortn	33,400	116,000	106,700	104,300	109,600	116,100	116,100	116,900
Income Before Taxes	95,400	432,000	487,100	449,800	295,500	247,800	304,400	206,200
Income Taxes	17,500	138,400	120,000	121,800	70,300	55,000	56,300	49,800
Net Income	77,900	292,600	385,800	325,100	98,000	197,300	248,200	153,300
Average Shares	136,300	137,300	140,000	142,900	143,200	147,300	145,963	146,999
Balance Sheet								
Current Assets	1,814,100	1,766,500	1,324,900	1,311,200	1,429,600	1,281,700	1,339,100	1,224,000
Total Assets	3,692,400	3,550,800	2,984,100	2,967,600	3,140,600	3,108,100	3,254,900	2,915,100
Current Liabilities	978,100	976,200	706,600	701,200	992,200	829,500	731,000	586,000
Long-Term Obligations	1,239,000	1,097,900	956,200	945,400	766,700	688,400	853,900	833,300
Total Liabilities	2,496,500	2,360,600	1,892,500	1,882,000	1,994,100	1,716,800	1,820,400	1,617,900
Stockholders' Equity	1,195,900	1,190,200	1,091,600	1,085,600	1,146,500	1,391,300	1,434,500	1,297,200
Shares Outstanding	131,269	131,900	133,500	135,600	137,800	139,400	142,100	139,400
Statistical Record								
Return on Assets %	8.35	8.95	12.93	10.64	3.14	6.20	8.02	5.18
Return on Equity %	25.17	25.65	35.34	29.13	7.72	13.96	18.12	10.93
EBITDA Margin %	13.69	14.81	16.77	15.08	11.66	10.70	12.29	9.76
Net Margin %	7.57	7.42	10.29	8.30	2.59	5.27	6.67	4.22
Asset Turnover	1.18	1.21	1.26	1.28	1.21	1.18	1.20	1.23
Current Ratio	1.85	1.81	1.88	1.87	1.44	1.55	1.83	2.09
Debt to Equity	1.04	0.92	0.88	0.87	0.67	0.49	0.60	0.64
Price Range	54.04-41.80	54.04-43.50	54.53-37.79	51.00-40.68	42.95-29.06	34.19-27.22	27.85-19.49	26.37-17.87
P/E Ratio	25.98-20.10	25.37-20.42	19.76-13.69	22.37-17.84	63.16-42.74	25.51-20.31	16.38-11.46	25.36-17.18
Average Yield %	2.97	2.89	2.80	2.76	3.53	3.83	4.88	4.83

Address: No. 1 Leggett Road, Carthage, MO 64836	Web Site: www.leggett.com	Auditors: PricewaterhouseCoopers LLP
Telephone: 417-358-8131	Officers: Robert Ted Enloe - Chairman Karl G. Glassman - President, Chief Executive Officer, Executive Vice President, Chief Operating Officer	Investor Contact: 417-358-8131 Transfer Agents: Wells Fargo Shareowner Services, St. Paul, MN

LEIDOS HOLDINGS INC

Exchange	Symbol	Price	52Wk Range	Yield	P/E
NYS	LDOS	$59.00 (6/29/2018)	69.42-51.19	2.17	23.05

*7 Year Price Score 111.30 *NYSE Composite Index=100 *12 Month Price Score 97.63

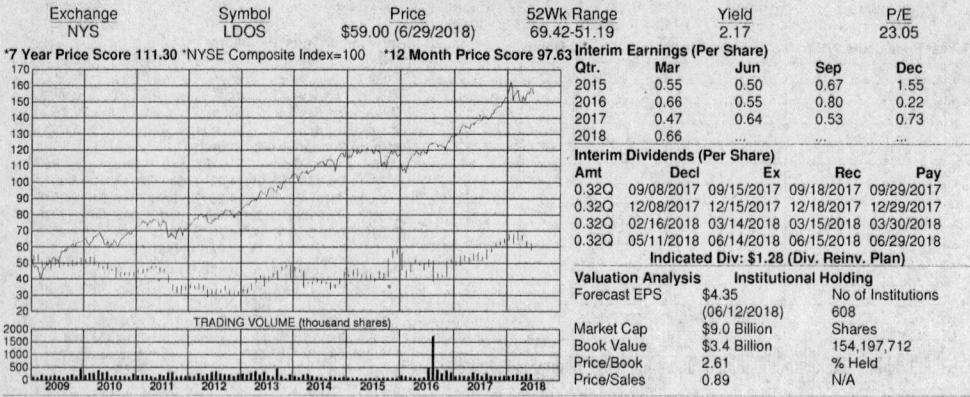

Interim Earnings (Per Share)

Qtr.	Mar	Jun	Sep	Dec
2015	0.55	0.50	0.67	1.55
2016	0.66	0.55	0.80	0.22
2017	0.47	0.64	0.53	0.73
2018	0.66	...	...	...

Interim Dividends (Per Share)

Amt	Decl	Ex	Rec	Pay
0.32Q	09/08/2017	09/15/2017	09/18/2017	09/29/2017
0.32Q	12/08/2017	12/15/2017	12/18/2017	12/29/2017
0.32Q	02/16/2018	03/14/2018	03/15/2018	03/30/2018
0.32Q	05/11/2018	06/14/2018	06/15/2018	06/29/2018

Indicated Div: $1.28 (Div. Reinv. Plan)

Valuation Analysis

		Institutional Holding	
Forecast EPS	$4.35 (06/12/2018)	No of Institutions	608
Market Cap	$9.0 Billion	Shares	
Book Value	$3.4 Billion	154,197,712	
Price/Book	2.61	% Held	
Price/Sales	0.89	N/A	

Business Summary: IT Services (MIC: 6.3.1 SIC: 7373 NAIC: 541330)

Leidos Holdings is a holding company. Through its subsidiaries, Co. provides technology and engineering services and solutions in the defense, intelligence, civil and health markets. Co. operates these segments: National Security Solutions, which deploys solutions in the areas of intelligence surveillance and reconnaissance, integrated systems and cybersecurity and global services; Information Systems & Global Solutions, which focuses on being a provider of information technology, management and engineering services; and Health and Infrastructure, which provides services and solutions focused on information technology and behavioral health and life sciences offerings.

Recent Developments: For the quarter ended Mar 30 2018, net income increased 37.8% to US$102.0 million from US$74.0 million in the year-earlier quarter. Revenues were US$2.44 billion, down 5.3% from US$2.58 billion the year before. Operating income was US$159.0 million versus US$141.0 million in the prior-year quarter, an increase of 12.8%. Direct operating expenses declined 6.6% to US$2.09 billion from US$2.23 billion in the comparable period the year before. Indirect operating expenses decreased 3.9% to US$198.0 million from US$206.0 million in the equivalent prior-year period.

Prospects: Our evaluation of Leidos Holdings Inc. as of Jan. 21, 2018 is the result of our systematic analysis on three basic characteristics: earnings strength, relative valuation, and recent stock price movement. The company has generated a negative trend in earnings per share over the past 5 quarters and while recent estimates for the company have been mixed, LDOS has posted better than expected results. Based on operating earnings yield, the company is undervalued when compared to all of the companies in our coverage universe. Share price changes over the past year indicates that LDOS will perform well over the near term.

Financial Data
(US$ in Millions)

	3 Mos	12/29/2017	12/30/2016	01/01/2016	01/30/2015	01/31/2014	01/31/2013	01/31/2012
Earnings Per Share	2.56	2.38	2.35	3.27	(4.36)	1.94	6.16	0.72
Cash Flow Per Share	4.18	3.47	4.38	5.94	5.37	2.35	4.13	9.19
Tang Book Value Per Share	N.M.	N.M.	N.M.	N.M.	N.M.	N.M.	2.73	2.10
Dividends Per Share	1.280	1.280	14.920	1.280	1.280	0.640	1.920	...
Dividend Payout %	50.00	53.78	634.89	39.14	...	32.99	31.17	...
Income Statement								
Total Revenue	2,443	10,170	7,043	4,712	5,063	5,772	11,173	10,587
EBITDA	168	575	432	437	(162)	237	855	430
Depn & Amortn	13	55	38	33	47	81	113	114
Income Before Taxes	121	380	308	355	(283)	88	658	207
Income Taxes	23	29	72	112	47	4	135	215
Net Income	102	366	244	242	(323)	164	525	59
Average Shares	154	154	104	74	74	83	83	84
Balance Sheet								
Current Assets	2,635	2,674	2,381	1,793	1,618	1,794	3,079	4,205
Total Assets	8,913	8,990	9,132	3,377	3,281	4,162	5,875	6,667
Current Liabilities	2,103	2,202	2,016	1,040	951	1,009	1,793	3,025
Long-Term Obligations	3,007	3,056	3,225	1,086	1,164	1,331	1,296	1,299
Total Liabilities	5,482	5,620	5,997	2,309	2,283	2,567	3,257	4,486
Stockholders' Equity	3,431	3,370	3,135	1,068	998	1,595	2,618	2,181
Shares Outstanding	152	151	150	72	74	80	85	85
Statistical Record								
Return on Assets %	4.39	4.05	3.91	6.97	N.M.	3.27	8.35	0.92
Return on Equity %	11.99	11.28	11.64	19.74	N.M.	7.79	21.82	2.53
EBITDA Margin %	6.88	5.65	6.13	9.27	N.M.	4.11	7.65	4.06
Net Margin %	4.18	3.60	3.46	5.14	N.M.	2.84	4.70	0.56
Asset Turnover	1.11	1.13	1.13	1.36	1.36	1.15	1.78	1.64
Current Ratio	1.25	1.21	1.18	1.72	1.70	1.78	1.72	1.39
Debt to Equity	0.88	0.91	1.03	1.02	1.02	0.83	0.50	0.60
Price Range	69.42-49.95	65.22-48.31	56.19-38.50	59.05-38.05	46.07-33.21	49.02-31.06	37.34-28.48	48.17-30.89
P/E Ratio	27.12-19.51	27.40-20.30	23.91-16.38	18.06-11.64	...	25.27-16.01	6.06-4.62	66.91-42.90
Average Yield %	2.16	2.29	31.53	2.83	3.26	1.55	5.91	...

Address: 11951 Freedom Drive, Reston, VA 20190	Web Site: www.leidos.com	Auditors: Deloitte & Touche LLP
Telephone: 571-526-6000	Officers: Roger A. Krone - Chairman, Chief Executive Officer James C. Reagan - Chief Financial Officer, Executive Vice President, Interim Principal Accounting Officer	Investor Contact: 703-676-2283 Transfer Agents: BNY Mellon Shareowner Services

LENNAR CORP

Exchange	Symbol	Price	52Wk Range	Yield	P/E
NYS	LEN	$52.50 (6/29/2018)	71.82-49.02	0.30	13.78

*7 Year Price Score 110.55 *NYSE Composite Index=100 *12 Month Price Score 91.33

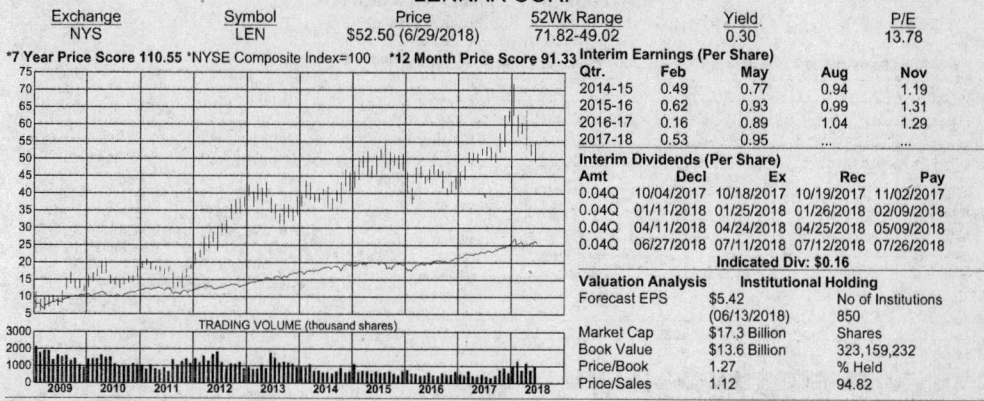

Interim Earnings (Per Share)

Qtr.	Feb	May	Aug	Nov
2014-15	0.49	0.77	0.94	1.19
2015-16	0.62	0.93	0.99	1.31
2016-17	0.16	0.89	1.04	1.29
2017-18	0.53	0.95	...	...

Interim Dividends (Per Share)

Amt	Decl	Ex	Rec	Pay
0.04Q	10/04/2017	10/18/2017	10/19/2017	11/02/2017
0.04Q	01/11/2018	01/25/2018	01/26/2018	02/09/2018
0.04Q	04/11/2018	04/24/2018	04/25/2018	05/09/2018
0.04Q	06/27/2018	07/11/2018	07/12/2018	07/26/2018

Indicated Div: $0.16

Valuation Analysis

		Institutional Holding	
Forecast EPS	$5.42	No of Institutions	
	(06/13/2018)	850	
Market Cap	$17.3 Billion	Shares	
Book Value	$13.6 Billion	323,159,232	
Price/Book	1.27	% Held	
Price/Sales	1.12	94.82	

TRADING VOLUME (thousand shares)

Business Summary: Builders (MIC: 2.2.5 SIC: 1521 NAIC: 236115)

Lennar is a homebuilder, a provider of real estate related financial services, a commercial real estate, investment management and finance company and a developer of multifamily rental properties. Co.'s homebuilding operations include the construction and sale of single-family attached and detached homes as well as the purchase, development and sale of residential land. Co.'s Lennar Financial Services Operations provides mortgage financing and title insurance and closing services; while its Rialto Operations primarily manages third-party capital and originates commercial mortgage loans. Co.'s Lennar Multifamily Operations develops, constructs and manages multifamily rental properties.

Recent Developments: For the quarter ended May 31 2018, net income increased 56.9% to US$314.8 million from US$200.7 million in the year-earlier quarter. Revenues were US$5.46 billion, up 67.4% from US$3.26 billion the year before. Direct operating expenses rose 73.6% to US$4.97 billion from US$2.86 billion in the comparable period the year before. Indirect operating expenses increased 62.9% to US$108.8 million from US$66.8 million in the equivalent prior-year period.

Prospects: Our evaluation of Lennar Corp. as of Jan. 21, 2018 is the result of our systematic analysis on three basic characteristics: earnings strength, relative valuation, and recent stock price movement. The company has enjoyed a very positive trend in earnings per share over the past 5 quarters and while recent estimates for the company have been raised by analysts, LEN has posted results that fell short of analysts expectations. Based on operating earnings yield, the company is undervalued when compared to all of the companies in our coverage universe. Share price changes over the past year indicates that LEN will perform poorly over the near term.

Financial Data

(US$ in Thousands)	6 Mos	3 Mos	11/30/2017	11/30/2016	11/30/2015	11/30/2014	11/30/2013	11/30/2012
Earnings Per Share	3.81	3.75	3.38	3.85	3.39	2.75	2.11	3.05
Cash Flow Per Share	3.66	3.05	4.20	2.27	(2.01)	(3.82)	(4.16)	(2.22)
Tang Book Value Per Share	30.13	28.91	31.99	29.21	26.05	23.08	19.99	17.48
Dividends Per Share	0.160	0.160	0.160	0.160	0.160	0.160	0.160	0.160
Dividend Payout %	4.20	4.26	4.73	4.15	4.72	5.83	7.59	5.25
Income Statement								
Total Revenue	8,439,852	2,980,791	12,646,365	10,949,999	9,474,008	7,779,812	5,935,095	4,104,706
EBITDA	644,514	271,899	1,217,769	1,344,728	1,180,426	992,888	783,815	351,191
Depn & Amortn	(11,984)	40	77,636	64,838	63,540	59,929	53,846	49,531
Income Before Taxes	656,498	271,859	1,140,133	1,275,264	1,104,432	896,408	636,056	207,307
Income Taxes	208,572	132,611	417,857	417,378	390,416	341,091	177,015	(435,218)
Net Income	446,472	136,215	810,480	911,844	802,894	638,916	479,674	679,124
Average Shares	326,818	254,448	237,156	235,326	235,428	232,804	230,438	223,068
Balance Sheet								
Current Assets	18,666,044	18,737,643	13,762,319	10,911,843	10,171,054	9,230,259	7,700,479	6,609,544
Total Assets	28,351,109	27,944,023	18,745,034	15,361,781	14,419,509	12,958,267	11,273,247	10,362,206
Current Liabilities	844,883	782,797	604,953	478,546	475,909	412,558	271,365	220,690
Long-Term Obligations	11,300,243	11,593,659	6,410,003	4,575,977	5,025,130	4,690,213	4,194,432	4,005,051
Total Liabilities	14,759,798	14,883,093	10,872,717	8,335,739	8,770,565	8,131,247	7,104,346	6,947,442
Stockholders' Equity	13,591,311	13,060,930	7,872,317	7,026,042	5,648,944	4,827,020	4,168,901	3,414,764
Shares Outstanding	329,478	325,684	239,964	239,164	215,368	209,140	208,500	195,378
Statistical Record								
Return on Assets %	4.46	4.11	4.75	6.11	5.87	5.27	4.43	6.94
Return on Equity %	9.61	9.01	10.88	14.35	15.33	14.20	12.65	22.16
EBITDA Margin %	7.64	9.12	9.63	12.28	12.46	12.76	13.21	8.56
Net Margin %	5.29	4.57	6.41	8.33	8.47	8.21	8.08	16.55
Asset Turnover	0.69	0.60	0.74	0.73	0.69	0.64	0.55	0.42
Current Ratio	22.09	23.94	22.75	22.80	21.37	22.37	28.38	29.95
Debt to Equity	0.83	0.89	0.81	0.65	0.89	0.97	1.01	1.17
Price Range	71.82-49.02	71.82-47.96	62.78-41.29	51.42-37.16	54.64-40.62	46.70-33.64	43.13-30.99	38.38-17.92
P/E Ratio	18.85-12.87	19.15-12.79	18.57-12.22	13.36-9.65	16.12-11.98	16.98-12.23	20.44-14.69	12.59-5.88
Average Yield %	0.28	0.29	0.32	0.36	0.33	0.41	0.43	0.57

Address: 700 Northwest 107th Avenue, Miami, FL 33172 **Telephone:** 305-559-4000	**Web Site:** www.lennar.com **Officers:** Stuart A. Miller - President, Chief Executive Officer, Chairman Richard (Rick) Beckwitt - President, Chief Executive Officer	**Auditors:** DELOITTE & TOUCHE LLP **Investor Contact:** 305-559-4000 **Transfer Agents:** ComputerShare Investor Services, Providence, RI

LENNOX INTERNATIONAL INC

Exchange	Symbol	Price	52Wk Range	Yield	P/E
NYS	LII	$200.15 (6/29/2018)	221.09-160.60	1.28	28.39

*7 Year Price Score 145.39 *NYSE Composite Index=100 *12 Month Price Score 102.65

Interim Earnings (Per Share)

Qtr.	Mar	Jun	Sep	Dec
2015	0.31	1.78	1.76	0.24
2016	0.56	2.51	2.33	0.94
2017	1.00	2.69	2.44	1.02
2018	0.90	...	...	...

Interim Dividends (Per Share)

Amt	Decl	Ex	Rec	Pay
0.51Q	09/14/2017	09/28/2017	09/29/2017	10/16/2017
0.51Q	12/07/2017	12/28/2017	12/29/2017	01/16/2018
0.51Q	03/16/2018	03/29/2018	04/02/2018	04/13/2018
0.64Q	05/15/2018	06/28/2018	06/29/2018	07/13/2018

Indicated Div: $2.56

Valuation Analysis | **Institutional Holding**

Forecast EPS	$10.15	No of Institutions
	(06/14/2018)	502
Market Cap	$8.3 Billion	Shares
Book Value	N/A	37,681,588
Price/Book	N/A	% Held
Price/Sales	2.13	60.61

Business Summary: Industrial Machinery & Equipment (MIC: 7.2.1 SIC: 3585 NAIC: 333415)

Lennox International is a provider of climate control solutions and designs, manufactures and markets products for the heating, ventilation, air conditioning, and refrigeration markets. Co. has three segments: Residential Heating and Cooling, which provides furnaces, air conditioners, heat pumps, packaged heating and cooling systems, and comfort control products, among others, for the residential replacement and new construction markets; Commercial Heating and Cooling, which manufactures and sells unitary heating and cooling equipment for light commercial applications; and Refrigeration, which provides condensing units, unit coolers, fluid coolers, and air-cooled condensers, among others.

Recent Developments: For the quarter ended Mar 31 2018, income from continuing operations decreased 12.9% to US$37.9 million from US$43.5 million in the year-earlier quarter. Net income decreased 12.9% to US$37.9 million from US$43.5 million in the year-earlier quarter. Revenues were US$834.8 million, up 5.2% from US$793.4 million the year before. Operating income was US$53.0 million versus US$60.8 million in the prior-year quarter, a decrease of 12.8%. Direct operating expenses rose 5.0% to US$611.6 million from US$582.5 million in the comparable period the year before. Indirect operating expenses increased 13.4% to US$170.2 million from US$150.1 million in the equivalent prior-year period.

Prospects: Our evaluation of Lennox International Inc. as of Jan. 21, 2018 is the result of our systematic analysis on three basic characteristics: earnings strength, relative valuation, and recent stock price movement. The company has managed to produce a neutral trend in earnings per share over the past 5 quarters and while recent estimates for the company have been mixed, LII has posted better than expected results. Based on operating earnings yield, the company is about fairly valued when compared to all of the companies in our coverage universe. Share price changes over the past year indicates that LII will perform in line with the market over the near term.

Financial Data

(US$ in Thousands)	3 Mos	12/31/2017	12/31/2016	12/31/2015	12/31/2014	12/31/2013	12/31/2012	12/31/2011
Earnings Per Share	7.05	7.14	6.32	4.09	4.23	3.39	1.75	1.65
Cash Flow Per Share	8.41	7.70	8.15	7.38	3.86	4.22	4.35	1.45
Tang Book Value Per Share	...	N.M.	N.M.	N.M.	N.M.	5.46	5.43	3.19
Dividends Per Share	2.040	1.960	1.650	1.380	1.140	0.920	0.760	0.720
Dividend Payout %	28.94	27.45	26.11	33.74	26.95	27.14	43.43	43.64
Income Statement								
Total Revenue	834,800	3,839,600	3,641,600	3,467,400	3,367,400	3,199,100	2,949,400	3,303,600
EBITDA	65,500	540,800	469,400	355,600	381,800	335,500	263,700	198,200
Depn & Amortn	16,600	64,600	58,100	62,800	60,800	58,900	55,400	60,400
Income Before Taxes	40,500	445,600	384,300	269,200	303,800	262,100	191,200	121,000
Income Taxes	6,100	156,900	124,100	95,400	109,500	94,400	66,700	42,300
Net Income	37,900	305,700	277,800	186,600	205,800	171,800	90,000	88,300
Average Shares	42,100	42,800	44,000	45,600	48,600	50,600	51,400	53,400
Balance Sheet								
Current Assets	1,346,800	1,137,300	1,005,900	938,200	1,014,000	902,400	987,100	903,200
Total Assets	2,086,100	1,891,500	1,760,300	1,680,200	1,764,300	1,626,700	1,691,900	1,705,700
Current Liabilities	712,800	654,500	888,600	824,000	827,300	714,000	639,600	572,900
Long-Term Obligations	1,258,300	970,500	615,700	508,600	675,000	233,200	351,000	459,600
Total Liabilities	2,188,700	1,841,400	1,722,700	1,579,000	1,755,900	1,141,800	1,195,100	1,237,900
Stockholders' Equity	(102,600)	50,100	37,600	101,200	8,400	484,900	496,800	467,800
Shares Outstanding	41,318	41,809	42,974	44,678	44,635	49,103	50,232	50,844
Statistical Record								
Return on Assets %	14.87	16.74	16.10	10.83	12.14	10.35	5.28	5.20
Return on Equity %	...	697.15	399.19	340.51	83.44	35.00	18.61	16.70
EBITDA Margin %	7.85	14.08	12.89	10.26	11.34	10.49	8.94	6.00
Net Margin %	4.54	7.96	7.63	5.38	6.11	5.37	3.05	2.67
Asset Turnover	1.92	2.10	2.11	2.01	1.99	1.93	1.73	1.94
Current Ratio	1.89	1.74	1.13	1.14	1.23	1.26	1.54	1.58
Debt to Equity	...	19.37	16.38	5.03	80.36	0.48	0.71	0.98
Price Range	221.09-160.60	210.66-148.51	163.16-113.97	137.79-93.85	96.04-73.66	85.12-52.52	53.84-34.74	53.63-25.29
P/E Ratio	31.36-22.78	29.50-20.80	25.82-18.03	33.69-22.95	22.70-17.41	25.11-15.49	30.77-19.85	32.50-15.33
Average Yield %	1.09	1.11	1.16	1.20	1.31	1.35	1.71	1.77

Address: 2140 Lake Park Blvd., Richardson, TX 75080
Telephone: 972-497-5000

Web Site: www.lennoxinternational.com
Officers: Todd M. Bluedorn - Chairman, Chief Executive Officer Joseph William Reitmeier - Executive Vice President, Chief Financial Officer, Division Officer

Auditors: KPMG LLP
Investor Contact: 972-497-6670
Transfer Agents: Computershare, Providence, RI

LIBERTY PROPERTY TRUST

Exchange	Symbol	Price	52Wk Range	Yield	P/E
NYS	LPT	$44.33 (6/29/2018)	45.29-38.63	3.61	17.25

*7 Year Price Score 91.54   *NYSE Composite Index=100   *12 Month Price Score 102.72

Interim Earnings (Per Share)

Qtr.	Mar	Jun	Sep	Dec
2015	0.21	0.24	0.61	0.54
2016	0.39	0.34	0.37	1.33
2017	0.29	0.35	0.40	0.87
2018	0.95	...	...	...

Interim Dividends (Per Share)

Amt	Decl	Ex	Rec	Pay
0.40Q	09/07/2017	09/29/2017	10/02/2017	10/15/2017
0.40Q	12/08/2017	12/29/2017	01/02/2018	01/15/2018
0.40Q	03/07/2018	03/29/2018	04/02/2018	04/15/2018
0.40Q	06/14/2018	06/29/2018	07/02/2018	07/15/2018

Indicated Div: $1.60 (Div. Reinv. Plan)

Valuation Analysis / Institutional Holding

Forecast EPS	$1.92 (06/13/2018)	No of Institutions	529
Market Cap	$6.6 Billion	Shares	181,930,976
Book Value	$3.2 Billion	% Held	101.16
Price/Book	2.06		
Price/Sales	8.92		

Business Summary: REITs (MIC: 5.3.1 SIC: 6798 NAIC: 525930)

Liberty Property Trust is a self-administered and self-managed real estate investment trust. Substantially all of Co.'s operations are conducted directly or indirectly, by its subsidiary, Liberty Property Limited Partnership. Co. provides leasing, property management, development and other tenant-related services for a portfolio of industrial and office properties. As of Dec 31 2017, Co. owned and operated 461 industrial and 48 office properties. At Dec 31 2017, Co. owned 20 properties under development, and 1,563 acres of developable land. Co. also had an ownership interest, through unconsolidated joint ventures, in 47 industrial and 18 office properties; and 347 acres of developable land.

Recent Developments: For the quarter ended Mar 31 2018, net income increased 224.8% to US$143.7 million from US$44.2 million in the year-earlier quarter. Revenues were US$190.2 million, up 14.7% from US$165.8 million the year before.

Prospects: Our evaluation of Liberty Property Trust as of Jan. 21, 2018 is the result of our systematic analysis on three basic characteristics: earnings strength, relative valuation, and recent stock price movement. The company has managed to produce a neutral trend in earnings per share over the past 5 quarters. Because the company lacks sufficient analyst estimate data, we place greater weight on the historical EPS trend as the measure of earnings strength. Based on operating earnings yield, the company is overvalued when compared to all of the companies in our coverage universe. Share price changes over the past year indicates that LPT will perform well over the near term.

Financial Data
(US$ in Thousands)

	3 Mos	12/31/2017	12/31/2016	12/31/2015	12/31/2014	12/31/2013	12/31/2012	12/31/2011
Earnings Per Share	2.57	1.91	2.43	1.60	1.47	1.60	1.17	1.59
Cash Flow Per Share	2.34	2.29	2.27	2.60	2.29	2.43	2.71	2.77
Tang Book Value Per Share	21.56	21.32	20.77	20.35	20.70	20.73	17.65	18.96
Dividends Per Share	1.600	1.600	1.900	1.900	1.900	1.900	1.900	1.900
Dividend Payout %	62.26	83.77	78.19	118.75	129.25	118.75	162.39	119.50
Income Statement								
Total Revenue	190,165	719,778	746,708	808,773	792,631	645,930	685,552	667,594
EBITDA	64,413	485,882	614,073	538,446	481,553	374,223	386,428	395,316
Depn & Amortn	967	148,900	166,800	181,000	179,100	162,500	140,600	144,300
Income Before Taxes	43,182	255,903	346,146	244,530	168,235	94,487	135,487	137,395
Income Taxes	554	1,992	1,971	3,233	2,967	2,799	976	1,020
Net Income	140,181	282,340	356,817	238,039	217,910	209,738	137,436	183,999
Average Shares	147,873	147,541	146,889	148,843	147,886	130,909	117,694	115,503
Balance Sheet								
Current Assets	52,513	152,056	179,264	177,501	213,061	328,726	189,119	193,063
Total Assets	6,414,631	6,439,757	5,992,813	6,557,629	6,625,536	6,775,560	5,177,971	4,989,673
Current Liabilities	163,872	161,731	159,293	149,323	148,809	167,506	109,260	104,523
Long-Term Obligations	2,806,278	2,909,545	2,556,936	3,147,016	3,163,395	3,253,519	2,657,398	2,222,862
Total Liabilities	3,229,380	3,352,399	2,989,422	3,604,701	3,597,864	3,739,716	3,086,959	2,886,079
Stockholders' Equity	3,185,251	3,087,358	3,003,391	2,952,928	3,027,672	3,035,844	2,091,012	2,103,594
Shares Outstanding	147,773	147,450	146,993	147,577	148,557	146,596	118,470	116,102
Statistical Record								
Return on Assets %	6.07	4.54	5.67	3.61	3.25	3.51	2.70	3.66
Return on Equity %	12.28	9.27	11.95	7.96	7.19	8.18	6.54	8.79
EBITDA Margin %	33.87	67.50	82.24	66.58	60.75	57.94	56.37	59.22
Net Margin %	73.72	39.23	47.79	29.43	27.49	32.47	20.05	27.56
Asset Turnover	0.12	0.12	0.12	0.12	0.12	0.11	0.13	0.13
Current Ratio	0.32	0.94	1.13	1.19	1.43	1.96	1.73	1.85
Debt to Equity	0.88	0.94	0.85	1.07	1.04	1.07	1.27	1.06
Price Range	45.29-38.55	45.29-37.56	42.25-27.30	41.42-29.91	40.08-32.77	44.70-32.12	38.57-30.91	36.06-26.16
P/E Ratio	17.62-15.00	23.71-19.66	17.39-11.23	25.89-18.69	27.27-22.29	27.94-20.07	32.97-26.42	22.68-16.45
Average Yield %	3.84	3.87	5.20	5.49	5.24	5.03	5.37	5.87

Address: 500 Chesterfield Parkway, Malvern, PA 19355 **Telephone:** 610-648-1700	**Web Site:** www.libertyproperty.com **Officers:** William P. Hankowsky - Chairman, President, Chief Executive Officer Christopher J. Papa - Executive Vice President, Chief Financial Officer	**Auditors:** Ernst & Young LLP **Investor Contact:** 610-648-1704 **Transfer Agents:** Wells Fargo Shareholder Services, St. Paul, MN

LIFE STORAGE INC

Exchange	Symbol	Price	52Wk Range	Yield	P/E
NYS	LSI	$97.31 (6/29/2018)	97.53-70.59	4.11	41.23

*7 Year Price Score 87.50   *NYSE Composite Index=100   *12 Month Price Score 110.11

Interim Earnings (Per Share)

Qtr.	Mar	Jun	Sep	Dec
2015	0.65	0.80	0.88	0.83
2016	0.73	1.03	(0.10)	0.38
2017	0.44	0.42	0.76	0.45
2018	0.73	...	...	...

Interim Dividends (Per Share)

Amt	Decl	Ex	Rec	Pay
1.00Q	10/03/2017	10/12/2017	10/13/2017	10/26/2017
1.00Q	01/03/2018	01/12/2018	01/16/2018	01/26/2018
1.00Q	04/03/2018	04/12/2018	04/13/2018	04/26/2018
1.00Q	07/05/2018	07/13/2018	07/16/2018	07/26/2018

Indicated Div: $4.00

Valuation Analysis

		Institutional Holding	
Forecast EPS	$3.19 (06/14/2018)	No of Institutions	403
Market Cap	$4.5 Billion	Shares	55,688,416
Book Value	$2.0 Billion	% Held	94.59
Price/Book	2.24		
Price/Sales	8.47		

Business Summary: REITs (MIC: 5.3.1 SIC: 6798 NAIC: 525930)

Life Storage is a self-administered and self-managed real estate investment trust that acquires, owns and manages self-storage properties. Co. owns its assets and conducts its operations via Life Storage LP (the Operating Partnership) and subsidiaries of the Operating Partnership. At Dec 31 2017, Co. had an ownership interest in and/or managed 706 self-storage properties in 28 states under the names Life Storage®. Co.'s self-storage facilities provides storage space to residential and commercial users on a month-to-month basis. Individual storage spaces are secured by a lock furnished by the customer to provide the customer with control of access to the space.

Recent Developments: For the quarter ended Mar 31 2018, net income increased 65.9% to US$34.0 million from US$20.5 million in the year-earlier quarter. Revenues were US$133.1 million, up 3.7% from US$128.3 million the year before. Revenues from property income rose 2.6% to US$121.6 million from US$118.6 million in the corresponding quarter a year earlier.

Prospects: Our evaluation of Life Storage Inc. as of Jan. 21, 2018 is the result of our systematic analysis on three basic characteristics: earnings strength, relative valuation, and recent stock price movement. The company has enjoyed a very positive trend in earnings per share over the past 5 quarters. Because the company lacks sufficient analyst estimate data, we place greater weight on the historical EPS trend as the measure of earnings strength. Based on operating earnings yield, the company is about fairly valued when compared to all of the companies in our coverage universe. Share price changes over the past year indicates that LSI will perform well over the near term.

Financial Data

(US$ in Thousands)	3 Mos	12/31/2017	12/31/2016	12/31/2015	12/31/2014	12/31/2013	12/31/2012	12/31/2011
Earnings Per Share	2.36	2.07	1.96	3.16	2.67	2.36	1.87	1.10
Cash Flow Per Share	5.39	5.36	5.21	5.26	4.42	3.85	3.36	2.90
Tang Book Value Per Share	43.06	43.57	44.96	32.75	28.61	26.76	23.93	22.64
Dividends Per Share	4.000	3.950	3.700	3.200	2.720	2.020	1.800	1.800
Dividend Payout %	169.49	190.82	188.78	101.27	101.87	85.59	96.26	163.64
Income Statement								
Total Revenue	133,094	529,750	462,608	366,602	326,080	273,507	236,007	211,156
EBITDA	51,168	299,624	262,497	206,481	174,200	147,864	123,689	108,097
Depn & Amortn	891	131,774	126,769	59,690	52,691	46,380	42,515	37,762
Income Before Taxes	33,077	93,495	81,291	109,672	86,971	69,524	48,012	31,869
Net Income	33,889	96,365	85,225	112,524	88,531	74,126	55,128	30,592
Average Shares	46,536	46,490	43,407	35,601	33,191	31,453	29,489	27,725
Balance Sheet								
Current Assets	33,299	24,857	37,026	20,747	21,417	22,298	16,508	14,905
Total Assets	3,868,914	3,876,774	3,857,984	2,122,172	1,854,800	1,561,875	1,484,441	1,344,735
Current Liabilities	209,574	102,315	84,832	55,350	50,841	44,449	43,083	38,559
Long-Term Obligations	1,622,157	1,726,763	1,653,552	830,993	801,127	626,254	684,251	625,423
Total Liabilities	1,849,577	1,848,451	1,769,490	919,857	878,931	691,166	755,711	689,196
Stockholders' Equity	2,019,337	2,028,323	2,088,494	1,202,315	975,869	870,709	728,730	655,539
Shares Outstanding	46,514	46,552	46,454	36,710	34,105	32,532	30,446	28,952
Statistical Record								
Return on Assets %	2.84	2.49	2.84	5.66	5.18	4.87	3.89	2.42
Return on Equity %	5.37	4.68	5.17	10.33	9.59	9.27	7.94	4.75
EBITDA Margin %	38.45	56.56	56.74	56.32	53.42	54.06	52.41	51.19
Net Margin %	25.46	18.19	18.42	30.69	27.15	27.10	23.36	14.49
Asset Turnover	0.14	0.14	0.15	0.18	0.19	0.18	0.17	0.17
Current Ratio	0.16	0.24	0.44	0.37	0.42	0.50	0.38	0.39
Debt to Equity	0.80	0.85	0.79	0.69	0.82	0.72	0.94	0.95
Price Range	91.12-70.59	91.12-70.59	117.95-79.15	110.00-86.13	88.94-63.30	78.83-60.67	62.78-43.10	44.60-34.27
P/E Ratio	38.61-29.91	44.02-34.10	60.18-40.38	34.81-27.26	33.31-23.71	33.40-25.71	33.57-23.05	40.55-31.15
Average Yield %	4.98	4.89	3.73	3.40	3.55	2.98	3.37	4.53

Address: 6467 Main Street, Williamsville, NY 14221 **Telephone:** 716-633-1850 **Fax:** 716-633-1860	**Web Site:** www.unclebobs.com **Officers:** Mark G. Barberio - Chairman Kenneth F. (Ken) Myszka - President, Chief Operating Officer	**Auditors:** Ernst & Young LLP **Investor Contact:** 716-633-1850 **Transfer Agents:** American Stock Transfer & Trust Company, Brooklyn, NY

LILLY (ELI) & CO

Exchange	Symbol	Price	52Wk Range	Yield	P/E
NYS	LLY	$85.33 (6/29/2018)	87.89-74.21	2.64	79.01

*7 Year Price Score 101.68 *NYSE Composite Index=100 *12 Month Price Score 100.42

Interim Earnings (Per Share)

Qtr.	Mar	Jun	Sep	Dec
2015	0.50	0.56	0.75	0.45
2016	0.41	0.71	0.73	0.73
2017	(0.10)	0.95	0.53	(1.56)
2018	1.16	...	...	...

Interim Dividends (Per Share)

Amt	Decl	Ex	Rec	Pay
0.52Q	10/16/2017	11/14/2017	11/15/2017	12/08/2017
0.563Q	12/11/2017	02/14/2018	02/15/2018	03/09/2018
0.563Q	05/07/2018	05/16/2018	05/17/2018	06/08/2018
0.563Q	06/18/2018	08/14/2018	08/15/2018	09/10/2018

Indicated Div: $2.25 (Div. Reinv. Plan)

Valuation Analysis		Institutional Holding	
Forecast EPS	$5.16	No of Institutions	
	(06/14/2018)	1913	
Market Cap	$92.6 Billion	Shares	
Book Value	$14.5 Billion	1,007,163,648	
Price/Book	6.38	% Held	
Price/Sales	3.97	72.59	

Business Summary: Pharmaceuticals (MIC: 4.1.1 SIC: 2834 NAIC: 325412)

Eli Lilly & Company is engaged in discovering, developing, manufacturing, and marketing products in two business segments: human pharmaceutical products and animal health products. Co.'s human pharmaceutical products include: endocrinology products, neurosciences products, oncology products, and cardiovascular products. Co.'s animal health products are comprised of products for animals, which include Rumensin, a cattle feed additive, and Tylan, an antibiotic used to control certain diseases in cattle, swine, and poultry; as well as products for companion animals, which include Trifexis and Comfortis, a chewable tablet that kills fleas and prevents flea infestations on dogs.

Recent Developments: For the quarter ended Mar 31 2018, net income amounted to US$1.22 billion versus a net loss of US$110.8 million in the year-earlier quarter. Revenues were US$5.70 billion, up 9.0% from US$5.23 billion the year before. Direct operating expenses rose 16.6% to US$1.57 billion from US$1.35 billion in the comparable period the year before. Indirect operating expenses decreased 29.3% to US$2.76 billion from US$3.90 billion in the equivalent prior-year period.

Prospects: Our evaluation of Lilly (Eli) & Co. as of Jan. 21, 2018 is the result of our systematic analysis on three basic characteristics: earnings strength, relative valuation, and recent stock price movement. The company has managed to produce a neutral trend in earnings per share over the past 5 quarters and while recent estimates for the company have been raised by analysts, LLY has posted better than expected results. Based on operating earnings yield, the company is undervalued when compared to all of the companies in our coverage universe. Share price changes over the past year indicates that LLY will perform well over the near term.

Financial Data
(US$ in Thousands)

	3 Mos	12/31/2017	12/31/2016	12/31/2015	12/31/2014	12/31/2013	12/31/2012	12/31/2011
Earnings Per Share	1.08	(0.19)	2.58	2.26	2.23	4.32	3.66	3.90
Cash Flow Per Share	5.45	5.34	4.57	2.61	4.08	5.31	4.75	6.49
Tang Book Value Per Share	5.71	2.90	5.16	4.97	9.66	11.91	8.75	7.27
Dividends Per Share	2.123	2.080	2.040	2.000	1.960	1.960	1.960	1.960
Dividend Payout %	196.53	...	79.07	88.50	87.89	45.37	53.55	50.26
Income Statement								
Total Revenue	5,700,000	22,871,300	21,222,100	19,958,700	19,615,600	23,113,100	22,603,400	24,286,500
EBITDA	1,879,500	3,018,200	4,166,700	3,581,800	3,787,200	6,704,500	6,235,000	6,188,000
Depn & Amortn	422,800	763,100	716,200	717,600	759,100	774,800	754,000	732,400
Income Before Taxes	1,441,000	2,197,400	3,374,000	2,790,000	3,000,300	5,889,300	5,408,200	5,349,500
Income Taxes	223,600	2,401,500	636,400	381,600	609,800	1,204,500	1,319,600	1,001,800
Net Income	1,217,400	(204,100)	2,737,600	2,408,400	2,390,500	4,684,800	4,088,600	4,347,700
Average Shares	1,049,800	1,052,023	1,061,825	1,065,720	1,074,286	1,084,766	1,117,294	1,113,967
Balance Sheet								
Current Assets	16,261,500	19,202,100	15,101,400	12,573,600	12,179,800	13,104,700	13,038,700	14,248,200
Total Assets	44,355,600	44,981,000	38,805,900	35,568,900	37,178,200	35,248,700	34,398,900	33,659,800
Current Liabilities	11,547,000	14,535,900	10,986,600	8,229,600	11,207,500	8,916,600	8,389,500	8,930,900
Long-Term Obligations	9,393,500	9,940,500	8,367,800	7,972,400	5,367,700	4,200,300	5,519,400	5,464,700
Total Liabilities	29,828,600	33,388,800	24,798,200	20,997,600	21,805,000	17,617,300	19,633,700	20,118,100
Stockholders' Equity	14,527,000	11,592,200	14,007,700	14,571,300	15,373,200	17,631,400	14,765,200	13,541,700
Shares Outstanding	1,085,430	1,100,008	1,100,875	1,105,267	1,110,627	1,116,795	1,143,643	1,157,791
Statistical Record								
Return on Assets %	2.74	N.M.	7.34	6.62	6.60	13.45	11.98	13.45
Return on Equity %	7.87	N.M.	19.11	16.09	14.49	28.92	28.81	33.49
EBITDA Margin %	32.97	13.20	19.63	17.95	19.31	29.01	27.58	25.48
Net Margin %	21.36	N.M.	12.90	12.07	12.19	20.27	18.09	17.90
Asset Turnover	0.57	0.55	0.57	0.55	0.54	0.66	0.66	0.75
Current Ratio	1.41	1.32	1.37	1.53	1.09	1.47	1.55	1.60
Debt to Equity	0.65	0.86	0.60	0.55	0.35	0.24	0.37	0.40
Price Range	87.89-74.21	87.89-74.58	84.26-65.97	89.98-68.41	72.83-50.73	58.33-47.65	53.81-38.49	41.75-33.63
P/E Ratio	81.38-68.71	...	32.66-25.57	39.81-30.27	32.66-22.75	13.50-11.03	14.70-10.52	10.71-8.62
Average Yield %	2.58	2.53	2.67	2.54	3.18	3.72	4.50	5.32

Address: Lilly Corporate Center, Indianapolis, IN 46285 Telephone: 317-276-2000	Web Site: www.lilly.com Officers: David A. Ricks - Chairman, President, Chief Executive Officer, Senior Vice President, Division Officer Jan M. Lundberg - Executive Vice President, Division Officer	Auditors: Ernst & Young LLP Investor Contact: 317-276-2000 Transfer Agents: Wells Fargo Shareowner Services, St. Paul, MN

LINCOLN NATIONAL CORP.

Exchange	Symbol	Price	52Wk Range	Yield	P/E
NYS	LNC	$62.25 (6/29/2018)	85.91-62.09	2.12	6.95

*7 Year Price Score 124.20 *NYSE Composite Index=100 *12 Month Price Score 90.15

Interim Earnings (Per Share)

Qtr.	Mar	Jun	Sep	Dec
2015	1.15	1.35	0.87	1.14
2016	0.82	1.35	2.00	0.87
2017	1.89	1.81	1.87	3.64
2018	1.64	...	...	...

Interim Dividends (Per Share)

Amt	Decl	Ex	Rec	Pay
0.29Q	08/10/2017	10/06/2017	10/10/2017	11/01/2017
0.33Q	11/01/2017	01/09/2018	01/10/2018	02/01/2018
0.33Q	02/22/2018	04/09/2018	04/10/2018	05/01/2018
0.33Q	05/25/2018	07/09/2018	07/10/2018	08/01/2018

Indicated Div: $1.32 (Div. Reinv. Plan)

Valuation Analysis | **Institutional Holding**

Forecast EPS	$8.46	No of Institutions	
	(06/14/2018)	1001	
Market Cap	$13.6 Billion	Shares	
Book Value	$16.0 Billion	230,677,696	
Price/Book	0.85	% Held	
Price/Sales	0.95	77.34	

Business Summary: Life & Health (MIC: 5.2.2 SIC: 6311 NAIC: 524113)

Lincoln National is a holding company. Co. operates multiple insurance and retirement businesses through its subsidiary companies. Co. sells a range of wealth protection, accumulation and retirement income products and solutions. These products include fixed and indexed annuities, variable annuities, universal life insurance (UL), variable universal life insurance, linked-benefit UL, indexed universal life insurance, term life insurance, employer-sponsored retirement plans and services, and group life, disability and dental. Co. provides products and services through its Annuities, Retirement Plan Services, Life Insurance and Group Protection segments.

Recent Developments: For the quarter ended Mar 31 2018, net income decreased 15.6% to US$367.0 million from US$435.0 million in the year-earlier quarter. Revenues were US$3.61 billion, up 3.1% from US$3.50 billion the year before. Net premiums earned were US$777.0 million versus US$807.0 million in the prior-year quarter, a decrease of 3.7%. Net investment income fell 0.4% to US$1.23 billion from US$1.24 billion a year ago.

Prospects: Our evaluation of Lincoln National Corp. (ID) as of Jan. 21, 2018 is the result of our systematic analysis on three basic characteristics: earnings strength, relative valuation, and recent stock price movement. The company has generated a negative trend in earnings per share over the past 5 quarters and while recent estimates for the company have been raised by analysts, LNC has posted better than expected results. Based on operating earnings yield, the company is undervalued when compared to all of the companies in our coverage universe. Share price changes over the past year indicates that LNC will perform poorly over the near term.

Financial Data

(US$ in Thousands)	3 Mos	12/31/2017	12/31/2016	12/31/2015	12/31/2014	12/31/2013	12/31/2012	12/31/2011
Earnings Per Share	8.96	9.22	5.03	4.51	5.67	4.52	4.56	0.92
Cash Flow Per Share	3.75	3.55	5.42	8.95	9.68	3.01	4.51	4.16
Tang Book Value Per Share	66.84	73.15	53.92	46.52	52.49	42.52	46.79	40.82
Dividends Per Share	1.200	1.160	1.000	0.800	0.640	0.480	0.320	0.200
Dividend Payout %	13.39	12.58	19.88	17.74	11.29	10.62	7.02	21.74
Income Statement								
Premium Income	777,000	3,256,000	2,987,000	3,246,000	2,988,000	2,687,000	2,462,000	2,294,000
Total Revenue	3,609,000	14,257,000	13,330,000	13,572,000	13,554,000	11,969,000	11,532,000	10,636,000
Benefits & Claims	1,358,000	5,160,000	4,692,000	5,044,000	4,679,000	3,862,000	3,538,000	3,345,000
Income Before Taxes	435,000	1,130,000	1,458,000	1,430,000	1,997,000	1,631,000	1,568,000	599,000
Income Taxes	68,000	(949,000)	266,000	276,000	483,000	387,000	282,000	297,000
Net Income	367,000	2,079,000	1,192,000	1,154,000	1,515,000	1,244,000	1,313,000	294,000
Average Shares	222,287	226,220	236,830	254,938	267,963	275,148	287,590	314,950
Balance Sheet								
Total Assets	279,237,000	281,763,000	261,627,000	251,937,000	253,377,000	236,945,000	218,869,000	202,906,000
Total Liabilities	263,252,000	264,441,000	247,149,000	238,320,000	237,637,000	223,493,000	203,896,000	188,742,000
Stockholders' Equity	15,985,000	17,322,000	14,478,000	13,617,000	15,740,000	13,452,000	14,973,000	14,164,000
Shares Outstanding	218,695	218,090	226,335	243,835	256,551	262,896	271,402	291,319
Statistical Record								
Return on Assets %	0.74	0.77	0.46	0.46	0.62	0.55	0.62	0.15
Return on Equity %	12.99	13.08	8.46	7.86	10.38	8.75	8.99	2.18
Loss Ratio %	174.77	158.48	157.08	155.39	156.59	143.73	143.70	145.82
Net Margin %	10.17	14.58	8.94	8.50	11.18	10.39	11.39	2.76
Price Range	85.91-63.23	78.54-63.23	68.48-30.78	61.65-46.07	58.80-45.67	51.95-25.90	27.29-19.29	32.49-14.32
P/E Ratio	9.59-7.06	8.52-6.86	13.61-6.12	13.67-10.22	10.37-8.05	11.49-5.73	5.98-4.23	35.32-15.57
Average Yield %	1.65	1.65	2.17	1.45	1.23	1.24	1.37	0.80

| **Address:** 150 N. Radnor Chester Road, Suite A305, Radnor, PA 19087 **Telephone:** 484-583-1400 | **Web Site:** www.lfg.com **Officers:** Dennis R. Glass - President, Chief Executive Officer Lisa M. Buckingham - Executive Vice President, Senior Vice President, Chief Human Resources Officer | **Auditors:** Ernst & Young LLP **Transfer Agents:** Computershare, Providence, RI |

LINDSAY CORP

Exchange	Symbol	Price	52Wk Range	Yield	P/E	Div Acheiver
NYS	LNN	$96.99 (6/29/2018)	101.46-84.54	1.28	46.86	15 Years

*7 Year Price Score 93.81   *NYSE Composite Index=100   *12 Month Price Score 104.32

Interim Earnings (Per Share)

Qtr.	Nov	Feb	May	Aug
2014-15	0.62	0.75	1.10	(0.24)
2015-16	0.62	(0.37)	0.90	0.72
2016-17	0.08	0.47	1.02	0.59
2017-18	0.30	0.16	...	...

Interim Dividends (Per Share)

Amt	Decl	Ex	Rec	Pay
0.30Q	10/12/2017	11/15/2017	11/16/2017	11/30/2017
0.30Q	12/08/2017	02/13/2018	02/14/2018	02/28/2018
0.30Q	05/04/2018	05/16/2018	05/17/2018	05/31/2018
0.31Q	06/27/2018	08/16/2018	08/17/2018	08/31/2018

Indicated Div: $1.24

Valuation Analysis   **Institutional Holding**

Forecast EPS	$3.23	No of Institutions	
	(06/14/2018)	238	
Market Cap	$1.0 Billion	Shares	
Book Value	$273.1 Million	14,795,580	
Price/Book	3.82	% Held	
Price/Sales	1.94	98.96	

Business Summary: Industrial Machinery & Equipment (MIC: 7.2.1 SIC: 3523 NAIC: 333111)

Lindsay is a provider of water management and road infrastructure products and services. Co.'s irrigation segment includes the manufacture and marketing of center pivot, lateral move, hose reel irrigation systems, and repair and replacement parts, and the design and manufacture of water pumping stations and controls for the agriculture, golf, landscape and municipal markets. Co.'s infrastructure segment includes the manufacture and marketing of moveable barriers, specialty barriers, crash cushions and end terminals, road marking and road safety equipment, large diameter steel tubing, and railroad signals and structures, and the provision of outsourced manufacturing and production services.

Recent Developments: For the quarter ended Nov 30 2017, net income increased 264.8% to US$3.2 million from US$873,000 in the year-earlier quarter. Revenues were US$124.5 million, up 12.8% from US$110.4 million the year before. Operating income was US$6.2 million versus US$2.7 million in the prior-year quarter, an increase of 126.7%. Direct operating expenses rose 12.3% to US$92.1 million from US$82.0 million in the comparable period the year before. Indirect operating expenses increased 2.2% to US$26.2 million from US$25.6 million in the equivalent prior-year period.

Prospects: Our evaluation of Lindsay Corp. as of Jan. 21, 2018 is the result of our systematic analysis on three basic characteristics: earnings strength, relative valuation, and recent stock price movement. The company has produced a positive trend in earnings per share over the past 5 quarters and while recent estimates for the company have been raised by analysts, LNN has posted results that fell short of analysts expectations. Based on operating earnings yield, the company is about fairly valued when compared to all of the companies in our coverage universe. Share price changes over the past year indicates that LNN will perform well over the near term.

Financial Data
(US$ in Thousands)

	6 Mos	3 Mos	08/31/2017	08/31/2016	08/31/2015	08/31/2014	08/31/2013	08/31/2012
Earnings Per Share	2.07	2.38	2.17	1.85	2.22	4.00	5.47	3.38
Cash Flow Per Share	1.85	2.46	3.70	3.02	4.12	7.15	4.48	4.12
Tang Book Value Per Share	14.42	14.03	14.03	12.00	14.16	25.21	23.87	20.11
Dividends Per Share	1.190	1.180	1.170	1.130	1.090	0.920	0.475	0.385
Dividend Payout %	57.49	49.58	53.92	61.08	49.10	23.00	8.68	11.39
Income Statement								
Total Revenue	254,865	124,526	517,985	516,411	560,181	617,933	690,848	551,255
EBITDA	20,712	9,988	51,494	45,594	60,446	88,913	116,915	74,696
Depn & Amortn	8,599	4,335	12,200	12,200	11,700	10,800	9,800	9,600
Income Before Taxes	10,468	4,792	35,715	29,288	46,751	78,655	107,307	65,108
Income Taxes	5,548	1,607	12,536	9,021	20,442	27,143	36,737	21,831
Net Income	4,920	3,185	23,179	20,267	26,309	51,512	70,570	43,277
Average Shares	10,765	10,740	10,694	10,930	11,855	12,882	12,901	12,810
Balance Sheet								
Current Assets	313,355	296,234	292,934	292,124	322,167	374,058	368,791	298,865
Total Assets	522,354	503,407	506,032	499,565	536,468	526,551	512,296	415,531
Current Liabilities	104,522	90,123	92,037	87,870	95,112	116,367	102,092	80,438
Long-Term Obligations	116,673	116,724	116,775	116,976	117,173	...	...	...
Total Liabilities	249,294	234,175	235,977	247,998	247,908	143,904	131,658	104,693
Stockholders' Equity	273,060	269,232	270,055	251,567	288,560	382,647	380,638	310,838
Shares Outstanding	10,758	10,722	10,697	10,630	11,290	12,440	12,873	12,723
Statistical Record								
Return on Assets %	4.39	5.18	4.61	3.90	4.95	9.92	15.21	10.83
Return on Equity %	8.44	9.85	8.89	7.48	7.84	13.50	20.41	14.72
EBITDA Margin %	8.13	8.02	9.94	8.83	10.79	14.39	16.92	13.55
Net Margin %	1.93	2.56	4.47	3.92	4.70	8.34	10.21	7.85
Asset Turnover	1.06	1.08	1.03	0.99	1.05	1.19	1.49	1.38
Current Ratio	3.00	3.29	3.18	3.32	3.39	3.21	3.61	3.72
Debt to Equity	0.43	0.43	0.43	0.46	0.41	...	...	...
Price Range	95.05-79.12	95.05-74.03	94.74-69.30	78.57-64.06	89.70-73.48	92.93-72.00	94.57-65.36	73.84-49.53
P/E Ratio	45.92-38.22	39.94-31.11	43.66-31.94	42.47-34.63	40.41-33.10	23.23-18.00	17.29-11.95	21.85-14.65
Average Yield %	1.35	1.38	1.43	1.60	1.33	1.12	0.60	0.63

Address: 2222 North 111th Street, Omaha, NE 68164
Telephone: 402-829-6800
Fax: 402-829-6834

Web Site: www.lindsay.com
Officers: Michael C. Nahl - Chairman Timothy L. Hassinger - President, Chief Executive Officer

Auditors: KPMG LLP
Investor Contact: 402-827-6579
Transfer Agents: Wells Fargo Shareowner Services, St. Paul, MN

LITHIA MOTORS INC

Exchange	Symbol	Price	52Wk Range	Yield	P/E
NYS	LAD	$94.57 (6/29/2018)	126.57-89.21	1.23	9.63

*7 Year Price Score 117.64 *NYSE Composite Index=100   *12 Month Price Score 89.59

TRADING VOLUME (thousand shares)

Interim Earnings (Per Share)

Qtr.	Mar	Jun	Sep	Dec
2015	1.53	1.93	1.64	1.81
2016	1.55	2.01	2.14	2.03
2017	2.01	2.12	2.07	3.56
2018	2.07	...	...	...

Interim Dividends (Per Share)

Amt	Decl	Ex	Rec	Pay
0.27Q	07/28/2017	08/09/2017	08/11/2017	08/25/2017
0.27Q	10/23/2017	11/09/2017	11/10/2017	11/24/2017
0.27Q	02/12/2018	03/08/2018	03/09/2018	03/23/2018
0.29Q	04/23/2018	05/10/2018	05/11/2018	05/25/2018

Indicated Div: $1.16

Valuation Analysis

		Institutional Holding	
Forecast EPS	$10.50 (06/14/2018)	No of Institutions	366
Market Cap	$2.4 Billion	Shares	32,470,520
Book Value	$1.1 Billion	% Held	84.77
Price/Book	2.10		
Price/Sales	0.22		

Business Summary: Retail - Automotive (MIC: 2.1.4 SIC: 5511 NAIC: 441110)

Lithia Motors is an operator of automotive franchises and a retailer of new and used vehicles and related services. As of Feb 23 2018, Co provided 30 brands of new and all brands of used vehicles in 171 stores and online at over 200 websites. Co. sells new and used cars and replacement parts; provide vehicle maintenance, warranty, paint and repair services; arrange related financing; and sell vehicle service contracts, vehicle protection products and credit insurance. Co.'s business segments are Domestic, Import and Luxury. The franchises in each segment also sell used vehicles, parts and automotive services, and automotive finance and insurance products.

Recent Developments: For the quarter ended Mar 31 2018, net income increased 2.6% to US$52.1 million from US$50.7 million in the year-earlier quarter. Revenues were US$2.66 billion, up 18.9% from US$2.24 billion the year before. Operating income was US$93.8 million versus US$86.1 million in the prior-year quarter, an increase of 8.8%. Direct operating expenses rose 18.9% to US$2.25 billion from US$1.89 billion in the comparable period the year before. Indirect operating expenses increased 23.0% to US$314.3 million from US$255.5 million in the equivalent prior-year period.

Prospects: Our evaluation of Lithia Motors Inc. as of Jan. 21, 2018 is the result of our systematic analysis on three basic characteristics: earnings strength, relative valuation, and recent stock price movement. The company has managed to produce a neutral trend in earnings per share over the past 5 quarters and while recent estimates for the company have been mixed, LAD has posted results that fell short of analysts expectations. Based on operating earnings yield, the company is undervalued when compared to all of the companies in our coverage universe. Share price changes over the past year indicates that LAD will perform in line with the market over the near term.

Financial Data
(US$ in Thousands)

	3 Mos	12/31/2017	12/31/2016	12/31/2015	12/31/2014	12/31/2013	12/31/2012	12/31/2011
Earnings Per Share	9.82	9.75	7.72	6.91	5.26	4.05	3.07	2.21
Cash Flow Per Share	2.84	5.94	3.40	2.82	1.16	1.24	(8.25)	(0.03)
Tang Book Value Per Share	34.85	25.63	18.58	17.44	12.31	15.99	12.99	11.14
Dividends Per Share	1.080	1.060	0.950	0.760	0.610	0.390	0.470	0.260
Dividend Payout %	11.00	10.87	12.31	11.00	11.60	9.63	15.31	11.76
Income Statement								
Total Revenue	2,659,679	10,086,510	8,678,157	7,864,252	5,390,326	4,005,749	3,316,487	2,699,360
EBITDA	111,991	478,903	381,630	343,329	261,461	206,546	168,208	129,635
Depn & Amortn	16,854	57,722	49,369	41,600	26,363	20,035	17,314	16,948
Income Before Taxes	69,797	347,069	283,523	262,704	210,495	165,788	128,457	89,175
Income Taxes	17,736	101,852	86,465	79,705	74,955	60,574	49,062	33,408
Net Income	52,061	245,217	197,058	182,999	138,720	106,000	80,362	58,860
Average Shares	25,158	25,145	25,521	26,490	26,382	26,191	26,170	26,664
Balance Sheet								
Current Assets	2,971,440	2,782,782	2,287,194	1,878,865	1,615,509	1,081,549	933,209	648,191
Total Assets	5,086,983	4,683,066	3,844,150	3,227,299	2,880,932	1,725,121	1,492,702	1,146,133
Current Liabilities	2,503,925	2,300,981	1,921,994	1,590,825	1,442,600	872,511	721,304	456,584
Long-Term Obligations	1,181,230	1,028,476	769,916	606,463	609,066	245,471	286,876	278,653
Total Liabilities	3,959,878	3,599,848	2,933,374	2,399,135	2,207,827	1,190,399	1,064,601	779,012
Stockholders' Equity	1,127,105	1,083,218	910,776	828,164	673,105	534,722	428,101	367,121
Shares Outstanding	24,985	24,968	25,144	26,218	26,233	25,891	25,678	25,957
Statistical Record								
Return on Assets %	5.55	5.75	5.56	5.99	6.02	6.59	6.07	5.56
Return on Equity %	23.74	24.60	22.60	24.38	22.97	22.02	20.16	17.13
EBITDA Margin %	4.21	4.75	4.40	4.37	4.85	5.16	5.07	4.80
Net Margin %	1.96	2.43	2.27	2.33	2.57	2.65	2.42	2.18
Asset Turnover	2.36	2.37	2.45	2.57	2.34	2.49	2.51	2.55
Current Ratio	1.19	1.21	1.19	1.18	1.12	1.24	1.29	1.42
Debt to Equity	1.05	0.95	0.85	0.73	0.90	0.46	0.67	0.76
Price Range	126.57-81.12	122.28-81.12	106.67-69.23	126.06-80.98	96.37-54.17	73.67-37.42	37.42-21.17	24.49-13.50
P/E Ratio	12.89-8.26	12.54-8.32	13.82-8.97	18.24-11.72	18.32-10.30	18.19-9.24	12.19-6.90	11.08-6.11
Average Yield %	1.02	1.04	1.11	0.72	0.80	0.69	1.66	1.48

Address: 150 N. Bartlett Street, Medford, OR 97501 **Telephone:** 541-776-6401	**Web Site:** www.lithia.com **Officers:** Sidney B. DeBoer - Executive Chairman, Chairman, Chief Executive Officer, Secretary Bryan B. DeBoer - President, Chief Executive Officer, Chief Operating Officer	**Auditors:** KPMG LLP **Investor Contact:** 877-331-3084 **Transfer Agents:** Broadridge Financial Solutions, Inc., Philadelphia, PA

LIVE NATION ENTERTAINMENT INC

Exchange	Symbol	Price	52Wk Range	Yield	P/E
NYS	LYV	$48.57 (6/29/2018)	48.73-34.01	N/A	N/A

*7 Year Price Score 147.86 *NYSE Composite Index=100 *12 Month Price Score 103.92

Interim Earnings (Per Share)

Qtr.	Mar	Jun	Sep	Dec
2015	(0.31)	0.06	0.38	(0.47)
2016	(0.29)	0.13	0.49	(0.57)
2017	(0.22)	0.29	0.53	(1.10)
2018	(0.24)	...	...	...

Interim Dividends (Per Share)

No Dividends Paid

Valuation Analysis   **Institutional Holding**

Forecast EPS	$0.08	No of Institutions
	(06/14/2018)	506
Market Cap	$10.1 Billion	Shares
Book Value	$1.1 Billion	163,063,040
Price/Book	8.92	% Held
Price/Sales	0.98	73.67

Business Summary: Entertainment (MIC: 2.3.2 SIC: 7929 NAIC: 711410)

Live Nation Entertainment is a live entertainment company. Co.'s reportable segments are: Concerts, which promotes live music events globally, produces music festivals, operates and manages music venues and creates associated content; Sponsorship and Advertising, which manages the development of strategic sponsorship programs, and sells international, national and local sponsorships and placement of advertising across Co.'s distribution network; Ticketing, which manages Co.'s global ticketing operations and is responsible for Co.'s primary websites, www.livenation.com and www.ticketmaster.com; and Artist Nation, which provides management services to music artists and other clients.

Recent Developments: For the quarter ended Mar 31 2018, net loss amounted to US$41.0 million versus a net loss of US$47.8 million in the year-earlier quarter. Revenues were US$1.48 billion, up 19.3% from US$1.24 billion the year before. Operating loss was US$6.0 million versus a loss of US$21.4 million in the prior-year quarter. Direct operating expenses rose 20.2% to US$932.1 million from US$775.3 million in the comparable period the year before. Indirect operating expenses increased 13.8% to US$556.3 million from US$489.0 million in the equivalent prior-year period.

Prospects: Our evaluation of Live Nation Entertainment, Inc. as of Jan. 21, 2018 is the result of our systematic analysis on three basic characteristics: earnings strength, relative valuation, and recent stock price movement. The company has suffered a very negative trend in earnings per share over the past 5 quarters. Because the company lacks sufficient analyst estimate data, we place greater weight on the historical EPS trend as the measure of earnings strength. Based on operating earnings yield, the company is overvalued when compared to all of the companies in our coverage universe. Share price changes over the past year indicates that LYV will perform very well over the near term.

Financial Data
(US$ in Thousands)

	3 Mos	12/31/2017	12/31/2016	12/31/2015	12/31/2014	12/31/2013	12/31/2012	12/31/2011
Earnings Per Share	(0.52)	(0.48)	(0.23)	(0.33)	(0.49)	(0.22)	(0.87)	(0.46)
Cash Flow Per Share	3.09	3.04	2.95	1.49	1.35	2.15	1.96	0.74
Income Statement								
Total Revenue	1,482,384	10,337,448	8,354,934	7,245,731	6,866,964	6,478,547	5,819,047	5,383,998
EBITDA	98,515	240,098	309,349	238,352	125,888	222,759	102,081	141,007
Depn & Amortn	107,816	149,634	139,288	134,148	127,168	122,164	124,593	129,177
Income Before Taxes	(37,859)	(10,541)	66,128	4,851	(103,986)	(5,993)	(142,082)	(104,369)
Income Taxes	6,884	(17,154)	28,029	22,122	4,630	30,878	29,736	(26,224)
Net Income	(33,906)	(6,015)	2,942	(32,508)	(90,807)	(43,378)	(163,227)	(83,016)
Average Shares	206,728	204,923	202,076	200,973	198,874	193,885	186,955	182,388
Balance Sheet								
Current Assets	4,644,690	3,152,742	2,673,551	2,288,315	2,267,691	2,160,104	1,812,812	1,576,790
Total Assets	9,117,548	7,504,263	6,764,266	6,156,241	5,988,361	5,683,521	5,290,806	5,087,771
Current Liabilities	4,438,713	3,577,000	2,460,344	2,101,206	2,010,781	2,255,518	1,768,172	1,492,553
Long-Term Obligations	2,747,399	1,952,366	2,259,736	2,002,662	2,015,915	1,530,484	1,677,955	1,663,056
Total Liabilities	7,979,877	6,323,067	5,638,250	4,919,288	4,691,407	4,274,293	3,935,388	3,626,668
Stockholders' Equity	1,137,671	1,181,196	1,126,016	1,236,953	1,296,954	1,409,228	1,355,418	1,461,103
Shares Outstanding	208,917	208,075	204,067	202,483	201,193	199,566	190,853	188,957
Statistical Record								
Return on Assets %	N.M.	N.M.	0.05	N.M.	N.M.	N.M.	N.M.	N.M.
Return on Equity %	N.M.	N.M.	0.25	N.M.	N.M.	N.M.	N.M.	N.M.
EBITDA Margin %	6.65	2.32	3.70	3.29	1.83	3.44	1.75	2.62
Net Margin %	N.M.	N.M.	0.04	N.M.	N.M.	N.M.	N.M.	N.M.
Asset Turnover	1.23	1.45	1.29	1.19	1.18	1.18	1.12	1.05
Current Ratio	1.05	0.88	1.09	1.09	1.13	0.96	1.03	1.06
Debt to Equity	2.41	1.65	2.01	1.62	1.55	1.09	1.24	1.14
Price Range	48.59-30.37	46.41-27.29	28.78-19.36	29.21-23.58	27.36-19.76	19.82-9.31	10.88-8.21	12.26-7.33

Address: 9348 Civic Center Drive,	Web Site: www.livenation.com; www.ticketmaster.com	Auditors: Ernst & Young LLP
Beverly Hills, CA 90210	Officers: Irving L. Azoff - Executive Chairman	Investor Contact: 310-867-7000
Telephone: 310-867-7000	Michael Rapino - President, Chief Executive Officer	Transfer Agents: Computershare, Providence, RI

LOCKHEED MARTIN CORP

Exchange	Symbol	Price	52Wk Range	Yield	P/E	Div Acheiver
NYS	LMT	$295.43 (6/29/2018)	361.00-277.61	2.71	35.59	15 Years

*7 Year Price Score 137.56 *NYSE Composite Index=100 *12 Month Price Score 96.88

TRADING VOLUME (thousand shares)

Interim Earnings (Per Share)

Qtr.	Mar	Jun	Sep	Dec
2015	2.74	2.94	2.77	3.01
2016	2.58	3.32	7.93	3.39
2017	2.61	3.23	3.24	(2.19)
2018	4.02	...	...	...

Interim Dividends (Per Share)

Amt	Decl	Ex	Rec	Pay
2.00Q	09/28/2017	11/30/2017	12/01/2017	12/29/2017
2.00Q	01/24/2018	02/28/2018	03/01/2018	03/23/2018
2.00Q	04/25/2018	05/31/2018	06/01/2018	06/22/2018
2.00Q	06/28/2018	08/31/2018	09/04/2018	09/28/2018

Indicated Div: $8.00 (Div. Reinv. Plan)

Valuation Analysis | **Institutional Holding**

Forecast EPS	$16.15	No of Institutions
	(06/14/2018)	1906
Market Cap	$84.4 Billion	Shares
Book Value	N/A	281,531,744
Price/Book	N/A	% Held
Price/Sales	1.63	83.15

Business Summary: Defense (MIC: 7.1.2 SIC: 3761 NAIC: 336414)

Lockheed Martin is a security and aerospace company. Co. has four segments: Aeronautics, designs, develops, manufactures, integrates, sustains, supports, and upgrades military aircraft; Missiles and Fire Control, provides air and missile defense systems, tactical missiles and air-to-ground precision strike weapon systems; Rotary and Mission Systems, designs, manufactures, services and supports military and civil helicopters, ship and submarine mission and combat systems; and Space Systems, engages in the research and development, design, engineering and production of satellites, strategic and defensive missile systems and space transportation systems.

Recent Developments: For the quarter ended Mar 25 2018, net income increased 46.6% to US$1.16 billion from US$789.0 million in the year-earlier quarter. Revenues were US$11.64 billion, up 3.8% from US$11.21 billion the year before. Operating income was US$1.73 billion versus US$1.40 billion in the prior-year quarter, an increase of 23.0%. Direct operating expenses rose 1.7% to US$9.98 billion from US$9.81 billion in the comparable period the year before. Indirect operating income amounted to US$67.0 million compared with an expense of US$4.0 million in the equivalent prior-year period.

Prospects: Our evaluation of Lockheed Martin Corp. as of Jan. 21, 2018 is the result of our systematic analysis on three basic characteristics: earnings strength, relative valuation, and recent stock price movement. The company has produced a positive trend in earnings per share over the past 5 quarters and while recent estimates for the company have been raised by analysts, LMT has posted results that fell short of analysts expectations. Based on operating earnings yield, the company is about fairly valued when compared to all of the companies in our coverage universe. Share price changes over the past year indicates that LMT will perform well over the near term.

Financial Data

(US$ in Millions)	3 Mos	12/31/2017	12/31/2016	12/31/2015	12/31/2014	12/31/2013	12/31/2012	12/31/2011
Earnings Per Share	8.30	6.89	17.49	11.46	11.21	9.13	8.36	7.81
Cash Flow Per Share	19.06	22.50	17.29	16.44	12.20	14.17	4.81	12.66
Dividends Per Share	7.640	7.460	6.770	6.150	5.490	4.780	4.150	3.250
Dividend Payout %	92.05	108.27	38.71	53.66	48.97	52.35	49.64	41.61
Income Statement								
Total Revenue	11,635	51,048	47,248	46,132	45,600	45,358	47,182	46,499
EBITDA	1,794	7,115	6,764	6,492	6,592	5,495	5,443	4,993
Depn & Amortn	279	1,195	1,215	1,026	994	990	988	1,008
Income Before Taxes	1,360	5,269	4,886	5,023	5,258	4,155	4,072	3,631
Income Taxes	203	3,340	1,133	1,418	1,644	1,205	1,327	964
Net Income	1,157	2,002	5,302	3,605	3,614	2,981	2,745	2,655
Average Shares	287	290	303	314	322	326	328	339
Balance Sheet								
Current Assets	17,816	17,461	15,108	16,198	12,329	13,329	13,855	14,094
Total Assets	46,634	46,521	47,806	49,128	37,073	36,188	38,657	37,908
Current Liabilities	13,974	12,637	12,542	14,057	11,112	11,120	12,155	12,130
Long-Term Obligations	13,473	13,513	14,282	14,305	6,169	6,152	6,158	6,460
Total Liabilities	46,816	47,204	46,295	46,031	33,673	31,270	38,618	36,907
Stockholders' Equity	(182)	(683)	1,511	3,097	3,400	4,918	39	1,001
Shares Outstanding	285	284	289	303	314	319	321	321
Statistical Record								
Return on Assets %	5.02	4.24	10.91	8.36	9.87	7.97	7.15	7.28
Return on Equity %	368.33	483.57	229.49	110.97	86.90	120.27	526.44	112.76
EBITDA Margin %	15.42	13.94	14.32	14.07	14.46	12.11	11.54	10.74
Net Margin %	9.94	3.92	11.22	7.81	7.93	6.57	5.82	5.71
Asset Turnover	1.08	1.08	0.97	1.07	1.24	1.21	1.23	1.27
Current Ratio	1.27	1.38	1.20	1.15	1.11	1.20	1.14	1.16
Debt to Equity	...	...	9.45	4.62	1.81	1.25	157.90	6.45
Price Range	361.00-266.98	322.82-250.90	267.62-206.08	226.43-185.52	196.84-146.07	148.84-86.70	94.87-79.98	82.27-66.87
P/E Ratio	43.49-32.17	46.85-36.42	15.30-11.78	19.76-16.19	17.56-13.03	16.30-9.50	11.35-9.57	10.53-8.56
Average Yield %	2.50	2.59	2.85	3.03	3.25	4.24	4.68	4.21

Address: 6801 Rockledge Drive, Bethesda, MD 20817-1877 **Telephone:** 301-897-6000	**Web Site:** www.lockheedmartin.com **Officers:** Marillyn A. Hewson - Chairman, President, President (frmr), President (frmr-frmr), Chief Executive Officer, Chief Executive Officer (frmr), Executive Vice President, Chief Operating Officer Bruce L. Tanner - Executive Vice President, Chief Financial Officer	**Auditors:** Ernst & Young LLP **Investor Contact:** 301-897-6584 **Transfer Agents:** Computershare Trust Company, N.A., Providence, RI

LOEWS CORP.

Exchange	Symbol	Price	52Wk Range	Yield	P/E
NYS	L	$48.28 (6/29/2018)	53.46-45.12	0.52	13.91

*7 Year Price Score 92.50 *NYSE Composite Index=100 *12 Month Price Score 99.66

Interim Earnings (Per Share)

Qtr.	Mar	Jun	Sep	Dec
2015	0.29	0.46	0.50	(0.53)
2016	0.30	(0.19)	0.97	0.85
2017	0.87	0.69	0.46	1.43
2018	0.89	...	...	...

Interim Dividends (Per Share)

Amt	Decl	Ex	Rec	Pay
0.063Q	08/08/2017	08/28/2017	08/30/2017	09/12/2017
0.063Q	11/14/2017	11/28/2017	11/29/2017	12/12/2017
0.063Q	02/13/2018	02/27/2018	02/28/2018	03/13/2018
0.063Q	05/08/2018	05/29/2018	05/30/2018	06/12/2018

Indicated Div: $0.25

Valuation Analysis

Forecast EPS	$3.50
	(06/14/2018)
Market Cap	$15.6 Billion
Book Value	$18.5 Billion
Price/Book	0.84
Price/Sales	1.11

Institutional Holding

No of Institutions	725
Shares	279,740,160
% Held	56.19

TRADING VOLUME (thousand shares)

Business Summary: General Insurance (MIC: 5.2.1 SIC: 6331 NAIC: 524126)

Loews is a holding company. Co. is engaged in: commercial property and casualty insurance, including surety through its 90.0% owned subsidiary, CNA Financial Corporation; operation of offshore oil and gas drilling rigs through its 53.0% owned subsidiary, Diamond Offshore Drilling, Inc.; transportation and storage of natural gas and natural gas liquids and gathering and processing of natural gas through its 53% owned subsidiary, Boardwalk Pipeline Partners, LP; and operation a chain of hotels in the U.S. and Canada through its Loews Hotels Holding Corporation subsidiary.

Recent Developments: For the quarter ended Mar 31 2018, net income decreased 2.8% to US$380.0 million from US$391.0 million in the year-earlier quarter. Revenues were US$3.58 billion, up 8.5% from US$3.30 billion the year before. Net premiums earned were US$1.79 billion versus US$1.65 billion in the prior-year quarter, an increase of 8.5%. Net investment income fell 16.2% to US$506.0 million from US$604.0 million a year ago.

Prospects: Our evaluation of Loews Corp. as of Jan. 21, 2018 is the result of our systematic analysis on three basic characteristics: earnings strength, relative valuation, and recent stock price movement. The company has generated a negative trend in earnings per share over the past 5 quarters and while recent estimates for the company have been raised by analysts, L has posted better than expected results. Based on operating earnings yield, the company is undervalued when compared to all of the companies in our coverage universe. Share price changes over the past year indicates that L will perform poorly over the near term.

Financial Data
(US$ in Thousands)

	3 Mos	12/31/2017	12/31/2016	12/31/2015	12/31/2014	12/31/2013	12/31/2012	12/31/2011
Earnings Per Share	3.47	3.45	1.93	0.72	1.55	1.53	1.43	2.63
Cash Flow Per Share	9.47	7.69	6.65	9.79	7.83	5.40	7.20	9.80
Tang Book Value Per Share	55.43	55.84	52.93	50.63	50.70	49.36	47.12	45.25
Dividends Per Share	0.250	0.250	0.250	0.250	0.250	0.250	0.250	0.250
Dividend Payout %	7.20	7.25	12.95	34.72	16.13	16.34	17.48	9.51
Income Statement								
Premium Income	1,785,000	6,988,000	6,924,000	6,921,000	7,212,000	7,271,000	6,882,000	6,603,000
Total Revenue	3,581,000	13,735,000	13,105,000	13,415,000	14,325,000	15,053,000	14,552,000	14,127,000
Benefits & Claims	1,339,000	5,310,000	5,283,000	5,384,000	5,591,000	5,947,000	5,896,000	5,489,000
Income Before Taxes	405,000	1,582,000	936,000	244,000	1,810,000	1,429,000	1,399,000	2,232,000
Income Taxes	25,000	170,000	220,000	(43,000)	457,000	360,000	289,000	536,000
Net Income	293,000	1,164,000	654,000	260,000	591,000	595,000	568,000	1,064,000
Average Shares	328,720	337,500	338,310	362,690	382,550	389,510	395,870	405,320
Balance Sheet								
Total Assets	80,786,000	79,586,000	76,594,000	76,029,000	78,367,000	79,939,000	80,021,000	75,375,000
Total Liabilities	62,254,000	60,382,000	58,431,000	58,468,000	59,087,000	60,481,000	60,562,000	56,540,000
Stockholders' Equity	18,532,000	19,204,000	18,163,000	17,561,000	19,280,000	19,458,000	19,459,000	18,835,000
Shares Outstanding	322,396	332,087	336,621	339,897	372,934	386,960	391,805	396,200
Statistical Record								
Return on Assets %	1.47	1.49	0.85	0.34	0.75	0.74	0.73	1.40
Return on Equity %	6.28	6.23	3.65	1.41	3.05	3.06	2.96	5.71
Loss Ratio %	75.01	75.99	76.30	77.79	77.52	81.79	85.67	83.13
Net Margin %	8.18	8.47	4.99	1.94	4.13	3.95	3.90	7.53
Price Range	53.46-45.12	50.65-45.12	47.90-34.21	42.53-35.36	48.24-39.07	49.20-40.75	43.17-37.31	44.26-33.50
P/E Ratio	15.41-13.00	14.68-13.08	24.82-17.73	59.07-49.11	31.12-25.21	32.16-26.63	30.19-26.09	16.83-12.74
Average Yield %	0.51	0.52	0.62	0.64	0.58	0.55	0.62	0.63

Address: 667 Madison Avenue, New York, NY 10065-8087 Telephone: 212-521-2000	Web Site: www.loews.com Officers: Andrew H. Tisch - Co-Chairman Jonathan M. Tisch - Co-Chairman	Auditors: DELOITTE & TOUCHE LLP Transfer Agents: Computershare Shareowner Services, Jersey City, NJ

LOUISIANA-PACIFIC CORP

Exchange	Symbol	Price	52Wk Range	Yield	P/E
NYS	LPX	$27.22 (6/29/2018)	31.06-23.45	1.91	9.35

*7 Year Price Score 126.62 *NYSE Composite Index=100 *12 Month Price Score 101.95

Interim Earnings (Per Share)

Qtr.	Mar	Jun	Sep	Dec
2015	(0.24)	(0.14)	(0.19)	(0.05)
2016	0.07	0.22	0.45	0.29
2017	0.38	0.65	0.75	0.89
2018	0.62	...	...	...

Interim Dividends (Per Share)

Amt	Decl	Ex	Rec	Pay
0.13Q	02/13/2018	02/23/2018	02/26/2018	03/13/2018
0.13Q	05/04/2018	05/17/2018	05/18/2018	06/01/2018

Indicated Div: $0.52

Valuation Analysis **Institutional Holding**

Forecast EPS	$3.04	No of Institutions
	(06/20/2018)	498
Market Cap	$4.0 Billion	Shares
Book Value	$1.7 Billion	167,111,552
Price/Book	2.36	% Held
Price/Sales	1.40	97.24

Business Summary: Paper & Forest Products (MIC: 8.1.2 SIC: 2493 NAIC: 321219)

Louisiana-Pacific is a manufacturer of building products. Co.'s products are used primarily in new home construction, repair and remodeling and outdoor structures. Co. operates in four segments: North America oriented strand board (OSB), which manufactures and distributes OSB structural panel products; siding, which includes SmartSide siding products and related accessories, and CanExel siding and accessories; engineered wood products, which manufactures and distributes laminated veneer lumber, I-Joists, laminated strand lumber and other related products; and South America, which manufactures and distributes OSB and siding products in South America and certain export markets.

Recent Developments: For the quarter ended Mar 31 2018, income from continuing operations increased 72.5% to US$94.9 million from US$55.0 million in the year-earlier quarter. Net income increased 65.3% to US$90.9 million from US$55.0 million in the year-earlier quarter. Revenues were US$691.3 million, up 13.2% from US$610.9 million the year before. Operating income was US$127.2 million versus US$75.4 million in the prior-year quarter, an increase of 68.7%. Direct operating expenses rose 6.6% to US$514.5 million from US$482.8 million in the comparable period the year before. Indirect operating expenses decreased 5.9% to US$49.6 million from US$52.7 million in the equivalent prior-year period.

Prospects: Our evaluation of Louisiana-Pacific Corp. as of Jan. 21, 2018 is the result of our systematic analysis on three basic characteristics: earnings strength, relative valuation, and recent stock price movement. The company has generated a negative trend in earnings per share over the past 5 quarters. However, while recent estimates for the company have been lowered by analysts, LPX has posted results that fell short of analysts expectations. Based on operating earnings yield, the company is undervalued when compared to all of the companies in our coverage universe. Share price changes over the past year indicates that LPX will perform well over the near term.

Financial Data

(US$ in Thousands)	3 Mos	12/31/2017	12/31/2016	12/31/2015	12/31/2014	12/31/2013	12/31/2012	12/31/2011
Earnings Per Share	2.91	2.66	1.03	(0.62)	(0.53)	1.23	0.20	(1.36)
Cash Flow Per Share	3.34	3.28	2.38	0.21	(0.37)	1.74	0.81	(0.30)
Tang Book Value Per Share	11.34	10.89	8.22	7.04	7.78	8.62	7.46	7.29
Dividends Per Share	0.130	...	...	...	...	...	...	...
Dividend Payout %	4.47	...	...	...	...	...	...	...
Income Statement								
Total Revenue	691,300	2,733,900	2,233,400	1,892,500	1,934,800	2,085,200	1,715,800	1,356,900
EBITDA	160,000	533,100	309,800	37,700	25,500	333,900	161,200	(48,300)
Depn & Amortn	31,000	3,600	112,800	101,900	100,700	91,300	73,900	78,900
Income Before Taxes	124,600	510,200	164,900	(95,400)	(105,000)	206,600	38,000	(184,100)
Income Taxes	29,700	119,100	19,800	(2,700)	(27,200)	41,100	7,600	(39,100)
Net Income	90,900	389,800	149,800	(88,100)	(75,400)	177,100	28,800	(181,300)
Average Shares	146,700	146,400	145,300	142,400	141,100	144,300	142,600	133,200
Balance Sheet								
Current Assets	1,405,600	1,359,600	1,016,500	769,100	950,300	1,034,200	995,600	656,800
Total Assets	2,499,200	2,448,500	2,031,200	2,176,300	2,353,500	2,493,300	2,331,000	2,139,900
Current Liabilities	237,600	270,100	228,800	143,000	172,700	166,200	239,300	139,500
Long-Term Obligations	351,100	350,800	374,400	751,800	759,500	762,700	782,700	715,900
Total Liabilities	826,800	844,000	835,500	1,159,300	1,237,700	1,267,000	1,297,200	1,139,000
Stockholders' Equity	1,672,400	1,604,500	1,195,700	1,017,000	1,115,800	1,226,300	1,033,800	1,000,900
Shares Outstanding	145,177	144,895	144,316	142,984	142,226	141,124	138,534	137,139
Statistical Record								
Return on Assets %	18.60	17.40	7.10	N.M.	N.M.	7.34	1.28	N.M.
Return on Equity %	29.10	27.84	13.50	N.M.	N.M.	15.67	2.82	N.M.
EBITDA Margin %	23.14	19.50	13.87	1.99	1.32	16.01	9.40	N.M.
Net Margin %	13.15	14.26	6.71	N.M.	N.M.	8.49	1.68	N.M.
Asset Turnover	1.23	1.22	1.06	0.84	0.80	0.86	0.77	0.60
Current Ratio	5.92	5.03	4.44	5.38	5.50	6.22	4.16	4.71
Debt to Equity	0.21	0.22	0.31	0.74	0.68	0.62	0.76	0.72
Price Range	30.74-22.28	29.14-18.83	20.86-13.78	18.70-14.19	18.79-12.61	22.18-14.75	19.32-7.68	11.57-4.63
P/E Ratio	10.56-7.66	10.95-7.08	20.25-13.38	...	...	18.03-11.99	96.60-38.40	...
Average Yield %	0.49	...	...	...	...	...	...	...

Address: 414 Union Street, Nashville, TN 37219	**Web Site:** www.lpcorp.com	**Auditors:** DELOITTE & TOUCHE LLP
Telephone: 615-986-5600	**Officers:** E. Gary Cook - Chairman William Bradley (Brad) Southern - Executive Vice President, Chief Operating Officer, Chief Executive Officer	**Transfer Agents:** Computershare Trust Company, N.A., Providence, RI
Fax: 615-986-5666		

LOWE'S COMPANIES INC

Exchange	Symbol	Price	52Wk Range	Yield	P/E	Div Acheiver
NYS	LOW	$95.57 (6/29/2018)	107.40-72.56	2.01	20.82	56 Years

*7 Year Price Score 119.20 *NYSE Composite Index=100 *12 Month Price Score 107.96

Interim Earnings (Per Share)

Qtr.	Apr	Jul	Oct	Jan
2015-16	0.70	1.20	0.80	0.03
2016-17	0.98	1.31	0.43	0.74
2017-18	0.70	1.68	1.05	0.67
2018-19	1.19	...	...	...

Interim Dividends (Per Share)

Amt	Decl	Ex	Rec	Pay
0.41Q	08/18/2017	10/24/2017	10/25/2017	11/08/2017
0.41Q	11/10/2017	01/23/2018	01/24/2018	02/07/2018
0.41Q	03/23/2018	04/24/2018	04/25/2018	05/09/2018
0.48Q	06/01/2018	07/24/2018	07/25/2018	08/08/2018

Indicated Div: $1.92 (Div. Reinv. Plan)

Valuation Analysis | **Institutional Holding**

Forecast EPS	$5.45	No of Institutions
	(06/14/2018)	2000
Market Cap	$78.6 Billion	Shares
Book Value	$5.7 Billion	805,358,976
Price/Book	13.67	% Held
Price/Sales	1.14	62.94

Business Summary: Retail - Hardware & Home Improvement (MIC: 2.1.8 SIC: 5211 NAIC: 444110)

Lowe's Companies is a home improvement retailer. As of Feb 2 2018, Co. operated 2,152 home improvement and hardware stores in the U.S., Canada and Mexico. Co. operated 87 Orchard Supply Hardware stores. Co. sells products in the following categories: Lumber and Building Materials; Tools and Hardware; Appliances; Fashion Fixtures; Rough Plumbing and Electrical; Seasonal Living; Lawn and Garden; Paint; Millwork; Flooring; Kitchens; Outdoor Power Equipment; and Home Fashions. Co.'s services includes installation services through independent contractors, and extended protection plans and repair services.

Recent Developments: For the quarter ended May 4 2018, net income increased 64.1% to US$988.0 million from US$602.0 million in the year-earlier quarter. Revenues were US$17.36 billion, up 3.0% from US$16.86 billion the year before. Operating income was US$1.47 billion versus US$1.56 billion in the prior-year quarter, a decrease of 6.0%. Direct operating expenses rose 2.6% to US$11.35 billion from US$11.06 billion in the comparable period the year before. Indirect operating expenses increased 7.2% to US$4.55 billion from US$4.24 billion in the equivalent prior-year period.

Prospects: Our evaluation of Lowe's Companies Inc. as of Jan. 21, 2018 is the result of our systematic analysis on three basic characteristics: earnings strength, relative valuation, and recent stock price movement. The company has generated a negative trend in earnings per share over the past 5 quarters. However, while recent estimates for the company have been mixed, LOW has posted better than expected results. Based on operating earnings yield, the company is about fairly valued when compared to all of the companies in our coverage universe. Share price changes over the past year indicates that LOW will perform very poorly over the near term.

Financial Data

(US$ in Thousands)	3 Mos	02/02/2018	02/03/2017	01/29/2016	01/30/2015	01/31/2014	02/01/2013	02/03/2012
Earnings Per Share	4.59	4.09	3.47	2.73	2.71	2.14	1.69	1.43
Cash Flow Per Share	6.30	6.05	6.28	5.17	5.00	3.89	3.28	3.37
Tang Book Value Per Share	5.42	5.50	6.18	8.41	10.38	11.51	12.48	13.32
Dividends Per Share	1.640	1.580	1.330	1.070	0.870	0.700	0.620	0.530
Dividend Payout %	35.73	38.63	38.33	39.19	32.10	32.71	36.69	37.06
Income Statement								
Total Revenue	17,360,000	68,619,000	65,017,000	59,074,000	56,223,000	53,417,000	50,521,000	50,208,000
EBITDA	1,852,000	7,522,000	7,346,000	6,455,000	6,277,000	5,611,000	5,083,000	4,757,000
Depn & Amortn	387,000	1,400,000	1,500,000	1,484,000	1,485,000	1,462,000	1,523,000	1,480,000
Income Before Taxes	1,305,000	5,489,000	5,201,000	4,419,000	4,276,000	3,673,000	3,137,000	2,906,000
Income Taxes	317,000	2,042,000	2,108,000	1,873,000	1,578,000	1,387,000	1,178,000	1,067,000
Net Income	988,000	3,447,000	3,093,000	2,546,000	2,698,000	2,286,000	1,959,000	1,839,000
Average Shares	826,000	840,000	881,000	929,000	990,000	1,061,000	1,152,000	1,273,000
Balance Sheet								
Current Assets	16,033,000	12,772,000	12,000,000	10,561,000	10,080,000	10,296,000	9,784,000	10,072,000
Total Assets	38,237,000	35,291,000	34,408,000	31,266,000	31,827,000	32,732,000	32,666,000	33,559,000
Current Liabilities	15,774,000	12,096,000	11,974,000	10,492,000	9,348,000	8,876,000	7,708,000	7,891,000
Long-Term Obligations	14,948,000	15,564,000	14,394,000	11,545,000	10,815,000	10,086,000	9,030,000	7,035,000
Total Liabilities	32,492,000	29,418,000	27,974,000	23,612,000	21,859,000	20,879,000	18,809,000	17,026,000
Stockholders' Equity	5,745,000	5,873,000	6,434,000	7,654,000	9,968,000	11,853,000	13,857,000	16,533,000
Shares Outstanding	822,000	830,000	866,000	910,000	960,000	1,030,000	1,110,000	1,241,000
Statistical Record								
Return on Assets %	10.11	9.92	9.27	8.09	8.38	7.01	5.93	5.38
Return on Equity %	67.99	56.17	43.20	28.98	24.80	17.83	12.93	10.44
EBITDA Margin %	10.67	10.96	11.30	10.93	11.16	10.50	10.06	9.47
Net Margin %	5.69	5.02	4.76	4.31	4.80	4.28	3.88	3.66
Asset Turnover	1.82	1.97	1.95	1.88	1.75	1.64	1.53	1.47
Current Ratio	1.02	1.06	1.00	1.01	1.08	1.16	1.27	1.28
Debt to Equity	2.60	2.65	2.24	1.51	1.08	0.85	0.65	0.43
Price Range	107.40-72.56	107.40-72.24	82.94-63.40	77.61-66.25	70.44-44.63	51.95-35.86	38.58-24.85	27.46-18.11
P/E Ratio	23.40-15.81	26.26-17.66	23.90-18.27	28.43-24.27	25.99-16.47	24.28-16.76	22.83-14.70	19.20-12.66
Average Yield %	1.95	1.93	1.79	1.49	1.64	1.59	2.03	2.24

Address: 1000 Lowe's Blvd., Mooresville, NC 28117
Telephone: 704-758-1000

Web Site: www.lowes.com
Officers: Richard W. Dreiling - Chairman Marvin R. Ellison - President, Chief Executive Officer

Auditors: Deloitte & Touche LLP
Investor Contact: 704-758-2033
Transfer Agents: Computershare Trust Company N.A., Providence, RI

L3 TECHNOLOGIES INC

Exchange	Symbol	Price	52Wk Range	Yield	P/E	Div Acheiver
NYS	LLL	$192.32 (6/29/2018)	217.46-167.08	1.66	21.37	13 Years

*7 Year Price Score 129.86 *NYSE Composite Index=100 *12 Month Price Score 98.92

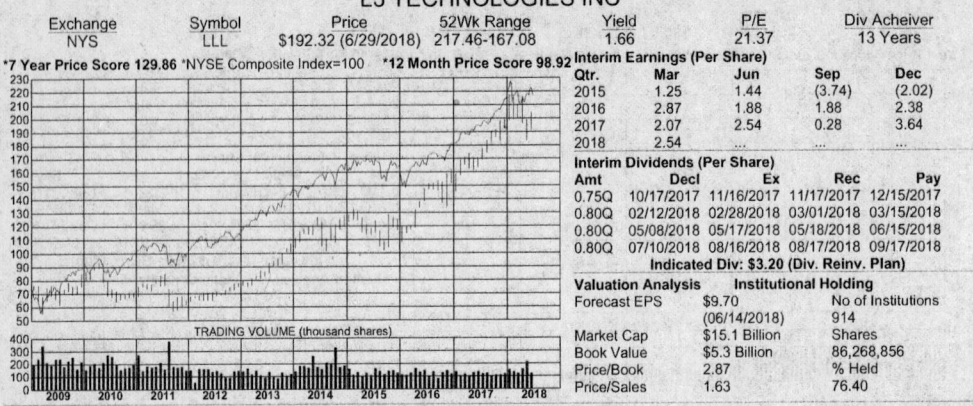

Interim Earnings (Per Share)

Qtr.	Mar	Jun	Sep	Dec
2015	1.25	1.44	(3.74)	(2.02)
2016	2.87	1.88	1.88	2.38
2017	2.07	2.54	0.28	3.64
2018	2.54	...	...	...

Interim Dividends (Per Share)

Amt	Decl	Ex	Rec	Pay
0.75Q	10/17/2017	11/16/2017	11/17/2017	12/15/2017
0.80Q	02/12/2018	02/28/2018	03/01/2018	03/15/2018
0.80Q	05/08/2018	05/17/2018	05/18/2018	06/15/2018
0.80Q	07/10/2018	08/16/2018	08/17/2018	09/17/2018

Indicated Div: $3.20 (Div. Reinv. Plan)

Valuation Analysis **Institutional Holding**

Forecast EPS	$9.70	No of Institutions
	(06/14/2018)	914
Market Cap	$15.1 Billion	Shares
Book Value	$5.3 Billion	86,268,856
Price/Book	2.87	% Held
Price/Sales	1.63	76.40

Business Summary: Aerospace (MIC: 7.1.1 SIC: 3812 NAIC: 334511)

L3 Technologies together with its subsidiaries, is a contractor in Intelligence, Surveillance and Reconnaissance systems, aircraft sustainment (including modifications, logistics and maintenance), simulation and training, night vision and image intensification equipment, and security and detection systems. Co. is also a provider of a range of communication and electronic systems and products used on military and commercial platforms. Co.'s customers include the U.S. Department of Defense and its contractors. Co. has three reportable segments: Electronic Systems, Aerospace Systems, and Communication Systems.

Recent Developments: For the quarter ended Mar 30 2018, income from continuing operations increased 22.3% to US$192.0 million from US$157.0 million in the year-earlier quarter. Net income increased 23.8% to US$208.0 million from US$168.0 million in the year-earlier quarter. Revenues were US$2.37 billion, up 2.2% from US$2.32 billion the year before. Operating income was US$251.0 million versus US$237.0 million in the prior-year quarter, an increase of 5.9%. Direct operating expenses declined 0.2% to US$1.72 billion from US$1.73 billion in the comparable period the year before. Indirect operating expenses increased 10.9% to US$397.0 million from US$358.0 million in the equivalent prior-year period.

Prospects: Our evaluation of L3 Technologies Inc. as of Jan. 21, 2018 is the result of our systematic analysis on three basic characteristics: earnings strength, relative valuation, and recent stock price movement. The company has generated a negative trend in earnings per share over the past 5 quarters. However, while recent estimates for the company have been mixed, LLL has posted better than expected results. Based on operating earnings yield, the company is about fairly valued when compared to all of the companies in our coverage universe. Share price changes over the past year indicates that LLL will perform in line with the market over the near term.

Financial Data

(US$ in Thousands)	3 Mos	12/31/2017	12/31/2016	12/31/2015	12/31/2014	12/31/2013	12/31/2012	12/31/2011
Earnings Per Share	9.00	8.51	9.01	(2.93)	7.56	8.54	8.30	9.03
Cash Flow Per Share	11.06	12.63	14.13	12.91	13.17	14.13	12.75	14.21
Dividends Per Share	3.050	3.000	2.800	2.600	2.400	2.200	2.000	1.800
Dividend Payout %	33.89	35.25	31.08	...	31.75	25.76	24.10	19.93
Income Statement								
Total Revenue	2,371,000	9,573,000	10,511,000	10,466,000	12,124,000	12,629,000	13,146,000	15,169,000
EBITDA	325,000	1,192,000	1,163,000	640,000	1,257,000	1,424,000	1,508,000	1,736,000
Depn & Amortn	74,000	172,000	162,000	166,000	172,000	166,000	170,000	173,000
Income Before Taxes	216,000	871,000	850,000	322,000	925,000	1,096,000	1,162,000	1,328,000
Income Taxes	24,000	102,000	189,000	25,000	248,000	309,000	374,000	360,000
Net Income	203,000	677,000	710,000	(240,000)	664,000	778,000	810,000	956,000
Average Shares	79,900	79,600	78,800	81,900	87,800	91,100	97,600	105,600
Balance Sheet								
Current Assets	4,480,000	4,448,000	3,697,000	4,232,000	4,737,000	4,649,000	4,571,000	5,244,000
Total Assets	12,873,000	12,729,000	11,865,000	12,085,000	13,836,000	14,009,000	13,826,000	15,497,000
Current Liabilities	2,335,000	2,379,000	2,135,000	2,879,000	2,525,000	2,523,000	2,597,000	2,690,000
Long-Term Obligations	3,349,000	3,346,000	3,338,000	3,153,000	3,940,000	3,645,000	3,653,000	4,135,000
Total Liabilities	7,620,000	7,646,000	7,312,000	7,730,000	8,551,000	7,986,000	8,363,000	8,862,000
Stockholders' Equity	5,253,000	5,083,000	4,553,000	4,355,000	5,285,000	6,023,000	5,463,000	6,635,000*
Shares Outstanding	78,387	77,876	77,232	78,133	82,040	85,828	90,433	98,979
Statistical Record								
Return on Assets %	5.72	5.51	5.91	N.M.	4.77	5.59	5.51	6.18
Return on Equity %	14.34	14.05	15.90	N.M.	11.74	13.55	13.35	14.27
EBITDA Margin %	13.71	12.45	11.06	6.12	10.37	11.28	11.47	11.44
Net Margin %	8.56	7.07	6.75	N.M.	5.48	6.16	6.16	6.30
Asset Turnover	0.74	0.78	0.88	0.81	0.87	0.91	0.89	0.98
Current Ratio	1.92	1.87	1.73	1.47	1.88	1.84	1.76	1.95
Debt to Equity	0.64	0.66	0.73	0.72	0.75	0.61	0.67	0.62
Price Range	217.46-160.69	199.05-145.71	161.56-108.05	132.87-101.90	128.34-101.39	107.13-74.86	77.91-64.17	84.70-56.53
P/E Ratio	24.16-17.85	23.39-17.12	17.93-11.99	...	16.98-13.41	12.54-8.77	9.39-7.73	9.38-6.26
Average Yield %	1.64	1.64	2.03	2.18	2.07	2.48	2.86	2.52

Address: 600 Third Avenue, New York, NY 10016 Telephone: 212-697-1111	Web Site: www.l-3com.com Officers: Christopher E. Kubasik - President, Chief Executive Officer, Chief Operating Officer Ralph G. D'Ambrosio - Senior Vice President, Chief Financial Officer, Vice President	Auditors: PricewaterhouseCoopers LLP Investor Contact: 212-697-1111 Transfer Agents: Computershare Trust Company, N.A, Providence, RI

M & T BANK CORP

Exchange	Symbol	Price	52Wk Range	Yield	P/E
NYS	MTB	$170.15 (6/29/2018)	196.81-142.47	1.88	19.34

*7 Year Price Score 113.77 *NYSE Composite Index=100 *12 Month Price Score 101.38

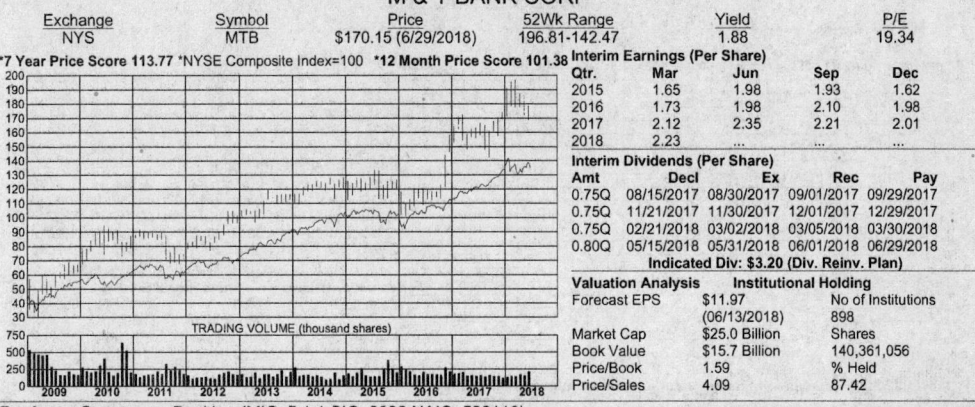

Interim Earnings (Per Share)

Qtr.	Mar	Jun	Sep	Dec
2015	1.65	1.98	1.93	1.62
2016	1.73	1.98	2.10	1.98
2017	2.12	2.35	2.21	2.01
2018	2.23	...	...	...

Interim Dividends (Per Share)

Amt	Decl	Ex	Rec	Pay
0.75Q	08/15/2017	08/30/2017	09/01/2017	09/29/2017
0.75Q	11/21/2017	11/30/2017	12/01/2017	12/29/2017
0.75Q	02/21/2018	03/02/2018	03/05/2018	03/30/2018
0.80Q	05/15/2018	05/31/2018	06/01/2018	06/29/2018

Indicated Div: $3.20 (Div. Reinv. Plan)

Valuation Analysis

		Institutional Holding	
Forecast EPS	$11.97 (06/13/2018)	No of Institutions	898
Market Cap	$25.0 Billion	Shares	140,361,056
Book Value	$15.7 Billion	% Held	87.42
Price/Book	1.59		
Price/Sales	4.09		

Business Summary: Banking (MIC: 5.1.1 SIC: 6022 NAIC: 522110)

M&T Bank is a bank holding company. Through subsidiaries, Co. provides individuals, corporations and other businesses, and institutions with commercial and retail banking services, including loans and deposits, trust, mortgage banking, asset management, insurance and other financial services. Banking activities are primarily focused on consumers residing in New York State, Maryland, New Jersey, Pennsylvania, Delaware, Connecticut, Virginia, West Virginia and the District of Columbia and on small and medium-size businesses in those areas. Certain subsidiaries also conduct activities in other areas. At Dec 31 2017, Co. had total assets of $118.59 billion and total deposits of $92.43 billion.

Recent Developments: For the quarter ended Mar 31 2018, net income increased 1.1% to US$352.6 million from US$348.9 million in the year-earlier quarter. Net interest income increased 6.7% to US$975.5 million from US$914.3 million in the year-earlier quarter. Provision for loan losses was US$43.0 million versus US$55.0 million in the prior-year quarter, a decrease of 21.8%. Non-interest income rose 2.7% to US$458.7 million from US$446.8 million, while non-interest expense advanced 18.5% to US$933.3 million.

Prospects: Our evaluation of M & T Bank Corp. as of Jan. 21, 2018 is the result of our systematic analysis on three basic characteristics: earnings strength, relative valuation, and recent stock price movement. The company has produced a positive trend in earnings per share over the past 5 quarters and while recent estimates for the company have been raised by analysts, MTB has posted better than expected results. Based on operating earnings yield, the company is undervalued when compared to all of the companies in our coverage universe. Share price changes over the past year indicates that MTB will perform poorly over the near term.

Financial Data

(US$ in Thousands)	3 Mos	12/31/2017	12/31/2016	12/31/2015	12/31/2014	12/31/2013	12/31/2012	12/31/2011
Earnings Per Share	8.80	8.70	7.78	7.18	7.42	8.20	7.54	6.35
Cash Flow Per Share	13.32	18.28	7.53	12.74	8.39	7.25	3.96	14.45
Tang Book Value Per Share	66.90	68.99	67.64	63.98	57.02	52.33	44.39	37.44
Dividends Per Share	3.000	3.000	2.800	2.800	2.800	2.800	2.800	2.800
Dividend Payout %	34.09	34.48	35.99	39.00	37.74	34.15	37.14	44.09
Income Statement								
Interest Income	1,082,150	4,167,795	3,895,871	3,170,844	2,956,877	2,957,334	2,941,685	2,792,087
Interest Expense	106,633	386,751	425,984	328,257	280,431	284,105	343,169	402,331
Net Interest Income	975,517	3,781,044	3,469,887	2,842,587	2,676,446	2,673,229	2,598,516	2,389,756
Provision for Losses	43,000	168,000	190,000	170,000	124,000	185,000	204,000	270,000
Non-Interest Income	458,696	1,851,143	1,825,996	1,839,304	1,795,945	1,881,331	1,688,781	1,607,143
Non-Interest Expense	933,344	3,140,325	3,047,485	2,822,932	2,742,857	2,635,885	2,509,260	2,478,068
Income Before Taxes	457,869	2,323,862	2,058,398	1,688,959	1,605,534	1,733,675	1,574,037	1,248,831
Income Taxes	105,259	915,556	743,284	595,025	522,616	579,069	523,028	365,121
Net Income	352,610	1,408,306	1,315,114	1,079,667	1,066,246	1,138,480	1,029,498	859,479
Average Shares	148,905	152,551	157,304	137,533	131,844	129,603	126,405	123,079
Balance Sheet								
Net Loans & Leases	86,691,078	86,971,785	89,864,419	86,533,507	65,749,394	63,156,483	65,645,097	59,187,715
Total Assets	118,622,824	118,593,487	123,449,206	122,787,884	96,685,535	85,162,391	83,008,803	77,924,287
Total Deposits	90,946,630	92,432,146	95,493,876	91,957,841	73,582,053	67,118,612	65,611,253	59,394,649
Total Liabilities	102,913,130	102,342,668	106,962,584	106,614,595	84,349,639	73,856,859	72,806,210	68,653,078
Stockholders' Equity	15,709,694	16,250,819	16,486,622	16,173,289	12,335,896	11,305,532	10,202,593	9,271,209
Shares Outstanding	146,798	150,084	156,180	159,563	132,312	130,516	128,176	125,683
Statistical Record								
Return on Assets %	1.17	1.16	1.07	0.98	1.17	1.35	1.28	1.18
Return on Equity %	8.85	8.60	8.03	7.57	9.02	10.59	10.54	9.75
Net Interest Margin %	90.15	90.72	89.07	89.65	90.52	90.39	88.33	85.59
Efficiency Ratio %	60.57	52.17	53.26	56.34	57.71	54.48	54.19	56.33
Loans to Deposits	0.95	0.94	0.94	0.94	0.89	0.94	1.00	1.00
Price Range	196.81-142.47	173.90-142.47	158.10-100.78	133.20-112.28	128.03-109.30	119.30-96.55	104.88-76.98	91.01-67.43
P/E Ratio	22.36-16.19	19.99-16.38	20.32-12.95	18.55-15.64	17.25-14.73	14.55-11.77	13.91-10.21	14.33-10.62
Average Yield %	1.80	1.87	2.35	2.28	2.32	2.57	3.18	3.44

Address: One M & T Plaza, Buffalo, NY 14203 **Telephone:** 716-635-4000	**Web Site:** www.mtb.com **Officers:** Rene F. Jones - Executive Vice President, Chief Financial Officer, Chairman, Chief Executive Officer Richard S. Gold - Executive Vice President, President, Chief Operating Officer	**Auditors:** PricewaterhouseCoopers LLP **Investor Contact:** 716-842-5138 **Transfer Agents:** Registrar and Transfer Company, Cranford, NJ

MACERICH CO (THE)

Exchange	Symbol	Price	52Wk Range	Yield	P/E
NYS	MAC	$56.83 (6/29/2018)	68.86-52.72	5.21	189.43

*7 Year Price Score 71.85 *NYSE Composite Index=100 *12 Month Price Score 95.30

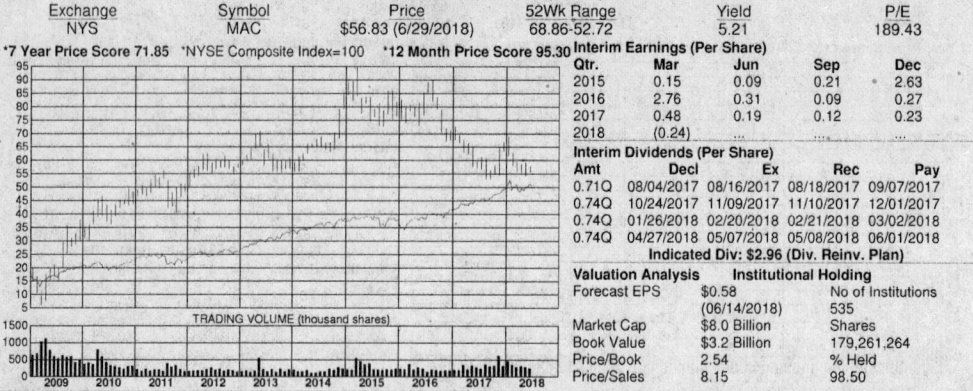

TRADING VOLUME (thousand shares)

Interim Earnings (Per Share)

Qtr.	Mar	Jun	Sep	Dec
2015	0.15	0.09	0.21	2.63
2016	2.76	0.31	0.09	0.27
2017	0.48	0.19	0.12	0.23
2018	(0.24)	...	...	...

Interim Dividends (Per Share)

Amt	Decl	Ex	Rec	Pay
0.71Q	08/04/2017	08/16/2017	08/18/2017	09/07/2017
0.74Q	10/24/2017	11/09/2017	11/10/2017	12/01/2017
0.74Q	01/26/2018	02/20/2018	02/21/2018	03/02/2018
0.74Q	04/27/2018	05/07/2018	05/08/2018	06/01/2018

Indicated Div: $2.96 (Div. Reinv. Plan)

Valuation Analysis   Institutional Holding

Forecast EPS	$0.58 (06/14/2018)	No of Institutions 535
Market Cap	$8.0 Billion	Shares
Book Value	$3.2 Billion	179,261,264
Price/Book	2.54	% Held
Price/Sales	8.15	98.50

Business Summary: REITs (MIC: 5.3.1 SIC: 6798 NAIC: 525930)

Macerich is a self-administered and self-managed real estate investment trust. Co. is involved in the acquisition, ownership, development, redevelopment, management and leasing of regional and community/power shopping centers. Co. is the sole general partner of, and owns a majority of the ownership interests in The Macerich Partnership, L.P. (the Operating Partnership). As of Dec 31 2017, the Operating Partnership owned or had an ownership interest in 48 regional shopping centers and seven community/power shopping centers. Co. conducts all of its operations through the Operating Partnership and its management companies.

Recent Developments: For the quarter ended Mar 31 2018, net loss amounted to US$34.4 million versus net income of US$74.8 million in the year-earlier quarter. Revenues were US$236.7 million, down 4.2% from US$247.0 million the year before. Revenues from property income fell 3.8% to US$222.9 million from US$231.8 million in the corresponding quarter a year earlier.

Prospects: Our evaluation of Macerich Co. as of Jan. 21, 2018 is the result of our systematic analysis on three basic characteristics: earnings strength, relative valuation, and recent stock price movement. The company has managed to produce a neutral trend in earnings per share over the past 5 quarters. Because the company lacks sufficient analyst estimate data, we place greater weight on the historical EPS trend as the measure of earnings strength. Based on operating earnings yield, the company is overvalued when compared to all of the companies in our coverage universe. Share price changes over the past year indicates that MAC will perform poorly over the near term.

Financial Data
(US$ in Thousands)

	3 Mos	12/31/2017	12/31/2016	12/31/2015	12/31/2014	12/31/2013	12/31/2012	12/31/2011
Earnings Per Share	0.30	1.02	3.52	3.08	10.45	3.00	2.51	1.18
Cash Flow Per Share	2.69	2.72	2.84	3.42	2.80	3.02	2.61	1.80
Tang Book Value Per Share	22.05	25.85	27.93	29.59	33.53	22.94	21.46	21.57
Dividends Per Share	2.900	2.870	2.750	6.630	2.510	2.360	2.230	2.050
Dividend Payout %	966.67	281.37	78.13	215.26	24.02	78.67	88.84	173.73
Income Statement								
Total Revenue	236,734	993,662	1,041,271	1,288,149	1,105,247	1,029,475	881,323	791,250
EBITDA	77,297	541,414	939,565	1,041,445	2,021,903	456,788	661,387	339,613
Depn & Amortn	78,864	277,917	277,270	354,977	289,178	269,790	271,025	235,884
Income Before Taxes	(54,202)	91,721	498,620	474,525	1,542,036	(10,249)	213,584	(91,556)
Income Taxes	(2,949)	15,594	722	(3,223)	(4,269)	(1,692)	(4,159)	(6,110)
Net Income	(33,573)	146,130	516,995	487,562	1,499,042	420,090	337,426	156,866
Average Shares	141,050	141,913	146,711	158,060	143,291	139,680	134,148	131,628
Balance Sheet								
Current Assets	489,218	255,758	280,995	257,901	230,463	186,055	271,862	269,801
Total Assets	9,157,273	9,605,862	9,958,148	11,258,576	13,121,778	9,075,250	9,311,209	7,938,549
Current Liabilities	352,877	384,113	427,481	815,382	684,122	440,099	388,425	371,968
Long-Term Obligations	4,903,841	5,170,264	4,965,900	5,283,742	6,292,400	4,582,727	5,261,370	4,206,074
Total Liabilities	5,999,513	5,924,284	5,852,261	6,543,162	7,481,658	5,716,501	6,233,680	5,125,212
Stockholders' Equity	3,157,760	3,681,578	4,105,887	4,715,414	5,640,120	3,358,749	3,077,529	2,813,337
Shares Outstanding	141,104	140,993	143,985	154,404	158,201	140,733	137,507	132,153
Statistical Record								
Return on Assets %	0.46	1.49	4.86	4.00	13.51	4.57	3.90	2.01
Return on Equity %	1.22	3.75	11.69	9.42	33.32	13.05	11.42	5.50
EBITDA Margin %	32.65	54.49	90.23	80.85	182.94	44.37	75.04	42.92
Net Margin %	N.M.	14.71	49.65	37.85	135.63	40.81	38.29	19.83
Asset Turnover	0.10	0.10	0.10	0.11	0.10	0.11	0.10	0.10
Current Ratio	1.39	0.67	0.66	0.32	0.34	0.42	0.70	0.73
Debt to Equity	1.55	1.40	1.21	1.12	1.12	1.36	1.71	1.50
Price Range	68.86-52.72	72.69-52.72	89.76-67.09	94.89-72.53	84.87-55.58	70.84-55.25	62.29-50.30	56.20-40.21
P/E Ratio	229.53-175.73	71.26-51.69	25.50-19.06	30.81-23.55	8.12-5.32	23.61-18.42	24.82-20.04	47.63-34.08
Average Yield %	4.86	4.69	3.52	8.13	3.80	3.86	3.89	4.18

Address: 401 Wilshire Boulevard, Suite 700, Santa Monica, CA 90401
Telephone: 310-394-6000

Web Site: www.macerich.com
Officers: Edward C. Coppola - President, Senior Executive Vice President, Chief Investment Officer Thomas E. O'Hern - Senior Executive Vice President, Executive Vice President, Senior Vice President, Chief Financial Officer, Treasurer, Chief Executive Officer

Auditors: KPMG LLP
Transfer Agents: Computershare Trust Company, N.A., Providence, RI

MACK CALI REALTY CORP

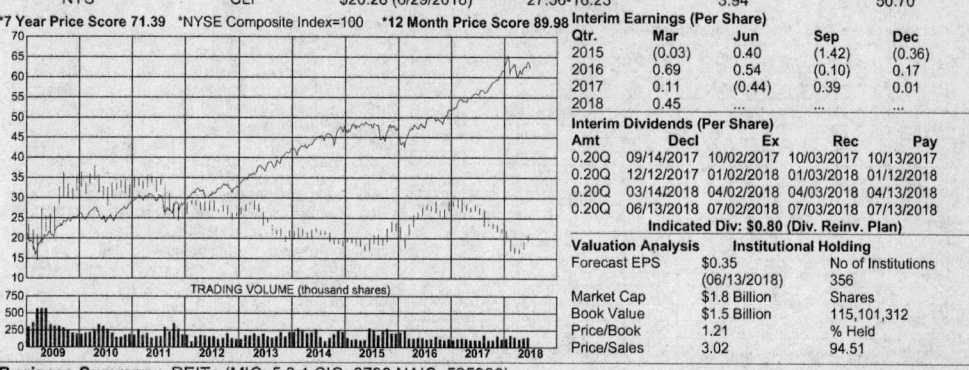

Exchange	Symbol	Price	52Wk Range	Yield	P/E
NYS	CLI	$20.28 (6/29/2018)	27.56-16.23	3.94	50.70

*7 Year Price Score 71.39   *NYSE Composite Index=100   *12 Month Price Score 89.98

Interim Earnings (Per Share)

Qtr.	Mar	Jun	Sep	Dec
2015	(0.03)	0.40	(1.42)	(0.36)
2016	0.69	0.54	(0.10)	0.17
2017	0.11	(0.44)	0.39	0.01
2018	0.45	...	...	...

Interim Dividends (Per Share)

Amt	Decl	Ex	Rec	Pay
0.20Q	09/14/2017	10/02/2017	10/03/2017	10/13/2017
0.20Q	12/12/2017	01/02/2018	01/03/2018	01/12/2018
0.20Q	03/14/2018	04/02/2018	04/03/2018	04/13/2018
0.20Q	06/13/2018	07/02/2018	07/03/2018	07/13/2018

Indicated Div: $0.80 (Div. Reinv. Plan)

Valuation Analysis

	Institutional Holding	
Forecast EPS	$0.35	No of Institutions
	(06/13/2018)	356
Market Cap	$1.8 Billion	Shares
Book Value	$1.5 Billion	115,101,312
Price/Book	1.21	% Held
Price/Sales	3.02	94.51

Business Summary: REITs (MIC: 5.3.1 SIC: 6798 NAIC: 525930)

Mack-Cali Realty is a self-administered and self-managed real estate investment trust that owns and operates a real estate portfolio comprised primarily of Class A office and office/flex properties located primarily in the Northeast. Co. operates in two business segments: commercial and other real estate and multi-family real estate and services. Co. provides leasing, property management, acquisition, development, construction and tenant-related services for its commercial and other real estate and multi-family real estate portfolio. As of Dec 31 2017, Co. owned or had interests in 157 properties, consisting of 69 office and 70 flex properties and 18 multi-family rental properties.

Recent Developments: For the quarter ended Mar 31 2018, net income increased 123.0% to US$50.7 million from US$22.7 million in the year-earlier quarter. Revenues were US$139.0 million, down 7.3% from US$149.9 million the year before. Revenues from property income fell 8.7% to US$130.4 million from US$142.8 million in the corresponding quarter a year earlier.

Prospects: Our evaluation of Mack Cali Realty Corp. as of Jan. 21, 2018 is the result of our systematic analysis on three basic characteristics: earnings strength, relative valuation, and recent stock price movement. The company has managed to produce a neutral trend in earnings per share over the past 5 quarters. Because the company lacks sufficient analyst estimate data, we place greater weight on the historical EPS trend as the measure of earnings strength. Based on operating earnings yield, the company is overvalued when compared to all of the companies in our coverage universe. Share price changes over the past year indicates that CLI will perform poorly over the near term.

Financial Data
(US$ in Thousands)

	3 Mos	12/31/2017	12/31/2016	12/31/2015	12/31/2014	12/31/2013	12/31/2012	12/31/2011
Earnings Per Share	0.40	0.06	1.30	(1.41)	0.32	(0.17)	0.47	0.81
Cash Flow Per Share	2.23	2.18	1.11	1.90	1.79	2.26	2.78	2.93
Tang Book Value Per Share	16.70	16.39	16.99	16.22	18.21	18.58	20.15	21.52
Dividends Per Share	0.750	0.700	0.600	0.600	0.900	1.500	1.800	1.800
Dividend Payout %	187.50	1,166.67	46.15	...	281.25	...	382.98	222.22
Income Statement								
Total Revenue	138,967	616,200	613,398	594,883	636,799	667,031	704,743	724,279
EBITDA	71,579	341,349	403,616	145,276	331,703	231,048	363,491	405,233
Depn & Amortn	3,516	210,928	198,835	181,899	188,626	197,609	198,966	199,932
Income Before Taxes	49,116	39,799	111,506	(138,880)	33,814	(87,359)	42,192	79,365
Net Income	43,036	23,185	117,224	(125,752)	28,567	(14,909)	40,922	71,420
Average Shares	100,604	100,703	100,498	100,222	100,041	99,785	99,996	98,962
Balance Sheet								
Current Assets	165,886	175,600	196,232	203,420	196,255	386,735	226,747	182,667
Total Assets	4,815,606	4,957,885	4,296,766	4,063,490	4,192,247	4,515,328	4,526,045	4,295,759
Current Liabilities	274,158	267,386	230,070	224,862	221,582	234,107	253,149	227,544
Long-Term Obligations	2,615,211	2,809,568	2,340,009	2,154,920	2,088,654	2,362,766	2,204,389	1,914,215
Total Liabilities	3,307,515	3,481,590	2,769,595	2,607,814	2,567,466	2,872,969	2,759,071	2,406,195
Stockholders' Equity	1,508,091	1,476,295	1,527,171	1,455,676	1,624,781	1,642,359	1,766,974	1,889,564
Shares Outstanding	90,136	89,914	89,696	89,583	89,076	88,247	87,536	87,799
Statistical Record								
Return on Assets %	0.95	0.50	2.80	N.M.	0.66	N.M.	0.93	1.65
Return on Equity %	3.05	1.54	7.84	N.M.	1.75	N.M.	2.23	3.92
EBITDA Margin %	51.51	55.40	65.80	24.42	52.09	34.64	51.58	55.95
Net Margin %	30.97	3.76	19.11	N.M.	4.49	N.M.	5.81	9.86
Asset Turnover	0.12	0.13	0.15	0.14	0.15	0.15	0.16	0.17
Current Ratio	0.61	0.66	0.85	0.90	0.89	1.65	0.90	0.80
Debt to Equity	1.73	1.90	1.53	1.48	1.29	1.44	1.25	1.01
Price Range	28.34-16.23	29.70-21.42	29.22-17.65	24.12-16.90	22.57-18.02	29.27-19.14	29.33-24.59	35.48-24.37
P/E Ratio	70.85-40.58	495.00-357.00	22.48-13.58	...	70.53-56.31	...	62.40-52.32	43.80-30.09
Average Yield %	3.20	2.73	2.38	3.02	4.38	6.12	6.58	5.78

Address: Harborside 3, 210 Hudson St., Ste. 400, Jersey City, NJ 07311 **Telephone:** 732-590-1010	**Web Site:** www.mack-cali.com **Officers:** William L. Mack - Chairman Michael J. DeMarco - President, Chief Executive Officer, Chief Operating Officer	**Auditors:** PricewaterhouseCoopers LLP **Transfer Agents:** Computershare Trust Company, N.A., Providence, RI

MACQUARIE INFRASTRUCTURE CORP

Exchange	Symbol	Price	52Wk Range	Yield	P/E
NYS	MIC	$42.20 (6/29/2018)	78.97-36.56	9.48	7.56

*7 Year Price Score 79.13 *NYSE Composite Index=100 *12 Month Price Score 66.58

Interim Earnings (Per Share)

Qtr.	Mar	Jun	Sep	Dec
2015	(1.22)	(0.80)	0.13	0.44
2016	0.28	0.24	0.51	0.82
2017	0.44	0.32	0.48	3.90
2018	0.88	...	...	...

Interim Dividends (Per Share)

Amt	Decl	Ex	Rec	Pay
1.38Q	08/02/2017	08/10/2017	08/14/2017	08/17/2017
1.42Q	11/01/2017	11/10/2017	11/13/2017	11/16/2017
1.44Q	02/21/2018	03/02/2018	03/05/2018	03/08/2018
1.00Q	05/02/2018	05/11/2018	05/14/2018	05/17/2018

Indicated Div: $4.00

Valuation Analysis / **Institutional Holding**

Forecast EPS	$2.21	No of Institutions
	(06/14/2018)	551
Market Cap	$3.6 Billion	Shares
Book Value	$3.1 Billion	75,683,872
Price/Book	1.15	% Held
Price/Sales	1.92	81.60

Business Summary: Business Services (MIC: 7.5.2 SIC: 4581 NAIC: 488119)

Macquarie Infrastructure is a holding company. Co. owns and operates a portfolio of businesses that provide services to other businesses, government agencies and individuals. The businesses that Co. owns and operates are: International-Matex Tank Terminals, which provides bulk liquid storage, handling and other services; Atlantic Aviation, which provides fuel, terminal, aircraft hangaring and other services to owners and operators of general aviation jet aircraft; Contracted Power, which comprises a gas-fired facility and controlling interests in wind and solar facilities; and MIC Hawaii, which includes an energy company that processes and distributes gas and provides related services.

Recent Developments: For the quarter ended Mar 31 2018, net income increased 43.4% to US$46.8 million from US$32.6 million in the year-earlier quarter. Revenues were US$501.6 million, up 11.1% from US$451.5 million the year before. Operating income was US$82.2 million versus US$79.0 million in the prior-year quarter, an increase of 4.1%. Direct operating expenses rose 19.3% to US$240.9 million from US$201.9 million in the comparable period the year before. Indirect operating expenses increased 4.6% to US$178.5 million from US$170.5 million in the equivalent prior-year period.

Prospects: Our evaluation of Macquarie Infrastructure Corp. as of Jan. 21, 2018 is the result of our systematic analysis on three basic characteristics: earnings strength, relative valuation, and recent stock price movement. The company has generated a negative trend in earnings per share over the past 5 quarters and while recent estimates for the company have been mixed, MIC has posted results that fell short of analysts expectations. Based on operating earnings yield, the company is about fairly valued when compared to all of the companies in our coverage universe. Share price changes over the past year indicates that MIC will perform poorly over the near term.

Financial Data
(US$ in Thousands)

	3 Mos	12/31/2017	12/31/2016	12/31/2015	12/31/2014	12/31/2013	12/31/2012	12/31/2011
Earnings Per Share	5.58	5.13	1.85	(1.39)	16.10	0.61	0.29	0.59
Cash Flow Per Share	6.43	6.36	6.91	4.89	3.99	3.02	4.66	1.98
Tang Book Value Per Share	1.72	2.02	0.48	0.98	N.M.	N.M.	N.M.	N.M.
Dividends Per Share	5.560	5.430	4.890	2.240	3.888	3.350	2.200	0.800
Dividend Payout %	99.64	105.85	264.32	...	24.15	549.18	758.62	135.59
Income Statement								
Income Before Taxes	63,574	221,958	226,126	(178,968)	988,518	7,008	(15,791)	28,843
Income Taxes	16,779	(234,154)	71,257	(65,161)	(24,374)	18,043	2,285	22,718
Net Income	76,834	451,202	156,381	(108,537)	1,042,028	31,254	13,321	27,343
Average Shares	92,793	91,073	82,218	77,997	64,925	51,396	46,655	46,021
Balance Sheet								
Total Assets	8,025,297	8,008,951	7,559,253	7,378,828	6,625,188	2,500,865	2,223,694	2,168,633
Total Liabilities	4,907,456	4,855,259	4,606,359	4,348,638	3,838,025	1,458,637	1,568,666	1,464,951
Stockholders' Equity	3,117,841	3,153,692	2,952,894	3,030,190	2,787,163	1,042,228	655,028	703,682
Shares Outstanding	84,902	84,733	82,047	80,006	71,089	56,295	47,453	46,338
Statistical Record								
Return on Assets %	6.32	5.80	2.09	N.M.	22.84	1.32	0.60	1.25
Return on Equity %	16.35	14.78	5.21	N.M.	54.42	3.68	1.96	3.92
Price Range	81.69-36.56	82.84-63.85	84.13-52.89	87.24-65.32	73.04-51.59	59.55-45.56	45.85-27.57	28.15-20.21
P/E Ratio	14.64-6.55	16.15-12.45	45.48-28.59	...	4.54-3.20	97.62-74.69	158.10-95.07	47.71-34.25
Average Yield %	8.07	7.23	6.62	2.84	6.18	6.27	6.03	3.26

Address: 125 West 55th Street, New York, NY 10019
Telephone: 212-231-1000

Web Site: www.macquarie.com/mic
Officers: Martin Stanley - Chairman, Alternate Chairman Christopher Frost - President, Chief Operating Officer, Chief Executive Officer

Auditors: KPMG LLP
Investor Contact: 212-231-1825
Transfer Agents: Computershare Shareowner Services LLC, Pittsburgh, PA

MACY'S INC

Exchange	Symbol	Price	52Wk Range	Yield	P/E
NYS	M	$37.43 (6/29/2018)	40.21-17.53	4.03	7.12

*7 Year Price Score 50.06 ***NYSE Composite Index=100** ***12 Month Price Score 132.68**

Interim Earnings (Per Share)

Qtr.	Apr	Jul	Oct	Jan
2015-16	0.56	0.64	0.36	1.66
2016-17	0.37	0.03	0.05	1.53
2017-18	0.23	0.38	0.12	4.31
2018-19	0.45	...	...	...

Interim Dividends (Per Share)

Amt	Decl	Ex	Rec	Pay
0.378Q	08/25/2017	09/14/2017	09/15/2017	10/02/2017
0.378Q	10/27/2017	12/14/2017	12/15/2017	01/02/2018
0.378Q	02/23/2018	03/14/2018	03/15/2018	04/02/2018
0.378Q	05/18/2018	06/14/2018	06/15/2018	07/02/2018

Indicated Div: $1.51 (Div. Reinv. Plan)

Valuation Analysis / Institutional Holding

Valuation Analysis		Institutional Holding	
Forecast EPS	$3.89 (06/20/2018)	No of Institutions	974
Market Cap	$11.5 Billion	Shares	344,814,912
Book Value	$5.8 Billion	% Held	N/A
Price/Book	1.97		
Price/Sales	0.46		

Business Summary: Retail - General Merchandise/Department Stores (MIC: 2.1.1 SIC: 5311 NAIC: 452111)

Macy's is an omnichannel retail organization operating stores, websites and mobile applications under three brands (Macy's, Bloomingdale's and Bluemercury) that sell a range of merchandise, including apparel and accessories (men's, women's and children's), cosmetics, home furnishings and other consumer goods. As of Feb 3 2018, Co. operated 852 stores in 44 states, the District of Columbia, Guam and Puerto Rico. As of Feb 3 2018, Co.'s operations were conducted through Macy's, Bloomingdale's, Bloomingdale's The Outlet, Macy's Backstage, bluemercury and Macy's China Limited.

Recent Developments: For the quarter ended May 5 2018, net income increased 70.1% to US$131.0 million from US$77.0 million in the year-earlier quarter. Revenues were US$5.70 billion, up 3.4% from US$5.51 billion the year before. Operating income was US$238.0 million versus US$219.0 million in the prior-year quarter, an increase of 8.7%. Direct operating expenses rose 2.4% to US$3.38 billion from US$3.30 billion in the comparable period the year before. Indirect operating expenses increased 4.5% to US$2.08 billion from US$1.99 billion in the equivalent prior-year period.

Prospects: Our evaluation of Macy's Inc. as of Jan. 21, 2018 is the result of our systematic analysis on three basic characteristics: earnings strength, relative valuation, and recent stock price movement. The company has enjoyed a very positive trend in earnings per share over the past 5 quarters and while recent estimates for the company have been raised by analysts, M has posted better than expected results. Based on operating earnings yield, the company is undervalued when compared to all of the companies in our coverage universe. Share price changes over the past year indicates that M will perform very poorly over the near term.

Financial Data
(US$ in Thousands)

	3 Mos	02/03/2018	01/28/2017	01/30/2016	01/31/2015	02/01/2014	02/02/2013	01/28/2012
Earnings Per Share	5.26	5.04	1.99	3.22	4.22	3.86	3.24	2.92
Cash Flow Per Share	6.63	6.26	5.85	6.06	7.65	6.76	5.49	4.94
Tang Book Value Per Share	4.66	4.23	N.M.	N.M.	3.34	5.42	4.51	3.84
Dividends Per Share	1.510	1.510	1.492	1.393	1.188	0.950	0.800	0.350
Dividend Payout %	28.71	29.96	75.00	43.25	28.14	24.61	24.69	11.99
Income Statement								
Total Revenue	5,698,000	24,837,000	25,778,000	27,079,000	28,105,000	27,931,000	27,686,000	26,405,000
EBITDA	484,000	2,763,000	2,359,000	3,086,000	3,814,000	3,690,000	3,557,000	3,481,000
Depn & Amortn	235,000	946,000	1,044,000	1,047,000	1,031,000	1,012,000	1,033,000	1,070,000
Income Before Taxes	183,000	1,507,000	952,000	1,678,000	2,390,000	2,290,000	2,102,000	1,968,000
Income Taxes	52,000	(29,000)	341,000	608,000	864,000	804,000	767,000	712,000
Net Income	139,000	1,547,000	619,000	1,072,000	1,526,000	1,486,000	1,335,000	1,256,000
Average Shares	309,400	306,800	310,800	333,000	361,700	384,800	412,200	430,400
Balance Sheet								
Current Assets	7,710,000	7,444,000	7,626,000	7,652,000	8,679,000	8,688,000	7,876,000	8,777,000
Total Assets	19,568,000	19,381,000	19,851,000	20,576,000	21,461,000	21,634,000	20,991,000	22,095,000
Current Liabilities	5,077,000	5,075,000	5,647,000	5,728,000	5,536,000	5,726,000	5,075,000	6,263,000
Long-Term Obligations	5,857,000	5,861,000	6,562,000	6,995,000	7,265,000	6,728,000	6,806,000	6,655,000
Total Liabilities	13,747,000	13,708,000	15,528,000	16,326,000	16,083,000	15,385,000	14,940,000	16,162,000
Stockholders' Equity	5,821,000	5,673,000	4,323,000	4,250,000	5,378,000	6,249,000	6,051,000	5,933,000
Shares Outstanding	306,370	304,765	304,062	310,256	340,573	364,935	387,701	414,181
Statistical Record								
Return on Assets %	8.24	7.76	3.07	5.11	7.10	6.99	6.10	5.90
Return on Equity %	31.93	30.45	14.48	22.33	26.32	24.23	21.92	21.97
EBITDA Margin %	8.49	11.12	9.15	11.40	13.57	13.21	12.85	13.18
Net Margin %	2.44	6.23	2.40	3.96	5.43	5.32	4.82	4.76
Asset Turnover	1.29	1.25	1.28	1.29	1.31	1.31	1.26	1.24
Current Ratio	1.52	1.47	1.35	1.34	1.57	1.52	1.55	1.40
Debt to Equity	1.01	1.03	1.52	1.65	1.35	1.08	1.12	1.12
Price Range	32.19-17.53	33.57-17.53	44.91-29.11	72.80-34.50	67.81-50.91	56.23-38.52	41.73-32.83	35.82-22.01
P/E Ratio	6.12-3.33	6.66-3.48	22.57-14.63	22.61-10.71	16.07-12.06	14.57-9.98	12.88-10.13	12.27-7.54
Average Yield %	6.23	6.09	3.99	2.43	2.00	2.03	2.09	1.26

Address: 151 West 34th Street, New York, NY 10001 **Telephone:** 212-494-1602 **Fax:** 212-494-1838	**Web Site:** www.macys.com **Officers:** Jeffrey (Jeff) Gennette - Chairman, President, Chief Executive Officer, Chief Merchandising Officer Harry A. (Hal) Lawton - President	**Auditors:** KPMG LLP **Investor Contact:** 513-579-7028 **Transfer Agents:** Computershare Shareowner Services, Pittsburgh, PA

MAGELLAN MIDSTREAM PARTNERS LP

Exchange	Symbol	Price	52Wk Range	Yield	P/E	Div Acheiver
NYS	MMP	$69.08 (6/29/2018)	75.19-57.08	5.43	18.42	16 Years

*7 Year Price Score 87.88 *NYSE Composite Index=100 *12 Month Price Score 100.35

Interim Earnings (Per Share)

Qtr.	Mar	Jun	Sep	Dec
2015	0.81	0.78	1.10	0.90
2016	0.91	0.82	0.85	0.93
2017	0.98	0.92	0.87	1.04
2018	0.92	...	...	...

Interim Dividends (Per Share)

Amt	Decl	Ex	Rec	Pay
0.89Q	07/20/2017	07/27/2017	07/31/2017	08/14/2017
0.905Q	10/19/2017	11/01/2017	11/02/2017	11/14/2017
0.92Q	01/23/2018	02/05/2018	02/06/2018	02/14/2018
0.938Q	04/26/2018	05/07/2018	05/08/2018	05/15/2018

Indicated Div: $3.75

Valuation Analysis | **Institutional Holding**

Forecast EPS	$4.08 (06/14/2018)	No of Institutions	843
Market Cap	$15.8 Billion	Shares	164,398,528
Book Value	N/A	% Held	58.21
Price/Book	N/A		
Price/Sales	6.20		

Business Summary: Equipment & Services (MIC: 9.1.3 SIC: 4613 NAIC: 486910)

Magellan Midstream Partners transports, stores and distributes refined petroleum products and crude oil. Co.'s segments are: refined products, which consists of its common carrier refined products pipeline system, independent terminals and its ammonia pipeline system; crude oil, which comprises crude oil pipelines and storage facilities and ships crude oil as a common carrier for customers including crude oil producers, end users such as refiners, and marketing and trading companies; and marine storage, which consists of marine terminals that provide distribution, storage, blending, inventory management and additive injection services for refiners, marketers, traders and other end users.

Recent Developments: For the quarter ended Mar 31 2018, net income decreased 5.3% to US$210.9 million from US$222.7 million in the year-earlier quarter. Revenues were US$678.8 million, up 5.7% from US$642.1 million the year before. Operating income was US$272.0 million versus US$271.5 million in the prior-year quarter, an increase of 0.2%. Direct operating expenses rose 12.6% to US$342.9 million from US$304.5 million in the comparable period the year before. Indirect operating expenses decreased 3.4% to US$63.9 million from US$66.1 million in the equivalent prior-year period.

Prospects: Our evaluation of Magellan Midstream Partners L.P. as of Jan. 21, 2018 is the result of our systematic analysis on three basic characteristics: earnings strength, relative valuation, and recent stock price movement. The company has generated a negative trend in earnings per share over the past 5 quarters. However, while recent estimates for the company have been mixed, MMP has posted results that fell short of analysts expectations. Based on operating earnings yield, the company is undervalued when compared to all of the companies in our coverage universe. Share price changes over the past year indicates that MMP will perform poorly over the near term.

Financial Data
(US$ in Thousands)

	3 Mos	12/31/2017	12/31/2016	12/31/2015	12/31/2014	12/31/2013	12/31/2012	12/31/2011
Earnings Per Share	3.75	3.81	3.52	3.59	3.69	2.56	1.92	1.83
Cash Flow Per Share	4.91	4.86	4.22	4.70	4.87	3.41	2.84	2.56
Dividends Per Share	3.587	3.523	3.245	2.915	2.505	2.098	1.784	1.556
Dividend Payout %	95.67	92.45	92.19	81.20	67.89	81.93	92.90	85.04
Income Statement								
Total Revenue	678,779	2,507,661	2,205,410	2,188,453	2,303,723	1,897,606	1,772,074	1,748,667
EBITDA	233,801	1,142,385	1,069,403	1,062,252	1,102,931	832,757	673,710	633,203
Depn & Amortn	5,069	196,300	176,700	164,100	159,000	136,400	126,700	118,900
Income Before Taxes	177,306	752,367	727,293	754,975	824,745	580,575	435,331	408,669
Income Taxes	934	3,830	3,218	2,336	4,620	4,613	2,622	1,866
Net Income	210,910	869,531	802,771	819,122	839,519	582,237	435,670	413,503
Average Shares	228,360	228,338	228,057	227,888	227,626	227,094	226,608	225,974
Balance Sheet								
Current Assets	493,192	611,839	370,394	338,854	402,667	396,733	700,278	612,190
Total Assets	7,376,049	7,394,375	6,772,073	6,041,567	5,517,285	4,820,812	4,420,067	4,045,001
Current Liabilities	788,540	836,510	481,656	713,072	536,155	638,276	392,620	311,055
Long-Term Obligations	4,272,747	4,273,518	4,087,192	3,189,287	2,982,895	2,435,316	2,393,408	2,151,775
Total Liabilities	5,236,862	5,264,722	4,679,968	4,019,831	3,649,052	3,173,370	2,904,365	2,581,598
Shares Outstanding	228,195	228,024	227,783	227,427	227,068	226,679	226,200	225,473
Statistical Record								
Return on Assets %	12.08	12.28	12.50	14.17	16.24	12.60	10.27	10.65
EBITDA Margin %	34.44	45.56	48.49	48.54	47.88	43.88	38.02	36.21
Net Margin %	31.07	34.67	36.40	37.43	36.44	30.68	24.59	23.65
Asset Turnover	0.36	0.35	0.34	0.38	0.45	0.41	0.42	0.45
Current Ratio	0.63	0.73	0.77	0.48	0.75	0.62	1.78	1.97
Price Range	77.40-57.08	81.46-64.06	77.40-56.97	85.01-55.08	89.12-60.52	63.27-43.19	45.34-32.51	34.48-26.59
P/E Ratio	20.64-15.22	21.38-16.81	21.99-16.18	23.68-15.34	24.15-16.40	24.71-16.87	23.61-16.93	18.84-14.53
Average Yield %	5.16	4.89	4.67	3.98	3.23	3.87	4.66	5.19

Address: One Williams Center, P.O. Box 22186, Tulsa, OK 74121-2186
Telephone: 918-574-7000

Web Site: www.magellanlp.com
Officers: Michael N. Mears - Chairman, President, Chief Executive Officer Michael J. Aaronson - Senior Vice President

Auditors: Ernst & Young LLP
Investor Contact: 918-574-7650
Transfer Agents: Computershare Trust Company, N.A., Providence, RI

MANPOWERGROUP INC

Exchange	Symbol	Price	52Wk Range	Yield	P/E
NYS	MAN	$86.06 (6/29/2018)	136.02-85.46	2.35	10.23

*7 Year Price Score 122.57 *NYSE Composite Index=100 *12 Month Price Score 78.88

Interim Earnings (Per Share)

Qtr.	Mar	Jun	Sep	Dec
2015	0.83	1.33	1.61	1.65
2016	0.98	1.60	1.87	1.85
2017	1.09	1.72	2.04	3.20
2018	1.45	...	...	...

Interim Dividends (Per Share)

Amt	Decl	Ex	Rec	Pay
0.86S	11/02/2016	11/29/2016	12/01/2016	12/15/2016
0.93S	05/02/2017	05/30/2017	06/01/2017	06/15/2017
0.93S	11/01/2017	11/30/2017	12/01/2017	12/15/2017
1.01S	05/04/2018	05/31/2018	06/01/2018	06/15/2018

Indicated Div: $2.02 (Div. Reinv. Plan)

Valuation Analysis / Institutional Holding

Forecast EPS	$8.90	No of Institutions
	(06/12/2018)	644
Market Cap	$5.7 Billion	Shares
Book Value	$2.9 Billion	86,116,448
Price/Book	1.99	% Held
Price/Sales	0.26	86.99

TRADING VOLUME (thousand shares)

Business Summary: Business Services (MIC: 7.5.2 SIC: 7363 NAIC: 561330)

ManpowerGroup provides a range of workforce solutions and services, which include recruitment and assessment, training and development, career management, outsourcing, and workforce consulting. Its brands and offerings include Manpower, Experis, Right Management and ManpowerGroup Solutions. Co.'s portfolio of recruitment services include permanent, temporary and contract recruitment of professionals, as well as administrative and industrial positions, which are provided under its Manpower and Experis brands. Experis focuses on the areas of information technology, engineering, and finance, while Right Management is focused on talent and career management workforce solutions.

Recent Developments: For the quarter ended Mar 31 2018, net income increased 30.4% to US$97.0 million from US$74.4 million in the year-earlier quarter. Revenues were US$5.52 billion, up 16.1% from US$4.76 billion the year before. Operating income was US$153.8 million versus US$127.9 million in the prior-year quarter, an increase of 20.3%. Direct operating expenses rose 16.8% to US$4.64 billion from US$3.97 billion in the comparable period the year before. Indirect operating expenses increased 10.9% to US$731.6 million from US$659.9 million in the equivalent prior-year period.

Prospects: Our evaluation of ManpowerGroup as of Jan. 21, 2018 is the result of our systematic analysis on three basic characteristics: earnings strength, relative valuation, and recent stock price movement. The company has managed to produce a neutral trend in earnings per share over the past 5 quarters and while recent estimates for the company have been mixed, MAN has posted better than expected results. Based on operating earnings yield, the company is undervalued when compared to all of the companies in our coverage universe. Share price changes over the past year indicates that MAN will perform well over the near term.

Financial Data
(US$ in Thousands)

	3 Mos	12/31/2017	12/31/2016	12/31/2015	12/31/2014	12/31/2013	12/31/2012	12/31/2011
Earnings Per Share	8.41	8.04	6.27	5.40	5.30	3.62	2.47	3.04
Cash Flow Per Share	2.29	5.97	8.54	6.66	3.85	5.09	4.16	0.85
Tang Book Value Per Share	18.48	17.37	12.36	14.25	20.24	19.08	14.73	14.31
Dividends Per Share	1.860	1.860	1.720	1.600	0.980	0.920	0.860	0.800
Dividend Payout %	22.12	23.13	27.43	29.63	18.49	25.41	34.82	26.32
Income Statement								
Total Revenue	5,522,400	21,034,300	19,654,100	19,329,900	20,762,800	20,250,500	20,678,000	22,006,000
EBITDA	171,800	855,100	820,900	771,900	796,900	603,200	504,100	619,800
Depn & Amortn	21,700	84,400	85,300	77,700	83,800	94,300	100,500	104,400
Income Before Taxes	137,700	737,300	701,300	660,700	681,600	475,500	368,400	479,900
Income Taxes	40,700	191,900	257,600	241,500	254,000	187,500	170,800	228,300
Net Income	97,000	545,400	443,700	419,200	427,600	288,000	197,600	251,600
Average Shares	66,900	67,900	70,800	77,700	80,700	79,600	80,100	82,800
Balance Sheet								
Current Assets	6,327,000	6,171,200	5,132,900	5,092,500	5,033,700	5,243,000	5,060,600	4,990,500
Total Assets	8,896,100	8,883,600	7,574,200	7,517,500	7,182,500	7,288,300	7,012,600	6,899,700
Current Liabilities	4,750,000	4,810,400	3,658,800	3,451,000	3,374,400	3,509,600	3,677,200	3,762,200
Long-Term Obligations	491,100	478,100	785,600	810,900	423,900	481,900	462,100	266,000
Total Liabilities	6,040,900	6,108,700	5,212,300	4,892,800	4,239,500	4,374,100	4,511,800	4,416,300
Stockholders' Equity	2,855,200	2,774,900	2,361,900	2,624,700	2,943,000	2,914,200	2,500,800	2,483,400
Shares Outstanding	65,966	66,077	66,969	73,038	78,114	79,355	76,647	79,903
Statistical Record								
Return on Assets %	6.85	6.63	5.86	5.70	5.91	4.03	2.83	3.69
Return on Equity %	21.43	21.24	17.75	15.06	14.60	10.64	7.91	10.31
EBITDA Margin %	3.11	4.07	4.18	3.99	3.84	2.98	2.44	2.82
Net Margin %	1.76	2.59	2.26	2.17	2.06	1.42	0.96	1.14
Asset Turnover	2.63	2.56	2.60	2.63	2.87	2.83	2.96	3.23
Current Ratio	1.33	1.28	1.40	1.48	1.49	1.49	1.38	1.33
Debt to Equity	0.17	0.17	0.33	0.31	0.14	0.17	0.18	0.11
Price Range	136.02-97.54	130.38-89.81	92.83-59.90	96.56-63.79	86.73-59.00	86.66-42.44	47.90-32.41	68.67-32.32
P/E Ratio	16.17-11.60	16.22-11.17	14.81-9.55	17.88-11.81	16.36-11.13	23.94-11.72	19.39-13.12	22.59-10.63
Average Yield %	1.61	1.70	2.18	1.89	1.28	1.45	2.18	1.56

Address: 100 Manpower Place, Milwaukee, WI 53212	**Web Site:** www.manpower.com	**Auditors:** Deloitte & Touche LLP
Telephone: 414-961-1000	**Officers:** Jonas Prising - Chairman, President, Chief Executive Officer, Executive Vice President Darryl Green - President, Chief Operating Officer, Executive Vice President, Region Officer	**Investor Contact:** 414-906-6807
Fax: 414-332-0796		**Transfer Agents:** ComputerShare, College Station, TX

MARATHON OIL CORP.

Exchange	Symbol	Price	52Wk Range	Yield	P/E
NYS	MRO	$20.86 (6/29/2018)	21.90-10.77	0.96	N/A

*7 Year Price Score 51.36 *NYSE Composite Index=100 *12 Month Price Score 127.59

Interim Earnings (Per Share)

Qtr.	Mar	Jun	Sep	Dec
2015	(0.41)	(0.57)	(1.11)	(1.17)
2016	(0.56)	(0.20)	(0.23)	(1.66)
2017	(5.84)	(0.16)	(0.70)	(0.03)
2018	0.42	...	...	...

Interim Dividends (Per Share)

Amt	Decl	Ex	Rec	Pay
0.05Q	07/26/2017	08/14/2017	08/16/2017	09/11/2017
0.05Q	10/25/2017	11/14/2017	11/15/2017	12/11/2017
0.05Q	01/30/2018	02/20/2018	02/21/2018	03/12/2018
0.05Q	04/26/2018	05/15/2018	05/16/2018	06/11/2018

Indicated Div: $0.20 (Div. Reinv. Plan)

Valuation Analysis | **Institutional Holding**

Forecast EPS	$0.86	No of Institutions
	(06/14/2018)	1037
Market Cap	$17.8 Billion	Shares
Book Value	$12.0 Billion	871,979,264
Price/Book	1.48	% Held
Price/Sales	3.28	76.21

Business Summary: Production & Extraction (MIC: 9.1.1 SIC: 1311 NAIC: 211111)

Marathon Oil is an exploration and production company. Co. has three segments: North America Exploration and Production (E&P), which explores for, produces and markets crude oil and condensate, natural gas liquids (NGLs) and natural gas in North America; International E&P, which explores for, produces and markets crude oil and condensate, NGLs and natural gas outside of North America; and Oil Sands Mining, which mines, extracts and transports bitumen from oil sands deposits in Alberta, Canada, and upgrades the bitumen to produce and market synthetic crude oil and vacuum gas oil. As of Dec 31 2017, Co. had total proved reserves of 2.00 billion barrels of oil equivalent.

Recent Developments: For the quarter ended Mar 31 2018, income from continuing operations was US$356.0 million compared with a loss of US$50.0 million in the year-earlier quarter. Net income amounted to US$356.0 million versus a net loss of US$4.96 billion in the year-earlier quarter. Revenues were US$1.73 billion, up 61.7% from US$1.07 billion the year before. Operating income was US$572.0 million versus US$72.0 million in the prior-year quarter, an increase of 694.4%. Direct operating expenses rose 25.7% to US$347.0 million from US$276.0 million in the comparable period the year before. Indirect operating expenses increased 12.4% to US$814.0 million from US$724.0 million in the equivalent prior-year period.

Prospects: Our evaluation of Marathon Oil Corp. as of Jan. 21, 2018 is the result of our systematic analysis on three basic characteristics: earnings strength, relative valuation, and recent stock price movement. The company has generated a negative trend in earnings per share over the past 5 quarters. Because the company lacks sufficient analyst estimate data, we place greater weight on the historical EPS trend as the measure of earnings strength. Based on operating earnings yield, the company is overvalued when compared to all of the companies in our coverage universe. Share price changes over the past year indicates that MRO will perform very poorly over the near term.

Financial Data

(US$ in Thousands)	3 Mos	12/31/2017	12/31/2016	12/31/2015	12/31/2014	12/31/2013	12/31/2012	12/31/2011
Earnings Per Share	(0.47)	(6.73)	(2.61)	(3.26)	4.46	2.47	2.23	4.13
Cash Flow Per Share	2.51	2.34	1.31	2.31	8.07	7.48	5.67	9.19
Tang Book Value Per Share	13.99	13.64	20.57	27.23	30.46	27.04	25.12	23.60
Dividends Per Share	0.200	0.200	0.200	0.680	0.800	0.720	0.680	0.800
Dividend Payout %	...	...	...	...	17.94	29.15	30.49	19.37
Income Statement								
Total Revenue	1,733,000	4,765,000	4,650,000	5,861,000	11,258,000	14,959,000	16,221,000	15,282,000
EBITDA	1,159,000	2,249,000	1,510,000	300,000	4,493,000	8,015,000	8,821,000	6,827,000
Depn & Amortn	590,000	2,372,000	2,395,000	2,957,000	2,861,000	2,790,000	2,478,000	2,266,000
Income Before Taxes	524,000	(454,000)	(1,235,000)	(2,958,000)	1,361,000	4,930,000	6,113,000	4,427,000
Income Taxes	168,000	376,000	905,000	(754,000)	392,000	3,337,000	4,531,000	2,720,000
Net Income	356,000	(5,723,000)	(2,140,000)	(2,204,000)	3,046,000	1,753,000	1,582,000	2,946,000
Average Shares	852,000	850,000	819,000	677,000	683,000	709,000	710,000	714,000
Balance Sheet								
Current Assets	2,902,000	2,566,000	3,665,000	2,590,000	4,593,000	2,975,000	3,762,000	3,224,000
Total Assets	21,634,000	22,012,000	31,094,000	32,311,000	36,011,000	35,620,000	35,306,000	31,371,000
Current Liabilities	1,909,000	1,968,000	2,240,000	1,729,000	4,379,000	4,333,000	5,081,000	4,394,000
Long-Term Obligations	5,495,000	5,494,000	6,589,000	7,276,000	5,323,000	6,394,000	6,512,000	4,674,000
Total Liabilities	9,600,000	10,304,000	13,553,000	13,758,000	14,991,000	16,276,000	17,023,000	14,219,000
Stockholders' Equity	12,034,000	11,708,000	17,541,000	18,553,000	21,020,000	19,344,000	18,283,000	17,152,000
Shares Outstanding	853,000	850,000	847,000	677,000	675,000	697,000	707,000	704,000
Statistical Record								
Return on Assets %	N.M.	N.M.	N.M.	N.M.	8.50	4.94	4.73	7.24
Return on Equity %	N.M.	N.M.	N.M.	N.M.	15.09	9.32	8.90	14.40
EBITDA Margin %	66.88	47.20	32.47	5.12	39.91	53.58	54.38	44.67
Net Margin %	20.54	N.M.	N.M.	N.M.	27.06	11.72	9.75	19.28
Asset Turnover	0.24	0.18	0.15	0.17	0.31	0.42	0.49	0.38
Current Ratio	1.52	1.30	1.64	1.50	1.05	0.69	0.74	0.73
Debt to Equity	0.46	0.47	0.38	0.39	0.25	0.33	0.36	0.27
Price Range	19.28-10.77	18.18-10.77	18.80-6.73	31.19-12.38	41.69-24.80	37.93-29.85	35.06-23.32	34.07-20.27
P/E Ratio	...	...	...	...	9.35-5.56	15.36-12.09	15.72-10.46	8.25-4.91
Average Yield %	1.40	1.40	1.49	2.99	2.25	2.25	2.32	2.81

Address: 5555 San Felipe Street,	Web Site: www.marathonoil.com	Auditors: PricewaterhouseCoopers LLP
Houston, TX 77056-2723	Officers: Lee M. Tillman - President, Chief Executive	Investor Contact: 713-296-4114
Telephone: 713-629-6600	Officer Patrick J. Wagner - Executive Vice President,	Transfer Agents: Computershare,
	Vice President, Interim Chief Financial Officer	Providence, RI

MARATHON PETROLEUM CORP.

Exchange	Symbol	Price	52Wk Range	Yield	P/E
NYS	MPC	$70.16 (6/29/2018)	82.93-49.45	2.62	10.39

*7 Year Price Score 123.72 *NYSE Composite Index=100 *12 Month Price Score 115.63

TRADING VOLUME (thousand shares)

Interim Earnings (Per Share)

Qtr.	Mar	Jun	Sep	Dec
2015	1.62	1.51	1.76	0.36
2016	0.00	1.51	0.27	0.43
2017	0.06	0.93	1.77	3.97
2018	0.08	...	...	...

Interim Dividends (Per Share)

Amt	Decl	Ex	Rec	Pay
0.40Q	07/26/2017	08/14/2017	08/16/2017	09/11/2017
0.40Q	10/25/2017	11/15/2017	11/16/2017	12/11/2017
0.46Q	01/29/2018	02/20/2018	02/21/2018	03/12/2018
0.46Q	04/25/2018	05/15/2018	05/16/2018	06/11/2018

Indicated Div: $1.84 (Div. Reinv. Plan)

Valuation Analysis | **Institutional Holding**

Forecast EPS	$4.49 (06/14/2018)	No of Institutions 1257
Market Cap	$32.8 Billion	Shares
Book Value	$15.0 Billion	445,905,792
Price/Book	2.19	% Held
Price/Sales	0.42	67.47

Business Summary: Refining & Marketing (MIC: 9.1.2 SIC: 1311 NAIC: 211111)

Marathon Petroleum is an independent petroleum refining, marketing, retail and transportation company. Co. has three segments: Refining and Marketing, which refines crude oil and other feedstocks at its refineries in the Gulf Coast and Midwest regions of the U.S., purchases refined products and ethanol for resale and distributes refined products; Speedway, which sells transportation fuels and convenience products in the retail market in the Midwest, East Coast and Southeast regions of the U.S.; and Midstream, which gathers, processes and transports natural gas; gathers, transports, fractionates, stores and markets natural gas liquids and transports and stores crude oil and refined products.

Recent Developments: For the quarter ended Mar 31 2018, net income increased 132.7% to US$235.0 million from US$101.0 million in the year-earlier quarter. Revenues were US$18.98 billion, up 15.8% from US$16.39 billion the year before. Operating income was US$440.0 million versus US$291.0 million in the prior-year quarter, an increase of 51.2%. Direct operating expenses rose 16.2% to US$17.51 billion from US$15.07 billion in the comparable period the year before. Indirect operating expenses were unchanged at US$1.03 billion versus the equivalent prior-year period.

Prospects: Our evaluation of Marathon Petroleum Corp. as of Jan. 21, 2018 is the result of our systematic analysis on three basic characteristics: earnings strength, relative valuation, and recent stock price movement. The company has enjoyed a very positive trend in earnings per share over the past 5 quarters and while recent estimates for the company have been mixed, MPC has posted better than expected results. Based on operating earnings yield, the company is undervalued when compared to all of the companies in our coverage universe. Share price changes over the past year indicates that MPC will perform poorly over the near term.

Financial Data

(US$ in Millions)	3 Mos	12/31/2017	12/31/2016	12/31/2015	12/31/2014	12/31/2013	12/31/2012	12/31/2011
Earnings Per Share	6.75	6.70	2.21	5.26	4.39	3.32	4.95	3.34
Cash Flow Per Share	11.26	13.04	7.53	7.55	5.46	5.40	6.59	4.65
Tang Book Value Per Share	24.42	21.50	18.88	17.36	16.76	16.80	16.16	12.13
Dividends Per Share	1.620	1.520	1.360	1.140	0.920	0.770	0.600	0.225
Dividend Payout %	24.00	22.69	61.54	21.67	20.96	23.19	12.13	6.75
Income Statement								
Total Revenue	18,984	75,369	63,364	72,258	98,102	100,254	82,492	78,759
EBITDA	450	6,056	4,355	6,302	5,356	4,624	6,317	4,632
Depn & Amortn	18	2,114	2,001	1,646	1,326	1,220	995	891
Income Before Taxes	257	3,344	1,822	4,374	3,835	3,246	5,238	3,719
Income Taxes	22	(460)	609	1,506	1,280	1,113	1,845	1,330
Net Income	37	3,432	1,174	2,852	2,524	2,112	3,389	2,389
Average Shares	480	512	530	542	574	634	684	714
Balance Sheet								
Current Assets	14,525	13,401	10,401	9,471	11,339	12,737	13,029	12,001
Total Assets	50,364	49,047	44,413	43,115	30,460	28,385	27,223	25,745
Current Liabilities	8,372	10,478	7,146	6,345	8,579	9,824	8,203	9,591
Long-Term Obligations	17,232	12,322	10,544	11,896	6,610	3,373	3,342	3,292
Total Liabilities	35,376	35,014	30,856	29,878	19,709	17,465	15,529	16,240
Stockholders' Equity	14,988	14,033	13,557	13,237	10,751	10,920	11,694	9,505
Shares Outstanding	467	486	528	531	548	594	666	714
Statistical Record								
Return on Assets %	7.15	7.34	2.68	7.75	8.58	7.60	12.76	9.76
Return on Equity %	24.51	24.88	8.74	23.78	23.29	18.68	31.89	26.92
EBITDA Margin %	2.37	8.04	6.87	8.72	5.46	4.61	7.66	5.88
Net Margin %	0.19	4.55	1.85	3.95	2.57	2.11	4.11	3.03
Asset Turnover	1.62	1.61	1.44	1.96	3.33	3.61	3.11	3.22
Current Ratio	1.73	1.28	1.46	1.49	1.32	1.30	1.59	1.25
Debt to Equity	1.15	0.88	0.78	0.90	0.61	0.31	0.29	0.35
Price Range	73.68-48.19	66.84-47.71	51.84-30.73	59.34-38.42	48.46-37.90	45.87-30.13	31.50-15.48	22.48-13.53
P/E Ratio	10.92-7.14	9.98-7.12	23.46-13.90	11.28-7.31	11.04-8.63	13.81-9.07	6.36-3.13	6.73-4.05
Average Yield %	2.76	2.81	3.38	2.25	2.11	2.02	2.57	1.26

Address: 539 South Main Street, Findlay, OH 45840-3229 Telephone: 419-422-2121	Web Site: www.marathonpetroleum.com Officers: Gary R. Heminger - Chairman, Chief Executive Officer, President Donald C. Templin - President, Division Officer, Senior Vice President, Chief Financial Officer	Auditors: PricewaterhouseCoopers LLP Investor Contact: 419-429-5640 Transfer Agents: Computershare, Canton, MA

MARKEL CORP (HOLDING CO)

Exchange	Symbol	Price	52Wk Range	Yield	P/E
NYS	MKL	$1084 (6/29/2018)	1182.13-969.00	N/A	61.72

*7 Year Price Score 121.76 *NYSE Composite Index=100 *12 Month Price Score 100.39

Interim Earnings (Per Share)

Qtr.	Mar	Jun	Sep	Dec
2015	13.49	6.72	7.39	14.14
2016	11.15	5.41	5.60	9.11
2017	3.90	10.31	(18.82)	30.33
2018	(4.25)	...	...	...

Interim Dividends (Per Share)

No Dividends Paid

Valuation Analysis

		Institutional Holding	
Forecast EPS	$36.00	No of Institutions	
	(06/06/2018)	625	
Market Cap	$15.1 Billion	Shares	
Book Value	$9.3 Billion	13,452,618	
Price/Book	1.62	% Held	
Price/Sales	2.42	75.91	

Business Summary: General Insurance (MIC: 5.2.1 SIC: 6331 NAIC: 524126)

Markel is a financial holding company. Co.'s principal business markets and underwrites specialty insurance products. Co. also owns interests in various industrial and service businesses that operate outside of the specialty insurance marketplace. Co. has three segments: U.S. Insurance, which includes all direct business and facultative placements written by Co.'s insurance subsidiaries domiciled in the U.S.; International Insurance, which includes all direct business and facultative placements written by Co.'s insurance subsidiaries domiciled outside of the U.S.; and Reinsurance, which includes property and casualty treaty reinsurance products provided through the broker market.

Recent Developments: For the quarter ended Mar 31 2018, net loss amounted to US$65.6 million versus net income of US$71.0 million in the year-earlier quarter. Revenues were US$1.58 billion, up 11.6% from US$1.41 billion the year before. Net premiums earned were US$1.15 billion versus US$982.6 million in the prior-year quarter, an increase of 17.1%. Net investment income rose 7.6% to US$108.0 million from US$100.4 million a year ago.

Prospects: Our evaluation of Markel Corp. as of Jan. 21, 2018 is the result of our systematic analysis on three basic characteristics: earnings strength, relative valuation, and recent stock price movement. The company has suffered a very negative trend in earnings per share over the past 5 quarters. However, while recent estimates for the company have been mixed, MKL has posted results that fell short of analysts expectations. Based on operating earnings yield, the company is overvalued when compared to all of the companies in our coverage universe. Share price changes over the past year indicates that MKL will perform well over the near term.

Financial Data
(US$ in Thousands)

	3 Mos	12/31/2017	12/31/2016	12/31/2015	12/31/2014	12/31/2013	12/31/2012	12/31/2011
Earnings Per Share	17.57	25.81	31.27	41.74	22.27	22.48	25.89	14.60
Cash Flow Per Share	64.90	61.48	38.05	46.58	51.26	59.46	40.61	32.14
Tang Book Value Per Share	447.45	458.23	472.67	420.80	418.50	367.58	294.88	261.92
Income Statement								
Premium Income	1,151,021	4,247,978	3,865,870	3,823,532	3,840,912	3,231,616	2,147,128	1,979,340
Total Revenue	1,575,471	6,061,659	5,612,026	5,369,983	5,133,667	4,323,083	3,000,112	2,629,950
Benefits & Claims	615,118	2,865,761	2,050,744	1,938,745	2,202,467	1,816,273	1,154,068	1,209,986
Income Before Taxes	42,837	87,295	629,920	742,105	440,378	361,743	312,050	190,196
Income Taxes	108,431	(313,463)	169,477	152,963	116,690	77,898	53,802	41,710
Net Income	(64,306)	395,269	455,689	582,772	321,182	281,021	253,385	142,026
Average Shares	13,959	14,006	14,078	14,061	14,057	12,586	9,666	9,726
Balance Sheet								
Total Assets	32,866,471	32,805,016	25,875,299	24,941,271	25,200,357	23,955,511	12,556,588	11,532,103
Total Liabilities	23,542,260	23,300,868	17,414,372	17,107,121	17,605,539	17,281,934	8,667,931	8,144,590
Stockholders' Equity	9,324,211	9,504,148	8,460,927	7,834,150	7,594,818	6,673,577	3,888,657	3,387,513
Shares Outstanding	13,895	13,903	13,954	13,959	13,961	13,985	9,629	9,620
Statistical Record								
Return on Assets %	0.88	1.35	1.79	2.32	1.31	1.54	2.10	1.27
Return on Equity %	2.90	4.40	5.58	7.55	4.50	5.32	6.95	4.33
Loss Ratio %	53.44	67.46	53.05	50.71	57.34	56.20	53.75	61.13
Net Margin %	(4.08)	6.52	8.12	10.85	6.26	6.50	8.45	5.40
Price Range	1182.13-943.33	1147.10-891.25	982.84-810.26	934.76-662.59	703.95-529.00	580.35-433.42	500.68-399.12	425.68-347.36
P/E Ratio	67.28-53.69	44.44-34.53	31.43-25.91	22.39-15.87	31.61-23.75	25.82-19.28	19.34-15.42	29.16-23.79

Address: 4521 Highwoods Parkway, Glen Allen, VA 23060-6148 **Telephone:** 804-747-0136	**Web Site:** www.markelcorp.com **Officers:** Alan I. Kirshner - Chairman, Chief Executive Officer Bradley James Kiscaden - President, Chief Administrative Officer	**Auditors:** KPMG LLP **Investor Contact:** 800-446-6671 **Transfer Agents:** American Stock Transfer & Trust Co., LLC, Brooklyn, NY

MARSH & McLENNAN COMPANIES INC.

Exchange	Symbol	Price	52Wk Range	Yield	P/E
NYS	MMC	$81.97 (6/29/2018)	85.97-76.88	2.03	26.27

*7 Year Price Score 121.58 ***NYSE Composite Index=100** ***12 Month Price Score 97.99**

Interim Earnings (Per Share)

Qtr.	Mar	Jun	Sep	Dec
2015	0.88	0.77	0.61	0.71
2016	0.91	0.90	0.73	0.84
2017	1.09	0.96	0.76	0.06
2018	1.34	...	...	...

Interim Dividends (Per Share)

Amt	Decl	Ex	Rec	Pay
0.375Q	09/19/2017	10/06/2017	10/10/2017	11/15/2017
0.375Q	01/17/2018	01/30/2018	01/31/2018	02/15/2018
0.375Q	03/21/2018	04/09/2018	04/10/2018	05/15/2018
0.415Q	05/17/2018	07/10/2018	07/11/2018	08/15/2018

Indicated Div: $1.66

Valuation Analysis / Institutional Holding

Forecast EPS	$4.35
	(06/13/2018)
Market Cap	$41.6 Billion
Book Value	$7.9 Billion
Price/Book	5.24
Price/Sales	2.87

No of Institutions	1102
Shares	537,543,616
% Held	84.96

TRADING VOLUME (thousand shares)

Business Summary: Brokers & Intermediaries (MIC: 5.2.3 SIC: 6411 NAIC: 524210)

Marsh & McLennan Companies is a holding company, engaged in providing clients advice and solutions in risk, strategy and people. Co.'s segments include: Risk and Insurance Services, which conducts its business through Marsh that provides, among others risk management, insurance program management services, risk consulting, and analytical modeling, and Guy Carpenter that creates and executes reinsurance and risk management solutions; and Consulting, which conducts its business through Mercer that operates in health, retirement, investments, and talent areas and Oliver Wyman Group that provides advisory services to clients through Oliver Wyman, Lippincott and NERA Economic Consulting.

Recent Developments: For the quarter ended Mar 31 2018, net income increased 20.4% to US$696.0 million from US$578.0 million in the year-earlier quarter. Revenues were US$4.00 billion, up 14.2% from US$3.50 billion the year before.

Prospects: Our evaluation of Marsh & McLennan Cos. Inc. as of Jan. 21, 2018 is the result of our systematic analysis on three basic characteristics: earnings strength, relative valuation, and recent stock price movement. The company has managed to produce a neutral trend in earnings per share over the past 5 quarters and while recent estimates for the company have been mixed, MMC has posted better than expected results. Based on operating earnings yield, the company is undervalued when compared to all of the companies in our coverage universe. Share price changes over the past year indicates that MMC will perform well over the near term.

Financial Data
(US$ in Thousands)

	3 Mos	12/31/2017	12/31/2016	12/31/2015	12/31/2014	12/31/2013	12/31/2012	12/31/2011
Earnings Per Share	3.12	2.87	3.38	2.98	2.65	2.43	2.13	1.79
Cash Flow Per Share	3.80	3.69	3.86	3.56	3.88	2.44	2.42	3.15
Tang Book Value Per Share	N.M.	N.M.	N.M.	N.M.	N.M.	0.99	N.M.	N.M.
Dividends Per Share	1.465	1.430	1.300	1.180	1.060	0.960	0.900	0.860
Dividend Payout %	46.96	49.83	38.46	39.60	40.00	39.51	42.25	48.04
Income Statement								
Total Revenue	4,000,000	14,024,000	13,211,000	12,893,000	12,951,000	12,261,000	11,924,000	11,526,000
EBITDA	1,019,000	3,040,000	2,794,000	2,566,000	2,287,000	2,194,000	1,925,000	1,640,000
Depn & Amortn	45,000	169,000	130,000	109,000	86,000	72,000	72,000	65,000
Income Before Taxes	916,000	2,643,000	2,480,000	2,307,000	2,057,000	1,973,000	1,696,000	1,404,000
Income Taxes	220,000	1,133,000	685,000	671,000	586,000	594,000	492,000	422,000
Net Income	690,000	1,492,000	1,768,000	1,599,000	1,465,000	1,357,000	1,176,000	993,000
Average Shares	514,000	519,000	524,000	536,000	553,000	558,000	552,000	551,000
Balance Sheet								
Current Assets	6,270,000	5,562,000	4,884,000	5,044,000	6,055,000	6,300,000	5,963,000	5,648,000
Total Assets	21,379,000	20,429,000	18,190,000	18,216,000	17,840,000	16,980,000	16,288,000	15,454,000
Current Liabilities	4,122,000	4,262,000	4,082,000	3,708,000	3,705,000	3,809,000	3,564,000	3,739,000
Long-Term Obligations	5,815,000	5,225,000	4,495,000	4,402,000	3,376,000	2,621,000	2,658,000	2,668,000
Total Liabilities	13,439,000	13,070,000	11,998,000	11,703,000	10,786,000	9,075,000	9,746,000	9,571,000
Stockholders' Equity	7,940,000	7,359,000	6,192,000	6,513,000	7,054,000	7,905,000	6,542,000	5,883,000
Shares Outstanding	507,931	508,711	514,491	521,897	540,142	546,759	545,507	539,178
Statistical Record								
Return on Assets %	8.00	7.73	9.69	8.87	8.41	8.16	7.39	6.46
Return on Equity %	22.29	22.02	27.76	23.57	19.59	18.79	18.88	16.21
EBITDA Margin %	25.48	21.68	21.15	19.90	17.66	17.89	16.14	14.23
Net Margin %	17.25	10.64	13.38	12.40	11.31	11.07	9.86	8.62
Asset Turnover	0.72	0.73	0.72	0.72	0.74	0.74	0.75	0.75
Current Ratio	1.52	1.31	1.20	1.36	1.63	1.65	1.67	1.51
Debt to Equity	0.73	0.71	0.73	0.68	0.48	0.33	0.41	0.45
Price Range	85.97-71.88	85.97-67.41	69.77-51.29	59.84-51.54	58.56-44.40	48.36-34.47	35.78-30.72	32.00-25.71
P/E Ratio	27.55-23.04	29.95-23.49	20.64-15.17	20.08-17.30	22.10-16.75	19.90-14.19	16.80-14.42	17.88-14.36
Average Yield %	1.83	1.85	2.04	2.10	2.07	2.34	2.72	2.93

Address: 1166 Avenue of the Americas, New York, NY 10036-2774
Telephone: 212-345-5000
Fax: 212-345-4809

Web Site: www.mmc.com
Officers: H. Edward Hanway - Chairman Daniel S. (Dan) Glaser - President, Chief Executive Officer, Chief Operating Officer, Division Officer

Auditors: Deloitte & Touche LLP
Investor Contact: 212-345-5462
Transfer Agents: Wells Fargo Shareowner Services, St. Paul, MN

MARTIN MARIETTA MATERIALS, INC.

Exchange	Symbol	Price	52Wk Range	Yield	P/E
NYS	MLM	$223.33 (6/29/2018)	239.96-193.30	0.79	20.77

*7 Year Price Score 121.23 *NYSE Composite Index=100 ***12 Month Price Score 100.78**

Interim Earnings (Per Share)

Qtr.	Mar	Jun	Sep	Dec
2015	0.07	1.22	1.74	1.26
2016	0.69	1.90	2.49	1.55
2017	0.67	2.25	2.39	5.95
2018	0.16	...	...	...

Interim Dividends (Per Share)

Amt	Decl	Ex	Rec	Pay
0.44Q	08/24/2017	08/31/2017	09/05/2017	09/29/2017
0.44Q	11/16/2017	11/30/2017	12/01/2017	12/29/2017
0.44Q	02/22/2018	03/02/2018	03/05/2018	03/29/2018
0.44Q	05/17/2018	05/31/2018	06/01/2018	06/29/2018

Indicated Div: $1.76

Valuation Analysis — **Institutional Holding**

Forecast EPS	$9.17 (05/14/2018)	No of Institutions 758
Market Cap	$14.1 Billion	Shares 73,144,864
Book Value	$4.7 Billion	% Held
Price/Book	3.01	101.75
Price/Sales	3.58	

Business Summary: Construction Materials (MIC: 8.5.1 SIC: 1411 NAIC: 212311)

Martin Marietta Materials is a supplier of aggregates products (crushed stone, sand, and gravel) used for the construction of infrastructure, nonresidential, and residential projects. Co.'s Aggregates business consists primarily of mining, processing, and selling granite, limestone, sand and gravel, as well as includes aggregates-related downstream product lines, its heavy building materials; Co.'s Cement business produces Portland and specialty cements; Co.'s Magnesia Specialties business manufactures and markets magnesia-based chemical products used in industrial, agricultural, and environmental applications, and dolomitic lime sold primarily to customers in the steel industry.

Recent Developments: For the quarter ended Mar 31 2018, net income decreased 76.3% to US$10.0 million from US$42.3 million in the year-earlier quarter. Revenues were US$802.0 million, down 5.0% from US$843.9 million the year before. Operating income was US$39.1 million versus US$77.2 million in the prior-year quarter, a decrease of 49.3%. Direct operating expenses declined 0.7% to US$691.6 million from US$696.8 million in the comparable period the year before. Indirect operating expenses increased 2.0% to US$71.3 million from US$69.9 million in the equivalent prior-year period.

Prospects: Our evaluation of Martin Marietta Materials Inc. as of Jan. 21, 2018 is the result of our systematic analysis on three basic characteristics: earnings strength, relative valuation, and recent stock price movement. The company has generated a negative trend in earnings per share over the past 5 quarters and while recent estimates for the company have been mixed, MLM has posted results that fell short of analysts expectations. Based on operating earnings yield, the company is about fairly valued when compared to all of the companies in our coverage universe. Share price changes over the past year indicates that MLM will perform very poorly over the near term.

Financial Data
(US$ in Thousands)

	3 Mos	12/31/2017	12/31/2016	12/31/2015	12/31/2014	12/31/2013	12/31/2012	12/31/2011
Earnings Per Share	10.75	11.25	6.63	4.29	2.71	2.61	1.83	1.78
Cash Flow Per Share	10.94	10.45	10.64	8.58	6.71	6.69	4.85	5.68
Tang Book Value Per Share	39.00	32.02	23.26	22.93	25.07	18.86	16.17	16.15
Dividends Per Share	1.740	1.720	1.640	1.600	1.600	1.600	1.600	1.600
Dividend Payout %	16.19	15.29	24.74	37.30	59.04	61.30	87.43	89.89
Income Statement								
Total Revenue	802,004	3,965,594	3,818,749	3,539,570	2,957,951	2,155,551	2,037,667	1,713,823
EBITDA	124,405	990,223	957,640	736,962	526,477	386,026	328,192	329,162
Depn & Amortn	76,821	279,808	268,935	246,874	211,242	168,333	171,940	169,974
Income Before Taxes	12,497	618,928	607,028	413,801	249,178	164,226	102,913	100,602
Income Taxes	2,457	(94,457)	181,584	124,863	94,847	44,045	16,950	20,986
Net Income	10,023	713,342	425,386	288,792	155,601	121,337	84,474	82,379
Average Shares	63,222	63,217	63,861	67,020	57,088	46,285	45,970	45,793
Balance Sheet								
Current Assets	2,601,930	2,631,160	1,086,385	1,082,168	1,288,816	755,366	700,401	657,850
Total Assets	8,948,050	8,992,511	7,300,905	6,961,732	7,464,392	3,259,826	3,160,926	3,147,822
Current Liabilities	650,979	694,216	546,588	367,191	396,648	210,549	173,335	173,712
Long-Term Obligations	2,728,102	2,727,294	1,506,153	1,553,649	1,571,059	1,018,518	1,042,183	1,052,902
Total Liabilities	4,271,420	4,312,911	3,160,927	2,904,448	3,113,226	1,721,949	1,750,381	1,738,501
Stockholders' Equity	4,676,630	4,679,600	4,139,978	4,057,284	4,351,166	1,537,877	1,410,545	1,409,321
Shares Outstanding	62,951	62,873	63,176	64,479	67,293	46,261	46,002	45,726
Statistical Record								
Return on Assets %	8.33	8.76	5.95	4.00	2.90	3.78	2.67	2.65
Return on Equity %	15.57	16.18	10.35	6.87	5.28	8.23	5.97	5.81
EBITDA Margin %	15.51	24.97	25.08	20.82	17.80	17.91	16.11	19.21
Net Margin %	1.25	17.99	11.14	8.16	5.26	5.63	4.15	4.81
Asset Turnover	0.48	0.49	0.53	0.49	0.55	0.67	0.64	0.55
Current Ratio	4.00	3.79	1.99	2.95	3.25	3.59	4.04	3.79
Debt to Equity	0.58	0.58	0.36	0.38	0.36	0.66	0.74	0.75
Price Range	239.96-195.54	242.00-195.54	233.52-117.00	176.51-104.58	134.91-98.70	112.09-93.56	95.59-64.56	93.00-61.62
P/E Ratio	22.32-18.19	21.51-17.38	35.22-17.65	41.14-24.38	49.78-36.42	42.95-35.85	52.23-35.28	52.25-34.62
Average Yield %	0.81	0.79	0.92	1.09	1.31	1.60	1.96	2.03

Address: 2710 Wycliff Road, Raleigh, NC 27607-3033	Web Site: www.martinmarietta.com	Auditors: PricewaterhouseCoopers LLP
Telephone: 919-781-4550	Officers: C. Howard Nye - Chairman, President, Chief Executive Officer James A.J. Nickolas - Chief Financial Officer, Senior Vice President	Investor Contact: 919-781-4550
		Transfer Agents: American Stock Transfer & Trust Company, LLC, Brooklyn, NY

MASCO CORP.

Exchange	Symbol	Price	52Wk Range	Yield	P/E
NYS	MAS	$37.42 (6/29/2018)	46.27-36.16	1.12	22.01

*7 Year Price Score 134.19 *NYSE Composite Index=100 *12 Month Price Score 93.49

Interim Earnings (Per Share)

Qtr.	Mar	Jun	Sep	Dec
2015	0.18	0.30	0.32	0.22
2016	0.32	0.45	0.40	0.30
2017	0.43	0.49	0.46	0.28
2018	0.47	...	...	...

Interim Dividends (Per Share)

Amt	Decl	Ex	Rec	Pay
0.105Q	09/22/2017	10/12/2017	10/13/2017	11/13/2017
0.105Q	12/14/2017	01/11/2018	01/12/2018	02/12/2018
0.105Q	03/23/2018	04/12/2018	04/13/2018	05/14/2018
0.105Q	06/22/2018	07/12/2018	07/13/2018	08/13/2018

Indicated Div: $0.42 (Div. Reinv. Plan)

Valuation Analysis / **Institutional Holding**

Forecast EPS	$2.52 (06/14/2018)	No of Institutions 895
Market Cap	$11.5 Billion	Shares 356,707,136
Book Value	N/A	% Held 83.35
Price/Book	N/A	
Price/Sales	1.48	

TRADING VOLUME (thousand shares)

Business Summary: Construction Materials (MIC: 8.5.1 SIC: 2434 NAIC: 337110)

Masco designs, manufactures and distributes home improvement and building products. Co. has four segments: Plumbing Products, which includes faucets, valves, showerheads, bathtubs, toilets, and spas; Architectural Products, which includes cabinet, door and window; Cabinetry Products, kitchen and bath cabinets; home office; entertainment centers; and storage products; and Windows and Other Specialty Products, which includes windows, window frame components, patio doors, staples, and other fastening tools.

Recent Developments: For the quarter ended Mar 31 2018, net income increased 8.8% to US$161.0 million from US$148.0 million in the year-earlier quarter. Revenues were US$1.92 billion, up 8.0% from US$1.78 billion the year before. Operating income was US$244.0 million versus US$257.0 million in the prior-year quarter, a decrease of 5.1%. Direct operating expenses rose 10.9% to US$1.30 billion from US$1.17 billion in the comparable period the year before. Indirect operating expenses increased 7.8% to US$375.0 million from US$348.0 million in the equivalent prior-year period.

Prospects: Our evaluation of Masco Corp. as of Jan. 21, 2018 is the result of our systematic analysis on three basic characteristics: earnings strength, relative valuation, and recent stock price movement. The company has generated a negative trend in earnings per share over the past 5 quarters and while recent estimates for the company have been mixed, MAS has posted results that fell short of analysts expectations. Based on operating earnings yield, the company is about fairly valued when compared to all of the companies in our coverage universe. Share price changes over the past year indicates that MAS will perform in line with the market over the near term.

Financial Data

(US$ in Thousands)	3 Mos	12/31/2017	12/31/2016	12/31/2015	12/31/2014	12/31/2013	12/31/2012	12/31/2011
Earnings Per Share	1.70	1.66	1.47	1.02	2.38	0.76	(0.33)	(1.66)
Cash Flow Per Share	2.73	2.39	2.22	2.07	1.72	1.84	0.80	0.69
Dividends Per Share	0.410	0.405	0.385	0.365	0.330	0.300	0.300	0.300
Dividend Payout %	24.12	24.40	26.19	35.78	13.87	39.47	...	...
Income Statement								
Total Revenue	1,920,000	7,644,000	7,357,000	7,142,000	8,521,000	8,173,000	7,745,000	7,467,000
EBITDA	241,000	1,279,000	1,183,000	1,030,000	956,000	842,000	497,000	27,000
Depn & Amortn	...	116,000	124,000	116,000	157,000	175,000	202,000	246,000
Income Before Taxes	200,000	885,000	830,000	689,000	575,000	434,000	42,000	(472,000)
Income Taxes	39,000	305,000	296,000	293,000	(333,000)	111,000	83,000	(49,000)
Net Income	149,000	533,000	491,000	355,000	856,000	272,000	(114,000)	(575,000)
Average Shares	313,000	318,000	330,000	341,000	352,000	352,000	349,000	348,000
Balance Sheet								
Current Assets	2,993,000	3,215,000	2,934,000	3,328,000	3,863,000	3,468,000	3,217,000	3,429,000
Total Assets	5,630,000	5,488,000	5,137,000	5,680,000	7,167,000	6,933,000	6,875,000	7,297,000
Current Liabilities	1,770,000	1,628,000	1,460,000	2,506,000	2,211,000	1,782,000	1,862,000	2,363,000
Long-Term Obligations	2,971,000	2,969,000	2,995,000	2,418,000	2,919,000	3,421,000	3,422,000	3,222,000
Total Liabilities	5,702,000	5,548,000	5,435,000	5,815,000	6,243,000	6,398,000	6,553,000	6,770,000
Stockholders' Equity	(72,000)	(60,000)	(298,000)	(135,000)	924,000	535,000	322,000	527,000
Shares Outstanding	308,000	310,400	318,000	330,500	345,000	349,500	349,000	347,900
Statistical Record								
Return on Assets %	10.07	10.03	9.05	5.53	12.14	3.94	N.M.	N.M.
Return on Equity %	...	...	...	89.99	117.34	63.48	N.M.	N.M.
EBITDA Margin %	12.55	16.73	16.08	14.42	11.22	10.30	6.42	0.36
Net Margin %	7.76	6.97	6.67	4.97	10.05	3.33	N.M.	N.M.
Asset Turnover	1.45	1.44	1.36	1.11	1.21	1.18	1.09	0.97
Current Ratio	1.69	1.97	2.01	1.33	1.75	1.95	1.73	1.45
Debt to Equity	...	...	...	...	3.16	6.39	10.63	6.11
Price Range	46.27-33.08	44.24-31.93	36.87-23.46	30.50-20.84	22.33-17.18	20.05-14.65	15.02-9.65	12.99-6.08
P/E Ratio	27.22-19.46	26.65-19.23	25.08-15.96	29.90-20.43	9.38-7.22	26.38-19.27	...	...
Average Yield %	1.04	1.09	1.22	1.45	1.67	1.69	2.48	3.03

Address: 17450 College Parkway, Livonia, MI 48152
Telephone: 313-274-7400

Web Site: www.masco.com
Officers: J. Michael Losh - Chairman Richard A. Manoogian - Chairman Emeritus, Executive Chairman, Chairman, President, Chief Executive Officer, Vice President

Auditors: PricewaterhouseCoopers LLP
Investor Contact: 313-792-5500
Transfer Agents: Computershare, Providence, RI

MASTERCARD INC

Exchange	Symbol	Price	52Wk Range	Yield	P/E
NYS	MA	$196.52 (6/29/2018)	203.21-120.78	0.51	48.29

*7 Year Price Score 148.24 *NYSE Composite Index=100 *12 Month Price Score 119.69

Interim Earnings (Per Share)

Qtr.	Mar	Jun	Sep	Dec
2015	0.89	0.81	0.86	0.79
2016	0.86	0.89	1.08	0.86
2017	1.00	1.10	1.34	0.22
2018	1.41	...	...	...

Interim Dividends (Per Share)

Amt	Decl	Ex	Rec	Pay
0.22Q	09/19/2017	10/05/2017	10/06/2017	11/09/2017
0.25Q	12/04/2017	01/08/2018	01/09/2018	02/09/2018
0.25Q	02/05/2018	04/06/2018	04/09/2018	05/09/2018
0.25Q	06/25/2018	07/06/2018	07/09/2018	08/09/2018

Indicated Div: $1.00

Valuation Analysis

		Institutional Holding	
Forecast EPS	$6.35 (06/14/2018)	No of Institutions	2039
Market Cap	$206.0 Billion	Shares	893,082,560
Book Value	$5.7 Billion	% Held	75.18
Price/Book	36.11		
Price/Sales	15.44		

Business Summary: Business Services (MIC: 7.5.2 SIC: 7389 NAIC: 561499)

MasterCard is a technology company in the global payments industry that connects consumers, financial institutions, merchants, governments and businesses worldwide, enabling them to use electronic forms of payment instead of cash and checks. Co. facilitates the switching (authorization, clearing and settlement) of payment transactions and delivers related products and services. Co. creates a range of payment solutions and services using its family of brands, including MasterCard®, Maestro® and Cirrus®. Co. also provides offerings such as safety and security products, information services and consulting, issuer and acquirer processing and loyalty and reward programs.

Recent Developments: For the quarter ended Mar 31 2018, net income increased 38.0% to US$1.49 billion from US$1.08 billion in the year-earlier quarter. Revenues were US$3.58 billion, up 30.9% from US$2.73 billion the year before. Operating income was US$1.83 billion versus US$1.51 billion in the prior-year quarter, an increase of 21.2%. Indirect operating expenses increased 42.9% to US$1.76 billion from US$1.23 billion in the equivalent prior-year period.

Prospects: Our evaluation of MasterCard Inc. as of Jan. 21, 2018 is the result of our systematic analysis on three basic characteristics: earnings strength, relative valuation, and recent stock price movement. The company has enjoyed a very positive trend in earnings per share over the past 5 quarters and while recent estimates for the company have been mixed, MA has posted better than expected results. Based on operating earnings yield, the company is about fairly valued when compared to all of the companies in our coverage universe. Share price changes over the past year indicates that MA will perform well over the near term.

Financial Data

(US$ in Thousands)	3 Mos	12/31/2017	12/31/2016	12/31/2015	12/31/2014	12/31/2013	12/31/2012	12/31/2011
Earnings Per Share	4.07	3.65	3.69	3.35	3.10	2.56	2.19	1.49
Cash Flow Per Share	5.56	5.21	4.07	3.57	2.92	3.41	2.35	2.10
Tang Book Value Per Share	1.41	1.25	2.94	2.99	3.95	4.76	4.18	3.30
Dividends Per Share	0.910	0.880	0.760	0.640	0.440	0.210	0.105	0.060
Dividend Payout %	22.36	24.11	20.60	19.10	14.19	8.20	4.79	4.04
Income Statement								
Total Revenue	3,580,000	12,497,000	10,776,000	9,667,000	9,473,000	8,346,000	7,391,000	6,714,000
EBITDA	2,133,000	6,861,000	5,893,000	5,150,000	5,208,000	4,573,000	4,000,000	2,804,000
Depn & Amortn	287,000	185,000	152,000	131,000	107,000	92,000	84,000	77,000
Income Before Taxes	1,803,000	6,522,000	5,646,000	4,958,000	5,079,000	4,500,000	3,932,000	2,746,000
Income Taxes	311,000	2,607,000	1,587,000	1,150,000	1,462,000	1,384,000	1,174,000	842,000
Net Income	1,492,000	3,915,000	4,059,000	3,808,000	3,617,000	3,116,000	2,759,000	1,906,000
Average Shares	1,057,000	1,072,000	1,101,000	1,137,000	1,169,000	1,215,000	1,260,000	1,280,000
Balance Sheet								
Current Assets	14,707,000	13,797,000	13,228,000	10,985,000	10,997,000	10,950,000	9,357,000	7,741,000
Total Assets	22,944,000	21,329,000	18,675,000	16,269,000	15,329,000	14,242,000	12,462,000	10,693,000
Current Liabilities	8,948,000	8,793,000	7,206,000	6,269,000	6,222,000	6,032,000	4,906,000	4,217,000
Long-Term Obligations	6,469,000	5,424,000	5,180,000	3,287,000	1,494,000	...	...	...
Total Liabilities	17,241,000	15,861,000	13,019,000	10,241,000	8,539,000	6,758,000	5,545,000	4,825,000
Stockholders' Equity	5,703,000	5,468,000	5,656,000	6,028,000	6,790,000	7,484,000	6,917,000	5,868,000
Shares Outstanding	1,048,000	1,054,000	1,081,000	1,116,000	1,152,561	1,194,188	1,232,439	1,268,637
Statistical Record								
Return on Assets %	20.84	19.57	23.17	24.10	24.46	23.34	23.77	19.52
Return on Equity %	76.47	70.39	69.29	59.42	50.68	43.27	43.04	34.43
EBITDA Margin %	59.58	54.90	54.69	53.27	54.98	54.79	54.12	41.76
Net Margin %	41.68	31.33	37.67	39.39	38.18	37.34	37.33	28.39
Asset Turnover	0.64	0.62	0.62	0.61	0.64	0.63	0.64	0.69
Current Ratio	1.64	1.57	1.84	1.75	1.77	1.82	1.91	1.84
Debt to Equity	1.13	0.99	0.92	0.55	0.22	...	...	...
Price Range	183.24-111.22	154.19-105.00	107.02-80.65	101.50-80.74	89.08-68.68	83.55-49.13	49.85-33.91	38.10-22.09
P/E Ratio	45.02-27.33	42.24-28.77	29.00-21.86	30.30-24.10	28.74-22.15	32.64-19.19	22.76-15.48	25.57-14.82
Average Yield %	0.64	0.69	0.80	0.70	0.69	0.57	0.34	0.24	0.20

Address: 2000 Purchase Street, Purchase, NY 10577 Telephone: 914-249-2000	Web Site: www.mastercard.com Officers: Richard Haythornthwaite - Chairman Ajaypal S. (Ajay) Banga - President, Chief Executive Officer	Auditors: PricewaterhouseCoopers LLP Investor Contact: 914-249-4565 Transfer Agents: Computershare, Jersey City, NJ

MATADOR RESOURCES CO

Exchange	Symbol	Price	52Wk Range	Yield	P/E
NYS	MTDR	$30.05 (6/29/2018)	34.28-21.06	N/A	22.43

*7 Year Price Score N/A   *NYSE Composite Index=100   *12 Month Price Score 104.20

Interim Earnings (Per Share)

Qtr.	Mar	Jun	Sep	Dec
2015	(0.68)	(1.89)	2.86	(2.76)
2016	(1.26)	(1.15)	0.13	1.17
2017	0.44	0.28	0.15	0.36
2018	0.55	...	...	...

Interim Dividends (Per Share)

No Dividends Paid

Valuation Analysis   **Institutional Holding**

Forecast EPS	$1.37	No of Institutions
	(06/14/2018)	341
Market Cap	$3.3 Billion	Shares
Book Value	$1.2 Billion	103,249,440
Price/Book	2.66	% Held
Price/Sales	5.47	N/A

TRADING VOLUME (thousand shares)

Business Summary: Production & Extraction (MIC: 9.1.1 SIC: 1311 NAIC: 211111)

Matador Resources is an independent energy company engaged in the exploration, development, production and acquisition of oil and natural gas resources. Additionally, Co. conducts midstream operations primarily, through its midstream joint venture, San Mateo Midstream, LLC, in support of its exploration, development and production operations and provides natural gas processing, natural gas, oil and salt water gathering services and salt water disposal services to third parties. As of Dec 31 2017, Co.'s estimated proved developed and undeveloped reserves were 86,743 thousand barrels of oil and 396.2 billion cubic feet of natural gas.

Recent Developments: For the quarter ended Mar 31 2018, net income increased 41.4% to US$64.9 million from US$45.9 million in the year-earlier quarter. Revenues were US$191.2 million, up 41.8% from US$134.8 million the year before. Operating income was US$73.4 million versus US$54.3 million in the prior-year quarter, an increase of 35.2%. Direct operating expenses rose 47.7% to US$44.2 million from US$29.9 million in the comparable period the year before. Indirect operating expenses increased 45.5% to US$73.7 million from US$50.6 million in the equivalent prior-year period.

Prospects: Our evaluation of Matador Resources Co as of Jan. 21, 2018 is the result of our systematic analysis on three basic characteristics: earnings strength, relative valuation, and recent stock price movement. The company has suffered a very negative trend in earnings per share over the past 5 quarters and while recent estimates for the company have been raised by analysts, MTDR has posted better than expected results. Based on operating earnings yield, the company is overvalued when compared to all of the companies in our coverage universe. Share price changes over the past year indicates that MTDR will perform very poorly over the near term.

Financial Data

(US$ in Thousands)	3 Mos	12/31/2017	12/31/2016	12/31/2015	12/31/2014	12/31/2013	12/31/2012	12/31/2011
Earnings Per Share	1.34	1.23	(1.07)	(8.34)	1.56	0.77	(0.62)	(0.25)
Cash Flow Per Share	3.43	2.93	1.47	2.56	3.58	3.05	2.30	1.45
Tang Book Value Per Share	11.28	10.66	6.94	5.70	11.81	8.67	6.82	6.35
Income Statement								
Total Revenue	191,180	544,276	264,422	316,169	431,036	260,889	165,156	79,244
EBITDA	73,780	342,385	53,302	(627,804)	313,855	158,648	46,541	16,292
Depn & Amortn	365	177,970	123,196	179,699	134,737	98,395	80,454	31,754
Income Before Taxes	64,924	129,850	(98,093)	(826,892)	175,129	54,791	(34,691)	(15,830)
Income Taxes	...	(8,157)	(1,036)	(147,368)	64,375	9,697	(1,430)	(5,521)
Net Income	59,894	125,867	(97,421)	(679,785)	110,771	45,094	(33,261)	(10,309)
Average Shares	109,412	102,543	91,273	81,537	70,906	58,929	53,852	41,686
Balance Sheet								
Current Assets	206,978	257,170	279,182	127,007	113,323	42,172	38,197	36,276
Total Assets	2,275,705	2,145,690	1,464,665	1,140,861	1,436,291	890,330	632,029	439,469
Current Liabilities	306,492	282,606	169,505	136,830	161,787	100,327	96,492	74,576
Long-Term Obligations	574,118	574,073	573,924	391,254	340,000	200,000	150,000	88,000
Total Liabilities	1,043,459	989,134	774,540	652,858	569,883	321,406	252,925	167,953
Stockholders' Equity	1,232,246	1,156,556	690,125	488,003	866,408	568,924	379,104	271,515
Shares Outstanding	109,261	108,510	99,511	85,564	73,342	65,652	55,577	42,768
Statistical Record								
Return on Assets %	7.16	6.97	N.M.	N.M.	9.52	5.92	N.M.	N.M.
Return on Equity %	13.60	13.63	N.M.	N.M.	15.43	9.51	N.M.	N.M.
EBITDA Margin %	38.59	62.91	20.16	N.M.	72.81	60.81	28.18	20.56
Net Margin %	31.33	23.13	N.M.	N.M.	25.70	17.28	N.M.	N.M.
Asset Turnover	0.30	0.30	0.20	0.25	0.37	0.34	0.31	0.20
Current Ratio	0.68	0.91	1.65	0.93	0.70	0.42	0.40	0.49
Debt to Equity	0.47	0.50	0.83	0.80	0.39	0.35	0.40	0.32
Price Range	33.30-20.30	31.35-20.30	26.64-12.58	29.35-18.30	29.28-14.44	23.72-7.72	12.07-7.88	...
P/E Ratio	24.85-15.15	25.49-16.50	...	...	18.77-9.26	30.81-10.03	...	...

Address: 5400 LBJ Freeway, Suite 1500, Dallas, TX 75240
Telephone: 972-371-5200

Web Site: www.matadorresources.com
Officers: Joseph Wm. Foran - Chairman, President, Chief Executive Officer, Secretary Matthew V. Hairford - President, Executive Vice President

Auditors: KPMG LLP
Transfer Agents: Registrar & Transfer Company, Cranford, NJ

MAXIMUS INC.

Exchange	Symbol	Price	52Wk Range	Yield	P/E
NYS	MMS	$62.11 (6/29/2018)	72.04-59.00	0.29	18.27

*7 Year Price Score 111.05 *NYSE Composite Index=100   *12 Month Price Score 96.09

Interim Earnings (Per Share)

Qtr.	Dec	Mar	Jun	Sep
2014-15	0.63	0.58	0.63	0.52
2015-16	0.40	0.74	0.79	0.76
2016-17	0.71	0.80	0.86	0.81
2017-18	0.89	0.84	...	...

Interim Dividends (Per Share)

Amt	Decl	Ex	Rec	Pay
0.045Q	10/12/2017	11/14/2017	11/15/2017	11/30/2017
0.045Q	01/11/2018	02/14/2018	02/15/2018	02/28/2018
0.045Q	04/11/2018	05/14/2018	05/15/2018	05/31/2018
0.045Q	07/06/2018	08/14/2018	08/15/2018	08/31/2018

Indicated Div: $0.18

Valuation Analysis | **Institutional Holding**

Forecast EPS	$3.35	No of Institutions
(06/12/2018)		457
Market Cap	$4.1 Billion	Shares
Book Value	$1.1 Billion	77,048,256
Price/Book	3.81	% Held
Price/Sales	1.65	94.59

TRADING VOLUME (thousand shares)

Business Summary: Business Services (MIC: 7.5.2 SIC: 7389 NAIC: 561499)

MAXIMUS is an operator of government health and human services programs. Co.'s segments are: Health Services, which provides business process services, assessments and appeals, and related consulting services, primarily for state, provincial and national government programs; U.S. Federal Services, which provides business process services for federal government programs, assessment and appeals services for both federal and similar state-based programs, and technology solutions for federal civilian programs; and Human Services, which provides national, state and local human services agencies with a variety of business process services and related consulting services for government programs.

Recent Developments: For the quarter ended Mar 31 2018, net income increased 3.8% to US$55.1 million from US$53.1 million in the year-earlier quarter. Revenues were US$612.8 million, down 1.5% from US$622.0 million the year before. Operating income was US$71.3 million versus US$80.3 million in the prior-year quarter, a decrease of 11.2%. Direct operating expenses declined 1.2% to US$464.0 million from US$469.7 million in the comparable period the year before. Indirect operating expenses increased 7.6% to US$77.5 million from US$72.0 million in the equivalent prior-year period.

Prospects: Our evaluation of Maximus Inc. as of Jan. 21, 2018 is the result of our systematic analysis on three basic characteristics: earnings strength, relative valuation, and recent stock price movement. The company has generated a negative trend in earnings per share over the past 5 quarters and while recent estimates for the company have remained steady, MMS has posted better than expected results. Based on operating earnings yield, the company is undervalued when compared to all of the companies in our coverage universe. Share price changes over the past year indicates that MMS will perform well over the near term.

Financial Data

(US$ in Thousands)	6 Mos	3 Mos	09/30/2017	09/30/2016	09/30/2015	09/30/2014	09/30/2013	09/30/2012
Earnings Per Share	3.40	3.36	3.17	2.69	2.35	2.11	1.67	1.10
Cash Flow Per Share	4.81	4.61	5.14	2.73	3.09	3.16	1.77	1.70
Tang Book Value Per Share	8.29	7.33	6.32	3.26	1.55	4.60	4.02	4.21
Dividends Per Share	0.180	0.180	0.180	0.180	0.180	0.180	0.180	0.180
Dividend Payout %	5.29	5.36	5.68	6.69	7.66	8.53	10.78	16.44
Income Statement								
Total Revenue	1,235,935	623,148	2,450,961	2,403,360	2,099,821	1,700,912	1,331,279	1,050,145
EBITDA	158,004	82,688	373,805	352,679	307,565	264,098	212,508	146,375
Depn & Amortn	5,321	2,718	57,408	62,577	46,348	38,790	26,300	18,800
Income Before Taxes	152,358	79,802	314,235	285,968	259,819	227,369	189,059	131,751
Income Taxes	37,300	19,850	102,053	105,808	99,770	81,973	71,934	55,652
Net Income	114,583	59,091	209,426	178,362	157,772	145,440	116,731	76,133
Average Shares	66,268	66,177	65,632	66,229	67,275	69,087	69,893	69,612
Balance Sheet								
Current Assets	759,032	718,849	657,242	620,980	580,899	532,460	489,599	448,684
Total Assets	1,430,500	1,401,530	1,350,662	1,348,819	1,280,171	900,996	857,978	695,293
Current Liabilities	279,351	279,256	316,266	340,756	356,380	265,321	262,307	199,136
Long-Term Obligations	...	12,050	527	165,338	210,618	...	1,319	1,558
Total Liabilities	367,920	400,422	410,577	599,738	667,793	345,034	328,470	244,187
Stockholders' Equity	1,062,580	1,001,108	940,085	749,081	612,378	555,962	529,508	451,106
Shares Outstanding	65,243	65,120	65,137	65,223	65,437	66,613	68,525	67,970
Statistical Record								
Return on Assets %	16.37	16.45	15.52	13.53	14.47	16.54	15.03	12.05
Return on Equity %	23.89	25.21	24.80	26.13	27.01	26.80	23.81	18.39
EBITDA Margin %	12.78	13.27	15.25	14.67	14.65	15.53	15.96	13.94
Net Margin %	9.27	9.48	8.54	7.42	7.51	8.55	8.77	7.25
Asset Turnover	1.79	1.83	1.82	1.82	1.93	1.93	1.71	1.66
Current Ratio	2.72	2.57	2.08	1.82	1.63	2.01	1.87	2.25
Debt to Equity	...	0.01	N.M.	0.22	0.34	...	N.M.	N.M.
Price Range	72.04-57.42	72.04-54.70	65.06-45.25	69.80-45.94	69.22-39.00	50.41-38.57	45.29-27.31	29.86-16.95
P/E Ratio	21.19-16.89	21.44-16.28	20.52-14.27	25.95-17.08	29.46-16.60	23.89-18.28	27.12-16.35	27.15-15.41
Average Yield %	0.28	0.29	0.30	0.32	0.30	0.41	0.50	0.80

Address: 1891 Metro Center Drive, Reston, VA 20190	**Web Site:** www.maximus.com	**Auditors:** Ernst & Young LLP
Telephone: 703-251-8500	**Officers:** Peter B. Pond - Chairman Bruce L. Caswell - President, Chief Executive Officer, Division Officer	**Investor Contact:** 703-251-8637
		Transfer Agents: American Stock Transfer & Trust Company, New York, NY

MCCORMICK & CO INC

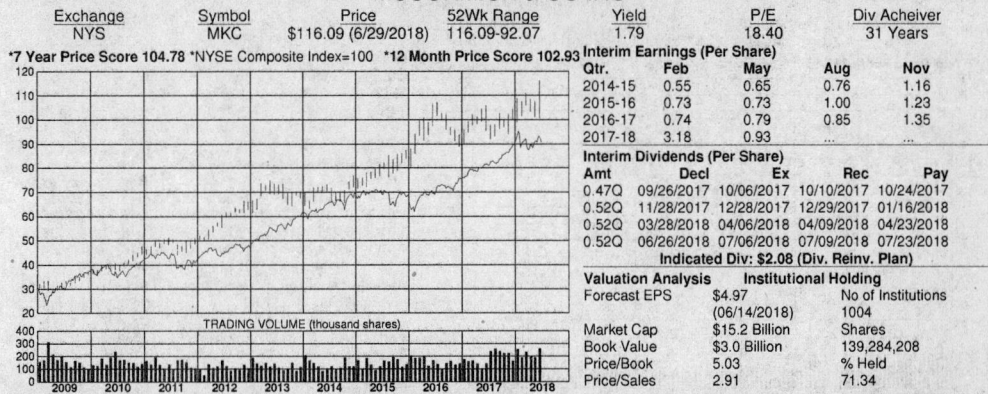

Exchange	Symbol	Price	52Wk Range	Yield	P/E	Div Acheiver
NYS	MKC	$116.09 (6/29/2018)	116.09-92.07	1.79	18.40	31 Years

*7 Year Price Score 104.78 *NYSE Composite Index=100 *12 Month Price Score 102.93

Interim Earnings (Per Share)

Qtr.	Feb	May	Aug	Nov
2014-15	0.55	0.65	0.76	1.16
2015-16	0.73	0.73	1.00	1.23
2016-17	0.74	0.79	0.85	1.35
2017-18	3.18	0.93	...	...

Interim Dividends (Per Share)

Amt	Decl	Ex	Rec	Pay
0.47Q	09/26/2017	10/06/2017	10/10/2017	10/24/2017
0.52Q	11/28/2017	12/28/2017	12/29/2017	01/16/2018
0.52Q	03/28/2018	04/06/2018	04/09/2018	04/23/2018
0.52Q	06/26/2018	07/06/2018	07/09/2018	07/23/2018

Indicated Div: $2.08 (Div. Reinv. Plan)

Valuation Analysis　　**Institutional Holding**

Forecast EPS	$4.97	No of Institutions
	(06/14/2018)	1004
Market Cap	$15.2 Billion	Shares
Book Value	$3.0 Billion	139,284,208
Price/Book	5.03	% Held
Price/Sales	2.91	71.34

TRADING VOLUME (thousand shares)

Business Summary: Food (MIC: 1.2.1 SIC: 2099 NAIC: 311942)

McCormick & Co. manufactures, markets and distributes spices, seasoning mixes, condiments and other flavorful products to the food industry-retailers, food manufacturers and foodservice businesses. The consumer segment sells to retailers, that include grocery, mass merchandise, warehouse clubs, discount and drug stores, and e-commerce retailers served directly and indirectly through distributors or wholesalers. In addition to marketing its branded products to these customers, Co. is also a supplier of private label items, also known as store brands.

Recent Developments: For the quarter ended May 31 2018, net income increased 23.3% to US$123.3 million from US$100.0 million in the year-earlier quarter. Revenues were US$1.33 billion, up 19.1% from US$1.11 billion the year before. Operating income was US$191.7 million versus US$132.6 million in the prior-year quarter, an increase of 44.6%. Direct operating expenses rose 12.3% to US$752.1 million from US$669.7 million in the comparable period the year before. Indirect operating expenses increased 22.9% to US$383.5 million from US$312.0 million in the equivalent prior-year period.

Prospects: Our evaluation of McCormick & Co. Inc. as of Jan. 21, 2018 is the result of our systematic analysis on three basic characteristics: earnings strength, relative valuation, and recent stock price movement. The company has enjoyed a very positive trend in earnings per share over the past 5 quarters and while recent estimates for the company have been mixed, MKC has posted better than expected results. Based on operating earnings yield, the company is about fairly valued when compared to all of the companies in our coverage universe. Share price changes over the past year indicates that MKC will perform well over the near term.

Financial Data

(US$ in Thousands)	6 Mos	3 Mos	11/30/2017	11/30/2016	11/30/2015	11/30/2014	11/30/2013	11/30/2012
Earnings Per Share	6.31	6.17	3.72	3.69	3.11	3.34	2.91	3.04
Cash Flow Per Share	6.64	5.72	6.43	5.18	4.61	3.88	3.52	3.42
Dividends Per Share	1.980	1.930	1.880	1.720	1.600	1.480	1.360	1.240
Dividend Payout %	31.38	31.28	50.54	46.61	51.45	44.31	46.74	40.79
Income Statement								
Total Revenue	2,564,400	1,237,100	4,834,100	4,411,500	4,296,300	4,243,200	4,123,400	4,014,200
EBITDA	452,500	221,800	836,600	753,900	655,400	706,800	658,700	683,500
Depn & Amortn	74,100	36,600	146,100	108,700	105,900	102,700	106,000	102,800
Income Before Taxes	292,400	143,400	594,800	589,200	496,200	554,400	499,400	526,100
Income Taxes	(238,000)	(271,100)	151,300	153,000	131,300	145,900	133,600	139,800
Net Income	545,900	422,600	477,400	472,300	401,600	437,900	389,000	407,800
Average Shares	132,900	132,900	128,400	128,000	129,200	131,000	133,600	134,300
Balance Sheet								
Current Assets	1,564,200	1,606,000	1,617,000	1,421,800	1,406,500	1,416,200	1,370,200	1,285,400
Total Assets	10,383,800	10,363,000	10,385,800	4,635,900	4,507,800	4,414,300	4,449,700	4,165,400
Current Liabilities	1,846,700	1,871,500	1,947,300	1,422,700	1,240,200	1,122,000	1,063,100	1,187,600
Long-Term Obligations	4,456,200	4,378,600	4,443,900	1,054,000	1,052,700	1,014,100	1,019,000	779,200
Total Liabilities	7,355,300	7,302,800	7,825,900	3,009,300	2,837,600	2,622,100	2,517,200	2,482,500
Stockholders' Equity	3,028,500	3,060,200	2,559,900	1,626,600	1,670,200	1,792,200	1,932,500	1,682,900
Shares Outstanding	131,267	131,256	131,000	125,300	127,300	128,400	131,100	132,500
Statistical Record								
Return on Assets %	10.88	10.67	6.36	10.30	9.00	9.88	9.03	9.86
Return on Equity %	34.38	-33.75	22.81	28.57	23.20	23.51	21.52	24.76
EBITDA Margin %	17.65	17.93	17.31	17.09	15.25	16.66	15.97	17.03
Net Margin %	21.29	34.16	9.88	10.71	9.35	10.32	9.43	10.16
Asset Turnover	0.69	0.67	0.64	0.96	0.96	0.96	0.96	0.97
Current Ratio	0.85	0.86	0.83	1.00	1.13	1.26	1.29	1.08
Debt to Equity	1.47	1.43	1.74	0.65	0.63	0.57	0.53	0.46
Price Range	110.74-92.07	108.77-92.07	105.92-88.78	107.07-79.78	86.03-71.39	74.33-63.03	74.76-61.23	66.37-48.54
P/E Ratio	17.55-14.59	17.63-14.92	28.47-23.87	29.02-21.62	27.66-22.95	22.25-18.87	25.69-21.04	21.83-15.97
Average Yield %	1.95	1.93	1.92	1.81	2.04	2.14	1.97	2.17

Address: 18 Loveton Circle, P. O. Box 6000, Sparks, MD 21152-6000	**Web Site:** www.mccormickcorporation.com	**Auditors:** Ernst & Young LLP
Telephone: 410-771-7301	**Officers:** Lawrence E. Kurzius - Chairman, President, Chief Executive Officer, Region Officer Michael R.	**Investor Contact:** 410-771-7244
Fax: 410-771-7462	Smith - Executive Vice President, Senior Vice President, Chief Financial Officer, Region Officer	**Transfer Agents:** Wells Fargo Bank, N.A. Shareowner Services, Mendota Heights, MN

MCDONALD'S CORP

Exchange	Symbol	Price	52Wk Range	Yield	P/E	Div Acheiver
NYS	MCD	$156.69 (6/29/2018)	178.36-148.27	2.58	23.63	41 Years

*7 Year Price Score 117.13 *NYSE Composite Index=100 *12 Month Price Score 98.63

TRADING VOLUME (thousand shares)

Interim Earnings (Per Share)

Qtr.	Mar	Jun	Sep	Dec
2015	0.84	1.26	1.40	1.31
2016	1.23	1.25	1.50	1.43
2017	1.47	1.70	2.32	0.89
2018	1.72	...	...	...

Interim Dividends (Per Share)

Amt	Decl	Ex	Rec	Pay
0.94Q	07/27/2017	08/30/2017	09/01/2017	09/18/2017
1.01Q	09/21/2017	11/30/2017	12/01/2017	12/15/2017
1.01Q	01/25/2018	02/28/2018	03/01/2018	03/15/2018
1.01Q	05/24/2018	06/01/2018	06/04/2018	06/18/2018

Indicated Div: $4.04 (Div. Reinv. Plan)

Valuation Analysis / Institutional Holding

Forecast EPS	$7.68	No of Institutions
	(06/14/2018)	2582
Market Cap	$123.0 Billion	Shares
Book Value	N/A	709,694,592
Price/Book	N/A	% Held
Price/Sales	5.52	60.51

Business Summary: Hotels, Restaurants & Travel (MIC: 2.2.1 SIC: 5812 NAIC: 722211)

McDonald's operates and franchises McDonald's restaurants. Co.'s menu includes hamburgers and cheeseburgers, Big Mac, Quarter Pounder with Cheese, Filet-O-Fish, several chicken sandwiches, Chicken McNuggets, wraps, french fries, salads, oatmeal, shakes, McFlurry desserts, sundaes, soft serve cones, pies, soft drinks, coffee, McCafé beverages and other beverages. Co.'s restaurants also provides breakfast menu that include Egg McMuffin, Sausage McMuffin with Egg, McGriddles, biscuit and bagel sandwiches and hotcakes. At Dec 31 2017, Co. had a total of 37,241 restaurants.

Recent Developments: For the quarter ended Mar 31 2018, net income increased 13.2% to US$1.38 billion from US$1.21 billion in the year-earlier quarter. Revenues were US$5.14 billion, down 9.5% from US$5.68 billion the year before. Operating income was US$2.14 billion versus US$2.03 billion in the prior-year quarter, an increase of 5.4%. Direct operating expenses declined 24.3% to US$2.13 billion from US$2.82 billion in the comparable period the year before. Indirect operating expenses increased 4.8% to US$864.9 million from US$825.5 million in the equivalent prior-year period.

Prospects: Our evaluation of McDonald's Corp. as of Jan. 21, 2018 is the result of our systematic analysis on three basic characteristics: earnings strength, relative valuation, and recent stock price movement. The company has managed to produce a neutral trend in earnings per share over the past 5 quarters and while recent estimates for the company have been mixed, MCD has posted results that fell short of analysts expectations. Based on operating earnings yield, the company is about fairly valued when compared to all of the companies in our coverage universe. Share price changes over the past year indicates that MCD will perform very well over the near term.

Financial Data
(US$ in Thousands)

	3 Mos	12/31/2017	12/31/2016	12/31/2015	12/31/2014	12/31/2013	12/31/2012	12/31/2011
Earnings Per Share	6.63	6.37	5.44	4.80	4.82	5.55	5.36	5.27
Cash Flow Per Share	7.15	6.88	7.07	6.96	6.86	7.13	6.88	6.93
Tang Book Value Per Share	...	...	...	5.04	10.51	13.26	12.46	11.49
Dividends Per Share	3.900	3.830	3.610	3.440	3.280	3.120	2.870	2.530
Dividend Payout %	58.82	60.13	66.36	71.67	68.05	56.22	53.54	48.01
Income Statement								
Total Revenue	5,138,900	22,820,400	24,621,900	25,413,000	27,441,300	28,105,700	27,567,000	27,006,000
EBITDA	2,439,500	10,538,600	9,086,700	8,778,800	9,490,700	10,147,000	9,854,300	9,656,600
Depn & Amortn	362,900	1,227,500	1,390,700	1,438,000	1,539,300	1,498,800	1,402,200	1,329,600
Income Before Taxes	1,845,300	8,389,800	6,811,200	6,702,500	7,380,900	8,126,300	7,935,500	7,834,200
Income Taxes	512,500	3,381,200	2,179,500	2,026,400	2,614,200	2,618,600	2,614,200	2,509,100
Net Income	1,375,400	5,192,100	4,686,500	4,529,300	4,757,800	5,585,900	5,464,800	5,503,100
Average Shares	798,700	815,500	861,200	944,600	986,300	1,006,000	1,020,200	1,044,900
Balance Sheet								
Current Assets	4,909,300	5,327,200	4,848,600	9,643,000	4,185,500	5,050,100	4,922,100	4,403,000
Total Assets	33,722,900	33,803,700	31,023,900	37,938,700	34,281,400	36,626,300	35,386,500	32,989,900
Current Liabilities	2,821,400	2,890,600	3,468,300	2,950,400	2,747,900	3,170,000	3,403,100	3,509,200
Long-Term Obligations	30,869,500	29,536,400	25,878,500	24,122,100	14,989,700	14,129,800	13,632,500	12,133,800
Total Liabilities	38,441,700	37,071,700	33,228,200	30,850,800	21,428,000	20,616,600	20,092,900	18,599,700
Stockholders' Equity	(4,718,800)	(3,268,000)	(2,204,300)	7,087,900	12,853,400	16,009,700	15,293,600	14,390,200
Shares Outstanding	785,200	794,100	819,300	906,800	962,900	990,400	1,002,700	1,021,400
Statistical Record								
Return on Assets %	16.26	16.02	13.55	12.54	13.42	15.51	15.94	16.94
Return on Equity %	...	...	191.40	45.43	32.97	35.69	36.72	37.92
EBITDA Margin %	47.47	46.18	36.90	34.54	34.59	36.10	35.75	35.76
Net Margin %	26.76	22.75	19.03	17.82	17.34	19.87	19.82	20.38
Asset Turnover	0.68	0.70	0.71	0.70	0.77	0.78	0.80	0.83
Current Ratio	1.74	1.84	1.40	3.27	1.52	1.59	1.45	1.25
Debt to Equity	...	...	...	3.40	1.17	0.88	0.89	0.84
Price Range	178.36-129.29	174.20-119.48	131.60-110.57	120.07-88.78	103.53-88.46	103.59-88.21	101.74-84.05	100.81-72.67
P/E Ratio	26.90-19.50	27.35-18.76	24.19-20.33	25.01-18.50	21.48-18.35	18.66-15.89	18.98-15.68	19.13-13.79
Average Yield %	2.46	2.57	3.00	3.43	3.40	3.21	3.10	3.01

Address: One McDonald's Plaza, Oak Brook, IL. 60523	Web Site: www.mcdonalds.com	Auditors: Ernst & Young LLP
Telephone: 630-623-3000	Officers: Enrique Hernandez - Chairman Stephen J. Easterbrook - President, Chief Executive Officer, Senior Executive Vice President, Region Officer	Investor Contact: 800-228-9623 Transfer Agents: Computershare, Providence, RI

MCKESSON CORP

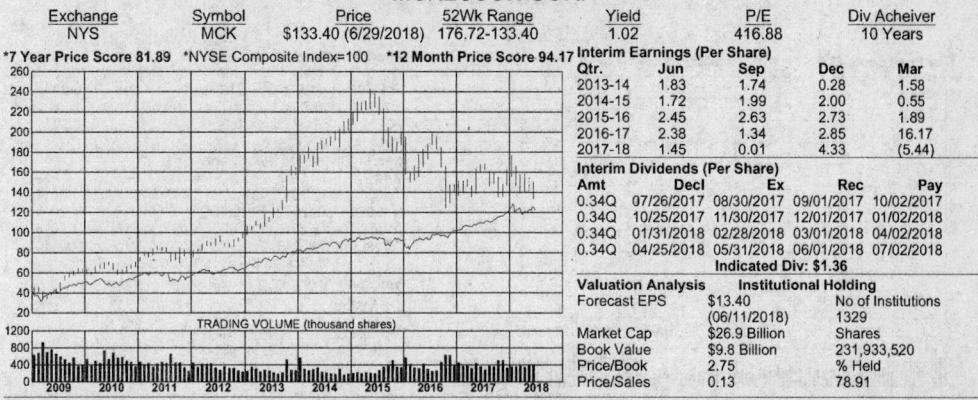

Exchange	Symbol	Price	52Wk Range	Yield	P/E	Div Acheiver
NYS	MCK	$133.40 (6/29/2018)	176.72-133.40	1.02	416.88	10 Years

*7 Year Price Score 81.89   *NYSE Composite Index=100   *12 Month Price Score 94.17

Interim Earnings (Per Share)

Qtr.	Jun	Sep	Dec	Mar
2013-14	1.83	1.74	0.28	1.58
2014-15	1.72	1.99	2.00	0.55
2015-16	2.45	2.63	2.73	1.89
2016-17	2.38	1.34	2.85	16.17
2017-18	1.45	0.01	4.33	(5.44)

Interim Dividends (Per Share)

Amt	Decl	Ex	Rec	Pay
0.34Q	07/26/2017	08/30/2017	09/01/2017	10/02/2017
0.34Q	10/25/2017	11/30/2017	12/01/2017	01/02/2018
0.34Q	01/31/2018	02/28/2018	03/01/2018	04/02/2018
0.34Q	04/25/2018	05/31/2018	06/01/2018	07/02/2018

Indicated Div: $1.36

Valuation Analysis

		Institutional Holding	
Forecast EPS	$13.40 (06/11/2018)	No of Institutions	1329
Market Cap	$26.9 Billion	Shares	231,933,520
Book Value	$9.8 Billion	% Held	78.91
Price/Book	2.75		
Price/Sales	0.13		

TRADING VOLUME (thousand shares)

Business Summary: Pharmaceuticals (MIC: 4.1.1 SIC: 5122 NAIC: 325412)

McKesson provides pharmaceuticals and medical supplies and services to its customers. Co. operates its business through two segments: McKesson Distribution Solutions and McKesson Technology Solutions. Co.'s Distribution Solutions segment distributes pharmaceutical drugs and other healthcare-related products internationally and provides practice management, technology, clinical support and business solutions to community-based oncology and other practices. Co.'s Technology Solutions segment provides clinical, financial and supply chain management solutions to healthcare organizations and includes its equity method investment in Change Healthcare, LLC.

Recent Developments: For the year ended Mar 31 2018, income from continuing operations decreased 94.5% to US$292.0 million from US$5.28 billion a year earlier. Net income decreased 94.2% to US$297.0 million from US$5.15 billion in the prior year. Revenues were US$208.36 billion, up 4.9% from US$198.53 billion the year before. Operating income was US$762.0 million versus US$7.11 billion in the prior year, a decrease of 89.3%. Direct operating expenses rose 5.3% to US$197.17 billion from US$187.26 billion in the comparable period the year before. Indirect operating expenses increased 150.4% to US$10.42 billion from US$4.16 billion in the equivalent prior-year period.

Prospects: Our evaluation of McKesson Corp. as of Jan. 21, 2018 is the result of our systematic analysis on three basic characteristics: earnings strength, relative valuation, and recent stock price movement. The company has generated a negative trend in earnings per share over the past 5 quarters and while recent estimates for the company have been raised by analysts, MCK has posted better than expected results. Based on operating earnings yield, the company is undervalued when compared to all of the companies in our coverage universe. Share price changes over the past year indicates that MCK will perform poorly over the near term.

Financial Data

(US$ in Thousands)	03/31/2018	03/31/2017	03/31/2016	03/31/2015	03/31/2014	03/31/2013	03/31/2012	03/31/2011
Earnings Per Share	0.32	22.73	9.70	6.27	5.41	5.59	5.59	4.57
Cash Flow Per Share	20.89	21.47	15.92	13.41	13.69	10.57	11.96	9.06
Tang Book Value Per Share	N.M.	N.M.	N.M.	N.M.	N.M.	N.M.	0.21	5.56
Dividends Per Share	1.300	1.120	1.080	0.960	0.920	0.800	0.800	0.720
Dividend Payout %	406.25	4.93	11.13	15.31	17.01	14.31	14.31	15.75
Income Statement								
Total Revenue	208,357,000	198,533,000	190,884,000	179,045,000	137,609,000	122,455,000	122,734,000	112,084,000
EBITDA	745,000	7,464,000	3,851,000	3,305,000	2,565,000	2,280,000	2,282,000	1,968,000
Depn & Amortn	303,000	324,000	281,000	306,000	186,000	146,000	140,000	139,000
Income Before Taxes	207,000	6,861,000	3,235,000	2,645,000	2,099,000	1,916,000	1,910,000	1,641,000
Income Taxes	(53,000)	1,614,000	908,000	815,000	742,000	581,000	516,000	505,000
Net Income	67,000	5,070,000	2,258,000	1,476,000	1,263,000	1,338,000	1,403,000	1,202,000
Average Shares	209,000	223,000	233,000	235,000	233,000	239,000	251,000	263,000
Balance Sheet								
Current Assets	37,136,000	36,948,000	38,437,000	36,670,000	32,573,000	23,170,000	23,603,000	22,357,000
Total Assets	60,381,000	60,969,000	56,563,000	53,870,000	51,759,000	34,786,000	33,093,000	30,886,000
Current Liabilities	36,685,000	35,612,000	35,071,000	33,497,000	29,501,000	21,357,000	21,686,000	18,726,000
Long-Term Obligations	6,751,000	7,305,000	6,535,000	8,180,000	8,949,000	4,521,000	3,072,000	3,587,000
Total Liabilities	50,577,000	49,874,000	47,639,000	45,869,000	43,237,000	27,716,000	26,262,000	23,666,000
Stockholders' Equity	9,804,000	11,095,000	8,924,000	8,001,000	8,522,000	7,070,000	6,831,000	7,220,000
Shares Outstanding	202,000	211,000	225,000	232,000	231,000	227,000	235,000	252,000
Statistical Record								
Return on Assets %	0.11	8.63	4.08	2.79	2.92	3.94	4.37	4.07
Return on Equity %	0.64	50.65	26.61	17.87	16.20	19.25	19.92	16.30
EBITDA Margin %	0.36	3.76	2.02	1.85	1.86	1.86	1.86	1.76
Net Margin %	0.03	2.55	1.18	0.82	-0.92	1.09	1.14	1.07
Asset Turnover	3.43	3.38	3.45	3.39	3.18	3.61	3.83	3.79
Current Ratio	1.01	1.04	1.10	1.09	1.10	1.08	1.09	1.19
Debt to Equity	0.69	0.66	0.73	1.02	1.05	0.64	0.45	0.50
Price Range	176.72-135.00	198.44-124.11	242.75-150.03	230.26-164.68	185.35-104.18	111.23-85.48	88.59-69.35	80.64-58.05
P/E Ratio	552.25-421.88	8.73-5.46	25.03-15.47	36.72-26.26	34.26-19.26	19.90-15.29	15.85-12.41	17.65-12.70
Average Yield %	0.85	0.68	0.54	0.48	0.66	0.85	1.00	1.06

Address: One Post Street, San Francisco, CA 94104 **Telephone:** 415-983-8300	**Web Site:** www.mckesson.com **Officers:** John H. Hammergren - Chairman, President, Chief Executive Officer James A. Beer - Executive Vice President, Chief Financial Officer, Principal Financial Officer	**Auditors:** DELOITTE & TOUCHE LLP **Investor Contact:** 415-983-8391 **Transfer Agents:** EQ Shareowner Services, Mendota Heights, MN

MDU RESOURCES GROUP INC

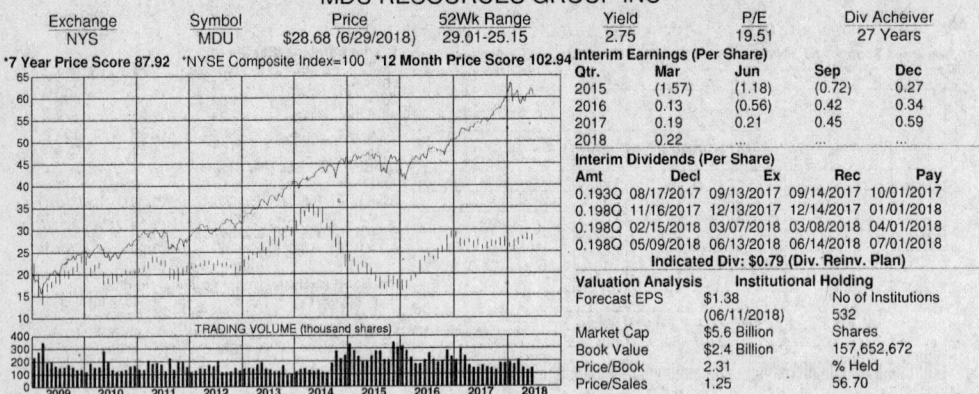

Exchange	Symbol	Price	52Wk Range	Yield	P/E	Div Acheiver
NYS	MDU	$28.68 (6/29/2018)	29.01-25.15	2.75	19.51	27 Years

*7 Year Price Score 87.92   *NYSE Composite Index=100   *12 Month Price Score 102.94

Interim Earnings (Per Share)

Qtr.	Mar	Jun	Sep	Dec
2015	(1.57)	(1.18)	(0.72)	0.27
2016	0.13	(0.56)	0.42	0.34
2017	0.19	0.21	0.45	0.59
2018	0.22	...	...	...

Interim Dividends (Per Share)

Amt	Decl	Ex	Rec	Pay
0.193Q	08/17/2017	09/13/2017	09/14/2017	10/01/2017
0.198Q	11/16/2017	12/13/2017	12/14/2017	01/01/2018
0.198Q	02/15/2018	03/07/2018	03/08/2018	04/01/2018
0.198Q	05/09/2018	06/13/2018	06/14/2018	07/01/2018

Indicated Div: $0.79 (Div. Reinv. Plan)

Valuation Analysis   Institutional Holding

Forecast EPS	$1.38	No of Institutions
	(06/11/2018)	532
Market Cap	$5.6 Billion	Shares
Book Value	$2.4 Billion	157,652,672
Price/Book	2.31	% Held
Price/Sales	1.25	56.70

TRADING VOLUME (thousand shares)

Business Summary: Electric Utilities (MIC: 3.1.1 SIC: 4911 NAIC: 221122)

MDU Resources Group is a regulated energy delivery and construction materials and services business. As of Dec 31 2017, Co.'s electric segment served 142,901 residential, commercial, industrial and municipal customers in 178 communities and adjacent rural areas, while its natural gas distribution operations served 938,867 residential, commercial and industrial customers in 335 communities and adjacent rural areas across eight states. Co.'s other businesses include pipeline and midstream, construction materials and contracting, construction services, as well as other, which includes the activities of Centennial Holdings Capital LLC, which insures various types of risks as a captive insurer.

Recent Developments: For the quarter ended Mar 31 2018, income from continuing operations increased 17.7% to US$42.0 million from US$35.6 million in the year-earlier quarter. Net income increased 13.7% to US$42.4 million from US$37.3 million in the year-earlier quarter. Revenues were US$976.3 million, up 4.1% from US$937.9 million the year before. Operating income was US$69.4 million versus US$65.8 million in the prior-year quarter, an increase of 5.5%. Direct operating expenses rose 4.1% to US$805.3 million from US$773.4 million in the comparable period the year before. Indirect operating expenses increased 2.9% to US$101.6 million from US$98.8 million in the equivalent prior-year period.

Prospects: Our evaluation of MDU Resources Group Inc. as of Jan. 21, 2018 is the result of our systematic analysis on three basic characteristics: earnings strength, relative valuation, and recent stock price movement. The company has generated a negative trend in earnings per share over the past 5 quarters and while recent estimates for the company have remained steady, MDU has posted results that fell short of analysts expectations. Based on operating earnings yield, the company is undervalued when compared to all of the companies in our coverage universe. Share price changes over the past year indicates that MDU will perform in line with the market over the near term.

Financial Data

(US$ in Thousands)	3 Mos	12/31/2017	12/31/2016	12/31/2015	12/31/2014	12/31/2013	12/31/2012	12/31/2011
Earnings Per Share	1.47	1.43	0.33	(3.20)	1.55	1.47	(0.01)	1.12
Cash Flow Per Share	2.39	2.29	2.36	3.29	3.20	3.93	3.09	3.32
Tang Book Value Per Share	9.17	9.18	8.52	8.91	12.74	11.40	10.49	11.15
Dividends Per Share	0.780	0.775	0.755	0.735	0.715	0.695	0.675	0.655
Dividend Payout %	53.06	54.20	228.79	...	46.13	47.28	...	58.48
Income Statement								
Total Revenue	976,293	4,443,351	4,128,828	4,191,549	4,670,558	4,462,404	4,075,431	4,050,492
EBITDA	122,687	640,301	630,394	501,095	899,555	886,523	385,054	756,282
Depn & Amortn	52,729	207,486	216,318	227,730	401,368	386,856	359,205	343,395
Income Before Taxes	49,511	350,027	326,228	180,297	411,171	415,750	(50,850)	331,533
Income Taxes	7,551	65,041	93,132	65,603	119,969	136,736	(31,146)	110,274
Net Income	42,437	281,203	64,433	(622,435)	298,233	278,933	(754)	213,026
Average Shares	195,982	195,687	195,618	194,986	192,587	189,693	188,826	188,905
Balance Sheet								
Current Assets	1,040,814	1,069,995	977,475	1,021,042	1,194,973	1,116,688	1,128,081	1,194,638
Total Assets	6,348,852	6,334,666	6,284,467	6,627,608	7,809,978	7,061,332	6,682,491	6,556,125
Current Liabilities	764,261	812,858	669,659	947,639	968,694	784,900	850,115	898,753
Long-Term Obligations	1,630,343	1,566,354	1,746,561	1,627,443	1,825,278	1,842,286	1,610,867	1,285,411
Total Liabilities	3,922,741	3,905,623	3,968,223	4,231,103	4,675,937	4,238,168	4,034,243	3,780,558
Stockholders' Equity	2,426,111	2,429,043	2,316,244	2,396,505	3,134,041	2,823,164	2,648,248	2,775,567
Shares Outstanding	195,304	195,304	195,304	195,265	194,215	189,329	188,830	188,793
Statistical Record								
Return on Assets %	4.58	4.46	1.00	N.M.	4.01	4.06	N.M.	3.31
Return on Equity %	12.08	11.85	2.73	N.M.	10.01	10.20	N.M.	7.79
EBITDA Margin %	12.57	14.41	15.27	11.95	19.26	19.87	9.45	18.67
Net Margin %	4.35	6.33	1.56	N.M.	6.39	6.25	N.M.	5.26
Asset Turnover	0.72	0.70	0.64	0.58	0.63	0.65	0.61	0.63
Current Ratio	1.36	1.32	1.46	1.08	1.23	1.42	1.33	1.33
Debt to Equity	0.67	0.64	0.75	0.68	0.58	0.65	0.61	0.46
Price Range	28.16-25.15	29.43-25.45	29.62-16.03	24.36-16.36	35.93-21.44	30.87-21.24	23.06-19.76	23.95-18.42
P/E Ratio	19.16-17.11	20.58-17.80	89.76-48.58	...	23.18-13.83	21.00-14.45	...	21.38-16.45
Average Yield %	2.92	2.88	3.34	3.70	2.31	2.62	3.09	3.06

Address: 1200 West Century Avenue, P.O. Box 5650, Bismarck, ND 58506-5650
Telephone: 701-530-1000

Web Site: www.mdu.com
Officers: Harry Jonathan Pearce - Chairman David L. Goodin - President, Chief Executive Officer

Auditors: Deloitte & Touche LLP
Investor Contact: 866-866-8919
Transfer Agents: Wells Fargo Bank, N.A., St. Paul, MN

MEDICAL PROPERTIES TRUST INC

Exchange	Symbol	Price	52Wk Range	Yield	P/E
NYS	MPW	$14.04 (6/29/2018)	14.16-11.88	7.12	16.33

*7 Year Price Score 83.22   *NYSE Composite Index=100   *12 Month Price Score 101.98

Interim Earnings (Per Share)

Qtr.	Mar	Jun	Sep	Dec
2015	0.17	0.11	0.10	0.25
2016	0.24	0.22	0.28	0.11
2017	0.21	0.21	0.21	0.19
2018	0.25	...	...	...

Interim Dividends (Per Share)

Amt	Decl	Ex	Rec	Pay
0.24Q	08/17/2017	09/13/2017	09/14/2017	10/12/2017
0.24Q	11/09/2017	12/06/2017	12/07/2017	01/11/2018
0.25Q	02/15/2018	03/14/2018	03/15/2018	04/12/2018
0.25Q	05/24/2018	06/13/2018	06/14/2018	07/12/2018

Indicated Div: $1.00

Valuation Analysis   **Institutional Holding**

Forecast EPS	$1.02	No of Institutions
	(06/13/2018)	496
Market Cap	$5.1 Billion	Shares
Book Value	$3.8 Billion	350,724,480
Price/Book	1.33	% Held
Price/Sales	6.80	80.66

Business Summary: REITs (MIC: 5.3.1 SIC: 6798 NAIC: 525930)

Medical Properties Trust is a self-advised real estate investment trust (REIT) focused on investing in and owning net-leased healthcare facilities across the U.S. and selectively in foreign jurisdictions. Co. acquires and develops healthcare facilities and leases the facilities to healthcare operating companies. Co. also makes mortgage loans to healthcare operators collateralized by their real estate assets. In addition, Co. selectively makes loans to certain of its operators through its REIT subsidiaries. At Feb 28 2018, Co.'s portfolio consisted of 275 properties, including 161 general acute care hospitals, 97 inpatient rehabilitation hospitals, and 17 long-term acute care hospitals.

Recent Developments: For the quarter ended Mar 31 2018, net income increased 33.5% to US$91.0 million from US$68.2 million in the year-earlier quarter. Revenues were US$205.0 million, up 31.1% from US$156.4 million the year before. Revenues from property income rose 26.7% to US$161.5 million from US$127.4 million in the corresponding quarter a year earlier.

Prospects: Our evaluation of Medical Properties Trust Inc. as of Jan. 21, 2018 is the result of our systematic analysis on three basic characteristics: earnings strength, relative valuation, and recent stock price movement. The company has produced a positive trend in earnings per share over the past 5 quarters. However, while recent estimates for the company have been mixed, MPW has posted results that fell short of analysts expectations. Based on operating earnings yield, the company is undervalued when compared to all of the companies in our coverage universe. Share price changes over the past year indicates that MPW will perform well over the near term.

Financial Data

(US$ in Thousands)	3 Mos	12/31/2017	12/31/2016	12/31/2015	12/31/2014	12/31/2013	12/31/2012	12/31/2011
Earnings Per Share	0.86	0.82	0.86	0.63	0.29	0.63	0.67	0.23
Cash Flow Per Share	1.08	1.04	1.01	0.95	0.88	0.93	0.79	0.72
Tang Book Value Per Share	10.53	10.48	10.13	8.88	8.00	8.33	7.70	7.48
Dividends Per Share	0.970	0.960	0.910	0.880	0.840	0.810	0.800	0.800
Dividend Payout %	112.79	117.07	105.81	139.68	289.66	128.57	119.40	347.83
Income Statement								
Total Revenue	205,046	704,745	541,137	441,878	312,532	242,523	201,397	143,319
EBITDA	94,007	599,315	485,035	336,782	201,521	195,915	171,405	107,913
Depn & Amortn	1,789	138,500	105,214	77,912	60,267	42,377	39,050	44,766
Income Before Taxes	92,218	283,861	220,224	138,581	48,579	86,473	72,450	19,431
Income Taxes	1,175	2,681	(6,830)	1,503	340	726	...	...
Net Income	90,601	289,793	225,048	139,598	50,522	96,991	89,900	26,536
Average Shares	365,343	350,441	261,072	218,304	170,540	152,598	132,333	110,629
Balance Sheet								
Current Assets	340,631	436,034	257,799	324,635	244,806	150,307	118,460	166,581
Total Assets	9,031,840	9,020,288	6,418,536	5,609,351	3,747,336	2,904,570	2,178,886	1,621,874
Current Liabilities	222,440	229,366	227,644	166,714	139,830	118,098	86,570	74,432
Long-Term Obligations	4,898,364	4,898,667	2,909,341	3,322,541	2,201,654	1,421,681	1,025,160	689,849
Total Liabilities	5,193,045	5,199,655	3,170,158	3,507,083	2,365,289	1,560,362	1,129,072	793,059
Stockholders' Equity	3,838,795	3,820,633	3,248,378	2,102,268	1,382,047	1,344,208	1,049,814	828,815
Shares Outstanding	364,695	364,424	320,514	236,744	172,743	161,310	136,335	110,786
Statistical Record								
Return on Assets %	3.95	3.75	3.73	2.98	1.52	3.82	4.72	1.79
Return on Equity %	8.82	8.20	8.39	8.01	3.71	8.10	9.54	3.07
EBITDA Margin %	45.85	85.04	89.63	76.22	64.48	80.78	85.11	75.30
Net Margin %	44.19	41.12	41.59	31.59	16.17	39.99	44.64	18.52
Asset Turnover	0.10	0.09	0.09	0.09	0.09	0.10	0.11	0.10
Current Ratio	1.53	1.90	1.13	1.95	1.75	1.27	1.37	2.24
Debt to Equity	1.28	1.28	0.90	1.58	1.59	1.06	0.98	0.83
Price Range	14.16-11.88	14.16-12.15	15.80-9.86	15.62-10.73	14.09-12.20	17.46-11.51	11.96-8.69	12.47-8.39
P/E Ratio	16.47-13.81	17.27-14.82	18.37-11.47	24.79-17.03	48.59-42.07	27.71-18.27	17.85-12.97	54.22-36.48
Average Yield %	7.39	7.31	6.72	6.78	6.70	6.36	5.80	7.91	7.43

Address: 1000 Urban Center Drive, Suite 501, Birmingham, AL 35242	**Web Site:** www.medicalpropertiestrust.com	**Auditors:** PricewaterhouseCoopers LLP
Telephone: 205-969-3755	**Officers:** Edward K. Aldag - Chairman, President, Chief Executive Officer William G. McKenzie - Vice-Chairman	**Investor Contact:** 205-397-8897
Fax: 205-969-3756		**Transfer Agents:** American Stock Transfer & Trust Company, New York, NY

MEDNAX, INC.

Exchange	Symbol	Price	52Wk Range	Yield	P/E
NYS	MD	$43.28 (6/29/2018)	60.58-41.19	N/A	12.19

*7 Year Price Score 72.31   *NYSE Composite Index=100   *12 Month Price Score 91.88

Interim Earnings (Per Share)

Qtr.	Mar	Jun	Sep	Dec
2015	0.72	0.90	0.97	0.99
2016	0.73	0.89	1.04	0.84
2017	0.59	0.69	0.71	1.47
2018	0.68	...	...	...

Interim Dividends (Per Share)

No Dividends Paid

Valuation Analysis   **Institutional Holding**

Forecast EPS	$4.13	No of Institutions
	(06/13/2018)	493
Market Cap	$4.1 Billion	Shares
Book Value	$3.1 Billion	110,928,984
Price/Book	1.30	% Held
Price/Sales	1.16	N/A

TRADING VOLUME (thousand shares)

Business Summary: Diagnostic & Health Related Services (MIC: 4.2.2 SIC: 8069 NAIC: 622310)

MEDNAX is a provider of physician services including newborn, anesthesia, maternal-fetal, teleradiology, pediatric cardiology and other pediatric subspecialty care. Co.'s network comprised of physicians who provide: neonatal clinical care to babies born prematurely or with medical complications; anesthesia care to patients in connection with surgical and other procedures, as well as pain management; maternal-fetal and obstetrical medical care to expectant mothers experiencing complicated pregnancies; pediatric intensive care; pediatric cardiology care; hospital-based pediatric care; pediatric surgical care; and pediatric ear, nose and throat and pediatric ophthalmology services.

Recent Developments: For the quarter ended Mar 31 2018, net income increased 16.0% to US$63.4 million from US$54.7 million in the year-earlier quarter. Revenues were US$901.9 million, up 7.9% from US$835.6 million the year before. Operating income was US$104.4 million versus US$106.0 million in the prior-year quarter, a decrease of 1.5%. Indirect operating expenses increased 9.3% to US$797.4 million from US$729.6 million in the equivalent prior-year period.

Prospects: Our evaluation of Mednax, Inc. as of Jan. 21, 2018 is the result of our systematic analysis on three basic characteristics: earnings strength, relative valuation, and recent stock price movement. The company has managed to produce a neutral trend in earnings per share over the past 5 quarters and while recent estimates for the company have been mixed, MD has posted better than expected results. Based on operating earnings yield, the company is undervalued when compared to all of the companies in our coverage universe. Share price changes over the past year indicates that MD will perform very poorly over the near term.

Financial Data
(US$ in Thousands)

	3 Mos	12/31/2017	12/31/2016	12/31/2015	12/31/2014	12/31/2013	12/31/2012	12/31/2011
Earnings Per Share	3.55	3.45	3.49	3.58	3.18	2.78	2.42	2.23
Cash Flow Per Share	4.52	5.53	4.79	3.96	4.29	4.09	3.34	2.84
Income Statement								
Total Revenue	901,857	3,458,312	3,183,159	2,779,996	2,438,913	2,154,012	1,816,612	1,588,248
EBITDA	106,986	517,929	602,706	581,912	531,627	469,327	407,216	371,884
Depn & Amortn	1,089	33,900	29,000	22,200	15,900	15,500	15,800	15,000
Income Before Taxes	85,962	409,470	510,614	536,602	506,836	448,412	388,171	353,245
Income Taxes	24,059	90,050	189,203	204,038	191,413	167,895	147,264	135,248
Net Income	63,428	320,372	324,914	336,320	317,281	280,517	240,907	217,997
Average Shares	93,505	92,958	93,109	93,960	99,887	100,969	99,382	97,592
Balance Sheet								
Current Assets	622,675	627,235	587,128	527,769	467,052	408,839	359,044	337,273
Total Assets	5,883,074	5,867,278	5,339,400	4,547,214	3,608,795	3,049,430	2,750,337	2,272,648
Current Liabilities	356,989	531,425	448,949	428,771	416,273	326,792	268,338	254,301
Long-Term Obligations	1,965,268	1,851,423	1,683,628	1,262,820	558,855	27,143	144,233	29,327
Total Liabilities	2,739,586	2,800,824	2,578,633	2,109,686	1,344,176	706,442	714,969	541,632
Stockholders' Equity	3,143,488	3,066,454	2,760,767	2,437,528	2,264,619	2,342,988	2,035,368	1,731,016
Shares Outstanding	94,388	93,721	93,718	93,739	96,030	101,207	100,038	97,866
Statistical Record								
Return on Assets %	5.82	5.72	6.55	8.25	9.53	9.67	9.57	10.12
Return on Equity %	11.14	11.00	12.47	14.30	13.77	12.81	12.76	13.72
EBITDA Margin %	11.86	14.98	18.93	20.93	21.80	21.79	22.42	23.41
Net Margin %	7.03	9.26	10.21	12.10	13.01	13.02	13.26	13.73
Asset Turnover	0.62	0.62	0.64	0.68	0.73	0.74	0.72	0.74
Current Ratio	1.74	1.18	1.31	1.23	1.12	1.25	1.34	1.33
Debt to Equity	0.63	0.60	0.61	0.52	0.25	0.01	0.07	0.02
Price Range	69.38-41.19	72.03-41.19	76.29-60.38	85.47-64.53	67.20-51.25	56.31-39.76	40.67-30.00	37.59-29.31
P/E Ratio	19.54-11.60	20.88-11.94	21.86-17.30	23.87-18.03	21.13-16.12	20.25-14.30	16.81-12.40	16.86-13.14

Address: 1301 Concord Terrace, Sunrise, FL 33323
Telephone: 954-384-0175

Web Site: www.mednax.com
Officers: Cesar L. Alvarez - Chairman Joseph M. Calabro - President, Chief Operating Officer

Auditors: PricewaterhouseCoopers LLP
Transfer Agents: ComputerShare Investor Services, Providence, RI

MEDTRONIC PLC

Exchange	Symbol	Price	52Wk Range	Yield	P/E
NYS	MDT	$85.61 (6/29/2018)	88.90-76.55	2.20	37.71

*7 Year Price Score 102.70 *NYSE Composite Index=100 *12 Month Price Score 102.20

Interim Earnings (Per Share)

Qtr.	Jul	Oct	Jan	Apr
2013-14	0.93	0.89	0.75	0.44
2014-15	0.87	0.83	0.98	(0.27)
2015-16	0.57	0.36	0.77	0.78
2016-17	0.66	0.80	0.59	0.84
2017-18	0.74	1.48	(1.03)	1.07

Interim Dividends (Per Share)

Amt	Decl	Ex	Rec	Pay
0.46Q	08/25/2017	09/28/2017	09/29/2017	10/20/2017
0.46Q	12/08/2017	12/28/2017	12/29/2017	01/19/2018
0.46Q	03/09/2018	03/22/2018	03/23/2018	04/13/2018
0.50Q	06/22/2018	07/05/2018	07/06/2018	07/25/2018

Indicated Div: $1.88 (Div. Reinv. Plan)

Valuation Analysis

Forecast EPS	N/A
Market Cap	$115.9 Billion
Book Value	$50.7 Billion
Price/Book	2.29
Price/Sales	3.87

Institutional Holding

No of Institutions	1545
Shares	1,222,324,224
% Held	N/A

Business Summary: Medical Instruments & Equipment (MIC: 4.3.1 SIC: 3845 NAIC: 334510)

Medtronic is a medical technology, services and solutions company. Co.'s operating segments are: Cardiac and Vascular, which include products for cardiac rhythm disorders and cardiovascular disease, as well as services to diagnose, treat, and manage heart and vascular-related disorders and diseases; Minimally Invasive Therapies, which provides products for surgical care and patient monitoring, patient care, renal care, and airway and ventilation; Restorative Therapies, which provides products focusing on the spine, bone graft substitutes, biologic products, trauma, implantable neurostimulation therapies and drug delivery systems; and Diabetes, which include products for diabetes management.

Recent Developments: For the year ended Apr 27 2018, net income decreased 23.1% to US$3.10 billion from US$4.02 billion in the prior year. Revenues were US$29.95 billion, up 0.8% from US$29.71 billion the year before. Operating income was US$6.65 billion versus US$5.33 billion in the prior year, an increase of 24.8%. Direct operating expenses declined 2.5% to US$9.06 billion from US$9.29 billion in the comparable period the year before. Indirect operating expenses decreased 5.6% to US$14.25 billion from US$15.09 billion in the equivalent prior-year period.

Prospects: Our evaluation of Medtronic PLC as of Sep. 17, 2017 is the result of our systematic analysis on three basic characteristics: earnings strength, relative valuation, and recent stock price movement. The company has managed to produce a neutral trend in earnings per share over the past 5 quarters. However, while recent estimates for the company have been lowered by analysts, MDT has posted better than expected results. Based on operating earnings yield, the company is undervalued when compared to all of the companies in our coverage universe. Share price changes over the past year indicates that MDT will perform in line with the market over the near term.

Financial Data
(US$ in Thousands)

	04/27/2018	04/28/2017	04/29/2016	04/24/2015	04/25/2014	04/26/2013	04/27/2012	04/29/2011
Earnings Per Share	2.27	2.89	2.48	2.41	3.02	3.37	3.41	2.86
Cash Flow Per Share	3.45	4.99	3.64	4.49	4.96	4.80	4.25	3.48
Tang Book Value Per Share	N.M.	N.M.	N.M.	N.M.	6.57	5.58	4.37	3.41
Dividends Per Share	1.840	1.720	1.520	1.220	1.120	1.040	0.970	0.900
Dividend Payout %	81.06	59.52	61.29	50.62	37.09	30.86	28.45	31.47
Income Statement								
Total Revenue	29,953,000	29,710,000	28,833,000	20,261,000	17,005,000	16,590,000	16,184,000	15,933,000
EBITDA	9,068,000	8,247,000	8,111,000	5,072,000	4,663,000	5,221,000	5,127,000	4,465,000
Depn & Amortn	2,644,000	2,917,000	2,820,000	1,306,000	850,000	819,000	833,000	464,000
Income Before Taxes	5,675,000	4,602,000	4,336,000	3,486,000	3,705,000	4,251,000	4,145,000	3,723,000
Income Taxes	2,580,000	578,000	798,000	811,000	640,000	784,000	730,000	627,000
Net Income	3,104,000	4,028,000	3,538,000	2,675,000	3,065,000	3,467,000	3,617,000	3,096,000
Average Shares	1,368,200	1,391,400	1,425,900	1,109,000	1,013,600	1,027,500	1,059,900	1,081,700
Balance Sheet								
Current Assets	22,980,000	24,873,000	23,600,000	30,844,000	21,210,000	17,793,000	9,515,000	9,117,000
Total Assets	91,393,000	99,816,000	99,782,000	106,685,000	37,943,000	34,841,000	33,083,000	30,424,000
Current Liabilities	10,084,000	14,220,000	7,165,000	9,173,000	5,559,000	3,891,000	5,857,000	4,714,000
Long-Term Obligations	23,699,000	25,921,000	30,247,000	33,752,000	10,315,000	9,741,000	7,359,000	8,112,000
Total Liabilities	40,673,000	49,522,000	47,719,000	53,455,000	18,500,000	16,170,000	15,970,000	14,456,000
Stockholders' Equity	50,720,000	50,294,000	52,063,000	53,230,000	19,443,000	18,671,000	17,113,000	15,968,000
Shares Outstanding	1,354,218	1,369,424	1,399,018	1,421,648	998,999	1,016,014	1,037,194	1,070,162
Statistical Record								
Return on Assets %	3.25	4.04	3.37	3.71	8.45	10.24	11.42	10.61
Return on Equity %	6.15	7.87	6.61	7.38	16.13	19.43	21.93	20.29
EBITDA Margin %	30.27	27.76	28.13	25.03	27.42	31.47	31.68	28.02
Net Margin %	10.36	13.56	12.27	13.20	18.02	20.90	22.35	19.43
Asset Turnover	0.31	0.30	0.27	0.28	0.47	0.49	0.51	0.55
Current Ratio	2.28	1.75	3.29	3.36	3.82	4.57	1.62	1.93
Debt to Equity	0.47	0.52	0.58	0.63	0.53	0.52	0.43	0.51
Price Range	89.30-76.55	88.92-70.61	79.78-64.52	79.25-58.21	62.31-46.36	47.72-35.89	43.20-30.41	44.13-31.21
P/E Ratio	39.34-33.72	30.77-24.43	32.17-26.02	32.88-24.15	20.63-15.35	14.16-10.65	12.67-8.92	15.43-10.91
Average Yield %	2.23	2.11	2.02	1.78	2.02	2.47	2.62	2.42

Address: 20 On Hatch, Lower Hatch Street, Dublin, 2
Telephone: 143-817-00

Web Site: www.medtronic.com
Officers: Chris Lee - Senior Vice President, Division Officer Omar Ishrak - Chairman, Chief Executive Officer

Auditors: PricewaterhouseCoopers LLP
Transfer Agents: Wells Fargo Shareowner Services, Mendota Heights, MN

MERCK & CO INC

Exchange	Symbol	Price	52Wk Range	Yield	P/E
NYS	MRK	$60.70 (6/29/2018)	66.16-53.27	3.16	104.66

*7 Year Price Score 90.57 *NYSE Composite Index=100 *12 Month Price Score 99.97

Interim Earnings (Per Share)
Qtr.	Mar	Jun	Sep	Dec
2015	0.33	0.24	0.64	0.34
2016	0.40	0.43	0.78	(0.21)
2017	0.56	0.71	(0.02)	(0.38)
2018	0.27	...	...	...

Interim Dividends (Per Share)
Amt	Decl	Ex	Rec	Pay
0.47Q	07/25/2017	09/14/2017	09/15/2017	10/06/2017
0.48Q	11/28/2017	12/14/2017	12/15/2017	01/08/2018
0.48Q	01/23/2018	03/14/2018	03/15/2018	04/06/2018
0.48Q	05/22/2018	06/14/2018	06/15/2018	07/09/2018

Indicated Div: $1.92 (Div. Reinv. Plan)

Valuation Analysis
Forecast EPS $4.22 (06/14/2018)
Market Cap $163.4 Billion
Book Value $33.7 Billion
Price/Book 4.85
Price/Sales 4.01

Institutional Holding
No of Institutions 2699
Shares 2,386,137,088
% Held N/A

Business Summary: Pharmaceuticals (MIC: 4.1.1 SIC: 2834 NAIC: 325412)

Merck & Co. is a health care company that provides health solutions through its prescription medicines, vaccines, biologic therapies and animal health products. Co.'s operations are comprised of three operating segments: pharmaceutical, which includes human health pharmaceutical and vaccine products marketed either directly by Co. or through joint ventures; animal health, which discovers, develops, manufactures and markets animal health products, including vaccines, which Co. sells to veterinarians, distributors and animal producers; and healthcare services.

Recent Developments: For the quarter ended Mar 31 2018, net income decreased 52.4% to US$741.0 million from US$1.56 billion in the year-earlier quarter. Revenues were US$10.04 billion, up 6.4% from US$9.43 billion the year before. Direct operating expenses rose 4.4% to US$3.18 billion from US$3.05 billion in the comparable period the year before. Indirect operating expenses increased 30.2% to US$5.80 billion from US$4.45 billion in the equivalent prior-year period.

Prospects: Our evaluation of Merck & Co. Inc. as of Jan. 21, 2018 is the result of our systematic analysis on three basic characteristics: earnings strength, relative valuation, and recent stock price movement. The company has generated a negative trend in earnings per share over the past 5 quarters and while recent estimates for the company have been mixed, MRK has posted better than expected results. Based on operating earnings yield, the company is undervalued when compared to all of the companies in our coverage universe. Share price changes over the past year indicates that MRK will perform poorly over the near term.

Financial Data
(US$ in Thousands)

	3 Mos	12/31/2017	12/31/2016	12/31/2015	12/31/2014	12/31/2013	12/31/2012	12/31/2011
Earnings Per Share	0.58	0.87	1.41	1.56	4.07	1.47	2.00	2.02
Cash Flow Per Share	2.71	2.36	3.74	4.41	2.72	3.93	3.29	4.03
Tang Book Value Per Share	0.69	0.69	1.68	1.56	5.38	4.67	3.90	2.65
Dividends Per Share	1.900	1.890	1.850	1.810	1.770	1.730	1.690	1.560
Dividend Payout %	327.59	217.24	131.21	116.03	43.49	117.69	84.50	77.23
Income Statement								
Total Revenue	10,037,000	40,122,000	39,807,000	39,498,000	42,237,000	44,033,000	47,267,000	48,047,000
EBITDA	2,634,000	8,348,000	6,538,000	7,179,000	19,992,000	12,666,000	15,557,000	14,701,000
Depn & Amortn	1,137,000	1,500,000	1,600,000	1,600,000	2,500,000	6,988,000	6,978,000	7,427,000
Income Before Taxes	1,397,000	6,479,000	4,573,000	5,196,000	17,026,000	5,141,000	8,097,000	6,724,000
Income Taxes	604,000	4,103,000	718,000	942,000	5,349,000	1,028,000	2,440,000	942,000
Net Income	736,000	2,394,000	3,920,000	4,442,000	11,920,000	4,404,000	6,168,000	6,272,000
Average Shares	2,710,000	2,748,000	2,787,000	2,841,000	2,928,000	2,996,000	3,076,000	3,094,000
Balance Sheet								
Current Assets	24,085,000	24,766,000	30,614,000	29,764,000	33,173,000	35,685,000	34,857,000	33,181,000
Total Assets	86,041,000	87,872,000	95,377,000	101,779,000	98,335,000	105,645,000	106,132,000	105,128,000
Current Liabilities	16,960,000	18,614,000	17,204,000	19,203,000	18,766,000	17,868,000	18,348,000	16,245,000
Long-Term Obligations	21,501,000	21,353,000	24,274,000	23,929,000	18,699,000	20,539,000	16,254,000	15,525,000
Total Liabilities	52,373,000	53,536,000	55,289,000	57,103,000	49,688,000	55,880,000	53,112,000	50,611,000
Stockholders' Equity	33,668,000	34,336,000	40,088,000	44,676,000	48,647,000	49,765,000	53,020,000	54,517,000
Shares Outstanding	2,692,482	2,696,612	2,748,732	2,781,128	2,838,140	2,927,527	3,026,636	3,040,839
Statistical Record								
Return on Assets %	1.73	2.61	3.97	4.44	11.69	4.16	5.82	5.95
Return on Equity %	4.30	6.43	9.22	9.52	24.22	8.57	11.44	11.52
EBITDA Margin %	26.24	20.81	16.42	18.18	47.33	28.76	32.91	30.60
Net Margin %	7.33	5.97	9.85	11.25	28.22	10.00	13.05	13.05
Asset Turnover	0.45	0.44	0.40	0.39	0.41	0.42	0.45	0.46
Current Ratio	1.42	1.33	1.78	1.55	1.77	2.00	1.90	2.04
Debt to Equity	0.64	0.62	0.61	0.54	0.38	0.41	0.31	0.28
Price Range	66.16-53.41	66.58-54.10	64.96-48.59	63.03-48.42	61.88-49.49	50.18-40.85	47.96-37.18	37.90-29.81
P/E Ratio	114.07-92.09	76.53-62.18	46.07-34.46	40.40-31.04	15.20-12.16	34.14-27.79	23.98-18.59	18.76-14.76
Average Yield %	3.14	3.04	3.22	3.20	3.10	3.73	4.09	4.57

Address: 2000 Galloping Hill Road, Keniworth, NJ 07033
Telephone: 908-740-4000
Fax: 908-735-1500

Web Site: www.merck.com
Officers: Kenneth C. Frazier - Chairman, President, Chief Executive Officer Robert M. Davis - Executive Vice President, Chief Financial Officer, Division Officer

Auditors: PricewaterhouseCoopers LLP
Investor Contact: 908-423-5881
Transfer Agents: Wells Fargo Shareowner Services, South St. Paul, MN

MERCURY GENERAL CORP.

Exchange	Symbol	Price	52Wk Range	Yield	P/E	Div Acheiver
NYS	MCY	$45.56 (6/29/2018)	59.89-42.31	5.49	33.50	31 Years

*7 Year Price Score 84.65   *NYSE Composite Index=100   *12 Month Price Score 88.73

Interim Earnings (Per Share)
Qtr.	Mar	Jun	Sep	Dec
2015	0.47	0.17	0.28	0.42
2016	0.42	0.88	0.49	(0.47)
2017	0.49	0.93	0.84	0.36
2018	(0.77)	...	...	...

Interim Dividends (Per Share)
Amt	Decl	Ex	Rec	Pay
0.623Q	07/31/2017	09/13/2017	09/14/2017	09/28/2017
0.625Q	10/30/2017	12/13/2017	12/14/2017	12/28/2017
0.625Q	02/05/2018	03/14/2018	03/15/2018	03/29/2018
0.625Q	04/30/2018	06/13/2018	06/14/2018	06/28/2018

Indicated Div: $2.50

Valuation Analysis
Forecast EPS	$2.00
	(06/10/2018)
Market Cap	$2.5 Billion
Book Value	$1.7 Billion
Price/Book	1.50
Price/Sales	0.75

Institutional Holding
No of Institutions	338
Shares	34,750,356
% Held	38.14

Business Summary: General Insurance (MIC: 5.2.1 SIC: 6331 NAIC: 524126)

Mercury General is an insurance holding company. Through its subsidiaries, Co. is primarily engaged in writing personal automobile insurance in 11 states, principally California. Co. also writes homeowners, commercial automobile, commercial property, mechanical breakdown, and umbrella insurance. Co. provides the following types of automobile coverage: collision, property damage, bodily injury, comprehensive, personal injury protection, underinsured and uninsured motorist, and other hazards. Co. provides the following types of homeowner's coverage: dwelling, liability, personal property, fire, and other hazards. Co. sells its policies through independent agents.

Recent Developments: For the quarter ended Mar 31 2018, net loss amounted to US$42.6 million versus net income of US$27.0 million in the year-earlier quarter. Revenues were US$783.2 million, down 7.6% from US$847.5 million the year before. Net premiums earned were US$808.1 million versus US$789.8 million in the prior-year quarter, an increase of 2.3%. Net investment income rose 1.1% to US$31.5 million from US$31.2 million a year ago.

Prospects: Our evaluation of Mercury General Corp. as of Jan. 21, 2018 is the result of our systematic analysis on three basic characteristics: earnings strength, relative valuation, and recent stock price movement. The company has suffered a very negative trend in earnings per share over the past 5 quarters. However, while recent estimates for the company have been mixed, MCY has posted better than expected results. Based on operating earnings yield, the company is about fairly valued when compared to all of the companies in our coverage universe. Share price changes over the past year indicates that MCY will perform in line with the market over the near term.

Financial Data
(US$ in Thousands)

	3 Mos	12/31/2017	12/31/2016	12/31/2015	12/31/2014	12/31/2013	12/31/2012	12/31/2011
Earnings Per Share	1.36	2.62	1.32	1.35	3.23	2.04	2.13	3.49
Cash Flow Per Share	6.24	6.17	5.19	3.45	4.48	3.82	2.69	2.89
Tang Book Value Per Share	29.31	30.69	30.46	31.66	32.60	31.62	31.90	32.10
Dividends Per Share	2.495	2.493	2.482	2.473	2.462	2.453	2.442	2.410
Dividend Payout %	183.46	95.13	188.07	183.15	76.24	120.22	114.67	69.05
Income Statement								
Premium Income	808,084	3,195,437	3,131,773	2,957,897	2,796,195	2,698,187	2,574,920	2,566,057
Total Revenue	783,184	3,415,962	3,227,683	3,009,300	3,011,773	2,821,041	2,783,370	2,777,285
Benefits & Claims	632,234	2,444,884	2,355,138	2,145,495	1,986,122	1,962,690	1,961,448	1,829,205
Income Before Taxes	(59,699)	167,085	70,724	70,567	247,425	132,096	135,310	245,099
Income Taxes	(17,092)	22,208	(2,320)	(3,912)	69,476	19,953	18,399	53,935
Net Income	(42,607)	144,877	73,044	74,479	177,949	112,143	116,911	191,164
Average Shares	55,335	55,327	55,302	55,209	55,020	54,964	54,922	54,845
Balance Sheet								
Total Assets	5,132,787	5,101,323	4,788,718	4,628,645	4,600,289	4,315,181	4,189,686	4,070,006
Total Liabilities	3,448,566	3,339,936	3,036,316	2,807,760	2,724,843	2,492,695	2,347,189	2,212,523
Stockholders' Equity	1,684,221	1,761,387	1,752,402	1,820,885	1,875,446	1,822,486	1,842,497	1,857,483
Shares Outstanding	55,332	55,332	55,289	55,164	55,121	54,975	54,922	54,856
Statistical Record								
Return on Assets %	1.51	2.93	1.55	1.61	3.99	2.64	2.82	4.62
Return on Equity %	4.39	8.25	4.08	4.03	9.62	6.12	6.30	10.47
Loss Ratio %	78.24	76.51	75.20	72.53	71.03	72.74	76.18	71.28
Net Margin %	(5.44)	4.24	2.26	2.47	5.91	3.98	4.20	6.88
Price Range	62.86-42.31	64.15-51.87	60.87-43.06	60.20-45.64	58.86-42.97	50.74-36.22	45.63-36.14	46.44-33.86
P/E Ratio	46.22-31.11	24.48-19.80	46.11-32.62	44.59-33.81	18.22-13.30	24.87-17.75	21.42-16.97	13.31-9.70
Average Yield %	4.61	4.37	4.66	4.56	5.03	5.60	5.85	5.97

Address: 4484 Wilshire Boulevard, Los Angeles, CA 90010 **Telephone:** 323-937-1060 **Fax:** 323-857-7116	**Web Site:** www.mercuryinsurance.com **Officers:** George Joseph - Chairman Gabriel Tirador - President, Chief Executive Officer	**Auditors:** KPMG LLP **Transfer Agents:** Computershare Trust Company, N.A., Canton, MA

MEREDITH CORP

Exchange	Symbol	Price	52Wk Range	Yield	P/E	Div Acheiver
NYS	MDP	$51.00 (6/29/2018)	71.80-47.85	4.27	20.90	24 Years

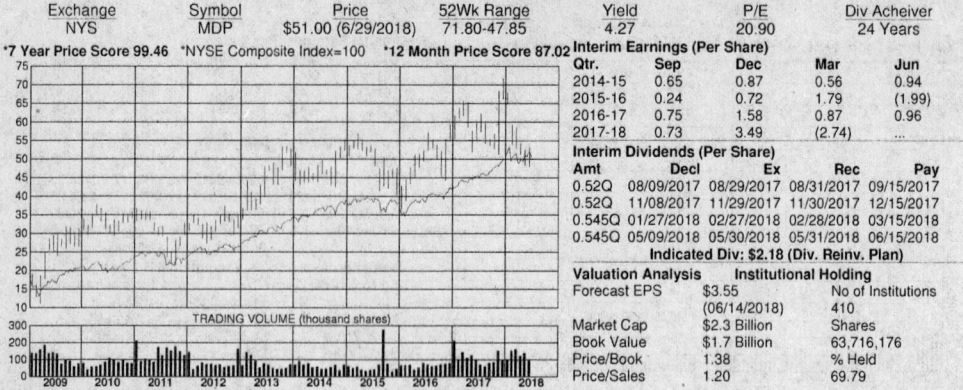

*7 Year Price Score 99.46   *NYSE Composite Index=100   *12 Month Price Score 87.02

Interim Earnings (Per Share)

Qtr.	Sep	Dec	Mar	Jun
2014-15	0.65	0.87	0.56	0.94
2015-16	0.24	0.72	1.79	(1.99)
2016-17	0.75	1.58	0.87	0.96
2017-18	0.73	3.49	(2.74)	...

Interim Dividends (Per Share)

Amt	Decl	Ex	Rec	Pay
0.52Q	08/09/2017	08/29/2017	08/31/2017	09/15/2017
0.52Q	11/08/2017	11/29/2017	11/30/2017	12/15/2017
0.545Q	01/27/2018	02/27/2018	02/28/2018	03/15/2018
0.545Q	05/09/2018	05/30/2018	05/31/2018	06/15/2018

Indicated Div: $2.18 (Div. Reinv. Plan)

Valuation Analysis   **Institutional Holding**

Forecast EPS	$3.55	No of Institutions
	(06/14/2018)	410
Market Cap	$2.3 Billion	Shares
Book Value	$1.7 Billion	63,716,176
Price/Book	1.38	% Held
Price/Sales	1.20	69.79

Business Summary: Advertising (MIC: 2.3.4 SIC: 2721 NAIC: 511120)

Meredith is a media company engaged in providing consumers with content and delivering the messages of Co.'s advertising and marketing partners. Co. operates two business segments: local media and national media. As of June 30 2017, Co.'s local media segment consisted of 17 television stations located across the U.S. in markets with related digital and mobile media assets. The national media segment includes national consumer media brands delivered via multiple media platforms including print magazines and digital and mobile media, brand licensing activities, database-related activities, and business-to-business marketing products and services.

Recent Developments: For the quarter ended Mar 31 2018, loss from continuing operations was US$95.4 million compared with income of US$39.8 million in the year-earlier quarter. Net loss amounted to US$110.1 million versus net income of US$39.8 million in the year-earlier quarter. Revenues were US$648.8 million, up 52.5% from US$425.4 million the year before. Operating loss was US$68.1 million versus an income of US$70.0 million in the prior-year quarter. Direct operating expenses rose 66.4% to US$249.5 million from US$149.9 million in the comparable period the year before. Indirect operating expenses increased 127.4% to US$467.4 million from US$205.5 million in the equivalent prior-year period.

Prospects: Our evaluation of Meredith Corp. as of Jan. 21, 2018 is the result of our systematic analysis on three basic characteristics: earnings strength, relative valuation, and recent stock price movement. The company has generated a negative trend in earnings per share over the past 5 quarters and while recent estimates for the company have remained steady, MDP has posted better than expected results. Based on operating earnings yield, the company is undervalued when compared to all of the companies in our coverage universe. Share price changes over the past year indicates that MDP will perform well over the near term.

Financial Data

(US$ in Thousands)	9 Mos	6 Mos	3 Mos	06/30/2017	06/30/2016	06/30/2015	06/30/2014	06/30/2013
Earnings Per Share	2.44	6.05	4.14	4.16	0.75	3.02	2.50	2.74
Cash Flow Per Share	3.07	4.54	5.26	4.92	5.07	4.32	3.99	4.25
Dividends Per Share	2.105	2.080	2.055	2.030	1.905	1.780	1.680	1.580
Dividend Payout %	86.27	34.38	49.64	48.80	254.00	58.94	67.20	57.66
Income Statement								
Total Revenue	1,459,300	810,469	392,771	1,713,361	1,649,628	1,594,176	1,468,708	1,471,340
EBITDA	97,500	128,794	74,219	361,473	186,774	297,606	230,927	254,101
Depn & Amortn	83,300	34,651	17,421	52,350	56,165	55,494	44,412	43,267
Income Before Taxes	(41,700)	83,894	51,720	290,334	110,207	222,760	174,339	197,404
Income Taxes	(139,000)	(108,855)	18,279	101,406	76,270	85,969	60,798	73,754
Net Income	82,600	192,749	33,441	188,928	33,937	136,791	113,541	123,650
Average Shares	45,000	45,601	45,620	45,447	45,357	45,323	45,410	45,085
Balance Sheet								
Current Assets	2,114,400	542,913	535,723	505,253	481,156	482,531	470,012	407,692
Total Assets	6,861,300	2,747,987	2,769,363	2,729,623	2,628,285	2,843,282	2,543,800	2,140,059
Current Liabilities	1,240,100	473,727	494,764	459,670	477,892	531,001	483,103	456,671
Long-Term Obligations	3,120,600	631,552	642,759	635,737	620,000	732,500	627,500	300,000
Total Liabilities	5,206,500	1,601,149	1,761,602	1,733,651	1,739,242	1,891,432	1,652,148	1,285,763
Stockholders' Equity	1,654,800	1,146,838	1,007,761	995,972	889,043	951,850	891,652	854,296
Shares Outstanding	44,869	44,735	44,676	44,552	44,556	44,620	44,476	44,566
Statistical Record								
Return on Assets %	2.66	10.16	6.97	7.05	1.24	5.08	4.85	5.95
Return on Equity %	9.59	26.24	19.70	20.05	3.68	14.84	13.01	14.97
EBITDA Margin %	6.68	15.89	18.90	21.10	11.32	18.67	15.72	17.27
Net Margin %	5.66	23.78	8.51	11.03	2.06	8.58	7.73	8.40
Asset Turnover	0.40	0.62	0.63	0.64	0.60	0.59	0.63	0.71
Current Ratio	1.71	1.15	1.08	1.10	1.01	0.91	0.97	0.89
Debt to Equity	1.89	0.55	0.64	0.64	0.70	0.77	0.70	0.35
Price Range	71.80-51.15	71.80-51.15	65.70-44.15	65.70-44.15	52.76-36.46	56.96-42.33	53.34-42.96	48.04-29.68
P/E Ratio	29.43-20.96	11.87-8.45	15.87-10.66	15.79-10.61	70.35-48.61	18.86-14.02	21.34-17.18	17.53-10.83
Average Yield %	3.59	3.51	3.59	3.60	4.12	3.51	3.56	4.35

Address: 1716 Locust Street, Des Moines, IA 50309-3023
Telephone: 515-284-3000

Web Site: www.meredith.com
Officers: Stephen M. Lacy - Chairman, President, Chief Executive Officer, Principal Accounting Officer, Principal Financial Officer, Acting Vice President, Executive Chairman D. Mell Meredith Frazier - Vice-Chairman

Auditors: KPMG LLP
Investor Contact: 515-284-3622
Transfer Agents: Wells Fargo Bank, N.A., St. Paul, MN

METLIFE INC

Exchange	Symbol	Price	52Wk Range	Yield	P/E
NYS	MET	$43.60 (6/29/2018)	55.73-43.60	3.85	10.77

*7 Year Price Score 95.18 *NYSE Composite Index=100 *12 Month Price Score 92.81

Interim Earnings (Per Share)

Qtr.	Mar	Jun	Sep	Dec
2015	1.87	0.92	1.06	0.71
2016	1.98	0.06	0.51	(1.92)
2017	0.75	0.77	(0.08)	2.17
2018	1.19	...	...	...

Interim Dividends (Per Share)

Amt	Decl	Ex	Rec	Pay
0.40Q	10/24/2017	11/03/2017	11/06/2017	12/13/2017
0.40Q	01/05/2018	02/02/2018	02/05/2018	03/13/2018
0.42Q	04/24/2018	05/04/2018	05/07/2018	06/13/2018
0.42Q	07/06/2018	08/03/2018	08/06/2018	09/13/2018

Indicated Div: $1.68

Valuation Analysis | **Institutional Holding**

Forecast EPS	$5.10 (06/14/2018)	No of Institutions 1550
Market Cap	$44.7 Billion	Shares 961,755,328
Book Value	$56.3 Billion	% Held
Price/Book	0.79	77.61
Price/Sales	0.70	

Business Summary: Life & Health (MIC: 5.2.2 SIC: 6311 NAIC: 524113)

MetLife is a holding company. Through its subsidiaries and affiliates, Co. is a provider of life insurance, annuities, employee benefits and asset management. In the U.S., Co. provides a range of insurance and financial services products, including life, dental, disability, property and casualty, guaranteed interest, stable value and annuities to both individuals and groups. Outside the U.S., Co. provides life, medical, dental, credit and other accident and health insurance, annuities, endowment and retirement and savings products to both individuals and groups. Co. has six segments: U.S.; Asia; Latin America; Europe, the Middle East and Africa; MetLife Holdings; and Brighthouse Financial.

Recent Developments: For the quarter ended Mar 31 2018, income from continuing operations increased 32.0% to US$1.26 billion from US$952.0 million in the year-earlier quarter. Net income increased 43.5% to US$1.26 billion from US$876.0 million in the year-earlier quarter. Revenues were US$14.81 billion, down 5.9% from US$15.74 billion the year before. Net premiums earned were US$10.57 billion versus US$10.33 billion in the prior-year quarter, an increase of 2.4%. Net investment income fell 27.9% to US$3.75 billion from US$5.20 billion a year ago.

Prospects: Our evaluation of MetLife Inc. as of Jan. 21, 2018 is the result of our systematic analysis on three basic characteristics: earnings strength, relative valuation, and recent stock price movement. The company has generated a negative trend in earnings per share over the past 5 quarters and while recent estimates for the company have been raised by analysts, MET has posted better than expected results. Based on operating earnings yield, the company is undervalued when compared to all of the companies in our coverage universe. Share price changes over the past year indicates that MET will perform in line with the market over the near term.

Financial Data

(US$ in Millions)	3 Mos	12/31/2017	12/31/2016	12/31/2015	12/31/2014	12/31/2013	12/31/2012	12/31/2011
Earnings Per Share	4.05	3.62	0.63	4.57	5.42	2.91	1.12	6.29
Cash Flow Per Share	11.08	11.48	13.44	12.64	14.51	14.59	15.98	9.71
Tang Book Value Per Share	45.48	47.04	53.02	53.32	55.02	46.25	50.03	45.34
Dividends Per Share	1.600	1.600	1.575	1.475	1.325	1.010	0.740	0.740
Dividend Payout %	39.51	44.20	250.00	32.28	24.45	34.71	66.07	11.76
Income Statement								
Premium Income	10,570	44,502	48,359	48,052	49,013	47,125	46,531	44,167
Total Revenue	14,805	62,308	63,476	69,951	73,316	68,199	68,150	70,262
Benefits & Claims	8,718	38,313	40,804	38,714	39,102	38,107	37,987	35,457
Income Before Taxes	1,656	3,536	(195)	7,470	8,804	4,052	1,442	10,026
Income Taxes	399	(1,470)	(999)	2,148	2,465	661	128	3,075
Net Income	1,253	4,010	800	5,310	6,309	3,368	1,324	6,981
Average Shares	1,044	1,078	1,108	1,128	1,142	1,116	1,076	1,068
Balance Sheet								
Total Assets	712,584	719,892	898,764	877,933	902,337	885,296	836,781	799,625
Total Liabilities	656,274	661,216	831,455	809,907	830,185	822,856	772,207	739,723
Stockholders' Equity	56,310	58,676	67,309	68,026	72,152	62,440	64,574	59,902
Shares Outstanding	1,024	1,043	1,095	1,098	1,131	1,122	1,091	1,057
Statistical Record								
Return on Assets %	0.55	0.50	0.09	0.60	0.71	0.39	0.16	0.91
Return on Equity %	7.14	6.37	1.18	7.58	9.38	5.30	2.12	12.85
Loss Ratio %	82.48	86.09	84.38	80.57	79.78	80.86	81.64	80.28
Net Margin %	8.46	6.44	1.26	7.59	8.61	4.94	1.94	9.94
Price Range	55.73-44.08	55.73-44.39	51.14-31.38	51.42-41.05	50.99-41.94	48.14-29.35	35.16-24.79	43.33-23.70
P/E Ratio	13.76-10.88	15.40-12.26	81.18-49.80	11.25-8.98	9.41-7.74	16.54-10.09	31.40-22.13	6.89-3.77
Average Yield %	3.26	3.27	3.94	3.22	2.81	2.56	2.44	2.13

Address: 200 Park Avenue, New York, NY 10166-0188 Telephone: 212-578-9500	Web Site: www.metlife.com Officers: Steven A. Kandarian - Chairman, President, Chief Executive Officer Ramy Tadros - Executive Vice President, Chief Risk Officer	Auditors: DELOITTE & TOUCHE LLP Transfer Agents: ComputerShare Investor Services, Providence, RI

METTLER-TOLEDO INTERNATIONAL, INC.

Exchange	Symbol	Price	52Wk Range	Yield	P/E
NYS	MTD	$578.63 (6/29/2018)	692.30-546.43	N/A	40.35

*7 Year Price Score 151.07 *NYSE Composite Index=100 *12 Month Price Score 92.24

TRADING VOLUME (thousand shares)

Interim Earnings (Per Share)

Qtr.	Mar	Jun	Sep	Dec
2015	2.19	2.73	3.16	4.41
2016	2.40	2.93	3.77	5.14
2017	3.48	3.84	3.99	2.93
2018	3.58	...	...	...

Interim Dividends (Per Share)

No Dividends Paid

Valuation Analysis		Institutional Holding	
Forecast EPS	$20.23	No of Institutions	
	(06/14/2018)	709	
Market Cap	$14.7 Billion	Shares	
Book Value	$560.7 Million	31,452,994	
Price/Book	26.20	% Held	
Price/Sales	5.26	84.02	

Business Summary: Industrial Machinery & Equipment (MIC: 7.2.1 SIC: 3826 NAIC: 334516)

Mettler-Toledo International is a supplier of precision instruments and services. Co. provides weighing instruments for use in laboratory, industrial and food retailing applications. Co. also provides analytical instruments for use in life science, reaction engineering and real-time analytic systems used in drug and chemical compound development, and process analytics instruments used for in-line measurement in production processes. In addition, Co. supplies end-of-line inspection systems used in production and packaging for food, pharmaceutical and other industries. Co. has five segments: U.S. Operations, Swiss Operations, Western European Operations, Chinese Operations, and Other.

Recent Developments: For the quarter ended Mar 31 2018, net income increased 0.9% to US$93.3 million in the year-earlier quarter. Revenues were US$660.8 million, up 11.1% from US$594.6 million the year before. Direct operating expenses rose 13.8% to US$285.9 million from US$251.2 million in the comparable period the year before. Indirect operating expenses increased 10.2% to US$251.5 million from US$228.3 million in the equivalent prior-year period.

Prospects: Our evaluation of Mettler-Toledo International Inc. as of Jan. 21, 2018 is the result of our systematic analysis on three basic characteristics: earnings strength, relative valuation, and recent stock price movement. The company has managed to produce a neutral trend in earnings per share over the past 5 quarters and while recent estimates for the company have been raised by analysts, MTD has posted better than expected results. Based on operating earnings yield, the company is about fairly valued when compared to all of the companies in our coverage universe. Share price changes over the past year indicates that MTD will perform very well over the near term.

Financial Data

(US$ in Thousands)	3 Mos	12/31/2017	12/31/2016	12/31/2015	12/31/2014	12/31/2013	12/31/2012	12/31/2011
Earnings Per Share	14.34	14.24	14.22	12.48	11.44	9.96	9.14	8.21
Cash Flow Per Share	20.63	20.08	16.66	15.42	14.50	11.55	10.53	8.81
Tang Book Value Per Share	N.M.	N.M.	N.M.	0.70	5.76	12.37	8.46	6.71
Income Statement								
Total Revenue	660,821	2,725,053	2,508,257	2,395,447	2,485,983	2,378,972	2,341,528	2,309,328
EBITDA	146,690	640,465	564,962	523,962	503,158	460,185	438,786	404,092
Depn & Amortn	20,892	33,458	32,743	33,087	33,617	34,765	33,421	31,689
Income Before Taxes	117,439	574,222	504,193	463,424	445,004	402,709	382,601	349,177
Income Taxes	24,135	198,250	119,823	110,604	106,763	96,615	91,754	79,684
Net Income	93,304	375,972	384,370	352,820	338,241	306,094	290,847	269,493
Average Shares	26,095	26,393	27,023	28,269	29,571	30,728	31,824	32,839
Balance Sheet								
Current Assets	927,372	1,006,723	896,784	862,815	849,430	913,987	864,920	1,018,863
Total Assets	2,511,907	2,549,805	2,166,777	2,018,485	2,009,110	2,152,819	2,117,400	2,203,474
Current Liabilities	636,882	689,673	587,515	595,127	678,890	564,188	562,677	609,844
Long-Term Obligations	978,715	960,170	875,056	576,984	335,790	395,960	347,131	476,715
Total Liabilities	1,951,160	2,002,525	1,731,834	1,438,028	1,289,515	1,217,767	1,290,181	1,422,337
Stockholders' Equity	560,747	547,280	434,943	580,457	719,595	935,052	827,219	781,150
Shares Outstanding	25,392	25,541	26,020	27,090	28,243	29,487	30,410	31,590
Statistical Record								
Return on Assets %	15.98	15.94	18.32	17.52	16.25	14.34	13.43	12.01
Return on Equity %	75.32	76.56	75.50	54.28	40.88	34.74	36.07	34.71
EBITDA Margin %	22.20	23.50	22.52	21.87	20.24	19.34	18.74	17.50
Net Margin %	14.12	13.80	15.32	14.73	13.61	12.87	12.42	11.67
Asset Turnover	1.18	1.16	1.20	1.19	1.19	1.11	1.08	1.03
Current Ratio	1.46	1.46	1.53	1.45	1.25	1.62	1.54	1.67
Debt to Equity	1.75	1.75	2.01	0.99	0.47	0.42	0.42	0.61
Price Range	692.30-473.87	689.11-414.52	429.91-298.14	346.92-277.62	305.89-223.80	253.27-193.30	195.00-148.68	191.95-130.12
P/E Ratio	48.28-33.05	48.39-29.11	30.23-20.97	27.80-22.25	26.74-19.56	25.43-19.41	21.33-16.27	23.38-15.85

Address: 1900 Polaris Parkway, Columbus, OH 43240	Web Site: www.mt.com	Auditors: PricewaterhouseCoopers LLP
Telephone: 614-438-4511	Officers: Robert F. Spoerry - Chairman Olivier A. Filliol - President, Chief Executive Officer	Investor Contact: 614-438-4748
Fax: 614-438-4646		Transfer Agents: Computershare Shareowner Services LLC, Jersey City, NJ

MFA FINANCIAL, INC.

Exchange	Symbol	Price	52Wk Range	Yield	P/E
NYS	MFA	$7.58 (6/29/2018)	8.87-6.83	10.55	9.47

*7 Year Price Score 82.58 *NYSE Composite Index=100 *12 Month Price Score 95.30

Interim Earnings (Per Share)

Qtr.	Mar	Jun	Sep	Dec
2015	0.21	0.20	0.20	0.19
2016	0.20	0.20	0.21	0.19
2017	0.20	0.20	0.15	0.25
2018	0.20	...	...	...

Interim Dividends (Per Share)

Amt	Decl	Ex	Rec	Pay
0.20Q	09/14/2017	09/27/2017	09/28/2017	10/31/2017
0.20Q	12/13/2017	12/27/2017	12/28/2017	01/31/2018
0.20Q	03/07/2018	03/28/2018	03/29/2018	04/30/2018
0.20Q	06/07/2018	06/28/2018	06/29/2018	07/31/2018

Indicated Div: $0.80

Valuation Analysis

		Institutional Holding	
Forecast EPS	$0.77	No of Institutions	
	(06/03/2018)	394	
Market Cap	$3.0 Billion	Shares	
Book Value	$3.2 Billion	377,996,160	
Price/Book	0.93	% Held	
Price/Sales	6.86	84.33	

Business Summary: REITs (MIC: 5.3.1 SIC: 6798 NAIC: 525930)

MFA Financial is a real estate investment trust holding company. Co. is primarily engaged in the real estate finance business. Co. engages in its business through subsidiaries that invest in residential mortgage assets, including Non-Agency mortgage-backed securities (MBS), which include Legacy Non-Agency MBS, and 3 Year Step-up securities; Agency MBS; residential whole loans, which are comprised of pools of fixed and adjustable rate residential mortgage loans acquired through consolidated trusts in secondary market transactions at discounted purchase prices; and CRT securities, which refer to credit risk transfer securities which are general obligations of Fannie Mae and Freddie Mac.

Recent Developments: For the quarter ended Mar 31 2018, net income increased 6.8% to US$83.4 million from US$78.1 million in the year-earlier quarter. Revenues were US$151.4 million, up 4.5% from US$144.8 million the year before.

Prospects: Our evaluation of MFA Financial, Inc. as of Jan. 21, 2018 is the result of our systematic analysis on three basic characteristics: earnings strength, relative valuation, and recent stock price movement. The company has generated a negative trend in earnings per share over the past 5 quarters. However, while recent estimates for the company have been mixed, MFA has posted results that fell short of analysts expectations. Based on operating earnings yield, the company is undervalued when compared to all of the companies in our coverage universe. Share price changes over the past year indicates that MFA will perform well over the near term.

Financial Data
(US$ in Thousands)

	3 Mos	12/31/2017	12/31/2016	12/31/2015	12/31/2014	12/31/2013	12/31/2012	12/31/2011
Earnings Per Share	0.80	0.79	0.80	0.80	0.81	0.78	0.83	0.90
Cash Flow Per Share	0.35	0.45	0.23	0.76	0.69	0.82	0.87	0.98
Tang Book Value Per Share	8.10	8.18	8.14	7.99	8.64	8.59	9.24	6.99
Dividends Per Share	0.800	0.800	0.800	0.800	0.800	1.640	0.880	1.005
Dividend Payout %	100.00	101.27	100.00	100.00	98.77	210.26	106.02	111.67
Income Statement								
Income Before Taxes	83,395	322,393	312,668	313,226	313,504	302,709	306,839	316,414
Net Income	83,395	322,393	312,668	313,226	313,504	302,709	306,839	316,414
Average Shares	398,317	388,357	371,122	372,114	369,048	362,399	356,762	341,627
Balance Sheet								
Total Assets	10,615,212	10,954,734	12,484,022	13,167,323	12,354,744	12,471,908	13,517,550	11,750,634
Total Liabilities	7,379,781	7,693,098	9,450,120	10,200,062	9,151,472	9,329,657	10,206,544	9,252,874
Stockholders' Equity	3,235,431	3,261,636	3,033,902	2,967,261	3,203,272	3,142,251	3,311,006	2,497,760
Shares Outstanding	398,429	397,831	371,854	370,584	370,084	365,125	357,546	356,112
Statistical Record								
Return on Assets %	2.91	2.75	2.43	2.45	2.53	2.33	2.42	3.10
Return on Equity %	10.42	10.24	10.39	10.15	9.88	9.38	10.54	13.33
Price Range	8.87-6.83	8.87-7.76	8.01-5.78	8.19-6.48	8.46-7.06	9.59-7.00	8.70-6.68	8.64-6.25
P/E Ratio	11.09-8.54	11.23-9.82	10.01-7.23	10.24-8.10	10.44-8.72	12.29-8.97	10.48-8.05	9.60-6.94
Average Yield %	9.80	9.65	11.15	10.67	9.97	19.93	11.28	13.21

Address: 350 Park Avenue, 20th Floor, New York, NY 10022 **Telephone:** 212-207-6400 **Fax:** 212-207-6420	**Web Site:** www.mfafinancial.com **Officers:** George H. Krauss - Chairman Bryan Wulfsohn - Senior Vice President	**Auditors:** KPMG LLP **Transfer Agents:** Computershare Shareowner Services LLC, Providence, RI

MGM RESORTS INTERNATIONAL

Exchange	Symbol	Price	52Wk Range	Yield	P/E
NYS	MGM	$29.03 (6/29/2018)	38.03-28.37	1.65	8.59

*7 Year Price Score 123.74 *NYSE Composite Index=100 *12 Month Price Score 93.56

Interim Earnings (Per Share)

Qtr.	Mar	Jun	Sep	Dec
2015	0.33	0.17	0.12	(1.43)
2016	0.12	0.83	0.93	0.04
2017	0.36	0.36	0.26	2.38
2018	0.38	...	...	...

Interim Dividends (Per Share)

Amt	Decl	Ex	Rec	Pay
0.11Q	07/26/2017	09/08/2017	09/11/2017	09/15/2017
0.11Q	11/07/2017	12/08/2017	12/11/2017	12/15/2017
0.12Q	02/19/2018	03/08/2018	03/09/2018	03/15/2018
0.12Q	04/25/2018	06/07/2018	06/08/2018	06/15/2018

Indicated Div: $0.48

Valuation Analysis

		Institutional Holding	
Forecast EPS	$1.42	No of Institutions	
	(06/13/2018)	732	
Market Cap	$16.2 Billion	Shares	
Book Value	$7.4 Billion	548,483,520	
Price/Book	2.19	% Held	
Price/Sales	1.48	65.66	

Business Summary: Hotels, Restaurants & Travel (MIC: 2.2.1 SIC: 7011 NAIC: 721120)

MGM Resorts International is a holding company. Through its subsidiaries, Co. owns and operates casino resorts, which provides gaming, hotel, convention, dining, entertainment, retail and other resort amenities. At Dec 31 2017, Co.'s domestic resorts consisted of the following casino resorts: Bellagio, MGM Grand Las Vegas, Mandalay Bay, The Mirage, Luxor, New York-New York, Excalibur, Monte Carlo and Circus Circus Las Vegas in Las Vegas, NV; MGM Grand Detroit in Detroit, MI; Beau Rivage in Biloxi, MS; Gold Strike in Tunica, MS; Borgata in Atlantic City, NJ; and MGM National Harbor in Prince George's County, MD.

Recent Developments: For the quarter ended Mar 31 2018, net income increased 5.4% to US$266.3 million from US$252.6 million in the year-earlier quarter. Revenues were US$2.82 billion, up 3.9% from US$2.72 billion the year before. Operating income was US$359.8 million versus US$496.5 million in the prior-year quarter, a decrease of 27.5%. Direct operating expenses rose 6.7% to US$1.64 billion from US$1.53 billion in the comparable period the year before. Indirect operating expenses increased 20.1% to US$827.3 million from US$688.7 million in the equivalent prior-year period.

Prospects: Our evaluation of MGM Resorts International as of Jan. 21, 2018 is the result of our systematic analysis on three basic characteristics: earnings strength, relative valuation, and recent stock price movement. The company has suffered a very negative trend in earnings per share over the past 5 quarters. However, while recent estimates for the company have been mixed, MGM has posted results that fell short of analysts expectations. Based on operating earnings yield, the company is about fairly valued when compared to all of the companies in our coverage universe. Share price changes over the past year indicates that MGM will perform poorly over the near term.

Financial Data
(US$ in Thousands)

	3 Mos	12/31/2017	12/31/2016	12/31/2015	12/31/2014	12/31/2013	12/31/2012	12/31/2011
Earnings Per Share	3.38	3.35	1.92	(0.82)	(0.31)	(0.32)	(3.62)	5.62
Cash Flow Per Share	4.21	3.86	2.69	1.85	2.30	2.68	1.85	1.38
Tang Book Value Per Share	3.14	3.40	0.55	N.M.	N.M.	N.M.	N.M.	N.M.
Dividends Per Share	0.450	0.440	...	...	...	...	...	...
Dividend Payout %	13.31	13.13	...	...	...	...	...	...
Income Statement								
Total Revenue	2,822,237	10,773,904	9,455,123	9,190,068	10,081,984	9,809,663	9,160,844	7,849,312
EBITDA	335,709	2,547,738	2,369,493	436,078	2,105,320	1,943,896	519,633	4,857,328
Depn & Amortn	9,634	1,026,476	890,020	866,163	853,415	884,506	1,001,086	910,946
Income Before Taxes	158,166	852,517	784,700	(1,227,664)	434,844	202,043	(1,597,811)	2,859,550
Income Taxes	(85,379)	(1,132,663)	22,299	(6,594)	283,708	31,263	(117,301)	(403,313)
Net Income	223,444	1,960,286	1,101,440	(447,720)	(149,873)	(156,606)	(1,767,691)	3,114,637
Average Shares	571,970	578,795	573,317	542,873	490,875	489,661	488,988	560,895
Balance Sheet								
Current Assets	2,392,713	2,374,627	2,229,587	2,408,749	3,027,160	2,719,439	2,507,092	2,812,720
Total Assets	29,298,270	29,159,178	28,173,301	25,215,178	26,702,511	26,110,185	26,284,738	27,766,276
Current Liabilities	3,586,888	3,092,382	2,293,421	2,237,951	3,407,925	2,215,328	1,925,671	1,744,764
Long-Term Obligations	12,742,861	12,751,052	12,979,220	12,368,311	12,913,882	13,447,230	13,589,283	13,470,167
Total Liabilities	21,927,480	21,546,526	21,953,121	20,095,251	22,611,594	21,879,006	21,919,190	21,679,698
Stockholders' Equity	7,370,790	7,612,652	6,220,180	5,119,927	4,090,917	4,231,179	4,365,548	6,086,578
Shares Outstanding	556,768	566,275	574,123	564,838	491,292	490,360	489,234	488,834
Statistical Record								
Return on Assets %	6.86	6.84	4.11	N.M.	N.M.	N.M.	N.M.	13.33
Return on Equity %	28.76	28.34	19.37	N.M.	N.M.	N.M.	N.M.	68.57
EBITDA Margin %	11.90	23.65	25.06	4.75	20.88	19.82	5.67	61.88
Net Margin %	7.92	18.19	11.65	N.M.	N.M.	N.M.	N.M.	39.68
Asset Turnover	0.38	0.38	0.35	0.35	0.38	0.37	0.34	0.34
Current Ratio	0.67	0.77	0.97	1.08	0.89	1.23	1.30	1.61
Debt to Equity	1.73	1.67	2.09	2.42	3.16	3.18	3.11	2.21
Price Range	38.03-27.12	34.27-25.43	29.95-16.56	24.14-17.57	28.39-18.01	23.52-11.64	14.74-9.00	16.76-8.23
P/E Ratio	11.25-8.02	10.23-7.59	15.60-8.63	...	...	...	...	2.98-1.46
Average Yield %	1.38	1.43	...	...	...	...	...	...

Address: 3600 Las Vegas Boulevard South, Las Vegas, NV 89109 **Telephone:** 702-693-7120	**Web Site:** www.mgmresorts.com **Officers:** James J. (Jim) Murren - Chairman, Chief Executive Officer William J. Hornbuckle - President, Chief Marketing Officer, Division Officer	**Auditors:** Deloitte & Touche LLP **Transfer Agents:** ComputerShare Investor Services, Providence, RI

MICHAEL KORS HOLDINGS LTD

Exchange	Symbol	Price	52Wk Range	Yield	P/E
NYS	KORS	$66.60 (6/29/2018)	69.06-33.25	N/A	17.43

*7 Year Price Score N/A *NYSE Composite Index=100 *12 Month Price Score 112.94

Interim Earnings (Per Share)

Qtr.	Jun	Sep	Dec	Mar
2013-14	0.61	0.71	1.11	0.78
2014-15	0.91	1.00	1.48	0.90
2015-16	0.87	1.01	1.59	0.99
2016-17	0.83	0.95	1.64	(0.11)
2017-18	0.80	1.32	1.42	0.29

Interim Dividends (Per Share)

No Dividends Paid

Valuation Analysis

		Institutional Holding	
Forecast EPS	N/A	No of Institutions	606
Market Cap	$10.0 Billion	Shares	
Book Value	$2.0 Billion	145,708,288	
Price/Book	4.94	% Held	83.12
Price/Sales	2.11		

Business Summary: Retail - Apparel and Accessories (MIC: 2.1.5 SIC: 3199 NAIC: 316999)

Michael Kors Holdings designs, markets, distributes and a retailer of branded women's apparel and accessories and men's apparel. Co. operates its business through three operating segments: Retail, which include women's apparel, accessories (handbags and small leather goods), men's apparel, footwear and licensed products, such as watches, jewelry, fragrances and beauty, and eyewear; Wholesale, which include accessories (handbags and small leather goods), footwear and women's and men's apparel; and Licensing, which includes royalties earned on licensed products and use of Co.'s trademarks, and rights granted to third parties for the right to operate retail stores and/or sell Co.'s products.

Recent Developments: For the year ended Mar 31 2018, net income increased 7.4% to US$592.1 million from US$551.5 million in the prior year. Revenues were US$4.72 billion, up 5.0% from US$4.49 billion the year before. Operating income was US$749.1 million versus US$689.9 million in the prior year, an increase of 8.6%. Direct operating expenses rose 1.5% to US$1.86 billion from US$1.83 billion in the comparable period the year before. Indirect operating expenses increased 7.0% to U$S2.11 billion from US$1.97 billion in the equivalent prior-year period.

Prospects: Our evaluation of Michael Kors Holdings Ltd. as of Sep. 17, 2017 is the result of our systematic analysis on three basic characteristics: earnings strength, relative valuation, and recent stock price movement. The company has generated a negative trend in earnings per share over the past 5 quarters. However, while recent estimates for the company have been lowered by analysts, KORS has posted better than expected results. Based on operating earnings yield, the company is undervalued when compared to all of the companies in our coverage universe. Share price changes over the past year indicates that KORS will perform very poorly over the near term.

Financial Data

(US$ in Thousands)	03/31/2018	04/01/2017	04/02/2016	03/28/2015	03/29/2014	03/30/2013	03/31/2012	04/02/2011
Earnings Per Share	3.82	3.29	4.44	4.28	3.22	1.97	0.78	0.40
Cash Flow Per Share	7.00	6.21	6.49	4.24	3.13	1.82	0.73	0.79
Tang Book Value Per Share	N.M.	6.77	10.80	10.85	8.54	5.02	2.22	0.73
Income Statement								
Total Revenue	4,718,600	4,493,700	4,712,100	4,371,469	3,310,843	2,181,732	1,302,254	803,339
EBITDA	946,400	890,400	1,346,200	1,387,438	1,084,640	681,351	286,311	158,680
Depn & Amortn	182,300	197,700	172,200	131,400	76,600	52,700	36,000	23,600
Income Before Taxes	741,800	688,600	1,172,300	1,255,823	1,007,647	627,127	248,816	133,219
Income Taxes	149,700	137,100	334,600	374,800	346,162	229,525	101,452	60,713
Net Income	591,900	552,500	839,100	881,023	661,485	397,602	147,364	72,506
Average Shares	155,102	168,123	189,054	205,865	205,638	201,540	189,299	179,177
Balance Sheet								
Current Assets	1,262,100	1,164,700	1,669,800	2,017,431	1,777,169	989,189	464,063	245,398
Total Assets	4,059,000	2,409,600	2,566,800	2,691,893	2,216,973	1,289,565	674,425	399,495
Current Liabilities	960,300	565,800	435,500	330,081	308,370	164,248	165,006	127,725
Long-Term Obligations	674,400	...	2,300	...	...	...	...	101,650
Total Liabilities	2,041,300	817,000	571,100	450,928	410,842	242,319	218,188	267,469
Stockholders' Equity	2,017,700	1,592,600	1,995,700	2,240,965	1,806,131	1,047,246	456,237	132,026
Shares Outstanding	149,698	155,833	176,441	199,656	204,261	201,454	192,731	140,554
Statistical Record								
Return on Assets %	18.35	22.27	31.40	35.99	37.83	40.60	27.52	21.34
Return on Equity %	32.88	30.88	38.97	43.66	46.49	53.04	50.24	77.45
EBITDA Margin %	20.06	19.81	28.57	31.74	32.76	31.23	21.99	19.75
Net Margin %	12.54	12.29	17.81	20.15	19.98	18.22	11.32	9.03
Asset Turnover	1.46	1.81	1.76	1.79	1.89	2.23	2.43	2.36
Current Ratio	1.31	2.06	3.83	6.11	5.76	6.02	2.81	1.92
Debt to Equity	0.33	...	N.M.	...	...	...	...	0.77
Price Range	68.14-33.05	56.35-36.02	66.26-35.57	97.01-64.33	99.84-52.36	64.84-36.04	49.59-24.10	...
P/E Ratio	17.84-8.65	17.13-10.95	14.92-8.01	22.67-15.03	31.01-16.26	32.91-18.29	63.58-30.90	...

Address: 33 Kingsway, London, WC2B 6UF	**Auditors:** Ernst & Young LLP
Telephone: 207-632-8600	**Investor Contact:** 203-682-8200
Web Site: www.michaelkors.com	**Transfer Agents:** American Stock Transfer & Trust Company, LLC, Brooklyn, NY
Officers: John D. Idol - Chairman, Chief Executive Officer Michael David Kors - Honorary Chairman, Chief Creative Officer	

MID-AMERICA APARTMENT COMMUNITIES INC

Exchange	Symbol	Price	52Wk Range	Yield	P/E
NYS	MAA	$100.67 (6/29/2018)	109.11-85.39	3.67	34.48

*7 Year Price Score 99.14   ***NYSE Composite Index=100**   ***12 Month Price Score 94.96**

Interim Earnings (Per Share)

Qtr.	Mar	Jun	Sep	Dec
2015	0.81	1.81	1.22	0.57
2016	0.58	0.60	1.12	0.40
2017	0.36	0.42	1.00	1.08
2018	0.42	...	...	...

Interim Dividends (Per Share)

Amt	Decl	Ex	Rec	Pay
0.87Q	09/26/2017	10/12/2017	10/13/2017	10/31/2017
0.922Q	12/05/2017	01/11/2018	01/12/2018	01/31/2018
0.922Q	03/13/2018	04/12/2018	04/13/2018	04/30/2018
0.922Q	05/22/2018	07/12/2018	07/13/2018	07/31/2018

Indicated Div: $3.69 (Div. Reinv. Plan)

Valuation Analysis   **Institutional Holding**

Forecast EPS	$1.89	No of Institutions
	(06/06/2018)	608
Market Cap	$11.5 Billion	Shares
Book Value	$6.3 Billion	123,300,952
Price/Book	1.82	% Held
Price/Sales	7.45	94.47

TRADING VOLUME (thousand shares)

Business Summary: REITs (MIC: 5.3.1 SIC: 6798 NAIC: 525930)

Mid-America Apartment Communities is a self-administered and self-managed real estate investment trust. Co. owns, operates, acquires and develops apartment communities mainly located in the Southeast and Southwest regions of the U.S. As of Dec 31 2017, Co.'s activities included full ownership and operation of 301 multi-family properties and four commercial properties located in Alabama, Arizona, Arkansas, Florida, Georgia, Kansas, Kentucky, Maryland, Mississippi, Missouri, Nevada, North Carolina, South Carolina, Tennessee, Texas, Virginia and Washington, D.C. Co.'s business is conducted principally through Mid-America Apartments, L.P., in which Co. is the sole general partner.

Recent Developments: For the quarter ended Mar 31 2018, net income increased 17.1% to US$50.8 million from US$43.4 million in the year-earlier quarter. Revenues were US$386.0 million, up 1.9% from US$378.9 million the year before.

Prospects: Our evaluation of Mid-America Apartment Communities Inc. as of Jan. 21, 2018 is the result of our systematic analysis on three basic characteristics: earnings strength, relative valuation, and recent stock price movement. The company has generated a negative trend in earnings per share over the past 5 quarters. Because the company lacks sufficient analyst estimate data, we place greater weight on the historical EPS trend as the measure of earnings strength. Based on operating earnings yield, the company is overvalued when compared to all of the companies in our coverage universe. Share price changes over the past year indicates that MAA will perform very well over the near term.

Financial Data

(US$ in Thousands)	3 Mos	12/31/2017	12/31/2016	12/31/2015	12/31/2014	12/31/2013	12/31/2012	12/31/2011
Earnings Per Share	2.92	2.86	2.69	4.41	1.97	2.25	2.56	1.31
Cash Flow Per Share	5.93	5.81	6.15	6.17	5.12	5.22	5.13	4.66
Tang Book Value Per Share	55.38	55.88	56.49	39.77	38.45	39.39	21.61	18.44
Dividends Per Share	3.533	3.480	3.280	3.080	2.920	2.780	2.640	2.510
Dividend Payout %	120.98	121.68	121.93	69.84	148.22	123.56	103.13	191.60
Income Statement								
Total Revenue	386,017	1,528,987	1,125,348	1,042,779	989,296	634,734	497,165	448,992
EBITDA	90,298	981,266	669,270	754,146	545,035	297,550	261,519	218,808
Depn & Amortn	(1,569)	484,730	313,463	279,382	280,462	183,803	131,428	118,969
Income Before Taxes	50,962	341,785	225,860	352,420	145,109	37,832	71,340	41,227
Income Taxes	640	2,619	1,699	1,673	2,050	893	...	...
Net Income	49,019	328,379	212,222	332,287	147,980	115,281	105,223	48,821
Average Shares	113,507	113,687	78,800	75,176	74,982	53,116	42,937	39,086
Balance Sheet								
Current Assets	82,110	88,867	121,800	63,641	53,582	133,694	9,883	58,679
Total Assets	11,417,376	11,491,919	11,604,491	6,847,781	6,831,028	6,841,925	2,751,068	2,530,468
Current Liabilities	...	...	30,799	17,545	18,921	24,337	11,255	8,401
Long-Term Obligations	4,498,851	4,502,057	4,499,712	3,427,568	3,524,515	3,472,718	1,673,848	1,649,755
Total Liabilities	5,118,352	5,141,599	5,190,599	3,847,434	3,934,593	3,890,064	1,832,303	1,808,100
Stockholders' Equity	6,299,024	6,350,320	6,413,892	3,000,347	2,896,435	2,951,861	918,765	722,368
Shares Outstanding	113,745	113,643	113,518	75,408	75,267	74,830	42,316	38,959
Statistical Record								
Return on Assets %	2.92	2.84	2.29	4.86	2.16	2.40	3.97	2.07
Return on Equity %	5.30	5.15	4.50	11.27	5.06	5.96	12.79	7.85
EBITDA Margin %	23.39	64.18	59.47	72.32	55.09	46.88	52.60	48.73
Net Margin %	12.70	21.48	18.86	31.87	14.96	18.16	21.16	10.87
Asset Turnover	0.13	0.13	0.12	0.15	0.14	0.13	0.19	0.19
Current Ratio	...	...	3.95	3.63	2.83	5.49	0.88	6.98
Debt to Equity	0.71	0.71	0.70	1.14	1.22	1.18	1.82	2.28
Price Range	110.32-85.39	110.32-93.78	109.67-84.64	92.40-71.15	76.24-60.74	74.41-59.70	70.20-58.49	73.25-55.35
P/E Ratio	37.78-29.24	38.57-32.79	40.77-31.46	20.95-16.13	38.70-30.83	33.07-26.53	27.42-22.85	55.92-42.25
Average Yield %	3.51	3.39	3.41	3.87	4.19	4.22	4.02	3.93

Address: 6584 Poplar Avenue, Memphis, TN 38138 **Telephone:** 901-682-6600 **Fax:** 901-682-6667	**Web Site:** www.maac.com **Officers:** H. Eric Bolton - Chairman, President, Chief Executive Officer Thomas L. Grimes - Executive Vice President, Chief Operating Officer	**Auditors:** Ernst & Young LLP **Investor Contact:** 901-682-6600 **Transfer Agents:** American Stock Transfer & Trust Company

MINERALS TECHNOLOGIES, INC.

Exchange	Symbol	Price	52Wk Range	Yield	P/E
NYS	MTX	$75.35 (6/29/2018)	76.95-62.95	0.27	13.38

*7 Year Price Score 102.28 *NYSE Composite Index=100 *12 Month Price Score 101.82

Interim Earnings (Per Share)

Qtr.	Mar	Jun	Sep	Dec
2015	1.01	0.76	0.83	0.48
2016	0.97	0.60	1.18	1.04
2017	0.97	1.21	1.17	2.13
2018	1.12	...	...	...

Interim Dividends (Per Share)

Amt	Decl	Ex	Rec	Pay
0.05Q	07/19/2017	08/23/2017	08/25/2017	09/07/2017
0.05Q	11/15/2017	11/24/2017	11/27/2017	12/08/2017
0.05Q	01/24/2018	02/15/2018	02/16/2018	03/08/2018
0.05Q	05/16/2018	05/30/2018	05/31/2018	06/14/2018

Indicated Div: $0.20

Valuation Analysis

		Institutional Holding	
Forecast EPS	$4.97 (06/05/2018)	No of Institutions	333
Market Cap	$2.7 Billion	Shares	42,092,484
Book Value	$1.3 Billion	% Held	93.01
Price/Book	2.05		
Price/Sales	1.57		

TRADING VOLUME (thousand shares)

Business Summary: Specialty Chemicals (MIC: 8.3.2 SIC: 2819 NAIC: 325188)

Minerals Technologies is a resource- and technology-based company. Co.'s segments are: Specialty Minerals, which provides synthetic mineral product precipitated calcium carbonate and processed mineral product quicklime, and mines mineral ores and processes and sells mineral products; Refractories, which provides monolithic and shaped refractory materials and specialty products, and calcium metal and metallurgical wire products; Performance Materials, which supplies bentonite and bentonite-related products; Construction Technologies, which provides products for non-residential construction, environmental and infrastructure projects; and Energy Services, which serves the oil and gas industry.

Recent Developments: For the quarter ended Apr 1 2018, net income increased 15.4% to US$41.1 million from US$35.6 million in the year-earlier quarter. Revenues were US$431.3 million, up 6.5% from US$405.0 million the year before. Operating income was US$62.6 million versus US$62.1 million in the prior-year quarter, an increase of 0.8%. Direct operating expenses rose 9.1% to US$317.8 million from US$291.3 million in the comparable period the year before. Indirect operating expenses decreased 1.4% to US$50.9 million from US$51.6 million in the equivalent prior-year period.

Prospects: Our evaluation of Minerals Technologies Inc. as of Jan. 21, 2018 is the result of our systematic analysis on three basic characteristics: earnings strength, relative valuation, and recent stock price movement. The company has managed to produce a neutral trend in earnings per share over the past 5 quarters and while recent estimates for the company have remained steady, MTX has posted better than expected results. Based on operating earnings yield, the company is undervalued when compared to all of the companies in our coverage universe. Share price changes over the past year indicates that MTX will perform very poorly over the near term.

Financial Data

(US$ in Thousands)	3 Mos	12/31/2017	12/31/2016	12/31/2015	12/31/2014	12/31/2013	12/31/2012	12/31/2011
Earnings Per Share	5.63	5.48	3.79	3.08	2.65	2.30	2.09	1.87
Cash Flow Per Share	6.42	5.90	6.43	7.78	9.01	3.89	3.95	3.71
Tang Book Value Per Share	9.30	7.80	0.67	N.M.	N.M.	22.80	20.73	19.17
Dividends Per Share	0.200	0.200	0.200	0.200	0.200	0.200	0.125	0.100
Dividend Payout %	3.55	3.65	5.28	6.49	7.55	8.70	5.98	5.36
Income Statement								
Total Revenue	431,300	1,675,700	1,638,000	1,797,600	1,725,000	1,018,181	1,005,619	1,044,853
EBITDA	81,000	309,900	300,100	283,400	246,200	168,657	155,799	152,987
Depn & Amortn	21,100	75,600	75,400	89,900	81,400	44,700	48,700	55,900
Income Before Taxes	49,200	190,900	170,300	132,600	123,000	123,710	107,046	97,740
Income Taxes	9,300	(6,600)	35,300	22,800	30,800	34,515	30,777	27,486
Net Income	39,900	195,100	133,400	107,900	92,400	80,330	74,147	67,521
Average Shares	35,700	35,600	35,200	35,000	34,800	34,976	35,529	36,236
Balance Sheet								
Current Assets	884,100	852,200	751,100	803,600	924,600	815,117	764,485	720,289
Total Assets	3,006,300	2,970,400	2,863,400	2,980,000	3,226,700	1,217,547	1,211,189	1,164,955
Current Liabilities	298,800	310,000	295,500	318,600	352,900	180,894	250,098	180,902
Long-Term Obligations	960,800	959,800	1,069,900	1,255,300	1,455,500	75,000	8,478	85,449
Total Liabilities	1,703,500	1,718,700	1,856,900	2,069,500	2,363,700	370,009	420,778	423,343
Stockholders' Equity	1,302,800	1,251,700	1,006,500	910,500	863,000	847,538	790,411	741,612
Shares Outstanding	35,364	35,374	34,969	34,784	34,649	34,350	34,949	35,309
Statistical Record								
Return on Assets %	6.79	6.69	4.55	3.48	4.16	6.61	6.22	5.92
Return on Equity %	16.99	17.28	13.88	12.17	10.80	9.81	9.65	9.02
EBITDA Margin %	18.78	18.49	18.32	15.77	14.27	16.56	15.49	14.64
Net Margin %	9.25	11.64	8.14	6.00	5.36	7.89	7.37	6.46
Asset Turnover	0.58	0.57	0.56	0.58	0.78	0.84	0.84	0.92
Current Ratio	2.96	2.75	2.54	2.52	2.62	4.51	3.06	3.98
Debt to Equity	0.74	0.77	1.06	1.38	1.69	0.09	0.01	0.12
Price Range	80.20-62.95	83.70-62.95	82.90-37.03	74.74-45.35	77.40-48.81	60.40-38.43	39.92-28.79	35.05-23.38
P/E Ratio	14.25-11.18	15.27-11.49	21.87-9.77	24.27-14.72	29.21-18.42	26.26-16.71	19.10-13.77	18.74-12.50
Average Yield %	0.28	0.27	0.32	0.33	0.32	0.32	0.37	0.33

Address: 622 Third Avenue, New York, NY 10017-6707
Telephone: 212-878-1800

Web Site: www.mineralstech.com
Officers: Duane R. Dunham - Chairman Douglas T. Dietrich - Chief Executive Officer, Interim Co-Chief Executive Officer, Chief Financial Officer, Senior Vice President, Vice President

Auditors: KPMG LLP
Investor Contact: 212-878-1831
Transfer Agents: Computershare Trust Company, N. A., Providence, RI

MOHAWK INDUSTRIES, INC.

Exchange	Symbol	Price	52Wk Range	Yield	P/E
NYS	MHK	$214.27 (6/29/2018)	284.82-204.04	N/A	16.38

*7 Year Price Score 127.13 *NYSE Composite Index=100 *12 Month Price Score 83.61

Interim Earnings (Per Share)

Qtr.	Mar	Jun	Sep	Dec
2015	0.30	2.53	2.89	2.58
2016	2.30	3.42	3.62	3.14
2017	2.68	3.48	3.61	3.21
2018	2.78	...	...	...

Interim Dividends (Per Share)

No Dividends Paid

Valuation Analysis

	Institutional Holding	
Forecast EPS	$15.26	No of Institutions
(06/14/2018)		814
Market Cap	$16.0 Billion	Shares
Book Value	$7.3 Billion	73,306,816
Price/Book	2.18	% Held
Price/Sales	1.65	82.98

TRADING VOLUME (thousand shares)

Business Summary: Construction Materials (MIC: 8.5.1 SIC: 2273 NAIC: 314110)

Mohawk Industries is a flooring manufacturer for residential and commercial spaces. Co. has three segments: Global Ceramic, which designs, manufactures, sources and markets a line of ceramic tile, porcelain tile, natural stone and other products; Flooring North America, which designs, manufactures, sources and markets its floor covering product lines, including carpets, rugs, carpet pad, hardwood, laminate and vinyl products, including vinyl tile; and Flooring Rest of the World, which designs, manufactures, sources, licenses and markets laminate, hardwood flooring, roofing elements, insulation boards, medium-density fiberboard, chipboards, other wood products and vinyl products.

Recent Developments: For the quarter ended Mar 31 2018, net income increased 4.1% to US$209.2 million from US$201.1 million in the year-earlier quarter. Revenues were US$2.41 billion, up 8.6% from US$2.22 billion the year before. Operating income was US$268.4 million versus US$274.8 million in the prior-year quarter, a decrease of 2.3%. Direct operating expenses rose 10.9% to US$1.71 billion from US$1.54 billion in the comparable period the year before. Indirect operating expenses increased 7.6% to US$436.3 million from US$405.6 million in the equivalent prior-year period.

Prospects: Our evaluation of Mohawk Industries Inc. as of Jan. 21, 2018 is the result of our systematic analysis on three basic characteristics: earnings strength, relative valuation, and recent stock price movement. The company has managed to produce a neutral trend in earnings per share over the past 5 quarters and while recent estimates for the company have been mixed, MHK has posted better than expected results. Based on operating earnings yield, the company is undervalued when compared to all of the companies in our coverage universe. Share price changes over the past year indicates that MHK will perform well over the near term.

Financial Data

(US$ in Thousands)	3 Mos	12/31/2017	12/31/2016	12/31/2015	12/31/2014	12/31/2013	12/31/2012	12/31/2011
Earnings Per Share	13.08	12.98	12.48	8.31	7.25	4.82	3.61	2.52
Cash Flow Per Share	16.26	16.05	17.87	12.40	9.09	7.32	8.49	4.38
Tang Book Value Per Share	52.67	49.66	35.96	21.97	28.96	26.32	25.74	20.87
Income Statement								
Total Revenue	2,412,202	9,491,290	8,959,087	8,071,563	7,803,446	7,348,754	5,787,980	5,642,258
EBITDA	387,055	1,757,614	1,647,905	1,148,433	1,077,938	814,249	596,598	522,071
Depn & Amortn	122,654	408,646	366,233	328,486	315,840	276,432	217,393	220,580
Income Before Taxes	256,873	1,317,857	1,241,125	748,861	663,891	445,571	304,492	199,874
Income Taxes	47,632	343,165	307,559	131,875	131,637	78,385	53,599	21,649
Net Income	208,766	971,638	930,362	615,302	531,965	348,786	250,258	173,922
Average Shares	74,929	74,839	74,568	74,043	73,363	72,301	69,306	68,964
Balance Sheet								
Current Assets	4,297,039	4,072,967	3,471,512	3,249,972	3,132,270	3,085,718	2,550,046	2,398,164
Total Assets	12,560,372	12,094,853	10,230,596	9,942,364	8,285,544	8,494,177	6,303,684	6,206,228
Current Liabilities	2,795,910	2,655,355	2,718,320	3,259,028	1,955,814	1,320,811	828,649	1,101,346
Long-Term Obligations	1,585,651	1,559,895	1,128,747	1,196,928	1,402,135	2,132,790	1,327,729	1,200,184
Total Liabilities	5,222,429	5,035,691	4,454,145	5,088,191	3,867,538	4,033,120	2,584,067	2,790,443
Stockholders' Equity	7,337,943	7,059,162	5,776,451	4,854,173	4,418,006	4,461,057	3,719,617	3,415,785
Shares Outstanding	74,533	74,421	74,168	73,929	72,913	72,686	69,153	68,781
Statistical Record								
Return on Assets %	8.42	8.70	9.20	6.75	6.34	4.71	3.99	2.83
Return on Equity %	14.63	15.14	17.46	13.27	11.98	8.53	7.00	5.20
EBITDA Margin %	16.05	18.52	18.39	14.23	13.81	11.08	10.31	9.25
Net Margin %	8.65	10.24	10.38	7.62	6.82	4.75	4.32	3.08
Asset Turnover	0.83	0.85	0.89	0.89	0.93	0.99	0.92	0.92
Current Ratio	1.54	1.53	1.28	1.00	1.60	2.34	3.08	2.18
Debt to Equity	0.22	0.22	0.20	0.25	0.32	0.48	0.36	0.35
Price Range	284.82-227.15	284.82-201.74	216.22-151.78	211.33-152.74	157.60-124.77	148.90-90.47	91.29-59.39	68.50-40.75
P/E Ratio	21.78-17.37	21.94-15.54	17.33-12.16	25.43-18.38	21.74-17.21	30.89-18.77	25.29-16.45	27.18-16.17

Address: 160 S. Industrial Blvd., Calhoun, GA 30701 Telephone: 706-629-7721	Web Site: www.mohawkind.com Officers: Jeffrey S. Lorberbaum - Chairman, Chief Executive Officer W. Christopher Wellborn - President, Chief Operating Officer	Auditors: KPMG LLP Investor Contact: 706-624-2695 Transfer Agents: American Stock Transfer and Trust Company, Addison, TX

MOLINA HEALTHCARE INC

Exchange	Symbol	Price	52Wk Range	Yield	P/E
NYS	MOH	$97.94 (6/29/2018)	101.48-56.78	N/A	N/A

*7 Year Price Score 126.75 *NYSE Composite Index=100 *12 Month Price Score 115.46

Interim Earnings (Per Share)

Qtr.	Mar	Jun	Sep	Dec
2015	0.56	0.72	0.77	0.51
2016	0.43	0.58	0.76	(0.85)
2017	1.37	(4.10)	(1.70)	(4.63)
2018	1.64	...	...	...

Interim Dividends (Per Share)

No Dividends Paid

Valuation Analysis

		Institutional Holding	
Forecast EPS	$4.58	No of Institutions	
	(06/14/2018)	382	
Market Cap	$6.1 Billion	Shares	
Book Value	$1.6 Billion	80,448,144	
Price/Book	3.91	% Held	
Price/Sales	0.31	74.21	

TRADING VOLUME (thousand shares)

2009 2010 2011 2012 2013 2014 2015 2016 2017 2018

Business Summary: Hospitals & Health Care Facilities (MIC: 4.2.1 SIC: 6324 NAIC: 524114)

Molina Healthcare provides managed health care services under the Medicaid and Medicare programs and through the state insurance marketplaces. Co. manages its operations through three reportable segments: Health Plans, which consists of Co.'s health plans; Molina Medicaid Solutions, which provides support to state government agencies in the administration of their Medicaid programs including business processing, information technology development, and administrative services; and Others, which includes primarily Co.'s Pathways behavioral health and social services provider.

Recent Developments: For the quarter ended Mar 31 2018, net income increased 39.0% to US$107.0 million from US$77.0 million in the year-earlier quarter. Revenues were US$4.65 billion, down 5.3% from US$4.90 billion the year before. Net premiums earned were US$4.43 billion versus US$4.76 billion in the prior-year quarter, a decrease of 7.0%.

Prospects: Our evaluation of Molina Healthcare Inc. as of Jan. 21, 2018 is the result of our systematic analysis on three basic characteristics: earnings strength, relative valuation, and recent stock price movement. The company has produced a positive trend in earnings per share over the past 5 quarters. Because the company lacks sufficient analyst estimate data, we place greater weight on the historical EPS trend as the measure of earnings strength. Based on operating earnings yield, the company is overvalued when compared to all of the companies in our coverage universe. Share price changes over the past year indicates that MOH will perform very poorly over the near term.

Financial Data
(US$ in Thousands)

	3 Mos	12/31/2017	12/31/2016	12/31/2015	12/31/2014	12/31/2013	12/31/2012	12/31/2011
Earnings Per Share	(8.79)	(9.07)	0.92	2.58	1.29	1.13	0.21	0.45
Cash Flow Per Share	7.98	14.36	12.20	21.63	22.59	4.16	7.48	4.93
Tang Book Value Per Share	21.02	18.03	15.60	16.36	13.06	12.28	11.84	10.90
Income Statement								
Total Revenue	4,646,000	19,883,000	17,782,000	14,178,000	9,666,601	6,588,934	6,028,763	4,769,940
EBITDA	219,000	(452,000)	351,000	437,000	226,715	159,817	56,334	97,673
Depn & Amortn	7,000	42,000	45,000	49,000	34,600	26,600	20,500	17,500
Income Before Taxes	179,000	(612,000)	205,000	322,000	135,304	81,146	19,065	64,654
Income Taxes	72,000	(100,000)	153,000	179,000	72,726	36,316	9,275	43,836
Net Income	107,000	(512,000)	52,000	143,000	62,223	52,929	9,790	20,818
Average Shares	65,000	56,000	56,000	56,000	48,340	46,862	46,999	46,425
Balance Sheet								
Current Assets	8,196,000	7,511,000	5,988,000	5,306,000	3,245,397	2,039,664	1,349,126	1,048,082
Total Assets	9,133,000	8,471,000	7,449,000	6,576,000	4,477,215	3,002,937	1,934,822	1,652,146
Current Liabilities	6,005,000	5,557,000	4,570,000	3,822,000	2,174,773	1,293,976	828,037	601,834
Long-Term Obligations	1,516,000	1,516,000	1,173,000	1,160,000	905,048	602,854	261,784	216,929
Total Liabilities	7,580,000	7,134,000	5,800,000	5,019,000	3,466,773	2,110,000	1,152,508	897,073
Stockholders' Equity	1,553,000	1,337,000	1,649,000	1,557,000	1,010,442	892,937	782,314	755,073
Shares Outstanding	62,000	60,000	57,000	56,000	49,727	45,871	46,762	45,815
Statistical Record								
Return on Assets %	N.M.	N.M.	0.74	2.59	1.66	2.14	0.54	1.32
Return on Equity %	N.M.	N.M.	3.24	11.14	6.54	6.32	1.27	2.82
EBITDA Margin %	4.71	N.M.	1.97	3.08	2.35	2.43	0.93	2.05
Net Margin %	2.30	N.M.	0.29	1.01	0.64	0.80	0.16	0.44
Asset Turnover	2.29	2:50	2.53	2.57	2.58	2.67	3.35	3.02
Current Ratio	1.36	1.35	1.31	1.39	1.49	1.58	1.63	1.74
Debt to Equity	0.98	1.13	0.71	0.75	0.90	0.68	0.33	0.29
Price Range	93.77-45.60	79.18-42.70	67.72-45.34	81.50-49.87	54.09-32.73	40.69-25.73	36.78-17.77	28.67-14.26
P/E Ratio	...	...	73.61-49.28	31.59-19.33	41.93-25.37	36.01-22.77	175.14-84.62	63.70-31.69

Address: 200 Oceangate, Suite 100, Long Beach, CA 90802	**Web Site:** www.molinahealthcare.com	**Auditors:** Ernst & Young LLP
Telephone: 562-435-3666	**Officers:** Joseph M. Zubretsky - President, Chief Executive Officer Thomas L. Tran - Chief Financial Officer, Treasurer	**Transfer Agents:** American Stock Transfer & Trust Company, New York, NY
Fax: 562-437-1335		

MOLSON COORS BREWING CO.

Exchange	Symbol	Price	52Wk Range	Yield	P/E
NYS	TAP	$68.04 (6/29/2018)	91.83-59.40	2.41	9.90

*7 Year Price Score 92.00   ***NYSE Composite Index=100**   ***12 Month Price Score 81.98**

Interim Earnings (Per Share)

Qtr.	Mar	Jun	Sep	Dec
2015	0.43	1.23	0.09	0.18
2016	0.78	0.80	0.94	6.73
2017	0.93	1.49	1.29	2.81
2018	1.28	...	...	...

Interim Dividends (Per Share)

Amt	Decl	Ex	Rec	Pay
0.41Q	11/16/2017	11/29/2017	11/30/2017	12/15/2017
0.41Q	02/22/2018	03/02/2018	03/05/2018	03/15/2018
0.41Q	05/24/2018	06/01/2018	06/04/2018	06/15/2018
0.41Q	07/12/2018	08/30/2018	08/31/2018	09/17/2018

Indicated Div: $1.64

Valuation Analysis   **Institutional Holding**

Forecast EPS	$4.86 (06/14/2018)	No of Institutions	812
Market Cap	$14.7 Billion	Shares	192,908,208
Book Value	$13.4 Billion	% Held	70.86
Price/Book	1.09		
Price/Sales	1.35		

TRADING VOLUME (thousand shares)

Business Summary: Beverages (MIC: 1.2.2 SIC: 2082 NAIC: 312120)

Molson Coors Brewing is a holding company. Co. is a brewer and has a portfolio of owned and partner brands, including primary brands Carling, Coors Light, Miller Lite, Molson Canadian and Staropramen, as well as craft and specialty beers such as the Blue Moon Brewing Company brands, Creemore Springs, Cobra and Doom Bar. Co.'s reporting segments include: MillerCoors LLC, operating in the U.S.; Molson Coors Canada, operating in Canada; Molson Coors Europe, operating in Bulgaria, Croatia, Czech Republic, Hungary, Montenegro, Republic of Ireland, Romania, Serbia, the U.K. and various other European countries; and Molson Coors International, operating in various other countries.

Recent Developments: For the quarter ended Mar 31 2018, net income increased 31.4% to US$282.5 million from US$215.0 million in the year-earlier quarter. Revenues were US$2.33 billion, down 4.8% from US$2.45 billion the year before. Operating income was US$429.5 million versus US$364.4 million in the prior-year quarter, an increase of 17.9%. Direct operating expenses rose 11.9% to US$1.54 billion from US$1.37 billion in the comparable period the year before. Indirect operating expenses decreased 48.6% to US$366.3 million from US$712.0 million in the equivalent prior-year period.

Prospects: Our evaluation of Molson Coors Brewing Co. as of Jan. 21, 2018 is the result of our systematic analysis on three basic characteristics: earnings strength, relative valuation, and recent stock price movement. The company has managed to produce a neutral trend in earnings per share over the past 5 quarters and while recent estimates for the company have been mixed, TAP has posted results that were in line with analysts expectations. Based on operating earnings yield, the company is undervalued when compared to all of the companies in our coverage universe. Share price changes over the past year indicates that TAP will perform poorly over the near term.

Financial Data

(US$ in Thousands)	3 Mos	12/31/2017	12/31/2016	12/31/2015	12/31/2014	12/31/2013	12/29/2012	12/31/2011
Earnings Per Share	6.87	6.53	9.26	1.93	2.76	3.08	2.44	3.63
Cash Flow Per Share	10.66	8.66	5.30	3.76	6.88	6.35	5.46	4.62
Tang Book Value Per Share	N.M.	N.M.	N.M.	1.70	N.M.	N.M.	N.M.	8.94
Dividends Per Share	1.640	1.640	1.640	1.640	1.480	1.280	1.280	1.240
Dividend Payout %	23.87	25.11	17.71	84.97	53.62	41.56	52.46	34.16
Income Statement								
Total Revenue	2,331,500	11,002,800	4,885,000	3,567,500	4,146,300	4,206,100	3,916,500	3,515,700
EBITDA	444,700	2,315,700	3,085,100	290,900	426,600	558,100	496,500	601,300
Depn & Amortn	4,100	590,700	306,300	284,500	268,400	272,500	230,300	177,000
Income Before Taxes	357,400	1,381,700	2,534,400	(105,600)	24,500	115,500	81,200	316,300
Income Taxes	74,900	(53,200)	1,050,700	51,800	69,000	84,000	154,500	99,400
Net Income	278,100	1,414,200	1,975,900	359,500	514,000	567,300	443,000	676,300
Average Shares	216,600	216,500	213,400	186,400	186,100	184,200	181,800	186,400
Balance Sheet								
Current Assets	2,137,000	2,189,700	2,169,600	1,258,800	1,578,900	1,537,700	1,748,000	2,118,000
Total Assets	30,184,500	30,246,900	29,341,500	12,276,300	13,996,300	15,580,100	16,212,200	12,423,800
Current Liabilities	4,128,400	3,399,300	3,157,500	1,217,200	2,325,300	2,142,100	2,598,700	1,277,200
Long-Term Obligations	9,527,000	10,598,700	11,387,700	2,908,700	2,337,100	3,213,000	3,422,500	1,914,900
Total Liabilities	16,738,600	17,020,800	17,922,800	5,233,300	6,133,000	6,941,200	8,245,300	4,775,900
Stockholders' Equity	13,445,900	13,226,100	11,418,700	7,043,000	7,863,300	8,638,900	7,966,900	7,647,900
Shares Outstanding	215,800	215,400	214,900	184,500	185,500	184,200	181,500	180,000
Statistical Record								
Return on Assets %	4.99	4.75	9.47	2.74	3.48	3.55	3.10	5.30
Return on Equity %	11.91	11.48	21.35	4.82	6.23	6.80	5.69	8.61
EBITDA Margin %	19.07	21.05	63.15	8.15	10.29	13.27	12.68	17.10
Net Margin %	11.93	12.85	40.45	10.08	12.40	13.49	11.31	19.24
Asset Turnover	0.36	0.37	0.23	0.27	0.28	0.26	0.27	0.28
Current Ratio	0.52	0.64	0.69	1.03	0.68	0.72	0.67	1.66
Debt to Equity	0.71	0.80	1.00	0.41	0.30	0.37	0.43	0.25
Price Range	96.86-72.16	101.59-76.52	111.25-83.63	95.14-65.19	77.75-51.32	56.15-41.83	46.00-38.28	50.19-38.00
P/E Ratio	14.10-10.50	15.56-11.72	12.01-9.03	49.30-33.78	28.17-18.59	18.23-13.58	18.85-15.69	13.83-10.47
Average Yield %	1.92	1.83	1.68	2.10	2.21	3.01	3.01	2.81

Address: 1555 Notre Dame Street East, Montreal, H2L 2R5 **Telephone:** 514-521-1786	**Web Site:** www.molsoncoors.com **Officers:** Geoffrey E. Molson - Chairman, Vice-Chairman Peter H. Coors - Chairman, Chairman (frmr), Vice-Chairman, Chief Customer Relations Officer	**Auditors:** PricewaterhouseCoopers LLP **Investor Contact:** 303-927-2448 **Transfer Agents:** CST Trust Company, Toronto, Ontario, Canada

MOODY'S CORP.

Exchange	Symbol	Price	52Wk Range	Yield	P/E
NYS	MCO	$170.56 (6/29/2018)	179.21-121.68	1.03	32.24

*7 Year Price Score 138.64 *NYSE Composite Index=100 *12 Month Price Score 111.50

Interim Earnings (Per Share)

Qtr.	Mar	Jun	Sep	Dec
2015	1.11	1.28	1.14	1.09
2016	0.93	1.30	1.31	(2.19)
2017	1.78	1.61	1.63	0.13
2018	1.92	...	...	...

Interim Dividends (Per Share)

Amt	Decl	Ex	Rec	Pay
0.38Q	10/24/2017	11/20/2017	11/21/2017	12/12/2017
0.44Q	01/24/2018	02/16/2018	02/20/2018	03/12/2018
0.44Q	04/24/2018	05/18/2018	05/21/2018	06/11/2018
0.44Q	07/09/2018	08/17/2018	08/20/2018	09/10/2018

Indicated Div: $1.76

Valuation Analysis **Institutional Holding**

Forecast EPS	$7.79	No of Institutions
	(06/12/2018)	896
Market Cap	$32.7 Billion	Shares
Book Value	$199.7 Million	215,136,336
Price/Book	163.92	% Held
Price/Sales	7.52	85.98

Business Summary: Business Services (MIC: 7.5.2 SIC: 7323 NAIC: 561450)

Moody's provides credit ratings; credit, capital markets and economic related research, data and analytical tools; software solutions and related risk management services; quantitative credit risk measures, financial services training and certification services; and research and analytical services to financial institution customers. Co. operates two segments: Moody's Investors Service, which publishes credit ratings on debt obligations and the entities that issue such obligations; and Moody's Analytics, which develops a range of products and services that support financial analysis and risk management activities of institutional participants in global financial markets.

Recent Developments: For the quarter ended Mar 31 2018, net income increased 8.9% to US$376.8 million from US$345.9 million in the year-earlier quarter. Revenues were US$1.13 billion, up 15.5% from US$975.2 million the year before. Operating income was US$490.8 million versus US$446.7 million in the prior-year quarter, an increase of 9.9%. Indirect operating expenses increased 20.3% to US$635.9 million from US$528.5 million in the equivalent prior-year period.

Prospects: Our evaluation of Moody's Corp. as of Jan. 21, 2018 is the result of our systematic analysis on three basic characteristics: earnings strength, relative valuation, and recent stock price movement. The company has generated a negative trend in earnings per share over the past 5 quarters and while recent estimates for the company have been raised by analysts, MCO has posted better than expected results. Based on operating earnings yield, the company is about fairly valued when compared to all of the companies in our coverage universe. Share price changes over the past year indicates that MCO will perform very well over the near term.

Financial Data

(US$ in Thousands)	3 Mos	12/31/2017	12/31/2016	12/31/2015	12/31/2014	12/31/2013	12/31/2012	12/31/2011
Earnings Per Share	5.29	5.15	1.36	4.63	4.61	3.60	3.05	2.49
Cash Flow Per Share	8.63	3.91	6.35	5.77	4.83	4.22	3.68	3.55
Dividends Per Share	1.580	1.520	1.480	1.360	1.120	0.900	0.640	0.535
Dividend Payout %	29.87	29.51	108.82	29.37	24.30	25.00	20.98	21.49
Income Statement								
Total Revenue	1,126,700	4,204,100	3,604,200	3,484,500	3,334,300	2,972,500	2,730,300	2,280,700
EBITDA	539,600	2,120,200	811,100	1,596,400	1,663,800	1,345,700	1,176,500	974,300
Depn & Amortn	49,100	158,300	126,700	113,500	95,600	93,400	93,500	79,200
Income Before Taxes	439,800	1,773,500	546,600	1,367,800	1,451,400	1,160,500	1,019,200	833,000
Income Taxes	64,300	779,100	282,200	430,000	455,000	353,400	324,300	261,800
Net Income	372,900	1,000,600	266,600	941,300	988,700	804,500	690,000	571,400
Average Shares	194,500	194,200	195,400	203,400	214,700	223,500	226,600	229,400
Balance Sheet								
Current Assets	2,818,800	2,580,600	3,253,100	3,243,100	2,686,400	2,968,800	2,525,700	1,424,400
Total Assets	9,014,000	8,594,200	5,327,300	5,123,400	4,669,000	4,395,100	3,960,900	2,876,100
Current Liabilities	1,920,900	2,063,300	2,428,200	1,218,500	1,199,700	1,141,300	1,164,900	1,134,000
Long-Term Obligations	5,118,000	5,111,100	3,063,000	3,401,000	2,547,300	2,101,800	1,607,400	1,172,500
Total Liabilities	8,814,300	8,921,900	6,552,300	5,688,400	4,856,600	4,058,100	3,575,700	3,045,100
Stockholders' Equity	199,700	(327,700)	(1,225,000)	(565,000)	(187,800)	337,000	385,200	(169,000)
Shares Outstanding	191,920	190,970	190,694	196,075	204,363	213,960	223,252	222,440
Statistical Record								
Return on Assets %	14.23	14.37	5.09	19.23	21.82	19.26	20.13	21.10
Return on Equity %	...	...	...	...	1,325.34	222.79	636.55	...
EBITDA Margin %	47.89	50.43	22.50	45.81	49.90	45.27	43.09	42.72
Net Margin %	33.10	23.80	7.40	27.01	29.65	27.06	25.27	25.05
Asset Turnover	0.60	0.60	0.69	0.71	0.74	0.71	0.80	0.84
Current Ratio	1.47	1.25	1.34	2.66	2.24	2.60	2.17	1.26
Debt to Equity	25.63	...	...	...	...	6.24	4.17	...
Price Range	170.20-111.38	152.57-94.67	110.16-78.45	112.90-89.32	101.84-72.65	78.47-43.37	51.54-34.09	41.75-26.54
P/E Ratio	32.17-21.05	29.63-18.38	81.00-57.68	24.38-19.29	22.09-15.76	21.80-12.05	16.90-11.18	16.77-10.66
Average Yield %	1.14	1.21	1.51	1.32	1.28	1.44	1.56	1.59

Address: 7 World Trade Center, 250 Greenwich Street, New York, NY 10007 **Telephone:** 212-553-0300	**Web Site:** www.moodys.com **Officers:** Henry A. McKinnell - Chairman Raymond W. McDaniel - Chairman, President, Chief Executive Officer	**Auditors:** KPMG LLP **Investor Contact:** 212-553-4857 **Transfer Agents:** American Stock Transfer & Trust Company, LLC, Brooklyn, NY

MORGAN STANLEY

Exchange	Symbol	Price	52Wk Range	Yield	P/E
NYS	MS	$47.40 (6/29/2018)	58.91-44.01	2.11	13.43

*7 Year Price Score 129.19 *NYSE Composite Index=100 *12 Month Price Score 99.04

Interim Earnings (Per Share)

Qtr.	Mar	Jun	Sep	Dec
2015	1.18	0.85	0.48	0.39
2016	0.55	0.75	0.81	0.81
2017	1.00	0.87	0.93	0.28
2018	1.45	...	...	...

Interim Dividends (Per Share)

Amt	Decl	Ex	Rec	Pay
0.25Q	07/19/2017	07/27/2017	07/31/2017	08/15/2017
0.25Q	10/17/2017	10/30/2017	10/31/2017	11/15/2017
0.25Q	01/18/2018	01/30/2018	01/31/2018	02/15/2018
0.25Q	04/18/2018	04/27/2018	04/30/2018	05/15/2018

Indicated Div: $1.00 (Div. Reinv. Plan)

Valuation Analysis   Institutional Holding

Forecast EPS	$4.68 (06/13/2018)	No of Institutions	1518
Market Cap	$84.1 Billion	Shares	1,838,956,928
Book Value	$78.0 Billion	% Held	77.91
Price/Book	1.08		
Price/Sales	1.84		

Business Summary: Finance Intermediaries & Services (MIC: 5.5.1 SIC: 6211 NAIC: 523110)

Morgan Stanley is a financial holding company. Through its subsidiaries and affiliates, Co. provides its products and services to corporations, governments, financial institutions and individuals. Co. has three segments: Institutional Securities, which provides capital raising and financial advisory services, sales and trading, lending, financing and market-making activities in equity, fixed income securities and related products; Wealth Management, which provides brokerage and investment advisory services; and Investment Management, which provides a range of investment strategies. As of Dec 31 2017, Co. had total assets of $851.73 billion and total deposits of $159.44 billion.

Recent Developments: For the quarter ended Mar 31 2018, income from continuing operations increased 35.8% to US$2.71 billion from US$1.99 billion in the year-earlier quarter. Net income increased 37.2% to US$2.70 billion from US$1.97 billion in the year-earlier quarter. Revenues were US$12.96 billion, up 18.5% from US$10.94 billion the year before. Direct operating expenses rose 57.9% to US$1.89 billion from US$1.19 billion in the comparable period the year before. Indirect operating expenses increased 10.4% to US$7.66 billion from US$6.94 billion in the equivalent prior-year period.

Prospects: Our evaluation of Morgan Stanley Dean Witter & Co. as of Jan. 21, 2018 is the result of our systematic analysis on three basic characteristics: earnings strength, relative valuation, and recent stock price movement. The company has managed to produce a neutral trend in earnings per share over the past 5 quarters and while recent estimates for the company have been raised by analysts, MS has posted better than expected results. Based on operating earnings yield, the company is undervalued when compared to all of the companies in our coverage universe. Share price changes over the past year indicates that MS will perform in line with the market over the near term.

Financial Data
(US$ in Thousands)

	3 Mos	12/31/2017	12/31/2016	12/31/2015	12/31/2014	12/31/2013	12/31/2012	12/31/2011
Earnings Per Share	3.53	3.07	2.92	2.90	1.60	1.36	(0.02)	1.23
Cash Flow Per Share	5.61	(2.53)	1.32	1.92	0.59	18.65	12.98	4.04
Tang Book Value Per Share	34.04	33.46	31.97	30.26	28.26	27.16	25.41	25.72
Dividends Per Share	0.950	0.900	0.700	0.550	0.350	0.200	0.200	0.200
Dividend Payout %	26.91	29.32	23.97	18.97	21.88	14.71	...	16.26
Income Statement								
Interest Income	2,860,000	8,997,000	7,016,000	5,835,000	5,413,000	5,209,000	5,725,000	7,264,000
Interest Expense	1,885,000	5,697,000	3,318,000	2,742,000	3,678,000	4,431,000	5,924,000	6,907,000
Net Interest Income	975,000	3,300,000	3,698,000	3,093,000	1,735,000	778,000	(199,000)	357,000
Non-Interest Income	10,102,000	34,645,000	30,933,000	32,062,000	32,540,000	31,639,000	26,311,000	32,046,000
Non-Interest Expense	7,657,000	27,542,000	25,783,000	26,660,000	30,684,000	27,935,000	25,597,000	26,289,000
Income Before Taxes	3,420,000	10,403,000	8,848,000	8,495,000	3,591,000	4,482,000	515,000	6,114,000
Income Taxes	714,000	4,168,000	2,726,000	2,200,000	(90,000)	826,000	(239,000)	1,418,000
Net Income	2,668,000	6,111,000	5,979,000	6,127,000	3,467,000	2,932,000	68,000	4,110,000
Average Shares	1,771,000	1,821,000	1,887,000	1,952,815	1,970,535	1,956,519	1,918,811	1,675,271
Balance Sheet								
Net Loans & Leases	109,135,000	104,126,000	94,248,000	85,759,000	66,577,000	42,874,000	29,046,000	15,369,000
Total Assets	858,495,000	851,733,000	814,949,000	787,465,000	801,510,000	832,702,000	780,960,000	749,898,000
Total Deposits	160,424,000	159,436,000	155,863,000	156,034,000	133,544,000	112,379,000	83,266,000	65,662,000
Total Liabilities	780,461,000	774,342,000	738,899,000	712,283,000	730,610,000	766,781,000	718,851,000	687,849,000
Stockholders' Equity	78,034,000	77,391,000	76,050,000	75,182,000	70,900,000	65,921,000	62,109,000	62,049,000
Shares Outstanding	1,773,934	1,788,086	1,852,481	1,920,024	1,950,980	1,944,868	1,974,042	1,926,986
Statistical Record								
Return on Assets %	0.81	0.73	0.74	0.77	0.42	0.36	0.01	0.53
Return on Equity %	8.78	7.97	7.89	8.39	5.07	4.58	0.11	6.89
Net Interest Margin %	34.09	36.68	52.71	53.01	32.05	14.94	N.M.	4.91
Efficiency Ratio %	59.07	63.11	67.94	70.35	80.85	75.81	79.90	66.88
Loans to Deposits	0.68	0.65	0.60	0.55	0.50	0.38	0.35	0.23
Price Range	58.91-40.69	53.85-40.69	43.73-21.69	40.54-31.01	39.00-28.47	31.62-19.12	21.17-12.36	30.99-12.47
P/E Ratio	16.69-11.53	17.54-13.25	14.98-7.43	13.98-10.69	24.38-17.79	23.25-14.06	...	25.20-10.14
Average Yield %	1.95	1.95	2.34	1.53	1.07	0.78	1.21	0.92

Address: 1585 Broadway, New York, NY 10036 **Telephone:** 212-761-4000	**Web Site:** www.morganstanley.com **Officers:** James P. Gorman - Chairman, President, Chief Executive Officer Thomas Colm Kelleher - President, Executive Vice President	**Auditors:** Deloitte & Touche LLP **Transfer Agents:** Computershare, Providence, RI

MOSAIC CO (THE)

Exchange	Symbol	Price	52Wk Range	Yield	P/E
NYS	MOS	$28.05 (6/29/2018)	29.68-19.39	0.36	N/A

*7 Year Price Score 47.41 *NYSE Composite Index=100 *12 Month Price Score 111.77

Interim Earnings (Per Share)

Qtr.	Mar	Jun	Sep	Dec
2015	0.80	1.08	0.45	0.45
2016	0.73	(0.03)	0.11	0.04
2017	0.00	0.28	0.65	(1.23)
2018	0.11	...	...	...

Interim Dividends (Per Share)

Amt	Decl	Ex	Rec	Pay
0.15Q	08/17/2017	09/06/2017	09/07/2017	09/21/2017
0.025Q	10/31/2017	12/06/2017	12/07/2017	12/21/2017
0.025Q	12/14/2017	02/28/2018	03/01/2018	03/15/2018
0.025Q	05/10/2018	06/06/2018	06/07/2018	06/21/2018

Indicated Div: $0.10

Valuation Analysis — **Institutional Holding**

Forecast EPS	$1.45	No of Institutions
	(06/14/2018)	829
Market Cap	$10.8 Billion	Shares
Book Value	$10.5 Billion	340,979,200
Price/Book	1.03	% Held
Price/Sales	1.39	N/A

Business Summary: Agricultural Chemicals (MIC: 8.3.3 SIC: 2874 NAIC: 325312)

Mosaic is a producer and marketer of concentrated phosphate and potash crop nutrients. Co. mines phosphate rock in Florida and processes rock into finished phosphate products at facilities in Florida and Louisiana; and mines potash in Saskatchewan and New Mexico. Co. is organized into three reportable business segments: Phosphates, which sells phosphate-based crop nutrients and animal feed ingredients; Potash, which sells potash, primarily as fertilizer, but also for use in industrial applications and, to a lesser degree, as animal feed ingredients; and International Distribution, which serves as a distribution outlet for Co.'s Phosphates and Potash segments.

Recent Developments: For the quarter ended Mar 31 2018, net income amounted to US$40.1 million versus a net loss of US$1.1 million in the year-earlier quarter. Revenues were US$1.93 billion, up 22.5% from US$1.58 billion the year before. Operating income was US$80.7 million versus US$30.1 million in the prior-year quarter, an increase of 168.1%. Direct operating expenses rose 16.8% to US$1.69 billion from US$1.45 billion in the comparable period the year before. Indirect operating expenses increased 62.2% to US$161.4 million from US$99.5 million in the equivalent prior-year period.

Prospects: Our evaluation of Mosaic Co as of Jan. 21, 2018 is the result of our systematic analysis on three basic characteristics: earnings strength, relative valuation, and recent stock price movement. The company has produced a positive trend in earnings per share over the past 5 quarters and while recent estimates for the company have been raised by analysts, MOS has posted better than expected results. Based on operating earnings yield, the company is undervalued when compared to all of the companies in our coverage universe. Share price changes over the past year indicates that MOS will perform very poorly over the near term.

Financial Data
(US$ in Thousands)

	3 Mos	12/31/2017	12/31/2016	12/31/2015	12/31/2014	12/31/2013	05/31/2013	05/31/2012
Earnings Per Share	(0.19)	(0.31)	0.85	2.78	2.68	0.80	4.42	4.42
Cash Flow Per Share	1.88	2.67	3.60	5.04	6.13	3.60	4.43	6.20
Tang Book Value Per Share	22.56	22.57	22.71	22.51	24.21	22.32	27.20	23.83
Dividends Per Share	0.350	0.600	1.100	1.075	1.000	0.500	1.000	0.275
Dividend Payout %	...	...	129.41	38.67	37.31	62.50	22.62	6.22
Income Statement								
Total Revenue	1,933,700	7,409,400	7,162,800	8,895,300	9,055,800	4,765,900	9,974,100	11,107,800
EBITDA	12,800	512,759	1,058,600	1,933,300	2,075,800	883,700	2,800,500	3,118,300
Depn & Amortn	(30,100)	659	703,800	732,200	750,900	386,200	604,800	508,100
Income Before Taxes	(6,500)	374,000	242,400	1,103,300	1,217,300	484,200	2,214,500	2,628,900
Income Taxes	(49,900)	494,900	(74,200)	99,100	184,700	152,600	341,000	711,400
Net Income	42,300	(107,200)	297,800	1,000,400	1,028,600	340,000	1,888,700	1,930,200
Average Shares	384,100	350,900	351,700	360,300	375,600	422,000	426,900	436,500
Balance Sheet								
Current Assets	3,841,400	4,616,500	3,057,700	4,144,700	5,364,200	8,105,800	6,880,500	6,581,100
Total Assets	20,452,300	18,633,400	16,840,700	17,412,400	18,283,000	19,554,000	18,086,000	16,690,400
Current Liabilities	2,220,500	2,031,100	1,476,800	2,048,300	1,600,400	3,265,900	1,764,900	1,917,700
Long-Term Obligations	4,823,100	4,878,100	3,779,300	3,791,100	3,778,000	3,008,900	1,009,600	1,010,000
Total Liabilities	9,997,300	9,015,900	7,256,100	7,880,600	7,579,900	8,251,700	4,660,600	4,707,300
Stockholders' Equity	10,455,000	9,617,500	9,584,600	9,531,800	10,703,100	11,302,300	13,425,400	11,983,100
Shares Outstanding	385,416	351,049	350,238	352,515	367,540	426,005	425,817	425,470
Statistical Record								
Return on Assets %	N.M.	N.M.	1.73	5.61	5.44	3.20	10.86	11.85
Return on Equity %	N.M.	N.M.	3.11	9.89	9.35	4.98	14.87	16.30
EBITDA Margin %	0.66	6.92	14.78	21.73	22.92	18.54	28.08	28.07
Net Margin %	2.19	N.M.	4.16	11.25	11.36	7.13	18.94	17.38
Asset Turnover	0.41	0.42	0.42	0.50	0.48	0.45	0.57	0.68
Current Ratio	1.73	2.27	2.07	2.02	3.35	2.48	3.90	3.43
Debt to Equity	0.46	0.51	0.39	0.40	0.35	0.27	0.08	0.08
Price Range	29.19-19.39	34.02-19.39	31.42-22.10	53.56-27.24	50.79-40.76	61.80-40.68	64.30-45.62	73.18-45.68
P/E Ratio	...	...	36.96-26.00	19.27-9.80	18.95-15.21	77.25-50.85	14.55-10.32	16.56-10.33
Average Yield %	1.47	2.40	4.12	2.57	2.13	1.04	1.75	0.47

Address: 3033 Campus Drive, Suite E490, Plymouth, MN 55441 Telephone: 800-918-8270 Fax: 763-577-2990	Web Site: www.mosaicco.com Officers: James C. (Joc) O'Rourke - President, Chief Executive Officer, Executive Vice President, Chief Operating Officer Mark J. Isaacson - Senior Vice President, Vice President, General Counsel, Corporate Secretary	Auditors: KPMG LLP Investor Contact: 763-577-8213 Transfer Agents: American Stock Transfer & Trust Company, New York, NY

MOTOROLA SOLUTIONS INC

Exchange	Symbol	Price	52Wk Range	Yield	P/E
NYS	MSI	$116.37 (6/29/2018)	117.71-83.02	1.79	N/A

*7 Year Price Score 116.17 ***NYSE Composite Index=100** ***12 Month Price Score 112.25**

TRADING VOLUME (thousand shares)

Interim Earnings (Per Share)

Qtr.	Mar	Jun	Sep	Dec
2015	0.34	0.68	0.57	1.44
2016	0.10	0.61	1.13	1.42
2017	0.45	0.78	1.25	(3.43)
2018	0.69	...	...	...

Interim Dividends (Per Share)

Amt	Decl	Ex	Rec	Pay
0.47Q	08/22/2017	09/14/2017	09/15/2017	10/13/2017
0.52Q	11/02/2017	12/14/2017	12/15/2017	01/12/2018
0.52Q	02/15/2018	03/14/2018	03/15/2018	04/13/2018
0.52Q	05/15/2018	06/14/2018	06/15/2018	07/13/2018

Indicated Div: $2.08

Valuation Analysis   **Institutional Holding**

Forecast EPS	$6.80	No of Institutions
	(06/14/2018)	958
Market Cap	$18.9 Billion	Shares
Book Value	N/A	321,289,184
Price/Book	N/A	% Held
Price/Sales	2.87	N/A

Business Summary: Manufacturing (MIC: 6.1.1 SIC: 3663 NAIC: 334220)

Motorola Solutions is a provider of communication infrastructure, devices, accessories, software and services. Co.'s Products segment provides a portfolio of infrastructure, devices, accessories, and software to government, public safety and first-responder agencies, municipalities, and commercial and industrial customers who operate private communications networks and manage a mobile workforce. Co.'s Services segment provides a set of service offerings for government, public safety, and commercial communication networks including: Integration services, Managed and Support services, and Integrated Digital Enhanced Network services.

Recent Developments: For the quarter ended Mar 31 2018, net income increased 50.0% to US$117.0 million from US$78.0 million in the year-earlier quarter. Revenues were US$1.47 billion, up 14.6% from US$1.28 billion the year before. Operating income was US$171.0 million versus US$173.0 million in the prior-year quarter, a decrease of 1.2%. Direct operating expenses rose 12.4% to US$799.0 million from US$711.0 million in the comparable period the year before. Indirect operating expenses increased 25.4% to US$498.0 million from US$397.0 million in the equivalent prior-year period.

Prospects: Our evaluation of Motorola Solutions Inc. as of Jan. 21, 2018 is the result of our systematic analysis on three basic characteristics: earnings strength, relative valuation, and recent stock price movement. The company has managed to produce a neutral trend in earnings per share over the past 5 quarters and while recent estimates for the company have been mixed, MSI has posted better than expected results. Based on operating earnings yield, the company is undervalued when compared to all of the companies in our coverage universe. Share price changes over the past year indicates that MSI will perform in line with the market over the near term.

Financial Data
(US$ in Millions)

	3 Mos	12/31/2017	12/31/2016	12/31/2015	12/31/2014	12/31/2013	12/31/2012	12/31/2011
Earnings Per Share	(0.71)	(0.95)	3.24	3.02	5.29	4.06	2.96	3.41
Cash Flow Per Share	4.36	8.26	6.85	5.04	(2.79)	3.55	3.65	2.54
Tang Book Value Per Share	...	...	...	...	10.60	8.11	5.96	11.73
Dividends Per Share	1.980	1.930	1.700	1.430	1.300	1.140	0.960	0.440
Dividend Payout %	...	...	52.47	47.35	24.57	28.08	32.43	12.90
Income Statement								
Total Revenue	1,468	6,380	6,038	5,695	5,881	8,696	8,698	8,203
EBITDA	267	1,620	1,344	1,240	(862)	1,486	1,489	1,177
Depn & Amortn	82	343	295	150	173	228	208	365
Income Before Taxes	139	1,076	844	917	(1,161)	1,145	1,215	738
Income Taxes	23	1,227	282	274	(465)	40	337	(3)
Net Income	117	(155)	560	610	1,299	1,099	881	1,158
Average Shares	170	162	173	201	245	270	297	339
Balance Sheet								
Current Assets	3,621	3,950	3,468	4,582	6,879	7,020	7,401	8,768
Total Assets	9,051	8,208	8,463	8,387	10,423	11,851	12,679	13,929
Current Liabilities	3,096	2,931	2,668	2,193	2,250	3,220	3,335	3,815
Long-Term Obligations	5,304	4,419	4,392	4,386	3,396	2,457	1,859	1,130
Total Liabilities	10,605	9,950	9,427	8,493	7,688	8,192	9,414	8,715
Stockholders' Equity	(1,554)	(1,742)	(964)	(106)	2,735	3,659	3,265	5,214
Shares Outstanding	162	161	164	174	219	254	276	318
Statistical Record								
Return on Assets %	N.M.	N.M.	6.63	6.49	11.66	8.96	6.60	5.86
Return on Equity %	...	...	46.41	40.63	31.74	20.72	14.39
EBITDA Margin %	18.19	25.39	22.26	21.77	N.M.	17.09	17.12	14.35
Net Margin %	7.97	N.M.	9.27	10.71	22.09	12.64	10.13	14.12
Asset Turnover	0.76	0.77	0.71	0.61	0.53	0.71	0.65	0.42
Current Ratio	1.17	1.35	1.30	2.09	3.06	2.18	2.22	2.30
Debt to Equity	...	...	...	...	1.24	0.67	0.57	0.22
Price Range	109.39-80.83	94.53-77.34	84.00-60.36	72.45-56.79	67.87-58.50	67.50-54.01	55.68-44.94	47.87-37.04
P/E Ratio	...	...	25.93-18.63	23.99-18.80	12.83-11.06	16.63-13.30	18.81-15.18	14.04-10.86
Average Yield %	2.17	2.24	2.34	2.21	2.02	1.90	1.93	1.02

Address: 500 West Monroe Street, Chicago, IL 60661 **Telephone:** 847-576-5000 **Fax:** 847-576-3477	**Web Site:** www.motorolasolutions.com **Officers:** Gregory Q. Brown - Chairman, President, Chief Executive Officer, Division Officer Gino A. Bonanote - Executive Vice President, Corporate Vice-President, Acting Chief Financial Officer, Chief Financial Officer, Acting Chief Financial Officer, Chief Financial Officer	**Auditors:** KPMG LLP **Investor Contact:** 847-576-6899 **Transfer Agents:** Computershare, Jersey City, NJ

MSA SAFETY INC

Exchange	Symbol	Price	52Wk Range	Yield	P/E	Div Acheiver
NYS	MSA	$96.34 (6/29/2018)	96.69-66.16	1.58	85.26	47 Years

*7 Year Price Score 122.82 *NYSE Composite Index=100 *12 Month Price Score 111.73

Interim Earnings (Per Share)

Qtr.	Mar	Jun	Sep	Dec
2015	0.26	0.63	0.42	0.55
2016	0.31	0.82	0.63	0.66
2017	0.37	0.32	0.83	(0.85)
2018	0.83	...	...	...

Interim Dividends (Per Share)

Amt	Decl	Ex	Rec	Pay
0.35Q	08/01/2017	08/14/2017	08/16/2017	09/10/2017
0.35Q	10/25/2017	11/13/2017	11/14/2017	12/10/2017
0.35Q	01/09/2018	02/13/2018	02/14/2018	03/10/2018
0.38Q	05/07/2018	05/18/2018	05/21/2018	06/10/2018

Indicated Div: $1.52

Valuation Analysis **Institutional Holding**

Forecast EPS	$4.50	No of Institutions
	(05/15/2018)	334
Market Cap	$3.7 Billion	Shares
Book Value	$635.9 Million	33,502,700
Price/Book	5.80	% Held
Price/Sales	2.94	N/A

Business Summary: Office Equipment & Furniture (MIC: 7.5.1 SIC: 3842 NAIC: 922160)

Mine Safety Appliances develops, manufactures and supplies safety products that protect people and facility infrastructures. Co. manufactures and sells safety products to protect the safety of workers and facility infrustructures in the oil and gas, fire service, construction, and mining industries. Co. also sells products designed for specific industrial and military applications. Co.'s products protect people against a variety of hazardous or life-threatening situations. Co.'s core products include fixed gas and flame detection systems, breathing apparatus, portable gas detection instruments, industrial head protection products, fire and rescue helmets, and fall protection devices.

Recent Developments: For the quarter ended Mar 31 2018, net income increased 121.2% to US$32.5 million from US$14.7 million in the year-earlier quarter. Revenues were US$325.9 million, up 22.6% from US$265.8 million the year before. Operating income was US$44.4 million versus US$18.6 million in the prior-year quarter, an increase of 138.7%. Direct operating expenses rose 22.3% to US$178.6 million from US$146.0 million in the comparable period the year before. Indirect operating expenses increased 1.8% to US$102.9 million from US$101.1 million in the equivalent prior-year period.

Prospects: Our evaluation of MSA Safety Inc. as of Jan. 21, 2018 is the result of our systematic analysis on three basic characteristics: earnings strength, relative valuation, and recent stock price movement. The company has produced a positive trend in earnings per share over the past 5 quarters and while recent estimates for the company have remained steady, MSA has posted better than expected results. Based on operating earnings yield, the company is about fairly valued when compared to all of the companies in our coverage universe. Share price changes over the past year indicates that MSA will perform well over the near term.

Financial Data

(US$ in Thousands)	3 Mos	12/31/2017	12/31/2016	12/31/2015	12/31/2014	12/31/2013	12/31/2012	12/31/2011
Earnings Per Share	1.13	0.67	2.42	1.87	2.33	2.34	2.42	1.87
Cash Flow Per Share	3.96	6.06	3.59	1.48	2.88	3.00	4.10	2.35
Tang Book Value Per Share	0.60	N.M.	3.82	2.21	6.58	7.20	5.43	4.66
Dividends Per Share	1.400	1.380	1.310	1.270	1.230	1.180	1.380	1.030
Dividend Payout %	123.89	205.97	54.13	67.91	52.79	50.43	57.02	55.08
Income Statement								
Total Revenue	325,894	1,196,809	1,149,530	1,129,922	1,136,650	1,111,883	1,179,895	1,178,608
EBITDA	56,446	69,539	192,495	148,780	163,246	157,910	177,332	151,763
Depn & Amortn	9,671	28,000	27,000	26,900	26,200	27,100	31,681	32,828
Income Before Taxes	41,994	29,775	151,911	111,026	127,195	120,133	134,290	104,818
Income Taxes	9,505	2,819	57,804	44,407	41,044	35,145	42,529	34,773
Net Income	32,371	26,027	91,936	70,807	88,506	88,247	90,637	69,852
Average Shares	38,778	38,697	37,986	37,710	37,728	37,450	37,042	36,831
Balance Sheet								
Current Assets	632,295	622,297	472,806	505,027	497,869	500,966	463,548	458,849
Total Assets	1,695,768	1,684,826	1,353,920	1,424,818	1,264,792	1,234,270	1,111,746	1,115,052
Current Liabilities	273,404	289,279	221,410	251,905	234,057	191,564	188,800	171,770
Long-Term Obligations	441,426	447,832	363,836	459,959	245,000	260,667	272,333	334,046
Total Liabilities	1,059,847	1,087,225	795,755	908,322	730,983	667,818	648,791	681,386
Stockholders' Equity	635,921	597,601	558,165	516,496	533,809	566,452	462,955	433,666
Shares Outstanding	38,303	38,222	37,736	37,372	37,448	37,202	37,007	36,692
Statistical Record								
Return on Assets %	2.98	1.71	6.60	5.27	7.08	7.52	8.12	6.04
Return on Equity %	7.26	4.50	17.06	13.48	16.09	17.15	20.16	15.79
EBITDA Margin %	17.32	5.81	16.75	13.17	14.36	14.20	15.03	12.88
Net Margin %	9.93	2.17	8.00	6.27	7.79	7.94	7.68	5.93
Asset Turnover	0.85	0.79	0.83	0.84	0.91	0.95	1.06	1.02
Current Ratio	2.31	2.15	2.14	2.00	2.13	2.62	2.46	2.67
Debt to Equity	0.69	0.75	0.65	0.89	0.46	0.46	0.59	0.77
Price Range	86.84-66.16	86.00-66.16	70.97-38.31	53.09-38.69	61.02-47.29	54.73-42.71	43.40-32.88	40.22-24.84
P/E Ratio	76.85-58.55	128.36-98.75	29.33-15.83	28.39-20.69	26.19-20.30	23.39-18.25	17.93-13.59	21.51-13.28
Average Yield %	1.79	1.83	2.49	2.72	2.28	2.41	3.62	3.11

Address: 1000 Cranberry Woods Drive, Cranberry Township, PA 16066-5207 **Telephone:** 724-776-8600	**Web Site:** www.msasafety.com **Officers:** Nishan J. Vartanian - President, Chief Executive Officer, Chief Operating Officer, Senior Vice President, Division Officer Kenneth D. Krause - Chief Financial Officer, Vice President, Vice President (frmr), Treasurer	**Auditors:** Ernst & Young LLP **Investor Contact:** 724-741-8534 **Transfer Agents:** Wells Fargo Shareowner Services, South St.Paul, MN

MSC INDUSTRIAL DIRECT CO INC

Exchange	Symbol	Price	52Wk Range	Yield	P/E	Div Acheiver
NYS	MSM	$84.85 (6/29/2018)	99.26-65.62	2.73	16.10	14 Years

*7 Year Price Score 87.80   *NYSE Composite Index=100   *12 Month Price Score 104.44

Interim Earnings (Per Share)

Qtr.	Nov	Feb	May	Aug
2014-15	0.91	0.83	1.03	0.96
2015-16	0.89	0.80	1.05	1.02
2016-17	0.95	0.93	1.09	1.07
2017-18	1.05	2.06	...	...

Interim Dividends (Per Share)

Amt	Decl	Ex	Rec	Pay
0.48Q	10/24/2017	11/13/2017	11/14/2017	11/28/2017
0.58Q	01/03/2018	01/12/2018	01/16/2018	01/30/2018
0.58Q	04/05/2018	04/16/2018	04/17/2018	05/01/2018
0.58Q	06/19/2018	07/09/2018	07/10/2018	07/24/2018

Indicated Div: $2.32

Valuation Analysis   Institutional Holding

Forecast EPS	$5.07	No of Institutions
	(06/14/2018)	460
Market Cap	$4.8 Billion	Shares
Book Value	$1.3 Billion	52,313,208
Price/Book	3.56	% Held
Price/Sales	1.58	81.21

Business Summary: Industrial Machinery & Equipment (MIC: 7.2.1 SIC: 5084 NAIC: 423830)

MSC Industrial Direct is a distributor of metalworking and maintenance, repair and operations (MRO) products and services. Co. serves a range of customers throughout the U.S., Canada and the U.K., from individual machine shops, to manufacturing companies, to government agencies such as the General Services Administration and the Department of Defense. Co.'s range of MRO products include cutting tools, measuring instruments, tooling components, metalworking products, fasteners, flat stock, raw materials, abrasives, machinery hand and power tools, safety and janitorial supplies, plumbing supplies, materials handling products, power transmission components, and electrical supplies.

Recent Developments: For the quarter ended Dec 2 2017, net income increased 9.8% to US$59.6 million from US$54.3 million in the year-earlier quarter. Revenues were US$768.6 million, up 12.0% from US$686.3 million the year before. Operating income was US$99.3 million versus US$90.6 million in the prior-year quarter, an increase of 9.6%. Direct operating expenses rose 14.8% to US$433.5 million from US$377.5 million in the comparable period the year before. Indirect operating expenses increased 8.1% to US$235.8 million from US$218.1 million in the equivalent prior-year period.

Prospects: Our evaluation of MSC Industrial Direct Co. Inc. as of Jan. 21, 2018 is the result of our systematic analysis on three basic characteristics: earnings strength, relative valuation, and recent stock price movement. The company has enjoyed a very positive trend in earnings per share over the past 5 quarters and while recent estimates for the company have been raised by analysts, MSM has posted results that fell short of analysts expectations. Based on operating earnings yield, the company is undervalued when compared to all of the companies in our coverage universe. Share price changes over the past year indicates that MSM will perform very poorly over the near term.

Financial Data

(US$ in Thousands)	6 Mos	3 Mos	09/02/2017	09/03/2016	08/29/2015	08/30/2014	08/31/2013	09/01/2012
Earnings Per Share	5.27	4.14	4.05	3.77	3.74	3.76	3.75	4.09
Cash Flow Per Share	4.76	4.50	4.37	6.48	4.09	4.40	5.21	3.69
Tang Book Value Per Share	10.75	9.19	8.53	6.52	9.56	10.24	9.53	13.48
Dividends Per Share	1.960	1.830	1.800	1.720	4.600	1.320	1.200	1.000
Dividend Payout %	37.19	44.20	44.44	45.62	122.99	35.11	32.00	24.45
Income Statement								
Total Revenue	1,537,548	768,561	2,887,744	2,863,505	2,910,379	2,787,122	2,457,649	2,355,918
EBITDA	228,357	114,619	434,060	433,936	431,509	430,714	421,645	436,863
Depn & Amortn	31,307	15,749	54,356	57,052	52,799	47,729	36,169	24,676
Income Before Taxes	190,639	95,796	367,992	371,731	373,141	379,525	383,429	412,142
Income Taxes	13,502	36,211	136,561	140,515	141,833	143,458	145,434	153,111
Net Income	177,137	59,585	231,431	231,216	231,308	236,067	237,995	259,031
Average Shares	56,892	56,504	56,971	61,076	61,487	62,339	63,011	62,803
Balance Sheet								
Current Assets	1,087,915	1,023,516	1,005,579	981,491	1,032,076	961,415	893,489	920,111
Total Assets	2,165,222	2,108,212	2,098,912	2,064,951	2,101,206	2,060,747	1,943,003	1,444,876
Current Liabilities	494,435	532,123	557,725	478,602	422,337	309,164	213,579	170,515
Long-Term Obligations	250,896	201,002	200,991	339,772	214,789	240,235	241,566	2,189
Total Liabilities	819,187	848,181	873,772	966,575	768,336	662,184	552,620	257,765
Stockholders' Equity	1,346,035	1,260,031	1,225,140	1,098,376	1,332,870	1,398,563	1,390,383	1,187,111
Shares Outstanding	56,482	56,455	56,391	56,581	61,658	61,618	63,434	62,800
Statistical Record								
Return on Assets %	14.26	11.53	11.15	10.92	11.15	11.82	14.09	18.95
Return on Equity %	23.80	19.78	19.98	18.71	16.98	16.98	18.52	23.38
EBITDA Margin %	14.85	14.91	15.03	15.15	14.83	15.45	17.16	18.54
Net Margin %	11.52	7.75	8.01	8.07	7.95	8.47	9.68	10.99
Asset Turnover	1.44	1.45	1.39	1.35	1.40	1.40	1.45	1.72
Current Ratio	2.20	1.92	1.80	2.05	2.44	3.11	4.18	5.40
Debt to Equity	0.19	0.16	0.16	0.31	0.16	0.17	0.17	N.M.
Price Range	105.03-65.62	105.50-65.62	105.50-65.62	77.76-55.01	91.09-65.04	96.13-75.55	87.79-67.18	84.27-56.13
P/E Ratio	19.93-12.45	25.48-15.85	26.05-16.20	20.63-14.59	24.36-17.39	25.57-20.09	23.41-17.91	20.60-13.72
Average Yield %	2.31	2.12	2.09	2.53	6.06	1.55	1.54	1.42

Address: 75 Maxess Road, Melville, NY 11747
Telephone: 516-812-2000
Fax: 516-349-7096

Web Site: www.mscdirect.com
Officers: Mitchell Jacobson - Chairman Erik Gershwind - President, Chief Executive Officer, Executive Vice President, Chief Operating Officer

Auditors: Ernst & Young LLP
Investor Contact: 516-812-1216
Transfer Agents: Computershare Trust Company, N.A., Providence, RI

MSCI INC

Exchange	Symbol	Price	52Wk Range	Yield	P/E
NYS	MSCI	$165.43 (6/29/2018)	172.75-102.28	0.92	44.00

*7 Year Price Score 166.03 *NYSE Composite Index=100 *12 Month Price Score 119.98

Interim Earnings (Per Share)

Qtr.	Mar	Jun	Sep	Dec
2015	0.39	0.50	0.59	0.56
2016	0.60	0.69	0.68	0.72
2017	0.80	0.89	0.93	0.70
2018	1.24	...	...	...

Interim Dividends (Per Share)

Amt	Decl	Ex	Rec	Pay
0.38Q	08/01/2017	08/16/2017	08/18/2017	08/31/2017
0.38Q	10/31/2017	11/16/2017	11/17/2017	11/30/2017
0.38Q	01/30/2018	02/15/2018	02/16/2018	03/15/2018
0.38Q	05/01/2018	05/17/2018	05/18/2018	05/31/2018

Indicated Div: $1.52

Valuation Analysis **Institutional Holding**

Forecast EPS	$5.25	No of Institutions
	(06/11/2018)	570
Market Cap	$14.9 Billion	Shares
Book Value	$421.4 Million	100,689,928
Price/Book	35.28	% Held
Price/Sales	11.23	94.51

TRADING VOLUME (thousand shares)

Business Summary: Publishing (MIC: 2.3.3 SIC: 7389 NAIC: 523999)

MSCI provides products and services to support the needs of institutional investors throughout their investment processes. Co. operates in four segments: Index, which used in many areas of the investment process, including index-linked product creation and performance benchmarking; Analytics, which provides institutional investors an integrated view of risk and return; environmental, social and governance, which include screening service that is designed to enable institutional investors to manage ESG standards and restrictions; and Real Estate, which provide real estate performance analysis for funds, investors, managers and lenders.

Recent Developments: For the quarter ended Mar 31 2018, net income increased 57.8% to US$115.1 million from US$73.0 million in the year-earlier quarter. Revenues were US$351.3 million, up 16.6% from US$301.2 million the year before. Operating income was US$167.2 million versus US$130.7 million in the prior-year quarter, an increase of 27.9%. Direct operating expenses rose 5.7% to US$71.3 million from US$67.5 million in the comparable period the year before. Indirect operating expenses increased 9.5% to US$112.8 million from US$103.0 million in the equivalent prior-year period.

Prospects: Our evaluation of MSCI Inc. as of Jan. 21, 2018 is the result of our systematic analysis on three basic characteristics: earnings strength, relative valuation, and recent stock price movement. The company has managed to produce a neutral trend in earnings per share over the past 5 quarters and while recent estimates for the company have been mixed, MSCI has posted better than expected results. Based on operating earnings yield, the company is about fairly valued when compared to all of the companies in our coverage universe. Share price changes over the past year indicates that MSCI will perform very well over the near term.

Financial Data
(US$ in Thousands)

	3 Mos	12/31/2017	12/31/2016	12/31/2015	12/31/2014	12/31/2013	12/31/2012	12/31/2011
Earnings Per Share	3.76	3.31	2.70	2.03	2.43	1.83	1.48	1.41
Cash Flow Per Share	5.06	4.47	4.52	2.80	2.64	2.67	2.84	2.11
Dividends Per Share	1.420	1.320	1.000	0.800	0.180	...	...	...
Dividend Payout %	37.77	39.88	37.04	39.41	7.41	...	...	...
Income Statement								
Total Revenue	351,316	1,274,172	1,150,669	1,075,013	996,680	1,035,667	950,141	900,941
EBITDA	186,615	656,630	566,016	488,585	413,624	451,358	426,881	403,589
Depn & Amortn	20,387	79,947	81,333	77,810	74,317	80,503	81,998	85,205
Income Before Taxes	139,438	466,899	385,938	349,554	308,338	345,621	289,409	263,413
Income Taxes	24,346	162,927	125,083	119,516	109,396	123,064	105,171	89,959
Net Income	115,092	303,972	260,855	223,648	284,113	222,557	184,238	173,454
Average Shares	92,587	91,914	96,540	109,926	116,706	121,074	123,204	122,276
Balance Sheet								
Current Assets	1,348,357	1,267,129	1,055,670	1,063,271	770,632	637,035	514,835	677,943
Total Assets	3,344,494	3,275,668	3,082,578	3,146,987	2,894,175	3,134,537	3,019,639	3,092,996
Current Liabilities	655,881	607,671	536,570	498,116	472,912	503,041	509,945	452,805
Long-Term Obligations	2,078,816	2,078,093	2,075,201	1,579,404	800,000	788,010	811,623	1,066,548
Total Liabilities	2,923,120	2,874,656	2,764,973	2,245,500	1,461,342	1,558,173	1,594,408	1,787,564
Stockholders' Equity	421,374	401,012	317,605	901,487	1,432,833	1,576,364	1,425,231	1,305,432
Shares Outstanding	89,859	90,104	91,279	101,013	112,072	118,083	120,114	121,212
Statistical Record								
Return on Assets %	10.90	9.56	8.35	7.40	9.43	7.23	6.01	5.64
Return on Equity %	98.86	84.60	42.68	19.16	18.88	14.83	13.46	14.41
EBITDA Margin %	53.12	51.53	49.19	45.45	41.50	43.58	44.93	44.80
Net Margin %	32.76	23.86	22.67	20.80	28.51	21.49	19.39	19.25
Asset Turnover	0.42	0.40	0.37	0.36	0.33	0.34	0.31	0.29
Current Ratio	2.06	2.09	1.97	2.13	1.63	1.27	1.01	1.50
Debt to Equity	4.93	5.18	6.53	1.75	0.56	0.50	0.57	0.82
Price Range	158.67-96.26	129.35-78.71	90.12-63.16	72.85-47.24	48.98-40.28	44.71-30.99	37.81-25.59	39.72-27.94
P/E Ratio	42.20-25.60	39.08-23.78	33.38-23.39	35.89-23.27	20.16-16.58	24.43-16.93	25.55-17.29	28.17-19.82
Average Yield %	1.19	1.24	1.29	1.29	0.40	...	...	...

Address: 7 World Trade Center, 250 Greenwich Street, 49th Floor, New York, NY 10007
Telephone: 212-804-3900

Web Site: www.msci.com
Officers: Henry A. Fernandez - Chairman, President, Chief Executive Officer C.D. Baer Pettit - President, Chief Operating Officer, Head

Auditors: PricewaterhouseCoopers LLP
Investor Contact: 212-804-3900
Transfer Agents: Broadridge Financial Solutions, Inc.

MURPHY OIL CORP

Interim Earnings (Per Share)

Qtr.	Mar	Jun	Sep	Dec
2015	(0.08)	(0.42)	(9.26)	(3.41)
2016	(1.16)	0.02	(0.09)	(0.36)
2017	0.34	(0.10)	(0.38)	(1.67)
2018	0.96	...	...	...

Interim Dividends (Per Share)

Amt	Decl	Ex	Rec	Pay
0.25Q	08/02/2017	08/10/2017	08/14/2017	09/01/2017
0.25Q	10/04/2017	11/10/2017	11/13/2017	12/01/2017
0.25Q	02/07/2018	02/16/2018	02/20/2018	03/05/2018
0.25Q	04/04/2018	05/11/2018	05/14/2018	06/01/2018

Indicated Div: $1.00

Valuation Analysis

		Institutional Holding	
Forecast EPS	$1.58	No of Institutions	
	(06/20/2018)	611	
Market Cap	$5.8 Billion	Shares	
Book Value	$4.7 Billion	197,843,968	
Price/Book	1.25	% Held	
Price/Sales	2.78	76.86	

Business Summary: Production & Extraction (MIC: 9.1.1 SIC: 2911 NAIC: 324110)

Murphy Oil is a holding company, engaged in oil and gas exploration and production company. Co. explores for and produces crude oil, natural gas and natural gas liquids. Co.'s principal exploration and production activities are conducted in the U.S. by wholly owned Murphy Exploration & Production Company - USA, in Malaysia, Australia, Brunei, and Vietnam by wholly owned Murphy Exploration & Production Company - International (Murphy Expro International) and its subsidiaries, and in Western Canada and offshore Eastern Canada by wholly-owned Murphy Oil Company Ltd. At Dec 31 2017, Co. had proved reserves of 328.10 million barrels of oil, and 1,927.10 billion cubic feet of natural gas.

Recent Developments: For the quarter ended Mar 31 2018, income from continuing operations increased 193.4% to US$168.7 million from US$57.5 million in the year-earlier quarter. Net income increased 187.8% to US$168.3 million from US$58.5 million in the year-earlier quarter. Revenues were US$585.6 million, down 13.5% from US$676.6 million the year before. Operating income was US$127.0 million versus US$214.5 million in the prior-year quarter, a decrease of 40.8%. Direct operating expenses rose 11.5% to US$148.7 million from US$133.4 million in the comparable period the year before. Indirect operating expenses decreased 5.7% to US$309.9 million from US$328.8 million in the equivalent prior-year period.

Prospects: Our evaluation of Murphy Oil Corp. as of Jan. 21, 2018 is the result of our systematic analysis on three basic characteristics: earnings strength, relative valuation, and recent stock price movement. The company has suffered a very negative trend in earnings per share over the past 5 quarters. Because the company lacks sufficient analyst estimate data, we place greater weight on the historical EPS trend as the measure of earnings strength. Based on operating earnings yield, the company is overvalued when compared to all of the companies in our coverage universe. Share price changes over the past year indicates that MUR will perform very poorly over the near term.

Financial Data

(US$ in Thousands)	3 Mos	12/31/2017	12/31/2016	12/31/2015	12/31/2014	12/31/2013	12/31/2012	12/31/2011
Earnings Per Share	(1.19)	(1.81)	(1.60)	(13.03)	5.03	5.94	4.99	4.49
Cash Flow Per Share	6.38	6.55	3.48	6.79	17.05	19.36	15.72	11.09
Tang Book Value Per Share	27.12	26.77	28.55	30.85	48.30	46.65	46.68	45.10
Dividends Per Share	1.000	1.000	1.200	1.400	1.325	1.250	3.675	1.100
Dividend Payout %	...	...	...	...	26.34	21.04	73.65	24.50
Income Statement								
Total Revenue	585,605	2,225,129	1,874,129	3,033,080	5,476,084	5,390,089	28,626,046	27,745,549
EBITDA	140,176	1,273,080	756,347	(1,462,455)	3,357,119	3,173,336	3,166,059	2,826,376
Depn & Amortn	13,168	1,019,495	1,101,292	1,702,432	1,989,030	1,628,749	1,528,145	1,234,693
Income Before Taxes	97,043	71,802	(493,115)	(3,282,262)	1,252,270	1,472,687	1,622,982	1,550,983
Income Taxes	(71,647)	382,738	(219,172)	(1,026,490)	227,297	584,550	658,936	810,051
Net Income	168,253	(311,789)	(275,970)	(2,270,833)	905,611	1,123,473	970,876	872,702
Average Shares	174,619	172,524	172,173	174,351	180,070	189,271	194,668	194,512
Balance Sheet								
Current Assets	1,308,043	1,371,603	1,559,183	1,448,416	3,279,149	3,508,643	4,108,583	3,447,671
Total Assets	9,938,210	9,860,942	10,295,860	11,493,812	16,742,307	17,509,484	17,522,643	14,138,138
Current Liabilities	866,071	834,207	1,502,432	1,674,629	3,147,887	3,224,031	3,409,081	2,824,928
Long-Term Obligations	2,898,850	2,906,520	2,422,750	3,040,594	2,536,238	2,936,563	2,245,201	249,553
Total Liabilities	5,245,903	5,240,751	5,379,181	6,187,084	8,168,873	8,913,754	8,580,608	5,359,741
Stockholders' Equity	4,692,307	4,620,191	4,916,679	5,306,728	8,573,434	8,595,730	8,942,035	8,778,397
Shares Outstanding	173,038	172,572	172,202	172,034	177,499	183,406	190,641	193,723
Statistical Record								
Return on Assets %	N.M.	N.M.	N.M.	N.M.	5.29	6.41	6.12	6.15
Return on Equity %	N.M.	N.M.	N.M.	N.M.	10.55	12.81	10.93	10.28
EBITDA Margin %	23.94	57.21	40.36	N.M.	61.31	58.87	11.06	10.19
Net Margin %	28.73	N.M.	N.M.	N.M.	16.54	20.84	3.39	3.15
Asset Turnover	0.21	0.22	0.17	0.21	0.32	0.31	1.80	1.96
Current Ratio	1.51	1.64	1.04	0.86	1.04	1.09	1.21	1.22
Debt to Equity	0.62	0.63	0.49	0.57	0.30	0.34	0.25	0.03
Price Range	34.95-22.63	32.18-22.63	36.24-15.76	51.77-21.71	67.75-44.33	65.55-51.20	55.89-37.67	66.86-36.33
P/E Ratio	...	...	...	...	13.47-8.83	11.04-8.62	11.20-7.55	14.89-8.09
Average Yield %	3.71	3.71	4.39	3.68	2.25	2.19	7.72	2.04

MURPHY USA INC

Exchange	Symbol	Price	52Wk Range	Yield	P/E
NYS	MUSA	$74.29 (6/29/2018)	88.59-62.57	N/A	9.22

*7 Year Price Score N/A   *NYSE Composite Index=100   *12 Month Price Score 94.85

Interim Earnings (Per Share)

Qtr.	Mar	Jun	Sep	Dec
2015	0.50	0.59	1.41	1.55
2016	2.08	1.17	1.16	1.15
2017	(0.08)	1.51	1.90	3.49
2018	1.16	...	...	...

Interim Dividends (Per Share)

No Dividends Paid

Valuation Analysis   **Institutional Holding**

Forecast EPS	$4.49	No of Institutions
	(06/12/2018)	N/A
Market Cap	$2.5 Billion	Shares
Book Value	$705.3 Million	N/A
Price/Book	3.50	% Held
Price/Sales	0.19	N/A

Business Summary: Retail - General Merchandise/Department Stores (MIC: 2.1.1 SIC: 5541 NAIC: 447110)

Murphy USA's business consists primarily of the marketing of retail motor fuel products and convenience merchandise through a chain of 1,446 as of Dec 31 2017 retail stores operated by Co. located in 26 states, primarily in the Southwest, Southeast and Midwest U.S. As of Dec 31 2017, of these stores, 1,158 were branded Murphy USA® and 288 were standalone Murphy Express locations. Co.'s business also includes certain product supply and wholesale assets, including product distribution terminals and pipeline positions. In addition to the motor fuel sold at its stores, Co.'s stores carry a selection of snacks, beverages, tobacco products and non-food merchandise.

Recent Developments: For the quarter ended Mar 31 2018, net income amounted to US$39.3 million versus a net loss of US$3.0 million in the year-earlier quarter. Revenues were US$3.24 billion, up 8.2% from US$3.00 billion the year before. Operating income was US$60.0 million versus a loss of US$600,000 in the prior-year quarter. Direct operating expenses rose 8.2% to US$3.04 billion from US$2.81 billion in the comparable period the year before. Indirect operating expenses decreased 24.2% to US$146.9 million from US$193.9 million in the equivalent prior-year period.

Prospects: Our evaluation of Murphy USA Inc. as of Jan. 21, 2018 is the result of our systematic analysis on three basic characteristics: earnings strength, relative valuation, and recent stock price movement. The company has produced a positive trend in earnings per share over the past 5 quarters and while recent estimates for the company have been raised by analysts, MUSA has posted better than expected results. Based on operating earnings yield, the company is undervalued when compared to all of the companies in our coverage universe. Share price changes over the past year indicates that MUSA will perform poorly over the near term.

Financial Data

(US$ in Thousands)	3 Mos	12/31/2017	12/31/2016	12/31/2015	12/31/2014	12/31/2013	12/31/2012	12/31/2011
Earnings Per Share	8.06	6.78	5.59	4.02	5.26	5.02	...	...
Cash Flow Per Share	12.97	7.92	8.57	4.97	6.63	7.63	...	...
Tang Book Value Per Share	21.22	21.66	18.87	19.01	18.79	14.04	...	...
Income Statement								
Total Revenue	3,244,200	12,826,553	11,594,553	12,699,411	17,209,919	18,083,335	19,655,436	19,273,455
EBITDA	91,800	402,339	489,767	336,211	485,059	345,217	222,695	407,623
Depn & Amortn	31,800	116,966	98,610	86,568	79,234	74,130	76,622	69,550
Income Before Taxes	47,300	240,022	352,031	218,289	369,423	257,677	145,740	337,557
Income Taxes	8,000	(5,242)	130,539	80,698	126,341	101,351	62,172	132,284
Net Income	39,300	245,264	221,492	176,340	243,863	235,033	83,568	324,020
Average Shares	34,062	36,156	39,646	43,794	46,417	46,858	...	...
Balance Sheet								
Current Assets	518,200	614,294	515,554	435,667	665,882	682,416	821,962	588,353
Total Assets	2,252,500	2,331,039	2,088,740	1,886,241	1,934,257	1,881,242	1,992,465	1,784,983
Current Liabilities	496,100	533,351	514,560	392,292	413,080	526,517	733,909	492,552
Long-Term Obligations	856,400	860,864	629,622	490,160	492,443	547,578	1,124	1,170
Total Liabilities	1,547,200	1,592,637	1,391,664	1,093,951	1,075,552	1,224,906	888,014	666,036
Stockholders' Equity	705,300	738,402	697,076	792,290	858,705	656,336	1,104,451	1,118,947
Shares Outstanding	33,231	34,091	36,935	41,678	45,710	46,743	...	...
Statistical Record								
Return on Assets %	13.52	11.10	11.11	9.23	12.78	...	4.41	...
Return on Equity %	41.74	34.17	29.66	21.36	32.19	...	7.50	...
EBITDA Margin %	2.83	3.14	4.22	2.65	2.82	1.91	1.13	2.11
Net Margin %	1.21	1.91	1.91	1.39	1.42	1.30	0.43	1.68
Asset Turnover	6.14	5.80	5.82	6.65	9.02	...	10.38	...
Current Ratio	1.04	1.15	1.00	1.11	1.61	1.30	1.12	1.19
Debt to Equity	1.21	1.17	0.90	0.62	0.57	0.83	N.M.	N.M.
Price Range	88.59-64.24	81.00-61.03	79.29-54.24	73.48-48.70	69.37-37.55	46.31-37.51	...	...
P/E Ratio	10.99-7.97	11.95-9.00	14.18-9.70	18.28-12.11	13.19-7.14	9.23-7.47	...	...

Address: 200 Peach Street, El Dorado, AR 71730-5836	**Web Site:** www.murphyusa.com	**Auditors:** KPMG LLP
Telephone: 870-875-7600	**Officers:** Robert Madison Murphy - Chairman R. Andrew Clyde - President, Chief Executive Officer	**Transfer Agents:** Computershare Trust Company, N.A.

NABORS INDUSTRIES LTD

Exchange	Symbol	Price	52Wk Range	Yield	P/E
NYS	NBR	$6.41 (6/29/2018)	8.62-5.48	3.74	N/A

*7 Year Price Score 40.24   *NYSE Composite Index=100   *12 Month Price Score 103.01

Interim Earnings (Per Share)

Qtr.	Mar	Jun	Sep	Dec
2015	0.42	(0.13)	(1.02)	(0.57)
2016	(1.41)	(0.65)	(0.39)	(1.18)
2017	(0.52)	(0.46)	(0.52)	(0.39)
2018	(0.46)	...	...	...

Interim Dividends (Per Share)

Amt	Decl	Ex	Rec	Pay
0.06Q	07/28/2017	09/11/2017	09/12/2017	10/03/2017
0.06Q	10/28/2017	12/12/2017	12/13/2017	01/03/2018
0.06Q	02/23/2018	03/12/2018	03/13/2018	04/03/2018
0.06Q	04/20/2018	06/11/2018	06/12/2018	07/03/2018

Indicated Div: $0.24

Valuation Analysis

		Institutional Holding	
Forecast EPS	N/A	No of Institutions	578
Market Cap	$2.0 Billion	Shares	
Book Value	$2.7 Billion		369,355,392
Price/Book	0.75	% Held	
Price/Sales	0.74		89.05

Business Summary: Production & Extraction (MIC: 9.1.1 SIC: 3533 NAIC: 333132)

Nabors Industries is a holding company. Co. owns and operates land-based drilling rig fleet and is a provider of offshore platform drilling rigs in the U.S. and multiple international markets. Co. also provides wellbore placement services, drilling software and performance tools, drilling equipment and technologies throughout the world's oil and gas markets. Co.'s Drilling & Rig Services business is comprised of its global land-based and offshore drilling rig operations and other rig services, consisting of equipment manufacturing and rig instrumentation. Co. also focuses on wellbore placement solutions and provides directional drilling and measurement while drilling systems and services.

Recent Developments: For the quarter ended Mar 31 2018, loss from continuing operations was US$143.6 million compared with a loss of US$147.6 million in the year-earlier quarter. Net loss amounted to US$143.7 million versus a net loss of US$148.1 million in the year-earlier quarter. Revenues were US$734.7 million, up 30.4% from US$563.3 million the year before. Direct operating expenses rose 22.6% to US$475.4 million from US$387.6 million in the comparable period the year before. Indirect operating expenses increased 8.7% to US$379.3 million from US$348.9 million in the equivalent prior-year period.

Prospects: Our evaluation of Nabors Industries Ltd. as of Sep. 17, 2017 is the result of our systematic analysis on three basic characteristics: earnings strength, relative valuation, and recent stock price movement. The company has produced a positive trend in earnings per share over the past 5 quarters. Because the company lacks sufficient analyst estimate data, we place greater weight on the historical EPS trend as the measure of earnings strength. Based on operating earnings yield, the company is overvalued when compared to all of the companies in our coverage universe. Share price changes over the past year indicates that NBR will perform very poorly over the near term.

Financial Data

(US$ in Thousands)	3 Mos	12/31/2017	12/31/2016	12/31/2015	12/31/2014	12/31/2013	12/31/2012	12/31/2011
Earnings Per Share	(1.83)	(1.90)	(3.64)	(1.29)	(2.28)	0.47	0.56	0.83
Cash Flow Per Share	0.13	0.22	1.92	3.03	6.13	4.82	5.37	5.07
Tang Book Value Per Share	7.99	8.70	10.85	14.64	16.36	18.71	19.08	17.93
Dividends Per Share	0.240	0.240	0.060	0.060	0.060	0.040	...	...
Dividend Payout %	...	...	...	...	...	8.51	...	...
Income Statement								
Total Revenue	734,661	2,565,486	2,007,108	3,791,664	6,809,727	6,248,631	6,751,390	6,136,938
EBITDA	(51,354)	478,705	(157,315)	734,970	729,004	1,457,981	1,592,526	1,750,307
Depn & Amortn	7,302	835,900	855,400	980,577	1,155,671	1,128,403	1,066,291	1,005,905
Income Before Taxes	(120,042)	(580,084)	(1,198,075)	(427,535)	(604,615)	106,160	274,683	487,769
Income Taxes	23,545	(82,970)	(186,831)	(98,038)	62,666	(55,181)	32,628	142,605
Net Income	(144,201)	(546,811)	(1,029,742)	(372,675)	(670,659)	139,982	164,034	243,679
Average Shares	308,788	280,653	276,475	282,982	290,694	296,592	292,323	292,484
Balance Sheet								
Current Assets	1,494,373	1,447,336	1,155,839	1,475,897	2,741,874	2,753,830	3,132,857	3,088,314
Total Assets	8,299,830	8,401,984	8,187,015	9,537,840	11,879,942	12,159,811	12,656,022	12,912,140
Current Liabilities	766,828	919,476	821,934	1,006,499	1,567,475	1,311,424	1,132,382	1,802,562
Long-Term Obligations	4,256,160	4,027,766	3,578,335	3,655,200	4,348,859	3,904,117	4,379,336	4,348,490
Total Liabilities	5,590,222	5,490,168	4,939,990	5,255,130	6,971,323	6,121,537	6,641,905	7,255,137
Stockholders' Equity	2,709,608	2,911,816	3,247,025	4,282,710	4,908,619	6,038,274	6,014,117	5,657,003
Shares Outstanding	317,520	314,710	283,925	281,184	289,408	295,297	290,399	287,628
Statistical Record								
Return on Assets %	N.M.	N.M.	N.M.	N.M.	N.M.	1.13	1.28	1.98
Return on Equity %	N.M.	N.M.	N.M.	N.M.	N.M.	2.32	2.80	4.41
EBITDA Margin %	N.M.	18.66	N.M.	19.38	10.71	23.33	23.59	28.52
Net Margin %	N.M.	N.M.	N.M.	N.M.	N.M.	2.24	2.43	3.97
Asset Turnover	0.33	0.31	0.23	0.35	0.57	0.50	0.53	0.50
Current Ratio	1.95	1.57	1.41	1.47	1.75	2.10	2.77	1.71
Debt to Equity	1.57	1.38	1.10	0.85	0.89	0.65	0.73	0.77
Price Range	14.18-5.48	18.19-5.48	17.49-5.53	16.70-7.73	30.04-10.00	18.14-14.45	22.31-12.65	32.06-11.74
P/E Ratio	...	...	...	...	...	38.60-30.74	39.84-22.59	38.63-14.14
Average Yield %	3.08	2.46	0.59	0.50	0.27	0.25	...	...

Address: Crown House, Second Floor, 4 Par-la-Ville Road, Hamilton, HM08 **Telephone:** 441-292-1510	**Web Site:** www.nabors.com **Officers:** Anthony G. Petrello - Chairman, President, Chief Executive Officer, Deputy Chairman, Chief Operating Officer William J. Restrepo - Chief Financial Officer	**Auditors:** PricewaterhouseCoopers LLP **Investor Contact:** 441-292-1510 **Transfer Agents:** Computershare Trust Company, N.A., Providence, RI

NACCO INDUSTRIES INC

Exchange	Symbol	Price	52Wk Range	Yield	P/E	Div Acheiver
NYS	NC	$33.75 (6/29/2018)	88.85-31.90	1.96	6.93	11 Years

*7 Year Price Score 72.14   *NYSE Composite Index=100   *12 Month Price Score 76.27

Interim Earnings (Per Share)

Qtr.	Mar	Jun	Sep	Dec
2015	0.14	(0.04)	0.45	2.58
2016	0.41	0.45	(0.07)	3.52
2017	0.73	0.99	1.23	1.47
2018	1.18	...	...	...

Interim Dividends (Per Share)

Amt	Decl	Ex	Rec	Pay
0.273Q	08/21/2017	08/30/2017	09/01/2017	09/15/2017
0.165Q	11/07/2017	11/30/2017	12/01/2017	12/15/2017
0.165Q	02/14/2018	02/28/2018	03/01/2018	03/15/2018
0.165Q	05/16/2018	05/31/2018	06/01/2018	06/15/2018

Indicated Div: $0.66

Valuation Analysis

Forecast EPS N/A

Market Cap	$234.2 Million
Book Value	$224.9 Million
Price/Book	1.04
Price/Sales	0.90

Institutional Holding

No of Institutions	126
Shares	4,004,500
% Held	46.18

Business Summary: Mining (MIC: 8.2.4 SIC: 1221 NAIC: 212111)

NACCO Industries is a holding company for The North American Coal Corporation. The North American Coal Corporation and its affiliated companies (NACoal) operate surface mines that supply coal primarily to power generation companies under long-term contracts, and provide other services to natural resource companies. In addition, its North American Mining business maintains and operates draglines and other equipment under contracts with sellers of aggregates. NACoal also provides coal handling, processing and drying services for a number of customers.

Recent Developments: For the quarter ended Mar 31 2018, income from continuing operations was unchanged at US$8.2 million compared with the year-earlier quarter. Net income increased 64.2% to US$8.2 million from US$5.0 million in the year-earlier quarter. Revenues were US$31.2 million, up 10.2% from US$28.3 million the year before. Operating income was US$9.7 million versus US$9.8 million in the prior-year quarter, a decrease of 0.9%. Direct operating expenses rose 8.6% to US$25.8 million from US$23.7 million in the comparable period the year before. Indirect operating income amounted to US$4.3 million compared with an income of US$5.2 million in the equivalent prior-year period.

Prospects: Our evaluation of NACCO Industries Inc. as of Jan. 21, 2018 is the result of our systematic analysis on three basic characteristics: earnings strength, relative valuation, and recent stock price movement. The company has generated a negative trend in earnings per share over the past 5 quarters. Because the company lacks sufficient analyst estimate data, we place greater weight on the historical EPS trend as the measure of earnings strength. Based on operating earnings yield, the company is undervalued when compared to all of the companies in our coverage universe. Share price changes over the past year indicates that NC will perform very well over the near term.

Financial Data

(US$ in Thousands)	3 Mos	12/31/2017	12/31/2016	12/31/2015	12/31/2014	12/31/2013	12/31/2012	12/31/2011
Earnings Per Share	4.87	4.41	4.32	3.13	(5.02)	5.47	12.92	19.28
Cash Flow Per Share	10.95	6.05	13.74	15.43	2.61	6.55	17.02	18.51
Tang Book Value Per Share	26.23	25.67	23.76	20.19	19.96	30.25	25.33	61.89
Dividends Per Share	0.875	0.978	1.065	1.045	1.023	1.000	5.378	2.120
Dividend Payout %	17.97	22.17	24.65	33.39	...	18.28	41.62	11.00
Income Statement								
Total Revenue	31,200	104,778	856,438	915,860	896,782	932,666	873,400	3,331,200
EBITDA	(6,160)	(17,342)	2,987	4,938	(89,464)	37,202	32,500	231,000
Depn & Amortn	84	12,723	19,284	23,687	28,100	24,568	15,200	45,600
Income Before Taxes	(6,890)	(33,505)	(21,989)	(25,673)	(125,130)	7,859	11,200	160,900
Income Taxes	804	639	4,863	2,815	(38,455)	11,270	15,800	51,700
Net Income	8,176	30,337	29,607	21,984	(38,118)	44,450	108,700	162,100
Average Shares	6,939	6,873	6,854	7,022	7,590	8,124	8,414	8,408
Balance Sheet								
Current Assets	162,289	176,988	381,732	361,434	465,713	461,290	486,800	1,375,100
Total Assets	374,176	389,552	668,021	655,408	770,520	809,956	776,300	1,801,400
Current Liabilities	40,839	53,976	221,828	191,746	254,681	238,119	227,200	891,200
Long-Term Obligations	34,687	42,021	120,295	160,113	191,431	152,431	135,400	129,100
Total Liabilities	149,294	170,104	447,728	454,270	559,046	512,176	494,900	1,225,200
Stockholders' Equity	224,882	219,448	220,293	201,138	211,474	297,780	281,400	576,200
Shares Outstanding	6,939	6,852	6,778	6,837	7,235	7,871	8,352	8,373
Statistical Record								
Return on Assets %	6.74	5.74	4.46	3.08	N.M.	5.60	8.41	9.37
Return on Equity %	14.92	13.80	14.01	10.66	N.M.	15.35	25.28	31.67
EBITDA Margin %	N.M.	N.M.	0.35	0.54	N.M.	3.99	3.72	6.93
Net Margin %	26.21	28.95	3.46	2.40	N.M.	4.77	12.45	4.87
Asset Turnover	0.52	0.20	1.29	1.28	1.13	1.18	0.68	1.93
Current Ratio	3.97	3.28	1.72	1.88	1.83	1.94	2.14	1.54
Debt to Equity	0.15	0.19	0.55	0.80	0.91	0.51	0.48	0.22
Price Range	88.85-31.90	88.85-31.90	97.55-42.20	62.37-40.48	63.56-47.69	66.35-48.54	60.69-31.20	43.53-20.73
P/E Ratio	18.24-6.55	20.15-7.23	22.58-9.77	19.93-12.93	...	12.13-8.87	4.70-2.41	2.26-1.08
Average Yield %	1.54	1.51	1.70	1.99	1.87	1.72	13.03	6.67

Address: 5875 Landerbrook Drive, Suite 220, Cleveland, OH 44124-4069 Telephone: 440-229-5151	Web Site: www.nacco.com Officers: J. C. Butler - Senior Vice President, Vice President, Chief Administrative Officer, Treasurer, President, Chief Executive Officer Lauren E. Miller - Vice President	Auditors: Ernst & Young LLP Investor Contact: 440-229-5130 Transfer Agents: Computershare, Canton, MA

NATIONAL FUEL GAS CO. (NJ)

Exchange	Symbol	Price	52Wk Range	Yield	P/E	Div Acheiver
NYS	NFG	$52.96 (6/29/2018)	59.84-49.10	3.21	11.56	46 Years

*7 Year Price Score 75.59   *NYSE Composite Index=100   *12 Month Price Score 93.51

Interim Earnings (Per Share)

Qtr.	Dec	Mar	Jun	Sep
2014-15	1.00	0.20	(3.44)	(2.25)
2015-16	(2.23)	(1.74)	0.10	0.44
2016-17	1.04	1.04	0.69	0.53
2017-18	2.30	1.06	...	...

Interim Dividends (Per Share)

Amt	Decl	Ex	Rec	Pay
0.415Q	09/14/2017	09/28/2017	09/29/2017	10/13/2017
0.415Q	12/07/2017	12/28/2017	12/29/2017	01/12/2018
0.415Q	03/08/2018	03/28/2018	03/29/2018	04/13/2018
0.425Q	06/14/2018	06/28/2018	06/29/2018	07/13/2018

Indicated Div: $1.70 (Div. Reinv. Plan)

Valuation Analysis

		Institutional Holding	
Forecast EPS	$3.26	No of Institutions	
	(06/11/2018)	559	
Market Cap	$4.5 Billion	Shares	
Book Value	$1.9 Billion	74,621,584	
Price/Book	2.37	% Held	
Price/Sales	2.85	63.54	

Business Summary: Gas Utilities (MIC: 3.3.1 SIC: 4924 NAIC: 221210)

National Fuel Gas is a holding company. Co. operates five segments: Exploration and Production, which is engaged in the exploration for, and the development and production of, natural gas and oil reserves; Pipeline and Storage, which provides interstate natural gas transportation and storage services; Gathering, which builds, owns and operates natural gas processing and pipeline gathering facilities; Utility, which sells natural gas or provides natural gas transportation services; and Energy Marketing, which markets natural gas. At Sept 30 2017, Co. had U.S. proved developed and undeveloped reserves of 30,207 thousand barrels of oil and 1,973,120 million cubic feet of natural gas.

Recent Developments: For the quarter ended Mar 31 2018, net income increased 2.9% to US$91.8 million from US$89.3 million in the year-earlier quarter. Revenues were US$540.9 million, up 3.6% from US$522.1 million the year before. Operating income was US$156.7 million versus US$170.0 million in the prior-year quarter, a decrease of 7.8%. Direct operating expenses rose 10.2% to US$300.2 million from US$272.6 million in the comparable period the year before. Indirect operating expenses increased 5.6% to US$84.0 million from US$79.5 million in the equivalent prior-year period.

Prospects: Our evaluation of National Fuel Gas Co. as of Jan. 21, 2018 is the result of our systematic analysis on three basic characteristics: earnings strength, relative valuation, and recent stock price movement. The company has generated a negative trend in earnings per share over the past 5 quarters and while recent estimates for the company have been raised by analysts, NFG has posted better than expected results. Based on operating earnings yield, the company is undervalued when compared to all of the companies in our coverage universe. Share price changes over the past year indicates that NFG will perform in line with the market over the near term.

Financial Data

(US$ in Thousands)	6 Mos	3 Mos	09/30/2017	09/30/2016	09/30/2015	09/30/2014	09/30/2013	09/30/2012
Earnings Per Share	4.58	4.56	3.30	(3.43)	(4.50)	3.52	3.08	2.63
Cash Flow Per Share	7.22	7.41	8.02	6.92	10.11	10.84	8.84	7.93
Tang Book Value Per Share	22.28	21.62	19.85	17.88	23.88	28.58	26.17	23.46
Dividends Per Share	1.660	1.650	1.640	1.600	1.560	1.520	1.480	1.440
Dividend Payout %	36.24	36.18	49.70	...	...	43.18	48.05	54.75
Income Statement								
Total Revenue	960,561	419,655	1,579,881	1,452,416	1,760,913	2,113,081	1,829,551	1,626,853
EBITDA	418,175	199,547	784,083	(157,281)	(266,856)	962,915	849,295	724,712
Depn & Amortn	116,985	55,830	224,195	249,417	336,158	383,781	326,760	271,530
Income Before Taxes	247,494	117,377	444,164	(523,507)	(698,563)	489,027	432,759	370,631
Income Taxes	(43,007)	(81,277)	160,682	(232,549)	(319,136)	189,614	172,758	150,554
Net Income	290,501	198,654	283,482	(290,958)	(379,427)	299,413	260,001	220,077
Average Shares	86,323	86,325	86,021	84,847	84,387	84,952	84,341	83,739
Balance Sheet								
Current Assets	592,993	521,552	818,280	413,031	513,001	377,332	448,677	355,576
Total Assets	5,914,573	5,791,932	6,103,320	5,636,387	6,702,139	6,739,597	6,218,347	5,935,142
Current Liabilities	379,895	365,288	646,039	303,737	446,140	490,576	302,171	734,479
Long-Term Obligations	2,085,012	2,084,465	2,083,681	2,086,252	2,084,009	1,649,000	1,649,000	1,149,000
Total Liabilities	3,995,386	3,932,009	4,399,585	4,109,383	4,676,699	4,328,914	4,023,618	3,975,047
Stockholders' Equity	1,919,187	1,859,923	1,703,735	1,527,004	2,025,440	2,410,683	2,194,729	1,960,095
Shares Outstanding	85,881	85,760	85,543	85,118	84,594	84,157	83,661	83,330
Statistical Record								
Return on Assets %	6.75	6.87	4.83	N.M.	N.M.	4.62	4.28	3.91
Return on Equity %	22.17	22.94	17.55	N.M.	N.M.	13.00	12.52	11.40
EBITDA Margin %	43.53	47.55	49.63	N.M.	N.M.	45.57	46.42	44.55
Net Margin %	30.24	47.34	17.94	N.M.	N.M.	14.17	14.21	13.53
Asset Turnover	0.27	0.28	0.27	0.23	0.26	0.33	0.30	0.29
Current Ratio	1.56	1.43	1.27	1.36	1.15	0.77	1.48	0.48
Debt to Equity	1.09	1.12	1.22	1.37	1.03	0.68	0.75	0.59
Price Range	60.83-49.10	60.91-53.32	60.91-50.68	59.45-37.90	71.90-48.82	78.30-65.45	68.76-48.69	63.58-42.17
P/E Ratio	13.28-10.72	13.36-11.69	18.46-15.36	...	...	22.24-18.59	22.32-15.81	24.17-16.03
Average Yield %	2.97	2.87	2.88	3.13	2.49	2.10	2.52	2.85

Address: 6363 Main Street,	Web Site: www.nationalfuelgas.com	Auditors: PricewaterhouseCoopers LLP
Williamsville, NY 14221	Officers: David F. Smith - Chairman, Chief Executive	Investor Contact: 716-857-6987
Telephone: 716-857-7000	Officer Ronald J. Tanski - President, Chief Operating	Transfer Agents: Wells Fargo
	Officer, Chief Executive Officer	Shareowner Services, Saint Paul, MN

NATIONAL HEALTH INVESTORS, INC.

Exchange	Symbol	Price	52Wk Range	Yield	P/E	Div Acheiver
NYS	NHI	$73.68 (6/29/2018)	80.81-63.33	5.43	19.97	15 Years

*7 Year Price Score 93.63 *NYSE Composite Index=100 *12 Month Price Score 97.28

Interim Earnings (Per Share)

Qtr.	Mar	Jun	Sep	Dec
2015	0.79	0.83	0.89	1.44
2016	0.85	1.16	0.83	1.03
2017	1.10	0.93	0.94	0.90
2018	0.92	...	...	...

Interim Dividends (Per Share)

Amt	Decl	Ex	Rec	Pay
0.95Q	08/09/2017	09/28/2017	09/29/2017	11/10/2017
0.95Q	11/08/2017	12/28/2017	12/29/2017	01/31/2018
1.00Q	02/16/2018	03/28/2018	03/30/2018	05/10/2018
1.00Q	05/08/2018	06/28/2018	06/29/2018	08/10/2018

Indicated Div: $4.00

Valuation Analysis

		Institutional Holding	
Forecast EPS	$3.83	No of Institutions	
	(06/05/2018)	320	
Market Cap	$3.1 Billion	Shares	
Book Value	$1.3 Billion	37,380,344	
Price/Book	2.32	% Held	
Price/Sales	10.74	68.67	

Business Summary: REITs (MIC: 5.3.1 SIC: 6798 NAIC: 525930)

National Health Investors is a real estate investment trust which focuses on sale-leaseback, joint-venture, mortgage and mezzanine financing of senior housing and medical investments. Co.'s portfolio consists of investments in independent living facilities, assisted living facilities, entrance-fee communities, senior living campuses, skilled nursing facilities, specialty hospitals and medical office buildings. At Dec 31 2017, Co. had investments in real estate, mortgage and other notes receivable involving 218 facilities located in 32 states. These investments involve senior housing properties, skilled nursing facilities, hospitals, medical office buildings and other notes receivable.

Recent Developments: For the quarter ended Mar 31 2018, net income decreased 13.1% to US$38.4 million from US$44.2 million in the year-earlier quarter. Revenues were US$72.7 million, up 9.6% from US$66.4 million the year before. Revenues from property income rose 9.7% to US$69.3 million from US$63.1 million in the corresponding quarter a year earlier.

Prospects: Our evaluation of National Health Investors Inc. as of Jan. 21, 2018 is the result of our systematic analysis on three basic characteristics: earnings strength, relative valuation, and recent stock price movement. The company has enjoyed a very positive trend in earnings per share over the past 5 quarters. Because the company lacks sufficient analyst estimate data, we place greater weight on the historical EPS trend as the measure of earnings strength. Based on operating earnings yield, the company is undervalued when compared to all of the companies in our coverage universe. Share price changes over the past year indicates that NHI will perform very well over the near term.

Financial Data

(US$ in Thousands)	3 Mos	12/31/2017	12/31/2016	12/31/2015	12/31/2014	12/31/2013	12/31/2012	12/31/2011
Earnings Per Share	3.69	3.87	3.87	3.95	3.04	3.74	3.26	2.92
Cash Flow Per Share	4.75	4.83	4.53	4.37	3.78	3.67	3.09	2.77
Tang Book Value Per Share	31.78	31.83	30.36	29.52	27.74	23.19	16.41	15.98
Dividends Per Share	3.850	3.800	3.600	3.400	3.080	3.120	2.640	2.715
Dividend Payout %	104.34	98.19	93.02	86.08	101.32	83.42	80.98	92.98
Income Statement								
Total Revenue	72,746	278,659	248,500	228,988	177,509	117,828	96,953	82,702
EBITDA	56,347	226,538	214,244	204,537	141,201	99,832	91,599	88,445
Depn & Amortn	17,915	67,173	59,565	53,163	38,078	20,658	16,981	11,992
Income Before Taxes	38,432	159,365	154,679	151,374	103,123	79,174	74,618	72,760
Income Taxes	...	...	749	(707)	...	...	...	...
Net Income	38,432	159,365	151,540	148,862	101,609	106,183	90,731	81,132
Average Shares	41,576	41,151	39,155	37,644	33,416	28,397	27,838	27,792
Balance Sheet								
Current Assets	114,239	100,422	77,350	73,063	38,441	30,003	21,542	25,776
Total Assets	2,559,428	2,545,821	2,403,633	2,146,349	1,982,960	1,455,820	705,981	579,563
Current Liabilities	79,321	56,932	55,866	52,784	47,582	34,904	33,350	37,105
Long-Term Obligations	1,160,226	1,145,497	1,115,981	926,257	862,726	617,080	203,250	97,300
Total Liabilities	1,239,547	1,223,704	1,194,043	1,013,057	943,035	689,274	248,799	136,078
Stockholders' Equity	1,319,881	1,322,117	1,209,590	1,133,292	1,039,925	766,546	457,182	443,485
Shares Outstanding	41,532	41,532	39,847	38,396	37,485	33,051	27,857	27,751
Statistical Record								
Return on Assets %	6.05	6.44	6.64	7.21	5.91	9.82	14.08	14.90
Return on Equity %	11.78	12.59	12.90	13.70	11.25	17.35	20.09	18.31
EBITDA Margin %	77.46	81.30	86.21	89.32	79.55	84.73	94.48	106.94
Net Margin %	52.83	57.19	60.98	65.01	57.24	90.12	93.58	98.10
Asset Turnover	0.11	0.11	0.11	0.11	0.10	0.11	0.15	0.15
Current Ratio	1.44	1.76	1.38	1.38	0.81	0.86	0.65	0.69
Debt to Equity	0.88	0.87	0.92	0.82	0.83	0.81	0.44	0.22
Price Range	80.81-63.33	80.81-69.30	82.39-55.73	76.46-54.10	71.19-55.13	72.30-53.28	57.14-43.70	49.19-38.03
P/E Ratio	21.90-17.16	20.88-17.91	21.29-14.40	19.36-13.70	23.42-18.13	19.33-14.25	17.53-13.40	16.85-13.02
Average Yield %	5.13	5.04	5.08	5.25	4.94	5.04	5.18	6.04

Address: 222 Robert Rose Drive, Murfreesboro, TN 37129 Telephone: 615-890-9100	Web Site: www.nhireit.com Officers: W. Andrew Adams - Chairman, Chief Executive Officer, Acting Chief Financial Officer Eric Mendelsohn - Interim President, Interim Chief Executive Officer, President, Chief Executive Officer	Auditors: BDO USA, LLP Investor Contact: 615-890-9100 Transfer Agents: Computershare Trust Company, N.A., Providence, RI

NATIONAL OILWELL VARCO INC

Exchange	Symbol	Price	52Wk Range	Yield	P/E
NYS	NOV	$43.40 (6/29/2018)	44.11-29.94	0.46	N/A

*7 Year Price Score 54.57 *NYSE Composite Index=100 *12 Month Price Score 114.52

Interim Earnings (Per Share)

Qtr.	Mar	Jun	Sep	Dec
2015	0.76	0.74	0.41	(3.91)
2016	(0.32)	(0.58)	(3.62)	(1.88)
2017	(0.32)	(0.20)	(0.07)	(0.04)
2018	(0.18)	...	...	...

Interim Dividends (Per Share)

Amt	Decl	Ex	Rec	Pay
0.05Q	08/17/2017	09/14/2017	09/15/2017	09/29/2017
0.05Q	11/16/2017	12/07/2017	12/08/2017	12/22/2017
0.05Q	02/23/2018	03/15/2018	03/16/2018	03/30/2018
0.05Q	05/11/2018	06/14/2018	06/15/2018	06/29/2018

Indicated Div: $0.20 (Div. Reinv. Plan)

Valuation Analysis   **Institutional Holding**

Forecast EPS	$0.09 (06/14/2018)	No of Institutions 997
Market Cap	$16.6 Billion	Shares
Book Value	$14.1 Billion	428,712,064
Price/Book	1.18	% Held
Price/Sales	2.25	86.41

Business Summary: Equipment & Services (MIC: 9.1.3 SIC: 3533 NAIC: 333132)

National Oilwell Varco is an oilfield equipment manufacturer and technology provider. Co. operates in four segments: Rig Systems, which designs, manufactures and sells land rigs, offshore drilling equipment packages, and drilling rig components; Rig Aftermarket, which provides aftermarket products and services to support land and offshore rigs, and drilling rig components; Wellbore Technologies, which designs, manufactures, rents, and sells equipment used to perform drilling operations; and Completion and Production Solutions, which designs, manufactures, and sells equipment and technologies for hydraulic fracture stimulation, well intervention, onshore production and offshore production.

Recent Developments: For the quarter ended Mar 31 2018, net loss amounted to US$66.0 million versus a net loss of US$120.0 million in the year-earlier quarter. Revenues were US$1.80 billion, up 3.1% from US$1.74 billion the year before. Operating loss was US$1.0 million versus a loss of US$97.0 million in the prior-year quarter. Direct operating expenses declined 1.6% to US$1.51 billion from US$1.53 billion in the comparable period the year before. Indirect operating expenses decreased 5.9% to US$288.0 million from US$306.0 million in the equivalent prior-year period.

Prospects: Our evaluation of National-Oilwell Inc. as of Jan. 21, 2018 is the result of our systematic analysis on three basic characteristics: earnings strength, relative valuation, and recent stock price movement. The company has produced a positive trend in earnings per share over the past 5 quarters. Because the company lacks sufficient analyst estimate data, we place greater weight on the historical EPS trend as the measure of earnings strength. Based on operating earnings yield, the company is overvalued when compared to all of the companies in our coverage universe. Share price changes over the past year indicates that NOV will perform very poorly over the near term.

Financial Data

(US$ in Thousands)	3 Mos	12/31/2017	12/31/2016	12/31/2015	12/31/2014	12/31/2013	12/31/2012	12/31/2011
Earnings Per Share	(0.49)	(0.63)	(6.41)	(1.99)	5.82	5.44	5.83	4.70
Cash Flow Per Share	1.57	2.21	2.55	3.44	6.11	7.97	1.45	5.08
Tang Book Value Per Share	12.18	12.01	11.47	14.78	18.40	18.97	19.50	17.45
Dividends Per Share	0.200	0.200	0.610	1.840	1.640	0.910	0.490	0.450
Dividend Payout %	...	...	...	...	28.18	16.73	8.40	9.57
Income Statement								
Total Revenue	1,795,000	7,304,000	7,251,000	14,757,000	21,440,000	22,869,000	20,041,000	14,658,000
EBITDA	125,000	49,000	(2,142,000)	(122,000)	3,936,000	3,774,000	3,809,000	3,177,000
Depn & Amortn	173,000	359,000	370,000	391,000	413,000	392,000	323,000	279,000
Income Before Taxes	(65,000)	(387,000)	(2,602,000)	(602,000)	3,436,000	3,283,000	3,447,000	2,876,000
Income Taxes	3,000	(156,000)	(207,000)	178,000	1,039,000	1,018,000	1,022,000	937,000
Net Income	(68,000)	(237,000)	(2,412,000)	(769,000)	2,502,000	2,327,000	2,491,000	1,994,000
Average Shares	377,000	377,000	376,000	387,000	430,000	428,000	427,000	424,000
Balance Sheet								
Current Assets	7,186,000	7,217,000	7,876,000	11,801,000	16,162,000	16,423,000	15,678,000	12,110,000
Total Assets	20,010,000	20,206,000	21,140,000	26,725,000	33,562,000	34,812,000	31,484,000	25,515,000
Current Liabilities	2,132,000	2,354,000	3,047,000	4,249,000	7,374,000	6,678,000	5,649,000	5,416,000
Long-Term Obligations	2,707,000	2,706,000	2,708,000	3,928,000	3,014,000	3,149,000	3,148,000	159,000
Total Liabilities	5,928,000	6,112,000	7,200,000	10,342,000	12,870,000	12,582,000	11,245,000	7,896,000
Stockholders' Equity	14,082,000	14,094,000	13,940,000	16,383,000	20,692,000	22,230,000	20,239,000	17,619,000
Shares Outstanding	381,900	380,104	378,637	375,764	418,977	428,433	426,928	423,390
Statistical Record								
Return on Assets %	N.M.	N.M.	N.M.	N.M.	7.32	7.02	8.72	8.21
Return on Equity %	N.M.	N.M.	N.M.	N.M.	11.66	10.96	13.12	11.95
EBITDA Margin %	6.96	0.67	N.M.	N.M.	18.36	16.50	19.01	21.67
Net Margin %	N.M.	N.M.	N.M.	N.M.	11.67	10.18	12.43	13.60
Asset Turnover	0.36	0.35	0.30	0.49	0.63	0.69	0.70	0.60
Current Ratio	3.37	3.07	2.58	2.78	2.19	2.46	2.78	2.24
Debt to Equity	0.19	0.19	0.19	0.24	0.15	0.14	0.16	0.01
Price Range	40.09-29.94	41.74-29.94	40.32-26.34	65.53-33.27	86.43-61.55	75.97-57.80	78.57-54.07	75.08-45.27
P/E Ratio	...	...	...	...	14.85-10.58	13.97-10.63	13.48-9.27	15.97-9.63
Average Yield %	0.58	0.57	1.84	4.01	2.22	1.38	0.73	0.70

Address: 7909 Parkwood Circle Drive, Houston, TX 77036-6565 Telephone: 713-346-7500	Web Site: www.nov.com Officers: Clay C. Williams - Chairman, President, Chief Executive Officer, Chief Operating Officer, Chief Financial Officer, Executive Vice President, Senior Vice President Craig L. Weinstock - Senior Vice President, Secretary, General Counsel	Auditors: Ernst & Young LLP Investor Contact: 713-346-7500 Transfer Agents: American Stock Transfer & Trust Company, New York, NY

NATIONAL RETAIL PROPERTIES INC

Exchange	Symbol	Price	52Wk Range	Yield	P/E	Div Acheiver
NYS	NNN	$43.96 (6/29/2018)	43.98-36.52	4.55	25.56	28 Years

*7 Year Price Score 88.12   *NYSE Composite Index=100   *12 Month Price Score 100.69

Interim Earnings (Per Share)

Qtr.	Mar	Jun	Sep	Dec
2015	0.34	0.28	0.34	0.24
2016	0.44	0.30	0.29	0.36
2017	0.35	0.33	0.35	0.42
2018	0.62	...	...	...

Interim Dividends (Per Share)

Amt	Decl	Ex	Rec	Pay
0.475Q	10/16/2017	10/30/2017	10/31/2017	11/15/2017
0.475Q	01/16/2018	01/30/2018	01/31/2018	02/15/2018
0.475Q	04/16/2018	04/27/2018	04/30/2018	05/15/2018
0.50Q	07/16/2018	07/30/2018	07/31/2018	08/15/2018

Indicated Div: $2.00 (Div. Reinv. Plan)

Valuation Analysis / **Institutional Holding**

Forecast EPS	$2.12	No of Institutions
	(05/27/2018)	477
Market Cap	$6.8 Billion	Shares
Book Value	$3.9 Billion	185,345,440
Price/Book	1.75	% Held
Price/Sales	11.34	N/A

Business Summary: REITs (MIC: 5.3.1 SIC: 6798 NAIC: 525930)

National Retail Properties is a real estate investment trust. Co.'s assets primarily include: real estate assets, mortgages and notes receivable. Co. acquires, owns, invests in and develops properties that are leased primarily to retail tenants under long-term net leases and are primarily held for investment. Co. owned 2,764 properties located in 48 states as of Dec 31 2017.

Recent Developments: For the quarter ended Mar 31 2018, net income increased 40.2% to US$103.3 million from US$73.6 million in the year-earlier quarter. Revenues were US$152.8 million, up 8.1% from US$141.4 million the year before. Revenues from property income rose 8.2% to US$152.8 million from US$141.2 million in the corresponding quarter a year earlier.

Prospects: Our evaluation of National Retail Properties Inc. as of Jan. 21, 2018 is the result of our systematic analysis on three basic characteristics: earnings strength, relative valuation, and recent stock price movement. The company has produced a positive trend in earnings per share over the past 5 quarters. Because the company lacks sufficient analyst estimate data, we place greater weight on the historical EPS trend as the measure of earnings strength. Based on operating earnings yield, the company is about fairly valued when compared to all of the companies in our coverage universe. Share price changes over the past year indicates that NNN will perform well over the near term.

Financial Data
(US$ in Thousands)

	3 Mos	12/31/2017	12/31/2016	12/31/2015	12/31/2014	12/31/2013	12/31/2012	12/31/2011
Earnings Per Share	1.72	1.45	1.38	1.20	1.24	1.10	1.11	0.96
Cash Flow Per Share	2.84	2.83	2.87	2.55	2.39	2.32	2.13	2.08
Tang Book Value Per Share	21.01	20.89	20.37	19.62	18.99	18.05	18.01	18.24
Dividends Per Share	1.880	1.860	1.780	1.710	1.650	1.600	1.560	1.530
Dividend Payout %	109.30	128.28	128.99	142.50	133.06	145.45	140.54	159.38
Income Statement								
Total Revenue	152,836	584,933	533,647	482,914	434,847	392,327	331,752	265,793
EBITDA	95,114	518,360	464,742	428,442	386,076	345,552	280,699	229,444
Depn & Amortn	3,844	180,857	156,236	140,714	121,221	106,304	83,096	65,017
Income Before Taxes	64,693	228,716	212,324	197,829	179,702	155,458	117,333	91,093
Income Taxes	...	...	...	10,318	(75)	618	(7,086)	779
Net Income	103,280	264,973	239,500	197,836	190,601	160,145	142,015	92,325
Average Shares	153,393	149,432	144,660	134,489	124,710	119,864	109,117	88,837
Balance Sheet								
Current Assets	34,226	31,597	323,059	43,133	39,276	30,389	30,646	29,418
Total Assets	6,660,656	6,560,534	6,334,151	5,460,044	4,926,714	4,454,523	3,988,026	3,434,429
Current Liabilities	212,779	140,811	19,665	20,113	17,396	63,542	191,727	80,708
Long-Term Obligations	2,460,542	2,459,707	2,311,689	1,975,944	1,741,054	1,523,659	1,412,764	1,273,509
Total Liabilities	2,796,476	2,719,941	2,417,352	2,117,910	1,844,199	1,677,478	1,691,741	1,431,931
Stockholders' Equity	3,864,180	3,840,593	3,916,799	3,342,134	3,082,515	2,777,045	2,296,285	2,002,498
Shares Outstanding	153,848	153,577	147,149	141,007	132,010	121,991	111,554	104,754
Statistical Record								
Return on Assets %	4.61	4.11	4.05	3.81	4.06	3.79	3.82	3.00
Return on Equity %	7.82	6.83	6.58	6.16	6.51	6.31	6.59	5.23
EBITDA Margin %	62.23	88.62	87.09	88.72	88.78	88.08	84.61	86.32
Net Margin %	67.58	45.30	44.88	40.97	43.83	40.82	42.81	34.74
Asset Turnover	0.09	0.09	0.09	0.09	0.09	0.09	0.09	0.09
Current Ratio	0.16	0.22	16.43	2.14	2.26	0.48	0.16	0.36
Debt to Equity	0.64	0.64	0.59	0.59	0.56	0.55	0.62	0.64
Price Range	45.53-36.52	46.13-36.72	53.46-39.00	44.24-33.99	40.34-30.33	41.89-30.09	32.25-26.10	27.30-22.92
P/E Ratio	26.47-21.23	31.81-25.32	38.74-28.26	36.87-28.33	32.53-24.46	38.08-27.35	29.05-23.51	28.44-23.88
Average Yield %	4.63	4.44	3.85	4.44	4.62	4.68	5.42	5.98

Address: 450 South Orange Avenue, Suite 900, Orlando, FL 32801 **Telephone:** 407-265-7348 **Fax:** 407-423-2894	**Web Site:** www.nnnreit.com **Officers:** Craig Macnab - Chairman, Chief Executive Officer Julian E. Whitehurst - President, Chief Executive Officer, Chief Operating Officer	**Auditors:** Ernst & Young LLP **Investor Contact:** 407-650-1228 **Transfer Agents:** American Stock Transfer & Trust Company, Brooklyn, NY

NAVISTAR INTERNATIONAL CORP.

Exchange	Symbol	Price	52Wk Range	Yield	P/E
NYS	NAV	$40.72 (6/29/2018)	47.45-26.23	N/A	24.53

*7 Year Price Score 104.22 *NYSE Composite Index=100 *12 Month Price Score 99.91

TRADING VOLUME (thousand shares)

Interim Earnings (Per Share)

Qtr.	Jan	Apr	Jul	Oct
2014-15	(0.52)	(0.78)	(0.34)	(0.61)
2015-16	(0.40)	0.05	(0.42)	(0.42)
2016-17	(0.76)	(0.86)	0.38	1.47
2017-18	(0.74)	0.55	...	...

Interim Dividends (Per Share)

No Dividends Paid

Valuation Analysis | Institutional Holding

Valuation Analysis		Institutional Holding	
Forecast EPS	$2.13	No of Institutions	
	(06/13/2018)	308	
Market Cap	$4.0 Billion	Shares	
Book Value	N/A	94,393,560	
Price/Book	N/A	% Held	
Price/Sales	0.44	100.88	

Business Summary: Autos- Manufacturing (MIC: 1.8.1 SIC: 3711 NAIC: 336211)
Navistar International, manufactures International® brand commercial and military trucks, diesel engines, IC Bus™ brand school and commercial buses, and provides service parts as well as retail, wholesale, and lease financing services for its trucks and parts. Co. operates four segments: Truck, which provides Class 4 through 8 trucks and buses; Parts, and other standard truck, trailer, and engine service parts; Global Operations, consisting of engine and truck operations in Brazil; and Financial Services.

Recent Developments: For the quarter ended Apr 30 2018, net income amounted to US$61.0 million versus a net loss of US$75.0 million in the year-earlier quarter. Revenues were US$2.42 billion, up 15.6% from US$2.10 billion the year before. Direct operating expenses rose 11.9% to US$1.99 billion from US$1.78 billion in the comparable period the year before. Indirect operating expenses decreased 6.1% to US$367.0 million from US$391.0 million in the equivalent prior-year period.

Prospects: Our evaluation of Navistar International Corp. as of Jan. 21, 2018 is the result of our systematic analysis on three basic characteristics: earnings strength, relative valuation, and recent stock price movement. The company has produced a positive trend in earnings per share over the past 5 quarters and while recent estimates for the company have been raised by analysts, NAV has posted better than expected results. Based on operating earnings yield, the company is overvalued when compared to all of the companies in our coverage universe. Share price changes over the past year indicates that NAV will perform very well over the near term.

Financial Data
(US$ in Millions)

	6 Mos	3 Mos	10/31/2017	10/31/2016	10/31/2015	10/31/2014	10/31/2013	10/31/2012
Earnings Per Share	1.66	0.25	0.32	(1.19)	(2.25)	(7.60)	(11.17)	(43.56)
Cash Flow Per Share	1.20	0.11	1.17	3.26	0.56	(4.13)	1.24	8.80
Income Statement								
Total Revenue	4,327	1,905	8,570	8,111	10,140	10,806	10,775	12,948
EBITDA	299	*91	482	368	274	63	(269)	(596)
Depn & Amortn	124	63	73	79	76	314	395	298
Income Before Taxes	17	(51)	58	(38)	(109)	(565)	(985)	(1,153)
Income Taxes	22	15	10	33	51	26	(171)	1,780
Net Income	(18)	(73)	30	(97)	(184)	(619)	(898)	(3,010)
Average Shares	99	98	93	81	81	81	80	69
Balance Sheet								
Current Assets	4,517	3,958	4,160	3,759	4,622	5,013	5,459	5,837
Total Assets	6,487	5,969	6,135	5,653	6,692	7,443	8,315	9,102
Current Liabilities	4,061	3,253	3,645	3,203	3,788	4,231	4,261	4,353
Long-Term Obligations	3,846	4,168	3,889	3,997	4,188	3,929	3,922	3,566
Total Liabilities	11,017	10,556	10,713	10,951	11,859	12,095	11,960	12,407
Stockholders' Equity	(4,530)	(4,587)	(4,578)	(5,298)	(5,167)	(4,652)	(3,645)	(3,305)
Shares Outstanding	98	98	98	81	81	81	80	79
Statistical Record								
Return on Assets %	2.48	0.33	0.51	N.M.	N.M.	N.M.	N.M.	N.M.
EBITDA Margin %	6.91	4.78	5.62	4.54	2.70	0.58	N.M.	N.M.
Net Margin %	N.M.	N.M.	0.35	N.M.	N.M.	N.M.	N.M.	N.M.
Asset Turnover	1.47	1.55	1.45	1.31	1.43	1.37	1.24	1.21
Current Ratio	1.11	1.22	1.14	1.17	1.22	1.18	1.28	1.34
Price Range	47.45-25.08	47.45-22.89	44.68-22.30	23.69-6.23	37.76-11.36	40.90-29.49	39.71-18.75	47.42-18.51
P/E Ratio	28.58-15.11	189.80-91.56	139.63-69.69	...	...	...	...	...

Address: 2701 Navistar Drive, Lisle, IL 60532	**Web Site:** www.navistar.com
Telephone: 331-332-5000	**Officers:** Troy A. Clarke - Chairman, President, Chief Executive Officer, Chief Operating Officer, Division Officer Persio V. Lisboa - Executive Vice President, Chief Operating Officer

Auditors: KPMG LLP
Investor Contact: 331-332-2143
Transfer Agents: Computershare Investor Services, Jersey City, NJ

NCR CORP

Exchange	Symbol	Price	52Wk Range	Yield	P/E
NYS	NCR	$29.98 (6/29/2018)	42.98-27.10	N/A	28.28

*7 Year Price Score 90.93 *NYSE Composite Index=100 *12 Month Price Score 87.80

Interim Earnings (Per Share)

Qtr.	Mar	Jun	Sep	Dec
2015	0.23	(2.03)	0.57	0.13
2016	0.16	0.49	0.68	0.35
2017	(0.14)	0.67	0.77	(0.44)
2018	0.06	...	...	...

Interim Dividends (Per Share)

No Dividends Paid

Valuation Analysis		Institutional Holding	
Forecast EPS	$3.30	No of Institutions	
	(06/12/2018)	603	
Market Cap	$3.5 Billion	Shares	
Book Value	$1.4 Billion	144,362,672	
Price/Book	2.50	% Held	
Price/Sales	0.54	92.22	

Business Summary: Computer Hardware & Equipment (MIC: 6.2.1 SIC: 3578 NAIC: 334119)

NCR is a provider of omni-channel technology solutions that help businesses connect, interact and transact with their customers. Co.'s offerings include automated teller machines, point of sale terminals and devices, self-service kiosks, omni-channel platform software and other software applications, and a complete suite of consulting, implementation, maintenance and managed services. Co. also resell third-party networking products and provide related service offerings in the telecommunications and technology sectors. Co. provides solutions for customers of varying sizes in a range of industries such as financial services, retail, hospitality, travel and telecommunications and technology.

Recent Developments: For the quarter ended Mar 31 2018, income from continuing operations decreased 1.8% to US$56.0 million from US$57.0 million in the year-earlier quarter. Net income decreased 63.2% to US$21.0 million from US$57.0 million in the year-earlier quarter. Revenues were US$1.52 billion, up 2.6% from US$1.48 billion the year before. Operating income was US$109.0 million versus US$115.0 million in the prior-year quarter, a decrease of 5.2%. Direct operating expenses rose 2.9% to US$1.10 billion from US$1.07 billion in the comparable period the year before. Indirect operating expenses increased 4.7% to US$311.0 million from US$297.0 million in the equivalent prior-year period.

Prospects: Our evaluation of NCR Corp. as of Jan. 21, 2018 is the result of our systematic analysis on three basic characteristics: earnings strength, relative valuation, and recent stock price movement. The company has generated a negative trend in earnings per share over the past 5 quarters. However, while recent estimates for the company have been lowered by analysts, NCR has posted better than expected results. Based on operating earnings yield, the company is undervalued when compared to all of the companies in our coverage universe. Share price changes over the past year indicates that NCR will perform very poorly over the near term.

Financial Data

(US$ in Thousands)	3 Mos	12/31/2017	12/31/2016	12/31/2015	12/31/2014	12/31/2013	12/31/2012	12/31/2011
Earnings Per Share	1.06	0.97	1.71	(1.09)	1.12	2.62	0.89	0.33
Cash Flow Per Share	5.77	6.19	7.10	4.06	3.12	1.70	(1.13)	2.37
Income Statement								
Total Revenue	1,517,000	6,516,000	6,543,000	6,373,000	6,591,000	6,123,000	5,730,000	5,443,000
EBITDA	190,000	728,000	635,000	164,000	395,000	719,000	282,000	153,000
Depn & Amortn	86,000	86,000	90,000	91,000	83,000	68,000	64,000	96,000
Income Before Taxes	63,000	482,000	379,000	(95,000)	137,000	554,000	182,000	49,000
Income Taxes	7,000	242,000	92,000	55,000	(48,000)	98,000	42,000	...
Net Income	20,000	232,000	270,000	(178,000)	191,000	443,000	146,000	53,000
Average Shares	123,800	127,000	157,400	167,600	171,200	169,300	163,800	161,000
Balance Sheet								
Current Assets	2,791,000	2,830,000	2,757,000	2,549,000	3,088,000	4,339,000	3,406,000	2,515,000
Total Assets	7,641,000	7,654,000	7,673,000	7,635,000	8,607,000	8,108,000	6,371,000	5,591,000
Current Liabilities	1,844,000	1,889,000	1,965,000	1,781,000	2,070,000	1,881,000	1,742,000	1,565,000
Long-Term Obligations	3,038,000	2,939,000	3,001,000	3,239,000	3,472,000	3,320,000	1,891,000	852,000
Total Liabilities	6,220,000	6,125,000	6,131,000	6,117,000	6,736,000	6,339,000	5,124,000	4,792,000
Stockholders' Equity	1,421,000	1,529,000	1,542,000	1,518,000	1,871,000	1,769,000	1,247,000	799,000
Shares Outstanding	118,300	122,000	124,600	133,000	168,600	166,600	162,800	157,600
Statistical Record								
Return on Assets %	2.54	3.03	3.52	N.M.	2.29	6.12	2.43	1.07
Return on Equity %	14.30	15.11	17.60	N.M.	10.49	29.38	14.23	6.30
EBITDA Margin %	12.52	11.17	9.71	2.57	5.99	11.74	4.92	2.81
Net Margin %	1.32	3.56	4.13	N.M.	2.90	7.24	2.55	0.97
Asset Turnover	0.85	0.85	0.85	0.78	0.79	0.85	0.96	1.09
Current Ratio	1.51	1.50	1.40	1.43	1.49	2.31	1.96	1.61
Debt to Equity	2.14	1.92	1.95	2.13	1.86	1.88	1.52	1.07
Price Range	45.68-29.57	49.59-29.57	41.75-19.08	34.73-22.39	37.50-23.54	41.56-25.48	25.64-16.48	20.83-15.31
P/E Ratio	43.09-27.90	51.12-30.48	24.42-11.16	...	33.48-21.02	15.86-9.73	28.81-18.52	63.12-46.39

Address: 864 Spring Street NW, Atlanta, GA 30308
Telephone: 937-445-5000

Web Site: www.ncr.com
Officers: Frank R. Martire - Executive Chairman
Michael D. Hayford - President, Chief Executive Officer

Auditors: PricewaterhouseCoopers LLP
Investor Contact: 212-589-8569
Transfer Agents: Wells Fargo Shareowner Services, St. Paul, MN

NEW JERSEY RESOURCES CORP

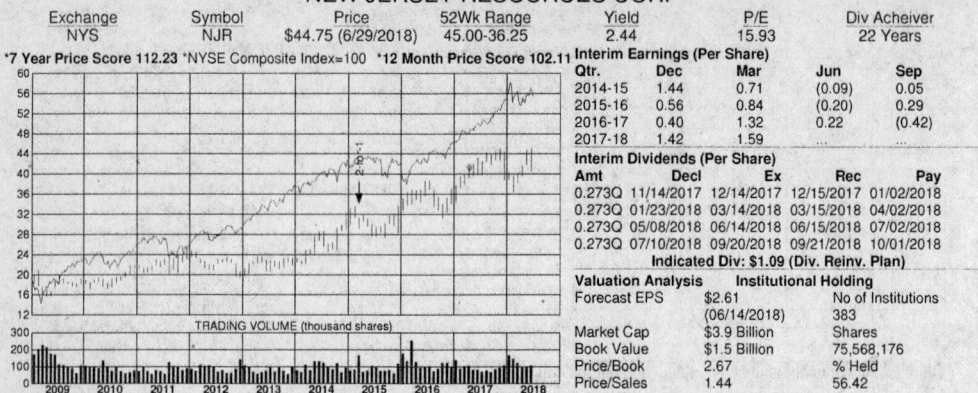

Exchange	Symbol	Price	52Wk Range	Yield	P/E	Div Acheiver
NYS	NJR	$44.75 (6/29/2018)	45.00-36.25	2.44	15.93	22 Years

*7 Year Price Score 112.23 *NYSE Composite Index=100 *12 Month Price Score 102.11

Interim Earnings (Per Share)

Qtr.	Dec	Mar	Jun	Sep
2014-15	1.44	0.71	(0.09)	0.05
2015-16	0.56	0.84	(0.20)	0.29
2016-17	0.40	1.32	0.22	(0.42)
2017-18	1.42	1.59	...	...

Interim Dividends (Per Share)

Amt	Decl	Ex	Rec	Pay
0.273Q	11/14/2017	12/14/2017	12/15/2017	01/02/2018
0.273Q	01/23/2018	03/14/2018	03/15/2018	04/02/2018
0.273Q	05/08/2018	06/14/2018	06/15/2018	07/02/2018
0.273Q	07/10/2018	09/20/2018	09/21/2018	10/01/2018

Indicated Div: $1.09 (Div. Reinv. Plan)

Valuation Analysis / **Institutional Holding**

Forecast EPS	$2.61
	(06/14/2018)
Market Cap	$3.9 Billion
Book Value	$1.5 Billion
Price/Book	2.67
Price/Sales	1.44

No of Institutions 383
Shares 75,568,176
% Held 56.42

Business Summary: Gas Utilities (MIC: 3.3.1 SIC: 4924 NAIC: 221210)

New Jersey Resources is an energy services holding company whose principal business is the distribution of natural gas through a regulated utility. Co.'s business segments are: Natural Gas Distribution, which consists of regulated natural gas services, off-system sales, capacity and storage management operations; Clean Energy Ventures, which consists of capital investments in clean energy projects; Energy Services, which consists of unregulated wholesale energy operations; and Midstream, which consists of investments in the midstream natural gas market, such as natural gas transportation and storage facilities.

Recent Developments: For the quarter ended Mar 31 2018, net income increased 22.3% to US$140.3 million from US$114.7 million in the year-earlier quarter. Revenues were US$1.02 billion, up 38.9% from $733.5 million the year before. Operating income was US$177.8 million versus US$139.7 million in the prior-year quarter, an increase of 27.3%. Direct operating expenses rose 43.9% to US$797.2 million from US$554.1 million in the comparable period the year before. Indirect operating expenses increased 10.5% to US$44.0 million from US$39.8 million in the equivalent prior-year period.

Prospects: Our evaluation of New Jersey Resources Corp. as of Jan. 21, 2018 is the result of our systematic analysis on three basic characteristics: earnings strength, relative valuation, and recent stock price movement. The company has suffered a very negative trend in earnings per share over the past 5 quarters and while recent estimates for the company have been raised by analysts, NJR has posted results that fell short of analysts expectations. Based on operating earnings yield, the company is undervalued when compared to all of the companies in our coverage universe. Share price changes over the past year indicates that NJR will perform well over the near term.

Financial Data

(US$ in Thousands)	6 Mos	3 Mos	09/30/2017	09/30/2016	09/30/2015	09/30/2014	09/30/2013	09/30/2012
Earnings Per Share	2.81	2.54	1.52	1.52	2.10	1.67	1.38	1.12
Cash Flow Per Share	4.44	3.11	2.87	1.66	4.55	4.24	1.37	0.61
Tang Book Value Per Share	16.48	14.98	13.81	13.55	12.94	11.45	10.57	9.78
Dividends Per Share	1.073	1.055	1.038	0.975	0.915	0.855	0.810	0.770
Dividend Payout %	38.17	41.54	68.26	64.14	43.57	51.20	58.91	69.06
Income Statement								
Total Revenue	1,724,348	705,305	2,268,617	1,880,905	2,733,987	3,738,145	3,198,068	2,248,923
EBITDA	279,855	85,563	263,281	249,431	316,395	261,483	211,324	152,461
Depn & Amortn	17,911	3,391	81,800	72,700	61,399	52,742	47,310	41,643
Income Before Taxes	238,241	70,267	136,595	145,687	227,275	183,278	140,035	89,974
Income Taxes	(19,267)	(50,168)	18,343	23,530	59,724	51,840	35,575	7,729
Net Income	263,965	123,699	132,065	131,672	180,960	141,970	114,809	92,879
Average Shares	87,989	87,347	87,144	86,731	86,265	84,922	83,628	83,264
Balance Sheet								
Current Assets	814,625	826,079	579,444	607,264	544,511	682,731	745,898	647,344
Total Assets	3,960,740	4,186,928	3,928,507	3,727,082	3,339,038	3,158,804	3,004,783	2,770,005
Current Liabilities	694,468	991,001	802,918	571,608	436,100	791,086	851,833	653,139
Long-Term Obligations	997,925	1,001,183	997,080	1,063,550	843,595	598,209	512,886	525,169
Total Liabilities	2,493,366	2,839,158	2,691,864	2,560,491	2,232,082	2,192,638	2,117,399	1,956,140
Stockholders' Equity	1,467,374	1,347,770	1,236,643	1,166,591	1,106,956	966,166	887,384	813,865
Shares Outstanding	87,656	87,475	86,555	86,086	85,531	84,356	83,923	83,239
Statistical Record								
Return on Assets %	6.30	5.43	3.45	3.72	5.57	4.61	3.98	3.42
Return on Equity %	17.90	17.44	10.99	11.55	17.46	15.32	13.50	11.65
EBITDA Margin %	16.23	12.13	11.61	13.26	11.57	6.99	6.61	6.78
Net Margin %	15.31	17.54	5.82	7.00	6.62	3.80	3.59	4.13
Asset Turnover	0.70	0.60	0.59	0.53	0.84	1.21	1.11	0.83
Current Ratio	1.17	0.83	0.72	1.06	1.25	0.86	0.88	0.99
Debt to Equity	0.68	0.74	0.81	0.91	0.76	0.62	0.58	0.65
Price Range	45.00-36.25	45.00-34.25	44.25-31.07	38.71-28.14	33.48-24.81	28.66-21.30	23.60-19.50	25.00-20.39
P/E Ratio	16.01-12.90	17.72-13.48	29.11-20.44	25.47-18.51	15.94-11.81	17.16-12.75	17.10-14.13	22.33-18.20
Average Yield %	2.60	2.57	2.68	2.85	3.10	3.50	3.72	3.38

Address: 1415 Wyckoff Road, Wall, NJ 07719	**Web Site:** www.njresources.com	**Auditors:** DELOITTE & TOUCHE LLP
Telephone: 732-938-1480	**Officers:** Laurence M. Downes - Chairman, President, Chief Executive Officer Stephen D. Westhoven - Executive Vice President, Chief Operating Officer	**Investor Contact:** 732-378-4967
		Transfer Agents: Wells Fargo Shareowner Services, St. Paul, MN

NEW RESIDENTIAL INVESTMENT CORP

Exchange	Symbol	Price	52Wk Range	Yield	P/E
NYS	NRZ	$17.49 (6/29/2018)	18.68-15.30	11.44	3.87

*7 Year Price Score N/A   *NYSE Composite Index=100   *12 Month Price Score 103.27

Interim Earnings (Per Share)

Qtr.	Mar	Jun	Sep	Dec
2015	0.25	0.37	0.24	0.47
2016	0.48	0.30	0.41	0.93
2017	0.42	1.04	0.73	0.94
2018	1.81	...	...	...

Interim Dividends (Per Share)

Amt	Decl	Ex	Rec	Pay
0.50Q	09/22/2017	09/29/2017	10/02/2017	10/27/2017
0.50Q	12/18/2017	12/28/2017	12/29/2017	01/30/2018
0.50Q	03/22/2018	03/29/2018	04/02/2018	04/27/2018
0.50Q	06/21/2018	06/29/2018	07/02/2018	07/27/2018

Indicated Div: $2.00

Valuation Analysis / **Institutional Holding**

Forecast EPS	$2.20	No of Institutions
	(05/28/2018)	397
Market Cap	$5.9 Billion	Shares
Book Value	$5.7 Billion	222,978,912
Price/Book	1.04	% Held
Price/Sales	2.19	61.45

Business Summary: REITs (MIC: 5.3.1 SIC: 6798 NAIC: 525930)

New Residential Investment is a real estate investment trust primarily focused on investing in, and managing investments related to residential real estate. Co.'s portfolio is composed of: mortgage servicing related assets, which provides a mortgage servicer with the right to service a pool of residential mortgage loans; residential mortgage backed securities, which includes Government-Sponsored Enterprise and Government Guaranteed Loans, and Non-GSE or Government Guaranteed Loans; residential mortgage loans, which packaged into pools held in securitization entities; and other investments, which include investment in consumer loans.

Recent Developments: For the quarter ended Mar 31 2018, net income increased 347.9% to US$614.4 million from US$137.2 million in the year-earlier quarter. Revenues were US$865.3 million, up 162.7% from US$329.4 million the year before.

Prospects: Our evaluation of New Residential Investment Corp. as of Jan. 21, 2018 is the result of our systematic analysis on three basic characteristics: earnings strength, relative valuation, and recent stock price movement. The company has suffered a very negative trend in earnings per share over the past 5 quarters and while recent estimates for the company have been mixed, NRZ has posted better than expected results. Based on operating earnings yield, the company is undervalued when compared to all of the companies in our coverage universe. Share price changes over the past year indicates that NRZ will perform well over the near term.

Financial Data
(US$ in Thousands)

	3 Mos	12/31/2017	12/31/2016	12/31/2015	12/31/2014	12/31/2013	12/31/2012	12/31/2011
Earnings Per Share	4.52	3.15	2.12	1.32	2.53	2.06	...	...
Cash Flow Per Share	(0.02)	(2.98)	2.35	1.60	1.14	1.21	...	...
Tang Book Value Per Share	16.85	15.26	13.00	12.13	11.28	10.00	2.99	...
Dividends Per Share	2.000	1.980	1.840	1.750	0.380	0.990	...	...
Dividend Payout %	44.25	62.86	86.79	132.58	15.02	48.06	...	...
Income Statement								
Total Revenue	865,333	2,151,814	1,257,241	687,101	721,945	328,575	51,182	1,627
EBITDA	430,081	150,896	(126,305)	(254,417)	186,648	251,715	35,908	714
Depn & Amortn	(177,371)	(1,031,384)	(747,932)	(525,298)	(278,408)	(13,908)	(5,339)	...
Income Before Taxes	607,452	1,182,280	621,627	270,881	465,056	265,623	41,247	714
Income Taxes	(6,912)	167,628	38,911	(11,001)	22,957	...	...	...
Net Income	604,253	957,533	504,453	268,636	352,877	265,949	41,247	714
Average Shares	333,380	304,381	238,486	202,907	139,565	128,684		
Balance Sheet								
Current Assets	419,370	2,002,241	1,978,390	1,788,417	212,985	271,994	...	...
Total Assets	22,011,941	22,213,562	18,365,035	15,192,722	8,093,690	5,958,658	534,876	43,971
Current Liabilities	16,128,691	10,201,086	6,805,056	4,937,019	3,301,202	1,956,965	156,520	4,163
Long-Term Obligations	...	7,084,391	7,990,605	7,249,568	2,913,209	2,488,618	...	...
Total Liabilities	16,348,005	17,523,357	15,104,935	12,396,789	6,497,601	4,692,808	156,520	4,163
Stockholders' Equity	5,663,936	4,690,205	3,260,100	2,795,933	1,596,089	1,265,850	378,356	39,808
Shares Outstanding	336,135	307,361	250,773	230,471	141,434	126,598	126,512	...
Statistical Record								
Return on Assets %	6.85	4.72	3.00	2.31	5.02	8.19	14.21	...
Return on Equity %	29.50	24.09	16.61	12.23	24.66	32.35	19.67	...
EBITDA Margin %	49.70	7.01	N.M.	N.M.	25.85	76.61	70.16	43.88
Net Margin %	69.83	44.50	40.12	39.10	48.88	80.94	80.59	43.88
Asset Turnover	0.13	0.11	0.07	0.06	0.10	0.10	0.18	...
Current Ratio	0.03	0.20	0.29	0.36	0.06	0.14	...	...
Debt to Equity	...	1.51	2.45	2.59	1.83	1.97	...	...
Price Range	18.30-15.30	18.30-15.15	16.36-9.86	17.78-10.43	13.72-11.58	14.00-11.70	...	...
P/E Ratio	4.05-3.38	5.81-4.81	7.72-4.65	13.47-7.90	5.42-4.58	6.80-5.68	...	...
Average Yield %	11.84	11.84	13.97	12.18	3.00	7.58	...	...

Address: 1345 Avenue of the Americas, New York, NY 10105 **Telephone:** 212-798-3150	**Web Site:** www.newresi.com **Officers:** Wesley Robert Edens - Chairman Kenneth M. Riis - President, Chief Executive Officer	**Auditors:** Ernst & Young LLP **Transfer Agents:** American Stock Transfer & Trust Company, LLC

NEW YORK COMMUNITY BANCORP INC.

Exchange	Symbol	Price	52Wk Range	Yield	P/E
NYS	NYCB	$11.04 (6/29/2018)	14.48-11.04	6.16	12.40

*7 Year Price Score 70.45 *NYSE Composite Index=100 *12 Month Price Score 90.11

Interim Earnings (Per Share)

Qtr.	Mar	Jun	Sep	Dec
2015	0.27	0.28	0.26	(0.91)
2016	0.27	0.26	0.26	0.23
2017	0.21	0.22	0.21	0.26
2018	0.20	...	...	...

Interim Dividends (Per Share)

Amt	Decl	Ex	Rec	Pay
0.17Q	07/26/2017	08/03/2017	08/07/2017	08/18/2017
0.17Q	10/24/2017	11/06/2017	11/07/2017	11/21/2017
0.17Q	01/31/2018	02/12/2018	02/13/2018	02/27/2018
0.17Q	04/24/2018	05/07/2018	05/08/2018	05/22/2018

Indicated Div: $0.68 (Div. Reinv. Plan)

Valuation Analysis | **Institutional Holding**

Forecast EPS	$0.81	No of Institutions
	(06/13/2018)	641
Market Cap	$5.4 Billion	Shares
Book Value	$6.8 Billion	400,683,296
Price/Book	0.80	% Held
Price/Sales	3.02	53.36

Business Summary: Banking (MIC: 5.1.1 SIC: 6036 NAIC: 522120)

New York Community Bancorp is a bank holding company. Co. has two subsidiaries: New York Community Bank (Community Bank), which provides multi-family loans, commercial real estate loans, and acquisition, development, and construction loans, among others; and New York Commercial Bank (Commercial Bank), which provides installment loans, revolving lines of credit, cash management services, and online banking, among others. As of Dec 31 2017, the Community Bank had 225 branches in Metro New York, New Jersey, Ohio, Florida, and Arizona, and the Commercial Bank had 30 branches in Metro New York. At Dec 31 2017, Co. had total assets of $49.13 billion and total deposits of $29.10 billion.

Recent Developments: For the quarter ended Mar 31 2018, net income increased 2.5% to US$106.6 million from US$104.0 million in the year-earlier quarter. Net interest income decreased 8.3% to US$270.3 million from US$294.9 million in the year-earlier quarter. Provision for loan losses was US$9.6 million versus a credit for loan losses of US$4.0 million in the prior-year quarter. Non-interest income fell 28.3% to US$22.9 million from US$31.9 million, while non-interest expense declined 16.7% to US$139.1 million.

Prospects: Our evaluation of New York Community Bancorp Inc. as of Jan. 21, 2018 is the result of our systematic analysis on three basic characteristics: earnings strength, relative valuation, and recent stock price movement. The company has produced a positive trend in earnings per share over the past 5 quarters and while recent estimates for the company have been mixed, NYCB has posted results that fell short of analysts expectations. Based on operating earnings yield, the company is undervalued when compared to all of the companies in our coverage universe. Share price changes over the past year indicates that NYCB will perform very poorly over the near term.

Financial Data
(US$ in Thousands)

	3 Mos	12/31/2017	12/31/2016	12/31/2015	12/31/2014	12/31/2013	12/31/2012	12/31/2011
Earnings Per Share	0.89	0.90	1.01	(0.11)	1.09	1.08	1.13	1.09
Cash Flow Per Share	2.26	2.72	1.55	(0.94)	1.64	3.13	1.31	1.90
Tang Book Value Per Share	7.82	7.88	7.09	6.70	7.03	6.90	6.93	6.77
Dividends Per Share	0.680	0.680	0.680	1.000	1.000	1.000	1.000	1.000
Dividend Payout %	76.40	75.56	67.33	...	91.74	92.59	88.50	91.74
Income Statement								
Interest Income	404,325	1,582,239	1,674,869	1,691,584	1,683,067	1,708,098	1,791,101	1,866,664
Interest Expense	134,027	452,236	387,487	1,283,509	542,714	541,482	631,080	666,243
Net Interest Income	270,298	1,130,003	1,287,382	408,075	1,140,353	1,166,616	1,160,021	1,200,421
Provision for Losses	9,571	37,242	4,180	(15,004)	(18,587)	30,758	62,988	100,420
Non-Interest Income	22,857	216,880	145,572	210,763	201,593	218,830	297,353	235,325
Non-Interest Expense	139,107	641,218	649,255	760,511	579,170	591,778	593,833	574,683
Income Before Taxes	144,477	668,215	777,128	(132,013)	773,066	747,126	780,909	734,577
Income Taxes	37,925	202,014	281,727	(84,857)	287,669	271,579	279,803	254,540
Net Income	106,552	466,201	495,401	(47,156)	485,397	475,547	501,106	480,037
Average Shares	488,140	487,073	485,150	448,982	440,988	439,251	437,712	436,143
Balance Sheet								
Net Loans & Leases	38,759,685	38,265,183	39,308,016	38,011,995	35,647,639	32,727,507	31,580,636	30,152,154
Total Assets	49,654,874	49,124,195	48,926,555	50,317,796	48,559,217	46,688,287	44,145,100	42,024,302
Total Deposits	29,235,434	29,102,163	28,887,903	28,426,758	28,328,734	25,660,992	24,877,521	22,274,130
Total Liabilities	42,874,157	42,328,819	42,802,564	44,383,100	42,777,402	40,952,625	38,488,836	36,458,598
Stockholders' Equity	6,780,717	6,795,376	6,123,991	5,934,696	5,781,815	5,735,662	5,656,264	5,565,704
Shares Outstanding	490,379	488,490	487,056	484,943	442,587	440,809	439,050	437,344
Statistical Record								
Return on Assets %	0.95	0.95	1.00	N.M.	1.02	1.05	1.16	1.15
Return on Equity %	6.98	7.22	8.19	N.M.	8.43	8.35	8.91	8.66
Net Interest Margin %	66.85	71.42	76.86	24.12	67.75	68.30	64.77	64.31
Efficiency Ratio %	32.56	35.64	35.66	39.98	30.73	30.71	28.43	27.34
Loans to Deposits	1.33	1.31	1.36	1.34	1.26	1.28	1.27	1.35
Price Range	14.48-11.70	16.22-11.70	17.30-13.78	19.16-15.25	17.34-14.82	16.85-12.96	14.95-11.57	18.97-11.32
P/E Ratio	16.27-13.15	18.02-13.00	17.13-13.64	...	15.91-13.60	15.60-12.00	13.23-10.24	17.40-10.39
Average Yield %	5.18	5.06	4.49	5.81	6.30	6.86	7.61	6.69

Address: 615 Merrick Avenue,	Web Site: www.mynycb.com	Auditors: KPMG LLP
Westbury, NY 11590	Officers: Joseph R. Ficalora - Chairman, President,	Transfer Agents: Computershare,
Telephone: 516-683-4100	Chief Executive Officer Thomas R. Cangemi - Senior	Providence, RI
	Executive Vice President, Chief Financial Officer	

NEW YORK TIMES CO.

Exchange	Symbol	Price	52Wk Range	Yield	P/E
NYS	NYT	$25.90 (6/29/2018)	26.60-17.10	0.62	323.75

*7 Year Price Score 129.44 *NYSE Composite Index=100 *12 Month Price Score 113.06

Interim Earnings (Per Share)

Qtr.	Mar	Jun	Sep	Dec
2015	(0.09)	0.10	0.06	0.31
2016	(0.05)	0.00	0.00	0.23
2017	0.08	0.09	0.20	(0.34)
2018	0.13	...	...	...

Interim Dividends (Per Share)

Amt	Decl	Ex	Rec	Pay
0.04Q	09/20/2017	10/03/2017	10/04/2017	10/19/2017
0.04Q	12/14/2017	01/09/2018	01/10/2018	01/25/2018
0.04Q	02/21/2018	04/03/2018	04/04/2018	04/19/2018
0.04Q	06/28/2018	07/10/2018	07/11/2018	07/26/2018

Indicated Div: $0.16 (Div. Reinv. Plan)

Valuation Analysis   **Institutional Holding**

Forecast EPS	$0.89	No of Institutions
	(05/26/2018)	373
Market Cap	$4.3 Billion	Shares
Book Value	$958.0 Million	178,901,680
Price/Book	4.46	% Held
Price/Sales	2.53	77.19

Business Summary: Publishing (MIC: 2.3.3 SIC: 2711 NAIC: 511110)

New York Times principal business consists of distributing content generated by its newsroom through its print, web and mobile platforms. In addition, Co. distributes selected content on third-party platforms. Co.'s businesses include: newspaper, The New York Times; websites, including NYTimes.com; mobile applications, including The Times's core news applications, as well as interest-specific applications such as NYT Cooking, Crossword and others; and related businesses, such as The Times news services division, product review and recommendation websites The Wirecutter and The Sweethome, digital archive distribution, NYT Live and other products and services under The Times brand.

Recent Developments: For the quarter ended Apr 1 2018, net income increased 67.1% to US$21.9 million from US$13.1 million in the year-earlier quarter. Revenues were US$413.9 million, up 3.8% from US$398.8 million the year before. Operating income was US$34.1 million versus US$27.8 million in the prior-year quarter, an increase of 22.4%. Direct operating expenses rose 0.7% to US$154.3 million from US$153.3 million in the comparable period the year before. Indirect operating expenses increased 3.6% to US$225.6 million from US$217.7 million in the equivalent prior-year period.

Prospects: Our evaluation of New York Times Co. as of Jan. 21, 2018 is the result of our systematic analysis on three basic characteristics: earnings strength, relative valuation, and recent stock price movement. The company has generated a negative trend in earnings per share over the past 5 quarters and while recent estimates for the company have remained steady, NYT has posted better than expected results. Based on operating earnings yield, the company is about fairly valued when compared to all of the companies in our coverage universe. Share price changes over the past year indicates that NYT will perform in line with the market over the near term.

Financial Data

(US$ in Thousands)	3 Mos	12/31/2017	12/25/2016	12/27/2015	12/28/2014	12/29/2013	12/30/2012	12/25/2011
Earnings Per Share	0.08	0.03	0.18	0.38	0.20	0.41	0.87	(0.27)
Cash Flow Per Share	0.45	0.53	0.59	1.07	0.54	0.23	0.53	0.50
Tang Book Value Per Share	4.93	4.65	4.43	4.45	4.06	4.78	3.43	N.M.
Dividends Per Share	0.160	0.160	0.160	0.160	0.160	0.040	...	...
Dividend Payout %	200.00	533.33	88.89	42.11	80.00	9.76	...	...
Income Statement								
Total Revenue	413,948	1,675,639	1,555,342	1,579,215	1,588,528	1,577,230	1,990,080	2,323,401
EBITDA	47,068	174,237	163,327	198,182	171,403	241,564	426,890	197,951
Depn & Amortn	15,041	61,871	61,723	61,597	79,455	85,477	103,775	116,454
Income Before Taxes	27,150	92,583	66,799	97,535	38,218	98,014	260,300	(3,746)
Income Taxes	5,251	103,956	4,421	33,910	(3,541)	37,892	103,482	36,506
Net Income	21,912	4,296	29,068	63,246	33,307	65,105	133,173	(39,669)
Average Shares	166,237	164,263	162,817	166,423	161,323	157,774	152,693	147,190
Balance Sheet								
Current Assets	740,015	749,699	796,178	862,532	1,148,095	1,172,267	1,308,408	748,589
Total Assets	2,097,094	2,099,780	2,185,395	2,417,690	2,566,474	2,572,552	2,806,335	2,883,450
Current Liabilities	370,429	415,657	398,737	563,585	600,508	348,511	422,577	513,308
Long-Term Obligations	251,092	250,209	246,978	242,851	426,458	684,142	696,914	698,220
Total Liabilities	1,139,103	1,202,501	1,337,580	1,590,939	1,840,146	1,729,642	2,173,835	2,377,090
Stockholders' Equity	957,991	897,279	847,815	826,751	726,328	842,910	632,500	506,360
Shares Outstanding	164,850	162,209	161,152	161,389	150,337	149,927	148,605	147,846
Statistical Record								
Return on Assets %	0.61	0.20	1.27	2.54	1.30	2.43	4.61	N.M.
Return on Equity %	1.43	0.48	3.48	8.17	4.26	8.85	23.01	N.M.
EBITDA Margin %	11.37	10.40	10.50	12.55	10.79	15.32	21.45	8.52
Net Margin %	5.29	0.26	1.87	4.00	2.10	4.13	6.69	N.M.
Asset Turnover	0.79	0.77	0.68	0.64	0.62	0.59	0.69	0.76
Current Ratio	2.00	1.80	2.00	1.53	1.91	3.36	3.10	1.46
Debt to Equity	0.26	0.28	0.29	0.29	0.59	0.81	1.10	1.38
Price Range	25.35-14.20	20.00-13.05	14.10-10.80	14.46-11.56	17.26-11.22	15.47-8.18	10.88-5.98	10.90-5.65
P/E Ratio	316.88-177.50	666.67-435.00	78.33-60.00	38.05-30.42	86.30-56.10	37.73-19.95	12.51-6.87	...
Average Yield %	0.84	0.95	1.28	1.20	1.13	0.36	...	...

Address: 620 Eighth Avenue, New York, NY 10018 **Telephone:** 212-556-1234	**Web Site:** www.nytco.com **Officers:** Mark Thompson - President, Chief Executive Officer Meredith A. Kopit Levien - Executive Vice President, Chief Operating Officer, Chief Revenue Officer	**Auditors:** Ernst & Young LLP **Investor Contact:** 212-556-4317 **Transfer Agents:** Computershare, Providence, RI

NEWELL BRANDS INC

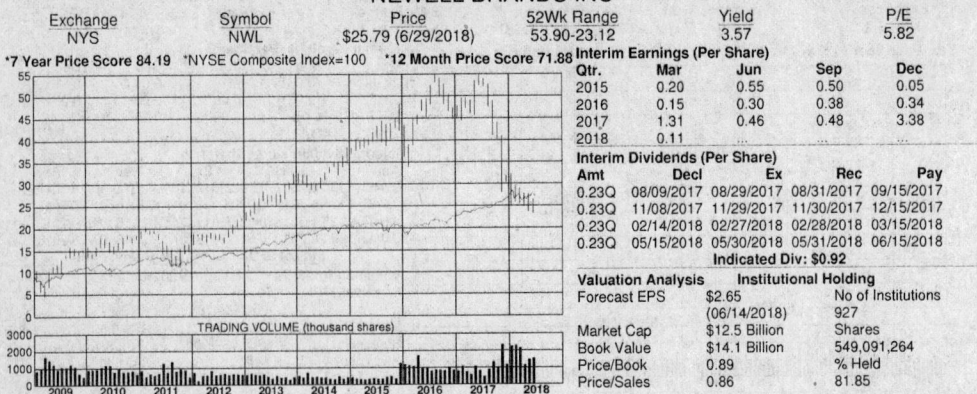

Exchange	Symbol	Price	52Wk Range	Yield	P/E
NYS	NWL	$25.79 (6/29/2018)	53.90-23.12	3.57	5.82

*7 Year Price Score 84.19 *NYSE Composite Index=100 *12 Month Price Score 71.88

Interim Earnings (Per Share)

Qtr.	Mar	Jun	Sep	Dec
2015	0.20	0.55	0.50	0.05
2016	0.15	0.30	0.38	0.34
2017	1.31	0.46	0.48	3.38
2018	0.11	...	...	...

Interim Dividends (Per Share)

Amt	Decl	Ex	Rec	Pay
0.23Q	08/09/2017	08/29/2017	08/31/2017	09/15/2017
0.23Q	11/08/2017	11/29/2017	11/30/2017	12/15/2017
0.23Q	02/14/2018	02/27/2018	02/28/2018	03/15/2018
0.23Q	05/15/2018	05/30/2018	05/31/2018	06/15/2018

Indicated Div: $0.92

Valuation Analysis

		Institutional Holding	
Forecast EPS	$2.65	No of Institutions	927
	(06/14/2018)		
Market Cap	$12.5 Billion	Shares	549,091,264
Book Value	$14.1 Billion	% Held	81.85
Price/Book	0.89		
Price/Sales	0.86		

Business Summary: Plastics (MIC: 8.4.2 SIC: 3089 NAIC: 326299)

Newell Brands is a marketer of consumer and commercial products. Co.'s key brands in each of its segment include: Writing, which includes Sharpie®, Paper Mate®, Expo® and Prismacolor®; Home Solutions, which includes Rubbermaid® and Contigo®; Tools, which includes Irwin® and Lenox®; Commercial Products, which includes Rubbermaid Commercial Products®; Baby and Parenting, which includes Graco® and Baby Jogger®; Branded Consumables, which includes Yankee Candle® and Diamond®; Consumer Solutions, which includes Crock-Pot® and FoodSaver®; Outdoor Solutions, which includes Coleman® and Jostens®; and Process Solutions, which includes Jarden Plastic Solutions and Jarden Applied Materials.

Recent Developments: For the quarter ended Mar 31 2018, net income decreased 91.7% to US$53.3 million from US$638.5 million in the year-earlier quarter. Revenues were US$3.02 billion, down 7.6% from US$3.27 billion the year before. Operating income was US$117.1 million versus US$154.0 million in the prior-year quarter, a decrease of 24.0%. Direct operating expenses declined 6.4% to US$2.01 billion from US$2.15 billion in the comparable period the year before. Indirect operating expenses decreased 7.8% to US$888.3 million from US$963.2 million in the equivalent prior-year period.

Prospects: Our evaluation of Newell Brands Inc. as of Jan. 21, 2018 is the result of our systematic analysis on three basic characteristics: earnings strength, relative valuation, and recent stock price movement. The company has managed to produce a neutral trend in earnings per share over the past 5 quarters and while recent estimates for the company have remained steady, NWL has posted results that fell short of analysts expectations. Based on operating earnings yield, the company is undervalued when compared to all of the companies in our coverage universe. Share price changes over the past year indicates that NWL will perform poorly over the near term.

Financial Data

(US$ in Thousands)	3 Mos	12/31/2017	12/31/2016	12/31/2015	12/31/2014	12/31/2013	12/31/2012	12/31/2011
Earnings Per Share	4.43	5.63	1.25	1.29	1.35	1.63	1.37	0.42
Cash Flow Per Share	1.69	1.91	4.33	2.10	2.30	2.10	2.12	1.91
Dividends Per Share	0.920	0.880	0.760	0.760	0.660	0.600	0.430	0.290
Dividend Payout %	20.77	15.63	60.80	58.91	48.89	36.81	31.39	69.05
Income Statement								
Total Revenue	3,017,400	14,742,200	13,264,000	5,915,700	5,727,000	5,692,500	5,902,700	5,864,600
EBITDA	186,000	2,181,900	1,433,100	503,800	615,700	700,200	750,100	350,800
Depn & Amortn	67,900	284,000	214,100	93,000	93,200	100,400	106,700	110,600
Income Before Taxes	2,000	1,429,000	814,500	330,900	462,100	539,500	567,300	154,000
Income Taxes	(51,300)	(1,319,800)	286,000	78,200	89,100	122,100	166,300	17,900
Net Income	53,300	2,748,800	527,800	350,000	377,800	474,600	401,300	125,200
Average Shares	487,000	488,000	423,100	271,500	278,900	291,800	293,600	296,200
Balance Sheet								
Current Assets	8,471,300	6,078,000	7,484,500	2,493,500	2,426,600	2,285,600	2,271,100	2,148,000
Total Assets	33,469,400	33,135,500	33,837,500	7,278,000	6,681,100	6,069,700	6,222,000	6,160,900
Current Liabilities	4,917,900	4,316,800	4,292,000	1,988,600	1,890,700	1,604,500	1,570,800	1,660,900
Long-Term Obligations	9,623,500	9,889,600	11,290,900	2,687,600	2,084,500	1,661,600	1,706,500	1,809,300
Total Liabilities	19,338,500	18,990,800	22,488,700	5,455,100	4,829,700	3,998,200	4,225,300	4,311,800
Stockholders' Equity	14,130,900	14,144,700	11,348,800	1,822,900	1,851,400	2,071,500	1,996,700	1,849,100
Shares Outstanding	485,700	485,200	482,500	267,200	269,200	278,600	286,900	288,300
Statistical Record								
Return on Assets %	6.48	8.21	2.56	5.01	5.93	7.72	6.46	1.99
Return on Equity %	16.56	21.56	7.99	19.05	19.26	23.33	20.81	6.68
EBITDA Margin %	6.16	14.80	10.80	8.52	10.75	12.30	12.71	5.98
Net Margin %	1.77	18.65	3.98	5.92	6.60	8.34	6.80	2.13
Asset Turnover	0.43	0.44	0.64	0.85	0.90	0.93	0.95	0.93
Current Ratio	1.72	1.41	1.74	1.25	1.28	1.42	1.45	1.29
Debt to Equity	0.68	0.70	0.99	1.47	1.13	0.80	0.85	0.98
Price Range	54.85-24.81	54.85-27.97	54.89-33.76	48.16-36.77	38.41-28.49	32.41-21.80	22.27-16.23	20.21-11.14
P/E Ratio	12.38-5.60	9.74-4.97	43.91-27.01	37.33-28.50	28.45-21.10	19.88-13.37	16.26-11.85	48.12-26.52
Average Yield %	2.26	1.94	1.63	1.85	2.04	2.25	2.30	1.79

Address: 221 River Street, Hoboken, NJ 07030	**Web Site:** www.newellrubbermaid.com	**Auditors:** PricewaterhouseCoopers LLP
Telephone: 201-610-6600	**Officers:** Patrick D. Campbell - Chairman Michael B. Polk - President, President (frmr), Chief Executive Officer	**Investor Contact:** 800-424-1941
		Transfer Agents: ComputerShare Investor Services, Providence, RI

NEWFIELD EXPLORATION CO

Exchange	Symbol	Price	52Wk Range	Yield	P/E
NYS	NFX	$30.25 (6/29/2018)	34.80-22.94	N/A	N/A

*7 Year Price Score 68.17 *NYSE Composite Index=100 *12 Month Price Score 100.29

Interim Earnings (Per Share)

Qtr.	Mar	Jun	Sep	Dec
2015	(3.30)	(6.09)	(7.52)	(4.01)
2016	(3.52)	(3.36)	0.24	0.14
2017	0.73	0.49	0.44	0.47
2018	0.43	...	...	...

Interim Dividends (Per Share)

No Dividends Paid

Valuation Analysis — **Institutional Holding**

Forecast EPS	$3.37	No of Institutions
(06/20/2018)		694
Market Cap	$6.0 Billion	Shares
Book Value	$1.5 Billion	231,501,024
Price/Book	4.01	% Held
Price/Sales	N/A	92.95

Business Summary: Production & Extraction (MIC: 9.1.1 SIC: 1311 NAIC: 211111)

Newfield Exploration is an independent energy company engaged in the exploration, development and production of crude oil, natural gas and natural gas liquids. Co.'s principal areas of operation are the Anadarko and Arkoma basins of Oklahoma, the Williston Basin of North Dakota and the Uinta Basin of Utah. In addition, Co. has oil producing assets offshore China. As of Dec 31 2017, Co. had proved reserves of 680.0 million barrels of oil equivalent, which consisted of 250.0 million barrels of oil and condensate, 1,704.00 billion cubic feet of natural gas, and 146 million barrels of natural gas liquids.

Recent Developments: For the quarter ended Mar 31 2018, net income decreased 41.5% to US$86.0 million from US$147.0 million in the year-earlier quarter. Revenues were US$580.0 million, up 39.1% from US$417.0 million the year before. Operating income was US$232.0 million versus US$121.0 million in the prior-year quarter, an increase of 91.7%. Direct operating expenses rose 12.7% to US$160.0 million from US$142.0 million in the comparable period the year before. Indirect operating expenses increased 22.1% to US$188.0 million from US$154.0 million in the equivalent prior-year period.

Prospects: Our evaluation of Newfield Exploration Co. as of Jan. 21, 2018 is the result of our systematic analysis on three basic characteristics: earnings strength, relative valuation, and recent stock price movement. The company has suffered a very negative trend in earnings per share over the past 5 quarters and while recent estimates for the company have been raised by analysts, NFX has posted better than expected results. Based on operating earnings yield, the company is undervalued when compared to all of the companies in our coverage universe. Share price changes over the past year indicates that NFX will perform very poorly over the near term.

Financial Data

(US$ in Thousands)	3 Mos	12/31/2017	12/31/2016	12/31/2015	12/31/2014	12/31/2013	12/31/2012	12/31/2011
Earnings Per Share	1.83	2.13	(6.36)	(21.18)	6.52	0.94	(8.80)	3.99
Cash Flow Per Share	...	4.78	4.27	7.60	10.12	10.70	8.47	11.86
Tang Book Value Per Share	7.54	7.05	4.71	8.43	28.35	21.70	20.54	29.11
Income Statement								
Total Revenue	580,000	1,767,000	1,472,000	1,557,000	2,288,000	1,789,000	2,567,000	2,471,000
EBITDA	255,000	942,000	(533,000)	(3,899,000)	2,082,000	1,252,000	104,000	1,700,000
Depn & Amortn	133,000	467,000	572,000	917,000	903,000	930,000	955,000	767,000
Income Before Taxes	99,000	386,000	(1,208,000)	(4,947,000)	1,032,000	170,000	(988,000)	840,000
Income Taxes	13,000	(41,000)	22,000	(1,585,000)	382,000	62,000	196,000	301,000
Net Income	86,000	427,000	(1,230,000)	(3,362,000)	900,000	147,000	(1,184,000)	539,000
Average Shares	200,000	200,000	193,000	159,000	138,000	136,000	135,000	135,000
Balance Sheet								
Current Assets	646,000	746,000	949,000	625,000	940,000	901,000	866,000	775,000
Total Assets	5,122,000	4,961,000	4,312,000	4,768,000	9,598,000	9,321,000	7,912,000	8,991,000
Current Liabilties	844,000	818,000	684,000	647,000	1,101,000	1,290,000	959,000	932,000
Long-Term Obligations	2,434,000	2,434,000	2,431,000	2,467,000	2,892,000	3,694,000	3,045,000	3,006,000
Total Liabilities	3,617,000	3,553,000	3,374,000	3,389,000	5,705,000	6,365,000	5,132,000	5,071,000
Stockholders' Equity	1,505,000	1,408,000	938,000	1,379,000	3,893,000	2,956,000	2,780,000	3,920,000
Shares Outstanding	199,726	199,704	198,954	163,490	137,328	136,221	135,314	134,684
Statistical Record								
Return on Assets %	...	9.21	N.M.	N.M.	9.51	1.71	N.M.	6.54
Return on Equity %	...	36.40	N.M.	N.M.	26.28	5.13	N.M.	14.84
EBITDA Margin %	43.97	53.31	N.M.	N.M.	91.00	69.98	4.05	68.80
Net Margin %	14.83	24.17	N.M.	N.M.	39.34	8.22	N.M.	21.81
Asset Turnover	...	0.38	0.32	0.22	0.24	0.21	0.30	0.30
Current Ratio	0.77	0.91	1.39	0.97	0.85	0.70	0.90	0.83
Debt to Equity	1.62	1.73	2.59	1.79	0.74	1.25	1.10	0.77
Price Range	37.14-22.94	43.67-24.51	47.88-22.31	41.05-22.73	44.98-23.56	31.68-19.84	42.25-23.88	76.45-35.81
P/E Ratio	20.30-12.54	20.50-11.51	...	...	6.90-3.61	33.70-21.11	...	19.16-8.97

Address: 4 Waterway Square Place, Suite 100, The Woodlands, TX 77380	Web Site: www.newfield.com	Auditors: PricewaterhouseCoopers LLP
Telephone: 281-210-5100	Officers: Lee K. Boothby - Chairman, President, Chief Executive Officer Gary D. Packer - Executive Vice President, Chief Operating Officer	Investor Contact: 281-210-5201
Fax: 281-210-5101		Transfer Agents: American Stock Transfer & Trust Company, New York, NY

NEWMARKET CORP

Exchange	Symbol	Price	52Wk Range	Yield	P/E	Div Acheiver
NYS	NEU	$404.50 (6/29/2018)	467.36-361.42	1.73	25.00	11 Years

*7 Year Price Score 94.61   *NSYE Composite Index=100   *12 Month Price Score 92.78

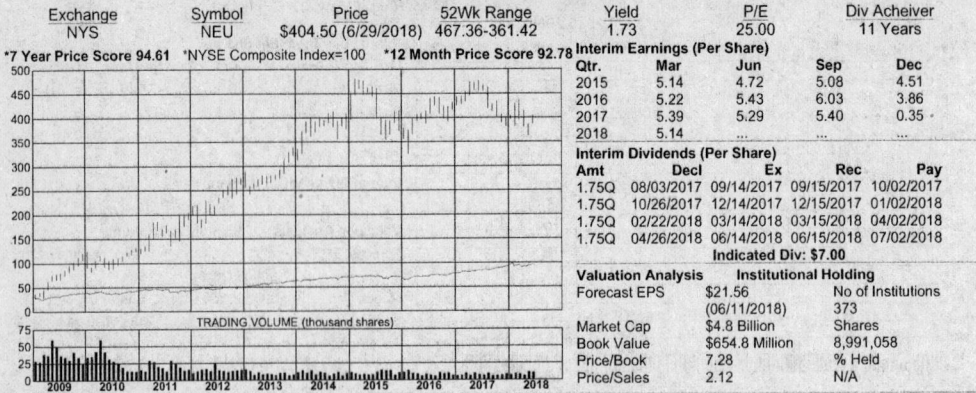

TRADING VOLUME (thousand shares)

Interim Earnings (Per Share)

Qtr.	Mar	Jun	Sep	Dec
2015	5.14	4.72	5.08	4.51
2016	5.22	5.43	6.03	3.86
2017	5.39	5.29	5.40	0.35
2018	5.14	...	...	...

Interim Dividends (Per Share)

Amt	Decl	Ex	Rec	Pay
1.75Q	08/03/2017	09/14/2017	09/15/2017	10/02/2017
1.75Q	10/26/2017	12/14/2017	12/15/2017	01/02/2018
1.75Q	02/22/2018	03/14/2018	03/15/2018	04/02/2018
1.75Q	04/26/2018	06/14/2018	06/15/2018	07/02/2018

Indicated Div: $7.00

Valuation Analysis

		Institutional Holding	
Forecast EPS	$21.56 (06/11/2018)	No of Institutions	373
Market Cap	$4.8 Billion	Shares	8,991,058
Book Value	$654.8 Million	% Held	N/A
Price/Book	7.28		
Price/Sales	2.12		

Business Summary: Specialty Chemicals (MIC: 8.3.2 SIC: 2869 NAIC: 325199)

NewMarket is a holding company and is the parent company of Afton Chemical Corporation (Afton), Ethyl Corporation (Ethyl), NewMarket Services Corporation (NewMarket Services), and NewMarket Development Corporation (NewMarket Development). Afton manufactures and sells petroleum additives, while Ethyl represents the sale of tetraethyl lead in North America and certain contracted manufacturing and services. NewMarket Development manages the property that Co. owns in Virginia. NewMarket Services provides various administrative services to Co., Afton, Ethyl, and NewMarket Development. Co.'s business is composed of one segment, petroleum additives.

Recent Developments: For the quarter ended Mar 31 2018, net income decreased 5.3% to US$60.6 million from US$63.9 million in the year-earlier quarter. Revenues were US$589.2 million, up 8.6% from US$542.8 million the year before. Operating income was US$81.6 million versus US$90.2 million in the prior-year quarter, a decrease of 9.6%. Direct operating expenses rose 15.6% to US$432.5 million from US$374.0 million in the comparable period the year before. Indirect operating expenses decreased 4.3% to US$75.2 million from US$78.6 million in the equivalent prior-year period.

Prospects: Our evaluation of NewMarket Corp. as of Jan. 21, 2018 is the result of our systematic analysis on three basic characteristics: earnings strength, relative valuation, and recent stock price movement. The company has generated a negative trend in earnings per share over the past 5 quarters and while recent estimates for the company have remained steady, NEU has posted results that fell short of analysts expectations. Based on operating earnings yield, the company is undervalued when compared to all of the companies in our coverage universe. Share price changes over the past year indicates that NEU will perform in line with the market over the near term.

Financial Data
(US$ in Thousands)

	3 Mos	12/31/2017	12/31/2016	12/31/2015	12/31/2014	12/31/2013	12/31/2012	12/31/2011
Earnings Per Share	16.18	16.08	20.54	19.45	18.38	19.90	17.85	15.09
Cash Flow Per Share	18.59	20.53	29.80	21.90	18.54	20.92	20.30	13.47
Tang Book Value Per Share	43.49	38.82	39.91	31.52	32.47	41.92	27.70	38.16
Dividends Per Share	7.000	7.000	6.400	5.800	4.700	3.800	28.000	2.390
Dividend Payout %	43.26	43.53	31.16	29.82	25.57	19.10	156.86	15.84
Income Statement								
Total Revenue	589,245	2,198,404	2,049,451	2,140,830	2,335,405	2,280,355	2,223,309	2,149,558
EBITDA	104,140	388,298	401,993	388,623	389,666	394,107	386,206	355,537
Depn & Amortn	17,665	51,000	42,000	35,000	34,000	35,000	34,000	33,000
Income Before Taxes	81,311	315,442	343,208	338,971	339,099	341,311	341,391	303,717
Income Taxes	20,746	124,933	99,767	100,368	105,844	98,964	101,798	96,810
Net Income	60,565	190,509	243,441	238,603	233,255	264,742	239,593	206,907
Average Shares	11,762	11,824	11,828	12,241	12,671	13,286	13,405	13,712
Balance Sheet								
Current Assets	886,490	833,654	836,883	774,767	797,191	897,319	735,495	679,731
Total Assets	1,779,465	1,712,154	1,416,436	1,289,915	1,231,925	1,327,274	1,257,510	1,191,662
Current Liabilities	303,027	316,793	294,590	263,680	259,674	247,614	216,671	216,024
Long-Term Obligations	624,894	602,900	507,275	494,586	363,526	349,467	424,407	232,601
Total Liabilities	1,124,680	1,110,505	933,185	902,351	810,884	754,826	855,305	642,069
Stockholders' Equity	654,785	601,649	483,251	387,564	421,041	572,448	402,205	549,593
Shares Outstanding	11,787	11,779	11,845	11,948	12,446	13,099	13,417	13,404
Statistical Record								
Return on Assets %	11.22	12.18	17.94	18.92	18.23	20.48	19.51	18.36
Return on Equity %	31.56	35.12	55.76	59.02	46.96	54.33	50.21	39.74
EBITDA Margin %	17.67	17.66	19.61	18.15	16.69	17.28	17.37	16.54
Net Margin %	10.28	8.67	11.88	11.15	9.99	11.61	10.78	9.63
Asset Turnover	1.35	1.41	1.51	1.70	1.83	1.76	1.81	1.91
Current Ratio	2.93	2.63	2.84	2.94	3.07	3.62	3.39	3.15
Debt to Equity	0.95	1.00	1.05	1.28	0.86	0.61	1.06	0.42
Price Range	476.18-381.01	476.18-381.23	442.62-324.89	480.33-354.59	413.39-311.61	337.22-241.65	277.43-173.46	203.71-119.76
P/E Ratio	29.43-23.55	29.61-23.71	21.55-15.82	24.70-18.23	22.49-16.95	16.95-12.14	15.54-9.72	13.50-7.94
Average Yield %	1.64	1.61	1.54	1.36	1.23	1.35	12.43	1.48

Address: 330 South Fourth Street, Richmond, VA 23219-4350
Telephone: 804-788-5000
Web Site: www.newmarket.com
Officers: Thomas E. (Teddy) Gottwald - Chairman, President, Chief Executive Officer Brian D. Paliotti - Chief Financial Officer, Vice President
Auditors: PricewaterhouseCoopers LLP
Investor Contact: 804-788-5555
Transfer Agents: ComputerShare Investor Services, Providence, RI

NEWMONT MINING CORP (HOLDING CO)

Exchange	Symbol	Price	52Wk Range	Yield	P/E
NYS	NEM	$37.71 (6/29/2018)	41.94-31.89	1.14	419.00

*7 Year Price Score 85.67   *NYSE Composite Index=100   *12 Month Price Score 101.31

Interim Earnings (Per Share)

Qtr.	Mar	Jun	Sep	Dec
2015	0.37	0.14	0.42	(0.50)
2016	0.10	0.04	(0.67)	(0.65)
2017	0.09	0.33	0.38	(0.98)
2018	0.36	...	...	...

Interim Dividends (Per Share)

Amt	Decl	Ex	Rec	Pay
0.075Q	07/19/2017	09/13/2017	09/14/2017	09/28/2017
0.075Q	10/24/2017	12/07/2017	12/08/2017	12/28/2017
0.14Q	02/20/2018	03/07/2018	03/08/2018	03/22/2018
0.14Q	04/24/2018	06/06/2018	06/07/2018	06/21/2018
		Indicated Div: $0.43		

Valuation Analysis — **Institutional Holding**

Forecast EPS	$1.39	No of Institutions	
	(06/12/2018)	1005	
Market Cap	$20.1 Billion	Shares	
Book Value	$10.6 Billion	567,220,800	
Price/Book	1.90	% Held	
Price/Sales	2.68	71.32	

Business Summary: Mining (MIC: 8.2.4 SIC: 1041 NAIC: 212221)

Newmont Mining is primarily a gold producer with operations and/or assets in the U.S., Australia, Peru, Ghana and Suriname. Co. is also engaged in the production of copper, principally through Boddington in Australia and Phoenix in the U.S. Co.'s regions include: North America, which consists primarily of Carlin, Phoenix, Twin Creeks and Long Canyon in the state of Nevada and Cripple Creek &Victor in the state of Colorado; South America, which consists primarily of Yanacocha in Peru and Merian in Suriname; Asia Pacific, which consists primarily of Boddington, Tanami and Kalgoorlie in Australia; and Africa, which consists primarily of Ahafo and Akyem in Ghana.

Recent Developments: For the year ended Dec 31 2017, loss from continuing operations was US$49.0 million compared with a loss of US$790.0 million a year earlier. Net loss amounted to US$87.0 million versus a net loss of US$923.0 million in the prior year. Revenues were US$7.35 billion, up 9.5% from US$6.71 billion the year before. Direct operating expenses rose 7.1% to US$4.04 billion from US$3.77 billion in the comparable period the year before. Indirect operating expenses decreased 31.1% to US$2.03 billion from US$2.95 billion in the equivalent prior-year period.

Prospects: Our evaluation of Newmont Mining Corp. as of Jan. 21, 2018 is the result of our systematic analysis on three basic characteristics: earnings strength, relative valuation, and recent stock price movement. The company has managed to produce a neutral trend in earnings per share over the past 5 quarters and while recent estimates for the company have been mixed, NEM has posted better than expected results. Based on operating earnings yield, the company is about fairly valued when compared to all of the companies in our coverage universe. Share price changes over the past year indicates that NEM will perform poorly over the near term.

Financial Data

(US$ in Thousands)	3 Mos	12/31/2017	12/31/2016	12/31/2015	12/31/2014	12/31/2013	12/31/2012	12/31/2011
Earnings Per Share	0.09	(0.18)	(1.18)	0.43	1.02	(4.94)	3.63	0.73
Cash Flow Per Share	4.17	4.38	5.24	4.16	2.88	3.10	4.77	7.26
Tang Book Value Per Share	19.82	19.90	20.21	21.14	20.17	19.91	27.08	25.39
Dividends Per Share	0.340	0.250	0.125	0.100	0.225	1.225	1.400	1.000
Dividend Payout %	377.78	...	...	23.26	22.06	...	38.57	136.99
Income Statement								
Total Revenue	1,817,000	7,348,000	6,711,000	7,729,000	7,292,000	8,322,000	9,868,000	10,358,000
EBITDA	626,000	2,554,000	1,279,000	2,530,000	2,092,000	(1,933,000)	4,383,000	3,079,000
Depn & Amortn	301,000	1,249,000	1,220,000	1,239,000	1,229,000	1,362,000	1,032,000	1,036,000
Income Before Taxes	283,000	1,092,000	(214,000)	966,000	506,000	(3,585,000)	3,114,000	1,810,000
Income Taxes	105,000	1,125,000	563,000	644,000	133,000	(813,000)	869,000	713,000
Net Income	192,000	(98,000)	(627,000)	220,000	508,000	(2,462,000)	1,809,000	366,000
Average Shares	535,000	535,000	532,000	516,000	499,000	498,000	499,000	504,000
Balance Sheet								
Current Assets	4,938,000	5,066,000	4,677,000	4,983,000	5,439,000	4,874,000	5,945,000	5,388,000
Total Assets	20,483,000	20,563,000	21,031,000	25,182,000	24,916,000	24,764,000	29,650,000	27,474,000
Current Liabilities	1,181,000	1,395,000	1,750,000	1,416,000	2,198,000	2,740,000	3,141,000	3,940,000
Long-Term Obligations	4,088,000	4,061,000	4,049,000	6,087,000	6,480,000	6,145,000	6,288,000	3,624,000
Total Liabilities	9,908,000	9,954,000	10,310,000	13,832,000	14,642,000	14,623,000	15,877,000	14,578,000
Stockholders' Equity	10,575,000	10,609,000	10,721,000	11,350,000	10,274,000	10,141,000	13,773,000	12,896,000
Shares Outstanding	533,486	533,085	530,465	529,650	498,670	497,678	496,723	494,727
Statistical Record								
Return on Assets %	0.23	N.M.	N.M.	0.88	2.05	N.M.	6.32	1.38
Return on Equity %	0.45	N.M.	N.M.	2.03	4.98	N.M.	13.53	2.79
EBITDA Margin %	34.45	34.76	19.06	32.73	28.69	N.M.	44.42	29.73
Net Margin %	10.57	N.M.	N.M.	2.85	6.97	N.M.	18.33	3.53
Asset Turnover	0.36	0.35	0.29	0.31	0.29	0.31	0.34	0.39
Current Ratio	4.18	3.63	2.67	3.52	2.47	1.78	1.89	1.37
Debt to Equity	0.39	0.38	0.38	0.54	0.63	0.61	0.46	0.28
Price Range	41.57-31.89	39.60-31.89	45.86-16.31	27.69-15.55	27.09-17.78	46.90-22.49	64.04-43.39	72.13-50.39
P/E Ratio	461.89-354.33	...	...	64.40-36.16	26.56-17.43	...	17.64-11.95	98.81-69.03
Average Yield %	0.94	0.71	0.38	0.47	0.96	3.74	2.75	1.70

Address: 6363 South Fiddler's Green Circle, Greenwood Village, CO 80111	**Web Site:** www.newmont.com	**Auditors:** Ernst & Young LLP
Telephone: 303-863-7414	**Officers:** Noreen Doyle - Chair Gary J. Goldberg - President, Chief Executive Officer, Executive Vice President, Chief Operating Officer	**Investor Contact:** 303-837-5362
Fax: 303-837-5837		**Transfer Agents:** Computershare, Providence, RI

NEXTERA ENERGY INC

Exchange	Symbol	Price	52Wk Range	Yield	P/E	Div Acheiver
NYS	NEE	$167.03 (6/29/2018)	168.08-138.82	2.66	9.63	22 Years

*7 Year Price Score 121.68 *NYSE Composite Index=100 *12 Month Price Score 103.45

TRADING VOLUME (thousand shares)

Interim Earnings (Per Share)

Qtr.	Mar	Jun	Sep	Dec
2015	1.45	1.59	1.93	1.09
2016	1.41	1.16	1.62	2.06
2017	3.37	1.68	1.79	4.55
2018	9.32	...	...	...

Interim Dividends (Per Share)

Amt	Decl	Ex	Rec	Pay
0.983Q	07/27/2017	08/23/2017	08/25/2017	09/15/2017
0.983Q	10/13/2017	11/22/2017	11/24/2017	12/15/2017
1.11Q	02/16/2018	02/26/2018	02/27/2018	03/15/2018
1.11Q	05/24/2018	06/04/2018	06/05/2018	06/15/2018

Indicated Div: $4.44 (Div. Reinv. Plan)

Valuation Analysis — **Institutional Holding**

Forecast EPS	$7.75	No of Institutions	1888
	(06/14/2018)		
Market Cap	$78.7 Billion	Shares	
Book Value	$32.7 Billion		445,089,120
Price/Book	2.41	% Held	
Price/Sales	4.60	N/A	

Business Summary: Electric Utilities (MIC: 3.1.1 SIC: 4911 NAIC: 221121)

NextEra Energy is a holding company. Co. is an electric power company in North America and a generator of renewable energy from the wind and sun. Co. also owns and/or operates generation, transmission and distribution facilities to support its services to retail and wholesale customers, and has investments in gas infrastructure assets. Co. operates mainly through two subsidiaries, Florida Power & Light Company (FPL) and NextEra Energy Resources, LLC (NEER). FPL is engaged primarily in the generation, transmission, distribution and sale of electric energy in Florida. NEER focuses on the development, acquisition and operation of long-term contracted assets with a focus on renewable projects.

Recent Developments: For the quarter ended Mar 31 2018, net income increased 140.8% to US$3.83 billion from US$1.59 billion in the year-earlier quarter. Revenues were US$3.86 billion, down 2.7% from US$3.97 billion the year before. Operating income was US$1.05 billion versus US$2.36 billion in the prior-year quarter, a decrease of 55.7%. Direct operating expenses declined 8.1% to US$1.60 billion from US$1.74 billion in the comparable period the year before. Indirect operating expenses amounted to US$1.22 billion compared with an income of US$127.0 million in the equivalent prior-year period.

Prospects: Our evaluation of NextEra Energy Inc. as of Jan. 21, 2018 is the result of our systematic analysis on three basic characteristics: earnings strength, relative valuation, and recent stock price movement. The company has managed to produce a neutral trend in earnings per share over the past 5 quarters and while recent estimates for the company have been mixed, NEE has posted better than expected results. Based on operating earnings yield, the company is undervalued when compared to all of the companies in our coverage universe. Share price changes over the past year indicates that NEE will perform very well over the near term.

Financial Data

(US$ in Thousands)	3 Mos	12/31/2017	12/31/2016	12/31/2015	12/31/2014	12/31/2013	12/31/2012	12/31/2011
Earnings Per Share	17.34	11.38	6.25	6.06	5.60	4.47	4.56	4.59
Cash Flow Per Share	13.47	13.68	13.64	13.58	12.66	12.03	9.55	9.78
Tang Book Value Per Share	69.44	59.89	52.01	48.97	44.96	41.47	37.90	35.92
Dividends Per Share	4.058	3.930	3.480	3.080	2.900	2.640	2.400	2.200
Dividend Payout %	23.40	34.53	55.68	50.83	51.79	59.06	52.63	47.93
Income Statement								
Total Revenue	3,863,000	17,195,000	16,155,000	17,486,000	17,021,000	15,136,000	14,256,000	15,341,000
EBITDA	5,158,000	8,540,000	8,542,000	8,141,000	7,592,000	5,997,000	5,247,000	5,158,000
Depn & Amortn	67,000	2,629,000	3,377,000	3,203,000	2,896,000	2,521,000	1,772,000	1,844,000
Income Before Taxes	4,883,000	4,526,000	4,240,000	3,883,000	3,552,000	2,496,000	2,590,000	2,397,000
Income Taxes	1,249,000	(653,000)	1,383,000	1,228,000	1,176,000	801,000	692,000	529,000
Net Income	4,428,000	5,378,000	2,912,000	2,762,000	2,469,000	1,908,000	1,911,000	1,923,000
Average Shares	474,300	472,500	465,800	454,000	440,100	427,000	419,200	419,000
Balance Sheet								
Current Assets	5,612,000	7,157,000	7,409,000	6,795,000	6,944,000	5,842,000	5,237,000	4,872,000
Total Assets	94,284,000	97,827,000	89,993,000	82,479,000	74,929,000	69,306,000	64,439,000	57,188,000
Current Liabilities	9,579,000	11,232,000	10,919,000	10,107,000	9,663,000	9,189,000	8,879,000	6,719,000
Long-Term Obligations	28,062,000	31,463,000	27,818,000	26,681,000	24,367,000	23,969,000	23,177,000	20,810,000
Total Liabilities	61,578,000	69,619,000	65,652,000	59,905,000	55,013,000	51,266,000	48,371,000	42,245,000
Stockholders' Equity	32,706,000	28,208,000	24,341,000	22,574,000	19,916,000	18,040,000	16,068,000	14,943,000
Shares Outstanding	471,000	471,000	468,000	461,000	443,000	435,000	424,000	416,000
Statistical Record								
Return on Assets %	8.87	5.73	3.37	3.51	3.42	2.85	3.13	3.49
Return on Equity %	28.26	20.47	12.38	13.00	13.01	11.19	12.29	13.08
EBITDA Margin %	133.52	49.67	52.88	46.56	44.60	39.62	36.81	33.62
Net Margin %	114.63	31.28	18.03	15.80	14.51	12.61	13.40	12.54
Asset Turnover	0.18	0.18	0.19	0.22	0.24	0.23	0.23	0.28
Current Ratio	0.59	0.64	0.68	0.67	0.72	0.64	0.59	0.73
Debt to Equity	0.86	1.12	1.14	1.18	1.22	1.33	1.44	1.39
Price Range	163.33-128.37	159.25-118.35	130.89-103.57	111.66-94.62	110.50-84.25	89.06-69.19	72.05-58.79	61.08-50.17
P/E Ratio	9.42-7.40	13.99-10.40	20.94-16.57	18.43-15.61	19.73-15.04	19.92-15.48	15.80-12.89	13.31-10.93
Average Yield %	2.74	2.79	2.91	3.00	3.01	3.31	3.65	3.96

Address: 700 Universe Boulevard, Juno Beach, FL 33408
Telephone: 561-694-4000
Fax: 561-694-4620

Web Site: www.nexteraenergy.com
Officers: James L. Robo - Chairman, President, Chief Executive Officer, Chief Operating Officer Armando Pimentel - Executive Vice President, Chief Financial Officer

Auditors: DELOITTE & TOUCHE LLP
Investor Contact: 561-694-4697
Transfer Agents: Computershare Trust Company, N.A., Canton, MA

NGL ENERGY PARTNERS LP

Exchange	Symbol	Price	52Wk Range	Yield	P/E
NYS	NGL	$12.50 (6/29/2018)	17.20-8.70	12.48	N/A

*7 Year Price Score 42.87 *NYSE Composite Index=100 *12 Month Price Score 95.20

Interim Earnings (Per Share)

Qtr.	Jun	Sep	Dec	Mar
2013-14	(0.35)	(0.05)	0.27	0.54
2014-15	(0.61)	(0.34)	(0.26)	0.88
2015-16	(0.56)	(0.41)	0.03	(1.46)
2016-17	1.38	(0.71)	(0.07)	0.13
2017-18	(0.61)	(1.56)	0.32	0.76

Interim Dividends (Per Share)

Amt	Decl	Ex	Rec	Pay
0.39Q	07/20/2017	08/02/2017	08/04/2017	08/14/2017
0.39Q	10/19/2017	11/03/2017	11/06/2017	11/14/2017
0.39Q	01/23/2018	02/05/2018	02/06/2018	02/14/2018
0.39Q	04/24/2018	05/04/2018	05/07/2018	05/15/2018

Indicated Div: $1.56

Valuation Analysis

		Institutional Holding	
Forecast EPS	$-0.18 (06/12/2018)	No of Institutions	140
Market Cap	$1.5 Billion	Shares	82,131,800
Book Value	$82.6 Million	% Held	48.85
Price/Book	18.41		
Price/Sales	0.09		

TRADING VOLUME (thousand shares)

Business Summary: Refining & Marketing (MIC: 9.1.2 SIC: 5172 NAIC: 424720)

NGL Energy Partners is a limited partnership company. At Mar 31 2017, Co.'s operations include: crude oil logistics segment, which purchases crude oil from producers and transports it to refineries or for resale; water solutions segment, which provides services for the treatment and disposal of wastewater generated from crude oil and natural gas production; liquids segment, which supplies natural gas liquids to retailers, wholesalers, refiners, and petrochemical plants; retail propane segment, which sells propane, distillates, equipment and supplies to end users; and refined products and renewables segment, which conducts gasoline, diesel, ethanol, and biodiesel marketing operations.

Recent Developments: For the year ended Mar 31 2018, net loss amounted to US$69.6 million versus net income of US$143.9 million in the prior year. Revenues were US$17.28 billion, up 32.7% from US$13.02 billion the year before. Operating income was US$138.3 million versus US$255.1 million in the prior year, a decrease of 45.8%. Direct operating expenses rose 34.2% to US$16.54 billion from US$12.32 billion in the comparable period the year before. Indirect operating expenses increased 36.7% to US$608.4 million from US$445.2 million in the equivalent prior-year period.

Prospects: On April 17, 2017, we entered into a purchase and sale agreement with the party owning the 50% noncontrolling interest in NGL Solids Solutions, LLC. Total consideration was $23.1 million, which consisted of cash of $20.0 million and the termination of a non-compete agreement that we valued at $3.1 million and in return we received the following, the remaining 50% interest in NGL Solids Solutions, LLC; and two parcels of land to develop saltwater disposal wells.

Financial Data
(US$ in Thousands)

	03/31/2018	03/31/2017	03/31/2016	03/31/2015	03/31/2014	03/31/2013	03/31/2012	03/31/2011
Earnings Per Share	(1.08)	0.95	(2.35)	(0.29)	0.51	0.96	0.32	1.16
Cash Flow Per Share	1.14	(0.25)	3.34	3.04	1.38	3.20	5.94	6.24
Dividends Per Share	1.560	1.560	2.538	2.366	2.014	1.688	0.854	...
Dividend Payout %	...	164.21	...	...	394.85	175.78	267.00	...
Income Statement								
Total Revenue	17,282,718	13,022,228	11,742,110	16,802,057	9,699,274	4,417,767	1,310,473	622,232
EBITDA	252,267	412,914	66,442	229,982	166,551	120,994	25,893	17,788
Depn & Amortn	128,808	119,707	136,938	105,700	59,900	39,196	10,573	2,848
Income Before Taxes	(76,111)	142,729	(203,585)	14,159	47,797	50,065	8,465	12,679
Income Taxes	1,458	1,939	(367)	(3,622)	937	1,875	601	...
Net Income	(70,875)	137,042	(198,929)	16,661	47,655	47,940	7,876	12,679
Average Shares	120,991	111,850	104,838	86,359	61,970	41,353	15,169	10,933
Balance Sheet								
Current Assets	1,799,758	1,484,207	1,028,480	1,645,344	1,309,299	762,119	198,624	76,821
Total Assets	6,151,122	6,320,379	5,560,155	6,547,501	4,167,223	2,291,347	749,137	163,833
Current Liabilities	1,116,382	938,598	706,017	1,112,996	995,792	659,288	144,419	50,544
Long-Term Obligations	2,682,628	2,963,483	2,912,837	2,745,299	1,629,834	740,436	199,177	65,541
Total Liabilities	4,065,954	4,116,433	3,903,797	4,421,707	2,640,644	1,407,669	344,236	116,480
Stockholders' Equity	82,576	63,890	...	...	...	...	...	...
Shares Outstanding	121,594	120,299	104,273	103,898	79,420	53,676	29,244	10,933
Statistical Record								
Return on Assets %	N.M.	2.31	N.M.	0.31	1.48	3.15	1.72	31.04
EBITDA Margin %	1.46	3.17	0.57	1.37	1.72	2.74	1.98	2.86
Net Margin %	N.M.	1.05	N.M.	0.10	0.49	1.09	0.60	2.04
Asset Turnover	2.77	2.19	1.93	3.14	3.00	2.91	2.86	15.23
Current Ratio	1.61	1.58	1.46	1.48	1.31	1.16	1.38	1.52
Debt to Equity	32.49	46.38	...	...	...	...	...	...
Price Range	23.15-8.70	25.75-7.18	33.63-5.70	45.67-23.44	37.72-26.65	26.90-20.15	23.15-18.40	...
P/E Ratio	...	27.11-7.56	...	...	73.96-52.25	28.02-20.99	72.34-57.50	...
Average Yield %	11.71	8.47	12.60	6.56	6.37	7.14	4.07	...

Address: 6120 South Yale Avenue, Suite 805, Tulsa, OK 74136
Telephone: 918-481-1119

Web Site: www.nglenergypartners.com
Officers: H. Michael Krimbill - Chief Executive Officer, Chief Financial Officer Robert W. (Trey) Karlovich - Executive Vice President, Chief Financial Officer, Treasurer, Associate/Affiliate Company Officer

Auditors: Grant Thornton LLP
Investor Contact: 918-481-1119
Transfer Agents: Wells Fargo Bank, N.A., St. Paul, MN

NIELSEN HOLDINGS PLC

Exchange	Symbol	Price	52Wk Range	Yield	P/E
NYS	NLSN	$30.93 (6/29/2018)	43.25-29.74	4.53	25.56

'7 Year Price Score 73.40 'NYSE Composite Index=100 '12 Month Price Score 83.74

Interim Earnings (Per Share)

Qtr.	Mar	Jun	Sep	Dec
2015	0.17	0.31	0.38	0.68
2016	0.27	0.31	0.36	0.45
2017	0.20	0.37	0.41	0.23
2018	0.20	...	...	...

Interim Dividends (Per Share)

Amt	Decl	Ex	Rec	Pay
0.34Q	07/20/2017	08/22/2017	08/24/2017	09/07/2017
0.34Q	10/19/2017	11/20/2017	11/21/2017	12/05/2017
0.34Q	02/22/2018	03/06/2018	03/07/2018	03/21/2018
0.35Q	04/19/2018	06/05/2018	06/06/2018	06/20/2018

Indicated Div: $1.40

Valuation Analysis

Forecast EPS	N/A
Market Cap	$11.0 Billion
Book Value	$4.3 Billion
Price/Book	2.59
Price/Sales	1.66

Institutional Holding

No of Institutions	543
Shares	426,583,520
% Held	80.75

Business Summary: Business Services (MIC: 7.5.2 SIC: 7389 NAIC: 561499)

Nielsen Holdings is an information and measurement company that provides clients with consumer behavior. Co. delivers media and marketing information, analytics and manufacturer and retailer insight about what and where consumers buy and what consumers read, watch and listen to. Co. has two segments: Buy and Watch. Co.'s Buy segment provides retail transactional measurement data, consumer behavior information and analytics primarily to businesses in the consumer packaged goods industry. Co.'s Watch segment provides viewership and listening data and analytics primarily to the media and advertising industries across the television, radio, online and mobile viewing and listening platforms.

Recent Developments: For the quarter ended Mar 31 2018, net income increased 2.7% to US$75.0 million from US$73.0 million in the year-earlier quarter. Revenues were US$1.61 billion, up 5.5% from US$1.53 billion the year before. Operating income was US$207.0 million versus US$205.0 million in the prior-year quarter, an increase of 1.0%. Direct operating expenses rose 8.8% to US$719.0 million from US$661.0 million in the comparable period the year before. Indirect operating expenses increased 3.6% to US$684.0 million from US$660.0 million in the equivalent prior-year period.

Prospects: Our evaluation of Nielsen Holdings PLC as of Sep. 17, 2017 is the result of our systematic analysis on three basic characteristics: earnings strength, relative valuation, and recent stock price movement. The company has produced a positive trend in earnings per share over the past 5 quarters and while recent estimates for the company have remained steady, NLSN has posted better than expected results. Based on operating earnings yield, the company is about fairly valued when compared to all of the companies in our coverage universe. Share price changes over the past year indicates that NLSN will perform poorly over the near term.

Financial Data
(US$ in Millions)

	3 Mos	12/31/2017	12/31/2016	12/31/2015	12/31/2014	12/31/2013	12/31/2012	12/31/2011
Earnings Per Share	1.21	1.20	1.39	1.54	1.00	1.94	0.75	0.24
Cash Flow Per Share	3.23	3.67	3.60	3.21	2.88	2.40	2.16	1.82
Dividends Per Share	1.360	1.330	1.210	0.280	0.950	0.720	...	...
Dividend Payout %	112.40	110.83	87.05	18.18	95.00	37.11	...	...
Income Statement								
Total Revenue	1,610	6,572	6,309	6,172	6,288	5,703	5,612	5,532
EBITDA	375	1,369	1,310	1,428	1,080	996	1,000	746
Depn & Amortn	167	171	165	160	162	169	183	171
Income Before Taxes	114	828	816	961	621	520	408	104
Income Taxes	39	388	309	383	236	91	140	22
Net Income	72	429	502	570	384	740	273	84
Average Shares	357	358	362	370	384	380	366	357
Balance Sheet								
Current Assets	2,264	2,282	2,222	1,908	2,019	2,134	1,676	1,665
Total Assets	16,923	16,866	15,730	15,303	15,376	15,530	14,585	14,504
Current Liabilities	1,839	1,697	1,594	1,687	1,798	1,535	1,751	1,692
Long-Term Obligations	8,286	8,357	7,738	7,028	6,465	6,492	6,229	6,619
Total Liabilities	12,665	12,621	11,628	10,870	10,320	9,801	9,655	9,871
Stockholders' Equity	4,258	4,245	4,102	4,433	5,056	5,729	4,930	4,633
Shares Outstanding	356	355	357	362	372	378	362	359
Statistical Record								
Return on Assets %	2.59	2.63	3.23	3.72	2.48	4.91	1.87	0.58
Return on Equity %	10.26	10.28	11.73	12.01	7.12	13.88	5.69	2.23
EBITDA Margin %	23.29	20.83	20.76	23.14	17.18	17.46	17.82	13.49
Net Margin %	4.47	6.53	7.96	9.24	6.11	12.98	4.86	1.52
Asset Turnover	0.40	0.40	0.41	0.40	0.41	0.38	0.38	0.38
Current Ratio	1.23	1.34	1.39	1.13	1.12	1.39	0.96	0.98
Debt to Equity	1.95	1.97	1.89	1.59	1.28	1.13	1.26	1.43
Price Range	43.25-31.51	45.50-35.67	55.81-41.95	49.06-42.20	49.51-41.04	45.93-30.59	31.80-25.03	32.06-25.00
P/E Ratio	35.74-26.04	37.92-29.73	40.15-30.18	31.86-27.40	49.51-41.04	23.68-15.77	42.40-33.37	133.58-104.17
Average Yield %	3.57	3.32	2.42	0.61	2.10	2.01	...	...

Address: 85 Broad Street, New York, NY 10004 **Telephone:** 646-654-5000	**Web Site:** www.nielsen.com **Officers:** Dwight M. (Mitch) Barns - Chief Executive Officer, Division Officer Jamere Jackson - Chief Financial Officer	**Auditors:** Ernst & Young LLP **Investor Contact:** 646-654-4602 **Transfer Agents:** Computershare

NIKE INC

Exchange	Symbol	Price	52Wk Range	Yield	P/E	Div Acheiver
NYS	NKE	$79.68 (6/29/2018)	79.68-50.83	1.00	75.17	16 Years

*7 Year Price Score 113.29 *NYSE Composite Index=100 *12 Month Price Score 114.49

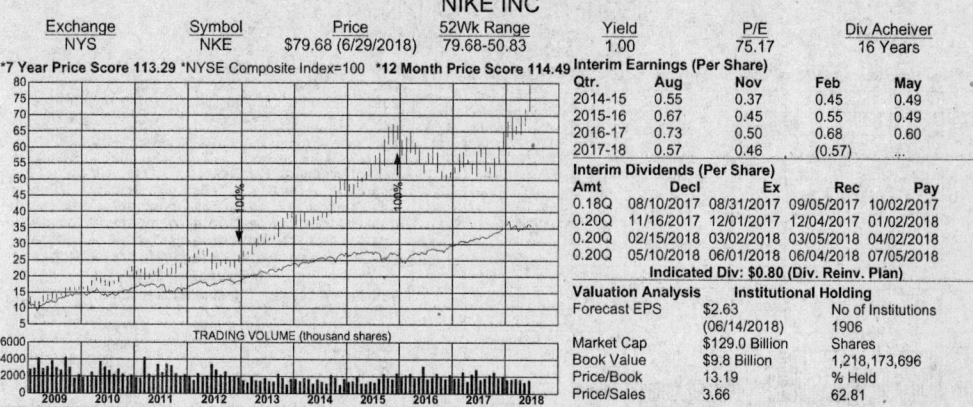

Interim Earnings (Per Share)

Qtr.	Aug	Nov	Feb	May
2014-15	0.55	0.37	0.45	0.49
2015-16	0.67	0.45	0.55	0.49
2016-17	0.73	0.50	0.68	0.60
2017-18	0.57	0.46	(0.57)	...

Interim Dividends (Per Share)

Amt	Decl	Ex	Rec	Pay
0.18Q	08/10/2017	08/31/2017	09/05/2017	10/02/2017
0.20Q	11/16/2017	12/01/2017	12/04/2017	01/02/2018
0.20Q	02/15/2018	03/02/2018	03/05/2018	04/02/2018
0.20Q	05/10/2018	06/01/2018	06/04/2018	07/05/2018

Indicated Div: $0.80 (Div. Reinv. Plan)

Valuation Analysis — **Institutional Holding**

Forecast EPS	$2.63	No of Institutions
	(06/14/2018)	1906
Market Cap	$129.0 Billion	Shares
Book Value	$9.8 Billion	1,218,173,696
Price/Book	13.19	% Held
Price/Sales	3.66	62.81

TRADING VOLUME (thousand shares)

Business Summary: Apparel, Footwear & Accessories (MIC: 1.4.2 SIC: 3021 NAIC: 316211)

NIKE is mainly engaged in the design, development, marketing and selling of athletic footwear, apparel, equipment, accessories and services. Co. sells its products to retail accounts, via Co.-owned retail stores, internet websites, and mobile applications (which Co. refers to as its Direct to Consumer operations), and via a mix of independent distributors and licensees throughout the world. Co. focuses its NIKE Brand offerings in nine key categories: Running, NIKE Basketball, the Jordan Brand, Football (Soccer), Men's Training, Women's Training, Action Sports, Sportswear (its sports lifestyle products) and Golf. Men's Training includes Co.'s baseball and American football product offerings.

Recent Developments: For the quarter ended Feb 28 2018, net loss amounted to US$921.0 million versus net income of US$1.14 billion in the year-earlier quarter. Revenues were US$8.98 billion, up 6.5% from US$8.43 billion the year before. Direct operating expenses rose 7.8% to US$5.05 billion from US$4.68 billion in the comparable period the year before. Indirect operating expenses increased 14.5% to US$2.78 billion from US$2.43 billion in the equivalent prior-year period.

Prospects: Our evaluation of NIKE Inc. as of Jan. 21, 2018 is the result of our systematic analysis on three basic characteristics: earnings strength, relative valuation, and recent stock price movement. The company has generated a negative trend in earnings per share over the past 5 quarters. However, while recent estimates for the company have been lowered by analysts, NKE has posted better than expected results. Based on operating earnings yield, the company is about fairly valued when compared to all of the companies in our coverage universe. Share price changes over the past year indicates that NKE will perform poorly over the near term.

Financial Data
(US$ in Thousands)

	9 Mos	6 Mos	3 Mos	05/31/2017	05/31/2016	05/31/2015	05/31/2014	05/31/2013
Earnings Per Share	1.06	2.31	2.35	2.51	2.16	1.85	1.49	1.36
Cash Flow Per Share	2.20	2.37	2.13	2.20	1.82	2.72	1.70	1.69
Tang Book Value Per Share	5.78	6.98	7.07	7.29	7.04	7.17	5.98	5.95
Dividends Per Share	0.740	0.720	0.780	0.680	0.620	0.540	0.465	0.405
Dividend Payout %	69.81	31.17	29.79	27.09	28.70	29.19	31.31	29.89
Income Statement								
Total Revenue	26,608,000	17,624,000	9,070,000	34,350,000	32,376,000	30,601,000	27,799,000	25,313,000
EBITDA	3,726,000	2,356,000	1,273,000	5,651,000	5,291,000	4,839,000	4,095,000	3,707,000
Depn & Amortn	574,000	376,000	185,000	706,000	649,000	606,000	518,000	438,000
Income Before Taxes	3,110,000	1,951,000	1,072,000	4,886,000	4,623,000	4,205,000	3,544,000	3,272,000
Income Taxes	2,314,000	234,000	122,000	646,000	863,000	932,000	851,000	808,000
Net Income	796,000	1,717,000	950,000	4,240,000	3,760,000	3,273,000	2,693,000	2,485,000
Average Shares	1,623,500	1,660,900	1,676,900	1,692,000	1,742,500	1,768,800	1,811,600	1,832,800
Balance Sheet								
Current Assets	15,355,000	16,582,000	16,192,000	16,061,000	15,025,000	15,976,000	13,696,000	13,626,000
Total Assets	22,552,000	24,055,000	23,647,000	23,259,000	21,396,000	21,600,000	18,594,000	17,584,000
Current Liabilities	5,783,000	6,750,000	6,056,000	5,474,000	5,358,000	6,334,000	5,027,000	3,926,000
Long-Term Obligations	3,469,000	3,472,000	3,472,000	3,471,000	2,010,000	1,079,000	1,199,000	1,210,000
Total Liabilities	12,770,000	12,297,000	11,654,000	10,852,000	9,138,000	8,893,000	7,770,000	6,428,000
Stockholders' Equity	9,782,000	11,758,000	11,993,000	12,407,000	12,258,000	12,707,000	10,824,000	11,156,000
Shares Outstanding	1,619,000	1,624,000	1,637,000	1,643,000	1,682,000	1,714,000	1,740,000	1,788,000
Statistical Record								
Return on Assets %	7.89	16.55	17.59	18.99	17.44	16.29	14.89	15.04
Return on Equity %	16.03	32.11	32.63	34.38	30.04	27.82	24.50	23.08
EBITDA Margin %	14.00	13.37	14.04	16.45	16.34	15.81	14.73	14.64
Net Margin %	2.99	9.74	10.47	12.34	11.61	10.70	9.69	9.82
Asset Turnover	1.54	1.49	1.53	1.54	1.50	1.52	1.54	1.53
Current Ratio	2.66	2.46	2.67	2.93	2.80	2.52	2.72	3.47
Debt to Equity	0.35	0.30	0.29	0.28	0.16	0.08	0.11	0.11
Price Range	69.65-50.83	60.42-50.07	60.14-49.62	60.22-49.62	67.17-50.67	52.49-37.27	39.93-29.98	32.95-21.95
P/E Ratio	65.71-47.95	26.16-21.68	25.59-21.11	23.99-19.77	31.09-23.46	28.37-20.15	26.80-20.12	24.23-16.14
Average Yield %	1.29	1.31	1.28	1.25	1.04	1.20	1.30	1.55

Address: One Bowerman Drive, Beaverton, OR 97005-6453 **Telephone:** 503-671-6453	**Web Site:** www.nike.com **Officers:** Mark G. Parker - Chairman, President, Chief Executive Officer Eric D. Sprunk - Chief Operating Officer, Vice President	**Auditors:** PricewaterhouseCoopers LLP **Transfer Agents:** Computershare Trust Company, N.A., Providence, RI

NISOURCE INC. (HOLDING CO.)

Exchange	Symbol	Price	52Wk Range	Yield	P/E
NYS	NI	$26.28 (6/29/2018)	27.58-22.51	2.97	47.78

*7 Year Price Score 119.77 *NYSE Composite Index=100 *12 Month Price Score 97.20

Interim Earnings (Per Share)

Qtr.	Mar	Jun	Sep	Dec
2015	0.85	(0.11)	(0.02)	0.19
2016	0.56	0.09	0.08	0.27
2017	0.65	(0.14)	0.04	(0.16)
2018	0.81	...	...	...

Interim Dividends (Per Share)

Amt	Decl	Ex	Rec	Pay
0.175Q	08/08/2017	10/30/2017	10/31/2017	11/20/2017
0.195Q	01/26/2018	02/08/2018	02/09/2018	02/20/2018
0.195Q	03/27/2018	04/27/2018	04/30/2018	05/18/2018
0.195Q	05/08/2018	07/30/2018	07/31/2018	08/20/2018

Indicated Div: $0.78

Valuation Analysis

Forecast EPS	$1.28 (06/14/2018)	**Institutional Holding**
		No of Institutions 703
Market Cap	$8.9 Billion	Shares 359,518,880
Book Value	$4.5 Billion	
Price/Book	1.97	% Held 86.63
Price/Sales	1.76	

Business Summary: Equipment & Services (MIC: 9.1.3 SIC: 4923 NAIC: 221210)

NiSource is an energy holding company. Through its subsidiaries, Co. is a natural gas distribution company. Co.'s reportable segments are: Gas Distribution Operations and Electric Operations. At Dec 31 2017, Co.'s natural gas distribution operations served approximately 3.5 million customers in seven states and operated approximately 60,000 miles of pipeline. Through its electric operations, Co. generates, transmits and distributes electricity through its subsidiary, Northern Indiana Public Service Company, and engages in wholesale and transmission transactions. At Dec 31 2017, the electric operations served approximately 469,000 customers in 20 counties in the northern part of Indiana.

Recent Developments: For the quarter ended Mar 31 2018, net income increased 30.7% to US$276.1 million from US$211.3 million in the year-earlier quarter. Revenues were US$1.75 billion, up 9.5% from US$1.60 billion the year before. Operating income was US$400.6 million versus US$415.4 million in the prior-year quarter, a decrease of 3.6%. Direct operating expenses rose 31.2% to US$724.4 million from US$552.3 million in the comparable period the year before. Indirect operating expenses decreased 0.8% to US$625.8 million from US$630.9 million in the equivalent prior-year period.

Prospects: Our evaluation of NiSource Inc. as of Jan. 21, 2018 is the result of our systematic analysis on three basic characteristics: earnings strength, relative valuation, and recent stock price movement. The company has generated a negative trend in earnings per share over the past 5 quarters and while recent estimates for the company have remained steady, NI has posted results that were in line with analysts expectations. Based on operating earnings yield, the company is undervalued when compared to all of the companies in our coverage universe. Share price changes over the past year indicates that NI will perform very well over the near term.

Financial Data

(US$ in Thousands)	3 Mos	12/31/2017	12/31/2016	12/31/2015	12/31/2014	12/31/2013	12/31/2012	12/31/2011
Earnings Per Share	0.55	0.39	1.02	0.90	1.67	1.70	1.39	1.03
Cash Flow Per Share	2.13	2.25	2.49	4.58	4.19	4.60	4.36	3.10
Tang Book Value Per Share	7.66	7.11	6.62	5.95	7.10	6.20	5.13	3.63
Dividends Per Share	0.720	0.700	0.640	0.830	1.020	0.980	0.940	0.920
Dividend Payout %	130.91	179.49	62.75	92.22	61.08	57.65	67.63	89.32
Income Statement								
Total Revenue	1,750,800	4,874,600	4,492,500	4,651,800	6,470,600	5,657,300	5,061,200	6,019,100
EBITDA	576,600	1,369,400	1,411,000	1,252,400	1,849,800	1,714,800	1,578,600	1,372,000
Depn & Amortn	144,700	577,700	554,700	533,100	615,500	586,700	571,600	547,100
Income Before Taxes	338,800	443,100	510,200	339,900	794,500	716,900	593,900	452,500
Income Taxes	62,700	314,500	182,100	141,300	310,400	261,900	215,500	163,300
Net Income	276,100	128,500	331,500	286,500	530,000	532,100	416,100	299,100
Average Shares	339,000	330,800	323,500	319,836	316,600	313,600	300,400	288,500
Balance Sheet								
Current Assets	1,633,800	1,763,300	1,762,100	1,577,200	2,466,500	2,159,200	2,352,400	2,248,200
Total Assets	20,098,500	19,961,700	18,691,900	17,492,500	24,866,300	22,653,900	21,844,700	20,708,300
Current Liabilities	3,226,200	3,178,400	3,452,200	2,657,500	3,954,900	3,178,400	3,301,600	3,646,400
Long-Term Obligations	7,286,800	7,512,200	6,058,200	5,948,500	8,155,900	7,593,200	6,819,100	6,267,100
Total Liabilities	15,592,300	15,641,600	14,620,700	13,649,000	18,691,000	16,767,300	16,290,400	15,710,100
Stockholders' Equity	4,506,200	4,320,100	4,071,200	3,843,500	6,175,300	5,886,600	5,554,300	4,997,300
Shares Outstanding	337,598	337,015	323,159	319,110	316,037	313,675	310,280	281,853
Statistical Record								
Return on Assets %	1.00	0.66	1.83	1.35	2.23	2.39	1.95	1.47
Return on Equity %	4.45	3.06	8.35	5.72	8.79	9.30	7.87	6.03
EBITDA Margin %	32.93	28.09	31.41	26.92	28.59	30.31	31.19	22.79
Net Margin %	15.77	2.64	7.38	6.16	8.19	9.41	8.22	4.97
Asset Turnover	0.26	0.25	0.25	0.22	0.27	0.25	0.24	0.30
Current Ratio	0.51	0.55	0.51	0.59	0.62	0.68	0.71	0.62
Debt to Equity	1.62	1.74	1.49	1.55	1.32	1.29	1.23	1.25
Price Range	27.58-22.51	27.58-21.84	26.77-19.46	19.83-16.10	17.41-12.69	12.92-9.78	10.15-8.83	9.38-6.92
P/E Ratio	50.15-40.93	70.72-56.00	26.25-19.08	22.03-17.88	10.43-7.60	7.60-5.75	7.30-6.35	9.11-6.72
Average Yield %	2.84	2.78	2.76	4.67	6.85	8.43	9.77	11.53

Address: 801 East 86th Avenue, Merrillville, IN 46410	**Web Site:** www.nisource.com	**Auditors:** Deloitte & Touche LLP
Telephone: 877-647-5990	**Officers:** Richard L. Thompson - Chairman Joseph Hamrock - President, Chief Executive Officer, Division Officer	**Investor Contact:** 219-647-5200
		Transfer Agents: Computershare, Providence, R.I.

NOBLE ENERGY INC

*7 Year Price Score 52.13   *NYSE Composite Index=100   *12 Month Price Score 116.51

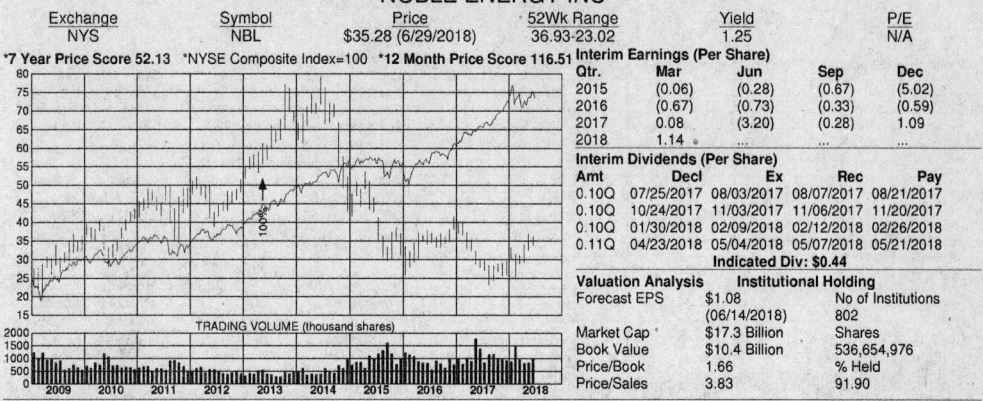

Interim Earnings (Per Share)

Qtr.	Mar	Jun	Sep	Dec
2015	(0.06)	(0.28)	(0.67)	(5.02)
2016	(0.67)	(0.73)	(0.33)	(0.59)
2017	0.08	(3.20)	(0.28)	1.09
2018	1.14	...	...	...

Interim Dividends (Per Share)

Amt	Decl	Ex	Rec	Pay
0.10Q	07/25/2017	08/03/2017	08/07/2017	08/21/2017
0.10Q	10/24/2017	11/03/2017	11/06/2017	11/20/2017
0.10Q	01/30/2018	02/09/2018	02/12/2018	02/26/2018
0.11Q	04/23/2018	05/04/2018	05/07/2018	05/21/2018
		Indicated Div: $0.44		

Valuation Analysis | **Institutional Holding**

Forecast EPS	$1.08	No of Institutions	
	(06/14/2018)	802	
Market Cap	$17.3 Billion	Shares	
Book Value	$10.4 Billion	536,654,976	
Price/Book	1.66	% Held	
Price/Sales	3.83	91.90	

Business Summary: Production & Extraction (MIC: 9.1.1 SIC: 1311 NAIC: 211111)

Noble Energy is engaged in crude oil, natural gas and natural gas liquids exploration and production. Co.'s properties consist primarily of interests in developed and undeveloped crude oil and natural gas leases and concessions. Co. also owns natural gas processing plants, gathering systems and other pipeline systems. Co. has operations in these areas: the DJ Basin, the Marcellus Shale, Eagle Ford Shale, Permian Basin, the deepwater Gulf of Mexico, offshore West Africa and Eastern Mediterranean. As of Dec 31 2017, Co. had total proved reserves of 1.97 billion barrels of oil equivalent (BoE), of which 1,097.0 million BoE are proved undeveloped and 868.0 million BoE are proved developed.

Recent Developments: For the quarter ended Mar 31 2018, net income increased to US$574.0 million from US$47.0 million in the year-earlier quarter. Revenues were US$1.29 billion, up 24.1% from US$1.04 billion the year before. Operating income was US$708.0 million versus US$35.0 million in the prior-year quarter, an increase of. Direct operating expenses rose 5.9% to US$321.0 million from US$303.0 million in the comparable period the year before. Indirect operating expenses decreased 63.2% to US$257.0 million from US$698.0 million in the equivalent prior-year period.

Prospects: Our evaluation of Noble Energy Inc. as of Jan. 21, 2018 is the result of our systematic analysis on three basic characteristics: earnings strength, relative valuation, and recent stock price movement. The company has generated a negative trend in earnings per share over the past 5 quarters. Because the company lacks sufficient analyst estimate data, we place greater weight on the historical EPS trend as the measure of earnings strength. Based on operating earnings yield, the company is overvalued when compared to all of the companies in our coverage universe. Share price changes over the past year indicates that NBL will perform very poorly over the near term.

Financial Data

(US$ in Thousands)	3 Mos	12/31/2017	12/31/2016	12/31/2015	12/31/2014	12/31/2013	12/31/2012	12/31/2011
Earnings Per Share	(1.25)	(2.38)	(2.32)	(6.07)	3.27	2.69	2.86	1.27
Cash Flow Per Share	4.10	4.16	3.13	5.13	9.71	8.18	8.22	6.16
Tang Book Value Per Share	17.64	17.61	21.43	24.02	26.61	23.78	21.29	18.45
Dividends Per Share	0.400	0.400	0.400	0.720	0.680	0.545	0.455	0.400
Dividend Payout %	...	...	...	...	20.80	20.26	15.94	31.50
Income Statement								
Total Revenue	1,286,000	4,256,000	3,491,000	3,133,000	5,101,000	5,015,000	4,223,000	3,763,000
EBITDA	1,084,000	216,000	1,065,000	288,000	3,679,000	3,072,000	2,883,000	1,737,000
Depn & Amortn	468,000	2,053,000	2,509,000	2,244,000	1,759,000	1,570,000	1,403,000	965,000
Income Before Taxes	543,000	(2,191,000)	(1,772,000)	(2,219,000)	1,710,000	1,344,000	1,356,000	715,000
Income Taxes	(31,000)	(1,141,000)	(787,000)	222,000	496,000	437,000	391,000	262,000
Net Income	554,000	(1,118,000)	(998,000)	(2,441,000)	1,214,000	978,000	1,027,000	453,000
Average Shares	488,000	469,000	430,000	402,000	367,000	363,000	360,000	358,000
Balance Sheet								
Current Assets	2,594,000	2,203,000	1,955,000	2,276,000	3,075,000	2,611,000	2,771,000	2,418,000
Total Assets	22,448,000	21,476,000	21,011,000	24,196,000	22,553,000	19,642,000	17,554,000	16,444,000
Current Liabilities	2,214,000	1,739,000	1,478,000	1,805,000	2,522,000	2,342,000	2,532,000	2,268,000
Long-Term Obligations	6,858,000	6,746,000	7,011,000	7,976,000	6,103,000	4,566,000	3,736,000	4,100,000
Total Liabilities	12,086,000	11,540,000	11,723,000	13,826,000	12,228,000	10,458,000	9,296,000	9,179,000
Stockholders' Equity	10,362,000	9,936,000	9,288,000	10,370,000	10,325,000	9,184,000	8,258,000	7,265,000
Shares Outstanding	489,000	489,956	433,399	431,792	364,693	359,905	358,000	356,000
Statistical Record								
Return on Assets %	N.M.	N.M.	N.M.	N.M.	5.75	5.26	6.03	3.05
Return on Equity %	N.M.	N.M.	N.M.	N.M.	12.45	11.21	13.20	6.42
EBITDA Margin %	84.29	5.08	30.51	9.19	72.12	61.26	68.27	46.16
Net Margin %	43.08	N.M.	N.M.	N.M.	23.80	19.50	24.32	12.04
Asset Turnover	0.21	0.20	0.15	0.13	0.24	0.27	0.25	0.25
Current Ratio	1.17	1.27	1.32	1.26	1.22	1.11	1.09	1.07
Debt to Equity	0.66	0.68	0.75	0.77	0.59	0.50	0.45	0.56
Price Range	35.36-23.02	40.30-23.02	41.64-25.72	53.47-29.58	79.23-43.00	77.13-50.87	52.28-38.80	49.84-34.28
P/E Ratio	...	...	...	...	24.23-13.15	28.67-18.91	18.28-13.56	39.24-27.00
Average Yield %	1.39	1.31	1.16	1.77	1.03	0.88	0.97	0.90

Address: 1001 Noble Energy Way, Houston, TX 77070	Web Site: www.nobleenergyinc.com	Auditors: KPMG LLP
Telephone: 281-872-3100	**Officers:** David L. Stover - Chairman, President, Chief Executive Officer, Chief Operating Officer Kenneth M. Fisher - Executive Vice President, Senior Vice President, Chief Financial Officer	**Investor Contact:** 281-.87-2.3125
Fax: 281-872-3111		**Transfer Agents:** Wells Fargo Bank, N.A., Mendota Heights, MN

NORDSTROM, INC.

Exchange	Symbol	Price	52Wk Range	Yield	P/E
NYS	JWN	$51.78 (6/29/2018)	53.56-38.30	2.86	18.97

*7 Year Price Score 67.78 *NYSE Composite Index=100 *12 Month Price Score 103.41

TRADING VOLUME (thousand shares)

Interim Earnings (Per Share)

Qtr.	Apr	Jul	Oct	Jan
2015-16	0.66	1.09	0.42	0.98
2016-17	0.26	0.67	(0.06)	1.15
2017-18	0.37	0.65	0.67	0.89
2018-19	0.52	...	...	...

Interim Dividends (Per Share)

Amt	Decl	Ex	Rec	Pay
0.37Q	08/16/2017	08/24/2017	08/28/2017	09/12/2017
0.37Q	11/15/2017	11/24/2017	11/27/2017	12/12/2017
0.37Q	02/21/2018	03/02/2018	03/05/2018	03/20/2018
0.37Q	05/08/2018	05/17/2018	05/18/2018	06/04/2018

Indicated Div: $1.48

Valuation Analysis

		Institutional Holding	
Forecast EPS	$3.46	No of Institutions	
	(06/13/2018)	849	
Market Cap	$8.7 Billion	Shares	
Book Value	$1.1 Billion	128,706,624	
Price/Book	8.12	% Held	
Price/Sales	0.55	50.77	

Business Summary: Retail - General Merchandise/Department Stores (MIC: 2.1.1 SIC: 5651 NAIC: 448140)

Nordstrom is a retailer that provides brands focused on apparel, shoes, cosmetics and accessories for women, men, young adults and children. Co. has two segments: Retail, which included 117 Nordstrom-branded stores in the U.S. and Nordstrom.com, 235 off-price Nordstrom Rack stores, six Canada stores, Nordstromrack.com/HauteLook, seven Trunk Club clubhouses and TrunkClub.com, two Jeffrey boutiques and two clearance stores that operate as Last Chance, as of Mar 19 2018; and Credit, which customers can access payment products and services, including a Nordstrom-branded private label card, two Nordstrom-branded Visa credit cards and a debit card for Nordstrom purchases.

Recent Developments: For the quarter ended May 5 2018, net income increased 38.1% to US$87.0 million from US$63.0 million in the year-earlier quarter. Revenues were US$3.56 billion, up 6.2% from US$3.35 billion the year before. Operating income was US$153.0 million versus US$151.0 million in the prior-year quarter, an increase of 1.3%. Direct operating expenses rose 6.2% to US$2.29 billion from US$2.16 billion in the comparable period the year before. Indirect operating expenses increased 6.9% to US$1.12 billion from US$1.05 billion in the equivalent prior-year period.

Prospects: Our evaluation of Nordstrom Inc. as of Jan. 21, 2018 is the result of our systematic analysis on three basic characteristics: earnings strength, relative valuation, and recent stock price movement. The company has managed to produce a neutral trend in earnings per share over the past 5 quarters and while recent estimates for the company have been mixed, JWN has posted better than expected results. Based on operating earnings yield, the company is undervalued when compared to all of the companies in our coverage universe. Share price changes over the past year indicates that JWN will perform very poorly over the near term.

Financial Data
(US$ in Thousands)

	3 Mos	02/03/2018	01/28/2017	01/30/2016	01/31/2015	02/01/2014	02/02/2013	01/28/2012
Earnings Per Share	2.73	2.59	2.02	3.15	3.72	3.71	3.56	3.14
Cash Flow Per Share	7.65	8.26	9.54	13.19	6.44	6.81	5.38	5.53
Tang Book Value Per Share	4.89	4.43	3.72	2.51	10.55	9.96	8.82	8.58
Dividends Per Share	1.480	1.480	1.480	6.330	1.320	1.200	1.080	0.920
Dividend Payout %	54.21	57.14	73.27	200.95	35.48	32.35	30.34	29.30
Income Statement								
Total Revenue	3,561,000	15,478,000	14,757,000	14,437,000	13,506,000	12,540,000	12,148,000	10,877,000
EBITDA	135,000	1,510,000	1,375,000	1,661,000	1,821,000	1,794,000	1,711,000	1,574,000
Depn & Amortn	(18,000)	584,000	570,000	560,000	498,000	444,000	366,000	325,000
Income Before Taxes	125,000	790,000	684,000	976,000	1,185,000	1,189,000	1,185,000	1,119,000
Income Taxes	38,000	353,000	330,000	376,000	465,000	455,000	450,000	436,000
Net Income	87,000	437,000	354,000	600,000	720,000	734,000	735,000	683,000
Average Shares	170,200	168,900	175,600	190,100	193,600	197,700	206,700	217,700
Balance Sheet								
Current Assets	3,563,000	3,503,000	3,242,000	3,014,000	5,224,000	5,228,000	5,081,000	5,560,000
Total Assets	8,016,000	8,115,000	7,858,000	7,698,000	9,245,000	8,574,000	8,089,000	8,491,000
Current Liabilities	3,255,000	3,289,000	3,029,000	2,911,000	2,800,000	2,541,000	2,226,000	2,575,000
Long-Term Obligations	2,680,000	2,681,000	2,763,000	2,795,000	3,123,000	3,106,000	3,124,000	3,141,000
Total Liabilities	6,946,000	7,138,000	6,988,000	6,827,000	6,805,000	6,494,000	6,176,000	6,535,000
Stockholders' Equity	1,070,000	977,000	870,000	871,000	2,440,000	2,080,000	1,913,000	1,956,000
Shares Outstanding	167,800	167,000	170,000	173,500	190,100	191,200	197,000	207,600
Statistical Record								
Return on Assets %	5.85	5.38	4.56	7.10	8.10	8.83	8.72	8.59
Return on Equity %	52.89	46.55	40.78	36.34	31.95	36.87	37.38	34.44
EBITDA Margin %	3.79	9.76	9.32	11.51	13.48	14.31	14.08	14.47
Net Margin %	2.44	2.82	2.40	4.16	5.33	5.85	6.05	6.28
Asset Turnover	1.99	1.91	1.90	1.71	1.52	1.51	1.44	1.37
Current Ratio	1.09	1.07	1.07	1.04	1.87	2.06	2.28	2.16
Debt to Equity	2.50	2.74	3.18	3.21	1.28	1.49	1.63	1.61
Price Range	53.56-38.30	52.82-38.30	61.49-36.20	82.32-45.45	79.78-55.38	63.43-52.45	58.20-46.80	52.77-37.45
P/E Ratio	19.62-14.03	20.39-14.79	30.44-17.92	26.13-14.43	21.45-14.89	17.10-14.14	16.35-13.15	16.81-11.93
Average Yield %	3.19	3.26	3.01	8.99	1.93	2.05	2.01	1.98

Address: 1617 Sixth Avenue, Seattle, WA 98101	Web Site: www.nordstrom.com	Auditors: Deloitte & Touche LLP
Telephone: 206-628-2111	Officers: Phillip G. Satre - Chairman Blake W. Nordstrom - Co-President, Interim Chief Financial Officer, President, Co-President (fmr), Executive Vice President	Investor Contact: 206-303-3200 Transfer Agents: Computershare, Providence, RI

NORFOLK SOUTHERN CORP.

Exchange	Symbol	Price	52Wk Range	Yield	P/E
NYS	NSC	$150.87 (6/29/2018)	156.28-112.48	1.91	7.91

*7 Year Price Score 116.61 *NYSE Composite Index=100 ***12 Month Price Score 108.84**

Interim Earnings (Per Share)

Qtr.	Mar	Jun	Sep	Dec
2015	1.00	1.41	1.49	1.20
2016	1.29	1.36	1.55	1.41
2017	1.48	1.71	1.75	13.68
2018	1.93	...	...	...

Interim Dividends (Per Share)

Amt	Decl	Ex	Rec	Pay
0.61Q	07/28/2017	08/03/2017	08/07/2017	09/11/2017
0.61Q	10/24/2017	11/02/2017	11/03/2017	12/11/2017
0.72Q	01/23/2018	02/01/2018	02/02/2018	03/10/2018
0.72Q	04/24/2018	05/03/2018	05/04/2018	06/11/2018

Indicated Div: $2.88 (Div. Reinv. Plan)

Valuation Analysis / Institutional Holding

Forecast EPS	$8.72	No of Institutions
	(06/14/2018)	1634
Market Cap	$42.6 Billion	Shares
Book Value	$16.4 Billion	259,167,600
Price/Book	2.60	% Held
Price/Sales	3.99	60.00

TRADING VOLUME (thousand shares)

Business Summary: Rail (MIC: 7.4.3 SIC: 4011 NAIC: 482111)

Norfolk Southern is a holding company engaged principally in the rail transportation business, operating primarily in the East and Midwest. Co.'s Norfolk Southern Railway Company subsidiary and its railroad subsidiaries transport raw materials, intermediate products and finished goods classified in the following commodity groups: intermodal; chemicals; agriculture/consumer products/government; coal; metals/construction; automotive; and, paper/clay/forest products. At Dec 31 2017, Co.'s railroad operated approximately 19,500 miles of road in 22 states and the District of Columbia. Co. also transports overseas freight through several Atlantic and Gulf Coast ports.

Recent Developments: For the quarter ended Mar 31 2018, net income increased 27.5% to US$552.0 million from US$433.0 million in the year-earlier quarter. Revenues were US$2.72 billion, up 5.5% from US$2.58 billion the year before. Operating income was US$835.0 million versus US$757.0 million in the prior-year quarter, an increase of 10.3%. Direct operating expenses rose 9.1% to US$873.0 million from US$800.0 million in the comparable period the year before. Indirect operating expenses decreased 0.9% to US$1.01 billion from US$1.02 billion in the equivalent prior-year period.

Prospects: Our evaluation of Norfolk Southern Corp. as of Jan. 21, 2018 is the result of our systematic analysis on three basic characteristics: earnings strength, relative valuation, and recent stock price movement. The company has managed to produce a neutral trend in earnings per share over the past 5 quarters and while recent estimates for the company have been raised by analysts, NSC has posted better than expected results. Based on operating earnings yield, the company is about fairly valued when compared to all of the companies in our coverage universe. Share price changes over the past year indicates that NSC will perform in line with the market over the near term.

Financial Data

(US$ in Thousands)	3 Mos	12/31/2017	12/31/2016	12/31/2015	12/31/2014	12/31/2013	12/31/2012	12/31/2011
Earnings Per Share	19.07	18.61	5.62	5.10	6.39	6.04	5.37	5.45
Cash Flow Per Share	11.37	11.30	10.30	9.53	9.22	9.87	9.53	9.34
Tang Book Value Per Share	58.11	57.57	42.73	40.93	40.25	36.55	31.08	30.00
Dividends Per Share	2.550	2.440	2.360	2.360	2.220	2.040	1.940	1.660
Dividend Payout %	13.37	13.11	41.99	46.27	34.74	33.77	36.13	30.46
Income Statement								
Total Revenue	2,717,000	10,551,000	9,888,000	10,511,000	11,624,000	11,245,000	11,040,000	11,172,000
EBITDA	1,115,000	4,741,000	4,171,000	4,042,000	4,638,000	4,374,000	4,142,000	4,205,000
Depn & Amortn	272,000	1,059,000	1,030,000	1,059,000	956,000	922,000	922,000	869,000
Income Before Taxes	707,000	3,128,000	2,582,000	2,442,000	3,134,000	2,923,000	2,724,000	2,887,000
Income Taxes	155,000	(2,276,000)	914,000	886,000	1,134,000	1,055,000	1,009,000	1,002,000
Net Income	552,000	5,404,000	1,668,000	1,556,000	2,000,000	1,910,000	1,749,000	1,916,000
Average Shares	285,900	290,300	296,000	304,400	312,500	315,500	325,200	351,300
Balance Sheet								
Current Assets	2,479,000	2,149,000	2,291,000	2,633,000	2,778,000	3,075,000	2,242,000	1,751,000
Total Assets	36,162,000	35,711,000	34,892,000	34,260,000	33,241,000	32,483,000	30,342,000	28,538,000
Current Liabilities	2,388,000	2,545,000	2,339,000	2,231,000	1,780,000	2,305,000	2,081,000	1,701,000
Long-Term Obligations	9,637,000	9,136,000	9,562,000	9,393,000	8,924,000	8,903,000	8,432,000	7,390,000
Total Liabilities	19,744,000	19,352,000	22,483,000	22,072,000	20,833,000	21,194,000	20,582,000	18,627,000
Stockholders' Equity	16,418,000	16,359,000	12,409,000	12,188,000	12,408,000	11,289,000	9,760,000	9,911,000
Shares Outstanding	282,541	284,157	290,417	297,795	308,240	308,878	314,034	330,386
Statistical Record								
Return on Assets %	15.49	15.31	4.81	4.61	6.09	6.08	5.92	6.75
Return on Equity %	38.16	37.57	13.53	12.65	16.88	18.15	17.73	18.62
EBITDA Margin %	41.04	44.93	42.18	38.45	39.90	38.90	37.52	37.64
Net Margin %	20.32	51.22	16.87	14.80	17.21	16.99	15.84	17.15
Asset Turnover	0.30	0.30	0.29	0.31	0.35	0.36	0.37	0.39
Current Ratio	1.04	0.84	0.98	1.18	1.56	1.33	1.08	1.03
Debt to Equity	0.59	0.56	0.77	0.77	0.72	0.79	0.86	0.75
Price Range	154.34-111.58	145.91-106.99	110.69-66.60	111.73-72.44	117.20-87.76	92.87-61.84	78.24-56.34	76.99-60.01
P/E Ratio	8.09-5.85	7.84-5.75	19.70-11.85	21.91-14.20	18.34-13.73	15.38-10.24	14.57-10.49	14.13-11.01
Average Yield %	1.98	1.99	2.67	2.54	2.18	2.65	2.83	2.41

Address: Three Commercial Place,	Web Site: www.norfolksouthern.com	Auditors: KPMG LLP
Norfolk, VA 23510-2191	Officers: James A. Squires - Chairman, President,	Investor Contact: 757-629-2861
Telephone: 757-629-2680	Chief Executive Officer, Executive Vice President,	Transfer Agents: American Stock
	Chief Financial Officer, Executive Vice President	Transfer & Trust Company, LLC,
	Michael Joseph Wheeler - Chief Operating Officer,	Brooklyn, NY
	Executive Vice President	

NORTHROP GRUMMAN CORP

Exchange	Symbol	Price	52Wk Range	Yield	P/E	Div Acheiver
NYS	NOC	$307.70 (6/29/2018)	360.03-256.71	1.56	25.54	14 Years

*7 Year Price Score 155.63 *NYSE Composite Index=100 *12 Month Price Score 102.85

Interim Earnings (Per Share)

Qtr.	Mar	Jun	Sep	Dec
2015	2.41	2.74	2.75	2.50
2016	3.03	2.85	3.35	2.96
2017	3.63	3.15	3.68	1.01
2018	4.21	...	...	...

Interim Dividends (Per Share)

Amt	Decl	Ex	Rec	Pay
1.00Q	08/16/2017	08/24/2017	08/28/2017	09/13/2017
1.00Q	11/15/2017	12/01/2017	12/04/2017	12/20/2017
1.10Q	01/25/2018	03/02/2018	03/05/2018	03/21/2018
1.20Q	05/15/2018	06/01/2018	06/04/2018	06/20/2018

Indicated Div: **$4.80 (Div. Reinv. Plan)**

Valuation Analysis | **Institutional Holding**

Forecast EPS	$16.60	No of Institutions
	(06/14/2018)	1414
Market Cap	$53.7 Billion	Shares
Book Value	$7.7 Billion	201,259,424
Price/Book	6.99	% Held
Price/Sales	2.04	72.08

Business Summary: Defense (MIC: 7.1.2 SIC: 3812 NAIC: 334511)

Northrop Grumman is a global security company. Co. has three segments: Aerospace Systems, which designs, develops, integrates and produces manned aircraft, autonomous systems, spacecraft, high-energy laser systems, microelectronics and other systems/subsystems; Mission Systems, which provides in advanced mission solutions and multifunction systems for Department of Defense, intelligence community, international, federal civil and commercial customers; and Technology Services, which provides logistics solutions supporting the life cycle of platforms and systems for global defense and federal-civil customers.

Recent Developments: For the quarter ended Mar 31 2018, net income increased 13.7% to US$739.0 million from US$650.0 million in the year-earlier quarter. Revenues were US$6.74 billion, up 5.1% from US$6.41 billion the year before. Operating income was US$854.0 million versus US$862.0 million in the prior-year quarter, a decrease of 0.9%. Direct operating expenses rose 6.6% to US$5.17 billion from US$4.85 billion in the comparable period the year before. Indirect operating expenses increased 1.9% to US$711.0 million from US$698.0 million in the equivalent prior-year period.

Prospects: Our evaluation of Northrop Grumman Corp. as of Jan. 21, 2018 is the result of our systematic analysis on three basic characteristics: earnings strength, relative valuation, and recent stock price movement. The company has generated a negative trend in earnings per share over the past 5 quarters and while recent estimates for the company have been raised by analysts, NOC has posted better than expected results. Based on operating earnings yield, the company is about fairly valued when compared to all of the companies in our coverage universe. Share price changes over the past year indicates that NOC will perform well over the near term.

Financial Data

(US$ in Thousands)	3 Mos	12/31/2017	12/31/2016	12/31/2015	12/31/2014	12/31/2013	12/31/2012	12/31/2011
Earnings Per Share	12.05	11.47	12.19	10.39	9.75	8.35	7.81	7.52
Cash Flow Per Share	16.15	14.98	15.68	11.41	12.42	10.81	10.59	7.64
Dividends Per Share	4.100	3.900	3.500	3.100	2.710	2.380	2.150	1.970
Dividend Payout %	34.02	34.00	28.71	29.84	27.79	28.50	27.53	26.20
Income Statement								
Total Revenue	6,735,000	25,803,000	24,508,000	23,526,000	23,979,000	24,661,000	25,218,000	26,412,000
EBITDA	1,136,000	3,884,000	3,680,000	3,558,000	3,681,000	3,615,000	3,625,000	3,766,000
Depn & Amortn	122,000	475,000	456,000	467,000	462,000	495,000	448,000	462,000
Income Before Taxes	871,000	3,049,000	2,923,000	2,790,000	2,937,000	2,863,000	2,965,000	3,083,000
Income Taxes	132,000	1,034,000	723,000	800,000	868,000	911,000	987,000	997,000
Net Income	739,000	2,015,000	2,200,000	1,990,000	2,069,000	1,952,000	1,978,000	2,118,000
Average Shares	175,400	175,600	180,500	191,600	212,100	233,900	253,400	281,600
Balance Sheet								
Current Assets	16,157,000	16,349,000	6,856,000	6,334,000	8,184,000	9,488,000	8,392,000	7,746,000
Total Assets	34,795,000	34,917,000	25,614,000	24,454,000	26,572,000	26,381,000	26,543,000	25,411,000
Current Liabilities	6,415,000	6,965,000	5,630,000	5,457,000	5,892,000	5,815,000	6,056,000	6,135,000
Long-Term Obligations	14,392,000	14,399,000	7,058,000	6,416,000	5,925,000	5,928,000	3,930,000	3,935,000
Total Liabilities	27,115,000	27,869,000	20,355,000	18,932,000	19,337,000	15,761,000	17,029,000	15,075,000
Stockholders' Equity	7,680,000	7,048,000	5,259,000	5,522,000	7,235,000	10,620,000	9,514,000	10,336,000
Shares Outstanding	174,382	174,085	175,068	181,303	198,930	217,599	239,209	253,889
Statistical Record								
Return on Assets %	7.02	6.66	8.76	7.80	7.81	7.38	7.59	7.45
Return on Equity %	31.94	32.75	40.70	31.20	23.18	19.39	19.88	17.73
EBITDA Margin %	16.87	15.05	15.02	15.12	15.35	14.66	14.37	14.26
Net Margin %	10.97	7.81	8.98	8.46	8.63	7.92	7.84	8.02
Asset Turnover	0.87	0.85	0.98	0.92	0.91	0.93	0.97	0.93
Current Ratio	2.52	2.35	1.22	1.16	1.39	1.63	1.39	1.26
Debt to Equity	1.87	2.04	1.34	1.16	0.82	0.56	0.41	0.38
Price Range	356.91-236.10	310.47-226.96	251.80-178.19	191.48-143.37	152.24-110.81	115.32-64.38	71.13-57.11	70.33-49.26
P/E Ratio	29.62-19.59	27.07-19.79	20.66-14.62	18.43-13.80	15.61-11.36	13.81-7.71	9.11-7.31	9.35-6.55
Average Yield %	1.42	1.48	1.65	1.85	2.16	2.76	3.37	3.30

Address: 2980 Fairview Park Drive, Falls Church, VA 22042 **Telephone:** 703-280-2900	**Web Site:** www.northropgrumman.com **Officers:** Wesley G. Bush - Chairman, President, Chief Executive Officer, Vice President, Chief Financial Officer, Chief Operating Officer Kathy J. Warden - President, Corporate Vice-President, Chief Operating Officer, Division Officer	**Auditors:** Deloitte & Touche LLP **Investor Contact:** 703-280-2268 **Transfer Agents:** Computershare, Providence, RI

NORTHWEST NATURAL GAS CO.

Exchange	Symbol	Price	52Wk Range	Yield	P/E	Div Acheiver
NYS	NWN	$63.80 (6/29/2018)	69.15-51.95	2.96	N/A	62 Years

*7 Year Price Score 98.10 *NYSE Composite Index=100 *12 Month Price Score 97.40

Interim Earnings (Per Share)

Qtr.	Mar	Jun	Sep	Dec
2015	1.04	0.08	(0.24)	1.08
2016	1.33	0.07	(0.29)	1.01
2017	1.40	0.10	(0.30)	(3.14)
2018	1.44	...	...	...

Interim Dividends (Per Share)

Amt	Decl	Ex	Rec	Pay
0.472Q	10/05/2017	10/30/2017	10/31/2017	11/15/2017
0.472Q	01/12/2018	01/31/2018	01/31/2018	02/15/2018
0.472Q	04/05/2018	04/27/2018	04/30/2018	05/15/2018
0.472Q	07/05/2018	07/30/2018	07/31/2018	08/15/2018

Indicated Div: $1.89 (Div. Reinv. Plan)

Valuation Analysis   Institutional Holding

Forecast EPS	$2.27	No of Institutions
	(06/07/2018)	325
Market Cap	$1.8 Billion	Shares
Book Value	$772.2 Million	26,091,268
Price/Book	2.38	% Held
Price/Sales	2.52	58.20

TRADING VOLUME (thousand shares)

Business Summary: Gas Utilities (MIC: 3.3.1 SIC: 4924 NAIC: 221210)

Northwest Natural Gas is engaged in the distribution of natural gas. Co. operates in two segments: local gas distribution, which is a regulated utility principally engaged in the purchase, sale, and delivery of natural gas and related services to customers in Oregon and southwest Washington; and gas storage, which includes natural gas storage services provided to customers primarily from two underground natural gas storage facilities, Co.'s Gill Ranch gas storage facility, and the non-utility portion of Co.'s Mist gas storage facility. At Dec 31 2017, Co. had 737,874 utility customers with approximately 89.0% of its customers located in Oregon and 11.0% located in Washington.

Recent Developments: For the quarter ended Mar 31 2018, net income increased 3.0% to US$41.5 million from US$40.3 million in the year-earlier quarter. Revenues were US$264.7 million, down 11.0% from US$297.3 million the year before. Operating income was US$67.3 million versus US$77.5 million in the prior-year quarter, a decrease of 13.1%. Direct operating expenses declined 24.7% to US$108.1 million from US$143.6 million in the comparable period the year before. Indirect operating expenses increased 17.2% to US$89.3 million from US$76.2 million in the equivalent prior-year period.

Prospects: Our evaluation of Northwest Natural Gas Co. as of Jan. 21, 2018 is the result of our systematic analysis on three basic characteristics: earnings strength, relative valuation, and recent stock price movement. The company has managed to produce a neutral trend in earnings per share over the past 5 quarters. However, while recent estimates for the company have been lowered by analysts, NWN has posted better than expected results. Based on operating earnings yield, the company is about fairly valued when compared to all of the companies in our coverage universe. Share price changes over the past year indicates that NWN will perform very well over the near term.

Financial Data

(US$ in Thousands)	3 Mos	12/31/2017	12/31/2016	12/31/2015	12/31/2014	12/31/2013	12/31/2012	12/31/2011
Earnings Per Share	(1.90)	(1.94)	2.12	1.96	2.16	2.24	2.22	2.39
Cash Flow Per Share	5.78	7.21	8.01	6.75	7.94	6.54	6.28	8.75
Tang Book Value Per Share	26.83	25.85	29.71	28.47	28.12	27.77	27.23	26.70
Dividends Per Share	1.885	1.883	1.873	1.863	1.845	1.825	1.790	1.750
Dividend Payout %	...	...	88.33	95.03	85.42	81.47	80.63	73.22
Income Statement								
Total Revenue	264,712	762,173	675,967	723,791	754,037	758,518	730,607	848,796
EBITDA	75,211	69,343	249,849	234,422	243,426	234,409	220,133	219,322
Depn & Amortn	8,697	117,222	111,112	102,427	98,528	86,994	73,017	70,004
Income Before Taxes	56,999	(86,380)	99,609	89,456	100,335	102,243	103,959	107,280
Income Taxes	15,462	(30,757)	40,714	35,753	41,643	41,705	44,104	43,382
Net Income	41,537	(55,623)	58,895	53,703	58,692	60,538	59,855	63,898
Average Shares	28,803	28,669	27,779	27,417	27,223	27,027	26,907	26,744
Balance Sheet								
Current Assets	241,694	269,936	288,053	332,063	362,560	330,448	283,699	348,689
Total Assets	3,029,339	3,039,746	3,079,801	3,076,692	3,064,945	2,970,911	2,818,753	2,746,574
Current Liabilities	316,853	381,850	274,517	477,714	469,410	432,791	368,436	414,464
Long-Term Obligations	683,497	683,184	679,334	576,700	621,700	681,700	691,700	641,700
Total Liabilities	2,257,134	2,296,970	2,229,304	2,295,720	2,297,624	2,219,039	2,085,720	2,032,086
Stockholders' Equity	772,205	742,776	850,497	780,972	767,321	751,872	733,033	714,488
Shares Outstanding	28,781	28,736	28,630	27,427	27,284	27,075	26,917	26,756
Statistical Record								
Return on Assets %	N.M.	N.M.	1.91	1.75	1.94	2.09	2.15	2.38
Return on Equity %	N.M.	N.M.	7.20	6.94	7.73	8.15	8.25	9.08
EBITDA Margin %	28.41	9.10	36.96	32.39	32.28	30.90	30.13	25.84
Net Margin %	15.69	N.M.	8.71	7.42	7.78	7.98	8.19	7.53
Asset Turnover	0.24	0.25	0.22	0.24	0.25	0.26	0.26	0.32
Current Ratio	0.76	0.71	1.05	0.70	0.77	0.76	0.77	0.84
Debt to Equity	0.89	0.92	0.80	0.74	0.81	0.91	0.94	0.90
Price Range	69.15-51.95	69.15-56.85	65.60-49.44	51.98-42.18	52.46-40.36	46.40-40.07	50.47-41.72	48.66-40.09
P/E Ratio	...	...	30.94-23.32	26.52-21.52	24.29-18.69	20.71-17.89	22.73-18.79	20.36-16.77
Average Yield %	3.06	3.02	3.28	4.01	4.14	4.21	3.83	3.86

Address: 220 N.W. Second Avenue, Portland, OR 97209 Telephone: 503-226-4211	Web Site: www.nwnatural.com Officers: Tod R. Hamachek - Chairman David H. Anderson - President, Chief Executive Officer, Executive Vice President, Chief Operating Officer, Executive Vice President (frmr), Senior Vice President, Chief Financial Officer	Auditors: PricewaterhouseCoopers LLP Investor Contact: 503-226-4211ext.24 Transfer Agents: American Stock Transfer & Trust Company, Brooklyn, NY

NORTHWESTERN CORP.

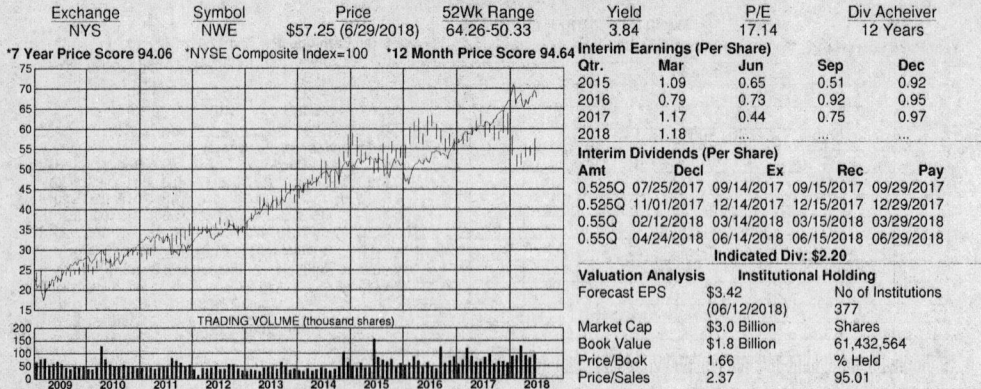

Exchange	Symbol	Price	52Wk Range	Yield	P/E	Div Acheiver	
NYS	NWE	$57.25 (6/29/2018)	64.26-50.33	3.84	17.14	12 Years	

*7 Year Price Score 94.06   *NYSE Composite Index=100   *12 Month Price Score 94.64

Interim Earnings (Per Share)

Qtr.	Mar	Jun	Sep	Dec
2015	1.09	0.65	0.51	0.92
2016	0.79	0.73	0.92	0.95
2017	1.17	0.44	0.75	0.97
2018	1.18	...	...	...

Interim Dividends (Per Share)

Amt	Decl	Ex	Rec	Pay
0.525Q	07/25/2017	09/14/2017	09/15/2017	09/29/2017
0.525Q	11/01/2017	12/14/2017	12/15/2017	12/29/2017
0.55Q	02/12/2018	03/14/2018	03/15/2018	03/29/2018
0.55Q	04/24/2018	06/14/2018	06/15/2018	06/29/2018

Indicated Div: $2.20

Valuation Analysis / **Institutional Holding**

Forecast EPS	$3.42 (06/12/2018)	No of Institutions	377
Market Cap	$3.0 Billion	Shares	61,432,564
Book Value	$1.8 Billion	% Held	95.01
Price/Book	1.66		
Price/Sales	2.37		

Business Summary: Electric Utilities (MIC: 3.1.1 SIC: 4931 NAIC: 221121)

Northwestern is engaged in providing electricity and natural gas to customers in Montana, South Dakota and Nebraska. Co. has two operating segments: Electric and Natural Gas. Co.'s regulated electric utility business in Montana includes generation, transmission and distribution, while its South Dakota electric utility business operates as a vertically integrated generation, transmission and distribution utility. Co.'s regulated natural gas utility business in Montana includes production, storage, transmission and distribution. As of Dec 31 2017, Co. provided electricity and natural gas to approximately 718,300 customers in Montana, South Dakota and Nebraska.

Recent Developments: For the quarter ended Mar 31 2018, net income increased 3.4% to US$58.5 million from US$56.6 million in the year-earlier quarter. Revenues were US$341.5 million, down 7.0% from US$367.3 million the year before. Operating income was US$84.5 million versus US$87.8 million in the prior-year quarter, a decrease of 3.7%. Direct operating expenses declined 19.8% to US$96.1 million from US$119.8 million in the comparable period the year before. Indirect operating expenses increased 0.7% to US$160.9 million from US$159.7 million in the equivalent prior-year period.

Prospects: Our evaluation of Northwestern Corp. as of Jan. 21, 2018 is the result of our systematic analysis on three basic characteristics: earnings strength, relative valuation, and recent stock price movement. The company has generated a negative trend in earnings per share over the past 5 quarters. However, while recent estimates for the company have been mixed, NWE has posted better than expected results. Based on operating earnings yield, the company is undervalued when compared to all of the companies in our coverage universe. Share price changes over the past year indicates that NWE will perform very well over the near term.

Financial Data
(US$ in Thousands)

	3 Mos	12/31/2017	12/31/2016	12/31/2015	12/31/2014	12/31/2013	12/31/2012	12/31/2011
Earnings Per Share	3.34	3.34	3.39	3.17	2.99	2.46	2.66	2.53
Cash Flow Per Share	6.88	6.66	5.97	7.18	6.23	5.08	6.80	6.45
Tang Book Value Per Share	27.84	29.19	27.28	25.79	23.93	17.44	15.55	13.89
Dividends Per Share	2.125	2.100	2.000	1.920	1.600	1.520	1.480	1.440
Dividend Payout %	63.62	62.87	59.00	60.57	53.51	61.79	55.64	56.92
Income Statement								
Total Revenue	341,502	1,305,652	1,257,247	1,214,299	1,204,863	1,154,519	1,070,342	1,117,316
EBITDA	84,554	434,471	410,831	418,101	311,992	291,601	287,601	270,406
Depn & Amortn	1,171	166,137	159,336	144,702	123,776	112,831	106,044	100,926
Income Before Taxes	60,413	176,071	156,525	181,246	110,414	108,284	116,495	102,621
Income Taxes	1,914	13,368	(7,647)	30,037	(10,272)	14,301	18,089	10,065
Net Income	58,499	162,703	164,172	151,209	120,686	93,983	98,406	92,556
Average Shares	49,416	48,655	48,475	47,642	40,431	38,227	37,040	36,547
Balance Sheet								
Current Assets	258,034	296,359	280,195	286,660	350,885	320,956	303,128	290,199
Total Assets	5,400,418	5,420,917	5,499,321	5,278,640	4,973,943	3,715,260	3,485,533	3,210,438
Current Liabilities	326,331	632,238	613,832	571,200	614,582	463,588	449,265	475,954
Long-Term Obligations	2,038,231	1,815,629	1,817,684	1,808,453	1,690,261	1,184,992	1,086,636	937,967
Total Liabilities	3,565,795	3,622,002	3,823,094	3,678,466	3,496,160	2,684,590	2,551,501	2,351,326
Stockholders' Equity	1,834,623	1,798,915	1,676,227	1,600,174	1,477,783	1,030,670	934,032	859,112
Shares Outstanding	53,051	49,372	48,331	48,172	46,914	38,745	37,221	36,278
Statistical Record								
Return on Assets %	3.02	2.98	3.04	2.95	2.78	2.61	2.93	2.96
Return on Equity %	9.29	9.36	9.99	9.83	9.62	9.57	10.95	11.02
EBITDA Margin %	24.76	33.28	32.68	34.43	25.89	25.26	26.87	24.20
Net Margin %	17.13	12.46	13.06	12.45	10.02	8.14	9.19	8.28
Asset Turnover	0.23	0.24	0.23	0.24	0.28	0.32	0.32	0.36
Current Ratio	0.79	0.47	0.46	0.50	0.57	0.69	0.67	0.61
Debt to Equity	1.11	1.01	1.08	1.13	1.14	1.15	1.16	1.09
Price Range	64.26-50.33	64.26-56.09	63.33-52.47	59.10-48.75	58.55-42.67	47.01-34.73	37.79-33.43	36.59-27.52
P/E Ratio	19.24-15.07	19.24-16.79	18.68-15.48	18.64-15.38	19.58-14.27	19.11-14.12	14.21-12.57	14.46-10.88
Average Yield %	3.63	3.52	3.44	3.60	3.31	3.67	4.17	4.52

Address: 3010 W. 69th Street, Sioux Falls, SD 57108 **Telephone:** 605-978-2900	**Web Site:** www.northwesternenergy.com **Officers:** Robert C. Rowe - President, Chief Executive Officer Brian B. Bird - Chief Financial Officer, Vice President	**Auditors:** Deloitte & Touche LLP **Investor Contact:** 605-978-2900

NOW INC

Exchange	Symbol	Price	52Wk Range	Yield	P/E
NYS	DNOW	$13.33 (6/29/2018)	16.57-9.41	N/A	N/A

*7 Year Price Score N/A *NYSE Composite Index=100 *12 Month Price Score 109.50

Interim Earnings (Per Share)

Qtr.	Mar	Jun	Sep	Dec
2015	(0.09)	(0.18)	(2.09)	(2.32)
2016	(0.59)	(0.40)	(0.53)	(0.66)
2017	(0.21)	(0.16)	(0.08)	(0.03)
2018	0.02	...	...	...

Interim Dividends (Per Share)

No Dividends Paid

Valuation Analysis | **Institutional Holding**

Forecast EPS	$0.19	No of Institutions
	(06/14/2018)	354
Market Cap	$1.4 Billion	Shares
Book Value	$1.2 Billion	140,034,288
Price/Book	1.21	% Held
Price/Sales	0.52	N/A

TRADING VOLUME (thousand shares)

Business Summary: Equipment & Services (MIC: 9.1.3 SIC: 3533 NAIC: 333132)

NOW is a distributor to the oil and gas and industrial markets. Co. operates primarily under the DistributionNOW and Wilson Export brands. Co.'s product offering includes consumable maintenance, repair and operating supplies, pipe, valves, fittings, flanges, gaskets, fasteners, electrical, instrumentation, pumps, paint and coatings, mill tools, safety supplies and spare parts. Co. operates through three reportable segments: U.S., which serve the upstream, midstream and downstream energy and industrial markets; Canada, which serves the energy exploration, production, mining and drilling business; and International, which provides inventory and support to drilling and exploration activities.

Recent Developments: For the quarter ended Mar 31 2018, net income amounted to US$2.0 million versus a net loss of US$23.0 million in the year-earlier quarter. Revenues were US$764.0 million, up 21.1% from US$631.0 million the year before. Operating income was US$7.0 million versus a loss of US$21.0 million in the prior-year quarter. Direct operating expenses rose 19.1% to US$616.0 million from US$517.0 million in the comparable period the year before. Indirect operating expenses increased 4.4% to US$141.0 million from US$135.0 million in the equivalent prior-year period.

Prospects: Our evaluation of NOW Inc. as of Jan. 21, 2018 is the result of our systematic analysis on three basic characteristics: earnings strength, relative valuation, and recent stock price movement. The company has generated a negative trend in earnings per share over the past 5 quarters. Because the company lacks sufficient analyst estimate data, we place greater weight on the historical EPS trend as the measure of earnings strength. Based on operating earnings yield, the company is overvalued when compared to all of the companies in our coverage universe. Share price changes over the past year indicates that DNOW will perform very poorly over the near term.

Financial Data

(US$ in Millions)	3 Mos	12/31/2017	12/31/2016	12/31/2015	12/31/2014	12/31/2013	12/31/2012	12/31/2011
Earnings Per Share	(0.25)	(0.48)	(2.18)	(4.68)	1.06	1.37	1.00	...
Cash Flow Per Share	(1.15)	(1.06)	2.19	3.03	1.01	...	...	...
Tang Book Value Per Share	6.48	6.40	6.40	9.67	14.45	...	...	...
Income Statement								
Total Revenue	764	2,648	2,107	3,010	4,105	4,296	3,414	1,641
EBITDA	14	(24)	(198)	(493)	194	233	173	132
Depn & Amortn	11	28	32	25	16	11	8	4
Income Before Taxes	3	(52)	(230)	(518)	178	222	165	128
Income Taxes	1	...	4	(16)	62	75	57	43
Net Income	2	(52)	(234)	(502)	116	147	108	85
Average Shares	108	108	107	107	108	107	107	...
Balance Sheet								
Current Assets	1,206	1,129	959	1,292	2,047	1,662	1,882	...
Total Assets	1,818	1,749	1,603	1,832	2,596	2,183	2,373	...
Current Liabilities	443	394	347	307	620	363	391	...
Long-Term Obligations	175	162	65	108	...	...	...	...
Total Liabilities	626	564	420	429	630	381	402	...
Stockholders' Equity	1,192	1,185	1,183	1,403	1,966	1,802	1,971	...
Shares Outstanding	108	108	107	107	107	...	...	...
Statistical Record								
Return on Assets %	N.M.	N.M.	N.M.	N.M.	4.85	6.45	...	...
EBITDA Margin %	1.83	N.M.	N.M.	N.M.	4.73	5.42	5.07	8.04
Net Margin %	0.26	N.M.	N.M.	N.M.	2.83	3.42	3.16	5.18
Asset Turnover	1.60	1.58	1.22	1.36	1.72	1.89	...	...
Current Ratio	2.72	2.87	2.76	4.21	3.30	4.58	4.81	...
Debt to Equity	0.15	0.14	0.05	0.08	...	...	...	...
Price Range	18.22-9.41	22.67-9.88	23.21-12.48	26.79-14.80	37.19-22.50	...	...	...
P/E Ratio	...	...	...	...	35.08-21.23	...	...	...

Address: 7402 North Eldridge Parkway, Houston, TX 77041 **Telephone:** 281-823-4700	**Web Site:** www.distributionnow.com **Officers:** J. Wayne Richards - Chairman Robert R. Workman - President, Chief Executive Officer	**Auditors:** Ernst & Young LLP **Transfer Agents:** American Stock Transfer & Trust Co., LLC , Brooklyn, NY

NRG ENERGY INC

Exchange	Symbol	Price	52Wk Range	Yield	P/E
NYS	NRG	$30.70 (6/29/2018)	34.91-16.12	0.39	N/A

*7 Year Price Score 98.52   *NYSE Composite Index=100   *12 Month Price Score 117.41

Interim Earnings (Per Share)

Qtr.	Mar	Jun	Sep	Dec
2015	(0.37)	(0.06)	0.18	(19.21)
2016	0.24	(0.61)	1.27	(3.13)
2017	(0.52)	(1.98)	0.53	(4.84)
2018	0.87	...	...	...

Interim Dividends (Per Share)

Amt	Decl	Ex	Rec	Pay
0.03Q	07/20/2017	07/28/2017	08/01/2017	08/15/2017
0.03Q	10/18/2017	10/31/2017	11/01/2017	11/15/2017
0.03Q	01/19/2018	01/31/2018	02/01/2018	02/15/2018
0.03Q	04/19/2018	04/30/2018	05/01/2018	05/15/2018

Indicated Div: $0.12

Valuation Analysis   **Institutional Holding**

Forecast EPS	$3.29 (06/13/2018)	No of Institutions 660
Market Cap	$9.7 Billion	Shares
Book Value	N/A	382,673,536
Price/Book	N/A	% Held
Price/Sales	0.91	101.23

TRADING VOLUME (thousand shares)

Business Summary: Electric Utilities (MIC: 3.1.1 SIC: 4911 NAIC: 221121)

NRG Energy is a power company, which produces, sells and delivers electricity and related products and services in power markets in the U.S. Co. owns and operates approx. 47,000 megawatt (MW) of generation; engages in the trading of wholesale energy, capacity and related products; transacts in and trades fuel and transportation services; and directly sells energy, services, and products and services to retail customers under the names NRG, Reliant and other retail brand names owned by Co.

Recent Developments: For the quarter ended Mar 31 2018; income from continuing operations was US$233.0 million compared with a loss of US$169.0 million in the year-earlier quarter. Net income amounted to US$233.0 million versus a net loss of US$203.0 million in the year-earlier quarter. Revenues were US$2.42 billion, up 1.6% from US$2.38 billion the year before. Operating income was US$406.0 million versus US$36.0 million in the prior-year quarter, an increase of. Direct operating expenses declined 16.3% to US$1.56 billion from US$1.86 billion in the comparable period the year before. Indirect operating expenses decreased 5.6% to US$457.0 million from US$484.0 million in the equivalent prior-year period.

Prospects: Our evaluation of NRG Energy Inc. as of Jan. 21, 2018 is the result of our systematic analysis on three basic characteristics: earnings strength, relative valuation, and recent stock price movement. The company has enjoyed a very positive trend in earnings per share over the past 5 quarters. However, while recent estimates for the company have been mixed, NRG has posted results that fell short of analysts' expectations. Based on operating earnings yield, the company is about fairly valued when compared to all of the companies in our coverage universe. Share price changes over the past year indicates that NRG will perform very well over the near term.

Financial Data

(US$ in Thousands)	3 Mos	12/31/2017	12/31/2016	12/31/2015	12/31/2014	12/31/2013	12/31/2012	12/31/2011
Earnings Per Share	(5.42)	(6.79)	(2.22)	(19.46)	0.23	(1.22)	2.35	0.78
Cash Flow Per Share	5.70	4.38	6.54	3.98	4.52	3.93	4.94	4.86
Tang Book Value Per Share	...	...	N.M.	N.M.	14.59	20.77	22.03	19.47
Dividends Per Share	0.120	0.120	0.235	0.580	0.540	0.450	0.180	...
Dividend Payout %	...	...	...	...	234.78	...	7.66	...
Income Statement								
Total Revenue	2,421,000	10,629,000	12,351,000	14,674,000	15,868,000	11,295,000	8,422,000	9,079,000
EBITDA	463,000	(660,000)	250,000	(3,921,000)	1,280,000	256,000	1,022,000	151,000
Depn & Amortn	62,000	108,000	91,000	81,000	64,000	49,000	146,000	167,000
Income Before Taxes	234,000	(1,658,000)	(902,000)	(5,130,000)	97,000	(641,000)	215,000	(681,000)
Income Taxes	(1,000)	8,000	16,000	1,342,000	3,000	(282,000)	(327,000)	(843,000)
Net Income	279,000	(2,153,000)	(774,000)	(6,382,000)	134,000	(386,000)	559,000	-197,000
Average Shares	322,000	317,000	316,000	329,000	339,000	323,000	234,000	241,000
Balance Sheet								
Current Assets	4,557,000	4,415,000	6,395,000	7,391,000	8,582,000	7,596,000	7,956,000	7,597,000
Total Assets	23,752,000	23,318,000	30,355,000	32,882,000	40,665,000	33,902,000	35,128,000	26,715,000
Current Liabilities	3,708,000	3,317,000	4,382,000	4,375,000	4,859,000	4,204,000	4,677,000	5,671,000
Long-Term Obligations	15,406,000	15,716,000	18,006,000	18,983,000	19,900,000	15,767,000	15,733,000	9,745,000
Total Liabilities	23,886,000	23,664,000	28,314,000	29,873,000	30,612,000	24,051,000	24,864,000	18,980,000
Stockholders' Equity	(134,000)	(346,000)	2,041,000	3,009,000	10,053,000	9,851,000	10,264,000	7,735,000
Shares Outstanding	314,886	316,743	315,443	314,190	336,662	323,779	322,606	227,519
Statistical Record								
Return on Assets %	N.M.	N.M.	N.M.	N.M.	0.36	N.M.	1.80	0.73
Return on Equity %	N.M.	N.M.	N.M.	N.M.	1.35	N.M.	6.19	2.46
EBITDA Margin %	19.12	N.M.	2.02	N.M.	8.07	2.27	12.13	1.66
Net Margin %	11.52	N.M.	N.M.	N.M.	0.84	N.M.	6.64	2.17
Asset Turnover	0.40	0.40	0.39	0.40	0.43	0.33	0.27	0.34
Current Ratio	1.23	1.33	1.46	1.69	1.77	1.81	1.70	1.34
Debt to Equity	...	...	8.82	6.31	1.98	1.60	1.53	1.26
Price Range	30.77-14.60	29.49-12.30	17.90-8.98	27.50-9.00	37.66-25.83	30.11-22.68	23.65-14.34	25.41-17.57
P/E Ratio	...	...	...	...163.74-112.30		...	10.06-6.10	32.58-22.53
Average Yield %	0.50	0.57	1.85	2.81	1.74	1.69	0.96	...

Address: 804 Carnegie Center, Princeton, NJ 08540	Web Site: www.nrgenergy.com	Auditors: KPMG LLP
Telephone: 609-524-4500	Officers: Lawrence S. Coben - Chairman Mauricio Gutierrez - President, Chief Executive Officer, Executive Vice President, Chief Operating Officer	Investor Contact: 609-524-4526 Transfer Agents: Computershare Shareowner Services LLC, College Station, TX

NU SKIN ENTERPRISES, INC.

Exchange	Symbol	Price	52Wk Range	Yield	P/E	Div Acheiver
NYS	NUS	$78.19 (6/29/2018)	83.66-53.70	1.87	31.40	16 Years

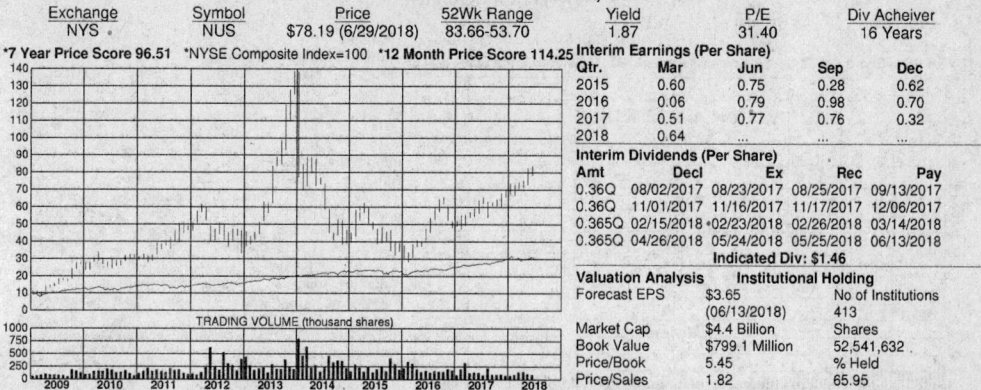

*7 Year Price Score 96.51 *NYSE Composite Index=100 *12 Month Price Score 114.25

Interim Earnings (Per Share)

Qtr.	Mar	Jun	Sep	Dec
2015	0.60	0.75	0.28	0.62
2016	0.06	0.79	0.98	0.70
2017	0.51	0.77	0.76	0.32
2018	0.64	...	...	...

Interim Dividends (Per Share)

Amt	Decl	Ex	Rec	Pay
0.36Q	08/02/2017	08/23/2017	08/25/2017	09/13/2017
0.36Q	11/01/2017	11/16/2017	11/17/2017	12/06/2017
0.365Q	02/15/2018	02/23/2018	02/26/2018	03/14/2018
0.365Q	04/26/2018	05/24/2018	05/25/2018	06/13/2018

Indicated Div: $1.46

Valuation Analysis   **Institutional Holding**

Forecast EPS	$3.65	No of Institutions
	(06/13/2018)	413
Market Cap	$4.4 Billion	Shares
Book Value	$799.1 Million	52,541,632
Price/Book	5.45	% Held
Price/Sales	1.82	65.95

Business Summary: Household & Personal Products (MIC: 1.7.1 SIC: 5122 NAIC: 424210)

NU Skin Enterprises develops and distributes consumer products, as well as providing a line of beauty and wellness solutions. Co. has two primary product categories, each operating under its own brand: Nu Skin, which provides anti-aging personal care products including ageLOC Me customized skin care system, ageLOC Spa systems and ageLOC Transformation anti-aging skin care system; and Pharmanex, with a product line that includes ageLOC Youth nutritional supplement, ageLOC TR90 weight management and body shaping system and LifePak nutritional supplements. As of Dec 31 2017, Co. sold and distributed its products in approximately 50 markets worldwide.

Recent Developments: For the quarter ended Mar 31 2018, net income increased 29.3% to US$35.5 million from US$27.5 million in the year-earlier quarter. Revenues were US$616.2 million, up 23.5% from US$499.1 million the year before. Operating income was US$59.0 million versus US$46.3 million in the prior-year quarter, an increase of 27.5%. Direct operating expenses rose 31.5% to US$146.3 million from US$111.3 million in the comparable period the year before. Indirect operating expenses increased 20.3% to US$410.9 million from US$341.6 million in the equivalent prior-year period.

Prospects: Our evaluation of NU Skin Enterprises Inc. as of Jan. 21, 2018 is the result of our systematic analysis on three basic characteristics: earnings strength, relative valuation, and recent stock price movement. The company has produced a positive trend in earnings per share over the past 5 quarters and while recent estimates for the company have been mixed, NUS has posted results that were in line with analysts expectations. Based on operating earnings yield, the company is undervalued when compared to all of the companies in our coverage universe. Share price changes over the past year indicates that NUS will perform well over the near term.

Financial Data

(US$ in Thousands)	3 Mos	12/31/2017	12/31/2016	12/31/2015	12/31/2014	12/31/2013	12/31/2012	12/31/2011
Earnings Per Share	2.49	2.36	2.55	2.25	3.11	5.94	3.52	2.38
Cash Flow Per Share	5.19	5.73	4.95	5.55	(0.96)	9.05	5.12	3.61
Tang Book Value Per Share	9.18	9.91	9.23	11.54	12.80	11.24	6.60	6.07
Dividends Per Share	1.445	1.440	1.420	1.400	1.380	1.200	0.800	0.590
Dividend Payout %	58.03	61.02	55.69	62.22	44.37	20.20	22.73	24.79
Income Statement								
Total Revenue	616,219	2,279,099	2,207,797	2,247,047	2,569,495	3,176,718	2,169,664	1,743,991
EBITDA	79,104	323,867	273,639	273,559	345,007	584,040	370,742	252,469
Depn & Amortn	18,907	58,300	60,800	61,600	46,500	27,100	25,500	25,700
Income Before Taxes	60,197	265,567	212,839	211,959	298,507	556,940	345,242	226,769
Income Taxes	24,658	136,130	69,753	78,913	109,331	192,052	123,597	73,439
Net Income	35,539	129,437	143,086	133,046	189,176	364,888	221,645	153,330
Average Shares	55,959	54,852	56,097	59,057	60,887	61,448	63,025	64,546
Balance Sheet								
Current Assets	833,801	777,789	714,337	706,392	834,667	1,118,334	599,403	530,087
Total Assets	1,774,669	1,589,872	1,474,045	1,505,843	1,614,434	1,821,062	1,152,907	990,956
Current Liabilities	734,448	447,370	399,011	407,597	418,329	776,792	320,103	241,171
Long-Term Obligations	107,275	310,790	334,165	181,745	164,567	113,852	154,963	107,944
Total Liabilities	975,541	885,276	809,975	680,222	671,996	962,443	562,295	416,720
Stockholders' Equity	799,128	704,596	664,070	825,621	942,438	858,619	590,612	574,236
Shares Outstanding	55,700	52,700	52,600	56,000	59,000	59,000	58,400	62,300
Statistical Record								
Return on Assets %	8.41	8.45	9.58	8.53	11.01	24.54	20.62	16.28
Return on Equity %	18.50	18.91	19.16	15.05	21.01	50.36	37.95	29.33
EBITDA Margin %	12.84	14.21	12.39	12.17	13.43	18.39	17.09	14.48
Net Margin %	5.77	5.68	6.48	5.92	7.36	11.49	10.22	8.79
Asset Turnover	1.47	1.49	1.48	1.44	1.50	2.14	2.02	1.85
Current Ratio	1.14	1.74	1.79	1.73	2.00	1.44	1.87	2.20
Debt to Equity	0.13	0.44	0.50	0.22	0.17	0.13	0.26	0.19
Price Range	74.35-53.70	69.97-47.22	65.89-28.13	62.20-31.89	138.22-38.28	138.66-37.05	61.50-33.05	51.61-27.81
P/E Ratio	29.86-21.57	29.65-20.01	25.84-11.03	27.64-14.17	44.44-12.31	23.34-6.24	17.47-9.39	21.68-11.68
Average Yield %	2.28	2.45	3.05	3.04	2.09	1.59	1.71	1.56

Address: 75 West Center Street, Provo, UT 84601
Telephone: 801-345-1000

Web Site: www.nuskinenterprises.com
Officers: Blake M. Roney - Chairman Steven J. Lund - Vice-Chairman

Auditors: PricewaterhouseCoopers LLP
Investor Contact: 801-345-2657
Transfer Agents: American Stock Transfer & Trust Co. LLC, Brooklyn, NY

NUCOR CORP.

Exchange	Symbol	Price	52Wk Range	Yield	P/E	Div Acheiver
NYS	NUE	$62.50 (6/29/2018)	70.18-53.48	2.43	15.28	45 Years

*7 Year Price Score 100.53 *NYSE Composite Index=100 *12 Month Price Score 103.85

Interim Earnings (Per Share)

Qtr.	Mar	Jun	Sep	Dec
2015	0.21	0.39	0.71	(0.19)
2016	0.22	0.73	0.84	0.69
2017	1.11	1.00	0.79	1.20
2018	1.10	...	...	...

Interim Dividends (Per Share)

Amt	Decl	Ex	Rec	Pay
0.378Q	09/14/2017	09/28/2017	09/29/2017	11/09/2017
0.38Q	12/01/2017	12/28/2017	12/29/2017	02/09/2018
0.38Q	02/20/2018	03/28/2018	03/29/2018	05/11/2018
0.38Q	06/07/2018	06/28/2018	06/29/2018	08/10/2018

Indicated Div: $1.52 (Div. Reinv. Plan)

Valuation Analysis **Institutional Holding**

Forecast EPS	$7.24 (06/13/2018)	No of Institutions 1141
Market Cap	$19.9 Billion	Shares 334,461,728
Book Value	$9.0 Billion	% Held 77.33
Price/Book	2.21	
Price/Sales	0.95	

Business Summary: Non-Precious Metals (MIC: 8.2.2 SIC: 3312 NAIC: 331111)

Nucor is engaged in the manufacturing of steel and steel products. Co. has three segments: steel mills, which produces and distributes sheet steel (hot-rolled, cold-rolled and galvanized), tubular products, plate steel, structural steel and bar steel; steel products, which produces steel joists and joist girders, steel deck, fabricated concrete reinforcing steel, cold finished steel, steel fasteners, metal building systems, steel grating, and wire and wire mesh; and raw materials, which produces direct reduced iron (DRI); brokers ferrous and nonferrous metals, pig iron, hot briquetted iron and DRI; supplies ferro-alloys; and processes ferrous and nonferrous scrap metal.

Recent Developments: For the quarter ended Mar 31 2018, net income increased 0.7% to US$380.1 million from US$377.6 million in the year-earlier quarter. Revenues were US$5.57 billion, up 15.6% from US$4.82 billion the year before. Direct operating expenses rose 19.4% to US$4.84 billion from US$4.05 billion in the comparable period the year before. Indirect operating expenses increased 3.4% to US$173.4 million from US$167.7 million in the equivalent prior-year period.

Prospects: Our evaluation of Nucor Corp. as of Jan. 21, 2018 is the result of our systematic analysis on three basic characteristics: earnings strength, relative valuation, and recent stock price movement. The company has suffered a very negative trend in earnings per share over the past 5 quarters. However, while recent estimates for the company have been mixed, NUE has posted better than expected results. Based on operating earnings yield, the company is undervalued when compared to all of the companies in our coverage universe. Share price changes over the past year indicates that NUE will perform very poorly over the near term.

Financial Data
(US$ in Thousands)

	3 Mos	12/31/2017	12/31/2016	12/31/2015	12/31/2014	12/31/2013	12/31/2012	12/31/2011
Earnings Per Share	4.09	4.10	2.48	1.11	2.22	1.52	1.58	2.45
Cash Flow Per Share	2.93	3.29	5.42	6.73	4.20	3.38	3.76	3.26
Tang Book Value Per Share	18.51	17.70	15.56	14.58	15.18	15.07	14.73	15.34
Dividends Per Share	1.515	1.513	1.502	1.492	1.482	1.472	1.462	1.452
Dividend Payout %	37.04	36.89	60.58	134.46	66.78	96.88	92.56	59.29
Income Statement								
Total Revenue	5,568,419	20,252,393	16,208,122	16,439,276	21,105,141	19,052,046	19,429,273	20,023,564
EBITDA	724,564	2,517,709	2,042,338	1,503,197	2,012,328	1,464,573	1,562,648	1,950,520
Depn & Amortn	181,118	635,833	613,192	625,757	652,000	535,852	534,010	522,571
Income Before Taxes	506,332	1,708,296	1,259,902	703,909	1,191,072	781,826	866,263	1,261,855
Income Taxes	135,800	369,386	398,243	213,154	388,787	205,594	259,814	390,828
Net Income	354,179	1,318,688	796,271	357,659	713,946	488,025	504,619	778,188
Average Shares	320,474	320,773	319,822	320,693	320,127	319,266	318,240	317,161
Balance Sheet								
Current Assets	7,079,216	6,824,420	6,506,393	5,754,380	6,441,888	6,410,046	5,661,364	6,708,081
Total Assets	16,121,246	15,841,246	15,223,518	14,250,399	15,615,927	15,203,283	14,152,059	14,570,350
Current Liabilities	2,844,581	2,824,764	2,389,966	1,385,173	2,097,776	1,960,216	2,029,568	2,396,059
Long-Term Obligations	3,242,865	3,242,242	3,739,141	4,360,600	4,360,600	4,376,900	3,380,200	3,630,200
Total Liabilities	7,145,219	7,102,222	7,343,653	6,833,521	7,843,457	7,557,514	6,510,488	7,095,465
Stockholders' Equity	8,976,027	8,739,036	7,879,865	7,416,878	7,772,470	7,645,769	7,641,571	7,474,885
Shares Outstanding	318,096	317,969	318,737	317,962	319,033	318,328	317,663	316,749
Statistical Record								
Return on Assets %	8.23	8.49	5.39	2.40	4.63	3.32	3.50	5.46
Return on Equity %	15.38	15.87	10.38	4.71	9.26	6.38	6.66	10.66
EBITDA Margin %	13.01	12.43	12.60	9.14	9.53	7.69	8.04	9.74
Net Margin %	6.36	6.51	4.91	2.18	3.38	2.56	2.60	3.89
Asset Turnover	1.31	1.30	1.10	1.10	1.37	1.30	1.35	1.41
Current Ratio	2.49	2.42	2.72	4.15	3.07	3.27	2.79	2.80
Debt to Equity	0.36	0.37	0.47	0.59	0.56	0.57	0.44	0.49
Price Range	70.18-53.48	64.73-53.48	66.75-34.86	49.77-37.00	58.09-46.62	54.62-42.23	45.41-34.39	48.88-30.91
P/E Ratio	17.16-13.08	15.79-13.04	26.92-14.06	44.84-33.33	26.17-21.00	35.93-27.78	28.74-21.77	19.95-12.62
Average Yield %	2.53	2.58	3.06	3.34	2.87	3.12	3.64	3.57

Address: 1915 Rexford Road, Charlotte, NC 28211 **Telephone:** 704-366-7000 **Fax:** 704-362-4208	**Web Site:** www.nucor.com **Officers:** John J. Ferriola - Chairman, President, Chief Executive Officer, Chief Operating Officer Leon J. Topalian - Executive Vice President	**Auditors:** PricewaterhouseCoopers LLP **Transfer Agents:** American Stock Transfer & Trust Company, LLC, New York, NY

NVR INC.

*7 Year Price Score 163.66 *NYSE Composite Index=100 ***12 Month Price Score 99.31**

TRADING VOLUME (thousand shares)

Interim Earnings (Per Share)

Qtr.	Mar	Jun	Sep	Dec
2015	9.22	21.91	27.11	31.67
2016	15.79	22.01	28.46	37.37
2017	25.12	35.19	38.02	28.44
2018	39.34	...	...	...

Interim Dividends (Per Share)

No Dividends Paid

Valuation Analysis — Institutional Holding

Forecast EPS	$196.56	No of Institutions
	(05/21/2018)	597
Market Cap	$10.7 Billion	Shares
Book Value	$1.5 Billion	3,864,127
Price/Book	7.33	% Held
Price/Sales	1.63	74.40

Business Summary: Builders (MIC: 2.2.5 SIC: 1531 NAIC: 236117)

NVR is engaged in the construction and sale of single-family detached homes, townhomes and condominium buildings, all of which are primarily constructed on a pre-sold basis. Co.'s homebuilding operations construct and sell single-family detached homes, townhomes and condominium buildings under three trade names: NVHomes and Heartland Homes, which are marketed primarily to move-up and up-scale buyers, and Ryan Homes, which is marketed primarily to first-time and first-time move-up buyers. Co. also operates a mortgage banking and title services business. Co.'s mortgage banking operations are operated primarily through a wholly owned subsidiary, NVR Mortgage Finance, Inc.

Recent Developments: For the quarter ended Mar 31 2018, net income increased 61.3% to US$166.0 million from US$102.9 million in the year-earlier quarter. Revenues were US$1.53 billion, up 19.8% from US$1.28 billion the year before. Direct operating expenses rose 18.1% to US$1.21 billion from US$1.03 billion in the comparable period the year before. Indirect operating expenses increased 7.4% to US$125.1 million from US$116.4 million in the equivalent prior-year period.

Prospects: Our evaluation of NVR Inc. as of Jan. 21, 2018 is the result of our systematic analysis on three basic characteristics: earnings strength, relative valuation, and recent stock price movement. The company has produced a positive trend in earnings per share over the past 5 quarters and while recent estimates for the company have been mixed, NVR has posted better than expected results. Based on operating earnings yield, the company is about fairly valued when compared to all of the companies in our coverage universe. Share price changes over the past year indicates that NVR will perform very well over the near term.

Financial Data

(US$ in Thousands)	3 Mos	12/31/2017	12/31/2016	12/31/2015	12/31/2014	12/31/2013	12/31/2012	12/31/2011
Earnings Per Share	140.99	126.77	103.61	89.99	63.50	54.81	35.12	23.01
Cash Flow Per Share	146.00	152.40	99.67	50.57	43.14	57.04	52.62	0.27
Tang Book Value Per Share	391.82	421.72	339.27	304.87	264.25	271.93	289.44	266.37
Income Statement								
Total Revenue	1,534,008	6,322,274	5,834,585	5,169,562	4,453,139	4,220,908	3,193,204	2,669,608
EBITDA	202,316	893,763	705,673	648,305	494,300	454,472	290,706	216,140
Depn & Amortn	5,036	22,667	22,269	21,534	17,614	13,391	8,100	6,672
Income Before Taxes	190,998	846,911	661,697	603,212	453,546	418,696	275,077	207,576
Income Taxes	24,949	309,390	236,435	220,285	171,916	152,219	94,489	78,156
Net Income	166,049	537,521	425,262	382,927	281,630	266,477	180,588	129,420
Average Shares	4,220	4,240	4,104	4,255	4,435	4,861	5,141	5,623
Balance Sheet								
Current Assets	1,816,329	1,934,687	1,506,923	1,430,852	1,414,424	1,604,150	1,830,732	1,013,482
Total Assets	2,846,065	2,989,279	2,643,943	2,515,131	2,351,335	2,486,148	2,604,842	1,779,485
Current Liabilities	467,140	444,830	405,847	370,693	337,174	304,483	283,819	213,267
Long-Term Obligations	597,220	597,066	596,455	599,260	599,230	602,440	603,562	6,596
Total Liabilities	1,379,257	1,383,787	1,339,502	1,275,966	1,227,080	1,224,796	1,124,365	404,686
Stockholders' Equity	1,466,808	1,605,492	1,304,441	1,239,165	1,124,255	1,261,352	1,480,477	1,374,799
Shares Outstanding	3,618	3,691	3,693	3,890	4,049	4,433	4,914	4,977
Statistical Record								
Return on Assets %	21.50	19.08	16.44	15.74	11.64	10.47	8.22	6.41
Return on Equity %	41.78	36.94	33.35	32.40	23.61	19.44	12.61	8.31
EBITDA Margin %	13.19	14.14	12.09	12.54	11.10	10.77	9.10	8.10
Net Margin %	10.82	8.50	7.29	7.41	6.32	6.31	5.66	4.85
Asset Turnover	2.35	2.24	2.26	2.12	1.84	1.66	1.45	1.32
Current Ratio	3.89	4.35	3.71	3.86	4.19	5.27	6.45	4.75
Debt to Equity	0.41	0.37	0.46	0.48	0.53	0.48	0.41	N.M.
Price Range		3700.00-2065.08	3525.73-1649.99	1830.00-1497.19	1720.00-1224.13	1276.68-997.49	1080.11-835.74	959.25-671.00	804.32-575.28
P/E Ratio		26.24-14.65	27.81-13.02	17.66-14.45	19.11-13.60	20.11-15.71	19.71-15.25	27.31-19.11	34.96-25.00

Address: 11700 Plaza America Drive, Suite 500, Reston, VA 20190 **Telephone:** 703-956-4000	**Web Site:** www.nvrinc.com **Officers:** Dwight C. Schar - Chairman Paul C. Saville - President, Chief Executive Officer	**Auditors:** KPMG LLP **Transfer Agents:** Computershare Trust Company, N.A., Providence, RI

OASIS PETROLEUM INC.

Exchange	Symbol	Price	52Wk Range	Yield	P/E
NYS	OAS	$12.97 (6/29/2018)	13.78-6.95	N/A	31.63

*7 Year Price Score 31.81   *NYSE Composite Index=100   *12 Month Price Score 131.89

Interim Earnings (Per Share)

Qtr.	Mar	Jun	Sep	Dec
2015	(0.17)	(0.39)	0.20	0.04
2016	(0.40)	(0.51)	(0.19)	(0.23)
2017	0.10	0.07	(0.18)	0.52
2018	0.00	...	...	...

Interim Dividends (Per Share)

No Dividends Paid

Valuation Analysis		Institutional Holding	
Forecast EPS	$0.41	No of Institutions	
	(06/24/2018)	370	
Market Cap	$4.1 Billion	Shares	
Book Value	$3.7 Billion	320,305,344	
Price/Book	1.10	% Held	
Price/Sales	2.97	106.96	

Business Summary: Production & Extraction (MIC: 9.1.1 SIC: 1311 NAIC: 211111)

Oasis Petroleum is an independent exploration and production company focused on the acquisition and development of unconventional oil and natural gas resources in the North Dakota and Montana regions of the Williston Basin. Co.'s subsidiary, Oasis Petroleum North America LLC, conducts Co.'s exploration and production activities and owns Co.'s proved and unproved oil and natural gas properties. Co. also operates a midstream services business through its subsidiary, Oasis Midstream Services LLC. As of Dec 31 2017, Co. had total estimated net proved reserves of 312.2 million barrels of oil equivalent, which comprised of 225.0 million barrels of oil and 523.50 billion cubic feet of natural gas.

Recent Developments: For the quarter ended Mar 31 2018, net income decreased 84.4% to US$3.7 million from US$23.8 million in the year-earlier quarter. Revenues were US$421.2 million, up 47.7% from US$285.1 million the year before. Operating income was US$113.0 million versus US$20.1 million in the prior-year quarter, an increase of 462.3%. Direct operating expenses rose 17.3% to US$130.2 million from US$111.0 million in the comparable period the year before. Indirect operating expenses increased 15.6% to US$178.1 million from US$154.0 million in the equivalent prior-year period.

Prospects: Our evaluation of Oasis Petroleum Inc. as of Jan. 21, 2018 is the result of our systematic analysis on three basic characteristics: earnings strength, relative valuation, and recent stock price movement. The company has produced a positive trend in earnings per share over the past 5 quarters. Because the company lacks sufficient analyst estimate data, we place greater weight on the historical EPS trend as the measure of earnings strength. Based on operating earnings yield, the company is overvalued when compared to all of the companies in our coverage universe. Share price changes over the past year indicates that OAS will perform very poorly over the near term.

Financial Data
(US$ in Thousands)

	3 Mos	12/31/2017	12/31/2016	12/31/2015	12/31/2014	12/31/2013	12/31/2012	12/31/2011
Earnings Per Share	0.41	0.52	(1.32)	(0.31)	5.05	2.44	1.66	0.86
Cash Flow Per Share	2.17	2.16	1.24	2.76	8.75	7.51	4.25	1.91
Tang Book Value Per Share	11.81	12.54	12.37	16.68	18.48	13.39	8.52	6.86
Income Statement								
Total Revenue	421,216	1,248,424	704,665	789,735	1,390,228	1,141,999	686,668	330,422
EBITDA	47,161	620,092	259,416	590,898	1,396,220	781,485	525,561	232,339
Depn & Amortn	5,475	549,113	490,665	497,621	423,362	311,303	209,544	76,542
Income Before Taxes	4,540	(75,858)	(371,554)	(56,371)	814,468	363,017	245,874	126,179
Income Taxes	828	(203,304)	(128,538)	(16,123)	307,591	135,058	92,486	46,789
Net Income	590	123,796	(243,016)	(40,248)	506,877	227,959	153,388	79,390
Average Shares	291,738	237,875	183,615	130,186	100,365	93,411	92,513	92,241
Balance Sheet								
Current Assets	418,857	407,835	238,549	365,286	696,607	447,606	492,686	623,640
Total Assets	7,638,930	6,615,130	6,178,632	5,649,375	5,938,412	4,711,924	2,528,794	1,727,382
Current Liabilities	670,013	623,480	381,115	370,568	795,128	466,418	330,785	182,584
Long-Term Obligations	2,696,532	2,097,606	2,297,214	2,302,584	2,700,000	2,535,570	1,200,000	800,000
Total Liabilities	3,890,398	3,239,439	3,255,475	3,330,033	4,066,111	3,363,375	1,733,789	1,093,144
Stockholders' Equity	3,748,532	3,375,691	2,923,157	2,319,342	1,872,301	1,348,549	795,005	634,238
Shares Outstanding	317,363	269,295	236,344	139,076	101,341	100,699	93,303	92,460
Statistical Record								
Return on Assets %	1.45	1.94	N.M.	N.M.	9.52	6.30	7.19	6.56
Return on Equity %	3.00	3.93	N.M.	N.M.	31.47	21.27	21.41	13.39
EBITDA Margin %	11.20	49.67	36.81	74.82	100.43	68.43	76.54	70.32
Net Margin %	0.14	9.92	N.M.	N.M.	36.46	19.96	22.34	24.03
Asset Turnover	0.20	0.20	0.12	0.14	0.26	0.32	0.32	0.27
Current Ratio	0.63	0.65	0.63	0.99	0.88	0.96	1.49	3.42
Debt to Equity	0.72	0.62	0.79	0.99	1.44	1.88	1.51	1.26
Price Range	14.50-6.95	16.22-6.95	16.55-4.29	18.72-6.45	57.42-11.05	56.72-31.80	35.43-22.37	35.76-20.26
P/E Ratio	35.37-16.95	31.19-13.37	...	...	11.37-2.19	23.25-13.03	21.34-13.48	41.58-23.56

Address: 1001 Fannin Street, Suite 1500, Houston, TX 77002 Telephone: 281-404-9500	Web Site: www.oasispetroleum.com Officers: Thomas B. Nusz - Chairman, President, Chief Executive Officer Taylor L. Reid - President, Executive Vice President, Chief Operating Officer	Auditors: PricewaterhouseCoopers LLP Investor Contact: 281-404-9600 Transfer Agents: Computershare Investor Services, Inc., Canton, MA

OCCIDENTAL PETROLEUM CORP

Exchange	Symbol	Price	52Wk Range	Yield	P/E	Div Acheiver
NYS	OXY	$83.68 (6/29/2018)	86.48-58.68	3.73	33.88	15 Years

*7 Year Price Score 70.95   *NYSE Composite Index=100   *12 Month Price Score 117.17

Interim Earnings (Per Share)

Qtr.	Mar	Jun	Sep	Dec
2015	(0.28)	0.23	(3.42)	(6.77)
2016	0.10	(0.18)	(0.32)	(0.35)
2017	0.15	0.66	0.25	0.64
2018	0.92	...	...	...

Interim Dividends (Per Share)

Amt	Decl	Ex	Rec	Pay
0.77Q	10/05/2017	12/08/2017	12/11/2017	01/16/2018
0.77Q	02/08/2018	03/08/2018	03/09/2018	04/16/2018
0.77Q	05/03/2018	06/08/2018	06/11/2018	07/16/2018
0.78Q	07/12/2018	09/07/2018	09/10/2018	10/15/2018

Indicated Div: $3.12 (Div. Reinv. Plan)

Valuation Analysis   **Institutional Holding**

Forecast EPS	$4.88	No of Institutions
	(06/14/2018)	1620
Market Cap	$64.1 Billion	Shares
Book Value	$20.7 Billion	782,282,816
Price/Book	3.09	% Held
Price/Sales	4.54	75.68

TRADING VOLUME (thousand shares)

Business Summary: Production & Extraction (MIC: 9.1.1 SIC: 1311 NAIC: 211111)

Occidental Petroleum conducts its operations through various subsidiaries and affiliates. Co.'s principal businesses consist of three segments: oil and gas, which explores for, develops and produces oil and condensate, natural gas liquids (NGLs) and natural gas; chemical, which manufactures and markets basic chemicals and vinyls; and midstream and marketing, which gathers, processes, transports, stores, purchases and markets oil, condensate, NGLs, natural gas, carbon dioxide and power. At Dec 31 2017, Co. had 2.60 billion barrels of oil equivalent of proved reserves, which consisted of 1.52 billion barrels of oil, 445.0 million barrels of NGLs and 3.83 trillion cubic feet of natural gas.

Recent Developments: For the quarter ended Mar 31 2018, net income increased 505.1% to US$708.0 million from US$117.0 million in the year-earlier quarter. Revenues were US$3.83 billion, up 28.4% from US$2.98 billion the year before. Direct operating expenses declined 4.4% to US$1.36 billion from US$1.43 billion in the comparable period the year before. Indirect operating expenses increased 6.6% to US$1.48 billion from US$1.39 billion in the equivalent prior-year period.

Prospects: Our evaluation of Occidental Petroleum Corp. as of Jan. 21, 2018 is the result of our systematic analysis on three basic characteristics: earnings strength, relative valuation, and recent stock price movement. The company has generated a negative trend in earnings per share over the past 5 quarters and while recent estimates for the company have been raised by analysts, OXY has posted better than expected results. Based on operating earnings yield, the company is overvalued when compared to all of the companies in our coverage universe. Share price changes over the past year indicates that OXY will perform poorly over the near term.

Financial Data

(US$ in Thousands)	3 Mos	12/31/2017	12/31/2016	12/31/2015	12/31/2014	12/31/2013	12/31/2012	12/31/2011
Earnings Per Share	2.47	1.70	(0.75)	(10.23)	0.79	7.32	5.67	8.32
Cash Flow Per Share	6.99	6.53	4.42	4.38	14.17	16.08	13.94	15.12
Tang Book Value Per Share	27.06	26.89	28.13	31.89	39.26	48.46	49.68	46.39
Dividends Per Share	3.070	3.060	3.020	2.970	2.880	2.560	2.160	1.840
Dividend Payout %	124.29	180.00	...	...	364.56	34.97	38.10	22.12
Income Statement								
Total Revenue	3,825,000	13,274,000	10,398,000	12,699,000	21,947,000	25,736,000	24,253,000	24,119,000
EBITDA	2,002,000	5,318,000	2,715,000	(4,993,000)	5,562,000	14,747,000	12,031,000	14,348,000
Depn & Amortn	921,000	4,002,000	4,268,000	4,544,000	4,261,000	5,347,000	4,511,000	3,591,000
Income Before Taxes	984,000	971,000	(1,845,000)	(9,684,000)	1,224,000	9,282,000	7,390,000	10,459,000
Income Taxes	339,000	17,000	(662,000)	(1,330,000)	1,685,000	3,755,000	3,118,000	4,201,000
Net Income	708,000	1,311,000	(574,000)	(7,829,000)	616,000	5,903,000	4,598,000	6,771,000
Average Shares	767,000	765,900	763,800	765,600	781,100	804,600	810,000	812,900
Balance Sheet								
Current Assets	8,894,000	8,270,000	8,428,000	9,402,000	13,873,000	11,323,000	9,492,000	11,542,000
Total Assets	42,808,000	42,026,000	43,109,000	43,437,000	56,259,000	69,443,000	64,210,000	60,044,000
Current Liabilities	7,070,000	7,400,000	6,362,000	6,842,000	8,244,000	8,434,000	7,290,000	7,947,000
Long-Term Obligations	10,309,000	9,328,000	9,819,000	6,883,000	6,838,000	6,939,000	7,023,000	5,871,000
Total Liabilities	22,086,000	21,454,000	21,612,000	19,087,000	21,300,000	26,317,000	24,194,000	22,424,000
Stockholders' Equity	20,722,000	20,572,000	21,497,000	24,350,000	34,959,000	43,126,000	40,016,000	37,620,000
Shares Outstanding	765,770	765,104	764,237	763,678	890,557	889,919	805,514	811,009
Statistical Record								
Return on Assets %	4.46	3.08	N.M.	N.M.	0.98	8.83	7.38	12.04
Return on Equity %	9.10	6.23	N.M.	N.M.	1.58	14.20	11.81	19.32
EBITDA Margin %	52.34	40.06	26.11	N.M.	25.34	57.30	49.61	59.49
Net Margin %	18.51	9.88	N.M.	N.M.	2.81	22.94	18.96	28.07
Asset Turnover	0.33	0.31	0.24	0.25	0.35	0.39	0.39	0.43
Current Ratio	1.26	1.12	1.32	1.37	1.68	1.34	1.30	1.45
Debt to Equity	0.50	0.45	0.46	0.28	0.20	0.16	0.18	0.16
Price Range	77.63-58.02	73.70-58.02	78.31-59.60	83.08-63.61	100.90-73.13	95.32-73.49	101.16-70.58	111.02-65.78
P/E Ratio	31.43-23.49	43.35-34.13	...	...	127.73-92.57	13.02-10.04	17.84-12.45	13.34-7.91
Average Yield %	4.73	4.77	4.20	3.99	3.18	2.99	2.56	2.01

Address: 5 Greenway Plaza, Suite 110, Houston, TX 77046
Telephone: 713-215-7000

Web Site: www.oxy.com
Officers: Eugene L. (Gene) Batchelder - Chairman
Vicki A. Hollub - President, Chief Executive Officer,
Chief Operating Officer, Senior Executive Vice
President, Division Officer

Auditors: KPMG LLP
Transfer Agents: American Stock
Transfer and Trust Company, LLC,
Brooklyn, NY

OCEANEERING INTERNATIONAL, INC.

Exchange	Symbol	Price	52Wk Range	Yield	P/E
NYS	OII	$25.46 (6/29/2018)	26.63-17.86	2.36	20.37

*7 Year Price Score 37.44 *NYSE Composite Index=100 *12 Month Price Score 105.83

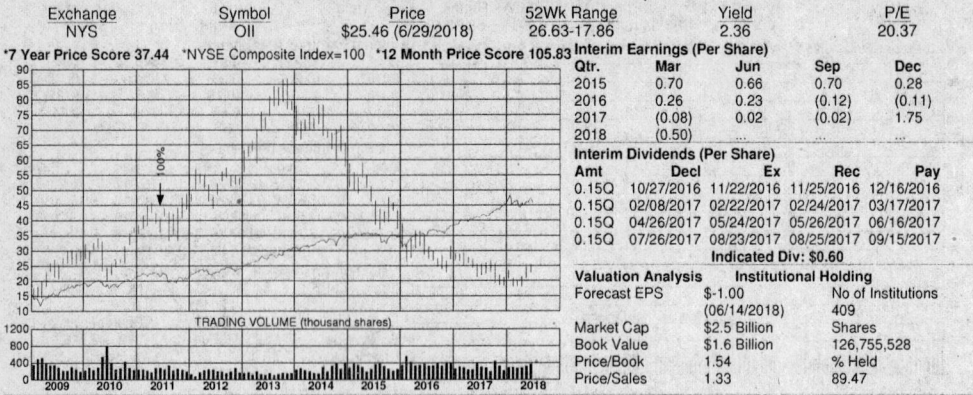

Interim Earnings (Per Share)

Qtr.	Mar	Jun	Sep	Dec
2015	0.70	0.66	0.70	0.28
2016	0.26	0.23	(0.12)	(0.11)
2017	(0.08)	0.02	(0.02)	1.75
2018	(0.50)	...	...	...

Interim Dividends (Per Share)

Amt	Decl	Ex	Rec	Pay
0.15Q	10/27/2016	11/22/2016	11/25/2016	12/16/2016
0.15Q	02/08/2017	02/22/2017	02/24/2017	03/17/2017
0.15Q	04/26/2017	05/24/2017	05/26/2017	06/16/2017
0.15Q	07/26/2017	08/23/2017	08/25/2017	09/15/2017

Indicated Div: $0.60

Valuation Analysis

		Institutional Holding	
Forecast EPS	$-1.00	No of Institutions	
	(06/14/2018)	409	
Market Cap	$2.5 Billion	Shares	
Book Value	$1.6 Billion	126,755,528	
Price/Book	1.54	% Held	
Price/Sales	1.33	89.47	

Business Summary: Equipment & Services (MIC: 9.1.3 SIC: 1389 NAIC: 213112)

Oceaneering International provides engineered services and products, primarily to the offshore oil and gas industry, with a focus on deepwater applications. Co. also serves the defense, aerospace and commercial theme park industries. Co.'s services and products include remotely operated vehicles, specialty subsea hardware, engineering and project management, subsea intervention services, including manned diving, survey and positioning services and asset integrity and nondestructive testing services. Co. operates two businesses: Oilfield business, which includes its Remotely Operated Vehicles, Subsea Products, Subsea Projects and Asset Integrity segments; and Advanced Technologies business.

Recent Developments: For the quarter ended Mar 31 2018, net loss amounted to US$49.1 million versus a net loss of US$7.5 million in the year-earlier quarter. Revenues were US$416.4 million, down 6.7% from US$446.2 million the year before. Operating loss was US$27.1 million versus a loss of US$150,000 in the prior-year quarter. Direct operating expenses declined 0.9% to US$397.6 million from US$401.3 million in the comparable period the year before. Indirect operating expenses increased 2.2% to US$46.0 million from US$45.0 million in the equivalent prior-year period.

Prospects: Our evaluation of Oceaneering International Inc. as of Jan. 21, 2018 is the result of our systematic analysis on three basic characteristics: earnings strength, relative valuation, and recent stock price movement. The company has enjoyed a very positive trend in earnings per share over the past 5 quarters. Because the company lacks sufficient analyst estimate data, we place greater weight on the historical EPS trend as the measure of earnings strength. Based on operating earnings yield, the company is overvalued when compared to all of the companies in our coverage universe. Share price changes over the past year indicates that OII will perform very poorly over the near term.

Financial Data

(US$ in Thousands)	3 Mos	12/31/2017	12/31/2016	12/31/2015	12/31/2014	12/31/2013	12/31/2012	12/31/2011
Earnings Per Share	1.25	1.68	0.25	2.34	4.00	3.42	2.66	2.16
Cash Flow Per Share	0.84	1.39	3.46	5.69	6.77	4.89	4.05	2.66
Tang Book Value Per Share	11.37	11.38	10.05	10.81	12.70	15.07	13.46	11.33
Dividends Per Share	0.300	0.450	0.960	1.080	1.030	0.840	0.690	0.450
Dividend Payout %	24.00	26.79	384.00	46.15	25.75	24.56	25.94	20.83
Income Statement								
Total Revenue	416,413	1,921,507	2,271,603	3,062,754	3,659,624	3,287,019	2,782,604	2,192,663
EBITDA	18,505	218,120	314,767	599,709	857,722	746,071	599,015	485,519
Depn & Amortn	54,128	213,519	250,247	241,235	229,779	202,228	176,483	151,227
Income Before Taxes	(42,402)	(15,861)	43,102	334,031	623,528	542,203	420,249	334,084
Income Taxes	5,888	(184,242)	18,760	105,250	195,148	170,836	132,905	102,227
Net Income	(49,133)	166,398	24,586	231,011	428,329	371,500	289,017	235,658
Average Shares	98,383	98,764	98,424	98,808	107,091	108,731	108,617	109,001
Balance Sheet								
Current Assets	1,105,745	1,187,402	1,262,595	1,517,493	1,713,550	1,433,275	1,202,990	984,122
Total Assets	2,928,681	3,023,950	3,130,315	3,429,536	3,511,701	3,128,500	2,768,118	2,400,544
Current Liabilities	372,522	435,797	508,364	615,956	679,137	727,088	617,185	501,375
Long-Term Obligations	785,068	792,312	793,058	795,836	750,000	...	94,000	120,000
Total Liabilities	1,295,832	1,364,786	1,613,672	1,850,802	1,854,081	1,085,060	952,658	842,582
Stockholders' Equity	1,632,849	1,659,164	1,516,643	1,578,734	1,657,620	2,043,440	1,815,460	1,557,962
Shares Outstanding	98,529	98,279	98,065	97,849	99,613	108,197	107,907	108,034
Statistical Record								
Return on Assets %	4.15	5.41	0.75	6.66	12.90	12.60	11.15	10.64
Return on Equity %	7.99	10.48	1.58	14.28	23.15	19.25	17.09	15.99
EBITDA Margin %	4.44	11.35	13.86	19.58	23.44	22.70	21.53	22.14
Net Margin %	N.M.	8.66	1.08	7.54	11.70	11.30	10.39	10.75
Asset Turnover	0.63	0.62	0.69	0.88	1.10	1.11	1.07	0.99
Current Ratio	2.97	2.72	2.48	2.46	2.52	1.97	1.95	1.96
Debt to Equity	0.48	0.48	0.52	0.50	0.45		0.05	0.08
Price Range	27.87-17.86	29.35-18.28	38.78-22.75	59.12-37.06	78.88-57.49	86.68-53.79	57.42-43.76	48.78-33.16
P/E Ratio	22.30-14.29	17.47-10.88	155.12-91.00	25.26-15.84	19.72-14.37	25.35-15.73	21.59-16.45	22.58-15.35
Average Yield %	1.32	1.83	3.24	2.27	1.48	1.14	1.34	1.10

Address: 11911 FM 529, Houston, TX 77041	Web Site: www.oceaneering.com	Auditors: Ernst & Young LLP
Telephone: 713-329-4500	Officers: John R. Huff - Chairman Roderick A. Larson - President, Chief Executive Officer, Chief Operating Officer, Senior Vice President	Investor Contact: 713-329-4500 Transfer Agents: Computershare Trust Company, N.A., Providence, RI

OGE ENERGY CORP.

Exchange	Symbol	Price	52Wk Range	Yield	P/E	Div Acheiver
NYS	OGE	$35.21 (6/29/2018)	37.23-29.60	3.78	11.04	11 Years

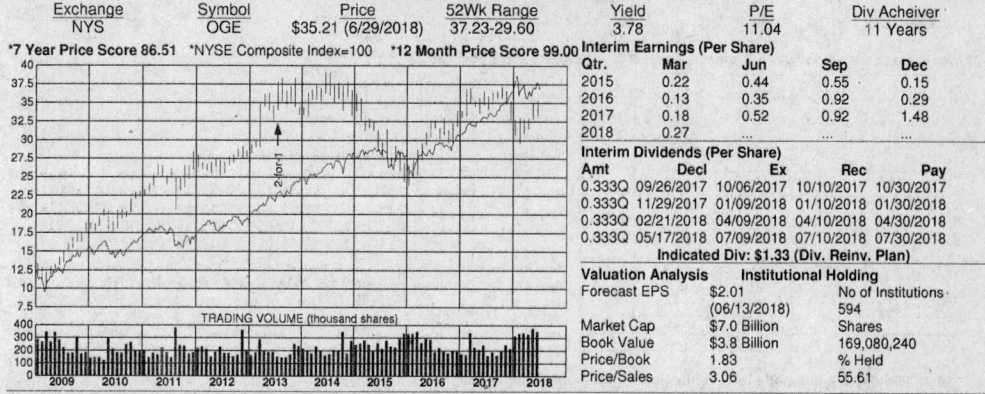

*7 Year Price Score 86.51 ***NYSE Composite Index=100** ***12 Month Price Score 99.00**

Interim Earnings (Per Share)

Qtr.	Mar	Jun	Sep	Dec
2015	0.22	0.44	0.55	0.15
2016	0.13	0.35	0.92	0.29
2017	0.18	0.52	0.92	1.48
2018	0.27	...	...	...

Interim Dividends (Per Share)

Amt	Decl	Ex	Rec	Pay
0.333Q	09/26/2017	10/06/2017	10/10/2017	10/30/2017
0.333Q	11/29/2017	01/09/2018	01/10/2018	01/30/2018
0.333Q	02/21/2018	04/09/2018	04/10/2018	04/30/2018
0.333Q	05/17/2018	07/09/2018	07/10/2018	07/30/2018

Indicated Div: $1.33 (Div. Reinv. Plan)

Valuation Analysis / Institutional Holding

Valuation Analysis		Institutional Holding	
Forecast EPS	$2.01	No of Institutions	594
	(06/13/2018)		
Market Cap	$7.0 Billion	Shares	169,080,240
Book Value	$3.8 Billion		
Price/Book	1.83	% Held	55.61
Price/Sales	3.06		

Business Summary: Electric Utilities (MIC: 3.1.1 SIC: 4911 NAIC: 221121)

OGE Energy is a holding company. Through its subsidiaries, Co. is an energy and energy services provider providing physical delivery and related services for both electricity and natural gas primarily in the south central U.S. Co. conducts these activities through two business segments: electric utility, which generates, transmits, distributes and sells electric energy in Oklahoma and western Arkansas; and natural gas midstream operations, which consist of Co.'s investment in Enable Midstream Partners, LP (Enable). Enable is engaged in the business of gathering, processing, transporting and storing natural gas. Enable also owns a crude oil gathering business in the Bakken shale formation.

Recent Developments: For the quarter ended Mar 31 2018, net income increased 52.8% to US$55.0 million from US$36.0 million in the year-earlier quarter. Revenues were US$492.7 million, up 8.0% from US$456.0 million the year before. Operating income was US$60.5 million versus US$45.7 million in the prior-year quarter, an increase of 32.4%. Direct operating expenses rose 5.6% to US$408.1 million from US$386.4 million in the comparable period the year before. Indirect operating expenses increased 0.8% to US$24.1 million from US$23.9 million in the equivalent prior-year period.

Prospects: Our evaluation of OGE Energy Corp. as of Jan. 21, 2018 is the result of our systematic analysis on three basic characteristics: earnings strength, relative valuation, and recent stock price movement. The company has generated a negative trend in earnings per share over the past 5 quarters. However, while recent estimates for the company have been mixed, OGE has posted results that fell short of analysts expectations. Based on operating earnings yield, the company is undervalued when compared to all of the companies in our coverage universe. Share price changes over the past year indicates that OGE will perform very well over the near term.

Financial Data

(US$ in Thousands)	3 Mos	12/31/2017	12/31/2016	12/31/2015	12/31/2014	12/31/2013	12/31/2012	12/31/2011
Earnings Per Share	3.19	3.10	1.69	1.36	1.98	1.94	1.79	1.73
Cash Flow Per Share	4.31	3.93	3.22	4.34	3.62	3.14	5.29	4.26
Tang Book Value Per Share	19.24	19.28	17.24	16.65	16.27	15.30	13.16	12.17
Dividends Per Share	1.270	1.240	1.127	1.025	0.925	0.835	0.785	0.750
Dividend Payout %	39.81	40.00	66.72	75.37	46.72	43.04	43.85	43.48
Income Statement								
Total Revenue	492,700	2,261,100	2,259,200	2,196,900	2,453,100	2,867,700	3,671,200	3,915,900
EBITDA	148,600	865,800	849,200	810,100	825,800	868,300	1,058,400	971,800
Depn & Amortn	78,800	283,500	322,600	307,900	281,400	298,600	374,800	307,100
Income Before Taxes	31,200	438,500	384,500	353,200	396,000	422,200	520,100	524,300
Income Taxes	10,100	(49,300)	148,100	97,400	172,800	130,300	135,100	160,700
Net Income	55,000	619,000	338,200	271,300	395,800	387,600	355,000	342,900
Average Shares	200,200	200,000	199,900	199,600	199,900	199,400	198,200	198,400
Balance Sheet								
Current Assets	493,500	497,000	549,500	570,200	705,800	694,600	794,200	652,700
Total Assets	10,436,400	10,412,700	9,939,600	9,597,400	9,527,800	9,134,700	9,922,200	8,906,000
Current Liabilities	1,215,200	950,500	1,027,200	752,800	573,300	1,093,800	1,276,400	998,500
Long-Term Obligations	2,500,100	2,749,600	2,405,800	2,645,600	2,755,300	2,300,100	2,848,600	2,737,100
Total Liabilities	6,594,300	6,561,600	6,495,800	6,271,400	6,283,400	6,097,600	7,155,000	6,342,700
Stockholders' Equity	3,842,100	3,851,100	3,443,800	3,326,000	3,244,400	3,037,100	2,767,200	2,563,300
Shares Outstanding	199,731	199,700	199,700	199,700	199,400	198,500	197,600	196,200
Statistical Record								
Return on Assets %	6.20	6.08	3.45	2.84	4.24	4.07	3.76	4.14
Return on Equity %	17.51	16.97	9.96	8.26	12.60	13.36	13.28	14.13
EBITDA Margin %	30.16	38.29	37.59	36.87	33.66	30.28	28.83	24.82
Net Margin %	11.16	27.38	14.97	12.35	16.13	13.52	9.67	8.76
Asset Turnover	0.22	0.22	0.23	0.23	0.26	0.30	0.39	0.47
Current Ratio	0.41	0.52	0.53	0.76	1.23	0.64	0.62	0.65
Debt to Equity	0.65	0.71	0.70	0.80	0.85	0.76	1.03	1.07
Price Range	37.23-29.60	37.23-32.66	33.89-23.86	36.20-24.37	39.08-33.18	38.36-28.16	29.09-25.20	28.41-20.58
P/E Ratio	11.67-9.28	12.01-10.54	20.05-14.12	26.62-17.92	19.74-16.76	19.77-14.51	16.25-14.08	16.42-11.90
Average Yield %	3.69	3.52	3.77	3.42	2.56	2.44	2.90	3.03

Address: 321 North Harvey, P.O. Box 321, Oklahoma City, OK 73101-0321
Telephone: 405-553-3000

Web Site: www.oge.com
Officers: Sean Trauschke - Chairman, President, Chief Executive Officer Stephen E. Merrill - Vice President, Chief Financial Officer

Auditors: Ernst & Young LLP
Investor Contact: 405-553-3966
Transfer Agents: Computershare, Providence, RI

OIL-DRI CORP. OF AMERICA

Exchange	Symbol	Price	52Wk Range	Yield	P/E	Div Acheiver
NYS	ODC	$42.14 (6/29/2018)	50.33-35.52	2.28	45.80	15 Years

*7 Year Price Score 106.41 *NYSE Composite Index=100 *12 Month Price Score 96.22

Interim Earnings (Per Share)

Qtr.	Oct	Jan	Apr	Jul
2014-15	0.30	0.39	0.19	0.71
2015-16	0.75	0.53	(0.13)	0.72
2016-17	0.28	0.58	0.44	0.18
2017-18	0.41	(0.15)	0.48	...

Interim Dividends (Per Share)

Amt	Decl	Ex	Rec	Pay
0.23Q	10/18/2017	11/16/2017	11/17/2017	12/01/2017
0.23Q	12/13/2017	02/15/2018	02/16/2018	03/02/2018
0.23Q	03/21/2018	05/17/2018	05/18/2018	06/01/2018
0.24Q	06/21/2018	08/16/2018	08/17/2018	08/31/2018

Indicated Div: $0.96

Valuation Analysis · **Institutional Holding**

Forecast EPS	N/A	No of Institutions 96
Market Cap	$308.3 Million	Shares 4,259,920
Book Value	$129.0 Million	% Held 52.88
Price/Book	2.39	
Price/Sales	1.16	

Business Summary: Household & Personal Products (MIC: 1.7.1 SIC: 3999 NAIC: 339999)

Oil-Dri Corp of America is engaged in developing, manufacturing and/or marketing sorbent products. Co.'s sorbent products are mainly produced from hydrated aluminosilicate minerals, primarily consisting of calcium bentonite, attapulgite and diatomaceous shale, which it refers to collectively as its clay or its minerals. Co.'s sorbent technologies include absorbent and adsorbent products, which draw liquids up into their pores. Co. also sells some nonclay-based products. Co.'s products include agricultural and horticultural products, animal health and nutrition products, bleaching clay and purification aid products, cat litter products, industrial and automotive products and sports products.

Recent Developments: For the quarter ended Apr 30 2018, net income increased 11.6% to US$3.6 million from US$3.2 million in the year-earlier quarter. Revenues were US$64.8 million, up 0.2% from US$64.7 million the year before. Operating income was US$3.1 million versus US$3.7 million in the prior-year quarter, a decrease of 16.9%. Direct operating expenses rose 0.3% to US$47.1 million from US$47.0 million in the comparable period the year before. Indirect operating expenses increased 4.2% to US$14.6 million from US$14.0 million in the equivalent prior-year period.

Prospects: Our evaluation of Oil-Dri Corp. of America as of Jan. 21, 2018 is the result of our systematic analysis on three basic characteristics: earnings strength, relative valuation, and recent stock price movement. The company has suffered a very negative trend in earnings per share over the past 5 quarters. Because the company lacks sufficient analyst estimate data, we place greater weight on the historical EPS trend as the measure of earnings strength. Based on operating earnings yield, the company is about fairly valued when compared to all of the companies in our coverage universe. Share price changes over the past year indicates that ODC will perform very well over the near term.

Financial Data

(US$ in Thousands)	9 Mos	6 Mos	3 Mos	07/31/2017	07/31/2016	07/31/2015	07/31/2014	07/31/2013
Earnings Per Share	0.92	0.88	1.61	1.47	1.87	1.59	1.17	2.07
Cash Flow Per Share	1.22	5.86	3.96	3.80	3.57	3.87	2.33	3.40
Tang Book Value Per Share	15.88	15.47	15.69	15.43	13.95	13.44	12.36	13.79
Dividends Per Share	0.910	0.900	0.890	0.880	0.840	0.800	0.760	0.720
Dividend Payout %	98.91	102.27	55.28	59.86	44.92	50.31	64.96	34.78
Income Statement								
Total Revenue	200,387	135,540	66,646	262,307	262,313	261,402	266,313	250,583
EBITDA	12,459	9,134	3,961	26,882	26,145	25,835	22,172	28,177
Depn & Amortn	(96)	(57)	(25)	11,544	10,782	10,352	9,289	8,939
Income Before Taxes	12,205	8,910	3,839	14,545	14,357	14,169	11,337	17,499
Income Taxes	6,666	6,956	789	3,753	744	2,801	2,981	2,913
Net Income	5,539	1,954	3,050	10,792	13,613	11,368	8,356	14,586
Average Shares	7,222	7,139	7,211	7,158	7,094	7,037	7,004	6,927
Balance Sheet								
Current Assets	87,132	94,154	88,901	97,017	91,173	82,643	83,516	103,372
Total Assets	198,010	205,535	206,917	212,575	204,933	190,031	186,204	183,559
Current Liabilities	35,719	33,334	27,747	32,954	30,740	28,888	29,500	31,447
Long-Term Obligations	6,099	6,092	6,085	9,161	12,333	15,417	18,900	22,400
Total Liabilities	68,997	79,273	78,807	86,538	89,382	79,503	81,896	80,621
Stockholders' Equity	129,013	126,262	128,110	126,037	115,551	110,528	104,308	102,938
Shares Outstanding	7,315	7,317	7,318	7,296	7,260	7,068	7,071	7,021
Statistical Record								
Return on Assets %	3.35	3.15	5.81	5.17	6.87	6.04	4.52	8.15
Return on Equity %	5.45	5.26	9.66	8.93	12.01	10.58	8.06	15.50
EBITDA Margin %	6.22	6.74	5.94	10.25	9.97	9.88	8.33	11.24
Net Margin %	2.76	1.44	4.58	4.11	5.19	4.35	3.14	5.82
Asset Turnover	1.30	1.29	1.29	1.26	1.32	1.39	1.44	1.40
Current Ratio	2.44	2.82	3.20	2.94	2.97	2.86	2.83	3.29
Debt to Equity	0.05	0.05	0.05	0.07	0.11	0.14	0.18	0.22
Price Range	50.33-34.10	50.33-33.56	50.33-32.82	43.58-32.82	38.30-22.11	33.85-24.60	40.64-28.97	31.88-21.00
P/E Ratio	54.71-37.07	57.19-38.14	31.26-20.39	29.65-22.33	20.48-11.82	21.29-15.47	34.74-24.76	15.40-10.14
Average Yield %	2.23	2.23	2.28	2.35	2.62	2.62	2.26	2.79

Address: 410 North Michigan Avenue, Suite 400, Chicago, IL 60611-4213	**Web Site:** www.oildri.com	**Auditors:** GRANT THORNTON LLP
Telephone: 312-321-1515	**Officers:** Richard M. Jaffee - Chairman Daniel S. Jaffee - President, Chief Executive Officer	**Investor Contact:** 312-321-1515
Fax: 312-321-9525		**Transfer Agents:** ComputerShare Investor Services, Chicago, IL

OLD REPUBLIC INTERNATIONAL CORP.

Exchange	Symbol	Price	52Wk Range	Yield	P/E	Div Acheiver
NYS	ORI	$19.91 (6/29/2018)	22.21-18.11	3.92	12.93	36 Years

*7 Year Price Score 105.17 *NYSE Composite Index=100 *12 Month Price Score 99.76

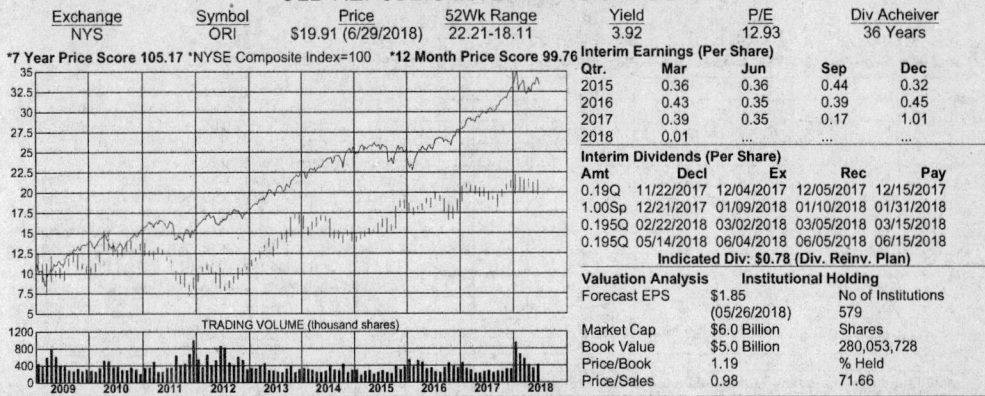

Interim Earnings (Per Share)

Qtr.	Mar	Jun	Sep	Dec
2015	0.36	0.36	0.44	0.32
2016	0.43	0.35	0.39	0.45
2017	0.39	0.35	0.17	1.01
2018	0.01	...	...	...

Interim Dividends (Per Share)

Amt	Decl	Ex	Rec	Pay
0.19Q	11/22/2017	12/04/2017	12/05/2017	12/15/2017
1.00Sp	12/21/2017	01/09/2018	01/10/2018	01/31/2018
0.195Q	02/22/2018	03/02/2018	03/05/2018	03/15/2018
0.195Q	05/14/2018	06/04/2018	06/05/2018	06/15/2018

Indicated Div: $0.78 (Div. Reinv. Plan)

Valuation Analysis / Institutional Holding

Forecast EPS	$1.85 (05/26/2018)	No of Institutions	579
Market Cap	$6.0 Billion	Shares	280,053,728
Book Value	$5.0 Billion	% Held	71.66
Price/Book	1.19		
Price/Sales	0.98		

Business Summary: General Insurance (MIC: 5.2.1 SIC: 6351 NAIC: 524113)

Old Republic International is a holding company engaged in the business of insurance underwriting and related services. Through its regulated insurance company subsidiaries, Co. conducts its operations in three main segments: General Insurance Group, which is a commercial lines insurance business focused on liability insurance coverages; Title Insurance Group, which consists mainly of the issuance of policies to real estate purchasers and investors based upon searches of the public records, which contain information concerning interests in real property; and the Republic Financial Indemnity Group Run-off Business, which consists of mortgage guaranty and consumer credit indemnity operations.

Recent Developments: For the quarter ended Mar 31 2018, net income decreased 96.5% to US$4.0 million from US$113.1 million in the year-earlier quarter. Revenues were US$1.33 billion, down 7.9% from US$1.44 billion the year before. Net premiums earned were US$1.23 billion versus US$1.20 billion in the prior-year quarter, an increase of 2.5%. Net investment income rose 4.4% to US$105.7 million from US$101.2 million a year ago.

Prospects: Our evaluation of Old Republic International Corp. as of Jan. 21, 2018 is the result of our systematic analysis on three basic characteristics: earnings strength, relative valuation, and recent stock price movement. The company has generated a negative trend in earnings per share over the past 5 quarters. However, while recent estimates for the company have been mixed, ORI has posted better than expected results. Based on operating earnings yield, the company is undervalued when compared to all of the companies in our coverage universe. Share price changes over the past year indicates that ORI will perform in line with the market over the near term.

Financial Data
(US$ in Thousands)

	3 Mos	12/31/2017	12/31/2016	12/31/2015	12/31/2014	12/31/2013	12/31/2012	12/31/2011
Earnings Per Share	1.54	1.92	1.62	1.48	1.44	1.74	(0.27)	(0.55)
Cash Flow Per Share	1.57	1.73	2.45	2.65	(0.70)	2.67	2.07	(0.37)
Tang Book Value Per Share	16.71	17.58	17.02	14.81	15.04	14.49	13.86	14.55
Dividends Per Share	1.765	0.760	0.750	0.740	0.730	0.720	0.710	0.700
Dividend Payout %	114.61	39.58	46.30	50.00	50.69	41.38	...	...
Income Statement								
Premium Income	1,231,000	5,080,200	4,868,900	4,758,800	4,446,300	4,456,600	4,043,800	3,695,500
Total Revenue	1,330,400	6,263,100	5,900,500	5,766,100	5,530,700	5,442,700	4,970,100	4,645,500
Benefits & Claims	...	2,459,200	2,329,800	2,441,300	2,500,000	2,223,000	2,747,400	2,730,600
Income Before Taxes	(6,000)	725,400	686,000	631,800	...	...	...	...
Income Taxes	(10,100)	164,800	219,000	209,600	199,700	225,000	(59,800)	(96,100)
Net Income	4,000	560,500	466,900	422,100	409,700	447,800	(68,600)	(140,500)
Average Shares	279,528	299,387	296,379	296,088	295,073	293,684	255,812	255,045
Balance Sheet								
Total Assets	18,998,800	19,403,500	18,591,600	17,110,500	16,988,100	16,534,400	16,226,800	16,050,400
Total Liabilities	13,950,200	14,670,200	14,119,900	13,229,600	13,064,000	12,759,400	12,630,600	12,277,800
Stockholders' Equity	5,048,600	4,733,300	4,471,600	3,880,800	3,924,000	3,775,000	3,596,200	3,772,500
Shares Outstanding	302,185	269,238	262,719	261,968	260,946	260,462	259,490	259,328
Statistical Record								
Return on Assets %	2.38	2.95	2.61	2.48	2.44	2.73	N.M.	N.M.
Return on Equity %	9.36	12.18	11.15	10.82	10.64	12.15	N.M.	N.M.
Loss Ratio %	...	48.41	47.85	51.30	56.23	49.88	67.94	73.89
Net Margin %	0.30	8.95	7.91	7.32	7.41	8.23	(1.38)	(3.02)
Price Range	22.21-18.11	21.46-18.11	19.98-16.58	19.02-13.87	17.27-13.74	17.36-10.65	11.19-7.83	13.84-7.18
P/E Ratio	14.42-11.76	11.18-9.43	12.33-10.23	12.85-9.37	11.99-9.54	9.98-6.12	...	...
Average Yield %	8.77	3.80	4.07	4.61	4.67	5.15	7.27	6.36

Address: 307 North Michigan Avenue, Chicago, IL 60601 **Telephone:** 312-346-8100	**Web Site:** www.oldrepublic.com **Officers:** Aldo C. Zucaro - Chairman, Chief Executive Officer R. Scott Rager - President, Senior Vice President, Chief Operating Officer, Division Officer	**Auditors:** KPMG LLP **Investor Contact:** 800-468-9716 **Transfer Agents:** Wells Fargo Shareholder Services, St. Paul, MN

OLIN CORP.

Exchange	Symbol	Price	52Wk Range	Yield	P/E
NYS	OLN	$28.72 (6/29/2018)	38.60-28.26	2.79	8.73

*7 Year Price Score 106.40 *NYSE Composite Index=100 *12 Month Price Score 93.92

Interim Earnings (Per Share)

Qtr.	Mar	Jun	Sep	Dec
2015	0.17	0.54	0.08	(0.79)
2016	(0.23)	(0.01)	0.11	0.11
2017	0.08	(0.04)	0.31	2.90
2018	0.12	...	...	...

Interim Dividends (Per Share)

Amt	Decl	Ex	Rec	Pay
0.20Q	07/27/2017	08/08/2017	08/10/2017	09/11/2017
0.20Q	10/25/2017	11/09/2017	11/10/2017	12/11/2017
0.20Q	01/26/2018	02/08/2018	02/09/2018	03/09/2018
0.20Q	04/26/2018	05/09/2018	05/10/2018	06/11/2018

Indicated Div: $0.80 (Div. Reinv. Plan)

Valuation Analysis / Institutional Holding

Forecast EPS	$1.99
(06/13/2018)	
Market Cap	$4.8 Billion
Book Value	$2.8 Billion
Price/Book	1.74
Price/Sales	0.75
No of Institutions	505
Shares	178,454,384
% Held	95.53

TRADING VOLUME (thousand shares)

Chart years: 2009 2010 2011 2012 2013 2014 2015 2016 2017 2018

Business Summary: Diversified Chemicals (MIC: 8.3.1 SIC: 2812 NAIC: 325181)

Olin is a manufacturer with three segments. The Chlor Alkali Products and Vinyls segment manufactures and sells chlorine and caustic soda, ethylene dichloride and vinyl chloride monomer, methyl chloride, methylene chloride, chloroform, carbon tetrachloride, perchloroethylene, trichloroethylene and vinylidene chloride, hydrochloric acid, hydrogen, bleach products and potassium hydroxide. The Epoxy segment produces and sells epoxy materials, including allyl chloride, epichlorohydrin, liquid epoxy resins and converted epoxy resins. The Winchester segment produces and sells sporting ammunition, reloading components, small caliber military ammunition and components, and industrial cartridges.

Recent Developments: For the quarter ended Mar 31 2018, net income increased 56.0% to US$20.9 million from US$13.4 million in the year-earlier quarter. Revenues were US$1.71 billion, up 9.1% from US$1.57 billion the year before. Operating income was US$84.9 million versus US$61.1 million in the prior-year quarter, an increase of 39.0%. Direct operating expenses rose 9.4% to US$1.53 billion from US$1.40 billion in the comparable period the year before. Indirect operating expenses decreased 10.9% to US$96.7 million from US$108.5 million in the equivalent prior-year period.

Prospects: Our evaluation of Olin Corp. as of Jan. 21, 2018 is the result of our systematic analysis on three basic characteristics: earnings strength, relative valuation, and recent stock price movement. The company has enjoyed a very positive trend in earnings per share over the past 5 quarters and while recent estimates for the company have been mixed, OLN has posted better than expected results. Based on operating earnings yield, the company is about fairly valued when compared to all of the companies in our coverage universe. Share price changes over the past year indicates that OLN will perform well over the near term.

Financial Data

(US$ in Thousands)	3 Mos	12/31/2017	12/31/2016	12/31/2015	12/31/2014	12/31/2013	12/31/2012	12/31/2011
Earnings Per Share	3.29	3.26	(0.02)	(0.01)	1.33	2.21	1.85	2.99
Cash Flow Per Share	3.77	3.90	3.64	2.10	2.03	3.97	3.48	2.70
Tang Book Value Per Share	0.46	0.33	N.M.	N.M.	1.84	2.72	1.23	4.23
Dividends Per Share	0.800	0.800	0.800	0.800	0.800	0.800	0.800	0.800
Dividend Payout %	24.32	24.54	...	...	60.15	36.20	43.24	26.76
Income Statement								
Total Revenue	1,710,300	6,268,400	5,550,600	2,854,400	2,241,200	2,515,000	2,184,700	1,961,100
EBITDA	237,000	796,100	662,100	324,800	342,600	420,500	358,500	498,300
Depn & Amortn	146,700	465,100	509,500	223,900	139,100	135,300	110,900	99,300
Income Before Taxes	27,000	115,400	(35,900)	5,000	161,000	247,200	222,200	369,800
Income Taxes	6,600	(432,300)	(30,300)	8,100	57,700	71,400	75,600	137,700
Net Income	20,900	549,500	(3,900)	(1,400)	105,700	178,600	149,600	241,700
Average Shares	169,200	168,500	165,200	103,400	79,700	80,900	81,000	80,800
Balance Sheet								
Current Assets	1,699,000	1,699,200	1,546,200	1,933,400	816,100	839,900	749,100	780,300
Total Assets	9,160,200	9,218,300	8,762,600	9,321,800	2,698,100	2,802,800	2,777,700	2,449,600
Current Liabilities	971,000	954,300	922,600	1,147,700	377,700	407,500	434,000	399,100
Long-Term Obligations	3,534,700	3,611,300	3,537,100	3,675,200	658,700	678,400	690,100	524,200
Total Liabilities	6,397,100	6,464,600	6,489,600	6,903,000	1,684,800	1,701,700	1,779,300	1,463,800
Stockholders' Equity	2,763,100	2,753,700	2,273,000	2,418,800	1,013,300	1,101,100	998,400	985,800
Shares Outstanding	167,200	167,100	165,400	165,100	77,400	79,400	80,200	80,100
Statistical Record								
Return on Assets %	6.20	6.11	N.M.	N.M.	3.84	6.40	5.71	10.75
Return on Equity %	22.13	21.86	N.M.	N.M.	10.00	17.01	15.04	26.62
EBITDA Margin %	13.86	12.70	11.93	11.38	15.29	16.72	16.41	25.41
Net Margin %	1.22	8.77	N.M.	N.M.	4.72	7.10	6.85	12.32
Asset Turnover	0.71	0.70	0.61	0.47	0.81	0.90	0.83	0.87
Current Ratio	1.75	1.78	1.68	1.68	2.16	2.06	1.73	1.96
Debt to Equity	1.28	1.31	1.56	1.52	0.65	0.62	0.69	0.53
Price Range	38.60-28.24	37.15-25.98	26.83-12.78	32.41-15.82	28.85-21.22	29.03-21.59	23.19-18.51	26.40-16.71
P/E Ratio	11.73-8.58	11.40-7.97	...	...	21.69-15.95	13.14-9.77	12.54-10.01	8.83-5.59
Average Yield %	2.44	2.51	3.88	3.31	3.03	3.32	3.80	3.87

Address: 190 Carondelet Plaza, Suite 1530, Clayton, MO 63105	**Web Site:** www.olin.com	**Auditors:** KPMG LLP
Telephone: 314-480-1400	**Officers:** John E. Fischer - Chairman, President, Chief Executive Officer, Chief Operating Officer, Senior Vice President, Vice President, Controller, Chief Financial Officer John L. McIntosh - Executive Vice President, Executive Vice President (frmr), Senior Vice President (frmr)	**Investor Contact:** 314-480-1452 **Transfer Agents:** EQ Shareowner Services, Mendota Heights, MN

OMEGA HEALTHCARE INVESTORS, INC.

Exchange	Symbol	Price	52Wk Range	Yield	P/E	Div Acheiver
NYS	OHI	$31.00 (6/29/2018)	33.70-25.36	8.52	77.50	15 Years

*7 Year Price Score 76.60   *NYSE Composite Index=100   *12 Month Price Score 101.97

Interim Earnings (Per Share)

Qtr.	Mar	Jun	Sep	Dec
2015	0.32	0.22	0.43	0.32
2016	0.29	0.57	0.40	0.64
2017	0.53	0.33	(0.67)	0.32
2018	0.42	...	...	...

Interim Dividends (Per Share)

Amt	Decl	Ex	Rec	Pay
0.65Q	10/12/2017	10/30/2017	10/31/2017	11/15/2017
0.66Q	01/16/2018	01/30/2018	01/31/2018	02/15/2018
0.66Q	04/13/2018	04/27/2018	04/30/2018	05/15/2018
0.66Q	07/13/2018	07/30/2018	07/31/2018	08/15/2018

Indicated Div: $2.64 (Div. Reinv. Plan)

Valuation Analysis **Institutional Holding**

Forecast EPS	$1.61	No of Institutions	
	(06/14/2018)	579	
Market Cap	$6.2 Billion	Shares	
Book Value	$3.5 Billion	194,293,568	
Price/Book	1.74	% Held	
Price/Sales	6.86	101.87	

Business Summary: REITs (MIC: 5.3.1 SIC: 6798 NAIC: 525930)

Omega Healthcare Investors is a real estate investment trust, investing in healthcare facilities, mainly long-term care facilities in the U.S. and the U.K. Co. provides lease or mortgage financing to operators of skilled nursing facilities (SNFs), assisted living facilities (ALFs), independent living facilities and rehabilitation and acute care facilities. Dec. 31, 2017, Co.'s portfolio of investments included 983 healthcare facilities located in 41 states and the U.K. that are operated by 74 third-party operators, comprising: 775 SNFs, 119 ALFs, 15 specialty facilities and one medical office building; fixed rate mortgages on 47 SNFs and four ALFs; and 22 facilities closed or held-for-sale.

Recent Developments: For the quarter ended Mar 31 2018, net income decreased 19.4% to US$87.9 million from US$109.1 million in the year-earlier quarter. Revenues were US$220.2 million, down 5.0% from US$231.7 million the year before. Revenues from property income rose 0.7% to US$193.9 million from US$192.5 million in the corresponding quarter a year earlier.

Prospects: Our evaluation of Omega Healthcare Investors Inc. as of Jan. 21, 2018 is the result of our systematic analysis on three basic characteristics: earnings strength, relative valuation, and recent stock price movement. The company has generated a negative trend in earnings per share over the past 5 quarters. Because the company lacks sufficient analyst estimate data, we place greater weight on the historical EPS trend as the measure of earnings strength. Based on operating earnings yield, the company is undervalued when compared to all of the companies in our coverage universe. Share price changes over the past year indicates that OHI will perform well over the near term.

Financial Data

(US$ in Thousands)	3 Mos	12/31/2017	12/31/2016	12/31/2015	12/31/2014	12/31/2013	12/31/2012	12/31/2011
Earnings Per Share	0.40	0.51	1.90	1.29	1.74	1.46	1.12	0.46
Cash Flow Per Share	2.60	2.92	3.25	2.69	2.67	2.39	1.93	1.66
Tang Book Value Per Share	14.57	14.68	16.39	16.50	10.98	10.52	9.00	8.50
Dividends Per Share	2.580	2.540	2.360	2.180	2.020	1.860	1.690	1.550
Dividend Payout %	645.00	498.04	124.21	168.99	116.09	127.40	150.89	336.96
Income Statement								
Total Revenue	220,199	908,385	900,827	743,617	504,787	418,714	350,460	292,204
EBITDA	137,750	636,501	838,040	661,266	482,537	385,700	350,947	245,496
Depn & Amortn	(444)	310,604	278,319	243,817	134,363	121,172	124,182	106,031
Income Before Taxes	88,525	105,921	384,333	234,526	221,349	172,521	120,698	52,606
Income Taxes	543	3,248	1,405	1,211	...	...	...	...
Net Income	84,220	100,419	366,415	224,524	221,349	172,521	120,698	52,606
Average Shares	207,816	206,790	201,635	180,508	127,294	118,100	108,011	102,177
Balance Sheet								
Current Assets	398,812	376,142	347,311	223,893	201,741	181,879	163,551	135,127
Total Assets	8,792,629	8,773,305	8,949,260	8,019,009	3,921,645	3,462,216	2,982,005	2,557,312
Current Liabilities	910,019	17,747	9,906	15,352	...	...	...	...
Long-Term Obligations	3,733,660	4,572,158	4,366,854	3,569,086	2,378,503	2,024,418	1,824,932	1,551,400
Total Liabilities	5,254,181	5,218,214	5,090,515	4,281,023	2,520,318	2,162,113	1,970,676	1,678,828
Stockholders' Equity	3,538,448	3,555,091	3,858,745	3,737,986	1,401,327	1,300,103	1,011,329	878,484
Shares Outstanding	198,595	198,309	196,142	187,399	127,606	123,530	112,393	103,410
Statistical Record								
Return on Assets %	0.91	1.13	4.31	3.76	6.00	5.35	4.35	2.16
Return on Equity %	2.17	2.71	9.62	8.74	16.39	14.93	12.74	5.59
EBITDA Margin %	62.56	70.07	93.03	88.93	95.59	92.12	100.14	84.02
Net Margin %	38.25	11.05	40.68	30.19	43.85	41.20	34.44	18.00
Asset Turnover	0.10	0.10	0.11	0.12	0.14	0.13	0.13	0.12
Current Ratio	0.44	21.19	35.06	14.58	...	...	...	...
Debt to Equity	1.06	1.29	1.13	0.95	1.70	1.56	1.80	1.77
Price Range	34.98-25.36	34.98-26.78	38.02-27.46	45.16-32.08	40.29-29.56	37.61-23.85	24.75-19.19	24.27-14.42
P/E Ratio	87.45-63.40	68.59-52.51	20.01-14.45	35.01-24.87	23.16-16.99	25.76-16.34	22.10-17.13	52.76-31.35
Average Yield %	8.54	8.06	7.12	5.91	5.68	6.10	7.59	7.73

Address: 303 International Circle, Suite 200, Hunt Valley, MD 21030	**Web Site:** www.omegahealthcare.com	**Auditors:** Ernst & Young LLP
Telephone: 410-427-1700	**Officers:** Bernard J. Korman - Chairman C. Taylor Pickett - President, Chief Executive Officer	**Investor Contact:** 410-427-1700
Fax: 410-427-8800		**Transfer Agents:** Registrar and Transfer Company, Cranford , NJ

OMNICOM GROUP, INC.

Exchange	Symbol	Price	52Wk Range	Yield	P/E
NYS	OMC	$76.27 (6/29/2018)	83.24-65.52	3.15	15.99

*7 Year Price Score 87.63   *NYSE Composite Index=100   *12 Month Price Score 97.80

Interim Earnings (Per Share)

Qtr.	Mar	Jun	Sep	Dec
2015	0.83	1.26	0.97	1.35
2016	0.90	1.36	1.06	1.47
2017	1.02	1.40	1.13	1.10
2018	1.14	...	...	...

Interim Dividends (Per Share)

Amt	Decl	Ex	Rec	Pay
0.55Q	07/13/2017	09/21/2017	09/22/2017	10/10/2017
0.60Q	12/04/2017	12/18/2017	12/19/2017	01/09/2018
0.60Q	02/15/2018	03/08/2018	03/09/2018	04/09/2018
0.60Q	05/22/2018	06/13/2018	06/14/2018	07/12/2018

Indicated Div: $2.40

Valuation Analysis / **Institutional Holding**

Forecast EPS	$5.62 (06/14/2018)	No of Institutions 1050
Market Cap	$17.3 Billion	Shares
Book Value	$2.6 Billion	306,838,432
Price/Book	6.60	% Held
Price/Sales	1.13	82.86

Business Summary: Advertising (MIC: 2.3.4 SIC: 7311 NAIC: 541810)

Omnicom Group is a holding company, engaged in providing advertising, marketing and corporate communications services. Co.'s networks and agencies provide a range of services in four fundamental disciplines: advertising, customer relationship management, public relations and specialty communications. Services in these disciplines include: advertising, brand consultancy, content marketing, corporate social responsibility consulting, crisis communications, custom publishing, data analytics, database management, direct marketing, entertainment marketing, environmental design, experiential marketing, field marketing, graphic arts/digital imaging, and instore design, among others.

Recent Developments: For the quarter ended Mar 31 2018, net income increased 8.5% to US$284.7 million from US$262.4 million in the year-earlier quarter. Revenues were US$3.63 billion, up 1.2% from US$3.59 billion the year before. Operating income was US$421.7 million versus US$415.7 million in the prior-year quarter, an increase of 1.4%. Direct operating expenses rose 1.4% to US$3.03 billion from US$2.99 billion in the comparable period the year before. Indirect operating expenses decreased 3.6% to US$174.8 million from US$181.3 million in the equivalent prior-year period.

Prospects: Our evaluation of Omnicom Group Inc. as of Jan. 21, 2018 is the result of our systematic analysis on three basic characteristics: earnings strength, relative valuation, and recent stock price movement. The company has managed to produce a neutral trend in earnings per share over the past 5 quarters. However, while recent estimates for the company have been lowered by analysts, OMC has posted better than expected results. Based on operating earnings yield, the company is undervalued when compared to all of the companies in our coverage universe. Share price changes over the past year indicates that OMC will perform poorly over the near term.

Financial Data

(US$ in Thousands)	3 Mos	12/31/2017	12/31/2016	12/31/2015	12/31/2014	12/31/2013	12/31/2012	12/31/2011
Earnings Per Share	4.77	4.65	4.78	4.41	4.24	3.71	3.61	3.33
Cash Flow Per Share	6.94	8.71	8.10	8.90	5.82	6.99	5.39	4.71
Dividends Per Share	2.300	2.250	2.150	2.000	1.900	1.600	1.200	1.000
Dividend Payout %	48.22	48.39	44.98	45.35	44.81	43.13	33.24	30.03
Income Statement								
Total Revenue	3,629,600	15,273,600	15,416,900	15,134,400	15,317,800	14,584,500	14,219,400	13,872,500
EBITDA	491,100	2,341,800	2,301,800	2,211,200	2,238,500	2,110,100	2,086,900	1,944,800
Depn & Amortn	69,400	282,100	292,900	291,100	294,400	284,800	282,700	273,700
Income Before Taxes	374,800	1,884,900	1,841,800	1,778,600	1,810,000	1,660,900	1,659,600	1,549,000
Income Taxes	90,900	696,200	600,500	583,600	593,100	565,200	527,100	505,800
Net Income	264,100	1,088,400	1,148,600	1,093,900	1,104,000	991,100	998,300	952,600
Average Shares	231,500	233,900	239,200	245,200	255,300	260,400	270,000	283,300
Balance Sheet								
Current Assets	12,338,500	14,116,000	12,722,000	11,980,500	11,190,500	11,652,300	11,661,400	10,421,500
Total Assets	23,513,100	24,931,200	23,165,400	22,110,700	21,559,700	22,098,700	22,151,900	20,505,400
Current Liabilities	13,598,800	15,108,900	14,010,900	14,219,600	12,061,100	12,277,700	11,875,800	11,671,000
Long-Term Obligations	4,885,000	4,912,900	4,920,500	3,564,200	4,562,600	4,033,400	4,448,500	3,182,900
Total Liabilities	20,886,700	22,316,100	21,003,400	19,658,300	18,709,700	18,516,300	18,691,100	17,001,100
Stockholders' Equity	2,626,400	2,615,100	2,162,000	2,452,400	2,850,000	3,582,400	3,460,800	3,504,300
Shares Outstanding	227,289	230,100	234,700	239,700	246,700	257,600	262,000	273,400
Statistical Record								
Return on Assets %	4.86	4.53	5.06	5.01	5.06	4.48	4.67	4.75
Return on Equity %	46.66	45.57	49.65	41.26	34.33	28.14	28.59	26.89
EBITDA Margin %	13.53	15.33	14.93	14.61	14.61	14.47	14.68	14.02
Net Margin %	7.28	7.13	7.45	7.23	7.21	6.80	7.02	6.87
Asset Turnover	0.67	0.64	0.68	0.69	0.70	0.66	0.66	0.69
Current Ratio	0.91	0.93	0.91	0.84	0.93	0.95	0.98	0.89
Debt to Equity	1.86	1.88	2.28	1.45	1.60	1.13	1.29	0.91
Price Range	86.21-65.52	87.39-65.52	88.47-67.94	80.52-64.79	78.41-64.93	74.37-49.96	54.23-44.04	50.90-35.95
P/E Ratio	18.07-13.74	18.79-14.09	18.51-14.21	18.26-14.69	18.49-15.31	20.05-13.47	15.02-12.20	15.29-10.80
Average Yield %	2.99	2.84	2.64	2.71	2.64	2.56	2.43	2.23

Address: 437 Madison Avenue, New York, NY 10022	Web Site: www.omnicomgroup.com	Auditors: KPMG LLP
Telephone: 212-415-3600	Officers: John D. Wren - Chairman, President, Chief Executive Officer Philip J. Angelastro - Executive Vice President, Senior Vice President, Chief Financial Officer, Controller	Investor Contact: 212-415-3393
Fax: 212-415-3393		Transfer Agents: Wells Fargo Bank, NA, South St. Paul, MN

ONE GAS, INC.

Exchange	Symbol	Price	52Wk Range	Yield	P/E
NYS	OGS	$74.74 (6/29/2018)	79.25-62.75	2.46	22.24

7 Year Price Score N/A   **NYSE Composite Index=100**   **12 Month Price Score 99.74**

Interim Earnings (Per Share)

Qtr.	Mar	Jun	Sep	Dec
2015	1.13	0.23	0.14	0.74
2016	1.22	0.38	0.24	0.80
2017	1.44	0.39	0.36	0.89
2018	1.72	...	...	...

Interim Dividends (Per Share)

Amt	Decl	Ex	Rec	Pay
0.42Q	07/24/2017	08/10/2017	08/14/2017	09/01/2017
0.42Q	10/30/2017	11/10/2017	11/13/2017	12/01/2017
0.46Q	01/16/2018	02/22/2018	02/23/2018	03/09/2018
0.46Q	04/30/2018	05/11/2018	05/14/2018	06/01/2018

Indicated Div: $1.84 (Div. Reinv. Plan)

Valuation Analysis

		Institutional Holding	
Forecast EPS	$3.13 (06/14/2018)	No of Institutions	392
Market Cap	$3.9 Billion	Shares	45,748,316
Book Value	$2.0 Billion	% Held	64.49
Price/Book	1.94		
Price/Sales	N/A		

Business Summary: Electric Utilities (MIC: 3.1.1 SIC: 4924 NAIC: 221210)

ONE Gas is a regulated natural gas distribution utility. Co. provide natural gas distribution services through its divisions in Oklahoma, Kansas and Texas through Oklahoma Natural Gas, Kansas Gas Service and Texas Gas Service, respectively. Co. serves residential, commercial, industrial and transportation customers in all three states. In addition, Co. also provides natural gas distribution services to wholesale and public authority customers. As of Dec 31 2017, Co. served a total of 2.0 million customers in Oklahoma, Kansas and Texas.

Recent Developments: For the quarter ended Mar 31 2018, net income increased 18.8% to US$90.8 million from US$76.5 million in the year-earlier quarter. Revenues were US$638.5 million, up 16.0% from US$550.4 million the year before. Operating income was US$130.3 million versus US$129.4 million in the prior-year quarter, an increase of 0.7%. Direct operating expenses rose 33.2% to US$350.4 million from US$263.2 million in the comparable period the year before. Indirect operating expenses were unchanged at US$157.8 million versus the equivalent prior-year period.

Prospects: Our evaluation of One Gas Inc. as of Jan. 21, 2018 is the result of our systematic analysis on three basic characteristics: earnings strength, relative valuation, and recent stock price movement. The company has generated a negative trend in earnings per share over the past 5 quarters. However, while recent estimates for the company have been lowered by analysts, OGS has posted better than expected results. Based on operating earnings yield, the company is about fairly valued when compared to all of the companies in our coverage universe. Share price changes over the past year indicates that OGS will perform very well over the near term.

Financial Data
(US$ in Thousands)

	3 Mos	12/31/2017	12/31/2016	12/31/2015	12/31/2014	12/31/2013	12/31/2012	12/31/2011
Earnings Per Share	3.36	3.08	2.65	2.24	2.07	...	...	...
Cash Flow Per Share	...	4.83	5.35	7.50	4.71	...	...	...
Tang Book Value Per Share	35.51	34.45	33.10	32.22	31.41	...	...	...
Dividends Per Share	1.720	1.680	1.400	1.200	0.840	...	...	...
Dividend Payout %	51.19	54.55	52.83	53.57	40.58	...	...	...
Income Statement								
Total Revenue	638,464	1,539,633	1,427,232	1,547,692	1,818,906	1,689,952	1,376,649	1,621,334
EBITDA	167,016	454,092	412,906	369,602	349,692	367,591	347,303	329,093
Depn & Amortn	38,890	151,889	143,829	133,023	125,722	144,758	130,150	132,212
Income Before Taxes	115,774	256,138	225,338	192,009	178,128	161,467	156,360	142,762
Income Taxes	24,939	93,143	85,243	72,979	68,338	62,272	59,851	56,004
Net Income	90,835	162,995	140,095	119,030	109,790	99,195	96,509	86,758
Average Shares	52,897	52,979	52,963	53,254	52,946	...	...	...
Balance Sheet								
Current Assets	501,696	588,994	568,923	482,845	667,501	602,184	457,094	...
Total Assets	5,159,093	5,206,878	4,942,791	4,644,410	4,649,210	3,846,475	3,491,332	...
Current Liabilities	844,706	673,330	443,933	304,221	392,433	769,077	578,702	...
Long-Term Obligations	893,463	1,193,257	1,192,446	1,201,305	1,201,311	1,028,949	1,028,954	...
Total Liabilities	3,138,145	3,246,669	3,054,511	2,802,855	2,855,173	2,607,452	2,336,535	...
Stockholders' Equity	2,020,948	1,960,209	1,888,280	1,841,555	1,794,037	1,239,023	1,154,797	...
Shares Outstanding	52,469	52,312	52,283	52,259	52,083	...	...	...
Statistical Record								
Return on Assets %	...	...	2.91	2.56	2.58	2.70	...	...
Return on Equity %	...	...	7.49	6.55	7.24	8.29	...	...
EBITDA Margin %	26.16	29.49	28.93	23.88	19.23	21.75	25.23	20.30
Net Margin %	14.23	10.59	9.82	7.69	6.04	5.87	7.01	5.35
Asset Turnover	...	...	0.30	0.33	0.43	0.46	...	...
Current Ratio	0.59	0.87	1.28	1.59	1.70	0.78	0.79	...
Debt to Equity	0.44	0.61	0.63	0.65	0.67	0.83	0.89	...
Price Range	79.25-62.75	79.25-62.30	66.59-48.40	51.34-39.38	44.19-32.25	...	...	...
P/E Ratio	23.59-18.68	25.73-20.23	25.13-18.26	22.92-17.58	21.35-15.58	...	...	...
Average Yield %	2.40	2.37	2.32	2.70	2.28	...	...	...

Address: 15 East Fifth Street, Tulsa, OK 74103 Telephone: 918-947-7000	Web Site: www.onegas.com Officers: John W. Gibson - Chairman Pierce H. Norton - President, Chief Executive Officer	Auditors: PricewaterhouseCoopers, LLP

ONEMAIN HOLDINGS INC

Exchange	Symbol	Price	52Wk Range	Yield	P/E
NYS	OMF	$33.29 (6/29/2018)	34.54-24.10	N/A	16.65

*7 Year Price Score N/A *NYSE Composite Index=100 *12 Month Price Score 111.76

Interim Earnings (Per Share)

Qtr.	Mar	Jun	Sep	Dec
2015	0.00	(0.09)	(0.08)	(1.71)
2016	1.13	0.19	0.19	0.20
2017	0.25	0.30	0.51	0.28
2018	0.91	...	...	...

Interim Dividends (Per Share)

No Dividends Paid

Valuation Analysis / Institutional Holding

Valuation Analysis		Institutional Holding	
Forecast EPS	$4.90	No of Institutions	
	(06/14/2018)	237	
Market Cap	$4.5 Billion	Shares	
Book Value	$3.4 Billion	131,298,944	
Price/Book	1.34	% Held	
Price/Sales	1.17	85.78	

TRADING VOLUME (thousand shares)

Business Summary: Credit & Lending (MIC: 5.4.1 SIC: 6141 NAIC: 522298)

OneMain Holdings is a financial services holding. Co.'s business segments are Consumer and Insurance, which originates and services personal loans through branch operations and centralized operations and provides credit insurance (life insurance, disability insurance, and involuntary unemployment insurance), non-credit insurance, and ancillary products; Acquisitions and Servicing, which consists of unsecured and secured loans by subordinate residential real estate mortgages and includes both closed-end accounts and open-end lines of credit; and Real Estate, which services and hold real estate loans secured by first or second mortgages on residential real estate.

Recent Developments: For the quarter ended Mar 31 2018, net income increased 275.8% to US$124.0 million from US$33.0 million in the year-earlier quarter. Net interest income increased 18.9% to US$662.0 million from US$557.0 million in the year-earlier quarter. Provision for loan losses was US$254.0 million versus US$245.0 million in the prior-year quarter, an increase of 3.7%. Non-interest income fell 2.8% to US$137.0 million from US$141.0 million, while non-interest expense declined 4.8% to US$377.0 million.

Prospects: Our evaluation of Onemain Holdings, Inc. as of Jan. 21, 2018 is the result of our systematic analysis on three basic characteristics: earnings strength, relative valuation, and recent stock price movement. The company has enjoyed a very positive trend in earnings per share over the past 5 quarters and while recent estimates for the company have been mixed, OMF has posted results that fell short of analysts expectations. Based on operating earnings yield, the company is undervalued when compared to all of the companies in our coverage universe. Share price changes over the past year indicates that OMF will perform very poorly over the near term.

Financial Data
(US$ in Thousands)

	3 Mos	12/31/2017	12/31/2016	12/31/2015	12/31/2014	12/31/2013	12/31/2012	12/31/2011
Earnings Per Share	2.00	1.35	1.59	(1.89)	4.38	(0.19)	(2.19)	(2.24)
Cash Flow Per Share	12.29	11.50	9.82	5.71	3.49	6.56	2.15	1.81
Tang Book Value Per Share	11.29	10.46	8.54	5.59	17.45	13.20	11.71	13.20
Income Statement								
Total Revenue	999,000	3,756,000	3,883,000	2,192,000	2,814,104	2,307,138	1,800,495	2,023,706
Income Before Taxes	168,000	431,000	356,000	(269,000)	904,496	77,557	(306,856)	(323,205)
Income Taxes	44,000	248,000	113,000	(147,000)	297,046	(16,185)	(88,222)	(99,049)
Net Income	124,000	183,000	215,000	(242,000)	504,636	(19,301)	(218,634)	(224,156)
Average Shares	135,897	135,678	135,135	127,910	115,265	102,917	100,000	100,000
Balance Sheet								
Total Assets	20,467,000	19,433,000	18,123,000	21,056,000	11,057,864	15,402,686	14,673,515	15,494,888
Total Liabilities	17,085,000	16,155,000	15,057,000	18,305,000	9,032,595	13,862,666	13,473,388	14,131,984
Stockholders' Equity	3,382,000	3,278,000	3,066,000	2,751,000	2,025,269	1,540,020	1,200,127	1,362,904
Shares Outstanding	135,696	135,349	134,867	134,494	114,832	114,788	100,000	100,000
Statistical Record								
Return on Assets %	1.43	0.97	1.09	N.M.	3.81	N.M.	N.M.	...
Return on Equity %	8.45	5.77	7.37	N.M.	28.31	N.M.	N.M.	...
Net Margin %	12.41	4.87	5.54	N.M.	17.93	N.M.	N.M.	N.M.
Asset Turnover	0.20	0.20	0.20	0.14	0.21	0.15	0.12	
Price Range	*34.53-22.38	32.61-22.03	41.54-16.90	53.83-31.60	39.86-22.35	25.28-19.26	...	...
P/E Ratio	17.27-11.19	24.16-16.32	26.13-10.63	...	9.10-5.10	...	...	...

Address: 601 N.W. Second Street, Evansville, IN 47708 **Telephone:** 812-424-8031	**Web Site:** www.onemainfinancial.com **Officers:** Jay N. Levine - President, Chief Executive Officer, Chairman Douglas H. (Doug) Shulman - President, Chief Executive Officer	**Auditors:** PricewaterhouseCoopers LLP **Transfer Agents:** American Stock Transfer & Trust Company, LLC

ONEOK INC

Exchange	Symbol	Price	52Wk Range	Yield	P/E	Div Acheiver
NYS	OKE	$69.83 (6/29/2018)	70.07-50.02	4.55	46.87	15 Years

*7 Year Price Score 95.15 *NYSE Composite Index=100 ***12 Month Price Score 115.08**

Interim Earnings (Per Share)

Qtr.	Mar	Jun	Sep	Dec
2015	0.29	0.36	0.39	0.12
2016	0.40	0.40	0.43	0.43
2017	0.41	0.33	0.43	0.09
2018	0.64	...	...	...

Interim Dividends (Per Share)

Amt	Decl	Ex	Rec	Pay
0.745Q	07/26/2017	08/03/2017	08/07/2017	08/14/2017
0.745Q	10/25/2017	11/03/2017	11/06/2017	11/14/2017
0.77Q	01/17/2018	01/26/2018	01/29/2018	02/14/2018
0.795Q	04/19/2018	04/27/2018	04/30/2018	05/15/2018

Indicated Div: $3.18 (Div. Reinv. Plan)

Valuation Analysis — **Institutional Holding**

Forecast EPS	$2.69	No of Institutions	1086
	(06/14/2018)		
Market Cap	$28.7 Billion	Shares	346,456,448
Book Value	$6.7 Billion	% Held	70.03
Price/Book	4.28		
Price/Sales	2.29		

Business Summary: Equipment & Services (MIC: 9.1.3 SIC: 4923 NAIC: 221210)

Oneok's operations is comprised of the following business segments: Natural Gas Gathering and Processing, which provides midstream services to contracted producers in North Dakota, Montana, Wyoming, Kansas and Oklahoma; Natural Gas Liquids (NGLs), which owns and operates facilities that gather, fractionate, treat and distribute NGLs and store NGL products, primarily in Oklahoma, Kansas, Texas, New Mexico and the Rocky Mountain region where it provides midstream services to producers of NGLs and delivers those products to the two primary market centers; and Natural Gas Pipelines, which provides transportation and storage services to end users through ONEOK Partners' wholly owned assets.

Recent Developments: For the quarter ended Mar 31 2018, net income increased 42.9% to US$266.0 million from US$186.2 million in the year-earlier quarter. Revenues were US$3.10 billion, up 12.8% from US$2.75 billion the year before. Operating income was US$419.7 million versus US$317.1 million in the prior-year quarter, an increase of 32.3%. Direct operating expenses rose 10.3% to US$2.65 billion from US$2.41 billion in the comparable period the year before. Indirect operating expenses increased 6.5% to US$28.9 million from US$27.2 million in the equivalent prior-year period.

Prospects: Our evaluation of Oneok Inc. as of Jan. 21, 2018 is the result of our systematic analysis on three basic characteristics: earnings strength, relative valuation, and recent stock price movement. The company has produced a positive trend in earnings per share over the past 5 quarters. However, while recent estimates for the company have been mixed, OKE has posted results that fell short of analysts expectations. Based on operating earnings yield, the company is about fairly valued when compared to all of the companies in our coverage universe. Share price changes over the past year indicates that OKE will perform very poorly over the near term.

Financial Data
(US$ in Thousands)

	3 Mos	12/31/2017	12/31/2016	12/31/2015	12/31/2014	12/31/2013	12/31/2012	12/31/2011
Earnings Per Share	1.49	1.29	1.66	1.16	1.49	1.27	1.71	1.68
Cash Flow Per Share	3.76	4.42	6.38	4.79	6.14	6.28	4.79	6.50
Tang Book Value Per Share	13.89	11.67	N.M.	N.M.	N.M.	5.59	5.53	5.93
Dividends Per Share	2.875	2.720	2.460	2.430	2.125	1.480	1.270	1.080
Dividend Payout %	192.95	210.85	148.19	209.48	142.62	116.54	74.27	64.29
Income Statement								
Total Revenue	3,102,077	12,173,907	8,920,934	7,763,206	12,195,091	14,602,717	12,632,559	14,805,794
EBITDA	521,595	1,773,516	1,679,502	1,167,983	1,441,071	1,348,409	1,459,579	1,465,610
Depn & Amortn	104,237	406,335	391,585	354,620	306,038	384,377	335,852	312,288
Income Before Taxes	301,633	881,523	818,266	396,576	778,870	629,826	821,422	856,316
Income Taxes	75,771	447,282	212,406	136,600	151,158	163,382	215,195	226,048
Net Income	264,508	387,841	352,039	244,977	314,107	266,533	360,619	360,594
Average Shares	412,173	299,780	212,383	210,541	210,427	209,695	210,710	214,498
Balance Sheet								
Current Assets	1,290,745	1,764,458	1,429,684	975,210	1,307,244	2,370,802	2,764,660	2,318,812
Total Assets	16,432,347	16,845,937	16,138,751	15,446,111	15,304,560	17,707,558	15,855,275	13,696,635
Current Liabilities	2,050,838	2,667,335	2,836,701	1,638,266	2,392,345	2,696,407	2,812,994	3,246,175
Long-Term Obligations	7,091,751	8,091,629	7,919,996	8,323,582	7,192,929	7,754,975	6,515,372	4,529,551
Total Liabilities	9,730,901	11,318,070	15,950,006	15,110,313	14,712,445	15,369,707	13,725,666	11,458,062
Stockholders' Equity	6,701,446	5,527,867	188,745	335,798	592,115	2,337,851	2,129,609	2,238,573
Shares Outstanding	411,073	388,703	210,681	209,731	208,322	206,618	204,935	206,509
Statistical Record								
Return on Assets %	3.48	2.35	2.22	1.59	1.90	1.59	2.43	2.75
Return on Equity %	16.28	13.57	133.86	52.80	21.44	11.93	16.47	15.39
EBITDA Margin %	16.81	14.57	18.83	15.05	11.82	9.23	11.55	9.90
Net Margin %	8.53	3.19	3.95	3.16	2.58	1.83	2.85	2.44
Asset Turnover	0.77	0.74	0.56	0.50	0.74	0.87	0.85	1.13
Current Ratio	0.63	0.66	0.50	0.60	0.55	0.88	0.98	0.71
Debt to Equity	1.06	1.46	41.96	24.79	12.15	3.32	3.06	2.02
Price Range	60.71-47.41	58.83-47.41	59.03-19.62	51.07-18.93	70.98-44.30	62.18-40.00	49.39-39.49	43.35-27.69
P/E Ratio	40.74-31.82	45.60-36.75	35.56-11.82	44.03-16.32	47.64-29.73	48.96-31.50	28.88-23.09	25.80-16.48
Average Yield %	5.31	5.08	5.99	6.22	3.44	2.96	2.92	3.11

Address: 100 West Fifth Street, Tulsa, OK 74103
Telephone: 918-588-7000
Fax: 918-588-7273

Web Site: www.oneok.com
Officers: Terry K. Spencer - President, Chief Executive Officer Robert F. Martinovich - Executive Vice President, Executive Vice President (frmr), Senior Vice President, Chief Administrative Officer, Chief Financial Officer, Treasurer

Auditors: PricewaterhouseCoopers LLP
Investor Contact: 918-588-7163
Transfer Agents: Wells Fargo Shareowner Services, St Paul, MN

ORACLE CORP

Exchange	Symbol	Price	52Wk Range	Yield	P/E
NYS	ORCL	$44.06 (6/29/2018)	52.97-42.82	1.72	48.96

*7 Year Price Score 101.64 *NYSE Composite Index=100 *12 Month Price Score 93.25

Interim Earnings (Per Share)

Qtr.	Aug	Nov	Feb	May
2013-14	0.47	0.56	0.56	0.80
2014-15	0.48	0.56	0.56	0.62
2015-16	0.40	0.52	0.50	0.66
2016-17	0.43	0.48	0.53	0.76
2017-18	0.52	0.52	(0.98)	0.80

Interim Dividends (Per Share)

Amt	Decl	Ex	Rec	Pay
0.19Q	09/12/2017	10/10/2017	10/11/2017	10/25/2017
0.19Q	12/13/2017	01/09/2018	01/10/2018	01/24/2018
0.19Q	03/16/2018	04/16/2018	04/17/2018	05/01/2018
0.19Q	06/19/2018	07/16/2018	07/17/2018	07/31/2018

Indicated Div: $0.76

Valuation Analysis | **Institutional Holding**

Forecast EPS	$3.34	No of Institutions
	(06/14/2018)	2460
Market Cap	$176.1 Billion	Shares
Book Value	$45.7 Billion	2,960,980,992
Price/Book	3.85	% Held
Price/Sales	4.42	53.04

Business Summary: Internet & Software (MIC: 6.3.2 SIC: 7372 NAIC: 511210)

Oracle provides products and services that address all aspects of corporate information technology environments: application, platform and infrastructure. Co. has three businesses that deliver its application, platform and infrastructure technologies. These businesses are: cloud and on-premise software, which is comprised of three operating segments: cloud software and on-premise software, cloud infrastructure as a service, and software license updates and product support; hardware systems, which is comprised of two operating segments: hardware products and hardware support; and services, which provides consulting services, support services and education services.

Recent Developments: For the year ended May 31 2018, net income decreased 59.0% to US$3.83 billion from US$9.34 billion in the prior year. Revenues were US$39.83 billion, up 5.6% from US$37.73 billion the year before. Operating income was US$13.68 billion versus US$12.71 billion in the prior year, an increase of 7.6%. Direct operating expenses rose 8.2% to US$8.08 billion from US$7.47 billion in the comparable period the year before. Indirect operating expenses increased 3.0% to US$18.07 billion from US$17.55 billion in the equivalent prior-year period.

Prospects: Our evaluation of Oracle Corp. as of Jan. 21, 2018 is the result of our systematic analysis on three basic characteristics: earnings strength, relative valuation, and recent stock price movement. The company has managed to produce a neutral trend in earnings per share over the past 5 quarters and while recent estimates for the company have been mixed, ORCL has posted better than expected results. Based on operating earnings yield, the company is undervalued when compared to all of the companies in our coverage universe. Share price changes over the past year indicates that ORCL will perform well over the near term.

Financial Data

(US$ in Thousands)	05/31/2018	05/31/2017	05/31/2016	05/31/2015	05/31/2014	05/31/2013	05/31/2012	05/31/2011
Earnings Per Share	0.90	2.21	2.07	2.21	2.38	2.26	1.96	1.67
Cash Flow Per Share	3.73	3.43	3.20	3.26	3.30	2.98	2.73	2.22
Tang Book Value Per Share	N.M.	0.76	1.88	1.88	2.48	2.30	2.18	2.04
Dividends Per Share	0.760	0.640	0.600	0.510	0.480	0.300	0.240	0.210
Dividend Payout %	84.44	28.96	28.99	23.08	20.17	13.27	12.24	12.57
Income Statement								
Total Revenue	39,831,000	37,728,000	37,047,000	38,226,000	38,275,000	37,180,000	37,121,000	35,622,000
EBITDA	16,635,000	15,082,000	14,996,000	16,602,000	17,361,000	17,501,000	16,532,000	14,949,000
Depn & Amortn	2,785,000	2,451,000	2,509,000	2,861,000	2,908,000	2,931,000	2,916,000	2,796,000
Income Before Taxes	13,026,000	11,635,000	11,558,000	12,947,000	13,802,000	14,010,000	13,081,000	11,508,000
Income Taxes	9,066,000	2,182,000	2,541,000	2,896,000	2,749,000	2,973,000	2,981,000	2,864,000
Net Income	3,825,000	9,335,000	8,901,000	9,938,000	10,955,000	10,925,000	9,981,000	8,547,000
Average Shares	4,238,000	4,217,000	4,304,999	4,502,999	4,603,999	4,843,999	5,094,999	5,127,999
Balance Sheet								
Current Assets	75,964,000	74,515,000	64,313,000	63,183,000	48,138,000	41,692,000	40,023,000	39,174,000
Total Assets	137,264,000	134,991,000	112,180,000	110,903,000	90,344,000	81,812,000	78,327,000	73,535,000
Current Liabilities	19,195,000	24,178,000	17,208,000	15,291,000	14,389,000	12,872,000	15,388,000	14,192,000
Long-Term Obligations	56,128,000	48,112,000	40,105,000	39,959,000	22,667,000	18,494,000	13,524,000	14,772,000
Total Liabilities	91,538,000	81,131,000	64,891,000	62,240,000	43,466,000	37,164,000	34,639,000	33,759,000
Stockholders' Equity	45,726,000	53,860,000	47,289,000	48,663,000	46,878,000	44,648,000	43,688,000	39,776,000
Shares Outstanding	3,997,000	4,137,000	4,131,000	4,342,999	4,463,999	4,645,999	4,904,999	5,067,999
Statistical Record								
Return on Assets %	2.81	7.55	7.96	9.88	12.73	13.64	13.11	12.65
Return on Equity %	7.68	18.46	18.50	20.80	23.94	24.74	23.85	24.22
EBITDA Margin %	41.76	39.98	40.48	43.43	45.36	47.07	44.54	41.97
Net Margin %	9.60	24.74	24.03	26.00	28.62	29.38	26.89	23.99
Asset Turnover	0.29	0.31	0.33	0.38	0.44	0.46	0.49	0.53
Current Ratio	3.96	3.08	3.74	4.13	3.35	3.24	2.60	2.76
Debt to Equity	1.23	0.89	0.85	0.82	0.48	0.41	0.31	0.37
Price Range	52.97-44.68	45.73-37.93	44.91-33.94	46.23-37.56	42.20-29.96	36.34-26.00	34.22-24.78	36.37-21.46
P/E Ratio	58.86-49.64	20.69-17.16	21.70-16.40	20.92-17.00	17.73-12.59	16.08-11.50	17.46-12.64	21.78-12.85
Average Yield %	1.56		1.54	1.55	1.22	1.34	0.93	0.81	0.73

Address: 500 Oracle Parkway, Redwood City, CA 94065 Telephone: 650-506-7000	Web Site: www.oracle.com Officers: Lawrence J. Ellison - Executive Chairman, Chief Technology Officer, Chairman, Chief Executive Officer Jeffrey O. Henley - Vice-Chairman, Chairman	Auditors: Ernst & Young LLP Investor Contact: 650-506-4073 Transfer Agents: American Stock Transfer & Trust Company, LLC, Brooklyn, NY

OSHKOSH CORP

Exchange	Symbol	Price	52Wk Range	Yield	P/E
NYS	OSK	$70.32 (6/29/2018)	96.24-66.94	1.37	13.71

*7 Year Price Score 134.40 *NYSE Composite Index=100 *12 Month Price Score 90.44

Interim Earnings (Per Share)

Qtr.	Dec	Mar	Jun	Sep
2014-15	0.43	0.69	1.13	0.65
2015-16	0.19	0.76	1.11	0.83
2016-17	0.26	0.58	1.69	1.23
2017-18	0.74	1.47	...	...

Interim Dividends (Per Share)

Amt	Decl	Ex	Rec	Pay
0.21Q	08/02/2017	08/16/2017	08/18/2017	09/01/2017
0.24Q	10/31/2017	11/15/2017	11/16/2017	11/30/2017
0.24Q	01/25/2018	02/09/2018	02/12/2018	02/26/2018
0.24Q	04/26/2018	05/11/2018	05/14/2018	05/29/2018

Indicated Div: $0.96 (Div. Reinv. Plan)

Valuation Analysis

		Institutional Holding	
Forecast EPS	$5.80	No of Institutions	
	(06/14/2018)	560	
Market Cap	$5.2 Billion	Shares	
Book Value	$2.3 Billion	80,057,160	
Price/Book	2.21	% Held	
Price/Sales	0.70	82.47	

Business Summary: Autos- Manufacturing (MIC: 1.8.1 SIC: 3711 NAIC: 336120)

Oshkosh is a designer, manufacturer and marketer a range of specialty vehicles and vehicle bodies. Co. has four reportable segments: access equipment, used in a variety of construction, agricultural, industrial, institutional and general maintenance applications to position workers and materials at elevated heights, as well as carriers and wreckers; defense, which manufacture tactical trucks, trailers and supply parts and services; fire and emergency, which manufacture custom and commercial firefighting vehicles and equipment; and commercial, which manufacture concrete mixers, refuse collection vehicles, portable and stationary concrete batch plants.

Recent Developments: For the quarter ended Mar 31 2018, net income increased 150.1% to US$110.8 million from US$44.3 million in the year-earlier quarter. Revenues were US$1.89 billion, up 16.6% from US$1.62 billion the year before. Operating income was US$155.9 million versus US$80.4 million in the prior-year quarter, an increase of 93.9%. Direct operating expenses rose 14.3% to US$1.55 billion from US$1.36 billion in the comparable period the year before. Indirect operating expenses decreased 0.8% to US$179.5 million from US$180.9 million in the equivalent prior-year period.

Prospects: Our evaluation of Oshkosh Corp. as of Jan. 21, 2018 is the result of our systematic analysis on three basic characteristics: earnings strength, relative valuation, and recent stock price movement. The company has managed to produce a neutral trend in earnings per share over the past 5 quarters and while recent estimates for the company have been raised by analysts, OSK has posted better than expected results. Based on operating earnings yield, the company is undervalued when compared to all of the companies in our coverage universe. Share price changes over the past year indicates that OSK will perform well over the near term.

Financial Data

(US$ in Thousands)	6 Mos	3 Mos	09/30/2017	09/30/2016	09/30/2015	09/30/2014	09/30/2013	09/30/2012
Earnings Per Share	5.13	4.24	3.77	2.91	2.90	3.61	3.55	2.51
Cash Flow Per Share	1.91	2.56	3.30	7.83	1.06	2.03	4.99	2.93
Tang Book Value Per Share	11.35	10.46	10.49	5.67	4.02	3.78	4.07	0.48
Dividends Per Share	0.900	0.870	0.840	0.740	0.680	0.150	...	...
Dividend Payout %	17.54	20.52	22.28	25.43	23.45	4.16	...	...
Income Statement								
Total Revenue	3,472,700	1,586,300	6,829,600	6,279,200	6,098,100	6,808,200	7,665,100	8,180,900
EBITDA	289,200	105,000	593,500	491,100	511,800	621,900	621,500	484,100
Depn & Amortn	59,800	30,700	127,300	125,800	118,100	120,600	121,900	123,300
Income Before Taxes	207,700	60,600	411,300	307,000	326,100	431,900	445,200	286,700
Income Taxes	40,900	4,700	127,200	92,400	99,200	125,000	131,700	57,400
Net Income	167,200	56,400	285,600	216,400	229,500	309,300	318,000	230,800
Average Shares	75,497	76,024	75,790	74,432	78,981	85,457	88,953	91,893
Balance Sheet								
Current Assets	3,153,600	2,916,600	3,039,800	2,417,500	2,429,300	2,384,300	2,553,400	2,694,500
Total Assets	5,194,500	4,962,100	5,098,900	4,513,800	4,613,000	4,586,700	4,765,700	4,947,800
Current Liabilities	1,739,800	1,565,400	1,683,100	1,367,600	1,458,100	1,311,600	1,380,700	1,704,500
Long-Term Obligations	818,800	803,400	807,900	826,200	855,000	875,000	890,000	955,000
Total Liabilities	2,844,900	2,668,700	2,791,500	2,537,300	2,701,900	2,601,700	2,657,900	3,094,300
Stockholders' Equity	2,349,600	2,293,400	2,307,400	1,976,500	1,911,100	1,985,000	2,107,800	1,853,500
Shares Outstanding	73,916	74,623	75,013	73,925	75,454	79,845	86,534	91,557
Statistical Record								
Return on Assets %	7.65	6.83	5.94	4.73	4.99	6.61	6.55	4.71
Return on Equity %	17.76	15.11	13.33	11.10	11.78	15.11	16.06	13.34
EBITDA Margin %	8.33	6.62	8.69	7.82	8.39	9.13	8.11	5.92
Net Margin %	4.81	3.56	4.18	3.45	3.76	4.54	4.15	2.82
Asset Turnover	1.47	1.52	1.42	1.37	1.33	1.46	1.58	1.67
Current Ratio	1.81	1.86	1.81	1.77	1.67	1.82	1.85	1.58
Debt to Equity	0.35	0.35	0.35	0.42	0.45	0.44	0.42	0.52
Price Range	96.24-62.45	92.10-62.45	82.68-52.58	56.90-30.33	54.90-35.23	60.03-44.15	49.12-26.85	29.76-14.51
P/E Ratio	18.76-12.17	21.72-14.73	21.93-13.95	19.55-10.42	18.93-12.15	16.63-12.23	13.84-7.56	11.86-5.78
Average Yield %	1.15	1.17	1.24	1.71	1.71	1.51	0.29	...

Address: P.O. Box 2566, Oshkosh, WI 54903-2566

Telephone: 920-235-9151

Web Site: www.oshkoshcorporation.com

Officers: Craig P. Omtvedt - Chairman Wilson R. Jones - President, Chief Executive Officer, Executive Vice President, Chief Operating Officer, Division Officer

Auditors: DELOITTE & TOUCHE LLP

Investor Contact: 920-966-5939

Transfer Agents: Computershare Investor Services, LLC, Providence, RI

OUTFRONT MEDIA INC

Exchange	Symbol	Price	52Wk Range	Yield	P/E
NYS	OUT	$19.45 (6/29/2018)	25.18-18.00	7.40	20.69

*7 Year Price Score N/A   *NYSE Composite Index=100   *12 Month Price Score 88.94

Interim Earnings (Per Share)

Qtr.	Mar	Jun	Sep	Dec
2015	0.01	0.16	0.15	(0.53)
2016	(0.02)	0.21	0.28	0.20
2017	0.02	0.27	0.36	0.25
2018	0.06	...	...	...

Interim Dividends (Per Share)

Amt	Decl	Ex	Rec	Pay
0.36Q	07/25/2017	09/07/2017	09/08/2017	09/29/2017
0.36Q	10/25/2017	12/07/2017	12/08/2017	12/29/2017
0.36Q	02/27/2018	03/08/2018	03/09/2018	03/30/2018
0.36Q	04/25/2018	06/07/2018	06/08/2018	06/29/2018

Indicated Div: $1.44

Valuation Analysis

		Institutional Holding	
Forecast EPS	$1.05	No of Institutions	
	(06/05/2018)	319	
Market Cap	$2.7 Billion	Shares	
Book Value	$1.1 Billion	158,293,744	
Price/Book	2.39	% Held	
Price/Sales	1.77	N/A	

Business Summary: REITs (MIC: 5.3.1 SIC: 6798 NAIC: 525930)

OUTFRONT Media is a real estate investment trust that provides advertising space on out-of-home advertising structures and sites in the U.S. and Canada. Co.'s inventory consists of billboard displays, which are mainly located on the heavily traveled highways and roadways, and transit advertising displays operated under multi-year contracts with municipalities in cities across the U.S. and Canada. As of Dec 31 2017, Co. had displays in 140 markets in the U.S. and Canada. Co.'s portfolio includes sites such as the Bay Bridge in San Francisco, various locations along Sunset Boulevard in Los Angeles, and sites in and around both Grand Central Station and Times Square in New York.

Recent Developments: For the quarter ended Mar 31 2018, net income increased 264.0% to US$9.1 million from US$2.5 million in the year-earlier quarter. Revenues were US$337.9 million, up 2.2% from US$330.6 million the year before.

Prospects: Our evaluation of OUTFRONT Media Inc. as of Jan. 21, 2018 is the result of our systematic analysis on three basic characteristics: earnings strength, relative valuation, and recent stock price movement. The company has managed to produce a neutral trend in earnings per share over the past 5 quarters and while recent estimates for the company have remained steady, OUT has posted better than expected results. Based on operating earnings yield, the company is about fairly valued when compared to all of the companies in our coverage universe. Share price changes over the past year indicates that OUT will perform in line with the market over the near term.

Financial Data
(US$ in Thousands)

	3 Mos	12/31/2017	12/31/2016	12/31/2015	12/31/2014	12/31/2013	12/31/2012	12/31/2011
Earnings Per Share	0.94	0.90	0.66	(0.21)	2.67	1.48	1.17	1.10
Cash Flow Per Share	2.01	1.80	2.08	2.13	2.30	2.87	3.20	3.53
Tang Book Value Per Share	N.M.	N.M.	N.M.	N.M.	N.M.	5.41	5.64	...
Dividends Per Share	1.440	1.440	1.360	1.420	5.670	...	...	...
Dividend Payout %	153.19	160.00	206.06	...	212.36	...	...	...
Income Statement								
Total Revenue	337,900	1,520,500	1,513,900	1,513,800	1,353,800	1,294,000	1,284,600	1,277,100
EBITDA	54,100	331,700	313,700	113,786,000	290,000	342,100	306,100	302,200
Depn & Amortn	22,500	89,700	108,900	113,700,000	107,200	104,500	105,900	109,000
Income Before Taxes	1,600	125,100	91,000	(28,800)	98,000	237,600	200,200	193,200
Income Taxes	(6,700)	4,100	5,400	5,400	(206,000)	96,600	89,000	87,800
Net Income	9,100	125,800	90,900	(29,400)	306,900	143,500	113,400	107,100
Average Shares	139,100	138,900	138,400	137,300	114,800	97,000	97,000	97,000
Balance Sheet								
Current Assets	354,400	376,000	378,200	416,600	355,300	317,200	315,000	...
Total Assets	3,770,700	3,808,200	3,738,500	3,845,200	4,023,600	3,355,500	3,464,900	...
Current Liabilities	304,700	299,600	251,500	265,600	255,200	212,200	205,600	...
Long-Term Obligations	2,156,400	2,145,300	2,136,800	2,251,700	2,198,300	...	...	...
Total Liabilities	2,638,900	2,627,100	2,505,600	2,632,600	2,578,100	601,100	621,000	...
Stockholders' Equity	1,131,800	1,181,100	1,232,900	1,212,600	1,445,500	2,754,400	2,843,900	...
Shares Outstanding	139,200	138,644	138,044	137,583	136,624	97,000	97,000	97,000
Statistical Record								
Return on Assets %	3.57	3.33	2.39	N.M.	8.32	4.21	...	...
Return on Equity %	11.43	10.42	7.41	N.M.	14.61	5.13	...	...
EBITDA Margin %	16.01	21.82	20.72	7,516.58	21.42	26.44	23.83	23.66
Net Margin %	2.69	8.27	6.00	N.M.	22.67	11.09	8.83	8.39
Asset Turnover	0.41	0.40	0.40	0.38	0.37	0.38	...	...
Current Ratio	1.16	1.26	1.50	1.57	1.39	1.49	1.53	...
Debt to Equity	1.91	1.82	1.73	1.86	1.52	...	...	...
Price Range	26.76-18.56	27.65-20.88	25.37-18.18	30.82-20.71	35.15-26.03	...	...	...
P/E Ratio	28.47-19.74	30.72-23.20	38.44-27.55	...	13.16-9.75	...	...	...
Average Yield %	6.30	5.95	6.10	5.50	18.34	...	...	...

Address: 405 Lexington Avenue, 17th Floor, New York, NY 10174
Telephone: 212-297-6400

Web Site: www.outfrontmedia.com
Officers: Jeremy J. Male - Chairman, Chief Executive Officer Matthew Siegel - Chief Financial Officer, Executive Vice President

Auditors: Pricewaterhouse Coopers LLP
Transfer Agents: Wells Fargo Bank, National Association

OWENS-ILLINOIS, INC.

Exchange	Symbol	Price	52Wk Range	Yield	P/E
NYS	OI	$16.81 (6/29/2018)	25.68-16.56	N/A	12.09

*7 Year Price Score 77.64 *NYSE Composite Index=100 *12 Month Price Score 81.24

Interim Earnings (Per Share)

Qtr.	Mar	Jun	Sep	Dec
2015	0.44	0.25	0.10	(1.26)
2016	0.41	0.64	0.66	(0.43)
2017	0.30	0.85	0.76	(0.81)
2018	0.59	...	...	...

Interim Dividends (Per Share)

No Dividends Paid

Valuation Analysis

		Institutional Holding	
Forecast EPS	$2.75	No of Institutions	
	(06/14/2018)	522	
Market Cap	$2.7 Billion	Shares	
Book Value	$989.0 Million	190,314,160	
Price/Book	2.75	% Held	
Price/Sales	0.39	93.05	

TRADING VOLUME (thousand shares)

Business Summary: Containers & Packaging (MIC: 8.1.3 SIC: 3221 NAIC: 327213)

Owens-Illinois is a manufacturer of glass containers. Co. produces glass containers for alcoholic beverages, including beer, flavored malt beverages, spirits and wine. Co. also produces glass packaging for a variety of food items, soft drinks, teas, juices and pharmaceuticals. Co. manufactures glass containers in a range of sizes, shapes and colors. Co. has four reportable segments based on its geographic locations: Europe, North America, South America and Asia Pacific.

Recent Developments: For the quarter ended Mar 31 2018, income from continuing operations increased 94.3% to US$103.0 million from US$53.0 million in the year-earlier quarter. Net income increased 94.3% to US$103.0 million from US$53.0 million in the year-earlier quarter. Revenues were US$1.74 billion, up 7.5% from US$1.62 billion the year before. Direct operating expenses rose 9.0% to US$1.42 billion from US$1.30 billion in the comparable period the year before. Indirect operating expenses decreased 5.1% to US$187.0 million from US$197.0 million in the equivalent prior-year period.

Prospects: Our evaluation of Owens-Illinois Inc. as of Jan. 21, 2018 is the result of our systematic analysis on three basic characteristics: earnings strength, relative valuation, and recent stock price movement. The company has managed to produce a neutral trend in earnings per share over the past 5 quarters and while recent estimates for the company have been mixed, OI has posted better than expected results. Based on operating earnings yield, the company is undervalued when compared to all of the companies in our coverage universe. Share price changes over the past year indicates that OI will perform very well over the near term.

Financial Data
(US$ in Thousands)

	3 Mos	12/31/2017	12/31/2016	12/31/2015	12/31/2014	12/31/2013	12/31/2012	12/31/2011
Earnings Per Share	1.39	1.10	1.28	(0.47)	0.45	1.11	1.11	(3.11)
Cash Flow Per Share	4.22	4.43	4.63	3.77	4.10	4.15	3.49	3.07
Income Statement								
Total Revenue	1,736,000	6,869,000	6,702,000	6,156,000	6,784,000	6,967,000	7,000,000	7,358,000
EBITDA	170,000	865,000	956,000	573,000	719,000	847,000	881,000	236,000
Depn & Amortn	(10,000)	399,000	388,000	323,000	335,000	350,000	378,000	405,000
Income Before Taxes	118,000	198,000	296,000	(1,000)	154,000	268,000	264,000	(472,000)
Income Taxes	32,000	70,000	119,000	106,000	92,000	120,000	108,000	85,000
Net Income	98,000	180,000	209,000	(74,000)	75,000	184,000	184,000	(510,000)
Average Shares	165,186	164,647	162,825	161,169	166,047	165,828	165,768	163,691
Balance Sheet								
Current Assets	2,768,000	2,420,000	2,254,000	2,334,000	2,371,000	2,550,000	2,648,000	2,694,000
Total Assets	10,281,000	9,756,000	9,135,000	9,421,000	7,858,000	8,419,000	8,598,000	8,926,000
Current Liabilities	2,078,000	2,280,000	2,060,000	2,122,000	2,328,000	2,254,000	2,162,000	2,245,000
Long-Term Obligations	5,640,000	5,121,000	5,133,000	5,345,000	2,972,000	3,245,000	3,454,000	3,627,000
Total Liabilities	9,292,000	8,948,000	8,881,000	8,955,000	6,700,000	6,963,000	7,717,000	8,087,000
Stockholders' Equity	989,000	808,000	254,000	466,000	1,158,000	1,456,000	881,000	839,000
Shares Outstanding	161,707	163,079	162,337	160,961	164,197	164,714	163,963	164,374
Statistical Record								
Return on Assets %	2.33	1.91	2.25	N.M.	0.92	2.16	2.09	N.M.
Return on Equity %	30.89	33.90	57.90	N.M.	5.74	15.75	21.34	N.M.
EBITDA Margin %	9.79	12.59	14.26	9.31	10.60	12.16	12.59	3.21
Net Margin %	5.65	2.62	3.12	N.M.	1.11	2.64	2.63	N.M.
Asset Turnover	0.71	0.73	0.72	0.71	0.83	0.82	0.80	0.79
Current Ratio	1.33	1.06	1.09	1.10	1.02	1.13	1.22	1.20
Debt to Equity	5.70	6.34	20.21	11.47	2.57	2.23	3.92	4.32
Price Range	25.68-19.87	25.68-17.95	20.18-12.06	26.99-16.94	35.78-23.53	35.78-21.27	24.83-17.07	33.01-14.04
P/E Ratio	18.47-14.29	23.35-16.32	15.77-9.42	...	79.51-52.29	32.23-19.16	22.37-15.38	...

Address: One Michael Owens Way, Perrysburg, OH 43551 **Telephone:** 567-336-5000	**Web Site:** www.o-i.com **Officers:** Andres Alberto Lopez - President, Chief Executive Officer, Chief Operating Officer, Division Officer Jan A. Bertsch - Senior Vice President, Chief Financial Officer	**Auditors:** Ernst & Young LLP **Investor Contact:** 567-336-2400 **Transfer Agents:** Computershare Trust Company, N.A., Providence, RI

OWENS CORNING

Exchange	Symbol	Price	52Wk Range	Yield	P/E
NYS	OC	$63.37 (6/29/2018)	96.36-61.76	1.33	25.55

*7 Year Price Score 134.62 *NYSE Composite Index=100 *12 Month Price Score 82.48

Interim Earnings (Per Share)

Qtr.	Mar	Jun	Sep	Dec
2015	0.15	0.77	0.95	0.92
2016	0.49	1.19	0.97	0.76
2017	0.89	0.85	0.85	(0.04)
2018	0.82	...	...	...

Interim Dividends (Per Share)

Amt	Decl	Ex	Rec	Pay
0.20Q	09/21/2017	10/13/2017	10/16/2017	11/02/2017
0.21Q	12/07/2017	12/29/2017	01/02/2018	01/17/2018
0.21Q	02/01/2018	03/08/2018	03/09/2018	04/03/2018
0.21Q	06/20/2018	07/16/2018	07/17/2018	08/02/2018

Indicated Div: $0.84

Valuation Analysis

		Institutional Holding	
Forecast EPS	$5.58	No of Institutions	
	(06/14/2018)	604	
Market Cap	$7.0 Billion	Shares	
Book Value	$4.1 Billion	130,850,544	
Price/Book	1.72	% Held	
Price/Sales	1.07	82.61	

TRADING VOLUME (thousand shares)

Business Summary: Construction Materials (MIC: 8.5.1 SIC: 3292 NAIC: 327910)

Owens Corning is a holding company. Through its subsidiaries, Co. produces glass fiber reinforcements and other materials for composites and of residential and commercial building materials. Co.'s products range from glass fiber used to reinforce composite materials for transportation, electronics, marine, infrastructure, wind-energy and other markets to insulation and roofing for residential, commercial and industrial applications. Co.'s segments are Composites, which includes Reinforcements and Downstream businesses; Insulation, which products include thermal and acoustical batts, and loosefill insulation; and Roofing, which main products are laminate and strip asphalt roofing shingles.

Recent Developments: For the quarter ended Mar 31 2018, net income decreased 8.9% to US$92.0 million from US$101.0 million in the year-earlier quarter. Revenues were US$1.69 billion, up 14.4% from US$1.48 billion the year before. Operating income was US$131.0 million versus US$170.0 million in the prior-year quarter, a decrease of 22.9%. Direct operating expenses rose 17.6% to US$1.34 billion from US$1.14 billion in the comparable period the year before. Indirect operating expenses increased 30.2% to US$224.0 million from US$172.0 million in the equivalent prior-year period.

Prospects: Our evaluation of Owens Corning as of Jan. 21, 2018 is the result of our systematic analysis on three basic characteristics: earnings strength, relative valuation, and recent stock price movement. The company has managed to produce a neutral trend in earnings per share over the past 5 quarters and while recent estimates for the company have been raised by analysts, OC has posted results that fell short of analysts expectations. Based on operating earnings yield, the company is undervalued when compared to all of the companies in our coverage universe. Share price changes over the past year indicates that OC will perform very well over the near term.

Financial Data

(US$ in Millions)	3 Mos	12/31/2017	12/31/2016	12/31/2015	12/31/2014	12/31/2013	12/31/2012	12/31/2011
Earnings Per Share	2.48	2.55	3.41	2.79	1.91	1.71	(0.16)	2.23
Cash Flow Per Share	8.24	9.11	8.22	6.33	3.75	3.54	2.76	2.36
Tang Book Value Per Share	2.38	11.61	12.20	13.57	12.79	13.47	11.41	12.27
Dividends Per Share	0.820	0.810	0.740	0.680	0.640	...	...	...
Dividend Payout %	33.06	31.76	21.70	24.37	33.51	...	...	...
Income Statement								
Total Revenue	1,691	6,384	5,677	5,350	5,276	5,295	5,172	5,335
EBITDA	240	1,006	1,016	831	629	695	402	757
Depn & Amortn	109	340	318	278	283	310	328	296
Income Before Taxes	103	559	590	453	232	273	(40)	353
Income Taxes	11	269	188	120	5	68	(28)	74
Net Income	92	289	393	330	226	204	(19)	276
Average Shares	112	113	115	118	118	119	119	123
Balance Sheet								
Current Assets	2,228	1,985	1,586	1,538	1,807	1,848	1,612	1,636
Total Assets	10,213	8,632	7,741	7,380	7,555	7,647	7,568	7,527
Current Liabilities	1,384	1,282	963	1,117	983	992	906	908
Long-Term Obligations	3,762	2,405	2,099	1,702	1,991	2,024	2,076	1,930
Total Liabilities	6,115	4,470	3,892	3,641	3,863	3,854	4,030	3,826
Stockholders' Equity	4,098	4,162	3,849	3,739	3,692	3,793	3,538	3,701
Shares Outstanding	111	111	112	115	117	117	118	120
Statistical Record								
Return on Assets %	3.08	3.53	5.18	4.42	2.97	2.68	N.M.	3.76
Return on Equity %	7.00	7.22	10.33	8.88	6.04	5.57	N.M.	7.51
EBITDA Margin %	14.19	15.76	17.90	15.53	11.92	13.13	7.77	14.19
Net Margin %	5.44	4.53	6.92	6.17	4.28	3.85	N.M.	5.17
Asset Turnover	0.73	0.78	0.75	0.72	0.69	0.70	0.68	0.73
Current Ratio	1.61	1.55	1.65	1.38	1.84	1.86	1.78	1.80
Debt to Equity	0.92	0.58	0.55	0.46	0.54	0.53	0.59	0.52
Price Range	96.36-59.67	92.75-51.66	56.03-40.52	48.08-35.04	46.05-29.00	44.95-35.62	37.05-26.13	38.51-20.55
P/E Ratio	38.85-24.06	36.37-20.26	16.43-11.88	17.23-12.56	24.11-15.18	26.29-20.83	...	17.27-9.22
Average Yield %	1.08	1.18	1.48	1.59	1.69	...	...	...

Address: One Owens Corning Parkway, Toledo, OH 43659 **Telephone:** 419-248-8000	**Web Site:** www.owenscorning.com **Officers:** Michael H. Thaman - Chairman, President, Chief Executive Officer Michael C. McMurray - Senior Vice President, Chief Financial Officer	**Auditors:** PricewaterhouseCoopers LLP **Investor Contact:** 419-248-5748 **Transfer Agents:** Wells Fargo Shareowner Services, Mendota Heights, MN

OWENS & MINOR, INC.

Exchange	Symbol	Price	52Wk Range	Yield	P/E	Div Acheiver
NYS	OMI	$16.71 (6/29/2018)	32.51-14.94	6.22	16.38	20 Years

*7 Year Price Score 54.66 *NYSE Composite Index=100 *12 Month Price Score 75.49

Interim Earnings (Per Share)

Qtr.	Mar	Jun	Sep	Dec
2015	0.30	0.39	0.45	0.51
2016	0.39	0.45	0.48	0.44
2017	0.31	0.33	0.18	0.38
2018	0.13	...	...	...

Interim Dividends (Per Share)

Amt	Decl	Ex	Rec	Pay
0.258Q	08/01/2017	09/14/2017	09/15/2017	09/29/2017
0.258Q	11/01/2017	12/14/2017	12/15/2017	12/29/2017
0.26Q	01/31/2018	03/14/2018	03/15/2018	03/30/2018
0.26Q	05/10/2018	06/14/2018	06/15/2018	07/02/2018

Indicated Div: $1.04 (Div. Reinv. Plan)

Valuation Analysis / **Institutional Holding**

Forecast EPS	$2.00	No of Institutions
	(06/11/2018)	404
Market Cap	$1.0 Billion	Shares
Book Value	$1.0 Billion	73,738,976
Price/Book	1.01	% Held
Price/Sales	0.11	65.15

Business Summary: Medical Instruments & Equipment (MIC: 4.3.1 SIC: 5047 NAIC: 423450)

Owens & Minor is a healthcare services company that connects medical products to the point of care. Co. provides supply chain assistance to the providers of healthcare services and the manufacturers of healthcare products, supplies and devices. Co. organizes its operations into three business units: Domestic, International and Clinical & Procedural Solutions (CPS). Co.'s Domestic unit is Co.'s U.S. distribution, logistics and services business, while the International unit is Co.'s European distribution, logistics and value-added services business. CPS provides product-related solutions, including surgical and procedural kitting and sourcing.

Recent Developments: For the quarter ended Mar 31 2018, net income decreased 56.6% to US$8.2 million from US$18.8 million in the year-earlier quarter. Revenues were US$2.37 billion, up 1.9% from US$2.33 billion the year before. Operating income was US$24.2 million versus US$35.5 million in the prior-year quarter, a decrease of 31.8%. Direct operating expenses was unchanged at US$2.05 billion versus the comparable period the year before. Indirect operating expenses increased 22.3% to US$300.5 million from US$245.7 million in the equivalent prior-year period.

Prospects: Our evaluation of Owens & Minor Inc. as of Jan. 21, 2018 is the result of our systematic analysis on three basic characteristics: earnings strength, relative valuation, and recent stock price movement. The company has produced a positive trend in earnings per share over the past 5 quarters and while recent estimates for the company have been mixed, OMI has posted results that fell short of analysts expectations. Based on operating earnings yield, the company is undervalued when compared to all of the companies in our coverage universe. Share price changes over the past year indicates that OMI will perform very poorly over the near term.

Financial Data

(US$ in Thousands)	3 Mos	12/31/2017	12/31/2016	12/31/2015	12/31/2014	12/31/2013	12/31/2012	12/31/2011
Earnings Per Share	1.02	1.20	1.76	1.65	1.06	1.76	1.72	1.81
Cash Flow Per Share	1.69	0.95	3.05	4.34	(0.06)	2.24	3.47	1.09
Tang Book Value Per Share	2.02	1.91	7.58	7.61	7.28	11.22	10.36	10.20
Dividends Per Share	1.033	1.030	1.020	1.010	1.000	0.960	0.880	0.800
Dividend Payout %	101.23	85.83	57.95	61.21	94.34	54.55	51.16	44.20
Income Statement								
Total Revenue	2,372,579	9,318,275	9,723,431	9,772,946	9,440,182	9,071,532	8,908,145	8,627,912
EBITDA	42,128	121,551	232,099	236,659	180,146	231,183	222,853	224,715
Depn & Amortn	17,911	32,300	32,500	36,300	35,500	33,100	26,100	21,200
Income Before Taxes	13,964	57,478	172,542	173,210	126,483	184,985	183,356	189,833
Income Taxes	5,813	(15,315)	63,755	69,801	59,980	74,103	74,353	74,635
Net Income	8,151	72,793	108,787	103,409	66,503	110,882	109,003	115,198
Average Shares	59,969	60,001	61,093	62,117	62,226	62,661	62,844	62,924
Balance Sheet								
Current Assets	2,187,773	2,181,905	1,962,039	1,974,700	1,870,706	1,725,932	1,628,894	1,525,825
Total Assets	3,391,554	3,376,293	2,717,752	2,777,840	2,735,406	2,324,042	2,207,701	1,946,815
Current Liabilities	1,325,980	1,309,733	1,034,638	1,063,589	1,004,555	989,179	924,287	732,365
Long-Term Obligations	897,071	900,744	564,583	572,559	608,551	213,815	215,383	212,681
Total Liabilities	2,372,636	2,360,814	1,757,714	1,785,250	1,744,568	1,300,129	1,235,175	1,028,728
Stockholders' Equity	1,018,918	1,015,479	960,038	992,590	990,838	1,023,913	972,526	918,087
Shares Outstanding	61,812	61,476	61,031	62,803	63,070	63,096	63,271	63,449
Statistical Record								
Return on Assets %	2.04	2.39	3.95	3.75	2.63	4.89	5.23	6.11
Return on Equity %	6.25	7.37	11.11	10.43	6.60	11.11	11.50	12.98
EBITDA Margin %	1.78	1.30	2.39	2.42	1.91	2.55	2.50	2.60
Net Margin %	0.34	0.78	1.12	1.06	0.70	1.22	1.22	1.34
Asset Turnover	3.07	3.06	3.53	3.55	3.73	4.00	4.28	4.58
Current Ratio	1.65	1.67	1.90	1.86	1.86	1.74	1.76	2.08
Debt to Equity	0.88	0.89	0.59	0.58	0.61	0.21	0.22	0.23
Price Range	34.80-14.94	36.95-18.10	41.20-31.94	39.02-31.94	37.49-31.72	38.23-28.51	31.28-27.01	35.48-26.67
P/E Ratio	34.12-14.65	30.79-15.08	23.41-18.15	23.65-19.36	35.37-29.92	21.72-16.20	18.19-15.70	19.60-14.73
Average Yield %	4.02	3.43	2.84	2.91	2.91	2.83	3.02	2.58

Address: 9120 Lockwood Boulevard, Mechanicsville, VA 23116	Web Site: www.owens-minor.com	Auditors: KPMG LLP
Telephone: 804-723-7000	Officers: Paul Cody Phipps - Chairman, President, Chief Executive Officer Nicholas J. Pace - Executive Vice President, Senior Vice President, General Counsel, Corporate Secretary	Investor Contact: 804-723-7555
Fax: 804-723-7100		Transfer Agents: Computershare Shareowner Services LLC, Providence, RI

PACKAGING CORP OF AMERICA

Exchange	Symbol	Price	52Wk Range	Yield	P/E
NYS	PKG	$111.79 (6/29/2018)	129.58-106.51	2.83	15.29

*7 Year Price Score 139.54 *NYSE Composite Index=100 *12 Month Price Score 100.07

Interim Earnings (Per Share)

Qtr.	Mar	Jun	Sep	Dec
2015	0.92	1.16	1.31	1.08
2016	1.09	1.23	1.26	1.17
2017	1.24	1.52	1.47	2.84
2018	1.48	...	...	...

Interim Dividends (Per Share)

Amt	Decl	Ex	Rec	Pay
0.63Q	08/25/2017	09/14/2017	09/15/2017	10/13/2017
0.63Q	12/14/2017	12/22/2017	12/26/2017	01/12/2018
0.63Q	02/27/2018	03/14/2018	03/15/2018	04/13/2018
0.79Q	05/15/2018	06/14/2018	06/15/2018	07/13/2018

Indicated Div: $3.16

Valuation Analysis **Institutional Holding**

Forecast EPS	$7.94	No of Institutions
	(06/13/2018)	762
Market Cap	$10.5 Billion	Shares
Book Value	$2.3 Billion	119,336,976
Price/Book	4.64	% Held
Price/Sales	1.60	84.54

TRADING VOLUME (thousand shares)

Business Summary: Containers & Packaging (MIC: 8.1.3 SIC: 2652 NAIC: 322213)

Packaging Corporation of America is a producer of containerboard products and uncoated freesheet. Co. has three reportable segments: Packaging, which produces corrugated packaging products, including shipping containers used to protect and transport manufactured goods, multi-color boxes and displays, as well as produces packaging for meat, fresh fruit and vegetables, processed food, beverages, and other industrial and consumer products; Paper, which manufactures and sells white papers, including both commodity and specialty papers; and Corporate and Other, which includes corporate support staff services.

Recent Developments: For the quarter ended Mar 31 2018, net income increased 19.3% to US$140.1 million from US$117.4 million in the year-earlier quarter. Revenues were US$1.69 billion, up 10.0% from US$1.54 billion the year before. Operating income was US$212.9 million versus US$203.4 million in the prior-year quarter, an increase of 4.7%. Direct operating expenses rose 11.4% to US$1.33 billion from US$1.20 billion in the comparable period the year before. Indirect operating expenses increased 6.2% to US$143.2 million from US$134.8 million in the equivalent prior-year period.

Prospects: Our evaluation of Packaging Corp. of America as of Jan. 21, 2018 is the result of our systematic analysis on three basic characteristics: earnings strength, relative valuation, and recent stock price movement. The company has produced a positive trend in earnings per share over the past 5 quarters and while recent estimates for the company have been mixed, PKG has posted results that fell short of analysts expectations. Based on operating earnings yield, the company is undervalued when compared to all of the companies in our coverage universe. Share price changes over the past year indicates that PKG will perform well over the near term.

Financial Data

(US$ in Thousands)	3 Mos	12/31/2017	12/31/2016	12/31/2015	12/31/2014	12/31/2013	12/31/2012	12/31/2011
Earnings Per Share	7.31	7.07	4.75	4.47	3.99	4.47	1.68	1.57
Cash Flow Per Share	9.56	9.16	8.55	7.89	7.59	6.30	4.18	3.48
Tang Book Value Per Share	10.51	9.43	6.95	8.51	6.92	4.85	8.80	8.60
Dividends Per Share	2.520	2.520	2.360	2.200	1.600	1.513	1.000	0.800
Dividend Payout %	34.47	35.64	49.68	49.22	40.10	33.84	59.52	50.96
Income Statement								
Total Revenue	1,690,600	6,444,900	5,779,000	5,741,700	5,852,600	3,665,308	2,843,877	2,620,111
EBITDA	309,800	1,279,000	780,624	1,073,000	1,050,900	664,807	609,459	434,249
Depn & Amortn	96,900	347,800	324	323,000	348,200	191,200	166,000	161,500
Income Before Taxes	186,600	828,600	688,500	664,500	614,300	415,332	380,559	243,504
Income Taxes	46,500	160,000	238,900	227,700	221,700	(20,951)	216,739	85,477
Net Income	140,100	668,600	449,600	436,800	392,600	436,283	163,820	158,027
Average Shares	93,800	93,700	93,700	96,700	97,100	97,547	97,497	100,376
Balance Sheet								
Current Assets	1,832,600	1,915,100	1,696,300	1,554,500	1,578,600	1,487,204	937,033	812,063
Total Assets	6,139,800	6,197,500	5,777,000	5,284,600	5,348,500	5,199,974	2,453,768	2,412,499
Current Liabilities	673,600	832,700	625,400	561,900	611,000	660,539	259,846	376,500
Long-Term Obligations	2,499,800	2,499,400	2,640,300	2,324,300	2,371,700	2,532,719	803,534	814,562
Total Liabilities	3,866,000	4,014,900	4,017,200	3,651,300	3,827,100	3,886,959	1,484,307	1,483,589
Stockholders' Equity	2,273,800	2,182,600	1,759,800	1,633,300	1,521,400	1,313,015	969,461	928,910
Shares Outstanding	94,300	94,350	94,213	96,129	98,368	98,172	98,142	98,322
Statistical Record								
Return on Assets %	11.54	11.17	8.11	8.22	7.44	11.40	6.71	6.82
Return on Equity %	33.73	33.92	26.43	27.69	27.70	38.23	17.21	16.31
EBITDA Margin %	18.32	19.85	13.51	18.69	17.96	18.14	21.43	16.57
Net Margin %	8.29	10.37	7.78	7.61	6.71	11.90	5.76	6.03
Asset Turnover	1.10	1.08	1.04	1.08	1.11	0.96	1.17	1.13
Current Ratio	2.72	2.30	2.71	2.77	2.58	2.25	3.61	2.16
Debt to Equity	1.10	1.15	1.50	1.42	1.56	1.93	0.83	0.88
Price Range	129.58-90.02	120.92-85.00	87.51-45.15	84.24-59.34	79.69-58.61	64.27-38.43	38.47-25.00	30.27-21.28
P/E Ratio	17.73-12.31	17.10-12.02	18.42-9.51	18.85-13.28	19.97-14.69	14.38-8.60	22.90-14.88	19.28-13.55
Average Yield %	2.25	2.40	3.38	3.12	2.32	2.97	3.22	2.98

Address: 1955 West Field Court, Lake Forest, IL 60045 **Telephone:** 847-482-3000	**Web Site:** www.packagingcorp.com **Officers:** Mark W. Kowlzan - Chairman, Chief Executive Officer, Senior Vice President Robert P. Mundy - Senior Vice President, Chief Financial Officer	**Auditors:** KPMG LLP **Investor Contact:** 877-454-2509 **Transfer Agents:** Computershare Trust Company N.A., Providence, RI

PALO ALTO NETWORKS, INC

Exchange	Symbol	Price	52Wk Range	Yield	P/E
NYS	PANW	$205.47 (6/29/2018)	215.56-127.72	N/A	N/A

*7 Year Price Score N/A   *NYSE Composite Index=100   *12 Month Price Score 124.71

TRADING VOLUME (thousand shares)

Interim Earnings (Per Share)

Qtr.	Oct	Jan	Apr	Jul
2014-15	(0.38)	(0.53)	(0.56)	(0.55)
2015-16	(0.45)	(0.72)	(0.80)	(0.61)
2016-17	(0.69)	(0.67)	(0.67)	(0.42)
2017-18	(0.70)	(0.38)	(0.51)	...

Interim Dividends (Per Share)

No Dividends Paid

Valuation Analysis   Institutional Holding

Forecast EPS	$3.88	No of Institutions
	(06/12/2018)	813
Market Cap	$19.1 Billion	Shares
Book Value	$749.8 Million	94,124,624
Price/Book	25.46	% Held
Price/Sales	8.99	82.37

Business Summary: IT Services (MIC: 6.3.1 SIC: 3577 NAIC: 423430)

Palo Alto Networks provides a platform that allows enterprises, service providers, and government entities to secure their organizations. Co.'s Next-Generation Security Platform consists of three elements: Next-Generation Firewall, which delivers application, user, and content visibility and control, and protection against cyber threats integrated within the firewall; Advanced Endpoint Protection, which prevents cyberattacks that aim to run malicious code or exploit software vulnerabilities; and Threat Intelligence Cloud, which provides central intelligence capabilities, security for software as a service applications, and automated delivery of preventative measures against cyberattacks.

Recent Developments: For the quarter ended Apr 30 2018, net loss amounted to US$46.7 million versus a net loss of US$60.9 million in the year-earlier quarter. Revenues were US$567.1 million, up 31.3% from US$431.8 million the year before. Operating loss was US$51.6 million versus a loss of US$49.1 million in the prior-year quarter. Direct operating expenses rose 29.3% to US$159.9 million from US$123.7 million in the comparable period the year before. Indirect operating expenses increased 28.4% to US$458.8 million from US$357.2 million in the equivalent prior-year period.

Prospects: Our evaluation of Palo Alto Networks, Inc as of Jan. 21, 2018 is the result of our systematic analysis on three basic characteristics: earnings strength, relative valuation, and recent stock price movement. The company has produced a positive trend in earnings per share over the past 5 quarters. However, while recent estimates for the company have been mixed, PANW has posted better than expected results. Based on operating earnings yield, the company is overvalued when compared to all of the companies in our coverage universe. Share price changes over the past year indicates that PANW will perform poorly over the near term.

Financial Data
(US$ in Thousands)

	9 Mos	6 Mos	3 Mos	07/31/2017	07/31/2016	07/31/2015	07/31/2014	07/31/2013
Earnings Per Share	(2.01)	(2.17)	(2.46)	(2.39)	(2.59)	(2.02)	(3.05)	(0.43)
Cash Flow Per Share	10.87	10.63	10.33	9.59	7.54	4.29	1.19	1.67
Tang Book Value Per Share	0.86	4.13	4.51	5.10	6.44	4.24	3.34	3.80
Income Statement								
Total Revenue	1,615,000	1,047,900	505,500	1,761,600	1,378,500	928,052	598,179	396,107
EBITDA	(31,600)	(19,700)	(21,400)	(125,900)	(139,200)	(105,052)	(203,346)	(9,229)
Depn & Amortn	87,800	56,700	28,100	58,400	42,500	28,200	16,931	9,911
Income Before Taxes	(138,600)	(89,100)	(55,800)	(194,100)	(205,100)	(155,577)	(222,160)	(18,656)
Income Taxes	7,000	9,800	8,200	22,500	20,800	9,405	4,292	10,590
Net Income	(145,600)	(98,900)	(64,000)	(216,600)	(225,900)	(164,982)	(226,452)	(29,246)
Average Shares	91,900	91,100	90,900	90,600	87,100	81,619	74,291	68,682
Balance Sheet								
Current Assets	2,205,500	2,210,200	2,039,500	1,976,300	1,719,100	1,074,030	958,326	529,699
Total Assets	3,908,300	3,627,500	3,486,500	3,438,300	2,761,200	1,965,178	1,478,466	585,606
Current Liabilities	1,943,100	1,856,400	1,743,000	1,201,300	846,800	1,032,227	348,171	206,102
Long-Term Obligations	...	...	...	524,700	508,200	...	466,875	...
Total Liabilities	3,158,500	2,960,900	2,781,800	2,678,700	1,971,300	1,389,363	1,009,883	313,186
Stockholders' Equity	749,800	666,600	704,700	759,600	789,900	575,815	468,583	272,420
Shares Outstanding	92,900	91,800	91,900	91,500	90,500	84,788	79,519	71,612
Statistical Record								
Asset Turnover	0.59	0.58	0.58	0.57	0.58	0.54	0.58	0.80
Current Ratio	1.14	1.19	1.17	1.65	2.03	1.04	2.75	2.57
Debt to Equity	...	...	...	0.69	0.64	...	1.00	...
Price Range	196.40-108.42	159.71-108.01	164.15-108.01	164.15-108.01	193.54-115.69	197.09-78.67	84.21-40.99	71.75-39.56

Address: 3000 Tannery Way, Santa Clara, CA 95054 **Telephone:** 408-753-4000	**Web Site:** www.paloaltonetworks.com **Officers:** Nikesh Arora - Chairman, Chief Executive Officer Mark F. Anderson - President, Senior Vice President	**Auditors:** Ernst & Young LLP **Investor Contact:** 408-753-3872 **Transfer Agents:** Computershare, Canton, MA

PANDORA MEDIA INC

Exchange	Symbol	Price	52Wk Range	Yield	P/E
NYS	P	$7.88 (6/29/2018)	9.83-4.13	N/A	N/A

*7 Year Price Score 35.64   *NYSE Composite Index=100   *12 Month Price Score 110.38

TRADING VOLUME (thousand shares)

Interim Earnings (Per Share)

Qtr.	Mar	Jun	Sep	Dec
2015	(0.23)	(0.08)	(0.40)	(0.08)
2016	(0.51)	(0.33)	(0.27)	(0.39)
2017	(0.56)	(1.20)	(0.34)	(0.19)
2018	(0.55)	...	...	...

Interim Dividends (Per Share)

No Dividends Paid

Valuation Analysis — Institutional Holding

Forecast EPS	$-0.48	No of Institutions
	(06/14/2018)	321
Market Cap	$2.0 Billion	Shares
Book Value	$543.5 Million	285,417,024
Price/Book	3.70	% Held
Price/Sales	1.37	98.02

Business Summary: Internet & Software (MIC: 6.3.2 SIC: 4832 NAIC: 515112)

Pandora Media is a music discovery platform providing music through earbuds, car speakers or live on stage. Co. provides local and national advertisers capabilities to deliver targeted messages to its listeners using a combination of audio, display and video advertisements. Co. has two models: Ad-Supported Service, which allows listeners to access Co.'s music and comedy catalogs and personalized playlist generating system; and Subscription Service, which subscription service, Pandora Plus and Pandora One are premium monthly or annual paid versions of the Pandora service, which include ad-free access, higher quality audio on supported devices and longer timeout-free listening.

Recent Developments: For the quarter ended Mar 31 2018, net loss amounted to US$131.7 million versus a net loss of US$132.3 million in the year-earlier quarter. Revenues were US$319.2 million, up 1.0% from US$316.0 million the year before. Operating loss was US$126.9 million versus a loss of US$124.8 million in the prior-year quarter. Direct operating expenses rose 5.6% to US$244.4 million from US$231.6 million in the comparable period the year before. Indirect operating expenses decreased 3.6% to US$201.7 million from US$209.2 million in the equivalent prior-year period.

Prospects: Our evaluation of Pandora Media Inc as of Jan. 21, 2018 is the result of our systematic analysis on three basic characteristics: earnings strength, relative valuation, and recent stock price movement. The company has produced a positive trend in earnings per share over the past 5 quarters. Because the company lacks sufficient analyst estimate data, we place greater weight on the historical EPS trend as the measure of earnings strength. Based on operating earnings yield, the company is overvalued when compared to all of the companies in our coverage universe. Share price changes over the past year indicates that P will perform in line with the market over the near term.

Financial Data
(US$ in Thousands)

	3 Mos	12/31/2017	12/31/2016	12/31/2015	12/31/2014	12/31/2013	01/31/2013	01/31/2012
Earnings Per Share	(2.28)	(2.29)	(1.49)	(0.79)	(0.15)	(0.15)	(0.23)	(0.19)
Cash Flow Per Share	(0.62)	(0.86)	(0.79)	(0.20)	0.10	(0.02)	(0.00)	0.06
Tang Book Value Per Share	1.78	2.20	0.67	1.46	2.76	2.56	0.57	0.64
Income Statement								
Total Revenue	319,233	1,466,812	1,384,826	1,164,043	920,802	600,233	427,145	274,340
EBITDA	(119,067)	(429,550)	(277,562)	(148,611)	(13,322)	(16,365)	(30,603)	(10,975)
Depn & Amortn	5,278	60,300	39,500	22,600	16,500	10,100	7,100	4,500
Income Before Taxes	(131,631)	(519,185)	(343,206)	(171,211)	(29,822)	(26,923)	(38,143)	(16,032)
Income Taxes	74	(790)	(228)	(1,550)	584	94	5	75
Net Income	(131,705)	(518,395)	(342,978)	(169,661)	(30,406)	(27,017)	(38,148)	(16,107)
Average Shares	252,934	243,637	230,693	213,790	205,273	180,968	168,294	105,955
Balance Sheet								
Current Assets	869,964	912,164	625,821	683,506	588,414	518,783	198,614	160,125
Total Assets	1,084,870	1,166,322	1,184,810	1,240,657	749,290	673,335	218,832	178,015
Current Liabilities	240,260	226,281	254,117	231,831	149,160	156,006	115,970	70,907
Long-Term Obligations	278,410	273,014	342,247	234,577	...	...	...	...
Total Liabilities	541,384	522,795	630,551	497,270	165,933	165,104	119,843	73,475
Stockholders' Equity	543,486	643,527	554,259	743,387	583,357	508,231	98,989	104,540
Shares Outstanding	255,044	250,867	235,162	224,970	209,071	195,395	172,506	163,569
Statistical Record								
Asset Turnover	1.35	1.25	1.14	1.17	1.29	1.54	2.15	...
Current Ratio	3.62	4.03	2.46	2.95	3.94	3.33	1.71	2.26
Debt to Equity	0.51	0.42	0.62	0.32	...	...	...	...
Price Range	11.98-4.13	13.58-4.49	14.77-7.88	21.98-11.51	39.43-16.90	31.56-11.36	14.66-7.18	20.04-9.79

Address: 2101 Webster Street, Suite 1650, Oakland, CA 94612 **Telephone:** 510-451-4100 **Fax:** 510-451-4286	**Web Site:** www.pandora.com **Officers:** Roger J. Lynch - President, Chief Executive Officer David Gerbitz - Executive Vice President	**Auditors:** Ernst & Young LLP **Investor Contact:** 510-451-4100 **Transfer Agents:** Computershare Trust Company, N.A.

PBF ENERGY INC

Exchange	Symbol	Price	52Wk Range	Yield	P/E
NYS	PBF	$41.93 (6/29/2018)	50.57-19.95	2.86	9.82

*7 Year Price Score N/A ***NYSE Composite Index=100** ***12 Month Price Score 137.12**

Interim Earnings (Per Share)

Qtr.	Mar	Jun	Sep	Dec
2015	1.00	1.57	0.49	(1.41)
2016	(0.30)	1.06	0.43	0.55
2017	(0.29)	(1.01)	2.85	2.16
2018	0.27	...	...	...

Interim Dividends (Per Share)

Amt	Decl	Ex	Rec	Pay
0.30Q	08/03/2017	08/11/2017	08/15/2017	08/31/2017
0.30Q	11/02/2017	11/10/2017	11/13/2017	11/29/2017
0.30Q	02/15/2018	02/27/2018	02/28/2018	03/14/2018
0.30Q	05/03/2018	05/14/2018	05/15/2018	05/30/2018

Indicated Div: $1.20

Valuation Analysis

		Institutional Holding	
Forecast EPS	$2.72	No of Institutions	
	(06/14/2018)	390	
Market Cap	$4.7 Billion	Shares	
Book Value	$2.3 Billion	122,138,848	
Price/Book	1.98	% Held	
Price/Sales	0.20	102.03	

Business Summary: Refining & Marketing (MIC: 9.1.2 SIC: 2911 NAIC: 324110)

PBF Energy is a holding company. Through its subsidiaries, Co. is engaged as an independent petroleum refiner and supplier of unbranded transportation fuels, heating oil, petrochemical feedstocks, lubricants and other petroleum products in the U.S. Co. operates in two business segments: refining, which Co. produces a variety of products at each of its refineries such as gasoline, ultra-low-sulfur diesel, heating oil, jet fuel, lubricants, petrochemicals and asphalt; and logistics, which through its PBF Logistics LP subsidiary, Co. owns or leases, operates, develops and acquires crude oil and refined petroleum products terminals, pipelines, storage facilities and similar logistics assets.

Recent Developments: For the quarter ended Mar 31 2018, net income amounted to US$41.8 million versus a net loss of US$20.0 million in the year-earlier quarter. Revenues were US$5.80 billion, up 22.0% from US$4.75 billion the year before. Operating income was US$95.7 million versus US$795,000 in the prior-year quarter, an increase of. Direct operating expenses rose 19.8% to US$5.64 billion from US$4.71 billion in the comparable period the year before. Indirect operating expenses increased 41.2% to US$65.6 million from US$46.5 million in the equivalent prior-year period.

Prospects: Our evaluation of PBF Energy Inc as of Jan. 21, 2018 is the result of our systematic analysis on three basic characteristics: earnings strength, relative valuation, and recent stock price movement. The company has enjoyed a very positive trend in earnings per share over the past 5 quarters. However, while recent estimates for the company have been mixed, PBF has posted better than expected results. Based on operating earnings yield, the company is undervalued when compared to all of the companies in our coverage universe. Share price changes over the past year indicates that PBF will perform well over the near term.

Financial Data

(US$ in Thousands)	3 Mos	12/31/2017	12/31/2016	12/31/2015	12/31/2014	12/31/2013	12/31/2012
Earnings Per Share	4.27	3.73	1.74	1.65	(0.51)	1.20	0.08
Cash Flow Per Share	6.91	6.25	6.61	6.36	6.13	8.97	34.47
Tang Book Value Per Share	21.15	21.13	18.54	16.84	14.86	16.47	17.76
Dividends Per Share	1.200	1.200	1.200	1.200	1.200	1.200	...
Dividend Payout %	28.10	32.17	68.97	72.73	...	100.00	...
Income Statement							
Total Revenue	5,802,776	21,786,637	15,920,424	13,123,929	19,828,155	19,151,455	20,138,687
EBITDA	183,944	1,100,420	629,842	483,226	269,542	403,963	978,888
Depn & Amortn	87,993	146,978	116,629	94,781	114,919	79,413	64,947
Income Before Taxes	52,753	799,015	363,168	282,258	55,859	230,766	805,312
Income Taxes	10,942	315,584	137,650	86,725	(22,412)	16,681	1,275
Net Income	30,366	415,517	170,811	146,401	(38,237)	39,540	1,956
Average Shares	115,193	113,898	103,606	94,138	74,464	33,061	97,230
Balance Sheet							
Current Assets	3,861,735	3,802,959	3,407,255	3,022,011	2,346,671	2,200,506	2,307,904
Total Assets	8,282,363	8,117,993	7,621,927	6,105,124	5,196,288	4,413,808	4,253,702
Current Liabilities	2,577,690	2,418,946	2,056,547	1,495,506	1,542,822	1,644,510	1,603,074
Long-Term Obligations	2,165,604	2,175,042	2,108,570	1,840,355	1,260,349	735,547	729,980
Total Liabilities	5,932,482	5,781,339	5,596,883	4,457,827	3,978,075	3,759,678	3,833,948
Stockholders' Equity	2,349,881	2,336,654	2,025,044	1,647,297	1,218,213	654,130	419,754
Shares Outstanding	111,119	110,565	109,204	97,781	81,981	39,665	23,571
Statistical Record							
Return on Assets %	6.04	5.28	2.48	2.59	N.M.	0.91	...
Return on Equity %	22.10	19.05	9.28	10.22	N.M.	7.36	...
EBITDA Margin %	3.17	5.05	3.96	3.68	1.36	2.11	4.86
Net Margin %	0.52	1.91	1.07	1.12	N.M.	0.21	0.01
Asset Turnover	2.89	2.77	2.31	2.32	4.13	4.42	...
Current Ratio	1.50	1.57	1.66	2.02	1.52	1.34	1.44
Debt to Equity	0.92	0.93	1.04	1.12	1.03	1.12	1.74
Price Range	36.36-19.32	35.59-19.32	37.67-19.82	41.48-22.95	32.24-22.12	41.98-20.98	29.05-26.25
P/E Ratio	8.52-4.52	9.54-5.18	21.65-11.39	25.14-13.91	...	34.98-17.48	363.13-328.13
Average Yield %	4.46	4.85	4.46	3.91	4.42	4.18	...

Address: One Sylvan Way, Second Floor, Parsippany, NJ 07054	**Web Site:** www.pbfenergy.com		**Auditors:** DELOITTE & TOUCHE LLP
Telephone: 973-455-7500	**Officers:** Thomas J. Nimbley - Chairman, Chief Executive Officer Matthew C. Lucey - President, Executive Vice President, Senior Vice President, Chief Financial Officer, Vice President		**Investor Contact:** 973-455-7578 **Transfer Agents:** American Stock Transfer & Trust Company, Brooklyn, NY

PARAMOUNT GROUP INC

Exchange	Symbol	Price	52Wk Range	Yield	P/E
NYS	PGRE	$15.40 (6/29/2018)	16.60-13.86	2.60	41.62

*7 Year Price Score N/A   ***NYSE Composite Index=100**   ***12 Month Price Score 96.80**

Interim Earnings (Per Share)
Qtr.	Mar	Jun	Sep	Dec
2015	(0.05)	(0.02)	0.01	0.04
2016	(0.03)	0.01	0.00	(0.03)
2017	0.00	0.44	(0.04)	(0.03)
2018	0.00	...	...	...

Interim Dividends (Per Share)
Amt	Decl	Ex	Rec	Pay
0.095Q	09/15/2017	09/28/2017	09/29/2017	10/13/2017
0.095Q	12/15/2017	12/28/2017	12/29/2017	01/12/2018
0.10Q	03/15/2018	03/28/2018	03/29/2018	04/13/2018
0.10Q	06/15/2018	06/28/2018	06/29/2018	07/13/2018

Indicated Div: $0.40

Valuation Analysis
		Institutional Holding	
Forecast EPS	$0.07 (06/13/2018)	No of Institutions	205
Market Cap	$3.7 Billion	Shares	
Book Value	$4.2 Billion	180,254,592	
Price/Book	0.89	% Held	
Price/Sales	5.13	N/A	

Business Summary: REITs (MIC: 5.3.1 SIC: 6798 NAIC: 525930)

Paramount Group is a real estate investment trust focused on owning, operating, managing, acquiring and redeveloping Class A office properties in select central business district submarkets of New York City, Washington, D.C. and San Francisco. Co. conducts its business through, and substantially all its interests in properties and investments are held by, Paramount Group Operating Partnership LP, a Delaware limited partnership (the Operating Partnership). Co. is the sole general partner of, and owned approximately 90.7% of, the Operating Partnership as of Dec 31 2017. As of Dec 31 2017, Co.'s portfolio consisted of 14 Class A office properties.

Recent Developments: For the quarter ended Mar 31 2018, net income increased 66.7% to US$2.7 million from US$1.6 million in the year-earlier quarter. Revenues were US$184.3 million, up 1.7% from US$181.2 million the year before.

Prospects: Our evaluation of Paramount Group Inc as of Jan. 21, 2018 is the result of our systematic analysis on three basic characteristics: earnings strength, relative valuation, and recent stock price movement. The company has produced a positive trend in earnings per share over the past 5 quarters. However, while recent estimates for the company have been mixed, PGRE has posted results that fell short of analysts expectations. Based on operating earnings yield, the company is overvalued when compared to all of the companies in our coverage universe. Share price changes over the past year indicates that PGRE will perform well over the near term.

Financial Data
(US$ in Thousands)	3 Mos	12/31/2017	12/31/2016	12/31/2015	12/31/2014	11/23/2014	12/31/2013	12/31/2012
Earnings Per Share	0.37	0.37	(0.05)	(0.02)	0.27	...	...	...
Cash Flow Per Share	0.87	0.80	0.66	(0.08)	(3.65)	...	...	...
Tang Book Value Per Share	15.92	15.91	15.55	15.32	15.28	...	...	...
Dividends Per Share	0.385	0.380	0.380	0.419	...	...	...	...
Dividend Payout %	104.05	102.70	...	...	...	...	...	...
Income Statement								
Total Revenue	184,271	718,967	683,341	662,408	66,135	227,389	419,890	246,815
EBITDA	52,642	341,162	249,601	319,807	134,409	164,557	345,606	191,228
Depn & Amortn	15,293	76,016	94,935	128,603	17,260	10,592	11,016	10,538
Income Before Taxes	3,192	112,353	3,854	23,709	73,227	127,859	313,868	146,722
Income Taxes	477	5,177	1,785	2,566	505	18,461	11,029	6,984
Net Income	1,114	86,381	(9,934)	(4,419)	57,308	21,510	16,514	2,295
Average Shares	240,338	236,401	218,053	212,106	212,107	...	...	...
Balance Sheet								
Current Assets	522,357	517,372	393,678	295,864	530,445	...	359,763	350,514
Total Assets	8,973,868	8,917,661	8,867,168	8,794,143	9,030,441	...	2,922,691	2,611,727
Current Liabilities	155,924	170,140	156,346	200,758	162,966	...	11,419	3,707
Long-Term Obligations	3,560,230	3,541,300	3,594,898	2,961,524	2,852,287	...	499,859	517,494
Total Liabilities	4,811,429	4,740,920	4,877,163	5,033,126	5,119,579	...	2,600,922	2,191,232
Stockholders' Equity	4,162,439	4,176,741	3,990,005	3,761,017	3,910,862	...	321,769	420,495
Shares Outstanding	240,505	240,427	230,015	212,112	212,106	...	...	...
Statistical Record								
Return on Assets %	0.98	0.97	N.M.	N.M.	9.21	...	0.60	...
Return on Equity %	2.14	2.12	N.M.	N.M.	26.01	...	4.45	...
EBITDA Margin %	28.57	47.45	36.53	48.28	203.23	72.37	82.31	77.48
Net Margin %	0.60	12.01	N.M.	N.M.	86.65	9.46	3.93	0.93
Asset Turnover	0.08	0.08	0.08	0.07	0.11	...	0.15	...
Current Ratio	3.35	3.04	2.52	1.47	3.25	...	31.51	94.55
Debt to Equity	0.86	0.85	0.90	0.79	0.73	...	1.55	1.23
Price Range	17.21-13.86	17.52-15.23	18.25-14.38	19.75-15.72	18.80-18.06	18.43-18.15	...	...
P/E Ratio	46.51-37.46	47.35-41.16	...	...	69.63-66.89	...	...	...
Average Yield %	2.45	2.35	2.33	2.31	...	...	...	...

Address: 1633 Broadway, Suite 1801, New York, NY 10019 **Telephone:** 212-237-3100	**Web Site:** www.paramount-group.com **Officers:** Albert P. Behler - Chairman, President, Chief Executive Officer Wilbur N. Paes - Chief Financial Officer, Executive Vice President, Treasurer, Senior Vice President, Chief Accounting Officer	**Auditors:** Deloitte & Touche LLP **Transfer Agents:** Computershare Trust Company, N.A.

PARKER HANNIFIN CORP

Exchange	Symbol	Price	52Wk Range	Yield	P/E
NYS	PH	$155.85 (6/29/2018)	210.94-153.96	1.95	21.15

*7 Year Price Score 120.64 *NYSE Composite Index=100   *12 Month Price Score 94.79

Interim Earnings (Per Share)

Qtr.	Sep	Dec	Mar	Jun
2014-15	1.85	1.80	2.02	1.29
2015-16	1.41	1.33	1.37	1.77
2016-17	1.55	1.78	1.75	2.16
2017-18	2.10	0.41	2.70	...

Interim Dividends (Per Share)

Amt	Decl	Ex	Rec	Pay
0.66Q	08/17/2017	08/24/2017	08/28/2017	09/08/2017
0.66Q	10/25/2017	11/09/2017	11/10/2017	12/01/2017
0.66Q	01/25/2018	02/08/2018	02/09/2018	03/02/2018
0.76Q	04/19/2018	05/09/2018	05/10/2018	06/01/2018

Indicated Div: $3.04 (Div. Reinv. Plan)

Valuation Analysis

		Institutional Holding	
Forecast EPS	$10.09 (06/14/2018)	No of Institutions	1029
Market Cap	$20.7 Billion	Shares	130,462,840
Book Value	$5.9 Billion	% Held	75.82
Price/Book	3.53		
Price/Sales	1.48		

TRADING VOLUME (thousand shares)

Business Summary: Industrial Machinery & Equipment (MIC: 7.2.1 SIC: 3492 NAIC: 332912)

Parker Hannifin is a manufacturer of motion and control technologies and systems, providing engineered solutions for a variety of mobile, industrial and aerospace markets. Co. has two reporting segments: Diversified Industrial and Aerospace Systems. Co.'s Diversified Industrial segment consist of a range of motion-control and fluid systems and components, which are categorized into the following groups: Engineered Materials, Filtration, Fluid Connectors, Motion Systems, and Instrumentation. The principal products of Co.'s Aerospace Systems Segment are used on commercial and military airframe and engine programs and include control actuation systems and components.

Recent Developments: For the quarter ended Mar 31 2018, net income increased 53.3% to US$366.1 million from US$238.8 million in the year-earlier quarter. Revenues were US$3.75 billion, up 20.2% from US$3.12 billion the year before. Direct operating expenses rose 18.5% to US$2.83 billion from US$2.38 billion in the comparable period the year before. Indirect operating expenses increased 7.3% to US$420.6 million from US$392.0 million in the equivalent prior-year period.

Prospects: Our evaluation of Parker Hannifin Corp. as of Jan. 21, 2018 is the result of our systematic analysis on three basic characteristics: earnings strength, relative valuation, and recent stock price movement. The company has managed to produce a neutral trend in earnings per share over the past 5 quarters and while recent estimates for the company have been raised by analysts, PH has posted better than expected results. Based on operating earnings yield, the company is about fairly valued when compared to all of the companies in our coverage universe. Share price changes over the past year indicates that PH will perform well over the near term.

Financial Data
(US$ in Thousands)	9 Mos	6 Mos	3 Mos	06/30/2017	06/30/2016	06/30/2015	06/30/2014	06/30/2013
Earnings Per Share	7.37	6.42	7.79	7.25	5.89	6.97	6.87	6.26
Cash Flow Per Share	10.66	10.21	10.72	9.77	8.62	9.11	9.31	7.98
Tang Book Value Per Share	N.M.	N.M.	N.M.	N.M.	5.59	8.29	15.44	8.20
Dividends Per Share	2.640	2.640	2.610	2.580	2.520	2.370	1.860	1.700
Dividend Payout %	35.82	41.12	33.50	35.59	42.78	34.00	27.07	27.16
Income Statement								
Total Revenue	10,484,915	6,735,324	3,364,651	12,029,312	11,360,753	12,711,744	13,215,971	13,015,704
EBITDA	1,716,499	1,075,427	543,964	1,693,945	1,441,553	1,753,422	1,854,251	1,616,275
Depn & Amortn	351,316	234,216	116,107	202,868	190,308	202,776	214,965	213,722
Income Before Taxes	1,204,350	734,523	374,302	1,328,641	1,114,728	1,432,240	1,556,720	1,311,001
Income Taxes	496,363	392,666	88,767	344,797	307,512	419,687	515,302	362,217
Net Income	707,545	341,556	285,397	983,412	806,840	1,012,140	1,041,048	948,427
Average Shares	135,768	136,194	135,794	135,559	136,911	145,112	151,444	151,588
Balance Sheet								
Current Assets	5,563,096	5,286,359	5,004,618	4,779,718	5,207,787	5,583,092	6,071,580	5,531,186
Total Assets	16,237,484	15,965,181	15,731,279	15,489,904	12,056,738	12,295,037	13,274,362	12,540,898
Current Liabilities	3,508,517	3,537,703	3,467,124	3,395,860	2,365,941	2,350,130	3,252,796	3,520,203
Long-Term Obligations	4,818,570	4,798,371	4,788,147	4,861,895	2,675,000	2,723,960	1,508,142	1,495,960
Total Liabilities	10,367,131	10,451,780	10,206,339	10,228,255	7,481,483	7,190,750	6,614,934	6,802,472
Stockholders' Equity	5,870,353	5,513,401	5,524,940	5,261,649	4,575,255	5,104,287	6,659,428	5,738,426
Shares Outstanding	132,959	133,048	133,226	133,191	134,012	138,558	148,902	149,288
Statistical Record								
Return on Assets %	6.34	6.31	7.64	7.14	6.61	7.92	8.07	8.00
Return on Equity %	18.86	17.40	20.82	19.99	16.63	17.21	16.79	17.84
EBITDA Margin %	16.37	15.97	16.17	14.08	12.69	13.79	14.03	12.42
Net Margin %	6.75	5.07	8.48	8.18	7.10	7.96	7.88	7.29
Asset Turnover	0.89	0.96	0.91	0.87	0.93	0.99	1.02	1.10
Current Ratio	1.59	1.49	1.44	1.41	2.20	2.38	1.87	1.57
Debt to Equity	0.82	0.87	0.87	0.92	0.58	0.53	0.23	0.26
Price Range	210.94-152.29	199.69-140.78	177.11-119.29	165.22-107.07	117.15-86.51	132.78-102.96	129.52-95.32	100.96-71.84
P/E Ratio	28.62-20.66	31.10-21.93	22.74-15.31	22.79-14.77	19.89-14.69	19.05-14.77	18.85-13.87	16.13-11.48
Average Yield %	1.51	1.60	1.72	1.84	2.38	1.96	1.61	1.95

Address: 6035 Parkland Boulevard, Cleveland, OH 44124-4141	Web Site: www.parker.com	Auditors: DELOITTE & TOUCHE LLP
Telephone: 216-896-3000	Officers: Thomas L. Williams - Chairman, Chief Executive Officer, Executive Vice President Lee C. Banks - President, Chief Operating Officer, Executive Vice President	Investor Contact: 216-896-2240 Transfer Agents: Wells Fargo Bank, N.A., St. Paul, MN

PARSLEY ENERGY INC

Exchange	Symbol	Price	52Wk Range	Yield	P/E
NYS	PE	$30.28 (6/29/2018)	32.84-21.74	N/A	48.84

'7 Year Price Score N/A **'NYSE Composite Index=100** **'12 Month Price Score 107.90**

TRADING VOLUME (thousand shares)

Interim Earnings (Per Share)

Qtr.	Mar	Jun	Sep	Dec
2015	(0.17)	(0.18)	0.01	(0.12)
2016	(0.14)	(0.13)	(0.02)	(0.18)
2017	0.13	0.17	(0.05)	0.18
2018	0.32	...	...	...

Interim Dividends (Per Share)

No Dividends Paid

Valuation Analysis

		Institutional Holding	
Forecast EPS	$1.59	No of Institutions	
	(06/13/2018)	417	
Market Cap	$10.0 Billion	Shares	
Book Value	$5.0 Billion	284,048,320	
Price/Book	1.99	% Held	
Price/Sales	8.63	N/A	

Business Summary: Production & Extraction (MIC: 9.1.1 SIC: 1311 NAIC: 211111)

Parsley Energy is a holding company. Co. is an independent oil and natural gas company focused on the acquisition and development of unconventional oil and natural gas reserves in the Permian Basin. The Permian Basin is located in West Texas and Southeastern New Mexico and is comprised of three primary sub-areas: the Midland Basin, the Central Basin Platform and the Delaware Basin. Co.'s properties are located in the Midland and Delaware Basins, where Co. focuses on horizontal development drilling. As of Dec 31 2017, Co.'s estimated proved reserves consisted of 248.5 million barrels (MMBbls) of oil, 451.7 billion cubic feet of natural gas, and 92.6 MMBbls of natural gas liquids.

Recent Developments: For the quarter ended Mar 31 2018, net income increased 175.4% to US$105.5 million from US$38.3 million in the year-earlier quarter. Revenues were US$392.7 million, up 95.5% from US$200.9 million the year before. Operating income was US$169.3 million versus US$72.5 million in the prior-year quarter, an increase of 133.4%. Direct operating expenses rose 105.9% to US$59.3 million from US$28.8 million in the comparable period the year before. Indirect operating expenses increased 64.9% to US$164.1 million from US$99.5 million in the equivalent prior-year period.

Prospects: Our evaluation of Parsley Energy Inc as of Jan. 21, 2018 is the result of our systematic analysis on three basic characteristics: earnings strength, relative valuation, and recent stock price movement. The company has suffered a very negative trend in earnings per share over the past 5 quarters and while recent estimates for the company have been raised by analysts, PE has posted better than expected results. Based on operating earnings yield, the company is overvalued when compared to all of the companies in our coverage universe. Share price changes over the past year indicates that PE will perform very poorly over the near term.

Financial Data
(US$ in Thousands)

	3 Mos	12/31/2017	12/31/2016	12/31/2015	12/31/2014	12/31/2013	12/31/2012	12/31/2011
Earnings Per Share	0.62	0.42	(0.46)	(0.45)	0.42	...	...	...
Cash Flow Per Share	3.37	2.88	1.41	1.55	3.36	...	...	...
Tang Book Value Per Share	15.24	14.99	10.07	7.49	5.61	...	...	...
Income Statement								
Total Revenue	392,741	967,044	457,773	266,057	301,757	121,018	37,679	10,834
EBITDA	277,293	559,873	176,092	122,395	132,949	44,046	19,571	12,358
Depn & Amortn	118,660	340,800	227,200	173,600	1,500	1,100	100	100
Income Before Taxes	128,788	129,628	(106,341)	(96,786)	92,842	29,232	13,186	11,800
Income Taxes	23,325	5,708	(17,424)	(23,755)	36,468	1,906	554	116
Net Income	82,890	106,774	(74,182)	(50,484)	23,429	27,510	12,899	11,820
Average Shares	261,639	296,512	161,793	111,271	55,239	...	...	...
Balance Sheet								
Current Assets	750,046	919,486	299,488	488,326	204,161	137,326	49,078	...
Total Assets	8,940,648	8,793,198	3,938,782	2,514,192	2,051,079	742,556	181,239	...
Current Liabilities	624,628	612,089	344,954	228,947	220,865	191,497	59,059	...
Long-Term Obligations	2,179,996	2,179,525	1,041,324	555,924	676,845	429,970	112,913	...
Total Liabilities	3,906,584	4,080,903	1,849,144	1,249,700	1,343,838	634,524	175,222	...
Stockholders' Equity	5,034,064	4,712,295	2,089,638	1,264,492	707,241	108,032	6,017	...
Shares Outstanding	330,240	314,388	207,599	168,768	126,046	...	...	...
Statistical Record								
Return on Assets %	2.05	1.68	N.M.	N.M.	1.68	5.96	...	...
Return on Equity %	3.51	3.14	N.M.	N.M.	5.75	48.24	...	...
EBITDA Margin %	70.60	57.90	38.47	46.00	44.06	36.40	51.94	114.07
Net Margin %	21.11	11.04	N.M.	N.M.	7.76	22.73	34.23	109.10
Asset Turnover	0.15	0.15	0.14	0.12	0.22	0.26	...	...
Current Ratio	1.20	1.50	0.87	2.14	0.92	0.72	0.83	...
Debt to Equity	0.43	0.46	0.50	0.44	0.96	3.98	18.77	...
Price Range	32.51-21.74	36.88-23.86	38.27-15.66	19.82-13.50	25.16-11.26	...	...	...
P/E Ratio	52.44-35.06	87.81-56.81	...	...	59.90-26.81	...	...	...

Address: 303 Colorado Street, Suite 3000, Austin, TX 78701 **Telephone:** 737-704-2300	**Web Site:** www.parsleyenergy.com **Officers:** Bryan Sheffield - Chairman, President, Chief Executive Officer Matthew (Matt) Gallagher - Vice President, Chief Operating Officer, President, Chief Executive Officer	**Auditors:** KPMG LLP **Transfer Agents:** American Stock Transfer & Trust Company, LLC

PENNEY (J.C.) CO.,INC. (HOLDING CO.)

Exchange	Symbol	Price	52Wk Range	Yield	P/E
NYS	JCP	$2.34 (6/29/2018)	5.56-2.30	N/A	N/A

*7 Year Price Score 22.05 *NYSE Composite Index=100 ***12 Month Price Score 74.57**

Interim Earnings (Per Share)

Qtr.	Apr	Jul	Oct	Jan
2015-16	(0.55)	(0.45)	(0.45)	(0.23)
2016-17	(0.22)	(0.18)	(0.22)	0.62
2017-18	(0.58)	(0.20)	(0.41)	0.82
2018-19	(0.25)	...	...	...

Interim Dividends (Per Share)

Dividend Payment Suspended

Valuation Analysis / Institutional Holding

Forecast EPS	$0.05	No of Institutions	
	(06/06/2018)	518	
Market Cap	$735.5 Million	Shares	
Book Value	$1.3 Billion	296,995,744	
Price/Book	0.56	% Held	
Price/Sales	0.06	63.32	

Business Summary: Retail - General Merchandise/Department Stores (MIC: 2.1.1 SIC: 5311 NAIC: 452111)

J.C. Penney Company is a holding company whose principal operating subsidiary is J. C. Penney Corporation, Inc. Co.'s business consists of selling merchandise and services to consumers through its department stores and its website at jcpenney.com. Co. sells family apparel and footwear, accessories, fine and fashion jewelry, beauty products through Sephora inside JCPenney and home furnishings. In addition, Co.'s department stores provide its customers with services such as styling salon, optical, portrait photography and custom decorating. As of Feb 3 2018, Co. operated 872 department stores in 49 states and Puerto Rico.

Recent Developments: For the quarter ended May 5 2018, net loss amounted to US$78.0 million versus a net loss of US$187.0 million in the year-earlier quarter. Revenues were US$2.67 billion, down 4.1% from US$2.78 billion the year before. Operating income was US$3.0 million versus a loss of US$6.0 million in the prior-year quarter. Direct operating expenses declined 0.8% to US$1.71 billion from US$1.73 billion in the comparable period the year before. Indirect operating expenses decreased 10.2% to US$956.0 million from US$1.07 billion in the equivalent prior-year period.

Prospects: Our evaluation of Penney (J.C.) Co.,Inc. as of Jan. 21, 2018 is the result of our systematic analysis on three basic characteristics: earnings strength, relative valuation, and recent stock price movement. The company has suffered a very negative trend in earnings per share over the past 5 quarters and while recent estimates for the company have been raised by analysts, JCP has posted better than expected results. Based on operating earnings yield, the company is undervalued when compared to all of the companies in our coverage universe. Share price changes over the past year indicates that JCP will perform very poorly over the near term.

Financial Data
(US$ in Thousands)

	3 Mos	02/03/2018	01/28/2017	01/30/2016	01/31/2015	02/01/2014	02/02/2013	01/28/2012
Earnings Per Share	(0.04)	(0.37)	...	(1.68)	(2.53)	(5.57)	(4.49)	(0.70)
Cash Flow Per Share	1.42	1.44	1.09	1.44	0.79	(7.30)	(0.04)	3.78
Tang Book Value Per Share	4.18	2.58	2.64	2.64	4.64	8.38	11.78	15.96
Dividends Per Share	...	...	...	...	...	...	0.200	0.800
Income Statement								
Total Revenue	2,671,000	12,506,000	12,547,000	12,625,000	12,257,000	11,859,000	12,985,000	17,260,000
EBITDA	140,000	653,000	974,000	517,000	289,000	(933,000)	(767,000)	516,000
Depn & Amortn	141,000	570,000	609,000	616,000	631,000	601,000	543,000	518,000
Income Before Taxes	(79,000)	(242,000)	2,000	(504,000)	(748,000)	(1,886,000)	(1,536,000)	(229,000)
Income Taxes	(1,000)	(126,000)	1,000	9,000	23,000	(498,000)	(551,000)	(77,000)
Net Income	(78,000)	(116,000)	1,000	(513,000)	(771,000)	(1,388,000)	(985,000)	(152,000)
Average Shares	313,900	311,100	313,000	305,900	305,200	249,300	219,200	217,400
Balance Sheet								
Current Assets	3,352,000	3,410,000	4,097,000	4,018,000	4,331,000	4,833,000	3,683,000	5,081,000
Total Assets	8,305,000	8,413,000	9,314,000	9,442,000	10,404,000	11,801,000	9,781,000	11,424,000
Current Liabilities	1,939,000	2,332,000	2,419,000	2,412,000	2,241,000	2,846,000	2,583,000	2,756,000
Long-Term Obligations	4,352,000	3,992,000	4,558,000	4,678,000	5,360,000	4,901,000	2,956,000	2,871,000
Total Liabilities	6,990,000	7,034,000	7,960,000	8,133,000	8,490,000	8,714,000	6,610,000	7,414,000
Stockholders' Equity	1,315,000	1,379,000	1,354,000	1,309,000	1,914,000	3,087,000	3,171,000	4,010,000
Shares Outstanding	314,300	312,000	308,300	306,100	304,900	304,600	219,300	215,900
Statistical Record								
Return on Assets %	N.M.	N.M.	0.01	N.M.	N.M.	N.M.	N.M.	N.M.
Return on Equity %	N.M.	N.M.	0.08	N.M.	N.M.	N.M.	N.M.	N.M.
EBITDA Margin %	5.24	5.22	7.76	4.10	2.36	N.M.	N.M.	2.99
Net Margin %	N.M.	N.M.	0.01	N.M.	N.M.	N.M.	N.M.	N.M.
Asset Turnover	1.48	1.39	1.34	1.28	1.11	1.10	1.20	1.41
Current Ratio	1.73	1.46	1.69	1.67	1.93	1.70	1.43	1.84
Debt to Equity	3.31	2.89	3.37	3.57	2.80	1.59	0.93	0.72
Price Range	5.71-2.37	7.31-2.37	11.86-6.45	9.98-6.31	11.20-5.08	22.47-5.77	43.13-16.28	41.42-23.81
Average Yield %	...	...	...	...	...	...	0.74	2.43

Address: 6501 Legacy Drive, Plano, TX 75024-3698 **Telephone:** 972-431-1000	**Web Site:** www.jcpenney.com **Officers:** Ronald W. Tysoe - Chairman Jeffrey A. Davis - Executive Vice President, Chief Financial Officer	**Auditors:** KPMG LLP **Investor Contact:** 972-431-5500 **Transfer Agents:** ComputerShare Investor Services, Providence, RI

PENTAIR PLC

Exchange	Symbol	Price	52Wk Range	Yield	P/E
NYS	PNR	$42.08 (6/29/2018)	49.78-40.79	1.66	11.34

*7 Year Price Score 93.69 *NYSE Composite Index=100 *12 Month Price Score 95.97

Interim Earnings (Per Share)

Qtr.	Mar	Jun	Sep	Dec
2015	0.62	0.81	0.63	(2.48)
2016	0.59	0.78	0.77	0.71
2017	0.48	1.43	0.68	1.03
2018	0.57	...	...	...

Interim Dividends (Per Share)

Amt	Decl	Ex	Rec	Pay
0.345Q	05/09/2017	07/19/2017	07/21/2017	08/04/2017
0.345Q	09/19/2017	10/19/2017	10/20/2017	11/03/2017
0.35Q	12/05/2017	01/25/2018	01/26/2018	02/09/2018
0.175Q	05/08/2018	07/19/2018	07/20/2018	08/03/2018

Indicated Div: $0.70

Valuation Analysis

		Institutional Holding	
Forecast EPS	N/A	No of Institutions	754
Market Cap	$7.5 Billion	Shares	174,074,704
Book Value	$4.7 Billion	% Held	
Price/Book	1.59	N/A	
Price/Sales	1.49		

TRADING VOLUME (thousand shares)

Business Summary: Industrial Machinery & Equipment (MIC: 7.2.1 SIC: 3559 NAIC: 333298)

Pentair is an industrial manufacturing company. Co. has three segments: Water Quality Systems, which designs, manufactures, markets and services water system products for filtration and fluid management in food and beverage, water, swimming pools and aquaculture applications; Flow & Filtration Solutions, which designs, manufactures, markets and services solutions for the filtration, separation, flow and fluid management in agriculture, food and beverage processing, water supply and disposal and industrial applications; and Technical Solutions, which designs, manufactures, markets and services products that guard and protect electrical and electronic equipment, and heat management solutions.

Recent Developments: For the quarter ended Mar 31 2018, income from continuing operations increased 29.1% to US$104.2 million from US$80.7 million in the year-earlier quarter. Net income increased 17.2% to US$102.9 million from US$87.8 million in the year-earlier quarter. Revenues were US$1.27 billion, up 7.3% from US$1.18 billion the year before. Operating income was US$152.3 million versus US$140.6 million in the prior-year quarter, an increase of 8.3%. Direct operating expenses rose 6.1% to US$807.7 million from US$761.2 million in the comparable period the year before. Indirect operating expenses increased 9.9% to US$309.7 million from US$281.7 million in the equivalent prior-year period.

Prospects: Our evaluation of Pentair PLC as of Sep. 17, 2017 is the result of our systematic analysis on three basic characteristics: earnings strength, relative valuation, and recent stock price movement. The company has enjoyed a very positive trend in earnings per share over the past 5 quarters and while recent estimates for the company have remained steady, PNR has posted results that fell short of analysts expectations. Based on operating earnings yield, the company is undervalued when compared to all of the companies in our coverage universe. Share price changes over the past year indicates that PNR will perform in line with the market over the near term.

Financial Data

(US$ in Thousands)	3 Mos	12/31/2017	12/31/2016	12/31/2015	12/31/2014	12/31/2013	12/31/2012	12/31/2011
Earnings Per Share	3.71	3.63	2.85	(0.42)	1.11	2.62	(0.84)	0.34
Cash Flow Per Share	3.12	3.41	4.74	4.10	5.29	4.55	0.53	3.26
Dividends Per Share	1.385	1.380	1.340	...	...	...	0.880	0.720
Dividend Payout %	37.33	38.02	47.02	...	...	...	...	211.76
Income Statement								
Total Revenue	1,269,700	4,936,500	4,890,000	6,449,000	7,039,000	7,479,700	4,416,146	3,456,686
EBITDA	191,800	660,400	781,400	313,500	990,400	942,600	(30,651)	234,752
Depn & Amortn	46,200	85,200	84,600	139,500	138,700	148,900	87,835	66,235
Income Before Taxes	131,800	487,900	556,700	71,300	783,100	724,600	(186,121)	109,682
Income Taxes	27,600	9,200	109,400	139,100	177,300	183,800	(79,353)	73,059
Net Income	102,900	666,500	522,200	(76,400)	214,900	536,800	(107,186)	34,222
Average Shares	181,500	183,700	183,100	182,600	193,700	204,600	127,368	99,753
Balance Sheet								
Current Assets	2,719,000	1,748,800	2,672,000	2,780,600	2,894,100	3,232,100	3,260,368	1,237,835
Total Assets	9,368,100	8,633,700	11,534,800	11,857,000	10,655,200	11,743,300	11,795,311	4,586,313
Current Liabilities	1,027,500	1,199,400	1,471,200	1,486,500	1,639,500	1,610,200	1,537,921	641,841
Long-Term Obligations	2,673,100	1,440,700	4,278,400	4,709,300	2,997,400	2,552,600	2,454,278	1,304,225
Total Liabilities	4,648,400	3,595,900	7,280,400	7,848,200	5,991,400	5,648,000	5,428,451	2,652,984
Stockholders' Equity	4,719,700	5,037,800	4,254,400	4,008,800	4,663,800	6,095,300	6,366,860	1,933,329
Shares Outstanding	178,386	180,306	181,800	180,500	182,500	228,600	206,137	98,622
Statistical Record								
Return on Assets %	6.43	6.61	4.45	N.M.	1.92	4.56	N.M.	0.80
Return on Equity %	14.99	14.35	12.60	N.M.	3.99	8.61	N.M.	1.70
EBITDA Margin %	15.11	13.38	15.98	4.86	14.07	12.60	N.M.	6.79
Net Margin %	8.10	13.50	10.68	N.M.	3.05	7.18	N.M.	0.99
Asset Turnover	0.47	0.49	0.42	0.57	0.63	0.64	0.54	0.81
Current Ratio	2.65	1.46	1.82	1.87	1.77	2.01	2.12	1.93
Debt to Equity	0.57	0.29	1.01	1.17	0.64	0.42	0.39	0.67
Price Range	49.78-40.79	47.79-37.99	44.84-28.79	46.17-32.37	55.61-40.18	52.16-33.01	33.07-22.91	28.37-20.20
P/E Ratio	13.42-10.99	13.17-10.47	15.73-10.10	...	50.10-36.20	19.91-12.60	...	83.45-59.41
Average Yield %	3.06	3.18	3.51	...	...	...	3.12	2.93

Address: 43 London Wall, London, 55416-1259	**Web Site:** www.pentair.com	**Auditors:** DELOITTE & TOUCHE LLP
Telephone: 207-347-8925	**Officers:** John L. Stauch - Chief Executive Officer, Chief Financial Officer, Executive Vice President Mark C. Borin - Senior Vice President, Chief Financial Officer, Chief Accounting Officer, Treasurer	**Investor Contact:** 763-656-5575 **Transfer Agents:** Wells Fargo

PERFORMANCE FOOD GROUP CO

Exchange	Symbol	Price	52Wk Range	Yield	P/E
NYS	PFGC	$36.70 (6/29/2018)	37.80-25.95	N/A	21.85

*7 Year Price Score N/A   *NYSE Composite Index=100   *12 Month Price Score 113.01

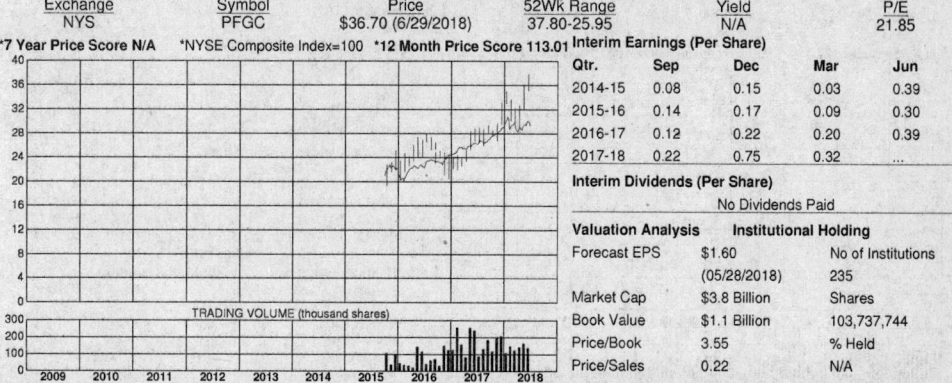

Interim Earnings (Per Share)

Qtr.	Sep	Dec	Mar	Jun
2014-15	0.08	0.15	0.03	0.39
2015-16	0.14	0.17	0.09	0.30
2016-17	0.12	0.22	0.20	0.39
2017-18	0.22	0.75	0.32	...

Interim Dividends (Per Share)

No Dividends Paid

Valuation Analysis   Institutional Holding

Forecast EPS	$1.60	No of Institutions	
	(05/28/2018)	235	
Market Cap	$3.8 Billion	Shares	
Book Value	$1.1 Billion	103,737,744	
Price/Book	3.55	% Held	
Price/Sales	0.22	N/A	

Business Summary: Retail - Food & Beverage, Drug & Tobacco (MIC: 2.1.2 SIC: 5141 NAIC: 445110)

Performance Food Group, through its subsidiaries, markets and distributes approximately 150,000 food and food-related products from 76 distribution centers to over 150,000 customer locations across the U.S. Co.'s products include a line of frozen foods, such as meats, fully prepared appetizers and entrees, fruits, vegetables, and desserts; a line of canned and dry foods; fresh meats; dairy products; beverage products; and imported specialties. Co. also supplies a variety of non-food items including paper products such as pizza boxes, disposable napkins, plates and cups; tableware such as china and silverware; cookware such as pots, pans, and utensils; restaurant; and cleaning supplies.

Recent Developments: For the quarter ended Mar 31 2018, net income increased 62.0% to US$33.7 million from US$20.8 million in the year-earlier quarter. Revenues were US$4.35 billion, up 2.7% from US$4.24 billion the year before. Operating income was US$60.1 million versus US$46.7 million in the prior-year quarter, an increase of 28.7%. Direct operating expenses rose 2.1% to US$3.79 billion from US$3.71 billion in the comparable period the year before. Indirect operating expenses increased 5.0% to US$498.6 million from US$474.7 million in the equivalent prior-year period.

Prospects: Our evaluation of Performance Food Group Company as of Jan. 21, 2018 is the result of our systematic analysis on three basic characteristics: earnings strength, relative valuation, and recent stock price movement. The company has managed to produce a neutral trend in earnings per share over the past 5 quarters and while recent estimates for the company have been raised by analysts, PFGC has posted better than expected results. Based on operating earnings yield, the company is about fairly valued when compared to all of the companies in our coverage universe. Share price changes over the past year indicates that PFGC will perform in line with the market over the near term.

Financial Data
(US$ in Thousands)

	9 Mos	6 Mos	3 Mos	07/01/2017	07/02/2016	06/27/2015	06/28/2014	06/29/2013
Earnings Per Share	1.68	1.56	1.03	0.93	0.70	0.64	0.18	0.10
Cash Flow Per Share	3.21	2.56	2.90	2.02	2.40	1.47	1.38	1.62
Tang Book Value Per Share	1.15	0.67	N.M.	0.06	N.M.	N.M.	N.M.	...
Dividends Per Share	...	...	...	...	...	...	...	2.530
Dividend Payout %	...	...	...	...	...	...	...	2,530.00
Income Statement								
Total Revenue	13,025,200	8,676,000	4,364,900	16,761,800	16,104,800	15,270,000	13,685,700	12,826,500
EBITDA	259,400	166,100	83,400	338,700	317,000	303,600	249,000	233,400
Depn & Amortn	99,400	66,100	32,600	126,100	118,600	121,300	132,700	120,000
Income Before Taxes	115,100	70,300	36,200	157,700	114,500	96,600	30,200	19,500
Income Taxes	(19,200)	(30,300)	13,600	61,400	46,200	40,100	14,700	11,100
Net Income	134,300	100,600	22,600	96,300	68,300	56,500	15,500	8,400
Average Shares	104,500	104,500	103,900	103,036	98,128	87,613	87,533	87,458
Balance Sheet								
Current Assets	2,183,600	2,140,000	2,132,800	2,084,900	1,938,900	1,900,300	1,727,300	...
Total Assets	3,932,500	3,882,600	3,883,300	3,804,100	3,455,400	3,390,900	3,239,800	...
Current Liabilities	1,447,100	1,280,100	1,375,200	1,383,300	1,316,700	1,277,000	1,170,400	...
Long-Term Obligations	1,246,300	1,406,100	1,351,800	1,285,900	1,143,100	1,429,600	1,449,000	...
Total Liabilities	2,871,100	2,867,100	2,933,900	2,878,600	2,652,600	2,897,900	2,805,700	...
Stockholders' Equity	1,061,400	1,015,500	949,400	925,500	802,800	493,000	434,100	...
Shares Outstanding	102,800	102,300	101,000	100,805	99,901	86,878	86,874	...
Statistical Record								
Return on Assets %	4.55	4.31	2.88	2.66	1.96	1.71	...	...
Return on Equity %	17.99	17.31	12.06	11.17	10.37	12.22	...	...
EBITDA Margin %	1.99	1.91	1.91	2.02	1.97	1.99	1.82	1.82
Net Margin %	1.03	1.16	0.52	0.57	0.42	0.37	0.11	0.07
Asset Turnover	4.55	4.61	4.61	4.63	4.63	4.62	...	...
Current Ratio	1.51	1.67	1.55	1.51	1.47	1.49	1.48	...
Debt to Equity	1.17	1.38	1.42	1.39	1.42	2.90	3.34	...
Price Range	35.00-23.30	33.20-21.90	29.40-20.45	28.85-20.45	27.43-19.20	...	...	...
P/E Ratio	20.83-13.87	21.28-14.04	28.54-19.85	31.02-21.99	39.19-27.43	...	...	...

Address: 12500 West Creek Parkway, Richmond, VA 23238 **Telephone:** 804-484-7700	**Web Site:** www.pfgc.com **Officers:** Douglas M. Steenland - Chairman George L. Holm - President, Chief Executive Officer	**Auditors:** DELOITTE & TOUCHE LLP **Transfer Agents:** Computershare Trust Company, N.A.

PERKINELMER, INC.

Exchange	Symbol	Price	52Wk Range	Yield	P/E
NYS	PKI	$73.23 (6/29/2018)	82.75-62.95	0.38	29.18

*7 Year Price Score 127.48 *NYSE Composite Index=100 *12 Month Price Score 101.98

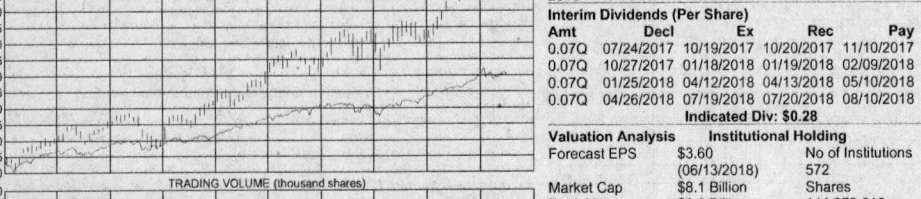

Interim Earnings (Per Share)

Qtr.	Mar	Jun	Sep	Dec
2015	0.36	0.43	0.48	0.60
2016	0.43	0.58	0.53	0.58
2017	0.35	1.84	0.82	(0.38)
2018	0.23	...	...	...

Interim Dividends (Per Share)

Amt	Decl	Ex	Rec	Pay
0.07Q	07/24/2017	10/19/2017	10/20/2017	11/10/2017
0.07Q	10/27/2017	01/18/2018	01/19/2018	02/09/2018
0.07Q	01/25/2018	04/12/2018	04/13/2018	05/10/2018
0.07Q	04/26/2018	07/19/2018	07/20/2018	08/10/2018

Indicated Div: $0.28

Valuation Analysis / Institutional Holding

Forecast EPS	$3.60	No of Institutions	
(06/13/2018)		572	
Market Cap	$8.1 Billion	Shares	
Book Value	$2.6 Billion	144,272,016	
Price/Book	3.17	% Held	
Price/Sales	3.39	88.52	

Business Summary: Biotechnology (MIC: 4.1.2 SIC: 3826 NAIC: 334516)

PerkinElmer is a provider of products, services and solutions to the diagnostics, research, environmental, industrial, food and laboratory services markets. The principal products and services of Co.'s two operating segments are: Diagnostics, which develops diagnostics, tools and applications focused on clinically-oriented customers, particularly within the reproductive health, market diagnostics and applied genomics markets; and Discovery & Analytical Solutions, which provides products and services targeted towards the environmental, industrial, food, life sciences research and laboratory services markets.

Recent Developments: For the quarter ended Apr 1 2018, income from continuing operations decreased 27.8% to US$26.0 million from US$36.1 million in the year-earlier quarter. Net income decreased 32.6% to US$26.0 million from US$38.6 million in the year-earlier quarter. Revenues were US$644.0 million, up 25.3% from US$514.1 million the year before. Operating income was US$39.9 million versus US$49.8 million in the prior-year quarter, a decrease of 19.8%. Direct operating expenses rose 28.2% to US$351.8 million from US$274.4 million in the comparable period the year before. Indirect operating expenses increased 32.8% to US$252.3 million from US$189.9 million in the equivalent prior-year period.

Prospects: Our evaluation of PerkinElmer Inc. as of Jan. 21, 2018 is the result of our systematic analysis on three basic characteristics: earnings strength, relative valuation, and recent stock price movement. The company has enjoyed a very positive trend in earnings per share over the past 5 quarters and while recent estimates for the company have remained steady, PKI has posted better than expected results. Based on operating earnings yield, the company is about fairly valued when compared to all of the companies in our coverage universe. Share price changes over the past year indicates that PKI will perform well over the near term.

Financial Data
(US$ in Thousands)

	3 Mos	12/31/2017	01/01/2017	01/03/2016	12/28/2014	12/29/2013	12/30/2012	01/01/2012
Earnings Per Share	2.51	2.64	2.12	1.87	1.39	1.47	0.61	0.07
Cash Flow Per Share	2.00	2.63	3.21	2.51	2.51	1.42	1.34	2.00
Dividends Per Share	0.280	0.280	0.280	0.280	0.280	0.280	0.280	0.280
Dividend Payout %	11.16	10.61	13.21	14.97	20.14	19.05	45.90	400.00
Income Statement								
Total Revenue	643,972	2,256,982	2,115,517	2,262,359	2,237,219	2,166,232	2,115,205	1,921,287
EBITDA	49,758	369,387	313,394	314,739	238,506	240,706	131,227	118,153
Depn & Amortn	9,823	31,300	28,500	33,400	33,300	38,100	35,600	30,900
Income Before Taxes	28,505	296,718	244,068	244,015	169,603	153,332	50,587	64,354
Income Taxes	2,470	139,828	28,362	31,327	8,437	(14,592)	(17,854)	63,182
Net Income	26,024	292,633	234,299	212,425	157,778	167,212	69,940	7,655
Average Shares	111,330	110,859	110,313	113,315	113,739	113,503	114,860	113,864
Balance Sheet								
Current Assets	1,234,004	1,199,955	1,189,931	1,033,161	1,068,551	1,044,838	971,754	862,218
Total Assets	6,126,186	6,091,463	4,276,683	4,166,295	4,134,075	3,946,712	3,901,762	3,834,198
Current Liabilities	925,984	950,902	603,355	561,485	597,310	602,796	581,100	600,066
Long-Term Obligations	1,859,698	1,788,803	1,045,254	1,011,762	1,051,892	932,104	938,824	944,908
Total Liabilities	3,570,934	3,588,275	2,123,113	2,055,854	2,091,973	1,952,225	1,961,950	1,991,982
Stockholders' Equity	2,555,252	2,503,188	2,153,570	2,110,441	2,042,102	1,994,487	1,939,812	1,842,216
Shares Outstanding	110,620	110,361	109,617	112,034	112,481	112,626	115,036	113,157
Statistical Record								
Return on Assets %	5.35	5.66	5.57	5.04	3.92	4.27	1.81	0.22
Return on Equity %	11.76	12.60	11.02	10.07	7.84	8.52	3.71	0.41
EBITDA Margin %	7.73	16.37	14.81	13.91	10.66	11.11	6.20	6.15
Net Margin %	4.04	12.97	11.08	9.39	7.05	7.72	3.31	0.40
Asset Turnover	0.46	0.44	0.50	0.54	0.56	0.55	0.55	0.55
Current Ratio	1.33	1.26	1.97	1.84	1.79	1.73	1.67	1.44
Debt to Equity	0.73	0.71	0.49	0.48	0.52	0.47	0.48	0.51
Price Range	82.75-56.95	73.84-51.57	56.92-41.45	54.36-42.66	48.25-39.83	41.18-30.35	32.29-20.37	28.46-17.47
P/E Ratio	32.97-22.69	27.97-19.53	26.85-19.55	29.07-22.81	34.71-28.65	28.01-20.65	52.93-33.39	406.57-249.57
Average Yield %	0.40	0.44	0.54	0.56	0.56	0.63	0.79	1.18

Address: 940 Winter Street, Waltham, MA 02451	**Web Site:** www.perkinelmer.com **Officers:** Robert F. Friel - Chairman, President, Chief Executive Officer James M. Mock - Senior Vice President, Chief Financial Officer	**Auditors:** DELOITTE & TOUCHE LLP **Investor Contact:** 781-663-6900 **Transfer Agents:** Computershare, Inc., Providence , RI
Telephone: 781-663-6900		
Fax: 781-663-6052		

PENSKE AUTOMOTIVE GROUP INC

Exchange	Symbol	Price	52Wk Range	Yield	P/E
NYS	PAG	$46.85 (6/29/2018)	54.55-39.04	2.99	6.31

*7 Year Price Score 94.25   *NYSE Composite Index=100   ***12 Month Price Score 102.17**

Interim Earnings (Per Share)

Qtr.	Mar	Jun	Sep	Dec
2015	0.83	1.04	0.96	0.79
2016	0.90	1.10	1.03	0.97
2017	0.96	1.23	1.10	3.84
2018	1.26	...	...	...

Interim Dividends (Per Share)

Amt	Decl	Ex	Rec	Pay
0.32Q	07/26/2017	08/08/2017	08/10/2017	09/01/2017
0.33Q	10/11/2017	11/09/2017	11/10/2017	12/01/2017
0.34Q	01/30/2018	02/09/2018	02/12/2018	03/01/2018
0.35Q	05/10/2018	05/18/2018	05/21/2018	06/01/2018

Indicated Div: $1.40

Valuation Analysis

		Institutional Holding	
Forecast EPS	$5.13	No of Institutions	
	(06/14/2018)	361	
Market Cap	$4.0 Billion	Shares	
Book Value	$2.5 Billion	100,599,776	
Price/Book	1.61	% Held	
Price/Sales	0.18	N/A	

Business Summary: Retail - Automotive (MIC: 2.1.4 SIC: 5511 NAIC: 441110)

Penske Automotive Group is a holding company. Through its subsidiaries, Co. operates in four segments: Retail Automotive, consisting of its retail automotive dealership operations; Retail Commercial Truck, consisting of its retail commercial truck dealership operations in the U.S. and Canada; Other, consisting of its commercial vehicle and power systems distribution operations and other non-automotive consolidated operations; and Non-Automotive Investments, consisting of its equity method investments in non-automotive operations. At Dec 31 2017, Co. operated 343 retail automotive franchises, of which 155 franchises were located in the U.S. and 188 franchises were located outside of the U.S.

Recent Developments: For the quarter ended Mar 31 2018, income from continuing operations increased 28.8% to US$107.7 million from US$83.6 million in the year-earlier quarter. Net income increased 29.9% to US$107.8 million from US$83.0 million in the year-earlier quarter. Revenues were US$5.75 billion, up 13.1% from US$5.08 billion the year before. Operating income was US$175.7 million versus US$150.2 million in the prior-year quarter, an increase of 17.0%. Direct operating expenses rose 13.4% to US$4.88 billion from US$4.31 billion in the comparable period the year before. Indirect operating expenses increased 10.4% to US$688.7 million from US$624.1 million in the equivalent prior-year period.

Prospects: Our evaluation of Penske Automotive Group Inc. as of Jan. 21, 2018 is the result of our systematic analysis on three basic characteristics: earnings strength, relative valuation, and recent stock price movement. The company has managed to produce a neutral trend in earnings per share over the past 5 quarters and while recent estimates for the company have been mixed, PAG has posted better than expected results. Based on operating earnings yield, the company is undervalued when compared to all of the companies in our coverage universe. Share price changes over the past year indicates that PAG will perform very poorly over the near term.

Financial Data

(US$ in Thousands)	3 Mos	12/31/2017	12/31/2016	12/31/2015	12/31/2014	12/31/2013	12/31/2012	12/31/2011
Earnings Per Share	7.43	7.14	3.99	3.63	3.17	2.70	2.05	1.94
Cash Flow Per Share	6.97	7.25	4.24	4.36	4.06	3.49	3.62	1.35
Tang Book Value Per Share	2.97	3.04	0.46	0.66	0.00	0.61	0.51	N.M.
Dividends Per Share	1.300	1.260	1.100	0.940	0.780	0.620	0.460	0.240
Dividend Payout %	17.50	17.65	27.57	25.90	24.61	22.96	22.44	12.37
Income Statement								
Total Revenue	5,746,900	21,386,900	20,118,500	19,284,900	17,177,200	14,705,400	13,163,517	11,556,232
EBITDA	201,300	706,500	664,600	644,500	590,100	497,900	401,100	347,093
Depn & Amortn	25,600	95,100	89,700	78,000	70,000	61,700	53,995	48,903
Income Before Taxes	127,000	440,600	438,600	452,600	421,200	344,700	261,416	222,937
Income Taxes	36,600	(64,800)	160,700	158,000	153,200	124,300	94,330	71,933
Net Income	108,100	613,300	342,900	326,100	286,700	244,200	185,540	176,881
Average Shares	85,992	85,877	86,000	89,759	90,354	90,330	90,342	91,274
Balance Sheet								
Current Assets	5,165,400	5,026,500	4,421,500	4,408,100	3,867,700	3,346,600	2,773,083	2,192,600
Total Assets	10,843,000	10,540,600	8,861,100	8,022,700	7,228,200	6,415,500	5,378,990	4,502,299
Current Liabilities	5,138,800	5,000,400	4,229,600	4,286,900	3,630,300	3,331,800	2,693,556	2,149,672
Long-Term Obligations	2,136,900	2,090,600	1,828,800	1,255,100	1,316,000	1,033,200	918,024	846,777
Total Liabilities	8,377,600	8,145,400	7,110,200	6,232,500	5,575,400	4,911,100	4,074,775	3,366,314
Stockholders' Equity	2,465,400	2,395,200	1,750,900	1,790,200	1,652,800	1,504,400	1,304,215	1,135,985
Shares Outstanding	84,975	85,787	85,214	89,524	90,244	90,243	90,294	90,277
Statistical Record								
Return on Assets %	6.31	6.32	4.05	4.28	4.20	4.14	3.75	4.13
Return on Equity %	29.48	29.58	19.31	18.94	18.16	17.39	15.17	16.25
EBITDA Margin %	3.50	3.30	3.30	3.34	3.44	3.39	3.05	3.00
Net Margin %	1.88	2.87	1.70	1.69	1.67	1.66	1.41	1.53
Asset Turnover	2.18	2.20	2.38	2.53	2.52	2.49	2.66	2.70
Current Ratio	1.01	1.01	1.05	1.03	1.07	1.00	1.03	1.02
Debt to Equity	0.87	0.87	1.04	0.70	0.80	0.69	0.70	0.75
Price Range	54.55-39.04	54.92-39.04	55.98-29.96	54.21-41.79	51.16-37.51	47.42-28.40	32.11-18.58	23.96-15.06
P/E Ratio	7.34-5.25	7.69-5.47	14.03-7.51	14.93-11.51	16.14-11.83	17.56-10.52	15.66-9.06	12.35-7.76
Average Yield %	2.84	2.72	2.71	1.89	1.72	1.72	1.78	1.23

Address: 2555 Telegraph Road,	Web Site: www.penskeautomotive.com	Auditors: Deloitte & Touche LLP
Bloomfield Hills, MI 48302-0954	Officers: Roger S. Penske - Chairman, Chief	Investor Contact: 866-715-5289
Telephone: 248-648-2500	Executive Officer Bud Denke - Executive Vice	Transfer Agents: ComputerShare
Fax: 248-648-2525	President	Investor Services, Providence, RI

PFIZER INC

Exchange	Symbol	Price	52Wk Range	Yield	P/E
NYS	PFE	$36.28 (6/29/2018)	39.02-32.67	3.75	10.08

*7 Year Price Score 94.78 *NYSE Composite Index=100 *12 Month Price Score 99.91

Interim Earnings (Per Share)

Qtr.	Mar	Jun	Sep	Dec
2015	0.38	0.42	0.34	(0.03)
2016	0.49	0.33	0.21	0.14
2017	0.51	0.51	0.47	2.03
2018	0.59	...	...	...

Interim Dividends (Per Share)

Amt	Decl	Ex	Rec	Pay
0.32Q	09/27/2017	11/09/2017	11/10/2017	12/01/2017
0.34Q	12/18/2017	02/01/2018	02/02/2018	03/01/2018
0.34Q	04/26/2018	05/10/2018	05/11/2018	06/01/2018
0.34Q	06/28/2018	08/02/2018	08/03/2018	09/04/2018

Indicated Div: $1.36

Valuation Analysis

		Institutional Holding	
Forecast EPS	$2.95 (06/14/2018)	No of Institutions	3080
Market Cap	$212.2 Billion	Shares	5,468,850,176
Book Value	$70.2 Billion	% Held	58.06
Price/Book	3.02		
Price/Sales	4.03		

Business Summary: Pharmaceuticals (MIC: 4.1.1 SIC: 2834 NAIC: 325412)

Pfizer is a research-based biopharmaceutical company involved in the discovery, development and manufacture of healthcare products. Co. manages its commercial operations through two distinct business segments: Pfizer Innovative Health (IH) and Pfizer Essential Health (EH). IH focuses on developing and commercializing medicines and vaccines that improve patients' lives, as well as products for consumer healthcare with key therapeutic areas that include internal medicine, vaccines, oncology, inflammation & immunology, rare diseases and consumer healthcare. EH includes legacy brands, branded generics, generic sterile injectable products, biosimilars and its contract manufacturing business.

Recent Developments: For the quarter ended Apr 1 2018, income from continuing operations increased 14.1% to US$3.57 billion from US$3.13 billion in the year-earlier quarter. Net income increased 14.1% to US$3.57 billion from US$3.13 billion in the year-earlier quarter. Revenues were US$12.91 billion, up 1.0% from US$12.78 billion the year before. Direct operating expenses rose 3.8% to US$2.56 billion from US$2.47 billion in the comparable period the year before. Indirect operating expenses decreased 2.3% to US$6.22 billion from US$6.36 billion in the equivalent prior-year period.

Prospects: Our evaluation of Pfizer Inc. as of Jan. 21, 2018 is the result of our systematic analysis on three basic characteristics: earnings strength, relative valuation, and recent stock price movement. The company has produced a positive trend in earnings per share over the past 5 quarters. However, while recent estimates for the company have been mixed, PFE has posted better than expected results. Based on operating earnings yield, the company is undervalued when compared to all of the companies in our coverage universe. Share price changes over the past year indicates that PFE will perform well over the near term.

Financial Data

(US$ in Thousands)	3 Mos	12/31/2017	12/31/2016	12/31/2015	12/31/2014	12/31/2013	12/31/2012	12/31/2011
Earnings Per Share	3.60	3.52	1.17	1.11	1.42	3.19	1.94	1.27
Cash Flow Per Share	2.83	2.76	2.60	2.35	2.66	2.61	2.29	2.59
Dividends Per Share	1.300	1.280	1.200	1.120	1.040	0.960	0.880	0.800
Dividend Payout %	36.11	36.36	102.56	100.90	73.24	30.09	45.36	62.99
Income Statement								
Total Revenue	12,906,000	52,546,000	52,824,000	48,851,000	49,605,000	51,584,000	58,986,000	67,425,000
EBITDA	5,556,000	17,942,000	13,123,000	13,421,000	17,214,000	21,326,000	18,396,000	19,570,000
Depn & Amortn	1,196,000	4,758,000	4,056,000	3,728,000	4,039,000	4,599,000	5,175,000	5,585,000
Income Before Taxes	4,127,000	12,305,000	8,351,000	8,965,000	12,240,000	15,716,000	12,080,000	12,762,000
Income Taxes	556,000	(9,049,000)	1,123,000	1,990,000	3,120,000	4,306,000	2,562,000	4,023,000
Net Income	3,561,000	21,308,000	7,215,000	6,960,000	9,135,000	22,003,000	14,570,000	10,009,000
Average Shares	6,056,999	6,057,999	6,158,999	6,256,999	6,423,999	6,895,001	7,508,001	7,870,001
Balance Sheet								
Current Assets	34,835,000	41,141,000	38,949,000	43,804,000	57,702,000	56,244,000	61,415,000	57,728,000
Total Assets	164,612,000	171,797,000	171,615,000	167,460,000	169,274,000	172,101,000	185,798,000	188,002,000
Current Liabilities	27,365,000	30,427,000	31,115,000	29,399,000	21,631,000	23,366,000	28,619,000	28,069,000
Long-Term Obligations	31,831,000	33,538,000	31,398,000	28,818,000	31,541,000	30,462,000	31,036,000	34,931,000
Total Liabilities	94,429,000	100,489,000	112,072,000	102,741,000	97,973,000	95,794,000	104,538,000	105,812,000
Stockholders' Equity	70,184,000	71,308,000	59,544,000	64,720,000	71,301,000	76,307,000	81,260,000	82,190,000
Shares Outstanding	5,849,570	5,978,999	6,069,999	6,174,999	6,290,999	6,398,999	7,276,001	7,575,001
Statistical Record								
Return on Assets %	13.05	12.41	4.24	4.13	5.35	12.30	7.77	5.23
Return on Equity %	33.82	32.57	11.58	10.23	12.38	27.93	17.78	11.78
EBITDA Margin %	43.05	34.15	24.84	27.47	34.70	41.34	31.19	29.02
Net Margin %	27.59	40.55	13.66	14.25	18.42	42.65	24.70	14.84
Asset Turnover	0.32	0.31	0.31	0.29	0.29	0.29	0.31	0.35
Current Ratio	1.27	1.35	1.25	1.49	2.67	2.41	2.15	2.06
Debt to Equity	0.45	0.47	0.53	0.45	0.44	0.40	0.38	0.43
Price Range	39.02-31.75	37.20-31.15	37.31-28.56	36.15-30.82	32.75-27.70	32.20-25.08	26.04-20.95	21.83-16.66
P/E Ratio	10.84-8.82	10.57-8.85	31.89-24.41	32.57-27.77	23.06-19.51	10.09-7.86	13.42-10.80	17.19-13.12
Average Yield %	3.73	3.76	3.66	3.32	3.43	3.31	3.79	4.10

Address: 235 East 42nd Street, New York, NY 10017 **Telephone:** 212-733-2323	**Web Site:** www.pfizer.com **Officers:** Ian C. Read - Chairman, President, Chief Executive Officer Frank A. D'Amelio - Executive Vice President, Senior Vice President, Chief Financial Officer	**Auditors:** KPMG LLP **Transfer Agents:** Computershare Trust Company, N.A., Canton, MA

PG&E CORP (HOLDING CO)

Exchange	Symbol	Price	52Wk Range	Yield	P/E
NYS	PCG	$42.56 (6/29/2018)	71.56-38.24	N/A	14.43

*7 Year Price Score 84.03 ***NYSE Composite Index=100** ***12 Month Price Score 80.46**

Interim Earnings (Per Share)

Qtr.	Mar	Jun	Sep	Dec
2015	0.06	0.83	0.63	0.26
2016	0.22	0.41	0.77	1.38
2017	1.13	0.79	1.07	0.23
2018	0.86	...	...	...

Interim Dividends (Per Share)

Amt	Decl	Ex	Rec	Pay
0.49Q	12/16/2016	12/28/2016	12/30/2016	01/15/2017
0.49Q	02/15/2017	03/29/2017	03/31/2017	04/15/2017
0.53Q	05/31/2017	06/28/2017	06/30/2017	07/15/2017
0.53Q	09/20/2017	09/28/2017	09/29/2017	10/15/2017

Valuation Analysis

		Institutional Holding	
Forecast EPS	$3.82	No of Institutions	925
	(06/14/2018)		
Market Cap	$22.0 Billion	Shares	491,276,640
Book Value	$19.7 Billion	% Held	90.34
Price/Book	1.11		
Price/Sales	1.30		

Business Summary: Electric Utilities (MIC: 3.1.1 SIC: 4931 NAIC: 221122)

PG&E is a holding company. Through its subsidiary, Pacific Gas and Electric Company (Utility), Co. is engaged in the sale and delivery of electricity and natural gas to customers. The Utility generates electricity and provides electricity transmission and distribution services throughout its service territory in northern and central California to residential, commercial, industrial, and agricultural customers. The Utility also provides natural gas transportation services to small commercial and residential customers and industrial, commercial, and natural gas-fired electric generation facilities that are connected to the Utility's gas system in its service territory.

Recent Developments: For the quarter ended Mar 31 2018, net income decreased 23.1% to US$445.0 million from US$579.0 million in the year-earlier quarter. Revenues were US$4.06 billion, down 5.0% from US$4.27 billion the year before. Operating income was US$599.0 million versus US$867.0 million in the prior-year quarter, a decrease of 30.9%. Direct operating expenses rose 0.6% to US$2.71 billion from US$2.69 billion in the comparable period the year before. Indirect operating expenses increased 5.6% to US$752.0 million from US$712.0 million in the equivalent prior-year period.

Prospects: Our evaluation of PG&E Corp. as of Jan. 21, 2018 is the result of our systematic analysis on three basic characteristics: earnings strength, relative valuation, and recent stock price movement. The company has generated a negative trend in earnings per share over the past 5 quarters. However, while recent estimates for the company have been mixed, PCG has posted better than expected results. Based on operating earnings yield, the company is undervalued when compared to all of the companies in our coverage universe. Share price changes over the past year indicates that PCG will perform very well over the near term.

Financial Data

(US$ in Thousands)	3 Mos	12/31/2017	12/31/2016	12/31/2015	12/31/2014	12/31/2013	12/31/2012	12/31/2011
Earnings Per Share	2.95	3.21	2.78	1.79	3.06	1.83	1.92	2.10
Cash Flow Per Share	11.49	11.67	8.81	7.75	7.86	7.72	11.48	9.32
Tang Book Value Per Share	38.24	37.34	35.39	33.69	33.09	31.41	30.35	29.35
Dividends Per Share	1.060	1.550	1.925	1.820	1.820	1.820	1.820	1.820
Dividend Payout %	35.93	48.29	69.24	101.68	59.48	99.45	94.79	86.67
Income Statement								
Total Revenue	4,056,000	17,135,000	17,666,000	16,833,000	17,090,000	15,598,000	15,040,000	14,956,000
EBITDA	1,459,000	5,882,000	5,023,000	4,237,000	4,953,000	3,879,000	4,035,000	4,206,000
Depn & Amortn	752,000	2,854,000	2,755,000	2,612,000	2,433,000	2,077,000	2,272,000	2,215,000
Income Before Taxes	496,000	2,171,000	1,462,000	861,000	1,795,000	1,096,000	1,067,000	1,298,000
Income Taxes	51,000	511,000	55,000	(27,000)	345,000	268,000	237,000	440,000
Net Income	445,000	1,660,000	1,407,000	888,000	1,450,000	828,000	830,000	858,000
Average Shares	516,000	513,000	501,000	487,000	470,000	445,000	425,000	402,000
Balance Sheet								
Current Assets	5,855,000	6,281,000	6,164,000	5,822,000	6,389,000	5,977,000	5,121,000	6,480,000
Total Assets	68,154,000	68,012,000	68,598,000	63,339,000	60,127,000	55,605,000	52,449,000	49,750,000
Current Liabilities	6,920,000	7,129,000	7,564,000	6,363,000	5,920,000	7,493,000	6,256,000	7,749,000
Long-Term Obligations	17,407,000	17,753,000	16,220,000	16,030,000	15,050,000	12,717,000	12,517,000	11,766,000
Total Liabilities	48,423,000	48,792,000	50,658,000	46,763,000	44,379,000	41,263,000	39,375,000	37,649,000
Stockholders' Equity	19,731,000	19,220,000	17,940,000	16,576,000	15,748,000	14,342,000	13,074,000	12,101,000
Shares Outstanding	516,003	514,755	506,891	492,025	475,913	456,670	430,718	412,257
Statistical Record								
Return on Assets %	2.22	2.43	2.13	1.44	2.51	1.53	1.62	1.79
Return on Equity %	8.01	8.93	8.13	5.49	9.64	6.04	6.58	7.34
EBITDA Margin %	35.97	34.33	28.43	25.17	28.98	24.87	26.83	28.12
Net Margin %	10.97	9.69	7.96	5.28	8.48	5.31	5.52	5.74
Asset Turnover	0.25	0.25	0.27	0.27	0.30	0.29	0.29	0.31
Current Ratio	0.85	0.88	0.81	0.91	1.08	0.80	0.82	0.84
Debt to Equity	0.88	0.92	0.90	0.97	0.96	0.89	0.96	0.97
Price Range	71.56-38.24	71.56-44.45	65.39-51.29	60.15-47.60	54.98-39.60	48.44-40.07	46.51-39.71	47.84-36.86
P/E Ratio	24.26-12.96	22.29-13.85	23.52-18.45	33.60-26.59	17.97-12.94	26.47-21.90	24.22-20.68	22.78-17.55
Average Yield %	1.80	2.43	3.22	3.44	3.97	4.21	4.23	4.23

Address: 77 Beale Street, P.O. Box 770000, San Francisco, CA 94177	**Web Site:** www.pgecorp.com	**Auditors:** DELOITTE & TOUCHE LLP
Telephone: 415-973-1000	**Officers:** Geisha J. Williams - President, Chief Economist John R. Simon - Executive Vice President, Senior Vice President, Executive Vice President, General Counsel	**Investor Contact:** 415-972-7080
Fax: 415-267-7265		**Transfer Agents:** American Stock Transfer and Trust Company, LLC, Brooklyn, NY

PHILIP MORRIS INTERNATIONAL INC

Exchange	Symbol	Price	52Wk Range	Yield	P/E
NYS	PM	$80.74 (6/29/2018)	121.62-76.85	5.65	20.92

*7 Year Price Score 91.63 *NYSE Composite Index=100 *12 Month Price Score 77.04

Interim Earnings (Per Share)

Qtr.	Mar	Jun	Sep	Dec
2015	1.16	1.21	1.25	0.80
2016	0.98	1.15	1.25	1.10
2017	1.02	1.14	1.27	0.45
2018	1.00	...	...	...

Interim Dividends (Per Share)

Amt	Decl	Ex	Rec	Pay
1.07Q	09/13/2017	09/26/2017	09/27/2017	10/12/2017
1.07Q	12/07/2017	12/20/2017	12/21/2017	01/11/2018
1.07Q	03/08/2018	03/21/2018	03/22/2018	04/11/2018
1.14Q	06/08/2018	06/21/2018	06/22/2018	07/11/2018

Indicated Div: $4.56

Valuation Analysis **Institutional Holding**

Forecast EPS	$5.17 (06/14/2018)	No of Institutions 2283
Market Cap	$125.5 Billion	Shares 1,333,952,256
Book Value	N/A	% Held
Price/Book	N/A	60.77
Price/Sales	1.83	

Business Summary: Tobacco Products (MIC: 1.3.1 SIC: 2111 NAIC: 312221)

Philip Morris International is a holding company. Through its subsidiaries and affiliates and their licensees, Co. manufactures and sells cigarettes, other tobacco products and other nicotine-containing products in markets outside the U.S. Co. has a range of premium, mid-price and low-price brands. Co.'s portfolio of international and local brands includes Marlboro, L&M, Bond Street, and Champion. Co. also focuses on the development and commercialization of Reduced-Risk Products that produces lower quantities of harmful compounds than found in cigarette smoke. Co.'s other tobacco products include tobacco for roll-your-own and make-your-own cigarettes, pipe tobacco, cigars and cigarillos.

Recent Developments: For the quarter ended Mar 31 2018, net income decreased 0.7% to US$1.65 billion from US$1.66 billion in the year-earlier quarter. Revenues were US$6.90 billion, up 13.7% from US$6.06 billion the year before. Operating income was US$2.43 billion versus US$2.42 billion in the prior-year quarter, an increase of 0.4%. Direct operating expenses rose 20.1% to US$2.62 billion from US$2.18 billion in the comparable period the year before. Indirect operating expenses increased 26.1% to US$1.86 billion from US$1.47 billion in the equivalent prior-year period.

Prospects: Our evaluation of Philip Morris International Inc. as of Jan. 21, 2018 is the result of our systematic analysis on three basic characteristics: earnings strength, relative valuation, and recent stock price movement. The company has produced a positive trend in earnings per share over the past 5 quarters and while recent estimates for the company have been mixed, PM has posted results that fell short of analysts expectations. Based on operating earnings yield, the company is about fairly valued when compared to all of the companies in our coverage universe. Share price changes over the past year indicates that PM will perform well over the near term.

Financial Data

(US$ in Thousands)	3 Mos	12/31/2017	12/31/2016	12/31/2015	12/31/2014	12/31/2013	12/31/2012	12/31/2011
Earnings Per Share	3.86	3.88	4.48	4.42	4.76	5.26	5.17	4.85
Cash Flow Per Share	6.08	5.74	5.19	5.08	4.94	6.25	5.55	5.98
Dividends Per Share	4.250	4.220	4.120	4.040	3.880	3.580	3.240	2.820
Dividend Payout %	110.10	108.76	91.96	91.40	81.51	68.06	62.67	58.14
Income Statement								
Total Revenue	6,896,000	78,098,000	74,953,000	73,908,000	80,106,000	80,029,000	77,393,000	76,346,000
EBITDA	2,442,000	12,378,000	11,558,000	11,377,000	12,591,000	14,397,000	14,744,000	14,325,000
Depn & Amortn	22,000	875,000	743,000	754,000	889,000	882,000	898,000	993,000
Income Before Taxes	2,193,000	10,589,000	9,924,000	9,615,000	10,650,000	12,542,000	12,987,000	12,532,000
Income Taxes	559,000	4,307,000	2,768,000	2,688,000	3,097,000	3,670,000	3,833,000	3,653,000
Net Income	1,556,000	6,035,000	6,967,000	6,873,000	7,493,000	8,576,000	8,800,000	8,591,000
Average Shares	1,554,000	1,553,000	1,551,000	1,549,000	1,566,000	1,622,000	1,692,000	1,762,000
Balance Sheet								
Current Assets	20,593,000	21,594,000	17,608,000	15,804,000	15,484,000	16,852,000	16,590,000	14,859,000
Total Assets	43,070,000	42,968,000	36,851,000	33,956,000	35,187,000	38,168,000	37,670,000	35,488,000
Current Liabilities	17,688,000	15,962,000	16,467,000	15,386,000	15,112,000	17,066,000	17,016,000	14,794,000
Long-Term Obligations	29,578,000	31,334,000	25,851,000	25,250,000	26,929,000	24,023,000	17,639,000	14,828,000
Total Liabilities	55,420,000	55,054,000	49,539,000	47,200,000	47,816,000	45,934,000	41,146,000	35,259,000
Stockholders' Equity	(12,350,000)	(12,086,000)	(12,688,000)	(13,244,000)	(12,629,000)	(7,766,000)	(3,476,000)	229,000
Shares Outstanding	1,554,466	1,553,217	1,551,385	1,549,344	1,546,899	1,589,002	1,653,612	1,725,908
Statistical Record								
Return on Assets %	15.06	15.12	19.63	19.88	20.43	22.62	23.99	24.36
Return on Equity %	...	...	...	...	...	...	...	460.03
EBITDA Margin %	35.41	15.85	15.42	15.39	15.72	17.99	19.05	18.76
Net Margin %	22.56	7.73	9.30	9.30	9.35	10.72	11.37	11.25
Asset Turnover	1.72	1.96	2.11	2.14	2.18	2.11	2.11	2.16
Current Ratio	1.16	1.35	1.07	1.03	1.02	0.99	0.97	1.00
Debt to Equity	...	...	...	...	...	...	...	64.75
Price Range	122.90-95.63	122.90-90.40	103.63-85.80	90.15-75.33	91.34-75.39	96.44-82.95	93.74-73.26	79.10-56.02
P/E Ratio	31.84-24.77	31.68-23.30	23.13-19.15	20.40-17.04	19.19-15.84	18.33-15.77	18.13-14.17	16.31-11.55
Average Yield %	3.84	3.82	4.29	4.86	4.60	4.01	3.74	4.21

Address: 120 Park Avenue, New York, NY 10017	**Web Site:** www.pmi.com	**Auditors:** PricewaterhouseCoopers SA
Telephone: 917-663-2000	**Officers:** Louis C. Camilleri - Chairman, Chief Executive Officer Marc S. Firestone - President, Senior Vice President, General Counsel	**Investor Contact:** 191-766-32233
Fax: 917-663-5372		**Transfer Agents:** ComputerShare LLC, Providence, RI

PHILLIPS 66

Exchange	Symbol	Price	52Wk Range	Yield	P/E
NYS	PSX	$112.31 (6/29/2018)	121.87-80.89	2.85	11.32

*7 Year Price Score N/A *NYSE Composite Index=100 *12 Month Price Score 117.35

TRADING VOLUME (thousand shares)

Interim Earnings (Per Share)

Qtr.	Mar	Jun	Sep	Dec
2015	1.79	1.84	2.90	1.21
2016	0.72	0.93	0.96	0.31
2017	1.02	1.06	1.60	6.19
2018	1.07	...	...	...

Interim Dividends (Per Share)

Amt	Decl	Ex	Rec	Pay
0.70Q	10/09/2017	11/16/2017	11/17/2017	12/01/2017
0.70Q	02/07/2018	02/16/2018	02/20/2018	03/01/2018
0.80Q	05/09/2018	05/18/2018	05/21/2018	06/01/2018
0.80Q	07/11/2018	08/20/2018	08/21/2018	09/04/2018

Indicated Div: $3.20

Valuation Analysis / Institutional Holding

Forecast EPS	$6.84	No of Institutions
	(06/14/2018)	1580
Market Cap	$52.3 Billion	Shares
Book Value	$21.9 Billion	368,294,208
Price/Book	2.39	% Held
Price/Sales	0.50	63.50

Business Summary: Refining & Marketing (MIC: 9.1.2 SIC: 2911 NAIC: 324110)

Phillips 66 is an energy manufacturing and logistics company with midstream, chemicals, refining, and marketing and specialties businesses. Co. has four segments: Midstream, which gathers, processes, transports and markets natural gas as well as transports, stores, fractionates and markets natural gas liquids; Chemicals, which manufactures and markets petrochemicals and plastics on a worldwide basis; Refining, which buys, sells and refines crude oil and other feedstocks into petroleum products (such as gasoline, distillates and aviation fuels); and Marketing and Specialties, which purchases for resale and markets refined petroleum products, mainly in the U.S. and Europe.

Recent Developments: For the quarter ended Mar 31 2018, net income increased 3.9% to US$585.0 million from US$563.0 million in the year-earlier quarter. Revenues were US$24.05 billion, up 1.4% from US$23.71 billion the year before. Direct operating expenses rose 18.1% to US$22.38 billion from US$18.95 billion in the comparable period the year before. Indirect operating expenses decreased 76.2% to US$945.0 million from US$3.97 billion in the equivalent prior-year period.

Prospects: Our evaluation of Phillips 66 Inc. as of Jan. 21, 2018 is the result of our systematic analysis on three basic characteristics: earnings strength, relative valuation, and recent stock price movement. The company has enjoyed a very positive trend in earnings per share over the past 5 quarters. However, while recent estimates for the company have been mixed, PSX has posted better than expected results. Based on operating earnings yield, the company is about fairly valued when compared to all of the companies in our coverage universe. Share price changes over the past year indicates that PSX will perform poorly over the near term.

Financial Data
(US$ in Thousands)

	3 Mos	12/31/2017	12/31/2016	12/31/2015	12/31/2014	12/31/2013	12/31/2012	12/31/2011
Earnings Per Share	9.92	9.85	2.92	7.73	8.33	6.02	6.48	...
Cash Flow Per Share	9.62	7.08	5.60	10.53	6.24	9.83	6.81	...
Tang Book Value Per Share	38.17	41.69	35.14	35.74	31.88	30.76	26.79	...
Dividends Per Share	2.800	2.730	2.450	2.180	1.890	1.327	0.450	...
Dividend Payout %	28.23	27.72	83.90	28.20	22.69	22.05	6.94	...
Income Statement								
Total Revenue	24,046,000	104,622,000	85,777,000	100,949,000	164,093,000	174,809,000	182,922,000	200,614,000
EBITDA	1,176,000	5,311,000	3,697,000	7,432,000	7,007,000	6,748,000	7,790,000	7,549,000
Depn & Amortn	336,000	1,318,000	1,168,000	1,078,000	995,000	947,000	913,000	908,000
Income Before Taxes	717,000	3,555,000	2,191,000	6,044,000	5,745,000	5,526,000	6,631,000	6,624,000
Income Taxes	132,000	(1,693,000)	547,000	1,764,000	1,654,000	1,844,000	2,500,000	1,844,000
Net Income	524,000	5,106,000	1,555,000	4,227,000	4,762,000	3,726,000	4,124,000	4,775,000
Average Shares	489,668	518,508	530,066	546,977	571,504	618,989	636,764	...
Balance Sheet								
Current Assets	12,125,000	14,390,000	12,680,000	12,256,000	16,696,000	19,237,000	17,962,000	13,948,000
Total Assets	52,132,000	54,371,000	51,653,000	48,580,000	48,741,000	49,798,000	48,073,000	43,211,000
Current Liabilities	9,236,000	10,107,000	9,463,000	7,531,000	11,094,000	12,931,000	12,482,000	12,384,000
Long-Term Obligations	11,579,000	10,069,000	9,588,000	8,843,000	7,842,000	6,131,000	6,961,000	361,000
Total Liabilities	30,209,000	29,286,000	29,263,000	25,480,000	27,151,000	27,848,000	27,298,000	19,947,000
Stockholders' Equity	21,923,000	25,085,000	22,390,000	23,100,000	21,590,000	21,950,000	20,775,000	23,264,000
Shares Outstanding	465,836	502,270	518,766	529,410	546,381	590,179	623,545	...
Statistical Record								
Return on Assets %	9.84	9.63	3.09	8.69	9.67	7.61	9.01	10.83
Return on Equity %	23.01	21.51	6.82	18.92	21.87	17.44	18.68	19.38
EBITDA Margin %	4.89	5.08	4.31	7.36	4.27	3.86	4.26	3.76
Net Margin %	2.18	4.88	1.81	4.19	2.90	2.13	2.25	2.38
Asset Turnover	2.03	1.97	1.71	2.07	3.33	3.57	4.00	4.55
Current Ratio	1.31	1.42	1.34	1.63	1.50	1.49	1.44	1.13
Debt to Equity	0.53	0.40	0.43	0.38	0.36	0.28	0.34	0.02
Price Range	106.90-75.33	102.06-75.33	90.16-72.90	93.68-59.09	87.51-65.09	77.13-50.58	53.58-29.35	...
P/E Ratio	10.78-7.59	10.36-7.65	30.88-24.97	12.12-7.64	10.51-7.81	12.81-8.40	8.27-4.53	...
Average Yield %	3.15	3.22	3.03	2.74	2.40	2.14	1.09	...

Address: 2331 CityWest Blvd., Houston, TX 77042 Telephone: 281-293-6600	Web Site: www.Phillips66.com Officers: Greg C. Garland - Chairman, President, Chief Executive Officer Paula Ann Johnson - Executive Vice President, Executive Vice President (frmr), Senior Vice President, General Counsel, Corporate Secretary	Auditors: Ernst & Young LLP Investor Contact: 800-624-6440 Transfer Agents: Computershare, Canton, MA

PIEDMONT OFFICE REALTY TRUST INC

Exchange	Symbol	Price	52Wk Range	Yield	P/E
NYS	PDM	$19.93 (6/29/2018)	21.42-16.78	4.21	16.07

*7 Year Price Score 82.43 *NYSE Composite Index=100 *12 Month Price Score 97.34

Interim Earnings (Per Share)

Qtr.	Mar	Jun	Sep	Dec
2015	0.12	0.20	(0.01)	0.84
2016	0.07	0.55	(0.09)	0.21
2017	0.10	0.16	0.87	(0.21)
2018	0.42	...	...	...

Interim Dividends (Per Share)

Amt	Decl	Ex	Rec	Pay
0.21Q	10/31/2017	11/22/2017	11/24/2017	01/04/2018
0.50Q	12/13/2017	12/22/2017	12/26/2017	01/09/2018
0.21Q	02/07/2018	02/22/2018	02/23/2018	03/16/2018
0.21Q	05/01/2018	05/22/2018	05/23/2018	06/15/2018

Indicated Div: $0.84

Valuation Analysis | **Institutional Holding**

Forecast EPS	$0.77	No of Institutions
	(06/13/2018)	305
Market Cap	$2.6 Billion	Shares
Book Value	$1.8 Billion	130,265,592
Price/Book	1.45	% Held
Price/Sales	4.66	69.36

Business Summary: REITs (MIC: 5.3.1 SIC: 6798 NAIC: 525930)

Piedmont Office Realty Trust is a self-managed real estate investment trust engaged in the acquisition, development, management, and ownership of commercial real estate properties. Co. conducts business primarily through Piedmont Operating Partnership, L.P., and performs the management of its buildings through two subsidiaries, Piedmont Government Services, LLC and Piedmont Office Management, LLC. As of Dec 31 2017, Co. owned and operated 67 office properties. Co.'s primary markets are Atlanta, Boston, Chicago, Dallas, Minneapolis, New York, Orlando, and Washington, D.C.

Recent Developments: For the quarter ended Mar 31 2018, net income increased 282.9% to US$57.8 million from US$15.1 million in the year-earlier quarter. Revenues were US$129.9 million, down 12.5% from US$148.5 million the year before.

Prospects: Our evaluation of Piedmont Office Realty Trust Inc. as of Jan. 21, 2018 is the result of our systematic analysis on three basic characteristics: earnings strength, relative valuation, and recent stock price movement. The company has managed to produce a neutral trend in earnings per share over the past 5 quarters. Because the company lacks sufficient analyst estimate data, we place greater weight on the historical EPS trend as the measure of earnings strength. Based on operating earnings yield, the company is overvalued when compared to all of the companies in our coverage universe. Share price changes over the past year indicates that PDM will perform in line with the market over the near

Financial Data

(US$ in Thousands)	3 Mos	12/31/2017	12/31/2016	12/31/2015	12/31/2014	12/31/2013	12/31/2012	12/31/2011
Earnings Per Share	1.24	0.92	0.74	1.15	0.28	0.60	0.55	1.30
Cash Flow Per Share	1.66	1.67	1.62	1.44	1.40	1.30	1.31	1.56
Tang Book Value Per Share	12.99	12.70	13.06	13.27	13.35	14.00	14.35	14.55
Dividends Per Share	1.340	1.340	0.840	0.840	0.810	0.800	0.800	1.260
Dividend Payout %	108.06	145.65	113.51	73.04	289.29	133.33	145.45	96.92
Income Statement								
Total Revenue	129,900	574,173	555,715	584,769	566,252	554,505	536,382	541,642
EBITDA	69,305	201,242	201,541	212,633	253,554	274,667	240,757	260,673
Depn & Amortn	42,928	119,288	127,733	134,503	138,679	123,566	113,649	109,730
Income Before Taxes	12,619	13,830	8,948	4,132	40,429	75,166	62,918	87,900
Net Income	57,830	133,564	107,887	172,990	43,348	98,728	93,204	225,041
Average Shares	136,182	145,379	145,634	150,880	154,585	165,137	170,441	172,980
Balance Sheet								
Current Assets	18,769	19,521	33,486	31,780	40,017	38,118	160,294	269,213
Total Assets	3,635,690	3,999,967	4,449,347	4,434,535	4,795,501	4,666,088	4,254,875	4,447,834
Current Liabilities	83,786	216,653	165,410	128,465	133,988	128,818	127,263	122,986
Long-Term Obligations	1,689,644	1,726,927	2,020,475	2,029,510	2,277,589	2,002,205	1,416,525	1,472,525
Total Liabilities	1,847,914	2,015,300	2,272,347	2,239,116	2,485,095	2,206,538	1,615,989	1,676,015
Stockholders' Equity	1,787,776	1,984,667	2,177,000	2,195,419	2,310,406	2,459,550	2,638,886	2,771,819
Shares Outstanding	130,024	142,358	145,235	145,511	154,324	157,460	167,556	172,629
Statistical Record								
Return on Assets %	4.41	3.16	2.42	3.75	0.92	2.21	2.14	5.10
Return on Equity %	9.10	6.42	4.92	7.68	1.82	3.87	3.44	8.13
EBITDA Margin %	53.35	35.05	36.27	36.36	44.78	49.53	44.89	48.13
Net Margin %	44.52	23.26	19.41	29.58	7.66	17.80	17.38	41.55
Asset Turnover	0.14	0.14	0.12	0.13	0.12	0.12	0.12	0.12
Current Ratio	0.22	0.09	0.20	0.25	0.30	0.30	1.26	2.19
Debt to Equity	0.95	0.87	0.93	0.92	0.99	0.81	0.54	0.53
Price Range	22.69-16.78	23.05-19.21	22.22-17.10	20.01-16.74	20.00-16.09	20.94-15.96	18.91-16.19	21.25-15.42
P/E Ratio	18.30-13.53	25.05-20.88	30.03-23.11	17.40-14.56	71.43-57.46	34.90-26.60	34.38-29.44	16.35-11.86
Average Yield %	6.66	6.41	4.17	4.56	4.43	4.33	4.59	6.70

Address: 11695 Johns Creek Parkway, Suite 350, Johns Creek, GA 30097 Telephone: 770-418-8800	Web Site: www.piedmontreit.com Officers: C. Brent Smith - Co-Chief Investment Officer, Chief Investment Officer Michael R. Buchanan - Chairman	Auditors: Ernst & Young LLP Transfer Agents: Computershare Inc.

PINNACLE FOODS INC.

Exchange	Symbol	Price	52Wk Range	Yield	P/E
NYS	PF	$65.06 (6/29/2018)	67.86-52.85	2.00	13.73

*7 Year Price Score N/A   *NYSE Composite Index=100   *12 Month Price Score 106.94

Interim Earnings (Per Share)

Qtr.	Mar	Jun	Sep	Dec
2015	0.35	0.37	0.41	0.67
2016	0.21	0.39	0.44	0.75
2017	0.19	0.16	0.39	3.71
2018	0.48	...	...	...

Interim Dividends (Per Share)

Amt	Decl	Ex	Rec	Pay
0.325Q	08/16/2017	08/25/2017	08/29/2017	10/09/2017
0.325Q	12/06/2017	12/18/2017	12/19/2017	01/10/2018
0.325Q	02/14/2018	02/26/2018	02/27/2018	04/11/2018
0.325Q	05/30/2018	06/11/2018	06/12/2018	07/12/2018

Indicated Div: $1.30

Valuation Analysis **Institutional Holding**

Forecast EPS	$2.90 (06/03/2018)	No of Institutions 433
Market Cap	$7.8 Billion	Shares
Book Value	$2.4 Billion	134,498,960
Price/Book	3.22	% Held
Price/Sales	2.46	92.87

Business Summary: Food (MIC: 1.2.1 SIC: 2099 NAIC: 311999)

Pinnacle Foods is a holding company. Co. is a manufacturer, marketer and distributor of convenience food products. Co.'s operations are managed and reported in four operating segments: the frozen segment, which is comprised of the retail businesses of Co.'s legacy frozen brands; the grocery segment, which is comprised of the retail businesses of Co.'s grocery brands; the boulder segment, which is comprised of the retail businesses of Co.'s health and wellness lifestyle brands; and the specialty segment, which includes Co.'s snack products (Tim's Cascade and Snyder of Berlin) and all of its U.S. foodservice and private label businesses.

Recent Developments: For the quarter ended Apr 1 2018, net income increased 145.9% to US$56.9 million from US$23.1 million in the year-earlier quarter. Revenues were US$778.8 million, up 1.7% from US$766.1 million the year before. Direct operating expenses rose 3.0% to US$572.4 million from US$555.5 million in the comparable period the year before. Indirect operating expenses decreased 8.3% to US$91.5 million from US$99.9 million in the equivalent prior-year period.

Prospects: Our evaluation of Pinnacle Foods Inc. as of Jan. 21, 2018 is the result of our systematic analysis on three basic characteristics: earnings strength, relative valuation, and recent stock price movement. The company has produced a positive trend in earnings per share over the past 5 quarters and while recent estimates for the company have been mixed, PF has posted better than expected results. Based on operating earnings yield, the company is about fairly valued when compared to all of the companies in our coverage universe. Share price changes over the past year indicates that PF will perform poorly over the near term.

Financial Data
(US$ in Thousands)

	3 Mos	12/31/2017	12/25/2016	12/27/2015	12/28/2014	12/29/2013	12/30/2012	12/25/2011
Earnings Per Share	4.74	4.45	1.79	1.81	2.13	0.82	0.61	(0.58)
Cash Flow Per Share	4.00	3.52	4.18	3.22	4.77	2.46	2.46	2.52
Dividends Per Share	1.260	1.220	1.080	0.980	0.890	0.570	...	...
Dividend Payout %	26.58	27.42	60.34	54.14	41.78	69.51	...	...
Income Statement								
Total Revenue	778,832	3,144,002	3,127,938	2,655,792	2,591,183	2,463,802	2,478,485	2,469,562
EBITDA	141,172	565,656	568,445	500,808	578,981	355,387	365,889	255,565
Depn & Amortn	25,471	117,000	88,800	76,106	66,710	62,350	82,295	72,299
Income Before Taxes	74,019	279,222	340,547	336,387	416,218	160,824	85,220	(24,811)
Income Taxes	17,105	(252,999)	129,430	123,879	167,800	71,475	32,701	22,103
Net Income	56,914	532,049	211,117	212,508	248,418	89,349	52,519	(46,914)
Average Shares	119,813	119,552	118,161	117,323	116,885	108,618	86,494	81,315
Balance Sheet								
Current Assets	873,733	1,032,317	1,150,515	857,634	715,709	792,309	705,277	725,482
Total Assets	6,423,042	6,578,264	6,739,645	5,340,083	5,200,945	5,081,191	4,399,988	4,451,621
Current Liabilities	593,975	561,311	571,696	405,647	383,436	331,304	333,724	334,148
Long-Term Obligations	2,703,733	2,925,594	3,140,496	2,272,932	2,285,984	2,476,167	2,576,386	2,738,650
Total Liabilities	4,017,782	4,199,132	4,791,637	3,534,554	3,486,956	3,483,150	3,511,262	3,606,269
Stockholders' Equity	2,405,260	2,379,132	1,948,008	1,805,529	1,713,989	1,598,041	888,726	845,352
Shares Outstanding	119,186	119,018	118,127	116,619	116,293	117,231	81,210	81,272
Statistical Record								
Return on Assets %	8.76	7.99	3.50	4.04	4.85	1.89	1.17	...
Return on Equity %	25.92	24.59	11.28	12.11	15.04	7.21	5.96	...
EBITDA Margin %	18.13	17.99	18.17	18.86	22.34	14.42	14.76	10.35
Net Margin %	7.31	16.92	6.75	8.00	9.59	3.63	2.12	N.M.
Asset Turnover	0.49	0.47	0.52	0.51	0.51	0.52	0.55	...
Current Ratio	1.47	1.84	2.01	2.11	1.87	2.39	2.11	2.17
Debt to Equity	1.12	1.23	1.61	1.26	1.33	1.55	2.90	3.24
Price Range	66.17-53.09	66.17-52.74	53.25-39.89	47.41-34.77	35.60-26.51	28.56-22.21	...	...
P/E Ratio	13.96-11.20	14.87-11.85	29.75-22.28	26.19-19.21	16.71-12.45	34.83-27.09	...	...
Average Yield %	2.16	2.11	2.32	2.35	2.86	2.21	...	...

Address: 399 Jefferson Road, Parsippany, NJ 07054
Telephone: 973-541-6620

Web Site: www.pinnaclefoods.com
Officers: Mark A. Clouse - Chief Executive Officer
Mark L. Schiller - Executive Vice President, Chief Commercial Officer, Division Officer

Auditors: DELOITTE & TOUCHE LLP
Transfer Agents: Computershare Trust Company, N.A.

PINNACLE WEST CAPITAL CORP

Exchange	Symbol	Price	52Wk Range	Yield	P/E
NYS	PNW	$80.56 (6/29/2018)	91.81-73.56	3.45	19.32

*7 Year Price Score 104.65 *NYSE Composite Index=100   *12 Month Price Score 92.33

Interim Earnings (Per Share)

Qtr.	Mar	Jun	Sep	Dec
2015	0.14	1.10	2.30	0.37
2016	0.04	1.08	2.35	0.48
2017	0.21	1.49	2.46	0.19
2018	0.03	...	...	...

Interim Dividends (Per Share)

Amt	Decl	Ex	Rec	Pay
0.695Q	10/18/2017	10/31/2017	11/01/2017	12/01/2017
0.695Q	12/20/2017	01/31/2018	02/01/2018	03/01/2018
0.695Q	04/18/2018	04/30/2018	05/01/2018	06/01/2018
0.695Q	06/20/2018	07/31/2018	08/01/2018	09/04/2018

Indicated Div: $2.78 (Div. Reinv. Plan)

Valuation Analysis / **Institutional Holding**

Forecast EPS	$4.46	No of Institutions 716
	(06/14/2018)	
Market Cap	$9.0 Billion	Shares 112,838,168
Book Value	$5.0 Billion	% Held 78.73
Price/Book	1.80	
Price/Sales	2.52	

Business Summary: Electric Utilities (MIC: 3.1.1 SIC: 4911 NAIC: 221122)

Pinnacle West Capital is a holding company. Through its subsidiary, Arizona Public Service Company, Co. provides either retail or wholesale electric service to most of the State of Arizona, with the exceptions of about one-half of the Phoenix metropolitan area, Tucson metropolitan area and Mohave County in northwestern Arizona. Co.'s business segment is its regulated electricity segment, which consists of regulated retail and wholesale electricity businesses (primarily electric service to Native Load customers) and related activities and includes electricity generation, transmission and distribution. As of Dec 31 2017, APS provided electric service to approximately 1.2 million customers.

Recent Developments: For the quarter ended Mar 31 2018, net income decreased 71.3% to US$8.1 million from US$28.2 million in the year-earlier quarter. Revenues were US$692.7 million, up 2.2% from US$677.7 million the year before. Operating income was US$31.3 million versus US$67.4 million in the prior-year quarter, a decrease of 53.5%. Direct operating expenses rose 5.5% to US$462.8 million from US$438.5 million in the comparable period the year before. Indirect operating expenses increased 15.6% to US$198.6 million from US$171.9 million in the equivalent prior-year period.

Prospects: Our evaluation of Pinnacle West Capital Corp. as of Jan. 21, 2018 is the result of our systematic analysis on three basic characteristics: earnings strength, relative valuation, and recent stock price movement. The company has generated a negative trend in earnings per share over the past 5 quarters and while recent estimates for the company have been mixed, PNW has posted better than expected results. Based on operating earnings yield, the company is undervalued when compared to all of the companies in our coverage universe. Share price changes over the past year indicates that PNW will perform very well over the near term.

Financial Data

(US$ in Thousands)	3 Mos	12/31/2017	12/31/2016	12/31/2015	12/31/2014	12/31/2013	12/31/2012	12/31/2011
Earnings Per Share	4.17	4.35	3.95	3.92	3.58	3.66	3.45	3.09
Cash Flow Per Share	10.22	10.00	9.16	9.86	9.94	10.49	10.66	10.32
Tang Book Value Per Share	44.85	44.80	43.14	41.30	39.50	38.07	36.20	34.98
Dividends Per Share	2.700	2.660	2.530	2.410	2.297	2.203	2.120	2.100
Dividend Payout %	64.75	61.15	64.05	61.48	64.18	60.18	61.45	67.96
Income Statement								
Total Revenue	692,714	3,565,296	3,498,682	3,495,443	3,491,632	3,454,628	3,301,804	3,241,379
EBITDA	77,139	1,556,270	1,372,772	1,344,624	1,366,128	1,379,467	1,219,262	1,099,652
Depn & Amortn	20,002	595,862	603,163	573,281	537,244	523,512	364,546	338,627
Income Before Taxes	6,829	766,221	584,743	593,131	644,401	670,557	656,310	539,238
Income Taxes	(1,265)	258,272	123,216	136,941	220,705	230,591	237,317	183,604
Net Income	3,221	488,456	442,034	437,257	397,595	406,074	381,542	339,473
Average Shares	112,493	112,367	112,046	111,552	111,178	110,806	110,527	109,864
Balance Sheet								
Current Assets	957,404	1,016,288	822,219	890,516	973,435	1,043,609	1,005,726	956,470
Total Assets	17,148,306	17,019,082	16,004,253	15,028,258	14,313,532	13,508,686	13,379,615	13,111,018
Current Liabilities	1,874,391	1,197,852	1,292,946	1,442,317	1,559,143	1,618,644	1,083,542	1,342,705
Long-Term Obligations	4,290,533	4,789,713	4,021,785	3,462,391	3,031,215	2,796,465	3,199,088	3,019,054
Total Liabilities	12,128,549	12,012,392	11,200,631	10,444,341	9,946,039	9,314,216	9,406,809	9,289,168
Stockholders' Equity	5,019,757	5,006,690	4,803,622	4,583,917	4,367,493	4,194,470	3,972,806	3,821,850
Shares Outstanding	111,932	111,751	111,336	110,980	110,571	110,181	109,742	109,245
Statistical Record								
Return on Assets %	2.81	2.96	2.84	2.98	2.86	3.02	2.87	2.67
Return on Equity %	9.51	9.96	9.39	9.77	9.29	9.94	9.76	9.05
EBITDA Margin %	11.14	43.65	39.24	38.47	39.13	39.93	36.93	33.93
Net Margin %	0.46	13.70	12.63	12.51	11.39	11.75	11.56	10.47
Asset Turnover	0.21	0.22	0.22	0.24	0.25	0.26	0.25	0.25
Current Ratio	0.51	0.85	0.64	0.62	0.62	0.64	0.93	0.71
Debt to Equity	0.85	0.96	0.84	0.76	0.69	0.67	0.81	0.79
Price Range	91.81-74.34	91.81-76.44	82.56-63.26	72.47-56.31	70.63-51.28	61.48-50.98	54.32-46.06	48.71-37.98
P/E Ratio	22.02-17.83	21.11-17.57	20.90-16.02	18.49-14.36	19.73-14.32	16.80-13.93	15.74-13.35	15.76-12.29
Average Yield %	3.17	3.11	3.42	3.83	4.05	3.94	4.21	4.81

Address: 400 North Fifth Street, P.O. Box 53999, Phoenix, AZ 85072-3999
Telephone: 602-250-1000
Fax: 602-379-2625

Web Site: www.pinnaclewest.com
Officers: Donald E. Brandt - Chairman, President, Chief Executive Officer James R. Hatfield - Executive Vice President, Senior Vice President, Chief Financial Officer, Treasurer

Auditors: Deloitte & Touche LLP
Investor Contact: 602-250-5668
Transfer Agents: Computershare, Providence, RI

PIONEER NATURAL RESOURCES CO

Exchange	Symbol	Price	52Wk Range	Yield	P/E
NYS	PXD	$189.24 (6/29/2018)	212.31-127.94	0.17	30.82

*7 Year Price Score 89.91 ***NYSE Composite Index=100** ***12 Month Price Score 114.49**

Interim Earnings (Per Share)
Qtr.	Mar	Jun	Sep	Dec
2015	(0.52)	(1.46)	4.27	(4.15)
2016	(1.65)	(1.63)	0.13	(0.24)
2017	(0.25)	1.36	(0.13)	3.87
2018	1.04	...	...	...

Interim Dividends (Per Share)
Amt	Decl	Ex	Rec	Pay
0.04Q	08/25/2016	09/28/2016	09/30/2016	10/12/2016
0.04Q	02/28/2017	03/29/2017	03/31/2017	04/12/2017
0.04Q	08/24/2017	09/28/2017	09/29/2017	10/12/2017
0.16Q	02/06/2018	03/28/2018	03/29/2018	04/12/2018

Indicated Div: $0.32

Valuation Analysis
		Institutional Holding	
Forecast EPS	$7.22	No of Institutions	1037
	(06/14/2018)		
Market Cap	$32.3 Billion	Shares	175,197,136
Book Value	$11.4 Billion	% Held	95.92
Price/Book	2.83		
Price/Sales	5.25		

TRADING VOLUME (thousand shares)

Business Summary: Production & Extraction (MIC: 9.1.1 SIC: 1311 NAIC: 211111)

Pioneer Natural Resources is a holding company. Through its subsidiaries, Co. is engaged as an oil and gas exploration and production company. Co. explores for, develops and produces oil, natural gas liquids and gas within the U.S. Co.'s operations are primarily located in the Permian Basin in West Texas, the Eagle Ford Shale play in South Texas, the Raton field in southeast Colorado and the West Panhandle field in the Texas Panhandle. As of Dec 31 2017, Co. had proved reserves of 985.4 million barrels of oil equivalent.

Recent Developments: For the quarter ended Mar 31 2018, net income amounted to US$178.0 million versus a net loss of US$42.0 million in the year-earlier quarter. Revenues were US$2.15 billion, up 65.4% from US$1.30 billion the year before. Direct operating expenses rose 97.7% to US$1.70 billion from US$860.0 million in the comparable period the year before. Indirect operating expenses decreased 56.7% to US$222.0 million from US$513.0 million in the equivalent prior-year period.

Prospects: Our evaluation of Pioneer Natural Resources Co as of Jan. 21, 2018 is the result of our systematic analysis on three basic characteristics: earnings strength, relative valuation, and recent stock price movement. The company has generated a negative trend in earnings per share over the past 5 quarters and while recent estimates for the company have been raised by analysts, PXD has posted better than expected results. Based on operating earnings yield, the company is overvalued when compared to all of the companies in our coverage universe. Share price changes over the past year indicates that PXD will perform very poorly over the near term.

Financial Data
(US$ in Thousands)	3 Mos	12/31/2017	12/31/2016	12/31/2015	12/31/2014	12/31/2013	12/31/2012	12/31/2011
Earnings Per Share	6.14	4.85	(3.34)	(1.83)	6.38	(6.16)	1.50	6.88
Cash Flow Per Share	13.41	12.29	9.00	8.38	16.43	15.76	14.90	13.09
Tang Book Value Per Share	65.30	64.66	59.70	54.20	55.77	44.36	43.70	42.60
Dividends Per Share	0.200	0.080	0.080	0.080	0.080	0.080	0.080	0.080
Dividend Payout %	3.26	1.65	...	...	1.25	...	5.33	1.16
Income Statement								
Total Revenue	2,150,000	5,455,000	3,824,000	4,825,000	5,055,000	3,719,510	3,228,308	2,786,585
EBITDA	638,000	1,941,000	817,000	1,241,000	2,912,000	600,107	1,314,968	1,441,962
Depn & Amortn	374,000	1,479,000	1,569,000	1,475,000	1,131,000	978,076	830,689	603,896
Income Before Taxes	228,000	309,000	(959,000)	(421,000)	1,597,000	(561,719)	280,057	656,406
Income Taxes	50,000	(524,000)	(403,000)	(155,000)	556,000	(211,775)	92,384	197,644
Net Income	178,000	833,000	(556,000)	(273,000)	930,000	(838,414)	192,285	834,489
Average Shares	171,000	170,000	166,000	149,000	144,000	136,130	126,320	119,215
Balance Sheet								
Current Assets	2,824,000	3,010,000	3,298,000	3,194,000	2,359,000	1,728,434	1,050,355	1,479,297
Total Assets	17,323,000	17,003,000	16,459,000	15,154,000	14,926,000	12,292,788	13,069,030	11,524,161
Current Liabilities	2,250,000	2,128,000	1,566,000	1,462,000	1,580,000	1,250,106	1,034,790	1,011,798
Long-Term Obligations	2,284,000	2,283,000	2,728,000	3,207,000	2,665,000	2,653,059	3,721,193	2,528,905
Total Liabilities	5,926,000	5,729,000	6,055,000	6,786,000	6,345,000	5,691,204	7,379,676	6,035,367
Stockholders' Equity	11,397,000	11,274,000	10,404,000	8,368,000	8,581,000	6,601,584	5,689,354	5,488,794
Shares Outstanding	170,418	170,188	169,724	149,379	149,000	142,627	123,355	121,856
Statistical Record								
Return on Assets %	6.37	4.98	N.M.	N.M.	6.83	N.M.	1.56	7.87
Return on Equity %	9.69	7.69	N.M.	N.M.	12.25	N.M.	3.43	17.37
EBITDA Margin %	29.67	35.58	21.37	25.72	57.61	16.13	40.73	51.75
Net Margin %	8.28	15.27	N.M.	N.M.	18.40	N.M.	5.96	29.95
Asset Turnover	0.37	0.33	0.24	0.32	0.37	0.29	0.26	0.26
Current Ratio	1.26	1.41	2.11	2.18	1.49	1.38	1.02	1.46
Debt to Equity	0.20	0.20	0.26	0.38	0.31	0.40	0.65	0.46
Price Range	190.44-127.94	198.90-127.94	193.24-107.75	180.23-107.24	233.07-130.60	224.95-106.59	116.24-78.78	104.66-61.82
P/E Ratio	31.02-20.84	41.01-26.38	...	...	36.53-20.47	...	77.49-52.52	15.21-8.99
Average Yield %	0.12	0.05	0.05	0.06	0.04	0.05	0.08	0.09

Address: 5205 N. O'Connor Blvd., Suite 200, Irving, TX 75039	Web Site: www.pxd.com	Auditors: Ernst & Young LLP
Telephone: 972-444-9001	Officers: Timothy L. Dove - President, Chief Executive Officer, Chief Operating Officer Richard P. Dealy - Executive Vice President, Chief Financial Officer	Investor Contact: 972-444-9001
Fax: 972-969-3587		Transfer Agents: Continental Stock Transfer & Trust Company, New York, NY

PITNEY BOWES INC

Exchange	Symbol	Price	52Wk Range	Yield	P/E
NYS	PBI	$8.57 (6/29/2018)	15.96-8.45	8.75	6.49

*7 Year Price Score 53.26 *NYSE Composite Index=100 *12 Month Price Score 75.70

Interim Earnings (Per Share)

Qtr.	Mar	Jun	Sep	Dec
2015	0.40	0.75	0.44	0.44
2016	0.30	0.28	0.35	(0.44)
2017	0.35	0.26	0.31	0.47
2018	0.28	...	...	...

Interim Dividends (Per Share)

Amt	Decl	Ex	Rec	Pay
0.188Q	08/04/2017	08/23/2017	08/25/2017	09/12/2017
0.188Q	11/10/2017	11/20/2017	11/21/2017	12/12/2017
0.188Q	02/05/2018	02/15/2018	02/16/2018	03/12/2018
0.188Q	05/07/2018	05/24/2018	05/25/2018	06/11/2018

Indicated Div: $0.75 (Div. Reinv. Plan)

Valuation Analysis

		Institutional Holding	
Forecast EPS	$1.18	No of Institutions	
	(06/10/2018)	606	
Market Cap	$1.6 Billion	Shares	
Book Value	$214.9 Million	205,137,456	
Price/Book	7.46	% Held	
Price/Sales	0.43	84.94	

Business Summary: Office Equipment & Furniture (MIC: 7.5.1 SIC: 7372 NAIC: 511210)

Pitney Bowes is a technology company. Co.'s solutions include: Small and Medium Business Solutions, which provides a range of equipment, software, supplies and services that enable Co.'s clients to create physical and digital mail, evidence postage and print shipping labels for the sending of mail, flats and parcels; Enterprise Business Solutions, which includes equipment and services that enable large enterprises to process inbound and outbound mail; and Digital Commerce Solutions, which provide a range of solutions, including customer information management, location intelligence, customer engagement software and shipping management and cross border ecommerce solutions.

Recent Developments: For the quarter ended Mar 31 2018, net income decreased 17.8% to US$53.5 million from US$65.1 million in the year-earlier quarter. Revenues were US$983.2 million, up 17.5% from US$836.6 million the year before. Direct operating expenses rose 44.7% to US$522.8 million from US$361.2 million in the comparable period the year before. Indirect operating expenses increased 2.2% to US$387.3 million from US$378.9 million in the equivalent prior-year period.

Prospects: Our evaluation of Pitney Bowes Inc. as of Jan. 21, 2018 is the result of our systematic analysis on three basic characteristics: earnings strength, relative valuation, and recent stock price movement. The company has generated a negative trend in earnings per share over the past 5 quarters and while recent estimates for the company have remained steady, PBI has posted results that fell short of analysts expectations. Based on operating earnings yield, the company is undervalued when compared to all of the companies in our coverage universe. Share price changes over the past year indicates that PBI will perform very poorly over the near term.

Financial Data

(US$ in Thousands)	3 Mos	12/31/2017	12/31/2016	12/31/2015	12/31/2014	12/31/2013	12/31/2012	12/31/2011
Earnings Per Share	1.32	1.39	0.49	2.03	1.64	0.70	2.21	3.05
Cash Flow Per Share	2.27	2.66	2.60	2.58	3.25	3.10	3.29	4.56
Dividends Per Share	0.750	0.750	0.750	0.750	0.750	0.938	1.500	1.480
Dividend Payout %	56.82	53.96	153.06	36.95	45.73	133.93	67.87	48.52
Income Statement								
Total Revenue	983,182	3,549,948	3,406,575	3,578,060	3,821,504	3,869,401	4,904,015	5,277,974
EBITDA	166,990	596,151	528,581	906,199	765,646	751,541	1,003,999	825,547
Depn & Amortn	50,820	149,000	138,000	136,000	165,000	158,000	211,000	214,000
Income Before Taxes	73,092	282,989	246,370	610,825	431,196	403,177	604,613	414,281
Income Taxes	19,579	21,649	131,819	189,778	112,815	83,069	150,305	44,585
Net Income	53,513	261,340	92,805	407,943	333,755	142,835	445,163	617,480
Average Shares	188,175	187,435	188,975	200,945	203,961	202,957	201,366	202,766
Balance Sheet								
Current Assets	2,289,033	2,636,508	2,325,183	2,319,808	2,760,120	2,838,212	3,212,127	3,259,858
Total Assets	6,319,618	6,678,715	5,837,133	6,141,462	6,485,693	6,772,708	7,859,891	8,147,104
Current Liabilities	2,004,226	2,054,993	2,327,619	2,279,051	2,360,623	2,227,755	2,877,037	3,091,862
Long-Term Obligations	3,248,713	3,559,278	2,750,405	2,507,912	2,927,127	3,346,295	3,642,375	3,683,909
Total Liabilities	6,104,725	6,490,154	5,940,793	5,962,740	6,408,434	6,584,305	7,749,260	8,186,090
Stockholders' Equity	214,893	188,561	(103,660)	178,721	77,259	188,403	110,631	(38,986)
Shares Outstanding	187,143	186,603	185,668	195,521	201,027	202,082	200,884	199,751
Statistical Record								
Return on Assets %	4.14	4.18	1.55	6.46	5.03	1.95	5.55	7.44
Return on Equity %	296.31	615.63	246.60	318.73	251.26	95.53	1,239.30	...
EBITDA Margin %	16.98	16.79	15.52	25.33	20.04	19.42	20.47	15.64
Net Margin %	5.44	7.36	2.72	11.40	8.73	3.69	9.08	11.70
Asset Turnover	0.61	0.57	0.57	0.57	0.58	0.53	0.61	0.64
Current Ratio	1.14	1.28	1.00	1.02	1.17	1.27	1.12	1.05
Debt to Equity	15.12	18.88	...	14.03	37.89	17.76	32.92	...
Price Range	16.14-9.64	16.59-9.64	21.70-14.24	24.42-18.82	28.18-21.13	24.09-10.64	19.54-10.41	26.18-17.35
P/E Ratio	12.23-7.30	11.94-6.94	44.29-29.06	12.03-9.27	17.18-12.88	34.41-15.20	8.84-4.71	8.58-5.69
Average Yield %	5.71	5.53	4.13	3.45	2.93	5.67	10.01	6.71

Address: 3001 Summer Street, Stamford, CT 06926	**Web Site:** www.pb.com	**Auditors:** PricewaterhouseCoopers LLP
Telephone: 203-356-5000	**Officers:** Marc B. Lautenbach - President, Chief Executive Officer Michael Monahan - Executive Vice President, Chief Financial Officer, Chief Operating Officer	**Investor Contact:** 203-351-6349
Fax: 203-351-7336		**Transfer Agents:** Computershare Trust Company, N.A., Providence, RI

PLANTRONICS, INC.

Exchange	Symbol	Price	52Wk Range	Yield	P/E
NYS	PLT	$76.25 (6/29/2018)	77.69-41.36	0.79	N/A

*7 Year Price Score 95.65 ***NYSE Composite Index=100** ***12 Month Price Score 130.20**

Interim Earnings (Per Share)
Qtr.	Jun	Sep	Dec	Mar
2013-14	0.62	0.53	0.80	0.65
2014-15	0.68	0.65	0.71	0.60
2015-16	0.55	0.52	0.49	0.40
2016-17	0.62	0.63	0.68	0.59
2017-18	0.57	0.59	(1.54)	0.30

Interim Dividends (Per Share)
Amt	Decl	Ex	Rec	Pay
0.15Q	07/27/2017	08/16/2017	08/18/2017	09/08/2017
0.15Q	10/31/2017	11/17/2017	11/20/2017	12/08/2017
0.15Q	01/30/2018	02/16/2018	02/20/2018	03/09/2018
0.15Q	05/01/2018	05/17/2018	05/18/2018	06/08/2018

Indicated Div: $0.60

Valuation Analysis
		Institutional Holding	
Forecast EPS	$3.09	No of Institutions	
	(06/13/2018)	329	
Market Cap	$2.5 Billion	Shares	
Book Value	$353.0 Million	42,952,240	
Price/Book	7.18	% Held	
Price/Sales	2.96	86.01	

Business Summary: Manufacturing (MIC: 6.1.1 SIC: 3661 NAIC: 334210)

Plantronics designs, manufactures, and markets lightweight communications headsets, telephone headset systems, other communication endpoints, and accessories for the business and consumer markets. Co. also manufactures and markets specialty telephone products, such as telephones for the hearing impaired, and related products. Co.'s product categories are Enterprise, which includes headsets optimized for Unified Communications, other corded and cordless communication headsets, audio processors, and telephone systems; and Consumer, which includes Bluetooth and corded products for mobile device applications, personal computer, gaming headsets, and products for the hearing impaired.

Recent Developments: For the year ended Mar 31 2018, net loss amounted to US$869,000 versus net income of US$82.6 million in the prior year. Revenues were US$856.9 million, down 2.8% from US$881.2 million the year before. Operating income was US$123.5 million versus US$125.1 million in the prior year, a decrease of 1.3%. Direct operating expenses declined 5.0% to US$417.8 million from US$439.8 million in the comparable period the year before. Indirect operating expenses decreased 0.2% to US$315.6 million from US$316.3 million in the equivalent prior-year period.

Prospects: Our evaluation of Plantronics Inc. as of Jan. 21, 2018 is the result of our systematic analysis on three basic characteristics: earnings strength, relative valuation, and recent stock price movement. The company has generated a negative trend in earnings per share over the past 5 quarters and while recent estimates for the company have been mixed, PLT has posted better than expected results. Based on operating earnings yield, the company is undervalued when compared to all of the companies in our coverage universe. Share price changes over the past year indicates that PLT will perform very poorly over the near term.

Financial Data
(US$ in Thousands)	03/31/2018	03/31/2017	03/31/2016	03/31/2015	03/31/2014	03/31/2013	03/31/2012	03/31/2011
Earnings Per Share	(0.03)	2.51	1.96	2.63	2.59	2.49	2.41	2.21
Cash Flow Per Share	3.75	4.27	4.29	3.70	3.33	3.01	3.18	3.32
Tang Book Value Per Share	10.15	10.97	8.90	17.10	16.00	14.56	12.06	12.83
Dividends Per Share	0.600	0.600	0.600	0.600	0.400	0.400	0.200	0.200
Dividend Payout %	...	23.90	30.61	22.81	15.44	16.06	8.30	9.05
Income Statement								
Total Revenue	856,903	881,176	856,907	865,010	818,607	762,226	713,368	683,602
EBITDA	150,624	151,595	127,225	167,585	155,624	153,897	154,653	157,012
Depn & Amortn	21,100	20,700	19,900	18,500	15,500	15,800	13,300	16,300
Income Before Taxes	100,227	101,665	82,176	145,251	141,139	138,425	142,602	140,656
Income Taxes	101,096	19,066	13,784	32,950	28,722	32,023	33,566	31,413
Net Income	(869)	82,599	68,392	112,301	112,417	106,402	109,036	109,243
Average Shares	32,345	32,963	34,938	42,643	43,364	42,738	45,265	49,344
Balance Sheet								
Current Assets	899,726	698,977	596,995	602,654	556,287	566,490	524,174	617,720
Total Assets	1,076,887	1,017,159	933,437	876,042	811,815	764,605	672,470	744,647
Current Liabilities	125,514	117,170	109,167	94,822	97,607	103,486	86,193	93,602
Long-Term Obligations	492,509	491,059	489,609	34,500	...	...	37,000	...
Total Liabilities	723,917	635,003	621,038	148,645	113,151	118,158	145,226	109,795
Stockholders' Equity	352,970	382,156	312,399	727,397	698,664	646,447	527,244	634,852
Shares Outstanding	33,251	33,416	33,319	41,601	42,649	43,283	42,512	48,315
Statistical Record								
Return on Assets %	N.M.	8.47	7.54	13.31	14.26	14.81	15.35	15.61
Return on Equity %	N.M.	23.78	13.12	15.75	16.71	18.13	18.71	18.11
EBITDA Margin %	17.58	17.20	14.85	19.37	19.01	20.19	21.68	22.97
Net Margin %	N.M.	9.37	7.98	12.98	13.73	13.96	15.28	15.98
Asset Turnover	0.82	0.90	0.94	1.02	1.04	1.06	1.00	0.98
Current Ratio	7.17	5.97	5.47	6.36	5.70	5.47	6.08	6.60
Debt to Equity	1.40	1.28	1.57	0.05	...	...	0.07	...
Price Range	60.37-41.36	57.47-37.28	58.09-32.55	55.45-41.57	49.56-41.41	45.61-28.95	40.26-27.45	38.20-26.79
P/E Ratio	...	22.90-14.85	29.64-16.61	21.08-15.81	19.14-15.99	18.32-11.63	16.71-11.39	17.29-12.12
Average Yield %	1.17	1.22	1.19	1.24	0.89	1.12	0.58	0.60

Address: 345 Encinal Street, Santa Cruz, CA 95060	**Web Site:** www.plantronics.com	**Auditors:** PricewaterhouseCoopers LLP
Telephone: 831-426-5858	**Officers:** Robert C. (Bob) Hagerty - Chairman Marvin Tseu - Vice-Chairman	**Investor Contact:** 831-426-5858
Fax: 831-426-6098		**Transfer Agents:** Computershare Trust Company, N.A., Providence, RI

PLATFORM SPECIALTY PRODUCTS CORP

Exchange NYS	**Symbol** PAH	**Price** $11.60 (6/29/2018)	**52Wk Range** 14.58-9.33	**Yield** N/A	**P/E** N/A

*7 Year Price Score N/A   ***NYSE Composite Index=100**   ***12 Month Price Score 101.56**

Interim Earnings (Per Share)

Qtr.	Mar	Jun	Sep	Dec
2015	(0.14)	(0.06)	(0.58)	(0.71)
2016	(0.59)	(0.04)	(0.15)	0.06
2017	(0.09)	(0.21)	(0.24)	(0.50)
2018	0.13	...	...	...

Interim Dividends (Per Share)

No Dividends Paid

Valuation Analysis   **Institutional Holding**

Forecast EPS	$0.96 (06/13/2018)	No of Institutions	275
Market Cap	$3.3 Billion	Shares	
Book Value	$2.9 Billion		295,356,224
Price/Book	1.17	% Held	
Price/Sales	0.86		N/A

Business Summary: Specialty Chemicals (MIC: 8.3.2 SIC: 5169 NAIC: 325998)

Platform Specialty Products is a producer of chemical products. Co.'s business involves the formulation of a range of chemicals, which are sold into various industries, including agricultural, animal health, electronics, and graphic arts. Co. manages its business in two reportable segments: Performance Solutions, which formulates and markets chemistry solutions that are used in electronics, automotive production, oil and gas production, drilling, commercial packaging and printing; and Agricultural Solutions, which provides to growers a range crop protection solutions from weeds (herbicides), insects (insecticides) and diseases (fungicides), in foliar and seed treatment applications.

Recent Developments: For the quarter ended Mar 31 2018, net income amounted to US$38.0 million versus a net loss of US$23.6 million in the year-earlier quarter. Revenues were US$964.1 million, up 11.9% from US$861.8 million the year before. Operating income was US$104.2 million versus US$99.3 million in the prior-year quarter, an increase of 4.9%. Direct operating expenses rose 15.7% to US$559.4 million from US$483.4 million in the comparable period the year before. Indirect operating expenses increased 7.7% to US$300.5 million from US$279.1 million in the equivalent prior-year period.

Prospects: Our evaluation of Platform Specialty Products as of Jan. 21, 2018 is the result of our systematic analysis on three basic characteristics: earnings strength, relative valuation, and recent stock price movement. The company has suffered a very negative trend in earnings per share over the past 5 quarters and while recent estimates for the company have been mixed, PAH has posted results that fell short of analysts expectations. Based on operating earnings yield, the company is undervalued when compared to all of the companies in our coverage universe. Share price changes over the past year indicates that PAH will perform very poorly over the near term.

Financial Data
(US$ in Thousands)

	3 Mos	12/31/2017	12/31/2016	12/31/2015	12/31/2014	12/31/2013
Earnings Per Share	(0.82)	(1.04)	(0.65)	(1.52)	(1.94)	(2.10)
Cash Flow Per Share	0.49	0.64	0.76	1.58	0.73	0.08
Income Statement						
Total Revenue	964,100	3,775,900	3,585,900	2,542,300	843,200	118,239
EBITDA	201,000	130,900	402,600	33,500	26,300	(192,172)
Depn & Amortn	19,800	78,300	75,000	48,900	19,300	3,900
Income Before Taxes	103,000	(289,000)	(48,100)	(229,300)	(30,900)	(201,444)
Income Taxes	65,000	6,600	28,600	75,100	(6,700)	(5,819)
Net Income	37,300	(296,200)	(73,700)	(308,600)	(29,900)	(194,222)
Average Shares	293,800	286,100	272,300	203,200	135,300	92,563
Balance Sheet						
Current Assets	2,552,100	2,340,600	2,071,200	2,270,500	1,578,400	383,239
Total Assets	10,547,200	10,252,400	10,054,100	10,190,200	4,557,600	2,241,888
Current Liabilities	1,235,300	1,091,800	1,082,700	1,062,400	242,600	119,420
Long-Term Obligations	5,495,200	5,440,600	5,122,900	5,173,600	1,400,800	744,291
Total Liabilities	7,691,400	7,509,300	7,318,000	7,440,400	2,098,000	1,188,321
Stockholders' Equity	2,855,800	2,743,100	2,736,100	2,749,800	2,459,600	1,053,567
Shares Outstanding	288,109	287,399	284,221	229,464	182,066	103,571
Statistical Record						
EBITDA Margin %	20.85	3.47	11.23	1.32	3.12	N.M.
Net Margin %	3.87	N.M.	N.M.	N.M.	N.M.	N.M.
Asset Turnover	0.37	0.37	0.35	0.34	0.25	...
Current Ratio	2.07	2.14	1.91	2.14	6.51	3.21
Debt to Equity	1.92	1.98	1.87	1.88	0.57	0.71
Price Range	14.58-9.45	14.58-9.45	12.83-5.55	28.35-10.12	28.70-13.83	...

Address: 1450 Centrepark Boulevard, Suite 210, West Palm Beach, FL 33401 **Telephone:** 561-207-9600	**Web Site:** www.platformspecialtyproducts.com **Officers:** Martin E. Franklin - Chairman Rakesh Sachdev - Chief Executive Officer	**Auditors:** PricewaterhouseCoopers LLP

PNC FINANCIAL SERVICES GROUP (THE)

Exchange	Symbol	Price	52Wk Range	Yield	P/E
NYS	PNC	$135.10 (6/29/2018)	162.45-120.71	2.81	12.46

*7 Year Price Score 126.87 *NYSE Composite Index=100 *12 Month Price Score 100.58

Interim Earnings (Per Share)

Qtr.	Mar	Jun	Sep	Dec
2015	1.75	1.88	1.90	1.87
2016	1.68	1.82	1.84	1.97
2017	1.96	2.10	2.16	4.15
2018	2.43	...	...	...

Interim Dividends (Per Share)

Amt	Decl	Ex	Rec	Pay
0.75Q	10/03/2017	10/16/2017	10/17/2017	11/05/2017
0.75Q	01/04/2018	01/16/2018	01/17/2018	02/05/2018
0.75Q	04/04/2018	04/13/2018	04/16/2018	05/05/2018
0.95Q	07/05/2018	07/16/2018	07/17/2018	08/06/2018

Indicated Div: $3.80

Valuation Analysis

		Institutional Holding	
Forecast EPS	$10.57	No of Institutions	
	(06/14/2018)	1619	
Market Cap	$63.5 Billion	Shares	
Book Value	$47.0 Billion	467,776,576	
Price/Book	1.35	% Held	
Price/Sales	3.44	79.93	

Business Summary: Banking (MIC: 5.1.1 SIC: 6021 NAIC: 522110)

PNC Financial Services Group is a bank holding company and a financial services company that provides its products and services nationally. Co.'s main markets are in Pennsylvania, Ohio, New Jersey, Michigan, Illinois, Maryland, Indiana, Florida, North Carolina, Kentucky, Washington, D.C., Delaware, Virginia, Georgia, Alabama, Missouri, Wisconsin and South Carolina. Co. also provides certain products and services internationally. Co. has six segments: retail banking, corporate and institutional banking, asset management group, residential mortgage banking, BlackRock, and non-strategic assets portfolio. At Dec 31 2017, Co. had total assets of $380.77 billion and deposits of $265.05 billion.

Recent Developments: For the quarter ended Mar 31 2018, net income increased 15.4% to US$1.24 billion from US$1.07 billion in the year-earlier quarter. Net interest income increased 9.3% to US$2.36 billion from US$2.16 billion in the year-earlier quarter. Provision for loan losses was US$92.0 million versus US$88.0 million in the prior-year quarter, an increase of 4.5%. Non-interest income rose 1.5% to US$1.75 billion from US$1.72 billion, while non-interest expense advanced 5.2% to US$2.53 billion.

Prospects: Our evaluation of PNC Financial Services Group as of Jan. 21, 2018 is the result of our systematic analysis on three basic characteristics: earnings strength, relative valuation, and recent stock price movement. The company has enjoyed a very positive trend in earnings per share over the past 5 quarters and while recent estimates for the company have been raised by analysts, PNC has posted better than expected results. Based on operating earnings yield, the company is undervalued when compared to all of the companies in our coverage universe. Share price changes over the past year indicates that PNC will perform in line with the market over the near term.

Financial Data

(US$ in Thousands)	3 Mos	12/31/2017	12/31/2016	12/31/2015	12/31/2014	12/31/2013	12/31/2012	12/31/2011
Earnings Per Share	10.84	10.36	7.30	7.39	7.30	7.39	5.30	5.64
Cash Flow Per Share	14.82	11.85	7.34	10.69	10.50	10.52	12.94	11.52
Tang Book Value Per Share	76.11	77.18	71.83	59.89	56.71	50.99	46.48	42.26
Dividends Per Share	2.800	2.600	2.120	2.010	1.880	1.720	1.550	1.150
Dividend Payout %	25.83	25.10	29.04	27.20	25.75	23.27	29.25	20.39
Income Statement								
Interest Income	2,918,000	10,814,000	9,652,000	9,323,000	9,431,000	10,007,000	10,734,000	10,194,000
Interest Expense	557,000	1,706,000	1,261,000	1,045,000	906,000	860,000	1,094,000	1,494,000
Net Interest Income	2,361,000	9,108,000	8,391,000	8,278,000	8,525,000	9,147,000	9,640,000	8,700,000
Provision for Losses	92,000	441,000	433,000	255,000	273,000	643,000	987,000	1,152,000
Non-Interest Income	1,750,000	7,221,000	6,771,000	6,947,000	6,850,000	6,865,000	5,872,000	5,626,000
Non-Interest Expense	2,527,000	10,398,000	9,476,000	9,463,000	9,488,000	9,801,000	10,582,000	9,105,000
Income Before Taxes	1,492,000	5,490,000	5,253,000	5,507,000	5,614,000	5,568,000	3,943,000	4,069,000
Income Taxes	253,000	102,000	1,268,000	1,364,000	1,407,000	1,341,000	942,000	998,000
Net Income	1,229,000	5,338,000	3,903,000	4,106,000	4,184,000	4,220,000	3,013,000	3,056,000
Average Shares	476,000	486,000	500,000	521,000	537,000	532,000	529,000	526,000
Balance Sheet								
Net Loans & Leases	219,975,000	220,502,000	210,748,000	205,509,000	203,748,000	194,259,000	185,513,000	157,603,000
Total Assets	379,161,000	380,768,000	366,380,000	358,493,000	345,072,000	320,296,000	305,107,000	271,205,000
Total Deposits	264,704,000	265,053,000	257,164,000	249,002,000	232,234,000	220,931,000	213,142,000	187,966,000
Total Liabilities	332,192,000	333,255,000	320,681,000	313,783,000	300,521,000	277,888,000	266,104,000	237,152,000
Stockholders' Equity	46,969,000	47,513,000	45,699,000	44,710,000	44,551,000	42,408,000	39,003,000	34,053,000
Shares Outstanding	470,000	473,000	485,000	504,000	523,000	533,000	528,000	527,000
Statistical Record								
Return on Assets %	1.47	1.43	1.07	1.17	1.26	1.35	1.04	1.14
Return on Equity %	11.88	11.45	8.61	9.20	9.62	10.37	8.23	9.51
Net Interest Margin %	80.91	84.22	86.94	88.79	90.39	91.41	89.81	85.34
Efficiency Ratio %	54.13	57.65	57.70	58.16	58.28	58.09	63.72	57.55
Loans to Deposits	0.83	0.83	0.82	0.83	0.88	0.88	0.87	0.84
Price Range	162.45-115.80	146.26-113.93	118.31-77.88	99.86-82.42	92.93-76.60	78.20-58.31	67.33-53.69	64.94-42.98
P/E Ratio	14.99-10.68	14.12-11.00	16.21-10.67	13.51-11.15	12.73-10.49	10.58-7.89	12.70-10.13	11.51-7.62
Average Yield %	2.07	2.04	2.35	2.16	2.22	2.44	2.55	2.02

Address: The Tower at PNC Plaza, 300 Fifth Avenue, Pittsburgh, PA 15222-2401
Telephone: 412-762-2000
Fax: 412-762-5798

Web Site: www.pnc.com
Officers: William S. Demchak - Chairman, President, Chief Executive Officer Orlando C. Esposito - Executive Vice President, Division Officer

Auditors: PricewaterhouseCoopers LLP
Investor Contact: 412-762-8257
Transfer Agents: Computershare Trust Company, N. A., Canton, MA

PNM RESOURCES INC

Exchange	Symbol	Price	52Wk Range	Yield	P/E
NYS	PNM	$38.90 (6/29/2018)	45.50-33.80	2.72	42.75

*7 Year Price Score 113.52 *NYSE Composite Index=100 *12 Month Price Score 95.03

Interim Earnings (Per Share)

Qtr.	Mar	Jun	Sep	Dec
2015	0.18	0.40	0.76	(1.14)
2016	0.13	0.34	0.68	0.31
2017	0.29	0.47	0.92	(0.67)
2018	0.19	...	...	...

Interim Dividends (Per Share)

Amt	Decl	Ex	Rec	Pay
0.242Q	07/26/2017	08/03/2017	08/07/2017	08/14/2017
0.242Q	09/19/2017	10/27/2017	10/30/2017	11/14/2017
0.265Q	12/01/2017	01/17/2018	01/18/2018	02/01/2018
0.265Q	02/23/2018	05/01/2018	05/02/2018	05/16/2018

Indicated Div: $1.06

Valuation Analysis

Forecast EPS	$1.87 (06/14/2018)
Market Cap	$3.1 Billion
Book Value	$1.7 Billion
Price/Book	1.83
Price/Sales	2.16

Institutional Holding

No of Institutions	398
Shares	96,138,360
% Held	79.10

Business Summary: Electric Utilities (MIC: 3.1.1 SIC: 4911 NAIC: 221121)

PNM Resources is a holding company with two regulated utilities providing electricity and electric services in New Mexico and Texas. Co.'s primary subsidiaries are Public Service Company of New Mexico (PNM) and Texas-New Mexico Power Company (TNMP). PNM is an electric utility that provides electric generation, transmission, and distribution service to its rate-regulated customers in New Mexico. TNMP is a regulated utility engaged in providing transmission and distribution services in Texas under the provisions of Texas Electric Choice Act and the Texas Public Utility Regulatory Act. As of Dec 31 2017, PNM had 523,812 customers, while TNMP had 249,632 consumers.

Recent Developments: For the quarter ended Mar 31 2018, net income decreased 28.9% to US$18.8 million from US$26.4 million in the year-earlier quarter. Revenues were US$317.9 million, down 3.7% from US$330.2 million the year before. Operating income was US$46.1 million versus US$58.1 million in the prior-year quarter, a decrease of 20.6%. Direct operating expenses declined 4.1% to US$144.9 million from US$151.1 million in the comparable period the year before. Indirect operating expenses increased 4.9% to US$126.9 million from US$121.0 million in the equivalent prior-year period.

Prospects: Our evaluation of PNM Resources Inc. as of Jan. 21, 2018 is the result of our systematic analysis on three basic characteristics: earnings strength, relative valuation, and recent stock price movement. The company has generated a negative trend in earnings per share over the past 5 quarters. However, while recent estimates for the company have been mixed, PNM has posted better than expected results. Based on operating earnings yield, the company is undervalued when compared to all of the companies in our coverage universe. Share price changes over the past year indicates that PNM will perform very well over the near term.

Financial Data (US$ in Thousands)	3 Mos	12/31/2017	12/31/2016	12/31/2015	12/31/2014	12/31/2013	12/31/2012	12/31/2011
Earnings Per Share	0.91	1.00	1.46	0.20	1.45	1.25	1.31	1.96
Cash Flow Per Share	5.91	6.56	5.19	4.85	5.20	4.85	3.52	3.28
Tang Book Value Per Share	17.79	17.93	17.69	17.43	18.26	17.66	16.84	16.41
Dividends Per Share	0.993	0.970	0.880	0.800	0.740	0.640	0.560	0.500
Dividend Payout %	109.07	97.00	60.27	400.00	51.03	51.20	42.75	25.51
Income Statement								
Total Revenue	317,878	1,445,003	1,362,951	1,439,082	1,435,853	1,387,923	1,342,403	1,700,619
EBITDA	116,261	605,662	543,547	377,376	521,658	453,355	489,307	617,169
Depn & Amortn	67,748	268,194	242,033	222,861	209,867	166,881	206,499	195,366
Income Before Taxes	19,582	225,759	195,174	46,153	200,647	175,069	175,035	312,469
Income Taxes	783	130,340	63,278	15,075	69,738	59,513	54,910	121,535
Net Income	15,122	80,402	117,377	16,168	116,782	101,035	106,075	176,887
Average Shares	80,013	80,141	80,132	80,139	80,279	79,845	80,417	89,757
Balance Sheet								
Current Assets	277,299	294,420	378,039	385,570	432,817	401,539	442,191	462,819
Total Assets	6,676,393	6,646,103	6,471,080	6,009,328	5,829,325	5,500,210	5,372,583	5,204,613
Current Liabilities	782,753	835,644	805,108	641,120	704,282	492,671	434,103	373,268
Long-Term Obligations	2,271,984	2,180,750	2,119,364	1,966,969	1,642,024	1,670,420	1,669,760	1,671,626
Total Liabilities	4,981,250	4,939,321	4,783,599	4,342,986	4,096,250	3,815,112	3,752,867	3,619,099
Stockholders' Equity	1,695,143	1,706,782	1,687,481	1,666,342	1,733,075	1,685,098	1,619,716	1,585,514
Shares Outstanding	79,653	79,653	79,653	79,653	79,653	79,653	79,653	79,653
Statistical Record								
Return on Assets %	1.10	1.23	1.88	0.27	2.06	1.86	2.00	3.39
Return on Equity %	4.27	4.74	6.98	0.95	6.83	6.11	6.60	10.94
EBITDA Margin %	36.57	41.91	39.88	26.22	36.33	32.66	36.45	36.29
Net Margin %	4.76	5.56	8.61	1.12	8.13	7.28	7.90	10.40
Asset Turnover	0.22	0.22	0.22	0.24	0.25	0.26	0.25	0.33
Current Ratio	0.35	0.35	0.47	0.60	0.61	0.82	1.02	1.24
Debt to Equity	1.34	1.28	1.26	1.18	0.95	0.99	1.03	1.05
Price Range	45.50-33.80	45.50-33.45	36.05-29.35	31.17-24.60	31.39-23.53	24.29-20.28	22.32-17.52	19.11-12.98
P/E Ratio	50.00-37.14	45.50-33.45	24.69-20.10	155.85-123.00	21.65-16.23	19.43-16.22	17.04-13.37	9.75-6.62
Average Yield %	2.51	2.47	2.69	2.89	2.74	2.82	2.85	3.19

Address: 414 Silver Ave. S.W., Albuquerque, NM 87102-3289 Telephone: 505-241-2700	Web Site: www.pnmresources.com Officers: Patricia K. Vincent-Collawn - Chairman, President, Chief Executive Officer Charles N. Eldred - Executive Vice President, Chief Financial Officer	Auditors: KPMG LLP Investor Contact: 505-241-2211 Transfer Agents: Computershare, Providence, RI

556

POLARIS INDUSTRIES INC.

Exchange	Symbol	Price	52Wk Range	Yield	P/E	Div Acheiver
NYS	PII	$122.18 (6/29/2018)	135.34-87.30	1.96	34.13	22 Years

*7 Year Price Score 87.30   ***NYSE Composite Index=100**   ***12 Month Price Score 102.58**

Interim Earnings (Per Share)

Qtr.	Mar	Jun	Sep	Dec
2015	1.30	1.49	2.30	1.66
2016	0.71	1.09	0.50	0.97
2017	(0.05)	0.97	1.28	0.48
2018	0.85	...	...	...

Interim Dividends (Per Share)

Amt	Decl	Ex	Rec	Pay
0.58Q	07/26/2017	08/30/2017	09/01/2017	09/15/2017
0.58Q	10/26/2017	11/30/2017	12/01/2017	12/15/2017
0.60Q	02/02/2018	02/28/2018	03/01/2018	03/15/2018
0.60Q	04/25/2018	05/31/2018	06/01/2018	06/15/2018

Indicated Div: $2.40 (Div. Reinv. Plan)

Valuation Analysis   **Institutional Holding**

Forecast EPS	$6.53	No of Institutions
	(06/14/2018)	699
Market Cap	$7.7 Billion	Shares
Book Value	$984.8 Million	67,212,456
Price/Book	7.83	% Held
Price/Sales	1.38	73.89

Business Summary: Autos- Manufacturing (MIC: 1.8.1 SIC: 3799 NAIC: 336999)

Polaris Industries are engaged in the design, engineering, manufacturing and marketing of Off-Road Vehicles, which includes the RZR® sport side-by-side, the RANGER® utility side-by-side, the GENERALâ„¢crossover side-by-side, the Sportsman® ATV and the Polaris ACE®; Snowmobiles, which include covers, traction products, reverse kits, electric starters, tracks, bags, windshields, oil and lubricants; Motorcycles, which include saddle bags, handlebars, backrests, exhaust, windshields, seats, oil and various chrome accessories; and Global Adjacent Markets vehicles, which provides a military version ATV and side-by-side vehicles with features designed for ultra-light tactical military applications.

Recent Developments: For the quarter ended Mar 31 2018, net income amounted to US$55.7 million versus a net loss of US$2.9 million in the year-earlier quarter. Revenues were US$1.30 billion, up 12.5% from US$1.15 billion the year before. Operating income was US$83.3 million versus US$21.1 million in the prior-year quarter, an increase of 294.9%. Direct operating expenses rose 6.9% to US$974.0 million from US$911.3 million in the comparable period the year before. Indirect operating expenses increased 8.5% to US$240.2 million from US$221.4 million in the equivalent prior-year period.

Prospects: Our evaluation of Polaris Industries Inc. as of Jan. 21, 2018 is the result of our systematic analysis on three basic characteristics: earnings strength, relative valuation, and recent stock price movement. The company has produced a positive trend in earnings per share over the past 5 quarters and while recent estimates for the company have been mixed, PII has posted better than expected results. Based on operating earnings yield, the company is about fairly valued when compared to all of the companies in our coverage universe. Share price changes over the past year indicates that PII will perform in line with the market over the near term.

Financial Data

(US$ in Thousands)	3 Mos	12/31/2017	12/31/2016	12/31/2015	12/31/2014	12/31/2013	12/31/2012	12/31/2011
Earnings Per Share	3.58	2.69	3.27	6.75	6.65	5.35	4.40	3.20
Cash Flow Per Share	8.31	9.22	8.87	6.67	8.00	7.18	6.03	4.40
Tang Book Value Per Share	3.28	2.58	1.31	11.56	9.82	4.79	8.50	6.17
Dividends Per Share	2.340	2.320	2.200	2.120	1.920	1.680	1.480	0.900
Dividend Payout %	65.36	86.25	67.28	31.41	28.87	31.40	33.64	28.13
Income Statement								
Total Revenue	1,297,473	5,428,477	4,516,629	4,719,290	4,479,648	3,777,068	3,209,782	2,656,949
EBITDA	155,971	548,814	503,955	856,133	842,187	675,153	556,534	417,003
Depn & Amortn	52,720	191,108	167,512	152,138	127,507	92,100	70,580	66,390
Income Before Taxes	95,203	325,551	320,124	692,539	703,441	576,843	480,022	346,626
Income Taxes	17,978	146,299	100,303	230,376	245,288	193,360	167,533	119,051
Net Income	55,714	172,492	212,948	455,361	454,029	377,292	312,310	227,575
Average Shares	65,219	64,180	65,158	67,484	68,229	70,546	71,005	71,057
Balance Sheet								
Current Assets	1,384,586	1,253,504	1,190,989	1,154,725	1,096,555	865,698	1,017,841	878,676
Total Assets	3,219,607	3,089,593	3,099,597	2,387,462	2,074,935	1,685,488	1,486,492	1,228,024
Current Liabilities	1,114,495	1,130,311	959,751	826,783	850,810	748,070	631,029	615,531
Long-Term Obligations	964,234	865,266	1,138,063	458,220	223,620	284,342	104,292	104,660
Total Liabilities	2,234,847	2,146,217	2,223,829	1,396,340	1,200,140	1,141,462	795,962	727,968
Stockholders' Equity	984,760	943,376	875,768	991,122	874,795	544,026	690,530	500,056
Shares Outstanding	63,098	63,075	63,109	65,309	66,307	65,623	68,647	68,430
Statistical Record								
Return on Assets %	7.27	5.57	7.74	20.41	24.15	23.79	22.95	19.88
Return on Equity %	25.26	18.96	22.75	48.81	64.00	61.12	52.32	52.25
EBITDA Margin %	12.02	10.11	11.16	18.14	18.80	17.88	17.34	15.69
Net Margin %	4.29	3.18	4.71	9.65	10.14	9.99	9.73	8.57
Asset Turnover	1.75	1.75	1.64	2.12	2.38	2.38	2.36	2.32
Current Ratio	1.24	1.11	1.24	1.40	1.29	1.16	1.61	1.43
Debt to Equity	0.98	0.92	1.30	0.46	0.26	0.52	0.15	0.21
Price Range	135.34-78.82	133.70-78.82	101.03-69.61	157.62-83.30	158.43-119.98	145.78-83.24	88.35-54.67	65.53-35.75
P/E Ratio	37.80-22.02	49.70-29.30	30.90-21.29	23.35-12.34	23.82-18.04	27.25-15.56	20.08-12.43	20.48-11.17
Average Yield %	2.24	2.41	2.61	1.59	1.37	1.58	1.96	1.78

Address: 2100 Highway 55, Medina, MN 55340	Web Site: www.polaris.com	Auditors: Ernst & Young LLP
	Officers: Scott W. Wine - Chairman, Chief Executive Officer Michael T. Speetzen - Executive Vice President, Chief Financial Officer	Investor Contact: 763-513-3477
Telephone: 763-542-0500		Transfer Agents: Wells Fargo Shareowner Services, Mendota Heights, MN

POLYONE CORP.

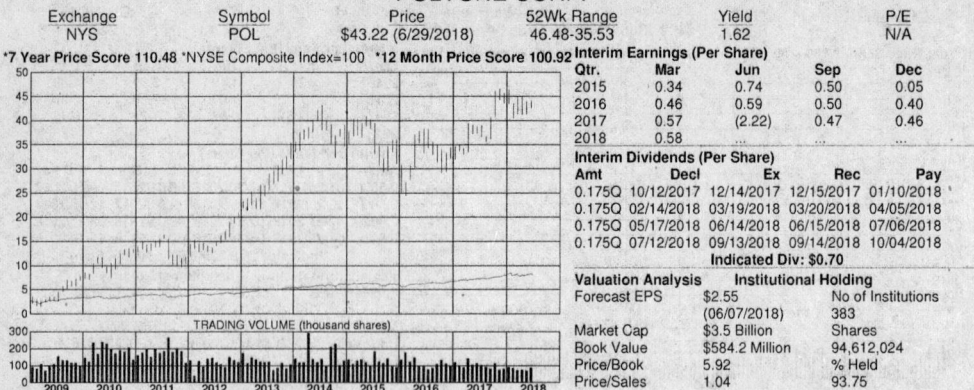

Exchange	Symbol	Price	52Wk Range	Yield	P/E
NYS	POL	$43.22 (6/29/2018)	46.48-35.53	1.62	N/A

*7 Year Price Score 110.48 *NYSE Composite Index=100 *12 Month Price Score 100.92

Interim Earnings (Per Share)

Qtr.	Mar	Jun	Sep	Dec
2015	0.34	0.74	0.50	0.05
2016	0.46	0.59	0.50	0.40
2017	0.57	(2.22)	0.47	0.46
2018	0.58	...	...	...

Interim Dividends (Per Share)

Amt	Decl	Ex	Rec	Pay
0.175Q	10/12/2017	12/14/2017	12/15/2017	01/10/2018
0.175Q	02/14/2018	03/19/2018	03/20/2018	04/05/2018
0.175Q	05/17/2018	06/14/2018	06/15/2018	07/06/2018
0.175Q	07/12/2018	09/13/2018	09/14/2018	10/04/2018

Indicated Div: $0.70

Valuation Analysis

		Institutional Holding	
Forecast EPS	$2.55	No of Institutions	
	(06/07/2018)	383	
Market Cap	$3.5 Billion	Shares	
Book Value	$584.2 Million	94,612,024	
Price/Book	5.92	% Held	
Price/Sales	1.04	93.75	

TRADING VOLUME (thousand shares)

Business Summary: Plastics (MIC: 8.4.2 SIC: 2821 NAIC: 325211)

PolyOne is a provider of polymer materials, services and solutions. Co. has five segments: Color, Additives and Inks, which provide color and additive concentrates in solid and liquid form, dispersions, as well as specialty inks, plastisols, and vinyl slush molding solutions; Specialty Engineered Materials, which provide polymer formulations, services and solutions; Designed Structures and Solutions, which produce sheet, custom rollstock and film, laminate and acrylic solutions; Performance Products and Solutions, which comprised of the Geon performance Materials and producer services business units; and PolyOne Distribution, which distributes engineering and commodity grade resins.

Recent Developments: For the quarter ended Mar 31 2018, income from continuing operations decreased 1.2% to US$47.7 million from US$48.3 million in the year-earlier quarter. Net income was unchanged at US$46.9 million versus US$46.9 million the year-earlier quarter. Revenues were US$901.6 million, up 13.2% from US$796.7 million the year before. Operating income was US$78.8 million versus US$82.0 million in the prior-year quarter, a decrease of 3.9%. Direct operating expenses rose 14.4% to US$703.1 million from US$614.5 million in the comparable period the year before. Indirect operating expenses increased 19.5% to US$119.7 million from US$100.2 million in the equivalent prior-year period.

Prospects: Our evaluation of PolyOne Corp. as of Jan. 21, 2018 is the result of our systematic analysis on three basic characteristics: earnings strength, relative valuation, and recent stock price movement. The company has produced a positive trend in earnings per share over the past 5 quarters and while recent estimates for the company have been mixed, POL has posted better than expected results. Based on operating earnings yield, the company is undervalued when compared to all of the companies in our coverage universe. Share price changes over the past year indicates that POL will perform well over the near term.

Financial Data

(US$ in Thousands)	3 Mos	12/31/2017	12/31/2016	12/31/2015	12/31/2014	12/31/2013	12/31/2012	12/31/2011
Earnings Per Share	(0.71)	(0.70)	1.95	1.63	0.85	2.53	0.80	1.83
Cash Flow Per Share	3.14	2.48	2.63	2.59	2.26	1.14	1.20	0.79
Tang Book Value Per Share	N.M.	N.M.	N.M.	N.M.	N.M.	0.55	N.M.	N.M.
Dividends Per Share	0.620	0.580	0.495	0.420	0.340	0.260	0.200	0.160
Dividend Payout %	...	...	25.38	25.77	40.00	10.28	25.00	8.74
Income Statement								
Total Revenue	901,600	3,229,900	3,339,800	3,377,600	3,835,500	3,771,200	2,992,600	2,863,500
EBITDA	102,300	334,300	364,100	316,200	255,300	278,600	197,000	134,100
Depn & Amortn	22,400	61,200	82,000	84,400	104,700	91,000	56,600	53,700
Income Before Taxes	64,400	212,300	222,300	167,700	88,400	124,100	89,600	46,700
Income Taxes	16,700	38,700	57,300	23,000	11,200	58,100	41,200	26,100
Net Income	46,900	(57,700)	165,200	144,600	79,200	243,800	71,900	172,600
Average Shares	81,300	82,100	84,600	88,700	93,500	96,500	89,800	94,300
Balance Sheet								
Current Assets	1,035,300	1,066,600	949,500	960,800	1,042,700	1,253,600	866,900	843,500
Total Assets	2,743,900	2,705,300	2,723,300	2,595,100	2,711,200	2,944,100	2,128,000	2,080,500
Current Liabilities	571,900	570,600	509,600	498,100	601,200	608,900	459,800	442,400
Long-Term Obligations	1,318,800	1,276,400	1,239,800	1,128,000	962,000	976,200	703,100	704,000
Total Liabilities	2,159,700	2,106,800	1,998,600	1,890,900	1,934,900	1,967,300	1,498,900	1,492,200
Stockholders' Equity	584,200	598,500	724,700	704,200	776,300	976,800	629,100	588,300
Shares Outstanding	79,971	80,900	82,600	85,300	89,300	95,100	89,500	88,800
Statistical Record								
Return on Assets %	N.M.	N.M.	6.20	5.45	2.80	9.61	3.41	9.20
Return on Equity %	N.M.	N.M.	23.06	19.53	9.04	30.36	11.78	31.26
EBITDA Margin %	11.35	10.35	10.90	9.36	6.66	7.39	6.58	4.68
Net Margin %	5.20	N.M.	4.95	4.28	2.06	6.46	2.40	6.03
Asset Turnover	1.21	1.19	1.25	1.27	1.36	1.49	1.42	1.53
Current Ratio	1.81	1.87	1.86	1.93	1.73	2.06	1.89	1.91
Debt to Equity	2.26	2.13	1.71	1.60	1.24	1.00	1.12	1.20
Price Range	46.48-33.33	46.48-31.83	38.21-24.30	40.89-29.27	43.14-32.19	35.44-20.42	20.74-11.77	16.34-9.63
P/E Ratio	...	...	19.59-12.46	25.09-17.96	50.75-37.87	14.01-8.07	25.92-14.71	8.93-5.26
Average Yield %	1.54	1.53	1.53	1.17	0.90	0.97	1.30	1.22

Address: 33587 Walker Road, Avon Lake, OH 44012
Telephone: 440-930-1000

Web Site: www.polyone.com
Officers: Robert M. Patterson - Chairman, President, Chief Executive Officer, Senior Vice President, Chief Financial Officer, Chief Operating Officer Bradley C. Richardson - Executive Vice President, Chief Financial Officer

Auditors: Ernst & Young LLP
Investor Contact: 440-930-1226
Transfer Agents: Wells Fargo Shareowner Services, Mendota Heights, MN

PORTLAND GENERAL ELECTRIC CO.

Exchange	Symbol	Price	52Wk Range	Yield	P/E	Div Acheiver
NYS	POR	$42.76 (6/29/2018)	49.72-39.11	3.39	21.38	11 Years

*7 Year Price Score 100.68 ***NYSE Composite Index=100** ***12 Month Price Score 92.62**

Interim Earnings (Per Share)

Qtr.	Mar	Jun	Sep	Dec
2015	0.62	0.44	0.40	0.57
2016	0.68	0.42	0.38	0.67
2017	0.82	0.36	0.44	0.48
2018	0.72	...	...	...

Interim Dividends (Per Share)

Amt	Decl	Ex	Rec	Pay
0.34Q	07/26/2017	09/22/2017	09/25/2017	10/16/2017
0.34Q	10/25/2017	12/22/2017	12/26/2017	01/16/2018
0.34Q	02/14/2018	03/23/2018	03/26/2018	04/16/2018
0.362Q	04/25/2018	06/22/2018	06/25/2018	07/16/2018

Indicated Div: $1.45

Valuation Analysis — **Institutional Holding**

Forecast EPS	$2.21	No of Institutions
	(06/14/2018)	433
Market Cap	$3.8 Billion	Shares
Book Value	$2.4 Billion	111,777,328
Price/Book	1.56	% Held
Price/Sales	1.93	105.94

TRADING VOLUME (thousand shares)

Business Summary: Electric Utilities (MIC: 3.1.1 SIC: 4911 NAIC: 221122)

Portland General Electric is an electric utility engaged in the generation, wholesale purchase, transmission, distribution, and retail sale of electricity in the state of Oregon. Co. also participates in the wholesale market by purchasing and selling electricity and natural gas to its retail customers. Co.'s service area includes 51 incorporated cities in Oregon, principally in Portland and Salem, within a state-approved service area allocation of approximately 4,000 square miles. As of Dec 31 2017, Co. served a total of 875,000 retail customers.

Recent Developments: For the quarter ended Mar 31 2018, net income decreased 12.3% to US$64.0 million from US$73.0 million in the year-earlier quarter. Revenues were US$493.0 million, down 7.0% from US$530.0 million the year before. Operating income was US$100.0 million versus US$124.0 million in the prior-year quarter, a decrease of 19.4%. Direct operating expenses declined 10.4% to US$199.0 million from US$222.0 million in the comparable period the year before. Indirect operating expenses increased 5.4% to US$194.0 million from US$184.0 million in the equivalent prior-year period.

Prospects: Our evaluation of Portland General Electric Co. as of Jan. 21, 2018 is the result of our systematic analysis on three basic characteristics: earnings strength, relative valuation, and recent stock price movement. The company has generated a negative trend in earnings per share over the past 5 quarters and while recent estimates for the company have been mixed, POR has posted better than expected results. Based on operating earnings yield, the company is undervalued when compared to all of the companies in our coverage universe. Share price changes over the past year indicates that POR will perform very well over the near term.

Financial Data

(US$ in Millions)	3 Mos	12/31/2017	12/31/2016	12/31/2015	12/31/2014	12/31/2013	12/31/2012	12/31/2011
Earnings Per Share	2.00	2.10	2.16	2.04	2.18	1.35	1.87	1.95
Cash Flow Per Share	6.97	6.70	6.20	6.14	6.63	7.08	6.53	6.01
Tang Book Value Per Share	27.45	27.11	26.35	25.43	24.43	23.29	22.87	22.07
Dividends Per Share	1.360	1.340	1.260	1.180	1.115	1.095	1.075	1.055
Dividend Payout %	68.00	63.81	58.33	57.84	51.15	81.11	57.49	54.10
Income Statement								
Total Revenue	493	2,009	1,923	1,898	1,900	1,810	1,805	1,813
EBITDA	195	439	399	369	356	248	334	334
Depn & Amortn	92	46	44	38	25	22	22	19
Income Before Taxes	72	273	243	217	235	125	204	205
Income Taxes	8	86	50	45	61	21	64	58
Net Income	64	187	193	172	175	105	141	147
Average Shares	89	89	89	84	80	77	75	75
Balance Sheet								
Current Assets	532	526	463	557	699	591	622	716
Total Assets	7,892	7,838	7,527	7,221	7,042	6,101	5,670	5,733
Current Liabilities	393	432	577	626	873	393	521	614
Long-Term Obligations	2,426	2,426	2,200	2,071	2,126	1,916	1,536	1,635
Total Liabilities	5,443	5,422	5,183	4,963	5,131	4,282	3,942	4,070
Stockholders' Equity	2,449	2,416	2,344	2,258	1,911	1,819	1,728	1,663
Shares Outstanding	89	89	88	88	78	78	75	75
Statistical Record								
Return on Assets %	2.30	2.43	2.61	2.41	2.66	1.78	2.47	2.62
Return on Equity %	7.36	7.86	8.36	8.25	9.38	5.92	8.29	9.03
EBITDA Margin %	39.55	21.85	20.75	19.44	18.74	13.70	18.50	18.42
Net Margin %	12.98	9.31	10.04	9.06	9.21	5.80	7.81	8.11
Asset Turnover	0.25	0.26	0.26	0.27	0.29	0.31	0.32	0.32
Current Ratio	1.35	1.22	0.80	0.89	0.80	1.50	1.19	1.17
Debt to Equity	0.99	1.00	0.94	0.92	1.11	1.05	0.89	0.98
Price Range	49.72-39.11	49.72-42.83	45.04-35.80	40.79-33.16	40.09-29.07	32.72-27.36	27.99-24.33	25.97-21.49
P/E Ratio	24.86-19.56	23.68-20.40	20.85-16.57	20.00-16.25	18.39-13.33	24.24-20.27	14.97-13.01	13.32-11.02
Average Yield %	3.01	2.92	3.06	3.26	3.26	3.35	3.67	4.12	4.38

Address: 121 S.W. Salmon Street, Portland, OR 97204	**Web Site:** www.portlandgeneral.com	**Auditors:** Deloitte & Touche LLP
Telephone: 503-464-8000	**Officers:** Jack E. Davis - Chairman James F. Lobdell -	**Investor Contact:** 503-464-8586
Fax: 503-464-2676	Chief Financial Officer, Senior Vice President, Treasurer, Vice President	**Transfer Agents:** American Stock Transfer & Trust Company, New York, NY

POST HOLDINGS INC

Exchange	Symbol	Price	52Wk Range	Yield	P/E
NYS	POST	$86.02 (6/29/2018)	88.35-71.63	N/A	20.24

*7 Year Price Score N/A   *NYSE Composite Index=100   *12 Month Price Score 98.34

TRADING VOLUME (thousand shares)

Interim Earnings (Per Share)

Qtr.	Dec	Mar	Jun	Sep
2014-15	(2.04)	0.45	0.33	(1.31)
2015-16	0.15	0.02	0.00	(0.58)
2016-17	1.22	(0.11)	(0.93)	0.16
2017-18	3.82	1.20	...	...

Interim Dividends (Per Share)

No Dividends Paid

Valuation Analysis — **Institutional Holding**

Forecast EPS	$4.36	No of Institutions
	(06/12/2018)	391
Market Cap	$5.8 Billion	Shares
Book Value	$3.1 Billion	82,317,152
Price/Book	1.86	% Held
Price/Sales	1.01	N/A

Business Summary: Food (MIC: 1.2.1 SIC: 2041 NAIC: 311211)

Post Holdings is a consumer packaged goods holding company. Co. operates in five segments:Post Consumer Brands segment includes the North American ready-to-eat (RTE) cereal and granola businesses, inclusive of the Weetabix North American RTE cereal business; Michael Foods Group segment includes foodservice and food ingredient egg, potato and pasta businesses and a retail cheese business; Active Nutrition segment includes protein shakes, bars and powders and nutritional supplements; Private Brands segment primarily consists of peanut and other nut butters and dried fruit and nuts; and the Weetabix segment includes the international (primarily the U.K.) RTE cereal and muesli business.

Recent Developments: For the quarter ended Mar 31 2018, net income amounted to US$91.8 million versus a net loss of US$2.1 million in the year-earlier quarter. Revenues were US$1.59 billion, up 26.3% from US$1.26 billion the year before. Operating income was US$164.3 million versus US$137.5 million in the prior-year quarter, an increase of 19.5%. Direct operating expenses rose 24.6% to US$1.11 billion from US$891.3 million in the comparable period the year before. Indirect operating expenses increased 37.4% to US$311.4 million from US$226.6 million in the equivalent prior-year period.

Prospects: Our evaluation of Post Holdings Inc. as of Jan. 21, 2018 is the result of our systematic analysis on three basic characteristics: earnings strength, relative valuation, and recent stock price movement. The company has enjoyed a very positive trend in earnings per share over the past 5 quarters and while recent estimates for the company have been raised by analysts, POST has posted results that fell short of analysts expectations. Based on operating earnings yield, the company is about fairly valued when compared to all of the companies in our coverage universe. Share price changes over the past year indicates that POST will perform in line with the market over the near term.

Financial Data

(US$ in Thousands)	6 Mos	3 Mos	09/30/2017	09/30/2016	09/30/2015	09/30/2014	09/30/2013	09/30/2012
Earnings Per Share	4.25	2.94	0.50	(0.41)	(2.33)	(9.03)	0.30	1.45
Cash Flow Per Share	10.13	9.32	5.70	7.28	7.96	4.61	3.65	4.20
Income Statement								
Total Revenue	3,019,200	1,433,100	5,225,800	5,026,800	4,648,200	2,411,100	1,034,100	958,900
EBITDA	432,300	171,400	712,300	579,200	393,000	(87,400)	184,600	203,900
Depn & Amortn	87,900	41,500	323,100	302,800	272,800	155,800	76,800	63,200
Income Before Taxes	155,100	39,400	74,400	(30,100)	(167,300)	(426,900)	22,300	80,400
Income Taxes	(231,900)	(255,800)	26,100	(26,800)	(52,000)	(83,700)	7,100	30,500
Net Income	386,400	294,900	48,300	(3,300)	(115,300)	(343,200)	15,200	49,900
Average Shares	76,000	77,300	69,900	68,800	56,700	39,700	33,000	34,500
Balance Sheet								
Current Assets	1,551,500	3,049,600	2,615,900	2,076,900	1,781,700	1,219,000	668,100	209,700
Total Assets	12,673,200	12,279,800	11,876,800	9,360,600	9,220,400	7,731,100	3,473,800	2,732,300
Current Liabilities	693,500	752,200	704,400	634,000	611,000	519,900	146,000	126,400
Long-Term Obligations	7,392,600	7,512,600	7,149,100	4,551,200	4,511,400	3,830,500	1,408,600	930,300
Total Liabilities	9,553,800	9,249,400	9,096,800	6,352,000	6,244,400	5,447,900	1,975,200	1,500,800
Stockholders' Equity	3,119,400	3,030,400	2,780,000	3,008,600	2,976,000	2,283,200	1,498,600	1,231,500
Shares Outstanding	67,288	65,576	66,100	64,900	60,300	43,000	30,900	32,650
Statistical Record								
Return on Assets %	3.03	2.29	0.45	N.M.	N.M.	N.M.	0.49	...
Return on Equity %	11.17	8.17	1.67	N.M.	N.M.	N.M.	1.11	...
EBITDA Margin %	14.32	11.96	13.63	11.52	8.45	N.M.	17.85	21.26
Net Margin %	12.80	20.58	0.92	N.M.	N.M.	N.M.	1.47	5.20
Asset Turnover	0.51	0.50	0.49	0.54	0.55	0.43	0.33	...
Current Ratio	2.24	4.05	3.71	3.28	2.92	2.34	4.58	1.66
Debt to Equity	2.37	2.48	2.57	1.51	1.52	1.68	0.94	0.76
Price Range	88.41-71.63	88.41-76.24	88.41-70.68	87.85-53.86	69.73-31.67	60.18-33.18	49.14-30.05	33.98-26.02
P/E Ratio	20.80-16.85	30.07-25.93	176.82-141.36	...	...	...	163.80-100.17	23.43-17.94

Address: 2503 S. Hanley Road, St. Louis, MO 63144
Telephone: 314-644-7600

Web Site: www.postholdings.com
Officers: Robert V. Vitale - President, Chief Executive Officer, Chief Financial Officer Jeff A. Zadoks - Executive Vice President, Senior Vice President, Chief Financial Officer, Chief Accounting Officer, Principal Financial Officer, Principal Accounting Officer, Corporate Controller

Auditors: PricewaterhouseCoopers LLP
Investor Contact: 314-644-7600
Transfer Agents: Computershare Trust Company, N.A., Providence, RI

PPG INDUSTRIES INC

Exchange	Symbol	Price	52Wk Range	Yield	P/E	Div Acheiver
NYS	PPG	$103.73 (6/29/2018)	121.47-100.43	1.74	16.68	46 Years

*7 Year Price Score 99.72 *NYSE Composite Index=100 ***12 Month Price Score 92.68**

Interim Earnings (Per Share)

Qtr.	Mar	Jun	Sep	Dec
2015	1.17	1.23	1.59	1.16
2016	1.29	1.37	(0.69)	1.30
2017	1.29	1.94	2.36	0.59
2018	1.33	...	...	...

Interim Dividends (Per Share)

Amt	Decl	Ex	Rec	Pay
0.45Q	07/20/2017	08/08/2017	08/10/2017	09/12/2017
0.45Q	10/19/2017	11/09/2017	11/10/2017	12/12/2017
0.45Q	01/18/2018	02/15/2018	02/16/2018	03/12/2018
0.45Q	04/19/2018	05/09/2018	05/10/2018	06/12/2018

Indicated Div: $1.80 (Div. Reinv. Plan)

Valuation Analysis — **Institutional Holding**

Forecast EPS	$6.35	No of Institutions	
	(06/11/2018)	1199	
Market Cap	$25.3 Billion	Shares	
Book Value	$5.3 Billion	229,496,864	
Price/Book	4.72	% Held	
Price/Sales	1.68	63.31	

Business Summary: Specialty Chemicals (MIC: 8.3.2 SIC: 2851 NAIC: 325510)

PPG Industries manufactures and distributes a range of coatings and specialty materials. Co. has three segments: Performance Coatings, which primarily supplies a variety of protective and decorative coatings, sealants and finishes along with paint strippers, stains and related chemicals, as well as transparencies and transparent armor; Industrial Coatings, which primarily supplies a variety of protective and decorative coatings and finishes along with adhesives, sealants, metal pretreatment products, optical monomers and coatings, precipitated silicas and other specialty materials; and Glass, which primarily supplies continuous-strand fiber glass products.

Recent Developments: For the quarter ended Mar 31 2018, income from continuing operations decreased 0.6% to US$334.0 million from US$336.0 million in the year-earlier quarter. Net income decreased 0.6% to US$340.0 million from US$342.0 million in the year-earlier quarter. Revenues were US$3.78 billion, up 8.5% from US$3.49 billion the year before. Direct operating expenses rose 14.7% to US$2.18 billion from US$1.90 billion in the comparable period the year before. Indirect operating expenses increased 3.6% to US$1.18 billion from US$1.14 billion in the equivalent prior-year period.

Prospects: Our evaluation of PPG Industries Inc. as of Jan. 21, 2018 is the result of our systematic analysis on three basic characteristics: earnings strength, relative valuation, and recent stock price movement. The company has managed to produce a neutral trend in earnings per share over the past 5 quarters. However, while recent estimates for the company have been mixed, PPG has posted better than expected results. Based on operating earnings yield, the company is undervalued when compared to all of the companies in our coverage universe. Share price changes over the past year indicates that PPG will perform well over the near term.

Financial Data

(US$ in Thousands)	3 Mos	12/31/2017	12/31/2016	12/31/2015	12/31/2014	12/31/2013	12/31/2012	12/31/2011
Earnings Per Share	6.22	6.17	3.28	5.14	7.51	11.14	3.03	3.44
Cash Flow Per Share	5.33	6.12	4.98	6.77	5.52	6.24	5.81	4.56
Tang Book Value Per Share	N.M.	N.M.	N.M.	N.M.	N.M.	2.11	0.71	N.M.
Dividends Per Share	1.750	1.700	1.560	1.415	1.310	1.210	1.170	1.130
Dividend Payout %	28.14	27.55	47.56	27.53	17.43	10.87	38.61	32.90
Income Statement								
Total Revenue	3,781,000	14,750,000	14,751,000	15,330,000	15,360,000	15,108,000	15,200,000	14,885,000
EBITDA	529,000	2,412,000	1,255,000	2,320,000	1,802,000	2,006,000	1,917,000	2,074,000
Depn & Amortn	87,000	331,000	341,000	363,000	350,000	356,000	355,000	346,000
Income Before Taxes	421,000	1,996,000	815,000	1,871,000	1,315,000	1,497,000	1,391,000	1,560,000
Income Taxes	87,000	616,000	241,000	456,000	259,000	333,000	338,000	385,000
Net Income	334,000	1,591,000	877,000	1,406,000	2,102,000	3,231,000	941,000	1,095,000
Average Shares	251,400	257,800	267,400	273,600	279,600	290,200	310,200	318,600
Balance Sheet								
Current Assets	7,110,000	6,477,000	6,452,000	6,554,000	6,850,000	7,214,000	7,715,000	6,694,000
Total Assets	17,544,000	16,538,000	15,769,000	17,076,000	17,583,000	15,863,000	15,878,000	14,382,000
Current Liabilities	4,030,000	3,894,000	4,240,000	4,656,000	4,876,000	4,135,000	4,461,000	3,702,000
Long-Term Obligations	5,199,000	4,134,000	3,787,000	4,042,000	3,544,000	3,372,000	3,368,000	3,574,000
Total Liabilities	12,198,000	10,980,000	10,943,000	12,093,000	12,403,000	10,931,000	11,815,000	11,133,000
Stockholders' Equity	5,346,000	5,558,000	4,826,000	4,983,000	5,180,000	4,932,000	4,063,000	3,249,000
Shares Outstanding	243,474	251,174	257,330	266,876	271,964	277,292	307,132	303,777
Statistical Record								
Return on Assets %	9.44	9.85	5.33	8.11	12.57	20.36	6.20	7.46
Return on Equity %	30.20	30.64	17.83	27.67	41.57	71.84	25.67	31.80
EBITDA Margin %	13.99	16.35	8.51	15.13	11.73	13.28	12.61	13.93
Net Margin %	8.83	10.79	5.95	9.17	13.68	21.39	6.19	7.36
Asset Turnover	0.89	0.91	0.90	0.88	0.92	0.95	1.00	1.01
Current Ratio	1.76	1.66	1.52	1.41	1.40	1.74	1.73	1.81
Debt to Equity	0.97	0.74	0.78	0.81	0.68	0.68	0.83	1.10
Price Range	121.47-100.73	118.67-95.25	116.55-89.27	118.85-84.51	116.23-88.30	94.83-65.04	67.67-42.16	48.24-34.34
P/E Ratio	19.53-16.19	19.23-15.44	35.53-27.22	23.12-16.44	15.48-11.76	8.51-5.84	22.33-13.92	14.02-9.98
Average Yield %	1.57	1.58	1.53	1.31	1.31	1.54	2.19	2.68

Address: One PPG Place, Pittsburgh, PA 15272	Web Site: www.ppg.com	Auditors: PricewaterhouseCoopers LLP
Telephone: 412-434-3131	Officers: Michael H. McGarry - Chairman, Chief Executive Officer, President, Executive Vice President, Senior Vice President, Chief Operating Officer Vincent J. Morales - Senior Vice President, Chief Financial Officer	Investor Contact: 412-434-3740 Transfer Agents: Computershare, Providence, R.I.

PPL CORP

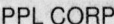

Exchange	Symbol	Price	52Wk Range	Yield	P/E	Div Acheiver
NYS	PPL	$28.55 (6/29/2018)	39.83-25.61	5.74	16.79	18 Years

*7 Year Price Score 84.98   *NYSE Composite Index=100   *12 Month Price Score 82.28

Interim Earnings (Per Share)

Qtr.	Mar	Jun	Sep	Dec
2015	0.96	(1.13)	0.58	0.59
2016	0.71	0.71	0.69	0.68
2017	0.59	0.43	0.51	0.11
2018	0.65	...	...	...

Interim Dividends (Per Share)

Amt	Decl	Ex	Rec	Pay
0.395Q	08/25/2017	09/07/2017	09/08/2017	10/02/2017
0.395Q	11/17/2017	12/07/2017	12/08/2017	01/02/2018
0.41Q	02/22/2018	03/08/2018	03/09/2018	04/02/2018
0.41Q	05/16/2018	06/07/2018	06/08/2018	07/02/2018

Indicated Div: $1.64 (Div. Reinv. Plan)

Valuation Analysis		Institutional Holding	
Forecast EPS	$2.31	No of Institutions	
	(06/14/2018)	1145	
Market Cap	$19.9 Billion	Shares	
Book Value	$11.2 Billion	599,146,496	
Price/Book	1.78	% Held	
Price/Sales	2.61	N/A	

Business Summary: Electric Utilities (MIC: 3.1.1 SIC: 4911 NAIC: 221122)

PPL is a utility holding company. Through its regulated utility subsidiaries, Co. delivers electricity to customers in the U.K., Pennsylvania, Kentucky, Virginia and Tennessee; delivers natural gas to customers in Kentucky; and generates electricity from power plants in Kentucky. Co. has three segments: U.K. Regulated, which has regulated electricity distribution operations in the U.K; Kentucky Regulated, which is engaged in the regulated generation, transmission, distribution and sale of electricity in Kentucky, Virginia and Tennessee, and the distribution and sale of natural gas in Kentucky; and Pennsylvania Regulated, which delivers electricity in eastern and central Pennsylvania.

Recent Developments: For the quarter ended Mar 31 2018, net income increased 12.2% to US$452.0 million from US$403.0 million in the year-earlier quarter. Revenues were US$2.13 billion, up 9.0% from US$1.95 billion the year before. Operating income was US$851.0 million versus US$758.0 million in the prior-year quarter, an increase of 12.3%. Direct operating expenses rose 5.4% to US$923.0 million from US$876.0 million in the comparable period the year before. Indirect operating expenses increased 11.0% to US$352.0 million from US$317.0 million in the equivalent prior-year period.

Prospects: Our evaluation of PPL Corp. as of Jan. 21, 2018 is the result of our systematic analysis on three basic characteristics: earnings strength, relative valuation, and recent stock price movement. The company has managed to produce a neutral trend in earnings per share over the past 5 quarters and while recent estimates for the company have been mixed, PPL has posted better than expected results. Based on operating earnings yield, the company is undervalued when compared to all of the companies in our coverage universe. Share price changes over the past year indicates that PPL will perform well over the near term.

Financial Data

(US$ in Thousands)	3 Mos	12/31/2017	12/31/2016	12/31/2015	12/31/2014	12/31/2013	12/31/2012	12/31/2011
Earnings Per Share	1.70	1.64	2.79	1.01	2.61	1.76	2.60	2.70
Cash Flow Per Share	4.16	3.59	4.25	3.90	5.21	4.69	4.75	4.55
Tang Book Value Per Share	10.28	9.82	9.03	8.44	13.06	11.57	9.27	9.77
Dividends Per Share	1.595	1.580	1.520	1.500	1.490	1.470	1.440	1.400
Dividend Payout %	93.82	96.34	54.48	148.51	57.09	83.52	55.38	51.85
Income Statement								
Total Revenue	2,126,000	7,447,000	7,517,000	7,669,000	11,499,000	11,860,000	12,286,000	12,737,000
EBITDA	1,098,000	3,819,000	4,361,000	3,822,000	4,620,000	3,473,000	4,146,000	4,053,000
Depn & Amortn	290,000	1,008,000	926,000	883,000	1,237,000	1,161,000	1,100,000	961,000
Income Before Taxes	569,000	1,912,000	2,550,000	2,072,000	2,364,000	1,309,000	2,090,000	2,201,000
Income Taxes	117,000	784,000	648,000	469,000	781,000	180,000	545,000	691,000
Net Income	452,000	1,128,000	1,902,000	682,000	1,737,000	1,130,000	1,526,000	1,495,000
Average Shares	695,322	687,334	680,446	672,586	665,973	663,073	581,626	550,952
Balance Sheet								
Current Assets	2,490,000	2,294,000	2,067,000	2,646,000	6,159,000	5,153,000	5,068,000	6,426,000
Total Assets	42,388,000	41,479,000	38,315,000	39,301,000	48,864,000	46,259,000	43,634,000	42,648,000
Current Liabilities	4,238,000	4,023,000	3,837,000	3,876,000	7,443,000	4,912,000	5,625,000	5,255,000
Long-Term Obligations	20,214,000	19,847,000	17,808,000	18,563,000	18,856,000	20,592,000	18,725,000	17,993,000
Total Liabilities	31,212,000	30,718,000	28,416,000	29,382,000	35,236,000	33,793,000	33,154,000	31,820,000
Stockholders' Equity	11,176,000	10,761,000	9,899,000	9,919,000	13,628,000	12,466,000	10,480,000	10,828,000
Shares Outstanding	697,383	693,398	679,731	673,857	665,849	630,321	581,944	578,405
Statistical Record								
Return on Assets %	2.89	2.83	4.89	1.55	3.65	2.51	3.53	3.96
Return on Equity %	11.06	10.92	19.14	5.79	13.31	9.85	14.28	15.71
EBITDA Margin %	51.65	51.28	58.02	49.84	40.18	29.28	33.75	31.82
Net Margin %	21.26	15.15	25.30	8.89	15.11	9.53	12.42	11.74
Asset Turnover	0.19	0.19	0.19	0.17	0.24	0.26	0.28	0.34
Current Ratio	0.59	0.57	0.54	0.68	0.83	1.05	0.90	1.22
Debt to Equity	1.81	1.84	1.80	1.87	1.38	1.65	1.79	1.66
Price Range	40.06-27.13	40.06-30.76	39.68-32.19	34.75-29.14	35.21-27.46	30.97-26.40	27.98-24.84	28.06-22.60
P/E Ratio	23.56-15.96	24.43-18.76	14.22-11.54	34.41-28.85	13.49-10.52	17.60-15.00	10.76-9.55	10.39-8.37
Average Yield %	4.45	4.24	4.25	4.68	4.80	5.19	5.47	5.50

Address: Two North Ninth Street, Allentown, PA 18101-1179 **Telephone:** 610-774-5151	**Web Site:** www.pplweb.com **Officers:** William H. Spence - Chairman, President, Chief Executive Officer, Chief Operating Officer Joanne H. Raphael - Senior Vice President, Secretary, General Counsel	**Auditors:** DELOITTE & TOUCHE LLP **Transfer Agents:** Equiniti Trust Company, Shareowner Services, Mendota Heights, MN

PRAXAIR INC

Exchange	Symbol	Price	52Wk Range	Yield	P/E
NYS	PX	$158.15 (6/29/2018)	165.69-127.44	2.09	34.68

*7 Year Price Score 98.52   *NYSE Composite Index=100   ***12 Month Price Score 104.85**

Interim Earnings (Per Share)

Qtr.	Mar	Jun	Sep	Dec
2015	1.43	1.06	1.40	1.47
2016	1.24	1.39	1.18	1.41
2017	1.35	1.41	1.45	0.11
2018	1.59	...	...	...

Interim Dividends (Per Share)

Amt	Decl	Ex	Rec	Pay
0.787Q	07/27/2017	09/07/2017	09/08/2017	09/15/2017
0.787Q	10/26/2017	12/06/2017	12/07/2017	12/15/2017
0.825Q	01/25/2018	03/06/2018	03/07/2018	03/15/2018
0.825Q	04/26/2018	06/06/2018	06/07/2018	06/15/2018

Indicated Div: $3.30 (Div. Reinv. Plan)

Valuation Analysis		Institutional Holding	
Forecast EPS	$6.76	No of Institutions	
	(06/14/2018)	1466	
Market Cap	$45.4 Billion	Shares	
Book Value	$6.4 Billion	304,222,016	
Price/Book	7.14	% Held	
Price/Sales	3.88	83.25	

Business Summary: Specialty Chemicals (MIC: 8.3.2 SIC: 2819 NAIC: 325188)

Praxair is an industrial gas company in North and South America. Co.'s primary products in its industrial gases business are atmospheric gases (oxygen, nitrogen, argon, rare gases) and process gases (carbon dioxide, helium, hydrogen, electronic gases, specialty gases, acetylene). Co. also designs, engineers, and builds equipment that produces industrial gases primarily for internal use. Co.'s surface technologies segment supplies wear-resistant and high-temperature corrosion-resistant metallic and ceramic coatings and powders. Co.'s subsidiary, Praxair Surface Technologies, supplies wear-resistant and high-temperature corrosion-resistant metallic and ceramic coatings and powders.

Recent Developments: For the quarter ended Mar 31 2018, net income increased 16.8% to US$472.0 million from US$404.0 million in the year-earlier quarter. Revenues were US$3.00 billion, up 9.9% from US$2.73 billion the year before. Operating income was US$653.0 million versus US$567.0 million in the prior-year quarter, an increase of 15.2%. Direct operating expenses rose 8.3% to US$1.68 billion from US$1.55 billion in the comparable period the year before. Indirect operating expenses increased 9.3% to US$669.0 million from US$612.0 million in the equivalent prior-year period.

Prospects: Our evaluation of Praxair Inc. as of Jan. 21, 2018 is the result of our systematic analysis on three basic characteristics: earnings strength, relative valuation, and recent stock price movement. The company has managed to produce a neutral trend in earnings per share over the past 5 quarters and while recent estimates for the company have been mixed, PX has posted better than expected results. Based on operating earnings yield, the company is about fairly valued when compared to all of the companies in our coverage universe. Share price changes over the past year indicates that PX will perform well over the near term.

Financial Data

(US$ in Thousands)	3 Mos	12/31/2017	12/31/2016	12/31/2015	12/31/2014	12/31/2013	12/31/2012	12/31/2011
Earnings Per Share	4.56	4.32	5.21	5.35	5.73	5.87	5.61	5.45
Cash Flow Per Share	10.50	10.62	9.68	9.34	9.81	9.87	9.20	8.12
Tang Book Value Per Share	8.86	7.78	4.64	2.93	6.56	9.58	11.42	9.88
Dividends Per Share	3.188	3.150	3.000	2.860	2.600	2.400	2.200	2.000
Dividend Payout %	69.90	72.92	57.58	53.46	45.38	40.89	39.22	36.70
Income Statement								
Total Revenue	2,999,000	11,437,000	10,534,000	10,776,000	12,273,000	11,925,000	11,224,000	11,252,000
EBITDA	962,000	3,632,000	3,360,000	3,427,000	3,778,000	3,734,000	3,438,000	3,471,000
Depn & Amortn	311,000	1,184,000	1,122,000	1,106,000	1,170,000	1,109,000	1,001,000	1,003,000
Income Before Taxes	605,000	2,287,000	2,048,000	2,160,000	2,395,000	2,447,000	2,296,000	2,323,000
Income Taxes	148,000	1,026,000	551,000	612,000	691,000	649,000	586,000	641,000
Net Income	462,000	1,247,000	1,500,000	1,547,000	1,694,000	1,755,000	1,692,000	1,672,000
Average Shares	290,809	289,114	287,757	289,055	295,608	298,965	301,845	306,722
Balance Sheet								
Current Assets	3,329,000	3,285,000	2,880,000	2,626,000	2,839,000	2,916,000	2,792,000	2,607,000
Total Assets	20,592,000	20,436,000	19,332,000	18,319,000	19,802,000	20,255,000	18,090,000	16,356,000
Current Liabilities	3,534,000	3,307,000	2,478,000	1,893,000	2,490,000	2,664,000	2,479,000	2,535,000
Long-Term Obligations	7,336,000	7,783,000	8,917,000	8,975,000	8,669,000	8,026,000	6,685,000	5,838,000
Total Liabilities	14,224,000	14,418,000	14,311,000	13,930,000	14,179,000	13,646,000	12,026,000	10,868,000
Stockholders' Equity	6,368,000	6,018,000	5,021,000	4,389,000	5,623,000	6,609,000	6,064,000	5,488,000
Shares Outstanding	287,369	286,776	284,900	284,879	289,261	294,133	296,229	298,530
Statistical Record								
Return on Assets %	6.56	6.27	7.95	8.12	8.46	9.15	9.80	10.57
Return on Equity %	22.19	22.59	31.79	30.90	27.70	27.70	29.21	29.65
EBITDA Margin %	32.08	31.76	31.90	31.80	30.78	31.31	30.63	30.85
Net Margin %	15.41	10.90	14.24	14.36	13.80	14.72	15.07	14.86
Asset Turnover	0.58	0.58	0.56	0.57	0.61	0.62	0.65	0.71
Current Ratio	0.94	0.99	1.16	1.39	1.14	1.09	1.13	1.03
Debt to Equity	1.15	1.29	1.78	2.04	1.54	1.21	1.10	1.06
Price Range	165.69-117.47	156.36-115.67	123.92-96.13	130.28-99.17	134.67-118.81	130.03-107.69	116.47-102.09	111.30-88.93
P/E Ratio	36.34-25.76	36.19-26.78	23.79-18.45	24.35-18.54	23.50-20.73	22.15-18.35	20.76-18.20	20.42-16.32
Average Yield %	2.26	2.39	2.64	2.45	2.01	2.04	2.03	2.00

Address: 10 Riverview Drive, Danbury, CT 06810-6268 Telephone: 203-837-2000	Web Site: www.praxair.com Officers: Stephen F. Angel - Chairman, Chief Executive Officer Matthew J. White - Senior Vice President, Vice President, Controller, Chief Financial Officer	Auditors: PricewaterhouseCoopers LLP Investor Contact: 203-837-2210 Transfer Agents: Registrar and Transfer Company, Cranford, NJ

PRESTIGE BRANDS HOLDINGS INC

Exchange	Symbol	Price	52Wk Range	Yield	P/E
NYS	PBH	$38.38 (6/29/2018)	53.63-28.49	N/A	6.05

*7 Year Price Score 95.88 *NYSE Composite Index=100 *12 Month Price Score 80.90

Interim Earnings (Per Share)

Qtr.	Jun	Sep	Dec	Mar
2013-14	0.40	0.63	0.06	0.31
2014-15	0.32	0.31	0.40	0.45
2015-16	0.49	0.60	0.53	0.26
2016-17	(0.10)	0.60	0.59	0.21
2017-18	0.63	0.57	5.88	(0.74)

Interim Dividends (Per Share)

No Dividends Paid

Valuation Analysis	Institutional Holding	
Forecast EPS	$2.90	No of Institutions
	(06/14/2018)	364
Market Cap	$2.0 Billion	Shares
Book Value	$1.2 Billion	79,873,152
Price/Book	1.73	% Held
Price/Sales	1.96	101.66

Business Summary: Pharmaceuticals (MIC: 4.1.1 SIC: 2834 NAIC: 325412)

Prestige Brands Holdings is a holding company. Through its subsidiaries, Co. develops, manufactures, markets, sells and distributes over-the-counter (OTC) healthcare and household cleaning products to mass merchandisers and drug, food, dollar, convenience, and club stores in North America (the U.S. and Canada) and in Australia and certain other international markets. Co.'s portfolio of OTC Healthcare products includes, among others, DenTek oral care products, Monistat women's health products, Nix lice treatment, Chloraseptic sore throat treatments, as well as Clear Eyes eye care products. Co.'s portfolio of Household Cleaning brands includes the Chore Boy, Comet and Spic and Span brands.

Recent Developments: For the year ended Mar 31 2018, net income increased 389.3% to US$339.6 million from US$69.4 million in the prior year. Revenues were US$1.04 billion, up 18.0% from US$882.1 million the year before. Operating income was US$215.9 million versus US$205.6 million in the prior year, an increase of 5.0%. Direct operating expenses rose 21.7% to US$464.7 million from US$381.8 million in the comparable period the year before. Indirect operating expenses increased 22.4% to US$360.6 million from US$294.7 million in the equivalent prior-year period.

Prospects: Our evaluation of Prestige Brands Holdings Inc. as of Jan. 21, 2018 is the result of our systematic analysis on three basic characteristics: earnings strength, relative valuation, and recent stock price movement. The company has managed to produce a neutral trend in earnings per share over the past 5 quarters and while recent estimates for the company have been mixed, PBH has posted results that fell short of analysts expectations. Based on operating earnings yield, the company is undervalued when compared to all of the companies in our coverage universe. Share price changes over the past year indicates that PBH will perform poorly over the near term.

Financial Data
(US$ in Thousands)

	03/31/2018	03/31/2017	03/31/2016	03/31/2015	03/31/2014	03/31/2013	03/31/2012	03/31/2011
Earnings Per Share	6.34	1.30	1.88	1.49	1.39	1.27	0.73	0.58
Cash Flow Per Share	3.96	2.79	3.30	3.00	2.16	2.72	1.34	1.73
Income Statement								
Total Revenue	1,041,179	882,060	806,247	714,623	601,881	623,597	441,085	336,510
EBITDA	223,065	210,193	247,545	212,492	173,530	192,041	103,177	87,698
Depn & Amortn	10,100	6,000	5,200	3,800	3,200	1,600	700	11,853
Income Before Taxes	107,086	110,850	157,185	127,458	101,748	106,034	61,157	48,528
Income Taxes	(232,484)	41,455	57,278	49,198	29,133	40,529	23,945	19,349
Net Income	339,570	69,395	99,907	78,260	72,615	65,505	37,212	29,220
Average Shares	53,526	53,362	53,143	52,670	52,349	51,440	50,748	50,338
Balance Sheet								
Current Assets	303,477	334,434	249,013	201,707	177,185	164,173	147,035	107,582
Total Assets	3,760,612	3,911,348	2,948,791	2,669,405	1,795,663	1,739,799	1,758,276	1,056,918
Current Liabilities	123,199	162,009	106,684	99,037	84,358	96,668	63,923	54,208
Long-Term Obligations	1,992,952	2,193,732	1,625,309	1,588,711	934,414	970,900	1,123,908	486,945
Total Liabilities	2,582,002	3,088,799	2,204,455	2,041,781	1,232,303	1,261,856	1,355,548	695,086
Stockholders' Equity	1,178,610	822,549	744,336	627,624	563,360	477,943	402,728	361,832
Shares Outstanding	53,043	52,955	52,760	52,296	51,815	51,130	50,285	50,116
Statistical Record								
Return on Assets %	8.85	2.02	3.55	3.51	4.11	3.75	2.64	3.16
Return on Equity %	33.94	8.86	14.52	13.14	13.95	14.88	9.71	8.46
EBITDA Margin %	21.42	23.83	30.70	29.73	28.83	30.80	23.39	26.06
Net Margin %	32.61	7.87	12.39	10.95	12.06	10.50	8.44	8.68
Asset Turnover	0.27	0.26	0.29	0.32	0.34	0.36	0.31	0.36
Current Ratio	2.46	2.06	2.33	2.04	2.10	1.70	2.30	1.98
Debt to Equity	1.69	2.67	2.18	2.53	1.66	2.03	2.79	1.35
Price Range	57.89-32.94	57.92-45.28	54.19-39.25	42.89-26.38	36.14-25.70	25.78-13.24	17.73-8.33	12.59-7.08
P/E Ratio	9.13-5.20	44.55-34.83	28.82-20.88	28.79-17.70	26.00-18.49	20.30-10.43	24.29-11.41	21.71-12.21

Address: 660 White Plains Road, Tarrytown, NY 10591	Web Site: www.prestigebrands.com	Auditors: PricewaterhouseCoopers LLP
Telephone: 914-524-6800	Officers: Ronald M. Lombardi - Chairman, President, Chief Executive Officer, Chief Financial Officer Christine Sacco - Chief Financial Officer	Investor Contact: 914-524-6819 Transfer Agents: Computershare Ltd., Canton, MA

PRIMERICA INC

Exchange	Symbol	Price	52Wk Range	Yield	P/E
NYS	PRI	$99.60 (6/29/2018)	106.45-72.15	1.00	12.51

*7 Year Price Score 147.01 *NYSE Composite Index=100 *12 Month Price Score 104.82

Interim Earnings (Per Share)

Qtr.	Mar	Jun	Sep	Dec
2015	0.82	0.94	0.98	0.97
2016	0.92	1.23	1.22	1.22
2017	1.11	1.36	1.46	3.68
2018	1.46	...	...	...

Interim Dividends (Per Share)

Amt	Decl	Ex	Rec	Pay
0.20Q	08/07/2017	08/16/2017	08/18/2017	09/15/2017
0.20Q	11/06/2017	11/16/2017	11/17/2017	12/15/2017
0.25Q	02/07/2018	02/14/2018	02/15/2018	03/16/2018
0.25Q	05/08/2018	05/21/2018	05/22/2018	06/15/2018

Indicated Div: $1.00

Valuation Analysis

		Institutional Holding	
Forecast EPS	$7.05	No of Institutions	
	(06/12/2018)	358	
Market Cap	$4.4 Billion	Shares	
Book Value	$1.4 Billion	46,819,212	
Price/Book	3.07	% Held	
Price/Sales	2.51	68.33	

Business Summary: Life & Health (MIC: 5.2.2 SIC: 6311 NAIC: 524113)

Primerica is a holding company. Through its subsidiaries, Co. distributes financial products to households in the U.S. and Canada. Co. has three operating segments: Term Life Insurance, which provides term life insurance to clients in the U.S., its territories, the District of Columbia and Canada; Investment and Savings Products, which includes mutual funds and annuities, segregated funds, and an individual annuity savings product that it underwrites in Canada; and Corporate and Other Distributed Products, which provides other products, including prepaid legal services, auto and homeowners' insurance referrals, credit information services, long-term care insurance and health insurance.

Recent Developments: For the quarter ended Mar 31 2018, net income increased 26.2% to US$65.7 million from US$52.1 million in the year-earlier quarter. Revenues were US$459.9 million, up 13.5% from US$405.2 million the year before. Net premiums earned were US$261.8 million versus US$227.9 million in the prior-year quarter, an increase of 14.9%. Net investment income fell 4.4% to US$19.0 million from US$19.9 million a year ago.

Prospects: Our evaluation of Primerica Inc as of Jan. 21, 2018 is the result of our systematic analysis on three basic characteristics: earnings strength, relative valuation, and recent stock price movement. The company has produced a positive trend in earnings per share over the past 5 quarters and while recent estimates for the company have been mixed, PRI has posted better than expected results. Based on operating earnings yield, the company is undervalued when compared to all of the companies in our coverage universe. Share price changes over the past year indicates that PRI will perform well over the near term.

Financial Data
(US$ in Thousands)

	3 Mos	12/31/2017	12/31/2016	12/31/2015	12/31/2014	12/31/2013	12/31/2012	12/31/2011
Earnings Per Share	7.96	7.61	4.59	3.70	3.29	2.83	2.71	2.36
Cash Flow Per Share	8.55	8.52	6.15	5.09	4.36	3.37	1.96	1.22
Tang Book Value Per Share	31.30	30.91	25.51	22.52	22.68	21.03	21.39	20.82
Dividends Per Share	0.840	0.780	0.700	0.640	0.480	0.440	0.240	0.100
Dividend Payout %	10.55	10.25	15.25	17.30	14.59	15.55	8.86	4.24
Income Statement								
Total Revenue	459,923	1,689,102	1,519,084	1,405,314	1,340,030	1,267,448	1,190,715	1,103,093
Income Before Taxes	82,963	379,520	337,595	290,981	275,722	251,198	266,888	275,844
Income Taxes	17,248	29,265	118,181	101,110	95,888	88,473	93,082	97,568
Net Income	65,715	350,255	219,414	189,871	181,412	162,725	173,806	178,276
Average Shares	44,855	45,689	47,453	50,913	54,598	56,625	62,401	73,107
Balance Sheet								
Total Assets	12,492,739	12,460,703	11,438,943	10,612,119	10,738,114	10,329,950	10,337,877	9,998,544
Total Liabilities	11,066,238	11,041,602	10,217,569	9,466,347	9,492,988	9,107,923	9,062,461	8,575,903
Stockholders' Equity	1,426,501	1,419,101	1,221,374	1,145,772	1,245,126	1,222,027	1,275,416	1,422,641
Shares Outstanding	43,953	44,251	45,721	48,297	52,169	54,834	56,374	64,883
Statistical Record								
Return on Assets %	3.01	2.93	1.98	1.78	1.72	1.57	1.70	1.79
Return on Equity %	27.23	26.53	18.49	15.88	14.71	13.03	12.85	12.49
Net Margin %	14.29	20.74	14.44	13.51	13.54	12.84	14.60	16.16
Asset Turnover	0.14	0.14	0.14	0.13	0.13	0.12	0.12	0.11
Price Range	106.45-71.45	105.30-69.95	72.50-39.93	55.09-41.01	55.60-39.51	43.97-30.01	30.26-23.34	25.98-19.28
P/E Ratio	13.37-8.98	13.84-9.19	15.80-8.70	14.89-11.08	16.90-12.01	15.54-10.60	11.17-8.61	11.01-8.17
Average Yield %	0.96	0.95	1.31	1.34	1.01	1.18	0.89	0.44

Address: 1 Primerica Parkway, Duluth, GA 30099 **Telephone:** 770-381-1000	**Web Site:** www.primerica.com **Officers:** Peter W. Schneider - President, Executive Vice President, Chief Administrative Officer, Corporate Secretary, General Counsel Glenn J. Williams - President, Chief Executive Officer	**Auditors:** KPMG LLP **Investor Contact:** 866-694-0420 **Transfer Agents:** American Stock Transfer & Trust Company, Brooklyn, NY

PROASSURANCE CORP

Exchange	Symbol	Price	52Wk Range	Yield	P/E
NYS	PRA	$35.45 (6/29/2018)	63.00-35.35	3.50	24.62

*7 Year Price Score 87.14   *NYSE Composite Index=100   *12 Month Price Score 75.69

Interim Earnings (Per Share)

Qtr.	Mar	Jun	Sep	Dec
2015	0.67	0.60	0.19	0.65
2016	0.36	0.81	0.63	1.02
2017	0.77	0.36	0.54	0.32
2018	0.22	...	...	...

Interim Dividends (Per Share)

Amt	Decl	Ex	Rec	Pay
4.69Sp	11/29/2017	12/20/2017	12/21/2017	01/10/2018
0.31Q	11/29/2017	12/20/2017	12/21/2017	01/10/2018
0.31Q	03/07/2018	03/28/2018	03/29/2018	04/18/2018
0.31Q	05/23/2018	06/21/2018	06/22/2018	07/10/2018

Indicated Div: $1.24

Valuation Analysis

		Institutional Holding	
Forecast EPS	$1.76	No of Institutions	
	(06/13/2018)	355	
Market Cap	$1.9 Billion	Shares	
Book Value	$1.6 Billion	53,097,124	
Price/Book	1.21	% Held	
Price/Sales	2.25	74.89	

Business Summary: General Insurance (MIC: 5.2.1 SIC: 6331 NAIC: 524126)

ProAssurance is a holding company for property and casualty insurance companies. Co. has four segments: Specialty Property and Casualty, which includes its professional liability business and its medical technology and life sciences business; Workers' Compensation, which includes its workers' compensation business provided to employers, groups and associations in the Mid-Atlantic, Southeast, Midwest, and Gulf South regions of the continental U.S.; Lloyd's Syndicate, which provides property and casualty insurance and reinsurance lines through Lloyd's of London Syndicate 1729; and Corporate, which includes Co.'s investment operations, which are managed at the corporate level.

Recent Developments: For the quarter ended Mar 31 2018, net income decreased 71.4% to US$11.9 million from US$41.5 million in the year-earlier quarter. Revenues were US$201.0 million, down 9.9% from US$223.0 million the year before. Net premiums earned were US$187.2 million versus US$182.9 million in the prior-year quarter, an increase of 2.3%. Net investment income fell 5.0% to US$22.0 million from US$23.2 million a year ago.

Prospects: Our evaluation of ProAssurance Corp. as of Jan. 21, 2018 is the result of our systematic analysis on three basic characteristics: earnings strength, relative valuation, and recent stock price movement. The company has generated a negative trend in earnings per share over the past 5 quarters and while recent estimates for the company have been mixed, PRA has posted better than expected results. Based on operating earnings yield, the company is about fairly valued when compared to all of the companies in our coverage universe. Share price changes over the past year indicates that PRA will perform well over the near term.

Financial Data
(US$ in Thousands)

	3 Mos	12/31/2017	12/31/2016	12/31/2015	12/31/2014	12/31/2013	12/31/2012	12/31/2011
Earnings Per Share	1.44	2.00	2.83	2.11	3.30	4.80	4.46	4.66
Cash Flow Per Share	3.06	2.79	3.17	2.04	1.62	0.63	1.48	2.61
Tang Book Value Per Share	23.83	24.34	28.24	31.17	32.66	35.64	33.34	31.93
Dividends Per Share	5.930	5.930	5.930	2.240	3.860	1.050	3.125	0.250
Dividend Payout %	411.81	296.50	209.54	106.16	116.97	21.88	70.07	5.37
Income Statement								
Premium Income	187,159	738,531	733,281	694,149	699,731	527,919	550,664	565,415
Total Revenue	201,032	866,149	870,214	772,079	852,326	740,178	715,854	716,784
Benefits & Claims	129,786	...	515,242	456,862	379,232	243,015	161,726	151,270
Income Before Taxes	8,434	128,623	176,201	128,855	262,005	397,159	395,966	414,598
Income Taxes	(3,422)	21,359	25,120	12,658	65,440	99,636	120,496	127,502
Net Income	11,856	107,264	151,081	116,197	196,565	297,523	275,470	287,096
Average Shares	53,682	53,611	53,448	55,017	59,525	62,020	61,833	61,684
Balance Sheet								
Total Assets	4,678,924	4,929,197	5,065,181	4,908,163	5,169,160	5,150,891	4,876,578	4,998,878
Total Liabilities	3,109,755	3,334,402	3,266,479	2,949,809	3,011,216	2,756,477	2,605,998	2,834,425
Stockholders' Equity	1,569,169	1,594,795	1,798,702	1,958,354	2,157,944	2,394,414	2,270,580	2,164,453
Shares Outstanding	53,593	53,457	53,251	53,100	56,533	61,196	61,623	61,107
Statistical Record								
Return on Assets %	1.63	2.15	3.02	2.31	3.81	5.93	5.56	5.82
Return on Equity %	4.58	6.32	8.02	5.65	8.64	12.76	12.39	14.28
Loss Ratio %	69.35	...	70.27	65.82	54.20	46.03	29.37	26.75
Net Margin %	5.90	12.38	17.36	15.05	23.06	40.20	38.48	40.05
Price Range	63.00-47.35	63.00-51.30	62.85-46.22	53.42-43.73	48.48-42.90	55.28-42.19	46.48-39.35	40.60-28.98
P/E Ratio	43.75-32.88	31.50-25.65	22.21-16.33	25.32-20.73	14.69-13.00	11.52-8.79	10.42-8.82	8.71-6.22
Average Yield %	10.44	10.21	11.41	4.69	8.52	2.18	7.12	0.72

Address: 100 Brookwood Place, Birmingham, AL 35209
Telephone: 205-877-4400
Fax: 205-802-4799

Web Site: www.proassurance.com
Officers: W. Stancil Starnes - Chairman, Chief Executive Officer Edward L. (Ned) Rand - Executive Vice President, Senior Vice President, Chief Financial Officer, Chief Operating Officer, Chief Accounting Officer

Auditors: Ernst & Young LLP
Investor Contact: 205-877-4461
Transfer Agents: Mellon Investor Services, LLC, Ridgefield Park, NJ

PROCTER & GAMBLE COMPANY (THE)

Exchange	Symbol	Price	52Wk Range	Yield	P/E	Div Acheiver
NYS	PG	$78.06 (6/29/2018)	94.40-70.94	3.68	20.71	64 Years

*7 Year Price Score 86.51   *NYSE Composite Index=100   *12 Month Price Score 86.73

Interim Earnings (Per Share)

Qtr.	Sep	Dec	Mar	Jun
2014-15	0.69	0.82	0.75	0.18
2015-16	0.91	1.12	0.97	0.69
2016-17	0.96	2.88	0.93	0.83
2017-18	1.06	0.93	0.95	...

Interim Dividends (Per Share)

Amt	Decl	Ex	Rec	Pay
0.69Q	10/10/2017	10/19/2017	10/20/2017	11/15/2017
0.69Q	01/09/2018	01/18/2018	01/19/2018	02/15/2018
0.717Q	04/10/2018	04/19/2018	04/20/2018	05/15/2018
0.717Q	07/10/2018	07/19/2018	07/20/2018	08/15/2018

Indicated Div: $2.87 (Div. Reinv. Plan)

Valuation Analysis — **Institutional Holding**

Valuation Analysis		Institutional Holding	
Forecast EPS	$4.18	No of Institutions	
	(06/14/2018)	3071	
Market Cap	$196.3 Billion	Shares	
Book Value	$54.3 Billion	1,967,427,712	
Price/Book	3.61	% Held	
Price/Sales	2.96	56.86	

Business Summary: Household & Personal Products (MIC: 1.7.1 SIC: 2841 NAIC: 325611)

Procter & Gamble provides consumer packaged goods. Co.'s products are sold mainly through mass merchandisers, grocery stores, membership club stores, drug stores, department stores, distributors, wholesalers, baby stores, beauty stores, e-commerce, high-frequency stores and pharmacies. At June 30 2017, Co. had five reportable segments: Beauty, which includes hair care, and skin and personal care products; Grooming, which includes shave care products; Health Care, which includes oral care and personal health care products; Fabric and Home Care, which includes fabric and home care products; and Baby, Feminine and Family Care, which includes baby care, feminine care and family care products.

Recent Developments: For the quarter ended Mar 31 2018, income from continuing operations decreased 0.6% to US$2.54 billion from US$2.56 billion in the year-earlier quarter. Net income decreased 0.6% to US$2.54 billion from US$2.56 billion in the year-earlier quarter. Revenues were US$16.28 billion, up 4.3% from US$15.61 billion the year before. Operating income was US$3.30 billion versus US$3.36 billion in the prior-year quarter, a decrease of 1.9%. Direct operating expenses rose 6.5% to US$8.34 billion from US$7.84 billion in the comparable period the year before. Indirect operating expenses increased 5.3% to US$4.64 billion from US$4.41 billion in the equivalent prior-year period.

Prospects: Our evaluation of Procter & Gamble Co. as of Jan. 21, 2018 is the result of our systematic analysis on three basic characteristics: earnings strength, relative valuation, and recent stock price movement. The company has managed to produce a neutral trend in earnings per share over the past 5 quarters and while recent estimates for the company have been raised by analysts, PG has posted better than expected results. Based on operating earnings yield, the company is undervalued when compared to all of the companies in our coverage universe. Share price changes over the past year indicates that PG will perform well over the near term.

Financial Data

(US$ in Millions)	9 Mos	6 Mos	3 Mos	06/30/2017	06/30/2016	06/30/2015	06/30/2014	06/30/2013
Earnings Per Share	3.77	3.75	5.70	5.59	3.69	2.44	4.01	3.86
Cash Flow Per Share	5.69	5.54	5.24	4.91	5.70	5.39	5.13	5.42
Dividends Per Share	2.758	2.738	2.718	2.698	2.658	2.594	2.448	2.288
Dividend Payout %	73.17	73.02	47.69	48.27	72.04	106.30	61.05	59.26
Income Statement								
Total Revenue	50,329	34,048	16,653	65,058	65,299	76,279	83,062	84,167
EBITDA	13,307	9,274	4,509	16,371	16,844	15,455	18,635	18,405
Depn & Amortn	2,084	1,368	692	2,820	3,078	3,134	3,141	2,982
Income Before Taxes	11,037	7,784	3,751	13,257	13,369	11,846	14,885	14,843
Income Taxes	3,066	2,353	881	3,063	3,342	2,916	3,178	3,441
Net Income	7,859	5,348	2,853	15,326	10,508	7,036	11,643	11,312
Average Shares	2,646	2,670	2,691	2,741	2,845	2,884	2,905	2,931
Balance Sheet								
Current Assets	27,960	31,214	28,096	26,494	33,782	29,646	31,617	23,990
Total Assets	124,369	126,644	122,851	120,406	127,136	129,495	144,266	139,263
Current Liabilities	30,711	33,107	30,724	30,210	30,770	29,790	33,726	30,037
Long-Term Obligations	22,437	22,186	20,188	18,038	18,945	18,329	19,811	19,111
Total Liabilities	70,054	72,532	68,033	65,222	69,795	67,076	75,052	71,199
Stockholders' Equity	54,315	54,112	54,818	55,184	57,341	62,419	69,214	68,064
Shares Outstanding	2,515	2,522	2,537	2,554	2,669	2,715	2,711	2,743
Statistical Record								
Return on Assets %	8.31	8.28	12.28	12.38	8.17	5.14	8.21	8.33
Return on Equity %	18.63	18.82	27.35	27.24	17.50	10.69	16.96	17.20
EBITDA Margin %	26.44	27.24	27.08	25.16	25.80	20.26	22.44	21.87
Net Margin %	15.62	15.71	17.13	23.56	16.09	9.22	14.02	13.44
Asset Turnover	0.55	0.54	0.52	0.53	0.51	0.56	0.59	0.62
Current Ratio	0.91	0.94	0.91	0.88	1.10	1.00	0.94	0.80
Debt to Equity	0.41	0.41	0.37	0.33	0.33	0.29	0.29	0.28
Price Range	94.40-75.91	94.40-83.49	94.40-81.86	91.67-81.86	84.67-68.06	93.46-77.32	85.41-75.59	82.54-61.19
P/E Ratio	25.04-20.14	25.17-22.26	16.56-14.36	16.40-14.64	22.95-18.44	38.30-31.69	21.30-18.85	21.38-15.85
Average Yield %	3.13	3.06	3.08	3.08	3.09	3.39	3.06	3.18

Address: One Procter & Gamble Plaza, Cincinnati, OH 45202	Web Site: www.pg.com	Auditors: Deloitte & Touche LLP
Telephone: 513-983-1100	Officers: David S. Taylor - Chairman, President, Chief Executive Officer, Division Officer Jon R. Moeller - Vice-Chairman, Chief Financial Officer	Investor Contact: 800-742-6253
		Transfer Agents: Computershare, Canton, MA

PROGRESSIVE CORP. (OH)

Exchange	Symbol	Price	52Wk Range	Yield	P/E
NYS	PGR	$59.15 (6/29/2018)	63.00-43.73	1.90	18.37

*7 Year Price Score 140.18 *NYSE Composite Index=100 *12 Month Price Score 111.45

Interim Earnings (Per Share)

Qtr.	Mar	Jun	Sep	Dec
2015	0.50	0.62	0.47	0.55
2016	0.44	0.33	0.34	0.65
2017	0.73	0.63	0.38	0.99
2018	1.22	...	...	...

Interim Dividends (Per Share)

Amt	Decl	Ex	Rec	Pay
0.686A	12/19/2014	02/02/2015	02/04/2015	02/13/2015
0.888A	12/04/2015	02/01/2016	02/03/2016	02/12/2016
0.681A	12/02/2016	02/01/2017	02/03/2017	02/10/2017
1.125A	12/08/2017	02/01/2018	02/02/2018	02/09/2018

Indicated Div: $1.12

Valuation Analysis — **Institutional Holding**

Forecast EPS	$4.28
(06/14/2018)	
Market Cap	$34.4 Billion
Book Value	$10.3 Billion
Price/Book	3.34
Price/Sales	1.23

No of Institutions	963
Shares	567,636,416
% Held	69.20

Business Summary: General Insurance (MIC: 5.2.1 SIC: 6331 NAIC: 524126)

Progressive is an insurance holding company. Through its insurance subsidiaries and affiliates, Co. provides personal and commercial auto insurance, residential property insurance, and other specialty property-casualty insurance and related services. Co.'s Personal Lines segment writes insurance for personal autos and recreational and other vehicles, while its commercial lines business writes primary liability, physical damage, and other auto-related insurance for automobiles and trucks owned and/or operated mainly by businesses as a part of the commercial auto market. Co.'s service businesses primarily include: Commercial Auto Insurance Procedures/Plans and its commission-based businesses.

Recent Developments: For the quarter ended Mar 31 2018, net income increased 69.6% to US$729.8 million from US$430.3 million in the year-earlier quarter. Revenues were US$7.43 billion, up 17.5% from US$6.32 billion the year before. Net premiums earned were US$7.17 billion versus US$6.03 billion in the prior-year quarter, an increase of 19.0%. Net investment income rose 28.7% to US$166.3 million from US$129.2 million a year ago.

Prospects: Our evaluation of Progressive Corp. as of Jan. 21, 2018 is the result of our systematic analysis on three basic characteristics: earnings strength, relative valuation, and recent stock price movement. The company has generated a negative trend in earnings per share over the past 5 quarters and while recent estimates for the company have been raised by analysts, PGR has posted better than expected results. Based on operating earnings yield, the company is about fairly valued when compared to all of the companies in our coverage universe. Share price changes over the past year indicates that PGR will perform very well over the near term.

Financial Data
(US$ in Thousands)

	3 Mos	12/31/2017	12/31/2016	12/31/2015	12/31/2014	12/31/2013	12/31/2012	12/31/2011
Earnings Per Share	3.22	2.72	1.76	2.15	2.15	1.93	1.48	1.59
Cash Flow Per Share	7.53	6.47	4.63	3.92	2.92	3.17	2.80	2.37
Tang Book Value Per Share	15.50	14.55	12.20	10.88	11.79	10.39	9.94	9.47
Dividends Per Share	1.125	0.681	0.888	0.686	1.493	0.284	1.407	0.399
Dividend Payout %	34.93	25.03	50.47	31.92	69.44	14.74	95.08	25.08
Income Statement								
Premium Income	7,174,000	25,729,900	22,474,000	19,899,100	18,398,500	17,103,400	16,018,000	14,902,800
Total Revenue	7,430,100	26,839,000	23,441,400	20,853,800	19,391,400	18,170,900	17,083,900	15,508,100
Benefits & Claims	4,870,800	18,808,000	16,879,600	14,342,000	13,306,200	12,472,400	11,948,000	10,634,800
Income Before Taxes	910,800	2,138,900	1,470,700	1,911,600	1,907,400	1,720,000	1,317,700	1,487,000
Income Taxes	181,000	540,800	413,500	611,100	626,400	554,600	415,400	471,500
Net Income	718,000	1,592,200	1,031,000	1,267,600	1,281,000	1,165,400	902,300	1,015,500
Average Shares	585,600	585,700	585,000	589,200	594,800	603,600	607,800	636,900
Balance Sheet								
Total Assets	41,330,900	38,701,200	33,427,500	29,819,300	25,787,600	24,408,200	22,694,700	21,844,800
Total Liabilities	31,007,700	29,416,400	25,470,400	22,529,900	18,859,000	18,218,700	16,687,700	16,038,100
Stockholders' Equity	10,323,200	9,284,800	7,957,100	7,289,400	6,928,600	6,189,500	6,007,000	5,806,700
Shares Outstanding	582,400	581,700	579,900	583,600	587,800	595,800	604,600	613,000
Statistical Record								
Return on Assets %	4.95	4.41	3.25	4.56	5.10	4.95	4.04	4.72
Return on Equity %	20.01	18.47	13.49	17.83	19.53	19.11	15.23	17.13
Loss Ratio %	67.90	73.10	75.11	72.07	72.32	72.92	74.59	71.36
Net Margin %	9.66	5.93	4.40	6.08	6.61	6.41	5.28	6.55
Price Range	62.33-38.87	56.51-35.53	35.74-29.49	33.64-25.85	27.35-22.59	28.14-21.10	23.30-19.24	21.94-17.09
P/E Ratio	19.36-12.07	20.78-13.06	20.31-16.76	15.65-12.02	12.72-10.51	14.58-10.93	15.74-13.00	13.80-10.75
Average Yield %	2.29	1.53	2.72	2.37	5.96	1.12	6.64	2.02

Address: 6300 Wilson Mills Road, Mayfield Village, OH 44143
Telephone: 440-461-5000
Fax: 440-446-7168

Web Site: www.progressive.com
Officers: Susan Patricia (Tricia) Griffith - President, Chief Executive Officer, Personal Lines Chief Operating Officer, Division Officer John Peter Sauerland - Vice President, Chief Financial Officer, Division Officer

Auditors: PricewaterhouseCoopers LLP
Investor Contact: 440-395-2222
Transfer Agents: American Stock Transfer & Trust Company, Brookly, NY

PROLOGIS INC

Exchange	Symbol	Price	52Wk Range	Yield	P/E
NYS	PLD	$65.69 (6/29/2018)	67.40-56.94	2.92	19.55

*7 Year Price Score 116.18 *NYSE Composite Index=100 *12 Month Price Score 100.86

Interim Earnings (Per Share)
Qtr.	Mar	Jun	Sep	Dec
2015	0.65	0.27	0.49	0.23
2016	0.39	0.52	0.52	0.83
2017	0.38	0.50	1.63	0.55
2018	0.68	...	...	...

Interim Dividends (Per Share)
Amt	Decl	Ex	Rec	Pay
0.44Q	09/07/2017	09/15/2017	09/18/2017	09/29/2017
0.44Q	12/07/2017	12/15/2017	12/18/2017	12/29/2017
0.48Q	02/22/2018	03/14/2018	03/15/2018	03/29/2018
0.48Q	05/02/2018	06/13/2018	06/14/2018	06/29/2018

Indicated Div: $1.92

Valuation Analysis | Institutional Holding
Forecast EPS	$1.93	No of Institutions
	(06/14/2018)	59
Market Cap	$35.0 Billion	Shares
Book Value	$15.7 Billion	10,207,956
Price/Book	2.23	% Held
Price/Sales	13.05	N/A

Business Summary: REITs (MIC: 5.3.1 SIC: 6798 NAIC: 525930)

Prologis is a real estate investment trust. Co. owns, manages and develops logistics facilities. The majority of Co.'s consolidated properties are in the U.S.; while outside the U.S., Co.'s properties are generally held in co-investment ventures. Co. is principally an owner-operator in the U.S. and a manager-developer outside the U.S. Co. has two operating segments: Real Estate Operations, which represents the ownership and development of operating properties, and includes development activities that lead to rental operations, including land held for development and properties under development; and Strategic Capital, which represents the management of unconsolidated co-investment ventures.

Recent Developments: For the quarter ended Mar 31 2018, net income increased 77.6% to US$392.0 million from US$220.7 million in the year-earlier quarter. Revenues were US$693.7 million, up 10.3% from US$629.2 million the year before. Revenues from property income fell 1.9% to US$555.9 million from US$566.9 million in the corresponding quarter a year earlier.

Prospects: Our evaluation of Prologis Inc. as of Jan. 21, 2018 is the result of our systematic analysis on three basic characteristics: earnings strength, relative valuation, and recent stock price movement. The company has generated a negative trend in earnings per share over the past 5 quarters. Because the company lacks sufficient analyst estimate data, we place greater weight on the historical EPS trend as the measure of earnings strength. Based on operating earnings yield, the company is overvalued when compared to all of the companies in our coverage universe. Share price changes over the past year indicates that PLD will perform very well over the near term.

Financial Data
(US$ in Thousands)	3 Mos	12/31/2017	12/31/2016	12/31/2015	12/31/2014	12/31/2013	12/31/2012	12/31/2011
Earnings Per Share	3.36	3.06	2.27	1.64	1.24	0.64	(0.18)	(0.51)
Cash Flow Per Share	3.16	3.18	2.69	1.85	1.41	1.00	1.01	0.56
Tang Book Value Per Share	29.28	28.86	27.70	27.82	27.28	27.29	27.04	28.52
Dividends Per Share	1.800	1.760	1.680	1.520	1.320	1.120	1.120	1.120
Dividend Payout %	53.57	57.52	74.01	92.68	106.45	175.00	...	...
Income Statement								
Total Revenue	693,656	2,618,134	2,533,135	2,197,074	1,760,787	1,750,486	2,005,961	1,533,291
EBITDA	379,078	2,626,626	2,258,082	1,853,116	1,548,602	1,265,568	1,151,775	801,552
Depn & Amortn	(12,046)	798,870	822,240	787,894	686,145	674,147	788,467	647,440
Income Before Taxes	345,855	1,567,001	1,140,797	789,343	579,340	239,042	(121,298)	(302,618)
Income Taxes	16,552	54,609	54,564	23,090	(25,656)	106,733	3,580	1,776
Net Income	367,378	1,652,325	1,209,932	869,439	636,183	342,921	(39,720)	(153,414)
Average Shares	554,123	552,300	546,666	533,944	506,391	491,546	459,895	370,534
Balance Sheet								
Current Assets	458,099	630,036	1,026,999	454,456	548,355	758,629	448,820	396,063
Total Assets	29,671,485	29,481,075	30,249,932	31,394,767	25,818,223	24,572,307	27,310,145	27,723,912
Current Liabilities	692,853	979,614	847,034	994,282	895,883	1,074,229	611,770	639,490
Long-Term Obligations	9,460,177	9,412,631	10,608,294	11,626,831	9,380,199	9,011,216	11,790,794	11,382,408
Total Liabilities	13,991,410	13,849,917	15,258,851	16,726,832	11,842,714	10,861,149	14,241,128	14,062,273
Stockholders' Equity	15,680,075	15,631,158	14,991,081	14,667,935	13,975,509	13,711,158	13,069,017	13,661,639
Shares Outstanding	533,107	532,186	528,671	524,512	509,498	498,799	461,770	458,597
Statistical Record								
Return on Assets %	6.10	5.53	3.91	3.04	2.53	1.32	N.M.	N.M.
Return on Equity %	11.93	10.79	8.14	6.07	4.60	2.56	N.M.	N.M.
EBITDA Margin %	54.65	100.32	89.14	84.34	87.95	72.30	57.42	52.28
Net Margin %	52.96	63.11	47.76	39.57	36.13	19.59	N.M.	N.M.
Asset Turnover	0.09	0.09	0.08	0.08	0.07	0.07	0.07	0.09
Current Ratio	0.66	0.64	1.21	0.46	0.61	0.71	0.73	0.62
Debt to Equity	0.60	0.60	0.71	0.79	0.67	0.66	0.90	0.83
Price Range	67.40-51.88	67.40-48.44	54.61-35.57	47.13-36.45	43.64-36.51	44.77-34.78	36.91-28.50	37.26-22.63
P/E Ratio	20.06-15.44	22.03-15.83	24.06-15.67	28.74-22.23	35.19-29.44	69.95-54.34	...	...
Average Yield %	2.94	3.01	3.52	3.67	3.26	2.87	3.33	3.55

Address: Pier 1, Bay 1, San Francisco, CA 94111	Web Site: www.prologis.com	Auditors: KPMG LLP
Telephone: 415-394-9000	Officers: Hamid R. Moghadam - Chairman, Chief Executive Officer, Co-Chief Executive Officer Thomas S. Olinger - Chief Financial Officer, Chief Integration Officer	Investor Contact: 415-733-9565
Fax: 415-394-9001		Transfer Agents: Computershare Investor Services, Canton, MA

PROSPERITY BANCSHARES INC.

Exchange	Symbol	Price	52Wk Range	Yield	P/E	Div Acheiver
NYS	PB	$68.36 (6/29/2018)	78.70-56.46	2.11	17.05	18 Years

*7 Year Price Score 101.57 *NYSE Composite Index=100 *12 Month Price Score 103.56

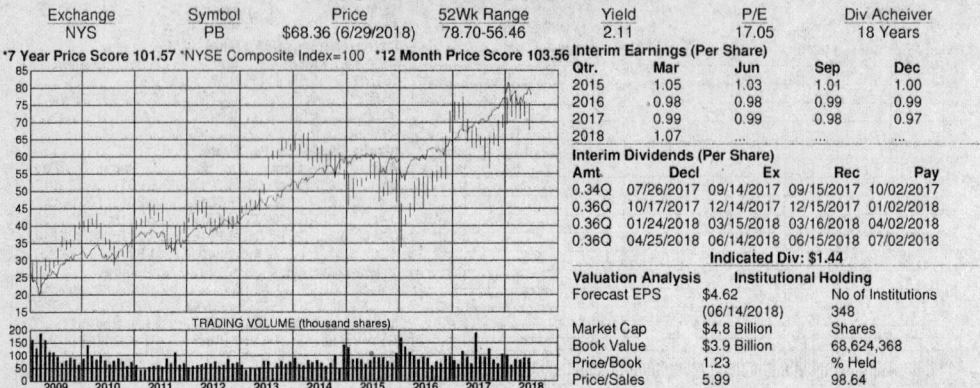

Interim Earnings (Per Share)

Qtr.	Mar	Jun	Sep	Dec
2015	1.05	1.03	1.01	1.00
2016	0.98	0.98	0.99	0.99
2017	0.99	0.99	0.98	0.97
2018	1.07	...	...	...

Interim Dividends (Per Share)

Amt.	Decl	Ex	Rec	Pay
0.34Q	07/26/2017	09/14/2017	09/15/2017	10/02/2017
0.36Q	10/17/2017	12/14/2017	12/15/2017	01/02/2018
0.36Q	01/24/2018	03/15/2018	03/16/2018	04/02/2018
0.36Q	04/25/2018	06/14/2018	06/15/2018	07/02/2018

Indicated Div: $1.44

Valuation Analysis   Institutional Holding

Forecast EPS	$4.62	No of Institutions	
	(06/14/2018)	348	
Market Cap	$4.8 Billion	Shares	
Book Value	$3.9 Billion	68,624,368	
Price/Book	1.23	% Held	
Price/Sales	5.99	98.64	

Business Summary: Banking (MIC: 5.1.1 SIC: 6022 NAIC: 522110)

Prosperity Bancshares is a financial holding company. Through its subsidiary, Prosperity Bank®, Co. provides financial products and services to small and medium-sized businesses and consumers. Co. is a real estate lender with commercial real estate and one-four family residential loans. Co. also provides commercial loans, loans for automobiles and other consumer durables, home equity loans, debit and credit cards, internet banking and other cash management services, mobile banking, trust and wealth management, retail brokerage services, mortgage banking services and automated telephone banking. As of Dec 31 2017, Co. had total assets of $22.59 billion and total deposits of $17.82 billion.

Recent Developments: For the quarter ended Mar 31 2018, net income increased 8.5% to US$74.4 million from US$68.6 million in the year-earlier quarter. Net interest income increased 0.5% to US$153.2 million from US$152.4 million in the year-earlier quarter. Provision for loan losses was US$9.0 million versus US$2.7 million in the prior-year quarter, an increase of 236.4%. Non-interest income fell 9.4% to US$27.9 million from US$30.8 million, while non-interest expense advanced 2.6% to US$80.1 million.

Prospects: Our evaluation of Prosperity Bancshares Inc. as of Jan. 21, 2018 is the result of our systematic analysis on three basic characteristics: earnings strength, relative valuation, and recent stock price movement. The company has managed to produce a neutral trend in earnings per share over the past 5 quarters and while recent estimates for the company have been raised by analysts, PB has posted better than expected results. Based on operating earnings yield, the company is undervalued when compared to all of the companies in our coverage universe. Share price changes over the past year indicates that PB will perform poorly over the near term.

Financial Data
(US$ in Thousands)

	3 Mos	12/31/2017	12/31/2016	12/31/2015	12/31/2014	12/31/2013	12/31/2012	12/31/2011
Earnings Per Share	4.01	3.92	3.94	4.09	4.32	3.65	3.23	3.01
Cash Flow Per Share	4.64	5.62	4.79	4.44	5.06	5.09	4.04	4.65
Tang Book Value Per Share	27.76	27.12	24.40	22.06	18.80	16.25	14.99	13.25
Dividends Per Share	1.400	1.380	1.240	1.117	0.993	0.885	0.800	0.720
Dividend Payout %	34.91	35.20	31.47	27.32	22.97	24.25	24.77	23.92
Income Statement								
Interest Income	171,018	677,355	675,779	669,701	714,795	539,297	419,842	371,908
Interest Expense	17,795	60,492	43,159	39,191	43,641	40,471	39,136	45,240
Net Interest Income	153,223	616,863	632,620	630,510	671,154	498,826	380,706	326,668
Provision for Losses	9,000	14,325	24,000	7,560	18,275	17,240	6,100	5,200
Non-Interest Income	27,938	116,633	118,425	120,781	120,832	95,427	74,887	53,958
Non-Interest Expense	80,054	313,101	318,387	313,536	327,962	247,196	198,457	156,559
Income Before Taxes	92,107	406,070	408,658	430,195	445,749	329,817	251,684	213,766
Income Taxes	17,746	133,905	134,192	143,549	148,308	108,419	83,783	72,017
Net Income	74,361	272,165	274,466	286,646	297,441	221,398	167,901	141,749
Average Shares	69,768	69,484	69,680	70,049	68,911	60,578	51,941	47,017
Balance Sheet								
Net Loans & Leases	9,927,816	9,936,732	9,536,734	9,357,205	9,163,421	7,707,939	5,127,376	3,714,312
Total Assets	22,472,314	22,587,292	22,331,072	22,037,216	21,507,733	18,642,028	14,583,573	9,822,671
Total Deposits	17,332,879	17,821,460	17,307,302	17,681,119	17,693,158	15,291,271	11,641,844	8,060,254
Total Liabilities	18,596,169	18,763,138	18,688,761	18,574,306	18,262,907	15,855,210	12,494,184	8,255,406
Stockholders' Equity	3,876,145	3,824,154	3,642,311	3,462,910	3,244,826	2,786,818	2,089,389	1,567,265
Shares Outstanding	69,819	69,490	69,491	70,021	69,779	66,048	56,447	46,910
Statistical Record								
Return on Assets %	1.24	1.21	1.23	1.32	1.48	1.33	1.37	1.47
Return on Equity %	7.35	7.29	7.70	8.55	9.86	9.08	9.16	9.39
Net Interest Margin %	89.59	91.07	93.61	94.15	93.89	92.50	90.68	87.84
Efficiency Ratio %	40.24	39.43	40.09	39.66	39.25	38.95	40.11	36.76
Loans to Deposits	0.57	0.56	0.55	0.53	0.52	0.50	0.44	0.46
Price Range	78.70-56.46	77.47-56.46	73.20-33.73	59.23-45.79	67.00-53.21	65.07-42.00	47.31-39.10	46.50-31.67
P/E Ratio	19.63-14.08	19.76-14.40	18.58-8.56	14.48-11.20	15.51-12.32	17.83-11.51	14.65-12.11	15.45-10.52
Average Yield %	2.07	2.06	2.38	2.13	1.65	1.64	1.89	1.79

Address: Prosperity Bank Plaza, 4295 San Felipe, Houston, TX 77027
Telephone: 281-269-7199
Web Site: www.prosperitybankusa.com
Officers: David Zalman - Chairman, President, Chief Executive Officer H. E. Timanus - Vice-Chairman
Auditors: Deloitte & Touche LLP
Investor Contact: 713-693-9300
Transfer Agents: Computershare Investor Services, Golden, Co

PRUDENTIAL FINANCIAL INC

Exchange	Symbol	Price	52Wk Range	Yield	P/E
NYS	PRU	$93.51 (6/29/2018)	126.02-93.22	3.85	5.22

*7 Year Price Score 108.56 *NYSE Composite Index=100 *12 Month Price Score 90.03

Interim Earnings (Per Share)

Qtr.	Mar	Jun	Sep	Dec
2015	4.37	3.03	3.16.	1.61
2016	2.93	2.04	4.07	0.69
2017	3.09	1.12	5.09	8.57
2018	3.14	...	...	...

Interim Dividends (Per Share)

Amt	Decl	Ex	Rec	Pay
0.75Q	08/08/2017	08/18/2017	08/22/2017	09/14/2017
0.75Q	11/14/2017	11/24/2017	11/27/2017	12/14/2017
0.90Q	02/07/2018	02/20/2018	02/21/2018	03/15/2018
0.90Q	05/08/2018	05/21/2018	05/22/2018	06/14/2018

Indicated Div: $3.60

Valuation Analysis / Institutional Holding

Forecast EPS	$12.18 (06/14/2018)	No of Institutions	1389
Market Cap	$39.4 Billion	Shares	343,922,720
Book Value	$51.8 Billion	% Held	60.34
Price/Book	0.76		
Price/Sales	0.66		

TRADING VOLUME (thousand shares)

Business Summary: Life & Health (MIC: 5.2.2 SIC: 6311 NAIC: 524113)

Prudential Financial is a holding company. Through its subsidiaries and affiliates, Co. provides financial products and services, including life insurance, annuities, retirement-related services, mutual funds and investment management. The U.S. Retirement Solutions and Investment Management division consists of Co.'s Individual Annuities, Retirement and Asset Management segments. The U.S. Individual Life and Group Insurance division consists of Co.'s Individual Life and Group Insurance segments. The International Insurance division consists of Co.'s International Insurance segment. As of Dec 31 2017, Co. had operations in the U.S., Asia, Europe and Latin America.

Recent Developments: For the quarter ended Mar 31 2018, net income decreased 0.6% to US$1.36 billion from US$1.37 billion in the year-earlier quarter. Revenues were US$13.76 billion, up 0.6% from US$13.67 billion the year before. Net premiums earned were US$7.31 billion versus US$6.48 billion in the prior-year quarter, an increase of 12.8%. Net investment income fell 1.6% to US$4.00 billion from US$4.06 billion a year ago.

Prospects: Our evaluation of Prudential Financial Inc. as of Jan. 21, 2018 is the result of our systematic analysis on three basic characteristics: earnings strength, relative valuation, and recent stock price movement. The company has managed to produce a neutral trend in earnings per share over the past 5 quarters and while recent estimates for the company have been raised by analysts, PRU has posted better than expected results. Based on operating earnings yield, the company is undervalued when compared to all of the companies in our coverage universe. Share price changes over the past year indicates that PRU will perform poorly over the near term.

Financial Data

(US$ in Millions)	3 Mos	12/31/2017	12/31/2016	12/31/2015	12/31/2014	12/31/2013	12/31/2012	12/31/2011
Earnings Per Share	17.92	17.86	9.71	12.17	3.23	(1.55)	0.94	7.22
Cash Flow Per Share	33.41	31.49	33.63	30.76	42.30	18.24	44.78	25.77
Tang Book Value Per Share	123.10	127.96	106.76	93.69	91.84	76.19	82.95	79.19
Dividends Per Share	3.150	3.000	2.800	2.440	2.170	1.730	1.600	1.450
Dividend Payout %	17.58	16.80	28.84	20.05	67.18	...	170.21	20.08
Income Statement								
Premium Income	7,311	32,091	30,964	28,521	29,293	26,237	65,354	24,338
Total Revenue	13,757	59,689	58,779	57,119	54,105	41,461	84,815	49,045
Benefits & Claims	7,675	33,794	33,632	30,627	31,587	26,733	65,131	23,614
Income Before Taxes	1,693	6,487	5,705	7,769	1,759	(1,684)	676.	5,117
Income Taxes	352	(1,438)	1,335	2,072	349	(1,058)	204	1,599
Net Income	1,363	7,863	4,368	5,642	1,381	(667)	469	3,666
Average Shares	430	436	446	460	467	463	468	488
Balance Sheet								
Total Assets	829,677	831,921	783,962	757,388	766,655	731,781	709,298	624,521
Total Liabilities	777,847	777,852	738,099	715,498	724,885	696,503	670,723	587,298
Stockholders' Equity	51,830	54,069	45,863	41,890	41,770	35,278	38,575	37,223
Shares Outstanding	421	422	429	447	454	463	465	470
Statistical Record								
Return on Assets %	0.97	0.97	0.57	0.74	0.18	N.M.	0.07	0.63
Return on Equity %	15.93	15.74	9.93	13.49	3.58	N.M.	1.23	10.53
Loss Ratio %	104.98	105.31	108.62	107.38	107.83	101.89	99.66	97.03
Net Margin %	9.91	13.17	7.43	9.88	2.55	(1.61)	0.55	7.47
Price Range	126.02-98.65	117.15-98.65	107.10-58.00	91.68-74.22	93.16-77.61	92.43-53.33	64.65-44.74	67.32-43.91
P/E Ratio	7.03-5.51	6.56-5.52	11.03-5.97	7.53-6.10	28.84-24.03	...	68.78-47.60	9.32-6.08
Average Yield %	2.88	2.77	3.53	2.93	2.51	2.41	2.93	2.55

Address: 751 Broad Street, Newark, NJ 07102
Telephone: 973-802-6000

Web Site: www.investor.prudential.com
Officers: John R. Strangfeld - Chairman, President, Chief Executive Officer Mark B. Grier - Vice-Chairman

Auditors: PricewaterhouseCoopers LLP
Transfer Agents: Computershare Trust Company, N.A., Providence, RI

PUBLIC SERVICE ENTERPRISE GROUP INC

Exchange	Symbol	Price	52Wk Range	Yield	P/E
NYS	PEG	$54.14 (6/29/2018)	54.24-41.85	3.32	13.60

*7 Year Price Score 100.58 *NYSE Composite Index=100 *12 Month Price Score 104.42

Interim Earnings (Per Share)

Qtr.	Mar	Jun	Sep	Dec
2015	1.15	0.68	0.87	0.60
2016	0.93	0.37	0.64	(0.19)
2017	0.23	0.22	0.78	1.88
2018	1.10	...	...	...

Interim Dividends (Per Share)

Amt	Decl	Ex	Rec	Pay
0.43Q	07/18/2017	09/07/2017	09/08/2017	09/29/2017
0.43Q	11/21/2017	12/07/2017	12/08/2017	12/29/2017
0.45Q	02/20/2018	03/07/2018	03/08/2018	03/30/2018
0.45Q	04/17/2018	06/07/2018	06/08/2018	06/29/2018

Indicated Div: $1.80

Valuation Analysis / **Institutional Holding**

Forecast EPS	$3.10	No of Institutions
	(06/14/2018)	1098
Market Cap	$27.3 Billion	Shares
Book Value	$14.1 Billion	422,203,968
Price/Book	1.93	% Held
Price/Sales	2.93	63.36

Business Summary: Electric Utilities (MIC: 3.1.1 SIC: 4931 NAIC: 221119)

Public Service Enterprise Group is a holding company. Through its subsidiaries, Co. is engaged in the energy industry. Co. conducts its business through two subsidiaries, Public Service Electric and Gas Company (PSE&G) and PSEG Power LLC (Power). PSE&G is a public utility, which is engaged in the transmission of electricity and distribution of electricity and natural gas in certain areas of New Jersey, and Power is a multi-regional energy supply company that integrates the operations of its merchant nuclear and fossil generating assets with its power marketing businesses through energy sales in energy markets and fuel supply functions primarily in the Northeast and Mid-Atlantic U.S.

Recent Developments: For the quarter ended Mar 31 2018, net income increased 389.5% to US$558.0 million from US$114.0 million in the year-earlier quarter. Revenues were US$2.82 billion, up 8.8% from US$2.59 billion the year before. Operating income was US$832.0 million versus US$178.0 million in the prior-year quarter, an increase of 367.4%. Direct operating expenses rose 7.6% to US$1.71 billion from US$1.59 billion in the comparable period the year before. Indirect operating expenses decreased 66.2% to US$280.0 million from US$828.0 million in the equivalent prior-year period.

Prospects: Our evaluation of Public Service Enterprise Group Inc. as of Jan. 21, 2018 is the result of our systematic analysis on three basic characteristics: earnings strength, relative valuation, and recent stock price movement. The company has generated a negative trend in earnings per share over the past 5 quarters and while recent estimates for the company have been mixed, PEG has posted results that fell short of analysts expectations. Based on operating earnings yield, the company is undervalued when compared to all of the companies in our coverage universe. Share price changes over the past year indicates that PEG will perform well over the near term.

Financial Data

(US$ in Thousands)	3 Mos	12/31/2017	12/31/2016	12/31/2015	12/31/2014	12/31/2013	12/31/2012	12/31/2011
Earnings Per Share	3.98	3.10	1.75	3.30	2.99	2.45	2.51	2.96
Cash Flow Per Share	6.36	6.46	6.54	7.76	6.25	6.24	5.49	7.03
Tang Book Value Per Share	27.69	27.16	25.78	25.63	23.89	22.85	21.21	20.01
Dividends Per Share	1.740	1.720	1.640	1.560	1.480	1.440	1.420	1.370
Dividend Payout %	43.72	55.48	93.71	47.27	49.50	58.78	56.57	46.28
Income Statement								
Total Revenue	2,818,000	9,084,000	9,061,000	10,415,000	10,886,000	9,968,000	9,781,000	11,079,000
EBITDA	881,000	3,408,000	2,945,000	4,114,000	3,816,000	3,449,000	3,264,000	3,635,000
Depn & Amortn	50,000	1,986,000	1,476,000	1,214,000	1,227,000	1,178,000	1,054,000	976,000
Income Before Taxes	758,000	1,254,000	1,202,000	2,668,000	2,443,000	2,044,000	1,999,000	2,380,000
Income Taxes	202,000	(306,000)	326,000	1,001,000	938,000	812,000	736,000	977,000
Net Income	558,000	1,574,000	887,000	1,679,000	1,518,000	1,243,000	1,275,000	1,503,000
Average Shares	507,000	507,000	508,000	508,000	508,000	507,525	507,086	506,982
Balance Sheet								
Current Assets	2,806,000	3,312,000	3,254,000	3,494,000	4,119,000	3,614,000	3,869,000	3,911,000
Total Assets	42,790,000	42,716,000	40,070,000	37,535,000	35,333,000	32,522,000	31,725,000	29,821,000
Current Liabilities	3,948,000	4,168,000	3,276,000	3,575,000	3,478,000	3,063,000	3,777,000	2,957,000
Long-Term Obligations	12,072,000	12,068,000	10,895,000	8,834,000	8,261,000	7,862,000	6,687,000	7,461,000
Total Liabilities	28,686,000	28,869,000	26,940,000	24,469,000	23,148,000	20,914,000	20,945,000	19,551,000
Stockholders' Equity	14,104,000	13,847,000	13,130,000	13,066,000	12,185,000	11,608,000	10,780,000	10,270,000
Shares Outstanding	504,000	505,000	504,866	505,282	505,836	505,857	505,892	505,945
Statistical Record								
Return on Assets %	4.89	3.80	2.28	4.61	4.47	3.87	4.13	5.03
Return on Equity %	14.89	11.67	6.75	13.30	12.76	11.10	12.08	15.10
EBITDA Margin %	31.26	37.52	32.50	39.50	35.05	34.60	33.37	32.81
Net Margin %	19.80	17.33	9.79	16.12	13.94	12.47	13.04	13.57
Asset Turnover	0.23	0.22	0.23	0.29	0.32	0.31	0.32	0.37
Current Ratio	0.71	0.79	0.99	0.98	1.18	1.18	1.02	1.32
Debt to Equity	0.86	0.87	0.83	0.68	0.68	0.68	0.62	0.73
Price Range	53.07-41.85	53.07-41.85	47.32-38.42	44.30-37.02	43.53-31.33	36.61-29.78	34.00-29.09	34.81-28.84
P/E Ratio	13.33-10.52	17.12-13.50	27.04-21.95	13.42-11.22	14.56-10.48	14.94-12.16	13.55-11.59	11.76-9.74
Average Yield %	3.69	3.74	3.78	3.80	3.93	4.36	4.54	4.24

Address: 80 Park Plaza, Newark, NJ 07102	**Web Site:** www.pseg.com	**Auditors:** DELOITTE & TOUCHE LLP
Telephone: 973-430-7000	**Officers:** Ralph Izzo - Chairman, President, Chief Executive Officer Daniel J. Cregg - Executive Vice President, Chief Financial Officer	**Investor Contact:** 973-430-6565
		Transfer Agents: Wells Fargo Bank, N.A., Mendota Heights, MN

PULTEGROUP INC

Exchange	Symbol	Price	52Wk Range	Yield	P/E
NYS	PHM	$28.75 (6/29/2018)	35.15-24.16	1.25	16.43

*7 Year Price Score 125.22 *NYSE Composite Index=100 *12 Month Price Score 101.85

Interim Earnings (Per Share)

Qtr.	Mar	Jun	Sep	Dec
2015	0.15	0.28	0.30	0.63
2016	0.24	0.34	0.37	0.81
2017	0.28	0.32	0.58	0.26
2018	0.59	...	...	...

Interim Dividends (Per Share)

Amt	Decl	Ex	Rec	Pay
0.09Q	09/06/2017	09/18/2017	09/19/2017	10/03/2017
0.09Q	12/01/2017	12/11/2017	12/12/2017	01/03/2018
0.09Q	02/08/2018	03/15/2018	03/16/2018	04/03/2018
0.09Q	05/10/2018	06/06/2018	06/07/2018	07/05/2018

Indicated Div: $0.36

Valuation Analysis — **Institutional Holding**

Forecast EPS	$3.30	No of Institutions	800
	(06/14/2018)		
Market Cap	$8.2 Billion	Shares	301,186,464
Book Value	$4.3 Billion	% Held	77.73
Price/Book	1.92		
Price/Sales	0.92		

TRADING VOLUME (thousand shares)

Business Summary: Builders (MIC: 2.2.5 SIC: 1531 NAIC: 236117)

PulteGroup is engaged in the homebuilding business. Homebuilding, its main business, includes the acquisition and development of land primarily for residential purposes within the U.S. and the construction of housing on such land. Through its brands, which include Centex, Pulte Homes, Del Webb, DiVosta Homes, and John Wieland Homes and Neighborhoods, Co. provides home designs, including single-family detached, townhouses, condominiums, and duplexes. Co. Homebuilding operations has six segment: Northeast, Southeast, Florida, Midwest, Texas, and West. Co. also has a reportable segment for its financial services operations, which consist principally of mortgage banking and title operations.

Recent Developments: For the quarter ended Mar 31 2018, net income increased 86.6% to US$170.8 million from US$91.5 million in the year-earlier quarter. Revenues were US$1.97 billion, up 20.9% from US$1.63 billion the year before. Direct operating expenses rose 20.4% to US$1.50 billion from US$1.25 billion in the comparable period the year before. Indirect operating expenses increased 0.4% to US$242.2 million from US$241.3 million in the equivalent prior-year period.

Prospects: Our evaluation of Pultegroup Inc. as of Jan. 21, 2018 is the result of our systematic analysis on three basic characteristics: earnings strength, relative valuation, and recent stock price movement. The company has enjoyed a very positive trend in earnings per share over the past 5 quarters and while recent estimates for the company have been mixed, PHM has posted results that fell short of analysts expectations. Based on operating earnings yield, the company is undervalued when compared to all of the companies in our coverage universe. Share price changes over the past year indicates that PHM will perform very well over the near term.

Financial Data

(US$ in Thousands)	3 Mos	12/31/2017	12/31/2016	12/31/2015	12/31/2014	12/31/2013	12/31/2012	12/31/2011
Earnings Per Share	1.75	1.44	1.75	1.36	1.26	6.72	0.54	(0.55)
Cash Flow Per Share	2.76	2.17	0.20	(0.98)	0.83	2.30	1.99	0.05
Tang Book Value Per Share	14.47	13.99	14.12	13.32	12.67	11.84	5.28	4.64
Dividends Per Share	0.360	0.360	0.360	0.330	0.230	0.150	...	...
Dividend Payout %	20.57	25.00	20.57	24.26	18.25	2.23	...	...
Income Statement								
Total Revenue	1,970,093	8,573,250	7,668,476	5,981,964	5,822,363	5,679,595	4,819,998	4,136,690
EBITDA	226,259	989,779	976,963	852,549	717,400	541,509	192,301	(298,338)
Depn & Amortn	3,450	51,000	54,000	46,200	39,833	18,500	16,900	19,000
Income Before Taxes	223,230	940,813	925,513	808,668	681,350	526,692	179,495	(313,596)
Income Taxes	53,440	491,607	331,147	321,933	215,420	(2,092,294)	(22,591)	(99,912)
Net Income	170,751	447,221	602,703	494,090	474,338	2,620,116	206,145	(210,388)
Average Shares	288,026	306,814	342,123	359,793	374,102	386,866	384,564	379,877
Balance Sheet								
Current Assets	7,649,815	7,528,646	7,534,903	6,332,065	5,854,026	5,752,801	5,844,850	6,008,765
Total Assets	9,706,395	9,686,649	10,178,200	8,967,160	8,569,410	8,734,143	6,734,409	6,885,620
Current Liabilities	870,835	854,848	745,133	652,636	547,715	629,884	571,133	552,688
Long-Term Obligations	3,334,670	3,444,771	3,460,919	2,387,982	1,981,057	2,163,832	2,648,408	3,088,344
Total Liabilities	5,431,738	5,532,623	5,518,837	4,207,835	3,764,456	4,085,191	4,544,793	4,947,005
Stockholders' Equity	4,274,657	4,154,026	4,659,363	4,759,325	4,804,954	4,648,952	2,189,616	1,938,615
Shares Outstanding	285,878	286,752	319,089	349,148	369,458	381,299	386,608	382,607
Statistical Record								
Return on Assets %	5.36	4.50	6.28	5.63	5.48	33.88	3.02	N.M.
Return on Equity %	11.78	10.15	12.76	10.33	10.03	76.63	9.96	N.M.
EBITDA Margin %	11.48	11.54	12.74	14.25	12.32	9.53	3.99	N.M.
Net Margin %	8.67	5.22	7.86	8.26	8.15	46.13	4.28	N.M.
Asset Turnover	0.91	0.86	0.80	0.68	0.67	0.73	0.71	0.57
Current Ratio	8.78	8.81	10.11	9.70	10.69	9.13	10.23	10.87
Debt to Equity	0.78	0.83	0.74	0.50	0.41	0.47	1.21	1.59
Price Range	35.15-22.15	34.44-18.46	22.11-15.36	23.24-17.18	21.72-16.66	24.25-15.11	18.61-6.52	8.69-3.54
P/E Ratio	20.09-12.66	23.92-12.82	12.63-8.78	17.09-12.63	17.24-13.22	3.61-2.25	34.46-12.07	...
Average Yield %	1.30	1.42	1.91	1.63	1.18	0.80	...	...

Address: 3350 Peachtree Road NE, Suite 150, Atlanta, GA 30326
Telephone: 404-978-6400

Web Site: www.pultegroupinc.com
Officers: Ryan R. Marshall - President, Region Officer, Chief Executive Officer Robert T. O'Shaughnessy - Executive Vice President, Chief Financial Officer

Auditors: Ernst & Young LLP
Investor Contact: 248-433-4502
Transfer Agents: Computershare Trust Company N.A., Providence, RI

PVH CORP

Exchange	Symbol	Price	52Wk Range	Yield	P/E
NYS	PVH	$149.72 (6/29/2018)	168.16-110.88	0.10	18.15

*7 Year Price Score 103.75 *NYSE Composite Index=100 *12 Month Price Score 111.60

TRADING VOLUME (thousand shares)

Interim Earnings (Per Share)

Qtr.	Apr	Jul	Oct	Jan
2015-16	1.37	1.22	2.67	1.63
2016-17	2.83	1.11	1.56	1.27
2017-18	0.89	1.52	3.05	1.39
2018-19	2.29	...	...	...

Interim Dividends (Per Share)

Amt	Decl	Ex	Rec	Pay
0.037Q	07/27/2017	08/22/2017	08/24/2017	09/22/2017
0.037Q	10/24/2017	11/21/2017	11/22/2017	12/20/2017
0.037Q	02/06/2018	02/27/2018	02/28/2018	03/28/2018
0.037Q	04/22/2018	05/16/2018	05/17/2018	06/21/2018

Indicated Div: $0.15

Valuation Analysis

		Institutional Holding	
Forecast EPS	$9.16	No of Institutions	743
	(06/11/2018)		
Market Cap	$11.6 Billion	Shares	
Book Value	$5.6 Billion		84,520,200
Price/Book	2.08	% Held	
Price/Sales	1.25	N/A	

Business Summary: Apparel, Footwear & Accessories (MIC: 1.4.2 SIC: 2321 NAIC: 315211)

PVH is an apparel company that designs and markets branded dress shirts, neckwear, sportswear, jeanswear, accessories, footwear and other related products and licenses its owned brands over a range of products. Co.'s brand portfolio includes CALVIN KLEIN and Tommy Hilfiger, as well as Van Heusen, IZOD, ARROW, Warner's, Olga and Eagle, which are owned brands, and Speedo, Geoffrey Beene, Kenneth Cole New York, Kenneth Cole Reaction, Sean John, MICHAEL Michael Kors, Michael Kors Collection and Chaps, which are licensed, as well as various other owned, licensed and private label brands. Co. aggregates its segments into three main businesses: Calvin Klein, Tommy Hilfiger and Heritage Brands.

Recent Developments: For the quarter ended May 6 2018, net income increased 155.2% to US$178.9 million from US$70.1 million in the year-earlier quarter. Revenues were US$2.31 billion, up 16.4% from US$1.99 billion the year before. Direct operating expenses rose 12.7% to US$1.02 billion from US$908.2 million in the comparable period the year before. Indirect operating expenses increased 8.5% to US$1.05 billion from US$968.0 million in the equivalent prior-year period.

Prospects: Our evaluation of PVH Corp. as of Jan. 21, 2018 is the result of our systematic analysis on three basic characteristics: earnings strength, relative valuation, and recent stock price movement. The company has produced a positive trend in earnings per share over the past 5 quarters. However, while recent estimates for the company have been mixed, PVH has posted better than expected results. Based on operating earnings yield, the company is undervalued when compared to all of the companies in our coverage universe. Share price changes over the past year indicates that PVH will perform well over the near term.

Financial Data

(US$ in Thousands)	3 Mos	02/04/2018	01/29/2017	01/31/2016	02/01/2015	02/02/2014	02/03/2013	01/29/2012
Earnings Per Share	8.25	6.84	6.79	6.89	5.27	1.74	5.87	4.36
Cash Flow Per Share	8.03	8.87	11.94	10.95	9.60	5.09	7.96	7.33
Dividends Per Share	0.150	0.150	0.150	0.150	0.150	0.150	0.150	0.150
Dividend Payout %	1.82	2.19	2.21	2.18	2.85	8.62	2.56	3.44
Income Statement								
Total Revenue	2,314,600	8,914,800	8,203,100	8,020,300	8,241,200	8,186,351	6,042,999	5,890,624
EBITDA	323,700	874,500	1,017,500	954,700	713,800	695,081	777,339	670,781
Depn & Amortn	83,200	252,200	228,400	210,800	193,800	189,675	122,424	112,495
Income Before Taxes	212,100	500,100	674,100	630,900	381,500	320,710	537,665	430,198
Income Taxes	37,000	(25,900)	125,500	75,100	(47,500)	185,284	109,272	113,684
Net Income	179,400	537,800	549,000	572,400	439,000	143,537	433,840	317,881
Average Shares	78,200	78,600	80,900	83,100	83,300	82,618	73,876	72,923
Balance Sheet								
Current Assets	3,041,600	3,030,800	2,879,600	2,812,600	2,901,200	2,998,592	2,437,006	1,739,235
Total Assets	11,714,600	11,885,700	11,067,900	10,696,400	10,931,800	11,575,578	7,781,549	6,752,361
Current Liabilities	1,727,100	1,871,600	1,564,800	1,527,200	1,428,600	1,552,397	1,162,447	1,043,871
Long-Term Obligations	3,013,200	3,061,300	3,197,300	3,054,300	3,438,700	3,878,221	2,211,642	1,832,925
Total Liabilities	6,150,000	6,349,300	6,263,400	6,144,100	6,567,500	7,240,399	4,528,980	4,036,912
Stockholders' Equity	5,564,600	5,536,400	4,804,500	4,552,300	4,364,300	4,335,179	3,252,569	2,715,449
Shares Outstanding	77,165	77,178	78,551	81,487	82,512	82,166	72,910	68,048
Statistical Record								
Return on Assets %	5.72	4.61	5.06	5.31	3.91	1.49	5.87	4.73
Return on Equity %	12.39	10.23	11.77	12.87	10.12	3.79	14.30	12.36
EBITDA Margin %	13.99	9.81	12.40	11.90	8.66	8.49	12.86	11.39
Net Margin %	7.75	6.03	6.69	7.14	5.33	1.75	7.18	5.40
Asset Turnover	0.82	0.76	0.76	0.74	0.73	0.85	0.82	0.88
Current Ratio	1.76	1.62	1.84	1.84	2.03	1.93	2.10	1.67
Debt to Equity	0.54	0.55	0.67	0.67	0.79	0.89	0.68	0.67
Price Range	162.25-97.47	156.25-85.48	114.00-70.46	118.98-66.41	133.66-107.87	137.62-103.85	120.86-72.70	77.94-51.47
P/E Ratio	19.67-11.81	22.84-12.50	16.79-10.38	17.27-9.64	25.36-20.47	79.09-59.68	20.59-12.39	17.88-11.81
Average Yield %	0.11	0.13	0.15	0.15	0.12	0.12	0.16	0.23

Address: 200 Madison Avenue, New York, NY 10016
Telephone: 212-381-3500

Web Site: www.pvh.com
Officers: Emanuel (Manny) Chirico - Chairman, Chief Executive Officer Michael A. Shaffer - Executive Vice President, Chief Financial Officer, Chief Operating Officer

Auditors: Ernst & Young LLP
Transfer Agents: Wells Fargo Bank, N.A., St. Paul, MN

QEP RESOURCES INC

Exchange	Symbol	Price	52Wk Range	Yield	P/E
NYS	QEP	$12.26 (6/29/2018)	13.56-7.09	N/A	20.78

*7 Year Price Score 34.62 *NYSE Composite Index=100 *12 Month Price Score 125.21

Interim Earnings (Per Share)

Qtr.	Mar	Jun	Sep	Dec
2015	(0.32)	(0.43)	0.12	(0.22)
2016	(4.55)	(0.90)	0.21	(0.47)
2017	0.32	0.19	(0.01)	0.63
2018	(0.22)	...	...	...

Interim Dividends (Per Share)

Dividend Payment Suspended

Valuation Analysis		Institutional Holding	
Forecast EPS	$-0.40	No of Institutions	
	(06/13/2018)	432	
Market Cap	$2.9 Billion	Shares	
Book Value	$3.7 Billion	272,991,264	
Price/Book	0.80	% Held	
Price/Sales	1.81	90.15	

TRADING VOLUME (thousand shares)

Business Summary: Production & Extraction (MIC: 9.1.1 SIC: 1311 NAIC: 211111)

QEP Resources is an independent crude oil and natural gas exploration and production company focused in two regions of the U.S.: the Northern Region (primarily in North Dakota, Wyoming and Utah) and the Southern Region (primarily in Texas and Louisiana). Co. sells gas volumes to wholesale marketers, industrial users, local distribution companies and utilities. Co. sells oil and natural gas liquids volumes to refiners, marketers and other companies. As of Dec 31 2017, Co. had estimated proved reserves of 684.7 million barrels of oil equivalent, consisting of 320.5 million barrels of oil, 1,793.60 billion cubic feet of gas, and 65.2 million barrels of natural gas liquids.

Recent Developments: For the quarter ended Mar 31 2018, net loss amounted to US$53.6 million versus net income of US$76.9 million in the year-earlier quarter. Revenues were US$428.9 million, up 2.1% from US$420.1 million the year before. Operating income was US$21.4 million versus a loss of US$5.2 million in the prior-year quarter. Direct operating expenses declined 22.9% to US$153.7 million from US$199.4 million in the comparable period the year before. Indirect operating expenses increased 12.4% to US$253.8 million from US$225.9 million in the equivalent prior-year period.

Prospects: Our evaluation of QEP Resources Inc. as of Jan. 21, 2018 is the result of our systematic analysis on three basic characteristics: earnings strength, relative valuation, and recent stock price movement. The company has generated a negative trend in earnings per share over the past 5 quarters. Because the company lacks sufficient analyst estimate data, we place greater weight on the historical EPS trend as the measure of earnings strength. Based on operating earnings yield, the company is overvalued when compared to all of the companies in our coverage universe. Share price changes over the past year indicates that QEP will perform very poorly over the near term.

Financial Data

(US$ in Thousands)	3 Mos	12/31/2017	12/31/2016	12/31/2015	12/31/2014	12/31/2013	12/31/2012	12/31/2011
Earnings Per Share	0.59	1.12	(5.62)	(0.85)	4.36	0.89	0.72	1.50
Cash Flow Per Share	2.53	2.49	2.99	2.73	8.58	6.65	7.27	7.32
Tang Book Value Per Share	15.38	15.76	14.62	22.33	23.23	18.87	17.97	18.34
Dividends Per Share	...	...	...	0.080	0.080	0.080	0.080	0.080
Dividend Payout %	...	...	...	...	1.83	8.99	11.11	5.33
Income Statement								
Total Revenue	428,900	1,622,900	1,377,100	2,018,600	3,414,300	2,935,800	2,349,800	3,159,200
EBITDA	(30,500)	854,000	(958,100)	786,900	561,300	1,465,900	1,218,200	1,274,700
Depn & Amortn	1,300	760,700	877,500	887,300	1,047,300	1,022,400	910,200	769,500
Income Before Taxes	(67,500)	(42,900)	(1,953,200)	(243,000)	(642,300)	285,400	191,700	419,300
Income Taxes	(13,900)	(312,200)	(708,200)	(93,600)	(232,500)	119,800	66,500	154,400
Net Income	(53,600)	269,300	(1,245,000)	(149,400)	784,400	159,400	128,300	267,200
Average Shares	240,900	240,600	221,700	176,600	179,800	179,500	178,700	178,400
Balance Sheet								
Current Assets	149,800	165,400	640,100	931,800	2,001,500	519,000	649,700	818,600
Total Assets	7,608,600	7,394,800	7,245,400	8,425,500	9,286,800	9,376,800	9,108,500	7,442,700
Current Liabilities	613,000	577,300	514,800	641,600	1,344,800	641,500	761,900	637,800
Long-Term Obligations	2,458,100	2,160,800	2,020,900	2,042,000	2,218,100	2,997,500	3,206,900	1,679,400
Total Liabilities	3,911,900	3,596,900	3,742,700	4,477,600	5,211,500	6,000,200	5,842,500	4,141,200
Stockholders' Equity	3,696,700	3,797,900	3,502,700	3,947,900	4,075,300	3,376,600	3,266,000	3,301,500
Shares Outstanding	240,300	241,000	239,600	176,800	175,400	178,900	178,400	176,800
Statistical Record								
Return on Assets %	1.87	3.68	N.M.	N.M.	8.41	1.72	1.55	3.76
Return on Equity %	3.81	7.38	N.M.	N.M.	21.05	4.80	3.90	8.47
EBITDA Margin %	N.M.	52.62	N.M.	38.98	16.44	49.93	51.84	40.35
Net Margin %	N.M.	16.59	N.M.	N.M.	22.97	5.43	5.46	8.46
Asset Turnover	0.22	0.22	0.18	0.23	0.37	0.32	0.28	0.44
Current Ratio	0.24	0.29	1.24	1.45	1.49	0.81	0.85	1.28
Debt to Equity	0.66	0.57	0.58	0.52	0.54	0.89	0.98	0.51
Price Range	12.88-7.09	19.23-7.09	20.45-9.29	23.76-11.31	35.57-18.64	33.48-26.86	34.90-24.52	45.15-24.82
P/E Ratio	21.83-12.02	17.17-6.33	...	...	8.16-4.28	37.62-30.18	48.47-34.06	30.10-16.55
Average Yield %	...	...	...	0.46	0.27	0.27	0.27	0.22

Address: 1050 17th Street, Suite 800, Denver, CO 80265	Web Site: www.qepres.com	Auditors: PricewaterhouseCoopers LLP
Telephone: 303-672-6900	Officers: Charles B. Stanley - Chairman, President, Chief Executive Officer Richard J. Doleshek - Executive Vice President, Chief Financial Officer, Chief Accounting Officer, Treasurer	Investor Contact: 303-405-6665 Transfer Agents: Wells Fargo Shareowner Services, Saint Paul, MN

QUAKER CHEMICAL CORP.

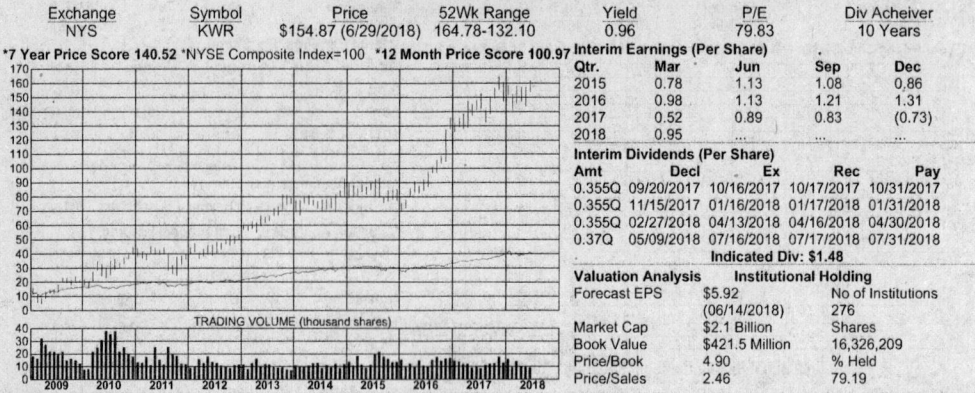

Exchange	Symbol	Price	52Wk Range	Yield	P/E	Div Acheiver
NYS	KWR	$154.87 (6/29/2018)	164.78-132.10	0.96	79.83	10 Years

*7 Year Price Score 140.52 *NYSE Composite Index=100 ***12 Month Price Score 100.97**

Interim Earnings (Per Share)

Qtr.	Mar	Jun	Sep	Dec
2015	0.78	1.13	1.08	0.86
2016	0.98	1.13	1.21	1.31
2017	0.52	0.89	0.83	(0.73)
2018	0.95	...	...	...

Interim Dividends (Per Share)

Amt	Decl	Ex	Rec	Pay
0.355Q	09/20/2017	10/16/2017	10/17/2017	10/31/2017
0.355Q	11/15/2017	01/16/2018	01/17/2018	01/31/2018
0.355Q	02/27/2018	04/13/2018	04/16/2018	04/30/2018
0.37Q	05/09/2018	07/16/2018	07/17/2018	07/31/2018

Indicated Div: $1.48

Valuation Analysis | **Institutional Holding**

Forecast EPS	$5.92	No of Institutions
	(06/14/2018)	276
Market Cap	$2.1 Billion	Shares
Book Value	$421.5 Million	16,326,209
Price/Book	4.90	% Held
Price/Sales	2.46	79.19

Business Summary: Specialty Chemicals (MIC: 8.3.2 SIC: 2999 NAIC: 324199)

Quaker Chemical develops, produces, and markets a range of formulated chemical specialty products and provides chemical management services for various heavy industrial and manufacturing applications in a global portfolio throughout its four regions: the North America region, the Europe, Middle East and Africa region, the Asia/Pacific region and the South America region. Co.'s products and services include rolling lubricants, machining and grinding compounds, hydraulic fluids, corrosion preventives, specialty greases, metal finishing compounds, forming compounds, chemical milling maskants for the aerospace industry, construction products, bio-lubricants, and die casting lubricants.

Recent Developments: For the quarter ended Mar 31 2018, net income increased 67.9% to US$12.8 million from US$7.6 million in the year-earlier quarter. Revenues were US$212.1 million, up 8.8% from US$194.9 million the year before. Operating income was US$20.2 million versus US$13.8 million in the prior-year quarter, an increase of 47.0%. Direct operating expenses rose 10.1% to US$136.6 million from US$124.0 million in the comparable period the year before. Indirect operating expenses decreased 3.3% to US$55.2 million from US$57.1 million in the equivalent prior-year period.

Prospects: Our evaluation of Quaker Chemical Corp. as of Jan. 21, 2018 is the result of our systematic analysis on three basic characteristics: earnings strength, relative valuation, and recent stock price movement. The company has managed to produce a neutral trend in earnings per share over the past 5 quarters. However, while recent estimates for the company have been mixed, KWR has posted better than expected results. Based on operating earnings yield, the company is about fairly valued when compared to all of the companies in our coverage universe. Share price changes over the past year indicates that KWR will perform in line with the market over the near term.

Financial Data

(US$ in Thousands)	3 Mos	12/31/2017	12/31/2016	12/31/2015	12/31/2014	12/31/2013	12/31/2012	12/31/2011
Earnings Per Share	1.94	1.52	4.63	3.84	4.26	4.27	3.63	3.47
Cash Flow Per Share	4.47	4.90	5.60	5.56	4.17	5.66	4.87	1.62
Tang Book Value Per Share	19.81	18.79	18.74	16.60	15.72	18.70	14.44	12.30
Dividends Per Share	1.410	1.400	1.330	1.240	1.100	0.990	0.970	0.950
Dividend Payout %	72.68	92.11	28.73	32.29	25.82	23.19	26.72	27.38
Income Statement								
Total Revenue	212,055	820,082	746,665	737,555	765,860	729,395	708,226	683,231
EBITDA	24,909	81,871	104,302	90,198	94,521	89,879	81,339	76,189
Depn & Amortn	5,047	19,845	19,441	19,007	16,398	15,117	14,700	13,227
Income Before Taxes	18,659	60,668	84,000	70,230	78,293	72,826	62,948	59,377
Income Taxes	5,556	41,653	23,226	17,785	23,539	20,489	15,575	14,256
Net Income	12,732	20,278	61,403	51,180	56,492	56,339	47,405	43,569
Average Shares	13,278	13,245	13,160	13,214	13,148	13,069	12,930	12,318
Balance Sheet								
Current Assets	429,300	406,586	376,468	365,853	351,518	328,847	277,810	259,549
Total Assets	744,465	722,126	692,028	685,513	665,526	584,146	536,634	505,521
Current Liabilities	157,437	154,743	127,411	124,555	124,901	130,856	107,792	106,649
Long-Term Obligations	69,648	61,068	65,769	81,439	75,328	17,321	30,000	46,701
Total Liabilities	322,964	314,454	289,268	312,468	308,051	247,992	255,534	256,772
Stockholders' Equity	421,501	407,672	402,760	373,045	357,475	336,154	281,100	248,749
Shares Outstanding	13,322	13,307	13,277	13,288	13,300	13,196	13,094	12,911
Statistical Record								
Return on Assets %	3.58	2.87	8.89	7.58	9.04	10.05	9.07	9.12
Return on Equity %	6.25	5.00	15.79	14.01	16.29	18.25	17.84	20.31
EBITDA Margin %	11.75	9.98	13.97	12.23	12.34	12.32	11.48	11.15
Net Margin %	6.00	2.47	8.22	6.94	7.38	7.72	6.69	6.38
Asset Turnover	1.15	1.16	1.08	1.09	1.23	1.30	1.36	1.43
Current Ratio	2.73	2.63	2.95	2.94	2.81	2.51	2.58	2.43
Debt to Equity	0.17	0.15	0.16	0.22	0.21	0.05	0.11	0.19
Price Range	164.78-128.57	164.78-125.48	135.85-69.57	93.16-75.74	92.67-66.71	81.41-53.86	53.86-36.15	45.18-24.45
P/E Ratio	84.94-66.27	108.41-82.55	29.34-15.03	24.26-19.72	21.75-15.66	19.07-12.61	14.84-9.96	13.02-7.05
Average Yield %	0.96	0.98	1.49	1.49	1.44	1.49	2.18	2.53

Address: One Quaker Park, 901 E. Hector Street, Conshohocken, PA 19428-2380 **Telephone:** 610-832-4000 **Fax:** 610-832-8682	Web Site: www.quakerchem.com **Officers:** Michael F. Barry - Chairman, President, Chief Executive Officer, Interim Chief Financial Officer Mary Dean Hall - Chief Financial Officer, Vice President, Treasurer	Auditors: PricewaterhouseCoopers LLP **Transfer Agents:** American Stock Transfer & Trust Company, LLC, Brooklyn, NY

QUANTA SERVICES, INC.

Exchange	Symbol	Price	52Wk Range	Yield	P/E
NYS	PWR	$33.40 (6/29/2018)	39.86-32.50	N/A	17.31

*7 Year Price Score 101.28 *NYSE Composite Index=100 *12 Month Price Score 96.30

Interim Earnings (Per Share)

Qtr.	Mar	Jun	Sep	Dec
2015	0.25	0.22	1.15	0.06
2016	0.13	0.11	0.48	0.56
2017	0.31	0.41	0.56	0.72
2018	0.24	...	...	...

Interim Dividends (Per Share)

No Dividends Paid

Valuation Analysis   Institutional Holding

Forecast EPS	$2.75	No of Institutions	
	(06/14/2018)	697	
Market Cap	$5.0 Billion	Shares	
Book Value	$3.6 Billion	178,596,976	
Price/Book	1.37	% Held	
Price/Sales	0.51	87.23	

Business Summary: Construction Services (MIC: 7.5.4 SIC: 1731 NAIC: 238210)

Quanta Services provides contracting services, including infrastructure solutions to the electric power and oil and gas industries in the U.S., Canada and Australia and other international markets. Co.'s services include the design, installation, upgrade, repair and maintenance of infrastructure within the industries that it serves, such as electric power transmission and distribution networks, substation facilities, renewable energy facilities, pipeline transmission and distribution systems and facilities, and infrastructure services for the offshore and inland water energy markets. Co. operates two segments: Electric Power Infrastructure Services and Oil and Gas Infrastructure Services.

Recent Developments: For the quarter ended Mar 31 2018, net income decreased 20.3% to US$38.6 million from US$48.4 million in the year-earlier quarter. Revenues were US$2.42 billion, up 11.0% from US$2.18 billion the year before. Operating income was US$75.2 million versus US$75.1 million in the prior-year quarter, an increase of 0.2%. Direct operating expenses rose 10.7% to US$2.12 billion from US$1.91 billion in the comparable period the year before. Indirect operating expenses increased 18.2% to US$225.8 million from US$191.1 million in the equivalent prior-year period.

Prospects: Our evaluation of Quanta Services Inc. as of Jan. 21, 2018 is the result of our systematic analysis on three basic characteristics: earnings strength, relative valuation, and recent stock price movement. The company has generated a negative trend in earnings per share over the past 5 quarters and while recent estimates for the company have been mixed, PWR has posted better than expected results. Based on operating earnings yield, the company is undervalued when compared to all of the companies in our coverage universe. Share price changes over the past year indicates that PWR will perform in line with the market over the near term.

Financial Data

(US$ in Thousands)	3 Mos	12/31/2017	12/31/2016	12/31/2015	12/31/2014	12/31/2013	12/31/2012	12/31/2011
Earnings Per Share	1.93	2.00	1.26	1.59	1.35	1.87	1.44	0.62
Cash Flow Per Share	2.57	2.39	2.42	3.17	1.41	2.08	0.78	1.03
Tang Book Value Per Share	9.82	10.79	10.24	8.31	10.65	10.38	9.59	7.49
Income Statement								
Total Revenue	2,417,576	9,466,478	7,651,319	7,572,436	7,851,250	6,522,842	5,920,269	4,623,829
EBITDA	122,658	589,876	523,014	433,320	668,480	687,408	622,762	363,178
Depn & Amortn	59,412	216,005	201,885	197,648	194,007	161,615	157,991	146,053
Income Before Taxes	56,614	353,757	308,665	229,141	473,449	526,505	462,496	216,370
Income Taxes	18,003	35,532	107,246	97,472	157,408	217,940	158,859	71,954
Net Income	37,614	314,978	198,383	310,907	296,714	401,921	306,629	132,515
Average Shares	157,556	157,155	157,288	195,120	219,690	214,978	212,835	213,168
Balance Sheet								
Current Assets	2,957,069	2,869,907	2,288,745	2,277,519	2,553,976	2,313,318	2,201,727	1,765,154
Total Assets	6,653,402	6,480,154	5,354,059	5,213,543	6,312,024	5,793,245	5,140,757	4,699,114
Current Liabilities	1,549,639	1,492,067	1,205,228	1,203,744	1,137,325	1,043,520	881,179	781,076
Long-Term Obligations	882,795	670,721	353,562	475,364	72,489	...	...	...
Total Liabilities	3,010,050	2,688,583	2,014,632	2,128,049	1,797,551	1,559,057	1,374,209	1,317,162
Stockholders' Equity	3,643,352	3,791,571	3,339,427	3,085,494	4,514,473	4,234,188	3,766,548	3,381,952
Shares Outstanding	149,600	153,828	151,226	159,783	218,145	216,442	213,179	210,112
Statistical Record								
Return on Assets %	4.99	5.32	3.74	5.40	4.90	7.35	6.22	2.93
Return on Equity %	8.65	8.83	6.16	8.18	6.78	10.05	8.56	3.93
EBITDA Margin %	5.07	6.23	6.84	5.72	8.51	10.54	10.52	7.85
Net Margin %	1.56	3.33	2.59	4.11	3.78	6.16	5.18	2.87
Asset Turnover	1.59	1.60	1.44	1.31	1.30	1.19	1.20	1.02
Current Ratio	1.91	1.92	1.90	1.89	2.25	2.22	2.50	2.26
Debt to Equity	0.24	0.18	0.11	0.15	0.02	...	...	...
Price Range	39.86-30.66	39.50-30.66	35.67-17.29	30.41-18.74	37.20-25.53	31.56-25.74	27.60-20.34	24.03-15.46
P/E Ratio	20.65-15.89	19.75-15.33	28.31-13.72	19.13-11.79	27.56-18.91	16.88-13.76	19.17-14.13	38.76-24.94

Address: 2800 Post Oak Boulevard, Suite 2600, Houston, TX 77056 **Telephone:** 713-629-7600	**Web Site:** www.quantaservices.com **Officers:** David M. McClanahan - Chairman Earl C. (Duke) Austin - President, Chief Executive Officer, Chief Operating Officer, Division Officer	**Auditors:** PricewaterhouseCoopers LLP **Investor Contact:** 713-341-7260 **Transfer Agents:** American Stock Transfer & Trust Company, New York, NY

QUEST DIAGNOSTICS, INC.

Exchange	Symbol	Price	52Wk Range	Yield	P/E
NYS	DGX	$109.94 (6/29/2018)	113.14-90.86	1.82	19.60

*7 Year Price Score 113.45 *NYSE Composite Index=100 *12 Month Price Score 103.60

Interim Earnings (Per Share)

Qtr.	Mar	Jun	Sep	Dec
2015	0.42	0.81	2.35	1.29
2016	0.70	1.37	1.34	1.09
2017	1.16	1.37	1.15	1.82
2018	1.27	...	...	...

Interim Dividends (Per Share)

Amt	Decl	Ex	Rec	Pay
0.45Q	08/18/2017	10/02/2017	10/03/2017	10/18/2017
0.45Q	11/29/2017	01/08/2018	01/09/2018	01/24/2018
0.50Q	02/01/2018	04/03/2018	04/04/2018	04/18/2018
0.50Q	05/14/2018	07/06/2018	07/09/2018	07/23/2018

Indicated Div: $2.00

Valuation Analysis

Forecast EPS	$6.61 (06/14/2018)
Market Cap	$15.0 Billion
Book Value	$5.0 Billion
Price/Book	2.97
Price/Sales	1.94

Institutional Holding

No of Institutions	949
Shares	165,869,264
% Held	93.41

Business Summary: Diagnostic & Health Related Services (MIC: 4.2.2 SIC: 8071 NAIC: 621511)

Quest Diagnostics is a provider of diagnostic information services. Co. is comprised of two businesses: Diagnostic Information Services and Diagnostic Solutions. Co.'s Diagnostic Information Services business develops and delivers diagnostic testing information and services, providing insights that empower and enable a range of customers, including patients, clinicians, hospitals, IDNs, health plans, employers and accountable care organizations. Co.'s Diagnostic Solutions group includes its risk assessment services business, which provides solutions for insurers, and its healthcare information technology businesses, which provides solutions for healthcare providers.

Recent Developments: For the quarter ended Mar 31 2018, net income increased 8.0% to US$189.0 million from US$175.0 million in the year-earlier quarter. Revenues were US$1.88 billion, up 3.7% from US$1.82 billion the year before. Operating income was US$272.0 million versus US$279.0 million in the prior-year quarter, a decrease of 2.5%. Direct operating expenses rose 5.2% to US$1.23 billion from US$1.17 billion in the comparable period the year before. Indirect operating expenses increased 3.5% to US$386.0 million from US$373.0 million in the equivalent prior-year period.

Prospects: Our evaluation of Quest Diagnostics Inc. as of Jan. 21, 2018 is the result of our systematic analysis on three basic characteristics: earnings strength, relative valuation, and recent stock price movement. The company has generated a negative trend in earnings per share over the past 5 quarters and while recent estimates for the company have been mixed, DGX has posted better than expected results. Based on operating earnings yield, the company is undervalued when compared to all of the companies in our coverage universe. Share price changes over the past year indicates that DGX will perform poorly over the near term.

Financial Data
(US$ in Thousands)

	3 Mos	12/31/2017	12/31/2016	12/31/2015	12/31/2014	12/31/2013	12/31/2012	12/31/2011
Earnings Per Share	5.61	5.50	4.51	4.87	3.81	5.54	3.46	2.92
Cash Flow Per Share	8.52	8.58	7.61	5.63	6.47	4.29	7.47	5.64
Dividends Per Share	1.800	1.800	1.580	1.470	1.290	1.200	0.680	0.400
Dividend Payout %	32.09	32.73	35.03	30.18	33.86	21.66	19.65	13.70
Income Statement								
Total Revenue	1,884,000	7,709,000	7,515,000	7,493,000	7,435,000	7,146,000	7,382,562	7,510,490
EBITDA	344,000	1,255,000	1,301,000	1,337,000	1,081,000	1,562,000	1,488,506	1,278,963
Depn & Amortn	74,000	74,000	72,000	81,000	94,000	79,000	281,047	281,102
Income Before Taxes	229,000	1,030,000	1,086,000	1,103,000	823,000	1,324,000	1,042,770	827,278
Income Taxes	52,000	241,000	429,000	373,000	262,000	500,000	401,897	349,000
Net Income	177,000	772,000	645,000	709,000	556,000	849,000	555,721	470,567
Average Shares	139,000	140,000	142,000	145,000	145,000	153,000	160,065	160,172
Balance Sheet								
Current Assets	1,371,000	1,306,000	1,531,000	1,501,000	1,603,000	1,383,000	1,560,997	1,401,260
Total Assets	10,695,000	10,503,000	10,100,000	9,962,000	9,877,000	8,948,000	9,283,863	9,313,379
Current Liabilities	1,117,000	1,057,000	981,000	1,173,000	1,709,000	1,132,000	1,047,603	1,561,159
Long-Term Obligations	3,718,000	3,748,000	3,728,000	3,492,000	3,244,000	3,120,000	3,354,173	3,370,522
Total Liabilities	5,665,000	5,582,000	5,472,000	5,278,000	5,576,000	5,000,000	5,120,816	5,620,507
Stockholders' Equity	5,030,000	4,921,000	4,628,000	4,684,000	4,301,000	3,948,000	4,163,047	3,692,872
Shares Outstanding	136,000	135,000	137,000	143,000	144,000	144,000	158,331	157,420
Statistical Record								
Return on Assets %	7.55	7.49	6.41	7.15	5.91	9.31	5.96	5.28
Return on Equity %	16.25	16.17	13.82	15.78	13.48	20.93	14.11	12.18
EBITDA Margin %	18.26	16.28	17.31	17.84	14.54	21.86	20.16	17.03
Net Margin %	9.39	10.01	8.58	9.46	7.48	11.88	7.53	6.27
Asset Turnover	0.74	0.75	0.75	0.76	0.79	0.78	0.79	0.84
Current Ratio	1.23	1.24	1.56	1.28	0.94	1.22	1.49	0.90
Debt to Equity	0.74	0.76	0.81	0.75	0.75	0.79	0.81	0.91
Price Range	111.16-90.86	111.16-90.54	92.60-60.54	79.60-60.51	68.10-50.80	63.70-52.79	64.68-54.62	60.83-46.02
P/E Ratio	19.81-16.20	20.21-16.46	20.53-13.42	16.34-12.43	17.87-13.33	11.50-9.53	18.69-15.79	20.83-15.76
Average Yield %	1.76	1.79	2.01	2.08	2.18	2.03	1.15	0.73

Address: 500 Plaza Drive, Secaucus, NJ 07094	Web Site: www.QuestDiagnostics.com	Auditors: PricewaterhouseCoopers LLP
Telephone: 973-520-2700	Officers: Stephen H. Rusckowski - Chairman, President, Chief Executive Officer Stephen H. Rusckowski - Chairman, President, Chief Executive Officer	Investor Contact: 973-520-2900
		Transfer Agents: Computershare, Providence, RI

RALPH LAUREN CORP

Exchange	Symbol	Price	52Wk Range	Yield	P/E
NYS	RL	$125.72 (6/29/2018)	142.90-70.53	1.99	63.82

*7 Year Price Score 61.05   *NYSE Composite Index=100   *12 Month Price Score 124.84

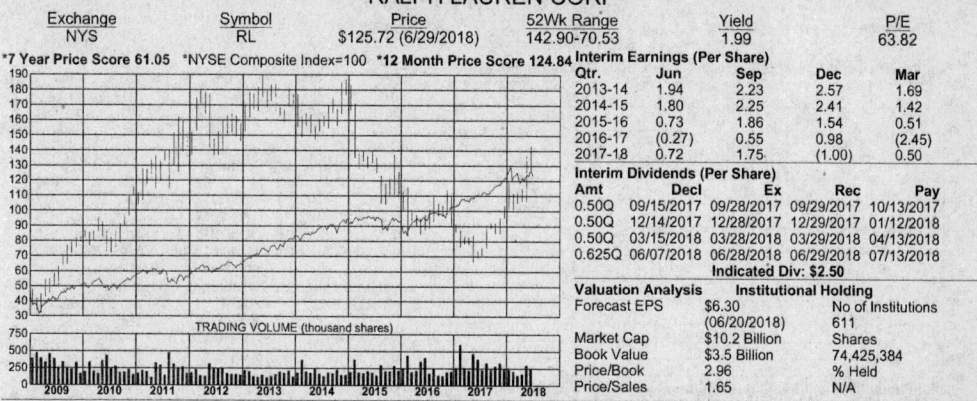

Interim Earnings (Per Share)

Qtr.	Jun	Sep	Dec	Mar
2013-14	1.94	2.23	2.57	1.69
2014-15	1.80	2.25	2.41	1.42
2015-16	0.73	1.86	1.54	0.51
2016-17	(0.27)	0.55	0.98	(2.45)
2017-18	0.72	1.75	(1.00)	0.50

Interim Dividends (Per Share)

Amt	Decl	Ex	Rec	Pay
0.50Q	09/15/2017	09/28/2017	09/29/2017	10/13/2017
0.50Q	12/14/2017	12/28/2017	12/29/2017	01/12/2018
0.50Q	03/15/2018	03/28/2018	03/29/2018	04/13/2018
0.625Q	06/07/2018	06/28/2018	06/29/2018	07/13/2018

Indicated Div: $2.50

Valuation Analysis

		Institutional Holding	
Forecast EPS	$6.30	No of Institutions	
	(06/20/2018)	611	
Market Cap	$10.2 Billion	Shares	
Book Value	$3.5 Billion	74,425,384	
Price/Book	2.96	% Held	
Price/Sales	1.65	N/A	

Business Summary: Apparel, Footwear & Accessories (MIC: 1.4.2 SIC: 2329 NAIC: 315211)

Ralph Lauren designs, markets, and distributes lifestyle products, including apparel, accessories, home furnishings, and other licensed product categories. Co.'s brand names include Ralph Lauren, Ralph Lauren Collection, Ralph Lauren Purple Label, Polo Ralph Lauren, Double RL, Lauren Ralph Lauren, Polo Ralph Lauren Children, Chaps, and Club Monaco, among others. At Mar 31 2018, Co. sold directly to customers via its 472 retail stores, 632 concession-based shop-within-shops, and through its various e-commerce sites; and its international licensing partners operated 88 Ralph Lauren stores, 54 Ralph Lauren concession shops, and 136 Club Monaco stores and shops.

Recent Developments: For the year ended Mar 31 2018, net income amounted to US$162.8 million versus a net loss of US$99.3 million in the prior year. Revenues were US$6.18 billion, down 7.1% from US$6.65 billion the year before. Operating income was US$498.2 million versus a loss of US$92.3 million in the prior year. Direct operating expenses declined 19.0% to US$2.43 billion from US$3.00 billion in the comparable period the year before. Indirect operating expenses decreased 13.1% to US$3.25 billion from US$3.74 billion in the equivalent prior-year period.

Prospects: Our evaluation of Ralph Lauren Corp. as of Jan. 21, 2018 is the result of our systematic analysis on three basic characteristics: earnings strength, relative valuation, and recent stock price movement. The company has enjoyed a very positive trend in earnings per share over the past 5 quarters and while recent estimates for the company have been raised by analysts, RL has posted better than expected results. Based on operating earnings yield, the company is undervalued when compared to all of the companies in our coverage universe. Share price changes over the past year indicates that RL will perform very poorly over the near term.

Financial Data

(US$ in Thousands)	03/31/2018	04/01/2017	04/02/2016	03/28/2015	03/29/2014	03/30/2013	03/31/2012	04/02/2011
Earnings Per Share	1.97	(1.20)	4.62	7.88	8.43	8.00	7.13	5.75
Cash Flow Per Share	11.97	11.55	11.63	10.16	10.03	11.19	9.58	7.19
Tang Book Value Per Share	28.52	26.85	31.15	31.53	31.24	27.38	24.70	20.11
Dividends Per Share	2.000	2.000	2.000	1.850	1.700	1.600	0.800	0.500
Dividend Payout %	101.52	...	43.29	23.48	20.17	20.00	11.22	8.70
Income Statement								
Total Revenue	6,182,300	6,652,800	7,405,000	7,620,000	7,450,000	6,944,800	6,859,500	5,660,300
EBITDA	790,300	(69,600)	602,000	1,034,000	1,157,000	1,142,000	1,066,800	869,100
Depn & Amortn	295,200	24,100	24,000	25,000	35,000	26,800	28,900	25,400
Income Before Taxes	489,200	(99,700)	563,000	998,000	1,105,000	1,098,800	1,024,400	833,100
Income Taxes	326,400	(5,600)	156,000	285,000	320,000	339,300	334,100	257,800
Net Income	162,800	(99,300)	396,000	702,000	776,000	750,000	681,000	567,600
Average Shares	82,500	82,700	85,900	89,100	92,000	93,700	95,500	98,700
Balance Sheet								
Current Assets	3,548,400	2,954,500	3,053,000	3,324,000	3,329,000	2,962,800	2,899,900	2,478,000
Total Assets	6,143,300	5,652,000	6,213,000	6,106,000	6,090,000	5,418,200	5,416,400	4,981,100
Current Liabilities	1,587,200	1,159,900	1,198,000	1,186,000	970,000	1,121,300	946,200	832,000
Long-Term Obligations	524,400	839,100	863,000	536,000	555,000	38,400	312,700	332,300
Total Liabilities	2,685,900	2,352,400	2,469,000	2,215,000	2,056,000	1,633,600	1,763,900	1,676,400
Stockholders' Equity	3,457,400	3,299,600	3,744,000	3,891,000	4,034,000	3,784,600	3,652,500	3,304,700
Shares Outstanding	81,300	81,000	82,900	86,300	88,700	90,900	92,700	94,500
Statistical Record								
Return on Assets %	2.77	N.M.	6.33	11.54	13.52	13.88	13.14	11.82
Return on Equity %	4.83	N.M.	10.21	17.76	19.90	20.22	19.63	17.73
EBITDA Margin %	12.78	N.M.	8.13	13.57	15.53	16.44	15.55	15.35
Net Margin %	2.63	N.M.	5.35	9.21	10.42	10.80	9.93	10.03
Asset Turnover	1.05	1.12	1.18	1.25	1.30	1.29	1.32	1.18
Current Ratio	2.24	2.55	2.55	2.80	3.43	2.64	3.06	2.98
Debt to Equity	0.15	0.25	0.23	0.14	0.14	0.01	0.09	0.10
Price Range	118.87-66.11	113.68-75.98	140.26-83.18	186.73-127.66	189.56-148.71	178.06-136.60	179.87-114.16	127.98-71.93
P/E Ratio	60.34-33.56	...	30.36-18.00	23.70-16.20	22.49-17.64	22.26-17.07	25.23-16.01	22.26-12.51
Average Yield %	2.24	2.12	1.70	1.15	1.00	1.01	0.56	0.52

Address: 650 Madison Avenue, New York, NY 10022 **Telephone:** 212-318-7000	**Web Site:** www.RalphLauren.com **Officers:** Ralph Lauren - Executive Chairman, Chairman, Chief Executive Officer, Chief Creative Officer David R. Lauren - Vice-Chairman, Chief Innovation Officer, Executive Vice President	**Auditors:** Ernst & Young LLP **Transfer Agents:** The Bank of New York Mellon, Jersey City, NJ

RANGE RESOURCES CORP

Exchange	Symbol	Price	52Wk Range	Yield	P/E
NYS	RRC	$16.73 (6/29/2018)	23.49-12.71	0.48	19.68

*7 Year Price Score 26.33 ***NYSE Composite Index=100** ***12 Month Price Score 90.80**

Interim Earnings (Per Share)

Qtr.	Mar	Jun	Sep	Dec
2015	0.16	(0.71)	(1.81)	(1.93)
2016	(0.55)	(1.35)	(0.23)	(0.66)
2017	0.69	0.28	(0.52)	0.89
2018	0.20	...	...	...

Interim Dividends (Per Share)

Amt	Decl	Ex	Rec	Pay
0.02Q	09/01/2017	09/14/2017	09/15/2017	09/29/2017
0.02Q	12/01/2017	12/14/2017	12/15/2017	12/29/2017
0.02Q	03/01/2018	03/15/2018	03/16/2018	03/30/2018
0.02Q	06/01/2018	06/14/2018	06/15/2018	06/29/2018

Indicated Div: $0.08

Valuation Analysis | **Institutional Holding**

Forecast EPS	$0.94	No of Institutions
	(06/13/2018)	686
Market Cap	$4.2 Billion	Shares
Book Value	$5.8 Billion	315,896,224
Price/Book	0.71	% Held
Price/Sales	1.62	97.94

Business Summary: Production & Extraction (MIC: 9.1.1 SIC: 1311 NAIC: 211111)

Range Resources is a natural gas, natural gas liquids and oil company, engaged in the exploration, development and acquisition of natural gas and oil properties. Co.'s properties in the Appalachian Region are located in the Appalachian Basin in the northeastern U.S., principally in Pennsylvania. Co.'s reserves are primarily in the Marcellus Shale formation, the Utica/Point Pleasant, Medina and Upper Devonian formations. Co.'s other operations include drilling, production and field operations in the Texas Panhandle, the Anadarko Basin of western Oklahoma, the Nemaha Uplift of Northern Oklahoma and Kansas. As of Dec 31 2017, Co. had total proved reserve of 15.3 trillion cubic feet equivalent.

Recent Developments: For the quarter ended Mar 31 2018, net income decreased 71.1% to US$49.2 million from US$170.1 million in the year-earlier quarter. Revenues were US$742.6 million, down 4.4% from US$776.7 million the year before. Direct operating expenses rose 29.8% to US$348.3 million from US$268.4 million in the comparable period the year before. Indirect operating expenses increased 34.0% to US$302.4 million from US$225.8 million in the equivalent prior-year period.

Prospects: Our evaluation of Range Resources Corp. as of Jan. 21, 2018 is the result of our systematic analysis on three basic characteristics: earnings strength, relative valuation, and recent stock price movement. The company has suffered a very negative trend in earnings per share over the past 5 quarters and while recent estimates for the company have been mixed, RRC has posted better than expected results. Based on operating earnings yield, the company is overvalued when compared to all of the companies in our coverage universe. Share price changes over the past year indicates that RRC will perform very poorly over the near term.

Financial Data

(US$ in Thousands)	3 Mos	12/31/2017	12/31/2016	12/31/2015	12/31/2014	12/31/2013	12/31/2012	12/31/2011
Earnings Per Share	0.85	1.34	(2.75)	(4.29)	3.79	0.70	0.08	0.36
Cash Flow Per Share	3.91	3.33	2.03	4.11	5.83	4.63	4.05	4.00
Tang Book Value Per Share	16.83	16.66	15.19	16.30	20.50	14.78	14.51	14.85
Dividends Per Share	0.080	0.080	0.080	0.160	0.160	0.160	0.160	0.160
Dividend Payout %	9.41	5.97	...	...	4.22	22.86	200.00	44.44
Income Statement								
Total Revenue	742,599	2,611,030	1,099,939	1,598,068	2,711,695	1,862,719	1,457,704	1,218,656
EBITDA	315,189	285,499	(625,525)	(874,023)	1,212,762	339,336	207,054	219,515
Depn & Amortn	170,890	7,700	8,400	11,900	12,900	13,200	13,200	16,200
Income Before Taxes	91,914	82,120	(802,138)	(1,052,362)	1,030,885	149,579	25,056	78,263
Income Taxes	42,676	(251,026)	(280,750)	(338,677)	396,503	33,857	12,054	35,557
Net Income	49,238	333,146	(521,388)	(713,685)	634,382	115,722	13,002	58,026
Average Shares	246,594	245,458	189,868	166,389	164,403	161,407	160,307	159,441
Balance Sheet								
Current Assets	337,947	429,234	281,883	439,074	570,292	248,301	327,614	315,263
Total Assets	11,730,168	11,728,841	11,282,245	6,900,031	8,746,780	7,299,086	6,728,735	5,845,470
Current Liabilities	678,846	755,473	702,653	351,720	755,264	495,561	455,143	511,932
Long-Term Obligations	4,081,694	4,108,806	3,773,517	2,651,303	3,073,000	3,140,516	2,878,185	1,974,967
Total Liabilities	5,895,576	5,954,569	5,873,877	4,140,373	5,289,351	4,884,634	4,371,343	3,453,050
Stockholders' Equity	5,834,592	5,774,272	5,408,368	2,759,658	3,457,429	2,414,452	2,357,392	2,392,420
Shares Outstanding	249,222	248,129	247,144	169,316	168,628	163,342	162,514	161,131
Statistical Record								
Return on Assets %	1.83	2.90	N.M.	N.M.	7.91	1.65	0.21	1.02
Return on Equity %	3.72	5.96	N.M.	N.M.	21.61	4.85	0.55	2.51
EBITDA Margin %	42.44	10.93	N.M.	N.M.	44.72	18.22	14.20	18.01
Net Margin %	6.63	12.76	N.M.	N.M.	23.39	6.21	0.89	4.76
Asset Turnover	0.22	0.23	0.12	0.20	0.34	0.27	0.23	0.21
Current Ratio	0.50	0.57	0.40	1.25	0.76	0.50	0.72	0.62
Debt to Equity	0.70	0.71	0.70	0.96	0.89	1.30	1.22	0.83
Price Range	29.90-12.71	35.71-15.63	46.45-20.45	64.75-21.17	93.70-52.28	84.31-62.05	73.28-54.02	74.40-44.74
P/E Ratio	35.18-14.95	26.65-11.66	...	...	24.72-13.79	120.44-88.64	916.00-675.25	206.67-124.28
Average Yield %	0.41	0.34	0.22	0.37	0.20	0.21	0.25	0.28

Address: 100 Throckmorton Street, Suite 1200, Fort Worth, TX 76102 **Telephone:** 817-870-2601	**Web Site:** www.rangeresources.com **Officers:** Jeffrey L. (Jeff) Ventura - Chairman, President, Chief Executive Officer, Chief Operating Officer David P. Poole - Senior Vice President, General Counsel, Corporate Secretary	**Auditors:** Ernst & Young LLP **Investor Contact:** 817-870-2601 **Transfer Agents:** Computershare Investor Services, LLC, Cleveland, OH

RAYMOND JAMES FINANCIAL, INC.

Exchange	Symbol	Price	52Wk Range	Yield	P/E
NYS	RJF	$89.35 (6/29/2018)	101.73-74.81	1.34	17.94

*7 Year Price Score 129.12 *NYSE Composite Index=100 ***12 Month Price Score 106.12**

Interim Earnings (Per Share)

Qtr.	Dec	Mar	Jun	Sep
2014-15	0.87	0.77	0.91	0.88
2015-16	0.73	0.87	0.87	1.18
2016-17	1.00	0.77	1.24	1.31
2017-18	0.80	1.63	...	...

Interim Dividends (Per Share)

Amt	Decl	Ex	Rec	Pay
0.22Q	08/23/2017	09/29/2017	10/02/2017	10/16/2017
0.25Q	11/29/2017	01/02/2018	01/03/2018	01/17/2018
0.25Q	02/23/2018	03/29/2018	04/02/2018	04/16/2018
0.30Q	05/22/2018	06/29/2018	07/02/2018	07/16/2018

Indicated Div: $1.20

Valuation Analysis

		Institutional Holding	
Forecast EPS	$6.78	No of Institutions	702
	(06/14/2018)		
Market Cap	$13.0 Billion	Shares	131,103,096
Book Value	$5.9 Billion	% Held	74.90
Price/Book	2.19		
Price/Sales	1.85		

Business Summary: Finance Intermediaries & Services (MIC: 5.5.1 SIC: 6211 NAIC: 523110)

Raymond James Financial is a financial holding company whose broker-dealer subsidiaries are engaged in various financial services businesses. The operating segments are: Private Client Group, which provides financial planning and securities transaction services to client accounts; Capital Markets, which conducts institutional sales, securities trading, equity research and investment banking, syndicate; Asset Management, which provides investment advisory and asset management services to individual and institutional investment portfolios, and sponsors mutual funds under the name Eagle; and Raymond James Bank, N.A. provides corporate loans, securities based loans and residential loans.

Recent Developments: For the quarter ended Mar 31 2018, net income increased 123.5% to US$242.6 million from US$108.5 million in the year-earlier quarter. Revenues were US$1.86 billion, up 16.1% from US$1.60 billion the year before. Direct operating expenses rose 21.6% to US$44.6 million from US$36.7 million in the comparable period the year before. Indirect operating expenses increased 5.6% to US$1.48 billion from US$1.40 billion in the equivalent prior-year period.

Prospects: Our evaluation of Raymond James Financial Inc. as of Jan. 21, 2018 is the result of our systematic analysis on three basic characteristics: earnings strength, relative valuation, and recent stock price movement. The company has managed to produce a neutral trend in earnings per share over the past 5 quarters and while recent estimates for the company have been raised by analysts, RJF has posted better than expected results. Based on operating earnings yield, the company is undervalued when compared to all of the companies in our coverage universe. Share price changes over the past year indicates that RJF will perform in line with the market over the near term.

Financial Data
(US$ in Thousands)

	6 Mos	3 Mos	09/30/2017	09/30/2016	09/30/2015	09/30/2014	09/30/2013	09/30/2012
Earnings Per Share	4.98	4.12	4.33	3.65	3.43	3.32	2.58	2.20
Cash Flow Per Share	8.26	5.70	9.11	(3.65)	6.31	3.63	4.79	2.98
Tang Book Value Per Share	36.37	34.76	35.31	31.15	29.00	26.82	23.66	21.11
Dividends Per Share	0.940	0.660	0.880	0.800	0.720	0.640	0.560	0.520
Dividend Payout %	18.88	16.02	20.32	21.92	20.99	19.28	21.71	23.64
Income Statement								
Total Revenue	3,622,826	1,765,592	6,524,875	5,520,344	5,308,164	4,965,460	4,595,798	3,897,900
EBITDA	637,459	311,188	984,538	824,744	802,483	757,307	579,638	483,904
Depn & Amortn	(5,314)	(496)	56,560	47,373	25,771	41,359	(14,272)	15,983
Income Before Taxes	642,773	311,684	927,978	777,371	776,712	715,948	593,910	467,921
Income Taxes	280,925	192,401	289,111	271,293	296,034	267,797	197,033	175,656
Net Income	361,689	118,842	636,235	529,350	502,140	480,248	367,154	295,869
Average Shares	149,037	148,261	146,647	144,513	145,939	143,589	140,541	131,791
Balance Sheet								
Current Assets	12,328,620	12,975,153	12,249,371	11,515,382	9,427,793	8,496,359	10,560,162	8,694,956
Total Assets	36,030,871	36,084,899	34,883,456	31,593,733	26,479,684	23,325,652	23,186,122	21,160,265
Current Liabilities	28,138,562	28,376,464	26,737,453	24,142,242	19,930,688	17,157,683	17,930,339	16,069,177
Long-Term Obligations	1,549,128	1,548,975	2,452,652	2,301,575	1,762,898	1,734,713	1,257,446	1,410,836
Total Liabilities	30,089,884	30,388,151	29,301,743	26,679,637	21,957,653	19,184,416	19,523,198	17,891,325
Stockholders' Equity	5,940,987	5,696,748	5,581,713	4,914,096	4,522,031	4,141,236	3,662,924	3,268,940
Shares Outstanding	145,551	145,153	144,096	141,544	142,918	141,203	139,557	137,736
Statistical Record								
Return on Assets %	2.14	1.80	1.91	1.82	2.02	2.07	1.66	1.51
Return on Equity %	13.25	11.29	12.12	11.19	11.59	12.31	10.59	10.08
EBITDA Margin %	17.60	17.63	15.09	14.94	15.12	15.25	12.61	12.41
Net Margin %	9.98	6.73	9.75	9.59	9.46	9.67	7.99	7.59
Asset Turnover	0.20	0.20	0.20	0.19	0.21	0.21	0.21	0.20
Current Ratio	0.44	0.46	0.46	0.48	0.47	0.50	0.59	0.54
Debt to Equity	0.26	0.27	0.44	0.47	0.39	0.42	0.34	0.43
Price Range	98.75-71.78	90.64-69.68	85.37-57.41	59.32-40.43	61.29-48.56	56.07-40.04	48.12-36.54	38.59-24.11
P/E Ratio	19.83-14.41	22.00-16.91	19.72-13.26	16.25-11.08	17.87-14.16	16.89-12.06	18.65-14.16	17.54-10.96
Average Yield %	1.12	0.83	1.18	1.53	1.28	1.27	1.33	1.56

Address: 880 Carillon Parkway, St. Petersburg, FL 33716 **Telephone:** 727-567-1000	**Web Site:** www.raymondjames.com **Officers:** Paul C. Reilly - Chairman, Chief Executive Officer Francis S. Godbold - Vice-Chairman	**Auditors:** KPMG LLP **Investor Contact:** 727-567-5133 **Transfer Agents:** Computershare Inc., College Station, TX

RAYONIER INC.

Exchange	Symbol	Price	52Wk Range	Yield	P/E
NYS	RYN	$38.69 (6/29/2018)	39.55-27.80	2.79	32.51

*7 Year Price Score 83.16   ***NYSE Composite Index=100**   ***12 Month Price Score 116.51**

Interim Earnings (Per Share)

Qtr.	Mar	Jun	Sep	Dec
2015	0.14	(0.01)	0.16	0.09
2016	0.12	0.89	0.32	0.40
2017	0.27	0.20	0.19	0.49
2018	0.31	...	...	...

Interim Dividends (Per Share)

Amt	Decl	Ex	Rec	Pay
0.25Q	07/21/2017	09/14/2017	09/15/2017	09/29/2017
0.25Q	10/20/2017	12/14/2017	12/15/2017	12/29/2017
0.25Q	02/23/2018	03/16/2018	03/16/2018	03/29/2018
0.27Q	05/21/2018	06/14/2018	06/15/2018	06/29/2018

Indicated Div: $1.08

Valuation Analysis

		Institutional Holding	
Forecast EPS	$0.73 (06/12/2018)	No of Institutions	500
Market Cap	$5.0 Billion	Shares	
Book Value	$1.6 Billion		145,455,712
Price/Book	3.06	% Held	
Price/Sales	5.98		75.17

Business Summary: REITs (MIC: 5.3.1 SIC: 6798 NAIC: 525930)

Rayonier is a timberland real estate investment trust. Co. has five business segments: The Southern Timber, Pacific Northwest Timber and New Zealand Timber, which reflect activities related to the harvesting of timber and other activities, such as recreational licenses; Real Estate, which reflects U.S. land sales comprised of: Improved Development, Unimproved Development, Rural, Non-Strategic/ Timberlands, and Large Dispositions; and Trading, which reflects the log trading activities that support Co.'s New Zealand operations. At Dec 31 2017, Co. owned, leased or managed approximately 2.6 million acres of timberlands located in the U.S. South, U.S. Pacific Northwest and New Zealand.

Recent Developments: For the quarter ended Mar 31 2018, net income increased 21.7% to US$42.7 million from US$35.1 million in the year-earlier quarter. Revenues were US$203.2 million, up 4.5% from US$194.5 million the year before.

Prospects: Our evaluation of Rayonier Inc. as of Jan. 21, 2018 is the result of our systematic analysis on three basic characteristics: earnings strength, relative valuation, and recent stock price movement. The company has generated a negative trend in earnings per share over the past 5 quarters. However, while recent estimates for the company have been mixed, RYN has posted better than expected results. Based on operating earnings yield, the company is overvalued when compared to all of the companies in our coverage universe. Share price changes over the past year indicates that RYN will perform in line with the market over the near term.

Financial Data

(US$ in Thousands)	3 Mos	12/31/2017	12/31/2016	12/31/2015	12/31/2014	12/31/2013	12/31/2012	12/31/2011
Earnings Per Share	1.19	1.16	1.73	0.37	0.76	2.86	2.17	2.20
Cash Flow Per Share	2.33	2.01	1.66	1.41	2.50	4.34	3.62	3.55
Tang Book Value Per Share	12.63	12.35	11.49	10.49	11.74	13.16	11.66	10.84
Dividends Per Share	1.000	1.000	1.000	1.000	2.030	1.860	1.680	1.232
Dividend Payout %	84.03	86.21	57.80	270.27	267.11	65.03	77.42	56.00
Income Statement								
Total Revenue	203,196	819,596	788,278	544,874	603,521	1,707,822	1,571,000	1,488,642
EBITDA	57,233	343,522	372,970	195,499	264,622	636,770	585,435	508,963
Depn & Amortn	159	128,031	117,193	117,715	166,333	214,518	174,534	156,765
Income Before Taxes	49,642	183,260	222,834	43,082	44,842	380,864	366,526	302,274
Income Taxes	6,936	21,681	5,064	(859)	(9,601)	49,661	88,391	30,357
Net Income	40,539	148,842	211,972	46,165	99,337	371,896	278,685	276,005
Average Shares	129,552	127,809	122,812	125,900	131,038	130,105	128,702	125,394
Balance Sheet								
Current Assets	196,494	183,527	164,804	105,685	214,363	519,094	566,274	344,502
Total Assets	2,878,372	2,858,481	2,685,760	2,319,263	2,453,115	3,685,501	3,122,951	2,569,348
Current Liabilities	65,517	68,548	91,966	59,457	202,002	276,112	307,823	178,251
Long-Term Obligations	996,145	1,022,004	1,030,205	833,879	621,849	1,461,724	1,120,052	819,229
Total Liabilities	1,246,599	1,265,458	1,274,150	1,031,179	964,645	2,024,331	1,684,947	1,246,275
Stockholders' Equity	1,631,773	1,593,023	1,411,610	1,288,084	1,488,470	1,661,170	1,438,004	1,323,073
Shares Outstanding	129,174	128,970	122,904	122,770	126,773	126,257	123,332	122,035
Statistical Record								
Return on Assets %	5.37	5.37	8.45	1.93	3.24	10.92	9.76	11.19
Return on Equity %	9.74	9.91	15.66	3.33	6.31	24.00	20.13	21.44
EBITDA Margin %	28.17	41.91	47.31	35.88	43.85	37.29	37.27	34.19
Net Margin %	19.95	18.16	26.89	8.47	16.46	21.78	17.74	18.54
Asset Turnover	0.29	0.30	0.31	0.23	0.20	0.50	0.55	0.60
Current Ratio	3.00	2.68	1.79	1.78	1.06	1.88	1.84	1.93
Debt to Equity	0.61	0.64	0.73	0.65	0.42	0.88	0.78	0.62
Price Range	35.77-27.27	31.78-27.03	28.25-18.63	29.87-21.97	36.35-25.91	45.01-30.74	38.68-31.06	33.71-26.13
P/E Ratio	30.06-22.92	27.40-23.30	16.33-10.77	80.73-59.38	47.83-34.09	15.74-10.75	17.83-14.31	15.32-11.88
Average Yield %	3.30	3.45	3.98	3.97	6.20	4.60	4.83	4.02

Address: 1 Rayonier Way, Yulce, FL 32097	Web Site: www.rayonier.com	Auditors: Ernst & Young LLP
Telephone: 904-357-9100	Officers: Richard D. Kincaid - Chairman David L. Nunes - President, Chief Executive Officer, Chief Operating Officer	Investor Contact: 904-357-9177
		Transfer Agents: Computershare, Providence, R.I.

RAYTHEON CO.

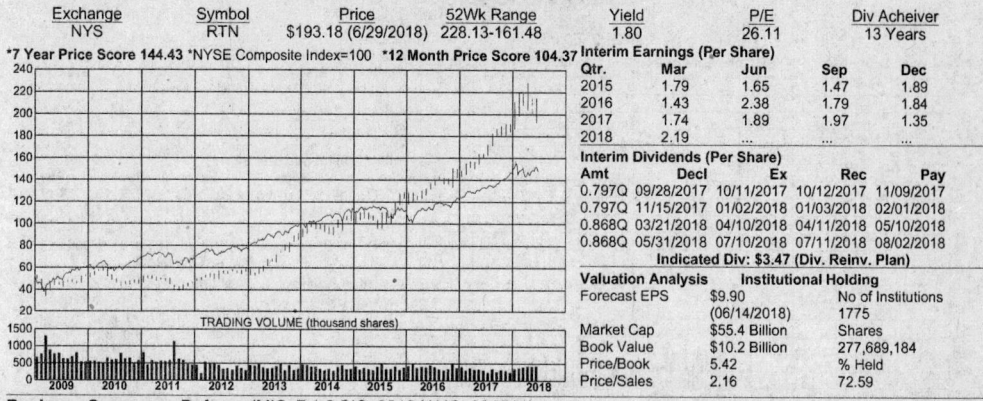

Exchange	Symbol	Price	52Wk Range	Yield	P/E	Div Acheiver
NYS	RTN	$193.18 (6/29/2018)	228.13-161.48	1.80	26.11	13 Years

*7 Year Price Score 144.43 *NYSE Composite Index=100 *12 Month Price Score 104.37

Interim Earnings (Per Share)

Qtr.	Mar	Jun	Sep	Dec
2015	1.79	1.65	1.47	1.89
2016	1.43	2.38	1.79	1.84
2017	1.74	1.89	1.97	1.35
2018	2.19	...	...	...

Interim Dividends (Per Share)

Amt	Decl	Ex	Rec	Pay
0.797Q	09/28/2017	10/11/2017	10/12/2017	11/09/2017
0.797Q	11/15/2017	01/02/2018	01/03/2018	02/01/2018
0.868Q	03/21/2018	04/10/2018	04/11/2018	05/10/2018
0.868Q	05/31/2018	07/10/2018	07/11/2018	08/02/2018

Indicated Div: $3.47 (Div. Reinv. Plan)

Valuation Analysis   **Institutional Holding**

Forecast EPS	$9.90
	(06/14/2018)
Market Cap	$55.4 Billion
Book Value	$10.2 Billion
Price/Book	5.42
Price/Sales	2.16

No of Institutions: 1775
Shares: 277,689,184
% Held: 72.59

Business Summary: Defense (MIC: 7.1.2 SIC: 3812 NAIC: 334511)

Raytheon, together with its subsidiaries, is a technology company, engaged in defense and other government markets. Co. has five segments: Integrated Defense Systems, which is engages in integrated air and missile defense; large land- and sea-based radar solutions; command, control, communications, computers, cyber and intelligence solutions; Intelligence, Information and Services, which provides technical and services to intelligence, defense, federal and commercial customers; Missile Systems, which provides missile and combat systems; Space and Airborne Systems, which provides integrated sensor and communication systems for missions; and Forcepoint, which develops cybersecurity products.

Recent Developments: For the quarter ended Apr 1 2018, income from continuing operations increased 25.6% to US$624.0 million from US$497.0 million in the year-earlier quarter. Net income increased 24.6% to US$623.0 million from US$500.0 million in the year-earlier quarter. Revenues were US$6.27 billion, up 4.5% from US$6.00 billion the year before. Operating income was US$1.04 billion versus US$948.0 million in the prior-year quarter, an increase of 9.8%. Direct operating expenses rose 3.8% to US$4.53 billion from US$4.37 billion in the comparable period the year before. Indirect operating expenses increased 1.2% to US$694.0 million from US$686.0 million in the equivalent prior-year period.

Prospects: Our evaluation of Raytheon Co. as of Jan. 21, 2018 is the result of our systematic analysis on three basic characteristics: earnings strength, relative valuation, and recent stock price movement. The company has produced a positive trend in earnings per share over the past 5 quarters. However, while recent estimates for the company have been mixed, RTN has posted better than expected results. Based on operating earnings yield, the company is about fairly valued when compared to all of the companies in our coverage universe. Share price changes over the past year indicates that RTN will perform well over the near term.

Financial Data

(US$ in Thousands)	3 Mos	12/31/2017	12/31/2016	12/31/2015	12/31/2014	12/31/2013	12/31/2012	12/31/2011
Earnings Per Share	7.40	6.95	7.44	6.80	7.18	6.16	5.65	5.28
Cash Flow Per Share	10.64	9.43	9.59	7.74	7.00	7.35	5.86	5.99
Dividends Per Share	3.190	3.125	2.868	2.615	2.365	2.150	1.930	1.665
Dividend Payout %	43.11	34.42	48.39	38.46	25.28	35.71	35.40	39.68
Income Statement								
Total Revenue	6,267,000	25,348,000	24,069,000	23,247,000	22,826,000	23,706,000	24,414,000	24,857,000
EBITDA	932,000	3,647,000	3,562,000	3,316,000	3,487,000	3,258,000	3,289,000	3,159,000
Depn & Amortn	135,000	350,000	316,000	307,000	301,000	303,000	318,000	314,000
Income Before Taxes	757,000	3,113,000	3,030,000	2,787,000	2,983,000	2,757,000	2,779,000	2,690,000
Income Taxes	133,000	1,114,000	857,000	733,000	790,000	808,000	878,000	793,000
Net Income	633,000	2,024,000	2,211,000	2,074,000	2,244,000	1,996,000	1,888,000	1,866,000
Average Shares	288,800	291,400	296,800	305,200	312,600	324,200	334,200	353,600
Balance Sheet								
Current Assets	10,960,000	11,326,000	10,678,000	9,812,000	10,292,000	9,816,000	9,246,000	9,309,000
Total Assets	30,497,000	30,860,000	30,052,000	29,281,000	27,900,000	25,967,000	26,686,000	25,854,000
Current Liabilities	6,779,000	7,348,000	6,427,000	6,126,000	5,930,000	5,810,000	5,902,000	6,130,000
Long-Term Obligations	4,751,000	4,750,000	5,335,000	5,330,000	5,330,000	4,734,000	4,731,000	4,605,000
Total Liabilities	20,260,000	20,897,000	19,986,000	19,153,000	18,375,000	14,932,000	18,660,000	17,673,000
Stockholders' Equity	10,237,000	9,963,000	10,066,000	10,128,000	9,525,000	11,035,000	8,026,000	8,181,000
Shares Outstanding	287,000	288,000	293,000	299,000	307,000	315,000	328,000	339,000
Statistical Record								
Return on Assets %	7.13	6.65	7.43	7.25	8.33	7.58	7.17	7.42
Return on Equity %	20.86	20.21	21.84	21.11	21.83	20.94	23.23	20.81
EBITDA Margin %	14.87	14.39	14.80	14.26	15.28	13.74	13.47	12.71
Net Margin %	10.10	7.98	9.19	8.92	9.83	8.42	7.73	7.51
Asset Turnover	0.85	0.83	0.81	0.81	0.85	0.90	0.93	0.99
Current Ratio	1.62	1.54	1.66	1.60	1.74	1.69	1.57	1.52
Debt to Equity	0.46	0.48	0.53	0.53	0.56	0.43	0.59	0.56
Price Range	219.86-149.95	191.38-142.90	150.54-117.62	127.95-95.57	110.47-88.13	91.04-52.67	59.28-47.99	52.51-38.83
P/E Ratio	29.71-20.26	27.54-20.56	20.23-15.81	18.82-14.05	15.39-12.27	14.78-8.55	10.49-8.49	9.95-7.35
Average Yield %	1.75	1.42	2.69	2.39	1.86	3.17	3.70	4.47

Address: 870 Winter Street, Waltham, MA 02451	Web Site: www.raytheon.com	Auditors: PricewaterhouseCoopers LLP
Telephone: 781-522-3000	Officers: Thomas Anthony Kennedy - Chairman, Chief Executive Officer, Executive Vice President, Chief Operating Officer, Vice President, Division Officer David C. Wajsgras - Senior Vice President, Vice President, Chief Financial Officer, Division Officer	Investor Contact: 877-786-7070
		Transfer Agents: American Stock Transfer & Trust Co. Brooklyn, NY

REALOGY HOLDINGS CORP

Exchange	Symbol	Price	52Wk Range	Yield	P/E
NYS	RLGY	$22.80 (6/29/2018)	34.98-22.73	1.58	8.11

*7 Year Price Score N/A   *NYSE Composite Index=100   *12 Month Price Score 83.89

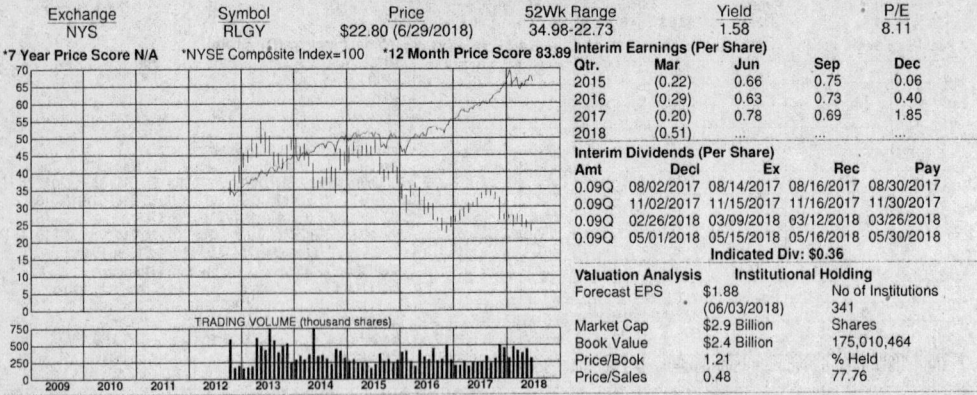

Interim Earnings (Per Share)

Qtr.	Mar	Jun	Sep	Dec
2015	(0.22)	0.66	0.75	0.06
2016	(0.29)	0.63	0.73	0.40
2017	(0.20)	0.78	0.69	1.85
2018	(0.51)	...	...	...

Interim Dividends (Per Share)

Amt	Decl	Ex	Rec	Pay
0.09Q	08/02/2017	08/14/2017	08/16/2017	08/30/2017
0.09Q	11/02/2017	11/15/2017	11/16/2017	11/30/2017
0.09Q	02/26/2018	03/09/2018	03/12/2018	03/26/2018
0.09Q	05/01/2018	05/15/2018	05/16/2018	05/30/2018
		Indicated Div: $0.36		

Valuation Analysis   **Institutional Holding**

Forecast EPS	$1.88	No of Institutions
	(06/03/2018)	341
Market Cap	$2.9 Billion	Shares
Book Value	$2.4 Billion	175,010,464
Price/Book	1.21	% Held
Price/Sales	0.48	77.76

Business Summary: Property, Real Estate & Development (MIC: 5.3.2 SIC: 6531 NAIC: 531210)

Realogy Holdings is a holding company. Through its subsidiaries, Co. is a provider of residential real estate services. Co. has four segments: real estate franchise services, which include brokerage brands such as Century 21®, Coldwell Banker®, Coldwell Banker Commercial®, and ERA®; Co.-owned real estate brokerage services, which operates real estate brokerage business under the Coldwell Banker®, Corcoran Group®, Sotheby's International Realty®, ZipRealty® and Citi Habitatssm brand names; relocation services, which is a provider of outsourced employee relocation services; and title and settlement services, which provides title and settlement (i.e., closing and escrow) services to customers.

Recent Developments: For the quarter ended Mar 31 2018, net loss amounted to US$67.0 million versus a net loss of US$28.0 million in the year-earlier quarter. Revenues were US$1.23 billion, up 2.2% from US$1.20 billion the year before.

Prospects: Our evaluation of Realogy Holdings Corp as of Jan. 21, 2018 is the result of our systematic analysis on three basic characteristics: earnings strength, relative valuation, and recent stock price movement. The company has generated a negative trend in earnings per share over the past 5 quarters and while recent estimates for the company have been mixed, RLGY has posted results that fell short of analysts expectations. Based on operating earnings yield, the company is undervalued when compared to all of the companies in our coverage universe. Share price changes over the past year indicates that RLGY will perform well over the near term.

Financial Data (US$ in Millions)	3 Mos	12/31/2017	12/31/2016	12/31/2015	12/31/2014	12/31/2013	12/31/2012	12/31/2011
Earnings Per Share	2.81	3.11	1.46	1.24	0.97	2.99	(14.41)	(55.00)
Cash Flow Per Share	4.21	4.88	4.05	3.71	2.90	3.38	(2.72)	(23.95)
Dividends Per Share	0.360	0.360	0.180	...	...	...	...	...
Dividend Payout %	12.81	11.58	12.33	...	...	...	...	...
Income Statement								
Total Revenue	1,229	6,114	5,810	5,706	5,328	5,289	4,672	4,093
EBITDA	(45)	605	612	597	566	523	30	307
Depn & Amortn	4	96	89	84	74	67	65	74
Income Before Taxes	(82)	351	349	282	225	175	(563)	(433)
Income Taxes	(19)	(65)	144	110	87	(242)	39	32
Net Income	(67)	431	213	184	143	438	(543)	(441)
Average Shares	130	138	145	148	147	146	37	8
Balance Sheet								
Current Assets	760	789	818	961	1,026	917	978	806
Total Assets	7,325	7,337	7,421	7,531	7,538	7,326	7,445	7,810
Current Liabilities	1,081	955	1,050	1,605	878	911	1,015	1,436
Long-Term Obligations	3,263	3,221	3,265	2,962	3,891	3,886	4,256	6,825
Total Liabilities	4,900	4,719	4,957	5,113	5,359	5,316	5,929	9,320
Stockholders' Equity	2,425	2,618	2,464	2,418	2,179	2,010	1,516	(1,510)
Shares Outstanding	128	131	140	146	146	146	145	8
Statistical Record								
Return on Assets %	5.35	5.84	2.84	2.44	1.92	5.93	N.M.	N.M.
Return on Equity %	16.35	16.96	8.70	8.01	6.83	24.84	N.M.	...
EBITDA Margin %	N.M.	9.90	10.53	10.46	10.62	9.89	0.64	7.50
Net Margin %	N.M.	7.05	3.67	3.22	2.68	8.28	N.M.	N.M.
Asset Turnover	0.84	0.83	0.78	0.76	0.72	0.72	0.61	0.52
Current Ratio	0.70	0.83	0.78	0.60	1.17	1.01	0.96	0.56
Debt to Equity	1.35	1.23	1.33	1.22	1.79	1.93	2.81	...
Price Range	34.98-23.97	34.98-25.41	36.96-22.20	49.53-36.48	49.98-33.86	54.85-40.67	42.03-33.50	...
P/E Ratio	12.45-8.53	11.25-8.17	25.32-15.21	39.94-29.42	51.53-34.91	18.34-13.60	...	...
Average Yield %	1.21	1.20	0.61	...	...	...	...	...

Address: 175 Park Avenue, Madison, NJ 07940
Telephone: 973-407-2000

Web Site: www.realogy.com
Officers: Michael J. Williams - Chairman Ryan M. Schneider - President, Chief Executive Officer, Chief Operating Officer

Auditors: PricewaterhouseCoopers LLP
Investor Contact: 973-407-4669
Transfer Agents: Computershare Trust Company, N.A.

REALTY INCOME CORP

Exchange	Symbol	Price	52Wk Range	Yield	P/E	Div Acheiver
NYS	O	$53.79 (6/29/2018)	59.90-47.56	4.91	48.03	23 Years

7 Year Price Score 90.51 **NYSE Composite Index=100** **12 Month Price Score 96.43**

Interim Earnings (Per Share)

Qtr.	Mar	Jun	Sep	Dec
2015	0.27	0.25	0.26	0.31
2016	0.25	0.27	0.27	0.33
2017	0.27	0.30	0.32	0.21
2018	0.29	...	...	...

Interim Dividends (Per Share)

Amt	Decl	Ex	Rec	Pay
0.22M	03/13/2018	03/29/2018	04/02/2018	04/13/2018
0.22M	04/17/2018	04/30/2018	05/01/2018	05/15/2018
0.22M	05/18/2018	05/31/2018	06/01/2018	06/15/2018
0.22M	06/19/2018	06/29/2018	07/02/2018	07/13/2018

Indicated Div: $2.64

Valuation Analysis / Institutional Holding

Forecast EPS	$1.26	No of Institutions
	(06/11/2018)	883
Market Cap	$15.3 Billion	Shares
Book Value	$7.3 Billion	245,513,136
Price/Book	2.10	% Held
Price/Sales	12.38	68.25

TRADING VOLUME (thousand shares)

Business Summary: REITs (MIC: 5.3.1 SIC: 6798 NAIC: 525930)

Realty Income is a real estate investment trust that invests in commercial real estate. Co. focuses on in-house acquisition, portfolio management, asset management, real estate research, credit research, legal, finance and accounting, information technology, and capital markets. As of Dec 31, 2017, Co, owned a portfolio of 5,172 properties, located in 49 states and Puerto Rico, with over 89.6 million sq. ft. of leasable space; and with an average leasable space per property of approximately 17,320 sq. ft.; approximately 12,060 sq. ft. per retail property and 224,340 sq. ft. per industrial property.

Recent Developments: For the quarter ended Mar 31 2018, net income decreased 6.4% to US$83.3 million from US$89.0 million in the year-earlier quarter. Revenues were US$318.3 million, up 6.8% from US$298.0 million the year before. Revenues from property income rose 7.0% to US$317.8 million from US$297.1 million in the corresponding quarter a year earlier.

Prospects: Our evaluation of Realty Income Corp. as of Jan. 21, 2018 is the result of our systematic analysis on three basic characteristics: earnings strength, relative valuation, and recent stock price movement. The company has enjoyed a very positive trend in earnings per share over the past 5 quarters. Because the company lacks sufficient analyst estimate data, we place greater weight on the historical EPS trend as the measure of earnings strength. Based on operating earnings yield, the company is overvalued when compared to all of the companies in our coverage universe. Share price changes over the past year indicates that O will perform well over the near term.

Financial Data
(US$ in Thousands)

	3 Mos	12/31/2017	12/31/2016	12/31/2015	12/31/2014	12/31/2013	12/31/2012	12/31/2011
Earnings Per Share	1.12	1.10	1.13	1.09	1.04	1.06	0.86	1.05
Cash Flow Per Share	3.09	3.20	3.14	2.94	2.87	2.71	2.45	2.37
Tang Book Value Per Share	21.07	21.68	21.79	21.89	20.27	21.37	17.95	16.80
Dividends Per Share	2.563	2.537	2.403	2.279	2.193	2.178	1.778	1.738
Dividend Payout %	228.79	230.64	212.65	209.08	210.85	205.46	206.73	165.51
Income Statement								
Total Revenue	318,295	1,215,768	1,103,172	1,023,285	933,505	778,375	475,510	421,059
EBITDA	89,393	846,788	787,179	709,192	654,665	509,159	306,334	282,042
Depn & Amortn	4,855	521,426	467,440	421,168	382,064	327,245	158,933	129,435
Income Before Taxes	84,538	325,362	319,739	288,024	272,601	181,914	147,401	152,607
Income Taxes	1,223	6,044	3,262	3,169	3,461	2,734	1,430	1,470
Net Income	83,163	318,798	315,571	283,766	270,635	245,564	159,152	157,032
Average Shares	284,345	273,936	255,624	236,208	218,767	191,781	132,884	126,189
Balance Sheet								
Current Assets	162,554	126,431	114,004	121,972	68,238	49,580	26,907	19,540
Total Assets	14,474,093	14,058,166	13,152,871	11,865,870	11,012,622	9,924,441	5,443,363	4,419,389
Current Liabilities	155,283	287,191	262,007	220,135	213,357	181,243	120,230	102,931
Long-Term Obligations	6,599,646	6,111,471	5,839,605	4,841,486	4,930,947	4,166,840	2,883,868	2,055,181
Total Liabilities	7,206,113	6,686,665	6,386,067	5,334,274	5,399,221	4,538,994	3,030,569	2,164,535
Stockholders' Equity	7,267,980	7,371,501	6,766,804	6,531,596	5,613,401	5,385,447	2,412,794	2,254,854
Shares Outstanding	284,380	284,213	260,168	250,416	224,881	207,485	133,452	133,223
Statistical Record								
Return on Assets %	2.24	2.34	2.52	2.48	2.59	3.20	3.22	3.95
Return on Equity %	4.38	4.51	4.73	4.67	4.92	6.30	6.80	7.66
EBITDA Margin %	28.08	69.65	71.36	69.31	70.13	65.41	64.42	66.98
Net Margin %	26.13	26.22	28.61	27.73	28.99	31.55	33.47	37.29
Asset Turnover	0.09	0.09	0.09	0.09	0.09	0.10	0.10	0.11
Current Ratio	1.05	0.44	0.44	0.55	0.32	0.27	0.22	0.19
Debt to Equity	0.91	0.83	0.86	0.74	0.88	0.77	1.20	0.91
Price Range	62.07-47.56	63.19-53.21	72.14-51.17	55.14-43.38	49.57-37.33	55.09-36.68	42.96-34.52	36.07-28.04
P/E Ratio	55.42-42.46	57.45-48.37	63.84-45.28	50.59-39.80	47.66-35.89	51.97-34.60	49.95-40.14	34.35-26.70
Average Yield %	4.62	4.41	3.90	4.68	5.05	5.03	4.51	5.12

Address: 11995 El Camino Real, San Diego, CA 92130 Telephone: 858-284-5000	Web Site: www.realtyincome.com Officers: Sumit Roy - President, Chief Operating Officer, Chief Investment Officer, Executive Vice President John P. Case - President, Co-President, Chief Executive Officer, Executive Vice President, Chief Investment Officer	Auditors: KPMG LLP Investor Contact: 760-741-2111 Transfer Agents: Wells Fargo Shareowner Services, St. Paul, MN

RED HAT INC

Exchange	Symbol	Price	52Wk Range	Yield	P/E
NYS	RHT	$134.37 (6/29/2018)	176.27-94.79	N/A	85.04

*7 Year Price Score 145.72 *NYSE Composite Index=100 *12 Month Price Score 121.65

Interim Earnings (Per Share)

Qtr.	May	Aug	Nov	Feb
2015-16	0.26	0.28	0.25	0.29
2016-17	0.33	0.32	0.37	0.37
2017-18	0.40	0.53	0.54	(0.08)
2018-19	0.59	...	...	...

Interim Dividends (Per Share)

No Dividends Paid

Valuation Analysis

		Institutional Holding	
Forecast EPS	$3.46	No of Institutions	
	(06/13/2018)	887	
Market Cap	$23.8 Billion	Shares	
Book Value	$1.4 Billion	203,227,888	
Price/Book	16.65	% Held	
Price/Sales	7.80	91.08	

TRADING VOLUME (thousand shares)

Business Summary: Internet & Software (MIC: 6.3.2 SIC: 7372 NAIC: 511210)

Red Hat is a provider of open source software solutions, using a community-powered approach to develop and provide operating system, virtualization, management, middleware, cloud, mobile and storage technologies. Co.'s software offerings include: Red Hat Enterprise Linux, an operating system built with open source software components; and Red Hat JBoss Middleware, a suite of offerings used to develop, deploy and manage applications, integrate applications, data and devices, and automate business processes across hybrid cloud environments. Co.'s offerings also include other technologies, such as a realtime operating system, distributed computing, directory services and user authentication.

Recent Developments: For the quarter ended May 31 2018, net income increased 50.3% to US$113.2 million from US$75.3 million in the year-earlier quarter. Revenues were US$813.5 million, up 20.2% from US$676.8 million the year before. Operating income was US$112.2 million versus US$89.7 million in the prior-year quarter, an increase of 25.0%. Direct operating expenses rose 21.9% to US$122.7 million from US$100.7 million in the comparable period the year before. Indirect operating expenses increased 19.0% to US$578.7 million from US$486.4 million in the equivalent prior-year period.

Prospects: Our evaluation of Red Hat Inc. as of Jan. 21, 2018 is the result of our systematic analysis on three basic characteristics: earnings strength, relative valuation, and recent stock price movement. The company has produced a positive trend in earnings per share over the past 5 quarters and while recent estimates for the company have been raised by analysts, RHT has posted better than expected results. Based on operating earnings yield, the company is overvalued when compared to all of the companies in our coverage universe. Share price changes over the past year indicates that RHT will perform very well over the near term.

Financial Data

(US$ in Thousands)	3 Mos	02/28/2018	02/28/2017	02/29/2016	02/28/2015	02/28/2014	02/28/2013	02/29/2012
Earnings Per Share	1.58	1.40	1.39	1.07	0.95	0.93	0.77	0.75
Cash Flow Per Share	5.70	5.21	4.36	3.91	3.34	2.85	2.41	2.02
Tang Book Value Per Share	N.M.	N.M.	0.39	0.89	1.24	3.85	3.56	3.67
Income Statement								
Total Revenue	813,530	2,920,461	2,411,803	2,052,230	1,789,489	1,534,615	1,328,817	1,133,103
EBITDA	116,543	545,094	384,158	335,222	304,557	278,072	240,325	231,214
Depn & Amortn	6,581	64,317	54,077	48,909	48,001	45,169	38,818	31,623
Income Before Taxes	111,477	474,701	320,180	274,865	255,498	239,548	209,752	208,009
Income Taxes	(1,713)	215,898	66,477	75,500	75,297	61,256	59,548	61,383
Net Income	113,190	258,803	253,703	199,365	180,201	178,292	150,204	146,626
Average Shares	190,739	184,602	182,961	186,119	189,246	192,036	195,804	196,451
Balance Sheet								
Current Assets	2,905,614	3,134,992	2,315,702	1,872,433	1,970,239	1,571,182	1,368,749	1,221,355
Total Assets	5,191,561	5,466,546	4,535,185	4,155,099	3,802,985	3,106,619	2,813,660	2,491,099
Current Liabilities	2,276,235	2,305,454	1,891,073	1,559,177	1,334,692	1,148,086	985,712	826,305
Long-Term Obligations	554,503	744,194	763,619	723,942	715,402	...	...	...
Total Liabilities	3,759,617	3,996,316	3,287,865	2,820,667	2,514,647	1,555,454	1,293,499	1,092,282
Stockholders' Equity	1,431,944	1,470,230	1,247,320	1,334,432	1,288,338	1,551,165	1,520,161	1,398,817
Shares Outstanding	177,472	177,073	176,901	181,185	183,551	189,712	193,021	192,654
Statistical Record								
Return on Assets %	6.16	5.18	5.84	5.00	5.22	6.02	5.66	6.24
Return on Equity %	21.83	19.05	19.65	15.16	12.69	11.61	10.29	10.87
EBITDA Margin %	14.33	18.66	15.93	16.33	17.02	18.12	18.09	20.41
Net Margin %	13.91	8.86	10.52	9.71	10.07	11.62	11.30	12.94
Asset Turnover	0.63	0.58	0.56	0.51	0.52	0.52	0.50	0.48
Current Ratio	1.28	1.36	1.22	1.20	1.48	1.37	1.39	1.48
Debt to Equity	0.39	0.51	0.60	0.54	0.56	...	...	...
Price Range	172.47-87.85	148.03-81.31	84.86-65.35	83.65-60.93	71.09-48.19	59.93-42.35	61.95-47.41	52.72-31.87
P/E Ratio	109.16-55.60	105.74-58.08	61.05-47.01	78.18-56.94	74.83-50.73	64.44-45.54	80.45-61.57	70.29-42.49

Address: 100 East Davie Street, Raleigh, NC 27601 **Telephone:** 919-754-3700	**Web Site:** www.redhat.com **Officers:** Narendra Kumar Gupta - Chairman James M. Whitehurst - President, Chief Executive Officer	**Auditors:** PricewaterhouseCoopers LLP **Investor Contact:** 919-754-3700 **Transfer Agents:** Computershare, Providence, RI

REGAL BELOIT CORP

Exchange	Symbol	Price	52Wk Range	Yield	P/E	Div Acheiver
NYS	RBC	$81.80 (6/29/2018)	86.75-69.75	1.37	16.26	13 Years

*7 Year Price Score 90.41   *NYSE Composite Index=100   *12 Month Price Score 100.36

Interim Earnings (Per Share)

Qtr.	Mar	Jun	Sep	Dec
2015	0.81	1.39	1.41	(0.43)
2016	0.93	1.26	1.32	1.01
2017	1.02	1.18	1.39	1.15
2018	1.31	...	...	...

Interim Dividends (Per Share)

Amt	Decl	Ex	Rec	Pay
0.26Q	07/26/2017	09/28/2017	09/29/2017	10/13/2017
0.26Q	10/27/2017	12/28/2017	12/29/2017	01/12/2018
0.26Q	01/20/2018	03/28/2018	03/29/2018	04/13/2018
0.28Q	04/30/2018	06/28/2018	06/29/2018	07/13/2018

Indicated Div: $1.12

Valuation Analysis | **Institutional Holding**

Forecast EPS	$5.85	No of Institutions
	(06/13/2018)	421
Market Cap	$3.6 Billion	Shares
Book Value	$2.4 Billion	51,912,304
Price/Book	1.51	% Held
Price/Sales	1.05	92.32

Business Summary: Electrical Equipment (MIC: 7.3.1 SIC: 3621 NAIC: 335312)

Regal Beloit is a manufacturer of electric motors, electrical motion controls, power generation and power transmission products. Co.'s segments are: Commercial and Industrial Systems, which designs, manufactures and sells primarily fractional, integral and large horsepower AC and DC motors and controls for commercial and industrial applications; Climate Solutions, which designs, manufactures and sells primarily fractional motors, electronic variable speed controls and blowers used in a variety of residential and light commercial air moving applications; and Power Transmission Solutions, which designs, manufactures and sells primarily mounted and unmounted bearings.

Recent Developments: For the quarter ended Mar 31 2018, net income increased 24.6% to US$59.3 million from US$47.6 million in the year-earlier quarter. Revenues were US$878.8 million, up 8.0% from US$813.5 million the year before. Operating income was US$88.2 million versus US$75.0 million in the prior-year quarter, an increase of 17.6%. Direct operating expenses rose 7.7% to US$643.9 million from US$598.0 million in the comparable period the year before. Indirect operating expenses increased 4.4% to US$146.7 million from US$140.5 million in the equivalent prior-year period.

Prospects: Our evaluation of Regal Beloit Corp. as of Jan. 21, 2018 is the result of our systematic analysis on three basic characteristics: earnings strength, relative valuation, and recent stock price movement. The company has managed to produce a neutral trend in earnings per share over the past 5 quarters. However, while recent estimates for the company have been mixed, RBC has posted better than expected results. Based on operating earnings yield, the company is undervalued when compared to all of the companies in our coverage universe. Share price changes over the past year indicates that RBC will perform in line with the market over the near term.

Financial Data

(US$ in Thousands)	3 Mos	12/30/2017	12/31/2016	01/02/2016	01/03/2015	12/28/2013	12/29/2012	12/31/2011
Earnings Per Share	5.03	4.74	4.52	3.18	0.69	2.64	4.64	3.79
Cash Flow Per Share	6.42	6.54	9.86	8.55	6.52	6.80	8.44	6.70
Tang Book Value Per Share	5.56	4.02	N.M.	N.M.	16.29	16.19	11.34	2.45
Dividends Per Share	1.040	1.020	0.950	0.910	0.860	0.790	0.750	0.710
Dividend Payout %	20.68	21.52	21.02	28.62	124.64	29.92	16.16	18.73
Income Statement								
Total Revenue	878,800	3,360,300	3,224,500	3,509,700	3,257,100	3,095,700	3,166,900	2,808,332
EBITDA	122,600	412,100	414,000	348,300	213,500	292,400	394,800	320,740
Depn & Amortn	34,800	82,000	93,400	95,500	92,000	84,400	82,000	65,027
Income Before Taxes	75,000	277,200	266,400	196,900	90,300	170,500	269,900	226,337
Income Taxes	15,700	59,100	57,100	48,400	54,200	44,500	69,600	68,317
Net Income	58,400	213,000	203,400	143,300	31,000	120,000	195,600	152,290
Average Shares	44,500	44,900	45,000	45,100	45,300	45,400	42,100	40,144
Balance Sheet								
Current Assets	1,686,100	1,574,400	1,532,000	1,635,200	1,652,000	1,725,900	1,539,900	1,291,121
Total Assets	4,507,200	4,388,200	4,358,500	4,591,700	3,407,600	3,643,500	3,569,100	3,266,515
Current Liabilities	713,200	712,000	701,600	612,800	561,300	700,900	533,900	524,496
Long-Term Obligations	1,081,500	1,039,900	1,310,900	1,715,600	625,400	609,000	754,700	909,159
Total Liabilities	2,118,100	2,062,700	2,319,700	2,654,400	1,473,200	1,587,300	1,615,700	1,730,584
Stockholders' Equity	2,389,100	2,325,500	2,038,800	1,937,300	1,934,400	2,056,200	1,953,400	1,535,931
Shares Outstanding	44,000	44,300	44,800	44,700	44,700	45,100	44,900	41,579
Statistical Record								
Return on Assets %	5.03	4.87	4.56	3.59	0.87	3.34	5.74	5.34
Return on Equity %	9.96	9.76	10.26	7.42	1.53	6.00	11.24	10.54
EBITDA Margin %	13.95	12.26	12.84	9.92	6.55	9.45	12.47	11.42
Net Margin %	6.65	6.34	6.31	4.08	0.95	3.88	6.18	5.42
Asset Turnover	0.77	0.77	0.72	0.88	0.91	0.86	0.93	0.99
Current Ratio	2.36	2.21	2.18	2.67	2.94	2.46	2.88	2.46
Debt to Equity	0.45	0.45	0.64	0.89	0.32	0.30	0.39	0.59
Price Range	86.75-69.75	86.75-69.45	75.10-49.38	80.95-55.46	80.02-63.13	84.67-62.35	75.00-52.05	76.04-42.97
P/E Ratio	17.25-13.87	18.30-14.65	16.62-10.92	25.46-17.44	115.97-91.49	32.07-23.62	16.16-11.22	20.06-11.34
Average Yield %	1.33	1.31	1.57	1.30	1.18	1.11	1.15	1.14

Address: 200 State Street, Beloit, WI 53511	Web Site: www.regal-beloit.com	Auditors: DELOITTE & TOUCHE LLP
Telephone: 608-364-8800	Officers: Mark J. Gliebe - Chairman, Chief Executive Officer Jonathan J. Schlemmer - Chief Operating Officer	Investor Contact: 608-364-8800 Transfer Agents: ComputerShare Investor Services, Providence, RI

REGENCY CENTERS CORP

Exchange	Symbol	Price	52Wk Range	Yield	P/E
NYS	REG	$62.08 (6/29/2018)	70.37-55.58	3.58	42.52

*7 Year Price Score 86.35 *NYSE Composite Index=100 *12 Month Price Score 93.32

Interim Earnings (Per Share)

Qtr.	Mar	Jun	Sep	Dec
2015	0.27	0.34	0.57	0.18
2016	0.49	0.35	0.05	0.54
2017	(0.26)	0.28	0.35	0.52
2018	0.31	...	...	...

Interim Dividends (Per Share)

Amt	Decl	Ex	Rec	Pay
0.53Q	08/02/2017	08/14/2017	08/16/2017	08/30/2017
0.53Q	10/31/2017	11/14/2017	11/15/2017	11/29/2017
0.555Q	02/06/2018	02/16/2018	02/20/2018	03/02/2018
0.555Q	04/30/2018	05/15/2018	05/16/2018	05/30/2018

Indicated Div: $2.22

Valuation Analysis

		Institutional Holding	
Forecast EPS	$1.48	No of Institutions	
	(06/20/2018)	521	
Market Cap	$10.5 Billion	Shares	
Book Value	$6.6 Billion	194,311,040	
Price/Book	1.60	% Held	
Price/Sales	9.85	104.58	

Business Summary: REITs (MIC: 5.3.1 SIC: 6798 NAIC: 525930)

Regency Centers is a real estate investment trust and the general partner of the Regency Centers, L.P. (Operating Partnership). Co. engages in the ownership, management, leasing, acquisition, and development of retail shopping centers through the Operating Partnership, and has no other assets or liabilities other than through its investment in the Operating Partnership. As of Dec 31 2017, Co., the Operating Partnership, and their controlled subsidiaries on a consolidated basis owned 311 retail shopping centers and held partial interests in an additional 115 retail shopping centers through unconsolidated investments in real estate partnerships.

Recent Developments: For the quarter ended Mar 31 2018, income from continuing operations was US$53.4 million compared with a loss of US$21.1 million in the year-earlier quarter. Net income amounted to US$53.5 million versus a net loss of US$20.7 million in the year-earlier quarter. Revenues were US$276.7 million, up 41.1% from US$196.1 million the year before. Revenues from property income rose 42.4% to US$205.3 million from US$144.1 million in the corresponding quarter a year earlier.

Prospects: Our evaluation of Regency Centers Corp. as of Jan. 21, 2018 is the result of our systematic analysis on three basic characteristics: earnings strength, relative valuation, and recent stock price movement. The company has enjoyed a very positive trend in earnings per share over the past 5 quarters. Because the company lacks sufficient analyst estimate data, we place greater weight on the historical EPS trend as the measure of earnings strength. Based on operating earnings yield, the company is about fairly valued when compared to all of the companies in our coverage universe. Share price changes over the past year indicates that REG will perform well over the near term.

Financial Data

(US$ in Thousands)	3 Mos	12/31/2017	12/31/2016	12/31/2015	12/31/2014	12/31/2013	12/31/2012	12/31/2011
Earnings Per Share	1.46	1.00	1.42	1.36	1.80	1.40	(0.08)	0.35
Cash Flow Per Share	3.45	2.95	2.86	2.92	3.01	2.74	2.86	2.48
Tang Book Value Per Share	34.18	36.34	20.62	16.77	16.32	16.02	15.14	16.81
Dividends Per Share	2.145	2.100	2.000	1.940	1.880	1.850	1.850	1.850
Dividend Payout %	146.92	210.00	140.85	142.65	104.44	132.14	...	528.57
Income Statement								
Total Revenue	276,693	984,326	614,371	569,763	537,898	489,007	496,920	500,417
EBITDA	74,095	551,665	322,075	351,959	366,206	305,850	241,606	307,803
Depn & Amortn	(5,710)	320,566	168,210	154,908	155,211	144,305	139,555	145,152
Income Before Taxes	43,020	98,470	63,153	94,429	101,504	52,579	(10,078)	39,006
Income Taxes	...	(9,737)	...	...	(996)	...	13,224	...
Net Income	52,660	176,077	164,922	150,056	187,390	149,804	25,867	51,370
Average Shares	170,959	159,960	101,285	94,856	92,404	91,409	89,669	88,249
Balance Sheet								
Current Assets	253,223	36,653	37,446	102,008	180,922	143,204	78,851	76,898
Total Assets	11,233,856	11,145,717	4,488,906	4,191,074	4,197,170	3,913,516	3,853,458	3,987,071
Current Liabilities	260,943	234,272	138,936	164,515	181,197	147,045	127,185	101,862
Long-Term Obligations	3,840,268	3,594,977	1,642,420	1,872,478	2,021,357	1,854,697	1,941,891	1,982,440
Total Liabilities	4,669,555	4,453,665	1,897,605	2,136,965	2,290,578	2,070,162	2,122,693	2,178,716
Stockholders' Equity	6,564,301	6,692,052	2,591,301	2,054,109	1,906,592	1,843,354	1,730,765	1,808,355
Shares Outstanding	169,036	170,998	104,149	96,794	93,682	91,960	90,059	89,583
Statistical Record								
Return on Assets %	2.24	2.25	3.79	3.58	4.62	3.86	0.66	1.29
Return on Equity %	3.76	3.79	7.08	7.58	9.99	8.38	1.46	2.93
EBITDA Margin %	26.78	56.04	52.42	61.77	68.08	62.55	48.62	61.51
Net Margin %	19.03	17.89	26.84	26.34	34.84	30.63	5.21	10.27
Asset Turnover	0.10	0.13	0.14	0.14	0.13	0.13	0.13	0.13
Current Ratio	0.97	0.16	0.27	0.62	1.00	0.97	0.62	0.75
Debt to Equity	0.59	0.54	0.63	0.91	1.06	1.01	1.12	1.10
Price Range	70.37-55.58	71.70-58.96	85.30-65.38	69.90-57.09	64.96-45.97	59.20-45.88	50.52-36.69	47.32-33.37
P/E Ratio	48.20-38.07	71.70-58.96	60.07-46.04	51.40-41.98	36.09-25.54	42.29-32.77	...	135.20-95.34
Average Yield %	3.38	3.21	2.68	2.99	3.44	3.63	4.05	4.49

Address: One Independent Drive, Suite 114, Jacksonville, FL 32202 **Telephone:** 904-598-7000	**Web Site:** www.regencycenters.com **Officers:** Martin E. (Hap) Stein - Chairman, Chief Executive Officer Lisa Palmer - President, Executive Vice President, Senior Vice President, Chief Financial Officer	**Auditors:** KPMG LLP **Investor Contact:** 904-598-7000 **Transfer Agents:** Broadridge Corporate Issuer Solutions, Inc., Philadelphia, PA

REGIONS FINANCIAL CORP

Exchange	Symbol	Price	52Wk Range	Yield	P/E
NYS	RF	$17.78 (6/29/2018)	20.11-13.17	2.02	15.88

*7 Year Price Score 133.41 ***NYSE Composite Index=100** ***12 Month Price Score 108.58**

Interim Earnings (Per Share)

Qtr.	Mar	Jun	Sep	Dec
2015	0.16	0.20	0.18	0.21
2016	0.20	0.20	0.24	0.22
2017	0.24	0.25	0.25	0.27
2018	0.35	...	...	...

Interim Dividends (Per Share)

Amt	Decl	Ex	Rec	Pay
0.09Q	07/27/2017	09/07/2017	09/08/2017	09/29/2017
0.09Q	10/19/2017	12/07/2017	12/08/2017	01/02/2018
0.09Q	02/08/2018	03/08/2018	03/09/2018	04/02/2018
0.09Q	04/25/2018	06/07/2018	06/08/2018	07/02/2018

Indicated Div: $0.36

TRADING VOLUME (thousand shares)

Valuation Analysis

		Institutional Holding	
Forecast EPS	$1.41	No of Institutions	
	(06/14/2018)	1028	
Market Cap	$20.0 Billion	Shares	
Book Value	$15.9 Billion	1,061,135,872	
Price/Book	1.26	% Held	
Price/Sales	3.24	67.51	

Business Summary: Banking (MIC: 5.1.1 SIC: 6021 NAIC: 522110)

Regions Financial is a financial holding company. Co. provides commercial, retail and mortgage banking services, as well as other financial services in the fields of asset management, wealth management, securities brokerage, insurance brokerage, trust services, merger and acquisition advisory services, and other specialty financing. At Dec 31 2017, Co. operated 1,900 Automated Teller Machines and 1,469 banking offices in Alabama, Arkansas, Florida, Georgia, Illinois, Indiana, Iowa, Kentucky, Louisiana, Mississippi, Missouri, North Carolina, South Carolina, Tennessee, and Texas. As of Dec 31 2017, Co. had total assets of $124.29 billion and total deposits of $96.89 billion.

Recent Developments: For the year ended Dec 31 2017, income from continuing operations increased 8.5% to US$1.26 billion from US$1.16 billion a year earlier. Net income increased 8.6% to US$1.26 billion from US$1.16 billion in the prior year. Net interest income increased 3.3% to US$3.62 billion from US$3.50 billion in the prior year. Provision for loan losses was US$150.0 million versus US$262.0 million in the prior year, a decrease of 42.7%. Non-interest income fell 2.2% to US$2.11 billion from US$2.15 billion, while non-interest expense declined 0.6% to US$3.70 billion.

Prospects: Our evaluation of Regions Financial Corp. as of Jan. 21, 2018 is the result of our systematic analysis on three basic characteristics: earnings strength, relative valuation, and recent stock price movement. The company has enjoyed a very positive trend in earnings per share over the past 5 quarters. Because the company lacks sufficient analyst estimate data, we place greater weight on the historical EPS trend as the measure of earnings strength. Based on operating earnings yield, the company is undervalued when compared to all of the companies in our coverage universe. Share price changes over the past year indicates that RF will perform poorly over the near term.

Financial Data

(US$ in Thousands)	3 Mos	12/31/2017	12/31/2016	12/31/2015	12/31/2014	12/31/2013	12/31/2012	12/31/2011
Earnings Per Share	1.12	1.00	0.87	0.75	0.80	0.77	0.71	(0.34)
Cash Flow Per Share	1.51	1.92	1.55	1.19	1.52	2.72	1.76	3.78
Tang Book Value Per Share	8.55	8.78	8.56	8.20	7.94	7.19	6.84	6.06
Dividends Per Share	0.340	0.315	0.255	0.230	0.180	0.100	0.040	0.040
Dividend Payout %	30.36	31.50	29.31	30.67	22.50	12.99	5.63	...
Income Statement								
Interest Income	1,047,000	3,988,000	3,814,000	3,603,000	3,588,000	3,646,000	3,903,000	4,252,000
Interest Expense	122,000	373,000	313,000	268,000	309,000	384,000	603,000	842,000
Net Interest Income	925,000	3,615,000	3,501,000	3,335,000	3,279,000	3,262,000	3,300,000	3,410,000
Provision for Losses	(10,000)	150,000	262,000	241,000	69,000	138,000	213,000	1,530,000
Non-Interest Income	507,000	2,105,000	2,153,000	2,071,000	1,821,000	2,019,000	2,100,000	2,143,000
Non-Interest Expense	900,000	3,699,000	3,720,000	3,635,000	3,432,000	3,556,000	3,526,000	3,862,000
Income Before Taxes	542,000	1,871,000	1,672,000	1,530,000	1,599,000	1,587,000	1,661,000	161,000
Income Taxes	128,000	614,000	514,000	455,000	457,000	452,000	482,000	(28,000)
Net Income	414,000	1,263,000	1,163,000	1,062,000	1,155,000	1,122,000	1,120,000	(215,000)
Average Shares	1,141,000	1,198,000	1,261,000	1,334,000	1,387,000	1,410,000	1,387,000	1,258,000
Balance Sheet								
Net Loans & Leases	79,434,000	79,361,000	79,722,000	80,504,000	76,745,000	74,323,000	73,459,000	76,042,000
Total Assets	122,913,000	124,294,000	125,968,000	126,050,000	119,679,000	117,396,000	121,347,000	127,050,000
Total Deposits	96,990,000	96,889,000	99,035,000	98,430,000	94,200,000	92,453,000	95,474,000	95,627,000
Total Liabilities	107,047,000	108,102,000	109,304,000	109,206,000	102,690,000	101,628,000	105,848,000	110,551,000
Stockholders' Equity	15,866,000	16,192,000	16,664,000	16,844,000	16,989,000	15,768,000	15,499,000	16,499,000
Shares Outstanding	1,125,557	1,134,068	1,214,580	1,297,330	1,353,941	1,377,720	1,413,339	1,258,816
Statistical Record								
Return on Assets %	1.11	1.01	0.92	0.86	0.97	0.94	0.90	N.M.
Return on Equity %	8.44	7.69	6.92	6.28	7.05	7.18	6.98	N.M.
Net Interest Margin %	88.35	90.65	91.79	92.56	91.39	89.47	84.55	80.20
Efficiency Ratio %	57.92	60.71	62.34	64.06	63.45	62.77	58.74	60.39
Loans to Deposits	0.82	0.82	0.80	0.82	0.81	0.80	0.77	0.80
Price Range	20.11-13.17	17.49-13.17	14.64-7.08	10.80-8.70	11.30-9.06	10.42-7.13	7.65-4.34	8.02-3.02
P/E Ratio	17.96-11.76	17.49-13.17	16.83-8.14	14.40-11.60	14.13-11.33	13.53-9.26	10.77-6.11	...
Average Yield %	2.15	2.13	2.22	2.63	2.36	1.75	1.11	0.70

Address: 1900 Fifth Avenue North,	Web Site: www.regions.com	Auditors: Ernst & Young LLP
Birmingham, AL 35203	Officers: O.B. Grayson Hall - Chairman, President,	Investor Contact: 205-801-0265
Telephone: 205-581-7890	Chief Executive Officer, Chief Operating Officer,	Transfer Agents: Computershare Trust
	Head John M. Turner - President, Senior Executive	Company, N.A., Providence, RI
	Vice President, Head, Chief Executive Officer	

REINSURANCE GROUP OF AMERICA, INC.

Exchange	Symbol	Price	52Wk Range	Yield	P/E
NYS	RGA	$133.48 (6/29/2018)	164.17-127.52	1.50	4.94

*7 Year Price Score 132.54 *NYSE Composite Index=100 *12 Month Price Score 97.52

TRADING VOLUME (thousand shares)

Interim Earnings (Per Share)

Qtr.	Mar	Jun	Sep	Dec
2015	1.81	1.94	1.25	2.45
2016	1.17	3.64	3.07	2.92
2017	2.22	3.54	3.47	18.48
2018	1.52	...	...	...

Interim Dividends (Per Share)

Amt	Decl	Ex	Rec	Pay
0.50Q	07/19/2017	08/04/2017	08/08/2017	08/29/2017
0.50Q	10/26/2017	11/06/2017	11/07/2017	11/28/2017
0.50Q	01/29/2018	02/07/2018	02/08/2018	03/01/2018
0.50Q	04/26/2018	05/07/2018	05/08/2018	05/29/2018

Indicated Div: $2.00

Valuation Analysis

		Institutional Holding	
Forecast EPS	$11.65	No of Institutions	
	(06/12/2018)	31	
Market Cap	$8.6 Billion	Shares	
Book Value	$9.0 Billion	784,655	
Price/Book	0.96	% Held	
Price/Sales	0.68	N/A	

Business Summary: Life & Health (MIC: 5.2.2 SIC: 6311 NAIC: 524130)

Reinsurance Group of America is an insurance holding company. Through its subsidiaries, Co. is engaged in providing traditional reinsurance, which includes individual and group life and health, disability, and critical illness reinsurance. Co. also provides financial solutions, which includes longevity reinsurance, asset-intensive products, primarily annuities, and financial reinsurance. Co. has five geographic-based and business-based operational segments: U.S. and Latin America; Canada; Europe, Middle East and Africa; Asia Pacific; and Corporate and Other. Geographic-based operations are further segmented into traditional and financial solutions businesses.

Recent Developments: For the quarter ended Mar 31 2018, net income decreased 31.1% to US$100.2 million from US$145.5 million in the year-earlier quarter. Revenues were US$3.17 billion, up 5.5% from US$3.01 billion the year before. Net premiums earned were US$2.58 billion versus US$2.37 billion in the prior-year quarter, an increase of 9.2%. Net investment income rose 0.4% to US$516.3 million from US$514.4 million a year ago.

Prospects: Our evaluation of Reinsurance Group of America Inc. as of Jan. 21, 2018 is the result of our systematic analysis on three basic characteristics: earnings strength, relative valuation, and recent stock price movement. The company has produced a positive trend in earnings per share over the past 5 quarters and while recent estimates for the company have been mixed, RGA has posted better than expected results. Based on operating earnings yield, the company is undervalued when compared to all of the companies in our coverage universe. Share price changes over the past year indicates that RGA will perform in line with the market over the near term.

Financial Data
(US$ in Thousands)

	3 Mos	12/31/2017	12/31/2016	12/31/2015	12/31/2014	12/31/2013	12/31/2012	12/31/2011
Earnings Per Share	27.01	27.71	10.79	7.46	9.78	5.78	8.52	8.09
Cash Flow Per Share	27.74	30.77	22.74	31.38	33.74	24.02	26.70	17.80
Tang Book Value Per Share	139.64	148.48	110.31	94.09	102.13	83.87	93.47	83.65
Dividends Per Share	1.910	1.820	1.560	1.400	1.260	1.080	0.840	0.600
Dividend Payout %	7.07	6.57	14.46	18.77	12.88	18.69	9.86	7.42
Income Statement								
Premium Income	2,582,551	9,841,130	9,248,871	8,570,741	8,669,854	8,254,027	7,906,596	7,335,687
Total Revenue	3,173,707	12,515,769	11,521,511	10,418,178	10,904,194	10,318,353	9,840,911	8,829,538
Benefits & Claims	...	8,518,917	7,993,375	7,489,382	7,406,641	7,304,332	6,665,999	6,224,800
Income Before Taxes	137,925	1,142,815	1,043,946	744,795	1,008,533	635,254	919,223	834,380
Income Taxes	37,695	(679,366)	342,503	242,629	324,486	216,417	287,330	234,760
Net Income	100,230	1,822,181	701,443	502,166	684,047	418,837	631,893	599,620
Average Shares	65,872	65,753	64,989	67,292	69,962	72,461	74,153	74,108
Balance Sheet								
Total Assets	60,954,823	60,514,818	53,097,879	50,383,152	44,679,611	39,674,473	40,360,438	32,104,032
Total Liabilities	51,946,562	50,945,283	46,004,797	44,247,771	37,656,159	33,738,946	33,450,251	25,966,927
Stockholders' Equity	9,008,261	9,569,535	7,093,082	6,135,381	7,023,452	5,935,527	6,910,187	6,137,105
Shares Outstanding	64,512	64,452	64,302	65,204	68,772	70,768	73,927	73,367
Statistical Record								
Return on Assets %	3.10	3.21	1.35	1.06	1.62	1.05	1.74	1.96
Return on Equity %	21.63	21.87	10.58	7.63	10.56	6.52	9.66	10.73
Loss Ratio %	...	86.56	86.43	87.38	85.43	88.49	84.31	84.86
Net Margin %	3.16	14.56	6.09	4.82	6.27	4.06	6.42	6.79
Price Range	164.17-122.13	164.17-122.13	128.28-78.61	98.57-82.81	89.22-71.51	77.41-53.52	60.01-48.64	63.79-44.99
P/E Ratio	6.08-4.52	5.92-4.41	11.89-7.29	13.21-11.10	9.12-7.31	13.39-9.26	7.04-5.71	7.89-5.56
Average Yield %	1.34	1.35	1.55	1.53	1.58	1.65	1.52	1.06

Address: 16600 Swingley Ridge Road, Chesterfield, MO 63017 **Telephone:** 636-736-7000	**Web Site:** www.rgare.com **Officers:** J. Cliff Eason - Chairman Anna Manning - President, Chief Executive Officer, Senior Executive Vice President	**Auditors:** DELOITTE & TOUCHE LLP **Investor Contact:** 636-300-8828

RELIANCE STEEL & ALUMINUM CO.

Exchange	Symbol	Price	52Wk Range	Yield	P/E
NYS	RS	$87.54 (6/29/2018)	96.56-69.11	2.28	9.60

*7 Year Price Score 99.93   *NYSE Composite Index=100   *12 Month Price Score 109.65

Interim Earnings (Per Share)

Qtr.	Mar	Jun	Sep	Dec
2015	1.30	1.20	0.69	0.95
2016	1.27	1.38	0.68	0.84
2017	1.52	1.40	1.32	4.10
2018	2.30	...	...	...

Interim Dividends (Per Share)

Amt	Decl	Ex	Rec	Pay
0.45Q	07/25/2017	08/16/2017	08/18/2017	09/08/2017
0.45Q	10/24/2017	11/16/2017	11/17/2017	12/08/2017
0.50Q	02/13/2018	03/15/2018	03/16/2018	03/30/2018
0.50Q	04/25/2018	05/24/2018	05/25/2018	06/15/2018

Indicated Div: $2.00

Valuation Analysis

Forecast EPS	$8.83
	(06/13/2018)
Market Cap	$6.3 Billion
Book Value	$4.8 Billion
Price/Book	1.33
Price/Sales	0.63

Institutional Holding

No of Institutions	501
Shares	71,081,280
% Held	82.41

Business Summary: Non-Precious Metals (MIC: 8.2.2 SIC: 5051 NAIC: 423510)

Reliance Steel & Aluminum is a metals service center company. Co. provides metals processing services and distributes a line of metal products, including alloy, aluminum, brass, copper, carbon steel, stainless steel, titanium and specialty steel products to customers in a range of industries, including general manufacturing, non-residential construction, transportation, aerospace and defense, energy, electronics and semiconductor fabrication, and heavy industry. Co. also services the auto industry, primarily through its toll processing operations. As of Dec 31 2017, Co.'s network of metals service centers operated more than 300 locations in 44 states in the U.S. and in 13 other countries.

Recent Developments: For the quarter ended Mar 31 2018, net income increased 50.9% from US$171.1 million from US$113.4 million in the year-earlier quarter. Revenues were US$2.76 billion, up 14.0% from US$2.42 billion the year before. Operating income was US$246.4 million versus US$190.2 million in the prior-year quarter, an increase of 29.5%. Direct operating expenses rose 14.1% to US$1.94 billion from US$1.70 billion in the comparable period the year before. Indirect operating expenses increased 7.9% to US$573.5 million from US$531.4 million in the equivalent prior-year period.

Prospects: Our evaluation of Reliance Steel & Aluminum Co. as of Jan. 21, 2018 is the result of our systematic analysis on three basic characteristics: earnings strength, relative valuation, and recent stock price movement. The company has generated a negative trend in earnings per share over the past 5 quarters and while recent estimates for the company have been mixed, RS has posted better than expected results. Based on operating earnings yield, the company is undervalued when compared to all of the companies in our coverage universe. Share price changes over the past year indicates that RS will perform poorly over the near term.

Financial Data
(US$ in Thousands)

	3 Mos	12/31/2017	12/31/2016	12/31/2015	12/31/2014	12/31/2013	12/31/2012	12/31/2011
Earnings Per Share	9.12	8.34	4.16	4.16	4.73	4.14	5.33	4.58
Cash Flow Per Share	5.95	5.48	8.63	13.83	4.58	8.24	7.98	3.14
Tang Book Value Per Share	24.67	23.58	16.10	14.83	14.49	12.51	17.19	13.38
Dividends Per Share	1.850	1.800	1.650	1.600	1.400	1.260	0.800	0.480
Dividend Payout %	20.29	21.58	39.66	38.46	29.60	30.43	15.01	10.48
Income Statement								
Total Revenue	2,757,100	9,721,000	8,613,400	9,350,500	10,451,600	9,223,800	8,442,300	8,134,700
EBITDA	298,600	942,600	796,200	817,900	890,900	792,700	859,900	741,700
Depn & Amortn	54,100	218,400	222,000	218,500	213,800	192,400	151,500	133,100
Income Before Taxes	225,200	583,800	428,500	458,700	544,100	476,000	607,200	509,400
Income Taxes	54,100	(37,200)	120,100	142,500	170,000	153,600	201,100	162,400
Net Income	169,000	613,400	304,300	311,500	371,500	321,600	403,500	343,800
Average Shares	73,450	73,539	73,120	74,902	78,615	77,646	75,694	75,041
Balance Sheet								
Current Assets	3,437,600	3,051,300	2,688,500	2,554,200	3,121,100	2,738,900	2,277,400	2,274,700
Total Assets	8,147,900	7,751,000	7,411,300	7,121,600	7,836,600	7,341,000	5,857,700	5,605,900
Current Liabilities	874,100	703,700	656,000	989,700	662,800	573,400	578,200	576,400
Long-Term Obligations	1,947,100	1,809,400	1,846,700	1,427,900	2,222,300	2,072,500	1,123,800	1,319,000
Total Liabilities	3,397,400	3,083,900	3,262,500	3,207,500	3,737,600	3,466,400	2,299,300	2,462,000
Stockholders' Equity	4,750,500	4,667,100	4,148,800	3,914,100	4,099,000	3,874,600	3,558,400	3,143,900
Shares Outstanding	72,342	72,609	72,682	71,739	77,337	77,492	76,042	75,007
Statistical Record								
Return on Assets %	8.45	8.09	4.18	4.16	4.90	4.87	7.02	6.69
Return on Equity %	14.91	13.92	7.53	7.77	9.32	8.65	12.01	11.52
EBITDA Margin %	10.83	9.70	9.24	8.75	8.52	8.59	10.19	9.12
Net Margin %	6.13	6.31	3.53	3.33	3.55	3.49	4.78	4.23
Asset Turnover	1.27	1.28	1.18	1.25	1.38	1.40	1.47	1.58
Current Ratio	3.93	4.34	4.10	2.58	4.71	4.78	3.94	3.95
Debt to Equity	0.41	0.39	0.45	0.36	0.54	0.53	0.32	0.42
Price Range	94.57-69.11	87.62-69.11	86.34-51.75	66.33-52.37	76.12-57.14	75.84-62.10	62.10-44.98	60.05-32.04
P/E Ratio	10.37-7.58	10.51-8.29	20.75-12.44	15.94-12.59	16.09-12.08	18.32-15.00	11.65-8.44	13.11-7.00
Average Yield %	2.34	2.32	2.31	2.71	2.02	1.82	1.57	1.00

Address: 350 South Grand Avenue, Suite 5100, Los Angeles, CA 90071
Telephone: 213-687-7700

Web Site: www.rsac.com
Officers: David H. Hannah - Chairman, Chief Executive Officer Gregg J. Mollins - President, Chief Executive Officer, Chief Operating Officer

Auditors: KPMG LLP
Investor Contact: 213-576-2428
Transfer Agents: American Stock Transfer & Trust Company, Brooklyn, NY

RENAISSANCERE HOLDINGS LTD.

Exchange	Symbol	Price	52Wk Range	Yield	P/E
NYS	RNR	$120.32 (6/29/2018)	148.48-116.61	1.10	N/A

*7 Year Price Score 103.22 *NYSE Composite Index=100 *12 Month Price Score 93.57

Interim Earnings (Per Share)

Qtr.	Mar	Jun	Sep	Dec
2015	4.14	1.59	1.66	2.09
2016	2.95	3.22	3.56	1.72
2017	2.25	4.24	(12.75)	(0.11)
2018	1.42	...	...	...

Interim Dividends (Per Share)

Amt	Decl	Ex	Rec	Pay
0.32Q	08/02/2017	09/14/2017	09/15/2017	09/29/2017
0.32Q	11/10/2017	12/14/2017	12/15/2017	12/29/2017
0.33Q	02/08/2018	03/14/2018	03/15/2018	03/29/2018
0.33Q	05/14/2018	06/14/2018	06/15/2018	06/29/2018
		Indicated Div: $1.32		

Valuation Analysis — **Institutional Holding**

Forecast EPS	N/A	No of Institutions
		449
Market Cap	$4.8 Billion	Shares
Book Value	$4.4 Billion	52,728,272
Price/Book	1.09	% Held
Price/Sales	2.36	75.82

Business Summary: General Insurance (MIC: 5.2.1 SIC: 6331 NAIC: 524126)

RenaissanceRe Holdings is a holding company. Together with its wholly owned and majority-owned subsidiaries and DaVinciRe Holdings Ltd, Co. is a global provider of reinsurance and insurance coverages and related services. Co.'s business consists of the following reportable segments: Property, which is comprised of catastrophe and other property reinsurance and insurance written on behalf of Co.'s operating subsidiaries and certain joint ventures managed by its ventures unit; and Casualty and Specialty, which is comprised of casualty and specialty reinsurance and insurance written on behalf of Co.'s operating subsidiaries and certain joint ventures managed by its ventures unit.

Recent Developments: For the quarter ended Mar 31 2018, net income decreased 30.3% to US$92.2 million from US$132.3 million in the year-earlier quarter. Revenues were US$418.0 million, down 11.5% from US$472.1 million the year before. Net premiums earned were US$440.3 million versus US$366.0 million in the prior-year quarter, an increase of 20.3%. Net investment income rose 4.0% to US$56.5 million from US$54.3 million a year ago.

Prospects: Our evaluation of RenaissanceRe Holdings Ltd. as of July 19, 2015 is the result of our systematic analysis on three basic characteristics: earnings strength, relative valuation, and recent stock price movement. The company has enjoyed a very positive trend in earnings per share over the past 5 quarters. However, while recent estimates for the company have been mixed, RNR has posted better than expected results. Based on operating earnings yield, the company is undervalued when compared to all of the companies in our coverage universe. Share price changes over the past year indicates that RNR will perform poorly over the near term.

Financial Data
(US$ in Thousands)

	3 Mos	12/31/2017	12/31/2016	12/31/2015	12/31/2014	12/31/2013	12/31/2012	12/31/2011
Earnings Per Share	(7.20)	(6.15)	11.43	9.28	12.60	14.87	11.23	(1.84)
Cash Flow Per Share	19.91	26.24	11.34	9.61	16.76	18.36	14.63	3.27
Tang Book Value Per Share	94.29	93.65	102.35	93.06	89.95	80.10	67.95	59.10
Dividends Per Share	1.290	1.280	1.240	1.200	1.160	1.120	1.080	1.040
Dividend Payout %	...	...	10.85	12.93	9.21	7.53	9.62	...
Income Statement								
Premium Income	440,282	1,717,575	1,403,430	1,400,551	1,062,416	1,114,626	1,069,355	951,049
Total Revenue	417,986	2,103,679	1,727,837	1,515,102	1,260,077	1,380,482	1,405,934	1,095,036
Income Before Taxes	88,800	(328,184)	630,388	496,376	686,864	841,038	748,091	(74,817)
Income Taxes	(3,407)	26,487	340	(45,866)	608	1,692	1,429	(315)
Net Income	62,308	(222,389)	502,962	431,192	532,718	690,624	600,909	(57,235)
Average Shares	39,599	39,854	41,559	43,526	39,968	44,128	49,603	50,747
Balance Sheet								
Total Assets	15,922,202	15,226,131	12,352,082	11,560,871	8,203,550	8,179,131	7,928,628	7,744,912
Total Liabilities	11,485,949	10,834,756	7,485,505	6,828,687	4,337,835	4,274,747	4,425,563	4,139,719
Stockholders' Equity	4,436,253	4,391,375	4,866,577	4,732,184	3,865,715	3,904,384	3,503,065	3,605,193
Shares Outstanding	40,245	40,023	41,187	43,701	38,441	43,646	45,542	51,542
Statistical Record								
Return on Assets %	N.M.	N.M.	4.20	4.36	6.50	8.58	7.65	N.M.
Return on Equity %	N.M.	N.M.	10.45	10.03	13.71	18.65	16.86	N.M.
Net Margin %	14.91	(10.57)	29.11	28.46	42.28	50.03	42.74	(5.23)
Price Range	148.48-116.61	150.35-123.88	136.45-108.93	115.47-94.50	108.42-89.80	97.34-80.20	82.76-71.69	75.05-60.13
P/E Ratio	...	...	11.94-9.53	12.44-10.18	8.60-7.13	6.55-5.39	7.37-6.38	...
Average Yield %	0.95	0.92	1.05	1.15	1.16	1.26	1.42	1.53

Address: Renaissance House, 12 Crow Lane, Pembroke, HM 19
Telephone: 441-295-4513
Fax: 441-295-9453

Web Site: www.renre.com
Officers: Kevin J. O'Donnell - President, Chief Executive Officer Robert (Bob) Qutub - Executive Vice President, Chief Financial Officer

Auditors: Ernst & Young Ltd.
Investor Contact: 441-295-4513
Transfer Agents: Computershare Shareowner Services LLC, Jersey City, NJ

REPUBLIC SERVICES INC

Exchange	Symbol	Price	52Wk Range	Yield	P/E	Div Acheiver
NYS	RSG	$68.36 (6/29/2018)	69.87-61.96	2.02	17.35	14 Years

*7 Year Price Score 123.69 *NYSE Composite Index=100 *12 Month Price Score 101.37

Interim Earnings (Per Share)

Qtr.	Mar	Jun	Sep	Dec
2015	0.49	0.54	0.61	0.49
2016	0.45	0.52	0.25	0.55
2017	0.55	0.60	0.66	1.96
2018	0.72	...	...	...

Interim Dividends (Per Share)

Amt	Decl	Ex	Rec	Pay
0.345Q	07/27/2017	09/29/2017	10/02/2017	10/16/2017
0.345Q	10/31/2017	12/29/2017	01/02/2018	01/16/2018
0.345Q	02/08/2018	03/29/2018	04/02/2018	04/16/2018
0.345Q	05/02/2018	06/29/2018	07/02/2018	07/16/2018

Indicated Div: $1.38

Valuation Analysis

		Institutional Holding	
Forecast EPS	$3.05 (06/14/2018)	No of Institutions	886
Market Cap	$22.5 Billion	Shares	309,402,368
Book Value	$7.9 Billion	% Held	65.21
Price/Book	2.84		
Price/Sales	2.23		

Business Summary: Sanitation Services (MIC: 7.5.3 SIC: 4953 NAIC: 562219)

Republic Services is a provider of non-hazardous solid waste collection, transfer, disposal, recycling, and energy services. As of Dec 31 2017, Co. operated in 40 states and Puerto Rico through 343 collection operations, 204 transfer stations, 195 active landfills, 90 recycling centers, seven treatment, recovery and disposal facilities, and 11 salt water disposal wells. Co. also operated 71 landfill gas and renewable energy projects and had post-closure responsibility for 124 closed landfills. Co. provides residential, small-container commercial, and large-container industrial solid waste collection services.

Recent Developments:
For the quarter ended Mar 31 2018, net income increased 26.7% to US$237.9 million from US$187.8 million in the year-earlier quarter. Revenues were US$2.43 billion, up 1.5% from US$2.39 billion the year before. Operating income was US$404.2 million versus US$388.1 million in the prior-year quarter, an increase of 4.1%. Direct operating expenses declined 1.0% to US$1.47 billion from US$1.48 billion in the comparable period the year before. Indirect operating expenses increased 6.3% to US$553.5 million from US$520.6 million in the equivalent prior-year period.

Prospects:
Our evaluation of Republic Services Inc. as of Jan. 21, 2018 is the result of our systematic analysis on three basic characteristics: earnings strength, relative valuation, and recent stock price movement. The company has managed to produce a neutral trend in earnings per share over the past 5 quarters and while recent estimates for the company have been mixed, RSG has posted better than expected results. Based on operating earnings yield, the company is about fairly valued when compared to all of the companies in our coverage universe. Share price changes over the past year indicates that RSG will perform in line with the market over the near term.

Financial Data
(US$ in Thousands)	3 Mos	12/31/2017	12/31/2016	12/31/2015	12/31/2014	12/31/2013	12/31/2012	12/31/2011
Earnings Per Share	3.94	3.77	1.78	2.13	1.53	1.62	1.55	1.56
Cash Flow Per Share	6.19	5.67	5.37	4.80	4.29	4.28	4.11	4.70
Dividends Per Share	1.355	1.330	1.240	1.160	1.080	0.990	0.910	0.840
Dividend Payout %	34.39	35.28	69.66	54.46	70.59	61.11	58.71	53.85
Income Statement								
Total Revenue	2,427,500	10,041,500	9,387,700	9,115,000	8,788,300	8,417,200	8,118,300	8,192,900
EBITDA	653,200	2,635,700	2,261,100	2,458,700	2,071,900	2,017,200	2,138,300	2,189,800
Depn & Amortn	248,000	965,300	919,800	898,700	838,500	806,700	926,900	843,600
Income Before Taxes	310,600	1,309,500	970,900	1,195,900	885,300	851,200	823,900	906,300
Income Taxes	72,700	3,100	351,600	445,500	337,400	262,100	251,800	317,400
Net Income	237,700	1,278,400	612,600	749,900	547,600	588,900	571,800	589,200
Average Shares	332,200	339,000	344,400	351,400	358,100	363,400	368,020	377,600
Balance Sheet								
Current Assets	1,354,000	1,436,800	1,284,500	1,230,300	1,391,000	1,421,900	1,231,300	1,265,700
Total Assets	21,108,700	21,147,000	20,629,600	20,577,200	20,094,000	19,949,200	19,616,900	19,551,500
Current Liabilities	2,560,200	2,634,800	1,812,000	1,834,800	1,826,000	1,717,100	1,695,000	1,897,500
Long-Term Obligations	7,499,700	7,480,700	7,653,100	7,568,700	7,050,800	7,002,400	7,051,100	6,887,000
Total Liabilities	13,196,900	13,188,200	12,938,300	12,803,100	12,348,700	12,045,700	11,913,600	11,870,200
Stockholders' Equity	7,911,800	7,958,800	7,691,300	7,774,100	7,745,300	7,903,500	7,703,300	7,681,300
Shares Outstanding	328,600	331,700	339,400	345,600	352,700	360,400	361,100	369,900
Statistical Record								
Return on Assets %	6.37	6.12	2.97	3.69	2.74	2.98	2.91	3.02
Return on Equity %	17.03	16.34	7.90	9.66	7.00	7.55	7.41	7.59
EBITDA Margin %	26.91	26.25	24.09	26.97	23.58	23.97	26.34	26.73
Net Margin %	9.79	12.73	6.53	8.23	6.23	7.00	7.04	7.19
Asset Turnover	0.48	0.48	0.45	0.45	0.44	0.43	0.41	0.42
Current Ratio	0.53	0.55	0.71	0.67	0.76	0.83	0.73	0.67
Debt to Equity	0.95	0.94	1.00	0.97	0.91	0.89	0.92	0.90
Price Range	69.30-61.25	67.61-56.42	57.50-42.20	45.25-39.04	40.89-31.53	35.44-29.33	31.14-25.39	32.94-24.76
P/E Ratio	17.59-15.55	17.93-14.97	32.30-23.71	21.24-18.33	26.73-20.61	21.88-18.10	20.09-16.38	21.12-15.87
Average Yield %	2.09	2.11	2.50	2.80	2.95	2.98	3.23	2.86

Address: 18500 North Allied Way, Phoenix, AZ 85054 Telephone: 480-627-2700	Web Site: www.republicservices.com Officers: Manuel Kadre - Chairman Donald W. Slager - President, Chief Executive Officer	Auditors: Ernst & Young LLP Transfer Agents: Wachovia Corp., Charlotte, NC

RESMED INC.

Exchange	Symbol	Price	52Wk Range	Yield	P/E
NYS	RMD	$103.58 (6/29/2018)	107.93-72.44	1.35	48.40

*7 Year Price Score 128.18 *NYSE Composite Index=100 ***12 Month Price Score 113.66**

TRADING VOLUME (thousand shares)

Interim Earnings (Per Share)

Qtr.	Sep	Dec	Mar	Jun
2014-15	0.58	0.64	0.64	0.61
2015-16	0.57	0.64	0.63	0.66
2016-17	0.54	0.54	0.62	0.71
2017-18	0.60	0.07	0.76	...

Interim Dividends (Per Share)

Amt	Decl	Ex	Rec	Pay
0.35Q	08/01/2017	08/15/2017	08/17/2017	09/21/2017
0.35Q	10/26/2017	11/08/2017	11/09/2017	12/14/2017
0.35Q	01/22/2018	02/07/2018	02/08/2018	03/15/2018
0.35Q	04/26/2018	05/09/2018	05/10/2018	06/14/2018

Indicated Div: $1.40

Valuation Analysis / Institutional Holding

Forecast EPS	$3.53	No of Institutions
	(06/13/2018)	603
Market Cap	$14.8 Billion	Shares
Book Value	$2.1 Billion	112,187,816
Price/Book	7.15	% Held
Price/Sales	6.50	54.68

Business Summary: Medical Instruments & Equipment (MIC: 4.3.1 SIC: 3841 NAIC: 339112)

ResMed is a holding company. Through its operating subsidiaries, Co. is engaged in the development, manufacturing, distribution and marketing of medical devices and cloud-based software applications that diagnose, treat and manage respiratory disorders including sleep disordered breathing (SDB), chronic obstructive pulmonary disease, neuromuscular disease and other chronic diseases. SDB includes obstructive sleep apnea, and other respiratory disorders that occur during sleep. Co.'s portfolio of products includes devices, diagnostic products, mask systems, headgear and other accessories, dental devices, portable oxygen concentrators and cloud-based software informatics solutions.

Recent Developments: For the quarter ended Mar 31 2018, net income increased 25.4% to US$110.1 million from US$87.8 million in the year-earlier quarter. Revenues were US$591.6 million, up 15.1% from US$514.2 million the year before. Operating income was US$136.4 million versus US$107.4 million in the prior-year quarter, an increase of 27.0%. Direct operating expenses rose 15.3% to US$247.3 million from US$214.5 million in the comparable period the year before. Indirect operating expenses increased 8.1% to US$207.9 million from US$192.3 million in the equivalent prior-year period.

Prospects: Our evaluation of ResMed Inc. as of Jan. 21, 2018 is the result of our systematic analysis on three basic characteristics: earnings strength, relative valuation, and recent stock price movement. The company has managed to produce a neutral trend in earnings per share over the past 5 quarters and while recent estimates for the company have been mixed, RMD has posted better than expected results. Based on operating earnings yield, the company is about fairly valued when compared to all of the companies in our coverage universe. Share price changes over the past year indicates that RMD will perform well over the near term.

Financial Data

(US$ in Thousands)	9 Mos	6 Mos	3 Mos	06/30/2017	06/30/2016	06/30/2015	06/30/2014	06/30/2013
Earnings Per Share	2.14	2.00	2.47	2.40	2.49	2.47	2.39	2.10
Cash Flow Per Share	3.61	3.04	2.97	2.93	3.90	2.73	2.77	2.82
Tang Book Value Per Share	5.31	4.95	5.10	4.46	2.39	9.08	10.15	9.06
Dividends Per Share	1.380	1.360	1.340	1.320	1.200	1.120	1.000	0.680
Dividend Payout %	64.49	68.00	54.25	55.00	48.19	45.34	41.84	32.38
Income Statement								
Total Revenue	1,716,566	1,124,932	523,659	2,066,737	1,838,713	1,678,912	1,554,973	1,514,457
EBITDA	424,362	279,055	123,183	476,472	457,835	424,154	415,704	362,775
Depn & Amortn	34,772	23,099	11,783	46,578	23,923	8,668	9,733	10,142
Income Before Taxes	380,394	250,250	108,485	418,743	439,566	435,916	431,078	385,119
Income Taxes	174,617	154,599	22,360	76,459	87,157	83,030	85,805	77,986
Net Income	205,777	95,651	86,125	342,284	352,409	352,886	345,273	307,133
Average Shares	143,985	143,855	143,480	142,453	141,669	142,687	144,359	146,410
Balance Sheet								
Current Assets	1,604,406	1,754,349	1,657,946	1,644,003	1,419,719	1,444,182	1,556,209	1,448,849
Total Assets	3,534,208	3,564,000	3,489,617	3,468,487	3,258,935	2,184,260	2,360,962	2,210,721
Current Liabilities	461,460	1,356,411	351,585	360,126	638,551	267,259	269,558	574,049
Long-Term Obligations	810,000	...	1,018,871	1,078,611	875,000	300,594	300,770	769
Total Liabilities	1,467,244	1,544,472	1,440,089	1,508,221	1,564,104	596,953	602,714	600,205
Stockholders' Equity	2,066,964	2,019,528	2,049,528	1,960,266	1,694,831	1,587,307	1,758,248	1,610,516
Shares Outstanding	142,723	142,174	142,263	142,174	140,660	140,474	140,304	142,013
Statistical Record								
Return on Assets %	8.84	8.28	10.34	10.18	12.91	15.53	15.10	14.13
Return on Equity %	15.68	15.29	18.44	18.73	21.42	21.10	20.50	19.09
EBITDA Margin %	24.72	24.81	23.52	23.05	24.90	25.26	26.73	23.95
Net Margin %	11.99	8.50	16.45	16.56	19.17	21.02	22.20	20.28
Asset Turnover	0.65	0.64	0.62	0.61	0.67	0.74	0.68	0.70
Current Ratio	3.48	1.29	4.72	4.57	2.22	5.40	5.77	2.52
Debt to Equity	0.39	...	0.50	0.55	0.52	0.19	0.17	N.M.
Price Range	102.82-67.46	86.44-61.87	81.38-57.34	78.91-57.34	64.08-49.43	74.82-46.25	57.11-42.03	51.17-30.63
P/E Ratio	48.05-31.52	43.22-30.93	32.95-23.21	32.88-23.89	25.73-19.85	30.29-18.72	23.90-17.59	24.37-14.59
Average Yield %	1.70	1.81	1.93	1.97	2.13	1.94	2.06	1.62

Address: 9001 Spectrum Center Blvd., San Diego, CA 92123	Web Site: www.resmed.com	Auditors: KPMG LLP
Telephone: 858-836-5000	Officers: Peter C. Farrell - Chairman, President, Chief Executive Officer Robert Andrew Douglas - President, Chief Operating Officer, Region Officer, Office of the Chief Executive Officer	Investor Contact: 858-836-5971 Transfer Agents: Computershare Trust Company N.A., Canton, MA

RETAIL PROPERTIES OF AMERICA INC

Exchange	Symbol	Price	52Wk Range	Yield	P/E
NYS	RPAI	$12.78 (6/29/2018)	13.66-10.92	5.18	9.98

*7 Year Price Score N/A   *NYSE Composite Index=100   *12 Month Price Score 96.07

Interim Earnings (Per Share)

Qtr.	Mar	Jun	Sep	Dec
2015	0.05	0.12	0.32	0.00
2016	0.19	0.11	0.30	0.06
2017	(0.05)	0.48	0.15	0.46
2018	0.19	...	...	...

Interim Dividends (Per Share)

Amt	Decl	Ex	Rec	Pay
0.166Q	07/25/2017	09/25/2017	09/26/2017	10/10/2017
0.166Q	10/26/2017	12/26/2017	12/27/2017	01/10/2018
0.166Q	02/08/2018	03/26/2018	03/27/2018	04/10/2018
0.166Q	04/24/2018	06/25/2018	06/26/2018	07/10/2018

Indicated Div: $0.66

Valuation Analysis | **Institutional Holding**

Forecast EPS	$0.37	No of Institutions
	(06/10/2018)	N/A
Market Cap	$2.8 Billion	Shares
Book Value	$1.9 Billion	N/A
Price/Book	1.48	% Held
Price/Sales	5.40	N/A

Business Summary: REITs (MIC: 5.3.1 SIC: 6798 NAIC: 525930)

Retail Properties of America is a real estate investment trust that owns and operates shopping centers in the U.S. As of Dec 31 2017, Co. owned 112 retail operating properties. Co.'s retail operating portfolio includes neighborhood and community centers, power centers, and lifestyle centers and multi-tenant retail-focused mixed-use properties, as well as single-user retail properties. In addition to its operating portfolio, as of Dec 31 2017, Co. owned two properties that were in active redevelopment and one property where Co. has begun activities in anticipation of future redevelopment.

Recent Developments: For the quarter ended Mar 31 2018, income from continuing operations was US$7.3 million compared with a loss of US$50.3 million in the year-earlier quarter. Net income amounted to US$41.8 million versus a net loss of US$9.1 million in the year-earlier quarter. Revenues were US$124.8 million, down 13.1% from US$143.7 million the year before.

Prospects: Our evaluation of Retail Properties of America as of Jan. 21, 2018 is the result of our systematic analysis on three basic characteristics: earnings strength, relative valuation, and recent stock price movement. The company has enjoyed a very positive trend in earnings per share over the past 5 quarters. However, while recent estimates for the company have been lowered by analysts, RPAI has posted better than expected results. Based on operating earnings yield, the company is overvalued when compared to all of the companies in our coverage universe. Share price changes over the past year indicates that RPAI will perform well over the near term.

Financial Data
(US$ in Thousands)

	3 Mos	12/31/2017	12/31/2016	12/31/2015	12/31/2014	12/31/2013	12/31/2012	12/31/2011
Earnings Per Share	1.28	1.03	0.66	0.49	0.14	0.02	...	(0.38)
Cash Flow Per Share	1.02	1.07	1.11	1.12	1.08	1.02	0.76	0.91
Tang Book Value Per Share	8.10	8.04	8.49	8.50	8.72	9.22	9.75	10.13
Dividends Per Share	0.662	0.662	0.662	0.662	0.662	0.662	0.662	0.630
Dividend Payout %	51.76	64.32	100.38	135.20	473.21	3,312.50	...	...
Income Statement								
Total Revenue	124,842	538,139	583,143	603,960	600,614	551,223	567,023	605,683
EBITDA	29,099	277,188	384,260	373,360	357,412	345,909	401,037	379,897
Depn & Amortn	3,073	217,580	237,420	230,590	220,892	240,713	229,800	244,854
Income Before Taxes	7,261	(86,484)	37,110	3,832	2,685	(41,609)	(7,928)	(96,694)
Net Income	41,780	251,491	166,817	125,096	43,300	13,626	(447)	(72,609)
Average Shares	219,403	230,927	236,951	236,382	236,187	234,134	220,464	192,456
Balance Sheet								
Current Assets	100,426	96,863	132,060	134,228	198,305	139,008	223,500	230,931
Total Assets	3,757,721	3,918,264	4,452,973	4,621,251	4,803,860	4,877,576	5,237,427	5,941,894
Current Liabilities	89,623	119,009	122,307	109,097	100,316	93,595	112,183	114,460
Long-Term Obligations	1,609,847	1,746,086	1,997,925	2,166,238	2,334,465	2,299,633	2,592,089	3,481,218
Total Liabilities	1,863,077	2,032,564	2,300,887	2,465,914	2,615,979	2,570,236	2,863,168	3,806,870
Stockholders' Equity	1,894,644	1,885,700	2,152,086	2,155,337	2,187,881	2,307,340	2,374,259	2,135,024
Shares Outstanding	219,489	219,237	236,770	237,267	236,602	236,302	230,643	193,529
Statistical Record								
Return on Assets %	7.35	6.01	3.67	2.65	0.89	0.27	N.M.	N.M.
Return on Equity %	15.13	12.46	7.72	5.76	1.93	0.58	N.M.	N.M.
EBITDA Margin %	23.31	51.51	65.89	61.82	59.51	62.75	70.73	62.72
Net Margin %	33.47	46.73	28.61	20.71	7.21	2.47	N.M.	N.M.
Asset Turnover	0.13	0.13	0.13	0.13	0.12	0.11	0.10	0.10
Current Ratio	1.12	0.81	1.08	1.23	1.98	1.49	1.99	2.02
Debt to Equity	0.85	0.93	0.93	1.01	1.07	1.00	1.09	1.63
Price Range	14.67-11.21	15.69-11.83	17.74-14.16	18.21-13.19	16.87-12.30	16.03-11.94	12.56-8.64	...
P/E Ratio	11.46-8.76	15.23-11.49	26.88-21.45	37.16-26.92	120.50-87.86	801.50-597.00	...	...
Average Yield %	5.17	4.90	4.16	4.34	4.48	4.70	6.26	...

Address: 2021 Spring Road, Suite 200, Oak Brook, IL 60523 **Telephone:** 630-634-4200	**Web Site:** www.rpai.com **Officers:** Gerald M. Gorski - Chairman Shane C. Garrison - President, Chief Operating Officer, Executive Vice President, Chief Investment Officer	**Auditors:** Deloitte & Touche LLP **Transfer Agents:** Registrar & Transfer Company, Cranford, NJ

RITE AID CORP

Exchange	Symbol	Price	52Wk Range	Yield	P/E
NYS	RAD	$1.73 (6/29/2018)	2.95-1.43	N/A	N/A

*7 Year Price Score 35.20 ***NYSE Composite Index=100** ***12 Month Price Score 87.89**

TRADING VOLUME (thousand shares)

Interim Earnings (Per Share)

Qtr.	May	Aug	Nov	Feb
2013-14	0.09	0.03	0.04	0.06
2014-15	0.04	0.13	0.10	1.81
2015-16	0.02	0.02	0.06	0.06
2016-17	0.00	0.01	0.01	(0.02)
2017-18	(0.07)	0.16	0.08	0.73

Interim Dividends (Per Share)

No Dividends Paid

Valuation Analysis		Institutional Holding	
Forecast EPS	$0.03	No of Institutions	
	(06/10/2018)	543	
Market Cap	$1.8 Billion	Shares	
Book Value	$1.6 Billion	649,663,296	
Price/Book	1.15	% Held	
Price/Sales	N/A	68.85	

Business Summary: Retail - Food & Beverage, Drug & Tobacco (MIC: 2.1.2 SIC: 5912 NAIC: 446110)

Rite Aid is a pharmacy retail healthcare company. Co. operates through its two reportable segments: Retail Pharmacy, which sells brand and generic prescription drugs, as well as an assortment of front-end products including health and beauty aids, personal care products, seasonal merchandise, and a private brand product line; and Pharmacy Services, which provides pharmacy benefit management (PBM) options through its EnvisionRxOption and MedTrak PBMs, as well as mail-order and specialty pharmacy services and cash pay infertility discount drug program via Design Rx, among others. As of Mar 3, 2018, Co. operated 2,550 stores in 19 states across the country and in the District of Columbia.

Recent Developments: For the year ended Mar 3 2018, loss from continuing operations was US$349.5 million compared with income of US$4.1 million a year earlier. Net income increased to US$943.5 million from US$4.1 million in the prior year. Revenues were US$21.53 billion, down 6.1% from US$22.93 billion the year before. Direct operating expenses declined 6.2% to US$16.75 billion from US$17.86 billion in the comparable period the year before. Indirect operating expenses decreased 3.8% to US$4.82 billion from US$5.02 billion in the equivalent prior-year period.

Prospects: Our evaluation of Rite Aid Corp. as of Jan. 21, 2018 is the result of our systematic analysis on three basic characteristics: earnings strength, relative valuation, and recent stock price movement. The company has enjoyed a very positive trend in earnings per share over the past 5 quarters. Because the company lacks sufficient analyst estimate data, we place greater weight on the historical EPS trend as the measure of earnings strength. Based on operating earnings yield, the company is overvalued when compared to all of the companies in our coverage universe. Share price changes over the past year indicates that RAD will perform very poorly over the near term.

Financial Data

(US$ in Thousands)	03/03/2018	03/04/2017	02/27/2016	02/28/2015	03/01/2014	03/02/2013	03/03/2012	02/26/2011
Earnings Per Share	...	...	0.16	2.08	0.23	0.12	(0.43)	(0.64)
Cash Flow Per Share	0.42	0.21	0.98	0.67	0.76	0.92	0.30	0.45
Income Statement								
Total Revenue	21,528,968	32,845,073	30,736,657	26,528,377	25,526,413	25,392,263	26,121,222	25,214,907
EBITDA	397,541	826,517	1,050,374	1,122,955	959,412	809,300	433,790	333,926
Depn & Amortn	238,318	346,081	322,396	298,523	284,603	286,374	296,792	331,927
Income Before Taxes	(43,545)	48,445	278,404	426,820	250,218	7,505	(392,257)	(545,582)
Income Taxes	305,987	44,392	112,939	(1,682,353)	804	(110,600)	(23,686)	9,842
Net Income	943,470	4,053	165,465	2,109,173	249,414	118,105	(368,571)	(555,424)
Average Shares	1,049,628	1,060,826	1,042,362	1,017,861	979,092	907,259	885,819	882,947
Balance Sheet								
Current Assets	4,735,291	5,065,288	4,550,727	4,221,758	4,285,125	4,409,047	4,504,586	4,411,365
Total Assets	8,989,327	11,593,752	11,277,010	8,863,252	6,944,871	7,078,719	7,364,291	7,555,850
Current Liabilities	3,464,065	3,005,248	2,996,895	2,485,000	2,507,452	2,578,270	2,570,319	2,420,323
Long-Term Obligations	3,370,874	7,307,358	6,967,288	5,544,567	5,707,969	5,996,220	6,248,780	6,156,820
Total Liabilities	7,388,317	10,979,682	10,695,582	8,806,196	9,058,573	9,538,153	9,951,047	9,767,217
Stockholders' Equity	1,601,010	614,070	581,428	57,056	(2,113,702)	(2,459,434)	(2,586,756)	(2,211,367)
Shares Outstanding	1,067,318	1,053,690	1,047,754	988,558	971,331	904,268	898,687	890,297
Statistical Record								
Return on Assets %	7.84	0.03	1.65	26.76	3.57	1.64	N.M.	N.M.
Return on Equity %	72.82	0.67	51.97	...	...	...	...	...
EBITDA Margin %	1.85	2.52	3.42	4.23	3.76	3.19	1.66	1.32
Net Margin %	4.38	0.01	0.54	7.95	0.98	0.47	N.M.	N.M.
Asset Turnover	1.79	2.83	3.06	3.37	3.65	3.53	3.44	3.24
Current Ratio	1.37	1.69	1.52	1.70	1.71	1.71	1.75	1.82
Debt to Equity	2.11	11.90	11.98	97.18	...	...	...	...
Price Range	5.23-1.43	8.70-5.25	9.32-6.05	8.50-4.51	6.74-1.65	2.05-0.97	1.67-0.91	1.74-0.87
P/E Ratio	5.81-1.59	N.M.	58.25-37.81	4.09-2.17	29.30-7.17	17.08-8.07	...	...

Address: 30 Hunter Lane, Camp Hill, PA 17011
Telephone: 717-761-2633
Fax: 717-975-5905

Web Site: www.riteaid.com
Officers: John T. Standley - Chairman, President, Chief Executive Officer, Chief Operating Officer Kermit R. Crawford - President, Chief Operating Officer

Auditors: DELOITTE & TOUCHE LLP
Investor Contact: 717-214-8867
Transfer Agents: American Stock Transfer & Trust Company, Brooklyn, NY

RLI CORP

Exchange	Symbol	Price	52Wk Range	Yield	P/E	Div Acheiver
NYS	RLI	$66.19 (6/29/2018)	69.71-51.02	1.33	30.22	41 Years

*7 Year Price Score 99.28   *NYSE Composite Index=100   *12 Month Price Score 108.61

Interim Earnings (Per Share)

Qtr.	Mar	Jun	Sep	Dec
2015	0.70	0.84	0.81	0.77
2016	0.71	0.65	0.50	0.73
2017	0.45	0.59	0.04	1.29
2018	0.27	...	...	...

Interim Dividends (Per Share)

Amt	Decl	Ex	Rec	Pay
1.75Sp	11/09/2017	11/29/2017	11/30/2017	12/27/2017
0.21Q	11/09/2017	11/29/2017	11/30/2017	12/27/2017
0.21Q	02/08/2018	02/27/2018	02/28/2018	03/20/2018
0.22Q	05/03/2018	05/30/2018	05/31/2018	06/20/2018

Indicated Div: $0.88 (Div. Reinv. Plan)

Valuation Analysis

		Institutional Holding	
Forecast EPS	$2.19 (05/21/2018)	No of Institutions	294
Market Cap	$2.9 Billion	Shares	47,481,060
Book Value	$832.9 Million	% Held	77.39
Price/Book	3.52		
Price/Sales	3.73		

Business Summary: General Insurance (MIC: 5.2.1 SIC: 6331 NAIC: 524126)

RLI is an insurance holding company. Through its subsidiaries, Co. is engaged in underwriting selected property and casualty insurance. Co. has three segments: casualty, which includes commerical and personal umbrella, general liability, commercial transportation, professional services, small commercial, executive products, medical professional liability, and other casualty; property, which includes commercial property, marine, specialty personal, property reinsurance, and crop reinsurance; and surety; which includes miscellaneous surety coverage, commercial surety bonds, bonds for small-to-medium sized contractors, and energy surety coverages.

Recent Developments: For the quarter ended Mar 31 2018, net income decreased 38.4% to US$12.2 million from US$19.8 million in the year-earlier quarter. Revenues were US$185.9 million, down 5.6% from US$196.9 million the year before. Net premiums earned were US$190.0 million versus US$183.3 million in the prior-year quarter, an increase of 3.7%. Net investment income rose 9.4% to US$14.2 million from US$13.0 million a year ago.

Prospects: Our evaluation of RLI Corp. as of Jan. 21, 2018 is the result of our systematic analysis on three basic characteristics: earnings strength, relative valuation, and recent stock price movement. The company has generated a negative trend in earnings per share over the past 5 quarters. However, while recent estimates for the company have been mixed, RLI has posted better than expected results. Based on operating earnings yield, the company is about fairly valued when compared to all of the companies in our coverage universe. Share price changes over the past year indicates that RLI will perform in line with the market over the near term.

Financial Data

(US$ in Thousands)	3 Mos	12/31/2017	12/31/2016	12/31/2015	12/31/2014	12/31/2013	12/31/2012	12/31/2011
Earnings Per Share	2.19	2.36	2.59	3.12	3.09	2.90	2.40	3.04
Cash Flow Per Share	4.56	4.49	3.97	3.52	2.86	3.16	0.85	2.80
Tang Book Value Per Share	17.58	17.99	17.28	17.27	17.92	17.54	16.94	17.92
Dividends Per Share	2.590	2.580	2.790	2.750	3.710	2.170	3.130	3.095
Dividend Payout %	118.26	109.32	107.72	88.14	120.06	74.83	130.69	101.64
Income Statement								
Premium Income	190,027	737,937	728,608	700,161	687,375	630,802	576,571	538,452
Total Revenue	185,891	797,224	816,328	794,634	775,165	705,601	660,774	619,169
Benefits & Claims	92,421	401,584	349,778	299,045	296,609	259,801	271,645	200,084
Income Before Taxes	9,212	67,365	146,249	185,768	177,149	164,751	133,879	183,232
Income Taxes	2,162	(20,439)	42,162	59,138	54,042	49,411	39,386	59,138
Net Income	12,216	105,028	114,920	137,544	135,445	126,255	103,346	130,591
Average Shares	44,650	44,500	44,432	44,131	43,819	43,514	43,160	42,868
Balance Sheet								
Total Assets	2,894,192	2,947,244	2,777,633	2,736,579	2,775,542	2,740,310	2,644,632	2,695,170
Total Liabilities	2,061,259	2,093,646	1,954,061	1,913,110	1,930,480	1,911,344	1,848,269	1,876,318
Stockholders' Equity	832,933	853,598	823,572	823,469	845,062	828,966	796,363	818,852
Shares Outstanding	44,253	44,148	43,944	43,544	43,102	42,982	42,525	42,324
Statistical Record								
Return on Assets %	3.44	3.67	4.16	4.99	4.91	4.69	3.86	5.01
Return on Equity %	11.59	12.52	13.92	16.49	16.18	15.54	12.76	16.22
Loss Ratio %	48.64	54.42	48.01	42.71	43.15	41.19	47.11	37.16
Net Margin %	6.57	13.17	14.08	17.31	17.47	17.89	15.64	21.09
Price Range	64.47-51.02	61.61-51.02	71.00-54.60	63.02-46.91	50.54-40.31	51.77-32.33	37.22-31.05	37.08-25.49
P/E Ratio	29.44-23.30	26.11-21.62	27.41-21.08	20.20-15.04	16.36-13.05	17.85-11.15	15.51-12.94	12.20-8.38
Average Yield %	4.47	4.50	4.31	5.14	8.25	5.42	9.18	10.04

Address: 9025 North Lindbergh Drive, Peoria, IL 61615 Telephone: 309-692-1000 Fax: 309-692-1068	Web Site: www.rlicorp.com Officers: Jonathan E. Michael - Chairman, President, Chief Executive Officer Aaron H. Jacoby - Vice President	Auditors: KPMG LLP Investor Contact: 309-693-5880 Transfer Agents: Wells Fargo Shareholder Services, St. Paul, MN

ROBERT HALF INTERNATIONAL INC.

Exchange	Symbol	Price	52Wk Range	Yield	P/E	Div Acheiver
NYS	RHI	$65.10 (6/29/2018)	70.07-43.24	1.72	26.14	13 Years

*7 Year Price Score 103.01 *NYSE Composite Index=100 ***12 Month Price Score 117.03**

Interim Earnings (Per Share)

Qtr.	Mar	Jun	Sep	Dec
2015	0.58	0.67	0.73	0.71
2016	0.64	0.71	0.71	0.61
2017	0.62	0.64	0.68	0.39
2018	0.78	...	...	...

Interim Dividends (Per Share)

Amt	Decl	Ex	Rec	Pay
0.24Q	08/01/2017	08/23/2017	08/25/2017	09/15/2017
0.24Q	10/31/2017	11/22/2017	11/24/2017	12/15/2017
0.28Q	02/13/2018	02/22/2018	02/23/2018	03/15/2018
0.28Q	05/01/2018	05/24/2018	05/25/2018	06/15/2018

Indicated Div: $1.12

Valuation Analysis | **Institutional Holding**

Forecast EPS	$3.34	No of Institutions
	(06/12/2018)	683
Market Cap	$8.0 Billion	Shares
Book Value	$1.1 Billion	139,905,552
Price/Book	7.22	% Held
Price/Sales	1.50	85.18

Business Summary: Business Services (MIC: 7.5.2 SIC: 7363 NAIC: 561320)

Robert Half International provides staffing and risk consulting services. Co.'s Accountemps, Robert Half Finance & Accounting, and Robert Half Management Resources divisions provide personnel in the fields of accounting and finance. Co.'s OfficeTeam division provides temporary administrative support personnel. Co.'s Robert Half Technology division provides project and technology personnel. Co.'s Robert Half Legal division provides staffing of lawyers, paralegals and legal support personnel. The Creative Group provides interactive, design, marketing, advertising and public relations professionals. Protiviti employs personnel focusing on risk, advisory and transactional services.

Recent Developments: For the quarter ended Mar 31 2018, net income increased 22.5% to US$96.2 million from US$78.5 million in the year-earlier quarter. Revenues were US$1.40 billion, up 8.4% from US$1.29 billion the year before. Direct operating expenses rose 8.1% to US$823.0 million from US$761.5 million in the comparable period the year before. Indirect operating expenses increased 9.3% to US$437.7 million from US$400.3 million in the equivalent prior-year period.

Prospects: Our evaluation of Robert Half International Inc. as of Jan. 21, 2018 is the result of our systematic analysis on three basic characteristics: earnings strength, relative valuation, and recent stock price movement. The company has managed to produce a neutral trend in earnings per share over the past 5 quarters. However, while recent estimates for the company have been mixed, RHI has posted results that fell short of analysts expectations. Based on operating earnings yield, the company is about fairly valued when compared to all of the companies in our coverage universe. Share price changes over the past year indicates that RHI will perform in line with the market over the near term.

Financial Data
(US$ in Thousands)

	3 Mos	12/31/2017	12/31/2016	12/31/2015	12/31/2014	12/31/2013	12/31/2012	12/31/2011
Earnings Per Share	2.49	2.33	2.67	2.69	2.26	1.83	1.50	1.04
Cash Flow Per Share	3.66	3.65	3.44	3.33	2.54	2.27	2.09	1.82
Tang Book Value Per Share	7.28	7.16	6.83	6.03	5.77	5.22	4.58	4.30
Dividends Per Share	1.000	0.960	0.880	0.800	0.720	0.640	0.600	0.560
Dividend Payout %	40.16	41.20	32.96	29.74	31.86	34.97	40.00	53.85
Income Statement								
Total Revenue	1,395,333	5,266,789	5,250,399	5,094,933	4,695,014	4,245,895	4,111,213	3,776,976
EBITDA	150,620	581,210	617,537	633,945	546,306	445,349	391,772	300,680
Depn & Amortn	16,716	65,493	64,315	53,465	49,681	48,772	48,724	51,415
Income Before Taxes	134,639	517,516	554,110	581,030	497,349	397,579	344,245	250,216
Income Taxes	38,472	226,932	210,721	223,234	191,421	145,384	134,303	100,294
Net Income	96,167	290,584	343,389	357,796	305,928	252,195	209,942	149,922
Average Shares	122,887	124,892	128,766	132,930	135,541	137,589	139,409	141,790
Balance Sheet								
Current Assets	1,468,456	1,431,869	1,284,234	1,343,681	1,323,283	1,172,528	1,064,685	1,006,678
Total Assets	1,893,860	1,867,454	1,777,971	1,702,960	1,647,267	1,490,271	1,381,271	1,311,836
Current Liabilities	764,440	747,896	679,896	655,549	623,362	535,853	501,637	473,001
Long-Term Obligations	608	657	840	1,007	1,159	1,300	1,428	1,545
Total Liabilities	779,063	762,189	691,372	699,179	667,409	570,628	539,260	511,331
Stockholders' Equity	1,114,797	1,105,265	1,086,599	1,003,781	979,858	919,643	842,011	800,505
Shares Outstanding	123,562	124,261	127,796	131,156	135,134	137,466	139,438	142,085
Statistical Record								
Return on Assets %	16.80	15.94	19.68	21.36	19.50	17.57	15.55	11.60
Return on Equity %	28.08	26.51	32.76	36.07	32.21	28.63	25.49	18.34
EBITDA Margin %	10.79	11.04	11.76	12.44	11.64	10.49	9.53	7.96
Net Margin %	6.89	5.52	6.54	7.02	6.52	5.94	5.11	3.97
Asset Turnover	2.93	2.89	3.01	3.04	2.99	2.96	3.04	2.92
Current Ratio	1.92	1.91	1.89	2.05	2.12	2.19	2.12	2.13
Price Range	60.51-43.24	57.04-43.24	49.24-34.57	63.00-44.95	58.99-39.17	42.10-31.33	31.82-25.24	33.85-20.06
P/E Ratio	24.30-17.37	24.48-18.56	18.44-12.95	23.42-16.71	26.10-17.33	23.01-17.12	21.21-16.83	32.55-19.29
Average Yield %	1.97	1.97	2.15	1.45	1.52	1.76	2.12	2.04

Address: 2884 Sand Hill Road, Suite 200, Menlo Park, CA 94025	Web Site: www.roberthalf.com	Auditors: PricewaterhouseCoopers LLP
Telephone: 650-234-6000	Officers: Harold M. Messmer - Chairman, President, Chief Executive Officer M. Keith Waddell - Vice-Chairman, President, Chief Financial Officer, Treasurer	Transfer Agents: Computershare Trust Company, N.A., Canton, MA

ROCKWELL COLLINS INC

Exchange	Symbol	Price	52Wk Range	Yield	P/E
NYS	COL	$134.68 (6/29/2018)	139.41-105.08	0.98	24.27

*7 Year Price Score 126.60 *NYSE Composite Index=100 *12 Month Price Score 101.86

Interim Earnings (Per Share)

Qtr.	Dec	Mar	Jun	Sep
2014-15	1.24	1.17	1.33	1.38
2015-16	1.02	1.29	1.63	1.58
2016-17	1.10	1.27	1.12	1.31
2017-18	1.69	1.43	...	...

Interim Dividends (Per Share)

Amt	Decl	Ex	Rec	Pay
0.33Q	08/01/2017	08/10/2017	08/14/2017	09/05/2017
0.33Q	10/31/2017	11/10/2017	11/13/2017	12/04/2017
0.33Q	02/01/2018	02/09/2018	02/12/2018	03/05/2018
0.33Q	04/19/2018	05/14/2018	05/15/2018	06/04/2018

Indicated Div: $1.32

Valuation Analysis

		Institutional Holding	
Forecast EPS	$7.24	No of Institutions	948
	(06/14/2018)		
Market Cap	$22.1 Billion	Shares	134,528,896
Book Value	$6.6 Billion	% Held	69.71
Price/Book	3.33		
Price/Sales	2.61		

Business Summary: Aerospace (MIC: 7.1.1 SIC: 3728 NAIC: 336413)

Rockwell Collins designs, produces and supports communications and aviation systems for commercial and military customers and provides information management services through voice and data communication networks and solutions worldwide. Co. also provides a range of services and support to its customers through a network of service centers, including equipment repair and overhaul, service parts, field service engineering, training, technical information services and aftermarket used equipment sales. As of Sept 30 2017, Co. served customer through its Interior Systems, Commercial Systems, Government Systems and Information Management Services operating segments.

Recent Developments: For the quarter ended Mar 31 2018, net income increased 41.1% to US$237.0 million from US$168.0 million in the year-earlier quarter. Revenues were US$2.18 billion, up 62.4% from US$1.34 billion the year before. Direct operating expenses rose 71.8% to US$1.60 billion from US$930.0 million in the comparable period the year before. Indirect operating expenses increased 54.2% to US$276.0 million from US$179.0 million in the equivalent prior-year period.

Prospects: Our evaluation of Rockwell Collins Inc. as of Jan. 21, 2018 is the result of our systematic analysis on three basic characteristics: earnings strength, relative valuation, and recent stock price movement. The company has enjoyed a very positive trend in earnings per share over the past 5 quarters and while recent estimates for the company have been raised by analysts, COL has posted results that were in line with analysts expectations. Based on operating earnings yield, the company is undervalued when compared to all of the companies in our coverage universe. Share price changes over the past year indicates that COL will perform very well over the near term.

Financial Data

(US$ in Millions)	6 Mos	3 Mos	09/30/2017	09/30/2016	09/30/2015	09/30/2014	09/30/2013	09/30/2012
Earnings Per Share	5.55	5.39	4.79	5.51	5.13	4.42	4.58	4.15
Cash Flow Per Share	7.23	6.77	8.69	5.53	5.66	4.89	4.52	3.67
Tang Book Value Per Share	N.M.	N.M.	N.M.	N.M.	N.M.	N.M.	4.08	1.32
Dividends Per Share	1.320	1.320	1.320	1.320	1.260	1.200	1.200	1.080
Dividend Payout %	23.78	24.49	27.56	23.96	24.56	27.15	26.20	26.02
Income Statement								
Total Revenue	4,191	2,011	6,822	5,259	5,244	4,979	4,610	4,726
EBITDA	916	437	1,286	1,143	1,172	1,075	1,061	1,044
Depn & Amortn	223	116	168	144	152	141	180	174
Income Before Taxes	563	257	931	935	959	875	855	846
Income Taxes	46	(23)	226	208	268	264	236	248
Net Income	517	280	705	728	686	604	632	609
Average Shares	165	165	147	132	133	136	138	146
Balance Sheet								
Current Assets	5,143	4,826	4,760	3,490	3,233	3,204	3,094	2,787
Total Assets	18,300	18,052	17,997	7,707	7,389	7,063	5,400	5,314
Current Liabilities	3,193	3,094	3,069	2,346	2,144	2,198	1,981	1,440
Long-Term Obligations	6,456	6,498	6,676	1,382	1,680	1,663	563	779
Total Liabilities	11,667	11,698	11,954	5,629	5,514	5,179	3,782	4,055
Stockholders' Equity	6,633	6,354	6,043	2,078	1,875	1,884	1,618	1,259
Shares Outstanding	164	163	162	130	131	134	135	142
Statistical Record								
Return on Assets %	6.97	6.52	5.49	9.62	9.49	9.69	11.80	11.35
Return on Equity %	20.14	19.64	17.36	36.73	36.50	34.49	43.93	43.66
EBITDA Margin %	21.86	21.73	18.85	21.73	22.35	21.59	23.02	22.09
Net Margin %	12.34	13.92	10.33	13.84	13.08	12.13	13.71	12.89
Asset Turnover	0.65	0.59	0.53	0.69	0.73	0.80	0.86	0.88
Current Ratio	1.61	1.56	1.55	1.49	1.51	1.46	1.56	1.94
Debt to Equity	0.97	1.02	1.10	0.67	0.90	0.88	0.35	0.62
Price Range	139.41-96.63	136.02-89.21	131.35-79.21	94.44-78.30	99.00-73.48	83.47-65.90	74.69-52.59	59.96-46.92
P/E Ratio	25.12-17.41	25.24-16.55	27.42-16.54	17.14-14.21	19.30-14.32	18.88-14.91	16.31-11.48	14.45-11.31
Average Yield %	1.07	1.16	1.30	1.51	1.43	1.57	1.91	2.01

Address: 400 Collins Road N.E., Cedar Rapids, IA 52498 **Telephone:** 319-295-1000	**Web Site:** www.rockwellcollins.com **Officers:** Robert K. Ortberg - Chairman, President, Chief Executive Officer, Executive Vice President, Division Officer Patrick E. Allen - Senior Vice President, Chief Financial Officer	**Auditors:** DELOITTE & TOUCHE LLP **Investor Contact:** 319-295-7575 **Transfer Agents:** Wells Fargo Shareowner Services, St. Paul, MN

599

ROCKWELL AUTOMATION, INC.

Exchange	Symbol	Price	52Wk Range	Yield	P/E
NYS	ROK	$166.23 (6/29/2018)	207.92-159.57	2.21	52.27

*7 Year Price Score 125.93 *NYSE Composite Index=100   *12 Month Price Score 95.20

Interim Earnings (Per Share)

Qtr.	Dec	Mar	Jun	Sep
2014-15	1.56	1.51	1.52	1.49
2015-16	1.40	1.28	1.46	1.43
2016-17	1.65	1.45	1.67	1.58
2017-18	(1.84)	1.77	...	...

Interim Dividends (Per Share)

Amt	Decl	Ex	Rec	Pay
0.835Q	11/01/2017	11/10/2017	11/13/2017	12/11/2017
0.835Q	02/07/2018	02/16/2018	02/20/2018	03/12/2018
0.92Q	04/25/2018	05/11/2018	05/14/2018	06/11/2018
0.92Q	06/06/2018	08/10/2018	08/13/2018	09/10/2018

Indicated Div: $3.68

Valuation Analysis   Institutional Holding

Forecast EPS	$7.90	No of Institutions	
	(06/14/2018)	1107	
Market Cap	$20.9 Billion	Shares	
Book Value	$1.9 Billion	117,864,336	
Price/Book	10.72	% Held	
Price/Sales	3.21	71.50	

Business Summary: Electrical Equipment (MIC: 7.3.1 SIC: 3829 NAIC: 334519)

Rockwell Automation is a provider of industrial automation and information. As of Sept 30 2017, Co. operated two operating segments: Architecture & Software and Control Products & Solutions. Co.'s Architecture & Software segment contains all of the hardware, software and communication components of Co.'s integrated control and information architecture which are of controlling the customer's industrial processes and connecting with their business enterprise. Co.'s Control Products & Solutions segment combines a portfolio of motor control and industrial control products, application knowledge and project management capabilities.

Recent Developments: For the quarter ended Mar 31 2018, net income increased 20.0% to US$227.4 million from US$189.5 million in the year-earlier quarter. Revenues were US$1.65 billion, up 6.2% from US$1.55 billion the year before. Direct operating expenses rose 5.9% to US$950.4 million from US$897.8 million in the comparable period the year before. Indirect operating expenses decreased 5.9% to US$401.2 million from US$426.2 million in the equivalent prior-year period.

Prospects: Our evaluation of Rockwell Automation Inc. as of Jan. 21, 2018 is the result of our systematic analysis on three basic characteristics: earnings strength, relative valuation, and recent stock price movement. The company has generated a negative trend in earnings per share over the past 5 quarters and while recent estimates for the company have been raised by analysts, ROK has posted results that fell short of analysts expectations. Based on operating earnings yield, the company is about fairly valued when compared to all of the companies in our coverage universe. Share price changes over the past year indicates that ROK will perform well over the near term.

Financial Data

(US$ in Thousands)	6 Mos	3 Mos	09/30/2017	09/30/2016	09/30/2015	09/30/2014	09/30/2013	09/30/2012
Earnings Per Share	3.18	2.86	6.35	5.56	6.09	5.91	5.36	5.13
Cash Flow Per Share	8.01	7.30	8.05	7.26	8.83	7.49	7.29	5.07
Tang Book Value Per Share	4.87	6.57	10.50	5.14	7.54	9.96	9.72	4.96
Dividends Per Share	3.190	3.115	3.040	2.900	2.600	2.320	1.980	1.745
Dividend Payout %	100.31	108.92	47.87	52.16	42.69	39.26	36.94	34.02
Income Statement								
Total Revenue	3,237,800	1,586,600	6,311,300	5,879,500	6,307,900	6,623,500	6,351,900	6,259,400
EBITDA	717,500	357,400	1,262,900	1,173,900	1,343,000	1,336,500	1,177,200	1,156,800
Depn & Amortn	82,800	39,600	168,900	172,200	162,500	152,500	145,200	138,600
Income Before Taxes	597,400	297,800	1,037,400	943,100	1,127,500	1,134,200	980,900	965,900
Income Taxes	606,400	534,200	211,700	213,400	299,900	307,400	224,600	228,900
Net Income	(9,000)	(236,400)	825,700	729,700	827,600	826,800	756,300	737,000
Average Shares	128,500	128,200	129,900	131,100	135,700	139,700	140,900	143,400
Balance Sheet								
Current Assets	3,940,900	4,533,900	4,420,700	4,185,000	4,048,000	3,934,200	3,679,900	3,387,500
Total Assets	6,513,600	7,158,700	7,161,700	7,101,200	6,404,700	6,229,500	5,844,600	5,636,500
Current Liabilities	1,877,800	2,286,600	2,145,800	1,975,900	1,327,700	1,692,100	1,544,700	1,531,600
Long-Term Obligations	1,229,800	1,239,300	1,243,400	1,516,300	1,500,900	905,600	905,100	905,000
Total Liabilities	4,566,400	5,002,500	4,498,100	5,111,100	4,147,900	3,571,400	3,259,100	3,784,800
Stockholders' Equity	1,947,200	2,156,200	2,663,600	1,990,100	2,256,800	2,658,100	2,585,500	1,851,700
Shares Outstanding	125,580	127,800	128,400	128,500	132,400	136,700	138,900	139,800
Statistical Record								
Return on Assets %	6.08	5.26	11.58	10.78	13.10	13.70	13.17	13.46
Return on Equity %	19.90	17.81	35.49	34.27	33.68	31.54	34.09	40.84
EBITDA Margin %	22.16	22.53	20.01	19.97	21.29	20.18	18.53	18.48
Net Margin %	N.M.	N.M.	13.08	12.41	13.12	12.48	11.91	11.77
Asset Turnover	0.96	0.90	0.88	0.87	1.00	1.10	1.11	1.14
Current Ratio	2.10	1.98	2.06	2.12	3.05	2.33	2.38	2.21
Debt to Equity	0.63	0.57	0.47	0.76	0.67	0.34	0.35	0.49
Price Range	207.92-148.43	200.83-137.74	178.21-115.20	122.34-89.71	126.89-98.60	127.83-104.39	109.13-68.73	84.55-54.55
P/E Ratio	65.38-46.68	70.22-48.16	28.06-18.14	22.00-16.13	20.84-16.19	21.63-17.66	20.36-12.82	16.48-10.63
Average Yield %	1.81	1.88	2.02	2.65	2.28	1.97	2.27	2.39

Address: 1201 South Second Street,	Web Site: www.rockwellautomation.com	Auditors: DELOITTE & TOUCHE LLP
Milwaukee, WI 53204	Officers: Keith D. Nosbusch - Chairman, President,	Investor Contact: 414-382-8510
Telephone: 414-382-2000	Chief Executive Officer Blake D. Moret - President,	Transfer Agents: Wells Fargo
	Chief Executive Officer, Senior Vice President	Shareowner Services, St. Paul, MN

ROLLINS, INC.

Exchange	Symbol	Price	52Wk Range	Yield	P/E	Div Acheiver
NYS	ROL	$52.58 (6/29/2018)	53.95-40.28	1.07	61.14	15 Years

*7 Year Price Score 148.45 *NYSE Composite Index=100 *12 Month Price Score 105.57

Interim Earnings (Per Share)

Qtr.	Mar	Jun	Sep	Dec
2015	0.14	0.21	0.21	0.15
2016	0.15	0.22	0.23	0.18
2017	0.18	0.25	0.24	0.15
2018	0.22	...	...	...

Interim Dividends (Per Share)

Amt	Decl	Ex	Rec	Pay
0.10Q	10/24/2017	11/09/2017	11/10/2017	12/11/2017
0.115Q	10/24/2017	11/09/2017	11/10/2017	12/11/2017
0.14Q	01/23/2018	02/08/2018	02/09/2018	03/09/2018
0.14Q	04/24/2018	05/09/2018	05/10/2018	06/11/2018

Indicated Div: $0.56

Valuation Analysis

		Institutional Holding	
Forecast EPS	$1.09	No of Institutions	426
	(06/07/2018)		
Market Cap	$11.5 Billion	Shares	101,796,240
Book Value	$662.8 Million	% Held	33.37
Price/Book	17.31		
Price/Sales	6.72		

Business Summary: Business Services (MIC: 7.5.2 SIC: 7342 NAIC: 561710)

Rollins provides pest and termite control services via its subsidiaries in North America, Australia, and Europe with international franchises in Central America, the Caribbean, the Middle East, Asia, the Mediterranean, Europe, Africa, Canada, Australia, and Mexico. Co.'s subsidiary, Orkin, LLC, provides pest control services and protection against termite damage, rodents and insects to homes and businesses. Co.'s other subsidiaries include Orkin Canada, a pest control provider in Canada; Western Pest Services, which is primarily a commercial pest control service company; and The Industrial Fumigant Company, which is a provider of pest management and sanitation services and products.

Recent Developments: For the quarter ended Mar 31 2018, net income increased 20.5% to US$48.5 million from US$40.3 million in the year-earlier quarter. Revenues were US$408.7 million, up 8.9% from US$375.2 million the year before. Direct operating expenses rose 9.0% to US$206.1 million from US$189.2 million in the comparable period the year before. Indirect operating expenses increased 11.3% to US$143.4 million from US$128.8 million in the equivalent prior-year period.

Prospects: Our evaluation of Rollins Inc. as of Jan. 21, 2018 is the result of our systematic analysis on three basic characteristics: earnings strength, relative valuation, and recent stock price movement. The company has produced a positive trend in earnings per share over the past 5 quarters and while recent estimates for the company have remained steady, ROL has posted results that fell short of analysts expectations. Based on operating earnings yield, the company is overvalued when compared to all of the companies in our coverage universe. Share price changes over the past year indicates that ROL will perform very well over the near term.

Financial Data

(US$ in Thousands)	3 Mos	12/31/2017	12/31/2016	12/31/2015	12/31/2014	12/31/2013	12/31/2012	12/31/2011
Earnings Per Share	0.86	0.82	0.77	0.70	0.63	0.56	0.51	0.46
Cash Flow Per Share	1.15	1.08	1.04	0.90	0.89	0.74	0.64	0.70
Tang Book Value Per Share	0.28	0.43	0.69	0.62	0.34	0.45	0.00	N.M.
Dividends Per Share	0.585	0.560	0.500	0.420	0.347	0.300	0.293	0.187
Dividend Payout %	68.02	68.29	64.94	60.00	55.32	53.57	57.89	40.58
Income Statement								
Total Revenue	408,742	1,673,957	1,573,477	1,485,305	1,411,566	1,337,374	1,270,909	1,205,064
EBITDA	76,168	321,643	285,176	262,418	235,857	205,636	191,868	176,716
Depn & Amortn	16,916	27,400	24,700	19,400	16,627	14,415	15,212	15,112
Income Before Taxes	59,194	294,502	260,636	243,178	219,484	191,606	176,642	161,096
Income Taxes	10,669	115,378	93,267	91,029	81,820	68,276	65,310	60,385
Net Income	48,525	179,124	167,369	152,149	137,664	123,330	111,332	100,711
Average Shares	218,163	217,988	218,244	218,583	218,694	219,121	219,459	220,419
Balance Sheet								
Current Assets	240,704	262,795	290,171	313,879	283,958	274,442	205,992	175,822
Total Assets	1,050,696	1,033,663	916,538	852,431	808,162	739,217	692,506	645,650
Current Liabilities	299,073	294,569	276,991	252,986	252,679	235,792	228,416	225,851
Total Liabilities	387,933	379,739	347,993	328,402	345,486	300,962	337,550	321,653
Stockholders' Equity	662,763	653,924	568,545	524,029	462,676	438,255	354,956	323,997
Shares Outstanding	218,186	217,992	217,791	218,753	218,482	218,796	219,022	219,376
Statistical Record								
Return on Assets %	18.97	18.37	18.87	18.32	17.79	17.23	16.59	15.93
Return on Equity %	30.07	29.31	30.55	30.84	30.56	31.10	32.71	32.38
EBITDA Margin %	18.63	19.21	18.12	17.67	16.71	15.38	15.10	14.66
Net Margin %	11.87	10.70	10.64	10.24	9.75	9.22	8.76	8.36
Asset Turnover	1.73	1.72	1.77	1.79	1.82	1.87	1.89	1.91
Current Ratio	0.80	0.89	1.05	1.24	1.12	1.16	0.90	0.78
Price Range	52.87-35.97	47.81-32.91	34.09-24.08	30.35-21.27	22.53-18.10	20.26-14.69	16.19-12.97	15.61-11.15
P/E Ratio	61.48-41.83	58.30-40.13	44.27-31.27	43.36-30.39	35.76-28.73	36.18-26.24	31.75-25.44	33.94-24.23
Average Yield %	1.31	1.35	1.75	1.62	1.72	1.75	1.99	1.40

Address: 2170 Piedmont Road, N.E., Atlanta, GA 30324 **Telephone:** 404-888-2000	**Web Site:** www.rollins.com **Officers:** R. Randall Rollins - Chairman Gary W. Rollins - Vice-Chairman, President, Chief Executive Officer, Chief Operating Officer	**Auditors:** GRANT THORNTON LLP **Investor Contact:** 404-888-2000 **Transfer Agents:** American Stock Transfer and Trust, Brooklyn, NY

ROPER TECHNOLOGIES INC

Exchange	Symbol	Price	52Wk Range	Yield	P/E	Div Acheiver
NYS	ROP	$275.91 (6/29/2018)	289.86-227.79	0.60	27.90	25 Years

*7 Year Price Score 130.45 *NYSE Composite Index=100 *12 Month Price Score 104.43

TRADING VOLUME (thousand shares)

Interim Earnings (Per Share)

Qtr.	Mar	Jun	Sep	Dec
2015	1.54	1.69	1.58	2.05
2016	1.48	1.54	1.63	1.78
2017	1.53	1.74	1.84	4.28
2018	2.03	...	...	...

Interim Dividends (Per Share)

Amt	Decl	Ex	Rec	Pay
0.35Q	09/25/2017	10/05/2017	10/06/2017	10/20/2017
0.412Q	12/18/2017	01/08/2018	01/09/2018	01/23/2018
0.412Q	03/12/2018	04/06/2018	04/09/2018	04/23/2018
0.412Q	06/11/2018	07/06/2018	07/09/2018	07/23/2018

Indicated Div: $1.65

Valuation Analysis / Institutional Holding

Forecast EPS	$11.31 (06/13/2018)	No of Institutions	942
Market Cap	$28.5 Billion	Shares	119,720,320
Book Value	$7.2 Billion	% Held	93.85
Price/Book	3.98		
Price/Sales	6.03		

Business Summary: Electrical Equipment (MIC: 7.3.1 SIC: 3823 NAIC: 334513)

Roper Technologies designs and develops software (both license and software-as-a-service) and engineered products and solutions. Co. has four segments: Medical and Scientific Imaging, which provides products and software in medical applications, and digital imaging products; Radio Frequency Technology, which provides radio frequency identification communication technology and software solutions; Industrial Technology, which produces fluid handling pumps, materials analysis equipment and consumables, and leak testing equipment, among others; and Energy Systems and Controls, which produces control systems, fluid properties testing equipment, and industrial valves and controls, among others.

Recent Developments: For the quarter ended Mar 31 2018, net income increased 33.6% to US$211.3 million from US$158.1 million in the year-earlier quarter. Revenues were US$1.20 billion, up 10.7% from US$1.09 billion the year before. Operating income was US$300.2 million versus US$258.3 million in the prior-year quarter, an increase of 16.2%. Direct operating expenses rose 8.0% to US$452.0 million from US$418.7 million in the comparable period the year before. Indirect operating expenses increased 10.0% to US$450.3 million from US$409.3 million in the equivalent prior-year period.

Prospects: Our evaluation of Roper Technologies Inc. as of Jan. 21, 2018 is the result of our systematic analysis on three basic characteristics: earnings strength, relative valuation, and recent stock price movement. The company has produced a positive trend in earnings per share over the past 5 quarters and while recent estimates for the company have been mixed, ROP has posted better than expected results. Based on operating earnings yield, the company is about fairly valued when compared to all of the companies in our coverage universe. Share price changes over the past year indicates that ROP will perform well over the near term.

Financial Data
(US$ in Thousands)

	3 Mos	12/31/2017	12/31/2016	12/31/2015	12/31/2014	12/31/2013	12/31/2012	12/31/2011
Earnings Per Share	9.89	9.39	6.43	6.85	6.40	5.37	4.86	4.34
Cash Flow Per Share	11.06	12.08	9.49	9.23	8.41	8.10	6.92	6.27
Dividends Per Share	1.462	1.400	1.200	1.000	0.800	0.495	0.715	0.440
Dividend Payout %	14.79	14.91	18.66	14.60	12.50	9.22	14.71	10.14
Income Statement								
Total Revenue	1,202,500	4,607,471	3,789,925	3,582,395	3,549,494	3,238,128	2,993,489	2,797,089
EBITDA	375,400	1,560,254	1,292,664	1,290,831	1,197,377	1,031,359	908,954	808,778
Depn & Amortn	76,900	344,965	240,453	204,261	197,284	189,190	154,748	140,143
Income Before Taxes	255,300	1,034,723	940,652	1,002,345	921,456	754,130	686,681	604,987
Income Taxes	44,000	62,951	282,007	306,278	275,423	215,837	203,321	177,740
Net Income	211,300	971,772	658,645	696,067	646,033	538,293	483,360	427,247
Average Shares	104,200	103,522	102,464	101,597	100,884	100,209	99,558	98,386
Balance Sheet								
Current Assets	1,502,000	1,759,402	1,776,501	1,618,047	1,512,105	1,373,337	1,245,542	1,115,473
Total Assets	14,074,100	14,316,413	14,324,927	10,168,365	8,412,934	8,184,981	7,071,104	5,319,417
Current Liabilities	2,047,500	2,029,409	1,445,272	720,128	627,947	643,091	1,086,210	554,196
Long-Term Obligations	3,820,700	4,354,611	5,808,561	3,264,417	2,203,031	2,453,836	1,503,107	1,015,110
Total Liabilities	6,918,600	7,452,849	8,536,062	4,869,418	3,657,574	3,971,931	3,383,378	2,124,321
Stockholders' Equity	7,155,500	6,863,564	5,788,865	5,298,947	4,755,360	4,213,050	3,687,726	3,195,096
Shares Outstanding	103,160	102,493	101,672	100,870	100,126	99,312	98,604	96,678
Statistical Record								
Return on Assets %	7.24	6.79	5.36	7.49	7.78	7.06	7.78	8.23
Return on Equity %	15.62	15.36	11.85	13.85	14.41	13.63	14.01	14.37
EBITDA Margin %	31.22	33.86	34.11	36.03	33.73	31.85	30.36	28.91
Net Margin %	17.57	21.09	17.38	19.43	18.20	16.62	16.15	15.27
Asset Turnover	0.33	0.32	0.31	0.39	0.43	0.42	0.48	0.54
Current Ratio	0.73	0.87	1.23	2.25	2.41	2.14	1.15	2.01
Debt to Equity	0.53	0.63	1.00	0.62	0.46	0.58	0.41	0.32
Price Range	289.86-205.01	267.21-184.93	189.79-158.89	194.83-145.75	160.48-128.99	138.68-111.48	113.14-88.02	88.45-65.91
P/E Ratio	29.31-20.73	28.46-19.69	29.52-24.71	28.44-21.28	25.07-20.15	25.82-20.76	23.28-18.11	20.38-15.19
Average Yield %	0.59	0.61	0.68	0.58	0.56	0.39	0.70	0.55

Address: 6901 Professional Parkway East, Suite 200, Sarasota, FL 34240 Telephone: 941-556-2601	Web Site: www.ropertech.com Officers: Brian D. Jellison - Chairman, President, Chief Executive Officer Laurence Neil Hunn - Executive Vice President, Chief Operating Officer	Auditors: PricewaterhouseCoopers LLP Investor Contact: 941-556-2601 Transfer Agents: American Stock Transfer & Trust Company, New York, NY

ROWAN COMPANIES PLC

| Exchange NYS | Symbol RDC | Price $16.22 (6/29/2018) | 52Wk Range 17.20-9.04 | Yield N/A | P/E N/A |

*7 Year Price Score 43.91   *NYSE Composite Index=100   *12 Month Price Score 112.51

Interim Earnings (Per Share)

Qtr.	Mar	Jun	Sep	Dec
2015	0.99	0.68	(1.92)	1.00
2016	0.98	1.72	0.04	(0.18)
2017	0.07	(0.23)	(0.17)	0.88
2018	(0.89)	...	...	...

Interim Dividends (Per Share)

Dividend Payment Suspended

Valuation Analysis   **Institutional Holding**

Forecast EPS	N/A	No of Institutions
		393
Market Cap	$2.1 Billion	Shares
Book Value	$5.3 Billion	159,559,184
Price/Book	0.39	% Held
Price/Sales	1.84	N/A

Business Summary: Equipment & Services (MIC: 9.1.3 SIC: 1381 NAIC: 213111)

Rowan Companies is a provider of offshore contract drilling services to the international oil and gas industry. As of Dec 31 2017, Co.'s fleet consisted of 23 self-elevating jack-up rigs and four ultra-deepwater drillships. Through a 50/50 joint venture, Co. also owns 5 self-elevating jack-up rigs. Co.'s fleet operates worldwide, including the U.S. Gulf of Mexico, the U.K. and Norwegian sectors of the North Sea, the Middle East and Trinidad. Co.'s ultra-deepwater drillships are self-propelled vessels equipped with computer-controlled dynamic-positioning systems, which allow them to maintain position without anchors through the use of their onboard propulsion and station-keeping systems.

Recent Developments: For the quarter ended Mar 31 2018, net loss amounted to US$112.3 million versus net income of US$10.3 million in the year-earlier quarter. Revenues were US$211.2 million, down 43.6% from US$374.3 million the year before. Operating loss was US$72.3 million versus an income of US$76.3 million in the prior-year quarter. Direct operating expenses declined 8.1% to US$157.4 million from US$171.3 million in the comparable period the year before. Indirect operating expenses decreased 0.5% to US$126.1 million from US$126.7 million in the equivalent prior-year period.

Prospects: Our evaluation of Rowan Cos. Plc as of Sep. 17, 2017 is the result of our systematic analysis on three basic characteristics: earnings strength, relative valuation, and recent stock price movement. The company has managed to produce a neutral trend in earnings per share over the past 5 quarters. Because the company lacks sufficient analyst estimate data, we place greater weight on the historical EPS trend as the measure of earnings strength. Based on operating earnings yield, the company is overvalued when compared to all of the companies in our coverage universe. Share price changes over the past year indicates that RDC will perform very poorly over the near term.

Financial Data

(US$ in Thousands)	3 Mos	12/31/2017	12/31/2016	12/31/2015	12/31/2014	12/31/2013	12/31/2012	12/31/2011
Earnings Per Share	(0.41)	0.57	2.55	0.75	(0.93)	2.03	1.46	5.83
Cash Flow Per Share	1.64	2.38	7.17	8.01	3.41	5.05	3.19	0.76
Tang Book Value Per Share	41.63	42.65	40.75	38.24	37.65	39.39	36.48	35.01
Income Statement								
Total Revenue	211,200	1,282,800	1,843,200	2,137,018	1,824,383	1,579,284	1,392,607	939,229
EBITDA	24,700	642,400	880,200	694,633	155,107	600,463	481,342	354,293
Depn & Amortn	97,900	403,700	402,900	392,735	322,641	271,008	247,900	204,872
Income Before Taxes	(104,800)	98,400	325,600	157,710	(269,607)	261,239	183,470	130,080
Income Taxes	6,200	26,600	5,000	64,399	(150,732)	8,663	(19,829)	(5,659)
Net Income	(112,300)	72,700	320,600	93,311	(114,852)	252,576	180,602	736,841
Average Shares	126,500	127,700	126,300	125,203	124,067	124,468	123,872	126,393
Balance Sheet								
Current Assets	1,432,200	1,560,400	1,580,300	921,275	941,096	1,528,878	1,552,550	821,715
Total Assets	8,328,000	8,458,300	8,675,600	8,347,267	8,411,192	7,975,761	7,699,487	6,597,845
Current Liabilities	237,500	257,400	483,800	328,671	333,221	354,584	294,094	348,371
Long-Term Obligations	2,510,500	2,510,300	2,553,400	2,692,419	2,807,324	2,008,700	2,009,598	1,089,335
Total Liabilities	3,044,800	3,072,200	3,561,700	3,574,808	3,719,793	3,082,000	3,167,763	2,271,858
Stockholders' Equity	5,283,200	5,386,100	5,113,900	4,772,459	4,691,399	4,893,761	4,531,724	4,325,987
Shares Outstanding	126,900	126,300	125,500	124,817	124,593	124,235	124,211	123,581
Statistical Record								
Return on Assets %	N.M.	0.85	3.76	1.11	N.M.	3.22	2.52	11.50
Return on Equity %	N.M.	1.38	6.47	1.97	N.M.	5.36	4.07	18.24
EBITDA Margin %	11.70	50.08	47.75	32.50	8.50	38.02	34.56	37.72
Net Margin %	N.M.	5.67	17.39	4.37	N.M.	15.99	12.97	78.45
Asset Turnover	0.13	0.15	0.22	0.26	0.22	0.20	0.19	0.15
Current Ratio	6.03	6.06	3.27	2.80	2.82	4.31	5.28	2.36
Debt to Equity	0.48	0.47	0.50	0.56	0.60	0.41	0.44	0.25
Price Range	17.20-9.04	20.19-9.04	20.90-11.23	24.88-15.15	35.36-19.81	38.30-30.50	38.78-28.99	44.19-29.12
P/E Ratio	...	35.42-15.86	8.20-4.40	33.17-20.20	...	18.87-15.02	26.56-19.86	7.58-4.99

Address: 2800 Post Oak Boulevard, Suite 5450, Houston, TX 77056-6189
Telephone: 713-621-7800
Fax: 713-960-7660

Web Site: www.rowancompanies.com
Officers: Thomas Peter Burke - President, Chief Executive Officer, Chief Operating Officer Stephen M. Butz - Executive Vice President, Chief Financial Officer, Treasurer

Auditors: Deloitte & Touche LLP
Investor Contact: 713-960-7517
Transfer Agents: Computershare Trust Company, N.A., Providence

ROYAL CARIBBEAN CRUISES LTD

Exchange	Symbol	Price	52Wk Range	Yield	P/E
NYS	RCL	$103.60 (6/29/2018)	134.98-102.15	2.32	13.70

*7 Year Price Score 142.92 *NYSE Composite Index=100   *12 Month Price Score 89.25

Interim Earnings (Per Share)

Qtr.	Mar	Jun	Sep	Dec
2015	0.20	0.84	1.03	0.94
2016	0.46	1.06	3.21	1.21
2017	0.99	1.71	3.49	1.34
2018	1.02	...	...	...

Interim Dividends (Per Share)

Amt	Decl	Ex	Rec	Pay
0.60Q	09/06/2017	09/21/2017	09/22/2017	10/11/2017
0.60Q	12/05/2017	12/20/2017	12/21/2017	01/05/2018
0.60Q	02/13/2018	03/06/2018	03/07/2018	04/05/2018
0.60Q	05/09/2018	06/01/2018	06/04/2018	07/03/2018

Indicated Div: $2.40

Valuation Analysis

	Institutional Holding	
Forecast EPS	N/A	No of Institutions 865
Market Cap	$21.9 Billion	Shares 175,222,640
Book Value	$10.6 Billion	% Held 50.11
Price/Book	2.06	
Price/Sales	2.49	

TRADING VOLUME (thousand shares)

Business Summary: Hotels, Restaurants & Travel (MIC: 2.2.1 SIC: 4489 NAIC: 487210)

Royal Caribbean Cruises is a cruise company. Co. owns and operates three cruise brands: Royal Caribbean International, Celebrity Cruises, and Azamara Club Cruises. Co. also owns a 50.0% joint venture interest in the German brand TUI Cruises, a 49.0% interest in the Spanish brand Pullmantur and a 36% interest in the Chinese brand SkySea Cruises. Together, these brands operated a combined 49 ships in the cruise vacation industry as of Dec 31 2017, operating on a selection of worldwide itineraries that call on approximately 540 destinations on all seven continents. Co.'s cruise brands provide a range of onboard services, amenities and activities.

Recent Developments: For the quarter ended Mar 31 2018, net income increased 1.8% to US$218.7 million from US$214.7 million in the year-earlier quarter. Revenues were US$2.03 billion, up 1.0% from US$2.01 billion the year before. Operating income was US$274.1 million versus US$279.5 million in the prior-year quarter, a decrease of 1.9%. Direct operating expenses was unchanged at US$1.18 billion versus the comparable period the year before. Indirect operating expenses increased 4.4% to US$577.6 million from US$553.2 million in the equivalent prior-year period.

Prospects: Our evaluation of Royal Caribbean Cruises Ltd. as of Aug. 2, 2015 is the result of our systematic analysis on three basic characteristics: earnings strength, relative valuation, and recent stock price movement. The company has generated a negative trend in earnings per share over the past 5 quarters and while recent estimates for the company have been mixed, RCL has posted better than expected results. Based on operating earnings yield, the company is about fairly valued when compared to all of the companies in our coverage universe. Share price changes over the past year indicates that RCL will perform very poorly over the near term.

Financial Data
(US$ in Thousands)

	3 Mos	12/31/2017	12/31/2016	12/31/2015	12/31/2014	12/31/2013	12/31/2012	12/31/2011
Earnings Per Share	7.56	7.53	5.93	3.02	3.43	2.14	0.08	2.77
Cash Flow Per Share	14.12	13.39	11.65	8.87	7.87	6.43	6.32	6.71
Tang Book Value Per Share	48.92	48.81	41.16	35.67	35.86	37.96	36.00	35.30
Dividends Per Share	...	2.160	1.710	1.350	1.100	0.740	0.440	...
Dividend Payout %	...	28.69	28.84	44.70	32.07	34.58	550.00	...
Income Statement								
Total Revenue	2,027,756	8,777,845	8,496,401	8,299,074	8,073,855	7,959,894	7,688,024	7,537,263
EBITDA	260,154	2,892,151	2,517,612	1,758,491	1,784,546	1,546,927	1,083,234	1,666,945
Depn & Amortn	10,108	997,137	947,710	827,008	772,445	754,711	730,493	702,426
Income Before Taxes	189,901	1,625,133	1,283,388	665,783	764,146	473,692	18,287	607,421
Net Income	218,653	1,625,133	1,283,388	665,783	764,146	473,692	18,287	607,421
Average Shares	213,602	215,694	216,316	220,689	223,044	220,941	219,457	219,229
Balance Sheet								
Current Assets	1,034,526	843,028	748,305	837,022	801,083	956,374	888,060	969,288
Total Assets	23,970,972	22,296,317	22,310,324	20,921,855	20,713,190	20,072,947	19,827,930	19,804,405
Current Liabilities	5,195,154	4,790,264	4,441,601	4,292,827	3,849,247	4,267,010	4,066,151	3,067,642
Long-Term Obligations	7,664,722	6,350,937	8,101,701	7,767,378	7,644,318	6,511,426	6,970,464	7,856,962
Total Liabilities	13,324,176	11,594,014	13,188,912	12,858,816	12,428,831	11,264,682	11,519,181	11,396,582
Stockholders' Equity	10,646,796	10,702,303	9,121,412	8,063,039	8,284,359	8,808,265	8,308,749	8,407,823
Shares Outstanding	211,730	213,337	214,594	217,993	219,297	220,473	218,771	217,057
Statistical Record								
Return on Assets %	7.08	7.29	5.92	3.20	3.75	2.37	0.09	3.08
Return on Equity %	16.36	16.40	14.90	8.15	8.94	5.53	0.22	7.43
EBITDA Margin %	12.83	32.95	29.63	21.19	22.10	19.43	14.09	22.12
Net Margin %	10.78	18.51	15.11	8.02	9.46	5.95	0.24	8.06
Asset Turnover	0.38	0.39	0.39	0.40	0.40	0.40	0.39	0.38
Current Ratio	0.20	0.18	0.17	0.19	0.21	0.22	0.22	0.32
Debt to Equity	0.72	0.59	0.89	0.96	0.92	0.74	0.84	0.93
Price Range	134.98-94.36	129.23-83.87	101.21-65.48	102.73-66.69	83.56-46.06	47.44-31.82	35.53-22.46	49.96-20.01
P/E Ratio	17.85-12.48	17.16-11.14	17.07-11.04	34.02-22.08	24.36-13.43	22.17-14.87	444.13-280.75	18.04-7.22
Average Yield %	...	1.96	2.25	1.59	1.86	1.98	1.54	...

Address: 1050 Caribbean Way, Miami, FL 33132 **Telephone:** 305-539-6000	**Web Site:** www.royalcaribbean.com **Officers:** Richard D. Fain - Chairman, Chief Executive Officer Adam M. Goldstein - President, Chief Operating Officer, Division Officer, Vice-Chairman	**Auditors:** PricewaterhouseCoopers LLP **Investor Contact:** 305-982-2625 **Transfer Agents:** American Stock Transfer and Trust Company, Brooklyn, NY

RPC, INC.

Exchange	Symbol	Price	52Wk Range	Yield	P/E
NYS	RES	$14.57 (6/29/2018)	26.73-13.65	2.75	15.02

7 Year Price Score 103.94 *NYSE Composite Index=100 *12 Month Price Score 78.38

Interim Earnings (Per Share)

Qtr.	Mar	Jun	Sep	Dec
2015	0.04	(0.16)	(0.16)	(0.18)
2016	(0.15)	(0.23)	(0.18)	(0.10)
2017	0.02	0.20	0.26	0.27
2018	0.24	...	...	...

Interim Dividends (Per Share)

Amt	Decl	Ex	Rec	Pay
0.07Q	10/25/2017	11/09/2017	11/10/2017	12/11/2017
0.07Q	10/25/2017	11/09/2017	11/10/2017	12/11/2017
0.10Q	01/24/2018	02/08/2018	02/09/2018	03/09/2018
0.10Q	04/25/2018	05/09/2018	05/10/2018	06/11/2018

Indicated Div: $0.40

Valuation Analysis

		Institutional Holding	
Forecast EPS	$1.19	No of Institutions	
	(06/14/2018)	379	
Market Cap	$3.1 Billion	Shares	
Book Value	$913.7 Million	87,886,880	
Price/Book	3.44	% Held	
Price/Sales	1.81	21.80	

Business Summary: Equipment & Services (MIC: 9.1.3 SIC: 1389 NAIC: 213112)

RPC is a holding company for several oilfield services companies. Co. provides oilfield services and equipment to oil and gas companies engaged in the exploration, production and development of oil and gas properties throughout the U.S., including the southwest, mid-continent, Gulf of Mexico, Rocky Mountain and Appalachian regions, and in selected international markets. The services and equipment provided include: Technical Services, such as pressure pumping services, coiled tubing services, snubbing services, nitrogen services, and firefighting and well control; and Support Services, such as the rental of drill pipe and other oilfield equipment and oilfield training and consulting.

Recent Developments: For the quarter ended Mar 31 2018, net income increased to US$52.1 million from US$3.6 million in the year-earlier quarter. Revenues were US$436.3 million, up 46.4% from US$298.1 million the year before. Operating income was US$60.8 million versus US$1.6 million in the prior-year quarter, an increase of. Direct operating expenses rose 36.7% to US$295.6 million from US$216.2 million in the comparable period the year before. Indirect operating expenses decreased 0.5% to US$79.9 million from US$80.3 million in the equivalent prior-year period.

Prospects: Our evaluation of RPC Inc. as of Jan. 21, 2018 is the result of our systematic analysis on three basic characteristics: earnings strength, relative valuation, and recent stock price movement. The company has enjoyed a very positive trend in earnings per share over the past 5 quarters and while recent estimates for the company have been mixed, RES has posted results that fell short of analysts expectations. Based on operating earnings yield, the company is about fairly valued when compared to all of the companies in our coverage universe. Share price changes over the past year indicates that RES will perform well over the near term.

Financial Data

(US$ in Thousands)	3 Mos	12/31/2017	12/31/2016	12/31/2015	12/31/2014	12/31/2013	12/31/2012	12/31/2011
Earnings Per Share	0.97	0.75	(0.66)	(0.47)	1.14	0.77	1.27	1.35
Cash Flow Per Share	1.20	0.62	0.47	2.22	1.50	1.70	2.59	1.77
Tang Book Value Per Share	4.09	4.06	3.56	4.24	4.83	4.28	3.98	3.34
Dividends Per Share	0.300	0.200	0.050	0.155	0.420	0.400	0.520	0.213
Dividend Payout %	30.93	26.67	...	...	36.84	51.95	40.94	15.84
Income Statement								
Total Revenue	436,334	1,595,227	728,974	1,263,840	2,337,413	1,861,489	1,945,023	1,809,807
EBITDA	104,341	398,648	(18,546)	123,308	634,198	493,073	659,465	662,150
Depn & Amortn	38,148	166,900	220,600	274,400	233,400	215,400	214,900	179,900
Income Before Taxes	66,490	232,816	(239,360)	(153,041)	399,386	276,270	442,619	478,815
Income Taxes	14,360	70,305	(98,114)	(53,480)	154,193	109,375	168,183	182,434
Net Income	52,130	162,511	(141,246)	(99,561)	245,193	166,895	274,436	296,381
Average Shares	213,293	214,303	214,227	213,632	215,889	216,733	216,796	220,249
Balance Sheet								
Current Assets	652,082	640,135	479,057	492,208	851,628	604,925	567,827	626,555
Total Assets	1,181,017	1,147,224	1,035,452	1,237,094	1,759,358	1,383,860	1,367,163	1,338,211
Current Liabilities	178,511	145,360	101,468	107,464	239,012	168,052	164,511	179,466
Long-Term Obligations	...	...	...	...	224,500	53,300	107,000	203,300
Total Liabilities	267,310	235,527	228,653	284,813	680,976	415,158	467,931	575,619
Stockholders' Equity	913,707	911,697	806,799	952,281	1,078,382	968,702	899,232	762,592
Shares Outstanding	215,469	216,543	217,489	216,991	216,539	218,985	220,144	221,187
Statistical Record								
Return on Assets %	18.92	14.89	N.M.	N.M.	15.60	12.13	20.23	26.63
Return on Equity %	24.52	18.91	N.M.	N.M.	23.96	17.87	32.94	45.54
EBITDA Margin %	23.91	24.99	N.M.	9.76	27.13	26.49	33.91	36.59
Net Margin %	11.95	10.19	N.M.	N.M.	10.49	8.97	14.11	16.38
Asset Turnover	1.55	1.46	0.64	0.84	1.49	1.35	1.43	1.63
Current Ratio	3.65	4.40	4.72	4.58	3.56	3.60	3.45	3.49
Debt to Equity	...	...	...	...	0.21	0.06	0.12	0.27
Price Range	26.73-17.05	26.73-16.83	21.63-10.35	16.27-8.54	24.91-11.86	18.56-12.24	14.45-8.96	18.03-10.08
P/E Ratio	27.56-17.58	35.64-22.44	...	...	21.85-10.40	24.10-15.90	11.38-7.06	13.36-7.47
Average Yield %	1.41	0.95	0.33	1.22	2.15	2.62	4.65	1.51

Address: 2801 Buford Highway, Suite 520, Atlanta, GA 30329	**Web Site:** www.rpc.net	**Auditors:** Grant Thornton LLP	
Telephone: 404-321-2140	**Officers:** R. Randall Rollins - Chairman Richard A. Hubbell - President, Chief Executive Officer	**Investor Contact:** 404-321-2140	
		Transfer Agents: American Stock Transfer & Trust Company, Brooklyn, NY	

RPM INTERNATIONAL INC (DE)

Exchange	Symbol	Price	52Wk Range	Yield	P/E	Div Acheiver
NYS	RPM	$58.32 (6/29/2018)	58.32-46.92	2.19	20.75	44 Years

*7 Year Price Score 99.81 *NYSE Composite Index=100 *12 Month Price Score 99.70

Interim Earnings (Per Share)

Qtr.	Aug	Nov	Feb	May
2014-15	0.73	0.52	(0.44)	0.94
2015-16	0.74	0.62	0.14	1.13
2016-17	0.83	(0.54)	0.09	0.95
2017-18	0.86	0.70	0.30	...

Interim Dividends (Per Share)

Amt	Decl	Ex	Rec	Pay
0.32Q	10/05/2017	10/13/2017	10/16/2017	10/31/2017
0.32Q	01/03/2018	01/16/2018	01/17/2018	01/31/2018
0.32Q	04/04/2018	04/16/2018	04/17/2018	04/30/2018
0.32Q	07/03/2018	07/16/2018	07/17/2018	07/31/2018

Indicated Div: $1.28 (Div. Reinv. Plan)

Valuation Analysis		Institutional Holding	
Forecast EPS	$3.07	No of Institutions	
	(06/13/2018)	630	
Market Cap	$7.8 Billion	Shares	
Book Value	$1.6 Billion	130,154,208	
Price/Book	4.77	% Held	
Price/Sales	1.48	67.27	

Business Summary: Specialty Chemicals (MIC: 8.3.2 SIC: 2851 NAIC: 325510)

RPM International, through its subsidiaries, manufactures, markets and sells various chemical product lines including paints, protective coatings, roofing systems, sealants and adhesives, focusing on the maintenance and improvement needs of the industrial, specialty and consumer markets. Co.'s family of products includes those marketed under brand names such as API, Betumat, Carboline, CAVE, DAP, Day-Glo, Dri-Eaz, Dryvit, Euclid, EUCO, Fibergrate, Fibregrid, Fibrecrete, Flecto, Flowcrete, Grupo PV, Hummervoll, illbruck, Mohawk, Prime Resins, and Rust-Oleum, among others. As May 31 2017, Co.'s subsidiaries marketed products in approximately 168 countries and territories.

Recent Developments: For the quarter ended Feb 28 2018, net income increased 220.0% to US$40.6 million from US$12.7 million in the year-earlier quarter. Revenues were US$1.10 billion, up 7.8% from US$1.02 billion the year before. Direct operating expenses rose 11.7% to US$663.2 million from US$593.9 million in the comparable period the year before. Indirect operating expenses decreased 2.0% to US$383.0 million from US$390.9 million in the equivalent prior-year period.

Prospects: Our evaluation of RPM Inc. as of Jan. 21, 2018 is the result of our systematic analysis on three basic characteristics: earnings strength, relative valuation, and recent stock price movement. The company has produced a positive trend in earnings per share over the past 5 quarters and while recent estimates for the company have been raised by analysts, RPM has posted better than expected results. Based on operating earnings yield, the company is undervalued when compared to all of the companies in our coverage universe. Share price changes over the past year indicates that RPM will perform in line with the market over the near term.

Financial Data

(US$ in Thousands)	9 Mos	6 Mos	3 Mos	05/31/2017	05/31/2016	05/31/2015	05/31/2014	05/31/2013
Earnings Per Share	2.81	2.60	1.36	1.36	2.63	1.78	2.18	0.74
Cash Flow Per Share	2.69	2.61	2.69	2.96	3.66	2.54	2.15	2.86
Dividends Per Share	1.240	1.220	1.200	1.175	1.085	1.020	0.945	0.890
Dividend Payout %	44.13	46.92	88.24	86.40	41.25	57.30	43.35	120.27
Income Statement								
Total Revenue	3,763,487	2,660,810	1,345,394	4,958,175	4,813,649	4,594,550	4,376,353	4,078,655
EBITDA	471,517	378,557	212,266	449,424	674,326	625,629	582,966	378,009
Depn & Amortn	96,201	63,631	31,376	113,770	107,232	95,088	86,743	83,415
Income Before Taxes	298,333	263,948	155,011	243,320	481,386	451,230	421,599	221,562
Income Taxes	45,814	51,704	38,381	59,662	126,008	224,925	118,503	67,040
Net Income	252,106	211,879	116,416	181,823	354,725	239,484	291,660	98,603
Average Shares	131,178	135,592	135,720	135,165	136,716	134,893	132,288	128,956
Balance Sheet								
Current Assets	2,357,344	2,395,056	2,362,948	2,397,436	2,138,342	2,099,846	2,062,295	1,886,272
Total Assets	5,135,925	5,144,671	5,108,916	5,090,449	4,776,041	4,694,240	4,378,365	4,115,526
Current Liabilities	922,113	1,074,993	1,095,147	1,235,394	1,002,191	903,236	937,086	928,030
Long-Term Obligations	2,179,658	1,883,272	1,868,229	1,836,437	1,646,332	1,654,037	1,345,965	1,369,176
Total Liabilities	3,502,547	3,537,918	3,549,805	3,654,388	3,403,706	3,402,848	2,995,521	2,914,668
Stockholders' Equity	1,633,378	1,606,753	1,559,111	1,436,061	1,372,335	1,291,392	1,382,844	1,200,858
Shares Outstanding	133,730	133,666	133,537	133,563	132,944	133,203	133,273	132,596
Statistical Record								
Return on Assets %	7.70	7.26	3.77	3.69	7.47	5.28	6.87	2.57
Return on Equity %	26.07	24.37	12.39	12.95	26.56	17.91	22.58	8.27
EBITDA Margin %	12.53	14.23	15.78	9.06	14.01	13.62	13.32	9.27
Net Margin %	6.70	7.96	8.65	3.67	7.37	5.21	6.66	2.42
Asset Turnover	1.07	1.07	1.03	1.01	1.01	1.01	1.03	1.06
Current Ratio	2.56	2.23	2.16	1.94	2.13	2.32	2.20	2.03
Debt to Equity	1.33	1.17	1.20	1.28	1.20	1.28	0.97	1.14
Price Range	56.26-47.98	56.26-48.31	56.26-46.29	56.26-46.29	51.45-37.38	51.82-40.22	44.14-31.20	34.03-25.07
P/E Ratio	20.02-17.07	21.64-18.58	41.37-34.04	41.37-34.04	19.56-14.21	29.11-22.60	20.25-14.31	45.99-33.88
Average Yield %	2.37	2.32	2.28	2.25	2.38	2.17	2.46	3.06

Address: P.O. Box 777, 2628 Pearl Road, Medina, OH 44258	Web Site: www.rpminc.com	Auditors: DELOITTE & TOUCHE LLP
Telephone: 330-273-5090	Officers: Frank C. Sullivan - Chairman, Chief Executive Officer Edward W. Moore - Senior Vice President, Vice President, Chief Compliance Officer, General Counsel, Secretary	Investor Contact: 800-776-4488
Fax: 330-225-8743		Transfer Agents: Wells Fargo Bank, N.A., St. Paul, MN

RSP PERMIAN INC

Exchange	Symbol	Price	52Wk Range	Yield	P/E
NYS	RSPP	$44.02 (6/29/2018)	50.31-29.37	N/A	24.32

*7 Year Price Score N/A   *NYSE Composite Index=100   *12 Month Price Score 114.39

Interim Earnings (Per Share)

Qtr.	Mar	Jun	Sep	Dec
2015	(0.01)	(0.07)	0.10	(0.24)
2016	(0.17)	(0.10)	0.01	0.03
2017	0.26	0.20	0.14	0.90
2018	0.57	...	...	...

Interim Dividends (Per Share)

No Dividends Paid

Valuation Analysis   Institutional Holding

Forecast EPS	$2.36	No of Institutions
	(06/24/2018)	404
Market Cap	$7.0 Billion	Shares
Book Value	$4.4 Billion	151,465,152
Price/Book	1.59	% Held
Price/Sales	7.71	69.23

TRADING VOLUME (thousand shares)

Business Summary: Production & Extraction (MIC: 9.1.1 SIC: 1311 NAIC: 211111)

RSP Permian is an independent oil and natural gas company focused on the acquisition, exploration, development and production of unconventional oil and natural gas reserves in the Permian Basin of West Texas. Co. designs and manages the well development and supervises operation and maintenance activities on a day-to-day basis. Independent contractors engaged by Co. provides all the equipment and personnel associated with these activities. As of Dec 31 2017, Co. had total proved reserves of 375.9 million barrels of oil equivalent, consisting of 261.3 million barrels of oil, 295.02 billion cubic feet of natural gas, and 65.4 million barrels of natural gas liquids.

Recent Developments: For the quarter ended Mar 31 2018, net income increased 130.1% to US$89.6 million from US$38.9 million in the year-earlier quarter. Revenues were US$276.3 million, up 62.6% from US$169.9 million the year before. Operating income was US$130.1 million versus US$55.4 million in the prior-year quarter, an increase of 134.8%. Direct operating expenses rose 38.8% to US$48.4 million from US$34.9 million in the comparable period the year before. Indirect operating expenses increased 22.8% to US$97.9 million from US$79.7 million in the equivalent prior-year period.

Prospects: Our evaluation of RSP Permian Inc. as of Jan. 21, 2018 is the result of our systematic analysis on three basic characteristics: earnings strength, relative valuation, and recent stock price movement. The company has generated a negative trend in earnings per share over the past 5 quarters and while recent estimates for the company have been raised by analysts, RSPP has posted better than expected results. Based on operating earnings yield, the company is overvalued when compared to all of the companies in our coverage universe. Share price changes over the past year indicates that RSPP will perform very poorly over the near term.

Financial Data
(US$ in Thousands)

	3 Mos	12/31/2017	12/31/2016	12/31/2015	12/31/2014	12/31/2013	12/31/2012	12/31/2011
Earnings Per Share	1.81	1.49	(0.23)	(0.21)	0.03	1.26	0.72	...
Cash Flow Per Share	3.62	3.23	1.54	2.52	3.10	2.30	2.27	...
Tang Book Value Per Share	27.67	27.25	24.07	18.44	17.02	...	...	...
Income Statement								
Total Revenue	276,322	803,708	353,857	283,992	281,925	123,042	104,427	63,989
EBITDA	135,078	480,859	206,202	169,859	263,381	119,120	87,846	151,806
Depn & Amortn	1,070	283,892	197,035	156,258	89,046	48,904	48,803	16,612
Income Before Taxes	111,505	114,508	(43,557)	(29,937)	160,304	65,000	35,569	131,722
Income Taxes	21,932	(117,628)	(18,706)	(11,683)	157,806	2,262	(339)	550
Net Income	89,573	232,136	(24,851)	(18,254)	2,498	62,738	35,908	131,172
Average Shares	158,309	155,526	107,324	86,770	71,898	31,934	31,933	...
Balance Sheet								
Current Assets	192,312	149,323	776,262	187,540	173,742	47,135	82,356	37,428
Total Assets	6,500,120	6,270,186	4,996,427	2,979,571	2,289,947	587,655	513,238	395,662
Current Liabilities	251,186	206,561	108,269	77,402	130,041	30,866	28,165	27,916
Long-Term Obligations	1,579,751	1,509,128	1,132,275	698,650	500,000	128,155	111,586	46,586
Total Liabilities	2,089,323	1,947,828	1,579,699	1,120,987	964,176	200,774	159,395	77,727
Stockholders' Equity	4,410,797	4,322,358	3,416,728	1,858,584	1,325,771	386,881	353,843	317,935
Shares Outstanding	159,423	158,596	141,923	100,807	77,903	...	...	...
Statistical Record								
Return on Assets %	4.63	4.12	N.M.	N.M.	...	...	7.88	...
Return on Equity %	6.63	6.00	N.M.	N.M.	...	...	10.66	...
EBITDA Margin %	48.88	59.83	58.27	59.81	93.42	96.81	84.12	237.24
Net Margin %	32.42	28.88	N.M.	N.M.	0.89	50.99	34.39	204.99
Asset Turnover	0.15	0.14	0.09	0.11	...	...	0.23	...
Current Ratio	0.77	0.72	7.17	2.42	1.34	1.53	2.92	1.34
Debt to Equity	0.36	0.35	0.33	0.38	0.38	0.33	0.32	0.15
Price Range	46.88-29.37	46.11-29.37	45.67-18.29	30.54-19.23	32.88-19.59	...	...	...
P/E Ratio	25.90-16.23	30.95-19.71	...	...	N.M.	...	...	...

Address: 3141 Hood Street, Suite 500, Dallas, TX 75219
Telephone: 214-252-2700

Web Site: www.rsppermian.com
Officers: Michael K. Grimm - Chairman Steven D. (Steve) Gray - Chief Executive Officer

Auditors: Grant Thornton LLP
Investor Contact: 214-252-2700
Transfer Agents: American Stock Transfer & Trust Company, LLC

RYDER SYSTEM, INC.

Exchange	Symbol	Price	52Wk Range	Yield	P/E	Div Acheiver
NYS	R	$71.86 (6/29/2018)	89.82-66.26	3.01	4.86	13 Years

*7 Year Price Score 90.78 *NYSE Composite Index=100 *12 Month Price Score 88.51

Interim Earnings (Per Share)

Qtr.	Mar	Jun	Sep	Dec
2015	0.99	1.59	1.69	1.43
2016	1.04	1.38	1.59	0.90
2017	0.71	0.96	1.11	12.10
2018	0.63	...	...	...

Interim Dividends (Per Share)

Amt	Decl	Ex	Rec	Pay
0.46Q	10/06/2017	11/17/2017	11/20/2017	12/15/2017
0.52Q	02/12/2018	02/16/2018	02/20/2018	03/16/2018
0.52Q	05/04/2018	05/18/2018	05/21/2018	06/15/2018
0.54Q	07/13/2018	08/17/2018	08/20/2018	09/21/2018

Indicated Div: $2.16 (Div. Reinv. Plan)

Valuation Analysis **Institutional Holding**

Forecast EPS	$5.65	No of Institutions	
(06/13/2018)		512	
Market Cap	$3.8 Billion	Shares	
Book Value	$2.9 Billion	65,121,456	
Price/Book	1.33	% Held	
Price/Sales	0.51	91.44	

TRADING VOLUME (thousand shares)

Business Summary: Trucking (MIC: 7.4.1 SIC: 7513 NAIC: 532120)

Ryder System is engaged in transportation and supply chain management solutions. Co. operates in three business segments: Fleet Management Solutions, which provides full service leasing, commercial rental, contract maintenance, and contract-related maintenance of trucks, tractors and trailers to customers principally in the U.S., Canada and the U.K.; Dedicated Transportation Solutions, which provides vehicles and drivers as part of a dedicated transportation solution in the U.S.; and Supply Chain Solutions, which provides supply chain solutions including distribution and transportation services in North America and Asia.

Recent Developments: For the quarter ended Mar 31 2018, income from continuing operations decreased 11.9% to US$33.9 million from US$38.5 million in the year-earlier quarter. Net income decreased 12.8% to US$33.5 million from US$38.4 million in the year-earlier quarter. Revenues were US$1.90 billion, up 9.6% from US$1.74 billion the year before. Direct operating expenses rose 10.4% to US$1.55 billion from US$1.41 billion in the comparable period the year before. Indirect operating expenses increased 12.3% to US$302.0 million from US$268.8 million in the equivalent prior-year period.

Prospects: Our evaluation of Ryder System Inc. as of Jan. 21, 2018 is the result of our systematic analysis on three basic characteristics: earnings strength, relative valuation, and recent stock price movement. The company has enjoyed a very positive trend in earnings per share over the past 5 quarters and while recent estimates for the company have been raised by analysts, R has posted better than expected results. Based on operating earnings yield, the company is undervalued when compared to all of the companies in our coverage universe. Share price changes over the past year indicates that R will perform in line with the market over the near term.

Financial Data

(US$ in Thousands)	3 Mos	12/31/2017	12/31/2016	12/31/2015	12/31/2014	12/31/2013	12/31/2012	12/31/2011
Earnings Per Share	14.80	14.87	4.90	5.71	4.11	4.53	4.09	3.28
Cash Flow Per Share	29.22	29.42	30.12	27.30	26.08	23.70	22.42	20.63
Tang Book Value Per Share	45.90	45.26	30.25	28.84	25.64	27.01	19.52	16.74
Dividends Per Share	1.880	1.800	1.700	1.560	1.420	1.300	1.200	1.120
Dividend Payout %	12.70	12.10	34.69	27.32	34.55	28.70	29.34	34.15
Income Statement								
Total Revenue	1,903,467	7,329,599	6,786,984	6,571,893	6,638,774	6,419,285	6,256,967	6,050,534
EBITDA	436,262	548,136	642,224	703,649	1,520,883	1,463,232	1,383,351	1,284,813
Depn & Amortn	350,381	94,000	88,000	84,000	1,040,259	957,141	939,677	872,262
Income Before Taxes	48,100	313,786	406,381	469,215	338,549	368,895	303,117	279,387
Income Taxes	14,168	(477,229)	141,741	163,226	118,090	125,699	102,218	108,019
Net Income	33,505	790,558	262,477	304,768	218,575	237,792	209,979	169,777
Average Shares	53,013	52,988	53,361	53,260	53,036	52,071	50,740	50,878
Balance Sheet								
Current Assets	1,311,521	1,322,282	1,101,557	1,098,302	1,076,197	1,062,493	1,040,237	1,088,173
Total Assets	11,736,157	11,452,231	10,902,454	10,967,809	9,675,986	9,103,782	8,318,979	7,617,835
Current Liabilities	1,809,280	2,012,778	1,744,069	1,680,255	1,093,591	1,231,139	1,272,665	1,173,823
Long-Term Obligations	4,999,770	4,583,582	4,599,864	4,883,326	4,500,275	3,929,987	3,452,821	3,107,779
Total Liabilities	8,877,342	8,617,215	8,850,179	8,980,698	7,856,512	7,207,068	6,851,492	6,299,682
Stockholders' Equity	2,858,815	2,835,016	2,052,275	1,987,111	1,819,474	1,896,714	1,467,487	1,318,153
Shares Outstanding	53,094	52,955	53,463	53,490	53,039	53,335	51,371	51,143
Statistical Record								
Return on Assets %	6.92	7.07	2.39	2.95	2.33	2.73	2.63	2.38
Return on Equity %	31.83	32.35	12.96	16.01	11.76	14.14	15.03	12.47
EBITDA Margin %	22.92	7.48	9.46	10.71	22.91	22.79	22.11	21.23
Net Margin %	1.76	10.79	3.87	4.64	3.29	3.70	3.36	2.81
Asset Turnover	0.66	0.66	0.62	0.64	0.71	0.74	0.78	0.85
Current Ratio	0.72	0.66	0.63	0.65	0.98	0.86	0.82	0.93
Debt to Equity	1.75	1.62	2.24	2.46	2.47	2.07	2.35	2.36
Price Range	89.82-63.04	85.02-63.04	84.69-47.79	99.58-54.03	95.52-68.76	73.78-49.93	57.18-33.40	59.35-35.45
P/E Ratio	6.07-4.26	5.72-4.24	17.28-9.75	17.44-9.46	23.24-16.73	16.29-11.02	13.98-8.17	18.09-10.81
Average Yield %	2.45	2.38	2.59	1.85	1.69	2.14	2.63	2.25

Address: 11690 N.W. 105th Street, Miami, FL 33178 **Telephone:** 305-500-3726	**Web Site:** www.ryder.com **Officers:** Robert E. Sanchez - Chairman, President, Chief Executive Officer, Chief Operating Officer, Division Officer Robert D. Fatovic - Executive Vice President, Chief Legal Officer, Corporate Secretary	**Auditors:** PricewaterhouseCoopers LLP **Investor Contact:** 305-500-4053 **Transfer Agents:** Wells Fargo Bank, N.A., St. Paul, MN

S&P GLOBAL INC

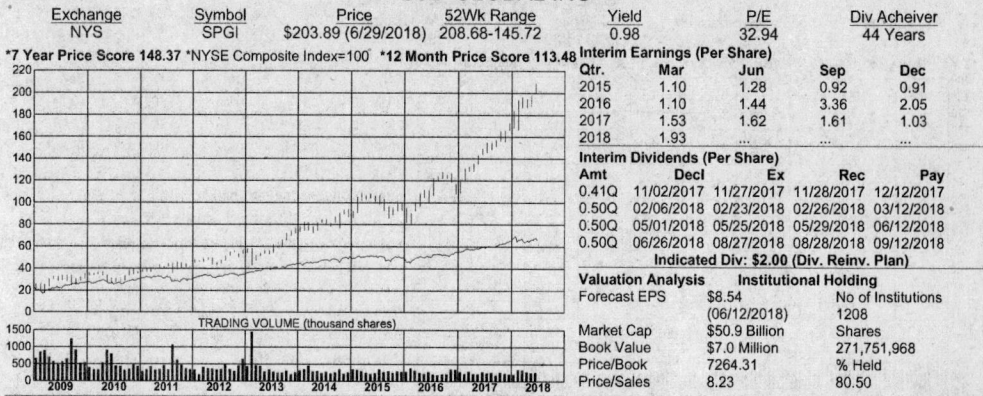

Exchange	Symbol	Price	52Wk Range	Yield	P/E	Div Acheiver
NYS	SPGI	$203.89 (6/29/2018)	208.68-145.72	0.98	32.94	44 Years

*7 Year Price Score 148.37 *NYSE Composite Index=100 ***12 Month Price Score 113.48**

Interim Earnings (Per Share)

Qtr.	Mar	Jun	Sep	Dec
2015	1.10	1.28	0.92	0.91
2016	1.10	1.44	3.36	2.05
2017	1.53	1.62	1.61	1.03
2018	1.93	...	...	...

Interim Dividends (Per Share)

Amt	Decl	Ex	Rec	Pay
0.41Q	11/02/2017	11/27/2017	11/28/2017	12/12/2017
0.50Q	02/06/2018	02/23/2018	02/26/2018	03/12/2018
0.50Q	05/01/2018	05/25/2018	05/29/2018	06/12/2018
0.50Q	06/26/2018	08/27/2018	08/28/2018	09/12/2018

Indicated Div: $2.00 (Div. Reinv. Plan)

Valuation Analysis   Institutional Holding

Forecast EPS	$8.54	No of Institutions
	(06/12/2018)	1208
Market Cap	$50.9 Billion	Shares
Book Value	$7.0 Million	271,751,968
Price/Book	7264.31	% Held
Price/Sales	8.23	80.50

TRADING VOLUME (thousand shares)

Business Summary: Credit & Lending (MIC: 5.4.1 SIC: 7323 NAIC: 561450)

S&P Global provides transparent and independent ratings, benchmarks, analytics and data to the capital and commodity markets worldwide. The capital markets include asset managers, investment banks, commercial banks, insurance companies, exchanges, and issuers; and the commodity markets include producers, traders and intermediaries within energy, metals, petrochemicals and agriculture. Co. has three segments: Ratings, which provides credit ratings, research and analytics to investors, issuers and other market participants; Market and Commodities Intelligence, which provides multi-asset-class data, research and analytical capabilities; and S&P Dow Jones Indices, which is an index provider.

Recent Developments: For the quarter ended Mar 31 2018, net income increased 24.2% to US$534.0 million from US$430.0 million in the year-earlier quarter. Revenues were US$1.57 billion, up 7.8% from US$1.45 billion the year before. Operating income was US$711.0 million versus US$639.0 million in the prior-year quarter, an increase of 11.3%. Direct operating expenses rose 6.8% to US$439.0 million from US$411.0 million in the comparable period the year before. Indirect operating expenses increased 3.5% to US$417.0 million from US$403.0 million in the equivalent prior-year period.

Prospects: Our evaluation of S&P Global Inc. as of Jan. 21, 2018 is the result of our systematic analysis on three basic characteristics: earnings strength, relative valuation, and recent stock price movement. The company has managed to produce a neutral trend in earnings per share over the past 5 quarters and while recent estimates for the company have been raised by analysts, SPGI has posted better than expected results. Based on operating earnings yield, the company is about fairly valued when compared to all of the companies in our coverage universe. Share price changes over the past year indicates that SPGI will perform very well over the near term.

Financial Data

(US$ in Thousands)	3 Mos	12/31/2017	12/31/2016	12/31/2015	12/31/2014	12/31/2013	12/31/2012	12/31/2011
Earnings Per Share	6.19	5.78	7.94	4.21	(0.42)	4.91	1.53	3.00
Cash Flow Per Share	8.02	7.87	5.56	0.72	4.45	2.97	2.67	4.51
Dividends Per Share	1.730	1.640	1.440	1.320	1.200	1.120	3.520	1.000
Dividend Payout %	27.95	28.37	18.14	31.35	...	22.81	230.07	33.33
Income Statement								
Total Revenue	1,567,000	6,063,000	5,661,000	5,313,000	5,051,000	4,875,000	4,450,000	6,246,000
EBITDA	760,000	2,790,000	3,550,000	2,074,000	247,000	1,542,000	1,352,000	1,609,000
Depn & Amortn	45,000	180,000	181,000	157,000	134,000	137,000	141,000	187,000
Income Before Taxes	681,000	2,461,000	3,188,000	1,815,000	54,000	1,346,000	1,130,000	1,347,000
Income Taxes	147,000	823,000	960,000	547,000	245,000	443,000	404,000	489,000
Net Income	491,000	1,496,000	2,106,000	1,156,000	(115,000)	1,376,000	437,000	911,000
Average Shares	258,400	258,900	265,200	274,600	271,500	279,800	284,600	304,000
Balance Sheet								
Current Assets	3,284,000	4,324,000	3,671,000	3,296,000	3,966,000	2,936,000	3,899,000	2,679,000
Total Assets	8,497,000	9,425,000	8,669,000	8,183,000	6,771,000	6,061,000	7,052,000	6,427,000
Current Liabilities	3,135,000	3,214,000	2,611,000	2,908,000	3,967,000	2,372,000	3,667,000	3,130,000
Long-Term Obligations	3,170,000	3,170,000	3,564,000	3,468,000	799,000	799,000	799,000	798,000
Total Liabilities	8,490,000	8,714,000	8,019,000	7,989,000	6,283,000	4,760,000	6,285,000	4,919,000
Stockholders' Equity	7,000	711,000	650,000	194,000	488,000	1,301,000	767,000	1,508,000
Shares Outstanding	249,400	253,700	258,300	265,200	272,000	271,000	279,000	276,000
Statistical Record								
Return on Assets %	18.52	16.54	24.93	15.46	N.M.	20.99	6.47	13.52
Return on Equity %	398.99	219.84	497.69	339.00	N.M.	133.08	38.31	49.00
EBITDA Margin %	48.50	46.02	62.71	39.04	4.89	31.63	30.38	25.76
Net Margin %	31.33	24.67	37.20	21.76	N.M.	28.23	9.82	14.59
Asset Turnover	0.72	0.67	0.67	0.71	0.79	0.74	0.66	0.93
Current Ratio	1.05	1.35	1.41	1.13	1.00	1.24	1.06	0.86
Debt to Equity	452.86	4.46	5.48	17.88	1.64	0.61	1.04	0.53
Price Range	195.96-128.28	172.57-108.39	127.56-80.77	108.59-85.40	93.71-71.98	78.20-42.67	56.65-42.40	45.57-35.35
P/E Ratio	31.66-20.72	29.86-18.75	16.07-10.17	25.79-20.29	...	15.93-8.69	37.03-27.71	15.19-11.78
Average Yield %	1.09	1.13	1.32	1.33	1.47	1.89	7.17	2.45

Address: 55 Water Street, New York, NY 10041	**Web Site:** www.spglobal.com	**Auditors:** Ernst & Young LLP
Telephone: 212-438-1000	**Officers:** Douglas L. Peterson - President, Chief Executive Officer, Division Officer Ewout L. Steenbergen - Executive Vice President, Chief Financial Officer	**Investor Contact:** 866-436-8502
		Transfer Agents: Computershare, Louisville, KY

SALESFORCE.COM INC

Exchange	Symbol	Price	52Wk Range	Yield	P/E
NYS	CRM	$136.40 (6/29/2018)	139.80-86.10	N/A	213.13

*7 Year Price Score 135.67 *NYSE Composite Index=100 *12 Month Price Score 119.09

TRADING VOLUME (thousand shares)

Interim Earnings (Per Share)

Qtr.	Apr	Jul	Oct	Jan
2015-16	0.01	0.00	(0.04)	(0.04)
2016-17	0.06	0.33	(0.05)	(0.07)
2017-18	(0.01)	0.02	0.07	0.09
2018-19	0.46	...	...	...

Interim Dividends (Per Share)

No Dividends Paid

Valuation Analysis		Institutional Holding	
Forecast EPS	$2.31	No of Institutions	
	(06/14/2018)	1394	
Market Cap	$100.1 Billion	Shares	
Book Value	$11.1 Billion	699,020,928	
Price/Book	9.05	% Held	
Price/Sales	9.02	97.37	

Business Summary: Internet & Software (MIC: 6.3.2 SIC: 7372 NAIC: 511210)

Salesforce.Com is a provider of enterprise cloud computing solutions. Co.'s service offerings include, among others: Sales Cloud, which enables companies to store data, monitor leads and progress, forecast opportunities, gain insights through relationship intelligence and collaborate around sale on desktop and mobile devices; Service Cloud, which enables companies to deliver more personalized customer service and support; Marketing Cloud, which enables companies to plan and personalize one-to-one customer interactions; and Analytics Cloud, which is an app for business intelligence and it enables companies to deploy sales, service, marketing and custom analytics apps using any data source.

Recent Developments: For the quarter ended Apr 30 2018, net income increased to US$344.0 million from US$1.0 million in the year-earlier quarter. Revenues were US$3.01 billion, up 25.4% from US$2.40 billion the year before. Operating income was US$191.0 million versus US$4.0 million in the prior-year quarter, an increase of. Direct operating expenses rose 17.8% to US$767.0 million from US$651.0 million in the comparable period the year before. Indirect operating expenses increased 17.6% to US$2.05 billion from US$1.74 billion in the equivalent prior-year period.

Prospects: Our evaluation of Salesforce.com Inc. as of Jan. 21, 2018 is the result of our systematic analysis on three basic characteristics: earnings strength, relative valuation, and recent stock price movement. The company has produced a positive trend in earnings per share over the past 5 quarters and while recent estimates for the company have remained steady, CRM has posted better than expected results. Based on operating earnings yield, the company is overvalued when compared to all of the companies in our coverage universe. Share price changes over the past year indicates that CRM will perform well over the near term.

Financial Data
(US$ in Thousands)

	3 Mos	01/31/2018	01/31/2017	01/31/2016	01/31/2015	01/31/2014	01/31/2013	01/31/2012
Earnings Per Share	0.64	0.17	0.26	(0.07)	(0.42)	(0.39)	(0.48)	(0.02)
Cash Flow Per Share	4.08	3.83	3.14	2.44	1.88	1.46	1.30	1.09
Tang Book Value Per Share	3.58	1.52	N.M.	0.74	N.M.	N.M.	0.98	1.15
Income Statement								
Total Revenue	3,006,000	10,480,012	8,391,984	6,667,216	5,373,586	4,071,003	3,050,195	2,266,539
EBITDA	692,000	661,851	437,171	438,764	106,752	(94,824)	4,254	69,328
Depn & Amortn	293,000	372,800	322,800	302,000	246,600	185,900	101,100	85,600
Income Before Taxes	385,000	202,108	25,383	64,279	(213,085)	(357,935)	(127,794)	(33,317)
Income Taxes	41,000	74,630	(154,249)	111,705	49,603	(125,760)	142,651	(21,745)
Net Income	344,000	127,478	179,632	(47,426)	(262,688)	(232,175)	(270,445)	(11,572)
Average Shares	754,000	734,598	700,217	661,647	624,148	597,613	564,896	541,208
Balance Sheet								
Current Assets	10,151,000	9,290,371	5,996,827	4,347,327	3,550,072	2,680,252	2,015,880	1,672,222
Total Assets	22,963,000	21,009,802	17,584,923	12,770,772	10,692,982	9,152,930	5,528,956	4,164,154
Current Liabilities	7,895,000	10,129,518	7,258,353	5,617,005	4,390,103	3,980,188	2,917,624	2,323,471
Long-Term Obligations	3,172,000	694,781	2,008,391	1,293,947	1,370,692	1,301,930	...	...
Total Liabilities	11,903,000	11,617,439	10,084,796	7,767,903	6,717,799	6,087,715	3,157,711	2,498,053
Stockholders' Equity	11,060,000	9,392,363	7,500,127	5,002,869	3,975,183	3,065,215	2,371,245	1,666,101
Shares Outstanding	733,900	729,853	707,460	670,929	650,596	610,143	585,626	548,146
Statistical Record								
Return on Assets %	2.40	0.66	1.18	N.M.	N.M.	N.M.	N.M.	N.M.
Return on Equity %	5.06	1.51	2.87	N.M.	N.M.	N.M.	N.M.	N.M.
EBITDA Margin %	23.02	6.32	5.21	6.58	1.99	N.M.	0.14	3.06
Net Margin %	11.44	1.22	2.14	N.M.	N.M.	N.M.	N.M.	N.M.
Asset Turnover	0.55	0.54	0.55	0.57	0.54	0.55	0.63	0.62
Current Ratio	1.29	0.92	0.83	0.77	0.81	0.67	0.69	0.72
Debt to Equity	0.29	0.07	0.27	0.26	0.34	0.42	...	...
Price Range	127.99-86.00	113.91-78.58	83.77-54.05	82.14-57.28	66.22-49.13	61.14-36.75	44.52-29.20	39.83-24.37
P/E Ratio	199.98-134.38	670.06-462.24	322.19-207.88	...	...	...	...	...

Address: The Landmark @ One Market, Suite 300, San Francisco, CA 94105 Telephone: 415-901-7000	Web Site: www.salesforce.com Officers: Marc Benioff - Chairman, Chief Executive Officer Keith G. Block - Co-Vice Chairman, President, Chief Operating Officer	Auditors: Ernst & Young LLP Investor Contact: 415-536-6250 Transfer Agents: Computershare, Providence, RI

SALLY BEAUTY HOLDINGS INC

Exchange	Symbol	Price	52Wk Range	Yield	P/E
NYS	SBH	$16.03 (6/29/2018)	21.14-14.81	N/A	8.39

*7 Year Price Score 56.12 ***NYSE Composite Index=100** ***12 Month Price Score 89.47**

Interim Earnings (Per Share)

Qtr.	Dec	Mar	Jun	Sep
2014-15	0.35	0.39	0.39	0.36
2015-16	0.28	0.41	0.46	0.36
2016-17	0.39	0.41	0.49	0.28
2017-18	0.65	0.49	...	...

Interim Dividends (Per Share)

No Dividends Paid

Valuation Analysis

		Institutional Holding	
Forecast EPS	$2.19	No of Institutions	
	(06/14/2018)	355	
Market Cap	$2.0 Billion	Shares	
Book Value	N/A	180,091,552	
Price/Book	N/A	% Held	
Price/Sales	0.50	93.12	

TRADING VOLUME (thousand shares)

Business Summary: Retail - Specialty (MIC: 2.1.3 SIC: 5999 NAIC: 446120)

Sally Beauty Holdings is a holding company. Through its subsidiaries, Co. is an international retailer and distributor of beauty supplies with operations primarily in North America, South America and Europe. Co. has two segments: Sally Beauty Supply, a retailer of beauty supplies providing beauty supplies to both retail consumers and salon professionals; and Beauty Systems Group (BSG), including its franchise-based business Armstrong McCall, a beauty supply distributor. As of Sep 30 2017, Sally Beauty Supply had 3,763 company-operated retail stores (generally under the Sally Beauty banner) while BSG had 1,200 company-operated retail stores (generally under the CosmoProf banner).

Recent Developments: For the quarter ended Mar 31 2018, net income increased 7.7% to US$61.4 million from US$57.0 million in the year-earlier quarter. Revenues were US$975.3 million, up 0.9% from US$966.5 million the year before. Operating income was US$111.1 million versus US$119.0 million in the prior-year quarter, a decrease of 6.7%. Direct operating expenses rose 2.2% to US$489.0 million from US$478.4 million in the comparable period the year before. Indirect operating expenses increased 1.7% to US$375.2 million from US$369.1 million in the equivalent prior-year period.

Prospects: Our evaluation of Sally Beauty Holdings Inc. as of Jan. 21, 2018 is the result of our systematic analysis on three basic characteristics: earnings strength, relative valuation, and recent stock price movement. The company has generated a negative trend in earnings per share over the past 5 quarters and while recent estimates for the company have been raised by analysts, SBH has posted results that fell short of analysts expectations. Based on operating earnings yield, the company is undervalued when compared to all of the companies in our coverage universe. Share price changes over the past year indicates that SBH will perform very poorly over the near term.

Financial Data
(US$ in Thousands)

	6 Mos	3 Mos	09/30/2017	09/30/2016	09/30/2015	09/30/2014	09/30/2013	09/30/2012
Earnings Per Share	1.91	1.83	1.56	1.50	1.49	1.51	1.48	1.24
Cash Flow Per Share	2.93	2.80	2.50	2.38	1.92	1.98	1.81	1.62
Income Statement								
Total Revenue	1,970,286	994,964	3,938,317	3,952,618	3,834,343	3,753,498	3,622,216	3,523,644
EBITDA	223,085	111,054	577,797	584,597	570,426	572,096	579,762	550,355
Depn & Amortn	1,851	921	99,200	86,300	75,100	65,100	59,400	51,000
Income Before Taxes	171,957	86,117	345,698	354,060	378,484	390,679	412,667	360,943
Income Taxes	27,322	2,853	130,622	131,118	143,397	144,686	151,516	127,879
Net Income	144,635	83,264	215,076	222,942	235,087	245,993	261,151	233,064
Average Shares	125,057	128,645	138,176	148,803	158,226	163,419	176,159	188,610
Balance Sheet								
Current Assets	1,154,161	1,163,675	1,170,503	1,172,827	1,187,102	1,104,149	1,015,817	1,163,907
Total Assets	2,100,150	2,113,321	2,123,093	2,132,063	2,094,351	2,029,973	1,950,086	2,065,800
Current Liabilities	545,828	590,002	574,565	488,665	491,699	463,537	542,653	477,388
Long-Term Obligations	1,769,841	1,771,299	1,771,853	1,783,294	1,786,839	1,810,667	1,612,685	1,615,322
Total Liabilities	2,415,179	2,455,956	2,486,709	2,408,229	2,392,172	2,377,026	2,253,565	2,180,885
Stockholders' Equity	(315,029)	(342,635)	(363,616)	(276,166)	(297,821)	(347,053)	(303,479)	(115,085)
Shares Outstanding	123,002	125,799	129,585	144,571	151,452	154,668	164,425	180,241
Statistical Record								
Return on Assets %	11.84	11.48	10.11	10.52	11.40	12.36	13.01	12.25
EBITDA Margin %	11.32	11.16	14.67	14.79	14.88	15.24	16.01	15.62
Net Margin %	7.34	8.37	5.46	5.64	6.13	6.55	7.21	6.61
Asset Turnover	1.89	1.86	1.85	1.87	1.86	1.89	1.80	1.85
Current Ratio	2.11	1.97	2.04	2.40	2.41	2.38	1.87	2.44
Price Range	21.14-15.14	26.80-15.14	29.12-17.38	32.75-22.13	34.88-23.44	30.67-24.14	31.57-22.76	28.07-16.28
P/E Ratio	11.07-7.93	14.64-8.27	18.67-11.14	21.83-14.75	23.41-15.73	20.31-15.99	21.33-15.38	22.64-13.13

Address: 3001 Colorado Boulevard, Denton, TX 76210 **Telephone:** 940-898-7500	**Web Site:** www.sallybeautyholdings.com **Officers:** Robert R. McMaster - Chairman Christian A. Brickman - President, Chief Executive Officer, Chief Operating Officer	**Auditors:** KPMG LLP **Investor Contact:** 940-297-3877 **Transfer Agents:** Computershare Trust Company N.A., Providence, RI

SANTANDER CONSUMER USA HOLDINGS INC

Exchange	Symbol	Price	52Wk Range	Yield	P/E
NYS	SC	$19.09 (6/29/2018)	20.41-12.69	1.05	5.35

7 Year Price Score N/A   **NYSE Composite Index=100**   **12 Month Price Score 113.16**

Interim Earnings (Per Share)

Qtr.	Mar	Jun	Sep	Dec
2015	0.81	0.79	0.62	0.08
2016	0.56	0.79	0.59	0.17
2017	0.40	0.74	0.55	1.61
2018	0.67	...	...	...

Interim Dividends (Per Share)

Amt	Decl	Ex	Rec	Pay
0.15Q	05/01/2014	05/08/2014	05/12/2014	05/30/2014
0.03Q	10/27/2017	11/06/2017	11/07/2017	11/17/2017
0.05Q	01/31/2018	02/09/2018	02/12/2018	02/22/2018
0.05Q	04/19/2018	05/03/2018	05/04/2018	05/14/2018

Indicated Div: $0.20

Valuation Analysis

		Institutional Holding	
Forecast EPS	$2.30	No of Institutions	259
	(06/14/2018)		
Market Cap	$6.9 Billion	Shares	380,920,064
Book Value	$6.7 Billion	% Held	N/A
Price/Book	1.02		
Price/Sales	1.04		

Business Summary: Credit & Lending (MIC: 5.4.1 SIC: 6141 NAIC: 522298)

Santander Consumer USA Holdings is a holding company. Through its subsidiaries, Co. is a consumer finance company focused on vehicle finance and third-party servicing. Co.'s primary business is the indirect origination and securitization of retail installment contracts, principally through manufacturer-franchised dealers in connection with their sale of new and used vehicles to retail consumers. Co. also originates vehicle loans through a web-based direct lending program, purchases vehicle retail installment contracts from other lenders, and services automobile and recreational and marine vehicle portfolios for other lenders.

Recent Developments: For the quarter ended Mar 31 2018, net income increased 68.9% to US$242.3 million from US$143.4 million in the year-earlier quarter. Net interest income decreased 7.9% to US$1.03 billion from US$1.11 billion in the year-earlier quarter. Provision for loan losses was US$459.0 million versus US$635.0 million in the prior-year quarter, a decrease of 27.7%. Non-interest income fell 54.8% to US$25.1 million from US$55.5 million, while non-interest expense declined 6.6% to US$292.3 million.

Prospects: Our evaluation of Santander Consumer USA Holdings Inc as of Jan. 21, 2018 is the result of our systematic analysis on three basic characteristics: earnings strength, relative valuation, and recent stock price movement. The company has enjoyed a very positive trend in earnings per share over the past 5 quarters. However, while recent estimates for the company have been mixed, SC has posted better than expected results. Based on operating earnings yield, the company is undervalued when compared to all of the companies in our coverage universe. Share price changes over the past year indicates that SC will perform well over the near term.

Financial Data
(US$ in Thousands)

	3 Mos	12/31/2017	12/31/2016	12/31/2015	12/31/2014	12/31/2013	12/31/2012	12/31/2011
Earnings Per Share	3.57	3.30	2.13	2.31	2.15	2.01	2.07	3.12
Cash Flow Per Share	11.47	10.47	12.45	10.98	11.18	6.13	4.16	6.32
Tang Book Value Per Share	18.34	17.69	14.30	12.01	9.83	7.38	5.99	6.04
Dividends Per Share	0.080	0.030	...	...	0.150	0.840	2.120	1.890
Dividend Payout %	2.24	0.91	...	...	6.98	41.79	102.42	60.58
Income Statement								
Total Revenue	1,650,605	6,665,126	6,623,142	6,697,184	6,127,331	4,245,587	3,244,191	3,047,042
Income Before Taxes	299,610	823,514	1,160,711	1,285,325	1,209,988	1,085,088	1,188,549	1,252,212
Income Taxes	57,311	(364,092)	394,245	458,032	443,639	389,418	453,615	464,034
Net Income	242,299	1,187,606	766,466	827,293	766,349	697,491	715,003	768,197
Average Shares	361,616	360,292	359,078	358,887	355,722	346,177	346,164	246,056
Balance Sheet								
Total Assets	40,045,188	39,422,304	38,539,104	36,570,373	32,342,176	26,401,896	18,741,644	19,404,371
Total Liabilities	33,319,173	32,941,803	33,300,485	32,145,410	28,783,827	23,715,064	16,542,110	17,187,687
Stockholders' Equity	6,726,015	6,480,501	5,238,619	4,424,963	3,558,349	2,686,832	2,199,534	2,216,684
Shares Outstanding	361,008	360,527	358,907	357,945	348,977	346,760	346,164	346,164
Statistical Record								
Return on Assets %	3.25	3.05	2.04	2.40	2.61	3.09	3.74	...
Return on Equity %	21.19	20.27	15.82	20.73	24.54	28.55	32.29	...
Net Margin %	14.68	17.82	11.57	12.35	12.51	16.43	22.04	25.21
Asset Turnover	0.17	0.17	0.18	0.19	0.21	0.19	0.17	...
Price Range	18.85-11.17	18.62-11.17	15.85-8.87	26.52-15.15	25.90-16.85			
P/E Ratio	5.28-3.13	5.64-3.38	7.44-4.16	11.48-6.56	12.05-7.84	...	...	...
Average Yield %	0.54	0.21	...	...	0.73	...	...	...

Address: 1601 Elm Street, Suite 800, Dallas, TX 75201 **Telephone:** 214-634-1110	**Web Site:** www.santanderconsumerusa.com **Officers:** William J. Rainer - Chairman Scott Powell - President, Chief Executive Officer	**Auditors:** PricewaterhouseCoopers LLP **Transfer Agents:** Computershare Trust Company, N.A.

SCANA CORP

Exchange	Symbol	Price	52Wk Range	Yield	P/E
NYS	SCG	$38.52 (6/29/2018)	67.56-34.02	1.28	N/A

*7 Year Price Score 68.28   *NYSE Composite Index=100   *12 Month Price Score 78.98

Interim Earnings (Per Share)

Qtr.	Mar	Jun	Sep	Dec
2015	2.80	0.69	1.04	0.69
2016	1.23	0.74	1.32	0.87
2017	1.19	0.85	0.24	(3.11)
2018	1.18	...	...	...

Interim Dividends (Per Share)

Amt	Decl	Ex	Rec	Pay
0.613Q	08/03/2017	09/08/2017	09/11/2017	10/01/2017
0.613Q	10/26/2017	12/11/2017	12/12/2017	01/01/2018
0.613Q	02/22/2018	03/09/2018	03/12/2018	04/01/2018
0.124Q	06/28/2018	07/09/2018	07/10/2018	07/18/2018

Indicated Div: $0.49 (Div. Reinv. Plan)

Valuation Analysis   **Institutional Holding**

Forecast EPS	$3.49	No of Institutions
	(06/12/2018)	727
Market Cap	$5.5 Billion	Shares
Book Value	$5.3 Billion	123,387,440
Price/Book	1.03	% Held
Price/Sales	N/A	55.39

TRADING VOLUME (thousand shares)

Business Summary: Electric Utilities (MIC: 3.1.1 SIC: 4931 NAIC: 221122)

SCANA is a holding company. Through its regulated subsidiaries, Co. is engaged in the generation, transmission, distribution and sale of electricity in South Carolina and in the purchase, transmission and sale of natural gas in North Carolina and South Carolina. Through nonregulated subsidiary, Co. markets natural gas to retail customers in Georgia and to wholesale customers in the southeast. A service company subsidiary of Co. provides primarily administrative and management services to Co. and its subsidiaries. As of Dec 31 2017, Co. distributed electricity to approximately 719,000 customers and the purchase, sale and transportation of natural gas to approximately 425,000 customers.

Recent Developments: For the quarter ended Mar 31 2018, net income decreased 1.2% to US$169.0 million from US$171.0 million in the year-earlier quarter. Revenues were US$1.18 billion, up 0.6% from US$1.17 billion the year before. Operating income was US$189.0 million versus US$320.0 million in the prior-year quarter, a decrease of 40.9%. Direct operating expenses rose 18.2% to US$818.0 million from US$692.0 million in the comparable period the year before. Indirect operating expenses increased 7.5% to US$173.0 million from US$161.0 million in the equivalent prior-year period.

Prospects: Our evaluation of SCANA Corp. as of Jan. 21, 2018 is the result of our systematic analysis on three basic characteristics: earnings strength, relative valuation, and recent stock price movement. The company has managed to produce a neutral trend in earnings per share over the past 5 quarters. However, while recent estimates for the company have been mixed, SCG has posted results that fell short of analysts expectations. Based on operating earnings yield, the company is undervalued when compared to all of the companies in our coverage universe. Share price changes over the past year indicates that SCG will perform very poorly over the near term.

Financial Data

(US$ in Thousands)	3 Mos	12/31/2017	12/31/2016	12/31/2015	12/31/2014	12/31/2013	12/31/2012	12/31/2011
Earnings Per Share	(0.84)	(0.83)	4.16	5.22	3.79	3.39	3.15	2.97
Cash Flow Per Share	...	8.17	7.62	7.41	5.14	7.57	6.38	6.30
Tang Book Value Per Share	37.37	35.28	38.59	36.62	33.48	31.45	29.73	28.15
Dividends Per Share	2.450	2.450	2.300	2.180	2.100	2.030	1.980	1.940
Dividend Payout %	...	...	55.29	41.76	55.41	59.88	62.86	65.32
Income Statement								
Total Revenue	1,180,000	4,407,000	4,227,000	4,380,000	4,951,000	4,495,000	4,176,000	4,409,000
EBITDA	330,000	582,000	1,652,000	1,868,000	1,546,000	1,441,000	1,309,000	1,233,000
Depn & Amortn	13,000	450,000	446,000	414,000	448,000	450,000	412,000	394,000
Income Before Taxes	220,000	(231,000)	864,000	1,136,000	786,000	694,000	602,000	555,000
Income Taxes	51,000	(112,000)	269,000	390,000	248,000	223,000	182,000	168,000
Net Income	169,000	(119,000)	595,000	746,000	538,000	471,000	420,000	387,000
Average Shares	143,000	143,000	142,900	142,900	141,900	139,100	133,300	130,200
Balance Sheet								
Current Assets	1,447,000	1,851,000	1,506,000	1,378,000	2,145,000	1,421,000	1,527,000	1,491,000
Total Assets	18,584,000	18,739,000	18,707,000	17,146,000	16,852,000	15,164,000	14,616,000	13,534,000
Current Liabilities	1,775,000	2,113,000	2,065,000	1,952,000	2,533,000	1,442,000	1,811,000	1,642,000
Long-Term Obligations	6,001,000	5,906,000	6,473,000	5,882,000	5,531,000	5,395,000	4,949,000	4,622,000
Total Liabilities	13,240,000	13,484,000	12,982,000	11,703,000	11,865,000	10,500,000	10,462,000	9,645,000
Stockholders' Equity	5,344,000	5,255,000	5,725,000	5,443,000	4,987,000	4,664,000	4,154,000	3,889,000
Shares Outstanding	143,000	143,000	142,900	142,900	142,700	141,000	132,000	130,000
Statistical Record								
Return on Assets %	...	N.M.	3.31	4.39	3.36	3.16	2.98	2.92
Return on Equity %	...	N.M.	10.63	14.30	11.15	10.68	10.42	10.20
EBITDA Margin %	27.97	13.21	39.08	42.65	31.23	32.06	31.35	27.97
Net Margin %	14.32	N.M.	14.08	17.03	10.87	10.48	10.06	8.78
Asset Turnover	...	0.24	0.24	0.26	0.31	0.30	0.30	0.33
Current Ratio	0.82	0.88	0.73	0.71	0.85	0.99	0.84	0.91
Debt to Equity	1.12	1.12	1.13	1.08	1.11	1.16	1.19	1.19
Price Range	71.22-35.60	73.28-37.39	76.12-60.08	65.36-50.00	63.18-45.67	54.20-44.86	49.65-43.71	45.34-35.12
P/E Ratio	...	...	18.30-14.44	12.52-9.58	16.67-12.05	15.99-13.23	15.76-13.88	15.27-11.82
Average Yield %	4.58	4.05	3.29	3.90	4.06	4.16	4.24	4.78

Address: 100 SCANA Parkway, Cayce, SC 29033	Web Site: www.scana.com	Auditors: Deloitte & Touche LLP
Telephone: 803-217-9000	**Officers:** Jimmy E. Addison - Executive Vice President, Senior Vice President, Chief Financial Officer, Chief Executive Officer Randal M. Senn - Senior Vice President, Vice President, Chief Information Officer	**Investor Contact:** 803-217-7512 **Transfer Agents:** SCANA Corporation, Columbia, SC

SCHLUMBERGER LTD

Exchange	Symbol	Price	52Wk Range	Yield	P/E
NYS	SLB	$67.03 (6/29/2018)	79.79-61.31	2.98	N/A

*7 Year Price Score 68.69 ***NYSE Composite Index=100** ***12 Month Price Score 101.42**

Interim Earnings (Per Share)

Qtr.	Mar	Jun	Sep	Dec
2015	0.76	0.88	0.78	(0.79)
2016	0.40	(1.56)	0.13	(0.14)
2017	0.20	(0.05)	0.39	(1.62)
2018	0.38	...	...	...

Interim Dividends (Per Share)

Amt	Decl	Ex	Rec	Pay
0.50Q	07/19/2017	09/01/2017	09/06/2017	10/13/2017
0.50Q	10/18/2017	12/05/2017	12/06/2017	01/12/2018
0.50Q	01/17/2018	02/06/2018	02/07/2018	04/13/2018
0.50Q	04/18/2018	06/05/2018	06/06/2018	07/13/2018

Indicated Div: $2.00

Valuation Analysis **Institutional Holding**

Forecast EPS	$1.90	No of Institutions
	(06/14/2018)	2388
Market Cap	$92.8 Billion	Shares
Book Value	$36.9 Billion	1,318,984,064
Price/Book	2.51	% Held
Price/Sales	2.94	74.32

TRADING VOLUME (thousand shares)

Business Summary: Equipment & Services (MIC: 9.1.3 SIC: 1389 NAIC: 213112)

Schlumberger is a provider of technology for reservoir characterization, drilling, production and processing to the oil and gas industry. Co. operates in the oilfield service markets, managing its business through four Groups: Reservoir Characterization, which include WesternGeco®, Wireline, Testing and Process; Drilling, which comprises Bits and Drilling Tools, M-I SWACO®, Drilling and Measurements, Land Rigs and Integrated Drilling Services; Production, which includes Well Services, Completions, Artificial Lift, Integrated Production Services and Schlumberger Production Management; and Cameron, which includes OneSubsea®, Surface Systems, Drilling Systems, and Valves and Measurement.

Recent Developments: For the quarter ended Mar 31 2018, net income increased 86.6% to US$530.0 million from US$284.0 million in the year-earlier quarter. Revenues were US$7.87 billion, up 13.4% from US$6.94 billion the year before. Direct operating expenses rose 11.9% to US$6.80 billion from US$6.08 billion in the comparable period the year before. Indirect operating expenses decreased 19.6% to US$426.0 million from US$530.0 million in the equivalent prior-year period.

Prospects: Our evaluation of Schlumberger Ltd. as of Jan. 21, 2018 is the result of our systematic analysis on three basic characteristics: earnings strength, relative valuation, and recent stock price movement. The company has produced a positive trend in earnings per share over the past 5 quarters. Because the company lacks sufficient analyst estimate data, we place greater weight on the historical EPS trend as the measure of earnings strength. Based on operating earnings yield, the company is overvalued when compared to all of the companies in our coverage universe. Share price changes over the past year indicates that SLB will perform very poorly over the near term.

Financial Data

(US$ in Thousands)	3 Mos	12/31/2017	12/31/2016	12/31/2015	12/31/2014	12/31/2013	12/31/2012	12/31/2011
Earnings Per Share	(0.90)	(1.08)	(1.24)	1.63	4.16	5.05	4.10	3.67
Cash Flow Per Share	4.03	4.08	4.60	6.95	8.64	7.40	5.11	4.57
Tang Book Value Per Share	1.87	1.71	4.48	12.30	13.89	15.34	11.57	9.17
Dividends Per Share	2.000	2.000	2.000	2.000	1.600	1.250	1.100	1.000
Dividend Payout %	...	...	...	122.70	38.46	24.75	26.83	27.25
Income Statement								
Total Revenue	7,871,000	30,664,000	28,010,000	35,711,000	48,871,000	46,459,000	42,321,000	39,669,000
EBITDA	1,309,000	1,683,000	1,365,000	6,427,000	11,208,000	12,182,000	10,431,000	9,336,000
Depn & Amortn	523,000	2,300,000	2,700,000	3,200,000	3,200,000	3,100,000	2,900,000	2,700,000
Income Before Taxes	643,000	(1,183,000)	(1,905,000)	2,881,000	7,639,000	8,691,000	7,191,000	6,338,000
Income Taxes	113,000	330,000	(278,000)	746,000	1,928,000	1,848,000	1,723,000	1,545,000
Net Income	525,000	(1,505,000)	(1,687,000)	2,072,000	5,438,000	6,732,000	5,490,000	4,997,000
Average Shares	1,394,000	1,388,000	1,357,000	1,275,000	1,308,000	1,333,000	1,339,000	1,361,000
Balance Sheet								
Current Assets	18,055,000	18,497,000	23,927,000	26,912,000	24,694,000	26,225,000	24,156,000	20,539,000
Total Assets	71,478,000	71,987,000	77,956,000	68,005,000	66,904,000	67,100,000	61,547,000	55,201,000
Current Liabilities	16,195,000	15,282,000	15,059,000	14,121,000	14,176,000	13,525,000	12,368,000	10,538,000
Long-Term Obligations	13,526,000	14,875,000	16,463,000	14,442,000	10,565,000	10,393,000	9,509,000	8,556,000
Total Liabilities	34,554,000	35,145,000	36,878,000	32,372,000	29,054,000	27,631,000	26,796,000	23,938,000
Stockholders' Equity	36,924,000	36,842,000	41,078,000	35,633,000	37,850,000	39,469,000	34,751,000	31,263,000
Shares Outstanding	1,385,133	1,383,932	1,391,475	1,256,367	1,275,312	1,307,330	1,328,255	1,333,775
Statistical Record								
Return on Assets %	N.M.	N.M.	N.M.	3.07	8.12	10.47	9.38	9.34
Return on Equity %	N.M.	N.M.	N.M.	5.64	14.07	18.14	16.59	15.99
EBITDA Margin %	16.63	5.49	4.87	18.00	22.93	26.22	24.65	23.53
Net Margin %	6.67	N.M.	N.M.	5.80	11.13	14.49	12.97	12.60
Asset Turnover	0.43	0.41	0.38	0.53	0.73	0.72	0.72	0.74
Current Ratio	1.11	1.21	1.59	1.91	1.74	1.94	1.95	1.95
Debt to Equity	0.37	0.40	0.40	0.41	0.28	0.26	0.27	0.27
Price Range	79.79-61.31	87.48-61.31	86.38-61.06	94.61-67.34	117.95-79.90	94.46-69.30	79.85-59.67	95.04-57.72
P/E Ratio	...	...	...	58.04-41.31	28.35-19.21	18.70-13.72	19.48-14.55	25.90-15.73
Average Yield %	2.94	2.82	2.59	2.44	1.62	1.55	1.55	1.24

Address: 42 Rue Saint-Dominique, Paris, 75007	Web Site: www.slb.com	Auditors: PricewaterhouseCoopers LLP
Telephone: 713-513-2000	Officers: Paal Kibsgaard - Chairman, Chief Executive Officer Simon Ayat - Executive Vice President, Chief Financial Officer	Investor Contact: 713-375-3535 Transfer Agents: Computershare Trust Company, N.A., Providence, RI

SCHWAB (CHARLES) CORP (THE)

Exchange	Symbol	Price	52Wk Range	Yield	P/E
NYS	SCHW	$51.10 (6/29/2018)	59.59-38.11	0.78	29.03

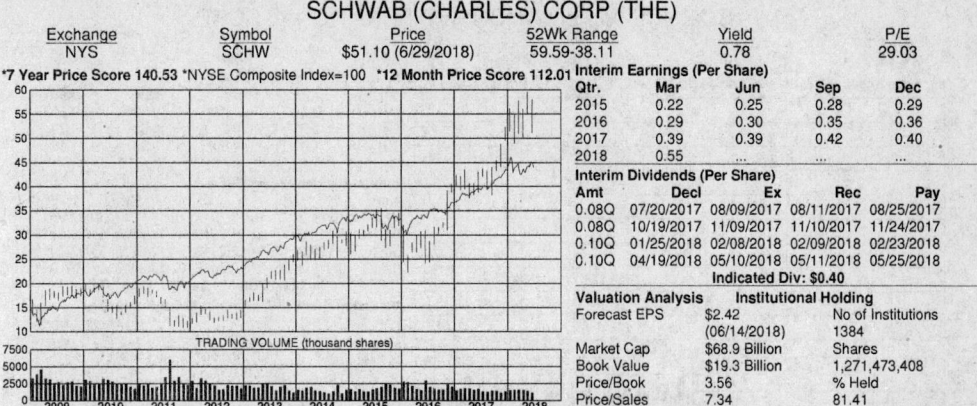

*7 Year Price Score 140.53 *NYSE Composite Index=100 *12 Month Price Score 112.01

Interim Earnings (Per Share)

Qtr.	Mar	Jun	Sep	Dec
2015	0.22	0.25	0.28	0.29
2016	0.29	0.30	0.35	0.36
2017	0.39	0.39	0.42	0.40
2018	0.55	...	...	...

Interim Dividends (Per Share)

Amt	Decl	Ex	Rec	Pay
0.08Q	07/20/2017	08/09/2017	08/11/2017	08/25/2017
0.08Q	10/19/2017	11/09/2017	11/10/2017	11/24/2017
0.10Q	01/25/2018	02/08/2018	02/09/2018	02/23/2018
0.10Q	04/19/2018	05/10/2018	05/11/2018	05/25/2018

Indicated Div: $0.40

Valuation Analysis   **Institutional Holding**

Forecast EPS	$2.42	No of Institutions
	(06/14/2018)	1384
Market Cap	$68.9 Billion	Shares
Book Value	$19.3 Billion	1,271,473,408
Price/Book	3.56	% Held
Price/Sales	7.34	81.41

Business Summary: Finance Intermediaries & Services (MIC: 5.5.1 SIC: 6211 NAIC: 523120)

Charles Schwab is a savings and loan holding company. Co. is engaged, through its subsidiaries, in wealth management, securities brokerage, banking, money management and financial advisory services. Co. provides financial services to individuals and institutional clients in two segments: Investor Services, which provides retail brokerage and banking services, retirement plan services, and other corporate brokerage services; and Advisor Services, which provides custodial, trading, and support services as well as retirement business services.

Recent Developments: For the quarter ended Mar 31 2018, net income increased 38.8% to US$783.0 million from US$564.0 million in the year-earlier quarter. Revenues were US$2.56 billion, up 19.7% from US$2.14 billion the year before. Direct operating expenses rose 187.3% to US$158.0 million from US$55.0 million in the comparable period the year before. Indirect operating expenses increased 12.8% to US$1.40 billion from US$1.24 billion in the equivalent prior-year period.

Prospects: Our evaluation of Schwab (Charles) Corp. as of Jan. 21, 2018 is the result of our systematic analysis on three basic characteristics: earnings strength, relative valuation, and recent stock price movement. The company has managed to produce a neutral trend in earnings per share over the past 5 quarters and while recent estimates for the company have been raised by analysts, SCHW has posted better than expected results. Based on operating earnings yield, the company is about fairly valued when compared to all of the companies in our coverage universe. Share price changes over the past year indicates that SCHW will perform poorly over the near term.

Financial Data

(US$ in Thousands)	3 Mos	12/31/2017	12/31/2016	12/31/2015	12/31/2014	12/31/2013	12/31/2012	12/31/2011
Earnings Per Share	1.76	1.61	1.31	1.03	0.95	0.78	0.69	0.70
Cash Flow Per Share	1.37	0.94	2.01	0.95	1.80	1.29	0.99	2.01
Tang Book Value Per Share	11.28	10.70	9.20	7.98	7.23	6.18	5.62	4.90
Dividends Per Share	0.340	0.320	0.270	0.240	0.240	0.240	0.240	0.240
Dividend Payout %	19.32	19.88	20.61	23.30	25.26	30.77	34.78	34.29
Income Statement								
Total Revenue	2,556,000	8,960,000	7,649,000	6,512,000	6,160,000	5,540,000	5,033,000	4,866,000
EBITDA	1,098,000	3,882,000	3,190,000	2,458,000	2,270,000	1,859,000	1,599,000	1,683,000
Depn & Amortn	96,000	232,000	197,000	179,000	155,000	154,000	149,000	291,000
Income Before Taxes	1,002,000	3,650,000	2,993,000	2,279,000	2,115,000	1,705,000	1,450,000	1,392,000
Income Taxes	219,000	1,296,000	1,104,000	832,000	794,000	634,000	522,000	528,000
Net Income	783,000	2,354,000	1,889,000	1,447,000	1,321,000	1,071,000	928,000	864,000
Average Shares	1,362,000	1,353,000	1,334,000	1,327,000	1,315,000	1,293,000	1,275,000	1,229,000
Balance Sheet								
Current Assets	36,192,000	51,120,000	51,334,000	50,004,000	48,798,000	46,258,000	55,559,000	46,608,000
Total Assets	248,320,000	243,274,000	223,383,000	183,718,000	154,642,000	143,642,000	133,637,000	108,553,000
Current Liabilities	222,394,000	217,186,000	201,755,000	165,275,000	139,124,000	129,772,000	120,775,000	97,441,000
Long-Term Obligations	4,128,000	4,753,000	2,876,000	2,890,000	1,899,000	1,903,000	1,632,000	2,001,000
Total Liabilities	228,990,000	224,749,000	206,962,000	170,316,000	142,839,000	133,261,000	124,048,000	100,839,000
Stockholders' Equity	19,330,000	18,525,000	16,421,000	13,402,000	11,803,000	10,381,000	9,589,000	7,714,000
Shares Outstanding	1,348,217	1,345,332	1,332,749	1,320,337	1,310,722	1,296,886	1,277,529	1,271,164
Statistical Record								
Return on Assets %	1.08	1.01	0.93	0.86	0.89	0.77	0.76	0.86
Return on Equity %	14.17	13.47	12.63	11.48	11.91	10.73	10.70	12.40
EBITDA Margin %	42.96	43.33	41.70	37.75	36.85	33.56	31.77	34.59
Net Margin %	30.63	26.27	24.70	22.22	21.44	19.33	18.44	17.76
Asset Turnover	0.04	0.04	0.04	0.04	0.04	0.04	0.04	0.05
Current Ratio	0.16	0.24	0.25	0.30	0.35	0.36	0.46	0.48
Debt to Equity	0.21	0.26	0.18	0.22	0.16	0.18	0.17	0.26
Price Range	57.76-37.53	52.28-37.53	40.47-22.22	35.42-25.96	30.78-23.65	26.00-14.36	15.38-11.61	19.45-10.75
P/E Ratio	32.82-21.32	32.47-23.31	30.89-16.96	34.39-25.20	32.40-24.89	33.33-18.41	22.29-16.83	27.79-15.36
Average Yield %	0.75	0.75	0.90	0.77	0.88	1.19	1.81	1.58

Address: 211 Main Street, San Francisco, CA 94105
Telephone: 415-667-7000
Fax: 415-627-8894

Web Site: www.aboutschwab.com
Officers: Charles R. Schwab - Chairman Walter W. Bettinger - President, Chief Executive Officer

Auditors: DELOITTE & TOUCHE LLP
Investor Contact: 415-667-1841
Transfer Agents: Wells Fargo Bank, N.A., St. Paul, MN

SCIENCE APPLICATIONS INTERNATIONAL CORP

Exchange	Symbol	Price	52Wk Range	Yield	P/E
NYS	SAIC	$80.93 (6/29/2018)	90.10-61.06	1.53	19.88

*7 Year Price Score N/A *NYSE Composite Index=100 *12 Month Price Score 111.76

Interim Earnings (Per Share)

Qtr.	Apr	Jul	Oct	Jan
2015-16	0.69	0.46	0.72	0.60
2016-17	0.71	0.81	0.91	0.79
2017-18	1.08	0.80	0.98	1.16
2018-19	1.13	...	...	...

Interim Dividends (Per Share)

Amt	Decl	Ex	Rec	Pay
0.31Q	10/04/2017	10/12/2017	10/13/2017	10/27/2017
0.31Q	12/14/2017	01/11/2018	01/12/2018	01/26/2018
0.31Q	03/29/2018	04/12/2018	04/13/2018	04/27/2018
0.31Q	06/12/2018	07/12/2018	07/13/2018	07/27/2018

Indicated Div: $1.24 (Div. Reinv. Plan)

Valuation Analysis **Institutional Holding**

Forecast EPS	$4.50	No of Institutions
	(06/11/2018)	333
Market Cap	$3.5 Billion	Shares
Book Value	$325.0 Million	33,249,548
Price/Book	10.71	% Held
Price/Sales	0.77	N/A

TRADING VOLUME (thousand shares)

Business Summary: IT Services (MIC: 6.3.1 SIC: 7373 NAIC: 541512)

Science Applications International is a provider of technical, engineering and enterprise information technology (IT) services primarily to the U.S. government. Co. provides engineering, systems integration and information technology offerings for government projects. Co.'s offerings include: engineering; technology and equipment platform integration; maintenance of ground and maritime systems; logistics; training and simulation; operation and program support services; and end-to-end services spanning the design, development, integration, deployment, management and operations, sustainment and security of its customers' entire IT infrastructure.

Recent Developments: For the year ended Feb 2 2018, net income increased 25.2% to US$179.0 million from US$143.0 million in the prior year. Revenues were US$4.45 billion, up 0.3% from US$4.44 billion the year before. Operating income was US$256.0 million versus US$263.0 million in the prior year, a decrease of 2.7%. Direct operating expenses rose 1.0% to US$4.04 billion from US$4.00 billion in the comparable period the year before. Indirect operating expenses decreased 11.9% to US$155.0 million from US$176.0 million in the equivalent prior-year period.

Prospects: Our evaluation of Science Applications International Corp. as of Jan. 21, 2018 is the result of our systematic analysis on three basic characteristics: earnings strength, relative valuation, and recent stock price movement. The company has generated a negative trend in earnings per share over the past 5 quarters. However, while recent estimates for the company have been mixed, SAIC has posted better than expected results. Based on operating earnings yield, the company is undervalued when compared to all of the companies in our coverage universe. Share price changes over the past year indicates that SAIC will perform poorly over the near term.

Financial Data
(US$ in Thousands)

	3 Mos	02/02/2018	02/03/2017	01/29/2016	01/30/2015	01/31/2014	01/31/2013	01/31/2012
Earnings Per Share	4.07	4.02	3.22	2.47	2.91	2.27	...	...
Cash Flow Per Share	5.12	5.03	6.04	4.95	5.92	3.77	...	...
Dividends Per Share	1.240	1.240	1.240	1.210	1.120	0.560	...	...
Dividend Payout %	30.47	30.85	38.51	48.99	38.49	24.67	...	...
Income Statement								
Total Revenue	1,175,000	4,454,000	4,450,000	4,315,000	3,885,000	4,121,000	4,781,000	4,733,000
EBITDA	78,000	281,000	296,000	253,000	259,000	196,000	294,000	313,000
Depn & Amortn	11,000	23,000	24,000	26,000	19,000	13,000	13,000	15,000
Income Before Taxes	55,000	214,000	220,000	183,000	223,000	176,000	281,000	298,000
Income Taxes	6,000	35,000	72,000	66,000	82,000	63,000	99,000	116,000
Net Income	49,000	179,000	148,000	117,000	141,000	113,000	182,000	182,000
Average Shares	43,400	44,500	45,900	47,400	48,500	49,700	...	...
Balance Sheet								
Current Assets	930,000	950,000	901,000	952,000	943,000	994,000	835,000	923,000
Total Assets	2,061,000	2,073,000	2,042,000	2,122,000	1,398,000	1,447,000	1,271,000	1,371,000
Current Liabilities	695,000	695,000	615,000	688,000	577,000	564,000	664,000	702,000
Long-Term Obligations	971,000	983,000	1,022,000	1,013,000	457,000	489,000	1,000	4,000
Total Liabilities	1,736,000	1,746,000	1,688,000	1,742,000	1,053,000	1,070,000	675,000	715,000
Stockholders' Equity	325,000	327,000	354,000	380,000	345,000	377,000	596,000	656,000
Shares Outstanding	43,000	43,000	44,000	45,000	46,000	49,000	...	...
Statistical Record								
Return on Assets %	8.71	8.72	6.99	6.67	9.94	8.31	13.74	...
Return on Equity %	54.16	52.71	39.67	32.36	39.17	23.23	28.99	...
EBITDA Margin %	6.64	6.31	6.65	5.86	6.67	4.76	6.15	6.61
Net Margin %	4.17	4.02	3.33	2.71	3.63	2.74	3.81	3.85
Asset Turnover	2.20	2.17	2.10	2.46	2.74	3.03	3.61	...
Current Ratio	1.34	1.37	1.47	1.38	1.63	1.76	1.26	1.31
Debt to Equity	2.99	3.01	2.89	2.67	1.32	1.30	N.M.	0.01
Price Range	86.30-61.06	89.24-61.06	88.65-40.50	55.70-39.89	52.13-34.65	39.03-30.94	...	...
P/E Ratio	21.20-15.00	22.20-15.19	27.53-12.58	22.55-16.15	17.91-11.91	17.19-13.63	...	...
Average Yield %	1.68	1.66	1.97	2.46	2.58	1.60	...	...

Address: 12010 Sunset Hills Road, Reston, VA 20190
Telephone: 703-676-4300

Web Site: www.saic.com
Officers: Edward J. Sanderson - Chairman Anthony J. Moraco - Chief Executive Officer, Division Officer, Holding/Parent Company Officer

Auditors: Ernst & Young LLP

SCOTTS MIRACLE-GRO CO (THE)

Exchange	Symbol	Price	52Wk Range	Yield	P/E
NYS	SMG	$83.16 (6/29/2018)	109.47-77.52	2.55	19.71

*7 Year Price Score 114.27 *NYSE Composite Index=100 *12 Month Price Score 88.36

Interim Earnings (Per Share)

Qtr.	Dec	Mar	Jun	Sep
2014-15	(1.23)	2.01	2.14	(0.38)
2015-16	(1.32)	3.38	3.44	(0.41)
2016-17	(1.09)	2.73	2.53	(0.53)
2017-18	(0.37)	2.59	...	...

Interim Dividends (Per Share)

Amt	Decl	Ex	Rec	Pay
0.53Q	08/01/2017	08/23/2017	08/25/2017	09/08/2017
0.53Q	11/01/2017	11/22/2017	11/24/2017	12/08/2017
0.53Q	01/26/2018	02/22/2018	02/23/2018	03/09/2018
0.53Q	04/30/2018	05/24/2018	05/25/2018	06/08/2018

Indicated Div: $2.12

Valuation Analysis

		Institutional Holding	
Forecast EPS	$3.83	No of Institutions	
	(06/13/2018)	513	
Market Cap	$4.6 Billion	Shares	
Book Value	$490.8 Million	47,161,696	
Price/Book	9.42	% Held	
Price/Sales	1.91	72.46	

Business Summary: Agricultural Chemicals (MIC: 8.3.3 SIC: 2879 NAIC: 325320)

Scotts Miracle-Gro provides consumer lawn and garden products in the following categories: lawn care, which includes lawn fertilizer products, grass seed products, and lawn-related weed, pest and disease control products as well as spreaders and outdoor cleaners; gardening and landscape, which includes water-soluble plant foods, continuous-release plant foods, potting mixes and garden soils, mulch and decorative groundcover products, plant-related pest and disease control products, organic garden products, live goods and seeding solutions as well as hydroponic gardening products; and controls, which includes insect control products, rodent control products and weed control products.

Recent Developments: For the quarter ended Mar 31 2018, income from continuing operations decreased 0.9% to US$152.7 million from US$154.1 million in the year-earlier quarter. Net income decreased 9.8% to US$149.0 million from US$165.2 million in the year-earlier quarter. Revenues were US$1.01 billion, down 6.6% from US$1.08 billion the year before. Operating income was US$232.3 million versus US$285.3 million in the prior-year quarter, a decrease of 18.6%. Direct operating expenses declined 2.6% to US$604.1 million from US$620.3 million in the comparable period the year before. Indirect operating expenses decreased 1.2% to US$176.9 million from US$179.0 million in the equivalent prior-year period.

Prospects: Our evaluation of Scotts Co. as of Jan. 21, 2018 is the result of our systematic analysis on three basic characteristics: earnings strength, relative valuation, and recent stock price movement. The company has managed to produce a neutral trend in earnings per share over the past 5 quarters and while recent estimates for the company have been raised by analysts, SMG has posted better than expected results. Based on operating earnings yield, the company is about fairly valued when compared to all of the companies in our coverage universe. Share price changes over the past year indicates that SMG will perform in line with the market over the near term.

Financial Data

(US$ in Thousands)	6 Mos	3 Mos	09/30/2017	09/30/2016	09/30/2015	09/30/2014	09/30/2013	09/30/2012
Earnings Per Share	4.22	4.36	3.63	5.09	2.57	2.65	2.57	1.71
Cash Flow Per Share	6.53	6.13	5.96	3.87	4.04	3.91	5.54	2.51
Tang Book Value Per Share	N.M.	N.M.	N.M.	N.M.	N.M.	N.M.	1.79	N.M.
Dividends Per Share	2.090	2.060	2.030	1.910	1.820	3.763	1.413	1.225
Dividend Payout %	49.53	47.25	55.92	37.52	70.82	141.98	54.96	71.64
Income Statement								
Total Revenue	1,234,900	221,500	2,642,100	2,836,100	3,016,500	2,841,300	2,816,500	2,826,100
EBITDA	193,300	(49,600)	505,700	533,500	378,200	378,500	387,500	314,200
Depn & Amortn	39,600	19,800	95,700	86,900	83,600	74,600	74,300	70,600
Income Before Taxes	113,300	(87,200)	343,900	384,900	244,100	256,600	254,000	181,800
Income Taxes	(17,300)	(66,600)	116,600	139,400	85,400	91,200	92,800	68,600
Net Income	127,700	(21,200)	218,300	315,300	159,800	166,500	161,100	106,500
Average Shares	57,400	57,600	60,200	62,000	62,200	62,700	62,600	62,100
Balance Sheet								
Current Assets	1,639,300	982,900	881,700	991,700	948,600	935,000	881,000	1,000,000
Total Assets	3,575,500	2,910,800	2,747,000	2,808,800	2,527,200	2,058,300	1,937,200	2,074,400
Current Liabilities	906,100	471,100	544,500	593,100	613,100	544,700	509,800	433,600
Long-Term Obligations	1,937,700	1,697,000	1,258,000	1,131,100	1,028,500	692,400	478,100	781,100
Total Liabilities	3,084,700	2,408,000	2,098,200	2,093,600	1,906,500	1,504,600	1,226,700	1,472,500
Stockholders' Equity	490,800	502,800	648,800	715,200	620,700	553,700	710,500	601,900
Shares Outstanding	55,600	57,200	58,100	60,300	61,400	60,700	62,000	61,300
Statistical Record								
Return on Assets %	6.64	8.79	7.86	11.79	6.97	8.33	8.03	5.15
Return on Equity %	42.08	48.46	32.01	47.08	27.21	26.34	24.55	18.29
EBITDA Margin %	15.65	N.M.	19.14	18.81	12.54	13.32	13.76	11.12
Net Margin %	10.34	N.M.	8.26	11.12	5.30	5.86	5.72	3.77
Asset Turnover	0.65	0.88	0.95	1.06	1.32	1.42	1.40	1.37
Current Ratio	1.81	2.09	1.62	1.67	1.55	1.72	1.73	2.31
Debt to Equity	3.95	3.38	1.94	1.58	1.66	1.25	0.67	1.30
Price Range	109.47-83.37	106.99-83.37	97.37-82.95	83.62-60.82	68.99-54.71	63.30-53.09	55.66-39.77	55.00-38.17
P/E Ratio	25.94-19.76	24.54-19.12	26.82-22.85	16.43-11.95	26.84-21.29	23.89-20.03	21.66-15.47	32.16-22.32
Average Yield %	2.20	2.18	2.21	2.70	2.92	6.44	3.03	2.69

Address: 14111 Scottslawn Road, Marysville, OH 43041	**Web Site:** www.scotts.com	**Auditors:** DELOITTE & TOUCHE LLP
Telephone: 937-644-0011	**Officers:** James Hagedorn - Chairman, Chief Executive Officer Michael C. Lukemire - President, Chief Operating Officer, Region Officer	**Investor Contact:** 937-644-0011
Fax: 937-644-7614		**Transfer Agents:** Wells Fargo Shareowner Services

SEALED AIR CORP

Exchange	Symbol	Price	52Wk Range	Yield	P/E
NYS	SEE	$42.45 (6/29/2018)	49.66-41.12	1.51	12.82

*7 Year Price Score 101.86 *NYSE Composite Index=100 *12 Month Price Score 97.15

Interim Earnings (Per Share)

Qtr.	Mar	Jun	Sep	Dec
2015	0.46	0.13	0.42	0.61
2016	0.46	0.25	0.83	0.87
2017	(0.22)	0.45	4.15	(0.08)
2018	(1.21)	...	...	...

Interim Dividends (Per Share)

Amt	Decl	Ex	Rec	Pay
0.16Q	10/05/2017	11/30/2017	12/01/2017	12/15/2017
0.16Q	02/14/2018	03/01/2018	03/02/2018	03/16/2018
0.16Q	05/17/2018	05/31/2018	06/01/2018	06/15/2018
0.16Q	07/13/2018	09/06/2018	09/07/2018	09/21/2018

Indicated Div: $0.64

Valuation Analysis **Institutional Holding**

Forecast EPS	$2.51 (06/14/2018)	No of Institutions	705
Market Cap	$6.9 Billion	Shares	202,817,984
Book Value	N/A	% Held	91.25
Price/Book	N/A		
Price/Sales	1.50		

Business Summary: Containers & Packaging (MIC: 8.1.3 SIC: 2671 NAIC: 322221)

Sealed Air is engaged in food safety and security, facility hygiene and product protection. Co. has three reportable segments: Food Care, which provides a range of integrated system solutions that improve the management of contamination risk and facility hygiene, extend product shelf life through packaging technologies, and improve merchandising, ease-of-use, and back-of-house preparation processes; Diversey Care, which provides Diversey®-branded system solutions for facility hygiene, food safety and security, and infection control; and Product Care, which provides tailored packaging solutions. Co.'s other category include its Medical Applications, which sells medical applications product.

Recent Developments: For the quarter ended Mar 31 2018, loss from continuing operations was US$208.0 million compared with a loss of US$53.7 million in the year-earlier quarter. Net loss amounted to US$200.6 million versus a net loss of US$43.2 million in the year-earlier quarter. Revenues were US$1.13 billion, up 9.6% from US$1.03 billion the year before. Operating income was US$167.5 million versus US$131.1 million in the prior-year quarter, an increase of 27.8%. Direct operating expenses rose 8.6% to US$757.0 million from US$696.8 million in the comparable period the year before. Indirect operating expenses increased 1.1% to US$206.5 million from US$204.3 million in the equivalent prior-year period.

Prospects: Our evaluation of Sealed Air Corp. as of Jan. 21, 2018 is the result of our systematic analysis on three basic characteristics: earnings strength, relative valuation, and recent stock price movement. The company has generated a negative trend in earnings per share over the past 5 quarters and while recent estimates for the company have been mixed, SEE has posted results that fell short of analysts expectations. Based on operating earnings yield, the company is about fairly valued when compared to all of the companies in our coverage universe. Share price changes over the past year indicates that SEE will perform in line with the market over the near term.

Financial Data
(US$ in Thousands)

	3 Mos	12/31/2017	12/31/2016	12/31/2015	12/31/2014	12/31/2013	12/31/2012	12/31/2011
Earnings Per Share	3.31	4.29	2.46	1.62	1.20	0.58	(7.31)	0.80
Cash Flow Per Share	2.26	2.27	4.65	4.75	(0.96)	3.21	2.09	2.35
Dividends Per Share	0.640	0.640	0.610	0.520	0.520	0.520	0.520	0.520
Dividend Payout %	19.34	14.92	24.80	32.10	43.33	89.66	...	65.00
Income Statement								
Total Revenue	1,131,000	4,461,600	6,778,300	7,031,500	7,750,500	7,690,800	7,648,100	5,640,900
EBITDA	188,300	697,600	981,400	853,400	806,100	810,200	(1,197,900)	610,500
Depn & Amortn	32,800	120,100	215,400	213,300	266,700	283,400	304,000	189,500
Income Before Taxes	113,500	393,300	565,900	425,900	267,200	176,800	(1,874,600)	212,900
Income Taxes	321,500	330,500	79,500	90,500	9,100	84,000	(261,900)	67,000
Net Income	(200,600)	814,900	486,400	335,400	258,100	124,200	(1,410,300)	149,100
Average Shares	165,300	188,900	197,200	206,700	213,900	213,500	192,800	185,400
Balance Sheet								
Current Assets	1,665,200	1,866,400	2,215,300	2,215,600	2,691,600	3,417,700	3,222,400	3,262,600
Total Assets	5,041,100	5,280,300	7,389,100	7,426,000	8,041,700	9,134,200	9,437,200	11,496,700
Current Liabilities	1,422,800	1,378,200	2,118,900	1,807,100	1,730,900	2,700,800	2,333,600	2,383,500
Long-Term Obligations	3,247,900	3,230,500	3,938,300	4,302,700	4,282,500	4,116,400	4,540,800	5,010,900
Total Liabilities	5,405,900	5,128,000	6,779,400	6,898,900	6,878,900	7,745,100	7,993,400	8,539,200
Stockholders' Equity	(364,800)	152,300	609,700	527,100	1,162,800	1,389,100	1,443,800	2,957,500
Shares Outstanding	161,616	168,595	193,482	196,013	210,531	196,198	194,557	192,062
Statistical Record								
Return on Assets %	10.29	12.86	6.55	4.34	3.01	1.34	N.M.	1.76
Return on Equity %	557.48	213.88	85.34	39.69	20.23	8.77	N.M.	5.56
EBITDA Margin %	16.65	15.64	14.48	12.14	10.40	10.53	N.M.	10.82
Net Margin %	N.M.	18.26	7.18	4.77	3.33	1.61	N.M.	2.64
Asset Turnover	0.73	0.70	0.91	0.91	0.90	0.83	0.73	0.67
Current Ratio	1.17	1.35	1.05	1.23	1.56	1.27	1.38	1.37
Debt to Equity	...	21.21	6.46	8.16	3.68	2.96	3.15	1.69
Price Range	49.66-41.12	50.22-41.72	52.68-38.36	55.40-39.42	43.47-29.86	34.13-17.51	21.04-13.11	28.52-15.61
P/E Ratio	15.00-12.42	11.71-9.72	21.41-15.59	34.20-24.33	36.23-24.88	58.84-30.19	...	35.65-19.51
Average Yield %	1.43	1.41	1.32	1.09	1.51	2.03	3.06	2.34

Address: 2415 Cascade Pointe Boulevard, Charlotte, NC 28208
Telephone: 980-221-3235
Fax: 201-703-4205

Web Site: www.sealedair.com
Officers: Jerry R. Whitaker - Chairman Edward L. (Ted) Doheny - President, Chief Executive Officer - Designate, Chief Operating Officer

Auditors: Ernst & Young LLP
Investor Contact: 201-791-7600
Transfer Agents: ComputerShare Investor Services, Providence, RI

SEMPRA ENERGY

Exchange	Symbol	Price	52Wk Range	Yield	P/E
NYS	SRE	$116.11 (6/29/2018)	122.23-100.71	3.08	193.52

*7 Year Price Score 97.17 *NYSE Composite Index=100 *12 Month Price Score 95.12

TRADING VOLUME (thousand shares)

Interim Earnings (Per Share)

Qtr.	Mar	Jun	Sep	Dec
2015	1.74	1.17	0.99	1.46
2016	1.27	0.06	2.46	1.53
2017	1.75	1.03	0.22	(1.98)
2018	1.33	...	...	...

Interim Dividends (Per Share)

Amt	Decl	Ex	Rec	Pay
0.823Q	09/08/2017	09/21/2017	09/22/2017	10/15/2017
0.823Q	12/15/2017	12/28/2017	12/29/2017	01/15/2018
0.895Q	02/22/2018	03/22/2018	03/23/2018	04/15/2018
0.895Q	06/20/2018	06/29/2018	07/02/2018	07/15/2018

Indicated Div: $3.58

Valuation Analysis

		Institutional Holding	
Forecast EPS	$5.40 (06/14/2018)	No of Institutions	964
Market Cap	$30.7 Billion	Shares	290,718,048
Book Value	$15.8 Billion	% Held	69.69
Price/Book	1.93		
Price/Sales	2.75		

Business Summary: Electric Utilities (MIC: 3.1.1 SIC: 4932 NAIC: 221210)

Sempra Energy is a holding company. Co.'s principal operating units are: Sempra Utilities, which includes Co.'s San Diego Gas & Electric Company, Southern California Gas Company and Sempra South American Utilities reportable segments; as well as Sempra Infrastructure, which includes Co.'s Sempra Mexico, Sempra Renewables and Sempra liquefied natural gas (LNG) & Midstream reportable segments. Sempra LNG & Midstream develops and invests in liquefied natural gas (LNG)-related infrastructure in North America, develops and operates natural gas storage facilities in Alabama and Mississippi and owns a 50.2% interest in a liquefaction project in Louisiana.

Recent Developments: For the quarter ended Mar 31 2018, net income decreased 20.8% to US$358.0 million from US$452.0 million in the year-earlier quarter. Revenues were US$2.96 billion, down 2.3% from US$3.03 billion the year before. Direct operating expenses declined 3.2% to US$1.76 billion from US$1.82 billion in the comparable period the year before. Indirect operating expenses increased 7.0% to US$503.0 million from US$470.0 million in the equivalent prior-year period.

Prospects: Our evaluation of Sempra Energy as of Jan. 21, 2018 is the result of our systematic analysis on three basic characteristics: earnings strength, relative valuation, and recent stock price movement. The company has generated a negative trend in earnings per share over the past 5 quarters. However, while recent estimates for the company have been mixed, SRE has posted results that fell short of analysts expectations. Based on operating earnings yield, the company is undervalued when compared to all of the companies in our coverage universe. Share price changes over the past year indicates that SRE will perform very well over the near term.

Financial Data

(US$ in Thousands)	3 Mos	12/31/2017	12/31/2016	12/31/2015	12/31/2014	12/31/2013	12/31/2012	12/31/2011
Earnings Per Share	0.60	1.01	5.46	5.37	4.63	4.01	3.48	5.62
Cash Flow Per Share	13.91	14.41	9.24	11.70	8.79	7.32	8.34	7.79
Tang Book Value Per Share	42.23	38.50	40.13	42.63	40.51	39.10	36.04	34.82
Dividends Per Share	3.362	3.290	3.020	2.800	2.640	2.520	2.400	1.920
Dividend Payout %	560.42	325.74	55.31	52.14	57.02	62.84	68.97	34.16
Income Statement								
Total Revenue	2,962,000	11,207,000	10,183,000	10,231,000	11,035,000	10,557,000	9,647,000	10,036,000
EBITDA	1,209,000	3,583,000	3,042,000	3,379,000	3,125,000	3,046,000	2,820,000	2,850,000
Depn & Amortn	386,000	1,422,000	1,312,000	1,250,000	1,156,000	1,113,000	1,090,000	978,000
Income Before Taxes	667,000	1,551,000	1,207,000	1,600,000	1,443,000	1,399,000	1,262,000	1,435,000
Income Taxes	289,000	1,276,000	389,000	341,000	300,000	366,000	59,000	366,000
Net Income	375,000	257,000	1,371,000	1,350,000	1,162,000	1,009,000	865,000	1,365,000
Average Shares	259,490	252,300	251,155	250,923	250,655	249,332	246,693	241,523
Balance Sheet								
Current Assets	3,394,000	3,341,000	3,110,000	2,891,000	4,184,000	3,997,000	3,695,000	2,332,000
Total Assets	60,485,000	50,454,000	47,786,000	41,150,000	39,732,000	37,244,000	36,499,000	33,356,000
Current Liabilities	9,109,000	6,635,000	5,927,000	4,612,000	5,069,000	4,369,000	4,258,000	4,163,000
Long-Term Obligations	20,898,000	16,445,000	14,429,000	13,134,000	12,167,000	11,253,000	11,621,000	10,078,000
Total Liabilities	44,641,000	37,784,000	34,835,000	29,341,000	28,406,000	26,236,000	26,217,000	23,518,000
Stockholders' Equity	15,844,000	12,670,000	12,951,000	11,809,000	11,326,000	11,008,000	10,282,000	9,838,000
Shares Outstanding	264,000	251,358	250,152	248,298	246,330	244,461	242,368	239,934
Statistical Record								
Return on Assets %	0.35	0.52	3.07	3.34	3.02	2.74	2.47	4.29
Return on Equity %	1.31	2.01	11.04	11.67	10.41	9.48	8.57	14.47
EBITDA Margin %	40.82	31.97	29.87	33.03	28.32	28.85	29.23	28.40
Net Margin %	12.66	2.29	13.46	13.20	10.53	9.56	8.97	13.60
Asset Turnover	0.20	0.23	0.23	0.25	0.29	0.29	0.28	0.32
Current Ratio	0.37	0.50	0.52	0.63	0.83	0.91	0.87	0.56
Debt to Equity	1.32	1.30	1.11	1.11	1.07	1.02	1.13	1.02
Price Range	122.23-103.36	122.23-100.82	114.50-87.00	115.08-90.09	115.85-88.44	92.10-70.84	72.74-54.83	55.50-45.59
P/E Ratio	203.72-172.27	121.02-99.82	20.97-15.93	21.43-16.78	25.02-19.10	22.97-17.67	20.90-15.76	9.88-8.11
Average Yield %	2.97	2.92	2.92	2.71	2.61	3.04	3.71	3.65

Address: 488 8th Avenue, San Diego, CA 92101
Telephone: 619-696-2000

Web Site: www.sempra.com
Officers: Debra L. Reed - Chairman, President, Chief Executive Officer, Executive Vice President Joseph A. Householder - President, Corporate Group President, Chief Financial Officer, Executive Vice President, Senior Vice President, Chief Accounting Officer, Controller, Chief Operating Officer

Auditors: DELOITTE & TOUCHE LLP
Transfer Agents: American Stock Transfer & Trust Company, LLC, Brooklyn, NY

SENSIENT TECHNOLOGIES CORP.

Exchange	Symbol	Price	52Wk Range	Yield	P/E	Div Acheiver
NYS	SXT	$71.55 (6/29/2018)	82.71-66.48	1.84	27.31	12 Years

*7 Year Price Score 103.02 *NYSE Composite Index=100 *12 Month Price Score 93.08

Interim Earnings (Per Share)

Qtr.	Mar	Jun	Sep	Dec
2015	0.64	0.63	0.60	0.43
2016	0.69	0.63	0.79	0.71
2017	0.30	0.69	0.73	0.31
2018	0.89	...	...	...

Interim Dividends (Per Share)

Amt	Decl	Ex	Rec	Pay
0.30Q	07/20/2017	08/02/2017	08/04/2017	09/01/2017
0.33Q	10/19/2017	11/03/2017	11/06/2017	12/01/2017
0.33Q	01/26/2018	02/05/2018	02/06/2018	03/01/2018
0.33Q	04/26/2018	05/10/2018	05/11/2018	06/01/2018

Indicated Div: $1.32

Valuation Analysis — Institutional Holding

Forecast EPS	$3.73	No of Institutions
	(06/11/2018)	392
Market Cap	$3.0 Billion	Shares
Book Value	$827.5 Million	59,393,680
Price/Book	3.66	% Held
Price/Sales	2.20	86.09

Business Summary: Specialty Chemicals (MIC: 8.3.2 SIC: 2816 NAIC: 325131)

Sensient Technologies is a manufacturer and marketer of colors, flavors and fragrances. Co.'s three reportable segments are: the Flavors & Fragrances Group, which is a developer, manufacturer and supplier of flavor and fragrance systems for the food, beverage, personal care and household-products industries; Color Group, which provides natural and synthetic color systems for use in foods, beverages and pharmaceuticals; colors and other ingredients for cosmetic; and Asia Pacific Group, which provides a range of products from its Flavors & Fragrances Group and Color Group, as well as products developed by regional technical teams.

Recent Developments: For the quarter ended Mar 31 2018, net income increased 189.5% to US$38.2 million from US$13.2 million in the year-earlier quarter. Revenues were US$356.5 million, up 4.4% from US$341.4 million the year before. Operating income was US$55.7 million versus US$24.0 million in the prior-year quarter, an increase of 131.6%. Direct operating expenses rose 5.9% to US$233.4 million from US$220.5 million in the comparable period the year before. Indirect operating expenses decreased 30.5% to US$67.4 million from US$96.9 million in the equivalent prior-year period.

Prospects: Our evaluation of Sensient Technologies Corp. as of Jan. 21, 2018 is the result of our systematic analysis on three basic characteristics: earnings strength, relative valuation, and recent stock price movement. The company has managed to produce a neutral trend in earnings per share over the past 5 quarters. However, while recent estimates for the company have been lowered by analysts, SXT has posted better than expected results. Based on operating earnings yield, the company is undervalued when compared to all of the companies in our coverage universe. Share price changes over the past year indicates that SXT will perform in line with the market over the near term.

Financial Data
(US$ in Thousands)

	3 Mos	12/31/2017	12/31/2016	12/31/2015	12/31/2014	12/31/2013	12/31/2012	12/31/2011
Earnings Per Share	2.62	2.03	2.82	2.31	1.51	2.27	2.49	2.41
Cash Flow Per Share	3.76	4.12	4.98	2.79	3.90	3.09	2.80	2.87
Tang Book Value Per Share	9.32	.10.10	10.04	9.74	12.95	15.54	13.91	11.86
Dividends Per Share	1.260	1.230	1.110	1.040	0.980	0.910	0.870	0.840
Dividend Payout %	48.09	60.59	39.36	45.02	64.90	40.09	34.94	34.85
Income Statement								
Total Revenue	356,477	1,362,265	1,383,210	1,375,964	1,447,821	1,467,550	1,459,050	1,430,789
EBITDA	68,259	214,762	231,323	213,035	180,890	223,078	238,200	235,594
Depn & Amortn	12,578	46,956	45,714	46,694	50,225	50,716	46,992	44,771
Income Before Taxes	50,126	148,423	167,285	149,396	114,598	156,215	174,307	171,384
Income Taxes	11,932	58,823	44,372	42,149	32,827	42,920	50,399	50,900
Net Income	38,194	89,600	126,256	106,785	73,646	113,295	123,908	120,484
Average Shares	43,034	44,031	44,843	46,204	48,819	49,934	49,822	49,937
Balance Sheet								
Current Assets	761,941	733,475	717,061	753,343	759,389	789,825	751,354	706,870
Total Assets	1,775,388	1,724,340	1,667,860	1,711,437	1,765,206	1,870,734	1,776,643	1,654,164
Current Liabilities	203,238	216,323	213,675	212,922	224,905	222,893	204,236	207,275
Long-Term Obligations	691,265	604,159	582,780	613,877	451,011	348,124	333,979	312,422
Total Liabilities	947,932	872,039	832,119	866,310	718,271	628,050	622,745	604,954
Stockholders' Equity	827,456	852,301	835,741	845,127	1,046,935	1,242,684	1,153,898	1,049,210
Shares Outstanding	42,336	43,195	44,238	44,780	47,424	49,849	49,690	49,916
Statistical Record								
Return on Assets %	6.69	.5.28	7.45	6.14	4.05	6.21	7.20	7.41
Return on Equity %	13.67	10.62	14.98	11.29	6.43	9.45	11.22	11.85
EBITDA Margin %	19.15	15.77	16.72	15.48	12.49	15.20	16.33	16.47
Net Margin %	10.71	6.58	9.13	7.76	5.09	7.72	8.49	8.42
Asset Turnover	0.80	0.80	0.82	0.79	0.80	0.80	0.85	0.88
Current Ratio	3.75	3.39	3.36	3.54	3.38	3.54	3.68	3.41
Debt to Equity	0.84	0.71	0.70	0.73	0.43	0.28	0.29	0.30
Price Range	83.35-67.56	83.35-71.84	83.11-53.92	70.25-57.39	62.98-46.74	53.32-35.56	40.92-33.81	39.45-30.92
P/E Ratio	31.81-25.79	41.06-35.39	29.47-19.12	30.41-24.84	41.71-30.95	23.49-15.67	16.43-13.58	16.37-12.83
Average Yield %	1.65	1.58	1.61	1.60	1.80	2.13	2.37	2.36

Address: 777 East Wisconsin Avenue, Milwaukee, WI 53202-5304 **Telephone:** 414-271-6755 **Fax:** 414-347-4795	**Web Site:** www.sensient.com **Officers:** Paul Manning - President, Chief Executive Officer, Division Officer Stephen J. Rolfs - Senior Vice President, Vice President, Chief Financial Officer	**Auditors:** Ernst & Young LLP **Investor Contact:** 414-347-3779 **Transfer Agents:** Wells Fargo Bank Minnesota, N.A., St. Paul, MN

SERVICE CORP. INTERNATIONAL

Exchange	Symbol	Price	52Wk Range	Yield	P/E
NYS	SCI	$35.79 (6/29/2018)	40.13-32.99	1.90	15.17

*7 Year Price Score 128.05 *NYSE Composite Index=100 ***12 Month Price Score 98.77**

Interim Earnings (Per Share)

Qtr.	Mar	Jun	Sep	Dec
2015	0.30	0.25	0.23	0.36
2016	0.24	0.08	0.24	0.34
2017	0.91	0.36	0.29	1.28
2018	0.43	...	...	...

Interim Dividends (Per Share)

Amt	Decl	Ex	Rec	Pay
0.15Q	08/07/2017	09/14/2017	09/15/2017	09/29/2017
0.15Q	11/08/2017	12/14/2017	12/15/2017	12/29/2017
0.17Q	02/13/2018	03/14/2018	03/15/2018	03/30/2018
0.17Q	05/09/2018	06/14/2018	06/15/2018	06/29/2018

Indicated Div: $0.68

Valuation Analysis / Institutional Holding

Valuation Analysis		Institutional Holding	
Forecast EPS	$1.82	No of Institutions	
	(05/28/2018)	523	
Market Cap	$6.6 Billion	Shares	
Book Value	$1.5 Billion	186,803,120	
Price/Book	4.36	% Held	
Price/Sales	2.12	80.35	

Business Summary: Miscellaneous Consumer Services (MIC: 2.2.3 SIC: 7261 NAIC: 812210)

Service Corporation International provides deathcare products and services. Co.'s funeral service and cemetery operations consist of funeral service locations, cemeteries, funeral/cemetery combination locations, crematoria, and other related businesses. Funeral service locations provide services related to funerals and cremations, including the use of funeral home facilities and motor vehicles, arranging and directing services, removal, preparation, embalming, cremations, memorialization, and catering. Co.'s cemeteries provide cemetery property interment rights, including developed lots, lawn crypts, mausoleum spaces, niches, and other cremation memorialization and interment options.

Recent Developments: For the quarter ended Mar 31 2018, net income decreased 53.0% to US$82.0 million from US$174.7 million in the year-earlier quarter. Revenues were US$794.5 million, up 2.2% from US$777.7 million the year before. Operating income was US$163.7 million versus US$139.9 million in the prior-year quarter, an increase of 17.0%. Direct operating expenses declined 0.3% to US$598.7 million from US$600.5 million in the comparable period the year before. Indirect operating expenses decreased 14.1% to US$32.1 million from US$37.3 million in the equivalent prior-year period.

Prospects: Our evaluation of Service Corp. International as of Jan. 21, 2018 is the result of our systematic analysis on three basic characteristics: earnings strength, relative valuation, and recent stock price movement. The company has generated a negative trend in earnings per share over the past 5 quarters and while recent estimates for the company have been mixed, SCI has posted better than expected results. Based on operating earnings yield, the company is about fairly valued when compared to all of the companies in our coverage universe. Share price changes over the past year indicates that SCI will perform in line with the market over the near term.

Financial Data

(US$ in Thousands)	3 Mos	12/31/2017	12/31/2016	12/31/2015	12/31/2014	12/31/2013	12/31/2012	12/31/2011
Earnings Per Share	2.36	2.84	0.90	1.14	0.81	0.67	0.70	0.61
Cash Flow Per Share	2.84	2.68	2.39	2.36	1.51	1.82	1.71	1.66
Dividends Per Share	0.620	0.580	0.510	0.440	0.340	0.270	0.280	0.190
Dividend Payout %	26.27	20.42	56.67	38.60	41.98	40.30	40.00	31.15
Income Statement								
Total Revenue	794,482	3,095,031	3,031,137	2,986,380	2,994,012	2,556,382	2,410,481	2,316,040
EBITDA	175,391	750,174	572,619	606,869	671,628	453,386	450,118	300,357
Depn & Amortn	21,446	180,791	178,189	172,915	167,186	138,198	137,660	25,591
Income Before Taxes	110,369	400,258	326,658	370,351	402,600	245,719	245,683	225,636
Income Taxes	28,321	(146,589)	149,353	135,027	225,980	96,615	91,548	79,404
Net Income	81,988	546,663	177,038	233,772	172,469	143,848	152,546	144,903
Average Shares	189,923	192,246	196,042	204,450	214,200	216,014	219,066	236,669
Balance Sheet								
Current Assets	351,005	481,296	354,396	308,409	396,856	393,747	286,199	328,093
Total Assets	12,429,008	12,864,503	12,038,149	11,718,888	11,923,644	12,906,070	9,683,568	9,327,812
Current Liabilities	591,805	828,979	537,870	519,396	552,008	642,584	412,104	385,608
Long-Term Obligations	3,316,695	3,135,316	3,196,616	3,071,738	2,963,794	3,155,548	1,916,621	1,861,116
Total Liabilities	10,917,263	11,455,113	10,945,436	10,534,196	10,554,918	11,491,840	8,340,541	7,935,718
Stockholders' Equity	1,511,745.	1,409,390	1,092,713	1,184,692	1,368,726	1,414,230	1,343,027	1,392,094
Shares Outstanding	184,011	186,614	189,405	195,772	204,866	212,316	211,046	222,955
Statistical Record								
Return on Assets %	3.68	4.39	1.49	1.98	1.39	1.27	1.60	1.56
Return on Equity %	33.71	43.70	15.50	18.31	12.39	10.43	11.12	10.09
EBITDA Margin %	22.08	24.24	18.89	20.32	22.43	17.74	18.67	12.97
Net Margin %	10.32	17.66	5.84	7.83	5.76	5.63	6.33	6.26
Asset Turnover	0.25	0.25	0.25	0.25	0.24	0.23	0.25	0.25
Current Ratio	0.59	0.58	0.66	0.59	0.72	0.61	0.69	0.85
Debt to Equity	2.19	2.22	2.93	2.59	2.17	2.23	1.43	1.34
Price Range	40.13-30.25	38.00-28.81	28.67-21.65	31.94-22.29	23.22-16.82	19.24-13.81	14.54-10.55	12.01-8.12
P/E Ratio	17.00-12.82	13.38-10.14	31.86-24.06	28.02-19.55	28.67-20.77	28.72-20.61	20.77-15.07	19.69-13.31
Average Yield %	1.76	1.75	1.96	1.61	1.67	1.56	2.26	1.83

Address: 1929 Allen Parkway,	Web Site: www.sci-corp.com	Auditors: PricewaterhouseCoopers LLP
Houston, TX 77019	Officers: Thomas L. (Tom) Ryan - Chairman,	Transfer Agents: Computershare
Telephone: 713-522-5141	President, Chief Executive Officer Michael R. Webb -	Shareowner Services, Providence, RI
	President, Executive Vice President, Chief Operating	
	Officer	

SERVICEMASTER GLOBAL HOLDINGS, INC

Exchange	Symbol	Price	52Wk Range	Yield	P/E
NYS	SERV	$59.47 (6/29/2018)	60.40-38.95	N/A	15.77

*7 Year Price Score N/A   *NYSE Composite Index=100   *12 Month Price Score 112.85

Interim Earnings (Per Share)

Qtr.	Mar	Jun	Sep	Dec
2015	0.20	0.49	0.36	0.12
2016	0.28	0.11	0.51	0.23
2017	0.29	0.63	0.59	2.25
2018	0.30	...	...	...

Interim Dividends (Per Share)

No Dividends Paid

Valuation Analysis		Institutional Holding	
Forecast EPS	$2.55	No of Institutions	
	(06/03/2018)	307	
Market Cap	$8.1 Billion	Shares	
Book Value	$1.2 Billion	157,705,056	
Price/Book	6.50	% Held	
Price/Sales	2.73	N/A	

Business Summary: Miscellaneous Consumer Services (MIC: 2.2.3 SIC: 8741 NAIC: 551112)

ServiceMaster Global Holdings is holding company. Co. is a provider of residential and commercial services, operating through a service network and franchised and licensed agreements. Co.'s portfolio of brands includes Terminix (termite and pest control), American Home Shield (home warranties), ServiceMaster Restore (disaster restoration), ServiceMaster Clean (janitorial), Merry Maids (residential cleaning), Furniture Medic (cabinet and wood furniture repair) and AmeriSpec (home inspection). Co. operates in three segments: Terminix, American Home Shield, and the Franchise Services Group (which includes ServiceMaster Restore, ServiceMaster Clean, Merry Maids, Furniture Medic and AmeriSpec).

Recent Developments: For the quarter ended Mar 31 2018, income from continuing operations increased 5.3% to US$40.0 million from US$38.0 million in the year-earlier quarter. Net income increased 2.6% to US$40.0 million from US$39.0 million in the year-earlier quarter. Revenues were US$675.0 million, up 5.0% from US$643.0 million the year before. Direct operating expenses rose 4.3% to US$361.0 million from US$346.0 million in the comparable period the year before. Indirect operating expenses increased 8.1% to US$214.0 million from US$198.0 million in the equivalent prior-year period.

Prospects: Our evaluation of ServiceMaster Global Holding as of Jan. 21, 2018 is the result of our systematic analysis on three basic characteristics: earnings strength, relative valuation, and recent stock price movement. The company has managed to produce a neutral trend in earnings per share over the past 5 quarters and while recent estimates for the company have been raised by analysts, SERV has posted better than expected results. Based on operating earnings yield, the company is about fairly valued when compared to all of the companies in our coverage universe. Share price changes over the past year indicates that SERV will perform well over the near term.

Financial Data
(US$ in Millions)

	3 Mos	12/31/2017	12/31/2016	12/31/2015	12/31/2014	12/31/2013	12/31/2012	12/31/2011
Earnings Per Share	3.77	3.76	1.13	1.17	(0.50)	(5.49)	(7.77)	0.50
Cash Flow Per Share	3.17	1.53	2.40	2.49	2.24	2.26	1.13	0.80
Income Statement								
Total Revenue	675	2,912	2,746	2,594	2,457	2,293	2,214	2,105
EBITDA	117	592	449	475	344	373	254	280
Depn & Amortn	26	76	61	47	48	48	42	38
Income Before Taxes	54	370	241	270	84	86	(26)	(13)
Income Taxes	14	(139)	85	107	40	43	(8)	(6)
Net Income	40	510	155	160	(57)	(507)	(714)	46
Average Shares	135	135	137	136	113	92	92	92
Balance Sheet								
Current Assets	739	1,242	998	933	1,044	1,213	1,085	...
Total Assets	5,383	5,646	5,386	5,098	5,134	5,905	6,415	...
Current Liabilities	761	1,174	1,042	955	905	972	899	...
Long-Term Obligations	2,676	2,643	2,772	2,698	3,017	3,867	3,881	...
Total Liabilities	4,143	4,479	4,700	4,553	4,775	5,882	5,880	...
Stockholders' Equity	1,239	1,167	686	545	359	23	535	...
Shares Outstanding	135	135	135	135	134	98	98	98
Statistical Record								
Return on Assets %	9.48	4.62	2.95	3.13	N.M.	N.M.	...	...
Return on Equity %	53.12	27.49	25.11	35.40	N.M.	N.M.	...	...
EBITDA Margin %	17.33	20.33	16.35	18.31	14.00	16.27	11.47	13.30
Net Margin %	5.93	17.51	5.64	6.17	N.M.	N.M.	N.M.	2.19
Asset Turnover	0.55	0.26	0.52	0.51	0.45	0.37	...	...
Current Ratio	0.97	1.06	0.96	0.98	1.15	1.25	1.21	...
Debt to Equity	2.16	2.26	4.04	4.95	8.40	168.13	7.25	...
Price Range	55.12-36.45	52.32-36.45	42.21-32.75	39.65-26.03	27.30-17.57	...	...	...
P/E Ratio	14.62-9.67	13.91-9.69	37.35-28.98	33.89-22.25	...	...	...	...

Address: 150 Peabody Place, Memphis, TN 38103 **Telephone:** 901-597-1400	**Web Site:** www.servicemaster.com **Officers:** Nikhil Madhukar Varty - Chief Executive Officer Anthony D. (Tony) DiLucente - Senior Vice President, Chief Financial Officer	**Auditors:** DELOITTE & TOUCHE LLP **Transfer Agents:** Computershare Trust Company, N.A.

SERVICENOW INC

Exchange	Symbol	Price	52Wk Range	Yield	P/E
NYS	NOW	$172.47 (6/29/2018)	186.42-103.58	N/A	N/A

*7 Year Price Score N/A   *NYSE Composite Index=100   *12 Month Price Score 123.62

Interim Earnings (Per Share)

Qtr.	Mar	Jun	Sep	Dec
2015	(0.38)	(0.40)	(0.26)	(0.23)
2016	(2.06)	(0.30)	(0.22)	(0.19)
2017	(0.24)	(0.33)	(0.14)	(0.16)
2018	0.06	...	...	...

Interim Dividends (Per Share)

No Dividends Paid

Valuation Analysis   Institutional Holding

Forecast EPS	$2.30	No of Institutions
	(06/13/2018)	624
Market Cap	$30.5 Billion	Shares
Book Value	$865.2 Million	188,559,232
Price/Book	35.20	% Held
Price/Sales	14.46	92.98

Business Summary: IT Services (MIC: 6.3.1 SIC: 7372 NAIC: 511210)

ServiceNow provides enterprise cloud computing solutions that define, structure, manage and automate services for global enterprises. Co. markets its services to enterprises in a variety of industries, including financial services, consumer products, information technology services, health care, government, education and technology. Co. sells its subscription services primarily through direct sales and, to a lesser extent, through indirect channel sales. Co. also provides a portfolio of professional services to customers through its professional services and a network of partners.

Recent Developments: For the quarter ended Mar 31 2018, net income amounted to US$10.6 million versus a net loss of US$21.5 million in the year-earlier quarter. Revenues were US$589.2 million, up 37.4% from US$428.8 million the year before. Operating loss was US$20.3 million versus a loss of US$21.8 million in the prior-year quarter. Direct operating expenses rose 23.6% to US$143.5 million from US$116.1 million in the comparable period the year before. Indirect operating expenses increased 39.3% to US$466.0 million from US$334.5 million in the equivalent prior-year period.

Prospects: Our evaluation of ServiceNow Inc as of Jan. 21, 2018 is the result of our systematic analysis on three basic characteristics: earnings strength, relative valuation, and recent stock price movement. The company has produced a positive trend in earnings per share over the past 5 quarters and while recent estimates for the company have remained steady, NOW has posted better than expected results. Based on operating earnings yield, the company is overvalued when compared to all of the companies in our coverage universe. Share price changes over the past year indicates that NOW will perform well over the near term.

Financial Data
(US$ in Thousands)

	3 Mos	12/31/2017	12/31/2016	12/31/2015	12/31/2014	12/31/2013	12/31/2012	12/31/2011
Earnings Per Share	(0.57)	(0.87)	(2.75)	(1.27)	(1.23)	(0.54)	(0.51)	(0.33)
Cash Flow Per Share	4.02	3.76	0.97	2.02	0.96	0.60	0.66	1.24
Tang Book Value Per Share	3.70	2.11	1.42	2.91	2.13	2.71	1.93	0.48
Income Statement								
Total Revenue	589,222	1,933,026	1,390,513	1,005,480	682,563	424,650	243,712	73,375
EBITDA	79,752	11,486	(339,908)	(106,065)	(109,735)	(43,667)	(24,084)	(2,163)
Depn & Amortn	75,183	112,900	82,900	60,300	42,100	22,600	13,500	2,000
Income Before Taxes	(7,360)	(149,004)	(450,051)	(193,012)	(175,540)	(71,197)	(35,980)	(5,609)
Income Taxes	(17,982)	126	1,753	5,414	3,847	2,511	1,368	1,075
Net Income	10,622	(149,130)	(451,804)	(198,426)	(179,387)	(73,708)	(37,348)	(6,684)
Average Shares	190,249	171,175	164,533	155,706	145,355	135,415	73,908	21,104
Balance Sheet								
Current Assets	2,489,926	2,410,564	1,342,535	1,085,635	906,986	797,749	422,089	130,507
Total Assets	3,704,485	3,397,904	2,033,767	1,807,052	1,425,079	1,168,476	478,114	156,323
Current Liabilities	2,098,016	2,100,631	1,071,498	731,636	506,997	328,088	211,627	126,561
Long-Term Obligations	637,795	630,018	507,812	474,534	443,764	414,777	...	...
Total Liabilities	2,839,322	2,813,772	1,646,806	1,240,238	996,404	774,217	234,709	145,577
Stockholders' Equity	865,163	584,132	386,961	566,814	428,675	394,259	243,405	10,746
Shares Outstanding	176,562	174,275	167,430	160,785	149,509	140,354	126,367	22,229
Statistical Record								
EBITDA Margin %	13.54	0.59	N.M.	N.M.	N.M.	N.M.	N.M.	N.M.
Net Margin %	1.80	N.M.	N.M.	N.M.	N.M.	N.M.	N.M.	N.M.
Asset Turnover	0.72	0.71	0.72	0.62	0.53	0.52	0.77	1.40
Current Ratio	1.19	1.15	1.25	1.48	1.79	2.43	1.99	1.03
Debt to Equity	0.74	1.08	1.31	0.84	1.04	1.05	...	...
Price Range		175.34-84.49	130.69-75.66	87.91-47.14	89.99-63.63	70.81-46.42	58.37-26.07	40.37-23.74	...

Address: 2225 Lawson Lane, Santa Clara, CA 95054 **Telephone:** 408-501-8550	**Web Site:** www.servicenow.com **Officers:** Frederic B. Luddy - Chief Products Officer, Chairman John J. Donahoe - President, Chief Executive Officer	**Auditors:** PricewaterhouseCoopers LLP **Investor Contact:** 408-961-2349 **Transfer Agents:** Computershare Trust Company, N.A

SHERWIN-WILLIAMS CO (THE)

Exchange	Symbol	Price	52Wk Range	Yield	P/E	Div Achiever
NYS	SHW	$407.57 (6/29/2018)	432.84-328.97	0.84	21.74	38 Years

*7 Year Price Score 130.91 ***NYSE Composite Index=100** ***12 Month Price Score 100.32**

TRADING VOLUME (thousand shares)

Interim Earnings (Per Share)

Qtr.	Mar	Jun	Sep	Dec
2015	1.38	3.70	3.97	2.12
2016	1.57	3.99	4.08	2.14
2017	2.53	3.36	3.33	9.44
2018	2.62	...	...	...

Interim Dividends (Per Share)

Amt	Decl	Ex	Rec	Pay
0.85Q	07/19/2017	08/16/2017	08/18/2017	09/08/2017
0.85Q	10/18/2017	11/16/2017	11/17/2017	12/08/2017
0.86Q	02/14/2018	02/23/2018	02/26/2018	03/09/2018
0.86Q	04/18/2018	05/17/2018	05/18/2018	06/01/2018

Indicated Div: $3.44 (Div. Reinv. Plan)

Valuation Analysis / Institutional Holding

Valuation Analysis		Institutional Holding	
Forecast EPS	$18.85	No of Institutions	
	(06/14/2018)	1168	
Market Cap	$38.1 Billion	Shares	
Book Value	$3.7 Billion	95,239,248	
Price/Book	10.33	% Held	
Price/Sales	2.36	70.75	

Business Summary: Specialty Chemicals (MIC: 8.3.2 SIC: 5231 NAIC: 444120)

Sherwin-Williams is engaged in the development, manufacture, distribution and sale of paint, coatings and related products to professional, industrial, commercial and retail customers primarily in North and South America with additional operations in the Caribbean region, Europe and Asia. Co. has three reportable operating segments: The Americas Group, Consumer Brands Group and Performance Coatings Group. As of Dec 31 2017, there were 4,620 company-operated specialty paint stores in Americas Group. The Consumer Brands Group consisted of operations in the United States and subsidiaries in 6 foreign countries. The Performance Coating Group operated 290 company-operated branches.

Recent Developments: For the quarter ended Mar 31 2018, net income increased 4.6% to US$250.1 million from US$239.2 million in the year-earlier quarter. Revenues were US$3.97 billion, up 43.6% from US$2.76 billion the year before. Direct operating expenses rose 60.6% to US$2.28 billion from US$1.42 billion in the comparable period the year before. Indirect operating expenses increased 28.0% to US$1.30 billion from US$1.02 billion in the equivalent prior-year period.

Prospects: Our evaluation of Sherwin-Williams Co: as of Jan. 21, 2018 is the result of our systematic analysis on three basic characteristics: earnings strength, relative valuation, and recent stock price movement. The company has produced a positive trend in earnings per share over the past 5 quarters and while recent estimates for the company have been raised by analysts, SHW has posted better than expected results. Based on operating earnings yield, the company is about fairly valued when compared to all of the companies in our coverage universe. Share price changes over the past year indicates that SHW will perform very well over the near term.

Financial Data

(US$ in Thousands)	3 Mos	12/31/2017	12/31/2016	12/31/2015	12/31/2014	12/31/2013	12/31/2012	12/31/2011
Earnings Per Share	18.75	18.67	11.99	11.16	8.78	7.26	6.02	4.14
Cash Flow Per Share	18.14	20.28	14.21	15.70	11.24	10.74	8.71	7.11
Tang Book Value Per Share	N.M.	N.M.	5.34	N.M.	N.M.	2.42	1.81	N.M.
Dividends Per Share	3.410	3.400	3.360	2.680	2.200	2.000	1.560	1.460
Dividend Payout %	18.19	18.21	28.02	24.01	25.06	27.55	25.91	35.27
Income Statement								
Total Revenue	3,965,006	14,983,788	11,855,602	11,339,304	11,129,533	10,185,532	9,534,462	8,765,699
EBITDA	552,904	2,274,880	1,942,072	1,807,920	1,518,381	1,333,224	1,126,386	961,238
Depn & Amortn	159,389	491,761	197,711	198,562	198,945	187,794	179,202	180,904
Income Before Taxes	303,586	1,528,219	1,595,233	1,548,966	1,258,226	1,085,958	907,309	741,548
Income Taxes	53,459	(285,583)	462,530	495,117	392,339	333,397	276,275	299,688
Net Income	250,127	1,772,262	1,132,703	1,053,849	865,887	752,561	631,034	441,860
Average Shares	95,546	94,927	94,488	94,024	98,075	103,048	103,930	105,671
Balance Sheet								
Current Assets	4,886,903	4,465,840	3,627,298	2,658,874	2,566,780	3,158,717	3,149,238	2,261,593
Total Assets	20,367,686	19,958,427	6,752,521	5,791,855	5,706,052	6,382,507	6,234,737	5,229,252
Current Liabilities	4,327,152	3,987,180	2,829,179	2,141,859	2,680,666	2,528,557	1,876,436	2,162,661
Long-Term Obligations	9,891,017	9,885,745	1,211,326	1,920,196	1,122,715	1,122,373	1,632,165	639,231
Total Liabilities	16,677,640	16,266,239	4,874,080	4,923,945	4,709,582	4,607,972	4,442,933	3,712,333
Stockholders' Equity	3,690,046	3,692,188	1,878,441	867,910	996,470	1,774,535	1,791,804	1,516,919
Shares Outstanding	93,545	93,883	93,013	92,246	94,704	100,129	103,270	103,854
Statistical Record								
Return on Assets %	13.04	13.27	18.01	18.33	14.33	11.93	10.98	8.50
Return on Equity %	61.97	63.63	82.26	113.05	62.50	42.20	38.04	28.27
EBITDA Margin %	13.94	15.18	16.38	15.94	13.64	13.09	11.81	10.97
Net Margin %	6.31	11.83	9.55	9.29	7.78	7.39	6.62	5.04
Asset Turnover	1.18	1.12	1.89	1.97	1.84	1.61	1.66	1.69
Current Ratio	1.13	1.12	1.28	1.24	0.96	1.25	1.68	1.05
Debt to Equity	2.68	2.68	0.64	2.21	1.13	0.63	0.91	0.42
Price Range	432.84-308.35	414.34-274.54	312.10-239.35	292.44-218.94	264.93-175.60	195.07-153.82	158.59-91.00	90.08-69.57
P/E Ratio	23.08-16.45	22.19-14.70	26.03-19.96	26.20-19.62	30.17-20.00	26.87-21.19	26.34-15.12	21.76-16.80
Average Yield %	0.92	0.99	1.21	0.99	1.04	1.13	1.22	1.78

Address: 101 West Prospect Avenue, Cleveland, OH 44115-1075 **Telephone:** 216-566-2000 **Fax:** 216-566-3310	**Web Site:** www.sherwin.com **Officers:** John G. Morikis - Chairman, President, President (frmr), Chief Executive Officer, Chief Operating Officer Allen J. Mistysyn - Senior Vice President, Vice President, Chief Financial Officer, Corporate Controller	**Auditors:** Ernst & Young LLP **Investor Contact:** 216-566-2244 **Transfer Agents:** EQ Shareowner Services, St. Paul, MN

SIGNET JEWELERS LTD

Exchange	Symbol	Price	52Wk Range	Yield	P/E
NYS	SIG	$55.75 (6/29/2018)	76.58-35.46	2.65	N/A

*7 Year Price Score 54.06 ***NYSE Composite Index=100** ***12 Month Price Score 83.56**

TRADING VOLUME (thousand shares)

Interim Earnings (Per Share)

Qtr.	Apr	Jul	Oct	Jan
2015-16	1.48	0.78	0.19	3.42
2016-17	1.87	1.06	0.20	3.90
2017-18	1.03	1.33	(0.20)	5.20
2018-19	(8.48)	...	...	...

Interim Dividends (Per Share)

Amt	Decl	Ex	Rec	Pay
0.31Q	08/24/2017	10/26/2017	10/27/2017	11/30/2017
0.31Q	01/10/2018	02/01/2018	02/02/2018	03/02/2018
0.37Q	03/14/2018	05/03/2018	05/04/2018	06/01/2018
0.37Q	06/06/2018	08/02/2018	08/03/2018	08/31/2018

Indicated Div: $1.48

Valuation Analysis   Institutional Holding

Forecast EPS	N/A	No of Institutions 461
Market Cap	$3.3 Billion	Shares 84,663,728
Book Value	$2.5 Billion	% Held
Price/Book	1.32	N/A
Price/Sales	0.52	

Business Summary: Retail - Specialty (MIC: 2.1.3 SIC: 5944 NAIC: 448310)

Signet Jewelers is a holding company. Through its subsidiaries, Co. is a retailer of diamond jewelry. Co. operates retail jewelry stores in a variety of real estate formats including mall-based, free-standing, strip center and outlet store locations. At Feb 3 2018, the Sterling Jewelers division operated 1,586 stores in all 50 U.S. states; the Zale division, which consists of two segments: Zale Jewelry, which operated 868 jewelry stores in shopping malls in North America, and Piercing Pagoda, which operated 598 mall-based kiosks in U.S. shopping malls; and the U.K. Jewelry division operated 504 stores in shopping malls and off-mall locations principally as H.Samuel and Ernest Jones.

Recent Developments: For the year ended Feb 3 2018, net income decreased 4.4% to US$519.3 million from US$543.2 million in the prior year. Revenues were US$6.25 billion, down 2.4% from US$6.41 billion the year before. Operating income was US$579.9 million versus US$763.2 million in the prior year, a decrease of 24.0%. Direct operating expenses rose 0.4% to US$4.06 billion from US$4.05 billion in the comparable period the year before. Indirect operating expenses increased 0.8% to US$1.61 billion from US$1.60 billion in the equivalent prior-year period.

Prospects: Our evaluation of Signet Jewelers Limited as of Sep. 17, 2017 is the result of our systematic analysis on three basic characteristics: earnings strength, relative valuation, and recent stock price movement. The company has managed to produce a neutral trend in earnings per share over the past 5 quarters and while recent estimates for the company have been raised by analysts, SIG has posted better than expected results. Based on operating earnings yield, the company is undervalued when compared to all of the companies in our coverage universe. Share price changes over the past year indicates that SIG will perform very poorly over the near term.

Financial Data

(US$ in Thousands)	3 Mos	02/03/2018	01/28/2017	01/30/2016	01/31/2015	02/01/2014	02/02/2013	01/28/2012
Earnings Per Share	(2.15)	7.44	7.08	5.87	4.75	4.56	4.35	3.73
Cash Flow Per Share	32.13	30.30	9.13	5.59	3.55	2.94	3.74	3.78
Tang Book Value Per Share	27.94	29.92	31.73	26.67	22.97	31.62	28.32	26.32
Dividends Per Share	1.300	1.240	1.040	0.880	0.720	0.600	0.480	0.200
Dividend Payout %	...	16.67	14.69	14.99	15.16	13.16	11.03	5.36
Income Statement								
Total Revenue	1,480,600	6,253,000	6,408,400	6,550,200	5,736,300	4,209,200	3,983,400	3,749,200
EBITDA	(575,200)	515,900	655,700	865,100	716,700	680,700	659,900	599,800
Depn & Amortn	(1,600)	194,100	175,000	161,400	140,100	110,200	99,400	92,400
Income Before Taxes	(582,500)	527,200	713,800	657,800	540,600	566,500	556,900	502,100
Income Taxes	(85,900)	7,900	170,600	189,900	159,300	198,500	197,000	177,700
Net Income	(496,600)	519,300	543,200	467,900	381,300	368,000	359,900	324,400
Average Shares	59,500	69,800	76,700	79,700	80,400	80,700	82,800	87,000
Balance Sheet								
Current Assets	3,366,300	3,446,100	4,642,600	4,589,900	4,407,300	3,257,600	3,032,900	3,016,300
Total Assets	5,272,900	5,839,600	6,597,800	6,474,400	6,327,600	4,029,200	3,715,800	3,611,400
Current Liabilities	1,108,400	1,037,200	1,203,700	1,152,900	1,338,300	900,700	868,700	867,200
Long-Term Obligations	679,700	688,200	1,317,900	1,328,700	1,363,800	...	...	...
Total Liabilities	2,766,300	2,726,200	3,495,700	3,413,700	3,517,200	1,466,100	1,385,900	1,332,300
Stockholders' Equity	2,506,600	3,113,400	3,102,100	3,060,700	2,810,400	2,563,100	2,329,900	2,279,100
Shares Outstanding	59,200	60,500	68,300	79,400	80,300	80,200	81,400	86,600
Statistical Record								
Return on Assets %	N.M.	8.22	8.33	7.33	7.38	9.53	9.66	9.71
Return on Equity %	N.M.	16.44	17.68	15.98	14.23	15.08	15.36	15.42
EBITDA Margin %	N.M.	8.25	10.23	13.21	12.49	16.17	16.57	16.00
Net Margin %	N.M.	8.30	8.48	7.14	6.65	8.74	9.03	8.65
Asset Turnover	1.08	0.99	0.98	1.03	1.11	1.09	1.07	1.12
Current Ratio	3.04	3.32	3.86	3.98	3.29	3.62	3.49	3.48
Debt to Equity	0.27	0.22	0.42	0.43	0.49	...	...	...
Price Range	76.58-35.46	79.16-47.88	124.03-73.16	150.94-113.39	132.12-75.28	80.86-59.64	63.43-41.27	48.01-31.26
P/E Ratio	...	10.64-6.44	17.52-10.33	25.71-19.32	27.81-15.85	17.73-13.08	14.58-9.49	12.87-8.38
Average Yield %	2.33	1.99	1.11	0.68	0.65	0.85	0.98	0.47

Address: Clarendon House, 2 Church Street, Hamilton, HM11	**Web Site:** www.signetjewelers.com	**Auditors:** KPMG LLP
Telephone: 441-296-5872	**Officers:** H. Todd Stitzer - Chairman Sebastian Hobbs - President, Chief Customer Officer	**Investor Contact:** 440-207-3179700
		Transfer Agents: Capita Registrars, Kent, United Kingdom

SIMON PROPERTY GROUP, INC.

Exchange	Symbol	Price	52Wk Range	Yield	P/E
NYS	SPG	$170.19 (6/29/2018)	172.85-146.74	4.44	25.36

*7 Year Price Score 78.67   *NYSE Composite Index=100   *12 Month Price Score 100.05

Interim Earnings (Per Share)

Qtr.	Mar	Jun	Sep	Dec
2015	1.16	1.52	1.36	1.84
2016	1.55	1.45	1.61	1.26
2017	1.53	1.23	1.65	1.83
2018	2.00	...	...	...

Interim Dividends (Per Share)

Amt	Decl	Ex	Rec	Pay
1.80Q	08/01/2017	08/15/2017	08/17/2017	08/31/2017
1.85Q	10/27/2017	11/15/2017	11/16/2017	11/30/2017
1.95Q	01/31/2018	02/13/2018	02/14/2018	02/28/2018
1.95Q	04/27/2018	05/16/2018	05/17/2018	05/31/2018

Indicated Div: $7.55

Valuation Analysis

Forecast EPS	$7.15	No of Institutions	
	(06/14/2018)	1044	
Market Cap	$52.7 Billion	Shares	
Book Value	$3.7 Billion	393,112,896	
Price/Book	14.22	% Held	
Price/Sales	9.42	96.18	

Institutional Holding

TRADING VOLUME (thousand shares)

Business Summary: REITs (MIC: 5.3.1 SIC: 6798 NAIC: 525930)

Simon Property Group is a self-administered and self-managed real estate investment trust. Co. owns, develops and manages retail real estate properties, which consist primarily of malls, Premium Outlets®, and The Mills®. As of Dec 31 2017, Co. owned or held an interest in 207 income-producing properties in the U.S., which consisted of 107 malls, 68 Premium Outlets, 14 Mills, four lifestyle centers, and 14 other retail properties in 37 states and Puerto Rico. Internationally, as of Dec 31 2017, Co. had ownership interests in nine Premium Outlets in Japan, four Premium Outlets in South Korea, two Premium Outlets in Canada, two Premium Outlets in Malaysia, and one Premium Outlet in Mexico.

Recent Developments: For the quarter ended Mar 31 2018, net income increased 29.8% to US$715.5 million from US$551.1 million in the year-earlier quarter. Revenues were US$1.40 billion, up 4.0% from US$1.35 billion the year before. Revenues from property income rose 1.6% to US$1.27 billion from US$1.25 billion in the corresponding quarter a year earlier.

Prospects: Our evaluation of Simon Property Group Inc. as of Jan. 21, 2018 is the result of our systematic analysis on three basic characteristics: earnings strength, relative valuation, and recent stock price movement. The company has enjoyed a very positive trend in earnings per share over the past 5 quarters. Because the company lacks sufficient analyst estimate data, we place greater weight on the historical EPS trend as the measure of earnings strength. Based on operating earnings yield, the company is about fairly valued when compared to all of the companies in our coverage universe. Share price changes over the past year indicates that SPG will perform in line with the market over the near term

Financial Data

(US$ in Thousands)	3 Mos	12/31/2017	12/31/2016	12/31/2015	12/31/2014	12/31/2013	12/31/2012	12/31/2011
Earnings Per Share	6.71	6.24	5.87	5.88	4.52	4.24	4.72	3.48
Cash Flow Per Share	11.76	11.54	10.76	9.75	8.79	8.71	8.27	6.83
Tang Book Value Per Share	11.83	11.32	13.16	13.50	15.33	17.98	17.87	15.57
Dividends Per Share	7.350	7.150	6.500	6.050	5.150	4.650	4.100	3.500
Dividend Payout %	109.54	114.58	110.73	102.89	113.94	109.67	86.86	100.57
Income Statement								
Total Revenue	1,399,814	5,538,640	5,435,229	5,266,103	4,870,818	5,170,138	4,880,084	4,306,432
EBITDA	1,165,662	4,011,377	3,966,872	4,017,480	3,673,776	3,816,420	4,016,054	3,260,626
Depn & Amortn	334,672	1,357,351	1,327,946	1,239,214	1,285,784	1,332,950	1,301,304	1,112,438
Income Before Taxes	625,498	1,844,633	1,781,372	1,854,569	1,395,391	1,346,331	1,587,725	1,164,662
Net Income	621,488	1,947,962	1,838,896	1,827,720	1,408,588	1,319,641	1,434,496	1,024,799
Average Shares	310,583	311,517	312,690	310,102	310,731	310,255	303,138	293,573
Balance Sheet								
Current Assets	1,053,365	2,224,981	1,224,678	1,325,739	1,192,479	2,298,345	1,705,819	1,285,381
Total Assets	31,017,860	32,257,638	31,103,578	30,650,673	29,532,330	33,324,574	32,586,606	26,216,925
Current Liabilities	1,180,851	2,675,568	2,573,760	2,692,345	2,426,844	2,465,704	2,098,916	1,787,281
Long-Term Obligations	23,647,623	24,632,463	22,977,104	22,502,173	20,852,993	23,588,531	23,113,007	18,446,410
Total Liabilities	27,310,274	28,380,990	26,655,368	26,153,672	24,413,616	27,284,683	26,497,997	21,299,314
Stockholders' Equity	3,707,586	3,876,648	4,448,210	4,497,001	5,118,714	6,039,891	6,088,609	4,917,611
Shares Outstanding	309,697	320,330	313,074	309,420	310,787	310,608	309,903	293,856
Statistical Record								
Return on Assets %	6.75	6.15	5.94	6.07	4.48	4.00	4.87	4.01
Return on Equity %	52.39	46.80	41.00	38.02	25.25	21.76	26.00	20.84
EBITDA Margin %	83.27	72.43	72.98	76.29	75.42	73.82	82.29	75.72
Net Margin %	44.40	35.17	33.83	34.71	28.92	25.52	29.39	23.80
Asset Turnover	0.18	0.17	0.18	0.18	0.15	0.16	0.17	0.17
Current Ratio	0.89	0.83	0.48	0.49	0.49	0.93	0.81	0.72
Debt to Equity	6.38	6.35	5.17	5.00	4.07	3.91	3.80	3.75
Price Range	174.73-150.46	186.83-152.26	227.60-174.20	206.19-171.00	187.46-141.62	169.56-134.02	153.76-119.15	123.17-89.65
P/E Ratio	26.04-22.42	29.94-24.40	38.77-29.68	35.07-29.08	41.47-31.33	39.99-31.61	32.58-25.24	35.39-25.76
Average Yield %	4.56	4.31	3.25	3.21	3.13	3.10	2.92	3.27

Address: 225 West Washington Street, Indianapolis, IN 46204 Telephone: 317-636-1600 Fax: 317-685-7336	Web Site: www.simon.com Officers: David Simon - Chairman, Chief Executive Officer Herbert Simon - Chairman Emeritus, Co-Chairman, Chief Executive Officer	Auditors: Ernst & Young LLP Investor Contact: 800-461-3439 Transfer Agents: Computershare, Pittsburgh, PA

SIX FLAGS ENTERTAINMENT CORP

Exchange	Symbol	Price	52Wk Range	Yield	P/E
NYS	SIX	$70.05 (6/29/2018)	72.76-51.90	4.45	22.74

*7 Year Price Score 115.47 *NYSE Composite Index=100 *12 Month Price Score 104.56

Interim Earnings (Per Share)

Qtr.	Mar	Jun	Sep	Dec
2015	(0.75)	0.67	1.64	0.00
2016	(0.51)	0.64	1.09	0.02
2017	(0.63)	0.59	2.11	1.12
2018	(0.74)	...	...	...

Interim Dividends (Per Share)

Amt	Decl	Ex	Rec	Pay
0.64Q	08/17/2017	08/29/2017	08/31/2017	09/11/2017
0.70Q	11/08/2017	11/29/2017	11/30/2017	12/11/2017
0.78Q	02/07/2018	02/15/2018	02/19/2018	03/05/2018
0.78Q	05/03/2018	05/30/2018	05/31/2018	06/11/2018

Indicated Div: $3.12

Valuation Analysis — **Institutional Holding**

Forecast EPS	$2.87	No of Institutions
	(06/12/2018)	452
Market Cap	$5.9 Billion	Shares
Book Value	N/A	107,070,176
Price/Book	N/A	% Held
Price/Sales	4.21	N/A

Business Summary: Sporting & Recreational (MIC: 2.2.4 SIC: 7996 NAIC: 713110)

Six Flags Entertainment is a regional theme park operator. As of Dec 31 2017, Co. has 20 regional theme and water parks, 17 are located in the U.S., two are located in Mexico and one is located in Montreal, Canada. Co.'s parks generally provides a range selection of thrill rides, water attractions, themed areas, concerts and shows, restaurants, game venues and retail outlets. During 2017, Co.'s parks offered approximately 850 rides, including over 140 roller coasters. Co. holds exclusive long-term licenses for theme park usage of certain Warner Bros. and DC Comics characters, including Bugs Bunny, Daffy Duck, Tweety Bird, Yosemite Sam, Batman, Superman, The Joker, Wonder Woman and others.

Recent Developments: For the quarter ended Mar 31 2018, net loss amounted to US$62.3 million versus a net loss of US$57.5 million in the year-earlier quarter. Revenues were US$129.0 million, up 29.6% from US$99.5 million the year before. Direct operating expenses rose 12.4% to US$113.0 million from US$100.5 million in the comparable period the year before. Indirect operating expenses decreased 5.2% to US$70.2 million from US$74.1 million in the equivalent prior-year period.

Prospects: Our evaluation of Six Flags Entertainment Corp. as of Jan. 21, 2018 is the result of our systematic analysis on three basic characteristics: earnings strength, relative valuation, and recent stock price movement. The company has produced a positive trend in earnings per share over the past 5 quarters and while recent estimates for the company have been mixed, SIX has posted better than expected results. Based on operating earnings yield, the company is about fairly valued when compared to all of the companies in our coverage universe. Share price changes over the past year indicates that SIX will perform in line with the market over the near term.

Financial Data
(US$ in Thousands)

	3 Mos	12/31/2017	12/31/2016	12/31/2015	12/31/2014	12/31/2013	12/31/2012	12/31/2011
Earnings Per Share	3.08	3.09	1.25	1.58	0.77	1.18	3.19	(0.20)
Cash Flow Per Share	5.72	5.13	5.00	5.06	4.15	3.80	3.44	2.50
Dividends Per Share	2.760	2.620	2.380	2.140	1.930	1.820	1.350	0.090
Dividend Payout %	89.61	84.79	190.40	135.44	250.65	154.24	42.32	...
Income Statement								
Total Revenue	128,964	1,359,074	1,319,398	1,263,938	1,175,793	1,109,930	1,070,332	1,013,174
EBITDA	(26,820)	537,268	419,428	443,915	338,049	391,752	392,855	223,159
Depn & Amortn	29,315	109,206	104,290	104,788	105,449	113,682	132,397	150,952
Income Before Taxes	(82,020)	329,052	233,266	263,224	160,011	203,925	213,834	6,990
Income Taxes	(19,675)	16,026	76,539	70,369	46,522	47,601	(172,228)	(8,065)
Net Income	(62,345)	273,816	118,302	154,690	76,022	118,552	354,009	(22,660)
Average Shares	84,457	88,494	94,398	97,981	98,139	100,371	110,936	110,150
Balance Sheet								
Current Assets	189,182	221,072	278,791	227,977	300,924	353,858	763,474	309,529
Total Assets	2,443,991	2,456,676	2,487,672	2,428,440	2,534,919	2,607,814	3,056,391	2,648,178
Current Liabilities	505,572	297,840	315,952	272,058	231,671	216,810	181,863	221,749
Long-Term Obligations	2,021,675	2,021,178	1,624,487	1,498,022	1,389,215	1,394,334	1,398,966	921,940
Total Liabilities	3,142,166	2,961,788	2,674,162	2,404,224	2,311,024	2,234,477	2,164,172	1,884,700
Stockholders' Equity	(698,175)	(505,112)	(186,490)	24,216	223,895	373,337	892,219	763,478
Shares Outstanding	83,536	84,488	90,849	91,550	92,937	94,857	107,637	109,283
Statistical Record								
Return on Assets %	11.04	11.08	4.80	6.23	2.96	4.19	12.38	N.M.
Return on Equity %	...	...	...	124.69	25.46	18.74	42.65	N.M.
EBITDA Margin %	N.M.	39.53	31.79	35.12	28.75	35.30	36.70	22.03
Net Margin %	N.M.	20.15	8.97	12.24	6.47	10.68	33.07	N.M.
Asset Turnover	0.57	0.55	0.54	0.51	0.46	0.39	0.37	0.38
Current Ratio	0.37	0.74	0.88	0.84	1.30	1.63	4.20	1.40
Debt to Equity	...	...	...	61.86	6.20	3.73	1.57	1.21
Price Range	69.55-51.91	67.58-51.90	61.33-46.74	54.96-42.34	43.24-33.15	39.98-30.55	32.42-20.43	20.69-12.90
P/E Ratio	22.58-16.85	21.87-16.80	49.06-37.39	34.78-26.80	56.16-43.05	33.88-25.89	10.16-6.40	
Average Yield %	4.49	4.36	4.34	4.49	4.94	5.14	5.15	0.53

Address: 924 Avenue J East, Grand Prairie, TX 75050 **Telephone:** 972-595-5000	**Web Site:** www.sixflags.com **Officers:** James W.P. Reid-Anderson - Executive Chairman, Chairman, President, Chief Executive Officer Marshall Barber - Chief Financial Officer	**Auditors:** KPMG LLP **Investor Contact:** 972-595-5000 **Transfer Agents:** Computershare

SKECHERS USA INC

Exchange	Symbol	Price	52Wk Range	Yield	P/E
NYS	SKX	$30.01 (6/29/2018)	42.45-24.03	N/A	23.26

*7 Year Price Score 133.59 *NYSE Composite Index=100 *12 Month Price Score 88.12

Interim Earnings (Per Share)

Qtr.	Mar	Jun	Sep	Dec
2015	0.37	0.52	0.43	0.19
2016	0.63	0.48	0.42	0.04
2017	0.60	0.38	0.59	(0.43)
2018	0.75	...	...	...

Interim Dividends (Per Share)

Amt	Decl	Ex	Rec	Pay
200%	08/21/2015	10/16/2015	10/02/2015	10/15/2015

Valuation Analysis

		Institutional Holding	
Forecast EPS	$2.12	No of Institutions	468
	(06/14/2018)		
Market Cap	$4.7 Billion	Shares	
Book Value	$1.9 Billion		138,261,184
Price/Book	2.41	% Held	
Price/Sales	1.08		76.25

Business Summary: Apparel, Footwear & Accessories (MIC: 1.4.2 SIC: 3149 NAIC: 316219)

Skechers U.S.A. designs and markets Skechers-branded lifestyle footwear for men, women and children, and performance footwear for men and women under the Skechers GO brand name. Co.'s brands are sold through department and specialty stores, athletic and independent retailers, boutiques and internet retailers. In addition to wholesale distribution, Co.'s footwear is available at its e-commerce website and its own retail stores. As of Feb 15 2018, Co. owned and operated 117 concept stores, 170 factory outlet stores and 162 warehouse outlet stores in the U.S., and 120 concept stores, 67 factory outlet stores, and 9 warehouse outlet stores internationally.

Recent Developments: For the quarter ended Mar 31 2018, net income increased 28.7% to US$137.3 million from US$106.6 million in the year-earlier quarter. Revenues were US$1.26 billion, up 16.6% from US$1.08 billion the year before. Operating income was US$148.8 million versus US$124.4 million in the prior-year quarter, an increase of 19.6%. Direct operating expenses rose 11.9% to US$667.0 million from US$596.3 million in the comparable period the year before. Indirect operating expenses increased 23.4% to US$439.8 million from US$356.3 million in the equivalent prior-year period.

Prospects: Our evaluation of Skechers U.S.A Inc. as of Jan. 21, 2018 is the result of our systematic analysis on three basic characteristics: earnings strength, relative valuation, and recent stock price movement. The company has enjoyed a very positive trend in earnings per share over the past 5 quarters and while recent estimates for the company have been raised by analysts, SKX has posted better than expected results. Based on operating earnings yield, the company is about fairly valued when compared to all of the companies in our coverage universe. Share price changes over the past year indicates that SKX will perform poorly over the near term.

Financial Data

(US$ in Thousands)	3 Mos	12/31/2017	12/31/2016	12/31/2015	12/31/2014	12/31/2013	12/31/2012	12/31/2011
Earnings Per Share	1.29	1.14	1.57	1.50	0.91	0.36	0.06	(0.46)
Cash Flow Per Share	1.58	1.02	2.34	1.52	1.08	0.66	(0.02)	1.13
Tang Book Value Per Share	12.43	11.70	10.35	8.64	7.05	6.12	5.78	5.74
Income Statement								
Total Revenue	1,255,600	4,180,826	3,577,196	3,159,068	2,386,668	1,854,095	1,567,425	1,613,574
EBITDA	155,203	485,027	443,750	344,030	252,466	137,761	66,880	(88,693)
Depn & Amortn	3,001	96,510	79,182	527	49,457	44,497	43,642	36,352
Income Before Taxes	151,879	384,260	359,484	333,497	191,380	82,215	10,473	(131,047)
Income Taxes	14,621	149,156	74,125	72,450	39,184	21,347	(39)	(63,467)
Net Income	117,652	179,190	243,493	231,912	138,811	54,788	9,512	(67,484)
Average Shares	157,630	156,523	155,084	154,200	153,078	151,689	149,826	145,473
Balance Sheet								
Current Assets	2,293,154	2,105,024	1,827,766	1,570,467	1,285,014	1,014,593	940,312	887,351
Total Assets	2,935,984	2,735,082	2,393,670	2,047,408	1,674,918	1,408,570	1,340,220	1,281,888
Current Liabilities	674,020	597,348	621,730	577,013	505,737	310,422	292,541	308,466
Long-Term Obligations	70,646	71,103	67,159	68,942	15,081	116,488	128,517	76,531
Total Liabilities	989,814	906,018	790,037	719,852	599,669	478,248	464,251	429,327
Stockholders' Equity	1,946,170	1,829,064	1,603,633	1,327,556	1,075,249	930,322	875,969	852,561
Shares Outstanding	156,577	156,329	154,931	153,602	152,271	151,674	150,885	147,768
Statistical Record								
Return on Assets %	7.59	6.99	10.94	12.46	9.00	3.99	0.72	N.M.
Return on Equity %	11.10	10.44	16.57	19.30	13.84	6.07	1.10	N.M.
EBITDA Margin %	12.36	11.60	12.40	10.89	10.58	7.43	4.27	N.M.
Net Margin %	9.37	4.29	6.81	7.34	5.82	2.95	0.61	N.M.
Asset Turnover	1.63	1.63	1.61	1.70	1.55	1.35	1.19	1.25
Current Ratio	3.40	3.52	2.94	2.72	2.54	3.27	3.21	2.88
Debt to Equity	0.04	0.04	0.04	0.05	0.01	0.13	0.15	0.09
Price Range	41.40-22.99	38.66-22.54	34.06-18.98	53.43-18.42	21.36-8.97	11.46-5.80	7.42-3.82	7.82-3.96
P/E Ratio	32.09-17.82	33.91-19.77	21.69-12.09	35.62-12.28	23.48-9.85	31.82-16.11	123.61-63.67	...

Address: 228 Manhattan Beach Blvd., Manhattan Beach, CA 90266
Telephone: 310-318-3100

Web Site: www.skechers.com
Officers: Robert Greenberg - Chairman, Chief Executive Officer Michael Greenberg - President

Auditors: BDO USA, LLP
Investor Contact: 310-829-5400
Transfer Agents: American Stock Transfer & Trust Company, Brooklyn, NY

628

SJW GROUP

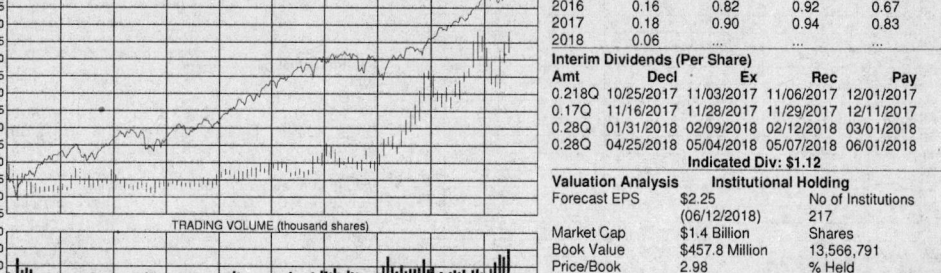

Exchange	Symbol	Price	52Wk Range	Yield	P/E	Div Acheiver
NYS	SJW	$66.22 (6/29/2018)	68.15-48.46	1.69	24.26	50 Years

7 Year Price Score 134.40 *NYSE Composite Index=100 *12 Month Price Score 106.39

Interim Earnings (Per Share)

Qtr.	Mar	Jun	Sep	Dec
2015	0.23	0.36	0.46	0.79
2016	0.16	0.82	0.92	0.67
2017	0.18	0.90	0.94	0.83
2018	0.06	...	...	...

Interim Dividends (Per Share)

Amt	Decl	Ex	Rec	Pay
0.218Q	10/25/2017	11/03/2017	11/06/2017	12/01/2017
0.17Q	11/16/2017	11/28/2017	11/29/2017	12/11/2017
0.28Q	01/31/2018	02/09/2018	02/12/2018	03/01/2018
0.28Q	04/25/2018	05/04/2018	05/07/2018	06/01/2018

Indicated Div: $1.12

Valuation Analysis — **Institutional Holding**

Forecast EPS	$2.25	No of Institutions
	(06/12/2018)	217
Market Cap	$1.4 Billion	Shares
Book Value	$457.8 Million	13,566,791
Price/Book	2.98	% Held
Price/Sales	3.45	56.55

TRADING VOLUME (thousand shares)

Business Summary: Water Utilities (MIC: 3.2.1 SIC: 4941 NAIC: 221310)

SJW is a holding company with four subsidiaries: San Jose Water Company, is a public utility in the business of providing water service to approximately 229,000 connections that serve a population of approximately 1.0 million people in an area; SJWTX, Inc., which providing water service to approximately 13,000 connections that serve approximately 39,000 people; SJW Land Company, which owns and operates commercial buildings in the states of California and Tennessee; and Texas Water Alliance Limited, is undertaking activities to develop a water supply project in Texas.

Recent Developments: For the quarter ended Mar 31 2018, net income decreased 65.0% to US$1.3 million from US$3.7 million in the year-earlier quarter. Revenues were US$75.0 million, up 8.7% from US$69.0 million the year before. Operating income was US$7.3 million versus US$11.7 million in the prior-year quarter, a decrease of 37.4%. Direct operating expenses rose 14.9% to US$30.4 million from US$26.5 million in the comparable period the year before. Indirect operating expenses increased 20.8% to US$37.3 million from US$30.9 million in the equivalent prior-year period.

Prospects: Our evaluation of SJW Group as of Jan. 21, 2018 is the result of our systematic analysis on three basic characteristics: earnings strength, relative valuation, and recent stock price movement. The company has produced a positive trend in earnings per share over the past 5 quarters. Because the company lacks sufficient analyst estimate data, we place greater weight on the historical EPS trend as the measure of earnings strength. Based on operating earnings yield, the company is about fairly valued when compared to all of the companies in our coverage universe. Share price changes over the past year indicates that SJW will perform very well over the near term.

Financial Data

(US$ in Thousands)	3 Mos	12/31/2017	12/31/2016	12/31/2015	12/31/2014	12/31/2013	12/31/2012	12/31/2011
Earnings Per Share	2.73	2.86	2.57	1.85	2.54	1.12	1.18	1.11
Cash Flow Per Share	4.64	4.93	5.57	4.78	3.26	3.21	3.98	3.46
Tang Book Value Per Share	22.24	22.57	20.61	18.83	17.75	15.92	14.71	14.20
Dividends Per Share	1.103	1.040	0.810	0.780	0.750	0.730	0.710	0.690
Dividend Payout %	40.38	36.36	31.52	42.16	29.53	65.18	60.17	62.16
Income Statement								
Total Revenue	75,042	389,225	339,706	305,082	319,668	276,869	261,547	238,955
EBITDA	20,917	165,878	150,878	121,573	132,989	89,057	89,050	84,260
Depn & Amortn	14,160	46,456	42,659	38,233	35,424	32,616	31,005	29,141
Income Before Taxes	705	96,493	86,381	61,154	76,777	36,519	37,860	35,444
Income Taxes	(580)	35,393	33,542	23,272	24,971	14,135	15,542	14,566
Net Income	1,285	59,204	52,839	37,882	51,806	22,384	22,318	20,878
Average Shares	20,701	20,685	20,588	20,515	20,416	19,971	18,839	18,794
Balance Sheet								
Current Assets	61,060	66,858	99,611	73,376	68,093	39,652	42,911	68,915
Total Assets	1,463,874	1,458,001	1,443,376	1,340,963	1,269,304	1,109,986	1,087,499	1,038,810
Current Liabilities	95,360	85,052	63,573	79,623	44,694	59,195	49,107	28,288
Long-Term Obligations	431,175	431,092	433,335	380,825	384,365	334,997	335,598	343,848
Total Liabilities	1,006,044	994,792	1,021,730	957,180	909,149	788,811	812,895	774,806
Stockholders' Equity	457,830	463,209	421,646	383,783	360,155	321,175	274,604	264,004
Shares Outstanding	20,585	20,520	20,456	20,381	20,286	20,169	18,670	18,592
Statistical Record								
Return on Assets %	3.92	4.08	3.79	2.90	4.35	2.04	2.09	2.12
Return on Equity %	12.92	13.38	13.08	10.18	15.21	7.51	8.26	8.04
EBITDA Margin %	27.87	42.62	44.41	39.85	41.60	32.17	34.05	35.26
Net Margin %	1.71	15.21	15.55	12.42	16.21	8.08	8.53	8.74
Asset Turnover	0.27	0.27	0.24	0.23	0.27	0.25	0.25	0.24
Current Ratio	0.64	0.79	1.57	0.92	1.52	0.67	0.87	2.44
Debt to Equity	0.94	0.93	1.03	0.99	1.07	1.04	1.22	1.30
Price Range	68.13-45.74	68.13-45.74	56.69-29.35	35.60-27.64	32.87-25.64	30.03-24.58	26.62-22.69	26.47-21.10
P/E Ratio	24.96-16.75	23.82-15.99	22.06-11.42	19.24-14.94	12.94-10.09	26.81-21.95	22.56-19.23	23.85-19.01
Average Yield %	1.98	1.93	2.01	2.53	2.65	2.65	2.96	2.94

Address: 110 West Taylor Street, San Jose, CA 95110	**Web Site:** www.sjwcorp.com	**Auditors:** KPMG LLP
Telephone: 408-279-7800	**Officers:** W. Richard Roth - Chairman, President, Chief Executive Officer James P. Lynch - Chief Financial Officer, Treasurer	**Investor Contact:** 800-250-5147
		Transfer Agents: American Stock Transfer & Trust Company, LLC, Brooklyn, NY

SL GREEN REALTY CORP

Exchange	Symbol	Price	52Wk Range	Yield	P/E
NYS	SLG	$100.53 (6/29/2018)	107.52-90.61	3.23	53.47

*7 Year Price Score 81.49 ***NYSE Composite Index=100** ***12 Month Price Score 98.29**

Interim Earnings (Per Share)

Qtr.	Mar	Jun	Sep	Dec
2015	0.44	(0.39)	1.64	1.02
2016	0.23	1.33	0.34	0.44
2017	0.11	0.08	0.40	0.28
2018	1.12	...	...	...

Interim Dividends (Per Share)

Amt	Decl	Ex	Rec	Pay
0.775Q	09/19/2017	09/29/2017	10/02/2017	10/16/2017
0.813Q	12/01/2017	12/29/2017	01/02/2018	01/16/2018
0.813Q	03/22/2018	03/29/2018	04/02/2018	04/16/2018
0.813Q	06/15/2018	06/28/2018	06/29/2018	07/16/2018

Indicated Div: $3.25

Valuation Analysis / Institutional Holding

Forecast EPS	$2.19	No of Institutions	
	(06/21/2018)	534	
Market Cap	$9.1 Billion	Shares	
Book Value	$6.8 Billion	132,466,304	
Price/Book	1.34	% Held	
Price/Sales	6.31	104.33	

Business Summary: REITs (MIC: 5.3.1 SIC: 6798 NAIC: 525930)

SL Green Realty is a self-managed real estate investment trust, with in-house capabilities in property management, acquisitions and dispositions, financing, development and redevelopment, construction and leasing. As of Dec 31 2017, Co. owned interests in properties in the New York Metropolitan area, primarily in midtown Manhattan. Co.'s investments in the New York Metropolitan area also include investments in Brooklyn, Long Island, Westchester County, Connecticut and New Jersey. As of Dec 31 2017, Co. had 57 consolidated commercial properties; 3 consolidated residental properties; 23 unconsolidated commerical properties and 12 unconsolidated residential properties.

Recent Developments: For the quarter ended Mar 31 2018, net income increased to US$113.8 million from US$924,000 in the year-earlier quarter. Revenues were US$301.7 million, down 20.1% from US$377.4 million the year before. Revenues from property income fell 25.7% to US$241.8 million from US$325.5 million in the corresponding quarter a year earlier.

Prospects: Our evaluation of SL Green Realty Corp. as of Jan. 21, 2018 is the result of our systematic analysis on three basic characteristics: earnings strength, relative valuation, and recent stock price movement. The company has generated a negative trend in earnings per share over the past 5 quarters. Because the company lacks sufficient analyst estimate data, we place greater weight on the historical EPS trend as the measure of earnings strength. Based on operating earnings yield, the company is overvalued when compared to all of the companies in our coverage universe. Share price changes over the past year indicates that SLG will perform well over the near term.

Financial Data
(US$ in Thousands)

	3 Mos	12/31/2017	12/31/2016	12/31/2015	12/31/2014	12/31/2013	12/31/2012	12/31/2011
Earnings Per Share	1.88	0.87	2.34	2.70	5.20	1.10	1.74	7.33
Cash Flow Per Share	5.53	5.56	6.32	5.30	5.12	4.19	3.95	3.74
Tang Book Value Per Share	72.82	67.94	73.63	73.50	69.73	66.88	66.49	65.37
Dividends Per Share	3.175	3.138	2.935	2.520	2.100	1.490	1.080	0.550
Dividend Payout %	168.88	360.63	125.43	93.33	40.38	135.45	62.07	7.50
Income Statement								
Total Revenue	301,695	1,511,473	1,863,981	1,662,829	1,519,978	1,469,077	1,400,255	1,263,428
EBITDA	237,068	685,356	1,327,727	1,121,708	870,139	760,751	717,855	1,161,173
Depn & Amortn	72,925	365,300	783,500	523,800	338,800	309,400	306,800	254,500
Income Before Taxes	116,227	63,011	223,028	274,038	213,939	121,136	80,486	620,756
Net Income	105,504	101,374	249,896	284,084	518,056	135,371	196,405	647,410
Average Shares	95,256	103,403	104,881	103,734	99,696	95,266	92,873	86,244
Balance Sheet								
Current Assets	807,921	724,625	966,884	1,107,032	914,062	836,223	744,306	568,181
Total Assets	13,380,870	13,982,904	15,857,787	19,857,941	17,096,587	14,959,001	14,387,754	13,483,852
Current Liabilities	600,542	328,349	380,410	554,909	441,887	374,074	317,459	343,328
Long-Term Obligations	5,465,265	5,897,975	6,523,798	10,447,108	8,199,609	6,967,579	6,557,938	6,052,509
Total Liabilities	6,591,500	7,456,076	8,231,302	12,287,960	10,088,098	8,384,046	7,918,402	7,506,305
Stockholders' Equity	6,789,370	6,526,828	7,626,485	7,569,981	7,008,489	6,574,955	6,469,352	5,977,547
Shares Outstanding	90,190	92,803	100,562	99,975	97,325	94,993	91,249	85,782
Statistical Record								
Return on Assets %	1.31	0.68	1.40	1.54	3.23	0.92	1.41	5.22
Return on Equity %	2.67	1.43	3.28	3.90	7.63	2.08	3.15	11.93
EBITDA Margin %	78.58	45.34	71.23	67.46	57.25	51.78	51.27	91.91
Net Margin %	34.97	6.71	13.41	17.08	34.08	9.21	14.03	51.24
Asset Turnover	0.10	0.10	0.10	0.09	0.09	0.10	0.10	0.10
Current Ratio	1.35	2.21	2.54	1.99	2.07	2.24	2.34	1.65
Debt to Equity	0.80	0.90	0.86	1.38	1.17	1.06	1.01	1.01
Price Range	109.73-90.61	113.75-94.15	119.20-80.54	134.00-100.95	123.10-90.96	98.15-76.65	85.14-68.16	90.01-55.14
P/E Ratio	58.37-48.20	130.75-108.22	50.94-34.42	49.63-37.39	23.67-17.49	89.23-69.68	48.93-39.17	12.28-7.52
Average Yield %	3.15	3.03	2.83	2.12	1.97	1.69	1.40	0.75

Address: 420 Lexington Avenue, New York, NY 10170 **Telephone:** 212-594-2700	**Web Site:** www.slgreen.com **Officers:** Marc Holliday - Incoming Chairman, Chief Executive Officer Stephen L. Green - Executive Chairman, Chairman Emeritus	**Auditors:** Ernst & Young LLP **Transfer Agents:** Computershare Shareowner Services, Providence, RI

SM ENERGY CO.

Exchange	Symbol	Price	52Wk Range	Yield	P/E
NYS	SM	$25.69 (6/29/2018)	27.18-12.79	0.39	36.70

*7 Year Price Score 33.73   *NYSE Composite Index=100   *12 Month Price Score 119.89

Interim Earnings (Per Share)

Qtr.	Mar	Jun	Sep	Dec
2015	(0.79)	(0.85)	0.05	(5.02)
2016	(5.10)	(2.48)	(0.52)	(2.12)
2017	0.67	(1.08)	(0.80)	(0.23)
2018	2.81	...	...	...

Interim Dividends (Per Share)

Amt	Decl	Ex	Rec	Pay
0.05S	09/23/2016	10/19/2016	10/21/2016	11/02/2016
0.05S	03/29/2017	04/19/2017	04/21/2017	05/03/2017
0.05S	09/27/2017	10/19/2017	10/20/2017	11/01/2017
0.05S	03/29/2018	04/26/2018	04/27/2018	05/09/2018

Indicated Div: $0.10

Valuation Analysis

		Institutional Holding	
Forecast EPS	$0.10	No of Institutions	
	(06/14/2018)	433	
Market Cap	$2.9 Billion	Shares	
Book Value	$2.7 Billion	150,331,168	
Price/Book	1.06	% Held	
Price/Sales	1.88	N/A	

Business Summary: Production & Extraction (MIC: 9.1.1 SIC: 1311 NAIC: 211111)

SM Energy is an independent energy company engaged in the acquisition, exploration, development, and production of crude oil and condensate, natural gas, and natural gas liquids in onshore North America. Co.'s operations are concentrated in three onshore operating areas in the U.S.: the South Texas & Gulf Coast Region; the Permian Region; and the Rocky Mountain Region. As of Dec 31 2017, Co. had total proved reserves of 468.1 million barrels of oil equivalent, consisting of 158.2 million barrels of oil, 1,280.1 billion cubic feet of natural gas, and 96.5 million barrels of natural gas liquids.

Recent Developments: For the quarter ended Mar 31 2018, net income increased 326.4% to US$317.4 million from US$74.4 million in the year-earlier quarter. Revenues were US$769.6 million, up 106.5% from US$372.7 million the year before. Operating income was US$459.1 million versus US$166.2 million in the prior-year quarter, an increase of 176.3%. Direct operating expenses declined 8.9% to US$251.4 million from US$275.9 million in the comparable period the year before. Indirect operating expenses amounted to US$59.2 million compared with an income of US$69.3 million in the equivalent prior-year period.

Prospects: Our evaluation of SM Energy Co. as of Jan. 21, 2018 is the result of our systematic analysis on three basic characteristics: earnings strength, relative valuation, and recent stock price movement. The company has suffered a very negative trend in earnings per share over the past 5 quarters. Because the company lacks sufficient analyst estimate data, we place greater weight on the historical EPS trend as the measure of earnings strength. Based on operating earnings yield, the company is overvalued when compared to all of the companies in our coverage universe. Share price changes over the past year indicates that SM will perform very poorly over the near term.

Financial Data
(US$ in Thousands)

	3 Mos	12/31/2017	12/31/2016	12/31/2015	12/31/2014	12/31/2013	12/31/2012	12/31/2011
Earnings Per Share	0.70	(1.44)	(9.90)	(6.61)	9.79	2.51	(0.83)	3.19
Cash Flow Per Share	4.66	4.63	7.20	14.45	21.67	20.09	14.12	11.93
Tang Book Value Per Share	24.28	21.44	22.44	27.21	33.89	23.96	21.37	22.84
Dividends Per Share	0.100	0.100	0.100	0.100	0.100	0.100	0.100	0.100
Dividend Payout %	14.29	...	...	...	1.02	3.98	...	3.13
Income Statement								
Total Revenue	769,595	1,129,376	1,217,450	1,556,965	2,522,307	2,293,374	1,505,102	1,603,318
EBITDA	463,343	408,756	(242,548)	334,007	1,936,931	1,196,517	714,629	913,786
Depn & Amortn	3,866	573,312	800,683	928,719	773,678	828,262	734,646	529,402
Income Before Taxes	416,392	(343,813)	(1,201,916)	(722,861)	1,064,699	278,611	(83,517)	339,001
Income Taxes	98,991	(182,970)	(444,172)	(275,151)	398,648	107,676	(29,268)	123,585
Net Income	317,401	(160,843)	(757,744)	(447,710)	666,051	170,935	(54,249)	215,416
Average Shares	112,870	111,428	76,568	67,723	68,044	67,998	65,138	67,564
Balance Sheet								
Current Assets	923,192	549,115	224,642	518,989	745,043	647,501	340,564	463,204
Total Assets	6,659,988	6,176,776	6,393,511	5,621,643	6,516,700	4,705,165	4,199,529	3,798,980
Current Liabilities	649,176	559,212	415,172	302,525	784,660	639,131	541,546	505,805
Long-Term Obligations	2,912,248	2,908,770	2,897,575	2,517,970	2,366,000	1,600,000	1,440,000	985,069
Total Liabilities	3,947,891	3,782,168	3,896,378	3,769,242	4,230,045	3,098,344	2,785,063	2,336,040
Stockholders' Equity	2,712,097	2,394,608	2,497,133	1,852,401	2,286,655	1,606,821	1,414,466	1,462,940
Shares Outstanding	111,687	111,687	111,257	68,075	67,463	67,056	66,195	64,064
Statistical Record								
Return on Assets %	1.26	N.M.	N.M.	N.M.	11.87	3.84	N.M.	6.58
Return on Equity %	3.08	N.M.	N.M.	N.M.	34.21	11.32	N.M.	16.07
EBITDA Margin %	60.21	36.19	N.M.	21.45	76.79	52.17	47.48	56.99
Net Margin %	41.24	N.M.	N.M.	N.M.	26.41	7.45	N.M.	13.44
Asset Turnover	0.23	0.18	0.20	0.26	0.45	0.52	0.38	0.49
Current Ratio	1.42	0.98	0.54	1.72	0.95	1.01	0.63	0.92
Debt to Equity	1.07	1.21	1.16	1.36	1.03	1.00	1.02	0.67
Price Range	26.89-12.79	36.08-12.79	41.27-7.60	59.01-18.22	89.58-30.17	91.98-52.21	83.35-41.80	86.85-56.04
P/E Ratio	38.41-18.27	...	...	...	9.15-3.08	36.65-20.80	...	27.23-17.57
Average Yield %	0.52	0.48	0.36	0.25	0.14	0.14	0.17	0.14

Address: 1775 Sherman Street, Suite 1200, Denver, CO 80203 Telephone: 303-861-8140 Fax: 303-861-0934	Web Site: www.sm-energy.com Officers: William D. Sullivan - Chairman Javan D. Ottoson - President, Chief Executive Officer, Executive Vice President, Chief Operating Officer	Auditors: Ernst & Young LLP Investor Contact: 303-861-8140 Transfer Agents: Computershare Trust Company NA, Golden, Co

SMITH (A O) CORP

Exchange	Symbol	Price	52Wk Range	Yield	P/E	Div Acheiver
NYS	AOS	$59.15 (6/29/2018)	67.84-53.46	1.22	33.42	25 Years

*7 Year Price Score 151.32 *NYSE Composite Index=100 *12 Month Price Score 100.94

Interim Earnings (Per Share)

Qtr.	Mar	Jun	Sep	Dec
2015	0.33	0.40	0.41	0.45
2016	0.41	0.49	0.47	0.47
2017	0.50	0.53	0.54	0.13
2018	0.57	...	...	...

Interim Dividends (Per Share)

Amt	Decl	Ex	Rec	Pay
0.14Q	10/09/2017	10/30/2017	10/31/2017	11/15/2017
0.18Q	01/19/2018	01/30/2018	01/31/2018	02/15/2018
0.18Q	04/09/2018	04/27/2018	04/30/2018	05/15/2018
0.18Q	07/09/2018	07/30/2018	07/31/2018	08/15/2018

Indicated Div: $0.72 (Div. Reinv. Plan)

Valuation Analysis

		Institutional Holding	
Forecast EPS	$2.60 (06/13/2018)	No of Institutions	655
Market Cap	$10.1 Billion	Shares	158,957,440
Book Value	$1.7 Billion	% Held	70.64
Price/Book	5.93		
Price/Sales	3.32		

Business Summary: Household Appliances, Electronics & Goods (MIC: 1.5.1 SIC: 3639 NAIC: 335228)

A.O. Smith is comprised of two reporting segments: North America and Rest of World. The Rest of World segment is primarily comprised of China, Europe and India. Both segments manufacture and market lines of residential and commercial gas, gas tankless and electric water heaters, as well as water treatment products. Both segments primarily manufacture and market in their respective regions of the world. The North America segment also manufactures and globally markets specialty commercial water heating equipment, condensing and non-condensing boilers and water systems tanks. Co. also manufactures and markets in-home air purification products in China.

Recent Developments: For the quarter ended Mar 31 2018, net income increased 12.7% to US$98.8 million from US$87.7 million in the year-earlier quarter. Revenues were US$788.0 million, up 6.5% from US$740.0 million the year before. Direct operating expenses rose 6.2% to US$466.5 million from US$439.1 million in the comparable period the year before. Indirect operating expenses increased 8.6% to US$196.1 million from US$180.5 million in the equivalent prior-year period.

Prospects: Our evaluation of Smith (A.O.) Corp. as of Jan. 21, 2018 is the result of our systematic analysis on three basic characteristics: earnings strength, relative valuation, and recent stock price movement. The company has managed to produce a neutral trend in earnings per share over the past 5 quarters and while recent estimates for the company have been mixed, AOS has posted better than expected results. Based on operating earnings yield, the company is about fairly valued when compared to all of the companies in our coverage universe. Share price changes over the past year indicates that AOS will perform in line with the market over the near term.

Financial Data

(US$ in Thousands)	3 Mos	12/31/2017	12/31/2016	12/31/2015	12/31/2014	12/31/2013	12/31/2012	12/31/2011
Earnings Per Share	1.77	1.70	1.85	1.58	1.14	0.92	0.85	1.64
Cash Flow Per Share	2.22	1.89	2.55	1.94	1.46	1.52	0.78	0.32
Tang Book Value Per Share	5.19	4.80	4.13	4.15	3.60	3.13	2.27	1.63
Dividends Per Share	0.600	0.560	0.480	0.380	0.300	0.230	0.180	0.150
Dividend Payout %	33.90	32.94	25.95	24.05	26.32	25.14	21.11	9.13
Income Statement								
Total Revenue	788,000	2,996,700	2,685,900	2,536,500	2,356,000	2,153,800	1,939,300	1,710,500
EBITDA	145,600	601,000	534,900	472,900	352,200	301,800	297,600	217,800
Depn & Amortn	17,900	70,100	65,100	63,000	59,800	59,700	54,600	47,000
Income Before Taxes	125,400	520,800	462,500	402,500	286,700	236,400	233,800	161,500
Income Taxes	26,600	224,300	136,000	119,600	78,900	66,700	71,200	50,300
Net Income	98,800	296,500	326,500	282,900	207,800	169,700	158,700	305,700
Average Shares	173,350	174,605	176,825	179,009	181,973	185,575	186,216	186,298
Balance Sheet								
Current Assets	1,669,100	1,766,800	1,562,000	1,455,300	1,319,000	1,205,600	1,107,200	1,208,700
Total Assets	3,106,900	3,197,300	2,891,000	2,646,500	2,515,300	2,391,500	2,265,200	2,349,000
Current Liabilities	766,900	788,500	765,600	653,200	605,200	590,900	499,000	519,900
Long-Term Obligations	285,800	402,900	316,400	236,100	210,100	177,700	225,100	443,000
Total Liabilities	1,398,500	1,548,500	1,375,700	1,204,200	1,134,000	1,062,800	1,071,100	1,263,200
Stockholders' Equity	1,708,400	1,648,800	1,515,300	1,442,300	1,381,300	1,328,700	1,194,100	1,085,800
Shares Outstanding	171,142	171,663	173,441	175,896	178,799	182,478	184,853	183,306
Statistical Record								
Return on Assets %	10.17	9.74	11.76	10.96	8.47	7.29	6.86	13.71
Return on Equity %	18.79	18.74	22.02	20.04	15.34	13.45	13.88	31.08
EBITDA Margin %	18.48	20.06	19.92	18.64	14.95	14.01	15.35	12.73
Net Margin %	12.54	9.89	12.16	11.15	8.82	7.88	8.18	17.87
Asset Turnover	1.01	0.98	0.97	0.98	0.96	0.93	0.84	0.77
Current Ratio	2.18	2.24	2.04	2.23	2.18	2.04	2.22	2.32
Debt to Equity	0.17	0.24	0.21	0.16	0.15	0.13	0.19	0.41
Price Range	67.84-49.56	63.42-47.19	51.41-31.03	40.43-27.11	28.40-22.34	27.44-15.77	15.90-10.26	11.16-7.61
P/E Ratio	38.33-28.00	37.31-27.76	27.79-16.77	25.59-17.16	24.91-19.60	29.83-17.14	18.70-12.07	6.81-4.64
Average Yield %	1.02	1.02	1.13	1.11	1.21	1.11	1.42	1.52

Address: 11270 West Park Place, Milwaukee, WI 53224-9508
Telephone: 414-359-4000
Fax: 414-359-4115

Web Site: www.aosmith.com
Officers: Ajita G. Rajendra - Chairman, President, Chief Executive Officer, Chief Operating Officer, Executive Vice President, Senior Vice President, Division Officer, Executive Chairman Kevin J. Wheeler - President, Chief Operating Officer, Senior Vice President, Region Officer, Chief Executive Officer

Auditors: Ernst & Young LLP
Investor Contact: 414-359-4130
Transfer Agents: Wells Fargo Shareowner Services, N.A., St. Paul, MN

SOTHEBY'S

Exchange	Symbol	Price	52Wk Range	Yield	P/E
NYS	BID	$54.34 (6/29/2018)	59.67-42.97	N/A	23.83

*7 Year Price Score 103.49 *NYSE Composite Index=100 *12 Month Price Score 107.13

Interim Earnings (Per Share)

Qtr.	Mar	Jun	Sep	Dec
2015	0.07	0.96	(0.26)	(0.16)
2016	(0.41)	1.52	(0.99)	1.13
2017	(0.21)	1.43	(0.45)	1.42
2018	(0.12)	...	...	...

Interim Dividends (Per Share)

Dividend Payment Suspended

Valuation Analysis		Institutional Holding	
Forecast EPS	$2.72	No of Institutions	
	(06/10/2018)	340	
Market Cap	$2.8 Billion	Shares	
Book Value	$590.8 Million	68,009,368	
Price/Book	4.81	% Held	
Price/Sales	2.85	105.86	

Business Summary: Miscellaneous Consumer Services (MIC: 2.2.3 SIC: 7389 NAIC: 453920)

Sotheby's is a global art business whose operations are organized under two segments: Agency and Finance. The Agency segment matches buyers and sellers of authenticated fine art, decorative art, jewelry, wine and collectibles (collectively, art or works of art or artwork or property) through the auction or private sale process. Agency segment activities also include the sale of artworks that are principally acquired incidental to the auction process and the activities of RM Sotheby's, an equity investee that operates as an auction house for investment-quality automobiles. The Finance segment provides art-related financing activities by making loans that are secured by works of art.

Recent Developments: For the quarter ended Mar 31 2018, net loss amounted to US$6.5 million versus a net loss of US$11.3 million in the year-earlier quarter. Revenues were US$195.8 million, down 1.8% from US$199.3 million the year before. Operating income was US$6.9 million versus a loss of US$14.1 million in the prior-year quarter. Direct operating expenses declined 45.2% to US$53.5 million from US$97.7 million in the comparable period the year before. Indirect operating expenses increased 17.1% to US$135.4 million from US$115.6 million in the equivalent prior-year period.

Prospects: Our evaluation of Sotheby's Holdings Inc. as of Jan. 21, 2018 is the result of our systematic analysis on three basic characteristics: earnings strength, relative valuation, and recent stock price movement. The company has managed to produce a neutral trend in earnings per share over the past 5 quarters and while recent estimates for the company have been mixed, BID has posted better than expected results. Based on operating earnings yield, the company is about fairly valued when compared to all of the companies in our coverage universe. Share price changes over the past year indicates that BID will perform very well over the near term.

Financial Data

(US$ in Thousands)	3 Mos	12/31/2017	12/31/2016	12/31/2015	12/31/2014	12/31/2013	12/31/2012	12/31/2011
Earnings Per Share	2.28	2.20	1.27	0.63	1.68	1.88	1.57	2.46
Cash Flow Per Share	4.35	6.95	2.77	2.28	0.64	3.47	(0.96)	5.99
Tang Book Value Per Share	9.94	10.57	8.34	12.05	12.51	16.27	14.43	13.19
Dividends Per Share	...	...	...	0.400	4.740	0.200	0.520	0.230
Dividend Payout %	...	...	...	63.49	282.14	10.64	33.12	9.35
Income Statement								
Total Revenue	195,796	989,389	805,377	961,494	938,053	853,678	768,492	831,836
EBITDA	(2,069)	194,820	145,650	219,768	246,927	245,004	220,215	286,085
Depn & Amortn	451	22,100	19,900	19,500	20,600	19,400	17,900	17,200
Income Before Taxes	(11,468)	141,686	96,734	169,299	193,021	185,693	159,436	231,389
Income Taxes	(4,136)	25,415	25,957	131,145	75,761	55,702	51,395	60,032
Net Income	(6,522)	118,796	74,112	43,727	117,795	130,006	108,292	171,416
Average Shares	52,464	53,101	57,653	68,121	69,606	69,175	68,527	68,850
Balance Sheet								
Current Assets	1,264,579	1,902,089	1,268,853	2,109,739	2,039,522	1,972,273	1,671,123	1,693,296
Total Assets	2,415,910	3,087,307	2,504,426	3,274,129	3,134,820	2,893,546	2,575,095	2,399,414
Current Liabilities	1,009,304	1,516,626	742,975	1,197,583	1,429,207	1,142,489	964,879	964,312
Long-Term Obligations	715,988	849,503	1,163,941	1,156,267	745,000	515,148	515,197	464,552
Total Liabilities	1,825,096	2,470,552	1,999,008	2,467,702	2,257,123	1,754,228	1,582,269	1,495,747
Stockholders' Equity	590,814	616,755	505,418	806,427	877,697	1,139,318	992,826	903,667
Shares Outstanding	52,303	52,461	52,971	65,791	68,991	69,131	67,779	67,407
Statistical Record								
Return on Assets %	5.11	4.25	2.56	1.36	3.91	4.75	4.34	7.49
Return on Equity %	22.87	21.17	11.27	5.19	11.68	12.19	11.39	20.47
EBITDA Margin %	N.M.	19.69	18.08	22.86	26.32	28.70	28.66	34.39
Net Margin %	N.M.	12.01	9.20	4.55	12.56	15.23	14.09	20.61
Asset Turnover	0.41	0.35	0.28	0.30	0.31	0.31	0.31	0.36
Current Ratio	1.25	1.25	1.71	1.76	1.43	1.73	1.73	1.76
Debt to Equity	1.21	1.38	2.30	1.43	0.85	0.45	0.52	0.51
Price Range	57.70-42.97	57.70-38.72	41.65-19.13	46.93-25.76	53.51-35.30	53.20-33.03	40.51-27.74	54.41-25.84
P/E Ratio	25.31-18.85	26.23-17.60	32.80-15.06	74.49-40.89	31.85-21.01	28.30-17.57	25.80-17.67	22.12-10.50
Average Yield %	...	...	...	1.03	11.32	0.47	1.56	0.58

Address: 1334 York Avenue, New York, NY 10021
Telephone: 212-606-7000

Web Site: www.sothebys.com
Officers: Domenico De Sole - Chairman The Duke of Devonshire - Deputy Chairman

Auditors: Deloitte & Touche LLP
Investor Contact: 800-700-6321
Transfer Agents: BNY Mellon Shareowner Services, Pittsburg, PA

SMUCKER (J.M.) CO.

Exchange	Symbol	Price	52Wk Range	Yield	P/E	Div Acheiver
NYS	SJM	$107.48 (6/29/2018)	131.53-99.99	3.16	9.12	20 Years

*7 Year Price Score 86.50 ***NYSE Composite Index=100** ***12 Month Price Score 92.82**

Interim Earnings (Per Share)

Qtr.	Jul	Oct	Jan	Apr
2013-14	1.19	1.46	1.59	1.18
2014-15	1.14	1.55	1.58	(0.95)
2015-16	1.14	1.47	1.55	1.60
2016-17	1.46	1.52	1.16	0.96
2017-18	1.12	1.71	7.32	1.63

Interim Dividends (Per Share)

Amt	Decl	Ex	Rec	Pay
0.78Q	10/20/2017	11/09/2017	11/10/2017	12/01/2017
0.78Q	01/19/2018	02/08/2018	02/09/2018	03/01/2018
0.78Q	04/20/2018	05/10/2018	05/11/2018	06/01/2018
0.85Q	07/13/2018	08/16/2018	08/17/2018	09/04/2018

Indicated Div: $3.40 (Div. Reinv. Plan)

Valuation Analysis

Forecast EPS	$8.45
	(06/14/2018)
Market Cap	$12.2 Billion
Book Value	$7.9 Billion
Price/Book	1.55
Price/Sales	1.66

Institutional Holding

No of Institutions	1104
Shares	108,076,832
% Held	59.87

Business Summary: Food (MIC: 1.2.1 SIC: 2033 NAIC: 311421)

Smucker (J.M.) manufactures and markets food and beverage products. Co.'s principal products are coffee, pet food, pet snacks, peanut butter, fruit spreads, shortening and oils, baking mixes and ready-to-spread frostings, frozen sandwiches, flour and baking ingredients, juices and beverages, and portion control products. Co. has three segments: U.S. Retail Coffee, U.S. Retail Consumer Foods, and U.S. Retail Pet Foods. The U.S. Retail Coffee segment primarily includes the domestic sales of Folgers, Dunkin' Donuts®, and Cafe Bustelo® branded coffee; and the U.S. Retail Consumer Foods segment primarily includes domestic sales of Jif®, Smucker's®, Crisco®, and Pillsbury® branded products.

Recent Developments: For the year ended Apr 30 2018, net income increased 126.0% to US$1.34 billion from US$592.3 million in the prior year. Revenues were US$7.36 billion, down 0.5% from US$7.39 billion the year before. Operating income was US$1.04 billion versus US$1.03 billion in the prior year, an increase of 0.4%. Direct operating expenses declined 0.8% to US$4.52 billion from US$4.56 billion in the comparable period the year before. Indirect operating expenses were unchanged at US$1.80 billion versus the equivalent prior-year period.

Prospects: Our evaluation of Smucker (J.M.) Co. as of Jan. 21, 2018 is the result of our systematic analysis on three basic characteristics: earnings strength, relative valuation, and recent stock price movement. The company has enjoyed a very positive trend in earnings per share over the past 5 quarters. However, while recent estimates for the company have been mixed, SJM has posted better than expected results. Based on operating earnings yield, the company is undervalued when compared to all of the companies in our coverage universe. Share price changes over the past year indicates that SJM will perform very poorly over the near term.

Financial Data

(US$ in Thousands)	04/30/2018	04/30/2017	04/30/2016	04/30/2015	04/30/2014	04/30/2013	04/30/2012	04/30/2011
Earnings Per Share	11.78	5.10	5.76	3.33	5.42	5.00	4.06	4.05
Cash Flow Per Share	10.78	9.17	12.23	7.12	8.27	7.93	6.50	3.35
Dividends Per Share	3.090	2.920	2.650	2.500	2.260	2.040	1.880	1.640
Dividend Payout %	26.23	57.25	46.01	75.08	41.70	40.80	46.31	40.49
Income Statement								
Total Revenue	7,357,100	7,392,300	7,811,200	5,692,700	5,610,600	5,897,700	5,525,782	4,825,743
EBITDA	1,241,400	1,253,200	1,370,700	760,400	1,086,600	1,064,800	939,886	950,041
Depn & Amortn	206,300	211,700	221,700	157,500	157,500	154,100	158,936	165,795
Income Before Taxes	861,000	878,400	977,900	523,000	849,700	817,300	701,158	717,164
Income Taxes	(477,600)	286,100	289,200	178,100	284,500	273,100	241,414	237,682
Net Income	1,338,600	592,300	688,700	344,900	565,200	544,200	459,744	479,482
Average Shares	113,000	115,578	118,959	103,043	103,518	107,904	112,262	117,119
Balance Sheet								
Current Assets	1,555,000	1,641,800	1,573,400	2,052,300	1,539,100	1,595,200	1,643,465	1,636,999
Total Assets	15,301,200	15,639,700	15,984,100	16,882,600	9,072,100	9,031,800	9,115,226	8,324,585
Current Liabilities	1,033,800	1,832,600	1,213,000	1,022,600	891,000	596,800	616,972	482,676
Long-Term Obligations	4,688,000	4,445,500	5,146,000	5,944,900	1,879,800	1,967,800	2,020,543	1,304,039
Total Liabilities	7,410,100	8,789,500	8,975,600	9,795,700	4,042,500	3,883,000	3,951,840	3,032,222
Stockholders' Equity	7,891,100	6,850,200	7,008,500	7,086,900	5,029,600	5,148,800	5,163,386	5,292,363
Shares Outstanding	113,572	113,439	116,306	119,577	101,697	106,486	110,284	114,172
Statistical Record								
Return on Assets %	8.65	3.75	4.18	2.66	6.24	6.00	5.26	5.88
Return on Equity %	18.16	8.55	9.75	5.69	11.11	10.55	8.77	9.03
EBITDA Margin %	16.87	16.95	17.55	13.36	19.37	18.05	17.01	19.69
Net Margin %	18.19	8.01	8.82	6.06	10.07	9.23	8.32	9.94
Asset Turnover	0.48	0.47	0.47	0.44	0.62	0.65	0.63	0.59
Current Ratio	1.50	0.90	1.30	2.01	1.73	2.67	2.66	3.39
Debt to Equity	0.59	0.65	0.73	0.84	0.37	0.38	0.39	0.25
Price Range	131.53-99.99	156.23-124.74	132.52-105.59	118.20-96.45	114.36-91.81	105.00-73.65	81.44-67.68	75.07-54.75
P/E Ratio	11.17-8.49	30.63-24.46	23.01-18.33	35.50-28.96	21.10-16.94	21.00-14.73	20.06-16.67	18.54-13.52
Average Yield %	2.61	2.14	2.23	2.38	2.19	2.38	2.46	2.59

Address: One Strawberry Lane, Orrville, OH 44667-0280
Telephone: 330-682-3000

Web Site: www.jmsmucker.com
Officers: Richard K. Smucker - Executive Chairman, Executive Chairman (frmr), President, Chief Executive Officer, Co-Chief Executive Officer Mark R. Belgya - Vice-Chairman, Senior Vice President, Chief Financial Officer

Auditors: Ernst & Young LLP
Investor Contact: 330-684-3838
Transfer Agents: Computershare, Louisville, KY

SNAP-ON, INC.

Exchange	Symbol	Price	52Wk Range	Yield	P/E
NYS	SNA	$160.72 (6/29/2018)	183.76-141.51	2.04	16.14

*7 Year Price Score 103.13 *NYSE Composite Index=100   *12 Month Price Score 95.99

TRADING VOLUME (thousand shares)

Interim Earnings (Per Share)

Qtr.	Mar	Jun	Sep	Dec
2015	1.87	2.03	1.98	2.22
2016	2.16	2.36	2.22	2.46
2017	2.39	2.60	2.29	2.25
2018	2.82	...	...	...

Interim Dividends (Per Share)

Amt	Decl	Ex	Rec	Pay
0.71Q	08/03/2017	08/16/2017	08/18/2017	09/08/2017
0.82Q	11/06/2017	11/16/2017	11/17/2017	12/08/2017
0.82Q	02/15/2018	03/01/2018	03/02/2018	03/16/2018
0.82Q	04/26/2018	05/18/2018	05/21/2018	06/08/2018

Indicated Div: $3.28

Valuation Analysis

		Institutional Holding	
Forecast EPS	$11.65	No of Institutions	
	(06/11/2018)	839	
Market Cap	$9.1 Billion	Shares	
Book Value	$3.1 Billion	81,754,560	
Price/Book	2.95	% Held	
Price/Sales	2.24	84.10	

Business Summary: Industrial Machinery & Equipment (MIC: 7.2.1 SIC: 3429 NAIC: 332510)

Snap-on is a manufacturer and marketer of tools, equipment, diagnostics, repair information and systems solutions. Products and services include hand and power tools, tool storage, diagnostic software, information and management systems, shop equipment and solutions, for vehicle dealerships and repair centers, as well as for the aviation and aerospace, agriculture, construction, government and military, mining, natural resources, power generation and technical education industries. Co. also provides financing programs to facilitate the sales of its products. Co.'s segments are: Commercial & Industrial Group; Snap-on Tools Group; Repair Systems & Information Group; and Financial Services.

Recent Developments: For the quarter ended Mar 31 2018, net income increased 15.0% to US$166.8 million from US$145.1 million in the year-earlier quarter. Revenues were US$1.02 billion, up 5.7% from US$963.9 million the year before. Operating income was US$234.6 million versus US$222.7 million in the prior-year quarter, an increase of 5.3%. Direct operating expenses rose 5.8% to US$490.0 million from US$463.1 million in the comparable period the year before. Indirect operating expenses increased 5.7% to US$293.9 million from US$278.1 million in the equivalent prior-year period.

Prospects: Our evaluation of Snap-On Inc. as of Jan. 21, 2018 is the result of our systematic analysis on three basic characteristics: earnings strength, relative valuation, and recent stock price movement. The company has managed to produce a neutral trend in earnings per share over the past 5 quarters and while recent estimates for the company have remained steady, SNA has posted better than expected results. Based on operating earnings yield, the company is undervalued when compared to all of the companies in our coverage universe. Share price changes over the past year indicates that SNA will perform poorly over the near term.

Financial Data

(US$ in Thousands)	3 Mos	12/30/2017	12/31/2016	01/02/2016	01/03/2015	12/28/2013	12/29/2012	12/31/2011
Earnings Per Share	9.96	9.52	9.20	8.10	7.14	5.93	5.20	4.71
Cash Flow Per Share	11.44	10.63	9.94	8.57	6.74	6.76	5.67	2.21
Tang Book Value Per Share	33.41	31.33	26.52	24.58	20.54	18.65	13.86	9.39
Dividends Per Share	3.060	2.950	2.540	2.200	1.850	1.580	1.400	1.300
Dividend Payout %	30.72	30.99	27.61	27.16	25.91	26.64	26.92	27.60
Income Statement								
Total Revenue	1,018,500	4,000,300	3,711,800	3,593,100	3,492,600	3,237,500	3,099,200	2,996,500
EBITDA	261,300	967,200	938,600	844,400	762,800	658,500	592,100	547,300
Depn & Amortn	24,000	93,200	85,600	82,500	79,500	76,700	76,700	74,600
Income Before Taxes	223,800	821,900	801,400	710,500	630,900	526,200	460,200	412,900
Income Taxes	57,600	250,900	244,300	221,200	199,500	166,700	148,200	133,700
Net Income	163,000	557,700	546,400	478,700	421,900	350,300	306,100	276,300
Average Shares	57,765	58,600	59,400	59,100	59,100	59,100	58,900	58,700
Balance Sheet								
Current Assets	2,168,400	2,119,300	1,884,000	1,898,100	1,858,600	1,796,200	1,669,000	1,530,700
Total Assets	5,317,600	5,249,100	4,723,200	4,486,900	4,310,100	4,110,000	3,902,300	3,672,900
Current Liabilities	951,600	1,193,300	989,500	670,500	718,700	715,400	589,200	583,800
Long-Term Obligations	946,300	753,600	708,800	861,700	862,700	858,900	970,400	967,900
Total Liabilities	2,233,700	2,295,200	2,106,000	2,074,200	2,102,300	1,996,800	2,100,200	2,142,000
Stockholders' Equity	3,083,900	2,953,900	2,617,200	2,412,700	2,207,800	2,113,200	1,802,100	1,530,900
Shares Outstanding	56,595	56,690	57,949	58,086	58,113	58,115	58,254	58,224
Statistical Record								
Return on Assets %	11.36	11.22	11.90	10.91	9.86	8.77	8.10	7.49
Return on Equity %	19.86	20.08	21.79	20.78	19.21	17.94	18.42	18.98
EBITDA Margin %	25.66	24.18	25.29	23.50	21.84	20.34	19.10	18.26
Net Margin %	16.00	13.94	14.72	13.32	12.08	10.82	9.88	9.22
Asset Turnover	0.80	0.80	0.81	0.82	0.82	0.81	0.82	0.81
Current Ratio	2.28	1.78	1.90	2.83	2.59	2.51	2.83	2.62
Debt to Equity	0.31	0.26	0.27	0.36	0.39	0.41	0.54	0.63
Price Range	183.76-141.51	181.53-141.51	176.20-135.41	174.09-131.45	139.35-97.23	108.88-77.06	80.03-51.12	64.09-42.45
P/E Ratio	18.45-14.21	19.07-14.86	19.15-14.72	21.49-16.23	19.52-13.62	18.36-12.99	15.39-9.83	13.61-9.01
Average Yield %	1.91	1.82	1.61	1.41	1.55	1.72	2.12	2.35

Address: 2801 80th Street, Kenosha, WI 53143	Web Site: www.snapon.com	Auditors: DELOITTE & TOUCHE LLP
Telephone: 262-656-5200	Officers: Nicholas T. Pinchuk - Chairman, President, Chief Executive Officer Aldo John Pagliari - Senior Vice President, Chief Financial Officer	Investor Contact: 262-656-6121
Fax: 262-656-5577		Transfer Agents: Computershare Trust Company, N.A., Providence, RI

SONIC AUTOMOTIVE, INC.

Exchange	Symbol	Price	52Wk Range	Yield	P/E
NYS	SAH	$20.60 (6/29/2018)	23.35-16.40	1.17	10.05

*7 Year Price Score 77.43 *NYSE Composite Index=100 *12 Month Price Score 107.02

Interim Earnings (Per Share)

Qtr.	Mar	Jun	Sep	Dec
2015	0.27	0.29	0.52	0.62
2016	0.31	0.50	0.40	0.84
2017	(0.01)	0.27	0.44	1.39
2018	(0.05)	...	...	...

Interim Dividends (Per Share)

Amt	Decl	Ex	Rec	Pay
0.05Q	07/28/2017	09/14/2017	09/15/2017	10/13/2017
0.05Q	10/24/2017	12/14/2017	12/15/2017	01/12/2018
0.06Q	02/27/2018	03/14/2018	03/15/2018	04/13/2018
0.06Q	04/26/2018	06/14/2018	06/15/2018	07/13/2018

Indicated Div: $0.24

Valuation Analysis

		Institutional Holding	
Forecast EPS	$2.26	No of Institutions	
	(06/11/2018)	226	
Market Cap	$879.0 Million	Shares	
Book Value	$768.7 Million	38,650,072	
Price/Book	1.14	% Held	
Price/Sales	0.09	63.79	

Business Summary: Retail - Automotive (MIC: 2.1.4 SIC: 5511 NAIC: 441110)

Sonic Automotive is an automotive retailer. As of Dec 31 2017, Co. operated 114 new vehicle franchises in 13 states (representing 25 different brands of cars and light trucks), 18 collision repair centers and nine pre-owned vehicle stores. Co. has two segments: Franchised Dealerships, which provides comprehensive services, including sales of both new and used cars and light trucks; sales of replacement parts and performance of vehicle maintenance, manufacturer warranty repairs, and related services; and Pre-Owned Stores Segment provides the same services in stand-alone pre-owned vehicle specialty retail locations and includes Co.'s EchoPark stores.

Recent Developments: For the quarter ended Mar 31 2018, loss from continuing operations was US$2.0 million compared with a loss of US$20,000 in the year-earlier quarter. Net loss amounted to US$2.2 million versus a net loss of US$541,000 in the year-earlier quarter. Revenues were US$2.40 billion, up 4.9% from US$2.29 billion the year before. Operating income was US$20.2 million versus US$36.4 million in the prior-year quarter, a decrease of 44.6%. Direct operating expenses rose 5.7% to US$2.05 billion from US$1.94 billion in the comparable period the year before. Indirect operating expenses increased 5.9% to US$332.3 million from US$313.9 million in the equivalent prior-year period.

Prospects: Our evaluation of Sonic Automotive Inc. as of Jan. 21, 2018 is the result of our systematic analysis on three basic characteristics: earnings strength, relative valuation, and recent stock price movement. The company has enjoyed a very positive trend in earnings per share over the past 5 quarters and while recent estimates for the company have been mixed, SAH has posted results that were in line with analysts expectations. Based on operating earnings yield, the company is undervalued when compared to all of the companies in our coverage universe. Share price changes over the past year indicates that SAH will perform very poorly over the near term.

Financial Data

(US$ in Thousands)	3 Mos	12/31/2017	12/31/2016	12/31/2015	12/31/2014	12/31/2013	12/31/2012	12/31/2011
Earnings Per Share	2.05	2.09	2.04	1.70	1.84	1.53	1.53	1.29
Cash Flow Per Share	3.23	3.70	4.73	1.38	3.09	2.41	(1.25)	2.93
Tang Book Value Per Share	3.97	4.32	3.86	3.54	2.10	0.94	0.03	N.M.
Dividends Per Share	0.210	0.200	0.200	0.113	0.100	0.100	0.100	0.100
Dividend Payout %	10.24	9.57	9.80	6.62	5.43	6.54	6.54	7.75
Income Statement								
Total Revenue	2,400,773	9,867,208	9,731,779	9,624,299	9,197,099	8,843,168	8,365,468	7,871,274
EBITDA	21,031	289,170	314,159	289,522	295,331	264,744	279,127	269,462
Depn & Amortn	754	92,127	81,125	72,130	61,621	58,284	58,350	55,628
Income Before Taxes	(3,856)	108,124	155,212	145,156	161,727	129,021	141,233	126,029
Income Taxes	(1,842)	13,971	60,696	57,065	63,168	44,343	49,972	48,382
Net Income	(2,194)	92,983	93,193	86,311	97,217	81,618	89,101	76,254
Average Shares	42,789	44,358	45,948	50,883	52,563	52,941	60,406	65,464
Balance Sheet								
Current Assets	1,958,540	2,019,797	2,031,044	2,083,112	1,768,959	1,732,185	1,611,033	1,180,729
Total Assets	3,788,495	3,818,518	3,639,336	3,562,381	3,183,135	3,051,170	2,776,722	2,339,629
Current Liabilities	1,887,067	1,954,832	1,936,880	1,914,621	1,647,006	1,594,536	1,524,155	1,156,675
Long-Term Obligations	1,004,657	963,389	839,675	781,145	742,610	730,157	610,798	536,011
Total Liabilities	3,019,778	3,031,758	2,914,172	2,833,333	2,516,417	2,437,531	2,250,177	1,816,887
Stockholders' Equity	768,717	786,760	725,164	729,048	666,718	613,639	526,545	522,742
Shares Outstanding	42,671	43,195	44,733	49,940	50,919	52,713	53,239	52,629
Statistical Record								
Return on Assets %	2.47	2.49	2.58	2.56	3.12	2.80	3.47	3.32
Return on Equity %	12.25	12.30	12.78	12.37	15.19	14.32	16.94	15.44
EBITDA Margin %	0.88	2.93	3.23	3.01	3.21	2.99	3.34	3.42
Net Margin %	N.M.	0.94	0.96	0.90	1.06	0.92	1.07	0.97
Asset Turnover	2.70	2.65	2.70	2.85	2.95	3.03	3.26	3.43
Current Ratio	1.04	1.03	1.05	1.09	1.07	1.09	1.06	1.02
Debt to Equity	1.31	1.22	1.16	1.07	1.11	1.19	1.16	1.03
Price Range	22.45-16.40	25.95-16.40	24.00-15.91	27.04-20.35	27.81-21.33	25.15-20.11	20.89-12.16	16.21-10.47
P/E Ratio	10.95-8.00	12.42-7.85	11.76-7.80	15.91-11.97	15.11-11.59	16.44-13.14	13.65-7.95	12.57-8.12
Average Yield %	1.08	1.00	1.09	0.47	0.41	0.44	0.58	0.73

Address: 4401 Colwick Road,	Web Site: www.sonicautomotive.com	Auditors: KPMG LLP
Charlotte, NC 28211	Officers: O. Bruton Smith - Executive Chairman,	Investor Contact: 888-766-4218
Telephone: 704-566-2400	Chairman, Chief Executive Officer David Bruton	Transfer Agents: American Stock
Fax: 704-536-5116	Smith - Executive Vice-Chairman, Chief Strategy	Transfer & Trust Company, New York,
	Officer, Vice-Chairman, Executive Vice President	NY

SONOCO PRODUCTS CO.

Exchange	Symbol	Price	52Wk Range	Yield	P/E	Div Acheiver
NYS	SON	$52.50 (6/29/2018)	55.45-46.60	3.12	27.06	34 Years

*7 Year Price Score 97.99 *NYSE Composite Index=100 *12 Month Price Score 100.53

Interim Earnings (Per Share)

Qtr.	Mar	Jun	Sep	Dec
2015	0.86	0.63	0.43	0.54
2016	0.59	0.55	0.64	1.03
2017	0.54	0.43	0.72	0.06
2018	0.73	...	...	...

Interim Dividends (Per Share)

Amt	Decl	Ex	Rec	Pay
0.39Q	07/19/2017	08/09/2017	08/11/2017	09/08/2017
0.39Q	10/16/2017	11/09/2017	11/10/2017	12/08/2017
0.39Q	02/14/2018	02/27/2018	02/28/2018	03/09/2018
0.41Q	04/18/2018	05/10/2018	05/11/2018	06/08/2018

Indicated Div: $1.64 (Div. Reinv. Plan)

Valuation Analysis

		Institutional Holding	
Forecast EPS	$3.29	No of Institutions	
	(06/11/2018)	562	
Market Cap	$5.2 Billion	Shares	
Book Value	$1.8 Billion	92,944,544	
Price/Book	2.95	% Held	
Price/Sales	1.01	69.34	

Business Summary: Containers & Packaging (MIC: 8.1.3 SIC: 2671 NAIC: 322221)

Sonoco Products is a manufacturer of industrial and consumer packaging products and a provider of packaging services. Co. has four segments: Consumer Packaging, which include round composite cans, shaped rigid paperboard containers, fiber caulk/adhesive tubes, and peelable membrane easy-open closures for composite and metal cans; Paper and Industrial Converted Products, which include Recycled paperboard, chipboard, tubeboard, and lightweight corestock; Display and Packaging, which include printed backer cards, thermoformed blisters and heat sealing equipment; and Protective Solutions, which include custom-engineered, paperboard-based and expanded foam protective packaging and components.

Recent Developments: For the quarter ended Apr 1 2018, net income increased 37.9% to US$74.9 million from US$54.3 million in the year-earlier quarter. Revenues were US$1.30 billion, up 11.2% from US$1.17 billion the year before. Operating income was US$110.1 million versus US$93.7 million in the prior-year quarter, an increase of 17.6%. Direct operating expenses rose 11.0% to US$1.05 billion from US$949.3 million in the comparable period the year before. Indirect operating expenses increased 8.6% to US$140.5 million from US$129.3 million in the equivalent prior-year period.

Prospects: Our evaluation of Sonoco Products Co. as of Jan. 21, 2018 is the result of our systematic analysis on three basic characteristics: earnings strength, relative valuation, and recent stock price movement. The company has enjoyed a very positive trend in earnings per share over the past 5 quarters and while recent estimates for the company have been mixed, SON has posted better than expected results. Based on operating earnings yield, the company is undervalued when compared to all of the companies in our coverage universe. Share price changes over the past year indicates that SON will perform poorly over the near term.

Financial Data

(US$ in Thousands)	3 Mos	12/31/2017	12/31/2016	12/31/2015	12/31/2014	12/31/2013	12/31/2012	12/31/2011
Earnings Per Share	1.94	1.74	2.81	2.44	2.32	2.12	1.91	2.13
Cash Flow Per Share	4.00	3.49	3.93	4.46	4.09	5.25	3.96	2.43
Tang Book Value Per Share	1.98	1.35	2.17	1.26	0.43	3.60	1.01	0.08
Dividends Per Share	1.560	1.540	1.460	1.370	1.270	1.230	1.190	1.150
Dividend Payout %	80.41	88.51	51.96	56.15	54.74	58.02	62.30	53.99
Income Statement								
Total Revenue	1,304,187	5,036,650	4,782,877	4,964,369	5,014,534	4,848,092	4,786,129	4,498,932
EBITDA	168,457	545,348	666,129	562,432	561,422	530,695	518,964	485,678
Depn & Amortn	58,068	178,049	173,295	179,888	169,911	169,400	171,905	163,198
Income Before Taxes	97,034	314,554	441,277	327,946	339,120	304,569	287,074	284,406
Income Taxes	23,356	146,589	164,631	87,738	108,922	96,203	103,759	78,423
Net Income	74,055	175,345	286,434	250,136	239,165	219,113	196,010	217,517
Average Shares	100,896	100,852	101,782	102,392	103,172	103,248	102,573	102,173
Balance Sheet								
Current Assets	1,664,036	1,563,636	1,348,768	1,307,378	1,390,283	1,378,474	1,499,896	1,312,791
Total Assets	4,653,069	4,557,721	3,923,203	4,020,269	4,209,996	3,979,291	4,176,065	3,986,170
Current Liabilities	1,035,374	999,970	802,616	922,516	905,445	867,225	1,044,235	836,483
Long-Term Obligations	1,289,045	1,288,002	1,020,698	1,021,854	1,200,885	946,257	1,099,454	1,232,960
Total Liabilities	2,880,906	2,850,655	2,390,845	2,507,340	2,702,873	2,268,554	2,687,079	2,574,375
Stockholders' Equity	1,772,163	1,707,066	1,532,358	1,512,929	1,507,123	1,710,737	1,488,986	1,411,795
Shares Outstanding	99,563	99,414	99,193	100,944	100,603	102,147	100,847	100,211
Statistical Record								
Return on Assets %	4.43	4.14	7.19	6.08	5.84	5.37	4.79	5.99
Return on Equity %	11.66	10.83	18.76	16.57	14.86	13.70	13.48	14.98
EBITDA Margin %	12.92	10.83	13.93	11.33	11.20	10.95	10.84	10.80
Net Margin %	5.68	3.48	5.99	5.04	4.77	4.52	4.10	4.83
Asset Turnover	1.17	1.19	1.20	1.21	1.22	1.19	1.17	1.24
Current Ratio	1.61	1.56	1.68	1.42	1.54	1.59	1.44	1.57
Debt to Equity	0.73	0.75	0.67	0.68	0.80	0.55	0.74	0.87
Price Range	55.45-46.60	55.45-47.15	55.25-37.01	47.44-37.26	44.50-37.55	41.72-29.73	34.49-29.20	36.80-27.34
P/E Ratio	28.58-24.02	31.87-27.10	19.66-13.17	19.44-15.27	19.18-16.19	19.68-14.02	18.06-15.29	17.28-12.84
Average Yield %	3.06	2.98	2.98	3.01	3.18	3.06	3.39	3.46

Address: 1 N. Second St., Hartsville, SC 29550	Web Site: www.sonoco.com	Auditors: PricewaterhouseCoopers LLP
Telephone: 843-383-7000	**Officers:** Harris E. DeLoach - Chairman, Chief Executive Officer Robert C. (Rob) Tiede - President, Chief Executive Officer, Executive Vice President, Chief Operating Officer, Division Officer	**Investor Contact:** 843-339-6018
Fax: 843-383-7008		**Transfer Agents:** Continental Stock Transfer & Trust Company, New York, NY

SOUTH JERSEY INDUSTRIES, INC.

Exchange	Symbol	Price	52Wk Range	Yield	P/E	Div Acheiver
NYS	SJI	$33.47 (6/29/2018)	36.34-26.11	3.35	38.03	18 Years

*7 Year Price Score 89.63 *NYSE Composite Index=100 *12 Month Price Score 99.44

Interim Earnings (Per Share)

Qtr.	Mar	Jun	Sep	Dec
2015	0.79	0.19	(0.18)	0.74
2016	0.95	(0.06)	0.12	0.59
2017	0.47	(0.10)	(0.47)	0.05
2018	1.40	...	...	...

Interim Dividends (Per Share)

Amt	Decl	Ex	Rec	Pay
0.28Q	11/20/2017	12/08/2017	12/11/2017	12/27/2017
0.28Q	01/22/2018	03/16/2018	03/19/2018	04/03/2018
0.28Q	05/14/2018	06/08/2018	06/11/2018	07/03/2018
0.28Q	07/05/2018	09/07/2018	09/10/2018	10/02/2018

Indicated Div: $1.12 (Div. Reinv. Plan)

Valuation Analysis | **Institutional Holding**

Forecast EPS	$1.60 (06/14/2018)	No of Institutions 326
Market Cap	$2.9 Billion	Shares
Book Value	$1.3 Billion	74,109,392
Price/Book	2.23	% Held
Price/Sales	2.14	66.45

Business Summary: Gas Utilities (MIC: 3.3.1 SIC: 4924 NAIC: 221210)

South Jersey Industries is a holding company. Co. operates via its subsidiaries: South Jersey Gas Co., which is a regulated natural gas utility; South Jersey Energy Co., which acquires and markets natural gas and electricity to retail end users; South Jersey Resources Group, LLC, which markets natural gas storage assets; South Jersey Exploration, LLC, which owns oil, gas and mineral rights in the Marcellus Shale region of Pennsylvania; Marina Energy, LLC, which develops and operates energy-related projects; South Jersey Energy Service Plus, LLC, which services residential and small commercial HVAC systems; and SJI Midstream, LLC, which invests in infrastructure and other midstream projects.

Recent Developments: For the quarter ended Mar 31 2018, income from continuing operations increased 194.9% to US$111.3 million from US$37.7 million in the year-earlier quarter. Net income increased 194.9% to US$111.2 million from US$37.7 million in the year-earlier quarter. Revenues were US$521.9 million, up 22.6% from US$425.8 million the year before. Operating income was US$157.9 million versus US$68.9 million in the prior-year quarter, an increase of 129.2%. Direct operating expenses rose 1.9% to US$337.0 million from US$330.6 million in the comparable period the year before. Indirect operating expenses increased 2.7% to US$27.1 million from US$26.4 million in the equivalent prior-year period.

Prospects: Our evaluation of South Jersey Industries Inc. as of Jan. 21, 2018 is the result of our systematic analysis on three basic characteristics: earnings strength, relative valuation, and recent stock price movement. The company has generated a negative trend in earnings per share over the past 5 quarters. However, while recent estimates for the company have been mixed, SJI has posted results that fell short of analysts expectations. Based on operating earnings yield, the company is about fairly valued when compared to all of the companies in our coverage universe. Share price changes over the past year indicates that SJI will perform well over the near term.

Financial Data

(US$ in Thousands)	3 Mos	12/31/2017	12/31/2016	12/31/2015	12/31/2014	12/31/2013	12/31/2012	12/31/2011
Earnings Per Share	0.88	(0.04)	1.56	1.53	1.46	1.27	1.49	1.49
Cash Flow Per Share	2.59	2.39	3.42	2.72	2.43	2.49	1.91	3.19
Tang Book Value Per Share	14.80	14.79	15.96	14.19	13.65	12.64	11.63	10.33
Dividends Per Share	1.105	1.097	1.064	1.018	0.960	0.900	0.825	0.749
Dividend Payout %	125.57	...	68.19	66.50	65.75	70.59	55.56	50.42
Income Statement								
Total Revenue	521,945	1,243,068	1,036,500	959,568	886,996	731,421	706,280	828,560
EBITDA	185,293	120,602	289,654	238,855	202,426	130,252	162,338	172,998
Depn & Amortn	24,662	100,718	90,389	72,451	63,004	49,637	41,336	35,749
Income Before Taxes	146,659	(34,135)	167,816	134,782	109,862	61,790	102,016	113,171
Income Taxes	36,415	(24,937)	54,151	1,360	4,449	(19,014)	11,479	22,502
Net Income	111,240	(3,490)	118,810	105,107	97,046	81,593	91,608	89,291
Average Shares	79,724	79,541	76,475	68,931	66,428	64,092	61,648	60,172
Balance Sheet								
Current Assets	413,506	438,993	473,313	431,274	566,697	482,898	394,837	340,609
Total Assets	3,890,080	3,865,086	3,730,567	3,480,900	3,349,425	2,924,855	2,631,440	2,247,510
Current Liabilities	924,180	883,082	952,624	832,476	850,185	764,973	651,834	587,971
Long-Term Obligations	974,749	1,122,999	808,005	1,006,394	859,491	680,400	601,400	424,213
Total Liabilities	2,608,583	2,672,677	2,441,327	2,443,361	2,416,993	2,097,855	1,895,226	1,623,396
Stockholders' Equity	1,281,497	1,192,409	1,289,240	1,037,539	932,432	827,000	736,214	624,114
Shares Outstanding	85,502	79,549	79,478	70,965	68,334	65,430	63,306	60,424
Statistical Record								
Return on Assets %	1.83	N.M.	3.29	3.08	3.09	2.94	3.74	4.13
Return on Equity %	5.41	N.M.	10.18	10.67	11.03	10.44	13.43	14.95
EBITDA Margin %	35.50	9.70	27.95	24.89	22.82	17.81	22.98	20.88
Net Margin %	21.31	N.M.	11.46	10.95	10.94	11.16	12.97	10.78
Asset Turnover	0.35	0.33	0.29	0.28	0.28	0.26	0.29	0.38
Current Ratio	0.45	0.50	0.50	0.52	0.67	0.63	0.61	0.58
Debt to Equity	0.76	0.94	0.63	0.97	0.92	0.82	0.82	0.68
Price Range	38.12-26.11	38.12-30.78	34.68-22.63	30.30-12.96	30.61-26.00	31.13-25.16	28.47-23.18	28.75-21.72
P/E Ratio	43.32-29.67	...	22.23-14.51	19.80-8.47	20.97-17.81	24.51-19.81	19.10-15.55	19.29-14.58
Average Yield %	3.34	3.35	3.64	3.94	3.41	3.15	3.23	2.81

Address: 1 South Jersey Plaza, Folsom, NJ 08037	Web Site: www.sjiindustries.com	Auditors: DELOITTE & TOUCHE LLP
Telephone: 609-561-9000	Officers: Walter M. Higgins - Chairman Michael J. Renna - President, Vice President, Chief Operating Officer, Chief Executive Officer	Investor Contact: 609-561-9000Ext.42 Transfer Agents: Computershare, Canton, MA

SOUTHERN COMPANY (THE)

Exchange	Symbol	Price	52Wk Range	Yield	P/E	Div Acheiver
NYS	SO	$46.31 (6/29/2018)	53.25-42.73	5.18	42.10	16 Years

*7 Year Price Score 82.33   *NYSE Composite Index=100   *12 Month Price Score 93.42

TRADING VOLUME (thousand shares)

Interim Earnings (Per Share)

Qtr.	Mar	Jun	Sep	Dec
2015	0.56	0.69	1.05	0.29
2016	0.53	0.65	1.16	0.19
2017	0.66	(1.37)	1.06	0.49
2018	0.92	...	...	...

Interim Dividends (Per Share)

Amt	Decl	Ex	Rec	Pay
0.58Q	07/17/2017	08/17/2017	08/21/2017	09/06/2017
0.58Q	10/16/2017	11/17/2017	11/20/2017	12/06/2017
0.58Q	01/19/2018	02/16/2018	02/20/2018	03/06/2018
0.60Q	04/16/2018	05/18/2018	05/21/2018	06/06/2018

Indicated Div: $2.40 (Div. Reinv. Plan)

Valuation Analysis | **Institutional Holding**

Forecast EPS	$2.90 (06/14/2018)	No of Institutions 1660
Market Cap	$46.8 Billion	Shares 690,329,280
Book Value	$25.0 Billion	% Held
Price/Book	1.87	49.30
Price/Sales	1.98	

Business Summary: Electric Utilities (MIC: 3.1.1 SIC: 4911 NAIC: 221119)

Southern is a holding company. Through its subsidiaries, Alabama Power Company, Georgia Power Company, Gulf Power Company and Mississippi Power Company, each of which is an operating public utility company, Co. supplies electric service in the states of Alabama, Georgia, Florida, and Mississippi. In addition, Co. owns all of the common stock of Southern Power Company, which is also an operating public utility company that constructs, acquires, owns, and manages generation assets, including renewable energy projects, and sells electricity at market-based rates in the wholesale market.

Recent Developments: For the quarter ended Mar 31 2018, net income increased 40.8% to US$936.0 million from US$665.0 million in the year-earlier quarter. Revenues were US$6.37 billion, up 10.4% from US$5.77 billion the year before. Operating income was US$1.38 billion versus US$1.25 billion in the prior-year quarter, an increase of 9.9%. Direct operating expenses rose 13.8% to US$3.83 billion from US$3.37 billion in the comparable period the year before. Indirect operating expenses increased 1.2% to US$1.17 billion from US$1.15 billion in the equivalent prior-year period.

Prospects: Our evaluation of Southern Company as of Jan. 21, 2018 is the result of our systematic analysis on three basic characteristics: earnings strength, relative valuation, and recent stock price movement. The company has generated a negative trend in earnings per share over the past 5 quarters. However, while recent estimates for the company have been mixed, SO has posted better than expected results. Based on operating earnings yield, the company is undervalued when compared to all of the companies in our coverage universe. Share price changes over the past year indicates that SO will perform very well over the near term.

Financial Data

(US$ in Thousands)	3 Mos	12/31/2017	12/31/2016	12/31/2015	12/31/2014	12/31/2013	12/31/2012	12/31/2011
Earnings Per Share	1.10	0.84	2.55	2.59	2.18	1.87	2.67	2.55
Cash Flow Per Share	6.93	6.39	5.13	6.89	6.48	6.95	5.61	6.89
Tang Book Value Per Share	17.72	17.22	17.83	22.72	22.39	21.85	21.52	20.75
Dividends Per Share	2.320	2.300	2.223	2.152	2.083	2.013	1.942	1.873
Dividend Payout %	210.91	273.81	87.16	83.11	95.53	107.62	72.75	73.43
Income Statement								
Total Revenue	6,372,000	23,031,000	19,896,000	17,489,000	18,467,000	17,087,000	16,537,000	17,657,000
EBITDA	2,339,000	4,690,000	7,240,000	6,841,000	6,117,000	5,662,000	6,713,000	6,392,000
Depn & Amortn	873,000	2,034,000	2,502,000	2,395,000	2,293,000	2,298,000	2,145,000	2,048,000
Income Before Taxes	1,008,000	962,000	3,421,000	3,629,000	3,008,000	2,559,000	3,749,000	3,487,000
Income Taxes	113,000	142,000	951,000	1,194,000	977,000	849,000	1,334,000	1,219,000
Net Income	942,000	880,000	2,493,000	2,421,000	2,031,000	1,710,000	2,415,000	2,268,000
Average Shares	1,016,000	1,008,000	958,000	914,000	901,000	881,000	879,000	864,000
Balance Sheet								
Current Assets	9,524,000	10,072,000	9,722,000	6,526,000	6,370,000	5,599,000	6,162,000	6,272,000
Total Assets	111,567,000	111,005,000	109,697,000	78,318,000	70,923,000	64,546,000	63,149,000	59,267,000
Current Liabilities	13,630,000	13,594,000	12,917,000	9,129,000	8,967,000	5,536,000	7,014,000	6,577,000
Long-Term Obligations	44,446,000	44,462,000	42,629,000	24,688,000	20,841,000	21,344,000	19,274,000	18,647,000
Total Liabilities	86,567,000	86,514,000	84,212,000	56,999,000	49,622,000	44,407,000	43,770,000	40,607,000
Stockholders' Equity	25,000,000	24,491,000	25,485,000	21,319,000	21,301,000	20,139,000	19,379,000	18,660,000
Shares Outstanding	1,011,625	1,007,603	990,394	911,721	907,777	887,086	867,768	865,125
Statistical Record								
Return on Assets %	1.04	0.80	2.64	3.24	3.00	2.68	3.93	3.97
Return on Equity %	4.53	3.52	10.62	11.36	9.80	8.65	12.66	12.62
EBITDA Margin %	36.71	20.36	36.39	39.12	33.12	33.14	40.59	36.20
Net Margin %	14.78	3.82	12.53	13.84	11.00	10.01	14.60	12.84
Asset Turnover	0.21	0.21	0.21	0.23	0.27	0.27	0.27	0.31
Current Ratio	0.70	0.74	0.75	0.71	0.71	1.01	0.88	0.95
Debt to Equity	1.78	1.82	1.67	1.16	0.98	1.06	0.99	1.00
Price Range	53.25-42.92	53.25-46.78	54.54-46.45	52.79-41.61	50.88-40.40	48.65-40.12	48.42-42.03	46.59-36.80
P/E Ratio	48.41-39.02	63.39-55.69	21.39-18.22	20.38-16.07	23.34-18.53	26.02-21.45	18.13-15.74	18.27-14.43
Average Yield %	4.78	4.64	4.43	4.78	4.78	4.70	4.61	4.64

Address: 30 Ivan Allen Jr. Boulevard, N.W., Atlanta, GA 30308	Web Site: www.southerncompany.com	Auditors: DELOITTE & TOUCHE LLP
Telephone: 404-506-5000	Officers: Thomas A. Fanning - Chairman, President, Chief Executive Officer, Chief Operating Officer, Executive Vice President W. Paul Bowers - Executive Vice President	Transfer Agents: ComputerShare, College Station, TX
Fax: 404-506-0455		

SOUTHERN COPPER CORP

Exchange	Symbol	Price	52Wk Range	Yield	P/E
NYS	SCCO	$46.87 (6/29/2018)	57.34-34.63	2.11	40.76

*7 Year Price Score 113.22 *NYSE Composite Index=100 *12 Month Price Score 106.55

Interim Earnings (Per Share)

Qtr.	Mar	Jun	Sep	Dec
2015	0.35	0.37	0.12	0.08
2016	0.24	0.29	0.26	0.22
2017	0.41	0.39	0.52	(0.37)
2018	0.61	...	...	...

Interim Dividends (Per Share)

Amt	Decl	Ex	Rec	Pay
0.14Q	07/20/2017	08/07/2017	08/09/2017	08/23/2017
0.25Q	10/19/2017	11/07/2017	11/08/2017	11/22/2017
0.30Q	01/25/2018	02/12/2018	02/13/2018	02/27/2018
0.30Q	04/19/2018	05/08/2018	05/09/2018	05/23/2018

Indicated Div: $0.99

Valuation Analysis **Institutional Holding**

Forecast EPS	$2.46 (06/14/2018)	No of Institutions 461
Market Cap	$36.2 Billion	Shares 74,829,048
Book Value	$6.3 Billion	% Held
Price/Book	5.71	N/A
Price/Sales	5.24	

Business Summary: Mining (MIC: 8.2.4 SIC: 1021 NAIC: 212234)

Southern Copper produces copper, molybdenum, zinc and silver. Co.'s mining, smelting and refining facilities are located in Peru and Mexico and Co. conducts its exploration activities in those countries and in Argentina, Chile and Ecuador. Co.'s Peruvian copper operations involve mining, milling and flotation of copper ore to produce copper concentrates and molybdenum concentrates; the smelting of copper concentrates to produce blister and anode copper; and the refining of anode copper to produce copper cathodes. Co.'s Mexican operations are conducted via its Minera Mexico S.A. de C.V. subsidiary, which engages in the mining and processing of copper, molybdenum, zinc, silver, gold and lead.

Recent Developments: For the quarter ended Mar 31 2018, net income increased 49.7% to US$471.9 million from US$315.3 million in the year-earlier quarter. Revenues were US$1.84 billion, up 16.2% from US$1.58 billion the year before. Operating income was US$773.3 million versus US$570.4 million in the prior-year quarter, an increase of 35.6%. Direct operating expenses rose 3.9% to US$876.5 million from US$843.8 million in the comparable period the year before. Indirect operating expenses increased 12.7% to US$191.3 million from US$169.7 million in the equivalent prior-year period.

Prospects: Our evaluation of Southern Copper Corp. as of Jan. 21, 2018 is the result of our systematic analysis on three basic characteristics: earnings strength, relative valuation, and recent stock price movement. The company has enjoyed a very positive trend in earnings per share over the past 5 quarters and while recent estimates for the company have been raised by analysts, SCCO has posted better than expected results. Based on comparing earnings yield, the company is about fairly valued when compared to all of the companies in our coverage universe. Share price changes over the past year indicates that SCCO will perform poorly over the near term.

Financial Data

(US$ in Thousands)	3 Mos	12/31/2017	12/31/2016	12/31/2015	12/31/2014	12/31/2013	12/31/2012	12/31/2011
Earnings Per Share	1.15	0.94	1.00	0.93	1.61	1.92	2.28	2.76
Cash Flow Per Share	2.76	2.56	1.19	1.11	1.64	2.20	2.36	2.45
Tang Book Value Per Share	8.01	7.70	7.35	6.60	7.06	6.13	5.26	4.64
Dividends Per Share	0.810	0.590	0.180	0.340	0.460	0.680	3.710	2.460
Dividend Payout %	70.43	62.77	18.00	36.56	28.57	35.42	162.72	89.13
Income Statement								
Total Revenue	1,841,100	6,654,500	5,379,800	5,045,900	5,787,694	5,952,943	6,669,266	6,818,721
EBITDA	933,000	3,268,400	2,178,700	1,892,700	2,634,999	2,942,818	3,164,216	3,907,380
Depn & Amortn	162,000	665,200	639,100	503,600	443,000	393,600	33,500	286,000
Income Before Taxes	704,400	2,302,700	1,256,000	1,189,200	2,068,706	2,372,598	2,973,542	3,448,688
Income Taxes	236,600	1,593,400	501,100	464,900	754,629	769,300	1,080,872	1,104,335
Net Income	470,700	728,500	776,500	736,400	1,332,973	1,618,517	1,934,632	2,336,424
Average Shares	773,000	773,000	773,600	794,700	828,199	842,668	848,346	845,901
Balance Sheet								
Current Assets	3,317,200	3,170,100	2,566,100	2,484,200	2,489,789	3,416,050	4,287,959	3,101,503
Total Assets	14,038,100	13,780,100	13,234,300	12,953,200	11,551,910	11,210,422	10,383,749	8,062,701
Current Liabilities	1,179,800	1,168,300	999,000	920,200	1,150,905	783,584	857,135	992,877
Long-Term Obligations	5,957,800	5,957,100	5,954,200	5,951,500	4,006,000	4,204,900	4,203,900	2,735,700
Total Liabilities	7,691,300	7,672,400	7,402,000	7,330,300	5,747,450	5,676,760	5,618,609	4,047,397
Stockholders' Equity	6,346,800	6,107,700	5,832,300	5,262,900	5,804,460	5,533,662	4,765,140	4,015,304
Shares Outstanding	773,028	773,028	773,016	773,707	806,690	884,596	884,596	840,980
Statistical Record								
Return on Assets %	6.42	5.39	6.00	6.10	11.71	14.99	20.92	28.86
Return on Equity %	14.23	12.20	13.96	13.31	23.51	31.43	43.95	59.11
EBITDA Margin %	50.68	49.12	40.50	37.51	45.53	49.43	47.44	57.30
Net Margin %	25.57	10.95	14.43	14.59	23.03	27.19	29.01	34.26
Asset Turnover	0.50	0.49	0.42	0.42	0.51	0.55	0.72	0.84
Current Ratio	2.81	2.71	2.57	2.70	2.16	4.36	5.00	3.12
Debt to Equity	0.94	0.98	1.02	1.13	0.69	0.76	0.88	0.68
Price Range	55.85-33.01	47.63-32.38	34.98-22.29	33.14-24.40	33.54-26.08	41.96-24.78	38.94-28.16	49.59-23.99
P/E Ratio	48.57-28.70	50.67-34.45	34.98-22.29	35.63-26.24	20.83-16.20	21.85-12.91	17.08-12.35	17.97-8.69
Average Yield %	1.93	1.43	0.66	1.19	1.53	2.17	11.20	7.04

Address: 1440 East Missouri Avenue, Suite 160, Phoenix, AZ 85014 Telephone: 602-264-1375 Fax: 602-264-1397	Web Site: www.southerncoppercorp.com Officers: German Larrea Mota Velasco - Chairman Oscar Gonzalez Rocha - President, Chief Executive Officer	Auditors: Galaz, Yamazaki, Ruiz Urquiza, S.C. Investor Contact: 602-264-1375 Transfer Agents: Computershare, Jersey City, NJ

SOUTHWEST AIRLINES CO

Exchange	Symbol	Price	52Wk Range	Yield	P/E
NYS	LUV	$50.88 (6/29/2018)	66.29-50.32	1.26	8.47

*7 Year Price Score 142.75 *NYSE Composite Index=100 *12 Month Price Score 89.92

Interim Earnings (Per Share)

Qtr.	Mar	Jun	Sep	Dec
2015	0.66	0.90	0.88	0.82
2016	0.79	1.28	0.62	0.85
2017	0.57	1.23	0.84	3.15
2018	0.79	...	...	...

Interim Dividends (Per Share)

Amt	Decl	Ex	Rec	Pay
0.125Q	08/03/2017	08/22/2017	08/24/2017	09/14/2017
0.125Q	11/16/2017	12/06/2017	12/07/2017	01/04/2018
0.125Q	01/31/2018	03/06/2018	03/07/2018	03/28/2018
0.16Q	05/16/2018	06/05/2018	06/06/2018	06/27/2018

Indicated Div: $0.64

Valuation Analysis

		Institutional Holding	
Forecast EPS	$4.27	No of Institutions	
	(06/14/2018)	1271	
Market Cap	$29.5 Billion	Shares	
Book Value	$9.6 Billion	566,974,912	
Price/Book	3.07	% Held	
Price/Sales	1.39	68.84	

Business Summary: Airlines/Air Freight (MIC: 7.4.4 SIC: 4512 NAIC: 481111)

Southwest Airlines operates Southwest Airlines, a passenger airline that provides scheduled air transportation in the U.S. and near-international markets. At Dec 31 2017, Co. operated a total of 706 Boeing 737 aircraft and served 100 destinations in 40 states, the District of Columbia, Puerto Rico, and 10 near-international countries: including Mexico, Jamaica, The Bahamas, Aruba, the Dominican Republic, Costa Rica, Belize, Cuba, Cayman Islands, Turks and Caicos. Co. complements its short-haul routes with long-haul nonstop service between markets such as Los Angeles and Nashville, Las Vegas and Orlando, San Diego and Baltimore, Houston and New York LaGuardia, and Oakland and Baltimore.

Recent Developments: For the quarter ended Mar 31 2018, net income increased 36.6% to US$463.0 million from US$339.0 million in the year-earlier quarter. Revenues were US$4.94 billion, up 1.9% from US$4.85 billion the year before. Operating income was US$616.0 million versus US$606.0 million in the prior-year quarter, an increase of 1.7%. Direct operating expenses rose 6.2% to US$1.61 billion from US$1.51 billion in the comparable period the year before. Indirect operating expenses decreased 0.5% to US$2.72 billion from US$2.74 billion in the equivalent prior-year period.

Prospects: Our evaluation of Southwest Airlines Co as of Jan. 21, 2018 is the result of our systematic analysis on three basic characteristics: earnings strength, relative valuation, and recent stock price movement. The company has produced a positive trend in earnings per share over the past 5 quarters. However, while recent estimates for the company have been mixed, LUV has posted better than expected results. Based on operating earnings yield, the company is undervalued when compared to all of the companies in our coverage universe. Share price changes over the past year indicates that LUV will perform well over the near term.

Financial Data

(US$ in Thousands)	3 Mos	12/31/2017	12/31/2016	12/31/2015	12/31/2014	12/31/2013	12/31/2012	12/31/2011
Earnings Per Share	6.01	5.79	3.55	3.27	1.64	1.05	0.56	0.23
Cash Flow Per Share	5.63	6.54	6.83	4.90	4.22	3.49	2.74	1.79
Tang Book Value Per Share	14.21	15.37	11.45	9.15	8.06	8.85	8.06	7.45
Dividends Per Share	0.500	0.475	0.375	0.285	0.220	0.130	0.035	0.018
Dividend Payout %	8.32	8.20	10.56	8.72	13.41	12.38	6.16	7.83
Income Statement								
Total Revenue	4,944,000	21,171,000	20,425,000	19,820,000	18,605,000	17,699,000	17,088,000	15,658,000
EBITDA	889,000	4,499,000	4,819,000	4,575,000	2,854,000	2,177,000	1,636,000	1,197,000
Depn & Amortn	277,000	1,218,000	1,221,000	1,015,000	938,000	867,000	832,000	702,000
Income Before Taxes	602,000	3,251,000	3,547,000	3,479,000	1,816,000	1,209,000	685,000	323,000
Income Taxes	139,000	(237,000)	1,303,000	1,298,000	680,000	455,000	264,000	145,000
Net Income	463,000	3,488,000	2,244,000	2,181,000	1,136,000	754,000	421,000	178,000
Average Shares	588,000	603,000	633,000	669,000	696,000	718,000	757,000	775,000
Balance Sheet								
Current Assets	4,801,000	4,815,000	4,498,000	4,024,000	4,404,000	4,456,000	4,227,000	4,345,000
Total Assets	25,503,000	25,110,000	23,286,000	21,312,000	20,200,000	19,345,000	18,596,000	18,068,000
Current Liabilities	7,162,000	6,905,000	6,844,000	7,406,000	5,923,000	5,676,000	4,650,000	4,533,000
Long-Term Obligations	3,227,000	3,320,000	2,821,000	2,541,000	2,434,000	2,191,000	2,883,000	3,107,000
Total Liabilities	15,884,000	14,680,000	14,845,000	13,954,000	13,425,000	12,009,000	11,604,000	11,191,000
Stockholders' Equity	9,619,000	10,430,000	8,441,000	7,358,000	6,775,000	7,336,000	6,992,000	6,877,000
Shares Outstanding	579,803	588,550	615,160	647,601	675,594	700,474	730,319	772,560
Statistical Record								
Return on Assets %	14.61	14.41	10.04	10.51	5.75	3.97	2.29	1.06
Return on Equity %	40.40	36.97	28.33	30.86	16.10	10.52	6.05	2.71
EBITDA Margin %	17.98	21.25	23.59	23.08	15.34	12.30	9.57	7.64
Net Margin %	9.36	16.48	10.99	11.00	6.11	4.26	2.46	1.14
Asset Turnover	0.86	0.87	0.91	0.95	0.94	0.93	0.93	0.93
Current Ratio	0.67	0.70	0.66	0.54	0.74	0.79	0.91	0.96
Debt to Equity	0.34	0.32	0.33	0.35	0.36	0.30	0.41	0.45
Price Range	66.29-50.71	66.09-49.46	50.89-34.72	49.58-32.36	42.32-18.84	18.95-10.24	10.56-7.88	13.32-7.35
P/E Ratio	11.03-8.44	11.41-8.54	14.34-9.78	15.16-9.90	25.80-11.49	18.05-9.75	18.86-14.07	57.91-31.96
Average Yield %	0.86	0.84	0.84	0.70	0.70	0.92	0.39	0.17

Address: P.O. Box 36611, Dallas, TX 75235-1611	**Web Site:** www.southwest.com	**Auditors:** Ernst & Young LLP
Telephone: 214-792-4000	**Officers:** Gary C. Kelly - Chairman, Chief Executive Officer, President Ron Ricks - Vice-Chairman, Executive Vice President, Chief Regulatory Officer, Executive Vice President (frmr), Corporate Secretary	**Investor Contact:** 214-792-4415
Fax: 214-792-5015		**Transfer Agents:** Wells Fargo Shareowner Services, Mendota Heights, MN

SOUTHWEST GAS HOLDINGS INC

Exchange	Symbol	Price	52Wk Range	Yield	P/E	Div Acheiver
NYS	SWX	$76.27 (6/29/2018)	86.23-64.14	2.73	18.07	11 Years

*7 Year Price Score 105.53 *NYSE Composite Index=100   *12 Month Price Score 96.23

TRADING VOLUME (thousand shares)

Interim Earnings (Per Share)

Qtr.	Mar	Jun	Sep	Dec
2015	1.53	0.10	(0.10)	1.39
2016	1.58	0.19	0.05	1.36
2017	1.45	0.37	0.21	2.01
2018	1.63	...	...	...

Interim Dividends (Per Share)

Amt	Decl	Ex	Rec	Pay
0.495Q	09/26/2017	11/14/2017	11/15/2017	12/01/2017
0.495Q	11/13/2017	02/14/2018	02/15/2018	03/01/2018
0.52Q	02/23/2018	05/14/2018	05/15/2018	06/01/2018
0.52Q	05/02/2018	08/14/2018	08/15/2018	09/04/2018

Indicated Div: $2.08 (Div. Reinv. Plan)

Valuation Analysis / Institutional Holding

Forecast EPS	$3.68	No of Institutions
	(05/21/2018)	400
Market Cap	$3.7 Billion	Shares
Book Value	$1.9 Billion	48,288,020
Price/Book	1.96	% Held
Price/Sales	1.39	77.03

Business Summary: Gas Utilities (MIC: 3.3.1 SIC: 4923 NAIC: 221210)

Southwest Gas Holdings is a holding company. Through its subsidiaries, Co. operates two business segments: natural gas operations (Southwest) and construction services (Centuri). Southwest focuses on the business of purchasing, distributing, and transporting natural gas. As of Dec 31 2017, Southwest purchased and distributed or transported natural gas to 2.0.15 million residential, commercial, and industrial customers in portions of Arizona, Nevada, and California. Co.'s subsidiary, Centuri Construction Group Inc., provides installation, replacement, repair, and maintenance of energy distribution systems, and developing industrial construction solutions for energy services utilities.

Recent Developments:

For the quarter ended Mar 31 2018, net income increased 13.5% to US$78.3 million from US$69.0 million in the year-earlier quarter. Revenues were US$754.3 million, up 15.2% from US$654.7 million the year before. Operating income was US$129.6 million versus US$124.3 million in the prior-year quarter, an increase of 4.2%. Direct operating expenses rose 31.2% to US$444.7 million from US$338.8 million in the comparable period the year before. Indirect operating expenses decreased 6.0% to US$180.1 million from US$191.6 million in the equivalent prior-year period.

Prospects:

Our evaluation of Southwest Gas Holdings Inc. as of Jan. 21, 2018 is the result of our systematic analysis on three basic characteristics: earnings strength, relative valuation, and recent stock price movement. The company has produced a positive trend in earnings per share over the past 5 quarters. However, while recent estimates for the company have been mixed, SWX has posted better than expected results. Based on operating earnings yield, the company is undervalued when compared to all of the companies in our coverage universe. Share price changes over the past year indicates that SWX will perform very well over the near term.

Financial Data

(US$ in Thousands)	3 Mos	12/31/2017	12/31/2016	12/31/2015	12/31/2014	12/31/2013	12/31/2012	12/31/2011
Earnings Per Share	4.22	4.04	3.18	2.92	3.01	3.11	2.86	2.43
Cash Flow Per Share	8.03	7.71	12.57	11.64	7.45	7.47	8.35	5.50
Tang Book Value Per Share	35.23	34.01	32.09	30.99	28.92	30.51	28.39	26.68
Dividends Per Share	1.980	1.485	1.755	1.580	1.425	1.285	1.150	1.045
Dividend Payout %	46.92	36.76	55.19	54.11	47.34	41.32	40.21	43.00
Income Statement								
Total Revenue	754,330	2,548,792	2,460,490	2,463,625	2,121,707	1,950,782	1,927,778	1,887,188
EBITDA	186,056	518,034	515,013	486,953	483,348	471,337	457,623	416,895
Depn & Amortn	62,478	187,075	214,037	201,233	194,360	185,283	182,612	172,712
Income Before Taxes	102,366	255,682	229,165	216,014	219,521	222,815	207,915	175,066
Income Taxes	24,301	65,088	78,468	79,902	78,373	77,942	75,276	63,303
Net Income	79,091	193,841	152,041	138,317	141,126	145,320	133,331	112,287
Average Shares	48,459	47,991	47,814	47,383	46,944	46,758	46,555	46,291
Balance Sheet								
Current Assets	663,933	657,032	533,307	558,174	606,783	494,672	458,417	461,632
Total Assets	6,327,633	6,237,066	5,581,126	5,358,685	5,214,515	4,565,174	4,488,057	4,276,007
Current Liabilities	602,851	815,881	628,375	535,045	470,117	434,164	535,129	847,568
Long-Term Obligations	1,998,127	1,798,576	1,549,983	1,551,204	1,637,592	1,381,327	1,268,373	930,858
Total Liabilities	4,448,095	4,422,298	3,917,636	3,764,277	3,725,992	3,150,651	3,177,878	3,049,987
Stockholders' Equity	1,879,538	1,814,768	1,663,490	1,594,408	1,488,523	1,414,523	1,310,179	1,226,020
Shares Outstanding	48,336	48,090	47,482	47,377	46,523	46,356	46,147	45,956
Statistical Record								
Return on Assets %	3.43	3.28	2.77	2.62	2.89	3.21	3.03	2.72
Return on Equity %	11.33	11.15	9.31	8.97	9.72	10.67	10.49	9.38
EBITDA Margin %	24.67	20.32	20.93	19.77	22.78	24.16	23.74	22.09
Net Margin %	10.48	7.61	6.18	5.61	6.65	7.45	6.92	5.95
Asset Turnover	0.45	0.43	0.45	0.47	0.43	0.43	0.44	0.46
Current Ratio	1.10	0.81	0.85	1.04	1.29	1.14	0.86	0.54
Debt to Equity	1.06	0.99	0.93	0.97	1.10	0.98	0.97	0.76
Price Range	86.23-64.14	86.27-72.83	78.83-53.86	63.38-50.78	64.04-47.62	55.91-42.24	45.94-39.52	43.00-32.24
P/E Ratio	20.43-15.20	21.35-18.03	24.79-16.94	21.71-17.39	21.28-15.82	17.98-13.58	16.06-13.82	17.70-13.27
Average Yield %	2.54	1.85	2.64	2.77	2.53	2.62	2.69	2.78

Address: 5241 Spring Mountain Road, Post Office Box 98510, Las Vegas, NV 89193-8510
Telephone: 702-876-7237
Fax: 702-873-3820

Web Site: www.swgasholdings.com; www.swgas.com
Officers: Michael J. Melarkey - Chairman John P. Hester - President, Chief Executive Officer, Executive Vice President, Senior Vice President

Auditors: PricewaterhouseCoopers LLP
Investor Contact: 702-876-7237
Transfer Agents: Wells Fargo Shareowner Services, St. Paul, MN

SOUTHWESTERN ENERGY COMPANY

Exchange	Symbol	Price	52Wk Range	Yield	P/E
NYS	SWN	$5.30 (6/29/2018)	6.67-3.50	N/A	3.71

*7 Year Price Score 17.09   *NYSE Composite Index=100   *12 Month Price Score 90.81

Interim Earnings (Per Share)

Qtr.	Mar	Jun	Sep	Dec
2015	0.12	(2.13)	(4.62)	(5.60)
2016	(3.03)	(1.61)	(1.52)	(0.30)
2017	0.57	0.45	0.09	0.53
2018	0.36	...	...	...

Interim Dividends (Per Share)

No Dividends Paid

Valuation Analysis

		Institutional Holding	
Forecast EPS	$0.81	No of Institutions	
	(06/13/2018)	651	
Market Cap	$3.1 Billion	Shares	
Book Value	$2.2 Billion	595,129,472	
Price/Book	1.42	% Held	
Price/Sales	0.95	93.29	

Business Summary: Production & Extraction (MIC: 9.1.1 SIC: 1311 NAIC: 211111)

Southwestern Energy is a holding company and an independent natural gas and oil company. Co.'s primary business is the exploration for and production of natural gas and oil, with its operations principally focused within the U.S. on development of unconventional natural gas reservoirs located in Pennsylvania, West Virginia and Arkansas. Through its affiliated midstream subsidiaries, Co. is engaged in natural gas gathering activities in Arkansas and Louisiana. As of Dec 31 2017, Co. had total estimated proved reserves of 14.78 trillion cubic feet equivalent, comprised of 11.13 trillion cubic feet of natural gas, 65.6 million barrels (MMBbls) of oil and 542.4 MMBbls of natural gas liquids.

Recent Developments: For the quarter ended Mar 31 2018, net income decreased 40.7% to US$208.0 million from US$351.0 million in the year-earlier quarter. Revenues were US$920.0 million, up 8.7% from US$846.0 million the year before. Operating income was US$255.0 million versus US$266.0 million in the prior-year quarter, a decrease of 4.1%. Direct operating expenses rose 11.6% to US$444.0 million from US$398.0 million in the comparable period the year before. Indirect operating expenses increased 21.4% to US$221.0 million from US$182.0 million in the equivalent prior-year period.

Prospects: Our evaluation of Southwestern Energy Company as of Jan. 21, 2018 is the result of our systematic analysis on three basic characteristics: earnings strength, relative valuation, and recent stock price movement. The company has suffered a very negative trend in earnings per share over the past 5 quarters. However, while recent estimates for the company have been mixed, SWN has posted results that fell short of analysts expectations. Based on operating earnings yield, the company is undervalued when compared to all of the companies in our coverage universe. Share price changes over the past year indicates that SWN will perform very poorly over the near term.

Financial Data
(US$ in Thousands)

	3 Mos	12/31/2017	12/31/2016	12/31/2015	12/31/2014	12/31/2013	12/31/2012	12/31/2011
Earnings Per Share	1.43	1.63	(6.32)	(12.25)	2.62	2.00	(2.03)	1.82
Cash Flow Per Share	2.01	2.20	1.14	4.15	6.64	5.45	4.73	5.01
Tang Book Value Per Share	3.74	3.86	1.85	5.85	13.15	10.26	8.65	11.37
Income Statement								
Total Revenue	920,000	3,203,000	2,436,000	3,133,000	4,038,000	3,371,145	2,715,043	2,952,906
EBITDA	249,000	1,601,000	(2,134,000)	(5,360,000)	2,460,000	2,022,524	(299,836)	1,783,031
Depn & Amortn	2,000	513,000	450,000	1,145,000	952,000	790,553	814,710	707,966
Income Before Taxes	208,000	953,000	(2,672,000)	(6,561,000)	1,449,000	1,190,377	(1,150,203)	1,050,990
Income Taxes	...	(93,000)	(29,000)	(2,005,000)	525,000	486,874	(443,139)	413,221
Net Income	208,000	1,046,000	(2,643,000)	(4,556,000)	924,000	703,503	(707,064)	637,769
Average Shares	573,844	500,804	435,337	380,521	352,410	350,465	348,610	349,921
Balance Sheet								
Current Assets	1,488,000	1,509,000	1,872,000	393,000	1,115,000	644,175	808,912	978,278
Total Assets	7,713,000	7,521,000	7,076,000	8,110,000	14,925,000	8,047,726	6,737,527	7,902,897
Current Liabilities	732,000	780,000	1,064,000	707,000	5,428,000	688,011	767,771	884,913
Long-Term Obligations	4,393,000	4,391,000	4,612,000	4,728,000	2,466,000	1,950,096	1,668,273	1,342,100
Total Liabilities	5,520,000	5,542,000	6,159,000	5,828,000	10,263,000	4,425,696	3,701,655	3,933,593
Stockholders' Equity	2,193,000	1,979,000	917,000	2,282,000	4,662,000	3,622,030	3,035,872	3,969,304
Shares Outstanding	586,833	512,103	495,217	390,091	354,477	352,928	351,035	348,959
Statistical Record								
Return on Assets %	12.11	14.33	N.M.	N.M.	8.04	9.52	N.M.	9.16
Return on Equity %	52.03	72.24	N.M.	N.M.	22.31	21.13	N.M.	18.39
EBITDA Margin %	27.07	49.98	N.M.	N.M.	60.92	60.00	N.M.	60.38
Net Margin %	22.61	32.66	N.M.	N.M.	22.88	20.87	N.M.	21.60
Asset Turnover	0.44	0.44	0.32	0.27	0.35	0.46	0.37	0.42
Current Ratio	2.03	1.93	1.76	0.56	0.21	0.94	1.05	1.11
Debt to Equity	2.00	2.22	5.03	2.07	0.53	0.54	0.55	0.34
Price Range	8.59-3.50	10.32-5.05	15.44-5.62	29.25-5.15	48.93-27.24	40.18-32.09	36.60-25.82	49.00-31.94
P/E Ratio	6.01-2.45	6.33-3.10	...	...	18.68-10.40	20.09-16.05	...	26.92-17.55

Address: 10000 Energy Drive, Spring, TX 77389
Telephone: 832-796-1000

Web Site: www.swn.com
Officers: William J. Way - President, Executive Vice President, Chief Operating Officer Clayton A. Carrell - Executive Vice President, Chief Operating Officer

Auditors: PricewaterhouseCoopers LLP
Investor Contact: 281-.61-8.4847
Transfer Agents: Computershare Trust Company, N.A, Providence, RI

SPECTRUM BRANDS HOLDINGS INC (NEW)

Exchange	Symbol	Price	52Wk Range	Yield	P/E
NYS	SPB	$80.80 (6//29/2018)	117.84-68.64	N/A	5.89

*7 Year Price Score N/A   *NYSE Composite Index=100   *12 Month Price Score N/A

Interim Earnings (Per Share)

Qtr.	Dec	Mar	Jun	Sep
2014-15	(3.47)	(7.19)	(2.36)	(4.46)
2015-16	(1.05)	(1.12)	(4.09)	(0.25)
2016-17	6.57	(2.54)	0.06	(0.81)
2017-18	15.57	(1.12)	...	...

Interim Dividends (Per Share)

No Dividends Paid

Valuation Analysis		Institutional Holding	
Forecast EPS	N/A	No of Institutions	
		247	
Market Cap	N/A	Shares	
Book Value	$691.6 Million	219,335,360	
Price/Book	N/A	% Held	
Price/Sales	N/A	N/A	

TRADING VOLUME (thousand shares)

Business Summary: Household & Personal Products (MIC: 1.7.1 SIC: 3691 NAIC: 335911)

HRG Group is a holding company. Co.'s principal operating subsidiaries include the following: Spectrum Brands Holdings, Inc., its subsidiary that provides global branded consumer products; Fidelity & Guaranty Life, its subsidiary that provides life insurance and annuity products; and Front Street Re (Delaware) Ltd., its subsidiary engaged in the business of providing long-term reinsurance, including reinsurance to the specialty insurance sector of fixed, deferred and payout annuities.

Recent Developments: For the quarter ended Mar 31 2018, loss from continuing operations was US$37.3 million compared with a loss of US$7.8 million in the year-earlier quarter. Net loss amounted to US$36.6 million versus a net loss of US$51.4 million in the year-earlier quarter. Revenues were US$766.1 million, up 1.1% from US$757.4 million the year before. Operating income was US$28.9 million versus US$95.3 million in the prior-year quarter, a decrease of 69.7%. Direct operating expenses rose 11.0% to US$494.8 million from US$445.6 million in the comparable period the year before. Indirect operating expenses increased 12.0% to US$242.4 million from US$216.5 million in the equivalent prior-year period.

Prospects: Our evaluation of HRG Group Inc. as of Jan. 21, 2018 is the result of our systematic analysis on three basic characteristics: earnings strength, relative valuation, and recent stock price movement. The company has enjoyed a very positive trend in earnings per share over the past 5 quarters. Because the company lacks sufficient analyst estimate data, we place greater weight on the historical EPS trend as the measure of earnings strength. Based on operating earnings yield, the company is overvalued when compared to all of the companies in our coverage universe. Share price changes over the past year indicates that HRG will perform very poorly over the near term.

Financial Data

(US$ in Thousands)	6 Mos	3 Mos	09/30/2017	09/30/2016	09/30/2015	09/30/2014	09/30/2013	09/30/2012
Earnings Per Share	13.71	12.28	3.29	(6.14)	(17.43)	(3.16)	(4.15)	0.93
Cash Flow Per Share	16.76	21.60	26.05	28.47	8.88	23.14	23.16	27.46
Income Statement								
Total Revenue	1,412,600	646,500	5,008,500	5,215,400	5,815,900	5,963,000	5,543,400	4,480,716
EBITDA	105,700	50,200	606,500	812,700	210,800	740,200	806,600	384,068
Depn & Amortn	49,000	22,600	95,200	183,700	221,900	205,100	176,400	107,650
Income Before Taxes	(86,400)	(47,900)	151,200	231,900	(440,800)	213,200	118,300	25,386
Income Taxes	(127,200)	(126,000)	48,300	41,500	71,600	111,500	187,300	(85,282)
Net Income	470,300	507,400	106,000	(198,800)	(556,800)	(10,300)	(45,800)	89,556
Average Shares	32,516	32,626	32,249	32,508	31,951	26,275	22,552	22,546
Balance Sheet								
Current Assets	3,805,300	4,636,900	1,615,400	3,444,600	2,802,700	2,724,400	3,381,000	2,797,438
Total Assets	8,240,300	9,080,000	35,849,700	35,792,800	32,334,100	30,100,200	27,908,800	25,200,491
Current Liabilities	1,222,500	2,120,600	1,115,600	989,800	1,137,700	1,033,000	1,012,700	679,265
Long-Term Obligations	5,248,400	4,888,400	5,774,100	5,430,900	6,382,700	5,157,800	4,896,100	2,150,625
Total Liabilities	7,548,700	8,259,600	35,091,700	35,154,700	31,747,400	28,658,600	26,854,700	23,703,669
Stockholders' Equity	691,600	820,400	758,000	638,100	586,700	1,441,600	1,054,100	1,496,822
Shares Outstanding	32,751	32,548	32,351	32,378	32,474	32,621	22,959	22,605
Statistical Record								
Return on Assets %	1.99	1.79	0.30	N.M.	N.M.	N.M.	N.M.	0.37
Return on Equity %	68.83	58.63	15.19	N.M.	N.M.	N.M.	N.M.	6.67
EBITDA Margin %	7.48	7.76	12.11	15.58	3.62	12.41	14.55	8.57
Net Margin %	33.29	78.48	2.12	N.M.	N.M.	N.M.	N.M.	2.00
Asset Turnover	0.18	0.20	0.14	0.15	0.19	0.21	0.21	0.18
Current Ratio	3.11	2.19	1.45	3.48	2.46	2.64	3.34	4.12
Debt to Equity	7.59	5.96	7.62	8.51	10.88	3.58	4.64	1.44

Address: 450 Park Avenue, 29th Floor, New York, NY 10022 **Telephone:** 212-906-8555	**Web Site:** www.harbingergroupinc.com **Officers:** David M. Maura - Executive Chairman, Chief Executive Officer Douglas L. Martin - Executive Vice President, Chief Financial Officer	**Auditors:** KPMG LLP **Investor Contact:** 212-905-8560 **Transfer Agents:** American Stock Transfer & Trust, New York, NY

SPIRIT AEROSYSTEMS HOLDINGS INC

Exchange	Symbol	Price	52Wk Range	Yield	P/E
NYS	SPR	$85.91 (6/29/2018)	102.93-57.94	0.56	29.22

*7 Year Price Score 153.88 *NYSE Composite Index=100 *12 Month Price Score 103.30

Interim Earnings (Per Share)

Qtr.	Mar	Jun	Sep	Dec
2015	1.30	1.11	2.24	1.02
2016	1.29	0.35	1.16	0.90
2017	1.17	(0.48)	1.26	1.06
2018	1.10	...	...	...

Interim Dividends (Per Share)

Amt	Decl	Ex	Rec	Pay
0.10Q	07/25/2017	09/15/2017	09/18/2017	10/10/2017
0.10Q	10/25/2017	12/15/2017	12/18/2017	01/08/2018
0.10Q	01/24/2018	03/16/2018	03/19/2018	04/09/2018
0.12Q	04/25/2018	06/15/2018	06/18/2018	07/09/2018

Indicated Div: $0.48

Valuation Analysis | **Institutional Holding**

Forecast EPS	$6.30	No of Institutions
	(06/14/2018)	542
Market Cap	$9.8 Billion	Shares
Book Value	$1.6 Billion	137,437,632
Price/Book	6.22	% Held
Price/Sales	1.39	90.53

Business Summary: Aerospace (MIC: 7.1.1 SIC: 3728 NAIC: 336413)

Spirit AeroSystems Holdings provides manufacturing and design expertise in a range of products and services for aircraft original equipment manufacturers. Co. has three segments: Fuselage Systems, which includes forward, mid and rear fuselage sections and systems; Propulsion Systems, which includes nacelles, struts/pylons and engine structural components; and Wing Systems, which includes wings, wing components, flight control surfaces and other miscellaneous structural parts. In addition to providing aerostructures for commercial aircraft, Co. designs, engineers and manufactures structural components for military aircraft such as Rotorcraft.

Recent Developments: For the quarter ended Mar 29 2018, net income decreased 11.5% to US$125.4 million from US$141.7 million in the year-earlier quarter. Revenues were US$1.74 billion, up 2.5% from US$1.69 billion the year before. Operating income was US$159.5 million versus US$204.4 million in the prior-year quarter, a decrease of 22.0%. Direct operating expenses rose 6.3% to US$1.51 billion from US$1.42 billion in the comparable period the year before. Indirect operating expenses decreased 4.5% to US$65.6 million from US$68.7 million in the equivalent prior-year period.

Prospects: Our evaluation of Spirit AeroSystems Holdings Inc. as of Jan. 21, 2018 is the result of our systematic analysis on three basic characteristics: earnings strength, relative valuation, and recent stock price movement. The company has produced a positive trend in earnings per share over the past 5 quarters. However, while recent estimates for the company have been mixed, SPR has posted results that were in line with analysts expectations. Based on operating earnings yield, the company is undervalued when compared to all of the companies in our coverage universe. Share price changes over the past year indicates that SPR will perform in line with the market over the near term.

Financial Data

(US$ in Thousands)	3 Mos	12/31/2017	12/31/2016	12/31/2015	12/31/2014	12/31/2013	12/31/2012	12/31/2011
Earnings Per Share	2.94	3.01	3.70	5.66	2.53	(4.40)	0.24	1.35
Cash Flow Per Share	5.57	4.91	5.67	9.32	2.58	1.84	3.86	(0.34)
Tang Book Value Per Share	13.73	15.70	15.82	15.59	11.45	10.17	13.80	13.63
Dividends Per Share	0.400	0.400	0.100	...	...	...	...	...
Dividend Payout %	13.61	13.29	2.70	...	...	...	...	...
Income Statement								
Total Revenue	1,736,100	6,983,000	6,792,900	6,643,900	6,799,200	5,961,000	5,397,700	4,863,800
EBITDA	162,500	589,100	732,800	875,600	368,200	(341,400)	112,700	486,700
Depn & Amortn	100	19,200	18,600	16,900	18,300	19,600	18,600	129,200
Income Before Taxes	152,300	534,600	660,500	808,100	262,400	(430,800)	11,400	280,300
Income Taxes	27,500	180,000	192,100	20,600	(95,900)	191,100	(24,100)	86,900
Net Income	125,400	354,900	469,700	788,700	358,800	(621,400)	34,800	192,400
Average Shares	114,100	117,900	127,000	139,400	141,600	141,300	142,700	142,300
Balance Sheet								
Current Assets	2,603,700	2,651,100	2,910,400	3,299,100	3,052,100	2,944,200	3,355,400	3,155,800
Total Assets	5,370,300	5,267,800	5,405,200	5,777,500	5,162,700	5,107,200	5,415,300	5,042,400
Current Liabilities	1,701,900	1,621,000	1,544,200	1,459,000	1,258,800	1,335,600	1,067,000	913,500
Long-Term Obligations	1,112,600	1,119,900	1,060,000	1,097,600	1,144,100	1,150,500	1,165,900	1,152,000
Total Liabilities	3,797,800	3,466,800	3,476,900	3,658,000	3,541,200	3,626,700	3,418,900	3,078,200
Stockholders' Equity	1,572,500	1,801,000	1,928,300	2,119,500	1,621,500	1,480,500	1,996,400	1,964,200
Shares Outstanding	113,803	114,447	121,642	135,617	141,089	144,798	143,697	142,865
Statistical Record								
Return on Assets %	6.25	6.65	8.38	14.42	6.99	N.M.	0.66	3.79
Return on Equity %	19.04	19.03	23.14	42.17	23.13	N.M.	1.75	10.19
EBITDA Margin %	9.36	8.44	10.79	13.18	5.42	N.M.	2.09	10.01
Net Margin %	7.22	5.08	6.91	11.87	5.28	N.M.	0.64	3.96
Asset Turnover	1.30	1.31	1.21	1.21	1.32	1.13	1.03	0.96
Current Ratio	1.53	1.64	1.88	2.26	2.42	2.20	3.14	3.45
Debt to Equity	0.71	0.62	0.55	0.52	0.71	0.78	0.58	0.59
Price Range	102.93-52.96	87.25-52.96	61.26-40.50	57.16-41.89	45.32-26.51	34.18-15.94	25.85-14.04	26.16-14.40
P/E Ratio	35.01-18.01	28.99-17.59	16.56-10.95	10.10-7.40	17.91-10.48	...	107.71-58.50	19.38-10.67
Average Yield %	0.54	0.60	0.21	...	...	...	...	...

Address: 3801 South Oliver, Wichita, KS 67210	**Web Site:** www.spiritaero.com	**Auditors:** Ernst & Young LLP
Telephone: 316-526-9000	**Officers:** Robert D. Johnson - Chairman Thomas C. Gentile - President, Chief Executive Officer, Executive Vice President, Chief Operating Officer	**Investor Contact:** 316-523-7040 **Transfer Agents:** Computershare, Pittsburgh, PA

SPIRE INC

Exchange	Symbol	Price	52Wk Range	Yield	P/E	Div Acheiver
NYS	SR	$70.65 (6/29/2018)	82.25-61.30	3.18	15.53	14 Years

*7 Year Price Score 108.51 *NYSE Composite Index=100 ***12 Month Price Score 94.78**

Interim Earnings (Per Share)

Qtr.	Dec	Mar	Jun	Sep
2014-15	1.09	2.18	0.32	(0.43)
2015-16	1.08	2.31	0.24	(0.36)
2016-17	0.99	2.36	0.45	(0.32)
2017-18	2.39	2.03	...	...

Interim Dividends (Per Share)

Amt	Decl	Ex	Rec	Pay
0.525Q	07/27/2017	09/08/2017	09/11/2017	10/03/2017
0.563Q	11/15/2017	12/08/2017	12/11/2017	01/03/2018
0.563Q	02/01/2018	03/09/2018	03/12/2018	04/03/2018
0.563Q	05/02/2018	06/08/2018	06/11/2018	07/03/2018

Indicated Div: $2.25

Valuation Analysis / **Institutional Holding**

Forecast EPS	$3.69 (06/14/2018)	No of Institutions	348
Market Cap	$3.4 Billion	Shares	47,176,496
Book Value	$2.2 Billion	% Held	64.47
Price/Book	1.59		
Price/Sales	1.75		

Business Summary: Gas Utilities (MIC: 3.3.1 SIC: 4924 NAIC: 221210).

Spire is a public utility holding company. Co. operates two business segments: Gas Utility and Gas Marketing. Co.'s Gas Utility segment includes the operations of Co.'s subsidiaries: Spire Missouri Inc., which is engaged in the purchase, retail distribution and sale of natural gas; Spire Alabama Inc., which is engaged in the purchase, retail distribution and sale of natural gas; and Spire Gulf Inc. and Spire Mississippi Inc., which is engaged the purchase, retail distribution and sale of natural gas; gas marketing. Co.'s Gas Marketing segment includes Co.'s subsidiary, Spire Marketing Inc., which is engaged in the marketing of natural gas and related activities on a non-regulated basis.

Recent Developments: For the quarter ended Mar 31 2018, net income decreased 9.1% to US$98.2 million from US$108.0 million in the year-earlier quarter. Revenues were US$813.4 million, up 22.6% from US$663.4 million the year before. Operating income was US$141.8 million versus US$180.4 million in the prior-year quarter, a decrease of 21.4%. Direct operating expenses rose 39.0% to US$671.6 million from US$483.0 million in the comparable period the year before.

Prospects: Our evaluation of Spire Inc. as of Jan. 21, 2018 is the result of our systematic analysis on three basic characteristics: earnings strength, relative valuation, and recent stock price movement. The company has managed to produce a neutral trend in earnings per share over the past 5 quarters and while recent estimates for the company have remained steady, SR has posted better than expected results. Based on operating earnings yield, the company is undervalued when compared to all of the companies in our coverage universe. Share price changes over the past year indicates that SR will perform very well over the near term.

Financial Data
(US$ in Thousands)

	6 Mos	3 Mos	09/30/2017	09/30/2016	09/30/2015	09/30/2014	09/30/2013	09/30/2012
Earnings Per Share	4.55	4.88	3.43	3.24	3.16	2.35	2.02	2.79
Cash Flow Per Share	7.71	6.14	6.15	7.42	7.46	3.42	6.33	5.74
Tang Book Value Per Share	20.29	18.79	16.98	13.22	14.48	13.21	24.44	26.69
Dividends Per Share	2.175	2.138	2.100	1.960	1.840	1.760	1.700	1.660
Dividend Payout %	47.80	43.80	61.22	60.49	58.23	74.89	84.16	59.50
Income Statement								
Total Revenue	1,375,200	561,800	1,740,700	1,537,300	1,976,400	1,627,200	1,017,019	1,125,475
EBITDA	331,700	147,700	482,400	428,200	404,300	246,400	147,133	153,904
Depn & Amortn	81,900	40,400	154,100	137,500	130,800	83,300	49,283	41,339
Income Before Taxes	200,000	82,900	239,200	213,500	198,900	116,900	70,336	88,929
Income Taxes	(14,200)	(33,100)	77,600	69,300	62,000	32,300	17,578	26,289
Net Income	214,200	116,000	161,600	144,200	136,900	84,600	52,758	62,640
Average Shares	48,400	48,400	47,000	44,300	43,300	35,900	25,952	22,340
Balance Sheet								
Current Assets	718,300	852,500	725,500	569,600	530,100	604,900	475,880	343,016
Total Assets	6,586,800	6,701,100	6,546,700	6,077,400	5,290,200	5,074,000	3,125,386	1,880,262
Current Liabilities	928,000	1,211,300	1,097,900	1,161,300	853,800	782,800	353,178	252,124
Long-Term Obligations	2,073,900	2,030,400	1,995,100	1,833,300	1,771,500	1,851,000	912,712	339,416
Total Liabilities	4,433,300	4,621,900	4,555,400	4,309,200	3,716,600	3,565,600	2,079,104	1,278,651
Stockholders' Equity	2,153,500	2,079,200	1,991,300	1,768,200	1,573,600	1,508,400	1,046,282	601,611
Shares Outstanding	48,400	48,300	48,263	45,650	43,335	43,183	32,696	22,539
Statistical Record								
Return on Assets %	3.47	3.57	2.56	2.53	2.64	2.06	2.11	3.41
Return on Equity %	11.03	11.99	8.60	8.61	8.88	6.62	6.40	10.63
EBITDA Margin %	24.12	26.29	27.71	27.85	20.46	15.14	14.47	13.67
Net Margin %	15.58	20.65	9.28	9.38	6.93	5.20	5.19	5.57
Asset Turnover	0.30	0.28	0.28	0.27	0.38	0.40	0.41	0.61
Current Ratio	0.77	0.70	0.66	0.49	0.62	0.77	1.35	1.36
Debt to Equity	0.96	0.98	1.00	1.04	1.13	1.23	0.87	0.56
Price Range	82.25-61.30	82.25-62.60	77.40-59.97	70.84-54.53	56.02-46.15	49.56-44.24	48.16-37.70	43.27-37.37
P/E Ratio	18.08-13.47	16.85-12.83	22.57-17.48	21.86-16.83	17.73-14.60	21.09-18.83	23.84-18.66	15.51-13.39
Average Yield %	3.00	2.98	3.09	3.09	3.54	3.78	3.96	4.12

Address: 700 Market Street, St. Louis, MO 63101
Telephone: 314-342-0500

Web Site: www.spireenergy.com
Officers: Edward L. Glotzbach - Chairman Suzanne Sitherwood - President, Chief Executive Officer

Auditors: DELOITTE & TOUCHE LLP
Investor Contact: 314-342-0878
Transfer Agents: Computershare Trust Company, N.A., Providence, RI

SPIRIT AIRLINES INC

Exchange	Symbol	Price	52Wk Range	Yield	P/E
NYS	SAVE	$36.35 (6/29/2018)	53.46-32.09	N/A	7.36

*7 Year Price Score N/A   *NYSE Composite Index=100   *12 Month Price Score N/A

Interim Earnings (Per Share)

Qtr.	Mar	Jun	Sep	Dec
2015	0.94	1.05	1.35	1.04
2016	0.86	1.03	1.17	0.71
2017	0.46	1.12	0.87	3.61
2018	(0.66)	...	...	...

Interim Dividends (Per Share)

No Dividends Paid

Valuation Analysis　　**Institutional Holding**

Forecast EPS	$3.25	No of Institutions	
	(06/14/2018)	327	
Market Cap	$3.1 Billion	Shares	
Book Value	$1.7 Billion	79,115,880	
Price/Book	1.79	% Held	
Price/Sales	1.11	93.66	

Business Summary: Airlines/Air Freight (MIC: 7.4.4 SIC: 4512 NAIC: 481111)

Spirit Airlines is an ultra low-cost, low-fare airline that offers affordable travel to price-conscious customers. As of Dec 31, 2017, Co.'s all-Airbus Fit Fleet operated more than 450 daily flights to 60 destinations in the United States, Caribbean and Latin America. Co.'s ultra low-cost carrier business model allows Co. to compete principally by offering customers its Bare Fares, which are unbundled base fares that remove components traditionally included in the price of an airline ticket. Co. then gives customers Frill Control, which provides customers the freedom to save by paying only for the options they choose such as bags, advance seat assignments and refreshments.

Recent Developments: For the quarter ended Mar 31 2018, net loss amounted to US$44.9 million versus net income of US$31.3 million in the year-earlier quarter. Revenues were US$704.1 million, up 19.4% from US$590.0 million the year before. Operating loss was US$38.8 million versus an income of US$58.3 million in the prior-year quarter. Direct operating expenses rose 26.1% to US$364.8 million from US$289.4 million in the comparable period the year before. Indirect operating expenses increased 56.1% to US$378.1 million from US$242.2 million in the equivalent prior-year period.

Prospects: Our evaluation of Spirit Airlines Inc as of Jan. 21, 2018 is the result of our systematic analysis on three basic characteristics: earnings strength, relative valuation, and recent stock price movement. The company has produced a positive trend in earnings per share over the past 5 quarters and while recent estimates for the company have been raised by analysts, SAVE has posted better than expected results. Based on operating earnings yield, the company is undervalued when compared to all of the companies in our coverage universe. Share price changes over the past year indicates that SAVE will perform very poorly over the near term.

Financial Data

(US$ in Thousands)	3 Mos	12/31/2017	12/31/2016	12/31/2015	12/31/2014	12/31/2013	12/31/2012	12/31/2011
Earnings Per Share	4.94	6.06	3.76	4.38	3.08	2.42	1.49	1.43
Cash Flow Per Share	6.19	6.14	6.72	6.55	3.58	2.69	1.57	3.22
Tang Book Value Per Share	25.20	26.06	20.12	17.13	13.78	10.60	8.04	6.44
Income Statement								
Total Revenue	704,138	2,647,666	2,321,956	2,141,463	1,931,580	1,654,385	1,318,388	1,071,186
EBITDA	(46,507)	536,521	550,001	584,180	399,444	313,398	188,085	150,860
Depn & Amortn	1,624	148,096	106,868	75,073	46,786	31,389	14,426	6,713
Income Before Taxes	(59,662)	353,652	419,460	502,403	352,994	282,410	174,584	122,831
Income Taxes	(14,740)	(66,954)	154,581	185,183	127,530	105,492	66,124	46,383
Net Income	(44,922)	420,606	264,879	317,220	225,464	176,918	108,460	76,448
Average Shares	68,222	69,377	70,508	72,426	73,294	72,999	72,590	53,515
Balance Sheet								
Current Assets	1,298,841	1,280,260	975,845	1,026,340	731,141	649,075	547,357	442,708
Total Assets	4,654,431	4,143,950	3,151,927	2,530,545	1,602,981	1,180,765	919,884	745,813
Current Liabilities	1,047,326	647,026	531,950	466,240	365,624	335,993	276,894	227,064
Long-Term Obligations	1,570,926	1,387,500	897,400	596,700	135,800	...	...	...
Total Liabilities	2,934,626	2,366,871	1,757,361	1,305,242	599,889	411,648	337,349	279,107
Stockholders' Equity	1,719,805	1,777,081	1,394,607	1,225,310	1,003,075	769,117	582,535	466,706
Shares Outstanding	68,250	68,196	69,326	71,541	72,775	72,566	72,470	72,522
Statistical Record								
Return on Assets %	8.49	11.53	9.30	15.35	16.20	16.84	12.99	12.52
Return on Equity %	21.84	26.52	20.17	28.47	25.44	26.18	20.62	42.28
EBITDA Margin %	N.M.	20.26	23.69	27.28	20.68	18.94	14.27	14.08
Net Margin %	N.M.	15.89	11.41	14.81	11.67	10.69	8.23	7.14
Asset Turnover	0.68	0.73	0.82	1.04	1.39	1.58	1.58	1.75
Current Ratio	1.24	1.98	1.84	2.20	2.00	1.93	1.98	1.95
Debt to Equity	0.91	0.78	0.64	0.49	0.14	...	...	...
Price Range	59.74-32.09	59.74-32.09	59.50-36.53	82.03-33.57	84.47-44.76	46.45-17.50	24.11-14.19	17.03-10.44
P/E Ratio	12.09-6.50	9.86-5.30	15.82-9.72	18.73-7.66	27.43-14.53	19.19-7.23	16.18-9.52	11.91-7.30

Address: 2800 Executive Way, Miramar, FL 33025	**Web Site:** www.spirit.com	**Auditors:** Ernst & Young LLP
Telephone: 954-447-7920	**Officers:** H. McIntyre (Mac) Gardner - Chairman Robert L. Fornaro - President, Chief Executive Officer	**Investor Contact:** 954-447-7920 **Transfer Agents:** Wells Fargo Shareholder Services

SPIRIT REALTY CAPITAL INC

Exchange	Symbol	Price	52Wk Range	Yield	P/E
NYS	SRC	$8.03 (6/29/2018)	8.32-6.56	8.97	42.26

*7 Year Price Score N/A   *NYSE Composite Index=100   *12 Month Price Score 103.55

Interim Earnings (Per Share)

Qtr.	Mar	Jun	Sep	Dec
2015	0.06	0.14	0.04	0.02
2016	0.06	0.10	0.06	0.00
2017	0.03	0.05	0.01	0.07
2018	0.06	...	...	...

Interim Dividends (Per Share)

Amt	Decl	Ex	Rec	Pay
0.18Q	12/08/2017	12/28/2017	12/29/2017	01/12/2018
0.18Q	03/05/2018	03/28/2018	03/30/2018	04/13/2018
0.00Q	05/01/2018	06/01/2018	05/18/2018	05/31/2018
0.18Q	06/05/2018	06/28/2018	06/29/2018	07/13/2018

Indicated Div: $0.72

Valuation Analysis

		Institutional Holding	
Forecast EPS	$0.26	No of Institutions	381
	(06/14/2018)		
Market Cap	$3.5 Billion	Shares	483,122,848
Book Value	$3.2 Billion	% Held	76.59
Price/Book	1.11		
Price/Sales	N/A		

Business Summary: REITs (MIC: 5.3.1 SIC: 6512 NAIC: 531120)

Spirit Realty Capital is a self-administered and self-managed real estate investment trust with in-house capabilities, including acquisition, portfolio management, asset management, credit research, real estate research, legal, finance and accounting and capital markets. Co. primarily invests in single-tenant, operationally essential real estate throughout the U.S., with business operations within mainly retail, but also office and industrial property types. Co.'s operations are carried out through an operating partnership, Spirit Realty, L.P. As of Dec 31 2017, Co.'s real estate portfolio consisted of 2,392 owned properties located in 49 states as well as in the U.S. Virgin Islands.

Recent Developments: For the quarter ended Mar 31 2018, net income increased 139.4% to US$30.7 million from US$12.8 million in the year-earlier quarter. Revenues were US$165.3 million, down 0.1% from US$165.4 million the year before. Revenues from property income fell 0.8% to US$162.5 million from US$163.8 million in the corresponding quarter a year earlier.

Prospects: Our evaluation of Spirit Realty Capital Inc as of Jan. 21, 2018 is the result of our systematic analysis on three basic characteristics: earnings strength, relative valuation, and recent stock price movement. The company has generated a negative trend in earnings per share over the past 5 quarters. However, while recent estimates for the company have been mixed, SRC has posted results that fell short of analysts expectations. Based on operating earnings yield, the company is about fairly valued when compared to all of the companies in our coverage universe. Share price changes over the past year indicates that SRC will perform poorly over the near term.

Financial Data

(US$ in Thousands)	3 Mos	12/31/2017	12/31/2016	12/31/2015	12/31/2014	12/31/2013	12/31/2012	12/31/2011
Earnings Per Share	0.19	0.16	0.21	0.26	(0.09)	...	0.12	0.26
Cash Flow Per Share	...	0.83	0.77	0.86	0.57	0.54	0.56	0.55
Tang Book Value Per Share	5.39	5.55	6.12	6.05	5.92	5.96	5.16	5.53
Dividends Per Share	0.720	0.720	0.705	0.685	0.669	0.302	...	...
Dividend Payout %	378.95	450.00	335.71	263.46	...	...	...	...
Income Statement								
Total Revenue	165,278	668,955	685,974	667,335	602,871	419,467	282,852	279,345
EBITDA	90,181	482,050	520,195	519,458	422,864	332,359	214,751	243,004
Depn & Amortn	7,541	279,487	277,563	270,892	253,016	185,151	82,588	81,758
Income Before Taxes	31,575	12,436	46,046	25,665	(50,222)	(32,059)	24,200	53,060
Income Taxes	252	394	965	601	673	1,113	...	...
Net Income	30,718	77,148	97,446	114,730	(33,799)	1,677	25,397	53,809
Average Shares	445,102	467,942	469,246	432,545	386,809	255,020	210,077	209,693
Balance Sheet								
Current Assets	10,989	8,798	10,059	21,790	176,181	66,588	93,772	122,419
Total Assets	7,202,820	7,263,511	7,677,971	7,918,996	8,017,001	7,231,045	3,289,536	3,430,322
Current Liabilities	141,898	148,919	148,915	142,475	123,298	114,679	30,172	28,326
Long-Term Obligations	3,741,020	3,639,680	3,664,628	4,092,787	4,369,634	3,778,218	1,757,322	1,767,591
Total Liabilities	4,034,097	3,943,902	3,995,863	4,429,165	4,698,900	4,113,011	1,922,109	1,944,127
Stockholders' Equity	3,168,723	3,319,609	3,682,108	3,489,831	3,318,101	3,118,034	1,367,427	1,486,195
Shares Outstanding	436,561	448,868	483,624	441,819	411,350	370,363	208,597	210,151
Statistical Record								
Return on Assets %	...	1.03	1.25	1.44	N.M.	0.03	0.75	...
Return on Equity %	...	2.20	2.71	3.37	N.M.	0.07	1.78	...
EBITDA Margin %	54.56	72.06	75.83	77.84	70.14	79.23	75.92	86.99
Net Margin %	18.59	11.53	14.21	17.19	N.M.	0.40	8.98	19.26
Asset Turnover	...	0.09	0.09	0.08	0.08	0.08	0.08	...
Current Ratio	0.08	0.06	0.07	0.15	1.43	0.58	3.11	4.32
Debt to Equity	1.18	1.10	1.00	1.17	1.32	1.21	1.29	1.19
Price Range	9.41-6.01	10.10-6.01	12.44-8.15	11.64-8.10	10.77-8.81	20.39-7.56	15.93-13.44	...
P/E Ratio	49.52-31.65	63.12-37.58	59.23-38.83	44.77-31.16	...	...	N.M. 132.77-112.01	...
Average Yield %	9.72	9.01	6.74	7.08	6.65	2.24	...	...

Address: 2727 North Harwood Street, Suite 300, Dallas, TX 75201
Telephone: 972-476-1900

Web Site: www.spiritrealty.com
Officers: Richard I. Gilchrist - Chairman Jackson Hsieh - President, Chief Operating Officer, Chief Executive Officer

Auditors: Ernst & Young LLP
Investor Contact: 480-606-0820

SPRINT CORP

Exchange	Symbol	Price	52Wk Range	Yield	P/E
NYS	S	$5.44 (6/29/2018)	8.87-4.85	N/A	2.94

*7 Year Price Score N/A   ***NYSE Composite Index=100**   ***12 Month Price Score 82.48**

Interim Earnings (Per Share)

Qtr.	Jun	Sep	Dec	Mar
2014-15	0.01	(0.19)	(0.60)	(0.06)
2015-16	(0.01)	(0.15)	(0.21)	(0.14)
2016-17	(0.08)	(0.04)	(0.12)	(0.07)
2017-18	0.05	(0.01)	1.76	0.06

Interim Dividends (Per Share)

No Dividends Paid

Valuation Analysis   Institutional Holding

Forecast EPS	$-0.03	No of Institutions
	(06/14/2018)	675
Market Cap	$21.8 Billion	Shares
Book Value	$26.4 Billion	783,290,048
Price/Book	0.83	% Held
Price/Sales	0.67	N/A

TRADING VOLUME (thousand shares)

Business Summary: Services (MIC: 6.1.2 SIC: 4813 NAIC: 517110)

Sprint is a holding company. Through its subsidiaries, Co. is a communications company providing wireless and wireline communications products and services to consumers, businesses, government subscribers, and resellers. Co. has two segments: Wireless, which provides wireless services on a postpaid and prepaid payment basis to retail subscribers and also on a wholesale basis, including the sale of wireless services that utilize Co.'s network but are sold under the wholesaler's brand; and Wireline, which provides wireline voice and data communication services to other communications companies and business subscribers, as well as voice, data and internet protocol communication services.

Recent Developments: For the year ended Mar 31 2018, net income amounted to US$7.38 billion versus a net loss of US$1.21 billion in the prior year. Revenues were US$32.41 billion, down 2.8% from US$33.35 billion the year before. Operating income was US$2.73 billion versus US$1.76 billion in the prior year, an increase of 54.6%. Direct operating expenses declined 13.1% to US$13.40 billion from US$15.42 billion in the comparable period the year before. Indirect operating expenses increased 0.7% to US$16.28 billion from US$16.16 billion in the equivalent prior-year period.

Prospects: Our evaluation of Sprint Corp as of Jan. 21, 2018 is the result of our systematic analysis on three basic characteristics: earnings strength, relative valuation, and recent stock price movement. The company has enjoyed a very positive trend in earnings per share over the past 5 quarters. Because the company lacks sufficient analyst estimate data, we place greater weight on the historical EPS trend as the measure of earnings strength. Based on operating earnings yield, the company is overvalued when compared to all of the companies in our coverage universe. Share price changes over the past year indicates that S will perform poorly over the near term.

Financial Data

(US$ in Thousands)	03/31/2018	03/31/2017	03/31/2016	03/31/2015	03/31/2014	12/31/2013	12/31/2012
Earnings Per Share	1.85	(0.30)	(0.50)	(0.85)	(0.04)	(0.54)	...
Cash Flow Per Share	2.52	1.05	0.98	0.62	0.54	(0.02)	...
Tang Book Value Per Share	N.M.	N.M.	N.M.	N.M.	N.M.	N.M.	1,001.29
Income Statement							
Total Revenue	32,406,000	33,347,000	32,180,000	34,532,000	8,875,000	16,891,000	
EBITDA	10,436,000	8,822,000	6,122,000	1,929,000	1,289,000	1,129,000	(23,000)
Depn & Amortn	7,768,000	7,098,000	5,794,000	3,797,000	868,000	2,026,000	...
Income Before Taxes	303,000	(771,000)	(1,854,000)	(3,919,000)	(95,000)	(1,815,000)	(23,000)
Income Taxes	(7,074,000)	435,000	141,000	(574,000)	56,000	45,000	4,000
Net Income	7,389,000	(1,206,000)	(1,995,000)	(3,345,000)	(151,000)	(1,860,000)	(27,000)
Average Shares	4,078,000	3,981,000	3,969,000	3,953,000	3,949,000	3,475,000	...
Balance Sheet							
Current Assets	14,253,000	14,117,000	6,833,000	9,777,000	11,579,000	13,058,000	11,000
Total Assets	85,459,000	85,123,000	78,975,000	83,030,000	84,689,000	86,095,000	3,115,000
Current Liabilities	10,800,000	12,458,000	11,963,000	10,940,000	9,698,000	10,669,000	4,000
Long-Term Obligations	37,463,000	35,878,000	29,268,000	32,531,000	31,787,000	32,017,000	...
Total Liabilities	59,103,000	66,315,000	59,192,000	61,320,000	59,377,000	60,511,000	5,000
Stockholders' Equity	26,356,000	18,808,000	19,783,000	21,710,000	25,312,000	25,584,000	3,110,000
Shares Outstanding	4,005,000	3,989,000	3,974,000	3,966,000	3,941,000	3,934,000	3,106
Statistical Record							
Return on Assets %	8.66	N.M.	N.M.	N.M.	N.M.	N.M.	...
Return on Equity %	32.72	N.M.	N.M.	N.M.	N.M.	N.M.	...
EBITDA Margin %	32.20	26.46	19.02	5.59	14.52	6.68	...
Net Margin %	22.80	N.M.	N.M.	N.M.	N.M.	N.M.	...
Asset Turnover	0.38	0.41	0.40	0.41	0.42	0.38	...
Current Ratio	1.32	1.13	0.57	0.89	1.19	1.22	2.75
Debt to Equity	1.42	1.91	1.48	1.50	1.26	1.25	...
Price Range	9.11-4.86	9.43-3.40	5.30-2.45	9.71-3.81	10.75-7.69	10.79-5.74	...
P/E Ratio	4.92-2.63	...	...	...	...	...	...

Address: 6200 Sprint Parkway, Overland Park, KS 66251 **Telephone:** 855-848-3280	**Web Site:** www.sprint.com **Officers:** Raul Marcelo Claure - Executive Chairman, President, Chief Executive Officer, Associate/Affiliate Company Officer Michel Combes - President, Chief Executive Officer, Chief Financial Officer	**Auditors:** DELOITTE & TOUCHE LLP

SQUARE INC

Exchange	Symbol	Price	52Wk Range	Yield	P/E
NYS	SQ	$61.64 (6/29/2018)	67.59-22.83	N/A	N/A

*7 Year Price Score N/A   *NYSE Composite Index=100   *12 Month Price Score 140.67

TRADING VOLUME (thousand shares)

Interim Earnings (Per Share)

Qtr.	Mar	Jun	Sep	Dec
2015	(0.33)	(0.20)	(0.35)	(0.36)
2016	(0.29)	(0.08)	(0.09)	(0.04)
2017	(0.04)	(0.04)	(0.04)	(0.04)
2018	(0.06)	...	...	...

Interim Dividends (Per Share)

No Dividends Paid

Valuation Analysis   Institutional Holding

Forecast EPS	$0.46	No of Institutions
	(06/14/2018)	562
Market Cap	$24.7 Billion	Shares
Book Value	$810.0 Million	222,160,928
Price/Book	30.47	% Held
Price/Sales	10.19	N/A

Business Summary: IT Services (MIC: 6.3.1 SIC: 7372 NAIC: 511210)

Square is a commerce ecosystem that combines software with hardware to enable sellers to turn mobile devices and computing devices into payment and point-of-sale solutions. Co.'s products and services including: Managed Payments Solutions, which sellers can accept payments in person via the swipe, dip, or tap of a card, online; In-person/card present payments, which its custom-designed hardware can process all card payment forms, including magnetic stripe; Square Cash, which is an personal finance app that allows anyone to send and receive money electronically; and Square Point of Sale, which includes Square Dashboard, Co.'s cloud-based reporting and analytics tool.

Recent Developments: For the quarter ended Mar 31 2018, net loss amounted to US$24.0 million versus a net loss of US$15.1 million in the year-earlier quarter. Revenues were US$668.6 million, up 44.9% from US$461.6 million the year before. Operating loss was US$21.0 million versus a loss of US$14.1 million in the prior-year quarter. Direct operating expenses rose 43.5% to US$413.4 million from US$288.1 million in the comparable period the year before. Indirect operating expenses increased 47.3% to US$276.2 million from US$187.5 million in the equivalent prior-year period.

Prospects: Our evaluation of Square Inc as of Jan. 21, 2018 is the result of our systematic analysis on three basic characteristics: earnings strength, relative valuation, and recent stock price movement. The company has managed to produce a neutral trend in earnings per share over the past 5 quarters and while recent estimates for the company have remained steady, SQ has posted better than expected results. Based on operating earnings yield, the company is overvalued when compared to all of the companies in our coverage universe. Share price changes over the past year indicates that SQ will perform very well over the near term.

Financial Data

(US$ in Thousands)	3 Mos	12/31/2017	12/31/2016	12/31/2015	12/31/2014	12/31/2013	12/31/2012
Earnings Per Share	(0.18)	(0.17)	(0.50)	(1.24)	(1.08)	(0.82)	(0.71)
Cash Flow Per Share	0.34	0.34	0.07	0.16	(0.77)	(0.47)	(0.36)
Tang Book Value Per Share	1.84	1.81	1.37	1.27	...	...	...
Income Statement							
Total Revenue	668,603	2,214,253	1,708,721	1,267,118	850,192	552,433	203,449
EBITDA	(13,662)	(24,506)	(141,753)	(154,808)	(135,095)	(95,792)	(81,694)
Depn & Amortn	10,149	29,700	28,700	20,100	16,500	8,200	3,500
Income Before Taxes	(23,811)	(62,664)	(169,673)	(176,071)	(152,653)	(103,980)	(85,199)
Income Taxes	175	149	1,917	3,746	1,440	513	...
Net Income	(23,986)	(62,813)	(171,590)	(179,817)	(154,093)	(104,493)	(85,199)
Average Shares	395,948	379,344	341,555	170,498	142,042	127,845	119,220
Balance Sheet							
Current Assets	1,990,383	1,778,294	1,001,425	705,563	409,867	253,802	...
Total Assets	2,379,612	2,187,270	1,211,362	894,772	541,888	318,341	...
Current Liabilities	1,131,732	972,827	577,464	334,202	191,106	129,741	...
Long-Term Obligations	362,965	358,572	...	...	30,000	...	...
Total Liabilities	1,569,632	1,400,937	635,209	386,724	268,216	156,047	...
Stockholders' Equity	809,980	786,333	576,153	508,048	273,672	162,294	...
Shares Outstanding	400,384	395,194	364,547	334,949	154,603	138,017	132,969
Statistical Record							
Asset Turnover	1.22	1.30	1.62	1.76	1.98	...	...
Current Ratio	1.76	1.83	1.73	2.11	2.14	1.96	...
Debt to Equity	0.45	0.46	...	...	0.11	...	...
Price Range	57.69-16.69	48.86-13.81	15.48-8.37	13.09-11.90	...	...	...

Address: 1455 Market Street, Suite 600, San Francisco, CA 94103
Telephone: 415-375-3176

Web Site: www.squareup.com
Officers: Jack Dorsey - Chairman, President, Chief Executive Officer Sarah Friar - Chief Financial Officer, Chief Accounting Officer

Auditors: KPMG LLP
Transfer Agents: American Stock Transfer & Trust Company, LLC, Brooklyn, NY

STANLEY BLACK & DECKER INC

Exchange	Symbol	Price	52Wk Range	Yield	P/E	Div Acheiver
NYS	SWK	$132.81 (6/29/2018)	175.91-132.81	1.90	20.25	50 Years

*7 Year Price Score 123.11 *NYSE Composite Index=100 *12 Month Price Score 90.89

Interim Earnings (Per Share)

Qtr.	Mar	Jun	Sep	Dec
2015	1.04	1.49	1.52	1.76
2016	1.28	1.84	1.68	1.70
2017	2.59	1.82	1.80	1.83
2018	1.11	...	...	...

Interim Dividends (Per Share)

Amt	Decl	Ex	Rec	Pay
0.63Q	07/19/2017	08/30/2017	09/01/2017	09/19/2017
0.63Q	10/18/2017	11/30/2017	12/01/2017	12/19/2017
0.63Q	02/27/2018	03/08/2018	03/09/2018	03/20/2018
0.63Q	04/19/2018	06/05/2018	06/06/2018	06/19/2018

Indicated Div: $2.52

Valuation Analysis — **Institutional Holding**

Forecast EPS	$8.41	No of Institutions
	(06/14/2018)	1076
Market Cap	$20.5 Billion	Shares
Book Value	$8.4 Billion	153,728,816
Price/Book	2.43	% Held
Price/Sales	1.56	N/A

TRADING VOLUME (thousand shares)

Business Summary: Industrial Machinery & Equipment (MIC: 7.2.1 SIC: 3423 NAIC: 332212)

Stanley Black & Decker is a provider of hand tools, power tools and related accessories, mechanical access solutions (for example, automatic doors and commercial locking systems), electronic security and monitoring systems, healthcare solutions, engineered fastening systems and products and services for various industrial applications. Co. has three segments: Tools & Storage, which is comprised of the Power Tools and Hand Tools, Accessories & Storage businesses; Security, which is comprised of the Convergent Security Solutions and the Mechanical Access Solutions businesses; and Industrial, which is comprised of the Engineered Fastening and Infrastructure businesses.

Recent Developments: For the quarter ended Mar 31 2018, net income decreased 56.8% to US$170.1 million from US$393.7 million in the year-earlier quarter. Revenues were US$3.21 billion, up 12.4% from US$2.86 billion the year before. Direct operating expenses rose 14.1% to US$2.04 billion from US$1.79 billion in the comparable period the year before. Indirect operating expenses increased 54.2% to US$913.9 million from US$592.6 million in the equivalent prior-year period.

Prospects: Our evaluation of Stanley Black & Decker, Inc. as of Jan. 21, 2018 is the result of our systematic analysis on three basic characteristics: earnings strength, relative valuation, and recent stock price movement. The company has enjoyed a very positive trend in earnings per share over the past 5 quarters and while recent estimates for the company have been raised by analysts, SWK has posted better than expected results. Based on operating earnings yield, the company is about fairly valued when compared to all of the companies in our coverage universe. Share price changes over the past year indicates that SWK will perform well over the near term.

Financial Data
(US$ in Thousands)

	3 Mos	12/30/2017	12/31/2016	01/02/2016	01/03/2015	12/28/2013	12/29/2012	12/31/2011
Earnings Per Share	6.56	8.04	6.51	5.79	4.76	3.09	5.30	3.97
Cash Flow Per Share	8.07	9.51	10.20	8.00	8.17	5.61	5.94	6.04
Dividends Per Share	2.470	2.420	2.260	2.140	2.040	1.980	1.800	1.640
Dividend Payout %	37.65	30.10	34.72	36.96	42.86	64.08	33.96	41.31
Income Statement								
Total Revenue	3,209,300	12,747,200	11,406,900	11,171,800	11,338,600	11,001,200	10,190,500	10,376,400
EBITDA	341,500	2,169,300	1,805,400	1,730,000	1,698,200	1,175,500	1,107,000	1,303,200
Depn & Amortn	42,300	460,700	408,000	414,000	449,800	441,300	445,300	410,100
Income Before Taxes	251,800	1,526,100	1,226,100	1,150,800	1,084,000	586,600	527,600	779,800
Income Taxes	81,700	300,500	261,200	248,600	227,100	69,300	78,900	88,600
Net Income	170,600	1,226,000	965,300	883,700	760,900	490,300	883,800	674,600
Average Shares	153,905	152,449	148,207	152,706	159,737	158,776	166,701	170,105
Balance Sheet								
Current Assets	5,077,900	4,566,100	4,788,500	3,662,100	3,948,800	3,968,700	4,098,300	4,322,700
Total Assets	19,683,200	19,079,900	15,634,900	15,172,300	15,849,100	16,535,100	15,844,000	15,949,000
Current Liabilities	4,810,200	4,361,800	2,807,500	2,802,600	2,832,000	3,221,000	3,073,400	3,268,500
Long-Term Obligations	2,827,600	2,843,000	3,815,500	3,836,600	3,839,800	3,799,400	3,526,500	2,925,800
Total Liabilities	11,244,000	10,782,800	9,267,900	9,360,700	9,420,000	9,735,900	9,176,900	8,945,400
Stockholders' Equity	8,439,200	8,297,100	6,367,000	5,811,600	6,429,100	6,799,200	6,667,100	7,003,600
Shares Outstanding	154,309	154,038	152,559	153,944	157,125	155,479	159,952	169,045
Statistical Record								
Return on Assets %	5.23	7.08	6.28	5.71	4.62	3.04	5.57	4.35
Return on Equity %	13.16	16.77	15.90	14.48	11.32	7.30	12.97	9.65
EBITDA Margin %	10.64	17.02	15.83	15.49	14.98	10.69	10.86	12.56
Net Margin %	5.32	9.62	8.46	7.91	6.71	4.46	8.67	6.50
Asset Turnover	0.69	0.74	0.74	0.72	0.69	0.68	0.64	0.67
Current Ratio	1.06	1.05	1.71	1.31	1.39	1.23	1.33	1.32
Debt to Equity	0.34	0.34	0.60	0.66	0.60	0.56	0.53	0.42
Price Range	175.91-130.57	170.03-115.75	125.78-90.14	110.17-90.51	97.36-75.64	92.36-73.97	81.34-59.25	77.29-47.83
P/E Ratio	26.82-19.90	21.15-14.40	19.32-13.85	19.03-15.63	20.45-15.89	29.89-23.94	15.35-11.18	19.47-12.05
Average Yield %	1.63	1.70	2.01	2.11	2.35	2.45	2.55	2.43

Address: 1000 Stanley Drive, New Britain, CT 06053 **Telephone:** 860-225-5111 **Fax:** 860-827-3895	**Web Site:** www.stanleyblackanddecker.com **Officers:** George W. Buckley - Chairman James M. Loree - President, Chief Executive Officer, Executive Vice President, Chief Operating Officer	**Auditors:** Ernst & Young LLP **Transfer Agents:** Computershare Investor Services, Canton, MA

STARWOOD PROPERTY TRUST INC.

Exchange	Symbol	Price	52Wk Range	Yield	P/E
NYS	STWD	$21.71 (6/29/2018)	22.55-19.72	8.84	14.47

*7 Year Price Score 76.92   *NYSE Composite Index=100   *12 Month Price Score 100.16

Interim Earnings (Per Share)

Qtr.	Mar	Jun	Sep	Dec
2015	0.52	0.49	0.49	0.40
2016	0.11	0.47	0.44	0.50
2017	0.39	0.44	0.33	0.35
2018	0.38	...	...	...

Interim Dividends (Per Share)

Amt	Decl	Ex	Rec	Pay
0.48Q	08/09/2017	09/28/2017	09/29/2017	10/13/2017
0.48Q	11/08/2017	12/28/2017	12/29/2017	01/15/2018
0.48Q	02/28/2018	03/28/2018	03/30/2018	04/13/2018
0.48Q	05/04/2018	06/28/2018	06/29/2018	07/13/2018

Indicated Div: $1.92

Valuation Analysis / Institutional Holding

Forecast EPS	$2.20 (06/12/2018)	No of Institutions	499
Market Cap	$5.7 Billion	Shares	213,712,656
Book Value	$4.5 Billion	% Held	89.80
Price/Book	1.28		
Price/Sales	6.04		

Business Summary: REITs (MIC: 5.3.1 SIC: 6798 NAIC: 525930)

Starwood Property Trust is a holding company. Co. conducts its operations as a real estate investment trust. Co. originates, acquires, finances and manages commercial mortgage loans and other commercial real estate debt investments, commercial mortgage-backed securities, and other commercial real estate investments in both the U.S. and Europe. Co.'s target assets include commercial real estate mortgage loans, other commercial real estate-related debt investments, residential mortgage-backed securities, certain residential mortgage loans, distressed or non-performing commercial loans, commercial properties subject to net leases and equity interests in commercial real estate.

Recent Developments: For the quarter ended Mar 31 2018, net income increased 1.9% to US$104.8 million from US$102.9 million in the year-earlier quarter. Revenues were US$260.6 million, up 31.1% from US$198.7 million the year before. Revenues from property income rose 42.2% to US$81.1 million from US$57.0 million in the corresponding quarter a year earlier.

Prospects: Our evaluation of Starwood Properties Trust Inc. as of Jan. 21, 2018 is the result of our systematic analysis on three basic characteristics: earnings strength, relative valuation, and recent stock price movement. The company has generated a negative trend in earnings per share over the past 5 quarters and while recent estimates for the company have remained steady, STWD has posted better than expected results. Based on operating earnings yield, the company is undervalued when compared to all of the companies in our coverage universe. Share price changes over the past year indicates that STWD will perform in line with the market over the near term.

Financial Data
(US$ in Thousands)

	3 Mos	12/31/2017	12/31/2016	12/31/2015	12/31/2014	12/31/2013	12/31/2012	12/31/2011
Earnings Per Share	1.50	1.52	1.50	1.91	2.24	1.82	1.76	1.38
Cash Flow Per Share	0.16	(0.95)	2.33	2.62	1.03	1.96	2.33	0.93
Tang Book Value Per Share	15.80	15.90	16.05	15.99	16.00	20.28	20.07	18.88
Dividends Per Share	1.920	1.920	1.920	1.920	1.920	1.820	1.860	1.740
Dividend Payout %	128.00	126.32	128.00	100.52	85.71	100.00	105.68	126.09
Income Statement								
Total Revenue	260,587	879,888	784,667	735,877	702,875	565,695	306,980	204,973
EBITDA	104,634	545,509	453,700	505,396	548,394	357,077	210,374	124,789
Depn & Amortn	(3,016)	131,725	99,428	62,681	42,141	31,535	5,669	3,780
Income Before Taxes	107,650	413,784	354,272	442,715	506,253	325,542	204,705	121,398
Income Taxes	2,856	31,522	8,344	17,206	24,096	24,053	1,023	790
Net Income	99,932	400,770	365,186	450,697	495,021	305,030	201,195	119,377
Average Shares	262,124	262,079	241,794	234,142	218,781	167,322	114,633	86,409
Balance Sheet								
Current Assets	420,674	499,918	768,340	471,289	370,621	432,078	214,447	142,019
Total Assets	61,126,855	62,941,289	77,256,266	85,738,138	116,099,297	110,770,575	4,324,373	2,997,447
Current Liabilities	373,188	389,602	364,931	317,903	298,932	357,530	112,259	74,482
Long-Term Obligations	7,881,220	7,972,476	6,200,670	5,432,278	4,685,252	3,436,649	1,393,705	1,156,716
Total Liabilities	56,668,323	58,462,875	72,733,992	81,597,822	112,238,441	106,488,047	1,605,027	1,237,959
Stockholders' Equity	4,458,532	4,478,414	4,522,274	4,140,316	3,860,856	4,282,528	2,719,346	1,759,488
Shares Outstanding	261,955	261,376	259,286	237,490	223,538	195,513	135,499	93,185
Statistical Record								
Return on Assets %	0.61	0.57	0.45	0.45	0.44	0.53	5.48	4.68
Return on Equity %	8.89	8.91	8.41	11.27	12.16	8.71	8.96	7.73
EBITDA Margin %	40.15	62.00	57.82	68.68	78.02	63.12	68.53	60.88
Net Margin %	38.35	45.55	46.54	61.25	70.43	53.92	65.54	58.24
Asset Turnover	0.01	0.01	0.01	0.01	0.01	0.01	0.08	0.08
Current Ratio	1.13	1.28	2.11	1.48	1.24	1.21	1.91	1.91
Debt to Equity	1.77	1.78	1.37	1.31	-1.21	0.80	0.51	0.66
Price Range	22.97-19.72	22.97-21.32	23.30-16.93	24.67-19.74	30.67-21.78	28.55-22.96	24.35-18.57	23.39-16.40
P/E Ratio	15.31-13.15	15.11-14.03	15.53-11.29	12.92-10.34	13.69-9.72	15.69-12.62	13.84-10.55	16.95-11.88
Average Yield %	8.85	8.67	9.28	8.54	8.01	7.01	8.63	8.60

Address: 591 West Putnam Avenue, Greenwich, CT 06830 Telephone: 203-422-7700	Web Site: www.starwoodpropertytrust.com Officers: Barry S. Sternlicht - Chairman, Chief Executive Officer Jeffrey F. DiModica - President	Auditors: DELOITTE & TOUCHE LLP Investor Contact: 202-422-7700 Transfer Agents: American Stock Transfer & Trust Company, LLC

STATE STREET CORP.

Exchange	Symbol	Price	52Wk Range	Yield	P/E
NYS	STT	$93.09 (6/29/2018)	112.71-89.73	1.80	16.33

*7 Year Price Score 116.27 *NYSE Composite Index=100 *12 Month Price Score 98.74

Interim Earnings (Per Share)

Qtr.	Mar	Jun	Sep	Dec
2015	0.90	0.94	1.32	1.31
2016	0.79	1.47	1.29	1.43
2017	1.15	1.53	1.66	0.89
2018	1.62	...	...	...

Interim Dividends (Per Share)

Amt	Decl	Ex	Rec	Pay
0.42Q	07/20/2017	09/29/2017	10/02/2017	10/16/2017
0.42Q	12/14/2017	12/29/2017	01/02/2018	01/17/2018
0.42Q	02/15/2018	03/29/2018	04/02/2018	04/16/2018
0.42Q	05/16/2018	06/29/2018	07/02/2018	07/17/2018

Indicated Div: $1.68

Valuation Analysis

		Institutional Holding	
Forecast EPS	$7.69	No of Institutions	
	(06/14/2018)	1303	
Market Cap	$34.0 Billion	Shares	
Book Value	$22.4 Billion	395,521,824	
Price/Book	1.52	% Held	
Price/Sales	2.79	76.47	

Business Summary: Banking (MIC: 5.1.1 SIC: 6022 NAIC: 522110)

State Street is a financial holding company. Through its subsidiaries, Co. provides financial products and services to institutional investors. Co. has two lines of business: Investment Servicing, which provides, among others, custody, product- and participant-level accounting, daily pricing and administration, master trust and master custody, record-keeping, cash management, foreign exchange, brokerage and other trading services; and Investment Management, which provides investment management, investment research and investment advisory services to corporations, public funds and other investors. At Dec 31 2017, Co. had total assets of $238.43 billion and total deposits of $184.90 billion.

Recent Developments: For the quarter ended Mar 31 2018, net income increased 31.7% to US$661.0 million from US$502.0 million in the year-earlier quarter. Net interest income increased 29.0% to US$658.0 million from US$510.0 million in the year-earlier quarter. Provision for loan losses was nil versus a credit for loan losses of US$2.0 million in the prior-year quarter. Non-interest income rose 9.4% to US$2.36 billion from US$2.16 billion, while non-interest expense advanced 8.1% to US$2.26 billion.

Prospects: Our evaluation of State Street Corp. as of Jan. 21, 2018 is the result of our systematic analysis on three basic characteristics: earnings strength, relative valuation, and recent stock price movement. The company has produced a positive trend in earnings per share over the past 5 quarters and while recent estimates for the company have been raised by analysts, STT has posted better than expected results. Based on operating earnings yield, the company is undervalued when compared to all of the companies in our coverage universe. Share price changes over the past year indicates that STT will perform in line with the market over the near term.

Financial Data

(US$ in Thousands)	3 Mos	12/31/2017	12/31/2016	12/31/2015	12/31/2014	12/31/2013	12/31/2012	12/31/2011
Earnings Per Share	5.70	5.24	4.97	4.47	4.57	4.62	4.20	3.79
Cash Flow Per Share	22.48	18.50	5.83	(3.44)	(1.32)	(4.42)	3.84	6.85
Tang Book Value Per Share	31.63	31.24	27.38	27.43	28.09	26.47	25.87	22.14
Dividends Per Share	1.640	1.600	1.440	1.320	1.160	1.040	0.960	0.720
Dividend Payout %	28.77	30.53	28.97	29.53	25.38	22.51	22.86	19.00
Income Statement								
Interest Income	857,000	2,908,000	2,512,000	2,488,000	2,652,000	2,714,000	3,014,000	2,946,000
Interest Expense	199,000	604,000	428,000	400,000	392,000	411,000	476,000	613,000
Net Interest Income	658,000	2,304,000	2,084,000	2,088,000	2,260,000	2,303,000	2,538,000	2,333,000
Provision for Losses	...	2,000	10,000	12,000	10,000	6,000	(3,000)	...
Non-Interest Income	2,361,000	8,866,000	8,123,000	8,272,000	8,035,000	7,581,000	7,111,000	7,261,000
Non-Interest Expense	2,256,000	8,269,000	8,077,000	8,050,000	7,827,000	7,192,000	6,886,000	7,058,000
Income Before Taxes	763,000	2,899,000	2,120,000	2,298,000	2,458,000	2,686,000	2,766,000	2,536,000
Income Taxes	102,000	722,000	(22,000)	318,000	421,000	550,000	705,000	616,000
Net Income	661,000	2,177,000	2,143,000	1,980,000	2,037,000	2,136,000	2,061,000	1,920,000
Average Shares	372,619	380,213	396,090	413,638	432,007	455,155	481,129	496,072
Balance Sheet								
Net Loans & Leases	29,528,000	23,240,000	19,704,000	18,753,000	18,161,000	13,458,000	12,285,000	10,031,000
Total Assets	250,286,000	238,425,000	242,698,000	245,192,000	274,119,000	243,291,000	222,582,000	216,827,000
Total Deposits	191,517,000	184,896,000	187,163,000	191,627,000	209,040,000	182,268,000	164,181,000	157,287,000
Total Liabilities	227,887,000	216,108,000	221,479,000	224,089,000	252,646,000	222,913,000	201,713,000	197,429,000
Stockholders' Equity	22,399,000	22,317,000	21,219,000	21,103,000	21,473,000	20,378,000	20,869,000	19,398,000
Shares Outstanding	365,407	367,649	381,939	399,651	415,195	434,128	458,662	487,423
Statistical Record								
Return on Assets %	0.96	0.90	0.88	0.76	0.79	0.92	0.94	1.02
Return on Equity %	10.69	10.00	10.10	9.30	9.73	10.36	10.21	10.33
Net Interest Margin %	76.78	79.23	82.96	83.92	85.22	84.86	84.21	79.19
Efficiency Ratio %	70.11	70.23	75.95	74.81	73.24	69.86	68.01	69.15
Loans to Deposits	0.15	0.13	0.11	0.10	0.09	0.07	0.07	0.06
Price Range	112.71-77.30	99.29-75.97	81.44-50.79	80.84-64.73	80.33-63.19	73.39-47.01	47.01-38.78	50.06-30.38
P/E Ratio	19.77-13.56	18.95-14.50	16.39-10.22	18.09-14.48	17.58-13.83	15.89-10.18	11.19-9.23	13.21-8.02
Average Yield %	1.74	1.82	2.24	1.78	1.65	1.62	2.22	1.73

Address: One Lincoln Street, Boston, MA 02111 Telephone: 617-786-3000	Web Site: www.statestreet.com Officers: Joseph L. Hooley - Chairman, Chief Executive Officer, President, Chief Operating Officer Ronald P. (Ron) O'Hanley - Vice-Chairman, President, Chief Operating Officer	Auditors: Ernst & Young LLP Investor Contact: 617-664-3477 Transfer Agents: American Stock Transfer & Trust Company, LLC, Brooklyn, NY

STEPAN CO.

Exchange	Symbol	Price	52Wk Range	Yield	P/E	Div Acheiver
NYS	SCL	$78.01 (6/29/2018)	91.52-68.42	1.15	20.21	50 Years

*7 Year Price Score 110.31 *NYSE Composite Index=100 *12 Month Price Score 90.95

Interim Earnings (Per Share)

Qtr.	Mar	Jun	Sep	Dec
2015	0.93	0.74	1.09	0.56
2016	1.21	1.21	0.89	0.42
2017	1.37	1.19	0.94	0.42
2018	1.31	...	...	...

Interim Dividends (Per Share)

Amt	Decl	Ex	Rec	Pay
0.205Q	07/25/2017	08/29/2017	08/31/2017	09/15/2017
0.225Q	10/24/2017	11/29/2017	11/30/2017	12/15/2017
0.225Q	02/21/2018	03/02/2018	03/05/2018	03/15/2018
0.225Q	04/23/2018	05/30/2018	05/31/2018	06/15/2018

Indicated Div: $0.90

Valuation Analysis — **Institutional Holding**

Forecast EPS	$4.76 (06/11/2018)	No of Institutions	272
Market Cap	$1.8 Billion	Shares	18,688,060
Book Value	$774.6 Million	% Held	61.54
Price/Book	2.28		
Price/Sales	0.90		

Business Summary: Specialty Chemicals (MIC: 8.3.2 SIC: 2843 NAIC: 325613)

Stepan is engaged in the production of specialty and intermediate chemicals, which are sold to other manufacturers for use in a variety of end products. Co. has three reportable segments: surfactants, polymers and specialty products. Surfactants are used in a variety of consumer and industrial cleaning compounds as well as in agricultural products, lubricating ingredients, oil field chemicals and other applications. Polymers are used primarily in plastics, building materials, refrigeration systems and coatings, adhesives, sealants and elastomers applications. Specialty products are used in food, flavoring, nutritional supplement and pharmaceutical applications.

Recent Developments: For the quarter ended Mar 31 2018, net income decreased 3.7% to US$30.7 million from US$31.9 million in the year-earlier quarter. Revenues were US$499.3 million, up 6.6% from US$468.3 million the year before. Operating income was US$39.7 million versus US$46.2 million in the prior-year quarter, a decrease of 14.2%. Direct operating expenses rose 8.9% to US$409.8 million from US$376.2 million in the comparable period the year before. Indirect operating expenses increased 8.8% to US$49.9 million from US$45.9 million in the equivalent prior-year period.

Prospects: Our evaluation of Stepan Co. as of Jan. 21, 2018 is the result of our systematic analysis on three basic characteristics: earnings strength, relative valuation, and recent stock price movement. The company has managed to produce a neutral trend in earnings per share over the past 5 quarters and while recent estimates for the company have remained steady, SCL has posted results that fell short of analysts expectations. Based on operating earnings yield, the company is undervalued when compared to all of the companies in our coverage universe. Share price changes over the past year indicates that SCL will perform in line with the market over the near term.

Financial Data
(US$ in Thousands)

	3 Mos	12/31/2017	12/31/2016	12/31/2015	12/31/2014	12/31/2013	12/31/2012	12/31/2011
Earnings Per Share	3.86	3.92	3.73	3.32	2.49	3.18	3.49	6.42
Cash Flow Per Share	8.52	8.67	9.28	8.06	3.60	6.64	5.11	7.47
Tang Book Value Per Share	32.31	30.94	26.17	23.69	22.61	23.15	21.01	36.12
Dividends Per Share	0.860	0.840	0.775	0.730	0.690	0.650	0.580	0.530
Dividend Payout %	22.28	21.43	20.78	21.99	27.71	20.44	16.62	8.26
Income Statement								
Total Revenue	499,335	1,925,007	1,766,166	1,776,167	1,927,213	1,880,786	1,803,737	1,843,092
EBITDA	60,763	229,703	201,988	191,359	155,788	167,724	181,339	164,704
Depn & Amortn	19,948	79,022	74,967	66,985	63,804	56,400	51,294	47,099
Income Before Taxes	37,664	139,237	113,816	109,841	80,543	100,966	120,446	108,510
Income Taxes	6,948	47,690	27,618	26,819	18,454	23,293	36,035	32,292
Net Income	30,723	91,578	86,191	75,968	57,101	72,828	79,396	71,976
Average Shares	23,389	23,377	23,094	22,858	22,917	22,924	22,730	11,220
Balance Sheet								
Current Assets	782,010	788,736	685,541	619,573	575,556	608,550	523,078	479,742
Total Assets	1,480,633	1,470,861	1,353,890	1,239,661	1,162,014	1,167,202	985,478	901,118
Current Liabilities	299,554	320,253	297,265	243,244	249,513	268,993	247,167	233,226
Long-Term Obligations	268,173	268,299	288,859	313,817	246,897	235,246	149,564	164,967
Total Liabilities	706,050	730,765	719,286	682,677	626,468	614,916	506,493	499,907
Stockholders' Equity	774,583	740,096	634,604	556,984	535,546	552,286	478,985	401,211
Shares Outstanding	22,645	22,509	22,424	22,280	22,255	22,332	21,965	10,246
Statistical Record								
Return on Assets %	6.34	6.48	6.63	6.33	4.90	6.77	8.39	8.41
Return on Equity %	12.49	13.32	14.43	13.91	10.50	14.12	17.99	19.18
EBITDA Margin %	12.17	11.93	11.44	10.77	8.08	8.92	10.05	8.94
Net Margin %	6.15	4.76	4.88	4.28	2.96	3.87	4.40	3.91
Asset Turnover	1.37	1.36	1.36	1.48	1.65	1.75	1.91	2.15
Current Ratio	2.61	2.46	2.31	2.55	2.31	2.26	2.12	2.06
Debt to Equity	0.35	0.36	0.46	0.56	0.46	0.43	0.31	0.41
Price Range	91.52-69.52	91.52-70.75	86.38-41.88	55.18-37.74	66.47-37.02	66.85-52.58	55.54-39.17	41.59-31.55
P/E Ratio	23.71-18.01	23.35-18.05	23.16-11.23	16.62-11.37	26.69-14.87	21.02-16.53	15.91-11.22	6.48-4.91
Average Yield %	1.05	1.03	1.23	1.57	1.31	1.11	1.26	1.46

Address: Edens & Winnetka Road, Northfield, IL 60093 Telephone: 847-446-7500	Web Site: www.stepan.com Officers: F. Quinn Stepan - Chairman, President, Chief Executive Officer Scott R. Behrens - Vice President, Division Officer	Auditors: DELOITTE & TOUCHE LLP Investor Contact: 847-446-7500 Transfer Agents: Computershare Investor Services, LLC, Chicago, IL

STERIS PLC

Exchange	Symbol	Price	52Wk Range	Yield	P/E
NYS	STE	$105.01 (6/29/2018)	107.54-80.83	1.18	30.98

*7 Year Price Score 125.33 *NYSE Composite Index=100 *12 Month Price Score 111.20

Interim Earnings (Per Share)

Qtr.	Jun	Sep	Dec	Mar
2013-14	0.54	0.50	0.48	0.65
2014-15	0.41	0.52	0.63	0.69
2015-16	0.40	0.14	0.26	0.76
2016-17	0.56	0.47	(0.06)	0.31
2017-18	0.68	0.75	1.11	0.86

Interim Dividends (Per Share)

Amt	Decl	Ex	Rec	Pay
0.31Q	08/08/2017	08/25/2017	08/29/2017	09/28/2017
0.31Q	11/01/2017	11/21/2017	11/22/2017	12/20/2017
0.31Q	01/30/2018	02/27/2018	02/28/2018	03/28/2018
0.31Q	05/04/2018	06/07/2018	06/08/2018	06/28/2018

Indicated Div: $1.24

Valuation Analysis

		Institutional Holding	
Forecast EPS	N/A	No of Institutions	N/A
Market Cap	$8.9 Billion	Shares	N/A
Book Value	$3.2 Billion	% Held	N/A
Price/Book	2.78		
Price/Sales	3.40		

Business Summary: Medical Instruments & Equipment (MIC: 4.3.1 SIC: 3842 NAIC: 339113)

STERIS is a provider of infection prevention and other procedural products and services. Co. has four segments: Healthcare Products, which provides infection prevention and procedural solutions, including capital equipment and related maintenance and installation services, as well as consumables; Healthcare Specialty Services, which provides a range of services for healthcare providers including hospital sterilization services and instrument and scope repairs; Life Sciences, which provides capital equipment and consumable products, and equipment maintenance and specialty services; and Applied Sterilization Technologies, which provides contract sterilization and laboratory services.

Recent Developments: For the year ended Mar 31 2018, net income increased 163.6% to US$291.6 million from US$110.6 million in the prior year. Revenues were US$2.62 billion, up 0.3% from US$2.61 billion the year before. Operating income was US$403.5 million versus US$227.6 million in the prior year, an increase of 77.3%. Direct operating expenses declined 3.9% to US$1.53 billion from US$1.59 billion in the comparable period the year before. Indirect operating expenses decreased 13.4% to US$690.8 million from US$798.0 million in the equivalent prior-year period.

Prospects: Our evaluation of Steris PLC as of Sep. 17, 2017 is the result of our systematic analysis on three basic characteristics: earnings strength, relative valuation, and recent stock price movement. The company has enjoyed a very positive trend in earnings per share over the past 5 quarters and while recent estimates for the company have remained steady, STE has posted better than expected results. Based on operating earnings yield, the company is about fairly valued when compared to all of the companies in our coverage universe. Share price changes over the past year indicates that STE will perform in line with the market over the near term.

Financial Data

(US$ in Thousands)	03/31/2018	03/31/2017	03/31/2016	03/31/2015	03/31/2014	03/31/2013	03/31/2012	03/31/2011
Earnings Per Share	3.39	1.28	1.56	2.25	2.17	2.72	2.31	0.85
Cash Flow Per Share	5.38	4.96	3.59	4.14	3.56	3.91	2.55	1.99
Tang Book Value Per Share	0.53	N.M.	N.M.	3.54	4.93	4.09	8.38	7.93
Dividends Per Share	1.210	1.090	0.980	0.900	0.820	0.740	0.660	0.560
Dividend Payout %	35.69	85.16	62.82	40.00	37.79	27.21	28.57	65.88
Income Statement								
Total Revenue	2,619,996	2,612,756	2,238,764	1,850,263	1,622,252	1,501,902	1,406,810	1,207,448
EBITDA	511,591	347,131	306,885	288,692	263,844	297,914	275,296	132,984
Depn & Amortn	108,137	119,536	93,958	61,481	57,037	55,085	52,980	47,772
Income Before Taxes	354,982	184,646	171,884	208,820	188,376	227,098	211,108	73,819
Income Taxes	63,360	74,015	60,299	73,756	58,934	67,121	74,993	22,554
Net Income	290,915	109,965	110,763	135,064	129,442	159,977	136,115	51,265
Average Shares	85,713	86,094	71,184	60,045	59,745	58,844	58,963	60,148
Balance Sheet								
Current Assets	989,657	1,017,802	972,525	720,432	674,745	613,940	651,883	705,806
Total Assets	5,200,334	4,924,455	5,346,416	2,099,466	1,887,162	1,761,109	1,405,696	1,426,685
Current Liabilities	398,462	381,583	400,606	283,331	254,506	218,837	278,395	344,746
Long-Term Obligations	1,316,001	1,478,361	1,567,796	623,250	493,480	492,290	210,000	210,000
Total Liabilities	1,994,374	2,125,853	2,323,382	1,027,834	848,457	816,167	584,295	639,116
Stockholders' Equity	3,205,960	2,798,602	3,023,034	1,071,632	1,038,705	944,942	821,401	787,569
Shares Outstanding	84,747	84,948	85,920	59,675	58,968	58,759	57,733	59,122
Statistical Record								
Return on Assets %	5.75	2.14	2.97	6.78	7.10	10.10	9.59	3.85
Return on Equity %	9.69	3.78	5.40	12.80	13.05	18.11	16.87	6.65
EBITDA Margin %	19.53	13.29	13.71	15.60	16.26	19.84	19.57	11.01
Net Margin %	11.10	4.21	4.95	7.30	7.98	10.65	9.68	4.25
Asset Turnover	0.52	0.51	0.60	0.93	0.89	0.95	0.99	0.91
Current Ratio	2.48	2.67	2.43	2.54	2.65	2.81	2.34	2.05
Debt to Equity	0.41	0.53	0.52	0.58	0.48	0.52	0.26	0.27
Price Range	95.85-69.22	73.90-63.28	77.73-61.96	70.38-47.64	49.76-39.02	41.61-29.01	36.72-27.38	37.83-28.35
P/E Ratio	28.27-20.42	57.73-49.44	49.83-39.72	31.28-21.17	22.93-17.98	15.30-10.67	15.90-11.85	44.51-33.35
Average Yield %	1.42	1.57	1.43	1.54	1.83	2.17	2.08	1.67

Address: Rutherford House Stephensons Way Chaddesden, Derby, 44060-1834 **Telephone:** 133-238-7100	**Web Site:** www.steris.com **Officers:** Mohsen M. Sohi - Chairman Walter M. Rosebrough - President, Chief Executive Officer	**Auditors:** Ernst & Young LLP **Investor Contact:** 440-392-7245 **Transfer Agents:** Computershare, Providence, RI

STERLING BANCORP (DE)

Exchange	Symbol	Price	52Wk Range	Yield	P/E
NYS	STL	$23.50 (6/29/2018)	26.25-21.15	1.19	32.64

*7 Year Price Score 132.28 *NYSE Composite Index=100 *12 Month Price Score 100.56

Interim Earnings (Per Share)

Qtr.	Mar	Jun	Sep	Dec
2015	0.19	(0.08)	0.19	0.28
2016	0.18	0.29	0.29	0.31
2017	0.29	0.31	0.33	(0.35)
2018	0.43	...	...	...

Interim Dividends (Per Share)

Amt	Decl	Ex	Rec	Pay
0.07Q	07/25/2017	08/03/2017	08/07/2017	08/21/2017
0.07Q	10/24/2017	11/03/2017	11/06/2017	11/20/2017
0.07Q	01/23/2018	02/02/2018	02/05/2018	02/20/2018
0.07Q	04/24/2018	05/04/2018	05/07/2018	05/21/2018

Indicated Div: $0.28

Valuation Analysis / **Institutional Holding**

Forecast EPS	$1.96 (06/11/2018)	No of Institutions 80
Market Cap	$5.3 Billion	Shares
Book Value	$4.3 Billion	17,654,872
Price/Book	1.24	% Held
Price/Sales	5.84	N/A

TRADING VOLUME (thousand shares)

Business Summary: Banking (MIC: 5.1.1 SIC: 6021 NAIC: 522110)

Sterling is a bank holding company and financial holding company. Through its principal subsidiary, Sterling National Bank, Co. operates as a regional bank providing a range of deposit, lending and wealth management products to commercial, consumer and municipal clients in its market area within the New York Metro Market, which includes Manhattan and Long Island; and the New York Suburban Market, which includes Rockland, Orange, Sullivan, Ulster, Putnam and Westchester counties in New York and Bergen County in New Jersey. As of Dec 31 2017, Co. had total assets of $30.36 billion and total deposits of $20.54 billion.

Recent Developments: For the quarter ended Mar 31 2018, net income increased 153.1% to US$98.9 million from US$39.1 million in the year-earlier quarter. Net interest income increased 115.4% to US$234.4 million from US$108.8 million in the year-earlier quarter. Provision for loan losses was US$13.0 million versus US$4.5 million in the prior-year quarter, an increase of 188.9%. Non-interest income rose 45.7% to US$18.7 million from US$12.8 million, while non-interest expense advanced 85.2% to US$111.7 million.

Prospects: Our evaluation of Sterling Bancorp as of Jan. 21, 2018 is the result of our systematic analysis on three basic characteristics: earnings strength, relative valuation, and recent stock price movement. The company has generated a negative trend in earnings per share over the past 5 quarters and while recent estimates for the company have been mixed, STL has posted results that fell short of analysts expectations. Based on operating earnings yield, the company is undervalued when compared to all of the companies in our coverage universe. Share price changes over the past year indicates that STL will perform in line with the market over the near term.

Financial Data
(US$ in Thousands)

	3 Mos	12/31/2017	12/31/2016	12/31/2015	12/31/2014	09/30/2014	09/30/2013	09/30/2012
Earnings Per Share	0.72	0.58	1.07	0.60	0.20	0.34	0.58	0.52
Cash Flow Per Share	1.08	1.54	1.52	0.83	(1.03)	1.59	0.52	0.65
Tang Book Value Per Share	10.68	10.53	8.08	7.05	6.47	6.30	7.08	7.26
Dividends Per Share	0.280	0.280	0.280	0.280	0.070	0.270	0.240	0.240
Dividend Payout %	38.89	48.28	26.17	46.67	35.00	79.41	41.38	46.15
Income Statement								
Interest Income	281,346	682,449	461,551	348,141	68,087	246,906	132,061	115,037
Interest Expense	46,976	106,306	57,282	36,925	7,850	28,918	19,894	18,573
Net Interest Income	234,370	576,143	404,269	311,216	60,237	217,988	112,167	96,464
Provision for Losses	13,000	26,000	20,000	15,700	3,000	19,100	12,150	10,612
Non-Interest Income	18,707	64,202	70,987	62,751	13,957	47,370	27,692	32,152
Non-Interest Expense	111,749	433,375	247,902	260,318	45,814	208,428	91,041	91,957
Income Before Taxes	128,328	180,970	207,354	97,949	25,380	37,830	36,668	26,047
Income Taxes	29,456	87,939	67,382	31,835	8,376	10,152	11,414	6,159
Net Income	98,872	93,031	139,972	66,114	17,004	27,678	25,254	19,888
Average Shares	225,264	158,124	131,234	110,329	84,194	80,534	43,783	38,428
Balance Sheet								
Net Loans & Leases	19,901,593	19,936,322	9,505,497	7,843,325	4,819,866	4,737,672	2,385,032	2,098,695
Total Assets	30,468,780	30,359,541	14,178,447	11,955,952	7,424,822	7,337,387	4,049,172	4,022,982
Total Deposits	20,623,233	20,538,204	10,068,259	8,580,007	5,212,325	5,298,654	2,962,294	3,111,151
Total Liabilities	26,195,025	26,119,363	12,323,264	10,290,879	6,449,622	6,376,249	3,566,306	3,531,860
Stockholders' Equity	4,273,755	4,240,178	1,855,183	1,665,073	975,200	961,138	482,866	491,122
Shares Outstanding	225,466	224,782	135,257	130,006	83,927	83,628	44,351	44,173
Statistical Record								
Return on Assets %	0.68	0.42	1.07	0.68	1.18	0.49	0.63	0.55
Return on Equity %	4.96	3.05	7.93	5.01	9.25	3.83	5.19	4.30
Net Interest Margin %	83.30	84.42	87.59	89.39	88.47	88.29	84.94	83.85
Efficiency Ratio %	37.24	58.04	46.55	63.35	55.84	70.83	56.99	62.48
Loans to Deposits	0.97	0.97	0.94	0.91	0.92	0.89	0.81	0.67
Price Range	26.25-21.15	26.05-21.15	24.40-13.57	17.61-12.97	14.49-12.55	13.47-10.80	11.31-8.67	9.65-5.51
P/E Ratio	36.46-29.37	44.91-36.47	22.80-12.68	29.35-21.62	72.45-62.75	39.62-31.76	19.50-14.95	18.56-10.60
Average Yield %	1.18	1.19	1.62	1.93	0.52	2.20	2.52	3.08

Address: 400 Rella Boulevard, Montebello, NY 10901 Telephone: 845-369-8040	Web Site: www.sterlingbancorp.com Officers: Richard L. O'Toole - Chairman Jack L. Kopnisky - President, Chief Executive Officer	Auditors: Crowe Horwath LLP Investor Contact: 845-369-8040 Transfer Agents: Registrar and Transfer Company, Crandford, NJ

STORE CAPITAL CORP

Exchange	Symbol	Price	52Wk Range	Yield	P/E
NYS	STOR	$27.40 (6/29/2018)	27.40-21.75	4.53	28.25

*7 Year Price Score N/A   *NYSE Composite Index=100   *12 Month Price Score 104.79

Interim Earnings (Per Share)

Qtr.	Mar	Jun	Sep	Dec
2015	0.15	0.17	0.18	0.18
2016	0.18	0.21	0.24	0.20
2017	0.19	0.35	0.15	0.21
2018	0.26	...	...	...

Interim Dividends (Per Share)

Amt	Decl	Ex	Rec	Pay
0.31Q	09/12/2017	09/28/2017	09/29/2017	10/16/2017
0.31Q	12/15/2017	12/28/2017	12/29/2017	01/16/2018
0.31Q	03/15/2018	03/28/2018	03/30/2018	04/16/2018
0.31Q	06/15/2018	06/28/2018	06/29/2018	07/16/2018

Indicated Div: $1.24

Valuation Analysis / Institutional Holding

Forecast EPS	$0.91	No of Institutions
	(06/14/2018)	333
Market Cap	$5.4 Billion	Shares
Book Value	$3.3 Billion	202,625,040
Price/Book	1.66	% Held
Price/Sales	11.53	N/A

Business Summary: REITs (MIC: 5.3.1 SIC: 6798 NAIC: 525930)

STORE Capital is an internally managed net-lease real estate investment trust that is engaged in the acquisition, investment and management of Single Tenant Operational Real Estate. As of Dec 31 2017, Co. owned a portfolio that consisted of investments in 1,921 property locations operated by 400 customers across 48 states. Co.'s customers operate across a range of industries within the service, retail and manufacturing sectors, with restaurants, early childhood education centers, movie theaters, health clubs and furniture stores representing the key industries in Co.'s portfolio. From time to time, Co. also provides mortgage financing to its customers.

Recent Developments: For the quarter ended Mar 31 2018, net income increased 59.2% to US$50.0 million from US$31.4 million in the year-earlier quarter. Revenues were US$125.8 million, up 16.6% from US$108.0 million the year before. Revenues from property income rose 17.7% to US$119.9 million from US$101.9 million in the corresponding quarter a year earlier.

Prospects: Our evaluation of STORE Capital Corp as of Jan. 21, 2018 is the result of our systematic analysis on three basic characteristics: earnings strength, relative valuation, and recent stock price movement. The company has managed to produce a neutral trend in earnings per share over the past 5 quarters and while recent estimates for the company have remained steady, STOR has posted results that fell short of analysts expectations. Based on operating earnings yield, the company is about fairly valued when compared to all of the companies in our coverage universe. Share price changes over the past year indicates that STOR will perform well over the near term.

Financial Data
(US$ in Thousands)

	3 Mos	12/31/2017	12/31/2016	12/31/2015	12/31/2014	12/31/2013	12/31/2012	12/31/2011
Earnings Per Share	0.97	0.90	0.82	0.68	0.61	0.52	0.30	(0.11)
Cash Flow Per Share	1.68	1.73	1.65	1.52	1.38	1.10	0.82	0.09
Tang Book Value Per Share	16.47	16.36	15.58	14.62	13.74	12.29	11.76	...
Dividends Per Share	1.220	1.200	1.120	1.040	0.114	...	...	...
Dividend Payout %	125.77	133.33	136.59	152.94	18.67	...	...	...
Income Statement								
Total Revenue	125,842	452,847	376,343	284,762	190,441	108,904	40,610	3,860
EBITDA	73,339	411,553	349,550	264,361	177,110	97,991	32,458	(44)
Depn & Amortn	3,569	168,188	133,907	99,857	66,465	36,338	13,619	1,530
Income Before Taxes	40,431	122,887	110,463	82,722	42,686	22,473	7,367	(2,694)
Income Taxes	49	453	358	274	180	155	70	5
Net Income	49,960	162,038	123,325	83,770	48,139	26,313	8,176	(2,022)
Average Shares	194,876	178,656	149,124	122,207	78,454	49,893	27,338	18,706
Balance Sheet								
Current Assets	35,116	42,937	54,200	67,115	136,313	61,814	64,752	...
Total Assets	6,128,848	5,899,777	4,941,668	3,911,388	2,913,612	1,786,100	979,833	...
Current Liabilities	141,553	350,068	94,209	246,670	43,609	20,481	175,477	...
Long-Term Obligations	2,724,625	2,306,901	2,303,671	1,597,505	1,284,151	991,577	306,581	...
Total Liabilities	2,866,178	2,728,835	2,458,413	1,851,595	1,330,928	1,012,186	482,919	...
Stockholders' Equity	3,262,670	3,170,942	2,483,255	2,059,793	1,582,684	773,914	496,914	...
Shares Outstanding	198,044	193,766	159,341	140,858	115,212	62,966	42,247	18,703
Statistical Record								
Return on Assets %	3.14	2.99	2.78	2.45	2.05	1.90	...	...
Return on Equity %	6.02	5.73	5.41	4.60	4.09	4.14	...	...
EBITDA Margin %	58.28	90.88	92.88	92.84	93.00	89.98	79.93	N.M.
Net Margin %	39.70	35.78	32.77	29.42	25.28	24.16	20.13	N.M.
Asset Turnover	0.08	0.08	0.08	0.08	0.08	0.08	...	...
Current Ratio	0.25	0.12	0.58	0.27	3.13	3.02	0.37	...
Debt to Equity	0.84	0.73	0.93	0.78	0.81	1.28	0.62	...
Price Range	26.37-19.77	26.37-19.77	31.19-22.38	23.77-19.79	22.04-19.50	...	...	...
P/E Ratio	27.19-20.38	29.30-21.97	38.04-27.29	34.96-29.10	36.13-31.97	...	...	...
Average Yield %	5.07	4.99	4.21	4.77	0.55	...	...	...

Address: 8377 East Hartford Drive, Suite 100, Scottsdale, AZ 85255 Telephone: 480-256-1100	Web Site: www.storecapital.com Officers: Morton H. Fleischer - Chairman Christopher H. Volk - President, Chief Executive Officer	Auditors: Ernst & Young LLP Transfer Agents: American Stock Transfer & Trust Company, LLC

STRYKER CORP

Exchange	Symbol	Price	52Wk Range	Yield	P/E	Div Acheiver
NYS	SYK	$168.86 (6/29/2018)	179.78-138.22	1.11	63.24	25 Years

*7 Year Price Score 133.73 ***NYSE Composite Index=100** ***12 Month Price Score 108.02**

Interim Earnings (Per Share)

Qtr.	Mar	Jun	Sep	Dec
2015	0.58	1.03	0.79	1.38
2016	1.07	1.00	0.94	1.34
2017	1.17	1.03	1.14	(0.66)
2018	1.16	...	...	...

Interim Dividends (Per Share)

Amt	Decl	Ex	Rec	Pay
0.425Q	08/01/2017	09/28/2017	09/29/2017	10/31/2017
0.47Q	12/06/2017	12/28/2017	12/29/2017	01/31/2018
0.47Q	02/07/2018	03/28/2018	03/29/2018	04/30/2018
0.47Q	05/02/2018	06/28/2018	06/29/2018	07/31/2018

Indicated Div: $1.88

Valuation Analysis / Institutional Holding

Forecast EPS	$7.23	No of Institutions	1569
	(06/13/2018)		
Market Cap	$63.1 Billion	Shares	341,402,080
Book Value	$9.2 Billion	% Held	
Price/Book	6.85		69.99
Price/Sales	4.96		

Business Summary: Medical Instruments & Equipment (MIC: 4.3.1 SIC: 3841 NAIC: 339112)

Stryker is a medical technology company. Co. segregates its operations into three reportable business segments, Orthopaedics, MedSurg, and Neurotechnology and Spine. The Orthopaedics segment includes reconstructive (hip and knee) and trauma implant systems and other related products. The MedSurg segment includes surgical equipment and surgical navigation systems; endoscopic and communications systems; patient handling, emergency medical equipment, intensive care disposable products and reprocessed and remanufactured medical devices and other related products. The Neurotechnology and Spine segment includes neurovascular products, spinal implant systems and other related products.

Recent Developments: For the quarter ended Mar 31 2018, net income decreased 0.2% to US$443.0 million from US$444.0 million in the year-earlier quarter. Revenues were US$3.24 billion, up 9.7% from US$2.96 billion the year before. Operating income was US$591.0 million versus US$556.0 million in the prior-year quarter, an increase of 6.3%. Direct operating expenses rose 11.4% to US$1.10 billion from US$991.0 million in the comparable period the year before. Indirect operating expenses increased 9.8% to US$1.55 billion from US$1.41 billion in the equivalent prior-year period.

Prospects: Our evaluation of Stryker Corp. as of Jan. 21, 2018 is the result of our systematic analysis on three basic characteristics: earnings strength, relative valuation, and recent stock price movement. The company has managed to produce a neutral trend in earnings per share over the past 5 quarters and while recent estimates for the company have been mixed, SYK has posted better than expected results. Based on operating earnings yield, the company is about fairly valued when compared to all of the companies in our coverage universe. Share price changes over the past year indicates that SYK will perform well over the near term.

Financial Data
(US$ in Thousands)

	3 Mos	12/31/2017	12/31/2016	12/31/2015	12/31/2014	12/31/2013	12/31/2012	12/31/2011
Earnings Per Share	2.67	2.68	4.35	3.78	1.34	2.63	3.39	3.45
Cash Flow Per Share	4.56	4.17	4.83	2.39	4.71	4.98	4.34	3.71
Tang Book Value Per Share	N.M.	N.M.	N.M.	6.92	6.33	8.50	13.24	10.94
Dividends Per Share	1.790	1.745	1.565	1.415	1.260	1.100	0.902	0.752
Dividend Payout %	67.04	65.11	35.98	37.43	94.03	41.83	26.62	21.81
Income Statement								
Total Revenue	3,241,000	12,444,000	11,325,000	9,946,000	9,675,000	9,021,000	8,657,000	8,307,000
EBITDA	718,000	2,705,000	2,467,000	2,132,000	1,538,000	1,519,000	1,982,000	1,968,000
Depn & Amortn	176,000	642,000	546,000	397,000	378,000	307,000	277,000	282,000
Income Before Taxes	542,000	2,063,000	1,921,000	1,735,000	1,160,000	1,212,000	1,705,000	1,686,000
Income Taxes	99,000	1,043,000	274,000	296,000	645,000	206,000	407,000	341,000
Net Income	443,000	1,020,000	1,647,000	1,439,000	515,000	1,006,000	1,298,000	1,345,000
Average Shares	380,700	380,100	378,500	380,900	382,800	382,100	383,000	389,500
Balance Sheet								
Current Assets	7,851,000	7,993,000	7,861,000	7,944,000	9,673,000	8,335,000	8,148,000	7,211,000
Total Assets	22,133,000	22,197,000	20,435,000	16,247,000	17,713,000	15,743,000	13,206,000	12,405,000
Current Liabilities	4,800,000	3,485,000	3,148,000	3,503,000	4,464,000	2,657,000	1,876,000	1,828,000
Long-Term Obligations	5,920,000	6,590,000	6,686,000	3,253,000	3,246,000	2,739,000	1,746,000	1,751,000
Total Liabilities	12,919,000	12,231,000	10,885,000	7,736,000	9,118,000	6,696,000	4,609,000	4,722,000
Stockholders' Equity	9,214,000	9,966,000	9,550,000	8,511,000	8,595,000	9,047,000	8,597,000	7,683,000
Shares Outstanding	373,710	374,400	375,000	373,000	378,000	378,000	380,000	381,000
Statistical Record								
Return on Assets %	4.78	4.79	8.96	8.47	3.08	6.95	10.11	11.55
Return on Equity %	10.77	10.45	18.19	16.82	5.84	11.40	15.90	18.11
EBITDA Margin %	22.15	21.74	21.78	21.44	15.90	16.84	22.89	23.69
Net Margin %	13.67	8.20	14.54	14.47	5.32	11.15	14.99	16.19
Asset Turnover	0.60	0.58	0.62	0.59	0.58	0.62	0.67	0.71
Current Ratio	1.64	2.29	2.50	2.27	2.17	3.14	4.34	3.94
Debt to Equity	0.64	0.66	0.70	0.38	0.38	0.30	0.20	0.23
Price Range	168.91-129.93	159.74-117.75	122.82-87.53	104.53-90.07	96.61-74.63	75.39-54.82	56.57-49.84	65.07-43.80
P/E Ratio	63.26-48.66	59.60-43.94	28.23-20.12	27.65-23.83	72.10-55.69	28.67-20.84	16.69-14.70	18.86-12.70
Average Yield %	1.21	1.25	1.42	1.48	1.52	1.62	1.34	1.37

Address: 2825 Airview Boulevard, Kalamazoo, MI 49002	**Web Site:** www.stryker.com	**Auditors:** Ernst & Young LLP
Telephone: 269-385-2600	**Officers:** Kevin A. Lobo - Chairman, President, Chief Executive Officer Glenn S. Boehnlein - Vice President, Chief Financial Officer	**Investor Contact:** 269-385-2600
Fax: 269-385-1062		**Transfer Agents:** American Stock Transfer & Trust Company, LLC, New York, NY

SUN COMMUNITIES INC

Exchange	Symbol	Price	52Wk Range	Yield	P/E
NYS	SUI	$97.88 (6/29/2018)	98.29-83.96	2.90	104.13

*7 Year Price Score 118.89 *NYSE Composite Index=100 *12 Month Price Score 104.15

Interim Earnings (Per Share)

Qtr.	Mar	Jun	Sep	Dec
2015	0.13	0.23	0.54	1.62
2016	0.14	(0.12)	0.27	(0.04)
2017	0.29	0.16	0.31	0.09
2018	0.38	...	...	...

Interim Dividends (Per Share)

Amt	Decl	Ex	Rec	Pay
0.67Q	09/05/2017	09/28/2017	09/29/2017	10/16/2017
0.67Q	12/11/2017	12/28/2017	12/29/2017	01/16/2018
0.71Q	03/06/2018	03/28/2018	03/29/2018	04/16/2018
0.71Q	05/22/2018	06/28/2018	06/29/2018	07/16/2018

Indicated Div: $2.84

Valuation Analysis — **Institutional Holding**

Forecast EPS	$1.47	No of Institutions
	(06/14/2018)	401
Market Cap	$7.8 Billion	Shares
Book Value	$2.6 Billion	89,243,792
Price/Book	2.99	% Held
Price/Sales	7.77	96.47

Business Summary: REITs (MIC: 5.3.1 SIC: 6798 NAIC: 525930)

Sun Communities is a self-administered and self-managed real estate investment trust. Co. is in the business of acquiring, operating, developing and expanding manufactured housing and recreational vehicle (RV) communities. Co. leases individual parcels of land with utility access for placement of manufactured homes and RVs to its customers. Co., through its subsidiary, Sun Home Services, Inc. (SHS), is engaged in the marketing, selling, and leasing of new and pre-owned homes to residents in Co.'s communities. At Dec 31 2017, Co. owned, operated or had an interest in a portfolio of 350 properties in 29 states and Ontario, Canada, while SHS had 11,074 occupied leased homes in its portfolio.

Recent Developments: For the quarter ended Mar 31 2018, net income increased 31.5% to US$33.6 million from US$25.5 million in the year-earlier quarter. Revenues were US$257.9 million, up 10.0% from US$234.4 million the year before. Revenues from property income rose 7.6% to US$210.2 million from US$195.4 million in the corresponding quarter a year earlier.

Prospects: Our evaluation of Sun Communities Inc. as of Jan. 21, 2018 is the result of our systematic analysis on three basic characteristics: earnings strength, relative valuation, and recent stock price movement. The company has managed to produce a neutral trend in earnings per share over the past 5 quarters. Because the company lacks sufficient analyst estimate data, we place greater weight on the historical EPS trend as the measure of earnings strength. Based on operating earnings yield, the company is overvalued when compared to all of the companies in our coverage universe. Share price changes over the past year indicates that SUI will perform very well over the near term.

Financial Data
(US$ in Thousands)

	3 Mos	12/31/2017	12/31/2016	12/31/2015	12/31/2014	12/31/2013	12/31/2012	12/31/2011
Earnings Per Share	0.94	0.85	0.26	2.52	0.54	0.31	0.18	(0.05)
Cash Flow Per Share	3.45	3.44	3.61	3.39	3.23	3.30	3.19	3.00
Tang Book Value Per Share	32.73	33.15	32.27	26.35	18.36	10.53	6.47	...
Dividends Per Share	2.720	2.680	2.600	2.600	2.600	2.520	2.520	3.150
Dividend Payout %	289.36	315.29	1,000.00	103.17	481.48	812.90	1,400.00	...
Income Statement								
Total Revenue	257,916	982,570	833,778	674,731	471,675	415,222	339,616	289,185
EBITDA	131,622	213,839	168,999	435,978	241,255	202,632	163,630	140,645
Depn & Amortn	66,437	1,914	600	160,969	132,059	107,923	88,106	75,191
Income Before Taxes	33,428	81,683	46,084	164,131	32,215	18,132	4,344	(2,485)
Income Taxes	(173)	(136)	283	1,158	219	234	249	150
Net Income	31,507	76,764	31,321	160,419	31,444	19,430	8,313	136
Average Shares	79,464	76,711	66,321	53,702	41,805	34,747	27,272	21,147
Balance Sheet								
Current Assets	245,315	10,127	8,164	45,086	83,459	4,753	29,508	5,857
Total Assets	6,149,653	6,111,957	5,870,776	4,190,551	2,937,692	1,999,236	1,754,117	1,367,974
Current Liabilities	3,008,965	41,257	100,095	25,000	5,794	181,383	29,781	129,034
Long-Term Obligations	179,138	3,037,981	3,009,947	2,320,049	1,826,293	1,311,437	1,423,720	1,268,191
Total Liabilities	3,535,115	3,470,460	3,508,221	2,651,944	2,045,953	1,618,729	1,561,595	1,494,583
Stockholders' Equity	2,614,538	2,641,497	2,362,555	1,538,607	891,739	380,507	192,522	(126,609)
Shares Outstanding	79,885	79,679	73,206	58,395	48,573	36,140	29,755	21,810
Statistical Record								
Return on Assets %	1.39	1.28	0.62	4.50	1.27	1.04	0.53	0.01
Return on Equity %	3.37	3.07	1.60	13.20	4.94	6.78	25.16	...
EBITDA Margin %	51.03	21.76	20.27	64.62	51.15	48.80	48.18	48.63
Net Margin %	12.22	7.81	3.76	23.78	6.67	4.68	2.45	0.05
Asset Turnover	0.17	0.16	0.17	0.19	0.19	0.22	0.22	0.23
Current Ratio	0.08	0.25	0.08	1.80	14.40	0.03	0.99	0.05
Debt to Equity	0.07	1.15	1.27	1.51	2.05	3.45	7.40	...
Price Range	95.60-80.03	95.60-76.13	81.55-63.81	71.27-60.66	63.97-41.98	56.89-39.87	47.29-36.16	39.92-31.16
P/E Ratio	101.70-85.14	112.47-89.56	313.65-245.42	28.28-23.99	118.46-77.74	183.52-128.61	262.72-200.89	...
Average Yield %	3.07	3.10	3.58	3.93	5.15	5.45	5.94	8.71

Address: 27777 Franklin Rd., Suite 200, Southfield, MI 48034 **Telephone:** 248-208-2500	**Web Site:** www.suncommunities.com **Officers:** Gary A. Shiffman - Chairman, President, Chief Executive Officer John B. McLaren - President, Executive Vice President, Chief Operating Officer	**Auditors:** GRANT THORNTON LLP **Investor Contact:** 248-208-2500 **Transfer Agents:** Computershare Trust Company, N.A., Providence, RI

SUNTRUST BANKS INC

Exchange	Symbol	Price	52Wk Range	Yield	P/E
NYS	STI	$66.02 (6/29/2018)	72.85-52.30	2.42	13.61

*7 Year Price Score 127.35 *NYSE Composite Index=100 *12 Month Price Score 105.59

TRADING VOLUME (thousand shares)

Interim Earnings (Per Share)

Qtr.	Mar	Jun	Sep	Dec
2015	0.78	0.89	1.00	0.91
2016	0.84	0.94	0.91	0.90
2017	0.91	1.03	1.06	1.47
2018	1.29	...	...	...

Interim Dividends (Per Share)

Amt	Decl	Ex	Rec	Pay
0.40Q	08/08/2017	08/29/2017	08/31/2017	09/15/2017
0.40Q	11/15/2017	11/29/2017	11/30/2017	12/15/2017
0.40Q	02/13/2018	02/27/2018	02/28/2018	03/15/2018
0.40Q	04/24/2018	05/30/2018	05/31/2018	06/15/2018

Indicated Div: $1.60 (Div. Reinv. Plan)

Valuation Analysis / Institutional Holding

Forecast EPS	$5.34 (06/14/2018)	No of Institutions	1197
Market Cap	$31.0 Billion	Shares	520,093,632
Book Value	$24.3 Billion	% Held	78.59
Price/Book	1.28		
Price/Sales	3.15		

Business Summary: Banking (MIC: 5.1.1 SIC: 6021 NAIC: 522110)

SunTrust Banks is a financial holding company. Through its subsidiary, SunTrust Bank (the Bank), Co. provides a line of financial services for consumers, businesses, corporations, and institutions, and not-for-profit entities, both through its branches. In addition to deposit, credit, mortgage banking, and trust and investment services provided by the Bank, other subsidiaries of Co. provide asset and wealth management, securities brokerage, and capital market services. Co. operates three business segments: Consumer Banking and Private Wealth Management, Wholesale Banking, and Mortgage Banking. As of Dec 31 2017, Co. had total assets of $205.96 billion and total deposits of $160.78 billion.

Recent Developments: For the quarter ended Mar 31 2018, net income increased 37.2% to US$645.0 million from US$470.0 million in the year-earlier quarter. Net interest income increased 5.5% to US$1.44 billion from US$1.37 billion in the year-earlier quarter. Provision for loan losses was US$28.0 million versus US$119.0 million in the prior-year quarter, a decrease of 76.5%. Non-interest income fell 6.0% to US$796.0 million from US$847.0 million, while non-interest expense declined 3.3% to US$1.42 billion.

Prospects: Our evaluation of SunTrust Banks Inc. as of Jan. 21, 2018 is the result of our systematic analysis on three basic characteristics: earnings strength, relative valuation, and recent stock price movement. The company has enjoyed a very positive trend in earnings per share over the past 5 quarters. Because the company lacks sufficient analyst estimate data, we place greater weight on the historical EPS trend as the measure of earnings strength. Based on operating earnings yield, the company is undervalued when compared to all of the companies in our coverage universe. Share price changes over the past year indicates that STI will perform in line with the market over the near term.

Financial Data
(US$ in Thousands)

	3 Mos	12/31/2017	12/31/2016	12/31/2015	12/31/2014	12/31/2013	12/31/2012	12/31/2011
Earnings Per Share	4.85	4.47	3.60	3.58	3.23	2.41	3.59	0.94
Cash Flow Per Share	6.85	11.45	(1.36)	6.79	(2.24)	7.88	3.75	8.83
Tang Book Value Per Share	29.63	30.91	29.31	28.60	27.12	24.24	24.00	23.15
Dividends Per Share	1.460	1.320	1.000	0.920	0.700	0.350	0.200	0.120
Dividend Payout %	30.10	29.53	27.78	25.70	21.67	14.52	5.57	12.77
Income Statement								
Interest Income	1,668,000	6,387,000	5,778,000	5,265,000	5,384,000	5,388,000	5,867,000	6,181,000
Interest Expense	227,000	754,000	557,000	501,000	544,000	535,000	765,000	1,116,000
Net Interest Income	1,441,000	5,633,000	5,221,000	4,764,000	4,840,000	4,853,000	5,102,000	5,065,000
Provision for Losses	28,000	409,000	444,000	165,000	342,000	553,000	1,395,000	1,513,000
Non-Interest Income	796,000	3,354,000	3,383,000	3,268,000	3,323,000	3,214,000	5,373,000	3,421,000
Non-Interest Expense	1,417,000	5,764,000	5,468,000	5,160,000	5,543,000	5,880,000	6,307,000	6,237,000
Income Before Taxes	792,000	2,814,000	2,692,000	2,707,000	2,278,000	1,634,000	2,757,000	739,000
Income Taxes	147,000	532,000	805,000	764,000	493,000	273,000	773,000	79,000
Net Income	643,000	2,273,000	1,878,000	1,933,000	1,774,000	1,344,000	1,958,000	647,000
Average Shares	473,620	486,954	503,466	520,586	533,391	539,093	538,061	527,618
Balance Sheet								
Net Loans & Leases	143,301,000	143,736,000	145,758,000	136,528,000	134,407,000	127,532,000	122,695,000	122,391,000
Total Assets	204,885,000	205,962,000	204,875,000	190,817,000	190,328,000	175,335,000	173,442,000	176,859,000
Total Deposits	162,379,000	160,780,000	160,398,000	149,830,000	140,567,000	129,759,000	132,316,000	127,922,000
Total Liabilities	180,616,000	180,808,000	181,257,000	167,380,000	167,323,000	153,913,000	152,457,000	156,793,000
Stockholders' Equity	24,269,000	25,154,000	23,618,000	23,437,000	23,005,000	21,422,000	20,985,000	20,066,000
Shares Outstanding	469,708	470,931	491,188	508,712	524,540	536,097	538,959	536,967
Statistical Record								
Return on Assets %	1.19	1.11	0.95	1.01	0.97	0.77	1.11	0.37
Return on Equity %	10.26	9.32	7.96	8.32	7.99	6.34	9.51	3.00
Net Interest Margin %	86.39	88.19	90.36	90.48	89.90	90.07	86.96	81.94
Efficiency Ratio %	57.51	59.17	59.69	60.47	63.66	68.36	56.11	64.96
Loans to Deposits	0.88	0.89	0.91	0.91	0.96	0.98	0.93	0.96
Price Range	72.85-52.30	66.03-52.30	56.39-31.36	45.35-36.71	42.69-34.73	36.81-27.12	30.31-18.52	32.59-15.80
P/E Ratio	15.02-10.78	14.77-11.70	15.66-8.71	12.67-10.25	13.22-10.75	15.27-11.25	8.44-5.16	34.67-16.81
Average Yield %	2.41	2.29	2.35	2.20	1.81	1.10	0.81	0.50

Address: 303 Peachtree Street, N.E., Atlanta, GA 30308 **Telephone:** 800-786-8787	**Web Site:** www.suntrust.com **Officers:** William H. Rogers - Chairman, President, Chief Executive Officer Mark A. Chancy - Vice-Chairman, Co-Chief Operating Officer, Division Officer, Executive Vice President	**Auditors:** Ernst & Young LLP **Investor Contact:** 877-930-8971 **Transfer Agents:** Computershare, Providence, RI

SUPERIOR ENERGY SERVICES, INC.

Exchange	Symbol	Price	52Wk Range	Yield	P/E
NYS	SPN	$9.74 (6/29/2018)	12.47-7.89	N/A	N/A

*7 Year Price Score 37.94   *NYSE Composite Index=100   *12 Month Price Score 108.11

Interim Earnings (Per Share)

Qtr.	Mar	Jun	Sep	Dec
2015	(0.07)	(5.22)	(5.45)	(1.57)
2016	(0.57)	(3.11)	(0.78)	(1.39)
2017	(0.60)	(0.42)	(0.39)	0.06
2018	(0.39)	...	...	...

Interim Dividends (Per Share)

Dividend Payment Suspended

Valuation Analysis   Institutional Holding

Forecast EPS	$-0.79	No of Institutions
	(06/14/2018)	448
Market Cap	$1.5 Billion	Shares
Book Value	$1.1 Billion	194,906,384
Price/Book	1.39	% Held
Price/Sales	0.77	95.04

Business Summary: Equipment & Services (MIC: 9.1.3 SIC: 1389 NAIC: 213112)
Superior Energy Services provide a range of services and products to the energy industry. Co. serves major, national and independent oil and natural gas exploration and production companies. Co. reports its operating results in four business segments: Drilling Products and Services, which includes downhole drilling tools and surface rentals; Onshore Completion and Workover Services, which include pressure pumping, fluid handling and workover and maintenance services; Production Services, which include intervention services; and Technical Solutions, which include well containment systems, completion tools and services and end-of-life services.

Recent Developments: For the quarter ended Mar 31 2018, loss from continuing operations was US$59.9 million compared with a loss of US$89.7 million in the year-earlier quarter. Net loss amounted to US$59.7 million versus a net loss of US$91.7 million in the year-earlier quarter. Revenues were US$482.3 million, up 20.3% from US$400.9 million the year before. Operating loss was US$42.7 million versus a loss of US$110.8 million in the prior-year quarter. Direct operating expenses rose 6.7% to US$343.5 million from US$322.0 million in the comparable period the year before. Indirect operating expenses decreased 4.3% to US$181.5 million from US$189.8 million in the equivalent prior-year period.

Prospects: Our evaluation of Superior Energy Services Inc. as of Jan. 21, 2018 is the result of our systematic analysis on three basic characteristics: earnings strength, relative valuation, and recent stock price movement. The company has enjoyed a very positive trend in earnings per share over the past 5 quarters. Because the company lacks sufficient analyst estimate data, we place greater weight on the historical EPS trend as the measure of earnings strength. Based on operating earnings yield, the company is overvalued when compared to all of the companies in our coverage universe. Share price changes over the past year indicates that SPN will perform very poorly over the near term.

Financial Data
(US$ in Thousands)

	3 Mos	12/31/2017	12/31/2016	12/31/2015	12/31/2014	12/31/2013	12/31/2012	12/31/2011
Earnings Per Share	(1.14)	(1.35)	(5.85)	(12.33)	1.65	(0.70)	2.42	1.76
Cash Flow Per Share	0.79	0.68	0.40	4.20	6.66	5.61	6.91	6.19
Tang Book Value Per Share	1.74	2.12	3.29	7.10	10.76	10.51	10.76	10.85
Dividends Per Share	...	...	0.080	0.320	0.320	0.080	...	...
Dividend Payout %	...	...	...	...	19.39	...	...	...
Income Statement								
Total Revenue	482,318	1,874,076	1,450,047	2,774,565	4,556,622	4,611,824	4,568,068	2,070,166
EBITDA	61,303	142,904	(520,688)	(1,378,365)	1,159,523	625,391	1,185,081	497,523
Depn & Amortn	105,719	419,200	486,900	584,100	620,600	593,000	480,000	224,600
Income Before Taxes	(69,303)	(377,751)	(1,100,341)	(2,059,783)	442,189	(71,585)	590,569	205,306
Income Taxes	(9,355)	(190,740)	(267,001)	(252,020)	161,399	39,833	225,020	79,146
Net Income	(59,724)	(205,921)	(886,899)	(1,854,718)	257,817	(111,418)	365,935	142,554
Average Shares	154,121	152,933	151,558	150,461	156,726	159,206	151,106	81,095
Balance Sheet								
Current Assets	732,365	760,819	781,551	1,295,125	1,728,811	1,476,429	1,460,357	883,222
Total Assets	3,064,763	3,110,225	3,470,255	4,914,244	7,377,389	7,411,307	7,802,886	4,048,145
Current Liabilities	393,116	375,197	344,534	448,576	712,047	639,400	772,065	393,533
Long-Term Obligations	1,280,569	1,279,771	1,284,600	1,588,263	1,627,842	1,646,535	1,814,500	1,685,087
Total Liabilities	1,986,594	1,977,796	2,166,335	2,703,432	3,297,651	3,279,863	3,571,807	2,594,546
Stockholders' Equity	1,078,169	1,132,429	1,303,920	2,210,812	4,079,738	4,131,444	4,231,079	1,453,599
Shares Outstanding	154,237	153,263	151,861	150,861	149,708	159,158	157,933	80,425
Statistical Record								
Return on Assets %	N.M.	N.M.	N.M.	N.M.	3.49	N.M.	6.16	4.10
Return on Equity %	N.M.	N.M.	N.M.	N.M.	6.28	N.M.	12.84	10.43
EBITDA Margin %	12.71	7.63	N.M.	N.M.	25.45	13.56	25.94	24.03
Net Margin %	N.M.	N.M.	N.M.	N.M.	5.66	N.M.	8.01	6.89
Asset Turnover	0.61	0.57	0.34	0.45	0.62	0.61	0.77	0.60
Current Ratio	1.86	2.03	2.27	2.89	2.43	2.31	1.89	2.24
Debt to Equity	1.19	1.13	0.99	0.72	0.40	0.40	0.43	1.16
Price Range	14.90-7.89	19.03-7.89	19.50-8.59	26.28-12.59	36.69-17.19	28.86-20.72	30.98-17.89	41.89-23.52
P/E Ratio	...	...	...	...	...	22.24-10.42	...	12.80-7.39	23.80-13.36
Average Yield %	...	...	0.53	1.70	1.08	0.31	...	...

Address: 1001 Louisiana Street, Suite 2900, Houston, TX 77002 **Telephone:** 713-654-2200	**Web Site:** www.superiorenergy.com **Officers:** Terence E. Hall - Chairman, President, Chief Executive Officer David D. (Dave) Dunlap - President, Chief Executive Officer	**Auditors:** KPMG LLP **Investor Contact:** 281-999-0047 **Transfer Agents:** Jones, Walker, LLP

SUPERVALU INC

Exchange	Symbol	Price	52Wk Range	Yield	P/E
NYS	SVU	$20.52 (6/29/2018)	26.18-13.73	N/A	17.39

*7 Year Price Score 37.05 *NYSE Composite Index=100 *12 Month Price Score 98.63

TRADING VOLUME (thousand shares)

Interim Earnings (Per Share)

Qtr.	Jun	Sep	Nov	Feb
2014-15	1.19	0.77	2.10	1.05
Qtr.	Jun	Sep	Dec	Feb
2015-16	1.61	0.77	0.91	1.33
2016-17	1.19	0.84	(0.70)	15.68
2017-18	0.28	(0.65)	0.67	0.87

Interim Dividends (Per Share)

Dividend Payment Suspended

Valuation Analysis	Institutional Holding	
Forecast EPS	$1.85	No of Institutions
	(06/12/2018)	382
Market Cap	$779.8 Million	Shares
Book Value	$505.0 Million	113,004,048
Price/Book	1.54	% Held
Price/Sales	0.06	90.27

Business Summary: Retail - Food & Beverage, Drug & Tobacco (MIC: 2.1.2 SIC: 5411 NAIC: 445110)

Supervalu is a public company grocery distributor to wholesale customers across the U.S. Co.'s business is classified by management into two reportable segments: Wholesale, which provides wholesale customers a range of food and non-food products, including national and regional brands, and Co.'s owns extensive lines of private label products; and Retail, which provides a range of nationally advertised brand name and private-label products, including grocery (both perishable and nonperishable), general merchandise, home, health and beauty care, and pharmacy.

Recent Developments: For the year ended Feb 24 2018, income from continuing operations increased 40.0% to US$49.0 million from US$35.0 million a year earlier. Net income decreased 93.0% to US$46.0 million from US$654.0 million in the prior year. Revenues were US$14.16 billion, up 29.7% from US$10.91 billion the year before. Operating income was US$193.0 million versus US$195.0 million in the prior year, a decrease of 1.0%. Direct operating expenses rose 33.5% to US$12.71 billion from US$9.52 billion in the comparable period the year before. Indirect operating expenses increased 4.8% to US$1.26 billion from US$1.20 billion in the equivalent prior-year period.

Prospects: Our evaluation of SUPERVALU Inc. as of Jan. 21, 2018 is the result of our systematic analysis on three basic characteristics: earnings strength, relative valuation, and recent stock price movement. The company has managed to produce a neutral trend in earnings per share over the past 5 quarters and while recent estimates for the company have been raised by analysts, SVU has posted better than expected results. Based on operating earnings yield, the company is undervalued when compared to all of the companies in our coverage universe. Share price changes over the past year indicates that SVU will perform in line with the market over the near term.

Financial Data

(US$ in Thousands)	02/24/2018	02/25/2017	02/27/2016	02/28/2015	02/22/2014	02/23/2013	02/25/2012	02/26/2011
Earnings Per Share	1.18	17.01	4.62	5.11	4.90	(48.37)	(34.37)	(49.91)
Cash Flow Per Share	3.56	9.56	11.32	10.81	0.52	29.73	34.96	38.51
Dividends Per Share	...	...	...	...	...	0.613	2.450	2.450
Income Statement								
Total Revenue	14,157,000	12,480,000	17,529,000	17,820,000	17,155,000	17,097,000	36,100,000	37,534,000
EBITDA	363,000	362,000	702,000	682,000	693,000	176,000	271,000	(151,000)
Depn & Amortn	170,000	179,000	248,000	258,000	275,000	333,000	790,000	825,000
Income Before Taxes	61,000	2,000	258,000	181,000	11,000	(426,000)	(1,028,000)	(1,523,000)
Income Taxes	28,000	(20,000)	85,000	58,000	5,000	(163,000)	12,000	(13,000)
Net Income	45,000	650,000	178,000	192,000	182,000	(1,466,000)	(1,040,000)	(1,510,000)
Average Shares	38,000	38,285	38,285	37,714	36,857	30,285	30,285	30,285
Balance Sheet								
Current Assets	1,861,000	1,541,000	1,635,000	1,700,000	1,543,000	2,970,000	3,225,000	3,420,000
Total Assets	4,387,000	3,580,000	4,370,000	4,485,000	4,374,000	11,034,000	12,053,000	13,758,000
Current Liabilities	1,548,000	1,229,000	1,572,000	1,533,000	1,491,000	4,350,000	3,590,000	3,786,000
Long-Term Obligations	1,873,000	1,449,000	2,400,000	2,693,000	2,732,000	2,815,000	5,868,000	6,348,000
Total Liabilities	3,882,000	3,204,000	4,811,000	5,131,000	5,112,000	12,449,000	12,032,000	12,418,000
Stockholders' Equity	505,000	376,000	(441,000)	(646,000)	(738,000)	(1,415,000)	21,000	1,340,000
Shares Outstanding	38,000	38,285	37,857	37,142	36,571	30,428	30,285	30,285
Statistical Record								
Return on Assets %	1.13	16.40	4.03	4.26	2.37	N.M.	N.M.	N.M.
Return on Equity %	10.24	...	...	...	...	...	N.M.	N.M.
EBITDA Margin %	2.56	2.90	4.00	3.83	4.04	1.03	0.75	N.M.
Net Margin %	0.32	5.21	1.02	1.08	1.06	N.M.	N.M.	N.M.
Asset Turnover	3.56	3.15	3.97	3.96	2.23	1.49	2.80	2.49
Current Ratio	1.20	1.25	1.04	1.11	1.03	0.68	0.90	0.90
Debt to Equity	3.71	3.85	...	...	...	...	279.43	4.74
Price Range	29.54-13.73	41.79-25.69	83.30-28.56	73.01-42.84	58.80-26.32	46.34-12.11	79.66-44.80	122.29-50.61
P/E Ratio	25.03-11.64	2.46-1.51	18.03-6.18	14.29-8.38	12.00-5.37	...	...	...
Average Yield %	...	...	...	...	...	2.31	4.24	3.02

Address: 11840 Valley View Road,	Web Site: www.supervalu.com	Auditors: KPMG LLP
Eden Prairie, MN 55344	Officers: Mark Gross - President, Chief Executive	Investor Contact: 952-828-4000
Telephone: 952-828-4000	Officer Robert N. Woseth - Chief Financial Officer,	Transfer Agents: Wells Fargo
	Executive Vice President, Chief Strategy Officer	Shareowner Services, St. Paul, MN

SYNCHRONY FINANCIAL

Exchange	Symbol	Price	52Wk Range	Yield	P/E
NYS	SYF	$33.38 (6/29/2018)	40.21-28.55	1.80	12.69

*7 Year Price Score N/A   *NYSE Composite Index=100   *12 Month Price Score 99.70

TRADING VOLUME (thousand shares)

Interim Earnings (Per Share)

Qtr.	Mar	Jun	Sep	Dec
2015	0.66	0.65	0.69	0.65
2016	0.70	0.58	0.73	0.70
2017	0.61	0.61	0.70	0.49
2018	0.83	...	...	...

Interim Dividends (Per Share)

Amt	Decl	Ex	Rec	Pay
0.15Q	07/26/2017	08/03/2017	08/07/2017	08/17/2017
0.15Q	10/25/2017	11/03/2017	11/06/2017	11/16/2017
0.15Q	01/23/2018	02/02/2018	02/05/2018	02/15/2018
0.15Q	04/25/2018	05/04/2018	05/07/2018	05/17/2018

Indicated Div: $0.60

Valuation Analysis

		Institutional Holding	
Forecast EPS	$3.42	No of Institutions	
	(06/14/2018)	826	
Market Cap	$25.4 Billion	Shares	
Book Value	$14.4 Billion	740,881,152	
Price/Book	1.77	% Held	
Price/Sales	1.49	N/A	

Business Summary: Banking (MIC: 5.1.1 SIC: 6141 NAIC: 522291)

Synchrony Financial is a savings and loan holding company. Co. provides a range of credit products through programs it has established with a group of national and regional retailers, local merchants, manufacturers, buying groups, industry associations and healthcare service providers. Co. provides its credit products primarily through its wholly-owned subsidiary, Synchrony Bank (the Bank). Through the Bank, Co. provides deposit products insured by the Federal Deposit Insurance Corporation, including certificates of deposit, individual retirement accounts, money market accounts and savings accounts. At Dec 31 2017, Co. had total assets of $95.81 billion and total deposits of $56.49 billion.

Recent Developments: For the quarter ended Mar 31 2018, net income increased 28.3% to US$640.0 million from US$499.0 million in the year-earlier quarter. Net interest income increased 7.1% to US$3.84 billion from US$3.59 billion in the year-earlier quarter. Provision for loan losses was US$1.36 billion versus US$1.31 billion in the prior-year quarter, an increase of 4.3%. Non-interest income fell 19.4% to US$75.0 million from US$93.0 million, while non-interest expense advanced 7.3% to US$1.71 billion.

Prospects: Our evaluation of Synchrony Financial as of Jan. 21, 2018 is the result of our systematic analysis on three basic characteristics: earnings strength, relative valuation, and recent stock price movement. The company has generated a negative trend in earnings per share over the past 5 quarters. Because the company lacks sufficient analyst estimate data, we place greater weight on the historical EPS trend as the measure of earnings strength. Based on operating earnings yield, the company is undervalued when compared to all of the companies in our coverage universe. Share price changes over the past year indicates that SYF will perform poorly over the near term.

Financial Data
(US$ in Millions)

	3 Mos	12/31/2017	12/31/2016	12/31/2015	12/31/2014	12/31/2013	12/31/2012	12/31/2011
Earnings Per Share	2.63	2.42	2.71	2.65	2.78	2.81	3.00	...
Cash Flow Per Share	11.89	11.21	8.21	7.42	7.05	...	...	...
Tang Book Value Per Share	16.55	16.21	15.34	13.14	10.81	...	...	...
Dividends Per Share	0.580	0.560	0.260	...	...	...	...	...
Dividend Payout %	22.05	23.14	9.59	...	...	...	...	...
Income Statement								
Total Revenue	4,319	16,695	15,122	13,620	12,727	11,813	10,793	9,638
Income Before Taxes	847	3,324	3,570	3,531	3,386	3,142	3,376	3,010
Income Taxes	207	1,389	1,319	1,317	1,277	1,163	1,257	1,120
Net Income	640	1,935	2,251	2,214	2,109	1,979	2,119	1,890
Average Shares	770	799	831	835	757	...	...	...
Balance Sheet								
Total Assets	95,559	95,808	90,207	84,135	75,707	59,085	53,462	...
Total Liabilities	81,203	81,574	76,011	71,531	65,229	53,125	48,880	...
Stockholders' Equity	14,356	14,234	14,196	12,604	10,478	5,960	4,582	...
Shares Outstanding	760	770	817	833	833	...	...	...
Statistical Record								
Return on Assets %	2.25	2.08	2.58	2.77	3.13	3.52	...	...
Return on Equity %	14.46	13.61	16.75	19.18	25.66	37.55	...	...
Net Margin %	14.82	11.59	14.89	16.26	16.57	16.75	19.63	19.61
Asset Turnover	0.18	0.18	0.17	0.17	0.19	0.21	...	...
Price Range	40.21-26.50	38.97-26.50	37.26-23.36	35.99-28.52	30.50-22.93	...	...	...
P/E Ratio	15.29-10.08	16.10-10.95	13.75-8.62	13.58-10.76	10.97-8.25	...	...	...
Average Yield %	1.77	1.73	0.89	...	...	...	...	...

Address: 777 Long Ridge Road, Stamford, CT 06902 **Telephone:** 203-585-2400	**Web Site:** www.synchronyfinancial.com **Officers:** Margaret M. Keane - President, Chief Executive Officer Brian D. Doubles - Executive Vice President, Chief Financial Officer, Treasurer, Division Officer	**Auditors:** KPMG LLP **Transfer Agents:** Computershare Trust Company, N.A.

SYNNEX CORP

Exchange	Symbol	Price	52Wk Range	Yield	P/E
NYS	SNX	$96.51 (6/29/2018)	140.70-95.31	1.45	14.67

*7 Year Price Score 129.83 *NYSE Composite Index=100 *12 Month Price Score 88.09

Interim Earnings (Per Share)

Qtr.	Feb	May	Aug	Nov
2014-15	1.16	1.30	1.21	1.56
2015-16	1.17	1.11	1.47	2.13
2016-17	1.54	1.83	1.87	2.27
2017-18	0.61	...	...	...

Interim Dividends (Per Share)

Amt	Decl	Ex	Rec	Pay
0.30Q	09/25/2017	10/12/2017	10/13/2017	10/27/2017
0.35Q	01/09/2018	01/18/2018	01/19/2018	01/31/2018
0.35Q	03/29/2018	04/12/2018	04/13/2018	04/27/2018
0.35Q	06/28/2018	07/12/2018	07/13/2018	07/27/2018

Indicated Div: $1.40

Valuation Analysis

		Institutional Holding	
Forecast EPS	$10.07	No of Institutions	
	(06/11/2018)	346	
Market Cap	$3.8 Billion	Shares	
Book Value	$2.3 Billion	35,367,216	
Price/Book	1.66	% Held	
Price/Sales	0.21	74.40	

Business Summary: IT Services (MIC: 6.3.1 SIC: 5045 NAIC: 334119)

Synnex is a business process services company, providing a range of distribution, logistics and integration services for the technology industry and providing outsourced services focused on customer engagement strategy to a range of enterprises. Co. has two segments: Technology Solutions, which distributes a range of information technology systems and products and also provides systems design and integration solutions; and Concentrix, which provides a portfolio of strategic solutions and end-to-end global business outsourcing services focused on customer engagement strategy, process optimization, technology innovation, front and back-office automation and business transformation to clients.

Recent Developments: For the year ended Nov 30 2017, net income increased 28.2% to US$301.2 million from US$235.0 million in the prior year. Revenues were US$17.05 billion, up 21.2% from US$14.06 billion the year before. Operating income was US$509.0 million versus US$379.6 million in the prior year, an increase of 34.1%. Direct operating expenses rose 21.3% to US$15.49 billion from US$12.78 billion in the comparable period the year before. Indirect operating expenses increased 15.3% to US$1.04 billion from US$903.4 million in the equivalent prior-year period.

Prospects: Our evaluation of Synnex Corp. as of Jan. 21, 2018 is the result of our systematic analysis on three basic characteristics: earnings strength, relative valuation, and recent stock price movement. The company has generated a negative trend in earnings per share over the past 5 quarters and while recent estimates for the company have been raised by analysts, SNX has posted better than expected results. Based on generated earnings yield, the company is undervalued when compared to all of the companies in our coverage universe. Share price changes over the past year indicates that SNX will perform well over the near term.

Financial Data

(US$ in Thousands)	3 Mos	11/30/2017	11/30/2016	11/30/2015	11/30/2014	11/30/2013	11/30/2012	11/30/2011
Earnings Per Share	6.58	7.51	5.88	5.24	4.57	3.06	3.99	4.08
Cash Flow Per Share	8.99	4.47	8.29	16.48	(6.10)	0.97	6.62	6.12
Tang Book Value Per Share	22.31	20.87	30.17	34.04	28.51	32.22	30.06	25.87
Dividends Per Share	1.150	1.050	0.850	0.575	0.125	...	...	...
Dividend Payout %	17.48	13.98	14.46	10.97	2.74	...	...	...
Income Statement								
Total Revenue	4,552,370	17,045,700	14,061,837	13,338,397	13,839,590	10,845,164	10,285,507	10,409,840
EBITDA	132,678	590,793	450,860	457,001	401,168	279,629	284,113	279,896
Depn & Amortn	21,924	80,705	65,803	103,510	91,699	24,462	24,630	24,673
Income Before Taxes	93,303	464,731	356,064	327,195	284,282	238,052	236,553	229,718
Income Taxes	68,869	163,558	121,059	118,588	104,132	85,730	84,050	79,165
Net Income	24,434	301,173	234,946	208,525	180,034	152,237	151,376	150,331
Average Shares	39,978	39,758	39,530	39,352	38,845	37,800	37,908	36,833
Balance Sheet								
Current Assets	5,525,766	5,739,778	4,045,109	3,649,781	3,899,989	2,931,733	2,580,461	2,438,415
Total Assets	7,457,783	7,698,526	5,223,263	4,444,147	4,713,042	3,325,889	2,963,262	2,833,295
Current Liabilities	3,741,173	4,041,207	2,477,828	1,918,157	2,721,729	1,789,378	1,494,707	1,372,253
Long-Term Obligations	1,121,206	1,136,089	603,229	638,798	264,246	65,405	81,152	223,822
Total Liabilities	5,142,344	5,414,831	3,247,487	2,644,766	3,059,484	1,914,667	1,644,239	1,674,916
Stockholders' Equity	2,315,439	2,283,695	1,975,776	1,799,381	1,653,558	1,411,222	1,319,023	1,158,379
Shares Outstanding	39,714	39,673	39,477	39,189	38,924	37,210	36,628	36,164
Statistical Record								
Return on Assets %	4.20	4.66	4.85	4.55	4.48	4.84	5.21	5.64
Return on Equity %	12.12	14.14	12.41	12.08	11.75	11.15	12.19	13.98
EBITDA Margin %	2.91	3.47	3.21	3.43	2.90	2.58	2.76	2.69
Net Margin %	0.54	1.77	1.67	1.56	1.30	1.40	1.47	1.44
Asset Turnover	2.88	2.64	2.90	2.91	3.44	3.45	3.54	3.90
Current Ratio	1.48	1.42	1.63	1.90	1.43	1.64	1.73	1.78
Debt to Equity	0.48	0.50	0.31	0.36	0.16	0.05	0.06	0.19
Price Range	140.70-103.37	137.33-103.37	118.71-78.16	96.10-68.43	76.94-52.36	66.42-32.60	43.89-28.42	36.60-23.20
P/E Ratio	21.38-15.71	18.29-13.76	20.19-13.29	18.34-13.06	16.84-11.46	21.71-10.65	11.00-7.12	8.97-5.69
Average Yield %	0.95	0.87	0.89	0.72	0.19	...	...	...

Address: 44201 Nobel Drive, Fremont, CA 94538
Telephone: 510-656-3333

Web Site: www.synnex.com
Officers: Kevin M. Murai - Chairman, President, Chief Executive Officer, Co-Chief Executive Officer Dennis Polk - Chief Operating Officer, President, Chief Executive Officer

Auditors: KPMG LLP
Transfer Agents: Computershare Trust Company, Providence, RI

SYNOVUS FINANCIAL CORP

Exchange	Symbol	Price	52Wk Range	Yield	P/E
NYS	SNV	$52.83 (6/29/2018)	57.07-40.52	1.89	21.56

*7 Year Price Score 139.56 *NYSE Composite Index=100 *12 Month Price Score 110.37

Interim Earnings (Per Share)

Qtr.	Mar	Jun	Sep	Dec
2015	0.38	0.40	0.42	0.42
2016	0.39	0.46	0.51	0.53
2017	0.56	0.60	0.78	0.23
2018	0.84	...	...	...

Interim Dividends (Per Share)

Amt	Decl	Ex	Rec	Pay
0.15Q	09/08/2017	09/20/2017	09/21/2017	10/02/2017
0.15Q	12/08/2017	12/20/2017	12/21/2017	01/02/2018
0.25Q	03/01/2018	03/14/2018	03/15/2018	04/02/2018
0.25Q	06/08/2018	06/20/2018	06/21/2018	07/02/2018

Indicated Div: $1.00 (Div. Reinv. Plan)

Valuation Analysis

		Institutional Holding	
Forecast EPS	$3.58 (06/14/2018)	No of Institutions	482
Market Cap	$6.3 Billion	Shares	183,430,336
Book Value	$3.0 Billion	% Held	80.93
Price/Book	2.12		
Price/Sales	4.06		

TRADING VOLUME (thousand shares)

Business Summary: Banking (MIC: 5.1.1 SIC: 6021 NAIC: 522110)

Synovus Financial is a financial services company and a bank holding company. Through its subsidiary bank, Synovus Bank, Co. provides financial services, including commercial and retail banking, financial management, insurance, and mortgage services to its customers in Georgia, Alabama, South Carolina, Florida, and Tennessee. In addition to its banking operations, Co., through other non-bank subsidiaries, also provides various other financial services such as portfolio management and investment banking, trust, asset management and financial planning services, as well as mortgage services. As of Dec 31 2017, Co. had total assets of $31.22 billion and total deposits of $26.15 billion.

Recent Developments: For the quarter ended Mar 31 2018, net income increased 43.6% to US$103.2 million from US$71.9 million in the year-earlier quarter. Net interest income increased 14.3% to US$274.3 million from US$239.9 million in the year-earlier quarter. Provision for loan losses was US$12.8 million versus US$8.7 million in the prior-year quarter, an increase of 47.3%. Non-interest income fell 6.7% to US$67.0 million from US$71.8 million, while non-interest expense declined 1.1% to US$195.2 million.

Prospects: Our evaluation of Synovus Financial Corp. as of Jan. 21, 2018 is the result of our systematic analysis on three basic characteristics: earnings strength, relative valuation, and recent stock price movement. The company has enjoyed a very positive trend in earnings per share over the past 5 quarters and while recent estimates for the company have been mixed, SNV has posted better than expected results. Based on operating earnings yield, the company is undervalued when compared to all of the companies in our coverage universe. Share price changes over the past year indicates that SNV will perform in line with the market over the near term.

Financial Data

(US$ in Thousands)	3 Mos	12/31/2017	12/31/2016	12/31/2015	12/31/2014	12/31/2013	12/31/2012	12/31/2011
Earnings Per Share	2.45	2.17	1.89	1.62	1.33	0.91	5.95	(1.05)
Cash Flow Per Share	4.89	5.30	3.75	3.38	2.79	4.74	4.19	5.76
Tang Book Value Per Share	23.27	23.27	22.32	22.00	21.24	20.12	22.98	16.47
Dividends Per Share	0.700	0.600	0.480	0.420	0.240	0.280	0.280	...
Dividend Payout %	28.57	27.65	25.40	25.93	18.05	30.77	4.71	...
Income Statement								
Interest Income	313,134	1,162,497	1,022,803	945,962	928,692	929,014	1,004,140	1,141,756
Interest Expense	38,850	139,188	123,623	118,644	109,408	118,822	150,023	217,602
Net Interest Income	274,284	1,023,309	899,180	827,318	819,284	810,192	854,117	924,154
Provision for Losses	12,776	67,185	28,000	19,010	33,831	69,598	320,369	418,795
Non-Interest Income	67,046	345,327	273,194	267,920	260,537	253,242	309,285	341,213
Non-Interest Expense	195,179	821,313	755,923	717,655	743,431	741,208	811,556	906,104
Income Before Taxes	133,375	480,138	388,451	358,573	302,559	252,628	31,477	(59,532)
Income Taxes	30,209	204,664	141,667	132,491	107,310	93,245	(798,732)	1,312
Net Income	103,166	275,474	246,784	226,082	195,249	159,383	830,209	(60,624)
Average Shares	119,321	122,012	125,078	133,201	139,154	134,225	130,014	112,181
Balance Sheet								
Net Loans & Leases	24,625,273	24,549,552	23,604,633	22,177,069	20,839,988	19,760,923	19,178,975	19,573,475
Total Assets	31,501,028	31,221,837	30,104,002	28,792,653	27,051,231	26,201,604	26,760,012	27,162,845
Total Deposits	26,253,507	26,147,900	24,648,060	23,242,661	21,531,700	20,876,790	21,057,044	22,411,752
Total Liabilities	28,544,533	28,260,271	27,176,078	25,792,457	24,009,961	23,252,619	23,190,581	24,335,393
Stockholders' Equity	2,956,495	2,961,566	2,927,924	3,000,196	3,041,270	2,948,985	3,569,431	2,827,452
Shares Outstanding	118,702	118,897	122,266	129,547	136,122	138,907	112,368	112,185
Statistical Record								
Return on Assets %	0.99	0.90	0.84	0.81	0.73	0.60	3.07	N.M.
Return on Equity %	10.37	9.35	8.30	7.48	6.52	4.89	25.89	N.M.
Net Interest Margin %	87.59	88.03	87.91	87.46	88.22	87.21	85.06	80.94
Efficiency Ratio %	51.34	54.47	58.33	59.12	62.51	62.69	61.79	61.10
Loans to Deposits	0.94	0.94	0.96	0.95	0.97	0.95	0.91	0.87
Price Range	52.88-39.11	50.13-39.11	41.78-25.95	33.56-24.49	27.51-21.84	25.20-17.08	17.85-10.71	20.34-6.86
P/E Ratio	21.58-15.96	23.10-18.02	22.11-13.73	20.72-15.12	20.68-16.42	27.69-18.77	3.00-1.80	...
Average Yield %	1.53	1.38	1.51	1.42	0.99	1.33	1.92	...

Address: 1111 Bay Avenue, Suite 500, Columbus, GA 31901 **Telephone:** 706-649-2311	**Web Site:** www.synovus.com **Officers:** Kessel D. Stelling - Chairman, President, Chief Executive Officer Kevin S. Blair - Executive Vice President, Chief Financial Officer	**Auditors:** KPMG LLP **Investor Contact:** 706-649-3555 **Transfer Agents:** American Stock Transfer & Trust Company, LLC., Brooklyn, NY

SYSCO CORP

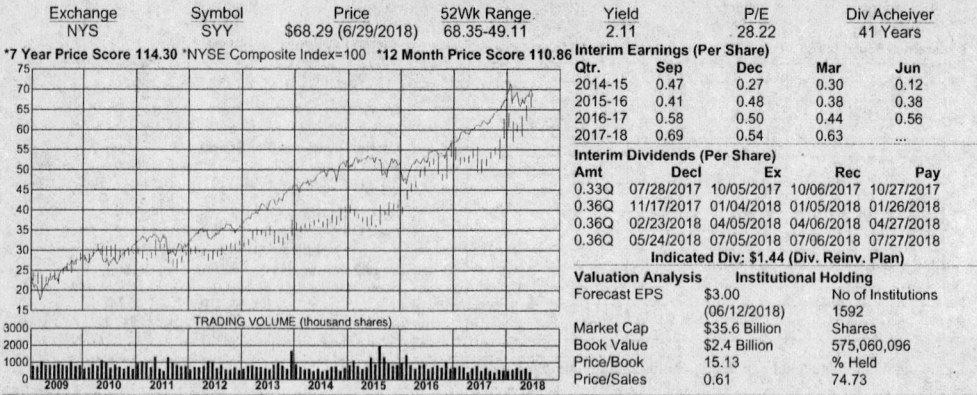

Exchange	Symbol	Price	52Wk Range	Yield	P/E	Div Acheiver
NYS	SYY	$68.29 (6/29/2018)	68.35-49.11	2.11	28.22	41 Years

*7 Year Price Score 114.30 *NYSE Composite Index=100 *12 Month Price Score 110.86

Interim Earnings (Per Share)

Qtr.	Sep	Dec	Mar	Jun
2014-15	0.47	0.27	0.30	0.12
2015-16	0.41	0.48	0.38	0.38
2016-17	0.58	0.50	0.44	0.56
2017-18	0.69	0.54	0.63	...

Interim Dividends (Per Share)

Amt	Decl	Ex	Rec	Pay
0.33Q	07/28/2017	10/05/2017	10/06/2017	10/27/2017
0.36Q	11/17/2017	01/04/2018	01/05/2018	01/26/2018
0.36Q	02/23/2018	04/05/2018	04/06/2018	04/27/2018
0.36Q	05/24/2018	07/05/2018	07/06/2018	07/27/2018

Indicated Div: $1.44 (Div. Reinv. Plan)

Valuation Analysis

		Institutional Holding	
Forecast EPS	$3.00	No of Institutions	
	(06/12/2018)	1592	
Market Cap	$35.6 Billion	Shares	
Book Value	$2.4 Billion	575,060,096	
Price/Book	15.13	% Held	
Price/Sales	0.61	74.73	

Business Summary: Retail - Food & Beverage, Drug & Tobacco (MIC: 2.1.2 SIC: 5141 NAIC: 424410)

Sysco is a distributor of food and related products primarily to the foodservice or food-away-from-home industry. Co.'s segments are: U.S. Foodservice Operations, which includes U.S. Broadline operations, custom-cut meat and seafood companies, FreshPoint and European Imports; International Foodservice Operations, which includes broadline operations that distribute a line of food products and non-food products to international customers; and SYGMA, which consists of operating companies that distribute a line of food products and non-food products to certain chain restaurant customer locations. Co.'s other segment consists of its hotel supply operations and Sysco Labs technology solutions.

Recent Developments: For the quarter ended Mar 31 2018, net income increased 38.5% to US$330.1 million from US$238.3 million in the year-earlier quarter. Revenues were US$14.35 billion, up 6.1% from US$13.52 billion the year before. Operating income was US$485.9 million versus US$436.0 million in the prior-year quarter, an increase of 11.5%. Direct operating expenses rose 6.2% to US$11.67 billion from US$10.99 billion in the comparable period the year before. Indirect operating expenses increased 4.4% to US$2.19 billion from US$2.10 billion in the equivalent prior-year period.

Prospects: Our evaluation of Sysco Corp. as of Jan. 21, 2018 is the result of our systematic analysis on three basic characteristics: earnings strength, relative valuation, and recent stock price movement. The company has enjoyed a very positive trend in earnings per share over the past 5 quarters and while recent estimates for the company have been raised by analysts, SYY has posted better than expected results. Based on operating earnings yield, the company is about fairly valued when compared to all of the companies in our coverage universe. Share price changes over the past year indicates that SYY will perform poorly over the near term.

Financial Data

(US$ in Thousands)	9 Mos	6 Mos	3 Mos	07/01/2017	07/02/2016	06/27/2015	06/28/2014	06/29/2013
Earnings Per Share	2.42	2.23	2.19	2.08	1.64	1.15	1.58	1.67
Cash Flow Per Share	4.36	4.80	3.81	4.02	3.32	2.63	2.55	2.57
Tang Book Value Per Share	N.M.	N.M.	N.M.	N.M.	2.06	5.29	5.36	5.29
Dividends Per Share	1.350	1.320	1.300	1.280	1.230	1.180	1.140	1.100
Dividend Payout %	55.79	59.19	59.36	61.54	75.00	102.61	72.15	65.87
Income Statement								
Total Revenue	43,411,418	29,061,914	14,650,424	55,371,139	50,366,919	48,680,752	46,516,712	44,411,233
EBITDA	1,687,178	1,179,449	634,532	2,834,508	2,347,853	1,758,754	2,093,165	2,149,450
Depn & Amortn	21,095	14,395	7,192	765,400	608,700	495,800	493,800	473,500
Income Before Taxes	1,363,068	998,184	546,456	1,766,230	1,433,007	1,008,147	1,475,624	1,547,455
Income Taxes	381,230	346,431	178,816	623,727	483,385	321,374	544,091	555,028
Net Income	981,838	651,753	367,640	1,142,503	949,622	686,773	931,533	992,427
Average Shares	527,990	527,249	533,063	548,545	577,391	596,849	590,216	592,675
Balance Sheet								
Current Assets	8,715,871	8,272,168	8,597,002	8,033,438	10,053,899	11,494,304	6,681,972	6,207,427
Total Assets	18,629,142	18,219,370	18,418,590	17,756,655	16,721,804	17,989,281	13,167,950	12,663,947
Current Liabilities	6,046,199	5,982,970	6,140,282	6,095,886	4,434,456	9,399,615	4,367,630	3,749,282
Long-Term Obligations	8,835,156	8,312,489	8,426,359	7,660,877	7,336,930	2,271,825	2,384,167	2,639,986
Total Liabilities	16,277,929	15,950,768	16,183,336	15,375,139	13,242,196	12,729,057	7,901,255	7,472,137
Stockholders' Equity	2,351,213	2,268,602	2,235,254	2,381,516	3,479,608	5,260,224	5,266,695	5,191,810
Shares Outstanding	520,755	521,410	521,661	530,039	559,597	594,317	586,124	586,106
Statistical Record								
Return on Assets %	7.04	6.67	6.51	6.65	5.38	4.42	7.23	8.04
Return on Equity %	54.98	50.38	45.14	39.09	21.38	13.08	17.86	20.15
EBITDA Margin %	3.89	4.06	4.33	5.12	4.66	3.61	4.50	4.84
Net Margin %	2.26	2.24	2.51	2.06	1.89	1.41	2.00	2.23
Asset Turnover	3.16	3.18	3.08	3.22	2.86	3.13	3.61	3.60
Current Ratio	1.44	1.38	1.40	1.32	2.27	1.22	1.53	1.66
Debt to Equity	3.76	3.66	3.77	3.22	2.11	0.43	0.45	0.51
Price Range	64.12-49.11	62.64-49.11	56.61-47.26	56.61-47.26	50.74-35.68	41.25-35.54	37.85-31.16	35.24-28.31
P/E Ratio	26.50-20.29	28.09-22.02	25.85-21.58	27.22-22.72	30.94-21.76	35.87-30.90	23.96-19.72	21.10-16.95
Average Yield %	2.43	2.45	2.47	2.47	2.88	3.09	3.26	3.44

Address: 1390 Enclave Parkway, Houston, TX 77077-2099
Telephone: 281-584-1390
Fax: 281-584-2880

Web Site: www.sysco.com
Officers: Jacquelyn M. Ward - Chairman Thomas L. Bene - President, Executive Vice President, Chief Operating Officer, Chief Commercial Officer, Chief Executive Officer

Auditors: Ernst & Young LLP
Investor Contact: 281-584-1308
Transfer Agents: American Stock Transfer & Trust Company, New York, NY

TABLEAU SOFTWARE INC

Exchange	Symbol	Price	52Wk Range	Yield	P/E
NYS	DATA	$97.75 (6/29/2018)	104.48-61.16	N/A	N/A

*7 Year Price Score N/A   *NYSE Composite Index=100   *12 Month Price Score 120.67

Interim Earnings (Per Share)

Qtr.	Mar	Jun	Sep	Dec
2015	(0.14)	(0.27)	(0.19)	(0.58)
2016	(0.62)	(0.64)	(0.40)	(0.27)
2017	(0.71)	(0.54)	(0.59)	(0.52)
2018	(0.57)	...	...	...

Interim Dividends (Per Share)

No Dividends Paid

Valuation Analysis   Institutional Holding

Forecast EPS	$-0.16	No of Institutions
	(06/13/2018)	362
Market Cap	$8.0 Billion	Shares
Book Value	$909.9 Million	71,733,248
Price/Book	8.76	% Held
Price/Sales	8.63	58.43

Business Summary: Internet & Software (MIC: 6.3.2 SIC: 7372 NAIC: 511210)

Tableau Software provides software products that enable a population of business users to engage with data, ask questions, and solve problems. Co. provides five products: Tableau Desktop, a self-service analytics product; Tableau Server, a business intelligence platform for organizations; Tableau Online, a hosted software-as-a-service version of Tableau Server; Tableau Public, a cloud-based platform for analyzing and sharing public data; and Vizable, an application used to analyze data on a tablet. Co.'s products are built on a foundation of proprietary technologies, such as VizQL, its Live Query Engine and In-Memory Data Engine, which work together to develop its Hybrid Data Architecture.

Recent Developments: For the quarter ended Mar 31 2018, net loss amounted to US$46.5 million versus a net loss of US$54.6 million in the year-earlier quarter. Revenues were US$246.2 million, up 23.2% from US$199.9 million the year before. Operating loss was US$50.4 million versus a loss of US$53.5 million in the prior-year quarter. Direct operating expenses rose 21.6% to US$32.4 million from US$26.7 million in the comparable period the year before. Indirect operating expenses increased 16.5% to US$264.2 million from US$226.8 million in the equivalent prior-year period.

Prospects: Our evaluation of Tableau Software, Inc. as of Jan. 21, 2018 is the result of our systematic analysis on three basic characteristics: earnings strength, relative valuation, and recent stock price movement. The company has suffered a very negative trend in earnings per share over the past 5 quarters and while recent estimates for the company have remained steady, DATA has posted results that fell short of analysts expectations. Based on operating earnings yield, the company is overvalued when compared to all of the companies in our coverage universe. Share price changes over the past year indicates that DATA will perform very well over the near term.

Financial Data

(US$ in Thousands)	3 Mos	12/31/2017	12/31/2016	12/31/2015	12/31/2014	12/31/2013	12/31/2012	12/31/2011
Earnings Per Share	(2.22)	(2.35)	(1.92)	(1.17)	0.08	0.12	...	0.04
Cash Flow Per Share	2.41	2.88	2.32	1.91	1.32	0.75	0.42	0.39
Tang Book Value Per Share	10.73	8.93	10.12	10.03	9.62	3.93	0.87	0.60
Income Statement								
Total Revenue	246,207	877,059	826,943	653,587	412,616	232,440	127,733	62,360
EBITDA	(48,799)	(133,999)	(94,427)	(27,107)	20,682	9,765	8,004	6,002
Depn & Amortn	118	44,700	43,000	23,700	13,500	6,900	3,800	2,100
Income Before Taxes	(48,917)	(178,699)	(137,427)	(50,807)	7,182	2,865	4,204	3,902
Income Taxes	(2,445)	6,861	7,022	32,893	1,309	(4,211)	2,777	523
Net Income	(46,472)	(185,560)	(144,449)	(83,700)	5,873	7,076	1,427	3,379
Average Shares	81,039	78,869	75,162	71,701	74,319	59,092	39,652	39,431
Balance Sheet								
Current Assets	1,097,601	1,089,218	1,151,624	944,739	810,261	332,181	76,161	45,440
Total Assets	1,430,656	1,398,795	1,287,199	1,030,711	865,662	354,927	86,992	51,277
Current Liabilities	445,185	562,729	428,721	272,601	180,274	104,289	51,930	28,259
Total Liabilities	520,783	645,172	495,351	296,766	193,656	110,267	57,018	31,523
Stockholders' Equity	909,873	753,623	791,848	733,945	672,006	244,660	29,974	19,754
Shares Outstanding	81,535	80,462	76,718	73,204	69,868	62,198	34,317	33,084
Statistical Record								
Return on Assets %	N.M.	N.M.	N.M.	N.M.	0.96	3.20	2.06	...
Return on Equity %	N.M.	N.M.	N.M.	N.M.	1.28	5.15	5.72	...
EBITDA Margin %	N.M.	N.M.	N.M.	N.M.	5.01	4.20	6.27	9.62
Net Margin %	N.M.	N.M.	N.M.	N.M.	1.42	3.04	1.12	5.42
Asset Turnover	0.69	0.65	0.71	0.69	0.68	1.05	1.84	...
Current Ratio	2.47	1.94	2.69	3.47	4.49	3.19	1.47	1.61
Price Range	86.64-49.55	82.17-43.32	94.30-37.22	128.74-77.58	100.28-54.13	74.75-48.53	...	...
P/E Ratio	...	...	...	...	N.M.	622.92-404.42	...	...

Address: 1621 North 34th Street, Seattle, WA 98103 **Telephone:** 206-633-3400	**Web Site:** www.tableau.com **Officers:** Christian Chabot - Chairman, Chief Executive Officer, Co-Founder Adam Selipsky - President, Chief Executive Officer	**Auditors:** PricewaterhouseCoopers LLP **Transfer Agents:** American Stock Transfer & Trust Company

TAHOE RESOURCES INC.

Exchange	Symbol	Price	52Wk Range	Yield	P/E
NYS	TAHO	$4.92 (6/29/2018)	8.62-3.84	N/A	N/A

*7 Year Price Score 29.10   *NYSE Composite Index=100   *12 Month Price Score 100.04

TRADING VOLUME (thousand shares)

Interim Earnings (Per Share)

Qtr.	Mar	Jun	Sep	Dec
2015	0.22	(0.04)	0.06	(0.53)
2016	0.17	0.05	0.20	(0.01)
2017	0.24	0.11	(0.03)	(0.06)
2018	(0.02)	...	...	...

Interim Dividends (Per Share)

Dividend Payment Suspended

Valuation Analysis		Institutional Holding	
Forecast EPS	$0.12	No of Institutions	
	(06/21/2018)	244	
Market Cap	$1.5 Billion	Shares	
Book Value	$2.6 Billion	213,479,616	
Price/Book	0.59	% Held	
Price/Sales	2.47	49.98	

Business Summary: Precious Metals (MIC: 8.2.1 SIC: 1044 NAIC: 212222)

Tahoe Resources is engaged in the operation of mineral properties for the mining of precious metals and the acquisition, exploration and development of mineral interests in the Americas.

Recent Developments: For the quarter ended Mar 31 2018, net loss amounted to US$6.9 million versus net income of US$74.7 million in the year-earlier quarter. Revenues were US$139.9 million, down 44.3% from US$251.0 million the year before. Operating loss was US$550,000 versus an income of US$88.3 million in the prior-year quarter. Direct operating expenses declined 14.3% to US$125.9 million from US$146.9 million in the comparable period the year before. Indirect operating expenses decreased 8.4% to US$14.5 million from US$15.9 million in the equivalent prior-year period.

Prospects: Our evaluation of Tahoe Resources Inc. as of Jan. 21, 2018 is the result of our systematic analysis on three basic characteristics: earnings strength, relative valuation, and recent stock price movement. The company has suffered a very negative trend in earnings per share over the past 5 quarters and while recent estimates for the company have been mixed, TAHO has posted results that fell short of analysts expectations. Based on operating earnings yield, the company is undervalued when compared to all of the companies in our coverage universe. Share price changes over the past year indicates that TAHO will perform poorly over the near term.

Financial Data
(US$ in Thousands)

	3 Mos	12/31/2017	12/31/2016	12/31/2015	12/31/2014	12/31/2013	12/31/2012	12/31/2011
Earnings Per Share	...	0.26	0.41	(0.35)	0.61	(0.45)	(0.65)	(0.48)
Cash Flow Per Share	...	0.75	0.86	0.80	0.81	(0.45)	(0.61)	(0.35)
Tang Book Value Per Share	8.02	8.03	7.90	7.06	5.95	5.30	5.71	6.36
Dividends Per Share	...	0.140	0.240	0.240	0.020	...	...	...
Dividend Payout %	...	53.85	58.54	...	3.28	...	...	...
Income Statement								
Total Revenue	139,942	733,557	784,503	519,721	350,265	...	...	...
EBITDA	37,052	292,445	349,397	(1,601)	168,418	(50,947)	(86,894)	(67,560)
Depn & Amortn	37,658	169,336	137,021	84,945	47,088	13,029	6,869	1,200
Income Before Taxes	(2,034)	119,827	208,732	(88,232)	115,690	(63,976)	(93,763)	(68,760)
Income Taxes	4,828	38,034	90,856	(16,321)	24,900	1,621	(310)	406
Net Income	(6,862)	81,793	117,876	(71,911)	90,790	(65,597)	(93,453)	(69,166)
Average Shares	313,192	312,833	289,988	207,810	147,992	145,842	144,634	142,798
Balance Sheet								
Current Assets	228,720	299,075	359,442	228,201	134,584	35,811	166,270	350,113
Total Assets	3,036,318	3,080,638	3,071,253	2,002,461	975,628	883,333	852,943	922,005
Current Liabilities	123,924	155,830	150,436	150,880	91,875	104,965	16,925	9,811
Long-Term Obligations	386	1,608	42,250	7,711	...	...	...	...
Total Liabilities	417,165	455,750	499,099	338,430	97,568	109,179	21,646	10,351
Stockholders' Equity	2,619,153	2,624,888	2,572,154	1,664,031	878,060	774,154	831,297	911,654
Shares Outstanding	312,775	312,775	311,362	227,401	147,644	146,094	145,565	143,427
Statistical Record								
Return on Assets %	0.01	2.66	4.63	N.M.	9.77	N.M.	N.M.	N.M.
Return on Equity %	0.01	3.15	5.55	N.M.	10.99	N.M.	N.M.	N.M.
EBITDA Margin %	26.48	39.87	44.54	N.M.	48.08	...	...	...
Net Margin %	N.M.	11.15	15.03	N.M.	25.92	...	...	...
Asset Turnover	0.20	0.24	0.31	0.35	0.38	...	...	...
Current Ratio	1.85	1.92	2.39	1.51	1.46	0.34	9.82	35.69
Debt to Equity	N.M.	N.M.	0.02	N.M.	...	...	...	...
Price Range	9.47-3.84	11.18-4.18	16.62-6.83	15.34-7.47	27.31-11.43	19.45-12.05	24.00-12.02	25.35-13.15
P/E Ratio	N.M.	43.00-16.08	40.54-16.66	...	44.77-18.74	...	...	...
Average Yield %	...	2.04	2.04	2.04	0.09	...	...	...

Address: 5310 Kietzke Lane, Suite 200, Reno, NV 89511	**Web Site:** www.tahoeresources.com	**Auditors:** Deloitte LLP
Telephone: 775-448-5800	**Officers:** C. Kevin McArthur - Executive Chairman, Chief Executive Officer, President, Vice-Chairman	**Investor Contact:** 775-448-5807
Fax: 775-398-7020	Ronald W. Clayton - President, Chief Operating Officer, Vice President	**Transfer Agents:** Computershare Investor Services Inc., Vancouver, British Columbia, Canada

TANGER FACTORY OUTLET CENTERS, INC.

Exchange	Symbol	Price	52Wk Range	Yield	P/E	Div Acheiver
NYS	SKT	$23.49 (6/29/2018)	27.67-20.04	5.96	33.08	24 Years

*7 Year Price Score 59.81   ***NYSE Composite Index=100**   ***12 Month Price Score 91.05**

Interim Earnings (Per Share)

Qtr.	Mar	Jun	Sep	Dec
2015	0.36	0.26	0.46	1.12
2016	0.28	0.76	0.72	0.25
2017	0.23	0.31	(0.17)	0.33
2018	0.24	...	...	...

Interim Dividends (Per Share)

Amt	Decl	Ex	Rec	Pay
0.343Q	10/05/2017	10/30/2017	10/31/2017	11/15/2017
0.343Q	01/11/2018	01/30/2018	01/31/2018	02/15/2018
0.35Q	04/12/2018	04/27/2018	04/30/2018	05/15/2018
0.35Q	07/12/2018	07/30/2018	07/31/2018	08/15/2018

Indicated Div: $1.40 (Div. Reinv. Plan)

Valuation Analysis   **Institutional Holding**

Forecast EPS	$0.96	No of Institutions
	(06/14/2018)	416
Market Cap	$2.2 Billion	Shares
Book Value	$563.7 Million	119,557,872
Price/Book	3.93	% Held
Price/Sales	4.52	99.38

Business Summary: REITs (MIC: 5.3.1 SIC: 6798 NAIC: 525930)

Tanger Factory Outlet Centers, along with its subsidiaries owns and operates outlet centers in the U.S. and Canada. Co. is a self-administered and self-managed real estate investment trust, which, through its controlling interest in Tanger Properties Limited Partnership and subsidiaries, focuses on developing, acquiring, owning, operating and managing outlet shopping centers. As of Feb 1 2018, Co.'s consolidated portfolio consisted of 36 outlet centers. Co. also had partial ownership interests in eight unconsolidated outlet centers, including four outlet centers in Canada. Each of Co.'s outlet centers, except one joint venture property, carries the Tanger brand name.

Recent Developments: For the quarter ended Mar 31 2018, net income increased 0.7% to US$23.7 million from US$23.5 million in the year-earlier quarter. Revenues were US$123.5 million, up 1.8% from US$121.4 million the year before. Revenues from property income rose 2.1% to US$121.9 million from US$119.4 million in the corresponding quarter a year earlier.

Prospects: Our evaluation of Tanger Factory Outlet Centers Inc. as of Jan. 21, 2018 is the result of our systematic analysis on three basic characteristics: earnings strength, relative valuation, and recent stock price movement. The company has managed to produce a neutral trend in earnings per share over the past 5 quarters. Because the company lacks sufficient analyst estimate data, we place greater weight on the historical EPS trend as the measure of earnings strength. Based on operating earnings yield, the company is about fairly valued when compared to all of the companies in our coverage universe. Share price changes over the past year indicates that SKT will perform poorly over the near term.

Financial Data

(US$ in Thousands)	3 Mos	12/31/2017	12/31/2016	12/31/2015	12/31/2014	12/31/2013	12/31/2012	12/31/2011
Earnings Per Share	0.71	0.71	2.01	2.20	0.77	1.13	0.57	0.52
Cash Flow Per Share	2.63	2.68	2.51	2.33	2.01	2.01	1.80	1.64
Tang Book Value Per Share	5.97	3.77	4.47	3.81	2.96	2.78	3.85	5.31
Dividends Per Share	1.370	1.353	1.260	1.305	0.945	0.885	0.830	0.794
Dividend Payout %	192.96	190.49	62.69	59.32	122.73	78.32	145.61	152.64
Income Statement								
Total Revenue	123,535	488,234	465,834	439,369	418,558	385,009	356,997	315,223
EBITDA	38,737	242,609	349,911	350,808	206,336	228,597	183,285	164,136
Depn & Amortn	1,446	107,845	96,813	85,900	80,100	74,700	73,700	66,200
Income Before Taxes	21,491	69,939	193,457	210,684	69,099	102,281	59,771	52,554
Net Income	22,838	68,002	193,744	211,200	74,011	107,557	53,228	44,641
Average Shares	93,644	94,522	95,345	94,759	93,839	94,247	92,661	84,129
Balance Sheet								
Current Assets	3,427	6,101	12,222	142,864	62,880	15,241	10,335	7,894
Total Assets	2,505,858	2,540,105	2,526,214	2,326,707	2,097,660	2,006,456	1,672,425	1,621,815
Current Liabilities	66,405	90,416	78,143	125,784	97,946	87,850	48,233	51,413
Long-Term Obligations	1,772,055	1,763,651	1,687,866	1,563,806	1,443,194	1,328,049	1,093,537	1,025,542
Total Liabilities	1,942,200	1,958,527	1,855,998	1,751,570	1,600,841	1,484,197	1,189,816	1,161,253
Stockholders' Equity	563,658	581,578	670,216	575,137	496,819	522,259	482,609	460,562
Shares Outstanding	94,382	94,560	96,095	95,880	95,509	94,505	94,061	86,727
Statistical Record								
Return on Assets %	2.72	2.68	7.96	9.55	3.61	5.85	3.22	3.15
Return on Equity %	11.17	10.86	31.03	39.40	14.53	21.41	11.26	10.79
EBITDA Margin %	31.36	49.69	75.11	79.84	49.30	59.37	51.34	52.07
Net Margin %	18.49	13.93	41.59	48.07	17.68	27.94	14.91	14.16
Asset Turnover	0.19	0.19	0.19	0.20	0.20	0.21	0.22	0.22
Current Ratio	0.05	0.07	0.16	1.14	0.64	0.17	0.21	0.15
Debt to Equity	3.14	3.03	2.52	2.72	2.90	2.54	2.27	2.23
Price Range	33.49-21.47	37.17-22.19	41.74-29.67	40.55-30.58	37.65-32.02	38.57-30.14	34.43-28.10	29.82-22.39
P/E Ratio	47.17-30.24	52.35-31.25	20.77-14.76	18.43-13.90	48.90-41.58	34.13-26.67	60.40-49.30	57.35-43.06
Average Yield %	5.37	4.82	3.47	3.79	2.70	2.58	2.63	2.96

Address: 3200 Northline Avenue, Suite 360, Greensboro, NC 27408. **Telephone:** 336-292-3010 **Fax:** 336-297-0931	**Web Site:** www.tangeroutlet.com **Officers:** Thomas J. Guerrieri - Vice President, Chief Accounting Officer, Controller Steven B. Tanger - President, Chief Executive Officer	**Auditors:** Deloitte & Touche LLP **Investor Contact:** 336-834-6892 **Transfer Agents:** Computershare Trust Company, NA, Providence, RI

TAPESTRY INC

Exchange	Symbol	Price	52Wk Range	Yield	P/E
NYS	TPR	$46.71 (6/29/2018)	54.64-38.87	2.89	39.92

*7 Year Price Score 78.66 ***NYSE Composite Index=100** ***12 Month Price Score 99.29**

Interim Earnings (Per Share)

Qtr.	Sep	Dec	Mar	Jun
2014-15	0.43	0.66	0.32	0.04
2015-16	0.35	0.61	0.40	0.29
2016-17	0.42	0.71	0.43	0.53
2017-18	(0.06)	0.22	0.48	...

Interim Dividends (Per Share)

Amt	Decl	Ex	Rec	Pay
0.338Q	08/15/2017	09/07/2017	09/08/2017	10/02/2017
0.338Q	11/15/2017	12/07/2017	12/08/2017	01/02/2018
0.338Q	02/15/2018	03/08/2018	03/09/2018	04/02/2018
0.338Q	05/17/2018	06/07/2018	06/08/2018	07/02/2018

Indicated Div: $1.35

Valuation Analysis **Institutional Holding**

Forecast EPS	$2.60	No of Institutions
(06/14/2018)		1002
Market Cap	$13.4 Billion	Shares
Book Value	$3.1 Billion	315,961,728
Price/Book	4.28	% Held
Price/Sales	2.43	83.44

TRADING VOLUME (thousand shares)

Business Summary: Apparel, Footwear & Accessories (MIC: 1.4.2 SIC: 3171 NAIC: 316992)

Tapestry is a marketer of accessories and gifts for women and men. Co.'s product offerings include women's and men's bags, leather goods, footwear, jewelry, travel bags, sunwear, watches and fragrance. Co.'s segments include: North America, which includes sales to North American consumers through Co.-operated stores, including the Internet, and sales to wholesale customers and distributors; International, which includes sales to consumers through Co.-operated stores, concession shop-in-shops and through the Internet; and Stuart Weitzman, which includes sales generated by the Stuart Weitzman brand, through numerous department stores, within third party distributors and operated stores.

Recent Developments: For the quarter ended Mar 31 2018, net income increased 14.8% to US$140.3 million from US$122.2 million in the year-earlier quarter. Revenues were US$1.32 billion, up 32.9% from US$995.2 million the year before. Operating income was US$159.0 million versus US$151.1 million in the prior-year quarter, an increase of 5.2%. Direct operating expenses rose 42.8% to US$413.5 million from US$289.5 million in the comparable period the year before. Indirect operating expenses increased 35.2% to US$749.9 million from US$554.6 million in the equivalent prior-year period.

Prospects: Our evaluation of Tapestry Inc. as of Jan. 21, 2018 is the result of our systematic analysis on three basic characteristics: earnings strength, relative valuation, and recent stock price movement. The company has managed to produce a neutral trend in earnings per share over the past 5 quarters and while recent estimates for the company have been raised by analysts, TPR has posted better than expected results. Based on operating earnings yield, the company is undervalued when compared to all of the companies in our coverage universe. Share price changes over the past year indicates that TPR will perform poorly over the near term.

Financial Data

(US$ in Thousands)	9 Mos	6 Mos	3 Mos	07/01/2017	07/02/2016	06/27/2015	06/28/2014	06/29/2013
Earnings Per Share	1.17	1.12	1.61	2.09	1.65	1.45	2.79	3.61
Cash Flow Per Share	3.18	3.36	2.78	3.05	2.69	3.41	3.56	5.02
Tang Book Value Per Share	N.M.	N.M.	N.M.	7.74	6.58	6.13	7.47	7.29
Dividends Per Share	1.350	1.350	1.350	1.350	1.350	1.350	1.350	1.238
Dividend Payout %	115.38	120.54	83.85	64.59	81.82	93.10	48.39	34.28
Income Statement								
Total Revenue	4,396,300	3,073,900	1,288,900	4,488,300	4,491,800	4,191,600	4,806,226	5,075,390
EBITDA	672,200	450,900	43,700	1,000,200	864,100	809,800	1,309,434	1,681,144
Depn & Amortn	188,600	126,300	65,500	212,800	210,600	191,800	189,360	162,987
Income Before Taxes	424,000	281,900	(42,300)	759,000	626,600	611,600	1,122,255	1,520,526
Income Taxes	238,200	236,400	(24,600)	168,000	166,100	209,200	340,919	486,106
Net Income	185,800	45,500	(17,700)	591,000	460,500	402,400	781,336	1,034,420
Average Shares	290,100	286,400	286,700	282,800	279,300	277,200	280,379	286,307
Balance Sheet								
Current Assets	2,288,300	3,282,300	3,022,300	3,953,300	2,172,900	2,506,500	1,855,217	2,070,947
Total Assets	6,588,000	7,481,200	7,454,400	5,831,600	4,892,700	4,666,900	3,663,131	3,531,897
Current Liabilities	860,100	1,731,400	1,734,900	753,800	826,700	834,700	813,118	722,510
Long-Term Obligations	1,599,500	1,887,500	1,888,200	1,579,500	861,200	879,100	...	485
Total Liabilities	3,450,000	4,531,800	4,514,400	2,829,700	2,209,800	2,177,000	1,242,478	1,122,739
Stockholders' Equity	3,138,000	2,949,400	2,940,000	3,001,900	2,682,900	2,489,900	2,420,653	2,409,158
Shares Outstanding	287,800	281,900	284,200	281,900	278,500	276,600	274,361	281,902
Statistical Record								
Return on Assets %	6.00	5.25	7.57	11.05	9.48	9.69	21.78	31.26
Return on Equity %	11.19	11.09	16.09	20.85	17.52	16.43	32.44	47.13
EBITDA Margin %	15.29	14.67	3.39	22.28	19.24	19.32	27.24	33.12
Net Margin %	4.23	1.48	N.M.	13.17	10.25	9.60	16.26	20.38
Asset Turnover	0.98	0.86	0.79	0.84	0.92	1.01	1.34	1.53
Current Ratio	2.66	1.90	1.74	5.24	2.63	3.00	2.28	2.87
Debt to Equity	0.51	0.64	0.64	0.53	0.32	0.35	...	N.M.
Price Range	53.24-38.74	48.74-34.99	48.74-34.24	47.34-34.24	42.00-27.44	43.56-33.00	59.55-34.02	62.60-46.50
P/E Ratio	45.50-33.11	43.52-31.24	30.27-21.27	22.65-16.38	25.45-16.63	30.04-22.76	21.34-12.19	17.34-12.88
Average Yield %	3.03	3.24	3.33	3.43	3.92	3.62	2.67	2.23

Address: 10 Hudson Yards, New York, NY 10001
Telephone: 212-594-1850
Fax: 212-594-1682

Web Site: www.tapestry.com
Officers: Jide James Zeitlin - Chairman Todd Kahn - President, Chief Administrative Officer, Executive Vice President, Senior Vice President, General Counsel, Secretary

Auditors: Deloitte & Touche LLP
Investor Contact: 212-629-2618
Transfer Agents: Mellon Investor Services, Jersey City, NJ

TARGET CORP

Exchange	Symbol	Price	52Wk Range	Yield	P/E	Div Acheiver
NYS	TGT	$76.12 (6/29/2018)	79.07-50.18	3.36	13.99	46 Years

*7 Year Price Score 80.32   *NYSE Composite Index=100   *12 Month Price Score 112.40

Interim Earnings (Per Share)

Qtr.	Apr	Jul	Oct	Jan
2015-16	0.98	1.18	0.87	2.28
2016-17	1.05	1.16	1.06	1.44
2017-18	1.23	1.22	0.88	2.01
2018-19	1.33	...	...	...

Interim Dividends (Per Share)

Amt	Decl	Ex	Rec	Pay
0.62Q	09/21/2017	11/14/2017	11/15/2017	12/10/2017
0.62Q	01/11/2018	02/20/2018	02/21/2018	03/10/2018
0.62Q	03/15/2018	05/15/2018	05/16/2018	06/10/2018
0.64Q	06/12/2018	08/15/2018	08/15/2018	09/10/2018

Indicated Div: $2.56 (Div. Reinv. Plan)

Valuation Analysis

		Institutional Holding	
Forecast EPS	$5.28	No of Institutions	
	(06/14/2018)	1769	
Market Cap	$40.6 Billion	Shares	
Book Value	$11.2 Billion	583,536,576	
Price/Book	3.64	% Held	
Price/Sales	0.56	78.54	

Business Summary: Retail - General Merchandise/Department Stores (MIC: 2.1.1 SIC: 5331 NAIC: 452990)

Target sells a range of general merchandise and food. The majority of Co.'s general merchandise stores sell an edited food assortment, including perishables, dry grocery, dairy, and frozen items. Co.'s digital channels include a range of general merchandise, including items found in Co.'s stores, along with a complementary assortment such as additional sizes and colors sold only online. Co. also sells merchandise through periodic design and partnerships and provides in-store amenities such as Target Cafe and Target Photo, and leased or licensed departments such as Target Optical, Starbucks, and other food service offerings. As of Jan 28 2017, Co. had 1,802 stores in the U.S.

Recent Developments: For the quarter ended May 5 2018, income from continuing operations increased 6.2% to US$717.0 million from US$675.0 million in the year-earlier quarter. Net income increased 5.9% to US$718.0 million from US$678.0 million in the year-earlier quarter. Revenues were US$16.78 billion, up 3.4% from US$16.22 billion the year before. Operating income was US$1.04 billion versus US$1.16 billion in the prior-year quarter, a decrease of 9.9%. Direct operating expenses rose 3.8% to US$11.63 billion from US$11.20 billion in the comparable period the year before. Indirect operating expenses increased 6.4% to US$4.12 billion from US$3.87 billion in the equivalent prior-year period.

Prospects: Our evaluation of Target Corp. as of Jan. 21, 2018 is the result of our systematic analysis on three basic characteristics: earnings strength, relative valuation, and recent stock price movement. The company has managed to produce a neutral trend in earnings per share over the past 5 quarters and while recent estimates for the company have been raised by analysts, TGT has posted better than expected results. Based on operating earnings yield, the company is undervalued when compared to all of the companies in our coverage universe. Share price changes over the past year indicates that TGT will perform very poorly over the near term.

Financial Data

(US$ in Millions)	3 Mos	02/03/2018	01/28/2017	01/30/2016	01/31/2015	02/01/2014	02/02/2013	01/28/2012
Earnings Per Share	5.44	5.33	4.70	5.31	(2.56)	3.07	4.52	4.28
Cash Flow Per Share	11.42	12.46	9.44	9.34	7.01	10.29	7.98	8.02
Tang Book Value Per Share	20.94	20.17	19.23	21.06	21.39	25.08	25.31	23.28
Dividends Per Share	2.460	2.440	2.320	2.160	1.900	1.580	1.320	1.100
Dividend Payout %	45.22	45.78	49.36	40.68	...	51.47	29.20	25.70
Income Statement								
Total Revenue	16,781	71,879	69,495	73,785	72,618	72,596	73,301	69,865
EBITDA	1,679	6,741	7,249	7,721	6,643	6,427	7,491	7,429
Depn & Amortn	631	2,429	2,280	2,191	2,108	2,198	2,120	2,107
Income Before Taxes	927	3,646	3,965	4,923	3,653	3,103	4,609	4,456
Income Taxes	210	718	1,296	1,602	1,204	1,132	1,610	1,527
Net Income	718	2,934	2,737	3,363	(1,636)	1,971	2,999	2,929
Average Shares	541	550	582	632	640	641	663	683
Balance Sheet								
Current Assets	10,876	12,564	11,990	14,130	14,087	11,573	16,388	16,449
Total Assets	38,929	38,999	37,431	40,262	41,404	44,553	48,163	46,630
Current Liabilities	12,044	13,201	12,708	12,622	11,736	12,777	14,031	14,287
Long-Term Obligations	11,107	11,317	11,031	11,945	12,705	12,622	14,654	13,697
Total Liabilities	27,771	27,290	26,478	27,305	27,407	28,322	31,605	30,809
Stockholders' Equity	11,158	11,709	10,953	12,957	13,997	16,231	16,558	15,821
Shares Outstanding	532	541	556	602	640	632	645	669
Statistical Record								
Return on Assets %	7.80	7.55	7.07	8.26	N.M.	4.26	6.23	6.50
Return on Equity %	26.79	25.47	22.96	25.02	N.M.	12.06	18.22	18.76
EBITDA Margin %	10.01	9.38	10.43	10.46	9.15	8.85	10.22	10.63
Net Margin %	4.28	4.08	3.94	4.56	N.M.	2.72	4.09	4.19
Asset Turnover	1.91	1.85	1.79	1.81	1.69	1.57	1.52	1.55
Current Ratio	0.90	0.95	0.94	1.12	1.20	0.91	1.17	1.15
Debt to Equity	1.00	0.97	1.01	0.92	0.91	0.78	0.89	0.87
Price Range	78.58-50.18	78.58-50.18	83.98-63.70	85.01-67.59	77.13-55.07	73.32-56.64	65.44-50.33	55.56-46.33
P/E Ratio	14.44-9.22	14.74-9.41	17.87-13.55	16.01-12.73	...	23.88-18.45	14.48-11.13	12.98-10.82
Average Yield %	3.94	4.14	3.16	2.77	3.03	2.38	2.21	2.16

Address: 1000 Nicollet Mall, Minneapolis, MN 55403 Telephone: 612-304-6073	Web Site: www.target.com Officers: Brian C. Cornell - Chairman, Chief Executive Officer John J. Mulligan - Interim President, Interim Chief Executive Officer, Executive Vice President, Chief Operating Officer, Chief Financial Officer	Auditors: Ernst & Young LLP Investor Contact: 800-775-3110 Transfer Agents: Mellon Investor Services, South Hackensack, N.J.

TARGA RESOURCES CORP

Exchange	Symbol	Price	52Wk Range	Yield	P/E
NYS	TRGP	$49.49 (6/29/2018)	51.44-40.35	7.36	109.98

*7 Year Price Score 59.49 ***NYSE Composite Index=100** ***12 Month Price Score 102.63**

TRADING VOLUME (thousand shares)

Interim Earnings (Per Share)

Qtr.	Mar	Jun	Sep	Dec
2015	0.07	0.27	0.23	0.49
2016	(0.06)	(0.33)	(0.23)	(1.12)
2017	(0.77)	0.14	(0.91)	1.25
2018	(0.03)	...	...	...

Interim Dividends (Per Share)

Amt	Decl	Ex	Rec	Pay
0.91Q	07/19/2017	07/28/2017	08/01/2017	08/15/2017
0.91Q	10/18/2017	10/31/2017	11/01/2017	11/15/2017
0.91Q	01/18/2018	01/31/2018	02/01/2018	02/15/2018
0.91Q	04/18/2018	04/30/2018	05/01/2018	05/15/2018

Indicated Div: $3.64

Valuation Analysis

		Institutional Holding	
Forecast EPS	$0.09 (06/14/2018)	No of Institutions	547
Market Cap	$10.8 Billion	Shares	221,843,296
Book Value	$6.3 Billion	% Held	
Price/Book	1.72		79.99
Price/Sales	1.18		

Business Summary: Refining & Marketing (MIC: 9.1.2 SIC: 4922 NAIC: 486210)

Targa Resources is a provider of midstream services and an independent midstream energy company. Co. operates two segments: Gathering and Processing, which consists of gathering, compressing, dehydrating, treating, conditioning, processing, and marketing natural gas and gathering crude oil; and Logistics and Marketing, which includes activities to convert mixed natural gas liquids (NGLs) into NGL products and provides certain services such as the fractionation, storage, terminaling, transportation, exporting, distribution and marketing of NGLs and NGL products, storing and terminaling of refined petroleum products and crude oil, as well as other natural gas supply and marketing activities.

Recent Developments: For the quarter ended Mar 31 2018, net income amounted to US$38.9 million versus a net loss of US$110.5 million in the year-earlier quarter. Revenues were US$2.46 billion, up 16.2% from US$2.11 billion the year before. Operating income was US$86.3 million versus US$50.5 million in the prior-year quarter, an increase of 70.9%. Direct operating expenses rose 17.1% to US$2.11 billion from US$1.81 billion in the comparable period the year before. Indirect operating expenses decreased 0.4% to US$255.1 million from US$256.0 million in the equivalent prior-year period.

Prospects: Our evaluation of Targa Resources Corp. as of Jan. 21, 2018 is the result of our systematic analysis on three basic characteristics: earnings strength, relative valuation, and recent stock price movement. The company has enjoyed a very positive trend in earnings per share over the past 5 quarters. Because the company lacks sufficient analyst estimate data, we place greater weight on the historical EPS trend as the measure of earnings strength. Based on operating earnings yield, the company is overvalued when compared to all of the companies in our coverage universe. Share price changes over the past year indicates that TRGP will perform very poorly over the near term.

Financial Data

(US$ in Thousands)	3 Mos	12/31/2017	12/31/2016	12/31/2015	12/31/2014	12/31/2013	12/31/2012	12/31/2011
Earnings Per Share	0.45	(0.31)	(1.80)	1.09	2.43	1.55	0.91	0.74
Cash Flow Per Share	4.46	4.54	5.41	19.34	18.14	9.20	10.42	9.25
Tang Book Value Per Share	17.99	18.18	19.36	N.M.	N.M.	N.M.	N.M.	3.73
Dividends Per Share	3.640	3.640	3.640	3.390	2.678	2.055	1.518	0.932
Dividend Payout %	808.89	...	...	311.01	110.19	132.58	166.76	125.89
Income Statement								
Total Revenue	2,455,600	8,814,900	6,690,900	6,658,600	8,616,500	6,556,000	5,885,700	6,994,500
EBITDA	32,900	579,100	610,300	663,000	982,900	656,600	530,900	538,900
Depn & Amortn	2,700	621,300	601,500	540,400	362,800	287,800	215,800	194,000
Income Before Taxes	46,300	(275,900)	(245,400)	(109,300)	473,000	234,700	194,300	233,200
Income Taxes	8,900	(397,100)	(100,600)	39,600	68,000	48,200	36,900	26,600
Net Income	22,900	54,000	(187,300)	58,300	102,300	65,100	38,100	30,700
Average Shares	218,700	206,900	154,400	53,600	42,100	42,100	41,800	41,400
Balance Sheet								
Current Assets	1,160,300	1,269,900	1,006,800	920,000	882,600	897,200	733,300	866,500
Total Assets	14,753,200	14,388,600	12,871,200	13,253,700	6,453,500	6,048,600	5,105,000	3,831,000
Current Liabilities	1,384,300	1,616,600	1,167,600	881,600	827,100	770,400	686,600	741,100
Long-Term Obligations	5,064,200	4,703,000	4,606,000	5,761,500	2,885,400	2,989,300	2,475,300	1,567,000
Total Liabilities	8,439,000	8,011,800	7,431,800	11,792,300	6,283,700	5,899,800	4,960,900	3,672,900
Stockholders' Equity	6,314,200	6,376,800	5,439,400	1,461,400	169,800	148,800	144,100	158,100
Shares Outstanding	218,832	217,566	184,720	56,020	42,143	42,162	42,294	42,398
Statistical Record								
Return on Assets %	1.38	0.40	N.M.	0.59	1.64	1.17	0.85	0.85
Return on Equity %	3.22	0.91	N.M.	7.15	64.22	44.45	25.15	20.30
EBITDA Margin %	1.34	6.57	9.12	9.96	11.41	10.02	9.02	7.70
Net Margin %	0.93	0.61	N.M.	0.88	1.19	0.99	0.65	0.44
Asset Turnover	0.64	0.65	0.51	0.68	1.38	1.18	1.31	1.94
Current Ratio	0.84	0.79	0.86	1.04	1.07	1.16	1.07	1.17
Debt to Equity	0.80	0.74	0.85	3.94	16.99	20.09	17.18	9.91
Price Range	59.90-40.35	61.35-40.35	58.20-15.43	107.22-25.74	150.62-85.34	88.46-52.84	52.84-39.62	41.05-26.68
P/E Ratio	133.11-89.67	...	...	98.37-23.61	61.98-35.12	57.07-34.09	58.07-43.54	55.47-36.05
Average Yield %	7.73	7.34	9.25	4.40	2.32	2.98	3.30	2.85

Address: 811 Louisiana St., Suite 2100, Houston, TX 77002 Telephone: 713-584-1000 Fax: 713-584-1100	Web Site: www.targaresources.com Officers: James W. Whalen - Executive Chairman, Advisor Matthew J. Meloy - President, Chief Financial Officer, Executive Vice President, Senior Vice President, Treasurer	Auditors: PricewaterhouseCoopers LLP Investor Contact: 713-584-1000 Transfer Agents: Computershare Trust Company, N.A.

TAUBMAN CENTERS INC

Exchange	Symbol	Price	52Wk Range	Yield	P/E
NYS	TCO	$58.76 (6/29/2018)	66.39-46.30	4.46	63.87

*7 Year Price Score 64.97 *NYSE Composite Index=100 *12 Month Price Score 98.22

Interim Earnings (Per Share)
Qtr.	Mar	Jun	Sep	Dec
2015	0.47	0.37	0.50	0.42
2016	0.41	0.57	0.31	0.48
2017	0.28	0.22	0.07	0.33
2018	0.30	...	...	...

Interim Dividends (Per Share)
Amt	Decl	Ex	Rec	Pay
0.625Q	09/01/2017	09/14/2017	09/15/2017	09/29/2017
0.625Q	12/04/2017	12/14/2017	12/15/2017	12/29/2017
0.655Q	03/02/2018	03/14/2018	03/15/2018	03/30/2018
0.655Q	05/31/2018	06/14/2018	06/15/2018	06/29/2018

Indicated Div: $2.62

Valuation Analysis / Institutional Holding
Forecast EPS	$1.32	No of Institutions
	(06/14/2018)	397
Market Cap	$3.6 Billion	Shares
Book Value	$6.9 Million	83,523,504
Price/Book	518.12	% Held
Price/Sales	5.59	104.85

TRADING VOLUME (thousand shares)

Business Summary: REITs (MIC: 5.3.1 SIC: 6798 NAIC: 525930)

Taubman Centers is a self-administered and self-managed real estate investment trust. The Taubman Realty Group Limited Partnership is a majority-owned partnership subsidiary of Co. that owns direct or indirect interests in all of Co.'s real estate properties. Co. owns, leases, acquires, disposes of, develops, expands, and manages regional shopping centers and interests therein. Co's owned portfolio of operating centers as of Dec 31 2017 consisted of 24 urban and suburban shopping centers operating in 11 U.S. states, Puerto Rico, South Korea, and China. The Consolidated Businesses consist of shopping centers and entities that are controlled by ownership or contractual agreements.

Recent Developments: For the quarter ended Mar 31 2018, net income increased 5.6% to US$34.6 million from US$32.8 million in the year-earlier quarter. Revenues were US$161.5 million, up 8.3% from US$149.1 million the year before. Revenues from property income rose 3.0% to US$89.5 million from US$86.9 million in the corresponding quarter a year earlier.

Prospects: Our evaluation of Taubman Centers Inc. as of Jan. 21, 2018 is the result of our systematic analysis on three basic characteristics: earnings strength, relative valuation, and recent stock price movement. The company has managed to produce a neutral trend in earnings per share over the past 5 quarters. Because the company lacks sufficient analyst estimate data, we place greater weight on the historical EPS trend as the measure of earnings strength. Based on operating earnings yield, the company is overvalued when compared to all of the companies in our coverage universe. Share price changes over the past year indicates that TCO will perform poorly over the near term.

Financial Data
(US$ in Thousands)	3 Mos	12/31/2017	12/31/2016	12/31/2015	12/31/2014	12/31/2013	12/31/2012	12/31/2011
Earnings Per Share	0.92	0.91	1.77	1.76	13.47	1.71	1.37	3.03
Cash Flow Per Share	4.13	4.61	5.04	5.01	5.75	5.84	5.40	4.75
Tang Book Value Per Share	0.11	0.37	1.19	1.87	5.03	...	...	...
Dividends Per Share	2.530	2.500	2.380	2.260	6.910	2.000	1.850	1.763
Dividend Payout %	275.00	274.73	134.46	128.41	51.30	116.96	135.04	58.17
Income Statement								
Total Revenue	161,492	629,165	612,557	557,172	679,129	767,154	747,974	644,918
EBITDA	80,897	315,160	337,347	299,983	312,736	412,835	391,803	345,422
Depn & Amortn	35,022	161,100	130,400	98,800	110,100	142,500	134,900	127,200
Income Before Taxes	15,052	45,488	120,662	138,142	111,833	140,312	114,287	95,945
Income Taxes	184	105	2,212	2,248	2,267	3,409	4,964	610
Net Income	24,973	80,705	132,613	134,127	893,013	132,590	106,174	192,871
Average Shares	60,917	61,040	60,829	62,161	64,921	64,575	61,376	58,529
Balance Sheet								
Current Assets	257,026	125,172	103,812	270,107	364,002	121,036	109,237	380,759
Total Assets	4,245,995	4,214,592	4,010,912	3,563,380	3,214,901	3,506,222	3,268,495	3,336,792
Current Liabilities	768,228	801,892	817,399	798,611	769,453	663,829	661,391	447,403
Long-Term Obligations	3,640,128	3,555,228	3,255,512	2,643,958	2,025,505	3,058,053	2,952,030	3,145,602
Total Liabilities	4,239,078	4,192,352	3,938,832	3,450,573	2,896,538	3,626,349	3,524,113	3,552,916
Stockholders' Equity	6,917	22,240	72,080	112,807	318,363	(120,127)	(255,618)	(216,124)
Shares Outstanding	60,991	60,832	60,430	60,233	63,324	63,101	63,310	58,022
Statistical Record								
Return on Assets %	1.98	1.96	3.49	3.96	26.57	3.91	3.21	6.56
Return on Equity %	232.76	171.13	143.06	62.22	900.96	...	...	...
EBITDA Margin %	50.09	50.09	55.07	53.84	46.05	53.81	52.38	53.56
Net Margin %	15.46	12.83	21.65	24.07	131.49	17.28	14.19	29.91
Asset Turnover	0.15	0.15	0.16	0.16	0.20	0.23	0.23	0.22
Current Ratio	0.33	0.16	0.13	0.34	0.47	0.18	0.17	0.85
Debt to Equity	526.26	159.86	45.17	23.44	6.36	...	...	...
Price Range	66.64-46.30	76.17-46.30	81.63-66.67	84.70-67.14	80.06-63.34	88.95-63.65	81.34-62.03	62.71-48.27
P/E Ratio	72.43-50.33	83.70-50.88	46.12-37.67	48.13-38.15	5.94-4.70	52.02-37.22	59.37-45.28	20.70-15.93
Average Yield %	4.37	4.16	3.27	3.03	9.43	2.68	2.46	3.13

| **Address:** 200 East Long Lake Road, Suite 300, Bloomfield Hills, MI 48304-2324 **Telephone:** 248-258-6800 | **Web Site:** www.taubman.com **Officers:** Robert S. Taubman - Chairman, President, Chief Executive Officer Paul A. Wright - Executive Vice President, Head | **Auditors:** KPMG LLP **Investor Contact:** 248-258-7367 **Transfer Agents:** Computershare, Providence, R.I. |

TC PIPELINES, LP

Exchange	Symbol	Price	52Wk Range	Yield	P/E	Div Acheiver
NYS	TCP	$25.95 (6/29/2018)	59.30-23.16	10.02	7.54	18 Years

*7 Year Price Score 73.25 *NYSE Composite Index=100 *12 Month Price Score 58.46

Interim Earnings (Per Share)

Qtr.	Mar	Jun	Sep	Dec
2015	0.88	0.66	0.70	(2.26)
2016	1.10	0.76	0.65	0.70
2017	1.05	0.73	0.61	0.78
2018	1.32	...	...	...

Interim Dividends (Per Share)

Amt	Decl	Ex	Rec	Pay
1.00Q	07/20/2017	07/28/2017	08/01/2017	08/11/2017
1.00Q	10/24/2017	11/02/2017	11/03/2017	11/14/2017
1.00Q	01/23/2018	02/01/2018	02/02/2018	02/13/2018
0.65Q	05/02/2018	05/08/2018	05/09/2018	05/15/2018

Indicated Div: $2.60

Valuation Analysis

		Institutional Holding	
Forecast EPS	$3.63	No of Institutions	
(05/29/2018)		247	
Market Cap	$1.9 Billion	Shares	
Book Value	N/A	53,338,468	
Price/Book	N/A	% Held	
Price/Sales	4.35	61.79	

Business Summary: Equipment & Services (MIC: 9.1.3 SIC: 4922 NAIC: 486210)

TC PipeLines is engaged in acquiring, owning and participating in the management of energy infrastructure businesses in North America. As of Dec 31 2017, Co. had ownership interests in eight pipelines that are collectively designed to transport approximately 10.4 billion cubic feet per day of natural gas from producing regions and import facilities to market hubs and consuming markets primarily in the Western, Midwestern and Eastern U.S. All of Co.'s pipeline systems, except Iroquois and the PNGTS joint facilities, are operated by subsidiaries of TransCanada Corporation and its subsidiaries.

Recent Developments: For the quarter ended Mar 31 2018, net income increased 22.9% to US$102.0 million from US$83.0 million in the year-earlier quarter. Revenues were US$115.0 million, up 2.7% from US$112.0 million the year before. Indirect operating expenses decreased 57.1% to US$12.0 million from US$28.0 million in the equivalent prior-year period.

Prospects: Our evaluation of TC PipeLines L.P. as of Jan. 21, 2018 is the result of our systematic analysis on three basic characteristics: earnings strength, relative valuation, and recent stock price movement. The company has enjoyed a very positive trend in earnings per share over the past 5 quarters. However, while recent estimates for the company have been mixed, TCP has posted results that fell short of analysts expectations. Based on operating earnings yield, the company is undervalued when compared to all of the companies in our coverage universe. Share price changes over the past year indicates that TCP will perform poorly over the near term.

Financial Data

(US$ in Thousands)	3 Mos	12/31/2017	12/31/2016	12/31/2015	12/31/2014	12/31/2013	12/31/2012	12/31/2011
Earnings Per Share	3.44	3.16	3.21	(0.03)	2.67	2.13	2.51	3.02
Cash Flow Per Share	5.66	5.43	5.78	4.60	4.91	4.62	2.85	3.31
Dividends Per Share	3.940	3.880	3.660	3.460	3.300	3.180	3.100	3.040
Dividend Payout %	114.53	122.78	114.02	...	123.60	149.30	123.51	100.66
Income Statement								
Total Revenue	115,000	422,000	357,000	344,000	336,000	341,000	65,000	70,400
EBITDA	93,000	318,000	278,000	61,000	249,000	252,000	41,000	31,500
Depn & Amortn	25,000	97,000	86,000	85,000	86,000	86,000	11,000	15,200
Income Before Taxes	44,000	140,000	128,000	(77,000)	116,000	124,000	8,000	3,900
Income Taxes	1,000	1,000	...	...	...	...	...	...
Net Income	96,000	252,000	244,000	13,000	172,000	155,000	137,000	157,400
Average Shares	71,200	69,200	67,400	63,900	62,700	58,900	53,500	51,100
Balance Sheet								
Current Assets	143,000	90,000	102,000	81,000	68,000	69,000	12,000	38,300
Total Assets	3,604,000	3,559,000	3,158,000	3,133,000	3,349,000	3,443,000	1,998,000	2,082,000
Current Liabilities	109,000	100,000	66,000	59,000	291,000	55,000	11,000	9,200
Long-Term Obligations	2,332,000	2,352,000	1,835,000	1,896,000	1,446,000	1,575,000	685,000	739,400
Total Liabilities	2,589,000	2,596,000	1,929,000	1,982,000	1,997,000	2,094,000	697,000	749,000
Stockholders' Equity	...	...	83,000	...	...	...	...	...
Shares Outstanding	71,300	72,473	69,354	66,217	63,561	62,327	53,472	53,472
Statistical Record								
Return on Assets %	8.01	7.50	7.74	0.40	5.06	5.70	6.70	8.43
EBITDA Margin %	80.87	75.36	77.87	17.73	74.11	73.90	63.08	44.74
Net Margin %	83.48	59.72	68.35	3.78	51.19	45.45	210.77	223.58
Asset Turnover	0.13	0.13	0.11	0.11	0.10	0.13	0.03	0.04
Current Ratio	1.31	0.90	1.55	1.37	0.23	1.25	1.09	4.16
Debt to Equity	...	...	22.11	...	...	...	...	...
Price Range	60.88-34.24	64.90-48.88	59.99-35.44	72.53-41.48	76.59-45.52	52.18-40.36	47.58-38.50	54.45-40.17
P/E Ratio	17.70-9.95	20.54-15.47	18.69-11.04	...	28.69-17.05	24.50-18.95	18.96-15.34	18.03-13.30
Average Yield %	7.39	6.94	7.04	5.94	5.92	6.75	7.05	6.36

Address: 700 Louisiana Street, Suite 700, Houston, TX 77002-2761 **Telephone:** 877-290-2772	**Web Site:** www.tcpipeleineslp.com **Officers:** Karl R. Johannson - Chairman, Holding/Parent Company Officer Brandon M. Anderson - President, Principal Executive Officer, Holding/Parent Company Officer	**Auditors:** KPMG LLP **Investor Contact:** 877-.29-0.2772 **Transfer Agents:** Computershare

TCF FINANCIAL CORP

Exchange	Symbol	Price	52Wk Range	Yield	P/E
NYS	TCF	$24.62 (6/29/2018)	27.20-14.76	2.44	15.48

*7 Year Price Score 109.04 *NYSE Composite Index=100 *12 Month Price Score 124.24

Interim Earnings (Per Share)

Qtr.	Mar	Jun	Sep	Dec
2015	0.21	0.29	0.29	0.29
2016	0.26	0.31	0.31	0.27
2017	0.25	0.33	0.29	0.58
2018	0.39	...	...	...

Interim Dividends (Per Share)

Amt	Decl	Ex	Rec	Pay
0.075Q	07/19/2017	08/11/2017	08/15/2017	09/01/2017
0.075Q	10/18/2017	11/14/2017	11/15/2017	12/01/2017
0.15Q	01/30/2018	02/14/2018	02/15/2018	03/01/2018
0.15Q	04/19/2018	05/14/2018	05/15/2018	06/01/2018

Indicated Div: $0.60 (Div. Reinv. Plan)

Valuation Analysis — **Institutional Holding**

Forecast EPS	$1.77	No of Institutions
	(06/14/2018)	424
Market Cap	$4.2 Billion	Shares
Book Value	$2.5 Billion	178,847,520
Price/Book	1.65	% Held
Price/Sales	2.76	81.69

Business Summary: Banking (MIC: 5.1.1 SIC: 6021 NAIC: 522110)

TCF Financial is a bank holding company. Through its subsidiary, TCF National Bank (TCF Bank), Co. provides retail banking products and commercial banking products. Co. also conducts commercial leasing and equipment finance business in all 50 states and, to a limited extent, in foreign countries; commercial inventory finance business in all 50 states and Canada and, to a limited extent, in other foreign countries and indirect auto finance business in all 50 states. Co.'s reportable segments are comprised of: Consumer Banking, Wholesale Banking and Enterprise Services. At Dec 31 2017, Co. had total assets of $23.00 billion and total deposits of $18.34 billion.

Recent Developments: For the quarter ended Mar 31 2018, net income increased 59.4% to US$73.8 million from US$46.3 million in the year-earlier quarter. Net interest income increased 9.5% to US$243.2 million from US$222.1 million in the year-earlier quarter. Provision for loan losses was US$11.4 million versus US$12.2 million in the prior-year quarter, a decrease of 6.8%. Non-interest income rose 8.4% to US$112.2 million from US$103.5 million, while non-interest expense advanced 0.8% to US$246.0 million.

Prospects: Our evaluation of TCF Financial Corp. as of Jan. 21, 2018 is the result of our systematic analysis on three basic characteristics: earnings strength, relative valuation, and recent stock price movement. The company has produced a positive trend in earnings per share over the past 5 quarters and while recent estimates for the company have been raised by analysts, TCF has posted results that fell short of analysts expectations. Based on operating earnings yield, the company is undervalued when compared to all of the companies in our coverage universe. Share price changes over the past year indicates that TCF will perform very poorly over the near term.

Financial Data

(US$ in Thousands)	3 Mos	12/31/2017	12/31/2016	12/31/2015	12/31/2014	12/31/2013	12/31/2012	12/31/2011
Earnings Per Share	1.59	1.44	1.15	1.07	0.94	0.82	(1.37)	0.71
Cash Flow Per Share	2.96	1.42	1.73	2.19	1.91	2.55	3.12	3.22
Tang Book Value Per Share	12.98	13.06	11.34	10.61	9.75	8.87	8.41	10.24
Dividends Per Share	0.375	0.300	0.300	0.225	0.200	0.200	0.200	0.200
Dividend Payout %	23.58	20.83	26.09	21.03	21.28	24.39	...	28.17
Income Statement								
Interest Income	275,262	1,019,057	930,730	891,930	874,229	864,540	884,623	937,951
Interest Expense	32,063	93,819	82,624	71,542	58,600	61,916	104,604	238,263
Net Interest Income	243,199	925,238	848,106	820,388	815,629	802,624	780,019	699,688
Provision for Losses	11,368	68,443	65,874	52,944	95,737	118,368	247,443	200,843
Non-Interest Income	112,204	448,299	465,900	441,998	433,267	404,058	490,423	444,434
Non-Interest Expense	245,980	1,059,934	909,887	894,747	871,777	845,269	1,362,554	764,451
Income Before Taxes	98,055	245,160	338,245	314,695	281,382	243,045	(339,555)	178,828
Income Taxes	21,631	(33,624)	116,528	108,872	99,766	84,345	(132,858)	64,441
Net Income	73,761	268,637	212,124	197,123	174,187	151,668	(212,884)	109,394
Average Shares	169,997	168,679	167,807	166,241	164,084	161,926	159,268	154,509
Balance Sheet								
Net Loans & Leases	19,266,157	19,068,281	17,952,390	17,437,570	16,369,743	15,674,477	15,168,885	13,908,904
Total Assets	23,385,052	23,002,159	21,441,326	20,691,704	19,394,611	18,379,840	18,225,917	18,979,388
Total Deposits	18,697,672	18,335,002	17,242,522	16,719,989	15,449,882	14,432,776	14,050,786	12,202,004
Total Liabilities	20,862,539	20,339,402	19,013,843	18,400,788	17,272,962	16,426,872	16,362,544	17,111,255
Stockholders' Equity	2,522,513	2,662,757	2,427,483	2,290,916	2,121,649	1,952,968	1,863,373	1,868,133
Shares Outstanding	169,415	171,669	170,991	169,844	167,461	165,122	163,386	160,323
Statistical Record								
Return on Assets %	1.31	1.21	1.00	0.98	0.92	0.83	N.M.	0.58
Return on Equity %	11.88	10.55	8.97	8.93	8.55	7.95	N.M.	6.55
Net Interest Margin %	88.35	90.79	91.12	91.98	93.30	92.84	88.18	74.60
Efficiency Ratio %	63.48	72.23	65.15	67.08	66.68	66.63	99.09	55.30
Loans to Deposits	1.03	1.04	1.04	1.04	1.06	1.09	1.08	1.14
Price Range	23.66-14.76	20.85-14.76	19.91-10.47	17.16-13.95	17.19-14.26	16.45-12.15	12.44-9.85	16.99-8.79
P/E Ratio	14.88-9.28	14.48-10.25	17.31-9.10	16.04-13.04	18.29-15.17	20.06-14.82	...	23.93-12.38
Average Yield %	2.07	1.76	2.16	1.44	1.26	1.37	1.77	1.54

Address: 200 Lake Street East, Wayzata, MN 55391-1693
Telephone: 952-745-2760

Web Site: www.tcfbank.com
Officers: Craig R. Dahl - Chairman, Vice-Chairman, President, Chief Executive Officer, Executive Vice President Thomas F. Jasper - Vice-Chairman, Chief Operating Officer, Executive Vice President, Chief Financial Officer

Auditors: KPMG LLP
Investor Contact: 952-745-2756
Transfer Agents: Computershare Trust Company, N.A., Providence, RI

TE CONNECTIVITY LTD

Exchange	Symbol	Price	52Wk Range	Yield	P/E
NYS	TEL	$90.06 (6/29/2018)	105.75-77.61	1.95	24.27

*7 Year Price Score 125.02 *NYSE Composite Index=100 *12 Month Price Score 101.16

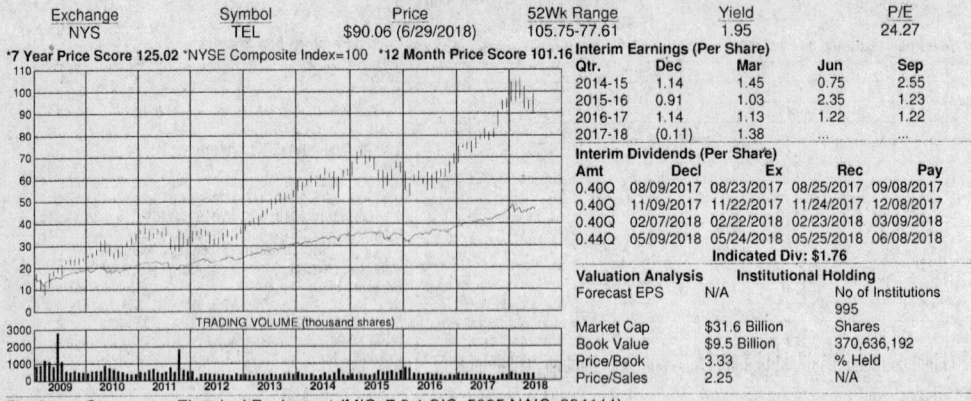

Interim Earnings (Per Share)

Qtr.	Dec	Mar	Jun	Sep
2014-15	1.14	1.45	0.75	2.55
2015-16	0.91	1.03	2.35	1.23
2016-17	1.14	1.13	1.22	1.22
2017-18	(0.11)	1.38	...	...

Interim Dividends (Per Share)

Amt	Decl	Ex	Rec	Pay
0.40Q	08/09/2017	08/23/2017	08/25/2017	09/08/2017
0.40Q	11/09/2017	11/22/2017	11/24/2017	12/08/2017
0.40Q	02/07/2018	02/22/2018	02/23/2018	03/09/2018
0.44Q	05/09/2018	05/24/2018	05/25/2018	06/08/2018

Indicated Div: $1.76

Valuation Analysis **Institutional Holding**

Forecast EPS	N/A	No of Institutions
		995
Market Cap	$31.6 Billion	Shares
Book Value	$9.5 Billion	370,636,192
Price/Book	3.33	% Held
Price/Sales	2.25	N/A

Business Summary: Electrical Equipment (MIC: 7.3.1 SIC: 5065 NAIC: 334111)

TE Connectivity operates three segments: Transportation Solutions, which engages in connectivity and sensor technologies, focusing on terminals and connector systems and components, sensors, relays, application tooling, and wire and heat shrink tubing; Industrial Solutions, which supplies products that connect and distribute power, data and signals, focusing on terminals and connector systems and components, heat shrink tubing, relays, and wire and cable; and Communications Solutions, which supplies electronics for the data and devices and appliances markets, focusing on terminals and connector systems and components, undersea telecommunication systems, heat shrink tubing, and antennas.

Recent Developments: For the quarter ended Mar 30 2018, income from continuing operations increased 21.2% to US$492.0 million from US$406.0 million in the year-earlier quarter. Net income increased 21.0% to US$490.0 million from US$405.0 million in the year-earlier quarter. Revenues were US$3.75 billion, up 16.1% from US$3.23 billion the year before. Operating income was US$624.0 million versus US$481.0 million in the prior-year quarter, an increase of 29.7%. Direct operating expenses rose 18.2% to US$2.50 billion from US$2.12 billion in the comparable period the year before. Indirect operating expenses decreased 1.6% to US$619.0 million from US$629.0 million in the equivalent prior-year period.

Prospects: Our evaluation of TE Connectivity Ltd. as of Sep. 17, 2017 is the result of our systematic analysis on three basic characteristics: earnings strength, relative valuation, and recent stock price movement. The company has generated a negative trend in earnings per share over the past 5 quarters and while recent estimates for the company have remained steady, TEL has posted better than expected results. Based on operating earnings yield, the company is undervalued when compared to all of the companies in our coverage universe. Share price changes over the past year indicates that TEL will perform well over the near term.

Financial Data

(US$ in Millions)	6 Mos	3 Mos	09/30/2017	09/30/2016	09/25/2015	09/26/2014	09/27/2013	09/28/2012
Earnings Per Share	3.71	3.46	4.70	5.44	5.89	4.27	3.02	2.59
Cash Flow Per Share	6.05	6.44	6.54	5.17	4.74	5.09	4.91	4.58
Tang Book Value Per Share	5.60	6.13	6.42	3.14	8.14	7.56	6.83	5.47
Dividends Per Share	1.600	1.570	1.540	1.400	1.240	1.080	0.920	0.780
Dividend Payout %	43.13	45.38	32.77	25.74	21.05	25.29	30.46	30.12
Income Statement								
Total Revenue	7,225	3,480	13,113	12,238	12,233	13,912	13,280	13,282
EBITDA	1,549	751	2,504	1,706	2,157	2,610	1,869	2,070
Depn & Amortn	341	168	466	436	463	502	496	502
Income Before Taxes	1,161	561	1,928	1,162	1,575	1,996	1,248	1,415
Income Taxes	708	600	255	(779)	337	207	(29)	249
Net Income	450	(40)	1,683	2,009	2,420	1,781	1,276	1,112
Average Shares	354	352	358	369	411	417	423	430
Balance Sheet								
Current Assets	5,960	5,733	5,926	4,775	7,887	7,544	6,309	6,503
Total Assets	19,247	18,811	19,403	17,608	20,608	20,152	18,461	19,306
Current Liabilities	4,164	3,635	3,847	3,066	3,577	3,954	3,924	4,004
Long-Term Obligations	3,335	3,317	3,634	3,739	3,403	3,281	2,303	2,696
Total Liabilities	9,767	9,180	9,652	9,123	11,023	11,145	10,081	11,335
Stockholders' Equity	9,480	9,631	9,751	8,485	9,585	9,007	8,380	7,971
Shares Outstanding	350	351	351	355	393	407	411	422
Statistical Record								
Return on Assets %	7.07	6.78	9.09	10.34	11.91	9.25	6.78	6.02
Return on Equity %	14.47	13.36	18.46	21.88	26.10	20.54	15.65	14.44
EBITDA Margin %	21.44	21.58	19.10	13.94	17.63	18.76	14.07	15.59
Net Margin %	6.23	N.M.	12.83	16.42	19.78	12.80	9.61	8.37
Asset Turnover	0.75	0.74	0.71	0.63	0.60	0.72	0.71	0.72
Current Ratio	1.43	1.58	1.54	1.56	2.20	1.91	1.61	1.62
Debt to Equity	0.35	0.34	0.37	0.44	0.36	0.36	0.27	0.34
Price Range	105.75-71.93	96.23-67.31	83.22-61.03	67.61-52.27	73.42-51.47	64.97-49.91	53.54-32.03	37.30-27.25
P/E Ratio	28.50-19.39	27.81-19.45	17.71-12.99	12.43-9.61	12.47-8.74	15.22-11.69	17.73-10.61	14.40-10.52
Average Yield %	1.83	1.95	2.08	2.30	1.92	1.86	2.18	2.32

Address: Rheinstrasse 20, Schaffhausen, CH-8200 **Telephone:** 526-336-661	**Web Site:** www.te.com **Officers:** Terrence R. Curtin - President, Chief Executive Officer, Executive Vice President, Vice President, Chief Financial Officer, Corporate Controller, Division Officer Heath A. Mitts - Executive Vice President, Chief Financial Officer	**Auditors:** Deloitte†& Touche†LLP **Investor Contact:** 610-893-9551 **Transfer Agents:** Computershare Shareowner Services LLC, Jersey City, NJ

TELEDYNE TECHNOLOGIES INC

Exchange	Symbol	Price	52Wk Range	Yield	P/E
NYS	TDY	$199.06 (6/29/2018)	213.77-127.65	N/A	27.57

*7 Year Price Score 140.69 *NYSE Composite Index=100 *12 Month Price Score 111.67

TRADING VOLUME (thousand shares)

Interim Earnings (Per Share)

Qtr.	Mar	Jun	Sep	Dec
2015	1.20	1.34	1.34	1.56
2016	1.10	1.31	1.46	1.47
2017	0.84	1.66	1.90	1.85
2018	1.81	...	...	...

Interim Dividends (Per Share)

No Dividends Paid

Valuation Analysis

		Institutional Holding	
Forecast EPS	$7.75	No of Institutions	
	(05/21/2018)	416	
Market Cap	$7.1 Billion	Shares	
Book Value	$2.1 Billion	41,330,444	
Price/Book	3.46	% Held	
Price/Sales	2.60	84.42	

Business Summary: Electronic Instruments & Related Products (MIC: 6.2.3 SIC: 3812 NAIC: 334511)

Teledyne Technologies provides technologies for industrial markets. Co. has four segments: Instrumentation; which provides monitoring and control instruments for marine, environmental, industrial and other applications, as well as electronic test and measurement equipment; Digital Imaging, which includes sensors, cameras and systems, as well as micro electro mechanical systems; Aerospace and Defense Electronics, which provide electronic components and subsystems and communications products; and Engineered Systems, which provide systems engineering and integration, technology development, as well as manufacturing solutions for defense, space, environmental and energy applications.

Recent Developments: For the quarter ended Apr 1 2018, net income increased 118.0% to US$66.5 million from US$30.5 million in the year-earlier quarter. Revenues were US$695.6 million, up 22.9% from US$566.1 million the year before. Operating income was US$88.4 million versus US$54.8 million in the prior-year quarter, an increase of 61.3%. Direct operating expenses rose 22.7% to US$438.2 million from US$357.0 million in the comparable period the year before. Indirect operating expenses increased 9.5% to US$169.0 million from US$154.3 million in the equivalent prior-year period.

Prospects: Our evaluation of Teledyne Technologies Inc. as of Jan. 21, 2018 is the result of our systematic analysis on three basic characteristics: earnings strength, relative valuation, and recent stock price movement. The company has generated a negative trend in earnings per share over the past 5 quarters and while recent estimates for the company have remained steady, TDY has posted better than expected results. Based on operating earnings yield, the company is about fairly valued when compared to all of the companies in our coverage universe. Share price changes over the past year indicates that TDY will perform well over the near term.

Financial Data
(US$ in Thousands)

	3 Mos	12/31/2017	01/01/2017	01/03/2016	12/28/2014	12/29/2013	12/30/2012	01/01/2012
Earnings Per Share	7.22	6.26	5.37	5.44	5.75	4.87	4.39	6.84
Cash Flow Per Share	11.04	10.67	9.19	5.86	7.78	5.49	5.18	5.93
Tang Book Value Per Share	N.M.	N.M.	3.60	N.M.	N.M.	4.34	N.M.	2.20
Income Statement								
Total Revenue	695,600	2,603,800	2,149,900	2,298,100	2,394,000	2,338,600	2,127,300	1,941,900
EBITDA	118,100	386,000	322,100	340,400	363,400	304,000	294,900	267,400
Depn & Amortn	28,800	65,900	57,600	58,300	62,300	59,600	48,900	39,600
Income Before Taxes	82,200	287,000	241,300	258,200	282,100	224,000	228,200	211,600
Income Taxes	15,700	59,800	50,400	62,700	66,500	39,500	65,400	69,500
Net Income	66,500	227,200	190,900	195,800	217,700	185,000	164,100	255,200
Average Shares	36,800	36,300	35,500	35,300	37,900	38,000	37,400	37,300
Balance Sheet								
Current Assets	1,060,200	1,011,900	846,200	828,200	941,700	799,100	744,800	602,700
Total Assets	3,920,100	3,846,400	2,774,400	2,718,500	2,862,200	2,751,100	2,406,400	1,826,100
Current Liabilities	555,200	540,600	501,800	393,600	539,000	418,100	407,300	334,200
Long-Term Obligations	1,019,200	1,069,300	515,800	762,900	618,900	549,000	556,200	311,400
Total Liabilities	1,864,200	1,899,100	1,220,000	1,374,400	1,434,900	1,279,400	1,258,600	846,800
Stockholders' Equity	2,055,900	1,947,300	1,554,400	1,344,100	1,427,300	1,471,700	1,147,800	979,300
Shares Outstanding	35,739	35,540	35,110	34,514	36,655	37,571	37,162	36,449
Statistical Record								
Return on Assets %	6.93	6.88	6.97	6.90	7.78	7.19	7.78	15.12
Return on Equity %	14.38	13.01	13.21	13.90	15.06	14.16	15.47	28.99
EBITDA Margin %	16.98	14.82	14.98	14.81	15.18	13.00	13.86	13.77
Net Margin %	9.56	8.73	8.88	8.52	9.09	7.91	7.71	13.14
Asset Turnover	0.72	0.79	0.78	0.81	0.86	0.91	1.01	1.15
Current Ratio	1.91	1.87	1.69	2.10	1.75	1.91	1.83	1.80
Debt to Equity	0.50	0.55	0.33	0.57	0.43	0.37	0.48	0.32
Price Range	199.49-121.96	186.24-121.11	128.89-76.61	111.48-83.47	108.50-88.48	92.99-65.07	65.76-55.22	58.56-43.93
P/E Ratio	27.63-16.89	29.75-19.35	24.00-14.27	20.49-15.34	18.87-15.39	19.09-13.36	14.98-12.58	8.56-6.42

Address: 1049 Camino Dos Rios, Thousand Oaks, CA 91360-2362	**Web Site:** www.teledyne.com	**Auditors:** Deloitte & Touche LLP
Telephone: 805-373-4545	**Officers:** Robert Mehrabian - Chairman, President, Chief Executive Officer Aldo (Al) Pichelli - President,	**Investor Contact:** 805-373-4542
Fax: 805-373-4775	Executive Vice President, Division Officer, Chief Operating Officer	**Transfer Agents:** Computershare, Jersey City, NJ

TELEFLEX INCORPORATED

Exchange	Symbol	Price	52Wk Range	Yield	P/E
NYS	TFX	$268.21 (6/29/2018)	287.65-203.01	0.51	74.30

*7 Year Price Score 153.94 *NYSE Composite Index=100 *12 Month Price Score 107.36

Interim Earnings (Per Share)

Qtr.	Mar	Jun	Sep	Dec
2015	0.81	0.93	1.25	2.10
2016	1.04	1.26	1.40	1.29
2017	0.86	1.67	1.65	(0.91)
2018	1.20	...	...	...

Interim Dividends (Per Share)

Amt	Decl	Ex	Rec	Pay
0.34Q	08/03/2017	08/11/2017	08/15/2017	09/15/2017
0.34Q	10/31/2017	11/14/2017	11/15/2017	12/15/2017
0.34Q	02/22/2018	03/01/2018	03/02/2018	03/15/2018
0.34Q	05/07/2018	05/14/2018	05/15/2018	06/15/2018

Indicated Div: $1.36 (Div. Reinv. Plan)

Valuation Analysis — **Institutional Holding**

Forecast EPS	$9.82 (06/13/2018)	No of Institutions	598
Market Cap	$12.6 Billion	Shares	53,696,508
Book Value	$2.6 Billion	% Held	94.56
Price/Book	4.92		
Price/Sales	5.61		

Business Summary: Medical Instruments & Equipment (MIC: 4.3.1 SIC: 3841 NAIC: 339112)

Teleflex is a provider of medical technology products. Co. designs, develops, manufactures and supplies single-use medical devices used by hospitals and healthcare providers for common diagnostic and therapeutic procedures in critical care and surgical applications. Co. has six segments: Vascular North America; Anesthesia North America; Surgical North America; Europe, the Middle East and Africa; Asia; and OEM. All of Co.'s segments, other than the OEM segment, design, manufacture and distribute medical devices used in critical care, surgical applications and cardiac care. Co.'s OEM segment designs, manufactures and supplies devices and instruments for other medical device manufacturers.

Recent Developments: For the quarter ended Apr 1 2018, income from continuing operations increased 36.1% to US$54.9 million from US$40.3 million in the year-earlier quarter. Net income increased 39.9% to US$56.2 million from US$40.2 million in the year-earlier quarter. Revenues were US$587.2 million, up 20.4% from US$487.9 million the year before. Operating income was US$86.8 million versus US$60.8 million in the prior-year quarter, an increase of 42.8%. Direct operating expenses rose 10.2% to US$256.0 million from US$232.3 million in the comparable period the year before. Indirect operating expenses increased 25.5% to US$244.4 million from US$194.7 million in the equivalent prior-year period.

Prospects: Our evaluation of Teleflex Inc. as of Jan. 21, 2018 is the result of our systematic analysis on three basic characteristics: earnings strength, relative valuation, and recent stock price movement. The company has generated a negative trend in earnings per share over the past 5 quarters. However, while recent estimates for the company have been mixed, TFX has posted better than expected results. Based on operating earnings yield, the company is overvalued when compared to all of the companies in our coverage universe. Share price changes over the past year indicates that TFX will perform well over the near term.

Financial Data

(US$ in Thousands)	3 Mos	12/31/2017	12/31/2016	12/31/2015	12/31/2014	12/31/2013	12/31/2012	12/31/2011
Earnings Per Share	3.61	3.27	4.98	5.10	4.04	3.45	(4.65)	7.92
Cash Flow Per Share	9.31	9.47	9.45	7.30	7.02	5.59	4.73	2.55
Dividends Per Share	1.360	1.360	1.360	1.360	1.360	1.360	1.360	1.360
Dividend Payout %	37.67	41.59	27.31	26.67	33.66	39.42	...	17.17
Income Statement								
Total Revenue	587,230	2,146,303	1,868,027	1,809,690	1,839,832	1,696,271	1,551,009	1,528,911
EBITDA	140,669	521,949	418,098	413,830	395,995	324,987	(16,907)	303,377
Depn & Amortn	53,826	155,263	117,906	108,393	111,133	92,976	80,468	85,617
Income Before Taxes	61,173	284,911	245,725	244,646	220,110	175,730	(165,369)	148,793
Income Taxes	6,242	129,648	8,074	7,838	28,650	23,547	16,413	27,000
Net Income	56,184	152,530	237,377	244,863	187,679	150,881	(190,057)	323,329
Average Shares	46,695	46,664	47,646	48,058	46,470	43,693	40,859	40,801
Balance Sheet								
Current Assets	1,205,159	1,128,807	1,183,393	1,006,431	1,053,209	1,200,554	1,069,079	1,280,256
Total Assets	6,300,600	6,181,492	3,891,213	3,878,516	3,977,255	4,209,007	3,739,497	3,924,103
Current Liabilities	551,742	483,876	427,646	666,712	634,899	635,120	274,405	271,007
Long-Term Obligations	2,154,217	2,162,927	850,252	646,000	700,000	930,000	965,280	954,809
Total Liabilities	3,740,100	3,750,961	1,751,872	1,869,244	2,065,946	2,295,480	1,960,547	1,943,515
Stockholders' Equity	2,560,500	2,430,531	2,139,341	2,009,272	1,911,309	1,913,527	1,778,950	1,980,588
Shares Outstanding	46,968	45,167	44,073	41,609	41,439	41,179	40,972	40,740
Statistical Record								
Return on Assets %	2.92	3.03	6.09	6.23	4.59	3.80	N.M.	8.55
Return on Equity %	7.05	6.68	11.41	12.49	9.81	8.17	N.M.	17.18
EBITDA Margin %	23.95	24.32	22.38	22.87	21.52	19.16	N.M.	19.84
Net Margin %	9.57	7.11	12.71	13.53	10.20	8.89	N.M.	21.15
Asset Turnover	0.39	0.43	0.48	0.46	0.45	0.43	0.40	0.40
Current Ratio	2.18	2.33	2.77	1.51	1.66	1.89	3.90	4.72
Debt to Equity	0.84	0.89	0.40	0.32	0.37	0.49	0.54	0.48
Price Range	287.65-192.50	270.19-158.86	188.35-126.00	140.26-109.41	119.15-90.94	98.82-71.31	71.38-57.73	63.81-49.51
P/E Ratio	79.68-53.32	82.63-48.58	37.82-25.30	27.50-21.45	29.49-22.51	28.64-20.67	...	8.06-6.25
Average Yield %	0.58	0.64	0.85	1.07	1.28	1.66	2.13	2.33

Address: 550 East Swedesford Road, Suite 400, Wayne, PA 19087
Telephone: 610-225-6800

Web Site: www.teleflex.com
Officers: Liam J. Kelly - President, Executive Vice President, Chief Operating Officer, Division Officer, Chief Executive Officer Thomas E. Powell - Executive Vice President, Senior Vice President, Chief Financial Officer

Auditors: PricewaterhouseCoopers LLP
Investor Contact: 610-948-2836
Transfer Agents: American Stock Transfer & Trust Company, New York, NY

TELEPHONE & DATA SYSTEMS INC

Exchange	Symbol	Price	52Wk Range	Yield	P/E	Div Acheiver
NYS	TDS	$27.42 (6/29/2018)	29.85-24.30	2.33	20.01	43 Years

*7 Year Price Score 84.70 *NYSE Composite Index=100 *12 Month Price Score 94.64

Interim Earnings (Per Share)

Qtr.	Mar	Jun	Sep	Dec
2015	1.33	0.21	0.46	(0.01)
2016	0.07	0.25	0.11	(0.05)
2017	0.33	0.09	(1.64)	2.58
2018	0.34	...	...	...

Interim Dividends (Per Share)

Amt	Decl	Ex	Rec	Pay
0.155Q	08/16/2017	09/14/2017	09/15/2017	09/29/2017
0.155Q	11/29/2017	12/14/2017	12/15/2017	12/28/2017
0.16Q	02/23/2018	03/15/2018	03/16/2018	03/29/2018
0.16Q	05/24/2018	06/14/2018	06/15/2018	06/29/2018

Indicated Div: $0.64

Valuation Analysis | **Institutional Holding**

Forecast EPS	$0.17	No of Institutions
	(06/12/2018)	393
Market Cap	$3.1 Billion	Shares
Book Value	$4.5 Billion	114,389,304
Price/Book	0.69	% Held
Price/Sales	0.61	N/A

Business Summary: Services (MIC: 6.1.2 SIC: 4813 NAIC: 517110)

Telephone and Data Systems is a telecommunications company. Co. provided communications services to approximately 5.1 million wireless customers and 1.2 million wireline and cable connections at Dec 31 2017. Co. conducts its wireless operations through its subsidiary, United States Cellular Corp. Co. provides broadband, video, voice and hosted and managed services, through its subsidiary, TDS Telecommunications Corporation. Co. has four business segments comprised of: U.S. Cellular, which provides a range of wireless devices such as handsets, tablets, mobile hotspots, home phones and routers; and TDS Telecom's Wireline, Cable, and Hosted and Managed Services operations.

Recent Developments:

For the quarter ended Mar 31 2018, net income increased 32.6% to US$57.0 million from US$43.0 million in the year-earlier quarter. Revenues were US$1.23 billion, down 1.1% from US$1.24 billion the year before. Operating income was US$80.0 million versus US$81.0 million in the prior-year quarter, a decrease of 1.2%. Direct operating expenses declined 3.3% to US$534.0 million from US$552.0 million in the comparable period the year before. Indirect operating expenses increased 1.0% to US$611.0 million from US$605.0 million in the equivalent prior-year period.

Prospects:

Our evaluation of Telephone and Data Systems Inc. as of Jan. 21, 2018 is the result of our systematic analysis on three basic characteristics: earnings strength, relative valuation, and recent stock price movement. The company has suffered a very negative trend in earnings per share over the past 5 quarters. Because the company lacks sufficient analyst estimate data, we place greater weight on the historical EPS trend as the measure of earnings strength. Based on operating earnings yield, the company is overvalued when compared to all of the companies in our coverage universe. Share price changes over the past year indicates that TDS will perform poorly over the near term.

Financial Data
(US$ in Thousands)

	3 Mos	12/31/2017	12/31/2016	12/31/2015	12/31/2014	12/31/2013	12/31/2012	12/31/2011
Earnings Per Share	1.37	1.37	0.39	1.98	(1.26)	1.29	0.75	1.83
Cash Flow Per Share	7.68	6.99	7.09	7.27	3.64	4.56	10.14	11.57
Tang Book Value Per Share	12.95	11.25	10.97	11.25	12.91	15.29	15.52	14.95
Dividends Per Share	0.625	0.620	0.592	0.564	0.536	0.510	0.490	0.470
Dividend Payout %	45.62	45.26	151.79	28.48	...	39.53	65.33	25.68
Income Statement								
Total Revenue	1,225,000	5,044,000	5,104,000	5,176,241	5,009,438	4,901,236	5,345,277	5,180,471
EBITDA	302,000	713,000	880,000	1,207,962	607,851	1,234,269	966,165	1,131,863
Depn & Amortn	221,000	817,000	820,000	810,500	797,600	984,400	785,300	741,600
Income Before Taxes	43,000	(259,000)	(48,000)	294,526	(284,189)	160,150	103,368	281,207
Income Taxes	24,000	(279,000)	40,000	171,992	(4,932)	126,043	73,582	113,503
Net Income	39,000	153,000	43,000	219,037	(136,355)	141,927	81,861	200,566
Average Shares	113,000	112,000	111,000	109,910	108,485	109,132	108,937	109,100
Balance Sheet								
Current Assets	2,043,000	1,966,000	2,059,000	2,158,343	1,766,955	2,087,337	1,763,437	1,705,680
Total Assets	9,481,000	9,295,000	9,446,000	9,422,462	8,906,939	8,904,147	8,623,900	8,201,005
Current Liabilities	750,000	918,000	887,000	944,384	1,063,256	1,191,756	924,608	874,133
Long-Term Obligations	2,431,000	2,437,000	2,433,000	2,439,827	1,993,586	1,720,074	1,721,571	1,529,857
Total Liabilities	5,009,000	5,026,000	5,301,000	5,296,088	4,979,837	4,785,486	4,611,539	4,238,014
Stockholders' Equity	4,472,000	4,269,000	4,145,000	4,126,374	3,927,102	4,118,661	4,012,361	3,962,991
Shares Outstanding	112,000	111,000	110,000	108,966	107,899	108,757	108,031	108,456
Statistical Record								
Return on Assets %	1.65	1.63	0.45	2.39	N.M.	1.62	0.97	2.51
Return on Equity %	3.58	3.64	1.04	5.44	N.M.	3.49	2.05	5.16
EBITDA Margin %	24.65	14.14	17.24	23.34	12.13	25.18	18.08	21.85
Net Margin %	3.18	3.03	0.84	4.23	N.M.	2.90	1.53	3.87
Asset Turnover	0.53	0.54	0.54	0.56	0.56	0.56	0.63	0.65
Current Ratio	2.72	2.14	2.32	2.29	1.66	1.75	1.91	1.95
Debt to Equity	0.54	0.57	0.59	0.59	0.51	0.42	0.43	0.39
Price Range	29.85-24.30	32.75-24.81	31.75-20.99	30.56-23.25	27.84-22.23	31.38-20.71	28.61-19.42	31.86-18.42
P/E Ratio	21.79-17.74	23.91-18.11	81.41-53.82	15.43-11.74	...	24.33-16.05	38.15-25.89	17.41-10.07
Average Yield %	2.27	2.22	2.22	2.14	2.10	2.00	2.08	1.81

Address: 30 North LaSalle Street, Suite 4000, Chicago, IL 60602	Web Site: www.teldta.com	Auditors: PricewaterhouseCoopers LLP
Telephone: 312-630-1900	Officers: LeRoy T. Carlson - President, Chief Executive Officer Douglas W. Chambers - Vice President, Corporate Controller, Senior Vice President, Chief Accounting Officer	Investor Contact: 312-592-5341
Fax: 312-630-1908		Transfer Agents: Computershare Trust Company, N.A., College Station, TX

TEMPUR SEALY INTERNATIONAL, INC.

Exchange	Symbol	Price	52Wk Range	Yield	P/E
NYS	TPX	$48.05 (6/29/2018)	67.63-41.78	N/A	18.77

*7 Year Price Score 82.12 *NYSE Composite Index=100 *12 Month Price Score 85.66

Interim Earnings (Per Share)

Qtr.	Mar	Jun	Sep	Dec
2015	0.38	0.34	0.64	(0.19)
2016	0.64	0.35	1.32	1.10
2017	0.62	0.45	0.81	0.88
2018	0.42	...	...	...

Interim Dividends (Per Share)

No Dividends Paid

Valuation Analysis | **Institutional Holding**

Forecast EPS	$3.37	No of Institutions	
	(06/14/2018)	386	
Market Cap	$2.6 Billion	Shares	
Book Value	$142.6 Million	79,423,624	
Price/Book	18.33	% Held	
Price/Sales	0.98	96.17	

Business Summary: Furniture (MIC: 1.6.2 SIC: 2515 NAIC: 337910)

Tempur Sealy International develops, manufactures, markets, and distributes bedding products. Co.'s brand portfolio includes TEMPUR®, Tempur-Pedic®, Sealy®, Sealy Posturepedic® and Stearns & Foster®. Co.'s products are: Bedding, which includes mattresses, foundations and adjustable foundations; and Other, which includes pillows, mattress covers, sheets, cushions and various other comfort products. TEMPUR® and Tempur-Pedic® are registered trademarks of Co. Co. also owns various trademarks, trade names, service marks, logos and design marks, including Sealy®, Stearns & Foster® and Sealy Posturepedic®. Co. also licenses the Bassett® trade name in various territories.

Recent Developments: For the quarter ended Mar 31 2018, net income decreased 28.8% to US$22.8 million from US$32.0 million in the year-earlier quarter. Revenues were US$648.0 million, down 10.3% from US$722.1 million the year before. Operating income was US$53.9 million versus US$59.5 million in the prior-year quarter, a decrease of 9.4%. Direct operating expenses declined 12.7% to US$380.1 million from US$435.5 million in the comparable period the year before. Indirect operating expenses decreased 5.8% to US$214.0 million from US$227.1 million in the equivalent prior-year period.

Prospects: Our evaluation of Tempur-Sealy International Inc. as of Jan. 21, 2018 is the result of our systematic analysis on three basic characteristics: earnings strength, relative valuation, and recent stock price movement. The company has generated a negative trend in earnings per share over the past 5 quarters and while recent estimates for the company have been mixed, TPX has posted better than expected results. Based on operating earnings yield, the company is undervalued when compared to all of the companies in our coverage universe. Share price changes over the past year indicates that TPX will perform well over the near term.

Financial Data
(US$ in Thousands)

	3 Mos	12/31/2017	12/31/2016	12/31/2015	12/31/2014	12/31/2013	12/31/2012	12/31/2011
Earnings Per Share	2.56	2.77	3.38	1.17	1.75	1.28	1.70	3.18
Cash Flow Per Share	2.69	4.13	2.80	3.80	3.70	1.63	3.08	3.71
Income Statement								
Total Revenue	648,000	2,754,400	3,127,300	3,151,200	2,989,800	2,464,300	1,402,900	1,417,938
EBITDA	58,700	346,100	411,300	337,800	316,200	293,800	278,900	369,258
Depn & Amortn	6,900	65,300	56,100	53,500	57,700	59,400	30,900	28,919
Income Before Taxes	28,900	172,800	270,000	188,200	166,600	123,600	229,200	328,391
Income Taxes	10,000	47,700	86,800	125,400	64,900	49,100	122,400	108,783
Net Income	23,100	151,400	202,100	73,500	108,900	78,600	106,800	219,608
Average Shares	54,900	54,700	59,800	62,600	62,100	61,600	62,900	69,149
Balance Sheet								
Current Assets	659,800	607,400	671,500	809,100	766,400	727,500	821,100	379,470
Total Assets	2,750,000	2,694,000	2,702,600	2,655,500	2,662,600	2,729,900	1,313,000	828,640
Current Liabilities	569,500	576,900	545,500	713,000	538,300	441,500	212,100	183,179
Long-Term Obligations	1,707,600	1,680,700	1,817,800	1,273,300	1,535,900	1,796,900	1,025,000	585,000
Total Liabilities	2,607,400	2,581,500	2,717,800	2,365,300	2,459,900	2,611,300	1,290,700	797,849
Stockholders' Equity	142,600	112,500	(15,200)	290,200	202,700	118,600	22,300	30,791
Shares Outstanding	54,395	54,200	54,400	62,400	60,900	60,600	59,700	63,770
Statistical Record								
Return on Assets %	5.18	5.61	7.52	2.76	4.04	3.89	9.95	28.43
Return on Equity %	225.32	311.20	146.58	29.82	67.79	111.57	401.23	280.07
EBITDA Margin %	9.06	12.57	13.15	10.72	10.58	11.92	19.88	26.04
Net Margin %	3.56	5.50	6.46	2.33	3.64	3.19	7.61	15.49
Asset Turnover	0.99	1.02	1.16	1.19	1.11	1.22	1.31	1.84
Current Ratio	1.16	1.05	1.23	1.13	1.42	1.65	3.87	2.07
Debt to Equity	11.97	14.94	...	4.39	7.58	15.15	45.96	19.00
Price Range	67.63-40.58	69.50-40.58	82.04-50.94	81.89-49.17	61.34-45.64	54.19-31.49	87.26-21.02	72.24-39.40
P/E Ratio	26.42-15.85	25.09-14.65	24.27-15.07	69.99-42.03	35.05-26.08	42.34-24.60	51.33-12.36	22.72-12.39

Address: 1000 Tempur Way, Lexington, KY 40511	**Web Site:** www.tempursealy.com	**Auditors:** Ernst & Young LLP
Telephone: 800-878-8889	**Officers:** Scott L. Thompson - Chairman, President, Chief Executive Officer Richard W. (Rick) Anderson - Executive Vice President, Region Officer	**Investor Contact:** 800-805-3635
		Transfer Agents: American Stock Transfer & Trust Company, LLC

TENET HEALTHCARE CORP.

Exchange	Symbol	Price	52Wk Range	Yield	P/E
NYS	THC	$33.57 (6/29/2018)	38.35-12.65	N/A	N/A

*7 Year Price Score 51.26   *NYSE Composite Index=100   *12 Month Price Score 165.69

Interim Earnings (Per Share)

Qtr.	Mar	Jun	Sep	Dec
2015	0.47	(0.61)	(0.29)	(0.98)
2016	(0.60)	(0.46)	(0.08)	(0.79)
2017	(0.53)	(0.55)	(3.64)	(2.27)
2018	0.96	...	...	...

Interim Dividends (Per Share)

No Dividends Paid

Valuation Analysis   **Institutional Holding**

Forecast EPS	$1.53	No of Institutions
	(06/14/2018)	421
Market Cap	$3.4 Billion	Shares
Book Value	N/A	197,417,376
Price/Book	N/A	% Held
Price/Sales	0.18	N/A

Business Summary: Hospitals & Health Care Facilities (MIC: 4.2.1 SIC: 8062 NAIC: 622110)

Tenet Healthcare is a healthcare services company. As of Dec 31 2017, Co. operated 76 hospitals, 20 surgical hospitals and over 470 outpatient centers, as well as nine facilities in the U.K. through its subsidiaries, partnerships and joint ventures, including USPI Holding Company, Inc. In addition, Co.'s Conifer Holdings, Inc. (Conifer) subsidiary provides healthcare business process services in the areas of hospital and physician revenue cycle management and care solutions to healthcare systems, as well as individual hospitals, physician practices, self-insured organizations, health plans and other entities. Co. has three segments: Hospital Operations and other; Ambulatory Care and Conifer.

Recent Developments: For the quarter ended Mar 31 2018, income from continuing operations increased 413.5% to US$190.0 million from US$37.0 million in the year-earlier quarter. Net income increased 430.6% to US$191.0 million from US$36.0 million in the year-earlier quarter. Revenues were US$4.72 billion, down 2.4% from US$4.84 billion the year before. Operating income was US$517.0 million versus US$267.0 million in the prior-year quarter, an increase of 93.6%. Indirect operating expenses decreased 8.0% to US$4.21 billion from US$4.58 billion in the equivalent prior-year period.

Prospects: Our evaluation of Tenet Healthcare Corp. as of Jan. 21, 2018 is the result of our systematic analysis on three basic characteristics: earnings strength, relative valuation, and recent stock price movement. The company has suffered a very negative trend in earnings per share over the past 5 quarters. However, while recent estimates for the company have been mixed, THC has posted better than expected results. Based on operating earnings yield, the company is overvalued when compared to all of the companies in our coverage universe. Share price changes over the past year indicates that THC will perform very poorly over the near term.

Financial Data
(US$ in Millions)

	3 Mos	12/31/2017	12/31/2016	12/31/2015	12/31/2014	12/31/2013	12/31/2012	12/31/2011
Earnings Per Share	(5.50)	(7.00)	(1.93)	(1.41)	0.12	(1.32)	1.30	0.48
Cash Flow Per Share	11.12	11.93	5.60	10.35	7.02	5.79	5.68	4.24
Income Statement								
Total Revenue	4,724	19,179	19,621	18,634	16,615	11,102	9,119	8,854
EBITDA	527	1,841	2,118	1,894	1,778	880	1,198	979
Depn & Amortn	11	914	891	838	877	564	452	443
Income Before Taxes	260	(101)	248	144	147	(158)	334	161
Income Taxes	70	219	67	68	49	(65)	125	61
Net Income	99	(704)	(192)	(140)	12	(134)	152	82
Average Shares	102	100	99	99	100	101	108	121
Balance Sheet								
Current Assets	5,634	5,573	5,257	5,171	4,717	3,710	2,681	2,357
Total Assets	23,184	23,385	24,701	23,682	18,141	16,130	9,044	8,462
Current Liabilities	4,561	4,332	4,034	4,308	3,577	2,928	1,763	1,815
Long-Term Obligations	14,223	14,791	15,064	14,383	11,695	10,690	5,158	4,294
Total Liabilities	23,249	23,532	24,284	22,991	17,490	15,375	7,901	7,039
Stockholders' Equity	(65)	(147)	417	691	651	755	1,143	1,423
Shares Outstanding	101	100	99	98	98	96	104	103
Statistical Record								
Return on Assets %	N.M.	N.M.	N.M.	N.M.	0.07	N.M.	1.73	0.97
Return on Equity %	N.M.	N.M.	N.M.	N.M.	1.71	N.M.	11.81	5.14
EBITDA Margin %	11.16	9.60	10.79	10.16	10.70	7.93	13.14	11.06
Net Margin %	2.10	N.M.	N.M.	N.M.	0.07	N.M.	1.67	0.93
Asset Turnover	0.80	0.80	0.81	0.89	0.97	0.88	1.04	1.04
Current Ratio	1.24	1.29	1.30	1.20	1.32	1.27	1.52	1.30
Debt to Equity	...	...	36.12	20.81	17.96	14.16	4.51	3.02
Price Range	25.12-12.65	22.67-12.65	32.61-14.38	60.78-27.23	63.27-38.75	49.25-32.47	33.50-17.56	30.52-14.36
P/E Ratio	...	...	...	...	527.25-322.92	...	25.77-13.51	63.58-29.92

Address: 1445 Ross Avenue, Suite 1400, Dallas, TX 75202
Telephone: 469-893-2200

Web Site: www.tenethealth.com
Officers: Ronald (Ron) A. Rittenmeyer - Executive Chairman, Chief Executive Officer Keith B. Pitts - Vice-Chairman

Auditors: Deloitte & Touche LLP
Transfer Agents: Computershare

TENNANT CO.

Exchange	Symbol	Price	52Wk Range	Yield	P/E	Div Acheiver
NYS	TNC	$79.00 (6/29/2018)	80.70-60.20	1.06	1580.00	45 Years

*7 Year Price Score 95.75   ***NYSE Composite Index=100**   ***12 Month Price Score 109.52**

Interim Earnings (Per Share)

Qtr.	Mar	Jun	Sep	Dec
2015	0.27	0.79	(0.05)	0.73
2016	0.25	0.85	0.64	0.85
2017	(0.22)	(0.15)	0.20	(0.18)
2018	0.18	...	...	...

Interim Dividends (Per Share)

Amt	Decl	Ex	Rec	Pay
0.21Q	08/17/2017	08/29/2017	08/31/2017	09/15/2017
0.21Q	11/09/2017	11/29/2017	11/30/2017	12/15/2017
0.21Q	02/15/2018	02/27/2018	02/28/2018	03/15/2018
0.21Q	04/25/2018	05/30/2018	05/31/2018	06/15/2018

Indicated Div: $0.84 (Div. Reinv. Plan)

Valuation Analysis   **Institutional Holding**

Forecast EPS	$1.95	No of Institutions	
(06/13/2018)		206	
Market Cap	$1.4 Billion	Shares	
Book Value	$305.5 Million		18,991,470
Price/Book	4.63	% Held	
Price/Sales	1.30		84.07

Business Summary: Industrial Machinery & Equipment (MIC: 7.2.1 SIC: 3589 NAIC: 333319)

Tennant is engaged in designing, manufacturing and marketing solutions. Co. provides products and solutions consisting of mechanized cleaning equipment, detergent-free and other sustainable cleaning technologies, aftermarket parts and consumables, equipment maintenance and repair service, specialty surface coatings, and business solutions such as financing, rental and leasing programs, and machine-to-machine asset management solutions. Co. markets and sells the following brands: Tennant®, Nobles®, Green Machines™, Alfa Uma Empresa Tennant™, IRIS® and Orbio®. Co.'s Orbio Technologies Group markets and sells Orbio-branded products and solutions.

Recent Developments: For the quarter ended Mar 31 2018, net income amounted to US$3.3 million versus a net loss of US$4.0 million in the year-earlier quarter. Revenues were US$272.8 million, up 42.8% from US$191.1 million the year before. Operating income was US$10.4 million versus a loss of US$2.7 million in the prior-year quarter. Direct operating expenses rose 45.7% to US$162.2 million from US$111.3 million in the comparable period the year before. Indirect operating expenses increased 21.7% to US$100.3 million from US$82.4 million in the equivalent prior-year period.

Prospects: Our evaluation of Tennant Co. as of Jan. 21, 2018 is the result of our systematic analysis on three basic characteristics: earnings strength, relative valuation, and recent stock price movement. The company has generated a negative trend in earnings per share over the past 5 quarters and while recent estimates for the company have remained steady, TNC has posted results that fell short of analysts expectations. Based on operating earnings yield, the company is overvalued when compared to all of the companies in our coverage universe. Share price changes over the past year indicates that TNC will perform poorly over the near term.

Financial Data
(US$ in Thousands)

	3 Mos	12/31/2017	12/31/2016	12/31/2015	12/31/2014	12/31/2013	12/31/2012	12/31/2011
Earnings Per Share	0.05	(0.35)	2.59	1.74	2.70	2.14	2.18	1.69
Cash Flow Per Share	3.98	3.06	3.29	2.51	3.26	3.27	2.56	3.02
Tang Book Value Per Share	N.M.	N.M.	14.19	13.09	13.40	12.22	10.50	9.39
Dividends Per Share	0.840	0.840	0.810	0.800	0.780	0.720	0.690	0.680
Dividend Payout %	1,680.00	...	31.27	45.98	28.89	33.64	31.65	40.24
Income Statement								
Total Revenue	272,847	1,003,066	808,572	811,799	821,983	752,011	738,980	753,998
EBITDA	23,420	64,950	85,331	68,115	88,652	78,935	79,410	68,304
Depn & Amortn	14,047	43,253	17,891	16,550	17,694	17,686	18,072	18,088
Income Before Taxes	4,377	(1,292)	66,491	50,424	69,538	59,878	59,890	48,730
Income Taxes	1,077	4,913	19,877	18,336	18,887	19,647	18,306	16,017
Net Income	3,274	(6,195)	46,614	32,088	50,651	40,231	41,584	32,713
Average Shares	18,245	17,695	17,976	18,493	18,740	18,833	19,102	19,360
Balance Sheet								
Current Assets	434,680	423,115	297,922	293,644	347,089	315,296	273,446	272,096
Total Assets	1,015,902	993,977	470,037	432,295	486,932	456,306	420,760	424,262
Current Liabilities	241,371	236,507	132,829	133,216	145,630	131,526	121,694	123,992
Long-Term Obligations	342,420	345,956	32,735	21,194	24,571	28,000	30,281	32,289
Total Liabilities	710,417	697,474	191,494	180,088	206,281	192,460	185,706	203,410
Stockholders' Equity	305,485	296,503	278,543	252,207	280,651	263,846	235,054	220,852
Shares Outstanding	17,910	17,881	17,688	17,744	18,415	18,491	18,464	18,834
Statistical Record								
Return on Assets %	0.14	N.M.	10.30	6.98	10.74	9.17	9.82	7.90
Return on Equity %	0.36	N.M.	17.52	12.04	18.60	16.13	18.19	14.97
EBITDA Margin %	8.58	6.48	10.55	8.39	10.79	10.50	10.75	9.06
Net Margin %	1.20	N.M.	5.76	3.95	6.16	5.35	5.63	4.34
Asset Turnover	1.46	1.37	1.79	1.77	1.74	1.71	1.74	1.82
Current Ratio	1.80	1.79	2.24	2.20	2.38	2.40	2.25	2.19
Debt to Equity	1.12	1.17	0.12	0.08	0.09	0.11	0.13	0.15
Price Range	76.30-60.20	76.30-60.40	76.50-46.54	72.17-54.49	76.52-58.21	68.70-43.95	48.45-35.30	44.25-32.92
P/E Ratio	N.M.	...	29.54-17.97	41.48-31.32	28.34-21.56	32.10-20.54	22.22-16.19	26.18-19.48
Average Yield %	1.23	1.21	1.37	1.28	1.15	1.35	1.67	1.73

Address: 701 North Lilac Drive, P.O. Box 1452, Minneapolis, MN 55440 **Telephone:** 763-540-1200	**Web Site:** www.tennantco.com **Officers:** H. Chris Killingstad - President, Chief Executive Officer Thomas Paulson - Chief Financial Officer, Senior Vice President	**Auditors:** KPMG LLP **Investor Contact:** 763-540-1204 **Transfer Agents:** Equiniti Trust Company, St. Paul, MN

TENNECO INC

Exchange	Symbol	Price	52Wk Range	Yield	P/E
NYS	TEN	$43.96 (6/29/2018)	65.29-43.96	2.27	11.10

*7 Year Price Score 89.88   *NYSE Composite Index=100   *12 Month Price Score 82.46

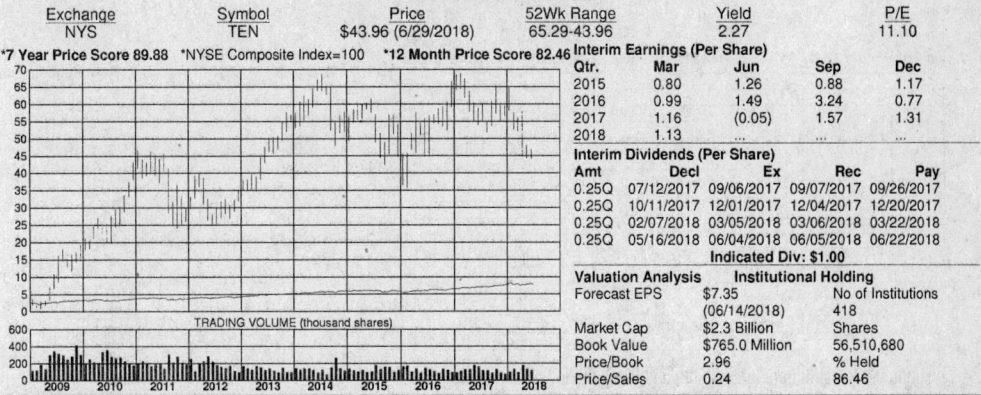

Interim Earnings (Per Share)

Qtr.	Mar	Jun	Sep	Dec
2015	0.80	1.26	0.88	1.17
2016	0.99	1.49	3.24	0.77
2017	1.16	(0.05)	1.57	1.31
2018	1.13	...	...	...

Interim Dividends (Per Share)

Amt	Decl	Ex	Rec	Pay
0.25Q	07/12/2017	09/06/2017	09/07/2017	09/26/2017
0.25Q	10/11/2017	12/01/2017	12/04/2017	12/20/2017
0.25Q	02/07/2018	03/05/2018	03/06/2018	03/22/2018
0.25Q	05/16/2018	06/04/2018	06/05/2018	06/22/2018

Indicated Div: $1.00

Valuation Analysis   Institutional Holding

Forecast EPS	$7.35	No of Institutions	418
	(06/14/2018)		
Market Cap	$2.3 Billion	Shares	56.510,680
Book Value	$765.0 Million	% Held	
Price/Book	2.96		86.46
Price/Sales	0.24		

TRADING VOLUME (thousand shares)

Business Summary: Auto Parts (MIC: 1.8.2 SIC: 3714 NAIC: 336330)

Tenneco is a producer of clean air and ride performance products and systems for light vehicle, commercial truck and off-highway applications. Co. serves both original equipment manufacturers and replacement markets. As a parts supplier, Co. produces individual component parts for vehicles as well as groups of components that are combined as modules or systems within vehicles. Co. has six operating segments: North America Clean Air, North America Ride Performance, Europe, South America and India Clean Air, Europe, South America and India Ride Performance, Asia Pacific Clean Air and Asia Pacific Ride Performance.

Recent Developments: For the quarter ended Mar 31 2018, net income decreased 1.4% to US$72.0 million from US$73.0 million in the year-earlier quarter. Revenues were US$2.57 billion, up 12.3% from US$2.29 billion the year before. Direct operating expenses rose 13.9% to US$2.20 billion from US$1.93 billion in the comparable period the year before. Indirect operating expenses increased 9.1% to US$253.0 million from US$232.0 million in the equivalent prior-year period.

Prospects: Our evaluation of Tenneco Automotive Inc. as of Jan. 21, 2018 is the result of our systematic analysis on three basic characteristics: earnings strength, relative valuation, and recent stock price movement. The company has generated a negative trend in earnings per share over the past 5 quarters. However, while recent estimates for the company have been mixed, TEN has posted better than expected results. Based on operating earnings yield, the company is undervalued when compared to all of the companies in our coverage universe. Share price changes over the past year indicates that TEN will perform poorly over the near term.

Financial Data
(US$ in Thousands)

	3 Mos	12/31/2017	12/31/2016	12/31/2015	12/31/2014	12/31/2013	12/31/2012	12/31/2011
Earnings Per Share	3.96	3.91	6.44	4.11	3.66	2.97	4.50	2.55
Cash Flow Per Share	12.46	11.91	8.72	8.66	5.61	8.32	6.07	4.09
Tang Book Value Per Share	13.50	12.15	9.44	6.09	6.63	5.49	2.30	...
Dividends Per Share	1.000	1.000	...	...	...	...	...	...
Dividend Payout %	25.25	25.58	...	...	...	...	...	...
Income Statement								
Total Revenue	2,574,000	9,274,000	8,599,000	8,209,000	8,420,000	7,964,000	7,363,000	7,205,000
EBITDA	176,000	641,000	740,000	722,000	700,000	629,000	633,000	586,000
Depn & Amortn	59,000	224,000	212,000	203,000	208,000	205,000	205,000	207,000
Income Before Taxes	97,000	344,000	436,000	452,000	401,000	344,000	323,000	271,000
Income Taxes	25,000	70,000	3,000	149,000	131,000	122,000	19,000	88,000
Net Income	58,000	207,000	363,000	247,000	226,000	183,000	275,000	157,000
Average Shares	51,501	53,026	56,407	60,193	61,782	61,594	61,083	61,520
Balance Sheet								
Current Assets	3,065,000	2,799,000	2,602,000	2,311,000	2,426,000	2,290,000	2,124,000	1,979,000
Total Assets	5,166,000	4,842,000	4,342,000	3,967,000	4,010,000	3,830,000	3,608,000	3,337,000
Current Liabilities	2,444,000	2,266,000	1,970,000	1,794,000	1,799,000	1,838,000	1,649,000	1,570,000
Long-Term Obligations	1,420,000	1,358,000	1,294,000	1,124,000	1,069,000	1,019,000	1,067,000	1,158,000
Total Liabilities	4,401,000	4,146,000	3,754,000	3,534,000	3,513,000	3,397,000	3,362,000	3,337,000
Stockholders' Equity	765,000	696,000	588,000	433,000	497,000	433,000	246,000	
Shares Outstanding	51,424	51,440	54,235	57,593	61,209	60,870	60,494	60,406
Statistical Record								
Return on Assets %	4.20	4.51	8.71	6.19	5.77	4.92	7.90	4.83
Return on Equity %	28.99	32.24	70.91	53.12	48.60	53.90	222.97	...
EBITDA Margin %	6.84	6.91	8.61	8.80	8.31	7.90	8.60	8.13
Net Margin %	2.25	2.23	4.22	3.01	2.68	2.30	3.73	2.18
Asset Turnover	1.95	2.02	2.06	2.06	2.15	2.14	2.11	2.22
Current Ratio	1.25	1.24	1.32	1.29	1.35	1.25	1.29	1.26
Debt to Equity	1.86	1.95	2.20	2.60	2.15	2.35	4.34	...
Price Range	65.29-51.74	68.71-51.74	66.52-35.59	61.53-42.24	68.60-47.93	57.53-34.57	39.76-24.72	46.58-23.90
P/E Ratio	16.49-13.07	17.57-13.23	10.33-5.53	14.97-10.28	18.74-13.10	19.37-11.64	8.84-5.49	18.27-9.37
Average Yield %	1.74	1.68	...	...	...	...	...	...

Address: 500 North Field Drive, Lake Forest, IL 60045
Telephone: 847-482-5000

Web Site: www.tenneco.com
Officers: Brian J. Kesseler - Chief Executive Officer, Chief Operating Officer Jason M. Hollar - Chief Financial Officer, Executive Vice President, Senior Vice President

Auditors: PricewaterhouseCoopers LLP
Investor Contact: 847-482-5162
Transfer Agents: Wells Fargo Bank, N.A. Shareowner Services, Mendota Heights, MN

TERADATA CORP (DE)

Exchange	Symbol	Price	52Wk Range	Yield	P/E
NYS	TDC	$40.15 (6/29/2018)	44.00-28.38	N/A	N/A

*7 Year Price Score 67.22 *NYSE Composite Index=100 *12 Month Price Score 109.36

Interim Earnings (Per Share)

Qtr.	Mar	Jun	Sep	Dec
2015	0.15	(1.87)	0.55	(0.37)
2016	(0.36)	0.49	0.37	0.44
2017	(0.02)	(0.03)	0.10	(0.58)
2018	(0.06)			

Interim Dividends (Per Share)

No Dividends Paid

Valuation Analysis

	Institutional Holding	
Forecast EPS	$1.41	No of Institutions
	(06/13/2018)	569
Market Cap	$4.8 Billion	Shares
Book Value	$644.0 Million	139,668,896
Price/Book	7.52	% Held
Price/Sales	2.23	89.34

TRADING VOLUME (thousand shares)

Business Summary: IT Services (MIC: 6.3.1 SIC: 7372 NAIC: 511210)

Teradata is a provider of analytic solutions and services. Co.'s services include analytics solutions, ecosystem architecture consulting and hybrid cloud solutions. These solutions include software and hardware technology components such as data warehousing, data, and tools for data integration, data discovery, and business intelligence. Co.'s services help companies architect, manage, and integrate their ever-changing analytic ecosystem, and include technology and data architecture consulting, analytic business consulting, open source consulting, and as-a-service services in the cloud. Additionally, Co. provides a set of support services.

Recent Developments: For the quarter ended Mar 31 2018, net loss amounted to US$7.0 million versus a net loss of US$2.0 million in the year-earlier quarter. Revenues were US$506.0 million, up 3.1% from US$491.0 million the year before. Operating loss was US$4.0 million versus an income of nil in the prior-year quarter. Direct operating expenses rose 6.4% to US$283.0 million from US$266.0 million in the comparable period the year before. Indirect operating expenses increased 0.9% to US$227.0 million from US$225.0 million in the equivalent prior-year period.

Prospects: Our evaluation of Teradata Corp. as of Jan. 21, 2018 is the result of our systematic analysis on three basic characteristics: earnings strength, relative valuation, and recent stock price movement. The company has generated a negative trend in earnings per share over the past 5 quarters and while recent estimates for the company have remained steady, TDC has posted better than expected results. Based on operating earnings yield, the company is overvalued when compared to all of the companies in our coverage universe. Share price changes over the past year indicates that TDC will perform well over the near term.

Financial Data

(US$ in Millions)	3 Mos	12/31/2017	12/31/2016	12/31/2015	12/31/2014	12/31/2013	12/31/2012	12/31/2011
Earnings Per Share	(0.57)	(0.53)	0.95	(1.53)	2.33	2.27	2.44	2.05
Cash Flow Per Share	2.14	2.58	3.43	2.87	4.38	3.12	3.41	3.05
Tang Book Value Per Share	0.95	1.03	2.93	1.97	2.87	3.56	2.95	2.68
Income Statement								
Total Revenue	506	2,156	2,322	2,530	2,732	2,692	2,665	2,362
EBITDA	28	128	350	(6)	616	612	667	514
Depn & Amortn	34	55	117	129	122	104	89	33
Income Before Taxes	(8)	58	221	(144)	494	508	578	481
Income Taxes	(1)	125	96	70	127	131	159	128
Net Income	(7)	(67)	125	(214)	367	377	419	353
Average Shares	121	125	131	139	157	166	171	171
Balance Sheet								
Current Assets	1,530	1,750	1,621	1,734	1,572	1,563	1,534	1,412
Total Assets	2,355	2,556	2,413	2,530	3,132	3,096	3,066	2,616
Current Liabilities	913	1,063	729	953	995	776	806	695
Long-Term Obligations	456	478	538	570	195	248	274	290
Total Liabilities	1,711	1,888	1,442	1,681	1,425	1,239	1,287	1,122
Stockholders' Equity	644	668	971	849	1,707	1,857	1,779	1,494
Shares Outstanding	120	121	130	130	147	159	165	167
Statistical Record								
Return on Assets %	N.M.	N.M.	5.04	N.M.	11.79	12.24	14.71	15.69
Return on Equity %	N.M.	N.M.	13.70	N.M.	20.59	20.74	25.53	26.31
EBITDA Margin %	5.53	5.94	15.07	N.M.	22.55	22.73	25.03	21.76
Net Margin %	N.M.	N.M.	5.38	N.M.	13.43	14.00	15.72	14.94
Asset Turnover	0.90	0.87	0.94	0.89	0.88	0.87	0.94	1.05
Current Ratio	1.68	1.65	2.22	1.82	1.58	2.01	1.90	2.03
Debt to Equity	0.71	0.72	0.55	0.67	0.11	0.13	0.15	0.19
Price Range	42.59-27.26	39.20-27.26	32.62-22.60	46.98-25.58	49.19-39.54	69.34-39.52	80.62-47.37	62.33-41.16
P/E Ratio	...	...	34.34-23.79	...	21.11-16.97	30.55-17.41	33.04-19.41	30.40-20.08

Address: 10000 Innovation Drive, Dayton, OH 45342	Web Site: www.teradata.com	Auditors: PricewaterhouseCoopers LLP
Telephone: 866-548-8348	Officers: James M. Ringler - Chairman Victor L. Lund - President, Chief Executive Officer	Investor Contact: 937-242-4878
		Transfer Agents: Computershare Shareowner Services

TERADYNE, INC.

Exchange	Symbol	Price	52Wk Range	Yield	P/E
NYS	TER	$38.07 (6/29/2018)	49.92-29.69	0.95	29.51

*7 Year Price Score 145.95 *NYSE Composite Index=100 *12 Month Price Score 92.60

Interim Earnings (Per Share)

Qtr.	Mar	Jun	Sep	Dec
2015	0.15	0.48	0.34	0.01
2016	0.24	(1.10)	0.31	0.33
2017	0.42	0.87	0.52	(0.53)
2018	0.43	...	...	...

Interim Dividends (Per Share)

Amt	Decl	Ex	Rec	Pay
0.07Q	08/24/2017	09/06/2017	09/07/2017	09/29/2017
0.07Q	11/14/2017	11/28/2017	11/29/2017	12/21/2017
0.09Q	01/24/2018	02/22/2018	02/23/2018	03/23/2018
0.09Q	05/08/2018	05/30/2018	05/31/2018	06/22/2018

Indicated Div: $0.36

Valuation Analysis — **Institutional Holding**

Forecast EPS	$1.94	No of Institutions
	(06/14/2018)	647
Market Cap	$7.4 Billion	Shares
Book Value	$1.9 Billion	231,743,104
Price/Book	3.87	% Held
Price/Sales	3.40	110.59

Business Summary: Semiconductors (MIC: 6.2.4 SIC: 3825 NAIC: 334515)

Teradyne is a global supplier of automation equipment for test and industrial applications. Co. designs, develops, manufactures and sells automatic test systems used to test semiconductors, wireless products, data storage and electronics systems in the consumer electronics, wireless, automotive, industrial, computing, communications, and aerospace and defense industries. Co.'s automatic test equipment and industrial automation products and services include: semiconductor test systems; defense/aerospace test instrumentation and systems, storage test systems, and circuit-board test and inspection systems; industrial automation products; and wireless test systems.

Recent Developments: For the quarter ended Apr 1 2018, net income increased 2.1% to US$87.0 million from US$85.2 million in the year-earlier quarter. Revenues were US$487.5 million, up 6.7% from US$456.9 million the year before. Operating income was US$97.5 million versus US$93.8 million in the prior-year quarter, an increase of 4.0%. Direct operating expenses rose 13.4% to US$217.6 million from US$191.9 million in the comparable period the year before. Indirect operating expenses increased 0.6% to US$172.3 million from US$171.2 million in the equivalent prior-year period.

Prospects: Our evaluation of Teradyne Inc. as of Jan. 21, 2018 is the result of our systematic analysis on three basic characteristics: earnings strength, relative valuation, and recent stock price movement. The company has generated a negative trend in earnings per share over the past 5 quarters and while recent estimates for the company have been mixed, TER has posted better than expected results. Based on operating earnings yield, the company is undervalued when compared to all of the companies in our coverage universe. Share price changes over the past year indicates that TER will perform well over the near term.

Financial Data
(US$ in Thousands)

	3 Mos	12/31/2017	12/31/2016	12/31/2015	12/31/2014	12/31/2013	12/31/2012	12/31/2011
Earnings Per Share	1.29	1.28	(0.21)	0.97	0.37	0.70	0.94	1.65
Cash Flow Per Share	3.10	3.16	2.19	1.95	2.43	1.40	2.16	1.48
Tang Book Value Per Share	7.97	8.30	7.56	6.08	7.46	7.15	5.91	4.14
Dividends Per Share	0.300	0.280	0.240	0.240	0.180	...	...	...
Dividend Payout %	23.26	21.88	...	24.74	48.65	...	...	...
Income Statement								
Total Revenue	487,467	2,136,606	1,753,250	1,639,578	1,647,824	1,427,933	1,656,750	1,429,061
EBITDA	122,269	624,900	56,729	385,017	240,251	320,359	415,868	327,254
Depn & Amortn	25,540	96,630	117,448	137,231	144,200	129,700	128,500	91,540
Income Before Taxes	95,820	524,412	(55,060)	253,124	95,376	201,922	265,976	218,637
Income Taxes	8,846	266,720	(11,639)	46,647	14,104	36,975	48,927	(129,256)
Net Income	86,974	257,692	(43,421)	206,477	81,272	164,947	217,049	373,809
Average Shares	203,484	201,641	202,578	213,321	222,550	235,599	230,246	226,820
Balance Sheet								
Current Assets	2,156,425	2,270,281	1,623,803	1,259,968	1,243,846	1,440,277	1,236,061	1,099,887
Total Assets	2,995,193	3,109,545	2,762,493	2,548,674	2,538,520	2,629,824	2,429,345	2,188,639
Current Liabilities	391,325	454,336	372,696	372,857	292,406	475,632	297,828	373,684
Long-Term Obligations	369,421	365,987	352,669	...	...	...	171,059	159,956
Total Liabilities	1,090,210	1,155,899	933,834	582,888	459,540	644,730	650,990	683,579
Stockholders' Equity	1,904,983	1,953,646	1,828,659	1,965,786	2,078,980	1,985,094	1,778,355	1,505,060
Shares Outstanding	193,808	195,548	199,177	203,641	216,613	191,731	187,908	183,587
Statistical Record								
Return on Assets %	8.89	8.78	N.M.	8.12	3.14	6.52	9.37	18.70
Return on Equity %	13.57	13.63	N.M.	10.21	4.00	8.77	13.18	28.46
EBITDA Margin %	25.08	29.25	3.24	23.48	14.58	22.44	25.10	22.90
Net Margin %	17.84	12.06	N.M.	12.59	4.93	11.55	13.10	26.16
Asset Turnover	0.74	0.73	0.66	0.64	0.64	0.56	0.72	0.71
Current Ratio	5.51	5.00	4.36	3.38	4.25	3.03	4.15	2.94
Debt to Equity	0.19	0.19	0.19	...	...	...	0.10	0.11
Price Range	49.92-29.69	44.43-25.38	26.25-17.55	21.48-16.78	20.72-16.16	18.56-14.30	17.39-13.05	19.07-10.55
P/E Ratio	38.70-23.02	34.71-19.83	...	22.14-17.30	56.00-43.68	26.51-20.43	18.50-13.88	11.56-6.39
Average Yield %	0.77	0.81	1.15	1.24	0.94	...	...	...

Address: 600 Riverpark Drive, North Reading, MA 01864
Telephone: 978-370-2700

Web Site: www.teradyne.com
Officers: Mark E. Jagiela - President, Chief Executive Officer, Vice President, Division Officer Gregory R. Beecher - Vice President, Chief Financial Officer, Treasurer

Auditors: PricewaterhouseCoopers LLP
Investor Contact: 978-370-2425
Transfer Agents: Broadridge Corporate Issue Services, Brentwood, NY

TEREX CORP.

Exchange	Symbol	Price	52Wk Range	Yield	P/E
NYS	TEX	$42.19 (6/29/2018)	49.79-35.84	0.95	20.09

*7 Year Price Score 115.58 *NYSE Composite Index=100 *12 Month Price Score 94.31

Interim Earnings (Per Share)

Qtr.	Mar	Jun	Sep	Dec
2015	0.01	0.78	0.40	0.15
2016	(0.65)	0.59	0.89	(2.46)
2017	(0.04)	1.04	0.66	(0.22)
2018	0.62	...	...	...

Interim Dividends (Per Share)

Amt	Decl	Ex	Rec	Pay
0.08Q	10/11/2017	11/08/2017	11/09/2017	12/19/2017
0.10Q	02/09/2018	03/08/2018	03/09/2018	03/19/2018
0.10Q	05/11/2018	06/07/2018	06/08/2018	06/19/2018
0.10Q	07/12/2018	08/08/2018	08/09/2018	09/19/2018

Indicated Div: $0.40

Valuation Analysis

		Institutional Holding	
Forecast EPS	$2.90	No of Institutions	510
	(06/13/2018)		
Market Cap	$3.2 Billion	Shares	101,815,712
Book Value	$1.1 Billion	% Held	91.37
Price/Book	2.97		
Price/Sales	0.69		

Business Summary: Industrial Machinery & Equipment (MIC: 7.2.1 SIC: 3537 NAIC: 333924)

Terex is a manufacturer of lifting and material processing products and services. Co. delivers lifecycle solutions to a range of industries, including the construction, infrastructure, manufacturing, shipping, transportation, refining, energy, utility, quarrying and mining industries. Co. has three business segments: Aerial Work Platforms, which provides aerial work platform equipment, telehandlers and light towers; Cranes, which provides mobile telescopic cranes, lattice boom crawler cranes, tower cranes, and utility equipment; and Materials Processing, which markets materials processing and specialty equipment, including crushers, washing systems, apron feeders, and recycling equipment.

Recent Developments: For the quarter ended Mar 31 2018, net income amounted to US$50.3 million versus a net loss of US$4.6 million in the year-earlier quarter. Revenues were US$1.26 billion, up 25.2% from US$1.01 billion the year before. Operating income was US$71.3 million versus a loss of US$4.7 million in the prior-year quarter. Direct operating expenses rose 20.5% to US$1.03 billion from US$854.6 million in the comparable period the year before. Indirect operating expenses increased 1.7% to US$159.6 million from US$157.0 million in the equivalent prior-year period.

Prospects: Our evaluation of Terex Corp. as of Jan. 21, 2018 is the result of our systematic analysis on three basic characteristics: earnings strength, relative valuation, and recent stock price movement. The company has produced a positive trend in earnings per share over the past 5 quarters and while recent estimates for the company have been mixed, TEX has posted better than expected results. Based on operating earnings yield, the company is about fairly valued when compared to all of the companies in our coverage universe. Share price changes over the past year indicates that TEX will perform very well over the near term.

Financial Data

(US$ in Thousands)	3 Mos	12/31/2017	12/31/2016	12/31/2015	12/31/2014	12/31/2013	12/31/2012	12/31/2011
Earnings Per Share	2.10	1.36	(1.63)	1.33	2.79	1.93	0.93	0.41
Cash Flow Per Share	3.82	1.65	3.39	1.98	3.74	1.70	2.64	0.17
Tang Book Value Per Share	10.34	11.65	11.49	5.61	5.21	4.55	2.62	1.18
Dividends Per Share	0.340	0.320	0.280	0.240	0.200	0.050	...	...
Dividend Payout %	16.19	23.53	...	18.05	7.17	2.59	...	...
Income Statement								
Total Revenue	1,260,900	4,363,400	4,443,100	6,543,100	7,308,900	7,084,000	7,348,400	6,504,600
EBITDA	87,600	232,500	(107,500)	430,600	527,500	523,600	421,400	302,700
Depn & Amortn	16,000	59,900	65,500	98,400	110,400	104,400	100,400	89,500
Income Before Taxes	59,000	112,000	(270,700)	226,600	297,200	291,300	155,600	84,500
Income Taxes	11,400	52,000	(77,400)	81,000	37,700	87,400	54,200	50,400
Net Income	50,300	128,700	(176,100)	145,900	319,000	226,000	105,800	45,200
Average Shares	81,700	94,900	107,900	109,600	114,200	117,000	113,900	110,700
Balance Sheet								
Current Assets	2,339,700	2,383,000	2,700,500	3,144,200	3,356,200	3,639,400	3,797,400	4,013,500
Total Assets	3,420,100	3,462,500	5,006,800	5,637,100	5,928,000	6,536,700	6,746,200	7,050,700
Current Liabilities	1,034,600	1,035,500	1,407,000	1,458,600	1,643,100	1,724,700	1,708,800	1,891,700
Long-Term Obligations	1,077,800	979,600	1,562,000	1,751,000	1,636,300	1,889,900	2,014,900	2,223,400
Total Liabilities	2,341,700	2,240,500	3,522,100	3,759,700	3,922,100	4,346,600	4,738,500	5,144,300
Stockholders' Equity	1,078,400	1,222,000	1,484,700	1,877,400	2,005,900	2,190,100	2,007,700	1,906,400
Shares Outstanding	76,000	80,200	105,000	107,700	105,400	109,900	109,900	108,800
Statistical Record								
Return on Assets %	4.84	3.04	N.M.	2.52	5.12	3.40	1.53	0.72
Return on Equity %	13.24	9.51	N.M.	7.51	15.20	10.77	5.39	2.27
EBITDA Margin %	6.95	5.33	N.M.	6.58	7.22	7.39	5.73	4.65
Net Margin %	3.99	2.95	N.M.	2.23	4.36	3.19	1.44	0.69
Asset Turnover	1.22	1.03	0.83	1.13	1.17	1.07	1.06	1.04
Current Ratio	2.26	2.30	1.92	2.16	2.04	2.11	2.22	2.12
Debt to Equity	1.00	0.80	1.05	0.93	0.82	0.86	1.00	1.17
Price Range	49.79-30.56	48.59-29.57	33.05-14.46	28.85-16.83	44.74-25.66	41.99-26.01	28.11-14.11	38.30-9.61
P/E Ratio	23.71-14.55	35.73-21.74	...	21.69-12.65	16.04-9.20	21.76-13.48	30.23-15.17	93.41-23.44
Average Yield %	0.84	0.85	1.18	1.03	0.54	0.15	...	...

Address: 200 Nyala Farm Road, Westport, CT 06880	Web Site: www.terex.com	Auditors: PricewaterhouseCoopers LLP
Telephone: 203-222-7170	Officers: John L. Garrison - President, Chief Executive Officer John D. Sheehan - Senior Vice President, Chief Financial Officer	Investor Contact: 203-222-5943
Fax: 203-222-7976		Transfer Agents: American Stock Transfer & Trust Company, New York, NY

TEGNA INC

Exchange	Symbol	Price	52Wk Range	Yield	P/E
NYS	TGNA	$10.85 (6/29/2018)	15.59-10.09	2.58	8.75

*7 Year Price Score 79.60   *NYSE Composite Index=100   *12 Month Price Score 83.57

Interim Earnings (Per Share)

Qtr.	Mar	Jun	Sep	Dec
2015	0.49	0.50	0.38	0.63
2016	0.38	0.45	0.54	0.61
2017	0.27	(0.60)	0.19	1.40
2018	0.25	...	...	...

Interim Dividends (Per Share)

Amt	Decl	Ex	Rec	Pay
0.07Q	07/25/2017	09/07/2017	09/08/2017	10/02/2017
0.07Q	11/02/2017	12/07/2017	12/08/2017	01/02/2018
0.07Q	02/22/2018	03/08/2018	03/09/2018	04/02/2018
0.07Q	04/25/2018	06/07/2018	06/08/2018	07/02/2018

Indicated Div: $0.28 (Div. Reinv. Plan)

Valuation Analysis

		Institutional Holding	
Forecast EPS	$1.73	No of Institutions	
	(06/10/2018)	615	
Market Cap	$2.3 Billion	Shares	
Book Value	$1.0 Billion	244,681,632	
Price/Book	2.26	% Held	
Price/Sales	1.20	83.11	

Business Summary: Radio & Television (MIC: 2.3.1 SIC: 2711 NAIC: 511110)

Tegna is involved in media and digital businesses that provide content and brands. Co. operates two reportable segments: Media, which includes 46 television stations operating in 38 markets, provides core advertising which includes local and national non-political advertising, political advertising, retransmission, digital which encompass digital marketing services and advertising on the stations' websites and tablet and mobile products; and Digital, which is comprised of three business units including; Cars.com, CareerBuilder, and G/O Digital businesses that operate in the automotive and human capital solutions industries.

Recent Developments: For the quarter ended Mar 31 2018, income from continuing operations increased 23.6% to US$55.2 million from US$44.7 million in the year-earlier quarter. Net income decreased 13.6% to US$55.2 million from US$63.9 million in the year-earlier quarter. Revenues were US$502.1 million, up 9.4% from US$459.1 million the year before. Operating income was US$137.0 million versus US$123.1 million in the prior-year quarter, an increase of 11.3%. Direct operating expenses rose 11.7% to US$258.5 million from US$231.4 million in the comparable period the year before. Indirect operating expenses increased 1.9% to US$106.6 million from US$104.6 million in the equivalent prior-year period.

Prospects: Our evaluation of Tegna Inc. as of Jan. 21, 2018 is the result of our systematic analysis on three basic characteristics: earnings strength, relative valuation, and recent stock price movement. The company has generated a negative trend in earnings per share over the past 5 quarters and while recent estimates for the company have been mixed, TGNA has posted better than expected results. Based on operating earnings yield, the company is undervalued when compared to all of the companies in our coverage universe. Share price changes over the past year indicates that TGNA will perform poorly over the near term.

Financial Data
(US$ in Thousands)

	3 Mos	12/31/2017	12/31/2016	12/31/2015	12/28/2014	12/29/2013	12/30/2012	12/25/2011
Earnings Per Share	1.24	1.26	1.99	2.00	4.58	1.66	1.79	1.89
Cash Flow Per Share	1.37	1.79	3.15	2.71	3.64	2.24	3.20	3.41
Dividends Per Share	0.280	0.350	0.560	0.680	0.800	0.800	0.800	0.240
Dividend Payout %	22.58	27.78	28.14	34.00	17.47	48.19	44.69	12.70
Income Statement								
Total Revenue	502,090	1,903,026	3,341,198	3,050,945	6,008,174	5,161,362	5,353,197	5,239,989
EBITDA	144,788	647,105	1,156,125	1,163,873	1,727,709	880,925	992,528	1,015,243
Depn & Amortn	20,253	136,507	204,490	262,244	265,724	189,572	194,039	197,373
Income Before Taxes	76,810	300,314	719,622	628,000	1,188,741	515,289	648,020	644,730
Income Taxes	20,385	(137,246)	216,979	202,314	225,600	113,200	195,400	152,800
Net Income	55,187	273,744	436,697	459,522	1,062,171	388,680	424,280	458,748
Average Shares	216,989	217,478	219,681	229,721	231,907	234,189	236,690	242,768
Balance Sheet								
Current Assets	507,295	636,923	790,688	805,159	1,480,465	1,923,485	1,072,720	1,075,545
Total Assets	5,145,329	4,962,115	8,542,725	8,537,758	11,205,455	9,240,706	6,379,886	6,616,450
Current Liabilities	272,863	325,352	619,181	606,783	1,127,936	1,007,192	934,516	901,937
Long-Term Obligations	3,196,070	3,007,041	4,042,749	4,200,816	4,488,028	3,707,010	1,432,100	1,760,363
Total Liabilities	4,108,693	3,967,074	6,271,307	6,345,787	7,950,541	6,547,608	4,029,272	4,288,559
Stockholders' Equity	1,036,636	995,041	2,271,418	2,191,971	3,254,914	2,693,098	2,350,614	2,327,891
Shares Outstanding	215,679	214,930	214,487	219,754	226,739	227,568	230,042	237,036
Statistical Record								
Return on Assets %	3.99	4.05	5.10	4.62	10.42	4.99	6.42	6.85
Return on Equity %	16.31	16.76	19.51	16.74	35.81	15.45	17.84	20.48
EBITDA Margin %	28.84	34.00	34.60	38.15	28.76	17.07	18.54	19.37
Net Margin %	10.99	14.38	13.07	15.06	17.68	7.53	7.93	8.75
Asset Turnover	0.29	0.28	0.39	0.31	0.59	0.66	0.81	0.78
Current Ratio	1:86	1.96	1.28	1.33	1.31	1.91	1.15	1.19
Debt to Equity	3.08	3.02	1.78	1.92	1.38	1.38	0.61	0.76
Price Range	16.73-11.27	16.92-11.78	16.35-11.55	21.12-14.00	17.70-13.29	15.01-9.23	9.72-6.32	8.81-4.38
P/E Ratio	13.49-9.09	13.43-9.35	8.22-5.80	10.56-7.00	3.87-2.90	9.04-5.56	5.43-3.53	4.66-2.32
Average Yield %	2.01	2.45	3.89	3.91	5.21	6.63	10.14	3.51

Address: 7950 Jones Branch Drive, McLean, VA 22107-0150 **Telephone:** 703-873-6600	**Web Site:** www.gannett.com **Officers:** David T. (Dave) Lougee - President, Chief Executive Officer, Division Officer Victoria D. Harker - Chief Financial Officer	**Auditors:** Ernst & Young LLP **Investor Contact:** 703-854-6917 **Transfer Agents:** Wells Fargo Bank, N.A., St Paul, MN

TEXTRON INC

Exchange	Symbol	Price	52Wk Range	Yield	P/E
NYS	TXT	$65.91 (6/29/2018)	69.32-47.10	0.12	43.94

*7 Year Price Score 120.94 *NYSE Composite Index=100 *12 Month Price Score 114.65

Interim Earnings (Per Share)

Qtr.	Mar	Jun	Sep	Dec
2015	0.46	0.60	0.63	0.82
2016	0.55	0.65	1.55	0.78
2017	0.37	0.57	0.60	(0.39)
2018	0.72	...	...	...

Interim Dividends (Per Share)

Amt	Decl	Ex	Rec	Pay
0.02Q	07/25/2017	09/14/2017	09/15/2017	10/01/2017
0.02Q	10/25/2017	12/14/2017	12/15/2017	01/01/2018
0.02Q	02/28/2018	03/09/2018	03/12/2018	04/01/2018
0.02Q	04/25/2018	06/14/2018	06/15/2018	07/01/2018

Indicated Div: $0.08

Valuation Analysis

		Institutional Holding	
Forecast EPS	$3.15	No of Institutions	
	(06/13/2018)	714	
Market Cap	$16.9 Billion	Shares	
Book Value	$5.7 Billion	249,600,544	
Price/Book	2.96	% Held	
Price/Sales	1.17	80.73	

Business Summary: Aerospace (MIC: 7.1.1 SIC: 3721 NAIC: 336411)

Textron has five operating segments: Textron Aviation, which manufactures, sells and services Beechcraft and Cessna aircraft, and services the Hawker brand of business jets; Bell, which supplies military and commercial helicopters, tiltrotor aircraft, and related spare parts and services; Textron Systems, which produces unmanned aircraft systems, marine and land systems, weapons and sensors, simulation, training and other defense and aviation mission support products and services; Industrial, which designs and manufactures fuel systems and functional components, specialized vehicles and equipment, and tools and test equipment; as well as Finance, which is a commercial finance business.

Recent Developments: For the quarter ended Mar 31 2018, income from continuing operations increased 89.0% to US$189.0 million from US$100.0 million in the year-earlier quarter. Net income increased 87.1% to US$189.0 million from US$101.0 million in the year-earlier quarter. Revenues were US$3.30 billion, up 6.6% from US$3.09 billion the year before. Direct operating expenses rose 5.3% to US$2.73 billion from US$2.59 billion in the comparable period the year before. Indirect operating expenses decreased 8.2% to US$349.0 million from US$380.0 million in the equivalent prior-year period.

Prospects: Our evaluation of Textron Inc. as of Jan. 21, 2018 is the result of our systematic analysis on three basic characteristics: earnings strength, relative valuation, and recent stock price movement. The company has produced a positive trend in earnings per share over the past 5 quarters and while recent estimates for the company have been mixed, TXT has posted better than expected results. Based on operating earnings yield, the company is about fairly valued when compared to all of the companies in our coverage universe. Share price changes over the past year indicates that TXT will perform in line with the market over the near term.

Financial Data
(US$ in Millions)

	3 Mos	12/30/2017	12/31/2016	01/02/2016	01/03/2015	12/28/2013	12/29/2012	12/31/2011
Earnings Per Share	1.50	1.14	3.53	2.50	2.13	1.75	2.00	0.79
Cash Flow Per Share	4.08	3.59	3.75	3.95	4.25	2.91	3.32	3.84
Tang Book Value Per Share	12.98	12.56	12.80	10.72	8.12	9.39	4.95	3.98
Dividends Per Share	0.080	0.080	0.080	0.080	0.080	0.080	0.080	0.080
Dividend Payout %	5.33	7.02	2.27	3.20	3.76	4.57	4.00	10.13
Income Statement								
Total Revenue	3,296	14,198	13,788	13,423	13,878	12,104	12,237	11,275
EBITDA	364	1,298	1,418	1,523	1,423	1,182	1,368	900
Depn & Amortn	105	362	368	383	379	335	315	317
Income Before Taxes	218	762	876	971	853	674	841	337
Income Taxes	29	456	33	273	248	176	260	95
Net Income	189	307	962	697	600	498	589	242
Average Shares	263	268	272	278	281	284	294	307
Balance Sheet								
Current Assets	6,821	7,027	7,053	6,478	6,273	5,572	5,389	5,263
Total Assets	14,968	15,340	15,358	14,708	14,605	12,944	13,033	13,615
Current Liabilities	3,349	3,660	3,893	3,792	3,638	3,003	3,512	2,931
Long-Term Obligations	3,902	3,898	3,317	3,348	3,866	3,179	3,453	4,780
Total Liabilities	9,276	9,693	9,784	9,744	10,333	8,560	10,042	10,870
Stockholders' Equity	5,692	5,647	5,574	4,964	4,272	4,384	2,991	2,745
Shares Outstanding	256	261	270	274	276	282	271	278
Statistical Record								
Return on Assets %	2.58	2.01	6.42	4.77	4.29	3.84	4.43	1.68
Return on Equity %	7.01	5.49	18.31	15.13	13.64	13.54	20.59	8.49
EBITDA Margin %	11.04	9.14	10.28	11.35	10.25	9.77	11.18	7.98
Net Margin %	5.73	2.16	6.98	5.19	4.32	4.11	4.81	2.15
Asset Turnover	0.94	0.93	0.92	0.92	0.99	0.93	0.92	0.78
Current Ratio	2.04	1.92	1.81	1.71	1.72	1.86	1.53	1.80
Debt to Equity	0.69	0.69	0.60	0.67	0.90	0.73	1.15	1.74
Price Range	61.22-45.37	57.18-45.37	49.04-31.11	46.86-37.00	44.23-32.28	37.29-24.79	28.89-18.64	28.50-14.88
P/E Ratio	40.81-30.25	50.16-39.80	13.89-8.81	18.74-14.80	20.77-15.15	21.31-14.17	14.45-9.32	36.08-18.84
Average Yield %	0.15	0.16	0.20	0.19	0.21	0.28	0.32	0.36

Address: 40 Westminster Street, Providence, RI 02903 Telephone: 401-421-2800	Web Site: www.textron.com Officers: Scott C. Donnelly - Chairman, President, Chief Executive Officer Frank T. Connor - Executive Vice President, Chief Financial Officer	Auditors: Ernst & Young LLP Investor Contact: 401-457-2288 Transfer Agents: American Stock Transfer & Trust Cmpany, LLC, Brooklyn, NY

THE GAP INC

*7 Year Price Score 75.72   *NYSE Composite Index=100   *12 Month Price Score 103.62

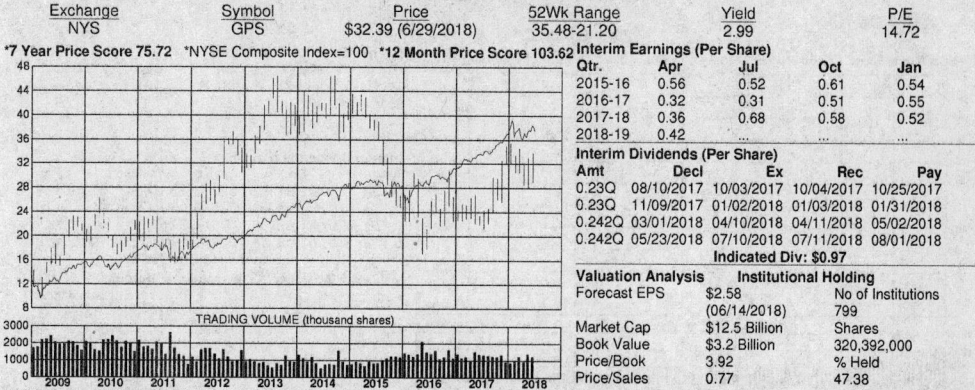

Interim Earnings (Per Share)

Qtr.	Apr	Jul	Oct	Jan
2015-16	0.56	0.52	0.61	0.54
2016-17	0.32	0.31	0.51	0.55
2017-18	0.36	0.68	0.58	0.52
2018-19	0.42	...	...	...

Interim Dividends (Per Share)

Amt	Decl	Ex	Rec	Pay
0.23Q	08/10/2017	10/03/2017	10/04/2017	10/25/2017
0.23Q	11/09/2017	01/02/2018	01/03/2018	01/31/2018
0.242Q	03/01/2018	04/10/2018	04/11/2018	05/02/2018
0.242Q	05/23/2018	07/10/2018	07/11/2018	08/01/2018

Indicated Div: $0.97

Valuation Analysis   **Institutional Holding**

Forecast EPS	$2.58	No of Institutions
	(06/14/2018)	799
Market Cap	$12.5 Billion	Shares
Book Value	$3.2 Billion	320,392,000
Price/Book	3.92	% Held
Price/Sales	0.77	47.38

Business Summary: Retail - Apparel and Accessories (MIC: 2.1.5 SIC: 5651 NAIC: 448140)

The Gap is a retailer providing apparel, accessories, and personal care products for men, women, and children under the Gap, Banana Republic, Old Navy, Athleta, and Intermix brands. Co. has stores in the U.S., Canada, the U.K., France, Ireland, Japan, Italy, China, Hong Kong, Taiwan, and Mexico, and has franchise agreements with unaffiliated franchisees to operate Gap, Banana Republic, and Old Navy stores throughout Asia, Europe, Latin America, the Middle East, and Africa. Under these agreements, third parties operate, or will operate, stores that sell apparel and related products under Co.'s brand names. At Feb 3 2018, Co. had 3,165 Co.-operated and 429 franchise store locations.

Recent Developments: For the quarter ended May 5 2018, net income increased 14.7% to US$164.0 million from US$143.0 million in the year-earlier quarter. Revenues were US$3.78 billion, up 10.0% from US$3.44 billion the year before. Operating income was US$229.0 million versus US$254.0 million in the prior-year quarter, a decrease of 9.8%. Direct operating expenses rose 10.2% to US$2.36 billion from US$2.14 billion in the comparable period the year before. Indirect operating expenses increased 14.2% to US$1.20 billion from US$1.05 billion in the equivalent prior-year period.

Prospects: Our evaluation of The Gap Inc. as of Jan. 21, 2018 is the result of our systematic analysis on three basic characteristics: earnings strength, relative valuation, and recent stock price movement. The company has managed to produce a neutral trend in earnings per share over the past 5 quarters and while recent estimates for the company have been mixed, GPS has posted better than expected results. Based on operating earnings yield, the company is undervalued when compared to all of the companies in our coverage universe. Share price changes over the past year indicates that GPS will perform well over the near term.

Financial Data
(US$ in Thousands)

	3 Mos	02/03/2018	01/28/2017	01/30/2016	01/31/2015	02/01/2014	02/02/2013	01/28/2012
Earnings Per Share	2.20	2.14	1.69	2.23	2.87	2.74	2.33	1.56
Cash Flow Per Share	3.14	3.45	4.32	3.89	4.91	3.71	3.95	2.58
Tang Book Value Per Share	8.26	7.56	6.77	5.73	6.44	6.17	5.57	5.32
Dividends Per Share	0.933	0.920	0.920	0.920	0.880	0.700	0.500	0.450
Dividend Payout %	42.39	42.99	54.44	41.26	30.66	25.55	21.46	28.85
Income Statement								
Total Revenue	3,783,000	15,855,000	15,516,000	15,797,000	16,435,000	16,148,000	15,651,000	14,549,000
EBITDA	215,000	2,035,000	1,781,000	2,112,000	2,643,000	2,679,000	2,497,000	2,026,000
Depn & Amortn	(14,000)	556,000	590,000	588,000	560,000	530,000	555,000	588,000
Income Before Taxes	219,000	1,424,000	1,124,000	1,471,000	2,013,000	2,093,000	1,861,000	1,369,000
Income Taxes	55,000	576,000	448,000	551,000	751,000	813,000	726,000	536,000
Net Income	164,000	848,000	676,000	920,000	1,262,000	1,280,000	1,135,000	833,000
Average Shares	393,000	396,000	400,000	413,000	440,000	467,000	488,000	533,000
Balance Sheet								
Current Assets	4,187,000	4,568,000	4,315,000	3,985,000	4,317,000	4,430,000	4,132,000	4,309,000
Total Assets	7,585,000	7,989,000	7,610,000	7,473,000	7,690,000	7,849,000	7,470,000	7,422,000
Current Liabilities	2,058,000	2,461,000	2,453,000	2,535,000	2,234,000	2,445,000	2,344,000	2,128,000
Long-Term Obligations	1,249,000	1,249,000	1,248,000	1,310,000	1,332,000	1,369,000	1,246,000	1,606,000
Total Liabilities	4,388,000	4,845,000	4,706,000	4,928,000	4,707,000	4,787,000	4,576,000	4,667,000
Stockholders' Equity	3,197,000	3,144,000	2,904,000	2,545,000	2,983,000	3,062,000	2,894,000	2,755,000
Shares Outstanding	387,000	389,000	399,000	397,000	421,000	446,000	463,000	485,000
Statistical Record								
Return on Assets %	11.59	10.70	8.99	12.17	16.29	16.76	15.00	11.53
Return on Equity %	28.68	27.59	24.88	33.38	41.87	43.10	39.53	24.44
EBITDA Margin %	5.68	12.84	11.48	13.37	16.08	16.59	15.95	13.93
Net Margin %	4.34	5.35	4.36	5.82	7.68	7.93	7.25	5.73
Asset Turnover	2.16	2.00	2.06	2.09	2.12	2.11	2.07	2.01
Current Ratio	2.03	1.86	1.76	1.57	1.93	1.81	1.76	2.02
Debt to Equity	0.39	0.40	0.43	0.51	0.45	0.45	0.43	0.58
Price Range	35.48-21.20	35.48-21.20	30.71-17.09	43.45-22.45	46.59-35.74	46.48-31.22	37.27-18.83	23.29-15.52
P/E Ratio	16.13-9.64	16.58-9.91	18.17-10.11	19.48-10.07	16.23-12.45	16.96-11.39	16.00-8.08	14.93-9.95
Average Yield %	3.31	3.49	3.78	2.70	2.15	1.78	1.64	2.33

Address: Two Folsom Street, San Francisco, CA 94105 **Telephone:** 415-427-0100	**Web Site:** www.gapinc.com **Officers:** Arthur L. (Art) Peck - President, Chief Executive Officer, Executive Vice President, Division Officer, Region Officer, Division Officer, President (frmr) Shawn Curran - Executive Vice President	**Auditors:** Deloitte & Touche LLP **Investor Contact:** 415-427-0100 **Transfer Agents:** Wells Fargo Bank, N.A., Mendota Heights, MN

THERMO FISHER SCIENTIFIC INC

Exchange	Symbol	Price	52Wk Range	Yield	P/E
NYS	TMO	$207.14 (6/29/2018)	224.11-171.74	0.33	36.79

*7 Year Price Score 132.60 *NYSE Composite Index=100 *12 Month Price Score 105.20

TRADING VOLUME (thousand shares)

Interim Earnings (Per Share)

Qtr.	Mar	Jun	Sep	Dec
2015	0.96	1.27	1.18	1.50
2016	1.01	1.30	1.19	1.59
2017	1.40	1.56	1.34	1.30
2018	1.43	...	...	...

Interim Dividends (Per Share)

Amt	Decl	Ex	Rec	Pay
0.15Q	11/09/2017	12/14/2017	12/15/2017	01/15/2018
0.17Q	01/31/2018	03/14/2018	03/15/2018	04/16/2018
0.17Q	05/24/2018	06/14/2018	06/15/2018	07/16/2018
0.17Q	07/12/2018	09/14/2018	09/17/2018	10/15/2018

Indicated Div: $0.68

Valuation Analysis / Institutional Holding

Forecast EPS	$10.90 (06/14/2018)	No of Institutions	1738
Market Cap	$83.3 Billion	Shares	433,343,392
Book Value	$26.1 Billion	% Held	90.66
Price/Book	3.19		
Price/Sales	3.79		

Business Summary: Biotechnology (MIC: 4.1.2 SIC: 3829 NAIC: 334519)

Thermo Fisher Scientific is a provider of analytical instruments, equipment, reagents and consumables, software and services for research, manufacturing, analysis, discovery and diagnostics. Markets served include pharmaceutical and biotech, academic and government, industrial and applied, as well as healthcare and diagnostics. Co. serves its customers through its five brands: Thermo Scientific, Applied Biosystems, Invitrogen, Fisher Scientific and Unity Lab Services. Co. has four business segments: Life Sciences Solutions, Analytical Instruments, Specialty Diagnostics and Laboratory Products and Services.

Recent Developments: For the quarter ended Mar 31 2018, net income increased 5.1% to US$579.0 million from US$551.0 million in the year-earlier quarter. Revenues were US$5.85 billion, up 22.8% from US$4.77 billion the year before. Operating income was US$786.0 million versus US$620.0 million in the prior-year quarter, an increase of 26.8%. Direct operating expenses rose 27.3% to US$3.27 billion from US$2.57 billion in the comparable period the year before. Indirect operating expenses increased 14.0% to US$1.79 billion from US$1.57 billion in the equivalent prior-year period.

Prospects: Our evaluation of Thermo Fisher Scientific Inc. as of Jan. 21, 2018 is the result of our systematic analysis on three basic characteristics: earnings strength, relative valuation, and recent stock price movement. The company has managed to produce a neutral trend in earnings per share over the past 5 quarters and while recent estimates for the company have been mixed, TMO has posted better than expected results. Based on operating earnings yield, the company is about fairly valued when compared to all of the companies in our coverage universe. Share price changes over the past year indicates that TMO will perform in line with the market over the near term.

Financial Data
(US$ in Thousands)

	3 Mos	12/31/2017	12/31/2016	12/31/2015	12/31/2014	12/31/2013	12/31/2012	12/31/2011
Earnings Per Share	5.63	5.59	5.09	4.92	4.71	3.48	3.21	3.46
Cash Flow Per Share	9.26	10.14	7.97	7.07	6.58	5.58	5.59	4.44
Dividends Per Share	0.620	0.600	0.600	0.600	0.600	0.600	0.540	...
Dividend Payout %	11.01	10.73	11.79	12.20	12.74	17.24	16.82	...
Income Statement								
Total Revenue	5,853,000	20,918,000	18,274,100	16,965,400	16,889,600	13,090,300	12,509,900	11,725,900
EBITDA	1,352,000	4,973,000	4,203,100	4,008,900	4,204,200	2,553,500	2,469,500	2,138,500
Depn & Amortn	575,000	2,033,000	1,758,000	1,688,200	1,684,800	999,900	983,700	863,500
Income Before Taxes	634,000	2,429,000	2,023,900	1,936,400	2,087,200	1,319,500	1,269,400	1,126,600
Income Taxes	55,000	201,000	(1,400)	(43,900)	191,700	40,400	11,000	107,000
Net Income	579,000	2,225,000	2,021,800	1,975,400	1,894,400	1,273,300	1,177,900	1,329,900
Average Shares	406,000	398,000	397,400	401,900	402,300	365,800	366,600	384,800
Balance Sheet								
Current Assets	9,588,000	9,421,000	7,021,000	5,741,200	6,539,800	9,880,700	4,834,800	4,821,900
Total Assets	56,580,000	56,669,000	45,907,500	40,889,000	42,852,100	31,863,400	27,444,600	26,833,700
Current Liabilities	7,072,000	7,048,000	4,865,800	4,147,300	5,349,800	3,126,000	2,093,300	3,113,100
Long-Term Obligations	18,122,000	18,873,000	15,372,400	11,473,900	12,351,600	9,499,600	7,031,200	5,755,200
Total Liabilities	30,457,000	31,256,000	24,368,200	19,538,800	22,304,000	15,007,300	11,979,900	11,795,600
Stockholders' Equity	26,123,000	25,413,000	21,539,300	21,350,200	20,548,100	16,856,100	15,464,700	15,038,100
Shares Outstanding	402,323	401,314	393,447	399,630	400,469	361,961	357,443	371,383
Statistical Record								
Return on Assets %	4.38	4.34	4.65	4.72	5.07	4.29	4.33	5.52
Return on Equity %	9.40	9.48	9.40	9.43	10.13	7.88	7.70	8.75
EBITDA Margin %	23.10	23.77	23.00	23.63	24.89	19.51	19.74	18.24
Net Margin %	9.89	10.64	11.06	11.64	11.22	9.73	9.42	11.34
Asset Turnover	0.43	0.41	0.42	0.41	0.45	0.44	0.46	0.49
Current Ratio	1.36	1.34	1.44	1.38	1.22	3.16	2.31	1.55
Debt to Equity	0.69	0.74	0.71	0.54	0.60	0.56	0.45	0.38
Price Range	224.11-152.18	200.37-140.98	159.56-121.94	143.03-118.13	129.29-109.63	111.35-63.78	65.28-45.95	65.57-43.54
P/E Ratio	39.81-27.03	35.84-25.22	31.35-23.96	29.07-24.01	27.45-23.28	32.00-18.33	20.34-14.31	18.95-12.58
Average Yield %	0.33	0.35	0.41	0.46	0.50	0.69	0.96	...

Address: 168 Third Avenue, Waltham, MA 02451	Web Site: www.thermofisher.com	Auditors: PricewaterhouseCoopers LLP
Telephone: 781-622-1000	Officers: Jim P. Manzi - Chairman, Chairman (frmr) Marc N. Casper - President, Chief Executive Officer, Executive Vice President (frmr), Senior Vice President, Chief Operating Officer	Investor Contact: 781-622-1111
Fax: 781-933-4476		Transfer Agents: American Stock Transfer & Trust Company, LLC, Brooklyn, NY

THOR INDUSTRIES, INC.

Exchange	Symbol	Price	52Wk Range	Yield	P/E
NYS	THO	$97.39 (6/29/2018)	157.02-92.60	1.52	11.16

*7 Year Price Score 151.81 *NYSE Composite Index=100 *12 Month Price Score 81.30

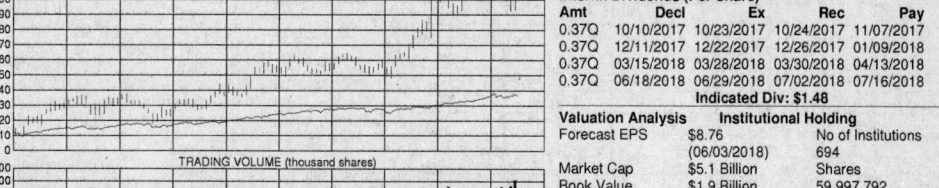

Interim Earnings (Per Share)

Qtr.	Oct	Jan	Apr	Jul
2014-15	0.73	0.54	1.17	1.30
2015-16	0.96	0.85	1.49	1.57
2016-17	1.49	1.23	2.11	2.26
2017-18	2.43	1.51	2.53	...

Interim Dividends (Per Share)

Amt	Decl	Ex	Rec	Pay
0.37Q	10/10/2017	10/23/2017	10/24/2017	11/07/2017
0.37Q	12/11/2017	12/22/2017	12/26/2017	01/09/2018
0.37Q	03/15/2018	03/28/2018	03/30/2018	04/13/2018
0.37Q	06/18/2018	06/29/2018	07/02/2018	07/16/2018

Indicated Div: $1.48

Valuation Analysis / **Institutional Holding**

Forecast EPS	$8.76	No of Institutions
	(06/03/2018)	694
Market Cap	$5.1 Billion	Shares
Book Value	$1.9 Billion	59,997,792
Price/Book	2.75	% Held
Price/Sales	0.61	83.49

Business Summary: Autos- Manufacturing (MIC: 1.8.1 SIC: 3716 NAIC: 336213)

Thor Industries, through its subsidiaries, manufactures a range of recreational vehicles and sells those vehicles in the U.S. and Canada. Co. has two reportable segments: towable recreational vehicles, which consists of the following operating segments that have been aggregated: Airstream (towable), Heartland (including Bison, CRV and DRV), Jayco (including Jayco towable, Starcraft and Highland Ridge), Keystone (including CrossRoads and Dutchmen) and KZ (including Livin' Lite); and motorized recreational vehicles, which consists of the following operating segments that have been aggregated: Airstream (motorized), Jayco (including Jayco motorized and Entegra Coach) and Thor Motor Coach.

Recent Developments: For the quarter ended Apr 30 2018, net income increased 20.2% to US$133.8 million from US$111.3 million in the year-earlier quarter. Revenues were US$2.25 billion, up 11.7% from US$2.02 billion the year before. Direct operating expenses rose 12.4% to US$1.93 billion from US$1.72 billion in the comparable period the year before. Indirect operating expenses increased 5.5% to US$133.3 million from US$126.3 million in the equivalent prior-year period.

Prospects: Our evaluation of Thor Industries Inc. as of Jan. 21, 2018 is the result of our systematic analysis on three basic characteristics: earnings strength, relative valuation, and recent stock price movement. The company has managed to produce a neutral trend in earnings per share over the past 5 quarters. However, while recent estimates for the company have been mixed, THO has posted better than expected results. Based on operating earnings yield, the company is undervalued when compared to all of the companies in our coverage universe. Share price changes over the past year indicates that THO will perform very well over the near term.

Financial Data

(US$ in Thousands)	9 Mos	6 Mos	3 Mos	07/31/2017	07/31/2016	07/31/2015	07/31/2014	07/31/2013
Earnings Per Share	8.73	8.31	8.03	7.09	4.88	3.74	3.35	2.88
Cash Flow Per Share	8.23	8.03	8.20	7.98	6.49	4.66	2.80	2.74
Tang Book Value Per Share	20.60	18.11	16.63	14.36	7.24	11.14	11.28	10.47
Dividends Per Share	1.440	1.400	1.360	1.320	1.200	1.080	1.920	2.220
Dividend Payout %	16.49	16.85	16.94	18.62	24.59	28.88	57.31	77.08
Income Statement								
Total Revenue	6,454,798	4,203,228	2,231,668	7,246,952	4,582,112	4,006,819	3,525,456	3,241,795
EBITDA	582,271	376,898	203,433	663,451	436,737	323,164	277,086	244,337
Depn & Amortn	70,683	46,758	15,311	98,258	52,575	31,381	25,834	24,987
Income Before Taxes	508,681	328,156	187,091	556,386	383,313	292,895	252,819	221,972
Income Taxes	166,735	119,998	58,685	182,132	125,291	90,886	77,303	70,296
Net Income	341,946	208,158	128,406	374,254	256,519	199,385	179,002	152,862
Average Shares	52,853	52,861	52,818	52,758	52,590	53,275	53,361	53,115
Balance Sheet								
Current Assets	1,427,361	1,334,202	1,317,588	1,180,167	1,016,858	775,841	844,049	830,704
Total Assets	2,866,482	2,708,959	2,709,966	2,557,931	2,325,464	1,503,248	1,408,718	1,328,268
Current Liabilities	855,565	817,117	877,385	781,046	651,652	378,335	370,715	361,672
Long-Term Obligations	80,000	80,000	90,000	145,000	360,000	...	...	...
Total Liabilities	1,000,856	961,030	1,025,861	981,391	1,060,242	438,061	431,021	435,654
Stockholders' Equity	1,865,626	1,747,929	1,684,105	1,576,540	1,265,222	1,065,187	977,697	892,614
Shares Outstanding	52,695	52,695	52,694	52,586	52,482	52,394	53,329	53,186
Statistical Record								
Return on Assets %	16.88	17.07	16.65	15.33	13.36	13.69	13.08	11.89
Return on Equity %	27.65	28.10	28.17	26.34	21.95	19.52	19.14	17.54
EBITDA Margin %	9.02	8.97	9.12	9.15	9.53	8.07	7.86	7.54
Net Margin %	5.30	4.95	5.75	5.16	5.60	4.98	5.08	4.72
Asset Turnover	3.07	3.17	3.05	2.97	2.39	2.75	2.58	2.52
Current Ratio	1.67	1.63	1.50	1.51	1.56	2.05	2.28	2.30
Debt to Equity	0.04	0.05	0.05	0.09	0.28	...	...	...
Price Range	157.02-90.53	157.02-89.41	136.22-74.53	115.42-74.53	76.54-48.06	64.38-50.03	64.16-49.03	55.27-27.22
P/E Ratio	17.99-10.37	18.90-10.76	16.96-9.28	16.28-10.51	15.68-9.85	17.21-13.38	19.15-14.64	19.19-9.45
Average Yield %	1.20	1.21	1.31	1.41	1.40	2.05	1.90	3.42	5.63

Address: 601 East Beardsley Ave.,	Web Site: www.thorindustries.com	Auditors: DELOITTE & TOUCHE LLP
Elkhart, IN 46514-3305	Officers: Peter B. Orthwein - Executive Chairman,	Transfer Agents: Computershare
Telephone: 574-970-7460	Chairman, President, Chief Executive Officer Robert	Investor Services
	W. Martin - President, Chief Executive Officer, Chief	
	Operating Officer, Division Officer	

3M CO

Exchange	Symbol	Price	52Wk Range	Yield	P/E	Div Acheiver
NYS	MMM	$196.72 (6/29/2018)	258.63-194.39	2.77	29.19	59 Years

*7 Year Price Score 120.45 *NYSE Composite Ihdex=100 *12 Month Price Score 90.13

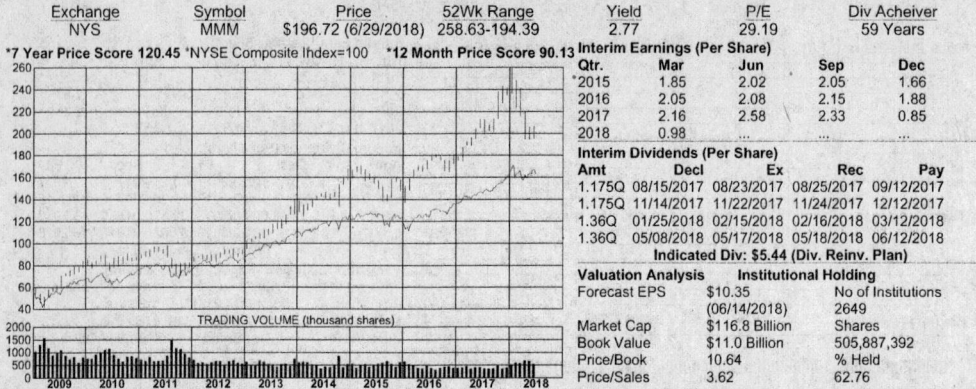

Interim Earnings (Per Share)

Qtr.	Mar	Jun	Sep	Dec
*2015	1.85	2.02	2.05	1.66
2016	2.05	2.08	2.15	1.88
2017	2.16	2.58	2.33	0.85
2018	0.98	...	...	...

Interim Dividends (Per Share)

Amt	Decl	Ex	Rec	Pay
1.175Q	08/15/2017	08/23/2017	08/25/2017	09/12/2017
1.175Q	11/14/2017	11/22/2017	11/24/2017	12/12/2017
1.36Q	01/25/2018	02/15/2018	02/16/2018	03/12/2018
1.36Q	05/08/2018	05/17/2018	05/18/2018	06/12/2018

Indicated Div: $5.44 (Div. Reinv. Plan)

Valuation Analysis | **Institutional Holding**

Forecast EPS	$10.35	No of Institutions
	(06/14/2018)	2649
Market Cap	$116.8 Billion	Shares
Book Value	$11.0 Billion	505,887,392
Price/Book	10.64	% Held
Price/Sales	3.62	62.76

Business Summary: Medical Instruments & Equipment (MIC: 4.3.1 SIC: 3841 NAIC: 339112)

3M is a technology company. Co. has five segments: Industrial, which provides tapes, coated, non-woven and bonded abrasives, and adhesives; Safety and Graphics, which provides personal protection products, traffic safety and security products and commercial graphics systems; Health Care, which provides medical and surgical supplies, skin health and infection prevention products and drug delivery systems; Electronics and Energy, which provides optical films solutions for electronic displays, packaging and interconnection devices, as well as insulating and splicing solutions; and Consumer, which provides sponges, scouring pads, cloths, consumer and office tapes.

Recent Developments: For the quarter ended Mar 31 2018, net income decreased 54.3% to US$606.0 million from US$1.33 billion in the year-earlier quarter. Revenues were US$8.28 billion, up 7.7% from US$7.69 billion the year before. Operating income was US$1.01 billion versus US$1.74 billion in the prior-year quarter, a decrease of 42.2%. Direct operating expenses rose 9.1% to US$4.24 billion from US$3.88 billion in the comparable period the year before. Indirect operating expenses increased 47.3% to US$3.04 billion from US$2.06 billion in the equivalent prior-year period.

Prospects: Our evaluation of 3M Co as of Jan. 21, 2018 is the result of our systematic analysis on three basic characteristics: earnings strength, relative valuation, and recent stock price movement. The company has produced a positive trend in earnings per share over the past 5 quarters. However, while recent estimates for the company have been mixed, MMM has posted better than expected results. Based on operating earnings yield, the company is about fairly valued when compared to all of the companies in our coverage universe. Share price changes over the past year indicates that MMM will perform well over the near term.

Financial Data
(US$ in Millions)

	3 Mos	12/31/2017	12/31/2016	12/31/2015	12/31/2014	12/31/2013	12/31/2012	12/31/2011
Earnings Per Share	6.74	7.93	8.16	7.58	7.49	6.72	6.32	5.96
Cash Flow Per Share	9.05	10.44	10.99	10.26	10.21	8.53	7.62	7.46
Tang Book Value Per Share	N.M.	N.M.	N.M.	N.M.	7.28	12.77	12.03	9.29
Dividends Per Share	4.885	4.700	4.440	4.100	3.420	2.540	2.360	2.200
Dividend Payout %	72.48	59.27	54.41	54.09	45.66	37.80	37.34	36.91
Income Statement								
Total Revenue	8,278	31,657	30,109	30,274	31,821	30,871	29,904	29,611
EBITDA	1,408	9,364	8,697	8,381	8,543	8,037	7,771	7,414
Depn & Amortn	382	1,544	1,474	1,435	1,408	1,371	1,288	1,236
Income Before Taxes	965	7,548	7,053	6,823	7,026	6,562	6,351	6,031
Income Taxes	359	2,679	1,995	1,982	2,028	1,841	1,840	1,674
Net Income	602	4,858	5,050	4,833	4,956	4,659	4,444	4,283
Average Shares	612	612	618	637	662	693	703	719
Balance Sheet								
Current Assets	14,818	14,277	11,726	10,986	11,765	12,733	13,630	12,240
Total Assets	38,575	37,987	32,906	32,718	31,269	33,550	33,876	31,616
Current Liabilities	8,959	7,687	6,219	7,118	5,998	7,498	6,200	5,441
Long-Term Obligations	12,211	12,156	10,723	8,799	6,790	4,384	4,987	4,563
Total Liabilities	27,598	26,424	22,608	21,010	18,160	16,048	16,301	16,196
Stockholders' Equity	10,977	11,563	10,298	11,708	13,109	17,502	17,575	15,420
Shares Outstanding	593	594	596	609	635	663	687	694
Statistical Record								
Return on Assets %	11.51	13.71	15.35	15.11	15.29	13.82	13.53	13.87
Return on Equity %	37.67	44.44	45.77	38.95	32.38	26.56	26.86	27.56
EBITDA Margin %	17.01	29.58	28.89	27.68	26.85	26.03	25.99	25.04
Net Margin %	7.27	15.35	16.77	15.96	15.57	15.09	14.86	14.46
Asset Turnover	0.90	0.89	0.92	0.95	0.98	0.92	0.91	0.96
Current Ratio	1.65	1.86	1.89	1.54	1.96	1.70	2.20	2.25
Debt to Equity	1.11	1.05	1.04	0.75	0.52	0.25	0.28	0.30
Price Range	258.63-188.65	243.14-174.18	181.42-136.96	170.50-137.58	167.27-123.90	140.25-92.85	95.37-82.51	97.97-70.93
P/E Ratio	38.37-27.99	30.66-21.96	22.23-16.78	22.49-18.15	22.33-16.54	20.87-13.82	15.09-13.06	16.44-11.90
Average Yield %	2.24	2.29	2.64	2.62	2.40	2.23	2.65	2.54

Address: 3M Center, St. Paul, MN 55144
Telephone: 651-733-1110
Fax: 651-733-9973

Web Site: www.3M.com
Officers: Inge G. Thulin - Executive Chairman, Chairman, President, Executive Vice President, Chief Executive Officer, Chief Operating Officer Hak Cheol Shin - Vice-Chairman, Executive Vice President, Executive Vice President (frmr)

Auditors: PricewaterhouseCoopers LLP
Investor Contact: 651-737-8503
Transfer Agents: Wells Fargo Shareowner Services, St. Paul, MN

. TIFFANY & CO.

Exchange	Symbol	Price	52Wk Range	Yield	P/E	Div Acheiver
NYS	TIF	$131.60 (6/29/2018)	137.89-87.55	1.67	39.17	15 Years

*7 Year Price Score 100.66 *NYSE Composite Index=100 *12 Month Price Score 121.47

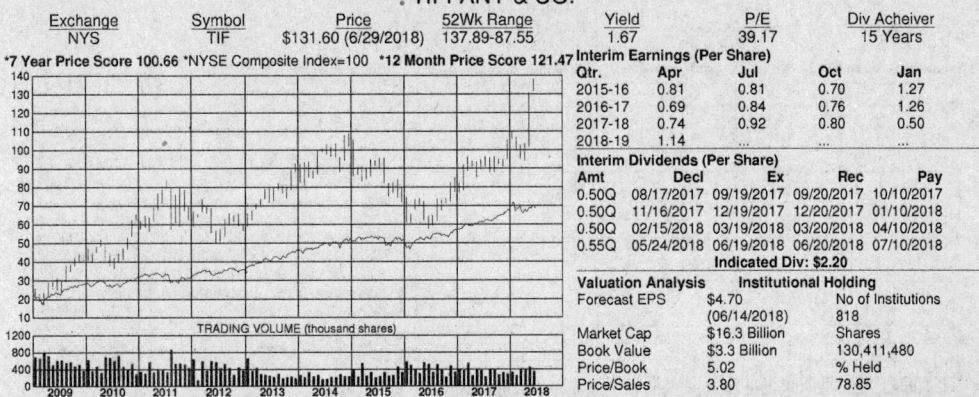

Interim Earnings (Per Share)

Qtr.	Apr	Jul	Oct	Jan
2015-16	0.81	0.81	0.70	1.27
2016-17	0.69	0.84	0.76	1.26
2017-18	0.74	0.92	0.80	0.50
2018-19	1.14	...	...	...

Interim Dividends (Per Share)

Amt	Decl	Ex	Rec	Pay
0.50Q	08/17/2017	09/19/2017	09/20/2017	10/10/2017
0.50Q	11/16/2017	12/19/2017	12/20/2017	01/10/2018
0.50Q	02/15/2018	03/19/2018	03/20/2018	04/10/2018
0.55Q	05/24/2018	06/19/2018	06/20/2018	07/10/2018

Indicated Div: $2.20

Valuation Analysis / Institutional Holding

Valuation Analysis		Institutional Holding	
Forecast EPS	$4.70	No of Institutions	
	(06/14/2018)	818	
Market Cap	$16.3 Billion	Shares	
Book Value	$3.3 Billion	130,411,480	
Price/Book	5.02	% Held	
Price/Sales	3.80	78.85	

Business Summary: Retail - Specialty (MIC: 2.1.3 SIC: 5944 NAIC: 448310)

Tiffany & Co. is a holding company that operates through its subsidiary companies. Its principal subsidiary, Tiffany and Company, is a jeweler and specialty retailer. Through its subsidiaries, Co. designs and manufactures products and operates TIFFANY & CO. retail stores worldwide, and also sells its products through internet, catalog, business-to-business and wholesale operations. Co. also sells timepieces, leather goods, sterling silverware, china, crystal, stationery, fragrances and accessories. Co. has four reportable segments: (i) Americas, (ii) Asia-Pacific, (iii) Japan and (iv) Europe. As of Jan 31 2018, Co. operated a total of 315 TIFFANY & CO. stores.

Recent Developments: For the quarter ended Apr 30 2018, net income increased 53.2% to US$142.3 million from US$92.9 million in the year-earlier quarter. Revenues were US$1.03 billion, up 14.9% from US$899.6 million the year before. Operating income was US$204.3 million versus US$149.6 million in the prior-year quarter, an increase of 36.6%. Direct operating expenses rose 12.3% to US$382.3 million from US$340.5 million in the comparable period the year before. Indirect operating expenses increased 9.1% to US$446.6 million from US$409.5 million in the equivalent prior-year period.

Prospects: Our evaluation of Tiffany & Co. as of Jan. 21, 2018 is the result of our systematic analysis on three basic characteristics: earnings strength, relative valuation, and recent stock price movement. The company has produced a positive trend in earnings per share over the past 5 quarters and while recent estimates for the company have been raised by analysts, TIF has posted better than expected results. Based on operating earnings yield, the company is about fairly valued when compared to all of the companies in our coverage universe. Share price changes over the past year indicates that TIF will perform in line with the market over the near term.

Financial Data

(US$ in Thousands)	3 Mos	01/31/2018	01/31/2017	01/31/2016	01/31/2015	01/31/2014	01/31/2013	01/31/2012
Earnings Per Share	3.36	2.96	3.55	3.59	3.73	1.41	3.25	3.40
Cash Flow Per Share	7.38	7.49	5.60	6.33	4.76	1.21	2.58	1.65
Tang Book Value Per Share	26.20	25.97	24.20	22.96	21.92	21.20	20.47	18.54
Dividends Per Share	2.000	1.950	1.750	1.580	1.480	1.340	1.250	1.120
Dividend Payout %	59.52	65.88	49.30	44.01	39.68	95.04	38.46	32.94
Income Statement								
Total Revenue	1,033,200	4,169,800	4,001,800	4,104,900	4,249,913	4,031,130	3,794,249	3,642,937
EBITDA	198,200	1,003,300	925,100	955,200	983,201	488,972	861,663	862,634
Depn & Amortn	(2,200)	200,800	202,500	196,300	182,761	171,452	159,018	149,109
Income Before Taxes	190,500	760,500	676,600	709,900	737,537	254,866	643,576	664,951
Income Taxes	48,200	390,400	230,500	246,000	253,358	73,497	227,419	225,761
Net Income	142,300	370,100	446,100	463,900	484,179	181,369	416,157	439,190
Average Shares	125,000	125,100	125,500	129,100	129,918	128,867	127,934	129,083
Balance Sheet								
Current Assets	3,980,200	3,983,300	3,573,600	3,508,400	3,611,387	3,228,388	3,151,589	2,889,675
Total Assets	5,450,600	5,468,100	5,097,600	5,129,700	5,180,603	4,752,351	4,630,850	4,158,992
Current Liabilities	684,300	724,800	632,800	729,900	658,033	696,740	586,592	626,677
Long-Term Obligations	882,900	882,900	878,400	798,100	882,535	751,154	765,238	538,352
Total Liabilities	2,196,900	2,234,700	2,084,100	2,218,300	2,345,544	2,031,914	2,032,118	1,810,087
Stockholders' Equity	3,253,700	3,233,400	3,013,500	2,911,400	2,835,059	2,720,437	2,598,732	2,348,905
Shares Outstanding	124,200	124,500	124,500	126,800	129,326	128,312	126,934	126,676
Statistical Record								
Return on Assets %	7.95	7.01	8.70	9.00	9.75	3.87	9.44	11.13
Return on Equity %	13.29	11.85	15.02	16.15	17.43	6.82	16.78	19.41
EBITDA Margin %	19.18	24.06	23.12	23.27	23.13	12.13	22.71	23.68
Net Margin %	13.77	8.88	11.15	11.30	11.39	4.50	10.97	12.06
Asset Turnover	0.82	0.79	0.78	0.80	0.86	0.86	0.86	0.92
Current Ratio	5.82	5.50	5.65	4.81	5.49	4.63	5.37	4.61
Debt to Equity	0.27	0.27	0.29	0.27	0.31	0.28	0.29	0.23
Price Range	109.88-85.03	109.88-78.00	85.06-57.48	95.70-60.93	108.67-80.88	92.78-62.17	73.27-50.29	83.82-56.27
P/E Ratio	32.70-25.31	37.12-26.35	23.96-16.19	26.66-16.97	29.13-21.68	65.80-44.09	22.54-15.47	24.65-16.55
Average Yield %	2.09	2.09	2.49	1.88	1.54	1.73	2.04	1.63

Address: 727 Fifth Avenue, New York, NY 10022 Telephone: 212-755-8000 Fax: 212-605-4465	Web Site: www.tiffany.com Officers: Michael J. Kowalski - Chairman, Chief Executive Officer, Interim Chief Executive Officer Alessandro Bogliolo - Chief Executive Officer	Auditors: PricewaterhouseCoopers LLP Investor Contact: 212-230-5301 Transfer Agents: Computershare, Providence, RI

TIMKEN CO. (THE)

Exchange	Symbol	Price	52Wk Range	Yield	P/E
NYS	TKR	$43.55 (6/29/2018)	55.50-42.75	2.57	14.00

*7 Year Price Score 99.47   *NYSE Composite Index=100   *12 Month Price Score 97.21

Interim Earnings (Per Share)

Qtr.	Mar	Jun	Sep	Dec
2015	(1.54)	0.43	0.75	(0.43)
2016	0.78	0.57	0.26	0.30
2017	0.48	1.04	0.68	0.37
2018	1.02	...	...	...

Interim Dividends (Per Share)

Amt	Decl	Ex	Rec	Pay
0.27Q	08/08/2017	08/18/2017	08/22/2017	09/01/2017
0.27Q	11/03/2017	11/16/2017	11/17/2017	12/01/2017
0.27Q	02/09/2018	02/16/2018	02/20/2018	03/02/2018
0.28Q	05/08/2018	05/17/2018	05/18/2018	06/04/2018

Indicated Div: $1.12

Valuation Analysis   Institutional Holding

Forecast EPS	$3.97	No of Institutions
	(06/12/2018)	508
Market Cap	$3.4 Billion	Shares
Book Value	$1.5 Billion	74,241,888
Price/Book	2.24	% Held
Price/Sales	1.06	68.91

Business Summary: Industrial Machinery & Equipment (MIC: 7.2.1 SIC: 3562 NAIC: 332991)

Timken engineers, manufactures and markets bearings, transmissions, gearboxes, belts, chain, couplings and related products and provides a range of power system rebuild and repair services. Co.'s products include: tapered roller bearings, which can increase power density and can include customized geometries, engineered surfaces and specialized sealing solutions; spherical and cylindrical roller bearings, which used in gear drives, rolling mills and other industrial and infrastructure development applications; Carlisle® belts, which used in industrial, commercial and consumer applications; and Drives® roller chain, which are used in a range of mobile and industrial machinery applications.

Recent Developments: For the quarter ended Mar 31 2018, net income increased 111.3% to US$80.5 million from US$38.1 million in the year-earlier quarter. Revenues were US$883.1 million, up 25.5% from US$703.8 million the year before. Operating income was US$116.1 million versus US$62.9 million in the prior-year quarter, an increase of 84.6%. Direct operating expenses rose 18.5% to US$618.2 million from US$521.6 million in the comparable period the year before. Indirect operating expenses increased 24.7% to US$148.8 million from US$119.3 million in the equivalent prior-year period.

Prospects: Our evaluation of Timken Co. as of Jan. 21, 2018 is the result of our systematic analysis on three basic characteristics: earnings strength, relative valuation, and recent stock price movement. The company has enjoyed a very positive trend in earnings per share over the past 5 quarters and while recent estimates for the company have been mixed, TKR has posted better than expected results. Based on operating earnings yield, the company is undervalued when compared to all of the companies in our coverage universe. Share price changes over the past year indicates that TKR will perform poorly over the near term.

Financial Data

(US$ in Thousands)	3 Mos	12/31/2017	12/31/2016	12/31/2015	12/31/2014	12/31/2013	12/31/2012	12/31/2011
Earnings Per Share	3.11	2.58	1.92	(0.84)	1.87	2.74	5.07	4.59
Cash Flow Per Share	1.88	3.05	5.11	4.43	3.40	4.53	6.46	2.17
Tang Book Value Per Share	7.48	6.57	8.35	9.04	12.16	22.11	17.40	14.94
Dividends Per Share	1.080	1.070	1.040	1.030	1.000	0.920	0.920	0.780
Dividend Payout %	34.73	41.47	54.17	...	53.48	33.58	18.15	16.99
Income Statement								
Total Revenue	883,100	3,003,800	2,669,800	2,872,300	3,076,200	4,341,200	4,987,000	5,170,200
EBITDA	154,200	391,800	349,200	(64,300)	343,800	615,500	973,200	906,500
Depn & Amortn	35,800	97,700	95,500	94,600	115,500	175,900	179,000	178,500
Income Before Taxes	108,800	259,900	222,100	(189,600)	204,000	417,100	766,000	696,800
Income Taxes	28,300	57,600	69,200	(121,600)	54,700	154,100	270,100	240,200
Net Income	80,200	203,400	152,600	(70,800)	170,800	262,700	495,500	454,300
Average Shares	79,013	78,911	79,234	84,631	91,224	95,823	97,602	98,655
Balance Sheet								
Current Assets	1,645,800	1,500,100	1,204,000	1,206,400	1,481,900	1,937,500	2,174,100	2,292,300
Total Assets	3,549,500	3,402,400	2,758,300	2,785,300	3,001,400	4,477,900	4,244,700	4,352,100
Current Liabilities	702,300	671,700	452,700	505,300	533,800	980,100	667,900	844,600
Long-Term Obligations	896,500	854,200	635,000	580,600	522,100	206,600	455,100	478,800
Total Liabilities	2,038,600	1,959,700	1,483,400	1,460,800	1,425,200	1,841,300	2,012,500	2,323,800
Stockholders' Equity	1,510,900	1,442,700	1,274,900	1,324,500	1,576,200	2,636,600	2,232,200	2,028,300
Shares Outstanding	77,596	77,703	77,449	80,263	88,591	93,122	95,898	97,666
Statistical Record								
Return on Assets %	7.71	6.60	5.49	N.M.	4.57	6.02	11.50	10.65
Return on Equity %	17.33	14.97	11.71	N.M.	8.11	10.79	23.20	22.98
EBITDA Margin %	17.46	13.04	13.08	N.M.	11.18	14.18	19.51	17.53
Net Margin %	9.08	6.77	5.72	N.M.	5.55	6.05	9.94	8.79
Asset Turnover	1.00	0.98	0.96	0.99	0.82	1.00	1.16	1.21
Current Ratio	2.34	2.23	2.66	2.39	2.78	1.98	3.26	2.71
Debt to Equity	0.59	0.59	0.50	0.44	0.33	0.08	0.20	0.24
Price Range	55.50-42.60	51.55-40.95	40.95-23.41	43.50-26.46	49.73-37.75	45.26-33.98	41.01-25.02	40.06-21.95
P/E Ratio	17.85-13.70	19.98-15.87	21.33-12.19	...	26.59-20.19	16.52-12.40	8.09-4.93	8.73-4.78
Average Yield %	2.29	2.32	3.14	2.88	2.30	2.31	2.85	2.44

Address: 4500 Mount Pleasant Street N.W., North Canton, OH 44720-5450 **Telephone:** 234-262-3000	**Web Site:** www.timken.com **Officers:** John M. Timken - Chairman Richard G. Kyle - President, Group President, Chief Executive Officer, Chief Operating Officer	**Auditors:** Ernst & Young LLP **Investor Contact:** 330-471-7446 **Transfer Agents:** Wells Fargo Shareowner Services, Saint Paul, MN

TJX COMPANIES, INC.

Exchange	Symbol	Price	52Wk Range	Yield	P/E	Div Acheiver
NYS	TJX	$95.18 (6/29/2018)	96.72-66.90	1.64	21.88	21 Years

*7 Year Price Score 102.35 *NYSE Composite Index=100 *12 Month Price Score 113.98

TRADING VOLUME (thousand shares)

Interim Earnings (Per Share)

Qtr.	Apr	Jul	Oct	Jan
2015-16	0.69	0.80	0.86	0.98
2016-17	0.76	0.84	0.83	1.03
2017-18	0.82	0.85	1.00	1.37
2018-19	1.13	...	...	...

Interim Dividends (Per Share)

Amt	Decl	Ex	Rec	Pay
0.313Q	09/15/2017	11/08/2017	11/09/2017	11/30/2017
0.313Q	12/05/2017	02/14/2018	02/15/2018	03/08/2018
0.39Q	04/04/2018	05/16/2018	05/17/2018	06/07/2018
0.39Q	06/06/2018	08/15/2018	08/16/2018	09/06/2018

Indicated Div: $1.56

Valuation Analysis / Institutional Holding

Forecast EPS	$4.85	No of Institutions
	(06/12/2018)	1627
Market Cap	$59.5 Billion	Shares
Book Value	$5.3 Billion	676,221,760
Price/Book	11.31	% Held
Price/Sales	1.62	81.69

Business Summary: Retail - Apparel and Accessories (MIC: 2.1.5 SIC: 5651 NAIC: 448140)

TJX Companies is an apparel and home fashions retailer. Co. operates its business in four main segments. In the U.S., Co.'s two segments are comprised of Marmaxx (T.J. Maxx, Marshalls and tjmaxx.com) and HomeGoods. The TJX Canada segment operates Winners, HomeSense and Marshalls in Canada, and the TJX International segment operates T.K. Maxx, HomeSense and tkmaxx.com in Europe and Trade Secret in Australia. All of Co.'s stores, with the exception of HomeGoods and HomeSense, sell family apparel and home fashions. HomeGoods and HomeSense provide home fashions. As of Feb 3 2018, Co. operated a total of 2,983 stores in the U.S.; 454 stores in Canada; and 595 stores in Europe and 38 in Australia.

Recent Developments: For the quarter ended May 5 2018, net income increased 33.6% to US$716.4 million from US$536.3 million in the year-earlier quarter. Revenues were US$8.69 billion, up 11.6% from US$7.78 billion the year before. Direct operating expenses rose 11.7% to US$6.18 billion from US$5.53 billion in the comparable period the year before. Indirect operating expenses increased 9.9% to US$1.55 billion from US$1.41 billion in the equivalent prior-year period.

Prospects: Our evaluation of TJX Companies Inc. as of Jan. 21, 2018 is the result of our systematic analysis on three basic characteristics: earnings strength, relative valuation, and recent stock price movement. The company has enjoyed a very positive trend in earnings per share over the past 5 quarters and while recent estimates for the company have been mixed, TJX has posted better than expected results. Based on operating earnings yield, the company is undervalued when compared to all of the companies in our coverage universe. Share price changes over the past year indicates that TJX will perform poorly over the near term.

Financial Data

(US$ in Thousands)	3 Mos	02/03/2018	01/28/2017	01/30/2016	01/31/2015	02/01/2014	02/02/2013	01/28/2012
Earnings Per Share	4.35	4.04	3.46	3.33	3.15	2.94	2.55	1.93
Cash Flow Per Share	5.27	4.67	5.51	4.37	4.35	3.64	4.08	2.52
Tang Book Value Per Share	8.26	8.04	6.68	5.97	5.78	5.56	4.63	4.06
Dividends Per Share	1.250	1.198	0.990	0.805	0.670	0.550	0.440	0.360
Dividend Payout %	28.74	29.64	28.61	24.17	21.27	18.71	17.25	18.65
Income Statement								
Total Revenue	8,688,720	35,864,664	33,183,744	30,944,938	29,078,407	27,422,696	25,878,372	23,191,455
EBITDA	1,153,406	4,614,133	4,425,373	4,321,396	4,178,646	3,899,393	3,108,226	2,449,262
Depn & Amortn	193,700	725,957	658,796	616,696	588,975	548,823	1,700	2,200
Income Before Taxes	955,558	3,856,588	3,723,043	3,658,300	3,549,884	3,319,489	3,077,351	2,411,414
Income Taxes	239,177	1,248,640	1,424,809	1,380,642	1,334,756	1,182,093	1,170,664	915,324
Net Income	716,381	2,607,948	2,298,234	2,277,658	2,215,128	2,137,396	1,906,687	1,496,090
Average Shares	634,436	646,105	664,432	683,251	703,545	726,376	747,555	773,772
Balance Sheet								
Current Assets	8,422,275	8,485,727	7,750,774	6,772,560	6,715,061	6,067,998	5,711,543	5,132,632
Total Assets	14,007,124	14,058,015	12,883,808	11,499,482	11,128,381	10,201,022	9,511,855	8,281,605
Current Liabilities	4,976,864	5,125,537	4,757,656	4,402,230	3,929,634	3,517,843	3,760,596	3,063,423
Long-Term Obligations	2,231,360	2,452,524	2,403,831	1,709,268	1,684,597	1,274,216	774,552	784,623
Total Liabilities	8,744,716	8,909,706	8,373,209	7,192,407	6,864,151	5,971,129	5,845,918	5,072,315
Stockholders' Equity	5,262,408	5,148,309	4,510,599	4,307,075	4,264,230	4,229,893	3,665,937	3,209,290
Shares Outstanding	625,202	628,009	646,319	663,495	684,733	705,016	723,902	746,702
Statistical Record								
Return on Assets %	20.83	19.05	18.90	20.19	20.83	21.74	21.08	18.46
Return on Equity %	56.81	53.13	52.27	53.29	52.30	54.29	54.57	47.56
EBITDA Margin %	13.27	12.87	13.34	13.96	14.37	14.22	12.01	10.56
Net Margin %	8.24	7.27	6.93	7.36	7.62	7.79	7.37	6.45
Asset Turnover	2.75	2.62	2.73	2.74	2.73	2.79	2.86	2.86
Current Ratio	1.69	1.66	1.63	1.54	1.71	1.72	1.52	1.68
Debt to Equity	0.42	0.48	0.53	0.40	0.40	0.30	0.21	0.24
Price Range	86.50-66.90	80.83-66.90	82.87-67.91	76.78-64.21	68.60-52.23	64.05-43.58	46.64-33.73	33.98-23.57
P/E Ratio	19.89-15.38	20.01-16.56	23.95-19.63	23.06-19.28	21.78-16.58	21.79-14.82	18.29-13.23	17.61-12.21
Average Yield %	1.66	1.61	1.30	1.16	1.12	1.03	1.05	1.30

Address: 770 Cochituate Road, Framingham, MA 01701 **Telephone:** 508-390-1000 **Fax:** 508-390-2091	**Web Site:** www.tjx.com **Officers:** Carol Meyrowitz - Executive Chairman, Chairman Ernie L. Herrman - President, Chief Executive Officer	**Auditors:** PricewaterhouseCoopers LLP **Investor Contact:** 508-390-2323 **Transfer Agents:** Computershare, Providence, RI

TOLL BROTHERS INC.

Exchange	Symbol	Price	52Wk Range	Yield	P/E
NYS	TOL	$36.99 (6/29/2018)	52.54-36.01	1.19	10.33

*7 Year Price Score 104.77 *NYSE Composite Index=100   *12 Month Price Score 91.13

Interim Earnings (Per Share)

Qtr.	Jan	Apr	Jul	Oct
2014-15	0.44	0.37	0.36	0.79
2015-16	0.40	0.51	0.61	0.66
2016-17	0.42	0.73	0.87	1.16
2017-18	0.83	0.72	...	...

Interim Dividends (Per Share)

Amt	Decl	Ex	Rec	Pay
0.08Q	09/19/2017	10/12/2017	10/13/2017	10/27/2017
0.08Q	12/13/2017	01/11/2018	01/12/2018	01/26/2018
0.11Q	03/13/2018	04/12/2018	04/13/2018	04/27/2018
0.11Q	06/19/2018	07/12/2018	07/13/2018	07/27/2018
		Indicated Div: $0.44		

Valuation Analysis

		Institutional Holding	
Forecast EPS	$4.40	No of Institutions	
	(06/14/2018)	669	
Market Cap	$5.6 Billion	Shares	
Book Value	$4.5 Billion	164,672,928	
Price/Book	1.25	% Held	
Price/Sales	0.89	86.35	

Business Summary: Builders (MIC: 2.2.5 SIC: 1531 NAIC: 236117)

Toll Brothers designs, builds, markets, sells and arranges financing for detached and attached homes in residential communities. Co. also builds and sells homes in urban infill markets through Toll Brothers City Living®. Co. is developing several land parcels for master planned communities. Co. also develops and operates for-rent apartments through joint ventures. Co. operates its own land development, architectural, engineering, mortgage, title, landscaping, security monitoring, lumber distribution, house component assembly, and manufacturing operations. In addition, Co. develops land for sale to other builders. Co. also develops, owns, and operates golf courses and country clubs.

Recent Developments: For the quarter ended Apr 30 2018, net income decreased 10.3% to US$111.8 million from US$124.6 million in the year-earlier quarter. Revenues were US$1.60 billion, up 17.3% from US$1.36 billion the year before. Operating income was US$134.4 million versus US$139.3 million in the prior-year quarter, a decrease of 3.5%. Direct operating expenses rose 20.5% to US$1.30 billion from US$1.08 billion in the comparable period the year before. Indirect operating expenses increased 13.6% to US$166.7 million from US$146.8 million in the equivalent prior-year period.

Prospects: Our evaluation of Toll Brothers Inc. as of Jan. 21, 2018 is the result of our systematic analysis on three basic characteristics: earnings strength, relative valuation, and recent stock price movement. The company has generated a negative trend in earnings per share over the past 5 quarters and while recent estimates for the company have been raised by analysts, TOL has posted results that fell short of analysts expectations. Based on operating earnings yield, the company is undervalued when compared to all of the companies in our coverage universe. Share price changes over the past year indicates that TOL will perform well over the near term.

Financial Data
(US$ in Thousands)

	6 Mos	3 Mos	10/31/2017	10/31/2016	10/31/2015	10/31/2014	10/31/2013	10/31/2012
Earnings Per Share	3.58	3.59	3.17	2.18	1.97	1.84	0.97	2.86
Cash Flow Per Share	2.45	3.77	5.92	0.88	0.34	1.76	(3.36)	(1.01)
Tang Book Value Per Share	29.50	29.03	28.82	26.14	24.15	22.02	19.68	18.51
Dividends Per Share	0.350	0.320	0.240	...	...	...	...	...
Dividend Payout %	9.78	8.91	7.57	...	...	...	...	...
Income Statement								
Total Revenue	2,774,667	1,175,468	5,815,058	5,169,508	4,171,248	3,911,602	2,674,299	1,882,781
EBITDA	252,130	96,809	710,957	561,336	528,204	486,440	278,515	111,936
Depn & Amortn	12,520	6,171	18,700	15,500	15,700	22,999	25,210	22,586
Income Before Taxes	242,902	92,718	698,245	548,279	514,443	463,441	253,305	89,350
Income Taxes	40,429	(509)	278,816	206,932	172,395	164,550	97,091	(374,204)
Net Income	243,917	132,107	535,495	382,095	363,167	340,032	170,606	487,146
Average Shares	155,129	158,897	169,487	175,973	184,703	185,875	177,963	170,154
Balance Sheet								
Current Assets	8,347,843	8,224,532	7,996,764	8,186,386	8,141,760	7,357,425	5,793,960	5,384,411
Total Assets	9,843,726	9,617,899	9,445,225	9,736,789	9,206,515	8,416,902	6,827,459	6,181,044
Current Liabilities	2,393,290	2,254,976	1,688,111	1,726,136	1,188,196	1,156,619	984,631	800,229
Long-Term Obligations	2,963,840	2,898,033	3,220,024	3,775,451	3,790,240	3,399,586	2,503,664	2,252,944
Total Liabilities	5,363,023	5,158,905	4,914,031	5,507,497	4,983,958	4,562,526	3,494,472	3,059,344
Stockholders' Equity	4,480,703	4,458,994	4,531,194	4,229,292	4,222,557	3,854,376	3,332,987	3,121,700
Shares Outstanding	151,864	153,602	157,205	161,783	174,847	175,046	169,353	168,637
Statistical Record								
Return on Assets %	5.93	6.24	5.58	4.02	4.12	4.46	2.62	8.65
Return on Equity %	13.09	13.61	12.23	9.02	8.99	9.46	5.29	17.02
EBITDA Margin %	9.09	8.24	12.23	10.86	12.66	12.44	10.41	5.95
Net Margin %	8.79	11.24	9.21	7.39	8.71	8.69	6.38	25.87
Asset Turnover	0.64	0.63	0.61	0.54	0.47	0.51	0.41	0.33
Current Ratio	3.49	3.65	4.74	4.74	6.85	6.36	5.88	6.73
Debt to Equity	0.66	0.65	0.71	0.89	0.90	0.88	0.75	0.72
Price Range	52.54-36.03	52.54-31.17	46.04-27.06	38.06-24.10	41.88-30.92	39.55-29.18	37.98-29.73	36.43-17.05
P/E Ratio	14.68-10.06	14.64-8.68	14.52-8.54	17.46-11.06	21.26-15.70	21.49-15.86	39.15-30.65	12.74-5.96
Average Yield %	0.82	0.79	0.66	...	...	...	...	...

Address: 250 Gibraltar Road, Horsham, PA 19044	Web Site: www.tollbrothers.com	Auditors: Ernst & Young LLP
Telephone: 215-938-8000	Officers: Robert I. Toll - Executive Chairman Richard T. Hartman - President, Chief Operating Officer	Investor Contact: 215-938-8312
Fax: 215-938-8023		Transfer Agents: American Stock Transfer and Trust Company, New York, NY

TOOTSIE ROLL INDUSTRIES INC

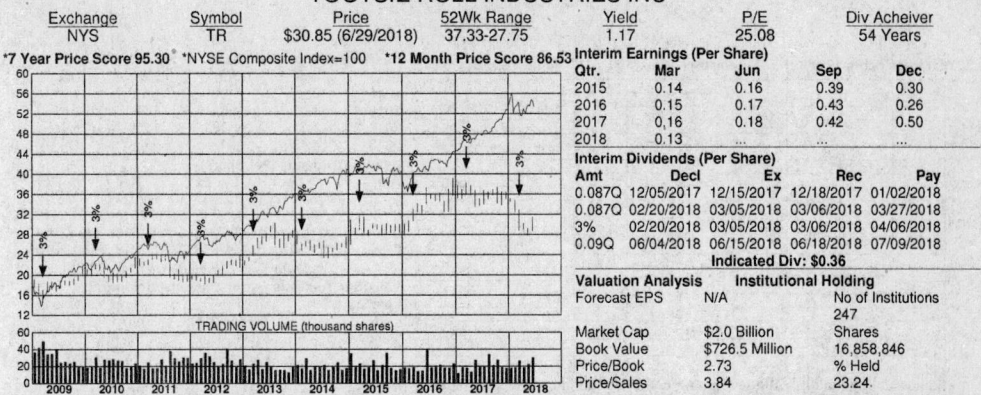

Exchange	Symbol	Price	52Wk Range	Yield	P/E	Div Acheiver
NYS	TR	$30.85 (6/29/2018)	37.33-27.75	1.17	25.08	54 Years

*7 Year Price Score 95.30 *NYSE Composite Index=100 ***12 Month Price Score 86.53**

Interim Earnings (Per Share)

Qtr.	Mar	Jun	Sep	Dec
2015	0.14	0.16	0.39	0.30
2016	0.15	0.17	0.43	0.26
2017	0.16	0.18	0.42	0.50
2018	0.13	...	...	...

Interim Dividends (Per Share)

Amt	Decl	Ex	Rec	Pay
0.087Q	12/05/2017	12/15/2017	12/18/2017	01/02/2018
0.087Q	02/20/2018	03/05/2018	03/06/2018	03/27/2018
3%	02/20/2018	03/05/2018	03/06/2018	04/06/2018
0.09Q	06/04/2018	06/15/2018	06/18/2018	07/09/2018

Indicated Div: $0.36

Valuation Analysis   **Institutional Holding**

Forecast EPS	N/A	No of Institutions
		247
Market Cap	$2.0 Billion	Shares
Book Value	$726.5 Million	16,858,846
Price/Book	2.73	% Held
Price/Sales	3.84	23.24

Business Summary: Food (MIC: 1.2.1 SIC: 2064 NAIC: 311340)

Tootsie Roll Industries and its consolidated subsidiaries are engaged in the manufacture and sale of confectionery products. This is the only industry segment in which Co. operates and is its only line of business. They are sold through candy and grocery brokers and by Co. itself to customers throughout the U.S. These customers include wholesale distributors of candy and groceries, supermarkets, variety stores, dollar stores, chain grocers, drug chains, discount chains, cooperative grocery associations, mass merchandisers, warehouse and membership club stores, vending machine operators, the U.S. military and fund-raising charitable organizations.

Recent Developments: For the quarter ended Mar 31 2018, net income decreased 19.1% to US$8.1 million from US$10.0 million in the year-earlier quarter. Revenues were US$101.8 million, down 2.5% from US$104.5 million the year before. Operating income was US$9.8 million versus US$11.9 million in the prior-year quarter, a decrease of 17.5%. Direct operating expenses rose 0.5% to US$66.1 million from US$65.8 million in the comparable period the year before. Indirect operating expenses decreased 3.2% to US$25.9 million from US$26.7 million in the equivalent prior-year period.

Prospects: Our evaluation of Tootsie Roll Industries Inc. as of Jan. 21, 2018 is the result of our systematic analysis on three basic characteristics: earnings strength, relative valuation, and recent stock price movement. The company has managed to produce a neutral trend in earnings per share over the past 5 quarters. Because the company lacks sufficient analyst estimate data, we place greater weight on the historical EPS trend as the measure of earnings strength. Based on operating earnings yield, the company is about fairly valued when compared to all of the companies in our coverage universe. Share price changes over the past year indicates that TR will perform in line with the market over the ne

Financial Data

(US$ in Thousands)	3 Mos	12/31/2017	12/31/2016	12/31/2015	12/31/2014	12/31/2013	12/31/2012	12/31/2011
Earnings Per Share	1.23	1.24	1.02	0.99	0.93	0.91	0.75	0.64
Cash Flow Per Share	0.63	0.66	1.49	1.36	1.30	1.64	1.45	0.73
Tang Book Value Per Share	7.44	7.51	7.06	6.77	6.54	6.49	5.78	6.09
Dividends Per Share	0.350	0.347	0.337	0.318	0.282	0.274	0.685	0.258
Dividend Payout %	28.48	27.92	33.09	32.19	30.25	30.24	91.87	40.59
Income Statement								
Total Revenue	101,800	519,289	521,100	540,112	543,525	543,383	549,870	532,505
EBITDA	10,819	100,845	115,514	111,621	110,569	104,155	93,707	79,175
Depn & Amortn	456	18,991	19,627	20,388	20,758	20,050	19,925	19,229
Income Before Taxes	10,363	84,561	97,912	92,578	91,294	85,458	75,014	60,912
Income Taxes	2,262	3,907	30,593	26,451	28,434	23,634	22,160	16,974
Net Income	8,125	80,864	67,510	66,089	63,298	60,849	52,004	43,938
Average Shares	64,434	65,074	66,029	67,138	68,163	67,118	70,141	69,126
Balance Sheet								
Current Assets	247,829	270,920	299,300	293,806	264,621	240,111	197,241	212,201
Total Assets	914,970	930,946	920,101	908,983	910,386	888,409	846,737	857,856
Current Liabilities	53,911	63,788	63,561	72,062	64,459	60,121	60,765	58,355
Long-Term Obligations	7,500	7,500	7,730	7,883	8,194	7,500	7,500	7,500
Total Liabilities	188,450	197,106	208,737	210,800	219,577	208,104	196,922	191,921
Stockholders' Equity	726,520	733,840	711,364	698,183	690,809	680,305	649,815	665,935
Shares Outstanding	64,273	64,648	65,604	66,485	67,636	66,619	69,497	68,578
Statistical Record								
Return on Assets %	8.65	8.74	7.36	7.27	7.04	7.01	6.08	5.11
Return on Equity %	11.02	11.19	9.55	9.52	9.23	9.15	7.88	6.58
EBITDA Margin %	10.63	19.42	22.17	20.67	20.34	19.17	17.04	14.87
Net Margin %	7.98	15.57	12.96	12.24	11.65	11.20	9.46	8.25
Asset Turnover	0.57	0.56	0.57	0.59	0.60	0.63	0.64	0.62
Current Ratio	4.60	4.25	4.71	4.08	4.11	3.99	3.25	3.64
Debt to Equity	0.01	0.01	0.01	0.01	0.01	0.01	0.01	0.01
Price Range	37.77-28.75	38.22-33.45	39.16-27.83	31.61-25.98	28.07-23.23	30.29-21.71	23.95-18.17	24.23-18.58
P/E Ratio	30.70-23.37	30.82-26.97	38.40-27.28	31.93-26.24	30.18-24.98	33.29-23.85	31.94-24.23	37.86-29.03
Average Yield %	1.00	0.97	1.00	1.09	1.10	1.03	3.35	1.19

Address: 7401 South Cicero Avenue, Chicago, IL 60629
Telephone: 773-838-3400
Fax: 773-838-3534

Web Site: www.tootsie.com
Officers: Ellen R. Gordon - Chairwoman, Chief Executive Officer G. Howard Ember - Vice President

Auditors: Grant Thornton LLP
Transfer Agents: American Stock Transfer & Trust Company, Brooklyn, NY

TORCHMARK CORP

Exchange	Symbol	Price	52Wk Range	Yield	P/E	Div Acheiver
NYS	TMK	$81.41 (6/29/2018)	93.32-74.68	0.79	6.46	12 Years

*7 Year Price Score 123.48 *NYSE Composite Index=100 ***12 Month Price Score 99.25**

Interim Earnings (Per Share)

Qtr.	Mar	Jun	Sep	Dec
2015	0.95	1.00	1.15	1.07
2016	1.01	1.13	1.25	1.11
2017	1.11	1.18	1.29	8.64
2018	1.49	...	...	...

Interim Dividends (Per Share)

Amt	Decl	Ex	Rec	Pay
0.15Q	08/28/2017	10/05/2017	10/06/2017	11/01/2017
0.15Q	11/13/2017	01/04/2018	01/05/2018	02/01/2018
0.16Q	03/01/2018	04/02/2018	04/03/2018	05/01/2018
0.16Q	05/11/2018	07/03/2018	07/05/2018	08/01/2018

Indicated Div: $0.64 (Div. Reinv. Plan)

TRADING VOLUME (thousand shares)

Valuation Analysis / Institutional Holding

Valuation Analysis		Institutional Holding	
Forecast EPS	$6.04	No of Institutions	
	(06/14/2018)	687	
Market Cap	$9.3 Billion	Shares	
Book Value	$5.8 Billion	108,167,896	
Price/Book	1.59	% Held	
Price/Sales	2.20	67.16	

Business Summary: Life & Health (MIC: 5.2.2 SIC: 6311 NAIC: 524113)

Torchmark is an insurance holding company for a group of insurance companies which market primarily individual life, and supplemental health insurance to middle income households. Co.'s segment comprised of Insurance, which consist of life, health, and annuities; and Investments, which consist of investment-grade securities. Life insurance products include traditional and interest-sensitive whole life insurance as well as term life insurance. Health insurance products are generally guaranteed-renewable and include Medicare Supplement, critical illness, accident, long-term care, and limited-benefit supplemental hospital and surgical coverages. Annuities include fixed-benefit contracts.

Recent Developments: For the quarter ended Mar 31 2018, income from continuing operations increased 26.6% to US$173.7 million from US$137.2 million in the year-earlier quarter. Net income increased 30.0% to US$173.6 million from US$133.5 million in the year-earlier quarter. Revenues were US$1.07 billion, up 4.6% from US$1.02 billion the year before. Net premiums earned were US$850.1 million versus US$820.6 million in the prior-year quarter, an increase of 3.6%. Net investment income rose 4.7% to US$218.1 million from US$208.3 million a year ago.

Prospects: Our evaluation of Torchmark Corp. as of Jan. 21, 2018 is the result of our systematic analysis on three basic characteristics: earnings strength, relative valuation, and recent stock price movement. The company has produced a positive trend in earnings per share over the past 5 quarters and while recent estimates for the company have been mixed, TMK has posted better than expected results. Based on operating earnings yield, the company is undervalued when compared to all of the companies in our coverage universe. Share price changes over the past year indicates that TMK will perform in line with the market over the near term.

Financial Data
(US$ in Thousands)

	3 Mos	12/31/2017	12/31/2016	12/31/2015	12/31/2014	12/31/2013	12/31/2012	12/31/2011
Earnings Per Share	12.60	12.22	4.49	4.16	4.09	3.79	3.61	3.15
Cash Flow Per Share	11.83	12.28	11.62	8.95	6.61	8.13	6.49	5.29
Tang Book Value Per Share	47.26	50.53	34.95	29.53	33.27	24.84	27.73	25.40
Dividends Per Share	0.600	0.590	0.555	0.405	0.493	0.439	0.380	0.296
Dividend Payout %	4.76	4.83	12.36	9.74	12.05	11.58	10.54	9.39
Income Statement								
Premium Income	850,106	3,282,935	3,137,034	2,998,720	3,209,420	3,052,274	2,856,462	2,656,318
Total Revenue	1,070,436	4,155,573	3,934,629	3,766,065	3,964,296	3,771,938	3,589,516	3,377,401
Benefits & Claims	569,889	2,227,875	2,128,748	2,016,212	2,219,200	2,088,846	1,955,682	1,793,276
Income Before Taxes	212,842	830,648	772,235	766,187	778,468	763,126	765,993	755,666
Income Taxes	39,131	(627,615)	232,645	249,894	235,529	234,654	236,669	237,326
Net Income	173,600	1,454,494	549,779	527,100	542,939	528,472	529,324	517,885
Average Shares	116,749	118,983	122,367	126,757	132,640	139,563	146,847	164,723
Balance Sheet								
Total Assets	23,182,343	23,474,985	21,436,087	19,853,213	20,214,730	18,191,744	18,776,910	17,156,391
Total Liabilities	17,362,042	17,243,564	16,869,226	15,797,661	15,517,264	14,415,402	14,415,124	12,927,483
Stockholders' Equity	5,820,301	6,231,421	4,566,861	4,055,552	4,697,466	3,776,342	4,361,786	4,228,908
Shares Outstanding	113,821	114,593	118,031	122,369	127,930	134,252	141,353	150,869
Statistical Record								
Return on Assets %	6.60	6.48	2.66	2.63	2.83	2.86	2.94	3.11
Return on Equity %	28.29	26.94	12.72	12.04	12.81	12.99	12.29	12.56
Loss Ratio %	67.04	67.86	67.86	67.24	69.15	68.44	68.47	67.51
Net Margin %	16.22	35.00	13.97	14.00	13.70	14.01	14.75	15.33
Price Range	93.32-74.11	91.16-73.00	74.83-48.58	63.12-50.07	55.68-48.37	52.35-34.45	35.31-28.91	30.16-22.12
P/E Ratio	7.41-5.88	7.46-5.97	16.67-10.82	15.17-12.04	13.61-11.83	13.81-9.09	9.78-8.01	9.57-7.02
Average Yield %	0.72	0.75	0.91	0.71	0.95	1.01	1.15	1.08

Address: 3700 South Stonebridge Drive, McKinney, TX 75070
Telephone: 972-569-4000

Web Site: www.torchmarkcorp.com
Officers: Larry M. Hutchison - Co-Chairman, Co-Chief Executive Officer, Executive Vice President, General Counsel Gary L. Coleman - Co-Chairman, Co-Chief Executive Officer, Executive Vice President, Chief Financial Officer

Auditors: Deloitte & Touche LLP
Investor Contact: 972-569-3627
Transfer Agents: Wells Fargo Shareowner Services, St. Paul, MN

TORO COMPANY (THE)

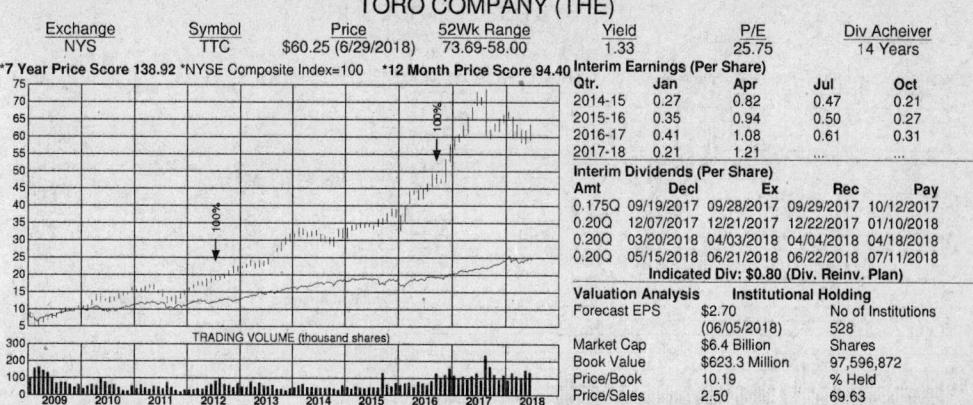

Exchange	Symbol	Price	52Wk Range	Yield	P/E	Div Acheiver
NYS	TTC	$60.25 (6/29/2018)	73.69-58.00	1.33	25.75	14 Years

*7 Year Price Score 138.92 *NYSE Composite Index=100 *12 Month Price Score 94.40

Interim Earnings (Per Share)

Qtr.	Jan	Apr	Jul	Oct
2014-15	0.27	0.82	0.47	0.21
2015-16	0.35	0.94	0.50	0.27
2016-17	0.41	1.08	0.61	0.31
2017-18	0.21	1.21	...	...

Interim Dividends (Per Share)

Amt	Decl	Ex	Rec	Pay
0.175Q	09/19/2017	09/28/2017	09/29/2017	10/12/2017
0.20Q	12/07/2017	12/21/2017	12/22/2017	01/10/2018
0.20Q	03/20/2018	04/03/2018	04/04/2018	04/18/2018
0.20Q	05/15/2018	06/21/2018	06/22/2018	07/11/2018

Indicated Div: $0.80 (Div. Reinv. Plan)

Valuation Analysis / **Institutional Holding**

Forecast EPS	$2.70	No of Institutions
(06/05/2018)		528
Market Cap	$6.4 Billion	Shares
Book Value	$623.3 Million	97,596,872
Price/Book	10.19	% Held
Price/Sales	2.50	69.63

Business Summary: Industrial Machinery & Equipment (MIC: 7.2.1 SIC: 3524 NAIC: 333112)

Toro designs, manufactures, and markets turf maintenance equipment and services, turf irrigation systems, landscaping equipment and lighting products, snow and ice management products, agricultural micro-irrigation systems, rental and construction equipment, and residential yard and snow thrower products. Co. has three segments: Professional, which consists of turf and landscape equipment, snow and ice management equipment, and irrigation products; Residential, which consists of walk power mowers, riding mowers, snow throwers, replacement parts, and home solutions products; and Distribution, which consists of its Co.-owned domestic distributorships.

Recent Developments: For the quarter ended May 4 2018, net income increased 9.0% to US$131.3 million from US$120.5 million in the year-earlier quarter. Revenues were US$875.3 million, up 0.3% from US$872.8 million the year before. Operating income was US$170.3 million versus US$159.3 million in the prior-year quarter, an increase of 6.9%. Direct operating expenses declined 0.9% to US$551.2 million from US$556.5 million in the comparable period the year before. Indirect operating expenses decreased 2.1% to US$153.8 million from US$157.0 million in the equivalent prior-year period.

Prospects: Our evaluation of Toro Co. as of Jan. 21, 2018 is the result of our systematic analysis on three basic characteristics: earnings strength, relative valuation, and recent stock price movement. The company has managed to produce a neutral trend in earnings per share over the past 5 quarters and while recent estimates for the company have been raised by analysts, TTC has posted better than expected results. Based on operating earnings yield, the company is about fairly valued when compared to all of the companies in our coverage universe. Share price changes over the past year indicates that TTC will perform in line with the market over the near term.

Financial Data

(US$ in Thousands)	6 Mos	3 Mos	10/31/2017	10/31/2016	10/31/2015	10/31/2014	10/31/2013	10/31/2012
Earnings Per Share	2.34	2.21	2.41	2.06	1.77	1.51	1.31	1.07
Cash Flow Per Share	3.09	3.30	3.33	3.29	2.13	1.62	1.92	1.56
Tang Book Value Per Share	2.73	2.56	2.88	2.28	1.35	2.63	2.10	1.62
Dividends Per Share	0.750	0.725	0.700	0.600	0.500	0.400	0.280	0.220
Dividend Payout %	32.05	32.81	29.05	29.13	28.17	26.49	21.37	20.56
Income Statement								
Total Revenue	1,423,526	548,246	2,505,176	2,392,175	2,390,875	2,172,691	2,041,431	1,958,690
EBITDA	275,230	86,429	415,657	392,736	351,263	311,280	283,586	253,226
Depn & Amortn	30,141	15,226	54,679	53,355	50,322	47,136	48,207	46,840
Income Before Taxes	235,551	66,385	343,224	320,872	282,678	249,183	219,616	190,266
Income Taxes	81,658	43,781	85,467	99,466	89,440	82,575	71,868	66,721
Net Income	153,893	22,604	267,717	230,994	201,591	173,870	154,845	129,541
Average Shares	108,835	109,855	111,252	111,987	113,514	115,256	118,210	121,236
Balance Sheet								
Current Assets	978,229	900,848	859,886	779,009	710,679	824,036	653,267	612,134
Total Assets	1,635,747	1,516,806	1,493,787	1,387,518	1,303,658	1,192,415	1,002,748	935,199
Current Liabilities	652,407	572,489	521,796	463,839	443,734	400,420	388,845	378,122
Long-Term Obligations	299,302	302,465	305,629	331,423	354,818	347,316	223,544	223,482
Total Liabilities	1,012,420	936,025	876,695	837,483	841,493	783,688	644,010	622,797
Stockholders' Equity	623,327	580,781	617,092	550,035	462,165	408,727	358,738	312,402
Shares Outstanding	105,456	106,434	106,882	108,427	109,301	111,356	113,577	116,532
Statistical Record								
Return on Assets %	15.84	16.81	18.58	17.12	16.15	15.84	15.98	14.31
Return on Equity %	41.61	44.86	45.88	45.52	46.30	45.31	46.14	44.61
EBITDA Margin %	19.33	15.76	16.59	16.42	14.69	14.33	13.89	12.93
Net Margin %	10.81	4.12	10.69	9.66	8.43	8.00	7.59	6.61
Asset Turnover	1.57	1.74	1.74	1.77	1.92	1.98	2.11	2.16
Current Ratio	1.50	1.57	1.65	1.68	1.60	2.06	1.68	1.62
Debt to Equity	0.48	0.52	0.50	0.60	0.77	0.85	0.62	0.72
Price Range	73.69-58.13	73.69-58.47	73.69-46.74	49.29-32.75	37.89-30.41	33.47-28.07	29.48-20.40	21.11-13.00
P/E Ratio	31.49-24.84	33.34-26.46	30.58-19.39	23.93-15.90	21.41-17.18	22.16-18.59	22.50-15.57	19.73-12.15
Average Yield %	1.15	1.12	1.12	1.41	1.48	1.29	1.18	1.25

Address: 8111 Lyndale Avenue South, Bloomington, MN 55420-1196 Telephone: 952-888-8801	Web Site: www.thetorocompany.com Officers: Richard M. Olson - Chairman, President, Chief Executive Officer, Vice President, Chief Operating Officer David H. Alkire - Vice President	Auditors: KPMG LLP Transfer Agents: Wells Fargo Shareowner Services, St. Paul, MN

TOTAL SYSTEM SERVICES, INC.

Exchange	Symbol	Price	52Wk Range	Yield	P/E
NYS	TSS	$84.52 (6/29/2018)	90.74-57.62	0.62	25.15

*7 Year Price Score 151.29 *NYSE Composite Index=100 *12 Month Price Score 109.67

Interim Earnings (Per Share)

Qtr.	Mar	Jun	Sep	Dec
2015	0.42	0.45	0.65	0.45
2016	0.49	0.38	0.46	0.40
2017	0.57	0.62	0.66	1.31
2018	0.77	...	...	...

Interim Dividends (Per Share)

Amt	Decl	Ex	Rec	Pay
0.13Q	07/25/2017	09/20/2017	09/21/2017	10/02/2017
0.13Q	12/11/2017	12/20/2017	12/21/2017	01/02/2018
0.13Q	03/07/2018	03/21/2018	03/22/2018	04/02/2018
0.13Q	06/05/2018	06/20/2018	06/21/2018	07/02/2018

Indicated Div: $0.52

Valuation Analysis — **Institutional Holding**

Forecast EPS	$4.35 (06/14/2018)	No of Institutions	747
Market Cap	$15.4 Billion	Shares	176,713,936
Book Value	$2.4 Billion	% Held	69.38
Price/Book	6.43		
Price/Sales	3.26		

Business Summary: Business Services (MIC: 7.5.2 SIC: 7389 NAIC: 561499)

Total System Services is a payment solutions provider that provides payment processing services, merchant services and related payment services to financial and nonfinancial institutions. Co. has four operating segments: Merchant Services, which provides merchant services to merchant acquirers and merchants; North America Services, and International Services, through which Co. processes information via its cardholder systems to financial and nonfinancial institutions throughout the U.S. and internationally; and NetSpend, which provides general purpose reloadable prepaid debit cards, payroll cards, and alternative financial service solutions to underbanked and other consumers and businesses.

Recent Developments: For the quarter ended Mar 31 2018, net income increased 33.6% to US$143.1 million from US$107.1 million in the year-earlier quarter. Revenues were US$987.2 million, down 16.7% from US$1.18 billion the year before. Operating income was US$188.3 million versus US$167.2 million in the prior-year quarter, an increase of 12.6%. Direct operating expenses declined 28.8% to US$613.4 million from US$861.9 million in the comparable period the year before. Indirect operating expenses increased 19.2% to US$185.5 million from US$155.7 million in the equivalent prior-year period.

Prospects: Our evaluation of Total System Services Inc. as of Jan. 21, 2018 is the result of our systematic analysis on three basic characteristics: earnings strength, relative valuation, and recent stock price movement. The company has generated a negative trend in earnings per share over the past 5 quarters and while recent estimates for the company have been mixed, TSS has posted better than expected results. Based on operating earnings yield, the company is about fairly valued when compared to all of the companies in our coverage universe. Share price changes over the past year indicates that TSS will perform well over the near term.

Financial Data

(US$ in Thousands)	3 Mos	12/31/2017	12/31/2016	12/31/2015	12/31/2014	12/31/2013	12/31/2012	12/31/2011
Earnings Per Share	3.36	3.16	1.73	1.97	1.72	1.29	1.29	1.15
Cash Flow Per Share	4.46	4.67	3.92	3.29	3.04	2.42	2.43	2.28
Tang Book Value Per Share	N.M.	N.M.	N.M.	N.M.	N.M.	N.M.	2.08	2.57
Dividends Per Share	0.490	0.460	0.400	0.400	0.400	0.400	0.400	0.310
Dividend Payout %	14.58	14.56	23.12	20.30	23.26	31.01	31.01	26.96
Income Statement								
Total Revenue	987,170	4,927,965	4,170,077	2,779,541	2,446,877	2,132,353	1,870,972	1,808,966
EBITDA	188,550	1,144,710	962,603	796,641	643,147	568,764	525,762	485,876
Depn & Amortn	1,268	411,120	387,866	260,502	250,218	212,845	170,908	169,325
Income Before Taxes	150,629	617,562	461,214	496,888	392,929	355,919	354,854	316,551
Income Taxes	18,135	65,878	161,175	151,364	129,761	112,369	115,102	102,597
Net Income	141,841	586,185	319,638	364,044	322,872	244,750	244,280	220,559
Average Shares	183,298	185,430	184,448	183,622	185,756	188,793	188,665	191,239
Balance Sheet								
Current Assets	1,178,279	1,079,244	1,022,689	882,902	690,553	653,933	574,726	650,181
Total Assets	7,531,717	6,331,689	6,366,177	3,908,300	3,733,581	3,686,568	2,023,838	1,858,392
Current Liabilities	1,217,870	989,092	420,353	339,218	296,513	297,215	230,519	380,576
Long-Term Obligations	3,326,536	2,628,002	3,313,276	1,383,634	1,405,106	1,435,751	192,014	63,593
Total Liabilities	5,137,143	4,090,696	4,266,257	2,065,282	2,040,819	2,105,491	598,628	557,103
Stockholders' Equity	2,394,574	2,240,993	2,099,920	1,843,018	1,692,762	1,581,077	1,425,210	1,301,289
Shares Outstanding	182,305	180,903	183,451	182,781	184,939	187,717	187,031	189,031
Statistical Record								
Return on Assets %	8.96	9.23	6.20	9.53	8.70	8.57	12.55	11.58
Return on Equity %	27.41	27.01	16.17	20.59	19.72	16.28	17.87	17.35
EBITDA Margin %	19.10	23.23	23.08	28.66	26.28	26.67	28.10	26.86
Net Margin %	14.37	11.90	7.67	13.10	13.20	11.48	13.06	12.19
Asset Turnover	0.68	0.78	0.81	0.73	0.66	0.75	0.96	0.95
Current Ratio	0.97	1.09	2.43	2.60	2.33	2.20	2.49	1.71
Debt to Equity	1.39	1.17	1.58	0.75	0.83	0.91	0.13	0.05
Price Range	90.74-52.12	79.99-50.32	56.43-37.96	56.37-33.27	34.41-28.70	33.30-21.42	24.39-19.40	20.42-15.38
P/E Ratio	27.01-15.51	25.31-15.92	32.62-21.94	28.61-16.89	20.01-16.69	25.81-16.60	18.91-15.04	17.76-13.37
Average Yield %	0.70	0.74	0.82	0.91	1.28	1.51	1.76	1.70

Address: One TSYS Way, P.O. 1755, Columbus, GA 31902	Web Site: www.tsys.com	Auditors: KPMG LLP
Telephone: 706-644-6081	Officers: M. Troy Woods - Chairman, President, President (frmr), Chief Executive Officer, Chief Operating Officer Paul M. Todd - Senior Executive Vice President, Chief Financial Officer	Investor Contact: 706-644-6081
Fax: 706-649-2456		Transfer Agents: American Stock Transfer & Trust Company, LLC, Brookly, NY

TRANSOCEAN LTD

Exchange	Symbol	Price	52Wk Range	Yield	P/E
NYS	RIG	$13.44 (6/29/2018)	13.75-7.28	N/A	N/A

*7 Year Price Score 28.81   ***NYSE Composite Index=100**   ***12 Month Price Score 120.00**

Interim Earnings (Per Share)

Qtr.	Mar	Jun	Sep	Dec
2015	(1.33)	0.93	0.88	1.67
2016	0.68	0.21	0.62	0.59
2017	0.23	(4.32)	(3.62)	(0.28)
2018	(0.48)	...	...	...

Interim Dividends (Per Share)

Amt	Decl	Ex	Rec	Pay
0.75Q	11/04/2014	11/12/2014	11/14/2014	12/17/2014
0.75Q	02/06/2015	02/18/2015	02/20/2015	03/18/2015
0.15Q	05/15/2015	05/27/2015	05/29/2015	06/17/2015
0.15Q	08/14/2015	08/21/2015	08/25/2015	09/23/2015

Valuation Analysis

		Institutional Holding	
Forecast EPS	N/A	No of Institutions	687
Market Cap	$6.2 Billion	Shares	
Book Value	$13.4 Billion		398,073,440
Price/Book	0.46	% Held	
Price/Sales	2.18		66.45

Business Summary: Equipment & Services (MIC: 9.1.3 SIC: 1389 NAIC: 213112)

Transocean is a provider of offshore contract drilling services for oil and gas wells. Co. contracts its drilling rigs, related equipment and work crews predominantly on a dayrate basis to drill oil and gas wells. Co. focuses on deepwater and harsh environment drilling services. At Feb 19 2018, Co. owned or had partial ownership interests in and operated 47 mobile offshore drilling units, including 30 ultra-deepwater floaters, seven harsh environment floaters, three deepwater floaters, six midwater floaters and 10 high-specification jackups. At Feb 19 2018, Co. had two ultra-deepwater drillships and two high-specification jackups under construction or under contract to be constructed.

Recent Developments: For the quarter ended Mar 31 2018, net loss amounted to US$212.0 million versus net income of US$95.0 million in the year-earlier quarter. Revenues were US$664.0 million, down 15.4% from US$785.0 million the year before. Operating loss was US$4.0 million versus an income of US$169.0 million in the prior-year quarter. Direct operating expenses rose 22.2% to US$424.0 million from US$347.0 million in the comparable period the year before. Indirect operating expenses decreased 9.3% to US$244.0 million from US$269.0 million in the equivalent prior-year period.

Prospects: Our evaluation of Transocean Ltd. as of Aug. 2, 2015 is the result of our systematic analysis on three basic characteristics: earnings strength, relative valuation, and recent stock price movement. The company has suffered a very negative trend in earnings per share over the past 5 quarters. Because the company lacks sufficient analyst estimate data, we place greater weight on the historical EPS trend as the measure of earnings strength. Based on operating earnings yield, the company is undervalued when compared to all of the companies in our coverage universe. Share price changes over the past year indicates that RIG will perform in line with the market over the near term.

Financial Data
(US$ in Millions)

	3 Mos	12/31/2017	12/31/2016	12/31/2015	12/31/2014	12/31/2013	12/31/2012	12/31/2011
Earnings Per Share	(8.70)	(8.00)	2.08	2.16	(5.29)	3.87	(0.62)	(17.79)
Cash Flow Per Share	2.43	2.93	5.19	9.49	6.13	5.33	7.59	5.54
Tang Book Value Per Share	26.76	32.48	40.58	39.83	37.74	37.99	35.49	35.72
Income Statement								
Total Revenue	664	2,973	4,161	7,386	9,174	9,484	9,196	9,142
EBITDA	207	(1,723)	2,216	2,388	(232)	3,290	1,491	(4,902)
Depn & Amortn	221	832	893	948	1,124	1,094	(42)	(45)
Income Before Taxes	(149)	(3,003)	934	1,030	(1,800)	1,664	866	(5,434)
Income Taxes	63	94	107	206	146	258	50	395
Net Income	(210)	(3,127)	778	791	(1,913)	1,407	(219)	(5,725)
Average Shares	438	391	367	363	362	360	356	322
Balance Sheet								
Current Assets	4,543	4,606	5,098	4,785	6,001	6,772	8,647	7,609
Total Assets	25,695	22,410	26,889	26,329	28,413	32,546	34,255	35,088
Current Liabilities	3,022	1,369	1,985	2,669	3,770	3,554	5,463	5,358
Long-Term Obligations	7,976	7,146	7,740	7,397	9,059	10,379	11,092	11,497
Total Liabilities	12,271	9,703	11,087	11,831	14,742	15,855	18,510	19,387
Stockholders' Equity	13,424	12,707	15,802	14,498	13,671	16,691	15,745	15,701
Shares Outstanding	461	391	389	364	362	360	359	349
Statistical Record								
Return on Assets %	N.M.	N.M.	2.92	2.89	N.M.	4.21	N.M.	N.M.
Return on Equity %	N.M.	N.M.	5.12	5.62	N.M.	8.68	N.M.	N.M.
EBITDA Margin %	31.17	N.M.	53.26	32.33	N.M.	34.69	16.21	N.M.
Net Margin %	N.M.	N.M.	18.70	10.71	N.M.	14.84	N.M.	N.M.
Asset Turnover	0.11	0.12	0.16	0.27	0.30	0.28	0.26	0.25
Current Ratio	1.50	3.36	2.57	1.79	1.59	1.91	1.58	1.42
Debt to Equity	0.59	0.56	0.49	0.51	0.66	0.62	0.70	0.73
Price Range	12.75-7.28	15.84-7.28	15.54-8.20	21.39-11.60	49.42-16.25	59.30-44.38	58.70-38.97	85.47-38.39
P/E Ratio	...	...	7.47-3.94	9.90-5.37	...	15.32-11.47	...	...

Address: Turmstrasse 30, Steinhausen, 6312	Web Site: www.deepwater.com	Auditors: Ernst & Young LLP
Telephone: 417-490-500	Officers: Merrill A. (Pete) Miller - Chairman Jeremy D. Thigpen - President, Chief Executive Officer	Investor Contact: 713-232-7551
		Transfer Agents: Computershare Shareowner Services LLC, Pittsburgh, PA

TRANSUNION

Exchange	Symbol	Price	52Wk Range	Yield	P/E
NYS	TRU	$71.64 (6/29/2018)	72.88-41.61	N/A	30.23

*7 Year Price Score N/A   *NYSE Composite Index=100   *12 Month Price Score 122.49

Interim Earnings (Per Share)

Qtr.	Mar	Jun	Sep	Dec
2015	(0.04)	(0.02)	(0.02)	0.12
2016	0.07	0.09	0.22	0.26
2017	0.33	0.34	0.36	1.29
2018	0.38	...	...	...

Interim Dividends (Per Share)

No Dividends Paid

Valuation Analysis		Institutional Holding	
Forecast EPS	$2.41	No of Institutions	
	(06/13/2018)	365	
Market Cap	$13.2 Billion	Shares	
Book Value	$1.8 Billion	187,708,848	
Price/Book	7.19	% Held	
Price/Sales	6.54	N/A	

TRADING VOLUME (thousand shares)

2009 2010 2011 2012 2013 2014 2015 2016 2017 2018

Business Summary: Miscellaneous Consumer Services (MIC: 2.2.3 SIC: 7323 NAIC: 561450)

TransUnion is a global risk and information solutions provider to businesses and consumers. Co. has three reportable segments: U.S. Information Services (USIS), which provide consumer reports, risk scores, analytical services and decisioning capabilities to businesses through three delivery platforms, online data services, marketing services and decision services; International, which provides services similar to Co.'s USIS segment to businesses in select regions outside the U.S.; and Consumer Interactive, which provides solutions that help consumers manage their personal finances and take precautions against identity theft through both direct and indirect channels.

Recent Developments: For the year ended Dec 31 2017, net income increased 243.7% to US$451.6 million from US$131.4 million in the prior year. Revenues were US$1.93 billion, up 13.4% from US$1.70 billion the year before. Operating income was US$464.7 million versus US$300.5 million in the prior year, an increase of 54.6%. Direct operating expenses rose 11.5% to US$645.7 million from US$579.1 million in the comparable period the year before. Indirect operating expenses decreased 0.2% to US$823.4 million from US$825.3 million in the equivalent prior-year period.

Prospects: Our evaluation of TransUnion as of Jan. 21, 2018 is the result of our systematic analysis on three basic characteristics: earnings strength, relative valuation, and recent stock price movement. The company has generated a negative trend in earnings per share over the past 5 quarters and while recent estimates for the company have been mixed, TRU has posted better than expected results. Based on operating earnings yield, the company is about fairly valued when compared to all of the companies in our coverage universe. Share price changes over the past year indicates that TRU will perform very well over the near term.

Financial Data

(US$ in Thousands)	3 Mos	12/31/2017	12/31/2016	12/31/2015	12/31/2014	12/31/2013	12/31/2012
Earnings Per Share	2.37	2.32	0.65	0.04	(0.08)	(0.24)	(0.06)
Cash Flow Per Share	2.73	2.57	2.13	1.87	1.05	0.98	0.37
Income Statement							
Total Revenue	537,400	1,933,800	1,704,900	1,506,800	1,304,700	1,183,200	767,000
EBITDA	122,500	513,400	345,400	208,500	229,100	200,300	145,600
Depn & Amortn	...	67,900	67,700	60,300	56,700	44,000	26,700
Income Before Taxes	100,700	363,400	196,800	17,800	(14,300)	(39,600)	(5,300)
Income Taxes	27,600	(79,100)	74,000	11,300	2,600	2,300	6,600
Net Income	73,100	441,200	120,600	5,900	(12,500)	(35,100)	(8,800)
Average Shares	190,100	189,900	184,600	166,800	147,296	146,496	146,230
Balance Sheet							
Current Assets	646,500	588,700	550,000	427,500	401,000	349,700	400,600
Total Assets	5,163,800	5,118,500	4,781,200	4,446,700	4,665,800	4,492,300	4,378,800
Current Liabilities	400,400	458,400	373,300	296,000	329,900	247,600	218,300
Long-Term Obligations	2,334,700	2,345,300	2,325,200	2,164,600	2,865,900	2,853,100	2,670,300
Total Liabilities	3,329,900	3,389,800	3,418,400	3,215,300	4,078,700	3,864,400	3,676,000
Stockholders' Equity	1,833,900	1,728,700	1,362,800	1,231,400	587,100	627,900	702,800
Shares Outstanding	184,000	183,200	183,200	182,300	147,829	146,896	146,763
Statistical Record							
Return on Assets %	9.12	8.91	2.61	0.13	N.M.	N.M.	...
Return on Equity %	28.24	28.54	9.27	0.65	N.M.	N.M.	...
EBITDA Margin %	22.79	26.55	20.26	13.84	17.56	16.93	18.98
Net Margin %	13.60	22.82	7.07	0.39	N.M.	N.M.	N.M.
Asset Turnover	0.41	0.39	0.37	0.33	0.28	0.27	...
Current Ratio	1.61	1.28	1.47	1.44	1.22	1.41	1.84
Debt to Equity	1.27	1.36	1.71	1.76	4.88	4.54	3.80
Price Range	61.35-37.97	56.21-30.96	35.43-20.98	27.98-23.19	...	...	...
P/E Ratio	25.89-16.02	24.23-13.34	54.51-32.28	699.50-579.75	...	...	...

Address: 555 West Adams, Chicago, IL 60661
Telephone: 312-985-2000

Web Site: www.transunion.com
Officers: Leo F. Mullin - Chairman James M. (Jim) Peck - President, Chief Executive Officer

Auditors: Ernst & Young LLP
Transfer Agents: American Stock Transfer & Trust Company, LLC

TRAVELERS COMPANIES INC (THE)

Exchange	Symbol	Price	52Wk Range	Yield	P/E	Div Acheiver
NYS	TRV	$122.34 (6/29/2018)	150.00-115.18	2.52	16.16	12 Years

*7 Year Price Score 109.19 *NYSE Composite Index=100 *12 Month Price Score 95.90

Interim Earnings (Per Share)

Qtr.	Mar	Jun	Sep	Dec
2015	2.55	2.53	2.97	2.84
2016	2.30	2.24	2.45	3.28
2017	2.17	2.11	1.05	1.99
2018	2.42	...	...	...

Interim Dividends (Per Share)

Amt	Decl	Ex	Rec	Pay
0.72Q	07/20/2017	09/07/2017	09/08/2017	09/29/2017
0.72Q	10/19/2017	12/08/2017	12/11/2017	12/29/2017
0.72Q	01/23/2018	03/08/2018	03/09/2018	03/30/2018
0.77Q	04/24/2018	06/07/2018	06/08/2018	06/29/2018

Indicated Div: $3.08 (Div. Reinv. Plan)

Valuation Analysis

		Institutional Holding	
Forecast EPS	$10.41	No of Institutions	
	(06/13/2018)	1550	
Market Cap	$33.1 Billion	Shares	
Book Value	$23.0 Billion	305,771,680	
Price/Book	1.44	% Held	
Price/Sales	1.13	N/A	

Business Summary: General Insurance (MIC: 5.2.1 SIC: 6331 NAIC: 524126)

Travelers Companies is a holding company. Through its subsidiaries, Co. provides a range of commercial and personal property and casualty insurance products and services. Co.'s segments include: Business and International Insurance, which provides a range of property and casualty insurance and insurance related services to its clients; Bond & Specialty Insurance, which provides surety, fidelity, management liability, professional liability, and other property and casualty coverages and related risk management services to a range of primarily domestic customers; and Personal Insurance, which writes a range of property and casualty insurance covering individuals' personal risks.

Recent Developments: For the quarter ended Mar 31 2018, net income increased 8.4% to US$669.0 million from US$617.0 million in the year-earlier quarter. Revenues were US$7.29 billion, up 5.0% from US$6.94 billion the year before. Net premiums earned were US$6.54 billion versus US$6.18 billion in the prior-year quarter, an increase of 5.7%. Net investment income fell 1.1% to US$603.0 million from US$610.0 million a year ago.

Prospects: Our evaluation of The Travelers Companies Inc. as of Jan. 21, 2018 is the result of our systematic analysis on three basic characteristics: earnings strength, relative valuation, and recent stock price movement. The company has generated a negative trend in earnings per share over the past 5 quarters. However, while recent estimates for the company have been mixed, TRV has posted better than expected results. Based on operating earnings yield, the company is undervalued when compared to all of the companies in our coverage universe. Share price changes over the past year indicates that TRV will perform well over the near term.

Financial Data
(US$ in Thousands)

	3 Mos	12/31/2017	12/31/2016	12/31/2015	12/31/2014	12/31/2013	12/31/2012	12/31/2011
Earnings Per Share	7.57	7.33	10.28	10.88	10.70	9.74	6.30	3.36
Cash Flow Per Share	13.07	13.63	14.55	11.06	10.90	10.31	8.34	5.22
Tang Book Value Per Share	69.13	71.62	69.29	66.73	64.93	58.87	57.39	52.65
Dividends Per Share	2.880	2.830	2.620	2.380	2.150	1.960	1.790	1.590
Dividend Payout %	38.04	38.61	25.49	21.88	20.09	20.12	28.41	47.32
Income Statement								
Premium Income	6,537,000	25,683,000	24,534,000	23,874,000	23,713,000	22,637,000	22,357,000	22,090,000
Total Revenue	7,286,000	28,902,000	27,625,000	26,800,000	27,162,000	26,191,000	25,740,000	25,446,000
Benefits & Claims	4,296,000	17,467,000	15,070,000	13,723,000	13,870,000	13,307,000	14,676,000	16,276,000
Income Before Taxes	778,000	2,730,000	4,053,000	4,740,000	5,089,000	4,945,000	3,166,000	1,352,000
Income Taxes	109,000	674,000	1,039,000	1,301,000	1,397,000	1,272,000	693,000	(74,000)
Net Income	669,000	2,056,000	3,014,000	3,439,000	3,692,000	3,673,000	2,473,000	1,426,000
Average Shares	273,900	278,600	291,000	313,900	342,500	374,300	389,800	420,500
Balance Sheet								
Total Assets	103,676,000	103,483,000	100,245,000	100,184,000	103,078,000	103,812,000	104,938,000	104,602,000
Total Liabilities	80,697,000	79,752,000	77,024,000	76,586,000	78,242,000	79,016,000	79,533,000	80,125,000
Stockholders' Equity	22,979,000	23,731,000	23,221,000	23,598,000	24,836,000	24,796,000	25,405,000	24,477,000
Shares Outstanding	270,200	271,400	279,600	295,900	322,200	353,500	377,400	392,800
Statistical Record								
Return on Assets %	2.06	2.02	3.00	3.38	3.57	3.52	2.35	1.36
Return on Equity %	9.05	8.76	12.84	14.20	14.88	14.63	9.89	5.71
Loss Ratio %	65.72	68.01	61.42	57.48	58.49	58.78	65.64	73.68
Net Margin %	9.18	7.11	10.91	12.83	13.59	14.02	9.61	5.60
Price Range	150.00-115.18	136.36-115.18	122.57-102.08	115.83-96.14	106.95-80.26	90.99-71.82	74.33-56.87	64.05-46.80
P/E Ratio	19.82-15.22	18.60-15.71	11.92-9.93	10.65-8.84	10.00-7.50	9.34-7.37	11.80-9.03	19.06-13.93
Average Yield %	2.22	2.26	2.31	2.25	2.33	2.35	2.78	2.81

Address: 485 Lexington Avenue, New York, NY 10017 Telephone: 917-778-6000	Web Site: www.travelers.com Officers: Alan D. Schnitzer - Chairman, Chief Executive Officer, Vice-Chairman, Chief Executive Officer - Designate, Executive Vice President, Chief Legal Officer Avrohom J. Kess - Vice-Chairman, Chief Legal Officer	Auditors: KPMG LLP Investor Contact: 917-778-9844 Transfer Agents: Wells Fargo Bank, N.A. Shareowner Services, St. Paul, MN

TREEHOUSE FOODS INC

Exchange	Symbol	Price	52Wk Range	Yield	P/E
NYS	THS	$52.51 (6/29/2018)	85.74-36.62	N/A	N/A

*7 Year Price Score 62.62 *NYSE Composite Index=100 *12 Month Price Score 84.32

Interim Earnings (Per Share)

Qtr.	Mar	Jun	Sep	Dec
2015	0.41	0.72	0.65	0.85
2016	(0.06)	0.27	0.65	(4.98)
2017	0.49	(0.60)	0.50	(5.41)
2018	(0.60)	...	...	...

Interim Dividends (Per Share)

No Dividends Paid

TRADING VOLUME (thousand shares)

Valuation Analysis

Institutional Holding	
Forecast EPS	$2.09
(06/13/2018)	
Market Cap	$3.0 Billion
Book Value	$2.2 Billion
Price/Book	1.33
Price/Sales	0.47

No of Institutions 399
Shares 72,664,016
% Held 100.89

Business Summary: Food (MIC: 1.2.1 SIC: 2033 NAIC: 311421)

TreeHouse Foods is a consumer packaged food and beverage manufacturer operating across the U.S., Canada, and Italy. Co.'s operating segments are: North American Retail Grocery, which sells branded and private label products, such as non-dairy powdered creamers, sweeteners, condensed, ready to serve, and powdered soups, broths and gravies, and refrigerated salad dressings and sauces, among others; Food Away From Home, which sells aseptic products, ready-to-eat and hot cereals, pasta, retail bakery products, and cookies, crackers, pretzels, and candy, among others; and Industrial and Export, which include Co.'s co-pack business and non-dairy powdered creamer sales to industrial customers.

Recent Developments: For the quarter ended Mar 31 2018, net loss amounted to US$34.1 million versus net income of US$28.2 million in the year-earlier quarter. Revenues were US$1.48 billion, down 3.6% from US$1.54 billion the year before. Operating loss was US$8.7 million versus an income of US$67.3 million in the prior-year quarter. Direct operating expenses was unchanged at US$1.25 billion versus the comparable period the year before. Indirect operating expenses increased 9.8% to US$240.6 million from US$219.1 million in the equivalent prior-year period.

Prospects: Our evaluation of TreeHouse Foods Inc. as of Jan. 21, 2018 is the result of our systematic analysis on three basic characteristics: earnings strength, relative valuation, and recent stock price movement. The company has generated a negative trend in earnings per share over the past 5 quarters and while recent estimates for the company have been mixed, THS has posted results that fell short of analysts expectations. Based on operating earnings yield, the company is undervalued when compared to all of the companies in our coverage universe. Share price changes over the past year indicates that THS will perform poorly over the near term.

Financial Data

(US$ in Thousands)	3 Mos	12/31/2017	12/31/2016	12/31/2015	12/31/2014	12/31/2013	12/31/2012	12/31/2011
Earnings Per Share	(6.11)	(5.01)	(4.10)	2.63	2.23	2.33	2.38	2.56
Cash Flow Per Share	8.59	8.86	8.57	6.63	5.39	5.95	5.64	4.36
Income Statement								
Total Revenue	1,481,200	6,307,100	6,175,088	3,206,405	2,946,102	2,293,927	2,182,125	2,049,985
EBITDA	27,400	(228,600)	98,007	275,271	240,916	245,329	239,875	241,437
Depn & Amortn	44,800	173,500	178,400	61,500	63,300	73,300	64,700	48,616
Income Before Taxes	(43,900)	(524,600)	(195,363)	171,264	136,570	124,910	124,209	139,798
Income Taxes	(9,800)	(238,400)	33,231	56,354	46,690	37,922	35,846	45,391
Net Income	(34,100)	(286,200)	(228,594)	114,910	89,880	86,988	88,363	94,407
Average Shares	56,500	57,100	55,717	43,709	40,238	37,396	37,118	36,950
Balance Sheet								
Current Assets	1,532,900	1,484,700	1,560,749	847,203	949,436	649,689	588,411	468,394
Total Assets	5,785,500	5,779,300	6,545,822	3,702,796	3,903,004	2,721,054	2,525,873	2,404,529
Current Liabilities	658,800	599,800	693,194	275,473	311,233	240,364	187,030	171,479
Long-Term Obligations	2,533,200	2,535,700	2,724,760	1,221,741	1,445,488	938,945	898,100	902,929
Total Liabilities	3,565,700	3,516,000	4,042,498	1,847,937	2,143,747	1,447,936	1,346,618	1,331,012
Stockholders' Equity	2,219,800	2,263,300	2,503,324	1,854,859	1,759,257	1,273,118	1,179,255	1,073,517
Shares Outstanding	56,400	56,638	56,759	43,125	42,662	36,493	36,196	35,921
Statistical Record								
Return on Assets %	N.M.	N.M.	N.M.	3.02	2.71	3.32	3.57	3.94
Return on Equity %	N.M.	N.M.	N.M.	6.36	5.93	7.09	7.82	9.20
EBITDA Margin %	1.85	N.M.	1.59	8.59	8.18	10.69	10.99	11.78
Net Margin %	N.M.	N.M.	N.M.	3.58	3.05	3.79	4.05	4.61
Asset Turnover	1.02	1.02	1.20	0.84	0.89	0.87	0.88	0.85
Current Ratio	2.33	2.48	2.25	3.08	3.05	2.70	3.15	2.73
Debt to Equity	1.14	1.12	1.09	0.66	0.82	0.74	0.76	0.84
Price Range	89.94-37.35	89.94-41.87	104.35-63.34	92.90-69.44	87.95-63.59	75.19-52.13	65.52-48.42	66.45-47.85
P/E Ratio	...	...	...	35.32-26.40	39.44-28.52	32.27-22.37	27.53-20.34	25.96-18.69

Address: 2021 Spring Road, Suite 600, Oak Brook, IL 60523 **Telephone:** 708-483-1300	**Web Site:** www.treehousefoods.com **Officers:** Gary D. Smith - Chairman Steven Oaklan - President, Chief Executive Officer	**Auditors:** DELOITTE & TOUCHE LLP **Transfer Agents:** BNY Mellon Shareowner Services, South Hackensack, NJ

TRI POINTE GROUP INC

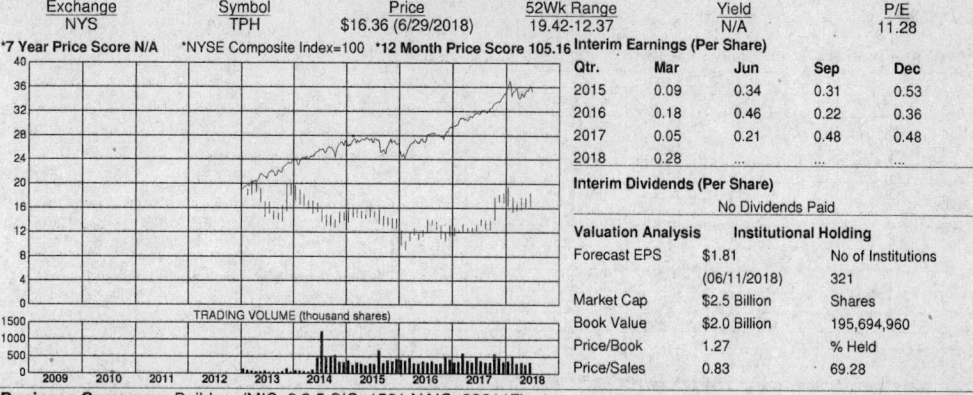

Exchange	Symbol	Price	52Wk Range	Yield	P/E	
NYS	TPH	$16.36 (6/29/2018)	19.42-12.37	N/A	11.28	

*7 Year Price Score N/A   *NYSE Composite Index=100   *12 Month Price Score 105.16

Interim Earnings (Per Share)

Qtr.	Mar	Jun	Sep	Dec
2015	0.09	0.34	0.31	0.53
2016	0.18	0.46	0.22	0.36
2017	0.05	0.21	0.48	0.48
2018	0.28	...	...	...

Interim Dividends (Per Share)

No Dividends Paid

Valuation Analysis   Institutional Holding

Forecast EPS	$1.81	No of Institutions	
	(06/11/2018)	321	
Market Cap	$2.5 Billion	Shares	
Book Value	$2.0 Billion	195,694,960	
Price/Book	1.27	% Held	
Price/Sales	0.83	69.28	

Business Summary: Builders (MIC: 2.2.5 SIC: 1531 NAIC: 236117)

TRI Pointe Group is engaged in the design, construction and sale of single-family detached and attached homes. As of Dec 31 2017, Co. had a portfolio of six homebuilding brands operating in 15 markets across eight states: Maracay Homes in Arizona, Pardee Homes in California and Nevada, Quadrant Homes in Washington, Trendmaker Homes in Texas, TRI Pointe Homes in California and Colorado and Winchester Homes in Maryland and Virginia. As of the same date, Co.'s operations consisted of 130 active selling communities and 27,312 lots owned or controlled. Co.'s operations are organized in two principal businesses: homebuilding and financial services.

Recent Developments: For the quarter ended Mar 31 2018, net income increased 421.8% to US$42.9 million from US$8.2 million in the year-earlier quarter. Revenues were US$583.7 million, up 48.4% from US$393.4 million the year before. Direct operating expenses rose 41.3% to US$451.6 million from US$319.6 million in the comparable period the year before. Indirect operating expenses increased 22.5% to US$75.2 million from US$61.4 million in the equivalent prior-year period.

Prospects: Our evaluation of Tri Pointe Group Inc as of Jan. 21, 2018 is the result of our systematic analysis on three basic characteristics: earnings strength, relative valuation, and recent stock price movement. The company has enjoyed a very positive trend in earnings per share over the past 5 quarters and while recent estimates for the company have been mixed, TPH has posted better than expected results. Based on operating earnings yield, the company is undervalued when compared to all of the companies in our coverage universe. Share price changes over the past year indicates that TPH will perform well over the near term.

Financial Data
(US$ in Thousands)

	3 Mos	12/31/2017	12/31/2016	12/31/2015	12/31/2014	12/31/2013	12/31/2012	12/31/2011
Earnings Per Share	1.45	1.21	1.21	1.27	0.58	0.50	...	...
Cash Flow Per Share	1.74	0.66	(0.98)	0.19	(0.78)	(7.16)	...	...
Tang Book Value Per Share	11.87	11.70	10.51	9.29	8.00	10.20	4.72	...
Income Statement								
Total Revenue	583,676	2,808,901	2,403,922	2,400,149	1,703,616	257,955	78,550	19,329
EBITDA	60,476	364,231	312,937	336,778	148,301	28,990	2,937	(3,835)
Depn & Amortn	3,470	19,406	15,699	20,209	20,049	3,237	431	758
Income Before Taxes	57,006	344,825	297,238	316,569	128,252	25,753	2,506	(4,593)
Income Taxes	14,660	152,267	106,094	112,079	43,767	10,379	...	...
Net Income	42,880	187,191	195,171	205,461	84,197	15,374	2,506	(4,593)
Average Shares	152,775	155,085	161,381	162,319	145,531	30,797	...	...
Balance Sheet								
Current Assets	3,599,230	3,590,480	3,325,007	2,908,125	2,628,751	497,211	214,455	92,258
Total Assets	3,846,761	3,805,381	3,564,640	3,138,071	2,913,524	506,035	217,516	93,776
Current Liabilities	198,683	161,770	125,901	125,409	135,272	45,617	10,995	4,412
Long-Term Obligations	1,473,074	1,471,302	1,382,033	1,172,947	1,171,691	138,112	57,368	6,873
Total Liabilities	1,883,117	1,875,659	1,735,193	1,473,388	1,459,344	183,729	68,363	11,285
Stockholders' Equity	1,963,644	1,929,722	1,829,447	1,664,683	1,454,180	322,306	149,153	82,491
Shares Outstanding	151,922	151,162	158,626	161,813	161,355	31,597	31,597	...
Statistical Record								
Return on Assets %	5.96	5.08	5.81	6.79	4.92	4.25	1.61	N.M.
Return on Equity %	11.67	9.96	11.14	13.18	9.48	6.52	2.16	N.M.
EBITDA Margin %	10.36	12.97	13.02	14.03	8.71	11.24	3.74	N.M.
Net Margin %	7.35	6.66	8.12	8.56	4.94	5.96	3.19	N.M.
Asset Turnover	0.81	0.76	0.72	0.79	1.00	0.71	0.50	0.31
Current Ratio	18.12	22.19	26.41	23.19	19.43	10.90	19.50	20.91
Debt to Equity	0.75	0.76	0.76	0.70	0.81	0.43	0.38	0.08
Price Range	19.42-12.09	18.44-11.37	14.07-9.05	16.05-12.50	19.93-12.73	20.51-13.66	...	...
P/E Ratio	13.39-8.34	15.24-9.40	11.63-7.48	12.64-9.84	34.36-21.95	41.02-27.32	...	...

Address: 19540 Jamboree Road, Suite 300, Irvine, CA 92612
Telephone: 949-438-1400

Web Site: www.tripointegroup.com
Officers: Steven J. Gilbert - Chairman Thomas J. Mitchell - President, Chief Operating Officer

Auditors: Ernst & Young LLP
Investor Contact: 949-478-8696
Transfer Agents: American Stock Transfer & Trust Company, LLC

TRIBUNE MEDIA CO

Exchange	Symbol	Price	52Wk Range	Yield	P/E
NYS	TRCO	$38.27 (6/29/2018)	43.58-34.92	2.61	7.99

*7 Year Price Score N/A   *NYSE Composite Index=100   *12 Month Price Score 89.94

Interim Earnings (Per Share)

Qtr.	Mar	Jun	Sep	Dec
2015	0.37	(0.04)	0.29	(4.01)
2016	0.12	(1.76)	1.61	0.21
2017	(0.99)	(0.35)	(0.21)	3.75
2018	1.60	...	...	...

Interim Dividends (Per Share)

Amt	Decl	Ex	Rec	Pay
0.25Q	08/02/2017	08/17/2017	08/21/2017	09/05/2017
0.25Q	10/26/2017	11/17/2017	11/20/2017	12/05/2017
0.25Q	02/21/2018	03/09/2018	03/12/2018	03/26/2018
0.25Q	05/08/2018	05/18/2018	05/21/2018	06/05/2018

Indicated Div: $1.00

Valuation Analysis

		Institutional Holding	
Forecast EPS	$2.63 (06/10/2018)	No of Institutions	290
Market Cap	$3.4 Billion	Shares	91,688,352
Book Value	$3.3 Billion	% Held	N/A
Price/Book	1.00		
Price/Sales	1.81		

TRADING VOLUME (thousand shares)

Business Summary: Radio & Television (MIC: 2.3.1 SIC: 4833 NAIC: 515120)

Tribune Media is a holding company. Through its subsidiaries, Co. is a diversified media and entertainment company. Co.'s reportable segment, Television and Entertainment, provides audiences with news, entertainment and sports programming, including content produced by Tribune Studios and its production partners, on Tribune Broadcasting's 42 local television stations as of Dec 31 2017 and their websites, a national general entertainment cable network (WGN America), a radio station and other digital assets. Co. also holds a variety of investments in cable and digital assets, including equity investments in Television Food Network, G.P. and CareerBuilder, LLC.

Recent Developments: For the quarter ended Mar 31 2018, income from continuing operations was US$141.2 million compared with a loss of US$101.2 million in the year-earlier quarter. Net income amounted to US$141.2 million versus a net loss of US$85.6 million in the year-earlier quarter. Revenues were US$443.6 million, up 0.8% from US$439.9 million the year before. Operating income was US$187.3 million versus a loss of US$21.0 million in the prior-year quarter. Direct operating expenses declined 15.8% to US$202.1 million from US$240.1 million in the comparable period the year before. Indirect operating expenses decreased 75.4% to US$54.2 million from US$220.8 million in the equivalent prior-year period.

Prospects: Our evaluation of Tribune Media Company as of Jan. 21, 2018 is the result of our systematic analysis on three basic characteristics: earnings strength, relative valuation, and recent stock price movement. The company has generated a negative trend in earnings per share over the past 5 quarters and while recent estimates for the company have been raised by analysts, TRCO has posted results that fell short of analysts expectations. Based on operating earnings yield, the company is overvalued when compared to all of the companies in our coverage universe. Share price changes over the past year indicates that TRCO will perform very well over the near term.

Financial Data

(US$ in Thousands)	3 Mos	12/31/2017	12/31/2016	12/31/2015	12/28/2014	12/29/2013	12/30/2007	12/31/2006
Earnings Per Share	4.79	2.20	0.16	(3.38)	4.75	2.41	...	2.14
Cash Flow Per Share	3.48	2.56	3.14	0.27	3.92	4.08	...	2.84
Dividends Per Share	1.000	6.770	1.000	7.480	...	...	...	0.720
Dividend Payout %	20.88	307.73	625.00	...	...	...	...	33.64
Income Statement								
Total Revenue	443,635	1,848,959	1,947,930	2,010,460	1,949,359	1,147,240	5,062,984	5,517,708
EBITDA	255,011	(39,957)	511,214	(205,835)	691,963	160,800	746,595	1,431,467
Depn & Amortn	57,530	56,314	72,409	74,289	29,000	8,000	228,070	229,343
Income Before Taxes	158,748	(255,658)	286,086	(444,554)	505,097	113,666	(63,115)	928,222
Income Taxes	56,702	(301,373)	347,202	22,323	278,699	95,965	(18,234)	348,142
Net Income	141,189	194,119	14,246	(319,918)	476,663	241,555	86,945	593,995
Average Shares	88,392	88,001	90,636	94,686	96,923	88,151	...	274,411
Balance Sheet								
Current Assets	1,349,904	1,292,991	1,296,300	1,021,945	2,160,823	1,735,280	1,385,023	1,377,430
Total Assets	8,047,704	8,169,328	9,401,051	9,758,535	11,396,455	11,476,009	13,149,719	13,400,772
Current Liabilities	440,181	654,267	550,853	547,417	684,180	798,837	2,189,966	2,546,714
Long-Term Obligations	2,920,882	2,919,185	3,391,627	3,452,544	3,490,897	3,760,475	11,840,206	3,576,211
Total Liabilities	4,702,607	4,952,192	5,861,285	5,932,337	6,201,024	6,550,448	16,663,659	9,081,156
Stockholders' Equity	3,345,097	3,217,136	3,539,766	3,826,198	5,195,431	4,925,561	(3,513,940)	4,319,616
Shares Outstanding	87,616	87,333	86,319	92,350	97,170	93,119	...	239,207
Statistical Record								
Return on Assets %	5.24	2.21	0.15	N.M.	4.18	...	0.66	4.18
Return on Equity %	13.48	5.75	0.39	N.M.	9.45	...	21.64	10.58
EBITDA Margin %	57.48	N.M.	26.24	N.M.	35.50	14.02	14.75	25.94
Net Margin %	31.83	10.50	0.73	N.M.	24.45	21.06	1.72	10.77
Asset Turnover	0.23	0.21	0.20	0.19	0.17	...	0.38	0.39
Current Ratio	3.07	1.98	2.35	1.87	3.16	2.17	0.63	0.54
Debt to Equity	0.87	0.91	0.96	0.90	0.67	0.76	...	0.83
Price Range	43.58-36.55	42.56-28.33	40.38-27.36	70.16-33.54	89.34-56.70	77.60-48.67	...	...
P/E Ratio	9.10-7.63	19.35-12.88	252.38-171.00	...	18.81-11.94	32.20-20.20	...	...
Average Yield %	2.45	17.47	2.76	15.04	...	...	...	...

Address: 515 North State Street, Chicago, IL 60654 **Telephone:** 646-563-8296	**Web Site:** www.tribune.com **Officers:** Peter M. Kern - Interim Chief Executive Officer Chandler Bigelow - Vice President, Interim Chief Financial Officer, Treasurer, Executive Vice President, Chief Financial Officer	**Auditors:** PricewaterhouseCoopers LLP **Investor Contact:** 212-210-2786 **Transfer Agents:** EquiServe Trust Company, Providence, RI

TRINITY INDUSTRIES, INC.

Exchange	Symbol	Price	52Wk Range	Yield	P/E
NYS	TRN	$34.26 (6/29/2018)	37.88-26.96	1.52	7.65

*7 Year Price Score 103.71 *NYSE Composite Index=100 *12 Month Price Score 102.20

Interim Earnings (Per Share)

Qtr.	Mar	Jun	Sep	Dec
2015	1.13	1.33	1.31	1.30
2016	0.64	0.62	0.55	0.44
2017	0.30	0.33	0.43	3.46
2018	0.26	...	...	...

Interim Dividends (Per Share)

Amt	Decl	Ex	Rec	Pay
0.13Q	09/06/2017	10/12/2017	10/13/2017	10/31/2017
0.13Q	12/12/2017	01/11/2018	01/12/2018	01/31/2018
0.13Q	03/08/2018	04/12/2018	04/13/2018	04/30/2018
0.13Q	05/08/2018	07/12/2018	07/13/2018	07/31/2018
		Indicated Div: $0.52		

Valuation Analysis | Institutional Holding

Forecast EPS	$1.40	No of Institutions
	(06/13/2018)	570
Market Cap	$5.2 Billion	Shares
Book Value	$4.5 Billion	162,755,136
Price/Book	1.15	% Held
Price/Sales	1.43	75.07

Business Summary: Industrial Machinery & Equipment (MIC: 7.2.1 SIC: 3743 NAIC: 336510)

Trinity Industries is an industrial company that owns a range of businesses providing products and services to the energy, chemical, agriculture, transportation, and construction sectors. Co. manufactures and sells a variety of products and services principally including: railcars and railcar parts; parts and steel components; the leasing, management, and maintenance of railcars; highway products; construction aggregates; inland barges; structural wind towers; and trench shields and shoring products. Co. serves its customers through five business groups: Rail Group, Railcar Leasing and Management Services Group, Construction Products Group, Inland Barge Group, and Energy Equipment Group.

Recent Developments: For the quarter ended Mar 31 2018, net income decreased 19.5% to US$41.6 million from US$51.7 million in the year-earlier quarter. Revenues were US$831.3 million, down 5.2% from US$877.3 million the year before. Operating income was US$98.6 million versus US$115.9 million in the prior-year quarter, a decrease of 14.9%. Direct operating expenses declined 4.6% to US$630.1 million from US$660.2 million in the comparable period the year before. Indirect operating expenses increased 1.4% to US$102.6 million from US$101.2 million in the equivalent prior-year period.

Prospects: Our evaluation of Trinity Industries Inc. as of Jan. 21, 2018 is the result of our systematic analysis on three basic characteristics: earnings strength, relative valuation, and recent stock price movement. The company has enjoyed a very positive trend in earnings per share over the past 5 quarters. However, while recent estimates for the company have been mixed, TRN has posted better than expected results. Based on operating earnings yield, the company is about fairly valued when compared to all of the companies in our coverage universe. Share price changes over the past year indicates that TRN will perform well over the near term.

Financial Data

(US$ in Thousands)	3 Mos	12/31/2017	12/31/2016	12/31/2015	12/31/2014	12/31/2013	12/31/2012	12/31/2011
Earnings Per Share	4.48	4.52	2.25	5.08	4.19	2.38	1.60	0.89
Cash Flow Per Share	4.85	5.13	7.33	6.26	5.43	4.33	3.40	0.67
Tang Book Value Per Share	24.44	24.66	20.79	18.97	14.28	13.72	11.46	10.21
Dividends Per Share	0.500	0.480	0.440	0.420	0.350	0.250	0.200	0.170
Dividend Payout %	11.16	10.62	19.56	8.27	8.35	10.53	12.54	19.21
Income Statement								
Total Revenue	831,300	3,662,800	4,588,300	6,392,700	6,170,000	4,365,300	3,811,900	3,075,100
EBITDA	174,200	717,700	899,500	1,586,800	1,385,600	904,700	772,800	614,200
Depn & Amortn	75,300	172,300	156,200	142,300	130,000	129,000	193,700	192,900
Income Before Taxes	56,500	372,000	566,800	1,252,000	1,064,100	590,500	385,900	237,500
Income Taxes	14,800	(341,600)	202,100	426,000	354,800	204,400	134,000	91,800
Net Income	40,200	702,500	343,600	796,500	678,200	375,500	255,200	142,200
Average Shares	153,700	152,000	148,600	152,200	156,700	153,000	155,000	155,600
Balance Sheet								
Current Assets	1,818,700	2,137,400	1,944,700	2,278,800	2,495,200	1,765,600	1,630,700	1,286,900
Total Assets	9,477,000	9,543,200	9,125,300	8,885,900	8,733,800	7,313,400	6,669,900	6,121,000
Current Liabilities	579,800	615,400	582,200	746,400	1,005,000	783,700	771,300	628,700
Long-Term Obligations	3,223,400	3,242,400	3,056,600	3,195,400	3,553,000	2,989,800	3,055,000	2,974,900
Total Liabilities	4,999,300	5,042,100	5,206,800	5,232,000	5,737,900	4,911,300	4,616,900	4,257,200
Stockholders' Equity	4,477,700	4,501,100	3,918,500	3,653,900	2,995,900	2,402,100	2,053,000	1,863,800
Shares Outstanding	150,900	150,900	152,200	152,900	155,600	154,800	158,200	160,400
Statistical Record								
Return on Assets %	7.48	7.53	3.80	9.04	8.45	5.37	3.98	2.39
Return on Equity %	16.52	16.69	9.05	23.96	25.13	16.86	13.00	7.84
EBITDA Margin %	20.96	19.59	19.60	24.82	22.46	20.72	20.27	19.97
Net Margin %	4.84	19.18	7.49	12.46	10.99	8.60	6.69	4.62
Asset Turnover	0.39	0.39	0.51	0.73	0.77	0.62	0.59	0.52
Current Ratio	3.14	3.47	3.34	3.05	2.48	2.25	2.11	2.05
Debt to Equity	0.72	0.72	0.78	0.87	1.19	1.24	1.49	1.60
Price Range	37.88-25.49	37.88-25.49	29.24-15.64	36.80-22.37	50.30-26.57	28.32-17.65	18.02-10.93	18.88-9.97
P/E Ratio	8.46-5.69	8.38-5.64	13.00-6.95	7.24-4.40	12.00-6.34	11.90-7.41	11.27-6.83	21.21-11.20
Average Yield %	1.61	1.64	2.04	1.48	0.93	1.16	1.33	1.14

Address: 2525 N. Stemmons Freeway, Dallas, TX 75207-2401 **Telephone:** 214-631-4420 **Fax:** 214-589-8501	**Web Site:** www.trin.net **Officers:** Timothy R. Wallace - Chairman, President, Chief Executive Officer James E. Perry - Senior Vice President, Vice President, Chief Financial Officer, Treasurer	**Auditors:** Ernst & Young LLP **Investor Contact:** 214-589-8909 **Transfer Agents:** American Stock Transfer & Trust Company

TRANSDIGM GROUP INC

Exchange	Symbol	Price	52Wk Range	Yield	P/E
NYS	TDG	$345.14 (6/29/2018)	346.00-250.43	N/A	26.73

*7 Year Price Score 118.34 *NYSE Composite Index=100 *12 Month Price Score 113.00

Interim Earnings (Per Share)

Qtr.	Dec	Mar	Jun	Sep
2014-15	1.63	1.96	1.75	2.50
2015-16	1.97	2.47	2.52	3.44
2016-17	0.41	2.78	3.08	1.65
2017-18	4.65	3.53	...	...

Interim Dividends (Per Share)

Amt	Decl	Ex	Rec	Pay
22.00U	07/03/2013	07/11/2013	07/15/2013	07/25/2013
25.00U	06/04/2014	06/12/2014	06/16/2014	06/26/2014
24.00U	10/14/2016	10/20/2016	10/24/2016	11/01/2016
22.00U	08/23/2017	08/31/2017	09/05/2017	09/12/2017

Valuation Analysis / Institutional Holding

Valuation Analysis		Institutional Holding	
Forecast EPS	$17.68	No of Institutions	587
	(06/14/2018)		
Market Cap	$18.1 Billion	Shares	65,963,164
Book Value	N/A	% Held	99.30
Price/Book	N/A		
Price/Sales	5.02		

TRADING VOLUME (thousand shares)

Business Summary: Aerospace (MIC: 7.1.1 SIC: 3728 NAIC: 336412)

TransDigm Group is a holding company. Through its subsidiaries, Co. designs, produces and supplies engineered aircraft components for use on commercial and military aircraft. Co.'s segments are: power & control, which include operations that primarily develop, produce and market systems and components that mainly provide power to or control power of the aircraft; airframe, which includes operations that primarily develop, produce and market systems and components that are used in non-power airframe applications utilizing airframe and cabin structure technologies; and non-aviation, which includes operations that primarily develop, produce and market products for non-aviation markets.

Recent Developments: For the quarter ended Mar 31 2018, income from continuing operations increased 29.6% to US$201.8 million from US$155.7 million in the year-earlier quarter. Net income increased 26.2% to US$196.3 million from US$155.5 million in the year-earlier quarter. Revenues were US$933.1 million, up 7.4% from US$868.7 million the year before. Operating income was US$409.1 million versus US$366.5 million in the prior-year quarter, an increase of 11.6%. Direct operating expenses rose 5.2% to US$399.0 million from US$379.3 million in the comparable period the year before. Indirect operating expenses increased 1.7% to US$125.0 million from US$122.9 million in the equivalent prior-year period.

Prospects: Our evaluation of Transdigm Group Inc. as of Jan. 21, 2018 is the result of our systematic analysis on three basic characteristics: earnings strength, relative valuation, and recent stock price movement. The company has managed to produce a neutral trend in earnings per share over the past 5 quarters and while recent estimates for the company have been raised by analysts, TDG has posted better than expected results. Based on operating earnings yield, the company is about fairly valued when compared to all of the companies in our coverage universe. Share price changes over the past year indicates that TDG will perform poorly over the near term.

Financial Data

(US$ in Thousands)	6 Mos	3 Mos	09/30/2017	09/30/2016	09/30/2015	09/30/2014	09/30/2013	09/30/2012
Earnings Per Share	12.91	12.16	7.88	10.39	7.84	3.16	2.39	5.97
Cash Flow Per Share	15.32	15.39	14.20	11.88	9.20	9.50	8.54	7.66
Dividends Per Share	22.000	22.000	46.000	...	...	25.000	34.850	...
Dividend Payout %	170.41	180.92	583.76	...	...	791.14	1,458.16	...
Income Statement								
Total Revenue	1,781,030	847,960	3,504,286	3,171,411	2,707,115	2,372,906	1,924,400	1,700,208
EBITDA	832,553	387,855	1,580,182	1,372,866	1,149,272	892,583	792,689	768,002
Depn & Amortn	72,203	35,958	140,163	120,900	93,663	96,385	73,515	68,227
Income Before Taxes	438,151	190,964	837,430	768,116	636,824	448,510	448,489	487,869
Income Taxes	(75,700)	(121,047)	208,889	181,702	189,612	141,600	145,700	162,900
Net Income	511,053	314,775	596,887	586,414	447,212	306,910	302,789	324,969
Average Shares	55,605	55,600	55,530	56,157	56,606	56,993	55,080	53,882
Balance Sheet								
Current Assets	2,470,104	2,271,333	2,133,552	2,930,697	1,831,962	1,689,576	1,320,495	1,050,531
Total Assets	10,394,677	10,112,127	9,975,661	10,726,277	8,427,050	6,756,848	6,148,879	5,459,617
Current Liabilities	812,835	823,421	870,994	752,603	658,215	585,907	322,500	233,915
Long-Term Obligations	11,365,790	11,378,320	11,393,620	9,943,191	8,183,502	7,233,836	5,700,193	3,598,625
Total Liabilities	12,704,014	12,711,840	12,926,865	11,377,767	9,465,356	8,312,947	6,485,260	4,240,783
Stockholders' Equity	(2,309,337)	(2,599,713)	(2,951,204)	(651,490)	(1,038,306)	(1,556,099)	(336,381)	1,218,834
Shares Outstanding	52,352	52,123	51,934	53,334	53,684	52,417	52,667	51,651
Statistical Record								
Return on Assets %	8.10	7.87	5.77	6.11	5.89	4.76	5.22	6.50
Return on Equity %	...	...	...	...	...	...	68.62	31.93
EBITDA Margin %	46.75	45.74	45.09	43.29	42.45	37.62	41.19	45.17
Net Margin %	28.69	37.12	17.03	18.49	16.52	12.93	15.73	19.11
Asset Turnover	0.35	0.35	0.34	0.33	0.36	0.37	0.33	0.34
Current Ratio	3.04	2.76	2.45	3.89	2.78	2.88	4.09	4.49
Debt to Equity	...	...	...	...	...	...	...	2.95
Price Range	317.37-218.76	287.60-210.04	289.86-210.04	291.81-187.29	244.35-171.82	197.00-137.86	162.48-125.52	145.61-77.38
P/E Ratio	24.58-16.95	23.65-17.27	36.78-26.65	28.09-18.03	31.17-21.92	62.34-43.63	67.98-52.52	24.39-12.96
Average Yield %	8.08	8.50	17.93	...	...	14.67	24.38	...

Address: 1301 East 9th Street, Suite 3000, Cleveland, OH 44114 Telephone: 216-706-2960	Web Site: www.transdigm.com Officers: W. Nicholas Howley - Executive Chairman, Chairman, Chief Executive Officer Robert S. Henderson - Vice-Chairman, Executive Vice President, Division Officer	Auditors: Ernst & Young LLP Investor Contact: 216-706-2945 Transfer Agents: Computershare, Providence, RI

TUPPERWARE BRANDS CORP

Exchange	Symbol	Price	52Wk Range	Yield	P/E
NYS	TUP	$41.24 (6/29/2018)	70.36-40.20	6.60	N/A

*7 Year Price Score 68.47 ***NYSE Composite Index=100** ***12 Month Price Score 77.12**

Interim Earnings (Per Share)

Qtr.	Mar	Jun	Sep	Dec
2015	0.59	1.23	0.72	1.15
2016	0.86	1.03	0.96	1.56
2017	0.93	(0.35)	0.61	(6.41)
2018	0.70	...	...	...

Interim Dividends (Per Share)

Amt	Decl	Ex	Rec	Pay
0.68Q	08/14/2017	09/19/2017	09/20/2017	10/05/2017
0.68Q	11/02/2017	12/19/2017	12/20/2017	01/05/2018
0.68Q	01/31/2018	03/19/2018	03/20/2018	04/05/2018
0.68Q	05/09/2018	06/19/2018	06/20/2018	07/06/2018

Indicated Div: $2.72

Valuation Analysis   **Institutional Holding**

Forecast EPS	$4.62	No of Institutions
	(06/13/2018)	588
Market Cap	$2.1 Billion	Shares
Book Value	N/A	60,578,232
Price/Book	N/A	% Held
Price/Sales	0.94	76.23

TRADING VOLUME (thousand shares)

Business Summary: Plastics (MIC: 8.4.2 SIC: 3089 NAIC: 326199)

Tupperware Brands manufactures and sells Tupperware® products and cosmetics and personal care products under trade names such as Avroy Shlain®, BeautiControl®, Fuller®, NaturCare®, Nutrimetics® and Nuvo® brands. Co. operates in three geographic regions: Europe (Europe, Africa and the Middle East), Asia Pacific and the Americas. The Tupperware product line consists of preparation, storage, and serving solutions for the kitchen and home, and cookware, knives, microwave products, microfiber textiles, and water-filtration related items. Co. also manufactures and distributes skin and hair care products, cosmetics, bath and body care, toiletries, fragrances, jewelry and nutritional products.

Recent Developments: For the quarter ended Mar 31 2018, net income decreased 24.7% to US$35.7 million from US$47.4 million in the year-earlier quarter. Revenues were US$542.6 million, down 2.2% from US$554.8 million the year before. Operating income was US$69.0 million versus US$77.0 million in the prior-year quarter, a decrease of 10.4%. Direct operating expenses rose 0.7% to US$179.0 million from US$177.7 million in the comparable period the year before. Indirect operating expenses decreased 1.8% to US$294.6 million from US$300.1 million in the equivalent prior-year period.

Prospects: Our evaluation of Tupperware Corp. as of Jan. 21, 2018 is the result of our systematic analysis on three basic characteristics: earnings strength, relative valuation, and recent stock price movement. The company has generated a negative trend in earnings per share over the past 5 quarters and while recent estimates for the company have been mixed, TUP has posted better than expected results. Based on operating earnings yield, the company is undervalued when compared to all of the companies in our coverage universe. Share price changes over the past year indicates that TUP will perform in line with the market over the near term.

Financial Data
(US$ in Thousands)

	3 Mos	12/30/2017	12/31/2016	12/26/2015	12/27/2014	12/28/2013	12/29/2012	12/31/2011
Earnings Per Share	(5.45)	(5.22)	4.41	3.69	4.20	5.17	3.42	3.55
Cash Flow Per Share	3.79	4.28	4.65	4.54	5.65	6.25	5.42	4.50
Tang Book Value Per Share	...	...	0.25	N.M.	N.M.	N.M.	2.64	1.68
Dividends Per Share	2.720	2.720	2.720	2.720	2.720	2.480	1.440	1.200
Dividend Payout %	...	...	61.68	73.71	64.76	47.97	42.11	33.80
Income Statement								
Total Revenue	542,600	2,255,800	2,213,100	2,283,800	2,606,100	2,671,600	2,583,800	2,585,000
EBITDA	68,800	279,300	396,600	357,300	393,400	448,000	352,800	388,000
Depn & Amortn	...	51,000	49,900	52,200	51,700	50,000	47,600	46,900
Income Before Taxes	58,400	185,100	301,300	259,900	298,200	360,400	272,800	295,300
Income Taxes	22,700	450,500	77,700	74,100	83,800	86,200	79,800	77,000
Net Income	35,700	(265,400)	223,600	185,800	214,400	274,200	193,000	218,300
Average Shares	51,300	50,800	50,700	50,400	51,000	53,100	56,400	61,400
Balance Sheet								
Current Assets	701,700	630,500	545,300	550,500	753,600	779,000	766,500	769,400
Total Assets	1,444,800	1,388,000	1,587,800	1,598,200	1,783,100	1,843,900	1,821,800	1,844,200
Current Liabilities	729,700	658,800	547,600	614,000	747,400	737,500	694,500	675,400
Long-Term Obligations	605,000	605,100	606,000	608,200	615,200	619,900	414,400	415,200
Total Liabilities	1,553,200	1,507,400	1,375,000	1,437,200	1,597,300	1,591,000	1,342,700	1,343,400
Stockholders' Equity	(108,400)	(119,400)	212,800	161,000	185,800	252,900	479,100	500,800
Shares Outstanding	51,117	51,057	50,637	50,436	49,682	50,324	54,059	56,507
Statistical Record								
Return on Assets %	N.M.	N.M.	13.81	11.02	11.85	15.00	10.56	11.13
Return on Equity %	N.M.	N.M.	117.70	107.45	98.01	75.12	39.50	33.28
EBITDA Margin %	12.68	12.38	17.92	15.64	15.10	16.77	13.65	15.01
Net Margin %	6.58	N.M.	10.10	8.14	8.23	10.26	7.47	8.44
Asset Turnover	1.44	1.52	1.37	1.35	1.44	1.46	1.41	1.32
Current Ratio	0.96	0.96	1.00	0.90	1.01	1.06	1.10	1.14
Debt to Equity	...	...	2.85	3.78	3.31	2.45	0.86	0.83
Price Range	73.52-46.21	73.52-53.86	66.72-43.97	72.68-48.42	95.54-59.64	96.00-64.00	66.56-51.16	71.45-45.63
P/E Ratio	...	...	15.13-9.97	19.70-13.12	22.75-14.20	18.57-12.38	19.46-14.96	20.13-12.85
Average Yield %	4.40	4.32	4.72	4.40	3.53	3.01	2.47	2.04

Address: 14901 South Orange Blossom Trail, Orlando, FL 32837	**Web Site:** www.tupperwarebrands.com	**Auditors:** PricewaterhouseCoopers LLP
Telephone: 407-826-5050	**Officers:** E. V. (Rick) Goings - Chairman, Chief Executive Officer, Executive Chairman Simon C. Hemus - Vice-Chairman, President, Chief Operating Officer	**Investor Contact:** 407-826-4475
		Transfer Agents: Equiniti Trust Company, Mendota Heights, MN

TWITTER INC

Exchange	Symbol	Price	52Wk Range	Yield	P/E
NYS	TWTR	$43.67 (6/29/2018)	46.76-15.75	N/A	4367.00

*7 Year Price Score N/A   *NYSE Composite Index=100   *12 Month Price Score 144.24

TRADING VOLUME (thousand shares)

Interim Earnings (Per Share)

Qtr.	Mar	Jun	Sep	Dec
2015	(0.25)	(0.21)	(0.20)	(0.13)
2016	(0.12)	(0.15)	(0.15)	(0.23)
2017	(0.09)	(0.16)	(0.03)	0.12
2018	0.08	...	...	...

Interim Dividends (Per Share)

No Dividends Paid

Valuation Analysis		Institutional Holding	
Forecast EPS	$0.75	No of Institutions	
	(06/14/2018)	778	
Market Cap	$32.8 Billion	Shares	
Book Value	$5.2 Billion	492,784,832	
Price/Book	6.30	% Held	
Price/Sales	12.83	90.26	

Business Summary: Internet & Software (MIC: 6.3.2 SIC: 7371 NAIC: 541511)

Twitter provides products and services for users, advertisers, developers and platform and data partners. Co.'s products and services for users include its Twitter platform for public self-expression and conversation in real time and its Periscope mobile application. Co.'s products and services for advertisers include Promoted Product for advertisers as well as MoPub mobile-focused advertising exchange and its Twitter Audience Platform. Co.'s products for developers include a set of tools, public application program interfaces (API) and embeddable widgets. Co.'s products for data partners include subscription access to its public data feed beyond its public API.

Recent Developments: For the quarter ended Mar 31 2018, net income amounted to US$61.0 million versus a net loss of US$61.6 million in the year-earlier quarter. Revenues were US$664.9 million, up 21.3% from US$548.3 million the year before. Operating income was US$74.9 million versus a loss of US$40.3 million in the prior-year quarter. Direct operating expenses rose 1.1% to US$222.8 million from US$220.3 million in the comparable period the year before. Indirect operating expenses decreased 0.3% to US$367.1 million from US$368.2 million in the equivalent prior-year period.

Prospects: Our evaluation of Twitter Inc as of Jan. 21, 2018 is the result of our systematic analysis on three basic characteristics: earnings strength, relative valuation, and recent stock price movement. The company has enjoyed a very positive trend in earnings per share over the past 5 quarters. However, while recent estimates for the company have been mixed, TWTR has posted better than expected results. Based on operating earnings yield, the company is overvalued when compared to all of the companies in our coverage universe. Share price changes over the past year indicates that TWTR will perform well over the near term.

Financial Data

(US$ in Thousands)	3 Mos	12/31/2017	12/31/2016	12/31/2015	12/31/2014	12/31/2013	12/31/2012	12/31/2011
Earnings Per Share	0.01	(0.15)	(0.65)	(0.79)	(0.96)	(6.82)	(0.68)	(1.60)
Cash Flow Per Share	1.16	1.13	1.08	0.58	0.14	0.01	(0.24)	(0.69)
Tang Book Value Per Share	5.29	5.10	4.61	4.47	4.51	4.40	4.39	4.96
Income Statement								
Total Revenue	664,871	2,443,299	2,529,619	2,218,032	1,403,002	1,329,780	316,933	106,313
EBITDA	95,438	359,019	(8,066)	(177,927)	(372,766)	(1,091,056)	(22,884)	(109,441)
Depn & Amortn	20,722	349,200	332,800	257,200	171,600	188,800	53,800	19,500
Income Before Taxes	63,882	(95,418)	(440,834)	(533,305)	(578,351)	(1,294,292)	(79,170)	(129,746)
Income Taxes	2,885	12,645	16,039	(12,274)	(531)	(3,646)	229	(1,444)
Net Income	60,997	(108,063)	(456,873)	(521,031)	(577,820)	(1,290,646)	(79,399)	(128,302)
Average Shares	765,861	732,702	702,135	662,424	604,990	379,020	117,401	102,544
Balance Sheet								
Current Assets	5,409,235	5,321,884	4,652,196	4,381,792	4,255,853	5,149,358	554,466	596,068
Total Assets	7,539,441	7,412,477	6,870,365	6,442,439	5,583,082	6,732,480	831,568	720,675
Current Liabilities	528,654	583,278	584,021	506,039	393,794	450,860	109,879	47,744
Long-Term Obligations	1,722,034	1,708,768	1,605,804	1,514,790	1,494,970	221,040	65,732	21,104
Total Liabilities	2,329,005	2,365,259	2,265,430	2,074,392	1,956,679	832,468	207,204	87,391
Stockholders' Equity	5,210,436	5,047,218	4,604,935	4,368,047	3,626,403	5,900,012	624,364	633,284
Shares Outstanding	752,037	746,902	721,572	694,132	642,385	1,139,844	125,597	118,967
Statistical Record								
Return on Assets %	0.20	N.M.	N.M.	N.M.	N.M.	N.M.	N.M.	...
Return on Equity %	0.29	N.M.	N.M.	N.M.	N.M.	N.M.	N.M.	...
EBITDA Margin %	14.35	14.69	N.M.	N.M.	N.M.	N.M.	N.M.	N.M.
Net Margin %	9.17	N.M.	N.M.	N.M.	N.M.	N.M.	N.M.	N.M.
Asset Turnover	0.35	0.34	0.38	0.37	0.23	0.35	0.41	...
Current Ratio	10.23	9.12	7.97	8.66	10.81	11.42	5.05	12.48
Debt to Equity	0.33	0.34	0.35	0.35	0.41	0.04	0.11	0.03
Price Range	36.60-14.29	25.20-14.29	24.87-14.01	52.87-22.14	69.00-30.50	73.31-39.06	...	...

Address: 1355 Market Street, Suite 900, San Francisco, CA 94103 Telephone: 415-222-9670	Web Site: www.twitter.com Officers: Omid R. Kordestani - Executive Chairman Jack Dorsey - Chairman, Chief Executive Officer, Interim Chief Executive Officer	Auditors: PricewaterhouseCoopers LLP Transfer Agents: Computershare Trust Company, N.A., Canton, MA

TYLER TECHNOLOGIES, INC.

Exchange	Symbol	Price	52Wk Range	Yield	P/E
NYS	TYL	$222.10 (6/29/2018)	239.16-167.49	N/A	51.53

*7 Year Price Score 138.22 *NYSE Composite Index=100 ***12 Month Price Score 116.12**

TRADING VOLUME (thousand shares)

Interim Earnings (Per Share)

Qtr.	Mar	Jun	Sep	Dec
2015	0.48	0.52	0.55	0.21
2016	0.44	0.49	0.58	1.31
2017	0.83	0.81	0.97	1.58
2018	0.95	...	...	...

Interim Dividends (Per Share)

No Dividends Paid

Valuation Analysis		Institutional Holding	
Forecast EPS	$4.78	No of Institutions	
	(06/11/2018)	437	
Market Cap	$8.5 Billion	Shares	
Book Value	$1.3 Billion	46,740,120	
Price/Book	6.74	% Held	
Price/Sales	9.85	98.79	

Business Summary: Internet & Software (MIC: 6.3.2 SIC: 7372 NAIC: 511210)

Tyler Technologies provides integrated information management solutions and services for the public sector, with a focus on local governments. Co. has two segments. The Enterprise Software Solutions segment provides municipal and county governments and schools with software systems and services to meet their information technology and automation needs for functions such as financial management and courts and justice processes. The Appraisal and Tax segment provides systems and software that automate the appraisal and assessment of real and personal property as well as property appraisal outsourcing services for local governments and taxing authorities.

Recent Developments: For the quarter ended Mar 31 2018, net income increased 15.4% to US$37.8 million from US$32.8 million in the year-earlier quarter. Revenues were US$221.2 million, up 10.7% from US$199.7 million the year before. Operating income was US$38.8 million versus US$36.8 million in the prior-year quarter, an increase of 5.4%. Direct operating expenses rose 12.5% to US$118.4 million from US$105.2 million in the comparable period the year before. Indirect operating expenses increased 10.9% to US$64.0 million from US$57.7 million in the equivalent prior-year period.

Prospects: Our evaluation of Tyler Technologies Inc. as of Jan. 21, 2018 is the result of our systematic analysis on three basic characteristics: earnings strength, relative valuation, and recent stock price movement. The company has generated a negative trend in earnings per share over the past 5 quarters and while recent estimates for the company have remained steady, TYL has posted better than expected results. Based on operating earnings yield, the company is overvalued when compared to all of the companies in our coverage universe. Share price changes over the past year indicates that TYL will perform in line with the market over the near term.

Financial Data

(US$ in Thousands)	3 Mos	12/31/2017	12/31/2016	12/31/2015	12/31/2014	12/31/2013	12/31/2012	12/31/2011
Earnings Per Share	4.31	4.18	2.82	1.77	1.66	1.13	1.00	0.83
Cash Flow Per Share	5.06	5.25	5.25	2.61	3.74	2.07	1.93	1.80
Tang Book Value Per Share	10.00	7.20	N.M.	N.M.	5.32	2.63	N.M.	N.M.
Income Statement								
Total Revenue	221,174	840,662	756,043	591,022	493,101	416,643	363,304	309,391
EBITDA	42,752	192,840	156,438	123,429	106,913	76,736	63,747	52,744
Depn & Amortn	3,315	31,212	27,131	15,005	12,446	10,917	9,879	8,631
Income Before Taxes	39,437	161,628	129,307	108,424	94,467	65,819	53,868	44,113
Income Taxes	1,612	(2,317)	19,450	43,555	35,527	26,718	20,874	16,556
Net Income	37,825	163,945	109,857	64,869	58,940	39,101	32,994	27,557
Average Shares	39,836	39,246	38,961	36,552	35,401	34,590	32,916	33,154
Balance Sheet								
Current Assets	532,636	496,800	282,960	268,215	346,710	217,235	122,757	107,092
Total Assets	1,625,624	1,589,592	1,357,945	1,356,570	573,982	444,488	338,315	295,391
Current Liabilities	319,549	382,310	361,501	337,572	232,839	192,110	169,795	151,640
Long-Term Obligations	...	...	10,000	66,000	...	...	18,000	60,700
Total Liabilities	364,410	422,498	442,420	497,713	237,009	198,169	193,016	217,281
Stockholders' Equity	1,261,214	1,167,094	915,525	858,857	336,973	246,319	145,299	78,110
Shares Outstanding	38,247	37,885	36,766	36,774	33,469	32,838	31,331	29,971
Statistical Record								
Return on Assets %	11.37	11.12	8.07	6.72	11.57	9.99	...	9.85
Return on Equity %	15.21	15.74	12.35	10.85	20.21	19.97	...	29.78
EBITDA Margin %	19.33	22.94	20.69	20.88	21.68	18.42	17.55	17.05
Net Margin %	17.10	19.50	14.53	10.98	11.95	9.38	9.08	8.91
Asset Turnover	0.58	0.57	0.56	0.61	0.97	1.06	...	1.11
Current Ratio	1.67	1.30	0.78	0.79	1.49	1.13	0.72	0.71
Debt to Equity	...	...	0.01	0.08	...	...	0.12	0.78
Price Range	212.48-152.58	184.11-144.77	175.47-119.50	180.61-104.17	114.09-76.00	104.62-48.44	49.00-30.34	32.65-20.28
P/E Ratio	49.30-35.40	44.05-34.63	62.22-42.38	102.04-58.85	68.73-45.78	92.58-42.87	49.00-30.34	39.34-24.43

Address: 5101 Tennyson Parkway,	Web Site: www.tylertech.com	Auditors: Ernst & Young LLP
Plano, TX 75024	Officers: John S. Marr - Chairman, President, Chief	Investor Contact: 972-713-3720
Telephone: 972-713-3700	Executive Officer H. Lynn Moore - President,	Transfer Agents: American Stock
	Executive Vice President, Secretary, General Counsel,	Transfer & Company, New York, NY
	Chief Executive Officer	

TYSON FOODS INC

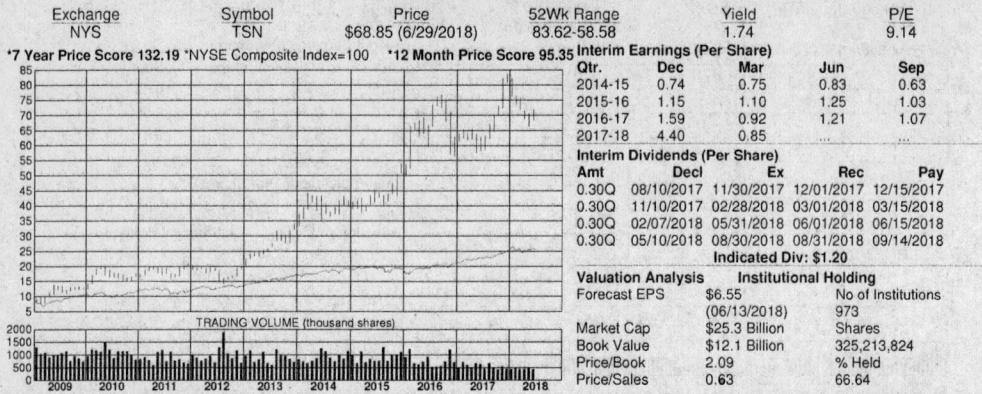

Exchange	Symbol	Price	52Wk Range	Yield	P/E
NYS	TSN	$68.85 (6/29/2018)	83.62-58.58	1.74	9.14

*7 Year Price Score 132.19 *NYSE Composite Index=100 *12 Month Price Score 95.35

Interim Earnings (Per Share)

Qtr.	Dec	Mar	Jun	Sep
2014-15	0.74	0.75	0.83	0.63
2015-16	1.15	1.10	1.25	1.03
2016-17	1.59	0.92	1.21	1.07
2017-18	4.40	0.85	...	...

Interim Dividends (Per Share)

Amt	Decl	Ex	Rec	Pay
0.30Q	08/10/2017	11/30/2017	12/01/2017	12/15/2017
0.30Q	11/10/2017	02/28/2018	03/01/2018	03/15/2018
0.30Q	02/07/2018	05/31/2018	06/01/2018	06/15/2018
0.30Q	05/10/2018	08/30/2018	08/31/2018	09/14/2018

Indicated Div: $1.20

Valuation Analysis

		Institutional Holding	
Forecast EPS	$6.55	No of Institutions	
	(06/13/2018)	973	
Market Cap	$25.3 Billion	Shares	
Book Value	$12.1 Billion	325,213,824	
Price/Book	2.09	% Held	
Price/Sales	0.63	66.64	

Business Summary: Food (MIC: 1.2.1 SIC: 2015 NAIC: 311615)

Tyson Foods operates a vertically-integrated chicken production process. Co.'s operations consist of breeding stock, contract growers, feed production, processing, further-processing, marketing and transportation of chicken and related allied products, including animal and pet food ingredients. Through its subsidiary, Cobb-Vantress, Inc., Co. is engaged in poultry breeding stock suppliers. Co. also process live fed cattle and hogs and fabricate dressed beef and pork carcasses into primal and sub-primal meat cuts, case ready beef and pork and fully-cooked meats. Co. produces a range of fresh, frozen and refrigerated food products. Co.'s segments are beef, pork, chicken, and prepared foods.

Recent Developments: For the quarter ended Mar 31 2018, net income decreased 7.3% to US$316.0 million from US$341.0 million in the year-earlier quarter. Revenues were US$9.77 billion, up 7.6% from US$9.08 billion the year before. Operating income was US$498.0 million versus US$571.0 million in the prior-year quarter, a decrease of 12.8%. Direct operating expenses rose 8.9% to US$8.75 billion from US$8.04 billion in the comparable period the year before. Indirect operating expenses increased 9.7% to US$522.0 million from US$476.0 million in the equivalent prior-year period.

Prospects: Our evaluation of Tyson Foods Inc. as of Jan. 21, 2018 is the result of our systematic analysis on three basic characteristics: earnings strength, relative valuation, and recent stock price movement. The company has managed to produce a neutral trend in earnings per share over the past 5 quarters and while recent estimates for the company have been raised by analysts, TSN has posted better than expected results. Based on operating earnings yield, the company is undervalued when compared to all of the companies in our coverage universe. Share price changes over the past year indicates that TSN will perform well over the near term.

Financial Data
(US$ in Thousands)

	6 Mos	3 Mos	09/30/2017	10/01/2016	10/03/2015	09/27/2014	09/28/2013	09/29/2012
Earnings Per Share	7.53	7.60	4.79	4.53	2.95	2.37	2.12	1.58
Cash Flow Per Share	7.53	7.08	7.12	7.07	6.24	3.34	3.74	3.28
Tang Book Value Per Share	N.M.	N.M.	N.M.	N.M.	N.M.	N.M.	12.10	11.12
Dividends Per Share	1.050	0.975	0.900	0.600	0.400	0.300	0.300	0.160
Dividend Payout %	13.94	12.83	18.79	13.25	13.56	12.66	14.15	10.13
Income Statement								
Total Revenue	20,002,000	10,229,000	38,260,000	36,881,000	41,373,000	37,580,000	34,374,000	33,278,000
EBITDA	1,894,000	1,157,000	3,542,000	3,458,000	2,814,000	1,871,000	1,869,000	1,714,000
Depn & Amortn	459,000	229,000	642,000	617,000	609,000	494,000	474,000	443,000
Income Before Taxes	1,265,000	842,000	2,628,000	2,598,000	*1,921,000	1,252,000	1,257,000	927,000
Income Taxes	(683,000)	(790,000)	850,000	826,000	697,000	396,000	409,000	351,000
Net Income	1,946,000	1,631,000	1,774,000	1,768,000	1,220,000	864,000	778,000	583,000
Average Shares	370,000	371,000	370,000	390,000	413,000	364,000	367,000	370,000
Balance Sheet								
Current Assets	5,990,000	5,993,000	6,258,000	4,888,000	5,381,000	6,221,000	5,604,000	5,403,000
Total Assets	28,091,000	28,046,000	28,066,000	22,373,000	23,004,000	23,956,000	12,177,000	11,896,000
Current Liabilities	3,838,000	3,978,000	4,032,000	2,762,000	3,535,000	3,797,000	3,010,000	2,830,000
Long-Term Obligations	8,872,000	8,875,000	9,297,000	6,200,000	6,010,000	7,535,000	1,895,000	1,917,000
Total Liabilities	15,955,000	16,091,000	17,525,000	12,765,000	13,313,000	15,066,000	5,976,000	5,884,000
Stockholders' Equity	12,136,000	11,955,000	10,541,000	9,608,000	9,691,000	8,890,000	6,201,000	6,012,000
Shares Outstanding	368,000	368,000	368,000	361,000	369,000	376,000	344,000	359,000
Statistical Record								
Return on Assets %	11.00	11.18	7.05	7.81	5.11	4.80	6.48	5.09
Return on Equity %	25.44	26.15	17.66	18.37	12.92	11.48	12.78	10.02
EBITDA Margin %	9.47	11.31	9.26	9.38	6.80	4.98	5.44	5.15
Net Margin %	9.73	15.94	4.64	4.79	2.95	2.30	2.26	1.75
Asset Turnover	1.58	1.56	1.52	1.63	1.73	2.09	2.86	2.91
Current Ratio	1.56	1.51	1.55	1.77	1.52	1.64	1.86	1.91
Debt to Equity	0.73	0.74	0.88	0.65	0.62	0.85	0.31	0.32
Price Range	83.62-57.34	83.62-57.34	75.10-56.17	76.76-43.10	45.01-37.12	44.01-27.56	31.83-16.02	20.91-14.17
P/E Ratio	11.10-7.61	11.00-7.54	15.68-11.73	16.94-9.51	15.26-12.58	18.57-11.63	15.01-7.56	13.23-8.97
Average Yield %	1.51	1.47	1.42	0.97	0.97	0.82	1.27	0.87

Address: 2200 West Don Tyson Parkway, Springdale, AR 72762-6999 **Telephone:** 479-290-4000 **Fax:** 479-290-7984	**Web Site:** www.tyson.com **Officers:** John Tyson - Chairman Thomas P. (Tom) Hayes - President, Chief Executive Officer	**Auditors:** PricewaterhouseCoopers LLP **Investor Contact:** 479-290-4235 **Transfer Agents:** Computershare, Inc., Providence , RI

UDR INC

Exchange	Symbol	Price	52Wk Range	Yield	P/E
NYS	UDR	$37.54 (6/29/2018)	40.05-32.92	3.44	N/A

*7 Year Price Score 97.48   *NYSE Composite Index=100   *12 Month Price Score 96.34

Interim Earnings (Per Share)

Qtr.	Mar	Jun	Sep	Dec
2015	0.28	0.33	0.05	0.63
2016	0.04	0.06	0.10	0.88
2017	0.09	0.03	0.06	0.26
2018	0.30	...	...	...

Interim Dividends (Per Share)

Amt	Decl	Ex	Rec	Pay
0.31Q	09/21/2017	10/06/2017	10/10/2017	10/31/2017
0.31Q	12/14/2017	01/09/2018	01/10/2018	01/31/2018
0.323Q	03/27/2018	04/06/2018	04/09/2018	04/30/2018
0.323Q	06/21/2018	07/09/2018	07/10/2018	07/31/2018

Indicated Div: $1.29

Valuation Analysis   **Institutional Holding**

Forecast EPS	$0.44	No of Institutions
	(06/14/2018)	536
Market Cap	$10.0 Billion	Shares
Book Value	$2.9 Billion	353,374,656
Price/Book	3.49	% Held
Price/Sales	N/A	N/A

TRADING VOLUME (thousand shares)

Business Summary: REITs (MIC: 5.3.1 SIC: 6798 NAIC: 525930)

UDR is a real estate investment trust that owns, operates, acquires, renovates, develops, redevelops, and manages multifamily apartment communities generally located in markets located throughout the U.S. Co. reports in two segments: Same-Store Communities and Non-Mature Communities/Other. As of Dec 31 2017, Co.'s consolidated real estate portfolio included 127 communities located in 19 markets, with a total of 39,998 completed apartment homes, which are held through its subsidiaries. In addition, Co. had an ownership interest in 29 communities containing 7,286 apartment homes through unconsolidated joint ventures or partnerships.

Recent Developments: For the quarter ended Mar 31 2018, income from continuing operations decreased 27.9% to US$18.9 million from US$26.3 million in the year-earlier quarter. Net income increased 214.2% to US$89.2 million from US$28.4 million in the year-earlier quarter. Revenues were US$253.3 million, up 3.9% from US$243.8 million the year before. Revenues from property income rose 3.8% to US$250.5 million from US$241.3 million in the corresponding quarter a year earlier.

Prospects: Our evaluation of UDR Inc. as of Jan. 21, 2018 is the result of our systematic analysis on three basic characteristics: earnings strength, relative valuation, and recent stock price movement. The company has managed to produce a neutral trend in earnings per share over the past 5 quarters. Because the company lacks sufficient analyst estimate data, we place greater weight on the historical EPS trend as the measure of earnings strength. Based on operating earnings yield, the company is overvalued when compared to all of the companies in our coverage universe. Share price changes over the past year indicates that UDR will perform well over the near term.

Financial Data
(US$ in Thousands)

	3 Mos	12/31/2017	12/31/2016	12/31/2015	12/31/2014	12/31/2013	12/31/2012	12/31/2011
Earnings Per Share	0.65	0.44	1.08	1.29	0.59	0.16	0.85	0.05
Cash Flow Per Share	...	1.94	2.02	1.67	1.56	1.36	1.32	1.21
Tang Book Value Per Share	10.58	10.38	11.40	10.90	10.54	11.03	11.78	9.95
Dividends Per Share	1.240	1.225	1.163	1.093	1.015	0.925	0.875	0.770
Dividend Payout %	190.77	278.41	107.64	84.69	172.03	578.13	102.94	1,540.00
Income Statement								
Total Revenue	253,305	995,791	959,861	894,638	818,046	758,926	729,363	708,685
EBITDA	161,344	633,818	613,658	558,885	490,693	465,151	472,016	440,799
Depn & Amortn	113,331	449,324	439,036	399,294	363,929	348,231	367,404	393,862
Income Before Taxes	20,829	57,754	53,521	39,267	8,168	(4,544)	(34,457)	(104,207)
Income Taxes	227	(240)	(3,774)	(3,886)	(15,098)	(7,299)	...	...
Net Income	81,756	121,558	292,718	340,383	154,334	44,812	212,177	20,023
Average Shares	269,208	268,830	267,311	263,752	253,445	249,969	238,851	201,294
Balance Sheet								
Current Assets	20,853	21,830	22,106	27,540	37,564	53,045	35,676	37,137
Total Assets	7,709,048	7,733,273	7,679,584	7,663,844	6,846,534	6,807,722	6,888,509	6,721,354
Current Liabilities	266,477	278,108	271,654	246,002	244,999	253,918	261,926	247,725
Long-Term Obligations	3,680,673	3,671,663	3,401,478	3,570,795	3,583,105	3,523,703	3,409,333	3,918,370
Total Liabilities	4,831,588	4,907,473	4,586,474	4,764,089	4,111,437	3,996,074	3,895,593	4,407,304
Stockholders' Equity	2,877,460	2,825,800	3,093,110	2,899,755	2,735,097	2,811,648	2,992,916	2,314,050
Shares Outstanding	267,583	267,822	267,259	261,844	255,114	250,749	250,139	219,650
Statistical Record								
Return on Assets %	...	1.58	3.81	4.69	2.26	0.65	3.11	0.33
Return on Equity %	...	4.11	9.74	12.08	5.56	1.54	7.97	1.02
EBITDA Margin %	63.70	63.65	63.93	62.47	59.98	61.29	64.72	62.20
Net Margin %	32.28	12.21	30.50	38.05	18.87	5.90	29.09	2.83
Asset Turnover	...	0.13	0.12	0.12	0.12	0.11	0.11	0.12
Current Ratio	0.08	0.08	0.08	0.11	0.15	0.21	0.14	0.15
Debt to Equity	1.28	1.30	1.10	1.23	1.31	1.25	1.14	1.69
Price Range	40.49-32.92	40.49-34.48	38.56-33.11	37.89-30.82	31.74-23.27	26.82-22.24	27.06-22.51	27.14-20.77
P/E Ratio	62.29-50.65	92.02-78.36	35.70-30.66	29.37-23.89	53.80-39.44	167.63-139.00	31.84-26.48	542.80-415.40
Average Yield %	3.28	3.23	3.27	3.24	3.66	3.80	3.47	3.17

Address: 1745 Shea Center Drive, Suite 200, Highlands Ranch, CO 80129
Telephone: 720-283-6120

Web Site: www.udrt.com
Officers: Thomas W. Toomey - Chairman, President, Chief Executive Officer Lynne B. Sagalyn - Vice-Chairman

Auditors: Ernst & Young LLP
Investor Contact: 720-348-7762
Transfer Agents: Wells Fargo Shareowner Services, Saint Paul, MN

UGI CORP.

Exchange	Symbol	Price	52Wk Range	Yield	P/E	Div Acheiver
NYS	UGI	$52.07 (6/29/2018)	52.24-42.53	2.00	14.67	30 Years

*7 Year Price Score 112.83 *NYSE Composite Index=100 *12 Month Price Score 103.69

Interim Earnings (Per Share)

Qtr.	Dec	Mar	Jun	Sep
2014-15	0.19	1.40	0.05	(0.05)
2015-16	0.65	1.33	0.34	(0.25)
2016-17	1.30	1.24	(0.11)	0.02
2017-18	2.07	1.57	...	...

Interim Dividends (Per Share)

Amt	Decl	Ex	Rec	Pay
0.25Q	07/25/2017	09/14/2017	09/15/2017	10/01/2017
0.25Q	11/29/2017	12/14/2017	12/15/2017	01/01/2018
0.25Q	01/25/2018	03/14/2018	03/15/2018	04/01/2018
0.26Q	04/24/2018	06/14/2018	06/15/2018	07/01/2018

Indicated Div: $1.04 (Div. Reinv. Plan)

Valuation Analysis	Institutional Holding	
Forecast EPS	$2.78	No of Institutions
	(06/12/2018)	656
Market Cap	$9.0 Billion	Shares
Book Value	$3.8 Billion	170,436,832
Price/Book	2.39	% Held
Price/Sales	1.25	79.32

Business Summary: Gas Utilities (MIC: 3.3.1 SIC: 4932 NAIC: 221210)

UGI is a holding company that, through its subsidiaries and affiliates, distributes, stores, transports and markets energy products and related services. In the U.S., Co. is the general partner and own limited partner interests in a retail propane marketing and distribution business; own and operate natural gas and electric distribution utilities; own all or a portion of electricity generation facilities; and own and operate an energy marketing, midstream infrastructure, storage, natural gas gathering, natural gas production and energy services business. Internationally, Co. markets and distributes propane and other liquefied petroleum gases in Europe.

Recent Developments: For the quarter ended Mar 31 2018, net income increased 30.8% to US$407.7 million from US$311.8 million in the year-earlier quarter. Revenues were US$2.81 billion, up 29.4% from US$2.17 billion the year before. Operating income was US$589.5 million versus US$513.2 million in the prior-year quarter, an increase of 14.9%. Direct operating expenses rose 45.6% to US$1.56 billion from US$1.07 billion in the comparable period the year before. Indirect operating expenses increased 12.4% to US$662.3 million from US$589.4 million in the equivalent prior-year period.

Prospects: Our evaluation of UGI Corp. as of Jan. 21, 2018 is the result of our systematic analysis on three basic characteristics: earnings strength, relative valuation, and recent stock price movement. The company has managed to produce a neutral trend in earnings per share over the past 5 quarters and while recent estimates for the company have been raised by analysts, UGI has posted better than expected results. Based on operating earnings yield, the company is undervalued when compared to all of the companies in our coverage universe. Share price changes over the past year indicates that UGI will perform well over the near term.

Financial Data

(US$ in Thousands)	6 Mos	3 Mos	09/30/2017	09/30/2016	09/30/2015	09/30/2014	09/30/2013	09/30/2012
Earnings Per Share	3.55	3.22	2.46	2.08	1.60	1.92	1.61	1.17
Cash Flow Per Share	5.52	5.00	5.55	5.58	6.72	5.82	4.69	4.18
Dividends Per Share	1.000	0.988	0.975	0.930	0.890	0.791	0.737	0.707
Dividend Payout %	28.17	30.67	39.63	44.71	55.63	41.19	45.85	60.23
Income Statement								
Total Revenue	4,937,200	2,125,200	6,120,700	5,685,700	6,691,100	8,277,300	7,194,700	6,519,200
EBITDA	1,159,500	482,500	1,276,200	1,277,500	1,148,500	1,307,700	1,130,300	769,800
Depn & Amortn	194,000	95,500	357,300	338,600	313,200	305,700	301,400	264,200
Income Before Taxes	849,200	328,800	697,100	710,200	594,200	767,900	590,800	286,500
Income Taxes	9,000	(104,400)	177,600	221,200	179,000	235,200	162,800	99,600
Net Income	641,900	365,900	436,600	364,700	281,000	337,200	278,100	199,400
Average Shares	176,350	176,948	177,159	175,572	175,667	175,231	173,281	170,148
Balance Sheet								
Current Assets	2,222,100	2,180,600	1,697,500	1,423,800	1,459,800	1,663,000	1,627,300	1,504,500
Total Assets	12,445,300	12,343,900	11,582,200	10,847,200	10,546,600	10,093,000	10,008,800	9,709,700
Current Liabilities	1,817,500	2,216,000	1,690,100	1,442,000	1,678,900	1,430,900	1,424,900	1,487,000
Long-Term Obligations	4,192,800	4,056,400	3,994,600	3,766,000	3,441,800	3,433,600	3,542,200	3,347,600
Total Liabilities	8,671,000	8,842,200	8,418,900	7,996,300	7,854,600	7,433,900	7,516,300	7,476,600
Stockholders' Equity	3,774,300	3,501,700	3,163,300	2,850,900	2,692,000	2,659,100	2,492,500	2,233,100
Shares Outstanding	173,118	173,997	173,143	172,960	172,388	172,273	171,643	168,930
Statistical Record								
Return on Assets %	5.27	4.84	3.89	3.40	2.72	3.35	2.82	2.43
Return on Equity %	18.10	17.62	14.52	13.12	10.50	13.09	11.77	9.45
EBITDA Margin %	23.48	22.70	20.85	22.47	17.16	15.80	15.71	11.81
Net Margin %	13.00	17.22	7.13	6.41	4.20	4.07	3.87	3.06
Asset Turnover	0.60	0.56	0.55	0.53	0.65	0.82	0.73	0.79
Current Ratio	1.22	0.98	1.00	0.99	0.87	1.16	1.14	1.01
Debt to Equity	1.11	1.16	1.26	1.32	1.28	1.29	1.42	1.50
Price Range	51.68-42.53	51.68-45.31	51.68-42.07	48.05-31.67	39.60-31.78	36.33-25.50	28.69-20.33	21.17-16.59
P/E Ratio	14.56-11.98	16.05-14.07	21.01-17.10	23.10-15.23	24.75-19.86	18.92-13.28	17.82-12.63	18.09-14.18
Average Yield %	2.09	2.04	2.04	2.34	2.50	2.61	2.99	3.68

Address: 460 North Gulph Road, King of Prussia, PA 19406
Telephone: 610-337-1000

Web Site: www.ugicorp.com
Officers: Marvin O. Schlanger - Chairman John L. Walsh - President, Chief Executive Officer, Chief Operating Officer

Auditors: Ernst & Young LLP
Investor Contact: 610-337-1000
Transfer Agents: ComputerShare Investor Services, Providence, RI

UNDER ARMOUR INC

Exchange NYS	**Symbol** UAA	**Price** $22.48 (6/29/2018)	**52Wk Range** 24.31-11.61	**Yield** N/A	**P/E** N/A

*7 Year Price Score 54.38 *NYSE Composite Index=100 *12 Month Price Score 122.58

Interim Earnings (Per Share)

Qtr.	Mar	Jun	Sep	Dec
2015	0.03	0.04	0.23	0.23
2016	0.04	(0.12)	0.29	0.24
2017	(0.01)	(0.03)	0.12	(0.31)
2018	(0.07)	...	...	...

Interim Dividends (Per Share)

No Dividends Paid

Valuation Analysis

		Institutional Holding	
Forecast EPS	$0.18	No of Institutions	657
	(06/13/2018)		
Market Cap	$10.0 Billion	Shares	
Book Value	$2.0 Billion		184,883,776
Price/Book	4.95	% Held	
Price/Sales	1.98		135.23

Business Summary: Apparel, Footwear & Accessories (MIC: 1.4.2 SIC: 5136 NAIC: 448110)

Under Armour is engaged in the development, marketing and distribution of apparel, footwear and accessories for men, women and youth. Co.'s apparel is provided in a range of styles and fits. Co. markets its apparel for consumers to choose HEATGEAR® when it is hot, COLDGEAR® when it is cold and ALLSEASONGEAR® between the extremes. Co.'s footwear offerings include frunning, basketball, cleated, slides and performance training, and outdoor footwear. Co.'s accessories primarily include the sale of gloves, bags and headwear. Co. also has agreements with its licensees to develop Under Armour apparel and accessories.

Recent Developments: For the quarter ended Mar 31 2018, net loss amounted to US$30.2 million versus a net loss of US$2.3 million in the year-earlier quarter. Revenues were US$1.19 billion, up 5.9% from US$1.12 billion the year before. Operating loss was US$28.7 million versus an income of US$7.5 million in the prior-year quarter. Direct operating expenses rose 8.2% to US$661.9 million from US$611.9 million in the comparable period the year before. Indirect operating expenses increased 10.3% to US$552.1 million from US$500.4 million in the equivalent prior-year period.

Prospects: Our evaluation of Under Armour Inc. as of Jan. 14, 2018 is the result of our systematic analysis on three basic characteristics: earnings strength, relative valuation, and recent stock price movement. The company has suffered a very negative trend in earnings per share over the past 5 quarters and while recent estimates for the company have been mixed, UAA has posted better than expected results. Based on operating earnings yield, the company is overvalued when compared to all of the companies in our coverage universe. Share price changes over the past year indicates that UAA will perform very poorly over the near term.

Financial Data
(US$ in Thousands)

	3 Mos	12/31/2017	12/31/2016	12/31/2015	12/31/2014	12/31/2013	12/31/2012	12/31/2011
Earnings Per Share	(0.29)	(0.22)	0.45	0.53	0.47	0.38	0.30	0.23
Cash Flow Per Share	0.65	1.07	1.39	(0.10)	0.51	0.28	0.48	0.04
Tang Book Value Per Share	3.17	3.20	3.20	2.33	2.81	2.14	1.94	1.52
Income Statement								
Total Revenue	1,185,370	4,976,553	4,825,335	3,963,313	3,084,370	2,332,051	1,834,921	1,472,684
EBITDA	(25,710)	188,529	545,416	488,413	411,145	312,226	248,422	193,403
Depn & Amortn	63	164,300	130,700	87,100	63,600	48,300	39,800	32,700
Income Before Taxes	(34,337)	(10,309)	388,282	386,685	342,210	260,993	203,439	156,862
Income Taxes	(4,093)	37,951	131,303	154,112	134,168	98,663	74,661	59,943
Net Income	(30,244)	(48,260)	256,979	232,573	208,042	162,330	128,778	96,919
Average Shares	443,052	219,254	221,944	441,736	438,760	431,916	425,520	420,208
Balance Sheet								
Current Assets	2,592,005	2,337,679	1,965,153	1,498,763	1,549,399	1,128,811	903,598	689,663
Total Assets	4,264,319	4,006,367	3,644,331	2,868,900	2,095,083	1,577,741	1,157,083	919,210
Current Liabilities	1,317,057	1,060,375	685,816	478,810	421,627	426,630	252,228	183,607
Long-Term Obligations	758,705	765,046	790,388	627,000	255,250	47,951	52,757	70,842
Total Liabilities	2,246,587	1,987,725	1,613,431	1,200,678	744,783	524,387	340,161	282,778
Stockholders' Equity	2,017,732	2,018,642	2,030,900	1,668,222	1,350,300	1,053,354	816,922	636,432
Shares Outstanding	444,040	442,082	438,438	432,192	427,791	423,257	419,044	413,969
Statistical Record								
Return on Assets %	N.M.	N.M.	7.87	9.37	11.33	11.87	12.37	12.16
Return on Equity %	N.M.	N.M.	13.86	15.41	17.31	17.36	17.67	17.10
EBITDA Margin %	N.M.	3.79	11.30	12.32	13.33	13.39	13.54	13.13
Net Margin %	N.M.	N.M.	5.33	5.87	6.75	6.96	7.02	6.58
Asset Turnover	1.29	1.30	1.48	1.60	1.68	1.71	1.76	1.85
Current Ratio	1.97	2.20	2.87	3.13	3.67	2.65	3.58	3.76
Debt to Equity	0.38	0.38	0.39	0.38	0.19	0.05	0.06	0.11
Price Range	23.14-11.61	30.71-11.61	46.99-29.05	53.78-33.17	37.55-21.18	22.55-11.85	15.51-9.32	11.11-6.82
P/E Ratio	...	...	104.42-64.56	101.46-62.59	79.89-45.06	59.34-31.17	51.68-31.07	48.29-29.64

Address: 1020 Hull Street, Baltimore, MD 21230 **Telephone:** 410-454-6428	**Web Site:** www.underarmour.com **Officers:** Kevin A. Plank - Chairman, President, Chief Executive Officer Patrik Frisk - President, Chief Operating Officer	**Auditors:** PricewaterhouseCoopers LLP **Transfer Agents:** American Stock Transfer & Trust Company, New York, NY

UNION PACIFIC CORP

Exchange	Symbol	Price	52Wk Range	Yield	P/E	Div Acheiver
NYS	UNP	$141.68 (6/29/2018)	147.02-101.40	2.06	10.32	11 Years

*7 Year Price Score 112.63 *NYSE Composite Index=100 *12 Month Price Score 111.10

Interim Earnings (Per Share)

Qtr.	Mar	Jun	Sep	Dec
2015	1.30	1.38	1.50	1.31
2016	1.16	1.17	1.36	1.39
2017	1.32	1.45	1.50	9.10
2018	1.68	...	...	...

Interim Dividends (Per Share)

Amt	Decl	Ex	Rec	Pay
0.605Q	07/27/2017	08/29/2017	08/31/2017	09/29/2017
0.665Q	11/16/2017	11/29/2017	11/30/2017	12/28/2017
0.73Q	02/08/2018	02/27/2018	02/28/2018	03/30/2018
0.73Q	05/10/2018	05/30/2018	05/31/2018	06/29/2018

Indicated Div: $2.92

Valuation Analysis / Institutional Holding

Forecast EPS	$7.66	No of Institutions
	(06/14/2018)	2199
Market Cap	$109.5 Billion	Shares
Book Value	$24.4 Billion	721,418,176
Price/Book	4.49	% Held
Price/Sales	5.07	74.39

TRADING VOLUME (thousand shares)

Business Summary: Rail (MIC: 7.4.3 SIC: 4011 NAIC: 482111)

Union Pacific, through its operating subsidiary, Union Pacific Railroad Company, is a Class I railroad operating in the U.S. As of Dec 31 2017, Co.'s network included 32,122 route miles, linking Pacific Coast and Gulf Coast ports with the Midwest and eastern U.S. gateways and providing several corridors to key Mexican gateways. Co. serves the western two-thirds of the country and maintains coordinated schedules with other rail carriers to move freight to and from the Atlantic Coast, the Pacific Coast, the Southeast, the Southwest, Canada, and Mexico. Co.'s six commodity groups includes agricultural, automotive, chemicals, coal, industrial products and intermodal.

Recent Developments: For the quarter ended Mar 31 2018, net income increased 22.2% to US$1.31 billion from US$1.07 billion in the year-earlier quarter. Revenues were US$5.48 billion, up 6.7% from US$5.13 billion the year before. Operating income was US$1.94 billion versus US$1.79 billion in the prior-year quarter, an increase of 8.4%. Direct operating expenses rose 11.7% to US$1.45 billion from US$1.30 billion in the comparable period the year before. Indirect operating expenses increased 2.0% to US$2.08 billion from US$2.04 billion in the equivalent prior-year period.

Prospects: Our evaluation of Union Pacific Corp. as of Jan. 21, 2018 is the result of our systematic analysis on three basic characteristics: earnings strength, relative valuation, and recent stock price movement. The company has managed to produce a neutral trend in earnings per share over the past 5 quarters and while recent estimates for the company have been raised by analysts, UNP has posted better than expected results. Based on operating earnings yield, the company is about fairly valued when compared to all of the companies in our coverage universe. Share price changes over the past year indicates that UNP will perform poorly over the near term.

Financial Data
(US$ in Thousands)

	3 Mos	12/31/2017	12/31/2016	12/31/2015	12/31/2014	12/31/2013	12/31/2012	12/31/2011
Earnings Per Share	13.73	13.36	5.07	5.49	5.75	4.71	4.13	3.36
Cash Flow Per Share	9.34	9.06	9.02	8.48	8.23	7.36	6.49	6.05
Tang Book Value Per Share	31.57	31.83	24.43	24.38	23.99	23.27	21.17	19.35
Dividends Per Share	2.605	2.480	2.255	2.200	1.910	1.480	1.245	0.965
Dividend Payout %	18.97	18.56	44.48	40.07	33.22	31.42	30.11	28.72
Income Statement								
Total Revenue	5,475,000	21,240,000	19,941,000	21,813,000	23,988,000	21,963,000	20,926,000	19,557,000
EBITDA	2,436,000	10,440,000	9,491,000	10,285,000	10,804,000	9,347,000	8,610,000	7,450,000
Depn & Amortn	543,000	2,105,000	2,038,000	2,012,000	1,904,000	1,777,000	1,760,000	1,617,000
Income Before Taxes	1,711,000	7,632,000	6,766,000	7,656,000	8,343,000	7,048,000	6,318,000	5,264,000
Income Taxes	401,000	(3,080,000)	2,533,000	2,884,000	3,163,000	2,660,000	2,375,000	1,972,000
Net Income	1,310,000	10,712,000	4,233,000	4,772,000	5,180,000	4,388,000	3,943,000	3,292,000
Average Shares	779,600	801,700	835,400	869,400	901,100	931,600	953,000	979,600
Balance Sheet								
Current Assets	3,897,000	4,006,000	3,596,000	4,130,000	4,679,000	3,990,000	3,614,000	3,727,000
Total Assets	57,789,000	57,806,000	55,718,000	54,600,000	52,716,000	49,731,000	47,153,000	45,096,000
Current Liabilities	4,746,000	3,939,000	3,640,000	3,206,000	3,765,000	3,791,000	3,119,000	3,317,000
Long-Term Obligations	15,697,000	16,144,000	14,249,000	13,607,000	11,018,000	8,872,000	8,801,000	8,697,000
Total Liabilities	33,400,000	32,950,000	35,786,000	33,898,000	31,527,000	28,506,000	27,276,000	26,518,000
Stockholders' Equity	24,389,000	24,856,000	19,932,000	20,702,000	21,189,000	21,225,000	19,877,000	18,578,000
Shares Outstanding	772,517	780,917	815,824	849,211	883,366	912,001	938,930	959,859
Statistical Record								
Return on Assets %	19.26	18.87	7.65	8.89	10.11	9.06	8.53	7.47
Return on Equity %	49.65	47.83	20.78	22.78	24.43	21.35	20.45	18.12
EBITDA Margin %	44.49	49.15	47.60	47.15	45.04	42.56	41.14	38.09
Net Margin %	23.93	50.43	21.23	21.88	21.59	19.98	18.84	16.83
Asset Turnover	0.38	0.37	0.36	0.41	0.47	0.45	0.45	0.44
Current Ratio	0.82	1.02	0.99	1.29	1.24	1.05	1.16	1.12
Debt to Equity	0.64	0.65	0.71	0.66	0.52	0.42	0.44	0.47
Price Range	141.97-101.40	136.32-101.40	106.33-68.79	123.83-75.43	123.31-82.58	84.00-62.86	64.22-52.49	53.38-39.91
P/E Ratio	10.34-7.39	10.20-7.59	20.97-13.57	22.56-13.74	21.45-14.36	17.83-13.35	15.55-12.71	15.89-11.88
Average Yield %	2.21	2.24	2.55	2.21	1.89	1.96	2.13	1.99

Address: 1400 Douglas Street, Omaha, NE 68179 Telephone: 402-544-5000	Web Site: www.up.com Officers: Lance M. Fritz - Chairman, President, Chief Executive Officer Robert M. Knight - Executive Vice President, Chief Financial Officer	Auditors: DELOITTE & TOUCHE LLP Investor Contact: 187-754-77261 Transfer Agents: Computershare Investor Services, LLC, Providence, RI

UNITED CONTINENTAL HOLDINGS INC

Exchange	Symbol	Price	52Wk Range	Yield	P/E
NYS	UAL	$69.73 (6/29/2018)	80.53-57.20	N/A	9.58

*7 Year Price Score 115.53 *NYSE Composite Index=100 *12 Month Price Score 103.54

Interim Earnings (Per Share)

Qtr.	Mar	Jun	Sep	Dec
2015	1.32	3.14	12.82	2.32
2016	0.88	1.78	3.01	1.28
2017	0.31	2.66	2.12	1.98
2018	0.52	...	...	...

Interim Dividends (Per Share)

No Dividends Paid

Valuation Analysis — **Institutional Holding**

Forecast EPS	$7.80	No of Institutions
	(06/14/2018)	786
Market Cap	$19.5 Billion	Shares
Book Value	$8.3 Billion	326,239,680
Price/Book	2.34	% Held
Price/Sales	0.51	N/A

Business Summary: Airlines/Air Freight (MIC: 7.4.4 SIC: 4512 NAIC: 481111)

United Continental Holdings is a holding company and its principal, wholly-owned subsidiary is United Airlines, Inc. (United). Co. is engaged in the transportation of people and cargo through its mainline and its regional operations. As of Dec 31 2017, Co., through United and its regional carriers, operated more than 4,500 flights a day to 338 airports across five continents from its hubs. Co. also has contractual relationships with various regional carriers to provide regional jet and turboprop service branded as United Express. Including aircraft operated by United's regional carriers, United's fleet consisted of 1,262 aircraft as of Dec 31 2017.

Recent Developments: For the quarter ended Mar 31 2018, net income increased 48.5% to US$147.0 million from US$99.0 million in the year-earlier quarter. Revenues were US$9.03 billion, up 7.2% from US$8.43 billion the year before. Operating income was US$276.0 million versus US$320.0 million in the prior-year quarter, a decrease of 13.8%. Direct operating expenses rose 13.3% to US$3.71 billion from US$3.27 billion in the comparable period the year before. Indirect operating expenses increased 4.4% to US$5.05 billion from US$4.83 billion in the equivalent prior-year period.

Prospects: Our evaluation of United Continental Holdings Inc. as of Jan. 21, 2018 is the result of our systematic analysis on three basic characteristics: earnings strength, relative valuation, and recent stock price movement. The company has generated a negative trend in earnings per share over the past 5 quarters and while recent estimates for the company have been raised by analysts, UAL has posted better than expected results. Based on operating earnings yield, the company is undervalued when compared to all of the companies in our coverage universe. Share price changes over the past year indicates that UAL will perform very poorly over the near term.

Financial Data
(US$ in Thousands)

	3 Mos	12/31/2017	12/31/2016	12/31/2015	12/31/2014	12/31/2013	12/31/2012	12/31/2011
Earnings Per Share	7.28	7.02	6.85	19.47	2.93	1.53	(2.18)	2.26
Cash Flow Per Share	16.20	11.28	16.75	15.94	7.10	4.15	2.82	7.32
Tang Book Value Per Share	1.05	2.59	1.60	0.84	N.M.	N.M.	N.M.	N.M.
Income Statement								
Total Revenue	9,032,000	37,736,000	36,556,000	37,864,000	38,901,000	38,279,000	37,152,000	37,110,000
EBITDA	865,000	3,618,000	4,427,000	4,907,000	1,870,000	1,324,000	132,000	1,875,000
Depn & Amortn	541,000	117,000	108,000	93,000	81,000	72,000	81,000	133,000
Income Before Taxes	184,000	2,999,000	3,819,000	4,219,000	1,128,000	539,000	(724,000)	845,000
Income Taxes	37,000	868,000	1,556,000	(3,121,000)	(4,000)	(32,000)	(1,000)	5,000
Net Income	147,000	2,131,000	2,263,000	7,340,000	1,132,000	571,000	(723,000)	840,000
Average Shares	284,900	303,600	330,300	377,000	390,000	390,000	331,000	383,000
Balance Sheet								
Current Assets	8,287,000	7,113,000	7,309,000	7,828,000	8,138,000	8,702,000	10,049,000	10,997,000
Total Assets	44,018,000	42,326,000	40,140,000	40,861,000	37,353,000	36,812,000	37,628,000	37,988,000
Current Liabilities	14,183,000	12,676,000	12,286,000	12,414,000	12,508,000	12,107,000	12,818,000	11,394,000
Long-Term Obligations	13,185,000	12,699,000	10,740,000	10,400,000	10,692,000	10,924,000	11,232,000	11,424,000
Total Liabilities	35,682,000	33,520,000	31,481,000	31,895,000	34,957,000	33,828,000	37,147,000	36,182,000
Stockholders' Equity	8,336,000	8,806,000	8,659,000	8,966,000	2,396,000	2,984,000	481,000	1,806,000
Shares Outstanding	279,410	286,973	314,612	364,609	374,525	362,283	332,472	330,906
Statistical Record								
Return on Assets %	5.11	5.17	5.57	18.77	3.05	1.53	N.M.	2.17
Return on Equity %	26.00	24.40	25.61	129.20	42.08	32.96	N.M.	47.55
EBITDA Margin %	9.58	9.59	12.11	12.96	4.81	3.46	0.36	5.05
Net Margin %	1.63	5.65	6.19	19.39	2.91	1.49	N.M.	2.26
Asset Turnover	0.90	0.92	0.90	0.97	1.05	1.03	0.98	0.96
Current Ratio	0.58	0.56	0.59	0.63	0.65	0.72	0.78	0.97
Debt to Equity	1.58	1.44	1.24	1.16	4.46	3.66	23.35	6.33
Price Range	82.03-57.20	82.03-57.20	76.05-37.75	73.62-50.78	66.89-37.73	39.83-23.38	25.17-17.48	27.48-15.53
P/E Ratio	11.27-7.86	11.69-8.15	11.10-5.51	3.78-2.61	22.83-12.88	26.03-15.28	....	12.16-6.87

Address: 233 South Wacker Drive, Chicago, IL 60606 Telephone: 872-825-4000	Web Site: www.unitedcontinentalholdings.com Officers: J. Scott Kirby - President Oscar Munoz - Chief Executive Officer, President, President (frmr-frmr), Chief Executive Officer (frmr)	Auditors: Ernst & Young LLP Investor Contact: 312-997-8610 Transfer Agents: ComputerShare Investor Services, Chicago, IL

UNITED PARCEL SERVICE INC

Exchange	Symbol	Price	52Wk Range	Yield	P/E
NYS	UPS	$106.23 (6/29/2018)	134.09-101.66	3.43	18.16

*7 Year Price Score 95.76   *NYSE Composite Index=100   *12 Month Price Score 97.00

TRADING VOLUME (thousand shares)

Interim Earnings (Per Share)

Qtr.	Mar	Jun	Sep	Dec
2015	1.12	1.35	1.39	1.48
2016	1.27	1.43	1.44	(0.26)
2017	1.32	1.58	1.45	1.27
2018	1.55	...	...	...

Interim Dividends (Per Share)

Amt	Decl	Ex	Rec	Pay
0.83Q	08/03/2017	08/10/2017	08/14/2017	08/30/2017
0.83Q	11/02/2017	11/10/2017	11/13/2017	11/29/2017
0.91Q	02/08/2018	02/16/2018	02/20/2018	03/07/2018
0.91Q	05/10/2018	05/18/2018	05/21/2018	06/06/2018

Indicated Div: $3.64

Valuation Analysis

Forecast EPS	$7.25 (06/13/2018)
Market Cap	$91.6 Billion
Book Value	$1.3 Billion
Price/Book	68.13
Price/Sales	1.35

Institutional Holding

No of Institutions	1969
Shares	588,211,200
% Held	50.50

Business Summary: Airlines/Air Freight (MIC: 7.4.4 SIC: 4215 NAIC: 492110)

United Parcel Service focuses its operations in the field of transportation services, primarily domestic and international letter and package delivery. Co. reports its operations in three segments: U.S. Domestic Package operations, which include the time-definite delivery of letters, documents and packages throughout the U.S.; International Package operations, which include shipments wholly outside the U.S., as well as shipments with either origin or destination outside the U.S.; and Supply Chain & Freight operations, which includes Co.'s Forwarding, Logistics, Coyote, Marken, UPS Mail Innovations, UPS Freight and other aggregated business units.

Recent Developments: For the quarter ended Mar 31 2018, net income increased 15.4% to US$1.35 billion from US$1.17 billion in the year-earlier quarter. Revenues were US$17.11 billion, up 10.3% from US$15.51 billion the year before. Operating income was US$1.52 billion versus US$1.62 billion in the prior-year quarter, a decrease of 6.0%. Direct operating expenses rose 21.7% to US$4.33 billion from US$3.56 billion in the comparable period the year before. Indirect operating expenses increased 9.0% to US$11.26 billion from US$10.34 billion in the equivalent prior-year period.

Prospects: Our evaluation of United Parcel Service Inc. as of Jan. 21, 2018 is the result of our systematic analysis on three basic characteristics: earnings strength, relative valuation, and recent stock price movement. The company has managed to produce a neutral trend in earnings per share over the past 5 quarters. However, while recent estimates for the company have been mixed, UPS has posted better than expected results. Based on operating earnings yield, the company is undervalued when compared to all of the companies in our coverage universe. Share price changes over the past year indicates that UPS will perform poorly over the near term.

Financial Data
(US$ in Millions)

	3 Mos	12/31/2017	12/31/2016	12/31/2015	12/31/2014	12/31/2013	12/31/2012	12/31/2011
Earnings Per Share	5.85	5.61	3.87	5.35	3.28	4.61	0.83	3.84
Cash Flow Per Share	6.13	1.70	7.31	8.25	6.25	7.77	7.50	7.21
Tang Book Value Per Share	N.M.	N.M.	N.M.	N.M.	N.M.	3.80	1.97	4.52
Dividends Per Share	3.400	3.320	3.120	2.920	2.680	2.480	2.280	2.080
Dividend Payout %	58.12	59.18	80.62	54.58	81.71	53.80	274.70	54.17
Income Statement								
Total Revenue	17,113	65,872	60,906	58,363	58,232	55,438	54,127	53,105
EBITDA	2,410	9,883	7,741	9,767	6,913	8,921	3,225	7,906
Depn & Amortn	596	2,282	2,224	2,084	1,923	1,867	1,858	1,782
Income Before Taxes	1,661	7,148	5,136	7,342	4,637	6,674	974	5,776
Income Taxes	316	2,238	1,705	2,498	1,605	2,302	167	1,972
Net Income	1,345	4,910	3,431	4,844	3,032	4,372	807	3,804
Average Shares	870	875	887	906	924	948	969	991
Balance Sheet								
Current Assets	13,620	15,548	13,849	13,208	11,808	13,387	15,591	12,284
Total Assets	44,464	45,403	40,377	38,311	35,471	36,212	38,863	34,701
Current Liabilities	11,149	12,708	11,730	10,696	8,639	7,131	8,390	6,514
Long-Term Obligations	20,409	20,278	12,394	11,316	9,864	10,824	11,089	11,095
Total Liabilities	43,120	44,403	39,972	35,841	33,330	29,738	34,210	27,666
Stockholders' Equity	1,344	1,000	405	2,470	2,141	6,474	4,653	7,035
Shares Outstanding	862	859	868	886	905	923	953	963
Statistical Record								
Return on Assets %	12.31	11.45	8.70	13.13	8.46	11.65	2.19	11.14
Return on Equity %	542.52	698.93	238.03	210.11	70.39	78.58	13.77	50.67
EBITDA Margin %	14.08	15.00	12.71	16.73	11.87	16.09	5.96	14.89
Net Margin %	7.86	7.45	5.63	8.30	5.21	7.89	1.49	7.16
Asset Turnover	1.63	1.54	1.54	1.58	1.62	1.48	1.47	1.56
Current Ratio	1.22	1.22	1.18	1.23	1.37	1.88	1.86	1.89
Debt to Equity	15.19	20.28	30.60	4.58	4.61	1.67	2.38	1.58
Price Range	134.09-101.66	123.72-102.87	120.16-88.70	114.25-94.46	112.45-93.62	105.08-73.73	81.11-70.02	76.47-61.70
P/E Ratio	22.92-17.38	22.05-18.34	31.05-22.92	21.36-17.66	34.28-28.54	22.79-15.99	97.72-84.36	19.91-16.07
Average Yield %	3.00	2.97	2.95	2.90	2.66	2.80	3.01	2.94

| **Address:** 55 Glenlake Parkway N.E., Atlanta, GA 30328
Telephone: 404-828-6000 | **Web Site:** www.ups.com
Officers: David P. Abney - Chairman, Chief Executive Officer, Senior Vice President, Chief Operating Officer Richard N. Peretz - Chief Financial Officer, Senior Vice President, Treasurer | **Auditors:** DELOITTE & TOUCHE LLP
Investor Contact: 404-828-6059
Transfer Agents: Computershare Shareowner Services, Pittsburgh, PA |

UNITED RENTALS INC

Exchange	Symbol	Price	52Wk Range	Yield	P/E
NYS	URI	$147.62 (6/29/2018)	189.40-107.26	N/A	8.89

*7 Year Price Score 150.49 ***NYSE Composite Index=100** ***12 Month Price Score 103.26**

TRADING VOLUME (thousand shares)

Interim Earnings (Per Share)

Qtr.	Mar	Jun	Sep	Dec
2015	1.16	0.88	2.25	1.80
2016	1.01	1.52	2.16	1.79
2017	1.27	1.65	2.33	10.47
2018	2.15	...	...	...

Interim Dividends (Per Share)

No Dividends Paid

Valuation Analysis — Institutional Holding

Forecast EPS	$15.21	No of Institutions
	(06/14/2018)	921
Market Cap	$12.4 Billion	Shares
Book Value	$3.1 Billion	101,166,968
Price/Book	4.05	% Held
Price/Sales	1.76	98.38

Business Summary: Construction Services (MIC: 7.5.4 SIC: 7359 NAIC: 532412)

United Rentals is an equipment rental company and operates throughout the U.S. and Canada. The types of equipment that Co. provides include general construction and industrial equipment, aerial work platforms, trench safety equipment, power and heating, ventilating and air conditioning equipment; pumps; and general tools and light equipment. Co.'s segments are: general rentals, which includes the rental of construction, aerial and industrial equipment, general tools and light equipment, and related services and activities; and trench, power and pump, which includes the rental of specialty construction products and related services.

Recent Developments: For the quarter ended Mar 31 2018, net income increased 67.9% to US$183.0 million from US$109.0 million in the year-earlier quarter. Revenues were US$1.73 billion, up 27.9% from US$1.36 billion the year before. Operating income was US$340.0 million versus US$257.0 million in the prior-year quarter, an increase of 32.3%. Direct operating expenses rose 29.2% to US$1.09 billion from US$842.0 million in the comparable period the year before. Indirect operating expenses increased 19.1% to US$306.0 million from US$257.0 million in the equivalent prior-year period.

Prospects: Our evaluation of United Rentals Inc. as of Jan. 21, 2018 is the result of our systematic analysis on three basic characteristics: earnings strength, relative valuation, and recent stock price movement. The company has produced a positive trend in earnings per share over the past 5 quarters and while recent estimates for the company have been raised by analysts, URI has posted better than expected results. Based on operating earnings yield, the company is undervalued when compared to all of the companies in our coverage universe. Share price changes over the past year indicates that URI will perform in line with the market over the near term.

Financial Data
(US$ in Thousands)

	3 Mos	12/31/2017	12/31/2016	12/31/2015	12/31/2014	12/31/2013	12/31/2012	12/31/2011
Earnings Per Share	16.60	15.73	6.45	6.07	5.15	3.64	0.79	1.38
Cash Flow Per Share	26.69	26.36	22.33	20.96	18.47	16.60	8.67	9.78
Income Statement								
Total Revenue	1,734,000	6,641,000	5,762,000	5,817,000	5,685,000	4,955,000	4,117,000	2,611,000
EBITDA	666,000	2,636,000	2,410,000	2,506,000	2,326,000	1,935,000	1,303,000	822,000
Depn & Amortn	325,000	1,124,000	990,000	976,000	921,000	852,000	699,000	423,000
Income Before Taxes	232,000	1,048,000	909,000	963,000	850,000	605,000	88,000	164,000
Income Taxes	49,000	(298,000)	343,000	378,000	310,000	218,000	13,000	63,000
Net Income	183,000	1,346,000	566,000	585,000	540,000	387,000	75,000	101,000
Average Shares	85,238	85,562	87,775	96,379	104,956	106,291	94,848	73,349
Balance Sheet								
Current Assets	1,590,000	1,772,000	1,361,000	1,294,000	1,546,000	1,362,000	1,343,000	723,000
Total Assets	14,688,000	15,030,000	11,988,000	12,083,000	12,467,000	11,231,000	11,026,000	4,143,000
Current Liabilities	1,641,000	1,668,000	1,184,000	1,233,000	1,478,000	1,286,000	1,351,000	864,000
Long-Term Obligations	8,412,000	8,717,000	7,193,000	7,555,000	7,434,000	6,569,000	6,734,000	2,647,000
Total Liabilities	11,630,000	11,924,000	10,340,000	10,607,000	10,669,000	9,383,000	9,452,000	4,040,000
Stockholders' Equity	3,058,000	3,106,000	1,648,000	1,476,000	1,798,000	1,848,000	1,574,000	103,000
Shares Outstanding	83,919	84,463	84,222	91,776	97,877	93,288	92,984	62,877
Statistical Record								
Return on Assets %	10.71	9.96	4.69	4.77	4.56	3.48	0.99	2.58
Return on Equity %	59.03	56.63	36.14	35.74	29.62	22.62	8.92	243.37
EBITDA Margin %	38.41	39.69	41.83	43.08	40.91	39.05	31.65	31.48
Net Margin %	10.55	20.27	9.82	10.06	9.50	7.81	1.82	3.87
Asset Turnover	0.53	0.49	0.48	0.47	0.48	0.45	0.54	0.67
Current Ratio	0.97	1.06	1.15	1.05	1.05	1.06	0.99	0.84
Debt to Equity	2.75	2.81	4.36	5.12	4.13	3.55	4.28	25.70
Price Range	189.40-101.62	173.33-101.62	109.12-43.34	105.13-59.48	119.02-74.46	77.95-45.52	46.82-27.23	34.09-13.11
P/E Ratio	11.41-6.12	11.02-6.46	16.92-6.72	17.32-9.80	23.11-14.46	21.41-12.51	59.27-34.47	24.70-9.50

Address: 100 First Stamford Place, Suite 700, Stamford, CT 06902 **Telephone:** 203-622-3131	**Web Site:** www.unitedrentals.com **Officers:** Jenne K. Britell - Chairman Matthew J. (Matt) Flannery - President, Chief Operating Officer, Executive Vice President, Senior Vice President	**Auditors:** Ernst & Young LLP **Investor Contact:** 203-618-7318 **Transfer Agents:** American Stock Transfer & Trust Company, New York, NY

UNITED STATES STEEL CORP.

Exchange	Symbol	Price	52Wk Range	Yield	P/E
NYS.	X	$34.75 (6/29/2018)	46.01-21.45	0.58	10.50

*7 Year Price Score 103.73 ***NYSE Composite Index=100** ***12 Month Price Score 108.89**

Interim Earnings (Per Share)

Qtr.	Mar	Jun	Sep	Dec
2015	(0.52)	(1.79)	(1.18)	(7.75)
2016	(2.32)	(0.32)	0.32	(0.59)
2017	(1.03)	1.48	0.83	0.90
2018	0.10			

Interim Dividends (Per Share)

Amt	Decl	Ex	Rec	Pay
0.05Q	07/25/2017	08/07/2017	08/09/2017	09/08/2017
0.05Q	10/31/2017	11/09/2017	11/10/2017	12/08/2017
0.05Q	01/31/2018	02/08/2018	02/09/2018	03/08/2018
0.05Q	04/26/2018	05/09/2018	05/10/2018	06/08/2018

Indicated Div: $0.20

Valuation Analysis | **Institutional Holding**

Forecast EPS	$5.43	No of Institutions	
	(06/13/2018)	684	
Market Cap	$6.1 Billion	Shares	
Book Value	$3.4 Billion	154,719,200	
Price/Book	1.79	% Held	
Price/Sales	0.48	77.12	

Business Summary: Non-Precious Metals (MIC: 8.2.2 SIC: 3312 NAIC: 331111)

United States Steel is a steel producer of flat-rolled and tubular products with major production operations in North America and Europe. Co. has three reportable operating segments: Flat-Rolled Products, which includes the production of slabs, strip mill plates, sheets and tin mill products, as well as all iron ore and coke production facilities; U. S. Steel Europe, which produces and sells slabs, sheet, strip mill plate, tin mill products and spiral welded pipe; and Tubular Products, which produces and sells seamless and electric resistance welded (welded) steel casing and tubing, standard and line pipe and mechanical tubing and serve customers in the oil, gas and petrochemical markets.

Recent Developments: For the quarter ended Mar 31 2018, net income amounted to US$18.0 million versus a net loss of US$180.0 million in the year-earlier quarter. Revenues were US$3.15 billion, up 15.6% from US$2.73 billion the year before. Operating income was US$137.0 million versus a loss of US$80.0 million in the prior-year quarter. Direct operating expenses rose 9.7% to US$2.81 billion from US$2.56 billion in the comparable period the year before. Indirect operating expenses decreased 17.1% to US$204.0 million from US$246.0 million in the equivalent prior-year period.

Prospects: Our evaluation of United States Steel Corp. as of Jan. 21, 2018 is the result of our systematic analysis on three basic characteristics: earnings strength, relative valuation, and recent stock price movement. The company has suffered a very negative trend in earnings per share over the past 5 quarters and while recent estimates for the company have been raised by analysts, X has posted better than expected results. Based on operating earnings yield, the company is undervalued when compared to all of the companies in our coverage universe. Share price changes over the past year indicates that X will perform very poorly over the near term.

Financial Data

(US$ in Millions)	3 Mos	12/31/2017	12/31/2016	12/31/2015	12/31/2014	12/31/2013	12/31/2012	12/31/2011
Earnings Per Share	3.31	2.19	(2.81)	(11.24)	0.69	(11.56)	(0.86)	(0.37)
Cash Flow Per Share	4.76	4.59	4.63	2.46	10.28	2.86	7.85	1.17
Tang Book Value Per Share	18.52	17.99	12.08	15.31	24.68	21.24	9.72	10.10
Dividends Per Share	0.200	0.200	0.200	0.200	0.200	0.200	0.200	0.200
Dividend Payout %	6.04	9.13	...	...	28.99	...	...	...
Income Statement								
Total Revenue	3,149	12,250	10,261	11,574	17,507	17,424	19,328	19,884
EBITDA	199	967	218	(739)	877	(1,325)	730	807
Depn & Amortn	128	501	507	547	627	684	661	681
Income Before Taxes	16	257	(514)	(1,497)	28	(2,272)	(138)	(58)
Income Taxes	1	(86)	24	183	68	(560)	131	80
Net Income	18	387	(440)	(1,642)	102	(1,672)	(124)	(53)
Average Shares	178	176	156	146	152	144	144	143
Balance Sheet								
Current Assets	4,830	4,755	4,356	3,917	6,431	6,078	5,374	5,774
Total Assets	10,026	9,862	9,160	9,190	12,314	13,143	15,217	16,073
Current Liabilities	2,959	2,721	2,331	2,148	3,569	3,245	2,990	3,649
Long-Term Obligations	2,571	2,700	2,981	3,116	3,120	3,616	3,936	3,828
Total Liabilities	6,588	6,542	6,886	6,754	8,515	9,795	11,740	12,573
Stockholders' Equity	3,438	3,320	2,274	2,436	3,799	3,348	3,477	3,500
Shares Outstanding	176	175	173	146	145	144	144	144
Statistical Record								
Return on Assets %	6.09	4.07	N.M.	N.M.	0.80	N.M.	N.M.	N.M.
Return on Equity %	20.85	13.84	N.M.	N.M.	2.85	N.M.	N.M.	N.M.
EBITDA Margin %	6.32	7.89	2.12	N.M.	5.01	N.M.	3.78	4.06
Net Margin %	0.57	3.16	N.M.	N.M.	0.58	N.M.	N.M.	N.M.
Asset Turnover	1.32	1.29	1.12	1.08	1.38	1.23	1.23	1.27
Current Ratio	1.63	1.75	1.87	1.82	1.80	1.87	1.80	1.58
Debt to Equity	0.75	0.81	1.31	1.28	0.82	1.08	1.13	1.09
Price Range	46.01-19.17	41.57-19.17	37.49-6.67	27.33-7.09	46.00-22.73	30.09-16.18	32.25-17.89	63.64-20.19
P/E Ratio	13.90-5.79	18.98-8.75	...	...	66.67-32.94	...	...	...
Average Yield %	0.69	0.71	1.08	1.07	0.66	0.95	0.85	0.50

Address: 600 Grant Street, Pittsburgh, PA 15219-2800 **Telephone:** 412-433-1121 **Fax:** 412-433-4818	**Web Site:** www.ussteel.com **Officers:** David B. Burritt - President, Chief Executive Officer, Chief Operating Officer, Chief Financial Officer, Executive Vice President Kevin P. Bradley - Executive Vice President, Chief Financial Officer	**Auditors:** PricewaterhouseCoopers LLP **Investor Contact:** 412-433-1121 **Transfer Agents:** Wells Fargo Bank Shareowner Services, St. Paul, MN

UNITEDHEALTH GROUP INC

Exchange	Symbol	Price	52Wk Range	Yield	P/E
NYS	UNH	$245.34 (6/29/2018)	255.98-185.42	1.47	21.60

*7 Year Price Score 157.09 *NYSE Composite Index=100 *12 Month Price Score 110.32

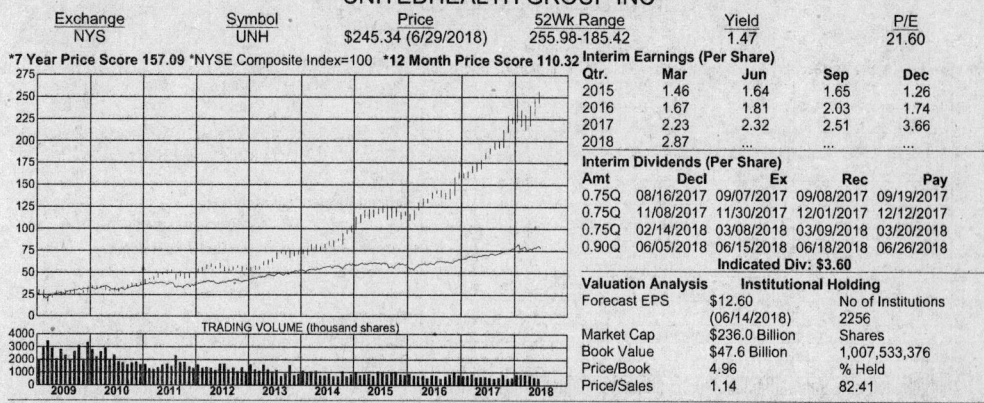

Interim Earnings (Per Share)

Qtr.	Mar	Jun	Sep	Dec
2015	1.46	1.64	1.65	1.26
2016	1.67	1.81	2.03	1.74
2017	2.23	2.32	2.51	3.66
2018	2.87	...	...	...

Interim Dividends (Per Share)

Amt	Decl	Ex	Rec	Pay
0.75Q	08/16/2017	09/07/2017	09/08/2017	09/19/2017
0.75Q	11/08/2017	11/30/2017	12/01/2017	12/12/2017
0.75Q	02/14/2018	03/08/2018	03/09/2018	03/20/2018
0.90Q	06/05/2018	06/15/2018	06/18/2018	06/26/2018

Indicated Div: $3.60

Valuation Analysis

		Institutional Holding	
Forecast EPS	$12.60	No of Institutions	
	(06/14/2018)	2256	
Market Cap	$236.0 Billion	Shares	
Book Value	$47.6 Billion	1,007,533,376	
Price/Book	4.96	% Held	
Price/Sales	1.14	82.41	

Business Summary: Life & Health (MIC: 5.2.2 SIC: 6324 NAIC: 524114)

UnitedHealth Group is a health and well-being company. Co. has four reportable segments across its two business platforms, UnitedHealthcare and Optum: UnitedHealthcare, which provides health care benefits to an array of customers and markets through its UnitedHealthcare Employer & Individual, UnitedHealthcare Medicare & Retirement, UnitedHealthcare Community & State and UnitedHealthcare Global; OptumHealth, which serves the physical, emotional and health-related financial needs of individuals; OptumInsight, which provides services, technology and health care expertise to main participants in the health care industry; and OptumRx, which provides pharmacy care services and programs.

Recent Developments: For the quarter ended Mar 31 2018, net income increased 33.5% to US$2.92 billion from US$2.19 billion in the year-earlier quarter. Revenues were US$55.19 billion, up 13.3% from US$48.72 billion the year before. Net premiums earned were US$44.08 billion versus US$38.94 billion in the prior-year quarter, an increase of 13.2%.

Prospects: Our evaluation of UnitedHealth Group Inc. as of Jan. 21, 2018 is the result of our systematic analysis on three basic characteristics: earnings strength, relative valuation, and recent stock price movement. The company has managed to produce a neutral trend in earnings per share over the past 5 quarters and while recent estimates for the company have been raised by analysts, UNH has posted better than expected results. Based on operating earnings yield, the company is about fairly valued when compared to all of the companies in our coverage universe. Share price changes over the past year indicates that UNH will perform in line with the market over the near term.

Financial Data
(US$ in Thousands)

	3 Mos	12/31/2017	12/31/2016	12/31/2015	12/31/2014	12/31/2013	12/31/2012	12/31/2011
Earnings Per Share	11.36	10.72	7.25	6.01	5.70	5.50	5.28	4.73
Cash Flow Per Share	16.05	14.10	10.26	10.22	8.28	6.95	6.95	6.51
Tang Book Value Per Share	N.M.	N.M.	N.M.	N.M.	N.M.	N.M.	N.M.	1.46
Dividends Per Share	3.000	2.875	2.375	1.875	1.405	1.053	0.800	0.613
Dividend Payout %	26.41	26.82	32.76	31.20	24.65	19.14	15.15	12.95
Income Statement								
Total Revenue	55,188,000	201,159,000	184,840,000	157,107,000	130,474,000	122,489,000	110,618,000	101,862,000
Income Before Taxes	3,724,000	14,023,000	11,863,000	10,231,000	9,656,000	8,915,000	8,622,000	7,959,000
Income Taxes	800,000	3,200,000	4,790,000	4,363,000	4,037,000	3,242,000	3,096,000	2,817,000
Net Income	2,836,000	10,558,000	7,017,000	5,813,000	5,619,000	5,625,000	5,526,000	5,142,000
Average Shares	987,000	985,000	968,000	967,000	986,000	1,023,000	1,046,000	1,087,000
Balance Sheet								
Total Assets	155,569,000	139,058,000	122,810,000	111,383,000	86,382,000	81,882,000	80,885,000	67,889,000
Total Liabilities	108,016,000	91,282,000	84,536,000	77,553,000	53,928,000	49,733,000	49,707,000	39,597,000
Stockholders' Equity	47,553,000	47,776,000	38,274,000	33,830,000	32,454,000	32,149,000	31,178,000	28,292,000
Shares Outstanding	962,000	969,000	952,000	953,000	954,000	988,000	1,019,000	1,039,000
Statistical Record								
Return on Assets %	7.67	8.06	5.98	5.88	6.68	6.91	7.41	7.85
Return on Equity %	25.09	24.54	19.41	17.54	17.40	17.76	18.53	19.00
Net Margin %	5.14	5.25	3.80	3.70	4.31	4.59	5.00	5.05
Price Range	248.47-164.01	228.17-157.62	163.94-109.23	125.86-98.92	103.04-69.74	75.30-51.40	60.26-50.35	53.13-36.11
P/E Ratio	21.87-14.44	21.28-14.70	22.61-15.07	20.94-16.46	18.08-12.24	13.69-9.35	11.41-9.54	11.23-7.63
Average Yield %	1.49	1.54	1.75	1.61	1.68	1.61	1.45	1.32

Address: UnitedHealth Group Center, 9900 Bren Road East, Minnetonka, MN 55343
Telephone: 952-936-1300

Web Site: www.unitedhealthgroup.com
Officers: Stephen J. Hemsley - Executive Chairman, President, Chief Executive Officer, Chief Operating Officer, Senior Executive Vice President David S. Wichmann - President, Chief Executive Officer, Chief Financial Officer, Executive Vice President, Division Officer

Auditors: DELOITTE & TOUCHE LLP
Investor Contact: 800-328-5979
Transfer Agents: Wells Fargo Shareowner Services, St. Paul, MN

UNITED STATES CELLULAR CORP

Exchange	Symbol	Price	52Wk Range	Yield	P/E
NYS	USM	$37.04 (6/29/2018)	41.49-32.76	N/A	102.89

*7 Year Price Score 76.48   *NYSE Composite Index=100   *12 Month Price Score 96.30

Interim Earnings (Per Share)

Qtr.	Mar	Jun	Sep	Dec
2015	1.89	0.23	0.75	(0.02)
2016	0.10	0.32	0.20	(0.07)
2017	0.31	0.14	(3.51)	3.21
2018	0.52	...	...	...

Interim Dividends (Per Share)

Dividend Payment Suspended

Valuation Analysis   Institutional Holding

Forecast EPS	$0.69	No of Institutions
	(06/13/2018)	175
Market Cap	$3.1 Billion	Shares
Book Value	$3.9 Billion	15,143,340
Price/Book	0.81	% Held
Price/Sales	0.81	14.61

TRADING VOLUME (thousand shares)

Business Summary: Services (MIC: 6.1.2 SIC: 4812 NAIC: 517212)

United States Cellular provides wireless telecommunications services. Co.'s postpaid customers are able to choose from a variety of national plans with voice, messaging and data usage options and pricing. Co. provides Shared Connect data plans which allow customers to share data usage among all users and devices connected to the plan. Co. also provides monthly prepaid service plans, which provide customers unlimited voice and unlimited messaging with a specified amount of high-speed data and unlimited data at lower speeds once the high-speed data limit is reached. Co. provides a range of wireless devices such as handsets, modems, mobile hotspots, home phone and tablets.

Recent Developments: For the quarter ended Mar 31 2018, net income increased 96.4% to US$55.0 million from US$28.0 million in the year-earlier quarter. Revenues were US$942.0 million, up 0.6% from US$936.0 million the year before. Operating income was US$65.0 million versus US$54.0 million in the prior-year quarter, an increase of 20.4%. Direct operating expenses declined 1.2% to US$398.0 million from US$403.0 million in the comparable period the year before. Indirect operating expenses were unchanged at US$479.0 million versus the equivalent prior-year period.

Prospects: Our evaluation of United States Cellular Corp. as of Jan. 21, 2018 is the result of our systematic analysis on three basic characteristics: earnings strength, relative valuation, and recent stock price movement. The company has managed to produce a neutral trend in earnings per share over the past 5 quarters. Because the company lacks sufficient analyst estimate data, we place greater weight on the historical EPS trend as the measure of earnings strength. Based on operating earnings yield, the company is overvalued when compared to all of the companies in our coverage universe. Share price changes over the past year indicates that USM will perform poorly over the near term.

Financial Data

(US$ in Thousands)	3 Mos	12/31/2017	12/31/2016	12/31/2015	12/31/2014	12/31/2013	12/31/2012	12/31/2011
Earnings Per Share	0.36	0.14	0.56	2.84	(0.51)	1.65	1.31	2.05
Cash Flow Per Share	7.01	5.52	5.88	6.59	2.05	3.46	10.60	11.64
Tang Book Value Per Share	19.72	17.11	16.21	16.08	17.70	19.03	22.04	19.56
Dividends Per Share	...	...	...	...	...	5.750	...	...
Dividend Payout %	...	...	...	...	...	348.48	...	...
Income Statement								
Total Revenue	942,000	3,890,000	3,939,000	3,996,853	3,892,747	3,918,836	4,452,084	4,343,346
EBITDA	223,000	300,000	605,000	908,908	449,970	956,809	751,138	856,575
Depn & Amortn	159,000	604,000	607,000	595,500	593,200	791,100	597,700	565,100
Income Before Taxes	39,000	(409,000)	(58,000)	263,546	(188,468)	125,707	114,689	229,256
Income Taxes	22,000	(287,000)	33,000	156,334	(11,782)	113,134	63,977	114,078
Net Income	45,000	12,000	48,000	241,347	(42,812)	140,038	111,006	175,041
Average Shares	86,000	86,000	85,000	84,891	84,213	84,730	85,067	85,335
Balance Sheet								
Current Assets	1,591,000	1,483,000	1,558,000	1,671,642	1,279,175	1,401,191	1,196,476	1,292,843
Total Assets	7,048,000	6,841,000	7,110,000	7,059,978	6,487,268	6,445,708	6,587,450	6,327,976
Current Liabilities	616,000	733,000	718,000	747,938	856,894	1,006,173	754,999	722,280
Long-Term Obligations	1,618,000	1,622,000	1,618,000	1,628,507	1,151,819	878,032	878,858	880,320
Total Liabilities	3,141,000	3,164,000	3,476,000	3,499,465	3,185,277	3,054,502	2,853,595	2,708,015
Stockholders' Equity	3,907,000	3,677,000	3,634,000	3,560,513	3,301,991	3,391,206	3,733,855	3,619,961
Shares Outstanding	85,000	85,000	85,000	84,359	84,080	84,205	84,168	84,557
Statistical Record								
Return on Assets %	0.44	0.17	0.68	3.56	N.M.	2.15	1.71	2.86
Return on Equity %	0.82	0.33	1.33	7.03	N.M.	3.93	3.01	4.93
EBITDA Margin %	23.67	7.71	15.36	22.74	11.56	24.42	16.87	19.72
Net Margin %	4.78	0.31	1.22	6.04	N.M.	3.57	2.49	4.03
Asset Turnover	0.55	0.56	0.55	0.59	0.60	0.60	0.69	0.71
Current Ratio	2.58	2.02	2.17	2.24	1.49	1.39	1.58	1.79
Debt to Equity	0.41	0.44	0.45	0.46	0.35	0.26	0.24	0.24
Price Range	40.91-32.76	45.67-32.95	45.87-33.97	43.36-34.42	44.45-31.93	48.80-32.62	47.61-33.76	51.99-36.07
P/E Ratio	113.64-91.00	326.21-235.36	81.91-60.66	15.27-12.12	...	29.58-19.77	36.34-25.77	25.36-17.60
Average Yield %	...	...	...	...	...	14.35	...	...

Address: 8410 West Bryn Mawr, Chicago, IL 60631 **Telephone:** 773-399-8900	**Web Site:** www.uscellular.com **Officers:** LeRoy T. Carlson - Chairman Kenneth R. Meyers - President, Chief Executive Officer, Vice President, Assistant Treasurer	**Auditors:** PricewaterhouseCoopers LLP **Investor Contact:** 312-592-5341 **Transfer Agents:** Computershare Trust Company, N.A., Louisville, KY

US BANCORP (DE)

Exchange	Symbol	Price	52Wk Range	Yield	P/E
NYS	USB	$50.02 (6/29/2018)	58.11-48.86	2.40	13.70

*7 Year Price Score 103.54 *NYSE Composite Index=100   *12 Month Price Score 94.51

Interim Earnings (Per Share)

Qtr.	Mar	Jun	Sep	Dec
2015	0.76	0.80	0.81	0.80
2016	0.76	0.83	0.84	0.81
2017	0.82	0.85	0.88	0.96
2018	0.96	...	...	...

Interim Dividends (Per Share)

Amt	Decl	Ex	Rec	Pay
0.30Q	09/19/2017	09/28/2017	09/29/2017	10/16/2017
0.30Q	12/19/2017	12/28/2017	12/29/2017	01/16/2018
0.30Q	03/19/2018	03/28/2018	03/29/2018	04/16/2018
0.30Q	06/19/2018	06/28/2018	06/29/2018	07/16/2018

Indicated Div: $1.20

Valuation Analysis / Institutional Holding

Valuation Analysis		Institutional Holding	
Forecast EPS	$4.05	No of Institutions	
	(06/13/2018)	2002	
Market Cap	$82.5 Billion	Shares	
Book Value	$49.2 Billion	1,479,725,568	
Price/Book	1.68	% Held	
Price/Sales	3.39	68.38	

TRADING VOLUME (thousand shares)

Business Summary: Banking (MIC: 5.1.1 SIC: 6021 NAIC: 522110)

U.S. Bancorp is a multi-state financial services holding company. Co. provides a range of financial services, including lending and depository services, cash management, capital markets, and trust and investment management services. Co. also engages in credit card services, merchant and automatic teller machine (ATM) processing, mortgage banking, insurance, brokerage and leasing. Banking and investment services are provided through a network of 3,067 banking offices principally operating in the Midwest and West regions of the U.S. At Dec 31 2017, Co. had total assets of $462.04 billion and deposits of $347.22 billion.

Recent Developments: For the quarter ended Mar 31 2018, net income increased 13.2% to US$1.68 billion from US$1.49 billion in the year-earlier quarter. Net interest income increased 6.3% to US$3.17 billion from US$2.98 billion in the year-earlier quarter. Provision for loan losses was US$341.0 million versus US$345.0 million in the prior-year quarter, a decrease of 1.2%. Non-interest income rose 0.6% to US$2.27 billion from US$2.26 billion, while non-interest expense advanced 5.0% to US$3.06 billion.

Prospects: Our evaluation of U.S. Bancorp as of Jan. 21, 2018 is the result of our systematic analysis on three basic characteristics: earnings strength, relative valuation, and recent stock price movement. The company has enjoyed a very positive trend in earnings per share over the past 5 quarters and while recent estimates for the company have been raised by analysts, USB has posted better than expected results. Based on operating earnings yield, the company is undervalued when compared to all of the companies in our coverage universe. Share price changes over the past year indicates that USB will perform in line with the market over the near term.

Financial Data

(US$ in Thousands)	3 Mos	12/31/2017	12/31/2016	12/31/2015	12/31/2014	12/31/2013	12/31/2012	12/31/2011
Earnings Per Share	3.65	3.51	3.24	3.16	3.08	3.00	2.84	2.46
Cash Flow Per Share	2.85	3.86	3.10	4.98	2.96	6.22	4.21	5.13
Tang Book Value Per Share	18.76	18.70	17.18	16.00	14.66	12.95	11.97	10.32
Dividends Per Share	1.180	1.160	1.070	1.010	0.965	0.885	0.780	0.500
Dividend Payout %	32.33	33.05	33.02	31.96	31.33	29.50	27.46	20.33
Income Statement								
Interest Income	3,791,000	14,385,000	13,167,000	12,402,000	12,228,000	12,285,000	12,883,000	12,639,000
Interest Expense	623,000	2,144,000	1,639,000	1,401,000	1,453,000	1,681,000	2,138,000	2,516,000
Net Interest Income	3,168,000	12,241,000	11,528,000	11,001,000	10,775,000	10,604,000	10,745,000	10,123,000
Provision for Losses	341,000	1,390,000	1,324,000	1,132,000	1,229,000	1,340,000	1,882,000	2,343,000
Non-Interest Income	2,272,000	9,611,000	9,577,000	9,092,000	9,164,000	8,774,000	9,319,000	8,760,000
Non-Interest Expense	3,055,000	12,945,000	11,676,000	10,931,000	10,715,000	10,274,000	10,456,000	9,911,000
Income Before Taxes	2,044,000	7,517,000	8,105,000	8,030,000	7,995,000	7,764,000	7,726,000	6,629,000
Income Taxes	362,000	1,264,000	2,161,000	2,097,000	2,087,000	2,032,000	2,236,000	1,841,000
Net Income	1,675,000	6,218,000	5,888,000	5,879,000	5,851,000	5,836,000	5,647,000	4,872,000
Average Shares	1,657,000	1,683,000	1,724,000	1,772,000	1,813,000	1,849,000	1,896,000	1,923,000
Balance Sheet								
Net Loans & Leases	278,770,000	280,061,000	274,220,000	260,170,000	248,604,000	234,253,000	226,881,000	212,238,000
Total Assets	460,119,000	462,040,000	445,964,000	421,853,000	402,529,000	364,021,000	353,855,000	340,122,000
Total Deposits	344,526,000	347,215,000	334,590,000	300,400,000	282,733,000	262,123,000	249,183,000	230,885,000
Total Liabilities	410,932,000	413,000,000	398,666,000	375,722,000	359,050,000	322,908,000	314,857,000	306,144,000
Stockholders' Equity	49,187,000	49,040,000	47,298,000	46,131,000	43,479,000	41,113,000	38,998,000	33,978,000
Shares Outstanding	1,648,977	1,655,645	1,696,912	1,745,190	1,785,866	1,824,748	1,869,431	1,909,821
Statistical Record								
Return on Assets %	1.41	1.37	1.35	1.43	1.53	1.63	1.62	1.50
Return on Equity %	13.24	12.91	12.57	13.12	13.83	14.57	15.43	15.35
Net Interest Margin %	83.57	85.10	87.55	88.70	88.12	86.32	83.40	80.09
Efficiency Ratio %	50.39	53.95	51.34	50.86	50.09	48.79	47.09	46.32
Loans to Deposits	0.81	0.81	0.82	0.87	0.88	0.89	0.91	0.92
Price Range	58.11-49.25	56.41-49.69	52.54-37.45	46.02-39.76	45.91-38.78	40.60-31.94	35.19-27.57	28.70-20.31
P/E Ratio	15.92-13.49	16.07-14.16	16.22-11.56	14.56-12.58	14.91-12.59	13.53-10.65	12.39-9.71	11.67-8.26
Average Yield %	2.22	2.20	2.49	2.33	2.30	2.47	2.45	1.97

Address: 800 Nicollet Mall, Minneapolis, MN 55402 Telephone: 651-466-3000	Web Site: www.usbank.com Officers: Andrew Cecere - Chairman, Vice-Chairman, President, Chief Executive Officer, Chief Operating Officer, Chief Financial Officer Terrance R. Dolan - Vice-Chairman, Vice-Chairman (frmr), Executive Vice President, Chief Financial Officer, Controller	Auditors: Ernst & Young LLP Investor Contact: 612-303-0778 Transfer Agents: Computershare, Providence, R.I.

UNITED TECHNOLOGIES CORP

Exchange	Symbol	Price	52Wk Range	Yield	P/E	Div Acheiver
NYS	UTX	$125.03 (6/29/2018)	138.32-109.55	2.24	22.37	24 Years

*7 Year Price Score 96.78 ***NYSE Composite Index=100** ***12 Month Price Score 99.57**

TRADING VOLUME (thousand shares)

Interim Earnings (Per Share)

Qtr.	Mar	Jun	Sep	Dec
2015	1.58	1.73	1.54	3.76
2016	1.43	1.65	1.78	1.26
2017	1.73	1.80	1.67	0.50
2018	1.62	...	...	...

Interim Dividends (Per Share)

Amt	Decl	Ex	Rec	Pay
0.70Q	10/11/2017	11/16/2017	11/17/2017	12/10/2017
0.70Q	02/05/2018	02/15/2018	02/16/2018	03/10/2018
0.70Q	04/30/2018	05/17/2018	05/18/2018	06/10/2018
0.70Q	06/13/2018	08/16/2018	08/17/2018	09/10/2018

Indicated Div: $2.80 (Div. Reinv. Plan)

Valuation Analysis / **Institutional Holding**

Forecast EPS	$7.15	No of Institutions
	(06/14/2018)	2419
Market Cap	$100.0 Billion	Shares
Book Value	$30.5 Billion	827,364,672
Price/Book	3.28	% Held
Price/Sales	1.63	81.55

Business Summary: Aerospace (MIC: 7.1.1 SIC: 3724 NAIC: 336412)

United Technologies provides technology products and services to the building systems and aerospace industries. Co. has four segments: Otis, which designs, manufactures, sells and installs passenger and freight elevators; UTC Climate, Controls & Security, which provides heating, ventilating, air conditioning and refrigeration solutions; Pratt & Whitney, which supplies aircraft engines for the commercial, military, business jet and general aviation market; and UTC Aerospace Systems, which provides aerospace products and aftermarket service solutions for aircraft manufacturers, airlines, regional, business and general aviation markets, military, space and undersea operations.

Recent Developments: For the quarter ended Mar 31 2018, net income decreased 6.4% to US$1.30 billion from US$1.39 billion in the year-earlier quarter. Revenues were US$15.24 billion, up 10.3% from US$13.82 billion the year before. Operating income was US$1.93 billion versus US$2.14 billion in the prior-year quarter, a decrease of 10.1%. Direct operating expenses rose 11.3% to US$11.28 billion from US$10.14 billion in the comparable period the year before. Indirect operating expenses increased 32.5% to US$2.03 billion from US$1.54 billion in the equivalent prior-year period.

Prospects: Our evaluation of United Technologies Corp. as of Jan. 21, 2018 is the result of our systematic analysis on three basic characteristics: earnings strength, relative valuation, and recent stock price movement. The company has managed to produce a neutral trend in earnings per share over the past 5 quarters and while recent estimates for the company have been raised by analysts, UTX has posted better than expected results. Based on operating earnings yield, the company is undervalued when compared to all of the companies in our coverage universe. Share price changes over the past year indicates that UTX will perform poorly over the near term.

Financial Data

(US$ in Millions)	3 Mos	12/31/2017	12/31/2016	12/31/2015	12/31/2014	12/31/2013	12/31/2012	12/31/2011
Earnings Per Share	5.59	5.70	6.12	8.61	6.82	6.25	5.66	5.49
Cash Flow Per Share	6.45	7.13	7.82	7.68	8.17	8.33	7.36	7.39
Tang Book Value Per Share	N.M.	N.M.	N.M.	N.M.	N.M.	N.M.	N.M.	0.02
Dividends Per Share	2.760	2.720	2.620	2.560	2.360	2.195	2.030	1.865
Dividend Payout %	49.37	47.72	42.81	29.73	34.60	35.12	35.87	33.97
Income Statement								
Total Revenue	15,242	59,837	57,244	56,098	65,100	62,626	57,708	58,190
EBITDA	2,700	9,850	9,277	8,359	10,891	10,259	8,604	8,989
Depn & Amortn	581	1,178	1,105	1,068	1,122	1,050	920	890
Income Before Taxes	1,890	7,763	7,133	6,467	8,887	8,312	6,911	7,605
Income Taxes	522	2,843	1,697	2,111	2,264	2,238	1,711	2,231
Net Income	1,297	4,552	5,055	7,608	6,220	5,721	5,130	4,979
Average Shares	800	799	826	883	911	915	906	906
Balance Sheet								
Current Assets	32,741	32,858	28,550	26,706	29,758	29,442	29,610	25,758
Total Assets	98,779	96,920	89,706	87,484	91,289	90,594	89,409	61,452
Current Liabilities	24,747	24,391	21,906	22,618	22,895	22,800	23,786	18,616
Long-Term Obligations	25,153	24,989	21,697	19,320	17,872	19,741	21,597	9,501
Total Liabilities	68,245	67,310	62,127	60,126	60,076	58,728	63,495	39,572
Stockholders' Equity	30,534	29,610	27,579	27,358	31,213	31,866	25,914	21,880
Shares Outstanding	800	799	808	838	909	916	918	907
Statistical Record								
Return on Assets %	4.72	4.88	5.69	8.51	6.84	6.36	6.78	8.30
Return on Equity %	15.36	15.92	18.35	25.98	19.72	19.80	21.41	23.02
EBITDA Margin %	17.71	16.46	16.21	14.90	16.73	16.38	14.91	15.45
Net Margin %	8.51	7.61	8.83	13.56	9.55	9.14	8.89	8.56
Asset Turnover	0.65	0.64	0.64	0.63	0.72	0.70	0.76	0.97
Current Ratio	1.32	1.35	1.30	1.18	1.30	1.29	1.24	1.38
Debt to Equity	0.82	0.84	0.79	0.71	0.57	0.62	0.83	0.43
Price Range	138.32-109.55	128.12-108.18	110.98-84.66	124.11-86.82	120.09-99.17	113.80-82.01	86.89-70.88	91.39-67.44
P/E Ratio	24.74-19.60	22.48-18.98	18.13-13.83	14.41-10.08	17.61-14.54	18.21-13.12	15.35-12.52	16.65-12.28
Average Yield %	2.26	2.32	2.59	2.39	2.11	2.22	2.59	2.33

Address: 10 Farm Springs Road, Farmington, CT 06032	Web Site: www.utc.com	Auditors: PricewaterhouseCoopers LLP
Telephone: 860-728-7000	Officers: Gregory J. (Greg) Hayes - Chairman, President, Chief Executive Officer, Senior Vice President, Chief Financial Officer Akhil Johri - Executive Vice President, Chief Financial Officer	Transfer Agents: Computershare Trust Company, N. A., Canton, MA
Fax: 860-728-7028		

UNIVAR INC

Exchange	Symbol	Price	52Wk Range	Yield	P/E
NYS	UNVR	$26.24 (6/29/2018)	31.65-25.85	N/A	22.82

*7 Year Price Score N/A   *NYSE Composite Index=100   *12 Month Price Score 93.01

Interim Earnings (Per Share)

Qtr.	Mar	Jun	Sep	Dec
2015	0.20	(0.12)	0.09	(0.03)
2016	0.10	0.29	(0.46)	(0.43)
2017	0.16	0.22	0.28	0.19
2018	0.46	...	...	...

Interim Dividends (Per Share)

No Dividends Paid

Valuation Analysis   Institutional Holding

Forecast EPS	$1.76	No of Institutions
	(06/13/2018)	233
Market Cap	$3.7 Billion	Shares
Book Value	$1.2 Billion	138,969,856
Price/Book	3.18	% Held
Price/Sales	0.44	N/A

TRADING VOLUME (thousand shares)

Business Summary: Specialty Chemicals (MIC: 8.3.2 SIC: 5169 NAIC: 325998)

Univar is a chemical and ingredients distributor and provider of specialty services. Co. purchases chemicals from chemical producers worldwide and warehouses, repackages, blends, dilutes, transports and sells those chemicals to more than 100,000 customer locations across approximately 150 countries. Co.'s operations are structured into four operating segments that represent the geographic areas under which it operates and manages its business: Univar USA; Univar Canada; Univar Europe and the Middle East and Africa; and Rest of World. The Rest of World segment includes developing businesses in Latin America (including Brazil and Mexico) and the Asia-Pacific region.

Recent Developments: For the quarter ended Mar 31 2018, net income increased 189.4% to US$65.4 million from US$22.6 million in the year-earlier quarter. Revenues were US$2.16 billion, up 8.0% from US$2.00 billion the year before. Operating income was US$107.9 million versus US$67.5 million in the prior-year quarter, an increase of 59.9%. Direct operating expenses rose 7.2% to US$1.67 billion from US$1.56 billion in the comparable period the year before. Indirect operating expenses increased 1.8% to US$378.7 million from US$371.9 million in the equivalent prior-year period.

Prospects: Our evaluation of Univar Inc as of Jan. 21, 2018 is the result of our systematic analysis on three basic characteristics: earnings strength, relative valuation, and recent stock price movement. The company has produced a positive trend in earnings per share over the past 5 quarters and while recent estimates for the company have been mixed, UNVR has posted better than expected results. Based on operating earnings yield, the company is overvalued when compared to all of the companies in our coverage universe. Share price changes over the past year indicates that UNVR will perform well over the near term.

Financial Data
(US$ in Thousands)

	3 Mos	12/31/2017	12/31/2016	12/31/2015	12/31/2014	12/31/2013	12/31/2012
Earnings Per Share	1.15	0.85	(0.50)	0.14	(0.20)	(0.83)	(2.01)
Cash Flow Per Share	1.56	1.99	3.25	2.98	1.27	2.91	0.16
Income Statement							
Total Revenue	2,158,000	8,253,700	8,073,700	8,981,800	10,373,900	10,324,600	9,747,100
EBITDA	143,900	451,800	232,600	370,200	348,200	330,500	258,000
Depn & Amortn	33,400	135,000	152,300	136,500	133,500	128,100	111,700
Income Before Taxes	75,600	168,800	(79,600)	26,700	(35,900)	(92,100)	(121,800)
Income Taxes	10,200	49,000	(11,200)	10,200	(15,800)	(9,800)	75,600
Net Income	65,400	119,800	(68,400)	16,500	(20,100)	(82,300)	(197,400)
Average Shares	142,000	141,400	137,800	120,100	99,718	99,299	98,355
Balance Sheet							
Current Assets	2,500,900	2,518,500	2,178,100	2,196,300	2,621,800	2,549,900	...
Total Assets	5,694,300	5,732,700	5,389,900	5,612,400	6,067,700	6,217,000	...
Current Liabilities	1,446,000	1,419,400	1,339,500	1,293,500	1,518,900	1,590,900	...
Long-Term Obligations	2,683,500	2,820,000	2,845,000	3,057,400	3,730,600	3,657,100	...
Total Liabilities	4,528,600	4,642,600	4,580,000	4,795,700	5,819,600	5,835,700	...
Stockholders' Equity	1,165,700	1,090,100	809,900	816,700	248,100	381,300	...
Shares Outstanding	141,300	141,100	138,800	138,000	100,190	99,956	99,781
Statistical Record							
Return on Assets %	2.88	2.15	N.M.	0.28	N.M.	...	...
Return on Equity %	15.93	12.61	N.M.	3.10	N.M.	...	...
EBITDA Margin %	6.67	5.47	2.88	4.12	3.36	3.20	2.65
Net Margin %	3.03	1.45	N.M.	0.18	N.M.	N.M.	N.M.
Asset Turnover	1.49	1.48	1.46	1.54	1.69	...	...
Current Ratio	1.73	1.77	1.63	1.70	1.73	1.60	...
Debt to Equity	2.30	2.59	3.51	3.74	15.04	9.59	...
Price Range	32.43-26.04	32.81-26.99	28.60-11.12	27.25-16.28	...	...	...
P/E Ratio	28.20-22.64	38.60-31.75	...	194.64-116.29	...	...	...

Address: 3075 Highland Parkway, Suite 200, Downers Grove, IL 60515 **Telephone:** 331-777-6000	**Web Site:** www.univar.com **Officers:** Stephen D. Newlin - Executive Chairman, Chairman, President, Chief Executive Officer David C. Jukes - President, Chief Executive Officer, Chief Operating Officer, Region Officer	**Auditors:** Ernst & Young LLP **Transfer Agents:** Wells Fargo Shareowner Services

UNIVERSAL CORP

Exchange	Symbol	Price	52Wk Range	Yield	P/E	Div Acheiver
NYS	UVV	$66.05 (6/29/2018)	67.00-46.35	4.54	15.95	47 Years

*7 Year Price Score 84.40 *NYSE Composite Index=100 *12 Month Price Score 108.27

Interim Earnings (Per Share)

Qtr.	Jun	Sep	Dec	Mar
2013-14	2.05	0.90	1.36	0.94
2014-15	(0.13)	0.48	1.87	1.63
2015-16	(0.43)	0.81	1.60	1.74
2016-17	(0.40)	0.90	1.92	(1.75)
2017-18	0.14	1.02	1.78	1.20

Interim Dividends (Per Share)

Amt	Decl	Ex	Rec	Pay
0.54Q	08/03/2017	10/06/2017	10/10/2017	11/06/2017
0.55Q	11/07/2017	01/05/2018	01/08/2018	02/05/2018
0.55Q	02/06/2018	04/06/2018	04/09/2018	05/07/2018
0.75Q	05/23/2018	07/06/2018	07/09/2018	08/06/2018

Indicated Div: $3.00 (Div. Reinv. Plan)

Valuation Analysis | **Institutional Holding**

Forecast EPS	N/A	No of Institutions
		284
Market Cap	$1.6 Billion	Shares
Book Value	$1.3 Billion	29,026,356
Price/Book	1.23	% Held
Price/Sales	0.81	93.05

TRADING VOLUME (thousand shares)

Business Summary: Tobacco Products (MIC: 1.3.1 SIC: 5159 NAIC: 424590)

Universal is a holding company. Through its subsidiary, Co. is engaged in supplying leaf tobacco. Co. has the following segments: North America, South America, Africa, Europe, Asia, which are primarily involved in flue-cured and burley leaf tobacco operations for supply to cigarette manufacturers; Dark Air-Cured, which supplies dark air-cured tobacco to manufacturers of cigars, pipe tobacco, and smokeless tobacco products; Oriental, which supplies oriental tobacco to cigarette manufacturers; and Special Services, which provides laboratory services, including physical and chemical product testing, electronic nicotine delivery system and e-liquid testing, and smoke testing for customers.

Recent Developments: For the year ended Mar 31 2018, net income increased 3.3% to US$116.2 million from US$112.5 million in the prior year. Revenues were US$2.03 billion, down 1.8% from US$2.07 billion the year before. Operating income was US$171.5 million versus US$178.4 million in the prior year, a decrease of 3.8%. Direct operating expenses declined 0.9% to US$1.66 billion from US$1.68 billion in the comparable period the year before. Indirect operating expenses decreased 7.3% to US$200.5 million from US$216.3 million in the equivalent prior-year period.

Prospects: Our evaluation of Universal Corp. as of Jan. 21, 2018 is the result of our systematic analysis on three basic characteristics: earnings strength, relative valuation, and recent stock price movement. The company has produced a positive trend in earnings per share over the past 5 quarters. Because the company lacks sufficient analyst estimate data, we place greater weight on the historical EPS trend as the measure of earnings strength. Based on operating earnings yield, the company is undervalued when compared to all of the companies in our coverage universe. Share price changes over the past year indicates that UVV will perform in line with the market over the near term.

Financial Data

(US$ in Thousands)	03/31/2018	03/31/2017	03/31/2016	03/31/2015	03/31/2014	03/31/2013	03/31/2012	03/31/2011
Earnings Per Share	4.14	0.88	3.92	4.06	5.25	4.66	3.25	5.42
Cash Flow Per Share	3.29	10.68	8.07	9.83	(0.15)	10.04	8.58	2.27
Tang Book Value Per Share	49.88	46.99	48.58	46.56	45.91	40.55	37.46	37.57
Dividends Per Share	2.170	2.130	2.090	2.050	2.010	1.970	1.930	1.890
Dividend Payout %	52.42	242.05	53.32	50.49	38.29	42.27	59.38	34.87
Income Statement								
Total Revenue	2,033,947	2,071,218	2,120,373	2,271,801	2,542,115	2,461,699	2,446,877	2,571,527
EBITDA	206,323	214,262	218,401	203,268	283,408	266,417	222,462	298,254
Depn & Amortn	34,836	35,911	36,754	35,394	37,257	43,408	42,158	43,654
Income Before Taxes	157,552	163,464	167,156	151,330	226,793	201,650	158,783	234,265
Income Taxes	50,509	56,732	54,430	38,006	75,535	66,366	61,159	78,349
Net Income	105,662	106,304	109,016	114,608	149,009	132,750	92,057	156,565
Average Shares	25,508	23,770	27,825	28,221	28,392	28,478	28,339	28,888
Balance Sheet								
Current Assets	1,589,043	1,561,399	1,638,546	1,634,610	1,673,247	1,745,973	1,690,629	1,578,234
Total Assets	2,168,632	2,123,405	2,232,797	2,198,473	2,270,907	2,306,155	2,266,919	2,227,867
Current Liabilities	267,720	267,996	246,270	270,913	454,977	622,597	392,708	512,351
Long-Term Obligations	369,086	368,733	370,000	370,000	240,000	181,250	392,500	320,193
Total Liabilities	826,203	836,916	818,575	835,748	892,677	1,047,584	1,083,468	1,042,261
Stockholders' Equity	1,342,429	1,286,489	1,414,222	1,362,725	1,378,230	1,258,571	1,183,451	1,185,606
Shares Outstanding	24,930	25,274	22,717	22,593	23,216	23,343	23,257	23,240
Statistical Record								
Return on Assets %	4.92	4.88	4.91	5.13	6.51	5.81	4.08	6.81
Return on Equity %	8.04	7.87	7.83	8.36	11.30	10.87	7.75	13.57
EBITDA Margin %	10.14	10.34	10.30	8.95	11.15	10.82	9.09	11.60
Net Margin %	5.19	5.13	5.14	5.04	5.86	5.39	3.76	6.09
Asset Turnover	0.95	0.95	0.95	1.02	1.11	1.08	1.09	1.12
Current Ratio	5.94	5.83	6.65	6.03	3.68	2.80	4.31	3.08
Debt to Equity	0.27	0.29	0.26	0.27	0.17	0.14	0.33	0.27
Price Range	75.60-46.35	81.35-52.33	58.41-46.80	56.82-38.53	63.36-48.43	58.36-44.03	48.60-35.11	55.92-35.44
P/E Ratio	18.26-11.20	92.44-59.47	14.90-11.94	14.00-9.49	12.07-9.22	12.52-9.45	14.95-10.80	10.32-6.54
Average Yield %	3.70	3.54	3.94	4.26	3.65	3.99	4.58	4.48

Address: 9201 Forest Hill Avenue, Richmond, VA 23235	**Web Site:** www.universalcorp.com	**Auditors:** Ernst & Young LLP
Telephone: 804-359-9311	**Officers:** George C. Freeman - Chairman, President, Chief Executive Officer, Principal Financial Officer Airton L. Hentschke - Senior Vice President, Chief Operating Officer	**Investor Contact:** 804-359-9311 **Transfer Agents:** Wells Fargo Bank, N.A., St. Paul, MN

UNIVERSAL HEALTH REALTY INCOME TRUST

Exchange	Symbol	Price	52Wk Range	Yield	P/E	Div Acheiver
NYS	UHT	$63.98 (6/29/2018)	84.23-55.36	4.19	36.98	30 Years

*7 Year Price Score 107.34 *NYSE Composite Index=100 ***12 Month Price Score 89.18**

Interim Earnings (Per Share)

Qtr.	Mar	Jun	Sep	Dec
2015	0.28	0.90	0.27	0.33
2016	0.33	0.34	0.28	0.33
2017	2.32	0.30	0.29	0.44
2018	0.70	...	...	...

Interim Dividends (Per Share)

Amt	Decl	Ex	Rec	Pay
0.66Q	09/07/2017	09/15/2017	09/18/2017	09/29/2017
0.665Q	12/06/2017	12/15/2017	12/18/2017	12/29/2017
0.665Q	03/15/2018	03/23/2018	03/26/2018	04/02/2018
0.67Q	06/13/2018	06/22/2018	06/25/2018	07/03/2018

Indicated Div: $2.68 (Div. Reinv. Plan)

Valuation Analysis | **Institutional Holding**

Forecast EPS	N/A	No of Institutions
		215
Market Cap	$878.8 Million	Shares
Book Value	$211.4 Million	10,543,175
Price/Book	4.16	% Held
Price/Sales	12.02	48.82

Business Summary: REITs (MIC: 5.3.1 SIC: 6798 NAIC: 525930)

Universal Health Realty Income Trust is real estate investment trust. Co. invests in health care and human service related facilities including acute care hospitals, rehabilitation hospitals, sub-acute facilities, surgery centers, free-standing emergency departments, childcare centers and medical office buildings (MOBs). As of Feb 28 2018, Co. had 68 real estate investments located in 20 states in the U.S. consisting of: six hospital facilities including three acute care, one rehabilitation and two sub-acute; 54 MOBs; fifty-four free-standing emergency departments, and; four preschool and childcare centers.

Recent Developments: For the quarter ended Mar 31 2018, net income decreased 69.6% to US$9.6 million from US$31.6 million in the year-earlier quarter. Revenues were US$18.5 million, up 4.4% from US$17.8 million the year before.

Prospects: Our evaluation of Universal Health Realty Income Trust as of Jan. 21, 2018 is the result of our systematic analysis on three basic characteristics: earnings strength, relative valuation, and recent stock price movement. The company has produced a positive trend in earnings per share over the past 5 quarters. Because the company lacks sufficient analyst estimate data, we place greater weight on the historical EPS trend as the measure of earnings strength. Based on operating earnings yield, the company is overvalued when compared to all of the companies in our coverage universe. Share price changes over the past year indicates that UHT will perform very well over the near term.

Financial Data
(US$ in Thousands)

	3 Mos	12/31/2017	12/31/2016	12/31/2015	12/31/2014	12/31/2013	12/31/2012	12/31/2011
Earnings Per Share	1.73	3.35	1.28	1.78	3.99	1.04	1.54	5.83
Cash Flow Per Share	3.45	3.38	3.02	2.87	2.54	2.47	2.42	1.69
Tang Book Value Per Share	13.98	13.83	12.31	13.15	13.64	11.26	11.93	12.69
Dividends Per Share	2.650	2.640	2.600	2.560	2.520	2.495	2.460	2.425
Dividend Payout %	153.18	78.81	203.13	143.82	63.16	239.90	159.74	41.60
Income Statement								
Total Revenue	18,539	72,348	67,081	63,950	59,786	54,280	53,950	29,494
EBITDA	11,633	78,218	44,897	51,352	78,162	36,956	44,439	80,444
Depn & Amortn	(10)	24,952	22,783	21,973	20,663	18,410	19,559	7,306
Income Before Taxes	9,175	43,203	12,759	21,155	49,123	11,074	17,112	70,736
Net Income	9,604	45,619	17,215	23,691	51,551	13,169	19,477	73,794
Average Shares	13,718	13,625	13,468	13,301	12,934	12,701	12,669	12,649
Balance Sheet								
Current Assets	13,716	12,489	11,542	10,302	10,166	8,700	7,872	15,687
Total Assets	489,585	490,008	524,750	458,901	428,866	373,145	383,038	370,929
Current Liabilities	184,492	540	626	504	545	491	539	473
Long-Term Obligations	70,781	256,409	315,717	252,704	213,155	199,987	197,936	174,836
Total Liabilities	278,229	279,447	333,473	263,859	224,285	207,515	205,367	182,068
Stockholders' Equity	211,356	210,561	191,277	195,042	204,581	165,630	177,671	188,861
Shares Outstanding	13,735	13,735	13,599	13,327	13,301	12,858	12,688	12,666
Statistical Record								
Return on Assets %	4.77	8.99	3.49	5.34	12.86	3.48	5.15	25.14
Return on Equity %	11.12	22.71	8.89	11.86	27.85	7.67	10.60	44.15
EBITDA Margin %	62.75	108.11	66.93	80.30	130.74	68.08	82.37	272.75
Net Margin %	51.80	63.05	25.66	37.05	86.23	24.26	36.10	250.20
Asset Turnover	0.15	0.14	0.14	0.14	0.15	0.14	0.14	0.10
Current Ratio	0.07	23.13	18.44	20.44	18.65	17.72	14.60	33.16
Debt to Equity	0.33	1.22	1.65	1.30	1.04	1.21	1.11	0.93
Price Range	84.23-55.36	84.23-60.01	65.59-47.26	56.87-43.54	49.13-40.06	58.85-38.52	50.61-37.77	43.38-32.21
P/E Ratio	48.69-32.00	25.14-17.91	51.24-36.92	31.95-24.46	12.31-10.04	56.59-37.04	32.86-24.53	7.44-5.52
Average Yield %	3.70	3.67	4.58	5.13	5.75	5.22	5.78	6.33

Address: Universal Corporate Center, 367 South Gulph Road, King of Prussia, PA 19406 **Telephone:** 610-265-0688 **Fax:** 610-768-3336	**Web Site:** www.uhrit.com **Officers:** Alan B. Miller - Chairman, President, Chief Executive Officer Charles F. Boyle - Vice President, Chief Financial Officer, Controller	**Auditors:** KPMG LLP **Transfer Agents:** Computershare, Providence, RI

UNIVERSAL HEALTH SERVICES, INC.

Exchange	Symbol	Price	52Wk Range	Yield	P/E
NYS	UHS	$111.44 (6/29/2018)	127.27-95.77	0.36	13.84

*7 Year Price Score 98.88 *NYSE Composite Index=100 *12 Month Price Score 100.58

Interim Earnings (Per Share)

Qtr.	Mar	Jun	Sep	Dec
2015	1.73	1.80	1.48	1.74
2016	1.93	1.89	1.54	1.78
2017	2.12	1.91	1.47	2.31
2018	2.36	...	...	...

Interim Dividends (Per Share)

Amt	Decl	Ex	Rec	Pay
0.10Q	07/19/2017	08/30/2017	09/01/2017	09/15/2017
0.10Q	11/15/2017	11/30/2017	12/01/2017	12/15/2017
0.10Q	01/17/2018	02/28/2018	03/01/2018	03/15/2018
0.10Q	05/16/2018	05/31/2018	06/01/2018	06/15/2018

Indicated Div: $0.40

Valuation Analysis   Institutional Holding

Forecast EPS	$9.45	No of Institutions
	(06/14/2018)	654
Market Cap	$10.5 Billion	Shares
Book Value	$5.2 Billion	107,493,320
Price/Book	2.02	% Held
Price/Sales	1.00	87.82

TRADING VOLUME (thousand shares)

Business Summary: Hospitals & Health Care Facilities (MIC: 4.2.1 SIC: 8062 NAIC: 622110)

Universal Health Services owns and operates, through its subsidiaries, acute care hospitals and outpatient facilities and behavioral health care facilities. Services provided by Co.'s hospitals include general and specialty surgery, internal medicine, obstetrics, emergency room care, radiology, oncology, diagnostic care, coronary care, pediatric services, pharmacy services and/or behavioral health services. As of Feb 28 2017, Co. owned and/or operated 319 inpatient facilities and 33 outpatient and other facilities including the following located in 37 states, Washington, D.C., the U.K., Puerto Rico and the U.S. Virgin Islands.

Recent Developments: For the quarter ended Mar 31 2018, net income increased 8.6% to US$228.7 million from US$210.5 million in the year-earlier quarter. Revenues were US$2.69 billion, up 2.9% from US$2.61 billion the year before. Operating income was US$333.8 million versus US$353.9 million in the prior-year quarter, a decrease of 5.7%. Indirect operating expenses increased 4.2% to US$2.35 billion from US$2.26 billion in the equivalent prior-year period.

Prospects: Our evaluation of Universal Health Services Inc. as of Jan. 21, 2018 is the result of our systematic analysis on three basic characteristics: earnings strength, relative valuation, and recent stock price movement. The company has managed to produce a neutral trend in earnings per share over the past 5 quarters and while recent estimates for the company have been raised by analysts, UHS has posted results that fell short of analysts expectations. Based on operating earnings yield, the company is undervalued when compared to all of the companies in our coverage universe. Share price changes over the past year indicates that UHS will perform poorly over the near term.

Financial Data
(US$ in Thousands)

	3 Mos	12/31/2017	12/31/2016	12/31/2015	12/31/2014	12/31/2013	12/31/2012	12/31/2011
Earnings Per Share	8.05	7.81	7.14	6.76	5.42	5.14	4.53	4.04
Cash Flow Per Share	11.29	12.36	13.22	10.33	10.48	9.02	8.40	7.39
Tang Book Value Per Share	14.54	12.36	7.75	6.65	4.51	2.04	N.M.	N.M.
Dividends Per Share	0.400	0.400	0.400	0.400	0.300	0.200	0.600	0.200
Dividend Payout %	4.97	5.12	5.60	5.92	5.54	3.89	13.25	4.95
Income Statement								
Total Revenue	2,687,516	10,409,865	9,766,210	9,043,451	8,065,326	7,283,822	6,961,400	7,500,198
EBITDA	446,948	1,668,578	1,632,211	1,596,895	1,377,805	1,301,063	1,213,081	1,165,628
Depn & Amortn	113,134	388,400	350,800	337,500	314,500	285,600	270,500	268,500
Income Before Taxes	296,238	1,135,009	1,156,358	1,145,901	929,667	869,332	763,663	696,336
Income Taxes	67,569	363,697	409,187	395,203	324,671	315,309	274,616	247,466
Net Income	223,832	752,303	702,409	680,528	545,343	510,733	443,446	398,167
Average Shares	94,683	96,325	98,380	100,694	100,544	99,361	97,711	98,537
Balance Sheet								
Current Assets	1,884,726	1,798,002	1,681,371	1,718,304	1,615,138	1,432,329	1,407,496	1,364,905
Total Assets	11,023,517	10,761,828	10,317,802	9,634,113	8,974,443	8,311,723	8,200,843	7,665,245
Current Liabilities	1,579,577	1,848,034	1,317,373	1,100,406	1,182,827	1,059,888	894,058	836,933
Long-Term Obligations	3,795,087	3,494,390	4,030,230	3,387,303	3,210,215	3,209,762	3,727,431	3,651,428
Total Liabilities	5,807,871	5,772,314	5,784,582	5,384,466	5,238,497	5,061,744	5,487,498	5,368,893
Stockholders' Equity	5,215,646	4,989,514	4,533,220	4,249,647	3,735,946	3,249,979	2,713,345	2,296,352
Shares Outstanding	94,406	94,227	96,630	98,296	98,716	98,311	97,591	96,609
Statistical Record								
Return on Assets %	7.17	7.14	7.02	7.31	6.31	6.19	5.57	5.24
Return on Equity %	15.48	15.80	15.95	17.04	15.61	17.13	17.66	18.63
EBITDA Margin %	16.63	16.03	16.71	17.66	17.08	17.86	17.43	15.54
Net Margin %	8.33	7.23	7.19	7.53	6.76	7.01	6.37	5.31
Asset Turnover	0.98	0.99	0.98	0.97	0.93	0.88	0.88	0.99
Current Ratio	1.19	0.97	1.28	1.56	1.37	1.35	1.57	1.63
Debt to Equity	0.73	0.70	0.89	0.80	0.86	0.99	1.37	1.59
Price Range	127.27-95.77	126.65-95.77	138.74-101.55	146.24-102.53	114.84-74.35	83.12-48.35	49.46-36.82	56.41-31.91
P/E Ratio	15.81-11.90	16.22-12.26	19.43-14.22	21.63-15.17	21.19-13.72	16.17-9.41	10.92-8.13	13.96-7.90
Average Yield %	0.35	0.35	0.33	0.32	0.32	0.29	1.43	0.45

Address: Universal Corporate Center, 367 South Gulph Road, King of Prussia, PA 19406 Telephone: 610-768-3300	Web Site: www.uhsinc.com Officers: Alan B. Miller - Chairman, Chief Executive Officer Marc D. Miller - President	Auditors: PricewaterhouseCoopers LLP Investor Contact: 610-768-3300 Transfer Agents: Computershare, Canton, MA

UNUM GROUP

Exchange	Symbol	Price	52Wk Range	Yield	P/E
NYS	UNM	$36.99 (6/29/2018)	58.59-36.64	2.49	8.04

*7 Year Price Score 117.49 *NYSE Composite Index=100 *12 Month Price Score 80.54

Interim Earnings (Per Share)

Qtr.	Mar	Jun	Sep	Dec
2015	0.84	0.90	0.83	0.93
2016	0.88	1.00	1.01	1.07
2017	1.00	1.07	1.12	1.18
2018	1.23	...	...	...

Interim Dividends (Per Share)

Amt	Decl	Ex	Rec	Pay
0.23Q	07/17/2017	07/27/2017	07/31/2017	08/18/2017
0.23Q	10/16/2017	10/27/2017	10/30/2017	11/17/2017
0.23Q	01/16/2018	01/26/2018	01/29/2018	02/16/2018
0.23Q	04/16/2018	04/27/2018	04/30/2018	05/18/2018

Indicated Div: $0.92

Valuation Analysis

		Institutional Holding	
Forecast EPS	$5.10	No of Institutions	
	(06/14/2018)	810	
Market Cap	$8.2 Billion	Shares	
Book Value	$9.5 Billion	270,717,280	
Price/Book	0.86	% Held	
Price/Sales	0.72	77.48	

TRADING VOLUME (thousand shares)

Business Summary: Life & Health (MIC: 5.2.2 SIC: 6321 NAIC: 524114)

Unum Group is an insurance holding company. Through its subsidiaries, Co. provides products such as disability, life, accident, and other related services. Co.'s segments are: Unum U.S., which includes group disability insurance, group life and accidental death and dismemberment products, and supplemental and voluntary lines of business; Unum U.K., which includes group disability and life, and supplemental lines of business; and Colonial Life, which includes insurance for accident, sickness, and disability products, life products, and cancer and critical illness products. Other segment includes the Closed Block, which consists of individual disability, group and individual long-term care.

Recent Developments: For the quarter ended Mar 31 2018, net income increased 19.0% to US$273.5 million from US$229.9 million in the year-earlier quarter. Revenues were US$2.90 billion, up 3.3% from US$2.81 billion the year before. Net premiums earned were US$2.25 billion versus US$2.14 billion in the prior-year quarter, an increase of 5.0%. Net investment income fell 0.0% to US$602.3 million from US$602.4 million a year ago.

Prospects: Our evaluation of UNUM Group as of Jan. 21, 2018 is the result of our systematic analysis on three basic characteristics: earnings strength, relative valuation, and recent stock price movement. The company has produced a positive trend in earnings per share over the past 5 quarters and while recent estimates for the company have been raised by analysts, UNM has posted better than expected results. Based on operating earnings yield, the company is undervalued when compared to all of the companies in our coverage universe. Share price changes over the past year indicates that UNM will perform well over the near term.

Financial Data

(US$ in Thousands)	3 Mos	12/31/2017	12/31/2016	12/31/2015	12/31/2014	12/31/2013	12/31/2012	12/31/2011
Earnings Per Share	4.60	4.37	3.95	3.50	1.61	3.23	3.17	0.78
Cash Flow Per Share	5.14	5.07	4.73	5.23	4.79	3.90	4.89	3.95
Tang Book Value Per Share	41.37	41.50	37.56	35.00	33.11	32.53	31.13	28.61
Dividends Per Share	0.890	0.860	0.770	0.700	0.620	0.550	0.470	0.395
Dividend Payout %	19.35	19.68	19.49	20.00	38.51	17.03	14.83	50.64
Income Statement								
Premium Income	2,250,000	8,597,100	8,357,700	8,082,400	7,797,200	7,624,700	7,716,100	7,514,200
Total Revenue	2,899,600	11,286,800	11,046,500	10,731,300	10,509,700	10,353,800	10,515,400	10,278,000
Income Before Taxes	341,100	1,404,000	1,347,700	1,238,300	527,200	1,205,200	1,249,500	257,200
Income Taxes	67,600	409,800	416,300	371,200	113,800	347,100	355,100	21,800
Net Income	273,500	994,200	931,400	867,100	413,400	858,100	894,400	235,400
Average Shares	222,577	227,335	235,979	247,854	256,652	265,949	281,756	303,571
Balance Sheet								
Total Assets	63,012,300	64,013,100	61,941,500	60,589,700	62,497,100	59,403,600	62,236,100	60,179,000
Total Liabilities	53,512,800	54,438,200	52,973,500	51,925,800	53,944,700	50,744,500	53,623,500	51,602,000
Stockholders' Equity	9,499,500	9,574,900	8,968,000	8,663,900	8,552,400	8,659,100	8,612,600	8,577,000
Shares Outstanding	221,168	222,547	229,822	240,917	252,309	260,017	270,205	292,715
Statistical Record								
Return on Assets %	1.65	1.58	1.52	1.41	0.68	1.41	1.46	0.40
Return on Equity %	11.16	10.72	10.54	10.07	4.80	9.94	10.38	2.69
Net Margin %	9.43	8.81	8.43	8.08	3.93	8.29	8.51	2.29
Price Range	58.59-43.80	57.49-43.80	44.60-24.07	37.61-31.05	36.81-30.71	35.16-20.82	24.68-18.36	26.90-19.91
P/E Ratio	12.74-9.52	13.16-10.02	11.29-6.09	10.75-8.87	22.86-19.07	10.89-6.45	7.79-5.79	34.49-25.53
Average Yield %	1.77	1.76	2.25	2.04	1.81	1.90	2.24	1.63

Address: 1 Fountain Square, Chattanooga, TN 37402
Telephone: 423-294-1011

Web Site: www.unum.com
Officers: Kevin T. Kabat - Chairman Richard P. McKenney - President, Chief Executive Officer, Executive Vice President, Chief Financial Officer

Auditors: Ernst & Young LLP
Transfer Agents: Computershare Trust Company, N.A., Providence, RI

URBAN EDGE PROPERTIES

Exchange	Symbol	Price	52Wk Range	Yield	P/E
NYS	UE	$22.87 (6/29/2018)	26.09-19.83	3.85	76.23

*7 Year Price Score N/A   *NYSE Composite Index=100   *12 Month Price Score 91.85

Interim Earnings (Per Share)

Qtr.	Mar	Jun	Sep	Dec
2015	(0.12)	0.16	0.19	0.15
2016	0.19	0.34	0.19	0.19
2017	0.50	0.13	0.15	(0.16)
2018	0.18	...	...	...

Interim Dividends (Per Share)

Amt	Decl	Ex	Rec	Pay
0.22Q	09/01/2017	09/14/2017	09/15/2017	09/29/2017
0.22Q	11/07/2017	12/14/2017	12/15/2017	12/29/2017
0.22Q	02/23/2018	03/14/2018	03/15/2018	03/30/2018
0.22Q	05/09/2018	06/14/2018	06/15/2018	06/29/2018

Indicated Div: $0.88 (Div. Reinv. Plan)

Valuation Analysis   Institutional Holding

Forecast EPS	$0.65	No of Institutions
	(06/03/2018)	261
Market Cap	$2.6 Billion	Shares
Book Value	$887.0 Million	123,102,736
Price/Book	2.94	% Held
Price/Sales	6.86	N/A

Business Summary: REITs (MIC: 5.3.1 SIC: 6798 NAIC: 525930)

Urban Edge Properties is a real estate investment trust. Co. is focused on managing, developing, redeveloping, and acquiring retail real estate in urban communities, primarily in the New York metropolitan region. Urban Edge Properties LP is a Delaware limited partnership formed to serve as Co.'s majority-owned partnership subsidiary and to own, through affiliates, all of Co.'s real estate properties and other assets. As of Dec 31 2017, Co.'s portfolio consisted of 85 shopping centers, four malls and a warehouse park adjacent to one of its centers.

Recent Developments: For the quarter ended Mar 31 2018, net income decreased 57.9% to US$23.0 million from US$54.7 million in the year-earlier quarter. Revenues were US$99.1 million, down 21.4% from US$126.1 million the year before. Revenues from property income rose 11.6% to US$69.7 million from US$62.5 million in the corresponding quarter a year earlier.

Prospects: Our evaluation of Urban Edge Properties as of Jan. 21, 2018 is the result of our systematic analysis on three basic characteristics: earnings strength, relative valuation, and recent stock price movement. The company has suffered a very negative trend in earnings per share over the past 5 quarters. Because the company lacks sufficient analyst estimate data, we place greater weight on the historical EPS trend as the measure of earnings strength. Based on operating earnings yield, the company is about fairly valued when compared to all of the companies in our coverage universe. Share price changes over the past year indicates that UE will perform well over the near term.

Financial Data
(US$ in Thousands)

	3 Mos	12/31/2017	12/31/2016	12/31/2015	12/31/2014	12/31/2013	12/31/2012
Earnings Per Share	0.30	0.61	0.91	0.39	0.66	1.10	0.70
Cash Flow Per Share	1.36	1.47	1.38	1.39	...	...	...
Tang Book Value Per Share	7.06	7.05	4.30	4.07	2.13	...	...
Dividends Per Share	0.880	0.880	0.820	0.800	...	...	...
Dividend Payout %	293.33	144.26	90.11	205.13	...	...	...
Income Statement							
Total Revenue	99,053	407,042	325,976	322,945	315,676	362,995	304,233
EBITDA	35,682	202,515	200,868	151,206	168,991	214,979	168,488
Depn & Amortn	(1,911)	75,885	52,232	53,130	46,551	47,766	43,522
Income Before Taxes	23,473	72,660	97,434	42,642	67,515	111,435	71,214
Income Taxes	434	(278)	804	1,294	1,721	2,100	1,364
Net Income	20,700	67,070	90,815	38,785	65,772	109,314	69,837
Average Shares	113,864	118,390	99,794	99,278	99,248	99,248	99,248
Balance Sheet							
Current Assets	594,225	617,859	245,902	285,688	123,447	120,767	...
Total Assets	2,803,378	2,820,808	1,904,138	1,918,931	1,741,529	1,749,965	...
Current Liabilities	71,061	69,595	48,842	45,331	26,924	30,538	...
Long-Term Obligations	1,552,543	1,564,542	1,197,513	1,233,983	1,288,535	1,200,762	...
Total Liabilities	1,916,399	1,930,889	1,443,832	1,481,011	1,483,007	1,408,700	...
Stockholders' Equity	886,979	889,919	460,306	437,920	258,522	341,265	...
Shares Outstanding	113,923	113,827	99,754	99,290	104,964	...	...
Statistical Record							
Return on Assets %	1.53	2.84	4.74	...	3.77	...	...
Return on Equity %	5.40	9.93	20.17	...	21.93	...	...
EBITDA Margin %	36.02	49.75	61.62	46.82	53.53	59.22	55.38
Net Margin %	20.90	16.48	27.86	12.01	20.84	30.11	22.96
Asset Turnover	0.16	0.17	0.17	...	0.18	...	...
Current Ratio	8.36	8.88	5.03	6.30	4.59	3.95	...
Debt to Equity	1.75	1.76	2.60	2.82	4.98	3.52	...
Price Range	27.65-20.45	28.85-23.44	30.15-22.22	25.00-20.12	...	...	...
P/E Ratio	92.17-68.17	47.30-38.43	33.13-24.42	64.10-51.59	...	...	...
Average Yield %	3.62	3.45	3.08	3.52	...	...	...

Address: 888 Seventh Avenue, New York, NY 10019 Telephone: 212-956-2556	Web Site: www.uedge.com Officers: Jeffrey S. Olson - Chairman, President, Chief Executive Officer Mark J. Langer - Executive President, Chief Financial Officer	Auditors: Deloitte & Touche LLP

URSTADT BIDDLE PROPERTIES INC

Exchange	Symbol	Price	52Wk Range	Yield	P/E	Div Acheiver
NYS	UBA	$22.63 (6/29/2018)	23.75-17.50	4.77	45.26	19 Years

*7 Year Price Score 82.35 *NYSE Composite Index=100 *12 Month Price Score 102.43

Interim Earnings (Per Share)

Qtr.	Jan	Apr	Jul	Oct
2014-15	0.06	0.10	0.13	0.62
2015-16	0.08	0.12	0.13	0.16
2016-17	0.08	0.57	0.14	0.01
2017-18	0.12	0.23	...	...

Interim Dividends (Per Share)

Amt	Decl	Ex	Rec	Pay
0.265Q	09/06/2017	10/05/2017	10/06/2017	10/20/2017
0.27Q	12/14/2017	01/04/2018	01/05/2018	01/19/2018
0.27Q	03/22/2018	03/29/2018	04/02/2018	04/16/2018
0.27Q	06/04/2018	07/05/2018	07/06/2018	07/20/2018

Indicated Div: $1.08

Valuation Analysis / **Institutional Holding**

Forecast EPS	$0.63	No of Institutions
	(06/14/2018)	41
Market Cap	$896.9 Million	Shares
Book Value	$589.1 Million	827,269
Price/Book	1.52	% Held
Price/Sales	6.66	2.95

Business Summary: REITs (MIC: 5.3.1 SIC: 6798 NAIC: 525930)

Urstadt Biddle Properties is a real estate investment trust engaged in the acquisition, ownership and management of commercial real estate. Co.'s sole business is the ownership of real estate investments, which consist principally of investments in income-producing properties, with primary emphasis on properties in the metropolitan New York tri-state area outside of the City of New York. At Oct 31 2017, Co. owned or had equity interests in 81 properties comprised of neighborhood and community shopping centers, office buildings, single tenant retail or restaurant properties and office/retail mixed use properties located in four states throughout the U.S.

Recent Developments: For the quarter ended Apr 30 2018, net income decreased 49.8% to US$14.0 million from US$27.9 million in the year-earlier quarter. Revenues were US$37.0 million, up 23.4% from US$30.0 million the year before. Revenues from property income rose 23.0% to US$35.8 million from US$29.1 million in the corresponding quarter a year earlier.

Prospects: Our evaluation of Urstadt Biddle Properties Inc. as of Jan. 21, 2018 is the result of our systematic analysis on three basic characteristics: earnings strength, relative valuation, and recent stock price movement. The company has suffered a very negative trend in earnings per share over the past 5 quarters. Because the company lacks sufficient analyst estimate data, we place greater weight on the historical EPS trend as the measure of earnings strength. Based on operating earnings yield, the company is undervalued when compared to all of the companies in our coverage universe. Share price changes over the past year indicates that UBA will perform well over the near term.

Financial Data
(US$ in Thousands)

	6 Mos	3 Mos	10/31/2017	10/31/2016	10/31/2015	10/31/2014	10/31/2013	10/31/2012
Earnings Per Share	0.50	0.84	0.80	0.49	0.90	1.42	0.31	0.41
Cash Flow Per Share	1.87	1.69	1.67	1.70	1.49	1.64	1.66	1.86
Tang Book Value Per Share	10.07	9.99	10.08	10.08	9.42	8.40	7.84	9.09
Dividends Per Share	1.070	1.065	1.060	1.040	1.020	1.010	1.000	0.990
Dividend Payout %	214.00	126.79	132.50	212.24	113.33	71.13	322.58	241.46
Income Statement								
Total Revenue	70,000	32,995	123,560	116,792	115,312	102,328	94,245	91,295
EBITDA	42,388	18,811	73,778	68,352	63,576	80,837	53,352	53,875
Depn & Amortn	13,917	6,949	26,512	23,025	22,435	19,249	17,816	16,721
Income Before Taxes	21,874	8,519	34,641	32,586	27,894	51,487	27,787	28,898
Net Income	20,644	7,984	52,933	33,716	49,264	65,151	29,795	28,260
Average Shares	38,681	9,058	38,529	36,022	35,060	31,963	31,740	29,168
Balance Sheet								
Current Assets	46,262	29,480	30,612	28,185	31,167	95,513	25,515	164,614
Total Assets	1,021,563	995,572	996,713	931,324	861,075	819,005	650,026	724,243
Current Liabilities	27,205	12,515	4,200	4,977	3,438	1,622	1,450	1,632
Long-Term Obligations	304,867	295,475	301,071	281,016	283,207	245,697	175,496	154,836
Total Liabilities	432,429	409,581	409,483	332,291	320,297	343,962	204,112	239,725
Stockholders' Equity	589,134	585,991	587,230	599,033	540,778	475,043	445,914	484,518
Shares Outstanding	39,633	39,637	39,393	39,141	35,721	32,805	32,565	32,315
Statistical Record								
Return on Assets %	3.86	5.56	5.49	3.75	5.86	8.87	4.34	4.33
Return on Equity %	6.47	9.12	8.92	5.90	9.70	14.15	6.40	6.38
EBITDA Margin %	60.55	57.01	59.71	58.52	55.13	79.00	56.61	59.01
Net Margin %	29.49	24.20	42.84	28.87	42.72	63.67	31.61	30.95
Asset Turnover	0.13	0.13	0.13	0.13	0.14	0.14	0.14	0.14
Current Ratio	1.70	2.36	7.29	5.66	9.07	58.89	17.60	100.87
Debt to Equity	0.52	0.50	0.51	0.47	0.52	0.52	0.39	0.32
Price Range	23.75-17.50	23.75-18.41	24.33-18.41	25.13-18.57	24.22-17.43	22.08-18.13	23.05-18.12	20.78-15.61
P/E Ratio	47.50-35.00	28.27-21.92	30.41-23.01	51.29-37.90	26.91-19.37	15.55-12.77	74.35-58.45	50.68-38.07
Average Yield %	5.24	5.07	4.98	4.87	4.89	5.02	4.88	5.25

Address: 321 Railroad Avenue, Greenwich, CT 06830 **Telephone:** 203-863-8200	**Web Site:** www.ubproperties.com **Officers:** Charles J. Urstadt - Chairman, Chief Executive Officer Willing L. Biddle - President, Chief Executive Officer, Chief Operating Officer	**Auditors:** PKF O'Connor Davies, LLP **Investor Contact:** 203-863-8200 **Transfer Agents:** BNY Mellon Shareowner Services, Jersey City, N

US FOODS HOLDING CORP

Exchange	Symbol	Price	52Wk Range	Yield	P/E
NYS	USFD	$37.82 (6/29/2018)	38.30-26.04	N/A	17.51

*7 Year Price Score N/A   *NYSE Composite Index=100   *12 Month Price Score 115.05

TRADING VOLUME (thousand shares)

Interim Earnings (Per Share)

Qtr.	Mar	Jun	Sep	Dec
2015	0.04	0.97	0.03	(0.06)
2016	0.08	(0.07)	0.59	0.35
2017	0.12	0.29	0.42	1.14
2018	0.31	...	...	...

Interim Dividends (Per Share)

No Dividends Paid

Valuation Analysis

		Institutional Holding	
Forecast EPS	$2.08	No of Institutions	
	(06/05/2018)	338	
Market Cap	$8.2 Billion	Shares	
Book Value	$2.8 Billion	220,226,832	
Price/Book	2.87	% Held	
Price/Sales	0.34	N/A	

Business Summary: Retail - Food & Beverage, Drug & Tobacco (MIC: 2.1.2 SIC: 5149 NAIC: 424490)

US Foods Holding is a holding company. Through its subsidiaries, Co. is engaged as a food company and a foodservice distributor. Co. supplies approximately 250,000 customer locations nationwide. They include independently owned single and multi-unit restaurants, regional restaurant concepts, national restaurant chains, hospitals, nursing homes, hotels and motels, country clubs, government and military organizations, colleges and universities, and retail locations. Co. provides approximately 400,000 fresh, frozen, and dry food stock-keeping units, as well as non-food items, sourced from over 5,000 suppliers.

Recent Developments: For the quarter ended Mar 31 2018, net income increased 151.0% to US$67.3 million from US$26.8 million in the year-earlier quarter. Revenues were US$5.82 billion, up 0.6% from US$5.79 billion the year before. Operating income was US$102.5 million versus US$75.8 million in the prior-year quarter, an increase of 35.1%. Direct operating expenses rose 0.7% to US$4.83 billion from US$4.80 billion in the comparable period the year before. Indirect operating expenses decreased 2.8% to US$889.4 million from US$915.5 million in the equivalent prior-year period.

Prospects: Our evaluation of US Foods Holding Corp as of Jan. 21, 2018 is the result of our systematic analysis on three basic characteristics: earnings strength, relative valuation, and recent stock price movement. The company has generated a negative trend in earnings per share over the past 5 quarters and while recent estimates for the company have been raised by analysts, USFD has posted better than expected results. Based on operating earnings yield, the company is about fairly valued when compared to all of the companies in our coverage universe. Share price changes over the past year indicates that USFD will perform poorly over the near term.

Financial Data

(US$ in Thousands)	3 Mos	12/30/2017	12/31/2016	01/02/2016	12/27/2014	12/28/2013
Earnings Per Share	2.16	1.97	1.03	0.98	(0.43)	(0.34)
Cash Flow Per Share	3.81	3.37	2.78	3.22	2.38	1.90
Income Statement						
Total Revenue	5,822,521	24,147,161	22,918,808	23,127,532	23,019,801	22,297,178
EBITDA	177,654	856,824	626,189	730,328	513,256	518,703
Depn & Amortn	72,030	283,000	266,000	253,000	261,000	240,000
Income Before Taxes	62,780	404,242	131,109	192,153	(36,946)	(27,384)
Income Taxes	(4,537)	(40,052)	(78,685)	24,635	35,968	29,822
Net Income	67,317	444,294	209,794	167,518	(72,914)	(57,206)
Average Shares	217,212	225,663	204,024	171,060	169,467	169,634
Balance Sheet						
Current Assets	2,931,112	2,819,381	2,789,171	3,060,433	2,820,099	...
Total Assets	9,173,774	9,037,158	8,944,450	9,239,359	9,022,538	...
Current Liabilities	2,218,225	2,002,882	1,969,285	1,802,823	1,825,587	...
Long-Term Obligations	3,509,757	3,648,055	3,705,751	4,682,149	4,661,697	...
Total Liabilities	6,327,887	6,285,795	6,406,800	7,327,741	7,357,822	...
Stockholders' Equity	2,845,887	2,751,363	2,537,650	1,911,618	1,664,716	...
Shares Outstanding	215,942	214,963	220,928	166,667	166,667	166,667
Statistical Record						
Return on Assets %	5.28	4.96	2.31	1.80	...	...
Return on Equity %	17.89	16.85	9.46	9.22	...	...
EBITDA Margin %	3.05	3.55	2.73	3.16	2.23	2.33
Net Margin %	1.16	1.84	0.92	0.72	N.M.	N.M.
Asset Turnover	2.64	2.69	2.53	2.49	...	...
Current Ratio	1.32	1.41	1.42	1.70	1.54	...
Debt to Equity	1.23	1.33	1.46	2.45	2.80	...
Price Range	34.66-26.04	31.93-25.77	27.48-22.38	...	...	...
P/E Ratio	16.05-12.06	16.21-13.08	26.68-21.73	...	...	...

Address: 9399 W. Higgins Road, Suite 500, Rosemont, IL 60018	Web Site: www.usfoods.com	Auditors: Deloitte & Touche LLP
Telephone: 847-720-8000	Officers: Pietro Satriano - President, Chief Executive Officer Dirk J. Locascio - Chief Financial Officer, Principal Financial Officer, Principal Accounting Officer	Transfer Agents: American Stock Transfer & Trust Company, LLC

USG CORP

Exchange	Symbol	Price	52Wk Range	Yield	P/E
NYS	USG	$43.12 (6/29/2018)	43.32-25.78	N/A	89.83

*7 Year Price Score 108.75 *NYSE Composite Index=100 *12 Month Price Score 115.98

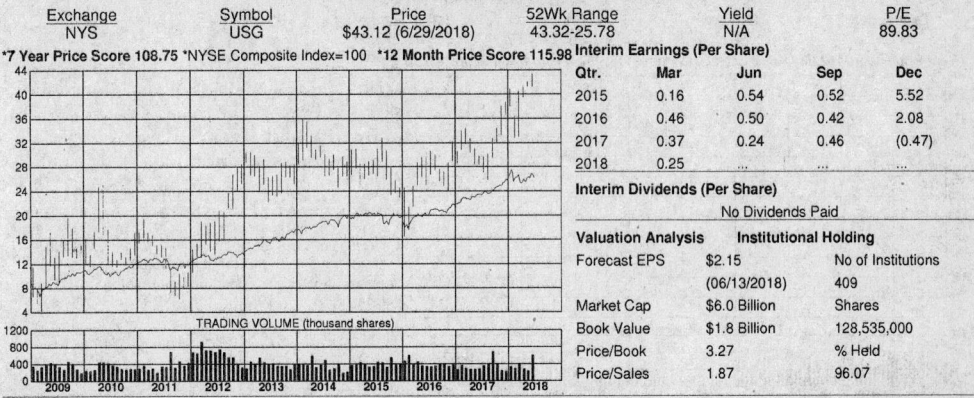

Interim Earnings (Per Share)

Qtr.	Mar	Jun	Sep	Dec
2015	0.16	0.54	0.52	5.52
2016	0.46	0.50	0.42	2.08
2017	0.37	0.24	0.46	(0.47)
2018	0.25	...	...	...

Interim Dividends (Per Share)

No Dividends Paid

Valuation Analysis

		Institutional Holding	
Forecast EPS	$2.15	No of Institutions	
	(06/13/2018)	409	
Market Cap	$6.0 Billion	Shares	
Book Value	$1.8 Billion	128,535,000	
Price/Book	3.27	% Held	
Price/Sales	1.87	96.07	

Business Summary: Construction Materials (MIC: 8.5.1 SIC: 3275 NAIC: 327420)

USG, through its subsidiaries, is a manufacturer of building systems. Co.'s operations are organized into three segments: Gypsum, which manufactures and markets gypsum and related products in the U.S., Canada and Mexico; Ceilings, which manufactures and markets interior systems products in the U.S., Canada, Mexico, and Latin America; as well as USG Boral Building Products, which consists of its 50/50 joint ventures, USG Boral Building Products Pte. Limited and USG Boral Building Products Pty Limited, which manufactures and distributes products for wall, ceiling, floor lining and exterior systems that utilize gypsum wallboard, mineral fiber ceiling tiles, steel grid and joint compound.

Recent Developments: For the quarter ended Mar 31 2018, income from continuing operations decreased 34.5% to US$36.0 million from US$55.0 million in the year-earlier quarter. Net income decreased 32.7% to US$37.0 million from US$55.0 million in the year-earlier quarter. Revenues were US$786.0 million, up 2.5% from US$767.0 million the year before. Operating income was US$46.0 million versus US$91.0 million in the prior-year quarter, a decrease of 49.5%. Direct operating expenses rose 7.3% to US$647.0 million from US$603.0 million in the comparable period the year before. Indirect operating expenses increased 27.4% to US$93.0 million from US$73.0 million in the equivalent prior-year period.

Prospects: Our evaluation of USG Corp. as of Jan. 21, 2018 is the result of our systematic analysis on three basic characteristics: earnings strength, relative valuation, and recent stock price movement. The company has produced a positive trend in earnings per share over the past 5 quarters and while recent estimates for the company have been mixed, USG has posted better than expected results. Based on operating earnings yield, the company is about fairly valued when compared to all of the companies in our coverage universe. Share price changes over the past year indicates that USG will perform in line with the market over the near term.

Financial Data

(US$ in Thousands)	3 Mos	12/31/2017	12/31/2016	12/31/2015	12/31/2014	12/31/2013	12/31/2012	12/31/2011
Earnings Per Share	0.48	0.60	3.46	6.73	0.25	0.42	(1.19)	(3.76)
Cash Flow Per Share	2.81	2.64	2.55	2.28	(10.61)	0.73	0.64	(1.87)
Tang Book Value Per Share	12.89	12.79	12.90	9.86	2.81	4.65	0.06	1.48
Income Statement								
Total Revenue	786,000	3,204,000	3,017,000	3,776,000	3,724,000	3,570,000	3,224,000	3,024,000
EBITDA	85,000	470,000	495,000	492,000	323,000	394,000	168,000	(51,000)
Depn & Amortn	36,000	129,000	129,000	130,000	134,000	135,000	136,000	144,000
Income Before Taxes	36,000	276,000	225,000	201,000	11,000	59,000	(170,000)	(400,000)
Income Taxes	9,000	238,000	63,000	(729,000)	7,000	11,000	12,000	(10,000)
Net Income	37,000	88,000	510,000	991,000	37,000	47,000	(126,000)	(390,000)
Average Shares	143,808	146,710	147,660	147,246	144,296	111,434	106,382	103,902
Balance Sheet								
Current Assets	956,000	991,000	949,000	1,400,000	1,152,000	1,700,000	1,327,000	1,226,000
Total Assets	3,831,000	3,851,000	3,869,000	4,736,000	3,994,000	4,121,000	3,723,000	3,719,000
Current Liabilities	400,000	415,000	422,000	991,000	563,000	568,000	551,000	525,000
Long-Term Obligations	1,078,000	1,078,000	1,083,000	1,675,000	2,205,000	2,292,000	2,305,000	2,297,000
Total Liabilities	1,992,000	2,006,000	1,983,000	3,300,000	3,587,000	3,483,000	3,717,000	3,563,000
Stockholders' Equity	1,839,000	1,845,000	1,886,000	1,436,000	407,000	638,000	6,000	156,000
Shares Outstanding	139,652	140,942	146,167	145,667	144,768	137,314	107,850	105,329
Statistical Record								
Return on Assets %	1.81	2.28	11.82	22.70	N.M.	1.20	N.M.	N.M.
Return on Equity %	3.67	4.72	30.62	107.54	N.M.	14.60	N.M.	N.M.
EBITDA Margin %	10.81	14.67	16.41	13.03	8.67	11.04	5.21	N.M.
Net Margin %	4.71	2.75	16.90	26.24	0.99	1.32	N.M.	N.M.
Asset Turnover	0.83	0.83	0.70	0.87	...	0.91	0.86	0.77
Current Ratio	2.39	2.39	2.25	1.41	2.05	2.99	2.41	2.34
Debt to Equity	0.59	0.58	0.57	1.17	5.42	3.59	384.17	14.72
Price Range	40.82-25.78	38.70-25.78	32.19-16.48	32.73-22.91	35.85-24.55	30.44-22.19	28.43-10.56	19.40-6.13
P/E Ratio	85.04-53.71	64.50-42.97	9.30-4.76	4.86-3.40	143.40-98.20	72.48-52.83	...	...

Address: 550 West Adams Street, Chicago, IL 60661-3676 Telephone: 312-436-4000	Web Site: www.usg.com Officers: Jennifer F. Scanlon - President, Chief Executive Officer Matthew F. Hilzinger - Executive Vice President, Chief Financial Officer	Auditors: DELOITTE & TOUCHE LLP Investor Contact: 312-436-6098 Transfer Agents: Computershare Trust Company, Providence, RI

VAIL RESORTS INC

Exchange	Symbol	Price	52Wk Range	Yield	P/E
NYS	MTN	$274.19 (6/29/2018)	285.05-199.09	2.14	28.35

*7 Year Price Score 162.88 *NYSE Composite Index=100 *12 Month Price Score 109.18

Interim Earnings (Per Share)

Qtr.	Oct	Jan	Apr	Jul
2014-15	(1.77)	3.10	3.56	(1.88)
2015-16	(1.63)	3.14	4.23	(1.75)
2016-17	(1.70)	3.63	4.40	(1.46)
2017-18	(0.71)	5.67	6.17	...

Interim Dividends (Per Share)

Amt	Decl	Ex	Rec	Pay
1.053Q	09/27/2017	10/06/2017	10/10/2017	10/27/2017
1.053Q	12/07/2017	12/26/2017	12/27/2017	01/10/2018
1.47Q	03/07/2018	03/26/2018	03/27/2018	04/11/2018
1.47Q	06/07/2018	06/26/2018	06/27/2018	07/12/2018

Indicated Div: $5.88

Valuation Analysis

		Institutional Holding	
Forecast EPS	$9.04 (06/13/2018)	No of Institutions	557
Market Cap	$11.1 Billion	Shares	47,987,064
Book Value	$1.8 Billion	% Held	99.85
Price/Book	6.24		
Price/Sales	5.50		

Business Summary: Sporting & Recreational (MIC: 2.2.4 SIC: 7999 NAIC: 713990)

Vail Resorts is a holding company and operates through various subsidiaries. Co. operates in three segments: Mountain, which operates mountain resort properties and urban ski areas, as well as ancillary services, primarily including ski school, dining and retail/rental operations; Lodging, which owns and/or manages hotels under its RockResorts brand, other lodging properties, condominiums located in proximity to its mountain resorts, National Park Service concessionaire properties including Grand Teton Lodge Company, a resort ground transportation company, and mountain resort golf courses; and Real Estate, which owns, develops and sells real estate in and around its resort communities.

Recent Developments: For the quarter ended Apr 30 2018, net income increased 38.3% to US$272.3 million from US$196.9 million in the year-earlier quarter. Revenues were US$844.5 million, up 6.3% from US$794.6 million the year before. Operating income was US$368.0 million versus US$320.1 million in the prior-year quarter, an increase of 15.0%. Direct operating expenses rose 3.2% to US$355.5 million from US$344.3 million in the comparable period the year before. Indirect operating expenses decreased 7.1% to US$121.1 million from US$130.3 million in the equivalent prior-year period.

Prospects: Our evaluation of Vail Resorts Inc. as of Jan. 21, 2018 is the result of our systematic analysis on three basic characteristics: earnings strength, relative valuation, and recent stock price movement. The company has generated a negative trend in earnings per share over the past 5 quarters. However, while recent estimates for the company have been mixed, MTN has posted better than expected results. Based on operating earnings yield, the company is about fairly valued when compared to all of the companies in our coverage universe. Share price changes over the past year indicates that MTN will perform well over the near term.

Financial Data

(US$ in Thousands)	9 Mos	6 Mos	3 Mos	07/31/2017	07/31/2016	07/31/2015	07/31/2014	07/31/2013
Earnings Per Share	9.67	7.90	5.86	5.22	4.01	3.07	0.77	1.03
Cash Flow Per Share	13.90	13.86	13.93	11.64	11.73	8.36	6.81	6.20
Tang Book Value Per Share	N.M.	N.M.	N.M.	N.M.	6.23	6.08	8.98	9.84
Dividends Per Share	4.629	4.212	3.969	3.726	2.865	2.075	1.245	0.790
Dividend Payout %	47.87	53.32	67.73	71.38	71.45	67.59	161.69	76.70
Income Statement								
Total Revenue	1,799,916	955,425	220,850	1,907,218	1,601,286	1,399,924	1,254,646	1,120,797
EBITDA	672,034	258,111	(61,533)	581,455	440,502	343,747	243,407	227,504
Depn & Amortn	154,132	100,028	48,624	180,800	156,800	144,000	136,600	130,200
Income Before Taxes	471,107	126,936	(125,331)	346,566	241,336	148,506	42,810	58,338
Income Taxes	(17,914)	(89,810)	(93,404)	116,731	93,165	34,718	15,866	21,619
Net Income	463,558	207,306	(28,385)	210,553	149,754	114,754	28,478	37,743
Average Shares	41,545	41,594	40,211	40,366	37,312	37,406	37,057	36,733
Balance Sheet								
Current Assets	519,660	481,009	395,703	433,070	322,865	288,143	275,046	343,469
Total Assets	4,075,435	4,156,806	4,008,616	4,110,718	2,482,018	2,489,621	2,173,849	2,275,422
Current Liabilities	497,814	659,493	709,596	604,557	506,481	398,647	324,206	313,335
Long-Term Obligations	1,078,005	1,182,349	1,262,325	1,234,024	686,909	806,676	625,600	795,928
Total Liabilities	2,304,762	2,511,478	2,607,211	2,539,562	1,607,478	1,623,053	1,353,006	1,451,554
Stockholders' Equity	1,770,673	1,645,328	1,401,405	1,571,156	874,540	866,568	820,843	823,868
Shares Outstanding	40,322	40,421	40,406	40,081	36,179	36,513	36,203	35,954
Statistical Record								
Return on Assets %	10.05	8.14	6.17	6.39	6.01	4.92	1.28	1.80
Return on Equity %	24.28	21.21	17.87	17.22	17.16	13.60	3.46	4.64
EBITDA Margin %	37.34	27.02	N.M.	30.49	27.51	24.55	19.40	20.30
Net Margin %	25.75	21.70	N.M.	11.04	9.35	8.20	2.27	3.37
Asset Turnover	0.50	0.48	0.49	0.58	0.64	0.60	0.56	0.53
Current Ratio	1.04	0.73	0.56	0.72	0.64	0.72	0.85	1.10
Debt to Equity	0.61	0.72	0.90	0.79	0.79	0.93	0.76	0.97
Price Range	236.71-198.75	236.71-171.54	232.28-154.44	215.36-142.60	144.80-101.26	111.48-74.23	78.79-64.90	66.98-49.00
P/E Ratio	24.48-20.55	29.96-21.71	39.64-26.35	41.26-27.32	36.11-25.25	36.31-24.18	102.32-84.29	65.03-47.57
Average Yield %	2.12	2.01	2.04	2.10	2.32	2.23	2.21	1.75

Address: 390 Interlocken Crescent, Broomfield, CO 80021 **Telephone:** 303-404-1800 **Fax:** 303-404-6415	**Web Site:** www.vailresorts.com **Officers:** Robert A. Katz - Chairman, Chief Executive Officer Michael Z. Barkin - Executive Vice President, Vice President, Chief Financial Officer	**Auditors:** PricewaterhouseCoopers LLP **Investor Contact:** 303-404-1820 **Transfer Agents:** Wells Fargo Shareowner Services, Saint Paul, MN

VALERO ENERGY CORP

Exchange	Symbol	Price	52Wk Range	Yield	P/E
NYS	VLO	$110.83 (6/29/2018)	124.44-64.55	2.89	11.56

*7 Year Price Score 136.28 *NYSE Composite Index=100 *12 Month Price Score 129.19

Interim Earnings (Per Share)

Qtr.	Mar	Jun	Sep	Dec
2015	1.87	2.66	2.79	0.69
2016	1.05	1.73	1.33	0.82
2017	0.68	1.23	1.91	5.36
2018	1.09	...	...	...

Interim Dividends (Per Share)

Amt	Decl	Ex	Rec	Pay
0.70Q	07/20/2017	08/07/2017	08/09/2017	09/07/2017
0.70Q	11/01/2017	11/20/2017	11/21/2017	12/12/2017
0.80Q	01/23/2018	02/12/2018	02/13/2018	03/06/2018
0.80Q	05/03/2018	05/16/2018	05/17/2018	06/05/2018

Indicated Div: $3.20

Valuation Analysis / Institutional Holding

Valuation Analysis		Institutional Holding	
Forecast EPS	$6.45	No of Institutions	
	(06/14/2018)	1546	
Market Cap	$47.8 Billion	Shares	
Book Value	$21.9 Billion	433,959,840	
Price/Book	2.18	% Held	
Price/Sales	0.48	75.04	

Business Summary: Refining & Marketing (MIC: 9.1.2 SIC: 2911 NAIC: 324110)

Valero Energy is a petroleum refiner and ethanol producer. Co. sells its refined petroleum products in both the wholesale rack and bulk markets, and outlets carry the Valero®, Diamond Shamrock®, Shamrock®, Ultramar®, Beacon®, and Texaco® brand names in the U.S., Canada, the U.K. and Ireland. As of Dec 31 2017, Co. had three segments: Refining, Ethanol and VLP. Refining includes Co.'s refining operations, the associated marketing activities, and logistics assets that support its refining operations. Ethanol includes Co.'s ethanol operations, the associated marketing activities, and logistics assets that support its ethanol operations. VLP includes the results of Valero Energy Partners LP.

Recent Developments: For the quarter ended Mar 31 2018, net income increased 81.3% to US$582.0 million from US$321.0 million in the year-earlier quarter. Revenues were US$26.44 billion, up 21.4% from US$21.77 billion the year before. Operating income was US$801.0 million versus US$528.0 million in the prior-year quarter, an increase of 51.7%. Direct operating expenses rose 20.6% to US$25.38 billion from US$21.04 billion in the comparable period the year before. Indirect operating expenses increased 27.9% to US$261.0 million from US$204.0 million in the equivalent prior-year period.

Prospects: Our evaluation of Valero Energy Corp. as of Jan. 21, 2018 is the result of our systematic analysis on three basic characteristics: earnings strength, relative valuation, and recent stock price movement. The company has produced a positive trend in earnings per share over the past 5 quarters. However, while recent estimates for the company have been mixed, VLO has posted better than expected results. Based on operating earnings yield, the company is undervalued when compared to all of the companies in our coverage universe. Share price changes over the past year indicates that VLO will perform poorly over the near term.

Financial Data

(US$ in Thousands)	3 Mos	12/31/2017	12/31/2016	12/31/2015	12/31/2014	12/31/2013	12/31/2012	12/31/2011
Earnings Per Share	9.59	9.16	4.94	7.99	6.85	4.97	3.75	3.68
Cash Flow Per Share	10.75	12.40	10.43	11.29	8.06	10.27	9.56	7.17
Tang Book Value Per Share	50.77	50.68	44.35	43.39	40.20	36.04	32.28	29.09
Dividends Per Share	2.900	2.800	2.400	1.700	1.050	0.850	0.650	0.300
Dividend Payout %	30.24	30.57	48.58	21.28	15.33	17.10	17.33	8.15
Income Statement								
Total Revenue	26,439,000	93,980,000	75,659,000	87,804,000	130,844,000	138,074,000	139,250,000	125,987,000
EBITDA	1,350,000	4,975,000	4,928,000	7,704,000	7,149,000	5,547,000	5,119,000	4,823,000
Depn & Amortn	498,000	1,300,000	1,300,000	1,300,000	1,200,000	1,200,000	1,100,000	1,100,000
Income Before Taxes	731,000	3,207,000	3,182,000	5,971,000	5,552,000	3,982,000	3,706,000	3,322,000
Income Taxes	149,000	(949,000)	765,000	1,870,000	1,777,000	1,254,000	1,626,000	1,226,000
Net Income	469,000	4,065,000	2,289,000	3,990,000	3,630,000	2,720,000	2,083,000	2,090,000
Average Shares	432,000	444,000	464,000	500,000	530,000	548,000	556,000	569,000
Balance Sheet								
Current Assets	18,260,000	19,312,000	16,800,000	14,972,000	16,614,000	19,277,000	16,460,000	15,972,000
Total Assets	49,376,000	50,158,000	46,173,000	44,343,000	45,550,000	47,260,000	44,477,000	42,783,000
Current Liabilities	10,752,000	11,071,000	8,328,000	7,360,000	9,980,000	13,123,000	11,929,000	12,708,000
Long-Term Obligations	8,086,000	8,750,000	7,886,000	7,250,000	5,780,000	6,261,000	6,463,000	6,732,000
Total Liabilities	27,499,000	28,167,000	26,149,000	23,816,000	24,873,000	27,800,000	26,445,000	26,360,000
Stockholders' Equity	21,877,000	21,991,000	20,024,000	20,527,000	20,677,000	19,460,000	18,032,000	16,423,000
Shares Outstanding	430,927	433,898	451,501	473,039	514,298	535,569	552,095	556,812
Statistical Record								
Return on Assets %	8.86	8.44	5.04	8.88	7.82	5.93	4.76	5.20
Return on Equity %	20.28	19.35	11.26	19.37	18.09	14.51	12.06	13.29
EBITDA Margin %	5.11	5.29	6.51	8.77	5.46	4.02	3.68	3.83
Net Margin %	1.77	4.33	3.03	4.54	2.77	1.97	1.50	1.66
Asset Turnover	2.07	1.95	1.67	1.95	2.82	3.01	3.18	3.13
Current Ratio	1.70	1.74	2.02	2.03	1.66	1.47	1.38	1.26
Debt to Equity	0.37	0.40	0.39	0.35	0.28	0.32	0.36	0.41
Price Range	98.95-61.47	92.30-61.47	72.09-47.24	73.03-44.07	58.51-43.76	50.40-31.17	31.41-17.91	28.07-15.68
P/E Ratio	10.32-6.41	10.08-6.71	14.59-9.56	9.14-5.52	8.54-6.39	10.14-6.27	8.37-4.78	7.63-4.26
Average Yield %	3.76	3.95	4.09	2.76	2.05	2.20	2.65	1.34

Address: One Valero Way, San Antonio, TX 78249
Telephone: 210-345-2000
Fax: 210-246-2646

Web Site: www.valero.com
Officers: Joseph W. Gorder - Chairman, President, Chief Executive Officer, Associate/Affiliate Company Officer, Executive Vice President, Chief Operating Officer, Chief Commercial Officer Donna M. Titzman - Executive Vice President, Chief Financial Officer, Senior Vice President, Vice President, Treasurer

Auditors: KPMG LLP
Investor Contact: 800-531-7911
Transfer Agents: ComputerShare Investor Services, Providence, RI

VALLEY NATIONAL BANCORP (NJ)

Exchange	Symbol	Price	52Wk Range	Yield	P/E
NYS	VLY	$12.16 (6/29/2018)	13.28-10.71	3.62	22.94

*7 Year Price Score 92.26 *NYSE Composite Index=100 *12 Month Price Score 104.02

Interim Earnings (Per Share)

Qtr.	Mar	Jun	Sep	Dec
2015	0.13	0.14	0.15	0.01
2016	0.14	0.15	0.16	0.19
2017	0.17	0.18	0.14	0.09
2018	0.12	...	...	...

Interim Dividends (Per Share)

Amt	Decl	Ex	Rec	Pay
0.11Q	08/22/2017	09/14/2017	09/15/2017	10/03/2017
0.11Q	11/28/2017	12/21/2017	12/22/2017	01/03/2018
0.11Q	03/01/2018	03/14/2018	03/15/2018	04/02/2018
0.11Q	05/22/2018	06/14/2018	06/15/2018	07/03/2018

Indicated Div: $0.44 (Div. Reinv. Plan)

Valuation Analysis **Institutional Holding**

Forecast EPS	$0.87	No of Institutions
	(06/11/2018)	390
Market Cap	$4.0 Billion	Shares
Book Value	$3.2 Billion	220,874,016
Price/Book	1.24	% Held
Price/Sales	3.94	55.59

Business Summary: Banking (MIC: 5.1.1 SIC: 6021 NAIC: 522110)

Valley National Bancorp is a bank holding company. Through its subsidiary, Valley National Bank (the Bank), Co. provides commercial, retail, insurance and wealth management financial services products. The Bank provides banking services including automated teller machines, telephone and internet banking, remote deposit capture, overdraft facilities, drive-in and night deposit services, and safe deposit facilities. The Bank also provides international banking services including standby letters of credit, documentary letters of credit and related products, and certain ancillary services. As of Dec 31 2017, Co. had total assets of $24.00 billion and total deposits of $18.15 billion.

Recent Developments: For the quarter ended Mar 31 2018, net income decreased 9.0% to US$42.0 million from US$46.1 million in the year-earlier quarter. Net interest income increased 28.3% to US$207.6 million from US$161.9 million in the year-earlier quarter. Provision for loan losses was US$10.9 million versus US$2.5 million in the prior-year quarter, an increase of 343.2%. Non-interest income rose 25.4% to US$32.3 million from US$25.7 million, while non-interest expense advanced 43.7% to US$173.8 million.

Prospects: Our evaluation of Valley National Bancorp as of Jan. 21, 2018 is the result of our systematic analysis on three basic characteristics: earnings strength, relative valuation, and recent stock price movement. The company has generated a negative trend in earnings per share over the past 5 quarters and while recent estimates for the company have been mixed, VLY has posted results that fell short of analysts expectations. Based on operating earnings yield, the company is undervalued when compared to all of the companies in our coverage universe. Share price changes over the past year indicates that VLY will perform poorly over the near term.

Financial Data
(US$ in Thousands)

	3 Mos	12/31/2017	12/31/2016	12/31/2015	12/31/2014	12/31/2013	12/31/2012	12/31/2011
Earnings Per Share	0.53	0.58	0.63	0.42	0.56	0.66	0.73	0.75
Cash Flow Per Share	1.93	2.35	1.64	0.66	0.89	1.43	1.63	1.07
Tang Book Value Per Share	5.65	6.01	5.80	5.36	5.38	5.39	5.26	5.19
Dividends Per Share	0.440	0.440	0.440	0.440	0.440	0.598	0.652	0.656
Dividend Payout %	83.02	75.86	69.84	104.76	78.57	90.53	89.29	87.20
Income Statement								
Interest Income	267,495	842,419	766,923	707,023	636,603	616,097	671,193	673,824
Interest Expense	59,897	174,107	148,774	156,754	161,846	168,377	181,312	199,013
Net Interest Income	207,598	668,312	618,149	550,269	474,757	447,720	489,881	474,811
Provision for Losses	10,948	9,942	11,869	8,101	1,884	16,095	25,552	53,335
Non-Interest Income	32,251	103,441	103,225	83,802	77,616	128,653	120,946	112,297
Non-Interest Expense	173,752	509,073	476,125	499,075	403,255	381,338	374,900	336,588
Income Before Taxes	55,149	252,738	233,380	126,895	147,234	178,940	210,375	197,185
Income Taxes	13,184	90,831	65,234	23,938	31,062	46,979	66,748	63,532
Net Income	41,965	161,907	168,146	102,957	116,172	131,961	143,627	133,653
Average Shares	332,465	264,889	255,268	234,437	205,716	199,309	197,354	178,426
Balance Sheet								
Net Loans & Leases	22,428,354	18,225,843	17,179,392	15,953,311	13,395,855	11,464,483	11,012,829	9,691,008
Total Assets	29,464,357	24,002,306	22,864,439	21,612,616	18,793,855	16,156,541	16,012,646	14,244,507
Total Deposits	21,959,846	18,153,462	17,730,708	16,253,551	14,034,116	11,319,262	11,264,018	9,673,102
Total Liabilities	26,219,354	21,469,141	20,487,283	19,405,525	16,930,838	14,615,501	14,510,269	12,978,259
Stockholders' Equity	3,245,003	2,533,165	2,377,156	2,207,091	1,863,017	1,541,040	1,502,377	1,266,248
Shares Outstanding	331,189	264,468	263,638	253,787	232,110	199,593	198,438	178,683
Statistical Record								
Return on Assets %	0.60	0.69	0.75	0.51	0.66	0.82	0.95	0.94
Return on Equity %	5.59	6.59	7.32	5.06	6.83	8.67	10.35	10.44
Net Interest Margin %	77.61	79.33	80.60	77.83	74.58	72.67	72.99	70.47
Efficiency Ratio %	57.97	53.82	54.72	63.11	56.46	51.20	47.33	42.82
Loans to Deposits	1.02	1.00	0.97	0.98	0.95	1.01	0.98	1.00
Price Range	13.28-10.71	12.76-10.71	11.97-8.31	11.14-9.05	10.80-9.21	10.65-8.85	12.59-8.72	13.52-9.42
P/E Ratio	25.06-20.21	22.00-18.47	19.00-13.19	26.52-21.55	19.29-16.45	16.14-13.41	17.25-11.95	18.03-12.56
Average Yield %	3.72	3.76	4.57	4.46	4.44	6.05	6.07	5.50

Address: 1455 Valley Road, Wayne, NJ 07470	**Web Site:** www.valleynationalbank.com	**Auditors:** KPMG LLP
Telephone: 973-305-8800	**Officers:** Gerald H. Lipkin - Chairman, Chief Executive Officer Dianne M. Grenz - Senior Executive Vice President	**Investor Contact:** 973-305-8800
		Transfer Agents: American Stock & Transfer & Trust Company, Brooklyn, NY

VALMONT INDUSTRIES INC

Exchange	Symbol	Price	52Wk Range	Yield	P/E
NYS	VMI	$150.75 (6/29/2018)	172.85-139.30	1.00	29.50

*7 Year Price Score 93.28   *NYSE Composite Index=100   *12 Month Price Score 94.72

Interim Earnings (Per Share)

Qtr.	Mar	Jun	Sep	Dec
2015	1.28	1.19	0.52	(1.29)
2016	1.45	1.85	1.24	3.09
2017	1.72	2.01	1.55	(0.17)
2018	1.72	...	...	...

Interim Dividends (Per Share)

Amt	Decl	Ex	Rec	Pay
0.375Q	09/05/2017	09/28/2017	09/29/2017	10/16/2017
0.375Q	12/04/2017	12/28/2017	12/29/2017	01/16/2018
0.375Q	03/05/2018	03/28/2018	03/29/2018	04/16/2018
0.375Q	06/04/2018	06/28/2018	06/29/2018	07/16/2018

Indicated Div: $1.50 (Div. Reinv. Plan)

Valuation Analysis — **Institutional Holding**

Forecast EPS	$8.05	No of Institutions
	(06/14/2018)	395
Market Cap	$3.4 Billion	Shares
Book Value	$1.1 Billion	26,577,920
Price/Book	2.97	% Held
Price/Sales	1.21	86.76

Business Summary: Construction Materials (MIC: 8.5.1 SIC: 3499 NAIC: 332323)

Valmont Industries is a producer of fabricated metal products. Co. has five segments: Engineered Support Structures, which provides engineered metal, wood, and composite structures and components; Utility Support Structures, which provides engineered steel and concrete structures; Energy and Mining, which provides access systems applications, forged steel grinding media, on and off shore oil, gas, and wind energy structures; Coatings, which consists of galvanizing, anodizing and powder coating services; and Irrigation, which provides agricultural irrigation equipment and related parts and services for the agricultural industry as well as tubular products for industrial customers.

Recent Developments: For the quarter ended Mar 31 2018, net income increased 1.3% to US$40.5 million from US$40.0 million in the year-earlier quarter. Revenues were US$698.7 million, up 9.6% from US$637.5 million the year before. Operating income was US$64.0 million versus US$64.7 million in the prior-year quarter, a decrease of 1.1%. Direct operating expenses rose 12.0% to US$529.4 million from US$472.9 million in the comparable period the year before. Indirect operating expenses increased 5.3% to US$105.3 million from US$99.9 million in the equivalent prior-year period.

Prospects: Our evaluation of Valmont Industries Inc. as of Jan. 21, 2018 is the result of our systematic analysis on three basic characteristics: earnings strength, relative valuation, and recent stock price movement. The company has managed to produce a neutral trend in earnings per share over the past 5 quarters and while recent estimates for the company have been mixed, VMI has posted results that fell short of analysts expectations. Based on operating earnings yield, the company is about fairly valued when compared to all of the companies in our coverage universe. Share price changes over the past year indicates that VMI will perform in line with the market over the near term.

Financial Data
(US$ in Thousands)

	3 Mos	12/30/2017	12/31/2016	12/26/2015	12/27/2014	12/28/2013	12/29/2012	12/31/2011
Earnings Per Share	5.11	5.11	7.63	1.71	7.09	10.35	8.75	8.60
Cash Flow Per Share	6.32	6.49	9.56	11.72	6.79	14.92	7.47	5.59
Tang Book Value Per Share	30.50	28.05	21.22	18.00	25.37	37.33	31.75	25.08
Dividends Per Share	1.500	1.500	1.500	1.500	1.375	0.975	0.855	0.705
Dividend Payout %	29.35	29.35	19.66	87.72	19.39	9.42	9.77	8.20
Income Statement								
Total Revenue	698,684	2,745,967	2,521,676	2,618,924	3,123,143	3,304,211	3,029,541	2,661,480
EBITDA	83,997	353,329	344,175	225,476	404,255	552,878	452,861	335,227
Depn & Amortn	21,178	84,957	82,417	91,144	89,328	77,436	70,218	74,560
Income Before Taxes	53,012	228,464	220,454	93,007	284,183	449,417	359,290	233,757
Income Taxes	12,532	106,145	42,063	47,427	94,894	157,781	126,502	4,590
Net Income	39,281	116,240	173,232	40,117	183,976	278,489	234,072	228,308
Average Shares	22,796	22,738	22,709	23,405	25,719	26,899	26,764	26,550
Balance Sheet								
Current Assets	1,523,343	1,472,565	1,253,216	1,226,852	1,392,941	1,597,840	1,425,940	1,252,943
Total Assets	2,618,064	2,602,250	2,391,731	2,399,428	2,729,668	2,776,494	2,568,551	2,306,076
Current Liabilities	374,262	402,998	349,848	366,554	397,214	436,580	412,433	408,070
Long-Term Obligations	753,647	753,888	754,795	763,964	766,654	470,907	472,593	474,415
Total Liabilities	1,472,823	1,489,414	1,448,249	1,480,987	1,527,835	1,254,469	1,218,639	1,159,114
Stockholders' Equity	1,145,241	1,112,836	943,482	918,441	1,201,833	1,522,025	1,349,912	1,146,962
Shares Outstanding	22,552	22,693	22,520	22,857	24,229	26,824	26,674	26,481
Statistical Record								
Return on Assets %	4.58	4.67	7.11	1.57	6.70	10.45	9.63	10.22
Return on Equity %	10.85	11.34	18.31	3.79	13.55	19.45	18.80	21.78
EBITDA Margin %	12.02	12.87	13.65	8.61	12.94	16.73	14.95	12.60
Net Margin %	5.62	4.23	6.87	1.53	5.89	8.43	7.73	8.58
Asset Turnover	1.10	1.10	1.04	1.02	1.14	1.24	1.25	1.19
Current Ratio	4.07	3.65	3.58	3.35	3.51	3.66	3.46	3.07
Debt to Equity	0.66	0.68	0.80	0.83	0.64	0.31	0.35	0.41
Price Range	172.85-142.35	172.85-136.05	155.40-98.95	130.26-93.99	161.11-123.75	164.50-132.08	141.13-92.07	110.26-74.27
P/E Ratio	33.83-27.86	33.83-26.62	20.37-12.97	76.18-54.96	22.72-17.45	15.89-12.76	16.13-10.52	12.82-8.64
Average Yield %	0.97	0.98	1.17	1.29	0.95	0.67	0.70	0.76

Address: One Valmont Plaza, Omaha, NE 68154-5215	**Web Site:** www.valmont.com	**Auditors:** DELOITTE & TOUCHE LLP
Telephone: 402-963-1000	**Officers:** Mogens C. Bay - Executive Chairman, Chairman, President, Chief Executive Officer Stephen G. Kaniewski - President, Chief Executive Officer, Chief Operating Officer	**Investor Contact:** 402-963-1000
Fax: 402-963-1198		**Transfer Agents:** Wells Fargo Shareowner Services, Mendota Heights, MN

VALVOLINE INC

Exchange	Symbol	Price	52Wk Range	Yield	P/E
NYS	VVV	$21.57 (6/29/2018)	25.40-20.02	1.38	20.16

*7 Year Price Score N/A ***NYSE Composite Index=100** ***12 Month Price Score 90.23**

TRADING VOLUME (thousand shares)

Interim Earnings (Per Share)

Qtr.	Dec	Mar	Jun	Sep
2015-16	0.32	0.34	0.44	0.11
2016-17	0.35	0.35	0.27	0.52
2017-18	(0.05)	0.33	...	...

Interim Dividends (Per Share)

Amt	Decl	Ex	Rec	Pay
0.049Q	07/27/2017	08/30/2017	09/01/2017	09/15/2017
0.074Q	11/14/2017	11/30/2017	12/01/2017	12/15/2017
0.074Q	01/31/2018	02/28/2018	03/01/2018	03/15/2018
0.074Q	04/18/2018	05/31/2018	06/01/2018	06/15/2018

Indicated Div: $0.30

Valuation Analysis		Institutional Holding	
Forecast EPS	$1.34	No of Institutions	
	(06/13/2018)	374	
Market Cap	$4.2 Billion	Shares	
Book Value	N/A	205,676,848	
Price/Book	N/A	% Held	
Price/Sales	1.94	N/A	

Business Summary: Specialty Chemicals (MIC: 8.3.2 SIC: 2992 NAIC: 324191)

Valvoline is a producer, marketer and supplier of engine and automotive maintenance products and services. Co.'s reportable segments are: Core North America, which sells Valvolineâ„¢ and other branded and private label products in the U.S. and Canada to both retailers for consumers to perform their own automotive maintenance, as well as to installer customers who use Co.'s products to service vehicles; Quick Lubes; which services the passenger car and light truck quick lube market through two platforms: Co.-owned and franchised Valvoline Instant Oil Changesm stores and Express Careâ„¢; and International, which sells Valvolineâ„¢ and other branded products outside the U.S. and Canada.

Recent Developments: For the quarter ended Mar 31 2018, net income decreased 5.6% to US$67.0 million from US$71.0 million in the year-earlier quarter. Revenues were US$569.0 million, up 10.7% from US$514.0 million the year before. Operating income was unchanged at US$100.0 million versus the prior-year quarter. Direct operating expenses rose 14.6% to US$362.0 million from US$316.0 million in the comparable period the year before. Indirect operating expenses increased 9.2% to US$107.0 million from US$98.0 million in the equivalent prior-year period.

Prospects: Our evaluation of Valvoline Inc as of Jan. 21, 2018 is the result of our systematic analysis on three basic characteristics: earnings strength, relative valuation, and recent stock price movement. The company has generated a negative trend in earnings per share over the past 5 quarters and while recent estimates for the company have been raised by analysts, VVV has posted better than expected results. Based on operating earnings yield, the company is undervalued when compared to all of the companies in our coverage universe. Share price changes over the past year indicates that VVV will perform in line with the market over the near term.

Financial Data
(US$ in Thousands)

	6 Mos	3 Mos	09/30/2017	09/30/2016	09/30/2015	09/30/2014	09/30/2013
Earnings Per Share	1.07	1.09	1.49	1.33	...	...	...
Cash Flow Per Share	(0.46)	(0.98)	(0.64)	1.51	...	...	...
Dividends Per Share	0.247	0.222	0.196	...	...	...	...
Dividend Payout %	23.08	20.32	13.15	...	...	...	...
Income Statement							
Total Revenue	1,114,000	545,000	2,084,000	1,929,000	1,966,900	2,041,300	1,996,200
EBITDA	233,000	109,000	574,000	468,000	334,400	301,200	415,700
Depn & Amortn	25,000	11,000	42,000	38,000	37,600	36,500	35,100
Income Before Taxes	178,000	84,000	490,000	421,000	296,800	264,700	380,600
Income Taxes	121,000	94,000	186,000	148,000	100,700	91,300	134,500
Net Income	57,000	(10,000)	304,000	273,000	196,100	173,400	246,100
Average Shares	200,000	202,000	204,000	205,000	...	...	...
Balance Sheet							
Current Assets	795,000	735,000	790,000	730,000	477,300	544,700	...
Total Assets	1,869,000	1,827,000	1,915,000	1,825,000	977,900	1,082,500	...
Current Liabilities	415,000	368,000	478,000	400,000	298,600	293,500	...
Long-Term Obligations	1,183,000	1,147,000	1,034,000	724,000	...	...	...
Total Liabilities	2,095,000	2,021,000	2,032,000	2,155,000	360,800	357,700	...
Stockholders' Equity	(226,000)	(194,000)	(117,000)	(330,000)	617,100	724,800	...
Shares Outstanding	197,000	201,000	203,000	205,000	...	...	...
Statistical Record							
Return on Assets %	11.55	12.03	16.26	19.43	19.04	...	...
Return on Equity %	...	...	...	189.66	29.23	...	...
EBITDA Margin %	20.92	20.00	27.54	24.26	17.00	14.76	20.82
Net Margin %	5.12	N.M.	14.59	14.15	9.97	8.49	12.33
Asset Turnover	1.16	1.16	1.11	1.37	1.91	...	...
Current Ratio	1.92	2.00	1.65	1.83	1.60	1.86	...
Price Range	25.40-21.17	25.06-21.17	24.66-18.90	23.98-23.10	...	...	...
P/E Ratio	23.74-19.79	22.99-19.42	16.55-12.68	18.03-17.37	...	...	...
Average Yield %	1.06	0.96	0.87	...	...	...	...

Address: 100 Valvoline Way, Lexington, KY 40509 Telephone: 859-357-7777	Web Site: www.valvoline.com Officers: Stephen F. Kirk - Chairman Samuel J. Mitchell - President, Chief Executive Officer	Auditors: Ernst & Young LLP Investor Contact: 859-357-7777 Transfer Agents: Wells Fargo Shareowner Services

VARIAN MEDICAL SYSTEMS INC

Exchange	Symbol	Price	52Wk Range	Yield	P/E
NYS	VAR	$113.72 (6/29/2018)	129.46-95.88	N/A	78.97

*7 Year Price Score 119.29 *NYSE Composite Index=100 *12 Month Price Score 103.82

Interim Earnings (Per Share)

Qtr.	Dec	Mar	Jun	Sep
2014-15	0.92	1.05	1.13	0.99
2015-16	0.91	1.01	1.04	1.24
2016-17	0.22	0.60	0.98	0.89
2017-18	(1.22)	0.79	...	...

Interim Dividends (Per Share)

No Dividends Paid

Valuation Analysis		Institutional Holding	
Forecast EPS	$4.46	No of Institutions	
	(06/14/2018)	861	
Market Cap	$10.4 Billion	Shares	
Book Value	$1.5 Billion	117,931,848	
Price/Book	7.18	% Held	
Price/Sales	3.71	81.85	

Business Summary: Medical Instruments & Equipment (MIC: 4.3.1 SIC: 3845 NAIC: 334510)

Varian Medical Systems is a manufacturer of medical devices and software for treating cancer and other medical conditions with radiotherapy, radiosurgery, proton therapy and brachytherapy. Co. has two segments: Oncology Systems, which designs, manufactures, sells and services hardware and software products for treating cancer with radiotherapy, and treatments such as fixed field intensity-modulated radiation therapy, image-guided radiation therapy, volumetric modulated arc therapy, stereotactic radiosurgery, stereotactic body radiotherapy and brachytherapy; and Imaging Components, which designs, manufactures, sells and services X-ray imaging components for use in a range of applications.

Recent Developments: For the quarter ended Mar 30 2018, income from continuing operations increased 5.3% to US$73.2 million from US$69.5 million in the year-earlier quarter. Net income increased 30.2% to US$73.2 million from US$56.2 million in the year-earlier quarter. Revenues were US$729.9 million, up 10.1% from US$663.2 million the year before. Operating income was US$94.3 million versus US$90.1 million in the prior-year quarter, an increase of 4.7%. Direct operating expenses rose 6.1% to US$411.4 million from US$387.6 million in the comparable period the year before. Indirect operating expenses increased 20.9% to US$224.2 million from US$185.5 million in the equivalent prior-year period.

Prospects: Our evaluation of Varian Medical Systems Inc. as of Jan. 21, 2018 is the result of our systematic analysis on three basic characteristics: earnings strength, relative valuation, and recent stock price movement. The company has produced a positive trend in earnings per share over the past 5 quarters. However, while recent estimates for the company have been lowered by analysts, VAR has posted results that fell short of analysts expectations. Based on operating earnings yield, the company is about fairly valued when compared to all of the companies in our coverage universe. Share price changes over the past year indicates that VAR will perform very well over the near term.

Financial Data
(US$ in Thousands)

	6 Mos	3 Mos	09/29/2017	09/30/2016	10/02/2015	09/26/2014	09/27/2013	09/28/2012
Earnings Per Share	1.44	1.25	2.68	4.19	4.09	3.83	3.98	3.76
Cash Flow Per Share	5.78	5.41	4.33	3.75	4.63	4.33	4.21	4.44
Tang Book Value Per Share	12.37	11.98	13.09	14.31	13.82	13.22	13.98	11.77
Income Statement								
Total Revenue	1,408,400	678,500	2,668,200	3,217,800	3,099,111	3,049,800	2,942,897	2,807,015
EBITDA	251,500	140,500	418,800	630,600	617,487	633,612	671,749	655,056
Depn & Amortn	35,800	19,100	76,900	79,800	68,520	62,457	62,859	60,982
Income Before Taxes	218,100	122,500	344,800	556,400	554,662	574,510	612,083	595,924
Income Taxes	257,100	234,700	87,700	153,700	142,644	170,807	173,835	168,875
Net Income	(39,100)	(112,300)	249,600	402,300	411,485	403,703	438,248	427,049
Average Shares	92,600	91,600	93,200	96,000	100,552	105,271	110,053	113,473
Balance Sheet								
Current Assets	2,345,400	2,351,600	2,190,300	2,616,000	2,525,045	2,494,165	2,704,783	2,170,515
Total Assets	3,307,500	3,299,800	3,179,400	3,816,000	3,600,748	3,357,290	3,468,474	2,878,726
Current Liabilities	1,530,200	1,616,400	1,550,100	1,614,000	1,382,904	1,201,654	1,160,579	1,236,531
Long-Term Obligations	25,000	...	...	287,500	337,500	387,500	450,000	6,250
Total Liabilities	1,855,300	1,913,200	1,684,400	2,075,500	1,889,148	1,740,870	1,754,627	1,368,950
Stockholders' Equity	1,452,200	1,386,600	1,495,000	1,740,500	1,711,600	1,616,420	1,713,847	1,509,776
Shares Outstanding	91,700	91,600	91,700	93,700	98,070	100,942	106,491	109,407
Statistical Record								
Return on Assets %	4.17	3.35	7.16	10.88	11.64	11.86	13.85	15.93
Return on Equity %	9.78	7.51	15.47	23.37	24.33	24.31	27.26	31.10
EBITDA Margin %	17.86	20.71	15.70	19.60	19.92	20.78	22.83	23.34
Net Margin %	N.M.	N.M.	9.35	12.50	13.28	13.24	14.89	15.21
Asset Turnover	0.87	0.78	0.76	0.87	0.88	0.90	0.93	1.05
Current Ratio	1.53	1.45	1.41	1.62	1.83	2.08	2.33	1.76
Debt to Equity	0.02	...	...	0.17	0.20	0.24	0.26	N.M.
Price Range	129.46-88.37	112.42-76.57	107.87-76.57	88.16-65.55	85.14-63.26	77.50-64.20	67.54-50.55	63.49-44.37
P/E Ratio	89.90-61.37	89.94-61.26	40.25-28.57	21.04-15.64	20.82-15.47	20.24-16.76	16.97-12.70	16.89-11.80

Address: 3100 Hansen Way, Palo Alto, CA 94304-1038	**Web Site:** www.varian.com	**Auditors:** PricewaterhouseCoopers LLP
Telephone: 650-493-4000	**Officers:** R. Andrew Eckert - Chairman Timothy E. Guertin - Vice-Chairman, President, Chief Executive Officer	**Investor Contact:** 650-424-5782
		Transfer Agents: Computershare Trust Company, N.A., Providence, RI

VECTOR GROUP LTD

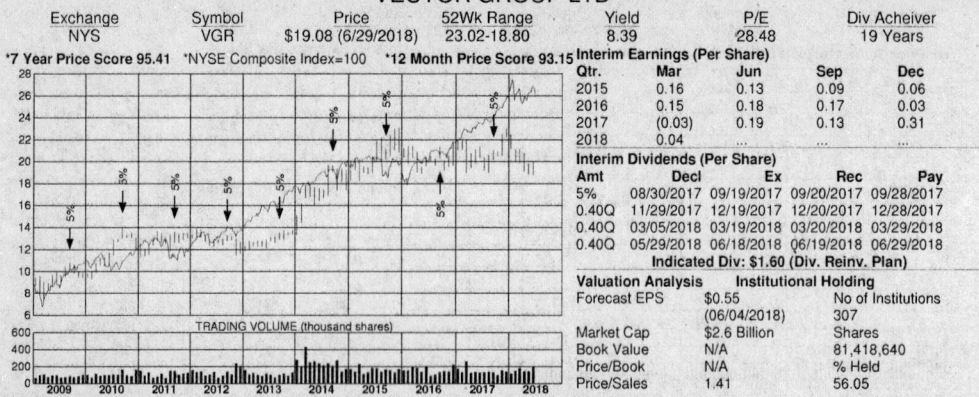

Exchange	Symbol	Price	52Wk Range	Yield	P/E	Div Acheiver
NYS	VGR	$19.08 (6/29/2018)	23.02-18.80	8.39	28.48	19 Years

*7 Year Price Score 95.41 *NYSE Composite Index=100 ***12 Month Price Score 93.15**

Interim Earnings (Per Share)

Qtr.	Mar	Jun	Sep	Dec
2015	0.16	0.13	0.09	0.06
2016	0.15	0.18	0.17	0.03
2017	(0.03)	0.19	0.13	0.31
2018	0.04	...	...	...

Interim Dividends (Per Share)

Amt	Decl	Ex	Rec	Pay
5%	08/30/2017	09/19/2017	09/20/2017	09/28/2017
0.40Q	11/29/2017	12/19/2017	12/20/2017	12/28/2017
0.40Q	03/05/2018	03/19/2018	03/20/2018	03/29/2018
0.40Q	05/29/2018	06/18/2018	06/19/2018	06/29/2018

Indicated Div: $1.60 (Div. Reinv. Plan)

Valuation Analysis **Institutional Holding**

Forecast EPS	$0.55	No of Institutions
	(06/04/2018)	307
Market Cap	$2.6 Billion	Shares
Book Value	N/A	81,418,640
Price/Book	N/A	% Held
Price/Sales	1.41	56.05

Business Summary: Tobacco Products (MIC: 1.3.1 SIC: 2111 NAIC: 312221)

Vector Group is a holding company. Co. is engaged principally in the manufacture and sale of cigarettes in the U.S. through its Liggett Group LLC and Vector Tobacco Inc. subsidiaries; and the real estate business through its New Valley LLC (New Valley) subsidiary. Co.'s business segments were Tobacco, E-Cigarettes and Real Estate. The Tobacco segment consists of the manufacture and sale of conventional cigarettes. The E-Cigarettes segment includes the operations of Co.'s e-cigarette business. The Real Estate segment includes Co.'s investment in New Valley, which includes Douglas Elliman, Escena, Sagaponack and investments in real estate ventures.

Recent Developments: For the quarter ended Mar 31 2018, net income amounted to US$3.7 million versus a net loss of US$4.2 million in the year-earlier quarter. Revenues were US$429.0 million, up 3.3% from US$415.2 million the year before. Operating income was US$48.1 million versus US$53.4 million in the prior-year quarter, a decrease of 10.0%. Direct operating expenses rose 6.7% to US$294.3 million from US$275.9 million in the comparable period the year before. Indirect operating expenses increased 0.9% to US$86.6 million from US$85.9 million in the equivalent prior-year period.

Prospects: Our evaluation of Vector Group Ltd. as of Jan. 21, 2018 is the result of our systematic analysis on three basic characteristics: earnings strength, relative valuation, and recent stock price movement. The company has produced a positive trend in earnings per share over the past 5 quarters and while recent estimates for the company have remained steady, VGR has posted results that fell short of analysts expectations. Based on operating earnings yield, the company is overvalued when compared to all of the companies in our coverage universe. Share price changes over the past year indicates that VGR will perform in line with the market over the near term.

Financial Data

(US$ in Thousands)	3 Mos	12/31/2017	12/31/2016	12/31/2015	12/31/2014	12/31/2013	12/31/2012	12/31/2011
Earnings Per Share	0.67	0.59	0.52	0.44	0.30	0.34	0.27	0.69
Cash Flow Per Share	1.09	0.99	0.75	1.11	0.90	0.47	0.78	0.34
Dividends Per Share	1.562	1.543	1.469	1.399	1.333	1.269	1.209	1.151
Dividend Payout %	232.95	261.50	280.52	314.83	440.88	376.32	440.87	165.92
Income Statement								
Total Revenue	428,966	1,807,476	1,690,949	1,657,197	1,591,315	1,056,200	1,084,546	1,133,380
EBITDA	55,035	252,311	281,729	242,461	255,976	181,706	145,924	215,363
Depn & Amortn	...	17,479	20,782	20,423	17,843	11,063	10,608	10,607
Income Before Taxes	11,010	68,538	123,983	108,385	77,142	38,496	25,214	104,050
Income Taxes	1,948	(1,582)	49,163	41,233	33,251	24,795	23,095	48,137
Net Income	7,211	84,572	71,127	59,198	36,978	38,944	30,622	75,020
Average Shares	132,978	132,672	130,472	129,866	119,226	111,515	108,092	105,702
Balance Sheet								
Current Assets	571,684	613,709	705,463	583,739	857,846	588,311	639,056	509,741
Total Assets	1,299,122	1,328,278	1,404,035	1,310,756	1,573,392	1,260,159	1,086,731	927,768
Current Liabilities	404,337	204,639	196,148	216,292	270,095	405,005	195,159	315,198
Long-Term Obligations	1,045,433	1,194,244	1,132,943	886,249	860,711	540,766	586,946	493,356
Total Liabilities	1,764,038	1,742,197	1,736,035	1,516,803	1,630,419	1,355,195	1,165,983	1,016,798
Stockholders' Equity	(464,916)	(413,919)	(332,000)	(206,047)	(57,027)	(95,036)	(79,252)	(89,030)
Shares Outstanding	134,365	134,365	134,126	129,981	132,549	118,491	114,735	106,459
Statistical Record								
Return on Assets %	7.15	6.19	5.23	4.11	2.61	3.32	3.03	7.99
EBITDA Margin %	12.83	13.96	16.66	14.63	16.09	17.20	13.45	19.00
Net Margin %	1.68	4.68	4.21	3.57	2.32	3.69	2.82	6.62
Asset Turnover	1.36	1.32	1.24	1.15	1.12	0.90	1.07	1.21
Current Ratio	1.41	3.00	3.60	2.70	3.18	1.45	3.27	1.62
Price Range	23.02-18.94	23.02-18.91	21.72-18.88	23.07-18.14	19.65-13.29	13.71-11.65	13.83-11.39	13.69-11.29
P/E Ratio	34.36-28.27	39.02-32.06	41.78-36.30	52.42-41.23	65.51-44.32	40.34-34.27	51.24-42.19	19.84-16.36
Average Yield %	7.52	7.42	7.28	6.88	7.68	9.89	9.42	9.05

Address: 4400 Biscayne Boulevard, Miami, FL 33137 Telephone: 305-579-8000	Web Site: www.vectorgroupltd.com Officers: Bennett S. LeBow - Chairman Howard M. Lorber - President, Chief Executive Officer	Auditors: Deloitte & Touche LLP Investor Contact: 212-687-8080 Transfer Agents: American Stock Transfer & Trust Company, LLC, Brooklyn, NY

VECTREN CORP

Exchange	Symbol	Price	52Wk Range	Yield	P/E	Div Acheiver
NYS	VVC	$71.45 (6/29/2018)	71.48-57.69	2.52	26.56	42 Years

*7 Year Price Score-121.09 *NYSE Composite Index=100 *12 Month Price Score 106.39

Interim Earnings (Per Share)

Qtr.	Mar	Jun	Sep	Dec
2015	0.69	0.43	0.48	0.79
2016	0.58	0.39	0.74	0.84
2017	0.67	0.45	0.75	0.73
2018	0.76	...	...	...

Interim Dividends (Per Share)

Amt	Decl	Ex	Rec	Pay
0.42Q	08/03/2017	08/11/2017	08/15/2017	09/01/2017
0.45Q	11/02/2017	11/14/2017	11/15/2017	12/01/2017
0.45Q	02/01/2018	02/14/2018	02/15/2018	03/01/2018
0.45Q	05/01/2018	05/14/2018	05/15/2018	06/01/2018

Indicated Div: $1.80 (Div. Reinv. Plan)

Valuation Analysis   **Institutional Holding**

Forecast EPS	$2.88	No of Institutions
	(06/12/2018)	524
Market Cap	$5.9 Billion	Shares
Book Value	$1.9 Billion	70,543,776
Price/Book	3.16	% Held
Price/Sales	2.21	57.29

Business Summary: Electric Utilities (MIC: 3.1.1 SIC: 4932 NAIC: 221210)

Vectren is an energy holding company. Co.'s subsidiary, Vectren Utility Holdings, Inc., served as the intermediate holding company for three public utilities that provides natural gas distribution and transportation services and electric transmission and distribution services. Co., through Vectren Enterprises, Inc. subsidiary, is involved in nonutility activities in two primary business areas: infrastructure services, which provides underground pipeline construction and repair to utility infrastructure; and energy services, which assists schools, hospitals, governmental facilities, and other private institutions with reducing energy and maintenance costs through Energy Systems Group, LLC.

Recent Developments: For the quarter ended Mar 31 2018, net income increased 14.6% to US$63.5 million from US$55.4 million in the year-earlier quarter. Revenues were US$658.4 million, up 5.4% from US$624.5 million the year before. Operating income was US$84.3 million versus US$101.4 million in the prior-year quarter, a decrease of 16.9%. Direct operating expenses rose 17.7% to US$254.2 million from US$215.9 million in the comparable period the year before. Indirect operating expenses increased 4.1% to US$319.9 million from US$307.2 million in the equivalent prior-year period.

Prospects: Our evaluation of Vectren Corp. as of Jan. 21, 2018 is the result of our systematic analysis on three basic characteristics: earnings strength, relative valuation, and recent stock price movement. The company has managed to produce a neutral trend in earnings per share over the past 5 quarters and while recent estimates for the company have remained steady, VVC has posted better than expected results. Based on operating earnings yield, the company is about fairly valued when compared to all of the companies in our coverage universe. Share price changes over the past year indicates that VVC will perform very well over the near term.

Financial Data
(US$ in Thousands)

	3 Mos	12/31/2017	12/31/2016	12/31/2015	12/31/2014	12/31/2013	12/31/2012	12/31/2011
Earnings Per Share	2.69	2.60	2.55	2.39	2.02	1.66	1.94	1.73
Cash Flow Per Share	5.13	6.01	6.31	6.11	5.92	7.13	4.71	5.10
Tang Book Value Per Share	19.05	18.74	17.79	16.79	15.94	15.68	15.37	14.69
Dividends Per Share	1.740	1.710	1.620	1.540	1.460	1.425	1.405	1.385
Dividend Payout %	64.68	65.77	63.53	64.44	72.28	85.84	72.42	80.06
Income Statement								
Total Revenue	658,400	2,657,300	2,448,300	2,434,700	2,611,700	2,491,200	2,232,800	2,325,200
EBITDA	164,700	600,400	646,000	616,400	595,100	621,600	607,900	604,800
Depn & Amortn	71,400	276,200	260,000	256,300	273,400	277,800	254,600	244,300
Income Before Taxes	69,800	263,500	323,100	293,600	247,500	263,400	264,800	260,000
Income Taxes	6,200	46,400	111,300	95,700	81,100	67,100	82,500	86,400
Net Income	63,500	216,000	211,600	197,300	166,900	136,600	159,000	141,600
Average Shares	83,100	83,000	82,800	82,700	82,500	82,400	82,100	81,800
Balance Sheet								
Current Assets	552,000	679,400	678,400	659,400	686,400	630,400	678,400	610,000
Total Assets	6,184,200	6,239,300	5,800,700	5,409,900	5,162,300	5,102,600	5,089,100	4,878,900
Current Liabilities	902,300	938,000	828,400	527,800	762,700	510,500	794,300	693,500
Long-Term Obligations	1,678,500	1,738,700	1,589,900	1,722,800	1,407,300	1,777,100	1,553,400	1,559,600
Total Liabilities	4,307,400	4,390,000	4,032,600	3,726,100	3,555,700	3,548,300	3,563,000	3,413,400
Stockholders' Equity	1,876,800	1,849,300	1,768,100	1,683,800	1,606,600	1,554,300	1,526,100	1,465,500
Shares Outstanding	83,100	83,000	82,900	82,800	82,600	82,400	82,200	81,900
Statistical Record								
Return on Assets %	3.77	3.59	3.76	3.73	3.25	2.68	3.18	2.94
Return on Equity %	12.23	11.94	12.23	11.99	10.56	8.87	10.60	9.75
EBITDA Margin %	25.02	22.59	26.39	25.32	22.79	24.95	27.23	26.01
Net Margin %	9.64	8.13	8.64	8.10	6.39	5.48	7.12	6.09
Asset Turnover	0.45	0.44	0.44	0.46	0.51	0.49	0.45	0.48
Current Ratio	0.61	0.72	0.82	1.25	0.90	1.23	0.85	0.88
Debt to Equity	0.89	0.94	0.90	1.02	0.88	1.14	1.02	1.06
Price Range	69.50-57.69	69.50-51.72	53.15-39.71	49.31-38.39	48.12-34.89	37.56-29.40	30.27-27.62	30.54-23.90
P/E Ratio	25.84-21.45	26.73-19.89	20.84-15.57	20.63-16.06	23.82-17.27	22.63-17.71	15.60-14.24	17.65-13.82
Average Yield %	2.77	2.79	3.31	3.59	3.63	4.17	4.83	5.06

Address: One Vectren Square,	Web Site: www.vectren.com	Auditors: DELOITTE & TOUCHE LLP
Evansville, IN 47708	Officers: Carl L. Chapman - Chairman, President,	Investor Contact: 812-491-4080
Telephone: 812-491-4000	Chief Executive Officer M. Susan Hardwick -	Transfer Agents: Wells Fargo
Fax: 812-491-4149	Executive Vice President, Chief Financial Officer,	Shareowner Services, St. Paul, MN
	Senior Vice President, Vice President, Controller,	
	Assistant Treasurer	

VEEVA SYSTEMS INC

Exchange	Symbol	Price	52Wk Range	Yield	P/E
NYS	VEEV	$76.86 (6/29/2018)	84.53-54.00	N/A	79.24

*7 Year Price Score N/A *NYSE Composite Index=100 *12 Month Price Score 117.34

Interim Earnings (Per Share)

Qtr.	Apr	Jul	Oct	Jan
2015-16	0.09	0.09	0.07	0.13
2016-17	0.09	0.09	0.15	0.15
2017-18	0.24	0.25	0.22	0.21
2018-19	0.29	...	...	...

Interim Dividends (Per Share)

No Dividends Paid

Valuation Analysis

Valuation Analysis		Institutional Holding	
Forecast EPS	$1.37	No of Institutions	
	(06/14/2018)	489	
Market Cap	$11.0 Billion	Shares	
Book Value	$974.4 Million	112,632,312	
Price/Book	11.29	% Held	
Price/Sales	15.22	28.65	

Business Summary: IT Services (MIC: 6.3.1 SIC: 7372 NAIC: 511210)

Veeva Systems provides industry cloud solutions for the life sciences industry. Veeva Commercial Cloud is a suite of multichannel customer relationship management applications, master data management applications, territory allocation and alignment applications and customer reference and data and services. Veeva Vault is Co.'s enterprise content management platform and suite of applications for managing both commercial content and research and development content and data, including content and data from the clinical, regulatory and quality functions of life sciences companies.

Recent Developments: For the quarter ended Apr 30 2018, net income increased 19.8% to US$44.3 million from US$37.0 million in the year-earlier quarter. Revenues were US$195.5 million, up 22.4% from US$159.8 million the year before. Operating income was US$44.0 million versus US$38.9 million in the prior-year quarter, an increase of 13.1%. Direct operating expenses rose 23.1% to US$60.2 million from US$48.9 million in the comparable period the year before. Indirect operating expenses increased 26.9% to US$91.4 million from US$72.0 million in the equivalent prior-year period.

Prospects: Our evaluation of Veeva Systems Inc as of Jan. 21, 2018 is the result of our systematic analysis on three basic characteristics: earnings strength, relative valuation, and recent stock price movement. The company has generated a negative trend in earnings per share over the past 5 quarters and while recent estimates for the company have remained steady, VEEV has posted better than expected results. Based on operating earnings yield, the company is overvalued when compared to all of the companies in our coverage universe. Share price changes over the past year indicates that VEEV will perform very well over the near term.

Financial Data
(US$ in Thousands)

	3 Mos	01/31/2018	01/31/2017	01/31/2016	01/31/2015	01/31/2014	01/31/2013	01/31/2012
Earnings Per Share	0.97	0.92	0.47	0.38	0.28	0.15	0.11	0.02
Cash Flow Per Share	2.04	1.66	1.06	0.61	0.53	0.81	1.47	0.27
Tang Book Value Per Share	5.93	5.24	3.76	2.70	3.02	2.14	1.05	0.29
Income Statement								
Total Revenue	195,547	685,571	544,043	409,221	313,222	210,151	129,548	61,262
EBITDA	52,035	156,151	110,058	77,100	68,586	39,400	29,593	6,953
Depn & Amortn	5,940	5,900	4,900	3,100	1,400	900	500	300
Income Before Taxes	46,095	158,634	109,635	78,617	67,186	38,500	29,093	6,653
Income Taxes	1,785	16,668	40,831	24,157	26,803	14,885	10,310	2,423
Net Income	44,310	141,966	68,804	54,460	40,383	23,615	18,783	4,230
Average Shares	154,935	153,681	147,578	144,977	144,204	68,024	30,599	24,776
Balance Sheet								
Current Assets	1,102,828	1,008,136	711,865	500,964	501,837	353,732	86,890	39,664
Total Assets	1,317,655	1,197,008	917,700	705,799	544,890	370,308	89,820	41,414
Current Liabilities	326,226	314,676	246,784	186,279	135,523	86,617	54,289	26,208
Total Liabilities	343,218	325,481	264,722	200,550	138,057	90,212	55,854	27,311
Stockholders' Equity	974,437	871,527	652,978	505,249	406,833	280,096	33,966	14,103
Shares Outstanding	143,176	142,069	137,886	133,545	131,067	124,791	24,843	22,620
Statistical Record								
Return on Assets %	12.99	13.43	8.45	8.71	8.82	10.26	28.55	...
Return on Equity %	17.85	18.62	11.85	11.94	11.76	15.04	77.94	...
EBITDA Margin %	26.61	22.78	20.23	18.84	21.90	18.75	22.84	11.35
Net Margin %	22.66	20.71	12.65	13.31	12.89	11.24	14.50	6.90
Asset Turnover	0.63	0.65	0.67	0.65	0.68	0.91	1.97	...
Current Ratio	3.38	3.20	2.88	2.69	3.70	4.08	1.60	1.51
Price Range	77.88-54.00	66.82-42.33	47.36-20.61	32.69-22.83	37.80-17.87	46.24-31.00	...	...
P/E Ratio	80.29-55.67	72.63-46.01	100.77-43.85	86.03-60.08	135.00-63.82	308.27-206.67	...	...

Address: 4280 Hacienda Drive, Pleasanton, CA 94588	Web Site: www.veeva.com	Auditors: KPMG LLP
Telephone: 925-452-6500	Officers: Gordon Ritter - Chairman Matthew J. Wallach - President	Transfer Agents: American Stock Transfer & Trust Company, LLC, Brooklyn, NY
Fax: 925-452-6504		

VENTAS INC

Exchange	Symbol	Price	52Wk Range	Yield	P/E
NYS	VTR	$56.95 (6/29/2018)	69.98-46.96	5.55	15.07

*7 Year Price Score 81.58   ***NYSE Composite Index=100**   ***12 Month Price Score 90.93**

Interim Earnings (Per Share)

Qtr.	Mar	Jun	Sep	Dec
2013	0.38	0.39	0.40	0.37
2014	0.41	0.47	0.37	0.36
2015	0.37	0.45	0.07	0.37
2016	0.44	0.42	0.42	0.58
2017	0.55	0.42	1.71	1.09

Interim Dividends (Per Share)

Amt	Decl	Ex	Rec	Pay
0.775Q	08/30/2017	09/11/2017	09/12/2017	09/29/2017
0.79Q	12/11/2017	12/29/2017	01/02/2018	01/12/2018
0.79Q	02/09/2018	03/29/2018	04/02/2018	04/12/2018
0.79Q	05/16/2018	06/29/2018	07/02/2018	07/12/2018

Indicated Div: $3.16

Valuation Analysis / Institutional Holding

Forecast EPS	$1.33	No of Institutions
	(06/13/2018)	971
Market Cap	$20.3 Billion	Shares
Book Value	$11.0 Billion	388,122,336
Price/Book	1.84	% Held
Price/Sales	5.68	96.39

Business Summary: REITs (MIC: 5.3.1 SIC: 6798 NAIC: 525930)

Ventas is a real estate investment trust, with a portfolio of seniors housing and healthcare properties located throughout the U.S., Canada and the U.K. Co.'s business segments include: triple-net leased properties, which acquires and owns seniors housing and healthcare properties throughout the U.S. and the U.K. and leases those properties to healthcare operating companies under triple-net or absolute-net leases that obligate the tenants to pay all property-related expenses; senior living operations, which invests in seniors housing communities throughout the U.S. and Canada; and office operations, which acquires, owns, develops, leases, and manages MOBs.

Recent Developments: For the year ended Dec 31 2017, income from continuing operations increased 16.2% to US$643.9 million from US$554.2 million a year earlier. Net income increased 108.9% to US$1.36 billion from US$651.5 million in the prior year. Revenues were US$3.57 billion, up 3.8% from US$3.44 billion the year before. Revenues from property income rose 3.2% to US$3.45 billion from US$3.34 billion in the corresponding earlier year.

Prospects: Our evaluation of Ventas Inc. as of Jan. 21, 2018 is the result of our systematic analysis on three basic characteristics: earnings strength, relative valuation, and recent stock price movement. The company has managed to produce a neutral trend in earnings per share over the past 5 quarters. However, while recent estimates for the company have been lowered by analysts, VTR has posted better than expected results. Based on operating earnings yield, the company is about fairly valued when compared to all of the companies in our coverage universe. Share price changes over the past year indicates that VTR will perform very well over the near term.

Financial Data

(US$ in Thousands)	12/31/2017	12/31/2016	12/31/2015	12/31/2014	12/31/2013	12/31/2012	12/31/2011	12/31/2010
Earnings Per Share	3.78	1.86	1.25	1.60	1.54	1.23	1.58	1.56
Cash Flow Per Share	4.06	3.96	4.21	4.27	4.08	3.39	3.38	2.86
Tang Book Value Per Share	28.03	27.16	26.02	28.08	28.91	29.73	30.87	15.18
Dividends Per Share	3.115	2.965	3.040	2.965	2.735	2.480	2.300	2.140
Dividend Payout %	82.41	159.41	243.20	185.31	177.60	201.63	145.57	137.18
Income Statement								
Total Revenue	3,574,149	3,443,522	3,286,398	3,075,746	2,810,053	2,485,299	1,764,991	1,016,867
EBITDA	1,916,376	1,827,193	1,673,771	1,634,643	1,550,817	1,281,227	1,001,682	614,934
Depn & Amortn	883,469	888,945	954,982	809,284	737,343	707,714	434,382	208,274
Income Before Taxes	584,711	518,508	351,675	448,517	478,990	280,112	330,493	227,797
Income Taxes	(59,799)	(31,343)	(39,284)	(8,732)	(11,828)	(6,282)	(31,137)	5,201
Net Income	1,356,470	649,231	417,843	475,767	453,509	362,800	364,493	246,167
Average Shares	358,566	348,390	334,007	296,677	295,110	294,488	230,790	157,657
Balance Sheet								
Current Assets	81,355	286,707	53,023	55,348	94,816	67,908	45,807	21,812
Total Assets	23,954,541	23,166,600	22,261,918	21,226,171	19,731,494	18,980,000	17,271,910	5,758,021
Current Liabilities	1,587,804	1,309,793	1,232,966	1,411,666	1,306,031	1,302,436	1,384,013	467,772
Long-Term Obligations	11,276,062	11,127,326	11,206,996	10,888,092	9,364,992	8,413,646	6,429,116	2,900,044
Total Liabilities	12,929,825	12,505,632	12,501,062	12,373,971	10,750,553	9,786,317	7,894,116	3,371,295
Stockholders' Equity	11,024,716	10,660,968	9,760,856	8,852,200	8,980,941	9,193,683	9,377,794	2,386,726
Shares Outstanding	356,186	354,124	334,342	298,471	294,189	291,866	288,809	157,265
Statistical Record								
Return on Assets %	5.76	2.85	1.92	2.32	2.34	2.00	3.17	4.33
Return on Equity %	12.51	6.34	4.49	5.34	4.99	3.90	6.20	10.15
EBITDA Margin %	53.62	53.06	50.93	53.15	55.19	51.55	56.75	60.47
Net Margin %	37.95	18.85	12.71	15.47	16.14	14.60	20.65	24.21
Asset Turnover	0.15	0.15	0.15	0.15	0.15	0.14	0.15	0.18
Current Ratio	0.05	0.22	0.04	0.04	0.07	0.05	0.03	0.05
Debt to Equity	1.02	1.04	1.15	1.23	1.04	0.92	0.69	1.22
Price Range	71.93-59.36	76.56-48.43	70.89-49.68	65.19-49.73	72.63-48.39	58.97-47.01	50.09-38.50	48.54-35.86
P/E Ratio	19.03-15.70	41.16-26.04	56.71-39.74	40.75-31.08	47.16-31.43	47.94-38.22	31.70-24.37	31.12-22.99
Average Yield %	4.80	4.59	5.14	5.23	4.64	4.65	4.96	5.01

Address: 353 N. Clark Street, Suite 3300, Chicago, IL 60654	Web Site: www.ventasreit.com	Auditors: KPMG LLP
Telephone: 877-483-6827	Officers: Debra A. Cafaro - Chairman, Chief Executive Officer Robert F. Probst - Executive Vice President, Chief Financial Officer, Acting Chief Accounting Officer	Investor Contact: 312-660-3848 Transfer Agents: Wells Fargo Shareowner Services, St. Paul, MN

VEREIT INC

Exchange	Symbol	Price	52Wk Range	Yield	P/E
NYS	VER	$7.44 (6/29/2018)	8.68-6.59	7.39	N/A

*7 Year Price Score N/A   ***NYSE Composite Index=100**   ***12 Month Price Score 92.48**

Interim Earnings (Per Share)

Qtr.	Mar	Jun	Sep	Dec
2015	(0.05)	(0.14)	(0.01)	(0.23)
2016	(0.15)	(0.02)	0.01	(0.14)
2017	0.00	0.02	0.00	(0.05)
2018	0.01	...	...	...

Interim Dividends (Per Share)

Amt	Decl	Ex	Rec	Pay
0.138Q	08/02/2017	09/28/2017	09/29/2017	10/16/2017
0.138Q	11/07/2017	12/28/2017	12/29/2017	01/16/2018
0.138Q	02/21/2018	03/28/2018	03/30/2018	04/16/2018
0.138Q	05/03/2018	06/28/2018	06/29/2018	07/16/2018

Indicated Div: $0.55

Valuation Analysis   **Institutional Holding**

Forecast EPS	$-0.01	No of Institutions
	(06/10/2018)	503
Market Cap	$7.2 Billion	Shares
Book Value	$7.7 Billion	953,764,864
Price/Book	0.93	% Held
Price/Sales	5.91	69.15

Business Summary: REITs (MIC: 5.3.1 SIC: 6798 NAIC: 525930)

VEREIT is a real estate operating company that operates two segments, its Real Estate Investment (REI) segment and its investment management segment, Cole Capital. Through its REI segment, Co. owns and manages a portfolio of retail, restaurant, office and industrial real estate properties. Through its Cole Capital segment, Co. is responsible for managing the affairs of certain non-traded real estate investment trusts on a day-to-day basis, identifying and making acquisitions and investments and recommending an approach for providing investors with liquidity. As of Dec 31 2017, Co. owned and managed a portfolio of 4,091 retail, restaurant, office and industrial real estate properties.

Recent Developments: For the quarter ended Mar 31 2018, net income increased 120.0% to US$32.5 million from US$14.8 million in the year-earlier quarter. Revenues were US$315.1 million, down 1.8% from US$320.9 million the year before. Revenues from property income fell 1.2% to US$290.6 million from US$294.2 million in the corresponding quarter a year earlier.

Prospects: Our evaluation of VEREIT Inc. as of Jan. 21, 2018 is the result of our systematic analysis on three basic characteristics: earnings strength, relative valuation, and recent stock price movement. The company has generated a negative trend in earnings per share over the past 5 quarters. Because the company lacks sufficient analyst estimate data, we place greater weight on the historical EPS trend as the measure of earnings strength. Based on operating earnings yield, the company is overvalued when compared to all of the companies in our coverage universe. Share price changes over the past year indicates that VER will perform well over the near term.

Financial Data

(US$ in Thousands)	3 Mos	12/31/2017	12/31/2016	12/31/2015	12/31/2014	12/31/2013	12/31/2012	12/31/2011
Earnings Per Share	(0.02)	(0.04)	(0.29)	(0.43)	(1.36)	(2.36)	(0.84)	(1.26)
Cash Flow Per Share	0.78	0.81	0.86	0.96	0.63	(0.04)	0.66	0.45
Tang Book Value Per Share	6.59	6.72	7.14	7.53	7.85	7.57	7.34	7.32
Dividends Per Share	0.550	0.550	0.550	0.275	1.076	0.907	0.884	0.219
Income Statement								
Total Revenue	315,074	1,252,285	1,454,823	1,556,017	1,579,257	240,496	16,822	3,175
EBITDA	272,066	1,090,879	909,616	865,146	448,900	(173,926)	6,874	720
Depn & Amortn	172,458	745,499	806,548	866,549	1,007,164	156,971	9,322	1,624
Income Before Taxes	29,183	55,614	(214,308)	(359,795)	(1,010,912)	(411,697)	(6,804)	(1,828)
Income Taxes	1,212	6,882	(3,701)	(36,303)	...	...	...	...
Net Income	31,795	31,818	(195,863)	(316,353)	(977,185)	(406,505)	(7,278)	(2,575)
Average Shares	996,707	974,098	931,422	903,360	793,150	174,052	9,150	2,045
Balance Sheet								
Current Assets	76,556	61,838	301,470	128,870	479,362	75,373	2,748	3,148
Total Assets	14,451,789	14,705,578	15,587,574	17,405,866	20,515,139	5,578,281	256,069	131,581
Current Liabilities	304,369	327,722	308,731	292,923	173,579	134,742	3,782	858
Long-Term Obligations	6,008,494	6,073,444	6,367,248	8,059,802	10,513,781	3,586,084	160,362	72,667
Total Liabilities	6,731,307	6,821,300	7,140,213	8,881,879	11,361,251	3,957,410	174,117	77,951
Stockholders' Equity	7,720,482	7,884,278	8,447,361	8,523,987	9,153,888	1,620,871	81,952	53,630
Shares Outstanding	968,154	974,208	974,146	904,884	905,530	202,344	11,157	7,323
Statistical Record								
Return on Assets %	0.33	0.21	N.M.	N.M.	N.M.	N.M.	N.M.	...
Return on Equity %	0.61	0.39	N.M.	N.M.	N.M.	N.M.	N.M.	...
EBITDA Margin %	86.35	87.11	62.52	55.60	28.42	N.M.	40.86	22.68
Net Margin %	10.09	2.54	N.M.	N.M.	N.M.	N.M.	N.M.	N.M.
Asset Turnover	0.08	0.08	0.09	0.08	0.12	0.08	0.09	...
Current Ratio	0.25	0.19	0.98	0.44	2.76	0.56	0.73	3.67
Debt to Equity	0.78	0.77	0.75	0.95	1.15	2.21	1.96	1.35
Price Range	8.92-6.66	9.12-7.49	11.06-7.07	10.10-7.67	14.88-7.70	17.82-12.20	13.48-10.00	12.75-10.05
Average Yield %	6.91	6.60	6.00	3.13	8.72	6.44	7.69	2.00

Address: 2325 E. Camelback Road, Suite 1100, Phoenix, AZ 85016
Telephone: 800-606-3610

Web Site: www.ir.vereit.com
Officers: Glenn J. Rufrano - Chief Executive Officer
Michael J. Bartolotta - Executive Vice President, Chief Financial Officer

Auditors: Deloitte & Touche LLP
Investor Contact: 800-606-3610
Transfer Agents: DST Systems, Inc.

VERIFONE SYSTEMS INC

Exchange	Symbol	Price	52Wk Range	Yield	P/E
NYS	PAY	$22.82 (6/29/2018)	23.03-15.00	N/A	N/A

*7 Year Price Score 55.10 *NYSE Composite Index=100 *12 Month Price Score 117.28

Interim Earnings (Per Share)

Qtr.	Jan	Apr	Jul	Oct
2014-15	0.12	0.15	0.08	0.32
2015-16	0.21	0.03	(0.28)	(0.04)
2016-17	(0.15)	(0.80)	(0.63)	0.03
2017-18	0.06	(0.15)	...	...

Interim Dividends (Per Share)

No Dividends Paid

Valuation Analysis | **Institutional Holding**

Forecast EPS	$1.48	No of Institutions
(06/13/2018)		417
Market Cap	$2.5 Billion	Shares
Book Value	$745.2 Million	136,799,728
Price/Book	3.39	% Held
Price/Sales	1.39	93.00

Business Summary: Electronic Instruments & Related Products (MIC: 6.2.3 SIC: 3578 NAIC: 334118)

VeriFone Systems is a holding company. Through its subsidiaries, Co. provides payments and commerce solutions at the point of sale (POS). Co. is engaged in designing, manufacturing, marketing and supplying a range of payment solutions and complementary services. Co.'s system solutions consist of POS electronic payment devices that run its operating systems, security and encryption software, and certified payment software, and that are designed to suit its clients' needs in a range of environments, including multilane and countertop implementations, self-service and unattended environments, in-vehicle and portable deployments, mobile point-of-sale solutions, as well as iPOS solutions.

Recent Developments: For the quarter ended Apr 30 2018, net loss amounted to US$16.8 million versus a net loss of US$89.7 million in the year-earlier quarter. Revenues were US$438.4 million, down 7.4% from US$473.7 million the year before. Operating income was US$6.8 million versus a loss of US$81.4 million in the prior-year quarter. Direct operating expenses declined 13.6% to US$259.9 million from US$300.9 million in the comparable period the year before. Indirect operating expenses decreased 32.4% to US$171.7 million from US$254.2 million in the equivalent prior-year period.

Prospects: Our evaluation of Verifone Systems Inc. as of Jan. 21, 2018 is the result of our systematic analysis on three basic characteristics: earnings strength, relative valuation, and recent stock price movement. The company has enjoyed a very positive trend in earnings per share over the past 5 quarters. However, while recent estimates for the company have been mixed, PAY has posted better than expected results. Based on operating earnings yield, the company is overvalued when compared to all of the companies in our coverage universe. Share price changes over the past year indicates that PAY will perform in line with the market over the near term.

Financial Data
(US$ in Thousands)

	6 Mos	3 Mos	10/31/2017	10/31/2016	10/31/2015	10/31/2014	10/31/2013	10/31/2012
Earnings Per Share	(0.69)	(1.34)	(1.55)	(0.08)	0.68	(0.34)	(2.73)	0.59
Cash Flow Per Share	1.49	1.55	1.48	1.74	2.19	1.78	2.18	2.03
Income Statement								
Total Revenue	875,200	436,797	1,870,976	1,992,149	2,000,457	1,868,874	1,702,221	1,865,971
EBITDA	48,795	30,626	26,100	189,425	245,595	159,868	88,346	256,479
Depn & Amortn	30,695	15,068	135,722	153,034	141,192	157,280	150,960	129,695
Income Before Taxes	(1,051)	6,641	(142,819)	1,827	72,948	(39,884)	(106,958)	68,353
Income Taxes	8,546	(514)	32,500	11,527	(7,409)	(3,442)	188,043	2,050
Net Income	(9,796)	7,249	(173,829)	(9,281)	79,097	(38,130)	(296,055)	65,033
Average Shares	110,508	112,196	111,817	110,829	115,934	111,586	108,609	110,315
Balance Sheet								
Current Assets	749,408	696,738	718,655	757,427	782,264	785,572	824,992	1,135,443
Total Assets	2,343,380	2,358,452	2,322,170	2,494,807	2,473,062	2,702,243	2,993,720	3,490,607
Current Liabilities	514,286	516,294	542,253	538,799	541,241	492,414	587,664	570,390
Long-Term Obligations	835,745	775,445	762,044	859,896	760,241	851,040	943,325	1,252,701
Total Liabilities	1,598,156	1,558,211	1,567,577	1,681,076	1,573,558	1,668,453	1,879,114	2,182,812
Stockholders' Equity	745,224	800,241	754,593	813,731	899,504	1,033,790	1,114,606	1,307,795
Shares Outstanding	110,723	110,352	112,367	111,261	112,684	113,314	110,160	107,930
Statistical Record								
Return on Assets %	N.M.	N.M.	N.M.	N.M.	3.06	N.M.	N.M.	2.23
Return on Equity %	N.M.	N.M.	N.M.	N.M.	8.18	N.M.	N.M.	5.18
EBITDA Margin %	5.58	7.01	1.39	9.51	12.28	8.55	5.19	13.75
Net Margin %	N.M.	1.66	N.M.	N.M.	3.95	N.M.	N.M.	3.49
Asset Turnover	0.77	0.77	0.78	0.80	0.77	0.66	0.53	0.64
Current Ratio	1.46	1.35	1.33	1.41	1.45	1.60	1.40	1.99
Debt to Equity	1.12	0.97	1.01	1.06	0.85	0.82	0.85	0.96
Price Range	23.03-15.00	21.31-17.13	21.31-15.41	31.11-15.04	38.93-26.20	37.53-22.41	35.94-15.75	54.45-27.85
P/E Ratio	...	...	...	...	57.25-38.53	...	...	92.29-47.20

Address: 88 West Plumeria Drive, San Jose, CA 95134 Telephone: 408-232-7800	Web Site: www.verifone.com Officers: Alex W. (Pete) Hart - Chairman Michael (Mike) Pulli - Chief Executive Officer	Auditors: Ernst & Young LLP Transfer Agents: Computershare, Canton, MA

VERITIV CORP

Exchange	Symbol	Price	52Wk Range	Yield	P/E
NYS	VRTV	$39.85 (6/29/2018)	45.05-22.65	N/A	N/A

*7 Year Price Score N/A   *NYSE Composite Index=100   *12 Month Price Score 107.94

Interim Earnings (Per Share)

Qtr.	Mar	Jun	Sep	Dec
2015	(0.14)	0.27	0.91	0.63
2016	0.21	0.49	0.34	0.26
2017	(0.14)	(0.58)	(0.91)	0.78
2018	(1.00)	...	...	...

Interim Dividends (Per Share)

No Dividends Paid

Valuation Analysis   Institutional Holding

Forecast EPS	$3.77	No of Institutions
	(05/23/2018)	219
Market Cap	$629.6 Million	Shares
Book Value	$537.7 Million	17,321,644
Price/Book	1.17	% Held
Price/Sales	0.07	N/A

TRADING VOLUME (thousand shares)

Business Summary: Industrial Machinery & Equipment (MIC: 7.2.1 SIC: 5111 NAIC: 424110)

Veritiv is a business to business distributor of packaging, facility solutions, print and publishing products and services. Co. also provides logistics and supply chain management solutions to its customers. Co.'s business is organized under four reportable segments: Packaging, which provides standard as well as custom packaging solutions; Facility Solutions, which sources and sells cleaning, break-room and other supplies such as towels and wipers; Print, which sells and distributes commercial printing, writing, copying, digital, format and specialty paper products, as well as graphics consumables; and Publishing, which sells and distributes coated and uncoated commercial printing papers.

Recent Developments: For the quarter ended Mar 31 2018, net loss amounted to US$15.8 million versus a net loss of US$2.2 million in the year-earlier quarter. Revenues were US$2.10 billion, up 5.3% from US$1.99 billion the year before. Operating loss was US$18.9 million versus an income of US$3.2 million in the prior-year quarter. Direct operating expenses rose 6.1% to US$1.73 billion from US$1.63 billion in the comparable period the year before. Indirect operating expenses increased 7.8% to US$390.4 million from US$362.1 million in the equivalent prior-year period.

Prospects: Our evaluation of Veritiv Corp. as of Jan. 21, 2018 is the result of our systematic analysis on three basic characteristics: earnings strength, relative valuation, and recent stock price movement. The company has generated a negative trend in earnings per share over the past 5 quarters. Because the company lacks sufficient analyst estimate data, we place greater weight on the historical EPS trend as the measure of earnings strength. Based on operating earnings yield, the company is undervalued when compared to all of the companies in our coverage universe. Share price changes over the past year indicates that VRTV will perform very poorly over the near term.

Financial Data

(US$ in Thousands)	3 Mos	12/31/2017	12/31/2016	12/31/2015	12/31/2014	12/31/2013	12/29/2012	12/31/2011
Earnings Per Share	(1.71)	(0.85)	1.30	1.67	(1.62)	...	...	...
Cash Flow Per Share	3.53	2.33	8.75	7.06	0.41	...	...	...
Tang Book Value Per Share	23.79	24.59	29.97	28.11	26.50	13.77	...	...
Income Statement								
Total Revenue	2,101,000	8,364,700	8,326,600	8,717,700	7,406,500	4,089,100	4,123,300	4,327,800
EBITDA	(7,700)	79,300	119,600	122,900	25,300	62,100	69,700	54,200
Depn & Amortn	700	50,000	51,300	51,000	32,900	21,900	22,200	21,300
Income Before Taxes	(17,700)	(1,900)	40,800	44,900	(21,600)	12,800	19,200	(33,800)
Income Taxes	(1,900)	11,400	19,800	18,200	(2,100)	(228,500)	15,200	(5,500)
Net Income	(15,800)	(13,300)	21,000	26,700	(19,600)	242,400	5,100	(27,100)
Average Shares	15,760	15,700	16,150	16,000	12,080	...	...	...
Balance Sheet								
Current Assets	2,093,100	2,114,100	1,948,600	1,925,200	1,959,100	870,600	882,200	...
Total Assets	2,700,900	2,708,400	2,483,700	2,476,900	2,574,500	1,215,200	1,039,200	...
Current Liabilities	862,000	907,400	867,800	814,200	851,100	344,400	396,600	...
Long-Term Obligations	1,149,800	1,089,900	925,300	998,300	1,067,400	371,300	371,600	...
Total Liabilities	2,163,200	2,158,700	1,941,900	1,946,800	2,062,000	815,700	878,400	...
Stockholders' Equity	537,700	549,700	541,800	530,100	512,500	399,500	160,800	...
Shares Outstanding	15,800	15,700	15,700	16,000	16,000	25,800	...	...
Statistical Record								
Return on Assets %	N.M.	N.M.	0.84	1.06	N.M.	21.39	...	...
Return on Equity %	N.M.	N.M.	3.91	5.12	N.M.	86.05	...	...
EBITDA Margin %	N.M.	0.95	1.44	1.41	0.34	1.52	1.69	1.25
Net Margin %	N.M.	N.M.	0.25	0.31	N.M.	5.93	0.12	N.M.
Asset Turnover	3.27	3.22	3.35	3.45	3.91	3.61	...	...
Current Ratio	2.43	2.33	2.25	2.36	2.30	2.53	2.22	...
Debt to Equity	2.14	1.98	1.71	1.88	2.08	0.93	2.31	...
Price Range	52.95-22.65	62.25-22.70	56.40-28.00	54.11-33.06	51.87-32.50	...	...	...
P/E Ratio	...	...	43.38-21.54	32.40-19.80	...	...	...	...

Address: 1000 Abernathy Road N.E., Building 400, Suite 1700, Atlanta, GA 30328 **Telephone:** 770-391-8200	**Web Site:** www.veritivcorp.com **Officers:** Mary A. Laschinger - Chairman, Chief Executive Officer, Holding/Parent Company Officer Stephen Joseph Smith - Senior Vice President, Chief Financial Officer	**Auditors:** Deloitte & Touche LLP **Transfer Agents:** Computershare Inc.

VERIZON COMMUNICATIONS INC

Exchange	Symbol	Price	52Wk Range	Yield	P/E	Div Acheiver
NYS	VZ	$50.31 (6/29/2018)	54.72-42.89	4.69	6.59	13 Years

*7 Year Price Score 83.67 ***NYSE Composite Index=100** ***12 Month Price Score 97.48**

Interim Earnings (Per Share)

Qtr.	Mar	Jun	Sep	Dec
2015	1.02	1.04	0.99	1.32
2016	1.06	0.17	0.89	1.10
2017	0.84	1.07	0.89	4.56
2018	1.11	...	...	...

Interim Dividends (Per Share)

Amt	Decl	Ex	Rec	Pay
0.59Q	09/07/2017	10/06/2017	10/10/2017	11/01/2017
0.59Q	12/07/2017	01/09/2018	01/10/2018	02/01/2018
0.59Q	03/06/2018	04/09/2018	04/10/2018	05/01/2018
0.59Q	06/07/2018	07/09/2018	07/10/2018	08/01/2018

Indicated Div: $2.36 (Div. Reinv. Plan)

Valuation Analysis | **Institutional Holding**

Forecast EPS	$4.57
	(06/14/2018)
Market Cap	$207.9 Billion
Book Value	$50.8 Billion
Price/Book	4.09
Price/Sales	1.62

Institutional Holding:
No of Institutions 2879
Shares 3,215,964,160
% Held 89.79

TRADING VOLUME (thousand shares)

Business Summary: Services (MIC: 6.1.2 SIC: 4813 NAIC: 517110)

Verizon Communications is a holding company. Through its subsidiaries, Co. provides communications, information and entertainment products and services to consumers, businesses and governmental agencies. Co. operates in two segments: Wireless, which include wireless voice and data services and equipment sales, which are provided to consumer, business and government customers across the U.S.; and Wireline, which include voice, data and video communications products and enhanced services including broadband video and data, corporate networking solutions, data center and cloud services, security and managed network services and local and long distance voice services.

Recent Developments: For the quarter ended Mar 31 2018, net income increased 31.3% to US$4.67 billion from US$3.55 billion in the year-earlier quarter. Revenues were US$31.77 billion, up 6.6% from US$29.81 billion the year before. Operating income was US$7.35 billion versus US$6.96 billion in the prior-year quarter, an increase of 5.6%. Direct operating expenses rose 10.0% to US$13.26 billion from US$12.05 billion in the comparable period the year before. Indirect operating expenses increased 3.4% to US$11.17 billion from US$10.81 billion in the equivalent prior-year period.

Prospects: Our evaluation of Verizon Communications Inc. as of Jan. 21, 2018 is the result of our systematic analysis on three basic characteristics: earnings strength, relative valuation, and recent stock price movement. The company has enjoyed a very positive trend in earnings per share over the past 5 quarters. However, while recent estimates for the company have been mixed, VZ has posted better than expected results. Based on operating earnings yield, the company is undervalued when compared to all of the companies in our coverage universe. Share price changes over the past year indicates that VZ will perform in line with the market over the near term.

Financial Data

(US$ in Thousands)	3 Mos	12/31/2017	12/31/2016	12/31/2015	12/31/2014	12/31/2013	12/31/2012	12/31/2011
Earnings Per Share	7.63	7.36	3.21	4.37	2.42	4.00	0.31	0.85
Cash Flow Per Share	7.38	6.20	5.55	9.53	7.71	13.54	11.01	10.51
Dividends Per Share	2.335	2.322	2.273	2.215	2.140	2.075	2.015	1.962
Dividend Payout %	30.60	31.56	70.79	50.69	88.43	51.88	650.00	230.88
Income Statement								
Total Revenue	31,772,000	126,034,000	125,980,000	131,620,000	127,079,000	120,550,000	115,846,000	110,875,000
EBITDA	11,582,000	40,063,000	39,628,000	47,454,000	33,263,000	46,757,000	27,007,000	27,789,000
Depn & Amortn	4,324,000	14,741,000	14,227,000	14,323,000	14,966,000	15,019,000	14,920,000	14,991,000
Income Before Taxes	6,073,000	20,671,000	21,084,000	28,326,000	13,490,000	29,135,000	9,573,000	10,039,000
Income Taxes	1,388,000	(9,956,000)	7,378,000	9,865,000	3,314,000	5,730,000	(660,000)	285,000
Net Income	4,545,000	30,101,000	13,127,000	17,879,000	9,625,000	11,497,000	875,000	2,404,000
Average Shares	4,107,000	4,089,000	4,086,000	4,093,000	3,981,000	2,874,000	2,862,000	2,839,000
Balance Sheet								
Current Assets	31,025,000	29,913,000	26,395,000	22,280,000	29,623,000	70,994,000	21,235,000	30,939,000
Total Assets	264,516,000	257,143,000	244,180,000	244,640,000	232,708,000	274,098,000	225,222,000	230,461,000
Current Liabilities	31,615,000	33,037,000	30,340,000	35,052,000	28,064,000	27,050,000	26,956,000	30,761,000
Long-Term Obligations	112,734,000	113,642,000	105,433,000	103,705,000	110,536,000	89,658,000	47,618,000	50,303,000
Total Liabilities	213,735,000	214,047,000	221,656,000	228,212,000	220,410,000	235,262,000	192,065,000	194,491,000
Stockholders' Equity	50,781,000	43,096,000	22,524,000	16,428,000	12,298,000	38,836,000	33,157,000	35,970,000
Shares Outstanding	4,131,897	4,079,477	4,076,684	4,073,175	4,154,964	2,862,000	2,858,569	2,834,016
Statistical Record								
Return on Assets %	12.20	12.01	5.36	7.49	3.80	4.61	0.38	1.07
Return on Equity %	84.00	91.74	67.22	124.48	37.65	31.94	2.52	6.45
EBITDA Margin %	36.45	31.79	31.46	36.05	26.18	38.79	23.31	25.06
Net Margin %	14.31	23.88	10.42	13.58	7.57	9.54	0.76	2.17
Asset Turnover	0.50	0.50	0.51	0.55	0.50	0.48	0.51	0.49
Current Ratio	0.98	0.91	0.87	0.64	1.06	2.62	0.79	1.01
Debt to Equity	2.22	2.64	4.68	6.31	8.99	2.31	1.44	1.40
Price Range	54.72-42.89	54.64-42.89	56.53-44.15	50.55-42.84	51.97-45.42	53.91-41.51	47.26-36.80	40.12-33.12
P/E Ratio	7.17-5.62	7.42-5.83	17.61-13.75	11.57-9.80	21.48-18.77	13.48-10.38	152.45-118.71	47.20-38.96
Average Yield %	4.84	4.87	4.42	4.42	4.70	4.40	4.27	4.78	5.36

Address: 1095 Avenue of the Americas, New York, NY 10036 Telephone: 212-395-1000	Web Site: www.verizon.com Officers: Lowell C. McAdam - Chairman, Chief Executive Officer, President, Chief Operating Officer Hans E. Vestberg - Executive Vice President, Chief Technology Officer, Division Officer, Chief Executive Officer	Auditors: Ernst & Young LLP

VERSUM MATERIALS INC

Exchange	Symbol	Price	52Wk Range	Yield	P/E
NYS	VSM	$37.15 (6/29/2018)	42.50-31.35	0.65	23.07

*7 Year Price Score N/A   *NYSE Composite Index=100   *12 Month Price Score 100.87

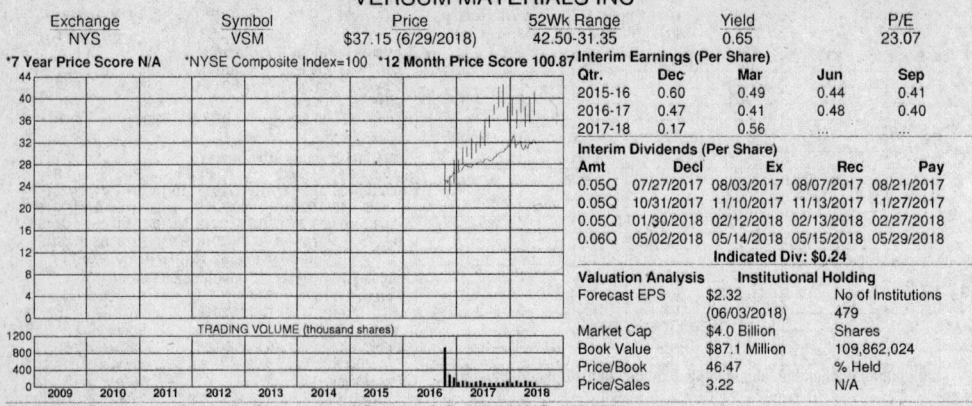

Interim Earnings (Per Share)

Qtr.	Dec	Mar	Jun	Sep
2015-16	0.60	0.49	0.44	0.41
2016-17	0.47	0.41	0.48	0.40
2017-18	0.17	0.56	...	...

Interim Dividends (Per Share)

Amt	Decl	Ex	Rec	Pay
0.05Q	07/27/2017	08/03/2017	08/07/2017	08/21/2017
0.05Q	10/31/2017	11/10/2017	11/13/2017	11/27/2017
0.05Q	01/30/2018	02/12/2018	02/13/2018	02/27/2018
0.06Q	05/02/2018	05/14/2018	05/15/2018	05/29/2018

Indicated Div: $0.24

Valuation Analysis / Institutional Holding

Forecast EPS	$2.32	No of Institutions	479
	(06/03/2018)		
Market Cap	$4.0 Billion	Shares	109,862,024
Book Value	$87.1 Million	% Held	N/A
Price/Book	46.47		
Price/Sales	3.22		

Business Summary: Specialty Chemicals (MIC: 8.3.2 SIC: 2869 NAIC: 325998)

Versum Materials is a provider of solutions to the semiconductor and display industries with knowledge in the development, manufacturing, transportation and handling of specialty materials. Co. has two segments: Materials, which provides specialty materials focusing on Integrated Circuit and flat-panel display customers, including specialty process gas, cleaners and etchants, slurries, organosilanes and organometallics deposition films; and Delivery Systems and Services, which designs, manufactures, installs, operates, and maintains chemical and gas delivery and distribution systems enabling the use of specialty gases and chemicals delivered directly to Co.'s customers' manufacturing tools.

Recent Developments: For the quarter ended Mar 31 2018, net income increased 35.3% to US$63.3 million from US$46.8 million in the year-earlier quarter. Revenues were US$340.7 million, up 25.8% from US$270.8 million the year before. Operating income was US$89.4 million versus US$69.9 million in the prior-year quarter, an increase of 27.9%. Direct operating expenses rose 26.8% to US$195.9 million from US$154.5 million in the comparable period the year before. Indirect operating expenses increased 19.4% to US$55.4 million from US$46.4 million in the equivalent prior-year period.

Prospects: Our evaluation of Versum Materials Inc. as of Jan. 21, 2018 is the result of our systematic analysis on three basic characteristics: earnings strength, relative valuation, and recent stock price movement. The company has generated a negative trend in earnings per share over the past 5 quarters and while recent estimates for the company have remained steady, VSM has posted results that fell short of analysts expectations. Based on operating earnings yield, the company is undervalued when compared to all of the companies in our coverage universe. Share price changes over the past year indicates that VSM will perform very well over the near term.

Financial Data

(US$ in Thousands)	6 Mos	3 Mos	09/30/2017	09/30/2016	09/30/2015	09/30/2014	09/30/2013
Earnings Per Share	1.61	1.46	1.76	1.95	...	...	...
Cash Flow Per Share	2.08	1.94	2.41	2.32	...	...	...
Dividends Per Share	0.200	0.150	0.100	...	...	...	...
Dividend Payout %	12.42	10.27	5.68	...	...	...	...
Income Statement							
Total Revenue	671,500	330,800	1,126,900	970,100	1,009,300	942,500	852,800
EBITDA	200,100	98,400	338,500	348,300	270,100	209,500	(100)
Depn & Amortn	23,900	11,600	38,400	69,400	48,100	48,300	46,400
Income Before Taxes	153,000	75,500	252,700	278,500	221,900	160,900	(46,800)
Income Taxes	69,100	54,900	52,800	58,800	31,700	31,900	29,100
Net Income	80,200	18,600	193,000	212,000	184,100	123,600	(80,600)
Average Shares	109,700	109,700	109,400	108,700	...	...	...
Balance Sheet							
Current Assets	651,800	652,300	606,900	468,000	295,000	358,000	...
Total Assets	1,345,400	1,322,100	1,246,800	1,043,800	887,400	1,034,000	...
Current Liabilities	128,100	158,000	158,000	104,300	89,600	94,400	...
Long-Term Obligations	976,100	977,100	977,000	980,300	...	4,400	...
Total Liabilities	1,258,300	1,299,700	1,256,800	1,181,100	178,700	198,000	...
Stockholders' Equity	87,100	22,400	(10,000)	(137,300)	708,700	836,000	...
Shares Outstanding	108,943	108,928	108,815	108,675	...	...	...
Statistical Record							
Return on Assets %	14.40	13.35	16.85	21.90	19.16	...	...
Return on Equity %	...	...	...	74.00	23.84	...	...
EBITDA Margin %	29.80	29.75	30.04	35.90	26.76	22.23	N.M.
Net Margin %	11.94	5.62	17.13	21.85	18.24	13.11	N.M.
Asset Turnover	1.02	0.99	0.98	1.00	1.05	...	...
Current Ratio	5.09	4.13	3.84	4.49	3.29	3.79	...
Debt to Equity	11.21	43.62	...	...	...	0.01	...
Price Range	42.50-28.91	42.50-26.78	38.82-22.46	...	...	...	...
P/E Ratio	26.40-17.96	29.11-18.34	22.06-12.76	...	...	...	...
Average Yield %	0.56	0.44	0.33	...	...	...	...

Address: 8555 South River Parkway, Tempe, AZ 85284 Telephone: 602-282-1000	Web Site: www.versummaterials.com Officers: Guillermo Novo - President, Chief Executive Officer George G. Bitto - Executive Vice President, Chief Financial Officer, Senior Vice President	Auditors: KPMG LLP Transfer Agents: Broadridge Corporate Issuer Solutions, Inc.

VF CORP.

Exchange	Symbol	Price	52Wk Range	Yield	P/E	Div Acheiver
NYS	VFC	$81.52 (6/29/2018)	84.47-55.72	2.26	49.41	45 Years

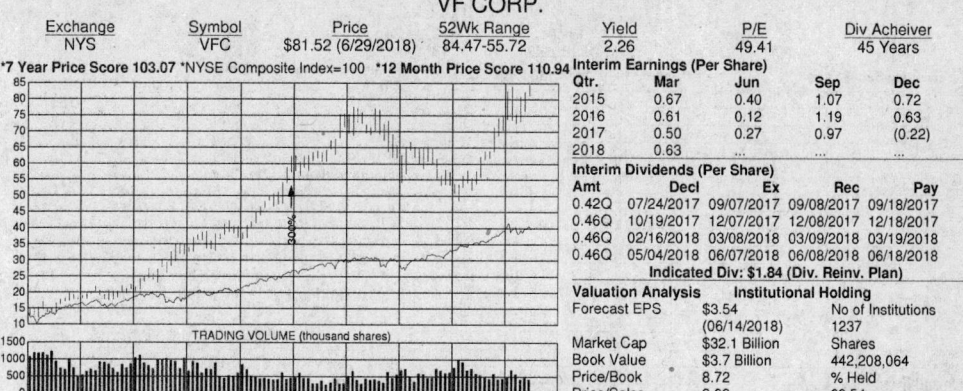

*7 Year Price Score 103.07 *NYSE Composite Index=100 *12 Month Price Score 110.94

Interim Earnings (Per Share)

Qtr.	Mar	Jun	Sep	Dec
2015	0.67	0.40	1.07	0.72
2016	0.61	0.12	1.19	0.63
2017	0.50	0.27	0.97	(0.22)
2018	0.63	...	...	...

Interim Dividends (Per Share)

Amt	Decl	Ex	Rec	Pay
0.42Q	07/24/2017	09/07/2017	09/08/2017	09/18/2017
0.46Q	10/19/2017	12/07/2017	12/08/2017	12/18/2017
0.46Q	02/16/2018	03/08/2018	03/09/2018	03/19/2018
0.46Q	05/04/2018	06/07/2018	06/08/2018	06/18/2018

Indicated Div: $1.84 (Div. Reinv. Plan)

Valuation Analysis

Forecast EPS	$3.54	No of Institutions	
	(06/14/2018)	1237	
Market Cap	$32.1 Billion	Shares	
Book Value	$3.7 Billion	442,208,064	
Price/Book	8.72	% Held	
Price/Sales	2.62	99.54	

Institutional Holding

Business Summary: Apparel, Footwear & Accessories (MIC: 1.4.2 SIC: 2329 NAIC: 315228)

VF is an apparel and footwear company. Co. designs, produces, procures, markets and distributes a range of products, including jeanswear, outerwear, footwear, backpacks, luggage, sportswear, and occupational and performance apparel. Products are marketed primarily under Co.-owned brand names. Co.'s products are marketed to consumers shopping in specialty stores, department stores, national chains, mass merchants and its own direct-to-consumer operations. Co. is organized by groupings of businesses called coalitions that consist of the following: Outdoor & Action Sports, Jeanswear, Imagewear and Sportswear. As of Dec 30 2017, Co. operated 1,518 retail stores.

Recent Developments: For the quarter ended Mar 31 2018, income from continuing operations increased 22.5% to US$261.2 million from US$213.3 million in the year-earlier quarter. Net income increased 20.9% to US$252.8 million from US$209.2 million in the year-earlier quarter. Revenues were US$3.05 billion, up 21.8% from US$2.50 billion the year before. Operating income was US$311.4 million versus US$289.7 million in the prior-year quarter, an increase of 7.5%. Direct operating expenses rose 21.1% to US$1.51 billion from US$1.24 billion in the comparable period the year before. Indirect operating expenses increased 27.0% to US$1.23 billion from US$967.1 million in the equivalent prior-year period.

Prospects: Our evaluation of VF Corp. as of Jan. 21, 2018 is the result of our systematic analysis on three basic characteristics: earnings strength, relative valuation, and recent stock price movement. The company has enjoyed a very positive trend in earnings per share over the past 5 quarters and while recent estimates for the company have been mixed, VFC has posted better than expected results. Based on operating earnings yield, the company is about fairly valued when compared to all of the companies in our coverage universe. Share price changes over the past year indicates that VFC will perform well over the near term.

Financial Data

(US$ in Thousands)	3 Mos	12/30/2017	12/31/2016	01/02/2016	01/03/2015	12/28/2013	12/29/2012	12/31/2011
Earnings Per Share	1.65	1.52	2.54	2.85	2.38	2.71	2.42	2.00
Cash Flow Per Share	3.65	3.70	3.56	2.70	3.86	3.44	2.91	2.47
Tang Book Value Per Share	N.M.	N.M.	2.82	3.06	2.78	2.21	0.29	N.M.
Dividends Per Share	1.760	1.720	1.530	1.330	1.107	0.915	0.757	0.652
Dividend Payout %	106.67	113.16	60.24	46.67	46.53	33.76	31.24	32.71
Income Statement								
Total Revenue	3,045,446	11,811,177	12,019,003	12,376,744	12,282,161	11,419,648	10,879,855	9,459,232
EBITDA	386,830	1,792,878	1,782,804	1,934,726	1,646,684	1,846,719	1,709,025	1,406,454
Depn & Amortn	71,532	290,503	281,577	272,075	214,504	203,597	196,898	168,911
Income Before Taxes	294,133	1,416,495	1,415,591	1,580,389	1,352,366	1,562,490	1,421,875	1,164,743
Income Taxes	32,969	695,286	243,064	348,796	304,861	352,371	335,737	274,350
Net Income	252,793	614,923	1,074,106	1,231,593	1,047,505	1,210,119	1,085,999	888,089
Average Shares	401,276	403,559	422,081	432,079	440,153	446,809	447,616	445,152
Balance Sheet								
Current Assets	4,683,323	4,392,124	4,293,098	4,163,136	4,185,854	3,882,982	3,449,583	3,187,944
Total Assets	10,311,310	9,958,502	9,739,287	9,639,542	9,980,140	10,315,443	9,633,021	9,313,136
Current Liabilities	3,138,829	2,745,200	1,785,400	1,941,713	1,620,241	1,568,001	1,732,212	1,666,032
Long-Term Obligations	2,212,555	2,187,789	2,039,180	1,401,820	1,423,581	1,426,829	1,429,166	1,831,781
Total Liabilities	6,623,214	6,238,602	4,798,366	4,254,704	4,349,258	4,238,405	4,507,396	4,787,135
Stockholders' Equity	3,688,096	3,719,900	4,940,921	5,384,838	5,630,832	6,077,038	5,125,625	4,525,991
Shares Outstanding	394,313	395,821	414,012	426,614	432,859	440,310	440,818	442,227
Statistical Record								
Return on Assets %	6.73	6.26	11.12	12.59	10.16	12.17	11.50	11.26
Return on Equity %	16.34	14.24	20.86	22.42	17.60	21.66	22.57	21.18
EBITDA Margin %	12.70	15.18	14.83	15.63	13.41	16.17	15.71	14.87
Net Margin %	8.30	5.21	8.94	9.95	8.53	10.60	9.98	9.39
Asset Turnover	1.26	1.20	1.24	1.27	1.19	1.15	1.15	1.20
Current Ratio	1.49	1.60	2.40	2.14	2.58	2.48	1.99	1.91
Debt to Equity	0.60	0.59	0.41	0.26	0.25	0.23	0.28	0.40
Price Range	83.94-51.62	74.61-48.32	66.75-53.07	77.61-61.81	75.46-55.99	62.08-36.44	42.22-32.42	35.26-20.34
P/E Ratio	50.87-31.28	49.09-31.79	26.28-20.89	27.23-21.69	31.71-23.53	22.91-13.44	17.44-13.40	17.63-10.17
Average Yield %	2.68	2.88	2.54	1.87	1.73	1.94	2.05	2.38

Address: 105 Corporate Center Boulevard, Greensboro, NC 27408 **Telephone:** 336-424-6000	**Web Site:** www.vfc.com **Officers:** Steven E. Rendle - Chairman, President, Chief Executive Officer, Vice President, Chief Operating Officer, Division Officer Scott A. Roe - Vice President, Chief Financial Officer, Chief Accounting Officer, Controller	**Auditors:** PricewaterhouseCoopers LLP **Transfer Agents:** Computershare Trust Company, N.A, Providence, RI

VISA INC

Exchange	Symbol	Price	52Wk Range	Yield	P/E
NYS	V	$132.45 (6/29/2018)	136.28-93.25	0.63	33.62

*7 Year Price Score 143.43 *NYSE Composite Index=100 *12 Month Price Score 112.82

Interim Earnings (Per Share)

Qtr.	Dec	Mar	Jun	Sep
2014-15	0.63	0.63	0.69	0.62
2015-16	0.80	0.71	0.17	0.79
2016-17	0.86	0.18	0.86	0.90
2017-18	1.07	1.11	...	...

Interim Dividends (Per Share)

Amt	Decl	Ex	Rec	Pay
0.165Q	07/17/2017	08/16/2017	08/18/2017	09/05/2017
0.195Q	10/17/2017	11/16/2017	11/17/2017	12/05/2017
0.21Q	01/30/2018	02/15/2018	02/16/2018	03/06/2018
0.21Q	04/17/2018	05/17/2018	05/18/2018	06/05/2018

Indicated Div: $0.84

Valuation Analysis / Institutional Holding

Forecast EPS	$4.50 (06/14/2018)	No of Institutions 2539
Market Cap	$271.1 Billion	Shares 1,846,064,256
Book Value	$34.1 Billion	% Held 84.72
Price/Book	7.95	
Price/Sales	14.01	

Business Summary: Business Services (MIC: 7.5.2 SIC: 7389 NAIC: 561499)

Visa is a payments technology company that enables electronic payments across more than 200 countries and territories. Co. facilitates global commerce through the transfer of value and information among a network of consumers, merchants, financial institutions, businesses, strategic partners, and government entities. Co.'s transaction processing network, VisaNet, enables authorization, clearing, and settlement of payment transactions and allows Co. to provide its financial institution and merchant clients with a range of products, platforms, and services. Co. operates in a four party model, which includes card issuing financial institutions, acquirers, and merchants.

Recent Developments: For the quarter ended Mar 31 2018, net income increased 505.8% to US$2.61 billion from US$430.0 million in the year-earlier quarter. Revenues were US$5.07 billion, up 13.3% from US$4.48 billion the year before. Operating income was US$3.34 billion versus US$2.81 billion in the prior-year quarter, an increase of 18.8%. Indirect operating expenses increased 4.1% to US$1.74 billion from US$1.67 billion in the equivalent prior-year period.

Prospects: Our evaluation of Visa Inc. as of Jan. 21, 2018 is the result of our systematic analysis on three basic characteristics: earnings strength, relative valuation, and recent stock price movement. The company has managed to produce a neutral trend in earnings per share over the past 5 quarters and while recent estimates for the company have been raised by analysts, V has posted better than expected results. Based on operating earnings yield, the company is about fairly valued when compared to all of the companies in our coverage universe. Share price changes over the past year indicates that V will perform in line with the market over the near term.

Financial Data
(US$ in Thousands)

	6 Mos	3 Mos	09/30/2017	09/30/2016	09/30/2015	09/30/2014	09/30/2013	09/30/2012
Earnings Per Share	3.94	3.01	2.80	2.48	2.58	2.15	1.90	0.79
Cash Flow Per Share	6.61	5.22	4.38	2.56	2.96	2.34	0.95	1.54
Tang Book Value Per Share	N.M.	N.M.	N.M.	N.M.	3.00	1.39	1.23	1.40
Dividends Per Share	0.735	0.690	0.660	0.560	0.480	0.400	0.330	0.220
Dividend Payout %	18.65	22.92	23.57	22.58	18.60	18.56	17.39	27.85
Income Statement								
Total Revenue	9,935,000	4,862,000	18,358,000	15,082,000	13,880,000	12,702,000	11,778,000	10,421,000
EBITDA	7,061,000	3,538,000	12,757,000	8,891,000	9,426,000	8,093,000	7,585,000	2,426,000
Depn & Amortn	298,000	145,000	500,000	452,000	431,000	369,000	328,000	265,000
Income Before Taxes	6,456,000	3,239,000	11,694,000	8,012,000	8,995,000	7,724,000	7,257,000	2,207,000
Income Taxes	1,329,000	717,000	4,995,000	2,021,000	2,667,000	2,286,000	2,277,000	65,000
Net Income	5,127,000	2,522,000	6,699,000	5,991,000	6,328,000	5,438,000	4,980,000	2,144,000
Average Shares	2,337,000	2,353,000	2,395,000	2,414,000	2,457,000	2,524,000	2,624,000	2,712,000
Balance Sheet								
Current Assets	18,536,000	17,287,000	19,023,000	14,313,000	10,892,000	9,562,000	7,822,000	11,786,000
Total Assets	69,042,000	67,154,000	67,977,000	64,035,000	40,236,000	38,569,000	35,956,000	40,013,000
Current Liabilities	9,551,000	8,363,000	9,994,000	8,046,000	5,374,000	6,006,000	4,335,000	7,954,000
Long-Term Obligations	16,624,000	16,621,000	16,618,000	15,882,000	...	...	...	...
Total Liabilities	34,939,000	33,753,000	35,217,000	31,123,000	10,394,000	11,156,000	9,086,000	12,383,000
Stockholders' Equity	34,103,000	33,401,000	32,760,000	32,912,000	29,842,000	27,413,000	26,870,000	27,630,000
Shares Outstanding	2,047,000	2,062,000	2,076,000	2,133,000	2,215,000	3,048,000	3,120,000	3,244,000
Statistical Record								
Return on Assets %	14.10	10.96	10.15	11.46	16.06	14.59	13.11	5.72
Return on Equity %	28.75	21.96	20.40	19.04	22.10	20.04	18.28	7.91
EBITDA Margin %	71.07	72.77	69.49	58.95	67.91	63.71	64.40	23.28
Net Margin %	51.61	51.87	36.49	39.72	45.59	42.81	42.28	20.57
Asset Turnover	0.29	0.29	0.28	0.29	0.35	0.34	0.31	0.28
Current Ratio	1.94	2.07	1.90	1.78	2.03	1.59	1.80	1.48
Debt to Equity	0.49	0.50	0.51	0.48	...	...	...	...
Price Range	126.32-88.68	114.35-79.50	106.21-75.43	83.36-67.77	76.38-50.06	58.25-45.63	49.71-34.00	33.75-21.07
P/E Ratio	32.06-22.51	37.99-26.41	37.93-26.94	33.61-27.33	29.60-19.40	27.09-21.22	26.16-17.89	42.72-26.66
Average Yield %	0.69	0.71	0.73	0.73	0.72	0.76	0.79	0.78

Address: P.O. Box 8999, San Francisco, CA 94128-8999	Web Site: www.corporate.visa.com	Auditors: KPMG LLP
Telephone: 650-432-3200	Officers: Ryan McInerney - President Alfred F. Kelly - Chief Executive Officer, Chief Executive Officer - Designate	Investor Contact: 650-432-7644 Transfer Agents: Wells Fargo Shareowner Services, St. Paul, MN

VISHAY INTERTECHNOLOGY, INC.

Exchange	Symbol	Price	52Wk Range	Yield	P/E
NYS	VSH	$23.20 (6/29/2018)	24.70-16.50	1.47	2320.00

*7 Year Price Score 116.17 *NYSE Composite Index=100 *12 Month Price Score 105.60

Interim Earnings (Per Share)

Qtr.	Mar	Jun	Sep	Dec
2015	0.20	0.17	(0.19)	(0.92)
2016	0.19	0.22	0.24	(0.33)
2017	0.24	0.36	0.41	(1.15)
2018	0.39	...	...	...

Interim Dividends (Per Share)

Amt	Decl	Ex	Rec	Pay
0.063Q	08/22/2017	09/14/2017	09/15/2017	09/28/2017
0.068Q	11/15/2017	12/06/2017	12/07/2017	12/21/2017
0.068Q	02/15/2018	03/13/2018	03/14/2018	03/29/2018
0.085Q	05/07/2018	06/12/2018	06/13/2018	06/28/2018

Indicated Div: $0.34

Valuation Analysis

		Institutional Holding	
Forecast EPS	$1.78	No of Institutions	
	(06/14/2018)	425	
Market Cap	$3.3 Billion	Shares	
Book Value	$1.5 Billion	197,018,176	
Price/Book	2.21	% Held	
Price/Sales	1.23	98.20	

Business Summary: Electrical Equipment (MIC: 7.3.1 SIC: 3679 NAIC: 334419)

Vishay Intertechnology is a manufacturer and supplier of discrete semiconductors and passive components. Semiconductors include MOSFETs, diodes, and optoelectronic components, which are used for various functions, including power control, power conversion, power management, signal switching, signal routing, signal blocking, signal amplification, data transfer, remote control, and circuit isolation. Passive components include resistive products, capacitors, and inductors, which are used to restrict current flow, suppress voltage increases, store and discharge energy, control alternating current and voltage, filter out unwanted electrical signals, and perform other functions.

Recent Developments: For the quarter ended Mar 31 2018, net income increased 69.3% to US$62.5 million from US$36.9 million in the year-earlier quarter. Revenues were US$716.8 million, up 18.5% from US$604.8 million the year before. Operating income was US$104.1 million versus US$67.6 million in the prior-year quarter, an increase of 54.0%. Direct operating expenses rose 15.4% to US$511.5 million from US$443.1 million in the comparable period the year before. Indirect operating expenses increased 7.5% to US$101.2 million from US$94.2 million in the equivalent prior-year period.

Prospects: Our evaluation of Vishay Intertechnology Inc. as of Jan. 21, 2018 is the result of our systematic analysis on three basic characteristics: earnings strength, relative valuation, and recent stock price movement. The company has produced a positive trend in earnings per share over the past 5 quarters and while recent estimates for the company have remained steady, VSH has posted better than expected results. Based on current earnings yield, the company is undervalued when compared to all of the companies in our coverage universe. Share price changes over the past year indicates that VSH will perform in line with the market over the near term.

Financial Data
(US$ in Thousands)

	3 Mos	12/31/2017	12/31/2016	12/31/2015	12/31/2014	12/31/2013	12/31/2012	12/31/2011
Earnings Per Share	0.01	(0.14)	0.32	(0.73)	0.77	0.81	0.79	1.42
Cash Flow Per Share	2.58	2.53	2.01	1.66	2.01	2.02	1.92	2.35
Tang Book Value Per Share	8.96	8.44	9.18	9.36	10.13	11.54	10.15	9.48
Dividends Per Share	0.260	0.255	0.250	0.240	0.240	...	...	...
Dividend Payout %	2,600.00	...	78.13		31.17	...	...	...
Income Statement								
Total Revenue	716,795	2,603,522	2,323,431	2,300,488	2,493,282	2,370,979	2,230,097	2,594,029
EBITDA	138,218	455,727	260,096	250,368	347,465	350,033	338,816	505,029
Depn & Amortn	40,558	148,883	144,521	154,340	160,804	155,064	153,801	165,022
Income Before Taxes	92,019	285,476	94,216	74,740	167,143	176,405	170,037	331,116
Income Taxes	29,474	298,924	44,843	182,473	49,300	52,636	46,506	91,119
Net Income	62,366	(20,344)	48,792	(108,514)	117,629	122,980	122,738	238,821
Average Shares	159,502	145,633	150,697	147,700	153,716	151,417	155,844	168,514
Balance Sheet								
Current Assets	2,294,945	2,192,290	1,864,472	1,887,492	1,926,450	1,980,680	1,791,263	1,830,676
Total Assets	3,570,510	3,459,189	3,077,801	3,152,986	3,298,773	3,237,139	3,016,277	2,993,730
Current Liabilities	529,043	564,335	456,850	457,724	456,739	449,065	412,170	439,788
Long-Term Obligations	406,385	370,470	357,023	436,738	454,922	364,911	392,931	399,054
Total Liabilities	2,057,615	2,031,032	1,512,284	1,530,510	1,473,407	1,364,383	1,392,949	1,390,724
Stockholders' Equity	1,512,895	1,428,157	1,565,517	1,622,476	1,825,366	1,872,756	1,623,328	1,603,006
Shares Outstanding	144,215	144,003	145,976	147,590	147,453	147,331	143,272	157,188
Statistical Record								
Return on Assets %	0.16	N.M.	1.56	N.M.	3.60	3.93	4.07	8.01
Return on Equity %	0.34	N.M.	3.05	N.M.	6.36	7.04	7.59	15.43
EBITDA Margin %	19.28	17.50	11.19	10.88	13.94	14.76	15.19	19.47
Net Margin %	8.70	N.M.	2.10	N.M.	4.72	5.19	5.50	9.21
Asset Turnover	0.81	0.80	0.74	0.71	0.76	0.76	0.74	0.87
Current Ratio	4.34	3.88	4.08	4.12	4.22	4.41	4.35	4.16
Debt to Equity	0.27	0.26	0.23	0.27	0.25	0.19	0.24	0.25
Price Range	23.85-15.50	23.20-15.50	16.60-10.28	14.59-9.30	16.17-12.68	15.32-10.28	12.74-8.18	19.08-8.09
P/E Ratio	N.M.	...	51.88-32.13	...	21.00-16.47	18.91-12.69	16.13-10.35	13.44-5.70
Average Yield %	1.38	1.42	1.91	1.98	1.66	...	...	...

Address: 63 Lancaster Avenue, Malvern, PA 19355-2143
Telephone: 610-644-1300

Web Site: www.vishay.com
Officers: Marc Zandman - Executive Chairman, Chief Business Development Officer Gerald Paul - President, Chief Executive Officer, Chief Technical Officer

Auditors: Ernst & Young LLP
Investor Contact: 610-644-1300
Transfer Agents: American Stock Transfer & Trust Company, New York, NY

VISTRA ENERGY CORP

Exchange	Symbol	Price	52Wk Range	Yield	P/E
NYS	VST	$23.66 (6/29/2018)	24.67-15.88	N/A	N/A

*7 Year Price Score N/A *NYSE Composite Index=100 *12 Month Price Score 120.52

TRADING VOLUME (thousand shares)

Interim Earnings (Per Share)

Qtr.	Mar	Jun	Sep	Dec
2017	0.18	(0.06)	0.64	(1.35)
2018	(0.71)	...	...	...

Interim Dividends (Per Share)

Amt	Decl	Ex	Rec	Pay
2.32U	12/08/2016	12/15/2016	12/19/2016	12/30/2016

Valuation Analysis

		Institutional Holding	
Forecast EPS	$0.94	No of Institutions	
	(06/13/2018)	311	
Market Cap	$10.1 Billion	Shares	
Book Value	$6.1 Billion	471,013,056	
Price/Book	1.67	% Held	
Price/Sales	2.10	N/A	

Business Summary: Electric Utilities (MIC: 3.1.1 SIC: 4911 NAIC: 221122)

Vistra Energy is a holding company. Co. is an energy company operating an integrated power business in Texas. Through its TXU Energy Retail Company LLC and Luminant subsidiaries, Co.'s operations consist of electricity solutions, including retail sales of electricity and related products to end users, power generation (including operations and maintenance and outage and project management) and sales of electricity in the wholesale marketplace, asset optimization and commodity risk management performed on an integrated basis for Co.'s retail and wholesale positions, and fuel logistics and management. Co. operates solely in the Electric Reliability Council of Texas, Inc. electricity market.

Recent Developments: For the quarter ended Mar 31 2018, net loss amounted to US$306.0 million versus net income of US$78.0 million in the year-earlier quarter. Revenues were US$765.0 million, down 43.6% from US$1.36 billion the year before. Operating loss was US$394.0 million versus an income of US$155.0 million in the prior-year quarter. Direct operating expenses declined 5.9% to US$844.0 million from US$897.0 million in the comparable period the year before. Indirect operating expenses increased 3.3% to US$315.0 million from US$305.0 million in the equivalent prior-year period.

Prospects: On October 10, 2017, subsidiaries of Co. entered into a Settlement Agreement with Alcoa Corporation and Alcoa USA Corp. The terminated agreements were scheduled to terminate in 2038 absent the Settlement Agreement. The Alcoa Parties made a cash payment to the Vistra Parties in the amount of $237.5 million and transferred certain real property and related assets to the Vistra Parties, the Vistra Parties agreed to assume and be responsible for certain liabilities and asset retirement obligations related to Sandow Unit 4, the Three Oaks Mine and other property transferred from Alcoa and both parties released one another from any obligations and claims under the terminated agreements.

Financial Data

(US$ in Millions)	3 Mos	12/31/2017	12/31/2016	10/02/2016	12/31/2015	12/31/2014
Earnings Per Share	(1.48)	(0.59)	(0.38)	...	...	...
Cash Flow Per Share	2.85	3.24	0.77	...	...	...
Tang Book Value Per Share	4.00	4.45	3.47	...	...	...
Dividends Per Share	...	...	2.320	...	...	...
Income Statement						
Total Revenue	765	5,430	1,191	4,255	5,704	5,989
EBITDA	(171)	664	(120)	23,031	(3,501)	(5,646)
Depn & Amortn	180	236	54	401	767	1,154
Income Before Taxes	(395)	250	(233)	21,584	(5,556)	(8,549)
Income Taxes	(89)	504	(70)	(1,267)	(879)	(2,320)
Net Income	(306)	(254)	(163)	22,851	(4,677)	(6,229)
Average Shares	428	427	427	...	...	...
Balance Sheet						
Current Assets	2,699	2,673	2,473	...	3,450	...
Total Assets	14,776	14,600	15,167	...	15,658	...
Current Liabilities	1,557	1,351	1,504	...	2,812	...
Long-Term Obligations	4,366	4,379	4,577	...	3	...
Total Liabilities	8,716	8,258	8,570	...	38,542	...
Stockholders' Equity	6,060	6,342	6,597	...	(22,884)	...
Shares Outstanding	428	428	427	...	...	...
Statistical Record						
EBITDA Margin %	N.M.	12.23	N.M.	541.27	N.M.	N.M.
Net Margin %	N.M.	N.M.	N.M.	537.04	N.M.	N.M.
Asset Turnover	0.33	0.36	0.31	...	...	...
Current Ratio	1.73	1.98	1.64	...	1.23	...
Debt to Equity	0.72	0.69	0.69	...	...	...
Price Range	21.13-14.59	20.49-14.59	16.40-13.60	...	...	...
Average Yield %	...	...	15.49	...	...	...

Address: 6555 Sierra Drive, Irving, TX 75039	Web Site: www.vistraenergy.com	Auditors: DELOITTE & TOUCHE LLP
Telephone: 214-812-4600	Officers: Scott B. Helm - Chairman Curtis A. (Curt) Morgan - President, Chief Executive Officer	Investor Contact: 214-812-0046 Transfer Agents: American Stock Transfer & Trust Company, LLC

VMWARE INC

Exchange	Symbol	Price	52Wk Range	Yield	P/E
NYS	VMW	$146.97 (6/29/2018)	152.18-85.89	N/A	47.26

*7 Year Price Score 108.87 *NYSE Composite Index=100 ***12 Month Price Score 116.88**

Interim Earnings (Per Share)

Qtr.	Mar	Jun	Sep	Dec
2016	0.38	0.62	0.75	1.03
2017-18	0.56	0.81	1.07	(1.06)
2018-19	2.29	...	...	...

Interim Dividends (Per Share)

No Dividends Paid

Valuation Analysis

		Institutional Holding	
Forecast EPS	$6.14	No of Institutions	
	(06/14/2018)	715	
Market Cap	$59.7 Billion	Shares	
Book Value	$9.7 Billion	95,459,736	
Price/Book	6.18	% Held	
Price/Sales	7.29	22.08	

Business Summary: Internet & Software (MIC: 6.3.2 SIC: 7372 NAIC: 511210)

VMware is a provider of virtualization and cloud infrastructure solutions. Co.'s virtualization infrastructure solutions are designed to deliver a software-defined data center, run on desktop computers and servers and support operating system and application environments, as well as networking and storage infrastructures. Co. has three product groups: Software-Defined Data Center, which are the basis for the private cloud environment; Hybrid Cloud Computing, which is comprised of VMware vCloud Air Network and VMware vCloud Air offerings; and End-User Computing solution that consists of VMware Workspace ONE, its digital workspace platform, which includes VMware AirWatch and VMware Horizon.

Recent Developments: For the quarter ended May 4 2018, net income increased 284.5% to US$942.0 million from US$245.0 million in the year-earlier quarter. Revenues were US$2.01 billion, up 13.8% from US$1.77 billion the year before. Operating income was US$382.0 million versus US$261.0 million in the prior-year quarter, an increase of 46.4%. Direct operating expenses rose 2.4% to US$296.0 million from US$289.0 million in the comparable period the year before. Indirect operating expenses increased 9.5% to US$1.33 billion from US$1.22 billion in the equivalent prior-year period.

Prospects: Our evaluation of VMware Inc. as of Jan. 21, 2018 is the result of our systematic analysis on three basic characteristics: earnings strength, relative valuation, and recent stock price movement. The company has enjoyed a very positive trend in earnings per share over the past 5 quarters and while recent estimates for the company have remained steady, VMW has posted better than expected results. Based on operating earnings yield, the company is about fairly valued when compared to all of the companies in our coverage universe. Share price changes over the past year indicates that VMW will perform very well over the near term.

Financial Data

(US$ in Thousands)	3 Mos	02/02/2018	02/03/2017	12/31/2016	12/31/2015	12/31/2014	12/31/2013	12/31/2012
Earnings Per Share	3.11	1.38	(0.02)	2.78	2.34	2.04	2.34	1.72
Cash Flow Per Share	8.72	7.92	9.48	5.65	4.48	5.07	5.91	4.44
Tang Book Value Per Share	11.14	6.52	8.97	8.69	7.84	6.68	7.39	5.04
Income Statement								
Total Revenue	2,008,000	7,922,000	496,000	7,093,000	6,571,000	6,035,000	5,207,000	4,605,047
EBITDA	1,365,000	2,070,000	(3,000)	1,714,000	1,429,000	1,262,000	1,292,000	1,028,668
Depn & Amortn	156,000	195,000	29,000	215,000	190,000	190,000	141,000	130,900
Income Before Taxes	1,175,000	1,801,000	(34,000)	1,473,000	1,213,000	1,048,000	1,147,000	893,114
Income Taxes	233,000	1,231,000	(26,000)	287,000	216,000	162,000	133,000	147,412
Net Income	942,000	570,000	(8,000)	1,186,000	997,000	886,000	1,014,000	745,702
Average Shares	410,932	413,368	408,625	423,994	426,547	434,513	433,415	433,974
Balance Sheet								
Current Assets	14,101,000	13,734,000	9,851,000	10,335,000	9,360,000	9,130,000	7,681,000	6,120,039
Total Assets	22,088,000	20,622,000	16,397,000	16,643,000	15,746,000	15,216,000	12,327,000	10,596,392
Current Liabilities	4,637,000	5,033,000	4,289,000	4,554,000	4,129,000	3,996,000	3,293,000	2,960,234
Long-Term Obligations	4,236,000	4,234,000	1,500,000	1,500,000	1,500,000	1,500,000	450,000	450,000
Total Liabilities	12,428,000	12,846,000	8,181,000	8,546,000	7,827,000	7,635,000	5,511,000	4,856,411
Stockholders' Equity	9,660,000	7,776,000	8,216,000	8,097,000	7,919,000	7,581,000	6,816,000	5,739,981
Shares Outstanding	406,434	403,776	410,060	408,351	421,947	429,359	430,349	428,688
Statistical Record								
Return on Assets %	6.68	3.09	N.M.	7.30	6.44	6.43	8.85	7.72
Return on Equity %	14.44	7.15	N.M.	14.77	12.86	12.31	16.15	14.15
EBITDA Margin %	67.98	26.13	N.M.	24.16	21.75	20.91	24.81	22.34
Net Margin %	46.91	7.20	N.M.	16.72	15.17	14.68	19.47	16.19
Asset Turnover	0.43	0.43	0.32	0.44	0.42	0.44	0.45	0.48
Current Ratio	3.04	2.73	2.30	2.27	2.27	2.28	2.33	2.07
Debt to Equity	0.44	0.54	0.18	0.19	0.19	0.20	0.07	0.08
Price Range	150.00-85.89	150.00-85.89	88.95-78.88	82.58-43.84	91.14-55.42	111.80-76.43	99.00-65.53	114.62-80.29
P/E Ratio	48.23-27.62	108.70-62.24	...	29.71-15.77	38.95-23.68	54.80-37.47	42.31-28.00	66.64-46.68

Address: 3401 Hillview Avenue, Palo Alto, CA 94304	**Web Site:** www.vmware.com	**Auditors:** PricewaterhouseCoopers LLP
Telephone: 650-427-5000	**Officers:** Michael S. Dell - Chairman Michael S. Dell - Chairman	**Investor Contact:** 650-427-2892
		Transfer Agents: American Stock Transfer & Trust Co., New York, NY

VORNADO REALTY TRUST

Exchange	Symbol	Price	52Wk Range	Yield	P/E
NYS	VNO	$73.92 (6/29/2018)	80.56-65.01	3.41	144.94

*7 Year Price Score 81.92 *NYSE Composite Index=100 *12 Month Price Score 95.17

Interim Earnings (Per Share)

Qtr.	Mar	Jun	Sep	Dec
2015	0.45	0.87	1.05	1.22
2016	(0.61)	1.16	0.35	3.43
2017	0.25	0.61	(0.15)	0.14
2018	(0.09)	...	...	...

Interim Dividends (Per Share)

Amt	Decl	Ex	Rec	Pay
0.60Q	07/27/2017	08/03/2017	08/07/2017	08/18/2017
0.60Q	10/26/2017	11/03/2017	11/06/2017	11/20/2017
0.63Q	01/17/2018	01/26/2018	01/29/2018	02/15/2018
0.63Q	04/25/2018	05/04/2018	05/07/2018	05/18/2018

Indicated Div: $2.52

Valuation Analysis

		Institutional Holding	
Forecast EPS	$0.89 (06/14/2018)	No of Institutions	686
Market Cap	$14.1 Billion	Shares	225,913,648
Book Value	$4.4 Billion	% Held	91.41
Price/Book	3.22		
Price/Sales	6.31		

Business Summary: REITs (MIC: 5.3.1 SIC: 6798 NAIC: 525930)

Vornado Realty Trust is a real estate investment trust. Co. conducts its business through, and substantially all of its interests in properties are held by, Vornado Realty L.P. Co. owns and operates office and retail properties in New York and Washington, DC/ Northern Virginia area. As of Dec 31 2017, Co. owned all or portions of, among others: office space in 36 properties, retail space in 71 properties, 12 residential properties, Hotel Pennsylvania in NY, a 32.4% interest in Alexander's, Inc. that owned seven properties in NY, theMart in Chicago, a 70.0% controlling interest in an office complex in San Francisco, 25% interest in Vornado Capital Partners and 32.5% interest in Toys "R" Us.

Recent Developments: For the quarter ended Mar 31 2018, income from continuing operations decreased 98.9% to US$645,000 from US$58.5 million in the year-earlier quarter. Net income decreased 99.6% to US$282,000 from US$73.8 million in the year-earlier quarter. Revenues were US$536.4 million, up 5.5% from US$508.6 million the year before. Revenues from property income rose 5.6% to US$500.4 million from US$473.9 million in the corresponding quarter a year earlier.

Prospects: Our evaluation of Vornado Realty Trust as of Jan. 14, 2018 is the result of our systematic analysis on three basic characteristics: earnings strength, relative valuation, and recent stock price movement. The company has generated a negative trend in earnings per share over the past 5 quarters. Because the company lacks sufficient analyst estimate data, we place greater weight on the historical EPS trend as the measure of earnings strength. Based on operating earnings yield, the company is overvalued when compared to all of the companies in our coverage universe. Share price changes over the past year indicates that VNO will perform well over the near term.

Financial Data
(US$ in Thousands)

	3 Mos	12/31/2017	12/31/2016	12/31/2015	12/31/2014	12/31/2013	12/31/2012	12/31/2011
Earnings Per Share	0.51	0.85	4.34	3.59	4.15	2.09	2.94	3.23
Cash Flow Per Share	4.34	4.54	5.28	3.57	6.05	5.57	4.43	3.81
Tang Book Value Per Share	17.44	17.30	29.97	27.54	27.63	27.58	28.06	29.65
Dividends Per Share	2.540	2.620	2.520	2.520	2.920	2.920	3.760	2.760
Dividend Payout %	498.04	308.24	58.06	70.19	70.36	139.71	127.89	85.45
Income Statement								
Total Revenue	536,437	2,084,126	2,506,202	2,502,267	2,635,940	2,760,909	2,766,457	2,915,665
EBITDA	93,146	1,097,835	1,761,684	1,499,334	1,377,389	1,324,381	900,561	1,486,619
Depn & Amortn	(10,581)	483,036	542,068	487,154	536,622	509,122	503,529	517,946
Income Before Taxes	20,810	300,006	841,275	661,022	400,282	369,708	(70,331)	476,098
Income Taxes	1,454	41,090	8,312	(84,695)	11,002	(6,406)	8,132	24,827
Net Income	9,680	227,416	906,917	760,434	864,852	475,971	617,260	662,302
Average Shares	190,081	191,258	190,173	189,564	188,690	187,709	186,530	186,021
Balance Sheet								
Current Assets	2,416,990	2,156,264	1,897,493	2,192,565	1,715,456	1,153,509	1,737,481	1,617,740
Total Assets	16,864,483	17,397,934	20,814,847	21,143,293	21,248,320	20,097,224	21,965,975	20,446,487
Current Liabilities	431,094	415,794	458,694	443,955	499,702	422,276	484,746	423,512
Long-Term Obligations	9,774,477	9,729,487	10,611,685	11,091,010	10,898,859	9,978,718	11,296,190	10,562,002
Total Liabilities	12,504,391	13,060,282	13,916,328	14,445,698	14,502,894	13,331,992	15,115,040	13,618,171
Stockholders' Equity	4,360,092	4,337,652	6,898,519	6,697,595	6,745,426	6,765,232	6,850,935	6,828,316
Shares Outstanding	190,169	189,983	189,100	188,576	187,887	187,284	186,734	185,080
Statistical Record								
Return on Assets %	0.92	1.19	4.31	3.59	4.18	2.26	2.90	3.23
Return on Equity %	3.09	4.05	13.30	11.31	12.80	6.99	9.00	10.08
EBITDA Margin %	17.36	52.68	70.29	59.92	52.25	47.97	32.55	50.99
Net Margin %	1.80	10.91	36.19	30.39	32.81	17.24	22.31	22.72
Asset Turnover	0.12	0.11	0.12	0.12	0.13	0.13	0.13	0.14
Current Ratio	5.61	5.19	4.14	4.94	3.43	2.73	3.58	3.82
Debt to Equity	2.24	2.24	1.54	1.66	1.62	1.48	1.65	1.55
Price Range	83.29-65.15	89.58-72.38	87.03-64.77	92.74-68.53	87.30-64.88	66.69-56.16	64.46-53.60	72.17-51.21
P/E Ratio	163.31-127.75	105.39-85.15	20.05-14.92	25.83-19.09	21.04-15.63	31.91-26.87	21.93-18.23	22.34-15.86
Average Yield %	3.39	3.32	3.32	3.23	3.09	3.86	4.68	4.41

Address: 888 Seventh Avenue, New York, NY 10019 Telephone: 212-894-7000	Web Site: www.vno.com Officers: Steven Roth - Chairman, Chief Executive Officer Joseph Macnow - Chief Financial Officer, Executive Vice President, Executive Vice President (frmr), Chief Administrative Officer	Auditors: Deloitte & Touche LLP Investor Contact: 201-587-1000 Transfer Agents: American Stock Transfer & Trust Co., New York, NY

VOYA FINANCIAL INC

Exchange	Symbol	Price	52Wk Range	Yield	P/E
NYS	VOYA	$47.00 (6/29/2018)	55.15-36.18	0.09	N/A

*7 Year Price Score N/A ***NYSE Composite Index=100** ***12 Month Price Score 110.42**

Interim Earnings (Per Share)

Qtr.	Mar	Jun	Sep	Dec
2015	0.77	1.24	0.18	(0.43)
2016	0.92	0.79	(1.24)	(2.64)
2017	(0.75)	0.89	0.81	(17.17)
2018	2.50	...	...	...

Interim Dividends (Per Share)

Amt	Decl	Ex	Rec	Pay
0.01Q	07/27/2017	08/29/2017	08/31/2017	09/28/2017
0.01Q	10/26/2017	11/29/2017	11/30/2017	12/28/2017
0.01Q	02/01/2018	02/27/2018	02/28/2018	03/28/2018
0.01Q	04/25/2018	05/25/2018	05/29/2018	06/28/2018

Indicated Div: $0.04

Valuation Analysis

		Institutional Holding	
Forecast EPS	$4.23	No of Institutions	
	(06/14/2018)	487	
Market Cap	$8.1 Billion	Shares	
Book Value	$9.4 Billion	202,165,216	
Price/Book	0.86	% Held	
Price/Sales	0.96	N/A	

Business Summary: Life & Health (MIC: 5.2.2 SIC: 6311 NAIC: 524210)

Voya Financial is a holding company. Through a number of direct and indirect subsidiaries, Co. is a retirement, investment and insurance company. Co.'s segments include: Retirement, which provides, among others, retirement services and products, providing tax-deferred; Investment Management, which provides domestic and international fixed income, equity, multi-asset and alternative investment products and solutions; Annuities, which provides fixed and indexed annuities, and other investment products and payout; Individual Life, which provides wealth protection and transfer opportunities; and Employee Benefits, which provides stop loss, voluntary employee-paid and disability products.

Recent Developments: For the quarter ended Mar 31 2018, net income amounted to US$446.0 million versus a net loss of US$142.0 million in the year-earlier quarter. Revenues were US$1.97 billion, down 4.4% from US$2.06 billion the year before. Net premiums earned were US$539.0 million versus US$547.0 million in the prior-year quarter, a decrease of 1.5%. Net investment income fell 2.4% to US$823.0 million from US$843.0 million a year ago.

Prospects: Our evaluation of Voya Financial Inc. as of Jan. 21, 2018 is the result of our systematic analysis on three basic characteristics: earnings strength, relative valuation, and recent stock price movement. The company has generated a negative trend in earnings per share over the past 5 quarters. However, while recent estimates for the company have been lowered by analysts, VOYA has posted results that fell short of analysts expectations. Based on operating earnings yield, the company is undervalued when compared to all of the companies in our coverage universe. Share price changes over the past year indicates that VOYA will perform very poorly over the near term.

Financial Data
(US$ in Thousands)

	3 Mos	12/31/2017	12/31/2016	12/31/2015	12/31/2014	12/31/2013	12/31/2012	12/31/2011
Earnings Per Share	(12.97)	(16.25)	(2.13)	1.80	9.02	2.38	2.06	(0.38)
Cash Flow Per Share	11.77	8.57	17.81	14.40	14.34	13.02	...	...
Tang Book Value Per Share	54.66	58.20	65.63	63.06	65.42	49.48	58.81	52.05
Dividends Per Share	0.040	0.040	0.040	0.040	0.040	0.020	...	...
Dividend Payout %	...	...	...	2.22	0.44	0.84	...	...
Income Statement								
Total Revenue	1,967,000	8,618,000	10,782,200	11,341,200	11,070,900	8,758,500	9,615,300	9,718,800
Income Before Taxes	21,000	528,000	(613,400)	584,500	785,200	758,100	606,000	277,800
Income Taxes	4,000	740,000	(214,700)	45,900	(1,752,200)	(32,500)	(5,200)	175,000
Net Income	446,000	(2,992,000)	(428,000)	408,300	2,299,700	600,500	473,000	(88,100)
Average Shares	178,400	184,100	200,800	227,400	255,100	251,800	...	...
Balance Sheet								
Total Assets	219,824,000	222,532,000	214,235,100	218,249,600	226,951,400	221,023,200	216,394,200	203,572,800
Total Liabilities	210,446,000	212,523,000	201,241,200	204,813,800	210,843,500	207,751,000	202,519,300	191,218,900
Stockholders' Equity	9,378,000	10,009,000	12,993,900	13,435,800	16,107,900	13,272,200	13,874,900	12,353,900
Shares Outstanding	171,555	171,982	194,639	209,095	241,875	261,675	230,000	230,000
Statistical Record								
Return on Assets %	N.M.	N.M.	N.M.	0.18	1.03	0.27	0.22	...
Return on Equity %	N.M.	N.M.	N.M.	2.76	15.65	4.42	3.60	...
Net Margin %	22.67	N.M.	N.M.	3.60	20.77	6.86	4.92	N.M.
Asset Turnover	0.04	0.04	0.05	0.05	0.05	0.04	0.05	...
Price Range	54.43-34.18	52.07-34.18	41.00-23.38	48.14-36.04	43.07-33.11	35.89-20.67	...	...
P/E Ratio	...	...	...	26.74-20.02	4.77-3.67	15.08-8.68	...	...
Average Yield %	0.09	0.10	0.13	0.09	0.11	0.07	...	...

Address: 230 Park Avenue, New York, NY 10169 **Telephone:** 212-309-8200	**Web Site:** www.ing.us **Officers:** Rodney Owen Martin - Chairman, Chief Executive Officer Michael S. Smith - Chief Financial Officer, Chief Risk Officer, Division Officer	**Auditors:** Ernst & Young LLP **Transfer Agents:** Computershare Trust Company, N.A, Canton, MA

VULCAN MATERIALS CO (HOLDING COMPANY)

Exchange	Symbol	Price	52Wk Range	Yield	P/E
NYS	VMC	$129.06 (6/29/2018)	141.11-110.92	0.87	28.55

*7 Year Price Score 123.28 *NYSE Composite Index=100 *12 Month Price Score 100.90

Interim Earnings (Per Share)

Qtr.	Mar	Jun	Sep	Dec
2015	(0.30)	0.36	0.91	0.66
2016	0.14	0.91	1.04	1.00
2017	0.33	0.89	0.81	2.43
2018	0.39	...	...	...

Interim Dividends (Per Share)

Amt	Decl	Ex	Rec	Pay
0.25Q	10/13/2017	11/21/2017	11/22/2017	12/08/2017
0.28Q	02/09/2018	02/22/2018	02/23/2018	03/09/2018
0.28Q	05/11/2018	05/23/2018	05/24/2018	06/08/2018
0.28Q	07/13/2018	08/21/2018	08/22/2018	09/07/2018

Indicated Div: $1.12 (Div. Reinv. Plan)

Valuation Analysis — **Institutional Holding**

Forecast EPS	$4.49	No of Institutions
	(06/14/2018)	840
Market Cap	$17.1 Billion	Shares
Book Value	$4.9 Billion	165,302,832
Price/Book	3.47	% Held
Price/Sales	4.31	88.33

Business Summary: Mining (MIC: 8.2.4 SIC: 1429 NAIC: 212319)

Vulcan Materials is a supplier of construction aggregates (primarily crushed stone, sand and gravel) and a producer of asphalt mix and ready-mixed concrete. Co. has four operating (and reportable) segments: the Aggregates segment, which produces and sells aggregates (crushed stone, sand and gravel, sand, and other aggregates) and related products and services (transportation and other); the Asphalt Mix segment, which produces and sells asphalt mix in four states; the Concrete segment, which produces and sells ready-mixed concrete in six states, Washington D.C. and the Bahamas; and the Calcium segment, which consists of a Florida facility that mines, produces and sells calcium products.

Recent Developments: For the quarter ended Mar 31 2018, income from continuing operations increased 22.7% to US$53.4 million from US$43.5 million in the year-earlier quarter. Net income increased 17.9% to US$53.0 million from US$44.9 million in the year-earlier quarter. Revenues were US$854.5 million, up 8.5% from US$787.3 million the year before. Operating income was US$81.2 million versus US$70.4 million in the prior-year quarter, an increase of 15.4%. Direct operating expenses rose 10.5% to US$695.1 million from US$629.1 million in the comparable period the year before. Indirect operating expenses decreased 11.0% to US$78.2 million from US$87.8 million in the equivalent prior-year period.

Prospects: Our evaluation of Vulcan Materials Co. as of Jan. 21, 2018 is the result of our systematic analysis on three basic characteristics: earnings strength, relative valuation, and recent stock price movement. The company has produced a positive trend in earnings per share over the past 5 quarters and while recent estimates for the company have been mixed, VMC has posted results that were in line with analysts expectations. Based on operating earnings yield, the company is overvalued when compared to all of the companies in our coverage universe. Share price changes over the past year indicates that VMC will perform very poorly over the near term.

Financial Data

(US$ in Thousands)	3 Mos	12/31/2017	12/31/2016	12/31/2015	12/31/2014	12/31/2013	12/31/2012	12/31/2011
Earnings Per Share	4.52	4.46	3.09	1.64	1.54	0.19	(0.41)	(0.55)
Cash Flow Per Share	4.85	4.87	4.83	3.78	1.98	2.74	1.83	1.31
Tang Book Value Per Share	5.46	5.92	5.35	4.45	2.45	1.22	N.M.	0.06
Dividends Per Share	1.030	1.000	0.800	0.400	0.220	0.040	0.040	0.760
Dividend Payout %	22.79	22.42	25.89	24.39	14.29	21.05	...	...
Income Statement								
Total Revenue	854,474	3,890,296	3,592,667	3,422,181	2,994,169	2,770,709	2,567,310	2,564,550
EBITDA	167,705	903,236	918,763	776,966	780,856	469,122	392,654	391,518
Depn & Amortn	81,439	250,835	238,237	228,866	239,611	271,180	301,146	328,072
Income Before Taxes	48,492	361,316	547,257	327,857	298,838	(3,703)	(120,418)	(153,738)
Income Taxes	(4,903)	(232,075)	124,851	94,943	91,692	(24,459)	(66,492)	(78,483)
Net Income	52,979	601,185	419,491	221,177	204,923	24,382	(52,593)	(70,778)
Average Shares	134,359	134,878	135,790	135,093	132,991	131,467	129,745	129,381
Balance Sheet								
Current Assets	1,011,199	1,180,101	1,137,182	1,084,591	920,469	951,496	984,972	863,100
Total Assets	9,453,211	9,504,891	8,471,475	8,301,632	8,061,902	8,259,143	8,126,599	8,229,314
Current Liabilities	583,307	442,872	372,244	353,479	451,878	299,135	436,411	406,253
Long-Term Obligations	2,775,687	2,813,482	1,982,751	1,980,334	1,855,447	2,522,243	2,526,401	2,680,677
Total Liabilities	4,540,001	4,535,998	3,898,999	3,847,444	3,885,203	4,321,037	4,365,537	4,437,697
Stockholders' Equity	4,913,210	4,968,893	4,572,476	4,454,188	4,176,699	3,938,106	3,761,062	3,791,617
Shares Outstanding	132,290	132,324	132,339	133,172	131,907	130,200	129,721	129,245
Statistical Record								
Return on Assets %	6.70	6.69	4.99	2.70	2.51	0.30	N.M.	N.M.
Return on Equity %	12.92	12.60	9.27	5.13	5.05	0.63	N.M.	N.M.
EBITDA Margin %	19.63	23.22	25.57	22.70	26.08	16.93	15.29	15.27
Net Margin %	6.20	15.45	11.68	6.46	6.84	0.88	N.M.	N.M.
Asset Turnover	0.43	0.43	0.43	0.42	0.37	0.34	0.31	0.31
Current Ratio	1.73	2.66	3.05	3.07	2.04	3.18	2.26	2.12
Debt to Equity	0.56	0.57	0.43	0.44	0.44	0.64	0.67	0.71
Price Range	141.11-111.30	135.28-112.50	136.04-81.60	105.70-64.98	69.01-55.28	59.49-45.59	53.25-32.57	46.98-26.19
P/E Ratio	31.22-24.62	30.33-25.22	44.03-26.41	64.45-39.62	44.81-35.90	313.11-239.95	...	...
Average Yield %	0.83	0.82	0.72	0.45	0.35	0.08	0.09	2.02

Address: 1200 Urban Center Drive, Birmingham, AL 35242	Web Site: www.vulcanmaterials.com	Auditors: DELOITTE & TOUCHE LLP
Telephone: 205-298-3000	Officers: J. Thomas (Tom) Hill - Chairman, President, Chief Executive Officer, Executive Vice President, Chief Operating Officer Stanley G. Bass - Chief Growth Officer	Investor Contact: 205-298-3220
Fax: 205-298-2963		Transfer Agents: Computershare Shareowner Services LLC, Providence, RI

WABTEC CORP

<table>
<thead>
<tr><th>Exchange</th><th>Symbol</th><th>Price</th><th>52Wk Range</th><th>Yield</th><th>P/E</th></tr>
</thead>
<tbody>
<tr><td>NYS</td><td>WAB</td><td>$98.58 (6/29/2018)</td><td>102.97-69.70</td><td>0.49</td><td>34.35</td></tr>
</tbody>
</table>

*7 Year Price Score 95.46   *NYSE Composite Index=100   *12 Month Price Score 117.19

Interim Earnings (Per Share)

Qtr.	Mar	Jun	Sep	Dec
2015	0.99	1.04	1.02	1.05
2016	1.02	1.00	0.91	0.42
2017	0.77	0.75	0.70	0.50
2018	0.92	...	...	...

Interim Dividends (Per Share)

Amt	Decl	Ex	Rec	Pay
0.12Q	10/31/2017	11/10/2017	11/13/2017	11/27/2017
0.12Q	01/29/2018	02/08/2018	02/09/2018	02/23/2018
0.12Q	04/19/2018	05/10/2018	05/11/2018	05/25/2018
0.12Q	05/15/2018	08/09/2018	08/10/2018	08/24/2018

Indicated Div: $0.48

Valuation Analysis

		Institutional Holding	
Forecast EPS	$3.86	No of Institutions	
	(06/14/2018)	595	
Market Cap	$9.5 Billion	Shares	
Book Value	$3.0 Billion	128,056,016	
Price/Book	3.19	% Held	
Price/Sales	2.36	88.05	

Business Summary: Construction Services (MIC: 7.5.4 SIC: 3743 NAIC: 336510)

Westinghouse Air Brake Technologies is a provider of technology-based products and services for the rail industry. Co. has two segments: the Freight Segment, which manufactures and services components for new and existing locomotive and freight cars; supplies rail control and infrastructure products; overhauls locomotives; and provides heat exchangers and cooling systems for rail and other industrial markets; and the Transit Segment, which manufactures and services components for new and existing passenger transit vehicles; supplies rail control and infrastructure products; builds new commuter locomotives; and refurbishes passenger transit vehicles.

Recent Developments: For the quarter ended Mar 31 2018, net income increased 21.5% to US$87.5 million from US$72.0 million in the year-earlier quarter. Revenues were US$1.06 billion, up 15.3% from US$916.0 million the year before. Operating income was US$131.3 million versus US$114.5 million in the prior-year quarter, an increase of 14.6%. Direct operating expenses rose 15.3% to US$745.3 million from US$646.3 million in the comparable period the year before. Indirect operating expenses increased 15.7% to US$179.6 million from US$155.2 million in the equivalent prior-year period.

Prospects: Our evaluation of Wabtec Corp. as of Jan. 21, 2018 is the result of our systematic analysis on three basic characteristics: earnings strength, relative valuation, and recent stock price movement. The company has enjoyed a very positive trend in earnings per share over the past 5 quarters and while recent estimates for the company have been mixed, WAB has posted better than expected results. Based on operating earnings yield, the company is about fairly valued when compared to all of the companies in our coverage universe. Share price changes over the past year indicates that WAB will perform poorly over the near term.

Financial Data

(US$ in Thousands)	3 Mos	12/31/2017	12/31/2016	12/31/2015	12/31/2014	12/31/2013	12/31/2012	12/31/2011
Earnings Per Share	2.87	2.72	3.34	4.10	3.62	3.01	2.60	1.75
Cash Flow Per Share	2.50	1.98	4.96	4.67	4.93	2.47	2.48	2.60
Tang Book Value Per Share	N.M.	N.M.	N.M.	4.36	5.42	4.31	3.17	2.09
Dividends Per Share	0.460	0.440	0.360	0.280	0.200	0.130	0.080	0.040
Dividend Payout %	16.03	16.18	10.78	6.83	5.52	4.32	3.08	2.28
Income Statement								
Total Revenue	1,056,177	3,881,756	2,931,188	3,307,998	3,044,454	2,566,392	2,391,122	1,967,637
EBITDA	161,090	484,888	502,498	645,356	564,229	469,928	420,509	300,221
Depn & Amortn	27,854	66,700	47,100	43,100	38,800	33,500	28,900	29,900
Income Before Taxes	112,952	349,484	412,837	585,368	507,855	421,087	377,358	255,314
Income Taxes	26,124	89,773	99,433	186,740	156,175	128,852	125,626	85,165
Net Income	88,366	262,261	304,887	398,628	351,680	292,235	251,732	170,149
Average Shares	96,371	96,125	91,141	97,006	96,885	96,832	96,742	96,658
Balance Sheet								
Current Assets	2,465,814	2,265,113	2,867,631	1,612,448	1,637,864	1,333,047	1,092,938	1,055,782
Total Assets	6,875,781	6,579,980	6,581,018	3,300,335	3,303,841	2,821,997	2,351,542	2,158,953
Current Liabilities	1,648,048	1,573,330	1,446,639	664,776	738,802	579,400	553,059	541,385
Long-Term Obligations	1,871,076	1,823,303	1,762,967	695,294	520,403	450,288	317,853	395,805
Total Liabilities	3,906,663	3,771,112	4,375,041	1,600,728	1,496,599	1,236,738	1,074,712	1,113,764
Stockholders' Equity	2,969,118	2,808,868	2,205,977	1,699,607	1,807,242	1,585,259	1,276,830	1,045,189
Shares Outstanding	96,227	96,034	95,425	91,836	96,274	95,909	95,407	95,892
Statistical Record								
Return on Assets %	4.29	3.99	6.15	12.07	11.48	11.30	11.13	8.59
Return on Equity %	10.40	10.46	15.57	22.73	20.73	20.42	21.62	17.50
EBITDA Margin %	15.25	12.49	17.14	19.51	18.53	18.31	17.59	15.26
Net Margin %	8.37	6.76	10.40	12.05	11.55	11.39	10.53	8.65
Asset Turnover	0.62	0.59	0.59	1.00	0.99	0.99	1.06	0.99
Current Ratio	1.50	1.44	1.98	2.43	2.22	2.30	1.98	1.95
Debt to Equity	0.63	0.65	0.80	0.41	0.29	0.28	0.25	0.38
Price Range	92.51-69.70	92.51-69.70	88.12-60.58	102.39-68.89	91.24-70.82	74.27-43.77	44.34-34.40	35.78-25.07
P/E Ratio	32.23-24.29	34.01-25.63	26.38-18.14	24.97-16.80	25.20-19.56	24.67-14.54	17.06-13.23	20.45-14.33
Average Yield %	0.58	0.55	0.48	0.31	0.25	0.25	0.21	0.13

Address: 1001 Air Brake Avenue, Wilmerding, PA 15148
Telephone: 412-825-1000
Fax: 412-825-1019

Web Site: www.wabtec.com
Officers: Albert J. Neupaver - Chairman, Executive Chairman, Chairman (frmr), President, Chief Executive Officer Emilio A. Fernandez - Vice-Chairman

Auditors: Ernst & Young LLP
Transfer Agents: Wells Fargo Shareowner Services, St Paul, MN

WALMART INC

Exchange	Symbol	Price	52Wk Range	Yield	P/E	Div Acheiver
NYS	WMT	$85.65 (6/29/2018)	109.55-73.23	2.43	28.55	42 Years

*7 Year Price Score 96.49   *NYSE Composite Index=100   ***12 Month Price Score 95.21**

Interim Earnings (Per Share)

Qtr.	Apr	Jul	Oct	Jan
2015-16	1.03	1.08	1.03	1.44
2016-17	0.98	1.21	0.98	1.22
2017-18	1.00	0.96	0.58	0.74
2018-19	0.72	...	...	...

Interim Dividends (Per Share)

Amt	Decl	Ex	Rec	Pay
0.52Q	02/20/2018	03/08/2018	03/09/2018	04/02/2018
0.52Q	02/20/2018	05/10/2018	05/11/2018	06/04/2018
0.52Q	02/20/2018	12/06/2018	12/07/2018	01/02/2019
0.52Q	02/20/2018	08/09/2018	08/10/2018	09/04/2018

Indicated Div: $2.08 (Div. Reinv. Plan)

Valuation Analysis		Institutional Holding	
Forecast EPS	$4.86	No of Institutions	
	(06/13/2018)	2542	
Market Cap	$252.8 Billion	Shares	
Book Value	$75.6 Billion	1,187,523,200	
Price/Book	3.35	% Held	
Price/Sales	0.50	27.91	

Business Summary: Retail - General Merchandise/Department Stores (MIC: 2.1.1 SIC: 5331 NAIC: 452990)

Walmart operates retail and other stores in various formats. Co.'s operations comprise of three business segments: Walmart U.S., which is a merchandiser of consumer products, operating under the Walmart or Wal-Mart brands, as well as walmart.com., and operating retail stores in all 50 states, Washington D.C. and Puerto Rico.; Walmart International, which consists of operations in 27 countries outside of the U.S. and includes numerous formats divided into three categories: retail, wholesale and other; and Sam's Club, which operates membership-only warehouse clubs, as well as samsclub.com, in the U.S., and its members include both business owners and individual consumers.

Recent Developments: For the quarter ended Apr 30 2018, net income decreased 27.8% to US$2.28 billion from US$3.15 billion in the year-earlier quarter. Revenues were US$122.69 billion, up 4.4% from US$117.54 billion the year before. Operating income was US$5.15 billion versus US$5.24 billion in the prior-year quarter, a decrease of 1.6%. Direct operating expenses rose 4.6% to US$91.71 billion from US$87.69 billion in the comparable period the year before. Indirect operating expenses increased 4.9% to US$25.83 billion from US$24.62 billion in the equivalent prior-year period.

Prospects: Our evaluation of Wal-Mart Stores Inc. as of Jan. 21, 2018 is the result of our systematic analysis on three basic characteristics: earnings strength, relative valuation, and recent stock price movement. The company has produced a positive trend in earnings per share over the past 5 quarters and while recent estimates for the company have been raised by analysts, WMT has posted better than expected results. Based on operating earnings yield, the company is about fairly valued when compared to all of the companies in our coverage universe. Share price changes over the past year indicates that WMT will perform well over the near term.

Financial Data
(US$ in Thousands)

	3 Mos	01/31/2018	01/31/2017	01/31/2016	01/31/2015	01/31/2014	01/31/2013	01/31/2012
Earnings Per Share	3.00	3.28	4.38	4.57	5.05	4.88	5.02	4.52
Cash Flow Per Share	9.53	9.46	10.14	8.54	8.84	7.11	7.56	7.01
Tang Book Value Per Share	19.21	20.20	19.93	20.19	19.61	17.55	16.85	14.82
Dividends Per Share	2.050	2.040	2.000	1.960	1.920	1.880	1.590	1.460
Dividend Payout %	68.33	62.20	45.66	42.89	38.02	38.52	31.67	32.30
Income Statement								
Total Revenue	122,690,000	500,343,000	485,873,000	482,130,000	485,651,000	476,294,000	469,162,000	446,950,000
EBITDA	5,987,000	27,801,000	32,764,000	33,505,000	36,247,000	35,672,000	36,201,000	34,658,000
Depn & Amortn	2,678,000	10,500,000	10,000,000	9,400,000	9,100,000	8,800,000	8,400,000	8,100,000
Income Before Taxes	2,822,000	15,123,000	20,497,000	21,638,000	24,799,000	24,656,000	25,737,000	24,398,000
Income Taxes	546,000	4,600,000	6,204,000	6,558,000	7,985,000	8,105,000	7,981,000	7,944,000
Net Income	2,134,000	9,862,000	13,643,000	14,694,000	16,363,000	16,022,000	16,999,000	15,699,000
Average Shares	2,967,000	3,010,000	3,112,000	3,217,000	3,243,000	3,283,000	3,389,000	3,474,000
Balance Sheet								
Current Assets	59,242,000	59,664,000	57,689,000	60,239,000	63,278,000	61,185,000	59,940,000	54,975,000
Total Assets	204,927,000	204,522,000	198,825,000	199,581,000	203,706,000	204,751,000	203,105,000	193,406,000
Current Liabilities	80,757,000	78,521,000	66,928,000	64,619,000	65,272,000	69,345,000	71,818,000	62,300,000
Long-Term Obligations	36,305,000	36,825,000	42,018,000	44,030,000	43,692,000	44,559,000	41,417,000	47,079,000
Total Liabilities	129,375,000	126,653,000	121,027,000	119,035,000	122,312,000	128,496,000	126,762,000	122,091,000
Stockholders' Equity	75,552,000	77,869,000	77,798,000	80,546,000	81,394,000	76,255,000	76,343,000	71,315,000
Shares Outstanding	2,951,000	2,952,000	3,048,000	3,162,000	3,228,000	3,233,000	3,314,000	3,418,000
Statistical Record								
Return on Assets %	4.43	4.89	6.83	7.29	8.01	7.86	8.55	8.39
Return on Equity %	12.00	12.67	17.19	18.15	20.76	21.00	22.96	22.45
EBITDA Margin %	4.88	5.56	6.74	6.95	7.46	7.49	7.72	7.75
Net Margin %	1.74	1.97	2.81	3.05	3.37	3.36	3.62	3.51
Asset Turnover	2.50	2.48	2.43	2.39	2.38	2.34	2.36	2.39
Current Ratio	0.73	0.76	0.86	0.93	0.97	0.88	0.83	0.88
Debt to Equity	0.48	0.47	0.54	0.55	0.54	0.58	0.54	0.66
Price Range	109.55-73.23	109.55-66.23	74.30-63.15	87.33-56.42	90.47-72.66	81.21-68.76	77.15-57.36	61.47-48.41
P/E Ratio	36.52-24.41	33.40-20.19	16.96-14.42	19.11-12.35	17.91-14.39	16.64-14.09	15.37-11.43	13.60-10.71
Average Yield %	2.36	2.49	2.86	2.78	2.46	2.48	2.33	2.67

Address: 702 S.W. 8th Street, Bentonville, AR 72716 Telephone: 479-273-4000	Web Site: www.stock.walmart.com Officers: Gregory B. Penner - Chairman C. Douglas (Doug) McMillon - President, Chief Executive Officer, Executive Vice President, Division Officer	Auditors: Ernst & Young LLP Investor Contact: 479-273-8446 Transfer Agents: Computershare Trust Company, N.A., Providence, RI

WASTE MANAGEMENT, INC. (DE)

Exchange	Symbol	Price	52Wk Range	Yield	P/E	Div Acheiver
NYS	WM	$81.34 (6/29/2018)	89.71-73.35	2.29	17.53	14 Years

*7 Year Price Score 124.97 *NYSE Composite Index=100 ***12 Month Price Score 99.82**

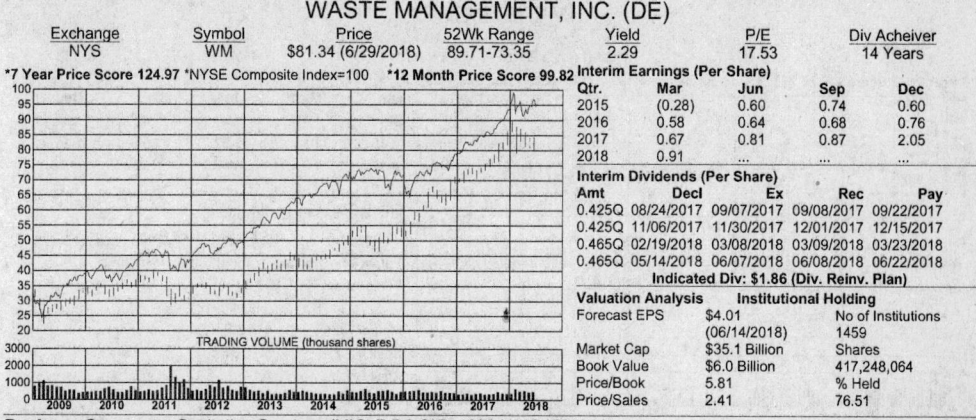

TRADING VOLUME (thousand shares)

Interim Earnings (Per Share)

Qtr.	Mar	Jun	Sep	Dec
2015	(0.28)	0.60	0.74	0.60
2016	0.58	0.64	0.68	0.76
2017	0.67	0.81	0.87	2.05
2018	0.91	...	...	...

Interim Dividends (Per Share)

Amt	Decl	Ex	Rec	Pay
0.425Q	08/24/2017	09/07/2017	09/08/2017	09/22/2017
0.425Q	11/06/2017	11/30/2017	12/01/2017	12/15/2017
0.465Q	02/19/2018	03/08/2018	03/09/2018	03/23/2018
0.465Q	05/14/2018	06/07/2018	06/08/2018	06/22/2018

Indicated Div: $1.86 (Div. Reinv. Plan)

Valuation Analysis **Institutional Holding**

Valuation Analysis		Institutional Holding	
Forecast EPS	$4.01	No of Institutions	
	(06/14/2018)	1459	
Market Cap	$35.1 Billion	Shares	
Book Value	$6.0 Billion	417,248,064	
Price/Book	5.81	% Held	
Price/Sales	2.41	76.51	

Business Summary: Sanitation Services (MIC: 7.5.3 SIC: 4953 NAIC: 562211)

Waste Management is a holding company. Through its subsidiaries, Co. is a provider of waste management environmental services. Co. partners with its residential, commercial, industrial and municipal customers and the communities it serves to manage and reduce waste at each stage from collection to disposal, while recovering resources and creating renewable energy. Co.'s Solid Waste business provides collection, transfer, disposal, and recycling and resource recovery services. Through its subsidiaries, Co. is also a developer, operator and owner of landfill gas-to-energy facilities. At Dec 31 2017, Co. owned or operated 244 solid waste landfills and five hazardous waste landfills.

Recent Developments: For the quarter ended Mar 31 2018, net income increased 33.0% to US$395.0 million from US$297.0 million in the year-earlier quarter. Revenues were US$3.51 billion, up 2.1% from US$3.44 billion the year before. Operating income was US$608.0 million versus US$558.0 million in the prior-year quarter, an increase of 9.0%. Direct operating expenses rose 0.8% to US$2.18 billion from US$2.17 billion in the comparable period the year before. Indirect operating expenses increased 0.4% to US$719.0 million from US$716.0 million in the equivalent prior-year period.

Prospects: Our evaluation of Waste Management Inc. as of Jan. 21, 2018 is the result of our systematic analysis on three basic characteristics: earnings strength, relative valuation, and recent stock price movement. The company has managed to produce a neutral trend in earnings per share over the past 5 quarters and while recent estimates for the company have been mixed, WM has posted better than expected results. Based on comparing earnings yield, the company is about fairly valued when compared to all of the companies in our coverage universe. Share price changes over the past year indicates that WM will perform in line with the market over the near term.

Financial Data

(US$ in Thousands)	3 Mos	12/31/2017	12/31/2016	12/31/2015	12/31/2014	12/31/2013	12/31/2012	12/31/2011
Earnings Per Share	4.64	4.41	2.65	1.65	2.79	0.21	1.76	2.04
Cash Flow Per Share	7.54	7.25	6.66	5.52	5.04	5.25	4.94	5.26
Dividends Per Share	1.740	1.700	1.640	1.540	1.500	1.460	1.420	1.360
Dividend Payout %	37.50	38.55	61.89	93.33	53.76	695.24	80.68	66.67
Income Statement								
Total Revenue	3,511,000	14,485,000	13,609,000	12,961,000	13,996,000	13,983,000	13,649,000	13,378,000
EBITDA	956,000	3,902,000	3,015,773	2,652,000	3,484,000	2,258,000	3,061,000	3,202,000
Depn & Amortn	347,000	1,280,000	773,773	1,169,000	1,214,000	1,253,000	1,228,000	1,178,000
Income Before Taxes	518,000	2,259,000	1,866,000	1,098,000	1,804,000	528,000	1,349,000	1,551,000
Income Taxes	116,000	242,000	642,000	308,000	413,000	364,000	443,000	511,000
Net Income	396,000	1,949,000	1,182,000	753,000	1,298,000	98,000	817,000	961,000
Average Shares	435,800	441,900	446,500	455,900	465,600	469,800	464,400	471,400
Balance Sheet								
Current Assets	2,491,000	2,624,000	2,376,000	2,345,000	3,641,000	2,499,000	2,423,000	2,379,000
Total Assets	22,106,000	21,829,000	20,859,000	20,419,000	21,412,000	22,603,000	23,097,000	22,569,000
Current Liabilities	3,373,000	3,262,000	2,794,000	2,510,000	3,485,000	3,014,000	3,036,000	3,068,000
Long-Term Obligations	8,901,000	8,752,000	8,893,000	8,728,000	8,345,000	9,500,000	9,173,000	9,125,000
Total Liabilities	16,062,000	15,810,000	15,562,000	15,074,000	15,546,000	16,896,000	16,743,000	16,499,000
Stockholders' Equity	6,044,000	6,019,000	5,297,000	5,345,000	5,866,000	5,707,000	6,354,000	6,070,000
Shares Outstanding	431,771	433,318	439,315	447,177	458,537	464,320	464,220	460,532
Statistical Record								
Return on Assets %	9.58	9.13	5.71	3.60	5.90	0.43	3.57	4.36
Return on Equity %	35.41	34.45	22.15	13.43	22.43	1.63	13.12	15.59
EBITDA Margin %	27.23	26.94	22.16	20.46	24.89	16.15	22.43	23.93
Net Margin %	11.28	13.46	8.69	5.81	9.27	0.70	5.99	7.18
Asset Turnover	0.68	0.68	0.66	0.62	0.64	0.61	0.60	0.61
Current Ratio	0.74	0.80	0.85	0.93	1.04	0.83	0.80	0.78
Debt to Equity	1.47	1.45	1.68	1.63	1.42	1.66	1.44	1.50
Price Range	89.71-70.50	86.30-69.18	71.14-51.52	55.18-46.35	51.58-40.41	46.10-33.74	36.08-30.96	39.61-28.17
P/E Ratio	19.33-15.19	19.57-15.69	26.85-19.44	33.44-28.09	18.49-14.48	219.52-160.67	20.50-17.59	19.42-13.81
Average Yield %	2.20	2.21	2.65	2.98	3.33	3.60	4.22	3.89

Address: 1001 Fannin Street, Houston, TX 77002	Web Site: www.wm.com	Auditors: Ernst & Young LLP
Telephone: 713-512-6200	**Officers:** James C. Fish - President, Executive Vice President, Chief Executive Officer, Chief Financial Officer Devina A. Rankin - Senior Vice President, Chief Financial Officer, Acting Chief Financial Officer, Vice President, Treasurer	**Investor Contact:** 713-265-1656
Fax: 713-512-6299		**Transfer Agents:** Computershare, Canton, MA

WATERS CORP.

Exchange	Symbol	Price	52Wk Range	Yield	P/E
NYS	WAT	$193.59 (6/29/2018)	218.70-172.58	N/A	569.38

*7 Year Price Score 126.26 *NYSE Composite Index=100 *12 Month Price Score 99.83

TRADING VOLUME (thousand shares)

Interim Earnings (Per Share)

Qtr.	Mar	Jun	Sep	Dec
2015	1.15	1.27	1.40	1.83
2016	1.15	1.57	1.53	2.15
2017	1.31	1.63	1.69	(4.38)
2018	1.40	...	...	...

Interim Dividends (Per Share)

No Dividends Paid

Valuation Analysis

Institutional Holding		
Forecast EPS	$8.20	No of Institutions
	(06/14/2018)	800
Market Cap	$15.2 Billion	Shares
Book Value	$2.1 Billion	90,771,352
Price/Book	7.17	% Held
Price/Sales	6.47	86.98

Business Summary: Biotechnology (MIC: 4.1.2 SIC: 3826 NAIC: 334516)

Waters is a holding company. Co. is an analytical instrument manufacturer that primarily designs, manufactures, sells and services high performance liquid chromatography, ultra performance liquid chromatography and mass spectrometry technology systems and support products, including chromatography columns, other consumable products and post-warranty service plans. In addition, Co. designs, manufactures, sells and services thermal analysis, rheometry and calorimetry instruments through its TA® product line. Co. is also a developer and supplier of software-based products that interface with its instruments, as well as other suppliers' instruments.

Recent Developments: For the quarter ended Mar 31 2018, net income increased 6.1% to US$112.0 million from US$105.6 million in the year-earlier quarter. Revenues were US$530.7 million, up 6.6% from US$498.0 million the year before. Operating income was US$144.4 million versus US$118.7 million in the prior-year quarter, an increase of 21.6%. Direct operating expenses rose 4.9% to US$221.4 million from US$211.1 million in the comparable period the year before. Indirect operating expenses decreased 2.0% to US$164.9 million from US$168.2 million in the equivalent prior-year period.

Prospects: Our evaluation of Waters Corp. as of Jan. 21, 2018 is the result of our systematic analysis on three basic characteristics: earnings strength, relative valuation, and recent stock price movement. The company has managed to produce a neutral trend in earnings per share over the past 5 quarters and while recent estimates for the company have been raised by analysts, WAT has posted better than expected results. Based on operating earnings yield, the company is about fairly valued when compared to all of the companies in our coverage universe. Share price changes over the past year indicates that WAT will perform well over the near term.

Financial Data
(US$ in Thousands)

	3 Mos	12/31/2017	12/31/2016	12/31/2015	12/31/2014	12/31/2013	12/31/2012	12/31/2011
Earnings Per Share	0.34	0.25	6.41	5.65	5.07	5.20	5.19	4.69
Cash Flow Per Share	8.86	8.74	7.77	6.80	6.07	5.68	5.10	5.48
Tang Book Value Per Share	19.42	20.74	21.78	18.21	15.72	13.84	10.77	8.29
Income Statement								
Total Revenue	530,670	2,309,078	2,167,423	2,042,332	1,989,344	1,904,218	1,843,641	1,851,184
EBITDA	173,361	767,860	720,788	657,438	612,139	595,463	580,321	594,987
Depn & Amortn	28,640	106,002	96,449	89,987	94,231	79,695	68,831	66,387
Income Before Taxes	140,549	641,097	600,114	541,919	490,740	490,105	487,625	509,252
Income Taxes	28,598	620,786	78,611	72,866	59,120	40,102	26,182	76,284
Net Income	111,951	20,311	521,503	469,053	431,620	450,003	461,443	432,968
Average Shares	79,715	80,604	81,417	83,087	85,151	86,546	88,979	92,325
Balance Sheet								
Current Assets	3,438,578	4,270,134	3,635,445	3,213,533	2,853,736	2,556,255	2,257,726	1,942,104
Total Assets	4,489,457	5,324,354	4,662,059	4,268,677	3,877,934	3,582,629	3,168,150	2,723,234
Current Liabilities	534,348	606,157	520,321	564,076	581,595	487,532	504,242	601,863
Long-Term Obligations	1,247,630	1,897,501	1,701,966	1,493,027	1,240,000	1,190,000	1,045,000	700,000
Total Liabilities	2,374,563	3,090,566	2,360,110	2,209,826	1,983,268	1,819,456	1,700,793	1,496,656
Stockholders' Equity	2,114,894	2,233,788	2,301,949	2,058,851	1,894,666	1,763,173	1,467,357	1,226,578
Shares Outstanding	78,319	79,337	80,023	81,472	83,147	84,819	86,390	88,996
Statistical Record								
Return on Assets %	0.57	0.41	11.65	11.52	11.57	13.33	15.62	17.14
Return on Equity %	1.18	0.90	23.85	23.73	23.60	27.86	34.16	37.73
EBITDA Margin %	32.67	33.25	33.26	32.19	30.77	31.27	31.48	32.14
Net Margin %	21.10	0.88	24.06	22.97	21.70	23.63	25.03	23.39
Asset Turnover	0.50	0.46	0.48	0.50	0.53	0.56	0.62	0.73
Current Ratio	6.44	7.04	6.99	5.70	4.91	5.24	4.48	3.23
Debt to Equity	0.59	0.85	0.74	0.73	0.65	0.67	0.71	0.57
Price Range		218.70-154.83	200.27-135.49	161.82-113.62	136.50-112.53	116.98-95.08	107.73-86.22	94.03-73.71	99.56-71.61
P/E Ratio		643.24-455.38	801.08-541.96	25.24-17.73	24.16-19.92	23.07-18.75	20.72-16.58	18.12-14.20	21.23-15.27

Address: 34 Maple Street, Milford, MA 01757	**Web Site:** www.waters.com	**Auditors:** PricewaterhouseCoopers LLP
Telephone: 508-478-2000	**Officers:** Christopher J. O'Connell - President, Chief Executive Officer Sherry L. Buck - Senior Vice President, Chief Financial Officer	**Investor Contact:** 508-482-2349
Fax: 508-872-1990		**Transfer Agents:** Computershare, Providence, RI

WATSCO INC.

Exchange	Symbol	Price	52Wk Range	Yield	P/E
NYS	WSO	$178.28 (6/29/2018)	191.35-142.30	3.25	29.86

*7 Year Price Score 120.01 *NYSE Composite Index=100 *12 Month Price Score 106.17

TRADING VOLUME (thousand shares)

Interim Earnings (Per Share)

Qtr.	Mar	Jun	Sep	Dec
2015	0.65	1.85	1.64	0.74
2016	0.71	1.82	1.78	0.83
2017	0.71	2.07	1.82	1.19
2018	0.89	...	...	...

Interim Dividends (Per Share)

Amt	Decl	Ex	Rec	Pay
1.25Q	10/02/2017	10/13/2017	10/16/2017	10/31/2017
1.25Q	01/02/2018	01/12/2018	01/16/2018	01/31/2018
1.45Q	04/02/2018	04/13/2018	04/16/2018	04/30/2018
1.45Q	07/02/2018	07/16/2018	07/17/2018	07/31/2018

Indicated Div: $5.80

Valuation Analysis

		Institutional Holding	
Forecast EPS	$6.75	No of Institutions	
	(06/13/2018)	464	
Market Cap	$6.7 Billion	Shares	
Book Value	$1.3 Billion	35,923,416	
Price/Book	5.15	% Held	
Price/Sales	1.51	71.73	

Business Summary: Industrial Machinery & Equipment (MIC: 7.2.1 SIC: 5075 NAIC: 423730)

Watsco is a distributor of air conditioning, heating and refrigeration equipment and related parts and supplies. The products Co. distributes consist of: equipment, including residential ducted and ductless air conditioners, gas, electric and oil furnaces, commercial air conditioning and heating equipment and systems, and other equipment; parts, including replacement compressors, evaporator coils, motors and other component parts; and supplies, including thermostats, insulation material, refrigerants, ductwork, grills, registers, sheet metal, tools, copper tubing, concrete pads, tape, adhesives and other ancillary supplies.

Recent Developments: For the quarter ended Mar 31 2018, net income increased 25.5% to US$42.4 million from US$33.8 million in the year-earlier quarter. Revenues were US$926.6 million, up 6.2% from US$872.1 million the year before. Operating income was US$53.9 million versus US$48.7 million in the prior-year quarter, an increase of 10.8%. Direct operating expenses rose 6.5% to US$695.7 million from US$653.5 million in the comparable period the year before. Indirect operating expenses increased 4.1% to US$176.9 million from US$169.9 million in the equivalent prior-year period.

Prospects: Our evaluation of Watsco Inc. as of Jan. 21, 2018 is the result of our systematic analysis on three basic characteristics: earnings strength, relative valuation, and recent stock price movement. The company has produced a positive trend in earnings per share over the past 5 quarters and while recent estimates for the company have been mixed, WSO has posted results that fell short of analysts expectations. Based on operating earnings yield, the company is about fairly valued when compared to all of the companies in our coverage universe. Share price changes over the past year indicates that WSO will perform in line with the market over the near term.

Financial Data
(US$ in Thousands)

	3 Mos	12/31/2017	12/31/2016	12/31/2015	12/31/2014	12/31/2013	12/31/2012	12/31/2011
Earnings Per Share	5.97	5.81	5.15	4.90	4.32	3.68	2.70	2.74
Cash Flow Per Share	6.73	9.34	8.50	6.83	4.49	4.67	5.46	2.00
Tang Book Value Per Share	20.20	20.26	13.16	11.85	8.86	7.02	3.81	12.36
Dividends Per Share	4.800	4.600	3.600	2.800	2.000	1.150	7.480	2.230
Dividend Payout %	80.40	79.17	69.90	57.14	46.30	31.25	277.04	81.39
Income Statement								
Total Revenue	926,577	4,341,955	4,220,702	4,113,239	3,944,540	3,743,330	3,431,712	2,977,759
EBITDA	57,837	370,644	360,485	350,550	317,905	282,886	235,894	208,414
Depn & Amortn	5,538	16,770	14,853	13,802	12,158	11,677	10,986	9,364
Income Before Taxes	53,372	347,511	341,919	331,201	300,541	265,379	220,243	194,592
Income Taxes	10,995	90,221	105,936	104,677	91,839	77,660	62,642	56,850
Net Income	34,219	208,221	182,810	172,929	151,387	127,723	103,334	90,450
Average Shares	34,320	32,862	32,616	32,480	32,358	32,258	31,744	30,753
Balance Sheet								
Current Assets	1,371,724	1,337,397	1,240,156	1,181,265	1,157,335	1,021,102	1,015,451	828,177
Total Assets	2,076,278	2,046,877	1,874,649	1,788,442	1,791,067	1,669,531	1,682,055	1,268,148
Current Liabilities	377,731	416,477	314,888	270,301	287,022	243,506	282,358	223,039
Long-Term Obligations	91,233	22,085	235,642	245,814	303,885	230,557	316,196	...
Total Liabilities	783,564	748,924	868,821	831,132	907,107	829,135	933,841	465,358
Stockholders' Equity	1,292,714	1,297,953	1,005,828	957,310	883,960	840,396	748,214	802,790
Shares Outstanding	37,359	37,228	35,530	35,311	35,006	34,727	34,521	33,005
Statistical Record								
Return on Assets %	10.78	10.62	9.95	9.66	8.75	7.62	6.99	7.22
Return on Equity %	19.04	18.08	18.57	18.78	17.56	16.08	13.29	11.54
EBITDA Margin %	6.24	8.54	8.54	8.52	8.06	7.56	6.87	7.00
Net Margin %	3.69	4.80	4.33	4.20	3.84	3.41	3.01	3.04
Asset Turnover	2.19	2.21	2.30	2.30	2.28	2.23	2.32	2.38
Current Ratio	3.63	3.21	3.94	4.37	4.03	4.19	3.60	3.71
Debt to Equity	0.07	0.02	0.23	0.26	0.34	0.27	0.42	...
Price Range	182.14-135.45	171.38-135.45	159.03-108.09	131.89-104.92	108.20-85.53	97.47-74.13	80.12-66.22	72.76-51.10
P/E Ratio	30.51-22.69	29.50-23.31	30.88-20.99	26.92-21.41	25.05-19.80	26.49-20.14	29.67-24.53	26.55-18.65
Average Yield %	3.04	3.02	2.65	2.30	2.05	1.32	10.29	3.54

Address: 2665 South Bayshore Drive, Suite 901, Miami, FL 33133 Telephone: 305-714-4100	Web Site: www.watsco.com Officers: Albert H. Nahmad - Chairman, President, Chief Executive Officer Aaron J. Nahmad - President, Vice President	Auditors: KPMG LLP Investor Contact: 305-714-4100 Transfer Agents: American Stock Transfer & Trust Company, New York, NY

WAYFAIR INC

Exchange	Symbol	Price	52Wk Range	Yield	P/E
NYS	W	$118.76 (6/29/2018)	118.76-57.85	N/A	N/A

*7 Year Price Score N/A   *NYSE Composite Index=100   *12 Month Price Score 117.86

TRADING VOLUME (thousand shares)

Interim Earnings (Per Share)

Qtr.	Mar	Jun	Sep	Dec
2015	(0.33)	(0.23)	(0.18)	(0.18)
2016	(0.49)	(0.57)	(0.72)	(0.52)
2017	(0.66)	(0.45)	(0.88)	(0.83)
2018	(1.22)	...	...	...

Interim Dividends (Per Share)

No Dividends Paid

Valuation Analysis   Institutional Holding

Forecast EPS	$-2.98	No of Institutions
	(06/14/2018)	272
Market Cap	$10.6 Billion	Shares
Book Value	N/A	69,848,720
Price/Book	N/A	% Held
Price/Sales	2.04	N/A

Business Summary: Retail - Furniture & Home Furnishings (MIC: 2.1.6 SIC: 5961 NAIC: 454111)

Wayfair is a holding company. Through its e-commerce business, Co. provides browsing, merchandising, and product discovery for products from approximately 8,000 products from over 10,000 suppliers. Co. provides five sites, including websites, mobile-optimized websites and mobile applications (collectively sites): Wayfair, Joss & Main, AllModern, DwellStudio, and Birch Lane. Wayfair is the only one of Co.'s sites that also operates internationally, operating as Wayfair.ca in Canada, Wayfair.co.uk in the U.K. and Wayfair.de in Germany. On its sites, Co. also feature certain products under its house brands, such as Three Postsâ,,¢ and Mercury Rowâ,,¢.

Recent Developments: For the quarter ended Mar 31 2018, net loss amounted to US$107.8 million versus a net loss of US$56.5 million in the year-earlier quarter. Revenues were US$1.40 billion, up 46.2% from US$960.8 million the year before. Operating loss was US$103.1 million versus a loss of US$56.2 million in the prior-year quarter. Direct operating expenses rose 49.2% to US$1.08 billion from US$723.9 million in the comparable period the year before. Indirect operating expenses increased 45.7% to US$426.9 million from US$293.1 million in the equivalent prior-year period.

Prospects: Our evaluation of Wayfair Inc as of Jan. 21, 2018 is the result of our systematic analysis on three basic characteristics: earnings strength, relative valuation, and recent stock price movement. The company has managed to produce a neutral trend in earnings per share over the past 5 quarters. Because the company lacks sufficient analyst estimate data, we place greater weight on the historical EPS trend as the measure of earnings strength. Based on operating earnings yield, the company is overvalued when compared to all of the companies in our coverage universe. Share price changes over the past year indicates that W will perform very well over the near term.

Financial Data

(US$ in Thousands)	3 Mos	12/31/2017	12/31/2016	12/31/2015	12/31/2014	12/31/2013	12/31/2012
Earnings Per Share	(3.38)	(2.81)	(2.29)	(0.92)	(2.97)	(0.99)	(0.80)
Cash Flow Per Share	0.75	0.39	0.74	1.61	0.08	0.83	0.10
Tang Book Value Per Share	...	...	0.88	2.83	3.60	0.92	1.36
Income Statement							
Total Revenue	1,404,269	4,720,895	3,380,360	2,249,885	1,318,951	915,843	601,028
EBITDA	(72,147)	(148,795)	(139,861)	(46,141)	(126,493)	(2,686)	(12,427)
Depn & Amortn	29,981	85,900	54,600	32,491	21,780	13,039	8,812
Income Before Taxes	(107,535)	(244,128)	(193,767)	(77,348)	(147,923)	(15,480)	(21,005)
Income Taxes	240	486	608	95	175	46	50
Net Income	(107,775)	(244,614)	(194,375)	(77,443)	(148,098)	(15,526)	(21,055)
Average Shares	88,467	86,983	84,977	83,726	50,641	41,331	41,271
Balance Sheet							
Current Assets	796,880	816,820	477,091	492,323	486,868	163,127	140,124
Total Assets	1,226,446	1,213,403	761,683	694,581	555,523	196,300	163,577
Current Liabilities	799,652	739,755	557,220	397,026	232,592	145,009	98,093
Long-Term Obligations	419,766	415,485	28,900	...	...	...	...
Total Liabilities	1,353,650	1,261,732	682,299	452,036	249,984	145,953	98,570
Stockholders' Equity	(127,204)	(48,329)	79,384	242,545	305,539	50,347	65,007
Shares Outstanding	88,853	88,208	85,830	84,310	83,182	44,904	44,818
Statistical Record							
Asset Turnover	5.25	4.78	4.63	3.60	3.51	5.09	...
Current Ratio	1.00	1.10	0.86	1.24	2.09	1.12	1.43
Debt to Equity	...	...	0.36	...	...	...	...
Price Range	97.52-40.21	83.77-35.18	48.25-31.89	53.58-19.12	37.72-18.40	...	...

Address: 4 Copley Place, 7th Floor, Boston, MA 02116 **Telephone:** 617-532-6100	**Web Site:** www.wayfair.com **Officers:** Niraj Shah - Co-Chairman, Chief Executive Officer Steven Conine - Co-Chairman, Chief Technology Officer	**Auditors:** Ernst & Young LLP **Transfer Agents:** Computershare Trust Company, N.A.

WEBSTER FINANCIAL CORP (WATERBURY, CONN)

Exchange	Symbol	Price	52Wk Range	Yield	P/E
NYS	WBS	$63.70 (6/29/2018)	67.70-44.50	2.07	22.04

*7 Year Price Score 129.20 *NYSE Composite Index=100 *12 Month Price Score 113.85

Interim Earnings (Per Share)

Qtr.	Mar	Jun	Sep	Dec
2015	0.52	0.55	0.54	0.55
2016	0.51	0.53	0.54	0.60
2017	0.62	0.64	0.67	0.73
2018	0.85	...	...	...

Interim Dividends (Per Share)

Amt	Decl	Ex	Rec	Pay
0.26Q	07/24/2017	08/03/2017	08/07/2017	08/21/2017
0.26Q	10/24/2017	11/06/2017	11/07/2017	11/21/2017
0.26Q	01/30/2018	02/12/2018	02/13/2018	02/27/2018
0.33Q	04/23/2018	05/04/2018	05/07/2018	05/21/2018

Indicated Div: $1.32 (Div. Reinv. Plan)

Valuation Analysis / **Institutional Holding**

Forecast EPS	$3.56	No of Institutions
(06/14/2018)		396
Market Cap	$5.9 Billion	Shares
Book Value	$2.7 Billion	104,111,760
Price/Book	2.15	% Held
Price/Sales	4.86	90.55

TRADING VOLUME (thousand shares)

Business Summary: Banking (MIC: 5.1.1 SIC: 6021 NAIC: 522110)

Webster Financial is a bank holding company and financial holding company. Co., through Webster Bank, National Association, provides financial services to individuals, families, and businesses. Co. provides business and consumer banking, mortgage lending, financial planning, trust, and investment services through 175 banking offices, 350 ATMs, mobile banking, and its internet website. Investment services include securities-related services, and brokerage and investment advice. Co. also provides equipment financing, commercial real estate lending, and asset-based lending across the Northeast. At Dec 31 2017, Co. had total assets of $26.49 billion and total deposits of $20.99 billion.

Recent Developments: For the quarter ended Mar 31 2018, net income increased 34.9% to US$80.2 million from US$59.5 million in the year-earlier quarter. Net interest income increased 11.2% to US$214.2 million from US$192.7 million in the year-earlier quarter. Provision for loan losses was US$11.0 million versus US$10.5 million in the prior-year quarter, an increase of 4.8%. Non-interest income rose 9.0% to US$68.7 million from US$63.0 million, while non-interest expense advanced 4.8% to US$171.6 million.

Prospects: Our evaluation of Webster Financial Corp. (CT) as of Jan. 14, 2018 is the result of our systematic analysis on three basic characteristics: earnings strength, relative valuation, and recent stock price movement. The company has managed to produce a neutral trend in earnings per share over the past 5 quarters. However, while recent estimates for the company have been mixed, WBS has posted better than expected results. Based on operating earnings yield, the company is about fairly valued when compared to all of the companies in our coverage universe. Share price changes over the past year indicates that WBS will perform poorly over the near term.

Financial Data

(US$ in Thousands)	3 Mos	12/31/2017	12/31/2016	12/31/2015	12/31/2014	12/31/2013	12/31/2012	12/31/2011
Earnings Per Share	2.89	2.67	2.16	2.15	2.08	1.86	1.86	1.61
Cash Flow Per Share	4.71	4.84	4.35	3.38	3.03	5.37	2.94	3.06
Tang Book Value Per Share	21.81	21.61	19.97	18.73	18.13	16.92	16.50	14.58
Dividends Per Share	1.040	1.030	0.980	0.890	0.750	0.550	0.350	0.160
Dividend Payout %	35.99	38.58	45.37	41.40	36.06	29.57	18.82	9.94
Income Statement								
Interest Income	245,921	913,605	821,913	760,040	718,941	687,640	693,502	699,723
Interest Expense	31,753	117,318	103,400	95,415	90,500	90,912	114,594	135,955
Net Interest Income	214,168	796,287	718,513	664,625	628,441	596,728	578,908	563,768
Provision for Losses	11,000	40,900	56,350	49,300	37,250	33,500	21,500	22,500
Non-Interest Income	68,747	259,478	264,478	239,545	202,108	191,050	192,758	177,042
Non-Interest Expense	171,615	661,075	623,191	554,554	502,138	498,059	501,804	510,976
Income Before Taxes	100,300	353,790	303,450	300,316	291,161	256,219	248,362	207,334
Income Taxes	20,075	98,351	96,323	93,976	91,409	76,670	74,665	57,951
Net Income	80,225	255,439	207,127	206,340	199,752	179,549	173,697	151,379
Average Shares	92,254	92,356	91,856	91,533	90,620	90,261	91,649	91,688
Balance Sheet								
Net Loans & Leases	17,619,953	17,344,752	16,899,845	15,533,836	13,808,713	12,568,005	11,959,200	11,049,308
Total Assets	26,752,147	26,487,645	26,072,529	24,677,820	22,533,010	20,852,999	20,146,765	18,714,340
Total Deposits	21,385,042	20,993,729	19,303,857	17,952,703	15,651,605	14,854,420	14,530,835	13,656,025
Total Liabilities	24,036,005	23,785,687	23,545,517	22,262,249	20,210,329	18,643,811	18,053,235	16,868,566
Stockholders' Equity	2,716,142	2,701,958	2,527,012	2,415,571	2,322,681	2,209,188	2,093,530	1,845,774
Shares Outstanding	91,880	92,021	91,752	91,561	90,381	89,959	84,963	87,215
Statistical Record								
Return on Assets %	1.05	0.97	0.81	0.87	0.92	0.88	0.89	0.82
Return on Equity %	10.47	9.77	8.36	8.71	8.82	8.35	8.79	8.37
Net Interest Margin %	87.09	87.16	87.42	87.45	87.41	86.78	83.48	80.57
Efficiency Ratio %	54.54	56.35	57.36	55.48	54.52	56.68	56.62	58.28
Loans to Deposits	0.82	0.83	0.88	0.86	0.88	0.85	0.82	0.81
Price Range	59.58-44.50	58.39-44.50	55.09-30.35	40.96-29.11	33.05-27.65	31.18-20.55	24.65-19.10	23.65-14.60
P/E Ratio	20.62-15.40	21.87-16.67	25.50-14.05	19.05-13.54	15.89-13.29	16.76-11.05	13.25-10.27	14.69-9.07
Average Yield %	1.97	1.98	2.55	2.43	2.46	2.17	1.62	0.80

Address: 145 Bank Street, Waterbury, CT 06702	**Web Site:** www.websterbank.com	**Auditors:** KPMG LLP
Telephone: 203-578-2202	**Officers:** James C. Smith - Chairman, President, Chief Executive Officer Joseph J. Savage - Executive Vice-Chairman, President, Executive Vice President	**Investor Contact:** 203-578-2202 **Transfer Agents:** Computershare, Pittsburgh, PA

WEC ENERGY GROUP INC

*7 Year Price Score 104.48 *NYSE Composite Index=100 *12 Month Price Score 95.99

Interim Earnings (Per Share)

Qtr.	Mar	Jun	Sep	Dec
2015	0.86	0.35	0.58	0.56
2016	1.09	0.57	0.68	0.61
2017	1.12	0.63	0.68	1.36
2018	1.23	...	...	...

Interim Dividends (Per Share)

Amt	Decl	Ex	Rec	Pay
0.52Q	07/20/2017	08/10/2017	08/14/2017	09/01/2017
0.52Q	10/19/2017	11/13/2017	11/14/2017	12/01/2017
0.552Q	12/07/2017	02/13/2018	02/14/2018	03/01/2018
0.552Q	04/19/2018	05/11/2018	05/14/2018	06/01/2018

Indicated Div: $2.21 (Div. Reinv. Plan)

Valuation Analysis **Institutional Holding**

Forecast EPS	$3.30	No of Institutions
	(06/12/2018)	1035
Market Cap	$20.4 Billion	Shares
Book Value	$9.7 Billion	275,080,992
Price/Book	2.10	% Held
Price/Sales	2.67	71.22

Business Summary: Electric Utilities (MIC: 3.1.1 SIC: 4931 NAIC: 221112)

WEC Energy Group is a holding company. Co. has six segments: Wisconsin, which is engaged mainly in the generation of electricity and the distribution of electricity and natural gas in Wisconsin; Illinois, which is engaged mainly in the distribution of natural gas in Illinois; Other states, which is engaged mainly in the distribution of natural gas in Minnesota and Michigan; Electric transmission, which includes its approximate 60% ownership interest in American Transmission Company LLC, an electric transmission company; We Power, which is engaged in the ownership of electric power generating facilities for lease to its subsidiary, Wisconsin Electric Power Company; and corporate and other.

Recent Developments: For the quarter ended Mar 31 2018, net income increased 9.4% to US$390.4 million from US$356.9 million in the year-earlier quarter. Revenues were US$2.29 billion, down 0.8% from US$2.30 billion the year before. Operating income was US$545.1 million versus US$614.7 million in the prior-year quarter, a decrease of 11.3%. Direct operating expenses rose 2.7% to US$1.48 billion from US$1.45 billion in the comparable period the year before. Indirect operating expenses increased 5.4% to US$257.4 million from US$244.2 million in the equivalent prior-year period.

Prospects: Our evaluation of WEC Energy Group Inc. as of Jan. 21, 2018 is the result of our systematic analysis on three basic characteristics: earnings strength, relative valuation, and recent stock price movement. The company has managed to produce a neutral trend in earnings per share over the past 5 quarters and while recent estimates for the company have been mixed, WEC has posted better than expected results. Based on operating earnings yield, the company is undervalued when compared to all of the companies in our coverage universe. Share price changes over the past year indicates that WEC will perform well over the near term.

Financial Data

(US$ in Thousands)	3 Mos	12/31/2017	12/31/2016	12/31/2015	12/31/2014	12/31/2013	12/31/2012	12/31/2011
Earnings Per Share	3.90	3.79	2.96	2.34	2.59	2.51	2.35	2.24
Cash Flow Per Share	7.16	6.59	6.65	4.77	5.31	5.41	5.09	4.27
Tang Book Value Per Share	21.06	20.40	18.74	17.93	17.77	16.78	16.12	15.28
Dividends Per Share	2.112	2.080	1.980	1.743	1.560	1.445	1.200	1.040
Dividend Payout %	54.17	54.88	66.89	74.48	60.23	57.57	51.06	46.43
Income Statement								
Total Revenue	2,286,500	7,648,500	7,472,300	5,926,100	4,997,100	4,519,000	4,246,400	4,486,400
EBITDA	761,200	2,648,400	2,525,500	1,892,900	1,544,900	1,499,100	1,406,800	1,286,400
Depn & Amortn	208,600	798,600	762,600	583,500	419,400	400,200	371,700	336,400
Income Before Taxes	445,900	1,434,100	1,360,200	978,000	884,000	846,800	786,900	714,200
Income Taxes	88,300	383,500	566,500	433,800	361,700	337,900	306,300	263,900
Net Income	390,400	1,204,900	940,200	640,300	588,300	577,400	546,300	526,200
Average Shares	316,900	317,200	316,900	272,700	227,500	229,700	232,800	235,400
Balance Sheet								
Current Assets	1,980,800	2,213,500	2,168,700	2,206,800	1,535,400	1,551,100	1,313,900	1,426,200
Total Assets	31,785,600	31,590,500	30,123,200	29,355,200	15,163,400	14,769,400	14,285,000	13,862,100
Current Liabilities	3,605,900	3,869,300	2,431,600	2,709,000	1,668,700	1,496,400	1,443,300	1,364,500
Long-Term Obligations	8,617,500	8,746,600	9,158,200	9,124,100	4,186,400	4,363,200	4,453,800	4,614,300
Total Liabilities	22,087,400	22,098,700	21,163,000	20,670,000	10,713,300	10,506,000	10,119,500	9,868,400
Stockholders' Equity	9,698,200	9,491,800	8,960,200	8,685,200	4,450,100	4,263,400	4,165,500	3,993,700
Shares Outstanding	315,538	315,574	315,614	315,683	225,517	225,962	229,039	230,486
Statistical Record								
Return on Assets %	4.01	3.90	3.15	2.88	3.93	3.97	3.87	3.91
Return on Equity %	13.14	13.06	10.63	9.75	13.50	13.70	13.35	13.45
EBITDA Margin %	33.29	34.63	33.80	31.94	30.92	33.17	33.13	28.67
Net Margin %	17.07	15.75	12.58	10.80	11.77	12.78	12.87	11.73
Asset Turnover	0.25	0.25	0.25	0.27	0.33	0.31	0.30	0.33
Current Ratio	0.55	0.57	0.89	0.81	0.92	1.04	0.91	1.05
Debt to Equity	0.89	0.92	1.02	1.05	0.94	1.02	1.07	1.16
Price Range	69.53-59.47	69.53-57.03	65.82-51.31	57.47-44.97	55.23-40.31	44.94-36.85	41.28-33.92	61.02-27.94
P/E Ratio	17.83-15.25	18.35-15.05	22.24-17.33	24.56-19.22	21.32-15.56	17.90-14.68	17.57-14.43	27.24-12.47
Average Yield %	3.32	3.31	3.36	3.49	3.41	3.49	3.23	2.90

WEINGARTEN REALTY INVESTORS

Exchange	Symbol	Price	52Wk Range	Yield	P/E
NYS	WRI	$30.81 (6/29/2018)	33.60-25.79	5.13	8.85

*7 Year Price Score 77.76   *NYSE Composite Index=100   *12 Month Price Score 95.13

Interim Earnings (Per Share)

Qtr.	Mar	Jun	Sep	Dec
2015	0.36	0.20	0.35	0.37
2016	0.85	0.28	0.40	0.34
2017	0.24	0.49	0.56	1.30
2018	1.13	...	...	...

Interim Dividends (Per Share)

Amt	Decl	Ex	Rec	Pay
0.385Q	10/24/2017	12/07/2017	12/08/2017	12/15/2017
0.75Sp	12/11/2017	12/22/2017	12/26/2017	12/29/2017
0.395Q	02/21/2018	03/07/2018	03/08/2018	03/15/2018
0.395Q	04/24/2018	06/07/2018	06/08/2018	06/15/2018

Indicated Div: $1.58 (Div. Reinv. Plan)

Valuation Analysis / Institutional Holding

Forecast EPS	$0.96	No of Institutions
(06/13/2018)		447
Market Cap	$4.0 Billion	Shares
Book Value	$1.7 Billion	155,047,984
Price/Book	2.29	% Held
Price/Sales	7.04	89.02

Business Summary: REITs (MIC: 5.3.1 SIC: 6798 NAIC: 525930)

Weingarten Realty Investors is a real estate investment trust, engaged in the ownership of shopping centers and other commercial real estate. Co.'s primary business is leasing space to tenants in the shopping centers Co. owns or leases. Co. also provides property management services. At Dec 31 2017, Co. owned or operated under long-term leases, either directly or through its interest in real estate joint ventures or partnerships, a total of 204 properties, which are located in 17 states. The portfolio of properties contains approximately 41.3 million square feet of gross leasable area. Co. also owned interests in 25 parcels of land held for development.

Recent Developments: For the quarter ended Mar 31 2018, income from continuing operations increased 93.5% to US$39.9 million from US$20.6 million in the year-earlier quarter. Net income increased 309.3% to US$149.0 million from US$36.4 million in the year-earlier quarter. Revenues were US$132.5 million, down 7.8% from US$143.7 million the year before. Revenues from property income fell 8.6% to US$128.7 million from US$140.8 million in the corresponding quarter a year earlier.

Prospects: Our evaluation of Weingarten Realty Investors as of Jan. 21, 2018 is the result of our systematic analysis on three basic characteristics: earnings strength, relative valuation, and recent stock price movement. The company has produced a positive trend in earnings per share over the past 5 quarters. Because the company lacks sufficient analyst estimate data, we place greater weight on the historical EPS trend as the measure of earnings strength. Based on operating earnings yield, the company is about fairly valued when compared to all of the companies in our coverage universe. Share price changes over the past year indicates that WRI will perform in line with the market over the near term.

Financial Data
(US$ in Thousands)

	3 Mos	12/31/2017	12/31/2016	12/31/2015	12/31/2014	12/31/2013	12/31/2012	12/31/2011
Earnings Per Share	3.48	2.60	1.87	1.29	2.25	1.50	0.90	(0.17)
Cash Flow Per Share	2.17	2.11	1.95	1.99	1.98	1.93	1.88	1.78
Tang Book Value Per Share	13.46	12.71	12.34	11.21	12.13	11.30	12.98	13.70
Dividends Per Share	2.300	2.290	1.460	1.380	1.550	1.220	1.160	1.100
Dividend Payout %	66.09	88.08	78.07	106.98	68.89	81.33	128.89	...
Income Statement								
Total Revenue	132,452	573,163	549,555	512,844	514,406	497,725	503,538	541,561
EBITDA	48,634	347,315	407,862	334,163	338,013	347,217	330,839	300,921
Depn & Amortn	781	169,891	165,097	148,590	154,257	150,147	147,251	162,505
Income Before Taxes	34,714	105,013	162,331	102,353	92,787	107,311	73,824	1,721
Income Taxes	783	(17)	6,856	52	(1,261)	7,051	79	395
Net Income	146,824	335,274	238,933	174,352	288,008	220,262	146,640	15,621
Average Shares	130,139	130,071	128,569	124,329	124,370	122,460	121,705	120,331
Balance Sheet								
Current Assets	175,329	117,576	110,723	106,950	100,970	173,927	99,144	100,172
Total Assets	4,109,166	4,196,639	4,426,928	3,901,945	3,814,094	4,223,929	4,184,784	4,588,226
Current Liabilities	88,024	116,463	116,859	112,205	112,479	108,535	119,699	124,888
Long-Term Obligations	1,928,570	2,081,152	2,356,528	2,113,277	1,938,188	2,299,844	2,204,030	2,531,837
Total Liabilities	2,381,239	2,563,911	2,846,992	2,512,483	2,328,908	2,845,754	2,607,654	2,932,846
Stockholders' Equity	1,727,927	1,632,728	1,579,936	1,389,462	1,485,186	1,378,175	1,577,130	1,655,380
Shares Outstanding	128,405	128,447	128,072	123,951	122,489	121,949	121,505	120,844
Statistical Record								
Return on Assets %	10.67	7.78	5.72	4.52	7.17	5.24	3.33	0.33
Return on Equity %	27.38	20.87	16.05	12.13	20.12	14.91	9.05	0.90
EBITDA Margin %	36.72	60.60	74.22	65.16	65.71	69.76	65.70	55.57
Net Margin %	110.85	58.50	43.48	34.00	55.99	44.25	29.12	2.88
Asset Turnover	0.13	0.13	0.13	0.13	0.13	0.12	0.11	0.12
Current Ratio	1.99	1.01	0.95	0.95	0.90	1.60	0.83	0.80
Debt to Equity	1.12	1.27	1.49	1.52	1.31	1.67	1.40	1.53
Price Range	35.27-26.48	36.70-29.37	43.44-32.48	38.41-30.43	36.96-27.42	35.84-26.77	28.85-21.56	26.80-19.35
P/E Ratio	10.14-7.61	14.12-11.30	23.23-17.37	29.78-23.59	16.43-12.19	23.89-17.85	32.06-23.96	...
Average Yield %	7.35	6.99	3.88	3.99	4.80	4.00	4.41	4.63

Address: 2600 Citadel Plaza Drive, Houston, TX 77292-4133
Telephone: 713-866-6000

Web Site: www.weingarten.com
Officers: Stanford Alexander - Chairman Andrew M. Alexander - President, Chief Executive Officer

Auditors: Deloitte & Touche LLP
Investor Contact: 713-866-6000
Transfer Agents: Computershare Trust Company, National Association, Canton, MA

WELBILT INC

Exchange	Symbol	Price	52Wk Range	Yield	P/E
NYS	WBT	$22.31 (6/29/2018)	23.60-18.57	N/A	22.31

*7 Year Price Score N/A   *NYSE Composite Index=100   *12 Month Price Score 95.89

Interim Earnings (Per Share)

Qtr.	Mar	Jun	Sep	Dec
2015	0.10	0.27	0.30	0.48
2016	0.13	0.11	0.18	0.15
2017	0.04	0.21	0.24	0.46
2018	0.09	...	...	...

Interim Dividends (Per Share)

No Dividends Paid

Valuation Analysis — **Institutional Holding**

Valuation Analysis		Institutional Holding	
Forecast EPS	$0.90 (06/07/2018)	No of Institutions	273
Market Cap	$3.1 Billion	Shares	130,909,944
Book Value	$132.3 Million	% Held	
Price/Book	23.58		
Price/Sales	2.13	N/A	

TRADING VOLUME (thousand shares)

Business Summary: Industrial Machinery & Equipment (MIC: 7.2.1 SIC: 3556 NAIC: 333294)

Welbilt is a commercial foodservice equipment company. Co. designs, manufactures and supplies food and beverage equipment for the commercial foodservice market. Co.'s portfolio of brands includes Clevelandâ,,¢, Convotherm®, Delfield®, fitKitchens®, Frymaster®, Garland®, Kolpak®, Lincolnâ,,¢, Manitowoc® Ice, Merco®, Merrychef® and Multiplex®. All of Co.'s products are supported by KitchenCare®, its aftermarket parts and repair service business. Co.'s products are used by commercial and institutional foodservice operators including restaurants, quick-service restaurant chains, hotels, caterers, supermarkets, convenience stores, business and industry, hospitals, schools and other institutions.

Recent Developments: For the quarter ended Mar 31 2018, net income increased 150.0% to US$12.5 million from US$5.0 million in the year-earlier quarter. Revenues were US$350.4 million, up 6.8% from US$328.0 million the year before. Operating income was US$41.6 million versus US$35.3 million in the prior-year quarter, an increase of 17.8%. Direct operating expenses rose 9.4% to US$224.2 million from US$205.0 million in the comparable period the year before. Indirect operating expenses decreased 3.5% to US$84.6 million from US$87.7 million in the equivalent prior-year period.

Prospects: Our evaluation of Welbilt Inc. as of Jan. 21, 2018 is the result of our systematic analysis on three basic characteristics: earnings strength, relative valuation, and recent stock price movement. The company has produced a positive trend in earnings per share over the past 5 quarters and while recent estimates for the company have been mixed, WBT has posted results that fell short of analysts expectations. Based on operating earnings yield, the company is about fairly valued when compared to all of the companies in our coverage universe. Share price changes over the past year indicates that WBT will perform well over the near term.

Financial Data

(US$ in Thousands)	3 Mos	12/31/2017	12/31/2016	12/31/2015	12/31/2014	12/31/2013
Earnings Per Share	1.00	0.95	0.57	1.15	1.17	1.07
Cash Flow Per Share	0.25	0.99	0.88	1.04	1.46	1.47
Income Statement						
Total Revenue	350,400	1,445,400	1,456,600	1,570,100	1,581,300	1,541,800
EBITDA	46,600	253,600	238,600	232,900	224,900	239,800
Depn & Amortn	13,500	47,900	48,500	51,000	53,000	51,400
Income Before Taxes	12,800	118,800	104,800	196,300	187,200	204,600
Income Taxes	300	(15,200)	25,300	39,300	25,900	55,300
Net Income	12,500	134,000	79,500	157,100	159,800	146,100
Average Shares	140,970	140,707	139,714	137,016	137,016	137,016
Balance Sheet						
Current Assets	446,700	383,700	308,200	252,600	289,500	...
Total Assets	1,898,800	1,840,400	1,769,100	1,754,000	1,898,300	...
Current Liabilities	278,000	290,100	313,100	321,300	368,600	...
Long-Term Obligations	1,279,500	1,232,200	1,278,700	2,300	3,600	...
Total Liabilities	1,766,500	1,730,000	1,812,600	545,300	646,900	...
Stockholders' Equity	132,300	110,400	(43,500)	1,208,700	1,251,400	...
Shares Outstanding	139,859	139,440	138,562	137,016	...	...
Statistical Record						
Return on Assets %	7.58	7.42	4.50	8.60	...	...
Return on Equity %	266.98	400.60	13.61	12.77	...	...
EBITDA Margin %	13.30	17.55	16.38	14.83	14.22	15.55
Net Margin %	3.57	9.27	5.46	10.01	10.11	9.48
Asset Turnover	0.79	0.80	0.82	0.86	...	...
Current Ratio	1.61	1.32	0.98	0.79	0.79	...
Debt to Equity	9.67	11.16	N.M.	N.M.	...	...
Price Range	23.60-18.55	23.51-18.25	19.33-13.80	...	...	...
P/E Ratio	23.60-18.55	24.75-19.21	33.91-24.21	...	...	...

Address: 2227 Welbilt Boulevard, New Port Richey, FL 34655
Telephone: 727-375-7010

Web Site: www.welbilt.com
Officers: Cynthia M. Egnotovich - Chairperson Hubertus M. Muehlhaeuser - President, Chief Executive Officer

Auditors: PricewaterhouseCoopers LLP
Transfer Agents: Computershare

WELLCARE HEALTH PLANS INC

Exchange	Symbol	Price	52Wk Range	Yield	P/E
NYS	WCG	$246.24 (6/29/2018)	246.24-164.15	N/A	27.18

*7 Year Price Score 165.16 ***NYSE Composite Index=100** ***12 Month Price Score 113.17**

TRADING VOLUME (thousand shares)

Interim Earnings (Per Share)

Qtr.	Mar	Jun	Sep	Dec
2015	0.39	1.17	0.82	0.29
2016	0.83	2.04	1.54	1.00
2017	1.50	1.65	3.82	1.34
2018	2.25	...	...	...

Interim Dividends (Per Share)

No Dividends Paid

Valuation Analysis — Institutional Holding

Forecast EPS	$10.26	No of Institutions
	(06/14/2018)	514
Market Cap	$11.0 Billion	Shares
Book Value	$2.5 Billion	55,716,764
Price/Book	4.40	% Held
Price/Sales	0.62	96.40

Business Summary: Hospitals & Health Care Facilities (MIC: 4.2.1 SIC: 6324 NAIC: 524114)

WellCare Health Plans is a managed care company with a focus on government-sponsored managed care services. Co. manages its business in three reportable segments: Medicaid Health Plans, which includes plans for beneficiaries of Temporary Assistance for Needy Families, and other state-based programs that are not part of the Medicaid program; Medicare Health Plans, which provides eligible persons age 65 and over and some disabled persons with a variety of hospital, medical and prescription drug benefits; and Medicare Prescription Drug Plans (PDPs), which provides stand-alone Medicare Part D coverage to Medicare-eligible beneficiaries in its Medicare PDPs segment.

Recent Developments: For the quarter ended Mar 31 2018, net income increased 51.1% to US$101.7 million from US$67.3 million in the year-earlier quarter. Revenues were US$4.65 billion, up 17.5% from US$3.95 billion the year before. Net premiums earned were US$4.63 billion versus US$3.95 billion in the prior-year quarter, an increase of 17.2%.

Prospects: Our evaluation of WellCare Health Plans Inc. as of Jan. 21, 2018 is the result of our systematic analysis on three basic characteristics: earnings strength, relative valuation, and recent stock price movement. The company has generated a negative trend in earnings per share over the past 5 quarters and while recent estimates for the company have been mixed, WCG has posted better than expected results. Based on operating earnings yield, the company is about fairly valued when compared to all of the companies in our coverage universe. Share price changes over the past year indicates that WCG will perform in line with the market over the near term.

Financial Data
(US$ in Thousands)

	3 Mos	12/31/2017	12/31/2016	12/31/2015	12/31/2014	12/31/2013	12/31/2012	12/31/2011
Earnings Per Share	9.06	8.31	5.43	2.67	1.44	3.98	4.22	6.10
Cash Flow Per Share	24.69	23.61	16.86	16.17	6.82	4.11	(0.71)	3.78
Tang Book Value Per Share	33.14	31.18	34.62	31.40	28.05	27.75	24.21	23.24
Income Statement								
Total Revenue	4,646,200	17,007,200	14,237,100	13,890,200	12,959,900	9,527,900	7,409,032	6,106,868
EBITDA	214,700	599,100	665,800	452,300	264,000	326,900	329,804	449,906
Depn & Amortn	36,400	87,700	77,200	62,000	46,800	36,700	29,243	24,922
Income Before Taxes	161,200	442,900	529,500	336,100	177,800	278,300	296,439	418,474
Income Taxes	56,800	87,900	287,400	217,500	114,100	103,000	111,711	154,228
Net Income	101,700	373,700	242,100	118,600	63,700	175,300	184,728	264,246
Average Shares	45,196	44,967	44,619	44,391	44,163	44,000	43,826	43,328
Balance Sheet								
Current Assets	7,177,200	5,819,200	5,119,600	4,268,500	3,526,300	2,692,700	2,100,710	2,119,894
Total Assets	9,671,400	8,364,600	6,152,800	5,193,600	4,495,000	3,450,700	2,675,516	2,488,111
Current Liabilities	5,679,800	4,443,200	3,055,800	2,441,600	1,935,700	1,237,100	1,113,426	1,123,140
Long-Term Obligations	1,183,000	1,182,400	997,600	912,100	900,000	600,000	120,000	135,000
Total Liabilities	7,169,000	5,947,900	4,152,700	3,465,300	2,899,100	1,932,800	1,352,352	1,371,265
Stockholders' Equity	2,502,400	2,416,700	2,000,100	1,728,300	1,595,900	1,517,900	1,323,164	1,116,846
Shares Outstanding	44,753	44,522	44,293	44,113	43,914	43,766	43,212	42,848
Statistical Record								
Return on Assets %	4.53	5.15	4.26	2.45	1.60	5.72	7.14	11.16
Return on Equity %	17.88	16.92	12.95	7.14	4.09	12.34	15.10	27.12
EBITDA Margin %	4.62	3.52	4.68	3.26	2.04	3.43	4.45	7.37
Net Margin %	2.19	2.20	1.70	0.85	0.49	1.84	2.49	4.33
Asset Turnover	1.97	2.34	2.50	2.87	3.26	3.11	2.86	2.58
Current Ratio	1.26	1.31	1.68	1.75	1.82	2.18	1.89	1.89
Debt to Equity	0.47	0.49	0.50	0.53	0.56	0.40	0.09	0.12
Price Range	218.79-140.21	212.99-136.63	141.40-70.06	98.51-72.85	84.25-56.64	74.76-45.78	74.24-45.90	58.45-29.90
P/E Ratio	24.15-15.48	25.63-16.44	26.04-12.90	36.90-27.28	58.51-39.33	18.78-11.50	17.59-10.88	9.58-4.90

Address: 8735 Henderson Road, Renaissance One, Tampa, FL 33634 Telephone: 813-290-6200	Web Site: www.wellcare.com Officers: Christian P. Michalik - Chairman Kenneth A. Burdick - President, Chief Executive Officer, Chief Operating Officer, Division Officer	Auditors: DELOITTE & TOUCHE LLP Investor Contact: 813-206-3916 Transfer Agents: Computershare Trust Company, N.A., Providence, RI

WELLS FARGO & CO.

Exchange	Symbol	Price	52Wk Range	Yield	P/E
NYS	WFC	$55.44 (6/29/2018)	65.93-49.58	2.81	13.66

*7 Year Price Score 96.80 *NYSE Composite Index=100 *12 Month Price Score 96.25

Interim Earnings (Per Share)
Qtr.	Mar	Jun	Sep	Dec
2015	1.04	1.03	1.05	1.00
2016	0.99	1.01	1.03	0.96
2017	1.00	1.07	0.84	1.19
2018	0.96	...	...	...

Interim Dividends (Per Share)
Amt	Decl	Ex	Rec	Pay
0.39Q	07/25/2017	08/02/2017	08/04/2017	09/01/2017
0.39Q	10/24/2017	11/02/2017	11/03/2017	12/01/2017
0.39Q	01/23/2018	02/01/2018	02/02/2018	03/01/2018
0.39Q	04/24/2018	05/03/2018	05/04/2018	06/01/2018

Indicated Div: $1.56 (Div. Reinv. Plan)

Valuation Analysis / Institutional Holding
Forecast EPS	$4.52 (06/14/2018)	No of Institutions 2857
Market Cap	$270.2 Billion	Shares 4,563,824,640
Book Value	$205.0 Billion	% Held
Price/Book	1.32	74.62
Price/Sales	2.73	

TRADING VOLUME (thousand shares)

Business Summary: Banking (MIC: 5.1.1 SIC: 6021 NAIC: 522110)

Wells Fargo is a financial holding company and a bank holding company.Co. has three operating segments: Community Banking; Wholesale Banking; and Wealth, Brokerage and Retirement. The Community Banking segment provides a line of financial products and services to consumers and businesses. The Wholesale Banking segment provides financial solutions to businesses across the U.S. and to financial institutions globally. The Wealth and Investment Management segment provides a range of personalized wealth management, investment and retirement products and services to clients across U.S. based businesses. At Dec 31 2017, Co. had total assets of $1.95 trillion and total deposits of $1.34 trillion.

Recent Developments: For the quarter ended Mar 31 2018, net income decreased 7.0% to US$5.33 billion from US$5.73 billion in the year-earlier quarter. Net interest income decreased 0.7% to US$12.24 billion from US$12.32 billion in the year-earlier quarter. Provision for loan losses was US$191.0 million versus US$605.0 million in the prior-year quarter, a decrease of 68.4%. Non-interest income fell 2.4% to US$9.70 billion from US$9.93 billion, while non-interest expense advanced 9.1% to US$15.04 billion.

Prospects: Our evaluation of Wells Fargo & Co. as of Jan. 21, 2018 is the result of our systematic analysis on three basic characteristics: earnings strength, relative valuation, and recent stock price movement. The company has produced a positive trend in earnings per share over the past 5 quarters and while recent estimates for the company have been raised by analysts, WFC has posted results that fell short of analysts expectations. Based on operating earnings yield, the company is undervalued when compared to all of the companies in our coverage universe. Share price changes over the past year indicates that WFC will perform poorly over the near term.

Financial Data
(US$ in Thousands)

	3 Mos	12/31/2017	12/31/2016	12/31/2015	12/31/2014	12/31/2013	12/31/2012	12/31/2011
Earnings Per Share	4.06	4.10	3.99	4.12	4.10	3.89	3.36	2.82
Cash Flow Per Share	4.25	3.77	0.03	2.88	3.35	10.90	11.04	2.59
Tang Book Value Per Share	27.59	28.28	26.17	25.21	23.42	20.10	18.81	15.34
Dividends Per Share	1.550	1.540	1.515	1.475	1.350	1.150	0.880	0.480
Dividend Payout %	38.18	37.56	37.97	35.80	32.93	29.56	26.19	17.02
Income Statement								
Interest Income	15,347,000	58,909,000	53,663,000	49,277,000	47,552,000	47,089,000	48,391,000	49,412,000
Interest Expense	3,109,000	9,352,000	5,909,000	3,976,000	4,025,000	4,289,000	5,161,000	6,649,000
Net Interest Income	12,238,000	49,557,000	47,754,000	45,301,000	43,527,000	42,800,000	43,230,000	42,763,000
Provision for Losses	191,000	2,528,000	3,770,000	2,442,000	1,395,000	2,309,000	7,217,000	7,899,000
Non-Interest Income	9,696,000	38,832,000	40,513,000	40,756,000	40,820,000	40,980,000	42,856,000	38,185,000
Non-Interest Expense	15,004,000	58,484,000	52,377,000	49,974,000	49,037,000	48,842,000	50,398,000	49,393,000
Income Before Taxes	6,701,000	27,377,000	32,120,000	33,641,000	33,915,000	32,629,000	28,471,000	23,656,000
Income Taxes	1,374,000	4,917,000	10,075,000	10,365,000	10,307,000	10,405,000	9,103,000	7,445,000
Net Income	5,136,000	22,183,000	21,938,000	22,894,000	23,057,000	21,878,000	18,897,000	15,869,000
Average Shares	4,930,699	5,017,299	5,108,329	5,209,799	5,324,399	5,371,199	5,351,499	5,323,399
Balance Sheet								
Net Loans & Leases	940,516,000	945,874,000	956,265,000	905,293,000	850,954,000	811,430,000	782,624,000	751,597,000
Total Assets	1,915,388,000	1,951,757,000	1,930,115,000	1,787,632,000	1,687,155,000	1,527,015,000	1,422,968,000	1,313,867,000
Total Deposits	1,303,689,000	1,335,991,000	1,306,079,000	1,223,312,000	1,168,310,000	1,079,177,000	1,002,835,000	920,070,000
Total Liabilities	1,710,436,000	1,744,821,000	1,730,534,000	1,594,634,000	1,502,761,000	1,356,873,000	1,265,414,000	1,173,626,000
Stockholders' Equity	204,952,000	206,936,000	199,581,000	192,998,000	184,394,000	170,142,000	157,554,000	140,241,000
Shares Outstanding	4,873,882	4,891,616	5,016,109	5,092,128	5,170,348	5,257,162	5,266,313	5,262,611
Statistical Record								
Return on Assets %	1.13	1.14	1.18	1.32	1.43	1.48	1.38	1.23
Return on Equity %	10.76	10.91	11.15	12.13	13.01	13.35	12.66	11.90
Net Interest Margin %	79.74	84.12	88.99	91.93	91.54	90.89	89.33	86.54
Efficiency Ratio %	59.91	59.84	55.62	55.51	55.49	55.46	55.23	56.39
Loans to Deposits	0.72	0.71	0.73	0.74	0.73	0.75	0.78	0.82
Price Range	65.93-49.58	61.61-49.58	57.29-43.75	58.52-50.02	55.71-44.23	45.54-34.18	36.13-28.43	34.10-22.88
P/E Ratio	16.24-12.21	15.03-12.09	14.36-10.96	14.20-12.14	13.59-10.79	11.71-8.79	10.75-8.46	12.09-8.11
Average Yield %	2.79	2.80	3.09	2.69	2.68	2.86	2.68	1.71

Address: 420 Montgomery Street, San Francisco, CA 94163 **Telephone:** 866-249-3302	**Web Site:** www.wellsfargo.com **Officers:** Elizabeth A. Duke - Chairman, Vice-Chairman Timothy J. Sloan - President, Chief Executive Officer, Chief Operating Officer, Head, Senior Executive Vice President, Chief Financial Officer, Chief Administrative Officer	**Auditors:** KPMG LLP **Investor Contact:** 415-371-2921 **Transfer Agents:** Wells Fargo Shareowners Services, St. Paul, MN

WELLTOWER INC

Exchange	Symbol	Price	52Wk Range	Yield	P/E	Div Acheiver
NYS	WELL	$62.69 (6/29/2018)	75.76-50.01	5.55	39.68	14 Years

*7 Year Price Score 79.06 *NYSE Composite Index=100 *12 Month Price Score 90.33

Interim Earnings (Per Share)

Qtr.	Mar	Jun	Sep	Dec
2015	0.56	0.89	0.52	0.37
2016	0.42	0.54	0.93	0.92
2017	0.86	0.51	0.20	(0.30)
2018	1.17	...	...	...

Interim Dividends (Per Share)

Amt	Decl	Ex	Rec	Pay
0.87Q	07/27/2017	08/04/2017	08/08/2017	08/21/2017
0.87Q	10/26/2017	11/06/2017	11/07/2017	11/20/2017
0.87Q	01/31/2018	02/12/2018	02/13/2018	02/21/2018
0.87Q	04/25/2018	05/07/2018	05/08/2018	05/23/2018

Indicated Div: $3.48 (Div. Reinv. Plan)

Valuation Analysis

		Institutional Holding	
Forecast EPS	$2.48	No of Institutions	
	(06/12/2018)	1045	
Market Cap	$23.3 Billion	Shares	
Book Value	$14.6 Billion	402,708,064	
Price/Book	1.60	% Held	
Price/Sales	5.36	95.30	

Business Summary: REITs (MIC: 5.3.1 SIC: 6798 NAIC: 525930)

Welltower is a real estate investment trust. As of Dec 31 2017, Co.'s portfolio consisted a total of 1,286 properties that comprised of 573 triple-net properties (independent living facilities and independent supportive living facilities, continuing care retirement communities, assisted living facilities, care homes with and without nursing, Alzheimer's/dementia care facilities, long-term/post-acute care facilities and hospitals); 443 seniors housing properties (independent living facilities and independent supportive living facilities, assisted living facilities, care homes and Alzheimer's/dementia care facilities); and 270 outpatient medical properties (outpatient medical buildings).

Recent Developments: For the quarter ended Mar 31 2018, income from continuing operations increased 23.4% to US$115.4 million from US$93.5 million in the year-earlier quarter. Net income increased 34.3% to US$453.6 million from US$337.6 million in the year-earlier quarter. Revenues were US$1.10 billion, up 3.3% from US$1.06 billion the year before. Revenues from property income fell 6.5% to US$343.4 million from US$367.1 million in the corresponding quarter a year earlier.

Prospects: Our evaluation of Welltower Inc. as of Jan. 21, 2018 is the result of our systematic analysis on three basic characteristics: earnings strength, relative valuation, and recent stock price movement. The company has managed to produce a neutral trend in earnings per share over the past 5 quarters. Because the company lacks sufficient analyst estimate data, we place greater weight on the historical EPS trend as the measure of earnings strength. Based on operating earnings yield, the company is about fairly valued when compared to all of the companies in our coverage universe. Share price changes over the past year indicates that HCN will perform well over the near term.

Financial Data

(US$ in Thousands)	3 Mos	12/31/2017	12/31/2016	12/31/2015	12/31/2014	12/31/2013	12/31/2012	12/31/2011
Earnings Per Share	1.58	1.26	2.81	2.34	1.45	0.28	0.98	0.90
Cash Flow Per Share	3.82	3.91	4.53	3.94	3.72	3.57	3.64	3.39
Tang Book Value Per Share	37.02	36.68	37.87	38.10	36.80	35.67	35.35	31.44
Dividends Per Share	3.480	3.480	3.440	3.300	3.180	3.060	2.960	2.835
Dividend Payout %	220.25	276.19	122.42	141.03	219.31	1,092.86	302.04	315.00
Income Statement								
Total Revenue	1,096,965	4,316,641	4,281,160	3,859,826	3,343,546	2,880,608	1,822,099	1,421,162
EBITDA	124,277	1,238,214	1,619,639	1,471,366	1,236,053	984,762	734,588	594,378
Depn & Amortn	4,889	938,598	910,386	835,249	851,840	882,517	548,935	437,949
Income Before Taxes	119,388	299,616	709,253	636,117	384,213	102,245	185,653	156,429
Income Taxes	1,588	20,128	(19,128)	6,451	(1,267)	7,491	7,612	1,388
Net Income	449,347	522,774	1,077,803	883,750	512,153	145,050	297,255	217,610
Average Shares	373,257	369,001	360,227	349,424	307,747	278,761	225,953	174,401
Balance Sheet								
Current Assets	264,119	698,471	949,798	818,252	553,423	231,601	1,141,421	233,102
Total Assets	27,746,169	27,944,445	28,865,184	29,023,845	25,014,296	23,083,957	19,549,109	14,924,606
Long-Term Obligations	11,349,840	11,731,936	12,358,245	12,967,686	10,828,013	10,652,014	8,531,899	7,240,752
Total Liabilities	13,188,224	13,521,298	14,058,791	14,433,285	11,839,143	11,669,374	9,254,308	7,799,842
Stockholders' Equity	14,558,435	14,423,147	14,806,393	14,590,560	13,175,153	11,414,583	10,294,801	7,124,764
Shares Outstanding	371,970	371,731	362,602	354,777	328,790	289,563	260,373	192,275
Statistical Record								
Return on Assets %	2.29	1.84	3.71	3.27	2.13	0.68	1.72	1.79
Return on Equity %	4.35	3.58	7.31	6.37	4.17	1.34	3.40	3.71
EBITDA Margin %	11.33	28.68	37.83	38.12	36.97	34.19	40.32	41.82
Net Margin %	40.96	12.11	25.18	22.90	15.32	5.04	16.31	15.31
Asset Turnover	0.16	0.15	0.15	0.14	0.14	0.14	0.11	0.12
Debt to Equity	0.78	0.81	0.83	0.89	0.82	0.93	0.83	1.02
Price Range	77.66-52.03	77.66-63.27	79.61-53.68	84.31-58.21	77.98-53.05	78.98-52.58	62.24-52.40	54.98-41.11
P/E Ratio	49.15-32.93	61.63-50.21	28.33-19.10	36.03-24.88	53.78-36.59	282.07-187.79	63.51-53.47	61.09-45.68
Average Yield %	5.16	4.96	4.94	4.68	4.97	4.75	5.16	5.62

Address: 4500 Dorr Street, Toledo, OH 43615 **Telephone:** 419-247-2800	**Web Site:** www.welltower.com **Officers:** Jeffrey H. Donahue - Chairman Thomas J. (Tom) DeRosa - Chief Executive Officer	**Auditors:** Ernst & Young LLP **Transfer Agents:** Computershare, Providence, RI

WESCO INTERNATIONAL, INC.

Exchange	Symbol	Price	52Wk Range	Yield	P/E
NYS	WCC	$57.10 (6/29/2018)	68.75-49.60	N/A	16.08

*7 Year Price Score 74.87   ***NYSE Composite Index=100**   ***12 Month Price Score 97.14**

Interim Earnings (Per Share)

Qtr.	Mar	Jun	Sep	Dec
2015	0.90	1.00	1.28	1.02
2016	0.77	1.02	(0.73)	0.97
2017	0.76	1.02	1.12	0.48
2018	0.93	...	...	...

Interim Dividends (Per Share)

No Dividends Paid

Valuation Analysis   Institutional Holding

Forecast EPS	$4.75	No of Institutions	
	(06/13/2018)	379	
Market Cap	$2.7 Billion	Shares	
Book Value	$2.1 Billion	54,958,740	
Price/Book	1.26	% Held	
Price/Sales	0.34	102.17	

TRADING VOLUME (thousand shares)

Business Summary: Electrical Equipment (MIC: 7.3.1 SIC: 5063 NAIC: 423610)

WESCO International is a distributor of products and provider of supply chain management and logistics services used primarily in industrial, construction, utility, and commercial, institutional and government markets. Co. is a provider of electrical, industrial, and communications maintenance, repair and operating and original equipment manufacturers products, construction materials, and supply chain management and logistics services. Co.'s primary product categories include general supplies, wire, cable and conduit, communications and security, electrical distribution and controls, lighting and sustainability, and automation, controls and motors.

Recent Developments: For the quarter ended Mar 31 2018, net income increased 13.7% to US$43.0 million from US$37.8 million in the year-earlier quarter. Revenues were US$1.99 billion, up 12.5% from US$1.77 billion the year before. Operating income was US$73.2 million versus US$66.6 million in the prior-year quarter, an increase of 9.9%. Direct operating expenses rose 13.5% to US$1.61 billion from US$1.42 billion in the comparable period the year before. Indirect operating expenses increased 8.2% to US$306.7 million from US$283.4 million in the equivalent prior-year period.

Prospects: Our evaluation of Wesco International Inc. as of Jan. 21, 2018 is the result of our systematic analysis on three basic characteristics: earnings strength, relative valuation, and recent stock price movement. The company has managed to produce a neutral trend in earnings per share over the past 5 quarters and while recent estimates for the company have been mixed, WCC has posted better than expected results. Based on operating earnings yield, the company is undervalued when compared to all of the companies in our coverage universe. Share price changes over the past year indicates that WCC will perform poorly over the near term.

Financial Data

(US$ in Thousands)	3 Mos	12/31/2017	12/31/2016	12/31/2015	12/31/2014	12/31/2013	12/31/2012	12/31/2011
Earnings Per Share	3.55	3.38	2.10	4.18	5.18	5.25	3.95	3.96
Cash Flow Per Share	3.28	3.12	6.79	6.52	5.65	7.14	6.58	3.88
Tang Book Value Per Share	0.62	N.M.	N.M.	N.M.	N.M.	N.M.	N.M.	4.17
Income Statement								
Total Revenue	1,993,915	7,679,021	7,336,017	7,518,487	7,889,626	7,513,342	6,579,301	6,125,718
EBITDA	89,120	337,190	225,226	391,542	484,717	483,658	343,801	345,479
Depn & Amortn	15,879	16,300	17,100	17,800	18,500	18,200	14,400	12,500
Income Before Taxes	53,458	252,440	131,551	303,910	384,153	379,851	281,639	279,376
Income Taxes	10,487	89,307	30,431	95,537	108,716	103,333	79,880	83,136
Net Income	44,421	163,460	101,588	210,687	275,906	276,430	201,777	196,251
Average Shares	47,608	48,361	48,333	50,373	53,258	52,650	51,133	49,623
Balance Sheet								
Current Assets	2,418,671	2,408,849	2,172,457	2,257,534	2,350,338	2,198,541	2,101,837	1,737,420
Total Assets	4,713,313	4,735,468	4,490,984	4,587,425	4,754,437	4,617,108	4,629,629	3,078,452
Current Liabilities	1,021,601	1,040,969	896,797	947,801	1,063,872	1,044,589	1,007,995	845,846
Long-Term Obligations	1,292,094	1,313,261	1,363,135	1,456,761	1,366,430	1,447,634	1,695,413	642,922
Total Liabilities	2,575,353	2,615,729	2,477,703	2,810,753	2,825,785	2,852,299	3,075,832	1,732,454
Stockholders' Equity	2,137,960	2,119,739	2,013,281	1,776,672	1,928,652	1,764,809	1,553,797	1,345,998
Shares Outstanding	47,075	47,009	48,611	42,173	44,489	44,267	44,061	43,424
Statistical Record								
Return on Assets %	3.69	3.54	2.23	4.51	5.89	5.98	5.22	6.65
Return on Equity %	8.10	7.91	5.35	11.37	14.94	16.66	13.88	15.73
EBITDA Margin %	4.47	4.39	3.07	5.21	6.14	6.44	5.23	5.64
Net Margin %	2.23	2.13	1.38	2.80	3.50	3.68	3.07	3.20
Asset Turnover	1.71	1.66	1.61	1.61	1.68	1.63	1.70	2.07
Current Ratio	2.37	2.31	2.42	2.38	2.21	2.10	2.09	2.05
Debt to Equity	0.60	0.62	0.68	0.82	0.71	0.82	1.09	0.48
Price Range	70.60-49.60	74.45-49.60	72.15-36.05	76.21-40.04	93.81-71.18	91.12-65.46	67.60-52.31	63.79-32.09
P/E Ratio	19.89-13.97	22.03-14.67	34.36-17.17	18.23-9.58	18.11-13.74	17.36-12.47	17.11-13.24	16.11-8.10

Address: 225 West Station Square Drive, Suite 700, Pittsburgh, PA 15219
Telephone: 412-454-2200

Web Site: www.wesco.com
Officers: John J. Engel - Chairman, President, Chief Executive Officer David S. Schulz - Senior Vice President, Chief Financial Officer

Auditors: PricewaterhouseCoopers LLP
Transfer Agents: Computershare, Providence, RI

WEST PHARMACEUTICAL SERVICES, INC.

Exchange	Symbol	Price	52Wk Range	Yield	P/E	Div Acheiver
NYS	WST	$99.29 (6/29/2018)	102.40-83.32	0.56	56.41	25 Years

*7 Year Price Score 137.13 *NYSE Composite Index=100 ***12 Month Price Score 98.89**

Interim Earnings (Per Share)

Qtr.	Mar	Jun	Sep	Dec
2015	0.45	0.38	0.02	0.45
2016	0.30	0.60	0.50	0.51
2017	0.81	0.51	0.67	0.00
2018	0.58	...	...	...

Interim Dividends (Per Share)

Amt	Decl	Ex	Rec	Pay
0.14Q	07/20/2017	10/17/2017	10/18/2017	11/01/2017
0.14Q	12/22/2017	01/17/2018	01/18/2018	02/01/2018
0.14Q	02/15/2018	04/17/2018	04/18/2018	05/02/2018
0.14Q	05/03/2018	07/17/2018	07/18/2018	08/01/2018

Indicated Div: $0.56 (Div. Reinv. Plan)

Valuation Analysis — **Institutional Holding**

Forecast EPS	$2.81 (06/12/2018)	No of Institutions	464
Market Cap	$7.3 Billion	Shares	85,600,968
Book Value	$1.3 Billion	% Held	90.19
Price/Book	5.60		
Price/Sales	4.49		

Business Summary: Rubber Products (MIC: 8.4.1 SIC: 3069 NAIC: 326299)

West Pharmaceutical Services is a manufacturer of packaging components and delivery systems for injectable drugs and healthcare products. Co.'s products include vial containment solutions, prefillable systems, self-injection platforms, cartridge systems and components, reconstitution and transfer systems, intradermal delivery solutions, specialty components, and contract manufacturing and analytical services. Proprietary Products segment provides proprietary packaging, containment and drug delivery products such as NovaPure® plungers. Contract-Manufactured Products segment includes a variety of custom contract-manufacturing and assembly solutions.

Recent Developments: For the quarter ended Mar 31 2018, net income decreased 28.4% to US$43.6 million from US$60.9 million in the year-earlier quarter. Revenues were US$415.7 million, up 7.2% from US$387.7 million the year before. Operating income was US$53.4 million versus US$60.5 million in the prior-year quarter, a decrease of 11.7%. Direct operating expenses rose 11.0% to US$281.3 million from US$253.5 million in the comparable period the year before. Indirect operating expenses increased 9.9% to US$81.0 million from US$73.7 million in the equivalent prior-year period.

Prospects: Our evaluation of West Pharmaceutical Services Inc. as of Jan. 21, 2018 is the result of our systematic analysis on three basic characteristics: earnings strength, relative valuation, and recent stock price movement. The company has produced a positive trend in earnings per share over the past 5 quarters and while recent estimates for the company have remained steady, WST has posted better than expected results. Based on operating earnings yield, the company is overvalued when compared to all of the companies in our coverage universe. Share price changes over the past year indicates that WST will perform well over the near term.

Financial Data

(US$ in Thousands)	3 Mos	12/31/2017	12/31/2016	12/31/2015	12/31/2014	12/31/2013	12/31/2012	12/31/2011
Earnings Per Share	1.76	1.99	1.91	1.30	1.75	1.57	1.15	1.08
Cash Flow Per Share	3.89	3.56	2.99	2.95	2.58	3.17	2.75	1.94
Tang Book Value Per Share	15.95	15.57	13.56	12.20	11.31	10.60	8.25	7.29
Dividends Per Share	0.540	0.530	0.490	0.450	0.410	0.385	0.365	0.345
Dividend Payout %	30.68	26.63	25.65	34.62	23.43	24.52	31.74	31.94
Income Statement								
Total Revenue	415,700	1,599,100	1,509,100	1,399,800	1,421,400	1,368,400	1,266,400	1,192,300
EBITDA	81,400	323,200	284,900	214,700	266,800	243,200	196,300	180,700
Depn & Amortn	26,400	94,300	88,100	86,100	84,800	81,000	72,800	71,100
Income Before Taxes	53,700	222,400	189,800	116,100	169,000	147,100	108,600	92,700
Income Taxes	12,500	80,900	54,400	26,300	47,200	40,200	32,700	23,500
Net Income	43,600	150,700	143,600	95,600	127,100	112,300	80,700	75,500
Average Shares	75,500	75,800	75,000	73,800	72,800	71,400	71,800	74,000
Balance Sheet								
Current Assets	743,500	743,500	641,900	673,700	659,300	650,700	557,300	472,000
Total Assets	1,869,600	1,862,800	1,716,700	1,695,100	1,670,900	1,671,600	1,564,000	1,399,100
Current Liabilities	263,400	279,500	241,000	314,300	252,500	236,900	261,800	243,200
Long-Term Obligations	198,000	197,000	226,200	228,900	309,500	371,300	378,800	299,300
Total Liabilities	564,300	582,900	599,200	671,200	714,000	765,200	835,100	744,200
Stockholders' Equity	1,305,300	1,279,900	1,117,500	1,023,900	956,900	906,400	728,900	654,900
Shares Outstanding	73,577	73,900	73,100	72,300	71,300	70,200	68,600	67,400
Statistical Record								
Return on Assets %	7.40	8.42	8.39	5.68	7.61	6.94	5.43	5.61
Return on Equity %	10.78	12.57	13.38	9.65	13.64	13.73	11.63	11.79
EBITDA Margin %	19.58	20.21	18.88	15.34	18.77	17.77	15.50	15.16
Net Margin %	10.49	9.42	9.52	6.83	8.94	8.21	6.37	6.33
Asset Turnover	0.90	0.89	0.88	0.83	0.85	0.85	0.85	0.89
Current Ratio	2.82	2.66	2.66	2.14	2.61	2.75	2.13	1.94
Debt to Equity	0.15	0.15	0.20	0.22	0.32	0.41	0.52	0.46
Price Range	102.40-78.61	101.65-78.61	85.30-54.64	64.13-49.19	55.08-39.26	50.08-27.38	27.86-18.90	23.72-17.82
P/E Ratio	58.18-44.66	51.08-39.50	44.66-28.61	49.33-37.84	31.47-22.43	31.90-17.44	24.23-16.43	21.96-16.50
Average Yield %	0.58	0.58	0.72	0.80	0.79	0.90	1.04	1.67

Address: 530 Herman O. West Drive, Exton, PA 19341-0645 **Telephone:** 610-594-2900	**Web Site:** www.westpharma.com **Officers:** Eric M. Green - President, Chief Executive Officer Karen A. Flynn - Senior Vice President, Chief Commercial Officer, Division Officer	**Auditors:** PricewaterhouseCoopers LLP **Investor Contact:** 610-594-3345 **Transfer Agents:** Broadbridge Corporate Issuer Solutions, Philadelphia, PA

WABCO HOLDINGS INC

Exchange	Symbol	Price	52Wk Range	Yield	P/E
NYS	WBC	$117.02 (6/29/2018)	161.00-116.90	N/A	14.83

*7 Year Price Score 117.01 *NYSE Composite Index=100 *12 Month Price Score 87.27

TRADING VOLUME (thousand shares)

Interim Earnings (Per Share)

Qtr.	Mar	Jun	Sep	Dec
2015	1.22	1.12	0.67	1.70
2016	(0.24)	1.33	1.76	1.14
2017	1.48	1.61	1.30	3.11
2018	1.87	...	...	...

Interim Dividends (Per Share)

No Dividends Paid

Valuation Analysis		Institutional Holding	
Forecast EPS	$7.73	No of Institutions	
	(06/13/2018)	515	
Market Cap	$6.3 Billion	Shares	
Book Value	$1.2 Billion	60,529,408	
Price/Book	5.15	% Held	
Price/Sales	1.76	91.05	

Business Summary: Construction Services (MIC: 7.5.4 SIC: 3711 NAIC: 336111)

WABCO engineers, develops, manufactures and sells systems controlling braking, stability, suspension, transmission automation, air compression and processing primarily for commercial vehicle. Co.'s key products include pneumatic anti-lock braking systems, electronic braking systems, electronic stability control, brake controls, automated manual transmission systems, and mechanical products such as air compressors and air control valves. Co. supplies commercial vehicle aftermarket distributors and service partners as well as fleet operators with replacement parts, fleet management solutions, diagnostic tools, training and other services. Co. provides remanufacturing services globally.

Recent Developments: For the quarter ended Mar 31 2018, net income increased 26.6% to US$106.7 million from US$84.3 million in the year-earlier quarter. Revenues were US$1.00 billion, up 34.3% from US$747.3 million the year before. Operating income was US$147.0 million versus US$108.5 million in the prior-year quarter, an increase of 35.5%. Direct operating expenses rose 36.9% to US$694.3 million from US$507.1 million in the comparable period the year before. Indirect operating expenses increased 23.0% to US$162.0 million from US$131.7 million in the equivalent prior-year period.

Prospects: Our evaluation of WABCO Holdings Inc. as of Jan. 21, 2018 is the result of our systematic analysis on three basic characteristics: earnings strength, relative valuation, and recent stock price movement. The company has managed to produce a neutral trend in earnings per share over the past 5 quarters and while recent estimates for the company have been raised by analysts, WBC has posted better than expected results. Based on operating earnings yield, the company is about fairly valued when compared to all of the companies in our coverage universe. Share price changes over the past year indicates that WBC will perform well over the near term.

Financial Data

(US$ in Thousands)	3 Mos	12/31/2017	12/31/2016	12/31/2015	12/31/2014	12/31/2013	12/31/2012	12/31/2011
Earnings Per Share	7.89	7.50	3.98	4.72	4.81	10.31	4.62	5.19
Cash Flow Per Share	8.49	7.82	7.26	6.84	5.25	10.66	5.59	4.98
Tang Book Value Per Share	2.27	0.37	4.10	6.10	5.86	11.85	4.23	2.90
Income Statement								
Total Revenue	1,003,300	3,304,200	2,810,000	2,627,500	2,851,000	2,720,500	2,477,400	2,794,100
EBITDA	173,000	752,600	455,000	369,200	434,400	703,500	396,400	468,300
Depn & Amortn	37,400	107,100	98,000	96,700	101,600	85,200	76,900	78,200
Income Before Taxes	132,600	629,500	344,300	265,400	333,000	623,200	318,000	388,400
Income Taxes	26,300	229,700	121,800	11,500	55,600	(21,000)	23,600	36,700
Net Income	100,700	406,100	223,000	275,200	291,500	653,200	302,000	357,000
Average Shares	53,890	54,139	55,981	58,274	60,546	63,382	65,323	68,829
Balance Sheet								
Current Assets	2,520,500	2,394,200	1,874,000	1,386,400	1,182,500	1,234,600	792,600	750,700
Total Assets	4,471,800	4,323,400	3,056,000	2,589,900	2,432,700	2,392,800	1,747,000	1,623,200
Current Liabilities	722,900	1,073,300	530,900	464,800	417,700	485,400	445,700	451,600
Long-Term Obligations	1,405,400	1,023,300	958,900	498,700	307,100	47,000	...	52,000
Total Liabilities	3,253,400	3,202,000	2,354,600	1,803,200	1,591,100	1,240,000	1,070,600	1,036,000
Stockholders' Equity	1,218,400	1,121,400	701,400	786,700	841,600	1,152,800	676,400	587,200
Shares Outstanding	53,596	53,735	54,491	56,759	58,425	61,359	62,747	64,765
Statistical Record								
Return on Assets %	11.20	11.01	7.88	10.96	12.08	31.56	17.87	22.68
Return on Equity %	43.05	44.56	29.89	33.80	29.23	71.42	47.67	71.44
EBITDA Margin %	17.24	22.78	16.19	14.05	15.24	25.86	16.00	16.76
Net Margin %	10.04	12.29	7.94	10.47	10.22	24.01	12.19	12.78
Asset Turnover	0.94	0.90	0.99	1.05	1.18	1.31	1.47	1.78
Current Ratio	3.49	2.23	3.53	2.98	2.83	2.54	1.78	1.66
Debt to Equity	1.15	0.91	1.37	0.63	0.36	0.04	...	0.09
Price Range	161.00-111.74	155.08-104.21	113.91-84.83	133.21-94.54	110.68-84.36	93.41-62.66	65.19-44.66	74.30-35.47
P/E Ratio	20.41-14.16	20.68-13.89	28.62-21.31	28.22-20.03	23.01-17.54	9.06-6.08	14.11-9.67	14.32-6.83

Address: Chaussée de la Hulpe 166, Brussels, 48309-3511 Telephone: 266-398-00 Fax: 267-543-42	Web Site: www.wabco-auto.com Officers: Jacques R. Esculier - Chairman, Chief Executive Officer Alexander De Bock - Interim Chief Financial Officer, Division Officer	Auditors: Ernst & Young Bedrijfsrevisoren BCVBA/ Reviseurs d'Entreprises SCCRL Investor Contact: 732-369-7477

WESTERN UNION CO

Exchange	Symbol	Price	52Wk Range	Yield	P/E
NYS	WU	$20.33 (6/29/2018)	21.49-18.47	3.74	N/A

*7 Year Price Score 86.71   ***NYSE Composite Index=100**   ***12 Month Price Score 101.63**

Interim Earnings (Per Share)

Qtr.	Mar	Jun	Sep	Dec
2015	0.39	0.36	0.45	0.42
2016	0.37	0.42	0.44	(0.72)
2017	0.33	0.35	0.51	(2.38)
2018	0.46	...	...	...

Interim Dividends (Per Share)

Amt	Decl	Ex	Rec	Pay
0.175Q	07/12/2017	09/14/2017	09/15/2017	09/29/2017
0.175Q	12/07/2017	12/15/2017	12/18/2017	12/29/2017
0.19Q	02/13/2018	03/15/2018	03/16/2018	03/30/2018
0.19Q	05/18/2018	06/14/2018	06/15/2018	06/29/2018

Indicated Div: $0.76

Valuation Analysis   **Institutional Holding**

Forecast EPS	$1.86	No of Institutions
	(06/14/2018)	890
Market Cap	$9.4 Billion	Shares
Book Value	N/A	596,905,664
Price/Book	N/A	% Held
Price/Sales	1.67	88.93

Business Summary: Business Services (MIC: 7.5.2 SIC: 7389 NAIC: 522320)

Western Union is a holding company. Through its subsidiaries, Co. is engaged in money movement and payment services. Co.'s segments are consumer-to-consumer, which facilitates money transfers between two consumers, through a network of third-party agents; consumer-to-business, which facilitates bill payments from consumers to businesses and other organizations, including utilities, auto finance companies, mortgage servicers, financial service providers and government agencies; and business solutions, which facilitates payment and foreign exchange solutions, primarily cross-border, cross-currency transactions, for small and medium size enterprises and other organizations and individuals.

Recent Developments: For the quarter ended Mar 31 2018, net income increased 32.1% to US$213.6 million from US$161.7 million in the year-earlier quarter. Revenues were US$1.39 billion, up 6.7% from US$1.30 billion the year before. Operating income was US$264.9 million versus US$240.1 million in the prior-year quarter, an increase of 10.3%. Direct operating expenses rose 3.2% to US$825.4 million from US$799.9 million in the comparable period the year before. Indirect operating expenses increased 14.0% to US$299.1 million from US$262.4 million in the equivalent prior-year period.

Prospects: Our evaluation of Western Union Co as of Jan. 21, 2018 is the result of our systematic analysis on three basic characteristics: earnings strength, relative valuation, and recent stock price movement. The company has produced a positive trend in earnings per share over the past 5 quarters. However, while recent estimates for the company have been mixed, WU has posted better than expected results. Based on operating earnings yield, the company is undervalued when compared to all of the companies in our coverage universe. Share price changes over the past year indicates that WU will perform poorly over the near term.

Financial Data

(US$ in Thousands)	3 Mos	12/31/2017	12/31/2016	12/31/2015	12/31/2014	12/31/2013	12/31/2012	12/31/2011
Earnings Per Share	(1.06)	(1.19)	0.51	1.62	1.59	1.43	1.69	1.84
Cash Flow Per Share	1.70	1.57	2.12	2.09	1.96	1.96	1.95	1.86
Dividends Per Share	0.715	0.700	0.640	0.620	0.500	0.500	0.425	0.310
Dividend Payout %	...	...	125.49	38.27	31.45	34.97	25.15	16.85
Income Statement								
Total Revenue	1,389,400	5,524,300	5,422,900	5,483,700	5,607,200	5,542,000	5,664,800	5,491,400
EBITDA	336,000	561,800	564,900	1,166,500	1,199,900	1,177,300	1,404,600	1,512,300
Depn & Amortn	66,700	77,100	74,200	67,700	66,600	64,200	61,700	61,000
Income Before Taxes	234,500	347,500	341,700	941,800	968,200	926,900	1,168,800	1,274,600
Income Taxes	20,900	904,600	88,500	104,000	115,800	128,500	142,900	109,200
Net Income	213,600	(557,100)	253,200	837,800	852,400	798,400	1,025,900	1,165,400
Average Shares	463,600	467,900	493,500	516,700	536,800	559,700	607,100	634,200
Balance Sheet								
Current Assets	934,300	958,700	1,004,400	1,399,300	1,846,200	2,157,000	1,849,000	1,443,800
Total Assets	9,188,000	9,231,400	9,419,600	9,458,900	9,890,400	10,121,300	9,465,700	9,069,900
Current Liabilities	2,866,500	2,143,500	1,622,800	1,090,500	1,071,700	1,200,100	1,157,100	1,557,700
Long-Term Obligations	2,133,400	3,033,600	2,786,100	3,225,600	3,720,400	4,213,000	4,029,200	3,286,200
Total Liabilities	9,563,800	9,722,800	8,517,400	8,054,000	8,590,000	9,016,600	8,525,100	8,175,100
Stockholders' Equity	(375,800)	(491,400)	902,200	1,404,900	1,300,400	1,104,700	940,600	894,800
Shares Outstanding	460,600	459,000	481,500	502,400	521,500	548,800	572,100	619,400
Statistical Record								
Return on Assets %	N.M.	N.M.	2.68	8.66	8.52	8.15	11.04	13.71
Return on Equity %	N.M.	N.M.	21.89	61.94	70.88	78.07	111.48	157.75
EBITDA Margin %	24.18	10.17	10.42	21.27	21.40	21.24	24.80	27.54
Net Margin %	15.37	N.M.	4.67	15.28	15.20	14.41	18.11	21.22
Asset Turnover	0.60	0.59	0.57	0.57	0.56	0.57	0.61	0.65
Current Ratio	0.33	0.45	0.62	1.28	1.72	1.80	1.60	0.93
Debt to Equity	...	...	3.09	2.30	2.86	3.81	4.28	3.67
Price Range	21.49-18.47	22.57-18.47	22.14-16.44	22.56-16.96	18.58-15.15	19.37-13.36	19.73-11.95	21.99-14.89
P/E Ratio	...	...	43.41-32.24	13.93-10.47	11.69-9.53	13.55-9.34	11.67-7.07	11.95-8.09
Average Yield %	3.66	3.57	3.25	3.19	2.98	3.05	2.52	1.64

Address: 12500 East Belford Avenue, Englewood, CO 80112
Telephone: 866-405-5012

Web Site: www.westernunion.com
Officers: Hikmet Ersek - President, Chief Executive Officer Rajesh K. Agrawal - Executive Vice President, Chief Financial Officer, Acting Chief Financial Officer, Division Officer

Auditors: Ernst & Young LLP
Transfer Agents: Wells Fargo Bank, National Association, South St. Paul, MN

WESTLAKE CHEMICAL CORP

Exchange	Symbol	Price	52Wk Range	Yield	P/E	Div Acheiver
NYS	WLK	$107.63 (6/29/2018)	123.67-65.85	0.78	9.63	13 Years

*7 Year Price Score 134.60 *NYSE Composite Index=100 *12 Month Price Score 114.87

TRADING VOLUME (thousand shares)

Interim Earnings (Per Share)

Qtr.	Mar	Jun	Sep	Dec
2015	1.10	1.54	1.39	0.84
2016	0.94	0.85	0.51	0.77
2017	1.06	1.17	1.61	6.20
2018	2.20	...	...	...

Interim Dividends (Per Share)

Amt	Decl	Ex	Rec	Pay
0.21Q	08/18/2017	08/30/2017	09/01/2017	09/18/2017
0.21Q	11/17/2017	11/24/2017	11/27/2017	12/11/2017
0.21Q	02/16/2018	02/26/2018	02/27/2018	03/13/2018
0.21Q	05/18/2018	05/29/2018	05/30/2018	06/13/2018
		Indicated Div: $0.84		

Valuation Analysis **Institutional Holding**

Forecast EPS	$9.17	No of Institutions
	(06/14/2018)	430
Market Cap	$13.9 Billion	Shares
Book Value	$5.1 Billion	44,900,968
Price/Book	2.71	% Held
Price/Sales	1.69	27.99

Business Summary: Specialty Chemicals (MIC: 8.3.2 SIC: 2869 NAIC: 325211)

Westlake Chemical operates a manufacturer and marketer of basic chemicals, vinyls, polymers and building products. Co. operates in two operating segments: Olefins and Vinyls. The Olefins segment manufactures and markets polyethylene, styrene monomer and various ethylene co-products. The Vinyls segment manufactures and markets polyvinyl chloride (PVC), vinyl chloride monomer, ethylene dichloride, chlor-alkali (chlorine and caustic soda), chlorinated derivative products and ethylene. Co. also manufactures and sells products fabricated from PVC, including siding, pipe, fittings, profiles, trim, mouldings, fence and decking products, window and door components and film and sheet products.

Recent Developments: For the quarter ended Mar 31 2018, net income increased 104.8% to US$297.0 million from US$145.0 million in the year-earlier quarter. Revenues were US$2.15 billion, up 10.7% from US$1.94 billion the year before. Operating income was US$401.0 million versus US$234.0 million in the prior-year quarter, an increase of 71.4%. Direct operating expenses rose 2.0% to US$1.61 billion from US$1.58 billion in the comparable period the year before. Indirect operating expenses increased 6.8% to US$141.0 million from US$132.0 million in the equivalent prior-year period.

Prospects: Our evaluation of Westlake Chemical Corp. as of Jan. 21, 2018 is the result of our systematic analysis on three basic characteristics: earnings strength, relative valuation, and recent stock price movement. The company has enjoyed a very positive trend in earnings per share over the past 5 quarters and while recent estimates for the company have been raised by analysts, WLK has posted better than expected results. Based on operating earnings yield, the company is undervalued when compared to all of the companies in our coverage universe. Share price changes over the past year indicates that WLK will perform very well over the near term.

Financial Data

(US$ in Thousands)	3 Mos	12/31/2017	12/31/2016	12/31/2015	12/31/2014	12/31/2013	12/31/2012	12/31/2011
Earnings Per Share	11.18	10.05	3.06	4.86	5.07	4.54	2.88	1.94
Cash Flow Per Share	12.40	11.91	6.43	8.18	7.76	5.65	4.69	2.75
Tang Book Value Per Share	26.06	23.84	13.88	23.44	20.27	16.95	13.63	12.83
Dividends Per Share	0.821	0.801	0.744	0.693	0.582	0.412	2.136	0.137
Dividend Payout %	7.34	7.97	24.32	14.26	11.48	9.08	74.30	7.09
Income Statement								
Total Revenue	2,150,000	8,041,000	5,075,456	4,463,336	4,415,350	3,759,484	3,571,041	3,619,848
EBITDA	449,000	1,797,000	931,091	1,195,092	1,286,092	1,081,476	743,688	556,937
Depn & Amortn	26,000	557,000	305,273	209,271	174,173	129,222	120,924	110,268
Income Before Taxes	386,000	1,081,000	554,766	957,199	1,078,035	937,258	583,725	398,542
Income Taxes	89,000	(258,000)	138,520	298,396	398,902	331,747	199,614	142,466
Net Income	287,000	1,304,000	398,859	646,010	678,523	610,425	385,555	258,966
Average Shares	130,190	129,540	129,974	132,301	133,643	133,779	133,282	132,600
Balance Sheet								
Current Assets	2,959,000	3,463,000	2,408,316	2,175,189	2,011,287	1,649,082	1,751,413	1,756,156
Total Assets	11,604,000	12,076,000	10,890,253	5,575,252	5,213,990	4,060,909	3,412,196	3,266,821
Current Liabilities	1,653,000	1,967,000	1,183,083	522,642	537,180	404,858	398,510	364,595
Long-Term Obligations	2,666,000	3,127,000	3,678,654	764,115	763,997	763,879	763,761	764,563
Total Liabilities	6,463,000	7,202,000	7,366,624	2,309,374	2,302,479	1,642,306	1,539,940	1,510,509
Stockholders' Equity	5,141,000	4,874,000	3,523,629	3,265,878	2,911,511	2,418,603	1,872,256	1,756,312
Shares Outstanding	129,593	129,418	128,925	130,218	132,891	133,327	133,805	133,064
Statistical Record								
Return on Assets %	13.01	11.36	4.83	11.98	14.63	16.34	11.51	8.33
Return on Equity %	33.02	31.06	11.72	20.92	25.46	28.45	21.19	15.88
EBITDA Margin %	20.88	22.35	18.34	26.78	29.13	28.77	20.83	15.39
Net Margin %	13.35	16.22	7.86	14.47	15.37	16.24	10.80	7.15
Asset Turnover	0.74	0.70	0.61	0.83	0.95	1.01	1.07	1.16
Current Ratio	1.79	1.76	2.04	4.16	3.74	4.07	4.39	4.82
Debt to Equity	0.52	0.64	1.04	0.23	0.26	0.32	0.41	0.44
Price Range	119.95-60.09	106.53-57.29	59.17-39.88	78.59-49.82	97.96-53.67	61.03-39.31	40.05-20.43	33.09-16.16
P/E Ratio	10.73-5.37	10.60-5.70	19.34-13.03	16.17-10.25	19.32-10.59	13.44-8.66	13.90-7.09	17.06-8.33
Average Yield %	0.97	1.09	1.53	1.10	0.78	0.84	6.67	0.59

Address: 2801 Post Oak Boulevard, Suite 600, Houston, TX 77056 **Telephone:** 713-960-9111	**Web Site:** www.westlake.com **Officers:** James Chao - Chairman Albert Chao - President, Chief Executive Officer	**Auditors:** PricewaterhouseCoopers LLP **Transfer Agents:** American Stock Transfer & Trust Company, New York, NY

WESTROCK CO

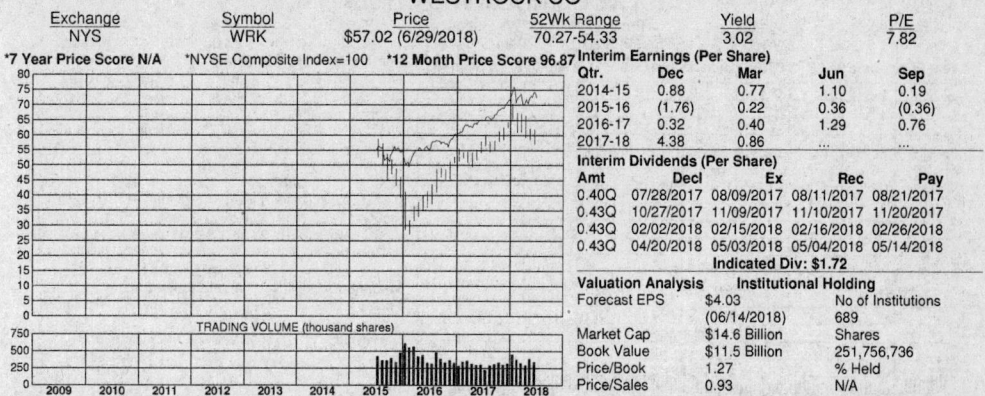

*7 Year Price Score N/A ***NYSE Composite Index=100** ***12 Month Price Score 96.87**

Interim Earnings (Per Share)

Qtr.	Dec	Mar	Jun	Sep
2014-15	0.88	0.77	1.10	0.19
2015-16	(1.76)	0.22	0.36	(0.36)
2016-17	0.32	0.40	1.29	0.76
2017-18	4.38	0.86	...	...

Interim Dividends (Per Share)

Amt	Decl	Ex	Rec	Pay
0.40Q	07/28/2017	08/09/2017	08/11/2017	08/21/2017
0.43Q	10/27/2017	11/09/2017	11/10/2017	11/20/2017
0.43Q	02/02/2018	02/15/2018	02/16/2018	02/26/2018
0.43Q	04/20/2018	05/03/2018	05/04/2018	05/14/2018

Indicated Div: $1.72

Valuation Analysis | **Institutional Holding**

Forecast EPS	$4.03	No of Institutions
	(06/14/2018)	689
Market Cap	$14.6 Billion	Shares
Book Value	$11.5 Billion	251,756,736
Price/Book	1.27	% Held
Price/Sales	0.93	N/A

TRADING VOLUME (thousand shares)

Business Summary: Containers & Packaging (MIC: 8.1.3 SIC: 2653 NAIC: 322211)

WestRock is a provider of paper and packaging solutions for consumer and corrugated packaging markets. Co.'s segments include: Corrugated Packaging, in which Co. operates an integrated corrugated packaging system that manufactures containerboard, corrugated sheets, corrugated packaging and preprinted linerboard for sale to consumer and industrial products manufacturers and corrugated box manufacturers; Consumer Packaging, in which Co. operates integrated virgin and recycled fiber paperboard mills and consumer packaging converting operations; Land and Development, in which Co. develops and sells real estate primarily in the Charleston, SC region.

Recent Developments: For the quarter ended Mar 31 2018, net income increased 128.6% to US$224.5 million from US$98.2 million in the year-earlier quarter. Revenues were US$4.02 billion, up 9.9% from US$3.66 billion the year before. Operating income was US$308.5 million versus US$187.0 million in the prior-year quarter, an increase of 65.0%. Direct operating expenses rose 8.0% to US$3.22 billion from US$2.98 billion in the comparable period the year before. Indirect operating expenses decreased 0.1% to US$488.1 million from US$488.4 million in the equivalent prior-year period.

Prospects: Our evaluation of WestRock Co. as of Jan. 21, 2018 is the result of our systematic analysis on three basic characteristics: earnings strength, relative valuation, and recent stock price movement. The company has produced a positive trend in earnings per share over the past 5 quarters. Because the company lacks sufficient analyst estimate data, we place greater weight on the historical EPS trend as the measure of earnings strength. Based on operating earnings yield, the company is about fairly valued when compared to all of the companies in our coverage universe. Share price changes over the past year indicates that WRK will perform poorly over the near term.

Financial Data
(US$ in Thousands)

	6 Mos	3 Mos	09/30/2017	09/30/2016	09/30/2015	09/30/2014	09/30/2013
Earnings Per Share	7.29	6.83	2.77	(1.54)	2.93	3.29	4.98
Cash Flow Per Share	7.10	6.85	7.54	6.63	7.06	8.02	7.17
Tang Book Value Per Share	10.35	10.04	5.83	9.37	9.36	12.07	...
Dividends Per Share	1.660	1.630	1.600	1.500	0.375	0.700	0.525
Dividend Payout %	22.77	23.87	57.76	...	12.80	21.28	10.54
Income Statement							
Total Revenue	7,911,000	3,894,000	14,859,700	14,171,800	11,381,300	9,895,100	9,545,400
EBITDA	578,700	193,800	1,952,200	1,340,500	1,477,700	1,338,500	1,274,300
Depn & Amortn	147,700	72,500	855,900	848,900	589,800	481,700	461,300
Income Before Taxes	287,900	56,500	818,600	234,900	755,200	761,500	706,100
Income Taxes	(1,054,400)	(1,073,200)	159,000	89,800	250,500	286,500	(21,800)
Net Income	1,358,300	1,135,100	708,200	(396,300)	507,100	479,700	727,300
Average Shares	260,300	259,200	255,700	257,900	173,300	146,000	146,100
Balance Sheet							
Current Assets	4,576,700	4,465,200	4,490,900	3,912,600	4,160,400	2,432,500	...
Total Assets	25,439,700	25,136,900	25,089,000	23,038,200	25,356,800	11,039,700	...
Current Liabilities	3,345,500	3,487,300	3,009,800	2,183,000	2,163,200	1,360,500	...
Long-Term Obligations	5,613,000	5,365,800	5,946,100	5,496,300	5,558,300	2,852,100	...
Total Liabilities	13,891,800	13,783,500	14,746,500	13,309,400	13,705,000	6,732,900	...
Stockholders' Equity	11,547,900	11,353,400	10,342,500	9,728,800	11,651,800	4,306,800	...
Shares Outstanding	256,400	254,900	254,500	251,000	257,000	140,000	...
Statistical Record							
Return on Assets %	7.78	7.34	2.94	N.M.	2.79	...	...
Return on Equity %	17.73	16.86	7.06	N.M.	6.36	...	...
EBITDA Margin %	7.32	4.98	13.14	9.46	12.98	13.53	13.35
Net Margin %	17.17	29.15	4.77	N.M.	4.46	4.85	7.62
Asset Turnover	0.65	0.64	0.62	0.58	0.63	...	...
Current Ratio	1.37	1.28	1.49	1.79	1.92	1.79	...
Debt to Equity	0.49	0.47	0.57	0.56	0.48	0.66	...
Price Range	70.27-49.34	64.42-49.34	59.73-45.05	51.93-27.01	58.62-45.07	...	...
P/E Ratio	9.64-6.77	9.43-7.22	21.56-16.26	...	20.01-15.38	...	...
Average Yield %	2.79	2.90	3.00	3.73	0.70	...	...

Address: 1000 Abernathy Road N.E., Atlanta, GA 30328 **Telephone:** 770-448-2193	**Web Site:** www.westrock.com **Officers:** John A. Luke - Chairman Steven C. Voorhees - President, Chief Executive Officer	**Auditors:** Ernst & Young LLP **Investor Contact:** 770-448-2193

WESTWOOD HOLDINGS GROUP, INC.

Exchange	Symbol	Price	52Wk Range	Yield	P/E	Div Acheiver
NYS	WHG	$59.54 (6/29/2018)	70.84-54.34	4.57	23.08	15 Years

*7 Year Price Score 94.95   ***NYSE Composite Index=100**   ***12 Month Price Score 93.62**

Interim Earnings (Per Share)

Qtr.	Mar	Jun	Sep	Dec
2015	0.71	1.23	0.87	0.55
2016	0.44	0.69	0.72	0.93
2017	0.73	0.83	0.49	0.33
2018	0.93	...	...	...

Interim Dividends (Per Share)

Amt	Decl	Ex	Rec	Pay
0.62Q	06/26/2017	09/07/2017	09/08/2017	10/02/2017
0.68Q	10/25/2017	12/07/2017	12/08/2017	01/02/2018
0.68Q	02/08/2018	03/08/2018	03/09/2018	04/02/2018
0.68Q	04/25/2018	06/07/2018	06/08/2018	07/02/2018

Indicated Div: $2.72

Valuation Analysis

		Institutional Holding	
Forecast EPS	N/A	No of Institutions	124
Market Cap	$536.9 Million	Shares	6,821,064
Book Value	$156.0 Million	% Held	66.27
Price/Book	3.44		
Price/Sales	3.98		

Price chart with TRADING VOLUME (thousand shares), years 2009–2018.

Business Summary: Wealth Management (MIC: 5.5.2 SIC: 6282 NAIC: 523930)

Westwood Holdings Group is a holding company. Co. manages investment assets and provides services via its subsidiaries. Westwood Management Corp., Westwood Advisors, LLC and Westwood International Advisors Inc. provide investment advisory services to institutional clients, Westwood Funds®, other mutual funds, an Ireland-domiciled fund formed pursuant to the European Union's Undertakings for Collective Investment in Transferable Securities, individuals and Westwood Trust's clients, while Westwood Trust provides trust and custodial services and participation in self-sponsored common trust funds to institutions and individuals. At Dec 31 2017, Co. had assets under management of $24.23 billion.

Recent Developments: For the year ended Dec 31 2017, net income decreased 11.7% to US$20.0 million from US$22.6 million in the prior year. Revenues were US$133.8 million, up 8.7% from US$123.0 million the year before. Indirect operating expenses increased 12.2% to US$99.9 million from US$89.0 million in the equivalent prior-year period.

Prospects: Our evaluation of Westwood Holdings Group Inc. as of Jan. 21, 2018 is the result of our systematic analysis on three basic characteristics: earnings strength, relative valuation, and recent stock price movement. The company has generated a negative trend in earnings per share over the past 5 quarters. Because the company lacks sufficient analyst estimate data, we place greater weight on the historical EPS trend as the measure of earnings strength. Based on operating earnings yield, the company is undervalued when compared to all of the companies in our coverage universe. Share price changes over the past year indicates that WHG will perform in line with the market over the near term.

Financial Data

(US$ in Thousands)	3 Mos	12/31/2017	12/31/2016	12/31/2015	12/31/2014	12/31/2013	12/31/2012	12/31/2011
Earnings Per Share	2.58	2.38	2.77	3.33	3.45	2.34	1.65	2.04
Cash Flow Per Share	4.77	5.89	5.94	7.12	3.53	2.96	1.92	2.66
Tang Book Value Per Share	13.20	12.30	11.07	9.67	11.47	9.00	7.61	7.12
Dividends Per Share	2.600	2.540	2.330	2.070	1.820	1.640	1.510	1.420
Dividend Payout %	100.78	106.72	84.12	62.16	52.75	70.09	91.52	69.61
Income Statement								
Total Revenue	33,567	133,785	123,021	130,936	113,241	91,825	77,495	68,909
EBITDA	11,118	36,809	36,939	44,816	42,974	29,038	20,847	23,871
Depn & Amortn	631	2,916	2,929	2,596	938	769	821	762
Income Before Taxes	10,487	33,893	34,010	42,220	42,036	28,269	20,026	23,109
Income Taxes	2,509	13,904	11,363	15,115	14,787	10,378	7,936	8,423
Net Income	7,978	19,989	22,647	27,105	27,249	17,891	12,090	14,686
Average Shares	8,539	8,400	8,165	8,149	7,906	7,643	7,338	7,208
Balance Sheet								
Current Assets	129,629	138,114	115,957	117,604	118,764	96,189	77,370	72,482
Total Assets	175,116	192,659	179,678	181,336	139,874	116,020	96,615	90,597
Current Liabilities	16,313	31,531	29,668	44,853	27,204	24,853	18,826	17,523
Total Liabilities	19,096	36,263	33,609	47,369	29,867	27,387	20,064	19,840
Stockholders' Equity	156,020	156,396	146,069	133,967	110,007	88,633	76,551	70,757
Shares Outstanding	9,017	8,899	8,810	8,630	8,308	8,176	8,031	7,707
Statistical Record								
Return on Assets %	12.84	10.74	12.51	16.88	21.30	16.83	12.88	17.99
Return on Equity %	14.56	13.22	16.13	22.22	27.44	21.66	16.37	22.35
EBITDA Margin %	33.12	27.51	30.03	34.23	37.95	31.62	26.90	34.64
Net Margin %	23.77	14.94	18.41	20.70	24.06	19.48	15.60	21.31
Asset Turnover	0.79	0.72	0.68	0.82	0.89	0.86	0.83	0.84
Current Ratio	7.95	4.38	3.91	2.62	4.37	3.87	4.11	4.14
Price Range	70.84-51.99	70.84-51.60	63.60-42.20	64.07-50.37	67.84-51.72	61.91-39.97	40.92-34.15	40.91-31.11
P/E Ratio	27.46-20.15	29.76-21.68	22.96-15.23	19.24-15.13	19.66-14.99	26.46-17.08	24.80-20.70	20.05-15.25
Average Yield %	4.29	4.26	4.26	3.55	3.09	3.47	3.97	3.87

Address: 200 Crescent Court, Suite 1200, Dallas, TX 75201	Web Site: www.westwoodgroup.com	Auditors: Deloitte & Touche, LLP
Telephone: 214-756-6900	Officers: Richard M. Frank - Chairman Susan M. Byrne - Vice-Chairman, Chief Investment Officer	Investor Contact: 214-756-6900
		Transfer Agents: American Stock Transfer & Trust Company, Brooklyn, NY

WEX INC

Exchange	Symbol	Price	52Wk Range	Yield	P/E
NYS	WEX	$190.48 (6/29/2018)	192.54-101.80	N/A	45.79

*7 Year Price Score 119.02 *NYSE Composite Index=100 *12 Month Price Score 127.06

TRADING VOLUME (thousand shares)

Interim Earnings (Per Share)

Qtr.	Mar	Jun	Sep	Dec
2015	0.57	0.68	0.83	0.54
2016	0.59	0.32	0.46	0.10
2017	0.68	0.40	0.79	1.85
2018	1.12	...	...	...

Interim Dividends (Per Share)

No Dividends Paid

Valuation Analysis   Institutional Holding

Forecast EPS	$8.05	No of Institutions
	(06/14/2018)	382
Market Cap	$8.2 Billion	Shares
Book Value	$1.8 Billion	56,411,976
Price/Book	4.66	% Held
Price/Sales	6.24	N/A

Business Summary: Miscellaneous Consumer Services (MIC: 2.2.3 SIC: 7389 NAIC: 561499)

Wex is a provider of corporate card payment solutions. Co. operates in three business segments: Fleet Solutions, which provides customers with fleet vehicle payment processing services specifically designed for the needs of commercial and government fleets; Travel and Corporate Solutions, which focuses on the complex payment environment of business-to-business payments, providing customers with payment processing solutions for their corporate payment and transaction monitoring needs; and Health and Employee Benefit Solutions, which is a provider of integrated software-as-a-service technologies and services for healthcare premium billing, payment and workflow management.

Recent Developments: For the quarter ended Mar 31 2018, net income increased 69.7% to US$49.3 million from US$29.1 million in the year-earlier quarter. Revenues were US$354.8 million, up 21.8% from US$291.4 million the year before. Operating income was US$78.4 million versus US$60.8 million in the prior-year quarter, an increase of 29.0%. Direct operating expenses rose 15.8% to US$134.9 million from US$116.4 million in the comparable period the year before. Indirect operating expenses increased 24.0% to US$141.6 million from US$114.2 million in the equivalent prior-year period.

Prospects: Our evaluation of Wex Inc. as of Jan. 21, 2018 is the result of our systematic analysis on three basic characteristics: earnings strength, relative valuation, and recent stock price movement. The company has produced a positive trend in earnings per share over the past 5 quarters and while recent estimates for the company have been mixed, WEX has posted better than expected results. Based on operating earnings yield, the company is about fairly valued when compared to all of the companies in our coverage universe. Share price changes over the past year indicates that WEX will perform poorly over the near term.

Financial Data

(US$ in Thousands)	3 Mos	12/31/2017	12/31/2016	12/31/2015	12/31/2014	12/31/2013	12/31/2012	12/31/2011
Earnings Per Share	4.16	3.72	1.48	2.62	5.18	3.82	2.48	3.43
Cash Flow Per Share	6.44	3.09	(3.69)	11.48	7.62	1.02	1.84	1.32
Tang Book Value Per Share	N.M.	N.M.	N.M.	N.M.	N.M.	N.M.	N.M.	1.29
Income Statement								
Total Revenue	354,829	1,250,548	1,018,460	854,637	817,647	717,463	623,151	553,076
EBITDA	89,049	406,901	241,137	273,613	378,456	300,895	260,025	259,427
Depn & Amortn	24,126	203,724	141,650	83,077	70,380	58,208	48,852	45,369
Income Before Taxes	64,923	178,695	87,101	184,908	301,639	238,400	206,183	208,605
Income Taxes	15,589	19,525	29,625	75,296	101,621	90,102	109,474	74,983
Net Income	48,633	160,266	60,637	111,317	202,211	149,208	96,922	133,622
Average Shares	43,450	43,105	40,914	38,843	39,000	39,103	39,092	38,998
Balance Sheet								
Current Assets	3,421,209	3,186,147	2,353,813	1,881,325	2,198,131	2,073,547	1,753,476	1,357,871
Total Assets	6,755,620	6,739,175	5,997,097	3,857,946	4,118,347	3,433,043	3,106,684	2,278,060
Current Liabilities	2,356,889	2,429,514	2,067,520	1,408,241	1,542,736	1,710,209	1,537,266	1,164,518
Long-Term Obligations	2,132,283	2,424,971	2,204,903	1,201,819	1,354,539	685,000	621,000	295,300
Total Liabilities	4,995,642	5,027,837	4,499,908	2,774,702	3,058,022	2,530,265	2,288,753	1,568,745
Stockholders' Equity	1,759,978	1,711,338	1,497,189	1,083,244	1,060,325	902,778	817,931	709,315
Shares Outstanding	43,072	43,022	42,841	38,746	38,897	38,987	38,908	38,765
Statistical Record								
Return on Assets %	2.78	2.52	1.23	2.79	5.36	4.56	3.59	6.11
Return on Equity %	10.88	9.99	4.69	10.39	20.60	17.34	12.66	21.07
EBITDA Margin %	25.10	32.54	23.68	32.02	46.29	41.94	41.73	46.91
Net Margin %	13.71	12.82	5.95	13.03	24.73	20.80	15.55	24.16
Asset Turnover	0.20	0.20	0.21	0.21	0.22	0.22	0.23	0.25
Current Ratio	1.45	1.31	1.14	1.34	1.42	1.21	1.14	1.17
Debt to Equity	1.21	1.42	1.47	1.11	1.28	0.76	0.76	0.42
Price Range	160.90-98.27	141.23-98.27	116.44-58.09	118.50-84.66	118.43-79.93	100.38-67.91	75.37-53.29	57.05-36.36
P/E Ratio	38.68-23.62	37.97-26.42	78.68-39.25	45.23-32.31	22.86-15.43	26.28-17.78	30.39-21.49	16.63-10.60

Address: 97 Darling Avenue, South Portland, ME 04106 Telephone: 207-773-8171	Web Site: www.wexinc.com Officers: Melissa D. Smith - President, Chief Executive Officer, Region Officer Kenneth W. Janosick - Senior Vice President, General Manager	Auditors: DELOITTE & TOUCHE LLP Investor Contact: 866-230-1633 Transfer Agents: American Stock Transfer & Trust Company, Brooklyn, NY

WEYERHAEUSER CO

Exchange	Symbol	Price	52Wk Range	Yield	P/E
NYS	WY	$36.46 (6/29/2018)	38.36-31.17	3.51	40.07

*7 Year Price Score 95.36 *NYSE Composite Index=100 *12 Month Price Score 103.50

Interim Earnings (Per Share)

Qtr.	Mar	Jun	Sep	Dec
2015	0.17	0.26	0.35	0.12
2016	0.11	0.21	0.30	0.75
2017	0.21	0.03	0.17	0.36
2018	0.35	...	...	...

Interim Dividends (Per Share)

Amt	Decl	Ex	Rec	Pay
0.31Q	08/24/2017	09/07/2017	09/08/2017	09/22/2017
0.32Q	11/09/2017	11/30/2017	12/01/2017	12/15/2017
0.32Q	02/08/2018	03/01/2018	03/02/2018	03/23/2018
0.32Q	05/17/2018	06/07/2018	06/08/2018	06/22/2018

Indicated Div: $1.28

Valuation Analysis / Institutional Holding

Forecast EPS	$1.48 (06/13/2018)	No of Institutions	1303
Market Cap	$27.6 Billion	Shares	710,391,296
Book Value	$9.0 Billion	% Held	88.32
Price/Book	3.07		
Price/Sales	3.74		

Business Summary: REITs (MIC: 5.3.1 SIC: 6798 NAIC: 525930)

Weyerhaeuser is a real estate investment trust. As of Dec. 31, 2017, Co. manages 12.4 million acres of private commercial timberlands where Co. owns 11.5 million of those acres and have leases on the other 900 thousand acres. In addition, Co. has renewable, long-term licenses on 14.0 million acres of Canadian timberlands. Co. has three segments: Timberlands, which include grade logs, fiber logs, timber, recreational leases and other products; Real Estate, Energy and Natural Resources, which maximizes the value of Co.'s timberland ownership through development of oil, natural gas, minerals and wind resources; and Wood Products, where Co. manufactures and distributes wood products.

Recent Developments: For the quarter ended Mar 31 2018, net income increased 71.3% to US$269.0 million from US$157.0 million in the year-earlier quarter. Revenues were US$1.87 billion, up 10.2% from US$1.69 billion the year before.

Prospects: Our evaluation of Weyerhaeuser Co. as of Jan. 21, 2018 is the result of our systematic analysis on three basic characteristics: earnings strength, relative valuation, and recent stock price movement. The company has enjoyed a very positive trend in earnings per share over the past 5 quarters and while recent estimates for the company have been mixed, WY has posted better than expected results. Based on operating earnings yield, the company is about fairly valued when compared to all of the companies in our coverage universe. Share price changes over the past year indicates that WY will perform well over the near term.

Financial Data

(US$ in Thousands)	3 Mos	12/31/2017	12/31/2016	12/31/2015	12/31/2014	12/31/2013	12/31/2012	12/31/2011
Earnings Per Share	0.91	0.77	1.39	0.89	3.18	0.95	0.71	0.61
Cash Flow Per Share	1.72	1.59	1.02	2.06	1.95	1.77	1.07	0.54
Tang Book Value Per Share	11.83	11.73	12.21	9.43	10.01	11.55	7.43	7.87
Dividends Per Share	1.260	1.250	1.240	1.200	1.020	0.810	0.620	0.600
Dividend Payout %	138.46	162.34	89.21	134.83	32.08	85.26	87.32	98.36
Income Statement								
Total Revenue	1,865,000	7,196,000	6,365,000	7,082,000	7,403,000	8,529,000	7,059,000	6,216,000
EBITDA	500,000	1,275,000	1,068,000	1,233,000	1,820,000	1,219,000	1,191,000	1,074,000
Depn & Amortn	120,000	206,000	198,000	314,000	500,000	472,000	456,000	480,000
Income Before Taxes	299,000	715,000	482,000	608,000	1,013,000	434,000	439,000	257,000
Income Taxes	30,000	134,000	89,000	(3,000)	185,000	(129,000)	55,000	(62,000)
Net Income	269,000	582,000	1,027,000	506,000	1,826,000	563,000	385,000	331,000
Average Shares	759,462	756,666	722,401	519,618	560,899	571,239	542,310	539,879
Balance Sheet								
Current Assets	1,919,000	1,715,000	1,622,000	2,174,000	3,033,000	2,326,000	2,140,000	2,068,000
Total Assets	17,885,000	18,059,000	19,243,000	12,486,000	13,457,000	14,498,000	12,592,000	12,598,000
Current Liabilities	911,000	1,165,000	1,206,000	875,000	918,000	1,128,000	1,230,000	941,000
Long-Term Obligations	6,230,000	6,232,000	6,840,000	5,402,000	5,402,000	5,407,000	3,951,000	4,466,000
Total Liabilities	8,894,000	9,160,000	10,063,000	7,617,000	8,153,000	7,703,000	8,522,000	8,335,000
Stockholders' Equity	8,991,000	8,899,000	9,180,000	4,869,000	5,304,000	6,795,000	4,070,000	4,263,000
Shares Outstanding	756,699	755,222	748,528	510,483	524,474	583,548	542,392	536,425
Statistical Record								
Return on Assets %	3.76	3.12	6.46	3.90	13.06	4.16	3.05	2.54
Return on Equity %	7.62	6.44	14.58	9.95	30.18	10.36	9.22	7.46
EBITDA Margin %	26.81	17.72	16.78	17.41	24.58	14.29	16.87	17.28
Net Margin %	14.42	8.09	16.14	7.14	24.67	6.60	5.45	5.32
Asset Turnover	0.40	0.39	0.40	0.55	0.53	0.63	0.56	0.48
Current Ratio	2.11	1.47	1.34	2.48	3.30	2.06	1.74	2.20
Debt to Equity	0.69	0.70	0.70	1.11	1.02	0.80	0.97	1.05
Price Range	37.85-31.17	36.55-30.21	33.12-22.22	36.69-26.87	36.64-27.72	32.60-26.65	28.52-18.69	25.20-15.25
P/E Ratio	41.59-34.25	47.47-39.23	23.83-15.99	41.22-30.19	11.52-8.72	34.32-28.05	40.17-26.32	41.31-25.00
Average Yield %	3.68	3.72	4.13	3.79	3.20	2.73	2.68	2.98

Address: 220 Occidental Avenue South, Seattle, WA 98104-7800	Web Site: www.weyerhaeuser.com	Auditors: KPMG LLP
Telephone: 206-539-3000	Officers: Rick R. Holley - Chairman Doyle R. Simons - President, Chief Executive Officer	Investor Contact: 253-924-2058
		Transfer Agents: Computershare Investor Services, Canton, MA

WHIRLPOOL CORP

Exchange	Symbol	Price	52Wk Range	Yield	P/E
NYS	WHR	$146.23 (6/29/2018)	198.34-143.89	3.15	36.47

*7 Year Price Score 95.44 ***NYSE Composite Index=100** ***12 Month Price Score 89.92**

TRADING VOLUME (thousand shares)

Interim Earnings (Per Share)

Qtr.	Mar	Jun	Sep	Dec
2015	2.38	2.21	2.95	2.29
2016	1.92	4.15	3.10	2.34
2017	2.01	2.52	3.72	(3.53)
2018	1.30	...	...	...

Interim Dividends (Per Share)

Amt	Decl	Ex	Rec	Pay
1.10Q	08/15/2017	08/23/2017	08/25/2017	09/15/2017
1.10Q	10/16/2017	11/16/2017	11/17/2017	12/15/2017
1.10Q	02/20/2018	03/01/2018	03/02/2018	03/15/2018
1.15Q	04/16/2018	05/17/2018	05/18/2018	06/15/2018

Indicated Div: $4.60

Valuation Analysis / Institutional Holding

Forecast EPS	$15.70	No of Institutions
	(06/14/2018)	906
Market Cap	$10.4 Billion	Shares
Book Value	$4.3 Billion	83,282,520
Price/Book	2.42	% Held
Price/Sales	0.49	89.99

Business Summary: Household Appliances, Electronics & Goods (MIC: 1.5.1 SIC: 3639 NAIC: 335228)

Whirlpool manufactures and markets a line of home appliances and related products. Co.'s principal products are laundry appliances, refrigerators and freezers, cooking appliances, dishwashers, mixers and other small domestic appliances. Co. also produces hermetic compressors for refrigeration systems. Co. manufactures and markets products under brand names such as Whirlpool, KitchenAid, Maytag, Consul, Brastemp, Amana, Bauknecht, Jenn-Air, Indesit, and Hotpoint. Co.'s reportable segments consist of North America, Europe, Middle East and Africa, Latin America and Asia.

Recent Developments: For the quarter ended Mar 31 2018, net income decreased 40.5% to US$94.0 million from US$158.0 million in the year-earlier quarter. Revenues were US$4.91 billion, up 2.6% from US$4.79 billion the year before. Operating income was US$143.0 million versus US$264.0 million in the prior-year quarter, a decrease of 45.8%. Direct operating expenses rose 3.5% to US$4.10 billion from US$3.96 billion in the comparable period the year before. Indirect operating expenses increased 19.0% to US$669.0 million from US$562.0 million in the equivalent prior-year period.

Prospects: Our evaluation of Whirlpool Corp. as of Jan. 21, 2018 is the result of our systematic analysis on three basic characteristics: earnings strength, relative valuation, and recent stock price movement. The company has produced a positive trend in earnings per share over the past 5 quarters. However, while recent estimates for the company have been mixed, WHR has posted results that fell short of analysts' expectations. Based on operating earnings yield, the company is undervalued when compared to all of the companies in our coverage universe. Share price changes over the past year indicates that WHR will perform in line with the market over the near term.

Financial Data

(US$ in Thousands)	3 Mos	12/31/2017	12/31/2016	12/31/2015	12/31/2014	12/31/2013	12/31/2012	12/31/2011
Earnings Per Share	4.01	4.70	11.50	9.83	8.17	10.24	5.06	4.99
Cash Flow Per Share	13.85	17.24	15.76	15.57	18.89	15.91	8.89	6.90
Tang Book Value Per Share	N.M.	N.M.	N.M.	N.M.	N.M.	19.35	10.34	9.12
Dividends Per Share	4.400	4.300	3.900	3.450	2.875	2.375	2.000	1.930
Dividend Payout %	109.73	91.49	33.91	35.10	35.19	23.19	39.53	38.68
Income Statement								
Total Revenue	4,911,000	21,253,000	20,718,000	20,891,000	19,872,000	18,769,000	18,143,000	18,666,000
EBITDA	163,000	1,790,000	2,009,000	1,953,000	1,748,000	1,789,000	1,420,000	1,350,000
Depn & Amortn	20,000	654,000	655,000	668,000	560,000	540,000	551,000	558,000
Income Before Taxes	109,000	887,000	1,114,000	1,031,000	881,000	917,000	558,000	(28,000)
Income Taxes	15,000	550,000	186,000	209,000	189,000	68,000	133,000	(436,000)
Net Income	94,000	350,000	888,000	783,000	650,000	827,000	401,000	390,000
Average Shares	72,100	74,400	77,200	79,700	79,600	80,800	79,300	78,100
Balance Sheet								
Current Assets	8,091,000	7,930,000	7,339,000	7,325,000	8,098,000	7,022,000	6,827,000	6,422,000
Total Assets	20,339,000	20,038,000	19,153,000	19,010,000	20,002,000	15,544,000	15,396,000	15,181,000
Current Liabilities	8,943,000	8,505,000	7,662,000	7,744,000	8,403,000	6,794,000	6,510,000	6,297,000
Long-Term Obligations	4,190,000	4,392,000	3,876,000	3,470,000	3,544,000	1,846,000	1,944,000	2,129,000
Total Liabilities	16,050,000	15,840,000	14,380,000	14,267,000	15,117,000	10,620,000	11,136,000	11,000,000
Stockholders' Equity	4,289,000	4,198,000	4,773,000	4,743,000	4,885,000	4,924,000	4,260,000	4,181,000
Shares Outstanding	71,000	71,000	74,465	77,221	77,956	77,417	78,407	76,451
Statistical Record								
Return on Assets %	1.46	1.79	4.64	4.01	3.66	5.35	2.62	2.54
Return on Equity %	6.39	7.80	18.61	16.27	13.25	18.01	9.48	9.28
EBITDA Margin %	3.32	8.42	9.70	9.35	8.80	9.53	7.83	7.23
Net Margin %	1.91	1.65	4.29	3.75	3.27	4.41	2.21	2.09
Asset Turnover	1.07	1.08	1.08	1.07	1.12	1.21	1.18	1.21
Current Ratio	0.90	0.93	0.96	0.95	0.96	1.03	1.05	1.02
Debt to Equity	0.98	1.05	0.81	0.73	0.73	0.37	0.46	0.51
Price Range	198.34-151.17	198.34-160.94	192.38-127.21	215.00-142.27	193.74-126.69	157.80-101.75	102.73-48.51	91.28-45.37
P/E Ratio	49.46-37.70	42.20-34.24	16.73-11.06	21.87-14.47	23.71-15.51	15.41-9.94	20.30-9.59	18.29-9.09
Average Yield %	2.52	2.43	2.33	1.93	1.88	1.86	2.69	2.75

Address: 2000 North M-63, Benton Harbor, MI 49022-2692	Web Site: www.whirlpoolcorp.com	Auditors: Ernst & Young LLP
Telephone: 269-923-5000	Officers: Jeff M. Fettig - Executive Chairman, Chief Executive Officer Marc R. Bitzer - Vice-Chairman, President, Chief Operating Officer, Chief Executive Officer, Region Officer	Investor Contact: 269-923-2641 Transfer Agents: Computershare Trust Company, N.A., Providence, RI

WHITE MOUNTAINS INSURANCE GROUP LTD

Exchange	Symbol	Price	52Wk Range	Yield	P/E
NYS	WTM	$906.61 (6/29/2018)	925.57-789.05	0.11	6.85

*7 Year Price Score 102.49 *NYSE Composite Index=100 *12 Month Price Score 103.13

Interim Earnings (Per Share)

Qtr.	Mar	Jun	Sep	Dec
2015	14.09	0.72	(10.01)	45.63
2016	2.34	66.79	18.80	(3.94)
2017	7.50	3.39	130.81	11.00
2018	(12.82)	...	...	...

Interim Dividends (Per Share)

Amt	Decl	Ex	Rec	Pay
1.00A	02/26/2015	03/12/2015	03/16/2015	03/25/2015
1.00A	02/26/2016	03/17/2016	03/21/2016	03/30/2016
1.00A	03/02/2017	03/16/2017	03/20/2017	03/29/2017
1.00A	03/02/2018	03/16/2018	03/19/2018	03/28/2018

Indicated Div: $1.00

Valuation Analysis

Forecast EPS	N/A
Market Cap	$3.4 Billion
Book Value	$3.4 Billion
Price/Book	0.99
Price/Sales	10.34

Institutional Holding

No of Institutions	318
Shares	4,147,356
% Held	76.85

TRADING VOLUME (thousand shares)

Business Summary: General Insurance (MIC: 5.2.1 SIC: 6331 NAIC: 524126)

White Mountains Insurance Group is an insurance holding company. Co.'s segments are MediaAlpha, a marketing technology company that develops technology that enables the programmatic buying and selling of vertical-specific, performance-based media between advertisers and publishers; HG Global/BAM, which consists of HG Global Ltd that provides 15%-of-par, first loss reinsurance protection for policies, and Build America Mutual Assurance Company, a mutual bond insurance company; and Other Operations, which consists of Co. and its intermediate holding companies, its wholly-owned investment management subsidiary and certain consolidated and unconsolidated private capital investments.

Recent Developments: For the quarter ended Mar 31 2018, loss from continuing operations was US$66.7 million compared with a loss of US$3.3 million in the year-earlier quarter. Net loss amounted to US$66.6 million versus net income of US$28.0 million in the year-earlier quarter. Revenues were US$42.1 million, down 52.6% from US$88.8 million the year before. Net premiums earned were unchanged at US$3.0 million versus the prior-year quarter. Net investment income rose 53.9% to US$19.7 million from US$12.8 million a year ago.

Prospects: Our evaluation of White Mountains Insurance Group Ltd. as of Sep. 17, 2017 is the result of our systematic analysis on three basic characteristics: earnings strength, relative valuation, and recent stock price movement. The company has produced a positive trend in earnings per share over the past 5 quarters. Because the company lacks sufficient analyst estimate data, we place greater weight on the historical EPS trend as the measure of earnings strength. Based on operating earnings yield, the company is overvalued when compared to all of the companies in our coverage universe. Share price changes over the past year indicates that WTM will perform in line with the market over the near term.

Financial Data

(US$ in Thousands)	3 Mos	12/31/2017	12/31/2016	12/31/2015	12/31/2014	12/31/2013	12/31/2012	12/31/2011
Earnings Per Share	132.38	146.06	82.19	50.60	51.21	51.89	30.50	97.44
Cash Flow Per Share	28.57	22.31	(31.29)	30.23	19.71	(16.53)	(33.57)	(14.66)
Tang Book Value Per Share	900.46	914.73	777.29	629.03	606.43	632.29	593.20	539.43
Dividends Per Share	...	1.000	1.000	1.000	1.000	1.000	1.000	1.000
Dividend Payout %	...	0.68	1.22	1.98	1.95	1.93	3.28	1.03
Income Statement								
Premium Income	3,000	10,400	1,114,000	1,188,200	2,058,900	1,987,300	2,063,600	1,927,800
Total Revenue	42,100	373,800	1,360,700	1,808,600	2,510,200	2,317,400	2,435,700	2,178,100
Benefits & Claims	...	1,100	664,000	708,900	1,169,300	1,040,500	1,193,900	1,206,900
Income Before Taxes	(66,000)	7,800	(40,400)	154,900	301,700	344,900	262,800	61,600
Income Taxes	700	(7,800)	(45,400)	(700)	53,300	76,600	(15,700)	(122,700)
Net Income	(48,000)	627,200	412,500	297,600	312,700	321,800	207,400	767,900
Average Shares	3,710	4,239	4,953	5,811	6,026	6,109	6,708	7,811
Balance Sheet								
Total Assets	3,587,000	3,659,200	6,544,700	10,284,500	10,456,900	12,144,300	12,895,400	14,064,000
Total Liabilities	148,000	166,700	2,941,400	6,371,300	6,460,300	8,238,800	9,163,600	9,976,300
Stockholders' Equity	3,439,000	3,492,500	3,603,300	3,913,200	3,996,600	3,905,500	3,731,800	4,087,700
Shares Outstanding	3,753	3,750	4,563	5,623	5,986	6,176	6,290	7,577
Statistical Record								
Return on Assets %	10.93	12.29	4.89	2.87	2.77	2.57	1.53	5.37
Return on Equity %	15.63	17.68	10.95	7.52	7.91	8.43	5.29	19.84
Loss Ratio %	...	10.58	59.61	59.66	56.79	52.36	57.86	62.61
Net Margin %	(114.01)	167.79	30.32	16.45	12.46	13.89	8.52	35.26
Price Range	895.90-789.05	947.00-839.51	868.00-699.47	808.00-618.00	674.71-559.26	610.50-515.00	547.67-439.94	453.46-335.60
P/E Ratio	6.77-5.96	6.48-5.75	10.56-8.51	15.97-12.21	13.18-10.92	11.77-9.92	17.96-14.42	4.65-3.44
Average Yield %	0.11	0.11	0.12	0.14	0.16	0.17	0.20	0.25

Address: 14 Wesley Street, 5th Floor, Hamilton, HM 11 **Telephone:** 441-278-3160 **Fax:** 441-278-3170	**Web Site:** www.whitemountains.com **Officers:** George Manning Rountree - Chief Executive Officer Reid T. Campbell - Executive Vice President, Chief Financial Officer	**Auditors:** PricewaterhouseCoopers LLP **Investor Contact:** 203-458-5850 **Transfer Agents:** Computershare Trust Company, N.A., Providence, RI, United States

WHITING PETROLEUM CORP

Exchange	Symbol	Price	52Wk Range	Yield	P/E
NYS	WLL	$52.72 (6/29/2018)	55.46-16.00	N/A	N/A

*7 Year Price Score 17.30   *NYSE Composite Index=100   *12 Month Price Score 165.95

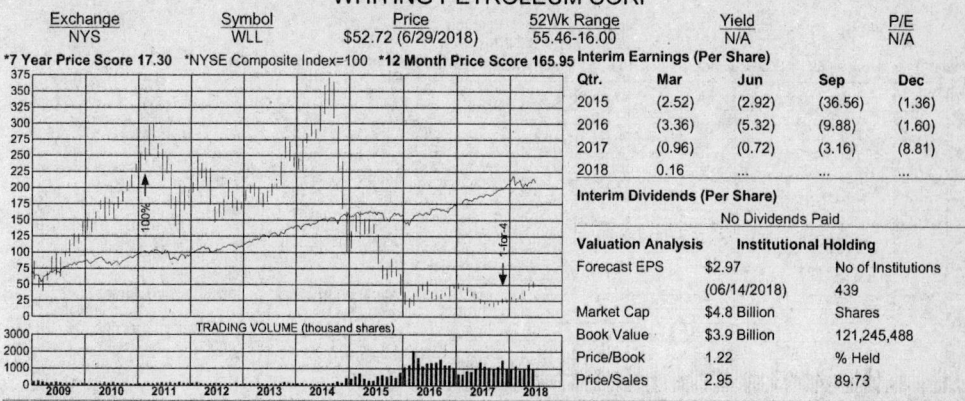

Interim Earnings (Per Share)

Qtr.	Mar	Jun	Sep	Dec
2015	(2.52)	(2.92)	(36.56)	(1.36)
2016	(3.36)	(5.32)	(9.88)	(1.60)
2017	(0.96)	(0.72)	(3.16)	(8.81)
2018	0.16	...	...	...

Interim Dividends (Per Share)

No Dividends Paid

Valuation Analysis

Valuation Analysis		Institutional Holding	
Forecast EPS	$2.97	No of Institutions	
	(06/14/2018)	439	
Market Cap	$4.8 Billion	Shares	
Book Value	$3.9 Billion	121,245,488	
Price/Book	1.22	% Held	
Price/Sales	2.95	89.73	

Business Summary: Production & Extraction (MIC: 9.1.1 SIC: 1311 NAIC: 211111)

Whiting Petroleum is an independent oil and gas company engaged in the development, acquisition, exploration and production of crude oil, natural gas liquids and natural gas primarily in the Rocky Mountains and Permian Basin regions of the U.S. Co. sells its oil and gas production to end users, marketers and other purchasers that have access to nearby pipeline facilities. As of Dec 31 2017, Co. had estimated total proved reserves of 617.6 million barrels of oil equivalent, consisting of 337.6 million barrels of oil, 138.9 million barrels of natural gas liquids and 846.5 billion cubic feet of natural gas.

Recent Developments: For the quarter ended Mar 31 2018, net income amounted to US$15.0 million versus a net loss of US$87.0 million in the year-earlier quarter. Revenues were US$515.1 million, up 38.7% from US$371.3 million the year before. Operating income was US$98.2 million versus a loss of US$77.5 million in the prior-year quarter. Direct operating expenses rose 6.5% to US$130.4 million from US$122.4 million in the comparable period the year before. Indirect operating expenses decreased 12.2% to US$286.5 million from US$326.4 million in the equivalent prior-year period.

Prospects: Our evaluation of Whiting Petroleum Corp. as of Jan. 21, 2018 is the result of our systematic analysis on three basic characteristics: earnings strength, relative valuation, and recent stock price movement. The company has suffered a very negative trend in earnings per share over the past 5 quarters. Because the company lacks sufficient analyst estimate data, we place greater weight on the historical EPS trend as the measure of earnings strength. Based on operating earnings yield, the company is overvalued when compared to all of the companies in our coverage universe. Share price changes over the past year indicates that WLL will perform very poorly over the near term.

Financial Data
(US$ in Thousands)

	3 Mos	12/31/2017	12/31/2016	12/31/2015	12/31/2014	12/31/2013	12/31/2012	12/31/2011
Earnings Per Share	(12.53)	(13.65)	(21.28)	(45.40)	2.12	12.24	13.92	16.56
Cash Flow Per Share	8.03	6.36	9.42	21.51	59.45	59.01	47.53	40.64
Tang Book Value Per Share	43.28	43.21	56.81	93.08	115.51	129.06	117.15	102.94
Income Statement								
Total Revenue	515,083	1,481,435	1,284,982	2,050,798	3,085,097	2,828,385	2,173,452	1,899,622
EBITDA	73,498	(1,522,017)	(860,671)	(2,649,706)	320,051	689,507	740,893	845,523
Depn & Amortn	6,467	7,536	8,479	9,664	5,494	4,700	3,672	2,688
Income Before Taxes	15,012	(1,720,641)	(1,426,770)	(2,993,495)	143,915	571,871	662,011	780,319
Income Taxes	...	(482,979)	(87,646)	(774,227)	79,170	205,868	247,912	288,691
Net Income	15,012	(1,237,648)	(1,339,102)	(2,219,182)	64,807	366,055	414,189	491,687
Average Shares	91,310	90,683	62,967	48,868	30,629	29,897	29,757	29,667
Balance Sheet								
Current Assets	328,529	1,189,628	622,602	535,190	842,999	1,069,618	384,412	298,703
Total Assets	7,532,708	8,403,034	9,876,142	11,389,085	14,019,504	8,833,470	7,272,419	6,045,609
Current Liabilities	567,984	1,553,328	478,331	599,813	1,208,516	777,685	636,979	567,034
Long-Term Obligations	2,861,428	2,764,716	3,535,303	5,197,704	5,628,782	2,653,834	1,800,000	1,380,000
Total Liabilities	3,597,095	4,483,892	4,734,912	6,638,481	8,324,530	5,004,903	3,827,431	3,024,752
Stockholders' Equity	3,935,613	3,919,142	5,141,230	4,750,604	5,694,974	3,828,567	3,444,988	3,020,857
Shares Outstanding	90,927	90,698	90,503	51,036	41,722	29,664	29,407	29,345
Statistical Record								
Return on Assets %	N.M.	N.M.	N.M.	N.M.	0.57	4.55	6.20	9.20
Return on Equity %	N.M.	N.M.	N.M.	N.M.	1.36	10.07	12.78	17.71
EBITDA Margin %	14.27	N.M.	N.M.	N.M.	10.37	24.38	34.09	44.51
Net Margin %	2.91	N.M.	N.M.	N.M.	2.10	12.94	19.06	25.88
Asset Turnover	0.19	0.16	0.12	0.16	0.27	0.35	0.33	0.36
Current Ratio	0.58	0.77	1.30	0.89	0.70	1.38	0.60	0.53
Debt to Equity	0.73	0.71	0.69	1.09	0.99	0.69	0.52	0.46
Price Range	38.68-16.00	52.40-16.00	55.40-14.12	163.80-33.24	370.64-100.16	279.00-169.92	249.88-145.64	298.00-122.64
P/E Ratio	...	...	...	...	174.83-47.25	22.79-13.88	17.95-10.46	18.00-7.41

Address: 1700 Broadway, Suite 2300, Denver, CO 80290-2300	**Web Site:** www.whiting.com	**Auditors:** Deloitte & Touche LLP
Telephone: 303-837-1661	**Officers:** Bradley J. Holly - President, Chief Executive Officer Bruce R. DeBoer - Senior Vice President, Vice President, Secretary, General Counsel	**Investor Contact:** 303-390-4051
Fax: 303-861-4023		

WILEY (JOHN) & SONS INC.

Exchange	Symbol	Price	52Wk Range	Yield	P/E	Div Acheiver
NYS	JW A	$62.40 (6/29/2018)	70.80-51.95	2.12	18.80	24 Years

*7 Year Price Score 93.69   *NYSE Composite Index=100   *12 Month Price Score 108.73

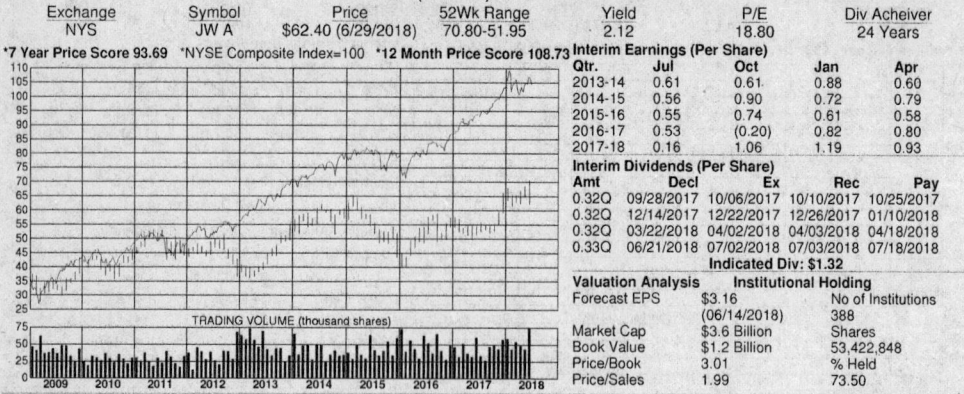

Interim Earnings (Per Share)

Qtr.	Jul	Oct	Jan	Apr
2013-14	0.61	0.61	0.88	0.60
2014-15	0.56	0.90	0.72	0.79
2015-16	0.55	0.74	0.61	0.58
2016-17	0.53	(0.20)	0.82	0.80
2017-18	0.16	1.06	1.19	0.93

Interim Dividends (Per Share)

Amt	Decl	Ex	Rec	Pay
0.32Q	09/28/2017	10/06/2017	10/10/2017	10/25/2017
0.32Q	12/14/2017	12/22/2017	12/26/2017	01/10/2018
0.32Q	03/22/2018	04/02/2018	04/03/2018	04/18/2018
0.33Q	06/21/2018	07/02/2018	07/03/2018	07/18/2018

Indicated Div: $1.32

Valuation Analysis

		Institutional Holding	
Forecast EPS	$3.16	No of Institutions	
	(06/14/2018)	388	
Market Cap	$3.6 Billion	Shares	
Book Value	$1.2 Billion	53,422,848	
Price/Book	3.01	% Held	
Price/Sales	1.99	73.50	

Business Summary: Publishing (MIC: 2.3.3 SIC: 2731 NAIC: 511130)

John Wiley & Sons is a global research and learning company. Co. has three segments: Research segment, which provides scientific, technical, medical, and scholarly journals, as well as related content and services to libraries and individual researchers, among others; Publishing, which provides scientific, professional, and education books and related content in print and digital formats, test preparation services and course workflow tools, to libraries, corporations, students, professionals, and researchers; and Solutions, which provides online program management services for higher education institutions and learning, development, and assessment services for businesses and professionals.

Recent Developments: For the year ended Apr 30 2018, net income increased 69.1% to US$192.2 million from US$113.6 million in the prior year. Revenues were US$1.80 billion, up 4.5% from US$1.72 billion the year before. Operating income was US$239.5 million versus US$206.2 million in the prior year, an increase of 16.2%. Direct operating expenses rose 5.3% to US$485.2 million from US$460.8 million in the comparable period the year before. Indirect operating expenses increased 1.9% to US$1.07 billion from US$1.05 billion in the equivalent prior-year period.

Prospects: Our evaluation of Wiley (John) & Sons Inc. as of Jan. 21, 2018 is the result of our systematic analysis on three basic characteristics: earnings strength, relative valuation, and recent stock price movement. The company has generated a negative trend in earnings per share over the past 5 quarters. However, while recent estimates for the company have been mixed; JW.A has posted better than expected results. Based on operating earnings yield, the company is undervalued when compared to all of the companies in our coverage universe. Share price changes over the past year indicates that JW.A will perform in line with the market over the near term.

Financial Data

(US$ in Thousands)	04/30/2018	04/30/2017	04/30/2016	04/30/2015	04/30/2014	04/30/2013	04/30/2012	04/30/2011
Earnings Per Share	3.32	1.95	2.48	2.97	2.70	2.39	3.47	2.80
Cash Flow Per Share	6.69	5.49	6.02	6.05	5.94	5.67	6.29	6.24
Dividends Per Share	1.280	1.240	1.200	1.160	1.000	0.960	0.800	0.640
Dividend Payout %	38.55	63.59	48.39	39.06	37.04	40.17	23.05	22.86
Income Statement								
Total Revenue	1,796,103	1,718,530	1,727,037	1,822,440	1,775,195	1,760,778	1,782,742	1,742,551
EBITDA	339,273	322,926	304,777	352,767	309,665	295,385	365,305	327,045
Depn & Amortn	112,557	116,352	116,191	113,286	103,000	97,999	87,147	81,085
Income Before Taxes	213,931	191,116	174,793	225,461	195,534	186,922	272,095	231,060
Income Taxes	21,745	77,473	29,011	48,593	35,024	42,697	59,349	59,171
Net Income	192,186	113,643	145,782	176,868	160,510	144,225	212,746	171,889
Average Shares	57,888	58,199	58,734	59,594	59,514	60,224	61,272	61,359
Balance Sheet								
Current Assets	479,971	359,735	670,679	740,919	789,662	634,971	574,600	527,490
Total Assets	2,839,451	2,606,217	2,921,096	3,004,243	3,077,365	2,806,375	2,532,946	2,430,141
Current Liabilities	874,311	787,856	781,807	803,683	729,587	667,169	640,930	756,365
Long-Term Obligations	360,000	365,000	605,007	650,090	700,100	673,000	475,000	330,500
Total Liabilities	1,648,894	1,603,080	1,883,990	1,949,203	1,895,117	1,818,019	1,515,378	1,452,252
Stockholders' Equity	1,190,557	1,003,137	1,037,106	1,055,040	1,182,248	988,356	1,017,568	977,889
Shares Outstanding	57,410	57,167	57,564	58,838	59,052	58,670	59,515	60,709
Statistical Record								
Return on Assets %	7.06	4.11	4.91	5.82	5.46	5.40	8.55	7.24
Return on Equity %	17.52	11.14	13.90	15.81	14.79	14.38	21.26	20.22
EBITDA Margin %	18.89	18.79	17.65	19.36	17.44	16.78	20.49	18.77
Net Margin %	10.70	6.61	8.44	9.71	9.04	8.19	11.93	9.86
Asset Turnover	0.66	0.62	0.58	0.60	0.60	0.66	0.72	0.73
Current Ratio	0.55	0.46	0.86	0.92	1.08	0.95	0.90	0.70
Debt to Equity	0.30	0.36	0.58	0.62	0.59	0.68	0.47	0.34
Price Range	67.85-49.75	58.80-48.46	58.66-40.21	65.21-51.45	58.83-38.15	51.32-36.09	53.00-42.35	52.64-35.59
P/E Ratio	20.44-14.98	30.15-24.85	23.65-16.21	21.96-17.32	21.79-14.13	21.47-15.10	15.27-12.20	18.80-12.71
Average Yield %	2.20	2.31	2.40	1.97	2.04	2.23	1.68	1.48

Address: 111 River Street, Hoboken, NJ 07030
Telephone: 201-748-6000

Web Site: www.wiley.com
Officers: Matthew S. Kissner - Chairman, Interim Chief Executive Officer, Interim President Brian A. Napack - President, Chief Executive Officer

Auditors: KPMG LLP
Investor Contact: 201-748-6874
Transfer Agents: Registrar and Transfer Company, Cranford, NJ

WILLIAMS COS INC (THE)

Exchange	Symbol	Price	52Wk Range	Yield	P/E
NYS	WMB	$27.11 (6/29/2018)	33.21-24.38	5.02	11.54

*7 Year Price Score 67.56 *NYSE Composite Index=100 *12 Month Price Score 92.32

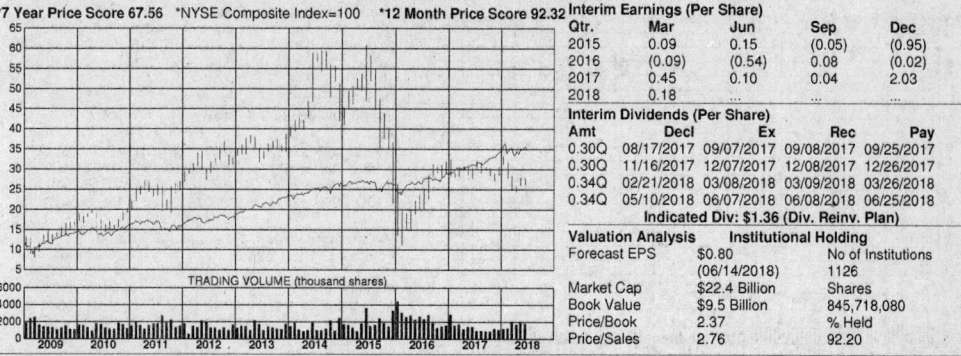

Interim Earnings (Per Share)

Qtr.	Mar	Jun	Sep	Dec
2015	0.09	0.15	(0.05)	(0.95)
2016	(0.09)	(0.54)	0.08	(0.02)
2017	0.45	0.10	0.04	2.03
2018	0.18	...	...	...

Interim Dividends (Per Share)

Amt	Decl	Ex	Rec	Pay
0.30Q	08/17/2017	09/07/2017	09/08/2017	09/25/2017
0.30Q	11/16/2017	12/07/2017	12/08/2017	12/26/2017
0.34Q	02/21/2018	03/08/2018	03/09/2018	03/26/2018
0.34Q	05/10/2018	06/07/2018	06/08/2018	06/25/2018

Indicated Div: $1.36 (Div. Reinv. Plan)

Valuation Analysis / Institutional Holding

Forecast EPS	$0.80	No of Institutions
	(06/14/2018)	1126
Market Cap	$22.4 Billion	Shares
Book Value	$9.5 Billion	845,718,080
Price/Book	2.37	% Held
Price/Sales	2.76	92.20

TRADING VOLUME (thousand shares)

Business Summary: Equipment & Services (MIC: 9.1.3 SIC: 4922 NAIC: 486210).

Williams Companies is an energy infrastructure company focused on connecting North America's hydrocarbon resource plays to markets for natural gas, natural gas liquids, and olefins. Co.'s operations are located in the U.S. As of Dec 31 2017, Co.'s interstate gas pipelines, midstream, and olefins production interests were largely held through Co.'s investment in Williams Partners L.P. Substantially all Co.'s operations are conducted through its subsidiaries. Co.'s business segments include Williams Partners, and Williams NGL & Petchem Services, and other, which include its Canadian construction services company.

Recent Developments: For the quarter ended Mar 31 2018, net income decreased 52.5% to US$270.0 million from US$569.0 million in the year-earlier quarter. Revenues were US$2.09 billion, up 5.0% from US$1.99 billion the year before. Operating income was US$491.0 million versus US$430.0 million in the prior-year quarter, an increase of 14.2%. Direct operating expenses rose 5.8% to US$1.01 billion from US$950.0 million in the comparable period the year before. Indirect operating expenses decreased 2.6% to US$592.0 million from US$608.0 million in the equivalent prior-year period.

Prospects: Our evaluation of Williams Cos Inc. as of Jan. 21, 2018 is the result of our systematic analysis on three basic characteristics: earnings strength, relative valuation, and recent stock price movement. The company has suffered a very negative trend in earnings per share over the past 5 quarters. However, while recent estimates for the company have been mixed, WMB has posted results that fell short of analysts expectations. Based on operating earnings yield, the company is overvalued when compared to all of the companies in our coverage universe. Share price changes over the past year indicates that WMB will perform poorly over the near term.

Financial Data
(US$ in Thousands)

	3 Mos	12/31/2017	12/31/2016	12/31/2015	12/31/2014	12/31/2013	12/31/2012	12/31/2011
Earnings Per Share	2.35	2.62	(0.57)	(0.76)	2.92	0.62	1.37	0.63
Cash Flow Per Share	3.20	3.09	4.87	3.57	2.94	3.25	2.95	5.84
Tang Book Value Per Share	1.00	1.05	N.M.	N.M.	N.M.	3.77	3.52	3.03
Dividends Per Share	1.240	1.200	1.680	2.450	1.958	1.438	1.196	0.775
Dividend Payout %	52.77	45.80	...	...	67.04	231.85	87.32	123.02
Income Statement								
Total Revenue	2,088,000	8,031,000	7,499,000	7,360,000	7,637,000	6,860,000	7,486,000	7,930,000
EBITDA	530,000	2,573,000	2,244,000	(981,000)	2,610,000	2,208,000	2,399,000	2,271,000
Depn & Amortn	14,000	1,389,000	1,407,000	1,382,000	967,000	752,000	712,000	658,000
Income Before Taxes	243,000	101,000	(342,000)	(3,407,000)	896,000	946,000	1,178,000	1,047,000
Income Taxes	55,000	(1,974,000)	(25,000)	(399,000)	1,249,000	401,000	360,000	124,000
Net Income	152,000	2,174,000	(424,000)	(571,000)	2,114,000	430,000	859,000	376,000
Average Shares	830,197	828,518	750,673	749,271	723,641	687,185	625,486	598,175
Balance Sheet								
Current Assets	2,399,000	2,179,000	1,462,000	1,527,000	1,890,000	1,683,000	1,924,000	1,894,000
Total Assets	47,052,000	46,352,000	46,835,000	49,020,000	50,563,000	27,142,000	24,327,000	16,502,000
Current Liabilities	2,164,000	2,646,000	2,949,000	2,497,000	2,567,000	1,983,000	1,549,000	1,675,000
Long-Term Obligations	21,379,000	20,434,000	22,624,000	23,812,000	20,888,000	11,353,000	10,735,000	8,369,000
Total Liabilities	37,579,000	36,696,000	42,192,000	42,872,000	41,786,000	22,278,000	19,575,000	14,709,000
Stockholders' Equity	9,473,000	9,656,000	4,643,000	6,148,000	8,777,000	4,864,000	4,752,000	1,793,000
Shares Outstanding	827,000	826,000	750,000	749,000	747,000	683,000	681,000	591,000
Statistical Record								
Return on Assets %	4.13	4.67	N.M.	N.M.	5.44	1.67	4.20	1.81
Return on Equity %	21.80	30.41	N.M.	N.M.	30.99	8.94	26.18	8.28
EBITDA Margin %	25.38	32.04	29.92	N.M.	34.18	32.19	32.05	28.64
Net Margin %	7.28	27.07	N.M.	N.M.	27.68	6.27	11.47	4.74
Asset Turnover	0.17	0.17	0.16	0.15	0.20	0.27	0.37	0.38
Current Ratio	1.11	0.82	0.50	0.61	0.74	0.85	1.24	1.13
Debt to Equity	2.26	2.12	4.87	3.87	2.38	2.33	2.26	4.67
Price Range	33.21-24.78	32.42-27.02	31.78-11.16	60.86-21.54	59.44-38.03	38.57-31.65	36.77-26.82	27.09-19.07
P/E Ratio	14.13-10.54	12.37-10.31	...	...	20.36-13.02	62.21-51.05	26.84-19.58	42.99-30.27
Average Yield %	4.17	4.06	7.14	5.37	4.00	4.05	3.79	3.26

Address: One Williams Center, Tulsa, OK 74172-0172 **Telephone:** 918-573-2000	**Web Site:** www.williams.com **Officers:** Joshua H. De Rienzis - Vice President, Corporate Secretary Stephen W. Bergstrom - Chairman	**Auditors:** PricewaterhouseCoopers LLP **Transfer Agents:** Computershare Trust Company, N.A., College Station, TX

WILLIAMS SONOMA INC

Exchange	Symbol	Price	52Wk Range	Yield	P/E	Div Acheiver
NYS	WSM	$61.38 (6/29/2018)	64.55-42.85	2.80	19.67	11 Years

*7 Year Price Score 75.00   *NYSE Composite Index=100   *12 Month Price Score 107.42

Interim Earnings (Per Share)

Qtr.	Apr	Jul	Oct	Jan
2015-16	0.48	0.58	0.77	1.55
2016-17	0.44	0.58	0.78	1.63
2017-18	0.45	0.61	0.84	1.13
2018-19	0.54	...	...	...

Interim Dividends (Per Share)

Amt	Decl	Ex	Rec	Pay
0.39Q	09/15/2017	10/26/2017	10/27/2017	11/22/2017
0.39Q	12/15/2017	01/24/2018	01/25/2018	02/23/2018
0.43Q	03/14/2018	04/26/2018	04/27/2018	05/25/2018
0.43Q	06/15/2018	07/19/2018	07/20/2018	08/24/2018

Indicated Div: $1.72

Valuation Analysis

		Institutional Holding	
Forecast EPS	$4.25	No of Institutions	594
	(06/14/2018)		
Market Cap	$5.1 Billion	Shares	118,712,600
Book Value	$1.2 Billion	% Held	84.38
Price/Book	4.27		
Price/Sales	0.95		

Business Summary: Retail - Furniture & Home Furnishings (MIC: 2.1.6 SIC: 5712 NAIC: 442110)

Williams-Sonoma is a retailer of products for the home. As of Jan 28 2018, the e-commerce channel had the following merchandising concepts: Williams Sonoma, Pottery Barn, Pottery Barn Kids, West Elm, PBteen, Williams Sonoma Home, Rejuvenation and Mark and Graham, which sell its products through its e-commerce websites and direct-mail catalogs. As of Jan 28 2018, Co. operated 631 stores comprising 586 stores in 43 states, Washington, D.C. and Puerto Rico, 26 stores in Canada, 19 stores in Australia and 2 stores in the U.K. Co. also operates 66 franchised stores and/or e-commerce websites in a number of countries in the Middle East, the Philippines, Mexico and South Korea.

Recent Developments: For the quarter ended Apr 29 2018, net income increased 14.2% to US$45.2 million from US$39.6 million in the year-earlier quarter. Revenues were US$1.20 billion, up 8.2% from US$1.11 billion the year before. Operating income was US$66.6 million versus US$62.5 million in the prior-year quarter, an increase of 6.5%. Direct operating expenses rose 7.7% to US$770.8 million from US$715.7 million in the comparable period the year before. Indirect operating expenses increased 9.7% to US$365.6 million from US$333.3 million in the equivalent prior-year period.

Prospects: Our evaluation of Williams-Sonoma Inc. as of Jan. 21, 2018 is the result of our systematic analysis on three basic characteristics: earnings strength, relative valuation, and recent stock price movement. The company has managed to produce a neutral trend in earnings per share over the past 5 quarters and while recent estimates for the company have been mixed, WSM has posted better than expected results. Based on operating earnings yield, the company is undervalued when compared to all of the companies in our coverage universe. Share price changes over the past year indicates that WSM will perform in line with the market over the near term.

Financial Data
(US$ in Thousands)

	3 Mos	01/28/2018	01/29/2017	01/31/2016	02/01/2015	02/02/2014	02/03/2013	01/29/2012
Earnings Per Share	3.12	3.02	3.41	3.37	3.24	2.82	2.54	2.22
Cash Flow Per Share	6.68	5.85	5.94	6.01	4.94	4.71	3.61	2.80
Tang Book Value Per Share	14.39	14.38	14.29	13.38	13.33	13.35	13.39	12.50
Dividends Per Share	1.600	1.560	1.480	1.400	1.320	1.240	0.880	0.730
Dividend Payout %	51.28	51.66	43.40	41.54	40.74	43.97	34.65	32.88
Income Statement								
Total Revenue	1,203,000	5,292,359	5,083,812	4,976,090	4,698,719	4,387,889	4,042,870	3,720,895
EBITDA	59,826	611,516	620,582	631,673	640,119	576,511	516,922	484,738
Depn & Amortn	(6,724)	157,705	147,983	143,039	137,854	124,413	107,759	103,006
Income Before Taxes	65,349	452,439	471,911	488,007	502,203	452,682	409,956	381,830
Income Taxes	20,181	192,894	166,524	177,939	193,349	173,780	153,226	144,899
Net Income	45,168	259,545	305,387	310,068	308,854	278,902	256,730	236,931
Average Shares	84,174	86,080	89,462	92,102	95,200	98,765	101,051	106,582
Balance Sheet								
Current Assets	1,523,217	1,636,445	1,367,180	1,336,100	1,391,923	1,419,103	1,316,772	1,276,366
Total Assets	2,656,905	2,785,749	2,476,879	2,417,427	2,330,277	2,336,734	2,187,679	2,060,838
Current Liabilities	882,821	1,007,823	961,256	996,427	875,948	861,096	657,127	571,799
Long-Term Obligations	299,472	299,422	...	...	...	1,968	3,753	5,478
Total Liabilities	1,459,671	1,582,183	1,228,659	1,219,201	1,105,571	1,080,732	878,541	805,576
Stockholders' Equity	1,197,234	1,203,566	1,248,220	1,198,226	1,224,706	1,256,002	1,309,138	1,255,262
Shares Outstanding	83,222	83,726	87,325	89,563	91,891	94,049	97,734	100,451
Statistical Record								
Return on Assets %	10.51	9.89	12.51	13.10	13.27	12.36	11.89	11.33
Return on Equity %	22.03	21.23	25.03	25.66	24.97	21.81	19.70	18.90
EBITDA Margin %	4.97	11.55	12.21	12.69	13.62	13.14	12.79	13.03
Net Margin %	3.75	4.90	6.01	6.23	6.57	6.36	6.35	6.37
Asset Turnover	2.13	2.02	2.08	2.10	2.02	1.94	1.87	1.78
Current Ratio	1.73	1.62	1.42	1.34	1.59	1.65	2.00	2.23
Debt to Equity	0.25	0.25	...	...	...	N.M.	N.M.	N.M.
Price Range	55.49-42.85	55.59-42.85	61.55-46.22	88.67-48.99	80.94-52.85	61.33-43.96	47.93-33.06	45.24-28.81
P/E Ratio	17.79-13.73	18.41-14.19	18.05-13.55	26.31-14.54	24.98-16.31	21.75-15.59	18.87-13.02	20.38-12.98
Average Yield %	3.20	3.14	2.80	1.87	1.96	2.28	2.20	1.98

Address: 3250 Van Ness Avenue, San Francisco, CA 94109	**Web Site:** www.williams-sonomainc.com	**Auditors:** DELOITTE & TOUCHE LLP
Telephone: 415-421-7900	**Officers:** Adrian D.P. Bellamy - Chairman Laura J. Alber - President, Chief Executive Officer	**Transfer Agents:** Wilson Sonsini Goodrich & Rosati Professional Corporation, Palo Alto, CA
Fax: 415-434-0881		

WORLDPAY INC

Exchange	Symbol	Price	52Wk Range	Yield	P/E
NYS	WP	$81.78 (6/29/2018)	85.40-59.93	N/A	314.54

*7 Year Price Score N/A   *NYSE Composite Index=100   *12 Month Price Score 107.82

Interim Earnings (Per Share)

Qtr.	Mar	Jun	Sep	Dec
2015	0.13	0.24	0.27	0.31
2016	0.25	0.38	0.41	0.28
2017	0.17	0.42	0.57	(0.37)
2018	(0.36)	...	...	...

Interim Dividends (Per Share)

No Dividends Paid

Valuation Analysis   Institutional Holding

Forecast EPS	$3.79	No of Institutions
	(06/14/2018)	594
Market Cap	$25.6 Billion	Shares
Book Value	$10.4 Billion	296,087,968
Price/Book	2.45	% Held
Price/Sales	6.47	103.83

Business Summary: Business Services (MIC: 7.5.2 SIC: 7389 NAIC: 561499)

Vantiv is a holding company. Through its subsidiaries, Co. provides electronic payment processing services to merchants and financial institutions. Co. operates two segments: Merchant Services, which provides merchant acquiring and payment processing services to national merchants, regional and small-to-mid sized businesses; and Financial Institution Services, which provides card issuer processing, payment network processing, fraud protection, card production, prepaid program management, automated teller machine driving and network gateway and switching services that utilize Co.'s proprietary Jeanie debit payment network to a set of financial institutions.

Recent Developments: For the quarter ended Mar 31 2018, net loss amounted to US$98.3 million versus net income of US$35.3 million in the year-earlier quarter. Revenues were US$850.7 million, down 8.3% from US$928.2 million the year before. Operating loss was US$27.7 million versus an income of US$73.8 million in the prior-year quarter. Direct operating expenses declined 100.0% to nil from US$458.1 million in the comparable period the year before. Indirect operating expenses increased 121.7% to US$878.4 million from US$396.3 million in the equivalent prior-year period.

Prospects: Our evaluation of Worldpay Inc. as of Jan. 21, 2018 is the result of our systematic analysis on three basic characteristics: earnings strength, relative valuation, and recent stock price movement. The company has generated a negative trend in earnings per share over the past 5 quarters. However, while recent estimates for the company have been mixed, WP has posted better than expected results. Based on operating earnings yield, the company is about fairly valued when compared to all of the companies in our coverage universe. Share price changes over the past year indicates that WP will perform in line with the market over the near term.

Financial Data
(US$ in Thousands)

	3 Mos	12/31/2017	12/31/2016	12/31/2015	12/31/2014	12/31/2013	12/31/2012	12/31/2011
Earnings Per Share	0.26	0.80	1.32	0.95	0.75	0.87	0.47	0.40
Cash Flow Per Share	2.65	4.87	4.27	5.23	4.18	3.46	2.51	2.61
Income Statement								
Total Revenue	850,700	4,026,477	3,578,991	3,159,938	2,577,203	2,108,077	1,863,239	1,622,421
EBITDA	29,800	1,050,273	602,758	479,742	384,868	389,602	252,883	260,354
Depn & Amortn	66,100	95,900	70,500	76,600	70,000	56,800	40,700	31,700
Income Before Taxes	(111,500)	813,712	422,724	297,406	235,167	291,900	157,611	117,119
Income Taxes	(13,200)	631,020	141,853	88,177	66,177	83,760	46,853	32,309
Net Income	(97,600)	130,110	213,208	147,946	125,292	133,572	57,610	36,240
Average Shares	274,098	162,807	162,115	200,934	199,170	206,027	122,747	89,514
Balance Sheet								
Current Assets	8,063,200	1,372,612	1,287,858	1,117,499	1,214,736	807,913	921,077	819,997
Total Assets	28,950,000	8,666,973	7,044,007	6,465,426	6,336,083	4,189,553	3,979,529	3,489,710
Current Liabilities	8,550,600	1,834,458	1,689,012	1,295,379	963,333	685,313	869,468	440,720
Long-Term Obligations	8,084,100	5,590,804	3,102,826	2,965,439	3,292,016	1,730,794	1,171,880	1,750,820
Total Liabilities	18,507,700	8,134,434	5,728,342	5,512,638	5,433,070	3,421,622	3,161,603	2,866,012
Stockholders' Equity	10,442,300	532,539	1,315,665	952,788	903,013	767,931	817,926	623,698
Shares Outstanding	312,660	177,848	196,177	190,531	188,497	190,581	211,484	89,514
Statistical Record								
Return on Assets %	0.02	1.66	3.15	2.31	2.38	3.27	1.54	1.06
Return on Equity %	0.06	14.08	18.75	15.94	15.00	16.85	7.97	5.95
EBITDA Margin %	3.50	26.08	16.84	15.18	14.93	18.48	13.57	16.05
Net Margin %	N.M.	3.23	5.96	4.68	4.86	6.34	3.09	2.23
Asset Turnover	0.22	0.51	0.53	0.49	0.49	0.52	0.50	0.47
Current Ratio	0.94	0.75	0.76	0.86	1.26	1.18	1.06	1.86
Debt to Equity	0.77	10.50	2.36	3.11	3.65	2.25	1.43	2.81
Price Range	85.03-59.88	75.87-59.88	59.73-43.20	52.84-33.25	34.82-28.79	32.61-19.97	24.03-19.50	...
P/E Ratio	327.04-230.31	94.84-74.85	45.25-32.73	55.62-35.00	46.43-38.39	37.48-22.95	51.13-41.49	...

Address: 8500 Governor's Hill Drive, Symmes Township, OH 45249
Telephone: 513-900-5250

Web Site: www.worldpay.com
Officers: Charles D. Drucker - Executive Chairman, President, Chief Executive Officer, Co-Chief Executive Officer Philip E.R. Jansen - Co-Chief Executive Officer

Auditors: DELOITTE & TOUCHE LLP
Investor Contact: 513-90-0.4811
Transfer Agents: American Stock Transfer & Trust Company, LLC

WORLD FUEL SERVICES CORP.

Exchange	Symbol	Price	52Wk Range	Yield	P/E
NYS	INT	$20.41 (6/29/2018)	39.81-20.18	1.18	N/A

*7 Year Price Score 56.25   *NYSE Composite Index=100   *12 Month Price Score 76.54

Interim Earnings (Per Share)

Qtr.	Mar	Jun	Sep	Dec
2015	0.78	0.42	0.71	0.74
2016	0.75	0.43	0.61	0.03
2017	0.45	0.44	(0.57)	(2.83)
2018	0.46	...	...	...

Interim Dividends (Per Share)

Amt	Decl	Ex	Rec	Pay
0.06Q	10/04/2017	10/13/2017	10/16/2017	11/06/2017
0.06Q	12/01/2017	12/14/2017	12/15/2017	01/05/2018
0.06Q	03/01/2018	03/15/2018	03/16/2018	04/06/2018
0.06Q	05/24/2018	06/07/2018	06/08/2018	07/06/2018

Indicated Div: $0.24

Valuation Analysis / Institutional Holding

Forecast EPS	$1.95	No of Institutions	
	(06/13/2018)	364	
Market Cap	$1.4 Billion	Shares	
Book Value	$1.8 Billion	84,042,248	
Price/Book	0.79	% Held	
Price/Sales	0.04	95.42	

Business Summary: Equipment & Services (MIC: 9.1.3 SIC: 5172 NAIC: 424720)

World Fuel Services is a global energy management company involved in providing energy procurement advisory services, supply fulfillment and transaction and payment management solutions to commercial and industrial customers. Co. primarily contracts with third parties for the delivery and storage of fuel products, however, Co. also operates storage facilities and transportation assets. Co. operates in three reportable segments: aviation, which provides fuel and related products and services; marine, which products and services include fuel, lubricants and related products and services to a base of customers; and land, which provides fuel, lubricants, power and natural gas solutions.

Recent Developments: For the quarter ended Mar 31 2018, net income increased 0.6% to US$31.3 million from US$31.1 million in the year-earlier quarter. Revenues were US$9.18 billion, up 12.0% from US$8.19 billion the year before. Operating income was US$57.2 million versus US$50.3 million in the prior-year quarter, an increase of 13.7%. Direct operating expenses rose 12.2% to US$8.94 billion from US$7.96 billion in the comparable period the year before. Indirect operating expenses increased 2.8% to US$186.2 million from US$181.1 million in the equivalent prior-year period.

Prospects: Our evaluation of World Fuel Services Corp. as of Jan. 21, 2018 is the result of our systematic analysis on three basic characteristics: earnings strength, relative valuation, and recent stock price movement. The company has enjoyed a very positive trend in earnings per share over the past 5 quarters. However, while recent estimates for the company have been mixed, INT has posted results that were in line with analysts expectations. Based on operating earnings yield, the company is undervalued when compared to all of the companies in our coverage universe. Share price changes over the past year indicates that INT will perform poorly over the near term.

Financial Data
(US$ in Thousands)

	3 Mos	12/31/2017	12/31/2016	12/31/2015	12/31/2014	12/31/2013	12/31/2012	12/31/2011
Earnings Per Share	(2.50)	(2.50)	1.81	2.64	3.11	2.83	2.64	2.71
Cash Flow Per Share	(2.38)	3.01	2.95	6.37	2.00	3.71	2.04	(2.02)
Tang Book Value Per Share	13.12	5.97	9.44	12.41	11.83	12.24	12.12	12.35
Dividends Per Share	0.240	0.240	0.240	0.240	0.150	0.150	0.150	0.150
Dividend Payout %	...	...	13.26	9.09	4.82	5.30	5.68	5:54
Income Statement								
Total Revenue	9,181,300	33,695,500	27,015,800	30,379,700	43,386,389	41,561,947	38,945,338	34,622,854
EBITDA	73,700	83,300	223,800	284,300	325,088	285,952	277,292	269,528
Depn & Amortn	18,800	44,100	42,500	35,100	30,300	22,000	18,600	15,500
Income Before Taxes	38,600	(21,100)	142,100	219,300	269,551	246,665	239,595	238,203
Income Taxes	7,300	149,200	15,700	36,300	51,144	39,505	38,244	39,001
Net Income	31,200	(170,200)	126,500	186,900	221,747	203,075	189,345	194,029
Average Shares	67,900	68,100	69,800	70,700	71,323	71,800	71,817	71,510
Balance Sheet								
Current Assets	3,770,700	3,940,400	3,836,600	3,254,600	3,674,843	3,815,501	3,281,377	3,122,227
Total Assets	5,472,100	5,587,800	5,412,600	4,549,400	4,879,980	4,739,277	4,107,751	3,697,246
Current Liabilities	2,670,100	2,718,600	2,182,700	1,762,800	2,241,354	2,514,515	2,149,298	2,026,142
Long-Term Obligations	800,800	884,600	1,170,800	746,700	671,954	449,064	354,253	269,348
Total Liabilities	3,717,000	3,865,800	3,487,600	2,638,000	3,024,622	3,065,379	2,590,577	2,364,285
Stockholders' Equity	1,755,200	1,721,900	1,925,000	1,911,400	1,855,358	1,673,898	1,517,174	1,332,961
Shares Outstanding	67,700	67,700	69,900	70,788	72,082	71,883	72,147	71,154
Statistical Record								
Return on Assets %	N.M.	N.M.	2.53	3.96	4.61	4.59	4.84	6.20
Return on Equity %	N.M.	N.M.	6.58	9.92	12.57	12.73	13.25	15.77
EBITDA Margin %	0.80	0.25	0.83	0.94	0.75	0.69	0.71	0.78
Net Margin %	0.34	N.M.	0.47	0.62	0.51	0.49	0.49	0.56
Asset Turnover	6.46	6.13	5.41	6.44	9.02	9.40	9.95	11.06
Current Ratio	1.41	1.45	1.76	1.85	1.64	1.52	1.53	1.54
Debt to Equity	0.46	0.51	0.61	0.39	0.36	0.27	0.23	0.20
Price Range	39.81-21.64	47.25-26.45	50.79-36.31	58.28-34.44	49.24-36.87	45.11-35.00	48.94-34.00	42.87-31.65
P/E Ratio	...	...	28.06-20.06	22.08-13.05	15.83-11.86	15.94-12.37	18.54-12.88	15.82-11.68
Average Yield %	0.75	0.67	0.53	0.51	0.34	0.38	0.38	0.40

Address: 9800 Northwest 41st Street, Miami, FL 33178	Web Site: www.wfscorp.com	Auditors: PricewaterhouseCoopers LLP
Telephone: 305-428-8000	Officers: Michael J. Kasbar - Chairman, President, Chief Operating Officer, Chief Executive Officer Ira M. Birns - Executive Vice President, Chief Financial Officer	Investor Contact: 305-428-8000
Fax: 305-392-5621		Transfer Agents: Wells Fargo Shareowner Services, St. Paul, MN

WORTHINGTON INDUSTRIES, INC.

Exchange	Symbol	Price	52Wk Range	Yield	P/E
NYS	WOR	$41.97 (6/29/2018)	53.14-39.65	2.19	12.17

*7 Year Price Score 107.69 *NYSE Composite Index=100 *12 Month Price Score 98.61

Interim Earnings (Per Share)

Qtr.	Aug	Nov	Feb	May
2014-15	0.63	0.43	(0.39)	0.43
2015-16	0.48	0.36	0.46	0.92
2016-17	1.02	0.72	0.55	0.86
2017-18	0.70	0.62	1.27	...

Interim Dividends (Per Share)

Amt	Decl	Ex	Rec	Pay
0.21Q	09/27/2017	12/14/2017	12/15/2017	12/29/2017
0.21Q	12/19/2017	03/14/2018	03/15/2018	03/29/2018
0.21Q	03/28/2018	06/14/2018	06/15/2018	06/29/2018
0.23Q	06/27/2018	09/13/2018	09/14/2018	09/28/2018

Indicated Div: $0.92

Valuation Analysis   Institutional Holding

Forecast EPS	$3.44	No of Institutions
	(06/11/2018)	339
Market Cap	$2.5 Billion	Shares
Book Value	$951.2 Million	41,614,376
Price/Book	2.64	% Held
Price/Sales	0.74	53.58

TRADING VOLUME (thousand shares)

Business Summary: Non-Precious Metals (MIC: 8.2.2 SIC: 3312 NAIC: 331111)

Worthington Industries is a metals manufacturing company, focused on steel processing and manufactured metal products. Co. operates three segments: Steel Processing, which buys coils of steel from steel mills and mini-mills and processes them to customer specifications; Pressure Cylinders, which manufactures and sells filled and unfilled pressure cylinders, tanks, hand torches, and oil and gas equipment with accessories and related products for end-use market applications; and Engineered Cabs, which designs and manufactures open and enclosed cabs and operator stations and custom fabrications for mobile equipment, and provides complementary products such as machined structural components.

Recent Developments: For the quarter ended Feb 28 2018, net income increased 101.0% to US$78.3 million from US$39.0 million in the year-earlier quarter. Revenues were US$841.7 million, up 19.6% from US$703.4 million the year before. Operating income was US$42.8 million versus US$34.3 million in the prior-year quarter, an increase of 24.6%. Direct operating expenses rose 20.6% to US$714.6 million from US$592.4 million in the comparable period the year before. Indirect operating expenses increased 9.9% to US$84.3 million from US$76.7 million in the equivalent prior-year period.

Prospects: Our evaluation of Worthington Industries Inc. as of Jan. 21, 2018 is the result of our systematic analysis on three basic characteristics: earnings strength, relative valuation, and recent stock price movement. The company has produced a positive trend in earnings per share over the past 5 quarters and while recent estimates for the company have been raised by analysts, WOR has posted results that fell short of analysts expectations. Based on operating earnings yield, the company is undervalued when compared to all of the companies in our coverage universe. Share price changes over the past year indicates that WOR will perform poorly over the near term.

Financial Data

(US$ in Thousands)	9 Mos	6 Mos	3 Mos	05/31/2017	05/31/2016	05/31/2015	05/31/2014	05/31/2013
Earnings Per Share	3.45	2.73	2.83	3.15	2.22	1.12	2.11	1.91
Cash Flow Per Share	4.69	4.65	4.77	5.38	6.60	3.23	3.32	3.94
Tang Book Value Per Share	6.06	5.42	5.71	9.89	7.33	6.10	6.73	6.74
Dividends Per Share	0.820	0.810	0.800	0.790	0.750	0.690	0.450	0.640
Dividend Payout %	23.77	29.67	28.27	25.08	33.78	61.61	21.33	33.51
Income Statement								
Total Revenue	2,561,160	1,719,503	848,237	3,014,108	2,819,714	3,384,234	3,126,426	2,612,244
EBITDA	217,202	147,601	67,938	290,153	202,205	126,018	215,060	186,596
Depn & Amortn	76,986	51,648	25,365	73,268	68,886	64,666	62,344	56,002
Income Before Taxes	111,596	77,108	33,766	187,089	101,649	25,552	126,045	106,676
Income Taxes	7,124	31,163	12,998	79,190	58,987	25,772	57,349	64,465
Net Income	164,025	84,937	45,534	204,515	143,715	76,785	151,300	136,442
Average Shares	62,345	63,468	64,590	64,874	64,755	68,483	71,664	71,314
Balance Sheet								
Current Assets	1,158,642	1,111,728	1,161,165	1,190,969	915,460	992,193	1,198,922	866,883
Total Assets	2,614,736	2,571,713	2,630,554	2,325,344	2,063,755	2,085,142	2,296,381	1,950,857
Current Liabilities	564,239	526,449	541,984	520,783	430,078	524,392	589,663	448,914
Long-Term Obligations	768,128	766,737	773,090	571,796	579,982	579,352	554,790	406,236
Total Liabilities	1,663,565	1,652,426	1,672,380	1,373,709	1,270,384	1,336,030	1,445,569	1,120,035
Stockholders' Equity	951,171	919,287	958,174	951,635	793,371	749,112	850,812	830,822
Shares Outstanding	59,802	60,755	62,144	62,802	61,533	64,141	67,408	69,752
Statistical Record								
Return on Assets %	9.07	7.52	7.67	9.32	6.91	3.50	7.12	7.13
Return on Equity %	23.84	19.66	20.34	23.44	18.58	9.60	17.99	17.86
EBITDA Margin %	8.48	8.58	8.01	9.63	7.17	3.72	6.88	7.14
Net Margin %	6.40	4.94	5.37	6.79	5.10	2.27	4.84	5.22
Asset Turnover	1.40	1.39	1.30	1.37	1.36	1.54	1.47	1.36
Current Ratio	2.05	2.11	2.14	2.29	2.13	1.89	2.03	1.93
Debt to Equity	0.81	0.83	0.81	0.60	0.73	0.77	0.65	0.49
Price Range	53.14-39.65	58.85-39.65	62.35-39.75	62.35-36.26	38.26-21.88	43.85-24.18	44.05-31.35	35.59-15.88
P/E Ratio	15.40-11.49	21.56-14.52	22.03-14.05	19.79-11.51	17.23-9.86	39.15-21.59	20.88-14.86	18.63-8.31
Average Yield %	1.77	1.71	1.66	1.70	2.48	2.02	1.19	2.54

Address: 200 Old Wilson Bridge Road, Columbus, OH 43085 **Telephone:** 614-438-3210 **Fax:** 614-438-3256	**Web Site:** www.worthingtonindustries.com **Officers:** John P. McConnell - Chairman, Chief Executive Officer Mark A. Russell - President, Chief Operating Officer	**Auditors:** KPMG LLP **Investor Contact:** 614-438-3077 **Transfer Agents:** Wells Fargo Shareowner Services, Saint Paul, MN

W.P. CAREY INC

Exchange	Symbol	Price	52Wk Range	Yield	P/E	Div Acheiver
NYS	WPC	$66.35 (6/29/2018)	72.32-59.24	6.15	25.32	19 Years

*7 Year Price Score 88.77 *NSYE Composite Index=100 *12 Month Price Score 98.39

TRADING VOLUME (thousand shares)

Interim Earnings (Per Share)

Qtr.	Mar	Jun	Sep	Dec
2015	0.34	0.59	0.20	0.48
2016	0.54	0.48	1.03	0.44
2017	0.53	0.59	0.74	0.69
2018	0.60	...	...	...

Interim Dividends (Per Share)

Amt	Decl	Ex	Rec	Pay
1.005Q	09/20/2017	09/29/2017	10/02/2017	10/16/2017
1.01Q	12/06/2017	12/28/2017	12/29/2017	01/16/2018
1.015Q	03/15/2018	03/28/2018	03/29/2018	04/16/2018
1.02Q	06/14/2018	06/28/2018	06/29/2018	07/16/2018

Indicated Div: $4.08 (Div. Reinv. Plan)

Valuation Analysis / Institutional Holding

Valuation Analysis		Institutional Holding	
Forecast EPS	$2.45	No of Institutions	
	(06/06/2018)	550	
Market Cap	$7.1 Billion	Shares	
Book Value	$3.1 Billion	64,702,376	
Price/Book	2.26	% Held	
Price/Sales	8.56	N/A	

Business Summary: REITs (MIC: 5.3.1 SIC: 6798 NAIC: 525930)

W. P. Carey is a self-managed diversified REIT and an owner and manager of commercial real estate, primarily net leased to companies in the U.S. and Europe on a long-term basis. Co.'s owned real estate portfolio, which is diversified by property type, tenant, tenant industry, and geographic location, is comprised primarily of single-tenant industrial, office, retail, and warehouse facilities. In addition to managing its owned real estate portfolio, Co. manages a series of non-traded public and private investment programs through its investment management business. As of Dec 31 2017, Co. had 210 corporate tenants and owned 887 properties in 17 countries.

Recent Developments: For the quarter ended Mar 31 2018, income from continuing operations increased 2.5% to US$61.3 million from US$59.8 million in the year-earlier quarter. Net income increased 13.8% to US$68.1 million from US$59.8 million in the year-earlier quarter. Revenues were US$201.8 million, down 7.9% from US$219.1 million the year before. Revenues from property income rose 5.2% to US$177.6 million from US$168.7 million in the corresponding quarter a year earlier.

Prospects: Our evaluation of W.P.Carey Inc. as of Jan. 21, 2018 is the result of our systematic analysis on three basic characteristics: earnings strength, relative valuation, and recent stock price movement. The company has produced a positive trend in earnings per share over the past 5 quarters. Because the company lacks sufficient analyst estimate data, we place greater weight on the historical EPS trend as the measure of earnings strength. Based on operating earnings yield, the company is about fairly valued when compared to all of the companies in our coverage universe. Share price changes over the past year indicates that WPC will perform very well over the near term.

Financial Data
(US$ in Thousands)

	3 Mos	12/31/2017	12/31/2016	12/31/2015	12/31/2014	12/31/2013	12/31/2012	12/31/2011
Earnings Per Share	2.62	2.56	2.49	1.61	2.39	1.41	1.28	3.42
Cash Flow Per Share	4.69	4.79	4.84	4.52	4.04	3.03	1.70	2.01
Tang Book Value Per Share	23.35	6.49	13.34	13.09	14.82	12.38	14.03	14.01
Dividends Per Share	4.030	4.010	3.929	3.826	3.685	3.500	2.440	2.190
Dividend Payout %	153.82	156.64	157.80	237.65	154.18	248.23	51.56	64.04
Income Statement								
Total Revenue	201,810	848,302	941,533	938,383	906,193	489,851	373,995	336,409
EBITDA	89,536	671,407	590,646	663,573	655,391	297,355	121,448	170,632
Depn & Amortn	11,455	316,466	265,179	303,906	292,606	152,213	48,509	23,325
Income Before Taxes	40,007	189,166	142,058	165,341	184,663	42,506	23,762	127,388
Income Taxes	(6,002)	2,711	3,288	37,621	17,609	1,252	6,783	37,228
Net Income	65,274	277,289	267,747	172,258	239,826	98,876	62,132	139,079
Average Shares	108,211	108,035	107,073	106,507	99,827	69,708	48,078	40,098
Balance Sheet								
Current Assets	171,331	267,620	455,092	219,445	233,160	149,553	159,906	67,666
Total Assets	8,287,871	8,231,402	8,453,954	8,754,673	8,637,328	4,678,950	4,609,042	1,462,623
Current Liabilities	357,447	372,819	374,007	445,089	393,924	273,171	335,791	149,152
Long-Term Obligations	4,389,131	4,265,267	4,440,814	4,492,793	4,088,546	2,067,410	1,968,397	589,369
Total Liabilities	5,138,837	5,039,141	5,152,287	5,327,430	4,886,439	2,774,535	2,581,896	780,042
Stockholders' Equity	3,149,034	3,192,261	3,301,667	3,427,243	3,750,889	1,904,415	2,027,146	682,581
Shares Outstanding	107,194	106,922	106,294	104,448	104,040	68,266	68,485	39,729
Statistical Record								
Return on Assets %	3.46	3.32	3.10	1.98	3.60	2.13	2.04	10.56
Return on Equity %	8.90	8.54	7.94	4.80	8.48	5.03	4.57	21.27
EBITDA Margin %	44.37	79.15	62.73	70.71	72.32	60.70	32.47	50.72
Net Margin %	32.34	32.69	28.44	18.36	26.47	20.18	16.61	41.34
Asset Turnover	0.10	0.10	0.11	0.11	0.14	0.11	0.12	0.26
Current Ratio	0.48	0.72	1.22	0.49	0.59	0.55	0.48	0.45
Debt to Equity	1.39	1.34	1.35	1.31	1.09	1.09	0.97	0.86
Price Range	72.32-59.24	72.32-59.64	72.87-51.87	73.58-56.23	72.84-57.87	78.58-51.89	54.70-41.65	44.34-29.85
P/E Ratio	27.60-22.61	28.25-23.30	29.27-20.83	45.70-34.93	30.48-24.21	55.73-36.80	42.73-32.54	12.96-8.73
Average Yield %	6.08		6.26	6.28	6.01	5.71	5.39	1.41	5.91

Address: 50 Rockefeller Plaza, New York, NY 10020	Web Site: www.wpcarey.com	Auditors: PricewaterhouseCoopers LLP
Telephone: 212-492-1100	Officers: John J. Park - President, Chief Financial Officer, Managing Director Jason E. Fox - President, Chief Executive Officer, Global Head	Investor Contact: 212-492-8920 Transfer Agents: Computershare Shareowner Services, LLC, Pittsburgh, PA

WPX ENERGY INC

Exchange	Symbol	Price	52Wk Range	Yield	P/E
NYS	WPX	$18.03 (6/29/2018)	19.17-9.27	N/A	N/A

*7 Year Price Score N/A   ***NYSE Composite Index=100**   ***12 Month Price Score 131.41**

TRADING VOLUME (thousand shares)

Interim Earnings (Per Share)

Qtr.	Mar	Jun	Sep	Dec
2015	0.32	(0.14)	(0.93)	(6.53)
2016	(0.06)	(0.68)	(0.72)	(0.51)
2017	0.22	0.18	(0.38)	(0.11)
2018	(0.30)	...	...	...

Interim Dividends (Per Share)

No Dividends Paid

Valuation Analysis   Institutional Holding

Forecast EPS	$0.08	No of Institutions
	(06/13/2018)	511
Market Cap	$7.2 Billion	Shares
Book Value	$4.0 Billion	442,226,560
Price/Book	1.80	% Held
Price/Sales	5.77	N/A

Business Summary: Production & Extraction (MIC: 9.1.1 SIC: 1311 NAIC: 211111)

WPX Energy is an independent oil and natural gas exploration and production company engaged in the exploitation and development of properties. Co.'s principal areas of operation are the Delaware Basin in Texas and New Mexico, the Williston Basin in North Dakota, and the San Juan Basin in New Mexico and Colorado. As of Dec 31 2017, Co. had total estimated proved reserves of 436 million barrels of oil equivalent, which comprised of 60.0% crude oil, 23.0% natural gas and 17.0% natural gas liquids.

Recent Developments: For the quarter ended Mar 31 2018, loss from continuing operations was US$26.0 million compared with income of US$95.0 million in the year-earlier quarter. Net loss amounted to US$115.0 million versus net income of US$92.0 million in the year-earlier quarter. Revenues were US$374.0 million, down 5.3% from US$395.0 million the year before. Operating income was US$6.0 million versus US$173.0 million in the prior-year quarter, a decrease of 96.5%. Direct operating expenses rose 78.0% to US$73.0 million from US$41.0 million in the comparable period the year before. Indirect operating expenses increased 63.0% to US$295.0 million from US$181.0 million in the equivalent prior-year period.

Prospects: Our evaluation of WPX Energy Inc. as of Jan. 21, 2018 is the result of our systematic analysis on three basic characteristics: earnings strength, relative valuation, and recent stock price movement. The company has managed to produce a neutral trend in earnings per share over the past 5 quarters. Because the company lacks sufficient analyst estimate data, we place greater weight on the historical EPS trend as the measure of earnings strength. Based on operating earnings yield, the company is overvalued when compared to all of the companies in our coverage universe. Share price changes over the past year indicates that WPX will perform very poorly over the near term.

Financial Data

(US$ in Millions)	3 Mos	12/31/2017	12/31/2016	12/31/2015	12/31/2014	12/31/2013	12/31/2012	12/31/2011
Earnings Per Share	(0.61)	(0.08)	(2.05)	(7.42)	0.80	(5.91)	(1.12)	(1.53)
Cash Flow Per Share	1.58	1.28	0.83	3.46	5.28	3.17	3.98	6.12
Tang Book Value Per Share	9.44	9.78	9.38	11.60	21.20	20.44	26.43	28.82
Income Statement								
Total Revenue	374	1,336	693	1,888	3,493	2,761	3,189	3,988
EBITDA	13	734	(63)	(1,392)	1,226	(794)	721	623
Depn & Amortn	8	705	667	975	899	972	1,001	956
Income Before Taxes	(41)	(159)	(937)	(2,554)	204	(1,869)	(374)	(441)
Income Taxes	(15)	(148)	(325)	(915)	75	(655)	(111)	(145)
Net Income	(115)	(16)	(601)	(1,727)	164	(1,185)	(223)	(302)
Average Shares	398	395	313	234	206	200	198	197
Balance Sheet								
Current Assets	1,161	638	754	850	1,869	922	772	1,674
Total Assets	8,127	8,207	7,264	8,350	8,798	8,429	9,456	10,432
Current Liabilities	925	839	677	690	1,209	1,007	726	1,156
Long-Term Obligations	2,576	2,575	2,575	3,189	2,280	1,916	1,508	1,503
Total Liabilities	4,121	4,080	3,798	4,815	4,479	4,320	4,188	4,754
Stockholders' Equity	4,006	4,127	3,466	3,535	4,319	4,109	5,268	5,678
Shares Outstanding	399	398	344	275	203	201	199	197
Statistical Record								
Return on Assets %	N.M.	N.M.	N.M.	N.M.	1.90	N.M.	N.M.	N.M.
Return on Equity %	N.M.	N.M.	N.M.	N.M.	3.89	N.M.	N.M.	N.M.
EBITDA Margin %	3.48	54.94	N.M.	N.M.	35.10	N.M.	22.61	15.62
Net Margin %	N.M.	N.M.	N.M.	N.M.	4.70	N.M.	N.M.	N.M.
Asset Turnover	0.16	0.17	0.09	0.22	0.41	0.31	0.32	0.39
Current Ratio	1.26	0.76	1.11	1.23	1.55	0.92	1.06	1.45
Debt to Equity	0.64	0.62	0.74	0.90	0.53	0.47	0.29	0.26
Price Range	15.76-8.71	15.26-8.71	15.54-3.56	14.55-5.16	26.62-10.27	23.45-14.19	19.67-13.37	...
P/E Ratio	...	...	...	...	33.27-12.84	...	...	...

Address: 3500 One Williams Center, Tulsa, OK 74172-0172	**Web Site:** www.wpxenergy.com	**Auditors:** Ernst & Young LLP
Telephone: 855-979-2012	**Officers:** Richard E. (Rick) Muncrief - Chairman, President, Chief Executive Officer Clay M. Gaspar - President, Senior Vice President, Chief Operating Officer	**Investor Contact:** 539-573-9360
		Transfer Agents: Computershare Trust Company, N.A., Canton, MA

WYNDHAM DESTINATIONS INC

Exchange	Symbol	Price	52Wk Range	Yield	P/E
NYS	WYND	$44.27 (6/29/2018)	57.47-43.39	3.70	5.97

*7 Year Price Score 120.98 *NYSE Composite Index=100 *12 Month Price Score 96.36

Interim Earnings (Per Share)

Qtr.	Mar	Jun	Sep	Dec
2015	1.00	1.33	1.61	1.21
2016	0.84	1.39	1.78	1.52
2017	1.33	0.75	1.97	4.35
2018	0.34	...	...	...

Interim Dividends (Per Share)

Amt	Decl	Ex	Rec	Pay
0.58Q	08/02/2017	08/23/2017	08/25/2017	09/08/2017
0.58Q	11/07/2017	11/24/2017	11/27/2017	12/11/2017
0.66Q	03/01/2018	03/14/2018	03/15/2018	03/30/2018
0.41Q	05/17/2018	06/14/2018	06/15/2018	06/29/2018

Indicated Div: $1.64

TRADING VOLUME (thousand shares)

Valuation Analysis

		Institutional Holding	
Forecast EPS	$4.70 (06/14/2018)	No of Institutions	807
Market Cap	$4.4 Billion	Shares	108,601,096
Book Value	$645.0 Million	% Held	77.35
Price/Book	6.84		
Price/Sales	0.89		

Business Summary: Hotels, Restaurants & Travel (MIC: 2.2.1 SIC: 7011 NAIC: 721110)

Wyndham Destinations is a hospitality company. Co. has three segments: hotel group, which franchises in the upscale, upper midscale, midscale, economy and extended stay segments with a concentration in economy brands, and provides property management services; destination network, which provides vacation accommodations; and vacation ownership, which develops and markets Vacation Ownership Interests (VOIs) to individual consumers, provides consumer financing in connection with the sale of VOIs and provides property management services at resorts. Co.'s brands include Wyndham Hotels and Resorts, Days Inn, Super 8, Howard Johnson, Wingate by Wyndham, and Dolce Hotels and Resorts, among others.

Recent Developments: For the quarter ended Mar 31 2018, income from continuing operations decreased 36.2% to US$81.0 million from US$127.0 million in the year-earlier quarter. Net income decreased 62.2% to US$34.0 million from US$90.0 million in the year-earlier quarter. Revenues were US$1.19 billion, up 3.1% from US$1.15 billion the year before. Operating income was US$159.0 million versus US$185.0 million in the prior-year quarter, a decrease of 14.1%. Direct operating expenses rose 0.5% to US$563.0 million from US$560.0 million in the comparable period the year before. Indirect operating expenses increased 14.4% to US$468.0 million from US$409.0 million in the equivalent prior-year period.

Prospects: Our evaluation of Wyndham Worldwide Corp. as of Jan. 21, 2018 is the result of our systematic analysis on three basic characteristics: earnings strength, relative valuation, and recent stock price movement. The company has generated a negative trend in earnings per share over the past 5 quarters and while recent estimates for the company have been mixed, WYN has posted better than expected results. Based on operating earnings yield, the company is undervalued when compared to all of the companies in our coverage universe. Share price changes over the past year indicates that WYN will perform well over the near term.

Financial Data
(US$ in Millions)

	3 Mos	12/31/2017	12/31/2016	12/31/2015	12/31/2014	12/31/2013	12/31/2012	12/31/2011
Earnings Per Share	7.41	8.40	5.53	5.14	4.18	3.21	2.75	2.51
Cash Flow Per Share	8.81	9.58	8.82	8.40	7.87	7.58	7.00	6.19
Dividends Per Share	2.400	2.320	2.000	1.680	1.400	1.160	0.920	0.600
Dividend Payout %	32.39	27.62	36.17	32.68	33.49	36.14	33.45	23.90
Income Statement								
Total Revenue	1,190	5,076	5,599	5,536	5,281	5,009	4,534	4,254
EBITDA	221	920	1,282	1,229	1,144	985	783	924
Depn & Amortn	56	181	214	197	196	180	31	146
Income Before Taxes	121	590	940	916	845	683	628	650
Income Taxes	40	(229)	328	304	316	250	229	233
Net Income	34	871	611	612	529	432	400	417
Average Shares	100	103	111	119	127	135	145	166
Balance Sheet								
Current Assets	3,682	2,964	1,812	1,869	1,867	1,940	1,866	1,730
Total Assets	11,099	10,403	9,819	9,716	9,679	9,741	9,463	9,023
Current Liabilities	3,099	2,539	2,032	1,957	1,859	1,790	1,931	1,563
Long-Term Obligations	5,972	5,686	5,283	4,955	4,792	4,608	4,018	3,773
Total Liabilities	10,454	9,525	9,105	8,766	8,424	8,118	7,533	6,791
Stockholders' Equity	645	878	714	950	1,255	1,623	1,930	2,232
Shares Outstanding	99	99	105	113	121	128	137	147
Statistical Record								
Return on Assets %	7.13	8.61	6.24	6.31	5.45	4.50	4.32	4.52
Return on Equity %	116.91	109.42	73.24	55.51	36.76	24.32	19.17	16.20
EBITDA Margin %	18.57	18.12	22.90	22.20	21.66	19.66	17.27	21.72
Net Margin %	2.86	17.16	10.91	11.05	10.02	8.62	8.82	9.80
Asset Turnover	0.46	0.50	0.57	0.57	0.54	0.52	0.49	0.46
Current Ratio	1.19	1.17	0.89	0.96	1.00	1.08	0.97	1.11
Debt to Equity	9.26	6.48	7.40	5.22	3.82	2.84	2.08	1.69
Price Range	57.47-37.91	52.65-34.27	36.46-27.81	42.47-31.67	39.16-30.97	33.26-24.01	24.84-16.64	17.19-11.45
P/E Ratio	7.76-5.12	6.27-4.08	6.59-5.03	8.26-6.16	9.37-7.41	10.36-7.48	9.03-6.05	6.85-4.56
Average Yield %	5.01	5.29	6.26	4.50	4.08	4.14	4.15	4.15

Address: 22 Sylvan Way, Parsippany, NJ 07054	**Web Site:** www.wyndhamworldwide.com	**Auditors:** DELOITTE & TOUCHE LLP
Telephone: 973-753-6000	**Officers:** Michael Dean Brown - Division Officer, President, Chief Executive Officer Scott G. McLester - Executive Vice President, General Counsel	**Investor Contact:** 973-753-5500
Fax: 973-496-8906		**Transfer Agents:** Wells Fargo Shareowner Services, St. Paul, MN

XEROX CORP

*7 Year Price Score 240.54 *NYSE Composite Index=100 ***12 Month Price Score 91.04**

Interim Earnings (Per Share)

Qtr.	Mar	Jun	Sep	Dec
2015	0.76	0.04	(0.16)	1.00
2016	0.12	0.60	0.68	(3.32)
2017	0.04	0.63	0.68	(0.75)
2018	0.08	...	...	...

Interim Dividends (Per Share)

Amt	Decl	Ex	Rec	Pay
0.25Q	10/17/2017	12/28/2017	12/29/2017	03/31/2018
0.25Q	02/22/2018	03/28/2018	03/30/2018	04/30/2018
0.25Q	05/14/2018	05/28/2018	06/29/2018	07/31/2018
0.25Q	07/19/2018	09/27/2018	09/28/2018	10/31/2018

Indicated Div: $1.00

TRADING VOLUME (thousand shares)

Valuation Analysis

		Institutional Holding	
Forecast EPS	$3.58	No of Institutions	
	(06/14/2018)	800	
Market Cap	$6.1 Billion	Shares	
Book Value	$5.8 Billion	452,351,968	
Price/Book	1.06	% Held	
Price/Sales	0.60	68.93	

Business Summary: Peripherals (MIC: 6.2.2 SIC: 3577 NAIC: 333315)

Xerox is a provider of digital print technology and related solutions. Co. operates in three main areas: Managed Document Services, which includes a continuum of solutions and services spanning from managing print to automating processes to managing content; Workplace Solutions, which is made up of two strategic product groups, Entry and Mid-Range, which share common technology, manufacturing and product platforms; and Graphic Communications, which are designed for customers in the graphic communications, enabling full-color, on-demand printing of a range of applications, including variable data for personalized content and one-to-one marketing.

Recent Developments: For the quarter ended Mar 31 2018, income from continuing operations decreased 45.8% to US$26.0 million from US$48.0 million in the year-earlier quarter. Net income decreased 38.1% to US$26.0 million from US$42.0 million in the year-earlier quarter. Revenues were US$2.44 billion, down 0.8% from US$2.45 billion the year before. Direct operating expenses declined 1.0% to US$1.43 billion from US$1.45 billion in the comparable period the year before. Indirect operating expenses decreased 15.0% to US$870.0 million from US$1.02 billion in the equivalent prior-year period.

Prospects: Our evaluation of Xerox Corp. as of Jan. 21, 2018 is the result of our systematic analysis on three basic characteristics: earnings strength, relative valuation, and recent stock price movement. The company has produced a positive trend in earnings per share over the past 5 quarters. However, while recent estimates for the company have been lowered by analysts, XRX has posted better than expected results. Based on operating earnings yield, the company is undervalued when compared to all of the companies in our coverage universe. Share price changes over the past year indicates that XRX will perform in line with the market over the near term.

Financial Data
(US$ in Thousands)

	3 Mos	12/31/2017	12/31/2016	12/31/2015	12/31/2014	12/31/2013	12/31/2012	12/31/2011
Earnings Per Share	0.64	0.71	(1.96)	1.68	3.24	3.64	3.52	3.60
Cash Flow Per Share	0.55	0.13	4.31	6.05	7.15	7.75	7.90	5.65
Tang Book Value Per Share	6.04	4.14	2.79	N.M.	N.M.	N.M.	N.M.	N.M.
Dividends Per Share	1.000	0.750	1.240	1.120	1.000	0.920	0.680	...
Dividend Payout %	156.25	105.63	...	66.67	30.86	25.27	19.32	...
Income Statement								
Total Revenue	2,435,000	10,265,000	10,771,000	18,045,000	19,540,000	21,435,000	22,390,000	22,626,000
EBITDA	208,000	1,003,000	1,078,000	1,344,000	2,212,000	2,470,000	2,822,000	2,828,000
Depn & Amortn	12,000	189,000	206,000	587,000	639,000	763,000	1,059,000	806,000
Income Before Taxes	134,000	570,000	568,000	412,000	1,206,000	1,312,000	1,348,000	1,565,000
Income Taxes	40,000	481,000	62,000	(23,000)	259,000	276,000	277,000	386,000
Net Income	23,000	195,000	(477,000)	474,000	969,000	1,159,000	1,195,000	1,295,000
Average Shares	254,660	256,570	255,994	269,056	299,640	318,381	332,296	360,943
Balance Sheet								
Current Assets	5,386,000	5,230,000	6,992,000	6,685,000	8,874,000	8,511,000	8,273,000	7,912,000
Total Assets	16,175,000	15,946,000	18,145,000	24,817,000	27,658,000	29,036,000	30,015,000	30,116,000
Current Liabilities	3,152,000	2,741,000	4,654,000	5,254,000	6,076,000	5,686,000	5,910,000	6,381,000
Long-Term Obligations	4,811,000	5,235,000	5,305,000	6,382,000	6,358,000	6,904,000	7,447,000	7,088,000
Total Liabilities	10,408,000	10,476,000	13,128,000	15,394,000	16,675,000	16,387,000	18,145,000	17,891,000
Stockholders' Equity	5,767,000	5,470,000	5,017,000	9,423,000	10,983,000	12,649,000	11,870,000	12,225,000
Shares Outstanding	254,679	254,613	253,593	253,209	279,186	297,080	305,943	334,335
Statistical Record								
Return on Assets %	1.11	1.14	N.M.	1.81	3.42	3.93	3.96	4.27
Return on Equity %	3.26	3.72	N.M.	4.65	8.20	9.45	9.89	10.54
EBITDA Margin %	8.54	9.77	10.01	7.45	11.32	11.52	12.60	12.50
Net Margin %	0.94	1.90	N.M.	2.63	4.96	5.41	5.34	5.72
Asset Turnover	0.64	0.60	0.50	0.69	0.69	0.73	0.74	0.75
Current Ratio	1.71	1.91	1.50	1.27	1.46	1.50	1.40	1.24
Debt to Equity	0.83	0.96	1.06	0.68	0.58	0.55	0.63	0.58
Price Range	34.13-6.88	33.95-6.88	7.41-5.72	9.22-6.12	9.43-6.78	8.06-4.49	5.77-4.10	7.71-4.43
P/E Ratio	53.33-10.75	47.82-9.69	...	5.49-3.64	2.91-2.09	2.21-1.23	1.64-1.17	2.14-1.23
Average Yield %	3.87	3.73	19.29	14.85	12.18	14.77	13.82	...

Address: P.O. Box 4505, 201 Merritt 7, Norwalk, CT 06851-1056
Telephone: 203-968-3000
Web Site: www.xerox.com
Officers: Keith Cozza - Chairman Giovanni (John) Visentin - Vice-Chairman, Chief Executive Officer
Auditors: PricewaterhouseCoopers LLP
Transfer Agents: Computershare Trust Company, N.A., Providence, RI

XL GROUP LTD

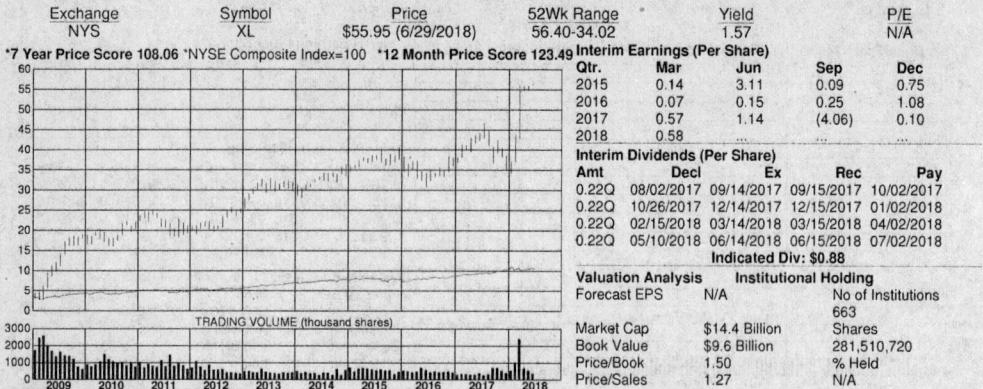

Exchange	Symbol	Price	52Wk Range	Yield	P/E
NYS	XL	$55.95 (6/29/2018)	56.40-34.02	1.57	N/A

*7 Year Price Score 108.06 *NYSE Composite Index=100 *12 Month Price Score 123.49

Interim Earnings (Per Share)

Qtr.	Mar	Jun	Sep	Dec
2015	0.14	3.11	0.09	0.75
2016	0.07	0.15	0.25	1.08
2017	0.57	1.14	(4.06)	0.10
2018	0.58	...	...	...

Interim Dividends (Per Share)

Amt	Decl	Ex	Rec	Pay
0.22Q	08/02/2017	09/14/2017	09/15/2017	10/02/2017
0.22Q	10/26/2017	12/14/2017	12/15/2017	01/02/2018
0.22Q	02/15/2018	03/14/2018	03/15/2018	04/02/2018
0.22Q	05/10/2018	06/14/2018	06/15/2018	07/02/2018

Indicated Div: $0.88

Valuation Analysis

Forecast EPS	N/A
Market Cap	$14.4 Billion
Book Value	$9.6 Billion
Price/Book	1.50
Price/Sales	1.27

Institutional Holding

No of Institutions	663
Shares	281,510,720
% Held	N/A

Business Summary: General Insurance (MIC: 5.2.1 SIC: 6331 NAIC: 524126)

XL Group is a holding company. Through its subsidiaries, Co. is an insurance and reinsurance company providing property, casualty and specialty products to industrial, commercial and professional firms, insurance companies and other enterprises. Co. is organized into two operating segments: insurance, which include four business groups: Global Casualty, Global Energy, Property and Construction, Global Professional and Global Specialt, as well as four regions: Americas; Europe, Middle East & Africa; U.K. & Ireland; and Asia Pacific; and reinsurance, which provides casualty, property risk, property catastrophe, specialty, and other reinsurance lines on a global basis.

Recent Developments: For the quarter ended Mar 31 2018, net income decreased 24.6% to US$161.2 million from US$213.8 million in the year-earlier quarter. Revenues were US$2.81 billion, up 2.2% from US$2.76 billion the year before. Net premiums earned were US$2.60 billion versus US$2.52 billion in the prior-year quarter, an increase of 3.1%. Net investment income rose 9.0% to US$218.5 million from US$200.5 million a year ago.

Prospects: Our evaluation of XL Group Ltd. as of Sep. 17, 2017 is the result of our systematic analysis on three basic characteristics: earnings strength, relative valuation, and recent stock price movement. The company has produced a positive trend in earnings per share over the past 5 quarters. However, while recent estimates for the company have been mixed, XL has posted better than expected results. Based on operating earnings yield, the company is undervalued when compared to all of the companies in our coverage universe. Share price changes over the past year indicates that XL will perform very well over the near term.

Financial Data
(US$ in Thousands)

	3 Mos	12/31/2017	12/31/2016	12/31/2015	12/31/2014	12/31/2013	12/31/2012	12/31/2011
Earnings Per Share	(2.24)	(2.16)	1.56	4.15	0.69	3.63	2.10	(1.52)
Cash Flow Per Share	(0.61)	0.13	3.27	2.15	3.61	2.71	3.43	1.05
Tang Book Value Per Share	28.66	29.77	32.73	32.12	37.56	34.45	33.82	28.57
Income Statement								
Premium Income	2,600,288	10,336,612	9,777,934	8,226,425	5,895,070	6,309,521	6,090,441	5,690,130
Total Revenue	2,814,942	11,328,157	10,546,086	9,308,926	6,602,267	7,541,234	7,230,480	6,696,803
Benefits & Claims	1,622,006	8,001,920	6,072,835	4,766,200	3,258,393	3,731,464	3,765,482	4,078,391
Income Before Taxes	182,853	(494,712)	567,877	909,031	258,517	1,094,348	708,606	(420,962)
Income Taxes	31,902	59,070	42,129	(19,161)	96,897	77,505	34,028	59,707
Net Income	152,648	(560,398)	440,968	1,207,152	188,340	1,059,916	651,134	(474,760)
Average Shares	261,176	259,894	282,758	290,999	271,527	292,069	310,282	312,896
Balance Sheet								
Total Assets	65,337,963	63,436,236	58,434,102	58,682,938	45,046,819	45,652,887	45,387,779	44,626,077
Total Liabilities	55,709,434	53,587,919	47,495,590	47,005,859	35,013,067	35,655,254	34,877,707	35,201,139
Stockholders' Equity	9,628,529	9,848,317	10,938,512	11,677,079	10,033,752	9,997,633	10,510,072	9,424,938
Shares Outstanding	258,171	256,033	266,889	294,745	255,182	278,253	298,681	315,645
Statistical Record								
Return on Assets %	N.M.	N.M.	0.75	2.33	0.42	2.33	1.44	N.M.
Return on Equity %	N.M.	N.M.	3.89	11.12	1.88	10.34	6.51	N.M.
Loss Ratio %	62.38	77.41	62.11	57.94	55.27	59.14	61.83	71.67
Net Margin %	5.42	(4.95)	4.18	12.97	2.85	14.05	9.01	(7.09)
Price Range	55.92-34.02	46.66-35.06	39.18-30.67	40.41-34.37	36.30-27.96	33.03-25.06	25.76-19.06	25.19-18.17
P/E Ratio	...	...	25.12-19.66	9.74-8.28	52.61-40.52	9.10-6.90	12.27-9.08	...

Address: O'Hara House, One Bermudiana Road, Hamilton, HM 08
Telephone: 441-292-8515

Web Site: www.xlgroup.com
Officers: Eugene M. (Gene) McQuade - Chairman
Michael S. McGavick - Chief Executive Officer

Auditors: PricewaterhouseCoopers LLP
Investor Contact: 203-964-3470
Transfer Agents: Mellon Investor Services, New Jersey

XPO LOGISTICS, INC.

Exchange	Symbol	Price	52Wk Range	Yield	P/E
NYS	XPO	$100.18 (6/29/2018)	114.18-54.99	N/A	36.04

*7 Year Price Score 188.09 *NYSE Composite Index=100 *12 Month Price Score 122.63

TRADING VOLUME (thousand shares)

Interim Earnings (Per Share)

Qtr.	Mar	Jun	Sep	Dec
2015	(0.20)	(0.89)	(0.94)	(0.55)
2016	(0.21)	0.35	0.11	0.23
2017	0.16	0.38	0.44	1.46
2018	0.50	...	...	...

Interim Dividends (Per Share)

No Dividends Paid

Valuation Analysis / Institutional Holding

Valuation Analysis		Institutional Holding	
Forecast EPS	$3.44	No of Institutions	
	(06/14/2018)	541	
Market Cap	$12.1 Billion	Shares	
Book Value	$3.7 Billion	148,140,256	
Price/Book	3.28	% Held	
Price/Sales	0.75	N/A	

Business Summary: Airlines/Air.Freight (MIC: 7.4.4 SIC: 4731 NAIC: 488510)

XPO Logistics is a transportation and logistics company. Co. has two segments: Transportation, which is a provider of freight brokerage provider, last mile logistics for heavy goods, less-than-truckload transportation, intermodal services and freight forwarder; and Logistics, which provide a range of contract logistics services, including engineered and customized solutions, warehousing and distribution, cold chain solutions and other inventory management solutions, including perform e-commerce fulfillment, warehousing, reverse logistics, storage, factory support, aftermarket support, manufacturing, distribution, packaging and labeling, as well as supply chain optimization services.

Recent Developments: For the quarter ended Mar 31 2018, net income increased 217.7% to US$79.1 million from US$24.9 million in the year-earlier quarter. Revenues were US$4.19 billion, up 18.4% from US$3.54 billion the year before. Operating income was US$141.0 million versus US$103.8 million in the prior-year quarter, an increase of 35.8%. Direct operating expenses rose 18.7% to US$3.60 billion from US$3.03 billion in the comparable period the year before. Indirect operating expenses increased 12.1% to US$450.2 million from US$401.7 million in the equivalent prior-year period.

Prospects: Our evaluation of XPO Logistics, Inc. as of Jan. 21, 2018 is the result of our systematic analysis on three basic characteristics: earnings strength, relative valuation, and recent stock price movement. The company has generated a negative trend in earnings per share over the past 5 quarters and while recent estimates for the company have been mixed, XPO has posted better than expected results. Based on operating earnings yield, the company is overvalued when compared to all of the companies in our coverage universe. Share price changes over the past year indicates that XPO will perform in line with the market over the near term.

Financial Data
(US$ in Thousands)

	3 Mos	12/31/2017	12/31/2016	12/31/2015	12/31/2014	12/31/2013	12/31/2012	12/31/2011
Earnings Per Share	2.78	2.45	0.53	(2.65)	(2.00)	(2.26)	(1.49)	(5.41)
Cash Flow Per Share	6.36	6.95	5.66	0.98	(0.40)	(2.91)	(1.54)	0.80
Tang Book Value Per Share	N.M.	N.M.	N.M.	N.M.	4.42	N.M.	6.90	4.85
Income Statement								
Total Revenue	4,191,500	15,380,800	14,619,400	7,623,200	2,356,600	702,303	278,591	177,076
EBITDA	309,200	1,032,700	933,900	137,200	(5,900)	(46,103)	(25,614)	2,378
Depn & Amortn	170,900	487,700	466,000	203,000	35,800	6,700	2,713	710
Income Before Taxes	78,900	260,700	106,800	(282,500)	(89,700)	(70,972)	(31,534)	1,477
Income Taxes	(200)	(99,500)	22,300	(90,900)	(26,100)	(22,442)	(11,195)	718
Net Income	72,600	340,200	69,000	(191,100)	(63,600)	(48,530)	(20,339)	759
Average Shares	133,400	127,800	122,800	92,800	53,600	22,752	15,694	8,246
Balance Sheet								
Current Assets	3,805,500	3,587,900	3,073,600	2,957,200	1,233,100	172,172	320,934	99,141
Total Assets	12,961,300	12,601,600	11,698,400	12,643,200	2,761,200	780,241	413,208	127,641
Current Liabilities	3,012,100	2,997,100	2,731,600	2,694,400	381,100	99,333	49,027	16,071
Long-Term Obligations	4,612,100	4,417,500	4,731,500	5,272,600	592,100	181,641	108,956	454
Total Liabilities	9,280,600	8,997,200	8,998,400	9,926,100	1,106,100	324,398	168,149	19,281
Stockholders' Equity	3,680,700	3,604,400	2,700,000	2,717,100	1,655,100	455,843	245,059	108,360
Shares Outstanding	120,600	119,920	111,087	109,523	77,421	30,538	17,957	8,365
Statistical Record								
Return on Assets %	3.18	2.80	0.57	N.M.	N.M.	N.M.	N.M.	0.82
Return on Equity %	12.19	10.79	2.54	N.M.	N.M.	N.M.	N.M.	1.07
EBITDA Margin %	7.38	6.71	6.39	1.80	N.M.	N.M.	N.M.	1.34
Net Margin %	1.73	2.21	0.47	N.M.	N.M.	N.M.	N.M.	0.43
Asset Turnover	1.30	1.27	1.20	0.99	1.33	1.18	1.03	1.92
Current Ratio	1.26	1.20	1.13	1.10	3.24	1.73	6.55	6.17
Debt to Equity	1.25	1.23	1.75	1.94	0.36	0.40	0.44	N.M.
Price Range	104.67-44.99	92.17-42.71	49.35-19.56	50.56-21.62	42.48-23.24	26.45-15.82	19.02-11.35	17.00-6.98
P/E Ratio	37.65-16.18	37.62-17.43	93.11-36.91	...	...	...	...	...

Address: Five American Lane,	Web Site: www.xpologistics.com	Auditors: KPMG LLP
Greenwich, CT 06831	Officers: Bradley S. Jacobs - Chairman, Chief	Investor Contact: 855-976-4696
Telephone: 855-976-6951	Executive Officer Troy A. Cooper - President, Chief	Transfer Agents: Computershare,
	Operating Officer, Senior Vice President	Canton, MA

XYLEM INC

Exchange	Symbol	Price	52Wk Range	Yield	P/E
NYS	XYL	$67.38 (6/29/2018)	79.48-54.34	1.25	34.55

*7 Year Price Score N/A ***NYSE Composite Index=100** ***12 Month Price Score 102.10**

Interim Earnings (Per Share)

Qtr.	Mar	Jun	Sep	Dec
2015	0.35	0.41	0.48	0.63
2016	0.37	0.39	0.41	0.28
2017	0.31	0.55	0.58	0.39
2018	0.43	...	...	...

Interim Dividends (Per Share)

Amt	Decl	Ex	Rec	Pay
0.18Q	08/17/2017	08/29/2017	08/31/2017	09/20/2017
0.18Q	10/12/2017	11/01/2017	11/02/2017	12/06/2017
0.21Q	01/31/2018	02/14/2018	02/15/2018	03/15/2018
0.21Q	05/10/2018	05/23/2018	05/24/2018	06/21/2018

Indicated Div: $0.84

Valuation Analysis **Institutional Holding**

Forecast EPS	$2.90 (06/13/2018)	No of Institutions 794
Market Cap	$12.1 Billion	Shares 179,165,472
Book Value	$2.5 Billion	% Held 84.10
Price/Book	4.77	
Price/Sales	2.50	

Business Summary: Industrial Machinery & Equipment (MIC: 7.2.1 SIC: 3561 NAIC: 333911)

Xylem is a water technology company. Co. designs, manufactures and services engineered solutions ranging across a variety of applications. Co. has three reportable business segments: Water Infrastructure, which supports the process that collects water from a source and distributes it to users, and then returns the wastewater to the environment through three linked applications; Applied Water, which encompasses the uses of water and serves a set of end markets including: residential, commercial, industrial and agricultural; as well as Sensus, which develops technology solutions that enable use and conservation of water and energy resources.

Recent Developments: For the quarter ended Mar 31 2018, net income increased 41.1% to US$79.0 million from US$56.0 million in the year-earlier quarter. Revenues were US$1.22 billion, up 13.6% from US$1.07 billion the year before. Operating income was US$113.0 million versus US$86.0 million in the prior-year quarter, an increase of 31.4%. Direct operating expenses rose 14.9% to US$757.0 million from US$659.0 million in the comparable period the year before. Indirect operating expenses increased 6.4% to US$347.0 million from US$326.0 million in the equivalent prior-year period.

Prospects: Our evaluation of Xylem Inc. as of Jan. 21, 2018 is the result of our systematic analysis on three basic characteristics: earnings strength, relative valuation, and recent stock price movement. The company has enjoyed a very positive trend in earnings per share over the past 5 quarters and while recent estimates for the company have been mixed, XYL has posted better than expected results. Based on operating earnings yield, the company is about fairly valued when compared to all of the companies in our coverage universe. Share price changes over the past year indicates that XYL will perform well over the near term.

Financial Data

(US$ in Millions)	3 Mos	12/31/2017	12/31/2016	12/31/2015	12/31/2014	12/31/2013	12/31/2012	12/31/2011
Earnings Per Share	1.95	1.83	1.45	1.87	1.83	1.22	1.59	1.50
Cash Flow Per Share	3.87	3.82	2.77	2.57	2.27	1.75	2.13	2.43
Tang Book Value Per Share	N.M.	N.M.	N.M.	0.36	0.33	0.19	N.M.	N.M.
Dividends Per Share	0.750	0.720	0.620	0.563	0.512	0.466	0.405	0.101
Dividend Payout %	38.46	39.34	42.73	30.12	27.98	38.16	25.46	6.75
Income Statement								
Total Revenue	1,217	4,707	3,771	3,653	3,916	3,837	3,791	3,803
EBITDA	183	651	492	541	566	447	529	486
Depn & Amortn	67	109	87	88	95	99	94	93
Income Before Taxes	95	463	337	400	419	296	384	379
Income Taxes	16	136	80	63	84	70	91	104
Net Income	79	331	260	340	337	228	297	279
Average Shares	181	180	180	181	184	186	186	185
Balance Sheet								
Current Assets	2,066	2,071	1,839	2,005	2,102	2,009	1,874	1,642
Total Assets	7,350	6,860	6,474	4,657	4,864	4,896	4,679	4,393
Current Liabilities	1,460	1,100	1,238	823	908	853	781	817
Long-Term Obligations	2,228	2,200	2,108	1,196	1,199	1,199	1,199	1,201
Total Liabilities	4,809	4,357	4,284	2,573	2,737	2,655	2,605	2,566
Stockholders' Equity	2,541	2,503	2,190	2,084	2,127	2,241	2,074	1,827
Shares Outstanding	180	179	179	178	182	184	185	184
Statistical Record								
Return on Assets %	5.10	4.96	4.66	7.14	6.91	4.76	6.53	...
Return on Equity %	14.77	14.11	12.13	16.15	15.43	10.57	15.19	...
EBITDA Margin %	15.04	13.83	13.05	14.81	14.45	11.65	13.95	12.78
Net Margin %	6.49	7.03	6.89	9.31	8.61	5.94	7.83	7.34
Asset Turnover	0.70	0.71	0.68	0.77	0.80	0.80	0.83	...
Current Ratio	1.42	1.88	1.49	2.44	2.31	2.36	2.40	2.01
Debt to Equity	0.88	0.88	0.96	0.57	0.56	0.54	0.58	0.66
Price Range	79.48-48.88	69.34-47.00	54.75-32.80	38.08-30.46	39.78-31.91	34.77-24.19	28.73-23.16	27.31-23.06
P/E Ratio	40.76-25.07	37.89-25.68	37.76-22.62	20.36-16.29	21.74-17.44	28.50-19.83	18.07-14.57	18.21-15.37
Average Yield %	1.19	1.27	1.38	1.59	1.39	1.63	1.57	0.41

Address: 1 International Drive, Rye Brook, NY 10573 Telephone: 914-323-5700 Fax: 914-323-5800	Web Site: www.xyleminc.com Officers: Markos I. Tambakeras - Chairman Patrick K. Decker - President, Chief Executive Officer	Auditors: DELOITTE & TOUCHE LLP Investor Contact: 914-323-5930 Transfer Agents: Wells Fargo Shareowner Services, St. Paul, MN

YUM! BRANDS INC

Exchange	Symbol	Price	52Wk Range	Yield	P/E
NYS	YUM	$78.22 (6/29/2018)	87.10-72.65	1.84	18.28

*7 Year Price Score 111.81 *NYSE Composite Index=100 *12 Month Price Score 101.71

Interim Earnings (Per Share)

Qtr.	Mar	Jun	Sep	Dec
2015	0.81	0.53	0.95	0.63
2016	0.93	0.81	1.56	0.76
2017	0.77	0.58	1.18	1.25
2018	1.27	...	...	...

Interim Dividends (Per Share)

Amt	Decl	Ex	Rec	Pay
0.30Q	05/19/2017	07/12/2017	07/14/2017	08/04/2017
0.30Q	10/23/2017	11/14/2017	11/15/2017	12/08/2017
0.36Q	01/26/2018	02/13/2018	02/14/2018	03/09/2018
0.36Q	04/25/2018	05/15/2018	05/16/2018	06/08/2018

Indicated Div: $1.44 (Div. Reinv. Plan)

Valuation Analysis — **Institutional Holding**

Forecast EPS	$3.45 (06/13/2018)	No of Institutions 1330
Market Cap	$25.6 Billion	Shares 319,259,616
Book Value	N/A	% Held 71.41
Price/Book	N/A	
Price/Sales	4.39	

Business Summary: Hotels, Restaurants & Travel (MIC: 2.2.1 SIC: 5812 NAIC: 722211)

Yum! Brands, through its three concepts of KFC, Pizza Hut and Taco Bell (the Concepts), develops, operates, franchises and licenses a worldwide system of restaurants which prepare, package and sell a menu of food items. Most restaurants in each Concept provide consumers the ability to dine in and/or carry out food. In addition, Taco Bell and KFC provide a drive-thru option in several stores. Pizza Hut provides a drive-thru option on a limited basis. Pizza Hut typically provides delivery service, as does KFC on a more limited basis primarily in China. Co.'s registered trademarks and service marks include Kentucky Fried Chicken®, KFC®, Pizza Hut® and Taco Bell® marks.

Recent Developments: For the quarter ended Mar 31 2018, net income increased 54.6% to US$433.0 million from US$280.0 million in the year-earlier quarter. Revenues were US$1.37 billion, down 3.2% from US$1.42 billion the year before. Operating income was US$553.0 million versus US$484.0 million in the prior-year quarter, an increase of 14.3%. Direct operating expenses declined 42.2% to US$438.0 million from US$758.0 million in the comparable period the year before. Indirect operating expenses increased 117.1% to US$380.0 million from US$175.0 million in the equivalent prior-year period.

Prospects: Our evaluation of Yum! Brands Inc. as of Jan. 21, 2018 is the result of our systematic analysis on three basic characteristics: earnings strength, relative valuation, and recent stock price movement. The company has managed to produce a neutral trend in earnings per share over the past 5 quarters and while recent estimates for the company have been mixed, YUM has posted better than expected results. Based on operating earnings yield, the company is about fairly valued when compared to all of the companies in our coverage universe. Share price changes over the past year indicates that YUM will perform well over the near term.

Financial Data
(US$ in Millions)

	3 Mos	12/31/2017	12/31/2016	12/26/2015	12/27/2014	12/28/2013	12/29/2012	12/31/2011
Earnings Per Share	4.28	3.77	4.04	2.92	2.32	2.36	3.38	2.74
Cash Flow Per Share	2.80	2.97	3.01	4.92	4.63	4.75	4.99	4.55
Tang Book Value Per Share	...	...	...	N.M.	1.22	1.44	0.95	1.83
Dividends Per Share	1.260	1.200	1.890	1.690	1.520	1.375	1.190	1.035
Dividend Payout %	29.44	31.83	46.78	57.88	65.52	58.26	35.21	37.77
Income Statement								
Total Revenue	1,371	5,878	6,366	13,105	13,279	13,084	13,633	12,626
EBITDA	653	2,952	1,919	2,592	2,229	2,458	2,876	2,367
Depn & Amortn	37	238	294	712	702	686	629	599
Income Before Taxes	509	2,274	1,318	1,746	1,397	1,525	2,098	1,612
Income Taxes	76	934	324	489	406	487	537	324
Net Income	433	1,340	1,619	1,293	1,051	1,091	1,597	1,319
Average Shares	340	355	400	443	453	461	473	481
Balance Sheet								
Current Assets	1,889	2,507	1,482	1,688	1,646	1,691	1,909	2,321
Total Assets	4,836	5,311	5,478	8,075	8,345	8,695	9,011	8,834
Current Liabilities	1,109	1,512	1,369	3,088	2,411	2,265	2,188	2,450
Long-Term Obligations	9,419	9,429	9,061	3,054	3,077	2,918	2,932	2,997
Total Liabilities	11,590	11,645	11,134	7,164	6,798	6,529	6,857	7,011
Stockholders' Equity	(6,754)	(6,334)	(5,656)	911	1,547	2,166	2,154	1,823
Shares Outstanding	327	332	355	420	434	443	451	460
Statistical Record								
Return on Assets %	29.90	24.84	23.51	15.79	12.37	12.36	17.95	15.13
Return on Equity %	...	...	...	105.50	56.77	50.65	80.53	76.36
EBITDA Margin %	47.63	50.22	30.14	19.78	16.79	18.79	21.10	18.75
Net Margin %	31.58	22.80	25.43	9.87	7.91	8.34	11.71	10.45
Asset Turnover	1.17	1.09	0.92	1.60	1.56	1.48	1.53	1.45
Current Ratio	1.70	1.66	1.08	0.55	0.68	0.75	0.87	0.95
Debt to Equity	...	...	...	3.35	1.99	1.35	1.36	1.64
Price Range	86.48-63.55	83.47-63.18	65.62-46.91	68.22-48.26	59.89-47.57	56.30-44.64	53.55-42.12	42.84-33.36
P/E Ratio	20.21-14.85	22.14-16.76	16.24-11.61	23.36-16.53	25.81-20.51	23.86-18.91	15.84-12.46	15.64-12.18
Average Yield %	1.65	1.66	3.18	2.93	2.85	2.74	2.46	2.73

Address: 1441 Gardiner Lane, Louisville, KY 40213 Telephone: 502-874-8300	Web Site: www.yum.com Officers: Greg Creed - Chief Executive Officer, Division Officer David E. (Dave) Russell - Senior Vice President, Vice President, Corporate Controller, Interim Chief Financial Officer, Vice President (frmr)	Auditors: KPMG LLP Investor Contact: 502-874-8006 Transfer Agents: American Stock Transfer & Trust Company, New York, NY

ZAYO GROUP HOLDINGS INC

Exchange	Symbol	Price	52Wk Range	Yield	P/E
NYS	ZAYO	$36.48 (6/29/2018)	37.62-29.92	N/A	114.00

*7 Year Price Score N/A   *NYSE Composite Index=100   *12 Month Price Score 98.85

Interim Earnings (Per Share)

Qtr.	Sep	Dec	Mar	Jun
2014-15	(0.50)	0.02	(0.22)	0.03
2015-16	(0.06)	(0.04)	(0.08)	(0.12)
2016-17	0.06	0.08	0.11	0.09
2017-18	0.09	0.05	0.09	...

Interim Dividends (Per Share)

No Dividends Paid

Valuation Analysis   **Institutional Holding**

Forecast EPS	$0.33	No of Institutions
	(06/14/2018)	412
Market Cap	$9.1 Billion	Shares
Book Value	$1.5 Billion	235,634,640
Price/Book	5.89	% Held
Price/Sales	3.51	N/A

Business Summary: Manufacturing (MIC: 6.1.1 SIC: 3669 NAIC: 334290)

Zayo Group Holdings is a holding company. Through its subsidiaries, Co. is a provider of bandwidth infrastructure in the U.S., Canada and Europe. Co. provides products and services through six segments: Fiber Solutions, which provides raw bandwidth infrastructure to customers; Transport, which provides lit bandwidth infrastructure solutions; Enterprise Networks, which provides communication solutions to medium and large enterprises; Zayo Colocation, which provides data center infrastructure solutions; Allstream, which provides Voice, SIP Trunking, Unified Communications and data services for businesses; and Other, which provides network and technical resources to customers.

Recent Developments: For the quarter ended Mar 31 2018, net income decreased 13.3% to US$23.4 million from US$27.0 million in the year-earlier quarter. Revenues were US$649.4 million, up 18.0% from US$550.2 million the year before. Operating income was US$105.3 million versus US$90.7 million in the prior-year quarter, an increase of 16.1%. Direct operating expenses rose 20.5% to US$234.9 million from US$195.0 million in the comparable period the year before. Indirect operating expenses increased 16.9% to US$309.2 million from US$264.5 million in the equivalent prior-year period.

Prospects: Our evaluation of Zayo Group Holdings Inc as of Jan. 21, 2018 is the result of our systematic analysis on three basic characteristics: earnings strength, relative valuation, and recent stock price movement. The company has generated a negative trend in earnings per share over the past 5 quarters. However, while recent estimates for the company have been mixed, ZAYO has posted results that fell short of analysts expectations. Based on operating earnings yield, the company is overvalued when compared to all of the companies in our coverage universe. Share price changes over the past year indicates that ZAYO will perform well over the near term.

Financial Data
(US$ in Thousands)

	9 Mos	6 Mos	3 Mos	06/30/2017	06/30/2016	06/30/2015	06/30/2014	06/30/2013
Earnings Per Share	0.32	0.34	0.37	0.35	(0.31)	(0.66)	(0.80)	(0.61)
Cash Flow Per Share	3.89	3.90	3.84	3.73	2.93	2.57	2.54	1.82
Income Statement								
Total Revenue	1,946,400	1,297,000	643,500	2,199,800	1,721,700	1,347,100	1,123,187	1,004,354
EBITDA	227,800	143,300	69,400	872,500	592,900	401,300	353,305	312,774
Depn & Amortn	(101,500)	(66,400)	(32,800)	526,900	440,500	351,400	294,125	280,128
Income Before Taxes	107,300	63,000	28,600	104,100	(67,700)	(164,100)	(144,349)	(169,818)
Income Taxes	49,200	28,300	5,400	18,400	8,500	(8,800)	37,295	(24,205)
Net Income	58,100	34,700	23,200	85,700	(76,200)	(155,300)	(179,294)	(137,217)
Average Shares	249,700	249,300	248,000	246,800	243,300	235,422	223,000	223,000
Balance Sheet								
Current Assets	697,300	606,400	610,200	514,600	397,100	567,900	544,979	303,496
Total Assets	9,241,500	8,935,900	8,862,400	8,739,400	6,727,500	6,094,600	5,049,066	4,251,240
Current Liabilities	627,000	611,600	671,500	620,300	486,500	386,900	344,886	281,760
Long-Term Obligations	5,813,900	5,628,400	5,629,800	5,626,300	4,130,200	3,680,500	3,242,529	2,821,072
Total Liabilities	7,701,100	7,425,600	7,382,900	7,328,900	5,508,300	4,883,400	4,632,681	3,644,987
Stockholders' Equity	1,540,400	1,510,300	1,479,500	1,410,500	1,219,200	1,211,200	416,385	606,253
Shares Outstanding	248,663	248,105	247,361	246,471	242,649	243,008	223,000	223,000
Statistical Record								
Return on Assets %	0.91	1.07	1.19	1.11	N.M.	N.M.	N.M.	...
Return on Equity %	5.64	6.07	6.81	6.52	N.M.	N.M.	N.M.	...
EBITDA Margin %	11.70	11.05	10.78	39.66	34.44	29.79	31.46	31.14
Net Margin %	2.98	2.68	3.61	3.90	N.M.	N.M.	N.M.	N.M.
Asset Turnover	0.29	0.31	0.30	0.28	0.27	0.24	0.24	...
Current Ratio	1.11	0.99	0.91	0.83	0.82	1.47	1.58	1.08
Debt to Equity	3.77	3.73	3.81	3.99	3.39	3.04	7.79	4.65
Price Range	37.62-29.92	37.07-29.92	35.55-29.71	35.22-27.56	29.43-21.89	32.03-22.00	...	...
P/E Ratio	117.56-93.50	109.03-88.00	96.08-80.30	100.63-78.74	...	...	...	...

Address: 1821 30th Street, Unit A, Boulder, CO 80301 **Telephone:** 303-381-4683	**Web Site:** www.zayo.com **Officers:** Daniel P. (Dan) Caruso - Chairman, Chief Executive Officer Matt Steinfort - Chief Financial Officer	**Auditors:** KPMG LLP **Transfer Agents:** American Stock Transfer & Trust Company LLC

ZENDESK INC

Exchange	Symbol	Price	52Wk Range	Yield	P/E
NYS	ZEN	$54.49 (6/29/2018)	59.43-25.48	N/A	N/A

*7 Year Price Score N/A   *NYSE Composite Index=100   *12 Month Price Score 139.88

Interim Earnings (Per Share)

Qtr.	Mar	Jun	Sep	Dec
2015	(0.25)	(0.25)	(0.22)	(0.28)
2016	(0.30)	(0.28)	(0.27)	(0.25)
2017	(0.28)	(0.29)	(0.28)	(0.26)
2018	(0.28)	...	...	...

Interim Dividends (Per Share)

No Dividends Paid

Valuation Analysis		Institutional Holding	
Forecast EPS	$0.10	No of Institutions	
	(06/24/2018)	276	
Market Cap	$5.7 Billion	Shares	
Book Value	$400.7 Million	112,903,712	
Price/Book	14.19	% Held	
Price/Sales	12.16	N/A	

TRADING VOLUME (thousand shares)

Business Summary: Internet & Software (MIC: 6.3.2 SIC: 7372 NAIC: 511210)

Zendesk is a software development company that provides software-as-a-service products. The primary product in Co.'s family, Zendesk Support, provides organizations with the ability to track, prioritize, and solve customer support tickets across multiple channels. Co.'s other available products integrate with Zendesk Support and include Zendesk Chat, Zendesk Talk, and Zendesk Help Center. Zendesk Chat is live chat software and Zendesk Talk is cloud-based call center software. In addition, Zendesk Help Center is a self-service destination that organizations can use to provide articles, interactive forums, and a community that help an organization's customers help themselves.

Recent Developments: For the quarter ended Mar 31 2018, net loss amounted to US$29.3 million versus a net loss of US$25.1 million in the year-earlier quarter. Revenues were US$129.8 million, up 38.2% from US$93.9 million the year before. Operating loss was US$33.6 million versus a loss of US$25.3 million in the prior-year quarter. Direct operating expenses rose 39.0% to US$39.1 million from US$28.1 million in the comparable period the year before. Indirect operating expenses increased 36.6% to US$124.4 million from US$91.0 million in the equivalent prior-year period.

Prospects: Our evaluation of Zendesk Inc as of Jan. 21, 2018 is the result of our systematic analysis on three basic characteristics: earnings strength, relative valuation, and recent stock price movement. The company has produced a positive trend in earnings per share over the past 5 quarters. Because the company lacks sufficient analyst estimate data, we place greater weight on the historical EPS trend as the measure of earnings strength. Based on operating earnings yield, the company is overvalued when compared to all of the companies in our coverage universe. Share price changes over the past year indicates that ZEN will perform in line with the market over the near term.

Financial Data
(US$ in Thousands)

	3 Mos	12/31/2017	12/31/2016	12/31/2015	12/31/2014	12/31/2013	12/31/2012
Earnings Per Share	(1.11)	(1.11)	(1.11)	(0.99)	(1.26)	(1.04)	(1.67)
Cash Flow Per Share	0.49	0.42	0.26	0.06	0.04	0.18	(0.26)
Tang Book Value Per Share	3.21	2.47	2.55	2.62	1.32	1.08	1.81
Income Statement							
Total Revenue	129,791	430,492	311,999	208,768	127,049	72,045	38,228
EBITDA	(21,085)	(91,856)	(86,606)	(72,514)	(61,578)	(19,450)	(23,144)
Depn & Amortn	11,530	20,300	16,200	11,200	6,100	2,900	1,100
Income Before Taxes	(32,615)	(112,156)	(102,806)	(83,714)	(67,678)	(22,350)	(24,244)
Income Taxes	(3,290)	(1,518)	993	338	(263)	221	121
Net Income	(29,325)	(110,638)	(103,799)	(84,052)	(67,415)	(22,571)	(24,365)
Average Shares	103,692	99,918	93,161	84,926	53,571	21,674	19,629
Balance Sheet							
Current Assets	837,140	328,207	279,818	283,231	139,005	73,859	54,661
Total Assets	1,112,523	560,204	475,285	422,686	205,788	92,736	64,058
Current Liabilities	261,297	230,724	167,218	117,399	78,149	42,153	21,137
Long-Term Obligations	439,953	...	...	...	3,911	23,405	374
Total Liabilities	711,870	238,563	175,857	129,396	92,082	67,643	22,943
Stockholders' Equity	400,653	321,641	299,428	293,290	113,706	25,093	41,115
Shares Outstanding	104,300	103,121	96,700	90,326	75,599	23,175	22,703
Statistical Record							
Asset Turnover	0.58	0.83	0.69	0.66	0.85	0.92	...
Current Ratio	3.20	1.42	1.67	2.41	1.78	1.75	2.59
Debt to Equity	1.10	...	...	...	0.03	0.93	0.01
Price Range	49.04-24.82	35.65-22.13	31.51-14.77	27.33-19.15	27.74-13.43	...	...

Address: 1019 Market Street, San Francisco, CA 94103
Telephone: 415-418-7506

Web Site: www.zendesk.com
Officers: Mikkel Svane - Chairman, Chief Executive Officer Adrian McDermott - President, Senior Vice President

Auditors: Ernst & Young LLP
Transfer Agents: Computershare Trust Company, N.A., Canton, Massachusetts

ZIMMER BIOMET HOLDINGS INC

Exchange	Symbol	Price	52Wk Range	Yield	P/E
NYS	ZBH	$111.44 (6/29/2018)	132.61-105.18	0.86	13.48

*7 Year Price Score 98.33   *NYSE Composite Index=100   *12 Month Price Score 95.23

Interim Earnings (Per Share)

Qtr.	Mar	Jun	Sep	Dec
2015	1.02	(0.91)	0.11	0.66
2016	0.52	(0.16)	0.78	0.34
2017	1.47	0.90	0.48	6.04
2018	0.85	...	...	...

Interim Dividends (Per Share)

Amt	Decl	Ex	Rec	Pay
0.24Q	08/07/2017	09/21/2017	09/22/2017	10/27/2017
0.24Q	12/18/2017	12/28/2017	12/29/2017	01/29/2018
0.24Q	03/12/2018	03/28/2018	03/29/2018	04/30/2018
0.24Q	06/14/2018	06/28/2018	06/29/2018	07/31/2018

Indicated Div: $0.96

Valuation Analysis   Institutional Holding

Forecast EPS	$7.66	No of Institutions	
	(06/14/2018)	1301	
Market Cap	$22.7 Billion	Shares	
Book Value	$12.0 Billion	234,602,224	
Price/Book	1.89	% Held	
Price/Sales	2.88	78.44	

Business Summary: Medical Instruments & Equipment (MIC: 4.3.1 SIC: 3842 NAIC: 339113)

Zimmer Biomet Holdings is engaged in musculoskeletal healthcare. Co. designs, manufactures and markets orthopaedic reconstructive products; sports medicine, biologics, extremities and trauma products; office based technologies; spine, craniomaxillofacial and thoracic (CMF) products; dental implants; and related surgical products. Co. manages its operations through three geographic operating segments: the Americas; Europe, the Middle East and Africa; and Asia Pacific. Co.'s four product category operating segments are as follows: Americas Spine; Office Based Technologies; CMF; and Dental.

Recent Developments: For the quarter ended Mar 31 2018, net income decreased 41.1% to US$176.2 million from US$299.3 million in the year-earlier quarter. Revenues were US$2.02 billion, up 2.3% from US$1.97 billion the year before. Operating income was US$305.0 million versus US$348.1 million in the prior-year quarter, a decrease of 12.4%. Direct operating expenses rose 12.3% to US$575.8 million from US$512.9 million in the comparable period the year before. Indirect operating expenses increased 2.3% to US$1.14 billion from US$1.11 billion in the equivalent prior-year period.

Prospects: Our evaluation of Zimmer Biomet Holdings Inc. as of Jan. 21, 2018 is the result of our systematic analysis on three basic characteristics: earnings strength, relative valuation, and recent stock price movement. The company has generated a negative trend in earnings per share over the past 5 quarters. However, while recent estimates for the company have been mixed, ZBH has posted results that fell short of analysts expectations. Based on operating earnings yield, the company is undervalued when compared to all of the companies in our coverage universe. Share price changes over the past year indicates that ZBH will perform in line with the market over the near term.

Financial Data

(US$ in Thousands)	3 Mos	12/31/2017	12/31/2016	12/31/2015	12/31/2014	12/31/2013	12/31/2012	12/31/2011
Earnings Per Share	8.27	8.90	1.51	0.77	4.19	4.43	4.29	4.03
Cash Flow Per Share	8.85	7.84	8.14	4.36	6.23	5.68	6.57	6.27
Tang Book Value Per Share	N.M.	N.M.	N.M.	N.M.	20.05	17.54	14.85	11.70
Dividends Per Share	0.960	0.960	0.960	0.880	0.880	0.800	0.720	...
Dividend Payout %	11.61	10.79	63.58	114.29	21.00	18.06	16.78	...
Income Statement								
Total Revenue	2,017,600	7,824,100	7,683,900	5,997,800	4,673,300	4,623,400	4,471,700	4,451,800
EBITDA	452,200	1,847,900	1,787,200	1,142,800	1,263,700	1,298,200	1,313,400	1,290,200
Depn & Amortn	150,800	1,058,000	1,032,600	712,400	268,600	262,600	266,000	266,100
Income Before Taxes	223,400	464,600	399,600	153,200	943,900	981,100	990,100	978,900
Income Taxes	47,200	(1,348,800)	95,000	7,000	224,900	221,900	237,200	218,900
Net Income	174,700	1,813,800	305,900	147,000	720,100	761,000	755,000	760,800
Average Shares	204,600	203,700	202,400	189,800	171,700	171,800	176,000	188,700
Balance Sheet								
Current Assets	5,775,300	4,515,300	4,663,600	5,862,900	4,289,000	4,197,700	3,708,700	3,276,600
Total Assets	27,181,200	25,964,500	26,684,400	27,219,500	9,634,700	9,580,600	9,012,400	8,515,300
Current Liabilities	3,424,500	3,020,200	2,381,500	1,617,900	1,038,000	1,031,600	866,000	867,100
Long-Term Obligations	9,486,900	8,917,500	10,665,800	11,556,300	1,425,500	1,672,300	1,720,800	1,576,000
Total Liabilities	15,182,800	14,228,700	17,015,500	17,331,600	3,113,900	3,283,300	3,151,500	3,008,100
Stockholders' Equity	11,998,400	11,735,800	9,668,900	9,887,900	6,520,800	6,297,300	5,860,900	5,507,200
Shares Outstanding	203,300	202,600	200,600	202,700	169,700	169,800	171,600	178,000
Statistical Record								
Return on Assets %	6.24	6.89	1.13	0.80	7.50	8.19	8.59	9.21
Return on Equity %	15.40	16.95	3.12	1.79	11.24	12.52	13.25	13.49
EBITDA Margin %	22.41	23.62	23.26	19.05	27.04	28.08	29.37	28.98
Net Margin %	8.66	23.18	3.98	2.45	15.41	16.46	16.88	17.09
Asset Turnover	0.29	0.30	0.28	0.33	0.49	0.50	0.51	0.54
Current Ratio	1.69	1.50	1.96	3.62	4.13	4.07	4.28	3.78
Debt to Equity	0.79	0.76	1.10	1.17	0.22	0.27	0.29	0.29
Price Range	132.61-107.44	132.61-103.33	133.09-91.68	121.76-92.41	115.05-90.87	93.43-66.66	68.80-53.21	69.69-47.42
P/E Ratio	16.04-12.99	14.90-11.61	88.14-60.72	158.13-120.01	27.46-21.69	21.09-15.05	16.04-12.40	17.29-11.77
Average Yield %	0.80	0.81	0.85	0.81	0.87	1.00	1.15	...

Address: 345 East Main Street,	Web Site: www.zimmer.com	Auditors: PricewaterhouseCoopers LLP
Warsaw, IN 46580	Officers: Bryan C. Hanson - President, Chief	Investor Contact: 574-267-6131
Telephone: 574-267-6131	Executive Officer Daniel P. Florin - Executive Vice	Transfer Agents: American Stock
	President, Interim Chief Executive Officer, Senior	Transfer & Trust Company LLC
	Vice President, Chief Financial Officer	

ZOETIS INC

Exchange	Symbol	Price	52Wk Range	Yield	P/E
NYS	ZTS	$85.19 (6/29/2018)	89.20-59.73	0.59	42.81

*7 Year Price Score N/A   *NYSE Composite Index=100   *12 Month Price Score 113.65

Interim Earnings (Per Share)

Qtr.	Mar	Jun	Sep	Dec
2015	0.33	(0.07)	0.38	0.05
2016	0.41	0.45	0.48	0.31
2017	0.48	0.50	0.61	0.16
2018	0.72	...	...	...

Interim Dividends (Per Share)

Amt	Decl	Ex	Rec	Pay
0.105Q	10/05/2017	11/08/2017	11/09/2017	12/01/2017
0.126Q	12/11/2017	01/18/2018	01/19/2018	03/01/2018
0.126Q	02/13/2018	04/19/2018	04/20/2018	06/01/2018
0.126Q	05/15/2018	07/19/2018	07/20/2018	09/04/2018

Indicated Div: $0.50

Valuation Analysis / Institutional Holding

Valuation Analysis		Institutional Holding	
Forecast EPS	$3.06	No of Institutions	
	(06/14/2018)	1065	
Market Cap	$41.3 Billion	Shares	
Book Value	$2.0 Billion	493,471,744	
Price/Book	21.07	% Held	
Price/Sales	7.59	89.05	

TRADING VOLUME (thousand shares)

Business Summary: Pharmaceuticals (MIC: 4.1.1 SIC: 2834 NAIC: 325412)

Zoetis engages in the discovery, development, manufacture and commercialization of animal health medicines and vaccines, with a focus on both livestock and companion animals. Co. organizes and operates its business in two segments: the U.S. and International. Co.'s main product categories are anti-infectives, vaccines, parasiticides, medicated feed additives, and other pharmaceutical products such as pain and sedation, oncology, antiemetic, allergy and dermatology, and reproductive products. Co.'s other product categories include nutritionals and agribusiness, as well as products and services in complementary areas, including biodevices, diagnostics and genetics.

Recent Developments: For the quarter ended Mar 31 2018, net income increased 46.4% to US$350.0 million from US$239.0 million in the year-earlier quarter. Revenues were US$1.37 billion, up 11.0% from US$1.23 billion the year before. Direct operating expenses rose 0.9% to US$447.0 million from US$443.0 million in the comparable period the year before. Indirect operating expenses increased 9.5% to US$460.0 million from US$420.0 million in the equivalent prior-year period.

Prospects: Our evaluation of Zoetis Inc as of Jan. 21, 2018 is the result of our systematic analysis on three basic characteristics: earnings strength, relative valuation, and recent stock price movement. The company has enjoyed a very positive trend in earnings per share over the past 5 quarters and while recent estimates for the company have been mixed, ZTS has posted better than expected results. Based on operating earnings yield, the company is about fairly valued when compared to all of the companies in our coverage universe. Share price changes over the past year indicates that ZTS will perform well over the near term.

Financial Data
(US$ in Millions)

	3 Mos	12/31/2017	12/31/2016	12/31/2015	12/31/2014	12/31/2013	12/31/2012	12/31/2011
Earnings Per Share	1.99	1.75	1.65	0.68	1.16	1.01	0.87	...
Cash Flow Per Share	3.33	2.75	1.43	1.33	1.25	1.36	0.91	...
Tang Book Value Per Share	N.M.	N.M.	N.M.	N.M.	N.M.	N.M.	4.35	...
Dividends Per Share	0.441	0.420	0.380	0.332	0.288	0.195	...	...
Dividend Payout %	22.16	24.00	23.03	48.82	24.83	19.31	...	...
Income Statement								
Total Revenue	1,366	5,307	4,888	4,765	4,785	4,561	4,336	4,233
EBITDA	547	1,933	1,624	865	1,138	1,009	938	499
Depn & Amortn	83	233	230	196	201	206	197	69
Income Before Taxes	417	1,525	1,228	545	820	690	710	394
Income Taxes	67	663	409	206	233	187	274	146
Net Income	352	864	821	339	583	504	436	245
Average Shares	489	493	498	502	502	500	500	...
Balance Sheet								
Current Assets	4,267	4,217	3,390	3,830	3,465	3,357	2,864	2,311
Total Assets	8,690	8,586	7,649	7,913	6,607	6,558	6,262	5,711
Current Liabilities	1,000	1,094	1,117	1,781	1,086	1,415	1,123	843
Long-Term Obligations	4,954	4,953	4,468	4,463	3,643	3,642	509	575
Total Liabilities	6,730	6,816	6,162	6,845	5,296	5,618	2,236	1,991
Stockholders' Equity	1,960	1,770	1,487	1,068	1,311	940	4,026	3,720
Shares Outstanding	484	486	492	497	501	500	500	...
Statistical Record								
Return on Assets %	11.97	10.64	10.52	4.67	8.86	7.86	...	4.46
Return on Equity %	54.81	53.05	64.09	28.50	51.80	20.30	...	6.94
EBITDA Margin %	40.04	36.42	33.22	18.15	23.78	22.12	21.63	11.79
Net Margin %	25.77	16.28	16.80	7.11	12.18	11.05	10.06	5.79
Asset Turnover	0.67	0.65	0.63	0.66	0.73	0.71	...	0.77
Current Ratio	4.27	3.85	3.03	2.15	3.19	2.37	2.55	2.74
Debt to Equity	2.53	2.80	3.00	4.18	2.78	3.87	0.13	0.15
Price Range	84.69-52.54	72.80-52.51	53.78-39.33	55.38-39.65	44.93-28.40	34.64-29.15	...	...
P/E Ratio	42.56-26.40	41.60-30.01	32.59-23.84	81.44-58.31	38.73-24.48	34.30-28.86	...	...
Average Yield %	0.66	0.69	0.79	0.72	0.85	0.61	...	...

Address: 10 Sylvan Way, Parsippany, NJ 07054	Web Site: www.zoetis.com	Auditors: KPMG LLP
Telephone: 973-822-7000	Officers: Michael B. McCallister - Chairman Catherine A. Knupp - President, Executive Vice President	Transfer Agents: Computershare Trust Company, N.A., College Station, TX

This Page left intentionally blank

CONDENSED

STATISTICAL

TABULATION

The tab section consists of statistical highlights for all U.S. companies listed on the New York Stock Exchange.

Statistics for companies whose fiscal year ends prior to June 30 are listed under the prior calendar year. Statistics for companies whose fiscal year ends June 30 or after are listed under the current calendar year. Dividends and price ranges are on a calendar year basis.

Because of editorial constraints a column for fourth quarter results was not included. At fiscal year-end, full fiscal year per share earnings are listed and quarterly figures are eliminated. Quarterly per share earnings are inserted as the company reports in the current fiscal year.

NOTE: Figures listed under "Earnings Per Share" for investment companies are net asset value per share.

For abbreviations, see the blue section of the Handbook.

SYMBOL	COMPANY	NATURE OF BUSINESS	FISCAL YEAR-END	TOTAL REV. $MILL	NET INCOME $MILL	TOTAL ASSETS $MILL	NET STK EQUITY $MILL	NO OF INST	INST. HOLDINGS (SHARES)
DDD	3D Systems Corp. (DE)	Computer Hardware & Equipment	12/31/17	646.1	-66.2	896.8	618.9	345	90529394
MMM	3M Co	Medical Instruments & Equipment	12/31/17	31657.0	4858.0	37987.0	11563.0	2645	506976188
WBAI	500.com Ltd.	Sporting & Recreational	12/31/17	131.3	-317.1	1754.6	1409.8	40	5164018
WUBA	58.com Inc	IT Services	12/31/17	10068.8	1384.6	28266.5	21329.9	274	90662102
EGHT	8x8 Inc	Internet & Software	3/31/18	296.5	-104.5	277.2	218.8	247	84051166
ATEN	A10 Networks Inc	Internet & Software	12/31/16	230.0	-20.9	221.3	86.1	142	52670135
AAC	AAC Holdings Inc	Diagnostic & Health Related Service	12/31/17	317.6	-20.6	428.3	151.0	5	557318
AIR	AAR Corp	Aerospace	5/31/18	1748.3	15.6	1524.7	936.3	269	41607961
AAN	Aaron's Inc	Retail - Furniture & Home Furnishing	12/31/17	3383.7	292.5	2692.3	1728.0	375	90622751
ABB	ABB Ltd	Electrical Equipment	12/31/17	34312.0	2213.0	43262.0	14819.0	558	172011812
ABT	Abbott Laboratories	Medical Instruments & Equipment	12/31/17	27390.0	477.0	76250.0	30897.0	2480	1552761601
ABBV	AbbVie Inc	Pharmaceuticals	12/31/17	28216.0	5309.0	70786.0	5097.0	2368	1266929335
ANF	Abercrombie & Fitch Co	Retail - Apparel and Accessories	2/3/18	3492.7	7.1	2325.7	1242.4	434	88703665
AGD	Aberdeen Global Dynamic Dividend	Holding and other Investment Office	10/31/17	11.0	9.4	146.7	143.4	44	2502772
AWP	Aberdeen Global Premier Propertie	Holding and other Investment Office	10/31/17	16.4	9.0	763.4	613.1	128	21863830
ACP	Aberdeen Income Credit Strategies	Finance Intermediaries & Services	10/31/16	24.5	19.1	289.9	191.3	33	4033554
JEQ	Aberdeen Japan Equity Fund Inc	Holding and other Investment Office	10/31/16	2.1	1.0	128.0	127.9	47	9525553
AOD	Aberdeen Total Dynamic Dividend F	Holding and other Investment Office	10/31/17	83.9	71.7	1105.8	1070.3	129	47216551
ABM	ABM Industries, Inc.	Sanitation Services	10/31/17	5453.6	3.8	3812.6	1375.7	293	78730097
AKR	Acadia Realty Trust	REITs	12/31/17	250.3	61.5	3960.2	1567.2	269	107025746
ACN	Accenture plc	Business Services	8/31/17	36765.5	3445.1	22689.9	8949.5	1583	550202401
ACCO	Acco Brands Corp	Office Equipment & Furniture	12/31/17	1948.8	131.7	2799.1	774.1	346	120368386
ATV	Acorn International Inc	Retail - Specialty	12/31/15	47.5	-40.2	240.7	178.3	10	290460
ATU	Actuant Corp	Industrial Machinery & Equipment	8/31/17	1095.8	-66.2	1517.0	500.5	271	85150959
AYI	Acuity Brands Inc (Holding Compan	Electrical Equipment	8/31/17	3505.1	321.7	2899.6	1665.6	620	56059599
GOLF	Acushnet Holdings Corp	Sporting & Recreational	12/31/17	1560.3	92.1	1727.3	814.7	130	38873482
ADX	Adams Diversified Equity Fund Inc	Holding and other Investment Office	12/31/16	28.3	18.9	1545.5	1513.5	149	23999134
PEO	Adams Natural Resources Fund Inc	Holding and other Investment Office	12/31/16	16.6	11.5	688.1	685.9	96	8766127
AGRO	Adecoagro SA	Agricultural Crop Production	12/31/17	1005.3	10.0	1607.2	639.7	137	50870290
ADNT	Adient Plc	Auto Parts	9/30/17	16213.0	877.0	13170.0	4279.0	503	96133280
ADT	ADT Inc (DE)	Services	12/31/17	4315.5	342.6	17014.8	3433.1	124	734537751
ATGE	Adtalem Global Education Inc	Educational Services	6/30/17	1809.8	122.3	2314.0	1669.0	373	73671223
AAP	Advance Auto Parts Inc	Retail - Automotive	12/30/17	9373.8	475.5	8482.3	3415.2	661	93193960
ADSW	Advanced Disposal Services Inc (D	Miscellaneous Consumer Services	12/31/17	1507.6	38.3	3493.3	884.6	161	90387179
WMS	Advanced Drainage Systems Inc	Plastics	3/31/18	1330.4	62.0	1043.2	417.1	146	47516890
ASIX	AdvanSix Inc	Plastics	12/31/17	1475.2	146.7	1050.3	376.3	472	27542813
AAV	Advantage Oil & Gas Ltd	Production & Extraction	12/31/17	225.4	95.0	1691.2	1311.7	-	0
AVK	Advent Claymore Convertible Secur	Holding and other Investment Office	10/31/17	26.8	16.0	583.7	353.4	86	6885898
AGC	Advent Claymore Convertible Secur	Holding and other Investment Office	10/31/17	14.2	6.8	315.3	184.1	56	10114581
LCM	Advent/Claymore Enhanced Growth	Holding and other Investment Office	10/31/17	5.4	2.1	124.9	86.8	36	3054537
ACM	AECOM	Construction Services	9/30/17	18203.4	339.4	14397.0	3996.1	447	156306902
ANW	Aegean Marine Petroleum Network	Equipment & Services	12/31/16	4076.2	51.9	1600.9	589.5	112	20811890
AEG	AEGON NV	Life & Health	12/31/17	50504.0	2469.0	395923.0	24082.0	336	204238662
AER	Aercap Holdings NV	Aerospace	12/31/17	5037.5	1076.2	42040.1	8579.7	440	142873049
HIVE	Aerohive Networks Inc	Internet & Software	12/31/17	152.9	-22.9	134.6	21.9	125	32270750
AJRD	Aerojet Rocketdyne Holdings Inc	Defense	12/31/17	1877.2	-9.2	2258.7	102.4	316	99327965
AES	AES Corp.	Electric Utilities	12/31/17	10530.0	-1161.0	33112.0	3302.0	761	789029537
AET	Aetna Inc	Life & Health	12/31/17	60535.0	1904.0	55151.0	15580.0	1420	368372038
AMG	Affiliated Managers Group Inc.	Wealth Management	12/31/17	2305.0	689.5	8702.1	3822.2	759	65911185
AFL	AFLAC Inc	Life & Health	12/31/17	21667.0	4604.0	137217.0	24598.0	1427	612451823
MITT	AG Mortgage Investment Trust Inc	REITs	12/31/17	172.5	118.6	3789.3	714.3	153	21684112
AGCO	AGCO Corp.	Industrial Machinery & Equipment	12/31/17	8306.5	186.4	7971.7	3029.6	573	85675795
A	Agilent Technologies, Inc.	Medical Instruments & Equipment	10/31/17	4472.0	684.0	8426.0	4831.0	1003	352533244
ATG PR	AGL Capital Trust II	Gas Utilities							0
AEM	Agnico Eagle Mines Ltd	Precious Metals	12/31/17	2242.6	243.9	7865.6	4947.0	447	153768007
ADC	Agree Realty Corp.	REITs	12/31/17	116.6	58.1	1494.6	908.7	284	35453223
AHC	AH Belo Corp	Publishing	12/31/17	248.6	10.2	162.8	97.7	86	16392223
AL	Air Lease Corp	Miscellaneous Transportation Servic	12/31/17	1516.4	756.2	15614.2	4127.4	373	98062813
APD	Air Products & Chemicals Inc	Specialty Chemicals	9/30/17	8187.6	3000.4	18467.2	10086.2	1384	250930542
AYR	Aircastle Ltd.	Aerospace	12/31/17	796.6	147.9	7199.1	1907.6	224	54481493
AKS	AK Steel Holding Corp.	Non-Precious Metals	12/31/17	6080.5	6.2	4296.1	-216.0	418	248210793
ALP PRQ	Alabama Power Co	Electric Utilities	12/31/17	6039.0	866.0	23864.0	7120.0		0
ALG	Alamo Group, Inc.	Industrial Machinery & Equipment	12/31/17	912.4	44.3	639.7	449.1	244	12097408
AGI	Alamos Gold (New)	Precious Metals	12/31/17	542.8	26.6	3313.8	2681.2	186	243805486
ALK	Alaska Air Group, Inc.	Airlines/Air Freight	12/31/17	7933.0	1034.0	10740.0	3721.0	726	121295875
AIN	Albany International Corp	Industrial Machinery & Equipment	12/31/17	863.7	33.1	1361.2	569.8	248	34902518
ALB	Albemarle Corp.	Specialty Chemicals	12/31/17	3072.0	54.8	7750.8	3674.5	809	119250198
AA	Alcoa Corporation	Metal Products	12/31/17	11652.0	217.0	17447.0	4523.0	533	165063022
ALEX	Alexander & Baldwin Inc (REIT)	REITs	12/31/17	425.5	228.3	2231.2	654.4		0
ALX	Alexander's Inc	REITs	12/31/17	230.6	80.5	1632.4	344.0	154	2140763
ARE	Alexandria Real Estate Equities Inc	REITs	12/31/17	1128.1	169.1	12104.0	5949.7	565	125836913
AQN	Algonquin Power & Utilities Corp	Water Utilities	12/31/17	1977.8	193.1	10533.6	3409.0	114	189589306
BABA	Alibaba Group Holding Ltd	Internet & Software	3/31/17	158273.0	43675.0	506812.0	281791.0	1518	1049234335
Y	Alleghany Corp.	General Insurance	12/31/17	6424.7	90.1	25384.3	8514.1	471	16078649
ATI	Allegheny Technologies, Inc.	Non-Precious Metals	12/31/17	3525.1	-91.9	5185.4	1739.4	497	160824058
ALLE	Allegion Plc	Services	12/31/17	2408.2	273.3	2542.0	401.6	578	96354341
AGN	Allergan PLC	Pharmaceuticals	12/31/17	15940.7	-4125.5	118341.9	73821.1	1286	302883541
ALE	Allete Inc.	Electric Utilities	12/31/17	1419.3	172.2	5080.0	2068.2	411	50697642
AKP	Alliance California Municipal Income	Holding and other Investment Office	10/31/17	7.8	5.1	209.7	161.5	35	1946759
ADS	Alliance Data Systems Corp.	Business Services	12/31/17	7719.4	788.7	30684.8	1855.3	793	67324995

EARNINGS PER SHARE QUARTERLY 1st	2nd	3rd	ANNUAL 2017	2016	2015	P/E RATIO	DIVIDENDS PER SHARE 2017	2016	2015	AV. YLD %	DIV. DECLARED AMOUNT	PAYABLE	PRICE RANGE 2017
-0.19	-	-	-0.59	-0.35	-5.85	-	-	-	-	-	-	-	18.6 - 8.1
0.98	-	-	7.93	8.16	7.58	32.6 - 24.5	4.70	4.44	4.10	2.1	1.360Y	18/78/27	258.6 - 194.4
-	-	-	-0.78	-0.49	-0.84	-	-	-	-	-	-	-	21.1 - 9.4
-	-	-	4.35	-2.73	-1.07	20.5 - 10.0	-	-	-	-	-	-	89.0 - 43.5
-	-	-0.96	-0.05	-0.06	0.02	-	-	-	-	-	-	-	22.6 - 12.2
-	-	-0.04	-	-0.32	-0.64	-	-	-	-	-	-	-	8.3 - 5.7
-0.01	-	-	-0.88	-0.03	0.48	-	-	-	-	-	-	-	12.9 - 6.1
-	-	0.44	1.64	1.37	0.24	29.7 - 21.1	0.30	0.30	0.30	0.7	0.0750Y	7/31/18	48.6 - 34.5
0.73	-	-	4.06	1.91	1.86	12.0 - 8.5	0.11	0.10	0.09	0.3	0.030Y	18/78/27	48.9 - 34.4
-	-	0.27	1.03	0.88	0.87	27.8 - 20.8	0.76	0.73	0.75	3.1	-	-	28.6 - 21.4
0.23	-	-	0.27	0.94	2.92	235.6 - 177.6	1.06	1.04	0.96	1.9	0.280Y	18/78/27	63.6 - 47.9
1.74	-	-	3.30	3.63	3.13	37.3 - 21.2	2.56	2.28	2.02	2.7	0.960Y	18/78/27	123.2 - 69.8
-0.62	-	-	0.06	0.51	0.71	477.3 - 148.2	0.80	0.80	0.80	4.3	0.20Y	6/18/18	28.6 - 8.9
-	-	-	0.75	0.70	0.80	15.4 - 13.5	0.78	0.78	0.77	7.3	0.0650	7/31/18	11.5 - 10.1
-	-	-	0.11	0.17	0.14	63.2 - 55.5	0.60	0.60	0.60	9.3	0.050	7/31/18	7.0 - 6.1
-	-	-	-	1.46	1.48	-	-	1.44	1.84	-	0.120	7/31/18	14.9 - 13.4
-	-	-	-	0.08	0.05	-	-	0.31	0.07	-	0.4218C	1/8/18	9.8 - 8.3
-	-	-	0.68	0.65	0.69	14.7 - 12.6	0.69	0.69	0.68	7.6	0.05750	7/31/18	10.0 - 8.6
-	0.40	-	0.07	1.01	1.33	-	0.68	0.66	0.64	-	0.1750Y	18/78/27	-
0.09	-	-	0.73	0.94	0.94	41.7 - 30.0	1.05	1.16	1.22	3.9	0.270Z	7/13/18	30.5 - 21.9
-	-	1.60	5.44	6.45	4.76	-	2.42	2.20	2.04	-	1.330	18/78/27	-
0.09	-	-	1.19	0.87	0.78	11.6 - 8.9	-	-	-	-	0.060Y	6/20/18	13.9 - 10.6
-	-	-0.13	-	-	-0.51	-	-	-	-	-	-	-	37.7 - 0.0
-	-	0.48	-1.11	-1.78	0.32	-	0.04	0.04	0.04	0.2	0.040Y	10/16/17	29.8 - 22.1
-	-	1.80	7.43	6.63	5.09	27.8 - 14.8	0.52	0.52	0.52	0.3	0.130Y	18/78/27	206.7 - 110.2
0.55	-	-	1.23	0.62	-0.74	20.7 - 12.7	0.48	-	-	2.3	0.130Y	6/15/18	25.4 - 15.6
-	-	-	-	0.19	0.13	-	-	0.99	0.93	-	0.050	8/31/18	16.1 - 14.3
-	-	-	-	0.41	0.37	-	-	1.14	1.38	-	0.10	8/31/18	21.4 - 17.7
-	-	-0.05	0.08	0.02	0.14	-	-	-	-	-	-	-	-
-	-1.80	-	9.34	-16.36	-	-	0.82	-	-	-	0.2750	8/15/18	-
-0.22	-	-	0.53	-0.84	-0.08	24.3 - 13.2	-	-	-	-	0.0350Y	18/78/27	12.9 - 7.0
-	-	0.63	1.91	-0.05	2.14	26.1 - 16.4	0.18	0.36	0.36	0.4	0.180Y	18/78/27	49.9 - 31.4
1.84	-	-	6.42	6.20	6.40	21.7 - 12.4	0.24	0.24	0.24	0.2	0.060Y	18/78/27	139.5 - 79.4
0.02	-	-	0.43	-0.44	-	59.4 - 50.3	-	-	-	-	-	-	25.6 - 21.6
-	-	0.51	0.50	0.27	-0.06	60.0 - 36.4	0.24	0.20	0.08	1.0	0.080Y	6/15/18	30.0 - 18.2
0.37	-	-	4.72	1.12	-	9.8 - 6.5	-	-	-	-	-	-	46.3 - 30.7
0.05	-	-	0.50	-0.09	0.12	18.3 - 5.5	-	-	-	-	-	-	9.2 - 2.8
-	-	-	-	0.75	0.65	-	1.24	1.13	1.13	7.8	0.11720	7/31/18	16.7 - 14.9
-	-	-	0.22	0.25	0.20	29.4 - 25.0	0.56	0.56	0.56	9.4	0.0470	7/31/18	6.5 - 5.5
-	-	-	0.17	0.26	0.21	52.1 - 45.4	0.84	0.84	0.84	10.1	0.210	5/31/18	8.9 - 7.7
-	-0.75	-	2.13	0.62	-1.04	18.6 - 14.3	-	-	-	-	0.010	4/4/18	39.6 - 30.5
-	-	-	-	1.11	0.73	-	-	0.08	0.08	-	0.010	4/4/18	-
-	-	0.21	1.14	0.15	0.27	6.5 - 4.6	0.26	0.26	0.24	4.1	0.40630Z	12/15/18	7.4 - 5.2
1.72	-	-	6.43	5.52	5.72	-	-	-	-	-	-	-	-
-0.13	-	-	-0.43	-0.73	-0.98	-	-	-	-	-	-	-	6.3 - 3.1
0.18	-	-	-0.13	0.27	0.10	-	-	-	-	-	0.030Y	5/28/04	35.7 - 21.3
1.03	-	-	-1.76	-1.71	0.44	-	0.48	0.44	0.40	4.2	0.130Y	18/78/27	13.5 - 10.1
3.67	-	-	5.68	6.41	6.78	34.1 - 26.7	1.75	1.00	1.00	1.0	0.50Y	18/78/27	193.7 - 151.4
2.77	-	-	12.03	8.57	9.28	17.9 - 12.4	0.80	-	-	0.4	0.30	18/78/27	215.8 - 148.7
0.91	-	-	5.77	3.21	2.92	8.0 - 6.7	0.87	0.83	0.79	2.0	0.260Y	18/78/27	45.9 - 38.6
0.17	-	-	3.77	1.80	0.01	5.2 - 4.3	2.00	1.90	2.27	10.8	0.50Z	7/31/18	19.7 - 16.4
0.30	-	-	2.32	1.96	3.06	32.5 - 25.5	0.56	0.52	0.48	0.8	0.150Y	18/78/27	75.5 - 59.2
-	0.63	-	2.10	1.40	1.20	35.6 - 27.9	0.53	0.46	0.40	0.8	0.1490Y	18/78/27	74.8 - 58.6
0.19	-	-	1.05	0.70	0.11	61.0 - 36.3	0.41	0.36	0.32	0.8	0.110	6/15/18	64.0 - 38.1
0.53	-	-	2.08	1.97	2.16	25.9 - 21.3	2.02	1.92	1.85	4.1	0.540Z	7/13/18	53.9 - 44.3
-0.19	-	-	0.46	-0.90	-0.84	12.5 - 9.5	0.46	0.32	0.32	9.3	0.080Y	9/7/18	5.8 - 4.3
1.00	-	-	6.82	3.44	2.34	7.4 - 5.6	0.33	0.23	0.17	0.8	0.10Y	18/78/27	50.3 - 37.9
-	1.89	-	13.65	2.89	5.88	12.7 - 10.4	3.62	2.53	3.20	2.3	1.10Y	18/78/27	174.0 - 142.1
0.73	-	-	1.87	1.92	1.50	-	1.06	0.98	0.90	-	0.280Y	6/15/18	-
0.09	-	-	0.02	-0.03	-2.86	339.0 - 207.0	-	-	-	-	0.050Y	18/78/27	6.8 - 4.1
-	-	-	-	-	-	-	0.39	-	-	1.5	0.31250Y	10/1/18	27.0 - 24.5
1.24	-	-	3.79	3.46	3.76	31.7 - 23.4	0.40	0.36	0.32	0.4	0.110Y	7/27/18	120.1 - 88.7
-	-	0.09	0.09	-0.07	-2.62	115.6 - 54.8	0.02	0.02	0.01	0.3	0.010	4/30/18	10.4 - 4.9
0.03	-	-	8.35	6.54	6.56	11.3 - 6.9	1.20	1.10	0.80	1.7	0.320	18/78/27	94.6 - 57.8
0.32	-	-	1.03	1.64	1.79	65.3 - 48.8	0.68	0.68	0.67	1.1	0.170Y	7/9/18	67.3 - 50.3
1.18	-	-	0.49	5.68	3.00	295.1 - 181.6	1.28	1.22	1.16	1.1	0.3350Y	18/78/27	144.6 - 89.0
0.80	-	-	1.16	-2.19	-	51.9 - 29.1	-	-	-	-	-	-	60.2 - 33.8
0.66	-	-	4.34	-0.18	0.54	10.8 - 4.8	15.92	0.25	-	49.2	15.92G7Z	18/78/27	46.9 - 20.9
-1.90	-	-	15.74	16.91	15.04	27.6 - 21.3	17.00	16.00	14.00	4.3	4.50Z	5/18/18	435.0 - 335.6
1.32	-	-	1.58	-1.99	1.63	84.8 - 72.5	3.45	3.23"	3.05	2.8	0.930Z	18/78/27	134.0 - 114.6
0.04	-	-	0.47	0.44	0.42	30.5 - 20.2	0.60	0.55	0.49	5.1	0.31250	7/3/18	14.4 - 9.5
-	-	9.20	16.97	27.89	9.70	12.4 - 8.3	-	-	-	-	-	-	210.9 - 141.0
11.04	-	-	5.85	29.59	35.13	108.3 - 89.4	-	-	-	-	10.0	18/78/27	633.8 - 523.2
0.42	-	-	-0.83	-5.97	-3.53	-	-	0.24	0.62	-	0.080Y	18/78/27	29.8 - 16.9
0.75	-	-	2.85	2.39	1.59	-	0.64	0.48	0.40	-	0.210	6/29/18	-
-0.99	-	-	-13.19	38.18	10.01	-	2.80	-	-	-	13.750	18/78/27	-
0.99	-	-	3.38	3.14	2.92	23.8 - 19.9	2.14	2.08	2.02	2.9	0.560Y	6/1/18	80.5 - 67.2
-	-	-	0.60	0.65	0.75	23.4 - 21.1	0.58	0.68	0.75	4.3	0.0421M	8/17/18	14.0 - 12.6
2.95	-	-	14.10	7.34	8.85	-	2.08	0.52	-	-	0.570	18/78/27	-

SYMBOL	COMPANY	NATURE OF BUSINESS	FISCAL YEAR-END	TOTAL REV. $MILL	NET INCOME $MILL	TOTAL ASSETS $MILL	NET STK EQUITY $MILL	NO OF INST	INST. HOLDINGS (SHARES)
AOI	Alliance One International Inc	Tobacco Products	3/31/18	1846.0	52.4	1966.6	271.9	110	16095250
AWF	AllianceBernstein Global High Inco	Holding and other Investment Office	3/31/17	82.6	70.7	1328.0	1195.9	154	19820199
AB	AllianceBernstein Holding LP	Wealth Management	12/31/17	232.4	207.4	1544.7		287	35597452
AFB	AllianceBernstein National Municipa	Holding and other Investment Office	10/31/17	26.4	18.9	697.7	521.6	82	7204622
LNT	Alliant Energy Corp	Electric Utilities	12/31/17	3382.2	467.5	14187.8	4182.2	674	202003453
NCV	AllianzGI Convertible & Income Fun	Holding and other Investment Office	2/28/17	72.0	64.3	968.9	962.2	99	14008702
NCZ	AllianzGI Convertible & Income Fun	Holding and other Investment Office	2/28/17	54.9	49.0	735.9	731.0	86	11862722
ACV	AllianzGI Diversified Income & Conv	Holding and other Investment Office	1/31/17	11.3	4.0	333.0	221.8		0
NIE	AllianzGI Equity & Convertible Inco	Holding and other Investment Office	1/31/17	17.5	11.2	597.8	596.9	81	6030906
NFJ	AllianzGI NFJ Dividend Interest & P	Holding and other Investment Office	1/31/17	46.5	32.8	1400.8	1395.1	146	29427816
ALSN	Allison Transmission Holdings Inc	Auto Parts	12/31/17	2262.0	504.0	4205.0	689.0	407	231610839
ALL	Allstate Corp	General Insurance	12/31/17	38524.0	3189.0	112422.0	22551.0	1404	374095757
ALLY	Ally Financial Inc	Credit & Lending	12/31/17	9866.0	929.0	167148.0	13494.0	500	470281071
AYX	Alteryx Inc	Internet & Software	12/31/17	131.6	-17.5	291.4	153.5	120	23575121
ATUS	Altice USA Inc	Radio & Television	12/31/17	9326.6	1520.0	34775.2	5725.6	135	132647875
ATUS	Altice USA Inc	Radio & Television	12/31/17	9326.6	1520.0	34775.2	5725.6	135	132647875
MO	Altria Group Inc	Tobacco Products	12/31/17	25576.0	10222.0	43202.0	15377.0	2324	1588977546
ACH	Aluminum Corp of China Ltd.	Non-Precious Metals	12/31/17	180080.8	1378.4	200146.6	39478.4	78	3161957
AMBR	Amber Road Inc	Internet & Software	12/31/17	79.1	-13.0	99.4	25.5	106	22191951
ABEV	Ambev SA	Beverages	12/31/17	47899.3	7332.0	86851.9	46008.8		0
AMC	AMC Entertainment Holdings Inc.	Entertainment	12/31/17	5079.2	-487.2	9805.9	2113.2	220	60274789
AEE	Ameren Corp	Electric Utilities	12/31/17	6177.0	523.0	25945.0	7184.0	774	211924297
AMRC	Ameresco Inc	Construction Services	12/31/17	717.2	37.5	984.0	336.6	114	14630168
AMX	America Movil SAB de CV	Services	12/31/17	1021633.5	29325.9	1486211.9	194164.3	492	303815502
AAT	American Assets Trust Inc	REITs	12/31/17	315.0	29.3	2259.9	833.7	243	56874951
AXL	American Axle & Manufacturing Hol	Auto Parts	12/31/17	6266.0	337.1	7882.8	1536.0	354	134698722
ACC	American Campus Communities Inc	REITs	12/31/17	796.4	69.0	6897.4	3485.0	466	166479709
AEO	American Eagle Outfitters, Inc.	Retail - Apparel and Accessories	2/3/18	3795.5	204.2	1816.3	1246.8	560	214575473
AEP	American Electric Power Company,	Electric Utilities	12/31/17	15424.9	1912.6	64729.1	18298.9	1363	430132232
AEL	American Equity Investment Life Ho	Life & Health	12/31/17	3891.7	174.6	62030.7	2850.2	383	104488652
AXP	American Express Co.	Credit & Lending	12/31/17	35583.0	2736.0	181159.0	18227.0	2045	891190665
AFG	American Financial Group Inc	General Insurance	12/31/17	6865.0	475.0	60658.0	5330.0	534	74121002
AMH	American Homes 4 Rent	REITs	12/31/17	960.4	81.0	8608.8	5149.6		0
AIG	American International Group Inc	General Insurance	12/31/17	49520.0	-6084.0	498301.0	65171.0	1428	1022277407
AMID	American Midstream Partners LP	Equipment & Services	12/31/17	651.4	-223.0	1923.5	317.2	70	32071058
ARL	American Realty Investors, Inc.	Property, Real Estate & Developmen	12/31/17	126.2	-8.4	1296.7	112.1	27	179958
ARA	American Renal Associates Holding	Diagnostic & Health Related Service	12/31/17	745.1	4.9	964.2	-56.4	103	29536198
AWR	American States Water Co	Water Utilities	12/31/17	440.6	69.4	1416.7	529.9	345	32959863
AMT	American Tower Corp (New)	REITs	12/31/17	6663.9	1238.9	33214.3	6241.5	1465	502130270
AVD	American Vanguard Corp	Agricultural Chemicals	12/31/17	355.0	20.3	535.6	305.1	194	29234155
AWK	American Water Works Co, Inc.	Water Utilities	12/31/17	3357.0	426.0	19482.0	5385.0	890	189389334
COLD	Americold Realty Trust	REITs	12/31/17	1543.6	-0.6	2395.2	185.9	98	89109143
APU	AmeriGas Partners LP	Gas Utilities	9/30/17	2453.5	162.1	4059.3		339	27561554
AMP	Ameriprise Financial Inc	Wealth Management	12/31/17	12027.0	1480.0	147470.0	5998.0	1143	166123949
ABC	AmerisourceBergen Corp.	Pharmaceuticals	9/30/17	153143.8	364.5	35316.5	2064.5	1056	199778830
AME	AMETEK Inc	Electrical Equipment	12/31/17	4300.2	681.5	7796.1	4027.6	796	237687503
ANFI	Amira Nature Foods Ltd	Food	3/31/17	551.9	25.1	574.6	262.5	44	6361326
AMN	AMN Healthcare Services Inc	Diagnostic & Health Related Service	12/31/17	1988.5	132.6	1254.0	562.5	412	68901888
AP	Ampco-Pittsburgh Corp.	Industrial Machinery & Equipment	12/31/17	432.4	-12.1	546.5	158.9	94	8052629
APH	Amphenol Corp.	Electrical Equipment	12/31/17	7011.3	650.5	10003.9	3989.8	888	347528051
AXR	AMREP Corp.	Business Services	4/30/18	40.2	0.2	105.9	86.6	39	1729580
APC	Anadarko Petroleum Corp	Production & Extraction	12/31/17	11908.0	-456.0	42086.0	10696.0	1319	621120640
ANDV	Andeavor	Refining & Marketing	12/31/17	34975.0	1528.0	28573.0	9815.0	885	154661293
ANDX	Andeavor Logistics LP	Production & Extraction	12/31/17	3213.0	349.0	8169.0		238	91194859
AU	AngloGold Ashanti Ltd	Precious Metals	12/31/17	4356.0	-191.0	7219.0	2663.0	237	207019763
BUD	Anheuser-Busch InBev SA/NV	Beverages	12/31/17	56444.0	7996.0	246126.0	72585.0		0
AXE	Anixter International Inc	Electrical Equipment	12/29/17	7927.4	109.0	4252.2	1459.0	333	41470494
NLY	Annaly Capital Management Inc	REITs	12/31/17	2808.5	1569.6	101760.0	14865.5	885	864418251
AMGP	Antero Midstream GP LP	Gas Utilities	12/31/17	69.7	2.3	29.8	15.6	149	140350077
AM	Antero Midstream Partners LP	Equipment & Services	12/31/17	772.5	237.6	3042.2		169	89925324
AR	Antero Resources Corp	Production & Extraction	12/31/17	3655.6	615.1	15261.5	8149.2	376	519684513
ANTM	Anthem Inc	Life & Health	12/31/17	90039.4	3842.8	70540.0	26502.9	1085	254922411
ANH	Anworth Mortgage Asset Corp.	REITs	12/31/17	152.6	54.4	5765.5	697.4	232	72223268
AON	Aon Plc	Brokers & Intermediaries	12/31/17	9998.0	1226.0	26088.0	4583.0	898	262013991
APA	Apache Corp	Production & Extraction	12/31/17	6423.0	1304.0	21922.0	7416.0	1207	479129246
AIV	Apartment Investment & Manageme	REITs	12/31/17	1005.4	315.8	6079.0	1663.1	501	208184715
APY	Apergy Corp	Industrial Machinery & Equipment	12/31/17	1009.6	110.6	1904.8	1635.3	39	1084644
APY	Apergy Corp	Industrial Machinery & Equipment	12/31/17	1009.6	110.6	1904.8	1635.3	39	1084644
ARI	Apollo Commercial Real Estate Fina	REITs	12/31/17	338.5	193.0	4088.6	2088.1	300	94718581
APO	Apollo Global Management LLC	Finance Intermediaries & Services	12/31/17	2610.2	629.1	6991.1	1462.9	301	152875929
AFT	Apollo Senior Floating Rate Fund In	Holding and other Investment Office	12/31/16	28.1	19.4	448.0	281.3	64	3556115
AIF	Apollo Tactical Income Fund Inc	Holding and other Investment Office	12/31/16	29.6	21.7	409.6	248.4	43	4807046
APLE	Apple Hospitality REIT Inc	REITs	12/31/17	1238.6	182.5	4902.3	3571.1	273	152119076
AIT	Applied Industrial Technologies, Inc.	Industrial Machinery & Equipment	6/30/17	2593.7	133.9	1387.6	745.3	352	45809001
ATR	AptarGroup Inc.	Plastics	12/31/17	2469.3	220.0	3137.8	1311.7	490	81079033
APTV	Aptiv PLC	Auto Parts	12/31/17	12884.0	1355.0	12169.0	3299.0	822	277126086
WTR	Aqua America Inc	Water Utilities	12/31/17	809.5	239.7	6332.5	1957.6	654	121589068
AQ	Aquantia Corp	Semiconductors	12/31/17	103.4	-5.4	110.4	90.9	86	7692062
WAAS	AquaVenture Holdings Ltd	Water Utilities	12/31/17	121.2	-25.8	554.6	352.1	94	8917486
ARMK	Aramark	Hotels, Restaurants & Travel	9/29/17	14604.4	373.9	11006.2	2459.1	419	258788929

| EARNINGS PER SHARE | | | | | | P/E | DIVIDENDS | | | AV. | DIV. DECLARED | | PRICE RANGE |
| QUARTERLY | | | ANNUAL | | | RATIO | PER SHARE | | | YLD | | | |
1st	2nd	3rd	2017	2016	2015		2017	2016	2015	%	AMOUNT	PAYABLE	2017
-	-	9.80	-	7.38	-1.70	-	-	-	-	-	0.030Y	9/23/05	28.8 - 9.9
-	-	-	0.82	0.89	1.00	16.0 - 14.0	0.95	1.11	1.44	7.7	0.06990	8/17/18	13.1 - 11.5
0.60	-	-	2.19	2.23	1.89	13.5 - 10.5	2.13	1.75	1.93	8.2	0.730	5/17/18	29.5 - 23.1
-	-	-	0.66	0.71	0.81	21.4 - 18.8	0.64	0.72	0.82	4.8	0.0458M	8/17/18	14.2 - 12.4
0.52	-	-	1.99	1.64	1.68	22.7 - 18.7	1.26	1.18	1.10	3.0	0.3350Y	18/78/27	45.2 - 37.1
-	-	-	0.73	0.83	0.87	9.9 - 9.1	0.78	0.93	1.08	11.2	0.0650	8/1/18	7.3 - 6.6
-	-	-	0.66	0.75	0.80	9.8 - 8.9	0.69	0.85	1.02	11.2	0.05750	8/1/18	6.5 - 5.8
-	-	-	0.39	0.18	-	61.8 - 52.4	2.00	1.17	-	9.0	0.1670	8/1/18	24.1 - 20.4
-	-	-	0.41	0.47	0.53	55.0 - 47.8	1.52	1.52	1.32	7.2	0.380	6/22/18	22.6 - 19.6
-	-	-	0.30	0.38	0.41	46.0 - 41.6	1.20	1.65	1.80	9.1	0.2250	6/22/18	13.8 - 12.5
1.08	-	-	3.36	1.27	1.03	13.5 - 9.9	0.60	0.60	0.60	1.5	0.150Y	18/78/27	45.3 - 33.2
2.63	-	-	8.36	4.67	5.05	12.5 - 10.3	1.48	1.32	1.20	1.6	0.460Y	18/78/27	104.9 - 86.5
0.57	-	-	2.04	2.15	-2.66	15.1 - 10.2	0.40	0.16	-	1.5	0.150Y	18/78/27	30.8 - 20.8
-0.09	-	-	-0.37	-0.95	-0.76	-	-	-	-	-	-	-	40.6 - 18.8
-0.17	-	-	2.188320.00	-	-	15.5 - 7.5	1.29	-	-	5.6	2.035G6	6/6/18	33.9 - 16.4
-0.17	-	-	2.188320.00	-	-	8.3 - 7.5	1.29	-	-	7.4	2.035G6	6/6/18	18.0 - 16.4
1.00	-	-	5.31	7.28	2.67	14.1 - 10.3	2.54	2.35	2.17	3.9	0.70Y	18/78/27	74.6 - 54.5
0.02	-	-	0.09	0.02	0.01	260.6 - 116.6	-	-	-	-	-	-	23.4 - 10.5
-0.11	-	-	-0.47	-0.70	-1.07	-	-	-	-	-	-	-	10.0 - 6.5
-	-	-	0.46	0.79	0.78	16.1 - 10.1	0.50	0.59	0.62	7.9	-	-	7.4 - 4.6
0.14	-	-	-3.80	1.13	1.06	-	0.80	0.80	0.80	5.2	0.20	6/25/18	23.2 - 11.0
0.62	-	-	2.14	2.68	2.59	30.2 - 24.6	1.78	1.72	1.66	3.1	0.45750Y	18/78/27	64.5 - 52.6
0.15	-	-	0.82	0.26	0.06	15.9 - 7.6	-	-	-	-	-	-	13.0 - 6.3
-	-	-	0.44	0.13	0.52	45.2 - 34.0	6.04	14.53	11.13	34.0	-	-	19.9 - 14.9
-0.01	-	-	0.62	0.72	0.86	66.7 - 51.2	1.05	1.01	0.95	2.8	0.270Z	6/28/18	41.4 - 31.7
0.78	-	-	3.21	3.06	3.02	6.1 - 4.2	-	-	-	-	0.020Y	12/29/08	19.6 - 13.6
0.18	-	-	0.50	0.75	1.02	98.0 - 69.6	1.74	1.66	1.58	4.1	0.460Z	18/78/27	49.0 - 34.8
0.22	-	-	1.16	1.11	0.42	21.8 - 9.2	0.50	0.50	0.50	2.9	0.13750Y	18/78/27	25.3 - 10.6
0.92	-	-	3.88	1.24	4.17	20.0 - 16.2	2.39	2.27	2.15	3.4	0.620Y	18/78/27	77.6 - 62.9
1.55	-	-	1.93	0.97	2.72	19.1 - 13.3	0.26	0.24	0.22	0.9	0.260Y	18/78/27	37.0 - 25.8
1.86	-	-	2.97	5.65	5.05	34.6 - 28.2	1.31	1.19	1.10	1.4	0.350Y	18/78/27	102.7 - 83.7
1.60	-	-	5.28	7.33	3.94	22.8 - 18.1	4.79	2.15	2.03	4.5	0.350Y	18/78/27	120.5 - 95.5
0.02	-	-	-0.08	-0.14	-0.40	-	0.20	0.20	0.20	0.9	0.36720Z	18/78/27	23.2 - 18.7
1.01	-	-	-6.54	-0.78	1.65	-	1.28	1.28	0.81	2.2	0.220Y	18/78/27	66.1 - 51.9
-0.42	-	-	-4.85	-1.11	-6.00	-	1.65	1.71	1.89	13.2	0.41250	5/15/18	15.1 - 9.6
-0.06	-	-	-0.61	-0.25	-0.21	-	-	-	-	-	-	-	20.5 - 0.0
-0.01	-	-	-0.24	-0.28	0.83	-	-	1.30	-	-	-	-	23.5 - 10.0
0.29	-	-	1.88	1.62	1.60	31.6 - 24.9	0.99	0.91	0.87	1.9	0.2550Y	18/78/27	59.5 - 46.7
0.63	-	-	2.67	1.98	1.41	57.2 - 49.0	2.62	2.17	1.81	1.9	0.770Z	18/78/27	152.7 - 130.9
0.16	-	-	0.68	0.44	0.23	35.1 - 25.5	0.06	0.03	0.02	0.3	0.020Y	7/12/18	23.9 - 17.4
0.59	-	-	2.38	2.62	2.64	38.8 - 32.0	1.62	1.47	1.33	1.9	0.4550Y	18/78/27	92.3 - 76.1
-0.08	-	-	-0.43	-0.35	-0.73	-	0.29	0.29	0.29	1.5	0.18750Z	7/16/18	22.7 - 17.5
-	1.44	-	1.25	1.77	1.91	38.6 - 31.8	3.78	3.72	3.60	8.6	0.950	18/78/27	48.2 - 39.8
3.91	-	-	9.44	7.81	8.48	19.3 - 13.7	3.24	2.92	2.59	2.1	0.90Y	18/78/27	182.0 - 129.2
-	1.29	-	1.64	6.32	-0.62	64.3 - 44.7	1.46	1.36	1.16	1.7	0.380Y	18/78/27	105.5 - 73.2
0.78	-	-	2.94	2.19	2.45	26.8 - 20.7	0.36	0.36	0.36	0.5	0.140Y	18/78/27	78.8 - 60.9
-	0.18	-	0.84	0.90	1.46	-	-	-	-	-	-	-	
0.87	-	-	2.68	2.15	1.68	25.3 - 13.3	-	-	-	-	-	-	67.8 - 35.5
0.08	-	-	-0.98	-6.68	0.13	-	0.18	0.45	0.72	1.4	0.090Y	4/28/17	18.3 - 8.8
0.84	-	-	2.06	2.61	2.41	45.2 - 35.2	0.70	0.58	0.53	0.8	0.230Y	18/78/27	93.1 - 72.5
-	-	-0.35	0.00	-1.27	1.43	-	-	-	-	-	1.7	8/24/07	7.7 - 0.0
0.22	-	-	-0.85	-5.90	-13.18	-	0.20	0.20	1.08	0.4	0.250Y	18/78/27	74.3 - 40.5
1.12	-	-	10.81	6.12	12.36	13.8 - 8.3	2.28	2.10	1.85	2.1	0.590Y	18/78/27	149.7 - 89.6
0.59	-	-	2.11	1.87	2.33	25.9 - 19.6	3.81	3.31	2.84	8.0	1.0150	5/15/18	54.8 - 41.4
-	-	-	-0.46	0.15	-0.20	-	0.09	-	-	0.9	-	-	11.7 - 7.9
0.52	-	-	3.98	0.71	4.96	31.7 - 23.2	4.08	1.70	-	3.7	-	-	126.0 - 92.3
0.94	-	-	3.21	3.59	3.81	27.4 - 17.7	-	-	-	-	5.7	18/78/27	88.0 - 56.8
1.12	-	-	1.37	1.39	0.42	9.2 - 7.3	2.49	3.17	3.17	22.0	0.30Z	18/78/27	12.5 - 10.0
0.07	-	-	0.03	-	-	734.0 - 509.7	0.09	-	-	0.5	0.1250	8/22/18	22.0 - 15.3
0.43	-	-	1.28	1.24	0.76	27.4 - 19.0	1.24	0.97	0.67	4.2	0.4150	8/17/18	35.0 - 24.3
0.05	-	-	1.94	-2.88	3.43	11.4 - 8.8	-	-	-	-	-	-	22.2 - 17.0
4.99	-	-	14.35	9.21	9.38	18.0 - 12.6	2.70	2.60	2.50	1.2	0.750Y	18/78/27	258.2 - 181.4
-0.05	-	-	0.47	0.17	0.08	13.2 - 9.7	0.60	0.60	0.60	11.1	0.140Z	7/30/18	6.2 - 4.6
2.37	-	-	4.70	5.16	4.88	-	1.41	1.29	1.15	-	0.40	5/15/18	
0.38	-	-	3.41	-3.71	-61.20	14.7 - 10.0	1.00	1.00	1.00	2.4	0.250Y	18/78/27	50.2 - 34.1
0.52	-	-	1.96	2.67	1.52	23.7 - 19.4	1.44	1.32	1.18	3.4	0.380Z	18/78/27	46.5 - 38.0
0.31	-	-	-	-	-	-	-	-	-	-	-	-	45.5 - 36.9
0.31	-	-	-	-	-	-	-	-	-	-	-	-	38.0 - 34.5
0.38	-	-	1.54	1.74	1.54	12.3 - 11.5	1.84	1.84	1.78	10.1	0.50Z	7/16/18	19.0 - 17.7
-0.34	-	-	3.10	2.11	0.61	11.9 - 8.5	1.85	1.25	1.96	6.0	0.3807GH	6/15/18	36.8 - 26.3
-	-	-	-	1.24	1.22	-	-	1.24	1.23	-	0.0960	8/31/18	17.2 - 16.1
-	-	-	-	1.50	1.48	-	-	1.52	1.56	-	0.1040	8/31/18	16.5 - 15.5
0.18	-	-	0.82	0.76	0.65	24.5 - 20.5	1.10	1.20	0.80	5.9	0.10Z	18/78/27	20.1 - 16.9
-	-	0.93	3.40	0.75	2.80	22.3 - 15.9	1.14	1.10	1.04	1.7	0.30Y	8/31/18	75.8 - 54.1
0.92	-	-	3.41	3.17	3.09	28.2 - 23.7	1.28	1.22	1.14	1.4	0.340Y	18/78/27	96.1 - 80.9
1.15	-	-	5.06	4.59	5.06	-	1.38	1.16	1.00	-	0.220	18/78/27	
0.29	-	-	1.35	1.32	1.14	29.1 - 24.0	0.79	0.74	0.69	2.3	0.2190Y	18/78/27	39.3 - 32.4
-0.04	-	-	-0.59	-0.10	-6.64	-	-	-	-	-	-	-	17.8 - 9.5
-0.24	-	-	-0.98	-0.28	-	-	-	-	-	-	-	-	
-	0.11	-	1.49	1.16	0.96	30.9 - 24.6	0.41	0.38	0.34	1.0	0.1050Y	18/78/27	46.0 - 36.6

SYMBOL	COMPANY	NATURE OF BUSINESS	FISCAL YEAR-END	TOTAL REV. $MILL	NET INCOME $MILL	TOTAL ASSETS $MILL	NET STK EQUITY $MILL	NO OF INST	INST. HOLDINGS (SHARES)
ABR	Arbor Realty Trust Inc	REITs	12/31/17	346.7	121.6	3625.9	695.8	156	37151119
ARC	ARC Document Solutions, Inc.	Printing	12/31/17	394.6	-21.5	339.4	130.2	140	39338871
MT	ArcelorMittal SA	Non-Precious Metals	12/31/17	68679.0	4568.0	85297.0	38789.0	7	1166729
ARCH	Arch Coal Inc	Mining	12/31/17	2324.6	238.4	1979.6	665.9	365	37945659
ADM	Archer Daniels Midland Co.	Food	12/31/17	60828.0	1595.0	39963.0	18313.0	1164	590181532
AROC	Archrock Inc	Equipment & Services	12/31/17	794.7	19.0	2408.0	777.0	283	84044550
ARNC	Arconic Inc	Non-Precious Metals	12/31/17	12960.0	-74.0	18718.0	4910.0	961	541786934
ARCO	Arcos Dorados Holdings Inc	Hotels, Restaurants & Travel	12/31/17	3319.5	129.2	1803.7	495.6	179	101360753
RCUS	Arcus Biosciences Inc	Biotechnology	12/31/17	1.4	-53.1	190.5	153.9	56	14775733
ARD	Ardagh Group SA	Containers & Packaging	12/31/17	7644.0	54.0	9298.0	-1148.0	94	17889288
ASC	Ardmore Shipping Corp	Shipping	12/31/17	195.9	-12.5	845.5	381.0	116	34416787
ACRE	Ares Commercial Real Estate Corp	REITs	12/31/17	97.5	30.4	1770.2	419.2	139	23474483
ARDC	Ares Dynamic Credit Allocation Fun	Finance Intermediaries & Services	10/31/16	39.5	28.5	594.1	391.8	63	8939460
ARES	Ares Management LP	Wealth Management	12/31/17	1415.5	76.2	8563.5	298.8	91	38999088
AGX	Argan Inc	Construction Services	1/31/18	892.8	72.0	603.4	358.1	232	13750238
ARGO	Argo Group International Holdings L	General Insurance	12/31/17	1774.1	50.3	8764.0	1819.7	249	36008461
ARGD	Argo Group US Inc	General Insurance							0
ANET	Arista Networks Inc	Computer Hardware & Equipment	12/31/17	1646.2	423.2	2460.9	1661.9	545	42308858
AI	Arlington Asset Investment Corp	Credit & Lending	12/31/17	127.1	17.4	4174.4	386.3	168	26779501
AHH	Armada Hoffler Properties Inc	REITs	12/31/17	302.8	21.0	1043.1	226.7	195	39800304
ARR	ARMOUR Residential REIT Inc.	REITs	12/31/17	311.5	181.2	8928.9	1326.1	195	31580736
AFI	Armstrong Flooring Inc	Plastics	12/31/17	1133.7	-41.8	879.5	550.0	143	26874026
AWI	Armstrong World Industries Inc	Construction Materials	12/31/17	893.6	154.8	1873.5	419.3	300	65134124
ARW	Arrow Electronics, Inc.	Electrical Equipment	12/31/17	26812.5	402.0	16462.8	4951.5	581	112749759
APAM	Artisan Partners Asset Management	Wealth Management	12/31/17	795.6	49.6	837.2	109.9	282	51606830
ASA	ASA Gold and Precious Metals Ltd	Holding and other Investment Office	11/30/17	1.4	-1.7	245.6	244.2	71	6391612
ABG	Asbury Automotive Group Inc	Retail - Automotive	12/31/17	6456.5	139.1	2356.7	394.2	276	27534197
ASX	ASE Technology Holding Co Ltd	Semiconductors	12/31/17	290441.2	22987.8	363857.8	190801.5	214	122260092
ASX	ASE Technology Holding Co Ltd	Semiconductors	12/31/17	290441.2	22987.8	363857.8	190801.5	214	122260092
ASGN	ASGN Inc	Business Services	12/31/17	2625.9	157.7	1810.1	991.4	369	54335653
AHT	Ashford Hospitality Trust Inc	REITs	12/31/17	1439.3	-67.0	4669.8	632.5	247	99864233
ASH	Ashland Global Holdings Inc	Specialty Chemicals	9/30/17	3260.0	1.0	8618.0	3406.0		0
APB	Asia Pacific Fund, Inc. (The)	Holding and other Investment Office	3/31/17	4.7	2.3	135.2	134.1	47	8012222
ASPN	Aspen Aerogels Inc	Construction Materials	12/31/17	111.6	-19.3	123.8	100.9	66	17984249
AHL	Aspen Insurance Holdings Ltd	General Insurance	12/31/17	2653.4	-267.7	12906.4	2925.8	344	72402244
ASB	Associated Banc-Corp	Banking	12/31/17	1219.3	229.3	30483.6	3237.4	389	155400089
AC	Associated Capital Group Inc	Brokers & Intermediaries	12/31/17	26.9	8.8	1006.9	918.1	70	3224720
AIZ	Assurant Inc	Life & Health	12/31/17	6415.0	519.6	31843.0	4270.6	589	66218696
AGO	Assured Guaranty Ltd	General Insurance	12/31/17	1739.0	730.0	14433.0	6839.0	423	141650475
AZN	AstraZeneca Plc	Pharmaceuticals	12/31/17	22465.0	3001.0	63354.0	14960.0	682	419271979
HOME	At Home Group Inc	Furniture	1/27/18	950.5	31.8	1373.3	590.9	161	29154726
T	AT&T Inc	Services	12/31/17	160546.0	29450.0	444097.0	140861.0	2967	4241972457
ATTO	Atento SA	Services	12/31/17	1921.7	-16.8	1330.3	368.4	77	71044246
ATH	Athene Holding Ltd	Life & Health	12/31/17	8727.0	1448.0	99747.0	9208.0	325	133624195
ATKR	Atkore International Group Inc	Electrical Equipment	9/30/17	1503.9	84.6	1215.1	360.9	170	47055629
AT	Atlantic Power Corp	Electric Utilities	12/31/17	431.0	-98.6	1158.8	-18.4		0
ATO	Atmos Energy Corp.	Gas Utilities	9/30/17	2759.7	396.4	10749.6	3898.7	606	104334094
AUO	AU Optronics Corp.	Electrical Equipment	12/31/17	341028.3	42609.5	430170.7	195749.3	170	73519220
ATHM	Autohome Inc	IT Services	12/31/17	6210.2	2001.6	12295.0	7951.6	253	53925116
ALV	Autoliv Inc	Auto Parts	12/31/17	10382.6	427.1	8549.9	4035.1	436	47617454
AN	AutoNation, Inc.	Retail - Automotive	12/31/17	21534.6	434.6	10271.5	2369.3	480	84539374
AZO	AutoZone, Inc.	Retail - Automotive	8/26/17	10888.7	1280.9	9259.8	-1428.4	872	30166653
AVLR	Avalara Inc	Internet & Software	12/31/17	213.2	-64.1	178.8	-22.7		0
AVB	AvalonBay Communities, Inc.	REITs	12/31/17	2158.6	876.9	18414.8	10388.0	742	161936093
AGR	Avangrid Inc	Electric Utilities	12/31/17	5963.0	381.0	31671.0	15077.0	290	46674635
AVNS	Avanos Medical Inc	Medical Instruments & Equipment	12/31/17	611.6	79.3	2195.9	1215.4	422	48938725
AVYA	Avaya Holdings Corp	Internet & Software	9/30/17	3272.0	-182.0	5898.0	-4429.0	122	96026887
AVY	Avery Dennison Corp	Containers & Packaging	12/30/17	6613.8	281.8	5136.9	1046.2	837	105917496
AVH	Avianca Holdings SA	Airlines/Air Freight	12/31/17	4441.7	82.0	6861.4	1415.6	60	8808301
AVA	Avista Corp	Electric Utilities	12/31/17	1445.9	115.9	5514.7	1729.8	362	68228276
AVP	Avon Products, Inc.	Household & Personal Products	12/31/17	5715.6	22.0	3697.9	-257.2	486	456604067
AVX	AVX Corp.	Electrical Equipment	3/31/18	1562.5	4.9	2672.8	2243.4	220	52870265
EQH	AXA Equitable Holdings Inc	General Insurance	12/31/17	12514.0	850.0	235648.0	13485.0		0
AXTA	Axalta Coating Systems Ltd	Miscellaneous Transportation Servic	12/31/17	4377.0	36.7	6832.2	1276.1	434	269022260
AXS	AXIS Capital Holdings Ltd	General Insurance	12/31/17	4591.6	-369.0	24760.2	5341.3	434	94723783
AZUL	Azul SA	Airlines/Air Freight	12/31/17	7789.5	529.0	10316.6	2833.6	96	34831208
AZRE	Azure Power Global Ltd	Electric Utilities	3/31/18	7700.6	-820.7	73984.1	12117.5	22	11455440
AZZ	AZZ Inc	Business Services	2/28/18	810.4	45.2	1028.2	565.2	218	29491916
BGS	B&G Foods Inc	Food	12/30/17	1668.1	217.5	3561.0	880.8	418	80893299
BW	Babcock & Wilcox Enterprises Inc	Industrial Machinery & Equipment	12/31/17	1557.7	-379.8	1322.2	182.1	146	42585080
BMI	Badger Meter Inc	Electronic Instruments & Related Pro	12/31/17	402.4	34.6	391.7	277.5	256	30465268
BHGE	Baker Hughes, A GE Company	Equipment & Services	12/31/17	17259.0	-73.0	57050.0	14709.0	586	398275354
BLL	Ball Corp	Metal Products	12/31/17	10983.0	374.0	17169.0	3941.0	733	335029425
BANC	Banc Of California Inc	Banking	12/31/17	433.9	57.7	10327.9	1012.3	227	64273155
BBVA	Banco Bilbao Vizcaya Argentaria S	Banking	12/31/17	43606.0	3519.0	690059.0	46343.0	375	217437944
BBD	Banco Bradesco SA	Banking	12/31/16	189109.1	17894.2	1192029.7	105302.4	312	936675729
BCH	Banco de Chile	Banking	12/31/17	2247831.0	572080.0	32561437.0	3545347.0	106	2232105
BLX	Banco Latinoamericano de Comerci	Banking	12/31/17	244.6	82.0	6267.7	1042.8	43	7009586
BMA	Banco Macro SA	Banking	12/31/17			202892.4		205	20364705
BSMX	Banco Santander (Mexico) SA, Insti	Banking	12/31/17	122.6	18.7	1329.2	115.4		0

1st	2nd	3rd	2017	2016	2015	P/E RATIO		2017	2016	2015	AV. YLD %	AMOUNT	PAYABLE	PRICE RANGE 2017	
0.42	-	-	1.12	0.83	0.90	9.3 -	7.1	0.72	0.62	0.58	8.4	0.53130Z	5/31/18	10.4 -	7.9
0.01	-	-	-0.47	-1.04	2.04									4.7 -	1.8
-	-	1.18	4.46	1.86	-13.29	8.4 -	5.2					0.3750Z	1/15/16	37.3 -	23.1
2.74	-	-	9.84	1.31	-136.86	10.2 -	7.0	1.05	-	-	1.3	0.40Y	6/15/18	100.7 -	68.8
0.70	-	-	2.79	2.16	2.98	16.7 -	14.0	1.28	1.20	1.12	3.0	0.3350Y	18/78/27	46.5 -	39.0
-0.06	-	-	0.26	-0.80	-1.55	49.2 -	32.1	0.48	0.50	0.60	4.5	0.120Y	5/15/18	12.8 -	8.3
0.29	-	-	-0.28	-2.31	-0.93			0.24	0.09	-	1.0	0.93750Y	18/78/27	30.8 -	16.9
-	-	-	0.61	0.37	-0.25							0.050	10/5/18		
-1.37	-	-	-29.03	-20.80	-							0.140		17.7 -	12.2
-	-	-	-	-	-			0.67	-	-		0.140	5/31/18		
-	-	-	-0.37	0.12	1.23							0.110	8/31/16		
0.33	-	-	1.07	1.41	1.20	13.2 -	11.3	1.08	1.04	1.00	8.3	0.280Z	7/17/18	14.1 -	12.1
-	-	-	-	1.23	1.21				1.30	1.40		0.10750	9/28/18	16.6 -	15.9
0.28	-	-	0.62	1.20	0.23	40.7 -	28.5	1.13	0.83	0.88	5.6	0.43750	6/30/18	25.3 -	17.7
0.31	-	-	4.50	2.42	2.05	15.5 -	7.8	1.00	0.70	0.70	2.0	0.250Y	7/31/18	69.6 -	35.3
0.71	-	-	1.43	4.13	4.52			0.94	0.75	0.63		0.270	6/15/18		
-	-	-	-	-	-							0.40630Z	9/15/18	25.5 -	0.0
1.79	-	-	5.35	2.50	1.67	57.6 -	26.8							308.0 -	143.5
-2.00	-	-	0.66	-1.79	-3.02	21.1 -	15.2	2.27	2.50	3.00	19.0	0.3750Y	7/31/18	13.9 -	10.1
0.11	-	-	0.50	0.85	0.75	31.7 -	25.5	0.76	0.72	0.68	5.4	0.20Z	7/5/18	15.9 -	12.7
0.96	-	-	4.17	-1.67	-1.09	6.5 -	5.1	2.28	3.02	1.65	9.3	0.16410Z	9/27/18	27.2 -	21.4
-0.40	-	-	-1.54	0.33	-									18.3 -	12.3
0.51	-	-	2.86	1.87	1.68	22.7 -	15.4					8.557	18/78/27	64.9 -	44.0
1.56	-	-	4.48	5.68	5.20	19.4 -	16.2					0.025	18/78/27	86.9 -	72.8
0.75	-	-	0.75	1.57	1.86	55.1 -	39.1	2.76	2.80	3.35	8.1	0.60	5/31/18	41.4 -	29.3
-	-	-	-0.09	-0.10	-0.09							0.020	5/25/18		
1.93	-	-	6.62	7.40	6.41	11.5 -	7.6					0.2250Y	18/78/27	75.8 -	50.1
-	-	0.57	2.62	2.37	2.51	2.4 -	2.1							6.3 -	5.5
-	-	0.57	2.62	2.37	2.51	2.1 -	1.7							5.5 -	4.5
0.55	-	-	2.97	1.81	1.84	28.8 -	15.2							85.5 -	45.1
-0.39	-	-	-1.30	-0.95	2.35			0.48	0.48	0.48	7.3	0.46880Z	7/16/18	8.1 -	5.5
-	1.15	-	0.01	-0.46	4.48	8001.0 -	6079.0	1.23	1.56	1.46	1.8	0.250Y	18/78/27	80.0 -	60.8
-	-	-	0.22	0.20	0.23	70.9 -	0.0	0.22	0.51	-	1.6	0.32B	1/5/18	15.6 -	0.0
-0.29	-	-	-0.83	-0.52	-0.28									5.4 -	4.0
0.38	-	-	-5.22	2.61	4.54							0.35160	18/78/27		
0.40	-	-	1.42	1.26	1.19	20.3 -	15.0	0.50	0.45	0.41	2.0	0.33590Y	18/78/27	28.9 -	21.3
-0.95	-	-	0.37	0.41	0.00	110.8 -	87.6	0.30	0.10	-	0.8	0.10Y	7/2/18	41.0 -	32.4
1.96	-	-	9.39	9.13	2.05	11.3 -	9.1	2.15	2.03	1.37	2.2	0.560Y	18/78/27	106.3 -	85.2
1.68	-	-	5.96	6.56	7.08			0.57	0.52	0.48		0.160	18/78/27		
-	-	0.54	2.37	2.76	2.23	15.6 -	12.2	1.37	1.37	1.38	4.0			37.0 -	28.9
0.28	-	-	0.48	0.07	-0.01	82.0 -	42.5							39.3 -	20.4
0.75	-	-	4.76	2.10	2.37	8.3 -	6.6	1.96	1.92	1.88	5.5	0.50Y	18/78/27	39.5 -	31.4
-	-	-	-0.18	0.01	0.66							0.34G	11/28/17		
1.36	-	-	7.37	4.21	3.21										
-	0.79	-	1.27	0.94	-0.08	19.1 -	12.5							24.2 -	15.9
0.12	-	-	-0.86	-1.02	-0.51					0.09		0.030	12/31/15	3.3 -	1.9
-	1.60	-	3.73	3.38	3.09	24.7 -	20.9	1.80	1.68	1.56	2.1	0.4850Y	18/78/27	92.3 -	78.0
-	-	-	4.27	1.02	0.70	1.2 -	0.9	3.89	2.20	3.19	91.1			5.0 -	3.7
-	-	-	16.95	10.58	8.57	7.0 -	2.7	5.08	-	-	6.7			118.9 -	45.6
1.45	-	-	4.87	6.42	5.17	23.6 -	15.6	2.38	2.30	2.22	2.5	0.620Y	18/78/27	115.1 -	76.0
1.01	-	-	4.43	4.15	3.89	14.0 -	8.7							62.0 -	38.7
-	-	13.42	44.07	40.70	36.03	18.1 -	11.2							797.0 -	493.1
-2.47	-	-	-11.39	-10.15	-16.96									53.4 -	44.1
1.03	-	-	6.35	7.52	5.51	30.6 -	24.2	5.68	5.40	5.00	3.3	1.470Y	18/78/27	194.3 -	153.9
0.79	-	-	1.23	2.04	1.05	44.1 -	35.3	1.73	1.73	-	3.5	0.440	18/78/27	54.3 -	43.4
0.43	-	-	1.69	0.85	-9.15	36.1 -	22.7							61.0 -	38.4
-	-1.18	-	-0.43	-1.54	-									23.5 -	16.4
1.40	-	-	3.13	3.54	2.95	39.2 -	28.4	1.76	1.60	1.46	1.7	0.520Y	18/78/27	122.7 -	88.8
-	-	-	0.05	0.04	-0.14	190.0 -	129.0	0.18	0.12	0.52	2.3			9.5 -	6.5
0.83	-	-	1.79	2.15	1.97	29.5 -	23.1	1.43	1.37	1.32	2.8	0.37250Y	6/15/18	52.8 -	41.4
-0.06	-	-	0.00	-0.29	-2.60			0.00	0.00	0.24	0.0	0.060Y	18/78/27	3.8 -	1.5
-	-	-0.55	0.75	0.60	1.34	26.2 -	19.5	0.43	0.42	0.40	2.5	0.1150Y	8/15/18	19.6 -	14.6
0.30	-	-	1.51	2.27	0.59	14.5 -	13.4							21.9 -	20.2
0.28	-	-	0.15	0.17	0.39										
0.75	-	-	-4.94	5.08	6.04			1.53	1.43	1.22		0.34380	7/16/18		
-	-	-	0.02	-0.55	-5.42	1737.5 -	818.0							34.8 -	16.4
-	-	-	-111.09	1722.09	1046.00										
0.60	-	-	2.33	2.96	2.52	24.5 -	17.0	0.64	0.60	0.58	1.4	0.170Y	7/31/18	57.1 -	39.6
0.31	-	-	3.26	1.73	1.22	12.0 -	6.8	1.86	1.73	1.38	6.0	0.4750Y	7/30/18	39.0 -	22.1
-2.73	-	-	-8.09	-2.31	0.36									11.9 -	1.7
0.26	-	-	1.19	1.11	0.90	43.4 -	33.0	0.49	0.43	0.39	1.1	0.130Y	18/78/27	51.6 -	39.3
0.17	-	-	-0.17	-2.08	-			0.35	-	-	1.1	0.180Y	6/1/18	37.9 -	25.9
0.35	-	-	1.05	0.81	1.00	40.9 -	33.6	0.36	0.26	0.26	0.9	0.10Y	18/78/27	42.9 -	35.3
0.06	-	-	0.71	1.94	1.34	32.5 -	24.2	0.52	0.49	0.48	2.6	0.43750Y	6/15/18	23.1 -	17.1
-	-	-	0.48	0.50	0.39	19.9 -	13.9	0.30	0.37	0.28	3.6			9.5 -	6.7
-	-	-	-	2.55	2.58				0.89	0.83				11.9 -	6.5
-	-	-	5.60	5.74	6.04	18.8 -	13.5	1420.27	1560.15	1583.10	1515.8			105.5 -	75.9
-	-	0.52	2.08	2.22	2.66			1.54	-	-		0.3850	8/15/18		
-	-	-	-	-	-									135.5 -	58.8
-	-	-	2.75	2.43	2.06	3.9 -	2.3							10.8 -	6.3

SYMBOL	COMPANY	NATURE OF BUSINESS	FISCAL YEAR-END	TOTAL REV. $MILL	NET INCOME $MILL	TOTAL ASSETS $MILL	NET STK EQUITY $MILL	NO OF INST	INST. HOLDINGS (SHARES)
BSBR	Banco Santander Brasil SA	Banking	12/31/17	88219.1	8924.1	645703.0	86650.7	138	66793758
BSAC	Banco Santander Chile	Banking	12/31/17	2407480.0	562801.0	35823605.0	3106037.0	194	101260563
SAN	Banco Santander SA (Spain)	Banking	12/31/17	77856.0	6619.0	1444305.0	94489.0	468	275676727
CIB	BanColombia SA	Banking	12/31/17	22171100.0	2615000.0	203908211.0	23112964.0	199	51671337
BXS	BancorpSouth Bank (Tupelo, MS)	Banking	12/31/17	781.0	153.0	15298.5	1713.5	285	82243074
BAC	Bank of America Corp	Banking	12/31/17	100264.0	18232.0	2281234.0	267146.0	2803	8277462879
BOH	Bank of Hawaii Corp	Banking	12/31/17	689.2	184.7	17089.1	1231.9	420	46460718
BMO	Bank of Montreal (Quebec)	Banking	10/31/17	28086.0	5348.0	709580.0	44354.0	576	321780037
BK	Bank of New York Mellon Corp	Banking	12/31/17	16617.0	4090.0	371758.0	41251.0	1472	964326471
BNS	Bank of Nova Scotia Halifax	Banking	10/31/17	36047.0	7876.0	915273.0	60033.0	530	677899977
NTB	Bank Of NT Butterfield & Son Ltd (T	Banking	12/31/17	464.7	153.3	10779.2	822.9		0
BKU	BankUnited Inc.	Banking	12/31/17	1362.4	614.3	30347.0	3026.1	336	129008581
BCS	Barclays PLC	Banking	12/31/17	27056.0	-1283.0	1133248.0	63905.0	382	149753191
MCI	Barings Corporate Investors	Holding and other Investment Office	12/31/16	28.2	22.2	321.9	281.6	64	2433314
BGH	Barings Global Short Duration High	Finance Intermediaries & Services	12/31/16	47.2	40.3	564.4	418.6		0
MPV	Barings Participation Investors	Holding and other Investment Office	12/31/16	12.8	10.3	155.8	136.6	38	1949855
BNED	Barnes & Noble Education Inc	Retail - Specialty	4/28/18	2203.6	-252.6	1039.2	468.0	183	39441400
BKS	Barnes & Noble Inc	Retail - Specialty	4/28/18	3662.3	-125.5	1749.6	412.0	276	57130807
B	Barnes Group Inc.	Industrial Machinery & Equipment	12/31/17	1436.5	59.4	2365.7	1260.3	364	61499381
ABX	Barrick Gold Corp.	Precious Metals	12/31/17	8374.0	1438.0	25308.0	9286.0	736	731490309
BAS	Basic Energy Services Inc	Equipment & Services	12/31/17	864.0	-96.7	820.5	338.7	191	31258036
BHC	Bausch Health Companies Inc	Pharmaceuticals	12/31/17	8724.0	2404.0	37497.0	5849.0	487	184003241
BAX	Baxter International Inc	Medical Instruments & Equipment	12/31/17	10561.0	717.0	17111.0	9124.0	1551	599704074
BTE	Baytex Energy Corp	Production & Extraction	12/31/17	849.6	87.2	4372.1	1914.9		0
BBT	BB&T Corp.	Banking	12/31/17	12156.0	2394.0	221642.0	29648.0	1369	589756952
BFR	BBVA Banco Frances SA (Argentin	Banking	12/31/17	38463.8	3878.3	225642.8	26056.5	94	33860956
BBX	BBX Capital Corp (New)	Hotels, Restaurants & Travel	12/31/17	815.8	82.2	1606.7	573.2	111	35109815
BCE	BCE Inc	Services	12/31/17	22719.0	2786.0	54263.0	19160.0	687	491204495
BZH	Beazer Homes USA, Inc.	Builders	9/30/17	1916.3	31.8	2221.0	682.4	258	43807847
BDX	Becton, Dickinson & Co	Medical Instruments & Equipment	9/30/17	12093.0	1100.0	37734.0	12948.0	1724	275368046
BDC	Belden Inc	Electrical Equipment	12/31/17	2388.6	93.2	3840.6	1434.2	369	65579114
BXE	Bellatrix Exploration Ltd	Production & Extraction	12/31/17	302.0	-91.4	1340.9	774.0	53	21245287
T 28A	BellSouth Telecommunications, Inc.	Services	12/31/99	17478.0	2770.0	25295.0	8805.0		0
BEL	Belmond Ltd	Hotels, Restaurants & Travel	12/31/17	560.8	-45.0	1653.6	698.5	213	113635738
BMS	Bemis Co Inc	Containers & Packaging	12/31/17	4046.2	94.0	3699.9	1201.2	525	99218511
BHE	Benchmark Electronics, Inc.	Electrical Equipment	12/31/17	2466.8	-32.0	2097.3	1328.8	309	60719355
WRB	Berkley (WR) Corp	General Insurance	12/31/17	7684.8	549.1	24299.9	5411.3	565	123692023
BRK A	Berkshire Hathaway Inc	General Insurance	12/31/17	242137.0	44940.0	702095.0	348296.0	2731	1026654111
BHLB	Berkshire Hills Bancorp Inc	Banking	12/31/17	485.9	55.2	11570.8	1496.3	258	35763837
BERY	Berry Global Group Inc	Plastics	9/30/17	7095.0	340.0	8476.0	1012.0	468	134187466
BBY	Best Buy Inc	Retail - Appliances and Electronics	2/3/18	42151.0	1000.0	13049.0	3612.0	918	297247966
BSTI	BEST Inc	Trucking	12/31/17	19989.6	-1227.9	10878.5	4391.8	75	48516597
BHP	BHP Billiton Ltd	Non-Precious Metals	6/30/17	38285.0	5890.0	117006.0	57258.0	623	73180029
BBL	BHP Billiton Plc	Production & Extraction	6/30/17	38285.0	5890.0	117006.0	57258.0	283	54710049
BIG	Big Lots, Inc.	Retail - General Merchandise/Depart	2/3/18	5271.0	189.8	1651.7	669.6	537	69310190
BH	Biglari Holdings Inc (New)	Hotels, Restaurants & Travel	12/31/17	839.8	50.1	1063.6	571.3		0
BIO	Bio-Rad Laboratories Inc	Biotechnology	12/31/17	2160.2	122.2	4273.0	2930.3	437	22995224
BHVN	Biohaven Pharmaceutical Holding C	Pharmaceuticals	12/31/17		-127.2	146.9	132.0	112	27439642
BITA	Bitauto Holdings Ltd	Internet & Software	12/31/17	8751.3	-1611.1	51515.7	11328.7	122	25075613
BJ	BJ's Wholesale Club Holdings Inc	Retail - General Merchandise/Depart	2/3/18	12754.6	50.3	3273.9	-1019.4		0
BKH	Black Hills Corporation	Electric Utilities	12/31/17	1680.3	177.0	6658.9	1709.0	383	67399583
BKI	Black Knight Inc	Internet & Software	12/31/17	1051.6	182.3	3655.9	1708.8	391	132991757
BSM	Black Stone Minerals LP	Production & Extraction	12/31/17	429.7	157.2	1576.5	322.4	88	23142403
BB	BlackBerry Ltd	Services	2/28/18	932.0	405.0	3780.0	2505.0	492	332658065
BJZ	Blackrock California Municipal 2018	Holding and other Investment Office	12/31/16	2.7	2.2	96.2	96.1	23	1549392
BFZ	BlackRock California Municipal Inco	Holding and other Investment Office	7/31/17	33.8	23.2	840.0	489.3	59	3518438
BHK	BlackRock Core Bond Trust	Holding and other Investment Office	8/31/17	50.0	40.8	1118.6	806.8	114	18512398
HYT	BlackRock Corporate High Yield Fu	Holding and other Investment Office	8/31/17	130.4	107.0	2215.2	1545.6	189	41347501
BTZ	BlackRock Credit Allocation Income	Holding and other Investment Office	10/31/17	106.1	86.8	2098.8	1598.0	160	55453249
DSU	BlackRock Debt Strategies Fund Inc	Holding and other Investment Office	2/28/17	55.9	45.7	1156.1	780.8	122	28166723
BGR	Blackrock Energy & Resources Trus	Holding and other Investment Office	12/31/16	13.4	8.0	494.6	487.1	106	7264941
CII	BlackRock Enhanced Capital & Inco	Holding and other Investment Office	12/31/16	11.7	5.6	677.5	665.2	97	10451650
BDJ	BlackRock Enhanced Equity Divide	Holding and other Investment Office	12/31/16	45.3	31.3	1773.9	1741.6	199	41702461
BOE	BlackRock Enhanced Global Divide	Holding and other Investment Office	12/31/16	20.5	10.7	943.3	929.9	125	20760883
EGF	BlackRock Enhanced Government	Holding and other Investment Office	12/31/16	3.7	2.6	114.1	90.1	25	4939454
BGY	BlackRock Enhanced International	Holding and other Investment Office	12/31/16	17.3	10.0	716.5	690.6	106	36838279
FRA	BlackRock Floating Rate Income Str	Holding and other Investment Office	8/31/17	38.7	28.3	834.4	556.0	121	10537989
BGT	BlackRock Floating Rate Income Tr	Holding and other Investment Office	10/31/17	23.8	17.2	521.1	342.9	76	6434356
BFO	BlackRock Florida Municipal 2020 T	Holding and other Investment Office	7/31/17	2.6	2.0	83.9	83.7	22	721797
BME	BlackRock Health Sciences Trust	Holding and other Investment Office	12/31/16	3.4	0.2	273.5	270.7	53	2548644
BLK	BlackRock Inc	Finance Intermediaries & Services	12/31/17	12491.0	4970.0	220217.0	31825.0	1526	159736806
BKT	BlackRock Income Trust Inc (The)	Holding and other Investment Office	8/31/16	22.8	18.0	622.6	444.9	90	39220647
BKN	BlackRock Investment Quality Muni	Holding and other Investment Office	4/30/17	18.7	13.6	423.0	264.6	74	2510144
BLW	Blackrock Limited Duration Income	Holding and other Investment Office	8/31/17	46.5	37.5	907.2	629.7	109	12641960
BTA	BlackRock Long-Term Municipal Ad	Holding and other Investment Office	4/30/17	12.4	9.0	277.6	164.7	43	3442661
BZM	BlackRock Maryland Municipal Bon	Holding and other Investment Office	8/31/17	1.9	1.2	50.3	31.9	22	181833
MHE	BlackRock Massachusetts Tax-Exe	Holding and other Investment Office	8/31/17	2.2	1.5	54.3	33.1	11	92661
BIT	Blackrock Multi-Sector Income Trust	Holding and other Investment Office	10/31/17	74.8	57.7	1271.4	765.9	83	13954725
MUI	BlackRock Muni Intermediate Durati	Holding and other Investment Office	4/30/17	36.2	24.8	931.3	580.9	105	12257036
MNE	BlackRock Muni New York Intermed	Holding and other Investment Office	7/31/17	3.8	2.4	103.9	65.1	29	546282

T8

EARNINGS PER SHARE — QUARTERLY			— ANNUAL —			P/E RATIO		DIVIDENDS PER SHARE			AV. YLD	DIV. DECLARED		PRICE RANGE	
1st	2nd	3rd	2017	2016	2015			2017	2016	2015	%	AMOUNT	PAYABLE	2017	
		176.00	11.32	9.29	1.24	1.1	0.6	1.44	0.79	0.96	15.0			12.0	7.3
		0.54	2.99	2.53	2.38	11.7	8.5	554.23	567.70	555.94	1782.4			34.9	25.5
		0.08	0.40	0.41	0.40	18.9	13.2	0.46	0.35	0.70	7.0	0.25560	6/5/18	7.5	5.3
			2780.00	3040.00	2680.00	0.0	0.0	3754.83	3500.05	3333.93	8511.4			50.8	37.0
0.54			1.67	1.41	1.33	21.1	16.5	0.14	0.45	0.35	0.4	0.140Y	18/78/27	35.2	27.6
0.62			1.56	1.50	1.31	21.1	14.7	0.39	0.25	0.20	1.4	1.750Y	18/78/27	32.8	22.9
1.28			4.33	4.23	3.70	20.5	17.3	2.04	1.89	1.80	2.4	0.60Y	18/78/27	88.6	75.0
	1.86		7.92	6.92	6.57	13.2	9.0	3.56	3.40	3.24	4.1	0.2750	8/27/18	104.7	71.4
1.10			3.72	3.15	2.71	15.7	13.5	0.86	0.72	0.68	1.6	0.3250Y	18/78/27	58.4	50.1
	1.70		6.49	5.77	5.67	13.1	8.7	3.05	2.88	2.72	4.3	0.30310	7/27/18	84.9	56.6
			2.76	1.18	1.23			1.28	0.40	0.50		0.380	5/15/18		
0.77			5.58	2.09	2.35	7.9	5.5	0.84	0.84	0.63	2.2	0.210Y	18/78/27	44.2	30.5
			-0.10	0.10	-0.02			0.12	0.18	0.25	1.1			12.4	9.4
				1.12	1.04				1.20	1.20		0.30	5/18/18	16.2	14.7
				1.57	1.90				1.85	2.19		0.14821	10/1/18	20.8	18.4
				1.00	0.95				1.08	1.08		0.270	5/18/18	15.5	13.9
	-6.04		0.11		0.33	97.8	45.5							10.8	5.0
	-0.87		0.30	-0.49	0.21	27.7	14.5	0.60	0.60		9.5	0.150Y	7/27/18	8.3	4.3
0.72			1.09	2.48	2.19	66.5	48.4	0.55	0.51	0.48	0.9	0.160Y	9/10/18	72.4	52.8
		-0.01	1.23	0.56	-2.44	18.3	9.3	0.12	0.08	0.14	0.7	0.030	6/15/18	22.5	11.4
-1.16			-3.72	-2.94	3403.46									29.0	11.1
-7.68			6.83	-6.94	-0.85	5.2	0.0					1.7	12/22/10	35.5	0.0
0.71			1.29	9.01	1.76	58.5	46.1	0.61	0.51	1.27	0.9	0.190Y	18/78/27	75.4	59.5
-0.27			0.37	-2.29	-5.72	16.4	6.1			0.80		0.10	9/15/15	6.1	2.2
0.94			2.74	2.77	2.56	20.4	15.9	1.26	1.15	1.05	2.5	0.35160Y	18/78/27	56.0	43.7
														26.6	12.3
0.11			0.79	0.32	1.40	12.7	7.6	0.03	0.01		0.4	0.010Y	7/20/18	10.0	6.0
0.73			3.11	3.33	2.98	20.2	13.0	2.87	2.73	2.60	5.6	0.17270	6/30/18	62.8	40.3
	0.35		0.99	0.15	10.83	22.2	13.3					0.46880Z	7/15/15	22.0	13.1
	-0.19		4.60	4.49	3.35	53.5	41.6	2.92	2.64	2.40	1.3	0.76560Y	18/78/27	246.3	191.6
-0.15			1.37	2.65	1.54	63.5	39.8	0.20	0.20	0.20	0.3	0.050Y	18/78/27	87.0	54.5
	-0.45		-1.85	-0.12	-11.55									3.9	1.0
-0.15			-0.44	0.35	0.16							0.0250	11/4/08		
0.52			1.02	2.48	2.44	48.3	40.2	1.20	1.16	1.12	2.7	0.310Y	18/78/27	49.2	41.0
-0.49			-0.64	1.29	1.83					0.10		0.150Y	7/12/18	35.6	26.3
1.30			4.26	4.68	3.87	18.4	14.7	1.55	1.51	0.47	2.2	0.150Y	18/78/27	78.3	62.5
-692.00			27326.00	4655.00	4656.00	11.9	9.3							825915.02	55400.0
0.55			1.39	1.88	1.73	31.3	23.8	0.84	0.80	0.76	2.2	0.220Y	8/23/18	43.5	33.1
	0.66		2.56	1.89	0.70	23.8	17.8							61.0	45.7
0.72			3.81	2.56	3.49	20.7	13.8	1.57	1.43	0.72	2.4	0.450Y	18/78/27	78.8	52.6
			-8.28	-93.51	-89.21									12.9	8.2
			1.10	-1.20	0.36	47.2	32.9	1.08	1.56	2.48	2.4			52.0	36.2
			1.10	-1.20	0.36	43.5	28.5	1.08	1.56	2.48	2.7			47.9	31.3
0.74			3.32	2.80	2.06	19.3	11.7	0.84	0.76	0.51	1.7	0.30Y	18/78/27	64.2	38.7
-5.15			40.77	81.28	-10.18	10.8	4.5							440.6	183.5
21.77			4.07	0.95	3.85	74.7	52.2							303.9	212.3
-2.32			-5.00	-5.05	-0.91										
			-23.16	-8.31	-7.30									53.2	19.1
0.15			0.48	0.26		49.3	45.8							23.6	22.0
2.46			3.21	1.37	-0.71	22.1	15.8	1.81	1.68	1.62	3.0	0.4750Y	18/78/27	70.8	50.7
0.29			1.47	0.67	0.29	37.0	28.6							54.4	42.0
0.23			1.01	0.26	-1.12	18.8	15.7	1.20	1.10	0.42	6.9	0.31250	5/24/18	19.0	15.9
-0.11			-2.30	-0.86	-0.58									17.9	8.6
				0.34	0.36				0.33	0.38		0.0025M	8/1/18	15.3	0.0
			0.73	0.83	0.83	20.2	17.6	0.77	0.86	0.87	5.6	0.047M	8/1/18	14.7	12.9
			0.76	0.79	0.86	18.8	16.6	0.78	0.84	1.08	5.8	0.0650	7/31/18	14.3	12.6
			0.85	0.82	0.87	13.5	12.3	0.89	0.99	0.97	8.2	0.0720	7/31/18	11.5	10.4
			0.81	0.88	0.96	16.8	14.9	0.84	0.92	0.97	6.5	0.0670	7/31/18	13.6	12.1
			0.73	0.78	0.87	16.2	15.3	0.21			1.8	0.06850	7/31/18	11.8	11.2
				0.27	0.29				1.00	1.50		0.07760	7/31/18	15.5	12.3
				0.13	0.11				1.15	1.20		0.08280	7/31/18	17.0	14.8
				0.17	0.17				0.56	0.56		0.04670	7/31/18	9.6	8.5
				0.15	0.11				1.05	1.16		0.0630	7/31/18	13.9	11.0
				0.36	0.41				0.53	0.62		0.0410	7/31/18	13.7	0.0
				0.09	0.08				0.52	0.59		0.0380	7/31/18	6.8	5.7
			0.76	0.76	0.81	19.2	18.0	0.81	0.75	0.81	5.7	0.06450	7/31/18	14.6	13.7
			0.73	0.74	0.78	19.6	17.9	0.77	0.70	0.81	5.6	0.06180	7/31/18	14.3	13.1
			0.37	0.46	0.42	40.9	0.0	0.42	0.38	0.44	3.0	0.026M	7/31/18	15.2	0.0
				0.02	-0.06				3.00	6.70		0.20	7/31/18	39.4	33.4
6.68			30.23	19.04	19.79	19.6	13.6	10.00	9.16	8.72	2.0	3.130Y	18/78/27	593.3	412.2
				0.28	0.32				0.34	0.40		0.02650	7/31/18	6.4	5.7
			0.79	0.88	0.90	19.9	17.1	1.11	0.91	0.95	7.7	0.057M	8/1/18	15.7	13.5
			1.01	1.32	1.16	16.1	14.7	1.27	1.30	1.29	8.2	0.07950	7/31/18	16.3	14.8
				0.68	0.69			0.66	0.70	0.72	5.6	0.0545M	8/1/18	12.5	11.1
			0.59	0.61	0.63	25.4	0.0	0.57	0.62	0.68	4.4	0.0474M	8/1/18	15.0	0.0
			0.62	0.65	0.68	23.2	0.0	0.64	0.68	0.71	5.7	0.044M	8/1/18	14.4	0.0
			1.51	1.69	1.55	12.4	11.1	1.77	1.64	1.48	9.9	0.11670	7/31/18	18.7	16.7
			0.65	0.73	0.77	22.2	19.9	0.82	0.96	0.82	6.0	0.0445M	8/1/18	14.4	13.0
			0.57	0.64	0.68	25.0	22.0	0.65	0.66	0.69	4.9	0.04M	8/1/18	14.2	12.5

SYMBOL	COMPANY	NATURE OF BUSINESS	FISCAL YEAR-END	TOTAL REV. $MILL	NET INCOME $MILL	TOTAL ASSETS $MILL	NET STK EQUITY $MILL	NO OF INST	INST. HOLDINGS (SHARES)
MUA	BlackRock MuniAssets Fund, Inc.	Holding and other Investment Office	4/30/17	29.8	25.3	576.4	505.3	71	2585350
BPK	Blackrock Municipal 2018 Term Tru	Holding and other Investment Office	12/31/16	6.9	5.7	243.3	239.2	56	5465477
BKK	BlackRock Municipal 2020 Term Tr	Holding and other Investment Office	4/30/17	13.2	11.0	332.2	315.8	62	2973648
BTT	BlackRock Municipal 2030 Target T	Holding and other Investment Office	7/31/17	88.3	63.4	2671.9	1679.8	107	11600533
BBK	Blackrock Municipal Bond Trust	Holding and other Investment Office	8/31/17	11.7	7.7	280.5	171.7	58	1255800
BAF	BlackRock Municipal Income Invest	Holding and other Investment Office	8/31/17	9.7	6.9	228.9	137.3	34	1137158
BBF	BlackRock Municipal Income Invest	Holding and other Investment Office	7/31/17	11.8	8.5	254.6	148.0	28	887988
BYM	BlackRock Municipal Income Qualit	Holding and other Investment Office	8/31/17	27.6	19.9	651.3	404.5	81	4421612
BFK	BlackRock Municipal Income Trust	Holding and other Investment Office	4/30/17	49.2	36.1	1060.2	638.0	90	5544672
BLE	BlackRock Municipal Income Trust I	Holding and other Investment Office	8/31/17	26.6	19.4	582.1	356.9	75	3089956
MEN	BlackRock MuniEnhanced Fund Inc	Holding and other Investment Office	4/30/17	25.4	19.1	565.6	349.0	63	5338000
MUC	BlackRock MuniHoldings California	Holding and other Investment Office	7/31/17	41.0	28.4	1089.9	636.9	73	5805978
MUH	BlackRock MuniHoldings Fund II Inc	Holding and other Investment Office	4/30/17	13.1	9.8	279.5	175.6	49	1725284
MHD	BlackRock MuniHoldings Fund Inc	Holding and other Investment Office	4/30/17	18.1	13.4	386.4	238.7	51	1581592
MFL	BlackRock MuniHoldings Investmen	Holding and other Investment Office	8/31/17	41.0	29.4	968.7	564.4	77	5449023
MUJ	BlackRock MuniHoldings New Jerse	Holding and other Investment Office	7/31/17	32.2	23.3	794.1	469.4	51	2544254
MHN	BlackRock MuniHoldings New York	Holding and other Investment Office	8/31/17	30.7	21.3	783.1	464.8	56	3284956
MUE	BlackRock MuniHoldings Quality Fu	Holding and other Investment Office	7/31/17	23.0	16.8	519.3	319.4	57	4175777
MUS	BlackRock MuniHoldings Quality Fu	Holding and other Investment Office	4/30/17	13.4	9.8	299.1	181.6	38	1992650
MVT	BlackRock MuniVest Fund II Inc	Holding and other Investment Office	4/30/17	25.4	19.2	524.9	321.9	52	1234572
MVF	BlackRock MuniVest Fund Inc	Holding and other Investment Office	8/31/17	48.0	35.9	1025.3	630.5	91	5825923
MZA	BlackRock MuniYield Arizona Fund	Holding and other Investment Office	7/31/17	4.7	3.3	108.0	67.3	15	208875
MYC	BlackRock MuniYield California Fun	Holding and other Investment Office	7/31/17	22.8	15.8	566.4	334.5	49	3073396
MCA	BlackRock MuniYield California Qua	Holding and other Investment Office	7/31/17	35.6	25.2	919.7	541.3	61	5390780
MYD	BlackRock MuniYield Fund Inc	Holding and other Investment Office	4/30/17	51.7	39.3	1112.5	687.9	83	5258566
MYF	BlackRock MuniYield Investment Fu	Holding and other Investment Office	7/31/17	16.0	11.9	348.3	204.4	39	1474611
MFT	BlackRock MuniYield Investment Q	Holding and other Investment Office	7/31/17	9.2	6.7	212.0	123.7	36	855937
MIY	BlackRock MuniYield Michigan Qual	Holding and other Investment Office	7/31/17	30.7	22.0	745.0	457.9	49	3579517
MYJ	BlackRock MuniYield New Jersey F	Holding and other Investment Office	7/31/17	16.1	11.7	389.7	228.3	36	1295143
MYN	BlackRock MuniYield New York Qu	Holding and other Investment Office	7/31/17	36.3	25.4	929.0	564.2	66	3842946
MPA	BlackRock MuniYield Pennsylvania	Holding and other Investment Office	7/31/17	14.2	10.2	352.0	210.2	44	1175337
MQT	BlackRock MuniYield Quality Fund I	Holding and other Investment Office	4/30/17	22.1	16.4	503.2	308.7	61	3971345
MYI	BlackRock MuniYield Quality Fund I	Holding and other Investment Office	7/31/17	70.7	52.5	1602.5	985.6	118	11783653
MQY	BlackRock MuniYield Quality Fund I	Holding and other Investment Office	4/30/17	34.7	26.1	781.8	477.8	85	5533735
BLH	Blackrock New York Municipal 2018	Holding and other Investment Office	12/31/16	1.2	0.8	54.2	54.1	15	653860
BQH	Blackrock New York Municipal Bond	Holding and other Investment Office	8/31/17	2.9	1.9	74.1	45.1	16	202819
BSE	BlackRock New York Municipal Inco	Holding and other Investment Office	8/31/17	6.1	4.1	160.1	98.1	30	1037653
BNY	BlackRock New York Municipal Inco	Holding and other Investment Office	7/31/17	12.9	8.7	324.1	195.0	35	1226658
BFY	BlackRock New York Municipal Inco	Holding and other Investment Office	8/31/17	5.3	3.6	131.6	78.6	22	572306
BCX	Blackrock Resources & Commoditie	Holding and other Investment Office	12/31/17	30.3	19.8	1046.5	1027.5	115	38764992
BST	Blackrock Science & Technology T	Holding and other Investment Office	12/31/16	4.0	0.1	456.7	452.4	53	4700802
BSD	Blackrock Strategic Municipal Trust	Holding and other Investment Office	4/30/17	7.9	5.7	175.3	103.8	36	775391
BBN	BlackRock Taxable Municipal Bond	Holding and other Investment Office	7/31/17	110.7	90.5	2075.9	1339.1	120	8226737
BUI	BlackRock Utilities, Infrastructure &	Holding and other Investment Office	12/31/17	13.3	9.5	359.4	357.8	45	1993520
BHV	BlackRock Virginia Municipal Bond	Holding and other Investment Office	8/31/17	1.8	1.2	41.6	25.2	17	88264
BGX	Blackstone / GSO Long-Short Credi	Holding and other Investment Office	12/31/16	23.1	17.8	361.2	215.2	47	4297202
BSL	Blackstone / GSO Senior Floating R	Holding and other Investment Office	12/31/16	25.5	18.9	427.5	268.2	48	3902204
BGB	Blackstone / GSO Strategic Credit F	Holding and other Investment Office	12/31/16	81.6	62.1	1255.5	749.9	76	19957137
BX	Blackstone Group LP (The)	Wealth Management	12/31/17	7119.1	1470.8	34428.9		856	374695513
BXMT	Blackstone Mortgage Trust Inc	REITs	12/31/17	537.9	217.6	10258.8	2911.1	348	74112173
HRB	Block (H & R), Inc.	Miscellaneous Consumer Services	4/30/18	3159.9	613.1	3140.9	393.7	710	273190683
APRN	Blue Apron Holdings Inc	Food	12/31/17	881.2	-210.1	517.7	223.8	102	22975127
BCRH	Blue Capital Reinsurance Holdings	General Insurance	12/31/17	49.4	-43.2	182.2	127.1	64	8037819
BXG	Bluegreen Vacations Corp	Property, Real Estate & Developmen	12/31/17	668.1	125.5	1236.4	382.2	68	13053878
BXC	BlueLinx Holdings Inc	Construction Services	12/30/17	1815.5	63.0	494.1	35.0	89	8955565
BA	Boeing Co. (The)	Aerospace	12/31/17	93392.0	8197.0	92333.0	355.0	2462	502745293
BCC	Boise Cascade Co. (DE)	Construction Materials	12/31/17	4432.0	83.0	1607.2	674.5	310	45731183
BCEI	Bonanza Creek Energy Inc	Production & Extraction	12/31/17	123.5	-5.0	830.4	688.3	152	24655956
BOOT	Boot Barn Holdings Inc	Retail - Apparel and Accessories	3/31/18	677.9	28.9	587.9	214.6	149	26062859
BAH	Booz Allen Hamilton Holding Corp.	Business Services	3/31/18	6171.9	305.1	3603.4	554.6	361	242359619
BWA	BorgWarner Inc	Auto Parts	12/31/17	9799.3	439.9	9787.6	3716.8	842	232461426
SAM	Boston Beer Co Inc (The)	Beverages	12/30/17	863.0	99.0	569.6	423.5	355	12179917
BXP	Boston Properties Inc.	REITs	12/31/17	2602.1	462.4	19372.2	5814.0	692	194238231
BSX	Boston Scientific Corp.	Medical Instruments & Equipment	12/31/17	9048.0	104.0	19042.0	7012.0	949	1478023428
BIF	Boulder Growth & Income Fund Inc.	Holding and other Investment Office	11/30/16	24.3	9.0	1204.7	1153.1	113	17082386
BOX	Box Inc	Internet & Software	1/31/18	506.1	-155.0	553.6	15.0	270	111365616
BYD	Boyd Gaming Corp.	Hotels, Restaurants & Travel	12/31/17	2383.7	189.2	4685.9	1101.0	354	97205524
BPMP	BP Midstream Partners LP	Gas Utilities	12/31/17	108.2	60.9	605.7		80	49160330
BP	BP PLC	Production & Extraction	12/31/17	243372.0	3389.0	276515.0	98491.0	1470	447537120
BPT	BP Prudhoe Bay Royalty Trust	Oil Royalty Traders	12/31/17	78.2	77.0	1.0	0.8	136	1331209
BRC	Brady Corp	Printing	7/31/17	1113.3	95.6	1050.2	700.1	269	51314383
BHR	Braemar Hotels & Resorts Inc	REITs	12/31/17	414.1	23.0	1423.8	487.4	153	25057783
BDN	Brandywine Realty Trust	REITs	12/31/17	520.5	120.8	3995.4	1829.2	377	244436949
BWG	BrandywineGLOBAL Global Income	Holding and other Investment Office	10/31/17	30.3	21.8	500.3	312.0	62	8366492
LND	Brasilagro Cia Brasileira De Proprie	Agricultural Crop Production	6/30/17	184.2	27.3	883.3	667.5	6	163240
BAK	Braskem S A	Refining & Marketing	12/31/15	47283.0	3140.3	59961.3	2022.6	145	25495984
BRFS	BRF S.A.	Food	12/31/17	33469.4	-1125.6	45228.5	11200.3	194	67599334
BPI	Bridgepoint Education, Inc.	Educational Services	12/31/17	478.4	10.5	287.5	128.5	138	51600936
BGG	Briggs & Stratton Corp.	Industrial Machinery & Equipment	7/2/17	1786.1	56.6	1451.0	559.3	297	46180565
BFAM	Bright Horizons Family Solutions, In	Services	12/31/17	1740.9	157.0	2468.6	749.1		0

| EARNINGS PER SHARE | | | | | | P/E RATIO | | DIVIDENDS PER SHARE | | | AV. YLD | DIV. DECLARED | | PRICE RANGE | |
| QUARTERLY | | | ANNUAL | | | | | | | | % | | | 2017 | |
1st	2nd	3rd	2017	2016	2015			2017	2016	2015		AMOUNT	PAYABLE		
-	-	-	-	0.72	0.73	-		0.70	0.74	0.76	4.9	0.0545M	8/1/18	15.8 -	13.1
-	-	-	-	0.36	0.41			-	0.37	0.60		0.005M	8/1/18	15.0 -	14.7
-	-	-	0.55	0.57	0.90	28.8 -	27.2	0.55	0.56	0.67	3.6	0.0318M	8/1/18	15.8 -	14.9
-	-	-	0.90	1.03	1.09	25.8 -	23.3	0.95	0.96	0.96	4.3	0.0624M	8/1/18	23.3 -	21.0
-	-	-	0.74	0.89	0.90	22.1 -	18.9	1.22	0.91	0.98	8.1	0.0635M	8/1/18	16.3 -	14.0
-	-	-	0.79	0.83	0.83	19.7 -	17.4	0.82	0.82	0.82	5.6	0.0585M	8/1/18	15.5 -	13.7
-	-	-	0.84	0.84	0.87	18.4 -	15.3	0.87	0.87	0.87	6.2	0.0605M	8/1/18	15.4 -	12.8
-	-	-	0.75	0.82	0.84	20.3 -	17.3	0.78	0.83	0.86	5.6	0.052M	8/1/18	15.2 -	13.0
-	-	-	0.81	0.87	0.88	18.1 -	15.7	0.84	0.90	0.91	6.1	0.0585M	8/1/18	14.7 -	12.7
-	-	-	0.83	0.93	0.92	19.0 -	16.1	0.89	0.93	0.96	6.2	0.058M	8/1/18	15.8 -	13.3
-	-	-	0.70	0.70	0.71	17.8 -	14.8	0.68	0.73	0.73	6.0	0.048M	8/1/18	12.5 -	10.4
-	-	-	0.69	0.77	0.78	22.0 -	18.8	0.74	0.80	0.82	5.3	0.0475M	8/1/18	15.2 -	13.0
-	-	-	0.86	0.91	0.93	18.9 -	15.8	0.90	0.94	0.97	6.1	0.0615M	8/1/18	16.3 -	13.6
-	-	-	0.95	1.00	1.03	19.1 -	15.7	0.98	1.06	1.06	6.0	0.07M	8/1/18	18.2 -	14.9
-	-	-	0.78	0.86	0.89	19.6 -	16.2	0.86	0.86	0.86	6.1	0.0565M	8/1/18	15.3 -	12.7
-	-	-	0.77	0.84	0.84	19.4 -	17.0	0.81	0.87	0.89	5.8	0.0525M	8/1/18	14.9 -	13.1
-	-	-	0.69	0.75	0.80	21.1 -	17.9	0.70	0.71	0.82	5.2	0.0445M	8/1/18	14.5 -	12.3
-	-	-	0.75	0.78	0.80	19.1 -	16.1	0.77	0.81	0.83	5.8	0.054M	8/1/18	14.3 -	12.0
-	-	z	0.75	0.80	0.80	18.9 -	16.4	0.80	0.81	0.81	6.1	0.0505M	8/1/18	14.2 -	12.3
-	-	-	0.91	0.98	0.99	17.7 -	15.3	0.94	1.00	1.04	6.2	0.0635M	8/1/18	16.1 -	13.9
-	-	-	0.56	0.61	0.62	17.7 -	15.4	0.57	0.63	0.64	6.1	0.041M	8/1/18	9.9 -	8.6
-	-	-	0.72	0.77	0.80	24.0 -	0.0	0.74	0.82	0.83	4.9	0.052M	8/1/18	17.3 -	0.0
-	-	-	0.74	0.86	0.87	21.2 -	17.7	1.10	1.01	0.90	7.6	0.052M	8/1/18	15.7 -	13.1
-	-	-	0.73	0.81	0.83	21.5 -	18.1	0.83	0.85	0.88	5.8	0.052M	8/1/18	15.7 -	13.2
-	-	-	0.84	0.90	0.91	18.7 -	15.5	0.87	0.93	0.95	6.1	0.061M	8/1/18	15.7 -	13.1
-	-	-	0.87	0.92	0.95	19.0 -	15.6	0.94	0.97	0.97	6.3	0.0695M	8/1/18	16.6 -	13.6
-	-	-	0.79	0.83	0.84	19.3 -	16.3	0.83	0.85	0.85	6.0	0.059M	8/1/18	15.3 -	12.9
-	-	-	0.75	0.79	0.83	19.1 -	17.3	0.77	0.83	0.86	5.6	0.052M	8/1/18	14.3 -	13.0
-	-	-	0.81	0.89	0.90	20.7 -	16.9	0.90	0.91	0.90	5.9	0.0605M	8/1/18	16.8 -	13.7
-	-	-	0.64	0.70	0.75	20.9 -	18.5	0.65	0.73	0.77	5.1	0.0425M	8/1/18	13.4 -	11.8
-	-	-	0.76	0.80	0.81	19.6 -	17.6	0.75	0.83	0.88	5.3	0.0555M	8/1/18	14.9 -	13.4
-	-	-	0.73	0.79	0.91	19.0 -	16.3	0.75	0.82	0.85	5.9	0.048M	8/1/18	13.9 -	11.9
-	-	-	0.77	0.84	0.87	19.3 -	16.1	0.82	0.88	0.89	6.1	0.0505M	8/1/18	14.9 -	12.4
-	-	-	0.84	0.90	0.92	19.1 -	16.3	0.87	0.95	0.96	5.8	0.056M	8/1/18	16.0 -	13.7
-	-	-	-	0.23	0.25			-	0.23	0.33		0.0025M	8/1/18	15.0 -	0.0
-	-	-	0.67	0.71	0.74	23.1 -	0.0	0.71	0.73	0.79	5.1	0.046M	8/1/18	15.4 -	0.0
-	-	-	0.63	0.68	0.70	21.8 -	19.4	0.63	0.68	0.73	4.8	0.0405M	8/1/18	13.7 -	12.2
-	-	-	0.67	0.75	0.79	23.1 -	19.0	0.72	0.80	0.83	5.1	0.0445M	8/1/18	15.5 -	12.7
-	-	-	0.71	0.81	0.82	22.2 -	18.0	0.76	0.83	0.84	5.3	0.049M	8/1/18	15.8 -	12.8
-	-	-	0.20	0.14	0.25	51.5 -	40.3	0.61	0.58	0.81	6.7	0.05160	7/31/18	10.3 -	8.1
-	-	-	-	0.00	0.03			-	1.20	1.20		0.150	7/31/18	35.3 -	22.2
-	-	-	0.78	0.82	1.04	19.5 -	16.0	0.79	0.85	0.88	5.8	0.057M	8/1/18	15.2 -	12.5
-	-	-	1.58	1.63	1.63	15.2 -	13.5	1.58	1.58	1.58	7.0	0.11880	7/31/18	23.9 -	21.3
-	-	-	0.56	0.56	0.47	38.8 -	34.4	1.45	1.45	1.45	7.0	0.1210	7/31/18	21.7 -	19.3
-	-	-	0.78	0.81	0.81	24.6 -	0.0	0.76	0.81	0.85	5.1	0.063M	8/1/18	19.2 -	0.0
-	-	-	-	1.40	1.22	-		-	1.43	1.27		0.1030	9/28/18	17.0 -	15.7
-	-	-	-	-	1.22			-	1.16	1.17		0.0970	9/28/18	18.5 -	17.0
-	-	-	1.39	1.48				-	1.34	1.37		0.1050	9/28/18	16.2 -	15.6
0.53	-	-	2.21	1.56	1.04	16.6 -	13.9	2.32	1.66	2.90	7.1	0.580	8/6/18	36.8 -	30.7
0.56	-	-	2.27	2.53	2.41	14.5 -	13.1	2.48	2.48	2.28	7.9	0.620Z	7/16/18	32.9 -	29.8
-	-	-1.18	1.91	1.49	1.71	16.5 -	11.8	0.88	0.80	0.80	3.3	0.250Y	18/78/27	31.5 -	22.5
-0.17	-	-	-1.64	-0.84	-0.92			-	-	-		-	-	9.7 -	1.8
0.06	-	-	-4.94	1.63	2.36			1.49	2.14	1.56		0.30	7/13/18	-	-
0.28	-	-	1.749510.003040.00			14.2 -	7.4	0.56	-	-	2.8	0.150Y	8/15/18	25.0 -	13.0
-1.47	-	-	6.81	1.77	-1.30	6.6 -	1.2	-	-	-		0.1250Y	12/28/07	45.1 -	8.0
4.15	-	-	13.43	7.61	7.44	27.7 -	14.8	5.68	4.36	3.64	1.9	1.710Y	18/78/27	371.6 -	198.6
0.94	-	-	2.12	0.98	1.33	23.2 -	13.3	0.07	-	-	0.2	0.070Y	6/15/18	49.1 -	28.2
0.68	-	-	-0.25	-4.04	-15.57	-		-	-	-		-	-	37.9 -	24.0
-	-	0.73	0.53	0.37	0.54	46.5 -	11.7	-	-	-		-	-	24.7 -	6.2
-	-	0.47	1.67	1.94	1.52	27.3 -	19.3	0.62	0.54	1.46	1.6	0.190Y	18/78/27	45.5 -	32.3
1.07	-	-	2.08	0.55	2.70	27.8 -	20.7	0.59	0.53	0.52	1.2	0.170Y	18/78/27	57.9 -	43.0
0.78	-	-	8.09	6.79	7.25	37.4 -	16.1	-	-	-		-	-	302.6 -	130.5
1.14	-	-	2.93	3.26	3.73	44.7 -	38.3	3.05	2.70	3.85	2.5	0.32810Z	18/78/27	131.0 -	112.1
0.21	-	-	0.08	0.25	-0.18	429.0 -	309.9	-	-	-		-	-	34.3 -	24.8
-	-	-	-	0.08	0.03			-	0.49	0.33		0.0340	7/31/18	11.8 -	9.7
-0.26	-	-	-1.19	-1.67	-11.48			-	-	-		-	-	29.0 -	17.5
0.36	-	-	1.64	3.63	0.42	24.3 -	14.9	0.15	-	-	0.5	0.060Y	7/15/18	39.9 -	24.4
0.58	-	-	0.42	-	-	53.6 -	40.4	0.18	-	-	0.9	0.26750	5/15/18	22.5 -	17.0
-	-	0.09	0.17	0.01	-0.35	281.1 -	200.0	2.38	2.38	2.38	5.9	-	-	47.8 -	34.0
-	-	-	3.60	2.04	5.86	8.5 -	5.2	3.60	2.04	5.86	16.3	1.40760	7/20/18	30.6 -	18.9
-	-	0.49	1.84	1.58	0.06	22.1 -	17.4	0.82	0.81	0.80	2.2	0.20750Y	18/78/27	40.6 -	31.9
0.07	-	-	0.51	0.55	-0.34	22.4 -	16.9	0.64	0.46	0.35	6.5	0.34380Z	7/16/18	11.4 -	8.6
0.25	-	-	0.65	0.19	-0.21	28.6 -	23.6	0.64	0.62	0.60	3.8	0.180Z	18/78/27	18.6 -	15.3
-	-	-	1.04	0.92	1.09	13.2 -	10.8	1.08	1.30	1.90	8.4	0.07650	9/4/18	13.7 -	11.2
-	-	-	0.47	0.18	3.10	9.3 -	0.0	0.49	1.36	-	16.2	-	-	4.3 -	0.0
-	-	-	-	-	3.95			-	-	1.11		-	-	32.6 -	20.4
-	-	0.33	-1.37	-0.46	3.72			-	0.61	1.25		-	-	15.3 -	4.7
0.08	-	-	0.32	-0.65	-1.54	45.7 -	17.0	-	-	-		-	-	14.6 -	5.5
-	-	0.74	1.31	0.60	1.00	20.8 -	13.3	0.56	0.54	0.50	2.5	0.140Y	6/29/18	27.2 -	17.4
0.62	-	-	2.59	1.55	1.50	41.7 -	29.3	-	-	-		-	-	108.1 -	75.8

SYMBOL	COMPANY	NATURE OF BUSINESS	FISCAL YEAR-END	TOTAL REV. $MILL	NET INCOME $MILL	TOTAL ASSETS $MILL	NET STK EQUITY $MILL	NO OF INST	INST. HOLDINGS (SHARES)
BEDU	Bright Scholar Education Holdings L	Educational Services	8/31/17	1328.4	172.0	2686.6	1416.1	59	18322252
BSIG	BrightSphere Investment Group PL	Finance Intermediaries & Services	12/31/17	887.4	4.2	1491.7	75.4	209	107172757
BV	BrightView Holdings Inc	Services	9/30/17	1713.6	-14.0	2858.6	696.3		0
EAT	Brinker International, Inc.	Hotels, Restaurants & Travel	6/28/17	3150.8	150.8	1413.7	-493.7	455	68887726
BCO	Brinks Co (The)	Business Services	12/31/17	3347.0	16.7	3059.6	317.4	429	59781677
BMY	Bristol-Myers Squibb Co.	Pharmaceuticals	12/31/17	20776.0	1007.0	33551.0	11741.0	2385	1449460256
BRS	Bristow Group Inc	Miscellaneous Transportation Servic	3/31/18	1445.0	-195.7	3165.0	1175.8	234	44748421
BTI	British American Tobacco Plc	Tobacco Products	12/31/17	20292.0	37533.0	141038.0	60804.0		0
BRX	Brixmor Property Group Inc	REITs	12/31/17	1283.2	300.3	9153.9	2908.3	394	338785638
BR	Broadridge Financial Solutions Inc	Finance Intermediaries & Services	6/30/17	4142.6	326.8	3149.8	1003.8	846	142596102
BKD	Brookdale Senior Living Inc	Hospitals & Health Care Facilities	12/31/17	4747.1	-571.4	7675.4	1530.7	338	216629204
BAM	Brookfield Asset Management Inc	Property, Real Estate & Developmen	12/31/17	40786.0	1462.0	192720.0	28244.0	591	670403921
BBU	Brookfield Business Partners LP	Construction Services	12/31/17	22823.0	-58.0	15804.0	1585.0	89	50548903
DTLA PR	Brookfield DTLA Fund Office Trust I	REITs	12/31/17	306.3	-23.1	2747.8	328.5	1	10000
INF	Brookfield Global Listed Infrastructu	Holding and other Investment Office	12/31/16	7.6	2.6	270.8	192.3	45	4311682
BIP	Brookfield Infrastructure Partners L	Electric Utilities	12/31/17	3535.0	124.0	29477.0	5587.0	326	151357240
RA	Brookfield Real Assets Income Fun	Holding and other Investment Office	12/31/17	78.3	63.4	1178.5	917.7	89	7752006
BEP	Brookfield Renewable Partners LP	Electric Utilities	12/31/17	2672.0	-32.0	30904.0	3956.0		0
BRO	Brown & Brown Inc	Brokers & Intermediaries	12/31/17	1881.3	399.6	5747.6	2582.7	437	225151065
BF B	Brown-Forman Corp	Beverages	4/30/18	3248.0	717.0	4976.0	1316.0	196	54144060
BRT	BRT Apartments Corp	REITs	9/30/17	105.8	13.6	993.9	166.0	62	5052407
BC	Brunswick Corp.	Leisure Equipment	12/31/17	4510.0	146.4	3358.2	1482.9	535	100776123
BT	BT Group Plc	Services	3/31/18	23723.0	2032.0	42759.0	10304.0	228	23816481
BPL	Buckeye Partners LP	Equipment & Services	12/31/17	3648.1	478.8	10304.7		516	118798689
BKE	Buckle, Inc. (The)	Retail - Apparel and Accessories	2/3/18	913.4	89.7	538.1	391.2	284	41024700
BBW	Build-A-Bear Workshop Inc	Retail - Specialty	12/30/17	357.9	7.9	198.0	107.3	126	17908945
BG	Bunge Ltd.	Food	12/31/17	45794.0	160.0	18871.0	7148.0	630	133169983
BURL	Burlington Stores Inc	Retail - Apparel and Accessories	2/3/18	6110.0	384.9	2812.8	86.8	456	78657579
BWXT	BWX Technologies inc	Industrial Machinery & Equipment	12/31/17	1687.7	147.8	1712.3	285.4	408	111599319
BY	Byline Bancorp Inc	Banking	12/31/17	186.9	21.7	3366.1	458.6	71	9337454
CJ	C&J Energy Services Inc (New)	Equipment & Services	12/31/17	1638.7	22.5	1608.9	1321.4	207	69150690
GYB	Cabco Series 2004-101 Trust Gold	Holding and other Investment Office						2	75600
CABO	Cable One Inc	Business Services	12/31/17	960.0	234.0	2218.3	671.4	291	5035753
CBT	Cabot Corp.	Specialty Chemicals	9/30/17	2717.0	241.0	3314.0	1480.0	439	67871176
COG	Cabot Oil & Gas Corp.	Production & Extraction	12/31/17	1764.2	100.4	4727.3	2523.9	796	502493727
CACI	CACI International Inc	IT Services	6/30/17	4354.6	163.7	3911.1	1793.6	404	30871618
WHD	Cactus Inc	Equipment & Services	12/31/17	341.2	66.5	266.5	-36.2	81	27793781
CADE	Cadence Bancorporation	Banking	12/31/17	496.7	102.4	10948.9	1359.1	118	29846532
CAE	CAE Inc	Aerospace	3/31/18	2830.0	347.0	5719.2	2298.2	224	156404503
CAI	CAI International Inc	Miscellaneous Transportation Servic	12/31/17	348.4	72.1	2430.4	563.8	172	17751908
CAL	Caleres Inc	Retail - Apparel and Accessories	2/3/18	2785.6	87.2	1489.4	717.5	270	52945498
CRC	California Resources Corp	Production & Extraction	12/31/17	2006.0	-266.0	6207.0	-814.0	350	39405390
CWT	California Water Service Group (DE	Water Utilities	12/31/17	666.9	67.2	2740.4	693.5	328	42075223
CALX	Calix Inc	Manufacturing	12/31/17	510.4	-83.0	295.1	145.0	131	37880251
ELY	Callaway Golf Co (DE)	Leisure Equipment	12/31/17	1048.7	40.8	991.2	649.6	350	103805653
CPE	Callon Petroleum Co. (DE)	Production & Extraction	12/31/17	365.5	120.4	2693.3	1856.0	392	289426173
CBM	Cambrex Corp	Pharmaceuticals	12/31/17	534.5	102.4	740.6	544.9	366	46934880
CPT	Camden Property Trust	REITs	12/31/17	928.7	196.4	6173.7	3405.4	511	108172986
CCJ	Cameco Corp.	Mining	12/31/17	2156.9	-204.9	7778.7	4859.3	429	263781800
CPB	Campbell Soup Co	Food	7/30/17	7890.0	887.0	7726.0	1637.0	879	199562853
CWH	Camping World Holdings Inc	Retail - Automotive	12/31/17	4285.3	28.4	2561.5	56.5	216	41296191
GOOS	Canada Goose Holdings Inc	Apparel, Footwear & Accessories	3/31/18	591.2	96.1	548.4	243.6	175	32965702
CM	Canadian Imperial Bank Of Comme	Banking	10/31/17	20896.0	4699.0	565264.0	31035.0	494	233654016
CNI	Canadian National Railway Co	Rail	12/31/17	13041.0	5484.0	37629.0	16656.0	837	497903984
CNQ	Canadian Natural Resources Ltd	Production & Extraction	12/31/17	16651.0	2397.0	73867.0	31653.0	574	828318829
CP	Canadian Pacific Railway Ltd	Rail	12/31/17	6554.0	2405.0	20135.0	6437.0	610	126141536
CNNE	Cannae Holdings Inc	Property, Real Estate & Developmen	12/31/17	1169.5	108.8	1487.2	1059.4		0
CAJ	Canon, Inc.	Leisure Equipment	12/31/17	4080015.0	241923.0	5198291.0	2870630.0	277	22390833
CGC	Canopy Growth Corp	Pharmaceuticals	3/31/17	39.9	-16.6	677.6	614.8		0
CMD	Cantel Medical Corp	Medical Instruments & Equipment	7/31/17	770.2	71.4	786.4	523.9	361	42435417
COF	Capital One Financial Corp	Banking	12/31/17	29999.0	1982.0	365693.0	48730.0	1281	523852232
CSU	Capital Senior Living Corp.	Hospitals & Health Care Facilities	12/31/17	467.0	-44.2	1182.7	80.4	142	36860513
CIC	Capitol Investment Corp IV	Business Services	12/31/17		-0.8	403.1	388.8	25	17482695
CMO	Capstead Mortgage Corp.	REITs	12/31/17	233.4	79.6	13733.4	1238.9	286	87091857
CRR	Carbo Ceramics Inc.	Equipment & Services	12/31/17	188.8	-253.1	540.6	405.8	228	29405711
CAH	Cardinal Health, Inc.	Pharmaceuticals	6/30/17	129976.0	1288.0	40112.0	6808.0	1064	350986263
CRCM	Care.com Inc	Services	12/30/17	174.1	10.7	164.4	139.7	175	30307508
CSL	Carlisle Companies Inc.	Rubber Products	12/31/17	4089.9	365.5	5299.8	2528.3	506	64274960
KMX	Carmax Inc.	Retail - Automotive	2/28/18	17120.2	664.1	17486.3	3316.8	735	218306188
CCL	Carnival Corp	Hotels, Restaurants & Travel	11/30/17	17510.0	2606.0	40778.0	24216.0	1174	498149621
CUK	Carnival Plc	Hotels, Restaurants & Travel	11/30/17	17510.0	2606.0	40778.0	24216.0	187	9685028
CRS	Carpenter Technology Corp.	Non-Precious Metals	6/30/17	1797.6	47.0	2878.1	1198.6	373	54089198
CSV	Carriage Services, Inc.	Miscellaneous Consumer Services	12/31/17	258.1	37.2	921.5	197.7	165	16623695
CARS	Cars.com Inc	IT Services	12/31/17	626.3	224.4	2511.0	1679.1	298	82327549
CRI	Carter's Inc	Apparel, Footwear & Accessories	12/30/17	3400.4	302.8	2068.0	857.1	547	60610477
CVNA	Carvana Co	Retail - Automotive	12/31/17	858.9	-62.8	641.1	125.7	108	22705031
CSLT	Castlight Health Inc	Internet & Software	12/31/17	131.4	-55.6	249.3	175.3	110	62303696
CTLT	Catalent Inc	Pharmaceuticals	6/30/17	2075.4	109.8	3454.3	723.5	338	157399120
CTT	Catchmark Timber Trust Inc	REITs	12/31/17	91.3	-13.5	740.2	402.4	199	41688211
CAT	Caterpillar Inc.	Construction Services	12/31/17	45462.0	754.0	76962.0	13697.0	2096	511477315

| EARNINGS PER SHARE | | | | | | P/E RATIO | | DIVIDENDS PER SHARE | | | AV. YLD | DIV. DECLARED | | PRICE RANGE | |
| QUARTERLY | | | ANNUAL | | | | | | | | % | | | 2017 | |
1st	2nd	3rd	2017	2016	2015			2017	2016	2015		AMOUNT	PAYABLE		
-	-	1.05	1.64	-0.38	-0.43	17.1 -	7.2	-	-	-	-	-	-	28.0 -	11.8
0.52	-	-	0.04	1.05	1.29	-	-	-	-	-	-	0.10	6/29/18	-	-
-	-	-	-0.18	-0.67	-0.52	-	-	-	-	-	-	-	-	21.9 -	21.4
-	-	1.02	2.94	3.42	3.05	17.7 -	10.2	1.36	1.28	1.12	3.6	0.380Y	18/78/27	52.1 -	29.9
0.43	-	-	0.32	0.68	-0.24	274.5 -	207.2	0.55	0.40	0.40	0.7	0.150Y	18/78/27	87.8 -	66.3
0.91	-	-	0.61	2.65	0.93	113.1 -	82.8	1.56	1.14	1.49	2.6	0.40Y	18/78/27	69.0 -	50.5
-	-	-0.23	-4.87	-2.12	2.37	-	-	0.28	1.09	1.28	2.3	0.070Y	6/22/17	18.7 -	6.5
-	-	-	18.30	2.49	2.30	3.9 -	2.6	2.27	1.58	1.52	3.7	-	-	71.5 -	48.3
0.20	-	-	0.98	0.91	0.65	20.4 -	14.3	1.04	0.98	0.90	6.0	0.2750Z	18/78/27	20.0 -	14.0
-	-	0.90	2.70	2.53	2.32	44.3 -	26.8	1.32	1.20	1.08	1.4	0.3650Y	18/78/27	119.6 -	72.3
-2.45	-	-	-3.07	-2.18	-2.48	-	-	-	-	-	-	0.250Y	18/78/27	14.7 -	6.5
0.84	-	-	1.37	1.55	2.26	41.2 -	27.7	0.56	0.52	0.47	1.2	0.29690	6/29/18	56.4 -	38.0
-	-	-	-1.04	0.06	-	-	-	-	-	-	-	0.06250	6/29/18	-	-
-	-	-	-	-	-	-	-	-	-	2.25	-	2.25GJ	1/4/16	30.0 -	0.0
-	-	-	0.18	0.28	-	-	-	-	1.40	1.40	-	0.08170	9/28/18	13.9 -	11.2
-	-	-0.04	-0.04	1.13	0.69	-	-	-	-	-	-	0.31250	6/29/18	-	-
-	-	-	1.74	0.15	-	14.0 -	12.4	2.39	0.20	-	10.3	0.1990	9/28/18	24.4 -	21.6
-	0.03	-	-0.18	-0.23	0.01	-	-	-	-	-	-	0.31250	7/31/18	-	-
0.32	-	-	1.41	0.91	0.85	20.3 -	15.1	0.28	0.25	0.23	1.1	0.0750Y	18/78/27	28.6 -	21.4
-	-	0.39	1.37	2.09	1.28	43.2 -	27.6	0.56	0.52	0.48	1.1	0.1580Y	18/78/27	59.2 -	37.8
-	1.75	-	0.97	2.23	-0.17	14.4 -	0.0	0.18	-	-	1.7	0.20Z	7/6/18	14.0 -	0.0
0.82	-	-	1.62	3.00	2.56	42.5 -	30.0	0.69	0.61	0.53	1.2	0.190Y	18/78/27	68.8 -	48.6
-	-	0.05	0.19	0.30	0.26	110.9 -	71.5	0.71	0.61	0.18	4.1	-	-	21.1 -	13.6
0.74	-	-	3.32	4.03	3.40	19.8 -	10.5	5.01	4.83	4.63	10.2	1.26250	18/78/27	65.9 -	34.9
0.38	-	-	2.03	3.06	3.38	14.0 -	6.7	1.75	1.94	3.66	8.6	0.250Y	7/27/18	28.4 -	13.7
0.02	-	-	0.50	0.09	1.59	21.9 -	14.7	-	-	-	-	-	-	10.9 -	7.3
-0.21	-	-	0.89	5.01	5.07	-	-	1.76	1.60	1.44	-	1.21880Z	18/78/27	-	-
1.20	-	-	3.01	1.99	0.87	52.0 -	26.7	-	-	-	-	-	-	156.4 -	80.3
0.66	-	-	1.47	1.76	1.22	48.3 -	33.1	0.42	0.36	0.32	0.7	0.160Y	18/78/27	70.9 -	48.6
0.22	-	-	0.38	3.27	-0.86	64.0 -	51.2	•	•	-	-	-	-	24.3 -	19.4
0.31	-	-	0.37	2.52	-8.48	97.6 -	62.0	-	-	-	-	-	-	36.1 -	22.9
-	-	-	-	-	-	-	-	-	-	-	-	0.20090Z	5/15/18	23.5 -	0.0
7.08	-	-	40.72	17.14	15.19	18.7 -	15.2	6.50	6.00	1.50	0.9	1.750Y	18/78/27	762.3 -	619.0
-	-2.80	-	3.80	2.36	-5.27	18.0 -	13.5	1.23	1.04	0.88	2.1	0.330Y	18/78/27	68.5 -	51.2
0.25	-	-	0.22	-0.91	-0.28	133.8 -	99.8	0.17	0.08	0.08	0.7	0.060Y	18/78/27	29.4 -	21.9
-	-	2.56	6.53	5.76	5.17	26.5 -	18.8	-	-	-	-	-	-	172.8 -	122.9
0.14	-	-	-1258.36	-224.00	306.88	0.0 -	0.0	-	-	-	-	-	-	36.2 -	20.3
0.46	-	-	1.25	0.87	0.52	25.0 -	16.4	-	-	-	-	0.150Y	9/17/18	31.2 -	20.5
-	-	0.44	0.93	0.85	0.76	30.1 -	17.2	0.32	0.29	0.27	1.6	0.090	6/29/18	28.0 -	16.0
0.83	-	-	3.68	0.31	1.28	10.6 -	5.3	-	-	-	-	0.6257GHY	7/16/18	38.9 -	19.6
0.40	-	-	1.52	1.85	1.89	23.7 -	14.9	0.28	0.28	0.28	0.9	0.070Y	7/2/18	36.0 -	22.7
-0.05	-	-	-6.26	6.76	-92.70	-	-	-	-	0.30	-	0.010Y	10/15/15	45.4 -	6.5
-0.05	-	-	1.40	1.01	0.94	32.6 -	25.3	0.72	0.69	0.67	1.8	0.18750Y	18/78/27	45.6 -	35.4
-0.23	-	-	-1.66	-0.56	-0.51	-	-	-	-	-	-	-	-	8.0 -	4.7
0.65	-	-	0.42	1.98	0.07	49.3 -	29.7	0.04	0.04	0.04	0.3	0.010Y	6/12/18	20.7 -	12.5
0.27	-	-	0.56	-0.78	-3.77	25.5 -	17.0	-	-	-	-	1.250Y	6/29/18	14.3 -	9.5
0.72	-	-	3.06	2.48	1.76	20.2 -	13.9	-	-	-	-	14.7	5/3/07	62.0 -	42.6
0.41	-	-	2.13	9.05	2.76	44.9 -	36.9	3.00	7.25	2.80	3.4	0.770Z	18/78/27	95.7 -	78.5
0.14	-	-	-0.52	-0.16	0.16	-	-	0.40	0.40	0.40	3.6	0.10	1/15/18	15.9 -	8.1
-	-	-1.31	2.89	1.81	2.21	18.8 -	11.5	1.40	1.25	1.25	3.1	0.350Y	18/78/27	54.2 -	33.2
0.08	-	-	1.07	0.09	-	44.1 -	17.6	0.74	0.08	-	2.1	0.07327Y	6/29/18	47.2 -	18.8
-	0.33	-	0.22	0.26	0.14	407.9 -	78.0	-	-	-	-	-	-	89.7 -	17.1
-	2.89	-	11.24	10.70	8.87	11.0 -	7.3	5.08	4.75	4.30	5.0	0.28130	7/27/18	124.0 -	81.8
1.00	-	-	7.24	4.67	4.39	15.1 -	9.8	1.65	1.50	1.25	1.8	0.4550	6/29/18	109.6 -	70.7
0.47	-	-	2.03	-0.19	-0.58	23.7 -	13.9	1.10	0.94	0.92	2.9	0.3350	7/1/18	48.2 -	28.2
2.41	-	-	16.44	10.63	8.40	15.6 -	9.2	2.19	1.85	1.40	1.1	0.650	7/30/18	256.0 -	151.3
-0.02	-	-	1.54	-0.09	-0.30	13.8 -	10.7	-	-	-	-	-	-	21.2 -	16.4
?	-	58.39	222.88	137.95	201.65	0.2 -	0.1	149.31	149.39	75.43	414.3	-	-	40.2 -	32.4
-0.03	-	-	-0.14	-0.05	-0.29	-	-	-	-	-	-	-	-	47.8 -	6.1
-	-	0.45	1.71	1.44	1.15	75.9 -	42.9	0.14	0.12	0.10	0.1	0.0850Y	7/31/18	129.8 -	73.3
2.62	-	-	3.49	6.89	7.07	30.3 -	22.4	1.60	1.60	1.50	1.7	0.3750Y	18/78/27	105.7 -	78.2
-0.24	-	-	-1.50	-0.97	-0.50	-	-	-	-	-	-	-	-	16.5 -	9.5
0.03	-	-	-0.07	-	-	-	-	-	-	-	-	-	-	-	-
0.16	-	-	0.65	0.70	0.97	16.3 -	12.6	0.80	0.95	1.14	8.7	0.46880Z	7/16/18	10.6 -	8.2
-0.83	-	-	-9.49	-3.29	-4.76	-	-	-	-	0.63	-	0.10Y	11/16/15	12.2 -	6.1
-	-	0.81	4.03	4.32	3.62	19.5 -	12.1	1.81	1.61	1.41	2.8	0.47630Y	18/78/27	78.7 -	48.8
0.05	-	-	0.22	0.10	-1.09	103.3 -	61.9	-	-	-	-	-	-	22.7 -	13.6
4.94	-	-	5.71	3.82	4.82	20.8 -	16.2	1.44	1.30	1.10	1.4	0.370Y	18/78/27	118.8 -	92.4
1.33	-	-	3.26	3.03	2.73	24.6 -	18.0	-	-	-	-	-	-	80.2 -	58.8
-	0.78	-	3.59	3.72	2.26	20.0 -	15.9	1.60	1.35	1.10	2.4	0.50Y	18/78/27	71.9 -	57.2
0.54	-	-	3.59	3.72	2.26	20.0 -	16.1	1.60	1.35	1.10	2.4	-	-	71.7 -	57.6
-	-	0.63	0.99	0.23	1.11	61.0 -	37.3	0.72	0.72	0.72	1.5	0.180Y	18/78/27	60.4 -	37.0
0.52	-	-	2.09	1.12	1.12	13.7 -	11.2	0.23	0.15	0.10	0.9	0.0750Y	6/1/18	28.6 -	23.3
0.01	-	-	3.13	1.37	-	10.2 -	7.0	-	-	-	-	-	-	32.0 -	22.0
0.89	-	-	6.24	5.08	4.50	19.7 -	13.5	1.48	1.32	0.88	1.4	0.450Y	18/78/27	122.8 -	84.3
-0.53	-	-	-1.31	-1.10	-0.42	-	*	-	-	-	-	-	-	43.7 -	12.5
-0.11	-	-	-0.44	-0.58	-0.85	-	-	-	-	-	-	-	-	4.5 -	3.2
-	-	0.14	0.87	0.89	1.75	54.5 -	38.8	-	-	-	-	-	-	47.4 -	33.8
-0.08	-	-	-0.34	-0.29	-0.21	-	-	0.54	0.53	0.50	4.3	0.1350Z	6/15/18	13.6 -	11.0
2.74	-	-	1.26	-0.11	3.50	135.6 -	84.5	3.10	3.08	2.94	2.2	0.860Y	18/78/27	170.9 -	106.5

SYMBOL	COMPANY	NATURE OF BUSINESS	FISCAL YEAR-END	TOTAL REV. $MILL	NET INCOME $MILL	TOTAL ASSETS $MILL	NET STK EQUITY $MILL	NO OF INST	INST. HOLDINGS (SHARES)
CATO	Cato Corp.	Retail - Apparel and Accessories	2/3/18	850.0	8.5	516.1	326.4	215	23571716
CBZ	CBIZ Inc	Business Services	12/31/17	855.3	50.4	1176.2	530.9	202	58870304
CBL	CBL & Associates Properties Inc	REITs	12/31/17	927.3	120.9	5704.8	1140.0	367	166434202
IGR	CBRE Clarion Global Real Estate In	Holding and other Investment Office	12/31/16	42.9	30.4	1103.8	1008.9	166	31492107
CBRE	CBRE Group Inc	Property, Real Estate & Developmen	12/31/17	14209.6	691.5	11483.8	4019.4	800	399177956
CBS	CBS Corp	Radio & Television	12/31/17	13692.0	357.0	20843.0	1978.0	1063	373802968
FUN	Cedar Fair LP	Sporting & Recreational	12/31/17	1322.0	215.5	2064.2		292	39316819
CDR	Cedar Realty Trust Inc	REITs	12/31/17	146.0	19.1	1252.4	628.3	230	104419224
CE	Celanese Corp (DE)	Specialty Chemicals	12/31/17	6140.0	843.0	9538.0	2887.0	676	152365153
CLS	Celestica Inc	Electrical Equipment	12/31/17	6110.5	105.0	2944.7	1350.7	209	109321631
CEL	Cellcom Israel Ltd	Services	12/31/17	3871.0	112.0	6087.0	1437.0	56	11882787
CPAC	Cementos Pacasmayo SAA (Peru)	Construction Materials	12/31/17	1225.6	93.8	2814.1	1506.6	22	4124691
CX	Cemex S.A.B. de C.V.	Construction Materials	12/31/17	258131.0	15221.0	567581.0	179539.0	463	560999592
CVE	Cenovus Energy Inc.	Production & Extraction	12/31/17	17043.0	3366.0	40933.0	19981.0	408	976544613
CNC	Centene Corp	Hospitals & Health Care Facilities	12/31/17	48382.0	828.0	21855.0	6850.0	859	186063206
CEN	Center Coast Brookfield MLP & Ene	Finance Intermediaries & Services	11/30/16	1.1	-4.8	364.7	233.1	43	5470971
CNP	CenterPoint Energy, Inc	Electric Utilities	12/31/17	9614.0	1792.0	22736.0	4688.0	826	419422843
EBR	Centrais Eletricas Brasileiras S.A.-E	Electric Utilities	12/31/17	37876.0	-1763.8	172975.4	42339.4	75	10150945
CEE	Central & Eastern Europe Fund Inc	Holding and other Investment Office	10/31/17	6.5	4.0	209.8	199.4	39	4508706
CPF	Central Pacific Financial Corp	Banking	12/31/17	219.1	41.2	5623.7	500.0	217	44643030
CEPU	Central Puerto SA (Argentina)	Electric Utilities	12/31/17	5956.6	3507.8	17079.0	7072.0	-	0
CCS	Century Communities Inc	Construction Services	12/31/17	1423.8	50.3	1735.0	735.2	175	26873601
CTL	CenturyLink Inc	Services	12/31/17	17656.0	1389.0	75611.0	23491.0	1067	926486518
CDAY	Ceridian HCM Holding Inc	IT Services	12/31/17	750.7	-9.2	6729.9	1091.2	-	0
CF	CF Industries Holdings Inc	Agricultural Chemicals	12/31/17	4130.0	358.0	13463.0	3579.0	763	262783321
CGG	CGG	Equipment & Services	12/31/17	1320.8	-514.9	4264.2	489.1	32	296806
GIB	CGI Group Inc	IT Services	9/30/17	10845.1	1035.2	11396.2	6202.6	305	195819168
ECOM	ChannelAdvisor Corp	IT Services	12/31/17	122.5	-16.6	140.5	81.9	102	23186001
CHAP	Chaparral Energy Inc (New)	Production & Extraction	12/31/17	227.1	-118.9	1139.3	842.8	-	0
CHRA	Charah Solutions Inc	Business Services	12/31/17	421.3	18.3	377.7	47.7	-	0
CRL	Charles River Laboratories Internati	Biotechnology	12/30/17	1857.6	123.4	2929.9	1045.1	496	63174725
CLDT	Chatham Lodging Trust	REITs	12/31/17	298.9	29.5	1392.2	803.2	220	45519124
CMCM	Cheetah Mobile Inc	Services	12/31/17	4974.8	1348.2	7448.9	4293.4	83	7684438
CHGG	Chegg Inc	Educational Services	12/31/17	255.1	-20.3	446.9	391.1	229	124612215
CHE	Chemed Corp	Diagnostic & Health Related Service	12/31/17	1666.7	98.2	920.0	540.4	422	21310705
CC	Chemours Co (The)	Specialty Chemicals	12/31/17	6183.0	746.0	7293.0	860.0	655	160939829
CHMI	Cherry Hill Mortgage Investment Co	REITs	12/31/17	82.4	47.4	2050.7	320.0	106	6705976
CHK	Chesapeake Energy Corp.	Production & Extraction	12/31/17	9496.0	949.0	12425.0	-496.0	794	631776704
CHKR	Chesapeake Granite Wash Trust	Oil Royalty Traders	12/31/17	15.7	13.3	28.4	27.6	-	0
CHSP	Chesapeake Lodging Trust	REITs	12/31/17	598.3	76.2	1975.4	1048.4	239	71198360
CPK	Chesapeake Utilities Corp.	Gas Utilities	12/31/17	617.6	58.1	1417.4	486.3	237	11959947
CVX	Chevron Corporation	Refining & Marketing	12/31/17	141722.0	9195.0	253806.0	148124.0	3017	1596199725
CHS	Chico's FAS Inc	Retail - Apparel and Accessories	2/3/18	2282.4	101.0	1087.6	656.4	405	161058592
CIM	Chimera Investment Corp	REITs	12/31/17	1168.3	524.7	21222.1	3635.0	392	198623886
DL	China Distance Education Holdings	Educational Services	9/30/17	131.0	14.9	224.6	48.8	40	38436232
CEA	China Eastern Airlines Corp., Ltd.	Airlines/Air Freight	12/31/17	101721.0	6352.0	227464.0	53106.0	42	1304060
CHN	China Fund, Inc. (The)	Holding and other Investment Office	10/31/17	7.6	2.9	376.9	366.5	69	12370497
CGA	China Green Agriculture Inc	Agricultural Chemicals	6/30/17	285.2	25.2	455.7	397.5	29	1371265
LFC	China Life Insurance Co Ltd	Life & Health	12/31/17	135095.0	32253.0	2897591.0	320933.0	177	19683501
CHL	China Mobile Limited	Services	12/31/17	740514.0	114279.0	1522113.0	985636.0	493	92031379
BORN	China New Borun Corp	Beverages	12/31/17	2140.9	176.7	3197.2	2045.6	22	950255
COE	China Online Education Group	Educational Services	12/31/17	848.0	-580.8	783.6	-668.4	12	5546661
SNP	China Petroleum & Chemical Corp	Production & Extraction	12/31/17	2360193.0	51119.0	1595504.0	727244.0	260	14412870
XRF	China Rapid Finance Ltd	Finance Intermediaries & Services	12/31/17	87.7	-36.6	137.5	59.0	40	6407664
ZNH	China Southern Airlines Co Ltd	Airlines/Air Freight	12/31/17	127489.0	5914.0	218329.0	49594.0	61	1390842
CHA	China Telecom Corp Ltd	Services	12/31/17	352285.0	18004.0	652368.0	315324.0	112	4713116
CHU	China Unicom (Hong Kong) Ltd	Services	12/31/17	274829.0	1828.0	571983.0	304050.0	159	35639410
CYD	China Yuchai International Ltd.	Auto Parts	12/31/17	16222.4	953.9	21015.1	8347.6	115	10996257
CMG	Chipotle Mexican Grill Inc	Hotels, Restaurants & Travel	12/31/17	4476.4	176.3	2045.7	1364.4	731	28738595
CHH	Choice Hotels International, Inc.	Hotels, Restaurants & Travel	12/31/17	1007.4	114.9	927.6	-212.1	284	34031297
CBK	Christopher & Banks Corp.	Retail - Apparel and Accessories	2/3/18	365.9	-22.0	119.4	50.4	109	21018971
CB	Chubb Ltd	General Insurance	12/31/17	32243.0	3861.0	167022.0	51172.0	1412	494089366
CHT	Chunghwa Telecom Co Ltd	Services	12/31/17	227514.2	40042.6	451123.1	364882.0	184	34971817
CHD	Church & Dwight Co Inc	Household & Personal Products	12/31/17	3776.2	743.4	6014.8	2218.0	970	238915865
CIEN	Ciena Corp	IT Services	10/31/17	2801.7	1262.0	3951.7	2136.3	493	179576249
CI	Cigna Corp	Life & Health	12/31/17	41616.0	2237.0	61753.0	13735.0	1242	262196795
XEC	Cimarex Energy Co	Production & Extraction	12/31/17	1918.2	494.3	5042.6	2568.3	731	113982618
CBB	Cincinnati Bell Inc	Services	12/31/17	1288.5	35.1	2162.4	-143.1	242	64375828
CNK	Cinemark Holdings Inc	Entertainment	12/31/17	2991.5	264.2	4470.9	1393.8	432	135094663
CINR	Ciner Resources LP	Mining	12/31/17	497.3	41.6	453.2		39	2072440
CIR	Circor International Inc	Industrial Machinery & Equipment	12/31/17	661.7	11.8	1906.8	602.0	180	21328423
CISN	Cision Ltd	IT Services	12/31/17	631.6	-123.0	1935.4	316.4	65	39069249
CIT	CIT Group Inc	Banking	12/31/17	3207.2	468.2	49278.7	6995.0	559	172261472
C	Citigroup Inc	Banking	12/31/17	87966.0	-6798.0	1842465.0	200740.0	2345	2696295561
CFG	Citizens Financial Group Inc (New)	Banking	12/31/17	6454.0	1652.0	152336.0	20270.0	740	532916320
CIA	Citizens, Inc. (Austin, TX)	Life & Health	12/31/17	252.6	-38.1	1644.5	223.5	80	13800466
CIO	City Office REIT Inc	REITs	12/31/17	106.5	5.8	896.5	359.6	157	25016613
CVEO	Civeo Corp (Canada)	Business Services	12/31/17	382.3	-105.7	853.9	476.3	135	112534009
CIVI	Civitas Solutions Inc	Hospitals & Health Care Facilities	9/30/17	1474.5	6.3	1049.4	162.9	108	34426468
CLH	Clean Harbors Inc	Sanitation Services	12/31/17	2945.0	100.7	3706.6	1188.2	373	66968483

EARNINGS PER SHARE — QUARTERLY — 1st	2nd	3rd	ANNUAL 2017	2016	2015	P/E RATIO	DIVIDENDS PER SHARE 2017	2016	2015	AV. YLD %	DIV. DECLARED AMOUNT	PAYABLE	PRICE RANGE 2017
0.94	-	-	1.72	2.39	2.15	15.0 - 6.3	1.29	1.20	1.20	8.3	0.330Y	6/25/18	25.8 - 10.9
0.64	-	-	0.91	0.75	0.65	25.4 - 15.9	-	-	-	-	-	-	23.1 - 14.4
-0.06	-	-	0.44	0.75	0.34	21.9 - 8.8	1.00	1.06	1.06	16.0	0.41410Z	7/2/18	9.6 - 3.9
-	-	-	-	0.26	0.27	-	-	0.60	0.57	-	0.050	7/31/18	8.0 - 7.2
0.44	-	-	2.03	1.69	1.63	24.2 - 17.2	-	-	-	-	-	-	49.0 - 34.9
1.32	-	-	0.88	2.81	2.89	76.8 - 55.4	0.72	0.66	0.60	1.3	0.180Y	18/78/27	67.6 - 48.7
-1.49	-	-	3.79	3.14	1.99	18.9 - 16.3	3.46	3.33	3.08	5.2	0.890	6/15/18	71.8 - 61.6
-0.26	-	-	-0.04	-0.08	0.09	-	0.20	0.20	0.20	4.0	0.40630Z	8/20/18	6.2 - 3.6
2.66	-	-	6.09	6.18	2.00	19.4 - 15.3	1.74	1.38	1.15	1.7	0.540Y	18/78/27	118.0 - 93.4
0.10	-	-	0.72	0.95	0.42	24.5 - 13.8	-	-	-	-	-	-	17.7 - 9.9
-	-	1.85	1.10	1.47	0.95	-	-	-	-	-	0.850	12/12/13	13.5 - 0.0
-	-	-	0.21	0.38	-	-	1.61	-	-	14.7	-	-	13.5 - 0.0
-	-	-	0.34	0.33	0.03	30.2 - 17.1	-	-	-	-	-	-	10.3 - 5.8
-0.53	-	-	3.05	-0.65	0.75	4.7 - 2.3	0.20	0.20	0.85	1.9	0.050	6/29/18	14.5 - 7.0
-	1.50	-	4.69	3.43	2.88	26.8 - 16.9	-	-	-	-	-	-	125.8 - 79.4
-	-	-	-0.24	-0.30	-	-	-	1.25	1.25	-	0.10420	9/28/18	11.5 - 8.3
0.38	-	-	4.13	1.00	-1.61	7.4 - 6.0	1.07	1.03	0.99	3.8	0.27750Y	18/78/27	30.4 - 24.9
-	-	-0.58	-1.30	2.62	-8.43	-	-	-	-	-	-	-	7.6 - 3.2
-	-	-	0.53	0.42	0.43	53.0 - 0.0	0.32	0.49	0.97	1.3	0.56150	1/26/18	28.1 - 0.0
0.48	-	-	1.34	1.50	1.40	24.5 - 20.5	0.70	0.60	0.82	2.3	0.210Y	6/15/18	32.8 - 27.5
-	-	-	2.33	1.17	6.66	7.9 - 4.2	0.85	7.40	-	5.5	-	-	18.4 - 9.9
0.67	-	-	2.03	2.33	1.88	17.5 - 10.8	-	-	-	-	-	-	35.5 - 21.9
0.11	-	-	2.21	1.16	1.58	10.8 - 6.2	2.16	2.16	2.16	11.7	0.540Y	18/78/27	24.0 - 13.6
-0.11	-	-	-0.46	-1.65	-1.61	-	-	-	-	-	-	-	52.1 - 30.5
0.27	-	-	1.53	-1.19	2.96	30.0 - 18.0	1.20	1.20	1.20	3.2	0.30Y	18/78/27	46.0 - 27.6
-	-	0.01	-11.18	-27.57	-238.50	-	-	-	-	-	0.2579E	3/19/18	6.7 - 0.0
-	0.94	-	3.41	3.42	3.04	24.6 - 14.4	-	-	-	-	-	-	83.8 - 49.2
-0.12	-	-	-0.63	-0.31	-0.84	-	-	-	-	-	-	-	15.2 - 8.4
-0.25	-	-	-2.64	-	-	-	-	-	-	-	-	-	25.9 - 0.0
0.02	-	-	-	-	-	-	-	-	-	-	-	-	12.0 - 10.3
1.08	-	-	2.54	3.23	3.13	46.5 - 38.1	-	-	-	-	-	-	118.1 - 96.7
0.06	-	-	0.73	0.81	0.86	32.5 - 24.9	1.32	1.38	1.20	6.3	0.110Z	8/31/18	23.8 - 18.2
-	-	-	0.94	-0.06	0.12	18.0 - 8.6	-	-	-	-	-	-	16.9 - 8.1
-0.02	-	-	-0.20	-0.47	-0.68	-	-	-	-	-	-	-	29.6 - 12.0
2.66	-	-	5.86	6.48	6.33	56.9 - 32.0	1.08	1.00	0.92	0.4	0.280Y	6/20/18	333.3 - 187.5
1.58	-	-	3.91	0.04	-0.50	14.6 - 9.7	0.12	0.12	0.58	0.2	0.170	18/78/27	57.2 - 38.1
2.64	-	-	3.98	3.30	1.76	4.9 - 4.1	1.96	2.11	1.98	10.9	0.51250Y	7/16/18	19.4 - 16.1
0.29	-	-	0.90	-6.45	-22.43	5.8 - 2.9	-	-	0.17	-	14.3750Y	18/78/27	5.2 - 2.6
0.08	-	-	0.36	0.36	1.52	6.8 - 3.3	0.36	0.42	1.52	18.8	0.04690	5/31/18	2.5 - 1.2
0.11	-	-	1.11	1.13	0.99	29.5 - 22.0	1.60	1.60	1.50	5.8	0.40Z	7/13/18	32.8 - 24.4
1.64	-	-	3.55	2.86	2.72	24.1 - 18.8	1.28	1.20	1.13	1.7	0.370Y	18/78/27	85.5 - 66.7
1.90	-	-	4.85	-0.27	2.45	27.5 - 21.2	4.32	4.29	4.28	3.7	1.120Y	18/78/27	133.6 - 103.0
0.23	-	-	0.69	0.01	0.42	15.7 - 10.4	0.32	0.31	0.30	3.6	0.0850Y	10/1/18	10.8 - 7.2
1.22	-	-	2.61	2.92	1.25	7.6 - 6.2	2.00	2.44	1.44	11.0	0.50Z	18/78/27	19.7 - 16.2
-	-	0.02	0.11	0.19	0.17	95.5 - 60.2	0.45	0.90	-	5.5	0.437	1/18/18	10.5 - 6.6
-	-	0.55	0.44	0.33	0.35	102.4 - 55.5	2.19	2.30	-	6.5	-	-	45.1 - 24.4
-	-	-	0.18	0.46	0.26	137.2 - 103.2	0.47	1.50	3.77	2.2	0.54930	1/4/18	24.7 - 18.6
-	-	0.19	0.66	0.67	0.93	2.4 - 1.7	-	-	0.10	-	0.1GY	1/31/15	1.6 - 1.1
0.48	-	-	1.13	0.66	1.22	15.7 - 11.2	0.93	1.77	2.00	6.1	-	-	17.8 - 12.7
-	-	-	5.58	5.31	5.30	10.1 - 7.8	23.20	10.33	10.59	46.8	-	-	56.5 - 43.7
-	-	0.42	6.87	2.48	5.01	0.2 - 0.2	-	-	-	-	-	-	1.5 - 1.2
-2.06	-	-	-1.93	-3.03	-5.57	-	-	-	-	-	-	-	19.4 - 9.7
0.16	-	-	0.42	0.39	0.27	251.2 - 166.2	23.82	12.34	17.88	29.1	-	-	105.5 - 69.8
-	-	-	-2.48	-2.46	-2.05	-	-	-	-	-	-	-	11.4 - 2.2
0.25	-	-	0.60	0.51	0.38	117.5 - 57.3	4.33	3.48	1.70	9.1	-	-	70.5 - 34.4
-	-	-	-	-	-	-	-	7.26	6.84	-	-	-	53.7 - 41.3
-	-	-	0.07	0.03	0.44	234.6 - 169.7	0.05	1.53	1.83	0.4	-	-	16.4 - 11.9
-	-	-	23.40	12.89	8.81	-	-	-	-	-	1.487	7/10/18	-
2.13	-	-	6.17	0.77	15.10	76.2 - 40.7	-	-	-	-	-	-	469.9 - 251.3
0.44	-	-	2.02	2.46	2.22	41.9 - 29.7	0.88	0.83	0.79	1.2	0.2150Y	18/78/27	84.6 - 60.0
-0.14	-	-	-0.48	-1.33	1.28	-	-	-	-	-	0.060Y	10/20/11	1.5 - 0.8
2.30	-	-	8.19	8.87	8.62	-	2.82	-	2.66	-	0.730	18/78/27	-
-	-	1.37	5.00	5.21	5.41	7.9 - 6.7	39.21	43.70	36.19	109.7	-	-	39.3 - 33.5
0.63	-	-	2.90	1.75	1.53	18.6 - 14.9	0.76	0.71	0.67	1.6	0.21750Y	18/78/27	53.8 - 43.3
-	0.09	-	7.53	0.51	0.10	3.7 - 2.6	-	-	-	-	-	-	27.5 - 19.6
3.72	-	-	8.77	7.19	8.04	25.8 - 18.7	0.04	0.04	0.04	0.0	0.040Y	18/78/27	226.2 - 164.0
1.96	-	-	5.19	-4.62	-25.92	24.8 - 16.1	0.32	0.40	0.64	0.3	0.160Y	18/78/27	128.7 - 83.7
-0.26	-	-	0.58	2.18	8.15	37.9 - 20.9	-	-	-	-	0.84380Y	7/2/18	22.0 - 12.2
0.53	-	-	2.26	2.19	1.87	19.2 - 14.3	1.16	1.08	1.00	3.2	0.320Y	18/78/27	43.3 - 32.3
0.51	-	-	2.07	2.08	2.58	13.9 - 11.4	2.27	2.26	2.17	8.7	0.5670	5/21/18	28.8 - 23.6
-0.88	-	-	0.70	0.61	0.58	86.8 - 52.4	0.15	0.15	0.15	0.3	0.03750Y	12/12/17	60.8 - 36.7
0.00	-	-	-1.63	-0.07	-0.01	-	-	-	-	-	-	-	-
0.74	-	-	2.80	-4.20	5.67	19.9 - 15.5	0.61	0.60	0.60	1.2	0.250Y	8/24/18	55.8 - 43.3
1.68	-	-	-2.98	4.72	5.40	-	0.96	0.42	0.16	1.3	0.53130Y	18/78/27	80.1 - 65.5
0.78	-	-	3.25	1.97	1.55	14.7 - 9.9	0.64	0.46	0.40	1.6	0.270Y	18/78/27	47.9 - 32.1
-	-	-	-0.77	0.04	-0.07	-	-	-	-	-	0.05640	3/20/79	8.7 - 6.7
1.24	-	-	-0.05	-0.13	-0.53	-	0.94	0.94	0.70	7.6	0.41410Z	7/25/18	13.8 - 10.0
-0.42	-	-	-0.82	-0.90	-1.24	-	-	-	-	-	-	-	4.4 - 1.6
-	-0.07	-	0.17	0.25	0.08	116.5 - 66.8	-	-	-	-	-	-	19.8 - 11.4
-0.22	-	-	1.76	-0.69	0.76	33.0 - 25.8	-	-	-	-	-	-	58.0 - 45.5

SYMBOL	COMPANY	NATURE OF BUSINESS	FISCAL YEAR-END	TOTAL REV. $MILL	NET INCOME $MILL	TOTAL ASSETS $MILL	NET STK EQUITY $MILL	NO OF INST	INST. HOLDINGS (SHARES)
CCO	Clear Channel Outdoor Holdings Inc	Advertising	12/31/17	2591.3	-639.7	4670.8	-1998.4	139	37953351
CBA	ClearBridge American Energy MLP	Finance Intermediaries & Services	11/30/16	1.2	-22.9	806.1	584.7	-	0
CEM	ClearBridge Energy MLP Fund Inc	Holding and other Investment Office	11/30/16	-1.0	-32.8	1842.0	1148.3	118	21591143
EMO	Clearbridge Energy MLP Opportunit	Holding and other Investment Office	11/30/16	-1.4	-12.4	650.8	431.7	54	8205739
CTR	ClearBridge Energy MLP Total Retu	Holding and other Investment Office	11/30/16	2.3	-12.0	744.3	532.9	59	7921148
CLW	Clearwater Paper Corp	Paper & Forest Products	12/31/17	1730.4	97.3	1802.3	575.4	198	17935734
CLF	Cleveland-Cliffs Inc (New)	Mining	12/31/17	2330.2	367.0	2953.4	-444.3	486	227109026
CLPR	Clipper Realty Inc	Property, Real Estate & Developmen	12/31/17	104.0	-2.4	1052.1	74.9	64	10085754
CLX	Clorox Co (The)	Household & Personal Products	6/30/17	5973.0	701.0	4573.0	542.0	1290	127597155
CLD	Cloud Peak Energy Inc	Mining	12/31/17	887.7	-6.6	1698.7	1007.8	200	75535871
CLDR	Cloudera Inc	Internet & Software	1/31/18	367.4	-385.8	689.2	323.0	165	108328577
CMS	CMS Energy Corp	Electric Utilities	12/31/17	6583.0	460.0	23050.0	4441.0	747	322201691
CNA	CNA Financial Corp	General Insurance	12/31/17	9542.0	899.0	56567.0	12244.0	300	275682380
CNHI	CNH Industrial NV	Industrial Machinery & Equipment	12/31/17	27361.0	295.0	48275.0	4390.0	226	345880724
CNO	CNO Financial Group Inc	Life & Health	12/31/17	4297.2	175.6	33110.3	4847.5	400	224684845
CEO	Cnooc Ltd.	Production & Extraction	12/31/17	186390.0	24677.0	617219.0	379975.0	293	10460641
CNXM	CNX Midstream Partners LP	Equipment & Services	12/31/17	233.8	115.0	926.6		84	13021126
CNX	CNX Resources Corp	Production & Extraction	12/31/17	1455.1	380.7	6931.9	3899.9	489	248214735
KO	Coca-Cola Co (The)	Beverages	12/31/17	35410.0	1248.0	87896.0	17072.0	2668	3336946593
CCE	Coca-Cola European Partners plc	Manufacturing	12/31/17	11062.0	688.0	18194.0	6685.0	-	0
KOF	Coca-Cola FEMSA SAB de CV	Beverages	12/31/17	203780.0	-12802.0	285677.0	122569.0	166	19016444
CDE	Coeur Mining Inc	Precious Metals	12/31/17	709.6	-1.3	1701.2	815.0	300	158380848
FOF	Cohen & Steers Closed-End Opport	Holding and other Investment Office	12/31/16	18.7	15.4	356.4	354.3	58	4293679
INB	Cohen & Steers Global Income Buil	Holding and other Investment Office	12/31/16	8.7	4.1	296.4	226.6	53	5490474
CNS	Cohen & Steers Inc	Wealth Management	12/31/17	378.2	91.9	410.1	275.5	229	28835040
UTF	Cohen & Steers Infrastructure Fund,	Holding and other Investment Office	12/31/16	102.2	58.8	2766.8	1876.7	174	19320063
LDP	Cohen & Steers Limited Duration Pr	Holding and other Investment Office	12/31/16	58.2	45.7	1051.1	733.8	73	6579814
MIE	Cohen & Steers MLP Income & Ene	Finance Intermediaries & Services	11/30/16	3.8	-4.6	424.4	318.1	43	5623651
RQI	Cohen & Steers Quality Income Re	Holding and other Investment Office	12/31/16	63.2	35.5	1946.3	1483.9	154	18495084
RNP	Cohen & Steers Reit & Preferred In	Holding and other Investment Office	12/31/16	66.2	48.9	1387.0	1034.6	116	9932778
PSF	Cohen & Steers Select Preferred & I	Holding and other Investment Office	12/31/16	27.2	21.8	445.5	311.2	45	1272253
RFI	Cohen & Steers Total Return Realty	Holding and other Investment Office	12/31/16	11.6	8.6	349.6	348.9	74	3159619
CFX	Colfax Corp	Industrial Machinery & Equipment	12/31/17	3300.2	151.1	6709.7	3500.4	285	96988382
CL	Colgate-Palmolive Co.	Household & Personal Products	12/31/17	15454.0	2024.0	12676.0	-60.0	2026	763164772
CLNY	Colony Capital Inc (New)	REITs	12/31/17	2796.7	-197.9	24785.6	8407.9	473	436280294
CLNC	Colony Credit Real Estate Inc	REITs	12/31/17	164.8	127.2	1839.4	1398.0	87	12722954
CXP	Columbia Property Trust Inc	REITs	12/31/17	289.0	176.0	4511.5	2531.9	296	103554940
STK	Columbia Seligman Premium Techn	Holding and other Investment Office	12/31/16	2.2	-0.8	275.2	273.2	48	1302850
CCZ	Comcast Holdings Corp	Radio & Television	12/31/04	8586.0	986.0	41942.0	19912.0	7	421299
CMA	Comerica, Inc.	Banking	12/31/17	3289.0	743.0	71567.0	7963.0	826	177398296
FIX	Comfort Systems USA Inc	Construction Services	12/31/17	1787.9	55.3	881.1	417.9	284	46940042
CMC	Commercial Metals Co.	Non-Precious Metals	8/31/17	4569.7	46.3	2975.1	1400.8	387	132296067
CBU	Community Bank System Inc	Banking	12/31/17	531.9	150.7	10746.2	1635.3	265	43496319
CYH	Community Health Systems, Inc.	Hospitals & Health Care Facilities	12/31/17	15353.0	-2459.0	17450.0	-767.0	349	145191646
CHCT	Community Healthcare Trust Inc	REITs	12/31/17	37.3	3.5	385.8	283.4	143	18634778
CBD	Companhia Brasileira de Distribuica	Retail - General Merchandise/Depart	12/31/15	69220.0	265.0	47241.0	10354.0	-	0
SBS	Companhia de Saneamento Basico	Water Utilities	12/31/17	14608.2	2519.3	39546.4	17513.0	277	125488219
CIG	Companhia Energetica de Minas G	Electric Utilities	12/31/17	21712.0	1001.0	42240.0	14326.0	208	97797362
ELP	Companhia Paranaense De Energia	Electric Utilities	12/31/16	13101.8	958.6	30434.2	14864.2	137	34482555
SID	Companhia Siderurgica Nacional	Non-Precious Metals	12/31/15	15331.9	1257.9	48650.0	7664.7	132	45344301
CCU	Compania Cervecerias Unidas S.A.	Beverages	12/31/17	1698360.8	129607.4	1976229.1	1101077.1	146	29926319
BVN	Compania de Minas Buenaventura	Precious Metals	12/31/17	1274.4	60.8	4332.8	2848.0	241	156030094
CODI	Compass Diversified Holdings	Miscellaneous Consumer Goods	12/31/17	1269.7	28.0	1820.3	873.2	170	27018154
CMP	Compass Minerals International Inc	Mining	12/31/17	1364.4	42.7	2571.0	694.6	472	50011138
CRK	Comstock Resources Inc	Production & Extraction	12/31/17	255.3	-111.4	930.4	-369.3	168	18782678
CAG	Conagra Brands Inc	Food	5/27/18	7938.3	808.4	10389.5	3676.2	1050	400763045
CXO	Concho Resources Inc	Production & Extraction	12/31/17	2586.0	956.0	13732.0	8915.0	681	166593096
CCM	Concord Medical Services Holdings	Diagnostic & Health Related Service	12/31/17	331.0	-284.3	3465.4	934.0	15	21742474
CNDT	Conduent Inc	Business Services	12/31/17	6022.0	181.0	7548.0	3671.0	358	196838347
COP	ConocoPhillips	Production & Extraction	12/31/17	32584.0	-855.0	73362.0	30607.0	2177	1088016216
CCR	CONSOL Coal Resources LP	Mining	12/31/17	322.8	40.5	494.2	213.2	24	6499723
CEIX	CONSOL Energy Inc (New)	Mining	12/31/17	1411.9	67.6	2707.1	204.3	244	26088343
CEIX	CONSOL Energy Inc (New)	Mining	12/31/17	1411.9	67.6	2707.1	204.3	244	26088343
ED	Consolidated Edison Inc	Electric Utilities	12/31/17	12033.0	1525.0	48111.0	15418.0	1194	223284562
STZ	Constellation Brands Inc	Beverages	2/28/18	7585.0	2318.9	20538.7	8046.1	1225	181136534
CSTM	Constellium N.V.	Non-Precious Metals	12/31/17	5237.0	-31.0	3711.0	-327.0	-	0
CMS PRB	Consumers Energy Co.	Electric Utilities	12/31/17	6222.0	632.0	21099.0	6488.0	-	0
TCS	Container Store Group, Inc	Retail - Furniture & Home Furnishing	3/31/18	857.2	19.4	749.4	248.7	121	41591979
CBPX	Continental Building Products Inc	Construction Materials	12/31/17	489.2	59.8	641.9	318.0	199	39870335
CLR	Continental Resources Inc.	Production & Extraction	12/31/17	3120.8	789.4	14199.7	5131.2	563	96722098
VLRS	Controladora Vuela Compania De A	Airlines/Air Freight	12/31/17	24845.4	-594.6	22666.3	10163.2	-	0
CVG	Convergys Corp	IT Services	12/31/17	2792.1	121.4	2414.7	1377.7	413	120178708
COO	Cooper Companies, Inc. (The)	Medical Instruments & Equipment	10/31/17	2139.0	372.9	4858.7	3175.7	660	61838297
CTB	Cooper Tire & Rubber Co.	Auto Parts	12/31/17	2854.7	95.4	2607.7	1127.1	358	72842161
CPS	Cooper-Standard Holdings Inc	Auto Parts	12/31/17	3618.1	135.3	2725.6	826.6	264	20469795
CPA	Copa Holdings S.A.	Airlines/Air Freight	12/31/17	2527.6	370.0	4252.9	2111.5	359	35967574
CLB	Core Laboratories N.V. (Netherland	Equipment & Services	12/31/17	659.8	83.1	584.8	144.8	515	59812144
CXW	CoreCivic Inc	REITs	12/31/17	1765.5	178.0	3272.4	1451.6	418	126360688
CLGX	CoreLogic Inc.	Business Services	12/31/17	1851.1	152.2	4077.4	1007.9	338	87610776
CORR	CorEnergy Infrastructure Trust Inc	REITs	12/31/17	88.7	32.6	633.4	461.8	151	10500962

T16

EARNINGS PER SHARE — QUARTERLY — 1st	2nd	3rd	— ANNUAL — 2017	2016	2015	P/E RATIO		DIVIDENDS PER SHARE 2017	2016	2015	AV. YLD %	DIV. DECLARED AMOUNT	PAYABLE	PRICE RANGE 2017	
-0.35	-	-	-1.77	0.39	-0.27	-		0.92	2.10	-	20.2	0.08247Y	1/24/18	5.3 -	3.8
				-0.39	-0.15				0.80	1.22		0.20	5/31/18	9.5 -	6.6
				-0.47	-0.16				1.42	1.71	-	0.3550	5/31/18	17.4 -	12.2
				-0.40	-0.18				1.28	1.50	-	0.320	5/31/18	13.2 -	9.7
				-0.31	-0.23				1.16	1.40	-	0.290	5/31/18	13.2 -	9.6
0.16	-	-	5.88	2.90	2.97	8.6 -	3.9							50.5 -	23.0
-0.29	-	-	1.26	0.87	-5.13	7.1 -	4.6					0.150Y	12/1/14	9.0 -	5.8
-0.21	-	-	-0.15	-0.34	-0.12			0.37	-	-	3.8	0.0950Z	5/29/18	12.4 -	7.7
		1.37	5.33	4.92	4.37	28.1 -	21.5	3.20	3.08	2.96	2.4	0.960Y	18/78/27	149.7 -	114.8
-0.10	-	-	-0.09	0.35	-3.36			-						5.5 -	2.9
-0.35	-	-	-5.15	-6.21				-						22.2 -	12.7
0.86	-	-	1.64	1.98	1.89	30.8 -	25.5	1.33	1.24	1.16	2.9	0.35750Y	18/78/27	50.5 -	41.8
1.07	-	-	3.30	3.17	1.77	16.7 -	13.7	3.10	3.00	3.00	6.1	0.30Y	18/78/27	55.1 -	45.2
0.14	-	-	0.22	-0.18	0.19			0.12	0.15	0.21		0.140	5/2/18		
0.50	-	-	1.02	2.01	1.39	25.9 -	18.6	0.35	0.31	0.27	1.5	0.10Y	6/25/18	26.4 -	18.9
-	-	-	0.55	0.01	0.45	419.1 -	0.0	32.80	28.08	41.50	34.3			230.5 -	0.0
0.40	-	-	1.72	1.58	1.20	12.2 -	9.1	1.15	1.00	0.88	6.3	0.32450	5/15/18	21.0 -	15.6
2.35	-	-	1.65	-3.70	-1.64	10.8 -	7.1	-	0.01	0.14		0.010Y	18/78/27	17.9 -	11.7
0.32	-	-	0.29	1.49	1.67	167.3 -	143.3	1.48	1.40	1.32	3.3	0.390Y	18/78/27	48.5 -	41.5
-	0.61	-	1.41	1.42	0.13							0.260	5/29/18		
-	-	-	-6.12	4.85				33.37	32.53	30.79	46.8			90.9 -	54.7
0.01	-	-	-0.01	0.34	-2.83									9.7 -	6.8
					0.60				1.04	1.04		0.0870	9/28/18	13.5 -	12.2
			0.18	0.17					0.92	1.12		0.0690	9/28/18	10.4 -	9.1
0.59	-	-	1.96	2.00	1.41	24.3 -	19.0	2.12	1.54	1.50	5.1	0.330Y	6/21/18	47.7 -	37.2
			0.69	0.68					2.03	1.60		0.1550	9/28/18	24.5 -	20.9
			1.59	1.68					1.88	1.87		0.1560	9/28/18	27.2 -	24.9
			-0.17	0.06					1.17	1.32		0.0770	9/28/18	11.3 -	8.9
			0.33	0.36	0.29	39.8 -	32.3	0.96	0.96	0.96	7.9	0.080	9/28/18	13.1 -	10.7
				1.03	0.91				1.48	1.48		0.1240	9/28/18	21.9 -	18.1
				1.82	1.96				2.45	2.19		0.1720	9/28/18	29.1 -	25.3
				0.33	0.28				0.96	1.30		0.080	9/28/18	12.8 -	11.6
0.20	-	-	1.22	1.04	1.34	35.4 -	24.5							43.2 -	29.8
0.72	-	-	2.28	2.72	1.52	34.0 -	27.0	1.59	1.55	1.50	2.3	0.420Y	18/78/27	77.5 -	61.6
-0.14	-	-	-0.64	0.21	0.60			2.21	0.40	0.40	22.1	0.44530Z	18/78/27	14.7 -	5.5
-0.05	-	-		0.85								0.1450	8/10/18	21.1 -	18.4
0.01	-	-	1.45	0.68	0.36	16.0 -	13.5	0.80	1.20	1.20	3.7	0.20Y	18/78/27	23.2 -	19.6
				-0.05	-0.04				1.85	1.85		0.46250	5/22/18	24.4 -	20.6
												0.39460Z	7/16/18	63.2 -	0.0
1.59	-	-	4.14	2.68	2.84	24.7 -	15.6	1.09	0.89	0.83	1.3	0.340Y	18/78/27	102.2 -	64.5
0.44	-	-	1.47	1.72	1.30	33.1 -	22.1	0.29	0.28	0.25	0.7	0.080Y	5/25/18	48.6 -	32.5
		0.34	0.39	0.47	1.20	67.0 -	43.8	0.48	0.48	0.48	2.3	0.120Y	18/78/27	26.1 -	17.1
0.78	-	-	3.03	2.32	2.19	20.5 -	16.2	1.32	1.26	1.22	2.4	0.340Y	18/78/27	62.0 -	49.1
-0.22	-	-	-22.00	-15.54	1.37							0.25G7	18/78/27	9.9 -	3.3
0.09	-	-	0.19	0.24	-0.31	157.2 -	118.1	1.56	1.52	0.52	5.9	0.40Z	6/1/18	29.9 -	22.4
					0.94					1.04				25.5 -	19.2
			3.69	4.31	0.78	3.2 -	1.6	0.90	0.21	0.27	9.1			11.8 -	5.8
		0.82	0.37	0.07	1.96	7.8 -	4.6	0.24	0.55	0.41	10.3			2.9 -	1.7
				3.35	4.16				1.08	0.86				9.5 -	5.4
					0.93					0.41				3.5 -	1.9
-	65.02	350.76	320.59	326.95		0.1 -	0.1	218.59	200.03	198.49	795.5			30.1 -	24.7
		0.26	0.24	-1.27	-1.25	69.6 -	47.0	0.08	0.03	-	0.6	0.02250	4/21/97	16.7 -	11.3
-0.09	-	-	-0.44	0.51	2.61			1.44	1.44	1.44	8.5	0.74GH	7/30/18	18.2 -	15.0
0.37	-	-	1.25	4.79	4.69	60.5 -	47.1	2.88	2.78	2.64	4.3	0.720Y	18/78/27	75.7 -	58.9
-2.78	-	-	-7.61	-11.52	-113.55							0.1250	12/15/14	11.5 -	4.1
		0.90	1.46	-1.56	-0.60	26.7 -	22.2	0.90	1.00	1.00	2.5	0.21250Y	18/78/27	38.9 -	32.4
5.58	-	-	6.41	-10.85	0.54	25.2 -	16.9							161.7 -	108.1
		0.20	-2.19	-2.00	-0.58					6.35				4.2 -	0.0
-0.26	-	-	0.83	-4.85		25.1 -	18.1							20.9 -	15.1
0.75	-	-	-0.70	-2.91	-3.58			1.06	1.00	2.94	1.9	0.2850Y	18/78/27	70.7 -	42.5
0.78	-	-	1.39	0.83	0.99	12.0 -	9.6	2.05	2.05	0.48	13.6	0.51250	5/15/18	16.6 -	13.3
2.20	-	-	2.40			10.4 -	0.0							25.0 -	0.0
2.20	-	-	2.40			19.7 -	8.2							47.4 -	19.6
1.37	-	-	4.94	4.12	4.05	18.1 -	14.5	2.76	2.68	2.60	3.4	0.7150Y	18/78/27	89.7 -	71.4
3.77	-	-	7.52	5.18	4.17	31.1 -	25.5	1.60	1.24	-	0.7	0.670	18/78/27	234.2 -	191.7
		0.43	-0.28	-0.04	-5.27										
								4.50	4.50	4.50	5.9	1.1250Y	7/1/18	106.0 -	0.0
		0.59	0.31	0.11	0.47	28.3 -	11.5							8.8 -	3.6
0.36	-	-	1.54	1.08	0.39	21.1 -	13.7							32.5 -	21.1
0.63	-	-	2.11	-1.08	-0.96	32.6 -	14.2							68.8 -	30.0
			-0.59	3.48	2.44									15.8 -	5.0
0.30	-	-	1.22	1.40	1.61	21.8 -	17.6	0.39	0.35	0.31	1.6	0.110Y	18/78/27	26.6 -	21.5
	1.23	-	7.52	5.59	4.14	33.9 -	29.0	0.06	0.06	0.06	0.0	0.030Y	18/78/27	254.9 -	217.9
0.16	-	-	1.81	4.51	3.69	22.3 -	13.3	0.42	0.42	0.42	1.3	0.1050Y	18/78/27	40.4 -	24.0
3.07	-	-	7.21	7.42	6.08	19.6 -	13.7							141.1 -	98.4
		2.45	8.72	7.90	-5.13							0.87G	6/15/18		
0.53	-	-	1.88	1.46	2.68			2.20	2.20	2.20		0.550	8/13/18		
0.32	-	-	1.50	1.87	1.88	19.4 -	12.7	1.68	2.04	2.16	7.2	0.430Z	18/78/27	29.0 -	19.0
0.34	-	-	1.78	1.19	1.41	31.2 -	23.8							55.5 -	42.4
0.45	-	-	2.07	2.14	0.79	18.8 -	15.4	3.00	3.00	2.75	8.3	0.750	5/31/18	39.0 -	31.9

SYMBOL	COMPANY	NATURE OF BUSINESS	FISCAL YEAR-END	TOTAL REV. $MILL	NET INCOME $MILL	TOTAL ASSETS $MILL	NET STK EQUITY $MILL	NO OF INST	INST. HOLDINGS (SHARES)
CPLG	CorePoint Lodging Inc	REITs	12/31/17	980.6	152.0	2953.1	825.7	4	249636
CPLG	CorePoint Lodging Inc	REITs	12/31/17	980.6	152.0	2953.1	825.7	4	249636
COR	CoreSite Realty Corp	REITs	12/31/17	481.8	74.9	1532.7	281.0	420	40226388
GLW	Corning Inc	Electrical Equipment	12/31/17	10116.0	-497.0	27494.0	15698.0	1554	819167033
CAAP	Corporacion America Airports SA	Services	12/31/17	1575.2	63.5	3801.2	461.8	34	16830964
CCT	Corporate Capital Trust Inc	Finance Intermediaries & Services	12/31/17	397.7	210.3	4221.5	2485.1	184	25370173
OFC	Corporate Office Properties Trust	REITs	12/31/17	612.8	70.1	3578.5	1386.0	398	129501080
CZZ	Cosan Ltd	Refining & Marketing	12/31/17	13582.5	551.0	55624.5	6038.8	174	76395275
CMRE	Costamare Inc	Shipping	12/31/17	412.4	72.9	2490.3	1218.5	142	29564718
COTV	Cotiviti Holdings Inc	Business Services	12/31/17	678.7	138.2	2099.2	1101.5	198	88484071
COT	Cott Corp	Beverages	12/30/17	2269.7	-1.4	4093.1	879.6	211	130044906
COTY	Coty, Inc.	Household & Personal Products	6/30/17	7650.3	-422.2	22548.2	9314.7	446	523541819
CUZ	Cousins Properties Inc	REITs	12/31/17	466.2	216.3	4204.6	2772.0	364	524377563
CVA	Covanta Holding Corp	Electric Utilities	12/31/17	1752.0	57.0	4441.0	427.0	367	140919210
CVIA	Covia Holdings Corp	Non-Precious Metals	12/31/17	1444.5	154.2	2022.8	1225.3	6	140706
CPL	CPFL Energia SA	Electric Utilities	12/31/17	26744.9	1179.8	41282.9	8961.5	100	5637389
CR	Crane Co.	Industrial Machinery & Equipment	12/31/17	2786.0	171.8	3593.5	1345.2	478	52922587
CRD B	Crawford & Co.	Brokers & Intermediaries	12/31/17	1163.7	27.7	787.9	182.3	68	11243056
BAP	CrediCorp Ltd.	Banking	12/31/17	17727.7	4091.8	170472.3	21756.6	372	61694147
CS	Credit Suisse Group AG	Banking	12/31/17	20900.0	-983.0	796289.0	41902.0	348	88164983
CPG	Crescent Point Energy Corp	Production & Extraction	12/31/17	2796.3	-124.0	16005.3	9162.9	198	215028311
CEQP	Crestwood Equity Partners LP	Equipment & Services	12/31/17	3880.9	-191.9	4284.9	-	190	57738769
CRH	CRH Plc	Construction Materials	12/31/17	25220.0	1895.0	31633.0	14491.0	225	41415636
CRT	Cross Timbers Royalty Trust	Oil Royalty Traders	12/31/17	6.6	6.1	10.8	9.3	54	811505
CAPL	CrossAmerica Partners LP	Equipment & Services	12/31/17	2094.8	23.2	947.2	0.0	70	11673175
CCI	Crown Castle International Corp (N	REITs	12/31/17	4355.6	444.5	32229.6	12339.1	1048	458409558
CCK	Crown Holdings Inc	Metal Products	12/31/17	8698.0	323.0	10663.0	601.0	579	152309558
CRY	CryoLife, Inc.	Medical Instruments & Equipment	12/31/17	189.7	3.7	589.7	277.1	168	32123139
CSS	CSS Industries, Inc.	Miscellaneous Consumer Goods	3/31/18	361.9	-36.5	365.2	253.7	119	8367078
CTS	CTS Corp	Electrical Equipment	12/31/17	423.0	14.4	539.7	343.8	184	40869131
CUBE	CubeSmart	REITs	12/31/17	558.9	134.3	3545.3	1629.1	376	249002254
CUB	Cubic Corp	Electronic Instruments & Related Pro	9/30/17	1485.9	-11.2	1336.3	689.6	248	33407807
CFR	Cullen/Frost Bankers, Inc.	Banking	12/31/17	1229.4	364.1	31747.9	3297.9	503	66739856
CULP	Culp Inc	Textiles	4/29/18	323.7	20.9	218.0	163.4	108	13641973
CMI	Cummins, Inc.	Auto Parts	12/31/17	20428.0	999.0	18075.0	7259.0	1376	166927506
CURO	CURO Group Holdings Corp	Finance Intermediaries & Services	12/31/17	963.6	49.2	859.7	-7.1	61	20066376
CW	Curtiss-Wright Corp.	Industrial Machinery & Equipment	12/31/17	2271.0	214.9	3236.3	1527.8	403	46999283
SRF	Cushing Energy Income Fund	Holding and other Investment Office	11/30/16	0.5	-0.3	30.0	27.8	26	561146
SRV	Cushing MLP & Infrastructure Total	Holding and other Investment Office	11/30/16	0.8	-2.0	149.8	100.0	34	2149226
SZC	Cushing Renaissance Fund (The)	Holding and other Investment Office	11/30/16	5.7	3.6	130.0	117.6	38	1630353
CUBI	Customers Bancorp Inc	Banking	12/31/17	451.8	78.8	9839.6	921.0	227	29130063
CVI	CVR Energy Inc	Refining & Marketing	12/31/17	5988.4	234.4	3806.7	918.8	225	95768074
UAN	CVR Partners LP	Agricultural Crop Production	12/31/17	330.8	-72.8	1234.3	-	78	37702132
CVRR	CVR Refining LP	Refining & Marketing	12/31/17	5664.2	88.8	2269.9	-	96	23712434
CVS	CVS Health Corporation	Retail - Food & Beverage, Drug & To	12/31/17	184765.0	6622.0	95131.0	37691.0	2252	1065894463
CELP	Cypress Energy Partners LP	Equipment & Services	12/31/17	286.3	-0.8	163.2	-	16	124442
CYS	CYS Investments Inc	REITs	12/31/17	318.9	181.3	13145.6	1574.2	250	123470113
DAN	Dana Inc	Auto Parts	12/31/17	7209.0	111.0	5644.0	1013.0	423	168492430
DHR	Danaher Corp	Medical Instruments & Equipment	12/31/17	18329.7	2492.1	46648.6	26358.2	1652	628083848
DAC	Danaos Corp	Shipping	12/31/17	451.7	83.9	2986.4	548.7	30	3934891
DQ	DAQO New Energy Corp	Semiconductors	12/31/17	352.9	92.8	748.8	391.7	90	4060392
DRI	Darden Restaurants, Inc.	Hotels, Restaurants & Travel	5/27/18	8080.1	596.0	5469.6	2194.8	921	144744562
DAR	Darling Ingredients Inc	Food	12/30/17	3662.3	128.5	4958.2	2244.9	394	205533354
DVA	DaVita Inc	Diagnostic & Health Related Service	12/31/17	10876.6	663.6	18948.2	4690.0	725	181678601
DCP	DCP Midstream LP	Equipment & Services	12/31/17	8462.0	229.0	13878.0	-	217	88348637
DCT	DCT Industrial Trust Inc	REITs	12/31/17	424.5	103.5	4010.7	1951.6	388	122656404
DDR	DDR Corp	REITs	12/31/17	921.6	-241.7	7170.1	2890.9	424	422023231
DF	Dean Foods Co.	Food	12/31/17	7795.0	61.6	2503.8	655.9	413	111241749
DECK	Deckers Outdoor Corp.	Apparel, Footwear & Accessories	3/31/18	1903.3	114.4	1264.4	940.8	450	40561523
DE	Deere & Co.	Industrial Machinery & Equipment	10/29/17	29737.7	2159.1	65786.3	9557.3	1662	273316572
DEX	Delaware Enhanced Global Dividen	Holding and other Investment Office	11/30/16	10.8	6.7	265.5	181.2	52	8223019
DDF	Delaware Investments Dividend & I	Holding and other Investment Office	11/30/16	4.9	3.2	130.0	88.7	37	1675526
DKL	Delek Logistics Partners LP	Equipment & Services	12/31/17	538.1	69.4	443.5	-	59	6248451
DK	Delek US Holdings Inc (New)	Refining & Marketing	12/31/17	7267.1	288.8	5935.2	1650.6	-	0
DVMT	Dell Technologies Inc	Computer Hardware & Equipment	2/2/18	78660.0	-3728.0	122281.0	9710.0	765	189470892
DVMT	Dell Technologies Inc - Common Cl	Internet & Software	2/2/18	7922.0	286.0	20622.0	-		0
DLPH	Delphi Technologies PLC	Manufacturing	12/31/17	4849.0	285.0	3793.0	68.0	479	77445301
DAL	Delta Air Lines Inc (DE)	Airlines/Air Freight	12/31/17	41244.0	3577.0	53292.0	13910.0	1312	759968766
DLX	Deluxe Corp	Printing	12/31/17	1965.6	230.2	2208.8	1015.0	505	55847477
DNR	Denbury Resources, Inc. (DE)	Production & Extraction	12/31/17	1129.8	163.2	4471.3	648.2	379	428268978
DESP	Despegar.com Corp	Hotels, Restaurants & Travel	12/31/17	523.9	42.4	738.7	218.0	78	50251501
DB	Deutsche Bank AG	Banking	12/31/17	38161.0	-751.0	1474732.0	67849.0	341	457749951
KMM	Deutsche Multi-Market Income Trus	Holding and other Investment Office	11/30/16	14.5	11.0	279.7	202.6	57	9753832
KST	Deutsche Strategic Income Trust	Holding and other Investment Office	11/30/16	3.9	2.7	76.7	54.9	34	2579340
DVN	Devon Energy Corp.	Production & Extraction	12/31/17	13949.0	898.0	30241.0	9254.0	1257	542482921
DHX	DHI Group Inc	Internet & Software	12/31/17	207.9	16.0	295.7	132.6	178	52211534
DHT	DHT Holdings Inc	Equipment & Services	12/31/17	355.1	6.6	1730.5	925.9	153	64516680
DEO	Diageo Plc	Beverages	6/30/17	12050.0	2662.0	28848.0	10313.0	1044	96384403
DO	Diamond Offshore Drilling, Inc.	Equipment & Services	12/31/17	1485.7	18.3	6250.6	3774.3	452	171562418
DRH	DiamondRock Hospitality Co.	REITs	12/31/17	870.0	91.9	3100.9	1833.6	343	308451840

| EARNINGS PER SHARE QUARTERLY | | | ANNUAL | | | P/E RATIO | DIVIDENDS PER SHARE | | | AV. YLD | DIV. DECLARED | | PRICE RANGE |
1st	2nd	3rd	2017	2016	2015		2017	2016	2015	%	AMOUNT	PAYABLE	2017
-0.13	-	-	1.30	-0.01	0.20	21.5 - 19.6	-	-					27.9 - 25.5
-0.13	-	-	1.30	-0.01	0.20	0.0 - 0.0							0.0 - 0.0
0.59	-	-	1.84	1.54	1.03	65.0 - 49.6	3.58	2.39	1.79	3.3	1.030Z	7/16/18	119.5 - 91.3
-0.72	-	-	-0.66	3.23	1.00	-	0.62	0.54	0.48	2.1	0.180Y	18/78/27	34.9 - 26.4
-	-	-	0.43	0.20	0.71	-							
0.57	-	-	1.54	1.55	1.55	12.3 - 9.5	0.37	1.80	1.80	2.2	0.40220	7/10/18	19.0 - 14.6
0.17	-	-	0.57	-0.03	1.74	62.2 - 43.8	1.10	1.10	1.10	3.7	0.2750Z	18/78/27	35.5 - 25.0
-	-	1.26	2.05	0.98	1.68		3.26				0.08220	5/17/18	
-	-	-	0.52	0.79	1.68		-				0.55470	7/16/18	
0.57	-	-	1.45	0.55	0.18	30.8 - 21.3	-						44.6 - 30.9
2.54	-	-	-0.01	-0.61	-0.03	-	0.24	0.24	0.24	1.4	0.060	6/13/18	22.7 - 13.8
-	-	-0.10	-0.66	0.44	0.64	-	0.65	0.25	0.20	3.7	0.1250	18/78/27	21.5 - 13.1
0.04	-	-	0.52	0.31	0.58	18.9 - 16.0	0.30	0.24	0.32	3.3	0.0650Z	7/16/18	9.8 - 8.3
1.53	-	-	0.44	-0.03	0.51	39.2 - 30.0	1.00	1.00	1.00	6.6	0.250Y	7/6/18	17.3 - 13.2
33.89	-	-	114.71	2.73	-53.84	0.2 - 0.2							24.5 - 18.6
-	-	-	1.15	0.87	0.83	15.3 - 9.3	0.37	0.36		2.5			17.6 - 10.7
1.13	-	-	2.84	2.07	3.89	35.2 - 25.4	1.32	1.32	1.32	1.5	0.350Y	18/78/27	99.9 - 72.2
0.16	-	-	0.52	0.67	-0.79	23.8 - 14.5	0.20	0.20	0.20	2.1	0.050Y	6/7/18	12.4 - 7.6
-	-	-	51.35	44.23	38.84		14.17				4.3040	5/11/18	
-	0.13	-	-0.41	-1.32	-1.73	-	1.18	0.70	1.17	7.1			20.0 - 14.4
-0.17	-	-	-0.23	-1.81	-1.82		0.36	0.50	2.11	4.2	0.030	8/15/18	11.6 - 6.4
0.21	-	-	-3.64	-3.55	-54.00		2.40	3.17		9.0	0.60	8/14/18	35.5 - 22.3
-	-	-	2.25	1.49	0.89	17.3 - 14.7	0.66	0.64	0.62	1.9			39.0 - 33.1
0.34	-	-	1.01	1.06	1.35	15.4 - 12.9	1.01	1.06	1.35	6.9	0.12510	8/14/18	15.6 - 13.1
-0.06	-	-	0.56	0.22	0.35	52.9 - 28.3	2.48	2.40	2.23	10.6	0.5250	8/13/18	29.6 - 15.8
0.21	-	-	1.01	0.95	4.42	112.9 - 95.7	3.90	3.61	3.35	3.7	1.050Y	18/78/27	114.0 - 96.6
0.67	-	-	2.38	3.56	2.82	25.7 - 18.2	-						61.2 - 43.3
-0.11	-	-	0.11	0.32	0.14	266.8 - 153.2			0.12		0.030Y	12/18/15	29.4 - 16.9
-	-	0.65	3.13	1.87	1.80	9.6 - 4.9	0.80	0.74	0.63	3.4	0.20Y	6/20/18	30.1 - 15.3
0.34	-	-	0.43	1.03	0.21	84.3 - 49.5	0.16	0.16	0.16	0.6	0.040Y	7/27/18	36.3 - 21.3
-	-	0.21	0.74	0.45	0.42	44.1 - 31.0	1.11	0.90	0.69	4.0	0.30Z	18/78/27	32.6 - 22.9
-	-0.07	-	-0.41	0.06	0.85	-	0.27	0.27	0.27	0.5	0.1350Y	3/12/18	71.8 - 40.2
1.61	-	-	5.51	4.70	4.28	21.9 - 14.8	2.25	2.15	2.10	2.2	0.33590Y	18/78/27	120.8 - 81.6
-	-	-0.06	1.78	1.36	1.21	19.0 - 13.8	0.51	0.66	0.62	1.7	0.090	7/16/18	33.9 - 24.6
1.96	-	-	5.97	8.23	7.84	32.2 - 22.2	4.21	4.00	3.51	2.6	1.140Y	18/78/27	192.5 - 132.3
0.49	-	-	1.25	1.69	0.46	20.9 - 11.0	-						26.1 - 13.7
0.98	-	-	4.80	4.15	3.05	29.6 - 19.1	0.56	0.52	0.52	0.5	0.150Y	18/78/27	142.1 - 91.8
-	-	-	-0.13	0.24		-		0.94	0.58		0.040	7/31/18	10.0 - 7.8
-	-	-	-0.29	-8.83		-		1.08	0.27		0.09030	7/31/18	12.9 - 10.2
-	-	-	-0.01	0.58		-		1.64	1.64		0.13670	7/31/18	21.2 - 15.5
0.64	-	-	1.97	2.31	1.96	16.8 - 12.7	-				0.3750Y	6/15/18	33.2 - 25.1
0.76	-	-	2.70	0.28	1.95	17.1 - 6.3	2.00	2.00	2.00	6.5	0.750Y	8/13/18	46.1 - 17.1
-0.17	-	-	-0.64	-0.26	0.85	-	0.02	0.71	1.25	0.6	0.020	5/15/17	4.2 - 2.6
0.99	-	-	0.60	0.10	1.97	42.3 - 11.3	0.94	-	3.12	6.8	0.510	5/14/18	25.4 - 6.8
0.98	-	-	6.44	4.90	4.63	13.0 - 9.4	2.00	1.70	1.40	2.8	0.50Y	18/78/27	83.6 - 60.6
0.06	-	-	0.29	0.13	0.35	28.3 - 19.1	1.04	1.63	1.63	15.1	0.210	5/15/18	8.2 - 5.5
-0.74	-	-	1.05	-0.04	-0.17	8.4 - 6.0	1.00	1.01	1.10	12.9	0.0909HZ	7/30/18	8.8 - 6.3
0.73	-	-	0.71	4.36	0.99	49.1 - 28.4	0.24	0.24	0.23	0.9	0.10Y	18/78/27	34.9 - 20.2
-	0.95	-	3.53	3.65	4.74	29.4 - 22.5	0.56	0.57	0.54	0.6	0.160Y	18/78/27	103.8 - 79.3
-	-	0.08	0.76	-3.34	1.07	-					0.4650	11/19/08	
-	-	-	0.34	0.16	0.05	200.7 - 58.1	-						68.2 - 19.8
-	-	1.73	3.80	2.90	5.47	28.7 - 20.3	2.24	2.10	2.20	2.5	0.750Y	18/78/27	108.9 - 77.0
0.58	-	-	0.77	0.62	0.48	26.4 - 20.3	-						20.4 - 15.6
0.98	-	-	3.47	4.29	1.25	23.1 - 15.5	-						80.0 - 53.9
0.08	-	-	0.43	1.64	0.91	98.8 - 70.0	3.12	3.12	3.12	8.7	0.780	5/15/18	42.5 - 30.1
0.52	-	-	1.11	1.03	1.05	60.4 - 47.1	1.29	1.18	1.13	2.2	0.360Z	18/78/27	67.1 - 52.3
-0.34	-	-	-1.48	0.20	-0.54	-	1.52	1.52		11.0	0.39060	18/78/27	17.8 - 11.0
-	-	-	0.67	1.31	-0.09	25.6 - 12.2	0.36	0.36	0.28	3.4	0.090Y	18/78/27	17.1 - 8.2
-	-	2.69	0.18	3.70	4.66	677.4 - 342.2	-						121.9 - 61.6
-	3.67	-	6.68	4.81	5.77	25.7 - 17.3	2.40	2.40	2.40	1.7	0.690Y	18/78/27	171.5 - 115.4
-	-	-	0.42	0.57				0.83	0.90		0.10290	7/27/18	12.7 - 11.2
-	-	-	0.38	0.44				0.59	0.63		0.09590	7/27/18	11.6 - 10.2
0.59	-	-	2.09	2.07	2.52	16.9 - 12.8	2.79	2.48	2.16	9.2	0.750	5/15/18	35.3 - 26.8
-0.43	-	-	4.00	-2.49	0.32	15.0 - 5.2	0.30	0.60	0.60	0.9	0.250Y	18/78/27	59.8 - 20.9
2.33	-	-	1.43	-2.72	-3.02	62.6 - 42.2	-						89.6 - 60.4
-	-	1.09	1.43	-	-	62.6 - 42.2	-						89.6 - 60.4
1.10	-	-	3.21	1.78	-						0.170	5/16/18	
-	1.47	-	4.95	5.79	5.63	12.1 - 9.1	1.01	0.68	0.45	1.9	0.350Y	18/78/27	60.1 - 45.2
1.31	-	-	4.72	4.65	4.36	16.5 - 14.0	1.20	1.20	1.20	1.7	0.30Y	18/78/27	77.7 - 66.2
0.09	-	-	0.41	-2.61	-12.57	11.9 - 2.3	-		0.19		0.06250	9/29/15	4.9 - 1.0
-	-	-	0.69	0.30	-1.49	-							
-	0.07	-	-0.53	-1.08	-5.06	-							
-	-	-	0.49	0.54		-		0.51	0.60		0.03250	7/31/18	9.0 - 8.7
-	-	-	0.62	0.69		-		0.65	0.95		0.0440	7/31/18	12.6 - 0.0
-0.38	-	-	1.70	-6.52	-35.55	26.4 - 17.4	0.24	0.42	0.96	0.7	0.080Y	18/78/27	44.8 - 29.5
0.07	-	-	0.33	-0.11	-0.21	9.4 - 3.8	-						3.1 - 1.3
-0.06	-	-	0.05	0.10	1.04	-					0.020	5/30/18	
-	-	-	1.05	0.89	0.95	141.5 - 112.6	2.35	2.29	2.09	1.7			148.6 - 118.3
0.14	-	-	0.13	-2.72	-2.00	163.2 - 78.6	-		0.50		0.1250Y	18/78/27	21.2 - 10.2
0.02	-	-	0.46	0.57	0.43	28.2 - 21.7	0.50	0.50	0.50	4.4	0.1250Z	7/12/18	12.9 - 10.0

SYMBOL	COMPANY	NATURE OF BUSINESS	FISCAL YEAR-END	TOTAL REV. $MILL	NET INCOME $MILL	TOTAL ASSETS $MILL	NET STK EQUITY $MILL	NO OF INST	INST. HOLDINGS (SHARES)
DSX	Diana Shipping Inc	Shipping	12/31/17	161.9	-511.7	1246.7	624.8	124	48374398
DKS	Dick's Sporting Goods, Inc	Retail - Specialty	2/3/18	8590.5	323.4	4203.9	1941.5	571	97531836
DBD	Diebold Nixdorf Inc	Computer Hardware & Equipment	12/31/17	4609.3	-233.1	5250.2	470.0	387	114165439
DLR	Digital Realty Trust Inc	REITs	12/31/17	2457.9	248.3	21404.3	10403.0	874	245386381
DDS	Dillard's Inc.	Retail - General Merchandise/Depart	2/3/18	6422.7	221.3	3673.2	1708.2	346	35004913
DIN	Dine Brands Global Inc	Retail - Food & Beverage, Drug & To	12/31/17	604.8	-330.5	1750.2	-146.7	288	23233923
DPLO	Diplomat Pharmacy Inc	Diagnostic & Health Related Service	12/31/17	4485.2	15.5	1940.4	749.5	264	67648981
DFS	Discover Financial Services	Credit & Lending	12/31/17	11545.0	2099.0	100087.0	10892.0	1168	391415766
DIS	Disney (Walt) Co. (The)	Entertainment	9/30/17	55137.0	8980.0	95789.0	41315.0	2798	1257367794
DHCP	Ditech Holding Corp	Credit & Lending	12/31/17	831.3	-426.9	14164.2	-449.2	87	16553970
DNI	Dividend & Income Fund	Holding and other Investment Office	12/31/16	4.9	2.6	179.1	151.0	52	4851968
DNP	DNP Select Income Fund Inc	Holding and other Investment Office	10/31/17	119.3	62.2	3890.0	2870.5	270	15937471
DLB	Dolby Laboratories Inc	Manufacturing	9/29/17	1081.5	201.8	2533.6	2136.7	422	65114982
DG	Dollar General Corp	Retail - General Merchandise/Depart	2/2/18	23471.0	1539.0	12516.9	6125.8	952	297161110
D	Dominion Energy Inc (New)	Electric Utilities	12/31/17	12586.0	2999.0	76585.0	17142.0	1602	540325552
DM	Dominion Energy Midstream Partne	Gas Utilities	12/31/17	480.2	115.7	7980.3		137	44584551
DPZ	Dominos Pizza Inc.	Hotels, Restaurants & Travel	12/31/17	2788.0	277.9	836.8	-2735.4	569	52607762
UFS	Domtar Corp	Paper & Forest Products	12/31/17	5157.0	-258.0	5212.0	2483.0		0
DCI	Donaldson Co. Inc.	Industrial Machinery & Equipment	7/31/17	2371.9	232.8	1979.7	850.1	508	130101693
RRD	Donnelley (RR) & Sons Company	Printing	12/31/17	6939.6	-34.4	3904.5	-217.6	402	104441290
DFIN	Donnelley Financial Solutions Inc	Business Services	12/31/17	1004.9	9.7	893.5	149.4	201	33015555
LPG	Dorian LPG Ltd.	Shipping	3/31/17	167.4	-1.4	1746.2	976.0	138	34439778
DSL	DoubleLine Income Solutions Fund	Holding and other Investment Office	9/30/17	228.8	177.8	3148.9	2214.0	170	27852339
DBL	Doubleline Opportunistic Credit Fun	Holding and other Investment Office	9/30/17	30.3	24.3	417.3	327.9	85	3752301
PLOW	Douglas Dynamics, Inc.	Industrial Machinery & Equipment	12/31/17	474.9	55.3	685.2	256.7	176	22470499
DEI	Douglas Emmett Inc	REITs	12/31/17	812.1	94.4	8292.6	2437.5	359	213111448
DOV	Dover Corp	Industrial Machinery & Equipment	12/31/17	7830.4	811.7	10657.7	4383.2	1000	169848173
DDE	Dover Downs Gaming & Entertainm	Hotels, Restaurants & Travel	12/31/17	176.9	-1.1	161.8	114.7	50	7668408
DVD	Dover Motorsports, Inc.	Sporting & Recreational	12/31/17	46.7	8.4	80.3	59.2	54	10284057
DWDP	DowDuPont Inc	Plastics	12/31/17	62484.0	1460.0	192164.0	100330.0	1964	1647052950
RDY	Dr. Reddy's Laboratories Ltd.	Pharmaceuticals	3/31/16	154708.0	20013.0	207650.0	128336.0	189	21515729
DRD	DRDGold Ltd	Precious Metals	6/30/17	2339.9	13.7	2287.4	1302.4	58	8293801
DHF	Dreyfus High Yield Strategies Fund	Holding and other Investment Office	3/31/17	26.1	20.8	382.5	258.7	84	10845719
DMB	Dreyfus Municipal Bond Infrastructu	Holding and other Investment Office	2/28/17	17.3	12.5	370.1	326.5	51	4457398
DSM	Dreyfus Strategic Municipal Bond F	Holding and other Investment Office	11/30/16	29.2	24.4	589.7	495.5	92	5703513
LEO	Dreyfus Strategic Municipals Inc	Holding and other Investment Office	9/30/17	39.2	31.9	828.4	678.5	92	5837788
DRQ	Dril-Quip Inc	Equipment & Services	12/31/17	455.5	-100.6	1399.8	1294.5	345	55526967
DS	Drive Shack Inc	Sporting & Recreational	12/31/17	292.6	-42.2	536.6	171.1	177	58282127
DSW	DSW Inc	Retail - Apparel and Accessories	2/3/18	2799.8	67.3	1413.6	950.4	389	91667146
DTE	DTE Energy Co	Electric Utilities	12/31/17	12607.0	1134.0	33767.0	9512.0	868	157451890
DTF	DTF Tax-Free Income, Inc.	Holding and other Investment Office	10/31/17	7.6	4.6	199.1	133.7	40	1339354
DCO	Ducommun Inc.	Aerospace	12/31/17	558.2	20.1	566.8	235.6	144	11549686
DPG	Duff & Phelps Global Utility Income	Holding and other Investment Office	10/31/17	32.3	15.4	933.2	662.7	69	6621993
DSE	Duff & Phelps Select Energy MLP F	Holding and other Investment Office	11/30/16	1.6	-2.7	274.9	192.9		0
DUC	Duff & Phelps Utility & Corporate Bo	Holding and other Investment Office	10/31/17	15.0	9.3	393.3	268.0	60	12930830
DUK	Duke Energy Corp	Electric Utilities	12/31/17	23565.0	3059.0	137914.0	41739.0	1823	549768358
DRE	Duke Realty Corp	REITs	12/31/17	780.9	1634.4	7388.2	4532.8	614	406610565
DNB	Dun & Bradstreet Corp (DE)	Business Services	12/31/17	1742.5	140.9	2480.9	-827.3	530	44702052
KTF	DWS Municipal Income Trust (New)	Holding and other Investment Office	11/30/16	38.0	29.6	823.3	491.5	91	6073815
KSM	DWS Strategic Municipal Income Tr	Holding and other Investment Office	11/30/16	11.7	8.9	229.9	136.0	40	1324627
DXC	DXC Technology Co	IT Services	3/31/18	24556.0	1751.0	33921.0	13487.0	917	241162399
DY	Dycom Industries, Inc.	Construction Services	1/27/18	1411.3	68.8	1841.0	725.0	447	42391172
DLNG	Dynagas LNG Partners LP	Equipment & Services	12/31/17	139.0	17.3	1054.3		48	5131208
DX	Dynex Capital, Inc.	REITs	12/31/17	94.5	33.9	3305.8	557.1	187	36013570
ELF	e.l.f. Beauty Inc	Household & Personal Products	12/31/17	269.9	33.5	417.2	193.9	119	41773677
EGIF	Eagle Growth & Income Opportuniti	Holding and other Investment Office	12/31/17	8.8	4.8	191.5	141.1	16	2427160
EXP	Eagle Materials Inc	Construction Materials	3/31/18	1386.5	256.6	2368.0	1417.7	489	55828072
ECC	Eagle Point Credit Company Inc	Holding and other Investment Office	12/31/16	55.8	31.4	448.4	288.0	30	11311247
ESTE	Earthstone Energy Inc	Production & Extraction	12/31/17	108.1	-12.5	834.4	279.2	86	11650606
DEA	Easterly Government Properties Inc	REITs	12/31/17	130.7	4.4	1425.3	667.8	206	49404892
EGP	EastGroup Properties Inc	REITs	12/31/17	274.1	83.2	1953.2	749.5	355	42238373
EMN	Eastman Chemical Co	Plastics	12/31/17	9549.0	1384.0	15999.0	5403.0	978	146517495
KODK	Eastman Kodak Co.	Leisure Equipment	12/31/17	1531.0	94.0	1707.0	221.0	210	45636429
ETN	Eaton Corp plc	Electrical Equipment	12/31/17	20404.0	2985.0	32623.0	17253.0	1216	390955253
EV	Eaton Vance Corp	Wealth Management	10/31/17	1529.0	282.1	2330.9	1011.4	539	111349471
EOI	Eaton Vance Enhanced Equity Inco	Holding and other Investment Office	9/30/17	10.5	4.4	570.4	566.8	83	5280441
EOS	Eaton Vance Enhanced Equity Inco	Holding and other Investment Office	12/31/16	8.4	1.2	654.0	651.1	92	7706505
EFF	Eaton Vance Floating Rate Income	Finance Intermediaries & Services	5/31/17	10.7	7.2	216.2	136.4	38	1726820
EFT	Eaton Vance Floating Rate Income	Holding and other Investment Office	5/31/17	49.5	34.5	979.7	620.8	119	14861967
EHT	Eaton Vance High Income 2021 Tar	Holding and other Investment Office	3/31/17	13.0	10.2	296.1	220.7	23	3027169
ETX	Eaton Vance Municipal Income 202	Holding and other Investment Office	1/31/18	13.4	9.0	353.3	221.5	42	2282901
EVN	Eaton Vance Municipal Income Trus	Holding and other Investment Office	11/30/16	25.2	18.2	538.9	321.9	76	3628545
EOT	Eaton Vance National Municipal Op	Holding and other Investment Office	3/31/17	18.6	15.5	378.2	330.2	51	1934429
ETJ	Eaton Vance Risk-Managed Diversi	Holding and other Investment Office	12/31/17	14.1	6.9	638.0	635.6	125	20348328
EFR	Eaton Vance Senior Floating Rate T	Holding and other Investment Office	10/31/17	44.7	33.1	879.8	656.3	111	8309825
EVF	Eaton Vance Senior Income Trust	Holding and other Investment Office	6/30/17	21.7	15.3	432.6	332.4	82	15276055
EVG	Eaton Vance Short Duration Diversif	Holding and other Investment Office	10/31/17	18.6	12.5	361.9	273.8	66	10594245
EVT	Eaton Vance Tax Advantaged Divid	Holding and other Investment Office	8/31/17	86.0	60.0	2073.8	1617.6	129	13562387
ETW	Eaton Vance Tax Managed Global	Holding and other Investment Office	12/31/16	30.2	17.4	1156.6	1139.6	139	22756799
ETG	Eaton Vance Tax-Advantage Global	Holding and other Investment Office	10/31/17	119.3	96.1	1859.9	1390.6	119	14256392

| EARNINGS PER SHARE | | | | | | P/E RATIO | | DIVIDENDS PER SHARE | | | AV. YLD | DIV. DECLARED | | PRICE RANGE | |
| QUARTERLY | | | ANNUAL | | | | | | | | | | | 2017 | |
1st	2nd	3rd	2017	2016	2015			2017	2016	2015	%	AMOUNT	PAYABLE		
-	-	-0.04	-5.41	-2.11	-0.89	-		-		-	-	0.55470	7/16/18	-	
0.59	-	-	2.56	2.83	2.84	15.8 -	9.5	0.60	0.55	0.50	1.9	0.2250Y	18/78/27	40.5 -	24.4
-0.94	-	-	-3.09	-0.48	1.12	-		0.40	0.96	1.15	2.3	0.10Y	18/78/27	28.0 -	11.5
0.42	-	-	0.99	2.20	1.56	127.3 -	98.9	3.72	3.52	3.40	3.3	0.41410Z	18/78/27	126.0 -	98.0
2.89	-	-	4.93	6.91	7.79	19.8 -	10.2	0.28	0.26	0.24	0.4	0.10Y	18/78/27	97.5 -	50.5
0.92	-	-	-18.28	5.33	5.52	-		3.88	3.73	3.54	7.0	0.630Y	7/6/18	82.2 -	37.3
-0.01	-	-	0.23	0.42	0.41	122.3 -	62.7	-		-	-	-		28.1 -	14.4
1.82	-	-	5.42	5.77	5.13	15.0 -	10.6	1.30	1.16	1.08	1.9	0.40Y	18/78/27	81.3 -	57.7
-	1.95	-	5.69	5.73	4.90	19.8 -	17.0	1.56	1.42	1.81	1.5	0.840Y	18/78/27	112.5 -	96.9
-12.73	-	-	-11.61	-14.71	-7.00	-		-		-	-	-		11.0 -	0.3
-	-	-	0.25	0.31		-		-	1.00	1.63	-	0.150	6/29/18	14.2 -	12.1
-	-	-	0.22	0.27	0.29	52.5 -	45.2	0.78	0.78	0.78	7.1	0.0650	10/10/18	11.5 -	9.9
-	0.66	-	1.95	1.81	1.75	36.0 -	24.7	0.56	0.48	0.40	0.9	0.160Y	18/78/27	70.2 -	48.3
1.36	-	-	4.43	3.95	3.49	23.8 -	15.6	1.00	0.88	-	1.1	0.290Y	18/78/27	105.3 -	69.0
0.77	-	-	4.72	3.44	3.20	18.0 -	13.1	3.04	2.80	2.59	4.1	0.8350Y	18/78/27	84.9 -	61.8
0.37	-	-	1.35	1.30	1.08	25.6 -	9.5	1.13	0.92	0.70	4.5	0.3340	5/15/18	34.5 -	12.8
2.00	-	-	5.83	4.30	3.47	50.2 -	28.9	1.84	1.52	1.24	0.9	0.550Y	18/78/27	292.4 -	168.7
0.86	-	-	-4.11	2.04	2.24	-		1.66	1.65	1.60	3.3	0.4350	18/78/27	64.6 -	36.7
-	-	0.53	1.74	1.42	1.49	30.0 -	24.9	0.70	0.69	0.67	1.5	0.190Y	18/78/27	52.2 -	43.4
-0.14	-	-	-0.49	-7.09	2.19	-		0.56	0.14	3.12	6.4	0.140Y	6/1/18	12.7 -	5.7
0.23	-	-	0.29	1.80		81.5 -	52.8	-		-	-	-		23.6 -	15.3
-	-	0.03	-0.03	2.29	0.45	-		-		-	-	-		-	
-	-	-	1.75	1.71	1.85	12.3 -	11.2	1.81	1.89	1.90	8.9	0.150	7/31/18	21.5 -	19.6
-	-	-	1.63	1.81	2.21	15.9 -	12.6	2.00	2.53	2.49	8.9	0.1670	7/31/18	26.0 -	20.6
-0.08	-	-	2.40	1.70	1.94	20.3 -	12.7	0.96	0.94	0.89	2.4	0.2650Y	6/29/18	48.8 -	30.6
0.17	-	-	0.58	0.55	0.39	71.4 -	60.2	0.94	0.89	0.85	2.4	0.250Z	18/78/27	41.4 -	34.9
-	0.91	-	5.15	3.25	5.46	16.8 -	12.8	1.82	1.72	1.64	2.4	0.470Y	18/78/27	86.4 -	65.9
-0.01	-	-	-0.03	0.02	0.06	-		-		-	-	0.020Y	12/10/12	2.2 -	0.9
-0.03	-	-	0.23	0.10	0.14	10.0 -	7.8	0.08	0.05	0.05	3.9	0.080Y	12/10/17	2.3 -	1.8
0.47	-	-	0.91	3.52	6.15	84.6 -	68.2	0.38	1.84	1.72	0.5	0.380Y	18/78/27	77.0 -	62.0
-	-	-	-	116.98	129.75	-		-	18.62	16.62	-	-		42.5 -	28.5
-0.03	-	-	0.03	0.15	0.17	136.0 -	75.0	0.97	4.87	0.16	31.2	-		4.1 -	2.3
-	-	-	0.29	0.30	0.32	12.3 -	10.8	0.32	0.35	0.36	9.6	0.02350	7/26/18	3.6 -	3.1
-	-	-	0.68	0.71	0.73	19.9 -	17.8	0.71	0.75	0.75	5.5	0.053M	8/1/18	13.5 -	12.1
-	-	-	-	0.50	0.52	-		-	0.50	0.50	-	0.035M	7/31/18	8.8 -	7.5
-	-	-	0.51	0.53	0.55	17.9 -	14.9	0.52	0.52	0.53	6.2	0.035M	7/31/18	9.2 -	7.6
-0.20	-	-	-2.69	2.47	4.98	-		-		-	-	-		56.4 -	36.2
-0.26	-	-	-0.71	1.07	0.24	-		0.00	0.48	0.48	0.0	0.52340Z	7/31/18	8.0 -	2.5
0.30	-	-	1.52	1.54	1.69	17.2 -	10.3	0.80	0.80	0.75	3.8	0.250Y	7/5/18	26.2 -	15.7
2.00	-	-	6.32	4.83	4.05	18.4 -	15.0	3.36	3.06	2.84	3.2	0.88250Y	18/78/27	116.0 -	94.7
-	-	-	-	0.57	0.69	-		0.75	0.88	0.84	5.4	0.05M	9/28/18	14.8 -	13.0
0.22	-	-	1.74	2.24	-6.63	20.4 -	14.8	-		-	-	0.0750Y	3/4/11	35.4 -	25.8
-	-	-	0.41	0.67	0.70	41.7 -	33.0	1.40	1.40	1.40	9.1	0.350	9/28/18	17.1 -	13.6
-	-	-	-	-0.10	-0.15	-		-	0.88	1.58	-	0.150	5/18/18	7.3 -	5.0
-	-	-	0.34	0.38	0.41	27.4 -	24.7	0.60	0.60	0.60	6.8	0.0350	9/28/18	9.3 -	8.4
0.88	-	-	4.36	3.11	4.05	20.9 -	16.5	3.49	3.36	3.24	4.3	0.92750Y	18/78/27	91.1 -	72.1
0.20	-	-	4.56	0.88	1.77	.6.6 -	5.4	1.62	0.73	0.89	5.9	0.20Z	18/78/27	30.1 -	24.5
1.71	-	-	3.79	2.65	4.64	35.2 -	27.8	2.01	1.93	1.85	1.7	0.52250Y	18/78/27	133.4 -	105.3
-	-	-	-	0.75	0.82	-		-	0.84	0.86	-	0.0525G	7/31/18	13.6 -	10.9
-	-	-	-	0.80	0.83	-		-	0.79	0.91	-	0.05G	7/31/18	12.8 -	10.7
-	-	2.68	-	-	-	-		-		-	-	0.190Y	7/17/18	92.8 -	65.7
0.53	-	-	4.92	3.89	2.41	25.0 -	15.5	-		-	-	0.0228G	18/78/27	122.8 -	76.1
-	-	-	0.27	1.69	1.60	-		-		-	-	0.250	7/19/18	-	
0.74	-	-	0.46	0.69	0.14	16.0 -	13.1	0.72	0.84	0.96	10.6	0.47660Z	7/16/18	7.4 -	6.0
0.01	-	-	0.68	-39.47	1560.00	39.7 -	22.4	-		-	-	-		27.0 -	15.2
-	-	-	0.67	0.69	0.35	25.8 -	22.2	0.98	1.13	0.55	6.1	0.0730	7/31/18	17.3 -	14.9
-	-	2.08	4.10	3.05	3.71	29.3 -	21.3	0.40	0.40	0.40	0.4	0.10Y	18/78/27	120.3 -	87.2
-	-	-	2.14	1.89		-		-	2.40	2.40	-	0.16150Y	9/28/18	21.6 -	17.8
0.19	-	-	-0.53	-2.92	-8.43	-		-		-	-	-		11.7 -	7.9
0.03	-	-	0.10	0.10	-0.08	220.9 -	190.4	1.00	0.92	0.54	4.9	0.260Y	6/28/18	22.1 -	19.0
0.83	-	-	2.44	2.93	1.49	39.3 -	32.0	2.52	2.44	2.34	2.9	0.640Z	6/29/18	96.0 -	78.2
2.00	-	-	9.47	5.75	5.66	11.7 -	8.7	2.09	1.89	1.66	2.2	0.560Y	18/78/27	110.8 -	82.8
-0.70	-	-	1.76	0.28	-1.91	6.6 -	1.7	-		-	-	0.250Y	12/12/08	11.6 -	3.0
1.10	-	-	6.68	4.21	4.23	-		2.40	2.28	2.20	-	0.660	18/78/27	-	
-	0.78	-	2.42	2.12	1.92	25.2 -	18.8	1.15	1.08	1.01	2.2	0.310Y	18/78/27	60.9 -	45.4
-	-	-	0.11	0.14	0.23	146.0 -	120.5	1.04	1.04	1.04	7.2	0.08640	7/31/18	16.1 -	13.3
-	-	-	-	0.03	0.13	-		-	1.05	1.05	-	0.08750	7/31/18	17.7 -	14.5
-	-	-	0.95	1.06	1.11	17.8 -	16.9	0.99	1.11	1.42	6.0	0.0760	7/31/18	16.9 -	16.1
-	-	-	0.86	0.91	0.88	17.8 -	16.3	0.87	0.90	0.89	5.9	0.0690	7/31/18	15.3 -	14.1
-	-	-	0.48	-		21.4 -	19.9	0.45	-		4.5	0.04750	7/19/18	10.2 -	9.6
-	-	-	0.87	0.94	0.92	24.2 -	21.7	0.85	0.85	0.85	4.3	0.0709M	7/31/18	21.0 -	18.9
-	-	-	-	0.77	0.89	-		-	0.77	0.89	-	0.0541M	7/19/18	13.1 -	11.4
-	-	-	1.02	1.06	1.09	23.0 -	19.6	1.24	1.03	1.03	5.7	0.0859M	7/31/18	23.5 -	20.0
-	-	-	0.11	0.20		-		-	1.12	1.12	-	0.0760	7/31/18	9.8 -	8.9
-	-	-	0.90	0.96	0.94	16.7 -	15.6	0.87	0.94	0.94	6.0	0.0720	7/31/18	15.0 -	14.0
-	-	-	0.40	0.42	0.40	17.1 -	15.9	0.39	0.41	0.40	5.9	0.0320	7/19/18	6.8 -	6.3
-	-	-	0.70	0.72	0.78	20.7 -	18.5	0.99	1.08	1.08	7.1	0.0650	7/31/18	14.5 -	12.9
-	-	-	0.82	0.74	0.81	29.5 -	25.9	1.74	1.74	1.45	7.7	0.1450	7/31/18	24.2 -	21.2
-	-	-	-	0.16	0.18	-		-	1.17	1.17	-	0.0910	7/31/18	12.5 -	11.4
-	-	-	1.26	1.27	1.16	14.5 -	13.1	1.23	1.23	1.23	7.2	0.10250	7/31/18	18.3 -	16.4

SYMBOL	COMPANY	NATURE OF BUSINESS	FISCAL YEAR-END	TOTAL REV. $MILL	NET INCOME $MILL	TOTAL ASSETS $MILL	NET STK EQUITY $MILL	NO OF INST	INST. HOLDINGS (SHARES)
EXD	Eaton Vance Tax-Advantaged Bond	Holding and other Investment Office	12/31/16	2.7	0.8	125.5	124.2	29	1897094
ETO	Eaton Vance Tax-Advantaged Glob	Holding and other Investment Office	10/31/17	13.6	7.1	480.1	357.8	56	2036410
ETB	Eaton Vance Tax-Managed Buy-Wri	Holding and other Investment Office	12/31/16	8.9	4.7	385.6	382.9	67	4872815
ETV	Eaton Vance Tax-Managed Buy-Wri	Holding and other Investment Office	12/31/16	17.3	7.6	907.2	899.0	144	12145283
ETY	Eaton Vance Tax-Managed Diversifi	Holding and other Investment Office	10/31/17	33.8	15.0	1797.5	1787.8	151	35105145
EXG	Eaton Vance Tax-Managed Global	Holding and other Investment Office	10/31/17	55.6	25.8	2901.2	2833.8	198	50146276
ECT	ECA Marcellus Trust I	Oil Royalty Traders	12/31/17	6.9	5.7	52.0	50.9	36	670331
ECR	Eclipse Resources Corp	Production & Extraction	12/31/17	383.7	8.5	1223.5	572.4	133	250691538
ECL	Ecolab Inc	Specialty Chemicals	12/31/17	13838.3	1508.4	19962.4	7618.5	1298	274084414
EC	Ecopetrol SA	Refining & Marketing	12/31/16	18485561.0	2447881.0	20437924.0	42026858.0	176	67319337
EPC	Edgewell Personal Care Co	Household & Personal Products	9/30/17	2298.4	5.7	4188.8	1741.7	510	68303809
EIX	Edison International	Electric Utilities	12/31/17	12320.0	565.0	52580.0	11671.0	934	316733274
EDR	Education Realty Trust Inc	REITs	12/31/17	331.1	47.4	3015.2	1844.7	341	115066254
EW	Edwards Lifesciences Corp	Medical Instruments & Equipment	12/31/17	3435.3	583.6	5695.8	2956.2	1071	201938433
EHIC	eHi Car Services Ltd	Miscellaneous Consumer Services	12/31/17	2739.5	122.2	10928.5	4206.5	53	18082032
EE	El Paso Electric Company	Electric Utilities	12/31/17	916.8	98.3	3484.4	1142.2	284	52040662
EGO	Eldorado Gold Corp	Precious Metals	12/31/17	391.4	-9.9	5090.3	3643.5	230	354144636
ELVT	Elevate Credit Inc	Credit & Lending	12/31/17	673.1	-6.9	687.5	96.2	65	23635610
ELLI	Ellie Mae Inc	Internet & Software	12/31/17	417.0	52.8	831.6	735.3	281	43237309
EFC	Ellington Financial LLC	Property, Real Estate & Developmen	12/31/17	94.0	35.2	2993.3	600.1	-	0
EARN	Ellington Residential Mortgaging Re	REITs	12/31/17	35.5	10.8	1887.1	192.7	81	8807150
AKO B	Embotelladora Andiña S.A.	Beverages	12/31/17	1848878.6	117835.8	2114859.5	791310.1	27	615225
ERJ	Embraer SA	Aerospace	12/31/17	5839.3	246.8	11936.2	4068.6	271	106759619
EME	EMCOR Group, Inc.	Construction Services	12/31/17	7687.0	227.2	3965.9	1673.3	500	75306722
EEX	Emerald Expositions Events Inc	Services	12/31/17	348.2	81.8	1637.9	761.2	88	25929906
EMES	Emerge Energy Services LP	Equipment & Services	12/31/17	364.3	-6.8	308.9		72	10604584
EBS	Emergent BioSolutions Inc	Biotechnology	12/31/17	560.9	82.6	1070.2	912.3	352	50798510
EMR	Emerson Electric Co.	Electrical Equipment	9/30/17	15264.0	1518.0	19589.0	8718.0	1998	577817217
ESRT	Empire State Realty Trust Inc	REITs	12/31/17	712.5	63.6	3931.3	1168.3	246	155933612
EIG	Employers Holdings Inc	General Insurance	12/31/17	801.4	101.2	3840.1	947.7	233	34028440
EDN	Empresa Distribuidora y Comerciali	Electric Utilities	12/31/17	24340.0	682.2	25304.9	1060.9	54	5047665
ENBL	Enable Midstream Partners L.P.	Equipment & Services	12/31/17	2803.0	436.0	11593.0		108	81791816
EEQ	Enbridge Energy Management LLC	Equipment & Services	12/31/17	-43.0	-29.0	1.0	1.0	207	87756211
EEP	Enbridge Energy Partners, L.P.	Equipment & Services	12/31/17	2428.0	282.0	14828.0		415	148049229
ENB	Enbridge Inc	Equipment & Services	12/31/17	44378.0	2859.0	162093.0	58135.0	1018	1129094905
ECA	Encana Corp	Production & Extraction	12/31/17	4443.0	827.0	15267.0	6728.0	589	726343601
EHC	Encompass Health Corp	Hospitals & Health Care Facilities	12/31/17	3919.0	256.3	4893.7	1181.7	500	124663410
EXK	Endeavour Silver Corp	Precious Metals	12/31/17	150.5	9.7	178.6	146.5	98	27111213
NDRO	Enduro Royalty Trust	Oil Royalty Traders	12/31/17	45.6	44.7	94.1	94.1	36	39074481
ENIA	Enel Americas SA	Electric Utilities	12/31/17	10540.3	709.0	20169.0	6480.5	195	107426790
ENIC	Enel Chile SA	Electric Utilities	12/31/17	2529346.9	349382.6	5694773.0	2983384.0	127	63632356
EOCC	Enel Generacion Chile SA	Electric Utilities	12/31/17	1634937.1	418453.8	3554462.2	1961517.7	129	7880777
EGN	Energen Corp.	Production & Extraction	12/31/17	961.0	306.8	5033.9	3438.5	515	109871325
ENR	Energizer Holdings Inc (New)	Household & Personal Products	9/30/17	1755.7	201.5	1823.6	85.1	437	68565923
TXU 19	Energy Future Holdings Corp	Electric Utilities	12/31/15	5370.0	-5342.0	23330.0	-25061.0	67	17905838
ETE	Energy Transfer Equity LP	Equipment & Services	12/31/17	40523.0	954.0	86246.0		539	548984801
ETP	Energy Transfer Partners LP (New)	Equipment & Services	12/31/17	29054.0	2081.0	77965.0		73	13673321
ERF	Enerplus Corp	Production & Extraction	12/31/17	935.0	237.0	2645.8	1600.8	325	133661891
ENS	Enersys	Electrical Equipment	3/31/18	2581.9	119.6	2486.9	1195.7	379	51509149
EGL	Engility Holdings Inc (New)	IT Services	12/31/17	1931.9	-35.2	2026.0	665.5	192	38918228
E	ENI S.p.A.	Production & Extraction	12/31/17	70977.0	3374.0	114928.0	48030.0	258	35017287
ENLC	EnLink Midstream LLC	Equipment & Services	12/31/17	5739.6	212.8	10537.8	1922.2	159	64074976
ENLK	EnLink Midstream Partners LP	Refining & Marketing	12/31/17	5739.6	148.9	9414.0		213	166047984
EBF	Ennis Inc	Printing	2/28/18	370.2	32.9	329.4	261.7	195	28865553
ENVA	Enova International Inc	Credit & Lending	12/31/17	843.7	29.2	1159.5	281.7	199	36209485
NPO	EnPro Industries Inc	Industrial Machinery & Equipment	12/31/17	1309.6	539.8	1886.1	902.8	290	25713963
ESV	Ensco plc	Equipment & Services	12/31/17	1843.0	-303.7	14625.9	8732.1	560	495071012
ETM	Entercom Communications Corp	Radio & Television	12/31/17	592.9	233.0	4539.2	1764.4	286	128142596
ETM	Entercom Communications Corp	Radio & Television	12/31/17	592.9	233.0	4539.2	1764.4	286	128142596
ETR	Entergy Corp	Electric Utilities	12/31/17	11074.5	425.4	46707.1	8190.3	893	185954789
ELC	Entergy Louisiana LLC (New)	Electric Utilities	12/31/17	4300.6	316.3	18448.9	5308.8	1	66887
EZT	Entergy Texas Inc	Electric Utilities	12/31/17	1544.9	76.2	4279.7	1260.2		0
EPD	Enterprise Products Partners L.P.	Equipment & Services	12/31/17	29241.5	2799.3	54418.1		1290	877819672
EVC	Entravision Communications Corp.	Radio & Television	12/31/17	536.0	176.3	766.0	348.9	216	74311069
ENV	Envestnet Inc	Internet & Software	12/31/17	683.7	-3.3	862.1	437.2	260	50179884
EVHC	Envision Healthcare Corp	Hospitals & Health Care Facilities	12/31/17	7819.3	-228.0	16572.6	6527.1		0
EVA	Enviva Partners LP	Paper & Forest Products	12/31/17	543.2	17.5	760.1		72	18527026
ENZ	Enzo Biochem, Inc.	Diagnostic & Health Related Service	7/31/17	107.8	-2.5	107.7	88.9	162	36518012
EOG	EOG Resources, Inc.	Production & Extraction	12/31/17	11208.3	2582.6	29833.1	16283.3	1451	576625026
EPE	EP Energy Corp.	Production & Extraction	12/31/17	1066.0	-194.0	4900.0	392.0	115	176175865
EPAM	Epam Systems, Inc.	Internet & Software	12/31/17	1450.4	72.8	1250.3	974.9	373	55214187
EPR	EPR Properties	REITs	12/31/17	576.0	263.0	6191.5	2927.3	496	89267837
EQT	EQT Corp	Production & Extraction	12/31/17	3378.0	1508.5	29522.6	13319.6	850	263129612
EQGP	EQT GP Holdings LP	Equipment & Services	12/31/17	834.1	262.0	3549.6		84	28017208
EQM	EQT Midstream Partners LP	Equipment & Services	12/31/17	834.1	571.9	3548.8		278	58792840
EFX	Equifax Inc	Business Services	12/31/17	3362.2	587.3	7223.4	3174.4	748	157304763
EQNR	Equinor ASA	Refining & Marketing	12/31/17	61187.0	4590.0	111100.0	39861.0	354	174148220
EQC	Equity Commonwealth	REITs	12/31/17	340.6	29.7	4236.9	3299.4	368	155214655
ELS	Equity Lifestyle Properties Inc	REITs	12/31/17	925.3	197.6	3610.0	1032.0	363	97472585
EQR	Equity Residential	REITs	12/31/17	2471.4	603.5	20570.6	10242.5	811	449316243

T22

EARNINGS PER SHARE QUARTERLY			ANNUAL			P/E RATIO		DIVIDENDS PER SHARE			AV. YLD %	DIV. DECLARED		PRICE RANGE 2017	
1st	2nd	3rd	2017	2016	2015			2017	2016	2015		AMOUNT	PAYABLE		
-	-	-	-	0.09	0.09	-		-	1.16	1.16		0.160	6/29/18	11.9 -	9.0
-	-	0.49	0.82	1.00		54.5 -	47.7	2.16	2.16	3.13	8.6	0.180	7/31/18	26.7 -	23.4
-	-	0.19	0.20	-				-	1.30	1.30		0.1080	7/31/18	17.1 -	15.4
-	-	0.12	0.11	-				-	1.33	1.33		0.11080	7/31/18	15.6 -	14.5
-	-	0.10	0.12	0.21		125.8 -	110.1	1.01	1.01	1.01	8.5	0.08430	7/31/18	12.6 -	11.0
-	-	0.09	0.20	0.13		109.1 -	98.0	0.93	0.98	0.98	10.0	0.0760	7/31/18	9.8 -	8.8
0.06	-	0.33	0.20	0.28		7.6 -	4.5	0.33	0.19	0.40	15.6	0.0590	5/31/18	2.5 -	1.5
-0.01	-	0.03	-0.84	-4.46		103.0 -	41.7	-						3.1 -	1.3
0.84	-	5.13	4.14	3.32		29.2 -	24.9	1.52	1.42	1.34	1.1	0.410Y	18/78/27	149.8 -	127.8
-	-	-	59.50	-175.00		-		-	-	2639.93				23.2 -	8.8
-	1.20	-	0.10	2.99	-4.44	763.3 -	414.0	-						76.3 -	41.4
0.67	-	1.72	3.97	3.10		48.0 -	33.8	2.23	1.98	1.73	3.2	0.6050Y	18/78/27	82.6 -	58.1
0.53	-	0.60	0.65	0.40		69.3 -	50.5	1.54	1.50	1.46	4.3	0.390Z	18/78/27	41.6 -	30.3
0.96	-	2.70	2.61	2.25		57.0 -	37.5	-						153.9 -	101.4
-	-	0.88	0.24	5.42		15.3 -	10.1	-						13.4 -	8.9
-0.17	-	2.42	2.39	2.03		25.2 -	20.0	1.31	1.23	1.17	2.4	0.360Y	9/28/18	60.9 -	48.4
0.01	-	-0.01	-0.48	-2.15		-		0.01	-	0.02	0.6	0.020	3/16/17	3.4 -	0.8
0.22	-	-0.20	-1.74	-1.59		-		-						9.4 -	6.0
0.06	-	1.48	1.15	0.72		78.3 -	54.6	-						115.8 -	80.9
0.33	-	1.10	1.09	1.98		14.9 -	12.8	1.76	1.95	2.45	11.4	0.410	6/15/18	16.4 -	14.1
-0.30	-	0.93	1.31	-		16.1 -	11.2	1.57	1.65	2.00	12.5	0.370Z	7/25/18	14.9 -	10.4
-	-	15.50	118.56	91.08	88.40	0.3 -	0.2	480.70	361.95	293.99	1714.7			31.6 -	22.5
-0.02	-	0.34	0.23	0.09		82.2 -	53.9	0.35	0.09	0.16	1.5			27.9 -	18.3
0.94	-	3.82	2.97	2.72		22.0 -	16.3	0.32	0.32	0.32	0.4	0.080Y	18/78/27	84.1 -	62.5
0.50	-	1.13	0.35	0.31		21.0 -	16.6	0.21	-	-	1.0	0.07250Y	5/29/18	23.7 -	18.8
0.05	-	-0.23	-2.92	-0.39		-		-	-	3.08		0.670	8/13/15	10.0 -	5.8
-0.10	-	1.71	1.13	1.41		32.5 -	19.7	-						55.6 -	33.7
-	0.76	-	2.35	2.52	3.99	31.5 -	24.7	1.92	1.90	1.88	2.9	0.4850Y	18/78/27	74.1 -	58.0
0.06	-	0.39	0.38	0.29		54.0 -	41.0	0.42	0.40	0.34	2.2	0.1050Z	18/78/27	21.1 -	16.0
-0.77	-	3.06	3.24	2.90		16.3 -	12.7	0.60	0.36	0.24	1.4	0.20Y	5/23/18	50.0 -	38.8
-	-	-0.62	0.76	-1.33	1.27	82.3 -	38.8	-						62.5 -	29.5
0.24	-	0.92	0.69	-1.78		19.6 -	14.2	1.27	1.27	1.26	8.5	0.3180	5/29/18	18.0 -	13.0
-0.02	-	-0.34	-1.54	-7.26		-		-						16.1 -	8.5
0.15	-	0.50	-1.08	-0.25		33.3 -	18.0	1.63	2.33	2.31	12.3	0.350	5/15/18	16.6 -	9.0
0.26	-	1.65	1.93	-0.04		32.0 -	17.7	2.41	2.12	1.86	5.8	0.39840	10/15/18	52.8 -	29.3
0.16	-	0.85	-1.07	-6.28		21.0 -	9.9	0.06	0.06	0.08	0.5	0.0150	6/29/18	17.8 -	8.4
0.84	-	2.69	2.59	1.91		25.7 -	15.8	0.98	0.94	0.88	1.9	0.270Y	18/78/27	69.2 -	42.5
0.02	-	0.08	0.03	-1.47		54.1 -	24.8	-						4.3 -	2.0
0.07	-	1.36	0.26	0.42		3.2 -	2.1	1.36	0.24	0.38	39.9	0.04320Z	8/14/18	4.3 -	2.8
-	-	0.01	7.70	13.48		1199.0 -	875.0	0.22	204.75	258.47	2.1			12.0 -	8.8
-	-	7.12	6.47	-		0.9 -	0.7	104.15	76.96	-	1783.8			6.5 -	4.8
-	-	51.02	57.62	47.90		0.6 -	0.4	786.49	359.31	485.80	3125.6			29.0 -	20.0
1.22	-	3.14	-1.77	-12.43		23.2 -	15.1	-	-	0.08		0.020Y	18/78/27	72.8 -	47.4
-	0.13	-	3.22	2.04	-0.06	19.6 -	12.8	1.10	1.00	0.25	2.2	0.290	18/78/27	63.0 -	41.1
0.31	-	0.83	0.92	1.11		23.1 -	17.1	1.15	1.14	1.02	6.8	0.3050	18/78/27	19.2 -	14.2
0.24	-	0.93	0.98	0.42		23.0 -	16.9	2.17	1.98	1.72	11.8	0.5650	18/78/27	21.4 -	15.7
0.12	-	0.96	1.72	-7.39		17.5 -	8.0	0.12	0.16	0.64	1.0	0.010Y	8/15/18	16.8 -	7.7
-	-	-0.61	3.64	2.99	3.77	22.5 -	16.9	0.70	0.70	0.70	1.0	0.1750	18/78/27	81.9 -	61.5
0.17	-	-0.96	-0.29	-7.02		-		-						35.6 -	22.3
-	-	1.10	0.94	-0.41	-2.44	42.6 -	31.4	1.16	1.14	1.35	3.4			40.1 -	29.5
0.07	-	1.17	-2.56	-2.17		16.9 -	11.8	1.02	1.02	0.98	6.1	0.2670	8/14/18	19.8 -	13.9
0.06	-	0.05	-1.99	-4.66		368.4 -	260.8	1.56	1.56	1.53	9.9	0.390	8/13/18	18.4 -	13.0
0.36	-	0.07	1.39	-1.72		302.9 -	254.3	2.20	0.70	0.70	11.2	0.2250Y	8/3/18	21.2 -	17.8
0.81	-	0.86	1.03	1.33		42.7 -	13.1	-						36.8 -	11.3
0.58	-	24.76	-1.86	-0.93		3.8 -	2.7	0.88	0.84	0.80	1.1	0.240	6/20/18	94.3 -	67.2
-0.32	-	-0.91	3.13	-6.88		-		0.04	0.04	0.60		0.010	18/78/27		
-0.10	-	4.38	0.91	0.73		2.8 -	1.5	0.52	0.23	-	5.1	0.090Y	6/28/18	12.3 -	6.4
-0.10	-	4.38	0.91	0.73		2.7 -	2.4	0.52	0.23	-	4.8	0.090Y	6/28/18	11.9 -	10.4
0.73	-	2.28	-3.26	-0.99		38.3 -	31.6	3.50	3.42	3.34	4.4	0.890Y	18/78/27	87.4 -	72.0
-	-	-	-	-		-		1.22	0.35	-	5.0	0.30470Z	9/4/18	25.1 -	23.1
-	-	-	-	-		-		1.41	1.41	1.41	5.6	0.35160Z	9/4/18	27.4 -	0.0
0.41	-	1.30	1.20	1.26		22.7 -	18.4	1.67	1.59	1.51	6.3	0.430	18/78/27	29.5 -	23.9
-0.02	-	1.92	0.22	0.28		4.0 -	2.1	0.16	0.13	0.11	2.7	0.050Y	6/29/18	7.8 -	4.0
0.17	-	-0.08	-1.30	0.12		-		-						59.8 -	37.5
-0.71	-	-1.93	-0.47	3.16		-		-				1.31250Y	7/3/17	62.9 -	24.8
-0.78	-	0.61	0.91	1.58		51.6 -	41.1	2.27	2.02	0.70	8.0	0.6250	5/29/18	31.4 -	25.1
-	-0.06	-0.05	0.97	-0.05		-		-						11.8 -	5.1
1.10	-	4.46	-1.98	-8.29		28.6 -	18.6	0.67	0.67	0.67	0.6	0.1850Y	18/78/27	127.5 -	83.2
0.07	-	-0.79	-0.11	-15.37		-		-						3.9 -	1.3
1.15	-	1.32	1.87	1.62		98.3 -	59.7	-						129.7 -	78.8
0.32	-	3.29	3.17	2.93		22.4 -	16.1	4.08	3.84	3.63	6.4	0.360Z	18/78/27	73.8 -	53.0
-5.99	-	8.04	-2.71	0.56		8.3 -	5.7	0.12	0.12	0.12	0.2	0.030Y	18/78/27	67.0 -	45.7
0.30	-	0.98	0.80	0.39		31.1 -	22.4	0.81	0.57	0.15	3.1	0.2580	5/24/18	30.5 -	22.0
1.61	-	5.19	5.21	4.70		15.0 -	9.9	3.65	3.05	2.50	5.4	1.0650	5/15/18	78.1 -	51.3
0.75	-	4.83	4.04	3.55		30.3 -	19.3	1.56	1.32	1.16	1.3	0.390Y	18/78/27	146.3 -	93.0
-	0.44	-	1.40	-0.91	-11.80	19.6 -	11.7	0.76	0.69	6.73	3.5			27.4 -	16.3
1.48	-	0.17	1.62	0.56		190.1 -	165.3	-				0.40630Z	8/15/18	32.3 -	28.1
0.68	-	2.17	1.92	1.54		42.7 -	37.6	1.95	1.70	1.50	2.2	0.550Z	18/78/27	92.6 -	81.5
0.57	-	1.63	11.68	2.36		43.2 -	33.9	2.02	13.02	2.21	3.2	1.03620Z	18/78/27	70.4 -	55.3

SYMBOL	COMPANY	NATURE OF BUSINESS	FISCAL YEAR-END	TOTAL REV. $MILL	NET INCOME $MILL	TOTAL ASSETS $MILL	NET STK EQUITY $MILL	NO OF INST	INST. HOLDINGS (SHARES)
EQS	Equus Total Return, Inc.	Holding and other Investment Office	12/31/17	0.6	-4.0	61.2	43.0	19	1409865
ERA	ERA Group Inc	Miscellaneous Transportation Servic	12/31/17	231.3	-28.2	792.1	445.7	137	20775046
EROS	Eros International Plc	Entertainment	3/31/17	253.0	3.8	1343.4	804.5	102	35192976
ESE	ESCO Technologies, Inc.	Industrial Machinery & Equipment	9/30/17	685.7	53.7	1260.4	671.9	240	31341740
ESNT	Essent Group Ltd	General Insurance	12/31/17	576.5	379.7	2674.4	1940.4	329	99697233
EPRT	Essential Properties Realty Trust In	Property, Real Estate & Developmen	12/31/17	54.5	6.3	942.2	181.4		0
ESS	Essex Property Trust Inc	REITs	12/31/17	1363.9	433.1	12495.7	6277.4	616	79099276
ESL	Esterline Technologies Corp	Electronic Instruments & Related Pro	9/29/17	2002.2	117.4	3130.3	1836.6	341	36398711
ETH	Ethan Allen Interiors, Inc.	Retail - Furniture & Home Furnishing	6/30/17	763.4	36.2	568.2	400.7	247	33268210
EURN	Euronav NV	Shipping	12/31/17	513.4	1.4	2811.0	1846.4	85	38513793
EEA	European Equity Fund Inc (The)	Holding and other Investment Office	12/31/16	2.0	0.9	72.9	72.1	39	3508763
EVR	Evercore Inc	Finance Intermediaries & Services	12/31/17	1704.3	125.5	1584.9	544.0	455	47719534
RE	Everest Re Group Ltd	General Insurance	12/31/17	6608.1	469.0	23591.8	8369.2	647	47493779
EVRG	Evergy Inc	Electric Utilities							0
EVRI	Everi Holdings Inc	Internet & Software	12/31/17	974.9	-51.9	1537.1	-140.6	223	81709937
ES	Eversource Energy	Electric Utilities	12/31/17	7752.0	988.0	36220.4	11086.2	131	24690998
EVTC	Evertec, Inc.	Business Services	12/31/17	407.1	55.1	902.8	144.1	205	66638831
EVH	Evolent Health Inc	Business Services	12/31/17	434.9	-60.7	1312.7	1010.9	193	83968401
AQUA	Evoqua Water Technologies Corp	Industrial Machinery & Equipment	9/30/17	1247.4	2.2	1473.3	211.4	132	57450843
XAN	Exantas Capital Corp	REITs	12/31/17	101.4	33.5	1912.1	671.5	157	25182069
EXC	Exelon Corp	Electric Utilities	12/31/17	33531.0	3770.0	116700.0	29857.0	1336	896188070
EXPR	Express Inc	Retail - Apparel and Accessories	2/3/18	2138.0	19.4	1187.6	654.0	261	97140455
EXTN	Exterran Corp	Equipment & Services	12/31/17	1215.3	33.9	1460.8	554.8	203	37106061
EXR	Extra Space Storage Inc	REITs	12/31/17	1105.0	479.0	7455.1	2350.8	594	168217796
XOM	Exxon Mobil Corp	Production & Extraction	12/31/17	244363.0	19710.0	348691.0	187688.0	3330	2966287962
FN	Fabrinet	Manufacturing	6/30/17	1420.5	97.1	1033.1	681.6	265	48506648
FDS	FactSet Research Systems Inc.	Business Services	8/31/17	1221.2	258.3	1413.3	559.7	581	48776621
FICO	Fair Isaac Corp	Internet & Software	9/30/17	932.2	128.3	1255.6	426.5	421	37600949
SFUN	Fang Holdings Ltd	Internet & Software	12/31/17	444.3	21.7	2000.3	739.6	148	198860666
FPAC U	Far Point Acquisition Corp	IT Services & Software	3/16/18		-0.0	0.1	0.0		0
FPI	Farmland Partners Inc	REITs	12/31/17	46.2	7.9	1166.1	468.7	136	17791569
FBK	FB Financial Corp	Banking	12/31/17	311.2	52.4	4727.7	596.7	118	12457355
FFG	FBL Financial Group Inc	Life & Health	12/31/17	735.5	194.3	10066.6	1388.8	138	9008672
FCB	FCB Financial Holdings Inc	Banking	12/31/17	409.1	125.2	10677.1	1179.2	222	46876858
AGM	Federal Agricultural Mortgage Corp	Credit & Lending	12/31/17	418.0	84.5	17792.3	708.1	184	8793795
FRT	Federal Realty Investment Trust (M	REITs	12/31/17	857.3	289.9	6275.8	2266.7	565	89793449
FSS	Federal Signal Corp.	Industrial Machinery & Equipment	12/31/17	898.5	61.6	992.3	457.4	256	66751719
FII	Federated Investors Inc (PA)	Wealth Management	12/31/17	1102.9	291.3	1231.4	761.2	489	118890016
FMN	Federated Premier Municipal Incom	Holding and other Investment Office	11/30/16	6.5	5.1	145.4	108.2	42	1628529
FDX	FedEx Corp	Airlines/Air Freight	5/31/18	65450.0	4572.0	52330.0	19416.0	1872	239511638
RACE	Ferrari NV (New)	Autos- Manufacturing	12/31/17	3416.9	535.4	4141.1	778.7	342	63182789
FGP	Ferrellgas Partners LP	Gas Utilities	7/31/17	1930.3	-54.2	1610.0		131	7815201
FOE	Ferro Corp	Specialty Chemicals	12/31/17	1396.7	57.1	1682.2	344.8	289	88608166
FCAU	Fiat Chrysler Automobiles NV	Autos- Manufacturing	12/31/17	110934.0	3491.0	96299.0	20819.0	351	509553039
FBR	Fibria Celulose SA	Paper & Forest Products	12/31/17	11739.2	1085.3	38693.3	14577.2	157	55836459
FNF	Fidelity National Financial Inc	General Insurance	12/31/17	7663.0	771.0	9151.0	4447.0	633	283584085
FNF	Fidelity National Financial Inc - FNF	General Insurance	12/31/15	9132.0	527.0	13931.0	5754.0		0
FIS	Fidelity National Information Service	Business Services	12/31/17	9123.0	1319.0	24517.0	10835.0	985	347262840
FMO	Fiduciary / Claymore MLP Opportun	Holding and other Investment Office	11/30/16	3.2	-4.8	805.1	496.8	96	7575169
FAF	First American Financial Corp	General Insurance	12/31/17	5772.4	423.0	9573.2	3480.0	472	108187621
FBP	First Bancorp	Banking	12/31/17	650.8	67.0	12261.3	1869.1	261	224484140
FCF	First Commonwealth Financial Corp	Banking	12/31/17	330.9	55.2	7308.5	888.1	243	85731565
FDC	First Data Corp (New)	IT Services	12/31/17	12052.0	1465.0	48269.0	3152.0	528	547865852
FHN	First Horizon National Corp	Banking	12/31/17	1480.1	165.5	41423.4	4285.1	507	320493076
FR	First Industrial Realty Trust Inc	REITs	12/31/17	396.4	201.5	2941.1	1427.8	392	156557977
AG	First Majestic Silver Corp	Precious Metals	12/31/17	252.3	-53.3	781.4	582.5	167	59203104
FRC	First Republic Bank (San Francisco,	Banking	12/31/17	2912.1	757.7	87780.5	7818.3	631	204928139
FEO	First Trust / Aberdeen Emerging Op	Holding and other Investment Office	12/31/16	4.9	3.4	90.1	83.7	34	1686096
FDEU	First Trust Dynamic Europe Equity I	Holding and other Investment Office	12/31/16	18.3	12.7	401.4	309.5	44	4483713
FIF	First Trust Energy Infrastructure Fu	Holding and other Investment Office	11/30/16	9.8	3.6	477.5	339.0	50	4835109
FFA	First Trust Enhanced Equity Income	Holding and other Investment Office	12/31/16	7.1	3.7	305.0	304.1	62	6057844
FSD	First Trust High Income Long/Short	Holding and other Investment Office	10/31/16	44.6	35.4	788.8	624.1	79	10964086
FPF	First Trust Intermediate Duration Pr	Finance Intermediaries & Services	10/31/16	144.0	117.5	2126.1	1459.9	98	10520934
FEI	First Trust MLP & Energy Income F	Finance Intermediaries & Services	10/31/16	11.5	-2.4	976.7	701.5	73	13435885
FMY	First Trust Mortgage Income Fund	Holding and other Investment Office	10/31/17	1.5	0.7	65.3	65.2	23	3183108
FPL	First Trust New Opportunities MLP	Finance Intermediaries & Services	10/31/16	5.2	21.6	418.3	307.9	50	5305819
FIV	First Trust Senior Floating Rate 202	Holding and other Investment Office	5/31/17	8.4	5.8	526.8	353.9	41	5960252
FCT	First Trust Senior Floating Rate Inco	Holding and other Investment Office	5/31/17	28.6	20.7	576.4	381.3	85	10279822
FGB	First Trust Specialty Finance and Fi	Holding and other Investment Office	11/30/16	11.2	9.5	125.6	97.8	36	1892607
FAM	First Trust/Aberdeen Global Opport	Holding and other Investment Office	12/31/16	17.3	12.6	291.9	208.5	57	4798415
FCFS	FirstCash Inc	Retail - Specialty	12/31/17	1779.8	143.9	2062.8	1475.3	335	53031785
FE	FirstEnergy Corp	Electric Utilities	12/31/17	14017.0	-1724.0	42257.0	3925.0	878	513713267
FIT	Fitbit Inc	Computer Hardware & Equipment	12/31/17	1615.5	-277.2	1582.1	824.0	270	149775104
FPH	Five Point Holdings LLC	Property, Real Estate & Developmen	12/31/17	139.4	73.2	2978.4	585.4	70	50381537
FBC	Flagstar Bancorp, Inc.	Credit & Lending	12/31/17	997.0	63.0	16912.0	1399.0	191	62849168
DFP	Flaherty & Crumrine Dynamic Prefe	Finance Intermediaries & Services	11/30/16	43.8	35.3	711.9	462.2	61	2227937
PFD	Flaherty & Crumrine Preferred Inco	Holding and other Investment Office	11/30/16	15.2	12.1	224.2	146.5	44	622956
PFO	Flaherty & Crumrine Preferred Inco	Holding and other Investment Office	11/30/16	13.8	10.9	209.1	136.8	53	1302610
FFC	Flaherty & Crumrine Preferred Secu	Holding and other Investment Office	11/30/16	82.8	69.3	1250.4	814.8	120	7517997
FLC	Flaherty & Crumrine Total Return F	Holding and other Investment Office	11/30/16	19.9	15.8	302.1	196.9	51	2189690

T24

EARNINGS PER SHARE QUARTERLY 1st	2nd	3rd	ANNUAL 2017	2016	2015	P/E RATIO		DIVIDENDS PER SHARE 2017	2016	2015	AV. YLD %	DIV. DECLARED AMOUNT	PAYABLE	PRICE RANGE 2017	
0.00	-	-	-0.30	-0.19	-0.19	-		-	-	-	-	0.1580	9/29/08	2.5 -	0.0
-0.06	-	-	-1.36	-0.39	0.42									13.9 -	8.3
-	-	-	0.05	0.05	0.72										
-	0.38	-	2.07	1.77	1.62	32.1 -	24.8	0.24	0.32	0.32	0.4	0.080Y	7/19/18	66.3 -	51.4
1.13	-	-	3.99	2.41	1.72										
-	-	-	-	-	-									13.7 -	13.5
1.38	-	-	6.57	6.27	3.49	41.0 -	33.2	7.00	6.40	5.76	2.8	1.860Z	18/78/27	269.4 -	217.8
-	0.80	-	3.91	3.42	1.91	25.6 -	17.5	-	-	-	-	0.09	18/78/27	100.1 -	68.5
-	-	0.09	1.29	2.00	1.27	25.2 -	17.1	0.72	0.59	0.46	2.6	0.190Y	7/25/18	32.5 -	22.1
-	-	-	0.01	1.29	2.22			0.12							
-	-	-	-	0.11	0.09			-	0.08	0.17	-	0.03020	6/26/18	10.7 -	9.2
2.10	-	-	2.80	2.43	0.98	40.0 -	25.1	1.42	1.27	1.15	1.6	0.50Y	18/78/27	112.1 -	70.3
5.11	-	-	11.36	23.68	22.10			5.05	4.70	4.00	-	1.30	18/78/27		
-	-	-	-	-	-									57.2 -	48.7
0.06	-	-	-0.78	-3.78	-1.59									8.9 -	6.2
0.85	-	-	3.11	2.96	2.76	21.2 -	17.0	1.90	1.78	1.67	3.1	0.5050Y	18/78/27	65.8 -	52.9
0.31	-	-	0.76	1.01	1.11	29.9 -	17.1	0.30	0.40	0.40	1.8	0.10Y	9/8/17	22.8 -	13.0
-0.18	-	-	-0.94	-3.55	6.93									26.9 -	10.5
-	0.10	-	0.02	0.11	-0.85	1259.5 -	925.5							25.2 -	18.5
-0.40	-	-	0.18	-1.73	-0.43	61.8 -	48.0	0.20	1.31	1.06	2.0	0.53910Z	7/30/18	11.1 -	8.6
0.60	-	-	3.97	1.22	2.54	10.7 -	8.9	1.31	1.26	1.24	3.4	0.3450Y	18/78/27	42.6 -	35.5
0.01	-	-	0.73	1.38	0.81	15.4 -	7.3	-	-	-	-	0.567	12/23/10	11.2 -	5.3
0.15	-	-	0.97	-6.59	1.35	34.1 -	24.2							33.1 -	23.5
0.70	-	-	3.76	2.91	1.56	26.9 -	19.7	3.12	2.93	2.24	3.7	0.860Z	18/78/27	101.0 -	74.1
1.09	-	-	4.63	1.88	3.85	19.2 -	15.7	3.06	2.98	2.88	3.8	0.820Y	18/78/27	89.1 -	72.8
-	-	0.55	2.57	1.68	1.21										
-	-	1.91	6.51	8.19	5.71	33.1 -	23.9	2.12	1.88	1.66	1.1	0.640Y	18/78/27	215.8 -	155.5
-	1.03	-	3.98	3.39	2.65	50.8 -	33.1	0.04	0.08	0.08	0.0	0.020Y	18/78/27	202.1 -	131.8
-	-	1.22	0.24	-1.81	-0.18	23.3 -	12.5	-	-	0.19	-			5.6 -	3.0
-	-	-	-	-	-									10.2 -	10.2
-0.08	-	-	0.03	0.09	0.08	317.7 -	241.0	0.51	0.51	0.50	6.0	0.3750Y	6/29/18	9.5 -	7.2
0.63	-	-	1.86	2.10	2.79	24.0 -	17.7	0.00	4.03	1.37	0.0	0.060Y	8/15/18	44.7 -	33.0
0.94	-	-	7.75	4.28	4.53	11.0 -	8.0	3.26	3.68	3.60	4.5	0.460Y	6/29/18	85.0 -	61.9
0.84	-	-	2.71	2.31	1.23	23.1 -	15.0	-	-	-	-			62.5 -	40.6
2.10	-	-	6.60	5.97	4.19	14.4 -	9.6	1.44	1.04	0.64	1.8	0.3750Y	7/17/18	95.3 -	63.3
0.81	-	-	3.97	3.50	3.03	34.0 -	27.2	3.96	3.84	3.62	3.2	0.31250Z	18/78/27	135.0 -	108.1
0.21	-	-	1.02	0.71	1.00	24.3 -	17.0	0.28	0.28	0.25	1.3	0.080Y	5/29/18	24.8 -	17.4
0.60	-	-	2.87	2.03	1.62	12.7 -	8.0	1.00	2.00	1.00	3.3	0.270Y	18/78/27	36.5 -	23.0
-	-	-	-	0.81	0.87			-	0.86	0.88	-	0.054M	8/1/18	15.1 -	13.2
-	-	7.59	11.07	6.51	3.65	24.8 -	18.4	1.60	1.00	0.80	0.7	0.650Y	18/78/27	274.3 -	203.6
-	-	0.74	2.82	2.11	1.52			-	-	-	-	0.710	5/2/18		
-	-	0.10	-0.55	-6.68	0.35			0.81	2.05	2.00	19.3	0.10	6/14/18	5.6 -	3.0
0.27	-	-	0.67	-0.25	0.72	37.8 -	26.7	-	-	-	-	0.010Y	3/10/09	25.4 -	17.9
0.65	-	-	2.24	1.18	-0.22							7.8750	12/15/16		
-	-	-	1.96	2.98	0.62	11.2 -	4.9	0.61	0.46	3.93	3.8			21.9 -	9.7
0.35	-	-	2.38	2.34	1.89	17.6 -	13.4	1.02	0.88	0.80	2.7	0.30Y	18/78/27	41.9 -	31.8
-	-	-	-	-	1.89			-	-	0.80	-	0.30Y	9/28/18	41.9 -	31.8
0.54	-	-	3.93	1.72	2.19	27.4 -	21.7	1.16	1.04	1.04	1.2	0.320Y	18/78/27	107.7 -	85.5
-	-	-	-	-0.14	-0.11			-	1.72	1.71	-	0.32310	5/31/18	15.3 -	10.4
0.67	-	-	3.76	3.09	2.62	16.5 -	11.7	1.44	1.20	1.00	2.7	0.380Y	18/78/27	62.1 -	44.1
0.15	-	-	0.30	0.43	0.10	27.1 -	15.5	-	-	-	-	0.14580	7/31/18	8.1 -	4.7
0.24	-	-	0.58	0.67	0.56	28.1 -	20.9	0.32	0.28	0.28	2.2	0.090Y	5/18/18	16.3 -	12.1
0.11	-	-	1.56	0.46	-7.70	14.1 -	9.6	-	-	-	-			21.9 -	15.0
0.27	-	-	0.65	0.94	0.34	31.7 -	24.7	0.36	0.28	0.24	1.9	0.38750Y	18/78/27	20.6 -	16.1
0.30	-	-	1.69	1.05	0.67	19.9 -	16.4	0.84	0.76	0.51	2.7	0.21750Z	18/78/27	33.7 -	27.8
-0.03	-	-	-0.32	0.05	-0.84			-	-	-	-			10.4 -	0.0
1.13	-	-	4.31	3.93	3.18	24.4 -	19.7	0.67	0.63	0.59	0.7	0.180Y	18/78/27	105.2 -	85.0
-	-	-	-	0.64	0.65			-	1.40	1.40	-	0.350	6/29/18	17.4 -	13.4
-	-	-	-	0.73	0.04			-	1.45	0.12	-	0.1210	8/15/18	20.0 -	16.0
-	-	-	-	0.21	0.34			-	1.66	1.32	-	0.110	8/15/18	19.2 -	14.8
-	-	-	-	0.19	0.20			-	0.95	0.94	-	0.2850	6/29/18	16.7 -	14.5
-	-	-	-	1.00	1.11			-	1.06	1.26	-	0.1050	8/15/18	17.2 -	14.7
-	-	-	-	1.94	1.96			-	1.95	2.11	-	0.14250	8/15/18	25.1 -	21.5
-	-	-	-	-0.05	0.07			-	1.42	1.38	-	0.11830	8/15/18	16.3 -	11.8
-	-	-	0.18	-0.02	1.02	80.4 -	0.0	0.71	0.91	1.02	5.2	0.060	8/15/18	14.5 -	0.0
-	-	-	-	0.91	-0.22			-	1.26	1.22	-	0.1050	8/15/18	13.3 -	9.6
-	-	-	0.17	-	-	59.1 -	53.2	0.13	-	-	1.4	0.04170	8/15/18	10.1 -	9.0
-	-	-	0.78	0.83	0.87	17.3 -	16.3	0.76	0.88	0.84	5.8	0.060	8/15/18	13.5 -	12.7
-	-	-	-	0.66	0.64			-	0.70	0.69	-	0.1750	5/31/18	7.3 -	5.9
-	-	-	-	0.73	0.82			-	0.90	1.14	-	0.070	8/15/18	12.0 -	9.9
0.90	-	-	3.00	1.72	2.14	31.7 -	19.3	0.77	0.56	-	1.1	0.220	5/31/18	95.2 -	57.9
2.54	-	-	-3.88	-14.49	1.37			1.44	1.44	1.44	4.4	0.360Y	18/78/27	36.5 -	29.1
-0.34	-	-	-1.19	-0.47	0.75									7.6 -	4.6
-0.10	-	-	0.18	-0.89	-0.07	83.9 -	59.0							15.1 -	10.6
0.60	-	-	1.09	2.66	2.24	36.0 -	27.4	-	-	-	-	0.50Y	12/31/07	39.2 -	29.9
-	-	-	-	1.84	1.79			-	1.92	1.92	-	0.1480	10/31/18	27.2 -	22.8
-	-	-	-	1.09	1.10			-	1.08	1.08	-	0.0780	10/31/18	15.9 -	13.3
-	-	-	-	0.88	0.90			-	0.88	0.88	-	0.0660	10/31/18	12.9 -	10.6
-	-	-	-	1.58	1.61			-	1.63	1.63	-	0.1140	10/31/18	22.3 -	18.3
-	-	-	-	1.60	1.65			-	1.63	1.63	-	0.1190	10/31/18	22.4 -	19.1

SYMBOL	COMPANY	NATURE OF BUSINESS	FISCAL YEAR-END	TOTAL REV. $MILL	NET INCOME $MILL	TOTAL ASSETS $MILL	NET STK EQUITY $MILL	NO. OF INST	INST. HOLDINGS (SHARES)
FLT	FleetCor Technologies Inc	Business Services	12/31/17	2249.5	740.2	11318.4	3676.5	548	92903083
FND	Floor & Decor Holdings Inc	Construction Materials	12/28/17	1384.8	102.8	1068.0	442.9	198	91470877
FTK	Flotek Industries Inc	Specialty Chemicals	12/31/17	317.1	-27.4	329.9	264.9	201	56189784
FLO	Flowers Foods, Inc.	Food	12/30/17	3920.7	150.1	2659.7	1250.7	464	165708362
FLS	Flowserve Corp	Industrial Machinery & Equipment	12/31/17	3660.8	2.7	4910.5	1654.6	613	158287216
FLR	Fluor Corp.	Construction Services	12/31/17	19521.0	191.4	9327.7	3342.3	790	142031631
FLY	Fly Leasing Ltd	Airlines/Air Freight	12/31/17	353.3	2.6	3595.6	543.7	105	21941563
FMC	FMC Corp.	Agricultural Chemicals	12/31/17	2878.6	535.8	9206.3	2681.8	779	137593615
FNB	FNB Corp	Banking	12/31/17	1232.8	199.2	31417.6	4409.2	435	297916672
FMX	Fomento Economico Mexicano, S A	Beverages	12/31/17	460456.0	42408.0	588541.0	250291.0	361	124746310
FL	Foot Locker, Inc.	Retail - Apparel and Accessories	2/3/18	7782.0	284.0	3961.0	2519.0	716	146262863
F	Ford Motor Co. (DE)	Autos- Manufacturing	12/31/17	156776.0	7602.0	257808.0	34890.0	1655	2910971955
F 12A	Ford Motor Credit Company LLC	Credit & Lending	12/31/17	4067.0	3007.0	160443.0	15884.0	1	2
FELP	Foresight Energy LP	Mining	12/31/17	724.1	-104.0	2606.6		30	9276083
FCE A	Forest City Realty Trust Inc	REITs	12/31/17	911.9	206.0	8063.3	3428.4	327	251529609
FOR	Forestar Group Inc (New)	Property, Real Estate & Developmen	12/31/17	114.3	50.3	761.9	604.2	157	16820774
FOR	Forestar Group Inc (New)	Property, Real Estate & Developmen	12/31/17	114.3	50.3	761.9	604.2	157	16820774
FTS	Fortis Inc	Electric Utilities	12/31/17	8301.0	963.0	47822.0	15003.0	·	0
FTV	Fortive Corp	Industrial Machinery & Equipment	12/31/17	6656.0	1044.5	10500.6	3790.3	930	299645471
FTAI	Fortress Transportation & Infrastruct	Miscellaneous Transportation Servic	12/31/17	217.7	0.1	1955.8	947.1	100	26525631
FSM	Fortuna Silver Mines Inc	Precious Metals	12/31/17	268.1	66.3	706.6	563.6	138	67072023
FBHS	Fortune Brands Home & Security, In	Household Appliances, Electronics &	12/31/17	5283.3	472.6	5511.4	2599.5	689	154773251
FET	Forum Energy Technologies Inc	Equipment & Services	12/31/17	818.6	-59.4	2195.2	1409.0	208	117080459
FBM	Foundation Building Materials Inc	Construction Materials	12/31/17	2060.9	82.5	1354.2	378.7	95	40000487
FCPT	Four Corners Property Trust Inc	REITs	12/31/17	133.2	71.4	1068.7	514.5	285	61533579
FEDU	Four Seasons Education (Cayman)	Educational Services	2/28/17	203.2	17.7	296.1	165.7	23	7702852
FNV	Franco-Nevada Corp	Precious Metals	12/31/17	675.0	194.7	4788.4	4705.5	·	0
FI	Frank's International NV	Equipment & Services	12/31/17	454.8	-159.5	1261.8	1115.9	133	80660083
FC	Franklin Covey Co	Business Services	8/31/17	185.3	-7.2	210.7	85.1	92	7679667
FSB	Franklin Financial Network Inc	Banking	12/31/17	147.2	28.1	3843.5	304.6	131	8579638
BEN	Franklin Resources, Inc.	Wealth Management	9/30/17	6392.2	1696.7	17534.0	12620.0	901	303937978
FT	Franklin Universal Trust	Holding and other Investment Office	8/31/17	13.5	9.6	268.0	207.0	59	7108919
FCX	Freeport-McMoRan Inc	Non-Precious Metals	12/31/17	16403.0	1817.0	37302.0	7977.0	1264	1231494502
FMS	Fresenius Medical Care AG & Co K	Diagnostic & Health Related Service	12/31/17	17783.6	1279.8	24025.1	9820.1	320	17547083
FDP	Fresh Del Monte Produce Inc.	Food	12/29/17	4085.9	120.8	2766.9	1767.4	227	36531459
RESI	Front Yard Residential Corp	REITs	12/31/17	94.2	-185.5	1974.5	644.6	144	50151362
FRO	Frontline Ltd	Equipment & Services	12/31/17	648.7	-264.9	3133.7	1187.3	173	28756701
FSIC	FS Investment Corp	Finance Intermediaries & Services	12/31/17	419.3	203.8	4104.3	2284.7	260	100676359
FCN	FTI Consulting Inc.	Business Services	12/31/17	1807.7	108.0	2257.2	1192.0	322	50341894
FTSI	FTS International Inc	Equipment & Services	12/31/17	1466.1	200.7	831.0	-468.5	89	68773805
FUL	Fuller (HB) Company	Specialty Chemicals	12/2/17	2306.0	58.2	4360.6	1043.6	338	69165983
FF	FutureFuel Corp	Specialty Chemicals	12/31/17	275.0	23.5	425.6	351.6	149	23018961
GCV	Gabelli Convertible and Income Sec	Holding and other Investment Office	12/31/16	2.9	1.7	99.2	98.7	22	2552252
GDV	Gabelli Dividend & Income Trust	Holding and other Investment Office	12/31/16	53.6	29.5	2445.4	2397.7	·	0
GAB	Gabelli Equity Trust Inc (The)	Holding and other Investment Office	12/31/16	33.6	15.4	1698.7	1693.4	164	29712396
GGZ	Gabelli Global Small & Mid Cap Val	Holding and other Investment Office	12/31/16	2.5	0.8	130.1	128.0	66	3293819
GRX	Gabelli Healthcare & WellnessRx Tr	Holding and other Investment Office	12/31/16	3.3	-0.5	283.9	282.6	81	6863887
GGT	Gabelli Multimedia Trust Inc	Holding and other Investment Office	12/31/16	4.0	1.4	233.3	232.4	62	3353573
GUT	Gabelli Utility Trust	Holding and other Investment Office	12/31/16	8.8	4.8	340.8	337.8	68	3926381
GFA	Gafisa SA	Builders	12/31/17	608.8	-849.9	2878.1	755.6	·	0
GCAP	GAIN Capital Holdings Inc	Finance Intermediaries & Services	12/31/17	308.6	-11.2	1448.6	285.7	140	26891271
AJG	Gallagher (Arthur J.) & Co.	Brokers & Intermediaries	12/31/17	6159.6	463.1	12897.4	4105.2	817	184970699
GBL	GAMCO Investors Inc	Finance Intermediaries & Services	12/31/17	360.5	77.8	128.3	-96.3	116	5818683
GNT	GAMCO Natural Resources, Gold &	Holding and other Investment Office	12/31/16	2.4	0.3	167.0	149.0	39	4206292
GME	GameStop Corp	Retail - Appliances and Electronics	2/3/18	9224.6	34.7	5041.6	2214.5	573	134817117
GCI	Gannett Co Inc (New)	Publishing	12/31/17	3146.5	6.9	2570.0	1017.4	306	122713034
GDI	Gardner Denver Holdings Inc	Manufacturing	12/31/17	2375.4	18.4	4621.2	1476.8	208	198701307
IT	Gartner Inc	IT Services	12/31/17	3311.5	3.3	7283.2	983.5	592	159017595
GLOG	GasLog Ltd	Equipment & Services	12/31/17	525.2	15.5	4634.9	918.0		0
GLOP	GasLog Partners LP	Equipment & Services	12/31/17	311.5	112.8	2110.4	910.2	93	16699419
GTES	Gates Industrial Corp PLC	Industrial Machinery & Equipment	12/30/17	3041.7	151.3	6853.7	1014.6	83	288379963
GATX	GATX Corp	Miscellaneous Transportation Servic	12/31/17	1376.9	502.0	7422.4	1792.7	366	56622139
GZT	Gazit-Globe Ltd	Property, Real Estate & Developmen	12/31/17	2831.0	493.0	48963.0	9936.0	45	12569824
GCP	GCP Applied Technologies Inc	Specialty Chemicals	12/31/17	1084.4	553.4	1703.0	490.2	231	65639730
GDL	GDL Fund (The)	Holding and other Investment Office	12/31/16	4.2	-6.6	415.5	216.8	56	10257122
GEGI 26	GE Global Insurance Holdings Corp	Brokers & Intermediaries	12/31/03	11621.0	656.0	52542.0	7943.0		0
GNK	Genco Shipping & Trading Ltd	Shipping	12/31/17	209.7	-58.7	1521.0	975.0	110	32422624
GNRC	Generac Holdings Inc	Electrical Equipment	12/31/17	1672.4	159.4	2020.0	559.6	331	70266431
GAM	General American Investors Co., In	Holding and other Investment Office	12/31/17	22.4	8.6	1276.4	1260.6	119	8941079
GD	General Dynamics Corp	Aerospace	12/31/17	30973.0	2912.0	35046.0	11435.0	1602	300038483
GE	General Electric Co	Electrical Equipment	12/31/17	122092.0	-5786.0	377945.0	64263.0	3009	6154001818
GIS	General Mills Inc	Food	5/27/18	15740.4	2131.0	30624.0	6141.1	1716	533903254
GM	General Motors Co	Autos- Manufacturing	12/31/17	145588.0	-3864.0	212482.0	35001.0	1377	1179103093
GM 26	General Motors Financial Co Inc	Credit & Lending	12/31/17		661.0	97015.0	10294.0	52	9475070
GCO	Genesco Inc.	Retail - Apparel and Accessories	2/3/18	2907.0	-111.8	1315.4	829.2	282	27965482
GWR	Genesee & Wyoming Inc.	Rail	12/31/17	2208.0	549.1	8034.9	3578.5	433	69497728
GEL	Genesis Energy L.P.	Equipment & Services	12/31/17	2028.4	82.6	7137.5	697.2	225	101237378
GEN	Genesis Healthcare Inc	Hospitals & Health Care Facilities	12/31/17	5373.7	-579.0	4787.9	-1084.2	28	1463447
GNE	Genie Energy Ltd	Electric Utilities	12/31/17	264.2	-7.0	125.8	84.0	74	6458220
G	Genpact Ltd	Business Services	12/31/17	2736.9	263.1	3449.6	1424.0	332	184131116

	EARNINGS PER SHARE					P/E RATIO		DIVIDENDS PER SHARE			AV. YLD	DIV. DECLARED		PRICE RANGE 2017	
1st	2nd	3rd	2017	2016	2015	2017		2017	2016	2015	%	AMOUNT	PAYABLE		
1.88	-	-	7.91	4.75	3.85	28.0-	17.5	-	-	-	-	-		221.7-	138.7
0.30	-	-	1.03	0.49	0.31	55.8-	32.0	-	-	-	-	-		57.5-	33.0
-	-	-	-0.48	-0.88	-0.25	-	-	-	-	-	-	-		9.3-	3.1
0.24	-	-	0.71	0.78	0.89	32.0-	23.9	1.29	0.63	0.57	6.6	0.180Y	18/78/27	22.7-	17.0
0.12	-	-	0.02	1.11	2.00	2394.0-	1879.0	0.57	0.76	0.72	1.3	0.190Y	18/78/27	47.9-	37.6
-0.13	-	-	1.36	2.00	2.81	45.3-	27.4	0.84	0.84	0.84	1.7	0.210Y	18/78/27	61.6-	37.2
-	0.09	-	0.09	-0.88	0.52	165.2-	129.1	-	-	1.00	-	-		14.9-	11.6
1.96	-	-	3.99	1.56	3.66	24.6-	18.3	0.66	0.66	0.66	0.8	0.1650Y	18/78/27	98.2-	73.1
0.26	-	-	0.63	0.78	0.86	23.4-	19.2	0.48	0.48	0.48	3.5	0.120Y	18/78/27	14.8-	12.1
-	-	-	2.11	1.05	0.88	49.0-	38.5	25.46	24.17	21.99	27.3	-		103.3-	81.2
1.38	-	-	4.91	3.84	3.56	12.0-	6.0	1.10	1.00	0.88	2.5	0.3450Y	18/78/27	58.9-	29.2
0.43	-	-	1.90	1.15	1.84	7.0-	5.4	0.65	0.85	0.60	5.6	0.150Y	18/78/27	13.2-	10.2
-0.12	-	-	-0.68	-1.37	-0.25	-	-	0.13	-	1.28	3.2	0.05650	5/31/18	4.9-	3.3
0.73	-	-	0.78	-0.61	1.97	33.6-	25.1	0.46	0.34	-	2.0	0.180Y	6/22/18	26.2-	19.6
0.11	-	-	1.19	1.38	-6.22	22.1-	0.0	-	-	-	-	-		26.4-	0.0
0.11	-	-	1.19	1.38	-6.22	14.1-	0.0	-	-	-	-	-		16.8-	0.0
0.76	-	-	2.31	1.89	2.59	16.5-	13.4	1.63	1.52	1.40	4.7	0.25620	6/1/18	38.1-	31.0
0.74	-	-	2.96	2.51	-	27.4-	21.0	0.28	0.14	-	0.4	0.070Y	18/78/27	81.1-	62.2
-0.01	-	-	-	-0.26	-0.18	-	-	1.32	1.32	0.48	7.6	0.330	5/29/18	20.0-	15.7
0.09	-	-	0.42	0.13	-0.08	18.1-	9.6	-	-	-	-	-		7.6-	4.0
0.49	-	-	3.03	2.62	1.93	24.1-	17.6	0.72	0.64	0.56	1.1	0.20Y	18/78/27	73.1-	53.3
0.25	-	-	-0.60	-0.90	-1.33	-	-	-	-	-	-	-		17.8-	10.4
-0.02	-	-	1.99	-0.95	-0.26	8.2-	5.7	-	-	-	-	-		16.3-	11.3
0.26	-	-	1.18	2.63	0.91	22.6-	18.1	1.00	9.29	-	4.1	0.2750Z	7/13/18	26.6-	21.3
-	-	-	0.94	-2.21	-	10.7-	5.7	-	-	-	-	-		10.1-	5.3
0.35	-	-	1.06	0.69	0.16	102.8-	63.2	0.91	0.87	0.83	1.1	0.240	6/28/18	109.0-	67.0
-0.19	-	-	-0.72	-0.77	0.50	-	-	0.23	0.45	0.60	-	0.0750	9/15/17	-	-
-	-	-0.18	-0.52	0.47	0.66	-	-	-	-	-	-	-		30.4-	17.5
0.73	-	-	2.04	2.42	1.54	20.5-	15.0	-	-	-	-	-		41.9-	30.6
-	0.78	-	3.01	2.94	3.29	15.7-	10.6	0.80	0.72	1.10	2.0	0.230Y	18/78/27	47.3-	31.8
-	-	-	0.38	0.39	0.45	19.3-	17.3	0.38	0.47	0.47	5.4	0.0320	8/15/18	7.3-	6.6
0.47	-	-	1.25	-3.16	-11.31	16.0-	9.5	-	-	0.57	-	0.050Y	18/78/27	20.0-	11.9
-	-	1.01	4.16	4.06	3.38	13.8-	10.8	0.34	0.31	0.30	0.7	-		57.5-	45.0
0.85	-	-	2.39	4.33	1.17	-	-	0.60	0.55	0.50	-	0.150	6/1/18	-	-
-0.51	-	-	-3.47	-4.18	-0.81	-	-	0.60	0.75	1.83	5.4	0.150Z	7/13/18	13.3-	9.6
-0.08	-	-	-1.56	0.75	1.29	-	-	0.30	1.05	0.25	-	0.150	6/21/17	-	-
0.21	-	-	0.83	0.85	1.10	11.2-	8.5	0.86	0.89	0.89	10.8	0.190	7/3/18	9.3-	7.0
1.04	-	-	2.75	2.05	1.58	23.5-	11.6	-	-	-	-	-		64.7-	31.9
5.68	-	-	-0.50	-6.93	-22.16	-	-	-	-	-	-	-		21.9-	14.2
0.92	-	-	1.13	2.42	1.69	51.9-	41.9	0.59	0.55	0.51	1.1	0.1550Y	18/78/27	58.6-	47.4
0.92	-	-	0.54	1.29	1.06	30.0-	21.3	0.24	2.53	0.24	1.7	0.060Y	12/17/18	16.2-	11.5
-	-	-	-	0.12	0.07	-	-	-	0.41	0.48	-	0.120	6/22/18	6.7-	4.9
-	-	-	-	0.36	0.30	-	-	-	1.32	1.24	-	0.110	9/21/18	24.9-	21.1
-	-	-	-	0.07	0.06	-	-	-	0.60	0.64	-	0.150	6/22/18	6.6-	6.0
-	-	-	-	0.10	-0.02	-	-	-	0.12	-	-	0.34060	6/26/18	13.5-	11.7
-	-	-	-	-0.02	-0.03	-	-	-	0.52	0.51	-	0.130	6/22/18	10.9-	9.2
-	-	-	-	0.05	0.03	-	-	-	0.83	0.94	-	0.32030	6/26/18	10.0-	8.5
-	-	-	-	0.11	0.13	-	-	-	0.60	0.60	-	0.050	9/21/18	7.2-	5.7
-	-	0.04	-31.60	-43.22	2.71	-	-	34.92	0.05	-	411.5	-		12.9-	5.3
0.35	-	-	-0.20	0.67	0.22	-	-	0.24	0.21	0.20	3.3	0.060Y	6/19/18	10.0-	6.1
1.48	-	-	2.54	2.32	2.06	28.6-	22.3	1.56	1.52	1.48	2.4	0.410Y	18/78/27	72.6-	56.8
0.94	-	-	2.60	3.92	3.24	12.3-	9.3	0.10	0.06	0.28	0.4	0.020Y	7/2/18	32.0-	24.3
-	-	-	-	0.01	0.02	-	-	-	0.84	0.84	-	0.050	9/21/18	7.2-	6.2
0.28	-	-	3.40	3.78	3.47	6.5-	3.7	1.48	1.44	1.32	8.5	0.380Y	18/78/27	22.2-	12.5
0.00	-	-	0.06	0.44	1.25	203.8-	132.5	0.64	0.64	0.32	6.4	0.160Y	6/25/18	12.2-	8.0
-	-	0.13	0.10	-0.25	-2.35	366.9-	206.7	-	-	-	-	-		36.7-	20.7
-0.22	-	-	0.04	2.31	2.06	3553.5-	2835.3	-	-	-	-	-		142.1-	113.4
-	-	0.03	0.07	-0.39	0.04	-	-	-	-	-	-	0.54690	7/2/18	-	-
-	-	-	2.09	2.17	2.38	-	-	-	-	-	-	0.51250Y	6/15/18	-	-
0.09	-	-	0.60	0.18	0.08	-	-	-	-	-	-	-		-	-
1.98	-	-	12.75	6.29	4.69	5.9-	4.4	1.68	1.60	1.52	2.6	0.440Y	18/78/27	75.8-	56.5
-	-	1.89	2.49	3.96	3.45	-	-	1.40	-	-	-	0.380	7/3/18	-	-
-0.09	-	-	7.74	1.02	0.57	4.4-	3.6	-	-	-	-	-		34.4-	27.7
-	-	-	-	-0.36	-0.44	-	-	-	0.64	0.64	-	0.10	6/22/18	10.3-	9.1
-1.61	-	-	-1.71	-30.03	-29.60	-	-	-	-	-	-	1.0Y	11/28/08	-	-
0.42	-	-	2.56	1.50	1.12	20.6-	14.0	-	-	-	-	5.7Y	6/21/13	52.8-	35.9
-	-	-	0.32	0.30	0.48	114.2-	102.3	3.29	3.18	1.15	9.5	0.37190Y	9/24/18	36.5-	32.7
2.65	-	-	9.56	9.52	9.08	24.1-	19.4	3.28	2.97	2.69	1.6	0.930Y	18/78/27	229.9-	185.9
-0.14	-	-	-0.72	0.89	-0.61	-	-	0.84	0.93	0.92	4.5	0.120Y	18/78/27	27.4-	12.8
-	-	1.62	2.77	2.77	1.97	21.7-	14.9	1.92	1.78	1.67	3.7	0.490Y	18/78/27	60.2-	41.2
0.72	-	-	-2.60	6.00	5.91	-	-	1.52	1.52	1.38	3.8	0.380Y	18/78/27	46.5-	34.8
-0.12	-	-	4.83	4.11	4.12	9.5-	4.4	-	-	-	-	0.3750Y	4/30/13	45.9-	21.1
1.19	-	-	8.79	2.42	3.89	9.5-	7.4	-	-	-	-	1.250	10/1/15	83.5-	65.1
-0.07	-	-	0.50	1.00	4.09	64.9-	37.6	2.65	2.72	2.47	11.1	0.530	8/14/18	32.4-	18.8
-0.70	-	-	-6.15	-0.82	-4.97	-	-	-	-	-	-	-		2.9-	0.7
0.24	-	-	-0.36	-1.14	-0.40	-	-	0.30	0.24	0.12	5.7	0.0750	5/23/18	7.2-	3.9
0.33	-	-	1.34	1.28	1.09	-	-	-	-	-	-	0.0750	18/78/27	-	-

SYMBOL	COMPANY	NATURE OF BUSINESS	FISCAL YEAR-END	TOTAL REV. $MILL	NET INCOME $MILL	TOTAL ASSETS $MILL	NET STK EQUITY $MILL	NO OF INST	INST. HOLDINGS (SHARES)
GPC	Genuine Parts Co.	Auto Parts	12/31/17	16308.8	616.8	12412.4	3412.2	995	143076089
GNW	Genworth Financial, Inc. (Holding C	Life & Health	12/31/17	8295.0	817.0	105297.0	13418.0	496	425741849
GEO	GEO Group Inc (The) (New)	REITs	12/31/17	2263.4	146.2	4226.9	1199.2	381	132035716
GPRK	GeoPark Ltd	Production & Extraction	12/31/17	330.1	-24.2	786.2	84.9	-	0
GPE PRA	Georgia Power Co	Electric Utilities	12/31/17	8310.0	1428.0	36779.0	11931.0	-	0
GGB	Gerdau S.A.	Non-Precious Metals	12/31/17	36917.6	-359.4	50301.8	23645.2	223	221504026
GTY	Getty Realty Corp.	REITs	12/31/17	120.2	47.2	1072.8	553.7	224	31681159
GGP	GGP Inc	REITs	12/31/17	2327.9	657.3	23350.0	8795.7	-	0
GIG U	GigCapital Inc	Business Services	10/11/17	-	-0.0	0.1	0.0	26	3410475
GIL	Gildan Activewear Inc	Apparel, Footwear & Accessories	12/31/17	2750.8	362.3	2980.7	2051.4	338	185513928
GKOS	Glaukos Corp	Medical Instruments & Equipment	12/31/17	159.3	-0.1	165.8	138.2	176	40583281
GSK	GlaxoSmithKline Plc	Pharmaceuticals	12/31/17	30186.0	1532.0	56381.0	-68.0	1129	342491857
BRSS	Global Brass & Copper Holdings Inc	Metal Products	12/31/17	1560.8	50.9	673.9	142.3	182	23401152
CO	Global Cord Blood Corp	Diagnostic & Health Related Service	3/31/18	936.8	237.1	5844.4	3113.4	54	23207071
GMRE	Global Medical REIT Inc	REITs	12/31/17	30.3	-0.1	474.6	246.3	110	9360950
GNL	Global Net Lease Inc	REITs	12/31/17	259.3	23.6	3038.6	1413.2	223	66573885
GLP	Global Partners LP	Equipment & Services	12/31/17	8920.6	58.8	2320.2	-	83	16933769
GPN	Global Payments Inc	Business Services	12/31/17	3975.2	468.4	12998.1	3794.5	703	177860996
GSL	Global Ship Lease, Inc.	Shipping	12/31/17	159.0	-74.3	675.2	251.6	-	0
GLOB	Globant SA	IT Services	12/31/17	413.4	30.5	357.2	263.4	146	27024245
GMED	Globus Medical Inc	Medical Instruments & Equipment	12/31/17	636.0	107.3	1078.5	967.8	-	0
GMS	GMS Inc	Construction Materials	4/30/18	2511.5	63.0	1454.5	579.5	181	30117601
GNC	GNC Holdings Inc	Retail - Food & Beverage, Drug & To	12/31/17	2453.0	-148.9	1516.6	-162.0	222	51974619
GDDY	GoDaddy Inc	Internet & Software	12/31/17	2231.9	136.4	5738.3	486.5	317	161194905
GOL	Gol Linhas Aereas Inteligentes SA	Airlines/Air Freight	12/31/16	9867.3	849.6	8404.4	-3650.0	94	25681544
GFI	Gold Fields Ltd.	Precious Metals	12/31/17	2761.8	-18.7	6620.1	3275.8	240	356718888
GG	Goldcorp Inc	Precious Metals	12/31/17	3423.0	658.0	21685.0	14184.0	614	549495777
GSBD	Goldman Sachs BDC Inc	Finance Intermediaries & Services	12/31/17	136.8	80.0	1298.6	725.8	89	14497207
GS	Goldman Sachs Group Inc	Finance Intermediaries & Services	12/31/17	42254.0	4286.0	916776.0	82243.0	1903	343018735
GER	Goldman Sachs MLP Energy Renai	Finance Intermediaries & Services	11/30/16	5.1	-10.3	857.6	597.6	-	0
GMZ	Goldman Sachs MLP Income Oppor	Finance Intermediaries & Services	11/30/16	7.8	-3.9	656.8	454.6	56	10912340
GRC	Gorman-Rupp Company (The)	Industrial Machinery & Equipment	12/31/17	379.4	26.6	395.0	325.5	153	16719878
GPX	GP Strategies Corp.	Business Services	12/31/17	509.2	12.9	365.0	188.1	120	16892357
GRA	Grace (WR) & Co	Specialty Chemicals	12/31/17	1716.5	11.2	2907.0	256.4	403	64468412
GGG	Graco Inc	Industrial Machinery & Equipment	12/29/17	1474.7	252.4	1379.2	723.1	570	161870676
EAF	GrafTech International Ltd	Electrical Equipment	12/31/17	550.8	8.0	1199.1	613.2	71	5718534
GHM	Graham Corp.	Industrial Machinery & Equipment	3/31/18	77.5	-9.8	143.3	103.3	122	10300219
GHC	Graham Holdings Co.	Educational Services	12/31/17	2591.8	302.0	4937.8	2915.1	364	4814146
GWW	Grainger (W.W.) Inc.	Electrical Equipment	12/31/17	10424.9	585.7	5804.3	1690.1	929	56463978
GPT	Gramercy Property Trust	REITs	12/31/17	545.2	85.3	6456.0	3138.6	340	185719490
GRAM	Grana y Montero SAA	Construction Services	12/31/15	7832.4	88.2	8991.8	2654.6	53	25090071
GVA	Granite Construction Inc	Construction Services	12/31/17	2989.7	69.1	1872.0	945.1	374	49799919
GPMT	Granite Point Mortgage Trust Inc	REITs	12/31/17	117.8	53.3	2499.1	829.6	210	29943657
GPMT	Granite Point Mortgage Trust Inc	REITs	12/31/17	117.8	53.3	2499.1	829.6	210	29943657
GRP U	Granite Real Estate Investment Tru	REITs	12/31/17	222.6	357.7	3206.4	2136.6	-	0
GPK	Graphic Packaging Holding Co	Containers & Packaging	12/31/17	4403.7	300.2	4863.0	1291.9	370	470734864
GTN	Gray Television Inc	Radio & Television	12/31/17	882.7	262.0	3260.9	992.9	286	87743468
AJX	Great Ajax Corp	REITs	12/31/17	93.9	28.9	1395.7	290.4	87	14249590
GWB	Great Western Bancorp Inc	Banking	9/30/17	497.7	144.8	11690.0	1755.0	234	69619034
GDOT	Green Dot Corp	Credit & Lending	12/31/17	890.2	85.9	2197.5	764.5	335	53925790
GBX	Greenbrier Companies Inc (The)	Rail	8/31/17	2169.2	116.1	2397.7	1018.1	368	41779922
GHL	Greenhill & Co Inc	Finance Intermediaries & Services	12/31/17	239.2	-26.7	610.8	208.3	248	36578231
GHG	GreenTree Hospitality Group Ltd	Hotels, Restaurants & Travel	12/31/17	778.1	285.4	1756.0	732.2	30	10705438
GEF	Greif Inc	Containers & Packaging	10/31/17	3638.2	118.6	3232.3	1042.4	327	29348709
GFF	Griffon Corp.	Construction Materials	9/30/17	1525.0	14.9	1873.5	398.8	184	36763663
GPI	Group 1 Automotive, Inc.	Retail - Automotive	12/31/17	11123.7	213.4	4871.1	1124.3	311	32117693
GRUB	GrubHub Inc	Internet & Software	12/31/17	683.1	99.0	1543.8	1117.8	368	104487431
PAC	Grupo Aeroportuario del Pacifico, S.	Airlines/Air Freight	12/31/17	12365.9	4649.1	39517.5	21028.2	138	7226993
ASR	Grupo Aeroportuario del Sureste SA	Airlines/Air Freight	12/31/17	12589.8	5834.5	56614.1	26040.1	145	10742929
AVAL	Grupo Aval Acciones Y Valores SA	Banking	12/31/17	8741833.0	1962414.0	236535540.0	16286996.0	62	75693028
SUPV	Grupo Supervielle SA	Banking	12/31/17	21492.8	2437.1	93971.3	15144.8	123	43068701
TV	Grupo Televisa SAB	Radio & Television	12/31/17	94274.2	4524.5	297220.1	85661.8	297	361303289
GSAH U	GS Acquisition Holdings Corp	Business Services	12/31/17	-	-0.0	0.0	0.0	-	0
GTT	GTT Communications, Inc.	Internet & Software	12/31/17	827.9	-71.5	1798.2	231.4	171	33154384
GSH	Guangshen Railway Co., Ltd.	Rail	12/31/17	18331.4	1015.4	33994.2	28684.7	45	1192193
GES	GUESS ?, Inc.	Retail - Apparel and Accessories	2/3/18	2363.8	-7.9	1655.6	916.8	331	80808098
GGM	Guggenheim Credit Allocation Fund	Holding and other Investment Office	5/31/17	16.5	12.8	231.6	158.7	35	855045
GPM	Guggenheim Enhanced Equity Inco	Holding and other Investment Office	12/31/16	4.4	1.2	233.1	159.2	72	10014556
GOF	Guggenheim Strategic Opportunitie	Holding and other Investment Office	5/31/17	38.7	30.3	538.0	410.5	66	3462223
GBAB	Guggenheim Taxable Municipal Ma	Holding and other Investment Office	5/31/17	33.9	27.7	521.8	405.8	49	3937870
GWRE	Guidewire Software Inc	Internet & Software	7/31/17	514.3	21.2	1078.9	893.3	339	95068306
HAE	Haemonetics Corp.	Medical Instruments & Equipment	3/31/18	903.9	45.6	1237.3	752.4	375	66797095
HK	Halcon Resources Corp	Production & Extraction	12/31/17	378.0	535.7	1643.6	1072.0	255	162278364
HAL	Halliburton Company	Equipment & Services	12/31/17	20620.0	-463.0	25085.0	8322.0	1521	866460394
HBB	Hamilton Beach Brands Holding Co	Household Appliances, Electronics &	12/31/17	740.7	17.9	326.2	46.4	91	5323559
HPS	Hancock John Preferred Income Fd	Holding and other Investment Office	7/31/17	57.4	45.2	928.8	616.7	57	3766794
HPF	Hancock John Preferred Income Fu	Holding and other Investment Office	7/31/17	43.4	34.0	705.1	465.6	58	1394622
HTD	Hancock John Tax-Advantaged Divi	Holding and other Investment Office	10/31/17	76.5	58.5	1366.0	934.9	112	7294451
HBI	HanesBrands Inc	Apparel, Footwear & Accessories	12/30/17	6471.4	61.9	6894.8	686.2	903	401815741
HASI	Hannon Armstrong Sustainable Infr	REITs	12/31/17	105.6	30.9	2250.2	639.2	212	44098041

T28

___ QUARTERLY ___			__ ANNUAL __			P/E RATIO		DIVIDENDS PER SHARE			AV. YLD	DIV. DECLARED		PRICE RANGE	
1st	2nd	3rd	2017	2016	2015	2017		2017	2016	2015	%	AMOUNT	PAYABLE	2017	
1.20	-	-	4.18	4.59	4.63	25.7 -	19.3	2.70	2.63	2.46	3.0	0.720Y	18/78/27	107.6 -	80.5
0.22	-	-	1.63	-0.56	-1.24	3.0 -	1.7							4.8 -	2.7
0.29	-	-	1.21	1.33	1.25	25.5 -	16.2	1.88	1.73	1.67	7.6	0.470Z	7/27/18	30.8 -	19.6
-	-	-	-0.40	-0.82	-4.05	-								28.3 -	0.0
-	-	-	-	-	-	-		1.25	1.53	1.53	4.8	0.31250Z	10/1/18	28.3 -	0.0
-	-	0.35	-0.21	-1.70	-2.69	-		0.04	0.04	0.17	1.0			5.3 -	3.0
0.25	-	-	1.26	1.12	1.11	23.7 -	18.0	1.16	1.03	1.15	4.4	0.320Z	7/5/18	29.8 -	22.7
0.06	-	-	0.68	1.34	1.43	35.4 -	28.0	0.88	1.06	0.71	4.1	0.39840Z	18/78/27	24.1 -	19.0
-	-0.06	-	-0.01	-	-	-								10.6 -	0.0
0.31	-	-	1.61	1.47	1.25	26.1 -	17.2	0.37	0.31	0.26	1.1	0.1120	6/11/18	42.1 -	27.8
-0.08	-	-	0.00	0.12	-2.13	-		-	-	-				44.5 -	24.5
-	-	0.25	0.31	0.19	1.72	138.0 -	111.8	1.60	1.92	1.55	4.1			42.8 -	34.7
0.71	-	-	2.30	1.49	1.66	15.7 -	12.3	0.20	0.15	0.15	0.6	0.060	5/25/18	36.2 -	28.2
-	-	0.70	1.59	1.25	1.36	-		-	-	-		0.08G	8/24/18	-	
0.02	-	-	-0.09	-0.68	-6.44	-		0.80	0.74	1.02	9.5	0.46880Z	7/31/18	9.8 -	6.5
0.03	-	-	0.30	0.81	-0.03	75.3 -	52.1	1.77	-	2.13	8.9	0.17750Y	9/17/18	22.6 -	15.6
1.73	-	-	1.74	-5.91	1.11	10.6 -	8.8	1.85	1.85	2.73	10.8	0.46250	18/78/27	18.4 -	15.3
0.57	-	-	3.01	0.81	2.06	39.4 -	29.3	0.04	0.02	0.04	0.0	0.010Y	18/78/27	118.5 -	88.3
-	-	0.15	-1.61	-1.42	-0.67	-		-	-	-		0.54690	7/2/18	-	
-	-	0.27	0.84	1.01	0.90	-								-	
0.39	-	-	1.10	1.08	1.17	52.2 -	25.7	-	-	-				57.4 -	28.3
-	-	0.47	1.19	0.38	-0.43	32.8 -	21.7	-	-	-				39.0 -	25.9
0.07	-	-	-2.16	-4.12	2.60	-		-	0.80	0.72		0.20Y	12/30/16	10.9 -	3.0
0.02	-	-	0.79	-0.21	-0.81	94.6 -	52.1	-	-	-				74.7 -	41.2
-	-	-	0.04	-0.21	-	-		-	-	-				14.1 -	4.5
-	-	-	-0.02	0.20	-0.45	-		0.06	0.04	0.02	1.5			4.7 -	3.4
0.08	-	-	0.76	0.19	-5.03	25.2 -	15.5	0.08	0.12	0.45	0.5	0.020	6/22/18	19.1 -	11.8
0.46	-	-	1.28	1.12	2.14	18.0 -	14.8	1.80	1.80	1.80	8.4	0.450	7/16/18	23.0 -	18.9
6.95	-	-	9.01	16.29	12.14	30.3 -	24.0	2.90	2.60	2.55	1.2	0.80Y	9/27/18	273.4 -	215.8
-	-	-	-	-0.13	0.09	-		-	0.64	1.33		0.160	5/29/18	7.4 -	5.4
-	-	-	-0.09	0.03	-	-		-	0.84	1.37		0.210	5/29/18	10.3 -	7.6
0.37	-	-	1.02	0.95	0.96	35.2 -	25.1	0.47	0.43	0.41	1.5	0.1250Y	18/78/27	35.9 -	25.6
0.16	-	-	0.76	1.21	1.09	40.9 -	23.2	-	-	-		0.025	2/1/89	31.1 -	17.6
0.64	-	-	0.16	1.33	1.99	478.7 -	376.7	0.84	0.51	-	1.2	0.240Y	18/78/27	76.6 -	60.3
0.49	-	-	1.45	0.24	1.95	33.8 -	24.3	0.48	0.44	0.40	1.1	0.13250Y	18/78/27	49.1 -	35.3
0.74	-	-	0.03	-	-0.88	684.3 -	481.7	-	-	-		0.0645GH	6/29/18	20.5 -	14.4
-	-	-1.19	0.52	0.61	1.45	52.7 -	34.7	0.36	0.33	0.20	1.7	0.090Y	6/27/18	27.4 -	18.0
7.78	-	-	53.89	29.80	-17.87	11.6 -	10.1	5.08	4.84	9.10	0.9	1.330Y	18/78/27	624.6 -	542.8
4.07	-	-	10.02	9.87	11.58	31.9 -	15.6	5.06	4.83	4.59	2.2	1.360Y	18/78/27	319.6 -	156.3
0.16	-	-	0.52	0.19	-0.90	59.8 -	41.1	1.50	1.37	-	5.5	0.3750Z	7/16/18	31.1 -	21.4
-	-	-	-	-	0.13	-		-	-	0.76				5.1 -	0.0
-0.29	-	-	1.71	1.42	1.52	39.7 -	27.7	0.52	0.52	0.52	0.9	0.130Y	18/78/27	67.8 -	47.4
0.33	-	-	0.60	0.52	-	32.2 -	27.3	0.70	-	-	3.9	0.40Z	7/18/18	19.3 -	16.4
0.33	-	-	0.60	0.52	-	31.3 -	0.0	0.70	-	-	4.8	0.40Z	7/18/18	18.8 -	0.0
-	-	-	-	-	-	-		2.61	2.43	2.30	5.8	0.2270	8/15/18	54.7 -	0.0
0.10	-	-	0.96	0.71	0.70	17.4 -	13.2	0.30	0.23	0.20	2.0	0.0750Y	18/78/27	16.7 -	12.7
0.22	-	-	3.55	0.86	0.57	5.0 -	3.0	-	-	-		0.030Y	10/15/08	17.8 -	10.8
0.38	-	-	1.51	1.65	1.68	9.7 -	8.5	1.13	0.99	0.64	8.2	0.30Y	5/30/18	14.6 -	12.8
-	0.69	-	2.45	2.14	1.90	18.6 -	13.7	0.74	0.56	0.36	1.8	0.250	5/23/18	45.5 -	33.5
1.29	-	-	1.61	0.80	0.72	48.7 -	24.0	-	-	-				78.4 -	38.6
-	1.91	-	3.65	5.73	5.93	14.8 -	11.5	0.86	0.81	0.60	1.8	0.250Y	8/9/18	54.2 -	41.9
0.21	-	-	-0.83	1.89	0.82	-		1.40	1.80	1.80	7.1	0.050Y	6/20/18	29.4 -	14.0
-	-	-	3.12	2.91	2.58	7.8 -	3.5	-	-	-				24.3 -	10.8
-	0.77	-	2.02	1.28	1.23	32.1 -	24.7	1.68	1.68	1.68	2.9	0.630Y	18/78/27	64.9 -	49.8
-	2.11	-	0.35	0.68	0.73	67.9 -	50.0	0.24	0.20	0.16	1.2	0.070Y	6/21/18	23.8 -	17.5
1.70	-	-	10.08	6.67	3.90	8.3 -	5.3	0.97	0.91	0.83	1.4	0.260Y	18/78/27	83.4 -	53.2
0.34	-	-	1.12	0.58	0.44	107.0 -	38.5	-	-	-				119.9 -	43.1
-	-	-	8.85	6.24	5.98	13.4 -	9.3	84.08	68.93	56.10	82.9			118.8 -	82.5
-	-	1.70	19.45	12.10	9.71	11.7 -	7.9	55.53	49.02	50.05	30.1			228.1 -	153.7
-	-	-	-	-	-	-		1177.18	1175.51	2019.35	13526.1			9.4 -	8.1
-	-	-	-	-	-	-		-	-	-				33.0 -	10.4
-	-	-	1.46	1.20	3.52	18.7 -	10.0	1.55	1.54	1.58	7.5			27.3 -	14.6
0.00	-	-	0.00	-0.02	-	-		-	-	-				10.3 -	10.2
-0.69	-	-	-1.71	0.14	0.54	-		-	-	-				61.9 -	28.4
0.06	-	-	0.14	0.16	0.15	267.3 -	177.4	3.46	3.48	2.16	11.8			37.4 -	24.8
-0.27	-	-	0.27	0.96	1.11	95.7 -	43.3	0.90	0.90	0.90	5.1	0.2250Y	6/29/18	25.9 -	11.7
-	-	-	1.91	2.02	1.95	12.3 -	11.1	2.18	2.18	2.16	9.7	0.18130	7/31/18	23.5 -	21.1
-	-	-	-	0.06	0.06	-		-	0.96	0.96		0.240	6/29/18	9.4 -	8.1
-	-	-	1.61	1.40	1.28	13.6 -	12.2	2.19	2.19	2.19	10.4	0.18210	7/31/18	21.9 -	19.6
-	-	-	1.59	1.48	1.48	14.6 -	13.2	1.55	1.66	1.66	7.0	0.12570	7/31/18	23.2 -	21.0
-	-	-0.62	0.28	0.20	0.14	339.5 -	243.7	-	-	-				95.1 -	68.3
-	-	-0.12	-0.51	-1.09	0.32	-		-	-	-				95.8 -	38.6
-0.02	-	-	3.65	-5.26	-633.60	2.3 -	1.1	-	-	-		14.3750	12/1/5	8.5 -	4.0
0.05	-	-	-0.53	-6.69	-0.79	-		0.72	0.72	0.72	1.6	0.180Y	18/78/27	56.8 -	38.7
-0.03	-	-	1.31	1.92	1.41	30.5 -	16.2	0.09	-	-	0.3	0.0850	6/15/18	39.9 -	21.2
-	-	-	1.43	1.41	1.44	13.5 -	11.9	1.47	1.47	1.47	8.0	0.12220	7/31/18	19.4 -	17.0
-	-	-	1.60	1.59	1.64	14.1 -	12.2	1.68	1.68	1.68	8.0	0.140	7/31/18	22.6 -	19.5
-	-	-	1.65	1.44	1.38	15.9 -	12.9	1.82	1.47	1.45	7.6	0.1380	7/31/18	26.2 -	21.3
0.22	-	-	0.17	1.40	1.06	151.0 -	97.1	0.60	0.44	0.40	2.8	0.150Y	18/78/27	25.7 -	16.5
-0.03	-	-	0.57	0.32	0.21	44.2 -	30.9	1.32	1.23	1.08	6.1	0.330Z	7/12/18	25.2 -	17.6

SYMBOL	COMPANY	NATURE OF BUSINESS	FISCAL YEAR-END	TOTAL REV. $MILL	NET INCOME $MILL	TOTAL ASSETS $MILL	NET STK EQUITY $MILL	NO OF INST	INST. HOLDINGS (SHARES)
THG	Hanover Insurance Group Inc	General Insurance	12/31/17	5184.4	186.2	15469.6	2997.7	445	52040190
HOG	Harley-Davidson Inc	Autos- Manufacturing	12/31/17	5647.2	521.8	9972.7	1844.3	803	199218362
HMY	Harmony Gold Mining Co. Ltd.	Precious Metals	6/30/17	1416.0	17.0	2966.0	2234.0	152	142984363
HRS	Harris Corp.	Defense	6/30/17	5900.0	553.0	10090.0	2928.0	1015	149944580
HSC	Harsco Corp.	Industrial Machinery & Equipment	12/31/17	1607.1	7.8	1578.7	170.5	389	83808055
HHS	Harte Hanks Inc	Advertising	12/31/17	383.9	-41.9	130.8	-34.6	110	10338071
HIG	Hartford Financial Services Group I	General Insurance	12/31/17	16974.0	-3131.0	225260.0	13494.0	994	430147243
HVT	Haverty Furniture Cos., Inc.	Retail - Furniture & Home Furnishing	12/31/17	820.0	21.1	461.3	294.1	184	20553943
HE	Hawaiian Electric Industries Inc	Electric Utilities	12/31/17	2555.6	167.2	13099.8	2131.7	403	67046865
HCHC	HC2 Holdings Inc	Business Services	12/31/17	1634.1	-46.9	3217.7	99.5	3	43552
HCA	HCA Healthcare Inc	Hospitals & Health Care Facilities	12/31/17	43614.0	2216.0	36593.0	-6806.0	814	293897349
HCI	HCI Group Inc	General Insurance	12/31/17	244.4	-6.9	842.3	194.0	145	7947629
HCP	HCP Inc	REITs	12/31/17	1848.4	414.2	14088.5	5301.0	901	527608494
HDB	HDFC Bank Ltd	Banking	3/31/15	602121.8	107000.5	6070965.2	633156.9	519	160922411
HR	Healthcare Realty Trust, Inc.	REITs	12/31/17	424.5	23.1	3193.6	1789.9	345	151684556
HTA	Healthcare Trust Of America Inc	REITs	12/31/17	614.0	63.9	6449.6	3278.8	373	245179221
HL	Hecla Mining Co	Precious Metals	12/31/17	577.8	-23.5	2365.0	1483.9	313	302619488
HEI	HEICO Corp	Aerospace	10/31/17	1524.8	186.0	2512.4	1161.1	364	35315978
HLX	Helix Energy Solutions Group Inc	Equipment & Services	12/31/17	581.4	30.1	2362.8	1567.4	316	158836838
HP	Helmerich & Payne, Inc.	Equipment & Services	9/30/17	1804.7	-128.2	6440.0	4164.6	802	139732937
HLF	Herbalife Nutrition Ltd	Household & Personal Products	12/31/17	4427.7	213.9	2895.1	-334.7	346	88777391
HRI	Herc Holdings Inc	Miscellaneous Transportation Servic	12/31/17	1754.5	160.3	3549.7	510.4	360	173732054
HTGC	Hercules Capital Inc	Holding and other Investment Office	12/31/17	172.2	96.4	1654.7	841.0	241	40468673
HRTG	Heritage Insurance Holdings Inc	General Insurance	12/31/17	406.6	-1.1	1771.2	379.8	142	23711738
HT	Hersha Hospitality Trust	REITs	12/31/17	498.2	99.9	2138.3	833.9	241	59233947
HSY	Hershey Company (The)	Food	12/31/17	7515.4	783.0	5553.7	915.3	1101	142896881
HTZ	Hertz Global Holdings Inc (New)	Miscellaneous Transportation Servic	12/31/17	8803.0	327.0	20058.0	1520.0	220	105544269
HES	Hess Corp	Production & Extraction	12/31/17	5405.0	-4074.0	23112.0	11051.0	835	342168845
HESM	Hess Midstream Partners LP	Equipment & Services	12/31/17	565.8	41.2	2635.1		66	14396015
HPE	Hewlett Packard Enterprise Co	IT Services	10/31/17	28871.0	344.0	61406.0	23466.0	897	1362969316
HXL	Hexcel Corp.	Plastics	12/31/17	1973.3	284.0	2780.9	1495.1	558	111014639
HF	HFF Inc	Property, Real Estate & Developmen	12/31/17	609.5	95.0	892.2	286.5	298	43483770
HCLP	Hi-Crush Partners LP	Mining	12/31/17	602.6	82.5	1123.1		140	26728746
PCF	High Income Securities Fund	Holding and other Investment Office	8/31/17	5.4	3.9	124.7	123.6	55	7450904
HPR	HighPoint Resources Corp	Production & Extraction						147	204802768
HIW	Highwoods Properties, Inc.	REITs	12/31/17	702.7	185.4	4623.8	2219.8	420	117414032
HIL	Hill International Inc	Business Services	12/31/16	520.8	-18.8	401.2	88.4	91	37086802
HRC	Hill-Rom Holdings, Inc.	Medical Instruments & Equipment	9/30/17	2743.7	133.6	4528.7	1358.2	27	4651596
HI	Hillenbrand Inc	Industrial Machinery & Equipment	9/30/17	1590.2	126.2	1956.5	751.4	360	60800283
HTH	Hilltop Holdings, Inc.	Banking	12/31/17	1712.2	132.5	13365.8	1912.1	252	69536578
HGV	Hilton Grand Vacations Inc	Hotels, Restaurants & Travel	12/31/17	1711.0	327.0	2384.0	518.0	309	119399726
HLT	Hilton Worldwide Holdings Inc	Hotels, Restaurants & Travel	12/31/17	9140.0	1259.0	14308.0	2072.0	562	352554461
HNI	HNI Corp	Office Equipment & Furniture	12/30/17	2175.9	89.8	1391.6	514.1	265	47984603
HMLP	Hoegh LNG Partners LP	Equipment & Services	12/31/17	143.5	48.8	1059.0	474.7	60	10751283
HEP	Holly Energy Partners LP	Equipment & Services	12/31/17	454.4	195.0	2154.1		145	37854602
HFC	HollyFrontier Corp	Refining & Marketing	12/31/17	14251.3	805.4	10692.2	5370.8	683	191507389
HD	Home Depot Inc	Retail - Hardware & Home Improvem	1/28/18	100904.0	8630.0	44529.0	1454.0	2771	1041825478
HMC	Honda Motor Co., Ltd.(Honda Giken	Autos- Manufacturing	3/31/18	5361146.0	1059337.0	19349164.0	7933538.0	366	47632668
HON	Honeywell International Inc	Auto Parts	12/31/17	40534.0	1655.0	59387.0	17281.0	2274	689388520
HMN	Horace Mann Educators Corp.	General Insurance	12/31/17	1171.6	169.5	11198.3	1501.6	276	51682332
HZN	Horizon Global Corp	Auto Parts	12/31/17	893.0	-3.5	661.0	141.9	152	24088337
HRL	Hormel Foods Corp.	Food	10/29/17	9167.5	846.7	6975.9	4935.9	767	251326985
HOS	Hornbeck Offshore Services Inc	Equipment & Services	12/31/17	191.4	27.4	2768.9	1437.9	146	31223470
DHI	Horton (DR) Inc	Builders	9/30/17	14091.0	1038.4	12184.6	7747.1	938	388760988
HST	Host Hotels & Resorts Inc	REITs	12/31/17	5387.0	564.0	11693.0	6973.0	772	961623955
HLI	Houlihan Lokey Inc	Wealth Management	3/31/18	963.4	172.3	1418.8	852.8	210	32778809
HOV	Hovnanian Enterprises, Inc.	Builders	10/31/17	2451.7	-332.2	1900.9	-460.4	228	76890957
HHC	Howard Hughes Corp	Property, Real Estate & Developmen	12/31/17	1100.1	168.4	6729.1	3183.0	343	42303487
HPQ	HP Inc	Computer Hardware & Equipment	10/31/17	52056.0	2526.0	32913.0	-3408.0	1532	1666921923
HSFC PR	HSBC Finance Corp	Credit & Lending	12/31/16	1414.0	-529.0	13882.0	5434.0		0
HSBC	HSBC Holdings Plc	Banking	12/31/17	82012.0	10798.0	2521771.0	190250.0	638	121420000
HUSI PR	HSBC USA, Inc.	Banking	12/31/17	6125.0	-179.0	187235.0	20094.0	1	80000
HMI	Huami Corp	Electronic Instruments & Related Pro	12/31/17	2048.9	167.7	1465.5	575.4		0
HNP	Huaneng Power International Inc	Electric Utilities	12/31/17	152459.4	1793.2	378693.7	75533.3	106	2903619
HUBB	Hubbell Inc.	Electrical Equipment	12/31/17	3668.8	243.1	3720.6	1634.2	468	56789536
HUBS	HubSpot Inc	Internet & Software	12/31/17	375.6	-39.7	712.2	210.4	266	39738756
HBM	Hudbay Minerals Inc	Precious Metals	12/31/17	1362.6	163.9	4648.7	2144.3	162	188192276
HUD	Hudson Ltd	Retail - General Merchandise/Depart	12/31/17	1802.5	-40.4	1457.8	493.7	76	35285617
HPP	Hudson Pacific Properties Inc	REITs	12/31/17	728.1	68.6	6622.1	3647.9	287	185533044
HGT	Hugoton Royalty Trust (TX)	Oil Royalty Traders	12/31/17	5.3	4.5	17.8	16.4	113	7050069
HUM	Humana Inc	Life & Health	12/31/17	53767.0	2448.0	27178.0	9842.0	982	161751788
HCFT	Hunt Companies Finance Trust Inc	REITs	12/31/17	86.6	4.7	2612.5	145.8	49	7275576
HII	Huntington Ingalls Industries, Inc.	Defense	12/31/17	7441.0	479.0	6374.0	1758.0	661	45190698
HUN	Huntsman Corp	Specialty Chemicals	12/31/17	8358.0	636.0	10244.0	2620.0	600	234587655
HUYA	HUYA Inc	IT Services	12/31/17	2184.8	-81.0	1300.5	569.9	4	4874
H	Hyatt Hotels Corp	Hotels, Restaurants & Travel	12/31/17	4685.0	249.0	7672.0	3535.0	307	47061718
HY	Hyster-Yale Materials Handling Inc	Autos- Manufacturing	12/31/17	2885.2	48.6	1647.9	565.5	195	10071879
IAG	IAMGold Corp	Precious Metals	12/31/17	1094.9	501.6	3966.9	2791.6	250	292677304
IBN	ICICI Bank Ltd (India)	Banking	3/31/17	1133976.3	101883.8	9860426.6	1046320.0	467	790170035
IDA	Idacorp Inc	Electric Utilities	12/31/17	1349.5	212.4	6045.4	2251.4	409	55118179

1st	2nd	3rd	2017	2016	2015	P/E high	P/E low	Div 2017	Div 2016	Div 2015	AV. YLD %	AMOUNT	PAYABLE	High	Low
1.57	-	-	4.33	3.59	7.40	28.5-	20.3	2.04	1.88	1.69	1.9	0.540Y	18/78/27	123.2-	87.9
1.03	-	-	3.02	3.83	3.69	18.5-	13.3	1.46	1.40	1.24	3.1	0.370Y	18/78/27	56.0-	40.0
0.03	-	-	0.04	0.15	-0.86	62.5-	38.0	0.06	-	-	3.2			2.5-	1.5
-	-	1.66	4.44	2.59	3.11	38.1-	24.7	2.12	2.00	1.88	1.5	0.570Y	18/78/27	169.0-	109.7
0.21	-	-	0.09	-1.07	0.08	293.9-	171.1	-	0.05	0.82	-	0.05120Y	2/16/16	26.4-	15.4
4.67	-	-	-6.76	-21.30	-27.70			-	0.90	3.40		0.0850Y	3/15/16	11.6-	0.0
1.64	-	-	-8.61	2.27	3.96			0.94	0.86	0.78	1.7	0.30Y	18/78/27	59.1-	50.3
0.57	-	-	0.98	1.30	1.22	27.6-	18.2	0.54	1.44	0.36	2.4	0.180Y	6/8/18	27.0-	17.9
0.37	-	-	1.52	2.29	1.50	25.2-	20.9	1.24	1.24	1.24	3.6	0.310Y	18/78/27	38.4-	31.7
-0.81	-	-	-1.16	-2.83	-1.50			-	-	-		8.57	8/27/13	7.0-	4.3
3.18	-	-	5.95	7.30	4.99	18.1-	12.5	-	-	-		0.350Y	18/78/27	107.8-	74.2
1.11	-	-	-0.75	2.92	5.90			1.40	1.20	1.20	3.7	0.3750Y	9/21/18	48.1-	28.9
0.08	-	-	0.88	1.34	-1.21	37.0-	24.6	1.48	2.10	2.26	5.7	0.370Z	18/78/27	32.5-	21.6
-	-	7.80	-	-	43.60			-	-	-				110.2-	87.3
0.07	-	-	0.18	0.78	0.70	192.5-	146.2	1.20	1.20	1.20	3.9	0.30Z	18/78/27	34.6-	26.3
0.05	-	-	0.34	0.33	0.26	93.5-	71.5	1.21	1.19	1.17	4.3	0.3050Z	18/78/27	31.8-	24.3
0.02	-	-	-0.06	0.18	-0.23			0.01	0.01	0.01	0.2	0.8750Y	7/2/18	5.5-	3.3
-	0.44	-	1.37	1.17	1.01	56.0-	34.4	0.12	0.10	0.09	0.2	0.060Y	18/78/27	76.7-	47.2
-0.02	-	-	0.20	-0.73	-3.58	43.4-	25.8	-	-	-				8.7-	5.2
-	-0.12	-	-1.20	-0.54	3.87			2.80	2.76	2.75	4.6	0.710Y	18/78/27	74.3-	42.3
0.54	-	-	1.29	1.51	1.99			-	-	-		0.30	18/78/27		
-0.36	-	-	5.60	-0.70	9.00	12.8-	6.5	-	-	-				71.5-	36.5
0.31	-	-	1.16	1.34	1.04	12.0-	10.3	1.24	1.24	1.24	9.8	0.32810Z	10/30/18	13.9-	11.9
0.55	-	-	-0.04	1.14	3.05			0.24	0.23	0.05	1.5	0.060Y	7/6/18	18.9-	9.3
-0.36	-	-	1.79	2.18	0.56	12.1-	9.4	1.32	0.84	0.84	7.1	0.40630Z	7/16/18	21.6-	16.8
1.65	-	-	3.66	3.34	2.32	31.5-	24.5	2.55	2.40	2.24	2.5	0.5960Y	18/78/27	115.5-	89.5
-2.43	-	-	3.94	-5.85	3.00	6.8-	2.8	-	-	-				26.7-	11.0
-0.38	-	-	-13.12	-19.92	-10.78			1.00	1.00	1.00	2.0	0.250Y	18/78/27	66.9-	38.1
0.30	-	-	0.75	-	-	30.4-	24.8	0.58	-	-	2.8	0.34520	8/13/18	22.8-	18.6
-	0.49	-	0.21	1.82	1.34	92.4-	62.2	0.26	0.22	-	1.7	0.11250Y	18/78/27	19.4-	13.1
0.68	-	-	3.09	2.65	2.44	23.7-	16.5	0.47	0.43	0.40	0.8	0.150Y	18/78/27	73.3-	51.0
0.42	-	-	2.39	1.99	2.18	21.5-	14.0	1.57	1.80	1.80	3.8	1.757Y	2/21/18	51.4-	33.4
0.59	-	-	0.96	-1.64	0.73	15.2-	7.7	0.15	-	1.83	1.4	0.750	8/14/18	14.6-	7.4
-	-	-	0.30	0.35	0.35	31.7-	28.8	0.37	0.37	0.37	4.1	0.02830Z	8/1/18	9.5-	8.6
-0.20	-	-	-	-	-			-	-	-				7.4-	2.8
0.31	-	-	1.78	5.30	1.00	29.7-	23.3	1.76	2.50	1.70	3.6	21.56250Z	18/78/27	52.9-	41.5
-	-	-0.08	-	-0.36	0.14			-	-	-				6.0-	4.3
-	0.42	-	1.99	1.86	0.82	47.4-	36.6	0.71	0.67	0.63	0.9	0.20Y	18/78/27	94.3-	72.8
-	-0.34	-	1.97	1.77	1.74	24.7-	17.8	0.82	0.81	0.80	1.9	0.20750Y	6/29/18	48.8-	35.1
0.25	-	-	1.36	1.48	2.09	20.2-	16.1	0.24	0.06	-	1.0	0.070	5/31/18	27.5-	21.8
0.30	-	-	3.28	1.70	-	14.4-	10.4	-	-	-				47.3-	34.0
0.51	-	-	3.85	1.05	4.26	22.8-	15.8	0.60	0.84	0.42	0.8	0.150Y	6/29/18	87.7-	60.8
0.06	-	-	2.00	1.88	2.32	21.4-	16.5	1.13	1.09	1.04	3.0	0.2950Y	18/78/27	42.9-	33.0
-	-	-	1.58	1.58	1.56			-	-	-		0.54690	8/15/18		
0.44	-	-	2.28	1.69	1.60	15.8-	11.6	2.50	2.32	2.17	7.9	0.660	8/9/18	36.0-	26.5
1.50	-	-	4.52	-1.48	3.90	18.1-	5.8	1.32	1.32	1.31	2.8	0.330Y	18/78/27	81.7-	26.2
2.08	-	-	6.45	5.46	4.71	32.1-	22.4	2.76	2.36	1.88	1.6	1.030Y	18/78/27	207.2-	144.6
-	-	318.50	342.10	191.16	282.66	0.1-	0.1	90.81	88.05	88.63	282.4			36.7-	27.2
-	1.68	-	2.14	6.20	6.04	77.1-	62.3	2.74	2.45	2.15	1.9	0.7450Y	18/78/27	165.0-	133.4
0.49	-	-	4.08	2.02	2.20	11.6-	8.3	1.10	1.06	1.00	2.6	0.2850Y	6/29/18	47.1-	34.0
-2.30	-	-	-0.14	-0.66	0.46			-	-	-				18.6-	5.3
-	0.44	-	1.57	1.64	1.27	24.0-	19.2	0.68	0.58	0.50	2.0	0.18750Y	18/78/27	37.7-	30.1
-1.04	-	-	0.73	-1.76	1.84	6.4-	3.0	-	-	-				4.7-	2.2
-	0.91	-	2.74	2.36	2.03	19.3-	12.5	0.40	0.32	0.25	0.9	0.1250Y	18/78/27	52.9-	34.4
0.34	-	-	0.76	1.02	0.74	29.3-	22.9	0.85	0.85	0.80	4.4	0.20Z	18/78/27	22.3-	17.4
-	-	0.93	1.63	1.10	135.88	32.2-	21.4	0.71	0.30	-	1.6	0.20Y	3/15/18	52.5-	34.9
-	-0.07	-	-2.25	-0.02	-0.11			-	-	-		0.47660Z	10/15/07	3.4-	1.6
0.03	-	-	3.91	4.73	1.60	35.8-	29.3	-	-	-				139.8-	114.5
-	0.64	-	1.48	1.43	2.48	16.7-	11.6	0.53	0.50	0.67	2.5	0.13930Y	18/78/27	24.6-	17.2
-	-	-	-	0.86	1.59			-	-	-		0.39750Y	6/15/16		
-	-	-	0.48	0.07	0.64	115.9-	97.0	2.55	2.55	2.50	5.1	0.50780	4/16/18	55.6-	46.6
-	-	-	-	-	-			-	0.49	1.02		0.40630Y	4/1/16		
-	-	-	0.65	-0.22	-1.22	21.6-	13.4	-	-	-				14.1-	8.7
0.08	-	-	0.11	0.58	0.94	277.3-	217.7	10.16	17.18	13.65	38.7			30.5-	23.9
1.05	-	-	4.39	5.24	4.77	31.7-	23.4	2.87	2.59	-	2.4	0.770Y	18/78/27	139.2-	102.5
-0.41	-	-	-1.08	-1.29	-1.39			-	-	-				142.1-	63.6
0.16	-	-	0.67	-0.15	-1.41	18.7-	8.1	0.02	0.02	0.02	0.2	0.010	3/29/18	12.5-	5.4
0.31	-	-	0.44	0.25	-0.19	81.8-	65.1	1.00	0.80	0.57	3.0	0.250Y	18/78/27	36.0-	28.6
0.01	-	-	0.11	0.05	0.19	17.3-	5.6	0.11	0.05	0.19	8.8	0.00930Z	3/14/18	1.9-	0.6
3.53	-	-	16.81	4.07	8.44	18.3-	13.7	1.89	0.87	1.15	0.7	0.50Y	18/78/27	306.9-	230.8
0.45	-	-	0.06	-0.79	-0.21	82.5-	46.2	0.60	2.05	1.35	15.8	0.18230	9/27/18	5.0-	2.8
3.48	-	-	10.46	12.14	8.36	25.9-	18.3	2.52	2.10	1.70	1.1	0.720Y	18/78/27	270.9-	191.4
1.11	-	-	2.61	1.36	0.38	13.5-	9.6	0.50	0.50	0.50	1.7	0.16250Y	18/78/27	35.3-	25.1
-	-	-	-1.01	-6.26	-			-	-	-				48.6-	16.1
3.40	-	-	1.98	1.52	0.86	42.5-	27.6	-	-	-		0.150Y	18/78/27	84.2-	54.6
0.90	-	-	2.94	2.61	4.57	30.6-	21.8	1.20	1.17	1.13	1.6	0.310Y	6/15/18	90.0-	64.0
0.09	-	-	1.07	0.12	-1.93	8.2-	4.6	-	-	-		0.1250	7/12/13	8.7-	4.9
3.17	-	-	17.43	17.41	20.94	0.6-	0.5	9.09	9.10	8.32	98.9			11.2-	7.9
0.72	-	-	4.21	3.94	3.87	23.5-	19.3	2.24	2.08	1.92	2.5	0.590Y	18/78/27	98.8-	81.0

SYMBOL	COMPANY	NATURE OF BUSINESS	FISCAL YEAR-END	TOTAL REV. $MILL	NET INCOME $MILL	TOTAL ASSETS $MILL	NET STK EQUITY $MILL	NO OF INST	INST. HOLDINGS (SHARES)
IEX	IDEX Corporation	Industrial Machinery & Equipment	12/31/17	2287.3	337.3	3399.6	1886.5	541	87851773
IDT	IDT Corp	Services	7/31/17	1501.7	8.2	519.0	145.7	136	14311366
ITW	Illinois Tool Works, Inc.	Industrial Machinery & Equipment	12/31/17	14314.0	1687.0	16780.0	4585.0	1680	364142163
IMAX	IMAX Corp.	Entertainment	12/31/17	380.8	2.3	866.6	527.7	237	66062749
ICD	Independence Contract Drilling Inc	Equipment & Services	12/31/17	90.0	-24.3	304.6	235.5	88	31286491
IHC	Independence Holding Company	Life & Health	12/31/17	320.5	42.0	1040.6	431.5	82	3776480
IRT	Independence Realty Trust Inc	REITs	12/31/17	161.2	30.2	1450.6	624.1	212	76711387
IFN	India Fund, Inc. (The)	Holding and other Investment Office	12/31/16	10.2	-0.1	734.5	689.7	147	10911641
IBA	Industrias Bachoco S.A.B. de C.V.	Food	12/31/17	58050.0	4948.2	50557.4	35619.0		0
INFY	Infosys Ltd.	IT Services	3/31/17	10208.0	2140.0	12854.0	10637.0	465	452663255
HIFR	InfraREIT Inc	REITs	12/31/17	134.6	12.3	1993.9	657.1	171	37862868
ING	ING Groep NV	Banking	12/31/17	45930.0	5464.0	843878.0	48429.0	431	155375369
IR	Ingersoll-Rand Plc	Industrial Machinery & Equipment	12/31/17	14197.6	1302.6	18173.3	7140.3	981	231978596
NGVT	Ingevity Corp	Specialty Chemicals	12/31/17	972.4	126.5	929.6	263.9	364	44442234
INGR	Ingredion Inc	Food	12/31/17	5832.0	519.0	6080.0	2891.0	714	86488033
IIPR	Innovative Industrial Properties Inc	Property, Real Estate & Developmen	12/31/17	6.4	-0.1	80.0	73.5	63	2848037
IPHI	Inphi Corp	Semiconductors	12/31/17	348.2	-74.9	917.5	411.4	237	61964182
INSI	Insight Select Income Fund	Holding and other Investment Office	3/31/17	11.0	9.4	223.1	222.3	53	2419087
NSP	Insperity Inc	Business Services	12/31/17	3300.2	84.4	1063.7	66.3	367	39806895
INSP	Inspire Medical Systems Inc	Medical Instruments & Equipment	12/31/17	28.6	-17.5	25.1	1.3		0
IBP	Installed Building Products Inc	Construction Services	12/31/17	1132.9	41.1	738.7	210.5	215	25025083
INST	Instructure Inc	Internet & Software	12/31/17	158.8	-49.8	135.4	4.4	170	30350176
ITGR	Integer Holdings Corp	Medical Instruments & Equipment	12/29/17	1461.9	66.7	2848.3	893.4	293	38707753
I	Intelsat SA	Services	12/31/17	2148.6	-178.7	12610.0	-3807.9		0
ICE	Intercontinental Exchange Inc	Finance Intermediaries & Services	12/31/17	5834.0	2514.0	78264.0	16924.0	957	569393031
IHG	InterContinental Hotels Group Plc	Hotels, Restaurants & Travel	12/31/17	1784.0	592.0	3175.0	-858.0	176	13514453
IBM	International Business Machines Co	IT Services	12/31/17	79139.0	5753.0	125356.0	17594.0	2787	708964987
IFF	International Flavors & Fragrances I	Specialty Chemicals	12/31/17	3398.7	295.7	4958.9	1684.2	747	92904047
IGT	International Game Technology PL	Entertainment	12/31/17	4939.0	-1068.6	15159.2	2005.0		0
IP	International Paper Co	Containers & Packaging	12/31/17	21743.0	2144.0	33903.0	6522.0	1232	446877240
INSW	International Seaways Inc	Miscellaneous Transportation Servic	12/31/17	290.1	-106.1	1664.5	1085.7	86	25593392
IPG	Interpublic Group of Companies Inc.	Advertising	12/31/17	7882.4	579.0	12695.2	2201.0	719	506188765
IPL PRD	Interstate Power & Light Co	Electric Utilities	12/31/17	1870.3	227.0	7606.0	2709.7		0
INXN	InterXion Holding NV	IT Services	12/31/17	489.3	39.1	1702.1	596.7	275	69847104
IPI	Intrepid Potash Inc	Agricultural Chemicals	12/31/17	157.6	-22.9	511.1	402.6	192	67399115
XON	Intrexon Corp	Biotechnology	12/31/17	231.0	-117.0	846.9	533.6		0
IVC	Invacare Corp	Medical Instruments & Equipment	12/31/17	966.5	-76.5	1066.0	423.3	233	56555874
VBF	Invesco Bond Fund	Holding and other Investment Office	2/28/17	10.7	9.5	230.1	227.5	50	2561777
VCV	Invesco California Value Municipal I	Holding and other Investment Office	2/28/17	44.3	33.4	1035.2	635.4	60	3884389
VTA	Invesco Dynamic Credit Opportuniti	Holding and other Investment Office	2/28/17	91.8	65.7	1619.0	981.8	124	29210599
IHIT	Invesco High Income 2023 Target T	Holding and other Investment Office	2/28/17	3.5	2.8	239.0	238.8	27	3437742
VLT	Invesco High Income Trust II	Holding and other Investment Office	2/28/17	10.9	8.8	182.4	132.8	43	3165870
IVZ	Invesco Ltd	Wealth Management	12/31/17	5160.3	1127.3	31668.8	8696.1	845	409572627
IVR	Invesco Mortgage Capital Inc	REITs	12/31/17	595.7	348.6	18657.3	2630.5	302	89960657
OIA	Invesco Municipal Income Opportun	Holding and other Investment Office	2/28/17	23.0	19.4	419.4	353.3	68	3344207
VMO	Invesco Municipal Opportunity Trust	Holding and other Investment Office	2/28/17	70.6	52.4	1547.4	903.9	138	10678566
VKQ	Invesco Municipal Trust	Holding and other Investment Office	2/28/17	56.0	41.9	1236.3	740.3	116	7151011
VPV	Invesco Pennsylvania Value Munici	Holding and other Investment Office	2/28/17	22.8	16.6	540.3	329.7	64	5199279
IQI	Invesco Quality Municipal Income T	Holding and other Investment Office	2/29/12	23.1	19.8	524.2	443.1		0
VVR	Invesco Senior Income Trust	Holding and other Investment Office	2/28/17	72.2	52.1	1423.7	888.3	155	73655218
VGM	Invesco Trust for Investment Grade	Holding and other Investment Office	2/28/17	59.0	43.3	1294.3	752.9	102	6089484
VTN	Invesco Trust For Investment Grade	Holding and other Investment Office	2/28/17	19.8	14.0	478.9	280.5	40	1731770
IIM	Invesco Value Municipal Income Tr	Holding and other Investment Office	2/29/16	50.2	40.2	1203.6	786.8		0
ITG	Investment Technology Group Inc.	Finance Intermediaries & Services	12/31/17	483.7	-39.4	784.9	363.2	227	40463762
IRET	Investors Real Estate Trust	REITs	4/30/18	169.7	116.8	1426.7	613.4	213	82655520
NVTA	Invitae Corp	Diagnostic & Health Related Service	12/31/17	68.2	-123.4	211.1	121.8	122	52662638
INVH	Invitation Homes Inc	Property, Real Estate & Developmen	12/31/17	1054.5	-105.3	18683.6	8498.1	314	548651185
IO	ION Geophysical Corp	Production & Extraction	12/31/17	197.6	-30.2	301.1	29.6	140	16615438
IQV	IQVIA Holdings Inc	Biotechnology	12/31/17	9739.0	1309.0	22742.0	8109.0	625	207856531
IRM	Iron Mountain Inc (New)	REITs	12/31/17	3845.6	183.8	10972.4	2297.4	663	281934135
IRS	IRSA Inversiones y Representacion	Property, Real Estate & Developmen	6/30/17	74172.0	3030.0	231242.0	25864.0	87	13830533
ICL	Israel Chemicals Ltd	Agricultural Chemicals	12/31/17	5418.0	364.0	8714.0	2859.0	105	98801909
STAR	iStar Inc	REITs	12/31/17	679.2	175.7	4731.1	879.7	253	72484247
ITCB	Itau CorpBanca	Banking	12/31/17	1643297.0	67821.0	28032773.0	3211477.0	46	1652071
ITUB	Itau Unibanco Holding S.A.	Banking	12/31/17	215798.0	23903.0	1434969.0	134840.0	458	858412315
ITT	ITT Inc	Industrial Machinery & Equipment	12/31/17	2585.3	113.5	3700.2	1596.1	604	112614933
IVH	Ivy High Income Opportunities Fund	Finance Intermediaries & Services	9/30/17	31.2	25.0	404.2	270.6	45	4367767
JAX	J Alexander's Holdings Inc	Hotels, Restaurants & Travel	12/31/17	233.3	7.3	169.7	108.7	129	13209411
JILL	J.Jill Inc	Retail - Apparel and Accessories	2/3/18	698.1	55.4	597.6	179.3	109	8082992
JBL	Jabil Inc	Electrical Equipment	8/31/17	19063.1	129.1	11096.0	2353.5	567	201648719
JEC	Jacobs Engineering Group, Inc.	Construction Services	9/29/17	10022.8	293.7	7380.9	4428.4	831	145284598
JAG	Jagged Peak Energy Inc	Production & Extraction	12/31/17	267.3	-76.5	1103.4	699.3	131	58600546
JHX	James Hardie Industries Plc	Construction Materials	3/31/17	1921.6	276.5	2012.7	-212.2	69	2449843
JHG	Janus Henderson Group Plc	Holding and other Investment Office	12/31/17	1743.7	655.5	7272.7	4837.3	217	102074988
JOF	Japan Smaller Capitalization Fund I	Holding and other Investment Office	2/28/17	6.8	3.3	342.9	342.5	74	21741596
JBGS	JBG SMITH Properties	REITs	12/31/17	543.0	-71.8	6071.8	2970.6	299	100649467
JBGS	JBG SMITH Properties	REITs	12/31/17	543.0	-71.8	6071.8	2970.6	299	100649467
JEF	Jefferies Financial Group Inc	Agricultural Livestock	12/31/17	11436.4	171.7	47169.1	10231.0	704	312458294
JELD	JELD-WEN Holding Inc	Manufacturing	12/31/17	3763.9	10.8	2862.9	792.0	203	68372196
JCAP	Jernigan Capital Inc	REITs	12/31/17	12.2	14.6	314.6	305.8	106	11166335

T32

1st	2nd	3rd	Ann 2017	Ann 2016	Ann 2015	P/E Hi	P/E Lo	Div 2017	Div 2016	Div 2015	Av. Yld %	Amount	Payable	Price Hi	Price Lo
1.27			4.36	3.53	3.62	34.5	25.8	1.45	1.34	1.24	1.1	0.430Y	18/78/27	150.4	112.7
		-0.14	0.35	1.03	3.63	44.8	14.0	0.76	0.75	2.03	6.9	0.090Y	6/29/18	15.7	4.9
1.90			4.86	5.70	5.13	36.8	27.9	2.86	2.40	2.07	1.9	0.780Y	18/78/27	178.9	135.6
0.13			0.04	0.42	0.78	660.0	442.5							26.4	17.7
-0.11			-0.64	-0.67	-0.33									5.2	2.8
0.46			2.63	7.09	1.71	14.8	7.8	0.16	0.15	0.08	0.6	0.150Y	6/18/18	39.0	20.6
0.04			0.41	-0.19	0.78	25.8	20.2	0.72	0.72	0.72	7.4	0.180Z	7/20/18	10.6	8.3
					0.01				1.71	1.82		0.710	6/29/18	28.8	23.8
		0.59	8.25	6.58	6.36	8.2	6.4	15.23	14.97	17.75	25.4			67.6	53.0
		0.35	0.94	0.90	0.88	20.7	15.2	0.55	0.97	1.49	3.3			19.4	14.3
0.29			0.28	1.14	0.31	82.8	63.5	1.00	1.00	0.81	4.8	0.250Z	7/19/18	23.2	17.8
			1.41	1.28	1.27	14.6	10.1	0.54	0.53	0.31	3.1	0.39840Z	12/15/18	20.6	14.2
0.48			5.05	5.65	2.48			1.70	1.36	1.16		0.530	18/78/27		
0.72			2.97	0.83	-	28.3	18.8							84.0	55.7
1.90			7.06	6.55	5.51	20.7	15.5	2.20	1.90	1.74	1.7	0.60Y	18/78/27	146.0	109.5
0.09			-0.13	-4.56				0.55			2.2	0.56250Z	7/16/18	38.8	16.1
-0.53			-1.78	2.25	-0.35									43.1	24.4
			0.88	0.93	0.98	23.6	20.7	0.90	1.01	1.06	4.6	0.20	8/22/18	20.8	18.2
1.18			2.01	1.54	0.79	50.4	17.4	1.58	0.48	0.42	2.6	0.20Y	6/25/18	101.3	35.0
-5.05			-14.88	-16.90	-20.74									39.5	24.1
0.20			1.30	1.23	0.85	59.7	39.3							77.6	51.0
-0.37			-1.69	-1.92	-6.07									46.7	28.6
0.25			2.09	0.19	-0.29	32.3	20.3							67.5	42.5
		-0.26	-1.50	8.36	-36.68							0.71880	5/2/16		
0.79			4.23	2.37	2.28	18.0	15.2	0.80	0.68	0.58	1.1	0.240Y	18/78/27	76.0	64.3
			3.05	1.94	5.13	22.6	16.1	0.33	4.61	0.58	0.6			68.9	49.1
1.81			6.14	12.38	13.42	27.5	22.4	5.90	5.50	5.00	3.9	1.570Y	18/78/27	169.1	137.5
1.63			3.72	5.05	5.16	42.2	32.8	2.66	2.40	2.06	1.9	0.690Y	18/78/27	156.9	122.1
		-3.95	-5.26	1.05	-0.39							0.20	6/19/18		
1.74			5.13	2.18	2.23	12.7	9.8	1.86	1.78	1.64	3.3	0.4750Y	18/78/27	65.1	50.1
-1.01			-3.64	-0.62	4256.92							0.53130Z	12/30/18		
-0.04			1.46	1.49	1.09	17.5	12.6	0.72	0.60	0.48	3.3	0.210Y	18/78/27	25.6	18.4
								1.27	1.27	1.27	5.1	0.31870Y	6/15/18	26.6	0.0
		-0.24	0.55	0.56	0.69										
0.01			-0.20	-0.88	-6.94							0.75G7	12/27/12	5.0	2.3
-0.33			-0.98	-1.58	-0.76									25.1	11.3
-0.43			-2.34	-1.32	-0.81			0.04	0.05	0.05	0.2	0.01140Y	7/20/18	19.8	12.7
			0.83	0.84	0.85	24.4	21.1	0.84	0.95	1.38	4.4	0.0690	7/31/18	20.3	17.5
			0.70	0.78	0.79	18.8	16.5	0.69	0.79	0.79	5.6	0.051M	7/31/18	13.2	11.5
			0.89	0.97	0.92	13.6	12.8	0.88	0.90	0.90	7.5	0.06250	7/31/18	12.1	11.4
			0.12	-	-	85.3	79.5	0.10			1.0	0.050	7/31/18	10.2	9.5
			1.08	1.14	1.18	14.1	12.5	1.13	1.24	1.29	7.8	0.0840	7/31/18	15.2	13.5
0.62			2.75	2.06	2.26			1.15	1.11	1.06		0.30	18/78/27		
0.37			2.75	1.98	0.67	6.8	5.6	1.63	1.60	1.70	9.7	0.48440Z	7/25/18	18.6	15.3
			0.41	0.42	0.40	20.0	17.9	0.40	0.39	0.40	5.2	0.0344M	7/31/18	8.2	7.4
			0.78	0.85	0.83	17.1	14.8	0.85	0.85	0.79	6.9	0.0554M	7/31/18	13.4	11.5
			0.76	0.83	0.80	17.1	15.2	0.78	0.82	0.81	6.4	0.0563M	7/31/18	13.0	11.6
			0.69	0.81	0.78	18.3	16.8	0.70	0.78	0.88	5.8	0.058M	7/31/18	12.6	11.6
												0.0574M	7/31/18	13.0	11.7
			0.29	0.31	0.32	15.9	14.8	0.29	0.32	0.32	6.6	0.01950	7/31/18	4.6	4.3
			0.80	0.89	0.86	17.3	15.1	0.81	0.88	0.89	6.3	0.0601M	7/31/18	13.8	12.1
			0.72	0.87	0.85	19.4	17.5	0.77	0.83	0.86	5.8	0.0583M	7/31/18	14.0	12.6
				0.85	0.86				0.84	0.90		0.062M	7/31/18	15.4	14.0
0.13			-1.19	-0.79	2.63			0.28	0.28	0.21	1.4	0.070	6/15/18	23.9	17.9
		1.12	0.26	0.49	0.11	25.8	17.9	0.46	0.52	0.52	8.1	0.41410Z	7/2/18	6.7	4.7
-0.66			-2.65	-3.02	-3.18									10.4	4.7
-0.03			-0.26	-0.32	-			0.22			1.0	0.110Y	18/78/27	24.1	20.6
-1.44			-2.55	-5.71	-2.29									31.6	3.3
0.32			5.88	0.76	3.08	18.5	14.9							108.6	87.6
0.16			0.69	0.42	0.58	60.1	44.8	2.24	2.00	1.91	6.2	0.58750Y	18/78/27	41.4	30.9
0.06			5.23	-2.18	-0.07	6.2	3.2			0.63				32.2	16.8
		0.31	0.29	-0.10	0.40			0.13							
0.35			1.56	0.55	-0.62	7.8	6.4					0.56250Z	6/15/18	12.2	9.9
	0.13		0.13	0.04	0.64	125.7	82.8	1.25	370.32	1224.66	8.7			16.3	10.8
		0.86	3.65	3.54	4.28	4.7	2.7	1.25	1.17	1.10	9.3			17.0	9.9
1.14			1.28	2.07	3.88	44.9	30.5	0.51	0.37	0.47	1.0	0.1340Y	18/78/27	57.4	39.0
			1.51	1.57	1.62	10.6	9.3	1.48	1.60	1.96	9.9	0.10	7/31/18	16.0	14.0
0.11			0.50	0.47	0.36	25.5	18.2							12.8	9.1
0.26			0.55	0.10	-0.04	23.1	7.7							12.7	4.3
	0.21		0.69	1.32	1.45	45.6	35.3	0.32	0.32	0.32	1.1	0.080Y	18/78/27	31.4	24.4
	0.34		2.42	1.73	2.40	29.4	20.5	0.45			0.7	0.150Y	18/78/27	71.0	49.6
-0.18			-0.36	-0.03	-									16.4	10.9
	0.12		0.62	0.55	0.65	30.0	22.0	0.30	0.98	1.48	1.8			18.6	13.6
0.82			3.93	1.66	2.78			0.64				0.360	6/1/18		
			0.12	0.06	0.06	114.5	94.5	0.94	0.88	0.13	7.6	0.0878B	12/21/17	13.7	11.3
-0.04			-0.70	-0.29				0.45			1.3	0.2250Y	18/78/27	38.5	31.0
-0.04			-0.70	-0.29				0.45			1.3	0.2250Y	18/78/27	37.2	31.8
0.34			0.45	0.34	0.74	62.2	48.4	0.33	0.25	0.25	1.3	0.10Y	18/78/27	28.0	21.8
0.37			0.00	-2.17	-15.88									41.8	27.1
0.12			1.10	2.42	-0.69	20.3	14.7	1.40	1.40	1.05	7.2	0.43750Z	7/13/18	22.3	16.1

SYMBOL	COMPANY	NATURE OF BUSINESS	FISCAL YEAR-END	TOTAL REV. $MILL	NET INCOME $MILL	TOTAL ASSETS $MILL	NET STK EQUITY $MILL	NO OF INST	INST. HOLDINGS (SHARES)
JT	Jianpu Technology Inc	Services	12/31/17	1445.8	-202.1	1913.5	1538.5	27	21776901
JKS	JinkoSolar Holding Co., Ltd.	Semiconductors	12/31/17	26472.9	141.7	28636.4	6689.3	109	9275249
JMP	JMP Group LLC	Finance Intermediaries & Services	12/31/17	154.6	-15.9	1076.6	96.3		0
JBT	John Bean Technologies Corp	Industrial Machinery & Equipment	12/31/17	1635.1	80.5	1391.4	441.9	317	39338453
DECR 19	John Deere Capital Corp.	Credit & Lending	10/29/17	2227.0	328.4	35002.8	3656.7		0
BTO	John Hancock Financial Opportuniti	Holding and other Investment Office	12/31/16	18.3	9.3	761.8	651.4	89	4693275
HEQ	John Hancock Hedged Equity & Inc	Holding and other Investment Office	12/31/16	7.5	5.1	205.9	205.5	38	1818374
JHS	John Hancock Income Securities Tr	Holding and other Investment Office	10/31/17	11.9	8.7	291.4	181.4	37	3088024
HTY	John Hancock Investment Trust	Holding and other Investment Office	8/31/92	3.9	2.6	119.5	119.5		0
JHI	John Hancock Investors Trust	Holding and other Investment Office	10/31/17	14.2	11.1	253.5	163.7	54	1199288
HPI	John Hancock Preferred Income Fu	Holding and other Investment Office	7/31/17	53.5	41.9	870.7	576.1	86	2434900
PDT	John Hancock Premium Dividend F	Holding and other Investment Office	10/31/17	70.9	53.6	1155.8	771.0	99	4597622
JNJ	Johnson & Johnson	Pharmaceuticals	12/31/17	76450.0	1300.0	157303.0	60160.0	3505	2325355470
JCI	Johnson Controls International plc	Miscellaneous Consumer Goods	9/30/17	30172.0	1611.0	51884.0	20447.0	1141	1020977992
JONE	Jones Energy Inc	Production & Extraction	12/31/17	188.6	-101.5	1710.1	559.3	103	84087550
JLL	Jones Lang LaSalle Inc	Property, Real Estate & Developmen	12/31/17	7932.4	254.2	8014.5	3243.2	553	52641444
JPM	JPMorgan Chase & Co	Banking	12/31/17	113899.0	24441.0	2533600.0	255693.0	3287	3202359166
JMEI	Jumei International Holding Ltd	Retail - Apparel and Accessories	12/31/17	5816.8	-37.0	4967.2	3875.2	72	26047430
JNPR	Juniper Networks Inc	Peripherals	12/31/17	5027.2	306.2	9833.8	4680.9	734	400110532
JP	Jupai Holdings Ltd	Wealth Management	12/31/17	1706.2	409.5	2626.1	1819.4	38	2687137
JE	Just Energy Group Inc	Electric Utilities	3/31/18	3626.6	509.3	1646.8	231.2		0
LRN	K12 Inc	Educational Services	6/30/17	888.5	0.5	735.3	574.3	194	39505656
KAI	Kadant Inc	Industrial Machinery & Equipment	12/30/17	515.0	31.1	761.1	331.0	251	14092449
KDMN	Kadmon Holdings Inc	Pharmaceuticals	12/31/17	12.3	-79.8	83.6	1.8	85	50614275
KAMN	Kaman Corp.	Industrial Machinery & Equipment	12/31/17	1805.9	49.8	1455.5	635.7	250	30564049
KSU	Kansas City Southern	Rail	12/31/17	2582.9	962.0	9198.7	4548.9	831	120000283
KS	KapStone Paper & Packaging Corp	Paper & Forest Products	12/31/17	3315.7	243.5	3324.0	1137.0	365	101264957
KAR	KAR Auction Services Inc.	Retail - Automotive	12/31/17	3458.0	362.0	6984.3	1484.9		0
KED	Kayne Anderson Energy Developm	Holding and other Investment Office	11/30/17	2.3	-4.3	289.2	174.2	65	3270418
KYE	Kayne Anderson Energy Total Retur	Holding and other Investment Office	11/30/17	21.6	4.4	562.2	384.2	88	9613890
KMF	Kayne Anderson Midstream/Energy	Holding and other Investment Office	11/30/17	17.0	3.2	439.3	311.8	67	6685393
KYN	Kayne Anderson MLP Investment C	Holding and other Investment Office	11/30/17	20.8	-51.4	3399.3	1826.2	251	36117501
KB	KB Financial Group, Inc.	Banking	12/31/16	3444829.0	2143744.0	756473656.0	30998044.0	222	26391826
KBH	KB HOME	Builders	11/30/17	4368.5	180.6	5041.5	1926.3	442	95295621
KBR	KBR Inc	Construction Services	12/31/17	4171.0	434.0	3674.0	1229.0	396	180066269
FRAC	Keane Group Inc	Equipment & Services	12/31/17	1542.1	-28.2	1043.1	513.1	159	94739969
K	Kellogg Co	Food	12/30/17	12923.0	1269.0	16350.0	2212.0	1067	461046778
KEM	KEMET Corp.	Electrical Equipment	3/31/18	1199.9	254.5	1218.3	463.0	302	50688255
KMPR	Kemper Corp (DE)	General Insurance	12/31/17	2723.4	120.9	8376.2	2115.6	303	40722699
KMT	Kennametal Inc.	Industrial Machinery & Equipment	6/30/17	2058.4	49.1	2415.5	1017.3	434	101744852
KW	Kennedy-Wilson Holdings Inc	Property, Real Estate & Developmen	12/31/17	810.6	100.5	7724.8	1365.6	4	2975087
KEN	Kenon Holdings Ltd	Energy	12/31/17	365.7	236.6	2525.9	983.1	13	732133
KDP	Keurig Dr Pepper Inc	Beverages	12/31/17	6690.0	1076.0	10022.0	2451.0	879	210452889
KEG	Key Energy Services Inc (DE)	Equipment & Services	12/31/17	436.2	-120.6	529.1	128.7	134	34421467
KEY	KeyCorp	Banking	12/31/17	6868.0	1296.0	137690.0	15023.0	1052	1022303659
KEYS	Keysight Technologies Inc	Industrial Machinery & Equipment	10/31/17	3189.0	102.0	5933.0	2310.0	483	182612424
KRC	Kilroy Realty Corp	REITs	12/31/17	719.0	164.6	6802.8	3700.8	390	139866607
KRP	Kimbell Royalty Partners LP	Oil Royalty Traders	12/31/17	30.3	1.7	295.3		29	3802063
KMB	Kimberly-Clark Corp.	Household & Personal Products	12/31/17	18259.0	2278.0	15151.0	690.0	1894	341533249
KIM	Kimco Realty Corp	REITs	12/31/17	1200.8	426.1	11763.7	5394.2	675	455637380
KMI	Kinder Morgan Inc.	Equipment & Services	12/31/17	13705.0	183.0	79055.0	33636.0	1329	1675425243
KFS	Kingsway Financial Services Inc	General Insurance	12/31/17	193.2	-15.5	484.6	44.1	33	8881550
KGC	Kinross Gold Corp.	Precious Metals	12/31/17	3303.0	445.4	8157.2	4583.6	383	756600377
KEX	Kirby Corp.	Shipping	12/31/17	2214.4	313.2	5127.4	3110.8	389	72594531
KL	Kirkland Lake Gold Ltd	Precious Metals	12/31/17	747.5	132.4	1485.8	1157.6		0
KRG	Kite Realty Group Trust	REITs	12/31/17	358.8	11.9	3512.5	1565.4	320	98306712
KKR	KKR & Co Inc	Finance Intermediaries & Services	12/31/17	3282.3	1018.3	45834.7		445	368080800
KIO	KKR Income Opportunities Fund	Finance Intermediaries & Services	10/31/17	31.8	24.2	407.0	280.4	62	5466817
KREF	KKR Real Estate Finance Trust Inc	REITs	12/31/17	100.8	59.1	7394.9	1060.1	64	38646584
KMG	KMG Chemicals, Inc.	Specialty Chemicals	7/31/17	333.4	23.6	792.4	173.7	195	15262331
KNX	Knight-Swift Transportation Holding	Trucking	12/31/17	2425.5	484.3	7683.4	5237.7	458	159082676
KNL	Knoll Inc	Office Equipment & Furniture	12/31/17	1132.9	80.2	861.0	358.5	233	59722631
KNOP	KNOT Offshore Partners LP	Equipment & Services	12/31/16	173.7	61.1	1292.3	521.7	63	14146922
KN	Knowles Corp	Electronic Instruments & Related Pro	12/31/17	744.2	68.3	1549.8	1132.1	338	121070239
KSS	Kohl's Corp.	Retail - General Merchandise/Depart	2/3/18	19095.0	859.0	13340.0	5426.0	996	224987746
PHG	Koninklijke Philips NV	Medical Instruments & Equipment	12/31/17	17780.0	1657.0	25315.0	11999.0	420	58547204
KOP	Koppers Holdings Inc	Paper & Forest Products	12/31/17	1475.5	29.1	1200.2	99.9	278	25135145
KEP	Korea Electric Power Corp	Electric Utilities	12/31/16	60190384.0	7048581.0	77837042.0	71723693.0	195	106202012
KF	Korea Fund Inc (The)	Holding and other Investment Office	6/30/17	4.2	1.1	273.6	260.0	49	4385814
KFY	Korn/Ferry International (DE)	Business Services	4/30/18	1819.5	133.8	2287.9	1216.6	353	64289765
KOS	Kosmos Energy Ltd	Production & Extraction	12/31/17	636.8	-222.8	3192.6	897.1	198	521899731
KRA	Kraton Corp	Plastics	12/31/17	1960.4	97.5	2932.5	635.5	277	35887962
KR	Kroger Co (The)	Retail - Food & Beverage, Drug & To	2/3/18	122662.0	1907.0	37197.0	6931.0	1140	866102689
KRO	Kronos Worldwide Inc	Specialty Chemicals	12/31/17	1729.0	354.5	1824.4	754.3	219	24670701
KT	KT Corp (Korea)	Services	12/31/16	22743665.0	711089.0	30587733.0	11441935.0	222	195772149
LB	L Brands, Inc	Retail - Apparel and Accessories	2/3/18	12632.0	983.0	8149.0	-753.0	803	253604143
LLL	L3 Technologies Inc	Aerospace	12/31/17	9573.0	677.0	12729.0	5083.0	911	86318255
LZB	La-Z-Boy Inc.	Furniture	4/28/18	1583.9	80.9	893.0	612.2	299	53357772
LH	Laboratory Corporation of America	Diagnostic & Health Related Service	12/31/17	10441.4	1268.2	16568.0	6830.0	1079	121576852
LADR	Ladder Capital Corp	REITs	12/31/17	450.1	95.3	6025.6	1235.0	209	66954061

| EARNINGS PER SHARE | | | | | | P/E RATIO | | DIVIDENDS PER SHARE | | | AV. YLD | DIV. DECLARED | | PRICE RANGE | |
| QUARTERLY | | | ANNUAL | | | | | PER SHARE | | | | | | 2017 | |
1st	2nd	3rd	2017	2016	2015			2017	2016	2015	%	AMOUNT	PAYABLE		
-	-	-	-0.57	-0.53	-0.57	-		-	-	-		-		8.8 -	4.9
-	-	1.10	1.08	14.03	5.35	27.7 -	10.9	-	-	-		-		29.9 -	11.8
-0.01	-	-	-0.74	0.13	-0.01	-		0.36	0.39	0.49	6.8	0.030	10/15/18	7.2 -	0.0
0.04	-	-	2.53	2.27	1.88	48.3 -	33.8	0.40	0.40	0.37	0.4	0.10Y	6/7/18	122.3 -	85.5
-	-	-	-	0.50	0.10	-		-	1.48	1.33		0.37010	6/29/18	40.8 -	31.8
-	-	-	-	0.42	0.39	-		-	1.50	1.50		0.3760	6/29/18	17.9 -	16.1
-	-	-	0.75	0.79	0.81	20.1 -	17.6	0.81	0.85	0.90	5.6	0.17650	6/29/18	15.0 -	13.2
-	-	-	-	-	-	-		-	-	-		0.220	6/29/18	9.7 -	8.3
-	-	-	1.28	1.32	1.41	14.7 -	12.4	1.30	1.39	1.49	7.5	0.31280	6/29/18	18.9 -	15.9
-	-	-	1.61	1.60	1.65	14.0 -	12.4	1.68	1.68	1.68	7.9	0.140	7/31/18	22.5 -	19.9
-	-	-	1.11	0.98	0.97	15.6 -	13.3	1.47	1.11	1.09	9.1	0.09750	7/31/18	17.3 -	14.8
1.60	-	-	0.47	5.93	5.48	315.2 -	254.0	3.32	3.15	2.95	2.5	0.90Y	18/78/27	148.1 -	119.4
-	0.47	-	1.71	-1.30	1.35	-		1.00	1.16	0.81		0.260	7/13/18	-	
-0.30	-	-	-1.51	-1.04	-0.08	-		-	-	-		0.830Z	5/15/17	2.0 -	0.3
0.88	-	-	5.55	6.98	9.65	31.9 -	21.0	0.72	0.64	0.56	0.5	0.410Y	18/78/27	177.3 -	116.7
2.37	-	-	6.31	6.19	6.00	18.8 -	14.0	2.04	1.84	1.68	2.0	0.560Y	18/78/27	118.8 -	88.4
-	-	-	-0.25	0.95	0.82	-		-	-	-		-		3.9 -	2.0
0.10	-	-	0.80	1.53	1.59	37.4 -	30.1	0.40	0.40	0.40	1.5	0.180	18/78/27	30.0 -	24.1
0.04	-	-	1.99	1.03	0.16	14.3 -	3.7	3.31	-	-	18.6	-		28.4 -	7.5
-	-1.13	-	2.42	0.43	-3.07	3.1 -	1.5	0.50	0.50	0.58	9.3	0.53130	6/29/18	7.4 -	3.5
-	-	0.32	0.01	0.23	0.29	1854.0 -	1296.0	-	-	-		-		18.5 -	13.0
0.96	-	-	2.75	2.88	3.10	41.3 -	27.5	0.82	0.74	0.66	0.9	0.220Y	8/9/18	113.6 -	75.5
-0.27	-	-	-1.42	-9.74	-18.10	-		-	-	-		-		5.8 -	2.1
0.50	-	-	1.75	2.10	2.17	42.7 -	27.4	0.80	0.72	0.72	1.4	0.20Y	7/5/18	74.7 -	47.9
-	1.45	-	9.16	4.43	4.40	12.4 -	11.1	1.38	1.32	1.32	1.3	0.250Y	18/78/27	113.7 -	101.3
0.33	-	-	2.47	0.88	1.09	14.2 -	8.4	0.40	0.40	0.40	1.4	0.10Y	7/11/18	35.0 -	20.7
0.66	-	-	2.62	1.60	1.51	21.6 -	15.4	1.31	1.19	1.08	2.6	0.350Y	18/78/27	56.6 -	40.3
-0.12	-	-	-0.40	-0.39	-0.20	-		1.68	1.92	2.12	10.0	0.40	7/13/18	18.8 -	14.4
-0.00	-	-	0.12	-0.05	0.30	95.1 -	70.7	1.00	1.08	1.94	10.0	0.250	7/13/18	11.4 -	8.5
-	-	-	0.14	-0.07	0.30	110.1 -	82.7	1.30	1.50	3.82	9.6	0.30	7/13/18	15.4 -	11.6
-0.11	-	-	-0.45	-0.61	-0.53	-		1.90	2.20	2.63	10.7	0.450	7/13/18	20.2 -	14.6
•	-	-1100.00	-	-5559.00	4376.00	-		-	968.55	765.23		-		63.9 -	44.6
-	0.57	-	1.85	1.12	0.85	20.9 -	11.2	0.10	0.10	0.10	0.4	0.0250Y	18/78/27	38.6 -	20.7
0.97	-	-	3.06	-0.43	1.40	7.1 -	4.8	0.32	0.32	0.32	1.8	0.080Y	18/78/27	21.6 -	14.7
-0.07	-	-	-0.34	-2.14	-	-		-	-	-		-		19.5 -	12.6
1.27	-	-	3.62	1.96	1.72	19.4 -	15.6	2.12	2.04	1.98	3.2	0.540Y	18/78/27	70.4 -	56.6
-	-	0.32	0.87	-1.17	-0.31	31.2 -	14.6	-	-	-		-		27.1 -	12.7
1.02	-	-	2.33	0.33	1.65	35.0 -	15.9	0.96	0.96	0.96	1.6	0.240Y	18/78/27	81.5 -	37.0
-	-	0.61	0.61	-2.83	-4.71	85.1 -	54.8	0.80	0.80	0.72	1.9	0.20Y	18/78/27	51.9 -	33.4
-0.02	-	-	0.83	0.01	0.66	25.8 -	19.5	0.70	0.56	0.48	3.7	0.190Z	7/5/18	21.4 -	16.1
-	-	-	4.40	-7.67	1.36	-		-	-	-		12.350	3/22/18	-	
0.88	-	-	5.89	4.54	3.97	-		2.32	2.12	1.92		103.757Y	7/10/18	-	
-1.23	-	-	-6.00	-0.51	-5.86	-		-	-	-		-		19.8 -	8.7
0.38	-	-	1.13	0.80	1.05	19.6 -	14.6	0.38	0.33	0.29	2.0	0.38280Y	18/78/27	22.1 -	16.5
-	0.34	-	0.56	1.95	3.00	110.6 -	69.1	-	-	-		-		61.9 -	38.7
0.36	-	-	1.51	2.97	2.42	51.2 -	42.2	1.65	3.38	1.40	2.3	0.4550Z	18/78/27	77.3 -	63.7
-3.23	-	-	0.10	-10.28	-51.83	230.0 -	0.0	0.84	-	-	4.8	0.420	5/14/18	23.0 -	0.0
-	1.30	-	6.40	5.99	2.77	20.1 -	15.4	3.88	3.68	3.52	3.4	1.0Y	18/78/27	128.7 -	98.5
0.30	-	-	0.87	0.79	2.00	24.2 -	15.2	1.09	1.03	0.97	6.3	0.32810Z	18/78/27	21.0 -	13.2
-	-0.08	-	0.01	0.25	0.10	2069.0 -	1481.0	0.50	0.50	1.93	2.8	0.20Y	18/78/27	20.7 -	14.8
-0.11	-	-	-0.73	0.02	0.04	-		-	-	-		0.080	6/30/09	8.0 -	0.0
0.08	-	-	0.35	-0.08	-0.86	16.9 -	10.1	-	-	-		0.080	3/28/13	5.9 -	3.5
0.54	-	-	5.62	2.62	4.11	16.6 -	10.7	-	-	-		0.05	18/78/27	93.3 -	60.0
-	-	0.20	0.63	0.34	-0.04	44.2 -	14.0	0.03	-	-	0.2	0.030	7/13/18	27.8 -	8.8
-0.21	-	-	0.14	0.01	0.18	152.7 -	101.3	1.21	1.14	1.08	6.8	0.31750Z	7/13/18	21.4 -	14.2
0.32	-	-	1.95	0.59	1.01	-		0.67	0.64	1.58		-		-	
-	-	-	1.59	1.61	1.47	11.5 -	9.7	1.59	1.50	1.65	9.6	0.1250	10/31/18	18.2 -	15.5
0.44	-	-	1.30	1.61	1.95	16.7 -	14.3	0.99	1.22	0.73	4.9	0.430Z	7/13/18	21.7 -	18.6
-	-	0.98	1.92	1.57	1.03	41.3 -	24.5	0.12	0.12	0.12	0.2	0.030Y	6/22/18	79.3 -	47.0
0.39	-	-	4.34	1.16	1.42	11.5 -	8.0	0.06	-	-	0.1	0.060Y	6/27/18	49.8 -	34.6
0.31	-	-	1.63	1.68	1.36	14.5 -	10.8	0.60	0.60	0.51	2.9	0.150Y	6/29/18	23.7 -	17.7
-	-	-	-	1.54	1.50	-		-	2.08	2.03		0.520	8/14/18	-	
-	-	-	0.75	-0.47	-2.69	22.5 -	14.7	-	-	-		-		16.9 -	11.0
0.45	-	-	3.11	3.46	4.24	25.2 -	11.8	2.00	1.80	1.56	3.7	0.610Y	18/78/27	78.3 -	36.6
-	-	0.40	1.75	1.56	0.70	24.7 -	20.3	0.70	0.67	0.68	1.8	-		43.2 -	35.5
0.81	-	-	1.32	1.39	-3.51	39.0 -	27.0	0.00	0.00	0.00	0.0	0.250Y	1/5/18	51.5 -	35.6
-	-2326.00	-	10980.00	20701.00	-			-	1572.05	248.49		0.08821	4/20/97	20.4 -	14.3
-	-	-	0.16	0.11	-0.02	279.0 -	0.0	0.33	4.35	-	0.8	3.7989C	1/5/18	44.6 -	0.0
-	-	0.48	1.47	0.58	1.76	44.2 -	21.7	0.40	0.40	0.10	0.9	0.10Y	7/13/18	64.9 -	31.9
-0.13	-	-	-0.57	-0.74	-0.18	-		-	-	-		-		52.8 -	31.7
0.68	-	-	3.07	3.43	-0.34	17.2 -	10.3	-	-	-		0.140Y	'18/78/27	31.3 -	19.9
2.37	-	-	2.05	2.06	1.72	15.3 -	9.7	0.45	0.40	0.34	1.8	0.140Y	18/78/27	31.3 -	19.9
0.61	-	-	3.06	0.37	-1.50	9.6 -	5.9	0.60	0.60	0.60	2.5	0.170Y	6/14/18	29.2 -	18.1
-	-	435.00	-	-2902.00	2258.00	-		-	250.38	-		-		18.6 -	12.9
0.17	-	-	3.98	4.22	3.50	15.8 -	8.0	4.40	4.00	2.36	10.1	0.60Y	18/78/27	63.0 -	31.7
2.54	-	-	8.51	9.01	-2.93	25.6 -	19.9	3.00	2.80	2.60	1.5	0.80Y	18/78/27	217.5 -	169.0
-	-	0.25	1.73	1.55	1.34	19.7 -	13.6	0.42	0.36	0.28	1.4	0.120Y	6/15/18	34.1 -	23.6
1.67	-	-	12.21	7.02	4.34	15.5 -	12.1	-	-	-		0.0826L	6/30/00	189.4 -	148.0
0.53	-	-	1.13	1.06	1.42	14.2 -	11.4	1.22	1.28	2.23	8.6	0.3250Z	7/2/18	16.0 -	12.9

T35

SYMBOL	COMPANY	NATURE OF BUSINESS	FISCAL YEAR-END	TOTAL REV. $MILL	NET INCOME $MILL	TOTAL ASSETS $MILL	NET STK EQUITY $MILL	NO OF INST	INST. HOLDINGS (SHARES)
LW	Lamb Weston Holdings Inc	Food	5/28/17	3168.0	326.9	2485.6	-647.2	603	132344478
LKB 04	Landesbank Baden-Wurttemberg	Banking	12/31/16	13453.0	10.0	243620.0	13081.0		0
LCI	Lannett Co., Inc.	Pharmaceuticals	6/30/17	633.3	-0.6	1603.3	561.1	250	43747230
LPI	Laredo Petroleum, Inc	Production & Extraction	12/31/17	822.2	549.0	2023.3	765.6	250	346133450
LVS	Las Vegas Sands Corp	Hotels, Restaurants & Travel	12/31/17	12882.0	2806.0	20687.0	6493.0	919	351300485
LHO	LaSalle Hotel Properties	REITs	12/31/17	1104.8	195.0	3814.9	2473.2	361	146539000
LTM	LATAM Airlines Group SA	Airlines/Air Freight	12/31/17	9613.9	155.3	18798.0	4176.1	116	22852982
LDF	Latin American Discovery Fund, Inc.	Holding and other Investment Office	12/31/16	1.6	0.6	73.0	72.4	30	3736668
EL	Lauder (Estee) Cos., Inc. (The)	Household & Personal Products	6/30/17	11824.0	1249.0	11568.0	4384.0	1088	241425364
LGI	Lazard Global Total Return & Incom	Holding and other Investment Office	12/31/16	6.4	3.9	177.2	151.0	44	3348137
LAZ	Lazard Ltd	Finance Intermediaries & Services	12/31/17	2697.8	253.6	4928.7	1199.8	478	111142118
LOR	Lazard World Dividend & Income Fu	Holding and other Investment Office	12/31/16	4.9	3.4	89.7	76.8	33	3340472
LCII	LCI Industries	Auto Parts	12/31/17	2147.8	132.9	945.9	652.7	346	29836995
LFGR	Leaf Group Ltd	Internet & Software	12/31/17	129.0	-31.1	83.2	58.5		0
LEA	Lear Corp.	Auto Parts	12/31/17	20467.0	1313.4	11945.9	4150.5	778	91103534
LEE	Lee Enterprises, Inc.	Publishing	9/24/17	566.9	27.5	620.9	-92.2	132	27809216
LGC	Legacy Acquisition Corp	Business Services	12/31/17		0.1	302.3	291.4	18	10264230
LM	Legg Mason, Inc.	Wealth Management	3/31/18	3140.3	285.1	8152.5	3824.4	588	112132991
LEG	Leggett & Platt, Inc.	Furniture	12/31/17	3943.8	292.6	3550.8	1190.2	685	134334119
LEH 06	Lehman Brothers, Inc.	Finance Intermediaries & Services	11/30/02	12124.0	740.0	196219.0	3152.0		0
LDOS	Leidos Holdings Inc	IT Services	12/29/17	10170.0	366.0	8990.0	3370.0	608	153174711
LEJU	Leju Holdings Ltd	Property, Real Estate & Developmen	12/31/17	362.5	-160.9	438.9	260.3	33	3466835
LC	LendingClub Corp	Credit & Lending	12/31/17	1176.8	-153.8	4640.8	922.5	215	376294990
LEN	Lennar Corp	Builders	11/30/17	12646.4	810.5	18745.0	7872.3	849	323813372
LII	Lennox International Inc	Industrial Machinery & Equipment	12/31/17	3839.6	305.7	1891.5	50.1	504	37593023
LHC	Leo Holdings Corp	Business Services	12/31/17		-0.0	0.4	0.0	1	116490
LXP	Lexington Realty Trust	REITs	12/31/17	391.6	85.6	3553.0	1323.9	367	231643453
LPL	LG Display Co Ltd	Electrical Equipment	12/31/16	26504074.0	906713.0	24884336.0	12955997.0	162	28621068
USA	Liberty All-Star Equity Fund	Holding and other Investment Office	12/31/16	20.2	8.4	1209.9	1161.0	185	58565143
ASG	Liberty All-Star Growth Fund Inc.	Holding and other Investment Office	12/31/16	1.2	-0.4	140.2	126.5	46	3184986
LBRT	Liberty Oilfield Services Inc	Equipment & Services	12/31/17	1489.9	168.5	852.1	435.3	85	126155405
LPT	Liberty Property Trust	REITs	12/31/17	719.8	282.3	6439.8	3087.4	531	181949952
LSI	Life Storage Inc	REITs	12/31/17	529.8	96.4	3876.8	2028.3	405	55697282
LITB	Lightinthebox Holding Co., Ltd.	Retail - Apparel and Accessories	12/31/17	319.9	-9.5	108.7	55.5	14	2963838
LLY	Lilly (Eli) & Co	Pharmaceuticals	12/31/17	22871.3	-204.1	44981.0	11592.2	1908	1006275392
LNC	Lincoln National Corp.	Life & Health	12/31/17	14257.0	2079.0	281763.0	17322.0	1000	230126431
LNN	Lindsay Corp	Industrial Machinery & Equipment	8/31/17	518.0	23.2	506.0	270.1	237	14774467
LN	LINE Corporation	IT Services	12/31/17	167147.0	8078.0	303439.0	185075.0	83	7614911
LKM	Link Motion Inc	IT Services	12/31/17	343.1	-127.6	853.6	385.8	72	10118803
LGF A	Lions Gate Entertainment Corp	Entertainment	3/31/18	4129.1	473.6	8967.6	3155.9	328	91210269
LAD	Lithia Motors Inc	Retail - Automotive	12/31/17	10086.5	245.2	4683.1	1083.2	365	32486361
LAC	Lithium Americas Corp (New)	Mining	12/31/17	4.3	-33.3	113.5	108.8	41	7007179
LYV	Live Nation Entertainment Inc	Entertainment	12/31/17	10337.4	-6.0	7504.3	1181.2	506	162710561
LYG	Lloyds Banking Group Plc	Banking	12/31/17	40713.0	3457.0	812109.0	48906.0	344	505659341
SCD	LMP Capital & Income Fund Inc	Holding and other Investment Office	11/30/16	13.1	9.0	363.1	275.8	56	5799731
LMT	Lockheed Martin Corp	Defense	12/31/17	51048.0	2002.0	46521.0	-683.0	1904	281731977
L	Loews Corp.	General Insurance	12/31/17	13735.0	1164.0	79586.0	19204.0	723	279737468
LOMA	Loma Negra Compania Industrial Ar	Manufacturing	12/31/17	15286.5	1590.8	12973.3	3822.6	98	48514493
LPX	Louisiana-Pacific Corp	Paper & Forest Products	12/31/17	2733.9	389.8	2448.5	1604.5	498	167111548
LOW	Lowe's Companies Inc	Retail - Hardware & Home Improvem	2/2/18	68619.0	3447.0	35291.0	5873.0	1998	805482121
LXU	LSB Industries, Inc.	Specialty Chemicals	12/31/17	427.5	-29.2	1189.2	613.2	168	22114829
LKSD	LSC Communications Inc	Printing	12/31/17	3603.0	-57.0	2014.0	248.0	215	32691705
LTC	LTC Properties, Inc.	REITs	12/31/17	168.1	87.3	1465.6	755.2	312	41851420
LUB	Luby's, Inc.	Hotels, Restaurants & Travel	8/30/17	376.0	-23.3	226.5	144.1	73	13252753
LL	Lumber Liquidators Holdings Inc	Retail - Hardware & Home Improvem	12/31/17	1028.9	-37.8	410.8	197.8	244	28533750
LXFR	Luxfer Holdings Plc	Industrial Machinery & Equipment	12/31/17	441.3	11.5	402.6	162.3	61	23058716
LXFT	Luxoft Holding, Inc.	IT Services	3/31/17	785.6	62.6	547.2	386.8	148	20887061
LDL	Lydall, Inc.	Industrial Machinery & Equipment	12/31/17	698.4	49.3	560.9	353.4	216	18181116
WLH	Lyon (William) Homes	Builders	12/31/17	1796.5	48.1	2061.1	780.5	218	35480841
LYB	LyondellBasell Industries NV	Diversified Chemicals	12/31/17	34484.0	4879.0	26206.0	8949.0	1069	336787308
MTB	M & T Bank Corp	Banking	12/31/17	6018.9	1408.3	118593.5	16250.8	900	140384867
MTB PRA	M & T Capital Trust IV	Banking						3	104665
MDC	M.D.C. Holdings, Inc.	Builders	12/31/17	2577.6	141.8	2780.3	1407.3	367	56360942
MHO	M/I Homes Inc	Builders	12/31/17	1962.0	72.1	1864.8	747.3	241	32252226
MAC	Macerich Co (The)	REITs	12/31/17	993.7	146.1	9605.9	3681.6	532	179218411
CLI	Mack Cali Realty Corp	REITs	12/31/17	616.2	23.2	4957.9	1476.3	355	115081480
MGU	Macquarie Global Infrastructure Tot	Holding and other Investment Office	11/30/16	18.9	11.2	411.5	287.7	68	5334335
MIC	Macquarie Infrastructure Corp	Business Services	12/31/17	1814.7	451.2	8009.0	3153.7	552	75498403
MFD	Macquarie/First Trust Global Infrastr	Holding and other Investment Office	11/30/16	12.3	9.6	157.0	108.3	39	1010031
M	Macy's Inc	Retail - General Merchandise/Depart	2/3/18	24837.0	1547.0	19381.0	5673.0	978	344204729
MCN	Madison Covered Call & Equity Stra	Holding and other Investment Office	12/31/16	2.3	0.6	169.5	162.1	49	7275463
MSG	Madison Square Garden Co (The) (	Sporting & Recreational	6/30/17	1318.5	-72.7	3712.8	2408.2	323	18499611
MSP	Madison Strategic Sector Premium	Holding and other Investment Office	12/31/16	1.0	0.3	76.1	72.8	24	2582476
MMP	Magellan Midstream Partners LP	Equipment & Services	12/31/17	2507.7	869.5	7394.4		843	164205270
MGA	Magna International Inc	Auto Parts	12/31/17	38946.0	2206.0	25393.0	11228.0	605	246263000
MX	MagnaChip Semiconductor Corp	Semiconductors	12/31/17	679.7	84.9	558.8	-39.6	114	33225112
MAIN	Main Street Capital Corp	Holding and other Investment Office	12/31/17	205.7	135.4	2265.4	1380.4	263	19925771
MMD	MainStay MacKay DefinedTerm Mu	Holding and other Investment Office	5/31/17	39.7	29.6	869.7	555.1		0
MNK	Mallinckrodt Plc	Pharmaceuticals	12/29/17	3221.6	2134.4	15280.9	6522.0	456	112651502
MZF	Managed Duration Investment Grad	Holding and other Investment Office	7/31/17	6.6	5.3	160.7	160.3	38	4491393

T36

EARNINGS PER SHARE QUARTERLY 1st	2nd	3rd	ANNUAL 2017	2016	2015	P/E RATIO	DIVIDENDS PER SHARE 2017	2016	2015	AV. YLD %	DIV. DECLARED AMOUNT	PAYABLE	PRICE RANGE 2017
		1.06	2.22			31.0 - 19.3	0.38			0.7	0.19130Y	8/31/18	68.7 - 42.7
		0.33	-0.02	1.20	4.04						0.0076	12/14/79	29.3 - 13.3
0.36			2.29	-1.16	-11.10	5.8 - 3.3							13.3 - 7.6
1.84			3.54	2.10	2.47	23.0 - 16.9	2.92	2.88	2.60	4.2	0.750Z	18/78/27	81.3 - 59.7
≤0.10			1.54	2.07	1.09	23.1 - 15.9	1.80	1.80	1.73	6.1	0.39370Z	18/78/27	35.6 - 24.4
0.15			0.26	0.13	-0.40	66.1 - 38.0	0.02			0.1			17.2 - 9.9
				0.09	0.05			0.07	0.03		0.05850	7/13/18	13.2 - 0.0
		0.99	3.35	2.96	2.82	47.2 - 28.0	1.32	1.14	0.92	1.0	0.380Y	18/78/27	158.0 - 93.9
				0.40	0.39			0.95	1.11		0.11560	8/23/18	19.3 - 16.1
1.21			1.91	2.92	7.40		2.81	2.69	2.35		0.440	18/78/27	
				0.50	0.51			0.69	0.92		0.07410	8/23/18	12.6 - 10.3
1.86			5.24	5.20	3.02	25.2 - 15.8	2.05	1.40	2.00	1.9	0.60Y	6/15/18	131.8 - 82.7
-0.26			-1.52	-0.10	-2.18								11.4 - 6.5
5.16			18.59	13.33	9.59	11.0 - 7.6	2.00	1.20	1.00	1.1	0.70Y	18/78/27	205.3 - 141.1
	0.04		0.50	0.64	0.43	5.8 - 3.6					0.190Y	10/1/08	2.9 - 1.8
0.02			0.00	-0.07									9.7 - 0.0
		1.58	2.18	-0.25	2.04	21.2 - 15.9	0.88	0.80	0.64	2.2	0.340Y	18/78/27	46.1 - 34.7
0.57			2.13	2.76	2.28	25.3 - 19.0	1.42	1.34	1.26	3.1	0.380Y	18/78/27	53.8 - 40.4
0.66			2.38	2.35	3.27	29.2 - 21.5	1.28	14.92	1.28	2.1	0.320Y	18/78/27	69.4 - 51.2
			-1.19	-0.07	0.26				0.18				2.0 - 1.0
-0.07			-0.38	-0.38	-0.01								6.5 - 2.6
	0.95		3.38	3.85	3.39	21.2 - 14.5	0.16	0.16	0.16	0.3	0.040Y	18/78/27	71.8 - 49.0
0.90			7.14	6.32	4.09	31.0 - 22.5	1.96	1.65	1.38	1.0	0.640Y	18/78/27	221.1 - 160.6
0.03			0.00										
-0.07			0.33	0.37	0.45	32.1 - 23.2	0.70	0.69	0.68	7.6	0.17750Z	7/16/18	10.6 - 7.7
1770.00				-2534.00	2701.00			246.60	250.23				16.9 - 7.9
				0.04	0.04			0.48	0.51		0.170	9/10/18	6.8 - 5.5
				-0.02	-0.03			0.36	0.77		0.120	9/10/18	6.7 - 4.8
0.34													23.4 - 16.2
0.95			1.91	2.43	1.60	23.7 - 20.2	1.60	1.90	1.90	3.8	0.40Z	18/78/27	45.3 - 38.6
0.73			2.07	1.96	3.16	47.1 - 34.1	3.95	3.70	3.20	4.7	1.0Z	18/78/27	97.5 - 70.6
		-0.02	-0.07	-0.07	-0.41								3.0 - 1.8
1.16			-0.19	2.58	2.26		2.08	2.04	2.00	2.5	0.56250Y	18/78/27	87.9 - 74.2
1.64			9.22	5.03	4.51	9.3 - 6.7	1.16	1.00	0.80	1.6	0.330Y	18/78/27	85.9 - 62.1
	0.16		2.17	1.85	2.22	46.8 - 39.0	1.17	1.13	1.09	1.3	0.310Y	18/78/27	101.5 - 84.5
-0.63			34.01	31.48	-39.12	1.4 - 1.0							46.9 - 34.0
	-0.01		-0.26	-0.00									4.4 - 0.7
		0.87	0.09	0.33	1.23	394.7 - 244.8	0.09	0.34	0.26	0.3	0.090Y	8/9/18	35.5 - 22.0
2.07			9.75	7.72	6.91	13.0 - 9.1	1.06	0.95	0.76	1.0	0.290Y	18/78/27	126.6 - 89.2
			-0.44	-0.45	-0.30								10.7 - 3.3
-0.24			-0.48	-0.23	-0.33								48.7 - 34.0
			0.04	0.02	0.01	104.8 - 81.0	0.13	0.16	0.10	3.6	0.48440	7/15/15	4.2 - 3.2
			0.50	0.58				1.24	1.12		0.310	7/2/18	14.8 - 12.3
4.02			6.89	17.49	11.46	52.4 - 40.5	7.46	6.77	6.15	2.3	2.0Y	18/78/27	361.0 - 278.9
0.89			3.45	1.93	0.72	15.5 - 13.1	0.25	0.25	0.25	0.5	0.06250Y	18/78/27	53.5 - 45.1
			2.79	0.87	0.61	9.0 - 3.7							25.0 - 10.3
0.62			2.66	1.03	-0.62	11.7 - 8.8					0.130Y	18/78/27	31.1 - 23.4
1.19			3.47	2.73	2.71	31.0 - 20.9	1.33	1.07	0.87	1.5	0.480Y	18/78/27	107.4 - 72.6
-0.49			-2.18	2.54	-1.67						10.0Y	4/1/10	11.6 - 4.9
-0.32			-1.69	3.23			1.00	0.25		6.3	0.260Y	9/5/18	21.7 - 11.7
0.51			2.20	2.21	1.94	23.9 - 15.8	2.28	2.19	2.07	5.2	0.190Z	9/28/18	52.6 - 34.9
	-0.37		-0.79	-0.35	-0.07						0.10	9/25/00	3.1 - 2.4
-0.07			-1.33	-2.51	-2.08								40.5 - 19.9
		0.60	0.43	0.82	0.59		0.50	0.50	0.40				
		0.73	1.88	2.06	1.91								
0.64			2.85	2.16	2.71	21.0 - 14.1					0.0194	9/15/82	60.0 - 40.3
0.21			1.24	1.55	1.48	26.2 - 17.8							32.4 - 22.1
3.11			12.23	9.13	9.59		-3.55	3.33	3.04		1.0	6/18/18	
2.23			8.70	7.78	7.18	22.6 - 16.4	3.00	2.80	2.80	1.7	0.80Y	18/78/27	196.8 - 142.5
											0.53130Z	12/16/13	
0.68			2.48	1.85	1.18	14.0 - 10.9	0.93	0.88	0.88	3.0	0.30Y	8/22/18	34.7 - 27.1
0.60			2.26	1.84	1.68	16.5 - 10.7					0.60940Y	9/15/17	37.3 - 24.3
-0.24			1.02	3.52	3.08	67.5 - 51.7	2.87	2.75	6.63	4.9	0.740Z	18/78/27	68.9 - 52.7
0.45			0.06	1.30	-1.41	459.3 - 270.5	0.70	0.60	0.60	3.3	0.20Z	18/78/27	27.6 - 16.2
			0.90	0.67				1.48	1.44		0.370	6/29/18	26.3 - 21.4
0.88			5.13	1.85	-1.39	15.4 - 7.1	5.43	4.89	2.24	9.2	1.0Y	18/78/27	79.0 - 36.6
				1.13	1.44			1.20	1.40		0.30	5/31/18	14.4 - 10.7
0.45			1.99	3.22	4.22	20.2 - 8.8	1.49	1.39	1.19	5.7	0.37750Y	18/78/27	40.2 - 17.5
			0.03	0.04				0.72	0.72		0.180	6/29/18	8.0 - 7.1
	0.38		-3.05	-3.12									310.2 - 191.2
			0.06	0.07				1.04	1.04		0.260	6/29/18	12.2 - 11.1
0.92			3.81	3.52	3.59	19.7 - 15.0	3.52	3.25	2.92	5.2	0.93750	18/78/27	75.2 - 57.1
1.83			5.90	5.16	4.88	14.7 - 7.7	1.10	1.00	0.88	1.7	0.330	6/8/18	86.7 - 45.6
0.08			2.02	-0.85	-2.47	6.5 - 4.5							13.2 - 9.0
0.59			2.39	2.23	2.18	17.4 - 14.8	2.79	2.73	2.66	7.2	0.190	9/14/18	41.5 - 35.4
			1.08	1.11	1.19	18.9 - 17.2	1.09	1.18	1.17	5.6	0.085M	9/28/18	20.4 - 18.6
-0.21			21.80	-1.45	2.75								
			0.78	0.84	0.88	18.4 - 16.8	0.61	0.73	0.76	4.5	0.040	7/31/18	14.4 - 13.1

SYMBOL	COMPANY	NATURE OF BUSINESS	FISCAL YEAR-END	TOTAL REV. $MILL	NET INCOME $MILL	TOTAL ASSETS $MILL	NET STK EQUITY $MILL	NO OF INST	INST. HOLDINGS (SHARES)
MANU	Manchester United Plc	Entertainment	6/30/17	581.2	39.2	1534.3	477.6	78	39031290
MTW	Manitowoc Company Inc (The)	Construction Services	12/31/17	1581.3	9.4	1607.8	677.5	343	56960153
MN	Manning & Napier Inc.	Wealth Management	12/31/17	201.5	3.6	205.2	-160.3	84	9743883
MAN	ManpowerGroup Inc	Business Services	12/31/17	21034.3	545.4	8883.6	2774.9	642	85729011
MFC	Manulife Financial Corp.	Life & Health	12/31/17	58323.0	2104.0	729533.0	41234.0	627	1088126021
MRO	Marathon Oil Corp.	Production & Extraction	12/31/17	4765.0	-5723.0	22012.0	11708.0	1041	873788343
MPC	Marathon Petroleum Corp.	Refining & Marketing	12/31/17	75369.0	3432.0	49047.0	14033.0	1259	445631589
MMI	Marcus & Millichap Inc	Property, Real Estate & Developmen	12/31/17	719.7	51.5	459.7	314.9	203	22566915
MCS	Marcus Corp. (The)	Hotels, Restaurants & Travel	12/28/17	622.7	65.0	1017.8	445.0	210	20917349
MPX	Marine Products Corp	Leisure Equipment	12/31/17	267.3	19.3	95.9	69.6	75	5728336
HZO	MarineMax Inc	Retail - Specialty	9/30/17	1052.3	23.5	640.0	302.2	211	30369593
MKL	Markel Corp (Holding Co)	General Insurance	12/31/17	6061.7	395.3	32805.0	9504.1	626	13475721
VAC	Marriott Vacations Worldwide Corp.	Hotels, Restaurants & Travel	12/31/17	1951.9	226.8	2906.2	1045.0	371	24289174
MMC	Marsh & McLennan Companies Inc.	Brokers & Intermediaries	12/31/17	14024.0	1492.0	20429.0	7359.0	1099	538108410
MLM	Martin Marietta Materials, Inc.	Construction Materials	12/31/17	3965.6	713.3	8992.5	4679.6	755	73262900
MAS	Masco Corp.	Construction Materials	12/31/17	7644.0	533.0	5488.0	-60.0	896	356513896
DOOR	Masonite International Corp (New)	Construction Materials	12/31/17	2032.9	151.7	1680.3	722.6	236	32673637
MTZ	MasTec Inc. (FL)	Construction Services	12/31/17	6607.0	347.2	4066.6	1430.8	446	78654840
MA	Mastercard Inc	Business Services	12/31/17	12497.0	3915.0	21329.0	5468.0	2037	893442441
MTDR	Matador Resources Co	Production & Extraction	12/31/17	544.3	125.9	2145.7	1156.6	341	103520611
MTRN	Materion Corp	Metal Products	12/31/17	1139.4	11.5	791.1	495.0	233	21969958
MATX	Matson Inc	Shipping	12/31/17	2046.9	232.0	2247.5	678.2	275	46150841
MLP	Maui Land & Pineapple Co., Inc.	Property, Real Estate & Developmen	12/31/17	24.4	10.9	44.8	31.1	80	4983406
MAXR	Maxar Technologies Ltd	Internet & Software	12/31/17	1631.2	100.4	6657.3	2013.6		0
MMS	MAXIMUS Inc.	Business Services	9/30/17	2451.0	209.4	1350.7	940.1	458	77018979
MXL	MaxLinear Inc	Semiconductors	12/31/17	420.3	-9.2	824.9	387.4	228	72125239
MBI	MBIA Inc.	General Insurance	12/31/17	433.0	-1605.0	9095.0	1413.0	318	130538454
MKC	McCormick & Co Inc	Food	11/30/17	4834.1	477.4	10385.8	2559.9	1007	139389692
MDR	McDermott International Inc (Panam	Equipment & Services	12/31/17	2984.8	178.5	3222.8	1760.7	505	373881027
MCD	McDonald's Corp	Hotels, Restaurants & Travel	12/31/17	22820.4	5192.3	33803.7	-3268.0	2579	710514927
MUX	McEwen Mining Inc	Precious Metals	12/31/17	67.7	-10.6	592.1	521.3	170	114554593
MCK	McKesson Corp	Pharmaceuticals	3/31/18	208357.0	67.0	60381.0	9804.0	1319	232048733
MDU	MDU Resources Group Inc	Electric Utilities	12/31/17	4443.4	281.2	6334.7	2429.0	537	157359189
MTL	Mechel PAO	Non-Precious Metals	12/31/17	299113.0	11557.0	319127.0	-253066.0	85	17707068
MRT	MedEquities Realty Trust Inc	REITs	12/31/17	61.1	20.4	581.6	353.8	117	30974735
MPW	Medical Properties Trust Inc	REITs	12/31/17	704.7	289.8	9020.3	3820.6	495	350624761
MED	Medifast Inc	Household & Personal Products	12/31/17	301.6	27.7	145.9	108.6	298	13448561
MCC	Medley Capital Corp	Holding and other Investment Office	9/30/17	96.3	36.4	959.6	460.4	124	18752466
MDLY	Medley Management Inc	Finance Intermediaries & Services	12/31/17	65.6	0.9	127.9	-8.0	63	3971495
MD	Mednax, Inc.	Diagnostic & Health Related Service	12/31/17	3458.3	320.4	5867.3	3066.5	493	110928818
MDT	Medtronic PLC	Medical Instruments & Equipment	4/27/18	29953.0	3104.0	91393.0	50720.0	1545	1221248439
MRK	Merck & Co Inc	Pharmaceuticals	12/31/17	40122.0	2394.0	87872.0	34336.0	2699	2386456185
MCY	Mercury General Corp.	General Insurance	12/31/17	3416.0	144.9	5101.3	1761.4	339	34722380
MDP	Meredith Corp	Advertising	6/30/17	1713.4	188.9	2729.6	996.0	409	64066958
MTH	Meritage Homes Corp	Builders	12/31/17	3241.0	143.3	3251.3	1576.8	299	46340554
MTOR	Meritor Inc	Auto Parts	9/30/17	3347.0	324.0	2782.0	268.0	358	96098758
MTR	Mesa Royalty Trust	Oil Royalty Traders	12/31/17	3.0	2.9	3.8	3.1	28	276261
MSB	Mesabi Trust	Non-Precious Metals	1/31/18	34.6	33.5	26.1	10.5	78	2696376
MEI	Methode Electronics Inc	Electrical Equipment	4/28/18	908.3	57.2	915.9	630.0	316	42424346
MET	MetLife Inc	Life & Health	12/31/17	62308.0	4010.0	719892.0	58676.0	1537	960537481
MCB	Metropolitan Bank Holding Corp	Banking	12/31/17	72.1	12.4	1759.9	236.9	66	4118496
MTD	Mettler-Toledo International, Inc.	Industrial Machinery & Equipment	12/31/17	2725.1	376.0	2549.8	547.3	707	31419570
MXE	Mexico Equity & Income Fund Inc (	Holding and other Investment Office	7/31/17	2.1	0.6	104.7	100.8	27	4274353
MXF	Mexico Fund, Inc.	Holding and other Investment Office	10/31/17	7.5	3.2	271.1	270.6	57	5539508
MFA	MFA Financial, Inc.	REITs	12/31/17	433.4	322.4	10954.7	3261.6	396	378120016
MFCB	MFC Bahcorp Ltd (Cayman Islands)	Finance Intermediaries & Services	12/31/17	274.0	-47.9	396.9	277.8	51	5397208
MCR	MFS Charter Income Trust	Holding and other Investment Office	11/30/16	28.7	24.0	584.4	477.1	87	22731614
MGF	MFS Government Markets Income	Holding and other Investment Office	11/30/16	6.4	5.1	192.2	174.4	57	23823413
CXE	MFS High Income Municipal Trust	Holding and other Investment Office	11/30/16	13.9	10.0	262.5	163.9	49	3606591
CMU	MFS High Yield Municipal Trust	Holding and other Investment Office	11/30/16	11.1	8.1	208.5	132.6	45	2185663
CIF	MFS Intermediate High Income Fun	Holding and other Investment Office	11/30/16	4.9	3.9	80.2	56.8	33	1032111
MIN	MFS Intermediate Income Trust	Holding and other Investment Office	10/31/17	14.5	11.2	528.0	524.9	112	57497802
CXH	MFS Investment Grade Municipal Tr	Holding and other Investment Office	11/30/16	8.5	6.2	174.1	117.6	41	2930152
MMT	MFS Multimarket Income Trust	Holding and other Investment Office	10/31/17	26.7	21.4	583.3	471.5	115	23498557
MFM	MFS Municipal Income Trust	Holding and other Investment Office	10/31/17	21.8	16.2	427.2	416.8	80	5205689
MFV	MFS Special Value Trust	Holding and other Investment Office	10/31/17	2.0	1.4	43.1	42.8	20	277368
MTG	MGIC Investment Corp. (WI)	Credit & Lending	12/31/17	1066.1	355.8	5619.5	3154.5	496	409281918
MGP	MGM Growth Properties LLC	REITs	12/31/17	765.7	41.8	10351.1	1624.6	202	72065804
MGM	MGM Resorts International	Hotels, Restaurants & Travel	12/31/17	10773.9	1960.3	29159.2	7612.7	737	549417806
KORS	Michael Kors Holdings Ltd	Retail - Apparel and Accessories	3/31/18	4718.6	591.9	4059.0	2017.7	605	144949801
MFGP	Micro Focus International Plc	Internet & Software	10/31/17	1234.5	106.3	17607.7	7624.6	457	100578766
MFGP	Micro Focus International Plc	Internet & Software	10/31/17	1234.5	106.3	17607.7	7624.6	457	100578766
MAA	Mid-America Apartment Communiti	REITs	12/31/17	1529.0	328.4	11491.9	6350.3	605	123386571
MSL	MidSouth Bancorp, Inc.	Banking	12/31/17	102.4	-11.8	1881.2	254.0	76	10246014
MPO	Midstates Petroleum Co Inc	Production & Extraction	12/31/17	228.8	-85.1	688.1	485.6	116	52588448
MCRN	Milacron Holdings Corp	Industrial Machinery & Equipment	12/31/17	1234.2	1.1	1858.8	520.7	170	114123589
MLR	Miller Industries Inc. (TN)	Auto Parts	12/31/17	615.1	23.0	317.2	203.1	118	10622887
HIE	Miller/Howard High Income Equity F	Holding and other Investment Office	10/31/17	8.3	4.3	237.3	167.9	37	2256738
MTX	Minerals Technologies, Inc.	Specialty Chemicals	12/31/17	1675.7	195.1	2970.4	1251.7	333	42091211
MP PRD	Mississippi Power Co	Electric Utilities	12/31/17	1187.0	-2588.0	4866.0	1391.0		0

EARNINGS PER SHARE						P/E RATIO	DIVIDENDS PER SHARE			AV. YLD %	DIV. DECLARED		PRICE RANGE 2017	
QUARTERLY			ANNUAL											
1st	2nd	3rd	2017	2016	2015		2017	2016	2015	%	AMOUNT	PAYABLE		
-0.00	-	-	0.24	0.22	-0.55	-	-	-	-	-	0.090	6/5/18	-	-
-0.28	-	-	0.26	-10.92	1.84	167.7 - 86.0	-	-	-	-	0.080Y	12/10/15	43.6 -	22.4
0.07	-	-	0.25	0.62	0.90	18.0 - 12.0	0.40	0.64	0.72	11.1	0.080	8/1/18	4.5 -	3.0
1.45	-	-	8.04	6.27	5.40	16.9 - 10.6	1.86	1.72	1.60	1.6	1.010Y	18/78/27	136.0 -	85.5
0.67	-	-	0.98	1.41	1.05	28.0 - 0.0	0.82	0.74	0.67	3.6	0.3831GH	6/19/18	27.5 -	0.0
0.42	-	-	-6.73	-2.61	-3.26	-	0.20	0.20	0.68	1.3	0.050Y	18/78/27	21.9 -	10.8
0.08	-	-	6.70	2.21	5.26	12.4 - 7.4	1.52	1.36	1.14	2.3	0.460Y	18/78/27	82.9 -	49.5
0.46	-	-	1.32	1.66	1.69	30.4 - 18.8	-	-	-	-	-	-	40.2 -	24.8
0.35	-	-	2.29	1.36	0.84	14.6 - 10.5	0.50	0.45	0.21	1.8	0.13640Y	6/15/18	33.4 -	24.1
0.22	-	-	0.55	0.44	0.39	32.8 - 23.2	0.33	0.24	0.20	2.2	0.10Y	6/11/18	18.1 -	12.7
-	0.27	-	0.95	0.91	1.92	25.9 - 14.9	-	-	-	-	-	-	24.6 -	14.2
-4.25	-	-	25.81	31.27	41.74	45.8 - 37.5	-	-	-	-	-	-	1182.1 -	969.0
1.32	-	-	8.18	4.83	3.82	18.6 - 13.3	1.45	1.25	1.05	1.1	0.40Y	6/11/18	152.5 -	108.7
1.34	-	-	2.87	3.38	2.98	30.0 - 26.8	1.43	1.30	1.18	1.8	0.4150Y	18/78/27	86.0 -	76.9
0.16	-	-	11.25	6.63	4.29	21.3 - 17.2	1.72	1.64	1.60	0.8	0.440Y	18/78/27	240.0 -	193.3
0.47	-	-	1.66	1.47	1.02	27.9 - 21.8	0.41	0.39	0.36	1.0	0.1050Y	18/78/27	46.3 -	36.2
0.73	-	-	5.09	3.17	-1.56	15.5 - 11.5	-	-	-	-	-	-	79.1 -	58.4
0.32	-	-	4.22	1.61	-0.98	13.0 - 9.2	-	-	-	-	-	-	54.8 -	38.8
1.41	-	-	3.65	3.69	3.35	55.7 - 33.1	0.88	0.76	0.64	0.5	0.250Y	18/78/27	203.2 -	120.8
0.55	-	-	1.23	-1.07	-8.34	27.9 - 17.1	-	-	-	-	-	-	34.3 -	21.1
0.51	-	-	0.56	1.27	1.58	102.1 - 66.1	0.40	0.38	0.35	0.8	0.1050Y	6/1/18	57.2 -	37.0
0.33	-	-	5.37	1.85	2.34	7.3 - 4.2	0.78	0.74	0.70	2.6	0.210Y	9/6/18	39.0 -	22.8
-	-	-0.03	0.57	1.15	0.36	48.0 - 18.5	-	-	-	-	0.1250	3/31/18	27.4 -	10.6
0.55	-	-	2.43	3.74	3.84	35.1 - 0.0	1.15	1.48	1.48	1.9	0.370	6/29/18	85.4 -	0.0
-	0.84	-	3.17	2.69	2.35	22.7 - 18.6	0.18	0.18	0.18	0.3	0.0450Y	18/78/27	72.0 -	59.0
0.03	-	-	-0.14	0.91	-0.79	-	-	-	-	-	-	-	28.8 -	15.6
-1.12	-	-	-13.50	-2.54	1.06	-	-	-	-	-	0.340Y	1/15/08	10.9 -	6.2
-	0.93	-	3.72	3.69	3.11	-	1.88	1.72	1.60	-	0.520Y	18/78/27	-	-
0.36	-	-	1.89	0.36	-0.24	14.3 - 8.9	-	-	-	-	0.01670	7/1/00	26.9 -	16.8
1.72	-	-	6.37	5.44	4.80	28.0 - 23.3	3.83	3.61	3.44	2.4	1.010Y	18/78/27	178.4 -	148.3
-0.02	-	-	-0.03	0.07	-0.07	-	0.01	0.01	0.01	0.4	0.005D	2/14/18	3.5 -	1.8
-	-	4.33	22.73	9.70	6.27	7.8 - 5.9	1.12	1.08	0.96	0.7	0.340Y	18/78/27	176.7 -	133.4
0.22	-	-	1.43	0.33	-3.20	20.3 - 17.6	0.78	0.76	0.73	2.9	0.19750Y	18/78/27	29.0 -	25.1
-	-	-	27.76	17.12	-276.65	0.2 - 0.1	-	-	-	-	-	-	5.8 -	3.0
0.16	-	-	0.64	-0.18	0.42	20.0 - 15.1	0.84	0.63	0.85	7.6	0.210Z	6/5/18	12.8 -	9.7
0.25	-	-	0.82	0.86	0.63	17.3 - 14.5	0.96	0.91	0.88	7.3	0.250Z	18/78/27	14.2 -	11.9
1.01	-	-	2.29	1.49	1.66	77.1 - 17.6	1.44	1.07	0.25	1.8	0.480Y	8/8/18	176.5 -	40.3
-	0.07	-	0.67	0.97	1.27	9.8 - 5.1	0.76	1.12	1.27	15.0	0.40630Z	10/30/18	6.6 -	3.4
-0.26	-	-	0.07	0.02	0.46	102.1 - 44.3	0.80	0.80	0.60	13.5	0.20Y	6/1/18	7.2 -	3.1
0.68	-	-	3.45	3.49	3.58	17.6 - 11.9	-	-	-	-	-	-	60.6 -	41.2
-	-	-1.03	2.89	2.48	2.41	-	1.72	1.52	1.22	-	0.50	18/78/27	-	-
0.27	-	-	0.87	1.41	1.56	76.0 - 61.2	1.89	1.85	1.81	3.2	0.480Y	18/78/27	66.2 -	53.3
-0.77	-	-	2.62	1.32	1.35	22.9 - 16.1	2.49	2.48	2.47	4.8	0.6250Y	18/78/27	59.9 -	42.3
-	-	-2.74	4.16	0.75	3.02	17.3 - 11.5	2.03	1.91	1.78	3.6	0.5450Y	18/78/27	71.8 -	47.9
1.07	-	-	3.41	3.55	3.09	16.1 - 11.5	-	-	-	-	-	-	55.0 -	39.0
-	0.63	-	3.59	6.23	0.64	8.2 - 4.6	-	-	-	-	0.10Y	12/8/08	29.5 -	16.7
0.34	-	-	1.58	0.65	1.03	12.4 - 7.3	1.51	0.65	1.03	10.0	0.0660Z	10/31/18	19.6 -	11.5
0.48	-	-	0.73	0.65	1.89	40.7 - 18.0	0.64	0.09	1.84	2.8	0.220	8/20/18	29.7 -	13.2
-	-	-0.65	2.48	2.20	2.57	19.3 - 15.0	0.36	0.36	0.36	0.9	0.110Y	7/27/18	47.8 -	37.1
1.19	-	-	3.62	0.63	4.57	15.4 - 12.0	1.60	1.58	1.48	3.3	0.420Y	18/78/27	55.7 -	43.6
0.75	-	-	2.34	0.43	1.54	23.3 - 15.8	-	-	-	-	-	-	54.6 -	37.0
3.58	-	-	14.24	14.22	12.48	48.6 - 38.4	-	-	-	-	-	-	692.3 -	546.4
-	-	-	0.09	0.01	-0.09	135.4 - 0.0	-	-	-	-	0.0480	12/28/17	12.2 -	0.0
-	-	-	0.21	0.17	0.09	86.5 - 67.2	0.53	1.05	2.20	3.2	0.150	7/26/18	18.2 -	14.1
0.20	-	-	0.79	0.80	0.80	11.2 - 8.6	0.80	0.80	0.80	10.0	0.20Z	18/78/27	8.9 -	6.8
-	0.55	-	-3.81	-2.00	-38.60	-	-	-	-	-	-	-	-	-
-	-	-	-	0.46	0.49	-	-	0.74	0.81	-	0.05850	7/31/18	8.7 -	7.9
-	-	-	-	0.16	0.17	-	-	0.41	0.43	-	0.0290	7/31/18	5.0 -	4.5
-	-	-	-	0.32	0.34	-	-	0.30	0.31	-	0.024M	7/31/18	5.5 -	4.8
-	-	-	-	0.29	0.31	-	-	0.27	0.28	-	0.0215M	7/31/18	4.9 -	4.4
-	-	-	-	0.19	0.20	-	-	0.26	0.24	-	0.02060	7/31/18	3.0 -	2.5
-	-	-	0.10	0.11	0.12	43.4 - 38.0	0.39	0.42	0.45	9.5	0.02940	7/31/18	4.3 -	3.8
-	-	-	-	0.53	0.55	-	-	0.49	0.51	-	0.039M	7/31/18	10.3 -	9.2
-	-	-	0.30	0.34	0.36	20.9 - 18.6	0.54	0.53	0.57	9.0	0.04170	7/31/18	6.3 -	5.6
-	-	-	0.39	0.41	0.42	18.9 - 16.5	0.38	0.38	0.39	5.5	0.03M	7/31/18	7.4 -	6.5
-	-	-	0.20	0.23	0.25	34.0 - 0.0	0.60	0.59	0.65	9.6	0.0470	7/31/18	6.8 -	0.0
0.38	-	-	0.95	0.86	2.60	16.6 - 10.5	-	-	-	-	0.0250Y	9/2/08	15.8 -	10.0
0.22	-	-	0.67	0.52	-	47.3 - 38.5	1.60	1.04	-	5.5	0.430Y	7/16/18	31.7 -	25.8
0.38	-	-	3.35	1.92	-0.82	11.4 - 8.5	0.44	-	-	1.3	0.120	18/78/27	38.0 -	28.4
-	-	1.42	3.29	4.44	4.28	-	-	-	-	-	-	-	-	-
-	-	-	0.35	0.77	0.61	102.5 - 37.1	0.58	0.67	0.48	2.2	-	-	35.9 -	13.0
-	-	-	0.35	0.77	0.61	84.9 - 79.6	0.58	0.67	0.48	2.0	-	-	29.7 -	27.9
0.42	-	-	2.86	2.69	4.41	38.2 - 29.9	3.48	3.28	3.08	3.5	0.92250Z	18/78/27	109.1 -	85.4
-0.03	-	-	-1.06	0.58	0.90	-	0.20	0.36	0.36	1.5	1.0Y	7/16/18	15.2 -	11.1
0.15	-	-	-3.39	0.39	-232.74	-	-	-	-	-	-	-	18.7 -	11.9
0.08	-	-	0.02	0.43	-0.65	1104.5 - 761.0	-	-	-	-	-	-	22.1 -	15.2
0.59	-	-	2.02	1.75	1.41	14.3 - 12.0	0.72	0.68	0.64	2.8	0.180Y	6/18/18	28.9 -	24.3
-	-	-	0.32	0.64	1.02	44.1 - 34.8	1.39	1.39	1.16	11.0	0.1160	9/28/18	14.1 -	11.2
1.12	-	-	5.48	3.79	3.08	14.0 - 11.5	0.20	0.20	0.20	0.3	0.050Y	18/78/27	77.0 -	63.0
-	-	-	-	-	-	-	1.31	1.31	1.31	7.2	0.32810Y	7/2/18	27.2 -	0.0

SYMBOL	COMPANY	NATURE OF BUSINESS	FISCAL YEAR-END	TOTAL REV. $MILL	NET INCOME $MILL	TOTAL ASSETS $MILL	NET STK EQUITY $MILL	NO OF INST	INST. HOLDINGS (SHARES)
MG	Mistras Group Inc	Business Services	12/31/17	701.0	-2.2	554.4	270.6	111	23256227
MUFG	Mitsubishi UFJ Financial Group Inc	Banking	3/31/18	4785786.0	1228160.0	300570312.0	14970182.0	327	179179096
MIXT	MiX Telematics Ltd	Miscellaneous Transportation Servic	3/31/17	1540.1	121.5	1906.7	1444.5	68	7492841
MFG	Mizuho Financial Group Inc	Banking	3/31/18		577608.0	204255642.0	8868421.0	149	59655724
MBT	Mobile TeleSystems PJSC	Services	12/31/17	442911.0	56042.0	551070.0	120126.0	359	366517935
MODN	Model N, Inc	IT Services	9/30/17	131.2	-39.5	171.9	41.3	121	24962663
MOD	Modine Manufacturing Co	Auto Parts	3/31/18	2103.1	22.2	1573.4	490.1	242	51997519
MC	Moelis & Co	Finance Intermediaries & Services	12/31/17	684.6	29.4	699.1	324.9	237	38712455
MHK	Mohawk Industries, Inc.	Construction Materials	12/31/17	9491.3	971.6	12094.9	7059.2	811	73422056
MOH	Molina Healthcare Inc	Hospitals & Health Care Facilities	12/31/17	19883.0	-512.0	8471.0	1337.0	386	80484494
TAP	Molson Coors Brewing Co.	Beverages	12/31/17	11002.8	1414.2	30246.9	13226.1	810	193435817
MNR	Monmouth Real Estate Investment	REITs	9/30/17	113.5	40.3	1443.0	712.9	256	59030897
MCO	Moody's Corp.	Business Services'	12/31/17	4204.1	1000.6	8594.2	-327.7	899	214923185
MOG A	Moog Inc	Industrial Machinery & Equipment	9/30/17	2497.5	141.3	3090.6	1214.3	308	36986181
MS	Morgan Stanley	Finance Intermediaries & Services	12/31/17	43642.0	6111.0	851733.0	77391.0	1522	1838745532
APF	Morgan Stanley Asia-Pacific Fund, I	Holding and other Investment Office	12/31/16	5.1	2.4	217.7	214.8	68	10267459
CAF	Morgan Stanley China A Share Fun	Holding and other Investment Office	12/31/16	10.6	2.1	456.6	454.7	95	9420597
MSD	Morgan Stanley Emerging Markets	Holding and other Investment Office	12/31/16	15.7	13.2	229.0	221.6	66	9192266
EDD	Morgan Stanley Emerging Markets	Holding and other Investment Office	10/31/17	58.8	42.4	851.0	585.0	107	18597272
MSF	Morgan Stanley Emerging Markets	Holding and other Investment Office	12/31/16	4.4	1.2	223.5	217.9	65	9559768
IIF	Morgan Stanley India Investment Fu	Holding and other Investment Office	12/31/16	4.9	-1.2	434.1	423.3	68	5860123
ICB	Morgan Stanley Trusts	Holding and other Investment Office	10/31/02	5.5	4.8	103.9	103.8		0
MOSC	Mosaic Acquisition Corp	Business Services	12/31/17		-0.2	346.2	334.0	36	17696134
MOS	Mosaic Co (The)	Agricultural Chemicals	12/31/17	7409.4	-107.2	18633.4	9617.5	828	340580302
MSI	Motorola Solutions Inc	Manufacturing	12/31/17	6380.0	-155.0	8208.0	-1742.0	962	321210165
MOV	Movado Group, Inc.	Miscellaneous Consumer Goods	1/31/18	568.0	-15.2	645.4	470.3	252	20448289
MPLX	MPLX LP	Equipment & Services	12/31/17	3867.0	830.0	19500.0	986.0	372	259665525
MRC	MRC Global Inc	Industrial Machinery & Equipment	12/31/17	3646.0	50.0	2340.0	1114.0	213	99117634
MSA	MSA Safety Inc	Office Equipment & Furniture	12/31/17	1196.8	26.0	1684.8	597.6	333	33295067
MSM	MSC Industrial Direct Co Inc	Industrial Machinery & Equipment	9/2/17	2887.7	231.4	2098.9	1225.1	461	52468454
MSCI	MSCI Inc	Publishing	12/31/17	1274.2	304.0	3275.7	401.0	567	100619368
MSGN	MSG Network Inc	Radio & Television	6/30/17	675.4	167.3	805.0	-944.2	289	71281493
MLI	Mueller Industries Inc	Industrial Machinery & Equipment	12/30/17	2266.1	85.6	1320.2	522.1	258	66857990
MWA	Mueller Water Products Inc	Industrial Machinery & Equipment	9/30/17	826.0	123.3	1258.3	488.4	330	160144878
MUR	Murphy Oil Corp	Production & Extraction	12/31/17	2225.1	-311.8	9860.9	4620.2	610	197674557
MUSA	Murphy USA Inc	Retail - General Merchandise/Depart	12/31/17	12826.6	245.3	2331.0	738.4		0
MVO	MV Oil Trust	Production & Extraction	12/31/17	9.1	8.3	17.0	17.0	44	1469251
MVC	MVC Capital Inc	Holding and other Investment Office	10/31/17	20.1	-5.6	403.4	279.5	95	12955744
MYE	Myers Industries Inc.	Plastics	12/31/17	547.0	-9.9	355.9	93.8	206	32508907
MYOV	Myovant Sciences Ltd	Pharmaceuticals	3/31/17		-83.4	185.3	166.8	49	13843336
NBR	Nabors Industries Ltd	Production & Extraction	12/31/17	2565.5	-546.8	8402.0	2911.8	581	373954276
NC	NACCO Industries Inc	Mining	12/31/17	104.8	30.3	389.6	219.4	127	3991162
NTP	Nam Tai Property Inc	Property, Real Estate & Developmen	12/31/17	1.9	3.9	262.1	244.4	77	10949309
NBHC	National Bank Holdings Corp	Banking	12/31/17	203.6	14.6	4843.5	532.4	163	33741106
NFG	National Fuel Gas Co. (NJ)	Gas Utilities	9/30/17	1579.9	283.5	6103.3	1703.7	559	74537777
NGG	National Grid plc	Electric Utilities	3/31/18	15250.0	3550.0	58787.0	18832.0	484	42258019
NHI	National Health Investors, Inc.	REITs	12/31/17	278.7	159.4	2545.8	1322.1	318	37404608
NOV	National Oilwell Varco Inc	Equipment & Services	12/31/17	7304.0	-237.0	20206.0	14094.0	998	428743527
NPK	National Presto Industries, Inc.	Defense	12/31/17	333.6	53.0	411.9	366.4	199	5905879
NNN	National Retail Properties Inc	REITs	12/31/17	584.9	265.0	6560.5	3840.6	480	185265499
NSA	National Storage Affiliates Trust	REITs	12/31/17	268.1	3.0	2266.7	841.0	222	52961932
NW PRC	National Westminster Bank Plc	Banking	12/31/17	9436.0	2065.0	340843.0	16286.0		0
NSM	Nationstar Mortgage Holdings Inc	Credit & Lending	12/31/17	1650.0	30.0	18036.0	1715.0	173	101134874
NGS	Natural Gas Services Group Inc	Equipment & Services	12/31/17	67.7	19.9	298.3	257.3	126	13969541
NGVC	Natural Grocers By Vitamin Cottage	Retail - Food & Beverage, Drug & To	9/30/17	769.0	6.9	300.0	133.9	104	8268312
NRP	Natural Resource Partners LP	Mining	12/31/17	378.0	88.7	1389.2	173.4	104	12721767
NTZ	Natuzzi S.p.A.	Furniture	12/31/17	449.6	-31.4	317.8	106.4	23	10152640
NLS	Nautilus Inc	Leisure Equipment	12/31/17	406.2	26.3	324.8	179.2	223	40332748
NCI	Navigant Consulting, Inc.	Business Services	12/31/17	1032.3	75.0	1080.3	687.3	259	53995632
NVGS	Navigator Holdings Ltd.	Miscellaneous Transportation Servic	12/31/17	298.6	5.3	1853.9	963.2		0
NNA	Navios Maritime Acquisition Corp	Equipment & Services	12/31/17	227.3	-78.9	1572.8	462.5	93	33842753
NM	Navios Maritime Holdings Inc	Shipping	12/31/17	487.8	-165.9	2630.0	516.1	120	32986749
NAP	Navios Maritime Midstream Partner	Shipping	12/31/17	83.1	14.6	456.5		29	1602961
NMM	Navios Maritime Partners LP	Shipping	12/31/17	211.7	-15.1	1305.3		104	37907654
NAV	Navistar International Corp.	Autos- Manufacturing	10/31/17	8570.0	30.0	6135.0	-4578.0	311	94601692
NCS	NCI Building Systems, Inc.	Metal Products	10/29/17	1770.3	54.7	1051.2	305.2	265	67840150
NCR	NCR Corp	Computer Hardware & Equipment	12/31/17	6516.0	232.0	7654.0	1529.0	604	143989894
NP	Neenah Inc	Paper & Forest Products	12/31/17	979.9	80.3	904.4	399.9	299	23184465
NNI	Nelnet Inc	Credit & Lending	12/31/17	1202.1	173.2	23964.4	2149.5	192	19143792
NPTN	NeoPhotonics Corp	Semiconductors	12/31/17	292.9	-53.3	403.0	194.5	130	43485773
NETS	Netshoes (Cayman) Ltd	Retail - Apparel and Accessories	12/31/17	1889.0	-169.7	1497.1	483.4	28	17903816
NVRO	Nevro Corp	Medical Instruments & Equipment	12/31/17	326.7	-36.7	454.1	249.2	238	35250895
HYB	New America High Income Fund, In	Holding and other Investment Office	12/31/16	21.4	17.4	324.7	231.1	65	11679596
NFC U	New Frontier Corp	Services	4/19/18		-0.0	0.1	0.0		0
GF	New Germany Fund, Inc.	Holding and other Investment Office	12/31/16	4.9	1.9	264.3	235.8	54	11075453
IRL	New Ireland Fund Inc (The)	Holding and other Investment Office	10/31/17	0.9	-0.5	58.4	58.2	44	1363088
NJR	New Jersey Resources Corp	Gas Utilities	9/30/17	2268.6	132.1	3928.5	1236.6	385	75767017
NEWM	New Media Investment Group Inc	Publishing	12/31/17	1342.0	-0.9	1283.5	674.4	213	55881812
NMFC	New Mountain Finance Corp	Wealth Management	12/31/17	197.8	102.2	1928.0	1035.0	175	35153980
EDU	New Oriental Education & Technolo	Educational Services	5/31/17	1799.5	274.5	2925.0	1680.9	389	138375416

EARNINGS PER SHARE QUARTERLY			ANNUAL			P/E RATIO		DIVIDENDS PER SHARE			AV. YLD %	DIV. DECLARED		PRICE RANGE 2017	
1st	2nd	3rd	2017	2016	2015			2017	2016	2015		AMOUNT	PAYABLE		
0.10	-	-	-0.08	0.32	0.54	-		-	-	-	-			23.6 -	17.1
21.50	-	-	14.68	57.51	107.50	0.5 -	0.4	18.30	17.75	17.79	273.9			8.1 -	5.6
-	-	-	0.19	0.23	0.19	108.9 -	40.3	1.51	2.83	-	11.7			20.7 -	7.7
4.66	-	-	14.28	33.50	31.64	0.3 -	0.2	15.17	15.30	13.83	419.7			4.0 -	3.4
-	-	9.09	28.66	24.35	24.87	0.4 -	0.3	51.79	51.09	46.79	504.3			12.6 -	7.8
-	-0.13	-	-1.38	-1.21	-0.76			-	-	-				18.9 -	12.7
-	-	-0.57	0.29	-0.03	0.45	86.6 -	53.3	-	-	-		0.10Y	12/5/08	25.1 -	15.4
0.75	-	-	0.78	1.58	1.55	85.8 -	49.1	2.48	3.29	1.00	5.1	1.57Y	9/12/18	67.0 -	38.3
2.78	-	-	12.98	12.48	8.31	21.9 -	15.7	-	-	-				284.8 -	204.0
1.64	-	-	-9.07	0.92	2.58			-	-	-				101.5 -	56.8
1.28	-	-	6.53	9.26	1.93	14.1 -	9.1	1.64	1.64	1.64	2.1	0.410Y	18/78/27	91.8 -	59.4
-	0.10	-	0.56	0.50	0.43	32.5 -	24.8	0.64	0.64	0.60	4.0	0.38280Z	9/17/18	18.2 -	13.9
1.92	-	-	5.15	1.36	4.63	34.8 -	23.7	1.52	1.48	1.36	1.0	0.440Y	18/78/27	179.2 -	122.0
-	0.39	-	3.90	3.47	3.35	23.6 -	18.6	-	-	-		0.250Y	6/1/18	92.0 -	72.5
1.45	-	-	3.07	2.92	2.90	19.2 -	14.3	0.90	0.70	0.55	1.8	0.30Y	18/78/27	58.9 -	44.0
-	-	-	-	0.17	0.16			-	0.15	0.14		0.02430	7/13/18	19.7 -	16.3
-	-	-	-	0.10	0.23			-	0.80	13.34		0.8323B	12/29/17	27.7 -	21.2
-	-	-	-	0.62	0.57			-	0.63	0.60		0.140	7/13/18	10.3 -	8.7
-	-	-	0.63	0.78	0.80	13.3 -	10.6	0.66	0.76	0.91	8.5	0.150	7/13/18	8.4 -	6.7
-	-	-	-	0.08	0.05			-	0.09	0.05		0.03210	1/10/18	19.9 -	15.8
-	-	-	-	-0.08	-0.16			-	1.14	0.04		0.0316B	7/13/18	36.8 -	25.7
-	-	-	-	-	-			-	-	-		0.0808C	5/25/18	19.1 -	0.0
0.03	-	-	0.00	-	-			-	-	-					
0.11	-	-	-0.31	0.85	2.78			0.60	1.10	1.08	2.4	0.0250Y	18/78/27	29.7 -	19.4
0.69	-	-	-0.95	3.24	3.02			1.93	1.70	1.43	2.0	0.520Y	18/78/27	117.7 -	83.0
0.35	-	-	1.51	1.90	2.02	35.1 -	14.4	0.52	0.44	0.40	1.6	0.20Y	6/25/18	53.0 -	21.8
0.61	-	-	1.06	-	1.22	36.9 -	30.3	2.21	2.03	1.70	6.3	0.61750	5/15/18	39.1 -	32.1
0.13	-	-	0.27	-1.10	-3.38	80.3 -	52.9	-	-	-				21.7 -	14.3
0.83	-	-	0.67	2.42	1.87	144.3 -	98.7	1.38	1.31	1.27	1.7	0.56250Y	18/78/27	96.7 -	66.2
-	-	1.39	4.05	3.77	3.74	24.5 -	16.2	1.80	1.72	4.60	2.1	0.580Y	18/78/27	99.3 -	65.6
1.24	-	-	3.31	2.70	2.03	52.2 -	30.9	1.32	1.00	0.80	1.0	0.380	18/78/27	172.8 -	102.3
-	-	0.62	2.21	0.10	3.28	11.7 -	7.4	-	-	-				25.8 -	16.4
0.42	-	-	1.49	1.74	1.54	24.8 -	17.1	3.40	0.38	0.30	10.9	0.10Y	6/15/18	37.0 -	25.4
-	0.06	-	0.76	0.39	0.19	17.0 -	12.8	0.15	0.10	0.07	1.3	0.050Y	5/21/18	12.9 -	9.7
0.96	-	-	-1.81	-1.60	-13.03			1.00	1.20	1.40	3.5	0.250Y	18/78/27	35.1 -	22.6
1.16	-	-	6.78	5.59	4.02	13.1 -	9.2	-	-	-				88.6 -	62.6
0.22	-	-	0.72	0.40	1.27	14.4 -	6.7	0.72	0.40	1.27	10.0	0.420Z	7/25/18	10.3 -	4.8
-	-	-	-0.25	0.85	0.41			0.56	0.71	0.54	5.4	0.150	7/31/18	11.0 -	9.5
0.22	-	-	-0.33	0.03	0.57			0.54	0.54	0.54	2.7	0.1350Y	7/3/18	24.4 -	16.0
-	-0.70	-	-1.70	-0.04				-	-						
-0.46	-	-	-1.90	-3.64	-1.29			0.24	0.06	0.06		0.060	18/78/27		
1.18	-	-	4.41	4.32	3.13	20.1 -	7.2	0.98	1.06	1.04	2.1	0.1650Y	18/78/27	88.8 -	31.9
-	-	0.40	0.11	-0.26	-0.32			0.28	0.28	0.08		0.070	1/19/18		
0.27	-	-	0.53	0.79	0.14	76.7 -	57.3	0.34	0.22	0.20	1.0	0.140Y	6/15/18	40.7 -	30.4
-	1.06	-	3.30	-3.43	-4.50	18.1 -	14.9	1.64	1.60	1.56	3.0	0.4250Y	18/78/27	59.8 -	49.1
-	-	-	2.06	0.69	0.53	31.7 -	25.0	0.44	0.43	0.43	0.7			65.4 -	51.6
0.92	-	-	3.87	3.87	3.95	20.9 -	16.4	3.80	3.60	3.40	5.2	1.0Z	18/78/27	80.8 -	63.3
-0.18	-	-	-0.63	-6.41	-1.99			0.20	0.61	1.84	0.6	0.050Y	18/78/27	44.1 -	29.9
1.57	-	-	7.58	6.39	5.83	17.8 -	12.0	5.50	5.05	4.05	5.2	5.6Y	3/15/18	135.0 -	90.8
0.62	-	-	1.45	1.38	1.20	30.3 -	25.2	1.86	1.78	1.71	4.6	0.50Z	18/78/27	44.0 -	36.5
0.09	-	-	0.01	0.31	0.17	3082.0 -	2124.0	1.04	0.88	0.54	4.1	0.3750Z	6/29/18	30.8 -	21.2
-	-	-	-	-	-			1.27	1.54	1.27	4.9			26.6 -	25.5
1.61	-	-	0.30	0.19	0.37	67.2 -	53.7	-	-	-				20.2 -	16.1
0.02	-	-	1.51	0.50	0.79	19.4 -	14.5	-	-	-				29.3 -	21.9
-	0.15	-	0.31	0.51	0.72	42.4 -	15.6	-	-	-				13.1 -	4.8
1.15	-	-	3.96	7.78	-45.75	9.3 -	5.8	1.80	1.35	-	6.3	0.450	5/14/18	37.0 -	23.0
-	-	-0.34	-0.57	-0.11	-0.30			-	-	-				2.8 -	0.0
0.26	-	-	0.85	1.09	0.84	22.4 -	13.7	-	-	-		0.10Y	9/10/07	19.1 -	11.7
0.25	-	-	1.55	1.19	1.23	16.2 -	9.4	-	-	-				25.0 -	14.6
-	-	-	0.10	0.80	1.76			-	-	-					
-	-0.41	-	-0.50	0.40	0.56			-	-	-		0.020	6/27/18		
-0.35	-	-	-1.50	-2.54	-1.42			-	-	-		0.060	9/25/15		
-4.14	-	-	0.70	1.19	1.33			1.69	-	-		0.1250	8/14/18		
-	-	-	-0.11	-0.62	0.48			-	-	-		0.020	5/14/18		
-	0.55	-	0.32	-1.19	-2.25	148.3 -	82.8	-	-	-				47.5 -	26.5
-	-0.09	-	0.77	0.70	0.24	29.9 -	17.2	-	-	-				23.0 -	13.3
0.06	-	-	0.97	1.71	-1.09	44.3 -	27.9	-	-	-				43.0 -	27.1
0.95	-	-	4.68	4.24	2.98	20.3 -	16.3	1.48	1.32	1.20	1.8	0.410Y	6/4/18	94.8 -	76.3
2.78	-	-	4.14	6.02	5.89	15.4 -	11.0	0.58	0.50	0.42	1.1	0.160Y	6/15/18	63.6 -	45.4
-0.41	-	-	-1.23	0.00	0.09			-	-	-				8.6 -	4.6
-	-	-	-5.95	-7.05	-4.66			-	-	-					
-0.59	-	-	-1.25	-1.12	-2.54			-	-	-				93.3 -	65.9
-	-	-	-	0.75	0.76			-	0.76	0.81		0.0550	7/31/18	10.0 -	8.6
-	-	-	-	0.12	0.13			-	1.18	1.23		0.0755B	6/26/18	21.3 -	16.7
-	-	-	-0.15	-0.06	0.21			1.14	2.22	1.13	8.9	0.2890	6/29/18	14.1 -	11.5
-	1.59	-	1.52	1.52	2.10	29.6 -	23.8	1.04	0.97	0.92	2.5	0.27250Y	18/78/27	45.0 -	36.3
-0.01	-	-	-0.02	0.70	1.52			1.42	1.34	1.29	8.9	0.370Y	5/16/18	18.9 -	13.2
0.30	-	-	1.38	1.60	0.55	10.7 -	9.1	1.36	1.36	1.36	9.9	0.340Y	6/29/18	14.7 -	12.6
0.81	-	-	1.74	1.43	1.23	61.1 -	40.8	-	0.40	-				106.3 -	71.0

SYMBOL	COMPANY	NATURE OF BUSINESS	FISCAL YEAR-END	TOTAL REV. $MILL	NET INCOME $MILL	TOTAL ASSETS $MILL	NET STK EQUITY $MILL	NO OF INST	INST. HOLDINGS (SHARES)
NEWR	New Relic Inc	Internet & Software	3/31/18	355.1	-45.3	443.3	215.1	273	43041178
NRZ	New Residential Investment Corp	REITs	12/31/17	2151.8	957.5	22213.6	4690.2	396	222958483
SNR	New Senior Investment Group Inc	REITs	12/31/17	449.1	12.2	2508.0	505.9	215	65638896
NWY	New York & Company Inc	Retail - Apparel and Accessories	2/3/18	926.9	5.7	303.0	86.9	96	57994052
NYCB	New York Community Bancorp Inc.	Banking	12/31/17	1799.1	466.2	49124.2	6795.4	642	400894356
NYRT	New York REIT Inc	REITs	12/31/17			1090.7		184	37703829
NYT	New York Times Co.	Publishing	12/31/17	1675.6	4.3	2099.8	897.3	372	178841471
NWL	Newell Brands Inc	Plastics	12/31/17	14742.2	2748.8	33135.5	14144.7	931	549400202
NFX	Newfield Exploration Co	Production & Extraction	12/31/17	1767.0	427.0	4961.0	1408.0	691	232822664
NEU	NewMarket Corp	Specialty Chemicals	12/31/17	2198.4	190.5	1712.2	601.6	374	8987371
NEM	Newmont Mining Corp (Holding Co)	Mining	12/31/17	7348.0	-98.0	20563.0	10609.0	1004	567341475
NR	Newpark Resources, Inc.	Equipment & Services	12/31/17	747.8	-6.1	902.7	547.5	261	108819419
NEXA	Nexa Resources SA	Metal Products	12/31/17	2449.5	126.9	5961.5	2486.8	63	19010232
NXRT	NexPoint Residential Trust Inc	REITs	12/31/17	144.2	53.4	1055.4	239.4	150	13965735
NHF	NexPoint Strategic Opportunities Fu	Holding and other Investment Office	12/31/16	77.0	65.3	562.7	414.8	77	8281688
NEE PRK	NextEra Energy Capital Holdings In	Electric Utilities							0
NEE	NextEra Energy Inc	Electric Utilities	12/31/17	17195.0	5378.0	97827.0	28208.0	1886	445162009
NEP	NextEra Energy Partners LP	Electric Utilities	12/31/17	807.0	-62.0	8395.0	2188.0	210	51026961
NGL	NGL Energy Partners LP	Refining & Marketing	3/31/18	17282.7	-70.9	6151.1	82.6	139	81805810
NLSN	Nielsen Holdings PLC	Business Services	12/31/17	6572.0	429.0	16866.0	4245.0	541	427873837
NKE	NIKE Inc	Apparel, Footwear & Accessories	5/31/17	34350.0	4240.0	23259.0	12407.0	1908	1215739430
NINE	Nine Energy Service Inc	Equipment & Services	12/31/17	543.7	-67.7	578.9	287.4	61	16982763
NI	NiSource Inc. (Holding Co.)	Equipment & Services	12/31/17	4874.6	128.5	19961.7	4320.1	701	359686834
NL	NL Industries, Inc.	Electrical Equipment	12/31/17	112.0	116.1	551.6	335.3	95	6322026
NOAH	Noah Holdings Ltd	Wealth Management	12/31/17	2826.9	762.9	6494.9	4429.3	141	29396296
NE	Noble Corp plc	Equipment & Services	12/31/17	1236.9	-516.5	10794.7	5276.2		0
NBL	Noble Energy Inc	Production & Extraction	12/31/17	4256.0	-1118.0	21476.0	9936.0	800	536664399
NBLX	Noble Midstream Partners LP	Equipment & Services	12/31/17	239.3	140.6	829.8	474.5	112	22206603
NOK	Nokia Corp	Manufacturing	12/31/17	23147.0	-1494.0	41024.0	16138.0	630	473613921
NOMD	Nomad Foods Ltd	Food	12/31/17	1956.6	136.5	4601.7	1852.6	215	143485616
NMR	Nomura Holdings Inc	Finance Intermediaries & Services	3/31/18	1030374.0	219343.0	40591329.0	2749320.0	158	35334441
OSB	Norbord Inc	Paper & Forest Products	12/31/17	2177.0	436.0	2103.0	1019.0		0
NAO	Nordic American Offshore Ltd (Ber	Equipment & Services	12/31/17	17.9	-29.3	387.7	248.3	76	9957443
NAT	Nordic American Tankers Ltd	Equipment & Services	12/31/17	297.1	-205.0	1141.1	711.1	224	40540921
JWN	Nordstrom, Inc.	Retail - General Merchandise/Depart	2/3/18	15478.0	437.0	8115.0	977.0	850	128440201
NSC	Norfolk Southern Corp.	Rail	12/31/17	10551.0	5404.0	35711.0	16359.0	1634	259214929
NOA	North American Construction Group	Equipment & Services	12/31/17	292.6	5.3	383.6	145.9	56	9727414
NRT	North European Oil Royalty Trust	Oil Royalty Traders	10/31/17	7.8	7.0	2.1	0.1	55	1512979
NOC	Northrop Grumman Corp	Defense	12/31/17	25803.0	2015.0	34917.0	7048.0	1411	202087015
NRE	NorthStar Realty Europe Corp	REITs	12/31/17	129.9	-31.1	1940.9	621.7	198	43552956
NWN	Northwest Natural Gas Co.	Gas Utilities	12/31/17	762.2	-55.6	3039.7	742.8	324	26463351
NWE	Northwestern Corp.	Electric Utilities	12/31/17	1305.7	162.7	5420.9	1798.9	376	61416973
NCLH	Norwegian Cruise Line Holdings Ltd	Hotels, Restaurants & Travel	12/31/17	5396.2	759.9	14094.9	5749.8	528	231618072
NVS	Novartis AG Basel	Pharmaceuticals	12/31/17	50135.0	7703.0	133079.0	74168.0	1404	302864894
NVO	Novo-Nordisk AS	Pharmaceuticals	12/31/17	111696.0	38130.0	102355.0	49815.0	751	182945400
DNOW	Now Inc	Equipment & Services	12/31/17	2648.0	-52.0	1749.0	1185.0	355	141535821
NRG	NRG Energy Inc	Electric Utilities	12/31/17	10629.0	-2153.0	23318.0	-346.0	661	384425518
NYLD	NRG Yield Inc	Electrical Equipment	12/31/17	1009.0	-8.0	8283.0	1747.0	231	60496544
NUS	NU Skin Enterprises, Inc.	Household & Personal Products	12/31/17	2279.1	129.4	1589.9	704.6	412	52116561
NUE	Nucor Corp.	Non-Precious Metals	12/31/17	20252.4	1318.7	15841.3	8739.0	1139	334799765
NS	NuStar Energy LP	Refining & Marketing	12/31/17	1814.0	148.0	6535.2		289	61868961
JMLP	Nuveen All Cap Energy MLP Opport	Finance Intermediaries & Services	11/30/16	1.6	-0.6	168.0	121.8	34	2130785
NVG	Nuveen AMT-Free Municipal Credit	Holding and other Investment Office	10/31/16	141.2	104.2	5294.1	3370.2	212	20349886
NUW	Nuveen AMT-Free Municipal Value	Holding and other Investment Office	10/31/16	12.4	10.6	256.2	247.4	34	1072628
NEA	Nuveen AMT-Free Quality Municipa	Holding and other Investment Office	10/31/16	102.0	73.6	6366.6	4037.2	239	45130705
NAZ	Nuveen Arizona Quality Municipal I	Holding and other Investment Office	2/28/17	11.1	7.8	259.0	165.1	31	693770
NBB	Nuveen Build America Bond Fund	Holding and other Investment Office	3/31/17	39.5	32.3	709.8	566.4	78	7764045
NBD	Nuveen Build America Bond Opport	Holding and other Investment Office	3/31/17	10.3	8.5	177.9	158.9		0
NKX	Nuveen California AMT-Free Qualit	Holding and other Investment Office	2/28/17	50.3	36.2	1170.9	732.6	67	4247154
NCB	Nuveen California Municipal Value	Holding and other Investment Office	2/28/17	3.0	2.5	54.0	53.6	16	199130
NCA	Nuveen California Municipal Value	Holding and other Investment Office	2/28/17	13.3	11.6	291.5	285.5	61	3289680
NAC	Nuveen California Quality Municipal	Holding and other Investment Office	2/28/17	127.7	93.9	3389.7	2221.6	103	10212451
NXC	Nuveen California Select Tax-Free I	Holding and other Investment Office	3/31/17	4.2	3.8	94.7	94.3	24	328909
NTC	Nuveen Connecticut Quality Munici	Holding and other Investment Office	5/31/17	12.6	8.3	331.4	205.5	53	2877941
JCE	Nuveen Core Equity Alpha Fund	Holding and other Investment Office	12/31/16	4.4	2.0	229.1	228.6	44	3288127
JQC	Nuveen Credit Strategies Income F	Holding and other Investment Office	7/31/17	103.2	70.7	2039.9	1265.4	187	56551836
JDD	Nuveen Diversified Dividend and In	Holding and other Investment Office	12/31/16	14.2	9.1	366.0	247.6	53	1614884
DIAX	Nuveen Dow 30SM Dynamic Overw	Holding and other Investment Office	12/31/16	15.1	9.8	608.6	597.2	87	5842916
JMF	Nuveen Energy MLP Total Return F	Holding and other Investment Office	11/30/16	2.5	-4.9	786.4	530.1	91	7149849
NEV	Nuveen Enhanced Municipal Value	Holding and other Investment Office	10/31/16	23.4	19.7	443.4	388.8	59	2906007
JFR	Nuveen Floating Rate Income Fund	Holding and other Investment Office	7/31/17	57.5	40.6	1081.3	663.9	121	15231874
JRO	Nuveen Floating Rate Income Oppo	Holding and other Investment Office	7/31/17	41.7	29.6	755.3	465.2	107	8986553
NKG	Nuveen Georgia Quality Municipal I	Holding and other Investment Office	5/31/17	8.9	5.8	234.2	145.6	30	1203520
JGH	Nuveen Global High Income Fund	Holding and other Investment Office	12/31/16	41.8	34.2	580.9	414.1	72	6292576
JHY	Nuveen High Income 2020 Target T	Finance Intermediaries & Services	12/31/17	11.4	9.2	198.8	154.6	25	2239325
JHA	Nuveen High Income December 20	Finance Intermediaries & Services	12/31/17	17.5	13.8	295.1	294.8		0
JHD	Nuveen High Income December 20	Finance Intermediaries & Services	12/31/17	19.6	15.5	339.5	275.6	38	5770111
NID	Nuveen Intermediate Duration Muni	Finance Intermediaries & Services	5/31/17	38.3	29.8	855.2	643.8	66	8485043
NIQ	Nuveen Intermediate Duration Quali	Holding and other Investment Office	5/31/17	8.8	6.5	240.1	182.7	41	2597547
NMY	Nuveen Maryland Quality Municipal	Holding and other Investment Office	5/31/17	21.3	14.2	571.7	342.4	62	3889168

1st	2nd	3rd	2017	2016	2015	P/E	RATIO	2017	2016	2015	AV. YLD %	AMOUNT	PAYABLE	2017 High	2017 Low
-	-	-0.14	-1.18	-1.39	-1.98	-	-	-	-	-	-	-	-	110.6	43.1
1.81	-	-	3.15	2.12	1.32	5.9	4.9	1.98	1.84	1.75	11.6	0.50Z	18/78/27	18.7	15.3
-0.16	-	-	0.15	-0.88	-1.08	69.7	46.1	1.04	1.04	0.75	12.4	0.260Z	6/22/18	10.5	6.9
0.05	-	-	-0.27	-0.16	-0.27	-	-	-	-	-	-	-	-	5.1	1.3
0.20	-	-	0.90	1.01	-0.11	16.1	12.3	0.68	0.68	1.00	5.3	0.170Y	18/78/27	14.5	11.0
-	-	-	-	-5.00	-2.40	-	-	-	3.80	4.60	-	4.85A	5/18/18	86.9	17.6
0.13	-	-	0.03	0.18	0.38	886.7	570.0	0.16	0.16	0.16	0.8	0.040Y	18/78/27	26.6	17.1
0.11	-	-	5.63	1.25	1.29	9.6	4.1	0.88	0.76	0.76	2.6	0.230Y	18/78/27	53.9	23.1
0.43	-	-	2.13	-6.36	-21.18	16.3	10.8	-	-	-	-	-	-	34.8	22.9
5.14	-	-	16.08	20.54	19.45	29.1	22.5	7.00	6.40	5.80	1.7	1.750Y	18/78/27	467.4	361.4
0.36	-	-	-0.18	-1.18	0.43	-	-	0.25	0.13	0.10	0.7	0.140Y	18/78/27	41.9	31.9
0.08	-	-	-0.07	-0.49	-1.10	-	-	-	-	-	-	-	-	11.3	7.0
-	-	-	1.09	-	-	-	-	-	-	-	-	0.6001G7	3/28/18	-	-
0.47	-	-	2.49	1.03	-0.51	11.7	9.3	0.91	0.84	0.62	3.5	0.250Z	6/29/18	29.2	23.1
-	-	-	-	4.08	8.75	-	-	-	2.80	0.72	-	0.20	7/31/18	25.5	21.9
-	-	-	-	-	-	-	-	-	-	-	-	0.32810Z	9/4/18	26.0	23.8
9.32	-	-	11.38	6.25	6.06	14.8	12.2	3.93	3.48	3.08	2.5	1.110Y	18/78/27	168.1	138.8
1.21	-	-	-1.20	1.88	0.46	-	-	1.49	1.30	0.91	3.7	0.420	5/15/18	46.7	36.8
-	-	0.32	0.95	-2.35	-0.29	18.1	9.2	1.56	2.54	2.37	12.8	0.390	18/78/27	17.2	8.7
0.20	-	-	1.20	1.39	1.54	-	-	1.33	1.21	0.28	-	0.350	18/78/27	-	-
-	-	-0.57	2.51	2.16	1.85	31.7	20.3	0.68	0.62	0.54	1.1	0.20Y	18/78/27	79.7	50.8
0.08	-	-	-4.55	-5.34	-2.97	-	-	-	-	-	-	-	-	38.5	23.0
0.81	-	-	0.39	1.02	0.90	70.7	57.7	0.70	0.64	0.83	2.8	0.1950Y	18/78/27	27.6	22.5
0.29	-	-	2.38	0.31	-0.49	6.4	3.0	-	-	-	-	0.1250Y	12/24/13	15.4	7.1
-	-	0.12	25.90	22.08	18.31	2.6	1.0	-	-	-	-	-	-	67.6	26.9
-0.58	-	-	-2.11	-3.82	2.06	-	-	-	0.20	1.28	-	0.020Y	8/8/16	-	-
1.14	-	-	-2.38	-2.32	-6.07	-	-	0.40	0.40	0.72	1.4	0.110Y	18/78/27	36.9	23.0
0.97	-	-	4.10	0.89	-	13.9	10.3	1.76	-	-	3.6	0.5110	5/14/18	56.9	42.2
-	-	-0.03	-0.26	-0.13	0.63	-	-	0.17	0.26	0.14	3.0	-	-	6.5	4.5
-	-	-	0.74	0.20	-2.32	-	-	-	-	-	-	-	-	-	-
15.77	-	-	65.65	35.52	60.03	0.1	0.1	11.99	22.72	14.94	207.2	-	-	6.8	4.8
1.09	-	-	5.03	2.13	-0.66	11.6	6.1	1.16	0.30	0.55	2.8	0.60	6/21/18	58.5	30.6
-	-	-	-0.53	-1.54	-0.47	-	-	0.08	-	-	-	0.010	6/8/18	-	-
-0.13	-	-	-1.97	-0.05	1.29	-	-	0.53	1.37	1.38	-	0.010	6/12/18	-	-
0.52	-	-	2.02	3.15	3.72	26.5	19.0	1.48	6.33	1.32	3.1	0.370Y	18/78/27	53.6	38.3
1.93	-	-	18.61	5.62	5.10	8.4	6.0	2.44	2.36	2.36	1.8	0.720Y	18/78/27	156.3	112.5
0.36	-	-	0.18	-0.01	-0.23	49.0	0.0	0.08	0.08	0.08	1.4	0.020	7/6/18	8.8	0.0
-	0.20	-	0.76	0.67	1.26	12.3	8.0	0.66	0.78	1.43	8.7	0.190Z	5/30/18	9.4	6.1
4.21	-	-	11.47	12.19	10.39	31.4	22.5	3.90	3.50	3.10	1.3	1.20Y	18/78/27	360.0	257.7
-0.02	-	-	-0.57	-1.07	-2.30	-	-	0.60	0.60	0.15	4.6	0.150Z	5/25/18	14.7	10.1
1.44	-	-	-1.94	2.12	1.96	-	-	1.88	1.87	1.86	3.1	0.47250Y	18/78/27	69.2	52.0
1.18	-	-	3.34	3.39	3.17	19.2	15.1	2.10	2.00	1.92	3.7	0.550Y	18/78/27	64.3	50.3
0.45	-	-	3.31	2.78	1.86	-	-	-	-	-	-	-	-	-	-
0.86	-	-	3.25	2.80	7.29	28.9	22.3	2.72	2.72	2.67	3.3	-	-	93.9	72.4
-	-	3.96	15.39	14.96	13.52	3.8	2.7	5.44	6.83	3.71	11.1	-	-	58.1	41.1
0.02	-	-	-0.48	-2.18	-4.68	-	-	-	-	-	-	-	-	16.6	9.4
0.87	-	-	-6.79	-2.22	-19.46	-	-	0.12	0.23	0.58	0.4	0.030Y	18/78/27	34.9	16.1
0.16	-	-	-0.16	0.58	0.40	-	-	1.10	0.94	0.63	6.1	0.3090Y	6/15/18	19.9	15.7
0.64	-	-	2.36	2.55	2.25	35.4	22.8	1.44	1.42	1.40	2.1	0.3650Y	18/78/27	83.7	53.7
1.10	-	-	4.10	2.48	1.11	17.1	13.0	1.51	1.50	1.49	2.5	0.380Y	18/78/27	70.2	53.5
1.15	-	-	0.64	1.27	3.30	74.5	30.7	4.38	4.38	4.38	14.1	0.56250	6/15/18	47.7	19.6
-	-	-	-0.05	-0.12	-	-	-	-	1.03	1.37	-	0.18750	8/15/18	9.6	6.9
-	-	-	0.73	0.77	-	-	-	-	0.88	0.85	-	0.0655M	8/1/18	15.8	14.3
-	-	-	0.76	0.80	-	-	-	-	0.79	0.79	-	0.056M	8/1/18	18.5	15.5
-	-	-	0.72	0.77	-	-	-	-	0.76	0.80	-	0.0535M	8/1/18	14.2	12.7
-	-	-	0.68	0.76	0.79	22.1	18.6	0.75	0.80	0.79	5.4	0.044M	8/1/18	15.0	12.6
-	-	-	1.22	1.29	1.37	18.1	16.4	1.28	1.35	1.39	6.1	0.1030	8/1/18	22.1	20.0
-	-	-	1.18	1.27	1.37	19.5	0.0	1.22	1.31	1.37	5.5	0.09550	8/1/18	23.1	0.0
-	-	-	0.76	0.82	0.85	21.3	17.5	0.87	0.87	0.85	5.9	0.056M	8/1/18	16.2	13.3
-	-	-	0.77	0.82	0.84	23.9	0.0	1.00	1.04	0.90	6.0	0.054M	8/1/18	18.4	0.0
-	-	-	0.42	0.45	0.46	25.5	21.9	0.44	0.47	0.47	4.4	0.0285M	8/1/18	10.7	9.2
-	-	-	0.78	0.88	0.87	19.9	16.9	0.87	0.93	0.93	6.1	0.0555M	8/1/18	15.6	13.2
-	-	-	0.60	0.64	0.66	27.0	22.6	0.72	0.67	0.80	4.9	0.044M	8/1/18	16.2	13.5
-	-	-	0.57	0.67	0.70	22.0	20.0	0.62	0.68	0.68	5.2	0.041M	8/1/18	12.5	11.4
-	-	-	-	0.13	0.09	-	-	-	1.14	2.75	-	0.27750	7/2/18	16.1	14.2
-	-	-	0.52	0.58	0.62	16.7	15.2	0.63	0.61	0.56	7.7	0.0370	8/1/18	8.7	7.9
-	-	-	-	0.46	0.46	-	-	-	1.08	1.08	-	0.240	7/2/18	13.1	11.6
-	-	-	-	0.27	0.25	-	-	-	1.04	1.06	-	0.310	7/2/18	19.9	0.0
-	-	-	-	-0.12	-0.08	-	-	-	1.35	1.34	-	0.250	8/15/18	13.6	9.8
-	-	-	-	0.85	0.93	-	-	-	0.95	0.97	-	0.062M	8/1/18	15.1	13.2
-	-	-	0.73	0.73	0.75	16.4	14.3	0.79	0.72	0.72	7.0	0.05750	8/1/18	11.9	10.4
-	-	-	0.76	0.77	0.79	15.6	13.6	0.83	0.76	0.76	7.4	0.0580	8/1/18	11.9	10.3
-	-	-	0.55	0.68	0.67	24.6	20.4	0.60	0.64	0.64	4.8	0.038M	8/1/18	13.6	11.2
-	-	-	-	1.47	1.58	-	-	-	1.54	1.57	-	0.1070	8/1/18	17.4	15.4
-	-	-	0.62	0.73	0.28	16.5	15.6	0.62	0.68	0.28	6.2	0.0420	8/1/18	10.2	9.7
-	-	-	0.47	0.60	0.04	21.5	20.8	0.50	0.61	-	5.0	0.0270	8/1/18	10.1	9.8
-	-	-	0.57	0.38	-	18.1	17.1	0.61	0.30	-	6.1	0.0350	8/1/18	10.3	9.8
-	-	-	0.63	0.68	0.69	21.7	19.6	0.67	0.68	0.68	5.2	0.0425M	8/1/18	13.7	12.3
-	-	-	0.49	0.53	0.58	27.4	25.2	0.51	0.58	0.60	4.0	0.033M	8/1/18	13.4	12.3
-	-	-	0.61	0.67	0.68	21.7	19.5	0.66	0.67	0.67	5.3	0.044M	8/1/18	13.2	11.9

SYMBOL	COMPANY	NATURE OF BUSINESS	FISCAL YEAR-END	TOTAL REV. $MILL	NET INCOME $MILL	TOTAL ASSETS $MILL	NET STK EQUITY $MILL	NO OF INST	INST. HOLDINGS (SHARES)
NMT	Nuveen Massachusetts Quality Mun	Holding and other Investment Office	5/31/17	8.6	6.0	212.1	137.6	28	517466
NUM	Nuveen Michigan Quality Municipal	Holding and other Investment Office	2/28/17	20.5	14.3	509.0	314.3	57	2407035
NMS	Nuveen Minnesota Quality Municipa	Holding and other Investment Office	5/31/17	6.0	3.9	139.0	84.7	19	417367
NOM	Nuveen Missouri Quality Municipal I	Holding and other Investment Office	5/31/17	2.3	1.5	51.5	32.7	14	87612
JLS	Nuveen Mortgage Opportunity Term	Holding and other Investment Office	12/31/17	34.4	24.8	545.9	397.6	54	5883012
JMT	Nuveen Mortgage Opportunity Term	Holding and other Investment Office	12/31/16	10.4	7.3	164.3	117.6	25	2440647
JMM	Nuveen Multi-Market Income Fund	Holding and other Investment Office	6/30/17	4.9	3.7	112.1	77.1	29	4285193
NHA	Nuveen Municipal 2021 Target Ter	Finance Intermediaries & Services	5/31/17	3.5	2.2	114.5	83.6	20	1567794
NZF	Nuveen Municipal Credit Income Fu	Holding and other Investment Office	10/31/16	109.2	80.6	3644.1	2321.8	170	14578275
NMZ	Nuveen Municipal High Income Opp	Holding and other Investment Office	10/31/16	57.0	47.3	1026.1	788.6	85	5569984
NMI	Nuveen Municipal Income Fund, Inc	Holding and other Investment Office	10/31/16	4.9	4.2	101.5	96.5	28	500918
NUV	Nuveen Municipal Value Fund, Inc.	Holding and other Investment Office	10/31/16	94.4	83.3	2178.4	2150.4	237	31377029
NJV	Nuveen New Jersey Municipal Valu	Holding and other Investment Office	2/28/17	1.0	0.8	26.4	24.1	21	229390
NXJ	Nuveen New Jersey Quality Municip	Holding and other Investment Office	2/28/17	35.6	25.6	980.1	647.6	64	4288891
NRK	Nuveen New York AMT-Free Qualit	Holding and other Investment Office	2/28/17	34.4	23.8	2028.3	1244.7	102	12781567
NYV	Nuveen New York Municipal Value	Holding and other Investment Office	2/28/17	0.7	0.6	36.5	36.3	17	142016
NNY	Nuveen New York Municipal Value	Holding and other Investment Office	2/28/17	2.8	2.4	154.2	150.4	35	1148441
NAN	Nuveen New York Quality Municipal	Holding and other Investment Office	2/28/17	13.0	9.1	730.2	462.2	55	3613352
NXN	Nuveen New York Select Tax-Free I	Holding and other Investment Office	3/31/17	2.4	2.2	57.5	55.1	15	280166
NNC	Nuveen North Carolina Quality Muni	Holding and other Investment Office	5/31/17	14.1	8.8	409.9	246.0	56	1940403
NUO	Nuveen Ohio Quality Municipal Inco	Holding and other Investment Office	2/28/17	19.4	13.8	459.8	302.7	55	2717765
NPN	Nuveen Pennsylvania Municipal Val	Holding and other Investment Office	2/28/17	0.8	0.6	19.6	18.5	11	63355
NQP	Nuveen Pennsylvania Quality Munic	ETFs	2/28/17	31.8	22.5	914.4	558.4	82	4070078
JPT	Nuveen Preferred & Income 2022 T	Holding and other Investment Office	7/31/17	6.4	5.0	218.4	174.8	24	456651
JPC	Nuveen Preferred & Income Opport	Holding and other Investment Office·	7/31/17	89.7	70.0	1694.6	1122.8	161	18951960
JPS	Nuveen Preferred & Income Securiti	Holding and other Investment Office	7/31/17	184.3	143.8	3183.9	2118.5	222	26207485
JPI	Nuveen Preferred & Income Term F	Holding and other Investment Office	7/31/17	50.7	39.8	826.4	591.0	76	4216656
NAD	Nuveen Quality Municipal Income F	Holding and other Investment Office	10/31/16	63.8	45.3	5037.2	3179.2	219	36721006
JRI	Nuveen Real Asset Income & Growt	Holding and other Investment Office	12/31/16	14.7	10.9	253.5	176.4	88	7477827
JRS	Nuveen Real Estate Income Fund	Holding and other Investment Office	12/31/16	17.5	11.3	476.1	329.1	73	4009485
BXMX	Nuveen S&P 500 Buy-Write Income	Holding and other Investment Office	12/31/16	31.0	18.3	1428.1	1399.9	134	20760548
SPXX	Nuveen S&P 500 Dynamic Overwrit	Holding and other Investment Office	12/31/16	5.5	3.3	246.5	242.0	50	3402453
NIM	Nuveen Select Maturities Municipal	Holding and other Investment Office	3/31/17	4.7	4.0	128.5	128.0	52	1945375
NXQ	Nuveen Select Tax Free Income Po	Holding and other Investment Office	3/31/17	10.3	9.5	257.2	256.3	60	2256156
NXP	Nuveen Select Tax-Free Income Po	Holding and other Investment Office	3/31/17	10.0	9.3	251.1	248.5	64	2177072
NXR	Nuveen Select Tax-Free Income Po	Holding and other Investment Office	3/31/17	8.1	7.4	202.8	199.5	51	1939513
NSL	Nuveen Senior Income Fund	Holding and other Investment Office	7/31/17	25.0	17.9	442.3	269.1	77	9535580
JSD	Nuveen Short Duration Credit Oppo	Holding and other Investment Office	7/31/17	17.6	13.0	300.3	182.5	47	2706811
JTD	Nuveen Tax-Advantaged Dividend	Holding and other Investment Office	5/31/17	12.5	7.9	348.1	224.5	50	2964918
JTA	Nuveen Tax-Advantaged Total Retu	Holding and other Investment Office	12/31/16	9.8	6.5	257.9	176.1	44	3542127
NTX	Nuveen Texas Quality Municipal Inc	Holding and other Investment Office	2/28/17	9.3	6.4	232.3	151.9	37	450288
NPV	Nuveen Virginia Quality Municipal In	Holding and other Investment Office	5/31/17	15.4	10.3	404.5	259.8	46	1206004
NVT	nVent Electric PLC	Industrial Machinery & Equipment	12/31/17	2097.9	361.7	4725.0	3791.3	45	1741337
NVR	NVR Inc.	Builders	12/31/17	6322.3	537.5	2989.3	1605.5	597	3884271
OAK	Oaktree Capital Group LLC	Wealth Management	12/31/17	1469.8	231.5	9014.8	869.0	258	43285527
OMP	Oasis Midstream Partners LP	Production & Extraction	12/31/17	182.2	11.6	709.9		41	7073764
OAS	Oasis Petroleum Inc.	Production & Extraction	12/31/17	1248.4	123.8	6615.1	3375.7	370	320305359
OBE	Obsidian Energy Ltd	Production & Extraction	12/31/17	431.0	-84.0	3008.0	2166.0	230	114798366
OXY	Occidental Petroleum Corp	Production & Extraction	12/31/17	13274.0	1311.0	42026.0	20572.0	1620	782412902
OII	Oceaneering International, Inc.	Equipment & Services	12/31/17	1921.5	166.4	3023.9	1659.2	408	126092739
OZM	Och-Ziff Capital Management Grou	Wealth Management	12/31/17	858.3	21.1	1639.4	-8.2	134	84496259
OCN	Ocwen Financial Corp	Credit & Lending	12/31/17		-128.0	8403.2	545.0	224	91584755
OFG	OFG Bancorp	Banking	12/31/17	424.3	52.6	6189.1	945.1	220	56565776
OGE	OGE Energy Corp.	Electric Utilities	12/31/17	2261.1	619.0	10412.7	3851.1	598	169031151
OIBR C	Oi SA	Services	12/31/15	27353.8	-9159.3	99334.6	15455.9	27	4486034
OIS	Oil States International, Inc.	Equipment & Services	12/31/17	670.6	-84.8	1301.5	1132.7	310	77842464
ODC	Oil-Dri Corp. of America	Household & Personal Products	7/31/17	262.3	10.8	212.6	126.0	96	4259955
ORI	Old Republic International Corp.	General Insurance	12/31/17	6263.1	560.5	19403.5	4733.3	581	281519042
OLN	Olin Corp.	Diversified Chemicals	12/31/17	6268.4	549.5	9218.3	2753.7	508	178633021
OHI	Omega Healthcare Investors, Inc.	REITs	12/31/17	908.4	100.4	8773.3	3555.1	577	196031985
OMC	Omnicom Group, Inc.	Advertising	12/31/17	15273.6	1088.4	24931.2	2615.1	1045	306288049
OMN	Omnova Solutions Inc	Specialty Chemicals	11/30/17	783.1	-87.8	612.8	38.2	164	45781273
ONDK	On Deck Capital Inc	Credit & Lending	12/31/17	350.9	-11.5	996.0	262.0	133	71588151
OGS	ONE Gas, Inc.	Electric Utilities	12/31/17	1539.6	163.0	5206.9	1960.2	389	45878542
OLP	One Liberty Properties, Inc.	REITs	12/31/17	75.9	24.1	742.6	296.8	155	9476888
OMAD U	One Madison Corp	Business Services	12/31/17		-0.0	0.9	0.1	14	6516586
OMF	OneMain Holdings Inc	Credit & Lending	12/31/17	3756.0	183.0	19433.0	3278.0	239	131399646
OKE	ONEOK Inc	Equipment & Services	12/31/17	12173.9	387.8	16845.9	5527.9	1089	345627060
ONE	OneSmart International Education	Educational Services	8/31/17	2057.6	258.8	2317.6	287.8	20	37641001
OOMA	OOMA Inc	Internet & Software	1/31/18	114.5	-13.1	73.4	37.1	88	15015940
OPY	Oppenheimer Holdings Inc	Finance Intermediaries & Services	12/31/17	920.3	22.8	2438.5	523.5	118	7277218
ORCL	Oracle Corp	Internet & Software	5/31/18	39831.0	3825.0	137264.0	45726.0	2455	2958230639
ORAN	Orange	Services	12/31/17	41102.0	1906.0	94714.0	30488.0	258	48649320
ORC	Orchid Island Capital, Inc.	REITs	12/31/17	54.8	2.0	4023.3	462.2	96	18896013
OEC	Orion Engineered Carbons SA	Specialty Chemicals	12/31/17	1177.2	66.8	974.6	83.3	162	54495298
ORN	Orion Group Holdings Inc	Construction Services	12/31/17	578.6	0.4	433.3	231.3	164	36597673
IX	Orix Corp. (Japan)	Credit & Lending	3/31/18	2862342.0	313135.0	11425982.0	2682424.0	201	5533628
ORA	Ormat Technologies Inc	Electric Utilities	12/31/17	692.8	155.5	2586.7	1236.1	274	40056930
OSK	Oshkosh Corp (New)	Autos- Manufacturing	9/30/17	6829.6	285.6	5098.9	2307.4	561	80252732
OR	Osisko Gold Royalties Ltd	Precious Metals	12/31/17	213.2	-42.5	2516.3	1894.4	-	0

T44

EARNINGS PER SHARE QUARTERLY			EARNINGS PER SHARE ANNUAL			P/E RATIO		DIVIDENDS PER SHARE			AV. YLD	DIV. DECLARED		PRICE RANGE 2017	
1st	2nd	3rd	2017	2016	2015			2017	2016	2015	%	AMOUNT	PAYABLE		
-	-	-	.64	.69	.65	23.4 -	0.0	.68	.71	.68	5.0	0.0445M	8/1/18	15.0 -	0.0
-	-	-	.68	.76	.80	20.6 -	18.4	.78	.78	.86	5.9	0.0445M	8/1/18	14.0 -	12.5
-	-	-	.70	.80	.74	23.0 -	0.0	.79	.81	.48	5.5	0.0550	8/1/18	16.1 -	0.0
-	-	-	.65	.72	.62	27.0 -	0.0	.71	.73	.73	6.0	0.043M	8/1/18	17.6 -	0.0
-	-	-	-	1.56	1.28	-		-	1.71	1.52		0.11350	8/1/18	26.3 -	23.3
-	-	-	-	-	1.20	-		-	1.67	1.53		0.11250	8/1/18	25.3 -	22.4
-	-	-	.39	.41	.47	19.8 -	0.0	.43	.48	.28	5.8	0.030	8/1/18	7.7 -	0.0
-	-	-	.26	.07	-	39.5 -	0.0	.30	.06		3.1	0.01650	8/1/18	10.3 -	0.0
-	-	-	-	.72	.83	-		-	.87	.78		0.066M	8/1/18	15.5 -	14.0
-	-	-	-	.86	.91	-		-	.91	.92		0.06M	8/1/18	13.9 -	12.3
-	-	-	-	.50	.51	-		-	.51	.51		0.036M	8/1/18	12.5 -	10.8
-	-	-	-	.40	.42	-		-	.39	.40		0.031M	8/1/18	10.4 -	9.3
-	-	-	.49	.62	.62	31.5 -	0.0	.67	.81	.81	4.9	0.045M	8/1/18	15.4 -	0.0
-	-	-	.60	.79	.67	23.3 -	21.4	.76	.82	.77	5.6	0.0545M	8/1/18	14.0 -	12.9
-	-	-	.27	.69	.72	49.7 -	44.0	.68	.70	.73	5.4	0.045M	8/1/18	13.4 -	11.9
-	-	-	.25	.81	.67	63.4 -	0.0	.29	.63	.64	2.1	0.0425M	8/1/18	15.9 -	0.0
-	-	-	.16	.41	.40	65.3 -	56.8	.39	.39	.39	4.0	0.03M	8/1/18	10.4 -	9.1
-	-	-	.29	.65	.71	50.0 -	42.8	.76	.79	.77	5.6	0.048M	8/1/18	14.5 -	12.4
-	-	-	.55	.57	.56	26.0 -	23.0	.55	.55	.57	4.1	0.042M	8/1/18	14.3 -	12.6
-	-	-	.53	.60	.61	25.7 -	22.8	.57	.60	.64	4.4	0.039M	8/1/18	13.6 -	12.1
-	-	-	.74	.81	.85	20.9 -	18.3	.75	.83	.93	5.2	0.0485M	8/1/18	15.4 -	13.5
-	-	-	.51	.68	.67	31.3 -	0.0	1.12	.62	.63	8.7	0.043M	8/1/18	15.9 -	0.0
-	-	-	-	.80	.81	-		.78	.83	.84	6.0	0.0505M	8/1/18	13.8 -	12.4
-	-	-	-	-	-	-		.64	-	-	2.6	0.11850	8/1/18	26.1 -	23.5
-	-	-	-	.77	.80	-		.78	.80	.77	7.7	0.0610	8/1/18	10.7 -	9.3
-	-	-	.71	.69	.64	14.7 -	12.4	.74	.70	.73	7.5	0.0560	8/1/18	10.5 -	8.8
-	-	-	1.75	1.86	1.96	14.6 -	13.1	1.84	2.13	1.94	7.5	0.13550	8/1/18	25.6 -	22.9
-	-	-	-	.71	.84	-		-	.85	.87		0.0575M	8/1/18	14.4 -	13.0
-	-	-	-	1.12	1.18	-		-	1.35	1.57		0.1060	8/1/18	18.8 -	16.0
-	-	-	-	.39	.38	-		-	.98	.96		0.2050	7/2/18	11.5 -	9.4
-	-	-	-	.18	.17	-		-	.93	1.00		0.2450	7/2/18	14.5 -	13.0
-	-	-	-	.20	.20	-		-	.98	1.04		0.280	7/2/18	19.3 -	15.1
-	-	-	.32	.32	.34	32.7 -	29.7	.32	.33	.34	3.2	0.026M	8/1/18	10.5 -	9.5
-	-	-	.53	.55	.58	27.0 -	25.1	.52	.54	.60	3.8	0.042M	8/1/18	14.3 -	13.3
-	-	-	.56	.58	.60	26.9 -	24.7	.55	.56	.61	3.8	0.0455M	8/1/18	15.1 -	13.9
-	-	-	.57	.58	.60	27.2 -	24.7	.53	.56	.61	3.6	0.0435M	8/1/18	15.5 -	14.1
-	-	-	.46	.45	.45	14.9 -	13.5	.46	.42	.42	7.0	0.03350	8/1/18	6.9 -	6.2
-	-	-	1.29	1.21	1.22	13.8 -	12.8	1.25	1.19	1.20	7.3	0.10050	8/1/18	17.8 -	16.5
-	-	-	-	-	.53	-		-	1.24	1.29		0.3350	7/2/18	18.4 -	15.9
-	-	-	-	.47	.47	-		-	1.01	1.09		0.270	7/2/18	14.6 -	12.7
-	-	-	-	-	.62	-		.65	.65	.68	4.7	0.0445M	8/1/18	14.8 -	0.0
-	-	-	.58	.66	.72	23.1 -	20.9	.59	.68	.75	4.6	0.046M	8/1/18	13.4 -	12.1
0.29	-	-	-	-	-	-		-	-	-		0.175G	8/17/18		
39.34	-	-	126.77	103.61	89.99	29.2 -	19.0	-	-	-		-		3700.0 -	2410.6
0.78	-	-	3.61	3.11	1.45	13.4 -	10.9	3.21	2.25	2.10	7.4	0.960	5/11/18	48.5 -	39.2
0.72	-	-	0.85	-	-	23.2 -	19.2	-	-	-		0.39250	5/29/18	19.7 -	16.3
0.00	-	-	0.52	-1.32	-0.31	26.5 -	13.4	-	-	-		-		13.8 -	7.0
-0.13	-	-	-0.17	-1.39	-5.27	-		-	-	.03		0.010	10/15/15	1.8 -	0.8
0.92	-	-	1.70	-0.75	-10.23	-		3.06	3.02	2.97		0.780Y	18/78/27		
-0.50	-	-	1.68	0.25	2.34	15.9 -	10.6	.45	.96	1.08	2.0	0.150Y	18/78/27	26.6 -	17.9
0.02	-	-	0.10	-0.73	0.14	39.2 -	19.2	.07	-	.87	2.6	0.020	5/21/18	3.9 -	1.9
0.02	-	-	-1.01	-1.61	-1.97	-		-	-	-		-		4.8 -	2.7
0.30	-	-	0.88	1.03	-0.37	16.8 -	9.0	.24	.24	.36	2.3	0.14580	10/1/18	14.8 -	7.9
0.27	-	-	3.10	1.69	1.36	12.0 -	9.5	1.24	1.13	1.02	3.6	0.33250Y	18/78/27	37.2 -	29.6
-	-	-	-	-	-12.55	-		-	-	-		-		9.5 -	4.4
-	-	-0.30	-1.69	-0.92	0.56	-		-	-	-		-		38.0 -	21.0
-	-	0.48	1.47	1.87	1.59	34.2 -	24.2	.88	.84	.80	2.1	0.180Y	18/78/27	50.3 -	35.5
0.01	-	-	1.92	1.62	1.48	11.6 -	9.4	.76	.75	.74	3.7	0.1950Y	18/78/27	22.2 -	18.1
0.12	-	-	3.26	-0.02	-0.01	11.8 -	8.7	.80	.80	.80	2.4	0.20Y	18/78/27	38.6 -	28.3
0.42	-	-	0.51	1.90	1.29	66.1 -	49.7	2.54	2.36	2.18	8.7	0.660Z	18/78/27	33.7 -	25.4
-	1.60	-	4.65	4.78	4.41	17.9 -	14.1	2.25	2.15	2.00	3.0	0.60Y	18/78/27	83.2 -	65.5
0.16	-	-	-1.98	-0.01	-0.39	-		-	-	-		0.050	5/31/01	11.7 -	8.6
-0.03	-	-	-0.16	-1.17	-0.02	-		-	-	-		-		7.6 -	4.1
1.72	-	-	3.08	2.65	2.24	25.7 -	20.4	1.68	1.40	1.20	2.3	0.460Y	18/78/27	79.3 -	62.8
0.30	-	-	1.28	1.39	1.22	21.3 -	17.0	1.74	1.66	1.58	7.1	0.450Z	7/6/18	27.3 -	21.8
0.02	-	-	0.00	-	-	-		-	-	-		-			
0.91	-	-	1.35	1.59	-1.89	25.6 -	17.9	-	-	-		-		34.5 -	24.1
0.64	-	-	1.29	1.66	1.16	54.3 -	38.8	2.72	2.46	2.43	4.7	0.7950Y	18/78/27	70.1 -	50.0
-0.30	-	-	0.06	0.04	0.01	263.0 -	163.5	-	-	-		-		15.8 -	9.8
-0.19	-	-	-0.74	-1.38	-2.81	-		-	-	-		-		14.2 -	7.6
0.48	-	-	1.67	-0.09	0.14	17.6 -	9.3	.44	.44	.44	1.9	0.110	5/25/18	29.4 -	15.6
-	-	-0.98	2.21	2.07	2.21	24.0 -	19.4	.64	.60	.51	1.3	0.190Y	18/78/27	53.0 -	42.8
-	-	-	0.62	1.04	0.92	29.8 -	25.8	.65	.61	.61	3.8	-		18.5 -	16.0
-0.31	-	-	0.05	0.08	0.05	208.6 -	140.0	1.68	1.68	1.92	19.3	0.090Z	8/10/18	10.4 -	7.0
-	-	-	1.10	0.74	0.72	-		-	-	-		0.20	9/28/18		
0.14	-	-	0.01	-0.13	-0.29	868.0 -	523.0	-	-	-		-		8.7 -	5.2
-	60.89	-	208.68	198.52	179.21	0.5 -	0.4	231.75	286.77	114.45	271.2	-		100.0 -	77.7
1.36	-	-	3.06	1.87	2.43	22.9 -	16.6	.41	.52	.26	0.7	0.10Y	5/30/18	70.1 -	50.8
-	1.47	-	3.77	2.91	2.90	25.5 -	17.8	.84	.74	.68	1.0	0.240Y	18/78/27	96.2 -	66.9
0.01	-	-	-0.33	0.40	0.32	-		.18	.16	.13	1.4	0.050	7/16/18	17.5 -	9.2

SYMBOL	COMPANY	NATURE OF BUSINESS	FISCAL YEAR-END	TOTAL REV. $MILL	NET INCOME $MILL	TOTAL ASSETS $MILL	NET STK EQUITY $MILL	NO OF INST	INST. HOLDINGS (SHARES)
OUT	OUTFRONT Media Inc	REITs	12/31/17	1520.5	125.8	3808.2	1181.1	318	158250685
OSG	Overseas Shipholding Group Inc (N	Equipment & Services	12/31/17	390.4	56.0	931.9	313.2	53	1749228
OMI	Owens & Minor, Inc.	Medical Instruments & Equipment	12/31/17	9318.3	72.8	3376.3	1015.5	403	73860430
OC	Owens Corning	Construction Materials	12/31/17	6384.0	289.0	8632.0	4162.0	606	131760791
OI	Owens-Illinois, Inc.	Containers & Packaging	12/31/17	6869.0	180.0	9756.0	808.0	524	190404402
OXM	Oxford Industries, Inc.	Apparel, Footwear & Accessories	2/3/18	1086.2	65.1	699.9	429.8	284	19093845
T 34D	Pacific Bell	Services	12/31/98	9406.0	1077.0	15093.0	3260.0	-	0
ROYT	Pacific Coast Oil Trust	Oil Royalty Traders	12/31/17	7.5	4.4	217.3	217.3	36	7627678
PKG	Packaging Corp of America	Containers & Packaging	12/31/17	6444.9	668.6	6197.5	2182.6	759	119090602
PAGS	PagSeguro Digital Ltd	Internet & Software	12/31/17	2523.4	0.0	4235.8	866.9	137	113586807
PANW	Palo Alto Networks, Inc	IT Services	7/31/17	1761.6	-216.6	3438.3	759.6	816	94518035
PAM	Pampa Energia SA	Electric Utilities	12/31/17	50347.0	4606.0	104467.0	16910.0	-	0
P	Pandora Media Inc	Internet & Software	12/31/17	1466.8	-518.4	1166.3	643.5	321	285323051
PHX	Panhandle Oil & Gas Inc	Production & Extraction	9/30/17	46.3	3.5	206.7	116.7	97	10900766
PARR	Par Pacific Holdings Inc	Refining & Marketing	12/31/17	2443.1	72.6	1347.4	447.7	210	46780874
PAR	Par Technology Corp.	Electronic Instruments & Related Pro	12/31/17	232.6	-3.4	114.6	69.0	63	5533853
PGRE	Paramount Group Inc	REITs	12/31/17	719.0	86.4	8917.7	4176.7	206	180879089
PKE	Park Electrochemical Corp.	Electrical Equipment	2/25/18	111.2	20.6	169.0	135.3	145	20444672
PK	Park Hotels & Resorts Inc	REITs	12/31/17	2791.0	2625.0	9714.0	6011.0	324	263292460
PKD	Parker Drilling Co	Equipment & Services	12/31/17	442.5	-118.7	990.3	296.1	171	111677608
PH	Parker Hannifin Corp	Industrial Machinery & Equipment	6/30/17	12029.3	983.4	15489.9	5261.6	1022	130637803
PE	Parsley Energy Inc	Production & Extraction	12/31/17	967.0	106.8	8793.2	4712.3	421	284214896
PRTY	Party City Holdco Inc	Retail - General Merchandise/Depart	12/31/17	2371.6	215.3	3454.8	972.0	168	106306954
PAYC	Paycom Software Inc	Internet & Software	12/31/17	433.0	66.8	1355.2	135.4	365	53593875
PBF	PBF Energy Inc	Refining & Marketing	12/31/17	21786.6	415.5	8118.0	2336.7	391	122537982
PBFX	PBF Logistics LP	Refining & Marketing	12/31/17	254.8	129.4	737.5	-14.8	65	14505213
PCM	PCM Fund Inc	Holding and other Investment Office	6/30/17	14.8	11.3	194.2	117.4	33	978440
BTU	Peabody Energy Corp (New)	Mining	12/31/17	4252.6	678.1	8181.2	3606.4	462	166573414
PSO	Pearson Plc	Publishing	12/31/17	4513.0	406.0	7888.0	4013.0	136	28170568
PEB	Pebblebrook Hotel Trust	REITs	12/31/17	769.3	99.9	2590.9	1498.9	290	102069652
PBA	Pembina Pipeline Corp	Equipment & Services	12/31/17	5453.0	891.0	25566.0	13789.0	403	242555384
JCP	Penney (J.C.) Co.,Inc. (Holding Co.)	Retail - General Merchandise/Depart	2/3/18	12506.0	-116.0	8413.0	1379.0	520	297403794
PEI	Pennsylvania Real Estate Investme	REITs	12/31/17	367.5	-29.3	2588.8	624.0	300	93274255
PFSI	Pennymac Financial Services Inc	Credit & Lending	12/31/17	1100.0	100.8	7368.1	469.4	121	26602397
PMT	Pennymac Mortgage Investment Tr	REITs	12/31/17	469.3	117.7	5604.9	1544.6	-	0
PAG	Penske Automotive Group Inc	Retail - Automotive	12/31/17	21386.9	613.3	10540.6	2395.2	360	99904960
PNR	Pentair PLC	Industrial Machinery & Equipment	12/31/17	4936.5	666.5	8633.7	5037.8	749	173924624
PEN	Penumbra Inc	Medical Instruments & Equipment	12/31/17	333.8	4.7	476.7	400.4	204	27597584
PFGC	Performance Food Group Co	Retail - Food & Beverage, Drug & To	7/1/17	16761.8	96.3	3804.1	925.5	234	103660683
PKI	PerkinElmer, Inc.	Biotechnology	12/31/17	2257.0	292.6	6091.5	2503.2	570	144198551
PBT	Permian Basin Royalty Trust	Oil Royalty Traders	12/31/17	30.6	29.3	4.0	0.5	104	6039963
PRT	PermRock Royalty Trust	Production & Extraction	12/31/17	27.5	19.9	0.0		-	0
PRGO	Perrigo Company plc	Pharmaceuticals	12/31/17	4946.2	119.6	11628.8	6170.5	-	0
PRSP	Perspecta Inc	IT Services	3/31/17	1073.0	36.0	1073.0	416.0	53	1204235
PRSP	Perspecta Inc	IT Services	3/31/17	1073.0	36.0	1073.0	416.0	53	1204235
PTR	PetroChina Co Ltd	Production & Extraction	12/31/17	2015890.0	22793.0	2404910.0	1193810.0	215	6079593
PBR	Petroleo Brasileiro SA	Production & Extraction	12/31/17	88827.0	-91.0	251366.0	79802.0	542	565861151
PFE	Pfizer Inc	Pharmaceuticals	12/31/17	52546.0	21308.0	171797.0	71308.0	3080	5467306072
PCG	P&G Corp (Holding Co)	Electric Utilities	12/31/17	17135.0	1660.0	68012.0	19220.0	922	489987611
GHY	PGIM Global Short Duration High Yi	Finance Intermediaries & Services	7/31/17	52.9	39.7	986.7	678.2	87	16025236
ISD	PGIM Short Duration High Yield Fu	Holding and other Investment Office	5/31/17	42.2	32.7	754.0	560.1	86	10155645
PGTI	PGT Innovations Inc	Metal Products	12/30/17	511.1	39.8	453.1	175.3	224	55557610
GLT	PH Glatfelter Co	Paper & Forest Products	12/31/17	1596.4	7.9	1730.8	708.9	208	50276395
PHH	PHH Corp	Credit & Lending	12/31/17	456.0	-217.0	1811.0	553.0	218	40989492
PM	Philip Morris International Inc	Tobacco Products	12/31/17	78098.0	6035.0	42968.0	-12086.0	2282	1336649070
PSX	Phillips 66	Refining & Marketing	12/31/17	104622.0	5106.0	54371.0	25085.0	1579	369184436
PSXP	Phillips 66 Partners LP	Equipment & Services	12/31/17	1169.0	524.0	5334.0	-1.0	201	52278964
FENG	Phoenix New Media Ltd	Radio & Television	12/31/17	1575.1	37.5	3599.1	2507.5	71	15581682
DOC	Physicians Realty Trust	REITs	12/31/17	343.6	38.1	4164.4	2473.2	335	198380587
PDM	Piedmont Office Realty Trust Inc	REITs	12/31/17	574.2	133.6	4000.0	1984.7	306	131642135
PIR	Pier 1 Imports Inc.	Retail - Furniture & Home Furnishing	3/3/18	1798.5	11.6	772.3	277.6	268	80217360
PCQ	Pimco California Municipal Income	Holding and other Investment Office	12/31/16	21.4	17.8	448.7	408.5	32	1099650
PCK	Pimco California Municipal Income	Holding and other Investment Office	12/31/16	23.7	19.7	481.1	430.6	41	2286651
PZC	Pimco California Municipal Income	Holding and other Investment Office	12/31/16	17.5	14.5	377.4	339.6	34	1092726
PTY	PIMCO Corpbrate & Income Opport	Holding and other Investment Office	7/31/17	99.0	87.9	1640.8	1378.7	128	8599896
PCN	PIMCO Corporate & Income Strateg	Holding and other Investment Office	7/31/15	32.9	28.2	760.1	739.1	-	0
PCI	PIMCO Dynamic Credit & Mortgage	Holding and other Investment Office	6/30/17	335.7	221.8	5935.7	3144.2	184	38692620
PDI	PIMCO Dynamic Income Fund	Holding and other Investment Office	6/30/17	172.7	121.1	2608.9	1372.7	129	10535886
PGP	PIMCO Global StocksPLUS & Inco	Holding and other Investment Office	6/30/17	15.8	12.3	182.6	119.5	43	769890
PHK	Pimco High Income Fund	Holding and other Investment Office	7/31/17	96.3	85.7	1180.0	986.9	134	9456133
PKO	PIMCO Income Opportunity Fund	Holding and other Investment Office	6/30/17	44.8	34.3	610.0	378.7	58	3147211
PFL	PIMCO Income Strategy Fund	Holding and other Investment Office	7/31/17	26.1	22.3	402.5	345.8	64	3971796
PFN	PIMCO Income Strategy Fund II	Holding and other Investment Office	7/31/17	54.8	47.5	794.6	704.8	103	12179759
PMF	Pimco Municipal Income Fund	Holding and other Investment Office	12/31/16	27.3	23.0	548.3	508.5	71	1991382
PML	Pimco Municipal Income Fund II	Holding and other Investment Office	12/31/16	57.4	48.4	1183.2	1094.5	98	6528497
PMX	Pimco Municipal Income Fund III	Holding and other Investment Office	12/31/16	29.9	25.3	579.3	538.4	58	1821083
PNI	Pimco New York Municipal Fund II	Holding and other Investment Office	12/31/16	9.7	7.9	216.3	197.8	23	562592
PNF	Pimco New York Municipal Income	Holding and other Investment Office	12/31/16	6.7	5.4	154.7	136.8	28	733927
PYN	Pimco New York Municipal Income	Holding and other Investment Office	12/31/16	4.1	3.2	91.0	83.0	17	414750
RCS	PIMCO Strategic Income Fund Inc	Holding and other Investment Office	6/30/17	34.5	29.5	1420.4	329.7	76	3506313

T46

| EARNINGS PER SHARE | | | | | | P/E RATIO | | DIVIDENDS PER SHARE | | | AV. YLD % | DIV. DECLARED | | PRICE RANGE 2017 | |
| QUARTERLY | | | ANNUAL | | | | | | | | | | | | |
1st	2nd	3rd	2017	2016	2015			2017	2016	2015		AMOUNT	PAYABLE		
0.06	-	-	0.90	0.66	-0.21	28.0-	20.0	1.44	1.36	1.42	6.7	0.360Y	18/78/27	25.2-	18.0
0.04	-	-	0.64	-3.25	-	6.3-	2.7					0.17970	5/13/16	4.0-	1.7
0.13	-	-	1.20	1.76	1.65	27.1-	12.4	1.03	1.02	1.01	4.8	0.260Y	18/78/27	32.5-	14.9
0.82	-	-	2.55	3.41	2.79	37.8-	24.2	0.81	0.74	0.68	1.0	0.210Y	18/78/27	96.4-	61.8
0.59	-	-	1.10	1.28	-0.47	23.3-	15.1					0.59380 Y	2/15/08	25.7-	16.6
1.23	-	-	3.15	1.85	2.78	29.4-	18.4	1.08	1.00	0.84	1.5	0.340Y	8/3/18	92.5-	57.8
0.08	-	-	0.11	0.01	0.26	24.8-	13.0	0.14	0.01	0.26	7.3	0.03640Z	7/23/18	2.7-	1.4
1.48	-	-	7.07	4.75	4.47	18.3-	15.1	2.52	2.36	2.20	2.2	0.790Y	18/78/27	129.6-	106.5
-	-	-	1.83	0.48	0.13			0.91							
-	-	-0.51	-2.39	-2.59	-2.02									215.6-	127.7
-	-	-	2.34	-0.01	2.28	30.6-	15.3							71.7-	35.8
-0.55	-	-	-2.29	-1.49	-0.79									9.8-	4.1
-	0.06	-	0.21	-0.61	0.56	118.6-	85.0	0.16	0.16	0.16	0.8	0.040Y	9/6/18	24.9-	17.9
0.33	-	-	1.57	-1.08	-1.06	13.5-	10.5							21.2-	16.4
0.00	-	-	-0.22	0.11	-0.06									17.7-	7.6
0.00	-	-	0.37	-0.05	-0.02	44.9-	37.5	0.38	0.38	0.42	2.5	0.10Z	18/78/27	16.6-	13.9
-	-	0.04	0.46	0.89	0.96	50.7-	36.0	0.40	0.40	1.90	2.1	0.10Y	8/7/18	23.3-	16.6
0.71	-	-	12.21	-	-	2.7-	2.0	4.63			16.4	0.457Z	7/16/18	32.4-	24.4
-0.21	-	-	-0.89	-1.86	-0.78							1.81250Y	6/30/18	1.4-	0.3
-	-	2.70	7.25	5.89	6.97	29.1-	21.2	2.58	2.52	2.37	1.5	0.760Y	18/78/27	210.9-	154.0
0.32	-	-	0.42	-0.46	-0.45	78.2-	51.8							32.8-	21.7
-0.01	-	-	1.79	0.98	0.09	9.2-	5.5							16.4-	9.8
0.70	-	-	1.13	0.74	0.36	104.1-	58.4							117.6-	66.0
0.27	-	-	3.73	1.74	1.65	13.6-	5.3	1.20	1.20	1.20	3.7	0.30Y	18/78/27	50.6-	19.9
0.43	-	-	2.17	2.01	2.18	10.1-	8.4	1.86	1.70	1.44	9.2	0.490	5/30/18	21.9-	18.2
-	-	-	0.98	1.22	0.44	12.3-	10.6	1.46	0.96	1.05	12.7	0.080	8/1/18	12.1-	10.4
0.82	-	-	3.67	-40.45	-109.98	12.9-	6.8			0.07		0.1250Y	8/23/18	47.5-	24.9
-	-	-	0.50	-2.87	1.01	24.9-	15.3	0.40	0.53	0.53	4.1			12.5-	7.6
0.29	-	-	1.19	0.64	0.95	34.8-	26.5	1.52	1.52	1.24	4.2	0.39840Z	7/16/18	41.5-	31.6
0.59	-	-	1.88	1.01	1.02	24.8-	16.0	2.04	1.90	1.80	5.3	0.30630	9/1/18	46.6-	30.1
-0.25	-	-	0.00	-1.68	-2.53							0.20Y	18/78/27	5.6-	2.3
-0.15	-	-	-0.89	-0.40	-1.93			0.84	0.84	0.84	7.9	0.42970Z	9/17/18	12.9-	9.0
0.67	-	-	4.03	2.94	2.17	6.2-	4.1							24.9-	16.6
0.35	-	-	1.48	1.08	1.16	13.0-	10.1	1.88	1.88	2.16	10.9	0.470Z	7/30/18	19.2-	15.0
1.26	-	-	7.14	3.99	3.63	7.6-	5.5	1.26	1.10	0.94	2.7	0.360Y	18/78/27	54.5-	39.0
0.57	-	-	3.63	2.85	-0.42			1.38	1.34			0.1750	18/78/27		
0.16	-	-	0.13	0.44	0.08	1276.5-	612.7							165.9-	79.7
-	-	0.32	0.93	0.70	0.64	40.6-	27.9							37.8-	25.9
0.23	-	-	2.64	2.12	1.87	31.3-	23.8	0.28	0.28	0.28	0.4	0.070Y	18/78/27	82.8-	63.0
0.20	-	-	0.63	0.42	0.34	16.3-	12.6	0.63	0.42	0.34	6.9	0.05750	8/14/18	10.2-	7.9
-	-	-										0.12920	8/14/18	16.3-	15.0
0.57	-	-	0.84	-28.01	0.04			0.64	0.58	0.25		0.190	6/19/18		
-	-	-										0.05GY	7/17/18	24.6-	20.0
-	-	-										0.05GY	7/17/18	26.7-	24.9
0.06	-	-	0.12	0.04	0.19	704.1-	507.8	9.26	3.91	14.12	13.3			84.5-	60.9
-	-	0.01	-0.01	-0.37	-0.65									17.1-	7.7
0.59	-	-	3.52	1.17	1.11	11.1-	9.3	1.28	1.20	1.12	3.6	0.340Y	18/78/27	39.0-	32.7
0.86	-	-	3.21	2.78	1.79	22.3-	11.9	1.55	1.93	1.82	2.9	0.530Y	18/78/27	71.6-	38.2
-	-	-	0.97	1.03	1.15	15.6-	14.1	1.19	1.34	1.75	8.3	0.08250	8/31/18	15.2-	13.7
-	-	-	0.98	1.06	1.20	15.7-	14.3	1.25	1.36	1.59	8.5	0.0850	8/31/18	15.4-	14.0
0.14	-	-	0.77	0.47	0.47	28.4-	16.3							21.9-	12.6
0.13	-	-	0.18	0.49	1.47	131.7-	90.7	0.39	0.50	0.48	2.0	0.130Y	8/1/18	23.7-	16.3
-0.92	-	-	-4.62	-3.77	-2.62									14.3-	8.1
1.00	-	-	3.88	4.48	4.42	31.3-	19.8	4.22	4.12	4.04	4.1	1.140Y	18/78/27	121.6-	76.8
1.07	-	-	9.85	2.92	7.73	12.4-	8.2	2.73	2.45	2.18	2.8	0.80Y	18/78/27	121.9-	80.9
0.87	-	-	2.59	2.20	3.26	21.7-	17.3	2.40	1.98	1.54	4.8	0.7520	8/13/18	56.2-	44.9
-	-	0.13	0.06	0.14	0.13	134.8-	41.0							8.1-	2.5
0.06	-	-	0.23	0.22	0.15	88.3-	62.5	0.91	0.90	0.90	5.4	0.230	7/18/18	20.3-	14.4
0.42	-	-	0.92	0.74	1.15	23.3-	18.2	1.34	0.84	0.84	6.9	0.210Z	18/78/27	21.4-	16.8
-0.36	-	-	0.37	0.46	0.82	15.8-	5.8	0.28	0.28	0.24	7.5	0.070Y	1/31/18	5.8-	2.2
-	-	-		0.95	0.65				0.92	0.92		0.077M	8/1/18	17.6-	14.4
-	-	-		0.62	0.38				0.61	0.65		0.035M	8/1/18	10.4-	8.0
-	-	-		0.65	0.17				0.72	0.72		0.045M	8/1/18	12.7-	9.6
-	-	-	1.21	1.30	0.68	15.6-	13.2	1.73	1.59	2.21	10.2	0.130	8/1/18	18.9-	16.0
-	-	-			0.73					1.70		0.11250	8/1/18	18.0-	16.1
-	-	-	1.62	2.01	0.76	14.6-	13.5	2.60	2.18	2.47	11.4	0.16410	8/1/18	23.6-	21.8
-	-	-	2.60	3.87	0.80	12.3-	11.1	4.10	5.24	4.19	13.4	0.22050	8/1/18	32.0-	29.0
-	-	-	1.15	1.15	0.34	15.9-	11.0	1.87	2.20	2.20	12.2	0.1220	8/1/18	18.3-	12.6
-	-	-	0.67	0.74	0.21	13.2-	11.0	1.10	1.26	1.46	13.8	0.08070	8/1/18	8.8-	7.3
-	-	-	2.28	2.33	1.54	12.2-	10.9	2.62	2.79	3.87	9.9	0.190	8/1/18	27.8-	24.8
-	-	-	0.88	0.88	0.79	14.2-	12.8	1.08	1.08	1.22	9.1	0.090	8/1/18	12.5-	11.3
-	-	-	0.80	0.87	0.70	13.6-	12.6	0.96	1.03	1.11	9.1	0.080	8/1/18	10.9-	10.1
-	-	-		0.90	0.65				0.97	0.97		0.0597M	8/1/18	14.2-	12.3
-	-	-		0.79	0.47				0.78	0.78		0.065M	8/1/18	13.5-	12.2
-	-	-		0.77	0.20				0.75	0.75		0.0558M	8/1/18	12.1-	10.8
-	-	-		0.72	0.43				0.80	0.80		0.0507M	8/1/18	12.5-	10.4
-	-	-		0.70	0.47				0.68	0.68		0.057M	8/1/18	13.5-	11.3
-	-	-		0.56	0.14				0.63	0.63		0.0423M	8/1/18	10.2-	8.5
-	-	-	0.70	0.76	0.30	15.1-	12.3	0.92	1.00	1.02	9.7	0.0720	8/1/18	10.6-	8.6

SYMBOL	COMPANY	NATURE OF BUSINESS	FISCAL YEAR-END	TOTAL REV. $MILL	NET INCOME $MILL	TOTAL ASSETS $MILL	NET STK EQUITY $MILL	NO OF INST	INST. HOLDINGS (SHARES)
PF	Pinnacle Foods Inc.	Food	12/31/17	3144.0	532.0	6578.3	2379.1	436	133853611
PNW	Pinnacle West Capital Corp	Electric Utilities	12/31/17	3565.3	488.5	17019.1	5006.7	713	113389689
PES	Pioneer Energy Services Corp	Production & Extraction	12/31/17	446.5	-75.1	766.9	210.1	192	71080781
PHD	Pioneer Floating Rate Trust	Holding and other Investment Office	11/30/16	25.1	19.2	481.3	309.3	81	7944397
PHT	Pioneer High Income Trust	Holding and other Investment Office	3/31/17	34.1	27.9	444.0	312.8	69	6634324
MAV	Pioneer Municipal High Income Adv	Holding and other Investment Office	3/31/17	22.4	19.1	434.2	433.5	56	2627301
MHI	Pioneer Municipal High Income Tru	Holding and other Investment Office	4/30/17	19.6	16.6	392.1	390.8	71	4914454
PXD	Pioneer Natural Resources Co	Production & Extraction	12/31/17	5455.0	833.0	17003.0	11274.0	1038	174990212
PJC	Piper Jaffray Companies	Finance Intermediaries & Services	12/31/17	895.2	-61.9	2024.7	693.3	301	15029882
PBI	Pitney Bowes Inc	Office Equipment & Furniture	12/31/17	3549.9	261.3	6678.7	188.6	605	204884422
PBI 08	Pitney-Bowes Credit Corp	Credit & Lending	12/31/01	587.8	160.1	5721.0	1476.4		0
PVTL	Pivotal Software Inc	IT Services	2/2/18	509.4	-163.5	1153.4	707.1	4	40760
PJT	PJT Partners Inc	Finance Intermediaries & Services	12/31/17	499.3	-32.6	559.0	-157.3		0
PAA	Plains All American Pipeline LP	Equipment & Services	12/31/17	26223.0	856.0	25351.0		567	370774239
PAGP	Plains GP Holdings LP	Equipment & Services	12/31/17	26223.0	-731.0	26753.0		311	143084517
PLNT	Planet Fitness Inc	Sporting & Recreational	12/31/17	429.9	33.1	1092.5	-119.5	273	98145031
PLT	Plantronics, Inc.	Manufacturing	3/31/18	856.9	-0.9	1076.9	353.0	330	42866828
PAH	Platform Specialty Products Corp	Specialty Chemicals	12/31/17	3775.9	-296.2	10252.4	2743.1	274	295066034
AGS	PlayAGS Inc	Industrial Machinery & Equipment	12/31/17	212.0	-45.1	697.2	-27.9	70	35509042
PHI	PLDT Inc	Services	12/31/17	159926.0	13371.0	459444.0	106842.0	123	19901037
PNC	PNC Financial Services Group (The	Banking	12/31/17	18035.0	5338.0	380768.0	47513.0	1617	467157027
PNM	PNM Resources Inc	Electric Utilities	12/31/17	1445.0	80.4	6646.1	1706.8	398	96116753
PII	Polaris Industries Inc.	Autos- Manufacturing	12/31/17	5428.5	172.5	3089.6	943.4	702	67092191
POL	PolyOne Corp.	Plastics	12/31/17	3229.9	-57.7	2705.3	598.5	379	94392670
POR	Portland General Electric Co.	Electric Utilities	12/31/17	2009.0	187.0	7838.0	2416.0	434	111579182
PKX	POSCO (South Korea)	Non-Precious Metals	12/31/17	60655099.6	2790105.7	79024959.1	43732877.3	295	20201417
POST	Post Holdings Inc	Food	9/30/17	5225.8	48.3	11876.8	2780.0	393	82324047
PPDF	PPDAI Group Inc	Brokers & Intermediaries	12/31/17	3880.6	1083.0	8603.7	3622.2	28	10415876
PPG	PPG Industries Inc	Specialty Chemicals	12/31/17	14750.0	1591.0	16538.0	5558.0	1194	229423679
PPL	PPL Corp	Electric Utilities	12/31/17	7447.0	1128.0	41479.0	10761.0	1140	599095903
PQG	PQ Group Holdings Inc	Chemicals	12/31/17	1472.1	57.6	4415.5	1628.0	86	92295853
PX	Praxair Inc	Specialty Chemicals	12/31/17	11437.0	1247.0	20436.0	6018.0	1465	303844355
PDS	Precision Drilling Corp.	Production & Extraction	12/31/17	1321.2	-132.0	3892.9	1810.3	214	159752002
APTS	Preferred Apartment Communities I	REITs	12/31/17	294.0	27.7	3252.4	1275.9	210	24806313
PBH	Prestige Brands Holdings Inc	Pharmaceuticals	3/31/18	1041.2	339.6	3760.6	1178.6	363	79865497
PVG	Pretium Resources Inc	Precious Metals	12/31/17	177.9	-16.5	1671.5	847.1		0
PRI	Primerica Inc	Life & Health	12/31/17	1689.1	350.3	12460.7	1419.1	355	46789245
PGZ	Principal Real Estate Income Fund	Finance Intermediaries & Services	10/31/16	13.0	9.3	193.3	131.3		0
PRA	ProAssurance Corp	General Insurance	12/31/17	866.1	107.3	4929.2	1594.8	351	53268747
PG	Procter & Gamble Company (The)	Household & Personal Products	6/30/17	65058.0	15326.0	120406.0	55184.0	3069	1973858261
PGR	Progressive Corp. (OH)	General Insurance	12/31/17	26839.0	1592.2	38701.2	9284.8	962	568611012
PLD	Prologis Inc	REITs	12/31/17	2618.1	1652.3	29481.1	15631.2	59	10207956
PUMP	ProPetro Holding Corp	Equipment & Services	12/31/17	981.9	12.6	719.0	413.3	211	71416587
PRO	Pros Holdings Inc	Internet & Software	12/31/17	168.8	-77.9	288.7	-47.0	159	37683042
PB	Prosperity Bancshares Inc.	Banking	12/31/17	794.0	272.2	22587.3	3824.2	349	68638210
PRLB	Proto Labs Inc	Manufacturing	12/31/17	344.5	51.8	518.7	461.2	313	32091591
PFS	Provident Financial Services Inc	Banking	12/31/17	379.5	93.9	9845.3	1298.7	240	54903518
PRU	Prudential Financial Inc	Life & Health	12/31/17	59689.0	7863.0	831921.0	54069.0	1388	343984588
PUK	Prudential Plc	Life & Health	12/31/17	86864.0	2389.0	493941.0	16087.0	297	25243434
PSB	PS Business Parks Inc	REITs	12/31/17	402.2	155.0	2100.2	1693.3	301	25151283
PEG 31	PSEG Power LLC	Electric Utilities	12/31/17	3930.0	479.0	12418.0	5967.0		0
TLK	PT Telekomunikasi Indonesia (Pers	Services	12/31/17	128256000.0	22120000.0	198185000.0	92467000.0	224	55915020
PEG	Public Service Enterprise Group Inc	Electric Utilities	12/31/17	9084.0	1574.0	42716.0	13847.0	1101	422171071
PSA	Public Storage	REITs	12/31/17	2668.5	1442.2	10732.9	8940.0	960	180013558
PHM	PulteGroup Inc	Builders	12/31/17	8573.3	447.2	9686.6	4154.0	800	301387145
PSTG	PURE Storage Inc	Internet & Software	1/31/18	1023.0	-177.6	1079.4	497.9	271	171791423
PMM	Putnam Managed Municipal Income	Holding and other Investment Office	10/31/17	25.9	21.2	568.6	526.3	109	7924706
PIM	Putnam Master Intermediate Incom	Holding and other Investment Office	9/30/17	16.7	14.1	508.2	269.5	81	22138342
PMO	Putnam Municipal Opportunities Tru	Holding and other Investment Office	4/30/17	32.0	26.3	723.0	673.4	103	7740405
PPT	Putnam Premier Income Trust	Holding and other Investment Office	7/31/17	36.2	30.8	1294.5	596.6	157	41900235
NEW	Puxin Ltd	Educational Services	12/31/17	1282.6	-397.3	2008.4	-152.8		0
PVH	PVH Corp	Apparel, Footwear & Accessories	2/4/18	8914.8	537.8	11885.7	5536.4	743	84487332
PZN	Pzena Investment Management Inc	Wealth Management	12/31/17	141.3	6.9	169.0	32.3	102	13571862
QTWO	Q2 Holdings Inc	Internet & Software	12/31/17	194.0	-26.2	212.8	106.6	212	42636858
QEP	QEP Resources Inc	Production & Extraction	12/31/17	1622.9	269.3	7394.8	3797.9	433	273117194
QGEN	Qiagen NV	Biotechnology	12/31/17	1417.5	40.4	5038.5	2541.0	333	162873543
QTS	QTS Realty Trust Inc	REITs	12/31/17	446.5	1.3	2415.1	877.4	264	62524036
QUAD	Quad/Graphics, Inc.	Printing	12/31/17	4131.4	107.2	2452.4	522.4	206	34462009
KWR	Quaker Chemical Corp.	Specialty Chemicals	12/31/17	820.1	20.3	722.1	407.7	273	16331755
QCP	Quality Care Properties Inc	REITs	12/31/17	318.5	-443.5	4392.1	2600.7	315	104655364
NX	Quanex Building Products Corp	Construction Materials	10/31/17	866.6	18.7	773.9	406.8	190	43724207
PWR	Quanta Services, Inc.	Construction Services	12/31/17	9466.5	315.0	6480.2	3791.6	697	180430802
QTM	Quantum Corp	Computer Hardware & Equipment	3/31/17	505.3	3.6	225.0	-116.0	162	73774163
QD	Qudian Inc	Finance Intermediaries & Services	12/31/17	4775.4	2164.5	19380.4	9540.4	102	16795335
DGX	Quest Diagnostics, Inc.	Diagnostic & Health Related Service	12/31/17	7709.0	772.0	10503.0	4921.0	949	165890061
QES	Quintana Energy Services Inc	Equipment & Services	12/31/17	438.0	-21.2	275.7	85.0	38	5574460
QHC	Quorum Health Corp	Hospitals & Health Care Facilities	12/31/17	2072.2	-114.2	1828.8	99.4	151	30442707
QUOT	Quotient Technology Inc	Internet & Software	12/31/17	322.1	-15.1	629.1	398.0	180	76532426
CTDD	Qwest Corp	Services	12/31/17	8550.0	1657.0	20869.0	9337.0	3	104248
RDN	Radian Group, Inc.	General Insurance	12/31/17	1221.6	121.1	5900.9	3000.0	383	243363594

T48

1st	2nd	3rd	2017	2016	2015	P/E Ratio 2017	Div 2017	Div 2016	Div 2015	Av Yld %	Amount	Payable	Price High	Price Low
0.48	-	-	4.45	1.79	1.81	15.2 - 11.9	1.22	1.08	0.98	2.1	0.3250Y	18/78/27	67.9	52.9
0.03	-	-	4.35	3.95	3.92	21.1 - 16.9	2.66	2.53	2.41	3.2	0.6950Y	18/78/27	91.8	73.6
-0.14	-	-	-0.97	-1.96	-2.41	-							6.2	1.7
-	-	-	-	0.77	0.76	-		0.72	0.69	-	0.060	7/31/18	12.2	11.2
-	-	-	0.95	1.19	1.36	10.7 - 9.8	0.97	1.34	1.61	10.0	0.0650	7/31/18	10.1	9.3
-	-	-	0.80	0.83	0.95	14.8 - 13.3	0.73	0.95	1.14	6.5	0.0525M	7/31/18	11.9	10.6
-	-	-	0.73	0.83	0.91	16.9 - 15.2	0.69	0.84	1.08	5.9	0.0525M	7/31/18	12.4	11.1
1.04	-	-	4.85	-3.34	-1.83	43.8 - 26.4	0.08	0.08	0.08	0.0	0.160Y	18/78/27	212.3	127.9
0.47	-	-	-5.07	-1.73	3.34	-	1.25	-	-	1.7	0.3750Y	6/15/18	99.7	53.0
0.28	-	-	1.39	0.49	2.03	11.5 - 6.1	0.75	0.75	0.75	6.3	0.18750Y	18/78/27	16.0	8.4
-0.31	-	-	-3.45	-4.42		-							28.9	15.7
0.24	-	-	-1.73	-0.17	-0.61	-	0.20	0.20		0.4	0.050Y	6/20/18	58.6	35.9
0.33	-	-	0.95	0.43	0.77	28.3 - 19.5	1.95	2.65	2.75	8.7	0.30	8/14/18	26.9	18.6
0.23	-	-	-5.03	0.94	1.41	-	1.95			8.5	0.30	8/14/18	27.6	19.6
0.23	-	-	0.42	0.50	0.11	111.2 - 53.0	-	2.78		-	2.78G7	12/5/16	46.7	22.2
-	-	-1.54	2.51	1.96	2.63	31.0 - 16.5	0.60	0.60	0.60	1.1	0.150Y	18/78/27	77.7	41.4
0.13	-	-	-1.04	-0.65	-1.52	-							14.6	9.3
-0.30	-	-	-1.94	-3.51	-1.92	-							27.1	18.5
-	-	42.72	61.61	92.33	101.85	0.6 - 0.4	76.41	106.49	151.70	255.0	0.8	10/14/94	34.6	21.8
2.43	-	-	10.36	7.30	7.39	15.7 - 11.7	2.60	2.12	2.01	1.8	0.33590Y	18/78/27	162.4	120.7
0.19	-	-	1.00	1.46	0.20	45.5 - 33.8	0.97	0.88	0.80	2.4	0.2650Y	18/78/27	45.5	33.8
0.85	-	-	2.69	3.27	6.75	50.3 - 32.5	2.32	2.20	2.12	2.1	0.60Y	18/78/27	135.3	87.3
0.58	-	-	-0.70	1.95	1.63	-	0.58	0.50	0.42	1.4	0.1750Y	18/78/27	46.5	35.5
0.72	-	-	2.10	2.16	2.04	23.7 - 18.6	1.34	1.26	1.18	3.1	0.36250Y	18/78/27	49.7	39.1
-	-	10764.09	4464.00	6627.00	1845.00	0.0 - 0.0	2543.46	2048.71	1983.43	3272.7			92.8	64.1
-	1.20	-	0.50	-0.41	-2.33	176.7 - 143.3					0.6250	8/15/18	88.3	71.6
-	-	-	-2.55	-0.09	-0.27	-							13.2	5.8
-	1.51	-	6.17	3.28	5.14	19.7 - 16.3	1.70	1.56	1.42	1.5	0.480Y	18/78/27	121.5	100.4
0.65	-	-	1.64	2.79	1.01	24.3 - 15.6	1.58	1.52	1.50	4.8	0.410Y	18/78/27	39.8	25.6
0.00	-	-	0.52	-21.01		34.6 - 25.2	-						18.0	13.1
1.59	-	-	4.32	5.21	5.35	38.4 - 29.5	3.15	3.00	2.86	2.1	0.8250Y	18/78/27	165.7	127.4
-0.06	-	-	-0.45	-0.53	-1.24	-			0.28	-	0.070	11/18/15	5.2	2.3
-0.14	-	-	-1.13	-2.11	-0.95	-	0.94	0.82	0.73	5.5	0.2550Z	7/16/18	21.9	13.7
-	-	5.88	1.30	1.88	1.49	41.3 - 21.9							53.6	28.5
-0.04	-	-	-0.09	-0.47	0.00	-							15.2	6.3
1.46	-	-	7.61	4.59	3.70	14.0 - 9.5	0.78	0.70	0.64	0.8	0.250Y	18/78/27	106.5	72.2
-	-	-	-	1.35	1.46	-		1.74	1.73	-	0.110	7/26/18	19.1	16.3
0.22	-	-	2.00	2.83	2.11	31.5 - 17.7	5.93	5.93	2.24	11.4	0.310Y	18/78/27	63.0	35.4
-	-	0.95	5.59	3.69	2.44	16.9 - 12.7	2.70	2.66	2.59	3.2	0.71720Y	18/78/27	94.4	70.9
1.22	-	-	2.72	1.76	2.15	23.2 - 16.1	0.68	0.89	0.69	1.3	1.12470Y	18/78/27	63.0	43.7
-	0.62	-	3.06	2.27	1.64	22.0 - 18.6	1.76	1.68	1.52	2.8	1.06750Z	18/78/27	67.4	56.9
0.42	-	-	0.16	-1.19	-1.31	140.6 - 69.2	-						22.5	11.1
-0.58	-	-	-2.46	-2.47	-2.23	-							38.0	22.4
1.07	-	-	3.92	3.94	4.09	20.1 - 14.4	1.38	1.24	1.12	2.0	0.360Y	18/78/27	78.7	56.5
0.66	-	-	1.93	1.61	1.77	70.6 - 34.9	-						136.3	67.3
0.43	-	-	1.45	1.38	1.33	20.0 - 16.2	0.93	0.71	0.65	3.5	0.20Y	5/31/18	28.9	23.5
3.14	-	-	17.86	9.71	12.17	7.1 - 5.2	3.00	2.80	2.44	2.8	0.90Y	18/78/27	126.0	93.2
-	-	-	0.93	0.75	1.01	59.3 - 48.7	0.94	1.00	0.78	1.9	0.40630Z	9/23/18	55.1	45.3
1.69	-	-	3.30	2.31	2.52	41.6 - 32.8	3.40	3.00	2.20	2.7	0.3250Z	6/28/18	137.4	108.3
-	-	-	223.30	195.98	157.38	0.2 - 0.1	11746.72	11188.16	8775.90	38464.2			36.1	23.8
1.10	-	-	3.10	1.75	3.30	17.5 - 13.5	1.72	1.64	1.56	3.5	0.450Y	18/78/27	54.2	41.9
1.65	-	-	6.73	6.81	6.07	34.0 - 26.8	8.00	7.30	6.50	3.9	0.31560Z	6/28/18	229.0	180.5
0.59	-	-	1.44	1.75	1.36	24.4 - 16.8	0.36	0.36	0.33	1.2	0.090Y	18/78/27	35.1	24.2
-0.29	-	-	-1.26	-2.59	-6.56	-							25.4	12.1
-	-	-	0.39	0.43	0.45	19.8 - 17.8	0.40	0.44	0.44	5.5	0.0289MZ	8/1/18	7.7	7.0
-	-	-	0.26	0.28	0.25	18.8 - 17.6	0.31	0.31	0.31	6.5	0.0220Z	8/1/18	4.9	4.6
-	-	-	0.69	0.74	0.73	18.6 - 16.7	0.68	0.71	0.71	5.6	0.0424MZ	8/1/18	12.8	11.5
-	-	-	0.28	0.31	0.28	20.0 - 18.1	0.31	0.31	0.31	5.8	0.0260Z	8/1/18	5.6	5.1
-3.05	-	-	-3.98	-1.29		-							30.0	18.8
2.29	-	-	6.79	6.89	5.27	24.8 - 16.3	0.15	0.15	0.15	0.1	0.03750Y	18/78/27	168.2	110.9
0.20	-	-	0.40	0.58	0.50	32.6 - 21.6	0.37	0.41	0.41	3.5	0.030Y	5/18/18	13.1	8.7
-0.14	-	-	-0.63	-0.92	-0.67	-							63.0	36.3
-0.22	-	-	1.12	-5.62	-0.85	12.1 - 6.3	-		0.08	-	0.020Y	18/78/27	13.6	7.1
-	0.06	-	0.17	0.34	0.56	-								
-0.02	-	-	0.01	0.46	0.53	6104.0 - 3227.0	1.56	1.44	1.28	3.3	0.44530Z	7/16/18	61.0	32.3
-0.07	-	-	2.07	0.90	-13.40	14.9 - 8.9	1.20	1.20	1.20	5.4	0.30Y	6/8/18	30.9	18.4
0.95	-	-	1.52	4.63	3.84	108.4 - 86.9	1.40	1.33	1.24	0.9	0.370Y	18/78/27	164.8	132.1
-	-	-0.36	-4.74	0.87		-							22.7	12.4
-	0.12	-	0.54	-0.05	0.47	44.5 - 30.7	0.16	0.16	0.16	0.8	0.040Y	6/30/18	24.1	16.6
0.24	-	-	2.00	1.26	1.59	19.9 - 16.3							39.9	32.5
-	-0.23	-	0.11	-2.24	0.48	78.2 - 18.7							8.6	2.1
-	-	-	7.09	1.90	-2.94	4.9 - 1.1							34.9	8.0
1.27	-	-	5.50	4.51	4.87	20.6 - 16.5	1.80	1.58	1.47	1.8	0.50Y	18/78/27	113.1	90.9
-0.44	-	-	-0.05	-0.37	-0.25	-							10.5	7.3
-3.48	-	-	-4.06	-12.24		-							9.8	2.9
-0.12	-	-	-0.17	-0.23	-0.32	-							17.6	10.5
-	-	-	-			-	1.07			4.6	0.40630Z	9/4/18	26.0	20.6
0.52	-	-	0.55	1.37	1.22	42.4 - 26.0	0.01	0.01	0.01	0.1	0.00250Y	6/4/18	23.3	14.3

SYMBOL	COMPANY	NATURE OF BUSINESS	FISCAL YEAR-END	TOTAL REV. $MILL	NET INCOME $MILL	TOTAL ASSETS $MILL	NET STK EQUITY $MILL	NO OF INST	INST. HOLDINGS (SHARES)
RL	Ralph Lauren Corp	Apparel, Footwear & Accessories	3/31/18	6182.3	162.8	6143.3	3457.4	613	74534657
RPT	Ramco-Gershenson Properties Trus	REITs	12/31/17	265.1	69.1	2030.4	864.3	235	98791494
RRC	Range Resources Corp	Production & Extraction	12/31/17	2611.0	333.1	11728.8	5774.3	685	315969063
RNGR	Ranger Energy Services Inc	Equipment & Services	12/31/17	154.0	-6.6	259.7	103.7		0
RJF	Raymond James Financial, Inc.	Finance Intermediaries & Services	9/30/17	6524.9	636.2	34883.5	5581.7	703	131119253
RYAM	Rayonier Advanced Materials Inc	Specialty Chemicals	12/31/17	961.3	325.0	2642.6	693.8	273	58210588
RYN	Rayonier Inc.	REITs	12/31/17	819.6	148.8	2858.5	1593.0	500	144258878
RTN	Raytheon Co.	Defense	12/31/17	25348.0	2024.0	30860.0	9963.0	1775	277226537
RMAX	Re/Max Holdings Inc	Property, Real Estate & Developmen	12/31/17	195.9	12.8	406.6	467.7	186	20174570
RLGY	Realogy Holdings Corp	Property, Real Estate & Developmen	12/31/17	6114.0	431.0	7337.0	2618.0	340	174888459
O	Realty Income Corp	REITs	12/31/17	1215.8	318.8	14058.2	7371.5	876	245519512
RHT	Red Hat Inc	Internet & Software	2/28/18	2920.5	258.8	5466.5	1470.2	885	203458388
RLH	Red Lions Hotels Corp	Hotels, Restaurants & Travel	12/31/17	171.9	0.6	330.3	162.9	98	18271078
RWT	Redwood Trust Inc	REITs	12/31/17	338.1	140.4	7039.8	1212.3	255	84724539
RBC	Regal Beloit Corp	Electrical Equipment	12/30/17	3360.3	213.0	4388.2	2325.5	422	51944922
RWGE	Regalwood Global Energy Ltd	Business Services	12/31/17		0.2	301.9	290.8	15	11480916
REG	Regency Centers Corp	REITs	12/31/17	984.3	176.1	11145.7	6692.1	517	194329446
RM	Regional Management Corp	Credit & Lending	12/31/17	272.5	30.0	829.5	239.4	116	11084491
RF	Regions Financial Corp	Banking	12/31/17	6093.0	1263.0	124294.0	16192.0	1029	1062657690
RGS	Regis Corp.	Miscellaneous Consumer Services	6/30/17	1691.9	-16.1	1011.5	508.2	226	59616012
RGA	Reinsurance Group of America, Inc.	Life & Health	12/31/17	12515.8	1822.2	60514.8	9569.5	31	784655
RS	Reliance Steel & Aluminum Co.	Non-Precious Metals	12/31/17	9721.0	613.4	7751.0	4667.1	503	71309021
RENX	RELX NV	Business Services	12/31/17		819.0	4466.0	4373.0	161	13273816
RELX	RELX PLC	Business Services	12/31/17			3232.0	3174.0	200	31253086
RNR	RenaissanceRe Holdings Ltd.	General Insurance	12/31/17	2103.7	-222.4	15226.1	4391.4	447	52813966
SOL	ReneSola Ltd	Semiconductors	12/31/17	103.0	34.5	335.7	90.5		0
RENN	Renren Inc	Internet & Software	12/31/17	202.1	-110.4	1194.2	674.8	63	5850351
RSG	Republic Services Inc	Sanitation Services	12/31/17	10041.5	1278.4	21147.0	7958.8	887	308945495
RMD	ResMed Inc.	Medical Instruments & Equipment	6/30/17	2066.7	342.3	3468.5	1960.3	603	112159384
REN	Resolute Energy Corp	Production & Extraction	12/31/17	303.5	-1.2	641.9	-74.4	155	26011213
RFP	Resolute Forest Products Inc	Paper & Forest Products	12/31/17	3513.0	-84.0	4147.0	1599.0	164	96143841
QSR	Restaurant Brands International Inc	Hotels, Restaurants & Travel	12/31/17	4576.1	648.8	21223.5	2226.4	382	195606133
RPAI	Retail Properties of America Inc	REITs	12/31/17	538.1	251.5	3918.3	1885.7		0
RVI	Retail Value Inc	Property, Real Estate & Developmen	12/31/17	322.9	-292.5	2326.6	1090.5		0
REVG	REV Group Inc	Auto Parts	10/31/17	2267.8	31.4	1254.4	572.4	146	64116029
REV	Revlon Inc	Household & Personal Products	12/31/17	2693.7	-183.2	3056.9	-770.4	110	13745589
REX	REX American Resources Corp	Refining & Marketing	1/31/18	452.6	39.7	478.9	381.5	190	7212252
REXR	Rexford Industrial Realty Inc	REITs	12/31/17	161.4	40.7	2111.4	1340.0	223	95927081
RXN	Rexnord Corp (New)	Industrial Machinery & Equipment	3/31/18	2066.0	75.9	3423.7	1212.7	262	130477670
RH	RH	Retail - Furniture & Home Furnishing	2/3/18	2440.2	2.2	1732.9	-7.3	307	31104813
RNG	RingCentral Inc	Internet & Software	12/31/17	501.5	-26.1	305.2	172.2	287	68647162
RIO	Rio Tinto Plc	Mining	12/31/17	40030.0	89.0	95726.0	44711.0	566	114487114
RBA	Ritchie Bros Auctioneers Inc	Business Services	12/31/17	610.5	75.0	2017.3	739.7	284	132266428
RAD	Rite Aid Corp	Retail - Food & Beverage, Drug & To	3/3/18	21529.0	943.5	8989.3	1601.0	543	649146956
RMPL PR	RiverNorth Marketplace Lending Co	Holding and other Investment Office	6/30/17	5.1	4.1	98.6	98.1		0
RIV	RiverNorth Opportunities Fund Inc	Finance Intermediaries & Services	10/31/16	3.6	2.6	74.3	74.0	20	409934
OPP	RiverNorth/DoubleLine Strategic Op	Holding and other Investment Office	6/30/17	12.2	8.7	292.9	220.8	35	2326701
RLI	RLI Corp	General Insurance	12/31/17	797.2	105.0	2947.2	853.6	293	47675365
RLJ	RLJ Lodging Trust	REITs	12/31/17	1356.3	75.3	6794.8	3547.4	318	211447049
RRTS	Roadrunner Transportation System	Miscellaneous Transportation Servic	12/31/17	2091.3	-91.2	876.0	110.8	165	46269277
RHI	Robert Half International Inc.	Business Services	12/31/17	5266.8	290.6	1867.5	1105.3	683	139896335
ROK	Rockwell Automation, Inc.	Electrical Equipment	9/30/17	6311.3	825.7	7161.7	2663.6	1105	117915677
COL	Rockwell Collins Inc	Aerospace	9/30/17	6822.0	705.0	17997.0	6043.0	945	134328335
RCI 14A	Rogers Cable Inc.	Radio & Television	12/31/06	3201.0	177.0	5245.0	419.0		0
RCI	Rogers Communications Inc	Services	12/31/17	14143.0	1711.0	28863.0	6347.0	388	299576215
ROG	Rogers Corp.	Plastics	12/31/17	821.0	80.5	1125.1	766.6	355	20501512
ROL	Rollins, Inc.	Business Services	12/31/17	1674.0	179.1	1033.7	653.9	426	101777652
ROP	Roper Technologies Inc	Electrical Equipment	12/31/17	4607.5	971.8	14316.4	6863.6	942	119771110
RST	Rosetta Stone Inc	Internet & Software	12/31/17	184.6	-1.5	194.8	2.4	136	23699175
RDC	Rowan Companies Plc	Equipment & Services	12/31/17	1282.8	72.7	8458.3	5386.1	395	159392711
RY	Royal Bank of Canada (Montreal, Q	Banking	10/31/17	50433.0	11428.0	1212853.0	73829.0	674	727858046
RBS	Royal Bank of Scotland Group Plc	Banking	12/31/17	16063.0	1146.0	738056.0	48330.0	172	36075460
RCL	Royal Caribbean Cruises Ltd	Hotels, Restaurants & Travel	12/31/17	8777.8	1625.1	22296.3	10702.3	864	172472409
RDS A	Royal Dutch Shell Plc	Production & Extraction	12/31/17	311870.0	12977.0	407097.0	194356.0	1401	334158593
RGT	Royce Global Value Trust Inc	ETFs	12/31/17	2.2	0.2	139.2	130.5	63	3813458
RMT	Royce Micro-Cap Trust, Inc.	Holding and other Investment Office	12/31/16	5.1	1.0	409.3	363.7	93	11828440
RVT	Royce Value Trust Inc	Holding and other Investment Office	12/31/16	18.0	9.7	1368.8	1296.0	175	24902634
RES	RPC, Inc.	Equipment & Services	12/31/17	1595.2	162.5	1147.2	911.7	379	86492630
RPM	RPM International Inc (DE)	Specialty Chemicals	5/31/18	5321.6	337.8	5271.8	1630.8	631	130068763
RUBI	Rubicon Project Inc	Internet & Software	12/31/17	155.5	-154.8	383.6	164.6	138	34181694
RTEC	Rudolph Technologies, Inc.	Semiconductors	12/31/17	255.1	32.9	385.9	333.2	277	38394689
RYB	RYB Education Inc	Educational Services	12/31/17	140.8	7.1	229.7	103.7	31	2415580
R	Ryder System, Inc.	Trucking	12/31/17	7329.6	790.6	11452.2	2835.0	511	65169041
RYI	Ryerson Holding Corp	Non-Precious Metals	12/31/17	3364.7	17.1	1711.9	-10.0	111	15686395
RHP	Ryman Hospitality Properties Inc	REITs	12/31/17	1184.7	176.1	2524.2	378.2	373	53272582
SPGI	S&P Global Inc	Credit & Lending	12/31/17	6063.0	1496.0	9425.0	711.0	1207	272050154
SBR	Sabine Royalty Trust	Oil Royalty Traders	12/31/17	37.2	34.7	5.3	4.6	108	1655515
SB	Safe Bulkers Inc	Shipping	12/31/17	148.0	-84.7	1035.1	456.3	109	24317369
SFE	Safeguard Scientifics, Inc.	Venture Capital	12/31/17		-88.6	176.5	81.8	157	27014535
SAFE	Safety, Income & Growth Inc	REITs	12/31/17	17.2	-3.7	728.5	355.9	58	7828100

T50

1st	2nd	3rd	2017	2016	2015	P/E RATIO	Div 2017	Div 2016	Div 2015	AV. YLD %	AMOUNT	PAYABLE	PRICE RANGE 2017
-	-	-1.00	-1.20	4.62	7.88	-	2.00	2.00	1.85	2.0	0.6250Y	18/78/27	142.9 - 70.5
0.07	-	-	0.78	0.66	0.73	19.0 - 14.4	0.88	0.86	0.82	6.8	0.90630Z	7/2/18	14.8 - 11.3
0.20	-	-	1.34	-2.75	-4.29	17.5 - 9.5	0.08	0.08	0.16	0.5	0.020Y	18/78/27	23.5 - 12.7
-0.68	-	-	-0.78	-1.79	-	-	-	-	-	-	-	-	15.5 - 6.9
-	1.63	-	4.33	3.65	3.43	23.5 - 17.3	0.88	0.80	0.72	1.0	0.30Y	18/78/27	101.7 - 74.8
0.38	-	-	5.81	1.55	1.30	3.8 - 2.3	0.28	0.28	0.28	1.6	0.070Y	9/28/18	22.3 - 13.2
0.31	-	-	1.16	1.73	0.37	34.1 - 24.0	1.00	1.00	1.00	3.1	0.270Z	18/78/27	39.5 - 27.8
2.19	-	-	6.95	7.44	6.80	32.8 - 23.4	2.39	3.60	2.62	1.2	0.86750Y	18/78/27	228.1 - 162.6
0.28	-	-	0.72	1.29	1.30	93.3 - 63.1	0.72	0.60	2.00	1.3	0.20Y	5/30/18	67.2 - 45.4
-0.51	-	-	3.11	1.46	1.24	11.2 - 7.3	0.36	0.18	-	1.3	0.090Y	18/78/27	35.0 - 22.7
0.29	-	-	1.10	1.13	1.09	54.5 - 43.2	2.54	* 2.40	2.28	4.7	0.220Z	18/78/27	59.9 - 47.6
0.59	-	-	1.39	1.07	0.95	126.8 - 68.2	-	-	-	-	-	-	176.3 - 94.8
0.10	-	-	0.02	-0.23	0.13	610.0 - 332.5	-	-	-	-	-	-	12.2 - 6.7
0.50	-	-	1.60	1.54	1.18	10.9 - 9.0	1.12	1.12	1.12	7.1	0.30Z	6/29/18	17.4 - 14.5
1.31	-	-	4.74	4.52	3.18	18.3 - 14.7	1.02	0.95	0.91	1.3	0.280Y	18/78/27	86.8 - 69.8
0.02	-	-	0.01	-	-	-	-	-	-	-	-	-	
0.31	-	-	1.00	1.42	1.36	70.4 - 55.6	2.10	2.00	1.94	3.4	0.5550Z	18/78/27	70.4 - 55.6
0.72	-	-	2.54	1.99	1.79	14.6 - 8.5	-	-	-	-	-	-	37.0 - 21.7
0.35	-	-	1.00	0.87	0.75	20.1 - 13.2	0.32	0.26	0.23	1.9	0.39840Y	18/78/27	20.1 - 13.2
-	-	-0.12	-0.35	-0.23	-0.62	-	-	-	-	-	0.060Y	11/19/13	18.3 - 10.0
1.52	-	-	27.71	10.79	7.46	5.9 - 4.6	1.82	1.56	1.40	1.2	0.50Y	18/78/27	164.2 - 127.5
2.30	-	-	8.34	4.16	4.16	11.6 - 8.3	1.80	1.65	1.60	2.2	0.50Y	18/78/27	96.6 - 69.1
-	-	-	-	-	-	-	0.38	0.35	0.83	1.8	-	-	23.3 - 20.1
-	-	-	-	-	-	-	0.37	0.32	0.84	1.7	-	-	24.0 - 20.3
1.42	-	-	-6.15	11.43	9.28	-	1.28	1.24	1.20	-	0.330	18/78/27	
-	-	-0.10	-	-0.17	-0.02	-	-	-	-	-	-	-	3.7 - 2.2
-	-	-0.02	-0.11	-0.18	-0.22	-	-	-	-	-	-	-	18.3 - 2.3
0.72	-	-	3.77	1.78	2.13	18.5 - 16.4	1.33	1.24	1.16	2.0	0.3450Y	18/78/27	69.9 - 62.0
-	-	0.76	2.40	2.49	2.47	45.0 - 30.2	1.32	1.20	1.12	1.5	0.350Y	18/78/27	107.9 - 72.4
-0.64	-	-	-0.35	-10.33	-49.55	-	-	-	-	-	20.31250Y	7/16/18	37.6 - 24.3
0.11	-	-	-0.93	-0.90	-2.78	-	-	-	-	-	-	-	15.0 - 0.0
0.59	-	-	2.54	1.45	0.50	33.9 - 21.1	0.78	0.62	0.44	1.1	0.450Y	7/3/18	86.2 - 53.5
0.19	-	-	1.03	0.66	0.49	13.3 - 10.6	0.66	0.66	0.66	5.3	0.16560Z	18/78/27	13.7 - 10.9
-	-	-	-	-	-	-	-	-	-	-	-	-	31.5 - 0.0
-	0.11	-	0.50	0.58	0.43	65.6 - 29.0	0.15	-	-	0.6	0.050Y	8/31/18	32.8 - 14.5
-1.71	-	-	-3.48	-0.42	1.07	-	-	-	-	-	0.16740Y	10/8/13	27.5 - 15.9
1.45	-	-	4.91	4.30	10.76	20.4 - 14.6	-	-	-	-	-	-	100.0 - 71.8
0.15	-	-	0.48	0.36	0.03	68.0 - 55.0	0.58	0.54	0.51	2.0	0.36720Y	6/29/18	32.7 - 26.4
-	-	0.67	0.64	0.66	0.80	47.9 - 35.4	-	-	-	-	0.71880Y	8/15/18	30.7 - 22.7
1.11	-	-	0.13	2.16	2.20	1237.5 - 347.4	-	-	-	-	-	-	160.9 - 45.2
-0.03	-	-	-0.34	-0.40	-0.46	-	-	-	-	-	-	-	80.3 - 34.5
-	-	-	4.87	2.55	-0.47	12.5 - 8.9	2.37	1.51	2.21	4.6	-	-	60.7 - 43.1
0.16	-	-	0.69	0.85	1.27	68.7 - 36.0	0.68	0.66	0.60	2.0	0.170	6/20/18	47.4 - 24.9
0.20	-	•	-	0.00	0.16	2.08	-	-	-	-	0.1150	18/78/27	2.7 - 1.4
-	-	-	2.32	-	-	11.0 - 0.0	-	-	-	-	0.36720	8/15/18	25.6 - 0.0
-	-	-	-	0.68	-	-	-	2.18	-	-	0.210	10/31/18	21.6 - 19.4
-	-	-	0.94	-	-	20.9 - 18.4	0.92	-	-	5.0	0.150	9/28/18	19.6 - 17.3
0.27	-	-	2.36	2.59	3.12	29.5 - 21.6	2.58	2.79	2.75	4.3	0.220Y	18/78/27	69.7 - 51.0
0.10	-	-	0.47	1.61	1.68	50.7 - 39.7	1.32	1.32	1.32	6.2	0.48750Z	7/31/18	23.8 - 18.7
-0.61	-	-	-2.37	-9.40	1.23	-	-	-	-	-	-	-	9.7 - 1.8
0.78	-	-	2.33	2.67	2.69	30.1 - 18.6	0.96	0.88	0.80	1.7	0.280Y	18/78/27	70.1 - 43.2
-	1.77	-	6.35	5.56	6.09	32.7 - 25.1	3.04	2.90	2.80	1.7	0.920Y	18/78/27	207.9 - 159.6
-	1.43	-	4.79	5.51	5.13	29.1 - 22.0	1.32	1.32	1.26	1.0	0.330	18/78/27	139.4 - 105.4
0.80	-	-	3.31	1.62	2.67	21.0 - 13.2	1.92	1.92	1.92	3.4	0.480	7/3/18	69.6 - 43.7
1.40	-	-	4.34	2.65	2.48	41.1 - 24.6	-	-	-	-	0.0075	2/12/92	178.5 - 106.7
0.22	-	-	0.82	0.77	0.70	65.8 - 49.1	0.56	0.50	0.42	1.2	0.140Y	18/78/27	54.0 - 40.3
2.03	-	-	9.39	6.43	6.85	30.9 - 24.3	1.40	1.20	1.00	0.5	0.41250Y	18/78/27	289.9 - 227.8
-0.29	-	-	-0.07	-1.25	-2.17	-	-	-	-	-	-	-	16.7 - 8.9
-0.89	-	-	0.57	2.55	0.75	-	-	-	-	-	0.10	18/78/27	
-	2.06	-	7.56	6.78	6.73	14.3 - 9.6	3.48	3.24	3.08	3.9	0.27810	8/24/18	108.1 - 72.9
-	-	-	0.06	-0.59	-0.17	145.0 - 106.2	-	-	-	-	0.53130	3/31/99	8.7 - 6.4
1.02	-	-	7.53	5.93	3.02	-	2.16	1.71	1.35	-	0.60	18/78/27	
-	-	0.49	1.56	0.58	0.30	47.2 - 33.8	3.76	3.76	3.76	5.9	-	-	73.6 - 52.8
-	-	-	0.02	0.06	0.10	585.5 - 478.0	0.11	0.14	-	1.0	0.110	12/27/17	11.7 - 9.6
-	-	-	0.03	0.03	-	-	-	0.64	1.26	-	0.180	6/27/18	10.4 - 8.2
-	-	-	-	0.12	0.12	-	-	1.02	1.24	-	0.30	6/27/18	17.1 - 14.2
0.24	-	-	0.75	-0.66	-0.47	35.6 - 18.2	0.20	0.05	0.16	1.0	0.10Y	18/78/27	26.7 - 13.7
-	-	0.30	1.36	2.63	1.78	42.9 - 34.5	1.18	1.09	1.02	2.3	0.320Y	18/78/27	58.3 - 46.9
-0.56	-	-	-3.17	-0.39	0.01	-	-	-	-	-	-	-	5.3 - 1.5
0.47	-	-	1.02	1.16	0.56	33.7 - 20.9	-	-	-	-	-	-	34.4 - 21.4
-	-	-	0.27	0.26	-0.22	115.3 - 58.1	-	-	-	-	-	-	31.1 - 15.7
0.63	-	-	14.87	4.90	5.71	6.0 - 4.5	1.80	1.70	1.56	2.3	0.540Y	18/78/27	89.8 - 66.3
0.28	-	-	0.46	0.54	-0.02	27.6 - 16.7	-	-	-	-	-	-	12.7 - 7.7
0.53	-	-	3.43	3.11	2.16	24.9 - 16.9	3.20	3.00	2.70	4.5	0.850	7/16/18	85.4 - 58.1
1.93	-	-	5.78	7.94	4.21	36.1 - 25.2	1.64	1.44	1.32	0.9	0.50Y	18/78/27	208.7 - 145.7
0.68	-	-	2.38	1.88	3.15	20.8 - 15.8	2.37	1.93	3.11	5.5	0.28120Z	7/30/18	49.5 - 37.7
0.03	-	-	-0.98	-0.83	-0.74	-	-	-	-	-	0.50	7/30/18	
-0.30	-	-	-4.34	-1.09	-2.85	-	-	-	-	-	0.02670	12/31/79	14.2 - 10.9
0.20	-	-	-0.25	-	-	-	0.31	-	-	1.7	0.150Z	7/13/18	19.9 - 15.6

SYMBOL	COMPANY	NATURE OF BUSINESS	FISCAL YEAR-END	TOTAL REV. $MILL	NET INCOME $MILL	TOTAL ASSETS $MILL	NET STK EQUITY $MILL	NO OF INST	INST. HOLDINGS (SHARES)
SAIL	SailPoint Technologies Holdings Inc	Services	12/31/17	186.1	-7.6	506.4	328.4	110	22150194
CRM	Salesforce.Com Inc	Internet & Software	1/31/18	10480.0	127.5	21009.8	9392.4	1399	700394802
SMM	Salient Midstream & MLP Fund	Holding and other Investment Office	11/30/16	8.2	2.0	352.2	254.6	49	5180740
SBH	Sally Beauty Holdings Inc	Retail - Specialty	9/30/17	3938.3	215.1	2123.1	-363.6	355	179923354
SJT	San Juan Basin Royalty Trust	Oil Royalty Traders	12/31/17	40.7	39.1	11.0	6.6	161	13597990
SN	Sanchez Energy Corp.	Production & Extraction	12/31/17	740.3	43.2	2470.6	-41.6	196	53681990
SD	SandRidge Energy Inc	Production & Extraction	12/31/17	357.3	47.1	1119.6	839.9	234	103535824
SDT	SandRidge Mississippian Trust I	Oil Royalty Traders	12/31/17	9.0	6.1	29.8	29.8	30	255239
SDR	SandRidge Mississippian Trust II	Oil Royalty Traders	12/31/17	15.6	11.6	46.8	46.8	29	505089
PER	SandRidge Permian Trust	Oil Royalty Traders	12/31/17	28.8	24.3	126.2	126.2		0
SNY	Sanofi	Pharmaceuticals	12/31/17	36204.0	8434.0	99826.0	58089.0	704	246815219
SC	Santander Consumer USA Holdings	Credit & Lending	12/31/17	6665.1	1187.6	39422.3	6480.5	261	380969371
SOV PRC	Santander Holdings USA Inc.	Banking	12/31/17	10715.7	561.1	128294.0	21182.7	56	9131130
SAP	SAP SE	Internet & Software	12/31/17	23461.0	4018.0	42497.0	25509.0	584	142646020
SAR	Saratoga Investment Corp	Holding and other Investment Office	2/28/18	38.6	12.7	360.3	143.7	36	3060301
SSL	Sasol Ltd.	Production & Extraction	6/30/17	172407.0	20374.0	398939.0	211711.0	206	24862427
BFS	Saul Centers Inc	REITs	12/31/17	227.3	48.3	1422.5	334.4	171	12214951
SCG	SCANA Corp	Electric Utilities	12/31/17	4407.0	-119.0	18739.0	5255.0	720	123727631
SLB	Schlumberger Ltd	Equipment & Services	12/31/17	30664.0	-1505.0	71987.0	36842.0	2369	1317835602
SNDR	Schneider National Inc (WI)	Trucking	12/31/17	4383.6	389.9	3330.5	1890.2	168	48349237
SCHW	Schwab (Charles) Corp (The)	Finance Intermediaries & Services	12/31/17	8960.0	2354.0	243274.0	18525.0	1381	1271027475
SWM	Schweitzer-Mauduit International In	Paper & Forest Products	12/31/17	982.1	34.5	1542.5	546.7	258	33081860
SAIC	Science Applications International C	IT Services	2/2/18	4454.0	179.0	2073.0	327.0	335	33276406
SALT	Scorpio Bulkers Inc	Shipping	12/31/17	162.2	-59.7	1643.4	917.4	113	34762997
STNG	Scorpio Tankers Inc	Equipment & Services	12/31/17	512.7	-158.2	4498.4	1685.3	205	206593234
SMG	Scotts Miracle-Gro Co (The)	Agricultural Chemicals	9/30/17	2642.1	218.3	2747.0	648.8	515	47036804
SE	Sea Ltd	IT Services	12/31/17	414.2	-560.5	1988.3	469.0	83	78727491
SA	Seabridge Gold Inc	Precious Metals	12/31/17		-10.3	382.9	355.6	121	16223103
CKH	SEACOR Holdings Inc	Shipping	12/31/17	577.9	61.6	1613.3	623.7	221	21195445
SMHI	SEACOR Marine Holdings Inc	Miscellaneous Transportation Servic	12/31/17	173.8	-32.9	1008.5	508.2	83	15695376
SDRL	Seadrill Ltd (New)	Production & Extraction	12/31/17	2088.0	-2973.0	17982.0	6560.0	268	73899320
SDLP	Seadrill Partners LLC	Production & Extraction	12/31/17	1128.4	141.2	6530.8		68	11612213
SEE	Sealed Air Corp	Containers & Packaging	12/31/17	4461.6	814.9	5280.3	152.3	698	202653351
SSW	Seaspan Corp	Shipping	12/31/17	831.3	175.2	5878.1	1949.4	173	25052407
SEAS	SeaWorld Entertainment Inc.	Sporting & Recreational	12/31/17	1263.3	-202.4	2085.8	287.5	206	94302656
WTTR	Select Energy Services Inc	Equipment & Services	12/31/17	692.5	-16.8	1356.4	656.6	124	47438973
SEM	Select Medical Holdings Corp	Hospitals & Health Care Facilities	12/31/17	4443.6	177.2	5127.2	823.4	253	122562251
SEMG	SemGroup Corp	Equipment & Services	12/31/17	2081.9	-17.1	5376.8	1658.4	225	91872733
SMI	Semiconductor Manufacturing Inter	Semiconductors	12/31/17	3101.2	179.7	11918.5	5233.0	57	6392609
SRE	Sempra Energy	Electric Utilities	12/31/17	11207.0	257.0	50454.0	12670.0	961	290553618
SEND	SendGrid Inc	Internet & Software	12/31/17	111.9	-6.3	223.3	179.8	88	17872133
ST	Sensata Technologies Holding PLC	Electrical Equipment	12/31/17	3306.7	408.4	6641.5	2345.6	397	212295032
SXT	Sensient Technologies Corp.	Specialty Chemicals	12/31/17	1362.3	89.6	1724.3	852.3	389	59339260
SQNS	Sequans Communications S A	Semiconductors	12/31/16	45.6	-24.8	65.1	8.9	42	32074806
SRG	Seritage Growth Properties	REITs	12/31/17	241.0	-73.8	2775.8	886.7	176	39266593
SCI	Service Corp. International	Miscellaneous Consumer Services	12/31/17	3095.0	546.7	12864.5	1409.4	523	186838308
SERV	ServiceMaster Global Holdings, Inc	Miscellaneous Consumer Services	12/31/17	2912.0	510.0	5646.0	1167.0	309	158158602
NOW	ServiceNow Inc	IT Services	12/31/17	1933.0	-149.1	3397.9	584.1	629	187855702
SHAK	Shake Shack Inc	Hotels, Restaurants & Travel	12/27/17	358.8	-0.3	470.6	169.5	210	33429995
SJR	Shaw Communications Inc	Radio & Television	8/31/17	4882.0	851.0	14373.0	6153.0	313	333487403
SHLX	Shell Midstream Partners LP	Equipment & Services	12/31/17	470.1	295.3	1366.5		197	126400478
SHW	Sherwin-Williams Co (The)	Specialty Chemicals	12/31/17	14983.8	1772.3	19958.4	3692.2	1161	95371611
SHG	Shinhan Financial Group Co. Ltd.	Banking	12/31/16	20298675.0	2774778.0	95680324.0	31109698.0	163	12600485
SFL	Ship Finance International Ltd	Equipment & Services	12/31/17	380.9	101.2	3012.1	1195.0	264	37489688
SHOP	Shopify Inc	IT Services	12/31/17	673.3	-40.0	1113.6	1001.1	393	61605543
SSTK	Shutterstock Inc	Internet & Software	12/31/17	557.1	16.7	577.8	314.6	194	22365607
SBGL	Sibanye-Stillwater	Mining	12/31/17	31240.7	3701.6	41721.3	16679.7	142	125555960
SIG	Signet Jewelers Ltd	Retail - Specialty	2/3/18	6253.0	519.3	5839.6	3113.4	465	84558073
SBOW	SilverBow Resources Inc	Production & Extraction	12/31/17	195.9	72.0	551.3	193.5	162	18384633
SPG	Simon Property Group, Inc.	REITs	12/31/17	5538.6	1948.0	32257.6	3876.6	1044	393058199
SSD	Simpson Manufacturing Co., Inc. (D	Construction Materials	12/31/17	977.0	92.6	1037.5	884.8	304	59410400
SHI	Sinopec Shanghai Petrochemical C	Refining & Marketing	12/31/17	92013.6	6141.6	39609.5	28256.3	92	1809074
SITE	SiteOne Landscape Supply Inc	Services	12/31/17	1861.7	54.6	910.7	212.8	217	45482255
SIX	Six Flags Entertainment Corp	Sporting & Recreational	12/31/17	1359.1	273.8	2456.7	-505.1	456	108489906
SJW	SJW Group	Water Utilities	12/31/17	389.2	59.2	1458.0	463.2	216	13591907
SKM	SK Telecom Co Ltd (South Korea)	Internet & Software	12/31/17	7520013.0	2599829.0	33428669.0	17842139.0	292	95480665
SKX	Skechers USA Inc	Apparel, Footwear & Accessories	12/31/17	4180.8	179.2	2735.1	1829.1	471	138142144
SKY	Skyline Champion Corp	Builders	5/31/17	236.5	0.0	55.6	25.3	73	5244592
SLG	SL Green Realty Corp	REITs	12/31/17	1511.5	101.4	13982.9	6526.8	534	132466308
SM	SM Energy Co.	Production & Extraction	12/31/17	1129.4	-160.8	6176.8	2394.6	430	150317713
SFS	Smart & Final Stores Inc	Retail - Food & Beverage, Drug & To	12/31/17	4570.6	-138.9	1809.9	403.0	112	77360884
SMAR	SmartSheet Inc	IT Services	1/31/18	111.3	-49.1	116.6	31.9		0
SNN	Smith & Nephew Plc	Medical Instruments & Equipment	12/31/17	4765.0	767.0	7866.0	4644.0	293	42034206
AOS	Smith (A O) Corp	Household Appliances, Electronics &	12/31/17	2996.7	296.5	3197.3	1648.8	659	159280048
SJM	Smucker (J.M.) Co.	Food	4/30/18	7357.1	1338.6	15301.2	7891.1	1103	108288657
SNAP	Snap Inc	Computer Hardware & Equipment	12/31/17	824.9	-3445.1	3421.6	2992.3	396	270726962
SNA	Snap-On, Inc.	Industrial Machinery & Equipment	12/30/17	4000.3	557.7	5249.1	2953.9	839	81676824
SNH PRZ	SNH Capital Trust I	REITs							0
IPOA	Social Capital Hedosophia Holdings	Business Services	12/31/17		1.3	693.6	669.1	84	55909562
SQM	Sociedad Química y Minera de Chil	Agricultural Chemicals	12/31/17	2157.3	427.7	4296.2	2187.8	332	35220639

EARNINGS PER SHARE QUARTERLY			ANNUAL			P/E RATIO		DIVIDENDS PER SHARE			AV. YLD	DIV. DECLARED		PRICE RANGE	
1st	2nd	3rd	2017	2016	2015	2017		2017	2016	2015	%	AMOUNT	PAYABLE	2017	
-0.07			-0.55	-0.58	-0.74									28.6-	13.0
0.46			0.26	-0.07	-0.42	537.7-	331.2							139.8-	86.1
				0.11	0.09				1.14	1.67		0.1710	5/30/18	12.1-	8.9
	0.49		1.56	1.50	1.49	13.6-	9.5							21.1-	14.8
0.13			0.84	0.30	0.36	12.1-	6.9	0.84	0.33	0.36	11.0	0.02910	8/14/18	10.2-	5.8
-0.30			-0.46	-4.63	-25.70							0.81250Y	7/2/18	7.5-	2.8
-1.18			1.44	-17.61	-7.16	15.0-	9.3					4.250Y	2/16/15	21.7-	13.3
0.04			0.22	0.54	1.24	9.9-	3.5	0.22	0.54	1.24	18.9	0.04880Z	5/25/18	2.2-	0.8
0.06			0.23	0.40	1.14	8.0-	3.4	0.23	0.40	1.14	18.7	0.0550Z	5/25/18	1.9-	0.8
0.11			0.46	0.54	1.90	6.7-	4.0	0.46	0.54	1.97	18.5	0.1250Z	5/25/18	3.1-	1.9
			6.66	3.63	3.25	7.6-	5.7	4.47	4.38	4.28	10.2			50.6-	37.6
0.67			3.30	2.13	2.31	6.2-	3.8	0.03			0.2	0.050	18/78/27	20.4-	12.7
								1.83	1.83	1.83	8.3	0.45620Y	8/15/18	26.6-	0.0
		0.82	3.35	3.04	2.56	36.2-	30.3	0.90	0.82	0.77	0.8			121.4-	101.7
			1.68	1.91	1.80	16.5-	11.7	1.93	2.36	0.40	8.9	0.510Y	6/27/18	27.7-	19.6
			33.27	21.66	48.70	1.1-	0.8	11.10	14.15	16.87	34.1			38.2-	27.3
0.31			1.63	1.52	1.42	40.1-	29.1	2.04	1.84	1.69	3.6	0.38280Z	7/16/18	65.3-	47.5
1.18			-0.83	4.16	5.22			2.45	2.30	2.18	5.4	0.12370Y	18/78/27	67.6-	34.0
0.38			-1.08	-1.24	1.63			2.00	2.00	2.00	3.0	0.50	18/78/27	79.8-	61.3
0.27			2.28	1.00	0.91	13.3-	9.0	0.15	0.20	0.16	0.6	0.060Y	7/9/18	30.2-	20.5
0.55			1.61	1.31	1.03	37.0-	23.7	0.32	0.27	0.24	0.6	0.3720Y	18/78/27	59.6-	38.1
0.67			1.12	2.70	2.94	42.7-	32.7	1.69	1.62	1.54	4.1	0.430Y	6/22/18	47.9-	36.7
1.13			3.22	2.47	2.91	28.0-	19.0	1.24	1.21	1.12	1.6	0.310	18/78/27	90.1-	61.1
			-0.83	-2.22	-23.86							0.020	8/31/18		
-0.10			-0.73	-0.15	1.20			0.04				0.51560Z	12/1/18		
	2.59		3.63	5.09	2.57	30.2-	21.4	2.03	1.91	1.82	2.2	0.530Y	18/78/27	109.5-	77.5
			-2.72	-1.30	-0.63									16.4-	10.3
		-0.03	-0.18	-0.14	-0.18									17.5-	9.8
0.04			3.31	-12.76	-3.94	17.7-	10.0					5.7Y	12/26/12	58.8-	33.0
-1.64			-1.87	-7.47	-1.54									24.3-	11.7
	-0.28		-5.89	-0.36	-1.49										
		0.48	1.88	3.20	2.45			0.40	0.70	1.70		0.10	5/15/18		
-1.21			4.29	2.46	1.62	11.6-	9.6	0.64	0.61	0.52	1.4	0.160Y	18/78/27	49.7-	41.1
		0.42	0.94	-1.89	1.46							0.49220	7/30/18		
-0.73			-2.36	-0.15	0.57				0.73	0.84		0.10	10/7/16	22.8-	10.6
0.15			-0.51	-0.05										21.7-	11.4
0.25			1.33	0.87	0.99	14.6-	11.3		0.00	0.10		0.10Y	3/11/15	19.4-	15.0
-0.48			-0.24	0.04	0.69			1.80	1.80	1.59	7.0	0.47250Y	5/25/18	30.8-	20.4
		0.00	0.04	0.08	0.10	227.7-	114.0							9.1-	4.6
1.33			1.01	5.46	5.37	121.0-	99.7	3.29	3.02	2.80	2.9	0.8950Y	18/78/27	122.2-	100.7
-0.03			-0.74	-0.52	-0.83									31.1-	18.0
0.52			2.37	1.53	2.03										
0.89			2.03	2.82	2.31	40.7-	32.7	1.23	1.11	1.04	1.7	0.330Y	18/78/27	82.7-	66.5
		-0.20		-0.39	-0.46									3.9-	1.5
0.26			-2.19	-1.64	-0.71			1.00	1.00	0.50	2.4	0.43750Z	7/16/18	49.0-	34.5
0.43			2.84	0.90	1.14	14.1-	11.6	0.58	0.51	0.44	1.6	0.170Y	18/78/27	40.1-	33.0
0.30			3.76	1.13	1.17	16.1-	10.4							60.4-	39.0
0.06			-0.87	-2.75	-1.27									186.4-	103.6
0.13			-0.01	0.53	-0.65									69.2-	30.6
	-0.33		1.71	2.51	1.79	17.5-	10.9	1.19	1.19	1.14	4.9	0.17440	10/1/18	29.9-	18.6
0.18			1.28	1.32	1.16	24.1-	15.8	1.19	0.97	0.67	4.6	0.3480	5/15/18	30.9-	20.3
2.62			18.67	11.99	11.16	23.2-	17.6	3.40	3.36	2.68	0.9	0.860Y	18/78/27	432.8-	329.0
	-1055.00			-5736.00	4789.00				1191.31	935.99				50.4-	38.1
			1.03	1.50	1.88			1.60	1.80	1.74		0.350	6/29/18		
-0.16			-0.42	-0.42	-0.30									229.3-	86.0
0.92			0.47	0.91	0.54	110.9-	67.0							52.1-	31.5
			3.78	0.74					5.08	2.19				6.3-	2.3
-8.48			7.08	5.87	4.75			1.04	0.88	0.72		0.370	18/78/27		
0.72			6.25	-15.61	-37.20	5.3-	3.3							33.3-	20.3
2.00			6.24	5.87	5.88	27.7-	21.7	7.15	6.50	6.05	4.5	1.04690Z	18/78/27	172.8-	146.7
0.54			1.94	1.86	1.38	34.6-	21.7	0.78	0.68	0.60	1.4	0.220Y	7/26/18	67.2-	42.0
0.16			0.57	0.55	0.30	129.8-	93.5	22.15	8.67		36.1			74.0-	53.3
-0.43			1.29	-3.01	-1.04	73.3-	37.5							94.5-	48.4
-0.74			3.09	1.25	1.58	23.5-	16.8	2.62	2.38	2.14	4.2	0.780Y	18/78/27	72.8-	51.9
0.06			2.86	2.57	1.85	23.8-	16.9	1.04	0.81	0.78	1.8	0.280Y	18/78/27	68.2-	48.5
		-7086.08	6582.00	3497.00	20988.00	0.0-	0.0	1109.69	1095.37	1027.39	4379.1			28.8-	22.8
0.75			1.14	1.57	1.50	37.2-	21.1							42.5-	24.0
		0.14	0.00	0.20	-1.24							0.62387Y	5/31/18	35.3-	5.7
1.12			0.87	2.34	2.70	123.6-	104.1	3.14	2.94	2.52	3.2	0.40630Z	18/78/27	107.5-	90.6
2.81			-1.44	-9.90	-6.61			0.10	0.40	0.10	0.5	0.050Y	18/78/27	27.2-	12.8
-0.10			-1.92	0.17	0.50									9.7-	4.5
-0.68			-1.00	-1.03										32.2-	18.9
		0.14	0.88	0.88	0.46	44.8-	38.5	0.37	0.63	0.60	1.0			39.4-	33.9
0.57			1.70	1.85	1.58	39.9-	31.4	0.56	0.48	0.38	0.9	0.180Y	18/78/27	67.8-	53.5
		7.32	5.10	5.76	3.33	25.8-	19.6	2.92	2.65	2.50	2.5	0.850Y	18/78/27	131.5-	100.0
-0.30			-2.95	-0.64	-0.51									20.8-	10.6
	3.12		9.52	9.20	8.10	19.3-	14.9	2.95	2.54	2.20	1.9	0.820Y	18/78/27	183.8-	141.5
-0.02			-0.04												
		0.53	1.63	1.06	0.81	39.2-	20.6	1.17	1.18	0.38	2.2			63.9-	33.6

SYMBOL	COMPANY	NATURE OF BUSINESS	FISCAL YEAR-END	TOTAL REV. $MILL	NET INCOME $MILL	TOTAL ASSETS $MILL	NET STK EQUITY $MILL	NO OF INST	INST. HOLDINGS (SHARES)
SOGO	Sogou Inc	IT & Communications	12/31/17	908.4	82.2	1321.0	908.2	87	22344675
SOI	Solaris Oilfield Infrastructure Inc	Industrial Machinery & Equipment	12/31/17	67.4	3.6	287.1	125.3	131	36216550
SAH	Sonic Automotive, Inc.	Retail - Automotive	12/31/17	9867.2	93.0	3818.5	786.8	226	38673950
SON	Sonoco Products Co.	Containers & Packaging	12/31/17	5036.6	175.3	4557.7	1707.1	554	92957161
SNE	Sony Corp	Household Appliances, Electronics &	3/31/18	8543982.0	490794.0	19065538.0	2967366.0	465	91327158
BID	Sotheby's	Miscellaneous Consumer Services	12/31/17	989.4	118.8	3087.3	616.8	341	68052773
SOR	Source Capital, Inc.	Holding and other Investment Office	12/31/16	7.1	3.5	357.6	355.3	85	4251535
SJI	South Jersey Industries, Inc.	Gas Utilities	12/31/17	1243.1	-3.5	3865.1	1192.4	325	74106979
SXE	Southcross Energy Partners LP	Gas Utilities	12/31/17	665.9	-67.6	1104.2		45	30489620
SO	Southern Company (The)	Electric Utilities	12/31/17	23031.0	880.0	111005.0	24491.0	1653	691240092
SCCO	Southern Copper Corp	Mining	12/31/17	6654.5	728.5	13780.1	6107.7	462	74755592
LUV	Southwest Airlines Co	Airlines/Air Freight	12/31/17	21171.0	3488.0	25110.0	10430.0	1270	568943360
SWX	Southwest Gas Holdings Inc	Gas Utilities	12/31/17	2548.8	193.8	6237.1	1814.8	398	48234057
SWN	Southwestern Energy Company	Production & Extraction	12/31/17	3203.0	1046.0	7521.0	1979.0	652	594120994
SPA	Sparton Corp	Electrical Equipment	7/2/17	397.6	1.3	217.1	81.9	111	8094190
SPE	Special Opportunities Fund Inc	Holding and other Investment Office	12/31/16	8.0	5.4	189.1	188.0	43	7161112
SEP	Spectra Energy Partners LP	Equipment & Services	12/31/17	1950.0	609.0	22056.0		339	72084936
SPB	Spectrum Brands Holdings Inc (Ne	Household & Personal Products	9/30/17	5008.5	106.0	35849.7	758.0	247	219349339
TRK	Speedway Motorsports, Inc.	Sporting & Recreational	12/31/17	453.6	148.2	1450.7	919.2	130	12630218
SR	Spire Inc	Gas Utilities	9/30/17	1740.7	161.6	6546.7	1991.3	346	47583886
SPR	Spirit AeroSystems Holdings Inc	Aerospace	12/31/17	6983.0	354.9	5267.8	1801.0	546	135948224
SAVE	Spirit Airlines Inc	Airlines/Air Freight	12/31/17	2647.7	420.6	4143.9	1777.1	328	79697588
SMTA	Spirit MTA REIT	REITs	12/31/17	231.8	-4.1	2357.7	390.9	10	89859
SMTA	Spirit MTA REIT	REITs	12/31/17	231.8	-4.1	2357.7	390.9	10	89859
SRC	Spirit Realty Capital Inc (New)	REITs	12/31/17	669.0	77.1	7263.5	3319.6	384	483895945
SPOT	Spotify Technology SA	Radio & Television	12/31/17	4090.0	-1235.0	3107.0	238.0	18	14818971
SRLP	Sprague Resources LP	Equipment & Services	12/31/17	2855.0	29.5	1363.0		49	5448272
S	Sprint Corp (New)	Services	3/31/18	32406.0	7389.0	85459.0	26356.0	673	783645217
SPXC	SPX Corp.	Industrial Machinery & Equipment	12/31/17	1425.8	89.3	2040.4	314.7	366	51416253
FLOW	SPX Flow Inc	Industrial Machinery & Equipment	12/31/17	1951.5	46.4	2689.0	964.3	241	42776303
SQ	Square Inc	IT Services	12/31/17	2214.3	-62.8	2187.3	786.3	566	222916450
JOE	St. Joe Co. (The)	Property, Real Estate & Developmen	12/31/17	98.8	59.6	921.0	577.6	215	93120447
STAG	STAG Industrial Inc	REITs	12/31/17	301.1	31.3	2680.7	1359.0	304	93367183
SSI	Stage Stores Inc	Retail - Apparel and Accessories	2/3/18	1592.3	-37.3	806.4	344.1	115	19985231
SMP	Standard Motor Products, Inc.	Auto Parts	12/31/17	1116.1	38.0	787.6	453.7	207	21626476
SXI	Standex International Corp.	Industrial Machinery & Equipment	6/30/17	755.3	46.5	867.7	408.7	226	15027903
SWK	Stanley Black & Decker Inc	Industrial Machinery & Equipment	12/30/17	12747.2	1226.0	19079.9	8297.1	1076	153657791
STN	Stantec Inc	Business Services	12/31/17	3417.3	97.0	3880.9	1896.3	1	6402
SGU	Star Group LP	Gas Utilities	9/30/17	1323.6	26.9	673.9		83	32767880
SCX	Starrett (LS) Co (The)	Industrial Machinery & Equipment	6/30/17	207.0	1.0	192.7	92.0	50	3184624
SRT	Startek, Inc.	Business Services	12/31/17	292.6	-1.3	96.0	46.9	91	7120194
STWD	Starwood Property Trust Inc.	REITs	12/31/17	879.9	400.8	62941.3	4478.4	497	213255285
STT	State Street Corp.	Banking	12/31/17	11774.0	2177.0	238425.0	22317.0	1304	395498555
SPLP PRA	Steel Partners Holdings LP	Metal Products	12/31/17	1372.0	-0.0	2164.0		31	9962492
SCS	Steelcase Inc.	Office Equipment & Furniture	2/23/18	3055.5	80.7	1859.2	813.3	299	92070952
SCM	Stellus Capital Investment Corp	Finance Intermediaries & Services	12/31/17	39.6	18.0	400.3	220.2	54	4431808
SCL	Stepan Co.	Specialty Chemicals	12/31/17	1925.0	91.6	1470.9	740.1	270	18742215
STE	Steris Plc	Medical Instruments & Equipment	3/31/18	2620.0	290.9	5200.3	3206.0		0
STL	Sterling Bancorp (DE)	Banking	12/31/17	746.7	93.0	30359.5	4240.2	80	17654994
STC	Stewart Information Services Corp	General Insurance	12/31/17	1955.7	48.7	1405.9	672.2	261	28498523
SF	Stifel Financial Corp	Finance Intermediaries & Services	12/31/17	2996.5	182.9	21384.0	2861.6	407	75028173
STM	STMicroelectronics NV	Semiconductors	12/31/17	8347.0	802.0	9681.0	5404.0	305	38575302
EDF	Stone Harbor Emerging Markets Inc	Holding and other Investment Office	11/30/16	27.4	22.5	332.9	217.9		0
EDI	Stone Harbor Emerging Markets Tot	Finance Intermediaries & Services	11/30/16	7.8	6.0	206.2	134.0	30	1254916
STON	StoneMor Partners L P	Miscellaneous Consumer Services	12/31/17	338.2	-75.2	1756.1		86	18662824
SRI	Stoneridge Inc.	Auto Parts	12/31/17	824.4	45.2	559.0	244.1	228	28797466
STOR	STORE Capital Corp	REITs	12/31/17	452.8	162.0	5899.8	3170.9	334	202462355
SYK	Stryker Corp	Medical Instruments & Equipment	12/31/17	12444.0	1020.0	22197.0	9966.0	1567	340931452
RGR	Sturm, Ruger & Co., Inc.	Leisure Equipment	FISCAL YEAR	522.3	52.1	284.3	230.1	295	20840088
SPH	Suburban Propane Partners LP	Gas Utilities	9/30/17	1187.9	38.0	2171.3		243	21564622
SMFG	Sumitomo Mitsui Financial Group In	Banking	3/31/18	4774506.0	759998.0	92175566.0	11262819.0		0
INN	Summit Hotel Properties Inc	REITs	12/31/17	515.4	99.2	2209.9	1274.5	282	120433947
SUM	Summit Materials Inc	Mining	12/30/17	1932.6	125.8	3787.3	1258.5	278	135194379
SMLP	Summit Midstream Partners LP	Equipment & Services	12/31/17	488.7	85.7	2894.8		95	38219965
SUI	Sun Communities Inc	REITs	12/31/17	982.6	76.8	6112.0	2641.5	400	89216066
SLF	Sun Life Financial Inc	Life & Health	12/31/17	29334.0	2242.0	269112.0	22971.0	419	295466088
SXC	SunCoke Energy Inc	Metal Products	12/31/17	1331.5	122.4	2060.1	426.2	261	67297239
SXCP	SunCoke Energy Partners LP	Metal Products	12/31/17	845.6	-18.1	1641.4			0
SU	Suncor Energy Inc	Refining & Marketing	12/31/17	32176.0	4458.0	89494.0	45383.0	846	1224313050
STG	Sunlands Online Education Group	IT & Communications							
SUN	Sunoco LP	Equipment & Services	12/31/17	11723.0	149.0	8344.0	2247.0	154	30148022
SHO	Sunstone Hotel Investors Inc	REITs	12/31/17	1193.6	145.4	3857.8	2533.7	307	309578145
STI 15	SunTrust Bank, Middle Georgia, N.	Banking							
STI	SunTrust Banks Inc	Banking	12/31/17	9741.0	2273.0	205962.0	25154.0	1195	521690243
SPN	Superior Energy Services, Inc.	Equipment & Services	12/31/17	1874.1	-205.9	3110.2	1132.4	447	194376662
SUP	Superior Industries International, Inc	Auto Parts	12/31/17	1108.1	-6.2	1551.3	538.5	192	27539966
SVU	Supervalu Inc	Retail - Food & Beverage, Drug & To	2/24/18	14157.0	45.0	4387.0	505.0	382	113044015
SLD	Sutherland Asset Management Cor	REITs	12/31/17	211.5	43.3	2523.5	536.1	83	10572069
SWZ	Swiss Helvetia Fund Inc (The)	Holding and other Investment Office	12/31/16	8.1	4.2	328.4	327.9	66	16102939
SWCH	Switch Inc	Services	12/31/17	378.3	-15.2	1434.8	108.9	123	36372019

| EARNINGS PER SHARE | | | | | | P/E RATIO | DIVIDENDS PER SHARE | | | AV. YLD % | DIV. DECLARED | | PRICE RANGE 2017 |
| QUARTERLY | | | ANNUAL | | | | | | | | | | |
1st	2nd	3rd	2017	2016	2015		2017	2016	2015	%	AMOUNT	PAYABLE	
-	-	-	0.20	0.11	-0.04	77.1 - 40.5	-	-	-	-	-	-	15.4 - 8.1
0.23	-	-	0.27	-0.23	-	86.9 - 42.1	-	-	-	-	-	-	23.5 - 11.4
-0.05	-	-	2.09	2.04	1.70	11.2 - 7.8	0.20	0.20	0.11	1.0	0.060Y	18/78/27	23.4 - 16.4
0.73	-	-	1.74	2.81	2.44	31.9 - 26.8	1.54	1.46	1.37	3.0	0.410Y	18/78/27	55.5 - 46.6
-	-	-228.91	56.89	117.49	-113.04	0.9 - 0.6	19.67	9.98	12.47	43.7	-	-	52.0 - 36.3
-0.12	-	-	2.20	1.27	0.63	27.1 - 19.5	-	-	0.40		0.10Y	18/78/27	59.7 - 43.0
-	-	-	0.40	0.02	-	-	-	35.23	4.00		0.250Y	6/15/18	42.7 - 38.7
1.40	-	-	-0.04	1.56	1.53	-	1.10	1.06	1.02	3.5	0.280Y	18/78/27	36.3 - 26.1
-0.21	-	-	-0.84	-1.48	-0.93	-	-	-	1.60		0.40	11/13/15	3.2 - 1.4
0.92	-	-	0.84	2.55	2.59	63.4 - 50.9	2.30	2.22	2.15	4.9	0.60Y	18/78/27	53.3 - 42.7
0.61	-	-	0.94	1.00	0.93	61.0 - 37.0	0.59	0.18	0.34	1.3	0.30	18/78/27	57.3 - 34.8
0.79	-	-	5.79	3.55	3.27	11.4 - 8.7	0.47	0.38	0.28	0.8	0.160Y	18/78/27	66.3 - 50.3
1.63	-	-	4.04	3.18	2.92	21.3 - 15.9	1.49	1.80	1.62	2.0	0.520Y	18/78/27	86.2 - 64.1
0.36	-	-	1.63	-6.32	-12.25	4.1 - 2.1	-	-	-		0.00750	18/78/27	6.7 - 3.5
-	-	0.06	0.13	-3.91	1.10	179.8 - 128.0	-	-	-		0.09070	10/5/05	23.4 - 16.6
-	-	-	-	0.63	0.41	-	-	0.81	1.19		0.21880Z	6/29/18	16.1 - 0.0
0.91	-	-	0.77	2.84	3.30	59.8 - 39.0	2.83	2.63	2.43	7.1	0.75120	5/30/18	46.0 - 30.0
-	-1.12	-	3.29	-6.14	-17.43	36.0 - 21.0	-	-	-		-	-	118.4 - 69.0
-0.07	-	-	3.61	0.96	-0.83	6.4 - 4.6	0.60	0.60	0.60	3.1	0.150Y	6/5/18	23.1 - 16.6
-	2.03	-	3.43	3.24	3.16	24.0 - 17.9	2.10	1.96	1.84	2.9	0.56250Y	18/78/27	82.3 - 61.3
1.10	-	-	3.01	3.70	5.66	34.2 - 19.4	0.40	0.10	-	0.5	0.120Y	18/78/27	102.9 - 58.3
-0.66	-	-	6.06	3.76	4.38	8.8 - 5.3	-	-	-		-	-	53.5 - 32.1
-	-	-	-	-	-	-	-	-	-		-	-	10.6 - 9.0
-	-	-	-	-	-	-	-	-	-		-	-	10.0 - 9.0
0.06	-	-	0.16	0.21	0.26	52.0 - 41.0	0.72	0.70	0.69	9.7	0.3750Z	18/78/27	8.3 - 6.6
-1.01	-	-	-8.14	-3.63	-1.62	-	-	-	-		-	-	-
3.21	-	-	1.13	0.38	3.65	24.9 - 19.4	2.40	2.16	1.92	9.6	0.65250	5/18/18	28.1 - 21.9
-	-	1.76	-0.30	-0.50	-0.85	-	-	-	-		-	-	8.9 - 4.8
0.28	-	-	2.03	-2.02	-2.03	18.6 - 11.6	-	-	0.75		0.3750Y	7/1/15	37.8 - 23.6
0.36	-	-	1.10	-9.23	2.14	49.5 - 28.6	-	-	-		-	-	54.5 - 31.5
-0.06	-	-	-0.17	-0.50	-1.24	-	-	-	-		-	-	67.6 - 22.8
0.01	-	-	0.84	0.21	-0.02	23.5 - 20.0	-	-	-		0.160Y	9/28/07	19.8 - 16.8
0.22	-	-	0.23	0.29	-0.61	125.3 - 98.2	1.41	1.39	1.37	5.3	0.42970Z	10/1/18	28.8 - 22.6
-1.14	-	-	-1.40	0.12	0.96	-	0.60	0.58	0.53	28.9	0.050Y	6/20/18	3.2 - 1.5
0.35	-	-	1.64	2.62	1.99	32.5 - 24.8	0.76	0.68	0.60	1.6	0.210Y	6/1/18	53.4 - 40.6
-	-	1.00	3.65	4.08	4.27	29.8 - 24.8	0.62	0.54	0.46	0.6	0.180Y	5/25/18	108.8 - 90.5
-	1.93	-	8.04	6.51	5.79	21.9 - 16.5	2.42	2.26	2.14	1.6	0.660Y	18/78/27	175.9 - 132.8
0.32	-	-	0.85	1.22	1.65	43.5 - 28.5	0.50	0.45	0.42	1.7	0.13750	7/12/18	37.0 - 24.2
-	0.81	-	0.46	0.70	0.59	24.7 - 19.6	0.42	0.40	0.36	4.1	0.11750	8/7/18	11.4 - 9.0
-	-	0.23	0.14	-2.01	0.75	65.9 - 42.5	0.40	0.40	0.40	5.2	0.10Z	12/29/17	9.2 - 6.0
-0.62	-	-	-0.08	0.02	-1.01	-	-	-	-		0.250Y	11/27/06	14.4 - 6.2
0.38	-	-	1.52	1.50	1.91	14.8 - 13.0	1.92	1.92	1.92	8.9	0.480Z	18/78/27	22.6 - 19.7
1.62	-	-	5.24	4.97	4.47	21.5 - 17.2	1.60	1.44	1.32	1.6	0.33430Y	18/78/27	112.7 - 90.2
-0.35	-	-	-	0.25	4.98	-	1.27	-	-	6.3	0.3750Z	6/15/18	22.5 - 0.0
0.14	-	-	1.03	1.36	0.68	15.3 - 12.1	0.48	0.45	0.42	3.4	0.1350Y	7/17/18	15.8 - 12.5
0.28	-	-	1.21	1.39	1.33	11.8 - 9.4	1.36	1.36	1.36	10.5	0.11330	10/15/18	14.3 - 11.3
1.31	-	-	3.92	3.73	3.32	23.3 - 17.5	0.84	0.78	0.73	1.1	0.2250Y	18/78/27	91.5 - 68.4
-	-	1.11	1.28	1.56	2.25	-	1.09	0.98	0.90		0.310	18/78/27	-
0.43	-	-	0.58	1.07	0.60	45.3 - 36.5	0.28	0.28	0.28	1.2	0.070Y	18/78/27	26.3 - 21.1
-0.16	-	-	2.06	1.85	-0.26	22.9 - 17.1	1.20	1.20	0.80	2.9	0.30Y	6/29/18	47.1 - 35.2
1.06	-	-	2.14	1.00	1.18	31.8 - 21.1	0.20	-	-	0.4	0.3250Z	10/15/18	68.0 - 45.2
-	-	0.26	0.89	0.19	0.12	29.5 - 16.1	0.20	0.24	0.34	0.9	-	-	26.2 - 14.3
-	-	-	1.42	2.24	-	-	-	2.16	2.16		0.180	10/25/18	17.3 - 12.9
-	-	-	0.63	1.96	-	-	-	1.81	1.81		0.15110Y	10/25/18	16.4 - 12.8
-	-	-0.25	-1.96	-0.94	-0.79	-	0.66	2.31	2.58	10.3	0.330	5/15/17	9.6 - 4.8
0.46	-	-	1.57	2.74	0.81	23.7 - 9.4	-	-	-		-	-	37.1 - 14.8
0.26	-	-	0.90	0.82	0.68	30.4 - 24.2	1.20	1.12	1.04	4.8	0.310	18/78/27	27.4 - 21.8
1.16	-	-	2.68	4.35	3.78	67.1 - 51.6	1.75	1.56	1.42	1.1	0.470Y	18/78/27	179.8 - 138.2
0.81	-	-	2.91	4.59	3.21	21.7 - 14.8	1.36	1.73	1.10	2.5	0.320Y	6/1/18	63.2 - 43.0
-	1.73	-	0.62	0.24	1.38	43.0 - 35.4	3.55	3.55	3.52	14.7	0.60	5/15/18	26.7 - 21.9
171.14	-	-	458.18	616.83	448.86	0.0 - 0.0	29.85	30.73	25.02	362.4	-	-	9.6 - 7.3
0.01	-	-	0.79	1.00	1.24	24.1 - 16.3	0.67	0.55	0.47	4.4	0.39060Z	5/31/18	19.0 - 12.9
-0.49	-	-	1.11	0.52	0.50	30.3 - 22.9	-	-	-		-	-	33.7 - 25.4
-0.18	-	-	0.98	-0.71	-6.08	25.2 - 13.4	2.30	2.30	2.27	12.1	0.5750	5/15/18	24.6 - 13.1
0.38	-	-	0.85	0.26	2.52	115.6 - 98.8	2.68	2.60	2.60	3.0	0.710Z	18/78/27	98.3 - 84.0
1.09	-	-	3.49	4.03	3.55	16.0 - 10.2	1.75	1.62	1.51	3.8	0.20820	6/29/18	55.8 - 35.7
0.13	-	-	1.88	0.22	-0.34	7.5 - 4.4	-	-	0.43		0.150	12/7/15	14.1 - 8.4
0.26	-	-	-0.54	2.07	1.92	-	2.38	2.38	2.29	13.6	0.40	9/4/18	21.7 - 14.8
0.48	-	-	2.68	0.28	-1.38	20.1 - 10.6	1.28	1.16	1.14	3.2	0.360	6/25/18	53.9 - 28.4
-	-	-	-	-	-	-	-	-	-		-	-	11.1 - 7.1
-3.74	-	-	0.34	-5.26	1.11	95.7 - 72.6	3.30	3.27	2.68	11.3	0.82550	5/15/18	32.5 - 24.7
0.15	-	-	0.59	0.55	1.62	29.7 - 24.3	0.73	0.68	1.41	4.5	0.40310Z	7/16/18	17.5 - 14.3
1.29	-	-	4.47	3.60	3.58	16.3 - 11.7	1.32	1.00	0.92	2.1	0.25560Y	18/78/27	72.8 - 52.3
-0.39	-	-	-1.35	-5.85	-12.33	-	-	0.08	0.32		0.080	18/78/27	12.5 - 7.9
0.07	-	-	-1.01	1.62	0.90	-	0.54	0.72	0.72	3.3	0.090Y	7/19/18	20.7 - 12.9
-	-	0.67	17.01	4.62	5.11	1.5 - 0.8	-	-	-		0.08750Y	18/78/27	26.2 - 13.7
0.56	-	-	1.38	1.85	-0.16	12.0 - 10.0	1.48	1.55	1.60	9.8	0.40Z	7/31/18	16.6 - 13.8
-	-	-	0.15	0.11	-	-	-	0.51	0.71		0.20250	6/29/18	13.7 - 12.0
0.02	-	-	-1.88	0.15	0.37	-	0.01	-	-	0.1	0.01470Y	6/8/18	20.8 - 12.1

SYMBOL	COMPANY	NATURE OF BUSINESS	FISCAL YEAR-END	TOTAL REV. $MILL	NET INCOME $MILL	TOTAL ASSETS $MILL	NET STK EQUITY $MILL	NO OF INST	INST. HOLDINGS (SHARES)
SYF	Synchrony Financial	Banking	12/31/17	16695.0	1935.0	95808.0	14234.0	824	738518482
SNX	Synnex Corp	IT Services	11/30/17	17045.7	301.2	7698.5	2283.7	349	35162068
SNV	Synovus Financial Corp	Banking	12/31/17	1507.8	275.5	31221.8	2961.6	486	183340362
SYY	Sysco Corp	Retail - Food & Beverage, Drug & To	7/1/17	55371.1	1142.5	17756.7	2381.5	1595	575272346
SYX	Systemax, Inc.	Retail - Appliances and Electronics	12/31/17	1265.4	40.4	551.4	211.8	142	12321291
DATA	Tableau Software Inc	Internet & Software	12/31/17	877.1	-185.6	1398.8	753.6	367	71994864
TAHO	Tahoe Resources Inc.	Precious Metals	12/31/17	733.6	81.8	3080.6	2624.9	244	213479608
TLRD	Tailored Brands Inc	Retail - Apparel and Accessories	2/3/18	3304.3	96.7	2000.0	2.2	323	62182978
TWN	Taiwan Fund, Inc. (The)	Holding and other Investment Office	8/31/17	4.7	1.7	198.6	197.6	37	8681003
TSM	Taiwan Semiconductor Manufacturi	Semiconductors	12/31/17	977442.7	343111.5	1991861.6	1522057.5	955	1183776397
TAL	TAL Education Group	Educational Services	2/28/18	1715.0	198.4	3054.6	1620.7	367	303649409
TGE	Tallgrass Energy LP	Equipment & Services	12/31/17	655.9	-128.7	4292.0		169	59786439
TALO	Talos Energy Inc	Production & Extraction							0
SKT	Tanger Factory Outlet Centers, Inc.	REITs	12/31/17	488.2	68.0	2540.1	581.6	415	119508141
TPR	Tapestry Inc	Apparel, Footwear & Accessories	7/1/17	4488.3	591.0	5831.6	3001.9	999	315181531
TRGP	Targa Resources Corp	Refining & Marketing	12/31/17	8819.8	54.0	14388.6	6376.8	545	221909413
TGT	Target Corp	Retail - General Merchandise/Depart	2/3/18	71879.0	2934.0	38999.0	11709.0	1762	583283269
TARO	Taro Pharmaceutical Industries Ltd.	Pharmaceuticals	3/31/18	661.9	211.1	2433.2	2205.2	160	6800947
TTM	Tata Motors Ltd	Autos- Manufacturing	3/31/17	2656495.1	61210.5	2666666.0	534197.0	367	76087175
TCO	Taubman Centers Inc	REITs	12/31/17	629.2	80.7	4214.6	22.2	396	83560251
TMHC	Taylor Morrison Home Corp	Builders	12/31/17	3885.3	91.2	4325.9	1596.1	244	116098240
TCP	TC PipeLines, LP	Equipment & Services	12/31/17	422.0	252.0	3559.0		246	53339227
TCF	TCF Financial Corp	Banking	12/31/17	1467.4	268.6	23002.2	2662.8	426	179076601
TSI	TCW Strategic Income Fund Inc	Holding and other Investment Office	12/31/16	14.6	12.2	284.4	277.1	89	21719533
TEL	TE Connectivity Ltd	Electrical Equipment	9/30/17	13113.0	1683.0	19403.0	9751.0	995	370604843
TISI	Team Inc	Equipment & Services	12/31/17	1200.2	-104.2	1055.8	457.5	225	45510797
FTI	TechnipFMC plc	Services	12/31/17	15056.9	113.3	28263.7	13387.9		0
TECK	Teck Resources Ltd	Mining	12/31/17	12048.0	2509.0	37058.0	19383.0	461	463200207
TK	Teekay Corp	Equipment & Services	12/31/17	1880.3	-163.3	8092.4	777.2	195	36990264
TGP	Teekay LNG Partners LP	Equipment & Services	12/31/17	432.7	63.9	5019.3		143	35947505
TOO	Teekay Offshore Partners LP	Equipment & Services	12/31/17	1110.3	-295.7	5637.8	132.2	108	316950255
TNK	Teekay Tankers Ltd	Equipment & Services	12/31/17	431.2	-58.0	2197.3	1006.6	156	91886619
TGNA	TEGNA Inc	Radio & Television	12/31/17	1903.0	273.7	4962.1	995.0	613	244640499
TRC	Tejon Ranch Co	Property, Real Estate & Developmen	12/31/17	35.7	-1.6	518.2	398.2	143	21831160
HQH	Tekla Healthcare Investors	Holding and other Investment Office	9/30/17	5.6	-5.2	1067.4	1057.6	121	9688797
THQ	Tekla Healthcare Opportunities Fun	Finance Intermediaries & Services	9/30/17	23.8	7.1	1120.7	875.7	77	8326139
HQL	Tekla Life Sciences Investors	Holding and other Investment Office	9/30/17	1.7	-3.9	468.3	466.4	73	3850803
THW	Tekla World Healthcare Fund	Holding and other Investment Office	9/30/17	13.2	3.6	602.0	479.9	55	4144932
TDOC	Teladoc Inc	Diagnostic & Health Related Service	12/31/17	233.3	-106.8	824.4	558.9	269	81673596
TLRA	Telaria Inc	Internet & Software	12/31/17	43.8	2.2	150.4	83.1	88	28257890
TEO	Telecom Argentina SA	Services	12/31/17	65319.0	7630.0	57588.0	23086.0	146	19043009
TI A	Telecom Italia SpA	Radio & Television	12/31/17	20977.0	1121.0	68783.0	21557.0	129	19934646
TDY	Teledyne Technologies Inc	Electronic Instruments & Related Pro	12/31/17	2603.8	227.2	3846.4	1947.3	416	41358124
TFX	Teleflex Incorporated	Medical Instruments & Equipment	12/31/17	2146.3	152.5	6181.5	2430.5	597	53772700
VIV	Telefonica Brasil SA	Services	12/31/17	43206.8	4608.8	101382.8	69461.4	268	179978864
TEF	Telefonica SA	Services	12/31/17	52008.0	3132.0	115066.0	16920.0	337	48853391
TDS	Telephone & Data Systems Inc	Services	12/31/17	5044.0	153.0	9295.0	4269.0	394	114428986
TU	TELUS Corp	Services	12/31/17	13202.0	1460.0	29548.0	8221.0	350	356408070
TDF	Templeton Dragon Fund, Inc.	Holding and other Investment Office	12/31/16	18.4	9.2	655.7	654.8	109	20577835
EMF	Templeton Emerging Markets Fund	Holding and other Investment Office	8/31/17	6.6	2.8	321.5	321.0	71	6401385
TEI	Templeton Emerging Markets Inco	Holding and other Investment Office	12/31/16	14.1	12.1	589.2	584.1	137	17545921
GIM	Templeton Global Income Fund (DE	Holding and other Investment Office	12/31/16	16.0	13.8	1017.0	984.4	195	46020928
TPX	Tempur Sealy International, Inc.	Furniture	12/31/17	2754.4	151.4	2694.0	112.5	386	79433174
TS	Tenaris SA	Equipment & Services	12/31/17	5288.5	544.7	14398.2	11482.2	306	115667511
THC	Tenet Healthcare Corp.	Hospitals & Health Care Facilities	12/31/17	19179.0	-704.0	23385.0	-147.0	420	197454676
TNC	Tennant Co.	Industrial Machinery & Equipment	12/31/17	1003.1	-6.2	994.0	296.5	205	18991685
TEN	Tenneco Inc	Auto Parts	12/31/17	9274.0	207.0	4842.0	696.0	416	56645120
TVC	Tennessee Valley Authority	Electric Utilities	9/30/17	10739.0	685.0	50017.0	9133.0		0
TDC	Teradata Corp (DE)	IT Services	12/31/17	2156.0	-67.0	2556.0	668.0	568	139653361
TER	Teradyne, Inc.	Semiconductors	12/31/17	2136.6	257.7	3109.5	1953.6	643	231367575
TEX	Terex Corp.	Industrial Machinery & Equipment	12/31/17	4363.4	128.7	3462.5	1222.0	510	101923990
TX	Ternium S A	Non-Precious Metals	12/31/17	9700.3	886.2	12122.6	5010.4	189	40057314
TRNO	Terreno Realty Corp	REITs	12/31/17	132.5	53.1	1567.9	1027.5	215	60154283
TTI	TETRA Technologies, Inc.	Equipment & Services	12/31/17	820.4	-39.0	1308.6	208.1	240	134822722
TEVA	Teva Pharmaceutical Industries Ltd.	Pharmaceuticals	12/31/17	22385.0	-16265.0	70615.0	17359.0	935	771189672
TPL	Texas Pacific Land Trust	Property, Real Estate & Developmen	12/31/17	132.3	76.4	127.5	79.2	178	4908588
TGH	Textainer Group Holdings Ltd	Shipping	12/31/17	490.8	19.4	4380.3	1152.5	177	16977166
TXT	Textron Inc	Aerospace	12/30/17	14198.0	307.0	15340.0	5647.0	715	249680650
GPS	The Gap Inc	Retail - Apparel and Accessories	2/3/18	15855.0	848.0	7989.0	3144.0	799	321924246
NWHM	The New Home Company Inc	Builders	12/31/17	751.2	17.2	644.5	264.0	89	13711925
TMO	Thermo Fisher Scientific Inc	Biotechnology	12/31/17	20918.0	2225.0	56669.0	25413.0	1741	433521167
THR	Thermon Group Holdings Inc	Electrical Equipment	3/31/18	308.6	11.9	662.5	334.9	132	39260069
TPRE	Third Point Reinsurance Ltd	General Insurance	12/31/17	939.0	277.8	4671.8	1764.3	197	82651427
TSLF	THL Credit Senior Loan Fund	Finance Intermediaries & Services	12/31/16	13.7	10.2	194.6	138.3	37	2266177
TRI	Thomson Reuters Corp	Publishing	12/31/17	11333.0	1395.0	26480.0	13077.0	446	216193704
THO	Thor Industries, Inc.	Autos- Manufacturing	7/31/17	7247.0	374.3	2557.9	1576.5	692	60061370
TDW	Tidewater Inc (New)	Equipment & Services	12/31/17	178.8	-39.3	1746.2	1019.7	213	37662190
TIER	Tier REIT Inc	REITs	12/31/17	216.5	84.3	1581.1	676.8	205	33834594
TIF	Tiffany & Co.	Retail - Specialty	1/31/18	4169.8	370.1	5468.1	3233.4	819	130864481
TLYS	Tilly's Inc	Retail - Apparel and Accessories	2/3/18	576.9	14.7	290.1	160.4	145	16114446

T56

| EARNINGS PER SHARE | | | | | | P/E RATIO | | DIVIDENDS PER SHARE | | | AV. YLD | DIV. DECLARED | | PRICE RANGE | |
| QUARTERLY | | | ANNUAL | | | | | | | | % | | | 2017 | |
1st	2nd	3rd	2017	2016	2015			2017	2016	2015		AMOUNT	PAYABLE		
0.83	-	-	2.42	2.71	2.65	16.6 -	11.8	0.56	0.26	-	1.7	0.150Y	18/78/27	40.2 -	28.6
0.61	-	-	7.51	5.88	5.24	18.7 -	12.7	1.05	0.85	0.57	0.9	0.350Y	18/78/27	140.7 -	95.3
0.84	-	-	2.17	1.89	1.62	26.3 -	18.7	0.60	0.48	0.42	1.2	0.250Y	18/78/27	57.1 -	40.5
-	-	0.63	2.08	1.64	1.15	32.9 -	23.6	0.97	1.23	1.18	1.7	0.360Y	18/78/27	68.3 -	49.1
0.38	-	-	1.07	-0.87	-2.69	36.8 -	16.9	0.35	0.10	-	1.2	1.7Y	7/2/18	39.4 -	18.1
-0.57	-	-	-2.35	-1.92	-1.17									104.5 -	61.2
-0.02	-	-	0.26	0.41	-0.35	42.1 -	14.8	0.14	0.24	0.24	2.5	0.020	18/78/27	10.9 -	3.8
0.27	-	-	0.51	-21.26	-0.01	68.9 -	20.0	0.72	0.72	0.72	3.5	0.180Y	9/28/18	35.2 -	10.2
-	-	-	0.20	0.12	0.07	111.3 -	97.7	-	-	2.63		0.660	1/9/18	22.3 -	19.5
-	-	3.47	13.23	12.89	11.68	3.5 -	2.6	27.95	24.45	17.90	69.9	-		46.4 -	34.5
-	0.15	-	0.66	0.60	0.41	70.9 -	30.6					-		46.8 -	20.2
0.29	-	-	-2.22	0.55	0.51			1.26	0.89	0.22	5.3	0.49750	8/14/18	28.3 -	17.6
-	-	-										-		36.4 -	30.8
0.24	-	-	0.71	2.01	2.20	39.0 -	28.2	1.35	1.26	1.30	5.7	0.350Z	18/78/27	27.7 -	20.0
-	-	0.48	2.09	1.65	1.45	26.1 -	18.6	1.35	1.35	1.35	3.0	0.33750Y	18/78/27	54.6 -	38.9
-0.03	-	-	-0.31	-1.80	1.09			3.64	3.64	3.39	7.9	23.750	18/78/27	51.4 -	40.4
1.33	-	-	4.70	5.31	-2.56	16.8 -	10.7	2.32	2.16	1.90	3.5	0.640Y	18/78/27	79.1 -	50.2
-	2.15	-	11.05	12.62	11.31							-			
-	-	3.51	18.00	28.40	39.40	2.0 -	-1.1	0.80	-	8.61	2.7			35.9 -	19.3
0.30	-	-	0.91	1.77	1.76	73.0 -	50.9	2.50	2.38	2.26	4.4	0.39060Z	18/78/27	66.4 -	46.3
0.41	-	-	1.47	1.69	1.85	19.3 -	13.5					-		28.4 -	19.8
1.32	-	-	3.16	3.21	-0.03	18.8 -	7.3	3.88	3.66	3.46	8.5	0.650	18/78/27	59.3 -	23.2
0.39	-	-	1.44	1.15	1.07	18.9 -	10.3	0.30	0.30	0.23	1.5	0.35630Y	18/78/27	27.2 -	14.8
-	-	-	0.26	0.22				-	0.28	0.21		0.06980	7/13/18	5.9 -	5.4
-	1.38	-	4.70	5.44	5.89			1.54	1.40	1.24		0.440Y	18/78/27		
-0.60	-	-	-3.49	-0.45	0.41							0.010	3/1/93	24.6 -	10.7
0.20	-	-	0.24	1932.42								0.130	6/6/18		
-	0.14	-	4.28	1.78	-4.29	9.0 -	4.1	0.60	0.10	0.20	2.1	0.050	6/29/18	38.6 -	17.6
-0.21	-	-	-1.89	-1.62	1.13			0.22	0.22	1.73		0.0550	8/15/18		
-	-	-	0.25	1.69	2.21			0.56	-			0.140	8/10/18		
0.03	-	-	-1.45	-0.25	0.32			0.14	0.44	2.18		0.55470	8/15/18		
-0.07	-	-	-0.31	0.40	1.35			0.12	0.18	0.24		0.030	3/9/18		
0.25	-	-	1.26	1.99	2.00	12.4 -	8.0	0.35	0.56	0.68	2.7	0.070Y	18/78/27	15.6 -	10.1
0.06	-	-	-0.07	0.03	0.14			-	-	-		0.0250	12/10/99	25.9 -	18.7
-	-	-	-0.13	-0.17	-0.22			1.96	3.10	2.61	8.4	0.470	6/29/18	26.2 -	20.5
-	-	-	0.16	0.18	0.11	118.3 -	100.6	1.35	1.65	1.35	7.7	0.11250	7/31/18	18.9 -	16.1
-	-	-	-0.18	-0.19	-0.25			1.59	2.85	2.09	7.9	0.40	6/29/18	22.2 -	18.1
-	-	-	0.12	0.09	-0.02	127.3 -	104.3	1.40	1.40	0.23	10.2	0.11670	7/31/18	15.3 -	12.5
-0.39	-	-	-1.93	-1.75	-2.91							-		62.4 -	28.1
-0.12	-	-	0.04	-0.40	-0.84	131.8 -	51.2					-		5.3 -	2.0
-	-	0.89	7.87	4.10	3.51	5.0 -	2.3	20.84	9.51	3.36	67.2	-		39.7 -	17.7
-	-	-	0.05	0.08	0.00	186.2 -	129.2					-		9.3 -	6.5
1.81	-	-	6.26	5.37	5.44	34.1 -	20.5					-		213.8 -	128.1
1.20	-	-	3.27	4.98	5.10	88.0 -	62.1	1.36	1.36	1.36	0.5	0.340Y	18/78/27	287.6 -	203.0
-	-	-	2.56	2.27	2.15	6.7 -	4.5	2.41	1.84	3.35	16.2	-		17.2 -	11.6
-	-	0.15	0.56	0.42	0.51	20.5 -	15.1	0.40	0.73	0.89	4.0	-		11.5 -	8.5
0.34	-	-	1.37	0.39	1.98	21.8 -	17.7	0.62	0.59	0.56	2.3	0.160Z	18/78/27	29.9 -	24.3
0.69	-	-	2.46	2.06	2.29	19.8 -	14.0	1.97	1.84	1.68	4.8	0.5250	7/3/18	48.8 -	34.4
-	-	-	0.27	0.30				-	1.69	4.01		1.366C	9/25/17	24.6 -	20.1
-	-	-	0.16	0.19	0.21	112.1 -	89.3	0.20	1.28	1.18	1.2	0.8687C	12/29/17	17.9 -	14.3
-	-	-	-	0.25	0.93			-	0.80	1.14		0.07190	7/31/18	11.9 -	10.2
-	-	-	-	0.10	0.33			-	0.30	0.64		0.03090Z	7/31/18	6.8 -	6.1
0.42	-	-	2.77	3.38	1.17	24.4 -	15.1					0.080Y	18/78/27	67.6 -	41.8
-	-	0.09	0.46	0.05	-0.07	87.7 -	56.5	0.82	0.86	0.90	2.5	-		40.4 -	26.0
0.96	-	-	-7.00	-1.93	-1.41							0.0267F	18/78/27	38.4 -	12.7
0.18	-	-	-0.35	2.59	1.74			0.84	0.81	0.80	1.2	0.210Y	18/78/27	80.7 -	60.2
1.13	-	-	3.91	6.44	4.11	16.7 -	11.2	1.00	-	-	1.8	0.250Y	18/78/27	65.3 -	44.0
-	-	-	-	-	-			0.84	0.84	0.95	3.3	0.22190Z	12/1/18	25.9 -	23.8
-0.06	-	-	-0.53	0.95	-1.53							-		44.0 -	28.4
0.43	-	-	1.28	-0.21	0.97	39.0 -	23.2	0.28	0.24	0.24	0.7	0.090Y	18/78/27	49.9 -	29.7
0.62	-	-	1.36	-1.63	1.33	36.6 -	26.4	0.32	0.28	0.24	0.8	0.10	18/78/27	49.8 -	35.8
-	-	0.05	0.45	0.30	0.00	93.8 -	60.4	1.00	0.90	0.90	3.0	-		42.2 -	27.2
0.18	-	-	0.95	0.26	0.26	41.1 -	33.8	0.84	0.76	0.66	2.3	0.220Z	7/20/18	39.0 -	32.1
-0.46	-	-	-0.34	-1.85	-1.59							-		4.8 -	1.9
1.03	-	-	-16.26	0.07	1.82			0.72	1.16	1.16	3.7	17.50	12/15/17	33.3 -	11.2
5.60	-	-	9.72	4.66	6.10	73.7 -	29.8	1.35	0.31	0.29	0.3	3.7Y	3/16/18	716.0 -	289.8
0.33	-	-	0.34	-0.89	1.87			-	0.51	1.65		0.03D	8/30/16		
0.72	-	-	1.14	3.53	2.50	60.8 -	41.6	0.08	0.08	0.08	0.1	0.020Y	18/78/27	69.3 -	47.4
0.42	-	-	1.69	2.23	2.87	21.0 -	12.6	0.92	0.92	0.88	3.1	0.24250Y	18/78/27	35.5 -	21.2
-0.03	-	-	0.82	1.01	1.28	16.4 -	11.8					-		13.4 -	9.7
1.43	-	-	5.59	5.09	4.92	40.1 -	30.7	0.60	0.60	0.60	0.3	0.170Y	18/78/27	224.1 -	171.7
-	-	0.02	0.45	0.71	1.52	54.8 -	35.5					-		24.7 -	16.0
-0.26	-	-	2.64	0.26	-0.84							-			
-	-	-	-	-	1.36			-	1.27	1.35		0.0960	7/31/18	18.1 -	16.4
-0.48	-	-	1.94	4.13	1.60	31.4 -	0.0	1.38	1.36	1.34	2.8	0.3450	6/15/18	60.9 -	0.0
-	-	2.53	7.09	4.88	3.74	22.1 -	13.1	1.32	1.20	1.08	1.1	0.370Y	18/78/27	157.0 -	92.6
-1.67	-	-	-1.82	-3.41	-1.34			-	0.75	1.00		-		35.1 -	0.7
0.17	-	-	1.75	-0.62	-0.66	13.7 -	9.9	0.72	0.72	0.36	3.7	0.180Y	6/29/18	24.0 -	17.2
1.14	-	-	3.55	3.59	3.73	38.8 -	24.7	1.75	1.58	1.48	1.7	0.550Y	18/78/27	137.9 -	87.5
0.04	-	-	0.40	0.27	0.50	41.3 -	21.5					1.7	2/20/18	16.5 -	8.6

SYMBOL	COMPANY	NATURE OF BUSINESS	FISCAL YEAR-END	TOTAL REV. $MILL	NET INCOME $MILL	TOTAL ASSETS $MILL	NET STK EQUITY $MILL	NO OF INST	INST. HOLDINGS (SHARES)
TSU	TIM Participacoes S.A.	Services	12/31/17	16234.0	1234.5	32600.4	18151.2	180	78625435
TKR	Timken Co. (The)	Industrial Machinery & Equipment	12/31/17	3003.8	203.4	3402.4	1442.7	506	74134286
TMST	Timkensteel Corp	Metal Products	12/31/17	1329.2	-43.8	1156.6	560.7	211	38972005
TWI	Titan International Inc	Industrial Machinery & Equipment	12/31/17	1468.9	-60.0	1290.1	320.9	231	69089414
TJX	TJX Companies, Inc.	Retail - Apparel and Accessories	2/3/18	35864.7	2607.9	14058.0	5148.3	1629	675816488
TOL	Toll Brothers Inc.	Builders	10/31/17	5815.1	535.5	9445.2	4531.2	664	164813367
TR	Tootsie Roll Industries Inc	Food	12/31/17	519.3	80.9	930.9	733.8	246	16874224
BLD	TopBuild Corp	Builders	12/31/17	1906.3	158.1	1749.5	996.5	341	40108131
TMK	Torchmark Corp	Life & Health	12/31/17	4155.6	1454.5	23475.0	6231.4	680	108057092
TTC	Toro Company (The)	Industrial Machinery & Equipment	10/31/17	2505.2	267.7	1493.8	617.1	527	97740770
TD	Toronto Dominion Bank	Banking	10/31/17	45583.0	10203.0	1278995.0	74207.0	791	1017119711
NDP	Tortoise Energy Independence Fun	Holding and other Investment Office	11/30/16	2.3	-1.8	319.3	246.1	44	2235161
TYG	Tortoise Energy Infrastructure Corp	Holding and other Investment Office	11/30/16	3.6	-38.0	2593.7	1412.3	222	19117710
NTG	Tortoise MLP Fund Inc	Holding and other Investment Office	11/30/16	0.4	-21.7	1514.4	904.9		0
TTP	Tortoise Pipeline & Energy Fund Inc	Holding and other Investment Office	11/30/16	6.0	0.4	304.0	234.5	48	2905258
TPZ	Tortoise Power & Energy Infrastruct	Holding and other Investment Office	11/30/16	8.0	5.0	217.4	166.1	52	1921651
TOT	Total SA	Production & Extraction	12/31/17	149099.0	8631.0	242631.0	111556.0	847	196248849
TSS	Total System Services, Inc.	Business Services	12/31/17	4928.0	586.2	6331.7	2241.0	746	176591059
TOWR	Tower International Inc	Auto Parts	12/31/17	1988.0	47.6	1260.1	269.9	195	20963207
TSQ	Townsquare Media Inc	Radio & Television	12/31/17	507.4	-11.2	1056.4	380.0	92	10019410
TM	Toyota Motor Corp	Autos- Manufacturing	3/31/18	29379510.0	2493983.0	50308249.0	19227956.0	509	15768104
TPGE	TPG Pace Energy Holdings Corp	Business Services	12/31/17		1.5	653.9	629.4	29	8992610
TPGH U	TPG Pace Holdings Corp	Business Services	12/31/17		-0.4	450.5	434.6	27	23003738
TRTX	TPG RE Finance Trust Inc	REITs	12/31/17	200.6	94.4	3355.4	1201.3	81	24156910
TSLX	TPG Specialty Lending Inc	Credit & Lending	12/31/17	210.9	120.3	1720.2	969.3	156	41003318
TAC	TransAlta Corp	Electric Utilities	12/31/17	2307.0	-160.0	10304.0	3326.0	126	175473565
TRP	TransCanada Corp	Equipment & Services	12/31/17	13449.0	3157.0	86101.0	25039.0	602	622644355
TCI	Transcontinental Realty Investors, I	Property, Real Estate & Development	12/31/17	125.2	-15.8	1313.4	189.2	39	235630
TDG	TransDigm Group Inc	Aerospace	9/30/17	3504.3	596.9	9975.7	-2951.2	588	65938557
TLP	TransMontaigne Partners LP	Equipment & Services	12/31/17	183.3	48.5	987.0		101	12523771
RIG	Transocean Ltd	Equipment & Services	12/31/17	2973.0	-3127.0	22410.0	12707.0	691	398431013
TGS	Transportadora de Gas del Sur S.A.	Equipment & Services	12/31/17	12246.7	2793.3	13666.9	5319.6		0
TRU	TransUnion	Miscellaneous Consumer Services	12/31/17	1933.8	441.2	5118.5	1728.7	363	187924737
TRV	Travelers Companies Inc (The)	General Insurance	12/31/17	28902.0	2056.0	103483.0	23731.0	1547	305674829
TVPT	Travelport Worldwide Ltd	Hotels, Restaurants & Travel	12/31/17	2447.3	142.5	2858.5	-202.3	278	135906823
TREC	Trecora Resources	Refining & Marketing	12/31/17	245.1	18.0	327.3	184.7	85	12661006
TG	Tredegar Corp.	Plastics	12/31/17	1013.0	38.3	755.7	343.8	197	25716473
THS	TreeHouse Foods Inc	Food	12/31/17	6307.1	-286.2	5779.3	2263.3	399	73526564
TREX	Trex Co Inc	Metal Products	12/31/17	565.2	95.1	326.2	231.3	374	33320311
TPH	TRI Pointe Group Inc	Builders	12/31/17	2808.9	187.2	3805.4	1929.7	321	195590251
TY	Tri-Continental Corp.	Holding and other Investment Office	12/31/17	59.3	51.6	1677.4	1675.2	135	11258017
TCAP	Triangle Capital Corp	Holding and other Investment Office	12/31/17	123.0	72.2	1223.1	641.3	158	25545355
TRCO	Tribune Media Co	Radio & Television	12/31/17	1849.0	194.1	8169.3	3217.1	292	91659310
TNET	Trinet Group Inc.	Services	12/31/17	3275.0	178.0	2593.0	206.0	244	67023020
TRN	Trinity Industries, Inc.	Industrial Machinery & Equipment	12/31/17	3662.8	702.5	9543.2	4501.1	575	162772484
TSE	Trinseo SA	Synthetic Materials	12/31/17	4448.1	328.3	2772.0	674.8	275	45168253
GTS	Triple-S Management Corp	Life & Health	12/31/17	2916.1	54.5	3116.8	913.4	165	23977709
TPVG	TriplePoint Venture Growth BDC Co	Finance Intermediaries & Services	12/31/17	51.5	26.3	510.3	234.9	63	7419498
TRTN	Triton International Ltd	Business Services	12/31/17	1200.9	344.6	9577.6	2076.3	240	55689798
TGI	Triumph Group Inc.	Aerospace	3/31/18	3199.0	-425.4	3807.1	450.5	342	81133511
TROX	Tronox Ltd	Specialty Chemicals	12/31/17	1698.0	-285.0	4864.0	829.0		0
TBI	TrueBlue Inc	Business Services	12/31/17	2508.8	55.5	1109.0	554.8	267	48905639
TNP	Tsakos Energy Navigation Ltd	Equipment & Services	12/31/17	529.2	7.6	3373.6	1494.3	109	25768399
TUP	Tupperware Brands Corp	Plastics	12/30/17	2255.8	-265.4	1388.0	-119.4	581	60348051
TKC	Turkcell Iletisim Hizmetleri AS	Services	12/31/17	17632.1	1979.1	33982.5	14989.2	175	36214460
TPB	Turning Point Brands Inc	Tobacco Products	12/31/17	285.8	20.2	282.3	53.3	80	4578360
TRQ	Turquoise Hill Resources Ltd.	Precious Metals	12/31/16	1203.3	210.6	12460.2	8726.9	245	737025962
TPC	Tutor Perini Corp	Construction Services	12/31/17	4757.2	148.4	4264.1	1713.3	25	447716
TWLO	Twilio Inc	Internet & Software	12/31/17	399.0	-63.7	449.8	359.8	274	60778114
TWTR	Twitter Inc	Internet & Software	12/31/17	2443.3	-108.1	7412.5	5047.2	785	491993077
TWO	Two Harbors Investment Corp	REITs	12/31/17	778.7	348.6	24789.3	3571.4	388	167439636
TWO	Two Harbors Investment Corp	REITs	12/31/17	778.7	348.6	24789.3	3571.4	388	167439636
TYL	Tyler Technologies, Inc.	Internet & Software	12/31/17	840.7	163.9	1589.6	1167.1	438	46700589
TSN	Tyson Foods Inc	Food	9/30/17	38260.0	1774.0	28066.0	10541.0	969	325523497
USPH	U.S. Physical Therapy, Inc.	Hospitals & Health Care Facilities	12/31/17	414.1	22.3	419.0	204.9	233	15523855
UBS	UBS Group AG	Holding and other Investment Office	12/31/17	36860.0	1053.0	915642.0	51214.0		0
UDR	UDR Inc	REITs	12/31/17	995.8	121.6	7733.3	2825.8	534	353268795
UGI	UGI Corp.	Gas Utilities	9/30/17	6120.7	436.6	11582.2	3163.3	659	169751205
UGP	Ultrapar Participacoes SA	Equipment & Services	12/31/17	80007.4	1574.3	28340.3	9381.3	144	34073402
UMH	UMH Properties Inc	REITs	12/31/17	112.6	12.7	823.9	421.2	161	22481046
UAA	Under Armour Inc	Apparel, Footwear & Accessories	12/31/17	4976.6	-48.3	4006.4	2018.6	655	183761065
UFI	Unifi, Inc.	Textiles	6/25/17	647.3	32.9	571.5	360.8	188	18207051
UNF	Unifirst Corp	Business Services	8/26/17	1591.0	70.2	1819.1	1453.2	293	20714341
UN	Unilever N.V.	Household & Personal Products	12/31/17	53715.0	6053.0	60285.0	13629.0	749	182084915
UL	Unilever Plc	Household & Personal Products	12/31/17	53715.0	6053.0	60285.0	13629.0	803	124910946
LTN	Union Acquisition Corp	Business Services	1/31/18		-0.0	0.2	0.0		0
UNP	Union Pacific Corp	Rail	12/31/17	21240.0	10712.0	57806.0	24856.0	2196	724033535
UIS	Unisys Corp	IT Services	12/31/17	2741.8	-65.3	2542.4	-1354.7	270	98041359
UNT	Unit Corp.	Production & Extraction	12/31/17	739.6	117.8	2581.5	1345.6	294	61748742
UAL	United Continental Holdings Inc	Airlines/Air Freight	12/31/17	37736.0	2131.0	42326.0	8806.0	782	326328174

| EARNINGS PER SHARE | | | | | | P/E RATIO | | DIVIDENDS PER SHARE | | | AV. YLD | DIV. DECLARED | | PRICE RANGE | |
| QUARTERLY | | | ANNUAL | | | | | | | | | | | 2017 | |
1st	2nd	3rd	2017	2016	2015			2017	2016	2015	%	AMOUNT	PAYABLE		
-	-	0.13	0.51	0.31	0.86	45.0-	29.2	0.50	0.89	0.66	2.6	-	-	22.9-	14.9
1.02	-	-	2.58	1.92	-0.84	21.5-	16.6	1.07	1.04	1.03	2.3	0.280Y	18/78/27	55.5-	42.8
-0.04	-	-	-0.99	-2.39	-1.63	-	-	-	-	0.42	-	0.140Y	9/10/15	19.7-	12.8
0.23	-	-	-1.12	-0.81	-1.74	-	-	0.02	0.02	0.02	0.2	0.0050Y	7/16/18	14.2-	8.1
1.13	-	-	3.46	3.33	3.15	28.0-	19.3	0.99	0.81	0.67	1.3	0.390Y	18/78/27	96.7-	66.9
-	0.72	-	3.17	2.18	1.97	16.6-	11.4	0.24	-	-	0.6	0.110Y	18/78/27	52.5-	36.0
0.13	-	-	1.24	1.02	0.99	30.1-	22.4	0.35	0.34	0.32	1.1	0.090Y	18/78/27	37.3-	27.8
0.74	-	-	4.32	1.92	2.09	20.1-	12.1	-	-	-	-	-	-	87.0-	52.3
1.49	-	-	12.22	4.49	4.16	7.6-	6.1	0.59	0.56	0.41	0.7	0.160Y	18/78/27	93.3-	74.7
-	1.21	-	2.41	2.06	1.77	30.6-	24.1	0.70	0.60	0.50	1.1	0.20Y	18/78/27	73.7-	58.0
-	1.54	-	5.50	4.67	4.21	14.0-	9.1	2.35	2.16	2.00	3.7	0.4475GH	7/31/18	77.0-	50.1
-	-	-	-0.12	-0.10	-	-	-	-	1.75	1.75	-	0.43750	5/31/18	14.9-	10.8
-	-	-	-0.78	-0.62	-	-	-	-	2.62	2.59	-	0.6550	5/31/18	32.1-	24.5
-	-	-	-0.46	-0.32	-	-	-	-	1.69	1.69	-	0.42250	8/31/18	21.1-	15.1
-	-	-	0.04	0.22	-	-	-	-	1.63	1.95	-	0.40750	5/31/18	20.2-	15.8
-	-	-	0.71	0.88	-	-	-	-	1.54	2.86	-	0.1250	8/31/18	21.7-	17.7
0.99	-	-	3.34	2.52	2.16	19.2-	14.5	2.82	2.70	2.70	5.0	-	-	64.2-	48.5
0.77	-	-	3.16	1.73	1.97	28.7-	18.2	0.46	0.40	0.40	0.6	0.130Y	18/78/27	90.7-	57.6
0.83	-	-	2.29	1.82	9.06	15.0-	9.4	0.45	0.41	0.10	1.6	0.120	9/7/18	34.3-	21.6
-1.44	-	-	-0.56	0.85	0.37	-	-	-	-	-	-	0.0750Y	8/15/18	11.4-	6.1
-	-	314.99	599.21	735.36	687.66	0.2-	0.2	417.35	448.34	351.14	331.4	-	-	140.7-	106.0
-0.02	-	-	0.02	-	-	543.5-	0.0	-	-	-	-	-	-	10.9-	0.0
0.02	-	-	-0.01	-	-	-	-	-	-	-	-	-	-	-	-
0.42	-	-	1.74	2.09	2.23	12.0-	10.6	0.71	1.99	2.41	3.6	0.430Z	7/25/18	20.9-	18.4
0.51	-	-	1.86	1.83	1.18	11.6-	9.4	1.75	1.56	1.56	8.9	0.390Y	7/13/18	21.6-	17.5
0.23	-	-	-0.66	0.41	-0.09	-	-	0.16	0.16	0.72	2.5	0.33120	9/30/18	8.4-	4.8
0.83	-	-	3.43	0.16	-1.75	18.9-	0.0	2.50	2.26	2.08	4.7	0.30630	5/31/18	64.7-	0.0
-0.05	-	-	-1.92	-0.10	-0.98	-	-	-	-	-	-	0.180	9/29/00	51.6-	0.0
-	3.53	-	7.88	10.39	7.84	43.9-	31.8	46.00	-	-	15.8	22.7Y	18/78/27	346.0-	250.4
0.52	-	-	2.20	2.14	2.12	21.6-	15.8	2.93	2.74	2.66	7.3	0.7950	8/8/18	47.5-	34.8
-0.48	-	-	-8.00	2.08	2.16	-	-	-	-	-	-	0.150	18/78/27	-	-
-	-	-0.06	3.52	1.17	-0.22	6.7-	3.4	-	0.41	-	-	-	-	23.7-	12.1
0.38	-	-	2.32	0.65	0.04	31.4-	17.9	-	-	-	-	0.075GY	18/78/27	72.9-	41.6
-	1.92	-	7.33	10.28	10.88	20.5-	15.7	2.83	2.62	2.38	2.1	0.770Y	18/78/27	150.0-	115.2
0.47	-	-	1.13	0.14	0.13	-	-	0.30	-	-	-	0.0750	6/21/18	-	-
0.09	-	-	0.72	0.78	0.74	20.7-	14.5	-	-	-	-	-	-	14.9-	10.4
0.55	-	-	1.16	0.75	-0.99	21.2-	12.8	0.44	0.44	0.42	2.4	0.110Y	7/1/18	24.6-	14.9
-0.60	-	-	-5.01	-4.10	2.63	-	-	-	-	-	-	-	-	85.7-	36.6
0.63	-	-	1.61	1.15	0.76	41.0-	21.0	-	-	-	-	-	-	66.0-	33.8
0.28	-	-	1.21	1.21	1.27	16.0-	10.2	-	-	-	-	-	-	19.4-	12.4
-	-	-	0.93	0.90	0.81	30.3-	26.1	1.17	0.91	0.81	4.5	0.2295C	6/28/18	28.2-	24.3
0.27	-	-	1.55	1.62	2.16	11.5-	6.0	1.65	1.89	2.36	13.6	1.786	8/3/18	17.8-	9.3
1.60	-	-	2.20	0.16	-3.38	19.8-	15.9	6.77	1.00	7.48	16.7	0.250	18/78/27	43.6-	34.9
0.75	-	-	2.49	0.85	0.45	22.8-	12.9	-	-	-	-	-	-	56.9-	32.2
0.26	-	-	4.52	2.25	5.08	8.4-	6.0	0.48	0.44	0.42	1.5	0.130Y	18/78/27	37.9-	27.0
2.71	-	-	7.30	6.70	2.73	-	-	1.38	-	-	-	0.40	7/25/18	-	-
0.17	-	-	2.26	0.71	2.02	19.2-	6.7	-	-	-	-	-	-	43.3-	15.2
0.34	-	-	1.61	1.42	1.46	8.8-	7.1	1.44	1.44	1.44	11.2	0.360	6/15/18	14.2-	11.5
1.00	-	-	4.52	-0.24	2.17	-	-	1.80	1.35	-	-	0.52D	6/22/18	-	-
-	-	-2.29	-0.87	-21.29	4.68	-	-	0.16	0.16	0.16	0.6	0.040Y	6/15/18	34.3-	18.7
-0.36	-	-	-2.39	-0.50	-2.75	-	-	0.18	-	-	-	0.0450	6/1/18	-	-
0.22	-	-	1.34	-0.37	1.71	21.9-	14.6	-	-	-	-	-	-	29.3-	19.6
0.25	-	-	-0.19	0.47	1.69	-	-	0.20	-	-	-	0.55470	7/30/18	-	-
0.70	-	-	-5.22	4.41	3.69	-	-	2.72	2.72	2.72	4.9	0.680Y	18/78/27	70.4-	40.2
-	-	0.16	0.90	0.68	0.94	12.4-	6.7	2.81	-	3.73	31.4	-	-	11.1-	6.0
0.15	-	-	1.04	1.49	1.10	30.8-	14.0	0.04	-	-	0.2	0.040Y	7/13/18	32.1-	14.5
0.04	-	-	-	0.10	0.16	-	-	-	-	-	-	-	-	4.5-	2.6
-0.24	-	-	2.92	1.92	0.91	10.2-	6.3	-	-	-	-	1.7Y	11/12/10	29.6-	18.4
-0.25	-	-	-0.70	-0.78	-2.19	-	-	-	-	-	-	-	-	61.6-	23.6
0.08	-	-	-0.15	-0.65	-0.79	-	-	-	-	-	-	-	-	46.8-	15.8
1.69	-	-	1.81	2.02	2.70	9.3-	7.9	0.47	1.86	2.08	3.0	0.1584HZ	7/30/18	16.8-	14.2
1.69	-	-	1.81	2.02	2.70	9.2-	0.0	0.47	1.86	2.08	3.6	0.1584HZ	7/30/18	16.7-	0.0
0.95	-	-	4.18	2.82	1.77	57.2-	40.1	-	-	-	-	-	-	239.2-	167.5
-	0.85	-	4.79	4.53	2.95	17.5-	12.2	0.90	0.60	0.40	1.3	0.270Y	18/78/27	83.6-	58.6
0.27	-	-	1.76	1.64	1.77	57.2-	32.3	0.80	0.68	0.60	1.1	0.230Z	6/8/18	100.8-	56.9
-	0.31	-	0.27	0.84	1.64	-	-	-	-	-	-	0.650	5/9/18	-	-
0.30	-	-	0.44	1.08	1.29	91.0-	74.8	1.23	1.16	1.09	3.3	0.32250Z	18/78/27	40.0-	32.9
-	1.57	-	2.46	2.08	1.60	21.2-	17.3	0.97	0.93	0.89	2.0	0.260Y	18/78/27	52.2-	42.5
-	-	0.61	2.88	2.86	2.74	9.0-	3.9	1.70	1.64	1.44	8.0	-	-	25.9-	11.4
-0.76	-	-	0.39	0.42	0.08	44.3-	29.9	0.72	0.72	0.72	4.9	0.39840Z	9/17/18	17.3-	11.7
-0.07	-	-	-0.22	0.45	0.53	-	-	-	-	-	-	-	-	24.3-	11.6
-	-	0.01	1.78	1.87	2.24	21.8-	16.6	-	-	-	-	0.140	5/8/98	38.9-	29.6
-	-	1.85	3.44	6.17	6.15	54.4-	39.8	0.15	0.15	0.15	0.1	0.090Y	9/28/18	187.1-	136.8
-	-	-	2.15	1.82	1.72	28.6-	24.2	1.23	1.26	1.20	2.2	-	-	61.4-	52.0
-	-	-	2.15	1.82	1.72	27.9-	23.8	1.37	1.26	1.18	2.5	-	-	59.9-	51.2
-0.07	-	-	-0.01	-	-	-	-	-	-	-	-	-	-	-	-
-	1.98	-	13.36	5.07	5.49	11.0-	7.6	2.48	2.25	2.20	2.0	0.730Y	18/78/27	147.0-	101.4
0.62	-	-	-1.30	-0.95	-2.20	-	-	-	-	-	-	1.56250Y	12/1/13	13.8-	7.0
0.15	-	-	2.28	-2.71	-21.12	11.6-	6.8	-	-	-	-	-	-	26.5-	15.4
-	2.48	-	7.02	6.85	19.47	11.5-	8.1	-	-	-	-	2.15G7Y	18/78/27	80.5-	57.2

SYMBOL	COMPANY	NATURE OF BUSINESS	FISCAL YEAR-END	TOTAL REV. $MILL	NET INCOME $MILL	TOTAL ASSETS $MILL	NET STK EQUITY $MILL	NO OF INST	INST. HOLDINGS (SHARES)
UMC	United Microelectronics Corp	Semiconductors	12/31/17	149284.7	9628.7	394099.2	213080.8	170	185679779
UPS	United Parcel Service Inc	Airlines/Air Freight	12/31/17	65872.0	4910.0	45403.0	1000.0	1967	588955347
URI	United Rentals Inc	Construction Services	12/31/17	6641.0	1346.0	15030.0	3106.0	920	101649939
USM	United States Cellular Corp	Services	12/31/17	3890.0	12.0	6841.0	3677.0	176	15195161
X	United States Steel Corp.	Non-Precious Metals	12/31/17	12250.0	387.0	9862.0	3320.0	687	154760620
UTX	United Technologies Corp	Aerospace	12/31/17	59837.0	4552.0	96920.0	29610.0	2414	828160613
UNH	UnitedHealth Group Inc	Life & Health	12/31/17	201159.0	10558.0	139058.0	47776.0	2253	1008368692
UTL	UNITIL Corp	Electric Utilities	12/31/17	406.2	29.0	1241.9	336.8	197	11576317
UNVR	Univar Inc	Specialty Chemicals	12/31/17	8253.7	119.8	5732.7	1090.1	231	138946726
UVV	Universal Corp	Tobacco Products	3/31/18	2033.9	105.7	2168.6	1342.4	286	28986826
UHT	Universal Health Realty Income Tru	REITs	12/31/17	72.3	45.6	490.0	210.6	215	10540911
UHS	Universal Health Services, Inc.	Hospitals & Health Care Facilities	12/31/17	10409.9	752.3	10761.8	4989.5	652	107530794
UVE	Universal Insurance Holdings, Inc	General Insurance	12/31/17	751.9	106.9	1455.0	440.0	256	29670518
UTI	Universal Technical Institute, Inc.	Educational Services	9/30/17	324.3	-8.1	274.1	125.8	95	20049991
UNM	Unum Group	Life & Health	12/31/17	11286.8	994.2	64013.1	9574.9	809	269627729
UE	Urban Edge Properties	REITs	12/31/17	407.0	67.1	2820.8	889.9	260	122917386
UBA	Urstadt Biddle Properties Inc	REITs	10/31/17	123.6	52.9	996.7	587.2	41	845903
USB	US Bancorp (DE)	Banking	12/31/17	23996.0	6218.0	462040.0	49040.0	1999	1480347133
USFD	US Foods Holding Corp	Retail - Food & Beverage, Drug & To	12/30/17	24147.2	444.3	9037.2	2751.4	341	220195467
SLCA	US Silica Holdings, Inc.	Mining	12/31/17	1240.9	145.2	2307.3	1396.5	412	91043796
USX	US Xpress Enterprises Inc	Trucking	12/31/06	1471.8	20.1	903.4	252.5	7	1143001
USAC	USA Compression Partners LP	Equipment & Services	12/31/17	280.2	11.4	1492.1		84	58556917
USNA	USANA Health Sciences Inc	Household & Personal Products	12/30/17	1047.3	62.5	519.3	363.2	236	13453368
USB PRI	USB Capital X	Banking						1	15070
USDP	USD Partners LP	Rail	12/31/17	111.3	22.2	307.4		35	8397700
USG	USG Corp	Construction Materials	12/31/17	3204.0	88.0	3851.0	1845.0	407	127797326
EGY	VAALCO Energy, Inc.	Production & Extraction	12/31/17	77.0	9.7	79.6	10.3	104	36827393
MTN	Vail Resorts Inc	Sporting & Recreational	7/31/17	1907.2	210.6	4110.7	1571.2	556	48097580
RIO 34	Vale Overseas Ltd	Finance Intermediaries & Services	12/31/05	84.1	0.0	1289.4	-0.0		0
VALE	Vale SA	Non-Precious Metals	12/31/17	33967.0	5507.0	99184.0	43458.0	583	1169891740
VALE	Vale SA	Non-Precious Metals	12/31/17	33967.0	5507.0	99184.0	43458.0	583	1169891740
VLO	Valero Energy Corp	Refining & Marketing	12/31/17	93980.0	4065.0	50158.0	21991.0	1540	434118117
VLP	Valero Energy Partners LP	Equipment & Services	12/31/17	452.0	238.4	1517.4		132	21229518
VHI	Valhi, Inc.	Specialty Chemicals	12/31/17	1904.6	207.5	2907.5	424.4	120	11929198
VLY	Valley National Bancorp (NJ)	Banking	12/31/17	945.9	161.9	24003.2	2533.2	390	220296560
VMI	Valmont Industries Inc	Construction Materials	12/30/17	2746.0	116.2	2602.3	1112.8	394	26578380
VVV	Valvoline Inc	Specialty Chemicals	9/30/17	2084.0	304.0	1915.0	-117.0	372	206586726
VAR	Varian Medical Systems Inc	Medical Instruments & Equipment	9/29/17	2668.2	249.6	3179.4	1495.0	857	117869815
VGR	Vector Group Ltd	Tobacco Products	12/31/17	1807.5	84.6	1328.3	-413.9	310	81433369
VVC	Vectren Corp	Electric Utilities	12/31/17	2657.3	216.0	6239.3	1849.3	524	70896210
VVC 13	Vectren Utility Holdings Inc.	Electric Utilities	12/31/17	1382.6	175.8	5497.8	1722.8	-	0
VEC	Vectrus Inc	Services	12/31/17	1114.8	59.5	495.6	183.4	213	11671329
VEDL	Vedanta Ltd	Non-Precious Metals	3/31/17	807518.4	55122.1	1990296.0	605001.1	169	48004125
VEEV	Veeva Systems Inc	IT Services	1/31/18	685.6	142.0	1197.0	871.5	491	113161987
VNTR	Venator Materials Plc	Manufacturing	12/31/17	2209.0	134.0	2847.0	1095.0	132	46130564
VTR	Ventas Inc	REITs	12/31/17	3574.1	1356.5	23954.5	11024.7	963	387905872
VNE	Veoneer Inc	Auto Parts	12/31/17	2322.2	-217.0	1662.5	835.6	4	18065
VER	VEREIT Inc	REITs	12/31/17	1252.3	31.8	14705.6	7884.3	500	952027907
PAY	VeriFone Systems Inc	Electronic Instruments & Related Pro	10/31/17	1871.0	-173.8	2322.2	754.6	417	136202166
VRTV	Veritiv Corp	Industrial Machinery & Equipment	12/31/17	8364.7	-13.3	2708.4	549.7	217	17297593
VZ	Verizon Communications Inc	Services	12/31/17	126034.0	30101.0	257143.0	43096.0	2882	3215255825
VET	Vermilion Energy Inc	Production & Extraction	12/31/17	1024.4	62.3	3975.0	1542.9	-	0
VRS	Verso Corp	Paper & Forest Products	12/31/17	2461.0	-30.0	1732.0	746.0	148	64641695
VSM	Versum Materials Inc	Specialty Chemicals	9/30/17	1126.9	193.0	1246.8	-10.0	478	109882593
VFC	VF Corp.	Apparel, Footwear & Accessories	12/30/17	11811.2	614.9	9958.5	3719.9	1232	441758193
VVI	Viad Corp.	Business Services	12/31/17	1307.0	57.7	919.9	429.1	249	23720180
VICI	VICI Properties Inc	REITs	12/31/17	187.6	42.7	9739.7	4691.5	169	364894220
VNCE	Vince Holding Corp	Retail - Apparel and Accessories	2/3/18	272.6	58.6	234.5	74.8	36	2313949
VIPS	Vipshop Holdings Ltd	Retail - Apparel and Accessories	12/31/17	72912.3	1949.7	37982.8	14294.5	345	345660080
ZTR	Virtus Global Dividend & Income Fu	Holding and other Investment Office	12/31/16	14.0	7.8	468.0	345.1	65	6511306
VGI	Virtus Global Multi-Sector Income F	Holding and other Investment Office	11/30/16	14.6	10.5	259.6	187.2	37	2458907
ZF	Virtus Total Return Fund Inc	Holding and other Investment Office	12/31/16	8.4	3.5	312.3	228.3	65	5250388
V	Visa Inc	Business Services	9/30/17	18358.0	6699.0	67977.0	32760.0	2540	1845826073
VSH	Vishay Intertechnology, Inc.	Electrical Equipment	12/31/17	2603.5	-20.3	3459.2	1428.2	426	197599276
VPG	Vishay Precision Group Inc.	Electronic Instruments & Related Pro	12/31/17	254.3	14.3	306.6	193.2	160	12770752
VSTO	Vista Outdoor Inc	Sporting & Recreational	3/31/18	2308.5	-60.2	2614.8	1217.5	234	70046130
VST	Vistra Energy Corp	Electric Utilities	12/31/17	5430.0	-254.0	14600.0	6342.0	317	471255135
VSI	Vitamin Shoppe Inc	Retail - Specialty	12/30/17	1178.7	-252.2	488.8	195.4	168	27457500
VAM	Vivaldi Opportunities Fund	Holding and other Investment Office	8/14/17		0.0	0.1	0.1	-	0
VSLR	Vivint Solar Inc	Electrical Equipment	12/31/17	268.0	209.1	2463.9	781.0	91	106862906
VMW	VMware Inc	Internet & Software	2/2/18	7922.0	570.0	20622.0	7776.0	713	95431720
VOC	VOC Energy Trust	Oil Royalty Traders	12/31/17	9.2	8.4	77.7	77.7	42	2745418
VCRA	Vocera Communications, Inc.	Computer Hardware & Equipment	12/31/17	162.5	-14.2	194.5	109.0	178	37760672
VG	Vonage Holdings Corp	Services	12/31/17	1002.3	-33.9	858.7	472.9	358	226687864
VNO	Vornado Realty Trust	REITs	12/31/17	2084.1	227.4	17397.9	4337.7	684	225659183
VJET	voxeljet AG	Industrial Machinery & Equipment	12/31/17	23.2	-8.5	67.0	43.8	39	2004767
IAE	VOYA Asia Pacific Dividend Equity I	Holding and other Investment Office	2/28/17	4.9	3.1	135.5	134.5	44	3778226
IHD	VOYA Emerging Markets High Divid	Holding and other Investment Office	2/28/17	5.9	3.5	177.1	175.7	38	6459255
VOYA	Voya Financial Inc	Life & Health	12/31/17	8618.0	-2992.0	222532.0	10009.0	489	202658408
IGA	VOYA Global Advantage & Premiu	Holding and other Investment Office	2/28/17	5.3	3.2	215.2	213.3	54	5380809

T60

EARNINGS PER SHARE — QUARTERLY			EARNINGS PER SHARE — ANNUAL			P/E RATIO		DIVIDENDS PER SHARE			AV. YLD %	DIV. DECLARED		PRICE RANGE 2017	
1st	2nd	3rd	2017	2016	2015			2017	2016	2015		AMOUNT	PAYABLE		
-	-	0.26	0.74	0.63	1.02	4.2 -	3.0	1.76	2.03	1.84	69.0	-	-	3.1 -	2.2
1.55	-	-	5.61	3.87	5.35	23.9 -	18.1	3.32	3.12	2.92	2.9	0.910Y	18/78/27	134.1 -	101.7
-	3.20	-	15.73	6.45	6.07	12.0 -	6.8	-	-	-	-	-	-	189.4 -	107.3
0.52	-	-	0.14	0.56	2.84	296.4 -	234.0	-	-	-	-	5.75GY	18/78/27	41.5 -	32.8
0.10	-	-	2.19	-2.81	-11.24	21.0 -	9.8	0.20	0.20	0.20	0.6	0.050Y	18/78/27	46.0 -	21.4
1.62	-	-	5.70	6.12	8.61	24.3 -	19.2	2.72	2.62	2.56	2.2	0.70Y	18/78/27	138.3 -	109.6
2.87	-	-	10.72	7.25	6.01	23.9 -	17.3	2.88	2.38	1.88	1.3	0.90Y	18/78/27	256.0 -	185.5
1.06	-	-	2.06	1.94	1.89	25.5 -	20.4	1.44	1.42	1.40	3.0	0.3650Y	5/29/18	52.5 -	42.0
0.46	-	-	0.85	-0.50	0.14	37.2 -	30.4	-	-	-	-	-	-	31.6 -	25.9
-	-	1.78	3.92	3.92	4.06	76.1 -	52.7	2.13	2.09	2.05	3.9	0.750Y	18/78/27	67.0 -	46.4
0.70	-	-	3.35	1.28	1.78	25.1 -	16.5	2.64	2.60	2.56	3.8	0.670Z	18/78/27	84.2 -	55.4
2.36	-	-	7.81	7.14	6.76	16.3 -	12.3	0.40	0.40	0.40	0.4	0.10Y	18/78/27	127.3 -	95.8
-	-	0.28	2.99	2.79	2.97	12.2 -	5.5	0.69	0.69	0.63	2.5	0.160Y	7/16/18	36.5 -	16.5
-	-0.40	-	-0.54	-2.02	-0.38			-	0.04	0.32	-	0.020Y	3/31/16	3.7 -	2.3
1.23	-	-	4.37	3.95	3.50	13.4 -	8.4	0.86	0.77	0.70	1.8	0.260Y	18/78/27	58.6 -	36.6
0.18	-	-	0.61	0.91	0.39	42.8 -	32.5	0.88	0.82	0.80	3.8	0.220Z	18/78/27	26.1 -	19.8
-	0.23	-	0.80	0.49	0.90	29.7 -	21.9	1.06	1.04	1.02	5.1	0.39060Z	18/78/27	23.8 -	17.5
0.96	-	-	3.51	3.24	3.16	16.6 -	13.9	1.16	1.07	1.01	2.2	25.6250Y	18/78/27	58.1 -	48.9
0.31	-	-	1.97	1.03	0.98	19.4 -	13.2	-	-	-	-	-	-	38.3 -	26.0
0.39	-	-	1.77	-0.63	0.22	21.6 -	13.6	0.25	0.25	0.44	0.8	0.06250Y	10/3/18	38.3 -	24.1
-	0.18	-	-	-	-			-	-	-	-	-	-	16.7 -	12.7
-0.23	-	-	0.16	0.27	-3.15	119.8 -	91.9	2.10	2.10	2.08	12.3	0.5250	8/10/18	19.2 -	14.7
1.19	-	-	2.53	3.99	3.59	47.3 -	21.5	-	-	-	-	-	-	119.6 -	54.4
0.24	-	-	0.88	1.06	0.83	13.5 -	10.5	1.35	1.25	1.11	12.3	0.35250	5/11/18	11.9 -	9.3
0.25	-	-	0.60	3.46	6.73	72.2 -	43.0	-	-	-	-	0.0250	18/78/27	43.3 -	25.8
0.15	-	-	0.16	-0.45	-2.72	18.1 -	4.2	-	-	-	-	0.001F	8/1/09	2.9 -	0.7
-	-	6.17	5.22	4.01	3.07	54.6 -	38.1	3.73	2.87	2.08	1.6	1.470Z	18/78/27	285.1 -	199.1
-	-	0.43	1.05	0.77	-2.35	14.4 -	8.3	0.34	0.04	0.25	2.9	-	-	15.1 -	8.7
-	-	0.43	1.05	0.77	-2.35	10.8 -	10.0	0.34	0.04	0.25	3.1	-	-	11.3 -	10.5
1.09	-	-	9.16	4.94	7.99	13.6 -	7.0	2.80	2.40	1.70	3.1	0.80Y	18/78/27	124.4 -	64.5
0.72	-	-	2.77	2.85	2.12	17.3 -	12.1	1.77	1.41	1.14	4.2	0.5510	8/13/18	48.0 -	33.6
0.26	-	-	0.61	-0.05	-0.39	14.4 -	3.2	0.08	0.08	0.08	1.6	0.020Y	6/21/18	8.8 -	2.2
0.12	-	-	0.58	0.63	0.42	22.9 -	18.5	0.44	0.44	0.44	3.7	0.34380Y	18/78/27	13.3 -	10.7
1.72	-	-	5.11	7.63	1.71	33.8 -	27.3	1.50	1.50	1.50	1.0	0.3750Y	18/78/27	172.8 -	139.3
-	0.33	-	1.49	1.33	-	17.0 -	13.4	0.20	-	-	0.9	0.07450Y	18/78/27	25.4 -	20.0
-	0.79	-	2.68	4.19	4.09	48.3 -	35.8	-	-	-	-	0.0250	18/78/27	129.5 -	95.9
0.04	-	-	0.59	0.52	0.44	39.0 -	31.9	1.54	1.47	1.40	7.5	0.40Y	18/78/27	23.0 -	18.8
0.76	-	-	2.60	2.55	2.39	27.5 -	22.2	1.71	1.62	1.54	2.6	0.450Y	18/78/27	71.5 -	57.7
0.54	-	-	5.31	2.16	2.86	7.5 -	4.9	-	-	-	-	-	-	39.9 -	25.8
-	-	-	18.60	-42.21	-43.29	1.2 -	0.7	5.86	20.79	-	31.6	-	-	21.9 -	13.2
0.29	-	-	0.47	0.38	0.28	179.9 -	114.9	-	-	-	-	-	-	84.5 -	54.0
0.73	-	-	1.26	-	-			-	-	-	-	-	-		
-	-	1.71	3.78	1.86	1.25	18.5 -	12.4	3.12	2.96	3.04	5.3	0.790Z	18/78/27	70.0 -	47.0
-	-	-	-	-	-			-	-	-	-	-	-	42.0 -	40.0
0.01	-	-	-0.04	-0.29	-0.43			0.55	0.55	0.28	7.2	0.13960Z	18/78/27	8.7 -	6.6
-	-0.15	-	-1.55	-0.08	0.68			-	-	-	-	-	-	23.0 -	15.0
-1.00	-	-	-0.85	1.30	1.67			-	-	-	-	-	-	45.0 -	22.6
1.11	-	-	7.36	3.21	4.37	7.4 -	5.8	2.32	2.27	2.21	4.8	0.590Y	18/78/27	54.7 -	42.9
0.20	-	-	0.51	-1.38	-1.98	98.2 -	0.0	2.58	2.58	2.58	6.6	0.230	8/15/18	50.1 -	
-0.06	-	-	-0.87	-0.93	-5.19			0.10	-	-	0.3	0.060Y	11/25/08	21.8 -	3.9
-	0.56	-	1.76	1.95	-	24.1 -	17.8	-	-	-	-	-	-	42.5 -	31.4
0.63	-	-	1.52	2.54	2.85	55.6 -	36.7	1.72	1.53	1.33	2.4	0.460Y	18/78/27	84.5 -	55.7
-0.47	-	-	2.83	2.09	1.32	21.7 -	16.4	0.40	0.40	0.40	0.7	0.10Y	7/2/18	61.4 -	46.5
0.33	-	-	0.19	-	-	121.0 -	93.9	-	-	-	-	0.26250Y	7/13/18	23.0 -	17.9
-0.49	-	-	-35.00	1.40	9.30			-	-	-	-	-	-	16.5 -	3.2
-	-	0.10	15.94	16.86	13.23	1.2 -	0.5	-	-	-	-	-	-	18.9 -	7.9
-	-	-	-	0.27	0.22			-	1.16	1.11	-	0.1130	9/21/18	14.1 -	10.7
-	-	-	-	0.93	0.91			-	1.87	2.02	-	0.1260	9/21/18	18.9 -	13.4
-	-	-	-	0.19	0.11			-	1.08	1.22	-	0.3610	7/19/18	13.1 -	10.5
-	1.11	-	2.80	2.48	2.58	48.7 -	33.3	0.66	0.56	0.48	0.6	0.210Y	18/78/27	136.3 -	93.3
0.39	-	-	-0.14	0.32	-0.73			0.26	0.25	0.24	1.3	0.0850	18/78/27	24.7 -	16.5
0.37	-	-	1.07	0.48	-0.96	37.2 -	15.5	-	-	-	-	-	-	39.8 -	16.6
-	0.94	-	-4.66	2.35	1.25			-	-	-	-	-	-	24.3 -	13.0
-0.71	-	-	-0.59	-0.38	-			-	2.32	-	-	2.32G7	18/78/27	24.7 -	15.9
-0.17	-	-	-10.90	1.04	1.82			-	-	-	-	0.0017B	12/21/17	11.9 -	3.5
-	-	-	-	-	-			-	-	-	-	-	-	15.2 -	0.0
-0.11	-	-	1.77	0.16	0.12	3.4 -	1.6	-	-	-	-	-	-	6.0 -	2.9
2.29	-	-	-0.02	2.78	2.34			-	-	-	-	-	-	152.2 -	85.9
0.11	-	-	0.50	0.28	0.47	13.0 -	6.6	0.50	0.28	0.47	10.9	0.20	8/14/18	6.5 -	3.3
-0.16	-	-	-0.50	-0.64	-0.66			-	-	-	-	-	-	31.9 -	22.9
0.10	-	-	-0.15	0.08	0.10			-	-	-	-	-	-	12.9 -	6.3
-0.09	-	-	0.85	4.34	3.59	94.8 -	76.5	2.62	2.52	2.52	3.6	0.32810Z	18/78/27	80.6 -	65.0
-	-	-	-2.29	-3.04	-2.58			-	-	-	-	-	-	6.0 -	3.1
-	-	-	0.25	0.29	0.27	45.4 -	39.4	0.97	1.15	1.28	9.2	0.2050	7/16/18	11.4 -	9.9
-	-	-	0.18	0.20	0.30	54.3 -	44.1	0.88	1.04	1.15	9.6	0.1850	7/16/18	9.8 -	7.9
2.50	-	-	-16.25	-2.13	1.80			0.04	0.04	0.04	0.1	0.010Y	18/78/27	55.1 -	36.2
-	-	-	0.18	0.17	0.17	65.6 -	58.7	1.06	1.12	1.12	9.4	0.2250	7/16/18	11.8 -	10.6

SYMBOL	COMPANY	NATURE OF BUSINESS	FISCAL YEAR-END	TOTAL REV. $MILL	NET INCOME $MILL	TOTAL ASSETS $MILL	NET STK EQUITY $MILL	NO OF INST	INST. HOLDINGS (SHARES)
IGD	VOYA Global Equity Dividend & Pre	Holding and other Investment Office	2/28/17	27.4	18.2	787.2	777.3	106	16385233
IDE	VOYA Infrastructure Industrials & M	Holding and other Investment Office	2/28/17	7.3	3.9	297.9	296.6	43	3593376
IID	VOYA International High Dividend E	Holding and other Investment Office	2/28/17	2.1	1.4	57.6	57.0	23	468852
IRR	Voya Natural Resources Equity Inco	Holding and other Investment Office	2/28/17	3.6	1.7	156.6	156.0	52	4993351
PPR	VOYA Prime Rate Trust	Holding and other Investment Office	2/28/17	64.6	45.7	1274.7	857.1	153	49936203
VMC	Vulcan Materials Co (Holding Comp	Mining	12/31/17	3890.3	601.2	9504.9	4968.9	836	166233025
WTI	W & T Offshore Inc	Production & Extraction	12/31/17	487.1	79.7	907.6	-573.5	214	85552356
WPC	W.P. Carey Inc	REITs	12/31/17	848.3	277.3	8231.4	3192.3	550	64800811
WNC	Wabash National Corp	Autos- Manufacturing	12/31/17	1767.2	111.4	1351.5	506.1	339	84963052
WBC	WABCO Holdings Inc	Construction Services	12/31/17	3304.2	406.1	4323.4	1121.4	514	60805271
WAB	Wabtec Corp	Construction Services	12/31/17	3881.8	262.3	6580.0	2808.9	598	128071363
WDR	Waddell & Reed Financial, Inc.	Finance Intermediaries & Services	12/31/17	1157.1	141.3	1384.4	872.9	384	108119367
WAGE	WageWorks Inc	Business Services	12/31/16	364.7	20.2	1343.4	408.1	304	50799263
WD	Walker & Dunlop Inc	Business Services	12/31/17	711.9	211.1	2208.4	809.4	262	30755132
WMT	Walmart Inc	Retail - General Merchandise/Depart	1/31/18	500343.0	9862.0	204522.0	77869.0	2535	1189651703
HCC	Warrior Met Coal Inc	Mining	12/31/17	1169.1	455.0	993.3	413.0	174	60685179
WPG	Washington Prime Group (New)	REITs	12/31/17	758.1	197.1	4451.4	1099.4	356	191635933
WRE	Washington Real Estate Investment	REITs	12/31/17	325.1	19.7	2359.4	1095.0	330	82633231
WCN	Waste Connections Inc (Canada)	Sanitation Services	12/31/17	4630.5	576.8	12014.7	6268.7	479	238544371
WM	Waste Management, Inc. (DE)	Sanitation Services	12/31/17	14485.0	1949.0	21829.0	6019.0	1454	417259259
WAT	Waters Corp.	Biotechnology	12/31/17	2309.1	20.3	5324.4	2233.8	798	90911475
WSO	Watsco Inc.	Industrial Machinery & Equipment	12/31/17	4342.0	208.2	2046.9	1298.0	464	36020586
WTS	Watts Water Technologies Inc	Industrial Machinery & Equipment	12/31/17	1456.7	73.1	1736.5	829.0	313	33149592
W	Wayfair Inc	Retail - Furniture & Home Furnishing	12/31/17	4720.9	-244.6	1213.4	-48.3	274	70232015
WFT	Weatherford International Plc	Equipment & Services	12/31/17	5699.0	-2813.0	9747.0	-626.0	431	1209141853
WBS	Webster Financial Corp (Waterbury,	Banking	12/31/17	1173.1	255.4	26487.6	2702.0	394	104138506
WEC	WEC Energy Group Inc	Electric Utilities	12/31/17	7648.5	1204.9	31590.5	9491.8	1031	275522427
WTW	Weight Watchers International, Inc.	Miscellaneous Consumer Services	12/30/17	1306.9	163.5	1246.0	-1016.0	343	70738193
WRI	Weingarten Realty Investors	REITs	12/31/17	573.2	335.3	4196.6	1632.7	443	155107875
WMK	Weis Markets, Inc.	Retail - Food & Beverage, Drug & To	12/30/17	3466.8	98.4	1441.7	992.8	166	12107427
WBT	Welbilt Inc	Industrial Machinery & Equipment	12/31/17	1445.4	134.0	1840.4	110.4	272	130782461
WCG	WellCare Health Plans Inc	Hospitals & Health Care Facilities	12/31/17	17007.2	373.7	8364.6	2416.7	519	55859020
WFC	Wells Fargo & Co.	Banking	12/31/17	97741.0	22183.0	1951757.0	206936.0	2851	4563996435
WSF	Wells Fargo Capital IV	Banking							0
EOD	Wells Fargo Global Dividend Opport	Holding and other Investment Office	10/31/17	17.7	13.8	352.1	303.7	64	9640948
WFE PRA	Wells Fargo Real Estate Investment	REITs	12/31/17	1353.1	1218.7	35945.6	32390.3		0
WELL	Welltower Inc	REITs	12/31/17	4316.6	522.8	27944.4	14423.1	1035	402490697
WAIR	Wesco Aircraft Holdings Inc.	Aerospace	9/30/17	1429.4	-237.3	1754.1	649.7	162	150592374
WCC	Wesco International, Inc.	Electrical Equipment	12/31/17	7679.0	163.5	4735.5	2119.7	378	54956221
WST	West Pharmaceutical Services, Inc.	Rubber Products	12/31/17	1599.1	150.7	1862.8	1279.9	465	85673243
WAL	Western Alliance Bancorporation	Banking	12/31/17	890.9	325.5	20329.1	2229.7	437	101778363
TLI	Western Asset Corporate Loan Fun	Holding and other Investment Office	9/30/17	9.6	7.1	178.8	113.0	41	4085572
EMD	Western Asset Emerging Markets D	Holding and other Investment Office	12/31/16	41.2	32.4	1336.2	1038.6	130	26070955
GDO	Western Asset Global Credit Define	Holding and other Investment Office	10/31/17	21.1	16.0	374.7	286.8	49	4017632
EHI	Western Asset Global High Income	Holding and other Investment Office	5/31/17	42.7	34.3	698.8	511.7	96	15346465
HIX	Western Asset High Income Fund II	Holding and other Investment Office	4/30/17	67.7	56.5	927.2	671.1	118	18935043
HIO	Western Asset High Income Opport	Holding and other Investment Office	9/30/17	51.5	44.8	747.3	730.5	131	50393852
HYI	Western Asset High Yield Defined	Holding and other Investment Office	5/31/17	22.6	20.0	393.5	385.8		0
WIA	Western Asset Inflation-Linked Inco	Holding and other Investment Office	11/30/16	12.5	7.9	545.1	369.1	75	18060083
WIW	Western Asset Inflation-Linked Opp	Holding and other Investment Office	11/30/16	30.8	21.0	1127.3	756.9	119	36913995
SBI	Western Asset Intermediate Muni F	Holding and other Investment Office	11/30/16	7.8	5.7	190.6	143.0	57	2836827
IGI	Western Asset Investment Grade D	Holding and other Investment Office	11/30/16	12.4	10.6	220.8	218.9	33	2172754
PAI	Western Asset Investment Grade In	Holding and other Investment Office	12/31/16	7.7	6.6	138.5	138.3	37	932391
MMU	Western Asset Managed Municipals	Holding and other Investment Office	5/31/16	39.4	31.6	889.1	659.3	98	6779589
WMC	Western Asset Mortgage Capital Co	REITs	12/31/17	177.6	85.1	3886.9	466.0	125	22352023
DMO	Western Asset Mortgage Defined O	Holding and other Investment Office	12/31/16	22.0	15.3	319.4	216.2	38	1471868
MHF	Western Asset Municipal High Inco	Holding and other Investment Office	10/31/17	8.1	6.9	173.0	171.5	55	3534416
MNP	Western Asset Municipal Partners F	Holding and other Investment Office	11/30/16	10.1	7.4	239.8	173.0	49	1878167
MTT	Western Asset Municipal Term Trus	Holding and other Investment Office	11/30/16	14.5	12.6	262.4	261.3	42	1228195
WEA	Western Asset Premier Bond Fund	Holding and other Investment Office	12/31/16	13.4	11.0	227.2	165.3	50	2567771
GFY	Western Asset Variable Rate Strate	Holding and other Investment Office	9/30/17	5.3	3.7	115.1	85.5	28	4785705
WGP	Western Gas Equity Partners LP	Equipment & Services	12/31/17	2248.4	376.6	8016.3		163	42107355
WES	Western Gas Partners LP	Equipment & Services	12/31/17	2333.5	567.5	8014.3			0
WU	Western Union Co	Business Services	12/31/17	5524.3	-557.1	9231.4	-491.4	885	597189680
WLK	Westlake Chemical Corp	Specialty Chemicals	12/31/17	8041.0	1304.0	12076.0	4874.0	431	44819277
WLKP	Westlake Chemical Partners LP	Specialty Chemicals	12/31/17	1173.0	48.7	1515.3		64	15213896
WMLP	Westmoreland Resource Partners L	Mining	12/31/17	315.6	-31.8	347.4		11	8724
WBK	Westpac Banking Corp	Banking	9/30/17	37518.0	7990.0	851875.0	61288.0	232	21815810
WRK	WestRock Co	Containers & Packaging	9/30/17	14859.7	708.2	25089.0	10342.5	688	251712739
WHG	Westwood Holdings Group, Inc.	Wealth Management	12/31/17	133.8	20.0	192.7	156.4	125	6859919
WEX	Wex Inc	Miscellaneous Consumer Services	12/31/17	1250.5	160.3	6739.2	1711.3	386	56420099
WY	Weyerhaeuser Co	REITs	12/31/17	7196.0	582.0	18059.0	8899.0	1299	709954657
WPM	Wheaton Precious Metals Corp	Precious Metals	12/31/17	843.2	57.7	5683.3	4899.7	491	262414111
WHR	Whirlpool Corp	Household Appliances, Electronics &	12/31/17	21253.0	350.0	20038.0	4198.0	905	83122404
WTM	White Mountains Insurance Group L	General Insurance	12/31/17	373.8	627.2	3659.2	3492.5	318	4154454
WSR	Whitestone REIT	REITs	12/31/17	126.0	8.3	1071.7	347.6	161	23238598
WLL	Whiting Petroleum Corp	Production & Extraction	12/31/17	1481.4	-1237.6	8403.0	3919.1	445	121256815
WOW	WideOpenWest Inc	Services	12/31/17	1188.1	159.5	2441.6	-204.4	102	52240655
WRD	WildHorse Resource Development	Production & Extraction	12/31/17	427.2	49.9	2778.1	1590.8	135	104123512
JW A	Wiley (John) & Sons Inc.	Publishing	4/30/18	1796.1	192.2	2839.5	1190.6	388	53197818

EARNINGS PER SHARE — QUARTERLY			EARNINGS PER SHARE — ANNUAL			P/E RATIO		DIVIDENDS PER SHARE			AV. YLD	DIV. DECLARED		PRICE RANGE 2017	
1st	2nd	3rd	2017	2016	2015			2017	2016	2015	%	AMOUNT	PAYABLE		
-	-	-	0.19	0.18	0.22	42.8 -	37.5	0.81	0.91	0.91	10.6	0.0610	8/15/18	8.1 -	7.1
-	-	-	0.20	0.23	0.26	87.4 -	73.5	1.39	1.54	1.62	8.8	0.290	7/16/18	17.5 -	14.7
-	-	-	0.17	0.20	0.22	46.2 -	39.1	0.79	0.83	0.83	10.8	0.0520	8/15/18	7.9 -	6.6
-	-	-	0.07	0.11	0.12	99.3 -	81.4	0.77	0.91	1.01	12.4	0.1620	7/16/18	7.0 -	5.7
-	-	-	0.31	0.32	0.33	17.4 -	16.2	0.32	0.33	0.35	6.2	0.02350	7/23/18	5.4 -	5.0
0.39	-	-	4.46	3.09	1.64	31.6 -	24.9	1.00	0.80	0.40	0.8	0.280Y	18/78/27	141.1 -	110.9
0.19	-	-	0.56	-2.60	-13.76	15.5 -	3.3	-	-	-		0.10Y	12/3/14	8.7 -	1.8
0.60	-	-	2.56	2.49	1.61	28.2 -	23.1	4.01	3.93	3.83	6.0	1.020Z	18/78/27	72.3 -	59.2
0.35	-	-	1.78	1.82	1.50	14.7 -	10.4	0.24	-	-	1.1	0.0750Y	7/26/18	26.2 -	18.4
1.87	-	-	7.50	3.98	4.72	21.5 -	15.6	-	-	-		0.070Y	18/78/27	161.0 -	116.9
0.92	-	-	2.72	3.34	4.10	37.9 -	25.6	0.44	0.36	0.28	0.5	0.120Y	18/78/27	103.0 -	69.7
0.56	-	-	1.69	1.78	2.94	13.9 -	10.6	1.84	1.84	1.72	9.2	0.250Y	8/1/18	23.4 -	17.9
-	-	0.24	-	0.54	0.63			-	-	-		-		67.0 -	41.0
1.16	-	-	6.56	3.65	2.65	9.3 -	6.9	-	-	-		0.250Y	6/5/18	61.2 -	45.4
0.72	-	-	4.38	4.57	5.05	25.0 -	16.7	2.00	1.96	1.92	2.3	0.520Y	18/78/27	109.6 -	73.2
3.36	-	-	8.62	-13.15		3.9 -	2.0	11.36	-	-	44.0	0.050Y	5/11/18	33.4 -	17.3
0.07	-	-	0.98	0.29	-0.55	9.8 -	5.7	1.00	1.00	1.00	13.4	0.42970Z	7/16/18	9.6 -	5.6
0.04	-	-	0.25	1.65	1.31	135.3 -	101.1	1.20	1.20	1.20	4.0	0.30Z	6/29/18	33.8 -	25.3
0.47	-	-	2.18	1.07	1.55	46.5 -	29.2	0.50	0.22	-	0.6	0.140	5/30/18	101.4 -	63.6
0.91	-	-	4.41	2.65	1.65	20.3 -	16.6	1.70	1.64	1.54	2.1	0.4650Y	18/78/27	89.7 -	73.4
1.40	-	-	0.25	6.41	5.65	874.8 -	690.3	-	-	-		-		218.7 -	172.6
0.89	-	-	5.81	5.15	4.90	32.9 -	24.5	4.60	3.60	2.80	2.7	1.450Y	18/78/27	191.3 -	142.3
0.82	-	-	2.12	2.44	-3.24	38.8 -	28.6	0.75	0.71	0.66	1.0	0.210Y	6/15/18	82.2 -	60.7
-1.22	-	-	-2.81	-2.29	-0.92			-	-	-		-		118.8 -	57.9
-0.25	-	-	-2.84	-3.82	-2.55			-	-	-		-			
0.85	-	-	2.67	2.16	2.15	25.4 -	16.7	1.03	0.98	0.89	1.8	0.32810Y	18/78/27	67.7 -	44.5
1.23	-	-	3.79	2.96	2.34	18.3 -	15.5	2.08	1.98	1.74	3.3	0.55250Y	18/78/27	69.5 -	58.6
0.56	-	-	2.40	1.03	0.56	43.0 -	13.5	-	-	0.00		0.1750Y	10/11/13	103.1 -	32.4
1.13	-	-	2.60	1.87	1.29	12.9 -	9.9	2.29	1.46	1.38	7.5	0.3950Z	18/78/27	33.6 -	25.8
0.60	-	-	3.66	3.24	2.21	15.5 -	9.3	1.20	1.20	1.20	2.7	0.30Y	8/13/18	56.7 -	34.0
0.09	-	-	0.95	0.57	1.15	24.8 -	19.5	-	-	-		-		23.6 -	18.6
2.25	-	-	8.31	5.43	2.67	29.6 -	19.8	-	-	-		-		246.2 -	164.2
0.96	-	-	4.10	3.99	4.12	16.1 -	12.1	1.54	1.51	1.48	2.8	0.390Y	18/78/27	65.9 -	49.6
-	-	-	0.30	0.62	0.68	21.7 -	18.5	0.60	0.58	0.72	10.0	0.16370	7/2/18	6.5 -	5.5
9.24	-	-	35.27	37.75	48.71	0.8 -	0.7	1.59	1.59	1.69	6.0	0.39840	7/2/18	27.3 -	25.4
1.17	-	-	1.26	2.81	2.34	60.1 -	39.7	3.48	3.44	3.30	5.5	0.81250Z	18/78/27	75.8 -	50.0
-	0.15	-	-2.40	0.93	-1.60			-	-	-				11.9 -	6.3
0.93	-	-	3.38	-2.10	4.18	20.3 -	14.7	-	-	-				68.8 -	49.6
0.58	-	-	1.99	1.91	1.30	51.5 -	41.9	0.53	0.49	0.45	0.6	0.140Y	18/78/27	102.4 -	83.3
-	-	0.79	3.10	2.50	2.03	20.4 -	14.5	-	-	-		0.39060Z	7/2/18	63.4 -	45.0
-	-	-	0.71	0.71	0.80	15.7 -	14.2	0.84	0.87	0.87	7.9	0.0530	9/4/18	11.2 -	10.1
-	-	-	-	1.01	1.05			-	1.26	1.31		0.10	9/4/18	16.1 -	13.2
-	-	-	1.07	1.20	1.23	17.4 -	15.3	1.36	1.36	1.36	7.8	0.1010	9/4/18	18.6 -	16.4
-	-	-	0.82	0.97	0.99	12.7 -	11.1	1.04	1.16	1.16	10.5	0.0610	9/4/18	10.4 -	9.1
-	-	-	0.66	0.73	0.79	11.1 -	9.8	0.69	0.82	0.83	10.0	0.04550	9/4/18	7.3 -	6.4
-	-	-	0.35	0.39	0.41	14.9 -	13.6	0.37	-	0.43	7.4	0.02650	9/4/18	5.2 -	4.8
-	-	-	0.88	1.28	1.30	17.9 -	16.4	1.27	1.32	1.32	8.4	0.08850	9/4/18	15.7 -	14.4
-	-	-	-	0.27	0.07			-	0.38	0.35		0.03450	7/31/18	12.0 -	11.1
-	-	-	-	0.34	0.25			-	0.40	0.37		0.0360	7/31/18	11.7 -	10.9
-	-	-	-	0.41	0.42			-	0.48	0.48		0.0295M	9/4/18	9.9 -	8.6
-	-	-	-	0.98	0.98			-	1.20	1.20		0.0850	9/4/18	22.9 -	20.1
-	-	-	-	0.70	0.70			-	0.69	0.69		0.05750	10/1/18	17.1 -	13.4
-	-	-	-	0.74	0.78			-	0.78	0.78		0.058M	9/4/18	14.5 -	12.6
0.52	-	-	2.03	-0.61	-0.25	5.4 -	4.3	1.24	1.38	2.49	12.3	0.310	7/26/18	10.9 -	8.8
-	-	-	-	1.47	2.13			-	3.00	3.32		0.190	9/4/18	27.1 -	23.0
-	-	-	0.32	0.31	0.36	25.2 -	22.2	0.28	0.33	0.35	3.8	0.0255M	9/4/18	8.1 -	7.1
-	-	-	-	0.76	0.81			-	0.87	0.87		0.0575M	9/4/18	16.2 -	14.0
-	-	-	-	1.04	1.11			-	1.05	1.01		0.0790	9/4/18	23.6 -	20.5
-	-	-	-	0.93	1.00			-	1.03	1.08		0.0650	10/1/18	14.4 -	12.5
-	-	-	0.80	0.79	0.69	21.9 -	0.0	0.93	0.93	0.88	5.5	0.07750Y	9/4/18	17.5 -	0.0
0.46	-	-	1.72	1.53	0.39	25.2 -	18.9	2.02	1.71	1.40	5.3	0.58250	8/23/18	43.3 -	32.5
0.38	-	-	1.30	1.74	-1.95	44.0 -	31.9	3.53	3.29	2.95	7.2	0.950	8/13/18	57.1 -	41.5
0.46	-	-	-1.19	0.51	1.62			0.70	0.64	0.62	3.6	0.190Y	18/78/27	21.5 -	18.5
2.20	-	-	10.05	3.06	4.86	12.3 -	6.6	0.80	0.74	0.69	0.8	0.210Y	18/78/27	123.7 -	65.8
0.36	-	-	1.72	1.50	1.47	14.8 -	12.4	1.44	1.29	1.15	6.2	0.39750	5/24/18	25.4 -	21.3
-0.56	-	-	-1.34	-1.51	-4.62			0.52	0.73	0.60	21.1	0.11550	11/14/17	3.9 -	1.0
-	-	-	2.29	2.18	2.49	11.5 -	9.0	1.84	2.07	1.74	7.7	-		26.3 -	20.6
-	0.86	-	2.77	-1.54	2.93	25.4 -	19.6	1.60	1.50	0.38	2.6	0.430	18/78/27	70.3 -	54.3
0.93	-	-	2.38	2.77	3.33	29.8 -	22.8	2.54	2.33	2.07	4.1	0.680Y	18/78/27	70.8 -	54.3
1.12	-	-	3.72	1.48	2.62	51.8 -	27.4	-	-	-		-		192.5 -	101.8
0.35	-	-	0.77	1.39	0.89	49.8 -	40.5	1.25	1.24	1.20	3.6	0.320Z	18/78/27	38.4 -	31.2
0.15	-	-	0.13	0.45	-0.41	225.5 -	141.1	0.33	0.21	0.20	1.4	0.090	6/7/18	29.3 -	18.3
1.30	-	-	4.70	11.50	9.83	42.2 -	30.6	4.30	3.90	3.45	2.6	1.150Y	18/78/27	198.3 -	143.9
-12.82	-	-	-146.06	82.19	50.60			1.00	1.00	1.00		1.0	18/78/27		
0.07	-	-	0.22	0.26	0.24	67.8 -	46.0	1.14	1.24	1.14	9.0	0.0950Z	9/14/18	14.9 -	10.1
0.16	-	-	-13.65	-21.28	-45.40			-	-	-		1.56250Y	6/17/13	55.5 -	16.0
-2.40	-	-	2.02	-	-	8.6 -	3.1	-	-	-		-		17.4 -	6.3
-1.24	-	-	0.32	-0.11	-	89.0 -	33.3	-	-	-		-		28.5 -	10.6
-	-	1.19	1.95	2.48	2.97	36.3 -	26.6	1.24	1.20	1.16	2.0	0.330Y	18/78/27	70.8 -	52.0

SYMBOL	COMPANY	NATURE OF BUSINESS	FISCAL YEAR-END	TOTAL REV. $MILL	NET INCOME $MILL	TOTAL ASSETS $MILL	NET STK EQUITY $MILL	NO OF INST	INST. HOLDINGS (SHARES)
WMB	Williams Cos Inc (The)	Equipment & Services	12/31/17	8031.0	2174.0	46352.0	9656.0	1126	845836631
WPZ	Williams Partners LP (New)	Equipment & Services	12/31/17	8010.0	871.0	45903.0		18	5221151
WSM	Williams Sonoma Inc	Retail - Furniture & Home Furnishing	1/28/18	5292.4	259.5	2785.7	1203.6	593	118813319
WGO	Winnebago Industries, Inc.	Autos- Manufacturing	8/26/17	1547.1	71.3	902.5	441.7	344	35310282
WIT	Wipro Ltd	IT Services	3/31/17	550402.0	84895.0	793516.0	520304.0	197	117223769
WNS	WNS (Holdings) Ltd	IT Services	3/31/18	758.0	86.4	759.6	495.0	193	48833592
WWW	Wolverine World Wide, Inc.	Apparel, Footwear & Accessories	12/30/17	2350.0	0.3	2399.0	949.6	408	120084521
WF	Woori Bank (Korea)	Banking	12/31/01	7459439.0	705352.0	77849060.0		63	2404775
WK	Workiva Inc	Internet & Software	12/31/17	207.9	-44.4	157.7	-16.9	131	20738314
INT	World Fuel Services Corp.	Equipment & Services	12/31/17	33695.5	-170.2	5587.8	1721.9	362	83968713
WWE	World Wrestling Entertainment Inc	Entertainment	12/31/17	801.0	32.6	614.5	253.0	281	53167889
WP	Worldpay Inc	Business Services	12/31/17	4026.5	130.1	8667.0	532.5	593	296195487
WOR	Worthington Industries, Inc.	Non-Precious Metals	5/31/17	3014.1	204.5	2325.3	951.6	340	41630204
WPP	WPP Plc (New)	Advertising	12/31/17	15265.4	1816.6	33668.7	9493.2	347	15590746
WPX	WPX Energy Inc	Production & Extraction	12/31/17	1336.0	-16.0	8207.0	4127.0	511	444870188
WYND	Wyndham Destinations Inc	Hotels, Restaurants & Travel	12/31/17	5076.0	871.0	10403.0	878.0	804	107361598
WH	Wyndham Hotels & Resorts Inc	Hotels, Restaurants & Travel	12/31/17	1347.0	243.0	2122.0	1300.0	56	2075853
WH	Wyndham Hotels & Resorts Inc	Hotels, Restaurants & Travel	12/31/17	1347.0	243.0	2122.0	1300.0	56	2075853
XFLT	XAI Octagon Floating Rate & Altern	Holding and other Investment Office	9/30/17		-0.0	71.2	71.0	11	695853
XHR	Xenia Hotels & Resorts Inc	REITs	12/31/17	945.3	98.9	3115.3	1614.9	290	90300984
XRM	Xerium Technologies Inc	Industrial Machinery & Equipment	12/31/17	481.0	-14.6	567.8	-136.5	98	12063640
XRX	Xerox Corp	Peripherals	12/31/17	10265.0	195.0	15946.0	5470.0	797	452369428
XIN	Xinyuan Real Estate Co Ltd	Property, Real Estate & Developmen	12/31/17	1976.9	63.6	6384.4	992.6	80	28639112
XL	XL Group Ltd	General Insurance	12/31/17	11328.2	-560.4	63436.2	9848.3	665	281871860
XOXO	XO Group Inc	Internet & Software	12/31/17	160.6	5.5	204.1	173.1	192	28144472
XPO	XPO Logistics, Inc.	Airlines/Air Freight	12/31/17	15380.8	340.2	12601.6	3604.4	540	148198666
XYL	Xylem Inc	Industrial Machinery & Equipment	12/31/17	4707.0	331.0	6860.0	2503.0	792	179359820
AUY	Yamana Gold Inc	Precious Metals	12/31/17	1803.8	-194.4	8763.3	4313.4	391	479436007
YELP	Yelp Inc	Internet & Software	12/31/17	846.8	152.9	1216.5	1099.6	321	82876344
YEXT	Yext Inc	Services	1/31/18	170.2	-66.6	203.5	81.5	100	45140453
YRD	Yirendai Ltd	Wealth Management	12/31/17	852.0	210.8	1155.6	456.5	97	7442652
YPF	YPF SA	Refining & Marketing	12/31/17	252813.0	12340.0	505718.0	152295.0	206	115430933
YUMC	Yum China Holdings Inc	Hotels, Restaurants & Travel	12/31/17	7144.0	403.0	4263.0	2782.0	750	368791122
YUM	Yum! Brands Inc	Hotels, Restaurants & Travel	12/31/17	5878.0	1340.0	5311.0	-6334.0	1328	319233100
ZAYO	Zayo Group Holdings Inc	Manufacturing	6/30/17	2199.8	85.7	8739.4	1410.5	412	235736357
ZEN	Zendesk Inc	Internet & Software	12/31/17	430.5	-110.6	560.2	321.6	276	112903712
ZBH	Zimmer Biomet Holdings Inc	Medical Instruments & Equipment	12/31/17	7824.1	1813.8	25964.5	11735.8	1295	234837722
ZOES	Zoe's Kitchen Inc	Hotels, Restaurants & Travel	12/25/17	314.1	-2.0	240.5	131.1	118	19582244
ZTS	Zoetis Inc	Pharmaceuticals	12/31/17	5307.0	864.0	8586.0	1770.0	1065	494170509
ZTO	ZTO Express (Cayman) Inc	Shipping	12/31/17	13060.1	3159.7	25827.6	21435.3	143	149505944
ZUO	Zuora Inc	Internet & Software	1/31/18	167.9	-47.2	155.4	26.7		0
ZYME	Zymeworks Inc	Pharmaceuticals	12/31/17	51.8	-10.4	132.0	116.4	21	1758579